Civil Costs: Law and Practice

Second Edition

Civil Costs: Law and Practice

Second Edition

Mark Friston MA (Cantab), MB BChir, MRCP(UK), FCL
of the Middle Temple, Barrister and Costs Lawyer
Kings Chambers, Manchester
Ely Place Chambers, London

JORDANS

Published by
Jordan Publishing Limited
21 St Thomas Street
Bristol BS1 6JS

British Library Cataloguing-in-Publication Data

A catalogue record for this book is available from the British Library.

ISBN 978 1 84661 312 8

Typeset by Letterpart Ltd, Reigate, Surrey

Printed in Great Britain by CPI Antony Rowe, Chippenham and Eastbourne

PREFACE TO THE SECOND EDITION

The preface to the first edition said that the law of costs is a paradox in that it can be both emotive and outstandingly dull at the same time. There are those who say that it has ceased to be dull: they would point to the globalisation of funding, the Jackson reforms, and the dozens of other policies and changes that are in the pipeline. They may have a point, but in order to *practise* costs, the topic needs to be approached in an orderly and pedestrian way. In a world of change, the winner will be the tortoise not the hare, hence this edition continues to focus on quotidian practical problems rather than glitzy policy issues.

That is not to say that this edition is uninspiring. There are those amongst the readership who will thrill at the thought of the tables at chapter 44, they will delight in the flowcharts in chapter 42, and they will be captivated by the newly-added references from Australian, US and even Canadian cases. There is much to excite the costs geek.

For those who have yet to develop such a passion for costs, this edition is merely a thorough and predictable update of the original. The updates are too numerous to summarise: they range from better cross-referencing through to new and rewritten chapters.

In addition to those who have already been mentioned in the preface to the first edition (to whom I repeat my thanks), I would like to thank the following persons: His Honour Judge Simon Brown QC, Master Colum Leonard, District Judge Ian Besford, District Judge Simon Bull, District Judge David Harris, District Judge Robert Hill, District Judge Lightman, Professor Dominic Regan, Mr Adam Aldred, Mr Daniel Claes, Mr Simon Gibbs, Mr Ian Stark, Mr Stephen Loxton, Mr Roger Mallalieu, Mr Roger Quick, Mr Anthony Rich, Ms Tracy Robinson, Mr Andrew Tollitt, Mr Andrew Walton, and Mr Gary 'Harry' Young.

Finally, in addition to my family (Sue, Emily and George), I owe a special debt of gratitude to Miss Erica Bedford (until recently, my assistant, now my colleague in chambers), Paul Hughes (member of the Kings Chambers Costs Team), Miss Elizabeth Love (costs lawyer at Keoghs), Kevin Latham (Costs Team), Mr Craig Ralph (Costs Team), and Matthew Smith (Costs Team), all of whom have been overly generous with their kindness and time.

The law is stated as at 15 April 2012. Any errors or omissions are entirely Emily and George's fault.

Mark Friston
Gurnett, 2012

PREFACE TO THE FIRST EDITION

The law of costs is a paradox in that it can be both emotive and outstandingly dull at the same time. It is a difficult area of the law because there are, and will always be, unanswered questions and diametrically competing interests. Perhaps as a result of these things, previous textbooks have been short and have sought to encourage the reader by providing an engaging, and often entertaining, commentary.

There will always remain a place for such textbooks, but there is also a need for a practitioners' text which is focused solely on the law rather than on policy, and which is detailed and fully referenced. This seeks to be such a textbook. Where appropriate, there is analysis and a discussion of the policy behind the law, but the author has taken care to avoid expressing his own views unless they are likely to be uncontentious. Where a point can be argued either way, this is stated and both arguments are set out. Most of the relevant law is included in such a way as to avoid the need to consult reports or other texts; this is in recognition of the fact that not all costs practitioners have access to the full range of law reports.

Whilst this book will be of use to any judge or lawyer who finds himself dealing with costs issues, it is has been written with the following species of lawyer particularly in mind:

- **Costs practitioners (such as costs lawyers, costs draftsmen, costs counsel, etc):** The chapters are broken down into subchapters dealing with real, practical issues. Subchapters include not only broad topics such 'limitation', 'apportionment', and 'oral retainers', but also day-to-day questions such as 'copying charges' and 'experts' fees'. Authorities are included in a way that makes them easy to find and include points of dispute or replies. Issues ancillary to the practice of costs (such as 'loss of lien', 'security for costs', etc) are also dealt with in sufficient detail to allow the costs practitioner to give sensible and accurate advice without having to consult other texts.

- **Solicitors with management responsibilities:** Now more than ever, financial success is dependent on practitioners having a firm grasp of the law of costs: that law pervades legal practice at all levels, and it is no longer sufficient to leave difficult costs issues to the end of the case to be sorted out by the costs practitioners (or, heaven forbid, trial counsel). All practitioners need to know not only how to avoid mantraps, but also how to deal with those traps once they have sprung. This book recognises that mistakes can happen. It provides sensible advice about how to limit the damage that mistakes can cause. This book complements the Solicitors' Code of Conduct 2007, but it also deals with lesser known regulations and rules, such as the Consumer Protection (Distance Selling) Regulations 2000 and the Solicitors' Financial Services (Conduct of Business) Rules 2001.

- **District judges:** The law of costs has become so complex that many district judges will not have the time to keep abreast of all recent developments. It can no longer be assumed that even diligent advocates will always be able to unearth all the relevant authorities. This book seeks to describe the relevant law in an even-handed and comprehensive way. Extensive authorities are included (usually in footnotes, and often with paragraph or page numbers). The true law often lies in the actual words used and, for this reason, authorities are frequently quoted verbatim. Usually, the name of the judge who gave the leading judgment is given, even if he or she is not quoted.

- **Counsel and solicitors with higher rights of audience:** In order to avoid snatching defeat from the jaws of victory, advocates need to know which authorities and principles are likely to persuade the court to make the order they seek. This book is designed so that specific questions can be answered relatively quickly, and case examples are given in such a way that the advocate can easily scan a list to find the most appropriate authority. Practical problems (such as 'exaggeration', or 'abandoned issues') are dealt with as discrete topics with cross-referencing where appropriate.

Whilst this book is a practitioners' text rather than a students' text, Parts IV onwards will be of use to students taking the Association of Costs Lawyers' Training Course. It will be of particular use to students seeking to do well in the written assignments of that course.

In addition to thanking the team at Jordan Publishing Ltd, I would like to thank the following people, some of whom have donated a considerable amount of their time: Mr Justice Kenneth Handley, Professor Paul Sweeting, Master John O'Hare, Master Christopher Wright, District Judge Duerden, Professor Andrew McGee, Mr Stephen Grime QC, Mr Michael Rawlinson QC, Mr Matthew Smith, Mr Andrew Grantham, Mr Paul Hughes, Mr Simon Gibbs, Mr Craig Ralph, Mr Kevin Latham, Mr Para Gorasia, Mr Sam Karim, Mr Carl Dray, Mr Kenneth Brown, Ms Anne Winyard, Mr Murray Heining, Mr Stephen Loxton, Mr Toby Brown, Mr Rocco Pirozzolo, Mr Frank Maher, Mr Nicholas Northrop, Mr Mark Balme, Mr Stephen Averill, Mr Martin Hoyle, Mr Brian Varney, Mr Geoffrey Claughton, and Ms Iram Akhtar. And finally, I thank (with much love) my long-suffering wife and children, Sue, Emily and George.

Mark Friston
Gurnett, 2010

CONTENTS

Part IV
The Practice of Costs (Between the Parties)

Chapter 21

TABLE OF CASES

References are to paragraph numbers.

TABLE OF STATUTES

References are to paragraph numbers.

TABLE OF STATUTORY INSTRUMENTS

References are to paragraph numbers.

TABLE OF PRACTICE DIRECTIONS AND PROTOCOLS

References are to paragraph numbers.

Costs Practice Direction—*continued*

Costs Practice Direction—*continued*

Part I
INTRODUCTION

Chapter 1

THE HISTORY OF COSTS

1.1   The history of costs has been a gradual evolution punctuated by repeated reinvention. It is said that if one waits long enough, every funding regime will come full circle in that the familiar or ancient will be recast into a supposedly 'new' form.[1] There is probably some truth in this, and it is therefore worth knowing where the law has been so that it can be seen where it is likely to go. This particularly true today; this is because change is imminent (see Chapter 42).

1.2   The language of costs has changed repeatedly during its history. Save where is otherwise obvious from the context, modern terminology is used in the main text, with relevant ancient terminology appearing in the footnotes.

1.3   This chapter is an overview discussing the evolution of costs as a distinct legal discipline.[2] In particular, the following developments are outlined:

- *13th century*: the emergence of 'costs' as a legal entity distinct from other monies recovered in litigation;
- *1605*: the emergence of consumer protection in the form of a need to deliver a bill supported by vouchers;
- *Circa 1606:* the arrival of two-way costs shifting (that being a facility for costs recovery by both claimants and defendants, rather than by just the claimants);
- *1630:* the development of a judicial awareness as to what constituted 'costs' (as opposed merely to monies spent as an incident of litigation);
- *Circa 1670*: the development of something akin to the modern concept of proportionality;
- *1728:* the emergence of a statutory right to a solicitor and client assessment and the enhancement of consumer protection by way of development of the Solicitors Acts;
- *1825 to 1845:* the gradual replacement of arbitrary measures of costs with costs to be assessed;
- *1865:* the emergence of the modern doctrine of the indemnity principle;
- *1870:* the development of 'business agreements' between clients and solicitors;
- *1883:* the development of the distinction between costs of contentious and non-contentious work;
- *1920:* the introduction of the ability to render gross sum bills;
- *1953:* the strengthening of consumer protection in the form of remuneration certificates and the introduction of the notion of assessment of 'fair and reasonable' costs for non-contentious work;
- *1959:* the introduction of the notion of assessment of what was 'necessary and proper' for contentious work;

---

[1]   See, for example, P Hurst 'Going Round in Circles' CJQ 2006, 25 (Oct), pp 546–556.

[2]   A detailed history can be found in R Quick *Quick on Costs* (Thomson Reuters). Much of what is set out herein is based on that history, which itself is based on Mr Quick's Master's dissertation.

- *1986:* the replacement of that test with costs on the 'standard' and 'indemnity' bases;
- *1990:* the introduction of the present funding regime under the CPR and the emergence of conditional funding;
- *2000:* the arrival of recoverable success fees and after-the-event (ATE) premiums between opposing parties;
- *2008:* the beginning of Lord Jackson's review into the funding of civil litigation; and
- *2011 to present day:* the implementation of reforms that will see the replacement of two-way costs shifting with one-way costs shifting, the abrogation of recoverable success fees and ATE premiums, and the strengthening of the concepts of case management, costs budgeting and costs management.

THE ANCIENT POSITION AT COMMON LAW

1.4   In ancient times, neither claimants nor defendants could recover costs by that name. Costs sanctions could be imposed, but those were a long way removed from a modern-day costs order. A claimant could be amerced (fined) for having wrongly brought an action or for having pleaded a case that was not true.[3] Hullock (a nineteenth century authority on the law of costs) had this to say:[4]

'Before the statute of Gloucester (1278) (6 Edw.1 cl.s.127) no person was entitled to recover any costs of suit either in plea real, personal, or mixed; but by the Common Law, if the plaintiff failed in his action, he was amersed (by the coroner and his jury) *pro falso clamore*,[5] if he succeeded, the defendant was in *misericordia* for his unjust detention of the plaintiff's rights.'

The amercement was given to the state (ie the King or the Lord) rather than to the defendant, so the defendant would not benefit directly from the amercement. In particular, the defendant would not be compensated in costs for having had a claim wrongly or dishonestly brought against him.

EARLY STATUTORY INTERVENTION AND THE NOTION OF 'COSTS' AS A SEPARATE LEGAL ENTITY

1.5   The Suits of Court Act 1267,[6] part of the Statute of Marlborough, introduced a number of categories of claim in which costs could be recovered. Further significant changes were enacted by the Recovery of Damages and Costs Act 1278[7] (this being part of the Statute of Gloucester). The relevant provisions in the 1278 Act read as follows:[8]

'The demandant in assise of novel disseisin, in writs of mort d'ancestor, cosinage, aiel and be sail, shall have damages. And the demandant shall have the costs of the writ purchased,

---

[3]   *Wharton's Law Lexicon* (14th edn, 1946), p 59; see also *Quick on Costs* (Thomson Reuters) at [2.30].

[4]   Hullock, *Costs in Civil Actions and Criminal Proceedings* (2nd edn, 1810)

[5]   A nominal amercement of a claimant for his false claim.

[6]   Otherwise known as the Statute of Marlborough (52 Hen III, c 9). This permitted a successful party his damages and his costs: 'tunc adjudicentur feoffatis damna sua, et misae suae' ('then the foeffees shall have their damages and costs'); see Coke's Second Institute (1641), p 109.

[7]   Otherwise known as the Statute of Gloucester (6 Edw I, c 1).

[8]   Translated from the original Latin.

together with damages, and this act shall hold place in all cases where the party recovers damages, and every person shall render damages where land is recovered against him upon his own intrusion, or his own act.'

Thus, legal expenses (limited to the costs of the writ) were recoverable by a claimant as costs – and by that name – but only in certain categories of litigation and then only when damages were also capable of being recovered.[9] Those monies were regarded as being an increase of damages, and as such were referred to as *costs de incremento* (meaning costs of increase).[10] The power of the jury to make such an allowance unquestionably existed where damages had been payable before the 1278 Act,[11] and if there ever was a rule that it would not apply to cases in which the right to damages arose after 1278,[12] that rule was not followed.[13] Where the claim was not for damages (such as claims relating to possession of land), costs could be recovered only to the extent provided for by statute,[14] but in time the ambit of the 1278 Act was given a wide interpretation; in particular, the ambit increased to include personal actions[15] and the whole of the costs of the claim[16] rather than merely the costs of the writ. There remained an important limitation, namely that where the successful party was the defendant, he was generally without remedy for any expenses he had incurred.[17] Put otherwise and in modern language, there was one-way rather than two-way costs shifting.

1.6   The notion of legal expenses being recoverable as costs spread to other jurisdictions. In 1324, for example, costs were for the first time allowed in France by an ordinance of Charles le Bel.

1.7   Even in the English jurisdiction the facility to recover costs was not something which applied uniformly in all courts. The law of equity developed alongside the common law and as a supplement to it, but the statutory provisions relating to the Court of Chancery tended to lag behind those in other courts. This was perhaps because the Court of Chancery considered itself to have the equitable power to award costs as damages according to *arbitrio boni viri* ('the judgment of the good man').[18] In 1393 the power to award costs in the Court of Chancery was put on a statutory footing[19] and in 1436 it was confirmed that such costs were payable as part of the damages,[20] but as the

---

[9]   Holdsworth, A History of English Law, (1971), Vol 4, p 537; see R Quick *Quick on Costs* (Thomson Reuters).

[10]   Bacon, A New Abridgement of the Law (1832), Vol II, pp 288–289.

[11]   *Robert Pilford's case* (1613), 10 CO Rep at 116A.

[12]   See *Robert Pilfold's Case* (1613) 10 Co Rep 115b; see R Quick *Quick on Costs*, (Thomson Reuters) at [2.30], footnote 3.

[13]   Gray, *A Treatise on the Law of Costs in Action and Other Proceedings in the Courts of Common Law at Westminster* (1853), pp 4 and 5.

[14]   Holdsworth, *A History of English Law*, (1971), Vol 4, p 537 (instancing proceedings in error).This princple continued to have an influence up until the nineteenth century, as demonstrated by *Dodd's Case* (1858) 44 ER 1087 (concenring habeus corpus), *R v Parlby* WN 190 at 191; see also *Quick on Costs* (Thomson Reuters) at [2.30].

[15]   *Readings and Moots at the Inns of Court in the Fifteenth Century* (1954) 71 *Selden Society* 153 at 154.

[16]   See Christian, A Short History of Solicitors (1896), p 25; see also *Reeves v Butler* [1726] Gilb Rep 195, 25 ER 136.

[17]   See *Hullock on Costs*, 2 2 Arch Pr 281.The Statute of Marlborough (1267) made limited provision for a defendant to recover costs on a claim for replevin and a suit upon a writ of error.

[18]   R Quick *Quick on Costs* (Thomson Reuters) at [2.100].

[19]   17 Ric II c 6.

[20]   15 Henry VI c 4.

jurisdiction developed, the extent to which that court relied on statute for its powers to award costs became less and less.[21] It was in this way that the early 'inherent jurisdiction' of the court came into being.

The early practice of costs

1.8   By modern standards the ancient system for quantifying costs lacked refinement. In particular, there was a tendency for lawyers to be paid according to the length of documents produced: the longer the document, the greater the fee. This resulted in lawyers having a direct financial interest in producing documents of undue length. There are those who say that the practice of adding 'recitals' to contracts and agreements arose not out of a desire to enhance the clarity of legal writing, but out of a need to increase the size of the document and hence the fee.[22]

1.9   There were concerns that the administration of justice was being put at risk by a system that paid fees by the folio, and perhaps as a result sixteenth-century judges developed some gratifyingly robust methods for discouraging disproportionate expenditure. In 1596, for example, a lawyer was fined and sent to prison for drafting a pleading which inappropriately ran to 120 pages; a hole was cut in his pleadings, and he was forced to poke his head through the hole and to parade around court 'bareheaded and barefaced'.[23]

THE EMERGENCE OF CONSUMER PROTECTION

1.10   As the facility for the recovery of costs developed, so too did the perception that lawyers had a tendency to abuse the system by excessive charging;[24] by the beginning of the seventeenth century the behaviour of some attorneys and solicitors was such that Parliament decided to impose a degree of state regulation,[25] this being in the form of the Attorneys Act 1605 (or, in the more expressive language of the day, an Act to 'reform the Multitudes and Misdemeanors of Attornies').[26] The mischief Parliament wished to regulate was identified in the following way:

> 'For that through the abuse of sundry attornies and solicitors by charging their clients with excessive fees and other unnecessary demands, such as were not, nor ought by them to have been employed or demanded, whereby the subjects grow to be overmuch burdened.'

It was enacted that attorneys and solicitors should obtain a 'ticket' (ie a receipt) for any fees paid to specified third parties, and that they must render a 'true bill' to their clients. Thus, the modern practice of delivering bills of costs supported by vouchers was born. The exercise of 'chancering' (ie, assessing) bills came into being.

---

[21]   See Blackstone, *Commentaries on the Laws of England* (a facsimile of the First Edition of 1765–1769 reprinted by the University of Chicago Press, 1979), Vol 3, pp 451–452; *Andrews v Barnes* (1888) 39 Ch D 133 at 138–139, per Fry LJ.

[22]   P Butt and R Castle *Modern Legal Drafting: A Guide to Using Clearer Language* (Cambridge University Press, 2nd edn, 2006), p 27.

[23]   *Mylward v Weldon* (1596) Tothill 102, 21 ER 136.

[24]   See Brooks, *Pettyfoggers and Vipers of the Commonwealth* (1986), pp 106, 138–140.

[25]   See W S Holdsworth *A History of English Law* (Methuen & Co, 3rd edn, 1923), vol III, p 392.

[26]   3 James I, CAP VII.

THE DEVELOPMENT OF COSTS FOR DEFENDANTS AND 'THE ENGLISH RULE'

1.11   In the meantime, there was a broadening of the spectrum of litigants who were able to benefit from an award of costs. Whilst claimants had been able to recover costs from defendants since the middle of the thirteenth century (see **1.4**), it was not until much later that provision was made for successful defendants. Limited provision was made in 1531 (that being limited to payment of costs in certain personal actions)[27] but it was not until the turn of the seventeenth century (ie, 1607) that general reciprocal provisions for defendants were made.[28] This was the emergence of two-way costs shifting. The system that the loser pays became so ingrained in the law of costs that it was said that it typified English costs law;[29] in the early seventeenth century, for example, Lord Coke commented that 'where costs are given the winner ought to be ordered to pay the loser's costs'[30] and similarly in the 1760 Blackstone made the following comments:[31]

'Thus much for judgments; to which costs are a necessary appendage; it being now as well the maxim of ours as of the civil law, that "victus victori in expensis condemnandus est".'

By the late nineteenth century the rule had reached a zenith in that in many cases a successful claimant could be deprived of costs only if there was 'good cause' to do so (which usually meant misconduct, omission or neglect on his part).[32] In so far as some types of litigation were concerned, that approach continued into the twentieth century.[33]

EARLY CONCEPTS OF PROPORTIONALITY AND AN AWARENESS OF WHAT WAS NOT 'COSTS'

1.12   In the early seventeenth century (and probably before this) judges began to interpret the relevant statutory law in such a way as to distinguish between 'costs' which were recoverable, and 'expenses' which were merely an incident of litigation. In 1628, for example, Lord Coke dealt with the distinction in this way:[34]

'Here [the Statute of Gloucester] is express mention made but of the costs of his writ, but it extendeth to all the legal cost of the suit, but not to the costs and expenses of his travel and loss of time, and therefore "costages" cometh of the verb "conster", and that again of the verb "constare", for these "costages" must "constare" to the court to be legal costs and expenses.'

---

[27]   23 Hen VIII c 15 *An Act that the Defendant shall recover Costs against the Plaintiff, if the Plaintiff be nonsuited, or if the Verdict pass against him*; see Bacon, *A New Abridgement of the Law* (7th edn, 1832), p 302.

[28]   4 James I, c 3, *Costs*. Those provisions were reciprocal in the sense that the defendant was able to recover costs only in those cases where the claimant would, if he had won, also have been able to recover costs: see Sayer, *The Law of Costs* (1768), p 68.

[29]   See the chapter entitled 'the English rule' in R Quick *Quick on Costs* (Thomson Reuters) at [2.30] *et seq*.

[30]   Coke *The Second Part of the Institutes of the Laws of England; Containing the Exposition of Many Ancient and Other Statutes*, p 289.

[31]   Blackstone, *Commentaries on the Laws of England* (a facsimile of the First Edition of 1765–1769 reprinted by the University of Chicago Press, 1979), Vol 3, p 399.

[32]   See *Jones v Curling* (1884) 13 QBD 262 at 265 and *Cooper v Whittingham* (1880) 15 Ch D 501 at 504; but see also *Forster v Farquhar* [1893] 1 QB 564.

[33]   In so far as copyright cases are concerned, see *W Savory Ltd v World of Golf Ltd* [1914] 2 Ch 566 at 571; more generaly, see Ord 65, r 1 up until the 1929 revision of the Rules of the Supreme Court.

[34]   *Institutes of the Laws of England; Containing the Exposition of Many Ancient and Other Statutes*, 2 Inst 288.

The distinction between what is and what is not 'costs' remains relevant today; indeed, Lord Coke's analysis is still occasionally cited.[35] The fact that there is no principle under English law of full recovery of the expenditure of the costs of litigation fashions costs policy even today.[36]

1.13 Returning to the chronology, by the seventeenth century the issue of disproportionate expenditure in litigation had become a concern, as had the inappropriate use of the courts in Westminster for cases for which the local courts were better suited. An Act was passed in 1601 limiting the recovery of costs by a method which took into account the value of the claim:[37] that Act provided that where a claim had been issued in Westminster, if less than 40 shillings was recovered, no greater amount could be recovered in costs. The restriction would apply only if the court certified that it should, however, and the reality was that this almost never happened; indeed, Gilbert B commented that the Act was 'pretty darkly penn'd and therefore I believe had very little or no effect'.[38] Successive Acts expanded the ambit of the rule to cover other cases[39]. Perhaps in response to the judicial apathy mentioned above, this was done in such a way as to change the requirement for a judicial certificate.[40] This did not have the effect it ought to have had, but the legislative intention to restrict costs was there, and the current Senior Costs Judge has commented (extrajudicially) that these provisions were the seventeenth century equivalent of the modern day fast-track case.[41]

FURTHER CONSUMER PROTECTION

1.14 The concept of a statutory right to a solicitor and client assessment (or 'taxation', as that procedure was then known) was the next significant development. Since long before statute intervened, the court had exercised an inherent jurisdiction over solicitors' costs as officers of the court,[42] but the first statute which contained provision for the court to order taxation of a solicitor's bill of costs was enacted in the early eighteenth century.[43] The solicitor was required to deliver a bill 'written in a common legible hand and in the English tongue (except law terms and names of writs) and in words at length[44] (except times and sums) which bill shall be subscribed with the proper hand of such attorney or solicitor respectively'.[45] The statutory right to an assessment represented a significant improvement in terms of consumer protection. One reason why this was progressive was because under the inherent jurisdiction the client was required to bring the amount of the disputed bill into court. A statutory assessment was possible without that money being brought into court.[46]

---

[35] See, for example, *McIlwraith v McIlwraith* [2005] EWHC 90010 (Costs) and the Irish case of *Dawson v Irish Brokers Association* [2002] IESC 36.

[36] See Sir Rupert Jackson's comments about the relatively recent 'myth' that clients are entitled to full costs recovery: R Jackson *A talk by Lord Justice Jackson to the Cambridge Law Faculty*, 5 September 2011 at p 5.

[37] 43 Eliz I c 6.

[38] *Reeves v Butler* (1726) Gilb Rep 195. See also Sayer, *The Law of Costs* (1768), p 12 and R Quick *Quick on Costs* (Thomson Reuters).

[39] Limitation Act 1623, s 6 (21 James I c 16) and then in 1670 22 & 23 Charles II, c 9, which in modern terminology would be known as the Duties on Law Proceedings Act 1670.

[40] See Sayer, *The Law of Costs* (1768), p 12 and R Quick *Quick on Costs* (Thomson Reuters).

[41] 'Going Round in Circles' CJQ 2006, 25 (Oct), pp 546–556.

[42] See the judgments of Lord Eldon LC in *Ex parte Earl of Uxbridge* (1801) 6 Ves 425 and of Lord Erskine LC in *Ex parte Arrowsmith* (1806) 13 Ves 124; see also *Chadwell v Bruer* (1728) 1 Barn KB 43.

[43] The Attorneys and Solicitors Act 1728 (2 Geo II, c 23).

[44] That is, not abbreviated.

[45] Solicitors Act 1728, s 23.

[46] See Solicitors Act 1728, s 23.

1.15 Provision was also made preventing a solicitor from bringing an action for his fees until after the expiration of one month or more from the delivery of his bill;[47] that provision has been repeated in subsequent Solicitors Acts, and survives today.

COSTS AS A SPECIALISM

1.16 The importance of costs as a distinct legal theme grew. One of the first textbooks on the topic (*Sayer's Law of Costs*) was published in 1768; this was the first of many.[48] In 1790 a man called Jefferson advised an aspiring lawyer that *Sayer's* was essential reading;[49] this was the same Jefferson who would later go on to become President of the United States. In 1792, Sir John Hullock published his *Law of Costs* which by 1796 had grown to be the *Law of Costs in Civil Actions and Criminal Proceedings*.

MORE COSTS, BETTER ASSESSMENTS AND GREATER CONSUMER PROTECTION

1.17 Despite all these developments, it continued to be the case that costs were recoverable only in certain types of claim. In 1797, the court broadened the array of cases in which costs were recoverable; this was done by finding that costs could be recovered by a successful claimant even in the absence of a specific statutory provision to that effect.[50] Interim costs orders also came into existence, this being as a result of the court exercising its inherent jurisdiction.[51]

1.18 In so far as costs between the parties were concerned, a system of awarding 'double' and 'treble' costs had developed.[52] This was in response to a perceived deficiency in the law that a litigant was not able to recover sufficient monies to compensate him for his reasonable expenditure. This system complemented a similar system of awarding multiple (ie, double or treble) damages.[53] The costs were awarded independently of the damages.[54] Not all costs awards were of multiple, however; not only did ordinary costs awards continue to be exist, but the Court of Chancery had developed a discretionary power to award costs as if they were between solicitor and client (this being the early forerunner of costs on the indemnity basis).[55]

1.19 Notwithstanding these seemingly modern concepts, the law of costs still lacked a coherent structure, and in particular, there continued to be uncertainty as to whether costs were an indemnity or a penalty. It was not unusual for costs to be awarded as if they were a penalty,[56] and at times, this worked in a sensible way that avoided the injustice arising out of what a modern-day lawyer would call a breach of the indemnity

---

[47] Attorneys and Solicitors Act 1728.
[48] See **3.52.**
[49] H Mews *Reader Instruction in Colleges and Universities: Teaching the Use of the Library* (Linnet Books, 1972).
[50] *Tyte v Globe* (1797) 7 TR 267.
[51] *Jones v Coxeter* (1742) 2 Atk 400.
[52] This topic is addressed in detail in R Quick *Quick on Costs* (Thomson Reuters) at [2.140].
[53] *Deacon v Morris* (1819) 2 B & Ald 393.
[54] Sayer, *The Law of Costs* (1768), p 195.
[55] *Andrews v Barnes* (1888) 39 Ch D 133 records the existnace of the power, and does so in such a way as to confirm that it existed at the time of abolition of the Court of Chancer by the Judicature Acts.
[56] See, for example, *Coan (Cone) v Bowles* (1690) 90 ER 709 and *Dibben v Cooke* (1698) 93 ER 998.

principle.[57] The fact that the court was able to award 'double' and 'treble' costs seemed naturally to lead to the conclusion that costs were penal rather than compensatory.[58] Sayer added his voice to those who supported the notion that costs were a penalty:[59]

> 'It is laid down in divers books, that every statute under which costs may be recovered is to be construed strictly; costs being a kind of penalty.'

Not everyone shared this view; in particular, Lord Mansfield said precisely the opposite, namely that costs were compensatory rather than in the nature of a penalty.[60] The dispute would not be resolved in the late nineteenth century. By that stage the number of statutes providing for multiple costs had become numerous.[61]

1.20   In the early nineteenth century there were concerns that litigation costs were getting out of control. This prompted Bentham to describe costs as 'the grand instrument of mischief in English practice'.[62] In 1828 those concerns prompted Lord Brougham to give a famously long speech – six hours – which was based on the premise that costs could be controlled by regulating lawyers' charges rather than restricting the recovery of costs:[63]

> '... How much nobler will be the Sovereign's [George IV] boast when he shall have it to say that he found law dear and left it cheap; found it a sealed book, left it a living letter; found it the patrimony of the rich, left it the inheritance of the poor; found it the two edged sword of craft and oppression, left it the staff of honesty and the shield of innocence.'

Lord Brougham's suggestions were not adopted by Parliament; instead, statutory provisions were made for assessing costs between opposing parties on a compensatory basis. In particular, the Limitation of Actions and Costs Act 1842[64] repealed provisions that allowed for payment of double costs, treble costs and costs as if between solicitor and client. In claims based on personal or local Acts, the 1842 Act made provision for party and party costs,[65] and in claims based on public Acts, it made provision for the following:[66]

> '[A] full and reasonable indemnity as to all costs, charges and expenses incurred in and about any action, suit or other legal proceeding, as shall be taxed by the proper officer in that behalf.'

Unsurprisingly, the law subsequently developed in such a way as to confirm that costs must be assessed in accordance with the indemnity principle.[67] In particular, it was realised that costs were not a penalty. There was uncertainty as to whether costs were an

---

57   *Richardson v Richardson* [1875] P 276 at 279: the recieving party was a pauper, and under the laws of the day this would have led to non-recovery of costs as compensation; the court avoided that restriction by awarding costs as a penalty.

58   See, for example, *Garnett v Bradley* [1878] 3 AC 944 at 957, per Lord Hatherley.

59   Sayer, *The Law of Costs* (1768), p 270; see R Quick *Quick on Costs* (Thomson Reuters) at [2.130].

60   *Ingle v Wordsworth* (1762) 97 ER 835, per Lord Mansfield.

61   See, for example, the description of the system in *Wilson v River Dun Navigation Co* (1839) 5 M & W 90.

62   Bentham, *Principles of Judicial Procedure* (1820–1827) as reprinted in Bowring (ed), *The Works of Jeremy Bentham*, Vol 7, p 111.

63   Brougham, *Hansard (NS)*, House of Commons, 7 February 1828, Vol 18.

64   Otherwise known as Pollock's Act of 1842 (5 & 6 Victoriae, c 97).

65   Limitation of Actions and Costs Act 1842, s 1.

66   Limitation of Actions and Costs Act 1842, s 2.

67   *Harold v Smith* (1865) H & N 381.

'indemnity' or whether they were just 'costs' (and whether there was a difference between these two), but Halsbury LC resolved that dispute by the expedient of finding that they were an indemnity as to costs.[68]

1.21   Along with the facility to assess costs between the parties came a need for sufficient judicial manpower to carry out those assessments; that need was addressed by the Court of Chancery Act 1842,[69] which created the posts of Taxing Masters (now referred to as Costs Judges). Taxing Masters of old obviously performed their duties well, because a few years later, the dramatist Herman Charles Merivale singled them out as being an 'exquisite and rational product of British law'.[70]

1.22   The Solicitors Act 1843 imposed for the first time a limit on the period of time during which a client may apply for an assessment of his costs, this being similar to the corresponding provisions in the modern day Solicitors Act 1974. It also introduced the one-fifth rule (or, as it was when first introduced, the one-sixth rule). That Act preserved the common law prohibition against conditional fee agreements.

1.23   It remained a concern that lawyers were producing overly long documents in order to enhance their fees (see **1.8**). In an attempt to deal with this problem, Parliament enacted various Acts including the Leases Act 1845, which provided[71] that fees should be based on 'not the Length of [the document in question], but only the Skill and Labour employed, and Responsibility incurred in the Preparation thereof.'

1.24   In stark contrast to the opinions of Merivale (**1.21**), from March 1852 to September 1853 Charles Dickens published his serialised novel *Bleak House*, which centred around the famous fictional case of *Jarndyce v Jarndyce;* that was a Chancery case that had droned on for so long that the original dispute had long since been forgotten and the lawyers – like 'maggots in nuts'[72] – fed upon the on-going wreckage of the costs. One would hope that Dickens overstated the malaise in the English legal system, but *Bleak House* certainly raised public awareness of the problems caused by inefficient legal practice, and it is possibly no coincidence that the in the late 1850s there were decisions aimed at increasing consumer protection. In particular, in 1857 it was determined that a bill ought to be drawn with a narrative sufficient to allow the client to know the fairness of the bill, to allow a solicitor to advise upon it, and the court to know the fairness of the items contained within.[73]

1.25   The Attorneys' and Solicitors' Act 1870 introduced the concept of agreements in writing (which were precursors of contentious and non-contentious business agreements). This provision permitted solicitors to agree terms of remuneration with their clients in such a way as to avoid the costs being assessed; such agreements were (and still are) subject to the scrutiny of the court.

---

[68]   *Reeve v Gibson* [1891] 1 QB 652 at 660.
[69]   5 & 6 Victoriae, c 103.
[70]   HC Merivale *Faucit Of Balliol* (1882), II.i.xvii.22.
[71]   At s 3.
[72]   Dickens C, *Bleak House*, Chapter 10.
[73]   *Haigh v Ousey* (1857) 7 E & B 578.

CONTENTIOUS AND NON-CONTENTIOUS WORK

1.26 In 1883, the Solicitors Remuneration Act 1881 impliedly brought about a statutory distinction between contentious and non-contentious work. This distinction was made because the Act related only to the following types of work, which were classified as being non-contentious:

> 'business connected with sales, purchases, leases, mortgages, settlements, and other matters of conveyancing, and in respect of other business not being business in any action, or transacted in any court, or in the chambers of any judge or master, and not being otherwise contentious business.'

The 1870 Act continued to govern contentious work.

CONSISTENCY BETWEEN THE COURTS AND THE 'PARTY AND PARTY' BASIS OF ASSESSMENT

1.27 In the meantime, the Judicature Acts of 1873 and 1875[74] had set up the Supreme Court of Judicature, and in doing so combined the administration of law and equity. The old courts, such as the Court of Chancery, were abolished, and two new courts, the Court of Appeal and the High Court, were created. The High Court was divided into divisions reflecting the old partition between common law and equity. The Court of Appeal had jurisdiction to hear a costs appeal on a discretionary issue only if the court below had granted permission.[75]

1.28 General rules of court were made shortly after the Supreme Court of Judicature was created, this being done by way of a schedule to the 1875 Act. This created the Supreme Court Rules. Those rules preserved aspects of the common law system (of allowing costs to the victor) and the equitable system (of costs being in the discretion of the judge but, where appropriate, with a presumption in favour of trustees: see **37.8**). Those rules were revised some years later when the General Order 1883 created the iconic 'Order 65', and in so doing introduced a scale of charges for some types of work. Scale costs were allowable on 'the lower scale' or 'the higher scale'; costs on the higher scale were allowed only if:

> 'On special grounds arising out of the nature and importance or the difficulty or urgency of the case the Judge ... so ordered.'

1.29 Where costs were to be assessed rather than fixed by reference to a scale, RSC Ord 65, r 29 provided that the appropriate measure was what was 'necessary and proper' for the attainment of justice:

> 'On every taxation the Taxing Master shall allow all such costs, charges and expenses as shall appear to him to have been necessary or proper for the attainment of justice or for defending the rights of any party, but save as against the party who incurred the same no costs shall be allowed which appear to the Taxing Master to have been incurred or increased through over

---

[74] Supreme Court of Judicature Act 1873 (36 & 37 Vict, c 66) and the Supreme Court of Judicature Act 1875 (38 & 39 Vict, c 77).

[75] See s 49 of the 1873 Act; the scope of this restriction was cut back the Court of Appeal taking a narror view as to what was 'discretionary' (see *Jones v Curling* (1884) 13 QBD 262 at 267 and 271).

caution, negligence or mistake or by payment of special fees to counsel or special charges or expenses to witnesses or other persons, or by other unusual expenses.'

This basis of assessment became known as the 'party and party' basis. That basis of assessment survived for over a century. It would seem, however, that costs practitioners of the time (who were unregulated) were not as familiar with the principles of assessment as perhaps they ought to have been; this much is apparent from the following extract from a case in which Chitty J made the following observations:[76]

> 'Very often neither counsel nor solicitors attend on the summons, but gentlemen come before me, subordinate clerks, who are not very competent to transact the business, and after a question or two as to the matters entrusted to them are found to be perfectly at sea, without rudder or compass.'

In any event, as is often the case when any new regime is introduced, there was a great deal of litigation concerning the interplay between the old and the new regime; specifically, there was much litigation concerning whether the provisions referred to in **1.13** and **1.18** (above) continued to play a role.[77]

FURTHER DEVELOPMENTS IN THE SOLICITORS ACTS AND ASSOCIATED LEGISLATION

1.30   The Rules of the Supreme Court (Solicitors' Remuneration) Rule 1920[78] sought to simplify matters by introducing a provision by which non-contentious work not covered by scale charges 'may at the option of the solicitor be by a gross sum in lieu of by detailed charges'. Thus, solicitors were permitted to render a gross sum bill in lieu of a bill containing detailed items. Before this, gross sum invoices existed, but they were not regarded as being statute bills.[79] The client's protection was preserved in that he could require that a bill containing detailed items of charges be delivered and assessed in lieu of the gross sum bill.

1.31   The Solicitors Act 1932 was a consolidating Act which was a precursor of the modern 1974 Act. The Solicitors' Remuneration (Gross Sum) Order 1934 repeated the option for the solicitor to charge by a gross sum in lieu of by detailed charges.

1.32   The 1920 Rules and 1934 Orders were revoked by the Solicitors Remuneration Order 1953,[80] which introduced two new concepts:

(1)   the remuneration certificate (or, rather, its 1950s' equivalent), and
(2)   a requirement to inform the client of the right to such a certificate.

The 1953 Order also introduced the 'fair and reasonable' basis for assessing costs. In particular, on any solicitor and client assessment of non-contentious costs it was the duty of the solicitor to satisfy the costs judge as to the fairness and reasonableness of his charges.

---

[76]   *Re Bethlehem and Bridewell Hospitals* (1885) 30 Ch D 542.
[77]   See R Quick *Quick on Costs* (Thomson Reuters) at [2.304]–[2.320].
[78]   SI 1920/683.
[79]   *Re Callis* (1901) 49 WR 316.
[80]   SI 1953/117.

1.33   The 1953 Order also provided that costs should be assessed with reference to certain prescribed factors (now, with biblical overtones,[81] known as 'the seven pillars of wisdom'); in order to deal with the perennial problem of overly long documents, express provision was made that non-contentious costs should be assessed by 'the number and importance of the documents prepared or perused, *without regard to length*' (emphasis added).

1.34   In 1955, Denning LJ observed that the distinction between contentious and non-contentious costs was in need of clarification.[82] Parliament duly responded by enacting the Solicitors (Amendment) Act 1956; this provided a statutory definition (albeit a somewhat circular one). A very similar definition survives in statutory form today.[83]

THE INTRODUCTION OF LEGAL AID

1.35   Legal aid in its modern form was introduced in 1949.[84] The need for legal aid came about because the number of practising solicitors fell during World War II,[85] and as a result there was insufficient capacity within the profession to carry out gratuitous work.[86] The responsibility for administering legal aid lay with the Law Society, although ultimately this responsibility was passed to the Legal Aid Board.[87] The legally aided person was afforded a degree of protection against costs orders being made against him.

DEVELOPMENTS IN THE MIDDLE OF THE TWENTIETH CENTURY

1.36   In 1959, changes were made to the party and party basis of assessment. The test of what was 'necessary and proper' was retained, but the breadth of the test was widened in the following way:[88]

> 'All such costs as were necessary or proper for the attainment of justice or for enforcing or defending the rights of the party whose costs are being taxed.'

Scale costs were also retained and fixed costs applied in certain circumstances.

1.37   In 1966, the Law Commission proposed that maintenance and champerty should be decriminalised; this was achieved in 1967.[89] At that stage the Law Commission continued to refuse to recommend making conditional fee agreements lawful,[90] but this had, at least, become a topic for discussion.

---

[81]   See Proverbs 9:1; the modern versions of the seven pillars are at CPR, r 44.5(3).
[82]   *In re a Solicitor* [1955] 2 QB 269.
[83]   See **5.17** onwards.
[84]   See the Legal Advice Act 1949.
[85]   From 17,000 in 1939 to 7,000 in 1944.
[86]   See Lord Rushcliffe's *Report of the Committee on Legal Aid and Legal Advice in England and Wales*, May 1944.
[87]   By the Legal Aid Act 1988.
[88]   RSC Ord 62, r 28(2).
[89]   See Criminal Law Act 1967, s 14(2).
[90]   *Proposals for Reform of the Law Relating to Champerty and Maintenance*, Law Com No 7 at para 19 and Law Commission *Sixth Annual Report 1970–1971* (Law Com No 47), pp 7–8, paras 33–35.

1.38 In response to calls for a wider availability of affordable legal advice,[91] the first publicly funded Law Centre was opened in 1970. The present Solicitors' Act was enacted in 1974.[92] The Association of Costs Lawyers (then known as the Association of Law Costs Draftsmen or 'ALCD') was established in 1977.

1.39 The party and party basis of assessment remained until 1986 when it was replaced by the standard basis of assessment;[93] this allowed recovery of 'a reasonable amount in respect of all costs reasonably incurred'. Costs on the indemnity basis were also possible. The reason for the change was because the perception was that costs on the party and party basis were too limited properly to compensate the receiving party for costs reasonably incurred. Scale charges were retained for a number of types of county court work.[94]

THE MODERN REGIME IN GENERAL

1.40 In 1988, the Report of the Review Body on Civil Justice suggested that the law of conditional fee agreements be reviewed[95] as attitudes towards them were beginning to change. In 1989, the political mood began to shift in favour of making conditional fee agreements lawful.[96] The relevant statutory provisions were swiftly made,[97] although it was some years before the requisite delegated legislation was made (see below).

1.41 The modern regime of solicitor and client assessments was ushered in by the Solicitors' (Non-Contentious Business) Remuneration Order 1994: this was (and, in its modern guise,[98] still is) similar to the 1953 Order, in that it provides that solicitors' costs were to be such sum as might be fair and reasonable to both solicitor and client. The client retained the right (recently revoked)[99] to a remuneration certificate; the solicitor retained the duty to inform his client of his rights to seek to obtain a remuneration certificate and to have the bill taxed.

1.42 In the early 1990s there was unease about the health of the civil litigation system in general and about its costs in particular.[100] The Lord Chancellor asked Lord Woolf to carry out a review of civil justice. In his Interim Report, Lord Woolf highlighted the problem of 'excessive and unaffordable costs' and of 'disproportionate costs'; he commented that 'the problem of costs is the most serious problem besetting our

---

91 Lord Chancellor's Advisory Committee on Legal Aid 1970.
92 Solicitors Act 1974.
93 See Rules of the Supreme Court (Amendment No 3) 1986 (SI 1986/2289).
94 CCR Ord 38, r 19(3).
95 (Cm 394), paras 384–389.
96 See the Lord Chancellor's Green Paper on *Contingency Fees* (1989) (Cm 571) and the White Paper, *Legal Services: A Framework for the Future* (1990) (Cm 740).
97 See s 58 of the Courts and Legal Services Act 1990 as originally enacted.
98 Solicitors (Non-Contentious Business) Remuneration Order 2009.
99 Ibid.
100 See, for example, Report of the General Council of the Bar and the Law Society of the United Kingdom *Civil Justice on Trial: The Case for Change* (1993).

litigation system'.[101] In his Final Report, Lord Woolf identified a number of objectives, including making costs more proportionate to the nature of the dispute, and making the amount of costs more predictable.[102]

1.43   Conditional fee agreements became a practical reality in 1995 when the necessary delegated legislation was made.[103] With certain limited exceptions, they were permitted only in personal injury work, insolvency and in cases before the European Commission of Human Rights.[104] In 1997, Lord Woolf's report was followed by a review of legal aid by the former banker Sir Peter Middleton, whose report recommended the wider implementation of conditional funding.[105] In 1998 legislation was enacted which effectively extended conditional funding to include all civil claims except family cases.[106] There was at that stage no provision for the recovery of a success fee from an unsuccessful opponent.

1.44   Lord Woolf's recommendations resulted in the introduction of the Civil Procedure Rules 1998 ('CPR') which became effective on 26 April 1999. The CPR retained the standard basis of assessment, but altered the way in which the costs were to be assessed; in particular, costs were to be the subject of a test of proportionality. The courts soon interpreted the CPR as encouraging a more liberal approach to the incidence of costs than had existed previously. Judges were encouraged not automatically to award the winner the entirety of his costs but to make separate orders which reflected the outcome of different issues.[107]

1.45   In April 2000, the statutory provisions relating to conditional fee agreements were amended to permit the recovery of success fees from unsuccessful opponents;[108] similar provisions were made for the recovery of after-the-event insurance premiums.[109] At about the same time, legal aid was, for all practical purposes, withdrawn for personal injury work (except clinical negligence), fatal accidents, and a whole swathe of other types of claim. This heralded a shift from public funding to conditional funding. The Legal Aid Board was replaced by the Legal Services Commission.[110]

1.46   In November 2000, collective conditional fee agreements became a reality.[111] These permitted unions (and similar bodies) to provide conditionally funded legal services to large numbers of clients.

---

[101]   Lord Woolf *Access to Justice, Interim Report to the Lord Chancellor on the civil justice system in England and Wales* (June 1995), chapter 3, paras 13–28.

[102]   Lord Woolf *Access to Justice, Final Report to the Lord Chancellor on the civil justice system in England and Wales* (July 1996), chapter 7.

[103]   See the Conditional Fee Agreements Regulations 1995 (SI 1995/1675) and the Conditional Fee Agreements Order 1995 (SI 1995/1674).

[104]   Conditional Fee Agreements Order 1995 (SI 1995/1674), art 2(1).

[105]   *Report to the Lord Chancellor by Sir Peter Middleton GCB*, September 1997, Executive Summary, para 10.

[106]   Conditional Fee Agreements Order 1998 (SI 1998/1860).

[107]   See *Phonographic Performance Limited v AEI Rediffusion Music Ltd* [1999] 1 WLR 1507 at 1522.

[108]   See the Conditional Fee Agreements Regulations 2000 (SI 2000/692) and the Conditional Fee Agreements Order 2000 (SI 2000/823).

[109]   See the Access to Justice Act 1999, s 29.

[110]   See the Access to Justice Act 1999, Part I.

[111]   See the Collective Conditional Fee Agreements Regulations 2000 (SI 2000/2988).

1.47   Provisions in 2003 introduced fixed fees for certain road traffic accidents.[112] Similar provisions were introduced in 2004 in relation to employers' liability claims and industrial disease claims.[113]

1.48   The regulations governing conditional fee agreements led to a surge in satellite litigation concerning costs. The result was the 'costs war' of the early 2000s.[114] In an attempt to bring it to an early end, simplified regulations were introduced for certain types of conditional fee agreement (ie 'CFAs Lite').[115] This did not have the impact that was intended, and in November 2005 the former regulations were revoked entirely.[116] Two years later, changes were made to the professional rules which govern solicitors; those changes made consumer protection in conditional funding a professional, rather than a regulatory, matter.[117] Whilst most practitioners would disagree, there are those who believe that the costs war is not yet over.[118]

1.49   In January 2009, the Master of the Rolls Sir Anthony Clarke appointed Sir Rupert Jackson to carry out a review of the rules and principles governing the costs of civil litigation. His final report was published in January 2010.[119] As was almost inevitable given the long history of costs, many of Jackson LJ's recommendations bore a resemblance to provisions which had gone before, but the overall regime was novel. As was almost inevitable given the long history of costs, many of Sir Rupert Jackson's recommendations bore a resemblance to provisions which had gone before, but the overall regime was novel. His reforms are addressed in Chapter 42.

1.50   Most of Sir Rupert Jackson's recommendations have historical pedigrees (some of which are remarkable for their antiquity). One way costs shifting,[120] for example, was the default position from about 1267 until 1606[121] and qualified one-way costs shifting was commonplace under the various public funding regimes, the first of which was first introduced in 1949.[122] A test of global proportionality[123] existed for several decades from 1670 (albeit in only limited circumstances),[124] and has cropped up from time to time in a number of different guises (some of which were rather curious, such as under the Slander of Women Act 1891).[125] Fixed costs[126] are the modern counterpart of scale charges, which were first introduced in 1883 (albeit initially for non-contentious work) and have existed in one guise or another right up until the introduction of the CPR.[127] Finally, Sir Rupert Jackson recommends success fees ought to be made irrecoverable between opposing parties;[128] that was the position between 1995 and 2000 (see **1.45**).

---

[112]   See CPR Part 45 III.
[113]   See CPR Part 45 IV and V.
[114]   The phrase 'costs war' was used by the Civil Justice Council in their Press Release, *Further Success for the Civil Justice Council – Helping to bring an end to the 'Costs War'*, October 2003; see also *Tankard v John Fredricks Plastics Ltd* [2008] EWCA Civ 1375 at [2].
[115]   Conditional Fee Agreements (Miscellaneous Amendments) Regulations 2003 (SI 2003/1240).
[116]   See the Conditional Fee Agreements (Revocation) Regulations 2005 (SI 2005/2305).
[117]   See rule 2 of the Solicitors' Code of Conduct 2007.
[118]   See, for example, (2008) 152 *Solicitors Journal* 16, pp 18–19.
[119]   R Jackson *Review of Civil Litigation Costs: Final Report* (TSO, 2009).
[120]   R Jackson *Review of Civil Litigation Costs: Final Report* (TSO, 2009), para 9.6.11.
[121]   See **1.11**.
[122]   See **1.39**.
[123]   R Jackson *Review of Civil Litigation Costs: Final Report* (TSO, 2009), para 3.6.1.
[124]   See **1.13**.
[125]   See **34.161**.
[126]   R Jackson *Review of Civil Litigation Costs: Final Report* (TSO, 2009), para 15.7.1.
[127]   Albeit only in the county courts: see **1.39**.
[128]   R Jackson *Review of Civil Litigation Costs: Final Report* (TSO, 2009), para 10.6.1.

1.51   Thus, the process of gradual evolution and reinvention which was mentioned in the opening paragraph of this chapter continues unabated and, it is to be hoped, to the benefit of everyone.

Chapter 2

THE LANGUAGE OF COSTS

COSTS TERMINOLOGY IN GENERAL

2.1   In the same way that costs regimes have a habit of reinventing themselves (see **1.1**), the language of costs has repeatedly has undergone stylistic changes: time after time, old wine has been decanted into new bottles bearing elegant new labels. Whilst the use of obsolete terminology is to be discouraged, echoes of expired terminology linger on, and the result is that it is often necessary to know the wine by both its old and new labels.

2.2   Whilst purists will object, modern nomenclature is used throughout this book regardless of whether the authorities referred to predate the CPR. Where appropriate, the expired terminology is also given (usually in the footnotes); this is particularly the case where the old terminology is still frequently still in use.

2.3   For obvious reasons, it is preferable to use modern terminology where it exists. Occasionally, however, a supposedly expired term will have no modern counterpart; an example is the vocabulary used to describe the anatomy of a bill of costs (such as 'the chronology'). Where no modern equivalent exists, this book has embraced the use of the supposedly expired term. It is a matter for the individual to decide whether or not to do the same.

2.4   Some phrases mean more than the sum total of their words and are best regarded as being terms of art. Examples include the phrases 'genuine issue'[1] (see **11.28**) and 'material breach'[2] (see **9.80**). Other phrases draw upon the name of the case which was seminal in the relevant area of the law, such as 'the *Bailey* presumption' (see **11.26**) and 'the *Pamplin* procedure' (see **24.28**). Such phrases are best described in context, so they are, on the whole, addressed in the main text rather than in this chapter.

CITATION OF COSTS AUTHORITIES

2.5   The remainder of this chapter is a 'costs lexicon' but, before that list begins, it is worth dealing with two topics concerning citation which are prone to cause confusion. The first is the nomenclature of the Costs Practice Direction ('CPD'), and the second is the use of neutral citation to refer to the decisions of costs judges.

---

[1]   This being a phrase which is often used as shorthand for the standard of evidence which is required to rebut a certain presumption concerning the weight that can be afforded to the certificate to a bill: see *Hazlett v Sefton Metropolitan Borough Council* [2000] 4 All ER 887.

[2]   This is a phrase which refers to a process whereby breaches of certain regulations which do not matter are distinguished from those which do matter: see *Hollins v Russell* [2003] EWCA Civ 718 at [221], per Brooke LJ.

The CPD

2.6   Unlike other practice directions, the practice directions on costs are not
designated 'Practice Direction 43', 'Practice Direction 44', etc. Instead, they exist as a
single 'Costs Practice Direction' (ie the CPD) which is comprises parts that are named
according to their collocation with the CPR Parts 43 to 48; thus, the practice direction
to CPR Part 47 is 'the Costs Practice Direction supplementing Part 47' rather than 'PD
47'.[3] Confusingly, the article numbers do not begin afresh with each new Part; instead,
they roll over from the previous Part. This means, for example, that the Practice
Direction supplementing Part 47 does not begin at art 1.1, but at art 28.1. It is often
easier (and clearer) to refer to a paragraph solely by article number (such as CPD,
art 40.10) rather than also by reference to the Part of the CPR to which it relates. In
order to avoid confusion, that is the convention which is used in this book, but other
methods of citation exist and will be encountered from time to time. Finally, the word
'article' is used to refer to the provisions in the CPD; this nomenclature is acceptable and
has been adopted to avoid confusion with provisions in the CPR. In practice, however,
the words 'paragraph' or 'direction' are more commonly used.

Neutral citation

2.7   A topic which often causes confusion is neutral citation of costs reports in the
Senior Courts Costs Office. The official neutral citation system was introduced in
January 2001[4] and operates for judgments in the Supreme Court, Privy Council, Court
of Appeal and all divisions of the High Court. Costs judgments from Costs Judges in
the Senior Courts Costs Office are often afforded a similar citation (such as '[2006]
EWHC 90052 (Costs)'). This citation is not official, but is promulgated by respected
sources such as BAILII;[5] the fact that a case bears a citation of 'EWHC' does not mean
that the case has been heard by a High Court judge, nor does it mean that a case has
been heard on appeal. Indeed, often the case will be a county court case. On a related
note, it should not be forgotten that where cases are to be cited in court, neutral citation
should not be used in preference to reported citation. In this regard, the requirements of
Practice Direction: Citation of Authorities [2012] 1 WLR 780[6] apply just as much to
costs litigation as they do to other legal disciplines. The relevant directions are set out in
the footnotes.[7]

---

[3]   See CPD, art 1.1; for an example of this terminology in practice, see *Gower Chemicals Group Litigation*
      [2008] EWHC 735 (QB) at [1].
[4]   *Practice Direction (Judgments: Form and Citation)* [2001] 1 WLR 194, issued on 11 January 2001.
[5]   The British and Irish Legal Information Institute.
[6]   Revoking *Practice Notes on Citation of Authorities (Court of Appeal) (Civil Division)* [1995] 1 WLR 1096
      and [1996] 1 WLR 854.
[7]   '6. Where a judgment is reported in the Official Law Reports (A.C., Q.B., Ch., Fam.) published by the
      Incorporated Council of Law Reporting for England and Wales, that report must be cited. These are the
      most authoritative reports; they contain a summary of the argument. Other series of reports and official
      transcripts of judgment may only be used when a case is not reported in the Official Law Reports. 7. If a
      judgment is not (or not yet) reported in the Official Law Reports but it is reported in the Weekly Law
      Reports (W.L.R.) or the All England Law Reports (All ER) that report should be cited. If the case is
      reported in both the W.L.R. and the All ER either report may properly be cited. 8. If a judgment is not
      reported in the Official Law Reports, the W.L.R, or the All ER, but it is reported in any of the authoritative
      specialist series of reports which contain a headnote and are made by individuals holding a Senior Courts
      qualification (for the purposes of section 115 of the Courts and Legal Services Act 1990), the specialist
      report should be cited. 9. Where a judgment is not reported in any of the reports referred to in
      paragraphs [6] to [8] above, but is reported in other reports, they may be cited. 10. Where a judgment has not
      been reported, reference may be made to the official transcript if that is available, not the handed-down text
      of the judgment, as this may have been subject to late revision after the text was handed down. Official

COSTS LEXICON

2.8   This lexicon lists costs vocabulary in alphabetical order. Many of the definitions are taken from CPR, r 43.2(1), which provides a list of essential definitions under the CPR; this lexicon includes all those definitions. It also includes a number of relevant common law definitions and definitions contained within relevant primary and delegated legislation. Where a term is in common usage but no such authoritative definition exists, a non-authoritative descriptive definition is given.

Acting as a solicitor

2.9   The phrase 'acting as a solicitor' is to be read as being limited to 'the doing of acts which only a solicitor may perform'.[8]

Additional liability

2.10   The phrase 'additional liability' is defined by CPR, r 43.2(o):

> '"Additional liability" means the percentage increase, the insurance premium, or the additional amount in respect of provision made by a membership organisation, as the case may be.'

2.11   CPR, r 43.2(l) and (m) provide the following additional guidance:

> '"Percentage increase" means the percentage by which the amount of a legal representative's fee can be increased in accordance with a conditional fee agreement which provides for a success fee; [and]
>
> "Insurance premium" means a sum of money paid or payable for insurance against the risk of incurring a costs liability in the proceedings, taken out after the event that is the subject matter of the claim.'

Admissible offer

2.12   An admissible offer is an offer to settle (which has usually been made without prejudice save as to costs) which is not an offer to which costs consequences under Part 36 apply and which is capable of being drawn to the court's attention.[9]

Advocacy services

2.13   Section 190(6) of the Legal Services Act 2007 (as amended) defines advocacy services in the following way:

> '"Advocacy services" means any services which it would be reasonable to expect a person who is exercising, or contemplating exercising, a right of audience in relation to any proceedings, or contemplated proceedings, to provide.'

The same words were used for the definition under the Courts and Legal Services Act 1990 (as amended).[10]

---

transcripts may be obtained from, for instance, BAILLI (http://www.bailii.org/). An unreported case should not usually be cited unless it contains a relevant statement of legal principle not found in reported authority.'

[8]   *Piper Double Glazing Ltd v DC Contracts* [1994] 1 WLR 777 at 786; this analysis was approved by Phillips MR in *R v Secretary of State for Transport ex p Factortame* [2002] EWCA Civ 932 at [26].

[9]   See CPR, r 44.3(4)(c).

[10]   Section 119(1) of the Courts and Legal Services Act 1990 (as amended).

After the event (ATE) insurance

2.14   ATE insurance is legal expenses insurance which is incepted after the event giving rise to the claim; it is usually specific to a single claim. It is to be distinguished from before the event (BTE) insurance (see **2.27**).

2.15   Whilst there is no statutory definition of ATE insurance, s 29 of the Access to Justice Act 1999 reads as follows:

> 'Where in any proceedings a costs order is made in favour of any party who has taken out an insurance policy against the risk of incurring a liability in those proceedings, the costs payable to him may ... include costs in respect of the premium of the policy.'

After the event (ATE) premium

2.16   An ATE premium is the premium payable under an ATE policy. On at least two occasions the Court of Appeal has approved of the following definition of a premium in the context of ATE insurance:[11]

> 'The consideration required of the assured in return for which the insurer undertakes his obligation under the contract of insurance.'

See also the definition of insurance premium at **2.65**.

Appropriate authorised body

2.17   See the definition of 'authorised body' at **2.24**.

Assisted person

2.18   Broadly speaking, an assisted person is a person who is in receipt of Legal Aid; this is to be distinguished from an LSC funded client (which is often truncated to just 'funded client') who is a person in receipt of CLS funding. In this regard, CPR, r 43.3(h) and (i) provide as follows:

> '"assisted person" means an assisted person within the statutory provisions relating to legal aid [and an] "LSC funded client" means an individual who receives services funded by the Legal Services Commission as part of the Community Legal Service within the meaning of Part I of the Access to Justice Act 1999.'

The definition of 'rights of audience' gives further details (see **2.98**). An authorised advocate should be distinguished from an authorised litigator (see **2.22–2.23**).

Authorised advocate

2.19   Up to 1 January 2010,[12] s 119(1) of the Courts and Legal Services Act 1990 (as amended) defined an authorised advocate in the following way:

> '"authorised advocate" means any person (including a barrister or solicitor) who has a right of audience granted by an authorised body in accordance with the provisions of this Act.'

---

[11]   Taken from *MacGillivray on Insurance Law* (9th edn, 1997), and approved of in *Claims Direct Litigation* [2003] EWCA Civ 136 at [25] and *The Accident Group Test Cases* [2004] EWCA Civ 575 at [17].

[12]   A complex timetable existed for commencement of the new Act: see **5.35**.

An authorised advocate should be distinguished from an authorised litigator. In any event, both of these terms have now been superseded by the term 'authorised person' (see **2.25**).

Authorised court officers

2.20   Despite the fact that they are often referred to as costs officers, the correct phrase is authorised *court* officer. An authorised court officer is a costs officer, but the reverse is not necessarily true (see **2.39**).

2.21   An authorised court officer is defined by CPR, r 43.2(d):

> '"Authorised court officer" means any officer of—
>
> > (i)   a county court;
> > (ii)   a district registry;
> > (iii) the Principal Registry of the Family Division; or
> > (iv)   the Costs Office, whom the Lord Chancellor has authorised to assess costs.'

Authorised litigator

2.22   As of 1 January 2010[13] this term has been superseded by the term 'authorised person' (see **2.25**), but prior to that date, s 119(1) of the Courts and Legal Services Act 1990 (as amended) defined an authorised litigator:

> '"Authorised litigator" means any person (including a solicitor) who has a right to conduct litigation granted by an authorised body in accordance with the provisions of this Act.'

2.23   Whilst not an exhaustive list, authorised litigators included the following: solicitors; Fellows of the Institute of Legal Executives; barristers; costs lawyers;[14] trade mark attorneys;[15] and officers of the Children and Family Court Advisory and Support Service.[16]

Authorised body and appropriate authorised body

2.24   As of 1 January 2010[17] this term has been superseded by the term 'relevant approved regulator'; prior to this date, s 119(1) of the Courts and Legal Services Act 1990 (as amended) provided the following definitions:

> '"Authorised body" and "appropriate authorised body"—
>
> > (a)   in relation to any right of audience or proposed right of audience, have the meanings given in section 27 [of the Courts and Legal Services Act 1990]; and
> > (b)   in relation to any right to conduct litigation or proposed right to conduct litigation, have the meanings given in section 28 [of that Act].'

For further details, see the definitions of 'right of audience' at **2.98** and 'authorised litigator' at **2.22–2.23**.

---

[13]   A complex timetable existed for commencement of the new Act: see **5.35**.
[14]   See the Association of Law Costs Draftsmen Order 2006 (SI 2006/333), art 3.
[15]   See the Institute of Trade Mark Attorneys Order 2005 (SI 2005/240), art 2.
[16]   See the Criminal Justice and Court Services Act 2000, s 15.
[17]   A complex timetable existed for commencement of the new Act: see **5.35**.

Authorised person

2.25   In the context of costs litigation the term 'authorised person' is generally a reference to the use of that phrase as contemplated by the Legal Services Act 2007. Section 18 of that Act defines an authorised person in these terms:

> '(1)   For the purposes of this Act "authorised person", in relation to an activity ("the relevant activity") which is a reserved legal activity, means—
>
> > (a)   a person who is authorised to carry on the relevant activity by a relevant approved regulator in relation to the relevant activity (other than by virtue of a licence under Part 5), or
> >
> > (b)   a licensable body which, by virtue of such a licence, is authorised to carry on the relevant activity by a licensing authority in relation to the reserved legal activity.'

Base costs

2.26   The CPD defines base costs in the following way (CPD, art 2.2):

> '"[B]ase costs" means costs other than the amount of any additional liability.'

The term 'basic costs' is also often used to mean the same thing.

Before the event (BTE) insurance/premium

2.27   BTE insurance is legal expenses insurance which is incepted before the event giving rise to the claim. It is to be distinguished from after the event (ATE) insurance (see **2.14**).

Bullock order

2.28   A *Bullock* order is a co-defendant order whereby the claimant is to pay the successful defendant's costs, but he is permitted to add those costs to the costs to be recovered from the unsuccessful defendant (see **7.27** *et seq*). It is named after *Bullock v London General Omnibus Co.*[18] It is also known as an indirect co-defendant order (cf direct co-defendant orders: see **2.100**).

Central funds

2.29   Schedule 1 of the Interpretation Act 1978 provides as follows:

> '"Central funds", in an enactment providing in relation to England and Wales for the payment of costs out of central funds, means money provided by Parliament.'

The reference to central funds is not the same as the Legal Aid Fund/CLS Fund; central funds rarely have any relevance to civil costs.

CFA Lite

2.30   See **9.9**.

---

[18]   [1907] 1 KB 264.

Collective conditional fee agreements

2.31   The now revoked Collective Conditional Fee Agreements Regulations 2000 defined a collective conditional fee agreement in the following way:

> 3.(1)   ... a collective conditional fee agreement is an agreement which—
>
> (a)   disregarding section 58(3)(c) of the Courts and Legal Services Act 1990, would be a conditional fee agreement; and
> (b)   does not refer to specific proceedings, but provides for fees to be payable on a common basis in relation to a class of proceedings, or, if it refers to more than one class of proceedings, on a common basis in relation to each class.

Although this definition no longer has legislative force, it continues to be used for the purposes of describing what is (and what is not) a collective conditional fee agreement. That said, the term is also now used to mean any form of conditional fee agreement where the detail is consigned to a separate document containing terms and conditions; to that extent, the expired regulatory definition is becoming less relevant.

Conditional fee agreements and collective conditional fee agreements

2.32   Section 58(2)(a) of the Courts and Legal Services Act 1990 (as amended) provides the following definition:

> '[A] conditional fee agreement is an agreement with a person providing advocacy or litigation services which provides for his fees and expenses, or any part of them, to be payable only in specified circumstances.'

Conditional retainer

2.33   See **9.36**.

Contentious business

2.34   Section 87 of the Solicitors Act 1974 defines contentious business as being:[19]

> 'Business done, whether as solicitor or advocate in or for the purpose of proceedings begun before a court or before an arbitrator ... not being business which falls within the definition of non-contentious or common form probate business[20] contained in section 128 of the Senior Courts Act 1981.'

2.35   The following clarification was given by Wynn-Parry J:[21]

> 'There is now a clear and, I should have thought, logical division between contentious and non-contentious business. All business is now to be regarded as contentious which is done before proceedings are begun provided that the business is done with a view to the proceedings being begun, and they are in fact begun, and also all business done in the course of the proceedings. All other business is non-contentious.'

A more detailed discussion of this definition may be found at **5.17–5.26**.

---

[19]   Section 87 of the Solicitors Act 1974.
[20]   Common form probate business of the type contained in s 128 of the Senior Courts Act 1981 relates to obtaining probate and administration where there is no contention as to the rights to probate.
[21]   *In re Simpkin Marshall Ltd* [1959] Ch 229 at 235.

Contentious business agreement

2.36   See **8.140**.

Contingency fee agreement

2.37   See **9.35**.

Costs

2.38   The word 'costs' is defined at CPR, r 43.2(1)(a) as including:

> 'fees, charges, disbursements, expenses, remuneration, reimbursement allowed to a litigant in person under rule 48.6, any additional liability incurred under a funding arrangement and any fee or reward charged by a lay representative for acting on behalf of a party in proceedings allocated to the small claims track.'

CPR, r 43.2 uses the word 'includes' to introduce this list; it does not, therefore, hold itself out as an exhaustive list.

Costs officers

2.39   The term 'costs officer' is a generic term which includes costs judges, district judges and authorised court officers. In this regard, CPR, r 43.2(1)(c) provides as follows:

> '"[C]osts officer" means—
>
> (i)   a costs judge;
> (ii)   a district judge; and
> (iii) an authorised court officer ...'

Costs judge

2.40   A costs judge is defined by CPR, r 43.2(b) as being a 'taxing master of the Senior Court' (see **21.71–21.73**). Since November 2005 there have been 'regional costs judges', who are district judges appointed to hear detailed assessment of bills of costs that fall within certain criteria (see **21.74–21.76**).

Costs Office

2.41   CPR, r 43.2(b) provides that 'Costs Office' means the Senior Courts Costs Office (which until October 2009 was known as the Supreme Court Costs Office).

Court

2.42   The Legal Services Act 2007 defines 'court' in the following way:

> '"court" includes—
>
> (a)   a tribunal that is (to any extent) a listed tribunal for, or for any of, the purposes of Schedule 7 to the Tribunals, Courts and Enforcement Act 2007 (functions etc of Administrative Justice and Tribunals Council);
> (b)   a court-martial;

(c)   a statutory inquiry within the meaning of section 16(1) of the Tribunals and Inquiries Act 1992 (c. 53);

(d)   an ecclesiastical court (including the Court of Faculties).'

Damages-based agreement (or damages-based conditional fee agreement)

2.43   See **9.20**.

Deemed orders

2.44   Deemed orders are orders which are deemed to be made on the happening of a specified event. They will arise in the following circumstances (see **7.74–7.98**):

- where a party allows court fees to remain unpaid after having been given notice to pay by the court;
- where a party accepts a Part 36 offer;
- where a party discontinues a claim; and
- where the court makes no order for costs in relation to a limited range of applications.

Default costs certificate

2.45   A default costs certificate is a costs certificate which is issued in default of a paying party not serving points of dispute (see **21.114**).

Detailed assessment

2.46   CPR, r 43.4 gives the following definition:

'"Detailed assessment" means the procedure by which the amount of costs is decided by a costs officer in accordance with Part 47.'

Detailed bill

2.47   A detailed bill is a statute bill (rendered to a client) which contains detailed items (see s 64(1) of the Solicitors Act 1974). It should be distinguished from a detailed breakdown (see **2.48**).

Detailed breakdown

2.48   In the context of costs between solicitor and client, a detailed breakdown is a document containing particulars of the costs which have already been claimed in a gross sum bill (see s 64(4) of the Solicitors Act 1974). It should not be confused with a detailed bill (see **2.47**).

Disbursement

2.49   See **31.1**.

Discounted conditional fee agreement

2.50 See **9.12**.

Final costs certificate

2.51 A final costs certificate is a document which states the amount of costs which have been assessed and, unless the court orders otherwise, will include an order to pay the costs to which it relates (see CPR, r 47.16(5)).

Fixed costs, fixed recoverable costs, etc

2.52 In idiomatic usage, the term 'fixed costs' is frequently used to refer to any or all of the costs regimes in CPR Parts 45 and 46. This usage is inaccurate; the term 'fixed costs' is highly specific, as is made clear by CPR, r 43.2(j):

> '"Fixed costs" means the amounts which are to be allowed in respect of solicitors' charges in the circumstances set out in Section I of Part 45.'

2.53 CPR Part 45 I pertains to a narrow category of costs which will apply when certain claims for specified sums are disposed of at the outset of proceedings; therefore, the term 'fixed costs' does not encompass fast track trial costs (allowable under CPR Part 46), fixed recoverable costs (allowable under CPR Part 45 II), or fixed percentage increases (or success fees) allowable under CPR Parts 45 III–V. It is a term which applies to fixed commencement costs (CPR, rr 45.2, 45.2A and 45.3), fixed costs on entry of judgment (CPR, rr 45.4 and 45.4A), miscellaneous fixed costs (CPR, r 45.5) and fixed enforcement costs (CPR, r 45.6).

2.54 The following terms are commonly used for describing the individual costs regimes referred to above:

- 'fixed recoverable costs' for costs allowable under CPR Part 45 II; these costs are often also referred to as 'fixed predictable costs';
- 'fixed percentage increases' (or 'fixed success fees') for costs allowable under CPR Parts 45 III–V; and
- 'fast track trial costs' for costs allowable under CPR, r 46.2.

Forthwith order

2.55 A forthwith order is an order made prior to the conclusion of proceedings for the purposes of allowing a party's costs to be assessed notwithstanding the general rule (in CPR, r 47.1) that the costs of any proceedings are not to be assessed by the detailed procedure until the conclusion of the proceedings.

Fund

2.56 The word 'fund' is defined by CPR, r 43.2(e) in the following way:

> '"Fund" includes any estate or property held for the benefit of any person or class of person and any fund to which a trustee or personal representative is entitled in his capacity.'

2.57 The word 'fund' is often also used to mean the Legal Aid Fund or the CLS Fund.

Funder

2.58   Save where the context suggests otherwise, the word 'funder' has nothing to do with a 'fund'. It is usually used to refer to a third party who has funded litigation (see **7.171–7.180** and **41.1**). Since 2000 the word has been defined (for certain purposes) in s 58B of the Courts and Legal Services Act 1990 (as amended) in the following way:

> '[A] person ("the funder") agrees to fund (in whole or in part) the provision of advocacy or litigation services (by someone other than the funder) to another person ("the litigant").'

2.59   The now revoked Collective Conditional Fee Agreements Regulations 2000 defined 'funder' in this way:[22]

> '"Funder" means the party to a collective conditional fee agreement who, under that agreement, is liable to pay the legal representative's fees.'

Funding arrangement

2.60   CPR, r 43.2(k) provides the following definition:

> '"Funding arrangement" means an arrangement where a person has—
>
> (i)   entered into a conditional fee agreement or a collective conditional fee agreement which provides for a success fee within the meaning of section 58(2) of the Courts and Legal Services Act 1990;
> (ii)   taken out an insurance policy to which section 29 of the Access to Justice Act 1999 (recovery of insurance premiums by way of costs) applies; or
> (iii) made an agreement with a membership organisation to meet his legal costs.'

2.61   Paradoxically (and unhelpfully), the term 'funding arrangement' has also taken on a colloquial meaning, namely: any arrangement relating to funding. It is perhaps because of this that real funding agreements are tautologically referred to as 'funding agreements within the meaning of CPR, r 43.2(k)'.

2.62   A funding arrangement should not be confused with a litigation funding agreement, which is the preferred name for what used to be called a third-party funding agreement; nor is it to be confused with that specific type of third-party funding as described by s 58B of the Courts and Legal Services Act 1990 (which is not yet in force) (see **2.71**).

Funded client

2.63   See 'assisted person' at **2.18**.

Gross sum bill

2.64   A gross sum bill is a statute bill which lacks detailed items (see s 64(1) of the Solicitors Act 1974); it is a term which is used only in relation to contentious business.

Insurance premium

2.65   In the context of costs, a reference to an insurance premium is usually a reference to an after the event insurance premium: see **2.14–2.15**. A detailed discussion of what is

---

[22]   At reg 1(2).

and is not insurance is beyond the scope of this book, but the following is generally accepted as outlining the requisite constituents:[23]

> 'The payment of one or more sums of money, commonly called premiums, by one party ("the policyholder"). In return for these payments the other party ("the insurer") undertakes to pay a sum of money on the happening of a specified event ... The event must be one which is adverse to the interests of the policyholder.'

There are circumstances where this definition would need modification,[24] but they would rarely be relevant in the context of the law of costs.

Indemnity basis

2.66   The indemnity basis is a basis of assessment by which the court will resolve any doubt as to whether the costs were reasonably incurred or were reasonable in amount in favour of the receiving party[25] (see **13.2–13.8**); under the CPR, the costs would not be subjected to a test of proportionality.

Interim costs certificate

2.67   An interim costs certificate is a certificate containing an order for an interim payment of costs; it is made after the receiving party has filed a request for a detailed assessment hearing[26] (see **21.284** *et seq*). It should be distinguished from an order for a payment on account (see **21.267** *et seq*).

Interim statute bill

2.68   An interim statute bill is a statute bill which is rendered prior to the conclusion of the retainer (see **17.5–17.8**). It should be distinguished from a request for payment on account (see **17.9**).

Legal representative (for the purposes of the CPR)

2.69   The CPR often refers to 'legal representatives' rather than solicitors. The term 'legal representative' is defined by CPR, r 2.3(1) as meaning:

> 'A barrister or a solicitor, solicitor's employee or other authorised litigator (as defined in the Courts and Legal Services Act 1990) who has been instructed to act for a party in relation to a claim.'

This is the definition used for the purposes of the CPR; other definitions may be appropriate for other purposes.

---

[23]   *Prudential Insurance Co v IRC* [1904] 2 KB 658, per Channell J.
[24]   The most obvious being that in contingency policies (such as life assurance) there is no requirement that the event be adverse to the interest of the policyholder.
[25]   See CPR, r 44.4(3).
[26]   See CPR, r 47.15.

Legal activities

2.70 The Legal Services Act 2007 (as amended) defines 'legal activities' in the following way:[27]

'(3) In this Act "legal activity" means—

    (a)   an activity which is a reserved legal activity within the meaning of this Act as originally enacted, and

    (b)   any other activity which consists of one or both of the following—

        (i)   the provision of legal advice or assistance in connection with the application of the law or with any form of resolution of legal disputes; .

        (ii)   the provision of representation in connection with any matter concerning the application of the law or any form of resolution of legal disputes.'

(4) But "legal activity" does not include any activity of a judicial or quasi-judicial nature (including acting as a mediator).

Litigation funding agreement

2.71 Section 58B(2) of the Courts and Legal Services Act 1990 (as amended) defines a litigation funding agreement:

'For the purposes of this section a litigation funding agreement is an agreement under which—

    (a)   a person ("the funder") agrees to fund (in whole or in part) the provision of advocacy or litigation services (by someone other than the funder) to another person ("the litigant"); and

    (b)   the litigant agrees to pay a sum to the funder in specified circumstances.'

The phrase 'litigation funding agreement' is now used to refer to any third-party funding agreement regardless of whether it falls within the ambit of this definition. In any event, at the time of writing s 58B was not in force.

Litigation services

2.72 Section 190(6) of the Legal Services Act 2007 (as amended) provides as follows:

'"litigation services" means any services which it would be reasonable to expect a person who is exercising, or contemplating exercising, a right to conduct litigation in relation to any proceedings, or contemplated proceedings, to provide.'

The same definition was used in the legislation that preceded that Act.[28]

LSC funded client

2.73 See 'assisted person' at **2.18**.

Membership organisation

2.74 CPR, r 43.3(n) provides the following definition:

'"Membership organisation" means a body prescribed for the purposes of section 30 of the

---

[27]   Legal Services Act 2007, ss 12(3) and (4); the definition does not include any activity of a judicial or quasi-judicial nature (including acting as a mediator): see s 12(4).

[28]   Section 119(1) of the Courts and Legal Services Act 1990 (as amended).

Access to Justice Act 1999 (recovery where body undertakes to meet costs liabilities).'

This definition has nothing to do with collective conditional fee agreements.

Non-contentious business

2.75   Non-contentious business is defined as being:[29]

> 'Any business done as a solicitor which is not contentious business as defined by this subsection.'

The definition of contentious business is addressed at **2.34–2.35**, and a more detailed discussion of the topic may be found at **5.16–5.27**.

Non-contentious business agreement

2.76   See **8.121**.

Non-party costs order

2.77   Non-party costs orders are orders against persons who are not parties to the litigation, but who are in some way connected to it. The term 'third-party costs order' is also used. An archetypal example is where an order is made against a non-party director who has used his party company for his own purposes (see **7.136** *et seq*).

Notional premium

2.78   CPR, r 43.2(o) refers to the additional amount payable to a membership organisation pursuant to s 30 of the Access to Justice Act 1999. The term 'notional premium' is gaining currency for the purpose of describing such monies.

Paying party

2.79   CPR, r 43.2(g) provides the following definition:

> '"paying party" means a party liable to pay costs.'

Payment on account

2.80   CPR, r 44.3(8) provides that where the court has ordered a party to pay costs, it may order an amount to be paid on account before the costs are assessed; a payment made pursuant to that power is a payment on account. It should be distinguished from a payment made pursuant to an interim costs certificate (see **2.67**, **21.267** *et seq* and **21.284** *et seq*).

Percentage increase

2.81   CPR, r 43.2(l) and (m) provide the following definition:[30]

---

[29]   See s 87 of the Solicitors Act 1974; Ward LJ described the definition as a 'fairly useless circular definition' in *Garry v Gwillim* [2002] EWCA Civ 1500.

[30]   A very similar definition existed in reg 3(3) of the now revoked Conditional Fee Agreements Regulations 2000: see **9.42**.

'"Percentage increase" means the percentage by which the amount of a legal representative's fee can be increased in accordance with a conditional fee agreement which provides for a success fee.'

Thus, the percentage increase is the correct term for a success fee expressed as a percentage uplift. Whilst strictly a misnomer, the term 'success fee' (see **2.103**) is almost universally used in preference; it would not be an exaggeration to say that the correct term is used so infrequently as to be close to falling out of the ordinary costs idiom.

Porrect

2.82 This is an ancient but useful word that, in a modern context, means to put forward or submit a bill of costs for examination or correction;[31] a receiving party would porrect his bill of costs at the time that he served and lodged it, and he would continue to porrect it when he made submissions in support of it at assessment hearing.

Postponement charge

2.83 This is also known as a 'postponement element'[32] or a 'charge for postponement'.[33] It is that part of the success fee which compensates the legal representative for the fact that where his fees are payable conditionally, he will not be able to issue interim statute bills of requests for payment on account (see **9.43**). In this regard, reg 3(1)(b) of the CFA Regulations 2000 impliedly provides the following definition:

'[That part] of the percentage increase, if any, [which] relates to the cost to the legal representative of the postponement of the payment of his fees and expenses.'

2.84 In so far as this book is concerned, the phrase is used to refer both to the charge itself, and to the percentage which is used to calculate it.

Pre-action protocol

2.85 A pre-action protocol may be defined as a statement of understanding between legal practitioners and others about pre-action practice; to be a pre-action protocol under the CPR that statement must be approved by a relevant practice direction.[34]

Proceedings

2.86 The word 'proceedings' is not defined under the Legal Services Act 2007. Prior to 1 January 2010[35] s 119(1) of the Courts and Legal Services Act 1990 stated that 'proceedings' meant proceedings in any court. That said, as John Leighton Williams QC[36] has observed, 'in statutory provisions as in conversation, context

---

[31]   *Oxford English Dictionary* 3rd edn, porrect, v. 3; see also *Wharton's Law Lex* (5th edn, 1872): 'Porrecting, producing for examination or taxation, as porrecting a [bill of costs], by a proctor'.

[32]   For an example of this phrase being used see *Sidhu v Sandu* [2008] EWHC 90108 (Costs) at [19].

[33]   See, for example, *Utting v McBain* [2007] EWHC 90085 (Costs) at [23].

[34]   See the Glossary to the CPR.

[35]   A complex timetable existed for commencement of the new Act: see **5.35**.

[36]   Sitting as a Deputy Judge of the High Court.

matters',[37] and this is palpably true with the word 'proceedings'; indeed, it is a word that has been given different meanings even within the same Part of the CPR.[38]

Profit costs

2.87   Profit costs are the fees charged by a solicitor for the legal services he has provided.

Publicly funded client

2.88   See 'assisted person' at **2.18**.

Receiving party

2.89   CPR, r 43.2(f) provides the following definition:

> '"Receiving party" means a party entitled to be paid costs.'

Regional costs judge

2.90   See 'costs judge' at **2.40**.

Regulated person

2.91   Section 21 of the Legal Services Act 2007 defines a regulated person in these terms:

> 'In this section "regulated persons", in relation to a body, means any class of persons which consists of or includes—
>
> (a)   persons who are authorised by the body to carry on an activity which is a reserved legal activity;
> (b)   persons who are not so authorised, but are employees of a person who is so authorised.'

Save where the context suggests otherwise, it is this which is the intended meaning when, in the context of costs litigation, a person is referred to as a regulated person.

Relevant lawyer

2.92   Section 190 of the Legal Services Act 2007 (as amended) defines 'relevant lawyer' in this way:

> '"Relevant lawyer" means an individual who is—
>
> (a)   a solicitor;
> (b)   a barrister;
> (c)   a solicitor in Scotland;
> (d)   an advocate in Scotland;
> (e)   a solicitor of the Court of Judicature of Northern Ireland;
> (f)   a member of the Bar of Northern Ireland;

---

[37]   *Thompson (a minor) and ors v Bruce* (unreported) 26 June 2011, QBD at [38].
[38]   Ibid: John Leighton Williams QC found that the meaning difference between CPR, r 36.10 and CPR, r 36.3.

(g) a registered foreign lawyer (within the meaning of section 89 of the Courts and Legal Services Act 1990 (c. 41));

(h) an individual not within paragraphs (a) to (g) who is an authorised person in relation to an activity which is a reserved legal activity; or

(i) a European lawyer (within the meaning of the European Communities (Services of Lawyers) Order 1978 (S.I. 1978/1910)).'

Remuneration certificate

2.93 See **19.2**; this term is now obsolete.

Request for payment on account

2.94 A request for payment on account is an invoice sent to a client requesting a payment on account of costs. It should be distinguished from an interim statute bill (see **2.68** and **17.9**).

Reserved instrument activities

2.95 The Legal Services Act 2007 (as amended) defines 'reserved instrument activities' in the following way:[39]

'(1) "Reserved instrument activities" means—

(a) preparing any instrument of transfer or charge for the purposes of the Land Registration Act 2002 (c. 9);

(b) making an application or lodging a document for registration under that Act;

(c) preparing any other instrument relating to real or personal estate for the purposes of the law of England and Wales or instrument relating to court proceedings in England and Wales.

The definition goes on to give further details concerning wills, leases, etc.

'(2) But "reserved instrument activities" does not include the preparation of an instrument relating to any particular court proceedings if, immediately before the appointed day, no restriction was placed on the persons entitled to carry on that activity.'

Reserved legal activities

2.96 The Legal Services Act 2007 (as amended) defines 'legal activities' in the following way:[40]

'(1) In this Act "reserved legal activity" means—

(a) the exercise of a right of audience;

(b) the conduct of litigation;

(c) reserved instrument activities;

(d) probate activities;

(e) notarial activities;

(f) the administration of oaths.'

Retainer

2.97 See **8.4–8.7**.

---

[39] Legal Services Act 2007 (as amended), Sch 2, para 5.
[40] Legal Services Act 2007 (as amended), s 12(1).

Right of audience and right to conduct litigation

2.98   Prior to 1 January 2010, s 119(1) of the Courts and Legal Services Act 1990 stated the following definitions:

> "'right of audience" means the right to exercise any of the functions of appearing before and addressing a court including the calling and examining of witnesses;
>
> "right to conduct litigation" means the right—
>
> (a)   to exercise all or any of the functions of issuing a writ or otherwise commencing proceedings before any court; and
>
> (b)   to perform any ancillary functions in relation to proceedings (such as entering appearances to actions).'

After that date, for most purposes concerning the Legal Services Act 2007[41] the following definitions apply:[42]

> '3 (1) A "right of audience" means the right to appear before and address a court, including the right to call and examine witnesses.
>
> (2) But a "right of audience" does not include a right to appear before or address a court, or to call or examine witnesses, in relation to any particular court or in relation to particular proceedings, if immediately before the appointed day no restriction was placed on the persons entitled to exercise that right.
>
> 4 (1) The "conduct of litigation" means—
>
> (a)   the issuing of proceedings before any court in England and Wales,
>
> (b)   the commencement, prosecution and defence of such proceedings, and
>
> (c)   the performance of any ancillary functions in relation to such proceedings (such as entering appearances to actions).
>
> (2) But the "conduct of litigation" does not include any activity within paragraphs (a) to (c) of sub-paragraph (1), in relation to any particular court or in relation to any particular proceedings, if immediately before the appointed day no restriction was placed on the persons entitled to carry on that activity.'

Rules of Court

2.99   Schedule 1 of the Interpretation Act 1978 defines Rules of Court in the following way:

> "'Rules of Court" in relation to any court means rules made by the authority having power to make rules or orders regulating the practice and procedure of that court ... and the power of the authority to make rules of court (as above defined) includes power to make such rules for the purpose of any Act which directs or authorises anything to be done by rules of court.'

Thus, the present Rules of Court are the CPR and, before those, they were the RSC and CCR. It should be noted, however, that in older authorities, the phrase 'rules of court' referred to rulings of the court in individual cases, and this was the case even where that phrase was used in statutes.[43]

---

[41]   Different definitions apply for certain housing disputes; see s 60A of the County Courts Act 1984, as amended by s 191 of the Legal Services Act 2007.

[42]   Legal Services Act 2007 (as amended), Sch 2, paras 3 and 4.

[43]   See *Jones v Williams* (1841) 8 M & W 349 at 538, per Parke B; see also *Legal Aid Board v Russell* [1991] 2 AC 317 at 819, per Lord Ackner.

Sanderson order

2.100 A *Sanderson* order is a co-defendant order by which the unsuccessful defendant pays the successful defendant's costs (see **7.27** *et seq*). It is also known as a direct co-defendant order (cf indirect co-defendant orders: see **2.28**). It is named after *Sanderson v Blyth Theatre Co*.[44]

Standard basis

2.101 The standard basis is a basis of assessment where the court will only allow costs which are proportionate to the matters in issue and will resolve any doubt as to whether costs were reasonably incurred or reasonable and proportionate in amount in favour of the paying party[45] (see **13.2–13.8**).

Statute bill

2.102 A statute bill is an invoice rendered to a client which is bona fide compliant with the requirements of s 69 of the Solicitors Act 1974 (see **17.33–17.71**).

Success fee

2.103 Section 58(2)(b) of the Courts and Legal Services Act 1990 (as amended) states the following definition:

> '[A] conditional fee agreement provides for a success fee if it provides for the amount of any fees to which it applies to be increased, in specified circumstances, above the amount which would be payable if it were not payable only in specified circumstances.'

Thus, a success fee is an amount rather than a percentage. Notwithstanding this, it is a phrase which is almost universally used to refer to the percentage by which fees are to be uplifted. As has been explained at **2.81**, the correct terminology for the percentage uplift is used so infrequently as to be close to falling beyond the ordinary costs idiom.

Summary assessment

2.104 CPR, r 43.3 defines summary assessment:

> '"Summary assessment" means the procedure by which the court, when making an order about costs, orders payment of a sum of money instead of fixed costs or "detailed assessment".'

Third-party costs order

2.105 See non-party costs order at **2.77**.

Unqualified person

2.106 The Solicitors Act 1974 defines an 'unqualified person' as being a person who has not been admitted as a solicitor and who does not hold a current practising

---

[44]   [1903] 2 KB 533.
[45]   See CPR, r 44.4(2).

certificate[46] (see **5.38**). Since 31 March 2009 the person must also be 'recognised' (or employed by a person who is recognised, or otherwise satisfying the requirements for in-house solicitors).[47]

Wasted costs

2.107 Wasted costs (see **7.207** *et seq*) are costs which are ordered against a legal representative (or which are disallowed, as the case may be);[48] CPD, art 53.9 reads:

> 'A wasted costs order is an order—
>
> (1)   that the legal representative pay a specified sum in respect of costs to a party; or
> (2)   for costs relating to a specified sum or items of work to be disallowed.'

---

[46]   See ss 1 and 87 of the Solicitors Act 1974.
[47]   See rule 12 of the Solicitors Code of Conduct 2007 and (from 1 July 2009) s 1B of the Solicitors Act 1974, as amended by the Legal Services Act 2007 and the Legal Services Act 2007 (Commencement No 5, Transitory and Transitional Provisions) Order 2009.
[48]   Section 51(6) and (7) of the Senior Courts Act 1981 refers to 'legal or other representatives'; therefore, it is possible that the wasted costs jurisdiction could be invoked in respect of representatives who are not legal representatives.

Chapter 3

THE STATUS OF THE RULES GOVERNING COSTS

THE SOURCES OF COSTS LAW

3.1   As is often the case with law which is largely adjectival, the sources of the law of costs are disparate and sundry; in addition to judge-made law, they include, but are not limited to, the following:

- primary legislation (such as the Solicitors Act 1974 and the Legal Services Act 2007);
- secondary (or 'delegated') legislation (such as the Solicitors (Non-Contentious Business) Remuneration Order 2009 and Civil Legal Aid (General) Regulations 1989);
- the SRA Code of Conduct 2011 (or, prior to 6 October 2011, the Solicitors' Code of Conduct 2007);
- other rules of professional conduct (such as the Code of Conduct of the Bar);
- the Funding Code published by the Legal Services Commission;
- rules of court (which at present are the Civil Procedure Rules 1998);
- rules of other tribunals (such as the Tribunal Procedure (Upper Tribunal) (Lands Chamber) Rules 2010);
- practice directions and, in particular, the Costs Practice Direction;
- pre-action protocols; and
- persuasive informal guidance (such as the Supreme Court Costs Office Guide 2006).

There is a degree of overlap between these various categories; thus (for example), the Tribunal Procedure (Upper Tribunal) (Lands Chamber) Rules 2010 were made by delegated legislation, as were the Civil Procedure Rules 1998.

3.2   Conflict or inconsistency between these sources of the law is the exception rather than the rule but, where it exists, it is necessary to be able to prioritise the status of sources in order to resolve that conflict or inconsistency. The status of primary legislation and secondary legislation is not discussed in this book as the reader is likely to have a good understanding of those issues.[1] Instead, this chapter focuses on the following:

- decided cases;
- the Codes of Conduct regulating solicitors;
- other rules of professional conduct;
- the Civil Procedure Rules 1998 ('CPR');

---

[1]   If the reader is not familiar with those issues, then a good place to start would be A T H Smith *Williams: Learning the Law* (Sweet & Maxwell, 13th edn, 2006), ISBN: 9780421925502.

- the Costs Practice Direction ('CPD');
- pre-action protocols; and
- persuasive informal guidance.

Each of these is dealt with in turn. It should be noted that it is only the status of these sources of the law that is addressed in this chapter: their contents are tackled elsewhere in this book.

DECIDED CASES AND PRECEDENCE

3.3   Judges are required to follow decisions that are binding upon them (this being the principle of *stare decisis*).[2] Only *ratio decidendi* (ie, 'rationale of judgment; a principle underlying and determining a judicial decision'[3]) is binding as a precedent; obiter dicta is not binding[4] (although it may be persuasive).[5] Where the court gives guidance that, technically, is obiter but which is considered and detailed (so called 'judicial dicta'), then it is often regarded as being highly persuasive;[6] this is especially true where the comments were made by a judge with an interest in the topic[7] or where all members of the court concur with the obiter.[8] Likewise, where the obiter is a recital of what the judge believes to be ratio of a previously-decided but unreported case, then that too is highly persuasive.[9] Precedence operates in the following way:

- ***Supreme Court and House of Lords:*** a decision of the House of Lords or Supreme Court is binding on all lower courts;[10]
- ***Privy Council:*** a decision of the Judicial Committee of the Privy Council is not, in theory, binding, but is usually given great weight;[11]
- ***European Court of Justice:*** a decision of the ECJ is, strictly speaking, binding only the court from which the case arose,[12] but the ECJ has held that where the issue is the interpretation of a Community instrument, its decisions ought to be followed generally;[13]
- ***European Court of Human Rights:*** where a domestic court decides a matter that relates to a guaranteed right it must take into account any relevant decision of the ECtHR;[14]
- ***Court of Appeal:*** a decision in the Court of Appeal will bind courts below it and, with limited exceptions, will bind itself;[15] the Court of Appeal is not, however,

---

2   This derives from Latin maxim *stare decisis et non quieta movere:* 'to stand by decisions and not disturb the undisturbed.'
3   *Oxford English Dictionary*, 3rd edn.
4   *Osborne v Rowlett* (1880) 13 Ch D 774 at 785.
5   *Tees Conservancy Comrs v James* [1935] Ch 544.
6   *G and C Kreglinger v New Patagonia Meat and Cold Storage Co Ltd* [1914] AC 25, HL
7   *Tees Conservancy Comrs v James* [1935] Ch 544.
8   *Mills v LCC* [1925] 1 KB 213, DC.
9   *Richard West & Partners (Inverness) Ltd v Dick* [1969] 2 Ch 424 at 431.
10   The Court of Appeal is not permitted to advise judges to disregard such decisions on the grounds that they are unworkable or wrong: *Cassell & Co Ltd v Broome* [1972] AC 1027.
11   See, for example, *Worcester Works Finance Ltd v Cooden Engineering Co Ltd* [1972] 1 QB 210.
12   *HP Bulmer Ltd v J Bollinger SA* [1974] Ch 401, [1974] 2 All ER 1226, CA.
13   *International Chemical Corpn v Amministrazione delle Finanze dello Stato* [1981] ECR 1191.
14   Human Rights Act 1998 s 2(1)(a) and (b).
15   *Re South Durham Iron Co, Smith's Case* (1879) 11 Ch D 579, CA.

bound to follow a decision that was given in ignorance of a conflicting decision of the House of Lords,[16] not is it required to follow a decision made in ignorance of legislation;[17]

- **Divisional Court:** a decision in the Divisional Court is binding upon itself[18] and upon judges deciding cases at first instance.[19]
- **High Court:** a decision of a High Court Judge will bind bind Masters, District Judges and Circuit Judges in the County Court;[20] High Court Judges do not bind each other,[21] but in practice they will regard appropriate first instance decisions at the same level as being persuasive (this being as a matter of judicial comity);[22] and
- **Circuit Judges, Masters and District Judges:** decisions at these judicial levels will bind no court; they ought not to be cited unless they have been reported or unless they contain a relevant statement of legal principle not found in reported authority.[23]

3.4   The following miscellaneous points can be made about case reports (the first of which is particularly relevant to the law of costs):

- **Discretionary decisions:** of importance in the context of the law of costs is the (often overlooked) principle that the exercise of discretion in one case is not to be taken as being a guide to the exercise of discretion in another case; Hodson LJ had this to say:[24]

    'It is dangerous in the exercise of discretion to take a reported case as a guide for that exercise in another case. This is specially true when the judgment on costs is taken apart from its context of the findings of fact which are contained in the same judgment.'

- **Unclear Ratio: Unclear Ratio:** if the *ratio* is not clear, then there is no duty upon the court to seek to spell the *ratio* out in order to apply it;[25] likewise, ratio from from lengthy judgments should not be taken out of context;[26]
- **Conflicting decision at the same judicial level:** as a matter of general principle, where there are conflicting decisions, the later decision will be given more weight if it has been reached after full consideration of the earlier decision;[27]
- **Longstanding decisions:** where a non-binding decision has stood the test of time and has been frequently cited, it will usually be regarded as being highly persuasive;[28]

---

[16]   *Huddersfield Police Authority v Watson* [1947] KB 842; mere misinterpretation of a decision in the House of Lords will not absolve the Court of Appeal from the duty subsequently to follow the decision in question, however: *Williams v Glasbrook Bros Ltd* [1947] 2 All ER 884, CA.

[17]   *Young v Bristol Aeroplane Co Ltd* [1944] KB 718, [1944] 2 All ER 293, CA.

[18]   *Huddersfield Police Authority v Watson* [1947] KB 842, [1947] 2 All ER 193, DC; the exception in the Court of Appeal apply: *Nicholas v Penny* [1950] 2 KB 466.

[19]   *John v John and Goff* [1965] P 289.

[20]   *Howard de Walden Estates Ltd v Aggio* [2007] EWCA Civ 499 (reversed on appeal, but on a different point).

[21]   The *Vera Cruz (No 2)* (1884) 9 PD 96, CA.

[22]   *Russian and English Bank v Baring Bros & Co Ltd* [1935] Ch 120, CA.

[23]   *Practice Direction: Citation of Authorities* [2012] 1 WLR 780 at [10].

[24]   *Bragg v Crosville Motor Services Ltd* [1959] 1 All ER 613 at 615.

[25]   *The Mostyn* [1928] AC 57, HL.

[26]   *Monk v Warbey* [1935] 1 KB 75, CA.

[27]   *Re Cromptons Leisure Machines Ltd* [2006] EWHC 3583 (Ch).

[28]   See, for example, *Astley v IRC* [1974] STC 367.

- **Decisions on applications for permission to appeal:** judgments given on applications for permission to appeal are not binding authorities; the court does not encourage reference to be made thereto;[29]
- **Judicial interjections:** interjections during argument are not binding;[30]
- **Multiple reasoning:** in general, where the court has given more than one reason for arriving at the decision reached, each will be capable of being ratio;[31] and
- **Citation of authorities:** see **2.7**.

THE CODES OF CONDUCT REGULATING SOLICITORS

3.5   The present incarnation of the code regulating solicitors[32] is the SRA Code of Conduct 2011 ('the Code of Conduct 2011'). Prior to 6 October 2011 it was the Solicitors' Code of Conduct 2007 ('the Code of Conduct 2007'), and prior 1 July 2007 it was the Solicitors' Practice Rules 1990 ('the SPR'). This chapter relies on law which was decided for the purposes of the previous provisions.[33] Some caution must be exercised in this regard: it is almost certainly true to say that the Code of Conduct 2011 will be afforded the same status in law as was the Code of Conduct 2007, but there are differences in the style and content of the two codes, and it is not yet known whether the new code will be afforded a similar status in practice.

Jurisdiction and vires

3.6   The Law Society's vires to make the SPR and the SRA's vires[34] to make the Codes of Conduct 2007 and 2011 derive from s 31 of the Solicitors Act 1974;[35] that provision enables the Law Society (or the SRA) to make rules which have the force of statute. This was explained by Lord Brightman in the following way:[36]

'The rules [in that case, the SPR] have the force of a statute ... just as much as if [they] were set out in a Schedule to the Act.'

So, when deciding what effect, if any, a breach of the SPR will have, the issue raised is one of legislative interpretation; the same is almost certainly true of the Code of Conduct 2011. The relevant provisions must be interpreted and applied as if they were set out in a Schedule to an Act. This principle was affirmed by Schiemann LJ in 1999[37]

---

[29]   *Clark v University of Lincolnshire and Humberside* [2000] 3 All ER 752 at 762 f, per Lord Woolf MR.

[30]   *Practice Note* [1942] WN 89, PC, per Viscount Simon C.

[31]   *Cheater v Cater* [1918] 1 KB 247, CA.

[32]   It is worth noting that the Code of Conduct 2011 regulates not just solicitors in traditional firms and in-house practice, but any person who chooses to be regulated by the Solicitors Regulation Authority ('SRA'), and this may include other species of lawyer as well as new entrants to the legal services market, such as non-lawyer managers of alternative business structures.

[33]   Generally speaking, what is said in this chapter about the Code of Conduct 2007/2011 is also true of the SPR and vice versa.

[34]   The SRA was established in January 2007 and was previously called the Law Society Regulation Board; it is part of the Law Society but acts independently of it.

[35]   '[The] Council [of the Law Society] may, if they think fit, make rules, with the concurrence of the Master of the Rolls, for regulating in respect of any matter the professional practice, conduct and discipline of solicitors and for empowering the Society to take such action as may be appropriate to enable the Society to ascertain whether or not the provisions of rules made, or of any code or guidance issued, by the Council are being complied with.'

[36]   *Swain v The Law Society* [1983] 1 AC 598 at 621.

[37]   In *Awwad v Geraghty & Co* [2000] 3 WLR 1041 at 1056.

and again by Arden LJ in 2005;[38] it is a principle which remains good law under the CPR[39] (not least because it is substantive law).

'Outcomes' and 'indicative behaviours'

3.7   Whilst it is almost certainly true to say that the Code of Conduct 2011 also has the force of statute (see **3.6**), it remains to be seen how this will apply in practice. There is uncertainty in this regard because the Code of Conduct 2011 is a move away from the traditional prescriptive method of regulating solicitors. It is based on 'outcomes-focused regulation' ('OFR'). Rather than containing prescriptive rules, supported by guidance, the new code comprises mandatory 'outcomes' and non-mandatory 'indicative behaviours':[40]

*   **Outcomes**: these describe what solicitors are expected to achieve in order to comply with the Principles in specific contexts; they are mandatory; and
*   **Indicative behaviours:** these provide non-mandatory examples of the kind of behaviours which may establish whether the relevant outcomes have been achieved and whether there has been compliance with the Principles.

OFR is not something that is achieved solely by the Code of Conduct 2011 in isolation, but is achieved by that code working in concert with certain other provisions which are set out in the SRA Handbook. From the point of view of the law of costs, the relevant parts are:

(i)   ten high-level Principles,[41]
(ii)   the Code of Conduct 2011 itself, and
(iii)   the Accounts Rules and rules dealing with financial services (see **3.17**).[42]

Whilst it is undoubtedly the case that the Code of Conduct 2011 is, in general terms, very different from Code of Conduct 2011, it is worth noting that in so far as client relations are concerned, the provisions are very similar; as such, it may well be that the differences may not be that great for the purposes of costs law. Transitional provisions exist.[43]

The effect of breaches of the Code of Conduct 2011

3.8   The fact that the Code of Conduct 2011 has the force of statute is only the starting point. Its effect is often mediated through the common law and, in particular, through a common law's interpretation of public policy. Broadly speaking, where something is done in breach of the Code of Conduct 2011, that breach will fall into one or both of two categories: first, there may be a failure in the performance of an obligation and, secondly, an act may be done (or an omission made) which is prohibited.

---

[38]   *Garbutt v Edwards* [2005] EWCA Civ 1206 at [31].
[39]   Ibid. Arden LJ explained that the SPR were there to protect the legitimate interests of the client and the administration of justice.
[40]   See para 3 of *Outcomes-focused regulation at a glance: Your quick guide to getting started with OFR and the new Handbook* (Law Society, 2011).
[41]   These are similar to the core principles in the Code of Conduct 2007;
[42]   Large parts of the Solicitors Accounts Rules 1998 have been retained. Nevertheless, some operational flexibility has been introduced, for example in relation to the payment of interest and signing on client account.
[43]   See Chapter 15 of the Code of Conduct 2011.

An example of the former would be a failure to provide a client with a proper estimate, and an example of the latter would be entering into a prohibited retainer, such as an unlawful contingency fee agreement. For the reasons set out below, the law takes more notice of the latter than the former.

Implied statutory prohibition

3.9   Whilst the starting point is to determine the meaning of the Code of Conduct 2011 by a process of legislative interpretation, the legal mechanism by which a breach gives rise to private law rights will vary from case to case. Those mechanisms may be placed in the categories of express and implied statutory prohibition (a detailed description of the mechanisms of statutory prohibition is given at **8.246–8.267**). (In this context the word 'prohibition' is used to include failing to do that which ought to have been done.) In the present context, express statutory prohibition is where a statute not only states what is or is not permissible, but also prescribes that in the event of a breach of that requirement, any associated contract or entitlement to costs will be prohibited. Implied statutory prohibition is where a prohibition exists, but is implied rather than expressly stated. In the context of costs law, express statutory prohibition is uncommon,[44] especially in so far as the Code of Conduct 2011 is concerned.

3.10   A prohibited contract or entitlement to costs may be such that the court's processes will not be used to enforce it (hence the term 'unenforceable'), but this will not always be the effect of the doctrine of implied statutory prohibition. In the context of general litigation rather than costs, Browne-Wilkinson J said:[45]

'The fact that a party has in the course of performing a contract committed an unlawful or immoral act will not by itself prevent him from further enforcing that contract unless the contract was entered into with the purpose of doing that unlawful or immoral act or the contract itself (as opposed to the mode of his performance) is prohibited by law.'

3.11   Where a breach of the Code of Conduct 2011 contains an implied statutory prohibition against a thing done or made, its effect is usually mediated via the common law concept of public policy. This can be illustrated by reference to the example of a contingency fee agreement under the Code of Conduct 2007; a contingency fee agreement was not made unenforceable as a direct result of a provision in that code, but instead it was made unenforceable by reason of it being contrary to public policy as reflected in that code.[46] As a matter of public policy the court's processes would not be used to enforce it. Whilst in a different league of culpability, an analogy may be drawn with a contract to commit a crime: a contract to rob a bank is unenforceable not because there is a statute which says that it unenforceable (ie express statutory prohibition), but because the common law will not allow the court to be used to enforce such an obnoxious contract (ie there is an implied statutory prohibition arising out of public policy).

---

[44]   A notable exception to this is s 58(1) of the Courts and Legal Services Act 1990 (as amended).
[45]   *Coral Leisure Group Ltd v Barnett* [1981] ICR 503.
[46]   See below for authorities on this point. See *Mohammed v Alaga & Co* [2000] 1 WLR 1815 at 1823 for an analogous situation involving a prohibited contract other than a retainer; see also *Awwad v Geraghty & Co* [2000] 3 WLR 1041 at 1056.

The role of discretion

3.12   Where the prohibition is implied, it is usually the case that the court has a considerable degree of discretion. The court will determine what is and what is not contrary to public policy and the consequences of the breach will then be very much in the discretion of the court (guided, of course, by precedent). At one extreme the court may ignore the breach entirely,[47] whilst at the other it may find that the breach is so bad that the entire solicitor and client relationship has been tainted with illegality.

3.13   The fact that the court has this type of discretion was explained by Lord Diplock in the following way:[48]

> 'The Council in exercising its powers under the Act to make rules and regulations and the Society in discharging functions vested in it by the Act or by such rules or regulations are acting in a public capacity and what they do in that capacity is governed by public law; and although the legal consequences of doing it may result in creating rights enforceable in private law, those rights are not necessarily the same as those that would flow in private law from doing a similar act otherwise than in the exercise of statutory powers.'

The relevance of public policy

3.14   In view of the fact that the effect of a breach of the Code of Conduct 2011 may be dependent on public policy, it is worth saying a word about the nature of public policy itself. In this regard, Bingham CJ commented:[49]

> 'When making such subordinate legislation [ie the Code of Conduct 2007/SPR], the Law Society is acting in the public interest and not (should there be any conflict) in the narrower interests of the solicitors' profession: see *Swain v The Law Society* [1983] 1 AC 598. The concurrence of the Master of the Rolls is required as a guarantee that the interests of the public are fully safeguarded.'

Thus, public policy is reflected in the Code of Conduct 2011. Put another way, the Code of Conduct 2011 ought to be regarded as being a measure of the public interest rather than a measure of what is in the interests of the solicitors' profession. The Code of Conduct 2011 does not, however, define what is in the public interest as the court may take other factors into account.

Other factors

3.15   In addition to taking into account the nature of the breach of the Code of Conduct 2011, the court may also consider the motives of the person seeking to rely on that breach. For obvious reasons the court would be more likely to give effect to a complaint made by the client than it would be to a stranger (such as a paying party seeking to take a technical point). In this regard, Arden LJ said:[50]

> 'In making these Rules, the Council of the Law Society is acting in the public interest ... The inference I would draw is that the Code is there to protect the legitimate interests of the client, and the administration of justice, rather than to relieve paying parties of their obligations to pay costs which have been reasonably incurred.'

---

[47]   See Arden LJ's analysis in *Garbutt v Edwards* [2005] EWCA Civ 1206 at [31].
[48]   *Swain v The Law Society* [1983] 1 AC 598 at 608.
[49]   *Mohammed v Alaga & Co* [2000] 1 WLR 1815 at 1823.
[50]   *Garbutt v Edwards* [2005] EWCA Civ 1206 at [36].

3.16 Thus, the effect and authority of the Code of Conduct 2011 will, in the absence of express statutory prohibition, depend on the facts of the case. It would be wrong simply to say that it has the force of statute and to assume that that is the answer to all issues; the approach of the court is far more nuanced than that.

OTHER RULES OF PROFESSIONAL CONDUCT

Financial and accounts rules

3.17 There are rules that are not within the Code of Conduct 2011 itself, but which are afforded a similar status. Examples include:

- the Solicitors' Accounts Rules 1998;
- the Solicitors' Financial Services (Scope) Rules 2001; and
- the Financial Services (Business) Rules 2001.

The Code of Conduct 2011 may, indeed, itself require compliance with these other rules.[51]

3.18 There are some aspects of the Solicitors' Financial Services (Scope) Rules 2001 and the Financial Services (Business) Rules 2001 which are examples of express statutory prohibition. This issue is beyond the scope of this chapter, but is dealt with in detail at **30.123–30.142**.

Guidance notes to the Code of Conduct 2011

3.19 The guidance notes to the Code of Conduct 2007 have not been made by statutory instrument and should not, therefore, be afforded the same status as the Code itself (see **3.54**). The guidance that accompanies the Code of Conduct 2011 is much more integrated with the that code than its forebear was with the Code of Conduct 2007, and it is difficult to see that code could be placed in context without taking that guidance in account; that said, there is, as at the time of writing, no authority as to the status of that guidance.

CIVIL PROCEDURE RULES 1998

3.20 The Civil Procedure Rules 1998 ('CPR') are particularly relevant to the law of costs because a great deal of costs law is based on procedure; that is, costs law is, to a large extent, adjectival law.

Jurisdiction and the procedure of making the CPR

3.21 The Civil Procedure Rules are made pursuant to s 1(1) of the Civil Procedure Act 1997 ('CPA 1997');[52] they apply in the civil division of the Court of Appeal, the High Court and county courts. In so far as the law of costs is concerned, the CPR may

---

[51] An example being r 5.01(1)(c), in respect of which the guidance notes make it clear that the Solicitors' Accounts Rules 1998 should be complied with in certain circumstances.

[52] The power is also governed by the Constitutional Reform Act 2005 and, in particular, by Sch 1 thereof.

also apply by analogy in other courts, such as the Supreme Court,[53] and in tribunals.[54] Where this is the case, the CPR will generally apply only to the extent that they do not conflict with rules specific to the tribunal or court in question.

3.22 CPA 1997 makes provisions about how the CPR are to be made.[55] Section 2 provides that proposed rules are formulated by the Civil Procedure Rule Committee (often loosely referred to as 'the Rules Committee') and that they may then be either allowed or disallowed by the Secretary of State for Justice (previously the Lord Chancellor). If the Secretary of State allows the proposed rules, CPA 1997, s 3(1)(b) provides that they are to be made by statutory instrument. Section 3(2) provides that they are subject to annulment by negative resolution of either House of Parliament: this means that they will be made unless one or other of the Houses objects.

Interpretation

3.23 Although they are usually referred to as being 'rules', the CPR as a whole are not only made by statutory instrument, but they *are* a statutory instrument;[56] that is, they are subordinate legislation.[57] This means that the interpretation of the CPR is a process of statutory interpretation which requires the application of ordinary canons of construction.[58] It also means that the court does not have the power to override the CPR (unless, of course, there is some contrary statutory provision, such as a provision under the Human Rights Act 1998).[59]

3.24 The court has a wide discretion to regulate its own procedure. Such regulation must be within the constraints imposed by the CPR but in view of the fact that CPR, r 3.1(2)(m) expressly confers the power to take any 'step or make any … order for the purpose of managing the case and furthering the overriding objective', the ambit of that discretion is wide indeed. Dyson LJ has noted that in many respects the CPR is 'open-textured' and that the court may 'fill in gaps left by those rules'; this further widens the ambit of that discretion.[60]

Henry VIII clause

3.25 The Secretary of State for Justice is advised by the Civil Justice Council.[61] He has significant powers to make or negate enactments in consequence of the CPR; this power arises out of a provision which is often referred to as a 'Henry VIII clause'. In particular, CPA 1997, s 4(1) allows the Lord Chancellor to amend, repeal or revoke any enactment to the extent that it is desirable in consequence of the CPR; if he wishes to do

---

[53] See para 1.4 of the Supreme Court Practice Direction 13 (Costs); see also Senior Courts Act 1981, s 1.

[54] See, for example, *Revenue & Customs Commissioners v Talentcore Ltd* (unreported) 19 November 2011, UT (Tax), Roth J.

[55] See also the Constitutional Reform Act 2005 and, in particular, Sch 1 thereof.

[56] See the Civil Procedure Rules 1998 (SI 1998/3132), which gave rise to the first version of the CPR; all subsequent amendments have been made by statutory instrument.

[57] See Interpretation Act 1978, s 21(1), which provides that '"subordinate legislation" means Orders in Council, orders, rules, regulations, schemes, warrants, byelaws and other instruments made by or under any Act.'

[58] *Vinos v Marks & Spencer plc* [2001] 3 All ER 784.

[59] *General Mediterranean Holdings SA v Patel* [1999] 2 Costs LR 10.

[60] *Leigh v Michelin Tyre plc* [2003] EWCA Civ 1766 at [21]. Whilst in a different context (ie purposive construction in a more general sense), Denning MR explained that that court 'will fill in gaps, quite unashamedly, without hesitation' (*James Buchanan & Co Ltd v Babco Forward and Shipping (UK) Ltd* [1977] QB 208); an analogy could be draw in with rules of court.

[61] See Civil Procedure Act 1997, s 6.

this, he must make the change by statutory instrument,[62] which may be subject to annulment by negative resolution of either House.[63] If he wishes, he may also amend, repeal or revoke relevant enactments made before the CPR came into force, but if he intends to do that, he must obtain the affirmative approval of both of the Houses of Parliament.[64]

Provisions made by directions

3.26 CPA 1997, Sch 1, para 6 provides that 'Civil Procedure Rules may refer to provisions made by directions.' Section 9(2) defines 'practice directions' as 'directions as to the practice and procedure of any court within the scope of the Civil Procedure Rules', so the CPR will, if they are so worded, incorporate provisions made in practice directions.[65] This does not mean that practice directions are ordinarily to be afforded the same status as the CPR; indeed, the opposite is generally true (see **3.31** onwards).

County Court Rules, RSC, etc

3.27 It is occasionally the case that rules of CPR still refer to rules which they replaced (ie the Rules of the Supreme Court 1965 and the County Court Rules 1981); where this is the case, the CPR may apply those rules to any extent, with or without modification.[66]

Overriding objective

3.28 When interpreting the CPR the court must seek to give effect to the overriding objective.[67] The intention of the original framers of the CPR was that the CPR were to be provisions which spoke for themselves so that there would be no need to refer to an ever-increasing body of authority in order to apply them.[68] Reference to pre-CPR case law is generally to be discouraged for the purposes of interpreting the CPR,[69] but may be instructive in appropriate circumstances.[70] Some provisions are a codification of pre-existing common law procedure and, in those circumstances, reference to pre-CPR authorities may be helpful.[71] Where two competing interpretations of a provision in the CPR are possible, it would be legitimate to take practice directions into account as an extrinsic aid to interpretation,[72] but May LJ has commented that they are 'at best a weak aid'.[73]

---

[62] See Constitutional Reform Act 2005, Sch 1, para 4(1)(b).
[63] See Constitutional Reform Act 2005, Sch 1, para 4(2).
[64] CPA 1997, s 4(2) and (5).
[65] An example is the last sentence of CPR, r 47.19, which defers to the CPD.
[66] CPA 1997, Sch 1, para 5.
[67] CPR, r 1.2.
[68] *ABCI v Banque Franco-Tunisienne & Ors* [2003] EWCA Civ 205 at [68].
[69] *Biguzzi v Rank Leisure plc* [1999] EWCA Civ 1972.
[70] *EI Du Pont De Nemours & Company v ST Dupont* [2003] EWCA Civ 1368 at [86].
[71] An example being the procedure as described in *Pamplin v Express Newspapers Ltd* [1985] 1 WLR 689, which is codified at CPD, art 40.14.
[72] *Van Aken v London Borough Of Camden* [2002] EWCA Civ 1724 at [36]. In some circumstances it may be possible to take *Hansard* into account: *Pepper v Hart* [1992] UKHL 3.
[73] *Godwin v Swindon Borough Council* [2001] EWCA Civ 1478 at [11].

Rules of evidence

3.29 Whilst it will rarely be relevant to the law of costs, the CPR may modify the rules of evidence as they apply to proceedings in any court within the scope of the rules.[74]

3.30 In summary, the CPR is a statutory instrument, and must be construed and applied as such.

THE STATUS OF PRACTICE DIRECTIONS

3.31 Practice directions may be defined as any directions as to the practice and procedure of any court within the scope of CPR.[75] As with the CPR, the Costs Practice Direction ('CPD') is particularly relevant to the law of costs as it is largely based on procedure almost to the point of it being adjectival law. For the reasons set out below, however, less weight should be given to practice directions than to the CPR themselves.

Vires to make practice directions

3.32 It is for the Lord Chief Justice, or a judicial office holder nominated by the Lord Chief Justice with the agreement of the Secretary of State for Justice, to make or give practice directions.[76] He has delegated his powers first to the Vice-Chancellor as Head of Civil Justice, and subsequently to the Deputy Head of Civil Justice.[77] Thus, practice directions are in fact usually made by the Lord Chief Justice, the Master of the Rolls (so far as they affect civil appeals), the Vice-Chancellor or the Head or Deputy Head of Civil Justice.

Bar against local practice directions

3.33 It is occasionally the case that county courts issue local practice directions; unless those directions are approved by the Secretary of State for Justice, the Lord Chief Justice or someone acting on their behalf, they are unlawful.[78] Prior to the coming into force of the CPA 1997 county courts had an inherent power to regulate their own practice and procedure,[79] but that power now exists only to the extent that approval has been given.[80]

Status of practice directions

3.34 The following discussion assumes that the provisions under scrutiny are not provisions which have been incorporated into the CPR themselves by their express wording. Where express incorporation has taken place, then the relevant provisions in the CPD must be afforded the same status as the CPR. The need to consign provisions

---

[74] CPA 1997, Sch 1, para 4.
[75] CPA 1997, Sch 1, para 9(2).
[76] See Constitutional Reform Act 2005, Sch 2, para 2(1)
[77] This is pursuant to the powers conferred by s 19 of the Constitutional Reform Act 2005.
[78] See s 5(2) of the Civil Procedure Act 1987, as amended by the Constitutional Reform Act 2005, Sch 2. Prior to 3 April 2006, see s 74A(2) of the County Courts Act 1984, as amended by CPA 1997, Sch 1, para 5. There are limited exceptions to the bar against local practice directions (see s 5(5) and (6) of the Constitutional Reform Act 2005).
[79] *Langley v North West Water Authority* [1991] 1 WLR 697.
[80] See s 5(2) of the Civil Procedure Act 1987, as amended.

to the CPD usually arises where there is too much detail to be conveniently set out in the CPR, or where there are details which may be subject to frequent change. An example is CPR, r 45.9(2), which relegates lists of certain geographical details to the CPD. The need to incorporate may also arise where the practice direction relates to temporary measures, such as transitional provisions and pilot schemes; see, for example, CPR, r 51.2 and the associated practice directions.

Not a source of law

3.35   Practice directions are made pursuant to CPA 1997, s 5. They may provide for any matter which may be provided for by the CPR. The fact that practice directions are made pursuant to a statutory power does not afford them the status of being subordinate legislation; in particular, practice directions do not meet the standard statutory definition of subordinate legislation.[81] In this regard, Hale LJ commented:[82]

> '[Practice directions] are probably not "made under" any Act at all: the fact that the CPR "may refer" to them does not mean that they are "made under" the [Civil Procedure Act] 1997.'

Consequently, practice directions (including the CPD) are not able to override the CPR or any other form of subordinate legislation.[83]

Poorly-drafted and ultra vires practice directions

3.36   Practice directions are not made by the Civil Procedure Rule Committee and are not laid before Parliament. Judges have been known to criticise the provisions in the CPD as being poorly constructed.[84] Hale LJ had the following to say on the topic:[85]

> 'They [practice directions] go through no democratic process at all, although if approved by the Lord Chancellor he will bear ministerial responsibility for them to Parliament. But there is a difference in principle between delegated legislation which may be scrutinised by Parliament and ministerial executive action. There is no ministerial responsibility for Practice Directions made for the Supreme Court by the Heads of Division. As Professor Jolowicz says ... "It is right that the court should retain its power to regulate its own procedure within the limits set by statutory rules, and to fill in gaps left by those rules; it is wrong that it should have power actually to legislate."'

3.37   In a similar vein but a different case, Brooke LJ developed the theme in this way:[86]

> 'It is sufficient for present purposes to say that a practice direction has no legislative force. Practice directions provide invaluable guidance to matters of practice in the civil courts, but in so far as they contain statements of the law which are wrong they carry no authority at all.'

---

81   See Interpretation Act 1978, s 21(1).
82   Per Hale LJ in *A Local Authority v A Mother and Child* [2001] 1 Costs LR 136 at 144.
83   See May LJ's comments in *Godwin v Swindon Borough Council* [2001] EWCA Civ 1478 at [11].
84   *Inline Logistics Ltd v UCI Logistics Ltd* [2002] 2 Costs LR 304.
85   *A Local Authority v A Mother and Child* [2001] 1 Costs LR 136.
86   *Ku v Liverpool City Council* [2005] EWCA Civ 475 at [47].

By reason of the fact that they carry no authority, the court has the vires to override a practice direction.[87]

Application of practice directions

3.38 Notwithstanding the above, practice directions should not be disregarded: the analysis set out above merely means that they are not a source of law. As mentioned at **3.24**, the court may need to fill in gaps left by the CPR, Where this is done by a practice direction, it will not necessarily create a clash between that practice direction and the rule it supplements.[88] In a similar vein, tribunals that apply the CPR by analogy may also apply the CPD by analogy.[89]

3.39 It is noticeable that the CPD largely reflects the CPR, but where this is not the case, it is usually because it is addressing administrative issues (which are not issues of law) or because it is describing – some may say codifying – the common law[90] (and therefore merely reflecting the law). Whilst an obvious point, the court may take non-compliance with practice directions into account when deciding the incidence or quantum of costs: for this reason alone it would be foolhardy to disregard practice directions without good reason. In this regard, it is not unlikely that the court would treat practice directions dealing with administrative steps as being similar to an order of the court.

3.40 In summary, practice directions (including the CPD) are not a source of law and at best are an extrinsic aid to interpretation, but they may fill in gaps in the CPR, and they are an important source of administrative guidance. Of particular importance in the context of costs is the fact that unjustified non-compliance with a practice direction may be a factor that the court takes into account when deciding either the incidence or quantum of costs.

PRE-ACTION PROTOCOLS

3.41 A pre-action protocol may be defined as a statement of best practice about pre-action conduct;[91] to qualify as a pre-action protocol under the CPR that statement must have been approved by the Head of Civil Justice and must be listed in Practice Direction (Pre-Action Conduct).[92]

3.42 There are a number of pre-action protocols; at the time of publication, they were as follows:

Pre-action Protocol	**Came into force**
Personal Injury	26 April 1999
Clinical Disputes	26 April 1999

---

[87] See, for example, *Ku v Liverpool City Council* [2005] EWCA Civ 475 at [47].

[88] *Leigh v Michelin Tyre plc* [2003] EWCA Civ 1766 at [21].

[89] See *Revenue & Customs Commissioners v Talentcore Ltd (t/a Team Spirits)* UT (Tax) (Roth J) 19 November 2011.

[90] An example being the procedure as described in *Pamplin v Express Newspapers Ltd* [1985] 1 WLR 689, which is codified at CPD, art 40.14.

[91] See the Glossary to the CPR.

[92] Ibid.

Pre-action Protocol	**Came into force**
Construction and Engineering	2 October 2000
Defamation	2 October 2000
Professional Negligence	16 July 2001
Judicial Review	4 March 2002
Disease and Illness	8 December 2003
Housing Disrepair	8 December 2003
Possession Claims Based on Rent Arrears	2 October 2006
Possession Claims Based on Mortgage Arrears etc	19 November 2008
Pre-Action Protocol for Low Value Personal Injury Claims in Road Traffic Accidents	30 April 2010
Pre-Action Protocol for Claims for Damages in Relation to the Physical State of Commercial Property at Termination of a Tenancy	1 January 2012

In addition to these specific protocols, there is a general Practice Direction – Pre-Action Conduct, which is often given a status similar to a protocol.

Relevance as to expectations of disputants

3.43   Whilst there are exceptions,[93] in the context of the law of costs the pre-action protocols and the practice direction which accompanies them will rarely be relevant as being a source of law. They are, nonetheless, relevant in that they create obligations and expectations which, if ignored or thwarted, may be reflected in either the incidence or quantum of costs; in this regard, CPR, r 44.5(5)(a) defines relevant conduct for the purposes of deciding the incidence of costs as including the extent to which the parties followed any relevant pre-action protocol. This issue is discussed in detail at **6.76–6.98**.

3.44   Pre-action protocols may also be relevant in the sense that the court may take a protocol into account when deciding what should be done generally for the purposes of better managing the class of claim to which the protocol relates. This may be an issue of deciding how best to make the protocol 'work', or of ensuring that the protocol is not used by a party as a reason to visit unfairness on an opponent.[94] In a similar vein, the court might take a pre-action protocol into account in such a way as to ensure that costs are dealt with in accordance with the protocol's broad objectives.[95]

---

[93]   An example being the requirements to give information about funding arrangements in Practice Directions and Protocols.

[94]   An example is *Birmingham City Council v Lee* [2008] EWCA Civ 891, in which the court found that a particular type of order was necessary if the protocol in question was not to operate as a means of preventing recovery of reasonably incurred legal costs.

[95]   See, for example, *McGlinn v Waltham Contractors Ltd* [2005] EWHC 1419 (TCC), where it was held that it would be wrong to make an award which would effectively penalise a claimant for having done what a pre-action protocol required, namely, to narrow the issues.

Substance over semantics

3.45   When taking pre-action protocols into account, the court tends to look at their substance and gist of what is written, rather than focusing on the protocols' technical or semantic aspects; in this regard, Aitkenhead J said:[96]

> 'The Court should be slow to allow the rules to be used in those circumstances for one party to obtain a tactical or costs advantage where in substance the principles of the Protocol have been complied with.'

Specific costs provisions

3.46   Some pre-action protocols themselves contain specific provisions and costs sanctions for non-compliance. For example, the Pre-action Protocol for Construction and Engineering Disputes suggests that a failure by a defendant to say at an early stage that it is the 'wrong' defendant may be taken into account when deciding the incidence of costs. Another example is that a defendant in a clinical negligence claim may face sanctions for not supplying clinical records in a timely fashion.[97] This is a topic which is addressed more fully at **6.87–6.88**.

3.47   In summary, whilst pre-action protocols would rarely be a source of law in the context of costs, they are often taken into account when the law is applied and, in particular, they may have a significant bearing on the incidence of costs.

THE STATUS OF PERSUASIVE INFORMAL GUIDANCE

3.48   There are many sources of informal guidance (such as guides, books and journals) but, in so far as the law of costs is concerned, they will usually be regarded as being instructive rather than authoritative. Such materials are often referred to as being 'secondary sources' of the law. This is in distinction to 'primary sources', which are themselves authoritative statements of the law. The authority of a secondary source has to be determined.

3.49   With the exception of textbooks such as *Chitty on Contracts*, it is not common for secondary sources of the law to be placed before the court and it is even rarer for the court to take such materials into account. Secondary sources are, however, often a convenient conduit via which primary sources can be found.

Court guides

3.50   The Senior Courts Costs Office publishes a lengthy court guide which is often referred to in court on matters of procedure. That guide, like most court guides, is a narrative document written or approved of by specialist judges acting in an extra-judicial capacity. Court guides provide a narrative to the CPR or other primary sources of the law, often explaining how they are to be applied in practice; court guides are not sources of law, however, and cannot override any provision in the CPR. Whilst there is no authority on the point, some commentators have said that where ambiguity

---

[96]   *TJ Brent Ltd v Black & Veatch Consulting Ltd* [2008] EWHC 1497 (TCC) at [45].
[97]   Pre-Action Protocol for the Resolution of Clinical Disputes, para 3.12.

exists in primary sources of the law, court guides may be used as being an extrinsic aid to interpretation.[98] There is, however, no authority to support that proposition.

Learned journals

3.51   Learned journals may be peer reviewed or not peer reviewed; for obvious reasons, the former will carry greater weight. Examples of peer-reviewed journals are the *Cambridge Law Review*, the *Oxford Journal of Legal Studies*, the *Law Quarterly Review* and the *Modern Law Review*. It is not common for articles on costs to appear in these journals. Instead, articles on costs normally appear in the *New Law Journal*, the *Law Gazette* and the *Solicitors Journal*. None of these are peer reviewed, and should be regarded as being nothing more than an aid to research.

Textbooks

3.52   Save for those rare exceptions that for present purposes can be disregarded,[99] textbooks can never be regarded as being a primary source of law; even where a textbook is properly cited as being persuasive,[100] it can never be binding. That said, costs disputes will often turn on the law of contract, and in those circumstances, it would be proper to cite books such as *Chitty on Contracts*; their value, however, derives from the fact that they can be trusted accurately to record and describe the law rather than from any intrinsic authority. It is not unknown for the court to cite textbooks on costs (such as *Cook on Costs*,[101] *Butterworths Costs Service*[102] and *Greenslade on Costs*[103]), but whilst such books are often regarded as correctly stating the law, they are not authoritative in the sense that they are a source of law. Textbooks may contain analysis and comment, and it may be that those comments are sufficiently correct to be adopted by the court post-publication.[104] Likewise, ancient textbooks will usually be given some weight if they are the only record of the law as it then stood; in this regard, modern readers may be surprised to learn that costs textbooks have been in existence for centuries.[105] As with any publication that is not a primary source of law, some caution ought to be exercised when citing textbooks; this is because no matter how careful the author may be, textbooks can contain errors.[106] As such, it is always good practice to cite the primary source of law where the circumstances permit.

---

[98]   See, for example, *Civil Procedure* (Sweet & Maxwell, 2009), Vol 1, para 2.3.6.

[99]   Whilst now rarely relied upon, there are about two dozen early textbooks which are collectively known as 'Books of Authority'; they are regarded as being intrinsically authoritative on the grounds that they are evidence of judicial decisions which are not otherwise recorded (ie, medieval and early modern decisions); see Blackstone M., Commentaries on the Laws of England, Book I, pp 72–73.

[100] Books such as 'The White Book', Chitty on Contracts, and other such esteemed works.

[101] See, for example, *Fourie v Le Roux & Ors Rev 1* [2007] UKHL 1, per Lord Carswell.

[102] See, for example, *Bensusan v Freedman* [2001] EWHC 9001 (Costs), per Master Hurst.

[103] See, for example, the Irish case of *Landers v Judge Patwell & Anor* [2006] IEHC 248, per Smyth J.

[104] See, for example, *Claims Direct Test Cases* [2003] EWCA Civ 136, where Brooke LJ adopted the 'ready reckoner' in *Cook on Costs (2003)* as being a useful tool for the purposes of assessing success fees.

[105] These include: Sayer *The Law of Costs* (1768); Baron Hullock *Costs in Civil Actions and Criminal Proceedings* (1796); Tidd *The law of costs in civil actions* (1793); Beames *A Summary of Doctrine of Courts of Equity with Respect to Costs, Deduced from Leading Cases* (1822); John Gray *A Treatise on the Law of Costs in Actions and other Proceedings in the Courts of Common Law at Westminster* (1853); and Dax *New Book of Costs in the Superior Courts of Common Law* (1847). Some of these are difficult to obtain, but the author would usually be able to assist in this regard.

[106] See, for example, *Carter-Ruck (a firm) v Mireskandari* [2011] EWHC 24 (QB) at [80] in which the court discovered an error that appeared in more than one textbook.

Consultation papers

3.53 Where there has been public consultation on an issue, consultation papers may have been drafted describing the background to, and history of, the legislation which was the subject of the consultation. Whilst there are examples of the court doing so without comment,[107] is a moot point whether the court is able to take consultation papers into account as an extrinsic aid to interpretation.[108] That said, they are often useful in other ways, such as identifying the law that was that was changed by the legislation in question or chronicling the history of the law in question.

Guidance in the Solicitors' Codes of Conduct

3.54 The Code of Conduct 2007 is accompanied by detailed guidance notes. Those notes have not been made by statutory instrument and should not, therefore, be afforded the same status as the Code of Conduct 2007 itself. Whilst there is no authority on the point, the guidance is probably admissible as an aid to interpretation of the Code of Conduct 2011. The guidance is probably also admissible on the point of what is acceptable practice and custom, this being a point which may be relevant to the terms to be implied into a retainer.

3.55 The guidance that accompanies the Code of Conduct 2011 is much more integrated with the that code than its forebear was with the Code of Conduct 2007, and it is difficult to see how the Code of Conduct 2011 could be placed in context without taking that guidance in account; that said, there is, as at the time of writing, no authority as to the status of that guidance.

---

[107] See, for example, *C v D* [2011] EWCA Civ 646 at [31].

[108] Examples do exist of the court taking consultation papers into account; in a costs context, see *Garrett v Halton Borough Council; Myatt v National Coal Board* [2006] EWCA Civ 1017 at [91] and [95]. However, Phillips MR seems to have indicated that they are not admissible, although this seems to have been for want of authority on the point: see *Callery v Gray* [2001] 1246 at [50].

Chapter 4

THE COURT'S POWERS

4.1   All judges stand in the place of the Crown, in whose name they conduct proceedings.[1] Whilst all the court's powers are derived from and can be traced to the authority of the Crown,[2] not all judges have the same range of powers; a full discussion of this issue is beyond the scope of this book, but a number of commonly encountered issues are discussed. This chapter focuses on the roles played by different types of judge. It deals only with jurisdictional issues; a discussion of the factors going to allocation within the judiciary can be found at **21.70–21.81**.

SENIOR COURTS: COSTS JUDGES

4.2   The comments under this heading refer to Masters sitting as costs judges in the courts listed at **4.4**; to avoid confusion with other types of costs judge, the word 'Master' will be used to refer to that type of judge sitting in that capacity. Where a Master sits as a deputy district judge of the county court, then the comments made at **4.8–4.10** would apply.

4.3   Masters are appointed by the Lord Chancellor with the concurrence of the Treasury.[3] There is a Senior Costs Judge who is appointed in a similar manner.[4] Masters are barred from legal practice.[5]

Range of jurisdiction

4.4   Masters assess all costs arising out of proceedings in the following courts and tribunals: Court of Appeal (Civil Division); the High Court; the Administrative Court; the Admiralty Registrar;[6] the Commercial Court; the Companies Court; the Technology and Construction Court and the Court of Protection; the Employment Appeal Tribunal; the Principal Registry of the Family Division; and Bankruptcy proceedings under the Insolvency Rules.

4.5   The Senior Costs Judge will make arrangements for proceedings to be assigned to individual Masters; they may vary such arrangements generally or in particular cases,

---

[1]   *John Russell & Co Ltd v Cayzer, Irvine & Co Ltd* [1916] 2 AC 298, HL at 302.

[2]   *United Engineering Workers' Union v Devanayagam* [1968] AC 356 at 382–383, per Lord Guest.

[3]   See Senior Courts Act 1981, s 89(1); this should be read in conjunction with the Transfer of Functions (Minister for the Civil Service and Treasury) Order 1981, which clarifies that the reference to the Minister is a reference to the Treasury.

[4]   See Senior Courts Act 1981, s 89(3)(c).

[5]   Courts and Legal Services Act 1990, s 75, and Sch 11.

[6]   The Master of the Administrative Court and the Admiralty Registrar both have powers to assess costs incurred in their respective courts, but since well before the introduction of the CPR they have requested the Masters to assess those costs on their behalf.

eg by transferring a case from a Master to whom it had been assigned to another Master.[7] A Master has the power to refer the matter to a High Court judge instead of dealing with it himself.[8]

Restrictions on vires

4.6   Where the CPR provide for the court to perform any act, then, except where an enactment, rule or practice direction provides otherwise, that act may be performed by a Master.[9] There are restrictions on what a Master can do,[10] but they usually arise out of restrictions which were not framed specifically with costs mind. They are, therefore, rarely of relevance in costs proceedings. Withal the following may be relevant from time to time:

- Masters are precluded from making orders or granting interim remedies relating to appeals from Masters or District Judges.[11]
- Masters are precluded from making orders or granting interim remedies relating to appeals against costs assessments, except on an appeal under r 47.20 against the decision of an authorised court officer.[12]
- Masters may not make injunctions or orders relating to injunctions, including those for specific performance where those involve an injunction[13] (those restrictions may not apply in certain limited circumstances, such as where the parties consent).[14]
- In proceedings in the Chancery Division, there is a restriction on dealing with the following without the consent of the Chancellor of the High Court:[15]
   — approving compromises:
      (i)   on behalf of a person under disability where that person's interest in a fund, or if there is no fund, the maximum amount of the claim, exceeds £100,000, and
      (ii)   on behalf of absent, unborn and unascertained persons;
   — making declarations, except in plain cases;
   — the proceedings are brought by a Part 8 claim form, seeking determination of any question of law or as to the construction of a document which is raised by the claim form;
   — giving permission to executors, administrators and trustees to bring or defend proceedings or to continue the prosecution or defence of proceedings, and granting an indemnity for costs out of the trust estate, except in plain cases;
   — granting an indemnity for costs out of the assets of a company on the application of minority shareholders bringing a derivative action, except in plain cases; and
   — making an order for rectification.

---

[7]   PD 2B, para 6.1; the fact that a case has been assigned to a particular Master does not prevent another Master from dealing with that case if circumstances require, whether at the request of the assigned Master or otherwise: see PD 2B, para 6.2.
[8]   PD 2B, para 1.2.
[9]   CPR, r 2.4(a).
[10]   They are summarised in PD 2B.
[11]   See PD 2B, para 2.3(d).
[12]   See PD 2B, para 2.3(e).
[13]   PD 2B, para 2.2.
[14]   See PD 2B, paras 2.3 and 2.4.
[15]   See PD 2B, para 5.1.

- There is a restriction on Masters hearing applications for declarations of incompatibility in accordance with s 4 of the Human Rights Act 1998.[16]

4.7   In practice, the only frequently incommodious restrictions are those concerning the powers of a Master to make declarations or to make an order for rectification. If a Master finds that he lacks the power to make the appropriate order, then he can either refer the matter to a High Court Judge,[17] or he can seek approval from the Chancellor of the High Court.[18]

COUNTY COURTS: COMMON LAW AND EQUITY

4.8   As they are entities created wholly by statute, county courts have only those powers which are conferred upon them by legislation. In proceedings dealing with the common law there is no limit to their powers, but this is not true of proceedings in which equitable remedies are sought.

Jurisdiction and 'the county court limit'

4.9   Section 23 of the County Courts Act 1984 confers an equitable jurisdiction on the county courts, but that jurisdiction is restricted (see below). It is not common that that jurisdiction needs to be invoked in the context of costs, but it may be necessary for the court to grant an equitable remedy from time to time: an example would be where a party seeks equitable rectification of a defective retainer. It may, thus, be relevant that the county courts' equitable jurisdiction is limited in the following way:[19]

> 'Proceedings for relief against fraud or mistake, where the damage sustained or the estate or fund in respect of which relief is sought does not exceed in amount or value the county court limit.'

So the county courts have an equitable jurisdiction only in those cases in which the relief sought does not exceed the 'county court limit'. That limit is currently £30,000[20] (this should not be confused with the limit which applies to solicitor and client assessments: see **4.12**). There is no reason to believe that this restriction will not apply when an SCCO Master sits as either a deputy district judge or a recorder of the county court.

4.10   Notwithstanding these restrictions, the parties may agree that a county court should have an equitable jurisdiction; that agreement must be recorded in a memorandum signed by the parties or by their respective agents or legal representatives.[21]

---

[16]   See PD 2B, para 7A.
[17]   See PD 2B, para 1.2.
[18]   See PD 2B, para 5.1.
[19]   See s 23(g) of the County Courts Act 1984.
[20]   The High Court and County Courts Jurisdiction Order 1991.
[21]   See s 24 of the County Courts Act 1984 (as amended by Courts and Legal Services Act 1990); see also s 18.

COUNTY COURTS: SOLICITOR AND CLIENT

4.11   The county courts have no jurisdiction to hear assessments in relation to non-contentious business.[22]

4.12   As to contentious business, s 69(3) of the Solicitors Act 1974 (as amended)[23] makes the following provisions:

> 'Where a bill of costs relates wholly or partly to contentious business done in a county court and the amount of the bill does not exceed £5,000, the powers and duties of the High Court under this section and sections 70 and 71 in relation to that bill may be exercised and performed by any county court in which any part of the business was done.'

Therefore, county courts do not have jurisdiction to hear bills relating to contentious business which exceeds £5,000. The parties may, however, extend jurisdiction by consent, but only if the parties sign a memorandum to that effect.[24]

4.13   An application made in the wrong court can be transferred (usually from a county court to the High Court).[25]

AUTHORISED COURT OFFICERS

4.14   The powers of an authorised court officer are significantly more restricted than the powers of a costs judge or a district judge. An authorised court officer does not have jurisdiction to hear claims for costs for more than £75,000 (inclusive of additional liability[26] but exclusive of VAT) or £30,000 in the case of a senior executive officer.[27] The parties may agree that the assessment should not be heard by an authorised court officer (see CPD, art 30.1(3)).

4.15   The powers of an authorised court officer are set out in CPR, r 47.3:

> '(1) An authorised court officer has all the powers of the court when making a detailed assessment, except—
>
> (a)   power to make a wasted costs order as defined in rule 48.7;
> (b)   power to make an order under—
>> (i)   rule 44.14 (powers in relation to misconduct);
>> (ii)   rule 47.8 (sanction for delay in commencing detailed assessment proceedings);
>> (iii) paragraph (2) (objection to detailed assessment by authorised court officer); and
> (c)   power to make a detailed assessment of costs payable to a solicitor by his client, unless the costs are being assessed under rule 48.5 (costs where money is payable to a child or protected party).
>
> (2) Where a party objects to the detailed assessment of costs being made by an authorised court officer, the court may order it to be made by a costs judge or a district judge.'

---

[22]   CPR, r 67.3(1).
[23]   By the High Court and County Courts Jurisdiction Order 1991, art 2(7), (8) and Schedule, Pt I.
[24]   See s 24 of the County Courts Act 1984 (as amended by Courts and Legal Services Act 1990); see also s 18. There are restrictions in family cases, chancery cases and admiralty cases.
[25]   CPR, r 30.1(2)(c).
[26]   See CPD, art 30.1(2).
[27]   See CPD, art 30.1(1).

Thus, an authorised court officer does not have penal powers, nor (for all practical purposes) is he able to hear a solicitor and client assessment under CPR, r 48.8.

THE COURT AS AN ARBITER

4.16   It occasionally happens that the parties are before the court not because the court has an express power to hear the matter, but because the parties agree that the court should act as arbiter. This can be done only to the extent that it is not prohibited by statute or rules of court.[28] In general litigation, examples are very few and far between, but this is not true of costs litigation. Examples include consensual compensation schemes and the quantification of ex gratia payments made to persons who are required to give evidence to non-statutory enquiries.[29] The court's involvement in those circumstances will usually be wholly as a result of the parties' consent. It is also done with the consent of the court: it is not possible for a person to impose on a judge the jurisdiction or duty to adjudicate on a matter where no statutory or common law right to an adjudication exists.[30]

4.17   For obvious reasons, where the parties are before the court consensually it will rarely be the case that they will dispute the court's powers. Where they do, the dispute will usually not be about the court's general power to hear the matter, but about whether the court is able to decide a particular issue. This will be an issue of contractual interpretation (ie interpretation of the agreement which has led the parties to be before the court), but the court will often be reluctant to give up jurisdiction in circumstances where the intervention would further the overriding objective. In a consensual compensation scheme involving a mammoth number of claimants, for example, Pill LJ found that the court had the power to impose sanctions on the basis that some of the claims (a very small percentage) had been issued and stayed. In the same case Arden LJ commented that CPR, r 3.1(2)(m) confers very wide powers on the court.[31] This seems to be in keeping with the way in which comparable matters are dealt with in litigation other than costs; in particular, Megarry J has found that where the agreed machinery for resolving a dispute had broken down, the court was not precluded from making an adjudication.[32]

THE PROVINCE OF PARLIAMENT

4.18   The court may, in appropriate circumstances, decline jurisdiction on the basis that an issue should properly be decided by Parliament. Whilst a dissenting judgment, and therefore only illustrative of the type of issues that are capable of being beyond the proper jurisdiction of the court, Buxton LJ made the following observations (in the context of protective costs orders ('PCOs')):[33]

> 'One of the criteria for making a PCO is effectively that the claimant is not eligible for Community Legal Service funding. The limits on such funding are very controversial, but

---

[28]   See, in a non-costs context, *Heyting v Dupont* [1964] 2 All ER 273.
[29]   Such as the Stephen Lawrence Inquiry.
[30]   *Re Hooker's Settlement, Heron v Public Trustee* [1955] Ch 55.
[31]   *AB & Ors v British Coal Corporation* [2006] EWCA Civ 987.
[32]   *Brown v Gould* [1972] Ch 53.
[33]   *R (Compton) v Wiltshire Primary Care Trust* [2008] EWCA Civ 749 at [70].

that controversy is about decisions taken by Parliament or under its authority. The court should in my view be very cautious in taking steps that extend support from public funds beyond that chosen by Parliament ...'

Thus, the extent of public funding is an area where the court will be cautious about intruding on the province of Parliament.

4.19   Another example of a court declining jurisdiction is *Willis v Nicolson*,[34] in which the Court of Appeal refused to issue guidance on costs capping. This was on the basis that the issues were best dealt with by the Civil Procedure Rule Committee following consultation. Where the Civil Procedure Rule Committee proposes rules, the proposed draft must be approved by the Lord Chancellor. Whilst it is not necessary for Parliament positively to affirm the proposed rules, they must be laid before the Houses and can be rejected by negative resolution of either House (see **3.22**). The Court of Appeal's decision to decline jurisdiction in *Willis* had the effect of requiring any appropriate guidance on the issue to be laid before Parliament.

4.20   In summary, whilst most courts will have the power to hear most costs disputes, some courts (the county courts in particular) may not be able to hear larger costs disputes or non-contentious solicitor and client disputes.

---

[34]   [2007] EWCA Civ 199.

Part II

THE LAW OF COSTS

Chapter 5

THE NATURE OF COSTS

GENERAL

5.1   This chapter discusses those identifying features that, firstly, allow monies to be recognised as being 'costs' (as opposed to damages or other monies), and, secondly, allow costs to be characterised as arising from contentious or non-contentious business. This chapter also examines the nature of lawyers' work: it explains why the professional exertions of lawyers tend to give rise to monetary losses which can be said to be 'costs' and why the same cannot generally be said of the monetary losses arising from the exertions of others. The emphasis is on costs between opposing parties, but much of what is said will also apply between solicitor and client.

5.2   The Solicitors Act 1974 defines costs as 'fees, charges, disbursements, expenses and remuneration'.[1] Similarly, the CPR provide the following definition:[2]

> '"Costs" includes fees, charges, disbursements, expenses, remuneration, reimbursement allowed to a litigant in person under rule 48.6, any additional liability incurred under a funding arrangement and any fee or reward charged by a lay representative for acting on behalf of a party in proceedings allocated to the small claims track.'

Neither of these definitions is fully inclusive in the sense that it will assist in deciding what cannot be categorised as being costs. It is therefore necessary to look to case law for assistance.

5.3   Not all monies occasioned by a person's involvement in litigation can be said to be costs. The realisation that this is true was made many centuries ago; there is, for example, a passage in Lord Coke's Commentary which acknowledges this distinction:[3]

> 'Here [the Statute of Gloucester] is express mention made but of the costs of his writ, but it extendeth to all the legal cost of the suit, but not to the costs and expenses of his travel and loss of time, and therefore "costages" cometh of the verb "conster", and that again of the verb "constare", for these "costages" must "constare" to the court to be legal costs and expenses.'

This was written in about 1628, but the fact that there is a distinction between monies which are and are not 'costs' remains relevant today; indeed, Lord Coke's analysis is still occasionally cited.[4]

---

[1]   Section 87(1).
[2]   CPR, r 43.2(1)(a).
[3]   The Second Part of the *Institutes of the Laws of England; Containing the Exposition of Many Ancient and Other Statutes*, 2 Inst 288.
[4]   See, for example, *McIlwraith v McIlwraith* [2005] EWHC 90010 (Costs) and the Irish case of *Dawson v Irish Brokers Association* [2002] IESC 36.

5.4   There is no single test which will determine whether monies can be said to be costs, but the factors described at **5.5–5.14** may, in an appropriate case, be relevant. Some of the factors relate to the nature of the monies in question, whereas other go to policy, or to the way in which the court quantifies costs; different factors may be relevant in different cases. A summary can be found at **5.16**.

Arise from litigation or professional work

5.5   In so far as the context of litigation is concerned, costs must arise from the litigation; Bowen LJ said:[5]

> 'Only legal costs which the Court can measure are to be allowed, and that such legal costs are to be treated as expenses necessarily arising from the litigation and necessarily caused by the course which it takes.'

The test of whether the monies in question have arisen from the litigation is only the starting point. Monies failing to satisfy that test will not be costs, but where that test is satisfied, the monies may or may not be costs depending on the factors set out below. Additionally, the monies must relate to professional work of providing legal services. This means that the following will not generate costs as they do not involve the provision of legal services: finding a business partner,[6] securing a loan,[7] collection of rent,[8] distributing monies in the context of winding up an estate,[9] dealing with administrative issues in the context of probate,[10] acting as a town clerk,[11] acting as an election agent,[12] and acting as a court official.[13] Disbursements are addressed at **31.2–31.5**. Counsel is addressed at **32.36**.

Costs not charges

5.6   The court assesses costs rather than charges. Put another way, it would be wrong to say that all fees and charges arising out of the litigation are costs. The identification of what monies are recoverable as costs and what are not is a matter for the court; put otherwise, that issue is not a mere function of the losses borne by the receiving party. In this regard, Purchas LJ made the following observations:[14]

> 'An award of costs has always ... ultimately been a matter of discretion in the court rather than the recognition by the court of a right possessed by a successful litigant.'

Brett MR had this to say on the topic:[15]

---

[5]   *London Scottish Benefit Society v Chorley* (1884) 13 QBD 872 at 877. See also the comments of Mecgarry V-C in *Re Gibson's Settlement Trusts* [1981] Ch 179 at 185.

[6]   *Sharp v Southern* [1905] VLR 223.

[7]   *Re Inderwick* (1885) 54 LJ Ch 72.

[8]   *Re Devereux* (1902) 46 SJ 320 and *In the Estate of Purton* (1935) 53 WN (NSW) 148; that said, see *Re Shilson Coode & Co* [1904] 1 Ch 837.

[9]   See the Australian case of *In the Estate of Purton* (1935) 53 WN (NSW) 148 (the writer is grateful to Roger Quick for assistance in finding the Australian cases).

[10]   See the Australian case of *In the Will of Douglas* (1951) 51 SR (NSW) 282.

[11]   *Bush v Martin* (1863) 2 H & C 311.

[12]   *Re Oliver* (1867) 36 LJ Ch 261, but only where that does not involve giving legal advice (see *Re Osborne* (1858) 25 Beav 353).

[13]   *Allen v Aldridge; Re Ward* (1843) 5 Beav 401.

[14]   *Hunt v RM Douglas (Roofing) Ltd*, CAT 18 November 1987, (1987) *The Times*, November 23 at p 21 of the official transcript, per Purchas LJ.

[15]   *London Scottish Benefit Society v Chorley* (1884) 13 QBD 872 at 875.

'I should have thought that the person wrongfully brought into litigation ought to be indemnified against the expenses to which he is unjustly put; but there cannot be a perfect indemnity, because it is impossible to determine how much of the costs is incurred through his own over-anxiety.'

The theme could be further developed by saying that costs are an assessment of what it is reasonable for the paying party to pay rather than what the receiving party might have incurred.[16]

Actually incurred

5.7   With one or two minor exceptions,[17] costs are limited to compensation for losses actually incurred. Put otherwise, most costs are limited to real losses rather than notional losses. Nourse LJ has commented that this was a 'cardinal requirement'.[18] The requirement that costs be actually incurred would not ordinarily prevent the court from assessing costs on the basis of a notional management (such as on the basis that counsel's advice ought to have been taken in writing rather than in conference); this, presumably, is permissible because the costs were actually incurred notwithstanding the notional management. There is a limit to which the court can do this, however; there is no authority for the proposition that the court can effectively re-write the bill of costs.

Calculable

5.8   This factor turns on whether losses can be computed in the sense that they can be expressed as a calculable sum. Purchas LJ rejected the notion that this was the only factor relevant for the purposes of deciding what are and are not costs.[19] The need for costs to be in a specifiable amount was another factor which Nourse LJ said was a 'cardinal requirement':

'The job of a taxing master is difficult enough without his having to worry his head over an item as foggy and suppositional as [an unquantified claim].'

In a similar vein, Bowen LJ remarked:[20]

'Professional skill and labour are recognised and can be measured by the law; private expenditure of labour and trouble by laymen cannot be measured. It depends on the zeal, assiduity, or the nervousness of the individual.'

---

[16]   *L v L* [1996] 1 FLR 873 at 885 per Neill LJ.

[17]   There are one or two exceptions. The Litigants in Person (Costs and Expenses) Act 1975, for example, permits recovery of notional monies, and even before that Act came into force it was held that a solicitor litigant in person was able to recover monies which would have been incurred had he instructed solicitors (see *H Tolputt & Co Ltd v Mole* [1911] 1 KB 87 and *London Scottish Benefit Society v Chorley* (1884) 13 QBD 872).

[18]   *Hunt v RM Douglas (Roofing) Ltd, CAT 18 November 1987,* (1987) *The Times,* November 23 at p 24 of the official transcript, per Purchas LJ.

[19]   *Hunt v RM Douglas (Roofing) Ltd, CAT 18 November 1987,* (1987) *The Times,* November 23 at p 21 of the official transcript, per Purchas LJ

[20]   *London Scottish Benefit Society v Chorley* (1884) 13 QBD 872 at 877.

No 'loss-of-opportunity' costs

5.9   Loss-of-opportunity costs are monies which, but for the litigation, the receiving party (as distinct from his lawyer) would have made or earned. They are similar to economic losses in the law of tort. Unless there is provision to the contrary, they are not recoverable as legal costs.[21]

Costs of being a litigant

5.10   The costs must arise from the litigation and not merely be costs of being a litigant. In this regard, Purchas LJ said:[22]

> 'Certain costs incurred by a litigant in person have never been considered as falling within the category of "legal costs". These are immediately discernible, e g the litigant's personal expenses of travel to court, his loss of time at court and his loss of earning or profit in whatever capacity he may operate. He has never been allowed to claim in a Bill of Costs these items where they arise solely from the occurrence of the litigation.'

5.11   In a slightly different context (ie the nature of the costs that a solicitor litigant in person can recover), Brett MR had this to say:[23]

> 'The unsuccessful adversary ... cannot be charged for what does not exist, he cannot be charged for the solicitor consulting himself, or instructing himself, or attending upon himself.'

The context in which these comments were made was such that Brett MR intended no allowance to be made in lieu of these matters: the implication is that the costs of being a litigant are not recoverable.

No test of remoteness

5.12   There is no test of remoteness in relation to legal costs.[24] Very remote costs are likely to have been unreasonably incurred, but would still, in principle, be 'costs'.

Not a punishment or a reward

5.13   Costs are neither punishment nor reward, but instead are an imperfect indemnity.[25] Bramwell B put it thus:[26]

> 'Costs as between party and party are given by the law as an indemnity to the person entitled to them: they are not imposed as a punishment on the party who pays them, nor given as a bonus to the party who receives them.'

---

[21]   *Hunt v RM Douglas (Roofing) Ltd, CAT 18 November 1987,* (1987) *The Times*, November 23 at p 23 of the official transcript, per Purchas LJ.

[22]   *Hunt v RM Douglas (Roofing) Ltd, CAT 18 November 1987,* (1987) *The Times*, November 23 at p 17 of the official transcript, per Purchas LJ.

[23]   *London Scottish Benefit Society v Chorley* (1884) 13 QBD 872 at 876.

[24]   *Hunt v RM Douglas (Roofing) Ltd, CAT 18 November 1987,* (1987) *The Times*, November 23 at p 18 of the official transcript, per Purchas LJ

[25]   *Malkinson v Trim* [2002] EWCA Civ 1273 at [11] per Chadwick LJ.

[26]   *Harold v Smith* (1860) 5 Hurlestone & Norman 381 at 385.

Likewise, Jessel MR said that the court had no power to order by way of a penalty that a party is to pay 'costs beyond the costs of the suit'.[27] This is the case even if the costs are described as being damages.[28] With one unimportant exception,[29] costs are not capable of being awarded as a punishment.[30] Older decisions (ie, before about 1850)[31] that imply the contrary are no longer good law. That said, commentators have noted that procedural abuses and defaults are often met with orders that have a flavour of penalty about them.[32]

Policy considerations

5.14   The rationale underlying decisions as to what are and are not costs may often turn on policy rather than legal principles; in this regard, Sedley J made the following comments about the recoverability of certain travelling expenses:[33]

> '[The restriction on the recovery of certain expenses was rather] regarded as a policy limitation than as a legal distinction. Certainly both in and after Coke's time, local courts were in chronic decline and the cost of coming to Westminster for justice was widely regarded as a scandal which was aggravated by the irrecoverability of the expenses: see Veall[34] ... where it is said that Coke himself estimated that litigants were spending a million pounds a year in coming to London for justice in the first quarter of the 17th Century. But the anomaly, if that is what it is, has become enshrined in the law.'

5.15   Finally, it is worth mentioning that the mere fact that monies cannot be characterised as being legal costs does not mean that the parties cannot agree that they will be treated as being recoverable costs: if a consent order specifically provides that certain monies will be recoverable, they will be recoverable even though they would not normally be thought of as being legal costs.[35]

---

27   *Willmott v Barber* (1881) WN 107 at 108. See also *Ross v York Newcastle & Berwick Railway Co* (1849) 18 LJR 199 at 200. Also see *Clarke & Chapman v Hart* (1868) 6 HLC 633 in which Cranworth LC said that costs are not a penalty but a necessary consequence of instituting litigation that has failed.

28   *Willmott v Barber* (1881) 17 Ch D 772, CA; *Re Vernon & Co (Pulp Products) Ltd's Patent* [1976] RPC 625; and *Cockburn v Edwards* (1881) 18 Ch D 449 at 459.

29   There is one minor exception to this rule, and even that is debatable under the CPR; this is where a non-party costs order is made against a legal representative, in which case the order can be seen as having a punitive element (see *Glasgow Harley (a firm) v McDonald* [2001] UKPC 18A and *Myers v Elman* [1940] AC 282.

30   See *Highgate Justices; Ex parte Petrou* [1954] 1 WLR 485; *Knight v Clifton* [1971] 1 Ch 700; *R v Tottenham Justices; Ex parte Joshi* [1982] 2 All ER 507. This rule holds good in other common law jurisdictions too: see, for example, *Armstrong v Boulton* [1990] VR 215 at 221 and *Cachia v Hanes* (1994) 179 CLR 4030. Whilst dealing with a criminal matter, the European Court of Human Rights has held that the fact that a litigant had elected to exercise his right to silence was something that could be taken into account as being a relevant factor without imposing a penalty: *Ashendon and Jones v United Kingdom* (2011) *The Times*, 22 September.

31   This is about the period that the efforts to move away from 'double' and 'treble' costs began to be recognised by the courts in the way that they analysed costs generally. See **1.19**; see R Quick *Quick on Costs* (Thomson Reuters) at [2.130].

32   Mause, *Winner Takes All: A Re-examination of the Indemnity System* (1969) 55 Iowa LR 26 at 37. See also the New South Wales case in which the following was said: 'Orders for costs are one of the ways, possibly one of the most effective ways, of a court controlling the standards of the profession and the efficiency of litigation': *Hermann v Charny* [1976] 1 NSWLR 261 at 268.

33   *R v Legal Aid Board ex p Eccleston* [1998] 1 WLR 1279.

34   Veall *The Popular Movement for Law Reform 1640–1660* (1970), pp 36–39.

35   See, for example, *Ruttle Plant Hire Ltd v DEFRA* [2007] EWHC 1633 (QB). This, presumably, would be subject to any affirmative restriction imposed by legislation: see **4.16**.

Summary

5.16   In summary, there is no single test that can be applied to determine what are and are not costs, but the following generalisations can be made:

- costs will generally arise from the litigation;
- costs will not be the expenses of being a litigant;
- costs will be calculable; and
- costs must have been actually incurred.

These factors help determine whether monies can be said to be costs; further considerations may need to be taken into account in deciding whether monies which are putatively costs are, in principle, recoverable as such.[36] Those considerations will usually depend on the nature of the monies in question. Examples of the types of question which may need to be asked can be found at **29.74–29.115**.

CONTENTIOUS AND NON-CONTENTIOUS BUSINESS

5.17   Whilst it is true to say that there are differences between contentious and non-contentious costs, that distinction is far less significant than one might expect. The law has developed with little regard to that distinction such that the present-day position is that those differences are, in general, limited to the following:

- contentious costs and non-contentious costs are assessed on different bases;[37]
- unwritten agreements between solicitor and client may be dealt with differently (see **8.222–8.225**); and
- conditional fee agreements (including contingency fee agreements) are unlawful at common law if and in so far as they relate to work which is contentious.

This final distinction has been significantly modified by statute (see **9.375–9.387** and **9.46** *et seq*); for most practical purposes the distinction remains relevant only to the extent that it has a bearing on whether damages-based agreements and other such agreements are lawful (see **9.309** onwards) and on whether unwritten agreements as to costs between solicitor and client can be enforced (see **8.222–8.225**). The distinction between contentious and non-contentious costs will become even less relevant as legislation intervenes to regulate damages-based agreements.[38]

Distinction between contentious and non-contentious business

5.18   Whether costs are contentious or non-contentious depends on the type of business from which they arose. Broadly speaking, the distinction between contentious and non-contentious business is as follows:

---

[36]   In *Re Gibson's Settlement Trusts* [1981] Ch 179 at 185 Megarry V-C identified three strands of reasoning that the court will take into account when gauging whether costs are *recoverable* in principle, but that is a slightly different topic which is dealt with at **29.75** *et seq*.

[37]   This can, albeit rarely, be significant: see, for example, *Bilkus v Stockler* [2010] EWCA Civ 101, where a finding that certain work was contentious deprived a solicitor of a £50,000 value element.

[38]   See Chapter 9.

- all business which is done in proceedings is contentious, as is all business done before proceedings are begun, provided that the business is done with a view to the proceedings being begun *and* provided they are in fact begun; and
- all other business is non-contentious, as is common form probate work.

In particular, Stanley Burnton LJ has explained the distinction does not depend on the nature of the work in hand but on whether it was done 'in or for the purposes of proceedings begun before a court or before an arbitrator';[39] therefore, even if highly disputed, work cannot be regarded as being intrinsically contentious by reason of its nature.

5.19 Taken in isolation, the legislative definitions are somewhat circular. Part of the definition of contentious business includes a reference to non-contentious business (see below), but non-contentious business is defined as being:[40]

'Any business done as a solicitor which is not contentious business as defined by this subsection.'

The definitions are, therefore, at the very least interdependent.

5.20 Prior to 1957, contentious business was defined as being '[a]ny business done by a solicitor in any court, whether as a solicitor or as an advocate.'[41] Thus, the definition of contentious business was a narrow definition which, for example, would not have included work ancillary to proceedings in court (such as conveyancing business done for the purposes of a claim).[42]

5.21 Since 1957,[43] however, contentious business has been defined as:[44]

'Business done, whether as solicitor or advocate in or for the purpose of proceedings begun before a court or before an arbitrator ..., not being business which falls within the definition of non-contentious or common form probate business[45] contained in section 128 of the Senior Courts Act 1981.'

This definition has been carried through to modern-day legislation;[46] it is wider than the previous definition in that it includes work done for the purpose of proceedings. This would include work such as conveyancing done for the purposes of a claim. In this regard, Wynn-Parry J had this to say:[47]

---

[39] This being the wording of s 87(1) of the Solicitors Act 1974.

[40] See Solicitors Act 1974, s 87; Ward LJ described the definition as a 'fairly useless circular definition' in *Garry v Gwillim* [2002] EWCA 1500.

[41] See Solicitors Act 1932, s 81(1).

[42] See *In re Simpkin Marshall Ltd* [1959] Ch 229 at 235.

[43] See the Solicitors Act 1957, which was probably in response to the following comments made by Denning LJ in *In re a Solicitor* [1955] 2 QB 269: 'Sir Hartley Shawcross asked us to draw a clear line for the guidance of the profession. We should have liked to accede to his request if we could. It seems to me that if a clear line is to be drawn there is only one possible place for it, namely, the issue of the writ or other originating process in the courts of law. All business before that date could be said to be non-contentious, and all business afterwards to be contentious. It would be very convenient if we could draw that line, but I do not think that we are at liberty to do so, for the simple reason that it is not the line drawn by Parliament.'

[44] Solicitors Act 1974, s 87.

[45] Common form probate business of the type contained in s 128 of the Senior Courts Act 1981 relates to obtaining probate and administration where there is no contention as to the rights to probate.

[46] See Solicitors Act 1974, s 87.

[47] *In re Simpkin Marshall Ltd* [1959] Ch 229 at 235.

'... There is now a clear and, I should have thought, logical division between contentious and non-contentious business. All business is now to be regarded as contentious which is done before proceedings are begun provided that the business is done with a view to the proceedings being begun, and they are in fact begun, and also all business done in the course of the proceedings. All other business is non-contentious.'

This oft-quoted passage does not convey the difficulty that Wynn-Parry J had in formulating his judgment. He candidly admitted that he found the question to be 'a really difficult one',[48] and he specifically commented that 'a different view could well be entertained'.[49] Stanley Burnton LJ has found that the phrase 'in or for the purposes of proceedings' must be read as a composite whole, and that it is permissible to look at the circumstances in which the work was being carried out; in the case before him, he found that work carried out for the purpose of valuing shares was contentious work in the context of it being carried out for litigation and under the direction of the court.[50]

5.22 Whilst not part of the definition, it is worth noting that s 51 of the Senior Courts Act 1981 states:

'Subject to the provisions of this or any other enactment and to rules of court, the costs of and incidental to all proceedings ... shall be in the discretion of the court.'

This provision is in keeping with Wynn-Parry J's analysis.

Examples of contentious business

5.23 The following are conventionally given as being examples of contentious business[51]:

- proceedings which have been begun in any court of record (not including a Coroner's Court);
- proceedings which have been begun before an arbitrator;
- proceedings which have been begun before the Lands Tribunal (more correctly known as Lands Chamber of the Upper Tribunal);[52]
- proceedings which have been begun before the Employment Appeals Tribunal (but not in the Employment Tribunal itself);
- proceedings which have been begun in the Upper Tribunal;[53]
- proceedings which have been begun which relate to contentious probate;
- proceedings which have been begun in the magistrates court relating to licensing; and
- any work which was done in anticipation of the above, but only where proceedings have actually been begun.

---

48   *In re Simpkin Marshall Ltd* [1959] Ch 229 at 236.
49   *In re Simpkin Marshall Ltd* [1959] Ch 229 at 239.
50   *Bilkus v Stockler* [2010] EWCA Civ 101 (Ch) at [44].
51   These list is based on, but not identical to, the list published by the Law Society in the booklet Non-contentious costs, Practice Advice Service, October 2010.
52   It is likely that at first instance this tribunal will, in due course, be assimilated into a body which will be known as Land, Property and Housing Chamber First Tier Tribunal.
53   This is a recent addition to this list, but it would seem to be a correct one given the fact that s 3(3) of the Tribunals, Courts and Enforcement Act 2007 provides that the Upper Tribunal is a superior court of record.

Examples of non-contentious business

5.24 Likewise, the following are conventionally given as being examples of non-contentious work:

- business done where no proceedings have been issued;
- business done where proceedings have been issued, but in a foreign court;
- non-contentious or common form probate;
- proceedings before the Criminal Injuries Compensation Authority;
- proceedings in inquires (including planning) or tribunals other than the Lands Tribunal, the Employment Appeals Tribunal, or a statutory inquiry; ;
- business done in respect of licensing relating where the body to whom representations are made is the Local Authority; and
- proceedings before a Coroner's Court (unless that work is for the purposes of a claim, which is subsequently brought).

Whilst not binding, Master Hurst has found that this conventional view has become so well-established that the aggregate consequences of adopting a different view would be worse than the aggregate consequences of allowing it to continue; specifically, he has rejected the submission that proceedings in Tribunals constituted before the coming into force of Tribunals, Courts and Enforcement Act 2007 should be regarded as being contentious.[54] He left open the issue of whether proceedings in the First Tier Tribunal should be regarded as contentious or non-contentious.[55]

Meaning of the word 'court'

5.25 There is no definition of the word 'court' in the Solicitors Act 1974 or in the Interpretation Act 1978. Whilst not binding, Master Hurst has found that the word 'court' means 'court of record';[56] this guidance has been adopted by the Law Society.[57] It is, perhaps, instructive that s 119 of the Courts and Legal Services Act 1990 (as amended)[58] refers to the following definition in the Legal Services Act 2007 (at paragraph 207):

> '"Court" includes—
>
> (a)   a tribunal that is (to any extent) a listed tribunal for, or for any of, the purposes of Schedule 7 to the Tribunals, Courts and Enforcement Act 2007 (functions etc of Administrative Justice and Tribunals Council);
>
> (b)   a court-martial;
>
> (c)   a statutory inquiry within the meaning of section 16(1) of the Tribunals and Inquiries Act 1992 (c 53); [and]
>
> (d)   an ecclesiastical court (including the Court of Faculties).'

It could well be that in the present day this is a definition to which weight should be given: there is, after all, no other relevant statutory definition. If this definition does apply, then it is possible that proceedings in the First Tier Tribunal will be regarded as

---

54   *Tel-Ka Talk Ltd v Revenue & Customs Commissioners* [2010] EWHC 90175 (Costs) at [145]. The Master did not specifically address the lists set out above (which are based on guidance issued by the Law Society), but his conclusion was that, in general terms, compatible with those list being a correct statement of the law.

55   *Tel-Ka Talk Ltd v Revenue & Customs Commissioners* [2010] EWHC 90175 (Costs) at [136].

56   *Tel-Ka Talk Ltd v Revenue & Customs Commissioners* [2010] EWHC 90175 (Costs) at [145].

57   See the booklet Non-contentious costs, Practice Advice Service, October 2010

58   In particular, as amended by the Tribunals, Courts and Enforcement Act 2007, para 15 of Sch 8.

being contentious.[59] The importance of this is that work which was formerly regarded as being non-contentious may become (and may already now be) contentious; this may have the effect of rendering unenforceable retainers which are of a type which hitherto have been regarded as being not only permissible, but the norm.[60] That said, this would be a significant change in so far as litigation funding is concerned, and there is a much force in the suggestion that it would be such an inconvenient change in the law that it ought to be rejected on grounds of policy.[61]

5.26   Whilst not binding, Master Hurst has found that the fact that a claim is subject to assessment under the CPR (or by analogy with the CPR) is not, of itself, reason to find that it is to be regarded as the subject of contentious work.[62] In a similar vein, Stanley Burnton LJ has found that work done after proceedings have concluded where such work was done not for the purpose of the proceedings, but in consequence of the proceedings.[63]

COSTS VERSUS DAMAGES

5.27   The distinction between costs and damages is not always easy to make.[64] Indeed, up until the mid-nineteenth century, costs were often regarded as being included as part of the damages.[65] This, however, was largely as a consequence of a now obsolete system by which 'double' or 'treble' damages were accompanied by 'double' or 'treble' costs (see **1.18**);[66] the relevance of this is that authorities decided before about 1850 ought to be treated with considerable caution.

5.28   As explained at **5.4–5.16**, not all losses and liabilities that arise during a claim will be costs. Where they have arisen as *part of* the claim or counterclaim (rather than *in consequence of* its prosecution or defence), they may best be categorised as being damages rather than costs; this will be the case even where the monies were spent purchasing legal services.[67] The distinction is often resolved by considering whether the

---

[59]   The list of supervised tribunals was previously set out in Sch 1 of the Tribunals and Inquiries Act 1992.

[60]   In brief, damages-based agreements (which are usually referred to as just 'contingency fee agreements') that might have been enforceable in proceedings before tribunals which were not under the aegis of the Council on Tribunals may well not be enforceable if and when that tribunal comes under the supervision of the Administrative Justice and Tribunals Council (unless, of course, the agreement complies with the relevant statutory provisions). Even if there is an argument to be had on the point, it will be relevant for only a short period of time because it is likely that legislation will shortly intervene to regulate damages-based agreements (see *Regulating damages based agreements: Response to consultation*, CP(R) 10/09 (Ministry of Justice, 27 October 2009)).

[61]   See, by analogy with old-style Tribunals, Master Hurst's analysis in *Tel-Ka Talk Ltd v Revenue & Customs Commissioners* [2010] EWHC 90175 (Costs) at [145].

[62]   In *Tel-Ka Talk Ltd v Revenue & Customs Commissioners* [2010] EWHC 90175 (Costs) at [137]–[142]; see also *Dean & Dean v Angel Airlines SA* [2007] EWHC 399 (QB) at [16] onwards, per McKay J.

[63]   *Bilkus v Stockler Brunton (a firm)* [2010] EWCA Civ 101 at [44]–[46].

[64]   Counter-intuitive examples exist: thus, a 'costs' order made against a solicitor under the inherent jurisdiction of the court is a summary procedure which is in lieu of the claim that could be brought for damages against the errant solicitor: see the Chapter 7 and, in particular, *Collen v Wright* (1857) 8 E&B 647.

[65]   See *Pilford's Case* (1613) 10 Co Rep 115b; 77 ER 1102 at 116b (Co Rep); see also *Ashmore v Ripley* (1617) 79 ER 359, and see Sayer *The Law of Costs* (1768), p 271.

[66]   See *Deacon v Morris* (1819) 2 B & Ald 393 and *Phillips v Bacon* (1808) 103 ER 587 at 304 (East) at 590 (ER).

[67]   An example would be where costs in foreign proceedings are claimed as damages or where non-contentious costs are claimed as damages. See, for example, *Berry v British Transport Commission* [1961] 3 All ER 65, *Seavision Investment SA v Norman Thomas Evennett, The Tiburon* [1992] 2 Lloyd's Rep 26, *British Racing Drivers' Club Ltd v Hextall Erskine & Co (a firm)* [1996] 3 All ER 667 and *Union Discount Co Ltd v Zoller* [2002] 1 All ER 693.

losses or liabilities arose as a natural consequence of the defendant's actions;[68] if they were, then the monies will usually be damages. Misclassification is troublesome because if costs are wrongly claimed as damages or vice versa, they may be disallowed entirely.[69] Sometimes the distinctions between costs and damages is extremely narrow; Sir Mark Waller, for example, acknowledged this fact when he explained that costs incurred by an owner of an arrested ship for the purposes of obtaining bail is truly a damages claim, but the costs of putting up a guarantee to avoid an arrest can properly be said to be costs.[70]

The fees of professional advisors

5.29   The issue of whether monies are costs or damages often arises where the monies in question are fees for professional advisors who were engaged for the purposes of dealing with the after effects of whichever wrong it was that led to the claim. An example might be the fees of a quantum surveyor who was instructed to advise on the costs of rebuilding a property destroyed by a defendant's carelessness: on one analysis the surveyor's fees could be thought of as being the costs of rebuilding the property, but a competing analysis would be that his fees are expert fees of preparing a report on quantum. If, for example, only 50% of the damages were recoverable as a result of contributory negligence, a dispute as to the nature of those fees would be more than merely academic.

5.30   Where the claimant seeks to recover such fees as damages, there would usually be no objection in principle (or if there were to be an objection, it would usually be dealt with by consent). This is because even if an objection were to be made and upheld, it would usually do nothing more than to move the fees from the claimant's schedule of special damages to his bill of costs. Any difficulties are further diminished by the fact that the court is able to treat the monies as costs notwithstanding the fact that they are claimed damages.[71] This, of course, assumes that there are no other factors at play. There is, for example, a general rule that a person may not bring an action for 'damages' where those monies are in truth costs which he has failed to recover in a previous claim against the same party;[72] likewise, a person may not claim costs as 'damages' if the reason he is doing so is because they would be disallowed if claimed as costs.[73] These principles apply only where the parties in the claim for damages are the same as the

---

[68]   See *Peak Construction (Liverpool) Ltd v McKinney Foundation* (1970) 1 Build LR 111; *Hutchinson v Harris* [1978] 10 BLR 19 at 39.

[69]   An example is where damages have wrongly been claimed as costs, but if they had been claimed as damages they would have been subject to a test of causation or remoteness.

[70]   *Ene 1 Kos Ltd v Petroleo Brasileiro SA* [2010] EWCA Civ 772 at [39]–[57].

[71]   That is, the court is able to delegate the task of ascertaining quantum to a costs judge who would 'assess' the monies on the standard basis: *Redbus LMDS Ltd v Jeffrey Green & Russell (a firm)* [2006] EWHC 2938 (Ch). Delegation to a costs judge would be particularly appropriate where the fees were those of a legal advisor and where those fees were extensive.

[72]   The seminal case on the point is *Quartz Hill Gold Mining Co v Eyre* (1883) 11 QBD at p 690, per Bowen LJ: 'If the judge refuses to give him costs, it is because he does not deserve them: if he deserves them, he will get them in the original action ...'; as a more modern example, see *Carroll v Kynaston* [2010] EWCA Civ 1404. See also *The 'Tiburon'* [1992] 2 Ll L Rep 26.

[73]   See *Cockburn v Edwards* (1881) 18 Ch D 449 at 462–463, *Harrison v McSheehan* (1885) WN 207; more recently see *Ross v Caunters* [1979] 3 All ER 580 at 600–601, per Megarry VC. The same principles apply to cross-claimants: *Penn v Bristol & West Building Society* [1997] 1 WLR 1356. Whilst an Australian case and therefore only persuasive, Hamilton J has been held that the principle also holds good in multi-party actions where there may be an attempt to claim costs not recovered from one person as damages against aother person: *Queanbeyan Leagues Club Ltd v Poldune Pty Ltd* [2000] NSWSC 1100; he had this to say: '[T]he best conclusion is that the rule should be that all costs of all parties in multi party proceedings should be dealt with by costs orders made in exercise of the court's discretionary power to make such orders'.

parties to the costs proceedings.[74] Moreover, these principles will not apply where the claim is a claim for a contractual indemnity.[75] Issues such as these seldom arise in the context of the law of costs; as such, further details are relegated to the footnotes.[76]

Consequences of misclassification

5.31 A finding that 'damages' ought to have been claimed as costs is often of little consequence because it will often be possible to transfer those monies to a bill of costs at the conclusion of the litigation. The more difficult situation, however, is where monies are claimed as 'costs' when they ought to have been claimed as damages; this is more problematic because it would often be too late to claim those monies as damages. Mocatta J had the following points to make about that topic:[77]

> 'The question has been raised whether the fees of a witness, which included expenditure that could have been claimed as damages in an action but were not included in the damages claimed, can be claimed instead as costs. I can see no reason why they should not be, provided that they were not recovered in the judgment by way of damages, provided that they are a proper item, and can be justified as to quantum.'

Thus there is no reason in principle why monies that are capable of being claimed as damages cannot be claimed as costs. This, however, is only where they are 'a proper item'; Mocatta J did not expand upon what he meant by a proper item, but a paying party would have good grounds for arguing that an item is not a proper item where he can show prejudice arising from the decision not to claim the monies as damages. It could, for example, be said that a fee cannot properly be claimed as costs if it would have been subject to reduction for contributory negligence as damages. Where – as is often the case – the fees are for professional advice concerning the damage sustained, it may be worth examining the nature of the evidence that has been adduced for the purposes of proving the claim;[78] that will usually reveal whether the monies were a natural consequence of the defendant's actions or a necessary part of proving the claim.

5.32 A professional's fees may be damages at one stage in the claim and costs at another. An example might be where the quantum surveyor mentioned above supervised the purchase of materials (in which case his fees would normally be damages), but then prepared an expert report on the costs of repair (in which case his fees would normally be costs). Whilst speaking in the context of an attempt to claim monies as damages rather than costs, Longmore LJ has said that where a party seeks to claim monies in

---

74   *Hammond v Bussey* (1888) 20 QBD 79.
75   The indemnity will apply only to the costs claimed, not to the costs of bringing the claim for the indemnity: *Simpson v British Industries Trust Ltd* (1923) 39 TLR 286.
76   The principle stated above (that costs may not be claimed as damages where in truth they are unrecovered costs) will usually apply, but not always: there is no rule of law that costs incurred in foreign proceedings are irrecoverable as damage in an English action between the same parties where a separate cause of action existed in relation to those costs: *Union Discount Co Ltd v Zoller (Costs)* [2001] EWCA Civ 1755, and *National Westminster Bank Plc v Rabobank Nederland* [2007] EWHC 3163 (Comm). Likewise, the rule does not apply where costs have been or could have been recovered in criminal proceedings and are now sought in a claim based on criminal conduct: see *Berry v British Transport Commission* [1962] 1 QB 306 in which the subsequent (ie, civil) claim was for malicious prosecution, false imprisonment and conspiracy).
77   *Manakee v Brattle* [1970] 1 WLR 1607.
78   See, for example, *Aerospace Publishing Ltd v Thames Water* [2007] EWCA Civ 3 at [86], which deals with the costs of employees diverted from their usual duties by the litigation.

different categories, he must prove that this is appropriate on clear evidence.[79] There are examples of the court making a distinction between costs and damages in respect of monies claimed in the same case.[80]

5.33   In summary, the question of whether monies are costs or damages is usually determined by considering whether they were incurred as a natural consequence of the defendant's actions. Where the distinction cannot fairly be made in this way, then the court may have to look at the issue of prejudice and to decide whether it is fair that monies are claimed in the form that the receiving party wishes to claim them. The issue of interest on costs recoverable as damages is addressed at **36.54–36.56**.

THE WORK OF LAWYERS

5.34   Save for the occasional anomalous case, the greater part of any bill will be the fees charged by the lawyers. In the present context the work of lawyers is relevant because there are categories of work which can be done only by 'authorised persons'[81] or 'exempt persons':[82] where that work has been carried out by someone else, it would usually be the case that no fees are recoverable for the work carried out. Most readers will not need to trouble themselves with the detail of the remainder of this chapter; this is because the conclusion that is reached (**5.68**) is very simple (this being in contrast to the route by which it is reached). That conclusion is that there is only a narrow class of work which can be carried out only by an authorised person or an exempt person, and work which does not fall within that category will not be irrecoverable by reason of it having been carried out by someone who was not an authorised person or exempt person.

5.35   As of 1 January 2010,[83] the question whether a person is entitled to carry on an activity which is a reserved legal activity is to be determined solely in accordance with the provisions of the Legal Services Act 2007 (as amended) ('LSA 2007').[84] That Act defines two categories of work, the wider of which wholly includes the narrower. The narrower category is that of 'reserved legal activities', which are defined in this way:[85]

'(1) In this Act [the Legal Services Act 2007] "reserved legal activity" means—

   (a)   the exercise of a right of audience;
   (b)   the conduct of litigation;
   (c)   reserved instrument activities;

---

[79]   *Aerospace Publishing Ltd v Thames Water* [2007] EWCA Civ 3 at [75].
[80]   *Wallace v Brian Gale & Associates* [1998] 2 Costs LR 53 at 56. See also the commentary in *Hutchinson v Harris* [1978] 10 BLR 19 at 23 and at 38–40.
[81]   See s 13(2)(a) of the Legal Services Act 2007.
[82]   See s 13(2)(b) of the Legal Services Act 2007.
[83]   Before this date, the issues were governed by the Courts and Legal Services Act 1990 (as amended). The relevant provisions were introduced in a staged way; the majority of the provisions came into force on 1 January 2010 (see the Legal Services Act 2007 (Commencement No 6, Transitory, Transitional and Saving Provisions) Order 2009 (SI 2009/3250)), but in so far as s 12 of the Act defines the term 'reserved legal activity' for the purposes of ss 1, 207, 69(4), Sch 1 para 2(3) to (5), Sch 15, para 2(3), (4), and Sch 22, para 2(6), (7)(b)), the relevant date was 7 March 2008 (see Legal Services Act 2007 (Commencement No 1 and Transitory Provisions) Order 2008 (SI 2008/222)), and in so far as s 12 defines that term for the purposes of the Administration of Justice Act 1985, ss 9, 32A), the relevant date was 31 March 2009 (see Legal Services Act 2007 (Commencement No 4, Transitory and Transitional Provisions and Appointed Day) Order 2009 (SI 2009/503)).
[84]   See s 13(1) of the Legal Services Act 2007.
[85]   Section 12(1) of the Legal Services Act 2007.

(d)   probate activities;
(e)   notarial activities;
(f)   the administration of oaths.'

These categories of work are those that only authorised persons or exempt persons are permitted to do.[86] The wider category is that of 'legal activity', which is defined in this way:[87]

'(3) In this Act "legal activity" means—

(a)   an activity which is a reserved legal activity within the meaning of this Act as originally enacted, and
(b)   any other activity which consists of one or both of the following—
        (i)   the provision of legal advice or assistance in connection with the application of the law or with any form of resolution of legal disputes;
        (ii)   the provision of representation in connection with any matter concerning the application of the law or any form of resolution of legal disputes.

(4) But "legal activity" does not include any activity of a judicial or quasi-judicial nature (including acting as a mediator).'

Whilst it is highly relevant for the purposes of regulation, this wider category is of little relevance to the law of costs; it is mentioned only for the sake of completeness. In particular, unlike reserved legal activities, the fact that a legal activity may have been carried out by a person who was neither authorised nor exempt would, of itself, have no bearing on the recoverability of the fees for that work.

Thus there are two questions which must be addressed when considering whether the costs of an activity are irrecoverable by reason of the status of the person who carried it out. The first is whether work in question – which is referred to as 'the relevant activity'[88] – was a reserved legal activity, and the second is whether the person who carried it out was an authorised person or an exempt person. There are three outcomes that need to be considered:

- ***Authorised or exempt Person:*** The relevant activity was carried out by an exempt person or an authorised person: in those circumstances the costs of performing the activity would not be irrecoverable by reason of the status of the person who carried it out, and this would be the case regardless of whether the relevant activity was or was not a reserved legal activity;
- ***Reserved legal activity and person not authorised or exempt:*** The relevant activity was a reserved legal activity and it was carried out by a person who was neither an authorised person nor an exempt person; in those circumstances the performance of the activity would have been an offence,[89] and by reason of the doctrine of implied statutory prohibition[90] (and, in some circumstances, also by reason of an express statutory prohibition[91]), this would mean that no fees would be recoverable in respect of that activity;
- ***Not a reserved legal activity:*** The relevant activity was not a reserved legal activity and it was carried out by a person who was neither an authorised person nor an

---

[86]   See s 13(2) of the Legal Services Act 2007.
[87]   Section 12(1) of the Legal Services Act 2007.
[88]   See, for example, s 14(1) of the Legal Services Act 2007.
[89]   See s 14 of the Legal Services Act 2007.
[90]   The reason for this would be 'implied statutory prohibition'; this is addressed in detail (albeit in a different context) at **8.247**.
[91]   See **5.40**; see Solicitors Act 1974, s 25.

exempt person; in those circumstances the costs of carrying out the task would not be irrecoverable by reason of the status of the person who carried out the work, but other factors may apply (see **5.69** onwards).

The rest of this section deals with the detail of the law, but – for the reasons set out above – most readers will not need to trouble themselves with the minutiae. There is an overview at **5.68**.

5.36   In a broad sense, costs – or, rather, profit costs, counsel's fees, costs lawyers' fees, etc – are the fees charged by lawyers for carrying out lawyers' work. What constitutes lawyers' work used to be governed by diverse and sundry sources of law, but since 1990 it has been a subject governed by statute. The first of the governing statutes was the Courts and Legal Services Act 1990 (as amended) ('CLSA 1990'), but on 1 January 2010 this was replaced by the LSA 2007.[92] Transitional provisions apply.[93] In the present context, the relevance of these Acts is that if work has been carried out lawfully, then a professional fee may be raised and costs would thereby be created, but if the work has been carried out unlawfully, then no fee may be raised and no costs would be created.[94] The issue is more complex than simply determining whether the work which has been done was work which would normally be done by lawyers: in some jurisdictions the test is, on occasion, as simple as that,[95] but in England and Wales a much more restrictive test applies.

5.37   Notwithstanding the fact that the present regime is now governed by LSA 2007, it is necessary to know about the old regime, this being because cost incurred under that regime will continue to be encountered for many years to come. As such, both regimes are described. In any event, both CLSA 1990 and LSA 2007 make frequent reference to the Solicitors Act 1974 ('SA 1974'), and as such it is convenient to deal with that Act first. It should be stressed, however, that in the present context, its relevance under the new regime (ie, under LSA 2007) is not particularly great.

The Solicitors Act 1974

5.38   The 1974 Act is concerned with solicitors rather than other categories of legal representative; that is, it does not define the entire range of persons who are authorised litigators.[96] The starting point is that SA 1974, s 20 prohibits any unqualified person from acting as a solicitor.[97] The Act defines an 'unqualified person' as being a person who has not been admitted as a solicitor and does not have in force a practising

---

[92] The introduction of this Act was staggered; see the footnotes to **5.35**.

[93] See the footnotes to **5.35** for an explanation of the staged introduction; transitional provisions are found at Sch 22 of the Legal Services Act 2007.

[94] If authority were needed for this assertion, it can be found (albeit only in relation to unqualified persons acting as a solicitor) at SA 1974, s 25.

[95] See, for example, the Australian case of *In re Sanderson* [1927] VLR 394, in which the following test was promulgated: 'What I do decide is that if a person does a thing usually done by a solicitor and does it in such a way as to lead to the reasonable inference that he is a solicitor – if he combines professing to be a solicitor with actions usually taken by a solicitor – I think he then acts as a solicitor.'

[96] See LSA 2007, s 207(1); prior to 1 January 2010, see CLSA 1990, s 119(1).

[97] This section was substituted by the Legal Services Act 2007, s 177, Sch 16, Pt 1, paras 1, 25: see the Legal Services Act 2007 (Commencement No 6, Transitory, Transitional and Saving Provisions) Order 2009 (SI 2009/3250), art 2(f)(ii).

certificate.[98] Since 31 March 2009 the person must, if a corporation, also be 'recognised', or employed by a person who is recognised, or must otherwise satisfy the requirements concerning recognition.[99]

5.39   Prior to 1 January 2010,[100] SA 1974, s 22 makes the following provisions:

'(1)   Subject to subsections (2) and (2A), any unqualified person who directly or indirectly—

(a)   draws or prepares any instrument of transfer or charge for the purposes of the Land Registration Act 2002, or makes any application or lodges any document for registration under that Act at the registry, or

(b)   draws or prepares any other instrument relating to real or personal estate, or any legal proceeding shall, unless he proves that the act was not done for or in the expectation of any fee, gain or reward, be guilty of an offence ...'

Following that date, this section was repealed;[101] the function of classifying instruments of this nature now falls to the LSA 2007 itself: see **5.58** *et seq.*[102]

5.40   SA 1974, s 25 provides:

'(1)   No costs in respect of anything done by any unqualified person acting as a solicitor shall be recoverable by him, or by any other person, in any action, suit or matter.'

Thus, there is an express statutory prohibition against the recovery of fees charged by an unqualified person acting as a solicitor. Whether that prohibition will apply is something that will be determined by the nature of the work done. SA 1974 created several classes of work for which costs could be recovered only if and to the extent that the work had been carried out by a practising solicitor, but the position was significantly altered by the CLSA 1990, which afforded other categories of legal representative the facility to charge a fee for providing certain legal services. Moreover, from 1 January 2010 onwards, LSA 2007 has applied, and the extent to which that Act refers back to the SA 1974 is limited. In any event, the practical effect of the express statutory probation mentioned above would be eclipsed by the implied statutory prohibition mentioned below (**5.46**), so in practical terms, the SA 1974 is of only passing relevance to the issue of whether the status of the person who carried out the work has a bearing on the recoverability of the costs relating to that work.

The Courts and Legal Services Act 1990

5.41   What is set out between here and **5.68** applies only to work done before 1 January 2010; transitional provisions apply.[103] Before that date, legal services were governed by CLSA 1990; that Act can be thought of acting in concert with SA 1974 to widen the category of persons who were able to claim fees for providing legal services. It achieved this in two stages: first, it defined categories of persons who were able to conduct

---

[98]   See SA 1974, ss 1 and 87.

[99]   See rule 12 of the Solicitors Code of Conduct 2007 and (from 1 July 2009) SA 1974, s 1B, as amended by the Legal Services Act 2007 and the Legal Services Act 2007 (Commencement No 5, Transitory and Transitional Provisions) Order 2009.

[100]   See the Legal Services Act 2007 (Commencement No 6, Transitory, Transitional and Saving Provisions) Order 2009 (SI 2009/3250), art 2(f)(ii).

[101]   Legal Services Act 2007, ss 177, 210, Sch 16, Pt 1, paras 1, 26(a), Sch 23.

[102]   See Legal Services Act 2007, Sch 2, para 5.

[103]   See the footnotes to **5.35** for an explanation of the staged introduction; transitional provisions are found at Sch 22 of the Legal Services Act 2007.

litigation or who had rights of audience (or both), and secondly, it disapplied the prohibition in SA 1974 against recovery of those persons' fees (see **5.40**). In particular, CLSA 1990 provided that a person who is able to conduct litigation or who has rights of audience will not be an 'unqualified person' for the purposes of the 1974 Act.[104] Instead, such a person would be an 'authorised litigator'.

5.42 Section 17 of CLSA 1990 introduced the twin concepts of 'the statutory objective' and 'the general principle':

'(1) The general objective of this Part is the development of legal services in England and Wales ... by making provision for new or better ways of providing such services and a wider choice of persons providing them, while maintaining the proper and efficient administration of justice.

(2) In this Act that objective is referred to as "the statutory objective".

(3) As a general principle the question whether a person should be granted a right of audience, or be granted a right to conduct litigation in relation to any court or proceedings, should be determined only by reference to—

(a)   whether he is qualified in accordance with the educational and training requirements appropriate to the court or proceedings;
(b)   whether he is a member of a professional or other body which—
  (i)   has rules of conduct (however described) governing the conduct of its members;
  (ii)   has an effective mechanism for enforcing the rules of conduct; and
  (iii)   is likely to enforce them;
(c)   ...
(d)   whether the rules of conduct are, in relation to the court or proceedings, appropriate in the interests of the proper and efficient administration of justice; and

(4) In this Act that principle is referred to as "the general principle".'

Thus, the CLSA 1990 created the 'general principle' that the issue of whether a person is able to conduct litigation or has rights of audience would be decided on the basis of:

(1)   the person's qualifications;
(2)   whether he was a member of a professional or other body; and
(3)   whether that body's own rules of conduct were in the interests of the administration of justice.

5.43 Section 28 of the 1990 Act dealt with the right to conduct litigation (see **5.54**). For persons entitled to conduct litigation, s 28(6) disapplied the prohibition against the recovery of fees created by SA 1974. The persons who were able to conduct litigation (ie 'authorised litigators') were defined in s 28(5) of CLSA 1990; the Act widened that category of persons. Section 27 of CLSA 1990 made similar provisions relating to rights of audience (see **5.55**).

5.44 Thus, there was considerable interplay between CLSA 1990 and SA 1974; Dyson LJ (giving judgment of the court) summarised that interplay in the following way:[105]

---

[104] See CLSA 1990, ss 27(10) and 28(6) and *Agassi v Robinson* [2005] EWCA Civ 1507 at [57].
[105] *Agassi v Robinson* [2005] EWCA Civ 1507 at [57].

'An authorised litigator is not an unqualified person within the meaning of the 1974 Act: section 28(6) of the 1990 Act. A person who is not an authorised litigator may not exercise the right to conduct litigation within the meaning of the 1990 Act and may not act as a solicitor within the meaning of section 20(1) of the 1974 Act and may not draw or prepare an instrument contrary to section 22(1) of the 1974 Act. If he purports to do any of these things, he will not be entitled to recover his costs for doing so. A person who does not have a current practising certificate and who is not an authorised litigator within the meaning of the 1990 Act acts as a solicitor in breach of section 20(1) of the 1974 Act at least if he (a) issues proceedings; (b) performs any ancillary functions in relation to proceedings or (c) draws or prepares an instrument relating to legal proceedings contrary to section 22(1) of the 1974 Act.'

5.45   For the reasons set out above (**5.40**), there was (subject to the provisions in CLSA 1990) an express statutory prohibition against the recovery of fees by a person acting as a solicitor where that person was not entitled so to do. The topic of what was meant by 'acting as a solicitor' will be dealt with in the next section (**5.48**), but there is another mechanism by which a fee may be negated by the operation of the law, and that is by a mechanism of implied statutory prohibition arising out of s 70 of the 1990 Act.

5.46   That mechanism turns not on whether a person was 'acting as a solicitor', but on whether they were 'conducting litigation' (or, for that matter, on whether the person was carrying out any activity that they were prohibiting from carrying out). CLSA, s 70 defined criminal offences; in particular:

- section 70(1) provided that a person not entitled to conduct litigation was guilty of an offence if he did any act in purported exercise of a right to conduct litigation in relation to any proceedings or contemplated proceedings; and
- section 70(3) provided that a person was guilty of an offence if he wilfully pretended to be entitled to exercise any right to conduct litigation.

These were relevant because, in addition to the express statutory prohibition mentioned above (**5.45**), there was an implied statutory prohibition that arose out of the fact that a person would have committed an offence if he carried out work which he was not permitted to do. The doctrine of implied statutory prohibition is a consequence of the fact that the court will not allow itself to be used for the purpose of enforcing unlawful bargains (see **8.247**). Whilst there is no express authority on this point, Dyson LJ has implied that this is the law.[106]

5.47   Two questions arise: the first is what is meant by 'acting as a solicitor', and the second is what is meant by 'conducting litigation'. These topics are dealt with in turn. There is a degree of overlap.

'Acting as a solicitor'

5.48   What is set out in the next few paragraphs applies to work done both before and after 1 January 2010, albeit in the context of different statutory regimes (see **5.35**); that said, its practical effect after 1 January 2010 is not great. The House of Lords has explained that if a step in proceedings is, by legislation, required to be done by the party or his solicitor, and if that step is taken by an unqualified person other than the party himself, that person would necessarily be acting as a solicitor.[107] The CPR have the force

---

[106]   *Agassi v Robinson* [2005] EWCA Civ 1507 at [28].
[107]   *The Law Society of the United Kingdom v Waterlow Brothers and Layton* (1883) 8 App Cas 407; this case

of statute: the relevance of this is that where the CPR require that an act be done by a person or his solicitor, it is an act which, if carried out by someone other than the party himself, would be an act carried out as a solicitor.

5.49   Thus, it may be relevant is the CPR refer to an act being carried by 'a solicitor'. The CPR, however, often refer to 'legal representatives' rather than 'solicitors'. The term 'legal representative' was, prior to 1 October 2008, defined by CPR, r 2.3(1) to mean:

> 'A barrister or a solicitor, solicitor's employee or other authorised litigator (as defined in the Courts and Legal Services Act 1990) who has been instructed to act for a party in relation to a claim.'

After that date,[108] CPR, r 2.3(1) read (and still does read) as follows:

> '"legal representative" means a –
>
> (a)   barrister;
> (b)   solicitor;
> (c)   solicitor's employee;
> (d)   manager of a body recognised under section 9 of the Administration of Justice Act 1985; or
> (e)   person who, for the purposes of the Legal Services Act 2007, is an authorised person in relation to an activity which constitutes the conduct of litigation (within the meaning of that Act),
>
> who has been instructed to act for a party in relation to proceedings.'

Thus, where the CPR require that an act be done by a party or his legal representative (as opposed to a 'solicitor') it cannot be said as a matter of textural interpretation that only a solicitor could carry out that act. For the reasons set out below, it is unlikely that carrying out an act which is required to be carried out by a 'legal representative' would be interpreted as 'acting as a solicitor'.

5.50   Nonetheless, it is possible to say that where the CPR says that an act must be performed by a solicitor, the performance of that act will be to act as a solicitor; whilst helpful, this does not provide a complete definition of what is meant by 'acting as a solicitor', this being because there may be other acts, not specified in the CPR, which also fall within the category of acting as a solicitor. There are old authorities which pointed to a plethora of such acts, but Dyson LJ has made it clear that they have been superseded.[109] Instead, he preferred the following analysis of Potter J:[110]

> 'So far as I am aware, the claim consultants [NB the receiving party was represented by a reputable claims consultant] have not at any stage held themselves out as solicitors, but have at all times acted specifically as "claims consultants" in relation to their representation of the claimant. Section 25 of the Solicitors Act 1974 is linked and, in my view, falls to be construed

---

related to a predecessor Act to the SA 1974, but on this specific point the principles are likely to be the same (but see **5.50**). An example would be in *In re Ainsworth ex p the Law Society* [1905] 2 KB 103, in which it was held that an unqualified person who gives notice of appearance is thereby acting in contravention of s 2 of the Solicitors Act 1843. In reaching this conclusion Lord Alverstone CJ was influenced by the fact that the relevant rule of court required a notice of appearance to be given either by the defendant himself or by his solicitor.

[108]   See the 47th Update to the CPR.

[109]   He has criticised them as containing little analysis of what is meant by the phrase 'acting as a solicitor': *Agassi v Robinson* [2005] EWCA Civ 1507 at [35] and [42].

[110]   *Piper Double Glazing Ltd v DC Contracts* [1994] 1 WLR 777 and 786; this analysis was approved by Phillips MR in *R v Secretary of State for Transport ex p Factortame* [2002] EWCA Civ 932 at [26].

with the sections which precede it. Those sections are penal in nature and relate to unqualified persons acting as solicitors (section 20), pretending to be solicitors (section 21), drawing or preparing instruments of transfer or charge etc, the drawing of which is limited to solicitors and certain other exempted professions (section 22) and preparing papers for probate, etc: section 23. By section 24 of the Act of 1974 those penal provisions are applied to bodies corporate. In these circumstances, it seems clear to me that the words "acting as a solicitor" are limited to the doing of acts which only a solicitor may perform and/or the doing of acts by a person pretending or holding himself out to be a solicitor. Such acts are not to be confused with the doing of acts of a kind commonly done by solicitors, but which involve no representation that the actor is acting as such. On that basis it seems plain to me that the claims consultants did not "act as a solicitor" in conducting the arbitration on behalf of the claimant. Accordingly, on the basis of the facts existing in this case, I answer the first preliminary issue in the affirmative.'

5.51   This means that the phrase 'acting as a solicitor' should be read as being limited to 'the doing of acts which only a solicitor may perform'.[111] This definition invites the obvious question of how the phrase 'acts which only a solicitor may perform' is to be construed. In *Agassi v Robinson*[112] the Court of Appeal was presented with a list of activities which counsel described as 'administrative support' and hence not acts which only a solicitor may perform. The court did not comment on the accuracy or otherwise of that list, but Dyson LJ did say that (because of the penal nature of s 20 of SA 1974), the definition of 'acting as a solicitor' should be read restrictively. In particular, he concluded that the act of merely giving legal advice would not fall within that definition.

5.52   Whilst there remains room for argument on the finer details, it seems that the definition of what amounts to acting as a solicitor is closely aligned with those acts which are required by legislation to be done by a solicitor or by the party himself. For obvious reasons the CPR – being the rules of procedure – contain most of the relevant provisions, but there are one or two further provisions which can be found elsewhere. In particular, prior to 1 January 2010,[113] s 22 of SA 1974, prohibited drawing an instrument for any legal proceedings in expectation of a fee (see **5.39**); in this regard, Waller LJ cited with approval the following passage:[114]

> 'In this context, "instrument" means any formal document. It would therefore be an offence for an unqualified person for or in expectation of a fee or reward, to settle a writ, statement of claim or defence or any other document of a similar character on behalf of another person.'

Thus, prior to 1 January 2010, the act of drawing of an instrument for a fee by an unqualified person would have been unlawful pursuant to the 1974 Act, and this would have been so regardless of what the CPR had to say on the matter. The function performed by s 22 of the SA 1974 is now performed by LSA 2007 (see **5.558** *et seq*).

5.53   Finally, the test of what is 'acting as a solicitor' does not vary from tribunal to tribunal (although the effect of that test may vary); this means that where the tribunal in question is a tribunal to which neither the CPR nor any similar rules apply, there may be no acts which would amount to 'acting as a solicitor'. Indeed, Potter J found that this

---

[111]   This view was also implicitly approved by Phillips MR (giving the judgment of the court) in another case: *R (Factortame Ltd and others) v Secretary of State for Transport, Local Government and Regions (No 8)* [2002] EWCA Civ 932, [2003] QB 381.
[112]   [2005] EWCA Civ 1507.
[113]   This was repealed by the Legal Services Act 2007, ss 177, 210, Sch 16, Pt 1, paras 1 and 26(a), Sch 23.
[114]   *Powell v Ely* (unreported) 19 May 1980, Divisional Court.

was true of arbitrations, and that therefore no part of the arbitral process could be said to involve acts which were 'acting as a solicitor'.[115] It could well be the case that the same is true of other tribunals.

'Conducting litigation'

5.54 What is set out in the next few paragraphs applies only to work carried out before 1 January 2010.[116] Section 119(1) of CLSA 1990 defined the right to conduct litigation as the right:

'(a) to issue proceedings before any court; and
(b) to perform any ancillary functions in relation to proceedings (such as entering appearances to actions).'

This means that there were two parts to the definition of 'conducting litigation': first, the act of issuing proceedings before any court; and, secondly, the act of performing any ancillary functions in relation to proceedings.

5.55 The concept of issuing proceedings presented no conceptual difficulties.[117] What amounted to the performance of ancillary functions was, however, not so obvious. The issue turns on what was meant by the phrase 'ancillary functions'. There are factors which pull in different directions: on the one hand, the need to protect the public from unqualified lawyers demanded a wide interpretation but, on the other hand, the punitive nature of the legislation called for a narrow interpretation. Dyson LJ preferred the latter:[118]

'The word "ancillary" indicates that it is not all functions in relation to proceedings that are comprised in the "right to conduct litigation". The usual meaning of "ancillary" is "subordinate". A clue to what was intended lies in the words in brackets "(such as entering appearances to actions)". These words show that it must have been intended that the ancillary functions would be formal steps required in the conduct of litigation. These would include drawing or preparing instruments within the meaning of section 22 of the 1974 Act and other formal steps. It is not necessary for the purposes of this case to decide the precise parameters of the definition of "the right to conduct litigation". It is unfortunate that this important definition is so unclear. But because there are potential penal implications, its very obscurity means that the words should be construed narrowly. Suffice it to say that we do not see how the giving of legal advice in connection with court proceedings can come within the definition.'

So the definition of what was and was not 'conducting litigation' was not precisely defined in the CLSA 1990, nor has it been precisely defined by case law. Given the fact that very similar wording appears in the LSA 2007, the same remains true in the present day.

---

[115] *Piper Double Glazing Ltd v DC Contracts* [1994] 1 WLR 777 and 786, as commented on by Dyson LJ in *Agassi v Robinson* [2005] EWCA Civ 1507 at [41] and [42].

[116] See **5.35**.

[117] It includes ancillary applications and appeals in the course of litigation: *Agassi v Robinson* [2005] EWCA Civ 1507 at [53].

[118] *Agassi v Robinson* [2005] EWCA Civ 1507 at [56].

'Rights of audience'

5.56   In so far as work carried out before 1 January 2010 is concerned, the approach is similar to that set out immediately above. The definition of 'right of audience' was as follows:[119]

"'right of audience" means the right to exercise any of the functions of appearing before and addressing a court including the calling and examining of witnesses.'

The position after that date is addressed at **5.60**.

The Legal Services Act 2007

5.57   What is set out below applies to work carried out on or after 1 January 2010; transitional provisions apply.[120] As of that date the matters discussed in this chapter were governed by the LSA 2007; that Act included the following as being its objectives:[121] protecting and promoting the public interest, protecting and promoting the interests of consumers, and improving access to justice. There is interplay with SA 1974, but it is not of great practical relevance.

5.58   A person is entitled to carry on a reserved legal activity where he is an authorised person or an exempt person in relation that activity.[122] It is an offence for a person to carry on such an activity without being entitled to do so;[123] the relevance of this is that it fees so incurred are almost certainly unenforceable (see, by analogy, **5.46**). Part 3 of LSA 2007 concerns 'reserved legal activities': these have been defined in general terms above (**5.35**). Those activities are categorised as being rights of audience, conduct of litigation, reserved instrument activities, probate activities, notarial activities and administration of oaths.[124] The precise provisions are qualified by transitional provisions.[125] What is set out herein is only a simplified summary of the first three reserved legal activities are addressed.

'Conduct of litigation'

5.59   Schedule 2 of the LSA 2007 defines 'conduct of litigation' in the following way:[126]

'(1) The "conduct of litigation" means –

(a)   the issuing of proceedings before any court in England and Wales,
(b)   the commencement, prosecution and defence of such proceedings, and
(c)   the performance of any ancillary functions in relation to such proceedings (such as entering appearances to actions).

(2) But the "conduct of litigation" does not include any activity within paragraphs (a) to (c) of sub-paragraph (1), in relation to any particular court or in relation to any particular proceedings, if immediately before the appointed day no restriction was placed on the persons entitled to carry on that activity.'

---

[119]   Courts and Legal Services Act 1990, s 119(1).
[120]   See the footnotes to **5.35** for an explanation of the staged introduction; transitional provisions are found at Sch 22 of the Legal Services Act 2007.
[121]   See the Legal Services Act 2007, s 1(1).
[122]   See the Legal Services Act 2007, s 13(2).
[123]   See the Legal Services Act 2007, s 14(1).
[124]   See the Legal Services Act 2007, Sch 2.
[125]   See the Legal Services Act 2007, Sch 2, Sch 22 and s 13.
[126]   At para 3.

Authorised persons will be able to conduct litigation to the extent of their authority, but a person who is not authorised may have the right conferred upon them by the court.[127] A litigant is an exempt person.[128] As to the way this definition is to be interpreted, see **5.55**. There is also a degree of overlap with 'reserved instrument activities' (see **5.60**).

'Rights of audience'

5.60   Schedule 2 of the LSA 2007 defines 'rights of audience' in the following way:[129]

'(1) A "right of audience" means the right to appear before and address a court, including the right to call and examine witnesses.

'(2) But a "right of audience" does not include a right to appear before or address a court, or to call or examine witnesses, in relation to any particular court or in relation to particular proceedings, if immediately before the appointed day no restriction was placed on the persons entitled to exercise that right.'

Authorised persons have rights of audience either in all courts (e g barristers) or only in some courts (or relating only to particular aspects of litigation). This is dealt with in detail in chapter 25 (albeit in the context of cost litigation). A person may become exempt person for the purposes of appearing in proceedings if he is granted a right of audience by the relevant court.[130] Employees may be exempt persons (see below). A litigant is an exempt person.[131]

'Reserved instrument activities'

5.61   In so far as it is likely to be relevant to the law of costs, Sch 2 of the LSA 2007 defines 'reserved instrument activities' in the following way:[132]

'(1) "Reserved instrument activities" means—

...

(c)   preparing any ... instrument relating to court proceedings in England and Wales.

(2) But "reserved instrument activities" does not include the preparation of an instrument relating to any particular court proceedings if, immediately before the appointed day, no restriction was placed on the persons entitled to carry on that activity.'

There are other provisions, such as those concerning instruments for the sale of land. As can be seen, however, the act of preparing an instrument relating to court proceedings is a 'reserved instrument activity'. Authorised persons will be able to carry out a reserved instrument activity to the extent of their authority. Lengthy provisions govern who is and who is not an exempt person,[133] but in essence, a person is exempt if he is employed by and supervised by a suitably authorised person.[134] A person is exempt if he is employed merely to engross the instrument or application.[135]

---

[127]   See Legal Services Act 2007, Sch 3, para 2(2).
[128]   See Legal Services Act 2007, Sch 3, para 2(4).
[129]   At para 2.
[130]   See Legal Services Act 2007, Sch 3, para 1(3).
[131]   See Legal Services Act 2007, Sch 3, para 1(6).
[132]   At para 5.
[133]   See Legal Services Act 2007, Sch 3, para 3.
[134]   Ibid.
[135]   See Legal Services Act 2007, Sch 3, para 3(9).

Agents, employers and employees

5.62   The issue that is addressed in the next few paragraphs is what should be made of the situation in which a person engages and assistant to carry out a reserved legal activity but only one of those persons is authorised to carry out the relevant activity. This usually arises in the context of employee and employer, but it may also arise in the context of principal and independent agent.

Unauthorised employer

5.63   Where an employee is authorised to carry out the relevant activity but his employer is not, then unless the provision of services is to the public (or a section of the public)[136] and unless it is part of the employer's business, the former will not carry on a reserved legal activity by virtue of the latter performing it in his capacity as employee.[137] This may be relevant if the fees in question are putatively payable to the employer.

Unauthorised employee or agent

5.64   In so far as the law of costs is concerned, the reverse situation is more commonly encountered (ie where the person assistant is the party who is not authorised but the person who gives the instructions is authorised).

5.65   The starting point is that where a person is an authorised to conduct of litigation, and where the person assisting him is under his supervision, then the assistant will be an exempt person for the purposes of exercising a right of audience, but this will be the case only if the proceedings are being heard in chambers and are not reserved family proceedings.[138] The word 'chambers' is not defined in the LSA 2007. Moreover, the CPR refer to 'in private' and 'in public' rather than 'in chambers' and 'in court'. As such, there is uncertainty as to what is meant by 'chambers'. Whilst not a source of law, PD 39A, para 1.14 may be an aid to interpretation of the word 'chambers':

> 'References to hearings being in public or private or in a judge's room contained in the Civil Procedure Rules (including the Rules of the Supreme Court and the County Court Rules scheduled to Part 50) and the practice directions which supplement them do not restrict any existing rights of audience or confer any new rights of audience in respect of applications or proceedings which under the rules previously in force would have been heard in court or in chambers respectively.'

Thus, whilst there is no authority on the point and whilst the contrary is easily arguable, it would seem that the CPR preserve the distinction between 'chambers' and 'in court' in such a way as to preserve (but not enlarge) the rights of audience that used to exist before the introduction of the CPR. In this regard it is relevant that solicitors have long been able to delegate certain tasks to unqualified staff.[139]

---

[136]   In general, this does not include the membership of a trade union: see Legal Services Act 2007, s 15(5); lengthy provision apply (see s 15(6)).

[137]   See Legal Services Act 2007, s 15(4).

[138]   See Legal Services Act 2007, Sch 3, para 1(7).

[139]   If authority were needed on to the point, the fact that certain work can be delegated to unadmitted staff was confirmed in *Sharratt v London Bus Co Ltd (The Accident Group Test Cases)* [2003] EWCA 718 at [196] and [212].

5.66   Whilst writing extra-judicially, the well-respected regional costs judge, District Judge Hill had this to say on the topic:[140]

> 'For many years persons employed by solicitors have been entitled to appear before the court when the court is sitting in chambers. This is recognised by long usage and it was not the purpose of the 1990 Act, nor is it of the 2007 Act, to restrict these long-established rights. But as I have already said, a disciplinary process is integral to a right of audience ... With a self-employed agent there is no employer or disciplinary body to which he can be reported if he were to behave in an inappropriate way.'

This highlights the distinction that between an employed assistant and an independent agent. Whilst it is not binding on any court and is not a source of law, District Judge Hill's analysis is often cited in support of the proposition that a more cautious approach is required under LSA 2007 than under the CLSA 1990.[141] The effect of this is that it is now an ordinary occurrence for the court to decline to hear from unqualified independent agents.[142] Where the person is qualified and supervised, however, then costs may be claimed (**12.10–12.14**); Burnett J has confirmed that this is the case were the employer is a costs lawyer.[143]

5.67   Whilst a defence of due diligence may be available,[144] an employer who unlawfully carries on a reserved legal activity through an employee would be guilty of an offence.[145]

Summary

5.68   To summarise, the following is *generally* correct:

- in so far as the law of costs are concerned, the relevance of what is and is not lawyers' work – i e what is and is not a 'legal activity' – is that if work in question – i e 'the relevant activity' – has been carried out unlawfully, then the doctrine of implied statutory prohibition will prevent recovery of fees (see **5.46**);
- Where the relevant activity was a 'reserved legal activity', the fees will be recoverable only if that person was an authorised or exempt person in relation to that activity; and
- For practical purposes, the three most important reserved legal activities are conducting litigation (see **5.59**), exercising a right of audience (see **5.60**), and reserved instrument activities (see **5.61**).

This means that reserved legal activities comprise only a narrow class of work, and work which does not fall within that category will not be irrecoverable by reason of it having been carried out by someone who was not an authorised person or exempt person.

---

[140]   R Hill 'In Practice: Benchmarks: Rights of audience' (2010) LS Gaz, 23 Sep, 20.

[141]   It is also in keeping with the concerns expressed in courts that deal in matters other than costs; see, for example, S Madge-Wyld 'Who may exercise a right of audience in claims for possession in the county court?' JHL (2011) Vol.14 No 1, pp 16–21. Also see **25.6**.

[142]   If costs are retrospectively claimed for such a person, it may be necessary to determine whether the assistant should be regarded as being an exempt person by implication (i e by reason of the court not having declined to hear him). That would be an arguable point to take, but there is a very powerful argument to the contrary, not least because there is no mention in the LSA 2007 of any such rights being conferred by implication.

[143]   *Kynaston v Carroll* [2011] EWHC 2179 (QB) at [6]–[8].

[144]   See Legal Services Act 2007, s 16(4).

[145]   See Legal Services Act 2007, s 16(2).

WORK DONE BY NON-LAWYERS

5.69 This section deals with the recoverability of fees levied by persons who represent others but who lack the status of being authorised persons (see **5.57** *et seq*); that class of person should be distinguished from the following:

* Persons who have been properly instructed by authorised persons (those persons are, as a result of their instruction, agents, which means that their fees are recoverable qua agency:[146] that issue is dealt with at **12.2–12.26**, but the points referred to at **5.64–5.67** may have a bearing in relation to some classes of work);
* Experts other than experts on the law of costs within the meaning of CPR, r 48.6(3)(b) (those persons are dealt with at **31.7–31.43**); and
* Employees of litigants (that issue is briefly dealt with at **11.88–11.101**).

The topics covered in this section will, with one unimportant exception,[147] relate exclusively to work done on behalf of persons who are litigants in person. This is because the person who seeks to represent the litigant would have no formal status, and this would mean that the litigant would be classed as being unrepresented. Where, in this section, reference is made to costs of litigants in person, this is a reference to fees for work done *for* a litigant in person (such as fees charged by a *McKenzie* friend) rather than costs for work done *by* a litigant in person.

5.70 Where a person who is not an authorised litigator conducts litigation, purports to exercise a right of audience, or draws a reserved instrument, the fees for that work are not recoverable for the reasons set out in the section above (see **5.58** *et seq*). Whilst there is no authority specifically relating to LSA 2007, if that Act is to be interpreted in the same way as CLSA 1990, then these categories are to be construed narrowly (see **5.55**); this would mean that in the ordinary run of things, fees for most of the work carried out by a non-lawyer would not be irrecoverable by reason of the effect of LSA 2007 (but as is explained in **5.73**, they are often irrecoverable for other reasons). Where an unauthorised person incurs disbursements with the client's express authority, those monies remain recoverable,[148] but this will, in general, not be the case in the absence of express authority (this being because an unauthorised person will, in general, not have any implied authority).[149] Furthermore, the fact that a partnership has as one of its members an unauthorised person will not prevent the remaining partners from recovering the fees for work done by them.[150]

5.71 This, however, is only the starting point. The CPR make a number of provisions which either affirm or qualify the law. Most of those qualifications arise out of the fact that where a person appears in court with a representative who is not a lawyer, that person will be a litigant in person. If small claims are disregarded for the moment,[151] CPR, r 48.6(3)(b) provides that a litigant in person may recover:

---

[146] See *In re Pomeroy & Tanner* [1897] 1 Ch 284, and the discussion in *Agassi v Robinson* [2005] EWCA Civ 1507 at [74] *et seq*.

[147] The only exception to this is where the litigant is represented by an authorised litigator but separately instructs a person who is not an authorised litigator without the authorised litigator's involvement; for obvious reasons, those circumstances will very rarely arise.

[148] *Hudgell Yeates & Co v Watson* [1978] 2 All ER 363 at 367.

[149] *Kent v Ward* (1894) 70 LT 612 at 613; and *Re Browne v Barber* [1913] 2 KB 553 at 573, 574 and 576.

[150] *Hudgell Yeates & Co v Watson* [1978] 2 All ER 363.

[151] Special provisions apply to costs on the small claims track (which is the arena in which the issues addressed in these paragraphs will most often arise); those provisions are dealt with below, but will usually overshadow the other factors.

(a)   payments reasonably made by him for legal services relating to the conduct of the proceedings; and

(b)   the costs of obtaining expert assistance in assessing the costs claim.

5.72   The costs of a solicitor, FILEX, etc will be recoverable, but so are the fees of the following:[152]

•   Fellows of the Association of Law Costs Draftsmen;[153]
•   costs draftsmen who are members of the Academy of Experts; and
•   costs draftsmen who are members of the Expert Witness Institute.

These persons may or may not be authorised litigators, but their fees will be recoverable in principle regardless of their status. This is not only by reason of the absence of any express or implied statutory prohibition, but also because of an affirmative provision within the CPR.

5.73   The next provision also arises out of status as a litigant in person but is restrictive rather than affirmative. The issue is whether the fees of a person who does not fall within any of the categories mentioned immediately above can be recovered as a general disbursement under CPR, r 48.6(3)(a)(ii). It is relevant that this provision restricts recovery to those disbursements which would have been allowed had the disbursements been made by a legal representative on the litigant in person's behalf. That restriction is important in that it often precludes recovery of the non-lawyer's fees; this is because those fees will not be recoverable if they related to work which a legal representative would normally have done. This is the conclusion that both Tuckey LJ[154] and Dyson LJ came to in different cases; Dyson LJ explained his reasoning in this way:[155]

> 'It is true that the rule refers to costs which would have been allowed as a disbursement if the disbursement had been made by a legal representative. But this does not require the court to make a fanciful hypothesis as to what disbursements a legal representative might have made. The rule contemplates allowing as costs only those categories of disbursements which would normally have been made by a legal representative. If the expenditure is for work which a legal representative would normally have done himself, it is not a disbursement within the language of CPR 48.6(3)(a)(ii).'

5.74   Dyson LJ went to explain that the services of some non-lawyers may, where appropriate, be characterised as being expert in nature (but, obviously, only where those services were not the type of work normally done by authorised persons):[156]

> 'It does not necessarily follow that [the receiving party] is not entitled to recover costs in respect of the ancillary assistance provided by [the non-lawyer] in these appeals. [The non-lawyer] is an accountant who has expertise in tax matters ... It may be appropriate to allow the appellant at least part of [the non-lawyer's] fees as a disbursement. It may be possible to argue that the cost of discussing the issues with counsel, assisting with the preparation of the skeleton argument etc is allowable as a disbursement, because the provision of this kind of assistance in a specialist esoteric area is not the kind of work that would normally be done by the solicitor instructed to conduct the appeals. Another way of

---

[152]   See CPD, art 52.1.
[153]   This still reads as this, even though the Association of Law Costs Draftsmen has become the Association of Costs Lawyers.
[154]   *United Building and Plumbing Contractors v Malkit Singh Kajila* [2002] EWCA Civ 628.
[155]   *Agassi v Robinson* [2005] EWCA Civ 1507 at [73].
[156]   *Agassi v Robinson* [2005] EWCA Civ 1507 at [76].

making the same point is that it may be possible to characterise these specialist services as those of an expert, and to say for that reason that the fees for these services are in principle recoverable as a disbursement.'

5.75   It is worth pausing here to summarise the position. Where the representative falls within one of the categories mentioned at **5.72**, his reasonable fees would – in the ordinary run of things and provided he is not carrying out reserved activities – be recoverable. Where he does not fall within one of those categories, his fees would be recoverable in theory, but in practice his client is likely to be a litigant in person, in which case his fees would be disallowed to the extent that they related to work which a solicitor would normally have carried out. This would normally preclude recovery of all of his fees (see **5.73**), but there is scope for fees to be recovered where the work relates to 'esoteric' matters and work that would not normally be done by solicitors (see **5.74**).

5.76   The following miscellaneous points can be made about certain specific circumstances, including where the representative was granted a right to be heard, where counsel was instructed by a person not entitled to conduct litigation, and where the claim is consigned to the small claims track.

Discretionary grant of right to be heard

5.77   Where a person appears in a court as a lay representative (often called a *McKenzie* friend),[157] he may be granted rights of audience or the right to conduct litigation for the purposes of that claim pursuant to LSA 2007 s 19 and Sch 3, para 1(2) (or, before 1 January 2010, pursuant to CLSA 1990, ss 27(2)(b) and 28(2)(c) respectively[158]). Whilst his decision is not binding on any court, Master Wright has found that where the court has exercised its discretion in this way, the fees of the *McKenzie* friend are, in principle, recoverable.[159]

Counsel

5.78   Where counsel has been instructed by a person who was not entitled to conduct litigation, counsel's fees are not recoverable in that litigation; this is because the prohibition created by SA 1974, s 25 relates not only to the unentitled person's own fees, but also to those of counsel whom he has instructed.[160]

Small claims

5.79   As mentioned above, particular provisions apply to cases allocated to the small claims track. Section 11 of the Courts and Legal Services Act 1990 provides that the Lord Chancellor may make an order granting lay representatives rights of audience in the county courts. The relevant order reads as follows:[161]

'(1)   Subject to paragraph (2), any person may exercise rights of audience in proceedings dealt with as a small claim in accordance with rules of court.

(2)   A lay representative may not exercise any right of audience—

---

[157]   *McKenzie v McKenzie* [1971] P 33.
[158]   An example is *Blakemore v Cummings* [2009] EWCA Civ 1276, in which Dyson LJ granted rights to a law costs draftsman to represent a litigant in the Court of Appeal.
[159]   *Fosberry & Anor v Revenue and Customs* [2006] EWHC 90061 (Costs).
[160]   *Westland Helicopters Ltd v Al-Hejailan* [2004] EWHC 1625 (Comm).
[161]   The Lay Representatives (Rights of Audience) Order 1999, SI 1999/1225, art 2.

    (a)   where his client does not attend the hearing;

    (b)   at any stage after judgment; or

    (c)   on any appeal brought against any decision made by the district judge in the proceedings.'

5.80   Thus, there is no reason in principle why a *McKenzie* friend should not recover costs in a small claim. This, of course, is subject to the small claims costs regime, which is an issue that is dealt with in more detail at **33.76–33.103**. In particular, however, CPR, r 27.14(4) reads as follows:

'The limits on costs imposed by this rule also apply to any fee or reward for acting on behalf of a party to the proceedings charged by a person exercising a right of audience by virtue of an order under section 11 of the Courts and Legal Services Act 1990 (a lay representative).'

5.81   In summary, special provisions apply to claims allocated to the small claims track. Where those provisions do not apply, the scope for recovery of the fees of persons who are not authorised litigators is narrow, but fees can be recovered where the assistance which has been rendered is of an esoteric nature. The fees can also be recovered if the representative is granted rights to conduct the particular case in hand.

Chapter 6

ORDERS FOR COSTS (JURISDICTION AND DISCRETION)

6.1 This chapter examines the principles governing the incidence of costs. Where the type of order in question is atypical (such as a wasted costs order, a non-party costs order, etc), then it ought to be read in conjunction with Chapter 7. The topics of indemnity and standard bases of assessment are dealt with in Chapter 13, and issues concerning joint costs orders are analysed at **12.27–12.66**.

The layout of this chapter is that, firstly, general principles are sketched out, and secondly, specific topics are studied in detail. The general principles include the following:

- the jurisdiction to make a costs order (**6.2-6.5**);
- factors to be taken into account (**6.13-6.24**)
- the range of orders which is available (**6.25-6.30**); and
- success and the 'general rule' (**6.31-6.53**).

And the specific topics include the following:

- the effect of offers (and, in particular, 'admissible offers') (**6.53-6.71**);
- conduct, including pre-proceedings conduct (**6.76-6.99**);
- the court's approach to 'issues' (**6.100-6.127**), including issues which have been abandoned (**6.126.137-6.137**);
- the court's approach to exaggeration (**6.138-6.154**);
- the effect of a refusal to mediate (**6.156-6.174**);
- the effect of a failure to respond to an offer (**6.175-6.179**);
- the effect of incurring disproportionate costs (**6.180**);
- the effects of a number of miscellaneous factor (**6.181-6.185**); and
- irrelevant factors and barely relevant factors (**6.186** *et seq*).

THE JURISDICTION TO MAKE AN ORDER

Statutory powers to award costs

6.2 With only limited exceptions (see **6.5**), the power to make costs orders in the civil courts derives from the Senior Courts Act 1981 (as amended), s 51 of which provides as follows:

'**51 Costs in civil division of Court of Appeal, High Court and county courts**

(1) Subject to the provisions of this or any other enactment and to rules of court, the costs of and incidental to all proceedings in—

(a)   the civil division of the Court of Appeal;

(b)   the High Court; and

(c)   any county court,

shall be in the discretion of the court.

(2)   Without prejudice to any general power to make rules of court, such rules may make provision for regulating matters relating to the costs of those proceedings including, in particular, prescribing scales of costs to be paid to legal or other representatives or for securing that the amount awarded to a party in respect of the costs to be paid by him to such representatives is not limited to what would have been payable by him to them if he had not been awarded costs.

(3)   The court shall have full power to determine by whom and to what extent the costs are to be paid.

(4)   In subsections (1) and (2) "proceedings" includes the administration of estates and trusts.

(5)   Nothing in subsection (1) shall alter the practice in any criminal cause, or in bankruptcy.'

Whilst this section expressly applies to the civil division of the Court of Appeal, the High Court and the county courts, it also applies in the Supreme Court, albeit only by analogy.[1]

6.3   The power to make a costs order is subject to rules of court and in particular to CPR, r 44.3; that rule provides as follows:

'(1)   The court has discretion as to—

(a)   whether costs are payable by one party to another;

(b)   the amount of those costs ...'

CPD, art 8.3 gives the following further guidance:

'(1)   The court may make an order about costs at any stage in a case.

(2)   In particular, the court may make an order about costs when it deals with any application, makes any order or holds any hearing and that order about costs may relate to the costs of that application, order or hearing.'

The court's power to make an award of costs is, therefore, almost unfettered. That power extends even so far as to permit the court to make orders against a person who is not a party to the proceedings in question. It also extends to those who have volunteered to become parties.[2]

6.4   But the courts' powers are not wholly without fetter. The court must act judicially. The powers conferred by s 51 of the Senior Courts Act 1981 are expressly stated to be subject to other legislation.[3] The person to whom or against whom costs are

---

[1]   The Supreme Court has power to determine any question necessary to be determined for the purposes of doing justice in an appeal to it under any enactment and its decisions are to be regarded as the decision of a court from which the appeal is heard (see ss 40(5) and 41(2) of the Constitutional Reform Act 2005).

[2]   See, for example, *Moore's (Wallisdown) Ltd v Pensions Ombudsman, Royal and Sun Alliance Life and Pensions Ltd v Pensions Ombudsman* [2002] 1 All ER 737; the fact that the party volunteered to become a party may, however, be taken into account when deciding whether an order should be made.

[3]   See *Conservative & Unionist Party (Claimant) v Election Commissioner* [2010] EWHC 285 (Admin) in which Keith J confirmed that the Representation of the People Act 1983, s 156 restricted the court's powers to make an order for costs against a non-party.

awarded must exist.[4] Moreover, the court exercising its discretion, it must act judicially. The court may make an award of costs only where costs exist, and it cannot award costs as a punishment or reward.[5] Bramwell B made that point in the following way:[6]

> 'Costs as between party and party are given by the law as an indemnity to the person entitled to them: they are not imposed as a punishment on the party who pays them, nor given as a bonus to the party who receives them.'

The court has no power to make an award in respect of monies which cannot be said to be costs; this is dealt with in more detail in Chapter 5.

Non-statutory powers to award costs

6.5   There is no general common law power to award costs.[7] This means that (save for the exceptions set out below) the power to award costs must be expressly provided for by statute[8] or by necessary implication.[9] This presents few problems in practice because s 51 of the Senior Courts Act 1981 (as amended) confers an almost boundless jurisdiction on the court, thus there is rarely any need for the court to rely on other powers. There are exceptions, but they are almost never encountered in modern-day practice: non-party costs awards against solicitors – which are not the same as wasted costs — are made under the court's 'inherent' jurisdiction,[10] and the fact that the House of Lords' power to make an award of costs derived from its inherent jurisdiction rather than from statute is now of only historical relevance.[11]

THE FORM OF THE ORDER

6.6   There are no formalities concerning the form of an order for costs, but the order must be tolerably clear and it must stand alone. It is not desirable that a costs order expresses itself by means of referring back to the judgment which preceded it; an order which does that may be struck down on appeal.[12] The words which give rise to the entitlement must be in the order itself; a provision contained within the schedule of a Tomlin order rather than in the order itself is not an order for costs and (absent a further order) does not give rise to a right to an assessment.[13]

---

[4]   A non-existent person cannot be ordered to pay costs or to receive them: *Russian Commercial and Industrial Bank v Comptoir d'Escompte de Mulhouse* [1923] 2 KB 630 (this decision was reversed on appeal, but that was on factual bases: [1925] AC 112, HL).

[5]   *Malkinson v Trim* [2002] EWCA Civ 1273 at [11].

[6]   *Harold v Smith* (1860) 5 Hurlestone & Norman 381 at 385.

[7]   *Garnett v Bradley* [1878] 3 AC 944 at 958; there used to be a free-standing equitable jurisdiction (see Garnett), but it is questionable whether it still survives.

[8]   This does not cause any difficulties in England and Wales because of the wide ambit of the s 51 of the Senior Courts Act 1981 (as amended), but the point does arise in other common law jurisdictions: see, for example, *Service v Flateau* (1900) 16 WN (NSW) 248. See R Quick *Quick on Costs* (Thomson Reuters) for a full discussion of the topic.

[9]   See *Queensland Fish Board v Bunney; Ex parte Queensland Fish Board* [1979] Qd R 301.

[10]   This is dealt with in detail at **7.191** onwards.

[11]   *West Ham Union Guardians v Churchwardens of St Matthew, Bethnal Green* [1896] AC 477, HL; see also *Bowes v Shand* (1877) 2 AC 455 at 472, 485 and *R v Chief Metropolitan Magistrate; Ex parte Osman* [1988] 3 All ER 173 at 175.

[12]   *Richardson Roofing Co Ltd (Claimant) v Ballast plc (Dissolved)* (Civ Div), 13 February 2009, CA (Jacob LJ, Aiken LJ, Sullivan LJ).

[13]   See, by analogy, *Horizon Technologies International v Lucky Wealth Consultants Ltd* [1992] 1 WLR 24.

THE IMPORTANCE AND MEANING OF THE ORDER

6.7   The order for costs is the cornerstone upon which subsequent costs proceedings will be based. Generally speaking, the parties will not be able to use the detailed assessment as an opportunity to revisit the entitlement to costs.[14] In particular, the costs judge would lack the vires to controvert the order (see **6.9**). It is not only what is in the order that is important; the costs judge can also take account of what is not in the order (albeit in only very limited circumstances). In particular, proportionality may prevent him from hearing an argument which ought to have been made at the time the order was made (see **12.141**). The relevant topics are briefly addressed under the headings 'No controversion' and 'Extent of opportunity to make further points'.

No controversion

6.8   The issue here is the extent to which a costs judge will regard himself as being constrained by the order (this being relevant to how the order should be phrased at the time it is made). As long as it stands and has not been successfully appealed or revised, an order will bind the costs judge such that he is obliged to give effect to it; moreover, he will not be able to assess costs in any way that is inconsistent with it. These principles were established in *Cope v United Dairies (London) Ltd*[15] and are entirely consistent with the way in which orders for assessment in other branches of the law are regarded.[16] *Cope* is such a well-known case that it is worth knowing the facts. The defendant was awarded costs against a legally aided claimant who was guilty of having failed to progress his claim following discharge of his certificate. The costs order did not distinguish between the claimant's liability for costs incurred before the discharge of his legal aid certificate and his liability for costs after discharge. The costs judge refused to assess those costs which had been incurred prior to the discharge of the legal aid certificate: he did this because he believed that part of the order to be ultra vires. The defendant successfully appealed that refusal. Megaw J held that a costs judge could not refuse to carry out an order for assessment on the ostensible basis that the costs judge considered it to be wrong or *ultra vires*.[17]

6.9   A costs judge lacks the power to rescind the order by varying or changing its intended effect.[18] Thus, Mann J has found that a costs judge lacks the power to assess an interim costs order at nil if that would controvert the order; the question Mann J had to address was:[19]

---

14   As to the finality of the order, see *Forbes-Smith v Forbes-Smith and Chadwick* [1901] P 258, CA; this case was disapproved in *Aiden Shipping Co Ltd v Interbulk Ltd* [1986] 2 All ER 409 at 412, but this was on a point which was different from the issue in hand, namely, whether a costs order can be regarded as being final.

15   (1968) Costs LR (Core vol) 23.

16   A common law judgment for damages to be assessed is binding on the court conducting the assessment: *Thomas v Bunn* [1991] AC 362. An enquiry as to title under a decree for specific performance is limited to the title which the vendor must show under the contract proved at the trial, and the officer of the court conducting the enquiry cannot consider whether a different contract exists which imposed a lesser obligation on the vendor: *McGrory v Alderdale Estate Ltd* [1918] AC 503 at 511, where Viscount Haldane said 'The terms of the decree have ... superseded and excluded all other evidence, and it is too late, if the decree remains unaltered, to try to import new terms in the course of inquiries which follow merely consequently.'

17   See p 24 of the report.

18   This is so even where the order has been made without judicial intervention by the operation of rules of court (so-called 'deemed orders': see *Lahey v Pirelli Tyres Limited* [2007] EWCA Civ 91 at [22].

19   *Business Environment Bow Lane Limited v Deanwater Estates Limited* [2009] EWHC 2014 at [1]. It should be noted that Mann J did not have the benefit of Waller LJ's guidance in *Drew v Whitbread* [2010] EWCA 53, CA and in *O'Beirne v Hudson* [2010] EWCA 52, CA. It is possible that his conclusion would have been different had he had this guidance.

'Where a claimant has picked up one or more costs orders in its favour on the way to a trial, but fails very badly at the trial (for example due to exaggeration), can the costs judge assess those costs at nil on the footing that they were not, as it turned out, reasonably incurred because they had been incurred in an action that sought an exaggerated sum which should never have been claimed?'

Mann J answered that question in the negative.[20] The costs judge does have a degree of freedom, however. Waller LJ has explained that without a 'special order', it would not be permissible for a costs judge to apply a fixed costs regime upon an assessment, but it would be permissible for a costs judge to carry out an item-by-item assessment on the basis that, properly managed, a fixed costs regime would have applied. Waller LJ accepted that the difference between these two approaches may be very fine.[21] The breadth of the costs judge's powers is illustrated by the fact that in an appropriate case he can take into account the fact that the claim belonged on the small claims track; whilst the small claims regime ought not to be directly applied in those circumstances, the costs judge would be able to take the existence of that regime into account when assessing the reasonableness of the costs; by that route the costs judge would, in appropriate case, be entitled to assess the profit costs at nil, or close to nil.[22]

6.10 Thus, whilst the order cannot be controverted and is of pivotal importance, it should not be forgotten that the costs judge does have significant powers. That range of powers is discussed in more detail at **12.103–12.141**.

Extent of opportunity to make further points

6.11 It may be that a party fails to raise a point at the time that the order was made and then wishes to raise it during the assessment. This topic is addressed in detail in Chapter 12, and in particular, at **21.160–21.160**. In appropriate circumstances a direction or special order may be required from the judge who made the order (see **21.160**);[23] thus, the costs judge's powers ought to be borne in mind when the order is made.

6.12 Whilst obiter, Waller LJ gave the following as an illustrative example of when a special order may be required: if it is to be argued that a witness in a long trial should never have been called because the evidence was irrelevant, a costs judge should not be required effectively to retry the case in order to adjudicate on the point: that is an issue which should be reflected in a special order.[24] The need to obtain the correct order is not a new requirement. It has, for example, always been the case that if a party fails to reserve his right to argue an issue which ought to have been mentioned in the order for costs, that party might be debarred from subsequently raising that issue.[25] For the

---

[20] See the footnote above.

[21] See *Drew v Whitbread* [2010] EWCA 53, CA at [41], in which Waller LJ said: 'I say to some extent this is what she did because in my view the costs judge was not entitled simply to rule that she was going to assess the costs of trial as if the case were on the fast track. To so rule does seem to me to rescind the Recorder's order. I cannot accept that in ruling as she did it can be said she was simply "assessing costs on the standard basis taking into account that the case should have been allocated to the fast track" which in my view is the permissible approach. It may in some cases be a distinction without a major difference.'

[22] *O'Beirne v Hudson* [2010] EWCA 52, CA at [19], per Waller; see also the comments of Hooper LJ at [22]. See also, in a different context, *Lahey v Pirelli* [2007] 1 WLR 998 at [19]–[22], per Dyson LJ. See also, in the context of Part 45, *Dockerill v Tullett* [2012] EWCA Civ 184.

[23] A striking example of the need to do this is where there are cross-orders as to costs (see **7.2** onwards and, in particular, the comments of Viscount Haldane recited at **7.14**).

[24] *Drew v Whitbread* [2010] EWCA 53, CA at [36].

[25] See, for example, *In re Frape ex p Perrett (No 2)* [1894] 2 Ch 295, in which the court found: 'The right of the

reasons set out in Chapter 12, however, it is now known that the rule in *Henderson v Henderson*[26] does not apply between trial judge and costs judge (see **12.130–12.135**), and the supposed rule in *Aaron v Shelton*[27] is no longer good law (see **12.138–12.139**).

FACTORS TO BE TAKEN INTO ACCOUNT

6.13   Whilst a trite point, it is worth stating that other than where specific provisions apply, each order for costs will be decided on the facts of the case in hand and in accordance with the relevant general principles set out in CPR, r 44.3. It is those principles which are described in this chapter.

6.14   In so far as it is relevant, CPR, r 44.3 makes the following provisions:

'(1)   ...

(2)   If the court decides to make an order about costs—

    (a)   the general rule is that the unsuccessful party will be ordered to pay the costs of the successful party; but

    (b)   the court may make a different order.

(3)   The general rule does not apply to the following proceedings—

    (a)   proceedings in the Court of Appeal on an application or appeal made in connection with proceedings in the Family Division; or

    (b)   proceedings in the Court of Appeal from a judgment, direction, decision or order given or made in probate proceedings or family proceedings.

(4)   In deciding what order (if any) to make about costs, the court must have regard to all the circumstances, including—

    (a)   the conduct of all the parties;

    (b)   whether a party has succeeded on part of his case, even if he has not been wholly successful; and

    (c)   any payment into court or admissible offer to settle made by a party which is drawn to the court's attention, and which is not an offer to which costs consequences under Part 36 apply.

(5)   The conduct of the parties includes—

    (a)   conduct before, as well as during, the proceedings and in particular the extent to which the parties followed any relevant pre-action protocol;

    (b)   whether it was reasonable for a party to raise, pursue or contest a particular allegation or issue;

    (c)   the manner in which a party has pursued or defended his case or a particular allegation or issue; and

    (d)   whether a claimant who has succeeded in his claim, in whole or in part, exaggerated his claim.'

---

    client to dispute the solicitor's retainer as to this bill in toto was not reserved in the order as it ought to have been, if he was to have that right'. See also *Skuse v Granada Television Limited* [1994] 1 WLR 1156, in which Drake J found that (on the facts of that particular case) the paying parties' failure to raise the issue of alleged maintenance at the time a costs order was made prevented them from raising the issue on the assessment.

[26]   *Henderson v Henderson* (1843) 3 Hare 100.

[27]   After *Aaron v Shelton* [2004] EWHC 1162 (QB).

Rules of court rather than case law

6.15 Generally speaking, it is to the rules of court rather than case law to which the court should look when making an order for costs. Brooke LJ has described these rules as 'the essential working tool' for resolving issues as to the incidence of costs.[28] Waller LJ has cautioned that in the area of the incidence of costs – where all cases are different and fact-specific – authorities other than those which lay down clear principles are of little assistance; it is to the CPR that one should go, he said, and it is by reference to the CPR that an appeal court should test whether a judge has gone wrong in any particular instance.[29] In a different case, Rix LJ (giving judgment of court) gave the following guidance:[30]

> 'It is trite to state but important to bear in mind that the rules prescribe the way in which the court's discretion as to costs should be exercised rather than any decision of this court on the facts of any particular case.'

This is, perhaps, an expression of the general (but often overlooked) principle that the exercise of discretion in one case is not to be taken as being a guide to how discretion should be exercised in another (see **3.4**).

The general rule

6.16 CPR, r 44.3(2) introduces 'the general rule',[31] namely, that the loser pays; it has been a feature of litigation in England and Wales for centuries.[32] The general rule is so fundamental to the operation of common law legal systems, that in an Australian case, it was found to be implied into legislation.[33] The general rule does not apply in all circumstance, however; in particular, it does not apply to certain family and probate cases in the Court of Appeal.[34] CPR, r 44.3(4) imposes a mandatory requirement that the court should take into account factors other than the general rule. Those factors are:

- the conduct of all the parties;
- whether a party has succeeded on part of his case, even if he has not been wholly successful; and
- any payment into court or admissible offer to settle made by a party which is drawn to the court's attention, and which is not an offer to which cost consequences under Part 36 apply.

These are referred to in this chapter as 'conduct', 'partial success' and 'admissible offers' respectively.

---

[28] *Groupama Insurance Co Ltd v Aon Ltd* [2003] EWCA Civ 1846 at [27].

[29] *Straker v Tudor Rose (a firm)* [2007] EWCA 368 at [10].

[30] *Kastor Navigation Co Ltd v AXA Global Risks (UK) Ltd* [2004] EWCA Civ 277 at [143].

[31] This rule is also often referred to as costs 'following the event', although that phrase should be used with caution as it can also mean other things.

[32] In about 1765 Blackstone recorded the maxim in this way: 'victus victori in expensis condemnandus est' (Blackstone, Commentaries on the Laws of England (a facsimile of the First Edition of 1765–1769 reprinted by the University of Chicago Press, 1979), Vol 3, p 399.) See *Quick on Costs* (Thomson Reuters) at [2.30] for a full discussion of the topic.

[33] See, for example *Hughes v Western Australian Cricket Assn (Inc)* (1986) ATPR 40-748 at 48 and 136

[34] See CPR, r 44.3(3).

All circumstances to be taken into account

6.17   CPD, art 8.4 emphasises that all circumstances should be taken into account when deciding the incidence of costs; it reads as follows:

> 'In deciding what order to make about costs the court is required to have regard to all the circumstances including any payment into court or admissible offer to settle made by a party which is drawn to the court's attention, and which is not an offer to which costs consequences under Part 36 apply.'

It is implicit from this guidance that the court's task is to identify all the relevant factors and then to make an award which balances those factors and which meets the justice of the situation.

6.18   Discretion should be exercised judicially: it cannot be exercised arbitrarily but must be based on fixed principles dictated by reason and justice.[35] The court should strive to give reasons for its order as to costs; Phillips MR had the following to say on this topic:[36]

> 'We understand that the costs were dealt with at the end of a long day and that the reasons were perfunctory. Costs are important, particularly where, as I fear in this case, they are disproportionate to what is at stake. Judges must be sure that their reasons for costs' orders are clear; they should not be left to inference, albeit that it is often possible to infer the reasons.'

6.19   All relevant factors should be taken into account. Although a pre-CPR decision, Buckley LJ explained the need to scan the 'whole battlefield', as he put it:[37]

> 'We have been referred to [authorities] for the proposition that we must have regard to all circumstances relevant to the issues in the action and the history of the action hitherto and the matters leading to the action. Those were both cases in which the orders for costs there under consideration were orders made at the trial of the actions. In such cases no doubt the relevant field to be scanned is the whole battlefield of the action and the whole of the conduct of the parties in relation to the matter in dispute may be relevant.'

No extraneous matters to be taken into account

6.20   The factors to be taken into account are the factors in the claim and not extraneous to it (such as unresolved suspicions or other unproven things). The oft-cited example of a court wrongly taking extraneous factors into account is where the costs of a motion for committal for contempt of an injunction were awarded against the alleged contemnor on the basis of his conduct, even though the court had found the allegations not proven.[38]

Not a mathematical approach

6.21   When making an order for costs which takes into account competing factors, the approach is not a mathematical approach, but one which does justice between the

---

[35]   *Ottway v Jones* [1955] 1 WLR 706, CA; *Bourne v Stanbridge* [1965] 1 WLR 189, CA.

[36]   *Lavelle v Lavelle* [2004] EWCA Civ 223 at [52].

[37]   *Scherer and another v Counting Instruments Ltd* [1986] 2 All ER 529 at 533.

[38]   *Knight v Clifton* [1971] 2 All ER 378, [1971] Ch 700.

parties; it is necessary to stand back and look at the effect of the proposed order. In this regard, Rix LJ (giving judgment of the court) commented:[39]

'The rules required [the judge] to have regard to all the circumstances of the case ... He should have stood back from the mathematical result and asked himself whether in all the circumstances, including the other factors to which we have referred, it was the right result.'

Chadwick LJ's guidance

6.22 Chadwick LJ has given the following guidance as to the general approach to making a costs order (with particular emphasis on cases involving more than one litigated issue):[40]

'The principles applicable in the present case may, I think, be summarised as follows:

(i)   Costs cannot be recovered except under an order of the court;

(ii)   the question whether to make any order as to costs – and, if so, what order – is a matter entrusted to the discretion of the trial judge;

(iii)   the starting point for the exercise of discretion is that costs should follow the event; nevertheless,

(iv)   the judge may make different orders for costs in relation to discrete issues – and, in particular, should consider doing so where a party has been successful on one issue but unsuccessful on another issue and, in that event, may make an order for costs against the party who has been generally successful in the litigation; and

(v)   the judge may deprive a party of costs on an issue on which he has been successful if satisfied that the party has acted unreasonably in relation to that issue;

(vi)   an appellate court should not interfere with a judge's exercise of discretion merely because it takes the view that it would have exercised that discretion differently.'

6.23 In so far as conduct is concerned, CPR, r 44.3(5) provides the following additional guidance:

- conduct before, as well as during, the proceedings and in particular the extent to which the parties followed any relevant pre-action protocol;
- whether it was reasonable for a party to raise, pursue or contest a particular allegation or issue;
- the manner in which a party has pursued or defended his case or a particular allegation or issue; and
- whether a claimant who has succeeded in his claim, in whole or in part, exaggerated his claim.

These things are referred to in this chapter as 'pre-proceedings conduct', 'issues', 'conduct generally' and 'exaggeration' respectively.

6.24 Thus, the following factors relevant to the incidence of costs can be identified:

- success and the 'general rule' (**6.31-6.53**).
- the effect of 'admissible offers' (**6.53-6.71**) and the effect of a failure to respond to an offer (**6.175-6.179**);
- conduct, including pre-proceedings conduct (**6.76-6.99**);

---

[39]   *Kastor Navigation Co Ltd v AXA Global Risks (UK) Ltd* [2004] EWCA Civ 277 at [153].
[40]   *Johnsey Estates (1990) Ltd v The Secretary of State for the Environment* [2001] EWCA Civ 535 at [21].

- the court's approach to 'issues' (**6.100-6.127**), including issues which have been abandoned (**6.128-6.137**);
- exaggeration (**6.138-6.154**);
- the effect of incurring disproportionate costs (**6.180**); and
- the other issues (**6.181-6.185**).

Once the range of costs orders available to the court has been described, each of these issues will be considered in turn.

THE RANGE OF ORDERS

6.25   The range of orders that the court may make is set out in CPR, r 44.3:

'(6)   The orders which the court may make under this rule include an order that a party must pay—

(a)   a proportion of another party's costs;

(b)   a stated amount in respect of another party's costs;

(c)   costs from or until a certain date only;

(d)   costs incurred before proceedings have begun;

(e)   costs relating to particular steps taken in the proceedings;

(f)   costs relating only to a distinct part of the proceedings; and

(g)   interest on costs from or until a certain date, including a date before judgment.

(7)   Where the court would otherwise consider making an order under paragraph (6)(f), it must instead, if practicable, make an order under paragraph (6)(a) or (c).

(8)   Where the court has ordered a party to pay costs, it may order an amount to be paid on account before the costs are assessed.

(9)   Where a party entitled to costs is also liable to pay costs the court may assess the costs which that party is liable to pay and either—

(a)   set off the amount assessed against the amount the party is entitled to be paid and direct him to pay any balance; or

(b)   delay the issue of a certificate for the costs to which the party is entitled until he has paid the amount which he is liable to pay.'

It is often said that the range of orders set out in CPR, r 44.3(6) is in decreasing order of desirability in that the judges should seek to make orders higher up the list in preference to orders lower down.[41] There probably is some truth in this (as confirmed by r 44.3(7), which specifically encourages the court to choose orders from the upper reaches of the list), but each case will have to be decided on its own facts. It would, for example, make little sense for a party to be awarded 5% of his costs (ie as per category (a) of the list) as opposed to his costs in respect of a particular part of the proceedings (as per category (f)), because the former would be an extremely inefficient method of assessing a relatively small amount of costs. However, it should be borne in mind that orders relating to particular steps or relating only to a distinct part of the proceedings (ie categories (e) and (f)) are prone to lead to disputes as to both the precise meaning and the precise effect of the order. It is perhaps for this reason that the Judicial Studies Board advises that a costs order in accordance with r 44.3(6)(e) or (f) should be made only exceptionally.[42]

---

[41]   See, for example, the Civil Bench Book, para 8.14.
[42]   The Civil Bench Book, para 8.14.

6.26 Where the court is minded to award a party costs but the intended award relates to only a distinct part of the proceedings, CPR, r 44.3(7) urges the court either to make an order that that party receives a proportion of its costs, or that the award is for costs from a certain date only; this would be in preference to an award of the costs of only a specified part of the proceedings. The circumstances in which this guidance would become relevant would be where a predominantly successful party has had more success on some issues than on others. The effect of r 44.3(7) is to discourage issues-based awards (but for the reasons set out elsewhere in this chapter, an issues-based *approach* to making awards is not discouraged; indeed, it is actively encouraged).

6.27 Percentage orders are orders that a party receives a percentage of his costs rather than the whole of his costs (see CPR, r 44.3(6)(a)). The Court of Appeal has emphasised that percentage orders are to be made where practicable.[43] Lord Phillips MR had the following to say on this matter:[44]

'We would emphasise that the CPR requires that an order which allows or disallows costs by reference to certain issues should be made only if other forms of order cannot be made which sufficiently reflect the justice of the case (see CPR 44.3(7)). In our view there are good reasons for this rule. An order which allows or disallows costs of certain issues creates difficulties at the stage of the assessment of costs because the Costs Judge will have to master the issue in detail to understand what costs were properly incurred in dealing with it and then analyse the work done by the receiving party's legal advisers to determine whether or not it was attributable to the issue the costs of which had been disallowed. All this adds to the costs of assessment and to the amount of time absorbed in dealing with costs on this basis. The costs incurred on assessment may thus be disproportionate to the benefit gained. In all the circumstances, contrary to what might be thought to be the case, a "percentage" order (under CPR 44.3(6)(a)) made by the Judge who heard the application will often produce a fairer result than an "issues based" order under CPR 44.3(6)(f). Moreover such an order is consistent with the overriding objective of the CPR.'

6.28 CPR, r 44.3(6) provides a list of available orders, but it is not an exhaustive list and other orders can be made if the court so wishes. Examples might include where a party is awarded its costs less a fixed sum[45] or where costs are capped at a certain level.[46] The court has considerable freedom in this regard, but unconventional orders should be made only where they can be justified on principled grounds.[47]

6.29 The words which are employed in costs orders are often terms of art. CPD, art 8.5 gives guidance as to what those terms mean. That guidance is stated to be in respect of orders made in proceedings before trial, but it is clear from the context in which it is given that it is of general applicability. The guidance is as follows:

---

[43] See *London Borough of Hackney v Campbell* [2005] EWCA Civ 613.
[44] *English v Emery Reimbold & Strick Ltd* [2002] EWCA Civ 605 at [115].
[45] See, for example, *Gil v Baygreen Properties Ltd* [2004] EWHC 2029 (Ch); see also *Wright v HSBC Bank plc* [2006] EWHC 1473 (Admin).
[46] See, for example, *SCT Finance v Bolton* [2002] EWCA Civ 56.
[47] Ibid.

Term	Effect
• Costs • Costs in any event	The party in whose favour the order is made is entitled to the costs in respect of the part of the proceedings to which the order relates, whatever other costs orders are made in the proceedings.
• Costs in the case • Costs in the application	The party in whose favour the court makes an order for costs at the end of the proceedings is entitled to his costs of the part of the proceedings to which the order relates.
• Costs reserved	The decision about costs is deferred to a later occasion, but if no later order is made the costs will be costs in the case.
• Claimant's/Defendant's costs in case/application	If the party in whose favour the costs order is made is awarded costs at the end the proceedings, that party is entitled to his costs of the part of the proceedings to which the order relates. If any other party is awarded costs at the end of the proceedings, the party in whose favour the final costs order is made is not liable to pay the costs of any other party in respect of the part of the proceedings to which the order relates.
• Costs thrown away	Where, for example, a judgment or order is set aside, the party in whose favour the costs order is made is entitled to the costs which have been incurred as a consequence. This includes the costs of – (a) preparing for and attending any hearing at which the judgment or order which has been set aside was made; (b) preparing for and attending any hearing to set aside the judgment or order in question; (c) preparing for and attending any hearing at which the court orders the proceedings or the part in question to be adjourned; (d) any steps taken to enforce a judgment or order which has subsequently been set aside.
• Costs of and caused by	Where, for example, the court makes this order on an application to amend a statement of case, the party in whose favour the costs order is made is entitled to the costs of preparing for and attending the application and the costs of any consequential amendment to his own statement of case.

Term	Effect
• Costs here and below	The party in whose favour the costs order is made is entitled not only to his costs in respect of the proceedings in which the court makes the order but also to his costs of the proceedings in any lower court. In the case of an appeal from a Divisional Court the party is not entitled to any costs incurred in any court below the Divisional Court.
• No order as to costs • Each party to pay his own costs	Each party is to bear his own costs of the part of the proceedings to which the order relates whatever costs order the court makes at the end of the proceedings.

6.30   In summary, there is a range of orders that can be made, some of which are to be preferred over others.

SUCCESS AND 'THE GENERAL RULE'

6.31   The 'general rule' is that the unsuccessful party will be ordered to pay the costs of the successful party.[48] This is an area of the law in respect of which an historical perspective is helpful. Prior to the introduction of the CPR, a party who had enjoyed substantial success could reasonably expect to be awarded the entirety of his costs. That state of affairs changed with the introduction of the CPR; even before the printers' ink was dry on the first edition, Lord Woolf MR was anxious to point out that a 'winner takes all' ethos was a thing of the past:[49]

> 'I draw attention to the new rules because, while they make clear that the general rule remains that the successful party will normally be entitled to costs, they at the same time indicate the wide range of considerations which will result in the court making different orders as to costs. From 26 April 1999 the "follow the event principle" will still play a significant role, but it will be a starting point from which a court can readily depart. This is also the position prior to the new rules coming into force. The most significant change of emphasis of the new rules is to require courts to be more ready to make separate orders which reflect the outcome of different issues. In doing this the new rules are reflecting a change of practice which has already started. It is now clear that a too robust application of the "follow the event principle" encourages litigants to increase the costs of litigation, since it discourages litigants from being selective as to the points they take. If you recover all your costs as long as you win, you are encouraged to leave no stone unturned in your effort to do so.'

Thus, under the CPR the court must take a more nuanced approach to the incidence of costs than merely looking at who has won. It should not be forgotten, however, that even before the introduction of the CPR, a claimant who recovered next to nothing would not expect to be awarded his costs.[50]

---

[48]   CPR, r 44.3(2)(a).

[49]   *Phonographic Performance Ltd v AEI Rediffusion Music Ltd* [1999] 1 WLR 1507 at 1522.

[50]   See, for example, *Anglo-Cyprian Trade Agencies Ltd v Paphos Wine Industries Ltd* [1951] 1 All ER 873; *Alltrans Express Ltd v C V Holdings Ltd* [1984] 1 WLR 394; and *Lipkin Gorman v Carpnale Ltd* [1989] 1 WLR 1340.

The meaning of success

6.32 Success must be real rather than technical. This was explained by Lightman J as follows:[51]

> 'For the purposes of the CPR, success [is not] a technical term but a result in real life, and the question as to who succeeded is a matter for the exercise of common sense.'

The difficulty is not normally knowing what success is, but measuring it. This is addressed under the next heading.

The measure of success

6.33 In most cases, it will be obvious who has won, but the following topics merit discussion:

- cases where there is more than one issue;
- starting points and finishing points;
- commercial litigation; and
- the effect of costs on success.

Whilst the court is not bound by the outcome of a dispute resolved in some way other than by the court,[52] it is possible for a party to succeed by way of compromise; this is addressed at **7.101–7.121**.

Cases with more than one issue

6.34 Cases in which it is not immediately apparent who has won are often also cases in which there is more than one issue. The following three points apply to the topic of how to determine success in those cases in which there is an abundance of issues.

One predominant issue

6.35 It would be wrong to confuse success on an issue (even an important one which took up a great deal of time) with success in the litigation taken as a whole. All of the facts need to be taken into account, and this includes issues which have been unsuccessfully litigated. It is because of the importance of context that Coulson J ruled that it would be wrong to make an immediate order following a preliminary-issues hearing without knowing the final result.[53] Longmore LJ (with whom Clarke and Ward LJJ agreed) has commented that it is not normally right to segregate a large element of the costs and thereafter to decide who the successful party is.[54] However,

---

[51] *BCCI v Ali & Ors* [2000] 2 Costs LR 243.

[52] An example of this is *Hudson v New Media Holding Co LLC* [2011] EWHC 3068 (QB) at [24], per Eady J. in which the court declined to accept that a finding of a court in the United States was determinative of the issue of whether the application in question had merit.

[53] *Perriam Limited v Wayne* [2011] EWHC 403 (QB) at [58]; in contrast, see *Fiona Trust & Holding Corporation v Privalov* [2011] EWHC 664 (Comm) at [14] where Andrew Smith J. explained that that the application of the general rule requires consideration of the overall relative success of the parties in respect of the relevant hearing(s) or stage(s) in the litigation, that is to say generally those in respect of which an award of costs is being considered, and the court is not concerned, for this purpose, about which party has won on individual issues.

[54] Longmore LJ in *A L Barnes v Time Talk (UK) Ltd* [2003] EWCA Civ 402 at [28], cited with approval in *Kastor Navigation Co Ltd v Axa Global Risks (UK) Ltd* [2004] EWCA Civ 277 at [146].

where a single issue has dominated the claim, it will be highly relevant. Ramsey J has said that where a party has succeeded on one claim and obtained the relief sought thereby, this carries with it not only the costs of that claim but also the common costs the successful party had to expend in order to pursue the proceedings;[55] in this regard Ramsey J seems to have gone further than Jackson J, who commented only that it would be open to the court deal with a case in that way.[56] A common example is where the court finds that there has been exaggeration; the fact that a claim was exaggerated usually governs the claim because it will impact upon the exaggerator's credibility. In this regard, Maurice Kay LJ (with whom Longmore LJ agreed) said:[57]

'To the question: who was the real winner in this litigation? there is, in my judgment, only one answer. The two-day hearing was concerned overwhelmingly with the issue of exaggeration, and the [defendant] won on that issue. [The claimant's] submission that that was only one issue, the other issue being the quantification of the claim, is not persuasive. Quite simply, that second issue was hardly an issue at all once the Recorder had found the exaggeration ...'

Unsurprisingly, the claimant in that case was ordered to pay the defendant's costs.

Many issues

6.36 Where the outcome of a claim is, in reality, one in which a party has succeed on a number of discrete issues but lost on others, the court must, in accordance with CPR, r 44.3(4)(b), consider whether an issues-based approach should be taken. Chadwick LJ held that it would be wrong in such circumstances to deprive the successful party of his costs on the basis that that party had obtained less than he had originally been claiming.[58] Whilst each case will turn on its own facts, Jackson LJ came to much the same conclusion in a case where the successful party had lost on a number of significant issues.[59] That said, where a party won on the facts but lost on a point of procedure that was said to be the 'main issue', Smith LJ said that no order for costs may be appropriate.[60]

Primary and secondary cases

6.37 If the parties each advance their own primary and alternative secondary cases, and if the primary cases both fail, leaving the parties to rely on their secondary cases, the court should look at who has won on the secondary cases as being the measure of success generally; it would be wrong in those circumstances to say that there has been a draw as a result of both parties having failed on their primary cases.[61]

---

[55]   *Mears Ltd v Leeds City Council* [2011] EWHC 2694 (TCC) at [28].
[56]   *Multiplex Constructions (UK) Limited v Cleveland Bridge UK Limited* [2008] EWHC 2280 (TCC) at [72(viii)].
[57]   *Painting v University of Oxford* [2005] EWCA Civ 161.
[58]   *Aspin v Metric Group Ltd* [2007] EWCA Civ 922 at [25]; where, however, the conduct of the claimant was such that he can be said to have exaggerated his claim, this this may justify depriving him of his costs: see, for example, *Abbott v Long*.
[59]   See *Naseem (t/a SH Builders and Contractors) v Kang* [2011] EWCA Civ 737 at [40].
[60]   *Owens v Noble* [2010] EWCA Civ 284 at [8].
[61]   *Day v Day* [2006] EWCA Civ 415; see also

Appeals

6.38   It would seem that where one of the issues is a point of law, the measure of success may change if an appeal is brought; in a case in which a point of general importance was taken on appeal, Lord Neuberger MR implied that there is a difference between hearings at first instance (where he dealt with the issue of success on the basis who had achieved the result that they were seeking) and hearings on appeal (where he distinguished between success on the facts and success on the point of principle).[62] This compares with the approach taken by Tomlinson LJ (sitting in the Commercial Court) in which he said that whilst an 'enthusiastic lawyer' might have believed that the case before him was about a point of law, ultimately it was about money.[63]

Starting points, offers, and finishing points

6.39   In addition to taking into account the findings that the court has made, it may also be relevant to take into account what the parties themselves had to say about the claim. To that extent, it may be necessary to look at what the parties claimed, and what they were prepared to accept and to concede.

Starting points and offers

6.40   It may be necessary to look at the points from which the parties started in order to see how far their opponent's efforts have caused them to shift (or to be shifted). Where the parties have advanced competing views as to the value of the claim, it may be necessary to take those competing views into account. In an appeal from a trial in which a claimant had recovered just under one-tenth of the sums that were claimed but still more than the defendant had offered, Auld LJ said:[64]

> 'In my view, the reality of this case is that [the defendant] was the winner. She was facing a claim substantially greater than the amount finally awarded. There were, as I have said, competing claims and offers, not only as to the manner of calculation of the amount due but as to the amount ... The sum ordered was arguably as limited a loss as it was a gain. And it emerged as a result, not only of [the claimant] losing the case on principle on the main issues in the case, but also as to the true amount due out of a very much larger claim. The disparity between what [the claimant] sought, including what he put [the defendant] through to get it, and what he received was so large as to put the relatively small amount finally awarded in the balance between two rival contentions into relative insignificance.'

Auld LJ went on to say that the defendant had won the case in principle, or as near as could be, given the large competing sums being canvassed between the parties and the wide issue between them as to the proper basis of the claim. Mummery LJ, who was also hearing the appeal, referred to these things as being 'special circumstances'. The appropriate order was that there be no order for costs. In a clinical negligence case in which the claimant recovered £2,000 out of a claim for £525,000, May and Tomlinson LJJ (Jackson LJ dissenting[65]) found that that constituted a win on the part of

---

[62]   *Manchester City Council v Pinnock (No 2)* [2011] UKSC 6 at [18].
[63]   *Pindell Ltd and another v Airasia Berhad (formerly known as Airasia SDN BHD)* [2010] EWHC 3238 (Comm) at [4].
[64]   *Islam v Ali* [2003] EWCA Civ 612 at [23].
[65]   This was primarily on the basis that the defendant ought to have made a Part 36 offer which is what they would have done had they followed the pre-CPR authority of *Oksuzoglu v Kay* [1998] 2 All ER 361: see *Marcus v Medway Primary Care Trust* [2011] EWCA Civ 750 at [21].

the defendant.[66] In different case, Mann J found that a defendant who was ordered to pay £6,750 in a claim where over £7m was claimed was the successful party (although ultimately he found that other factors prevailed).[67] Other case examples exist.[68]

6.41 In a similar vein, Lord Bingham MR noted:[69]

'The judge must look closely at the facts of the particular case before him and ask: who, as a matter of substance and reality, has won? Has the plaintiff won anything of value which he could not have won without fighting the action through to a finish? Has the defendant substantially denied the plaintiff the prize which the plaintiff fought the action to win?'

Lord Bingham's comments were made in the context of without prejudice offers, but there is no reason to believe that they would not also apply where the parties' positions are openly stated. Where a defendant is faced with a claim he believes to be significantly overvalued, it will not always be necessary to make an offer to avoid being condemned in costs: he could seek to rely on the notion that at the end of the day the court will ask itself 'who, as a matter of substance and reality, has won?'.[70] This would be a risk-laden tactic, however. Likewise, whilst every defendant should be aware of the need to keep offers under review (especially in cases involving expert evidence),[71] a failure in this regard will not inescapably result in an adverse order for costs. Where, for example, a low but protective offer could have been made but would certainly not have been accepted, the act of making an offer may be thought of as being a mere matter of ritual; whilst such an approach is supported by authority,[72] not all judges agree that it is correct,[73] and in view of the fact that an award of costs is very much a matter of discretion, a defendant would do well not to rely on the court making such a finding but instead to protect itself by making suitable offers.

6.42 A not uncommon scenario is that both parties turn out to have been over-optimistic in their Part 36 offers in that the claimant recovers more than the defendant has offered, but less than the claimant has offered to accept. Jackson LJ has explained that in such a case the claimant should normally be regarded as 'the successful party', this being because he will have been forced to bring proceedings in order to recover the sum awarded.[74]

Finishing points (concessions)

6.43 A party need not win at a hearing in order to be successful; success can be achieved by obtaining a concession. See **7.101–7.120.**

---

[66] *Marcus v Medway Primary Care Trust* [2011] EWCA Civ 750.

[67] *Fulham Leisure Holdings Ltd v Nicholson Graham & Jones* [2006] EWHC 2428 (Ch).

[68] *Bajwa v British Airways* [1999] PIQR 152 at para 38; for an example of the court making no order for costs, see *Hooper v Biddle & Co* [2006] EWHC 2995 (Ch), per Susan Prevezer QC.

[69] *Roache v Newsgroup Newspapers Ltd* [1998] EMLR 161.

[70] See *Marcus v Medway Primary Care Trust* [2011] EWCA Civ 750 at [46], per Tomlinson LJ who cited *Roache v Newsgroup Newspapers Ltd* [1998] EMLR 161.

[71] Whilst a pre-CPR case, see *Oksuzoglu v Kay* [1998] 2 All ER 361.

[72] See *Anglo-Cyprian Trade Agencies Limited v Paphos Wine Industries Limited* [1951] 1 All ER 873, per Devlin J, cited with approval by Tomlinson LJ in *Marcus v Medway Primary Care Trust* [2011] EWCA Civ 750 at [51]. See also *Alltrans Express Limited v CVA Holdings Limited* [1983] 1 WLR 394 at 402 (per Stephenson LJ) and at 404 (per Griffiths LJ).

[73] See *Marcus v Medway Primary Care Trust* [2011] EWCA Civ 750 at [21], per Jackson LJ.

[74] *Fox v Foundation Piling Limited* [2011] EWCA Civ 790 at [46].

Culpable exaggeration

6.44   The paragraphs immediately above assume that there has been no culpable exaggeration. If there has been exaggeration, then different considerations apply. These are discussed at **6.141–6.150**.

Commercial claims

6.45   Commercial claims are often complex in that there may be several components to both the claim and the counterclaim. Where this is so, Longmore LJ has explained that the measure of who has won is often who has been ordered to pay money to the other:[75]

> 'The most important thing is to identify the party who is to pay money to the other. That is the surest indication of success and failure.'

In a property claim concerning maintenance in which there was a claim and a counterclaim, Maurice Kay LJ has confirmed that it would be wrong to say that the claim was 'all about the counterclaim': there was one dispute, namely, whether one party owed the other any money.[76] Such an approach may not be appropriate where the claim was not a case of damages and past events (such as a trademark dispute where the question was of principle for the future), but even where the claim was not about damages, it is usually possible to decide who has achieved the most advantageous commercial benefit.[77]

6.46   Sitting as a deputy High Court judge, HHJ Coulson QC (now Coulson J) provided the following summary of the authorities relating to who has won and who has lost in commercial litigation:[78]

> '(a) The starting point for the exercise of the court's discretion is that costs follow the event. To work out who is the successful party, the court has to ask: "Who, as a matter of substance and reality, has won?"[79]

> (b) In a commercial case, it is important to identify which party is to pay money to the other.[80] Where there has been a payment into court, it is important to see whether or not that payment into court has been beaten.[81]

---

[75]   *A L Barnes Ltd v Time Talk (UK) Ltd* [2003] EWCA Civ 402 at [28]; see also *Pindell Ltd and another v Airasia Berhad (formerly known as Airasia SDN BHD)* [2010] EWHC 3238 (Comm) at [4]; *Burchell v Bullard & others* [2005] EWCA Civ 358 at [33]; *Day v Day* [2006] EWCA Civ 415 (which was not a commercial claim, but which was a claim about money); and *Whitecap Leisure Ltd v John H Rundle Ltd* [2008] EWCA Civ 1026. The concept is not a new one: see, for example, *Baines v Bromley* (1881) 6 QBD 691.

[76]   *Villa Agencies Spf Ltd v Kestrel Travel Consultancy Ltd*, unreported at the time of writing, 17 January 2012, CA (Civ Div).

[77]   *L'Oreal SA v Bellure NV* (unreported) 27 July 2010, CA, Civil Division (Jacob LJ and Sir David Keene); the substantive case was *L'Oreal SA v Bellure NV* [2010] EWCA Civ 535.

[78]   *McGlinn v Waltham Contractors Ltd* [2005] EWHC 1419 (TCC).

[79]   *Johnsey Estates (1990) Ltd v The Secretary of State for the Environment* [2001] EWCA Civ 535; *Painting v University of Oxford* [2005] EWCA Civ 161; *Roache v Newsgroup Newspapers Ltd* [1998] EMLR 161.

[80]   *A L Barnes v Time Talk(UK) Ltd* [2003] EWCA Civ 402.

[81]   *Johnsey Estates (1990) Ltd v The Secretary of State for the Environment* [2001] EWCA Civ 535.

(c) A defendant's failure to beat a payment into court will usually mean that he is treated by the court as the losing party, particularly if the case is not appropriate for an issue-based costs order.[82] However, such failure may not always be regarded as decisive.[83]

(d) Depending on the facts, the court may treat a defendant who has failed to beat the payment into court as the successful party, or make no order as to costs; although it is not possible to list all the circumstances in which this may be appropriate, they might include the situation where the claimant has only just beaten the payment into court; where the payment into court reflected much more closely the amount eventually recovered, as compared to the amount claimed; where the claimant's conduct made it difficult or even impossible to make an effective payment in; and where the trial was largely devoted to the failure of the claimant's exaggerated case.[84]

(e) It may not always be possible for the court to say, when considering the action as a whole, that one party should be regarded as the overall winner.[85] Indeed, even if it is possible to identify one party as the successful party, it may still be appropriate, depending on the circumstances, to make an issue-based costs order, so as to give effect to the substance of the result and to move away from too rigid an application of the "follow the event principle".'[86]

As can be seen from this analysis, it is necessary to take many factors into account when the issue of success is decided in commercial cases.

6.47 Following a review of all the relevant authorities, Jackson J offered the following guidance:[87]

'From this review of authority I derive the following eight principles.

(i) In commercial litigation where each party has claims and asserts that a balance is owing in its own favour, the party which ends up receiving payment should generally be characterised as the overall winner of the entire action.

(ii) In considering how to exercise its discretion the court should take as its starting point the general rule that the successful party is entitled to an order for costs.

(iii) The judge must then consider what departures are required from that starting point, having regard to all the circumstances of the case.

(iv) Where the circumstances of the case require an issue-based costs order, that is what the judge should make. However, the judge should hesitate before doing so, because of the practical difficulties which this causes and because of the steer given by rule 44.3(7).

(v) In many cases the judge can and should reflect the relative success of the parties on different issues by making a proportionate costs order.

(vi) In considering the circumstances of the case the judge will have regard not only to any Part 36 offers made but also to each party's approach to negotiations (insofar as admissible) and general conduct of the litigation.

---

[82] *Johnsey Estates (1990) Ltd v The Secretary of State for the Environment* [2001] EWCA Civ 535; *Firle v Datapoint* [2001] EWCA Civ 1106; *Jackson v The Ministry of Defence* [2006] EWCA Civ 46.

[83] *Bajwa v British Airways* [1999] PIQR 152.

[84] *Bajwa v British Airways* [1999] PIQR 152; *Roache v Newsgroup Newspapers Ltd* [1998] EMLR 161; *Molloy v Shell UK Ltd* [2001] EWCA Civ 1272.

[85] *Roache v Newsgroup Newspapers Ltd* [1998] EMLR 161.

[86] *National Westminster Bank plc v Angeli Kotonou* [2006] EWHC 1785 (Ch); *Summit Property Ltd v Pitmans* [2002] EWCA Civ 2020; *Fulham Leisure Holdings Ltd v Nicholson Graham & Jones* [2006] EWHC 2428 (Ch); *AEI Rediffusion Music Ltd v Phonographic Performance Ltd* [1999] 1 WLR 1507.

[87] *Multiplex Constructions (UK) Ltd v Cleveland Bridge UK Ltd* [2008] EWHC 2280 (TCC) at [72].

(vii) If (a) one party makes an offer under part 36 or an admissible offer within rule 44.3(4)(c) which is nearly but not quite sufficient, and (b) the other party rejects that offer outright without any attempt to negotiate, then it might be appropriate to penalise the second party in costs.

(viii) In assessing a proportionate costs order the judge should consider what costs are referable to each issue and what costs are common to several issues. It will often be reasonable for the overall winner to recover not only the costs specific to the issues which he has won but also the common costs.'

Warren J has commented that an unsuccessful party does not bear an onus to show that the adoption of the general rule would be unjust: instead, it is for the court to consider all the circumstances of the case and to make an order accordingly.[88]

Broadly equal degrees of success

6.48   In some cases, it can be said that both parties have benefited (or not) in equal measure and that the case is a draw; that would normally result in an order that there be no order for costs.[89] Ward LJ has commented that where there has been broadly equal success on both sides and both sides have conducted themselves badly, the court would be fully entitled to cast them away with no order for costs and a plague on both their houses.[90] Whilst very much the exception, circumstances may exist where the claim and counterclaim may need to be considered separately for the purposes of determining who is the victor.[91]

The effect of costs on success and vice versa

6.49   A party's putative success may be diminished or negated by the fact that he has to pay costs (either to the other side, or to his own lawyers). Two issues then arise: first, whether the court should try to preserve a party's success by not condemning him in costs, and secondly, whether a party's liability for costs should be taken into account when deciding who has won.

Preservation of a party's success

6.50   The application of the general rule will usually mean that a party who has been awarded damages will also be awarded costs. This means that the issue of diminution of damages by an award of costs will arise only where there is a proposed departure from the general rule, perhaps as a result of the otherwise successful party having lost on one or more issues. It would, generally speaking,[92] be wrong in those circumstances for the court to decline to make an issues-based award on the supposed basis that that would diminish the otherwise successful party's damages. In this regard, Potter LJ found that a trial judge had been wrong to take into account the possibility that the claimant, who had been awarded aggravated damages, might not get the full benefit of his award if an issue-based award was made.[93]

---

[88]   See *Southern Counties Fresh Foods v RWM Purchasers Ltd* [2011] EWHC 1370 (Ch) at [12].

[89]   See, for example, *Square Mile Partnership Ltd v Fitzmaurice McCall Ltd* [2006] EWHC 236 (Ch); see also the obiter comments of Mummery LJ in *Peakman v Linbrooke Services Ltd* [2008] EWCA Civ 1120.

[90]   *Cambertown Timber Merchants Ltd v Sidhu* [2011] EWCA Civ 1041 at [35],

[91]   See, for example, *Lloyds v Svenby* [2002] EWHC 576 (QB) at [5], per Stanley Burnton J; the circumtaneces in that case that justified that approach were that the costs of the counterclaim were negligible.

[92]   In family cases, however, decisions of the court as to financial matters as between the parties (including cost) should take into account the incidence of an order of costs and the effect upon the parties' means.

[93]   *Fleming v The Chief Constable of the Sussex Police Force* [2004] EWCA Civ 643.

The effect of costs on success

6.51   In some circumstances, the court may take into account the fact that a successful litigant has had to incur costs which are not recovered from a paying party. This will usually be a relevant factor where the successful claimant has beaten a defendant's Part 36 offer but has done so only narrowly. This issue is dealt with at **14.34–14.43**. As can be seen, following the introduction of CPR, r 36.14(1A), the scope for taking this factor into account is not significantly curtailed.

Partial success

6.52   'Partial success' is a phrase that will mean that one or both of the following situations will exist:

- a claimant has recovered much less than was claimed, or a defendant must pay only a modest amount more than had been conceded; or
- a party has succeeded generally, but lost on a number of issues.

The first of these topics has already been addressed at **6.39–6.44**; it is discussed further at **6.138–6.154**. The second topic is considered at **6.100–6.127**. It is worth recording that in some jurisdictions a method known as the Welamson doctrine applies.[94] Greatly simplified, this means that if a party recovers half of that which was in dispute, that should be regarded as being one half a loss and one half a win, and that as such, the appropriate order should be no order for costs. Likewise, if he recovers three-quarters of that which was in dispute, that should be regarded as being one quarter a loss, and three quarters a win, and as such, he should receive one half of his costs. The Welamson doctrine is mentioned simply because other jurisdictions (including arbitral jurisdictions) have shown an interest in it.[95] It is possible that at some stage domestic courts are asked to apply it.

ADMISSIBLE OFFERS

6.53   Negotiations or offers which have taken place on a basis that is expressly 'without prejudice save as to costs' are admissible on the question of entitlement to costs.[96] Where such an offer is admissible and where it is not an offer to which the costs consequences under Part 36 apply, it is referred to as an 'admissible offer';[97] withdrawn Part 36 offers are a species of admissible offer, as are offers that have fallen short of being Part 36 offers for technical reasons.[98] For present purposes, an admissible offer differs from a *Calderbank* offer[99] only in name. Extant Part 36 offers are dealt with at **14.28–14.57**. Part 36 offers that have been withdrawn and withdrawn offers generally are addressed at **14.73-14.74**. Special provisions apply to admiralty claims: see **6.74**.

---

[94]   See L Welamson *Principer om rattegangskostnader under debatt, Festskrift Till Olivecrona* 684-709 (1964) and J Gotanda *Awarding Costs and Attorneys' Fees in International Commercial Arbitrations*, Michigan Journal of International Law (1999) 1-50
[95]   See, for example, Quick, R Quick on Costs (Thomson Reuters) at [10.2361].
[96]   See *Reed Executive plc v Reed Business Information Ltd* [2004] EWCA Civ 887 at [20], which confirmed that *Calderbank v Calderbank* [1976] Fam 93 and *Cutts v Head* [1984] Ch 290 remained good law under the CPR.
[97]   See CPR, r 44.3(4)(c).
[98]   See, for example, *French v Groupama Insurance Co Ltd* [2011] EWCA Civ 1119 at [41] *et seq*, per Rix LJ and *Brown v Mcasso Music Production* [2005] EWCA Civ 1546, per Neuberger LJ.
[99]   Named after *Calderbank v Calderbank* [1976] Fam 93.

Admissibility

6.54   CPR, r 44.3(4)(c) provides that in deciding what order, if any, to make about costs, the court must have regard to all the circumstances, including any admissible offer which is drawn to the court's attention.[100] CPD, art 8.4 makes very similar provisions:

> 'In deciding what order to make about costs the court is required to have regard to all the circumstances including any payment into court or admissible offer to settle made by a party which is drawn to the court's attention, and which is not an offer to which costs consequences under Part 36 apply.'

6.55   It is implicit in CPR, r 44.3(4)(c) that not all offers to settle are admissible. There is nothing within r 44.3 which purports to regulate the existing law relating to without prejudice negotiations.[101] In particular, the reference to 'all the circumstances' should be read as meaning 'all the admissible circumstances'.[102] That said, CPR, r 44.3(4)(c) specifically excludes Part 36 offers from the ambit of admissible offers, and Ward LJ has confirmed that if the offer is one to which the costs consequences under Part 36 apply, then it cannot be taken into account under CPR Part 44; in this regard he said that 'Part 36 trumps Pt 44'.[103] If, however, the offer falls short of being a Part 36 offer or if it ceased to be a Part 36 offer by reason of it having been withdrawn, then it will be an admissible offer (see **6.72** and **14.73-14.74**). This would also be true of an offer which has not been beaten, in which case it may be taken into account under CPR, r 44.3 as being a relevant background fact.[104]

6.56   Negotiations or offers which have taken place on a basis that was without prejudice (as opposed to without prejudice save as to costs) are not admissible on the question of entitlement to costs; this rule (which can be analysed as being a rule of evidence, a rule relating to privilege, or a rule of law) was laid down in *Walker v Wilsher*,[105] in which Bowen LJ reasoned the matter in this way:

> '... [It] would be a bad thing and lead to serious consequences if the Courts allowed the action of litigants, on letters written to them "without prejudice", to be given in evidence against them or to be used as material for depriving them of costs. It is most important that the door should not be shut against compromises, as would certainly be the case if letters written "without prejudice" and suggesting methods of compromise were liable to be read when a question of costs arose.'

6.57   When they were made for the purposes of without prejudice negotiations, there is no distinction between an acknowledgement and an admission: both will be treated as being without prejudice.[106]

6.58   Thus, there is a general exclusory rule against the admission as evidence of without prejudice negotiations or offers. There are exceptions to this rule; in the context of civil proceedings (and costs in particular), those exceptions are:

---

[100]   See also, *Crouch v King's Healthcare NHS Trust* [2004] EWCA Civ 1332, which has been superseded by changes in CPR Part 36, but remains good law in so far as it confirms that *Calderbank* offers are admissible in money claims.

[101]   *Reed Executive plc v Reed Business Information Ltd* [2004] EWCA Civ 887 at [12].

[102]   *Reed Executive plc v Reed Business Information Ltd* [2004] EWCA Civ 887 at [31].

[103]   *Shovelar v Lane* [2011] EWCA Civ 802 at [52].

[104]   See, for example, *Straker v Tudor Rose (a firm)* [2007] EWCA Civ 368 at [3].

[105]   (1889) 23 QBD 225.

[106]   *Ofulue v Bossert* [2009] UKHL 16.

- where an offer was expressly stated to be without prejudice save as to costs (see above);
- where all relevant parties waive privilege;[107]
- where the court is required to decide whether the negotiations have led to a concluded compromise;[108]
- where the court is required to decide whether an apparent agreement should be set aside on the grounds of misrepresentation, fraud, or undue influence;[109]
- where the court is required to decide whether the negotiations have led to an estoppel;[110]
- where the exclusion of the evidence would act as a cloak for perjury, blackmail or unambiguous impropriety;[111] and
- where the court is required to rule on the effect of delay or apparent acquiescence (when, for example, an application is made to strike out for want of prosecution) and evidence of the negotiations is required to explain that delay or apparent acquiescence[112] (where this is done, the court will usually order that the without prejudice material is to be admitted only for the purpose of deciding the limited issue before the court).[113]

Withdrawn offers and failed attempts to accept offers

6.59   It is now settled law that (contrary to some older authorities)[114] if an admissible offer is withdrawn it may be taken into account as being part of the background facts and may be given considerable weight in that regard. This is addressed in detail at **14.73-14.74**. It may be that a party seeks to accept an offer made by an opponent but, for whatever reason, is not able to do this; Bernard Livesey QC (sitting as a Deputy Judge of the Chancery Division) has found that this is capable of being a form of admissible offer.[115]

Admissibility of offers to mediate

6.60   One type of offer that cannot be in the form of a Part 36 offer is an offer to mediate; if such an offer is to be taken into account at all, it could only be as an admissible offer. The effect of offers to mediate is dealt with in more detail at **6.156-6.174**.[116] In so far as admissibility is concerned, Jacob LJ (with whom Rix and Auld LJJ agreed) has emphasised that an offer to mediate may be taken into account if it is made without prejudice save as to costs, but it may not be taken into account if it is made on a merely 'without prejudice' basis; he explained as follows:[117]

---

[107]   An example being *Botham v Khan* [2004] EWHC 2602 (QB), where the parties waived privilege to allow the court to deal with an application pursuant to CPR, r 44.14.

[108]   See, for example, *Tomlin v Standard Telephones and Cables Ltd* [1969] 1 WLR 1378.

[109]   See, for example, the Ontario case of *Underwood v Cox* (1912) 4 DLR 66.

[110]   See *Hodgkinson & Corby Ltd v Wards Mobility Services Ltd* [1997] FSR 178 (a decision which was not disapproved on appeal).

[111]   See, for example, *Hawick Jersey International Ltd v Caplan* (1988) *The Times*, March 11.

[112]   In *Walker v Wilsher* (1889) 23 QBD 335 Lindley LJ regarded this exception as limited to 'the fact that such letters have been written and the dates at which they were written', but in *Unilever plc v Procter & Gamble Co* [2000] 1 WLR 2436 at 2445 Robert Walker LJ said (obiter) that 'fuller evidence [may be] needed in order to give the court a fair picture of the rights and wrongs of the delay'.

[113]   See, for example, *Family Housing Association v Hyde* [1993] 1 WLR 354.

[114]   See, for example, *The Toni* [1974] 1 Lloyd's Reports 489 at 496–497 in which Megaw LJ.

[115]   *Rowles-Davies v Call 24-7 Limited* [2010] EWHC 1695 (Ch) at [27]

[116]   See the line of cases beginning with *Halsey v Milton Keynes General NHS Trust* [2004] 3 Costs LR 393.

[117]   *Reed Executive plc v Reed Business Information Ltd* [2004] EWCA Civ 887 at [34]–[35].

'I therefore conclude that the rule in *Walker v Wilsher* remains good law and that the court cannot order disclosure of "without prejudice" negotiations against the wishes of one of the parties to those negotiations. This may (indeed does) mean in some cases the court when it comes to the question of costs cannot decide whether one side or the other was unreasonable in refusing mediation.

I do not regard such a conclusion as disastrous or damaging from the point of view of encouraging ADR. Far from it. Everyone knows the *Calderbank* Rules. It is open to either side to make open or *Calderbank* offers of ADR. These days there is no shame or sign of weakness in so doing. The opposite party can respond to such matters, either openly or in *Calderbank* form. If it does so and gives good reason(s) why it thinks ADR will not serve a useful purpose, then that is one thing. If it fails to do so, then that is a matter the court may consider relevant (not decisive, of course) in exercising its discretion as to costs. The reasonableness or otherwise of going to ADR may be fairly and squarely debated between the parties and under the *Calderbank* procedure made available to the court but only when it comes to consider costs.'

The effect of this is that a party may, if it so wishes, make an offer to mediate on a wholly without prejudice basis, in which case it will not be admissible for the purposes of deciding the incidence of costs.

Admissibility on the small claims track

6.61   A further type of offer that (assuming it to be admissible) can only be an admissible offer is an offer made in a claim which has been allocated to the small claims track; this is because CPR Part 36 does not apply to such claims. For reasons set out at **33.76–33.103**, costs will be awarded on that track only if a party has acted unreasonably; in this regard, CPR, r 27.14(3) gives the following guidance:

'A party's rejection of an offer in settlement will not of itself constitute unreasonable behaviour under paragraph (2)(g) but the court may take it into consideration when it is applying the unreasonableness test.'

An offeror will not, therefore, be able to rely on an admissible offer in isolation, but it may be a factor to be taken into account within a basket of other factors.

Effect of a refusal to waive privilege

6.62   If a party refuses to waive privilege in substantive litigation, it would be wrong to regard that refusal as giving rise to an adverse inference to be drawn against the refusing party.[118] There is no reason to believe that this principle does not apply to costs litigation (including decisions as to the incidence of costs) with just as much force as it does to substantive litigation.

Effect of an admissible offer on the incidence of costs

6.63   Whether the existence of an admissible offer will have a bearing on the incidence of costs will depend on the facts of the case in question. Generally speaking, the offeror will hope to rely on the offer for one or more the following purposes:

*   to demonstrate a willingness to narrow the issues and further the overriding objective;

---

[118]   *Reed Executive plc v Reed Business Information Ltd* [2004] EWCA Civ 887 at [36].

- to demonstrate a willingness to enter into negotiations and to dispel any allegation to the contrary;
- to highlight an opponent's reluctance to enter into negotiations; and
- to obtain an outcome which is at least as advantageous as the offer (either for the purposes of obtaining a favourable costs order, or for the purpose of obtain an award of costs on the indemnity basis).

There are seven scenarios which merit particular attention; they are:

(1) 'drop hands' offers;
(2) defendant's refusal to come to a commercial settlement;
(3) unrealistic offers;
(4) non-monetary offers;
(5) absent offers on alternative cases;
(6) very late offers; and
(7) withdrawn Part 36 offers and withdrawn offers generally.

Each of these topics is dealt with in turn. The antepenultimate topic (ie, number (5)) is somewhat arcane; it addresses the situation in which a party has to rely on an alternative case but has not made an offer based on the contingency that the primary case might fail.

6.64 The effect of an admissible offer may fall anywhere between having no effect on the incidence of costs all the way through to having an effect very similar to that which a Part 36 offer would have had.[119] Jackson LJ has explained that the court's discretion is wider where an admissible offer has been beaten than where a Part 36 offer has been beaten;[120] in the latter circumstances the court's discretion is modified by CPR, r 36.14, but in the former, no such restraint exists. Unlike under CPR Part 36, there are no prescribed rules as to the effect of an admissible offer; the presence (or, occasionally, absence) of an offer will merely be one factor amongst others to be taken into account. Thus, each case will turn on its own facts. One factor that might be relevant is the way the offer was regarded; thus, if the parties believed that an offer was a Part 36 offer and acted as if this was the case, then that would be a factor to be borne in mind even though they may have been mistaken.[121]

'Drop hands' offers

6.65 A 'drop hands' offer is an offer to leave the claim where it lies with each party bearing his own costs. If, for example, no monies have been paid in the claim to date it will be an offer that the claim be abandoned without the claimant having to pay the defendant's costs. Mann J has explained that where a party has made a drop hands offer, the correct approach is to consider what the appropriate costs order would have been in the absence of that offer, and then to compare that hypothetical position with the actual offer made.[122]

---

[119] As an example of the latter, see *Stokes Pension Fund Trustees v Western Power Distribution (South West) Plc* [2005] EWCA Civ 854; see also *Fox v Foundation Piling Limited* [2011] EWCA Civ 790 at [45].

[120] *Fox v Foundation Piling Limited* [2011] EWCA Civ 790 at [44] and [45].

[121] *Howell v Lees-Millais* [2011] EWCA Civ 786 at [24]–[28].

[122] *Fulham Leisure Holdings Ltd v Nicholson Graham & Jones* [2006] EWHC 2428 (Ch).

6.66   Where an admissible drop hands offer has been made and the court decides not to take it into account, reasons should be given. Chadwick LJ (with whom Rix and Thorpe LJJ agreed) commented on this matter:[123]

> 'If the judge was to deny the party who had been successful overall the costs, or any part of the costs, of his success, then he had to explain why the other party, who had refused to accept the "drop hands" proposal ... was entitled to ignore that proposal and run up further costs.'

This means that whilst a drop hands offer cannot be ignored, it would be capable of being disregarded for principled reasons.

Defendant's refusal to come to a commercial settlement

6.67   The fact that a successful defendant may have rejected a claimant's offer would not, in the ordinary run of things, lead to the defendant being penalised for not having previously agreed to compromise that claim on commercial grounds. Dyson LJ has said:[124]

> 'If defendants ... wish to take a stand and contest [unfounded claims] rather than make payments (even nuisance value payments) to buy them off, then the court should be slow to characterise such conduct as unreasonable so as to deprive defendants of their costs, if they are ultimately successful.'

Ward LJ added the following observations:[125]

> 'If the parties reasonably believe that they have a real prospect of success each is entitled fully and properly to advance his or her case or defence, but neither can then complain that the fight is taken to the bitter end of a judgment of the court. Each will have to accept that those who live by the sword must risk dying by the sword as well. That is the inevitable risk of litigation.'

Unrealistic offers

6.68   An offeror will usually hope to benefit from having made an offer, but where an admissible offer can be taken as being an indication of the level at which a litigant has pitched his case, it may be capable of working against the offeror.[126] This might happen where an unrealistic offer is regarded as evidence of expectations which were out of reach and unrealistic. In general, nonetheless, a party should not be penalised for pitching an offer too high (or too low), and the court should avoid getting drawn into an exercise of making an adjudication as to the reasonableness of offers.[127] In particular,there is nothing in CPR Part 36 which states that an offeror is to be prejudiced as to costs because he has expressed his willingness to accept less than his open position; Rix LJ commented that that would make the procedure a most dangerous one to use.[128]

---

[123]   *Bellamy v Sheffield Teaching Hospitals NHS Trust* [2003] EWCA Civ 1124 at [36].

[124]   *Daniels v Commissioner of Police for the Metropolis* [2005] EWCA Civ 1312 at [31].

[125]   *Daniels v Commissioner of Police for the Metropolis* [2005] EWCA Civ 1312 at [36].

[126]   See, for example, *Islam v Ali* [2003] EWCA Civ 612 at [18].

[127]   *Quorum v Schramm (No 2)* [2002] 2 Lloyd's Rep 72 and *Johnsey Estates (1990) Ltd v The Secretary of State for the Environment* [2001] EWCA Civ 535. Also see *Rolf v de Guerin* [2011] EWCA Civ 78.

[128]   *Rolf v De Guerin* [2011] EWCA Civ 78 at [34].

Non-monetary offers

6.69   Where a non-monetary offer is made (such as an offer to extend a lease), it may be taken into account as being an admissible offer. It may be appropriate to assess the effect of the offer by examining whether the offeror has 'secured broadly' a result which was better for him than that which he had offered.[129] There is a further discussion of non-monetary offers at **13.59** and **14.45–14.47**, that being in the context of CPR Part 36: most of what is said in that context also has resonance in the context of admissible offers.

Absent offers on alternative cases

6.70   Where a party advances a primary case but also advances an alternative case which, if successful, would be less advantageous to that party than the primary case, the existence of the alternative case would create a need for that party to consider making a protective offer based on that alternative case. In a dispute between a mother and son about the ownership of a house, Ward LJ had the following to say:[130]

> 'In my judgment the valuable use of payments into court and Part 36 offers to settle place an onus, in the first place, on the defendant. He had the ability to pay his fallback position into court and he could, if he took the view, have done so, confident that his greedy mother backed by his horrible brother would not have taken that money but would have fought him to the bitter end for the whole of the proceeds of sale, but that was his means of protecting his position. He failed to avail it, and it seems to me that that loses him the protection of the rules.'

These comments were made in the context of CPR Part 36, but there is no reason to believe that they would not also apply to admissible offers.

Very late offers

6.71   An offer made very late in the proceedings may be given little or no weight.[131]

Would-be, quasi and withdrawn Part 36 offers

6.72   Whilst offers to which the costs consequences in Part 36 apply are not themselves admissible offers,[132] withdrawn Part 36 offers are,[133] as are offers that have fallen short of being Part 36 offers for technical reasons.[134] Such an admissible offer will not have the same mechanistic effect as a Part 36 offer, however; in this regard, Rix LJ had this to say:[135]

---

[129]   *MBI Incorporated v Riminex Investments Ltd* [2002] EWHC 2856 (QB).
[130]   *Day v Day* [2006] EWCA Civ 415 at [20].
[131]   *London Tara Hotel Limited v Kensington Close Hotel Limited* [2011] EWHC 29 (Ch) at [30], per Roth J.
[132]   *Shovelar v Lane* [2011] EWCA Civ 802 at [52], per Ward LJ.
[133]   *Epsom College v Pierse Contracting Southern Ltd (formerly Biseley Construction Ltd) (in liq)* [2011] EWCA Civ 1449 at [54] *et seq*, per Rix LJ. Presumably the same is true of a Part 36 offer to which the costs consequences in Part 36 do not apply, such as where an offer has not been 'beaten': see *Straker v Tudor Rose (a firm)* [2007] EWCA Civ 368 at [3].
[134]   See, for example, *French v Groupama Insurance Co Ltd* [2011] EWCA Civ 1119 at [41] *et seq*, per Rix LJ and *Brown v Mcasso Music Production* [2005] EWCA Civ 1546, per Neuberger LJ.
[135]   *French v Groupama Insurance Co Ltd* [2011] EWCA Civ 1119 at [41]. Also see *Epsom College v Pierse Contracting Southern Ltd (formerly Biseley Construction Ltd) (in liq)* [2011] EWCA Civ 1449 at [54] *et seq*, per Rix LJ at [54], per Rix LJ.

'The question remains not merely whether the withdrawn offer be taken into account but whether Part 36 consequences should ordinarily flow where a Part 36 offer has been withdrawn . . . [It] has become hard to ignore the rules which state that the Part 36 costs consequences (viz the consequences of amended rule 36.14(2) and (3)) "do not apply" to even a Part 36 offer that has been withdrawn . . . After all, if a mechanistic rule that an offer which beats the judgment should result in all costs being switched to the offeree is to make sense, there needs to be sufficient formality about the making and maintenance of the offer. That formality is provided by the rules, and it is not altogether obvious to see why the mechanistic rule should prima facie survive when the formalities are not observed.'

Part 36 offers that have been withdrawn and withdrawn offers generally are addressed at **14.73-14.74**.

Conditional offers

6.73   A conditional offer to pay a sum of money on account (as opposed to pay a sum of money that if accepted would dispose of the dispute or part of the dispute) is not an offer to which much weight should be given; that said, Longmore LJ has confirmed that it is an offer that is admissible notwithstanding the fact that it would be afforded only limited weight.[136] On the facts of the case before him (in which the claim was probably exaggerated), he regarded it as being a factor that justified an order that there be no order as to costs.

Admiralty claims ('Part 61 offers')

6.74   The following provisions apply to collision claims:

'(10) The consequences set out in paragraph (11) apply where a party to a claim to establish liability for a collision claim (other than a claim for loss of life or personal injury)—

(a)   makes an offer to settle in the form set out in paragraph (12) not less than 21 days before the start of the trial;

(b)   that offer is not accepted; and

(c)   the maker of the offer obtains at trial an apportionment equal to or more favourable than his offer.

(11) Where paragraph (10) applies the parties will, unless the court considers it unjust, be entitled to the following costs—

(a)   the maker of the offer will be entitled to –

(i)   all his costs from 21 days after the offer was made; and

(ii)   his costs before then in the percentage to which he would have been entitled had the offer been accepted; and

(b)   all other parties to whom the offer was made –

(i)   will be entitled to their costs up to 21 days after the offer was made in the percentage to which they would have been entitled had the offer been accepted; but

(ii)   will not be entitled to their costs thereafter.

(12) An offer under paragraph (10) must be in writing and must contain—

(a)   an offer to settle liability at stated percentages;

(b)   an offer to pay costs in accordance with the same percentages;

(c)   a term that the offer remain open for 21 days after the date it is made; and

(d)   a term that, unless the court orders otherwise, on expiry of that period the offer remains open on the same terms except that the offeree should pay all the costs

---

[136]   *Ali v Stagecoach* [2011] EWCA Civ 1494 at [8] and [9].

from that date until acceptance.'

Teare J has found that the approach to interpreting putatively defective Part 61 offers is similar to that which is taken with Part 36 offers[137] (see **14.25**).

When to consider admissible offers

6.75 A party may make an offer and then have such a degree of success prior to conclusion of the proceedings as a whole that it is nearly inevitable that he will beat the offer; an example might be where there has been a trial on a preliminary issue. Where those are the circumstances, it does not follow that the court should determine the relevant costs straight away. This is not only because it will only be upon conclusion that the court can be sure that the offeror has truly beaten the offer, but also because his putative entitlement to costs may be influenced by factors such as set-off, the costs of issues, etc. It was for reasons such as these that Jack J has said that it would be only in the most exceptional case that the determination of costs should take place prior to the conclusion of the proceedings.[138] Jackson LJ commented that where a party raises the issue of an offer prior to the conclusion of a trial on a preliminary issue, the normal order would be to reserve costs.[139]

CONDUCT

6.76 It has long been established that for the purposes of costs the court is entitled to take into account the conduct of the parties, including pre-proceedings conduct (or 'anterior conduct', as it is sometimes known).[140] The CPR have not changed this.[141] The emphasis on 'front loading' and on pre-action protocols has, if anything, heightened the importance of conduct. The conduct must relate to the claim rather than to something merely ancillary to it.[142]

6.77 The authorities are not *ad idem* as to the extent to which pre-proceedings conduct should be taken into account. The matter is best analysed by drawing a distinction between procedural and non-procedural conduct. There is no doubt that the former can be taken into account in all courts, but in so far as the latter is concerned, there seems to be a divergence between practice in the Commercial Court and the practices in other

---

[137] See *Miom Ltd v Sea Echo ENE (No 2)* [2011] EWHC 2715 (Admlty).

[138] *Tullett Prebon plc v BGC Brokeers LP* [2010] EWHC 989 (QB) at [6]; see also *HSS Hire Services Group plc v Builders Merchants Ltd* [2005] 3 All E R 486, *Shepherds Investments Ltd v Walters* [2007] EWCA Civ 29, and *Multiplex Constructions (UK) Ltd v Cleveland Bridge (UK) Ltd* [2007] EWHC 659 (TCC) at [26].

[139] *Multiplex Constructions (UK) Ltd v Cleveland Bridge (UK) Ltd* [2007] EWHC 659 (TCC) at [26]; in a similar vein, Coulson J had this to say about preliminary points generally: 'The mere fact that a party has won a preliminary issue does not, of itself, entitle that party to its costs of that issue. Before knowing the overall outcome of the trial, it is always dangerous to give one party its costs of an issue merely because, through a sensible case management decision, one aspect of the substantive dispute was dealt with in advance of the others' (*Perriam Ltd v Wayne* [2011] EWHC 403 (QB) at [53]).

[140] *Hall v Rover Financial Services Ltd (GB)* [2002] EWCA Civ 1514 at [18]. It was originally believed that there needed to be a 'good cause' for pre-proceedings conduct to displace the rule that costs follow the event (*Angus v Clifford* [1891] 2 Ch 449; *Harnett v Vise* (1880) 5 Ex D 30; and *Bostock v Ransey UDC* [1900] 2 QB 616), but as long ago as the 1920s the House of Lords clarified that the court's discretion was unfettered in this respect (*Donald Campbell & Co Ltd v Pollak* [1927] AC 732).

[141] *Groupama Insurance Co Ltd v Aon Ltd* [2003] EWCA Civ 1846.

[142] See, for example, *Barr v Biffa Waste Services Limited* [2011] EWHC 1107 (TCC) at [19]–[21], this being a nuisance claim in which Coulson J declined to give weight to poor pre-proceedings conduct because it related to the Environment Agency rather than to the claim itself.

courts. Each of those types of court is considered in turn. It should not be forgotten that conduct may also be reflected in the basis of costs: this dealt with at **13.12** *et seq.*

Non-procedural conduct

6.78   The focus in this section is on pre-proceedings conduct. Whilst it may be an oversimplification to say that the Commercial Court tends to give less weight to the circumstances which led to the claim than do other courts, a complaint that a party brought litigation upon himself is less likely to find favour in that court than it would in other fora.

Commercial Court

6.79   Longmore LJ (with whom Tuckey LJ agreed) said:[143]

'The relevant conduct must be conduct in the proceedings themselves ... It is not, in my view, proper to disallow a successful party her costs simply because of anterior dishonest conduct which, while it may have been a part of the transaction which gives rise to the proceedings, cannot be characterised as misconduct in relation to the proceedings themselves.'

6.80   Commenting in a later case, Brooke LJ expressed doubt as to whether all the relevant authorities had been drawn to Longmore LJ's attention. He did not go so far as to cast doubt on the correctness of what his brother judges had said, preferring instead to distinguish the practice in the Commercial Court from the practices in other courts:[144]

'Longmore and Tuckey LJJ both have immense experience of practice in the Commercial Court, where issues of this kind arise very frequently, and in this passage Longmore LJ should be interpreted as doing no more than describing the contemporary practice of the judges of that court. In commercial transactions business people not infrequently do not follow the Queensberry Rules in their dealings with each other, but this in itself is not seen to be sufficient to deprive one of them, if successful in the ensuing litigation, of his costs of the litigation.'

Latham and Butler-Sloss LJJ agreed with that analysis.

Other courts

6.81   Brook LJ explained the practices in courts other than the Commercial Court in this way:[145]

'The philosophy of the Woolf Reforms is that the parties should lay their cards on the table as fully as possible and as early as possible, so that they can assess the desirability of a negotiated settlement (as against the risks of contested litigation) in a well-informed way. If they then decide to litigate (and to burden other parties with the costs of litigation), and to pursue the litigation to trial they must expect, as a general rule, to have to pay the costs of parties necessarily joined to the litigation if they lose.'

---

[143]   *Hall v Rover Financial Services Ltd (GB)* [2002] EWCA Civ 1514; this was a case in which the claimant had been guilty of 'moral blindness' in the transaction which led to the claim.

[144]   *Groupama Insurance Co Ltd v Aon Ltd* [2003] EWCA Civ 1846 at [39].

[145]   *Groupama Insurance Co Ltd v Aon Ltd* [2003] EWCA Civ 1846 at [39].

Case examples are given at **6.89–6.97**.

6.82   It seems, therefore, that pre-proceedings conduct may be relevant, especially if that conduct has been carried forward into the litigation itself. At this point, it is worth mentioning contributory negligence which, on one analysis, is a type of pre-proceedings conduct. The Civil Bench Book gives the following advice about contributory negligence:[146]

'As has always been the case, it is probable a proportion [of costs] only will be awarded in an accident claim where a claimant has been held to be partly responsible for what occurred, the starting point being a reduction equal to the percentage or proportion of the contributory negligence as found.'

This guidance is rarely followed and may, indeed, be wrong.[147] See **6.113**.

Procedural conduct

6.83   Procedural failings may be reflected in the incidence of costs in any court. This relates to both pre-proceedings conduct and conduct during the claim; indeed, the CPR specifically refer to the court taking into account conduct before the proceedings, including the extent to which the parties followed any pre-action protocol.[148] The court tends to look at the substance of the guidance given in the applicable protocol, rather than its technical or semantic aspects. Akenhead J had the following to say on this subject:[149]

'The Court should be slow to allow the rules to be used … for one party to obtain a tactical or costs advantage where in substance the principles of the Protocol have been complied with.'

6.84   Where there has been a breach of a pre-action protocol, it is often appropriate to deal with that breach at an early stage in the litigation, thereby putting the parties back into the positions they would have been in had there not been a breach.[150] This would militate against the court reserving such issues until the conclusion of the litigation. Sir Henry Brooke has cautioned against double jeopardy; where a breach of a pre-action protocol has been put right and has been reflected in an interim costs order, the court should avoid reflecting the same breach in the final costs award.[151]

6.85   Practice Direction – Pre-action Conduct gives the following guidance:[152]

---

[146]   Paragraph 8.14.

[147]   In support of the proposition that the guidance is wrong, see *Sonmez v Kebabery Wholesale Ltd* [2009] EWCA Civ 1386 at [22], per Ward LJ, and *Onay v Brown* [2009] EWCA Civ 775 at [29], per Goldring LJ.

[148]   See CPR, r 44.3(4)(a) and (5)(a).

[149]   *TJ Brent Ltd v Black & Veatch Consulting Ltd* [2008] EWHC 1497 (TCC) at [45]; see also para 4.3(1) of Practice Direction – Pre-Action Conduct.

[150]   *Charles Church Developments Ltd v Stent Foundations Ltd* [2007] EWHC 855 (TCC), Ramsey J; see also *Daejan Investments Ltd v The Park West Club Ltd* [2004] BLR 223.

[151]   *Thornhill v Nationwide Metal Recycling Limited* [2011] EWCA Civ 919 at [47].

[152]   Before 9 April 2009 similar, but not identical, guidance was given in Practice Direction – Protocols; if the conduct under consideration occurred before that date, it may be appropriate to refer to the contemporaneous requirements, where appropriate. There are, however, no transitional provisions in this regard.

'**4.   Compliance**

4.1   The CPR enable the court to take into account the extent of the parties' compliance with this Practice Direction or a relevant pre-action protocol (see paragraph 5.2) when ... making orders about who should pay costs (see CPR rule 44.3(5)(a)).

4.2   The court will expect the parties to have complied with this Practice Direction or any relevant pre-action protocol. The court may ask the parties to explain what steps were taken to comply prior to the start of the claim. Where there has been a failure of compliance by a party the court may ask that party to provide an explanation.

Assessment of compliance

4.3   When considering compliance the court will—

    (1)   be concerned about whether the parties have complied in substance with the relevant principles and requirements and is not likely to be concerned with minor or technical shortcomings;

    (2)   consider the proportionality of the steps taken compared to the size and importance of the matter;

    (3)   take account of the urgency of the matter. Where a matter is urgent (for example, an application for an injunction) the court will expect the parties to comply only to the extent that it is reasonable to do so ...

Examples of non-compliance

4.4   The court may decide that there has been a failure of compliance by a party because, for example, that party has—

    (1)   not provided sufficient information to enable the other party to understand the issues;

    (2)   not acted within a time limit set out in a relevant pre-action protocol, or, where no specific time limit applies, within a reasonable period;

    (3)   unreasonably refused to consider ADR (paragraph 8 in Part III of this Practice Direction and the pre-action protocols all contain similar provisions about ADR); or

    (4)   without good reason, not disclosed documents requested to be disclosed.

Sanctions for non-compliance

4.5   The court will look at the overall effect of non-compliance on the other party when deciding whether to impose sanctions.

4.6   If, in the opinion of the court, there has been non-compliance, the sanctions which the court may impose include—

    (1)   ....

    (2)   an order that the party at fault pays the costs, or part of the costs, of the other party or parties (this may include an order under rule 27.14(2)(g) in cases allocated to the small claims track);

    (3)   an order that the party at fault pays those costs on an indemnity basis (rule 44.4(3) sets out the definition of the assessment of costs on an indemnity basis) ...'

6.86   Thus, the court may ask a non-compliant party to explain his conduct. The court will look at the effect of the non-compliance, but will not be overly concerned about minor or technical shortcomings. Proportionality and the need for urgency may be taken into account.

6.87 A number of the pre-action protocols specifically provide that non-compliance may lead to costs sanctions being imposed. The Pre-action Protocol for Construction and Engineering Disputes, for example, says that a failure by a defendant to clarify at an early stage that it is the 'wrong' defendant may be taken into account. Another example is that a defendant in a clinical negligence claim may face sanctions for not supplying clinical records in a timely fashion.[153]

6.88 There are general provisions relating to claims not covered by specific pre-action protocols; in so far as those provisions mention costs at all, they do so by cautioning against excessive costs. The following is an illustrative extract from Practice Direction – Pre-action Conduct:

> '**6.1** The principles that should govern the conduct of the parties are that, unless the circumstances make it inappropriate, before starting proceedings the parties should—
>
> (1) exchange sufficient information about the matter to allow them to understand each other's position and make informed decisions about settlement and how to proceed;
> (2) make appropriate attempts to resolve the matter without starting proceedings, and in particular consider the use of an appropriate form of ADR in order to do so.
>
> **6.2** The parties should act in a reasonable and proportionate manner in all dealings with one another. In particular, the costs incurred in complying should be proportionate to the complexity of the matter and any money at stake. The parties must not use this Practice Direction as a tactical device to secure an unfair advantage for one party or to generate unnecessary costs.'

Case examples

6.89 The following are case examples of conduct (both pre-proceedings conduct and conduct during proceedings) being reflected in the incidence of costs; some relate to procedural default and others relate to non-procedural conduct. They are nothing more than examples, and should not be regarded as setting any form of precedent.

Criminality and reprehensible conduct

6.90 Whilst an extreme example, where a husband succeeded in his claim in respect of property jointly owned with his wife, he was deprived of his costs by reason of the fact that he had murdered her.[154] In a similar vein, a defendant in a criminal matter was denied an individual costs award (which is a matter to which the CPR apply) because had engaged in the systemic dishonest abuse, under assumed identities, of various persons; this was despite the fact that he was acquitted of the actual offences of which he was charged.[155]

Failure to send letter of claim, to respond to letter of claim (and delay)

6.91 In a case in which no letter of claim had been sent, Morritt V-C ordered the 'successful' claimants – if that is the correct word given the costs order he made – not only to pay the defendant's costs, but to do so on the indemnity basis.[156] In a case

---

[153] Pre-Action Protocol for the Resolution of Clinical Disputes, para 3.12.
[154] *McMinn v McMinn* [2003] 2 FLR 823.
[155] *In the matter of Olden v Crown Prosecution Service* [2010] EWCA Civ 961.
[156] *Phoenix Finance Ltd v Federation Internationale de l'Automobile* [2002] EWHC 1028 (Ch).

concerning a well-resourced defendant (the state), Park J discounted its costs by 15% to take account of the fact that the response to a letter had been about 6 weeks later than it should have been according to the applicable pre-action protocol.[157] Being late in providing a response will usually sound in the amount of costs rather than the incidence of costs, this being a reflection of the fact that the claimant will have to read into the matter again if a long period of time is allowed to lapse before he receives a response.[158] The fact that a person may be overworked and was putatively not able to respond to correspondence is not a factor that can properly be taken into account.[159]

Prematurity and aggression

6.92   Aggressive conduct on the part of a losing party may be reflected in a costs order on the indemnity basis (see **13.30**). Aggression and prematurity on the part of the successful party may result in an adjustment to the incidence of costs[160] but it is the conduct of both sides that is relevant, including the reaction of an opponent. Thus, if a defendant's reaction to supposedly premature issue is not to react straight away but to wait and then to deny liability, the putative prematurity would be irrelevant.[161] For premature issue in the context of fixed costs, see **33.29**. An overly aggressive attitude towards the recovery of costs can backfire and is capable of contributing to an adverse costs award, or even an adverse costs award on the indemnity basis.[162] In a case in which the claimant had brought an abusive claim, Tugdenhat J ruled the defendant should not have its costs pre-issue because it would not have been able to seek an order for those costs if the abusive claim had not been brought;[163] this somewhat at odds with the way such costs are treated on an assessment (see **29.34-29.35**) and as such is perhaps best regarded as being an illustration of the fact that each case must be determined on its own facts.

Fabricating evidence and dishonest cases

6.93   In a case in which a successful claimant had fabricated evidence, Mr Nicholas Davidson QC (sitting as a deputy judge of the Chancery Division) deducted £20,000 from her costs to take account of that behaviour (and to take account of the fact that she had failed to take advantage of a sensible opportunity to negotiate).[164] A party who might otherwise have been awarded costs on the indemnity basis may lose that benefit if he is found guilty of knowingly advancing a false case.[165] See also 'culpable exaggeration' (**6.141-6.150**).

---

[157]   *Aegis Group plc v Inland Revenue Commissioners* [2005] EWHC 1468 (Ch).
[158]   *Thompson (a minor) and ors v Bruce* (unreported) 26 June 2011, QBD at [58], per John Leighton Williams QC sitting as a Deputy Judge of the High Court.
[159]   *Bahta & Ors, R (on the application of) v Secretary of State for the Home Department & Ors* [2011] EWCA Civ 895 at [60], per Pill LJ.
[160]   See, for example, *Pathology Group v Reynolds* (unreported) 28 November 2011, QBD, HHJ Seymour QC sitting as a Judge of the High Court.
[161]   See *Roper v Auckland Risk Advisors Ltd* (unreported) 5 September 2011, QBD, Eder J.
[162]   *Hudson v New Media Holding Co LLC* [2011] EWHC 3068 (QB) at [30] per Eady.
[163]   *Citation Plc v Ellis Whittam Ltd* [2012] EWHC 764 (QB) at [28].
[164]   *Gil v Baygreen Properties Ltd* [2004] EWHC 2029 (Ch).
[165]   See, for example, *Bank of Tokyo-Mitsubishi UFJ Ltd v Baskan Gida Sanayi Ve Pazarlama AS* [2009] EWHC 1696 (Ch), per Briggs J; see also *Digicel (St Lucia) v Cable & Wireless plc* [2010] EWHC 774 (Ch), per Morgan J.

Departing from industry practice and from guidelines

6.94   Brooke LJ penalised a litigant for having altered a fax contrary to acceptable market practice.[166] Likewise, a breach of a director's duty and dishonest assistance were taken into account (amongst other things) when making a costs order.[167] Where a party wrongly failed to raise the possibility of arbitration in a case where that would have been expected and required, Coulson J found that that was a factor that the court was able to take into account.[168] If an organisation departs from its own guidelines, that may result in an adverse costs order.[169] A failure on the part of a defendant police force to keep up to date with a complaint that had been made by the claimant was found to be factor that could be taken into account.[170]

Allowing an opponent to proceed on an incorrect footing

6.95   A well-resourced defendant had allowed a litigant in person to proceed on a mistaken understanding as to which regulations applied. The defendant succeeded, but Jack J ordered that their costs be discounted by a fixed sum (£5,000) to take account of that conduct.[171] Whilst now a very old authority decided under a different regime to CPR, r 44.3,[172] Lord Sterndale MR has commented that because he is brought into litigation against his will and therefore has less control over this involvement, less weight should be attributed to such conduct on the part of a defendant.[173]

Refusal to pay costs properly incurred and pouncing on oversights

6.96   A refusal to pay costs properly incurred may itself be justification for an award of costs,[174] but the failure to pay needs to be relevant to the matter in hand, and as such it would be in only exceptional circumstances that an award would reflect the late payment of costs in another application.[175]

Taking advantage of an opponent by pouncing on a procedural mishap may result in an adverse costs award.[176] In this regard, it is relevant that procedural mishaps can often be remedied by consent and with the party not at fault being awarded its costs.[177]

---

[166]   *Groupama Insurance Co Ltd v Aon Ltd* [2003] EWCA Civ 1846.

[167]   *Grupo Torras SA v Sheikh Fahad Mohammed Al-Sabah* [1999] CLC 1469, QBD.

[168]   *Bovis Homes Ltd v Kendrick Construction Ltd* [2009] EWHC 1359 (TCC).

[169]   See, for example, *Atkins (deceased) v Revenue & Customs Commissioners* [2011] UKFTT 468 (TC) in which HHJ N Nowlan awarded costs against Revenue & Customs on the basis that it had failed to follow its own guidelines, thereby incurring expense unnecessarily.

[170]   *Zapello v Chief Constable Of Sussex Police* [2010] EWCA Civ 1417.

[171]   *Wright v HSBC Bank plc* [2006] EWHC 1473 (Admin).

[172]   Specifically, the regime (RSC Ord 65, r 1 in its pre-1929 guise) involved a test of whether there was 'good cause' to deprive the successful party of his costs.

[173]   *Ritter v Godfrey* [1920] 2 KB 47 at 52.

[174]   Although a very old case, *Thomas v Palin* (1882) 21 Ch D 360 illustrates this fact that, in an appropriate case, it may be reasonable to issue proceedings solely for the purposes of asking the court to rule on the recoverability of disputed costs.

[175]   *Hoque v Ali* (unreported) 15 February 2012, CA.

[176]   Whilst it did not relate to pre-proceedings conduct, Coulson J took a dim view of a party who had sought judgment in default when it was known that an extension was being sought: see *Roundstone Nurseries Ltd v Stephenson Holdings Ltd* [2009] EWHC 1431 (TCC).

[177]   See, for example, *Hannigan v Hannigan* [2000] 2 FCR 650.

Failure to give disclosure and failure to give evidence

6.97 A failure to give disclosure at an appropriate stage is capable of giving rise to adverse costs orders; whilst sitting as a Deputy Judge of the High Court, HHJ Simon Brown QC halved a successful party's costs to take account of such conduct.[178] Contrary examples do exist, however; whilst in a context other than the exercise of discretion under CPR, r 44.3[179], Floyd J commented that a party may escape criticism for not having accelerated its disclosure if resolution of the factual dispute between the parties would not have disposed of the claim generally.[180] Whilst a criminal case, the European Court of Human Rights has ruled that it would not be a breach of Art 6 of the ECHR for the court to take into account the fact that a defendant had exercised a right of silence;[181] there is no reason to believe that it would be a breach of Art 6 if the court were to take into account the fact that a party chose not to give evidence.

Putatively good conduct and cooperation

6.98 Whilst not binding and whilst technically obiter, HHJ Graham Jones has found that an assertion that good conduct should be reflected in the incidence of costs was novel and unsupported by authority.[182] Where the parties cooperate to a high degree, it is possible that their conduct could give rise to a tacit understanding that there will be no order for costs in respect of the issues over which they are cooperating.[183]

Procedure

6.99 It is open to the trial judge to make an order that the costs judge is to determine issues relating to conduct; this may be appropriate where those issues are particularly numerous and detailed.[184] Nonetheless, whilst it used to be thought that a failure to raise such issues at the time the order was made would preclude those issues being raised during the detailed assessment,[185] it is now known that this is not correct. (These issues are dealt with at **12.103–12.141**.) Notwithstanding this better understanding of the law, good practice requires that the trial judge is given opportunity to give directions which might assist the costs judge, and common sense dictates that this means that issues concerning conduct ought to be raised sooner rather than later.

ISSUES

6.100 The following discussion deals with the important topic of how the court deals with the costs of identifiable, discrete issues (ie separate contentions and arguments)

---

[178] *Earles v Barclays Bank plc* [2009] EWHC 2500 (QB) per HHJ Simon Brown QC.
[179] The context was whether to depart from the default position that a person who has discontinued should pay costs: see **7.82** *et seq*.
[180] See *Mobiqa Limited v Trinity Mobile Limited* [2010] EWHC 253 (Pat) at [25]; it was clear that there were other factors at play in that case, an in particular, the defendant had explained its case with great clarity.
[181] *Ashendon and Jones v United Kingdom* (2011) Times, 22 September; the court was careful to point out that the findings of the trial court were phrased in such a way as to make it clear that the costs award did not imply a suspicion that the defendant might have committed the offence.
[182] See *Various Claimants v Gower Chemicals Limited* (unreported) 27 August 2010, Cardiff County Court at [29], per HHJ Graham Jones.
[183] See, for example, *JSC BTA Bank v Solodchencko* (unreported) 23 January 2012, Ch D, per Henderson J.
[184] See, for example, *Re Dalmar Properties Ltd sub nom David Norman Kaye v Kingstars Ltd* [2008] EWHC 2753 (Ch).
[185] See *Aaron v Shelton* [2004] EWHC 1162 (QB), which is now known not to be good law.

which a party has advanced or defended; such issues will be referred to as 'unsuccessful issues' and 'successful issues' depending on whether they have been lost or won from the perspective of the party in question. Issues will also be referred to as 'reasonably argued' or 'unreasonably argued' depending on whether the party in question acted reasonably in advancing or defending the issue. Where a party abandons an issue, special considerations may apply. This is dealt with at **6.128–6.137**, which should be read in conjunction with this section.

Historical perspective

6.101 Some of the case law decided during the first two years of the CPR (1999 to 2001) can be put into context only if something is known of the history of the law. As explained above, the pre-CPR ethos was that the 'winner takes all'. Moreover, the fact that the winner may have raised issues that ultimately failed would not have prevented him from being awarded all of his costs (see *Re Elgindata (No 2)*).[186] This philosophy meant that issues-based costs orders were a rarity (although historically they were less of a rarity than some of the authorities referred to below seem to acknowledge[187]). The CPR brought about significant changes in this area. Speaking shortly before its introduction, Lord Woolf MR explained the new ethos:[188]

> 'The most significant change of emphasis of the new rules is to require courts to be more ready to make separate orders which reflect the outcome of different issues. In doing this, the new rules are reflecting a change of practice which has already started. It is now clear that a too robust application of the "follow the event principle" encourages litigants to increase the costs of litigation, since it discourages litigants from being selective as to the points they take. If you recover all your costs as long as you win, you are encouraged to leave no stone unturned in your effort to do so.'

6.102 Shortly thereafter, Jackson J expressed a similar view:[189]

> 'The straight jacket imposed on the Court by [*Elgindata*] is gone, and the search for justice is untrammelled by constraints beyond those laid down by the new code itself.'

Neuberger J echoed these comments: he said that, whilst *Elgindata* should not be overlooked, it could not be said that it represented the law under the CPR.[190]

6.103 Not all judges agreed that the introduction of the CPR had effected such radical changes. Rimer J opined that the court had always had the power to disallow costs of issues which had been unreasonably advanced and that the CPR merely spelt out more specifically those factors that the court was able to take into account.[191] Hale LJ commented that some of the reasoning in *Elgindata* was capable of applying post-CPR.[192]

---

[186]   [1992] 1 WLR 1207.
[187]   Early examples inlcluded *Myers v Defries* (1880) 5 Ex D 180 at 187 and *Reid Hewitt & Co v Joseph* [1918] AC 717 at 723; Porter & Wortham, *A Guide to Costs* (19th ed, 1932) at p 683 appears to record issues-bsed awards as being unremarkable and ordinary events.
[188]   *Phonographic Performance Ltd v AEI Rediffusion Music Ltd* [1999] 1 WLR 1507 at 1522.
[189]   *BCCI v Ali & Ors* [2000] 2 Costs LR 243.
[190]   *Harrison v Bloom Camillin (a firm)* (unreported) 4 February 2000, Ch D; see also *Antonelli v Allen* (2000) *The Times*, December 8, in which Neuberger J made an issues-based costs order shortly thereafter. See also *Liverpool City Council v Cahvassed Ltd* (unreported) 18 August 1999.
[191]   *Deg-Deutsche Investitions Und Entwicklungsgesellschaft MBH v Koshy & Ors* (2000) *The Times*, March 30.
[192]   *Universal Cycles v Grangebriar Ltd* (unreported) 8 February 2000, CA.

6.104 So, in the early days of the CPR there were two schools of thought: both schools accepted that the costs of unsuccessful issues could be disallowed, but one of those schools believed that this was the case only if those issues had been unreasonably argued. In the event, the latter school of thought was shown to be wrong.[193] Thomas J analysed the topic thus:[194]

> 'Under CPR 44.3(4) the court is bound to have regard to all the circumstances of the case, including two specific matters: (a) the conduct of all the parties, and (b) whether a party succeeded on part of this case. The conduct of the parties is defined under [CPR, r 44.3(5)]. Under paragraph (5), the definition includes the reasonableness of raising, pursuing and contesting a particular allegation or issues. However, it seems to me clear that under subparagraph (b) of CPR 44.3(4) the reasonableness of the party taking a particular point … is not necessarily relevant; that subparagraph is quite distinct from conduct of the parties and therefore the reasonableness of raising an issue does not necessarily have to be taken into account. Quite apart from the language of the CPR, it seems to me this construction gives effect to the particular purpose of encouraging litigants to be selective as to the points they take and thus decreasing costs of litigation.'

6.105 In view of the existence of two schools of thought up to about 2001 (and possibly early 2002), some caution ought to be exercised when considering authorities which were decided during that period.

The modern approach

Depriving a party of the costs of an unsuccessful issue

6.106 The modern approach is as follows:

- CPR, r 44.3(4)(b) specifically requires the court to have regard to whether a party has succeeded on part of his case, even if he has not been wholly successful;
- CPR, r 44.3(5) requires the court to consider whether it was reasonable for a party to raise, pursue or contest a particular issue, and the manner in which that party has pursued or defended that issue; and
- CPR, r 44.3(6) provides a range of orders that might be suitable for an issues-based approach.

The first and second of these bullet points describe different processes: for the reasons set out above, a party may be deprived of the costs of an issue upon which it has lost regardless of whether that issue was reasonably or unreasonably advanced or defended. This does not necessarily mean that the costs of an unsuccessful issue may be awarded against a party. (It is worth pausing here to note that an issues-based approach is not the same as an order which makes specific reference to the costs of issues; that is, an issues-based approach may, and usually will, give rise to an order which makes no mention of the issues themselves. Some authorities use the term 'issues-based' to mean an order which specifically refers to issues; they should be read accordingly.)

---

[193] See *Summit Property Ltd v Pitmans* [2002] EWCA Civ 2020; *Stena Rederi Aktiebolag* [2003] EWCA Civ 214; and *Kastor Navigation Co Ltd & Anor v AXA Global Risks (UK) Ltd & Ors* [2004] EWCA Civ 277.

[194] *Stocznia Gdanska SA v Latvian Shipping Co* (2001) *The Times*, May 8, Thomas J.

Requiring a party to pay the costs of an unsuccessful issue

6.107 Where an unsuccessful issue was unreasonably argued, then there are good reasons why a party may be condemned as to the costs of that issue. Simon Brown LJ explained it in this way:[195]

> 'For my part I have no doubt whatever that judges nowadays should be altogether readier than in times past to make costs orders which reflect not merely the overall outcome of proceedings but also the loss of particular issues. If, moreover, the "winning" party has not merely lost on an issue but has pursued an issue when clearly he should not have done, then there are two good reasons why that should be reflected in the costs order: first, as a sanction to deter such conduct in future; secondly, to relieve the "losing" party of at least part of his costs liability. It is one thing for the losing party to have to pay the costs of issues properly before the court, another that he should have to pay also for fighting issues which were hopeless and ought never to have been pursued.'

6.108 A related but distinct topic is whether the costs of an unsuccessful issue can be awarded against a party who reasonably argued the point. Longmore LJ (with whom Tuckey and Chadwick LJJ agreed) found that such an award could be made even in the absence of unreasonable conduct.[196] However, Longmore LJ introduced the notion that a case must be 'exceptional':[197]

> 'It is thus a matter of ordinary common sense that if it is appropriate to consider costs on an issue basis at all, it may be appropriate, in a suitably exceptional case, to make an order which not only deprives a successful party of his costs of a particular issue but also an order which requires him to pay the otherwise unsuccessful party's costs of that issue, without it being necessary for the court to decide that allegations have been made improperly or unreasonably.'

In a similar vein, whilst obiter, Lord Neuberger MR said that in 'an extreme case, he [the successful party] may even have to pay some of the unsuccessful party's costs'.[198]

6.109 Longmore LJ did not expand upon what might amount to an exceptional case, but in a subsequent case Warren J dealt with the topic as follows:[199]

> 'I note there the words "in a suitably exceptional case". I do not read those words "suitably exceptional case" as meaning that one goes back to *Elgindata* and has to find unreasonable or improper conduct or, because we know that is not what we have to find, something pretty close to it; but it does mean something out of the ordinary in some sort of relevant way.'

Warren J continued:[200]

> 'The task is to identify those cases where the loss on an issue carries the costs sanction ranging from deprivation of costs to an order against the losing party on that issue. The test ... is that one no longer has to find improper or unreasonable conduct. Instead, as Longmore LJ puts it [in *Summit*], one has to find a suitably exceptional case so far as concerns making adverse orders.'

---

[195] *Budgen v Andrew Gardner Partnership* [2002] EWCA Civ 1125 at [26].
[196] *Summit Property Ltd v Pitmans* [2002] EWCA Civ 2020.
[197] *Summit Property Ltd v Pitmans* [2002] EWCA Civ 2020 at [17].
[198] *M v Mayor and Burgesses of the London Borough of Croydon* [2012] EWCA Civ 595 at [45].
[199] *Activis Ltd v Merck & Co Inc* [2007] EWHC 1625 (Pat) at [15].
[200] At [26] and then at [30].

6.110 Thus, Warren J was able to find exceptionality in the fact that the issue was discrete and significant.[201] In a similar vein in a different case, Mann J said that (but for an offer which one of the parties had made) he would have found that the requirement for exceptionality had been made where a party had chosen, albeit reasonably, to defend its position without any affirmative supporting evidence.[202] It seems, therefore, that the requirement of exceptionality is not a significant fetter upon the court's discretion. This does not mean that the court will focus on every small issue which may have been lost and adjust the costs accordingly; in this regard, Coulson J had this to say in the context of a commercial claim:[203]

> 'In civil litigation it is almost inevitable that there will have been some point or argument, raised by the otherwise successful party but rejected by the judge, which will have added to the length of the trial. In my view, the mere fact that the successful party was not successful on every last issue cannot, of itself, justify an issue-based costs order.'

Likewise, Jackson LJ (with whom Sir Anthony Clarke MR and Dyson LJ agreed) came to much the same conclusion in the context of a personal injuries case.[204] In a different case, Jackson LJ appeared to draw a distinction between personal injury cases and other types of case:[205]

> 'In a personal injury action the fact that the claimant has won on some issues and lost on other issues along the way is not normally a reason for depriving the claimant of part of his costs . . . Indeed the fact that the claimant has deliberately exaggerated his claim may in certain instances not be a good reason for depriving him of part of his costs . . . Nevertheless in other cases . . . the fact that the successful party has failed on certain issues may constitute a good reason for modifying the costs order in his favour.'

6.111 It has been argued that if the court were to order parties to pay costs of issues which were unsuccessful but reasonably argued, the court's armoury would be left understocked for those cases in which there had been improper conduct. That argument did not find favour with Aldous, Chadwick or Munby LJJ.[206] Indeed, Tomlinson J has commented on the positive benefits that issues-based awards would bring in encouraging parties to be selective about the points that they take.[207]

6.112 It has also been argued that awarding costs against a party who had won the litigation but who had lost on an issue might do injustice by 'redefining who has won'. Rix LJ (giving judgment to which Tuckey and Neuberger LJJ had contributed) rejected that submission.[208]

---

[201] Coulson J rejected the submission that *Fleming v Chief Constable of Sussex Police Force* [2004] EWCA Civ 643 was authority for the proposition that an issues-based order was required where any discrete issue added significantly to the length of the trial: *J Murphy & Sons Ltd v Johnston Precast Ltd (Formerly Johnston Pipes Ltd) (No 2 Costs)* [2008] EWHC 3104 (TCC) at [9]. Cf *Shore v Sedgewick Financial Services Limited* [2007] EWHC 3054 (QB).

[202] *Fulham Leisure Holdings Ltd v Nicholson Graham & Jones* [2006] EWHC 2428 (Ch) at [10].

[203] *J Murphy & Sons Ltd v Johnson Precast Ltd (No 2) (Costs)* [2008] EWHC 3104 (TCC) at [10]. See also *Pindell Ltd and another v Airasia Berhad (formerly known as Airasia SDN BHD)* [2010] EWHC 3238 (Comm) at [12] and [19] per Tomlinson LJ (sitting in the Commercial Court).

[204] *Goodwin v Bennetts UK Limited* [2008] EWCA Civ 1658 at [21]; see also *Fox v Foundation Piling Limited* [2011] EWCA Civ 790 at [47].

[205] *Fox v Foundation Piling Limited* [2011] EWCA Civ 790 at [48]. Whilst a dissenting judgment, see also *Marcus v Medway Primary Care Trust* [2011] EWCA Civ 750 at [30], per Jackson LJ.

[206] *Stena Rederi Aktiebolag* [2003] EWCA Civ 214.

[207] *Base Metal Trading Ltd v Shamurin* [2003] EWHC 2606 (Comm).

[208] *Kastor Navigation Co Ltd & Anor v AXA Global Risks (UK) Ltd & Ors* [2004] EWCA Civ 277 at [143].

6.113 One particular issue merits specific mention: contributory negligence. In general, the court will not regard an allegation of contributory negligence as being a separate issue, as it is regarded as being part of the trial on liability in general; this is so even if contributory negligence is heard as a preliminary issue. Where the parties have treated liability and contributory negligence as being separate topics for the purposes of negotiation, that is something that can be taken into account as being part of the parties' conduct.[209]

Successful issues unreasonably argued ('costs building')

6.114 The concept of issues-based costs awards is not limited to unsuccessful issues; it may also relate to those which have been successful. Chadwick LJ explained this in these terms:[210]

> 'There will be cases ... where, on an issue by issue approach, a party who has been successful on an issue may still be denied his costs of that issue because, in the view of the court, he has pursued it unreasonably.'

And likewise, in a different case, he remarked:[211]

> '[The] judge may deprive a party of costs on an issue on which he has been successful if satisfied that the party has acted unreasonably in relation to that issue'.

6.115 The court may disallow the costs of a successful issue in instances such as where there was no need to litigate the point at all because it was not a necessary ingredient of a party's case, or where the issue was not likely to be contentious and did not need to be proved. The colloquial term 'costs building' is often applied to the practice of incurring costs unnecessarily.

Circumstances in which an issues-based approach should be taken

Mandatory consideration of an issues-based approach

6.116 Circumstances may arise in which the court would be required to consider making an issues-based order. This is particularly so in cases in which the issues are distinct. By way of illustration, Chadwick LJ made the following comments in a case in which the trial judge had (wrongly) failed to analyse the matter in an issues-based way:[212]

> 'This was a case in which, as it seems to me, the judge was required to consider whether to make an issue-based costs order; he had to consider that question if he were to comply with the guidance given in CPR 44.3 rule (4)(b) ... [Certain claims] clearly did raise quite separate issues: perhaps distinct from each other and clearly distinct from the [other] issues. The matters for consideration, and the evidence in relation to those two claims were, as it seems to me, quite distinct from the matters which had to be considered in relation to [those other issues].'

---

[209] See *Sonmez v Kebabery Wholesale Ltd* [2009] EWCA Civ 1386 at [22], per Ward LJ and *Onay v Brown* [2009] EWCA Civ 775 at [29], per Goldring LJ.

[210] *Summit Property Ltd v Pitmans* [2002] EWCA Civ 2020 at [27].

[211] *Johnsey Estates (1990) Ltd v Secretary of State for the Environment* [2001] EWCA Civ 535 at [21], per Chadwick LJ.

[212] *Aspin v Metric Group Ltd* [2007] EWCA Civ 922 at [23]. Also see *Rolf v de Guerin* [2011] EWCA Civ 78.

It is worth noting that CPR, r 44.3(4)(b) says that the court 'must' have regard to whether a party has succeeded on part of his case, even if he has not been wholly successful.

The exercise of discretion

6.117   When considering whether an issues-based approach is appropriate, Neuberger J has suggested that the following factors might be relevant:[213]

- the reasonableness of the successful party taking the point on which he was unsuccessful in that connection (CPR, r 44.3(5)(b));
- the manner in which the successful party took the point and conducted his case generally (CPR, r 44.2(5)(c));
- the reasonableness of the point, i e whether it reasonable for the successful party to have taken the point in the circumstances;
- the extra costs in terms of preparing for the trial and preparing witness statements, documents and so on;
- the extra time taken in court over the particular issues raised by the point;[214]
- the extent to which the point was interrelated in terms of evidence and argument with the points on which the successful party was successful; and
- standing back and looking at the matter globally, the extent to which it is just in all the circumstances to deprive the successful party of all or any of its costs because of the fact that it was unsuccessful on one or more points.

This list of factors (which was formulated in 2000) is very much in keeping with the guidance that Rix LJ would give 4 years later,[215] so the concerns mentioned under the heading 'historical perspective' probably do not apply.

Issues-based orders and Part 36 offers

6.118   While based on the 'old' Part 36, Rix LJ has found that the phrase 'his costs' in what was then CPR, r 36.21(3)(a) (which is analogous to the present r 36.14(3)(b)) should not be read as if it said 'all his costs'. Therefore, if the court wishes to deprive an otherwise successful litigant of costs of an unsuccessful issue, then the fact that that claimant has beaten a Part 36 offer will not prevent the court from giving effect to its wishes.[216] Although the jurisdiction to make such an order exists, where a party's entitlement to costs has arisen by reason of him having beaten a Part 36 Offer, the court would have to be persuaded that there was something unjust in applying the normal rule.[217] This is addressed in more detail at **14.53-14.57**.

Determination of the correct order

6.119   Regardless of the eventual form of the order, the process of making an issue-based order involves two stages. The first may be called the formulation stage, and the second the adjustment stage.

---

[213]   *Antonelli v Allen* (2000) *The Times*, December 8.

[214]   Where an issue arises only during the course of argument, it may be open to the court to find that it was too bound up with the rest of the issues to justify an issues-based award: see *Investec Bank (UK) Ltd v Zulman* [2010] EWCA Civ 675, 5th paragraph, per Longmore LJ.

[215]   *Kastor Navigation Co Ltd v AXA Global Risks (UK) Ltd* [2004] EWCA Civ 277.

[216]   *Kastor Navigation Co Ltd v AXA Global Risks (UK) Ltd* [2004] EWCA Civ 277 at [135]–[139].

[217]   *Fulham Leisure Holdings Ltd v Nicholson Graham & Jones* [2006] EWHC 2428 (Ch).

The formulation stage

6.120 This stage involves identifying the appropriate competing issues and formulating the approach to be taken; Chadwick LJ described the process as follows:[218]

> 'An issue based approach requires a judge to consider, issue by issue in relation to those issues to which that approach is to be applied, where the costs on each distinct or discrete issue should fall. If, in relation to any issue in the case before it the court considers that it should adopt an issue based approach to costs, the court must ask itself which party has been successful on that issue. Then, if the costs are to follow the event on that issue, the party who has been unsuccessful on that issue must expect to pay the costs of that issue to the party who has succeeded on that issue. That is the effect of applying the general principle on an issue by issue based approach to costs.'

A point that has not been addressed in any great detail under the CPR is what constitutes an issue. Whilst it is guidance that was considered under a very different regime to the CPR, it is perhaps worth noting that Bowen LJ referred to issues as being 'heads of controversy';[219] whilst also a case not decided under the CPR, Thomas J has referred to an issue as being 'identified parts of the litigation in respect of which the party's costs may be taxed'.[220]

The adjustment stage

6.121 This stage involves standing back and looking at the effect of the proposed order. Rix LJ (giving judgment of the court) had this to say on the subject:[221]

> 'The rules required [the judge] to have regard to all the circumstances of the case ... He should have stood back from the mathematical result and asked himself whether in all the circumstances, including the other factors to which we have referred, it was the right result.'

For obvious reasons, there will be a significant amount of overlap between the two stages. Rix LJ cautioned against an overly rigorous and mathematical approach to the formulation of orders.[222] In a similar vein, Ramsey J has commented (in the context of a percentage order) that there is no simple formula for establishing the award based on the number of issues, pages of evidence or paragraphs of submissions or judgments; he said that the decision must to some extent be impressionistic based on my knowledge of the case.[223]

Percentage orders

6.122 Percentage orders (otherwise known as 'fractional orders') are orders by which the receiving party is entitled to only a proportion of the costs incurred. They are by no means a modern concept,[224] nor is the notion that they are to be preferred to issues

---

[218] *Summit Property Ltd v Pitmans* [2002] EWCA Civ 2020 at [27].

[219] *Foster v Farquhar* [1893] 1 QB 564.

[220] *Colburt v Beard* [1992] 2 Ad R 67.

[221] *Kastor Navigation Co Ltd v AXA Global Risks (UK) Ltd* [2004] EWCA Civ 277 at [153].

[222] See, also, *Douglas v Hello! Limited* [2004] EWHC 63 (Ch), in which it was held that an overly rigorous issues-based approach would not properly reflect the amount of time taken up by the fact that so many issues were unnecessarily taken.

[223] *Mears Ltd v Leeds City Council* [2011] EWHC 2694 (TCC) at [28].

[224] The earliest example the writer has been able to find is *Willmott v Barber* [1880] 15 Ch D 96 at 105 where Fry J made an issues-based percentage order.

awards.[225] CPR, r 44.3(7) states that, where practicable, the court must make either a percentage order (or an order from or until a certain date) in preference to an order for the cost of a distinct part of the proceedings.[226] This guidance would apply to most issues-based orders. The benefit of such an approach was explained by Chadwick LJ:[227]

'That [a percentage order] would obviate the need for a detailed assessment of the separate costs of each issue. That, as it seems to me, is not only a proper approach: it is the approach which is positively required by the Rules.'

6.123 The fact that percentage orders are to be preferred to orders for the cost of a distinct part of the proceedings does not mean that CPR, r 44.6(f) should be disregarded entirely; Brooke LJ, for example, has commented that the ability to make an order which deals with only a part of the proceedings enabled a court to do greater justice if the successful party had caused costs to be incurred on an issue subsequently abandoned.[228] Whilst obiter, Akenhead J has commented that an issues order under CPR, r 44.6(f) may be appropriate where it is not possible to determine who has won overall.[229]

6.124 When making a percentage order, the correct approach is to identify the relevant factors and to make an order which takes them into account and which meets the justice if the situation. It is not a mathematical exercise (see **6.121**). If the factors pull in different directions, the task is to see whether one set of factors pulls more strongly than the other, and then to take that into account by adjusting the percentage within the appropriate range.[230] Rix LJ recognised that this approach, unlike a rigorously mathematical approach, might lead to uncertainty, but he explained that justice was to be preferred over certainty:[231]

'[We] think it was an error of approach by the judge simply to visit the mathematical outcome of the issue by issue approach on the owners. This took no account of the other factors to which we have referred. The rules required him to have regard to all the circumstances of the case and it does not seem to us that he did so, at least not in the way the rules required. He should have stood back from the mathematical result and asked himself whether in all the circumstances, including the other factors to which we have referred, it was the right result.'

6.125 At about the same time, Pumfrey J gave similar guidance; in doing so he drew on his experience of patent claims (which have long been the subject of issues-based orders).[232] His guidance can be summarised as follows:

- the court should decide whether, notwithstanding its overall success, the successful party should be deprived of some part of its costs;
- if the successful party is to be deprived of some part of its costs, the court should determine the matters to which those parts relate;
- the court should decide whether, in relation to those matters, it should not also pay the costs of the unsuccessful party;

---

[225] See, for example, *Cinema Press Ltd v Pictures & Pleasures Ltd* [1945] 1 All ER 440 at 444.
[226] See also *Enterprise Managed Services Ltd v McFadden Utilities Ltd* [2010] EWHC 1506 (TCC) at [8], per Akenhead J.
[227] *National Westminster Bank plc v Kotonou* [2007] EWCA Civ 223.
[228] *Winter v Winter* [2000] All ER (D) 1791.
[229] See also *Enterprise Managed Services Ltd v McFadden Utilities Ltd* [2010] EWHC 1506 (TCC) at 8, per Akenhead J at [10], subpara (a).
[230] *Kastor Navigation Co Ltd v AXA Global Risks (UK) Ltd* [2004] EWCA Civ 277 at [156].
[231] *Kastor Navigation Co Ltd v AXA Global Risks (UK) Ltd* [2004] EWCA Civ 277 at [153].
[232] *Apotex Europe Ltd v SmithKline Beecham plc* [2004] EWHC 964 (Ch) at [9]–[13].

- the court must then convert the conclusion into an award of costs based upon a percentage;
- this should be done only if it is clearly understood that the process being undertaken is not that of detailed assessment; and
- all costs are notionally allocated to the issues; the successful party is assumed to recover all its reasonable costs of the action, and the percentage deduction is made from that overall sum.

Pumfrey J made no mention of Rix LJ's guidance about standing back and asking whether the result was the right result (see above); it is entirely possible that Pumfrey J was not aware of Rix LJ's guidance (this being because it had been given only a few weeks beforehand). There is no reason to believe that Pumfrey J intended that there should not be a stage of standing back to look at the result.

6.126 In a different case, Pumfrey J explained that it is often convenient to treat both parties' costs of an issue as being equal in amount and to double the deduction, with the result that if a party fails to recover costs of an issue amounting to, say, 15% of his total costs, he will be deducted 30% of his costs if the court concludes that he should also pay the costs of that issue to the other.[233] These comments were made in the context of a patents claim; it is possible that this rule of thumb would be less useful in other types of claims, where, perhaps, the court might not be confident that the parties' costs of the issue in question are likely to be similar in amount. Akenhead J had this to say in the context of a commercial claim:[234]

'(a) The first step is obviously to determine which of the parties has been successful in overall terms; if one can not determine that, it may be that one needs to consider the issues-based approach.

(b) One needs to consider the overall context of the litigation, including the reasons which led to its genesis; that involves considering the conduct of the parties which led to the need for the litigation in the first place.

(c) The reasonableness, or unreasonableness, of each party taking the various points or issues upon which it lost, should be considered by the Court. The more unreasonable the position of the losing party, the more likely that, even if the court orders only standard, as opposed to indemnity, based costs, it will attach weight to this factor.

(d) Whilst one needs to have regard to the issues upon which each party has succeeded, a simple mathematical approach on the basis of the number of issues "won" by each party will often not be an appropriate basis for fixing the percentage; thus, simply because the overall successful party has won 3 out of 5 issues, should not mean automatically that it should recover 60% of its costs. One needs to have regard to the likely amount of resources applied as well as to the impact overall of the success or failure on the various issues.

(e) Similarly, the Court should be cautious about fixing a proportion by reference to the amount of time or space applied by the judge in his or her judgement to the issues upon which each party has been successful or unsuccessful. The judge may simply have had to take up more time and space in the written judgement to address what may be more complex issues. The fact that 80% of the judgement addresses a legal issue upon which the overall successful party lost should not, at least generally, mean that it can only recover 20% of its costs.

---

[233] *Monsanto Technology LLC v Cargill International SA* [2007] EWHC 3113 (Pat).
[234] *Enterprise Managed Services Ltd v McFadden Utilities Ltd* [2010] EWHC 1506 (TCC) at 10.

(f) The Court needs also to have regard to the fact that the overall unsuccessful party will have incurred cost in dealing with the issues upon which it has "won".

(g) Where the parties have put before the court summary costs bills for assessment, the Court can have regard to the likely cost and resource which each party will have applied in relation to the issues upon which they have won or lost.

(h) Where the parties can not put such information before the Court, and in any event, the Court must do the best that it can in fixing a proportion.'

6.127 In summary, the court is encouraged to make orders which are based on issues, but if the court wishes to award the costs of an issue against an otherwise successful party (as opposed to merely depriving him of those costs), the case must be 'exceptional'. Orders should, where practicable, be either a percentage order or an order from or until a certain date, but, in any event, the court must stand back and look at the effect of the order before finally making it.

ISSUES ABANDONED OR BARELY PURSUED

6.128 The costs of issues which have been abandoned (or barely pursued) merit special attention. Two cases are relevant, the first of which, *Shirley v Caswell*,[235] has been clarified by the second, *Dooley v Parker*.[236] Before those cases are addressed, it is worth saying (at the risk of stating the obvious) that the fact that an issue has not been pursued will not always mean that adverse costs consequences will be visited upon the party who raised it; by way of example, Tugendhat J has commented that the court should be careful not to discourage parties from keeping all their arguments under review and from sensibly deciding not to argue a point.[237] Also at risk of stating the obvious, it should be noted that only those issues that were part of the claim should be taken into account; it would not be appropriate to take into account issues that were in dispute but that were not part of the claim.[238]

6.129 The net effect of *Shirley* and *Dooley* is that the court should be careful not to penalise a receiving party twice for the same decision; ie a costs judge should not normally disallow costs because an issue was not pursued if the costs of that issue have already been taken into account when the costs order was made. (This must be distinguished from circumstances in which costs have been unreasonably or improperly incurred in pursuing an issue – such as where the issue was dishonestly advanced – in which case the court may take that conduct into account both at the time of making the order and when assessing the costs.)[239] *Shirley* and *Dooley* are relevant not only to how the order should be framed, but also to how the assessment should be conducted.

6.130 Reference is often made to *Shirley* in everyday practice, and it is therefore worth setting out the salient facts. *Shirley* was a claim in professional negligence against a barrister. The claimants won after a lengthy trial. They abandoned (or barely pursued) some of the issues that were originally pleaded. The trial judge took the view that these

---

[235]   [2001] 1 Costs LR 1.
[236]   [2002] EWCA Civ 1118.
[237]   *D Pride & Partners v Institute for Animal Health* [2009] EWHC 1617 (QB).
[238]   See, for example, *Naseem t/a SH Builders and Contractors v Kang* [2011] EWCA Civ 737 at [40].
[239]   *Northstar Systems v Fielding* [2006] EWCA Civ 1660; and *Nugent v Goss Aviation* [2002] EWHC 1281 (QB) at [50].

issues should be reflected in the costs order, so he ordered the defendant to pay 60% of claimants' costs and the claimants to pay 40% of defendant's costs. The claimants appealed that decision.

6.131 Chadwick LJ (with whom Buxton and Aldous LJJ agreed) found that there was no basis for disturbing the order that the claimants pay 40% of the defendant's costs. This order was justified as being 'costs thrown away'. Chadwick LJ found that the trial judge's order in relation to the claimants' costs should not stand, however. He said (at p 18):

> 'The costs of issues abandoned, or not pursued at trial, ought, prima facie, to be disallowed against the party incurring them on an assessment of the costs of that party by the costs judge because, again prima facie, they are costs which have been unnecessarily incurred in the litigation. To take them into account in making a special costs order carries the risk that the claimants will be doubly penalised. They will be deprived of costs under the order, and again deprived of the same costs on an assessment or taxation.'

Chadwick LJ implied that the appropriate way of dealing with the costs of abandoned issues was to disallow those costs at the assessment on the basis that those costs were unreasonably incurred. Waller LJ came to a similar conclusion in relation to the costs of medical reports which were abandoned and which went unused.[240]

6.132 In *Dooley* Dyson LJ (with whom Rix LJ and Wall J agreed) clarified Chadwick LJ's comments. *Dooley* concerned a dispute over certain rights over land; the claimant raised a number of issues, two of which were abandoned. The court was troubled to hear that *Shirley* was being perceived as laying down a principle that where a party had been successful generally but had abandoned issues, the court was prevented from awarding that party only a proportion of its costs. Dyson LJ strongly disagreed with that interpretation of *Shirley*. After having set out the relevant part of Chadwick LJ's judgment, he made these comments:[241]

> 'I do not read this passage as laying down any broad statement of principle other than the obvious one that an order should not penalise a party twice over. It is plain ... that there is jurisdiction to order the paying party to pay only a proportion of the receiving party's costs. That will commonly be appropriate where the receiving party has failed on one or more issues in the case having succeeded on others. Of course, if an order is made disallowing part of a receiving party's costs, then the costs judge must take account of that fact when making the assessment of costs and take great care to make sure that a double penalty is not imposed. There should be no difficulty about this, since the costs judge should know from the terms of the judgment of the trial judge ordering payment of a proportion of a party's costs, that that is what the trial judge did and the reasons why he or she did it.'

6.133 Some commentators have said that *Dooley* has confined *Shirley* to its own facts. It is suggested that a better analysis is that the question of whether abandoned issues are reflected in the order for costs will depend on the facts of each case and that the court is free to do what most effectively meets the justice of the situation. Where, as in *Shirley*, the task of disentangling and quantifying the costs of abandoned issues is likely to be a one which, if left to the costs judge, would result in the requisite reductions being made on the grounds of reasonableness, then it may well be appropriate for the trial judge to award the successful party costs without deduction. Where, on the other hand, it is not clear whether the costs would be disallowed on the assessment, or where there was a risk

---

[240] *Hall & Ors v Stone* [2007] EWCA Civ 1354 at [79].
[241] *Dooley v Parker* [2002] EWCA Civ 1118 at [32].

that significant costs would be incurred arguing that topic, then it may be appropriate (should the circumstances permit) for the order itself to reflect the costs of the issues abandoned. These are only examples: each case will turn on its own facts.

6.134 In the context of group litigation, David Steel J has commented that where the costs of abandoned issues are to be taken into account, a broad-brush approach would be appropriate.[242]

6.135 Whilst the court should be cautious not inadvertently to penalise a party twice over, it should not be forgotten that the costs judge's ordinary function is to disallow costs which have been unreasonably incurred. This was explained by Burton J:[243]

> 'On an assessment the costs judge, who will prima facie disallow costs in respect of issues abandoned or not pursued, as the Court of Appeal has directed to do in *Shirley v Caswell*, will in any event disallow the costs of any claims which were positively struck out.'

When Burton J's judgment is read in the light of *Dooley*, it is clear that the costs judge's precise role is not a matter of immutable principle, but will turn on the correct interpretation of the costs order. A corollary to this is that the costs judge's ordinary function ought to be borne in mind when the order is made.

6.136 In particular, it should be borne in mind that a costs judge will ordinarily disallow costs unreasonably incurred, and that this may be in addition to the costs affirmatively struck out in the costs order. This may be the intended effect of the order: whilst not relating specifically to the costs of abandoned issues, Waller LJ has made it clear that there is no reason in principle why the costs of an issue should not be taken into account both at the time the order was made and at the time of the assessment (in order to understand the following, it should be noted that Waller LJ was dealing with a successful party who had been dishonest):[244]

> 'Clearly there is no problem if the judge's order makes "no order as to costs", but if the judge orders a reduction by say 20% without more, what would be the natural construction of that order? My view is that the natural construction of such an order, unless the contrary is expressly stated, is that the party guilty of dishonesty should not be entitled to say on assessment, "my costs incurred in seeking to make a dishonest case can be taken as reasonably incurred because the judge has made a reduction". If the dishonest party was entitled to succeed on such an argument, he will hardly suffer any penalty at all.'

6.137 Finally, it will not always be obvious whether a party can be said to have abandoned an issue. In a case in which the defendant had made an offer putatively in respect of only one aspect of the claimant's injuries (this being on the basis that the other injuries had allegedly been caused by someone else), Stadlen J found that the offer was capable of being accepted in respect of the whole claim and that the Claimant was entitled to her costs accordingly.[245]

---

[242] *Colour Quest Ltd v Total Downstream UK plc* [2009] EWHC 823 (Comm).
[243] *Nugent v Goss Aviation* [2002] EWHC 1281 (QB) at [50].
[244] *Northstar Systems v Fielding* [2006] EWCA Civ 1660 at [33].
[245] *Sutherland v Turnbull* [2010] EWHC 2699 (QB) at [29]–[32].

EXAGGERATION

6.138 This section deals with exaggeration and the incidence of costs. The issue of how exaggeration is to be reflected in the assessment of costs is dealt with at **34.82–34.97**.

6.139 Where a person has advanced an exaggerated claim, the court is able to take that fact into account when making an award of costs. CPR, r 44.3(5)(d) makes specific mention of the court's ability to do this; indeed, the rule can be read as requiring the court to take that factor into account. The court is not limited to exercising its ordinary discretion as to costs; instead, in more egregious cases the court is able to invoke its powers in relation to misconduct[246] and, in extreme cases, the court is able to contemplate committal for contempt of court.[247] That is a topic which is beyond the scope of this book.

6.140 The word 'exaggeration' can be interpreted to mean two different things. No one would dispute that a claim which has been improperly or dishonestly inflated should be said to be exaggerated, but it could also be argued that an honest and proper claim which ultimately was allowed at a sum very much lower than it was originally put is also exaggerated. These two interpretations are referred to as 'culpable exaggeration' and 'innocent exaggeration' respectively. Jackson LJ has confirmed that different considerations may arise depending on whether the exaggeration has or has not been culpable.[248] The phrases 'intentional exaggeration' and 'unintentional exaggeration' are often used; Walker J has used the word, 'concoction' to describe the culpable exaggeration.[249]

Culpable exaggeration

6.141 Culpable exaggeration may be taken into account either at the time that the costs order is made or at the time that costs are assessed[250] or, if consistent with the terms of the order, both. Walker J has made it clear that the mere fact that a claim has settled for a figure that was considerably less than that which was claimed will not be sufficient to justify a finding of culpable exaggeration, even where it was known that the claimant had lied.[251]

6.142 In an early example of exaggeration being reflected in a costs order under the CPR (*Molloy v Shell (UK) Ltd*),[252] Laws LJ ordered a 'successful' claimant to pay the costs of a defendant notwithstanding that he recovered more than the defendant's Part 36 offer (£18,897 as against the defendant's Part 36 offer of £15,000). This was in the context of the claimant having sought more than £300,000. The trial judge had allowed 75% of the defendant's post-offer costs, but Laws LJ (with whom Mummery LJ agreed) increased that to 100% on appeal; he had the following to say on the topic:[253]

---

[246] See CPR, r 44.14 and Ward LJ's comments in *Widlake v BAA Ltd* [2009] EWCA Civ 1256 at [41]. It is not a jurisdiction which is commonly invoked outwith a detailed assessment, not least because there is no need: a trial judge would not need to rely on that jurisdiction to make an order against an exaggerator.

[247] See, for example, *Kirk v Walton* [2009] EWHC 703 (QB).

[248] *Fox v Foundation Piling Limited* [2011] EWCA Civ 790 at [48]–[63]. See also *Painting v University of Oxford* [2005] EWCA Civ 161 at [26], per Longmore LJ and *Vector v JD Williams* [2009] EWHC 3601 (TCC) at [75], per Ramsey J.

[249] *Morton v Portal Ltd* [2010] EWHC 1804 (QB) at [41], per Walker J.

[250] See, for example, *Booth v Britannia Hotels Ltd* [2002] EWCA Civ 579.

[251] *Morton v Portal Ltd* [2010] EWHC 1804 (QB) at [48]–[54], per Walker J.

[252] [2001] EWCA Civ 1272.

[253] [2001] EWCA Civ 1272 at [18].

'[The judge] fell into error ... The respondent's approach to this action has been nothing [short] of a cynical and dishonest abuse of the court's process. For my part I entertain considerable qualms as to whether, faced with manipulation of the civil justice system on so grand a scale, the court should once it knows the facts entertain the case at all save to make the dishonest claimant pay the defendant's costs. However, all that is sought here is an order for 100 per cent of the appellant's costs instead of 75 per cent, the costs in question being only those incurred after the date of the Part 36 payment. The appeal certainly cannot be resisted on that basis. I would allow it and make the order sought.'

Ward LJ (with whom Smith and Wilson LJJ agreed) has commented that *Molloy* should be treated with considerable caution.[254] He said that in so far as damages are concerned there is no rule of law that a genuine claim which has been exaggerated will be dismissed,[255] and it would be wrong to believe that such a rule existed for costs. Instead, the court should exercise its discretion, which is a process of determining who has won and of regarding the exaggeration as being one aspect of the parties' conduct. It may be appropriate to disallow the exaggerator's costs in pursuing the exaggerated aspects of the claim and to make an allowance for the corresponding costs incurred by his opponent.[256] Ward LJ determined that in the case before him (which related to only modest sums), the correct order was that there be no order for costs.

6.143 The court has a wide ambit of discretion. Recent examples exist of the court condemning exaggerators in costs rather than simply depriving them of their costs. In a personal injury claim (*Painting v University of Oxford*)[257] in which the claimant had been awarded £25,331 out of about £400,000 sought, Maurice Kay LJ (with whom Longmore LJ agreed) ordered costs against the claimant, thereby allowing the appeal. Maurice Kay LJ commented that the following factors were significant in that case:[258]

- when viewed objectively, the judgment was overwhelmingly favourable to the defendant, who was, in real terms, the winner;
- had there been no exaggeration, the claim would probably have been compromised at an early stage and with modest costs; and
- the claimant failed to demonstrate any willingness to negotiate or to put forward a proposal to accept a reasonable sum.

Facts such as these will not present themselves every day: a differently constituted Court of Appeal described *Painting* as 'extreme with a vastly exaggerated case supported by untruthful evidence.[259] Thus, whilst there is no suggestion that *Painting* has been confined to its own facts, it is clear that it should not be seen as setting a precedent.

6.144 At the other end of the spectrum, in a case in which about £1m was claimed but only £155,000 recovered (*Jackson v The Ministry of Defence*),[260] Tuckey LJ (with whom

---

[254] See *Widlake v BAA Ltd* [2009] EWCA Civ 1256 at [34].
[255] See *Ul-Haq v Shah* [2009] EWCA Civ 542.
[256] *Widlake v BAA Ltd* [2009] EWCA Civ 1256 at [34] onwards. As another example of this (this time in the context of a credit hire case in which the exaggerated claim was 6 times the amount recovered and the claimant's conduct was 'reprehensible', see *Abbott v Long* [2011] EWCA Civ 874.
[257] [2005] EWCA Civ 161.
[258] *Straker v Tudor Rose (a firm)* [2007] EWCA Civ 368.
[259] *Straker v Tudor Rose (a firm)* [2007] EWCA Civ 368.
[260] [2006] EWCA Civ 46.

Keene and Wilson LJJ agreed) refused to disturb the trial judge's award of 75% of the claimant's costs. This was in circumstances in which the defendant had made a Part 36 offer of £150,000. Tuckey LJ said:[261]

> 'The claimant was successful in the sense that he established a claim for substantial damages and beat the payment into court, albeit by a small margin. The defendant was perfectly able to protect itself against the fact that it faced an exaggerated claim.'

6.145 At first blush, it seems difficult to reconcile the fact that in *Jackson* the appeal was not allowed, but in *Painting* it was. Tuckey LJ explained that the difference between *Painting* and the case before him was that the trial judge in *Painting* had not addressed the question as to who was the overall winner, nor had he given appropriate weight to that fact, whereas the trial judge in the case before him had taken all relevant factors into account.

6.146 Mann J has made it clear that particular care needs to be taken to avoid applying hindsight.[262] Whilst exaggeration is a topic which is often articulated in terms of conduct generally, it is also a topic which, in appropriate cases, will lend itself to being dealt with as a discrete issue. This is because it is usually an issue which is well defined and easily identifiable (examples being the costs of obtaining evidence as to quantum or the costs of preparing the Schedule of Financial Losses). In some cases it will be seen as being the only issue; this is because where exaggeration exists it has a tendency to become the dominant issue. This is illustrated by the following extract from *Painting* (per Maurice Kay LJ):[263]

> 'To the question: who was the real winner in this litigation? there is, in my judgment, only one answer. The two-day hearing was concerned overwhelmingly with the issue of exaggeration, and the [defendant] won on that issue. [The claimant's] submission that that was only one issue, the other issue being the quantification of the claim, is not persuasive. Quite simply, that second issue was hardly an issue at all once the Recorder had found the exaggeration ...'

6.147 Another example of exaggeration being dealt with as a discrete issue was a case in which a party's unreasonable pursuance of an untenable counterclaim led to the claim being wrongly allocated to the multi-track when it ought to have been in the small claims track; that was a factor which Goldring LJ said ought to be given weight.[264]

6.148 As mentioned above, the effect of offers (or absence thereof) can be significant in cases involving exaggeration. In particular, if an exaggerator has made no offers to accept a reasonable sum, that might be a factor that would count against that party even if his opponent has failed to beat its own offers.[265] In this regard, Maurice Kay LJ said the following:[266]

---

[261] [2006] EWCA Civ 46 at [15].
[262] *Business Environment Bow Lane v Deanswater Estates Ltd* [2009] EWHC 2014.
[263] *Painting v University of Oxford* [2005] EWCA Civ 161 at [21].
[264] *Peakman v Linbrooke Services Ltd* [2008] EWCA Civ 1239 at [29]–[32]; whilst not binding, see also *Singh v Aqua Descaling Ltd* (unreported) 12 June 2008, Walsall County Court, in which HHJ Oliver-Jones QC found that the costs of a claim allocated to the multi-track ought to be restricted to the small claims track because that would have been the correct track had there been no exaggeration.
[265] See, for example, *Abbott v Long* [2011] EWCA Civ 874 at [8] *et seq*, per Arden LJ.
[266] *Painting v University of Oxford* [2005] EWCA Civ 161 at [22].

'At no stage did [the exaggerator] manifest any willingness to negotiate or to put forward a counter-proposal to the Part 36 payment. No-one can compel a claimant to take such steps. However to contest and lose an issue of exaggeration without having made ever a counter-proposal is a matter of some significance in this kind of litigation. It must not be assumed that beating a Part 36 payment is conclusive. It is a factor and will often be conclusive, but one has to have regard to all the circumstances of the case.'

Longmore LJ added his own comments:[267]

'[The claimant] herself made no attempt to negotiate, made no offer of her own and made no response to the offers of the University. That would not have mattered in pre-CPR days but, to my mind, that now matters very much.'

6.149 If an exaggerator accepts evidence of exaggeration and alters his position accordingly, then that can be a factor capable of negating the effect of the original exaggeration.[268] On the other hand, if his opponent fails to make an adequate offer to protect himself, then that too may be taken into account.[269] Indeed, the response of an exaggerator's opponent may be highly relevant. In a case in which an opponent of an exaggerator had not moved from its position of denying liability and had not engaged in making or considering Part 36 offers, Ramsey J found that the general rule that costs follow the event was not displaced.[270]

6.150 Walker J has explained that where exaggeration is alleged but not admitted, and where the court has not heard evidence, then considerable caution must be exercised before reaching, on a broad brush examination of documents alone, any conclusion adverse to the alleged exaggerator. Indeed, Walker J had this to say:[271]

'Lies are told in litigation every day up and down the country and quite rightly do not lead to a penalty being imposed in respect of them. There is a considerable difference between a concocted claim and an exaggerated claim and judges must be astute to measure how reprehensible the conduct is.'

Innocent exaggeration

6.151 Whilst Waller LJ did not agree, Smith LJ had the following to say on the topic of innocent exaggeration:[272]

'It seems to me that [CPR, r 44.3(4)] is designed to allow the judge to take into account on costs the fact that the losing party actually won on one (or more than one) issue in the case. I do not think it means that the judge can cut down the costs of the successful party merely because he has not done quite as well as he had hoped. But if the claimant's exaggeration was no more than to put his case rather high, it does not seem to me that a defendant who has not made an effective and admissible offer can be regarded as the victor.'

---

[267] *Painting v University of Oxford* [2005] EWCA Civ 161 at [27].
[268] *Morgan v UPS* [2008] EWCA Civ 1476.
[269] See, for example, *Widlake v BAA Ltd* [2009] EWCA Civ 1256 at [39]. See also *Fox v Foundation Piling Limited* [2011] EWCA Civ 790 at [48].
[270] *Biffa Waste Services Ltd v Maschinenfabrik Ernst Hese GmBH* [2008] EWHC 2657 (TCC); see also *Widlake v BAA Ltd* [2009] EWCA Civ 1256 at [39].
[271] *Morton v Portal Ltd* [2010] EWHC 1804 (QB) at [41], per Walker J.
[272] *Hall v Stone* [2007] EWCA Civ 1354 at [72]–[73].

So, the mere fact that a party has recovered less than he claimed is not a reason for disapplying the general rule. As to what may be sufficient to disapply the general rule, Smith LJ said (obiter):

> 'I would accept that exaggeration by a claimant may be taken into account as "conduct" under CPR 44.3(4)(a). However, for a defendant to regard himself as a winner or even partial winner on an issue of exaggeration, the exaggeration must be an important feature of the claim with costs consequences.'

Thus, if the exaggeration is innocent, an offer would usually have to be made to put the exaggerator at risk on costs. Lloyd LJ agreed with Smith LJ's analysis. Jackson (with whom Moore-Bick and Ward LJJ agreed) came to a very similar conclusion in a subsequent case.[273] That said, it would seem that there are limits to that analysis in that if the difference between the parties is so great as to render the chances of the defendant's offer being accepted close to nil, then the act of making an offer may be thought of as being 'a mere matter of ritual'. In those circumstances, the exaggerator may be found to be the loser even though he has not received any offers (see **6.41** for details). It has to be stressed, however, that there is significant divergence of judicial opinion on that point (see **6.41**), and that as such it would be a risky strategy to elect to rely on that argument in preference to making an offer.

6.152 There are case examples of innocent exaggeration displacing the general rule. *Hooper v Biddle & Co*, for example, was a commercial case in which a successful claimant was deprived of costs by reason of having recovered less than was claimed; he had claimed £3.75m but had recovered only £38,000.[274]

6.153 Where exaggeration is a factor which will be reflected in the costs order, this would be so regardless of which individual (ie lawyer, expert or client) was to blame. Ward LJ has said that a claim may still be categorised as being an exaggerated claim even though the fault lay with the professionals advising the claimant rather than the claimant himself.[275]

6.154 In summary, it seems that innocent exaggeration will, of itself, rarely result in the general rule being disapplied, but it may be a factor to be taken into account, and in appropriate circumstances may result in the exaggerator being deprived of his costs.

OTHER ISSUES RELEVANT TO THE INCIDENCE OF COSTS

6.155 The following miscellaneous issues are here considered in turn:

- refusal to mediate;
- failure to respond to an offer;
- incurring disproportionate costs;
- deplorable behaviour;
- commencing proceedings in the wrong venue;
- changes to statement of case;
- proving probate claims; and

---

[273] *Fox v Foundation Piling Limited* [2011] EWCA Civ 790 at [63].
[274] [2006] EWHC 2995 (Ch), per Susan Prevezer QC.
[275] *Carver v BAA plc* [2008] EWCA Civ 412 at [35].

- irrelevant factors.

Refusal to mediate

6.156 It is necessary to set out the development of the law in some detail, but the present state of the law has been pithily summed up by Akenhead J as: 'the real question is did [the losing party] act unreasonably in refusing ADR?'[276]

6.157 An historically early indication that a refusal to mediate could have adverse costs consequences was given by the Court of Appeal in *Dunnett v Railtrack plc*.[277] Whilst the case gave no detailed guidance about the principles to be applied, Brooke LJ made the following comments:[278]

> 'It is to be hoped that any publicity given to this part of the judgment of the court will draw the attention of lawyers to their duties to further the overriding objective in the way that is set out in Part 1 of the Rules and to the possibility that, if they turn down out of hand the chance of alternative dispute resolution when suggested by the court, as happened on this occasion, they may have to face uncomfortable costs consequence.'

Brooke LJ was correct to anticipate that his comments would attract publicity: for a period of time following *Dunnett* there was widespread anxiety that a refusal to mediate would result in 'uncomfortable' costs consequences. Indeed, some commentators even went so far as to say that a refusal to mediate would give rise to a presumption that there would be adverse costs consequences.[279]

6.158 It soon became apparent, however, that a reasonable and justifiable refusal to mediate would not result in adverse costs consequences. In a professional negligence claim against a barrister, Lightman J found that it had been appropriate for the defendant to have taken the view that the mediation was not likely to succeed; having made that finding, Lightman J rejected the claimant's submissions that the defendant should be deprived of his costs by reason of his refusal to mediate.[280] (It is worth noting, however, that the claimant accepted that his case was hopeless; indeed, one of his arguments was that his case was so bad that the mediation would have brought a swift end to the claim.)

6.159 Lightman J commented that his findings that the defendant had acted reasonably in refusing mediation were 'quite exceptional'. He had this to say on the topic:[281]

> 'If mediation can have no real prospect of success a party may, with impunity, refuse to proceed to mediation on this ground. But refusal is a high risk course to take, for if the court finds that there was a real prospect, the party refusing to proceed to mediation may, as I have said, be severely penalised. Further, the hurdle in the way of a party refusing to proceed to mediation on this ground is high, for in making this objective assessment of the prospects of mediation, the starting point must surely be the fact that the mediation process itself can and does often bring about a more sensible and more conciliatory attitude ...'

---

[276] *Corby Group Litigation* [2009] EWHC 2109 (TCC) at [23].
[277] [2002] EWCA Civ 303.
[278] *Dunnett v Railtrack plc* [2002] EWCA Civ 303 at [18].
[279] See, for example, 'The CPR Regime five years on' (2004) 154 NLJ 7126, pp 644–645.
[280] *Hurst v Leeming* [2002] EWHC 1051 (Ch).
[281] *Hurst v Leeming* [2002] EWHC 1051 (Ch) at [15].

6.160 Notwithstanding these comments, further cases were decided on the basis that a refusal to mediate was reasonable. Indeed, it was soon realised that an 'offer' to mediate could be little more than a tactical step, as Park J commented:[282]

'In my judgment it would be a grave injustice to [the party who seeks costs] to deprive them of any part of their costs on the ground that they declined [the other party's] self-serving invitations (demands would be a more accurate word) to participate in the mediation.'

6.161 In 2004, the Court of Appeal gave general guidance on the topic in *Halsey v Milton Keynes General NHS Trust*.[283] Those principles have been summarised by Jack J in this way:[284]

'(a) A party cannot be ordered to submit to mediation as that would be contrary to Article 6 of the European Convention on Human Rights [*Halsey* at paragraph 9].

(b) The burden is on the unsuccessful party to show why the general rule of costs following the event should not apply, and it must be shown that the successful party acted unreasonably in refusing to agree to mediation [paragraph 13].

(c) A party's reasonable belief that he has a strong case is relevant to the reasonableness of his refusal, for otherwise the fear of cost sanctions may be used to extract unmerited settlements [paragraph 18].

(d) Where a case is evenly balanced ... a party's belief that he would win should be given little or no weight in considering whether a refusal was reasonable ... his belief must be unreasonable [paragraph 19].

(e) The cost of mediation is a relevant factor ... [paragraph 21].

(f) Whether the mediation had a reasonable prospect of success is relevant to the reasonableness of a refusal to agree to mediation ... [paragraph 25].

(g) In considering whether the refusal to agree to mediation was unreasonable it is for the unsuccessful party to show that there was a reasonable prospect that the mediation would have been successful [paragraph 28].

(h) Where a party refuses to take part in mediation despite encouragement from the court to do so, that is a factor to be taken into account ... [paragraph 29].

(i) Public bodies are not in a special position [paragraph 34].'

6.162 In a different case, Ward LJ (with whom Rix LJ agreed) said:[285]

'The court has given its stamp of approval to mediation and it is now the legal profession which must become fully aware of and acknowledge its value. The profession can no longer with impunity shrug aside reasonable requests to mediate ... [litigants] can expect little sympathy if they blithely battle on regardless of the alternatives.'

---

[282] *Société Internationale de Télécommunications Aéronautiques SC v Wyatt Co (UK) Ltd* [2002] EWHC 2401 (Ch).

[283] [2004] EWCA Civ 576.

[284] *Hickman v Blake Lapthorn* [2006] EWHC 12 (QB), [2006] All ER (D) 67 at [21].

[285] *Burchell v Bullard* [2005] EWCA Civ 358 at [43].

6.163 A factor that may, at first blush, seem to be highly relevant is the amount of costs that mediation would have avoided. Jack J has found that whilst this is a factor to be taken into account, it should not be afforded such significance that a defendant is put in the position of being required to settle a claim for more than it is worth solely for the purposes of avoiding an adverse costs order.[286]

6.164 The following specific circumstances and case examples merit further mention (although they are, on the whole, only comments or case examples and ought not to be regarded as setting a precedent).

Attempts at other methods of ADR

6.165 In *Valentine v Allen* Peter Gibson LJ (with whom Chadwick LJ and Hale LJ agreed) noted that whilst the successful party had refused mediation, it had engaged in other forms of dispute resolution. In particular, generous offers had been made. *Dunnett* was, therefore, distinguished.[287]

Awaiting clarification of case and caution generally

6.166 A party may escape being penalised for refusing to mediate until after the issue of proceedings if that refusal was on the basis that it was necessary to know the full details of the parties' cases before seeking to settle the matter.[288] Whilst in the context other than the exercise of discretion under CPR, r 44.3,[289] Floyd J has commented that a party may escape criticism if the putative refusal was in reality a reasonable request to await exchange of expert evidence; this would be especially true if that party reasonably believed that given time the other side's case would collapse.[290] In a case in which a compromise had nearly been reached but there were some procedural issues that remained, Arden LJ has explained the court may fall into error if it seeks to impose its own view as to what would have been required to bring the matter to a close.[291]

Unrealistic demands

6.167 Whilst relating to informal negotiations rather than a formal mediation, in *RBG Resources plc (in liquidation)* Lightman J imposed a percentage reduction on a successful defendant to take account of the fact that he refused to enter into productive negotiations and instead insisted on a term of settlement that he knew, or ought to have known, was unrealistic.[292] Likewise, if a person fails to settle a case because he unreasonably holds out for his costs, that is a factor which may be reflected in an adverse costs award.[293] At the risk of stating the obvious, if a part refuses mediation because he wants his day in court, that might sound in costs.[294]

---

[286] *Hickman v Blake Lapthorn* [2006] EWHC 12 (QB), [2006] All ER (D) 67 at [21].

[287] *Valentine v Allen* [2003] EWCA Civ 1274.

[288] See, for example, *Wethered Estate Ltd v Davis* [2005] EWHC 1903 (Ch), Clive Freedman QC.

[289] The context was whether to depart from the default position that a person who has discontinued should pay costs: see **7.82** *et seq*.

[290] *Mobiqa Limited v Trinity Mobile Limited* [2010] EWHC 253 (Pat) at [27] and [28].

[291] *Carlisle & Cumbria United Independent Supports' Society Limited v CUFC Holding Limited at* [2010] EWCA Civ 463 at [13].

[292] [2005] EWHC 994 (Ch).

[293] *Strachey v Ramage* [2008] EWCA Civ 804.

[294] As an example of this in practice, see *Rolf v de Guerin* [2011] EWCA Civ 78; the refusal to mediate was just one factor amongst many in that case.

Lip service

6.168 A party who agreed to mediation but then took an unreasonable position in the mediation was in the same position as a party who unreasonably refused to mediate.[295] However, it will usually be the case that events of the mediation are entirely without prejudice, in which case the evidence of what happened during the mediation would be inadmissible.

Dispute between neighbours

6.169 In a dispute between neighbours about a garage roof, Thomas LJ commented (obiter) that if the order in the court below had not reflected a refusal to mediate, that would have been an error.[296] Whilst he did not expressly refer to the fact, it is likely that Thomas LJ took that view because disputes between neighbours are of a type in which mediation can be particularly effective.

Refusal by a claimant

6.170 Whilst there is no authority on the point, a claimant who refused to mediate would find it more difficult to justify his position than a defendant. This is because a defendant who offers mediation is presumably willing to negotiate, and a willingness to negotiate implies a willingness to settle. Thus, a claimant who refuses mediation would be giving up a chance to achieve the very thing that he had chosen to seek.

Pre-action protocols and court sanctioned schemes

6.171 Paragraph 4.4(3) of Practice Direction – Pre-action Conduct expressly provides that the court may take unreasonable refusal to mediate into account when deciding whether there has been compliance with a pre-action protocol. Where a refusal is in respect of a court sanctioned scheme and where that refusal is unreasonable, it would be open to the court to condemn the refusing party in costs on the indemnity basis.[297]

Government departments

6.172 In 2001, the Lord Chancellor's Department made a formal pledge committing government departments to ADR whenever the other side agreed to it. In a case in which a government department refused to mediate, Lewison J commented:[298]

> 'As I have said, however, the most important feature to my mind is the formal pledge given on behalf of the government and its various departments to use ADR in appropriate cases. The government did not abide by that pledge in this case. I am not in a position to form any real view of whether a mediation would or would not have succeeded. It may well have done, but in my judgment a failure to abide by the formal pledge given on part of the government, coupled with the fact that the defendant did not succeed on all the issues ... justifies a decision that the defendant should not recover any further costs from the claimant.'

---

[295] *Carleton, v Strutt & Parker (a partnership)* [2008] EWHC 424 (QB).
[296] *Seeff v Ho* [2011] EWCA Civ 186 at [49] and [50].
[297] *Virani v Manuel Revert y Cia Sa* [2003] EWCA Civ 1651.
[298] *Royal Bank of Canada v Secretary of State for Defence* [2003] EWHC 1841 (Ch) at [12].

Professional negligence

6.173 Lightman J has found that the fact that a claim was a professional negligence claim would not, of itself, make it inappropriate for mediation.[299]

Opponent's case waning

6.174 In a case where the claimant's negotiating position had progressed steadily downwards as the case had progressed, Floyd J found (albeit in a context other than the exercise of discretion under CPR, r 44.3)[300] that it was reasonable for the defendant to decline to mediate, this being on the basis (amongst others: see **6.166**) that given time, the claimant's case would collapse.[301]

Failure to respond to an offer

6.175 Failing to respond to an offer is conduct which can be taken into account for the purposes of determining the incidence of costs: an oft-cited example is *Painting v University of Oxford*[302] (see **6.143**), in which the failure to respond was one factor amongst others. It would be wrong to ascribe to *Painting* the status of a case laying down a point of principle. Indeed, the Court of Appeal has commented on *Painting* that the facts were 'extreme with a vastly exaggerated case supported by untruthful evidence from the claimant'.[303] Thus, it would not follow that the fact that a party has failed to respond to an offer would necessarily result in costs consequences for that party: each case must be decided on its own facts.

6.176 Unless CPR, r 36.14(1)(b) applies, a failure to respond to an offer would rarely merit an award of costs on the indemnity basis,[304] but again the failure may be a factor to be taken into account. Kay LJ made the following remarks which have resonance in this specific context notwithstanding the fact that they were made in a more general context:[305]

> 'The approach of the CPR is a relatively simple one: namely, if one party has made a real effort to find a reasonable solution to the proceedings and the other party has resisted that sensible approach, then the latter puts himself at risk that the order for costs may be on an indemnity basis.'

6.177 In *Hall v Stone*,[306] Smith LJ noted (at [82]):

> '... In these days where both sides are expected to conduct themselves in a reasonable way and to seek agreement where possible, it may be right to penalise a party to some degree for failing to accept a reasonable offer or for failing to come back with a counter offer.'

---

[299] *Hurst v Leeming* [2002] EWHC 1051 (Ch).
[300] The context was whether to depart from the default position that a person who has discontinued should pay costs: see **7.82** *et seq*
[301] *Mobiqa Limited v Trinity Mobile Limited* [2010] EWHC 253 (Pat) at [27] and [28].
[302] [2005] EWCA Civ 161.
[303] *Straker v Tudor Rose (a firm)* [2007] EWCA Civ 368.
[304] *Kiam v MGN Ltd (No 2)* [2002] EWCA Civ 66.
[305] *Reid Minty (a firm) v Taylor* [2001] EWCA Civ 1723 at [37], per Kay LJ.
[306] [2007] EWCA Civ 1354.

6.178 Jackson J has made the following comments about the situation where an offer has been made which was nearly but not quite sufficient, and where the offeree had rejected the offer without any attempt at negotiation:[307]

'If (a) one party makes an order offer under Pt 36 or an admissible offer within r 44.3(4)(c) which is nearly but not quite sufficient, and (b) the other party rejects that offer outright without any attempt to negotiate, then it might be appropriate to penalise the second party in costs.'

These comments were based on *Carver v BA plc*[308] and to that extent must be treated with some caution (this being because the ambit of that decision has been significantly curtailed by CPR, r 36.14(1A): see **14.34–14.43**), but the general principle (namely, of taking conduct into account, including whether there was a high-handed reaction to a reasonable offer) almost certainly remains good law.

6.179 In summary, whilst failing to respond to an offer will be a factor to be taken into account, it would not normally be a sufficiently prominent factor to oust the general rule, but instead would usually be a factor that may be reflected in the costs order 'to some degree'.

Incurring disproportionate costs and small claims

6.180 Where a judge believes that costs are disproportionate but nonetheless wishes to award that party only his proportionate costs, it would be wrong in principle to make an order that costs be assessed subject to a cap; this is because such an order might deprive that party of costs proportionately incurred.[309]

Deplorable behaviour

6.181 Whilst each case will be decided on its own facts, Longmore LJ declined to find that a successful litigant should be deprived of her costs solely by reason of the fact that she had engaged in correspondence which was deplorable in its tone and worthy of condemnation.[310] In sufficiently egregious cases, the fabrication of documents may, however, merit a disallowance of costs.[311] Whilst rarely invoked in practice, there is also the possibility of sanctions relating to misconduct under CPR, r 44.14.

Commencing proceedings in the wrong venue

6.182 Section 51 of the Senior Courts Act 1981 provides:

'(8)   Where—

(a)   a person has commenced proceedings in the High Court; but

(b)   those proceedings should, in the opinion of the court, have been commenced in a county court in accordance with any provision made under section 1 of the Courts and Legal Services Act 1990 or by or under any other enactment,

---

[307] *Multiplex Constructions (UK) Ltd v Cleveland Bridge UK Ltd* [2008] EWHC 2280 (TCC) at [72].

[308] *Multiplex Constructions (UK) Ltd v Cleveland Bridge UK Ltd* [2008] EWHC 2280 (TCC) at [71].

[309] *SCT Finance v Bolton* [2002] EWCA Civ 56 at [36].

[310] *Lawal v Northern Spirit* (unreported and without neutral citation) 19 February 2004, CA (Civ Div), Longmore, Laws and Peter Gibson LJJ.

[311] *Gil v Baygreen Properties Ltd (in liquidation)* [2004] EWHC 2029 (Ch), in which a fixed sum was disallowed from the successful party's costs.

the person responsible for determining the amount which is to be awarded to that person by way of costs shall have regard to those circumstances.

(9)   Where, in complying with subsection (8), the responsible person reduces the amount which would otherwise be awarded to the person in question—

  (a)   the amount of that reduction shall not exceed 25 per cent; and

  (b)   on any taxation of the costs payable by that person to his legal representative, regard shall be had to the amount of the reduction.'

So, if a person commences proceedings in the High Court which ought to have been commenced in the county court, that person's costs may be reduced, but that reduction will be limited to 25%.

Changes to statement of case

6.183 A failure properly to state the case is capable of leading to a successful party being deprived of costs. Where a late amendment is made and where that substantially changes the nature of the case, it would be usual for the party who made the amendment to bear the costs thrown away. It would normally be open to the court to make a percentage order.[312] It may be inappropriate to make an order at the time that permission is given for the amendment; the better solution may be to reserve costs and to allow the outcome of trial deal with the just allocation of costs.[313] If a party unreasonably opposes an amendment, he may be penalised in costs.[314]

Proving probate claims

6.184 There is a common law principle that where a defendant has given notice by which he requests a will to be proved in solemn form, costs would not follow the event if the circumstances had reasonably led to the defendant's request.[315] Scrutton LJ, however, added this salutary warning:[316]

> 'I should be reluctant to do anything to create the idea that unsuccessful litigants might get their costs out of the estate, without making a very strong case on [their] facts. The lure of 'costs out of the estate' is responsible for much unnecessary litigation.'

Henderson J had this to say about the modern application of the principles referred to above:[317]

> '... it is I think fair to say that the trend of the more recent authorities has been to encourage a very careful scrutiny of any case in which the first exception is said to apply, and to narrow rather than extend the circumstances in which it will be held to be engaged. There are at least two factors which have in my judgment contributed to this change of emphasis. First, less importance is attached today than it was in Victorian times to the independent duty of the court to investigate the circumstances in which a will was executed and to satisfy itself as to its validity. Secondly, the courts are increasingly alert to the dangers of encouraging

---

[312]   *Professional Information Technology Consultants Ltd v Jones* [2001] EWCA Civ 2103.

[313]   *Chadwick v Hollingsworth (No 2)* [2010] EWHC 2718 (QB) at [30], per Rix LJ (sitting in the QBD).

[314]   *La Chemise Lacoste SA v Sketchers USA Ltd* [2006] EWHC 3642 (Ch).

[315]   *Spiers v English* [1907] P 122 at p 126, per Sir Gorrell Barnes, this case articulating the principle first articulated by Sir JP Wilde in at *Mitchell & Mitchell v Gard & Kingwell* (1863) 3 Sw & Tr 275 at 278. See also *Twist v Tye* [1902] P 92 and *Re Cutliffe's Estate* [1959] P.

[316]   *Re Plant dec'd* [1926] P 139 at 152.

[317]   *Kostic v Chaplin* [2007] EWHC 2909 (Ch) at [21].

litigation, and discouraging settlement of doubtful claims at an early stage, if costs are allowed out of the estate to the unsuccessful party.'

6.185 These principles are reflected in CPR, r 57.7(5), which provides:

> '(a) A defendant may give notice in his defence that he does not raise any positive case, but insists on the will being proved in solemn form and, for that purpose, will cross-examine the witnesses who attested the will.
>
> (b) If a defendant gives such a notice, the court will not make an order for costs against him unless it considers that there was no reasonable ground for opposing the will.'

Thus the 'general rule' that costs follow the event will not necessarily apply in cases concerning probate.[318] The principle, known as 'the probate rule', that costs will not follow the event may require a different approach. The probate rule does not apply in all circumstances, however, as different considerations apply to cases having different jurisdictional origins. The probate rule does apply in the type of case that used to be heard in the Ecclesiastical Courts and the Probate Division.[319] Special provisions apply in the Court of Appeal.[320] The probate rule will not apply in a chancery action for a declaration of constructive trust; Ward LJ had this to say on that topic:[321]

> 'The probate rule is rooted in the inquisitorial exercise that was conducted by the Ecclesiastical Courts and the Probate Division where the court had to be satisfied of the validity of the will before it could pronounce for the will and admit it to probate. The effect of mutual wills upon the distribution of the estate under a later will which is admitted to probate is a matter for the Chancery Division applying the law of trusts; it is not a matter of probate law and practice. The nature of that litigation is not inquisitorial: it is adversarial and, not infrequently, very adversarial as the two families disunited by death battle for their perceived true inheritance.'

Irrelevant and barely relevant factors

6.186 Almost any admissible factor can be taken into account for the purposes of determining the incidence of costs, but a number of factors are usually regarded as being irrelevant or inadmissible for other reasons; they include, but are not limited to, the following.

Impecuniosity

6.187 A party's impecuniosity is usually[322] regarded as being irrelevant[323] (although it may be a factor which has a bearing on other factors, such as a party's perception of the value of a claim). In the context of a commercial claim, Colman J refused to make an

---

[318] See also *Kostic v Chaplin and Others* [2007] EWHC 2909 (Ch), which deals with conduct in contentious probate.

[319] *Shovelar v Lane* [2011] EWCA Civ 802 at [44].

[320] CPR, r 44.3(3)(b) provides that: 'the general rule does not apply in the following proceedings: proceedings in the Court of Appeal from a judgment, direction, decision or order given or made in probate proceedings'.

[321] *Shovelar v Lane* [2011] EWCA Civ 802 at [44].

[322] The most common exception to this is where a non-party costs order is sought against a director who has litigated for his own purposes through a worthless company: see **7.136** onwards; another exception is where the court takes the parties' solvency into account when determining the correct type of co-defendant order to make, see **7.42**.

[323] Whilst a pre-CPR case, see *Building Contractors Ltd v Ahmed* (1998) *The Independent*, November 23 (Hirst LJ and Cazalet J).

order against a Part 20 defendant where one of the principal reasons for asking for that order was the fact that the unsuccessful claimant was unable to pay.[324]

The availability of public funding

6.188 The fact that a party has the benefit of public funding is a factor which is, by the operation of statute, a factor that of itself is irrelevant.[325] Likewise, the fact that the court has the option to make an order against the LSC in respect of the costs incurred in a funded claim is largely irrelevant.[326] That said, the fact that a party may have public funding may, in some circumstances, be a relevant background fact in public law cases: the Supreme Court has held that when deciding what, if any, costs order to make in a public law case, the consequences for solicitors who do publicly funded work is a factor that may be taken into account. Their Lordships found that the court should be very slow to impose an order that each side must be liable for its own costs in a high cost case where either or both sides are publicly funded.[327]

The availability of funding other than public funding

6.189 The fact that a party may be funded by a well-financed funder, such as a union, would normally be regarded as being an irrelevant factor[328] (unless, of course, the issue was whether a non-party costs order should be made). Indeed, Lord Neuberger MR has had this to say on the topic:[329]

> 'The third principle is that the basis upon which the successful party's lawyers are funded, whether privately in the traditional way, under a "no win no fee" basis, by the Community Legal Service, by a Law Centre, or on a *pro bono* arrangement, will rarely, if ever, make any difference to that party's right to recover costs.'

The possible concerns of ATE insurers

6.190 Leveson LJ has explained that it would not be a reason to avoid making an issues-based costs order merely because the funding criteria of ATE insurers required that certain points be taken and that if costs were to be awarded on an issues basis this would discourage ATE insurers from providing insurance and impair access to justice.[330] Presumably, the same would apply to costs orders other than issues-based orders.

---

[324] *Arkin v Borchard* [2003] EWHC 3088 (Comm).

[325] See regs 3, 15(1) and (2) of of the Community Legal Services (Costs) Regulations 2000, and s 11 of the Access to Justice Act 1999. Also see *Boxall v Waltham Forest LBC* (2001) 4 CCL Rep 258 (Scott Baker J), *R (on the application of Kuzeva and another) v Southwark London Borough Council* [2002] EWCQ Civ 781 (Schiemann, Sedley and Hale LJJ), and *R (on the application of Scott) v London Borough of Hackney* [2009] EWCA Civ 217 (Sir Andrew Morritt C, Richards, Hallett LJJ).

[326] See reg 7(2) of the Community Legal Service (Cost Protection) Regulations 2000 (SI 2000/824), which provides as follows: 'Nothing in these Regulations shall be construed, in relation to proceedings where one of more parties are receiving, or have received, funded services, as: (a) requiring a court to make a costs order where it would not otherwise have made a costs order; or (b) affecting the court's power to make a wasted costs order against a legal representative.'

[327] *R (on the application of E) v Governing Body of JFS and the Admissions Appeal Panel of JFS* [2009] UKSC 1.

[328] Whilst a case in the Employment Tribunal rather than the civil courts, *Omar v Worldwide News Inc* [1998] IRLR 291 illustrates this principle.

[329] *M v Mayor and Burgesses of the London Borough of Croydon* [2012] EWCA Civ 595 at [46].

[330] *Kew v Bettamix Ltd* [2006] EWCA Civ 1535.

Litigant in person

6.191 The fact that a party acts in person is, by and large, not of itself regarded as being relevant to the incidence of costs,[331] but it may be a factor which has a bearing on other issues, such as conduct. In particular, in practice a litigant in person will usually be afforded more leeway than a person who was represented.

The amount of costs claimed

6.192 Whilst he was dealing with a matter to which Part 36 applied rather than Part 44, Ward LJ has confirmed that the court must assume that the sums claimed will be assessed, and as such, the fact that a seemingly excessive amount is not to be given weight, this being because the 'assessment will produce the right figure . . . [and the paying party] will be properly condemned in that sum and no greater sum'.[332]

Financial inequality

6.193 In so far as the incidence of costs in private law claims is concerned, in a commercial claim the fact that one party is financially stronger than another will not be a factor to which much weight will be given (although it may be a factor to which considerable weight may have been given in the management of the claim pursuant to the overriding objective). In this regard, Stanley Burnton LJ said this:[333]

'The claims between the parties arise out of their commercial relations. This context is very different from the public law cases in which a substantial defendant may be required to bear all parties' costs, or be deprived of its own costs on the issues on which it succeeds. The fact that the Appellant is a larger organisation than the Respondents does not in our view affect the costs issues.'

Contributions between defendants

6.194 Akenhead J has found that when deciding the incidence of costs in a case in which a contribution was sought between defendants, the court is not limited by the contribution made (or not made) between the defendants nor is it limited by any apportionment relating thereto.[334]

Late payment of other costs orders

6.195 Lord Neuberger MR has said that it would be in only exceptional circumstances that it would be appropriate for an award of costs to reflect the late payment of costs in another application;[335] presumably this would not be the case where the late payment directly led to the application in question.

---

[331] See *Building Contractors Ltd v Ahmed* (1998) *The Independent*, November 23, Hirst LJ and Cazalet J.

[332] *Shovelar v Lane* [2011] EWCA Civ 802 at [54].

[333] *AXA Sunlife Services plc v Campbell Martin Ltd* [2011] EWCA Civ 549 at [2].

[334] *Carillion JM Ltd v PHI Group Ltd* [2011] EWHC 1581 (TCC).

[335] *Hoque v Ali* (unreported) 15 February 2012, CA.

Chapter 7

ORDERS FOR COSTS (TYPES OF ORDER)

CROSS-ORDERS AND OTHER RECIPROCAL ENTITLEMENTS

7.1   This subchapter deals with cross-orders for costs and those situations where the court would have made cross orders for costs had it not decided to make a less intricate order. It ought to be read in conjunction with **12.67–12.102** on 'set-off'.

7.2   Cross-orders for costs will exist where parties reciprocally pay and receive costs. The following discussion addresses not only cross-orders themselves, but also the alternatives to cross-orders. Where the constituent parts of the cross-orders relate to entirely different subject matters (such as reciprocal orders for two separate claims), no conceptual difficulty will arise: each entitlement will be ascertained by the costs judge in the ordinary way, and there will be no need to consider whether any of the costs should be ascribed to any particular order. Likewise, other than considering whether to make an order for set-off, the judge making the costs order will not need to consider how the two entitlements interact.

7.3   The same is not true where the cross-orders touch upon similar subject matters (such as where disputed factual evidence went to both a claim and a counterclaim). In those circumstances it will be necessary for the court to consider how the two entitlements interrelate. Any interrelation can be taken into account at the stage of making the costs order, or at the stage of assessing the costs, or at both stages. In view of the fact that the order for costs will govern the way in which the court will assess the costs, the latter must be taken into account when considering the former. In view of this, while this chapter focuses on the incidence of costs, it necessarily also examines the way in which cross-orders are assessed.

7.4   Where the cross-orders touch upon similar subject matters (as in the example given immediately above), the court must decide what to do with those costs over which both parties could legitimately lay claim. Using a counterclaim as an example, the court would have to determine whether the costs are to be ascribed to the claim, or to the counterclaim, or to both. It may be necessary to split the costs. There are, in theory, two ways in which that might be done: costs may be divided if they fall into separately attributable components (ie components which may be separately attributed to the claim and the counterclaim), or the costs may be apportioned. For the reasons set out below, the notion of apportionment has, by and large, been relegated only to those cases in which 'special directions' have been given.

Orders relating to claim and counterclaim

7.5   In general, where cross-orders relate to claim and counterclaim, the costs are to be ascribed to the claim, save that where they can be categorised as applying solely to the counterclaim they will be ascribed to the counterclaim.

7.6   The principal authority on this topic is *Medway Oil and Storage Company Ltd v Continental Contractors Ltd*,[1] which, in brief, established that where both a claim and a counterclaim succeed, the true rule is that the claim shall be treated as if it stood alone and the counterclaim should bear only the amount by which it has caused the costs of the proceedings to be increased. Unless the trial judge gives 'special directions', there will be no apportionment of costs common to claim and counterclaim.

7.7   *Medway Oil* is complex, both in terms of the law it clarifies and in terms of the proceedings themselves. In order to be able to understand the House of Lords' guidance, it is necessary to know something of the procedural history of the case. It is also worth bearing in mind that the issue that the court ultimately had to decide was whether costs should be apportioned between claim and counterclaim, or whether they should generally be ascribed to one or the other, without apportionment.

7.8   The facts were that a claim and counterclaim were both dismissed with costs. The sums involved were substantial. At the first appeal the judge (who had also heard the trial itself) found that the defendant was entitled to the costs which it had incurred in defending the claim, and the claimant was entitled only to such costs as it would not have incurred had it not been compelled to meet the counterclaim (that is, the costs should not be apportioned between the claim and the counterclaim).

7.9   The Court of Appeal disagreed (but ultimately was shown to be wrong to do so); the Court of Appeal found that the costs should be apportioned. That court found that there was no reason why the claimants should not be allowed costs incurred in resisting the counterclaim merely because the facts they put forward were common to both claim and counterclaim. It was held that the costs judge ought to have apportioned to the counterclaim such portion of the common items as had arisen and been incurred by reason of the counterclaim.

7.10   That ruling (ie of the Court of Appeal) was at odds with existing authority (see below); the matter then went to the House of Lords on a further appeal where Viscount Haldane described the competing principles (ie apportionment and non-apportionment):

> 'One view is that as the costs of the issues were ... properly incurred in defeating the claim they should be given to the [defendant], the [claimant] getting only such extra costs as were incurred by reason of the counterclaim and but for it would not have been incurred. The other view is that the proper principle of [assessment] under a judgment such as the judgment in this case is that when one party has got the costs of a claim and another of a counterclaim, the [costs judge] ought to allow to each party all such costs as he has properly incurred in maintenance or resistance, as the case may be. When therefore the matters in controversy are common to both claim and counterclaim, the costs, so far as common to both claim and counterclaim, should be apportioned.'

7.11   The House of Lords considered a line of authority[2] that established that where there has been success (or failure) on both the claim and the counterclaim, costs should not be apportioned between the claim and the counterclaim, but (in the absence of special directions) should instead be assessed as if the claim stood by itself.

---

[1]   [1929] AC 88; whilst obiter, Ward LJ has confirmed that this case remains good law under the CPR: *Burchell v Bullard* [2005] EWCA Civ 358 at [26]–[27].

[2]   Beginning with *Saner v Bilton* (1879) 11 Ch D 416; and including *Mason v Brentini* (1880) 15 Ch D 287; *Baines v Bromley* (1881) 6 QBD 691; *In re Brown* (1883) 23 Ch D 377; *Shrapnel v Laing* (1888) 20 QBD 334; and *Atlas Metal Co v Miller* [1898] 2 QB 500 at 505.

7.12   The House of Lords noted that there were more recent authorities[3] which suggested a change of attitude; on the face of it, those authorities supported apportioning costs between the claim and the counterclaim. Viscount Haldane concluded that, properly analysed, those authorities did not support the practice of apportioning costs, but that they did support costs being *divided* between the claim and the counterclaim (assuming, of course, that the costs were capable of being so treated).[4] The distinction between division of costs and apportionment of costs depends on whether the item in question is divisible.[5] For example, a round trip to take counsel's advice on both the claim and counterclaim would not be divisible, but a trip of 100 miles to see a witness in the claim followed by a trip of 50 miles to see a witness in the counterclaim would be divisible.

7.13   The general principles of *Medway Oil* may be summarised as:

- Where there has been success on the claim and the counterclaim such that the claimant is awarded the costs of the claim and the defendant (ie the counterclaimant) the costs of the counterclaim, the claimant will be entitled to the costs of the claim as if the claim stood by itself, and the defendant will be entitled only to those costs attributable to the increase in costs which the counterclaim has caused.
- Where (as in *Medway Oil* itself) the positions are reversed such that both the claim and the counterclaim have failed (with costs), the defendant will be entitled to costs of the claim as if it stood by itself, and the claimant will be entitled only to those costs attributable to the increase in costs which the counterclaim has brought about.
- Unless the trial judge gives 'special directions', there will be no apportionment of costs between the claim and the counterclaim.
- This will not, however, prevent costs which are capable of division being divided between the claim and the counterclaim.

7.14   The House of Lords recognised that whilst these principles had the merit of being conceptually easy to apply upon an assessment, the result might be harsh on the unsuccessful party in the claim.[6] Viscount Haldane said:

'My Lords, in the authorities which I have now cited successive Courts of Appeal have laid down a principle which is not only intelligible, but capable of being easily applied by the [Costs Judge]. It may work out apparently harshly in exceptional cases. But when these threaten to occur the remedy is to apply at the trial for special directions as to issues and details. The advantage of the principle is that it is a definite one, which lifts the subject out of the somewhat vague regions of apportionment.'

7.15   It is not always necessary for a defendant to bring a formal counterclaim in order to have the court take the existence of a counterclaim into account. Thus, in a case in which the parties had agreed that the issue of liability would dispose of both the claim

---

[3]   *Christie v Platt* [1921] 2 KB 1 (the dissenting view as expressed in the Irish case of *Crean v M'Millan* [1922] 2 IR 105).

[4]   See *Medway Oil and Storage Company Ltd v Continental Contractors Ltd* [1929] AC 88 at 100 and 101–102.

[5]   For a discussion of the distinction between division and apportionment, see *Hay v Szterbin* [2010] EWHC 1967 (Ch) at [12] and [13], per Newey J.

[6]   See, for example, the facts of *Christie v Platt* [1921] 2 KB 17.

and the counterclaim and that there was no need formally to issue a counterclaim, Smith LJ found that it was open to the court to take the notional counterclaim into account.[7]

Orders other than those relating to claim and counterclaim

7.16 The rule in *Medway Oil* is also capable of applying in other situations where there are reciprocal entitlements to costs, such as where a successful claimant has to pay the costs of quantifying the damages from the date of an offer.[8] It will also apply where a party is successful overall but is ordered to pay costs of certain issues: in these circumstances, the rule in *Medway Oil* would usually apply in that apportionment would not be appropriate.[9] Nonetheless, whilst the principles in *Medway Oil* would apply under the CPR, the actual form of the order (ie cross-orders) ought to be avoided; in particular, Patten J has made it clear that cross-orders are unwieldy and ought to be avoided:[10]

> 'The implementation of orders of this kind [ie cross-orders as to costs of issues] or indeed for any kind of division of costs in relation to specific issues can involve the parties and the costs judge in extensive further litigation in the course of the detailed assessment, during which the whole history of the action is scrutinised in order to determine which part of any expenditure related to which issue. In the present case, [the costs judge] was sensibly asked by the parties to make certain preliminary rulings as to the principles on which the division of the common costs should be approached. But I am told that this process has so far generated tens of thousands of pounds in additional costs and that the hearing of the detailed assessment has been allocated a further four days of court time. There is therefore every prospect that the length of time taken in the assessment of costs will exceed the length of the trial itself and add vastly to the costs of the litigation in general. These matters need, I think, to be borne firmly in mind by a trial judge who is asked to make a complicated order for costs. There is much to be said for the application of the general rule that costs should follow the event and for keeping to the simple formula of orders for a stated proportion of the costs or a stated amount of costs in cases where recognition of a limited degree of success by one or other party is called for.'

7.17 In a similar vein, Morgan J has indicated that where each party unsuccessfully raised issues on an application and where those issues were similar in terms of complexity and degree of involvement, it would be appropriate to make no order for costs rather than to order that there be cross-assessments.[11]

7.18 Finally, it is worth mentioning that, in general, the court does not regard the fact that contributory negligence has been argued as being a discrete issue separate from the general issue of liability. This means that cross-orders as to costs would rarely be appropriate in respect of liability and contributory negligence.[12]

---

[7] *Parkes v Martin* [2009] EWCA Civ 883, Smith LJ and Rimer LJ.
[8] *Cinema Press Ltd v Pictures & Pleasures Ltd* [1945] KB 356.
[9] *Dyson Technology Ltd v Strutt* [2007] EWHC 1756 (Ch).
[10] *Dyson Technology Ltd v Strutt* [2007] EWHC 1756 (Ch) at [6].
[11] *Mastercigars Direct Ltd v Withers LLP* [2009] EWHC 1531 (Ch).
[12] See *Sonmez v Kebabery Wholesale Ltd* [2009] EWCA Civ 1386 at [22], per Ward LJ, and *Onay v Brown* [2009] EWCA Civ 775 at [29], per Goldring LJ.

Orders under the CPR and the alternatives to *Medway*

7.19 Having described the way in which cross-orders for costs are assessed, it is now possible to address the issue of when it is appropriate that cross-orders be made. This section should be read in conjunction with **6.31–6.31** on 'set-off' and **6.31–6.52** on 'success and the general rule'. In appropriate cases it would also be necessary to consider making an issues-based order, in which case the discussion at **6.100–6.127** would apply.

7.20 In practice, the court is often reluctant to make an order as per *Medway Oil*; this is not only because it can lead to unfair results, but also because the costs of a detailed assessment of both sides' costs are often far in excess of the net payment that one party has to make to the other. The court may therefore look at making a different order. Indeed, in a case which had no noticeably remarkable features, Ward LJ commented that it would be wrong for the court not to consider making other orders, such as a percentage order under CPR, r 43.6(a).[13] Where the court made such an order, the court would have to bear the *Medway Oil* principle in mind.

7.21 The whole gamut of possible orders ought to be considered. In some cases (commercial cases in particular), the court may decide not to look at success on the claim and the counterclaim in isolation, but to look at who won overall; it may be that the court regards the person who receives the cheque for the balance as being the winner. These issues are discussed in detail at **6.31–6.52**. In view of the practice under the CPR of making issues-based orders rather than orders based solely on who has won, it would not be uncommon for the *Medway Oil* point not to arise in the first place

7.22 Where the parties do legitimately have reciprocal claims for costs, orders the court may make are no order for costs[14] and an order that one party is entitled to only a percentage of its costs. If it is not possible to estimate the costs on each side at the time the order is made, it may not be appropriate to carry out this type of rough and ready set-off; it may be better to wait until the parties have turned the reciprocal entitlements into money amounts and then effect set-off at that level.[15] It would seem that the court is entitled to disregard the effect of success fees when considering whether to set-off at the stage of making the costs order; this lead to some curious results. In a claim in which a claimant and a defendant were found to be 65% and 35% responsible for a road traffic accident, Rafferty J declined to interfere with an order that each party pays the other side's costs: because the defendant claimed a success fee and the claimant did not, the effect of this was that the net result was that the claimant would make a significant net payment to the defendant.[16]

7.23 'Special orders' ought to be borne in mind: the order may, for example, provide for cross-orders, but also provide that the principle in *Medway Oil* should not apply and that costs may be apportioned. Whether this is the effect of an order is a matter of interpretation (which may include provisions which exist by implication); whilst not binding, an example of the court finding that the principles in *Medway Oil* did not apply is *Bateman v Joyce*, in which the court found that the parties did not have the principles in *Medway Oil* in mind at the time they agreed the order.[17]

---

[13] *Burchell v Bullard* [2005] EWCA Civ 358 at [29]–[30].
[14] See, for example, *Square Mile Partnership Ltd v Fitzmaurice McCall Ltd* [2006] EWHC 236 (Ch).
[15] Whilst he did not mention CPR, r 44.3(9) by that name, see *Amin v Amin* [2010] EWHC 827 (Ch) at [51], per Warren J.
[16] *Horth v Thompson* [2010] EWHC 1674 (QB) at [19].
[17] *Bateman v Joyce* [2008] EWHC 90100 (Costs), Master Campbell.

7.24   In summary, whilst *Medway Oil* remains good law, the modern philosophy is that an order that there be cross-orders is only one option amongst many, and that alternatives ought to be considered. In any event, the emphasis on issues-based orders means that, in practice, the conundrum of what to do about reciprocal claims for costs may never arise, as the form of the order may be dictated by considerations other than those in *Medway Oil*.

Set-off and CPR, r 44.3(9)

7.25   Again, this section should be read in conjunction with **21.289–21.289** on 'set-off' and with **21.289–21.303** on final costs certificates.

7.26   It used to be the case that where the court was minded to make cross orders as to costs, the costs judge would, in certain circumstances, be encouraged make separate awards without set-off.[18] This is no longer the case; the position is now governed by CPR, r 44.3(9), which provides as follows:

> 'Where a party entitled to costs is also liable to pay costs the court may assess the costs which that party is liable to pay and either—
>
> (a)   set off the amount assessed against the amount the party is entitled to be paid and direct him to pay any balance; or
>
> (b)   delay the issue of a certificate for the costs to which the party is entitled until he has paid the amount which he is liable to pay.'

Thus, the court has the power to ensure that a party does not take his costs without paying what he owes.

BULLOCK AND *SANDERSON* ORDERS, PASSING UP THE LINE AND CUT-THROUGH ORDERS

7.27   *Sanderson* and *Bullock* orders (which will be referred to as 'co-defendant orders') are an example of costs passing up the line to the person responsible for the claim; the more general issue of costs passing up the line is dealt with at **7.46–7.52**.

7.28   The basis of the discussion here is that there has been no costs sharing agreement between the co-defendants; where such an agreement exists, it is likely that the court would exercise its discretion in accordance with the agreement.

7.29   Co-defendant orders are available when a claimant sues two defendants and is successful against only one of them. The effect of these orders is to make the unsuccessful defendant bear the successful defendant's costs. Keene LJ explained the policy behind these orders:[19]

> '[W]here a plaintiff had behaved reasonably in suing both defendants he should not normally end up paying costs to either party even though he succeeded only against one of the defendants.'

---

[18]   See, for example, *Chell Engineering Ltd v Unit Tool and Engineering Co Ltd* [1950] 1 All ER 378.

[19]   *King v Zurich Insurance Company* [2002] EWCA Civ 598.

This type of situation is different from when a claimant sues two defendants and loses against both of them and the question is whether the claimant should pay the costs of any contribution proceedings between the defendants. This situation is addressed in at **7.44** *et seq.*

7.30   The difference between the two types of co-defendant order is that one achieves this aim directly, whereas the other does so indirectly:

- with the direct (*Sanderson*)[20] order, the unsuccessful defendant pays the successful defendant's costs;
- with the indirect (*Bullock*)[21] order, the claimant pays the successful defendant's costs, but the claimant is permitted to add those costs to those to be recovered from the unsuccessful defendant.

There is an historical explanation for the development of these two types of order. The indirect order developed as a result of a now obsolete but mandatory rule in jury trials that costs had to follow the event, and the direct order arose out of the need to do justice in cases against the Attorney-General, who in the nineteenth century was effectively immune against costs.[22] It is debateable whether there is still a pressing need for these two variants of the same type of order.[23]

7.31   A *Sanderson* order has the advantage of bypassing the claimant, and therefore may be preferable where, for example, the claimant is legally aided or insolvent.[24] It also has the advantage of avoiding the possibility of the successful defendant's costs being assessed twice.

The circumstances in which such orders should be made

7.32   The factors set out in CPR, r 44.3 are just as relevant to the exercise of the court's discretion as to *Bullock* orders and *Sanderson* orders as they are in respect of other types of costs order. The archetypal circumstances in which a co-defendant order would be appropriate are where the claimant has been injured in a collision between two vehicles and where he did not know which was at fault, but it was clear from the facts that one of them must have been responsible.[25]

7.33   An important consideration will be CPR, r 44.3(5)(b), which in the present context would include the reasonableness of the claimant's conduct in joining and pursuing a claim against the defendant against whom the claimant did not succeed.[26] The conduct of the other parties will also be relevant.

---

[20]   After *Sanderson v Blyth Theatre Co* [1903] 2 KB 533.

[21]   After *Bullock v London General Omnibus Co* [1907] 1 KB 264.

[22]   *Attorney-General v Corporation of Chester* (1851) 14 Beav 338; see also *Rudow v Great Britain Mutual Life Assurance Society* (1879) 17 Ch Div 600, which extended the application of the direct order following the Judicature Acts.

[23]   *Attorney-General v Corporation of Chester* (1851) 14 Beav 338; see also *Rudow v Great Britain Mutual Life Assurance Society* (1879) 17 Ch Div 600, which extended the application of the direct order following the Judicature Acts.

[24]   See the discussion of this topic by Colman J in *Arkin v Borchard Lines Ltd* (unreported) 16 December 2003, Ch D at [11]–[15].

[25]   *Besterman v British Motor Cab Company Ltd* [1914] 3 KB 181.

[26]   See *Irvine v Commissioner of the Police for the Metropolis* [2005] EWCA Civ 129 at [30].

7.34   The rationale behind *Bullock* and *Sanderson* is entirely adjectival and does not create any principle of law; therefore, each case must be decided on its own merits. In particular, there is no rule of law compelling the court to make a *Bullock* or *Sanderson* order.[27] Waller LJ had the following to say on the topic:[28]

> '[There] are no hard and fast rules as to when it is appropriate to make a *Bullock* or *Sanderson* order. The court takes into account the fact that, if a claimant has behaved reasonably in suing two defendants, it will be harsh if he ends up paying the costs of the defendant against whom he has not succeeded. Equally, if it was not reasonable to join one defendant because the cause of action was practically unsustainable, it would be unjust to make a co-defendant pay those defendant's costs. Those costs should be paid by a claimant. It will always be a factor whether one defendant has sought to blame another.'

7.35   That the power to make a co-defendant order has survived the introduction of the CPR was confirmed by Peter Gibson LJ, who went on to say that a co-defendant order is a 'strong order' which is capable of working injustice to the defendant against whom the claim has succeeded. He had the following to say:[29]

> 'There is no doubt that the jurisdiction to make a *Bullock* or *Sanderson* order has survived the introduction of the CPR, though the exercise of discretion to make such an order must be guided by the overriding objective and the specific provisions of Rule 44.3. The jurisdiction is a useful one. It is designed to avoid the injustice that when a claimant does not know which of two or more defendants should be sued for a wrong done to the claimant, he can join those whom it is reasonable to join and avoid having what he recovers in damages from the unsuccessful defendant eroded or eliminated by the order for costs against the claimant in respect of his action against the successful defendant or defendants. However, it must also be recognised that it is a strong order, capable of working injustice to the defendant against whom the claim has succeeded, to be made liable not only for the claimant's costs of the action against that defendant, but also the costs of the other defendants whom the claimant has chosen to join but against whom the claimant has failed.'

7.36   There are, however, certain factors that are relevant to the issue of whether the court should make an order, perhaps the most important of which is whether the claims against the defendants are connected. In this regard, Lord Goddard said:[30]

> 'It does not appear to us that it [ie a *Bullock* order] is an appropriate order to make where a plaintiff is alleging perfectly independent causes of action against two defendants where the breaches of duty alleged are in no way connected the one with the other.'

7.37   Thus, where the claims are unconnected, it will not ordinarily be appropriate to make a co-defendant order. The rationale behind Lord Goddard's guidance is that where a claimant pursues two unconnected claims, the general rule—that an unsuccessful party should pay the costs of the successful party—would suggest that the claimant should pay the costs of the unsuccessful claim. Moreover, it might be unfair to visit the costs of the successful defence on the unsuccessful defendant in circumstances where the unsuccessful defendant had no connection with the successful defence.

---

27   Whilst a pre-CPR case, *Hong v A&R Brown Ltd* [1948] 1 KB 515 is still informative in this regard.
28   *Moon v Garrett* [2006] EWCA Civ 1121.
29   *Irvine v Commissioner of the Police for the Metropolis* [2005] EWCA Civ 129.
30   *Hong v A&R Brown Ltd* [1948] 1 KB 515, cited with approval post CPR in *Irvine v Commissioner of the Police for the Metropolis* [2005] EWCA Civ 129 at [27].

7.38 Another relevant factor is whether the defendants have been sued 'in the alternative' (see below); whilst not an absolute requirement, *Bullock* and *Sanderson* orders are often said to be available only where this condition is met.[31]

7.39 It is usually said that 'in the alternative' means that the claimant was expected to succeed against one defendant, but not both. This notion seems to have arisen out of contract cases in which apportionment of liability would not normally be a realistic option;[32] this, of course, is different from claims in tort, where the court may find that both defendants are liable (albeit to only limited extents). It seems that the modern practice is not to regard the possibility of such a finding as being a bar to a co-defendant order. Indeed, while he was speaking in a pre-CPR context, Lord Goddard seemed to have regarded this as being the most common instance in which such an order might be appropriate (the emphasis is added):[33]

> 'A *Bullock* order is appropriate where a plaintiff is in doubt as to which of two persons is responsible for the act or acts of negligence which caused his injury, the most common instance being, of course, where a third person is injured in a collision between two vehicles and where the accident is, therefore, caused by the negligence of one or the other, *or both*.'

7.40 Whilst there is no authority on the point, a plausible analysis is that the issue is not whether the claim could have succeeded against one defendant but not both, but whether it was within the power of the unsuccessful defendant to dispose of the entirety of the matter by making an appropriate admission or offer. If this is correct, a claim should be regarded as having been brought 'in the alternative' if full settlement of one claim would have disposed of the other.

7.41 Whilst there is no binding authority on the point, first instance decisions suggest that co-defendant orders are not normally available where two defendants have been sued as a result of doubt about the law.

7.42 The next issue is whether an order should be a *Sanderson* order or a *Bullock* order. There are no rules of law in this regard, but the court must be aware of the real effect of the order. The court should consider those effects in what Lord Brandon called the 'balance of hardship'. He offered the following guidance:[34]

> 'The judge must have been aware of these matters. Having regard to them it seems to me impossible to say that the judge could not, in the judicial exercise of his discretion, have made a *Sanderson* order but was bound to make a *Bullock* order. On the contrary the balance of hardship seems to me, not to require the judge to make a *Sanderson* order than a *Bullock* order, but at least to provide a legitimate ground for him, in the judicial exercise of his discretion, to do so.'

Thus, contrary to the general principle that the court will regard impecuniosity as irrelevant to the incidence of costs,[35] the court may enquire as to the solvency of the claimant and the losing defendant before deciding the form of the order to make.

---

[31] See *Irvine v Commissioner of the Police for the Metropolis* [2005] EWCA Civ 129 at [26].
[32] See *Bankamerica Finance Ltd v Nock* [1988] AC 1002 at 1011; see also *Irvine v Commissioner of the Police for the Metropolis* [2005] EWCA Civ 129.
[33] *Mulready v JH & W Bell Ltd* [1953] 2 All ER 215.
[34] *Bankamerica Finance Ltd v Nock* [1988] AC 1002 at 1012.
[35] See **6.187**.

Colman J has commented that whilst the balance of hardship might be the determining factor, it is open to the court to take into account other factors when deciding the form of the order.[36]

7.43   The fact that a person is legally aided is not a factor that should be taken into account,[37] although such a person will often be impecunious. In this regard, Goff LJ had the following to say (albeit in the context of a passing-up-the-line order):[38]

> 'It cannot be right to deprive a third party of an order for costs to which he is otherwise entitled against the defendant, because the defendant when looking to the plaintiff for reimbursement finds a person not worth powder and shot.'

Failure against both defendants

7.44   Prior to the introduction of the CPR, neither type of co-defendant order would have been available where the claimant had failed against both defendants, In this regard, Stuart Smith LJ (with whom Peter Gibson and Balcombe LJJ agreed) said:[39]

> 'The fallacy of Mr Knight's argument is this: while an unsuccessful defendant, A, will normally be held liable to pay the costs of a successful defendant, B, whether directly or indirectly, whom he had blamed, that does not apply where the plaintiff fails against both. In such circumstances A is not ordered to pay the costs of B, even though he may have blamed him.'

7.45   It has been argued that this analysis is no longer good law under the CPR, which require a more flexible approach to costs. Sitting as a section 9 judge, HHJ Coulson QC (now Coulson J) rejected that notion:[40]

> 'It seems to me that it could only be in truly exceptional circumstances that a claimant, who has lost against both defendants, might recover the costs of pursuing one defendant against the other defendant. In my judgment, if the claimant has been unsuccessful against both defendants, the justification for a *Bullock/Sanderson* order simply does not arise. Thus I consider that this principle, succinctly explained by Stuart-Smith LJ in *Beoco*, remains good law, notwithstanding the greater flexibility of the CPR.'

It therefore remains the case that neither type of order is normally available in circumstances where the claimant has lost against both defendants. If, however, the defendants litigated issues as between themselves, then it may be appropriate to make an order as between them, and in some circumstances this may relieve the unsuccessful claimant of the burden of paying the whole of the defendants' costs.[41]

---

[36]   *Arkin v Borchard Lines Ltd* [2003] EWHC 3088 (Comm) at [18].
[37]   *Johnson v Ribbins* [1977] 1 WLR 1458 at 1463–1464.
[38]   *Johnson v Ribbins* [1977] 1 WLR 1458 at 1464; on the effect of legal aid on the incidence of costs generally, see *Boxall v Waltham Forest LBC* (2001) 4 CCL Rep 258.
[39]   *Beoco Ltd v Alfa Laval Co Ltd* [1995] 1 QB 137.
[40]   *McGlinn v Waltham Contractors Ltd* [2005] EWHC 1419 (TCC) at [21].
[41]   See, for example, *Green v Sunset & Vine Productions Ltd* (unreported) 4 November 2009, QBD at [7]–[9], per Ouseley J.

Passing up the line and cut-through orders

7.46   The costs of successful defendants brought in under what is now Part 20 of the rules of 1998 may pass up the line. In *Johnson v Ribbins* (which is pre-CPR case) Goff LJ had this to say:[42]

> 'In the exercise of that discretion ... in our judgment, the court should be guided by the principle that normally costs follow the event as is expressly provided by RSC Ord 62, r 3(2) and should, therefore, normally order the defendant, though successful in the action, to pay the costs of the third party if he also be successful. Then if in the circumstances of the case these costs ought fairly to be borne by the plaintiff the court will further order that they be added to the defendants' costs of the action as against the plaintiffs.'

The applicability of this line of thinking under the CPR has been confirmed.[43]

7.47   Similar logic applies to 'strings of contracts'. In a pre-CPR case concerning arbitrations, Diplock J had the following to say:[44]

> 'I think that I should make these observations about the way in which costs should be dealt with where third, fourth, fifth or sixth parties have been brought in these string contract cases which are very common ... In the ordinary way, however, where damages are claimed for breach of contract on one contract in a string of contracts, and the seller brings in his immediate seller as a third party, and the third party brings in his immediate seller as a fourth party, then, provided that the contracts are the same or substantially the same so that the issue whether the goods comply with a description is the same, the defendant (in this case it was the plaintiffs, because it was a counterclaim), if successful, should recover against the plaintiffs not only his costs but any costs of the third party which he has been ordered to pay: the third party in like manner should recover from the defendant his own costs and any costs of the fourth party which he has been compelled to pay, and so on down the string. That is the normal way in which costs should be dealt with in this kind of action where there is a string of contracts in substantially the same terms. In saying that, I am not excluding the possibility that there may be special reasons for departing from that normal practice. Whether it was reasonable for the defendant to bring in a third party at all is always a question to be considered, and that is a matter on which a lot of facts may be relevant.'

7.48   No difficulty arises if the parties are solvent, but where the claimant is insolvent, the difficult question arises of whether the Part 20 defendant should, with the defendant, share the burden of the claimant's impecuniosity. That would be achieved by making a 'cut-through order', which is an order that the successful Part 20 defendant would recover its costs directly from the claimant, essentially treating the defendant and the Part 20 defendant as if they were co-defendants. Colman J had the following to say on the topic:[45]

> 'The fact that it is the policy of the law to give effect to access to justice permitting an impecunious claimant to sue and so to expose an ultimately successful defendant to shoulder the burden of his own costs see *Hamilton v Al Fayed (No 2)* [2002] 3 All ER 641, per Simon Brown LJ at 658–659, raises the question whether, if that defendant, with knowledge of the claimant's lack of resources, then chooses to protect his position by joining a third party Part 20 defendant, it is in the interests of justice that the third party should be placed in a similar position as to the recovery of his costs, if successful, to that of the defendant who has

---

42   [1977] 1 WLR 1458 at 1463–1464.
43   *SCT Finance v Bolton* [2002] EWCA Civ 56 at [23]; and *Arkin v Borchard Lines Ltd* [2003] EWHC 3088 (Comm) at [22].
44   *L E Cattan Ltd v A Michaelides & Co* [1958] 1 WLR 717 at 719.
45   *Arkin v Borchard Lines Ltd* [2003] EWHC 3088 (Comm) at [32].

chosen to join him. It is indeed hard to see why the apparent injustice to the defendant by reason of his inability to recover his costs from the impecunious claimant should ordinarily be spread to the third party who has been sued involuntarily by a sufficiently resourced defendant. If, as it is ultimately decided, he has been wrongly sued and is under no liability to the defendant, to expose him by a costs order to the impecuniosity of the claimant would normally not only be unnecessary to do justice to the defendant but would do serious injustice to the third party. This, as I see it, represents a quite different position from that which arises where there are co-defendants both of whom have been sued by the same impecunious claimant. In such a case there is often a far stronger character of injustice if the successful defendant is deprived of his costs which can in appropriate cases be cured by a cut-through or *Sanderson* order causing them to be paid by the unsuccessful defendant.'

7.49   Coleman J went on to comment on the 'separability principle', which is the term he gave to the principle that a Part 20 claim is something separate from the original claim. He emphasised that this distinguished cut-through orders from co-defendant orders (where, conventionally, claims would have been brought against the co-defendants in the alternative).[46] He found that it was only in exceptional cases that there should be departure from the separability principle.

7.50   In any event, the court must consider whether it would work injustice on an unsuccessful defendant to make him liable for the costs of another defendant against whom the claimant has failed.[47]

7.51   Although the authorities on the point are now very old, it is generally thought that the principles set out in these few paragraphs will apply even where one or more of the litigants is a child.[48]

7.52   In summary, where there are co-defendants or there is a line of litigants, the court is able to make orders that pass the burden of the costs to the person responsible for the claim, but that must be in such a way as takes into account all the relevant factors and no irrelevant factors.

CONSENT ORDERS AND TOMLIN ORDERS

7.53   Consent orders (of which Tomlin orders are a specific type) may make provision as to costs. The CPR permit the parties to place a draft consent order before the court so that the court may make it in the agreed terms.[49] Where a costs order is made, it will usually (but not always) be possible to ask a court officer to enter and seal the order;[50] the notable exceptions are:[51]

- where one or more of the parties is a litigant in person;
- where one or more of the parties is a child; and
- where one or more of the parties is a patient.

---

[46]   This is not always the case, however: see **7.39**.
[47]   *Hong v A&R Brown Ltd* [1948] 1 KB 515.
[48]   *Short v Ridge* (1876) WN 47 at 48; and *Goldsmith v Russell* (1855) 5 De GM & G 547 at 556.
[49]   CPR, r 40.3(1)(d) and r 40.6(1).
[50]   See CPR, r 40.6(3)(b)(vii).
[51]   See CPR, r 40.6(2) and (3).

Where any of these circumstances exist, the order must be made by a judge upon application; that application may be heard in the absence of the parties.[52]

7.54 Certain formalities apply to consent orders. The order must be expressed as being 'by consent' and it must be signed by the legal representative acting for each of the parties, or by the party if he is a litigant in person.[53] This is counter-intuitive, because it is the party's legal representative who must sign (if there is one), not the party himself. Where the order is to go before a judge, a space must be left to allow the judge's name and judicial title to be inserted.[54]

7.55 Tomlin orders (which are named after a judge, not a case)[55] are a type of bipartite consent order comprising a schedule and a body; the schedule will usually contain the terms of the compromise, and the body will contain the procedural provisions (including the costs order). In some circumstances, the schedule may be kept confidential even from the court. The wording of a Tomlin order is usually as follows:

'IT IS ORDERED BY CONSENT

> **THAT UPON** the parties having agreed the terms set out in the attached schedule, all further proceedings in this claim be stayed except for the purpose of carrying such terms into effect
>
> **AND** for that purpose the parties have permission to apply.'

7.56 An agreement to pay costs which is contained within the schedule of a Tomlin order rather than in the order itself is not an order for costs; this means that without further order, it will not give rise to a right to an assessment.[56] Likewise, a provision for costs in the schedule of a Tomlin order will not attract judgment debt interest on those costs.[57] It is for these reasons that PD 40B, para 3.5(2) stipulates that any order for the payment or assessment of costs is to be contained in the body of the order and not in the schedule.

7.57 It is worth saying a word or two about the effect of a Tomlin order; this is because it is relevant to the issue of what a party can do if another party fails to abide by the terms of the agreement. The making of a Tomlin order leaves the underlying claim extant. As Denning MR said in *Cooper v Williams*:[58]

> '... I am of the opinion that the effect of a stay is that it is not equivalent to a discontinuance, or to a judgment for the plaintiff or the defendant. It is a stay which can be and may be removed if proper grounds are shown.'

7.58 Likewise, in *Rofa Sport Management AG v DHL International (UK) Ltd*[59] Neill LJ, giving the judgment of the court (with which Ralph Gibson and May LJJ agreed) held:

---

[52] See CPR, r 40.6(5) and (6) and PD 40B, para 3.3.
[53] CPR, r 40.6(7) and PD 40B, para 3.4.
[54] PD 40B, para 3.3(2).
[55] The judge was Tomlin J, and the phrase comes from his ruling in *Dashwood v Dashwood* [1927] WN 276, 64 LJNC 431.
[56] See, by analogy, *Horizon Technologies International v Lucky Wealth Consultants Ltd* [1992] 1 WLR 24.
[57] *Wills v Crown Estate Commissioners* [2003] EWHC 1718 (Ch) at [20].
[58] [1963] 2 QB 567 at 580.
[59] [1989] 1 WLR 902 at 911.

'In my judgment, for the sake of clarity and certainty the word "stay" in an order should not be treated as a possible equivalent of a dismissal or a discontinuance. There may well, of course, be cases, however, where the person who wishes to have the stay removed will face great difficulties. An action which has been stayed by consent following a compromise provides an obvious example. But, as it seems to me, the action following a stay remains technically in being. The action cannot proceed or resume its active life without an order of the court, but I do not consider that it can properly be regarded as dead in the same way as an action which has been dismissed or discontinued by order.'

7.59   The importance of this is that if a party fails to perform its obligations under the terms of the agreement as set out in the schedule, it is open to the court to lift the stay and to continue with the claim. This does not mean that the court will readily entertain such an application: this was made clear by Fox LJ in *Hollingsworth v Humphrey*,[60] in which he said:

'The first question, it seems to me, is the meaning of the agreement reached between the parties. That agreement, I think, consists not only of the schedule terms of the compromise but includes the provision for a stay itself which is an integral part of the compromise. The wording of the order is that "all further proceedings in this action except for the purpose of carrying the said terms into effect be stayed". As between the parties, therefore, it seems to me that, while the action is not continued or dismissed, the bargain was that the action would not be resorted to thereafter save for the purpose of enforcing the terms. That is the plain meaning of the language used. Moreover, it seems to me that there is no reason why the parties should have intended anything else.'

Fox LJ went on to say that the test was whether 'proper grounds had been shown' (as per *Cooper v Williams*) and added:

'In deciding whether "proper grounds are shown" (or "good cause" is shown) for lifting the stay it is necessary to consider all the circumstances of the case.'

7.60   Where a party is aggrieved by another party's refusal to comply with the terms of the compromise, and where the court does not lift the stay, that party's remedy is to sue upon the compromise.

7.61   The wording of CPR, r 40.6 is as follows:

'(1)   This rule applies where all the parties agree the terms in which a judgment should be given or an order should be made.

(2)   A court officer may enter and seal an agreed judgment or order if—

    (a)   the judgment or order is listed in paragraph (3);

    (b)   none of the parties is a litigant in person; and

    (c)   the approval of the court is not required by these Rules, a practice direction or any enactment before an agreed order can be made.

(3)   The judgments and orders referred to in paragraph (2) are—

    (a)   a judgment or order for—

        (i)   the payment of an amount of money (including a judgment or order for damages or the value of goods to be decided by the court); or

        (ii)   the delivery up of goods with or without the option of paying the value of the goods or the agreed value.

    (b)   an order for—

---

[60]   (1987) *The Independent*, December 21, CA.

> (i)   the dismissal of any proceedings, wholly or in part;
>
> (ii)   the stay of proceedings on agreed terms, disposing of the proceedings, whether those terms are recorded in a schedule to the order or elsewhere;
>
> (iii)   the stay of enforcement of a judgment, either unconditionally or on condition that the money due under the judgment is paid by instalments specified in the order;
>
> (iv)   the setting aside under Part 13 of a default judgment which has not been satisfied;
>
> (v)   the payment out of money which has been paid into court;
>
> (vi)   the discharge from liability of any party;
>
> (vii)   the payment, assessment or waiver of costs, or such other provision for costs as may be agreed.
>
> (4)   Rule 40.3 (drawing up and filing of judgments and orders) applies to judgments and orders entered and sealed by a court officer under paragraph (2) as it applies to other judgments and orders.
>
> (5)   Where paragraph (2) does not apply, any party may apply for a judgment or order in the terms agreed.
>
> (6)   The court may deal with an application under paragraph (5) without a hearing.
>
> (7)   Where this rule applies—
>
> (a)   the order which is agreed by the parties must be drawn up in the terms agreed;
>
> (b)   it must be expressed as being "By Consent";
>
> (c)   it must be signed by the legal representative acting for each of the parties to whom the order relates or, where paragraph (5) applies, by the party if he is a litigant in person.'

7.62   PD 40B, para 3 provides as follows:

> '**3.1**   Rule 40.6(3) sets out the types of consent judgments and orders which may be entered and sealed by a court officer. The court officer may do so in those cases provided that:
>
> (1)   none of the parties is a litigant in person, and
>
> (2)   the approval of the court is not required by the Rules, a practice direction or any enactment.
>
> **3.2**   If a consent order filed for sealing appears to be unclear or incorrect the court officer may refer it to a judge for consideration.
>
> **3.3**   Where a consent judgment or order does not come within the provisions of rule 40.6(2):
>
> (1)   an application notice requesting a judgment or order in the agreed terms should be filed with the draft judgment or order to be entered or sealed, and
>
> (2)   the draft judgment or order must be drawn so that the judge's name and judicial title can be inserted.
>
> **3.4**   A consent judgment or order must:
>
> (1)   be drawn up in the terms agreed,
>
> (2)   bear on it the words "By Consent", and
>
> (3)   be signed by
>
> (a)   solicitors or counsel acting for each of the parties to the order, or
>
> (b)   where a party is a litigant in person, the litigant.
>
> **3.5**   Where the parties draw up a consent order in the form of a stay of proceedings on agreed terms, disposing of the proceedings, and where the terms are recorded in a schedule to the order, any direction for:
>
> (1)   payment of money out of court, or

(2)   payment and assessment of costs

should be contained in the body of the order and not in the schedule.'

7.63   In summary, consent orders must be marked 'by consent' and must be signed. Where a consent order is in the form of a Tomlin order, the provision dealing with costs must be in the body of the order rather than the schedule.

SPLIT TRIALS AND 'FORTHWITH' ORDERS

7.64   Generally speaking, a detailed assessment cannot be begun unless the court so orders or unless the claim has been concluded. This used to be as a result of a common law rule,[61] but is now as a result of CPR, r 47.1:

'The general rule is that the costs of any proceedings or any part of the proceedings are not to be assessed by the detailed procedure until the conclusion of the proceedings but the court may order them to be assessed immediately.'

This general rule stems from the recommendations made in 1983 by the then equivalent of the Senior Costs Judge.[62] Those recommendations were intended to ensure that costs were assessed together at the conclusion of the proceedings rather than piecemeal during the currency of the proceedings.

7.65   The question of whether a forthwith order should be made usually arises where there is an order for a split trial (e g a trial on liability followed by a trial on quantum, or where there has been a trial on limitation to be followed by a trial on the claim itself). Less commonly, it may arise in protracted proceedings where the costs of an interlocutory step are substantial (although often the court would deal with those costs by carrying out a summary assessment).

7.66   If circumstances such as those arise, the receiving party may ask for its costs to be assessed forthwith (i e a party may ask for a 'forthwith' order). The effect of such an order is to permit the costs judge to assess the costs immediately, without further order.

7.67   The need for forthwith orders existed before the introduction of the CPR; the rationale was (and still is) to encourage deferral of assessment until the end of the claim so that all costs may be assessed by the same judge. In practical terms, the effect of that commendable objective is thwarted under the CPR because costs are now often dealt with piecemeal by summary assessment.

7.68   Forthwith orders will not normally encompass the success fee. CPD, art 14.5 gives the following guidance:

'Where there has been a trial of one or more issues separately from other issues, the court will not normally order detailed assessment of the additional liability until all issues have been tried unless the parties agree.'

---

[61]   This was in accordance with the maxim unica directio fiat damnorum, that there should be only one certification of the damages; this rule arose at a time when damages were considered to include costs: see *Phillips v Phillips* (1879) 5 QBD 60.

[62]   See para 30 of the report, dated 25 January 1983, of a working party on Order 62 chaired by Master Horne.

7.69 A request for a forthwith order may be refused if it would cause prejudice to the paying party. If, for example, the receiving party is a funded party and if the costs might be subject to set-off in the event of a subsequent costs order being made against that party, it would usually be appropriate that no forthwith order is made.[63]

7.70 Where a split trial on liability is determined in favour of the claimant and where a prior Part 36 offer has been made, it would usually be appropriate to postpone the determination of the costs generally until such time as the damages have been determined; this is to enable the court to take the Part 36 offer into account. As Waller LJ said:[64]

> 'The proper approach at the conclusion of a trial of a preliminary issue where there has been a Part 36 payment in or a Part 36 offer, should therefore normally be to adjourn the question of costs pending the resolution of all the issues including damages, at which stage the quantum of the Part 36 offer can be revealed and the discretion in relation to costs exercised in the knowledge of it.'

7.71 A costs judge may make a forthwith order, but (whilst there is no authority on the point) CPD, art 28.1(5) appears to be worded in such a way as to restrict the costs judge to making such an order only where there is no realistic prospect of the claim continuing. See **21.42** and **21.43** for more details..

7.72 Guidance is given in CPD, art 28.1 as follows:

> '(1) For the purposes of rule 47.1, proceedings are concluded when the court has finally determined the matters in issue in the claim, whether or not there is an appeal.
>
> (2) For the purposes of this rule, the making of an award of provisional damages under Part 41 will be treated as a final determination of the matters in issue.
>
> (3) The court may order or the parties may agree in writing that, although the proceedings are continuing, they will nevertheless be treated as concluded.
>
> (4)
>
> > (a) A party who is served with a notice of commencement ... may apply to a costs judge or a district judge to determine whether the party who served it is entitled to commence detailed assessment proceedings.
> >
> > (b) On hearing such an application the orders which the court may make include: an order allowing the detailed assessment proceedings to continue, or an order setting aside the notice of commencement.
>
> (5) A costs judge or a district judge may make an order allowing detailed assessment proceedings to be commenced where there is no realistic prospect of the claim continuing.'

A number of case examples can be found at **21.50—21.53**.

7.73 In summary, a detailed assessment cannot be begun unless the court so orders or unless the claim has been concluded; a 'forthwith order' may be made, but it will not be made in every instance.

---

[63]   See, for example, *Hicks v Russell Jones & Walker* [2001] CP Rep 25, CA.
[64]   *HSS Hire Services Group plc v BMB Builders Merchants Ltd & Anor* [2005] EWCA Civ 626 at [29].

DEEMED ORDERS

7.74 Deemed orders are orders which—without the intervention or the further intervention of the court—are automatically made on the happening of some event. They are orders for costs rather than mere procedural entitlements to costs.[65] They will arise in the following circumstances:

- where a party allows court fees to remain unpaid after having been given notice to pay by the court;
- where a party accepts a Part 36 offer;
- where a party discontinues a claim; and
- where the court makes no order for costs in relation to a limited range of applications.

The court may or may not have discretion to disapply the deemed order (see below).

7.75 The starting point is CPR, r 44.12, which provides:

'(1) Where a right to costs arises under—

    (a)   rule 3.7 (defendant's right to costs where claim struck out for non-payment of fees);

    (b)   rule 36.10(1) or (2) (claimant's entitlement to costs where a Part 36 offer is accepted);

    (c)   (*omitted*[66])

    (d)   rule 38.6 (defendant's right to costs where claimant discontinues),

a costs order will be deemed to have been made on the standard basis.

(2) Interest payable pursuant to section 17 of the Judgments Act 1838 or section 74 of the County Courts Act 1984 on the costs deemed to have been ordered under paragraph (1) shall begin to run from the date on which the event which gave rise to the entitlement to costs occurred.'

7.76 Each of these three circumstances is now dealt with in turn. It can be seen that a deemed order is on the standard basis, and that it gives rise to an entitlement to judgment-debt interest in exactly the same way as it would have done had it been made by the court.

Non-payment of court fees

7.77 If court fees go unpaid, there is a mechanism by which the court may give notice to the defaulting party; if that notice goes unheeded, then the claim will be automatically struck out and the defaulting party will become liable for costs.

7.78 The relevant provisions are in CPR, r 3.7, which, in so far as it is relevant, provides as follows:

---

[65] This may be relevant in so far as interest is concerned. The need for deemed orders was noted by Lord Ackner in *Legal Aid Board v Russell* [1991] 2 AC 317, in which the entitlement to costs arose out of a provision that fell short of creating an actual order for costs (and therefore failed to come within the ambit of ss 17 and 18 of the Judgments Act 1838); this led to the RSC being changed in October 1991 in such a way as to elevate the entitlement to the status of being an deemed order and to affirm the right to interest.

[66] This provision used to relate to claimant's Part 36 offers; it became otiose when Part 36 was redrafted in 2007. Now, CPR, r 44.12 makes no distinction between Part 36 offers made by claimants and those made by defendants.

'(1) This rule applies where—

(a) an allocation questionnaire or a pre-trial check list (listing questionnaire) is filed without payment of the fee specified by the relevant Fees Order;

(b) the court dispenses with the need for an allocation questionnaire or a pre-trial check list or both;

(c) these Rules do not require an allocation questionnaire or a pre-trial check list to be filed in relation to the claim in question; or

(d) the court has made an order giving permission to proceed with a claim for judicial review.

...

(2) The court will serve a notice on the claimant requiring payment of the fee specified in the relevant Fees Order if, at the time the fee is due, the claimant has not paid it or made an application for exemption or remission.

(3) The notice will specify the date by which the claimant must pay the fee.

(4) If the claimant does not—

(a) pay the fee; or

(b) make an application for an exemption from or remission of the fee,

by the date specified in the notice—

(i) the claim will automatically be struck out without further order of the court; and

(ii) the claimant shall be liable for the costs which the defendant has incurred unless the court orders otherwise.

(Rule 44.12 provides for the basis of assessment where a right to costs arises under this rule ...)

(5) Where an application for exemption from or remission of a fee is refused, the court will serve notice on the claimant requiring payment of the fee by the date specified in the notice.

(6) If the claimant does not pay the fee by the date specified in the notice—

(a) the claim will automatically be struck out without further order of the court; and

(b) the claimant shall be liable for the costs which the defendant has incurred unless the court orders otherwise.

(7) ...'

(CPR, r 3.7(7) goes on to provide a mechanism by which a defaulting party may apply for relief. Those details are not set out here.)

CPR Part 36

7.79 Where an offeree accepts a Part 36 offer, that creates a deemed order that the offeree will pay the offeror's costs on the standard basis.

7.80 In so far as it is relevant, CPR, r 36.10 provides:

'(1) Subject to paragraph (2) and paragraph (4)(a), where a Part 36 offer is accepted within the relevant period the claimant will be entitled to his costs of the proceedings up to the date on which notice of acceptance was served on the offeror.

(2) Where—

(a) a defendant's Part 36 offer relates to part only of the claim; and

(b) at the time of serving notice of acceptance within the relevant period the claimant abandons the balance of the claim, the claimant will be entitled to his costs of the proceedings up to the date of serving notice of acceptance unless the court orders otherwise.

(3) Costs under paragraphs (1) and (2) of this rule will be assessed on the standard basis if the amount of costs is not agreed.

(Rule 44.4(2) explains the standard basis for assessment of costs)

(4) Where—

    (a)   a Part 36 offer that was made less than 21 days before the start of trial is accepted; or

    (b)   a Part 36 offer is accepted after expiry of the relevant period,

if the parties do not agree the liability for costs, the court will make an order as to costs.'

7.81 The court has no jurisdiction to disapply a deemed order that arises from acceptance of a Part 36 offer. If an offeror does not wish acceptance of the offer to give rise to a deemed order, he should make his offer as an 'admissible offer' (see **6.53**) or as a commercial offer (for example, '£x,000 with no order for costs'). If it is the offeree who wishes to escape the effect of a deemed order (perhaps because he believes that he is entitled to costs on the indemnity basis rather than on the standard basis), he could wait until the expiry of the 21-day relevant period and then immediately accept the offer. That would have the effect of placing the costs at large and within the court's jurisdiction.

Discontinuance

7.82 Unless the court orders otherwise, discontinuance of a claim will result in the discontinuer being deemed to be liable for costs. This is the default position and as such does not need to be justified on a case-by-case basis,[67] but the justification of the policy is that the effect of discontinuance is to deprive the defendant of the opportunity of vindicating himself.[68]

Jurisdiction

7.83 CPR, r 38.6 provides:

'(1) Unless the court orders otherwise, a claimant who discontinues is liable for the costs which a defendant against whom he discontinues incurred on or before the date on which notice of discontinuance was served on him.

(2) If proceedings are only partly discontinued—

    (a)   the claimant is liable under paragraph (1) for costs relating only to the part of the proceedings which he is discontinuing; and

    (b)   unless the court orders otherwise, the costs which the claimant is liable to pay must not be assessed until the conclusion of the rest of the proceedings.

(3) This rule does not apply to claims allocated to the small claims track.

(Rule 44.12 provides for the basis of assessment where right to costs arises on discontinuance ...)'

---

[67] If there ever was a rule that the claimant would be required only to pay a defendant's costs on discontinuance if he was, in effect, surrendering and acknowledging defeat, that rule no longer applies under the CPR *In re Walker Wingsail Systems plc* [2005] EWCA Civ 247, overturning *Barretts & Baird (Wholesale) Ltd v Institute of Professional Civil Servants* [1987] IRLR 3.

[68] *Far Out Productions Inc v Unilever UK & CN Holdings Ltd* [2009] EWHC 3484 (Ch) at [4], per Mr N Strauss QC (seeing as Deputy Judge of the High Court).

Practical jurisdictional matters

7.84 Service of a notice of discontinuance brings an end to the claim, but issues concerning costs remain extant to the extent that they need to be determined (see CPR, r 38.5). The date of the deemed order is the date of service of the notice. The court may take into account any delay between that date and the application that the court should 'order otherwise'.[69]

7.85 Whether a claim has been discontinued will depend on the facts. Where the entire claim has been brought to an end, there will usually be no potential for dispute; this is because CPR, r 38.3(1) provides that in order to discontinue a claim, a claimant must file and serve a notice of discontinuance. Therefore, the issue will usually be a matter of straightforward fact (ie whether notice of discontinuance has been served). The issue can prove more troublesome if only parts of the claim have been brought to an end or if a claim is abandoned without notice being served; these things are dealt with below.

7.86 Where only a part of the claim has been discontinued, there may be a dispute as to whether CPR, r 38.6(2) should apply to the abandoned part of the claim (either directly or by analogy). The matter may be analysed in terms of constructive discontinuance; an example is where claimants amended their pleadings in such a way as to abandon their claim for damages; Park J found that this was capable of amounting to discontinuance.[70]

7.87 Moreover, there is such a thing as constructive discontinuance of the entire claim. That would occur where the court finds that the claimant has effectively abandoned the whole of his claim; this is dealt with in detail at **7.111–7.117**.

Discretion

7.88 Where a discontinuer makes an application for a deemed order not to apply, the burden will be on him to prove that there is 'good reason' why the court should accede to such a request.[71] Lewison LJ has explained that this is the case in all courts.[72] Mr N Strauss QC (sitting as Deputy Judge of the High Court) has said that whilst there is no invariable rule, a discontinuer would normally have to show a substantial change from the position which existed at the time the proceedings were commenced.[73] A mere change of heart on the part of the claimant, or a mere re-evaluation of the worth of the litigation would not be sufficient;[74] Chadwick LJ gave the following guidance:[75]

---

[69] See, for example, *Hoist UK Ltd v Reid Lifiting Ltd* [2010] EWHC 1922 (Ch) at [10], per Mr Roger Wyand QC sitting as a Deputy High Court Judge; in that case, the court did not give much weight to the fact that there had been delay (of about a month), this being because the discontinuer had given notice of the intention to make the application.

[70] *Isaac v Isaac (No 2)* [2005] EWHC 435 (Ch).

[71] *In re Walker Wingsail Systems plc* [2005] EWCA Civ 247 at [24], per Chadwick LJ.

[72] *Fresenius Kabi Deutschland GmbH v Carefusion 303 Inc* [2011] EWCA Civ 1288 at [12] *et seq*; this arose in the context of a practice that had arisen in patent cases of making 'Earth Closet Orders'; the court ruled that that practice should now stop (overruling *Baird v Moule's Patent Earth Closet Co Ltd* (1881) LR 17 Ch D 139).

[73] *Far Out Productions Inc v Unilever UK & CN Holdings Ltd* [2009] EWHC 3484 (Ch) at [2], per Mr N Strauss QC (seeing as Deputy Judge of the High Court).

[74] Ibid; see also *Teasdale v HSBC Bank plc, Brookes v HSBC Bank plc* [2010] EWHC 612 (QB), per HHJ Waksman QC (sitting as a Deputy High Court Judge) at [7]; HHJ Waksman QC's judgment was upheld on appeal (*Brookes v HSBC Bank plc; Jemitus v Bank of Scotland plc* [2011] EWCA Civ 354).

[75] *In re Walker Wingsail Systems plc* [2005] EWCA Civ 247 at [36].

'... [J]ustice will normally lead to the conclusion that a defendant who defends himself at substantial expense against a [claimant] who changes his mind in the middle of the action for no good reason – other than that he has re-evaluated the factors that have remained unchanged – should be compensated for his costs.'

If the claimant seeks to rely on the fact that there was new evidence or disclosure, the court may decline to make an order in the claimant's favour if that evidence or disclosure lacked causal significance (or, in the words of Pitchford J, if it was not a 'discrete clinching piece of evidence').[76] Similarly, it may be relevant that the claimant could have clarified the position in pre-action correspondence,[77] or that the claimant has failed to clarify the position in the context of delay in the claim generally.[78] At the other end of the spectrum, if the defendant can be shown to have perversely encouraged a claimant by concealing the existence of a defence, then he will be at risk.[79]

Conduct

7.89   The court may, in its discretion, reduce or negate a defendant's costs to take account of that party's conduct; case examples include the following:

- the defendant having an unreasonable attitude to negotiations,[80] or a perverse attitude towards disclosing his defence;[81]
- the defendant failing to discharge duties that because of his status or position he could be expected to discharge;[82]
- the defendant significantly changing its case such that the proceedings had to be discontinued in favour of proceedings in a different forum;[83]
- a failure on the part of the defendant to comply with pre-action protocol;[84] and
- an absence of evidence to support a defendant's contention that the claimant's challenge to a will was unreasonable.[85]

The fact that discontinuance has resulted in a saving of costs and time would not of itself justify a departure from the usual order.[86] Whilst obiter, Moore-Bick LJ has commented that whilst there may be cases in which it can be said that the defendant has

---

[76]   See, for example, *R (on the application of Allbutt) v Ministry of Defence* [2009] EWHC 3351 (Admin), per Pitchford J at [30].

[77]   Ibid.

[78]   *Far Out Productions Inc v Unilever UK & CN Holdings Ltd* [2009] EWHC 3484 (Ch) at [5], per Mr N Strauss QC (seeing as Deputy Judge of the High Court); delay during the claim will, of itself, usually have only a very limited influence on the final order: whilst not binding, see *In the matter of Smart-Tel (UK) plc, sub nom OR v Doshi* [2007] BCC 896, Companies Ct at [38], per Mr Registrar Baister

[79]   The obiter comments of Potter LJ in *RTZ Pension Property Trust Ltd v ARC Property Developments Ltd* [1999] 1 All ER 532 at 541 have been cited under the CPR as remaining good law (see *Teasdale v HSBC Bank plc, Brookes v HSBC Bank plc* [2010] EWHC 612 (QB), per HHJ Waksman QC (sitting as a Deputy High Court Judge) at [7(6)]. HHJ Waksman QC's judgment was upheld on appeal (*Brookes v HSBC Bank plc; Jemitus v Bank of Scotland plc* [2011] EWCA Civ 354).

[80]   *RBG Resources plc v Rastogi* [2004] EWHC 994 (Ch).

[81]   *RTZ Pension Property Trust Ltd v ARC Property Developments Ltd* [1999] 1 All ER 532 at 541 (see the footnotes above).

[82]   Whilst not binding, see In the matter of *Smart-Tel (UK) plc, sub nom OR v Doshi* [2007] BCC 896, Companies Ct at [42] in which Mr Registrar Baister reduced a defendant's entitlement to costs on the basis that he created difficulties by not fully discharging his duties as an accountant.

[83]   *Webb v Environment Agency* (unreported) 5 April 2011, QBD, Sweeney J.

[84]   *Aegis Group plc v Inland Revenue* [2005] EWHC 1468 (Ch).

[85]   *Wylde v Culver* [2006] EWHC 1313 (Ch) (Bompas QC).

[86]   *Messih v McMillan Williams* [2010] EWCA Civ 844 at [31], per Patten LJ; also see *Griffin v Smith et al* [2010] EWHC 3414 (Ch) at [19], per David Ricarhds J.

brought the litigation on himself, even that is unlikely to justify a departure from the rule if the claimant discontinues in circumstances which amount to a failure of the claim.[87]

7.90   Where a discontinuer has brought a claim unreasonably early and without having given adequate notice to the defendant, an application by the discontinuer not to pay the costs is likely to fail.[88] Likewise, if the defendant has given a clear account of its case that went beyond that which it was required to give under the relevant rules, directions or protocol, that will be a factor that the court will take into account.[89] Where the need for discontinuance arises by reason of carelessness, it is likely that the court would be unsympathetic to the discontinuer; an example might be where a claimant intends to bring proceedings against one natural person, but inadvertently sues the partnership of which he is a member.[90]

Supervening events

7.91   Where a claimant has to discontinue because of some supervening event beyond his control (such as an opponent becoming bankrupt for reasons unrelated to the claim), then the interests of justice might require that a deemed order is not made.[91] In these circumstances the court will usually have to decide the incidence of costs without having made any finding as to the substantive issues; this is a topic which is dealt with in detail at **7.106–7.108**, **7.115** and **7.120**. The following is the briefest of summaries:

- The burden of persuading the court to depart from the deemed order will lie with the claimant;[92] the test is not a threshold test, but is a matter of identifying all the relevant factors and weighing them up;[93]
- The default position is not that there shall be no order as to costs, but that the discontinuing party will bear the costs (see **7.107**);
- Where, however, an independent supervening event has made it unnecessary to continue with the claim, and where it is not possible to know who would have won or what would have happened had the supervening event not occurred, an order that there be no order to costs might be appropriate;[94]
- Where the claim has been discontinued as a result of a supervening event which was within the control of the defendant and which was in reality a capitulation on the part of the defendant, the appropriate order would usually be an award to the claimant;[95]
- Likewise, where a claimant has effectively achieved his aim by reason of interlocutory relief being afforded to him, the court may relieve him of the burden of paying costs if the court finds that there was reasonable justification for bringing the claim;[96]

---

[87]   *Brookes v HSBC Bank plc; Jemitus v Bank of Scotland plc* [2011] EWCA Civ 354 at [10].

[88]   *Reid v Capita Group plc* [2005] EWHC 2448 (Ch).

[89]   See, for example, *Mobiqa Limited v Trinity Mobile Limited* [2010] EWHC 253 (Pat) at [25]–[28], per Floyd J.

[90]   See, for example, *Brooks v AH Brooks & Co (a firm)* [2010] EWHC 2720 (Ch), per HHJ Cooke (sitting as a Judge of the High Court).

[91]   See, for example, *Everton v World Professional Billiards and Snooker Association (Promotions) Ltd* (unreported) 13 December 2001, Gray J; see also **7.115** *et seq*.

[92]   *In re Walker Wingsail Systems plc* [2005] EWCA Civ 247 at [24]. See **7.106**.

[93]   *Messih v McMillan Williams & Ors* [2010] EWCA Civ 844 at [27], per Patten LJ.

[94]   Although a pre-CPR case, *R v Liverpool City Council ex p Newman & Ors* [1993] 5 Admin LR 669 is an example of this. See **7.107**.

[95]   As an example, see *R v North & West Devon Health Authority & Ors ex p Bowhay & Ors* [2001] 60 BMLR 228.

[96]   *Ansol Ltd v Taylor Joynson Garrett (a firm)* [2002] All ER (D) 44 (Jan).

- Where the putative supervening event is, in reality, nothing more than the claimant becoming alive to the commercial wisdom of the matter, and where that realisation was based on factors that were, or could have been known at the outset of the claim, the burden of costs will generally lie with the claimant;[97] and
- Likewise, where the decision to discontinue was motivated by practical, pragmatic or financial reasons as opposed to a lack of confidence in the merits of the case, the burden of costs will also usually lie with the claimant.[98]

7.92   Putative supervening events that lack independence from the litigation will rarely be given weight (unless, of course, the event is a capitulation on the part of a defendant). If, for example, there are two defendants and if the claimant discontinues against one of them because he has achieved what amounts to the satisfaction of his whole claim against the other, that would not usually justify a departure from the ordinary rule that on discontinuance a claimant should pay the costs of the defendant against whom he has discontinued.[99]

Indemnity basis costs

7.93   A deemed order is on the standard basis, but there is no reason in principle why the court should not order that costs be payable on the indemnity basis.[100] The court has the power to make such an order regardless of purpose of the application; it is for this reason that Proudman J has warned that an application made by the claimant may inadvertently afford the defendant a forum in which to seek indemnity basis costs.[101] In any event, case examples in which indemnity basis costs were sought are as follows:

- in a case in which he had found that the discontinuer had deliberately sought to delay the trial of the matter before discontinuing, Blackburn J made an award of costs on the indemnity basis;[102]
- in a case in which the discontinuer served notice of discontinuance on the second day of the trial in circumstances where it had previously conceded that it was unlikely to succeed, Rattee J made an award of costs on the indemnity basis;[103] and
- In a case in which the discontinuer had advanced a hopeless claim, Henderson J made an order against him on the indemnity basis.[104]

7.94   A defendant has a right to apply to have the notice of discontinuance set aside (see CPR, r 38.4(1)); this right must be exercised within 28 days after the notice of discontinuance was served (r 38.8(2)).

---

[97]   *In re Walker Wingsail Systems plc* [2005] EWCA Civ 247; see also *Teasdale v HSBC Bank plc, Brookes v HSBC Bank plc* [2010] EWHC 612 (QB), per HHJ Waksman QC (sitting as a Deputy High Court Judge) at [7]. HHJ Waksman QC's judgment was upheld on appeal (*Brookes v HSBC Bank plc; Jemitus v Bank of Scotland plc* [2011] EWCA Civ 354). See **7.108**.

[98]   *Maini v Maini* [2009] EWHC 3036 (Ch) at [11]; see also *Teasdale v HSBC Bank plc, Brookes v HSBC Bank plc* [2010] EWHC 612 (QB), per HHJ Waksman QC (sitting as a Deputy High Court Judge) at [7(4)]

[99]   *Messih v McMillan Williams & Ors* [2010] EWCA Civ 844 at [28], per Patten LJ.

[100]   For a discussion of this, see *Hoist UK Ltd v Reid Lifiting Ltd* [2010] EWHC 1922 (Ch) at [6]–[9], per Mr Roger Wyand QC sitting as a Deputy High Court Judge.

[101]   *Maini v Maini* [2009] EWHC 3036 (Ch) at [7].

[102]   *Naskaris v ANS plc* [2002] EWHC 1782 (Ch).

[103]   *Atlantic Bar and Grill Ltd v Posthouse Hotels Ltd* [2000] CP Rep 32.

[104]   *Mireskandari v Law Society* [2009] EWHC 2224 (Ch), in particular at [73].

Small claims

7.95   Discontinuance of a claim on the small claims track will not result in a deemed costs order being made (see CPR, r 38.6(3)), but, where the discontinuer has behaved unreasonably, the court may make an award as a matter of discretion (see r 27.14(1)(g)).

Group litigation

7.96   Discontinuance in group litigation is often viewed in a different light from discontinuance in other claims; this is because there are many legitimate reasons why a claimant in those circumstances might choose to discontinue his claim other than his claim being flawed. Each order must, therefore, be decided on its own merits.

7.97   It is often the case that there is an order in the group litigation order which disapplies CPR, r 38.6 for cases on the group litigation register. This issue is dealt with in more detail at **39.40–39.41**.

Enforcement

7.98   It may happen that a claimant discontinues part of his claim, but fails to pay his opponent's costs. If these are the facts, the CPR provide a mechanism by which the claimant may be prevented from continuing with the remainder of his claim unless he pays what is due. CPR, r 38.8 makes the following provisions:

'(1) This rule applies where—

    (a)   proceedings are partly discontinued;

    (b)   a claimant is liable to pay costs under rule 38.6; and

    (c)   the claimant fails to pay those costs within 14 days of—

        (i)   the date on which the parties agreed the sum payable by the claimant; or

        (ii)   the date on which the court ordered the costs to be paid.

(2) Where this rule applies, the court may stay the remainder of the proceedings until the claimant pays the whole of the costs which he is liable to pay under rule 38.6.'

Deemed orders after applications

7.99   Generally speaking, where the court makes no order for costs, that will mean that no party is entitled to costs. There are exceptions, however, in that a deemed order[105] will arise in some situations, as follows:

- where the court makes an order granting permission to appeal;
- where the court makes an order granting permission to apply for judicial review; and
- where the court makes any order or direction sought by a party on an application without notice.

In all of those circumstances, where the court makes no order for costs, it will be deemed to include an order for the applicant's costs in the case.[106] Further details are given at **7.379–7.383**.

---

[105]   Some would argue that these were not proper deemed orders because they arise only if and when the court makes an order; even if this is correct, it is convenient to group them with proper deemed orders, as they are very similar.

[106]   See CPR, r 44.13(1A).

7.100 In summary, deemed costs orders will be made in four situations: a failure to pay a court fee; acceptance of a Part 36 offer; discontinuance; and following a limited range of applications. In so far as all but the second of these situations are concerned, the court may make some different order in its discretion.

COSTS-ONLY MATTERS (NO HEARING ON THE SUBSTANTIVE ISSUES)

7.101 This section deals with the topic of how a court should dispose of a dispute as to the incidence of costs if that is the only issue that the court is asked to determine.

Jurisdiction and discretion

7.102 The fact that all of the substantive issues (that is, the issues other than the incidence of costs) have been settled by consent would not deprive the court of the jurisdiction to adjudicate upon and make a costs order.[107] In this regard, the court's discretion is unfettered; in particular, there is no tradition in those circumstances of making no order for costs.[108] Indeed, as is set out below, the starting point is that if a winner can be identified on a proper basis of agreed or determined facts, the 'general rule' in CPR, r 44.3(2)(a) will apply.

Whether to make an order

7.103 The fact that the court has the power to make a costs order without having adjudicated upon the substantive issues does not mean that the court is obliged to make an order for costs. Indeed, the court is discouraged from doing so unless there is a proper basis of agreed or determined facts upon which the court can decide who has won.[109] Chadwick LJ had the following to say on the topic:[110]

> 'The first question for the court – in every case – is whether it is satisfied that it is in a position to make an order about costs at all ... In addressing that question the court must have regard to the need (if an order about costs is to be made) to have a proper basis of agreed or determined facts upon which to decide, in the light of the principles set out under the other provisions in CPR 44, what order should be made. The general rule, if the court decides to make an order about costs, is that the unsuccessful party will be ordered to pay the costs of the successful party – CPR 44.3(2)(a). But the court may make a different order – CPR 44.3(2)(b). Unless the court is satisfied that it has a proper basis of agreed or determined facts upon which to decide whether the case is one in which it should give effect to "the general rule" – or should make "a different order" (and, if so, what order) – it must accept that it is not in a position to make an order about costs at all. That is not an abdication of the court's function in relation to costs. It is a proper recognition that the course which the parties have adopted in the litigation has led to the position in which the right way in which to discharge that function is to decide not to make an order about costs.'

---

[107] *Brawley v Marczynski (No 1)* [2002] EWCA Civ 756; although pre-CPR, see also *Butcher v Wolfe* [1999] BLR 61.

[108] *Brawley v Marczynski (No 1)* [2002] EWCA Civ 756.

[109] As an example, of a case in which the court declined to exercise its jurisdiction, see *R (on the application of G) v Worcestershire County Council* [2005] EWHC 2332 (Admin). Everything had settled at mediation save for the costs; Collins J found that it was impossible to say that it was obvious that either party would have won.

[110] *BCT Software Solutions Ltd v C Brewer & Sons Ltd* [2003] EWCA Civ 939 at [22].

General approach

7.104 Chadwick LJ went on to give further guidance, which may be summarised as follows:

- the court should be slow to embark on a determination of disputed facts solely in order to put itself in a position to make a decision about costs;
- the court is entitled to say to the parties that if they have not reached an agreement on costs, they have not settled the dispute;
- if the court is unable to decide who is the winner or loser without effectively trying the action, it should make no order as to costs;
- there is no tradition of making no order for costs if the matter has settled without a judicial adjudication;
- it should be recognised that there is likely to be difficulty in deciding who is the winner and loser in more complex cases without embarking on a trial, for example, of cases involving a number of issues and claims for discretionary equitable relief; and
- in straightforward cases it will be reasonably clear from the terms of settlement which party has won or lost, but it will often be the case that neither side has won or lost.

Scott Baker J gave similar guidance for public law cases (see the footnotes);[111] Lord Neuberger MR has confirmed that the principles in public law cases are the same as in private law cases.[112] Thus, in both private and public law cases, much will turn on the ease with which the court is able to determine the facts about the claim and who has won.

Fact-finding and adjudication as to who has won

7.105 The fact that the court has not heard the substantive issues does not deprive the court of the ability to reflect the parties' conduct in the incidence of costs,[113] but if the court is to disapply the general rule that the loser pays,[114] clear findings or agreed facts are necessary.[115] Stanley Burnton LJ has said that it is important that both the work and costs involved in preparing the parties' submissions on costs are proportionate to the

---

[111] *Boxall v Waltham Forest LBC 21 December 2000* (2001) 4 CCL Rep 258 at [22] cited with approval by Pill LJ in *Bahta & Ors, R (on the application of) v Secretary of State for the Home Department & Ors* [2011] EWCA Civ 895 at [7] and by Lord Neuberger MR in *M v Mayor and Burgesses of the London Borough of Croydon* [2012] EWCA Civ 595 at [34]: 'Having considered the authorities, the principles I deduced to be applicable are as follows: (i) the court has power to make a costs order when the substantive proceedings have been resolved without a trial but the parties have not agreed about costs. (ii) it will ordinarily be irrelevant that the Claimant is legally aided; (iii) the overriding objective is to do justice between the parties without incurring unnecessary court time and consequently additional cost; (iv) at each end of the spectrum there will be cases where it is obvious which side would have won had the substantive issues been fought to a conclusion. In between, the position will, in differing degrees, be less clear. How far the court will be prepared to look into the previously unresolved substantive issues will depend on the circumstances of the particular case, not least the amount of costs at stake and the conduct of the parties. (v) in the absence of a good reason to make any other order the fall back is to make no order as to costs. (vi) the court should take care to ensure that it does not discourage parties from settling judicial review proceedings for example by a local authority making a concession at an early stage.' Pill LJ has clarified that (vi) will not allow a party to avoid the cosequenes of non-compliance with a pre-action protocol: *Bahta* at [64].

[112] *M v Mayor and Burgesses of the London Borough of Croydon* [2012] EWCA Civ 595 at [52] to [58].

[113] As examples of this, see *RBG Resources plc v Rastogi* (2005) EWHC 994 (Ch); and *In the matter of Smart-Tel (UK) plc, sub nom OR v Doshi* [2007] BCC 896, Companies Ct.

[114] See **6.31** *et seq.*

[115] *Straker v Tudor Rose (a firm)* [2007] EWCA 368 at [13].

amount at stake.[116] In a different case Rimer LJ explained that if a factual enquiry is required, no party has the right to insist on oral evidence being heard. He explained that the court is entitled to deal with such a matter summarily;[117] it is normally sufficient, he said, that the court reads the evidence and hears the parties' arguments. Whilst his guidance implied that the court would always have the freedom to deal with such issues in a summary way, Rimer LJ went on to say that in an exceptional case (such as where the costs in question are very considerable), it may be consistent with the overriding objective for the court to hear oral evidence.[118] In deciding whether to do this, the fact that the parties have not proceeded to a trial of the substantive issues is often afforded some weight.[119] Ramsey J cited the following pre-CPR judgment of Simon Browne LJ, who was giving a dissenting judgment in a case where the substantive issues had been appealed solely for the purposes of dealing with costs:[120]

> '[Where the only outstanding issues are those relating to costs] an altogether broader approach should be adopted. One which enables the court in a comparatively short time to decide, and decide, moreover, without giving a fully-reasoned judgment, into which general category of discontinuance the case falls. Can it really be an appropriate use of court time (not to mention the parties' ever escalating costs) to resolve in a series of decisions (including perhaps the House of Lords hereafter?) what, in all other respects, is a purely academic question, even if an important one, just so as to deal fairly and properly with the costs incurred by the parties before that question became academic? I would hold not. would suggest instead that the costs can and properly should be dealt with once only, and even then generally on a broad-brush approach.'

Stanley Burnton LJ has commented that no order for costs will be the default order when the judge cannot without disproportionate expenditure of judicial time, if at all, fairly and sensibly make an order in favour of either party.[121]

Discontinuance and consensual dismissal

7.106 A situation in which the court is commonly asked to decide the incidence of costs is where a claimant has discontinued a claim or abandoned a claim. There is a presumption that the discontinuer will pay costs (see **7.82–7.92**), but the court has the power to make a different order. The onus of proving that the court should make some different order lies with the discontinuer; this was explained by Chadwick LJ:[122]

> 'The form in which that Rule is expressed ... makes it clear that the normal order on discontinuance is that the claimant bears the Defendants' costs up to the date on which notice of discontinuance is served. [CPR, r 38.6(1)] makes it clear that the court may order otherwise; but the burden is on the party who seeks to persuade the court that some other consequence should follow; and the task of the court is to consider whether there is some good reason to depart from the normal order.'

---

[116]   *M v Mayor and Burgesses of the London Borough of Croydon* [2012] EWCA Civ 595 at [77].

[117]   *Coyne and another v DRC Distribution Ltd* [2008] EWCA Civ 488 at [68] and [69], per Rimer LJ.

[118]   *Coyne and another v DRC Distribution Ltd* [2008] EWCA Civ 488 at [69] *et seq*, per Rimer LJ.

[119]   By way of example, HHJ Stephen Davies (sitting as a High Court Judge), gave some weight to the fact that a party who alleged poor conduct had chosen not to withdraw a Part 36 Offer upon becoming aware of the facts that led to the allegation; this was one of the factors that persuaded him to deal with allegations summarily: *Pocklington Steel Structures Limited v Cordell Group Limited* (unreported) 9 December 2010, TCC, Manchester District Registry.

[120]   *Vector Investments v JD Williams* [2009] EWHC 3601 (TCC) [25], per Ramsay J, citing *R v Holderness Borough Council Ex parte James Robert Developments* [1993] 1 PLR 108 at 115–119, per Simon Browne LJ.

[121]   *M v Mayor and Burgesses of the London Borough of Croydon* [2012] EWCA Civ 595 at [77].

[122]   *In re Walker Wingsail Systems plc* [2005] EWCA Civ 247 at [24].

Proudman J has explained that the role of the court is limited, and that the court cannot as if by magic look into the hearts and minds of the parties to determine the ultimate truth behind the dispute:[123]

> 'A party who brings a claim takes the risks of the litigation ... The court decides a case on the evidence at trial. It is a misunderstanding of the role of the court to think that the judge can simply look into the parties' hearts and minds to determine the ultimate truth behind the dispute. If for whatever reason a Claimant cannot make good his case on the evidence at trial he must take the consequences of the litigation risk he assumed. It is unjust for the Defendant to bear the costs of an action which the Claimant cannot, for whatever reason ... prove at trial.'

This passage was paraphrased and approved by Moore-Bick LJ.[124]

Supervening events, etc

7.107 As set out above, where a discontinuer has discontinued his claim, the default position is not that there shall be no order as to costs, but that the discontinuing party will bear the costs. Different orders may be appropriate if the reason for discontinuance was an independent supervening event which rendered the outcome of the claim academic (see **7.111–7.113, 7.115**, and **7.118-7.121** for case examples). The event must be independent in the sense that claimant could not invoke such a change if it had resulted from the very fact of the claim; an example would be where the defendant had run out of money by defending the claim.[125] Moreover, the court should consider taking an issues-based approach in suitable cases.[126] Likewise, if the defendant's conduct is such that a discount in his costs should be made, then the fact that the claimant has discontinued should not prevent the court from making such an order; an example would be where a defendant failed to comply with the relevant pre-action protocol.[127] Another example would be where a defendant refused to enter into productive negotiations because of his unreasonable insistence on a term of settlement that he knew (or ought to have known) was unrealistic.[128] It would, however, be wrong to place too much weight on supposed failures to engage in negotiations.[129]

7.108 Where the supposed supervening event is, in reality, nothing more than the claimant becoming alive to the commercial wisdom of continuing with the claim, and where that realisation was based on factors that were, or could have been known at the outset of the claim, there would be no reason for the court relieve the discontinuer of the burden of paying costs.[130] Likewise, a decision to discontinue motivated by practical, pragmatic or financial reasons as opposed to a lack of confidence in the merits of the case will not, without more, assist the discontinuer.[131]

---

[123]　*Maini v Maini* [2009] EWHC 3036 (Ch) at [11].
[124]　*Brookes v HSBC Bank plc; Jemitus v Bank of Scotland plc* [2011] EWCA Civ 354 at [10].
[125]　*Teasdale v HSBC Bank plc, Brookes v HSBC Bank plc* [2010] EWHC 612 (QB), per HHJ Waksman QC (sitting as a Deputy High Court Judge) at [7(5)]. HHJ Waksman QC's judgment was upheld on appeal (*Brookes v HSBC Bank plc; Jemitus v Bank of Scotland plc* [2011] EWCA Civ 354).
[126]　*R v Westminster City Council ex p Chorion plc* [2002] EWCA Civ 1126.
[127]　*Aegis Group plc v Inland Revenue Commissioners* [2005] EWHC 1468.
[128]　*RBG Resources plc (in liquidation)* [2005] EWHC 994 (Ch).
[129]　See, for example, *Bray (t/a Building Co) v Bishop*, 19 June 2009, CA (Longmore and Lloyd LJJ).
[130]　*In re Walker Wingsail Systems plc* [2005] EWCA Civ 247; see also *Teasdale v HSBC Bank plc, Brookes v HSBC Bank plc* [2010] EWHC 612 (QB), per HHJ Waksman QC (sitting as a Deputy High Court Judge) at [7].
[131]　*Maini v Maini* [2009] EWHC 3036 (Ch) at [11]; see also *Teasdale v HSBC Bank plc, Brookes v HSBC*

7.109 Parties should be careful about how they put their arguments at first instance; this is because it is particularly difficult to prove that the court below was wrong within the meaning of CPR, r 52.11(3); and because the court will usually allow the appeal only if the decision of the court below was 'manifestly unjust').[132]

Concessions and compromises

7.110 At the other end of the scale from discontinuance is where the claimant secures concessions that make adjudication superfluous; in between those two extremes are compromises. The approach of the court will depend on the extent to which the claimant can be said to be the victor.[133] Lord Neuberger MR had this to say on the topic:[134]

> '[There is] a sharp difference between (i) a case where a Claimant has been wholly successful whether following a contested hearing or pursuant to a settlement, and (ii) a case where he has only succeeded in part following a contested hearing, or pursuant to a settlement, and (iii) a case where there has been some compromise which does not actually reflect the Claimant's claims. While in every case, the allocation of costs will depend on the specific facts, there are some points which can be made about these different types of case.
>
> In case (i), it is hard to see why the Claimant should not recover all his costs, unless there is some good reason to the contrary. Whether pursuant to judgment following a contested hearing, or by virtue of a settlement, the Claimant can, at least absent special circumstances, say that he has been vindicated, and, as the successful party, that he should recover his costs. In the latter case, the Defendants can no doubt say that they were realistic in settling, and should not be penalised in costs, but the answer to that point is that the Defendants should, on that basis, have settled before the proceedings were issued ...
>
> In case (ii), when deciding how to allocate liability for costs after a trial, the court will normally determine questions such as how reasonable the Claimant was in pursuing the unsuccessful claim, how important it was compared with the successful claim, and how much the costs were increased as a result of the Claimant pursuing the unsuccessful claim. Given that there will have been a hearing, the court will be in a reasonably good position to make findings on such questions. However, where there has been a settlement, the court will, at least normally, be in a significantly worse position to make findings on such issues than where the case has been fought out. In many such cases, the court will be able to form a view as to the appropriate costs order based on such issues; in other cases, it will be much more difficult. I would accept the argument that, where the parties have settled the Claimant's substantive claims on the basis that he succeeds in part, but only in part, there is often much to be said for concluding that there is no order for costs. ... However, where there is not a clear winner, so much would depend on the particular facts. In some such cases, it may help to consider who would have won if the matter had proceeded to trial, as, if it is tolerably clear, it may, for instance support or undermine the contention that one of the two claims was stronger than the other ...

Bank plc [2010] EWHC 612 (QB), per HHJ Waksman QC (sitting as a Deputy High Court Judge) at [7(4)]. HHJ Waksman QC's judgment was upheld on appeal (*Brookes v HSBC Bank plc; Jemitus v Bank of Scotland plc* [2011] EWCA Civ 354).

[132] *BCT Software Solutions Ltd v C Brewer & Sons Ltd* [2003] EWCA Civ 939.

[133] See *Harripaul v Lewisham LBC* [2012] EWCA Civ 266 at [10] in which a concession resulted in judgment being entered for the appellant; Rimer LJ confirmed that the appellant was to be regarded as the successful party and that the starting point was that she should be entitled to her costs; he went on to say that the making by the respondent of the concession is a factor that must be brought into consideration.

[134] *M v Mayor and Burgesses of the London Borough of Croydon* [2012] EWCA Civ 595 at [60] to [63].

In case (iii), the court is often unable to gauge whether there is a successful party in any respect, and, if so, who it is. In such cases, therefore, there is an even more powerful argument that the default position should be no order for costs. However, in some such cases, it may well be sensible to look at the underlying claims and inquire whether it was tolerably clear who would have won if the matter had not settled. If it is, then that may well strongly support the contention that the party who would have won did better out of the settlement, and therefore did win.'

Case examples may be divided into two groups: those in which there is a clear winner (ie, the first of Lord Neuberger MR's categories) and those in which it is not clear who has won (ie the second and third of those categories). Each is dealt with in turn.

Examples of cases where there was a clear winner or loser

Interim relief and undertakings

7.111 The first case example is *Fox Gregory Ltd v Hamptons Group Ltd*.[135] The claimant used to employ a third party ('the employee') who after leaving their employment took up employment with the defendant. The employee had removed confidential property before leaving the claimant's employment. The claimant asked for an undertaking for delivery of the property. This request was initially ignored but after a time the defendant indicated that it was looking into the matter. The claimant issued a claim for injunctive relief. The defendant then voluntarily gave the undertakings sought; the claim was dismissed by consent. The only outstanding issue was the costs.

7.112 The judge at first instance found that the defendant had won. Arden LJ disagreed:

> 'The next question is whether it would be possible to say who was the winner and who was the loser. The only issue, in my judgment, was whether interim relief in the form of the undertakings would have been given if the undertakings had not been given. That, as I see it, is the substance of the issue before the court on 29 November. As I have explained, no significant costs were incurred on the other matters. In my judgment, if one looks at that issue then it is clear that the winner was Fox Gregory, rather than Hamptons, because Hamptons had to give those undertakings, and for this reason I would take the view that the judge was wrong in principle to say that Hamptons was substantially the winner.'

Grant of lease

7.113 The next case example is *Lay v Drexler*.[136] The claimant brought a claim for the grant of a new tenancy; the dispute was not about the grant of a proposed new lease, but about its terms. About a year after issue of proceedings, the claimant indicated that it no longer wanted a new lease. The claim was dismissed by consent. The judge at first instance made no order for costs on the basis that the claim had been settled; he believed that there was insufficient material before him to allow him to exercise his discretion one way or the other. Evans-Lombe J (sitting in the Court of Appeal) disagreed. He found that the situation was analogous to discontinuance and that the claimant should therefore bear the costs.

---

[135] [2006] EWCA Civ 1544.
[136] [2007] EWCA Civ 464.

Split on liability

7.114 In *Onay v Brown* Goldring LJ (with whom Toulson and Carnworth LJJ agreed) found that a trial judge had erred in not giving adequate weight to the fact that acceptance of an offer to settle liability in a 75/25 split in the claimant's favour was a win; to describe it as anything else would be 'wholly artificial'.[137] In a different case, Mann J acknowledged the jurisdiction to make an issues-based costs order, but he declined to do so on the facts of the case before him.[138]

Non-financial goals

7.115 Where a supervening event has made it unnecessary to continue with a claim, and where it is not possible to know who would have won or what would have happened had the supervening event not occurred, an order that there be no order to costs might be appropriate.[139] Where, however, the claim has been discontinued as a result of a supervening event which was within the control of the defendant and which was in reality a capitulation to the claimant's strong case, the appropriate order would usually be an award to the claimant. An example would be where a claimant pursued a claim with the aim of keeping a building open; after the issue of proceedings, the defendant took steps that ensured exactly that which the claimant wanted; Crane J ordered the defendant to pay the claimant's costs.[140]

Concessions on appeal

7.116 A concession made on an appeal after permission has been given may also amount to success,[141] as may a concession in judicial review proceedings.[142] Where the concession has been made for commercial reasons unconnected with the judicial review, the claimant may find himself going without his costs.[143]

Compromise for far less than was claimed

7.117 Acceptance of an offer which was very significantly less than the amount claimed can amount to a sufficient absence of a win to displace the general rule that the successful party will be awarded costs.[144]

---

[137] *Onay v Brown* [2009] EWCA Civ 775 at [29(5)].
[138] *Rambus Inc v Hynx Semiconductor UK Ltd* [2004] EWHC 2313 (Pat).
[139] Although a pre-CPR case, *R v Liverpool City Council ex p Newman & Ors* [1993] 5 Admin LR 669 is an example of this.
[140] *R v North & West Devon Health Authority & Ors ex p Bowhay & Ors* [2001] 60 BMLR 228; in a similar vein, see *R (on the application of J) v Hackney London Borough Council* [2010] EWHC 3021 (Admin) (McKenna J). Another examples is *Thomas Brown Estates Ltd v Hunters Partners* [2012] EWHC 30 (QB), in which Eder J awarded a claimant its costs after it became unnecessary for it to continue its claim for declarations as the defendant had abandoned its case concerning the claimant's use of a trading name.
[141] *AB & Ors v British Coal Corporation* [2007] EWHC 1406 (QB).
[142] *Boxall v Waltham Forest LBC* (2001) 4 CCL Rep 258 (Scott Baker J).
[143] *Slater Ellison v Law Society* [2002] All ER (D) 335 (Feb).
[144] *Hooper v Biddle* [2006] EWHC 2995 (Ch).

Examples of cases where there was no clear winner or loser

Partial success: undertakings and damages

7.118 *Promar International Ltd v Clarke*[145] is an example of a case in which there was no clear winner or loser. The claimant (who was the defendant's former employer) brought proceedings for an injunction and damages for breach of a restrictive covenant. The claim was disputed but the covenant was accepted. An interim injunction was granted; this was soon replaced by undertaking until trial or further order. The trial took place on 15 December 2004. By that stage, the restrictive covenant had all but expired. The claimant sought damages of L133,000. During the course of opening submissions the defendant made an unconditional offer to give an undertaking. This satisfied the claimant, who then abandoned the claim for damages. The only issue that the parties were unable to resolve was the costs.

7.119 The judge made no order for costs (this was on the basis that the claimant had secured something of value, yet had not proceeded with the rest of the claim). The claimant appealed but lost that appeal. Hallett LJ said:

> 'The only message that this case may send out is to reiterate and reinforce the warnings given by this court in *BCT Software and Venture Finance* of the dangers of trial judges being persuaded to decide issues of costs when all issues, save costs, have been settled or resolved without the necessity for a judgment.'

Supervening insolvency

7.120 A claim may be discontinued not as a result of one or other party succeeding, but because some independent supervening event has made the outcome of the claim irrelevant (see **7.88** onwards). This was the case in *Everton v World Professional Billiards and Snooker Association (Promotions) Ltd*,[146] when the claimant became bankrupt: Gray J ordered that there be no order for costs. Where a claim was brought against several defendants but was discontinued because the insolvency of the main defendants made it uneconomic to continue, Lewison J declined to relieve the claimant of the obligation to pay costs; this was on the basis that the claimant had elected not to proceed against the remaining defendant.[147] Similarly, Norris J ordered a claimant to pay costs in a case where a case had been maintained against a secondary defendant; he found that the court should not 'do anything to encourage litigants to pursue multiple parties to cater for remote contingencies'.[148]

7.121 In summary, the fact that the court has not heard the substantive issues will not prevent the court from making a costs order, but the court ought to exercise some caution before making such an order. Where the court does make an order, that order would normally follow the general rule that the loser pays, but the court can make some different order if the circumstances merit such a step.

---

[145] [2006] EWCA Civ 332.

[146] *Everton v World Professional Billiards and Snooker Association (Promotions) Ltd* (unreported) 13 December 2001, QB.

[147] *Jass v Blackburn* [2003] EWHC 2963 (Ch).

[148] *Dhillon v Siddiqui et al* [2010] EWHC 1400 (Ch) at [36].

ORDERS WHERE PROCEEDINGS ARE NOT ISSUED

7.122 This section considers the topic of whether a party can obtain an order for costs where proceedings have not been issued. Where the parties agree the incidence of costs but cannot agree quantum, then the appropriate mechanism for assessing the costs is by bringing a Part 8 claim pursuant to CPR, r 44.12A, which is discussed at **7.384–7.398**.

Claimant

7.123 Where a claimant's opponent refuses to pay costs, then he must issue proceedings. If there is agreement as to the incidence of costs, then costs-only proceedings should be issued. Where there is no such agreement, the claimant will have to bring either a Part 7 or a Part 8 claim depending upon the cause of action that he has (see below).

7.124 If it has not been compromised, then it may be appropriate to bring a claim on the original cause of action. Where there has been a compromise, it may be appropriate to sue upon the compromise, depending on its terms.

7.125 The existence of costs-only proceedings does not detract from the availability of other means of bringing the matter before the court. CPD, art 17.11 makes the following provisions:

> 'Nothing in this rule [relating to costs-only proceedings] prevents a person from issuing a claim form under Part 7 or Part 8 to sue on an agreement made in settlement of a dispute where that agreement makes provision for costs, nor from claiming in that case an order for costs or a specified sum in respect of costs.'

7.126 Contrary to what was said in the first edition of the book, if a claim settled pre-issue by way of a Part 36 offer being accepted, it is not possible to rely on that acceptance as giving rise to a free-standing right to assessment; Moore-Bick LJ had this to say on the point:[149]

> 'An order for costs cannot exist in a vacuum divorced from any substantive proceedings and accordingly an order for costs cannot be deemed to have been made under rule 44.12(1)(b) if a Part 36 offer is made and accepted before any proceedings have been commenced.'

As such, costs-only proceedings must be brought to obtain an order, regardless of whether the pre-issue compromise was or was not in accordance with the procedure in Part 36.

7.127 If the person who is served with Notice of Commencement wished to contend that the claimant was not entitled to costs, he could make an application pursuant to CPD, art 28.1(4), which provides:

> '(a) A party who is served with a notice of commencement ... may apply to a costs judge or a district judge to determine whether the party who served it is entitled to commence detailed assessment proceedings.
>
> (b) On hearing such an application the orders which the court may make include: an order allowing the detailed assessment proceedings to continue, or an order setting aside the notice of commencement.'

---

[149] *Solomon v Cromwell Group Plc* [2011] EWCA Civ 1584 at [16].

Alternatively, an application could be made pursuant to CPR Part 11 (this being the procedure to dispute the court's jurisdiction), but only where the circumstances made such a course of action appropriate.

7.128 Occasionally the claimant will wish to argue that not only has the incidence of costs been agreed, but so has quantum; if those are the circumstances, it would not be appropriate to make an application pursuant to CPD, art 36.2 (which is a procedure for dealing with disputes as to compromise of costs); this is because that article is limited to purported agreement made 'in the course of proceedings'.

Defendant

7.129 If a defendant has successfully defeated a claim such that the claimant did not issue proceedings, it will be procedurally difficult for the defendant to obtain an order for his costs. This is because a defendant, unlike a claimant, would not normally be able to issue proceedings for the original cause of action.

7.130 The difficulty that such a defendant would face is highlighted by the way in which s 51(1) of the Senior Courts Act 1981 is worded. That section makes provision for the court to make orders for the costs 'of and incidental to proceedings': if there are no proceedings, that power will not exist. For the reasons set out below, a defendant would face almost insuperable procedural problems in securing an award of costs.

7.131 If there has been a compromise that the claimant will pay costs notwithstanding the fact that no proceedings have been issued, then the defendant could sue upon that compromise, but it would almost never happen that a claimant would agree to such a compromise in the first place.

7.132 In theory, a defendant could himself initiate proceedings—perhaps in the guise of a claim for costs payable as damages or just an unabashed claim for costs—but a defendant who wished to do that (or claimant as he would have become by that stage) would face arguments about such a claim being an abuse of process.

7.133 Even if the defendant/claimant were able to avoid having his claim struck out as being an abuse of process, he would still face difficulties in proving that the court has the power to make an award. This is because the pre-action costs will generally not be 'of or incidental' to the proceedings: they will be of or incidental to some other claim—a claim which was never brought.

7.134 This jurisdictional problem would not be the only difficulty a defendant/claimant would face. Even if the defendant/claimant were able to show that the court had jurisdiction to make an award of costs, he would still have difficulties in persuading the court to exercise its discretion in his favour. Whilst not binding on any court, HHJ Coulson QC (now Coulson J) considered a similar issue in a claim where the claimant had abandoned a significant part of its claim as a result of liaison with the defendant in accordance with a pre-action protocol. (Those abandoned issues were so significant that they amounted to a separate claim.) The issue was whether the defendant could recover the costs of the claim that was never brought. The judge found that the defendant could not recover those costs:[150]

---

[150] *McGlinn v Waltham Contractors Ltd* [2005] EWHC 1419 (TCC) at [14].

'It would be wrong in principle to penalise the Claimant for abandoning claims which the Defendants had demonstrated were not going to succeed, because to do so would be to penalise the Claimant for doing the very thing which the Protocol is designed to achieve.'

In other words, the purpose of the pre-action period is to allow the parties to try to settle the matter (by withdrawal, if appropriate), and it would not be right to penalise a claimant for having taken a sensible decision not to issue proceedings. HHJ Coulson QC went on to say that an order would be appropriate only where there were exceptional circumstances, such as unreasonable conduct.

7.135 The wasted costs jurisdiction does not apply to cases where proceedings have not been issued.[151] The combined effect of these things is that a defendant who has successfully defeated a claim prior to the issue of proceedings would find it almost impossible to get an order for his costs. It is perhaps because of this that it is not unknown for defendants to encourage claimants to issue proceedings before putting all their cards on the table; for obvious reasons such a practice is contrary to the overriding objective and is therefore not to be encouraged.

NON-PARTY COSTS ORDERS

7.136 Non-party costs orders, or 'third-party costs orders', as they are also known, are orders against persons who are not parties to the litigation, but who are in some way connected to it. An archetypal example is where an order is made against a non-party director who has used his party company for his own purposes. Broadly speaking, in order to obtain a non-party costs order, the court must be satisfied that such an 'exceptional' order is justified, and that the conduct of the non-party has caused the costs in question to be incurred. Different considerations apply to some types of non-party costs order, however, as will be explained in due course.

Jurisdiction

7.137 The power to make a non-party costs order most commonly arises out of s 51 of the Senior Courts Act 1981 (as amended) ('SCA 1981'). The House of Lords has clarified that s 51(3) of that Act[152] provided a sufficiently wide discretion to permit the court to make costs orders against a person who, at the material time, had not been a party to the litigation.[153] The Act was amended in 1990,[154] but those amendments did not diminish the ambit of the court's powers;[155] there is no reason to believe that subsequent amendments wrought any changes in this respect.

7.138 The jurisdiction is statutory and does not depend on the common law. In particular, it does not depend on the presence of champertous maintenance; if the relationship between a party and a non-party is champertous, then that will be merely a

---

[151] *Byrne v South Sefton Health Authority* [2001] EWCA Civ 1904.
[152] The relevant part reads as follows: '(3) The court shall have full power to determine by whom and to what extent the costs are to be paid.'
[153] *Aiden Shipping Ltd v Interbulk Ltd* [1986] 1 AC 965; early examples exist of the court exercising the jurisdiction: see *Bacal Contracting Ltd v Modern Engineering (Bristol) Ltd* [1980] 2 All ER 655.
[154] Courts and Legal Services Act 1990, s 4.
[155] *Nordstern Allgemeine Versicherungs AG v Internav Ltd* [1999] 2 Lloyd's Rep 139.

factor to be taken into account.[156] Indeed, it is worth emphasising that the jurisdiction is a simple matter of the exercise of a discretion to order a party to pay costs; as Laws LJ remarked:[157]

> '[It would not be desirable if] the exercise of this jurisdiction becomes over-complicated by reference to authority. Indeed I think it has become overburdened. Section 51 confers a discretion not confined by specific limitations. While the learning is, with respect, important in indicating the kind of considerations upon which the court will focus, it must not be treated as a rule-book.'

7.139 Powers other than under SCA 1981, s 51 exist (such as the power to make awards against solicitors arising out of the inherent jurisdiction of the court),[158] but it is rarely necessary to consider powers other than those conferred by statute, not least because the statutory powers are so wide-ranging. Under the CPR, the only circumstances in which those powers are relevant is when an order is sought against a legal representative, and even then it will be relevant in only very limited circumstances (see below).

Procedure

7.140 Procedural issues, defaults in particular, may be relevant to the exercise of the court's discretion. The relevant procedure is contained in CPR, r 48.2. In summary, the non-party must be added as a party to the proceedings for the purposes of addressing the issue of costs, and he must be given a reasonable opportunity to attend a hearing at which the court will consider the matter further. A failure to comply with those requirements may amount to a denial of the non-party's fundamental rights,[159] and that is capable of being a reason for the court refusing to hear the application.[160] It is desirable that there should be a concise statement of the grounds and essential allegations of fact relied on by the applicant. That concise statement could be amended or supplemented, if the need arose.[161] The application should normally be determined by the trial judge.[162]

7.141 Whilst not a formal procedural requirement, Balcombe LJ has commented that the applicant should, at the earliest opportunity, notify the non-party of the possibility that the applicant may seek to apply for costs against him.[163] Lewison J held that it was appropriate to restrict entitlement to such reasonable period of time after the notification as to allow the non-party to reflect upon his position.[164] Likewise, whilst there were also other factors at play, Sales J reversed a non-party costs order on the basis that the non-party had not been given proper notice that an order might be sought against him.[165] Nonetheless, Proudman J has explained that early warning is not a stand-alone requirement which will operate conclusively against the non-party; it is no

---

[156] *Nordstern Allgemeine Versicherungs AG v Internav Ltd* [1999] 2 Lloyd's Rep 139.
[157] *Petromec Inc v Petroleo Brasileiro* [2006] EWCA Civ 1038 at [19].
[158] For a description of this, see *Ridehalgh v Horsefield* [1994] Ch 205 at 211; as an example of that jurisdiction in action, see *Edwards v Edwards* [1958] 2 All ER 179.
[159] As a pre-Human Rights Act 1998 example of this, see *Re Land and Property Trust Co plc (No 4)* [1994] 1 BCLC 232, CA.
[160] See, for example, *Barndeal Ltd v Cherrywalk Properties Ltd* [2005] EWHC 1377 (QB), per Newman J.
[161] *Vaughan v (1) Jones & (2) Fowler* [2006] EWHC 2123 (Ch), per Richards J.
[162] *Equitas Ltd v Horace Holman & Co Ltd* [2008] EWHC 2287 (Comm), per Andrew Smith J; see also *Symphony Group plc v Hodgson* [1994] QB 193.
[163] *Symphony Group plc v Hodgson* [1994] QB 193.
[164] *Brampton Manor (Leisure) v McLean* [2007] EWHC 3340 (Ch).
[165] *Bank of Baroda v Patel* [2008] EWHC 3390 (Ch).

more than a material consideration, albeit a highly material consideration.[166] Sir Andrew Morritt C has confirmed that that the giving of prompt notice of a possible claim for a non-party costs order is not a condition of an order, but is a 'material consideration in determining whether to make one and, if so, to what extent'.[167]

Evidence

7.142 Notwithstanding its noteworthy nature, an application for a non-party costs order is still an application for costs and, therefore, there is a limit to the extent to which the court is able proportionately to determine contested issues of fact. This general principle does not stretch so far as to preclude the determination of contested issues of fact. Rather, the procedure is comparable to that on a summary judgment application or on a contested winding-up petition.[168] Unlike the jurisdiction to make a wasted costs order, there is no requirement that the issues must be capable of being dealt with summarily.[169] Burton J has said that there would be exceptional cases where, in the interests of fairness, the procedure can be adapted to allow evidence to be given orally and for witnesses to be cross-examined:[170]

> 'If I were to say ... that there can never be in a s 51 application an order for evidence to be given orally, in chief or cross examination ... then that would be, in my judgment, a licence for people to be able to give evidence in writing which they knew could never be tested. On the other hand, if this is the first time that an order is made and as a result orders will be sought on other occasions, that does not open too wide a floodgate, because I accompany it, and I am sure any other judge would accompany it, with a substantial reminder that the procedure is ordinarily summary, and that the procedure is ordinarily intended to reflect all the caveats which the s 51 jurisprudence and the reported cases have set up for us to bear in mind. One, these are ancillary proceedings, and should not grow out of control into satellite litigation. Two, proportionality must always be considered. Three, it must always be borne in mind that the ordinary process is a summary process.'

Burton J here identified three safeguards governing oral evidence. Those safeguards are that it must be borne in mind that the proceedings are ancillary proceedings and that they should not grow out of control into satellite litigation; that proportionality must always be considered; and that it must always be borne in mind that the ordinary process is a summary process. That said, circumstances will arise where cross-examination is mandatory; in a case in which the court below had made adverse findings as to a non-party's motives on the basis of statements alone, HHJ Anthony Thornton QC (sitting a Judge of the High Court) found that those findings were flawed because the non-parties had not been given opportunity to answer the criticisms in cross-examination.[171]

7.143 Where they were made in proceedings not involving the same parties, judicial findings are generally inadmissible as evidence of the facts (not being matters of record) upon which they were based.[172] This has the potential to cause difficulties in respect of findings made before the non-party was added as a party. In practice, the court is, in

---

[166]   *Europeans Ltd v Commissioners for HM Revenue and Customs* [2011] EWHC 948 (Ch) at [30].
[167]   *Farrell and another v Direct Accident Management Services Ltd* [2009] EWCA Civ 769 at [11].
[168]   *Total Spares & Supplies Ltd v Antares SRL* [2006] EWHC 1537 (Ch), per Richards J.
[169]   *Robertson Research International Ltd v ABG Exploration BV* (1999) *The Times*, November 3, QBD (Pat Ct), per Laddie J.
[170]   *Grecoair Inc v Tilling* [2009] EWHC 115 at [42].
[171]   *Dweck v Fostater (Defendant) and Rowbury et al (Third Parties)* [2010] EWHC 1874 (QB).
[172]   *Hollington v F Hewthorn & Co Ltd* [1943] KB 587.

appropriate circumstances, able to avoid the inconveniences that this principle might cause. This is because the procedure of deciding an application for a non-party costs award is summary and is not hidebound by the rules of evidence.[173] An unconstrained approach would be justified only where the non-party was sufficiently close to the original proceedings that he would be kept from injustice.[174]

Privilege and disclosure

7.144 In general there will be no disclosure for the purposes of deciding whether to make a non-party costs order, but this will not always be the case. That said, this will not always be the case; Blake J had this to say on the topic:[175]

> 'If the court decides that it is necessary and in the interests of justice to make a disclosure order, it may proceed to give a detailed order within its general powers under the CPR to remove outstanding issues that may be the source of delay and further expense if unaddressed. Such an order may include inspection of documents by the court where there is a clear issue as to whether privilege attaches to them.'

Drawing upon these comments and also upon Laddie J's comments that the court should exercise its considerable administrative powers to ensure that an application for a non-party costs order should be dealt with as speedily and inexpensively as possible,[176] Burton J approached the issue of disclosure by identifying the live issues and by limiting disclosure to those issues.[177] Burton J went on to conclude that communications passing between a legal representative and his client were not covered by legal professional privilege if the client acted for some criminal purpose; he found that this was the case regardless of whether it was the client himself who had the criminal intention, or whether some other person was using the client as his innocent tool.[178]

Categories of order

7.145 Non-party costs orders are categorised on the following way.

- *Category one: controllers*: where the non-party has had a hand in controlling the proceedings; this category will include directors and shadow directors, liquidators and receivers, 'active' shareholders, and office holders (see **7.155-7.170**).
- *Category two: funders*: where the non-party has maintained or financed the proceedings; this category will include pure funders, commercial funders, insurers, and unions (see **7.171-7.190**).
- *Category three: legal representatives*: where the non-party is a legal representative of a party (see **7.191-7.201**).
- *Category four: causative persons*: where the non-party has caused the proceedings (see **7.202**).

---

[173] *Brendon v Spiro* [1938] 1 KB 176 at 192, cited with approval in *Bahai v Rashidian* [1985] 1 WLR 1337 at 1343 and 1345H.

[174] *Globe Equities Ltd v Kotrie* [1999] BLR 232 at para 18(6).

[175] *Thomson v Berkhampsted Collegiate School* [2009] EWHC 2374 (QB) at [16].

[176] *Robertson Research International Ltd v ABG Exploration BV* (1999) *The Times*, November 3, QBD (Pat Ct) at [40]; Laddie J's comments were made in a context other than disclosure.

[177] *Owners and/or demise charterers of dredger 'Kamal XXVI' and barge 'Kamal XXIV' v Owners of ship 'Ariela'* [2010] EWHC 2531 (Comm) at [10]–[12].

[178] *Owners and/or demise charterers of dredger 'Kamal XXVI' and barge 'Kamal XXIV' v Owners of ship 'Ariela'* [2010] EWHC 2531 (Comm) at [25].

- **Category five: related persons**: where the non-party is a party to related proceedings which were heard at the same time as the index proceedings but which were not consolidated with them (see **7.203**).
- **Category six: group litigation**: where the non-party has an interest in the proceedings by reason of the claim being a test claim in group litigation or representative proceedings (see **7.204** and **.205**).

The categories, which were formulated by Balcombe LJ, are known as the *Symphony Group* categories;[179] they are not mutually exclusive. There is one further category that can be added, namely, tribunals.

7.146 Each of the *Symphony Group* categories is dealt with consecutively, but first there is a brief discussion of both the putative need for the circumstances to be exceptional, and of the relevance of causation between conduct and costs. Because of the abundance of authority on the topic, and because the very first category comprises those authorities, the focus is on non-party orders against directors. Even though he may be interested in one of the other *Symphony Group* categories, the reader would do no harm by reading 'category one: controllers'.

Exceptionality

7.147 In the days before the true law had been fully clarified, Balcombe LJ explained that a non-party costs order would always be 'exceptional' and that any application for such an order should be regarded with 'considerable caution'. Even at that stage, the court recognised that it was not a hidebound jurisdiction, in that Balcombe LJ implied that there were degrees of exceptionality.[180] In due course Phillips LJ made the following comments about what was meant by 'exceptional':[181]

> 'The test is whether they [ie the factors that are said to make the case exceptional] are extraordinary in the context of the entire range of litigation that comes to the courts.'

This affirmed the existence of the test, but—importantly—it made it clear that the test was whether the matter was extraordinary in the context of everything that the court sees, rather than extraordinary in the context of the particular class of claim which was in question.

7.148 The present understanding of the law seems to be that there is an exceptionality test,[182] but that it does not confine the court in any undesirable way; this is because it is merely a test of whether the case is out of the ordinary run of things.[183] Lord Brown, giving the judgment of their Lordships, said:[184]

> 'Although costs orders against non-parties are to be regarded as "exceptional", exceptional in this context means no more than outside the ordinary run of cases where parties pursue or defend claims for their own benefit and at their own expense. The ultimate question in any such "exceptional" case is whether in all the circumstances it is just to make the order. It

---

179   See *Symphony Group plc v Hodgson* [1994] QB 193 at 197.
180   *Symphony Group plc v Hodgson* [1994] QB 179.
181   *TGA Chapman Ltd v Christopher and Sun Alliance* [1998] 2 All ER 873 at 20.
182   See below; but compare this with *Globe Equities Ltd v Globe Legal Services Ltd* [1999] BLR 232, where it was said that the test of exceptionality should not be elevated into a precondition to the exercise of the power to make a costs order against a non-party.
183   *Mills v Birchall (sub nom Dolphin Quays Developments v Mills)* [2008] EWCA Civ 385 at [74], per Collins LJ.
184   *Dymocks Franchise Systems (NSW) Pty Ltd v Todd* [2004] UKPC 39 at [25(i)].

must be recognised that this is inevitably to some extent a fact-specific jurisdiction and that there will often be a number of different considerations in play, some militating in favour of an order, some against.'

Lord Brown's comments were not binding (he was hearing an appeal in the Privy Council), but they were soon taken up by the Court of Appeal,[185] which showed itself willing to lift the corporate veil in appropriate circumstances. That said, it remains the case that it will be genuinely exceptional for an order for the payment of costs to be made against a non-party where the applicant had a cause of action against the non-party and could have joined him as a party to the original proceedings. This is because joinder as a party to the proceedings gives the person concerned all the protection conferred by the rules.[186]

7.149 In practice, the test of exceptionality will often be satisfied merely by the situation which exists; in those circumstances the court's attention will be focused on the other factors, such as whether it would be just to make the order sought. Indeed, there are circumstances (such as where a director has funded and controlled a claim for his own benefit) where the making of a non-party order would be the 'ordinary consequence' of the state of affairs in hand.[187] Even in those circumstances, the issue of exceptionality would be relevant, because whether a case is 'exceptional' may be a factor to be taken into account in the exercise of the court's discretion.[188]

Causation

7.150 As the true law has gradually been discovered, the need for the court to find a direct causative link between conduct and costs has progressively diminished.[189] Whilst, in the majority of cases, there will be a direct causal link, it is now known that this is not a necessary ingredient. When the jurisdiction was first discovered, conventional teaching was that there must be a causal link; Simon Brown LJ spoke of it being a 'necessary precondition':[190]

'Proof of causation is a necessary pre-condition of the making of a section 51 order against a non-party, as to which there is ample authority and, as I understand it, no dispute.'

7.151 In any event, even when this was believed to be the law, there was never a 'but for' test (ie a test of 'but for' the conduct of the non-party, the costs would not have been incurred). In this regard, Morritt LJ had the following to say:[191]

'[Counsel for the non-party] submitted that the proper question was "but for the exceptional circumstances would the costs sought have been incurred". I do not accept that submission. I accept that the costs claimed must have been caused to some extent by the non-party against whom the order is sought for otherwise it is hard to envisage any circumstance in which it could be just to order the non-party to pay them. But I do not see why they must be caused by all the factors which render the case exceptional. For example, one of the factors

[185] *Goodwood Recoveries Ltd v Breen* [2005] EWCA Civ 414.
[186] *Oriakhel v Vickers* [2008] EWCA Civ 748 at [31], per Jacob LJ citing *Symphony Group plc v Hodgson* [1994] QB 193 at 203 with approval.
[187] See, for example, *Dymocks Franchise Systems (NSW) Pty Ltd v Todd* [2004] UKPC 39 at [25], per Lord Brown.
[188] *Globe Equities Ltd v Globe Legal Services Ltd* [1999] BLR 232.
[189] See P Gearon 'Third Parties Beware' (2006) 156 NLJ 7238, pp 1312–1313.
[190] *Hamilton v Al Fayed* [2003] QB 1175 at [54], per Simon Brown LJ.
[191] *Globe Equities Ltd v Globe Legal Services Ltd* [1999] BLR 232 at 241 (para 28).

likely to be present in most, if not all, cases where an order is made is that the litigation was for the benefit of the non-party; but that is no reason to require that the costs were all incurred in obtaining that benefit.'

7.152 In a similar vein, Rix LJ rejected the notion that the conduct had to be the 'effective cause' of the costs.[192]

7.153 The court's understanding of the law developed step by step, and in 2006 Richards J explained that circumstances might exist where a causative link between conduct and costs would not be an essential ingredient at all. His view was based on an analysis of the authorities; in particular he noted the following extract from *Dymocks Franchise System (NSW) Pty Ltd v Todd*:[193]

> 'Although the position may well be different when a number of non-parties act in concert, their Lordships are content to assume for the purposes of this application that a non-party could not *ordinarily* be made liable for costs if those costs would in any event have been incurred even without such non-party's involvement in the proceedings.'

The emphasis was Richards J's own; he went on to draw the following conclusion:[194]

> 'It cannot in my judgment any longer be said that causation is a necessary pre-condition to an order for costs against a non-party. Causation will often be a vital factor but there may be cases where, in accordance with principle, it is just to make an order for costs against a non-party who cannot be said to have caused the costs in question.'

7.154 Thus, it is not necessary to have a direct causal link, although it would be a mistake to believe that causation is no longer relevant: in many cases it will go to the very heart of the exercise of the court's discretion. It should be remembered that the factual situation which led Richards J to come to the conclusion that a causative link was not required was, on any analysis, unusual.[195] The relevance of this is that it would probably only be in unusual circumstances that the court would make an order in the absence of a causative link. Common sense dictates that, in most cases, it is likely to be one of only a handful of issues that the court will focus its attention on.

Category one: controllers

7.155 Where a non-party directs and manages a claim or a defence, he places himself at risk of being ordered to pay costs. Non-party costs orders are discretionary, and so the ultimate question is always whether in all the circumstances it would be just to make the order.[196] The court must take into account all the facts of the case, including the conduct of the proceedings.[197]

---

[192] *Goodwood Recoveries Ltd v Breen* [2005] EWCA Civ 414 at [65].
[193] *Total Spares & Supplies Ltd v Antares SRL* [2006] EWHC 1537 (Ch) at [52], per Richards J; the extract was originally from *Dymocks Franchise System (NSW) Pty Ltd v Todd* [2004] 1 WLR 2807 at [20].
[194] *Total Spares & Supplies Ltd v Antares SRL* [2006] EWHC 1537 (Ch) at [54], per Richards J.
[195] The conduct of the non-party was unrelated to control or funding of the proceedings; instead, he had moved assets away from one of the parties in such a way as to make it 'judgment proof'. That conduct could not in any sense be said to be causative of the costs of the litigation, but was clearly germane in a wider sense.
[196] See, for example, *Dymocks Franchise Systems (NSW) Pty Ltd v Todd* [2004] UKPC 39 at [25]; and *Mills v Birchall & Anor* [2008] EWCA Civ 385 at [30] and [74].
[197] *DNA Productions (Europe) Ltd v Manoukian* [2008] EWHC 2627 at [6(ii)].

7.156 The types of non-party who fall into this category include directors, receivers, liquidators, etc, but it can also include 'active' shareholders and, on occasion, persons such as family members[198] and even local authorities.[199] This diversity in the types of person against whom an order may be made illustrates the fact that it is not the status of the person that is determinative of the matter, but what that person does in the claim and what role he chooses to play. In this regard, a central concept is that of the 'real party' (otherwise know as the 'real party interested',[200] or the 'real litigant'),[201] which Evans-Lombe J described thus:[202]

> 'The fundamental contrast is between a director who bona fide pursues unsuccessful litigation in the name of the company for the benefit of the company, but where the company cannot pay the order for costs against it, for the benefit of its creditors, and where the director in question is the real litigant in the sense that the court can be satisfied that without his initiative and finance the litigation would not have been pursued by the company, and who stood, albeit with others including creditors, to benefit materially from its success.'

Where two or more people have conspired to become the real parties, then an order may be made against them that is joint and several.[203]

7.157 In a similar vein, Lord Brown said a real party was a person who was: 'not so much facilitating access to justice by the party funded as himself gaining access to justice for his own purposes'; Lord Brown also went on to explain that the real party need not be the only party with an interest in the matter.[204] It is often the case that the court's first task is to decide whether the non-party in question was, in truth, the real party (or, more accurately, *a* real party). It is instructive to examine this issue by focusing on company directors, but the principles are the same for other types of non-party.

7.158 The ability to identify a real-party director and to make a costs order against him is a method by which the corporate veil can be lifted. The existence of that ability does not snatch the veil away entirely, however, as directors who do nothing more than the performance of their ordinary functions will not be at risk. If, for example, a director causes costs to be incurred knowing that the company would not be able to meet its costs liabilities in the event that the claim is unsuccessful, then he would not be at risk if he acted for the company's benefit rather than his own. Something more would be required, such as the director having been advised that the company does not have a case.

7.159 For the reasons set out at **7.147–7.149** under the heading 'exceptionality', a non-party costs order would usually be made only in those cases which were out of the ordinary. This does not mean that non-party costs orders will be made only sporadically or in a way that is difficult to predict. Lord Brown has said that where a person has

---

[198] See, for example, *Thomson v Berkhampsted Collegiate School* [2009] EWHC 2374 (QB), per Blake J; the family interference in the claim also stretched to funding.

[199] See, for example, *R (on the application of Tallington Lakes Ltd) v Grantham Magistrates' Court* (unreported) 24 February 2011, QBD (Stephen Morris QC sitting as a Deputy Judge of the High Court) in which a local authority sought to use the magistrates' court for the purposes of enforcing a claim from rates.

[200] *Metalloy Supplies Ltd v MA (UK) Ltd* [1997] 1 WLR 1613 at 1620, per Millett LJ.

[201] *DNA Productions (Europe) Ltd v Manoukian* [2008] EWHC 2627 at [6(i)], per Evans-Lombe J.

[202] *DNA Productions (Europe) Ltd v Manoukian* [2008] EWHC 2627 at [6(i)].

[203] See, for example, *Ashley-Carter v Hofmann & Mountford Ltd* [2010] EWHC 2349 (QB), HHJ Thornton QC sitting as a judge of the High Court.

[204] *Dymocks Franchise Systems (NSW) Pty Ltd v Todd* [2004] UKPC 39 at [25(3)]; as an example of the court finding that there was more than one real party, see *Myatt v National Coal Board (No 2)* [2007] EWCA Civ 307.

funded and controlled the action and is to benefit from it, justice will 'ordinarily require' that, if the proceedings fail, he will pay the successful party's costs.[205] He went on to say:[206]

> '[Their] Lordships would hold that, generally speaking, where a non-party promotes and funds proceedings by an insolvent company solely or substantially for his own financial benefit, he should be liable for the costs if his claim or defence or appeal fails. As explained in the cases, however, that is not to say that orders will invariably be made in such cases, particularly, say, where the non-party is himself a director or liquidator who can realistically be regarded as acting in the interests of the company (and more especially its shareholders and creditors) than in his own interests.'

7.160 These comments were not binding (they were made in the Privy Council), but they were taken up in the Court of Appeal by Rix LJ, for example:[207]

> 'Where a non-party director can be described as the "real party", seeking his own benefit, controlling and/or funding the litigation, then even where he has acted in good faith or without any impropriety, justice may well demand that he be liable in costs on a fact-sensitive and objective assessment of the circumstances.'

7.161 It is clear from Rix LJ's comments that each case will be decided on its own facts. Any fact may be relevant, but there are certain issues upon which the court tends to focus. Whilst some of those issues (such as the non-party's conduct) are almost always taken into account, none of them should be regarded as having been elevated to conditions prerequisite for the making of a non-party costs order. The topics are as follows: conduct, the availability of alternative securities or remedies, the relevance of funding. This list is by no means exhaustive. Again, the focus is on directors, but the principles would apply to other non-parties.

Conduct

7.162 Traditional teaching is that non-party costs orders against directors are 'necessarily rare' and are made only in cases where the director has failed to act bona fide in the interest of the company.[208] The ambit of that category of case has gradually increased over the last decade or so. It was soon discovered that impropriety would suffice, and the court also allowed itself to look at what the non-party had expected to gain.[209] As the concept of the 'real party' became more widely received, the court began to look not merely at bona fide belief, but also at whether the director, qua alter ego, was

---

[205]   *Dymocks Franchise Systems (NSW) Pty Ltd v Todd* [2004] UKPC 39 at [25(3)].

[206]   *Dymocks Franchise Systems (NSW) Pty Ltd v Todd* [2004] UKPC 39 at [29].

[207]   *Goodwood Recoveries Ltd v Breen* [2005] EWCA Civ 414.

[208]   *Taylor v Pace Developments Ltd* [1991] BCC 406 at 409, per Lloyd J; see also *Floods of Queensferry Ltd v Shand Construction* [2002] EWCA Civ 918, in which the principles in *Taylor* were reaffirmed as representing the law. As an example of a case in which an order was made, see *Secretary of State for Trade and Industry v Backhouse* [2001] EWCA Civ 67, in which the director treated the companies money as his own. See also *Leverton Ltd v Crawford Offshore (Exploration) Services Ltd (in liquidation)* (1996) *Times*, 22 November, QBD, in which the director forged documents, manufactured and suppressed evidence, and eventually ended up controlling and financing the proceedings.

[209]   *Metalloy Supplies Ltd v MA (UK) Ltd* [1997] 1 WLR 1613 at 1620, per Millett LJ.

litigating for his own interests or his company's interests.[210] Over time, the true law was discovered – or, some might say, the law was changed – such that Lord Brown was able to say:[211]

> 'The authorities establish that, whilst any impropriety or the pursuit of speculative litigation may of itself support the making of an order against a non-party, its absence does not preclude the making of such an order.'

7.163 Thus, the presence of impropriety or unreasonableness will count against the non-party,[212] but its absence will not preclude the making of an order.[213] The same is true of bad faith.[214] Evans-Lombe J emphasised that impropriety may be an ingredient, but it is not a necessary ingredient:[215]

> 'It is not a requirement for the making of a non-party costs order against a director who has funded and controlled litigation consequent on a claim brought by his company at his instance, that impropriety must be shown in the way that the claim was prosecuted.'

7.164 Whilst it is not necessary that any of the requirements of champerty are present, 'wanton and officious intermeddling' in a dispute would be a factor relevant to the exercise of the court's discretion.[216]

7.165 Where poor conduct does exist, it will have the same capacity to sound in a non-party costs order as it would in any other type of costs order. In particular, where the conduct is sufficiently culpable, there is no reason why the award cannot be made on the indemnity basis.[217]

Availability of alternative securities or remedies

7.166 One factor that may be particularly relevant is whether the applicant could have taken steps to protect his position during the course of the proceedings. This usually means considering the availability of an order for security for costs.[218] The court would not be precluded from making a non-party costs order solely because the applicant failed to apply for security for costs.[219]

---

[210] *Re North West Holdings plc* [2001] EWCA Civ 67; as an example of a case in which the court found that the putative funder was not the 'real party', see *Lingfield Properties (Darlington) Ltd v Padgett Lavender Associates* [2008] EWHC 2795 (QB).

[211] *Dymocks Franchise Systems (NSW) Pty Ltd v Todd* [2004] UKPC 39 at [33].

[212] An example is *Bournemouth and Boscombe Athletic Football Club Ltd v Lloyds TSB Bank plc* [2004] EWCA Civ 935, in which a director of an impecunious football club persisted in bringing pointless claims against its bank.

[213] See also *Mills v Birchall (sub nom Dolphin Quays Developments v Mills)* [2008] EWCA Civ 385 at [69]; and *DNA Productions (Europe) Ltd v Manoukian* [2008] EWHC 2627 at [6(iii)].

[214] See, for example, *Kirby v Hoff* [2010] EWHC 3559 (QB) in which Davis J found that an order against a controlling non-party could be upheld notwithstanding the fact that that the court below had made an error in finding that she had acted in bad faith.

[215] In *BE Studios v Smith & Williamson* [2005] EWHC 2730 (Ch) at [18], per Evans-Lombe J.

[216] *Nordstern Allgemeine Versicherungs AG v Internav Ltd* [1999] 2 Lloyd's Rep 139 at 152, relying on *Giles v Thompson* (1994) 1 AC 142.

[217] See, for example, *Vellacott v The Convergance Group plc* [2007] EWHC 17874 (Ch), in which Rimer J made an order against a director who had controlled a 'hopeless' Part 20 claim solely for his personal benefit.

[218] *DNA Productions (Europe) Ltd v Manoukian* [2008] EWHC 2627 at [6(iv)].

[219] *Mills v Birchall (sub nom Dolphin Quays Developments v Mills)* [2008] EWCA Civ 385 at [62], per Collins LJ.

The relevance of funding

7.167 The issue of funding per se is dealt with in the second *Symphony Group* category (see below), but for many years it was believed that it was a prerequisite for a third-party costs order against a director that he should have funded the litigation. This was an incorrect understanding of the law. Whilst obiter, Longmore LJ explained the true law thus:[220]

> '[A]lthough funding took place in most of the reported cases, it is not, in my view, essential, in the sense of being a jurisdictional pre-requisite to the exercise of the court's discretion. If the evidence is that a respondent (whether director or shareholder or controller of a relevant company) has effectively controlled the proceedings and has sought to derive potential benefit from them, that will be enough to establish the jurisdiction. Whether such jurisdiction should be exercised is, of course, another matter entirely and the extent to which a respondent has, in fact, funded any proceedings may be very relevant to the exercise of discretion.'

7.168 Most of the comments made above relate to directors. The principles are broadly the same regardless of the status of the non-party. One or two other types of non-party merit a brief mention.

Active shareholders

7.169 Where the court is considering the extent to which the non-party has controlled the litigation, the court will take into account the extent to which he could have been expected to control the litigation by reason of his status; a sole director, for example, would have no choice but to be in control. Shareholders, on the other hand, would not, and this is the principal reason why 'active' shareholders often fare badly in so far as non-party costs orders are concerned. This was explained by Chadwick LJ:[221]

> '[A] shareholder is not under any duty to the company in relation to the conduct of litigation. He is not required to decide whether it is, or is not, in the interests and for the benefit of the company to bring or defend proceedings. He does not require the protection of the company's separate corporate personality to enable him to fulfil his role as shareholder in relation to the litigation. If he chooses to involve himself in the company's litigation – thereby usurping the role of the directors – he does so at his own risk.'

If confirmation of the correctness of these comments were needed, it may be found in the many examples which exist of the court making orders against 'active' shareholders.[222] The fact that the company may be insolvent would not prevent an order being made.[223]

Receivers, secured creditors and administrators

7.170 Following a lengthy and thorough analysis of the authorities, Lawrence Collins LJ concluded that there was the potential for injustice where, for the benefit of secured creditors, a receiver conducted litigation on behalf of an insolvent company. He concluded that the authorities confirmed that a non-party costs order could be made

---

[220] *Petromec Inc v Petroleo Brasileiro* [2006] EWCA Civ 1038 at [10].
[221] *CIBC Mellon Trust Company v Stolzenberg* [2005] EWCA Civ 628 at [24].
[222] See, for example, *I-Remit Inc* [2008] EWHC 939 (Ch), per David Richards J; and *Suisse Security Bank & Trust Ltd v Julian Francis* [2006] UKPC 41.
[223] See, for example, *Macaria Investments Ltd v Sanders* (unreported) 29 November 2011, Ch D, Newey J.

against a receiver or against the secured creditor, especially where the non-party was the real party. His analysis demonstrated that the court would give weight to the actions (or lack thereof) taken in respect of security for costs. He also made it clear that there must something about the case which lifted it out of the ordinary run of things.[224] Where an order is made against an administrator, the court has the power to issue an order preventing him from recouping his expenses from the company's assets.[225]

Category two: funders

7.171 The provision of funds is, potentially, in the public interest, as it enhances access to justice. Thus, there is a need to balance the desirable (ie encouraging access to justice) against the undesirable (ie the possibility that the opponent incurs irrecoverable costs which, without the funding, he would not have incurred). There as been a change in public perceptions of what is and is not to be encouraged,[226] and this has led to the recognition that there are two categories of funder: the person who provides assistance for non-commercial or altruistic reasons, and the person who has a commercial interest in the funded litigation. The law treats persons in these two categories differently. There are three other types of funder which merit a brief mention, and again, they all fall within a category where their activities are potentially in the public interest. They are insurers, unions, and membership organisations. Each is dealt with in turn, but, before this is done, it is worth noting that the distinction between pure funders and commercial funders is not a hard-and-fast distinction which separates those who are at risk of having orders made against them from those who are not. In this regard, Phillips MR commented:[227]

> 'We are not sure that the adjective "pure" assists in the analysis. It is, we believe, designed to draw a distinction between those who assist a litigant without ulterior motive and those who do so because they have a personal interest in the outcome of the litigation. Public policy now recognises that it is desirable, in order to facilitate access to justice, that third parties should provide assistance designed to ensure that those who are involved in litigation have the benefit of legal representation. Intervention to this end will not normally render the intervener liable to pay costs. If the intervener has agreed, or anticipates, some reward for his intervention, this will not necessarily expose him to liability for costs. Whether it does will depend upon what is just, having regard to the facts of the individual case. If the intervention is in bad faith, or for some ulterior motive, then the intervener will be at risk in relation to costs occasioned as a consequence of his intervention.'

Funders: pure funders

7.172 It is generally true to say that pure funders are unlikely to be at risk of having a non-party costs order made against them. Simply providing funds without more involvement in the matter would not, in general, expose the funder to the risk of an order being made.[228] Lord Brown explained:[229]

---

[224] *Mills v Birchall (sub nom Dolphin Quays Developments v Mills)* [2008] EWCA Civ 385 at [29] *et seq*, per Collins LJ.

[225] *Rubin v Cobalt Pictures Ltd et al* [2010] EWHC 3223 (Ch) at [100]–[104]; see also *Re Silver Valley Mines (Winding Up)* (1882) LR 21 Ch D 381, CA and *Mond v Hammond Suddards (No 2)* [2000] Ch 40, CA (Civ Div).

[226] See the discussion in *Gulf Azov Shipping Co Ltd v Idisi* [2004] EWCA Civ 292 at [35], per Phillips MR.

[227] *Gulf Azov Shipping Co Ltd v Idisi* [2004] EWCA Civ 292 at [54].

[228] *Gulf Azov Shipping Co Ltd v Idisi* [2004] EWCA Civ 292.

[229] *Dymocks Franchise Systems (NSW) Pty Ltd v Todd* [2004] UKPC 39 at [25].

'Generally speaking the discretion will not be exercised against "pure funders" ... as those with no personal interest in the litigation, who do not stand to benefit from it, are not funding it as a matter of business, and in no way seek to control its course. In their case the court's normal approach is to give priority to the public interest in the funded party getting access to justice over that of the successful unfunded party recovering his costs and so not having to bear the expense of vindicating his rights.'

7.173 Notwithstanding this, each case will turn on its own facts, and the fact that a non-party does not have a direct financial interest in the litigation will not prevent an order being made in appropriate cases. The archetypal example is a non-party funder whose interests have more to do with a personal acrimony than with money.[230] Unnecessary meddling in the litigation is another situation where an order can be made,[231] as is the 'pure' funder who is exposed as having an indirect commercial interest.[232]

7.174 The fact that a non-party has a financial interest in the litigation will not necessarily prevent that party from being classified as being a pure funder. HHJ Coulson QC (now Coulson J) found that a wife of a bankrupt had provided funding for his counsel out of natural love and affection rather than out of some interest of her own. This was despite the fact that there was an indirect financial link between the bankrupt and his non-party wife.[233] However, the court will not always regard funding within a marriage as being pure funding; where there is a commercial interest, that can result in the non-party spouse being regarded as a commercial funder.[234] Likewise, the fact that the funder is a close family member will by no means provide protection against an order being made, especially if the funder meddled in the matter.[235]

Funders: commercial funders

7.175 Statute has intervened,[236] but the provisions are not yet in force, so issues concerning commercial funding arrangements have to be decided under the common law. At common law, both in this country and abroad,[237] commercial funders can be found to be liable for the costs of the litigation which they have funded. There are two competing policies at play:

(1)   Access to justice: the need not to discourage commercial funders by exposing them to an unlimited liability for costs.
(2)   'Costs shifting': the need to compensate opponents for costs which have been incurred as a result of the funding.

---

[230]   See, for example, *Latimer Management Consultants Ltd v Ellingham Investments Ltd* [2006] EWHC 3662 (Ch).
[231]   See, for example, *Gulf Azov Shipping Co Ltd v Chief Humprey Irikefe Idisi* (unreported) 21 July 2003, QBD, Arthur Marriott QC sitting as a deputy High Court judge.
[232]   See, for example, *Princo v Phillips* [2003] EWHC 2589 (Ch), Pumfrey J.
[233]   *Jackson v Thakrar* [2007] EWHC 626 (TCC).
[234]   *PR Records v Vinyl 2000* [2008] EWHC 192 (Ch).
[235]   See, for example, *Thomson v Berkhampsted Collegiate School* [2009] EWHC 2374 (QB), per Blake J.
[236]   Whilst it is not yet in force, s 58B of the Courts and Legal Services Act 1990 (as amended) provides a formal structure for commercial funding arrangements; that structure provides a mechanism for the recovery of the funder's equivalent of a success fee.
[237]   See, for example, New Zealand, *Arklow Investments Ltd v MacLean* (unreported) 19 May 2000, High Court of New Zealand, per Fisher J: '[T]he overall rationale [is] that it is wrong to allow someone to fund litigation in the hope of gaining a benefit without a corresponding risk that that person will share in the costs of the proceedings if they ultimately fail . . .'; see, however, *Jeffery & Katauskas Pty Ltd v SST Consulting Pty Ltd; Jeffery & Katauskas Pty Ltd v Rickard Constructions Pty Ltd* [2009] HCA 43 in which the Australian High Court found that it was not appropriate to make an order against a funder.

7.176 The seminal case of *Arkin v Borchard*[238] sought to strike a balance between these two policies. Phillips MR had the following to say (he used the term 'professional funder' rather than 'commercial funder'):[239]

> '[The] existence of this rule [that costs should normally follow the event), and the reasons given to justify its existence, render it unjust that a funder who purchases a stake in an action for a commercial motive should be protected from all liability for the costs of the opposing party if the funded party fails in the action. Somehow or other a just solution must be devised whereby on the one hand a successful opponent is not denied all his costs while on the other hand commercial funders who provide help to those seeking access to justice which they could not otherwise afford are not deterred by the fear of disproportionate costs consequences if the litigation they are supporting does not succeed.
>
> If a professional funder contemplating funding a discrete part of an action were potentially liable for the entirety of the opponent's costs should the claim fail, no professional funder would be likely to take that risk. However there was a practicable solution which would reconcile the desirability of access to justice with the rule that costs generally follow the event.
>
> A professional funder who finances part of a litigant's costs of litigation should be potentially liable for the costs of the opposing party to the extent of the funding provided.'

7.177 Thus, a commercial funder will be at risk of a non-party costs order, but his potential liability would ordinarily be limited to the extent of his funding. Phillips MR commented that such an arrangement would have the following effects:

- commercial funders are likely to cap the funds that they provide in order to limit their exposure to a reasonable amount;
- this should have a salutary effect in keeping costs proportionate; and
- commercial funders will also have to consider with even greater care whether the prospects of the litigation are sufficiently good to justify the support that they are asked to give.

7.178 The restriction on the funder's liability would not apply if the agreement were to fall foul of the policy considerations that render an agreement champertous; in those circumstances, the funder may have an unlimited liability. Moreover, there have been instances of the court distinguishing *Arkin v Borchard* on the grounds that the funding was provided by a funder who, whilst a commercial entity, was not in the business of providing litigation funding. In this regard HHJ Mackie (sitting a judge of the High Court) made the following findings:[240]

> '[It has been] submitted that it would be unfair, if an order were made, for his clients to have to pay to the Claimants an amount greater then [sic] they had paid towards the cost of the defence. That submission derives from the decision of the Court of Appeal in *Arkin* and [counsel] says that it would be unfair for his clients to be put in a worse position than a professional litigation funder. I do not agree … That approach [in *Arkin*] makes it possible for people without money to obtain professional funding for part of their costs of conducting a case. The situation is very different from that in this case and is driven by more

---

[238] [2005] EWCA Civ 655. Not all common law jurisdictions approach this matter in the same way; see, for example, *Jeffrey & Katauskas Pty Ltd v SST Consulting Pty Ltd* [2009] HCA 43 (Australia), where it was held that there must be an element of abuse of process before an order could be made. See also *Saunders v Houghton* [2009] NZCA 610.

[239] *Arkin v Borchard* [2005] EWCA Civ 655 at [38] *et seq*.

[240] *Merchantbridge & Co Ltd v Safron General Partner 1 Ltd* [2011] EWHC 1524 (Comm) at [46].

obvious policy considerations that do not apply here, except to the limited extent to which access to justice has been relied on. I therefore see no reason to limit the obligations of the Defendants in the manner proposed by [counsel].'

It is possible that this case marks a change of direction that is unfavourable to litigation funders; this might be a reflection of the fact that there are those who believe that *Arkin* was overly indulgent of professional funders. Indeed, Jackson LJ (speaking extrajudicially) had these points to make on the topic:[241]

> 'It is perfectly possible for litigation funders to have business models which encompass full liability for adverse costs. This will remain the case, even if ATE insurance premiums (in those cases where ATE insurance is taken out) cease to be recoverable under costs orders ... In my view, it is wrong in principle that a litigation funder, which stands to recover a share of damages in the event of success, should be able to escape part of the liability for costs in the event of defeat.'

Thus, it is possible that *Arkin* will prove to have been the high point of costs protection enjoyed by funders, but it is worth mentioning that some common law jurisdictions have found that litigation funders should not suffer any exposure to adverse costs at all,[242] so there is a great deal of scope for funders to resist any shift away from *Arkin*.

7.179 As to procedure, Sir Donald Rattee has confirmed that the court has the inherent power to order a funded party to disclose the identity and address of its commercial funder, and that the court has the power to order that party to say whether funding has been provided in return for a share in the money or property recovered.[243]

7.180 There are many people who, as a result of their professional activities, may have a financial interest in the litigation in the sense that they may not get paid if the litigation goes against the party they have assisted, but this would not mean that they would all be commercial funders. The following categories merit a brief mention.

Lenders

7.181 Whilst an obvious point, a lender who has no involvement or interest in the proceedings cannot be categorised as being a commercial funder.[244]

Legal representatives

7.182 (The general topic of non-party costs orders against legal representatives is dealt with at **7.191** *et seq*; this section addresses the issue of whether a legal representative can be said to be a funder; a discussion of this topic is also found at **7.194**.) A legal representative will not become a commercial funder solely by reason of providing his legal services pro bono; on this point, Rose LJ said:[245]

---

[241] R Jackson, Review of Civil Litigation Costs: Final Report (December 2009), TSO, chapter 11, para 4.5 a.

[242] In *Jeffery & Katauskas Pty Ltd v SST Consulting Pty Ltd* [2009] HCA 43, the High Court of Australia found that the funder should not be liable to pay adverse costs.

[243] *Reeves v Sprecher* [2007] EWHC 3226 (Ch); in the case before him (ie prior to the issue of an application for security for costs) Sir Donald Rattee refused to order disclosure of the funding agreement itself, but he did not rule out disclosure in other circumstances.

[244] *Petroleo Brasileiro SA v Petromec Inc* [2005] EWHC 2430 (Comm) at [32].

[245] *Tolstoy-Miloslavsky v Lord Aldington* [1996] 2 All ER 556 at 565.

'There is in my judgment no jurisdiction to make an order for costs against a solicitor solely on the ground that he acted without fee. It is in the public interest and it has always been recognised that it is proper for counsel and solicitors to act without fee. The access to justice which this can provide, for example in cases outside the scope of legal aid, confers a benefit on the public.'

7.183 However, the provision of legal services is capable of contributing to a finding of funding; thus, in a case where the solicitors were acting in a dual role—partly for themselves and partly for their client—Lloyd LJ found that the provision of legal services for no fee was something which went to fund the claim.[246] Whilst not binding, HHJ Birse QC found that if the services were provided for the solicitors' benefit as well as those of the client, the solicitors may have a dual role even if instructed under a conditional fee agreement (albeit a damages-based agreement of sorts); he impliedly found that it is not a condition precedent to such a finding that the agreement is shown to be a sham.[247] A failure to obtain after the event insurance in circumstances where that was a gross breach of duty may contribute to a finding that the solicitor was a funder;[248] in this regard, the causal effect of such a failing may be that the claim would not have proceeded at all if the client had known the true risk that he was taking.

7.184 If an order is to be made against a legal representative acting in that capacity, then s 51(1) and (3) of the Senior Courts Act 1981 have no application (see **7.191–7.201** on legal representatives).

Peripherally interested persons

7.185 Even if the funder has a commercial motive, a non-party would not generally be condemned in costs if the litigation was merely ancillary to the purpose for which he provided funds to the litigant.[249]

Funders: insurers

7.186 There is a distinction to be drawn between legal expenses insurers and insurers who conduct litigation as a result of being subrogated to their insured's rights. Generally speaking, a legal expenses insurer would not be required to pay more than the limit of the cover provided for in the policy. As a result, a legal expenses insurer can be expected to indemnify its client up to the limit of cover, but the court would generally not make a non-party costs order against it for anything beyond that limit.[250] In a case in which the insurer had taken an ordinary, passive role in the litigation, Phillips LJ explained his conclusion by referring to the following factors:[251]

- The legal expenses insurer had no interest in the result of the litigation, save in so far as it affected its liability to pay costs.

---

[246] *Myatt v National Coal Board (No 2)* [2007] EWCA Civ 307 at [25].

[247] *Media Cat Ltd v Adams et al* [2011] EWPCC 010 at [96] and [97]. The agreement in that case was a damages-based agreement of sorts whereby the solicitor was entitled to 65 percent of the monies recovered.

[248] See, for example, *Adris v Royal Bank of Scotland plc and ors* [2010] EWHC 941 (QB), per HHJ Waksman QC sitting as Judge of the High Court; whilst not binding, see also *Clarke v Oldham MBC* (unreported) 14 April 2008, Oldham CC, per HHJ Armitage QC.

[249] See, for example, *Vaughan v Jones* [2006] EWHC 2123 (Ch), in which David Richards J declined to make an order against a 'funder' who had provided money to the litigant for the purposes of annulling the litigant's bankruptcy.

[250] *Murphy v Young's Brewery* [1997] 1 WLR 1592.

[251] *Murphy v Young's Brewery* [1997] 1 WLR 1592 at 1602.

- The legal expenses insurer had not initiated the litigation.
- The legal expenses insurer exercised no control over the conduct of the litigation.
- The legal expenses insurer could not have been accused of 'wanton and officious intermeddling' in the dispute.

7.187 It can be seen that Phillips LJ's decision was based on the facts, but most instances of BTE insurance would be very similar, as would many instances of ATE insurance. By way of example, HHJ Vosper QC declined to make an order against an ATE insurer who had cancelled a claimant's policy; that was on the basis that the insurer had no more control of the litigation than an insurer ordinarily would.[252] It is not difficult to envisage, however, that an unusually proactive legal expenses insurer might find that it is at risk of a non-party costs order being made which exceeds the limit of cover.

7.188 Liability insurers are in a different position. This is because they will usually fund litigation not in the interests of their client, but in their own interests. As a result, a liability insurer can be ordered to pay more than the limit of cover.[253] It would rarely be the case that an opponent would need to go to the trouble of seeking a formal non-party costs order, because the insurer would be contractually bound to provide an indemnity (at least up to the level of the limit). Examples do, however, exist.[254] Indeed, if the insurer litigates in such a way as to place its interests concerning the limit ahead of its client's interests, then that may of itself be a factor that the court is entitled to take into account.[255]

Funders: unions and membership organisations

7.189 Whilst it is a point which is almost never litigated, unless the proceedings are in the Employment Tribunal,[256] unions and membership organisations are particularly at risk of non-party costs orders being made against them (or, more accurately, if they were not almost universally in the habit of meeting their members' obligations, they would be at risk of non-party costs orders being made against them). As indicated by Denning MR:[257]

> 'Most of the actions in our courts are supported by some association or other, or by the state itself. Comparatively few litigants bring suits, or defend them, at their own expense. Most claims by workmen against their employers are paid for by a trade union. Most defences of motorists are paid for by insurance companies. This is perfectly justifiable and is accepted by everyone as lawful, provided always that the one who supports the litigation, if it fails, pays the costs of the other side.'

7.190 Section 30 of the Access to Justice Act 1999 provides a formal mechanism whereby unions and membership organisations can recover their costs of bearing the risk of having to pay an adverse costs order. This issue is dealt with elsewhere in this book.

---

[252] *Samuel v Swansea City & County Council* (unreported) 15 July 2008, Swansea CC.
[253] *TGA Chapman Ltd v Christopher and Sun Alliance* [1998] 2 All ER 873.
[254] See, for example, *Palmer v Estate of Palmer, Deceased* [EWCA] 2008 Civ 46.
[255] *Cormack v Washbourne (formerly trading as Washbourne & Co (a firm))* [2000] Lloyd's Rep PN 459.
[256] See *Carr v Allen-Bradley Electronics Ltd* [1980] ICR 603, [1980] IRLR 263, EAT, in which it was decided that given the special nature of the Employment Tribunal it would not be appropriate to follow the practice in the High Court.
[257] *Hill v Archbold* [1968] 1 QB 686 at 494.

Category three: legal representatives

7.191 The jurisdiction to make a non-party costs award against a legal representative (or, more accurately, a solicitor)[258] is different from the jurisdiction arising under the wasted costs regime. Unless the legal representative becomes a quasi-party (see **7.182-7.184** and **7.194**), the jurisdiction does not arise under s 51 of the SCA 1981, but instead arises out of the 'inherent' jurisdiction of the court. This means that there is more than one jurisdiction under which a non-party costs order can be made against a solicitor.

7.192 Indeed, if he were to be particularly misfortunate, a solicitor may suffer orders made against him under no fewer than three entirely separate jurisdictions. If, at the material time, he was acting as a legal representative for a client in proceedings, the only jurisdiction which may be used against him in that capacity would be the wasted costs regime under SCA 1981, s 51(7) (which is described at **7.207-7.332** on 'wasted costs'). If he was acting as legal representative but not with the authority of a client, then he may be at risk of a non-party order made under the inherent jurisdiction of the court. If he acts as a quasi-party (as may happen entirely properly if, for example, the dispute becomes a dispute solely about his fees), then he will be treated as if he were any other controlling/funding person and he would be at risk of an order under SCA 1981, s 51(3). Whilst an overly simplistic analysis which will not hold good in all circumstances but which is useful as a framework, the difference between the jurisdictions can be explained in the following way: the first jurisdiction generally arises where the legal representative has failed in his duty to his client (as well as, perhaps, to the court); the second arises where he has failed in his duty to the court; and the third arises where he has discharged his duty, but the duty was owed, at least in part, to himself.

7.193 Subject to what is said in the paragraph below about 'dual roles', the three jurisdictions are, for practical purposes, mutually exclusive.[259] The non-party costs jurisdictions (ie the second two jurisdictions mentioned above) cannot arise where a legal representative is acting on behalf of a client exclusively in that capacity; where this is so, it is the wasted costs jurisdiction that would need to be invoked.[260] The court's inherent jurisdiction cannot be invoked in such a way as to do something which is inconsistent with the CPR;[261] this means that the jurisdiction to make a non-party costs order against a legal representative cannot be used to make an award that would be precluded by the wasted costs regime.

7.194 The jurisdiction to make an order against a legal representative acting as a quasi-party is the same as that which has been described in the sections on 'controllers' and 'funders' above (see **7.182-7.184**). Ward LJ has confirmed that if a legal representative goes beyond conducting proceedings as a legal representative and behaves as a quasi-party, he will not be immune from a costs order under SCA 1981, s 51(3)

---

[258] It is a moot point whether the court's inherent jurisdiction applies to barristers; for a discussion of this topic in the context of New Zealand law, see *Harley v McDonald, Glasgow Harley (a firm) v McDonald* [2001] UKPC 18A at [41]–[47].

[259] There is an example of the court making orders under two of these jurisdictions at the same time, but it is not clear whether the court was asked to consider the issue of jurisdiction in any detail (see *Globe Equities Ltd v Kotrie* [1999] BLR 232, in which the Court of Appeal made no comment when they heard that an order had been made under both s 51(3) and under s 51(6) and (7) against the same person acting in the same case).

[260] *Hodgeson v Imperial Tobacco Ltd* [1998] 1 WLR 1056 at 1066, per Woolf LJ.

[261] *Tombstone Ltd v Raja* [2008] EWCA Civ 1444.

merely because he is a barrister or a solicitor.[262] In general, he would be treated as a funder. This may be particularly relevant in the context of costs litigation, because it will often be the case that the litigation is for the benefit of the legal representative rather than the client.[263] A legal representative may find himself acting in more than one role at the same time, ie it is possible for a legal representative to represent both himself and his client in circumstances where his interests can be regarded as being significant. Where this is so, then it is open to the court to find that he has a 'dual role', in which case the court may make an order which reflects that situation (such as a percentage order).[264] Case examples are given at **7.184**.

7.195 It is the court's inherent jurisdiction which is the focus of the remainder of these few paragraphs. The usual circumstance in which the non-party costs jurisdiction is exercised is when a solicitor commences or pursues proceedings without the authority of his client,[265] or on a misunderstanding as to what his instructions were,[266] or on behalf of a client who lacks capacity,[267] or on behalf of a 'client' who does not exist.[268] In other jurisdictions, awards have been made where a party has invoked a jurisdiction that does not exist.[269] Merely acting on instructions to bring a claim which did not exist (such as where the client is a bankrupt and the claim relates to property) would not necessarily be sufficient to justify such an order. McCowan LJ explained, albeit in the pre-CPR context, on what basis the solicitor's duty lies:[270]

> 'I see nothing ... to contradict the contention ... that a solicitor who lends his name to the commencement of proceedings is saying: (1) that he has a client; (2) that the client bears the name of the party to the proceedings; and (3) that that client has authorised the proceedings. He does not represent that the client has a good cause of action.'

7.196 Whilst McCowan LJ did not go so far as to say that this was the appropriate test or threshold criterion, he did allow the appeal which was before him on the basis that the solicitor could not be criticised for not having done more. It may be that other considerations will be appropriate in other cases, but, at the very least, McCowan LJ's three duties give an indication as to how the court should exercise its discretion. Waller LJ, in the same case, said that a relevant factor was whether there was a client against whom the court could make an order. He clarified that the jurisdiction can be exercised without any fault on the part of the solicitor other than the fact that the

---

[262] *Tolstoy-Miloslavsky v Lord Aldington* [1996] 2 All ER 556 at 570, per Ward LJ.

[263] See, for example, *Myatt v National Coal Board (No 2)* [2007] EWCA Civ 307.

[264] See *Myatt v National Coal Board (No 2)* [2007] EWCA Civ 307 at [27], distinguishing *Tolstoy-Miloslavsky v Lord Aldington* [1996] 2 All ER 556. Whilst not binding on any court, HHJ Armitage QC has made an award based on a 'dual role' in a case where solicitors had failed to take out ATE insurance and used their own money to fund a claim, partly for the purposes or re-covering profit costs (*Clarke v Oldham MBC* (unreported) 14 April 2008, Oldham CC).

[265] *Fricker v Van Grutten* [1896] 2 Ch 662.

[266] See, for example, *Edwards v Edwards* [1958] 2 All ER 179, in which Sachs J made an order against solicitors who had allowed proceedings to continue in circumstances where if they had taken account of certain items of disclosure, they would have realised that the proceedings were based on a misunderstanding.

[267] *Geilinger v Gibbs* [1897] 1 Ch 479, Kekewitch J.

[268] As a modern example, see *Padhiar v Patel* [2001] Lloyd's Rep PN 328; see also *Babury Ltd v London Industrial plc* (unreported) 20 October 1989, Steyn J; see also *Kleinwort Benson v De Montenegro* [1994] NPC 46, Aldous J.

[269] See *Pringle v Secretary of State of India* (1888) 40 Ch D 288; *Re Avonbank Dairy Co Pty Ltd* [1962] Tas SR 121.

[270] *Nelson v Nelson* [1997] 1 All ER 970 at 973, per McCowan LJ.

solicitor lacked authority to act.[271] Whilst obiter, he went on to confirm that the court does have a discretion, but he had the following to say about how the court should exercise it:[272]

> 'I should finally make clear two things. First, because even in the want of authority case the court is exercising its inherent jurisdiction, it must be right to say that the court ultimately has a discretion. But second, it is of such importance that solicitors do not commence proceedings without authority leaving the opposing party without even a person or entity against whom an order for costs can be obtained, that it is difficult to contemplate circumstances where, if the lack of authority leads to that result, the discretion would be exercised in favour of the solicitors.'

7.197 The conceptual basis for such an order is as breach of an implied contract or warranty given by the solicitor that he was authorised so to act by his client.[273] In modern terminology, the type of contract would be a collateral contract.[274] The nature of the remedy is a claim for damages and the measure of damages the costs thrown away by the opposite party.[275] Other common law jurisdictions have described the power as being a means to remedy a misuse of the court's process.[276]

7.198 Lord Bingham MR has explained, obiter, that the court's inherent jurisdiction is regulatory:[277]

> 'Procedures have changed over the years. The role of the courts (in the case of solicitors) and the Inns of Court (in the case of barristers) has in large measure been assumed by the professional bodies themselves. But the sanctions remain, not to compensate those who have suffered loss but to compel observance of prescribed standards of professional conduct.'

7.199 Although the jurisdiction is not primarily compensatory, an order may be expressed in those terms. Whilst not binding, Lord Hope explained that an order may be crafted to be both compensatory and regulatory (or punitive, as he put it):[278]

> 'The jurisdiction is compensatory in that the court directs its attention to costs that would not have been incurred but for the failure in duty. It is punitive in that the order is directed against the practitioner personally, not the party to the litigation who would otherwise have had to pay the costs.'

7.200 Rose LJ explained that there are six reasons why the court has no jurisdiction under SCA 1981, s 51(3) to make a costs order against a legal representative acting in

---

[271] *Nelson v Nelson* [1997] 1 All ER 970 at 977; see also *SEB Trygg Liv Holding Aktiebolag v Manches* [2005] EWCA Civ 1237.

[272] *Nelson v Nelson* [1997] 1 All ER 970 at 978.

[273] *Yonge v Toynbee* [1910] 1 KB 215; see also *Nelson v Nelson* [1997] 1 All ER 970.

[274] *SEB Trygg Liv Holding Aktiebolag v Manches* [2005] EWCA Civ 1237 at 57, per Buxton LJ.

[275] The court's inherent jurisdiction is usually exercised summarily, without the need for fresh proceedings to be brought by the 'opponent' against the solicitor; the summary process will be in lieu of the claim that could be brought pursuant to *Collen v Wright* (1857) 8 E&B 647.

[276] *R v Forbes; Ex parte Bevan* (1972) 127 CLR 1 at 8; see also *Darcey v Pre-Term Foundation Clinic* [1983] 2 NSWLR 497 at 504.

[277] *Ridehalgh v Horsefield* [1994] Ch 205 at 211.

[278] *Harley v McDonald; Glasgow Harley (a firm) v McDonald* [2001] UKPC 18A at [49]; see also the comments of Lord Wright in *Myers v Elman* [1940] AC 282 at 319.

that capacity (unless he is also acting as a quasi-party, in which case he may be found to have a dual role).[279] Those reasons give some insight into the nature of the jurisdiction:[280]

(1)   It is inconceivable that Parliament would have introduced the wasted costs regime if the court's powers under SCA 1981, s 51(3) were already sufficiently wide to enable it to make orders against solicitors.

(2)   Even prior to the introduction of the wasted costs regime there is no authority that s 51(3) conferred jurisdiction to award costs against legal representatives; indeed, there were obiter observations to the contrary.[281]

(3)   The provisions which introduced the wasted costs regime were not retrospective,[282] and there was no jurisdiction to make orders against a barrister prior to that amendment.[283]

(4)   The provisions that were introduced in the civil courts were mirrored by similar statutory provisions introduced in the criminal courts; this suggests that Parliament intended all legal representatives to be treated alike.[284]

(5)   Balcombe LJ's analysis in *Symphony Group* did not suggest that *Aiden Shipping* has any application to legal representatives.

(6)   The origins of the wasted cost regime lay in the provisions of procedural rules of court which reflected the court's inherent jurisdiction in relation to solicitors, but there is no such suggestion in relation to s 51(3).[285]

7.201 Procedurally, the court's inherent jurisdiction is summary and is not suited to resolution of factual disputes. That said, there have been instances of the court ordering disclosure against solicitors against whom an order was sought.[286] If the court concludes that further investigation is not appropriate, given the summary nature of the jurisdiction, that should not be seen as a surrender by the court of its responsibility; this is because it would be done in the knowledge of the client having other remedies, such as a complaint to the Law Society or a claim in negligence.[287]

Category four: causative persons

7.202 A person who causes litigation may find that he has to pay for it. An example of this is *Pritchard v JH Cobden Ltd*,[288] where the claimant suffered brain damage through the defendant's negligence. That resulted in a personality change which precipitated a divorce. The costs of the divorce proceedings were payable by the defendant (who, for obvious reasons, was not a party to the divorce proceedings). Another example is

---

[279]   *Myatt v National Coal Board (No 2)* [2007] EWCA Civ 307 at [27].

[280]   *Tolstoy-Miloslavsky v Lord Aldington* [1996] 1 WLR 736, CA at 743; in *Globe Equities Ltd v Kotrie* [1999] BLR 232 the Court of Appeal made no comment when they heard that an order had been made under both s 51(1) and (3) and s 51(6) and (7) against the same person acting in the same case; it seems, however, as if the court was not asked to consider this apparent incongruity.

[281]   *Gupta v Comer* [1991] 1 All ER 289 at 293.

[282]   *Fozal v Gofur* (1993) *The Times*, July 9, CA; and *Ridehalgh v Horsefield* [1994] Ch 205 at 250.

[283]   *Fozal v Gofur* (1993) *The Times*, July 9, CA; *Davy-Chiesman v Davy-Chiesman* [1984] 1 All ER 321 at 328; and *Orchard v South Eastern Electricity Board* [1987] QB 565 at 571–581, per Donaldson MR and Dillon LJ.

[284]   See Courts and Legal Services Act 1990, ss 111 and 112, which amended, respectively, the Prosecution of Offences Act 1985 and the Magistrates' Courts Act 1980 so as to introduce a wasted costs regime in those respective courts.

[285]   *Ridehalgh v Horsefield* [1994] Ch 205 at 226–231.

[286]   *Germany v Flatman* [2011] EWHC 2945 (QB) at [28] and [29].

[287]   *Harley v McDonald, Glasgow Harley (a firm) v McDonald* [2001] UKPC 18A at [54].

[288]   [1988] Fam 22.

Phillips v Symes,[289] in which an expert witness was ordered to pay costs. In that case, the expert, by his evidence, had caused significant expense to be incurred and did so in flagrant and reckless disregard of his duties to the court. Costs orders against tribunals may also fall into this category: special rules apply which are tribunal-specific and beyond the scope of this book.

Category five: related claims

7.203 An example of where the non-party is a party to related proceedings which were heard at the same time as the index proceedings but which were not consolidated with them would be the case of *Aiden Shipping Co Ltd v Interbulk Ltd*.[290]

Category six: group actions and representative claims

7.204 The common law position was established in *Davies v Eli Lilly & Co* [1987] 1 WLR 1136. CPR, r 48.6A is the result of an attempt to codify *Davies* and subsequent authorities; it is addressed in detail at **39.2–39.62**. Whether there has been agreement as to costs between the co-litigants will be a relevant factor; the court will regard the persons whom the party represents as being beneficiaries of the litigation in the sense that they will be bound by its outcome.[291] This common law position remains good law under the CPR,[292] and is reflected in r 19.6(4), which provides:

> '(4)   Unless the court otherwise directs any judgment or order given in a claim in which a party is acting as a representative under this rule—
>
> (a)   is binding on all persons represented in the claim; but
> (b)   may only be enforced by or against a person who is not a party to the claim with the permission of the court.'

7.205 Whilst these things are factors to be taken into account, they will not result in a costs order against the representative party being enforceable against the persons whom he represents. If the receiving party wishes to enforce against the persons whom the party represents (such as where the party was a member of an unincorporated association and the receiving party wishes to pursue the other members), then that is something which must be addressed in the order.[293]

Tribunals

7.206 If a tribunal represents itself on an appeal from or review of its own decision, the court has the vires to make an order against it;[294] such orders may or may not be non-party costs orders depending on whether the tribunal is made a party (other than solely for the purposes of costs). To the extent that such orders can be said to be non-party costs orders, they are treated very differently to other types of non-party costs order. Ferris J, for example, has found that where a tribunal makes itself a party to the litigation, it puts the tribunal at risk as to an order for costs, but whether such an order was actually made against it was a matter of discretion to be excercised in accordance

---

[289]   [2004] EWHC 2330 (Ch).
[290]   [1986] AC 965.
[291]   *Markt & Co Ltd v Knight Steamship Company Ltd* [1910] 2 KB 1201 at 1039; see also *Moon v Atherton* [1972] 2 QB 435.
[292]   *Howells v Dominion Insurance Co Ltd* [2005] EWHC 552 (QB).
[293]   *Howells v Dominion Insurance Co Ltd* [2005] EWHC 552 (QB).
[294]   *Providence Capitol Trustees Ltd v Ayres* [1996] 4 All ER 760, Ch D; as an example, see *R (on the application of Touche) v Inner London North Coroner* [2001] 2 All ER 752.

with the principles set out in the CPR, including the general rule that the unsuccessful party would be ordered to pay the costs of the successful party.[295] Ferris J declined to follow pre-CPR rule that the tribunal would be liable only for those costs that have been occasioned by its involvement.[296]

WASTED COSTS

7.207 Wasted costs are costs which are ordered against a legal representative (or which are disallowed, as the case may be);[297] the jurisdiction arises where the legal representative had been acting in that capacity, and where there has been an improper, unreasonable or negligent act or omission on the part of the legal representative or any employee of that person.[298] CPD, art 53.9 gives the following definition:

> 'A wasted costs order is an order—
>
> > (1)   that the legal representative pay a specified sum in respect of costs to a party; or
> > (2)   for costs relating to a specified sum or items of work to be disallowed.'

7.208 Whilst neither the relevant legislation nor the CPR make any express mention of it, the term 'wasted costs' is also used to refer to a costs indemnity that a legal representative may be ordered to provide for the benefit of one or more of the parties.

7.209 It is worth noting that in some circumstances (such as where the legal representative has acted as a quasi-party or where he was acting without authority), the jurisdiction to make non-party costs orders might be relevant; this is described in detail at **7.191–7.201**.

Jurisdiction

7.210 The jurisdiction to make a wasted costs order has its origins in the court's role in supervising officers of the court,[299] but it now arises[300] from SCA 1981, s 51(6) and (7) (as amended):[301]

> '(6)   In any proceedings mentioned in subsection (1), the court may disallow, or (as the case may be) order the legal or other representative concerned to meet, the whole of any wasted costs or such part of them as may be determined in accordance with rules of court.
>
> (7)   In subsection (6), "wasted costs" means any costs incurred by a party—

---

[295]   *Moore's (Wallisdown) Ltd v Pensions Ombudsman* [2002] 1 All ER 737 at 745, [25].
[296]   *Moore's (Wallisdown) Ltd v Pensions Ombudsman* [2002] 1 All ER 737 at 747, [38] in which Ferris J refused to follow *Elliott v Pensions Ombudsman* [1998] OPLR 21 and *University of Nottingham v Eyett (No 2)* [1999] 2 All ER 445.
[297]   Senior Courts Act 1981, s 51(6) and (7) refer to 'legal or other representatives', so it is possible that the wasted costs jurisdiction could be invoked in respect of representatives who are not legal representatives.
[298]   See Senior Courts Act 1981, s 51(6) and (7) and CPR, r 48.7(1).
[299]   See *Charles v Gillian Radford & Co* [2003] EWHC 3180 (Ch) at [22], in which Neuberger J referred to *Harley v McDonald, Glasgow Harley (a firm) v McDonald* [2001] UKPC 18, *Ridehalgh v Horsefield* [1994] Ch 205 at 232 and *Miles v Elman* [1940] AC 282.
[300]   The history and development of the jurisdiction can be traced through the following (which are in chronological order): *Myers v Elman* [1940] AC 282, Solicitors Act 1957, s 50(2); *Davy-Chiesman v Davy-Chiesman* [1984] Fam 48; RSC Ord 62, r 11(1); *Sinclair-Jones v Kay* [1989] 1 WLR 114; and *Gupta v Comer* [1991] 1 QB 629.
[301]   By Courts and Legal Services Act 1990, s 4.

(a)   as a result of any improper, unreasonable or negligent act or omission on the part of any legal or other representative or any employee of such a representative; or

(b)   which, in the light of any such act or omission occurring after they were incurred, the court considers it is unreasonable to expect that party to pay.'

7.211 The jurisdiction to make wasted costs orders is consistent with the European Convention on Human Rights.[302]

Relationship with other powers to make orders against legal representatives

7.212 It is possible for the court to make orders against legal representatives other than those made under SCA 1981, s 51(6) and (7), but this will usually be the case only where the court exercises its inherent power to control officers of the court or where the legal representative is not acting in that capacity. These topics are dealt with in detail at **7.192** *et seq.*

7.213 Where a legal representative is acting in that capacity the court has no jurisdiction to make an order pursuant to SCA 1981, s 51(1) and (3),[303] and therefore, unless the court exercises its inherent jurisdiction, the court must make a finding of an act or omission that was improper, unreasonable or negligent before any costs order can be made against that person.

Rules of court (substantive litigation)

7.214 As with all powers originating under SCA 1981, s 51, the powers are regulated by rules of court, which in this instance are the provisions in CPR, r 48.7:

'(1) This rule applies where the court is considering whether to make an order under section 51(6) of the Senior Courts Act 1981 (court's power to disallow or (as the case may be) order a legal representative to meet, "wasted costs").

(2) The court must give the legal representative a reasonable opportunity to attend a hearing to give reasons why it should not make such an order.

(3) Omitted.[304]

(4) When the court makes a wasted costs order, it must—

(a)   specify the amount to be disallowed or paid; or
(b)   direct a costs judge or a district judge to decide the amount of costs to be disallowed or paid.

(5) The court may direct that notice must be given to the legal representative's client, in such manner as the court may direct—

(a)   of any proceedings under this rule; or
(b)   of any order made under it against his legal representative.

---

[302] *X v Germany* No 7544/76 14 EComHR; and *B v United Kingdom* No 10615 38 EComHR confirming compliance with the European Convention for the Protection of Human Rights and Fundamental Freedoms 1950 (as set out in Sch 1 to the Human Rights Act 1998).

[303] *Tolstoy-Miloslavsky v Lord Aldington* [1996] 1 WLR 736, CA.

[304] This rule used to provide that the court may direct that privileged documents are to be disclosed to the court and, if the court so directs, to the other party to the application for an order; it was revoked by the Civil Procedure (Amendment No 3) Rules 2000 (SI 2000/1317) after Toulson J found it to be ultra vires in *General Mediterranean Holding SA v Patel* [1999] 2 Costs LR 10.

(6)   Before making a wasted costs order, the court may direct a costs judge or a district judge to inquire into the matter and report to the court.

(7)   The court may refer the question of wasted costs to a costs judge or a district judge, instead of making a wasted costs order.'

The effect of these rules is that the power to make an award against a legal representative may be exercised only once the court has given the representative reasonable opportunity to show cause why such an order should not be made; this is dealt with in detail at **7.316–7.319**.

Rules of court (detailed assessments)

7.215   In addition to the provisions in CPR, r 48.7, there are provisions in r 44.14 for costs orders to be made against legal representatives; those provisions are generally called into play where there has been a shortcoming during costs proceedings (as opposed to substantive proceedings), but this is not always the case. The relevant provisions are as follows:

'(1)   The court may make an order under this rule where—

(a)   a party or his legal representative, in connection with a summary or detailed assessment, fails to comply with a rule, practice direction or court order; or

(b)   it appears to the court that the conduct of a party or his legal representative, before or during the proceedings which gave rise to the assessment proceedings, was unreasonable or improper.

(2)   Where paragraph (1) applies, the court may—

(a)   ...

(b)   order the party at fault or his legal representative to pay costs which he has caused any other party to incur.'

7.216   Thus CPR, r 44.14(1)(a) will apply only to detailed assessment proceedings, but case examples do exist of the court making an order under r 44.14 during the course of the substantive litigation itself.[305] Even though that jurisdiction exists, there is little point in the court making an award under r 44.14 in substantive litigation because r 47.8 affords the court wider powers. Furthermore, Dyson LJ has given extensive obiter guidance that the word 'unreasonable' in r 44.14(1) is to be interpreted in a narrow way which is commensurate with the interpretation of the same word in SCA 1981, s 51(6);[306] the effect of this is that r 44.14(1) affords the court a power which adds very little to that already afforded by the general wasted costs provisions. Rule 44.14 is not, therefore, specifically addressed in any detail here. The issue of misconduct and r 44.14 is, however, considered in more detail at **34.99–34.124**.

7.217   Whilst there is no authority on the point, where the court is minded to make a wasted costs order against a legal representative in costs proceedings, there is no reason to believe that the existence of the powers in CPR, r 44.14 releases the court from the need to afford the legal representative those procedural safeguards embodied in r 48.7. If

---

[305]   See, for example, *R (on the application of (1) Gransian Ltd (2) Xon Yong Zhou) v Home Department* [2008] EWHC 3431 (Admin).

[306]   See *Lahey v Pirelli Tyres Ltd* [2007] EWCA Civ 91 at [28], which cites with approval the comments of Park J in *Haji-Ioannou v Frangos* [2006] EWCA Civ 1663 at [10].

case law under the pre-CPR equivalent of r 44.14 is of any continuing relevance, it demonstrates that a finding against a legal representative should be made only in limited circumstances; they are:[307]

- that the legal representative had wasted costs by his failure to conduct the proceedings with reasonable competence and expedition;
- that the costs claimed were caused by the above shortcomings; and
- that (given that a finding against a solicitor would affect his reputation) there was high standard of proof.[308]

Initiation of the inquiry

7.218 It will usually be one of the parties who will initiate an inquiry into whether a wasted costs order should be made, but in some circumstances, the court may act of its own volition;[309] CPD, art 53.2 makes the following provision:

> 'The court may make a wasted costs order against a legal representative on its own initiative.'

7.219 Lord Bingham MR has advised that the court should be slow to initiate an enquiry; this is because such a course of action may lead to difficult and often embarrassing issues concerning the costs of the enquiry.[310] Where, however, the proceedings are such that costs would not normally be sought in an adversarial fashion (as in some family proceedings) and where public funds are under consideration, it may be appropriate for the court to initiate an enquiry.[311]

7.220 There is nothing to prevent a party applying for a wasted costs order against his own legal representative.[312]

7.221 In order for a person to be made an award pursuant to SCA 1981, s 51(7), he must be a 'party'; not every person who has an interest in the proceedings will be a party. For example, Sedley J has found that a person who voluntarily appears at an ex parte hearing as a prospective respondent to a judicial review is not entitled to wasted costs, because they cannot be said to be a party.[313] Carnwath J, on the other hand, has interpreted the word 'party' broadly; he found that a respondent to a claim for interim relief must necessarily be a party 'in some sense', and that the jurisdiction to make a wasted costs order did, therefore, exist.[314]

7.222 Where a lawyer is not acting for a party (and therefore not acting as a legal representative) the jurisdiction to make a wasted costs order pursuant to SCA 1981,

---

[307] *Mainwaring v Goldtech Investments Ltd* (1991) *The Times*, February 19, CA, which relied in part on *Sinclair-Jones v Kay* [1988] 2 All ER 611, CA.

[308] See, however, **8.240**: Lord Carswell has now clarified that the standard itself is 'finite and invariable; but that where fraud or impropriety is alleged, the court will 'look more critically or more anxiously than in other [cases before it] can be satisfied to the requisite standard': *R (on the application of D) v Life Sentence Review Commissioners* [2008] UKHL 33 at [28].

[309] *Ridehalgh v Horsefield* [1994] Ch 205.

[310] *Ridehalgh v Horsefield* [1994] Ch 205 at 228.

[311] *Re G and others (children) (care proceedings: wasted costs)* [1999] 4 All ER 371 at 379–381.

[312] *Medcalf v Mardell* [2002] UKHL 27.

[313] *R v Camden London Borough Council, ex p Martin* [1997] 1 WLR 359.

[314] *Lubrizol v Tyndallwoods* [1998] All ER (D) 139.

s 51(6) and (7) will not exist,[315] but in those circumstances the court may make a non-party costs order, where that is appropriate;[316] this is covered in more detail at **7.191–7.201**.

7.223 In so far as it continues to exist, the immunity of advocates does not prevent a wasted costs order being made against counsel.[317] Whilst now of only historical interest, a wasted costs order cannot be made against counsel for acts or omissions before 1 October 1991.[318]

The circumstances in which the jurisdiction will be available

7.224 Chadwick LJ has found that the definitions[319] in s 119(1) of the Courts and Legal Services Act 1990 apply to s 51(6) and (7) of SCA 1981, and that therefore there is no jurisdiction to make a wasted costs order against a legal representative in a case in which no proceedings were ever issued.[320] The rationale for this is that the jurisdiction to make a wasted costs order is based on a duty to the court, so it will only exist where proceedings have been issued.

7.225 Where at the time of the act or omission complained of proceedings had not been issued, but where proceedings are subsequently issued and the legal representative then carries out work, Ward LJ has found that the jurisdiction to make a wasted costs order will exist.[321]

7.226 Where, however, the acts or omissions occurred prior to the issue of proceedings, Neuberger J has drawn a distinction between cases in which the legal representative does and does not carry out work after the issue of proceedings. He found that where the legal representative does not carry out work post-issue, a wasted costs order cannot be made for those acts and omissions unless there are 'special circumstances', about which he added:[322]

> '[A] solicitor can be liable for wasted costs as a result of some action on his part which was "immediately relevant" to the exercise of "the right to conduct litigation" prior to the actual issue of proceedings. However, as I see it, in light of authorities referred to, that does not detract from the requirement that the conduct must not only be "improper, unreasonable or negligent," but it must also amount in some way to "a breach of duty to the court".'

7.227 For the reasons set out under 'Causation' (**7.279** *et seq*), for most practical purposes the jurisdiction will not exist where the legal representative had ceased to act prior to the issue of proceedings. This, however, is not a jurisdictional restriction, it is merely an almost unavoidable consequence of the facts.

---

[315] *Globe Equities Ltd v Kotrie* [1999] BLR 232; the Court of Appeal made no comment when they heard that an order had been made under both s 51(1) and (3) and s 51(6) and (7) against the same person acting in the same case; it seems, however, as if the court was not asked to consider this apparent incongruity.

[316] See, for example, *Kleinwort Benson v De Montenegro* [1994] NPC 46, Aldous J.

[317] *Ridehalgh v Horsefield* [1994] Ch 205; *Brown v Bennett* [2002] 2 All ER 273 at 291.

[318] *Fozal v Gofur* (1993) *The Times*, July 9, CA; *Davy-Chiesman v Davy-Chiesman* [1984] 1 All ER 321 at 328; and *Orchard v South Eastern Electricity Board,* [1987] QB 565 at 571–581, per Donaldson MR and Dillon LJ.

[319] The right to conduct litigation is defined by s 119(1) of the Courts and Legal Services Act 1990 as the right to issue proceedings and to perform ancillary functions in relation to proceedings.

[320] *Byrne v South Sefton Health Authority* [2001] EWCA Civ 1904.

[321] *Wagstaff v Colls* [2003] EWCA Civ 469 at [73]–[75], distinguishing *Byrne v South Sefton Health Authority* [2001] EWCA Civ 1904.

[322] *Charles v Gillian Radford & Co* [2003] EWHC 3180 (Ch) at [20], [33] and [41]–[44].

7.228 The power to make an order under SCA 1981, s 51(6) and (7) is an additional power to that exercisable under s 51(1): thus, where an original costs order has been made between the parties in the substantive claim, this will not preclude a wasted costs order being made against a legal representative at a later stage.[323] An application for a wasted costs order may be made after the general costs order in the substantive claim has been perfected.[324] (Timing generally is addressed at **7.320-7.326**).

7.229 Where proceedings have been stayed by way of a Tomlin order, those proceedings will remain extant, so a wasted costs application could be made without having to lift the stay.[325] Where, however, proceedings have been brought to an end in such a way as to totally extinguish the possibility of any further steps being taken (such as by the whole proceedings being absorbed within the terms of a compromise), then there will be no jurisdiction.[326]

Discretion

7.230 The court applies a three-stage test:[327]

(1)   Has the legal representative of whom complaint is made acted improperly, unreasonably or negligently?
(2)   If so, did such conduct cause the applicant to incur unnecessary costs?
(3)   If so, is it in all the circumstances just to order the legal representative to compensate the applicant for the whole or any part of the relevant costs? (If so, the costs to be met must be specified and, in a criminal case, the amount of the costs).

(CPD, art 53.4 sets out these three stages in such a way as to reflect the common law.)

7.231 The first of these issues is dealt with in detail at **7.253–7.278** and the second at **7.279-7.283**. The third, more general, issue is discussed here. It should also be borne in mind that these three issues are dealt with in two arenas: that is the court will decide whether the respondent legal representative must show cause as to why he should not pay costs, and then, where appropriate, the court will hear that issue. Therefore, whilst the test is a three-stage test, the first question the court must ask itself is usually whether it should exercise its discretion to allow an enquiry to take place.

7.232 Three aspects of the issue of discretion merit particular attention: proportionality, the summary nature of the jurisdiction, and the status of the persons involved. Each of these is considered in turn.

---

[323]   *Melchior v Vittivel* [2002] CP Rep 24; see also *Gray v Going Places Leisure Travel Ltd* [2005] EWCA Civ 189 at [16].
[324]   *Wagstaff v Colls* [2003] EWCA Civ 469 at [49].
[325]   *Wagstaff v Colls* [2003] EWCA Civ 469.
[326]   *Sharma & anr v Hunters* [2011] EWHC 2546 (COP) at [28].
[327]   This test was first formulated in *In re A Barrister (Wasted Costs Order) (No 1 of 1991)* [1993] QB 293 and approved by Bingham MR (giving the judgment of the court) in *Ridehalgh v Horsefield* [1994] Ch 205.

Proportionality

7.233 The court will always take into account the costs of the proposed enquiry.[328] As to the need to avoid disproportionate satellite litigation, Lord Woolf MR remarked:[329]

'The wasted costs jurisdiction is salutary as long as it is not allowed to be a vehicle which generates substantial additional costs to the parties. It should not be used to create subordinate or satellite litigation, which is as expensive and as complex as the original litigation. It must be used as a remedy in cases where the need for a wasted costs order is reasonably obvious. It is a summary remedy which is to be used in circumstances where there is a clear picture which indicates that a professional adviser has been negligent etc.'

Wall J, on the other hand, has commented that it cannot be right for a respondent to seek to prevent an otherwise wholly meritorious application for wasted costs proceeding merely because the costs incurred in defending it will be substantial.[330] Likewise, a legal representative cannot escape the consequences of the wasted costs jurisdiction by the mere fact that the litigation in which his conduct is challenged is complex.[331]

7.234 The issue of proportionality may turn on the nature of the allegations that are made. The more serious the allegations the greater the risk that the court will exercise its discretion against the applicant on the grounds that the application is disproportionate.[332]

The summary nature of the jurisdiction

7.235 Both the House of Lords and the Court of Appeal have repeatedly stressed the summary nature of wasted costs applications. Lord Woolf MR commented on the extent to which the court can consider disputed issues of fact:[333]

'The ability of the court to make a wasted costs order can have advantages, but it will be of no advantage if it is going to result in complex proceedings which involve detailed investigation of facts. If a situation involves detailed investigation of facts, and indeed actions of dishonesty, then it may well be that the wasted costs procedure is largely inappropriate to cover the situation, except in what would be an exceptional case.'

---

[328] *Ridehalgh v Horsefield* [1994] Ch 205; see, for example, *Chief Constable of North Yorkshire v Audsley* [2000] Lloyds's Rep PN 675, in which Keene J refused to entertain an application where the costs of the application (estimated at £130,000) were not a great deal less than the sums claimed (£169,000); see also *Harrison v Harrison* [2009] EWHC 428 (QB).

[329] *Wall v Lefever* [1998] 1 FCR 605 at 614; see also *Chief Constable of North Yorkshire v Audley* [2000] Lloyd's Rep PN 675; *White v White* [2002] All ER (D) 454 (Mar) (in which an application was dismissed at the first stage because, amongst other things, the disposition of the issues would have required a further trial) and *Media Cat Ltd v Adams et al* [2011] EWPCC 010 at [9], [15], [29] and [31] (in which HHJ Peter Birse QC restricted the number of allegations that would be allowed to proceed to the second stage on the grounds that it would be too costly to investigate the entirety of the legal representative's behavior).

[330] *B v B (wasted costs)* [2001] 3 FCR 724 at [35].

[331] See Peter Gibson LJ's comments in *Medcalf v Mardell* [2001] LLR (PN) 146 at 159, which Ward LJ has confirmed remains good guidance notwithstanding the fact that the House of Lords allowed the subsequent appeal: *Wagstaff v Colls* [2003] EWCA Civ 469 at [59].

[332] *Wagstaff v Colls* [2003] EWCA Civ 469 at [81].

[333] *Manzanilla Ltd v Corton Property and Investments Ltd* [1997] 3 FCR 389, cited by Roch LJ in *Turner Page Music v Torres Design Associates Ltd* (1998) *The Times*, August 3, CA.

7.236 Whilst obiter, Roch LJ has commented that, if the situation involved allegations of breach of professional duty to the solicitor's client, that, too, may make the application one that is not suited to a summary procedure.[334]

The status of the persons involved

7.237 Whilst advocate immunity does not prevent a wasted costs order being made against an advocate, the policy underlying it should be borne in mind for the purposes of discretion. Lord Bingham MR gave the following guidance:[335]

> 'Any judge who is invited to make or contemplates making an order arising out of an advocate's conduct of court proceedings must make full allowance for the fact that an advocate in court, like a commander in battle, often has to make decisions quickly and under pressure, in the fog of war and ignorant of developments on the other side of the hill. Mistakes will inevitably be made, things done which the outcome shows to have been unwise. But advocacy is more an art than a science. It cannot be conducted according to formulae. Individuals differ in their style and approach. It is only when, with all allowances made, an advocate's conduct of court proceedings is quite plainly unjustifiable that it can be appropriate to make a wasted costs order against him.'

7.238 When exercising its discretion the court may take into account the effect that a wasted costs order would have on the legal representative. In a case in which he found that an order would lead to bankruptcy of the person involved (a solicitor advocate) Wyn Williams J decided that that would be a disproportionate consequence of her unreasonable conduct, and that the order should not, therefore, be made.[336] There have been calls for the court to take the size of firm into account, this being because (it is said) an order against a small firm may cause real difficulties to the firm in question.[337]

7.239 The fact that a party has the benefit of costs protection as a result of being publicly funded is not a factor to be taken into account; Lord Bingham MR has commented that it would subvert the benevolent purposes of public funding if legal representatives were subject to any unusual personal risk.[338] Moreover, there is nothing within the regime governing costs orders against the LSC which affects the court's power to make a wasted costs order against a legal representative.[339]

Evidential issues

7.240 The points made above about the summary nature of the jurisdiction are repeated: the court will not carry out in-depth analyses of the facts.

Burden of proof

7.241 As with any civil application, the legal burden lies with the party who seeks to persuade the court to take action.[340]

---

[334] *Turner Page Music v Torres Design Associates Ltd* (1998) *The Times*, August 3, CA.
[335] *Ridehalgh v Horsefield* [1994] Ch 205; see also *Brown v Bennett* [2002] 2 All ER 273.
[336] *R (on the application of Hide) v Staffordshire CC* [2007] EWHC 2441 (Admin).
[337] Cottam, H, Family Law Journal Fam LJ (2010) No 96 May pp 22–24.
[338] *Ridehalgh v Horsefield* [1994] Ch 205.
[339] Regulation 7(2)(b) of the Community Legal Service (Cost Protection) Regulations 2000 (SI 2000/824).
[340] *Dickinson v Minister of Pensions* [1953] 1 QB 228.

7.242 The fact that a respondent legal representative may be required to 'show cause' does not mean that the burden is on him to exculpate himself. It is for the applicant to prove that the order should be made (or, where the enquiry has been initiated by the court, it is for the court to satisfy itself that the order should be made).[341]

7.243 However, as with any civil application, the evidential burden may shift as the evidence unfolds.[342] A respondent legal representative will not be called upon to show cause unless an apparently strong prima facie case has been made out against him, and Bingham MR noted that the language of the then applicable rule of court (which is not dissimilar to the present rule) recognised a shift in the evidential burden.[343] Thus, Lord Bingham MR seems to have recognised that whilst the legal burden will at all time rest with the applicant, the evidential burden may, as the application proceeds, shift towards the respondent legal representative.

Privilege and inferences

7.244 Legal professional privilege is the client's, not the lawyers'; only the client can waive it. The issue may arise in two ways: the applicant's privilege and the respondent's privilege.

7.245 The applicant's privilege may be relevant to the issue of what the application would or would not have done had the respondent legal representative not acted in the manner complained of; if an applicant declines to waive privilege in relation to material relevant to that issue, adverse inferences may legitimately be drawn. In any event, difficulties do not usually arise, because the applicant and his lawyers generally act as one.

7.246 A respondent legal representative is in a different position; this is because a legal representative may wish to rely on material which his client wishes to remain privileged. However, privilege is not the legal representative's to waive.[344] This can give rise to tensions between the rights of the legal representative and his client.

7.247 There is the potential for injustice if a respondent legal representative is not able to prove or refer to the advice and guidance he gave his client. Lord Bingham MR had this to say on the topic:[345]

> 'Where a wasted costs order is sought against a practitioner precluded by legal professional privilege from giving his full answer to the application, the court should not make an order unless, proceeding with extreme care, it is (a) satisfied that there is nothing the practitioner could say, if unconstrained, to resist the order and (b) that it is in all the circumstances fair to make the order.'

Henderson J added the following emphasis:[346]

---

341 *Ridehalgh v Horsefield* [1994] Ch 205.
342 *Abrath v North Eastern Rly Co* (1883) 11 QBD 440.
343 *Ridehalgh v Horsefield* [1994] Ch 205 at 228.
344 *Ridehalgh v Horsefield* [1994] Ch 205.
345 *Medcalf v Mardell* [2002] UKHL 27 at [23].
346 *Sharma & anr v Hunters* [2011] EWHC 2546 (COP) at [20], per Henderson J.

'The court should make an order only if, proceeding "with extreme care", it is satisfied that there is *nothing* (my emphasis) the practitioner could say to resist the order, had privilege been waived, and, in addition, that it is in all the circumstances fair to make the order.'

In some cases the potential for prejudice may be mitigated by referring the matter to a costs judge,[347] who will be able to conduct the hearing in a forum where different rules apply, but Lord Bingham MR has commented that only in a small minority of cases would this procedure be appropriate. He has explained that a full allowance ought to be made for the inability of respondent lawyers to tell the whole story. Where there is room for doubt, the respondent lawyers are entitled to the benefit of that doubt;[348] the court may make assumptions in favour of the legal representatives where it is fairly possible to do so.[349] It is again only when, with all allowances made, a legal representative's conduct of proceedings is quite plainly unjustifiable that it would be appropriate to make a wasted costs order.[350]

7.248 The following are examples of the court giving the respondent legal representative the benefit if the doubt:

- Latham LJ found that it would not be proper to infer from the fact that public funding was granted that counsel had advised that the case had merit: the court would need to see counsel's advice (or, presumably, some other direct evidence) before it could come to that conclusion.[351]
- In the same case, Latham LJ gave another example: where a concession was made shortly after an authority was drawn to the respondent legal representative's attention, it would not be proper to infer that the legal representative was unaware of that authority.[352]
- In a New Zealand case before the Privy Council, Lord Hope has explained that it would almost always be unwise for the court to regard the pursuit of hopeless cases as a demonstration of incompetence.[353]

7.249 A respondent barrister may properly be asked whether he knew or saw documents; provided this caused no prejudice to his lay client, that question is permissible even if the non-privileged documents were in his brief. The barrister could not be compelled to answer such a question, but the question could properly be put.[354]

Evidence and procedure

7.250 Formal processes of disclosure are inappropriate.[355] Interrogation of a respondent lawyer is not generally permitted.[356]

---

[347] See CPR, r 48.7(7).

[348] *Ridehalgh v Horsefield* [1994] Ch 205; see also *Daly v Hubner* [2002] Lloyd's Rep PN 461 (Ch).

[349] *Daly v Hubner* [2002] Lloyd's Rep PN 461 (Ch) at [27].

[350] *Ridehalgh v Horsefield* [1994] Ch 205.

[351] *Dempsey v Johnstone* [2003] EWCA Civ 1134 at [32]; also *D Walter & Co Ltd v Neville Eckley & Co* [1997] BCC 331, in which Scott V-C said much the same.

[352] *Dempsey v Johnstone* [2003] EWCA Civ 1134 at [33].

[353] *Harley v McDonald, Glasgow Harley (a firm) v McDonald* [2001] UKPC 18.

[354] *Brown v Bennett* [2001] All ER (D) 246 (Dec), per Neuberger J.

[355] *Ridehalgh v Horsefield* [1994] Ch 205 at 238H.

[356] *Ridehalgh v Horsefield* [1994] Ch 205 at 238H.

Admissibility of judicial findings

7.251 Whilst judicial findings are generally inadmissible as evidence of the facts upon which they were based,[357] that restriction does not always apply to the determination of costs; this is because the procedure is summary and not hidebound by the rules of evidence.[358]

7.252 However, the departure from the general principles can be justified only where the non-party (ie the legal representative) was sufficiently close to the original proceedings that he will not suffer any injustice.[359] For obvious reasons, this will usually be the case where the judicial findings are said to be relevant to the issue of wasted costs.

The standard of conduct

7.253 The requisite conduct for a wasted costs order is that the legal representative must have acted improperly, unreasonably or negligently. There is a good deal of overlap between the three categories, as to which Lord Bingham MR said:[360]

> 'We were invited to give the three adjectives (improper, unreasonable and negligent) specific, self-contained meanings, so as to avoid overlap between the three. We do not read these very familiar expressions in that way. Conduct which is unreasonable may also be improper, and conduct which is negligent will very frequently be (if it is not by definition) unreasonable. We do not think any sharp differentiation between these expressions is useful or necessary or intended.'

Where the court finds that the standard of conduct is deficient, the court must give reasons.[361]

7.254 Each of the three types of failing is dealt with in turn. Two specific aspects of conduct are then considered: pursuing a hopeless case and sheltering behind counsel.

Impropriety

7.255 Lord Bingham MR explained the meaning of the word 'improper' in this way:[362]

> '"improper" ... covers, but is not confined to, conduct which would ordinarily be held to justify disbarment, striking off, suspension from practice or other serious professional penalty. It covers any significant breach of a substantial duty imposed by a relevant code of professional conduct. But it is not in our judgment limited to that. Conduct which would be regarded as improper according to the consensus of professional (including judicial) opinion can be fairly stigmatised as such whether or not it violates the letter of a professional code.'

---

[357] *Hollington v F Hewthorn & Co Ltd* [1943] KB 587.
[358] *Brendon v Spiro* [1938] 1 KB 176 at 192, cited with approval in *Bahai v Rashidian* [1985] 1 WLR 1337 at 1343D and 1345H.
[359] *Globe Equities Ltd v Kotrie* [1999] BLR 232 at para 18(6).
[360] *Ridehalgh v Horsefield* [1994] Ch 205.
[361] Whilst an Employment Tribunal matter, the general reasoning of Underhill J in *Neafsey v Small* (unreported) 9 December 2010, EAT, at [26] *et seq* applies.
[362] *Ridehalgh v Horsefield* [1994] Ch 205.

7.256 Peter Gibson LJ (with whom Mummery and Blackburne LJJ agreed) has made it clear that any impropriety has to be 'very serious'. There has to be something more than negligence; there has to be something akin to an abuse of process.[363]

7.257 Where improper conduct is calculated to prevent or inhibit the court from furthering the overriding objective, it would be proper to consider making an order under CPR, r 44.14;[364] for the reasons set out above, however, this jurisdiction would normally be exercised only in respect of costs proceedings.

7.258 Where it is said that the legal representative should not have pleaded fraud, it will not be for the legal representative to show that he had admissible evidence of fraud but only that material existed which allowed the allegations to be based.[365]

Unreasonableness

7.259 Lord Bingham MR explained the meaning of the word 'unreasonable' thus:[366]

> '"Unreasonable" … aptly describes conduct which is vexatious, designed to harass the other side rather than advance the resolution of the case, and it makes no difference that the conduct is the product of excessive zeal and not improper motive. But conduct cannot be described as unreasonable simply because it leads in the event to an unsuccessful result or because other more cautious legal representatives would have acted differently. The acid test is whether the conduct permits of a reasonable explanation. If so, the course adopted may be regarded as optimistic and as reflecting on a practitioner's judgment, but it is not unreasonable.'

7.260 In so far as acting on instructions is concerned, there is a distinction to be drawn between allowing a client to take a bad point and making representations to the court that the point is a good point; on this point, Chadwick J said:[367]

> 'I do not hold that a solicitor who, on his client's express instructions, presents a petition in those circumstances [knowing the petition will fail] must, necessarily, be said to have acted unreasonably or improperly. I do hold that a solicitor who, in swearing an affidavit … to support [the] petition, asserts on his oath a belief that [he believes the case to be sound], acts improperly if he does not have that belief; and acts unreasonably if there are no grounds upon which a competent solicitor could reach that view on the material available to him.'

7.261 Where unreasonable conduct is calculated to prevent or inhibit the court from furthering the overriding objective, it would be proper to consider making an order under CPR, r 44.14.[368]

Negligence

7.262 Lord Bingham MR explained the meaning of the word 'negligent':[369]

---

[363] *Persaud v Persaud* [2003] EWCA Civ 394.
[364] See CPD, art 18.1.
[365] *Medcalf v Mardell* [2002] UKHL 27.
[366] *Ridehalgh v Horsefield* [1994] Ch 205.
[367] *Re a Company (No 006798 of 1995)* [1996] 2 All ER 417 at 432.
[368] See CPD, art 18.1.
[369] *Ridehalgh v Horsefield* [1994] Ch 205; see also *Persaud v Persaud* [2003] EWCA Civ 394, in which the court declined to modify the test; see also *Sampson v John Buddy Timber Ltd*, *The Independent*, May 17, 1995.

'"negligent" should be understood in an untechnical way to denote failure to act with the competence reasonably to be expected of ordinary members of the profession. In adopting an untechnical approach to the meaning of negligence in this context, we would however wish firmly to discountenance any suggestion that an applicant for a wasted costs order under this head need prove anything less than he would have to prove in an action for negligence: "advice, acts or omissions in the course of their professional work which no member of the profession who was reasonably well-informed and competent would have given or done or omitted to do"; an error "such as no reasonably well-informed and competent member of that profession could have made".'

7.263 One of the most important differences between 'negligence' in the present sense and 'negligence' in the sense of a tort is that the former is based on a duty to the court whereas the latter is not. Neuberger J has commented that a bare finding of negligence would not be sufficient to found a wasted costs order: there must also be a breach of duty to the court.[370]

7.264 For example, merely advancing a hopeless case per se will not normally justify a wasted costs order.[371]

7.265 Where the court is examining the quality of advice given (such as where counsel has advised that a case qualifies for public funding), the test is whether no reasonably competent legal representative would have continued with the action.[372]

7.266 Where an allegation is based on a putative breach of requirement set out in a detailed statutory code such as those relating to public funding, the court should be slow to supplement the statutory or regulatory duties so as to require a legal representative to meet some higher standard than that set out in that code.[373] Where the requirement is a failure to comply with some procedural requirement, the fact that an opponent is a litigant in person may be of relevance.[374]

7.267 Negligence might be appropriate to describe the situation where it was clear that a legal representative had failed to appreciate that there was a binding authority that was fatal to a client's case and such negligence might justify the making of a wasted costs order.[375]

Hopeless cases

7.268 An oft-encountered aspect of allegedly negligent conduct is where it is said that a legal representative has pursued a hopeless case.

7.269 After having noted the 'cab rank' rule which binds barristers and the commendable tendency of solicitors act in a similar way, Lord Bingham MR made it clear that a legal representative is not to be held to have acted improperly, unreasonably or negligently simply because he acts for a party who pursues a claim or a defence which

---

[370]   *Charles v Gillian Radford & Co* [2003] EWHC 3180 (Ch) at [22], in which he referred to *Harley v McDonald, Glasgow Harley (a firm) v McDonald* [2001] UKPC 18, *Ridehalgh v Horsefield* [1994] Ch 205 at 232, and *Miles v Elman* [1940] AC 282.

[371]   *Persaud v Persaud* [2003] EWCA Civ 394.

[372]   *Dempsey v Johnstone* [2003] EWCA Civ 1134 at [28].

[373]   *Tate v Hart* [1999] PNLR 787.

[374]   *Godfrey Morgan Solicitors Ltd v Cobalt Systems Ltd Godfrey Morgan Solicitors Ltd v Cobalt Systems Ltd* [2011] 6 Costs LR 1006 at [21], per Underhill J (in the Employment Appeal Tribunal).

[375]   *Dempsey v Johnstone* [2003] EWCA Civ 1134.

is plainly doomed to fail.[376] This does not permit a legal representative to advance proceedings which are an abuse of the court (whether this is on instructions or not), as Bingham MR indicated:[377]

> 'A legal representative is not entitled to use litigious procedures for purposes for which they were not intended, as by issuing or pursuing proceedings for reasons unconnected with success in the litigation or pursuing a case known to be dishonest, nor is he entitled to evade rules intended to safeguard the interests of justice, as by knowingly failing to make full disclosure on ex parte application or knowingly conniving at incomplete disclosure of documents.'

7.270 Some cases may be so poor that they can be regarded as being an abuse of process. A clear distinction has to be drawn between a hopeless case being presented and the lending of assistance to a case which amounted to an abuse of process.[378]

7.271 Whilst he was dealing with a slightly different topic,[379] Lord Hope explained in a Privy Council case that it is not errors of judgment that attract the exercise of the jurisdiction to make a wasted costs order as a result of abuse, but errors of a duty owed to the court;[380] this would be a relevant consideration where a case can be said to have such poor chances of success that it was an abuse of process to advance it.

7.272 Where the conduct admits of no reasonable explanation, it will be no answer to an allegation of pursuing a case which is an abuse of process to rely on the lay client's refusal to waive privilege.[381]

Sheltering behind counsel

7.273 Where a solicitor instructs counsel and counsel gives advice which is incorrect, the solicitor may, in appropriate circumstances, be able to avoid a wasted costs order on the basis that he was following counsel's advice.[382]

7.274 However, a solicitor does not abdicate his professional responsibility when he seeks the advice of counsel.[383] A solicitor has to apply his 'own expert professional mind to the substance of the advice received'.[384] Where a solicitor has applied his own mind to the matter and had doubts about it, and where as a result of those doubts the solicitor has taken counsel's advice and acted upon that advice, Aldous LJ held that it would not be appropriate to find that the solicitor had acted negligently.[385]

---

[376] *Ridehalgh v Horsefield* [1994] Ch 205, relying on observations in *Rondel v Worsley* [1969] 1 AC 191 at 275.

[377] *Ridehalgh v Horsefield* [1994] Ch 205 at 232.

[378] *Persaud v Persaud* [2003] EWCA Civ 394.

[379] That being a non-English legal point which is more akin to non-party costs orders than wasted costs orders.

[380] *Harley v McDonald, Glasgow Harley (a firm) v McDonald* [2001] UKPC 18 at [57]; wasted costs orders in New Zealand cases are technically made under the court's inherent powers and as such are not wasted costs orders, but Lord Hope made the comment as commentary on *Ridehalgh v Horsefield* [1994] Ch 205, and therefore nothing seems to turn on this jurisdictional distinction. Neuberger J commented that *Harley* was of assistance in this regard in *Charles v Gillian Radford & Co* [2003] EWHC 3180 (Ch) at [24].

[381] *Morris v Roberts (HMIT) (wasted costs)* [2005] EWHC 1040 (Ch).

[382] See, for example, *Swedac Ltd v Magnet and Southern plc* [1989] FSR 243 QBD.

[383] *Locke v Camberwell Health Authority* [1991] 2 Med LR 249, approved of in *Ridehalgh v Horsefield* [1994] Ch 205; see also *Matrix Securities Ltd v Theodore Goddard* [1998] PNLR 290 at 322, where the specialist was a tax counsel.

[384] *Ridehalgh v Horsefield* [1994] Ch 205 at 228.

[385] *Reaveley v Safeway Stores plc* [1998] PNLR 526 at 532; see also *R v Oxfordshire County Council* [1987] NLJ Rep 542 QBD.

7.275 The more specialist the nature of the advice, the more reasonable is it likely to be for a solicitor to accept it and act on it.[386] Common sense dictates that the same can be said of advice obtained from very experienced counsel, but examples do exist of solicitors being criticised for failing to scrutinise work carried out by senior counsel.[387]

7.276 For obvious reasons, a solicitor will find it difficult to shelter behind counsel in circumstances where counsel has given incorrect advice as a result of being inadequately instructed.[388]

7.277 In addition to relying on counsel, a solicitor may also be able to rely on experts; in a case where the applicant complained that no reasonable solicitor would have advanced the case, for example, David Richards J refused to make an order on the basis that there was expert evidence which was capable of supporting the claim.[389]

7.278 Whilst a slightly different topic, it is perhaps worth saying that case examples do exist of the court making an order against solicitors for having failed to take counsel's advice in circumstances in which counsel's advice was required.[390]

Causation

7.279 The court has jurisdiction to make a wasted costs order only if and to the extent that the conduct complained of has caused costs to be wasted.[391]

7.280 The issue of causation should be dealt with on the balance of probabilities rather than on a loss-of-chance basis.[392]

7.281 Chadwick LJ has commented that the causation requirement will not often be met where the legal adviser had ceased to act by the time that the proceedings were brought.[393] Although obiter, Neuberger J has qualified this by saying that it was not an inflexible rule; the example he gave was that it would be curious if solicitors could avoid a wasted costs order merely by causing their client to instruct someone else for the purposes of issuing proceedings.[394]

7.282 The application may fail for want of causation where the court is satisfied that the costs will be paid by the respondent legal representative's lay client. Silber J, for example, refused to find that a causative link had been made out in a case in which a lay client had historically discharged its costs liabilities.[395] Mackay J came to a similar

---

[386] *B v B (wasted costs)* [2001] 3 FCR 724 at 737; *Davy-Chiesman v Davy-Chiesman* [1984] 1 All ER 321; and *Locke v Camberwell Health Authority* [1991] 2 Med LR 249 at 254; also approved of in *Ridehalgh v Horsefield* [1994] [1994] Ch 205.

[387] See, for example, *Tolstoy-Miloslavsky v Lord Aldington* [1996] 1 WLR 736, CA.

[388] See *Locke v Camberwell Health Authority* [1991] 2 Med LR 249, in which solicitors were criticised for not having given certain material (medical notes) to counsel; the decision to make an order for that reason was later reversed on the facts.

[389] *Marsh v Sofaer and Giffinhoofe & Co (a firm)* [2006] EWHC 1217 (Ch).

[390] See, for example, *D Walter & Co Ltd v Neville Eckley & Co* [1997] BCC 331.

[391] *In re A Barrister (Wasted Costs Order) (No 1 of 1991)* [1993] QB 293, approved by Bingham MR (giving the judgment of the court) in *Ridehalgh v Horsefield* [1994] Ch 205.

[392] *Brown v Bennett* [2002] 2 All ER 273 at 291.

[393] *Byrne v South Sefton Health Authority* [2001] EWCA Civ 1904 at [31].

[394] *Charles v Gillian Radford & Co* [2003] EWHC 3180 (Ch) at [47].

[395] *KOO Golden East Mongolia (a body corporate) v Bank of Nova Scotia* [2008] EWHC 1120 (QB) at [72].

conclusion in an application for wasted costs against a barrister in a case in which only a relatively modest amount remained outstanding under the substantive costs order and was, in any event, likely to be paid.[396]

7.283 Where a person has waived the right to recover the costs from a third party, the legal representative's conduct cannot be said to be causative of the costs thrown away; indeed, there would be a risk of double recovery in such circumstances.[397] Where the opponent could have taken steps to prevent costs being wasted but chose not to do so, it will be open to the court to find an absence of causative influence.[398]

Case examples

7.284 A number of case examples are given below, but this is done in the same breath as saying that each case must be decided on its own facts and that it is 'dangerous in the exercise of discretion to take a reported case as a guide for that exercise in another case' (per Hodson LJ).[399] In particular, unless the contrary is stated, none of the examples given below establishes any principle or rule of law.

Abusive proceedings

7.285 Where an appeal contained elements that rendered it incapable of succeeding, it was an abuse of the appellate process to bring an appeal: a legal representative who advised such a course of action would be acting both unreasonably and improperly.[400] In a case in which solicitors had had a hand in setting up a device designed to frustrate the proper operation of immigration law, Blake J made an order that those solicitors pay wasted costs.[401] In a case in which fraud was alleged, a wasted costs order was made against solicitors who knew that fraud had been admitted in other proceedings, but who had failed to disclose that fact.[402]

Frivolous proceedings

7.286 Where a misguided appeal had been begun and then frivolously proceeded with despite the fact that the tribunal had made it clear it was ill-advised, counsel and his instructing solicitors were ordered to pay the costs.[403]

Vexatious proceedings

7.287 A wasted costs order was made in a case which heaped 'fraud and perjury upon the vicious calumny of the allegation of being a war criminal'; this was in circumstances in which the court accepted the legal representatives' belief in the bona fides of their client.[404]

---

[396] *Harrison v Harrison* [2009] EWHC 428 (QB).

[397] *D v H (Costs)* [2008] EWHC 559 (Fam).

[398] An example being where a party could have applied to strike out: *CMCS Common Market Commercial Services AVV v Taylor* [2011] EWHC 324 (Ch) at [65]–[75], per Briggs J.

[399] *Bragg v Crosville Motor Services Ltd* [1959] 1 All ER 613 at 615.

[400] *B v B (wasted costs)* [2001] 3 FCR 724.

[401] *R (on the application of (1) Gransian Ltd (2) Xon Yong Zhou) v Home Department* [2008] EWHC 3431 (Admin).

[402] *General Mediterranean Holdings SA v Patel* [1999] 3 All ER 673 (Comm).

[403] *Abbassi v Secretary of State for the Home Department* [1992] Imm AR 349.

[404] *Tolstoy-Miloslavsky v Lord Aldington* [1996] 1 WLR 736, CA.

Pointless proceedings

7.288 A hopeless application to remove an order which itself had been put in place to manage the possibility of hopeless applications being made may result in an order being made.[405]

Failure to prepare

7.289 Where counsel had had insufficient time to prepare for a hearing, the court should give weight to the fact that counsel's hands may be tied by the 'cab rank rule' in such a way that there is little that counsel can do about the situation.[406]

Failure to liaise with court

7.290 Although in a criminal case, Hooper LJ has found that a failure by counsel to inform the court of a new time estimate for trial may result in a wasted costs order if that was as a result of an error that no reasonably well-informed member of the Bar would have made.[407] In a case in which a solicitor had informed the court of the need for an adjournment only a day before a hearing, the particular facts of the case (in which there were administrative difficulties with public funding) led the Court of Appeal to find that there had only been an error of judgment and that it would not be appropriate to make an order.[408]

Failure to liaise with experts

7.291 In a family case, Wall J found counsel to have been guilty of unreasonable conduct in failing properly to liaise with his client's expert in order to ensure that the expert was apprised of all the relevant issues in the case.[409]

Failure to liaise with opponents

7.292 In an administrative case, Bennett J refused to make an award against solicitors who had failed to keep an opponent abreast of the difficulties that the solicitors were having in obtaining instructions.[410]

Failure to assist an opponent

7.293 Whilst co-operation between parties is to be commended, a legal representative's duty is to his lay client, not to his opponent,[411] so a failure to inform an opponent of a court order or to assist an opponent would not lead to an order being made. However, an obstructive attitude or a personal vendetta against an opponent might be a factor that would justify an order.[412] Sir Andrew Morritt has found that where a person had

---

[405] *R (on the application of Santur v Home Department* [2007] EWHC 741 (Admin).
[406] *Antonelle v Wade Grey Farr (a firm)*, which was one of the appeals heard at the same time as *Ridehalgh v Horsefield* [1994] Ch 205.
[407] *Re Olugbade (a barrister)* [2008] EWCA Crim 2922.
[408] *Re a Solicitor (wasted costs order)* [1993] 2 FLR 959.
[409] *Re G and others (children) (care proceedings: wasted costs)* [1999] 4 All ER 371.
[410] *R (on the Application of Latchman) v Home Department* [2004] EWHC 2795 (Admin).
[411] *Fitzhugh Gates (a firm) v Sherman* [2003] EWCA Civ 886 at [64]; and *Connolly-Martin v Davies* [1999] Lloyd's Rep PN 790 at 795; see also *B v Pendlebury* [2002] EWHC 1797.
[412] *Fletamentos Maritimos v Effjohn International* [2003] Lloyd's Rep PN 26.

obtained a bankruptcy order against another person, but later discovered that there was no debt, he was not under a duty to contact the trustee in bankruptcy to prevent costs being incurred.[413]

Failure to heed issues drawn to a party's attention

7.294 Gross J upheld a wasted costs order in a case where the respondent solicitors had failed to apply the correct legal test, which had been drawn to their attention by their opponents.[414]

Advancing incorrect evidence

7.295 It was improper for a solicitor to swear an affidavit saying that he believed that a company was insolvent if he did not hold that belief, and it was unreasonable to swear such an affidavit if no reasonable solicitor would have held that belief.[415]

Failure to disclose

7.296 Where a solicitor failed to give full and frank disclosure when drafting an affidavit for use in an ex parte application, Rix J found that it was appropriate to make a wasted costs order regardless of whether the solicitor appreciated the significance of a non-disclosed fact.[416] Ward LJ found that the duty to give disclosure does not, for the purposes of wasted costs, extend to requiring legal representatives actually to inspect his client's documents (in that case, a CD-ROM) to verify his client's word.[417] A failure to supervise redaction may, however, fall below the requiste standard.[418]

Incredible witnesses

7.297 Where the claim turns on credibility, it would not be appropriate to make a wasted costs order against a legal representative for failing to realise that his witnesses would not do well.[419]

Specialist proceedings

7.298 Although obiter, Brooke J has indicated that a lack of familiarity with specialist proceedings would put a legal representative at risk of a wasted costs order if he held himself out as being competent in that specialist arena.[420]

---

[413]   *Redbridge London Borough Council v Mustafa* [2010] EWHC 1105 (Ch).

[414]   *The Isaacs Partnership (a firm) v Umm Al-Jawaby Oil Service Co Ltd* [2003] EWHC 2539 (QB).

[415]   *Re a Company (No 006798 of 1995)* [1996] 2 All ER 417; compare this with *Rybak v Langbar International* [2011] EWHC 451 (Ch) in which the solicitor was found not to be at fault for not ensuring that the evidence that his clients were giving was correct.

[416]   *Lowline (PLS) Ltd v Direct Aviation Ltd* (unreported) 8 March 1999, QB (Comm), Rix J.

[417]   *Hedrich v Standard Bank London Ltd* [2008] EWCA Civ 905.

[418]   See *CMCS Common Market Commercial Services AVV v Taylor* [2011] EWHC 324 (Ch) at [60] *et seq*, per Briggs J.

[419]   *Gandesha v Nandra* (unreported) 21 November 2001, Ch D, Jacob J.

[420]   *R v Horsham District Council and another ex p Wenman and others* [1995] 1 WLR 680.

Wrong proceedings

7.299 In an application in which the legal representatives had wrongly applied for a judicial review rather than a statutory review of a decision of an immigration judge, Collins J ordered those legal representatives to pay costs.[421]

Failure to realise client is a patient

7.300 In a family case in which a solicitor had failed to realise that the client was a patient, Cornell J commented that he would have made a wasted costs order only if the solicitor had ignored the need to consider that aspect of the matter.[422]

No instructions

7.301 In an EAT case, where a legal representative makes an accusation of bias without instructions, that may be grounds for a wasted costs order;[423] where the legal representative is acting completely without instructions, this would be grounds for the court making an order under its inherent jurisdiction (see **7.191–7.201**).

Inability to obtain instructions and pro bono

7.302 Where solicitors had been aware for a period of about 2 months that a claim (an application for judicial review) had been rendered academic, and where the claim was withdrawn only 4 days before the hearing, Bennett J declined to make a wasted costs order because the solicitors had tried, but failed, to obtain instructions.[424] The fact that the lawyer is acting pro bono is probably a factor that may be taken into account.[425]

Failure to observe time limits

7.303 Although obiter, Neuberger J commented on his decision not to make a wasted costs order in the case before him:[426]

> 'It should be emphasised that I am not suggesting that by failing to miss any time limit, so that he is in breach of his duty to his client, a solicitor could not be liable for a wasted costs order. Indeed there will be many occasions where such an order would be appropriate. For example, where a solicitor fails to serve a document on another party within a time limit laid down by a court order or by the CPR, through an oversight. In such a case, there would be a very strong case for saying that a solicitor should pay the costs of all parties to an application to extend time, or for relief from sanctions, which was necessary as a result of the oversight.'

---

[421] *R (on the application of Kamau) v Secretary of State for the Home Department* [2007] All ER (D) 111 (Apr).
[422] *Re O (a minor) (wasted costs application)* [1994] 2 FLR 842 at 847.
[423] *Highvogue Ltd and Morris v Davies* (2007) UKEAT/0093/07, Beatson J.
[424] *R (on the Application of Latchman) v Home Department* [2004] EWHC 2795 (Admin).
[425] Whilst an EAT based on rules specific to the Employment Tribunal, see *Jackson v Cambridgeshire County Council* (2011) PNLR 32 (EAT).
[426] *Charles v Gillian Radford & Co* [2003] EWHC 3180 (Ch) at [30].

Unacceptable delay

7.304 Unexplained and unacceptable delay may lead to an order being made.[427] Where an acceptable reason for the delay is advanced (such as funding difficulties), it would not be appropriate to make an order.[428]

Failure to serve notices

7.305 There are many instances of the court making wasted costs orders against solicitors who failed to serve notices of revocation or discharge of public funding.[429]

Failing to attend a hearing

7.306 Failing to attend a hearing may give rise to a wasted costs order, but if the solicitor reasonably relied on an assurance given by another solicitor that he would go on the record and attend, then that might amount to a defence even if the first solicitor remained on the record throughout.[430]

Raising new points at a late stage

7.307 The fact that a new point is raised at a late stage will not necessarily result in a finding of unreasonable conduct; failing to realise that some act may result in new avenues of argument being opened up will also not normally qualify as a shortcoming which is unreasonable.[431]

Trial overrunning

7.308 Where counsel had to seek an adjournment of a trial because another trial in which he was briefed had begun late, the Court of Appeal found that no order should be made; the court reminded itself of the need to bear in mind the demands of practice.[432]

Quantum

7.309 Quantum is assessed in the usual way (often by summary assessment).

7.310 The legal representative's liability is not limited only to those costs incurred whilst exercising rights of audience.[433]

7.311 The court will not be able to assess any additional liability payable by the respondent legal representative until the conclusion of the proceedings.[434]

---

[427] *Kilroy v Kilroy* [1997] PNLR 66.
[428] *Trill v Sacher (No 2)* [1992] 40 LS Gaz R 32, CA.
[429] See, for example, *Banks v Humphrey & Glasgow* [1997] PIQR P464 CA; as a counter-example, see *Tate v Hart* [1999] PNLR 787.
[430] See, for example, *Equity Solicitors v Javid* [2009] EWCA Civ 535 at [24], per Holman J (sitting the Court of Appeal).
[431] *Hallam-Peel & Co v Southwark LBC* [2008] EWCA Civ 1120.
[432] *Re a Barrister (wasted costs order No 4 of 1993)* (1995) *The Times*, April 21.
[433] *Medcalf v Mardell* [2002] UKHL 27.
[434] See CPD, art 53.10 and CPR, r 44.3A(1) and (2).

Procedural issues

7.312 The following topics are now discussed in turn: procedure generally; the two stages; timing; particulars; ancillary proceedings; notice; and settled applications.

Procedure generally

7.313 The procedure will be tailored to suit the needs of the case.[435] CPD, art 53.5 makes the following provisions:

> 'The court will give directions about the procedure that will be followed in each case in order to ensure that the issues are dealt with in a way which is fair and as simple and summary as the circumstances permit.'

7.314 CPD, art 53.3 stipulates the mechanisms by which an application may be made:

> 'A party may apply for a wasted costs order—
>
> (1)   by filing an application notice in accordance with Part 23; or
> (2)   by making an application orally in the course of any hearing.'

Oral applications for a wasted costs order should only be heard if the basis of the costs sought to be recovered was narrow and clear; where this is not the case, the court should require the applicant to make a written application, supported by evidence, if so advised.[436]

7.315 The application ought to be heard by the judge who heard the proceedings to which the application relates.[437] Where possible, this ought to be so even if his judgment on the substantive issues contained criticisms of the respondent legal representatives.[438]

The two stages

7.316 As a general rule, the court considers the issue in two stages, as explained by CPD, art 53.6:

> 'As a general rule the court will consider whether to make a wasted costs order in two stages—
>
> (1)   in the first stage, the court must be satisfied—
>   (a)   that it has before it evidence or other material which, if unanswered, would be likely to lead to a wasted costs order being made; and
>   (b)   the wasted costs proceedings are justified notwithstanding the likely costs involved.
> (2)   at the second stage (even if the court is satisfied under paragraph (1)) the court will consider, after giving the legal representative an opportunity to give reasons why the court should not make a wasted costs order, whether it is appropriate to make a wasted costs order in accordance with paragraph 53.4 above.'

7.317 It is not always necessary for there to be an adjournment between the two stages, as CPD, art 53.7 provides:

---

[435]   Although a pre-CPR case, this was explained in *Ridehalgh v Horsefield* [1994] Ch 205 at 238G.

[436]   *Regent Leisuretime Ltd v Skerrett* [2006] EWCA Civ 1032.

[437]   *Re Merc Property Ltd* [1999] 2 BCLC 286; and *Gray v Going Places Leisure Travel Ltd* [2005] EWCA Civ 189.

[438]   *In re Freudiana Holdings Ltd* (1995) *The Times*, December 4.

'On an application for a wasted costs order under Part 23 the court may proceed to the second stage described in paragraph 53.6 without first adjourning the hearing if it is satisfied that the legal representative has already had a reasonable opportunity to give reasons why the court should not make a wasted costs order. In other cases the court will adjourn the hearing before proceeding to the second stage.'

7.318 Where counsel acting on behalf of the respondent solicitors makes concessions that found a wasted costs order, and where those solicitors are present in court and do not object to counsel's concessions or ask for an adjournment, that hearing may, in appropriate circumstances be sufficient opportunity to show cause, in which case the court will not be obliged to insist on a full investigation of the solicitors' conduct.[439]

7.319 By analogy with criminal procedure, the court should not make a wasted costs order on the basis that the respondent legal representative has permission to apply to set it aside; the legal representative must be given an opportunity to make representations before the order is made, not after.[440]

Timing

7.320 Unless the proceedings are wholly extinguished (see **7.229**) the jurisdiction to make a wasted costs order may be made at any stage of the proceedings (see **7.228**), not least because it is a matter of case management.[441] CPD, art 53.1 provides as follows:

'Rule 48.7 deals with wasted costs orders against legal representatives. Such orders can be made at any stage in the proceedings up to and including the proceedings relating to the detailed assessment of costs. In general, applications for wasted costs are best left until after the end of the trial.'

7.321 Neuberger LJ (with whom Latham and Brooke LJJ agreed) gave the following guidance about the timing of applications for wasted costs:[442]

• The making of an order as to who should bear the costs and on what are part terms are part of the overall order made by the court at the conclusion of the trial.
• In the absence of at least a good reason to the contrary, the costs of proceedings should be dealt with by the tribunal which determines the issue which disposes of the case immediately after the judgment in disposing of the case.
• In principle, there is no difference in this connection between a costs order against a party and a costs order against a non-party; orders for wasted costs are all part of the costs allocation exercise which is to be implemented by the judge hearing the trial in relation to the costs of the action.
• Where a wasted costs order is sought in respect of an interlocutory matter before trial, it is often better for the application for wasted costs only to be made after the trial.
• It is, however, not mandatory that the application for wasted costs is made at the end of the trial. In many cases, a party considering an application for a wasted costs order will ask the judge for time to consider whether to make such an

---

[439] *Woolwich Building Society v Finberg* [1998] PNLR 216, CA.
[440] *Re Wiseman Lee (a firm) (wasted costs order) (No 5 of 2000)* [2001] EWCA Crim 707.
[441] Whilst it was in the Employment Appeal Tribunal and therefore not binding, see *Wilsons Solicitors (in a matter of wasted costs) v Johnson*, 9 February 2011, per Underhill J at [34].
[442] *Gray v Going Places Leisure Travel Ltd* [2005] EWCA Civ 189 at [11]–[16].

application and, even if such an application is made, the normal course is for the court to give directions in relation to the disposal of the application rather than to deal with it straightaway.

• The application for a wasted costs order can be made after the order in relation to the proceedings has been drawn up. That is not to say that the court entertaining the application late will necessarily grant it if there is no good reason for the delay.

Holman J has noted that applications are often made in a hasty and insufficiently considered manner and has warned that adverse costs consequences would often result from this.[443] Henderson J, however, has commented on the need for applications to be made promptly.[444]

7.322 Aldous J had the following to say:[445]

> 'Although the right to seek and obtain wasted costs orders is not limited under the statute, I envisage that it would rarely be wise or right to seek to obtain such an order until after trial. Further, I do not envisage that the right to seek and obtain such an order could or should be affected by waiting until after trial before making a claim; although on rare occasions it might be desirable to inform the legal representative that such an order might be sought.'

7.323 Lord Bingham MR agreed with the thrust of what Aldous J had to say, but has commented that it is impossible to lay down rules of universal application, and that circumstances may exist where an interlocutory battle resolves the real dispute between the parties.[446]

7.324 Wall J has commented that in certain family proceedings, it may be appropriate to hear an application before he conclusion of the case.[447]

7.325 In appropriate circumstances, a wasted costs order may be heard as late as on an appeal.[448]

7.326 The fact that the substantive proceedings may have been stayed will not prevent the court from hearing the application.[449]

Particulars

7.327 Fairness requires that the respondent legal representative is told clearly what it is alleged he has done wrong and what it is that is claimed.[450] It is for this reason that CPD, art 53.8 stipulates the following requirements:

> 'On an application for a wasted costs order under Part 23 the application notice and any evidence in support must identify—

---

[443] *Equity Solicitors v Javid* [2009] EWCA Civ 535 at [26], per Holman J (sitting the Court of Appeal).

[444] *Sharma & anr v Hunters* [2011] EWHC 2546 (COP) at [21], per Henderson J citing *Gray v Going Places Leisure Travel Limited* [2005] EWCA Civ 189 at [14]-[15].

[445] *Filmlab Systems International Ltd and another v Pennington* [1994] 4 All ER 673 at 679; and *Gray v Going Places Leisure Travel Ltd* [2005] EWCA Civ 189.

[446] *Ridehalgh v Horsefield* [1994] Ch 205 at 228.

[447] *B v B (wasted costs order)* [2001] 3 FCR 724.

[448] *Sherman v Perkins* [2002] WTLR 603, David Mackie QC.

[449] *Wagstaff v Colls* [2003] EWCA Civ 469.

[450] See, by way of analogy with criminal procedure, *Re P (a barrister) (wasted costs order)* [2001] EWCA Crim 1728; see also *Ridehalgh v Horsefield* [1994] Ch 205 at 238.

(1)   what the legal representative is alleged to have done or failed to do; and

(2)   the costs that he may be ordered to pay or which are sought against him.'

CPD, art 18.1 makes similar provisions relating to orders made under CPR, r 44.14.

7.328 Pumfrey J commented on the topic:[451]

'It seems to me that it is wrong in principle to make an order to "show cause" in the absence of a clear statement of what the respondent lawyer is said to have done wrong. Only then is it possible for the court to decide whether a sufficiently strong prima facie case exists to justify the order.'

7.329 Where fraud is alleged, this must be made clear.[452]

Ancillary proceedings

7.330 Where the court finds that a wasted costs order should be made, it would not normally be appropriate for the court to express a view as to whether the legal representative's conduct was a breach of his professional rules of conduct or whether his lay client had a civil claim against him; those were issues to be dealt with in the appropriate forums in a focused way, with the legal representative being given a proper opportunity to deal with any contested issue of fact or law.[453]

Giving notice of the possibility of an application

7.331 No potential applicant should threaten an opponent with a wasted costs application or use the spectre of an application as a means of intimidation.[454] There is nothing objectionable about alerting an opponent to the possibility, where appropriate.[455]

Settled applications

7.332 Where an application is settled, the parties should prepare a short and succinct written note explaining what had happened so far as the lawyers were concerned; that note should inform the court of the matters which are relevant to the reputation of the lawyers, which, as a result of the settlement which has been achieved, would otherwise not be brought to the court's attention. Lord Woolf MR explained that the purpose of such a note would be to avoid the need for further hearings after the parties had come to terms.[456]

Costs of the application

7.333 The costs of the application will be determined according to the usual principle in CPR, r 44.3. In a case in which the court had refused an application for wasted costs

---

[451] *S v M* [1998] 3 FCR 665 at 673.

[452] *Wagstaff v Colls* [2003] EWCA Civ 469 at [79].

[453] *Harley v McDonald, Glasgow Harley (a firm) v McDonald* [2001] UKPC 18 at [51].

[454] *Orchard v South Eastern Electricity Board* [1987] QB 565.

[455] *Ridehalgh v Horsefield* [1994] Ch 205.

[456] *Manzanilla Ltd v Corton Property and Investments Ltd* [1997] 3 FCR 389 at para 39.

on the basis that the application was disproportionate and frivolous, Evans-Lombe J found that the court below had erred in failing to award the costs of the application to the respondent.[457]

ORDERS AGAINST PUBLICLY FUNDED OPPONENTS

7.334 There are two methods by which a receiving party may obtain costs which have been incurred in litigation against a publicly funded opponent: costs may be sought against the publicly funded person personally, or they may be sought against the Legal Services Commission ('LSC'). In addition, where costs are payable by a publicly funded party who is also the recipient of costs or damages, those costs may be the subject of set-off: this issue is dealt with in detail at **12.67–12.102**.

7.335 This book deals primarily with the regime under the Access to Justice Act 1999 ('AJA 1999'). Different (but not wholly dissimilar) rules applied where the publicly funded person was awarded funding under the Legal Aid Act 1988. That old regime is still referred to from time to time, and is briefly mentioned below.

7.336 A person will have costs protection only if he and to the extent that he receives publically-funded legal services; the mere fact that he has a certificate is not itself sufficient to confer costs protection. If a certificate is discharged, costs protection will shield the funded party up to the date on which funded services ceased to be provided; this will not necessarily be the same date on which the certificate was formally discharged.[458] A litigant who has a certificate but who acts in person for a period and who gives notice of that fact, will not have costs protection for the period in question.[459] A certificate that is limited to certain steps in the litigation may become spent once those steps have been taken.[460] Where a person has costs protection the court will usually ask itself two questions: firstly, the court will decide whether the publicly funded person should be required personally to pay costs, and secondly the court will decide whether the LSC should pay any costs which the person himself has not been ordered to pay. Procedural details (such as which judge is to decide these matters and at what stage) differ markedly between the old and the current regimes.

The old regime

7.337 The old regime was governed by s 18 of the Legal Aid Act 1988. The Legal Aid Board ('LAB') would be ordered to pay costs if the court was satisfied that it was just and equitable that provision for the costs should have been made out of public funds. In cases at first instance, the unassisted party would be awarded costs only if he would suffer severe financial hardship if no order were made.[461] The award would then usually be sufficient to discharge the hardship rather than to meet the entire costs reasonably claimed.[462]

---

[457] *9MD Ltd v One Step Beyond* [2008] EWHC 3231 (Ch).
[458] *LSC (Burridge v Stafford: Khan v Ali* [2000] 1 WLR 927. See also *Re H (minors) (No 2) (abduction: custody rights)* [1992] 2 AC 303, HL.
[459] Whilst decided under the old regime, see *Mohamadi v Shellpoint Trustees Ltd* [2009] EWHC 1098 (Ch), per Briggs J.
[460] Whilst decided under the old regime, see *Turner v Plasplugs Ltd* [1996] 2 All ER 939, CA.
[461] See Legal Aid Act 1988, s 18(4).
[462] *Adams v Riley* [1988] QB 372, QBD.

7.338 The order against the LAB would be made at the same time that the court decided the incidence of costs between the parties. Put another way, the trial judge would make both the order against the paying party and the order against the LAB.[463] Before making an order the court had to determine how much, if anything, the assisted person should pay. In practice, what tended to happen was that an 'unless' order would be made that gave the LAB the opportunity to challenge the order.[464] Therefore, the costs judge's role under the old regime was limited to quantifying the costs; he would have played no part in deciding whether the order should be made against the LAB.

7.339 Costs were not be awarded against the LAB as a matter of course,[465] and where no order would have been made between the parties – such as in a family case – no order may be made against the LSC.[466] Examples of cases in which an order was made include cases in which the proceedings in question were misconceived and ought never to have been instituted.[467]

The current regime

7.340 The current regime requires the costs judge not only to quantify the costs, but also to decide whether the LSC is to pay the costs. It was introduced on 1 April 2000 when s 18 of the Legal Aid Act 1988 was repealed.[468] Two statutory instruments were brought into force; they were the Community Legal Service (Costs) Regulations 2000 (SI 2000/441) ('the Costs Regulations') and the Community Legal Service (Cost Protection) Regulations 2000 (SI 2000/824) (as amended) ('the Cost Protection Regulations').

7.341 Complex transitional provisions apply, the details of which are beyond the scope of this book; broadly speaking, most costs orders will now be subject to the procedures of the current regime.[469]

---

[463] The jurisdiction to make an order against the LSC (then the Legal Aid Board) to an unassisted party was conferred by s 18 of the Legal Aid Act 1988. Section 18(1)–(4) make the following provisions:

'(1) This section applies to proceedings to which a legally assisted person is a party and which are finally decided in favour of an unassisted party.

(2) In any proceedings to which this section applies the court by which the proceedings were so decided may, subject to subsections (3) and (4) below, make an order for the payment by the board to the unassisted party of the whole or any part of the costs incurred by him in the proceedings.

(3) Before making an order under this section, the court shall consider what order for costs should be made against the assisted party and for determining his liability in respect of such costs.

(4) An order under this section in respect of any costs may only be made if— (a) an order for costs would be made in the proceedings apart from this Act; (b) as respects the costs incurred in a court of first instance, those proceedings were instituted by the assisted party and the court is satisfied that the unassisted party will suffer severe financial hardship unless the order is made; and (c) in any case, the court is satisfied that it is just and equitable in all the circumstances of the case that provision for the costs should be made out of public funds.'

[464] The Court of Appeal in *Maynard v Osmond (No 2)* [1979] 1 WLR 31 devised that procedure, under which the court would make a provisional determination of: (a) the amount of costs to be paid by the funded party, if any, and (b) whether an order should be made for costs to be paid by the LSC. The order would not be drawn up for 10 weeks; this was to enable the LSC to make objections.

[465] *Din v Wandsworth London Borough Council (No 2)* [1982] 1 All ER 1022, HL.

[466] See Legal Aid Act 1988, s 18(4) and *K v K (legal aid: costs)* [1995] 2 FCR 189, CA.

[467] See, for example, *Aire Property Trust v Treeweek* [1989] 1 EGLR 61, CA in which Kerr LJ found that he was 'in no doubt' that an order should be made where funded party's appeal lacked jurisdiction.

[468] See AJA 1999, s 106 and Sch 15, Pt I.

[469] See art 8.3 of the Access to Justice Act 1999 (Commencement Number 3, Transitional Provisions and Savings Order) 2000 (SI 2000/774); see also CPD, art 22.3.

7.342 The relevant statutory provisions are contained in AJA 1999, s 11 (which is set out in full at **7.371**). The relevant regulatory provisions are set out in the Community Legal Services (Costs) Regulations 2000 and the Community Legal Services (Costs Protection) Regulations 2000 (which are set out at **7.372** and **7.374** respectively). When applying that regime, it is the position of the parties to the litigation which is relevant, not the position of third parties who may be affected by the litigation.[470]

Procedural issues

7.343 Philips MR has described the procedure as being a two-stage affair in which the trial judge is responsible for stage one and the costs judge discharges the court's duties under stage two[471] (see below). Phillips MR has noted that whilst it is arguable that the trial court has the power to discharge the duties under both stages, it should restrict its function to stage one only.[472]

Stage one

7.344 The trial judge has the following tasks to perform:

(1)   To decide whether to make an order for costs against a funded litigant ('the client').[473]
(2)   To decide whether it is in a position to specify the amount, if any, to be paid by the client.[474]
(3)   To make a costs order against the client which either:
    (a)   specifies the amount, if any, to be paid by the client and states the amount of the full costs; or
    (b)   does not specify the amount to be paid by the client.[475]
(4)   Where the order does not specify the amount to be paid by the client, to make, if it sees fit, findings of fact as to the parties' conduct, in the proceedings or otherwise, which are relevant to the determination of that amount.[476]

Stage two

7.345 Stage two is the province of the costs judge; the procedure is as follows:

(1)   The receiving party may, within 3 months of the making of the costs order, request a hearing to determine the costs payable to him;[477] that time limit may be extended only if there is good reason for the delay.[478]
(2)   The receiving party may, at the same time, seek a costs order against the commission.[479]

---

[470]   *Aehmed v Legal Services Commission* [2009] EWCA Civ 572.
[471]   *R v Secretary of State for the Home Department ex p Gunn* [2001] EWCA Civ 891.
[472]   *R v Secretary of State for the Home Department ex p Gunn* [2001] EWCA Civ 891 at [29].
[473]   Community Legal Service (Costs) Regulations 2000 (SI 2000/441), reg 9(1).
[474]   SI 2000/441, reg 9(2).
[475]   SI 2000/441, reg 9(3) and (4).
[476]   SI 2000/441, reg 9(6).
[477]   SI 2000/441, reg 10(2).
[478]   See SI 2000/441, reg 10(3)(b); and see reg 5(3)(b) of the Community Legal Service (Cost Protection) Regulations 2000 as amended by the para 4 of the Community Legal Service (Cost Protection) (Amendment No 2) Regulations 2001 (SI 2001/3812).
[479]   SI 2000/441, reg 10(3)(c); see also CPD, art 22.4.

(3)   The receiving party must, when making the request, file with the appropriate court office[480] and serve on the client and the regional director of the commission (if an order is sought against the commission):[481]

    (a)   a bill of costs;

    (b)   a statement of resources;[482] and

    (c)   a written notice that a costs order is sought against the commission.[483]

(4)   The publicly funded person must file a statement of resources and serve this on the receiving party and the regional director (where a claim is made on the commission);[484] where appropriate, points of dispute may also be served.[485]

(5)   The court sets a date for the hearing,[486] which will be listed as being in private.[487]

(6)   The court conducts the hearing, assesses the costs (if any) to be paid by the client and, where appropriate, makes a costs order against the commission.[488]

The court's power to make an order against the LSC in respect of a funded party is limited to orders made in accordance with the regime set out above.[489]

7.346 In an obiter footnote Walls LJ has made it clear that where the real dispute is about whether the LSC should pay the costs rather than whether a costs order under AJA 1999, s 11(1) should be made, the parties should act sensibly and agree an order that allows those arguments to be put to the costs judge.[490]

7.347 As to the interplay between the trial judge and the costs judge, Phillips MR has commented that it was open to the trial judge to make any findings in relation to the conduct of the parties or facts that have emerged in the course of the proceedings that have relevance to the task to be performed by the costs judge or district judge. Beyond this the trial court should not go, as to do so would be to usurp the functions of the costs judge.[491]

---

[480]   See CPD, arts 23.2 and 23.2A for detailed directions as to what is the appropriate office; in essence, the appropriate office is the court that made the order under AJA 1999, s 11(1), unless the court is in or around London, in which case it is the Supreme Court Costs Office.

[481]   See CPD, art 23.3(1).

[482]   CPD, art 22.1 provides that a 'statement of resources' means:

'(1)   a statement, verified by a statement of truth, made by a party to proceedings setting out:

(a)   his income and capital and financial commitments during the previous year and, if applicable, those of his partner;

(b)   his estimated future financial resources and expectations and, if applicable, those of his partner ('partner' is defined in paragraph 21.4, above);

(c)   a declaration that he and, if applicable, his partner, has not deliberately foregone or deprived himself of any resources or expectations;

(d)   particulars of any application for funding made by him in connection with the proceedings; and,

(e)   any other facts relevant to the determination of his resources; or

(2)   a statement, verified by a statement of truth, made by a client receiving funded services, setting out the information provided by the client under Regulation 6 of the Community Legal Service (Financial) Regulations 2000, and stating that there has been no significant change in the client's financial circumstances since the date on which the information was provided or, as the case may be, details of any such change.'

[483]   SI 2000/441, reg 10(3) and (4).

[484]   SI 2000/441, reg 10(6); the statement may be produced at the hearing: see CPD, art 22.4.

[485]   CPD, art 23.5.

[486]   SI 2000/441, reg 10(9).

[487]   CPD, art 23.8.

[488]   *R v Secretary of State for the Home Department ex p Gunn* [2001] EWCA Civ 891 at [38].

[489]   Community Legal Service (Cost Protection) Regulations 2000, reg 7(1); see also CPD, art 22.9.

[490]   *Wyatt v Portsmouth Hospitals NHS Trust* [2006] EWCA Civ 529 at [62].

[491]   *R v Secretary of State for the Home Department ex p Gunn* [2001] EWCA Civ 891 at [33]–[34].

Timing

7.348 Two issues concerning timing merit particular mention: the first is whether the court can make a s 11(1) order in circumstances where some aspects of the litigation remain to be decided, and the second is the 3-month time limit during which an application for an order against the LSC must be made.

'Finally decided'

7.349 Regulation 5(1)(b) of the Cost Protection Regulations provides that the regime described above will apply when 'proceedings are finally decided in favour of a non-funded party'. It is not always obvious whether the proceedings have been finally decided; an example would be where court has allowed an appeal but remitted the matter for a further determination. Such situations can cause difficulties because the court could, in theory, make an AJA 1999, s 11(1) order in circumstances where the costs judge would have no jurisdiction to make an order against the LSC until the conclusion of the entire proceedings. The receiving party could, therefore, be placed in the invidious position of having both to wait until the conclusion of the proceedings and of having to comply with the 3-month time limit during which an application must be made for the court to decide whether an order should be made against the LSC (see below). Chadwick LJ found that in those circumstances it would not usually be appropriate for the trial judge to adjourn making the s 11(1) costs order until the conclusion of the litigation; instead, the trial judge should make the order immediately on the basis that, if necessary, the costs judge could adjourn stage two, as appropriate.[492] In any event, Chadwick LJ approved a definition of proceedings which, for the purposes of orders out of public funds, defined proceedings in such a way as to be limited to the proceedings immediately to hand (which, in the case before him, was the appeal itself).[493]

The 3-month time limit

7.350 The receiving party must make its application for an order against the LSC within 3 months of the making of the AJA 1999, s 11(1) costs order.[494] Prior to 3 December 2001 the court had no discretion to extend or disapply that time limit:[495] practitioners came to refer to that time limit as 'the ten-two trap', which was named after reg 10(2) of the Costs Regulations. After that date the Cost Protection Regulations were amended in such a way as to allow the court to extend that period if there is good reason for the delay.[496] It is the writer's experience that the court will not usually accept ignorance of the rules as being good reason. If the application is made in the wrong court, it is open to the judge to find that the application has, thereby, been made out of

---

[492] *Masterman-Lister v Brutton & Co (No 2)* [2003] EWCA Civ 70; see also *Wyatt v Portsmouth Hospitals NHS Trust* [2006] EWCA Civ 529 at [25].

[493] *Masterman-Lister v Brutton & Co (No 2)* [2003] EWCA Civ 70, approving *General Accident Car and Life Assurance Corporation Ltd v Foster* [1972] 3 All ER 877; Chadwick LJ's analysis was applied by Wall LJ in *Wyatt v Portsmouth Hospitals NHS Trust* [2006] EWCA Civ 529.

[494] Community Legal Service (Cost Protection) Regulations 2000 (SI 2000/824), reg 5(3)(b).

[495] *R v Secretary of State for the Home Department ex p Gunn* [2001] EWCA Civ 891 at [27] *et seq*; see also CPD, art 23.4.

[496] Community Legal Service (Cost Protection) (Amendment No 2) Regulations 2001 (SI 2001/3812); as an example of this in practice, see *Floyd & Anor v Legal Services Commission* [2010] EWHC 906 (QB).

time.[497] Cox J has found that it is not open to a judge to extend time generally under CPR, r 3.1 as being a means by which to avoid the need to find that is a good reason for the delay.[498]

Government departments

7.351 The nature of public funding is that the litigation is often against government departments (or other publicly funded bodies). Where those are the circumstances it could be argued that the court should not make an order against the LSC because that would be merely to order that money is moved from one government coffer to another. Whilst the court has expressed some sympathy for that argument,[499] it has consistently and repeatedly rejected it.[500] In particular, the fact that the non-funded party is a government department does not remove jurisdiction to make an order against the commission in its favour,[501] nor does it affect the procedure to be adopted when the court is exercising its discretion.[502]

Discretion

Stage one

7.352 This section deals with the trial judge's discretion to make an AJA 1999, s 11(1) costs order. There are three components to the decision; they are: whether to make an order; whether to state the amount; and whether to make any comments which would assist the costs judge in stage two. Each of these is discussed in turn.

Whether to make an order

7.353 Where the court is considering whether to make a s 11(1) costs order, it shall consider whether, but for cost protection, it would have made a costs order against the client and, if so, whether it would, on making the costs order, have specified the amount to be paid under that order.[503]

7.354 There is nothing in the regime described here that should be taken as requiring the court to make a costs order where it would not otherwise have made one.[504]

7.355 CPR, r 44.17 states that CPR Parts 44–48 do not apply to the extent that s 11 of AJA 1999 and provisions made under that Act make different provision. Wall LJ has confirmed that r 44.17 does not oust the provisions in r 44.3, and that, therefore, the court may take the matters set out in that rule into account.[505]

7.356 Whilst the guidance was given in the context of litigation which putatively had the flavour of family litigation, Wall LJ firmly rejected the notion that the requisite

---

[497] *Liverpool Freeport Electronics Ltd v Habib Bank Ltd & Legal Services Commission* [2009] EWHC 861 (QB).
[498] *Floyd v S Floyd v Legal Services Commission* [2010] EWHC 906 (QB) at [21].
[499] *R v Secretary of State for the Home Department ex p Gunn* [2001] EWCA Civ 891 at [51].
[500] Historically, see *R v Greenwich LBC ex p Lovelace (No 2)* [1992] QB 155 and *In re O (Costs: Liability of Legal Aid Board)* [1997] 1 FLR 465.
[501] *R v Secretary of State for the Home Department ex p Gunn* [2001] EWCA Civ 891 at [38].
[502] *R v Secretary of State for the Home Department ex p Gunn* [2001] EWCA Civ 891 at [50].
[503] Community Legal Service (Costs) Regulations 2000, reg 9(1); see **7.372**.
[504] Community Legal Service (Cost Protection) Regulations 2000, reg 7(2)(a).
[505] *Wyatt v Portsmouth Hospitals NHS Trust* [2006] EWCA Civ 529 at [29].

'conduct' must be unreasonable or in some way discreditable; likewise, he rejected the idea that there must be 'exceptional circumstances'.[506]

7.357 Wall LJ has emphasised the need to separate the first stage and the second stage, and has commented that the first stage is a threshold test:[507]

> 'In our judgment, it is of crucial importance to remember throughout that we are not being asked to make an order for costs against the LSC, nor are we deciding the extent to which, if at all, the LSC should underwrite the Trust's costs. Those are matters for the costs judge at stage two of the regulatory procedure. It is for the costs judge to decide whether or not it is just and equitable to make an order against the LSC. What Parliament has done is to set a hypothetical threshold criterion without which the costs judge cannot entertain an application against the LSC. In our judgment, this case easily crosses that threshold.'

Wall LJ has implicitly made it clear that one factor the court can take into account is the effect that any order would have on the parties and their subsequent relationship;[508] this may be a particularly relevant factor where the litigation is a public interest case.

Whether to state the amount

7.358 When exercising its discretion to make a s 11(1) costs order, the options that the court has are as follows:[509]

- ***To make an unquantified costs order against the client***: If the court considers that it would have made a costs order against the client, but that it would not have specified the amount to be paid under it:[510]
  - (a) the court shall, when making the s 11(1) costs order specify the amount (if any) that the funded party is to pay under that order if, but only if—
    - (i) it considers that it has sufficient information before it to decide what amount is, in that case, a reasonable amount for the client to pay, in accordance with AJA 1999, s 11(1); and
    - (ii) it is satisfied that, if it were to determine the full costs at that time, they would exceed the amount referred to immediately above;
  - (b) otherwise, the court shall not specify the amount the client is to pay under the costs order.
- ***To make a quantified order against the client:*** If the court considers that it would have made a costs order against the client, and that it would have specified the amount to be paid under it, the court shall, when making the s 11(1) costs order:
  - (a) specify the amount (if any) that the client is to pay under that order if, but only if, it considers that it has sufficient information before it to decide what amount is, in that case, a reasonable amount for the client to pay, in accordance with s 11(1) of the Act;
  - (b) otherwise, it shall not specify the amount the client is to pay under the costs order.

  Any such order shall state the amount of the full costs.
- ***Findings of fact:*** Where the court makes a s 11(1) costs order that does not specify the amount which the funded party is to pay under it, the court may also make

---

[506] *Wyatt v Portsmouth Hospitals NHS Trust* [2006] EWCA Civ 529 at [43].
[507] *Wyatt v Portsmouth Hospitals NHS Trust* [2006] EWCA Civ 529 at [51].
[508] *Wyatt v Portsmouth Hospitals NHS Trust* [2006] EWCA Civ 529 at [60].
[509] See reg 9(2)–(6) of the Community Legal Service (Costs) Regulations 2000, discussed in *Wyatt v Portsmouth Hospitals NHS Trust* [2006] EWCA Civ 529 at [54]; also see CPD, arts 22.5 and 22.6.
[510] See also CPD, art 22.7, which makes very similar provisions.

findings of fact, as to the parties' conduct in the proceedings or otherwise, relevant to the determination of that amount, and those findings shall be taken into consideration in that determination.

The wording of the relevant provisions can be found at **7.372.**

7.359 Wall LJ has found that the trial court is entitled to accept assertions that the funded party is impecunious, and is, therefore, entitled to make a finding that the sum the funded party should personally pay is nil.[511]

7.360 Where an order specifying the costs payable is made and the LSC funded client does not have cost protection in respect of all of the costs awarded in that order, the order must identify the sum payable (if any) in respect of which the LSC funded client has cost protection and the sum payable (if any) in respect of which he does not have cost protection.[512]

7.361 Where an order is made, it may be appropriate if comments are also recorded to assist the costs judge. The CPD makes the following provisions:[513]

'If the court makes an order for costs to be determined it may also—

(1)   state the amount of full costs, or
(2)   make findings of facts, eg concerning the conduct of all the parties which are to be taken into account by the court in the subsequent determination proceedings.'

Stage two

7.362 There are two aspects to the court's discretion pertaining to stage two (ie the discretion exercised by the costs judge). Those aspects are: the extent to which the funded person should himself bear the costs; and whether and to what extent the LSC should bear the costs.

Personal liability

7.363 Costs ordered against a funded person shall not exceed the amount (if any) which is a reasonable one for him to pay having regard to all the circumstances, including:[514]

• the financial resources of all parties to the proceedings; and
• their conduct in connection with the dispute to which the proceedings relate.

The funded person's clothes, household furniture and the tools and implements of his trade shall not be taken into account, except so far as may be prescribed.[515]

---

[511]   *Wyatt v Portsmouth Hospitals NHS Trust* [2006] EWCA Civ 529 at [58].
[512]   CPD, art 22.8.
[513]   See also CPD, art 22.6.
[514]   AJA 1999, s 11(1).
[515]   AJA 1999, s 11(2).

LSC liability

7.364 The court may make an order against the LSC only where the following conditions are satisfied:[516]

(1)   the amount (if any) which the client is required personally to pay under that costs order is less than the amount of the full costs due under the s 11(1) order;

(2)   unless there is a good reason for the delay, the non-funded party has made a request for a determination of the LSC's liability within 3 months of the making of the s 11(1) order;

(3)   as regards costs incurred in a court of first instance, the proceedings were instituted by the funded party, the non-funded party is an individual and the court is satisfied that the non-funded party will suffer financial hardship unless the order is made; and

(4)   in any case, the court is satisfied that it is just and equitable in the circumstances that provision for the costs should be made out of public funds.

In considering these matters the costs judge is expressly required to consider the financial resources of the non-funded person and his partner.[517]

7.365 When giving judgment in the context of stage one rather than stage two, Wall LJ explained that the difference between first instance hearings and appeals is that a hearing at first instance is a necessary thing which is required to make findings of fact and to establish the parties' rights, but an appeal is a matter of choice.[518]

7.366 Where the non-funded party is acting in a representative, fiduciary or official capacity, the court shall have regard to the value of the property, estate or fund and the resources of the beneficiaries, if any.[519]

7.367 Where the costs judge is deciding whether to exercise his discretion in a case involving costs in the Court of Appeal, Phillips MR has confirmed that the following comments of Lord Woolf MR (which were made under the old regime) remain good law:[520]

'If the court comes to a conclusion that in those circumstances it would make the hypothetical order for costs, [ie a section 11(1) order] then in the case of an appeal the court will usually conclude in the absence of some special circumstance that for the purposes of section 18(4)(c) [of the Legal Aid Act 1988] it is just and equitable to make an order. Contrary to Mr Howard's submission a local authority, because it is a public body, is not at a disadvantage as compared with any other litigant in seeking an order against the board.'

Lord Phillips MR went on to say that:

'Costs judges should proceed on the premise that it is just and equitable that the commission should stand behind their "client", by definition under the Regulations the individual who receives funded services, unless they are aware of facts which render that result unjust or inequitable.'

---

[516]   Community Legal Service (Cost Protection) Regulations 2000 (SI 2000/824), reg 5(2) and (3).

[517]   SI 2000/824, reg 5(6).

[518]   *Wyatt v Portsmouth Hospitals NHS Trust* [2006] EWCA Civ 529 at [36]–[42].

[519]   SI 2000/824, reg 5(6).

[520]   *R v Secretary of State for the Home Department ex p Gunn* [2001] EWCA Civ 891 at [50], approving *In re O (Costs: Liability of Legal Aid Board)* [1997] 1 FLR 465.

In courts at first instance, it will be necessary for the non-funded party to show financial hardship.[521] Sharp J has commented that the question of whether the non-funded party would suffer financial hardship if their costs were not paid was a question of fact and degree; it is a question that must take into account the impact or the likely consequences to the non-funded person if his costs are not paid.[522] Sharp J found that the removal of the word 'severe' means that the wording of the regulations represented a deliberate and significant relaxation of the formerly stringent regime.[523]

7.368 Where the LSC funded client does not have cost protection in respect of all of the costs awarded, the order made by the costs judge or district judge must in addition to specifying the costs payable, identify the full costs in respect of which cost protection applies and the full costs in respect of which cost protection does not apply.[524]

Changes in circumstances and variation

7.369 The receiving party may apply to the court for a variation of the amount which the LSC funded client is required to pay on the ground that there has been a significant change in the client's circumstances since the date of the order.[525] The CPD gives detailed guidance as to the procedure.[526]

Revocation of the certificate

7.370 Where a legally-aided opponent has had his legal aid certificate revoked, it is open to the court to give effect to that revocation by varying any costs order which had been made against him in such a way as to remove the bar against immediate enforcement.[527]

The wording of the relevant provisions

7.371 Section 11 of AJA 1999 provides:

'(1) Except in prescribed circumstances, costs ordered against an individual in relation to any proceedings or part of proceedings funded for him shall not exceed the amount (if any) which is a reasonable one for him to pay having regard to all the circumstances including—

(a) the financial resources of all parties to the proceedings, and
(b) their conduct in connection with the dispute to which the proceedings relate; and for this purpose proceedings, or a part of the proceedings, are funded for an individual if services relating to the proceedings or part are funded for him by the commission as part of the Community Legal Service.

(2) In assessing for the purposes of subsection (1) the financial resources of an individual for whom services are funded by the commission as part of the Community Legal Service, his clothes and household furniture and the tools and implements of his trade shall not be taken into account, except so far as may be prescribed.

---

[521] Community Legal Service (Cost Protection) Regulations 2000 (SI 2000/824), reg 5(3).
[522] *Legal Services Commission v F, A, & V* [2011] EWHC 899 (QB) at [49].
[523] Ibid at [48].
[524] CPD, art 23.9.
[525] CPD, art 23.11.
[526] CPD, arts 23.11–23.17.
[527] *DEG-Deutsche Investitions und Entwicklungsgesellschaft mbH v Koshy* [2001] 3 All ER 878.

(3) Subject to subsections (1) and (2), regulations may make provision about costs in relation to proceedings in which services are funded by the commission for any of the parties as part of the Community Legal Service.

(4) The regulations may, in particular, make provision—

    (a)   specifying the principles to be applied in determining the amount of any costs which may be awarded against a party for whom services are funded by the commission as part of the Community Legal Service,

    (b)   limiting the circumstances in which, or extent to which, an order for costs may be enforced against such a party,

    (c)   as to the cases in which, and extent to which, such a party may be required to give security for costs and the manner in which it is to be given,

    (d)   requiring the payment by the commission of the whole or part of any costs incurred by a party for whom services are not funded by the commission as part of the Community Legal Service,

    (e)   specifying the principles to be applied in determining the amount of any costs which may be awarded to a party for whom services are so funded,

    (f)   requiring the payment to the commission, or the person or body by which the services were provided, of the whole or part of any sum awarded by way of costs to such a party, and

    (g)   as to the court, tribunal or other person or body by whom the amount of any costs is to be determined and the extent to which any determination of that amount is to be final.'

7.372 The relevant procedures are set out in regs 9 and 10 of the Costs Regulations, as amended:

'9(1) Where the court is considering whether to make a section 11(1) costs order, it shall consider whether, but for cost protection, it would have made a costs order against the client and, if so, whether it would, on making the costs order, have specified the amount to be paid under that order.

(2) If the court considers that it would have made a costs order against the client, but that it would not have specified the amount to be paid under it, the court shall, when making the section 11(1) costs order:

    (a)   specify the amount (if any) that the client is to pay under that order if, but only if:

        (i)   it considers that it has sufficient information before it to decide what amount is, in that case, a reasonable amount for the client to pay, in accordance with section 11(1) of the Act; and

        (ii)   it is satisfied that, if it were to determine the full costs at that time, they would exceed the amount referred to in sub-paragraph (i);

    (b)   otherwise, it shall not specify the amount the client is to pay under the costs order.

(3) If the court considers that it would have made a costs order against the client, and that it would have specified the amount to be paid under it, the court shall, when making the section 11(1) costs order:

    (a)   specify the amount (if any) that the client is to pay under that order if, but only if, it considers that it has sufficient information before it to decide what amount is, in that case, a reasonable amount for the client to pay, in accordance with section 11(1) of the Act;

    (b)   otherwise, it shall not specify the amount the client is to pay under the costs order.

(4) Any order made under paragraph (3) shall state the amount of the full costs.

(5) The amount (if any) to be paid by the client under an order made under paragraph (2)(b) or paragraph (3)(b), and any application for a costs order against the commission,

shall be determined in accordance with regulation 10, and at any such determination following an order made under paragraph (2)(b), the amount of the full costs shall also be assessed.

(6)   Where the court makes a section 11(1) costs order that does not specify the amount which the client is to pay under it, it may also make findings of fact, as to the parties' conduct in the proceedings or otherwise, relevant to the determination of that amount, and those findings shall be taken into consideration in that determination.

10(1)   The following paragraphs of this regulation apply where the amount to be paid under a section 11(1) costs order, or an application for a costs order against the Commission, is to be determined under this regulation, by virtue of regulation 9(5).

(2)   The receiving party may, within three months after a section 11(1) costs order is made, request a hearing to determine the costs payable to him.

(3)   A request under paragraph (2) shall be accompanied by:

   (a)   if the section 11(1) costs order does not state the full costs, the receiving party's bill of costs, which shall comply with any requirements of relevant rules of court relating to the form and content of a bill of costs where the court is assessing a party's costs;

   (b)   unless the conditions set out in paragraph (3A) are satisfied, a statement of resources; and

   (c)   if the receiving party is seeking, or, subject to the determination of the amount to be paid under the section 11(1) costs order, may seek, a costs order against the Commission, written notice to that effect.

(3A)   The conditions referred to in paragraph (3)(b) above are that—

   (a)   the court is determining an application for a costs order against the Commission;

   (b)   the costs were not incurred in a court of first instance.

(4)   The receiving party shall file the documents referred to in paragraph (3) with the court and at the same time serve copies of them:

   (a)   on the client, if a determination of costs payable under section 11(1) of the Act is sought; and

   (b)   on the ... Director, if notice has been given under paragraph (3)(c).

(5)   Where documents are served on the client under paragraph (4)(a), the client shall make a statement of resources.

(6)   The client shall file the statement of resources made under paragraph (5) with the court, and serve copies of it on the receiving party and, if notice has been given under paragraph (3)(c), on the ... Director, not more than 21 days after the client receives a copy of the receiving party's statement of resources.

(7)   The client may, at the same time as filing and serving a statement of resources under paragraph (6), file, and serve on the same persons, a statement setting out any points of dispute in relation to the bill of costs referred to in paragraph (3)(a).

(8)   If the client, without good reason, fails to file a statement of resources in accordance with paragraph (6), the court shall determine the amount which the client shall be required to pay under the section 11(1) costs order (and, if relevant, the full costs), having regard to the statement made by the receiving party, and the court need not hold an oral hearing for such determination.

(9)   If the client files a statement of resources in accordance with paragraph (6), or the period for filing such notice expires, or if the costs payable by the client have already been determined, the court shall set a date for the hearing and, at least 14 days before that date, serve notice of it on:

   (a)   the receiving party;

(b)   the client (unless the costs payable by the client have already been determined); and

(c)   if a costs order against the Commission is or may be sought, the ... Director.

(10)   The court's functions under this regulation may be exercised:

(a)   in relation to proceedings in the House of Lords, by the Clerk to the Parliaments;
(b)   in relation to proceedings in the Court of Appeal, High Court or a county court, a costs judge or a district judge;
(c)   in relation to proceedings in a magistrates' court, by a single justice or by the justices' clerk;
(d)   in relation to proceedings in the Employment Appeal Tribunal, by the Registrar of that Tribunal.

(11)   The amount of costs to be determined under this regulation may include the costs incurred in relation to a request made under this regulation.'

7.373 Regulation 10A empowers the court to order a funded party to pay an amount on account of costs and reg 13(1)(a) permits a regional director appointed by the commission to appear at any hearing in relation to which notice has been given under reg 10(3)(c).

7.374 Further provisions are made at reg 5 of the Cost Protection Regulations, which make the following provisions:

'(1)   The following paragraphs of this regulation apply where:

(a)   funded services are provided to a client in relation to proceedings;
(b)   those proceedings are finally decided in favour of a non-funded party; and
(c)   cost protection applies.

(2)   The court may, subject to the following paragraphs of this regulation, make an order for the payment by the Commission to the non-funded party of the whole or any part of the costs incurred by him in the proceedings (other than any costs that the client is required to pay under a section 11(1) costs order).

(3)   An order under paragraph (2) may only be made if all the conditions set out in sub-paragraphs (a), (b), (c) and (d) are satisfied:

(a)   a section 11(1) costs order is made against the client in the proceedings, and the amount (if any) which the client is required to pay under that costs order is less than the amount of the full costs;
(b)   unless there is a good reason for the delay, the non-funded party makes a request under regulation 10(2) of the Community Legal Service (Costs) Regulations 2000 within three months of the making of the section 11(1) costs order;
(c)   as regards costs incurred in a court of first instance, the proceedings were instituted by the client, the non-funded party is an individual, and the court is satisfied that the non-funded party will suffer ... financial hardship unless the order is made; and
(d)   in any case, the court is satisfied that it is just and equitable in the circumstances that provision for the costs should be made out of public funds.

(3A)   An order under paragraph (2) may be made—

(a)   in relation to proceedings in the House of Lords, by the Clerk to the Parliaments;
(b)   in relation to proceedings in the Court of Appeal, High Court or a county court, by a costs judge or a district judge;
(c)   in relation to proceedings in a magistrates' court, by a single justice or by the justices' clerk;
(d)   in relation to proceedings in the Employment Appeal Tribunal, by the Registrar of that tribunal.

(4) Where the client receives funded services in connection with part only of the proceedings, the reference in paragraph (2) to the costs incurred by the non-funded party in the relevant proceedings shall be construed as a reference to so much of those costs as is attributable to the part of the proceedings which are funded proceedings.

(5) Where a court decides any proceedings in favour of the non-funded party and an appeal lies (with or without permission) against that decision, any order made under this regulation shall not take effect:

    (a)   where permission to appeal is required, unless the time limit for applications for permission to appeal expires without permission being granted;

    (b)   where permission to appeal is granted or is not required, unless the time limit for appeal expires without an appeal being brought.

(6) Subject to paragraph (7), in determining whether the conditions in paragraph (3)(c) and (d) are satisfied, the court shall have regard to the resources of the non-funded party and of his partner.

(7) The court shall not have regard to the resources of the partner of the non-funded party if the partner has a contrary interest in the funded proceedings.

(8) Where the non-funded party is acting in a representative, fiduciary or official capacity and is entitled to be indemnified in respect of his costs from any property, estate or fund, the court shall, for the purposes of paragraph (3), have regard to the value of the property, estate or fund and the resources of the persons, if any, including that party where appropriate, who are beneficially interested in that property, estate or fund.'

7.375 Regulation 7 provides:

'(1) No order to pay costs in favour of a non-funded party shall be made against the commission in respect of funded proceedings except in accordance with these Regulations, and any costs to be paid under such an order shall be paid out of the Community Legal Service Fund.

(2) Nothing in these Regulations shall be construed, in relation to proceedings where one of more parties are receiving, or have received, funded services, as:

    (a)   requiring a court to make a costs order where it would not otherwise have made a costs order; or

    (b)   affecting the court's power to make a wasted costs order against a legal representative.'

7.376 CPR, r 44.17 is the only part of the CPR to make direct reference to AJA 1999, s 11(1) orders:

'This Part and Part 45 (fixed costs), Part 46 (fast track trial costs), Part 47 (procedure for detailed assessment of costs and default provisions) and Part 48 (special cases), do not apply to the assessment of costs in proceedings to the extent that—

    (a)   section 11 of the Access to Justice Act 1999, and provisions made under that Act, or

    (b)   regulations made under the Legal Aid Act 1988,

make different provision. (The costs practice direction sets out the procedure to be followed where a party was wholly or partially funded by the Legal Services Commission).'

7.377 The CPD contains extensive directions relating to AJA 1999, s 11(1) orders, and stage two in particular:

'SECTION 22 ORDERS FOR COSTS TO WHICH SECTION 11 OF THE ACCESS TO JUSTICE ACT 1999 APPLIES

22.1　In this Practice Direction:

"order for costs to be determined" means an order for costs to which Section 11 of the Access to Justice Act 1999 applies under which the amount of costs payable by the LSC funded client is to be determined by a costs judge or district judge under Section 23 of this Practice Direction.

"order specifying the costs payable" means an order for costs to which Section 11 of the Act applies and which specifies the amount which the LSC funded client is to pay.

"full costs" means, where an order to which Section 11 of the Act applies is made against a LSC funded client, the amount of costs which that person would, had cost protection not applied, have been ordered to pay.

"determination proceedings" means proceedings to which paragraphs 22.1 to 22.10 apply.

"Section 11(1) costs order" means an order for costs to be determined or an order specifying the costs payable other than an order specifying the costs payable which was made in determination proceedings.

"statement of resources" means

(1)　a statement, verified by a statement of truth, made by a party to proceedings setting out:

    (a)　his income and capital and financial commitments during the previous year and, if applicable, those of his partner;

    (b)　his estimated future financial resources and expectations and, if applicable, those of his partner ("partner" is defined in paragraph 21.4, above);

    (c)　a declaration that he and, if applicable, his partner, has not deliberately foregone or deprived himself of any resources or expectations;

    (d)　particulars of any application for funding made by him in connection with the proceedings; and,

    (e)　any other facts relevant to the determination of his resources; or

(2)　a statement, verified by a statement of truth, made by a client receiving funded services, setting out the information provided by the client under Regulation 6 of the Community Legal Service (Financial) Regulations 2000, and stating that there has been no significant change in the client's financial circumstances since the date on which the information was provided or, as the case may be, details of any such change.

"Regional Director" means any Regional Director appointed by the LSC and any member of his staff authorised to act on his behalf.

22.2　Regulations 8 to 13 of the Community Legal Service (Costs) Regulations 2000 as amended set out the procedure for seeking costs against a funded client and the LSC. The effect of these Regulations is set out in this section and the next section of this Practice Direction.

22.3　As from 5 June 2000, Regulations 9 to 13 of the Community Legal Service (Costs) Regulations 2000 as amended also apply to certificates issued under the Legal Aid Act 1988 where costs against the assisted person fall to be assessed under Regulation 124 of the Civil Legal Aid (General) Regulations 1989. In this section and the next section of this Practice Direction the expression 'LSC funded client' includes an assisted person (defined in rule 43.2).

22.4　Regulation 8 of the Community Legal Service (Costs) Regulations 2000 as amended provides that a party intending to seek an order for costs against a LSC funded client may at any time file and serve on the LSC funded client a statement of resources. If that statement is served 7 or more days before a date fixed for a hearing at which an order for costs may be made, the LSC funded client must also make a statement of resources and produce it at the hearing.

22.5 If the court decides to make an order for costs against a LSC funded client to whom cost protection applies it may either:

(1)   make an order for costs to be determined, or

(2)   make an order specifying the costs payable.

22.6 If the court makes an order for costs to be determined it may also

(1)   state the amount of full costs, or

(2)   make findings of facts, e g concerning the conduct of all the parties which are to be taken into account by the court in the subsequent determination proceedings.

22.7 The court will not make an order specifying the costs payable unless:

(1)   it considers that it has sufficient information before it to decide what amount is a reasonable amount for the LSC funded client to pay in accordance with Section 11 of the Act, and

(2)   either

    (a)   the order also states the amount of full costs, or

    (b)   the court considers that it has sufficient information before it to decide what amount is a reasonable amount for the LSC funded client to pay in accordance with Section 11 of the Act and is satisfied that, if it were to determine the full costs at that time, they would exceed the amounts specified in the order.

22.8 Where an order specifying the costs payable is made and the LSC funded client does not have cost protection in respect of all of the costs awarded in that order, the order must identify the sum payable (if any) in respect of which the LSC funded client has cost protection and the sum payable (if any) in respect of which he does not have cost protection.

22.9 The court cannot make an order under Regulations 8 to 13 of the Community Legal Service (Costs) Regulations 2000 as amended except in proceedings to which the next section of this Practice Direction applies.

SECTION 23 DETERMINATION PROCEEDINGS AND SIMILAR PROCEEDINGS UNDER THE COMMUNITY LEGAL SERVICE (COSTS) REGULATIONS 2000

23.1 This section of this Practice Direction deals with

(1)   proceedings subsequent to the making of an order for costs to be determined,

(2)   variations in the amount stated in an order specifying the amount of costs payable and

(3)   the late determination of costs under an order for costs to be determined;

(4)   appeals in respect of determination.

23.2 In this section of this Practice Direction "appropriate court office" means:

(1)   the district registry or county court in which the case was being dealt with when the Section 11(1) order was made, or to which it has subsequently been transferred; or

(2)   in all other cases, the Senior Courts Costs Office.

23.2A

(1) This paragraph applies where the appropriate office is any of the following county courts:
Barnet, Bow, Brentford, Bromley, Central London, Clerkenwell, Croydon, Edmonton, Ilford, Kingston, Lambeth, Mayors and City of London, Romford, Shoreditch, Uxbridge, Wandsworth, West London, Willesden and Woolwich.

(2) Where this paragraph applies:

    (i)   a receiving party seeking an order specifying costs payable by an LSC funded client and/or by the Legal Services Commission under this section must file his application in the Senior Courts Costs Office and, for all purposes relating to that application, the Senior Courts Costs Office will be treated as the appropriate office in that case; and

    (ii)   unless an order is made transferring the application to the Senior Courts Costs Office as part of the High Court, an appeal from any decision made by a costs judge shall lie to the Designated Civil Judge for the London Group of County Courts or such judge as he shall nominate. The appeal notice and any other relevant papers should be lodged at the Central London Civil Justice Centre.

23.3

(1) A receiving party seeking an order specifying costs payable by an LSC funded client and/or by the LSC may within 3 months of an order for costs to be determined, file in the appropriate court office an application in Form N244 accompanied by

    (a)   the receiving party's bill of costs (unless the full costs have already been determined);

    (b)   the receiving party's statement of resources (unless the court is determining an application against a costs order against the LSC and the costs were not incurred in the court of first instance); and

    (c)   if the receiving party intends to seek costs against the LSC, written notice to that effect.

(2) If the LSC funded client's liability has already been determined and is less than the full costs, the application will be for costs against the LSC only. If the LSC funded client's liability has not yet been determined, the receiving party must indicate if costs will be sought against the LSC if the funded client's liability is determined as less than the full costs.

(The LSC funded client's certificate will contain the addresses of the LSC funded client, his solicitor, and the relevant Regional Office of the LSC.)

23.4 The receiving party must file the above documents in the appropriate court office and (where relevant) serve copies on the LSC funded client and the Regional Director. In respect of applications for funded services made before 3 December 2001 a failure to file a request within the 3 months time limit specified in Regulation 10(2) is an absolute bar to the making of a costs order against the LSC. Where the application for funded services was made on or after 3 December 2001 the court does have power to extend the 3 months time limit, but only if the applicant can show good reason for the delay.

23.5 On being served with the application, the LSC funded client must respond by filing a statement of resources and serving a copy of it on the receiving party (and the Regional Director where relevant) within 21 days. The LSC funded client may also file and serve written points disputing the bill within the same time limit. (Under rule 3.1 the court may extend or shorten this time limit.)

23.6 If the LSC funded client fails to file a statement of resources without good reason, the court will determine his liability (and the amount of full costs if relevant) and need not hold an oral hearing for such determination.

23.7 When the LSC funded client files a statement or the 21 day period for doing so expires, the court will fix a hearing date and give the relevant parties at least 14 days notice. The court may fix a hearing without waiting for the expiry of the 21 day period if the application is made only against the LSC.

23.8 Determination proceedings will be listed for hearing before a costs judge or district judge. The determination of the liability on the LSC funded client will be listed as a private hearing.

23.9   Where the LSC funded client does not have cost protection in respect of all of the costs awarded, the order made by the costs judge or district judge must in addition to specifying the costs payable, identify the full costs in respect of which cost protection applies and the full costs in respect of which cost protection does not apply.

23.10   The Regional Director may appear at any hearing at which a costs order may be made against the LSC. Instead of appearing, he may file a written statement at court and serve a copy on the receiving party. The written statement should be filed and a copy served, not less than 7 days before the hearing.

Variation of an order specifying the costs payable

23.11

(1)   This paragraph applies where the amount stated in an order specifying the costs payable plus the amount ordered to be paid by the LSC is less than the full costs to which cost protection applies.

(2)   The receiving party may apply to the court for a variation of the amount which the LSC funded client is required to pay on the ground that there has been a significant change in the client's circumstances since the date of the order.

23.12   On an application under paragraph 23.11, where the order specifying the costs payable does not state the full costs

(1)   The receiving party must file with his application the receiving party's statement of resources and bill of costs and copies of these documents should be served with the application.

(2)   The LSC funded client must respond to the application by making a statement of resources which must be filed at court and served on the receiving party within 21 days thereafter. The LSC funded client may also file and serve written points disputing the bill within the same time limit.

(3)   The court will, when determining the application assess the full costs identifying any part of them to which cost protection does apply and any part of them to which cost protection does not apply.

23.13   On an application under paragraph 23.11 the order specifying the costs payable may be varied as the court thinks fit. That variation must not increase:

(1)   the amount of any costs ordered to be paid by the LSC, and

(2)   the amount payable by the LSC funded client,

to a sum which is greater than the amount of the full costs plus the costs of the application.

23.14

(1)   Where an order for costs to be determined has been made but the receiving party has not applied, within the three month time limit under paragraph 23.2, the receiving party may apply on any of the following grounds for a determination of the amount which the funded client is required to pay:

(a)   there has been a significant change in the funded client's circumstances since the date of the order for costs to be determined; or

(b)   material additional information about the funded client's financial resources is available which could not with reasonable diligence have been obtained by the receiving party at the relevant time; or

(c)   there were other good reasons for the failure by the receiving party to make an application within the time limit.

(2)   An application for costs payable by the LSC cannot be made under this paragraph.

23.15

(1)   Where the receiving party has received funded services in relation to the proceedings, the LSC may make an application under paragraphs 23.11 and 23.14 above.

(2)   In respect of an application under paragraph 23.11 made by the LSC, the LSC must file and serve copies of the documents described in paragraph 23.12(1)

23.16   An application under paragraph 23.11, 23.14 and 23.15 must be commenced before the expiration of 6 years from the date on which the court made the order specifying the costs payable, or (as the case may be) the order for costs to be determined.

23.17   Applications under paragraphs 23.11, 23.14 and 23.15 should be made in the appropriate court office and should be made in Form N244 to be listed for a hearing before a costs judge or district judge.

Appeals

23.18

(1)   Save as mentioned above any determination made under Regulation 9 or 10 of the Costs Regulations is final (Regulation 11(1)). Any party with a financial interest in the assessment of the full costs, other than a funded party, may appeal against that assessment in accordance with CPR Part 52 (Regulation 11(2) and CPR rule 47.20).

(2)   The receiving party or the Commission may appeal on a point of law against the making of a costs order against the Commission, against the amount of costs the Commission is required to pay or against the court's refusal to make such an order (Regulation 11(4)).'

ORDERS AGAINST THE CROWN

7.378   Where the Crown is a party to litigation, it will be treated in much the same way as any other party save that the nature of the proceedings and the character and circumstances in which they were brought may be different to those in other proceedings. There is legislation that requires the court to have regard to those matters: see **38.87**.[528]

NO ORDER AS TO COSTS

7.379   With one or two exceptions (see below), where the court makes no order for costs, that will mean that no party is entitled to costs.[529] The exceptions are:

- where the court makes an order granting permission to appeal;
- where the court makes an order granting permission to apply for judicial review; and
- where the court makes any order or direction sought by a party on an application without notice.

In all of those circumstances, where the court makes no order for costs it will be deemed to include an order for the applicant's costs in the case.[530]

---

[528]   The Administration of Justice (Miscellaneous Provisions) Act 1933.
[529]   CPR, r 44.13(1)(a).
[530]   CPR, r 44.13(1A); see also *A Practice Statement (Judicial Review: costs)* (2004) *The Times*, 20 May, QBD.

7.380 The fact that the court has not made an order for costs at the end of a hearing does not always mean that neither party will be entitled to costs at the conclusion of the claim: in particular, if the hearing was adjourned part heard (such as on the first day of a trial lasting more than one day), then the court would deal with the costs of that day upon conclusion of the trial.

7.381 Where, on the other hand, the court considers the issue of costs but makes no order, that will be a disposal of that issue on the basis that neither party is entitled to costs. This would prevent the court from making a subsequent order for costs in respect of the same matter (unless, of course, that were to be as a result of a successful appeal).[531]

7.382 Where no order for costs is made in respect of a hearing and the court makes no order relating to consequential costs (such as costs thrown away by an adjournment), that may be interpreted as disentitling the parties from those consequential costs.[532]

7.383 The wording of the relevant provision, CPR, r 44.13, is as follows:

'(1)   Where the court makes an order which does not mention costs—

(a)   subject to paragraphs (1A) and (1B), the general rule is that no party is entitled—
    (i)   to costs; or
    (ii)   to seek an order under section 194(3) of the Legal Services Act 2007,
    in relation to that order; but
(b)   this does not affect any entitlement of a party to recover costs out of a fund held by that party as trustee or personal representative, or pursuant to any lease, mortgage or other security.

(1A)   Where the court makes—

(a)   an order granting permission to appeal;
(b)   an order granting permission to apply for judicial review; or
(c)   any other order or direction sought by a party on an application without notice,

and its order does not mention costs, it will be deemed to include an order for applicant's costs in the case.

(1B)   Any party affected by a deemed order for costs under paragraph (1A) may apply at any time to vary the order.'

ORDERS IN SPECIFIC CIRCUMSTANCES

Costs-only proceedings

7.384 Costs-only proceedings are a mechanism by which parties may bring a disputed bill of costs before the court without the need to issue proceedings in the substantive claim. The procedure allows the recovery of those costs which would have been recoverable in the proceedings, had the proceedings been commenced.[533]

---

[531]   *Griffiths v Commissioner of Police for the Metropolis* [2003] EWCA Civ 313 at [6]–[11].
[532]   *Beahan v Stoneham* (unreported) 19 January 2001, QBD, Buckley J.
[533]   *Callery v Gray* [2001] EWCA Civ 1117 at [54], per Woolf CJ.

Availability

7.385 Where the parties have reached agreement on all issues (including the incidence of costs), but they have been unable to agree the quantum of costs, a CPR Part 8 claim may be brought solely for the purpose of obtaining an order for the disputed costs to be assessed.[534] Whilst it is usually the receiving party who brings such a claim, the CPR make provision for any party to issue proceedings;[535] it is not unknown for paying parties to issue proceedings in claims where the receiving party has delayed bringing proceedings.

Alternatives to costs-only proceedings

7.386 Where a costs-only claim has been dismissed under CPR, r 44.12A(4), that dismissal does not prevent the claimant from issuing another claim under CPR, Part 7 or Part 8, based on the agreement or alleged agreement to which the costs-only proceedings related.[536] Likewise, nothing in the costs-only provisions in the CPR prevents a person from issuing a claim form under Part 7 or Part 8 to sue on an agreement made in settlement of a dispute where that agreement makes provision for costs, nor from claiming in that case an order for costs or a specified sum in respect of costs.[537]

Procedure

7.387 The claim form must state the remedy sought (ie that the Part 8 claimant seeks an order for costs to be assessed).[538] The claim form must contain or be accompanied by the agreement or confirmation that costs are payable; that document or statement must be part of the evidence in support of the claim.[539] By analogy with litigation other than costs, it would seem that procedural errors in this regard will not necessarily lead to the claim being struck out[540] (although see **7.392**).

7.388 The claim should not be issued in the High Court unless the dispute to which the agreement related was of such a value or type that had proceedings been begun they would have been commenced in the High Court.[541] When a claim is to be issued in the High Court in the Royal Courts of Justice, it ought to be issued in the Senior Courts Costs Office.[542]

7.389 The claim form must:[543]

- identify the claim or dispute to which the agreement to pay costs relates;
- state the date and terms of the agreement on which the claimant relies;
- set out or have attached to it a draft of the order which the claimant seeks;
- state the amount of the costs claimed; and

---

[534] See CPR, r 44.12A(1) and (2).
[535] CPR, r 44.12A(2).
[536] CPD, art 17.9.
[537] CPD, art 17.11.
[538] See CPR, r 8.2(b)(ii) and CPD, art 17.3.
[539] CPR, r 44.12A(3) and CPD, art 17.4.
[540] See, for example, *Parnall v Hurst* (2003) *The Times*, 10 July in which HHJ Peter Langan QC declined to strike out a Part 8 claim where the evidence in support had not been served along with the claim form.
[541] CPD, art 17.1.
[542] CPD, art 17.2.
[543] CPD, art 17.3.

- state whether the costs are claimed on the standard or indemnity basis; if no basis is specified, the costs will be treated as being claimed on the standard basis.

7.390 Costs-only claims will not generally be allocated to a track; in particular, they will not be deemed to be allocated to the multi-track.[544]

7.391 It is not clear whether the court has a jurisdiction to make an order, other than by consent, that a payment on account of the costs to be assessed is made in costs-only proceedings.[545]

Disposal

7.392 The court may either dismiss the claim or make an order that the costs be assessed by way of detailed assessment, but the court must dismiss the claim if it is opposed:[546] the proceedings are, therefore, for all practical purposes, consensual. A claim will be treated as opposed if the defendant files an acknowledgement of service stating that he intends to contest the making of an order for costs or to seek a different remedy.[547] A claim will not be treated as opposed if the defendant files an acknowledgement of service stating that he disputes the amount of the claim for costs.[548]

7.393 When the time for filing the acknowledgement of service has expired, the CPR Part 8 claimant may request the court to make an order in the terms of his claim. The Part 8 claimant may not make such a request if the Part 8 defendant has filed an acknowledgement of service stating that he intends to contest the claim or to seek a different order. The request may be made by letter.[549]

7.394 If the parties agree an order which deals with the costs-only proceedings, the terms of the consent order need not be the same as those sought in the claim itself. Where the costs-only proceedings are dealt with by consent, the provisions in CPR, r 40.6 apply.[550]

The assessment

7.395 Although the costs which are the subject of costs-only proceedings are payable as a result of a contract, those costs are not the subject matter of the original dispute, so the provisions relating to costs payable under a contract[551] do not apply.[552] The costs will, therefore, be assessed on the standard basis (or the indemnity basis, as the case may be)[553] without any modification.

7.396 Whilst the costs that are the subject of costs-only proceedings are to be assessed, that assessment may reflect provisions for fixed costs. In particular, it is not possible to

---

[544] See CPD, art 17.10, which disapplies CPR, r 8.9.
[545] *Banchio v Lai* [2003] EWHC 9038 (Costs).
[546] See CPR, r 44.12A(4)(a) and (4)(b).
[547] CPD, art 17.9(1)(a).
[548] CPD, art 17.9(1)(b).
[549] CPD, art 17.6.
[550] CPD, art 17.7.
[551] See CPR, r 48.3, which introduces a certain presumption that costs incurred under the terms of a contract have been reasonably incurred.
[552] CPR, r 44.12A(5).
[553] See, also, CPD, art 17.8, which expressly provides that CPR, r 44.4 will apply.

avoid the operation of Section II of CPR Part 45 by issuing costs-only proceedings in the hope that the court will assess the costs on the basis of what is reasonable rather than on the basis of predictive costs; this is because in proceedings to which Part 45, Section II apply, the court shall assess the costs in the manner set out in that section.[554]

The wording of the relevant provisions

7.397 The CPR make the following provision in r 44.12A relating to costs-only proceedings:

'(1)   This rule sets out a procedure which may be followed where—

(a)   the parties to a dispute have reached an agreement on all issues (including which party is to pay the costs) which is made or confirmed in writing; but
(b)   they have failed to agree the amount of those costs; and
(c)   no proceedings have been started.

(2)   Either party to the agreement may start proceedings under this rule by issuing a claim form in accordance with Part 8.

(3)   The claim form must contain or be accompanied by the agreement or confirmation.

(4)   Except as provided in paragraph (4A), in proceedings to which this rule applies the court—

(a)   may
(i)   make an order for costs to be determined by detailed assessment; or
(ii)   dismiss the claim; and
(b)   must dismiss the claim if it is opposed.

(4A)   In proceedings to which Section II of Part 45 applies, the court shall assess the costs in the manner set out in that Section.

(5)   Rule 48.3 (amount of costs where costs are payable pursuant to a contract) does not apply to claims started under the procedure in this rule. (Rule 7.2 provides that proceedings are started when the court issues a claim form at the request of the claimant)

(Rule 8.1(6) provides that a practice direction may modify the Part 8 procedure)'.

7.398   The CPD gives the following guidance which supplements the CPR:

'SECTION 17 COSTS-ONLY PROCEEDINGS: RULE 44.12A

17.1   A claim form under this rule should not be issued in the High Court unless the dispute to which the agreement relates was of such a value or type that had proceedings been begun they would have been commenced in the High Court.

17.2   A claim form which is to be issued in the High Court at the Royal Courts of Justice will be issued in the Senior Courts Costs Office.

17.3   Attention is drawn to rule 8.2 (in particular to paragraph (b)(ii)) and to rule 44.12A(3). The claim form must:

(1)   identify the claim or dispute to which the agreement to pay costs relates;
(2)   state the date and terms of the agreement on which the claimant relies;
(3)   set out or have attached to it a draft of the order which the claimant seeks;
(4)   state the amount of the costs claimed; and,
(5)   state whether the costs are claimed on the standard or indemnity basis. If no basis is specified the costs will be treated as being claimed on the standard basis.

---

[554]   CPR, r 44.12A(4A).

17.4 The evidence to be filed and served with the claim form under Rule 8.5 must include copies of the documents on which the claimant relies to prove the defendant's agreement to pay costs.

17.5 A costs judge or a district judge has jurisdiction to hear and decide any issue which may arise in a claim issued under this rule irrespective of the amount of the costs claimed or of the value of the claim to which the agreement to pay costs relates. A costs officer may make an order by consent under paragraph 17.7, or an order dismissing a claim under paragraph 17.9 below.

17.6 When the time for filing the defendant's acknowledgement of service has expired, the claimant may by letter request the court to make an order in the terms of his claim, unless the defendant has filed an acknowledgement of service stating that he intends to contest the claim or to seek a different order.

17.7 Rule 40.6 applies where an order is to be made by consent. An order may be made by consent in terms which differ from those set out in the claim form.

17.8

    (1)   An order for costs made under this rule will be treated as an order for the amount of costs to be decided by a detailed assessment to which Part 47 and the practice directions relating to it apply. Rule 44.4(4) (determination of basis of assessment) also applies to the order.

    (2)   In cases in which an additional liability is claimed, the costs judge or district judge should have regard to the time when and the extent to which the claim has been settled and to the fact that the claim has been settled without the need to commence proceedings.

17.9

    (1)   For the purposes of rule 44.12A(4)(b)—

        (a)   a claim will be treated as opposed if the defendant files an acknowledgement of service stating that he intends to contest the making of an order for costs or to seek a different remedy; and

        (b)   a claim will not be treated as opposed if the defendant files an acknowledgement of service stating that he disputes the amount of the claim for costs.

    (2)   An order dismissing the claim will be made as soon as an acknowledgement of service opposing the claim is filed. The dismissal of a claim under rule 44.12A(4) does not prevent the claimant from issuing another claim form under Part 7 or Part 8 based on the agreement or alleged agreement to which the proceedings under this rule related.

17.10

    (1)   Rule 8.9 (which provides that claims issued under Part 8 shall be treated as allocated to the multi-track) shall not apply to claims issued under this rule. A claim issued under this rule may be dealt with without being allocated to a track.

    (2)   Rule 8.1(3) and Part 24 do not apply to proceedings brought under rule 44.12A.

17.11 Nothing in this rule prevents a person from issuing a claim form under Part 7 or Part 8 to sue on an agreement made in settlement of a dispute where that agreement makes provision for costs, nor from claiming in that case an order for costs or a specified sum in respect of costs.'

Interim costs orders

Jurisdiction

7.399 There is nothing within either s 51 of the Senior Courts Act 1981 or the CPR which prevents the court from making costs orders at times other than at the conclusion of the case; indeed, the provisions relating to summary assessment of costs implicitly acknowledge that such orders are available to the court.

7.400 In any event, CPR, r 44.3(6)(e) and (f) make express provision for the court to make an award of costs relating to particular steps taken in the proceedings or to a distinct part of the proceedings.

Available orders

7.401 There are no restrictions on the orders that are available to the court when making an order at an interlocutory stage, but the following orders may be particularly relevant:[555]

•	Costs reserved	The decision about costs is deferred to a later occasion, but if no later order is made the costs will be costs in the case.
•	Claimant's/defendant's costs in case/application	If the party in whose favour the costs order is made is awarded costs at the end the proceedings, that party is entitled to his costs of the part of the proceedings to which the order relates. If any other party is awarded costs at the end of the proceedings, the party in whose favour the final costs order is made is not liable to pay the costs of any other party in respect of the part of the proceedings to which the order relates.

Discretion

7.402 The exercise of the court's discretion at an interlocutory stage is much the same as at any other stage. There are some differences, however. In a pre-CPR case, Buckley LJ explained those differences in the following way:[556]

> '[H]ere we are concerned with the costs of an interlocutory application. Conduct which might be relevant to how the costs of the action should ultimately be borne may be quite irrelevant to whether a party was justified in making a particular interlocutory application. In such a context one naturally starts from a basis of considering whether the defendants were justified in launching their [interlocutory applications].'

Having set the scene, Buckley LJ continued:[557]

> 'When [the court is concerned with] an interlocutory step in an action, the circumstances may be such that it is not then possible to see on which side justice requires that the decision who should bear the costs of that step should ultimately fall. This may depend on how the issues in the action are eventually decided. Consequently, costs in interlocutory matters are often made costs in the cause or reserved.'

---

[555]   See the table at CPD, art 8.5.
[556]   *Scherer and another v Counting Instruments Ltd* [1986] 2 All ER 529 at 533.
[557]   *Scherer and another v Counting Instruments Ltd* [1986] 2 All ER 529 at 536.

Therefore, the interests of justice may require the court to defer making an order in respect of some interlocutory step until the conclusion of the claim. Where a prior Part 36 offer has been made, it would usually be appropriate to postpone the determination of the costs generally until such time as the outcome of the claim has been determined: see **7.70**.

The effect of interim costs orders

7.403 There is authority (albeit pre-CPR)[558] for the proposition that a final costs order does not negate the effect of earlier costs orders. By way of example, if the defendant is awarded the costs of a hearing, the fact that the claimant is subsequently awarded the costs of the claim in general would not negate the defendant's entitlement in principle to the costs of that hearing. It is possible that there is an exception to principle, however, in that Pill LJ had this to say of an appeal in which the claimant had discontinued in a claim after having been awarded the costs of a strike out application:[559]

> '[B]y discontinuing their claim, [the Claimant] accepted that it is not a valid claim against the Defendant. The position should be, and in my view the wording of the rule provides, that in those circumstances the Claimant is on the face of it liable for the ... Defendant's costs. That would have the effect of reversing the order for costs below. The Claimant should not normally have the luxury of bringing a claim now accepted as invalid and not meeting costs incurred along the way.'

Thus, the act of discontinuing is capable of giving rise to a reversal of interim costs orders previously made in the discontinuer's favour. Pill LJ's comments were made in the context of the interim order in question being the subject of an appeal; it is, therefore, possible that he intended his comments to be limited to situations in which the interim order had come back before the court by reason of it being appealed. That is certainly an arguable reading of the judgment, but the fact that Pill LJ went on to say that the effect of the discontinuance ought to have been the same even if the appeal had been dismissed rather suggests that his comments were intended to be of wider application.[560]

7.404 Unless the court makes a 'forthwith order', the beneficiary of an interim costs order will not be able to commence detailed assessment proceedings until the conclusion of the proceedings.[561] This issue is discussed in detail at **7.64–7.73**.

7.405 It is implicit from the examples given in the table at CPD, art 8.5 that where costs are reserved but where no subsequent order is expressly made, the reserved costs will be in the case (or in the application, as the case may be).

PRE-ACTION DISCLOSURE AND APPLICATIONS FOR DISCLOSURE AGAINST NON-PARTIES

7.406 The starting point for a discussion of the incidence of costs of applications for pre-action disclosure or disclosure against non parties is CPR, r 48.1, which provides:

'(1)   This paragraph applies where a person applies—

---

[558]   *Teheran-Europe Co Ltd v ST Belton (Tractors) Ltd* [1971] 2 QB 491 at 493, per Widgery LJ.
[559]   *Safeway v Twigger* [2010] EWCA Civ 1472, per Pill LJ at [58].
[560]   Ibid at [60].
[561]   See CPR, r 47.1.

(a)   for an order under—
        (i)   section 33 of the Senior Courts Act 1981; or
        (ii)   section 52 of the County Courts Act 1984,
(which give the court powers exercisable before commencement of proceedings); or
(b)   for an order under—
        (i)   section 34 of the Senior Courts Act 1981; or
        (ii)   section 53 of the County Courts Act 1984,
(which give the court power to make an order against a non-party for disclosure of documents, inspection of property etc).

(2)   The general rule is that the court will award the person against whom the order is sought his costs—

(a)   of the application; and
(b)   of complying with any order made on the application.

(3)   The court may however make a different order, having regard to all the circumstances, including—

(a)   the extent to which it was reasonable for the person against whom the order was sought to oppose the application; and
(b)   whether the parties to the application have complied with any relevant pre-action protocol.'

There is, therefore, a 'general rule' that the respondent will be awarded their costs, not only of the application, but also of the task of complying with any order which is made. This approach usually applies to all orders for disclosure against non-parties,[562] including those which are based on the *Norwich Pharmacal* principle.[563] In considering whether it should depart from that general rule the court may take into account the parties' conduct, including whether it was reasonable to oppose the application and whether there has been compliance with the relevant pre-action protocol. There is no requirement that the court should decide the issue of costs at the same time that the order regarding disclosure is made: where appropriate, for example, the costs may be reserved pending the conclusion of the trial.[564]

Deviation from the general rule

7.407 Moore-Bick LJ has explained that the aforesaid 'general rule' is a starting point, and that the onus will be on the applicant to persuade the court that some other order is appropriate:[565]

> 'By laying down a general rule that the respondent will be awarded his costs, therefore, I think that the Rules implicitly recognise that it will not usually be unreasonable for him to require the applicant to satisfy the court that he ought to be granted the relief which he seeks. The reason for that (if it be necessary to find one) lies, I think, in a recognition that a private person who is not a party to existing litigation which brings with it an obligation of disclosure is entitled to maintain the privacy of his papers unless sufficient grounds can be shown for overriding it and that it is for the person seeking to invade that privacy to justify doing so. At all events, the rule is clear in its terms and provides the point of departure for a judge dealing with the costs of an application of this kind.'

---

[562]   There is a further type of order that may be sought against non-parties against whom a non-party costs order was sought (*Germany v Flatman* [2011] EWHC 2945 (QB) at [28] and [29]); this is addressed in more detail at **7.199**.

[563]   See, for example, *Patel v Unite* (unreported) 26 January 2012, QBD, HHJ Parkes QC sitting as Judge of the High Court.

[564]   See, for example, *Microsoft Corporation v Datel Design and Development Ltd* [2011] EWHC 1986 (Ch).

[565]   *SES Contracting Ltd v UK Coal plc* [2007] EWCA Civ 791 at [17].

7.408 After having dismissed the suggestion that applications for pre-action disclosure are such an engrained aspect of litigation that opposition would, in general, be unreasonable, Moore-Bick LJ went on to pose the question that the court should ask itself:[566]

> 'The real question which arises in this case, therefore, is whether it was unreasonable for [the respondent] to oppose the application at all, and if not, whether its conduct in relation to the application was capable of justifying [an order which departed from the general rule mentioned above].'

7.409 Amongst other factors, Moore-Bick LJ took into account the nature of the claim, the fact that the application was not routine, the reasons given for opposing the application and the manner of the opposition. He explained that the court should make use of the range of orders available to it.

7.410 Moore-Bick LJ went on to confirm that it was not typically the case that the respondent should be ordered to pay costs; he explained that this was true even where his conduct could be criticised:[567]

> 'The fact is that, short of ordering [the respondent] to pay the costs of [the applicant] on the indemnity basis, the judge's order was the strongest available to him. If one is starting from the position set out in rule 48.1(2) one would expect an order of this kind to be made only in a case where it was clearly unreasonable for the respondent to oppose the application or where the manner of his opposition was so unreasonable as to make it appropriate to require him to bear the whole of both parties' costs.'

These comments were made in the context of the court below having ordered the respondent to bear the whole of the costs of the application. It would seem that such a strong order would be expected only where the opposition to the application was 'clearly unreasonable' or where the manner of the opposition would justify such an order. On the facts of the case before Moore-Bick LJ, the order against the respondent was substituted with no order for costs.

Case examples

7.411 In a different case (a commercial claim), Akenhead J found that it could be reasonable for a respondent carefully to consider its response to an application for disclosure.[568] Similarly, in a family matter in which a respondent NHS trust had concerns about disclosing a child's records, Sumner J commented that the respondent was entitled to present a proper argument to the court raising legitimate concerns and to ask the court to consider whether in the exercise of its discretion those concerns were or were not to prevail.[569] In a commercial claim, Waller LJ refused to interfere with an order condemning a respondent in costs in a case in which it had acted unreasonably in resisting an application 'root and branch'.[570] In an application in which electronic data had been destroyed because it was more than six years old, HHJ Seymour (sitting as a Judge of the High Court) found that the court below was wrong to deprive a solicitor of

---

[566] *SES Contracting Ltd v UK Coal plc* [2007] EWCA Civ 791 at [18].
[567] *SES Contracting Ltd v UK Coal plc* [2007] EWCA Civ 791 at [24].
[568] *Moduleco Ltd v Carillon Construction Ltd* [2009] EWHC 250 (TCC).
[569] *Re R (a child) (disclosure)* [2004] EWHC 2085 (Fam) at [71].
[570] *Bermuda International Securities Ltd v KPMG* [2001] EWCA Civ 269.

his costs merely because he had asserted privilege concerning the reasons as to why the file had been destroyed: he found that the solicitor's only obligation when he was asked for a file was to tell the truth.[571]

Costs of compliance

7.412 The general rule is that the court will award the person against whom the order is sought his costs of complying with any order made on the application.[572] If the respondent has already scanned the documents, Mance J has confirmed that it is open to the court to find that the costs of copying are limited to the costs of providing the copy disk as opposed to the original fee for scanning.[573]

CLARIFICATION AND REVISION OF ORDERS

7.413 It may be the case that one or more of the parties wish to return to the judge who made a costs order for the purposes of clarifying the order, correcting it, or for the purposes of asking the court to make a different order. Each of these things is dealt with in turn, followed by a short discussion of setting aside orders made by consent.

Clarification

7.414 There used to be a rule of practice whereby, once a costs order had been drawn up, there could be no further reference to the judge who made it.[574] Singleton LJ has made it clear that this rule is not in the public interest; where difficulty arises over the interpretation of an order, trouble and expense would be saved if the parties were able to go back to the judge, even after the order had been drawn up.[575] Singleton LJ's comments were made prior to the introduction of the CPR, but, if anything, the CPR have made his remarks even more apposite than they were when they were first made. In any event, the court has an inherent power to vary its own orders to make the meaning and intention of the court clear.[576]

Correction

7.415 The court may correct an accidental slip or omission in an order under what is colloquially known as the 'slip rule'.[577] The slip rule is limited to correcting clerical and administrative mistakes, and cannot be used to vary the substance of the order,[578] or to resolve a misunderstanding as to the effect of an order.[579] It is often the case that the court will ask the parties to draw up an order: where this happens, it does not matter

---

[571] *Beckett Bemrose & Hagan Solicitors v Future Mortgages Ltd* [2010] EWHC 1997 (QB) at [63].

[572] CPR, r 48.1(2)(b).

[573] *Grupo Torras SA v Al-Sabah* [1997] CLC 1553.

[574] *Kelly's Directories Ltd v Gavin & Lloyd* [1901] 2 Ch 763.

[575] *Korner v H Korner & Co Ltd* [1951] Ch 11.

[576] PD 40B, para 4.5.

[577] CPR, r 40.12(1); a right which also exists under the common law: see *Re Inchcape, Craigmyle v Inchcape* [1942] 2 All ER 157, *Thynne v Thynne* [1955] P 272, CA and *Bristol-Myers Squib Co v Baker Norton Pharmaceuticals Inc (No 2)* [2001] RPC 45 at [25], per Aldous LJ.

[578] *Preston Banking Co v William Allsup & Sons* [1895] 1 Ch 141, CA). Whilst obiter, see *Riva Bella SA v Tamsen Yachts GmBH* [2011] EWHC 2338 (Comm) at [22], per Elder J; see also *R v Cripps ex p Muldoon* [1984] 2 All ER 705.

[579] *Mölnlycke AB v Procter & Gamble Ltd (No 6)* [1993] FSR 154, Ch D.

that the error may have originated under counsel's hand,[580] nor does it matter if the error arose under the hand of one of the parties,[581] but an order may not admit an alteration if it was by consent and if it correctly recorded the intentions of the parties at the time it was sealed.[582] The application notice (which may be an informal document such as a letter) should describe the error and set out the correction required. An application may be dealt with without a hearing where the applicant so requests, with the consent of the parties, or where the court does not consider that a hearing would be appropriate.[583] If the application is opposed, it should, if practicable, be listed for hearing before the judge who gave the judgment or made the order.[584]

Review

7.416 A discussion of when an order can and cannot be reviewed is a hefty topic which is beyond the scope of this book; only the barest of outlines is given here. A costs order is a final judgment.[585] A judgment takes effect from the time when the judge pronounces it and the subsequent entry of it is in obedience to the rules of court.[586] The CPR make express provision for orders to be set aside or varied.[587] The existence of that power does not permit a judge to hear an appeal from himself.[588] On this point, Neuberger J has rejected the notion that the court should go behind its own costs order and act as an appellant court. He had the following to say on the topic:[589]

'It seems to me that when a court makes an order, only in the most exceptional circumstances, such as those involving fraud ... would the court revisit the order, even though it is for costs. The court cannot act as an appellate court in respect of its own orders.'

The parties may apply to set aside or vary an order, as may a non-party (such as a funder) who is directly affected by the order.[590]

7.417 The jurisdiction to review an order and to reverse a decision prior to the sealing of an order is often described as 'the *Barrell* jurisdiction'.[591] The relevant principles have been reviewed in detail by Wilson LJ;[592] a summary of that review is as follows:

- A judge's reversal of his decision is to be distinguished from his amplification of the reasons which he has given for it;

---

[580] *Riva Bella SA v Tamsen Yachts GmBH* [2011] EWHC 2338 (Comm), per Elder J.

[581] Whilst a pre-CPR case in a slightly different context to the present context, see *Navimpex Centrala Navala v George Moundreas & Co SA* (1983) 127 Sol Jo 392, CA.

[582] *Leo Pharma A/S v Sandoz Ltd* [2010] EWHC 1911 (Pat).

[583] PD 40, para 4.2.

[584] PD 40, para 4.4.

[585] As to the finality of the order, see *Forbes-Smith v Forbes-Smith and Chadwick* [1901] P 258, CA; this case was disapproved in *Aiden Shipping Co Ltd v Interbulk Ltd* [1986] 2 All ER 409 at 412, but this was on a point which was different from the issue in hand, namely, whether a costs order can be regarded as being final.

[586] *Holtby v Hodgson* (1889) 24 QBD 103.

[587] See CPR, r 3.1(7); the power also probably exists by virtue of r 3.1(2)(m); see *Lloyds Investment (Scandinavia) Ltd v Ager-Hanssen* [2003] EWHC 1740 (Ch).

[588] *Roult v North West Strategic Health Authority* [2009] EWCA Civ 444 and *Customs and Excise Commissioners v Anchor Foods Ltd (No 3)* (1999) *The Times*, September 28, Ch D.

[589] *Commissioner of Customs and Excise v Anchor Foods Limited (No 2)* (1999) *The Times*, September 28, Neuberger J.

[590] See CPR, r 40.9.

[591] After *Barrell Enterprises, Re* [1973] 1 WLR 1.

[592] *Paulin v Paulin* [2009] EWCA Civ 221 at [30].

- A Judge has jurisdiction to reverse his decision at any time until his order is 'perfected' but not afterwards;[593] the modern equivalent of an order being 'perfected' is it being sealed pursuant to CPR 40.2(2)(b);
- Contrary to pre-CPR thinking, a written reserved judgment might be less open to reversal than an *ex tempore* judgment;[594]
- If a written judgment had been disseminated only as a draft, it might be more open to reversal than if it had been handed down and thereby finally delivered;[595]
- The formula in *Barrell* governs the jurisdiction to reverse, and the requirement that there be 'exceptional circumstances' has been reaffirmed under the CPR;[596] but
- That formula is not a statutory definition and should not be turned into a straitjacket at the expense of the interests of justice;[597] a formula of 'strong reasons' was an acceptable alternative to that of 'exceptional circumstances'.[598]

It is now commonplace for judgments to be circulated to the parties' advocates prior to being handed down; this is not an opportunity to any party to reopen or reargue the case, but in exceptional circumstances, the court might properly be invited to reconsider the draft.[599]

7.418 In so far as costs are concerned, Jacob J has commented that the jurisdiction to vary an order should be exercised only for 'strong reasons' and in exceptional circumstances.[600] This may be appropriate if the order was made on a false basis.[601] An example of a case where a costs order was varied is where Bernard Livesey QC varied an order after learning that the court had been misled as to the financial positions of the parties and as to who was benefiting from the litigation.[602] Another example is where a legally aided party's financial circumstances changed in such a way as to make it appropriate to vary the order so as to remove a prohibition against immediate enforcement.[603] It would be wrong, however, to review interim orders on the basis of the outcome of the claim.[604]

7.419 In cases of orders obtained by fraud, the court may set aside the order, but it would usually be necessary fully to particularise the allegations of fraud in new

---

[593] *In Re Suffield and Watts* (1888) 20 QBD 693, 5 Morr 83, 36 WR 584
[594] *Stewart v Engel* [2000] 3 All ER 518, [2000] 1 WLR 2268, per Sir Christopher Slade at 2276A
[595] *Robinson v Fernsby* [2003] EWCA Civ 1820, per May LJ at 98 and Mance LJ at 113.
[596] See, for example, *Taylor v Lawrence* [2002] EWCA Civ 90.
[597] *Compagnie Noga D'Importation et D'Exportation SA v Abacha* [2001] 3 All ER 513.
[598] *Robinson v Fernsby* [2003] EWCA Civ 1820 at [94], where May LJ expressed approval of the formaula of 'strong reasons' as originally described in *Compagnie Noga D'Importation et D'Exportation SA v Abacha* [2001] 3 All ER 513 by Rix J.
[599] *R (on the application of Mohamed) v Secretary Of State for Foreign & Commonwealth Affairs* [2010] EWCA Civ 158. Also see *Robinson v Bird* [2003] EWCA Civ 1820 and *R (on the application of Edwards) v Environment Agency (No 2)* [2008] UKHL 22.
[600] *South Coast Investments Ltd v Axisa* [2002] All ER (D) 123 (Jan).
[601] Whilst obiter, see Mann J's comments in *Business Environment Bow Lane v Deanwater Estates Ltd* [2009] EWHC 2014 (Ch) at [40]; see, in a context other than costs, *Lloyds Investments (Scandinavia) Ltd v Ager-Hanssen* [2003] EWHC 1740 and *Collier v Williams* [2006] EWCA Civ 20; see also *Commissioners of Customs & Excise v Anchor Foods Ltd* (unreported) 8 July 1999, in which Neuberger J indicated that there must be fraud or slips.
[602] *Latimer Management Consultants Ltd v Ellingham Investments Ltd* [2006] EWHC 3662 (Ch).
[603] *DEG-Deutsche Investitions und Entwicklungsgesellschaft mbH v Koshy* [2001] EWCA Civ 79.
[604] *Compagnie Noga D'Importation et D'Exportation SA v Abacha* [2003] EWCA Civ 1101.

proceedings.[605] In cases of real injustice, the Court of Appeal has a residual jurisdiction to review an order,[606] but that jurisdiction is only very rarely exercised and has never been exercised solely in relation to costs.

7.420 Unless the CPR provide otherwise, the court has no power to set aside or vary an order that has been deemed to be made by the operation of the rules;[607] the CPR do provide otherwise where the deemed order arises out of discontinuance[608] or non-payment of court fees,[609] so the bar against revocation and variation of a deemed order applies only to orders deemed to be made as a result of acceptance of a CPR Part 36 offer.

Consent

7.421 Where an order has been made by consent, it may be set aside on any ground which would undermine a compromise itself. CPR, r 3.1(7) is applicable to case management decisions, and therefore does not apply where the order was based upon a final settlement agreed between the parties.[610] Whilst most do not relate to orders for costs, there are case examples of orders being set aside by reason of them being obtained by misrepresentation,[611] duress,[612] and mutual mistake of fact.[613] Neuberger J has confirmed that in so far as costs are concerned, the jurisdiction may be exercised only in exceptional circumstances.[614] Orders may also be set aside where they have been obtained without authority;[615] the fact that authority may have been given as a result of negligent legal advice would not be a ground for setting aside a consent order.[616] Likewise, a compromise based on a mistake of law would not usually be set aside for that reason.[617] A factor that the court will take into account when deciding whether to set a consent order aside is whether the application to set aside has been made promptly.[618] Another relevant factor is whether the order has been sealed:[619] once the order has been perfected, the judge making the order is *functus officio*[620] and should play no further role in respect of that order.[621]

---

[605] See *Jonesco v Beard* [1930] AC 298; see also *Kuwait Airways Corpn v Iraqi Airways Co (No 2)* [2001] 1 WLR 429, HL; and see *Jonesco v Beard* [1930] AC 298.

[606] *Taylor v Lawrence* [2002] EWCA Civ 90.

[607] See *Lahey v Pirelli Tyres Ltd* [2007] EWCA Civ 91 at [18], in which Dyson LJ approved the comments of Park J in *Walker Residential Ltd v Davis & another* [2005] EWHC 3483 (Ch) at [49].

[608] See CPR, r 38.6(1).

[609] See CPR, r 3.7(4)(b)(ii).

[610] *Roult v North West Strategic Health Authority* [2009] EWCA Civ 444.

[611] *Gilbert v Endean* (1878) 9 Ch D 259, CA.

[612] *Cumming v Ince* (1847) 11 QB 112.

[613] *Huddersfield Banking Co Ltd v Henry Lister & Son Ltd* [1895] 2 Ch 273, CA.

[614] *Centrehigh Ltd (t/a Shono UK) v Amen* (unreported) 18 July 2001, Ch D; see also *Customs and Excise Commissioners v Anchor Foods Ltd (No 3)* (1999) *The Times*, September 28, Ch D.

[615] See, *for example, Shepherd v Robinson* [1919] 1 KB 474, CA.

[616] *Tibbs v Dick* [1999] 2 FCR 322, CA.

[617] *Holsworthy UDC v Holsworthy RDC* [1907] 2 Ch 62.

[618] *Watt v Assets Co, Bain v Assets Co* [1905] AC 317, HL.

[619] *Huddersfield Banking Co Ltd v Henry Lister & Son Ltd* [1895] 2 Ch 273, CA.

[620] This means that the judge has 'performed his office', in which case he has no ongoing legal authority because his duties have been performed.

[621] *Re Suffield v Watts ex p Brown* (1888) 20 QBD 693, as considered in *Centrehigh Ltd (t/a Shono UK) v Amen* (unreported) 18 July 2001, Ch D.

Chapter 8

RETAINERS (GENERAL PRINCIPLES)

8.1   This chapter concerns retainers (see **8.4–8.7** for an explanation of that often-misunderstood term). Where appropriate, it should be read in conjunction with the chapters on erroneous retainers and on the indemnity principle. In particular, where the reader seeks guidance on whether there has been a breach of the indemnity principle between opposing parties, then the relevant part of this chapter should be read first, followed by those in Chapter 11 on the indemnity principle, and then, if appropriate, Chapter 10 on erroneous retainers. Conditional fee agreements are dealt with in Chapter 9.

TYPES OF RETAINER

8.2   Broadly speaking, retainers fall into the following categories:

- private retainers (**8.110–8.113**);
- business agreements (non-contentious and contentious) (**8.114–8.198**);
- implied retainers (**8.199–8.216**);
- oral retainers (8.217–8.218);
- conditional fee agreements (9.1–9.420); and
- statutory retainers.

There is another means by which a solicitor may be paid for his services, ie quantum meruit. Because that issue usually arises in the context of the indemnity principle, it is convenient to deal with that topic in Chapter 11.

8.3   In addition to these categories of retainer, it is worth mentioning situations in which problems can arise in practice:

- contracts made at a place other than the lawyer's place of business (8.324–8.394);
- retainers involving more than one client (8.402–8.431);
- retainers which are unlawful (8.231–8.241); and
- retainers which, by reason of error, are not as they should be (10.1–10.80).

This last of these topics is given its own chapter. The other topics are discussed in this chapter.

DISAMBIGUATION

8.4   In the context of costs law, a reference to a 'retainer' is not a reference to the engagement of a lawyer to provide legal services; instead, it is a reference to the legal mechanism by which a lawyer is afforded his right to claim a fee. In particular, the following differences should be noted:

- **Costs law:** a 'retainer' is the legal mechanism by which the solicitor gains his right to payment: In addition to contacts of retainer, the term also encompasses non-contractual retainers, such as statutory retainers arising out of public funding. A retainer (in the costs sense) will not necessarily set out the details as to how legal services are to be provided, or even which legal services are to be provided.
- **Professional liability:** a 'retainer' is the contract of engagement (or, as Bernard Livesey QC put it, "*the fons et origo* of a solicitor's duties ... [a] contract of engagement between himself and the client");[1] it will usually contain details as to how the legal services will be provided, and will usually contain client care information, etc.

8.5   In general usage, the word 'retainer' may mean something subtly different from the legal meanings set out above. The *Oxford English Dictionary* defines retainer as: 'The act or fact of retaining, withholding, or keeping for oneself; an authorization to do this'. In practice, this will often be thought of as being a reference to the terms of the engagement, and because those terms are usually contained in a client care letter, this is what many lawyers believe is 'the retainer. That is a different concept to a retainer in the context of the law of costs: whilst a client care letter may, from time to time, contain the written instrument that creates a retainer (in the costs sense), in many instances it will not.[2]

8.6   A retainer and the written instrument which purports to create the retainer are not necessarily the same thing. In the context of a contractual retainer, for example, the retainer – ie the true bargain struck between client and solicitor – may not be the same as the written instrument which purports to set out the relevant terms. In particular, the written instrument may contain errors, or it may have been qualified or amended by written or unwritten means.

8.7   Whilst not commonly encountered in modern practice, when applied to counsel the word 'retainer' may be a reference to a retaining fee, which is a sum of money paid to counsel for the purposes of securing his services. That type of retainer has nothing to do with the issues discussed in this chapter and must be distinguished therefrom.

---

[1]   *Phelps v Stewards (a firm)* [2007] EWHC 1561 (Ch), per Bernard Livesey QC, sitting as a Judge of the Chancery Division; the quote was originally from Jackson & Powell, 6th edn, at para 11-004.

[2]   An example would be where a solicitor has entered into a conditional fee agreement: the retainer would be the contract created by the conditional fee agreement, but the terms relating to the provision of legal services would probably be set out in the client care letter. A counter example would be where the details of the solicitor's remuneration are set out in the client care letter; in those circumstances the retainer and the client care letter would, for all practical purposes, be one and the same.

GENERAL PRINCIPLES

8.8   Regardless of the finer points of how they are classified, the purpose of retainers is to govern the payment of fees for legal services. There are several general points that need to be borne in mind when considering the nature and effect of a retainer (or, more accurately, when considering a contract of retainer); they are as follows:

-    *Entire contract*: The first issue is whether the retainer is an entire contract. This may be relevant because where a contract is an entire contract, unless the retainer provides otherwise the solicitor will not be able to render a bill until the conclusion of the matter to which the retainer relates. In some circumstances he will be debarred from claiming any fee at all until he has provided the entirety of the services he agreed to provide.
-    *Ambit*: The next issue is whether the scope of the retainer covers the case in hand and, if not, what the effect of that should be.
-    *Interim payments*: A further issue is whether the retainer permits of interim payments (be those final payments for discrete items of work, or merely payments on account) and, if so, on what terms.
-    *General provisions*: A small number of general provisions (such as those concerning 'unusual' costs and interest) may be included in any contract of retainer, regardless of its type. A solicitor should always consider these aspects of the matter, especially where the retainer relates to work done in the county court.
-    *Evidence*: Finally, the evidential principles which govern factual disputes between solicitor and client ought to be borne in mind.

Each will be considered in turn. The focus is on retainers made by solicitors, but on the whole the principles will also apply to retainers made by other species of lawyer.

Entire contracts

8.9   An entire contract (also known as a 'contract entire' or, in more modern parlance, an 'indivisible contract') is a contract that must be performed in its entirety (or, at least, substantially performed) before payment can be claimed. A memorable example is the undertaker who was not able to finish a funeral owing to the bursting of the coffin; he failed to perform the whole of his obligations under the contract, and so was not able to raise a fee.[3]

8.10   Some retainers are entire contracts under which a solicitor is obliged to provide a complete basket of services (such as legal representation for the entire duration of a claim). This is of potential significance for the following reasons:

(1)   Except under the doctrine of substantial performance (see below), a failure to perform the whole of the obligation to provide legal services may mean that the solicitor cannot demand performance of the client's obligations (ie payment of his fees).[4]
(2)   The solicitor would not normally be able to claim payment pro rata, nor can he ordinarily bring a claim in restitution.[5]

---

[3]   *Vigers v Cook* [1919] 2 KB 475, CA.
[4]   See, for example, *Wild v Simpson* [1919] 2 KB 544.
[5]   *Sumpter v Hedges* [1898] 1 QB 673, CA.

(3)   He would not be able assert that there was an implied term which contradicted the express terms that the contract was a contract entire and, therefore, he would not be able to say that it was an implied term that he would be paid for part performance.

(4)   For much the same reasons he cannot claim quantum meruit.[6]

The fact that the cause of the failure to perform the whole of the solicitor's obligations was beyond his control is not something that would normally[7] have a bearing on any of these things, so incomplete performance would not necessarily also amount to a breach of contract.[8] There are ways in which the solicitor may be able to be paid, but they would afford him only sketchy and erratic relief.[9]

8.11   In modern practice it will rarely be the case that a solicitor will feel the full force of these strictures, as nearly all modern retainers contain some sort of provision for payment in the event of incomplete performance, but the issue of whether a retainer is an entire contract can still be relevant. This is for the following reasons:

•   Even where a provision for such a payment exists, the fact that the retainer is an entire contract may have a bearing on when the solicitor is able to charge his fees.

•   The fact that the retainer is an entire contract may have a bearing on whether a client is entitled to an assessment; in particular, if an interim invoice has been paid for many months, the client may wish to argue that it was only a request for interim payment on account, and in support of that argument the client may wish to contend that this must have been the case because the retainer was an entire contract.

8.12   Thus, it is important to be able to distinguish between those retainers which are entire contracts and those which are not. That question can be fully addressed only if something is known of the history of the topic; this is because in ancient times there was a stark difference between the way in which the common law and the courts of chancery regarded retainers; that difference narrowed over time, so the history of the development of the law must be known in order to put authorities in their correct context.

8.13   At the end of the nineteenth century Lord Esher MR said the following about the way in which the common law looked at the issue:[10]

> 'When one considers the nature of a common law action, it seems obvious that the law must imply that the contract of the solicitor upon a retainer in the action is an entire contract to conduct the action to the end. When a man goes to a solicitor and instructs him for the purpose of bringing or defending such an action, he does not mean to employ the solicitor to take one step, and then give him fresh instructions to take another step, and so on; he instructs the solicitor as a skilled person to act for him in the action, to take all the necessary steps in it, and to carry it on to the end. If the meaning of the retainer is that the solicitor is to carry on the action to the end, it necessarily follows that the contract of the solicitor is an entire contract – that is, a contract to take all the steps which are necessary to bring the action to a conclusion.'

---

6   See **11.77** onwards.
7   The exceptions are set out at the end of this section.
8   See, for example, *Cutter v Powell* (1795) 6 Term Rep 320.
9   See **8.25** onwards.
10   *Underwood, Son & Piper v Lewis* [1894] 2 QB 306.

So, the position at common law was that a retainer was capable of being an entire contract, and indeed may well have been an entire contract if the instructions could be interpreted in that way; Lord Esher MR went on to say that (at common law) there was a presumption that a retainer would be an entire contract:

'When it is shewn that there were no special terms, but only the ordinary retainer for the purposes of the action, the implication I have mentioned is that which every reasonable person would make, and therefore the implication which the law makes in such a case ... There may be circumstances which justify the solicitor in putting an end to the contract, but ... he cannot do so without giving reasonable notice. The result ... seems to me to be that, though there may be valid reasons for giving such a notice, if no such notice is given, the contract of the solicitor is an entire contract, and he cannot sue for his costs before the termination of the action.'

8.14   Thus, at common law unless there were terms to the contrary, a retainer which had been entered into for the purposes of a claim would be presumed to be an entire contract. The solicitor could end the contract by giving reasonable notice, in which case he would not be able to charge a fee.[11]

8.15   As was explained by Sir George Jessel MR, the application of the concept of the entire contract had its limitations; in particular, it would have had only very limited application in a case which could properly have been said to have comprised a succession of matters:[12]

'If a man engages to carry a box of cigars from London to Birmingham, it is an entire contract, and he cannot throw the cigars out of the carriage half-way there, and ask for half the money; or if a shoemaker agrees to make a pair of shoes, he cannot offer you one shoe, and ask you to pay one half the price. That is intelligible. In my opinion, in the case of a solicitor there is not an implied contract of that kind. It bears no fair relation to the doctrine of entire contract. It is a series of services which, though nominally in relation to one matter, is in reality in relation to a succession of matters, and it is not within the doctrine of entire contract, because it is not within the mischief of it. It is not reasonable that a solicitor should engage to act on for an indefinite number of years, winding up estates, without receiving any payment on which he can maintain himself.'

Therefore, whilst in a short engagement the court would be ready to infer the existence of an entire contract, the same would not be true of a long-running matter. In any event, it is trite law that a contract may contain both divisible and indivisible obligations,[13] so it would be open to the court to find that a retainer is divisible to the extent that properly reflects the need of the solicitor to get paid in a long-running matter.

8.16   The position in respect of Chancery proceedings was different from that at common law. The difference arose not because equity offered a different legal exposition, but out of pragmatism; this is because Chancery proceedings were prone to last much longer than common law claims, a situation thus described by Lord Esher MR:[14]

---

[11]   As an aside, it is worth mentioning that in ancient times the solicitor was not able to end the contract at all: so, if he failed to perform his obligations, he would not only be unable to raise a fee, but he would be liable in damages for breach of contract.

[12]   *In re Hall v Barker* (1893) 9 Ch D 538 at 543.

[13]   See, for example, *Hoenig v Isaacs* [1952] 2 All ER 176.

[14]   *In Re Romer & Haslam* [1893] 2 QB 286 at 293.

'If a solicitor undertakes to carry through a legal transaction, the law is that he cannot send in a final bill of costs until that transaction is completed; the law on the point is the same in equity as at common law. But in equity the nature of many of the suits is such that they can be divided into stages, and the Court may treat the legal transaction as finished although the suit has not been carried to its final conclusion; this is a most important feature of Chancery proceedings. The ordinary procedure in equity is for the matter to go on to the stage of decree. In many suits there may be successive decrees; but the decision or decree has to be worked out – a process which may take years ... In an ordinary common law action, the duties of the solicitor are completed when judgment is pronounced: the client gets nothing by the action until that time; though the circumstances of each action may differ, the law applicable to them is the same.'

8.17   The position in Chancery proceedings and in common law claims were, therefore, at opposite ends of a spectrum. Each case was decided on its own facts, as was explained by Sir George Jessel MR:[15]

'Of course a suit in equity which might relate to a number of different matters might be continued to such a period of time that, if the doctrine extended to suits in equity, one might be compelled, if the case called for discussion and decision, to limit its application to some period or periods during the suit short of the final disposal of it.'

This analysis was approved by Lindley LJ, who commented that:[16]

'[It] is for those who maintain the contrary view to shew some good grounds.'

8.18   Thus, the position at the end of the nineteenth century was that different types of cases were dealt with in different ways, in that where there was an unremarkable common law case it was generally regarded as being conducted under an entire contract, but where the case was a long-running case, the court would look at each stage individually. However, there was a gradual evolution in the law which mitigated the rigid common law analysis. In 1980, Roskill LJ described the development of the law:[17]

'After the fusion of law and equity it is plain that gradually, as common law cases became more complicated, the former rigid common law rule was mitigated on pragmatic grounds.'

8.19   The modern approach is to decide the issue on the facts of each case; it is not clear whether any of the old presumptions continue to apply, but even if they do, in practice their effect would be greatly diminished by the following factors:

(1)   The prevalence of conditional fee agreements means that in many cases the solicitor will necessarily be paid only upon the conclusion of the matter; for obvious reasons, that type of retainer would generally be an entire contract, regardless of the type of claim to which they apply.[18]

(2)   In non-conditional cases, the solicitor's statutory right[19] to charge payments on account in contentious business often makes the issue of the nature of the retainer academic.

---

[15]   *In re Hall v Barker* (1893) 9 Ch D 538 at 543.
[16]   *Re Nelson, Son and Hastings* (1885) 30 Ch D 1.
[17]   *Davidsons v Jones-Fenleigh* (1980) Costs LR (Core vol) 70 at 72.
[18]   See **8.23**.
[19]   See Solicitors Act 1974, s 65(2).

(3) The prevalence of standard terms and conditions means that the issue is usually dealt with expressly in the retainer, so the nature of the retainer can usually be determined by examining the terms rather than by looking at the nature of the case to which the retainer relates.

8.20 A number of specific types of retainer merit discussion.

'General retainers'

8.21 Where a solicitor agrees 'to act generally' for a person, Slesser LJ has stated that it would not be correct to imply a contract that the solicitor is to continue to act without payment throughout the life of the client.[20]

Retainers relating to appeals

8.22 The position in respect of appeals is much the same as it is in respect of proceedings at first instance. Indeed, if a solicitor is instructed on an appeal and if he was instructed in the court below, the contract will generally cover both proceedings.[21]

Conditional fee agreements

8.23 Whilst there is no authority on the point, it is difficult to envisage a conditional fee agreement which is not an entire contract (or, at least, which does not have obligations which are non-divisible). A possible exception to this is discounted conditional fee agreements (where a discounted fee is payable regardless of whether the case is won), but even in those circumstances the agreement may be drafted in such a way as to make it a contract entire. Another possible exception would be where an agreement is so heavily qualified with contingent provisions that the reality is that payment would be made regardless of the stage at which the agreement terminated. A more common exception would be where the agreement provides for payment of disbursements regardless of the outcome of the claim; if that were the case, then it would be open to the court to find that the agreement is an entire contract but only in part (that is, that it contains both divisible and non-divisible obligations).

Options and stages

8.24 A retainer may have options to cover only certain aspects of the matter (such as an option that it may or may not apply beyond a particular stage in the proceedings); that does not necessarily mean that the retainer is not an entire contract in respect of those parts to which it does apply.[22] Where a contract is for the provision of services in a piecemeal way (ie many stages), then it would be open to the court to find that it was not a contract entire.[23]

---

[20] *Warmingtons v McMurray* [1937] 1 All ER 562. In a different case Tuckey LJ has stated that a 'general retainer' is an entire contract (*Donsland Ltd (a firm) v Van Hoogstraten* [2002] EWCA Civ 253); that, however, was in the context of considering whether the solicitors had authority to act rather than considering a solicitor's right to payment, and it probably should not be taken as being authority for the proposition that the retainer cannot be broken down into its constituent parts for the purpose of considering remuneration.

[21] *Harris v Quite* (1969) LR 4 QB 653.

[22] See, by analogy, *J Rosenthal & Sons Ltd v Esmail* [1965] 1 WLR 1117, HL at 1131, per Lord Pearson.

[23] Whilst it related to a surveyor's retainer rather than a solicitor's, see *Smales v Lea* [2011] EWCA Civ 1325.

The effect of a retainer being an entire contract

8.25   Where a retainer is an entire contract, the starting position is that the solicitor is entitled to payment only if he discharges the entirety of his obligations.[24] Nonetheless, most retainers will contain some provision for payment of a reasonable sum in the event of some unforeseen circumstances preventing the solicitor for performing his obligations. Even where no such provision exists, there are mechanisms which permit the solicitor to raise a charge in certain (but not all)[25] circumstances; they include the following.

Substantial performance

8.26   Where the obligations have been substantially performed such that there are only some minor or inconsequential matters outstanding, the doctrine of substantial performance may allow the solicitor to recover fees,[26] but this is subject to an allowance being made for those tasks that he has not completed.[27] An example might be where a solicitor has agreed to carry out a transaction for a fixed sum, but, whilst he has been able to effect the transaction, he is, by reason of events beyond his control, unable to deal with all of the formalities.

Acceptance of partial performance

8.27   Where the original retainer was an entire contract, but where it can be inferred that the client has agreed that a new retainer (or varied retainer) should be made for performance of lesser obligations, payment may be demanded upon performance of those lesser obligations.[28] The client must have had the opportunity to accept or reject the part performance (that is, the performance of the lesser obligations), and he must have chosen to accept it.[29] It is not relevant that the part performance may be as a result of the solicitor's own decision[30] (such as where a solicitor wishes to withdrawn from a case for personal reasons).

Partial performance under a contentious business agreement

8.28   Where a solicitor is prevented from performing his obligations under a contentious business agreement, s 63 of the Solicitors Act 1974 will, in some circumstances (ie death, incapacity, or disinstruction of the solicitor), permit the court to allow an appropriate amount; that amount will usually be assessed on a basis which takes the terms of the agreement into account. These issues are discussed at **8.189**.

---

[24]   See *Wild v Simpson* [1919] 2 KB 544; as a modern example of this principle in operation, see *Richard Buxton (a firm) v Mills-Owens* [2008] EWHC 1831 (QB); this decision was reversed on appeal on the grounds that the solicitor had been entitled to terminate (see *Richard Buxton (a firm) v Mills-Owen* [2010] EWCA Civ 122).

[25]   As a contrary example, see *Minkin v Cawdery Kaye Fireman & Taylor* [2011] EWHC 177 (QB) at [38] in which Cranston J found that termination for non-payment of fees disentitled the solicitor to payment, this being in circumstances in which the retainer provided that the client may withhold payment if he had reasonable justification for doing so (see **8.74**).

[26]   In a non-costs context, see *H Dakin & Co Ltd v Lee* [1916] 1 KB 566, CA.

[27]   *Hoenig v Isaacs* [1952] 2 All ER 176, CA.

[28]   See *Astilleros Canarios SA v Cape Hatteras Shipping Co SA, The Cape Hatteras* [1982] 1 Lloyd's Rep 518; *Appleby v Myers* (1867) LR 2 CP 651.

[29]   *Sumpter v Hedges* [1898] 1 QB 673, CA.

[30]   In a non-costs context, see *Appleby v Myers* (1867) LR 2 CP 651 at 65, per Blackburn J.

Frustration

8.29   Where a client frustrates the performance of his solicitor's duties, and where the solicitor has performed services which are of valuable benefit to the client, the solicitor may recover such sums as the court deems fit.[31] There are three stages to the process: the court must identify the benefit bestowed on the client (which will be provision of legal services); then it must value that benefit (ie assess the value of those services), and then it must award a sum which is just.[32]

8.30   Even where a contract is an entire contract, the solicitor is entitled to terminate that retainer without being in breach of contract (assuming, of course, that he acts reasonably). This is dealt with in more detail at **8.71–8.89**.

AMBIT AND AUTHORITY

8.31   This section discusses whether work can be said to fall within the ambit of a retainer, and if not, what effect this would have on the solicitor's ability to recover his fees.

8.32   Whether work is within the ambit of the retainer is a matter of contractual interpretation. Whilst no special principles apply, common sense dictates that the purpose of a retainer is to facilitate the provision of legal services and that, therefore, where the court is faced with two competing interpretations, one of which would embrace those services and one of which would not, a purposive construction would favour the former over the latter. An example of this is a 'general retainer' (which is a retainer to look after a person's affairs generally); Tuckey LJ has confirmed that the lack of specific instructions in those circumstances ought not to be construed as limiting the ambit of the retainer.[33]

8.33   Other case examples exist. Whilst not binding, Master Gordon-Saker found that a reference to the company who were handling a claim on behalf of one of the parties should be taken as being a reference which included that party; the effect of this was that the scope of the retainer included the work which had been carried out, notwithstanding the fact that the name of the person against whom the claim was brought was different from the opponent named in the agreement.[34] Similarly, whilst only a decision refusing permission to appeal and therefore not a decision that should be cited to any court, Maurice Kay LJ found that it was not incumbent upon a solicitor to draft his retainer in such a way as to embrace all areas into which the claim may develop.[35]

8.34   In addition to the ability to interpret the retainer in a purposive way, the court has other tools which may assist in avoiding an unjust outcome. It may, for example, be able to find an implied term which covers the work or, in appropriate cases, it may find

---

[31]   See Law Reform (Frustrated Contracts) Act 1943.
[32]   In an analagous context other than costs, see *BP Exploration Co (Libya) Ltd v Hunt (No 2)* [1979] 1 WLR 783 at 801, per Goff J.
[33]   *Donsland Ltd (a firm) v Van Hoogstraten* [2002] EWCA Civ 253 at [27]. This was in a context other than costs, but that part of Tuckey LJ's reasoning probably does apply to the ambit of the retainer for the purposes of costs.
[34]   *Brierley v Prescott* [2006] EWHC 90062 (Costs).
[35]   *Blair v Danesh* [2009] EWCA Civ 516.

whole implied retainers (see **8.199–8.216** and Chapter 10).[36] Thus, in order to avoid difficulties arising out of the rule that there can be no liability for the costs incurred without authority before the retainer was made,[37] it would be open to the court to rely on the presumption that authority may be implied by virtue of the fact that instructions were given.[38]

8.35   Retainers are not always so malleable, however. Although not binding, HHJ Stewart QC has found that where a conditional fee agreement was made to pursue a claim against a person A but the claim was pursued against a person B, the work done in respect of person B did not fall within the ambit of the retainer.[39] He rejected the notion that a purposive construction would permit the court to find otherwise. He also rejected the argument that the claimant elected to treat the contract as covering the claim against person B, and that it is not for a stranger to the contract (ie the paying party) to intervene with an argument to the contrary.[40]

8.36   There are examples (which, again, are not binding) of the court taking a similar approach to that taken by HHJ Stewart QC in circumstances where a claim was brought under the Fatal Accidents Act 1976 but the retainer was in respect of the Law Reform (Miscellaneous Provisions) Act 1934.[41]

8.37   It does not automatically follow that no liability will attach when fees are incurred beyond the ambit of the retainer. As mentioned above, the court may find that there is an implied retainer; it may also simply rely on the rebuttable presumption that a person who instructs a solicitor will be liable for the solicitor's reasonable costs.[42] Where the work has been carried out on a conditional fee basis, it would usually not be possible for the receiving party to rely on the existence of an implied retainer; this is because it is a statutory requirement that conditional fee agreements are in writing.[43] Contrary examples do exist, however.[44]

8.38   A common but misconceived argument is that the retainer was with a litigation friend but the work was done for the benefit of the person whom that friend represented. Not only is that objection susceptible to the two arguments set out below (ie agency and constructive trust), but it would usually also fail by reason of the litigation friend's non-contractual ability to recover his fees from the property of the person he represents. In particular, CPR, r 21.12 makes express provision for the recovery of expenses, including costs. Thus, the person whom the litigation friend represents would be liable for the costs not by reason of having a direct contractual liability, but by reason of the CPR making express provision that the litigation friend's fees can be recovered. Whilst there is no authority on the point, the mechanism by which that liability is created probably has more in common with a costs order than with an obligation arising out of a contract.

---

[36]   As an example, see *Meretz Investments Ltd v ACP Ltd* [2007] EWHC 2635 (Ch).
[37]   *Re Watson, ex p Phillips* (1887) 19 QBD 234, CA.
[38]   See, for example, *Bolden v Nicholay* (1857) 3 Jur NS 884; see also **11.23** *et seq.*
[39]   *Law v Liverpool City Council*, 10 May 2005, Liverpool County Court, HHJ Stewart QC.
[40]   This was an argument based on *King v Victoria Insurance Co* [1896] AC 250.
[41]   See, for example, *Pacey v The Ministry of Defence* [2009] EWHC 90138 (Costs).
[42]   As an example, see *Meretz Investments Ltd v ACP Ltd* [2007] EWHC 2635 (Ch).
[43]   See s 58(3)(a) of the Courts and Legal Services Act 1990 (as amended).
[44]   *Law v Liverpool City Council*, 10 May 2005, Liverpool County Court, HHJ Stewart QC, where the base costs were held to be recoverable, but that seems to have been as a result of an agreement between the parties.

8.39   In any event, whilst there are counter-arguments, it could be argued that the person who is acting in a representative capacity was acting as an agent. Another argument (which would apply only where a costs order has been made) is that the receiving party (ie the person who was being represented) holds the entitlement to costs on constructive trust for the person who was acting in a representative capacity. There is no authority to confirm whether either of these arguments is correct, however.

8.40   Another issue that may arise is whether work was carried out with the authority of a client. Authority may be express[45] or implied;[46] it may be given retrospectively by way of ratification.[47] An agent who has been given authority to act generally will have authority to instruct a solicitor.[48] This applies to insurers who appoint solicitors to on behalf of an insured.[49] It also applies to solicitors who themselves instruct agents,[50] but it not would permit a solicitor to instruct a different solicitor to act in his stead.[51]

INTERIM PAYMENTS, BREAKS AND TERMINATION

8.41   The following discussion addresses the contractual aspects of interim payments; other aspects (such as procedure, amount, etc) are addressed in Chapter 17. The retainer governs not only the size of a fee that a solicitor may charge, but also the stage at which he may claim that fee. In particular, a solicitor is not able to require payment as and when he pleases. Instead, either he must come to an accommodation with his client about when his fees are to be discharged, or he must wait until the appropriate stage is reached.

8.42   The circumstances in which a solicitor[52] may render a bill are:

- in accordance with s 65(2) of the Solicitors Act 1974;
- by express agreement;
- by implied agreement;
- where there is a 'natural break' in the matter; and
- upon termination of the retainer.

Each of these issues is dealt with in turn.

Payments on account in contentious business

8.43   In cases where a retainer relates to contentious business, the solicitor has a statutory right to ask for a payment on account;[53] this means that there is no need for a corresponding contractual provision. The statutory right is different from the other types of payment described here, for the following reasons:

---

[45]   See, for example, *Pickford v Ewington* (1835) 4 Dowl 453 and *May v Sherwin* (1883) 27 Sol Jo 278, CA.

[46]   See, for example, *Tomlinson v Broadsmith* [1896] 1 QB 386, CA. See also *Court v Berlin* [1897] 2 QB 396, CA.

[47]   *Terrell v Hutton* (1854) 4 HL Cas 1091 at 1099, per Lord Cranworth.

[48]   *Re Frampton, ex p Frampton* (1859) 1 De GF & J 263, CA.

[49]   See *Walsh v Julius* (1927) *The Times*, 13 July and *Luck v Meyler* (1928) 72 Sol Jo 337.

[50]   See *Re Bishop, ex p Langley, ex p Smith* (1879) 13 Ch D 110, CA. See also *Solley v Wood* (1852) 16 Beav 370.

[51]   *Re Becket, Purnell v Paine* [1918] 2 Ch 72, CA.

[52]   The statutory provisions set out under this heading do not apply to retainers with legal representatives other than solicitors; whilst there is no authority on the point, it is likely that if those provisions have any relevance in that situation, it would be only by analogy.

[53]   It is assumed that the reader knows the difference between interim statute bills and interim payments on account; these topics are dealt with in Chapter 17.

- the right is to ask for a payment on account, not to enforce it;
- the right relates to payments on account of fees incurred or yet to be incurred, rather than payments in final discharge of fees already incurred; and
- there are no fetters as to the time or times when requests may be made.

8.44   Interim payments on account are dealt with in more detail at **17.9–17.30**, but for present purposes – that is, deciding the nature of the retainer – it is sufficient to say that where, in a contentious matter, a client refuses or fails to make payment, the solicitor's remedy is to withdraw from the retainer. The relevance of this is set out below.

8.45   First, when the fact that a payment on account cannot be enforced is taken together with the fact that the solicitor's right to terminate is statutory, it can be seen that there is no pressing need for payments on account to be expressly mentioned in a retainer; thus the absence or presence of such provisions tells one very little about the nature of the retainer (unless, of course, the retainer expressly excludes such payments).

8.46   Secondly, notwithstanding this, many standard-term retainers do make express provision for payment on account; where such a facility exists, then that too will say very little about the nature of the retainer, and in particular it will say nothing about whether the retainer is an entire contract. That is because such a facility would not be for payments which may be kept in the event of non-performance of the entirety of the solicitor's obligations.[54] Thus, the absence or presence of a facility for payment on account will, in the event of his withdrawal from the retainer, rarely be relevant to the issue of whether the solicitor will be met with a defence of non-performance of his obligations.

8.47   Thirdly, where the facility is such that it purports to allow enforcement of payments on account, it would be likely that it would be for interim statute bills as opposed to payments on account. This means that the solicitor would rarely be without remedy in the event of non-payment: either the facility is for interim statute bills (in which case he can sue upon them), or it is not (in which case he can terminate the retainer).

8.48   It can be seen from the above that where a retainer makes provision for interim payments, the distinction that needs to be made is whether that provision is for payments on account, or for interim statute bills. That issue will turn on two things: first, what is said in the retainer, and secondly, what happens when a bill is rendered. The former is discussed here, and the latter at **17.9–17.30**.

Express provisions

8.49   Most standard form retainers provide a facility for regular payments, often on a set date of each calendar month or at intervals no more frequent than monthly. It is not always necessary to be so specific, although it is desirable from a consumer protection point of view to make the situation clear in an express and transparent way. Judge LJ had the following to say on that topic:[55]

---

[54]   This should be distinguished from a facility for interim statute bills, which would almost certainly mean that the retainer was not an entire contract.

[55]   *Abedi v Penningtons* [2000] 2 Costs LR 205 at 221.

'The desirability of such arrangements is likely to be reinforced by the increasing impact of the Civil Justice Reforms on a client's entitlement to be kept properly informed of his escalating financial obligations at each stage of the proceedings. As clients should know exactly where they stand throughout the process, it is reasonable to anticipate that questions of their own costs, and payment, should be arranged at an early stage in the process.'

Where the retainer distinguishes between 'interim bills' and 'requests for payment on account' the former will generally be taken to be a reference to interim statute bills.[56]

8.50   Many retainers hedge their bets in that provision is made both for interim statute bills and for payments on account. In particular, retainers will commonly stipulate that interim invoices are not to be treated as being interim statute bills unless they say upon their face that they are final bills: this provision is intended to allow revisions to be made to the sums claimed upon conclusion of the matter. It is also a retainer which can be adapted to suit the circumstances.

8.51   Highly-adaptable retainers such as those which provide for both payments on account and interim statute bills are not without their problems, however. This is because the adaptability goes hand-in-hand with the potential for error and the potential for disputes between solicitor and client. If, for example, a long series of detailed bills are rendered and paid, there may be a dispute about whether time has started to run for the purposes of s 70 of the Solicitors Act 1974; if some of those bills have been paid for more than a period of 12 months, that issue may determine whether the court has discretion to carry out a detailed assessment pursuant to that section.[57]

8.52   Where the retainer itself does not make express provision for interim payments (be those on account or otherwise), it may be varied or added to by subsequent agreement. Cases may arise in which it is said that there was an express agreement that interim statute bills may be rendered, but that that agreement was not rendered in writing. Where there is a dispute about such facts, Denning LJ made it clear that the solicitor may have to suffer the effects of having failed to record the true situation in writing.[58]

8.53   In summary, it is desirable (but not essential) that the retainer sets out expressly whether interim payments may be requested and, if so, whether they are to be regarded as being interim statute bills of requests for interim payments on account. Many retainers allow for both types of request but stipulate that in default of any provision to the contrary, an interim invoice will be a request for payment on account. Where there is not express provision, then the court must consider whether there is any implied provision. That is the subject of the next section.

Implied provisions

8.54   The question addressed under this heading is whether a retainer contains an implied term that interim statute bills may be rendered; see **17.14–17.22** for a discussion of what is and is not an interim statute bill. The topic of contractual implication in general is discussed at **8.199–8.216**. There is a great deal of overlap between this topic

---

[56]   See *R (on the application of Scott Halborg, trading under the style of Halborg & Co, Solicitors) v Law Society* [2010] EWHC 38 (Admin) at [23], per Keith J.

[57]   This is because there is an absolute bar to such assessments where a statute bill has been paid for more than 12 months: see **18.4**.

[58]   *Griffiths v Evans* [1953] 2 All ER 1364 at 1369. See also **8.103** onwards.

and the topic discussed under the next heading (natural breaks); indeed, the concept of 'natural breaks' may be seen as being a species of implied provision.

8.55 If a retainer does not make express provision for the delivery of interim statute bills, it may be possible, where the circumstances permit, to infer such a provision. Each case will turn on its own facts, but an implied agreement may arise:

- from a tacit acceptance of bills previously rendered;
- as a result of previous dealings between solicitor and client; and
- as a result of custom.

8.56 After a review of the authorities, Simon Brown LJ has confirmed that interim statute bills may become payable by virtue of what can be inferred from the circumstances as well as what was expressly agreed. In particular, payment of such bills may be a factor to be taken into account.[59] In a different case, Roskill LJ has emphasised that the intention of the parties is a relevant factor:[60]

> 'If the client's reaction is to pay the bill in its entirety without demur it is not difficult to infer an agreement that that bill is to be treated as a complete self-contained bill of costs to date ... Looking at each of [the bills], it seems to me, applying the principles laid down in [*In Re Romer & Haslam* [1893] 2 QB at 286], that there was a clear intention on the part of the [solicitors], and indeed a plain agreement to be inferred from the conduct of the parties that those bills should be treated as completely self-contained bills covering the period down to the relevant date given.'

Commenting on this extract from Roskill LJ's judgment, Simon Brown LJ has clarified that the mere fact of payment would not, of itself, usually be sufficient to allow agreement to be inferred.[61] This is particularly true in cases where the issue is not whether there was an implied agreement that interim payments would be made, but whether those interim payments were in respect of interim statute bills. In those circumstances, the issue will be the true nature of the payments, not whether there was agreement that they would be made. It should also be borne in mind that, in appropriate circumstances, a series of bills delivered over a short period of time may constitute a single bill;[62] again, this diminishes the potential importance of the fact that a client agreed to pay interim invoices.

8.57 Cogent evidence is required before the court will conclude that there is an implied provision that interim statute bills may be rendered. This is because the delivery of an interim statute bill starts time running for the purposes of s 70 of the Solicitors Act 1974.[63] Fulford J explained that the onus is on the solicitor to explain matters clearly to the client:[64]

> 'In particular the party must know what rights are being negotiated and dispensed with in the sense that the solicitor must make it plain to the client that the purpose of sending the bill at that time is that it is to be treated as a complete self-contained bill of costs to date'.

---

[59]   *Abedi v Penningtons* [2000] 2 Costs LR 205.
[60]   *Davidsons v Jones-Fenleigh* (1980) Costs LR (Core vol) 70 at 75.
[61]   *Abedi v Penningtons* [2000] 2 Costs LR 205 at 219, citing *In Re Romer & Haslam* [1893] 2 QB 286 at 298, per Bowen LJ. See also *R (on the application of Scott Halborg, trading under the style of Halborg & Co, Solicitors) v Law Society* [2010] EWHC 38 (Admin) at [25], per Keith J.
[62]   *Chamberlain v Boodle & King* [1982] 1 WLR 1443; see also *Re Cartwright* (1873) LR 16 Eq 469.
[63]   See **18.4**.
[64]   *Adams v Al Malik* [2003] EWHC 3232 (QB) at [48], per Fulford J.

8.58 Where there is a factual dispute about what was said and done, the solicitor may find the court prefers his client's evidence if he has not made a written record. However, where the disputed fact is something that would not normally be recorded in writing (such as an assurance made to an accounts department that a cheque is in the post), then this principle may have less relevance.[65]

8.59 Although there is no authority on the point, where the retainer was made before 6 October 2011there are two aspects of the Solicitors' Code of Conduct 2007 which may have a bearing on the issue. The first is the then requirement to give advice about the retainer, and the second is the then requirement to confirm that information in writing.[66] These requirements may make it more difficult for a solicitor to rely on implied terms than otherwise would have been the case, but a failure to comply with the Solicitors' Code of Conduct 2007 will not necessarily preclude the court finding that there is an implied provision.[67] The Solicitors' Code of Conduct 2007 seems not to contain the provision which existed previously that a solicitor must discuss when payment of his fees is to be made.[68]

8.60 The SRA Code of Conduct 2011 contains no express requirement that the terms of the retainer be in writing;[69] instead, it refers to the provision of information in 'a clear and accessible form which is appropriate to the needs and circumstances of the client' as being an 'indicative behaviour'.[70] It is possible that in most cases this would imply a need for the terms of the retainer to be in written form, but it is difficult to see how this would assist the court to any great extent when determining the terms of the retainer.

Natural breaks

8.61 The next question is whether the retainer is such that an interim statute bill may be rendered whenever there is a 'natural break' in the proceedings. This topic may be seen as being akin to and a development of the topic discussed above (implied provisions). It is a topic of some significance because if a client pays a bill and only subsequently learns that it was an interim statute bill, he may unknowingly set himself on a path which will lead to him losing the right to have that bill assessed.

8.62 A natural break will arise where one stage in the proceedings draws to a close and another begins; where this happens, the solicitor will be able to deliver an interim statute bill unless there is something that prevents him from doing so (such an express or implied term in the retainer). Lord Esher MR described a natural break in the following way:[71]

> '[The] conclusion of a definite and distinct part of the legal transaction as would entitle the solicitors to send in a final bill of costs'

---

[65] See **8.102** onwards.

[66] See rules 2.03(1) and 2.03(5) and, in respect of conditional fee agreements, rules 2.03(2).

[67] Whilst dealing with the indemnity principle and, in particular, hourly rates, see *Ghadami v Lyon Cole Insurance Group Limited* [2010] EWCA Civ 767 at [27], per Lloyd LJ.

[68] See para 4(j) of the Solicitors' Costs Information and Client Care Code 1999.

[69] There are provisions relating to complaints and service provision, but not to fees: see O(1.9) and O(1.10) of the SRA Code of Conduct 2011.

[70] See IB(1.19) of the SRA Code of Conduct 2011.

[71] *In Re Romer & Haslam* [1893] 2 QB 286 at 293.

Because of the lack of certainty that they inherently have, Cranston J has said that solicitors should rely on natural breaks as a basis for delivering interim statute bills in only the clearest of cases.[72]

8.63   Whether a retainer prohibits or permits the rendering of interim statute bills at times of natural breaks will be a matter of contractual interpretation. The following may be relevant.

Superseding provisions

8.64   It is often the case that a retainer will make express provision for the delivery of interim statute bills at regular intervals. Whilst such provisions would usually make the issue academic, it may be that the express provisions are so through as to leave no room for the notion of natural breaks.

Confirmatory provisions

8.65   It is often the case that a retainer will expressly confirm that interim statute bills may be delivered when there is a natural break; this is usually done by referring to bills being rendered 'at other times' (ie other than regular bills) or 'at an appropriate stage' rather than by referring to the phrase 'natural breaks'.

Implied provisions

8.66   A provision may be implied, especially by conduct. This is discussed at **8.54–8.60**. Indeed, on one analysis, a natural break is little more than a species of an implied contractual term.

Contrary provisions

8.67   Retainers may contain provisions which prevent interim statute bills being rendered at times of natural breaks. It is rare for a retainer to contain an express provision to that effect, but such a provision may exist by implication; this may arise where the retainer lists the situations in which interim statute bills may be delivered but makes no mention of natural breaks. This would be an example of the principle *expressio unius est exclusio alterius* (to express one thing is to exclude another).

The nature of the retainer

8.68   The nature of the retainer may be relevant; this is because some types of retainer (such as conditional fee agreements) do not easily lend themselves to the notion of payments on account, this being because monies would not ordinarily become payable until conclusion of the matter as a whole. Where a provision for an interim payment exists in such circumstances, it is usually because some particular part of the litigation has concluded by way of a natural break. An example would be where a conditional fee agreement provides for immediate payment of the costs where those costs are recovered from an opponent; the payment of those costs would usually be seen as being a natural break.

---

[72]   *Minkin v Cawdery Kaye Fireman & Taylor* [2011] EWHC 177 (QB) at [28], citing with approval from *Cordrey on Solicitors*.

8.69 Whilst the nature of the contract may be relevant, it will rarely be determinative of the issue of whether there has been a natural break. In particular, a finding that the retainer is an entire contract will be of only limited relevance. This is because the whole point of the doctrine of natural breaks is to allow interim payment of costs in circumstances where the retainer is an entire contract.

8.70 In summary, a retainer may or may not make provision for natural breaks. In practice, however, the exercise will usually be undertaken only when it is necessary to determine the nature of an interim invoice, and in those circumstances many factors may need to be taken into account, of which the retainer will usually only be one.

Termination

8.71 The termination of a retainer may have many consequences in so far as costs are concerned. It may also have other consequences, especially where the act of termination was made by the solicitor. No attempt is made in this book to address any issues other than the law of costs; in particular, issues of negligence are not discussed and issues of professional conduct are discussed only to the very limited extent that they are relevant to the law of costs. It should be noted that whilst it may be perfectly proper from the costs point of view to terminate a retainer, the same may not be true from the perspective of professional conduct.

The circumstances in which a retainer may be terminated

8.72 A retainer may be terminated in many ways, but the following merit specific mention:

* termination by the client;
* termination by the solicitor;
* termination by reason of death; and
* termination by reason of incapacity.

Bankruptcy and insolvency can be added to this list as they will, for practical purposes, result in a situation very similar to termination. Termination should be distingihsed from suspension; this is addressed at **8.88**.

8.73 A client may end the retainer at any time and for any reason.[73]

A client may end the retainer at any time and for any reason.[74] Many retainers contain an express provision to this effect.[75] In any event, unless it is an entire contract, the common law will give rise to the existence of an implied term.[76] Where he is a consumer, the client may also be given a statutory right to cancel the retainer,[77] as discussed at **8.324** *et seq*. A client may, where appropriate, treat a retainer as having been terminated

---

[73] See, for example, *Re Galland* (1885) 31 Ch D 296 at 300, CA, per Chitty J. See also para 8 of the guidance to rule 2.01 of the Solicitors' Code of Conduct 2007.

[74] See, for example, *Re Galland* (1885) 31 Ch D 296 at 300, CA, per Chitty J. See also para 8 of the guidance to rule 2.01 of the Solicitors' Code of Conduct 2007.

[75] See, for example, para 7 of the various incarnations of the Law Society model conditional fee agreement.

[76] *JH Milner & Son v Percy Bilton Ltd* [1966] 1 WLR 1582.

[77] See, for example, Cancellation of Contracts made in a Consumer's Home or Place of Work etc Regulations 2008 (SI 2008/1816).

if the solicitor is guilty of misconduct of a type that is incompatible with the solicitor carrying out the work.[78] Moreover, a disclaimer of liability under the retainer may be accepted as repudiation of it.[79]

8.74   Subject to giving reasonable notice, the solicitor may terminate only for good reason (or 'good cause' as it is referred to in the Solicitors Act 1974). A full discussion of what amounts to good reason is beyond the scope of this book, but an important contrary example is non-payment of fees under a retainer that provides that the client may withhold payment if there is reasonable justification to do so (this being a fairly common provision): Cranston J found that if the client declines to pay on *subjectively* reasonable grounds, the termination by the solicitors would be unlawful.[80] Examples of when it would be reasonable to give notice of an intention to terminate include a breakdown in confidence between solicitor and the client, where the solicitor believes the case to be not properly arguable,[81] where the client misleads the solicitor,[82] or where the solicitor is unable to obtain proper instructions.[83] A solicitor is professionally obliged to give reasonable notice of termination; the SRA Code of Conduct 2011 (which has applied from 6 October 2011) provides that 'ceasing to act for a client without good reason and without providing reasonable notice' may be an initiative behaviour demonstrating a failure to comply with the Principles.[84] If the termination took place before that date, then Solicitors' Code of Conduct 2007 would have applied:[85]

> 'If there is good reason to cease acting, you must give reasonable notice to the client. What amounts to reasonable notice will depend on the circumstances. For example, it would normally be unreasonable to stop acting for a client immediately before a court hearing where it is impossible for the client to find alternative representation ... There may be circumstances where it is reasonable to give no notice.'

The duty to give reasonable notice also exists in law;[86] a failure to give reasonable notice may amount to repudiatory breach of contract, which (where the retainer is an entire contract) may mean that no fees at all may be charged.[87]

8.75   From the costs point of view the most important 'good cause' arises out of SA 1974, s 65(2), which reads as follows:

> 'If a solicitor who has been retained by a client to conduct contentious business requests the client to make a payment of a sum of money, being a reasonable sum on account of the costs incurred or to be incurred in the conduct of that business and the client refuses or fails within a reasonable time to make that payment, the refusal or failure shall be deemed to be a good cause whereby the solicitor may, upon giving reasonable notice to the client, withdraw from the retainer.'

---

[78]   *Re Smith* (1841) 4 Beav 309.
[79]   *Hawkes v Cottrell* (1858) 3 H & N 243 at 245.
[80]   *Minkin v Cawdery Kaye Fireman & Taylor* [2011] EWHC 177 (QB) at [38] and [46].
[81]   *Richard Buxton (a firm) v Mills-Owen* [2010] EWCA Civ 122.
[82]   See, for example, *Kris Motor Spares Ltd v Fox Williams LLP* [2009] EWHC 2813 (QB).
[83]   See, for example, Solicitors' Code of Conduct 2007, para 8 of the guidance to rule 2.01.
[84]   See IB(1.26) of the SRA Code of Conduct 2011.
[85]   Solicitors' Code of Conduct 2007, para 9 of the guidance to rule 2.01.
[86]   See *Underwood, Son & Piper v Lewis*, at 313, per Lord Esher MR; at 315, per A L Smith LJ; more recently, see *Minkin v Cawdery Kaye Fireman & Taylor* [2011] EWHC 177 (QB) at [31].
[87]   *Minkin v Cawdery Kaye Fireman & Taylor* [2011] EWHC 177 (QB) at [38].

Crane J has found that the reference to a 'reasonable sum' is a reference to an amount which it was reasonable to request at that particular time.[88] Toulson J has found that a request by solicitors for 90% of outstanding costs was unreasonable in the context of those costs being disputed.[89]

8.76   The guidance to the Solicitors' Practice Rules 1990 stipulated that if a retainer is for the solicitor to be remunerated by an agreed fee, the solicitor may not terminate the retainer by reason of that work becoming unremunerative.[90] This provision was not repeated in the Solicitors' Code of Conduct 2007, nor is it repeated in the SRA Code of Conduct 2011. Those codes contain only general provisions relating to termination (see **8.74**).

8.77   A solicitor's right to terminate will exist regardless of whether the retainer is a private retainer or a conditional fee agreement. This was made clear by Lord Woolf MR:[91]

> 'The lawyer has however the right, if the need should arise, to cease to act for a client under a CFA in the same way as a lawyer can cease to act in the event of there being a conventional retainer.'

Termination by death

8.78   Although the death of a counterparty will not generally discharge a contract,[92] many retainers contain a provision that death is a stipulated event which will result in termination. Termination by death will not be a breach of contract.[93] Retainers often provide that the personal representative of the deceased client may continue the retainer by subsequent agreement. A personal representative may continue the retainer by adopting it, in which case, he will incur a personal liability.[94]

8.79   Where a contract is a general retainer (ie a contract arising out of instructions to do generally what is necessary in a person's affairs), the death of the client will not necessarily result in the retainer being terminated; the solicitors will remain instructed to the extent that they must continue to do what is necessary to protect and preserve their client's interests.[95] In any event, the solicitor will be entitled to sue for work already done if his client dies;[96] there is less certainty about whether the personal representatives of a deceased solicitor are entitled to sue for the fees incurred before the solicitor's death, but this situation will rarely arise in practice because few solicitors now practice as sole practitioners in their own names.[97]

---

[88]   *Collyer Bristow v Robichaux* (unreported) 20 July 2001, QBD.
[89]   In *Wong v Vizards* [1997] 2 Costs LR 46 at 52.
[90]   *The Guide to the Professional Conduct of Solicitors* (Law Society, 8th edn), section 13.03, para 5.
[91]   *Hodgson v Imperial Tobacco Ltd* [1998] 1 WLR 1056 at 1065. See also *Kris Motor Spares Ltd v Fox Williams LLP* [2009] EWHC 2813 (QB).
[92]   See, in a context other than costs, *Werner v Humphreys* (1841) 2 Man & G 853.
[93]   *Pool v Pool* (1889) 61 LT 401.
[94]   *Re Bentinck, Bentinck v Bentinck* (1893) 37 Sol Jo 233.
[95]   *Donsland Ltd (a firm) v Van Hoogstraten* [2002] EWCA Civ 253.
[96]   *Whitehead v Lord* (1852) 7 Exch 691.
[97]   See *Underwood, Son and Piper v Lewis* [1894] 2 QB 306 at 313, CA, per Lord Esher MR; that said, see also the Law Reform (Frustrated Contracts) Act 1943 s 1.

Termination by loss of capacity

8.80   Loss of mental capacity has, in the past, been regarded as being an event that terminates a contract of retainer,[98] but it cannot be said with certainty that this remains good law. The Guidance to the Solicitors' Code of Conduct 2007 stated that a retainer will automatically terminate if a client loses mental capacity,[99] but that guidance is not a source of law (see **5.53**). The SRA Code of Conduct 2011 refers to a need to have proper regard for a client's mental capacity or other vulnerability,[100] but is otherwise silent on the point.

Termination by insolvency

8.81   Where the client becomes bankrupt and where the solicitor carries out no work for the trustee or assignee that will usually give rise to termination,[101] that will not, as a rule, result in the retainer being terminated,[102] but in other circumstances, the retainer will pass to the trustee or assignee.[103] Any claim for costs against the client will become a bankruptcy debt,[104] which will be payable out of the property held by the trustee. Few solicitors would be prepared to continue acting on such terms, so the effect of a client's bankruptcy is to terminate the retainer. However, there would be nothing to prevent the solicitors entering into a new retainer with the trustee, if that is what they wished to do. In so far as corporate insolvency is concerned, solicitor's retainer is not terminated by the removal of the liquidator who retained him, and this is so even if at the relevant time no replacement has been appointed.[105]

8.82   Where the solicitor is practising on his own account and where he becomes bankrupt, the bankruptcy will usually result in a retainer being terminated, not as a result of a contractual provision, but as a result of the fact that he would lose his ability to practice.[106] The same is true of injury sufficient to prevent the solicitor practising,[107] disqualification from practice[108] and imprisonment.[109] The client may, however, subsequently enter into a new retainer with the intervener. Likewise, whilst there is authority for the proposition that where a solicitor transfers his business to someone else, that will terminate the retainer,[110] there is ample scope for the court to avoid injustice by finding that the retainer was novated or otherwise adopted by the new solicitors. Where a firm is dissolved, that will, in general, terminate the firm's retainer,[111] but again there is usually scope for the court to avoid injustice in that regard.

---

[98]   *Yonge v Toynbee* [1910] 1 KB 215, CA, overruling *Smout v Ilbery* (1842) 10 M & W 1, and approving *Collen v Wright* (1857) 8 E & B 647, Ex Ch.

[99]   See para 6(a)(iii) of the guidance to rule 2.01; for the reasons set out at **38.36–38.52** a retainer may exist and be enforceable in certain circumstances, but in view of the fact that the aforementioned guidance gives specific advice as to what should be done to protect the client's position in the event of a loss of capacity, there would be scope for the court to find that there was an implied term that those things would be done, and that, in order to do those things, the retainer must be terminated.

[100] See IB(1.6) of the SRA Code of Conduct 2011.

[101] *Re Moss* (1866) LR 2 Eq 345.

[102] In a context other than costs, see *Jennings' Trustee v King* [1952] Ch 899. See also *Re Moss* (1866) LR 2 Eq 345 at 438, per Lord Romily.

[103] See Insolvency Act 1986, s 283(1).

[104] See Insolvency Act 1986, s 322.

[105] See *R v Lord Mayor of London, ex p Boaler* [1893] 2 QB 146, DC.

[106] See the Solicitors Act 1974. s 15(1).

[107] *Forney v Bushe* (1954) 104 L Jo 604.

[108] See *Re Smith* (1861) 9 WR 396, per Kindersley V-C.

[109] Whilst it may no longer be good law, see *Scott v Fenning* (1845) 15 LJ Ch 88.

[110] *Colegrave v Manley* (1823) Turn & R 400.

[111] *Griffiths v Griffiths* (1843) 2 Hare 587; see also *Rawlinson v Moss* (1861) 30 LJ Ch 797.

The effect of termination

8.83   The effect of termination will be a matter of contractual interpretation, and so may differ from case to case. The following general points can be made:

- Lawful termination will not generally result in the client being discharged from the accrued rights under the retainer,[112] ie the solicitor's right to be paid for work already done.
- Termination of the retainer will not always bring the relationship between solicitor and client to an end; in particular, where a conditional fee agreement has been terminated, the client will often be placed under an ongoing contractual obligation to inform the solicitor if the case is subsequently won.
- Likewise, termination will not necessarily result in a final crystallisation of the client's liability for costs. The example given above illustrates this: it may be, for example, that whilst the client became liable to pay base costs immediately upon termination, he would become liable to pay a success fee if subsequently won the claim.

8.84   Another example of a terminated retainer continuing to have effect is where a solicitor is required to carry out 'run-off' work, such as preparing a detailed bill of costs, either for a solicitor and client assessment, or for use in recovering costs from an opposing party. Many retainers will expressly provide that such work is to be payable under the terms of the retainer. Likewise, if a client disinstructs a solicitor in circumstances in which the solicitor has a continuing duty the court, then it is likely that the solicitor would be able to charge for any work which he was required to do in discharge of that duty.[113]

8.85   One class of retainer merits specific mention. Most conditional fee agreements used by solicitors are based on the Law Society's model agreement (which has been published in several versions). Whilst the exact wording is subject to variation, that model agreement usually contains the following provision:

> 'You can end the agreement at any time. We then have the right to decide whether you must:
> - pay our basic charges and our disbursements including barristers' fees when we ask for them; or
> - pay our basic charges, and our disbursements including barristers' fees and success fees if you go on to win your claim for damages.'

This is known as an election provision. It is desirable for an election to be made not only expressly, but also at an early stage. This is because disputes can otherwise arise if the client loses the claim before an election is made. If, in those circumstances, the solicitor then claims base charges in accordance with the first limb of the election provision, he may be accused of having delayed his decision for the purposes having his cake and eating it.

Wrongful termination

8.86   Whilst the effect of wrongfully terminating a retainer may sound in damages, disciplinary action or both, from the point of view of the law of costs, the effect is

---

[112]   *Richard Buxton (a firm) v Mills-Owen* [2010] EWCA Civ 122; see also *Minkin v Cawdery Kaye Fireman & Taylor* [2011] EWHC 177 (QB) at [32].
[113]   See *Lady De la Pole v Dick* (1885) 29 Ch D 351 at 356–357, CA.

usually limited (unless the retainer is an entire contract: see below). In particular, the wrongfulness of a termination will rarely result in costs being made irrecoverable (unless, of course, that wrongfulness results in diminution by reason of set-off). Wrongful termination must be distinguished from suspension (see **8.88**).

8.87   The situation is different if the retainer is an entire contract; this is because the termination will go hand-in-hand with the failure to discharge the requisite obligations. This means that wrongful termination is capable of resulting in the solicitor being disentitled to raise a fee (see **8.25**).[114] Atkin LJ has explained that in those circumstances quantum meruit would also be prohibited on policy grounds.[115] Nelson J has commented, obiter, that if a solicitor charges more than he is entitled to charge and then terminates the retainer as a result of a refusal to pay, this would usually amount merely to a breach of contract and would not automatically disentitle the solicitor to his fees for the work already done.[116]

8.88   It is possible for a contract of retainer to contain a provision that it be suspended (i.e., a provision that the supply of legal services be put on hold pending some event, usually payment of fees). Whilst he acknowledged that there is a degree of overlap between suspension and termination, Ward LJ found that they should be regarded as being distinct and distinguishable concepts.[117] On the facts of the case before him (which were unremarkable save for the fact that the retainer made express provision for suspension), Ward LJ found that it was not necessary to imply a provision that the solicitor would suspend the retainer only after having given reasonable notice.[118]

8.89   Ward LJ went on to find that (assuming it to be in accordance with the terms of the retainer) suspension did not amount to termination the contract and that it would be wrong to regard suspension as absolving the client from performing his obligations under the contract.[119]

GENERAL PROVISIONS

8.90   There are many provisions which may be incorporated into a retainer for the purposes of clarification and for dealing with unusual and difficult situations. The following provisions may be incorporated into any contractual retainer, regardless of its type. They do not provide an exhaustive list. A skilled drafter would consider many more provisions than the ones set out below.[120]

'Unusual' costs

8.91   Where a client wishes to incur costs which would be regarded as being 'unusual' in the sense that they are not likely to be recovered from an opposing party, it is good

---

[114]   An example of this is *Minkin v Cawdery Kaye Fireman & Taylor* [2011] EWHC 177 (QB) at [38]., in which the solicitors wrongfully terminated for non-payment of fees: see **8.74**.
[115]   *Wild v Simpson* [1918–19] All ER Rep 682 at 693 (Duke LJ dissenting, albeit on other grounds).
[116]   *Wilson v William Sturges & Co* [2006] EWHC 792 (QB).
[117]   *Cawdery Kaye Fireman & Taylor v Minkin* [2012] EWCA Civ 546 at [30].
[118]   *Cawdery Kaye Fireman & Taylor v Minkin* [2012] EWCA Civ 546 at [30].
[119]   *Cawdery Kaye Fireman & Taylor v Minkin* [2012] EWCA Civ 546 at [44].
[120]   For pragmatic guidance as to drafting contracts generally, the reader would do well to read K Adams *A Manual of Style for Contract Drafting*, (2nd edn, 2008, American Bar Association Business Law Section, ISBN978-1-60442-028-9).

practice to obtain the client's consent to those costs being incurred. It is often the case that the client care letter contains an express warning that those fees are not likely to be recovered. The provisions of CPR, r 48.8(2)(c) are relevant in that regard (see below) because they are likely to be disallowed on a solicitor and client assessment if the client was not informed that they might not be recovered from an opposing party. Likewise, where the client wishes to incur costs in the county court which are not likely to be recovered in that court (see **26.10**), disputes can be avoided if it is recorded that the client agreed to that course of action. The relevant provisions in CPR, r 48.8 read as follows:

'(1A)   Section 74(3) of the Solicitors Act 1974 applies unless the solicitor and client have entered into a written agreement which expressly permits payment to the solicitor of an amount of costs greater than that which the client could have recovered from another party to the proceedings.

(2)   Subject to paragraph (1A), costs are to be assessed on the indemnity basis but are to be presumed—

...

(c)   to have been unreasonably incurred if—
(i)   they are of an unusual nature or amount; and
(ii)   the solicitor did not tell his client that as a result he might not recover all of them from the other party.'

8.92   Section 74(3) of the Solicitors Act 1974 reads:

'(3)   The amount which may be allowed on the taxation [assessment] of any costs or bill of costs in respect of any item relating to proceedings in a county court shall not, except in so far as rules of court may otherwise provide, exceed the amount which could have been allowed in respect of that item as between party and party in those proceedings, having regard to the nature of the proceedings and the amount of the claim and of any counterclaim.'

Where notice has been given, the details of that notice may need to be kept under review. In particular, it would not be appropriate to give general notice about 'unusual' expenditure, and then to rely solely on that general notice as and when specific unusual expenditure is made.

Destination of interest

8.93   It is often the case that express provision is made for interest. Where the solicitor wishes to charge interest on unpaid bills, it would, for obvious reasons, be usual to include the appropriate express provisions within the retainer. What is often omitted, however, is provision for the destination of interest recovered from an opposing party.

8.94   Where interest is recovered from an opposing party, it belongs to the client (as would be the case with any other type of costs recovery other than public funding). If the client had already paid his solicitors' fees during the course of the litigation, then no problem would arise: this is because the client is the correct person to compensate for having funded the litigation. If, on the other hand, it is the solicitor who has borne the brunt of funding the litigation, then he may have a legitimate claim to the interest. Disputes may be avoided by including an express provision which deals with that point. This is what Lord Acker had to say on the topic:[121]

---

[121]   *Hunt v RM Douglas (Roofing) Ltd* [1990] 1 AC 398, HL at 407.

'[In order for the solicitor to recover the interest the retainer must contain] an express agreement between the solicitor and his client that any interest recovered on costs and disbursements after judgment is pronounced but before the [costs judge's] certificate is obtained, which costs and disbursements have not in fact been paid prior to taxation, shall as to the interest on the costs belong to the solicitor and as to the interest on disbursements be held by him for and on behalf of the person or persons to whom the disbursements are ultimately paid.'

Lord Acker's speech was made before the rules of court were changed so as to allow interest to be recovered on costs for a period prior to the order being made. There is no reason to believe that his guidance would have been any different in respect of interest of that type.

Forum

8.95   It may be sensible to include a contractual provision expressly stating the jurisdiction in which any dispute concerning costs will be litigated. This would be particularly true where the client is out of the jurisdiction or where the litigation is conducted in a different jurisdiction. It should not be forgotten that Scotland is a different jurisdiction.

Severability clause

8.96   Some retainers contain a provision which permits an objectionable provision to be severed from the rest of the agreement in the event of the retainer being found to be unenforceable because of that objectionable provision. The prime reason this is included is not because of the possibility of a dispute arising between solicitor and client, but because of the possibility of an opposing party raising an argument on the indemnity principle. An example would be where the solicitor was anxious about the possibility of a particular provision being seen as an unlawful contingency fee agreement. Whilst the inclusion of a severability clause will rarely cause any harm, it is doubtful whether it is a provision which is capable of having its intended effect.[122]

Variation in writing clause

8.97   Some retainers contain a restriction that, to be effective, any variation should be in writing. The intention is to avoid factual disputes about the terms of the retainer. Where the counterparties are sure that the written retainer is exactly as they would like, the inclusion of such a restriction is unobjectionable. Harm can be caused, however, in circumstances where the client's needs change during the course of the litigation. An example would be where a retainer expressly states that it would not cover an appeal, but that this provision was supposedly overridden by a subsequent oral agreement that it would cover an appeal. If, as is often the case, no one turns their mind to the issue of whether a variation should be effected in writing, disputes can arise as to the ambit of the retainer (especially if the retainer was a conditional fee agreement, which must be in writing).

---

[122]   See **10.71**. Whilst not binding, see *Oyston v The Royal Bank of Scotland plc* [2006] EWHC 90053 (Costs) at [36]. See also *Aratra Potato Co Ltd v Taylor Joynson-Garrett* [1995] 4 All ER 695 at 710, per Garland J.

Deemed signature clause

8.98 It can often be the case that one or more of the counterparties has failed to sign the retainer. Equally, the original signed document may be lost. In order to deal with these contingencies it is possible to incorporate a term whereby the retainer will be deemed to have been signed in the event of the client continuing to give instructions after receipt of his copy of the retainer. It would be sensible to regard any such term as being only a back-up provision.

Deemed increase clause

8.99 Almost all written retainers make provision for the solicitor's hourly rates to be reviewed. It is possible to make provision for a deemed increase to be made automatically. Examples include linking the rates to the local guideline rates, or merely increasing the rate by a fixed percentage each year. It is possible to draft a retainer in such a way as to provide for a deemed increase to apply only if and to the extent that no agreed increase has been made.

ADR clause

8.100 Whilst they are far from common, some retainers include an express provision concerning the resolution of any dispute about the solicitor's fees. Examples include a provision for the matter to be decided by a barrister of more than 10 years call, or by mediation or by arbitration. Where the sums involved are likely to be small, it is also possible to provide that any claim (including an assessment) will be treated as a small claim and that the small-claims costs regime will apply. Whilst there is no authority on the topic, a solicitor would be well advised to take care not to impinge too much on the client's right to a detailed assessment; where it is proposed to restrict that right, thought ought to be given to making a formal business agreement.

FSA declaration

8.101 Whilst beyond the scope of this book, retainers often contain provisions concerning the solicitor's status with the Financial Services Authority (ie whether they are registered or not). The FSA publishes a standard paragraph that ought to be included. There is no need for those issues to be dealt with in the retainer itself.

Notices concerning the retainer

8.102 It may often be the case that where a retainer is made at a place which is not the solicitor's place of business certain notices must be made. This is discussed at **8.324–8.401**.

EVIDENCE: FACTUAL DISPUTES ABOUT RETAINERS

8.103 This section addresses the question of how the court would deal with a factual dispute between solicitor and client about the terms of a retainer. Where it is a paying party who wishes to challenge the retainer, he will usually (but not always) need to establish a 'genuine issue' or 'genuine concern' that there has been a breach of the indemnity principle. He will also have to overcome the rebuttable presumption that – broadly speaking – a person who instructs a solicitor will be liable for his fees. These issues are dealt with at **11.22–11.32**.

8.104 Factual disputes about retainers are dealt with in much the same way as any other factual dispute. The legal burden (otherwise known as the burden of persuasion) will at all times remain with the solicitor, who must prove the existence of an enforceable retainer as a condition for the recovery of his fees.[123]

8.105 The evidential burden (otherwise known as the burden of adducing evidence) will shift between the parties, depending on what is being asserted. There is, however, a presumption in favour of the solicitor that a client is liable for the fees of a solicitor whom he engages.[124] This presumption is rebuttable and, in effect, is a presumption that there will be an implied retainer unless the contrary can be shown. Whilst he was speaking in the context of costs between opposing parties rather than between solicitor and client, Lloyd J explained the presumption in the following terms:[125]

> 'Once it was shown ... that [the client] was indeed the client, then a presumption arose that he was to be personally liable for the costs. That presumption could, however, be rebutted if it were established that there was an express or implied agreement, binding on the solicitor, that [the receiving party] would not have to pay those costs in any circumstances.'[126]

This presumption has its limits, however, and is considered in more detail at **8.199–8.216**.

8.106 Where there is a dispute between a solicitor and a client concerning the terms or existence of a retainer, one factor that will be given weight is the presence or absence of a written instrument. If there is a written document, it will be taken into account in the usual way, but if it is absent, that will create a rebuttable evidential presumption in the client's favour. The principle was described by Denning LJ in this way:[127]

> 'On this question of retainer, I would observe that where there is a difference between a solicitor and his client on it, the courts have said for the last 100 years or more that the word of the client is to be preferred to the word of the solicitor, or, at any rate more weight is to be given to it: ... The reason is plain. It is because the client is ignorant and the solicitor is, or should be, learned. If the solicitor does not take the precaution of getting a written retainer, he has only himself to thank for being at variance with his client over it and must take the consequences.'

On a similar point, Rougier J said this:[128]

---

[123] This being a reflection of the generally applicable principle, as explained by Davies LJ in *Chapman v Oakleigh Animal Products Ltd* (1970) 8 KIR 1063, CA at 1072 that the onus of proof is on the claimant.

[124] See *Adams v London Improved Motor Builders Ltd* [1921] 1 KB 495 at 501; see also *R v Miller (Raymond)* [1983] 1 WLR 1056 at 1059–1062, which was cited with approval in *Bailey v IBC Vehicles Ltd* [1998] 3 All ER 570 at 574. See also *Hazlett v Sefton Metropolitan Borough Council* [2000] 4 All ER 887.

[125] *R v Miller* [1983] 1 WLR 1057 at 1061; following elevation, Lloyd LJ reaffirmed this principle *Ghadami v Lyon Cole Insurance Group Limited* [2010] EWCA Civ 767 at [10].

[126] The need to show 'an agreement ... not to have to pay those costs in any circumstances' is not a test of universal applicability; it only applies in cases in which the facts imply the existence of a retainer. See the discussion about *Byrne v Kunkel & Kunkel* [1999] 1 CL 349 elsewhere in this work.

[127] *Griffiths v Evans* [1953] 2 All ER 1364 at 1369.

[128] *Gray & Anr v Buss & Merton (a firm)* [1999] PNLR 882 at 892.

'It seems to me that the underlying basis for this principle must be that it is the client who actually knows what he wants the solicitor to do, and so it is the solicitor's business to ascertain the client's wishes accurately, bearing in mind the possibility that the client, through ignorance of the correct terminology, may not have correctly expressed it.'

Peter Smith J has confirmed that this principle is not limited to situations in which the solicitor ought to have recognised the possibility of misapprehension and sought clarification accordingly.[129]

8.107 This principle is ancient,[130] but Butterfield J has recently confirmed it as being good law.[131] Indeed, in modern practice Denning LJ's words may have particular resonance, this being because of the way in which the various codes of conduct have addressed the issue of written confirmation about costs. The exact provisions depend on when the work was done. Most contracts of retainer would, at the time of writing, have been made after 1 July 2007 but before 6 October 2011; where this is so, the following provisions in the Solicitors' Code of Conduct 2007[132] would apply:

'(5) Any information about the cost must be clear and confirmed in writing.'

The reference to 'the cost' was a reference to the cost to the client of instructing the solicitor; it included information about the retainer. The Solicitors' Code of Conduct 2007 imposed the following obligations:[133]

'2.03 Information about the cost

(1) You must give your client the best information possible about the likely overall cost of a matter both at the outset and, when appropriate, as the matter progresses. In particular you must:

    (a)   advise the client of the basis and terms of your charges;

    (b)   advise the client if charging rates are to be increased;

    (c)   advise the client of likely payments which you or your client may need to make to others;

    (d)   discuss with the client how the client will pay, in particular:

        (i)   whether the client may be eligible and should apply for public funding; and

        (ii)   whether the client's own costs are covered by insurance or may be paid by someone else such as an employer or trade union;

    (e)   advise the client that there are circumstances where you may be entitled to exercise a lien for unpaid costs;

    (f)   advise the client of their potential liability for any other party's costs; and

    (g)   discuss with the client whether their liability for another party's costs may be covered by existing insurance or whether specially purchased insurance may be obtained.'

8.108 In so far as retainers made before 1 July 2007 are concerned, similar provisions existed under the Solicitors Practice Rules 1990.[134] Contracts of retainer made on or

---

129 *Sibley & Co v Reachbyte Ltd* [2008] EWHC 2665 (Ch) at [44]–[50].

130 See *Re Paine* (1912) 28 TLR 201, per Warrington J. Older authorities exist (see, for example, *Allen v Bone* (1841) 4 Beav 493 and *Crossley v Crowther* (1851) 9 Hare 384), but they appear to suggest that there is a rule of law that operates against the solicitor; to the extent that they do that, those authorities are probably no longer good law.

131 *Fereidooni v Pettman Smith* [2001] EWHC 9007 (Costs).

132 Paragraph 2.03(5) of the Solicitors' Code of Conduct 2007.

133 Paragraph 2.03(1) of the Solicitors' Code of Conduct 2007.

134 See para 3(3) of the Solicitors' Costs Information and Client Care Code 1999.

after 6 October 2011 will be subject to the SRA Code of Conduct 2011; that code does not contain the same words as appeared in the previous codes,[135] but this does not mean that the principle described by Denning LJ is any less important. Indeed, the corresponding provisions in the SRA Code of Conduct 2011 include the following:

> **'Outcomes**
>
> You must achieve these outcomes:
>
> **O(1.1)** you treat your clients fairly;
>
> . . .
>
> **O(1.6)** you only enter into fee agreements with your clients that are legal, and which you consider are suitable for the client's needs and take account of the client's best interests;
>
> . . .
>
> **O(1.12)** clients are in a position to make informed decisions about the services they need, how their matter will be handled and the options available to them;
>
> **O(1.13)** clients receive the best possible information, both at the time of engagement and when appropriate as their matter progresses, about the likely overall cost of their matter;
>
> **O(1.14)** clients are informed of their right to challenge or complain about your bill and the circumstances in which they may be liable to pay interest on an unpaid bill;
>
> **O(1.15)** you properly account to clients for any financial benefit you receive as a result of your instructions;
>
> . . .
>
> **'Fee arrangements with your client**
>
> **IB(1.13)** discussing whether the potential outcomes of the client's matter are likely to justify the expense or risk involved, including any risk of having to pay someone else's legal fees;
>
> **IB(1.14)** clearly explaining your fees and if and when they are likely to change;
>
> **IB(1.15)** warning about any other payments for which the client may be responsible;
>
> **IB(1.16)** discussing how the client will pay, including whether public funding may be available, whether the client has insurance that might cover the fees, and whether the fees may be paid by someone else such as a trade union;
>
> **IB(1.17)** where you are acting for a client under a fee arrangement governed by statute, such as a conditional fee agreement, giving the client all relevant information relating to that arrangement;
>
> **IB(1.18)** where you are acting for a publicly funded client, explaining how their publicly funded status affects the costs;
>
> **IB(1.19)** providing the information in a clear and accessible form which is appropriate to the needs and circumstances of the client;
>
> **IB(1.20)** where you receive a financial benefit as a result of acting for a client, either:
>
> - paying it to the client;
> - offsetting it against your fees; or
> - keeping it only where you can justify keeping it, you have told the client the amount of the benefit (or an approximation if you do not know the exact amount) and the client has agreed that you can keep it;

---

[135]   See **8.59** above.

IB(1.21) ensuring that disbursements included in your bill reflect the actual amount spent or to be spent on behalf of the client.

...

IB(1.26) ceasing to act for a client without good reason and without providing reasonable notice;

IB(1.27) entering into unlawful fee arrangements such as an unlawful contingency fee.'

8.109 Where the retainer is a conditional fee agreement made before 6 October 2011, there were additional topics which ought to have been discussed (and, for the reasons set out above, recorded in writing):[136]

'(2)   Where you are acting for the client under a conditional fee agreement, (including a collective conditional fee agreement) in addition to complying with 2.03(1) above and 2.03(5) and (6) below, you must explain the following, both at the outset and, when appropriate, as the matter progresses:

(a)   the circumstances in which your client may be liable for your costs and whether you will seek payment of these from the client, if entitled to do so;

(b)   if you intend to seek payment of any or all of your costs from your client, you must advise your client of their right to an assessment of those costs; and

(c)   where applicable, the fact that you are obliged under a fee sharing agreement to pay to a charity any fees which you receive by way of costs from the client's opponent or other third party.'

Breach of these obligations would be most unlikely to have the effect of making a retainer unenforceable (especially when the challenge is made by a paying party),[137] but from an evidential point of view, a solicitor may find it difficult to explain the absence of a written record in the event that he is at odds with his client over a matter which ought to have been recorded in writing.

PRIVATE RETAINERS

8.110 A private retainer is an ordinary retainer, that being a retainer by which the client agrees to pay the solicitor for his work on an unconditional basis. Contentious and non-contentious business agreements are sometimes classified as being varieties of private retainer, but in order to avoid confusion that classification is not used in this book. The distinction between a private retainer and a business agreement can be a fine one, however (as is explained at **8.116**).

8.111 Private retainers are usually created by one or both of two documents:

- *Client care letters*: A client care letter is a letter which, as the name implies, sets out the basis upon which the solicitor will provide services to the client. It will usually deal with many issues other than costs (such as the details of the person, with conduct of the matter, the complaints procedure, etc). It may also give initial advice about the claim.
- *Terms and conditions*: This is usually a standard document which contains the terms and conditions upon which the solicitors will provide legal services. Standard form terms and conditions exist.

---

[136]   Paragraph 2.03(1) of the Solicitors' Code of Conduct 2007.
[137]   See *Garbutt v Edwards* [2005] EWCA Civ 1206.

At the time of writing, most retainers encountered in practice would have been made before 6 October 2011 but after 1 July 2007; as such, the Solicitors' Code of Conduct 2007 applied. That code required that certain information was given both orally and in writing (see **8.108** for the details); the requisite information was usually given in one or both of these documents.

8.112 The guidance to the Solicitors' Code of Conduct 2007 made it clear that the solicitor was not required to be inflexible about the information that he gave in an individual case. The code advised that over-complex or lengthy documents may not be helpful.[138] If and in so far as a need to confirm the terms of the retainer can be implied into the SRA Code of Conduct 2011, it is most unlikely that any such requirement would be any more demanding of a solicitor than that which existed previously; this is because the SRA Code of Conduct 2011 specifically refers to itself as being a flexible code which focuses on outcomes rather than on laying down prescriptive guidance. That said, solicitors would be storing up trouble for themselves if they were not to set themselves high standards in this regard; disregarding aspects of the SRA Code of Conduct 2011 would be a very risky strategy.[139]

8.113 When drafting a private retainer, the drafter would do well to consider whether any of the provisions mentioned in the section on general provisions (see **8.90–8.102**) need to be included.

BUSINESS AGREEMENTS (NON-CONTENTIOUS AND CONTENTIOUS)

8.114 Business agreements fall into two categories: non-contentious and contentious. Each has its own statutory regime.

8.115 Broadly speaking, business agreements differ from other retainers in that if they are not set aside, they are enforceable without the client having a right to a full assessment.[140] However, the court has many powers to regulate business agreements, one of which is to set the agreement aside on the basis that it is unfair or unreasonable. Clients should not assume that the court will readily intervene in this regard, however, as Mustill LJ said:[141]

> '[From] a practical point of view the agreement of the client is strongest evidence that the fee is reasonable.'

---

[138] Paragraphs 13 and 22 of the guidance to rule 2.01 of the Solicitors' Code of Conduct 2007.

[139] Whilst he was dealing with the Solicitors Practice Rules 1990 rather than the SRA Code of Conduct 2011, Auld LJ (sitting the Divisional Court) said that there was a heavy onus on a solicitor to establish that his client is so sophisticated in matters of litigation, and so attentive to the cost implications of the litigation in question, that the then requirements to give information about costs could be disregarded: *Darby v Law Society* [2003] EWHC 2270 (Admin) at [27].

[140] In the case of a non-contentious business agreement, the agreement will be enforceable without the client having the right to a remuneration certificate, and this will be the case even for bills rendered before 11 August 2009.

[141] *Walton v Egan* [1982] QB 1232.

Business agreements and agreements generally

8.116 The distinction between business agreements and other forms of retainer can sometimes be a fine one. A well-drafted client care letter that has been signed by both the solicitor and the client could easily (and inadvertently) be a contentious business agreement. In practice, it would be unlikely that a dispute as to the nature of such a document would arise because, for all practical purposes, the court's scrutiny of such an agreement pursuant to SA 1974, s 61(4B) (see below) would be almost indistinguishable from an assessment in which the hourly rate had been agreed.

8.117 Both contentious and non-contentious business agreements are governed by statute in the form of the Solicitors Act 1974. Certain requirements are stipulated in that Act (see **8.123–8.145**), but there is nothing which expressly stipulates what will happen in the event of non-compliance. That topic is most easily addressed by looking at the history of business agreements. It can be seen that non-compliance with the requisite provisions will result in the counterparties being denied the benefit of the putative non-contentious business agreement.

Purported compromises and agreements to restrict assessments

8.118 At common law an agreement by a solicitor to be paid a predicable sum (as opposed to a fee to be assessed) was not necessarily regarded as being void, but it was looked upon with suspicion.[142] It was not uncommon for such agreements to be found to be unenforceable.[143] The common law was described by Fletcher-Moulton in these terms:[144]

> 'At that date [that is, before the introduction of statutory regulation] agreements between a solicitor and his client as to the terms on which the solicitor's business was to be done were not necessarily unenforceable. They were, however, viewed with great jealousy by the Courts, because they were agreements between a man and his legal adviser as to the terms of the latter's remuneration, and there was so great an opportunity for the exercise of undue influence, that the Courts were very slow to enforce such agreements where they were favourable to the solicitor unless they were satisfied that they were made under circumstances that precluded any suspicion of an improper attempt on the solicitor's part to benefit himself at his client's expense.'

Thus, the position at common law was that agreements restricting the client's right to challenge his solicitor's fees were often not enforced and that this was often on grounds that were not dissimilar to presumed undue influence. A similar line of thought applied to agreements to settle accounts for costs already incurred by taking a gross sum before delivery of a bill (see **19.38**). In so far as costs yet to be incurred are concerned, a solicitor could not in general enter into a bare agreement that his costs would not be assessed[145], and any agreement to preclude the right to an assessment had to be shown to be favourable to the client in order to be enforceable.[146] In particular, there is no reason why a solicitor cannot agree to limit his fees.[147] Further, examples are given in the

---

[142] *In re Whitcombe* (1844) 8 Beav 140; many of the applicable cases dealt primarily with verbal agreements.

[143] For example, a textbook predating the introduction of statutory control records that such agreements were only 'not infrequently' held to be binding, which implies that they were also held not to be binding (*Cordery on Solicitors* (3rd edn), p 261).

[144] *Clare v Joseph* [1907] 2 KB 369 at 376.

[145] See, for example, *Balme v Paver* (1821) Jac Rep 305 and *Scougall v Campbell* (1826) 3 Russ 545.

[146] See *Re Newman* (1861) 30 Beav 196 and *Re Cawley & Whatley* (1870) 18 WR 1125.

[147] *Scarth v Rutland* (1866) LR 1 CP 642 at 643, per Earl CJ. This case is often cited as being authority for the

footnotes.[148] Where the court found against the solicitor in respect of an agreement to fix his costs, the only agreement that was found to be unenforceable was the agreement restricting the client's ability to challenge the level of fees: the retainer itself would not usually have been at risk. Therefore, if the court found the agreement to be unenforceable, the solicitor would still be able to recover his fees, but those fees would be subject to an assessment.[149]

8.119 When the statutory regime was first introduced, the position was much the same: agreements that did not comply with the legislative requirements were impeached;[150] where this happened, the then statutory regime expressly provided that the solicitor's costs would be taxed as if the agreement had never been made.[151]

8.120 The same is broadly true today. If an agreement falls short of being (say) a contentious business agreement, the solicitor will lose the benefit of SA 1974, s 60(1) and, as a result, the costs will be subject to an assessment. The failed agreement may form the basis of that assessment – and to this extent the costs will be assessed in accordance with that agreement even though it has failed – but (equally) those costs will be recovered only to the extent that they were reasonably incurred and reasonable in amount.

Non-contentious business agreements

8.121 Non-contentious business agreements (like contentious business agreements) are a creation of statute.[152] The principal characteristic of a non-contentious business agreement is that it is a retainer which, subject to certain safeguards, will allow the solicitor to recover his fees as if they were an ordinary debt. This means that the client would not ordinarily be entitled to an assessment of those fees. A lesser form of non-contentious business agreement exists, which permits only the hourly rate to be treated in this way, leaving the client free to ask the court to ascertain the reasonableness of the time claimed.

8.122 The modern legislation is at s 57 of the SA 1974 (as amended),[153] and provides:

---

proposition that if the client has failed to plead a defence of non-delivery of a detailed bill, the solicitor could recover in an action on the agreement; it is unlikely that this remains good law.

[148] The following is a list of agreements that have been found to be enforceable, but it is important to note that many of the in categories (i), (ii) and (iii) would be likely now be subject to statutory provisions concerning conditional fee agreements: (i) agreeing not to charge in the event of non-recovery of costs (*Jennings v Johnson* (1873) LR 8 CP 425); (ii) agreeing not to charge in the event of failure (*Tabram v Horne* (1827) 1 Man & Ry 228; *Galloway v Corporation of London* (1867) LR 4 Eq 90 at 97; *Turner v Tennant* (1846) 10 Jur 429; and *Gundry v Sainsbury* [1910] 1 KB 645); (iii) agreeing to charge disbursements only (*Jones v Reade* (1836) 5 A & E 529); and (iv) agreements to restrict costs (*Moon v Hall* (1864) 17 CB(NS) 760; and *Re Owen; Ex parte Payton* (1885) 52 LT 628); see also *Re a Solicitor (No 2)* [1956] 1 QB 155, which (obiter) affirmed Clare and Jennings as being good law. See also *Electrical Trades Union v Tarlo* [1964] Ch 720 (oral retainer related to both contentious and non-contentious work: contentious part found to be enforceable).

[149] See *Saunderson v Glass* (1742) 2 Atk 296, *Philby v Hazle* (1860) 8 CBNS 647 at 652, and *O'Brien v Lewis* (1863) 32 LT (Ch) 569.

[150] *In re Russell Son & Scott* [1885] 30 Ch D 114 at 116.

[151] Attorneys and Solicitors Act 1870 (33 & 34 Vict c 28), s 9.

[152] Whilst not given their modern title, they were first created by Attorneys and Solicitors Act 1870 (33 & 34 Vict c 28), s 2, and given something similar to their modern form in s 8 of the Solicitors' Remuneration Act 1881.

[153] By Courts and Legal Services Act 1990, s 98.

'(1)   Whether or not any order is in force under section 56,[154] a solicitor and his client may, before or after or in the course of the transaction of any non-contentious business by the solicitor, make an agreement as to his remuneration in respect of that business.

(2)   The agreement may provide for the remuneration of the solicitor by a gross sum or by reference to an hourly rate, or by a commission or percentage, or by a salary, or otherwise, and it may be made on the terms that the amount of the remuneration stipulated for shall or shall not include all or any disbursements made by the solicitor in respect of searches, plans, travelling, taxes, fees or other matters.

(3)   The agreement shall be in writing and signed by the person to be bound by it or his agent in that behalf.

(4)   Subject to subsections (5) and (7), the agreement may be sued and recovered on or set aside in the like manner and on the like grounds as an agreement not relating to the remuneration of a solicitor.

(5)   If on any assessment of costs the agreement is relied on by the solicitor and objected to by the client as unfair or unreasonable, the costs officer may enquire into the facts and certify them to the court, and if from that certificate it appears just to the court that the agreement should be set aside, or the amount payable under it reduced, the court may so order and may give such consequential directions as it thinks fit.

(6)   Subsection (7) applies where the agreement provides for the remuneration of the solicitor to be by reference to an hourly rate.

(7)   If, on the assessment of any costs, the agreement is relied on by the solicitor and the client objects to the amount of the costs (but is not alleging that the agreement is unfair or unreasonable), the costs officer may enquire into—

(a)   the number of hours worked by the solicitor; and
(b)   whether the number of hours worked by him was excessive.'

It is to be noted that the reference to payment by percentage expressly authorises agreements where the amount of the fee paid to the solicitor is based on results; this is a type of conditional fee agreement that is often referred to as a 'contingency fee agreement. The enforceability of such an agreement is expressly preserved by the legislation relating to conditional fee agreements.[155] This is addressed in detail at **9.303-9.308**.

The requirements of a non-contentious business agreement

8.123   The requirements of a non-contentious business agreement are that:

- it must be in writing;[156]
- it must be signed by the person to be bound by it or his agent in that behalf;[157] and
- it must state the terms of the remuneration (this being a provision implied by SA 1974, s 57(3)).[158]

Each of these requirements is considered in turn.

---

[154]   That order is the Solicitors' (Non-Contentious Business) Remuneration Order 2009 (SI 2009/1931).
[155]   See s 58(5) of the Courts and Legal Services Act 1990 (as amended).
[156]   SA 1974, s 57(7).
[157]   SA 1974, s 57(3).
[158]   *Bake v French (No 2)* [1907] 2 Ch 215.

Written form

8.124 SA 1974, s 57(3) provides that the agreement must be in writing. The absence of a written agreement will usually mean that the agreement is unenforceable;[159] this would usually be to the client's advantage and the solicitor's disadvantage, but this will not always be the case. Pearson J, for example, found that a client could not rely on an oral agreement that his solicitor would charge less than the ordinary rate of remuneration.[160] (Where it is said that there is an oral agreement as to the sums payable, there is an apparent anomaly between the way in which the law treats non-contentious and contentious costs: this is dealt with at **8.222–8.225**.) Stanley Burnton LJ has confirmed that there is no requirement that a non-contentious business agreement must not be in the same written instrument as a contentious business agreement.[161]

Signature

8.125 Section 57(3) also provides that the agreement must be signed by the 'person bound by it'; this does not necessarily mean that the agreement must be signed by both the solicitor and client, as indicated by Lindley LJ:[162]

> 'What is meant by an agreement signed by the person to be bound? The subsection does not mean signed by both parties, because only one is required to sign. It means that the person to sign is the person who seeks to get rid of the agreement, and who is sought to be bound by it. Here the client seeks to get rid of the agreement, and he is the person who signs it. In such a case it is sufficient for him to sign it whatever the solicitor may do.'

(The reference to getting 'rid of the agreement' was made in the context of an application by a client for assessment notwithstanding the existence of an agreement.) Thus, the agreement must be signed by the person against whom it is sought to be enforced.

Statement of terms

8.126 Section 57(2) (as amended) of SA 1974 specifies the methods by which payment may be calculated. It makes the following provisions:

- the agreement may or may not encompass disbursements;
- payment may be independent of outcome, such as by gross sum, reference to an hourly rate,[163] or a salary;
- payment may be dependent on outcome, such as payment of a percentage or of a commission; and
- other methods of payment may be used.

---

[159] See **8.222**.

[160] In *In re a Solicitor* [1956] 1 QB 157; whilst obiter, that case affirmed the view that oral agreements in relation to contentious work were enforceable.

[161] *Bilkus v Stockler Brunton (a firm)* [2010] EWCA Civ 101 at [50]–[53].

[162] *In re Frape ex p Perrett* [1893] 2 Ch 284 at 294.

[163] This provision came about as a result of the amendments effected by s 98 of the Courts and Legal Services Act 1990.

8.127 The terms of remuneration should be expressed in the agreement.[164] Where work has already been done, the words 'agreed costs' are not, of themselves, sufficient to satisfy that requirement,[165] but where the detail of the agreement could be implied, that phrase is capable of being sufficient.[166]

8.128 SA 1974 provides that an agreement may be made 'before or after or in the course of the transaction of any non-contentious business by the solicitor'; this means that the agreement may be retrospective in effect. It is not bar to the creation of an agreement, therefore, that the work to which it relates has already been completed or is in the process of being completed.

8.129 It is possible for a non-contentious business agreement to be formed without that being the intention of the counterparties. Whilst this can happen regardless of whether the agreement was made before, during or after the transaction to which it relates, the effect can be particularly expected when the agreement is retrospective.[167] An extreme example is a detailed receipted account, which, if sufficiently clear and detailed and if signed by the counterparties may be capable of giving rise to a binding agreement.[168] The mere taking of a bill of exchange will not be sufficient, however.[169] Another example is where a client waives his right to a bill in writing after having been given details about the costs; this can give rise to a binding agreement even where no bill has been delivered.[170] It should be borne in mind, however, that most of the authorities concerning unintended agreements are at least a century old, and it is possible that modern-day courts – with their greater emphasis on consumer protection – would be reluctant to find that a client has unintentionally agreed to forgo his right to a detailed assessment.

8.130 The terms of an agreement must be precise and unambiguous.[171] If the agreement contains a one-sided ambiguous provision which has been inserted by the solicitor, the *contra proferentum* rule may apply in the client's favour.[172]

8.131 A non-contentious business agreement does not necessarily need to be a single document; a series of documents may suffice.[173]

8.132 Agreements concerning security for a solicitor's fees do not fall within the ambit of SA 1974, s 57.[174] Mustill J has said, obiter, that s 57:[175]

---

[164] *Bake v French (No 2)* [1907] 2 Ch 215.
[165] *In re Bayliss* [1896] 2 Ch 107 at 119.
[166] *In re Frape ex p Perrett* [1893] 2 Ch 284.
[167] See SA 1974, s 57(1).
[168] See *In Re Thompson ex p Baylis* [1894] 1 QB 462; it should be noted, however, that despite the impression given in the Law Reports, the client in that case had already received a statute bill: see the report in the *Law Journal* (63 LJ (QB) 187), referred to by Chitty J in *In re Baylis* [1896] 2 Ch 109 at 114.
[169] *Ray v Newton* [1913] 1 KB 249; see also *Martin Boston & Co (a firm) v Levy* [1982] 1 WLR 1434.
[170] *Bake v French (No 2)* [1907] 2 Ch 215.
[171] *Chamberlain v Boodle & King* [1982] 3 All ER 188.
[172] *R a Debtor (No 1594 of 1992)* (1992) *The Times*, December 8.
[173] *Bake v French (No 2)* [1907] 2 Ch 215.
[174] *In re an undertaking by Wingfields, Halse and Trustram, Jonesco v Evening Standard Company* [1932] 2 KB 340 (this case related to law which did not distinguish between contentious and non-contentious law, however).
[175] *Walton v Egan* [1982] 3 WLR 352 at 357.

'seems to be concerned with the ascertainment of the amount of the remuneration, rather than the way in which it is to be paid – so that an agreement as to the source of the funds which are to be used for paying the bill lies outside the scope of the section.'

The effect of a non-contentious business agreement

8.133 The principal effect of a non-contentious business agreement is that it may be treated 'as an agreement not relating to the remuneration of a solicitor'; this means that the client may lose the right to challenge the level of fees by way of a detailed assessment.[176] If upon enquiry the court finds that the agreement is unfair or unreasonable, however, it may be set aside or the amount payable under it may be reduced.[177]

8.134 A non-contentious business agreement may provide for remuneration to be by reference to an hourly rate; where that is the case, the court may ascertain the number of hours worked by the solicitor.[178] That would be an exercise virtually indistinguishable from an ordinary assessment (except, of course, the hourly rate would not fall to be assessed). The court may carry out that ascertainment without making a finding that the agreement was unfair or unreasonable; if, however, either of those thresholds was met, the court could set aside the agreed rate, or might reduce it.[179]

8.135 A client who has entered into a non-contentious business agreement will not be able to apply for a remuneration certificate[180] even if the invoice was rendered before 11 August 2009.[181] Whilst there is no authority on the point, this would seem to be the case even where the agreement relates only to the hourly rate.

8.136 A solicitor may sue upon a non-contentious business agreement as if it were any other debt.[182] This is differs from contentious business agreements, where the court's approval is required to enforce the agreement.[183]

Termination of a non-contentious business agreement

8.137 A non-contentious business agreement may be terminated at will; there are no formalities required. A full discussion of the circumstances in which a solicitor may terminate his retainer is beyond the scope of this book, but the SRA Code of Conduct 2011 states that ceasing to act for a client 'without good reason and without providing reasonable notice' is an indicative behaviour that might indicate a failure to provide the requisite standard of care.[184] This echoed the advice given under the Solicitors' Code of Conduct 2007.[185] This issue is dealt with in more detail at **8.71–8.89**. The same law applies to non-contentious business agreements as it does to any other type of retainer.

---

[176]   SA 1974, s 57(4).
[177]   SA 1974, s 57(5).
[178]   SA 1974, s 57(5) and (6).
[179]   SA 1974, s 57(5).
[180]   The Solicitors' (Non-Contentious Business) Remuneration Order 1994 (SI 2009/1931), art 9(c).
[181]   SI 2009/1931, art 1(3).
[182]   SA 1974, s 57(4).
[183]   SA 1974, s 61(1).
[184]   See IB(1.26).
[185]   Solicitors' Code of Conduct 2007, para 8 of the guidance to rule 2.01.

The wording of the relevant statutory provisions

8.138 SA 1974, s 57 (as amended) provides as follows:

'57 Non-contentious business agreements

(1) Whether or not any order is in force under section 56, a solicitor and his client may, before or after or in the course of the transaction of any non-contentious business by the solicitor, make an agreement as to his remuneration in respect of that business.

(2) The agreement may provide for the remuneration of the solicitor by a gross sum or by reference to an hourly rate, or by a commission or percentage, or by a salary, or otherwise, and it may be made on the terms that the amount of the remuneration stipulated for shall or shall not include all or any disbursements made by the solicitor in respect of searches, plans, travelling, stamps, taxes, fees or other matters.

(3) The agreement shall be in writing and signed by the person to be bound by it or his agent in that behalf.

(4) Subject to subsections (5) and (7), the agreement may be sued and recovered on or set aside in the like manner and on the like grounds as an agreement not relating to the remuneration of a solicitor.

(5) If on any assessment of costs the agreement is relied on by the solicitor and objected to by the client as unfair or unreasonable, the costs officer may enquire into the facts and certify them to the court, and if from that certificate it appears just to the court that the agreement should be set aside, or the amount payable under it reduced, the court may so order and may give such consequential directions as it thinks fit.

(6) Subsection (7) applies where the agreement provides for the remuneration of the solicitor to be by reference to an hourly rate.

(7) If, on the assessment of any costs, the agreement is relied on by the solicitor and the client objects to the amount of the costs (but is not alleging that the agreement is unfair or unreasonable), the costs officer may enquire into—

(a) the number of hours worked by the solicitor; and

(b) whether the number of hours worked by him was excessive.'

Contentious business agreements

8.139 Contentious business agreements (like their non-contentious brethren) are a creation of statute.[186] They are often referred to as 'CBAs', but that abbreviation is not used in this book because it is prone to be confused with the abbreviation commonly used for conditional fee agreements. Whilst on the topic of conditional fee agreements, it is worth saying that, unlike the legislation governing non-contentious business agreements, there is nothing within the legislation governing contentious business agreements that would turn an otherwise unlawful conditional fee agreement into a lawful agreement[187]; this includes a contingency fee agreements. As such, what is set out in this section should not be regarded as being an alternative mechanism by which conditional free agreements may be found to be enforceable.

8.140 A contentious business agreement is a retainer which, subject to certain safeguards, will allow the solicitor to recover his fees for contentious work as if they

---

[186] SA 1974, ss 59–63.

[187] See SA 1974, s 59(2), which is set out at **8.146**. Whilst not binding, for a discussion on this topic see Master Hurst's judgment in *Tel-Ka Talk Ltd v Revenue & Customs Commissioners* [2010] EWHC 90175 (Costs) at [134] onwards.

were an ordinary debt. The principal effect of this is that the costs will not ordinarily be subject to assessment (or, if the agreement provides for payment by an hourly rate, the rate will not ordinarily be subject to assessment). However, judicial control continues to exist in an attenuated form, in that the court can set aside a contentious business agreement if it is found to be unfair or unreasonable.

8.141 The modern provisions are set out in SA 1974, ss 59–63. They were amended by the Courts and Legal Services Act 1990 to introduce an express facility to charge with reference to hourly rates. The wording of the modern provisions derives from the Solicitors Act 1957, but similar provisions existed well before this. In order to understand the effect of contentious business agreements, it is necessary to know something of the common law and of the history of the jurisdiction.

The relationship of SA 1974 with the common law

8.142 The original statutory provisions were introduced by the Attorneys and Solicitors Act 1870, which made no distinction between contentious and non-contentious work. But, notwithstanding this, s 4 of that Act was in many ways comparable with the provisions which govern the form, content and effect of modern contentious business agreements.[188]

8.143 By looking at the way in which the law regarded that early Act it is possible to see that the statutory provisions are purely enabling provisions: they are not intended in any way to be restrictive, as Fletcher Moulton LJ remarked:[189]

> 'It is to be remarked in the first place that this is a purely enabling, and not a disabling, section, and the Court would not, unless forced to do so, construe such a section so as to take away or alter powers already in existence, except indeed by extending them.'

He went on to say that:

> '... the specific provisions of s 4 did no more than provide and regulate a procedure for the control of such agreements; they did not in substance alter the law affecting them.'

8.144 The statutory provisions were, when they were first enacted at least, intended not to restrict the ability of clients and solicitors to negotiate the terms of engagement. The relevance of this is that where a retainer does not comply with the requisite statutory requirements, that retainer will be judged by the common law, and may or may not be found to be enforceable. This issue is discussed at **8.118**.

The form and content of contentious business agreements

8.145 The form and content of a modern contentious business agreement is governed by SA 1974, s 59 and by the authorities which clarify that section; the requirements are as follows:

- that the agreement is in writing;[190]

---

[188] SA 1974, s 59.
[189] *Clare v Joseph* [1907] 2 KB 376.
[190] SSA 1974, s 59(1).

- that it must contain terms going to the amount of costs, or to the method by which those costs are to be calculated;[191] and
- that it must be sufficiently specific to allow the client to know what is being proposed.[192]

It is a moot point whether the agreement needs to be signed; this is addressed below.

8.146 SA 1974, s 59 provides as follows:

'(1) Subject to subsection (2), a solicitor may make an agreement in writing with his client as to his remuneration in respect of any contentious business done, or to be done, by him (in this Act referred to as a "contentious business agreement") providing that he shall be remunerated by a gross sum or by reference to an hourly rate, or by a salary, or otherwise, and whether at a higher or lower rate than that at which he would otherwise have been entitled to be remunerated.

(2) Nothing in this section or in sections 60 to 63 shall give validity to—

(a) any purchase by a solicitor of the interest, or any part of the interest, of his client in any action, suit or other contentious proceeding; or

(b) any agreement by which a solicitor retained or employed to prosecute any action, suit or other contentious proceeding, stipulates for payment only in the event of success in that action, suit or proceeding; or

(c) any disposition, contract, settlement, conveyance, delivery, dealing or transfer which under the law relating to bankruptcy is invalid against a trustee or creditor in any bankruptcy or composition.'

Each of the requirements mentioned above is considered in turn.

Writing

8.147 Whether an agreement is in writing will be a matter of fact to be determined in the usual way. Oral agreements are discussed at **8.217–8.230**.

8.148 An agreement may be a contentious business agreement even if it is contained in several documents or letters, rather than one.[193] Stanley Burnton LJ has confirmed that there is no requirement that a contentious business agreement must not be in the same written instrument as a non-contentious business agreement.[194]

Terms as to costs

8.149 This requirement will overlap with the requirement that the agreement is sufficiently specific. Denning MR has explained that the agreement must relate to the solicitor's remuneration itself, rather than just to some variable aspect of the way in which his bill will be drawn up (see below). Mann J commented on this requirement:[195]

'The purpose of a [contentious business agreement] is to fix the fees, or provide a fixing mechanism, so that the parties (and in particular the client) knows where they stand.'

---

[191] SA 1974, s 59(1); see also *Chamberlain v Boodle & King* [1982] 1 WLR 1443 at 1445.
[192] *Chamberlain v Boodle & King* [1982] 1 WLR 1443 at 1445.
[193] *Chamberlain v Boodle & King* [1982] 1 WLR 1443 at 1445.
[194] *Bilkus v Stockler Brunton (a firm)* [2010] EWCA Civ 101 at [50]–[53].
[195] *Wilson v The Spectre Partnership* [2007] EWHC 133 (Ch) at [16(b)].

The retainer which was before Denning MR did little more than make provision for a number of different rates to be paid in respect of different fee earners and, even then, those rates were not fixed. He said this on the subject:[196]

> '... [It] seems to me that this is not an agreement as to remuneration at all. It is simply an indication of the rate of charging on which the solicitors propose to make up their bill. It is by no means an agreement in writing as to remuneration ... It is impossible to say that this was a contentious business agreement in writing such as to deprive the client of his right to have it taxed.'

(It should be noted that this was before the statutory provisions were changed so as expressly to include retainers dealing with hourly rates.)

8.150 It seems, therefore, that a contentious business agreement must be an agreement that can properly be said to be an agreement as to what will be charged, rather than just a general indication as to the way in which the costs will be calculated. Although they are based on nothing more reliable than the writer's opinion, the following two are examples which would probably fail to meet this requirement:

- Where a solicitor and client agree a limit on the number of hours that may be worked and where that limit is reached, the client could argue that there was no agreement that the solicitor may reach that limit, and that, therefore, the agreement was not sufficiently fixed.
- Where a solicitor and client agree an hourly rate, but where the agreement also provides for an increase in that rate which is conditional upon the existence of some complicating factor making the litigation harder to manage (such as a need for urgency), the client could argue that there was no agreement that that factor had come into existence.

8.151 Where there has been agreement as to the general way in which the costs will be calculated and where the court rejects the argument that that agreement amounts to a contentious business agreement, the agreed figures will still be relevant in the sense that they will be taken into account when considering the reasonableness of the costs.[197]

Sufficiently specific

8.152 For an agreement to comply with the requirements of SA 1974, s 59, Denning MR held that it:[198]

> 'must be sufficient specific – so as to tell the client what he is letting himself in for by way of costs.'

Mann J put the matter in this way:[199]

> 'The essence of a [contentious business agreement] is certainty ... Since the client is disadvantaged [by entering into a contentious business agreement], the agreement has to be in writing, and it has to be sufficiently certain.'

---

[196] *Chamberlain v Boodle & King* [1982] 1 WLR 1443 at 1445.
[197] See CPR, r 48.8(2)(a) and (b).
[198] *Chamberlain v Boodle & King* [1982] 1 WLR 1443 at 1445.
[199] *Wilson v The Spectre Partnership* [2007] EWHC 133 (Ch).

8.153 The requirement that the agreement is sufficiently specific is similar to (and may overlap with) the requirement that the amount or method be stated (see above), but there are differences, in that an agreement may lack specificity in a way that relates to something other than the quantum of the solicitor's fees. Each case will turn on its own facts, but the following are examples:

- where the retainer is a general retainer rather than a retainer relating to a specific case, and where it had not been adapted for use in the case in hand;[200]
- where the agreement contemplated the execution of a more formal document;[201]
- where the retainer afforded a facility for the solicitors fees to be adjusted to take account of the nature of the case;[202] and
- where the agreement was contained in a series of letters which had not been signed by the client.[203]

8.154 Whilst they are not express requirements, there are two other issues that merit attention, not least because they may be important factors in deciding whether the requirements have been satisfied. The first is the need for a signature, and the second is the extent to which the client must be put on notice that the agreement is intended to be a contentious business agreement.

Signature

8.155 There is no express statutory requirement that a contentious business agreement be signed. There is (old) obiter to the effect that a signature is necessary,[204] but it is doubtful if those authorities represent the modern law.[205] However, Denning MR has held that if a client is to be deprived of his right to an assessment, he should at least sign the agreement,[206] but that was in the context of the putative agreement being contained in letters rather than a specific document; it was also in the context of the agreement being found insufficiently specific to be a contentious business agreement.

8.156 Even if there is a requirement that a contentious business agreement is to be signed, a failure by the solicitor to sign will not necessarily prevent him from enforcing that agreement.[207] This would be on the basis that the client had signed it, so there can be no doubt that the client was prepared to be bound by its terms.

8.157 Although there is no specific authority on the point, it would be open to a client to argue that if the circumstances were such that he could reasonably have expected to have been given the opportunity to sign the retainer, it would be unfair to afford the solicitor the benefits of it being a contentious business agreement.[208]

---

[200] *Wilson v The Spectre Partnership* [2007] EWHC 133 (Ch).
[201] See, in a context other than costs, *Tiverton Estates Ltd v Wearwell Ltd* [1975] Ch 146, which was considered in *Martin Boston & Co (a firm) v Levy* [1982] 1 WLR 1434.
[202] *Wilson v The Spectre Partnership* [2007] EWHC 133 (Ch) at [16(b)].
[203] *Chamberlain v Boodle & King* [1982] 1 WLR 1443 at 1445.
[204] *In re Lewis ex p Munro* (1876) 1 QBD 724.
[205] See *In re Thompson ex p Bayliss* [1894] 1 QB 462.
[206] *Chamberlain v Boodle & King* [1982] 1 WLR 1443 at 1445.
[207] *Bake v French (No 2)* [1907] 2 Ch 215; *In re Thompson ex p Bayliss* [1894] 1 QB 462 at 464; and *In re Jones* [1895] 2 Ch 719. A contrary decision (*Pontifex v Farnham* (1892) 41 WR 238) was confined to its own facts in *Bake v French*.
[208] See, by way of analogy, *Martin Boston & Co (a firm) v Levy* [1982] 1 WLR 1434, in which there is a discussion about the effect of a client having a reasonable expectation of the agreement being executed in a more formal form.

Notice

8.158 Neither SA 1974 nor the authorities stipulate that the client must be put on notice that if he makes the agreement, he will not be able to claim an assessment as of right. That said, in so far as contracts made before 6 October 2011 are concerned, it is difficult to see how a solicitor could have complied with para 2.30 of the Solicitors' Code of Conduct 2007[209] without telling the client that his right to an assessment would be negated if he were to agree to enter into a contentious business agreement. The SRA Code of Conduct 2011 is less specific, however, (see **8.60**) and it is likely that the court would not find that code helpful in deciding what was and was not required for the purposes of creating a fully enforceable contract of retainer.

8.159 While the label given to a retainer may be a factor to be taken into account when construing that document, the presence or absence of a label is not determinative of the issue of whether the retainer is a contentious business agreement. In particular, the fact that a retainer is not referred to as being a contentious business agreement does preclude it from being one. Mann J has explained that the test is whether the retainer meets the criteria for a contentious business agreement, not whether the counterparties referred to it in that way.[210] Although there is no authority on the point, the court would probably place weight on a provision which expressly provided that the agreement was not a contentious business agreement; and even if it did, it would be open to the client to argue that in the light of that provision, the agreement was unfair within the meaning of SA 1974, s 61(2)(b) in that it gave misleading information.

8.160 There is no reason why a conditional fee agreement should not also be a contentious business agreement. Indeed, there is obiter comment to suggest that in appropriate circumstances this would be the case.[211] Where this is so, the agreement must comply with the legislation governing conditional fee agreements.

8.161 Most conditional fee agreements expressly state that they are not contentious business agreements. It is not clear what effect, if any, a statement such as that would have. If the issue were to arise, the client could argue that if the agreement was a contentious business agreement that aspect of it should be set aside pursuant to SA 1974, s 61(2)(b). The client could also argue that the solicitor should be estopped from denying the client's right to a detailed assessment. In practice, it is unlikely that these issues would ever arise because, even if the agreement were a contentious business agreement, the client would still be able to challenge the time and the success fee in the usual way.

8.162 An agreement which provides for security of payment (rather than for the method or the amount of payment) will not be a contentious business agreement simply because it is in writing, etc.[212] Mustill J commented, obiter, but while dealing with non-contentious rather than contentious work:[213]

---

[209] This provides that 'if you intend to seek payment of any or all of your costs from your client, you must advise your client of their right to an assessment of those costs.'

[210] *Wilson v The Spectre Partnership* [2007] EWHC 133 (Ch).

[211] *Hollins v Russell* [2003] 1 WLR 2487 at [93].

[212] *In re Jackson* [1915] 1 KB 371 (for present purposes that case did not distinguish between contentious and non-contentious work).

[213] *Walton v Egan* [1982] 3 WLR 352 at 357.

'[The statutory provisions] seem to be concerned with the ascertainment of the amount of the remuneration, rather than the way in which it is to be paid – so that an agreement as to the source of the funds which are to be used for paying the bill lies outside the scope of [those provisions].'

8.163 The provisions relating to contentious business agreements do not impose a requirement that agreements for security of payment be made in writing[214] (although, of course, other legislation may impose such an obligation, depending on the nature of the security which is involved).

8.164 In summary, a contentious business agreement must be in writing, it must state the amount or method for calculating the solicitor's fees, and it must be sufficiently specific and certain to inform the client of the proposed charges.

The effect of contentious business agreements

8.165 Broadly speaking, the effect of a contentious business agreement is that (unless the court finds that it is unfair or unreasonable) the client will lose the right to a detailed assessment of whichever fees have been agreed.[215] Moreover, the solicitor may commence proceedings for his fees without having to wait for the expiry of one month after the delivery of his bill.[216]

8.166 Not all contentious business agreements are intended to preclude assessment; this is because some agreements fix only certain aspects of the costs. Thus, whilst a contentious business agreement may contain provisions fixing all of the solicitor's fees (such as a fixed fee), it may also fix a only part of those fees (such as where it provides for payment by reference to an agreed hourly rate). Where an hourly rate has been set, the court may ascertain the number of hours worked by the solicitor,[217] and to that extent there may be an assessment. The court may carry out that exercise without making a finding that the agreement was unfair or unreasonable; if, however, the agreement was found to be unfair or unreasonable, then the court could set the rate aside or reduce it.[218]

Statutory provisions

8.167 A number of the relevant provisions are set out in SA 1974, s 60 (as amended), which reads:

'(1)   Subject to the provisions of this section and to sections 61 to 63, the costs of a solicitor in any case where a contentious business agreement has been made shall not be subject to assessment or (except in the case of an agreement which provides for the solicitor to be remunerated by reference to an hourly rate) to the provisions of section 69.

(2)   Subject to subsection (3), a contentious business agreement shall not affect the amount of, or any rights or remedies for the recovery of, any costs payable by the client to, or to the client by, any person other than the solicitor, and that person may, unless he has otherwise agreed, require any such costs to be assessed according to the rules for their assessment for the time being in force.

---

[214]   *In re an undertaking by Wingfields, Halse and Trustram, Jonesco v Evening Standard Company* [1932] 2 KB 340.
[215]   SA 1974, s 60(1).
[216]   See SA 1974, s 60(1), which sets aside s 69(1).
[217]   See SA 1974, s 61(4A) and (4B).
[218]   See SA 1974, s 61(2) and (4).

(3)   A client shall not be entitled to recover from any other person under an order for the payment of any costs to which a contentious business agreement relates more than the amount payable by him to his solicitor in respect of those costs under the agreement.

(4)   A contentious business agreement shall be deemed to exclude any claim by the solicitor in respect of the business to which it relates other than—

    (a)   a claim for the agreed costs; or
    (b)   a claim for such costs as are expressly excepted from the agreement.

(5)   A provision in a contentious business agreement that the solicitor shall not be liable for his negligence, or that of any employee of his, shall be void if the client is a natural person who, in entering that agreement, is acting for purposes which are outside his trade, business or profession.

(6)   A provision in a contentious business agreement that the solicitor shall be relieved from any responsibility to which he would otherwise be subject as a solicitor shall be void.'

8.168   The effect of these provisions may be summarised in the following way:

- *No assessment:* Subsection (1) precludes an assessment of fees which are the subject of a contentious business agreement (although this will not be the case if the court finds that the agreement should be set aside as being unfair or unreasonable: see below). Where the contentious business agreement provides for remuneration by reference to an hourly rate, the time claimed (but not the rate) may be assessed (see **8.166**).
- *Third parties:* Subsection (2) provides that a contentious business agreement does not affect the costs payable by or to a third party, and that he (the third party) may require the costs to be assessed. Where a third party is paying the solicitor's fees, the indemnity principle would usually apply, and in view of this the solicitor would not be able to seek more from the third party than he could from his own client; the effect of this is that for all practical purposes the third party can elect whether to have the costs assessed, or whether to pay the amount stipulated in the agreement.
- *Indemnity principle preserved:* Subsection (3) creates a statutory version of the indemnity principle. Hansard records that it was included in anticipation of the possibility of the indemnity principle being abolished.[219]
- *Ambit:* Subsection (4) limits the effect of a contentious business agreement to that which has been agreed.
- *Limitation on liability:* Subsection (5) restricts the extent to which a solicitor can limit his liability for negligence. Subsection (6) and the last twelve or so words of subsection (5) have been inserted by the Legal Services Act 2007 in order to regulate the growing trend to insert clauses which limit a liability in negligence.[220] These issues go beyond the remit of this book and are not discussed further.

Comparison between contentious business agreements and other retainers

8.169   In order to understand the effect of the statutory provisions mentioned above it is necessary to know how the law treats agreements which fix (or which were intended to fix) the quantum of a solicitor's fees but which are not regarded as being contentious business agreements. Oral agreements fall within this category (see **8.222**) and as such

---

[219]   *Hansard*, HL Deb, col GC64 (2 July 1972).
[220]   See 'Negligence claims: the ins and outs of limiting your liability' PILJ (2007) 58, September, pp 21–24.

are a fair comparator. By comparing the effect of the statutory provisions with that of the common law, it is possible to determine what difference the statutory provisions make.

8.170 As was set out above (**8.143**), Fletcher Moulton LJ has explained that the statutory provisions relating to contentious business agreements were intended to be enabling rather than disabling. In the case before him, Fletcher Moulton LJ went on to find that the oral agreement in question was enforceable by the client notwithstanding its unwritten form.[221] Similar conclusions have been reached in other cases in which the agreement in question has been found to fall short of being a contentious business agreement (see the footnotes to **8.118**).This is a reflection of the principle that the common law generally allows enforcement against the solicitor (**8.118** and **8.222**).

8.171 Where the solicitor intends to rely on an oral agreement as against the client, however, the common law will apply in that it will, in general, be enforceable only if favourable from the client's persepective.[222] In line with the principles set out in **8.223**, oral agreements cannot be relied upon against the client so as to act unfavourably from the client's point of view.[223] Thus, when compared with the position under the common law, the effect of compliance with the statutory provisions concerning contentious business agreements is to put the status of the agreement beyond doubt (subject, of course, to it not being unfair or unreasonable (**8.166**)), whereas without compliance, there is considerable potential for doubt as the uncertainties of the common law will prevail (see **8.143**)

Payment by salary and the indemnity principle

8.172 Provided that there is no infringement of the relevant rules of professional conduct, a solicitor may enter into an agreement to be paid a fixed salary as an employee. This is so even where the monies recovered beyond his fixed salary are to be paid to his employer.[224] By analogy with the authorities decided under the common law, it is likely that this principle has survived SA 1974, s 60(3); this would be on the basis that the costs are assessed as if an independent solicitor had carried out the work.[225]

Enforcement and examination of contentious business agreements

8.173 'Enforcement' in this context is used in the sense of the court adjudicating upon, rather than enforcing a judgment or order. The parallel jurisdiction is also examined, whereby the court can set an agreement aside if it is found to be unfair or unreasonable.

8.174 SA 1974, s 61 provides as follows:

'(1) No action shall be brought on any contentious business agreement, but on the application of any person who—

(a) is a party to the agreement or the representative of such a party; or

---

[221] The agreement that was found to be enforceable was a conditional fee agreement!

[222] *In re Fernandes* (1878) WN 57; and *In re Russell, Son v Scott* (1885) 30 Ch D 114. The second of these two

[223] *Chamberlain v Boodle & King* (1980) 124 SJ 186, subsequently upheld on appeal at [1982] 1 WLR 1443; *Martin Boston & Co (a firm) v Levy* [1982] 1 WLR 1434 (arguable defence to a claim by solicitors for fees for contentious work under oral agreement).

[224] *Galloway v Corporation of London* (1867) LR 4 EQ 90.

[225] For a discussion of this point in the context of the common law indemnity principle, see *In re Eastwood, deceased; Lloyds Bank Ltd v Eastwood* [1975] Ch 112.

(b)   is or is alleged to be liable to pay, or is or claims to be entitled to be paid, the costs due or alleged to be due in respect of the business to which the agreement relates,

the court may enforce or set aside the agreement and determine every question as to its validity or effect.

(2)   On any application under subsection (1), the court—

(a)   if it is of the opinion that the agreement is in all respects fair and reasonable, may enforce it;

(b)   if it is of the opinion that the agreement is in any respect unfair or unreasonable, may set it aside and order the costs covered by it to be assessed as if it had never been made;

(c)   in any case, may make such order as to the costs of the application as it thinks fit.

(3)   If the business covered by a contentious business agreement (not being an agreement to which section 62 applies) is business done, or to be done, in any action, a client who is a party to the agreement may make application to a costs officer of the court for the agreement to be examined.

(4)   A costs officer before whom an agreement is laid under subsection (3) shall examine it and may either allow it, or, if he is of the opinion that the agreement is unfair or unreasonable, require the opinion of the court to be taken on it, and the court may allow the agreement or reduce the amount payable under it, or set it aside and order the costs covered by it to be assessed as if it had never been made.

(4A)   Subsection (4B) applies where a contentious business agreement provides for the remuneration of the solicitor to be by reference to an hourly rate.

(4B)   If on the assessment of any costs the agreement is relied on by the solicitor and the client objects to the amount of the costs (but is not alleging that the agreement is unfair or unreasonable), the costs officer may enquire into—

(a)   the number of hours worked by the solicitor; and

(b)   whether the number of hours worked by him was excessive.

(5)   Where the amount agreed under any contentious business agreement is paid by or on behalf of the client or by any person entitled to do so, the person making the payment may at any time within twelve months from the date of payment, or within such further time as appears to the court to be reasonable, apply to the court, and, if it appears to the court that the special circumstances of the case require it to be re-opened, the court may, on such terms as may be just, re-open it and order the costs covered by the agreement to be assessed and the whole or any part of the amount received by the solicitor to be repaid by him.

(6)   In this section and in sections 62 and 63 "the court" means—

(a)   in relation to an agreement under which any business has been done in any court having jurisdiction to enforce and set aside agreements, any such court in which any of that business has been done;

(b)   in relation to an agreement under which no business has been done in any such court, and under which more than Ł50 is payable, the High Court;

(c)   in relation to an agreement under which no business has been done in any such court and under which not more than Ł50 is payable, any county court which would, but for the provisions of subsection (1) prohibiting the bringing of an action on the agreement, have had jurisdiction in any action on it;

and for the avoidance of doubt it is hereby declared that in paragraph (a) "court having jurisdiction to enforce and set aside agreements" includes a county court.'

Thus, there are three separate functions contained within the section: there is the jurisdiction to enforce (which is not contained in s 61(1) and (2)); there is the jurisdiction to examine (which is contained in s 61(3), (4), (4A) and (4B)); and there is the power to re-open an agreement as per s 61(5). The last of these topics (along with some other topics arising out of s 61) is considered at **8.197**.

8.175 Historically, the jurisdictions to enforce and to examine were entirely separate:[226] an application under one jurisdiction would not have precluded an application under the other.[227] This is still theoretically true, but as in most circumstances the issues would be almost identical under both jurisdictions, it is doubtful whether a court applying the overriding objective would suffer the same arguments to be put more than once.

8.176 SA 1974, s 61(1) precludes an action being brought on a contentious business agreement,[228] but provides an alternative mechanism by which an agreement may be enforced upon application. It is within the court's discretion whether to enforce it, that discretion turning on whether the agreement is fair and reasonable. If it is unfair or unreasonable, the court may set it aside and order the costs covered by it to be assessed as if it had never been made.[229] There is a similar jurisdiction which may be exercised upon examination of the agreement, under which, if the court finds that the agreement is unfair or unreasonable, it is given the power not only to set aside the agreement, but also to reduce the amount payable under it.[230]

8.177 There is some ambiguity as to how the jurisdiction to enforce operates: this is discussed at **8.194–8.195**. In particular, it is not wholly clear when the court's permission is required.

8.178 From the client's point of view, the effect of the two jurisdictions is that if a client is not content with his solicitor's costs, he is able to ask the court to determine whether the agreement is a fair and reasonable one.[231] If it is, then the court will allow the agreement (which, in effect, means that the court will permit it to be enforced without further enquiry), but if it is not, then the court will set aside the agreement, in which case the costs will be assessed in the usual way, or the court may reduce the amount payable under it.[232]

8.179 The setting aside of an agreement will not have the effect of automatically negating the solicitor's ability to recover costs. This is because there will usually be an underlying enforceable retainer which will allow the solicitor to recover his costs (subject to the court assessing those costs as being reasonable). Where there is doubt about this (such as where the contentious business agreement is also a conditional fee agreement, in which case it might be said that by setting that agreement aside, there could be no implied agreement to step into its place), it would be open to the court to make an order under SA 1974, s 61(4) to reduce the amount payable under the agreement.

---

[226] In Attorneys and Solicitors Act 1870 (33 & 34 Vict c 28) these powers were contained in separate sections of the Act.

[227] *In re Stuart ex p Cathcart* [1893] 2 QB 202 at 204; see also *In re Simmons & Politzer* [1954] 2 QB 296, in which is was held that a failure to comply with certain statutory requirements concerning examination by the court could be a reason to set aside upon reopening the matter (those statutory requirements no longer exist, and to that extent *Simmons & Politzer* is no longer good law).

[228] A solicitor is, however, able to bring an action for failure on the part of the client to instruct the solicitor under the terms of the agreement: *Rees v Williams* (1875) LR 10 Exch 200.

[229] SA 1974, s 61(2)(b).

[230] SA 1974, s 61(4).

[231] SA 1974, s 61(3); but also see s 61(1), which implies a similar jurisdiction.

[232] SA 1974, s 61(4); but also see s 61(2), which implies a similar jurisdiction.

8.180 Where the agreement provides for payment by way of an hourly rate, the court may assess the number of hours worked, and may do so without having to make a finding that the agreement is unfair or unreasonable.[233]

8.181 What is 'fair and reasonable' will depend on the facts of each case. The test is whether the agreement is fair and reasonable, so is in two parts: what is fair and what is reasonable, as noted by Esher MR:[234]

> 'With regard to the fairness of such an agreement, it appears to me that this refers to the mode of obtaining the agreement, and that if a solicitor makes an agreement with a client who fully understands and appreciates that agreement that satisfies the requirement as to fairness. But the agreement must also be reasonable, and in determining whether it is so the matters covered by the expression "fair" cannot be re-introduced.'

8.182 Whilst there is no authority on the point, it is likely that in deciding whether the agreement is 'fair' the court would take into account the prevailing standards that the client was entitled to expect the solicitor to meet, so the quality and content of the advice given pursuant to the prevailing codes of conduct may be relevant.

8.183 In considering what is reasonable, the court should not carry out a de facto detailed assessment,[235] although it is difficult to see how the court could decide whether the agreement is reasonable without coming to some approximate view of what would have been allowed had the agreement not existed.

8.184 In summary, if the court finds that a contentious business agreement is unfair or unreasonable it has the power to set aside the agreement or to reduce the amounts payable under it. Otherwise, the court may allow the agreement to be enforced.

Contentious business agreements where the client is acting in a representative capacity

8.185 It used to be the case that all contentious business agreements needed to be examined by the court before payment could be received.[236] That rule no longer applies, but the court does still have a role to play in certain circumstances in which the client is acting in a representative capacity.

8.186 SA 1974, s 62 provides as follows:

> **'62   Contentious business agreements by certain representatives**
>
> (1)   Where the client who makes a contentious business agreement makes it as a representative of a person whose property will be chargeable with the whole or part of the amount payable under the agreement, the agreement shall be laid before a costs officer of the court before payment.
>
> (2)   A costs officer before whom an agreement is laid under subsection (1) shall examine it and may either allow it, or, if he is of the opinion that it is unfair or unreasonable, require

---

[233]   SA 1974, s 61(4A) and (4B).
[234]   *In re Stuart ex p Cathcart* [1893] 2 QB 202 at 205.
[235]   *Re Templeton and Cox* (1909) 101 LT 144, CA.
[236]   See Solicitors Act, 1932, s 60 (which was the old requirement) and *In re Simmons & Politzer* [1954] 2 QB 296.

the opinion of the court to be taken on it, and the court may allow the agreement or reduce the amount payable under it, or set it aside and order the costs covered by it to be assessed as if it had never been made.

(3)   A client who makes a contentious business agreement as mentioned in subsection (1) and pays the whole or any part of the amount payable under the agreement without it being allowed by the officer or by the court shall be liable at any time to account to the person whose property is charged with the whole or any part of the amount so paid for the sum so charged, and the solicitor who accepts the payment may be ordered by the court to refund the amount received by him.

(4)   A client makes a contentious business agreement as the representative of another person if he makes it—

    (a)   as his guardian,
    (b)   as a trustee for him under a deed or will,
    (c)   as a deputy for him appointed by the Court of Protection with powers in relation to his property and affairs, or
    (d)   as another person authorised under that Act to act on his behalf.'

Thus, where a contentious business agreement is made by a client who is acting as a representative of another person, the court's approval must be sought before any payment is made under that agreement. If the court's approval is not sought, then the solicitor can be required to account for any monies paid, as can the representative person. These provisions protect the child or person who lacks capacity from abuse; they are comparable to the provisions requiring the compromise of a solicitor and client bill to be approved by the court.

8.187   SA 1974, s 62(4)(c) and (d) refer to persons who lack capacity. The reference to 'that Act' in s 62(4)(d) is not wholly clear; that subsection was inserted by the Mental Capacity Act 2005,[237] and is (possibly) a reference to that Act. If this is right, then a client will be acting in a representative capacity if he makes the agreement for another person authorised under the Mental Capacity Act 2005 to act on his behalf.

8.188   In summary, persons acting in a representative capacity are required to obtain the court's approval of the contentious business agreement before making any payments under it; if they fail to do this, they may be ordered to account to the person whom they represent for any monies paid.

Contentious business agreements where there is only partial performance

8.189   Where, by reason of death, loss of capacity or disinstruction, a solicitor is prevented from performing his obligations under a contentious business agreement, the court may make an allowance for the work done. This is as a consequence of SA 1974, s 63, which makes the following provision:

'**63   Effect on contentious business agreement of death, incapability or change of solicitor**

(1)   If, after some business has been done under a contentious business agreement but before the solicitor has wholly performed it—

    (a)   the solicitor dies, or becomes incapable of acting; or
    (b)   the client changes his solicitor (as, notwithstanding the agreement, he shall be entitled to do),

---

[237]   MCA 2005, s 67(1) and Sch 6, para 22(1) and (3).

any party to, or the representative of any party to, the agreement may apply to the court, and the court shall have the same jurisdiction as to enforcing the agreement so far as it has been performed, or setting it aside, as the court would have had if the solicitor had not died or become incapable of acting, or the client had not changed his solicitor.

(2) The court, notwithstanding that it is of the opinion that the agreement is in all respects fair and reasonable, may order the amount due in respect of business under the agreement to be ascertained by assessment, and in that case—

   (a)   the costs officer, in ascertaining that amount, shall have regard so far as may be to the terms of the agreement; and

   (b)   payment of the amount found by him to be due may be enforced in the same manner as if the agreement had been completely performed.

(3) If in such a case as is mentioned in subsection (1)(b) an order is made for the assessment of the amount due to the solicitor in respect of the business done under the agreement, the court shall direct the costs officer to have regard to the circumstances under which the change of solicitor has taken place, and the costs officer, unless he is of the opinion that there has been no default, negligence, improper delay or other conduct on the part of the solicitor, or any of his employees, affording the client reasonable ground for changing his solicitor, shall not allow to the solicitor the full amount of the remuneration agreed to be paid to him.'

8.190 One effect of these provisions is to limit the potentially harsh effect of a contentious business agreement being an entire contract. In particular, if a solicitor is unable to complete his obligations under the agreement because he dies, loses capacity, or because his client dismisses him without reasonable grounds, then the court will award a sum to be assessed (or, if circumstances permit, payment in full).

8.191 If, on the other hand, the client had reasonable grounds for terminating the retainer, the court will be able to assess the costs, and in doing so will be able to take the solicitor's default, negligence, improper delay or other conduct (if any) into account.

8.192 SA 1974, s 63(3) permits the court to take account of default or negligence, improper delay or other conduct on the part of the solicitor, or any of his employees, affording the client reasonable grounds for changing his solicitor. It is clear that the default of negligence can be taken into account in such a way as to reduce the solicitor's fees to a level which is lower than they would have been had the agreement been fully performed. What is less clear is whether the court is able to take that conduct into account in such a way as to allow a figure which is lower than the amount which is a reasonable amount: it is arguable that the court does have this power, but there is no authority on that point.

8.193 In summary, SA 1974, s 63 permits the court to allow a solicitor to be paid an appropriate sum in the event of the solicitor being unable fully to perform his obligations under a contentious business agreement by reason of death, disability or dismissal.

Procedural issues

Enforcement of a contentious business agreement

8.194 There is some ambiguity as to how the jurisdiction to enforce under SA 1974, s 61(1) operates. There are two schools of thought: the first is that the court's permission must be sought before any application is made to enforce, and the second is that the court's permission to enforce the agreement is required only if and when the agreement becomes contentious. In quoting a passage from *Cook on Costs*, Mann J commented:[238]

> '[One of the parties] drew my attention to a passage in Cook on Costs [2006] at para 6.9 in which the author suggests that an action could be commenced without what he calls the "permission" of the court to enforce the agreement, and that the statutory bar would only be called into play if the point was taken. He says "... it is only if the solicitor wishes to rely on the contentious business agreement that he needs permission to proceed". If the point were not taken then the solicitor would be able to benefit from a default or summary judgment (assuming, of course, that the conditions necessary for those forms of judgment existed) ... I confess I have difficulty understanding the passage in Cook. If there is a [contentious business agreement], and the solicitor sues for fees due under it, it seems to me that he would be enforcing the [contentious business agreement]. I do not understand how he can claim the fees due under it without enforcing it.'

On the facts of the case before him it was not necessary for Mann J to clarify the correct procedure, but it seems as if he subscribed to the first school of thought. In any event, the phrase 'no action shall be brought' in s 61(1) does not prevent a claim being brought for breach of a contentious business agreement.[239]

8.195 Any claim should be made by the CPR, Part 8 procedure (or, in existing proceedings, by application).[240] Where the claim is issued in the High Court in London, it *must* be issued in the SCCO,[241] unless it is a claim under SA 1974, s 63, in which case it *may* be issued in the SCCO.[242]

Challenging a contentious business agreement

8.196 The procedural points made above apply when the claim is to challenge the agreement. There are two sets of rules that govern the relevant procedure:

- **SA 1974 s 61(6)**: Where the agreement relates to business done in in a county court or where the amount payable under the agreement is less that £50, the appropriate court in which to bring the claim is the county court; in all other circumstances the appropriate court is the High Court;[243] and
- **CPR, r 67.3**: Where the claim relates to contentious business done in a county court, and is within the financial limit of the county court's jurisdiction specified in SA 1974, s 69(3) (currently £5,000), the claim may be made in *that* county court.[244] In every other case, it *must* be made in the High Court.[245]

There is a tension between these two provisions, but it is unlikely to give rise to problems in practice. If, however, a claim is issued in the county court when s 61(6) provides that it ought to have been brought in the High Court, the court will lack the vires to deal with the issue.[246]

---

[238] *Wilson v The Spectre Partnership* [2007] EWHC 133 (Ch) at [13].
[239] *Rees v Williams* (1875) LR 10 Ex 200.
[240] CPR, r 67.3(2).
[241] See PD 67, paras 2.1 and 1(2)–(5).
[242] See PD 67, paras 2.1 and 1(6).
[243] See SA 1974, s 61(6).
[244] CPR, r 67.3(1)(a).
[245] CPR, r 67.3(1)(b).
[246] See also *R (on the application of Srinivasans Solicitors) v Croydon County Court* [2011] EWHC 3615 (Admin).

Re-opening a contentious business agreement

8.197 If the liability under a contentious business agreement has been discharged, the person who made the payment may apply to the court for the matter to be re-opened and the costs assessed; the court may make such an order only if there are 'special circumstances' within the meaning of SA 1974, s 61(5). Unlike with bills in general, there is no absolute bar to an assessment after the expiry of 12 months following payment; in particular, the aforesaid section provides that the court may reopen the matter 'within such further time as appears to the court to be reasonable'. This gives rise to the somewhat anomalous situation that a client who has paid his solicitors costs for a period exceeding one year may be in a better position if he paid them under a formal contentious business agreement than he would have been in had there been no such agreement.

Seeking approval of a contentious business agreement

8.198 Where the client has been acting in a representative capacity and where he must seek the court's approval of the agreement, the procedure for laying the agreement before the court is the CPR, Part 8 procedure (or, in existing proceedings, by application).[247] Where the claim is issued in the High Court in London, it must be issued in the Senior Courts Costs Office.[248]

IMPLIED RETAINERS

8.199 This section addresses the issue of implication. Many of the principles discussed herein will also apply where the issue is whether an express retainer contains implied terms.[249] In the absence of an express retainer, the conduct of solicitor and client may imply the existence of an unwritten contract of retainer.

8.200 There are, in the present context, three modes of implication: implication arising out of the relationship between the counterparties (ie the solicitor and client), implication by law, and implication by custom or usage.

8.201 The first of these modes is often of pivotal relevance. A contract, including a contract for services such as a retainer, will be implied where it is a necessary inference from the words or conduct of the counterparties that it exists.[250] There is a rebuttable presumption that a client will be liable for the fees of the solicitor whom he engages.[251] Whilst it can be analysed in other ways, for practical purposes it is a presumption that there will be an implied retainer unless the contrary can be shown.

8.202 Lloyd J explained the presumption thus:[252]

---

[247] CPR, r 67.3(2) and PD 67, para 1(5).

[248] PD 67, para 2.1(1).

[249] The specific topic of whether a retainer contains an implied term that the solicitor may deliver an interim statute bill has already been addressed at **8.54–8.60**.

[250] See, for example, *Harrods Ltd v Harrods (Buenos Aires) Ltd* (1998) *The Times*, June 1, CA and *Re Chappell ex p Ford* (1885) 16 QBD 305, CA.

[251] See *Adams v London Improved Motor Builders Ltd* [1921] 1 KB 495 at 501; see also *R v Miller (Raymond)* [1983] 1 WLR 1056 at 1059–1062, which was cited with approval in *Bailey v IBC Vehicles Ltd* [1998] 3 All ER 570 at 574. See also *Hazlett v Sefton Metropolitan Borough Council* [2000] 4 All ER 887.

[252] *R v Miller [1983] 1 WLR 1057* at 1061; see also *Ghadami v Lyon Cole Insurance Group Limited* [2010] EWCA Civ 767 at [10] in which Lloyd LJ reaffirmed this principle.

'Once it was shown ... that [the receiving party] was indeed the client, then a presumption arose that he was to be personally liable for the costs. That presumption could, however, be rebutted if it were established that there was an express or implied agreement, binding on the solicitor, that [the client] would not have to pay those costs in any circumstances.'[253]

That presumption may be rebutted either upon evidence or by operation of the law (or both): see **11.24**.

8.203 The second mode of implication (namely, by law) may also have a role to play in the context of the law of costs. In particular, it is an implied term of a consumer contract for services that the person providing services will be paid reasonable remuneration for those services. Statute provides as follows:[254]

'15 Implied term about consideration

(1) Where, under a contract for the supply of a service, the consideration for the service is not determined by the contract, left to be determined in a manner agreed by the contract or determined by the course of dealing between the parties, there is an implied term that the party contracting with the supplier will pay a reasonable charge.

(2) What is a reasonable charge is a question of fact.'

This statutory provision implies only a term rather than an entire contract. It would, however, rarely be the case that the very existence of a retainer was in dispute, especially in the context of the presumption mentioned above (**8.202**).

8.204 The third mode of implication (by custom or usage) will most often be encountered in cases involving commercial clients, but it may also arise in other circumstances, such as where a private client habitually instructs his family's solicitor.[255] Where the counterparties are acting in the court of their business (ie where both the solicitor and the client are businesses and are acting in that capacity) evidence of custom and usage is admissible for the purposes of implying a term into a contract.[256]

8.205 A solicitor's claim for costs could not usually be founded upon estoppel by convention;[257] something more would usually be required than merely asserting that the client is estopped from denying the existence of a retainer by reason of his long-standing relationship with the solicitors. However, for the reasons set out above, the solicitor would be able to point to something more.

8.206 The analysis which follows focuses on the contractual relationship between solicitor and client, but the principles would also apply to a dispute between opposing parties. An opposing party would have the additional hurdle of proving a 'genuine issue': see **11.22–11.32**. In addition, an opposing party would face the challenge of

---

[253] The need to show 'an agreement ... not to have to pay those costs in any circumstances' is not a test of universal applicability; it only applies in cases in which the facts imply the existence of a retainer. See the discussion about *Byrne v Kunkel & Kunkel* [1999] 1 CL 349 elsewhere in this work.

[254] See s 15 of the Supply of Goods and Services Act 1982.

[255] By way of example, there is one term that would be implied by custom in almost every implied retainer, regardless of whether the client was a business or a private individual: that is the basis of charging by 6-minute units; that term would be implied on the basis that the court does not commonly use any other method for quantifying time.

[256] In a context other than costs, see *Cunliffe-Owen v Teather and Greenwood* [1967] 1 WLR 1421, which deals with the custom in the Stock Exchange.

[257] In a setting other than costs, see *Baird Textiles Holdings Ltd v Marks & Spencer plc* [2001] EWCA Civ 274; as to the requirement of necessity, see *The Aramis* [1989] 1 Lloyd's Rep 213.

having to garner evidence: even if he were to be successful in demonstrating a genuine issue, the paying party's task can often be burdensome by reason of the fact that the receiving party may claim privilege in respect of any material upon which he does not wish to rely.

8.207 A dispute between solicitor and client about the existence or terms of an enforceable retainer may turn on disputed facts; the topic of how the court deals with disputed facts of that nature is discussed at **8.106–8.107**: in essence, the client will be given the benefit of the fact that the solicitor failed to keep a written record of the retainer.

8.208 For the reasons set out in the extract from Lloyd J's judgment, the client would have to clear a high hurdle to rebut the presumption; this is because (subject to what is said below about the operation of the law) he must prove that there was an express or an implied term, binding on the solicitor, that he would not have to pay the solicitor's fees in any circumstances. The advantages that the presumption affords the solicitor are not, however, necessarily as great as they may at first appear. This is for the following reasons:

(1)   In view of the fact that solicitors are professionally obliged to confirm certain costs information in writing,[258] the fact that there is no written retainer is capable of being afforded significant weight. One could argue that this is a natural consequence of the court's desire to protect the client as a consumer. That said, there are instances of the court affording a breach of the Solicitors' prevailing codes of conduct very little weight.[259] Moreover, Slade J has said that the absence of a client care letter does not affect the liability of the client if he has acquiesced the instruction of the solicitors on his behalf by a third party.[260]

(2)   In appropriate cases it may also be relevant that the CPR and CPD require a solicitor to give certain information about the level of costs.[261]

(3)   The need to show 'an agreement ... not to have to pay those costs in any circumstances' is not a test of universal applicability; it only applies in cases in which the facts imply the existence of an enforceable contractual retainer.

8.209 The last of these points is illustrated by a decision of HHJ Cowell[262] (or, more accurately, by the way in which that case was commented upon by Burton J in a similar case).[263] In HHJ Cowell's case, the action was pursued to trial with all parties acting on the erroneous assumption that the receiving party was legally aided. In fact, there was no legal aid certificate and, as a result, the paying party argued that there was no retainer. HHJ Cowell came to the following conclusion:

> '[A] party is presumed to be liable for his costs until proved otherwise and [none of the parties] had discharged the burden upon them to prove the existence of an express or implied agreement between [the receiving party] and his former solicitors that he would never have to

---

[258]   See para 2.03(5) of the Solicitors' Code of Conduct 2007. In respect of work done prior to 1 July 2007, see paras 3(c) and 4(j) of the Solicitors' Costs Information and Client Care Code 1999.

[259]   *Ghadami v Lyon Cole Insurance Group Limited* [2010] EWCA Civ 767, both at [27] (per Lloyd) and also in general; the client had not received the client care documentation that he was entitled to, but the court found that that did not preclude liability and that the lack of a stated hourly rate did not prevent the court from allowing a reasonable rate.

[260]   *Culkin v Wirral Independent Appeals Panel* [2011] EWHC 1526 (QB) at [18].

[261]   See CPD, art 6.4(2).

[262]   *Byrne v Kunkel & Kunkel* [1999] 1 CL 349.

[263]   *Bridgewater v Griffiths* [2000] 1 WLR 524 at 533.

pay their costs in any circumstances ... In the absence of such an agreement, the mere lack of legal aid did not mean there was a breach of the indemnity principle ...'

Burton J, obiter, strongly disagreed with that analysis, essentially on the basis that the facts did not support the notion that the counterparties had intended to enter into a private retainer:[264]

> 'I cannot accept the judge's conclusion ... There surely cannot be a question, in a legal aid, or presumed legal aid, situation, that there has to be proved the existence of an express or implied agreement that the legally aided plaintiff would never have himself to pay his solicitor's costs (save any shortfall as referred to above): the burden must surely be exactly the reverse, namely, that there would have to be established an express or implied agreement, or at any rate a quasi-contractual obligation upon such a client, that he would be personally liable to pay his solicitor in some unforeseen situation ...'

8.210 Thus, the approach of the court is take into account all of the facts, including the nature of the retainer (if any) that was intended. If that retainer was something other than a private retainer, then it may not be open to the court to find that an implied private retainer takes its place. This, perhaps, is akin to the principle that terms which were expressly agreed may not be contradicted by implied terms.[265]

8.211 In any event, some retainers are not capable of being enforceable when they exist in an implied form; this is because the law stipulates that they must be in writing and that if they are not they are unenforceable. The most prominent example is a conditional fee agreement relating to contentious business, which must be in writing[266] and cannot be enforceable when it exists in unwritten form.[267] It could be argued that other examples exist.[268]

8.212 Some types of retainer are required to be in writing (such as contentious and non-contentious business agreements)[269] but will not be unenforceable solely by reason of being in unwritten form. It is a moot point whether a failed business agreement would default to a private retainer or to a non-complaint business agreement, but that distinction would be of academic interest only because the solicitor would still be entitled to be paid.

8.213 An implied retainer may fail because it has not made provision for rights that statute stipulates should have been afforded to the client. An example is where the retainer is made at the client's home and where no Notice of Cancellation was given in accordance with the Cancellation of Contracts made in a Consumer's Home or Place of Work etc Regulations 2008. Those topics are dealt with at **8.324** *et seq.*

8.214 An unwelcome feature of implied retainers is that they rarely contain any specific terms as to the solicitor's remuneration. In particular, it will not usually be possible to say that the counterparties had decided upon a specific hourly rate (although this may

---

[264] *Bridgewater v Griffiths* [2000] 1 WLR 524 at 533.
[265] Expressum facit cessare tacitum: 'what is expressed makes what is implied silent'; in a context other than costs, see *Lynch v Thorne* [1956] 1 WLR 303, CA.
[266] See the Courts and Legal Services Act 1990 (as amended), s 58(3)(a).
[267] See Courts and Legal Services Act 1990 (as amended), s 58(1).
[268] See the section on 'retainers made not at the solicitors' offices'; it can be seen that where some of those regulations apply, written notice must be given; it could be argued that this is an implied requirement that the retainer (or at least part of it) must be in writing.
[269] SA 1974, ss 57(3) and 59(2).

be possible if the client, without demur, discharged invoices which stated the rate). Where it is not possible to find that a specific rate was agreed, it is open to the court to find an implied term that the rate would be a reasonable rate.[270]

8.215 Applying an implied term as to the hourly rate will not always be a straightforward task; there may, for example, be a dispute about whether there is provision that the rates may be uplifted to take account of the complexity of the work.[271] On the whole, the court will be reluctant to allow a solicitor something such as an uplift that has not been expressly agreed.[272]

8.216 In summary, there is a rebuttable presumption that a client will be liable for the fees of the solicitor whom he engages. That presumption may be rebutted on evidence or by operation of the law. The court will take into account the nature of the retainer that the counterparties intended to be created, and where that intended retainer was a conditional fee agreement, the retainer will be unenforceable by reason of it being an unwritten conditional fee agreement.

ORAL RETAINERS

8.217 It is trite costs law that retainers do not need to be in writing.[273] Whilst oral retainers are, by definition, express contracts, specific terms will often need to be implied, and to that extent the discussion above on implied retainers will be relevant.

8.218 Whilst the meaning of the terms of an oral retainer is a matter of law, the wording of the terms themselves is a matter for the costs judge to decide sitting as the tribunal of fact. These two issues are considered in turn.

Issues of fact

8.219 Where the client disputes the terms of an oral retainer, the court will usually give weight to the fact that there is no written retainer (see **8.103–8.109**). In general terms, where the solicitor has failed to keep a written record of the retainer, there will be an evidential presumption in the client's favour. Older cases that suggest that this presumption was a rule of law rather than an evidential presumption[274] are now probably no longer good law.

8.220 A retainer may be part oral and part written; where this is the case, the evidential status of oral evidence may need to be considered. The rule against parol evidence would prevent the counterparties from relying on evidence as to their subjective intention. Where the written retainer was intended to be the whole of the contract, evidence may not be adduced to add to, vary or contradict it.[275]

---

[270] See *Ghadami v Lyon Cole Insurance Group Limited* [2010] EWCA Civ 767 at [27]; also see the statutory provisions mentioned at **8.203**.

[271] See, for example, *Adams v Mac Innes* [2001] EWHC 9014 (Costs).

[272] Whilst dealing with implied terms rather than implied retainers, see *Bilkus v Stockler Brunton (a firm)* [2010] EWCA Civ 101 at [54], per Stanley Burnton LJ.

[273] See, for example, *Owen v Ord* (1828) 3 C & P 349; *Wiggins v Peppin* (1839) 2 Beav 403; and *Bird v Harris* [1881] WN 5, CA.

[274] See *Allen v Bone* (1841) 4 Beav 493, per Lord Langdale MR; *Crossley v Crowther* (1851) 9 Hare 384; and *Atkinson v Abbot* (1855) 3 Drew 251.

[275] That said, evidence that the counterparties had agreed to suspend or disregard the written document may be

Issues of law

8.221 There are three types of oral retainer which merit particular attention: agreements which were intended to be business agreements; conditional fee agreements; and agreements made away from the solicitor's place of business.

Business agreements

8.222 The solicitor and client may have entered into an oral agreement that certain aspects of the remuneration are to be fixed or to be determined in a particular way (such as an agreement to apply a discount, or an agreement that there will be a fixed fee). Such an agreement will be analogous to a contentious business agreement or non-contentious business agreement, as the case may be. Whether such an agreement would be regarded as being a 'failed' business agreement, or as being merely akin to a business agreement is a moot point[276] but, regardless of this, even where such an agreement is found to be unenforceable (see below), it will be only the agreement as to the amount (or method of determining the amount) which will be of no effect: the underlying retainer will remain extant and enforceable.

8.223 The precise effect of such agreements will depend on whether the work to which an agreement relates is contentious or non-contentious. There are some inconsistencies and ambiguities in the authorities, but the following is fair description of law:

• **Contentious business:** Where the agreement relates to contentious business it cannot be relied upon against the client (in the sense that it causes an adverse result from the client's point of view)[277] but, in appropriate circumstances, it can be relied upon against the solicitor.[278] Put otherwise, where the agreement is favourable to the client, it may be enforced, but where it is not favourable to the client, then it will not be enforced (see **8.118**). The reason for this is that the legislation governing contentious business agreements is regarded as being enabling legislation that does not supplant the common law (see **8.143** and **8.170**), and as such, if the agreement 'fails', then it will be judged according to the common law, and specifically, to that body of law that developed before legislation was made (in 1870) that made provision for business agreements.[279] It is said that this applies to agreements for costs already incurred,[280] but it is possible that that principle is no longer good law, and certainly, other common law jurisdictions have moved away from it.[281]

---

adduced, this being an issue which may arise in circumstances where the client says that there was an agreement that the solicitor's standard terms and conditions would not apply: in a non-costs setting see *Pym v Campbell* (1856) 6 E&B 370.

[276] It is probably the former: see *Barclays plc v Villers* [2000] 1 All ER (Comm) 357 at 367.

[277] *Chamberlain v Boodle & King* (1980) 124 SJ 186, subsequently upheld on appeal at [1982] 1 WLR 1443; *Martin Boston & Co (a firm) v Levy* [1982] 1 WLR 1434 (arguable defence to a claim by solicitors for fees for contentious work under oral agreement).

[278] See, for example, *Gundry v Sainsbury* [1910] 1 KB 99 (verbal agreement that client would pay no costs). As an early example, see *Jennings v Johnson* (1873) LR 8 CP 425 (agreement similar to a modern-day CFA Lite); see also *Re a Solicitor (No 2)* [1956] 1 QB 155, which, obiter, affirmed *Clare* and *Jennings* as being good law; see also *Electrical Trades Union v Tarlo* [1964] Ch 720 (oral retainer related to both contentious and non-contentious work; contentious part found to be enforceable); see also *In re a Solicitor* [1956] 1 QB 157 (whilst obiter, that case affirmed the view that oral agreements in relation to contentious work were enforceable as against the solicitor).

[279] That being the Attorneys and Solicitors Act 1870.

[280] *Re Russell, Son & Scott* (1885) 30 Ch D 114

[281] See, for example, *Bear v Waxman* [1912] VLR 292; Anderson and Rowland JJ in *D'Alessandro & D'Angelo v*

- **Non-contentious Business:** Where the agreement relates to non-contentious business it would usually be held to be unenforceable as against both parties, even where it would otherwise be to the client's advantage.[282] This is because, in contrast to the legislation governing contentious business agreements, the legislation governing non-contentious business agreements[283] is generally regarded as being disabling in the sense that agreements that do not comply cannot be enforced.[284]

The distinction between these two types of agreement was illustrated by a case in which the agreement related in part to contentious business and in part to non-contentious business; Wilberforce J found that the part of the agreement that related to contentious work was enforceable by the client but that the remainder was unenforceable.[285]

8.224 It is not wholly clear whether the distinction between these two types of agreement is still good law; this is because it appears to have been founded on (or, at least, justified by) statutory provisions which are no longer in force. In particular, Pearson J[286] explained the difference on the basis that the then provisions relating to contentious business[287] were more liberal than those relating to non-contentious business.[288] The presently available authorities relating to oral agreements should, therefore, be viewed with some caution as it is arguable that the proper interpretation of the modern provisions (namely, s 57 of the Solicitors Act 1974) is not the same as set out above.

8.225 Where the agreement is found to be a contentious or non-contentious business agreement, the court has the power to set it aside if that is the fair thing to do.[289]

Conditional fee agreements

8.226 Whilst there is no authority directly on the point, it would seem that any oral conditional fee agreement would be unenforceable by reason of it not being in writing.[290] This will apparently be so even if it is in respect of non-contentious business; indeed, whilst its function was merely to describe the law rather than create it, the guidance to the (now revoked) Solicitors' Code of Conduct 2007 offered the following narrative:[291]

> 'It is acceptable to enter into a contingency fee arrangement for non-contentious matters ... but you should note that to be enforceable the arrangement must be contained in a non-contentious business agreement.'

      Cooper (unreported, WASC, Full Ct, Kennedy, Rowland and Anderson JJ, Lib No 960334, 21 June 1996) both found no bar to cost agreements in Western Australia covering past services.

[282] In *In re a Solicitor* [1956] 1 QB 157, for example, Pearson J found that a client could not rely on an oral agreement that his solicitor would charge less than the ordinary rate of remuneration.

[283] This, originally, being the Solicitors' Remuneration Act 1881, s 8(1).

[284] *In re a Solicitor* [1956] 1 QB 157.

[285] *Electrical Trades Union v Tarlo* [1964] Ch 731.

[286] *In re a Solicitor* [1956] 1 QB 157.

[287] Then s 4 of the Attorneys and Solicitors Act 1870, now s 59 of SA 1974.

[288] Then s 57 of the Solicitors Act 1932, now s 57 of SA 1974.

[289] See SA 1974, ss 57(5) and 61(4); see also *Re Heritage ex p Docker* (1878) 3 QBD 726 and *Ingrams v Sykes* (1987) 137 NLJ 1135; see also *Barclays plc v Villers* [2000] 1 All ER (Comm) 357 at 367.

[290] See s 58(1) and (3)(a) of the Courts and Legal Services Act 1990 (as amended).

[291] Paragraph 45 of the guidance to rule 2.04 of the Solicitors' Code of Conduct 2007.

8.227 This state of affairs has come about as a result of a combination of the common law and the express statutory prohibition[292] created by s 58(1) of the Courts and Legal Services Act 1990 (as amended); that provision renders unenforceable any conditional fee agreement which does not comply with the requirements of that section, one of which is that the agreement must be in writing. There is an exception to this prohibition in that s 58(5) of that Act reads:

> '(5) If a conditional fee agreement is an agreement to which section 57 of the Solicitors Act 1974 (non-contentious business agreements between solicitor and client) applies, subsection (1) shall not make it unenforceable.'

In view of the fact that one of the requirements of SA 1974, s 57 is that the agreement should be in writing, the exception does not operate in such a way as to permit of such a thing as an enforceable oral conditional fee agreement.

8.228 Even where the agreement is one to which s 58(1) of the Courts and Legal Services Act 1990 (as amended) does not relate, an unwritten conditional fee agreement in non-contentious work would be unenforceable as a result of the operation of the common law (see above).

Agreements made away from the solicitor's place of business

8.229 An oral retainer made at a place other than the solicitor's place of business may be unenforceable if there has been a failure to give written Notice of Cancellation in accordance with the Cancellation of Contracts made in a Consumer's Home or Place of Work etc Regulations 2008. That topic is discussed at **8.324** *et seq.*

8.230 In summary, an oral conditional fee agreement will be unenforceable. An oral agreement made at a place other than the solicitor's place of business may be unenforceable if there has also been a failure to give written Notice of Cancellation. Most other oral retainers will not be unenforceable by reason of them not being in writing, but agreements setting the quantum of costs may be unenforceable, especially against the client.

SHAM RETAINERS

8.231 A sham retainer will exist where the counterparties have created a written instrument which is intended give either the court or the paying party the appearance of having created legal rights and obligations different from the real legal rights and obligations which they intended to create.[293]

8.232 In the past, sham retainers usually arose in the context of the client being unable or unwilling to pay his solicitor's fees in the event of the claim being lost; a solicitor would often agree to charge only if the case was won, but would not make that agreement openly because such agreements were unlawful: the term 'speccing agreement' was applied to them.[294] Given the fact that conditional fee agreements are now lawful, speccing agreements are largely of historical interest only.

---

[292] See **8.246** for a discussion of the term 'express statutory prohibition'.

[293] This definition is adapted from *Snook v London & West Riding Investments Ltd* [1967] 2 QB 786 at 802.

[294] That term also applied to some types of informal conditional fee agreements which are not sham agreements.

8.233 Sham agreements are not wholly extinct, however. Current-day examples may include where the written instrument records an hourly rate that the client is not prepared to pay and has agreed this with his solicitor. Another example would be where the counterparties have retrospectively entered into a conditional fee agreement after the costs order was made in an attempt to recover a success fee to which there was no entitlement.

8.234 Although the category that is sham agreements will embrace criminal behaviour (such as the fraud mentioned immediately above), sham agreements may arise in surprisingly innocent circumstances. If, for example, it forms the basis of the retainer, an assurance 'not to worry' about fees may suffice.[295]

8.235 Whether an agreement is a sham will depend on the facts. Arden LJ gave the following guidance (which has been paraphrased and adapted to apply to the law of costs):[296]

- In the case of a written retainer, the court is not restricted to examining the four corners of the written instrument; it may examine external evidence, which may include the counterparties' explanations and the way in which the retainer was used.
- The test of intention is a subjective test; the counterparties must have intended to create different rights and obligations from those set out in the written instrument, and in addition they must have intended to give a false impression of those rights and obligations to third parties.
- The fact that the terms of the retainer are uncommercial or artificial does not mean that the retainer is a sham.
- The fact that parties subsequently depart from the terms of the retainer does not necessarily mean that they never intended the retainer to be effective and binding.
- The intention must be a common intention shared by both solicitor and client.

8.236 A distinction should be made between an intention which forms the basis of the retainer and an intention which is merely the exercise of discretion within the parameters of the retainer. Tuckey J had the following to say (obiter) on that topic (in the context of a putative speccing agreement):[297]

> 'If ... it is made clear that the client is liable for costs irrespective of the outcome of proceedings, there can be no objection to the solicitors agreeing that such liability need not be discharged until the end of those proceedings, if any, is known. At that stage, provided that it has not formed the basis of the agreement with the client, it would be open to the solicitors, if the circumstances warranted it, to decide not to enforce their right to be paid, in the event that some or all of their costs were unrecovered from the other party to the proceedings.'

Both Kennedy LJ and Jowitt J have approved of those comments, but in doing so remarked that if a solicitor always (or nearly always) waived his fees in the event of the claim being lost, the court could draw the inference that that formed the basis of the agreement.[298]

---

[295] *British Waterways Board v Norman* (1993) 26 HLR 232: whilst the Court of Appeal did not use the term 'sham agreement', that was clearly their conclusion.

[296] *Stone v Hitch* [2001] EWCA Civ 63.

[297] *British Waterways Board v Norman* (1993) 26 HLR 232 at 243.

[298] *Wells v Barnsley Metropolitan Borough Council* (1999) *The Times*, November 12, QBD.

8.237 The mere fact that the solicitor knows that the client will not be able to afford to pay him does not prove that the retainer is a sham, as Latham LJ (giving the judgment of the court) noted:[299]

> 'Whilst the client's impecuniosity may be relevant to determining what the true nature of the agreement was, the mere fact that the solicitor may have been conducting the action on credit or continuing an action in the knowledge of his client's lack of means does not justify a conclusion that he was unlawfully maintaining the action.'

8.238 Mustill LJ has commented that there nothing improper in a solicitor acting in a case for a meritorious client who to his knowledge cannot afford to pay his costs if the case is lost.[300] In a similar vein, Sir Christopher Bellamy found that the fact that a client was paying a monthly contribution which was far lower than the value of services being provided did not give rise to the inference that the retainer was a sham.[301]

8.239 The court will not usually allow a paying party to test the retainer by cross-examination unless there is substance in the allegations; this will not only be on the basis of the presumption afforded by the certificate,[302] but may also on the wider basis of proportionality. Indeed, it was in the context of a paying party wishing to prove the existence of a sham retainer that Latham LJ made the following (famous) comments:[303]

> 'Satellite litigation about costs has become a growth industry, and one that is a blot on the civil justice system. Costs Judges should be astute to prevent such proceedings from being protracted by allegations that are without substance.'

8.240 Where fraud or impropriety are alleged, the accused party may be able to rely on the rebuttable presumption that his acts have been in accordance with the law and what is ethically right.[304] Cogent evidence is required to prove fraud. Whilst some have said that where fraud is alleged the standard of proof approaches the criminal standard,[305] the better analysis is that the standard remains the same but the more serious the allegation the more unlikely it is and the more cogent the evidence needs to be to be capable of proving it.[306] In this regard, Lord Carswell has explained that the standard or proof (albeit in the context of a criminal matter) is 'finite and unvarying':[307]

> '[I]n some contexts a court or tribunal has to look at the facts more critically or more anxiously than in others before it can be satisfied to the requisite standard. The standard itself is, however, finite and unvarying. Situations which make such heightened examination necessary may be the inherent unlikelihood of the occurrence taking place, ... the seriousness of the allegation to be proved or, in some cases, the consequences which could follow from acceptance of proof of the relevant fact. The seriousness of the allegation requires no elaboration: a tribunal of fact will look closely into the facts grounding an allegation of

---

[299] *Burnstein v Times Newspapers Ltd* [2002] EWCA Civ 1739 at [21].
[300] *Singh v Observer Ltd (Note)* [1989] 3 All ER 777; see also *A Ltd v B Ltd* [1996] 1 WLR 665 and *Thai Trading Co (a firm) v Taylor* [1998] 3 All ER 65 at 72.
[301] *Albion Water v Water Services Regulation Authority* [2007] CAT 1; this case is not binding.
[302] This is discussed in detail at **11.22–11.32**.
[303] *Burnstein v Times Newspapers Ltd* [2002] EWCA Civ 1739 at [29].
[304] See, in a non-costs context, *Constantine Steamship Line Ltd v Imperial Smelting Corpn Ltd* [1942] AC 154 and *Low v Guthrie* [1909] AC 278, HL.
[305] See the discussion in *Hornal v Neuberger Products Ltd* [1957] 1 QB 247; see also *Miles v Cain* (1989) *The Times*, December 15, CA.
[306] *Dellow's Will Trusts, Lloyds Bank Ltd v Institute of Cancer Research* [1964] 1 All ER 771.
[307] *R (on the application of D) v Life Sentence Review Commissioners* [2008] UKHL 33 at [28].

fraud before accepting that it has been established. The seriousness of consequences is another facet of the same proposition: if it is alleged that a bank manager has committed a minor peculation, that could entail very serious consequences for his career, so making it the less likely that he would risk doing such a thing. These are all matters of ordinary experience, requiring the application of good sense on the part of those who have to decide such issues. They do not require a different standard of proof or a specially cogent standard of evidence, merely appropriately careful consideration by the tribunal before it is satisfied of the matter which has to be established.'

8.241 In summary, whilst sham agreements may still be encountered from time to time, they are much less common than they were before conditional fee agreements became lawful. The issue of whether a retainer is a sham is determined in exactly the same way as the issue of whether any other contract is a sham. Each case will turn on its own facts.

WAIVER

8.242 Whilst waiver of fees would clearly be a factor that the court could take into account for assessing the amount payable, if a client is to rely on waiver as negating the solicitor's contractual right to payment, the waiver must be supported by consideration. In this regard Tugendhat J that a promise did not become contractually binding simply because the making of the promise was potentially advantageous to the promisor.[308] Likewise, the act of writing costs off for taxation purposes would not extinguish the contractual right to payment.[309]

UNLAWFUL RETAINERS

8.243 The topic of unlawful retainers is dominated by the concepts of express and implied statutory prohibition. It is worth pausing at this juncture to note that there is a distinction between statutory prohibition (which will be determined by a process of statutory interpretation) and common-law prohibition (which is less well defined, and which will turn on issues of public policy). There is an overlap between these two things; in particular, the mechanism by which statute may prohibit a retainer may be mediated by public policy (see below for examples). The distinction between statutory interpretation and public policy may not always be clear (especially in the context of costs law, which is heavily regulated by statute). Some commentators have said that the distinction 'no longer serves any useful purpose, and ought to be abandoned'.[310] This may or may not be true, but it is certainly the case that in appropriate circumstances statute may be regarded as reflecting public policy and as being a measure of it.[311] This will be of obvious relevance when interpreting a provision in statute, but it may also be relevant when considering other supposed prohibitions: the fact that something is not prohibited by statute may be relevant in those circumstances.

---

[308] *Ashia Centur Ltd v Barker Gillette LLP* [2011] EWHC 148 (QB) at [20].
[309] *Slatter v Ronaldsons* [2002] 2 Costs LR 267.
[310] See Greig DW and Davis LJR *The Law of Contract* (1987), p 1116.
[311] See, for example, Steyn LJ's comments in *Giles v Thompson* [1993] 3 All ER 321 at 331 where, in the context of champerty, he said: 'There is, of course, no more cogent evidence of a change of public policy than the expression of the will of Parliament'; see also *Awwad v Geraghty* [2001] QB 570 at 600 and *Bevan Ashford v Geoff Yeandle (Contractors) Ltd (in Liquidation)* [1999] Ch 239.

Statutory prohibition in the context of costs

8.244 This area of the law has developed not in the context of costs, but in that of claims being brought against defendants who have sought to defend the claim on the basis that the contract is illegal. There are many conflicting decisions.

8.245 In general, there are two mechanisms by which a contract of retainer may be prohibited by statute: express statutory prohibition and implied statutory prohibition.

Express statutory prohibition

8.246 This will exist where a statute expressly provides that a contract is unlawful or unenforceable. An example is a conditional fee agreement for contentious business: if that agreement does not comply with the requirements of s 58 of the Courts and Legal Services Act 1990 (as amended), it will be rendered unenforceable as a direct result of the operation of statute. Where a statute expressly provides that a retainer is unenforceable, there is no need to inquire as to the meaning of that provision, because its meaning and effect will be evident from the express language used.[312]

Implied statutory prohibition

8.247 This differs from express statutory prohibition in that the effect of the statute will not be set out in express terms in the statute, so the court must ascertain the its meaning by a process of statutory interpretation. The reader is referred to textbooks on contract for a detailed analysis of the topic.

8.248 When considering whether a retainer is unenforceable by reason of implied statutory prohibition, the procedure is identical to that used in any other branch of the law. Devlin J clarified that procedure:[313]

(1)   it must be determined whether the statutory intention was to prohibit contracts at all; and
(2)   it must be determined whether the contract under consideration belongs to the class of contract which the statute intended to prohibit.

8.249 There are three ways in which a contact may be unlawful in the absence of express statutory prohibition:

(1)   The contract may be an agreement to inflict a legal wrong.
(2)   The agreement itself may be objectionable on the basis that it is unlawful or on the basis that the counterparties have inflicted a legal wrong while in the process of forming it.
(3)   The counterparties may inflict a legal wrong while in the process of performing the agreement.

8.250 The term 'legal wrong' is used in the sense that it includes both acts and omissions. In the context of costs, examples of these things would be:

---

[312]   See Williams 'The Legal Effect of Illegal Contracts (1942–1944)' 8 CLJ 51 at 58–69 for a discussion of this topic in general.
[313]   *St John Shipping Corporation v Joseph Rank Ltd* [1957] 1 QB 267.

- In the first category, an agreement with a claims referral company to provide unregulated and unlawful insurance (such as where the solicitor himself offers to act as the insurer).
- In the second category, failure to abide by the provisions in the Code of Conduct which prohibit certain forms of contingency fee agreement.
- In the third category, failing to declare a commission paid by an ATE insurer.

The effect of a retainer being in the first category will generally be greater than the effect of a retainer being in the third category.

8.251 In discussing each of these categories in turn the focus is on statutes and delegated legislation, but it is worth noting that the principles may, with the appropriate modifications, also apply to non-statutory forms of prohibition, such a failure to comply with non-statutory professional guidance.

The first category: contracts to commit a legal wrong

8.252 An agreement in the first of these categories will, unsurprisingly, not usually be enforced by the courts;[314] this is because the court will not be used as a vehicle to carry out illegal acts or otherwise to inflict legal wrongs. The principle may be summed up in the Latin phrase, *ex dolo malo non oritur actio*: 'no court will lend its aid to a man who founds his cause of action upon an immoral or illegal action'. Lord Bingham CJ explained the principle:[315]

> 'If the court were to allow its process to be used to enforce agreements of this kind, the risk would inevitably arise that such agreements would abound … to the detriment of the public.'

8.253 It would rarely be the case that a contract to commit a legal wrong would be the same contract as the retainer. This is because the supply of legal services is not an inherently unlawful activity. However, a contract which relates to legal funding but which is not a retainer may be an agreement to commit a legal wrong; an example might be an illegal agreement to share fees.[316] Where the facts are such that the objectionable contract is so entwined with the retainer that the two should stand or fall together, it may be said that the objectionable contract (or the objectionable part of the contract) is tainted with illegality.

8.254 A contract which falls within this category would usually be unenforceable. As is implied above, it is important to identify the correct contract when considering the issue of enforceability. If, for example, a solicitor has agreed with a claims management agency to provide unlawful insurance, the starting point would be that the agreement would be unenforceable rather than the contracts of insurance themselves.[317] Indeed, if those were the facts, statute would expressly provide the court with discretion to order that the obligations arising under the contract of insurance would be enforceable.[318]

---

[314] This does not mean that the entirety of the contractual obligations will become unenforceable, nor does it mean that the court would have no discretion; in the example which is given (unlawful insurance) the court has the power to exercise its discretion to allow the agreement to be enforced.

[315] *Mohammed v Alaga & Co* [2000] 1 WLR 1815 at 1824; strictly speaking, Bingham CJ was dealing with a case which was in the second category rather that the first.

[316] *Mohammed v Alaga & Co* [2000] 1 WLR 1815.

[317] For an example which dealt with similar issues, see *Dix v Townend & Anor* [2008] EWHC 90117 (Costs).

[318] See s 28 of the Financial Services and Markets Act 2000.

The second category: prohibited contracts and formation

8.255 An agreement in the second category may or may not be unenforceable, depending on how the statute, properly interpreted, applies to the facts of the case.

8.256 The mechanism by which statute may result in a contract in the second category being unenforceable was explained by Megarry J:[319]

'Where a contract is made in contravention of some statutory provision then, in addition to any criminal sanctions, the Courts may in some cases find that the contract itself is stricken with illegality ... If the statute ... provides that one of the parties must satisfy certain requirements ... before making any contract of the type in question, then the statutory prohibitional requirement may well be sufficiently linked to the contract for questions to arise of the illegality of any contract made in breach of the statutory requirement.'

The fact that this mechanism exists does not mean that the court will be quick to find that a contract will be 'stricken with illegality', as Megarry J put it. Devlin J noted:[320]

'If a contract has as its whole object the doing of the very act which the statute prohibits, it can be argued that you can hardly make sense of a statute which forbids an act and yet permits to be made a contract to do it; that is a clear implication. But unless you get a clear implication of that sort, I think that a court ought to be very slow to hold that a statute intends to interfere with the rights and remedies given by the ordinary law of contract. Caution in this respect is, I think, especially necessary in these times when so much of commercial life is governed by regulations of some sort or another; which may easily be broken without wicked intent.'

8.257 The court is, therefore, sympathetic to the plight of persons who are heavily regulated. In a similar vein Sachs LJ referred to persons 'flounder[ing] in a mass of statutes, orders and regulations governing their daily affairs'.[321] Some would say that those words have even more resonance in the context of costs than they had in the context in which they were originally spoken. The relevance of this sympathetic attitude is that it does not follow that merely because a retainer has been created in a way which breaches some statutory provision, it will be unenforceable.

8.258 Contracts which are prohibited by legislation commonly arise in the context of costs; they may be found to be unenforceable, but this will not always be the case. The mechanism by which a contract or retainer may be found to be unenforceable is not dissimilar to the mechanism by which contracts in the first of the three categories are found to be unenforceable. May LJ explained that there was no distinction of substance or quality between an unlawful retainer and an unlawful agreement to share professional fees,[322] for example.

8.259 As to the interplay between public policy and statutory prohibition, Phillips MR said, in the context of champerty:[323]

'Where the law expressly restricts the circumstances in which agreements in support of litigation are lawful, this provides a powerful indication of the limits of public policy in

---

[319] *Curragh Investments Ltd v Cook* [1974] 1 WLR 1559.
[320] *St John Shipping Corporation v Joseph Rank Ltd* [1957] 1 QB 267.
[321] *Shaw v Groom* [1970] 2 QB 504 at 522.
[322] *Awwad v Geraghty & Co* [2000] 1 Costs LR 105 at 140.
[323] *R v Secretary of State for Transport ex p Factortame* [2002] EWCA Civ 932 at [36].

analogous situations. Where this is not the case, then we believe one must today look at the facts of the particular case and consider whether those facts suggest that the agreement in question [is contrary to public policy].'

8.260   As was explained by Schiemann LJ,[324] the court defers to Parliament on issues as significant as what is and is not permissible in terms of conditional funding; the practical effect of this is that whilst the court recognises that there is a distinction between Parliament's role in enacting statutory regulation and the court's role in adjudicating upon issues of public policy, the court may conclude that public policy is reflected in statute. Lord Bingham CJ, as part of his reasoning for finding that a contract was unlawful as a result of it being in breach of the Solicitors Practice Rules 1990, said:[325]

> 'Section 31 [of the Solicitors Act 1974] confers power on the Law Society to make, with the concurrence of the Master of the Rolls, subordinate legislation governing the professional practice and conduct of solicitors ... When making such subordinate legislation, the Law Society is acting in the public interest and not (should there be any conflict) in the narrower interests of the solicitors' profession (see *Swain v Law Society*). The concurrence of the Master of the Rolls is required as a guarantee that the interests of the public are fully safeguarded.'

8.261   Where, instead of an express provision that a contract is unenforceable, statute imposes a penalty for a prohibited act or omission, one issue that will arise is whether that penalty is sufficient to uphold the purpose of that provision (or to defeat the mischief that the provision was enacted to address). In the context of costs, this will often mean examining the power that the Solicitors Regulation Authority has to punish solicitors and to award compensation to clients. These were factors that Arden LJ took into account when considering whether a failure to provide an estimate of costs should have the effect of making the retainer unenforceable:[326] her conclusion was that those powers were sufficient for upholding the purpose of the statute.

8.262   In summary, where a contract of retainer falls within the second category, it may or may not be enforceable depending on the facts and the statutory purpose.

The third category: performance

8.263   An agreement in the third category would rarely be unenforceable. In all areas of the law the court draws a distinction between the creation of a contract and its performance. This was explained by Browne-Wilkinson J:[327]

> 'The fact that a party has in the course of performing a contract committed an unlawful or immoral act will not by itself prevent him from further enforcing that contract unless the contract was entered into with the purpose of doing that unlawful or immoral act or the contract itself (as opposed to the mode of his performance) is prohibited by law.'

However, in the context of costs a failure in the performance of a contract may sound in the quantum of costs (see, for example, **8.189**).

---

[324]   *Awwad v Geraghty & Co* [2000] 1 Costs LR 105 at 132.
[325]   *Mohammed v Alaga & Co (a firm)* [2000] 1 WLR 1815 at 1823.
[326]   *Garbutt v Edwards* [2005] EWCA Civ 1206 at [39]–[41].
[327]   *Coral Leisure Group Ltd v Barnett* [1981] ICR 503.

8.264 Where a legal wrong occurs in the performance of a contract, the starting point is to recognise that the retainer is within the third rather than the second category. This may not always be as easy as it sounds, as a legal wrong which occurs in the performance of a retainer may occur at about the same time that the retainer itself comes into existence.[328] This can be an important issue because, as mentioned above, a retainer falling within the third category will not usually be unenforceable for that reason.

8.265 Where a contract falls within the third category, the phrase 'harmless collaterality'[329] has been used to describe the relationship between the legal wrong and the contract. Although she did not refer to it by that name, Arden LJ commented:[330]

'The fact that statute imposes a requirement to take some step ... is not of itself sufficient to render the performance of a contract in disregard of that step unlawful and unenforceable ... What the court has to do is to determine the effect of the requirement as a matter of the true construction of the statutory provision.'

8.266 Arden LJ was addressing harmless collaterality in the context of a contract of retainer, but there are many instances of the court coming to a very similar conclusion in other contexts.[331] The general approach is illustrated by a case in which auctioneers had sought to take a secret profit. The issue was whether that legal wrong disentitled them to their fee. The court found that it did not.[332]

8.267 In summary, where a case falls within the third category, the case may be labelled as being an instance of harmless collaterality; as that label suggests, this would not commonly result in the retainer being unenforceable.

The position of the paying party

8.268 Another factor which can have a bearing on the matter is whether the person who raises the issue of the supposed unenforceability of the retainer is the client or the paying party.

8.269 It is often said that the court is less willing to make a finding of unenforceability when the person who advances that argument is the paying party – a stranger to the contract who may be said to be seeking to catch a windfall – as opposed to the innocent client. This is a point of view,[333] but in so far as the bare issue of whether there is an implied statutory prohibition is concerned, it does not seem to be borne out by the authorities. It may be a highly relevant factor to the issue of whether the court will allow argument on the point[334] or whether to exercise its discretion in favour of allowing the retainer to be enforced.

8.270 Most of the authorities on implied statutory prohibition arose in the context of a defendant seeking to impugn the very same contract that he had sought to make. This is relevant because such persons were, if anything, in a morally more objectionable

---

[328] An example would be where a solicitor fails to account to a client for a commission.
[329] *Imageview Management Ltd v Jack* [2009] EWCA Civ 63.
[330] *Garbutt v Edwards* [2005] EWCA Civ 1206 at [35].
[331] See, for example, *Kelly v Cooper* [1993] AC 205; *Boardman v Phipps* [1967] 2 AC 46; and *The Peppy* [1997] 2 Lloyd's Rep 722.
[332] *Hippisley v Knee Bros* [1905] 1 KB 1.
[333] See, for example, the comments of Gilligan J in the Irish case of *Boyne v Dublin Bus* [2006] IEHC 209.
[334] See Chapter 11 on the law relating to the *Bailey* presumption, 'genuine issues', etc.

position than a paying party who seeks to rely on a breach of the indemnity principle. So it is worth examining the way in which the court dealt with the question of the justice of the situation.

8.271 The answer is that the law is largely unperturbed by the duplicity of the arguments and prefers to grant a windfall rather than giving either of the counterparties the benefit of an unlawful contract, as explained by Lord Mansfield:[335]

> 'The objection, that a contract is immoral or illegal as between plaintiff and defendant, sounds at all times very ill in the mouth of the defendant. It is not for his sake, however, that the objection is ever allowed; but it is founded in general principles of policy, which the defendant has the advantage of, contrary to the real justice, as between him and the plaintiff, by accident, if I may say so. The principle of public policy is this: *ex dolo malo non oritur actio*. No Court will lend its aid to a man who founds his cause of action upon an immoral or illegal act. If, from the plaintiff's own stating or otherwise, the cause of action appears to arise *ex turpi causa*, or the transgression of a positive law of this country, there the Court says he has no right to be assisted. It is upon that ground the Court goes; not for the sake of the defendant, but because they will not lend their aid to such a plaintiff. So if the plaintiff and defendant were to change sides, and the defendant was to bring his action against the plaintiff, the latter would then have the advantage of it; for where both are equally in fault, *potior est conditio defendentis*.'

Thus, in contexts other than the law of costs, an illegal contract will be found to be unenforceable, not because such a decision would bring justice to a wrongly pursued defendant, but because public policy requires that the contract itself should be struck down and that neither party should have the benefit of it.

8.272 The same appears to be true in the context of costs. In the well-known case of *Garbutt v Edwards*, Arden LJ did not make any distinction between the status of a client and the status of the paying party.[336] In so far as implied statutory prohibition was concerned, the only comments she made about the interests of the parties were as follows:[337]

> 'In making these rules [ie the SPR], the Council of the Law Society is acting in the public interest, and the rules have the force of subordinate legislation (see *Swain v Law Society* [1982] 2 All ER 827, [1983] AC 598). The inference I would draw is that the code is there to protect the legitimate interests of the client, and the administration of justice, rather than to relieve paying parties of their obligations to pay costs which have been reasonably incurred.'

In so far as the implied statutory prohibition itself was concerned, she took that distinction no further (although she did rely on that distinction in other contexts). The way in which Arden LJ dealt with the issue suggests that the position of the paying party is to be taken into account only for the purposes of interpreting the statute (such as in identifying the mischief); this would be entirely consistent with the approach in other areas of the law.

8.273 It is also worth noting that in a different context (the issue of whether a retainer could constructively be said to be a CFA Lite), Hughes LJ has confirmed that the source of the contention (ie whether the contention comes from the client or the paying party)

---

[335] *Holman v Johnson* (1775) 1 Cowp 341 at 343.
[336] *Garbutt v Edwards* [2005] EWCA Civ 1206: she did make this decision in relation to an alternative ground of appeal relating to the effect of an estimate of the issue of quantum, but that is a different matter.
[337] *Garbutt v Edwards* [2005] EWCA Civ 1206 at [31].

cannot alter the construction of the agreement: the contractual position as between the solicitor and the client must be the same, whoever takes the point.[338]

8.274 Where the court is afforded the power to exercise its discretion as to whether a retainer is or is not enforceable, the fact that the challenge was brought by the paying party rather than the client could well be a relevant factor.

8.275 In summary, where statute expressly provides that an act or omission will result in the retainer being unenforceable, then express statutory prohibition will be said to exist. In cases where no such consequence is expressly stated, the court must interpret the statue to determine two things: first, whether the statute intends to prohibit contracts at all; and secondly, whether the contract under consideration belongs to the class of contract which the statute intends to prohibit. When considering that issue, it is often useful to distinguish between formation and performance of a contract, as it is rare for a shortcoming in relation to the latter to result in a contract being rendered unenforceable.

Specific instances of express and implied statutory prohibition

Conditional fee agreements

8.276 This topic is discussed in detail in Chapter 9. It is mentioned here only as an example of express statutory prohibition. That example is created by s 58(1) of the Courts and Legal Services Act 1990 (as amended):

'A conditional fee agreement which satisfies all of the conditions applicable to it by virtue of this section shall not be unenforceable by reason only of its being a conditional fee agreement; but ... any other conditional fee agreement shall be unenforceable.'

Thus, this provision expressly states that non-compliance with the provision in that Act will lead to the disobedient contract of retainer being unenforceable (hence *express statutory prohibition*).

Contingency fee agreements

8.277 It has repeatedly been said that the Solicitors' Practice Rules 1990 ('the SPR') had a force equivalent to that of a schedule to a statute.[339] The same is true of the SPR's successor, namely, the Solicitors' Code of Conduct 2007 (see **3.5** *et seq*). That code has itself been replaced by the SRA Code of Conduct 2011, and no doubt the same general principle applies. Despite this, what is set out below applies only to contracts of retainer made before 6 October 2011; this is because the provisions referred to do *not* have their counterparts in the new SRA Code of Conduct 2011 (see **8.231**).

8.278 The Solicitors' Code of Conduct 2007 defined the phrase 'contingency fee' in the following way:[340]

---

[338] *Jones v Wrexham Borough Council* [2007] EWCA Civ 1356 at [83].
[339] See the relevant section of the chapter on the 'the status of the rules governing costs'; see, in particular, *Swain v The Law Society* [1983] 1 AC 598.
[340] Rule 24 of the Solicitors' Code of Conduct 2007; see also para 41 of the guidance to rule 2.04; Some caution ought to be exercised over the meaning of the phrase 'contingency fee agreement', as that phrase is often used to mean an agreement where the fees are quantitatively linked to the sums recovered as damages, debt

'A "contingency fee" is defined in rule 24 (Interpretation) as any sum (whether fixed, or calculated either as a percentage of the proceeds or otherwise) payable only in the event of success.'

The guidance to rule 2.04 of that code stated that this definition was sufficiently broad to include conditional fee agreements.[341]

8.279 Rule 2.04 of that code imposed the following prohibition:[342]

'(1) You must not enter into an arrangement to receive a contingency fee for work done in prosecuting or defending any contentious proceedings before a court of England and Wales, a British court martial or an arbitrator where the seat of the arbitration is in England and Wales, except as permitted by statute or the common law.

(2) You must not enter into an arrangement to receive a contingency fee for work done in prosecuting or defending any contentious proceedings before a court of an overseas jurisdiction or an arbitrator where the seat of the arbitration is overseas except to the extent that a lawyer of that jurisdiction would be permitted to do so.'

Thus, in so far as retainers made between 1 July 2007 and 6 October 2011 were concerned, contingency fees were prohibited save to the extent that they were permitted by statue or common law. The SPR imposed a very similar prohibition for work done after 8 January 1999,[343] and before that date, similar (but more restrictive) provisions applied.[344]

8.280 Thus, contingency fee agreements were prohibited. May LJ made the following comments about the provisions contained in the SPR (which, presumably, also apply to the provisions in the Solicitors' Code of Conduct 2007):[345]

'They are secondary legislation having the force of statute ... The Rules regulate professional practice, but breach of the Rules is unlawful in addition to being a breach of professional practice ... Although no doubt not every trifling breach of the Solicitors' Practice Rules would render a transaction with which it was concerned unenforceable, in my view an arrangement to receive a contingency fee contrary to rule 8(1) would make the fee agreement which it comprised unenforceable.'

---

or price paid; that usage is significantly narrower than the above definition; that type of agreement is referred to in this book as a damages-based conditional fee agreement and is dealt with in detail at **9.20–9.23** and **9.309–9.320**.

[341] See para 44 of that guidance; the definition in rule 24 certainly is wide enough to include most conditional fee agreements, but it could be argued that it does not include agreements by which the fees are payable in the event of some happening other than success.

[342] Similar provisions relating to overseas clients could be found at rule 15.02 (rule 2(4) of the Solicitors' Code of Conduct 2007.

[343] '(1) A solicitor who is retained or employed to prosecute or defend any action, suit or other contentious proceeding shall not enter into any arrangement to receive a contingency fee in respect of that proceeding, save one permitted under statute or by the common law.

(2) Paragraph (1) of this rule shall not apply to an arrangement in respect of an action, suit or other contentious proceeding in any country other than England and Wales to the extent that the local lawyer would be permitted to receive a contingency fee in respect of that proceeding.'

[344] A different more restrictive form of wording was used up until 8 January 1999: 'A solicitor who is retained or employed to prosecute any action, suit or other contentious proceeding shall not enter into any arrangement to receive a contingency fee in respect of that proceeding.'

[345] *Awwad v Geraghty & Co (a firm)* [2000] 1 All ER 608 at 633.

There is, therefore, an implied statutory prohibition against a contingency fee agreement relating to contentious business; the only exceptions to that prohibition are where the agreement is permitted by statute or the common law (see Chapter 9).

8.281 In summary, both the SPR and the Solicitors' Code of Conduct 2007 gave rise to an implied statutory prohibition that, save to the extent that they are permitted by statute or the common law, made contingency fee agreements, including conditional fee agreements, unenforceable. The link between the prohibition and the lack of enforceability was not expressly stated in the legislation, hence, *implied* legislative prohibition. (This was, however, of little practical relevance because it was eclipsed by the express statutory prohibition referred to in **8.276**.)

8.282 There is, in the writer's opinion, no implied statutory prohibition against contingency fee agreements arising out of the SRA Code of Conduct 2011; this is because that code says no more than that entering into unlawful fee arrangements such as an unlawful contingency fee is indicative of the solicitor not having complied with the Principles of that code.[346] As such, SRA Code of Conduct 2011 appears to follow the law rather than shape it. This is, however, only the writer's opinion and as such may be incorrect.

Consumer protection regulations

8.283 In the present context, there are two statutory instruments (the older of which has now been revoked by the newer) which make provision for express statutory prohibition of contracts which do not comply with certain consumer protection requirements. They are:

- the Consumer Protection (Cancellation of Contracts Concluded away from Business Premises) Regulations 1987 (SI 1987/2117) (as amended); and
- the Cancellation of Contracts made in a Consumer's Home or Place of Work etc Regulations 2008 (SI 2008/1816).

Broadly speaking, these will apply where a contract is made at the client's home or place of work. This is a topic which is dealt with in detail at **8.324** *et seq*.

Other breaches of the codes of conduct

8.284 The applicable principles are those explained at **8.247–8.251**. In particular, where a retainer is said to be unenforceable by reason of implied statutory prohibition, the correct way of addressing that issue is to apply Devlin J's two-stage test (see **8.248**).

8.285 Whilst the true meaning of each provision must be determined by a process of statutory interpretation, and whilst that meaning would be the same regardless of whether the argument was raised by the client or by the paying party, the general thrust of Arden LJ's judgment in *Garbutt v Edwards*[347] was that a failure strictly to adhere to the then Code of Conduct (in that instance the Solicitors' Practice Rules) would not render a contract of retainer unenforceable. The fact that other common law

---

[346] See IB(1.27 and OP(1.3).
[347] [2005] EWCA Civ 1206.

jurisdictions have come to similar conclusion strongly implies that that is a principle of general application and that as such it applies to the Solicitors' Code of Conduct 2007 and the SRA Code of Conduct 2011.[348]

8.286 One factor that appeared to have a bearing on Arden LJ's analysis was that, although the SPR made no provision for non-complaint retainers to be rendered unenforceable, it made express provision for compensation to be payable to the client for inadequate professional services (those provisions qualifying the power conferred by SA 1974, s 37A). It is, perhaps, relevant that the Solicitors' Code of Conduct 2007 had done nothing to diminish those powers. Those powers do not seem to be part of the SRA Code of Conduct Rules 2011 themselves (or the associated SRA Disciplinary Rules 2011), but the Legal Ombudsman has very similar powers.

8.287 In summary, whilst each case must be considered individually, a failure to comply with the requirements of the prevailing Code of Conduct would not generally result in the retainer being found to be unenforceable.

Provisions relating to insurance

8.288 The provisions relating to insurance are potentially relevant to a contract of insurance in two ways:

- **Quasi-insurance**: It has been argued that an agreement to provide an indemnity for adverse costs is an agreement to provide insurance, and that where a legal representative provides such an indemnity in an unregulated fashion, this has the effect of making his contract of retainer unenforceable; and
- **Ineptly provided ATE insurance**: It may be that where a solicitor carries out the task of arranging ATE insurance and where he does this ineptly, his ineptitude puts his own contract of retainer at risk.

The first of these topics is addressed immediately below; the second is addressed at **8.304** *et seq.*

Quasi-insurance

8.289 Two issues arise: the first being whether such an agreement is contrary to the rules of champerty, and the second being whether the agreement is contrary to the legislative provisions regulating insurance. For the reasons set out below, it is now known that there is almost no scope for the court to find that a contract of retainer is unenforceable for either of these reasons. The topic of champerty is addressed first. As is explained at **9.340** *et seq*, the law of champerty still very much applies to legal representatives acting in that capacity. It is, however, a necessary ingredient that the putative champerter is acting contrary to public policy. Lord Neuberger MR had this to say on this topic:[349]

> 'Access to justice is an essential ingredient of a modern civilised society, but it is difficult to achieve for the great majority of citizens, especially with the ever reducing availability of legal aid. This has been accompanied by a shift in legislative policy towards favouring the

---

[348] See, for example, *Boyne v Dublin Bus* [2006] IEHC 209 and *A & L Goodbody Solicitors v Colthurst* (unreported) 5 November 2003, High Court of Ireland.

[349] *Morris v London Borough of Southwark* [2011] EWCA Civ 25 at [49].

relaxation of previously tight professional ethical constraints, in order to enable a variety of more flexible funding arrangements (which some applaud and others believe give too much weight to consumerism and involve expensive regulation). In these circumstances, I find it hard to accept that, by shouldering the risk of an adverse order for costs against his client, a solicitor is acting contrary to public policy, which is, of course, the basis for the law of champerty.'

Lord Neuberger MR went on to say that he rejected the idea that such cases are to be dealt on a case-by-case basis.[350] There has been a degree of academic criticism of this decision, but Lord Neuberger MR readily pointed out that 'the rule against champerty is not entirely logical in its extent or limits';[351] as such, it is an analysis that is unashamedly based on current-day policy.

8.290 Lord Neuberger MR also considered whether an arrangement that a legal representative bears the risk of adverse costs orders could be said to be unlawful maintenance. He concluded that it could not, this being because maintenance involves an element of assisting one of the parties 'without justification or excuse', and as Lord Phillips had found before him,[352] Lord Neuberger MR could not envisage of a legal representative acting in that capacity doing so without justification or excuse.[353]

8.291 The next topic is the relevance of the legislation that governs insurance (a detailed discussion of which can be found at **30.124** *et seq*). That legislation provides for an express statutory prohibition which, subject to the court ordering otherwise, will prevent an unregulated contract of insurance from being enforced against the client. For the reasons set out below, the question of whether the express statutory prohibition applies will turn on whether, taking the contract as whole, it can be said to have as its principal object the provision of insurance. If the answer to that question is in the negative, then the contract will not be enforceable by reason of the express statutory prohibition. As will be explained below, Lord Neuberger MR has said that that question will almost always be answered in the negative.

8.292 The Financial Services and Markets Act 2000 creates an express statutory prohibition which it labels 'the general prohibition'. The general prohibition is part of the machinery which regulates 'regulated activities'. The general prohibition is a creation of FSMA 2000, s 19:

'(1) No person may carry on a regulated activity in the United Kingdom, or purport to do so, unless he is—

    (a)   an authorised person; or
    (b)   an exempt person.

(2)   The prohibition is referred to in this Act as the general prohibition.'

8.293 What is and is not a regulated activity is defined by the Financial Services and Markets Act 2000 (Regulated Activities) Order 2001 (SI 2001/544) ('the RAO'). Providing ATE insurance as a principle is a regulated activity. On 14 January 2005 the RAO was amended,[354] and from that date the act of giving advice about ATE insurance also became a regulated activity.

---

[350]   *Morris v London Borough of Southwark* [2011] EWCA Civ 25 at [57].
[351]   *Morris v London Borough of Southwark* [2011] EWCA Civ 25 at [51].
[352]   *R v Secretary of State for Transport ex p Factortame* [2002] EWCA Civ 932 at [76].
[353]   *Morris v London Borough of Southwark* [2011] EWCA Civ 25 at [53].
[354]   Financial Services and Markets Act 2000 (Regulated Activities) (Amendment) Order 2004, SI 2004/1610.

8.294 One aspect of the express prohibition is created by FSMA 2000, s 26, which (in so far as it is relevant) reads:

> '(1) An agreement made by a person in the course of carrying on a regulated activity in contravention of the general prohibition is unenforceable against the other party.
>
> ...
>
> (3) 'Agreement' means an agreement—
>
>   (a)   made after this section comes into force; and
>   (b)   the making or performance of which constitutes, or is part of, the regulated activity in question.'

Therefore, where a solicitor makes a contract in the course of carrying on a regulated activity in contravention of the general prohibition, that agreement will be rendered unenforceable against the client, but only if the making or performance of the contract constitutes, or is part of, the regulated activity in question.

8.295 FSMA 2000, s 26 relates to agreements made *by* a person in contravention of the general prohibition. Section 27 introduces a similar provision which relates to agreement made *through* such a person. In so far as it is relevant, it reads:

> '(1) An agreement made by an authorised person ("the provider")—
>
>   (a)   in the course of carrying on a regulated activity (not in contravention of the general prohibition), but
>   (b)   in consequence of something said or done by another person ("the third party") in the course of a regulated activity carried on by the third party in contravention of the general prohibition, is unenforceable against the other party.
>
> ...
>
> (3) "Agreement" means an agreement—
>
>   (a)   made after this section comes into force; and
>   (b)   the making or performance of which constitutes, or is part of, the regulated activity in question carried on by the provider.'

This creates an express statutory prohibition which is similar to the one described above, but which is one step removed in that the contract will be unenforceable not as an effect of the involvement of the person who made the contract, but as a result of the involvement of a person who said or did something which led to the creation of the contract.

8.296 Thus the question arises as to whether a contract of retainer which also provides for an indemnity for adverse costs falls within the ambit of these provisions.

8.297 This would be the case only if the contract in question could be said to be a contract of insurance. A detailed discussion of what is and is not insurance is beyond the scope of this book, but subject to what is said below at **8.300**, the following is generally accepted as describing the requisite constituents:[355]

> 'The payment of one or more sums of money, commonly called premiums, by one party ("the policyholder"). In return for these payments the other party ("the insurer") undertakes to pay a sum of money on the happening of a specified event ... The event must be one which is adverse to the interests of the policyholder.'

---

[355] *Prudential Insurance Co v IRC* [1904] 2 KB 658, per Channell J.

8.298 In so far as contracts of retainers are concerned, Lord Neuberger MR approved of the following findings in the court below:[356]

> '45. I have been referred to the following extract from McGillivray on Insurance Law. I do not apologise for quoting it, word-for-word, reflecting as it does my own view,
>
>> "It is sometimes necessary to decide, in the context of fiscal or regulatory legislation, whether a contract containing insurance and non-insurance elements should be classified wholly or partly as a contract of insurance. The inclusion of indemnity provisions within a contract, or the supply of services, neither makes the indemnifier an insurer, nor justifies describing the contract as wholly or partly one of insurance. Where a contract for sale, or for services, contains elements of insurance, it will be regarded as a contract of insurance only if, taking the contract as whole, it can be said to have as its principal object the provision of insurance."
>
> 46. In my judgment, this, on any view, was a contract for the provision of legal services. The indemnity clause, whether looked at individually or as part of the contract, was a subsidiary part of the contract. ... [T]his was a contract for the provision of legal services, with an indemnity clause whereby the solicitor undertook to pay the opponent's costs, in the event that that became necessary. To characterise it as a contract of insurance, albeit that the indemnity created some principles similar to an insurance contract, is to go too far ...'

8.299 Thus a contract of retainer could almost never be said to be a contract of the type that would engage the regulatory framework governing insurance. It is, perhaps, possible that a legal representative could cross the line and conduct his business in such a way as to make the provision of legal services a subsidiary element, but there are no instances of any such findings ever having been made.

8.300 Lord Neuberger MR's analysis has received a certain amount of academic criticism, but two points are worth making in this regard. The first is that the law has always avoided being overly rigid in its view of what is and is not insurance. In this regard, Templeman J had the following to say:[357]

> 'It does not follow that the definition given by Channell J [above at **8.297**] in a case based on the facts with which he was concerned and applied by me to the case in which I am now concerned is an exhaustive definition of insurance. There may well be some contracts of guarantee, some contracts of maintenance which might at first sight appear to have some resemblance to the definition laid down by Channell J and which, on analysis, are not found to be true contracts of insurance at all.'

8.301 The second point is that this is not the first time that the court has found that a contract for something that may, at first blush, appear to be insurance should not be regarded as being a contract of insurance. An example of this arose in the context of a scheme to give discretionary legal assistance to members of a mutual professional organisation. Megarry V-C drew a distinction between contracts *of* insurance, and contracts *for* insurance.[358] This was an analysis very similar to Lord Neuberger MR's analysis as set out above.

8.302 Nonetheless, it is still theoretically possible that a legal representative could cross the line and enter into an agreement that was not a contract of retainer, but was a

---

[356] *Morris v London Borough of Southwark* [2011] EWCA Civ 25 at [59].
[357] *Department of Trade and Industry v St Christopher Motorists Association Ltd* [1974] 1 All ER 395.
[358] *Medical Defence Union Ltd v Department of Trade* [1979] 2 All ER 421 at 431.

contract of insurance. Even if this were to happen, it would not necessarily follow that the contact would be unenforceable against the client. This is because the FSMA 2000, s 28 gives the court discretion to allow the contract to be enforced against the client:

'(1)   This section applies to an agreement which is unenforceable because of section 26 or 27.

...

(3)   If the court is satisfied that it is just and equitable in the circumstances of the case, it may allow—

(a)   the agreement to be enforced; or
(b)   money and property paid or transferred under the agreement to be retained.

(4)   In considering whether to allow the agreement to be enforced or (as the case may be) the money or property paid or transferred under the agreement to be retained the court must—

(a)   if the case arises as a result of section 26, have regard to the issue mentioned in subsection (5); or
(b)   if the case arises as a result of section 27, have regard to the issue mentioned in subsection (6).

(5)   The issue is whether the person carrying on the regulated activity concerned reasonably believed that he was not contravening the general prohibition by making the agreement.

(6)   The issue is whether the provider knew that the third party was (in carrying on the regulated activity) contravening the general prohibition.

(7)   If the person against whom the agreement is unenforceable—

(a)   elects not to perform the agreement, or
(b)   as a result of this section, recovers money paid or other property transferred by him under the agreement, he must repay any money and return any other property received by him under the agreement.

(8)   If property transferred under the agreement has passed to a third party, a reference in section 26 or 27 or this section to that property is to be read as a reference to its value at the time of its transfer under the agreement.

(9)   The commission of an authorisation offence does not make the agreement concerned illegal or invalid to any greater extent than is provided by section 26 or 27.'

Subsection (4) is worded in mandatory terms. In view of the guidance given by Lord Neuberger MR as set out at **8.289**, it is difficult to think of circumstances in which it could be argued that this provision would give rise to a breach of the indemnity principle. Examples might include where the contract was a tripartite agreement with an unregulated third-party that was in some way objectionable on public policy grounds.

8.303   In summary, whist it remains a theoretical possibility, for all practical purposes a contract of retainer would not be made unenforceable solely by reason of it containing a provision to provide an indemnity in respect of an opponent's costs.

Ineptly provided ATE insurance

8.304   This section addresses the steps that need to be taken to avoid a breach of the 'general prohibition' (see **8.292**); for the reasons set out above it is likely that the only circumstances in which a legal representative would need to concern himself with such issues would be where he is dealing with insurance provided by an insurer; this would usually arise in the context of the legal representative arranging ATE insurance. As is set out above (**8.294-8.2948.294**), a breach of the general prohibition is capable of rendering unenforceable a contract made 'in the course of carrying on a regulated activity' (**8.294**); it is not known whether this would be interpreted sufficiently widely to mean that a contract of retainer made at the same time as an ATE policy would be regarded as having been made 'in the course of carrying on a regulated activity'. Given the sentiments expressed by Lord Neuberger MR relating to quasi-insurance (see **8.298**) this would seem unlikely, but it cannot be ruled out entirely, and as such, compliance remains an issue that deserves to be addressed. In any event, it is desirable not to breach the general prohibition for reasons unrelated to retainers.

8.305 The relevant law follows a tortuous path through statute, delegated legislation and rules of professional conduct, but an overview is as follows:

- Effecting or carrying out a contract of ATE insurance as a principal is a regulated activity, as is giving advice about ATE insurance;
- Carrying out either of these activities without also complying with the relevant regulatory regime would amount to a breach of the general provision;
- Certain professionals are exempt from many of the requirements imposed by the FSMA 2000, but only if and to the extent that they comply with certain rules;
- In so far as solicitors are concerned, the task of formulating those rules is delegated to the Solicitors Regulation Authority in its role as a designated professional body; and
- Those rules have been formulated in such a way as to lie alongside the prevailing rules of professional conduct, and compliance with those rules will mean that the solicitor avoids breaching the general prohibition.

8.306 The starting point is FSMA 2000, s 327; this section exempts certain persons from the general prohibition, but only if:

- that person is a member of a profession (or controlled or managed by one or more such members);
- that person accounts to his client for any commission received;
- the activity in question is 'incidental to the provision by him of professional services';
- the activity is of a certain permitted type and is not of a prohibited type; and
- the activity is the only regulated activity carried on by that person (other than regulated activities in relation to which he is an exempt person).

These provisions permit certain firms to be treated as 'exempt professional firms' and to carry on activities known as 'exempt regulated activities'. These firms will not need to be regulated by the Financial Services Authority (FSA), but will be able to carry on exempt regulated activities under the supervision of a designated professional body. A designated professional body must formulate rules to regulate the way regulated activities are performed.

8.307 The Solicitors Regulation Authority is a designated professional body. There are two sets of relevant rules, both of which have been made by the procedure described above and both of which have the force of statute (see **3.5–3.19**). Firstly, there are the SRA Financial Services (Scope) Rules 2001 ('the Scope Rules'), and secondly there are the SRA Financial Services (Conduct of Business) Rules 2001 ('the Conduct of Business

Rules').[359] Both were amended on 14 January 2005 to include ATE insurance, then again on 1 July 2007 to take account of the introduction of the Solicitors Code of Conduct 2007, and then again on 6 October 2011 to take account of the SRA Code of Conduct 2011. They are referred to as rules governing 'specialist services' under the SRA Code of Conduct 2011.

8.308 The Scope Rules include the following:

• a list of prohibited activities;
• basic conditions which must be satisfied; and
• restrictions relating to particular types of activities.

8.309 Like the RAO, the Scope Rules were amended on 14 January 2005 to encompass ATE insurance. In the present context the most important provisions are:

• that a solicitor may provide 'insurance mediation activities' (a definition which includes giving advice about ATE insurance) only if registered with the FSA;
• that the advice must arise out of, or be complementary to, the provision of a professional service to the client; and
• that the solicitor must account to the client for any pecuniary reward or other advantage received from a third party.

8.310 Registration with the FSA is not the same as being regulated by the FSA; registration is a straightforward administrative process whereas regulation is much more involved. The issue of whether advice is complementary to the provision of legal services would depend on the facts of the case in hand; it is implicit that there will be a limit to what could be regarded as being complementary, but there is no authority as to where the line should be drawn.

8.311 As to the third of these requirements (accounting for any pecuniary reward), it is not unusual for solicitors to be paid a commission for recommending a contract of insurance. The requirement to account to the client does not mean that the commission necessarily has to be paid to the client; in this regard the SRA Code of Conduct 2011 reads as follows:[360]

> 'O(1.15) You must achieve these outcomes: you properly account to clients for any financial benefit you receive as a result of your instructions.'

> ... IB(1.20) where you receive a financial benefit as a result of acting for a client, either:

> (a)   paying it to the client;
> (b)   offsetting it against your fees; or
> (c)   keeping it only where you can justify keeping it, you have told the client the amount of the benefit (or an approximation if you do not know the exact amount) and the client has agreed that you can keep it.'

8.312 Up until 6 October 2011 the Solicitors' Code of Conduct 2007 made the following provisions:[361]

---

[359]   These used to be known as the Solicitors' Financial Services (Scope) Rules 2001 and the Solicitors' Financial Services (Conduct of Business) Rules 2001 respectively.
[360]   Provisions concerning overseas practice can be found at OP(1.1).
[361]   Rule 2.06 of the Solicitors' Code of Conduct 2007.

'If you are a principal in a firm you must ensure that your firm pays to your client commission received over Ł20 unless the client, having been told the amount, or if the precise amount is not known, an approximate amount or how the amount is to be calculated, has agreed that your firm may keep it.'

Even under those rules, however, the Ł20 limit did not apply to commissions paid on ATE insurance. This is because FSMA 2000, s 327(3) overrode that limit:

'P [ie the solicitor] must not receive from a person other than his client any pecuniary reward or other advantage, for which he does not account to his client, arising out of his carrying on of any of the activities.'

Solicitors, therefore, need to and have always needed to account for all ATE commissions, regardless of size.

8.313 The Conduct of Business Rules require that solicitors give 'status disclosure', which in essence means that the solicitor should explain that he is not authorised by the FSA, but that he is regulated by the Solicitors Regulation Authority. In particular, the solicitor is required to give the client the following information in writing:

- a statement that the firm is not authorised by the FSA;
- the name and address of the firm;
- the nature of the regulated activities carried on by the firm, and the fact that they are limited in scope;
- a statement that the firm is regulated by the Solicitors Regulation Authority; and
- a statement explaining that complaints and redress mechanisms are provided though Solicitors Regulation Authority regulation.

Moreover, the following statement must be made in writing:

'[This firm is]/[We are] not authorised by the Financial Services Authority. However, we are included on the register maintained by the Financial Services Authority so that we can carry on insurance mediation activity, which is broadly the advising on, selling and administration of insurance contracts. This part of our business, including arrangements for complaints or redress if something goes wrong, is regulated by Solicitors Regulation Authority. The register can be accessed via the Financial Services Authority website at www.fsa.gov.uk/register.'

The guidance notes to the Conduct of Business Rules suggest that this information may be given in the client care letter.

8.314 The Conduct of Business Rules provide that certain records must be kept.[362] In essence, the client's instructions need to be recorded, as must any relevant instructions given to any other person. A record most also be kept of the commissions received and of how that commission has been accounted. These records must be kept for at least 6 years.[363]

8.315 In so far as ATE insurance is concerned, the solicitor must comply with the provisions of Appendix 1 of the Conduct of Business Rules ('Appendix 1');[364] that appendix imposes three obligations: certain information must be disclosed, the client

---

[362] See rule 5 of the Solicitors' Financial Services (Conduct of Business) Rules 2001, which must be read in conjunction with rule 4.
[363] See rule 9 of the Solicitors' Financial Services (Conduct of Business) Rules 2001.
[364] See rule 8A of the Solicitors' Financial Services (Conduct of Business) Rules 2001.

must be advised whether the ATE insurance is suitable, and the client must be given a 'demands and needs statement'. Each of these things is addressed in turn.

Disclosure

8.316 The solicitor must take reasonable steps to communicate information to the client in a way that is 'clear, fair and not misleading',[365] and must declare the basis upon which any recommendation is made.[366]

8.317 The solicitor must elect whether to give advice which is based on an analysis of the ATE insurance market, or whether to give advice on some other basis. If the former, he must inform the client whether any recommendation he makes is given on the basis of a 'fair analysis' of a sufficiently large number of ATE policies to enable the firm to make a recommendation adequate to meet the client's needs.[367] If the latter, the firm must:[368]

- advise whether the firm is contractually obliged to conduct insurance mediation activities only with one or more insurance undertakings;
- advise the client that the client can request details of the insurance undertakings with which the firm conducts business; and
- provide the client with such details on request.

8.318 Many solicitors are contractually bound to recommend only one particular policy; this is justifiable because it avoids adverse selection of cases. In recognition of this, the Solicitors Regulation Authority has issued the following guidance:[369]

> 'The Law Society is aware that some firms have entered into contracts with introducers whereby they are obliged to effect for their client a particular type of insurance contract e g if there is a conditional fee agreement. These arrangements are acceptable provided, of course, that the particular insurance policy is suitable for the client's needs and the solicitor has informed the client of the constraint.'

Advice must be provided on paper or on any other durable medium which is available and accessible to the client.[370]

Suitability

8.319 Before a firm recommends an ATE policy, it must take reasonable steps to ensure that the recommendation is suitable to the client's demands and needs. In particular, solicitors must:[371]

- consider relevant information already held;
- obtain details of any relevant existing insurance;
- identify the client's requirements and explain to the client what the client needs to disclose;

---

[365] See art 1 of Appendix 1 of the Solicitors' Financial Services (Conduct of Business) Rules 2001.
[366] See arts 1(2) and (3) of Appendix 1 of the Solicitors' Financial Services (Conduct of Business) Rules 2001.
[367] Solicitors' Financial Services (Conduct of Business) Rules 2001, Appendix 1, art 1(2).
[368] Solicitors' Financial Services (Conduct of Business) Rules 2001, Appendix 1, art (3).
[369] The Solicitors Regulation Authority's Guidance on the Conduct of Business Rules (undated, but issued in 2005), para 9.7.
[370] Solicitors' Financial Services (Conduct of Business) Rules 2001, Appendix 1, art 1(4).
[371] Solicitors' Financial Services (Conduct of Business) Rules 2001, Appendix 1, art 2.

- assess whether the level of cover is sufficient for the risks that the client wishes to insure; and
- consider the relevance of any exclusions, excesses, limitations or conditions.

Where a solicitor is not able to recommend suitable insurance because it does not exist on the ATE market, that fact must be disclosed to the client.[372]

Demands and needs

8.320 Before the contract of insurance is finalised, the client must be provided with a 'demands and needs statement', which must address the following:[373]

- it must set out the client's demands and needs on the basis of the information provided by the client;
- it must explain the reason for recommending that contract of insurance;
- it must reflect the complexity of the insurance contract being proposed; and
- it must be on paper or on any other durable medium available and accessible to the client.

8.321 In summary, whilst it is extremely unlikely that it would ever operate in such a way as to render a contract of retainer unenforceable, there is a statutory mechanism that provides a means by which a contract of retainer could be found to be unenforceable by reason of it having been associated in some way with a breach of the 'general prohibition'.

Arguments in the alternative to implied statutory prohibition

8.322 For the sake of completeness it is also worth mentioning an argument that may arise when reliance is placed on an implied statutory prohibition. The points made in this section relate to retainers in general rather than to any particulate type of retainer.

8.323 Where it is said that a legal wrong should result in a retainer being found to be unlawful or unenforceable, it may also be said (in the alternative) that if the legal wrong had not occurred, the costs would have been lower.[374] Such an argument will go to quantum rather than the enforceability of the retainer.[375] There are three points to make about arguments of that type:

(1) That it is a different argument from the primary argument, and it should not be seen as being a lesser version of it. By way of example, Arden LJ rejected the

---

[372] Solicitors' Financial Services (Conduct of Business) Rules 2001, Appendix 1, art 2.
[373] Solicitors' Financial Services (Conduct of Business) Rules 2001, Appendix 1, art 3.
[374] Paradoxically, this can work against the paying party, as it did in a case in which Hughes LJ found that a failure properly to describe the terms of a seemingly defective conditional fee agreement contributed to the retainer being found to be a CFA Lite, and therefore enforceable: *Jones v Wrexham Borough Council* [2007] EWCA Civ 1356 at [94].
[375] Although it would rarely arise in the context of costs, it is possible for an implied statutory prohibition to sound in quantum rather than to have the effect of rendering the retainer unenforceable; an example would be where a solicitor has made a secret profit out of an illegal arrangement with a claims referrer; in those circumstances, legal mechanisms could be invoked that would either require the solicitor to account to the client for the secret profit, or to reduce the solicitor's fees by the same amount; such things are beyond the scope of this book; a discussion of the relevant mechanisms can be found in textbooks on contract.

notion that the failure to give an estimate should, by reason of a lesser form of statutory prohibition, sound in the application of a tariff reduction:[376]

> 'I have already concluded that the paying party cannot claim that the contract of retainer is unlawful because of the failure to give an estimate. In those circumstances, it would seem to me illogical to apply some sort of tariff as suggested by Mr Morgan. It would result in the paying party obtaining a part of the benefit he would have obtained if I had held that the contract of retainer was rendered unenforceable.'

(2)   That because it is a different argument, different considerations may apply. In particular, the court may have to consider the causative effect of the conduct complained of.

(3)   That because the argument is not based on express statutory prohibition there can be no question of the *Bailey* presumption undermining legislative policy; in view of this, the *Bailey* presumption will usually apply.[377]

It is, therefore, important to identify the arguments and to recognise them for what they are.

RETAINERS MADE NOT AT THE SOLICITORS' OFFICES

8.324 Where a solicitor enters into a contract of retainer which is not made in the solicitor's offices there are certain regulations that may apply:

- The Consumer Protection (Cancellation of Contracts Concluded away from Business Premises) Regulations 1987 (SI 1987/2117) (as amended).
- The Consumer Protection (Distance Selling) Regulations 2000 (SI 2000/2334) (as amended).
- The Electronic Commerce (EC Directive) Regulations 2002 (SI 2002/2013).
- The Cancellation of Contracts made in a Consumer's Home or Place of Work etc Regulations 2008 (SI 2008/1816).

These will be referred to as 'the 1987 Regulations', 'the 2000 Regulations', 'the 2002 Regulations' and 'the 2008 Regulations' respectively. Collectively this group will be referred to as 'the Regulations'. Relevant extracts from these Regulations are given at the end of this chapter.

8.325 At the time of publishing this was an area of the law that was in the process of being clarified, so the reader must carry out his own research to supplement what is in this chapter (including checking that none of the Regulations have been amended).

The general application of the Regulations

8.326 Whilst they may apply in other situations, one or other of the Regulations is likely to apply when a contract of retainer is made during or after the following types of interaction between solicitor and client:

- visits to the client's home;

---

[376]   *Garbutt v Edwards* [2005] EWCA Civ 1206 at [45].
[377]   *Garbutt v Edwards* [2005] EWCA Civ 1206 at [47].

- visits to the home of another person;
- visits to the client's place of work;
- excursions organised by the solicitor away from his offices; and
- negotiations concerning retainers carried out solely over the telephone, by post, or by email.

8.327 There are firms who organise their businesses in such a way that one or other of the Regulations will apply to almost all of their clients; in particular, firms involved in low-value personal injury work will often conduct all of their business over the telephone and by post. Other firms may also find that the Regulations apply when they did not expect this to be so; an example would be where a solicitor who usually sees clients in his offices offers to visit an injured or ill client at his home.

8.328 The above list is simplified and adapted for the purposes of allowing solicitors to take a view of whether they need to carry out further research; the actual applicability of the Regulations turns on many subtleties (see below), and solicitors are urged to read the applicable regulations for themselves.

Legislative background

8.329 The policy underlying the Regulations is consumer protection. That policy is broadly similar for all of the Regulations; the Consumer Protection (Cancellation of Contracts Concluded away from Business Premises) Regulations 1987 and the Cancellation of Contracts made in a Consumer's Home or Place of Work etc Regulations 2008 are taken as being illustrative.

8.330 All of the Regulations have their origins in the European Community. The 1987 Regulations, for example, came into being to give domestic effect to Council Directive 85/577/EEC;[378] this was achieved under the vires of s 2(2) of the European Communities Act 1972, which makes general provision for regulations to be made to implement any European Community obligation of the United Kingdom.[379]

8.331 All but the 2008 Regulations give effect to 'minimum harmonisation directives', in that they seek to reduce the disparity in the way in which different member states deal with consumer contracts made away from business premises. The 2008 Regulations go further than that, in that they deal with certain issues highlighted by a 2002 campaign initiated by the Citizens Advice Bureau; the 2008 Regulations are, therefore, specific to the United Kingdom.

8.332 When Directive 85/577/EEC was initially given domestic effect, it related only to unsolicited visits. As a result of the Citizens Advice Bureau's campaign, the protection afforded to consumers was extended in 2008 to include solicited visits; this was under the vires of ss 59 and 62(3)(f) of the Consumers, Estate Agents and Redress Act 2007. The policy underpinning that extension was explained by Baroness Vadera, Under-Secretary of State of the sponsoring department:[380]

---

[378] Council Directive 85/577/EEC of 20 December 1985 to protect the consumer in respect of contracts negotiated away from business premises [1985] OJ L 372/31.

[379] It is, perhaps, worth noting that in 2008 the European Commission published proposals for a new 'Consumer Rights Directive', which may eventually result in legislation which is less fragmented: see *Consumer Law Bulletin* No 257 (LexisNexis, 2008).

[380] *Hansard*, HL Deb, col GC80 (2 July 2008).

'The purpose of the proposed new regulations is to extend to solicited visits the cooling-off period and cancellation rights that currently apply to contracts made during unsolicited visits by traders; and to require that a notice of the right to cancel the contract be prominently and clearly displayed in the same document where the contract is completed wholly or partly in writing.'

Baroness Vadera went on to explain that certain contracts were excluded because other provisions (such as the Financial Services and Markets Act 2000) were considered adequate and satisfactory.

8.333 Before the Regulations are considered in detail, it is worth addressing the issue of whether they were intended to apply to solicitors.

Application to solicitors

8.334 Whilst the answer is probably that they do apply (see **8.337**), it is far from certain that the Regulations cover solicitors. With the possible exception of the 2002 Regulations it does seem that none of the Regulations was made with solicitors expressly in mind. The recital to Directive 85/577/EEC, for example, includes the following, which illustrates that its main target was trades people such as double-glazing salesmen:

'Whereas the special feature of contracts concluded away from the business premises of the trader is that as a rule it is the trader who initiates the contract negotiations, for which the consumer is unprepared or which he does not except [sic]; whereas the consumer is often unable to compare the quality and price of the offer with other offers; whereas this surprise element generally exists not only in contracts made at the doorstep but also in other forms of contract concluded by the trader away from his business premises.'

Indeed, the Directive used to be referred to as 'the Doorstep Selling Directive',[381] which alludes to an activity that few solicitors engage in.

8.335 Specifically in respect of the 2008 Regulations, during a Parliamentary debate in the House of Lords the sponsoring minister of the 2008 Regulations referred to complaints about home maintenance, improvements, repairs and doubling glazing sales.[382] Moreover, the consultation paper[383] which preceded the 2008 Regulations referred to doorstep selling and cold-calling, the latter of which was prohibited by the Solicitors' Code of Conduct 2007.

8.336 The writer is unable to find any mention in *Hansard* that contracts of retainer were intended to fall within the ambit of the Regulations. The same is true of the minutes of the House of Commons General Committee on Delegated Legislation.[384] In view of this, it would seem that it is possible that Parliament did not consider the prospect that the Regulations would apply to solicitors; this is despite the fact that focus groups did consider it.[385] This apparent failure by Parliament may simply have been a

---

[381] Discussion Paper on the Review of Directive 85/577/EEC, to Protect the Consumer in Respect of Contracts Negotiated Away From Business Premises (Doorstep Selling Directive) (Research Centre for Consumers Organisations, 3 December 2007).
[382] *Hansard*, HL Deb, col GC82 (2 July 2008), Baroness Vadera.
[383] 'Response to the Public Consultation on Doorstep Selling and Cold Calling' (DTI, September 2006).
[384] Second Delegated Legislation Committee, 30 June 2008.
[385] See, for example, CAB 'Door to Door – CAB clients' experience of doorstep selling' (September 2002), p 16.

natural consequence of the fact that most of the Regulations implemented minimum harmonisation directives and, therefore, did not need to be debated at length.

8.337 Notwithstanding the above, Directive 85/577/EEC defines a 'trader' as including a person acting in his professional capacity. This would appear to include solicitors. It is possible that the court will ultimately find that the word 'trader' should be read narrowly, but there are many reasons why the court could do otherwise. The court may, for example, draw an analogy with other putatively excepted contracts which are not expressly stated to be excepted in the Regulations: in those circumstances, the court has given weight to the fact that the Regulations are silent as to the contract in question yet make specific mention of other contracts (see **8.344**).[386] The court may also be persuaded by the principle that derogations from an individual right conferred by Directive 85/577/EEC will rarely be implied and will usually be interpreted narrowly,[387] especially where the right is for the benefit of a consumer.[388] The court may rely on the long-established principle that the nature of the services is barely relevant in that Directive 85/577/EEC is there to protect 'the consumer not because he purchases certain goods but because of the way in which the goods are purchased or the contract concluded'.[389] The court would probably be unsympathetic to an argument that there was uncertainty about the applicability of the Regulations: this is because the ECJ has commented that businesses which are in doubt about whether their activities are covered by Directive 85/577/EEC should take suitable measures to allow them to avoid bearing the consequences of the materialisation of any risks.[390] Exactly what the court will make of the Regulations remains to be seen. The remainder of this discussion is based on the premise that the Regulations do apply to solicitors, but (for the reasons set out at **8.334–8.336**) it is possible that the court will find otherwise.

The 2008 Regulations

8.338 The Cancellation of Contracts made in a Consumer's Home or Place of Work etc Regulations 2008 revoke and replace the Consumer Protection (Cancellation of Contracts Concluded away from Business Premises) Regulations 1987. They also expand the scope of regulatory control to include both solicited and unsolicited visits.

Vires

8.339 Whilst the 1987 Regulations merely gave domestic effect to Council Directive 85/577/EEC, the 2008 Regulations go further in that they address a number of purely domestic concerns. The 2008 Regulations are made under two discrete powers. The first (concerning unsolicited visits) is the vires created by para 2(2) of the European Communities Act 1972, and the second (concerning solicited visits) is the vires created by ss 59 and 62(3)(f) of the Consumers, Estate Agents and Redress Act 2007.

---

[386] This was a point that the ECJ took into account when considering any analogous argument that credit hire agreements should be excluded from the scope of Council Directive 85/577/EEC: see *Heininger and another v Bayerische Hypo und Vereinsbank AG* [2004] All ER (EC) 1 at [30]–[32].

[387] See, for example, *Johnston v Chief Constable of the Royal Ulster Constabulary: Case C-222/84* [1986] 3 All ER 135 at 158.

[388] *Veedfald v Århus Amtskommune Case C-203/99* [2001] ECR I-3569 at [15].

[389] Per Advocate General Alber in *Travel-Vac SL v Antelm Sanchis* [1999] All ER (EC) 656 at 662.

[390] *Schulte and another v Deutsche Bausparkasse Badenia AG* [2006] All ER (EC) 420 at [84]–[103].

8.340 Section 59 of the Consumers, Estate Agents and Redress Act 2007 does need to be set out, however, because it defines the ambit of the power to make purely domestic provisions:

> '(1) The Secretary of State may make regulations entitling a consumer who is a party to a protected contract to cancel the contract.
>
> (2) A protected contract is a contract between a consumer and a trader which is for the supply of goods or services to the consumer by a trader and is made—
>
> > (a) during a solicited visit by a trader to the consumer's home or place of work, or to the home of another individual, or
> > (b) after an offer made by the consumer during such a visit.
>
> (3) A visit is solicited if it is made at the express request of the consumer.
>
> (4) Regulations made under this section may make any provision which may be made by regulations under section 2(2) of the European Communities Act 1972 (c 68) (by virtue of section 2(4) of that Act).
>
> (5) The regulations may in particular make provision—
>
> > (a) as to the circumstances in which the consumer may cancel the contract and the effect of such a cancellation;
> > (b) requiring the trader to inform the consumer of the matters within paragraph (a);
> > (c) for the enforcement of any requirement imposed by virtue of paragraph (b).
>
> (6) For the purposes of this section, "consumer" and "trader" in relation to a contract have the same meaning as they have for the purposes of the relevant Directive in relation to transactions within that Directive.
>
> (7) "The relevant Directive" means—
>
> > (a) Council Directive 85/577/EEC to protect the consumer in respect of contracts negotiated away from business premises, as it has effect from time to time, or
> > (b) if that Directive is repealed and re-enacted (with or without modification), that Directive as re-enacted.'

Section 59 refers to 'consumers' and 'traders'; the definitions of these words are discussed below.

8.341 Section 62(3)(f) is merely a procedural provision which requires that regulations modifying any Act must be laid before Parliament.

Application

8.342 The 2008 Regulations do not apply to contracts which were made before 1 October 2008;[391] those contracts were governed, if at all, by the 1987 Regulations (see **8.364**).

8.343 Section 59 of the Consumers, Estate Agents and Redress Act 2007 defines 'consumer' and 'trader' by reference to Directive 85/577/EEC; that definition is given at Art 2 of that Directive:

> '–   "consumer" means a natural person who, in transactions covered by this Directive, is acting for purposes which can be regarded as outside his trade or profession;

---

[391] See Cancellation of Contracts made in a Consumer's Home or Place of Work etc Regulations 2008 (SI 2008/1816), reg 4(3).

- "trader" means a natural or legal person who, for the transaction in question, acts in his commercial or professional capacity, and anyone acting in the name or on behalf of a trader.'

The 2008 Regulations themselves include similar definitions at reg 2(1):

"'consumer" means a natural person who in making a contract to which these Regulations apply is acting for purposes which can be regarded as outside his trade or profession;

...

"'trader" means a person who, in making a contract to which these Regulations apply, is acting in his commercial or professional capacity and anyone acting in the name or on behalf of a trader.'

Thus, subject to the court finding that an unusually narrow definition of any of the relevant terms should apply (see **8.334–8.337**), the 2008 Regulations would apply where a solicitor supplies services to a natural person[392] who is not acting in the course of his trade or profession. There is, however, scope for arguing that these conditions will not be met if the supply of legal services is for a purpose which is connected with a person's trade or profession;[393] whilst there is no authority on the point, it is possible that this includes the situation where legal services are provided both to a client and to a funder, such as an insurer or a union.[394] Whilst he was addressing legislation which was only analogous to the Regulations,[395] Field J has found that where there are two linked contracts (a principal contract and contract which is ancillary to the principal contract), both must have been executed as a consumer for the Regulations to apply;[396] again, this may be of relevance where, for example, the retainer is formed ancillary to a contract of insurance or a contract of union membership.

8.344 Certain contracts are expressly excepted from the 2008 Regulations; whilst many of those contracts are, like retainers, subject to other forms of regulatory control, retainers are not amongst those which are excepted.[397] However, Sch 3, para 6 does except the following:

'Any contract not falling within paragraph 5 under which the total payments to be made by the consumer do not exceed £35.'

It may be the case that some conditional fee agreements fall within this category; in particular, this might include agreements which do not permit the solicitor in any circumstances to recover monies from his client beyond those which are recovered from the opponent. There is, however, no authority on this point, and the counter-arguments are easy to muster.

---

[392] This would seem not to include a person in a partnership, association or co-operative: see *Case C-215/08 E Friz GmbH v Carsten von der Heyden*, opinion of 8 September 2009 (unreported), AG Trstenjak.

[393] *Bayerische Hypothetken v Dietzinger: Case C-45/96* [1998] 1 WLR 1035 at [18]–[23], where the ECJ found that guaranteed repayment of a debt contracted by another person who, for his part, was active within the course of his trade or profession was sufficient to disapply Directive 85/577. See also *Barclays Bank plc v Kufner* [2008] EWHC 2319 (Comm) at [28], per Field J.

[394] That said, the ECJ has held that a contract which benefits a stranger standing outside the contract is not excluded from the scope of the directive on the sole ground that the benefit of the contract is intended for the use of that third party: see *Bayerische Hypothetken v Dietzinger: Case C-45/96* [1998] 1 WLR 1035.

[395] Unfair Terms in Consumer Contracts Regulations 1999.

[396] *Barclays Bank plc v Kufner* [2008] EWHC 2319 (Comm) at [28], per Field J.

[397] SI 2008/1816, reg 6.

8.345 The 2008 Regulations will apply to a contract which is made in the following circumstances:[398]

- during a visit by the trader to the consumer's home or place of work, or to the home of another individual;
- during an excursion organised by the trader away from his business premises; and
- after an offer made by the consumer during such a visit or excursion.

If one draws an analogy with cases concerning salesmen, the mere fact that a solicitor habitually visits a place (such as a union's offices) will not make that place his place of business.[399] There is no definition of 'excursion' within the 2008 Regulations, but the ECJ has found that where, in order to present the products and services he was offering, a trader invited a consumer to go to a specified place which was different from the premises where the trader usually carried on his business, any resulting contract had to be considered to have been concluded 'during an excursion organised by the trader';[400] therefore, the meaning of 'excursion' does not seem to be limited to activities which use travel as a leisure activity, such as coach trips, holidays, etc.

8.346 If a retainer is signed by both parties during the visit or excursion, then it will usually be clear that the retainer was made during that visit or excursion, but it is often the case that the retainer will not be signed by both parties at the same time. In particular, it is commonly the case that solicitors engage agents to obtain a signature during a home visit, but that the solicitor will sign it only once he has telephoned the client to explain the terms of the retainer and to enquire about alternative means of funding. If those are the circumstances, then it is arguable that what appeared to be an offer was, in truth, an invitation to treat. It may be argued that the negotiations carried out during the visit or excursion were merely the parties feeling their way to agreement as to the retainer; it could then be argued that no proposal was made during that visit or excursion which was capable of acceptance.

8.347 Although there is no authority on the point, that situation would be similar to circumstances in which a retail pharmacist advertises a medicine for sale in his shop, but the contract for sale can be concluded only once the pharmacist – a professional overseeing the transaction, just like a solicitor overseeing a retainer – decides that the sale should proceed; in those circumstances, the offer is made only when the sale is allowed to proceed.[401]

8.348 Whilst the 2008 Regulations draw a distinction between solicited and unsolicited visits, that distinction is not likely to be relevant to solicitors or their retainers (this being because the distinction matters only in respect of certain specified types of contracts, and that group does not include contracts of retainer).[402]

8.349 There is only limited scope to contract out of the provisions of the 2008 Regulations. In particular, any contractual term will be void if it is inconsistent with a regulatory provision for the protection of the consumer. This will be so where the

---

[398]   SI 2008/1816, reg 5.
[399]   See *In the matter of Tag World Services Ltd* [2008] EWHC 1866 (Ch) at [24].
[400]   *Travel-Vac SL v Antelm Sanchis* [1999] All ER (D) 408.
[401]   See *Pharmaceutical Society of Great Britain v Boots Cash Chemists (Southern) Ltd* [1953] 1 QB 401.
[402]   See SI 2008/1816, reg 6(d).

contractual term purports to impose an additional or different duty or liability on the consumer from those specified in the 2008 Regulations.[403]

The effect of compliance with the 2008 Regulations

8.350 Where there has been compliance with the 2008 Regulations, the retainer will not be unenforceable for want of compliance, but the client will have the right to cancel it during 'the cancellation period', which is 7 days.[404]

8.351 A cancelled retainer will be treated as if it had never been entered into by the client. A cancellation notice sent by post is taken to have been served at the time of posting, whether or not it is actually received. Where a cancellation notice is sent by email, it is taken to have been served on the day on which it was sent.[405]

8.352 Where a client enters into a 'specified contract' (the definition of which includes contracts of retainer) and where he wishes the solicitor to start work before the end of the cancellation period, he must request this in writing.[406] If the client subsequently cancels the retainer, he must 'pay in accordance with the reasonable requirements of the cancelled contract for ... services that were supplied before the cancellation'.[407] If the contract is a conditional fee agreement, it would be sensible to include such a provision so as to avoid the counterparties falling into a dispute about whether payment would be due in those circumstances.

8.353 If the client does not confirm that he wishes his solicitor to begin work immediately, and if he cancels the contract within the cancellation period, the solicitor will not be able to recover any fees. It is not permissible for the solicitor to charge a penalty or lump sum upon renunciation of the contract.[408]

8.354 Where a contract is cancelled, any monies paid on account are refundable, and any securities taken in respect of fees will be treated as never having been taken.[409] The provisions concerning payments on account permit the solicitor to deduct payment for services already rendered, but the same is not true of securities, which must be returned in whole. This, presumably, applies to lien, charging orders, and security for costs taken pursuant to SA 1974, s 65(1).

8.355 Cancellation of the retainer will have the effect of cancelling any related credit agreement (such as a disbursements funding loan).[410] Where this happens, the solicitor must tell the creditor, and any monies paid by the client must be reimbursed. There are also provisions concerning interest which are dependent on the nature of the credit agreement;[411] those provisions are beyond the scope of this book.

---

[403] SI 2008/1816, reg 15.
[404] SI 2008/1816, reg 7(1) and 2.
[405] SI 2008/1816, reg 8.
[406] SI 2008/1816, reg 9.
[407] SI 2008/1816, reg 9(2).
[408] *Travel-Vac SL v Antelm Sanchis* [1999] All ER (D) 408.
[409] SI 2008/1816, reg 10.
[410] SI 2008/1816, reg 11(1).
[411] SI 2008/1816, reg 12.

The requirements of the 2008 Regulations

8.356   Where the 2008 Regulations apply, the following requirements must be satisfied:

- The solicitor must give the client a written notice of his right to cancel the retainer; that notice must be given at the time the retainer is made, or, if the contract is made after the visit or excursion, at the time the offer is made.[412]
- That notice must:[413]
  - be dated;
  - indicate the right of the consumer to cancel the contract within the cancellation period;
  - be easily legible;
  - contain the following information: the identity of the solicitor, including trading name, if any; the solicitor's reference, code or other details to enable the contract or offer to be identified;
  - contain a cancellation form in the manner set out in Part II of Sch 4 of the 2008 Regulations, provided as a detachable slip and completed by or on behalf of the trader in accordance with the notes;
  - contain the name and address (including any electronic mail address as well as the postal address) of the person to whom a cancellation notice may be given;
  - contain a statement that the consumer has a right to cancel the contract if he wishes and that this right can be exercised by delivering, or sending (including by electronic mail) a cancellation notice to the person mentioned above at any time within the period of 7 days starting with the day of receipt of a notice in writing of the right to cancel the contract;
  - contain a statement that notice of cancellation is deemed to be served as soon as it is posted or sent to a trader or, in the case of an electronic communication, from the day it is sent to the trader;
  - contain a statement that the consumer can use the cancellation form provided, if he wishes;
  - indicate, if applicable, that the consumer may be required to pay for the services supplied if services are provided with his written agreement before the end of the cancellation period; and
  - indicate, if applicable, that a related credit agreement (such as a disbursement funding loan) will be automatically cancelled if the retainer is cancelled.

The notice mentioned above must be incorporated into the written instrument of retainer.[414] It must be set out in a separate box with the heading 'Notice of the Right to Cancel'. It must also have as much prominence as any other information in the retainer, apart from the heading and the names of the solicitor and client and any information inserted in handwriting.[415]

8.357   For the reasons set out at **8.352**, a solicitor who seeks to be paid for services provided prior to cancellation must ensure that the client has confirmed that fact in writing.

---

[412]   SI 2008/1816, reg 7(2).
[413]   SI 2008/1816, reg 7(3) and Sch 4.
[414]   SI 2008/1816, reg 7(4).
[415]   SI 2008/1816, reg 7(5).

Non-compliance with the 2008 Regulations

8.358 Regulation 7(6) of the 2008 Regulations reads as follows:

> 'A contract to which these Regulations apply shall not be enforceable against the consumer unless the trader has given the consumer a notice of the right to cancel and the information required in accordance with this regulation.'

This provision (which is the only provision in the 2008 Regulations concerning enforceability of the retainer) appears to be more subtle and specific than a bare statement that non-compliance will result in the contract being unenforceable. It remains to be seen how the court will deal with the issue, but it might be that it will overlook minor failings to give information in the exact form required by the 2008 Regulations in the sense that the court will look for substantial compliance rather than absolute compliance. Indeed, it is possible that the court will apply some form of test of materiality, akin to that which applies to putative breaches of the Conditional Fee Agreements Regulations 2000 (SI 2000/692). In this regard it is worth bearing in mind that the ECJ has confirmed that Arts 4 and 5 of Directive 85/577/EEC allowed member states some latitude regarding consumer protection when information on the right of cancellation was not provided by the trader and in determining the time limit and conditions of cancellation; nonetheless, the court commented that that latitude did not affect the precise and unconditional nature of the provisions of the Directive, or make it impossible to determine minimum rights.[416] It would, for example, not be open to the court to find that the effluxion of time negated the client's right to claim the benefit of Directive 85/577/EEC.[417]

8.359 Non-compliance is a criminal offence, but such issues are beyond the scope of this book. A defence of due diligence may apply.

The 2008 Regulations between the parties

8.360 It is not yet known whether the court will require a paying party to make out a 'genuine issue' before that party can challenge compliance with the 2008 Regulations. In support of this proposition is the fact that unlike regs 2, 3 and 5 of the Conditional Fee Agreements Regulations 2000, the issues that a receiving party's solicitor would need to certify would be almost exclusively factual issues. This means that there are grounds for distinguishing the train of thought that led Brooke LJ to conclude that there is no need for the court to find a 'genuine issue' before permitting the paying party to raise a challenge in respect of those regulations.[418] Indeed, to this extent compliance with the 2008 Regulations seems to be comparable to compliance with reg 4 of the Conditional Fee Agreements Regulations 2000, in respect of which a paying party must make out a 'genuine issue' if he is to bring a successful challenge.

8.361 What is also not clear is whether a receiving party is obliged to lodge documents proving compliance with the 2008 Regulations at court pursuant to CPD, art 40.2(i). This is because that provision requires lodging of documents 'explaining how the solicitor's charges are to be calculated'; it is a moot point whether cancellation notices, etc fall within this category. Given the fact that the cancellation notice must be in the

---

[416] *Faccini Dori v Recreb Srl* [1995] All ER (EC) 1.
[417] See, by analogy, the comments of *Advocate General Léger in Heininger and another v Bayerische Hypo und Vereinsbank AG* [2004] All ER (EC) 1 at [60]–[65]. Compare this with *Annelore Hamilton v Volksbank Filder eG*, Case C-412/06 [2008] ECR I-2383, ECJ at [46], however, where the ECJ distinguished *Heininger*.
[418] *Hollins v Russell* [2003] 1 WLR 2487 at [51]–[87].

same written instrument as the retainer, it is difficult to see how a receiving party could avoid lodging it, or, more importantly, avoid the court knowing that the notice is not where it should be.

8.362 There is no reason in principle why a paying party should not put CPR, Part 18 requests to a receiving party, but whether a receiving party would be required to answer those requests would be in the discretion of the court, to be decided on the facts of the case.

8.363 If a receiving party's solicitor knows that he is in breach of the requirements of the 2008 Regulations, and if he knows that as a result of that breach the retainer is unenforceable, then it would be improper for that solicitor to certify a bill of costs if that bill gives the contrary impression. Care should be taken in this regard, as improperly miscertifying a bill of costs is a serious disciplinary offence.[419] If a solicitor is in doubt about an issue such as this, he would do well to take specialist advice.

The 1987 Regulations

8.364 The Consumer Protection (Cancellation of Contracts Concluded away from Business Premises) Regulations 1987 came into force on 1 July 1988. On 1 October 2008 they were revoked and replaced by the 2008 Regulations. Transitional provisions apply: the 1987 Regulations continue to have effect in relation to a contracts of retainer entered into before 1 October 2008.[420] Accordingly, the 1987 Regulations apply to retainers made between 1 July 1988 and 1 October 2008.

Application

8.365 The 1987 Regulations are similar to the 2008 Regulations, but with one important difference: they appear not to apply to solicited visits.

8.366 In the context of costs, an 'unsolicited visit' is defined in the 1987 Regulations as meaning a visit by a solicitor, whether or not he is the solicitor who supplies the services, which does not take place at the express request of the client; it includes a visit which takes place after a solicitor telephones the client (otherwise than at his express request) indicating expressly or by implication that he is willing to visit the client.[421]

8.367 These circumstances would be a common occurrence in some firms, an example being where a solicitor offers during a telephone call to see a sick or injured client at home. Indeed, some high-volume personal injury firms have made it their policy that every client would be offered a home visit. It would seem, therefore, that many home visits (whether carried out by solicitors or agents) will be classified as being unsolicited visits.

---

[419]   *Bailey v IBC Vehicles Ltd* [1998] 3 All ER 570.
[420]   SI 2008/1816, reg 4(2).
[421]   SI 1987/2117, reg 3(3); this definition is one of the few things that is different from the corresponding provision in the 2008 Regulations.

8.368 Other than the fact that the visit must be unsolicited, the circumstances in which the 1987 Regulations apply are similar to those in which the 2008 Regulations apply.[422] The 1987 Regulations applied to excursions, regardless of whether they were solicited.

Requirements

8.369 A difference between the 1987 Regulations and the 2008 Regulations is that the requirements of the later Regulations were more onerous; this is a reflection of the fact that one of the reasons for introducing the 2008 Regulations was to increase the prominence of the information given to consumers.[423]

8.370 The requirements of the 1987 Regulations are as follows:[424]

- The client must be given a notice in writing which indicates the right to cancel the contract of retainer within 7 days.
- The notice shall be easily legible and if incorporated in the retainer or other document shall be afforded no less prominence than that given to any other information in the document, apart from the heading and the names of the parties to the contract and any information inserted in handwriting.
- The notice shall be dated and delivered to the client at the time the retainer is made or, if the contract is made after the visit or excursion, at the time the offer is made.
- The notice must contain:
  - the name of the solicitor;
  - the solicitor's reference number, code or other details to enable the retainer or offer to be identified;
  - the name and address of a person to whom notice of cancellation may be given;
  - a statement that the client has a right to cancel the contract if he wishes and that this right can be exercised by sending or taking a written notice of cancellation to the person mentioned above within the period of 7 days following the making of the retainer;
  - a statement that the consumer can use the cancellation form provided, if he wishes.
- A Cancellation Form in the form set out in Part II of the Schedule to the 1987 Regulations and completed in accordance with the footnotes.

The effect of compliance

8.371 In so far as unsolicited visits are concerned, the effect of the 1987 Regulations was almost identical to that of the 2008 Regulations. To this extent, the things set out in the section above are repeated. Likewise, the effect of cancellation is much the same as under the 2008 Regulations.

---

[422] There is one further circumstance, which concerns the client not knowing the trader's business, but it would almost never be the case that this would apply to solicitors (SI 1987/2117, reg 3(1)(b)) and can, therefore, be ignored for present purposes.

[423] *Hansard*, HL Deb, col GC80 (2 July 2008).

[424] SI 1987/2117, reg 4 and Schedule, Parts I and II.

The effect of non-compliance

8.372 The effect of non-compliance with the 1987 Regulations is broadly the same as that of non-compliance with the 2008 Regulations. The relevant provision reads:[425]

> 'No contract to which these Regulations apply shall be enforceable against the consumer unless the trader has delivered to the consumer notice in writing in accordance with paragraphs (3) and (4) below [ie shall be legible and delivered] indicating the right of the consumer to cancel the contract within the period of 7 days mentioned in paragraph (5) below containing both the information set out in Part I [ie the things set out above] of the Schedule to these Regulations and a Cancellation Form in the form set out in Part II of the Schedule and completed in accordance with the footnotes.'

Remedial action by receiving parties

8.373 To a large extent, the profession failed to pay attention to the 1987 Regulations until 2009, by which stage they had been revoked. Some standard terms and conditions do contain the requisite provisions, but (in the writer's experience) this tends to be the case only with firms that do commercial work. Even then, it is rare for retainers to include the requisite Cancellation Notice.

8.374 Where a claim has been concluded, most receiving parties may have little option but to rely on the arguments implied in the general discussion above. Where, however, the case has not concluded, it may be possible to take other steps. If a claimant-based firm finds itself in difficulties in respect of their retainers, they should consider:

- obtaining detailed evidence as to what exactly was discussed during home visits and/or initial telephone calls;
- obtaining detailed evidence as to what exactly was said during follow-up telephone calls;
- taking a view as to whether it can be said with reasonable certainty that no offers (as opposed to invitations to treat) were made during those visits and/or telephone calls;
- entering into bespoke retrospective retainers, but only where appropriate;
- recasting the retainers going forward, but only where appropriate;
- changing the way in which retainers are made, and considering terminating the use of agents;
- how best to discharge the obligations under CPD, art 40.2(i);
- a strategy in relation to 'genuine issues', certificates, disclosure and election pursuant to CPD, art 40.14;
- whether publicity material (such as websites) needs to be altered to reduce the risk of 'genuine issues' being proved;
- ADR in appropriate cases; and
- carrying out a risk assessment in relation to costs awaiting payment.

8.375 Recast and new retainers may be conditional fee agreements and are usually 'CFAs Lite'. This is not always the case, however; contentious business agreements and other non-conditional retainers have also been used.

8.376 Where a client is asked to enter into a new retainer, the receiving party's solicitor needs to take care to ensure that the paying party is not given the opportunity to argue

---

[425] SI 1987/2117, reg 4(1).

that the new retainer is, in reality, merely a continuation of the original retainer. Thought also ought to be given to the need for independent legal advice.

The 2000 Regulations

8.377 The Consumer Protection (Distance Selling) Regulations 2000 came into force on 31 October 2000, and were significantly amended on 6 April 2005; they implement Directive 97/7/EC.[426] In effect, they provide for a cooling-off period during which the client can cancel the retainer; where this happens, the retainer will be treated as if it had not been made.

8.378 For most purposes the relevance of the 2000 Regulations is that where a solicitor has failed to inform the client that the retainer may last more than 30 days, the retainer could, arguably, be rendered void *ab initio*. This, however, is on a strict reading of the 2000 Regulations, and there is no authority to confirm that this will happen in practice.

Application

8.379 The 2000 Regulations apply to retainers which are made exclusively by means of distance communication. Such arrangements are commonplace in low-value personal injury work. In so far as solicitors are concerned, distance communication is likely to include letters, telephone attendances, video attendances, email, and facsimile.[427] The use of distance communication must be exclusive: ie up to and including the moment at which the retainer is made, distance communication must have been the only means by which the solicitor communicated with the client.[428]

Requirements

8.380 The 2000 Regulations require the solicitor to provide the client with certain information. In so far as it relates to the provision of legal services, the requirements are as follows:

- In the case of a telephone communication, the identity of the solicitor and the commercial purpose of the call shall be made clear at the beginning of the conversation with the client.[429]
- The solicitor shall provide the following:[430]
  - the identity of the solicitors and, where the retainer requires payment in advance, the solicitor's address, including the address to which complaints should be made;[431]
  - a description of the main characteristics of the services to be provided;
  - the price of the services, including all taxes;
  - the arrangements for payment, delivery or performance;
  - the existence of a right of cancellation, and the conditions in which that right may be exercised;[432]
  - the period for which the offer of services remains valid.

---

[426] Directive 97/7/EC of the European Parliament and the Council of 20 May 1997 (OJ No L144, 4.6.97), p 19.
[427] Consumer Protection (Distance Selling) Regulations 2000 (SI 2000/2334), Sch 1.
[428] SI 2000/2334, reg 3(1) and 4.
[429] SI 2000/2334, reg 7(4).
[430] SI 2000/2334, reg 7(1)(a).
[431] SI 2000/2334, reg 8(2)(c).
[432] SI 2000/2334, reg 8(2)(e).

- The solicitor shall ensure that the information as set out above is provided in a clear and comprehensible manner appropriate to the means of distance communication used, with due regard in particular to the principles of good faith in commercial transactions and the principles governing the protection of those who are unable to give their consent, such as minors.[433]
- The solicitor shall ensure that his commercial purpose is made clear when providing the information required above.[434]

The information mentioned above must be supplied in writing or in another durable medium, and must be given either prior to the conclusion of the retainer (ie before the retainer is made) or in good time thereafter. In any event, it must be given prior to the termination of the retainer.[435]

8.381 Where a solicitor has begun work on a client's case, it would be a generous solicitor who would be willing to allow the contract to be cancelled without being paid for that work. The provisions relating to pre-cancellation work changed on 6 April 2005:

- *Pre-2005*: Where the solicitor wants to be paid for pre-cancellation work, then the client must be told in writing or other durable medium that he will not be able to cancel the retainer once work has begun.[436] The client's agreement to this provision will be implied by the client giving instructions to begin work.[437] (The client will, of course, still be able to terminate the retainer in the usual way.)
- *Post-2005*:[438] After that date the solicitor must inform the client in writing or other durable medium that if the client agrees to services starting within what otherwise would have been the cancellation period, the right to cancel will be lost. Where a solicitor provides that information before beginning work and where the client agrees to work beginning before the expiry of the cancellation period, there is no right to cancel.[439]

Other than as set out above, there shall be no contracting-out of the provisions of the 2000 Regulations.[440]

8.382 Unless there is agreement to the contrary, the solicitor must perform the retainer (ie finish his work) within 30 days of the retainer being made. For obvious reasons, this will rarely be possible. The 2000 Regulations provide that if there is no agreement that the work will take longer than 30 days and if the contract is not performed within 30 days, then, from the solicitor's point of view, the retainer will be treated as if it had not been made. With most retainers to which the 2000 Regulations apply, a failure to agree that the solicitor's work will take longer than 30 days may lead to difficulties in proving compliance with the indemnity principle. There is, however, no authority to confirm that the court will apply the 2000 Regulations in such a harsh way.[441]

---

[433] SI 2000/2334, reg 7(2).
[434] SI 2000/2334, reg 7(3).
[435] SI 2000/2334, reg 8.
[436] SI 2000/2334, reg 8(3).
[437] SI 2000/2334, reg 13(1)(a).
[438] The Consumer Protection (Distance Selling) (Amendment) Regulations 2005.
[439] SI 2000/2334, regs 8, 12 and 13, as amended.
[440] SI 2000/2334, reg 25.
[441] SI 2000/2334, reg 19.

Cancellation

8.383 The cancellation period varies depending on the circumstances; for the reasons set out above, however, after 6 April 2005 where there has been full compliance with the 2000 Regulations and where work has begun with the client's agreement during what otherwise would have been the cancellation period, the right to cancel is lost.

Full compliance

8.384 Where the requirements set out above have been complied with prior to the retainer being made, the cancellation period ends on the expiry of the period of 7 working days beginning with the day after the day on which the contract is concluded. (A 'working day' is defined as all days other than Saturdays, Sundays and public holidays.)[442]

Late compliance

8.385 In most circumstances,[443] if those requirements are met late, then the cancellation period ends on the expiry of the period of 7 working days beginning with the day after the day on which the client receives the requisite information. After 6 April 2005, however, if the work has been completed within 7 working days of the retainer being made, then the cancellation period ends on the date that work is completed.[444]

No compliance

8.386 In all other circumstances (ie where the requisite information is not given) the cancellation period ends on the expiry of the period of 3 months and 7 working days beginning with the day after the day on which the contract is concluded.[445]

Notice of cancellation

8.387 If the client gives notice of cancellation during the cancellation period, that notice shall operate to cancel the retainer. The retainer will be treated as if it had never been made.[446] The client will not be able to cancel the retainer if the solicitor has given notice prohibiting cancellation (see above).

8.388 Notice of cancellation may be given by post, fax, or email. Where the evidence is that it was sent by post, it is regarded as having been given regardless of whether it was received.[447]

8.389 If the retainer is cancelled, any sums paid on account must be returned, as must any securities which have been taken.[448] Any related credit agreement (such as a disbursement funding loan) may be automatically cancelled;[449] special provisions apply which are beyond the scope of this book.

---

[442] SI 2000/2334, regs 12(2) and 2(1).
[443] Where work has begun within the initial 7-day period, see SI 2000/2334, reg 12(3)(a).
[444] After 2005, see SI 2000/2334, reg 13(1)(a).
[445] SI 2000/2334, reg 12.
[446] SI 2000/2334, reg 10.
[447] SI 2000/2334, reg 10(4).
[448] SI 2000/2334, reg 14.
[449] SI 2000/2334, reg 15.

Failure to give the requisite information

8.390 Where the solicitor fails to provide the requisite information in accordance with the 2000 Regulations, the cancellation period is extended by 3 months. Unlike the other Regulations (and subject to what is set out above about the need to give notice of the time that the work will take), the retainer will not be unenforceable for want of compliance.

8.391 If a retainer has been cancelled in circumstances in which the solicitor has failed to give notice of the effect of beginning work during the first 7 days of the retainer (see above), then it is arguable that the solicitor is entitled to quantum meruit; this would be on the basis that the effect of cancellation is not to make the retainer unenforceable (in which case an action in quantum meruit would not lie), but to cancel the retainer *ab initio*. In those circumstances (ie valuable services being provided in the absence of a contract), the court might be willing to find that the solicitor is entitled to quantum meruit. However, whilst not directly on point, the comments of Schiemann LJ in *Awwad v Geragthy & Co*[450] would present the solicitor with some difficulties. These issues are discussed in more detail at **11.77–11.84**.

Remedial action in respect of the 2000 Regulations

8.392 As with the other Regulations, many solicitors have failed to heed the 2000 Regulations until as late as 2009. This is despite the fact that trade journals mentioned their relevance as early as March 2001.[451]

8.393 Generally speaking, many of the requirements will be met in most instances, even where the solicitor was unaware of the 2000 Regulations. This, however, is subject to a noteworthy exception: if the solicitor has failed to inform the client that the retainer may last more than 30 days, the retainer could, arguably, be rendered void *ab initio* (see above).

8.394 If a solicitor discovers that he has failed to comply with the 2000 Regulations, there are a number of remedial actions that could be considered; they include (but are not limited to):

- immediately giving the requisite information;
- ensuring that the client is given the requisite notices, which may be a notice that the client may not cancel the retainer and a notice that the work will take more than 30 days;
- entering into bespoke retrospective retainers, but only where appropriate;
- recasting the retainers going forward, but only where appropriate;
- considering changing the way in which retainers are made, and considering terminating the use of distance methods;
- considering how best to discharge the obligations under CPD, art 40.2(i);
- considering a strategy in relation to 'genuine issues', certificates, disclosure and election pursuant to CPD, art 40.14;
- considering whether publicity material (such as websites) needs to be altered to reduce the risk of 'genuine issues' being proven;
- considering ADR in appropriate cases; and

---

[450] [2001] QB 570 at 596.
[451] S Singleton 'Cancelling contracts with solicitors' (2001) 145 SJ 9, pp 204–206; and N Laver 'Going the Distance' (2001) 98 LSG 22, pp 30–31.

• carrying out a risk assessment in relation to costs awaiting payment.

The 2002 Regulations

8.395 The Electronic Commerce (EC Directive) Regulations 2002 are dealt with only briefly because they are highly specialised regulations which will apply to only a small number of firms. Broadly speaking, in so far as costs work are concerned, they may apply where a firm sells its services on the internet or by email, and where those services are themselves provided in this way. An example might include internet-based conveyancing.

8.396 The 2002 Regulations do not apply to the activities of a public notary or equivalent to the extent that those activities involve a direct and specific connection with the exercise of public authority.[452] They will also not apply to a retainer for defence.[453]

8.397 The 2002 Regulations give domestic effect to the provisions of Directive 2000/31/EC;[454] the purpose of that directive is to ensure free movement of 'information society services' across the European Community.

8.398 The 2002 Regulations provide that general information be given to the client; this includes: the name of the solicitors; the solicitors' geographical address; contact details; details of registration with the Law Society; details of how to access the prevailing Code of Conduct; and the solicitors' VAT number.

8.399 Specific information also has to be given; this includes information about the technical steps which must be taken to conclude the retainer and the means for identifying and correcting input errors.

8.400 Where some of these things are not done, the client will have the right to rescind the retainer, subject to the court ordering otherwise.[455] Where the court is conducting a solicitor and client assessment, this could result in the court finding that no costs are payable.

8.401 The same is not likely to be true when the court is carrying out a between the parties assessment. The extent to which a paying party would be able to rely on the 2002 Regulations for the purposes of proving a breach of the indemnity principle are probably significantly restricted, this being for the reasons given by Arden LJ in *Garbutt v Edwards*.[456] This topic is discussed at **8.268–8.275**.

RETAINERS INVOLVING MORE THAN ONE CLIENT

8.402 The principal focus of this section is on retainers in which two or more clients have given instructions for their own purposes. This is to be distinguished from retainers where a person has agreed to pay or is otherwise obliged to pay for legal services to be rendered to someone else: that issue is briefly considered at **8.432–8.434**.

---

[452] Electronic Commerce (EC Directive) Regulations 2002 (SI 2002/2013), reg 3(1).
[453] SI 2002/2013, reg 3.
[454] OJ L 178, 17 July 2000, p 1.
[455] SI 2002/2013, reg 15.
[456] [2005] EWCA Civ 1206 at [35] *et seq*.

Joint obligations

8.403 A retainer may take in more than one client in one of two ways: expressly and impliedly.

Express

8.404 The retainer may expressly refer to more than one client, either in a single document which refers to all of the client counterparties, or by way of a number of documents which refer to only one client each but which are expressly linked so as to form a collective whole. An example of the latter would be where a number of seemingly separate retainers in group litigation are expressly linked by an overarching fee-sharing agreement.

Implied

8.405 In contrast, the inclusion of more than one client may arise by implication. The context in which this usually arises is where several seemingly separate documents are implicitly linked in such a way that must each be read in the context of the others. An example would be where co-litigants each have their own retainer, but where their instructions are to incur costs which are to be shared amongst them.

Plurality of debtors

8.406 Regardless of the mechanism by which a retainer takes in more than one client, the retainer will be such that there will be a plurality of debtors. Where this is the case, there will be joint obligations. The law of joint obligations is not beyond criticism; in 1949 Glanville Williams remarked on the subject:[457]

> 'This [work] discusses a difficult and seriously defective part of the common law ... I do not suppose any lawyer can read the pages that follow without astonishment that the law can be so involved, inconvenient and unjust.'

Modern commentators much more learned than the writer have confirmed that this comment is still apposite today,[458] so the treatise here should only be regarded as a general overview of the topic; further legal research may be required in more demanding cases.

The nature of obligations where there is a plurality of debtors

8.407 Where there is a plurality of debtors (who in the present contest will be the clients), the obligation to discharge the debt may be joint, joint and several, or several. The nature of the obligation is a question of contractual interpretation, but some general rules can be discerned from the authorities. As with any form of contractual interpretation, the 'matrix of fact' will be relevant; in the context of retainers, two things will be particularly relevant: the nature of the instructions, and the nature of the subject matter of the instructions.

---

[457] GL Williams *Joint Obligations: a treatise on joint and joint and several liability in contract, quasi-contract and trusts in England* (Butterworth & Co, 1949).

[458] R Brownsword *Common Law Series: The Law of Contract* (LexisNexis Butterworths, 2007), para 6.336.

8.408 It is worth pausing here to consider the types of obligations that can arise when there is a plurality of debtors. Obligations can be 'several', in which case the debtor will be individually liable for his costs or his share of the costs. At the other end of the spectrum, the liability may be 'joint', in which case there would be only one obligation to pay costs, and that obligation would be owed by all the clients: the main advantage (from the solicitor's point of view) is that he would be able to recover the whole of his costs from any solvent client. Between these two extremes the liability may be 'joint and several', in which case there would be joint and individual promises to pay costs. These topics are covered in detail Chapter 12. which focuses on orders for costs between opposing parties, but the general principles are the same when the issue arises between solicitors and clients. For present purposes, however, it is necessary only to know that these three categories of obligation exist.

8.409 Contracts of retainer may contain more than one category of obligation to pay a solicitor's fees.[459] This is because the nature of the obligation to pay costs may vary depending on the task which was being undertaken. This is why costs may be categorised as being 'common costs' and 'individual costs',[460] and why the former would be apportioned in a bill of costs, whereas the latter would not. This is a topic which is dealt with in detail in Chapter 12 and (in the context of group litigation) Chapter 38.

8.410 Whether the obligation is joint, joint and several, or several will depend on the wording of the contract of retainer. There are two other factors that may be of relevance: first, the nature of instructions (ie whether the instructions were given jointly or separately) and, secondly, the nature of the subject matter of the instructions (ie whether the interest that the clients have in the matter is joint or several). Whilst these are only two factors against many, the following is a possible classification (which is only an invention of the writer, and which ought not to be given a status any greater than it deserves).

Separate instructions in separate matters

8.411 This situation would occur when the client's interests in the subject matter of the retainer are separate and where the instructions are also separate. For obvious reasons, it will usually follow that that client will bear the full liability for the costs incurred and that the obligation to pay will be several[461] (unless, of course, the retainer provides otherwise). Chadwick LJ has commented that this principle will apply where separate clients give separate instructions on discrete issues which can be said to be separate.[462]

Separate instructions in joint matters

8.412 This situation is dealt with in detail at **8.417–8.426**; in essence, it will arise where persons who are otherwise unconnected instruct a solicitor who then carries out work which is of benefit to all of them. An example is where several claimants pursue a claim based on similar facts against a single defendant and where the retainers are, on the face

---

[459] See *Bayliss v Kelly and Ors* [1997] 2 Costs LR 54 at 59, in which Chadwick LJ distinguished between the costs of issues in the context of the client's liability potentially being dealt with according to the issue involved.

[460] In the context of group litigation, see CPR, r 48.6A(2).

[461] This will not always be the case: where a client is a test-claimant in group litigation, for example, those costs may be categorised as being common costs: see CPR, r 48.6A(b)(ii).

[462] *Bayliss v Kelly and Ors* [1997] 2 Costs LR 54 at 59.

of it, separate; in those circumstances, each claimant will generally be liable only for the costs attributable to his own claim, together with his share of the costs which were common to the claim.

Joint instructions in separate matters

8.413 This situation would occur when the client's interests in the subject matter are separate, but where instructions are given jointly. The mere fact that the instructions are given jointly is not enough to allow a conclusion to be drawn that there is a joint retainer, as Amphlett B commented:[463]

> '... [T]he mere fact that the several defendants appear by the same solicitor, that they join in putting in the same answer, join in the same affidavits, and attend joint consultations, would not, to my mind, amount to evidence that there was any joint retainer.'

In the modern context these comments would still have resonance as a consequence of the need to ensure that clients are afforded an adequate degree of consumer protection; in particular, there is a need to ensure that a client does not become liable for the costs of others without realising that that is the case. A case example is where a solicitor was instructed by co-habitees to prepare wills conferring mutual benefits; the court found that the obligations were several.[464] Another case example is where a number of directors where sued in their personal capacities and where they gave joint instructions to a solicitor to 'take such steps as you may consider necessary in the matter'; the obligation was found to be several.[465]

8.414 It will, however, not always be the case that where the client's interests are separate, their obligations will also be separate. A case example is a retainer which took in two tenants in common (ie each owned a separate and distinct part of the property); in view of the nature of the instructions, the court found that the liability was joint and several.[466]

Joint instructions in joint matters

8.415 Where the solicitor is acting for litigants pursuing a joint cause of action upon the receipt of joint instructions, the starting point will be that the retainer imposes a joint liability unless the contrary can be shown.[467] For the reasons set out above, a distinction must be drawn between clients giving instructions jointly, and clients merely giving instructions to the same solicitor. Whilst there is no authority on the point, it would be in keeping with the modern emphasis on client care that a joint liability would be created only where the client was made aware of the fact that he was assuming a liability for all of the costs, including those for legal services which might be of benefit to others.

8.416 It will be clear from the case examples given above that each case will turn on its own facts. There is, however, one legal principle that dominates the topic of joint obligations, and that is the principle of equal apportionment.

---

[463]   *Burridge v Bellew* (1875) 32 LT 807 at 812; see also the New Zealand case of *Longreach Oil Ltd v Southern Cross Exploration NL* 1988 NSW Lexis 9762.

[464]   *Hall v Meyrick* [1957] 2 QB 455.

[465]   *Davies v Chatwood* (1879) 11 Ch D 244.

[466]   *Furlong v Scallan* (1875) IR 9 Eq 202.

[467]   *Starving v Cousins* (1835) 1 Gale 159; see, for example, *Burridge v Bellew* (1875) 32 LT 807.

The principle of equal apportionment

8.417 This section deals with the situation in which costs can fairly be said to have been incurred for the benefit of more than one client, but where the instructions were given separately. Where the instructions were given jointly, then (generally) the retainer would fall within the fourth category mentioned above, in which case the obligations would generally be joint. Where this is not the case (ie where each client has given his own instructions), the retainer would (generally) fall in the second category above. The most striking example of this is where there is group litigation in which a large number of clients instruct the same solicitor.

8.418 The starting point in these circumstances is that there will be 'equal apportionment'; this means that each client will be responsible for his share of the common costs (together, of course, with his individual costs). This is a principle which Donaldson MR has commented has age-old respectability, being based 'upon the Rhodian Law, the Rolls of Oleron and the maritime law of general average'.[468]

8.419 It is instructive to look at the development of the law of equal apportionment. This is necessary because older cases are often cited and it is necessary to be able to put those cases in context. In a mid-nineteenth-century case a Masters' Certificate[469] was obtained which explained the principle in this way:[470]

> 'If one solicitor appears for three defendants, and the bill [ie the claim] is dismissed with costs as to one of them, the plaintiff can only be compelled to pay the costs of such proceedings as exclusively relate to that defendant, and one-third of the costs of the proceedings taken jointly for all three defendants.'

The certificate went on to say:

> '... [B]ut, nevertheless, the extent of the liability of the client may vary according to the circumstances of each case; in other words, according to the retainer of the solicitor.'

The certificate was (with some reservations) accepted by the Court of Appeal in Chancery. Thus, whilst the principle of equal apportionment was something that could be expected to yield to what was recorded in the retainer, the practice in the courts of equity was that where there was no contractual provision to the contrary, costs incurred jointly would be apportioned equally on a several basis.

8.420 This principle of equal apportionment was both enduring and widespread.[471] According to Kelly CB (giving judgment in the late nineteenth century), there was no difference between the practice in the courts of law and the practice in the courts of equity.[472] He confirmed that if there was a joint contract of retainer between the solicitor and his clients, each client would be jointly liable for the whole costs, but that if there were separate contracts, each would be liable for his own costs and his own portion

---

[468] *Davies v Eli Lilly & Co* [1987] 1 WLR 1136.
[469] This was a document similar to a short statement by a court assessor; it was a method whereby the then equivalent of a costs judge could give guidance to an appeal court.
[470] *In re Colquhoun* (1854) 5 DM&G 35.
[471] See, for example, *Keen v Towler* (1924) 41 TLR 86 and *Davies v Chatwood* (1879) 40 LT 187.
[472] *Burridge v Bellew* (1875) 32 LT 807 at 812.

of the joint costs. As has already been mentioned, Amphlett B clarified (in the same case) that the fact that the litigation may be conducted jointly does not necessarily make the liability joint.[473]

8.421 An oft-quoted example of equal apportionment is *Beaumont v Senior and Bull*,[474] which is an early twentieth century case in which two defendants (D1 and D2) were represented by the same solicitor. It concerned costs between opposing parties, but it shed light on the retainer. D1's defence failed, but D2 was successful. There was no agreement as to how the costs should be shared. Costs followed the event in that both the claimant and D2 were awarded costs. D2's bill claimed all of the costs of the claim, but the costs judge allowed only those additional costs which had been caused by D2 being joined as a defendant (ie the costs of defending the claim against D1 and D2 were disallowed unless they had been caused solely by D2's involvement). D2 brought an appeal. The Divisional Court found that in the absence of any agreement between the defendants as to how the costs of the defence should be shared, the defendants were each liable for an equal proportion of the costs of the defence.

8.422 Similar decisions followed as the principle of equal apportionment became ingrained as established law. A few years later, for example, the principle was again approved by the Court of Appeal in *Ellingsen v Det Skandinaviske Compani*;[475] as in earlier cases,[476] the court expressed some reservations about the principle, but commented that it had by that stage become too well established to be disturbed. Subject to what is said below, that would appear to be the position today.

Deviation from equal apportionment

8.423 The principle of equal apportionment is capable of leading to injustice when applied rigidly and, in view of this, subsequent cases heralded a more flexible approach, although there are significant limits to the extent to which the court can deviate from the principle.

8.424 The case that is usually quoted as being an example of the flexible approach is *Korner v H Korner & Co Ltd*,[477] where the Court of Appeal found that the general principle of equal apportionment was a rule of thumb which was convenient to apply in ordinary cases, but should not be applied in every case if that would result in injustice. The court found that the principle of equal apportionment was not appropriate in the case before them; this, amongst other things, was because of the differences in the defences which had been raised by the defendants. Singleton LJ explained the court's reasoning:[478]

> 'I do not know of any authority which compels the court to follow the rule [of equal apportionment] which I have mentioned in every class of case, and even if to follow it would result in injustice. To do so would be to fly in the teeth of the generally accepted principle as stated in [*Ellingsen*] "that the successful party is to be recompensed the liability he has reasonably incurred in defending himself".'

---

[473] *Burridge v Bellew* (1875) 32 LT 807 at 813 and 814.
[474] *Beaumont v Senior and Bull* [1903] 1 KB 282.
[475] [1919] 2 KB 567; see also *Keen v Towler* (1924) 41 TLR 86, in which Darling LJ did the same.
[476] In particular, *In re Colquhoun* (1854) 5 DM&G 35.
[477] *Korner v H Korner & Co Ltd* [1951] Ch 11.
[478] *Korner v H Korner & Co Ltd* [1951] Ch 11 at 17

8.425 It should be noted that Singleton LJ did not say that an adjustment should be made so as to meet the justice of the situation: the adjustment that he made was based on the nature of cases each litigant had advanced and the different costs attributable thereto; it was not based on a broader discretionary notion of what was fair and just. Similarly, Chadwick J said:[479]

> '[There is] no support in [the authorities] for the proposition that a pro-rata apportionment of the general costs of the action should be modified or "adjusted" on the ground that one client is more important, or more prominent in the litigation, than others. If costs cannot be attributed to particular clients on the basis of separate defences or separate issues, then they must be apportioned equally between all those clients for whose benefit they have been incurred.'

Thus, Chadwick J found that there was no support for the proposition that the adjustment should take into account the relative importance or prominence of the parties: he found that it should be based solely on the issues raised and the costs which could be attributed to those issues.

8.426 The exercise of adjustment will be a largely factual exercise.[480] As can be seen from one of the authorities which are discussed below (*BCCI v Ali & Ors*), where a party has incurred costs that cannot fairly be attributed to his co-litigants, the court can take that fact into account, but only in a limited way.

Costs sharing agreements

8.427 Where litigation involves more than one client and where costs will be incurred in respect of issues which are common to the clients, or some of them, it may be appropriate to enter into a costs sharing agreement. This can be done by way of a simple agreement to share a part of the costs, or, in a more challenging case, it can be made more robust by way of a system of interlocking indemnities; the way in which this works is that all of the contributors are jointly and severally liable for all of the costs, but each contributor is able to rely on a full indemnity from the other contributors for all but his share of the costs.[481]

8.428 A costs sharing agreement would almost always deal with the clients' liability for their own solicitor's fees, but many agreements also make provision for sharing the burden of an adverse costs order. Where this is the case, care must be taken to ensure that the costs sharing agreement does not conflict with any provision that has been made for ATE insurance. In particular, care must be taken to ensure that the additional exposure that such an agreement may impose upon a litigant does not cause him to be exposed to a liability which exceeds the level of his ATE cover.

8.429 Where the retainer is such that the solicitors' fees, or part of them, are dependent on recovery of costs from the opponent (such as CFA Lite), the costs sharing agreement should make it clear whether the liability for an adverse costs order is to be set off against costs recovered, so that there should be no doubt whether it is the client or the solicitor who bears the brunt of that risk.

---

[479] *Bayliss v Kelly and Ors* [1997] 2 Costs LR 54 at 60.
[480] See *Meretz Investments Ltd v ACP Ltd* [2007] EWHC 2635 (Ch).
[481] This scheme has not been approved by any court, but equally, it has not ever been challenged.

8.430 In group litigation the costs sharing agreement may need to be approved by the court and, in any event, will be subject to the court's supervision. These issues are discussed in more detail in Chapter 38.

8.431 A costs sharing agreement can have a considerable bearing on the way in which the court deals with the incidence of costs; this issue is addressed at **34.151–34.159**. A precedent costs sharing agreement can be found at the end of this book. That precedent is, however, a very basic type of agreement; in particular, it does not incorporate the interlocking indemnities referred to above.

Guarantees, etc

8.432 The types of retainer which have been considered so far in this section are where two or more clients have given instructions for their own purposes. This is to be distinguished from retainers where a person has agreed to pay or is otherwise obliged to pay for legal services to be rendered to someone else, which may arise as a result of the following:

- where a person has provided a guarantee for another person's costs;
- where a tenant is contractually liable to pay his landlord's costs;
- where a mortgagor is liable to pay the mortgagee's costs;
- where a solicitor is liable to meet the costs of intervention in his practice;
- where a person agrees to pay costs as between solicitor and client as part of a compromise; and
- where there are any other circumstances in which a person is obliged to pay another person's costs.

Where these are the circumstances, the usual principles of indemnity, guarantee, etc will apply. Other than the fact that the person liable to pay will, in appropriate circumstances, be entitled to an assessment of the costs which is independent of the client's right to an assessment,[482] there is no real difference between guarantees, etc in the context of costs and in other contexts.

8.433 One species of retainer that merits particular mention is where litigation is pursued in the name of a small limited company but the retainer is also in the name of the director: the aim of such a retainer is to provide a personal guarantee in respect of the costs of the litigation. Where this is done, the solicitor would act wisely if he were to ensure compliance with the formalities relating to guarantees: in particular, he should note that a guarantee ought to be in writing and signed by the guarantor.[483]

8.434 In summary, the nature of the retainer is a question of contractual interpretation which will turn on the wording of the retainer, the nature of the instructions, the nature of the matter to which the instructions relate, and any other relevant factor. Where the instructions are given separately but relate to work which has to benefit all of the clients, the principle of equal apportionment will apply, but only if the retainer does not provide otherwise.

---

[482]   See **18.75–18.89** on s 71 of the Solicitors Act 1974.
[483]   Statute of Frauds 1677, s 4.

RETAINERS WITH SPECIFIC TYPES OF PERSON

Retainers with children and those who lack capacity

8.435 This is addressed in Chapter 37.

Retainers with companies and members

8.436 There is nothing in principle to prevent a company from instructing a solicitor.[484] The old provisions[485] that required a retainer to be in writing and made under seal no longer apply.[486] Whilst each case will be highly dependent on its own facts, authority exists for the proposition that where a company is not bound by a retainer, its individual members may be.[487]

Retainers with unincorporated associations

8.437 An unincorporated association may not make a contract of retainer as an entity in its own right; the retainer will be with the committee or the other persons who acted with authority in giving instructions to the solicitors.[488]

Retainers with trustees, executors, liquidators, etc

8.438 Unless it is expressly agreed otherwise,[489] a trustee or executor is personally liable for the monies payable under a retainer.[490] A trustee has a right to an indemnity from the fund: see **37.8**. Where there is more than one trustee, a retainer with one will bind the rest only if there is express authority to that effect.[491] A liquidator (unlike a trustee in bankruptcy[492]) is not personally liable for costs;[493] as such, it is desirable that it is expressly recorded that the solicitor will look only to the assets for his costs.[494]

RELEVANT EXTRACTS FROM THE REGULATIONS

8.439 Relevant extracts from the Regulations are given below, in chronological order. Only those regulations pertinent to costs in England and Wales have been included.

---

[484] If authority were needed on the point, see *A-G v Brecon Corpn* (1878) 10 Ch D 204.
[485] See *Arnold v Poole Corpn* (1842) 4 Man & G 860.
[486] See the Corporate Bodies' Contracts Act 1960, s 1.
[487] *Robinson v Price* (1886) 2 TLR 242.
[488] See *Flemyng v Hector* (1836) 2 M & W 172 and *Jones v Hope* [1880] WN 69, CA.
[489] *Blyth v Fladgate* [1891] 1 Ch 337 at 359, per Stirling J.
[490] *Staniar v Evans, Evans v Staniar* (1886) 34 Ch D 470 at 477, per North J.
[491] See *Luke v South Kensington Hotel Co* (1879) 11 Ch D 121, CA and *Brazier v Camp* (1894) 9 R 852, CA.
[492] The difference between a liquidator and a trustee in bankruptcy is that the assets are vested in the latter but not the former.
[493] *Re Anglo-Moravian Hungarian Junction Rly Co, ex p Watkin* (1875) 1 Ch D 130, CA.
[494] *Re Hermann Loog Ltd* (1887) 36 Ch D 502.

The Consumer Protection (Cancellation of Contracts Concluded away from Business Premises) Regulations 1987 (as amended)

Citation and commencement

1. These Regulations may be cited as the Consumer Protection (Cancellation of Contracts Concluded away from Business Premises) Regulations 1987 and shall come into force on 1st July 1988.

Interpretation

2.(1)   In these Regulations-

'business' includes a trade or profession;

'consumer' means a person, other than a body corporate, who, in making a contract to which these Regulations apply, is acting for purposes which can be regarded as outside his business;

...

'notice of cancellation' has the meaning given by regulation 4(5) below;

'security' in relation to a contract means a mortgage, charge, pledge, bond, debenture, indemnity, guarantee, bill, note or other right provided by the consumer, or at his request (express or implied), to secure the carrying out of his obligations under the contract;

'signed' has the same meaning as in the Consumer Credit Act 1974; and

'trader' means a person who, in making a contract to which these Regulations apply, is acting for the purposes of his business, and anyone acting in the name or on behalf of such a person.

...

Contracts to which the Regulations apply

3.(1)   These Regulations apply to a contract, other than an excepted contract, for the supply by a trader of goods or services to a consumer which is made—

(a)   during an unsolicited visit by a trade—
    (i)   to the consumer's home or to the home of another person; or
    (ii)   to the consumer's place of work;

(b)   during a visit by a trader as mentioned in paragraph (a)(i) or (ii) above at the express request of the consumer where the goods or services to which the contract relates are other than those concerning which the consumer requested the visit of the trader, provided that when the visit was requested the consumer did not know, or could not reasonably have known, that the supply of those other goods or services formed part of the trader's business activities;

(c)   after an offer was made by the consumer in respect of the supply by a trader of the goods or services in the circumstances mentioned in paragraph (a) or (b) above or (d) below; or

(d)   during an excursion organised by the trader away from premises on which he is carrying on any business (whether on a permanent or temporary basis).

(2)   For the purposes of this regulation an excepted contract means

...

(f)   any contract not falling within sub-paragraph (g) below under which the total payments to be made by the consumer do not exceed £35; and

(g)   any contract under which credit within the meaning of the Consumer Credit Act 1974 is provided not exceeding £35 other than a hire-purchase or conditional sale agreement.

(3) In this regulation 'unsolicited visit' means a visit by a trader, whether or not he is the trader who supplies the goods or services, which does not take place at the express request of the consumer and includes—

    (a)   a visit by a trader which takes place after he, or a person acting in his name or on his behalf, telephones the consumer (otherwise than at the consumer's express request) and indicates during the course of the telephone call (either expressly or by implication) that he, or the trader in whose name or on whose behalf he is acting, is willing to visit the consumer; and

    (b)   a visit by a trader which takes place after he, or a person acting in his name or on his behalf, visits the consumer (otherwise than at the consumer's express request) and indicates during the course of that visit (either expressly or by implication) that he, or the trader in whose name or on whose behalf he is acting, is willing to make a subsequent visit to the consumer.

Cancellation of Contract

4.(1) No contract to which these Regulations apply shall be enforceable against the consumer unless the trader has delivered to the consumer notice in writing in accordance with paragraphs (3) and (4) below indicating the right of the consumer to cancel the contract within the period of 7 days mentioned in paragraph (5) below containing both the information set out in Part I of the Schedule to these Regulations and a Cancellation Form in the form set out in Part II of the Schedule and completed in accordance with the footnotes.

...

(3) The information to be contained in the notice under paragraph (1) above shall be easily legible and if incorporated in the contract or other document shall be afforded no less prominence than that given to any other information in the document apart from the heading to the document and the names of the parties to the contract and any information inserted in handwriting.

(4) The notice shall be dated and delivered to the consumer—

    (a)   in the cases mentioned in regulation 3(1)(a), (b) and (d) above, at the time of the making of the contract; and

    (b)   in the case mentioned in regulation 3(1)(c) above, at the time of the making of the offer by the consumer.

(5) If within the period of 7 days following the making of the contract the consumer serves a notice in writing (a 'notice of cancellation') on the trader or any other person specified in a notice referred to in paragraph (1) above as a person to whom notice of cancellation may be given which, however expressed and whether or not conforming to the cancellation form set out in Part II of the Schedule to these Regulations, indicates the intention of the consumer to cancel the contract, the notice of cancellation shall operate to cancel the contract.

(6) Except as otherwise provided under these Regulations, a contract cancelled under paragraph (5) above shall be treated as if it had never been entered into by the consumer.

(7) Notwithstanding anything in section 7 of the Interpretation Act 1978, a notice of cancellation sent by post by a consumer shall be deemed to have been served at the time of posting, whether or not it is actually received.

...

Recovery of money paid by consumer

5.(1) Subject to regulation 7(2) below, on the cancellation of a contract under regulation 4 above, any sum paid by or on behalf of the consumer under or in contemplation of the contract shall become repayable.

(2)   If under the terms of the cancelled contract the consumer or any person on his behalf is in possession of any goods, he shall have a lien on them for any sum repayable to him under paragraph (1) above.

(3)   Where any security has been provided in relation to the cancelled contract, the security, so far as it is so provided, shall be treated as never having had effect and any property lodged with the trader solely for the purposes of the security as so provided shall be returned by him forthwith.

...

No contracting-out

10.(1)   A term contained in a contract to which these Regulations apply is void if, and to the extent that, it is inconsistent with a provision for the protection of the consumer contained in these Regulations.

(2)   Where a provision of these Regulations specifies the duty or liability of the consumer in certain circumstances a term contained in a contract to which these Regulations apply is inconsistent with that provision if it purports to impose, directly or indirectly, an additional duty or liability on him in those circumstances.

Service of documents

11.(1)   A document to be served under these Regulations on a person may be so served—

- (a)   by delivering it to him, or by sending it by post to him, or by leaving it with him, at his proper address addressed to him by name;
- (b)   if the person is a body corporate, by serving it in accordance with paragraph (a) above on the secretary or clerk of that body; or
- (c)   if the person is a partnership, by serving it in accordance with paragraph (a) above on a partner or on a person having the control or management of the partnership business.

(2)   For the purposes of these Regulations, a document sent by post to, or left at, the address last known to the server of the document as the address of a person shall be treated as sent by post to, or left at, his proper address.

The Consumer Protection (Distance Selling) Regulations 2000 (as amended)

Title, commencement and extent

1.(1)   These Regulations may be cited as the Consumer Protection (Distance Selling) Regulations 2000 and shall come into force on 31 October 2000.

...

Interpretation

3.(1)   In these Regulations—

'breach' means contravention by a supplier of a prohibition in, or failure to comply with a requirement of, these Regulations;
'business' includes a trade or profession;
'consumer' means any natural person who, in contracts to which these Regulations apply, is acting for purposes which are outside his business;
'court' in relation to England and Wales and Northern Ireland means a county court or the High Court, and in relation to Scotland means the Sheriff Court or the Court of Session;

'credit' includes a cash loan and any other form of financial accommodation, and for this purpose 'cash' includes money in any form;

...

'distance contract' means any contract concerning goods or services concluded between a supplier and a consumer under an organised distance sales or service provision scheme run by the supplier who, for the purpose of the contract, makes exclusive use of one or more means of distance communication up to and including the moment at which the contract is concluded;

...

'excepted contract' means a contract such as is mentioned in regulation 5(1);

'means of distance communication' means any means which, without the simultaneous physical presence of the supplier and the consumer, may be used for the conclusion of a contract between those parties; and an indicative list of such means is contained in Schedule 1;

'Member State' means a State which is a contracting party to the EEA Agreement;

...

'period for performance' has the meaning given by regulation 19(2);

'personal credit agreement' has the meaning given by regulation 14(8);

'related credit agreement' has the meaning given by regulation 15(5);

'supplier' means any person who, in contracts to which these Regulations apply, is acting in his commercial or professional capacity; and

'working days' means all days other than Saturdays, Sundays and public holidays.

(2) In the application of these Regulations to Scotland, for references to an 'injunction' or an 'interim injunction' there shall be substituted references to an 'interdict' or an 'interim interdict' respectively.

Contracts to which these Regulations apply

4. These Regulations apply, subject to regulation 6, to distance contracts other than excepted contracts.

...

Information required prior to the conclusion of the contract

7.(1) Subject to paragraph (4), in good time prior to the conclusion of the contract the supplier shall—

- (a) provide to the consumer the following information—
  - (i) the identity of the supplier and, where the contract requires payment in advance, the supplier's address;
  - (ii) a description of the main characteristics of the goods or services;
  - (iii) the price of the goods or services including all taxes;
  - (iv) delivery costs where appropriate;
  - (v) the arrangements for payment, delivery or performance;
  - (vi) the existence of a right of cancellation except in the cases referred to in regulation 13;
  - (vii) the cost of using the means of distance communication where it is calculated other than at the basic rate;
  - (viii) the period for which the offer or the price remains valid; and
  - (ix) where appropriate, the minimum duration of the contract, in the case of contracts for the supply of goods or services to be performed permanently or recurrently;
- (b) inform the consumer if he proposes, in the event of the goods or services ordered by the consumer being unavailable, to provide substitute goods or services (as the case may be) of equivalent quality and price; and

(c)   inform the consumer that the cost of returning any such substitute goods to the supplier in the event of cancellation by the consumer would be met by the supplier.

(2)   The supplier shall ensure that the information required by paragraph (1) is provided in a clear and comprehensible manner appropriate to the means of distance communication used, with due regard in particular to the principles of good faith in commercial transactions and the principles governing the protection of those who are unable to give their consent such as minors.

(3)   Subject to paragraph (4), the supplier shall ensure that his commercial purpose is made clear when providing the information required by paragraph (1).

(4)   In the case of a telephone communication, the identity of the supplier and the commercial purpose of the call shall be made clear at the beginning of the conversation with the consumer.

Written and additional information

8.(1)   Subject to regulation 9, the supplier shall provide to the consumer in writing, or in another durable medium which is available and accessible to the consumer, the information referred to in paragraph (2), either—

(a)   prior to the conclusion of the contract, or
(b)   thereafter, in good time and in any event—
  (i)   during the performance of the contract, in the case of services; and
  ...

(2)   The information required to be provided by paragraph (1) is—

(a)   the information set out in paragraphs (i) to (vi) of Regulation 7(1)(a);
(b)   information about the conditions and procedures for exercising the right to cancel under regulation 10, including—
  ...
  (iii)   in the case of a contract for the supply of services, information as to how the right to cancel may be affected by the consumer agreeing to performance of the services beginning before the end of the seven working day period referred to in regulation 12;
(c)   the geographical address of the place of business of the supplier to which the consumer may address any complaints;
(d)   information about any after-sales services and guarantees; and
(e)   the conditions for exercising any contractual right to cancel the contract, where the contract is of an unspecified duration or a duration exceeding one year.

(3)   Subject to regulation 9, prior to the conclusion of a contract for the supply of services, the supplier shall inform the consumer in writing or in another durable medium which is available and accessible to the consumer that, unless the parties agree otherwise, he will not be able to cancel the contract under regulation 10 once the performance of the services has begun with his agreement.

...

Right to cancel

10.(1)   Subject to regulation 13, if within the cancellation period set out in regulations 11 and 12, the consumer gives a notice of cancellation to the supplier, or any other person previously notified by the supplier to the consumer as a person to whom notice of cancellation may be given, the notice of cancellation shall operate to cancel the contract.

(2)   Except as otherwise provided by these Regulations, the effect of a notice of cancellation is that the contract shall be treated as if it had not been made.

(3) For the purposes of these Regulations, a notice of cancellation is a notice in writing or in another durable medium available and accessible to the supplier (or to the other person to whom it is given) which, however expressed, indicates the intention of the consumer to cancel the contract.

(4) A notice of cancellation given under this regulation by a consumer to a supplier or other person is to be treated as having been properly given if the consumer—

(a) leaves it at the address last known to the consumer and addressed to the supplier or other person by name (in which case it is to be taken to have been given on the day on which it was left);

(b) sends it by post to the address last known to the consumer and addressed to the supplier or other person by name (in which case, it is to be taken to have been given on the day on which it was posted);

(c) sends it by facsimile to the business facsimile number last known to the consumer (in which case it is to be taken to have been given on the day on which it is sent); or

(d) sends it by electronic mail, to the business electronic mail address last known to the consumer (in which case it is to be taken to have been given on the day on which it is sent).

(5) Where a consumer gives a notice in accordance with paragraph (4)(a) or (b) to a supplier who is a body corporate or a partnership, the notice is to be treated as having been properly given if—

(a) in the case of a body corporate, it is left at the address of, or sent to, the secretary or clerk of that body; or

(b) in the case of a partnership, it is left with or sent to a partner or a person having control or management of the partnership business.

...

Cancellation period in the case of contracts for the supply of services

12.(1) For the purposes of regulation 10, the cancellation period in the case of contracts for the supply of services begins with the day on which the contract is concluded and ends as provided in paragraphs (2) to (4).

(2) Where the supplier complies with regulation 8 on or before the day on which the contract is concluded, the cancellation period ends on the expiry of the period of seven working days beginning with the day after the day on which the contract is concluded.

(3) Subject to paragraph (3A) where a supplier who has not complied with regulation 8 on or before the day on which the contract is concluded provides to the consumer the information referred to in regulation 8(2), and does so in writing or in another durable medium available and accessible to the consumer, within the period of three months beginning with the day after the day on which the contract is concluded, the cancellation period ends on the expiry of the period of seven working days beginning with the day after the day on which the consumer receives the information.

(3A) Where the performance of the contract has begun with the consumer's agreement before the expiry of the period of seven working days beginning with the day after the day on which the contract was concluded and the supplier has not complied with regulation 8 on or before the day on which performance began, but provides to the consumer the information referred to in regulation 8(2) in good time during the performance of the contract, the cancellation period ends—

(a) on the expiry of the period of seven working days beginning with the day after the day on which the consumer receives the information; or

(b) if the performance of the contract is completed before the expiry of the period referred to in sub-paragraph (a), on the day when the performance of the contract is completed.

(4)   Where neither paragraph (2) to (3A) applies, the cancellation period ends on the expiry of the period of three months and seven working days beginning with the day after the day on which the contract is concluded.

Exceptions to the right to cancel

13.(1)   Unless the parties have agreed otherwise, the consumer will not have the right to cancel the contract by giving notice of cancellation pursuant to regulation 10 in respect of contracts—

    (a)   for the supply of services if the performance of the contract has begun with the consumer's agreement—

        (i)   before the end of the cancellation period applicable under regulation 12(2); and

        (ii)   after the supplier has provided the information referred to in regulation 8(2);

    (b)   for the supply of goods or services the price of which is dependent on fluctuations in the financial market which cannot be controlled by the supplier;

    (c)   for the supply of goods made to the consumer's specifications or clearly personalised or which by reason of their nature cannot be returned or are liable to deteriorate or expire rapidly;

    (d)   for the supply of audio or video recordings or computer software if they are unsealed by the consumer;

    (e)   for the supply of newspapers, periodicals or magazines; or

    (f)   for gaming, betting or lottery services.

Recovery of sums paid by or on behalf of the consumer on cancellation, and return of security

14.(1)   On the cancellation of a contract under regulation 10, the supplier shall reimburse any sum paid by or on behalf of the consumer under or in relation to the contract to the person by whom it was made free of any charge, less any charge made in accordance with paragraph (5).

(2)   The reference in paragraph (1) to any sum paid on behalf of the consumer includes any sum paid by a creditor who is not the same person as the supplier under a personal credit agreement with the consumer.

(3)   The supplier shall make the reimbursement referred to in paragraph (1) as soon as possible and in any case within a period not exceeding 30 days beginning with the day on which the notice of cancellation was given.

(4)   Where any security has been provided in relation to the contract, the security (so far as it is so provided) shall, on cancellation under regulation 10, be treated as never having had effect and any property lodged with the supplier solely for the purposes of the security as so provided shall be returned by him forthwith.

(5)   Subject to paragraphs (6) and (7), the supplier may make a charge, not exceeding the direct costs of recovering any goods supplied under the contract, where a term of the contract provides that the consumer must return any goods supplied if he cancels the contract under regulation 10 but the consumer does not comply with this provision or returns the goods at the expense of the supplier.

(6)   Paragraph (5) shall not apply where—

    (a)   the consumer cancels in circumstances where he has the right to reject the goods under a term of the contract, including a term implied by virtue of any enactment, or

    (b)   the term requiring the consumer to return any goods supplied if he cancels the contract is an 'unfair term' within the meaning of the Unfair Terms in Consumer Contracts Regulations 1999.

(7) Paragraph (5) shall not apply to the cost of recovering any goods which were supplied as substitutes for the goods ordered by the consumer.

(8) For the purposes of these Regulations, a personal credit agreement is an agreement between the consumer and any other person ('the creditor') by which the creditor provides the consumer with credit of any amount.

Automatic cancellation of a related credit agreement

15.(1)   Where a notice of cancellation is given under regulation 10 which has the effect of cancelling the contract, the giving of the notice shall also have the effect of cancelling any related credit agreement.

(2)   Where a related credit agreement is cancelled by virtue of paragraph (1), the supplier shall, if he is not the same person as the creditor under that agreement, forthwith on receipt of the notice of cancellation inform the creditor that the notice has been given.

(3)   Where a related credit agreement is cancelled by virtue of paragraph (1)—

- (a)   any sum paid by or on behalf of the consumer under, or in relation to, the credit agreement which the supplier is not obliged to reimburse under regulation 14(1) shall be reimbursed, except for any sum which, if it had not already been paid, would have to be paid under subparagraph (b);
- (b)   the agreement shall continue in force so far as it relates to repayment of the credit and payment of interest, subject to regulation 16; and
- (c)   subject to subparagraph (b), the agreement shall cease to be enforceable.

(4)   Where any security has been provided under a related credit agreement, the security, so far as it is so provided, shall be treated as never having had effect and any property lodged with the creditor solely for the purposes of the security as so provided shall be returned by him forthwith.

(5)   For the purposes of this regulation and regulation 16, a 'related credit agreement' means an agreement under which fixed sum credit which fully or partly covers the price under a contract cancelled under regulation 10 is granted—

- (a)   by the supplier, or
- (b)   by another person, under an arrangement between that person and the supplier.

(6)   For the purposes of this regulation and regulation 16—

- (a)   'creditor' is a person who grants credit under a related credit agreement;
- (b)   'fixed sum credit' has the same meaning as in section 10 of the Consumer Credit Act 1974;
- (c)   'repayment' in relation to credit means repayment of money received by the consumer, and cognate expressions shall be construed accordingly; and
- (d)   'interest' means interest on money so received.

Repayment of credit and interest after cancellation of a related credit agreement

16.(1)   This regulation applies following the cancellation of a related credit agreement by virtue of regulation 15(1).

(2)   If the consumer repays the whole or a portion of the credit—

- (a)   before the expiry of one month following the cancellation of the credit agreement, or
- (b)   in the case of a credit repayable by instalments, before the date on which the first instalment is due,

no interest shall be payable on the amount repaid.

(3)   If the whole of a credit repayable by instalments is not repaid on or before the date referred to in paragraph (2)(b), the consumer shall not be liable to repay any of the credit except on receipt of a request in writing, signed by the creditor, stating the amounts of the remaining instalments (recalculated by the creditor as nearly as may be in accordance with the agreement and without extending the repayment period), but excluding any sum other than principal and interest.

(4)   Where any security has been provided under a related credit agreement the duty imposed on the consumer to repay credit and to pay interest shall not be enforceable before the creditor has discharged any duty imposed on him by regulation 15(4) to return any property lodged with him as security on cancellation.

Restoration of goods by consumer after cancellation

17.(1)   This regulation applies where a contract is cancelled under regulation 10 after the consumer has acquired possession of any goods under the contract other than any goods mentioned in regulation 13(1)(b) to (e).

(2)   The consumer shall be treated as having been under a duty throughout the period prior to cancellation—

    (a)   to retain possession of the goods, and
    (b)   to take reasonable care of them.

(3)   On cancellation, the consumer shall be under a duty to restore the goods to the supplier in accordance with this regulation, and in the meanwhile to retain possession of the goods and take reasonable care of them.

(4)   The consumer shall not be under any duty to deliver the goods except at his own premises and in pursuance of a request in writing, or in another durable medium available and accessible to the consumer, from the supplier and given to the consumer either before, or at the time when, the goods are collected from those premises.

(5)   If the consumer—

    (a)   delivers the goods (whether at his own premises or elsewhere) to any person to whom, under regulation 10(1), a notice of cancellation could have been given; or
    (b)   sends the goods at his own expense to such a person,

he shall be discharged from any duty to retain possession of the goods or restore them to the supplier.

(6)   Where the consumer delivers the goods in accordance with paragraph (5)(a), his obligation to take care of the goods shall cease; and if he sends the goods in accordance with paragraph (5)(b), he shall be under a duty to take reasonable care to see that they are received by the supplier and not damaged in transit, but in other respects his duty to take care of the goods shall cease when he sends them.

(7)   Where, at any time during the period of 21 days beginning with the day notice of cancellation was given, the consumer receives such a request as is mentioned in paragraph (4), and unreasonably refuses or unreasonably fails to comply with it, his duty to retain possession and take reasonable care of the goods shall continue until he delivers or sends the goods as mentioned in paragraph (5), but if within that period he does not receive such a request his duty to take reasonable care of the goods shall cease at the end of that period.

(8)   Where—

    (a)   a term of the contract provides that if the consumer cancels the contract, he must return the goods to the supplier, and
    (b)   the consumer is not otherwise entitled to reject the goods under the terms of the contract or by virtue of any enactment,

paragraph (7) shall apply as if for the period of 21 days there were substituted the period of 6 months.

(9)   Where any security has been provided in relation to the cancelled contract, the duty to restore goods imposed on the consumer by this regulation shall not be enforceable before the supplier has discharged any duty imposed on him by regulation 14(4) to return any property lodged with him as security on cancellation.

(10)   Breach of a duty imposed by this regulation on a consumer is actionable as a breach of statutory duty.

Goods given in part-exchange

18.(1)   This regulation applies on the cancellation of a contract under regulation 10 where the supplier agreed to take goods in part-exchange (the 'part-exchange goods') and those goods have been delivered to him.

(2)   Unless, before the end of the period of 10 days beginning with the date of cancellation, the part-exchange goods are returned to the consumer in a condition substantially as good as when they were delivered to the supplier, the consumer shall be entitled to recover from the supplier a sum equal to the part-exchange allowance.

(3)   In this regulation the part-exchange allowance means the sum agreed as such in the cancelled contract, or if no such sum was agreed, such sum as it would have been reasonable to allow in respect of the part-exchange goods if no notice of cancellation had been served.

(4)   Where the consumer recovers from the supplier a sum equal to the part-exchange allowance, the title of the consumer to the part-exchange goods shall vest in the supplier (if it has not already done so) on recovery of that sum.

Performance

19.(1)   Unless the parties agree otherwise, the supplier shall perform the contract within a maximum of 30 days beginning with the day after the day the consumer sent his order to the supplier.

(2)   Subject to paragraphs (7) and (8), where the supplier is unable to perform the contract because the goods or services ordered are not available, within the period for performance referred to in paragraph (1) or such other period as the parties agree ('the period for performance'), he shall—

(a)   inform the consumer; and
(b)   reimburse any sum paid by or on behalf of the consumer under or in relation to the contract to the person by whom it was made.

(3)   The reference in paragraph (2)(b) to any sum paid on behalf of the consumer includes any sum paid by a creditor who is not the same person as the supplier under a personal credit agreement with the consumer.

(4)   The supplier shall make the reimbursement referred to in paragraph (2)(b) as soon as possible and in any event within a period of 30 days beginning with the day after the day on which the period for performance expired.

(5)   A contract which has not been performed within the period for performance shall be treated as if it had not been made, save for any rights or remedies which the consumer has under it as a result of the non-performance.

(6)   Where any security has been provided in relation to the contract, the security (so far as it is so provided) shall, where the supplier is unable to perform the contract within the period for performance, be treated as never having had any effect and any property lodged with the supplier solely for the purposes of the security as so provided shall be returned by him forthwith.

(7) Where the supplier is unable to supply the goods or services ordered by the consumer, the supplier may perform the contract for the purposes of these Regulations by providing substitute goods or services (as the case may be) of equivalent quality and price provided that—

    (a)   this possibility was provided for in the contract;

    (b)   prior to the conclusion of the contract the supplier gave the consumer the information required by regulation 7(1)(b) and (c) in the manner required by regulation 7(2).

(8) In the case of outdoor leisure events which by their nature cannot be rescheduled, paragraph 2(b) shall not apply where the consumer and the supplier so agree.

The Cancellation of Contracts made in a Consumer's Home or Place of Work etc Regulations 2008

Citation and commencement

1. These Regulations may be cited as the Cancellation of Contracts made in a Consumer's Home or Place of Work etc Regulations 2008 and shall come into force on 1 October 2008.

Interpretation

2.(1) In these Regulations:

'the 1974 Act' means the Consumer Credit Act 1974;

'cancellable agreement' has the same meaning as in section 189(1) of the 1974 Act;

'cancellation notice' means a notice in writing given by the consumer which indicates that he wishes to cancel the contract;

'cancellation period' means the period of 7 days starting with the date of receipt by the consumer of a notice of the right to cancel;

'consumer' means a natural person who in making a contract to which these Regulations apply is acting for purposes which can be regarded as outside his trade or profession;

'consumer credit agreement' means an agreement between the consumer and any other person by which the other person provides the consumer with credit of any amount;

'credit' includes a cash loan and any other form of financial accommodation, and for this purpose 'cash' includes money in any form;

'enforcement authority' means any person mentioned in regulation 21;

'fixed sum credit' has the same meaning as in section 10(1) of the 1974 Act;

'notice of the right to cancel' means a notice given in accordance with regulation 7;

'related credit agreement' means a consumer credit agreement under which fixed sum credit which fully or partly covers the price under a contract which may be cancelled under regulation 7 is granted—

    (i)   by the trader; or

    (ii)   by another person, under an arrangement made between that person and the trader;

'solicited visit' has the meaning given in regulation 6(3);

'specified contract' has the meaning given in regulation 9; and

'trader' means a person who, in making a contract to which these Regulations apply, is acting in his commercial or professional capacity and anyone acting in the name or on behalf of a trader.

(2)   Paragraph 8(2) of Schedule 3 has effect for the purposes of paragraphs 7 and 8(1).

Consequential amendments, revocations and saving

3.   Schedule 1 (Consequential Amendments) shall have effect.

4.(1)   Schedule 2 (Revocations) shall have effect.

(2)   The Consumer Protection (Cancellation of Contracts Concluded away from Business Premises) Regulations 1987 ('the 1987 Regulations') shall continue to have effect in relation to a contract to which they applied before their revocation by these Regulations.

(3)   These Regulations shall not apply to a contract to which the 1987 Regulations applied before their revocation.

Scope of application

5.   These Regulations apply to a contract, including a consumer credit agreement, between a consumer and a trader which is for the supply of goods or services to the consumer by a trader and which is made—

- (a)   during a visit by the trader to the consumer's home or place of work, or to the home of another individual;
- (b)   during an excursion organised by the trader away from his business premises; or
- (c)   after an offer made by the consumer during such a visit or excursion.

6.(1)   These Regulations do not apply to—

- (a)   any contracts listed in Schedule 3 (Excepted Contracts);
- (b)   a cancellable agreement;
- (c)   a consumer credit agreement which may be cancelled by the consumer in accordance with the terms of the agreement conferring upon him similar rights as if the agreement were a cancellable agreement; or
- (d)   a contract made during a solicited visit or a contract made after an offer made by a consumer during a solicited visit where the contract is—
    - ...

(2)   Where any agreement referred to in paragraph (1)(b), (c) or (d)(iii) is a related credit agreement the provisions of regulations 11 and 12 shall apply to the cancellation of that agreement.

(3)   A solicited visit means a visit by a trader, whether or not he is the trader who supplies the goods or services, to a consumer's home or place of work or to the home of another individual, which is made at the express request of the consumer but does not include—

- (a)   a visit by a trader which is made after he, or a person acting in his name or on his behalf—
    - (i)   telephones the consumer (otherwise than at the consumer's express request) and indicates during the course of the telephone call (either expressly or by implication) that he, or the trader in whose name or on whose behalf he is acting, is willing to visit the consumer; or
    - (ii)   visits the consumer (otherwise than at the consumer's express request) and indicates during the course of that visit (either expressly or by implication) that he, or the trader in whose name or on whose behalf he is acting, is willing to make a subsequent visit to the consumer; or
- (b)   a visit during which the contract which is made relates to goods and services other than those concerning which the consumer requested the visit of the trader, provided that when the visit was requested the consumer did not know, or could not reasonably have known, that the supply of such goods or services formed part of the trader's commercial or professional activities.

Right to cancel a contract to which these Regulations apply

7.(1)   A consumer has the right to cancel a contract to which these Regulations apply within the cancellation period.

(2)   The trader must give the consumer a written notice of his right to cancel the contract and such notice must be given at the time the contract is made except in the case of a contract to which regulation 5(c) applies in which case the notice must be given at the time the offer is made by the consumer.

(3)   The notice must—

    (a)   be dated;

    (b)   indicate the right of the consumer to cancel the contract within the cancellation period;

    (c)   be easily legible;

    (d)   contain—

        (i)   the information set out in Part I of Schedule 4; and

        (ii)   a cancellation form in the form set out in Part II of that Schedule provided as a detachable slip and completed by or on behalf of the trader in accordance with the notes; and

    (e)   indicate if applicable—

        (i)   that the consumer may be required to pay for the goods or services supplied if the performance of the contract has begun with his written agreement before the end of the cancellation period;

        (ii)   that a related credit agreement will be automatically cancelled if the contract for goods or services is cancelled.

(4)   Where the contract is wholly or partly in writing the notice must be incorporated in the same document.

(5)   If incorporated in the contract or another document the notice of the right to cancel must—

    (a)   be set out in a separate box with the heading 'Notice of the Right to Cancel'; and

    (b)   have as much prominence as any other information in the contract or document apart from the heading and the names of the parties to the contract and any information inserted in handwriting.

(6)   A contract to which these Regulations apply shall not be enforceable against the consumer unless the trader has given the consumer a notice of the right to cancel and the information required in accordance with this regulation.

Exercise of the right to cancel a contract

8.(1)   If the consumer serves a cancellation notice within the cancellation period then the contract is cancelled.

(2)   A contract which is cancelled shall be treated as if it had never been entered into by the consumer except where these Regulations provide otherwise.

(3)   The cancellation notice must indicate the intention of the consumer to cancel the contract and does not need to follow the form of cancellation notice set out in Part II of Schedule 4.

(4)   The cancellation notice must be served on the trader or another person specified in the notice of the right to cancel as a person to whom the cancellation notice may be given.

(5)   A cancellation notice sent by post is taken to have been served at the time of posting, whether or not it is actually received.

(6)   Where a cancellation notice is sent by electronic mail it is taken to have been served on the day on which it is sent.

Cancellation of specified contracts commenced before expiry of the right to cancel

9.(1) Where the consumer enters into a specified contract and he wishes the performance of the contract to begin before the end of the cancellation period, he must request this in writing.

(2) Where the consumer cancels a specified contract in accordance with regulation 8 he shall be under a duty to pay in accordance with the reasonable requirements of the cancelled contract for goods or services that were supplied before the cancellation.

(3) If the consumer fails to provide the request in writing referred to in paragraph (1) then—

- (a) the trader is not obliged to begin performance of the specified contract before the end of the cancellation period; and
- (b) the consumer is not bound by the duty referred to in paragraph (2) if he cancels the contract in accordance with regulation 8.

(4) For the purposes of this regulation and regulation 13, a 'specified contract' means a contract for any of the following—

- (a) the supply of newspapers, periodicals or magazines;
- (b) advertising in any medium;
- (c) the supply of goods the price of which is dependent on fluctuations in the financial markets which cannot be controlled by the trader;
- (d) the supply of goods to meet an emergency;
- (e) the supply of goods made to a customer's specifications or clearly personalised and any services in connection with the provision of such goods;
- (f) the supply of perishable goods;
- (g) the supply of goods which by their nature are consumed by use and which, before the cancellation, were so consumed;
- (h) the supply of goods which, before the cancellation, had become incorporated in any land or thing not comprised in the cancelled contract;
- (i) the supply of goods or services relating to a funeral; or
- (j) the supply of services of any other kind.

Recovery of money paid by consumer

10.(1) On the cancellation of a contract under regulation 8 any sum paid by or on behalf of the consumer in respect of the contract shall become repayable except where these Regulations provide otherwise.

(2) If the consumer or any person on his behalf is in possession of any goods under the terms of the cancelled contract then he shall have a lien on them for any sum repayable to him under paragraph (1).

(3) Where any security has been provided in relation to the cancelled contract, the security shall be treated as never having had effect for that purpose and the trader must immediately return any property lodged with him solely as security for the purposes of the cancelled contract.

Automatic cancellation of related credit agreement

11.(1) A cancellation notice which cancels a contract for goods or services shall have the effect of cancelling any related credit agreement.

(2) Subject to paragraphs (3) and (4), where a related credit agreement has been cancelled under paragraph (1)—

- (a) the trader must, if he is not the same person as the creditor under that agreement, immediately on receipt of the cancellation notice inform the creditor that the notice has been given;

(b)   any sum paid by or on behalf of the consumer in relation to the credit agreement must be reimbursed, except for any sum which would have to be paid under sub-paragraph (c);

(c)   the agreement shall continue in force so far as it relates to repayment of the credit and payment of interest in accordance with regulation 12, but shall otherwise cease to be enforceable; and

(d)   any security provided under the related credit agreement shall be treated as never having had effect for that purpose and the creditor must immediately return any property lodged with him solely as security for the purposes of the related credit agreement.

(3)   Where a related credit agreement is a cancellable agreement—

(a)   its cancellation under paragraph (1) shall take effect as if a notice of cancellation within the meaning of the 1974 Act had been served;

(b)   that Act shall apply in respect of the consequences of such cancellation;

(c)   paragraph (2)(b) to (d) and regulation 12 shall not apply in respect of its cancellation; and

(d)   regulations 13 and 14 shall not apply in respect of the cancellation of the related contract for goods or services.

(4)   Where a related credit agreement of a kind referred to in regulation 6(1)(c) is cancelled under paragraph (1)—

(a)   paragraph (2)(b) to (d) and regulation 12 shall not apply in respect of its cancellation; and

(b)   regulations 13 and 14 shall not apply in respect of the cancellation of the related contract for goods or services.

(5)   Where a related credit agreement of a kind referred to in regulation 6(1)(d)(iii) is cancelled under paragraph (1)—

(a)   the provisions of this regulation and regulation 12 shall apply in respect of its cancellation; and

(b)   the provisions of regulations 13 and 14 shall apply in respect of the cancellation of the related contract for goods or services.

(6)   For the purposes of this regulation and regulation 12 'creditor' is the person who grants credit under a related credit agreement.

Repayment of credit and interest

12.(1)   Where—

(a)   a contract under which credit is provided to the consumer is cancelled under regulation 8; or

(b)   a related credit agreement (other than a cancellable agreement or an agreement of a kind referred to in regulation 6(1)(c)) is cancelled as a result of the cancellation of a contract for goods or services,

the contract or agreement shall continue in force so far as it relates to repayment of the credit and payment of interest.

(2)   If, following the cancellation of a contract or related credit agreement to which paragraph (1) applies, the consumer repays the whole or a portion of the credit—

(a)   before the expiry of one month following service of the cancellation notice; or

(b)   in the case of a credit repayable by instalments, before the date on which the first instalment is due,

no interest shall be payable on the amount repaid.

(3) If the whole of a credit repayable by instalments is not repaid on or before the date specified in paragraph (2)(b), the consumer shall not be liable to repay any of the credit except on receipt of a request in writing signed by the trader stating the amounts of the remaining instalments (recalculated by the trader as nearly as may be in accordance with the contract and without extending the repayment period), but excluding any sum other than principal and interest.

(4) Repayment of a credit, or payment of interest, under a cancelled contract or related credit agreement shall be treated as duly made if it is made to any person on whom, under regulation 8(4), a cancellation notice could have been served.

(5) Where any security has been provided in relation to the contract or consumer credit agreement, the duty imposed on the consumer by this regulation shall not be enforceable before the trader or creditor has discharged any duty imposed on him by regulation 10(3) or 11(2)(d) respectively.

…

No contracting-out of contracts to which these Regulations apply

15.(1) A term contained in a contract is void if, and to the extent that, it is inconsistent with a provision for the protection of the consumer contained in these Regulations.

(2) Where a provision of these Regulations specifies the duty or liability of the consumer in certain circumstances, a term contained in a contract is inconsistent with that provision if it purports to impose, directly or indirectly, an additional or different duty or liability on the consumer in those circumstances.

Service of documents

16.(1) A document to be served under these Regulations on a person may be so served—

    (a)   by delivering it to him, or by leaving it at his proper address or by sending it to him at that address;

    (b)   if the person is a body corporate, by serving it in accordance with sub-paragraph (a) on the secretary or clerk of that body;

    (c)   if the person is a partnership, by serving it in accordance with sub-paragraph (a) on a partner or on a person having the control or management of the partnership business; and

    (d)   if the person is an unincorporated body, by serving it in accordance with sub-paragraph (a) on a person having control or management of that body.

(2) For the purposes of paragraph (1), the proper address of any person on whom a document is to be served under these Regulations is his last known address except that—

    (a)   in the case of service on a body corporate or its secretary or clerk, it is the address of the registered or principal office of the body corporate in the United Kingdom; and

    (b)   in the case of service on a partnership or partner or person having the control or management of a partnership business, it is the partnership's principal place of business in the United Kingdom.

(3) A person's electronic mail address may also be his proper address for the purposes of paragraph (1).

…

SCHEDULE 4
Notice of the right to cancel

This schedule has no associated Explanatory Memorandum

PART I
INFORMATION TO BE CONTAINED IN NOTICE OF THE RIGHT TO CANCEL

1. The identity of the trader including trading name if any.

2. The trader's reference number, code or other details to enable the contract or offer to be identified.

3. A statement that the consumer has a right to cancel the contract if he wishes and that this right can be exercised by delivering, or sending (including by electronic mail) a cancellation notice to the person mentioned in the next paragraph at any time within the period of 7 days starting with the day of receipt of a notice in writing of the right to cancel the contract.

4. The name and address, (including any electronic mail address as well as the postal address), of a person to whom a cancellation notice may be given.

5. A statement that the notice of cancellation is deemed to be served as soon as it is posted or sent to a trader or in the case of an electronic communication from the day it is sent to the trader.

6. A statement that the consumer can use the cancellation form provided if he wishes.

PART II
CANCELLATION NOTICE TO BE INCLUDED IN NOTICE OF THE RIGHT TO CANCEL

If you wish to cancel the contract you MUST DO SO IN WRITING and deliver personally or send (which may be by electronic mail) this to the person named below. You may use this form if you want to but you do not have to.

(Complete, detach and retirn this form ONLY IF YOU WISH TO CANCEL THE CONTRACT.)

To .... [trader to insert name and address of person to whom notice may be given.]

I/We (delete as appropriate) hereby give notice that I/we (delete as appropriate) wish to cancel my/our (delete as appropriate) contract .... [trader to insert reference number, code or other details to enable the contract or offer to be identified. He may also insert the name and address of the consumer.]

Signed
Name and Address
Date

Chapter 9

CONDITIONAL RETAINERS (CONDITIONAL FEE AGREEMENTS)

9.1   A conditional fee agreement may be defined as being a contract of retainer which provides that the legal representative's fee (or any part of it) is payable only in specified circumstances. Those circumstances are usually (indeed, almost invariably) related to the outcome of the matter to which the agreement relates. The statutory definition of a conditional fee agreement is dealt with in detail below (**9.46–9.55**).

9.2   This chapter discusses the topic in the following way. The current statutory law is outlined first because, to a large extent, the common law has been eclipsed by statute. Secondly, there is a discussion of the ways in which a conditional fee agreement can fall short of compliance with the statutory regime. Thirdly, the common law is described: this includes a short discussion of champerty and of conditional fee agreements in non-contentious work. And finally, a number of miscellaneous issues are addressed, such as how to tell whether the ambit of an agreement covers the work that is being undertaken.

9.3   Whilst the distinction between the statutory law and the common law is a useful framework, it is not adhered to rigidly. In particular, the topic of conditional fee agreements in non-contentious business spans both; this topic is discussed at **9.299** *et seq.*

TYPES OF CONDITIONAL FEE AGREEMENTS

9.4   Conditional fee agreements come in many different styles. This is an area of the law which is bedevilled by TFLAs (three- and four-letter acronyms). The following headings cover most types of conditional fee agreement (including one or two which are unlawful or of questionable validity).

Ordinary conditional fee agreements

Other names

9.5   This is what is usually meant by the acronym 'CFA'. Consumers often refer to this type of agreement as a 'no win, no fee' agreement. Where this type of agreement provides for a success fee, the terms 'enhanced fee agreement' and 'conditional uplift fee agreement' ('CUFA') are occasionally used, but in view of the fact that success fees are now almost ubiquitous, these terms have fallen into disuse.

Payment terms

9.6   If the claim is successful, the legal representative will be paid his full fees (usually together with a success fee), but if it is unsuccessful, no fees are payable. Disbursements may or may not be payable in the event of a win. If the client wins but fails to beat a Part 36 offer, fees incurred after the offer may or may not be payable, depending on the type of agreement; if fees are not payable, the agreement is said to provide for a quantum risk (see **9.44** for a further discussion of that term).

Pros and cons

9.7   This type of agreement is simple and easy to understand. The client must bear the risk of fees being incurred in the event of a win but not recovered in the litigation (those monies often being referred to as 'the shortfall'). In contrast to some other types of agreement (specifically, collective conditional fee agreements) this type of agreement can be administratively burdensome because a whole new written document will have to be produced for each retainer created.

Notes

9.8   All of the model agreements published by the Law Society over the last 10 years or so have been ordinary conditional fee agreements.[1]

CFA Lite

Other names

9.9   This is otherwise known as a 'simplified CFA'. A CFA Lite is often described by and to consumers as a 'no costs to you' agreement. The phrase 'CFA Lite' was originally a light-hearted term (which, for a short period, competed with the term 'Decaf CFA'), but it has gained currency and is now an accepted label.[2] The ambit of the definition has also changed (see below). In the past, such agreements would often have been referred to as *Thai Trading* agreements (se **9.32** *et seq*).

Payment terms

9.10   The main characteristic of a CFA Lite is that in ordinary circumstances the client will be liable only for those costs which are recovered in the litigation. The phrase 'CFA Lite' originally referred only to the type of agreement made under reg 3A of the Conditional Fee Agreements Regulations 2000 (as amended) ('the CFA Regulations 2000'): that type of agreement was one in which the client was 'liable to pay his legal representative's fees and expenses only to the extent that sums [were] recovered in respect of the relevant proceedings, whether by way of costs or otherwise'. The CFA Regulations 2000 were revoked on 1 November 2005, but the use of the term has continued; the term has, therefore, come to mean any conditional fee agreement where

---

[1]   The current version is for use following the revocation of the Conditional Fee Agreements Regulations 2000 (SI 2000/692); prior to that the Law Society's April 2000 model agreement had to be replaced 3 months later by their July 2000 model agreement; this was to make a change to a provision in the earlier model which has come under attack: see *Hollins v Russell* [2003] EWCA Civ 718 at [118]–[120] for a discussion of this.

[2]   See, for example, *Jones v Wrexham Borough Council* [2007] EWCA Civ 1356, in which Waller LJ repeatedly used the term; see also *Munkenbeck & Marshall v Harold* [2005] EWHC 356 (TCC) and the speech of Phillips MR made to Law Society Litigation conferences in 2003.

the legal representative's fees are limited to those costs recovered in the litigation. Many modern-day CFA Lites would not satisfy the original requirements: in particular, it is not uncommon for disbursements to be payable regardless of the outcome of the claim.

Pros and cons

9.11 This type of agreement is simple to understand: the legal representative must bear the burden of fees not being recovered in the litigation, but this is a burden that can be used to justify a higher success fee than would otherwise be the case (although this may change in the future following the Jackson reforms). As with any other type of agreement other than collective conditional fee agreements, a CFA Lite can be administratively burdensome because a new written instrument will have to be created for each retainer.

Discounted conditional fee agreements

Other names

9.12 This is often shortened to 'dCFA'; another term is a 'guaranteed fee agreement'. The term 'partial fee agreement' is occasionally used at the Bar.[3]

Payment terms

9.13 A discounted conditional fee agreement is an agreement where the legal representative's fees are payable in full if the case is won, but a discounted fee will apply if the case is lost. A success fee is often payable in addition, but this is very from always being the case.

Pros and cons

9.14 The legal representative has the comfort of knowing that he will be paid something regardless of the outcome of the litigation. The client has to bear the burden of paying those monies regardless of whether the case is successful. Otherwise, the pros and cons are very similar to ordinary conditional fee agreements (see **9.7**).

Notes

9.15 This type of agreement is particularly popular with solicitors who have a predominately defendant practice; it allows liability insurers to fund the litigation at a discount but in such a way as to ensure that the solicitor has an incentive to win. The fact that a success fee may be payable can be used to put pressure on an opponent to settle or discontinue: some legal representatives see that as a significant advantage. It is also used in combination with litigation (third-party) funding (see **41.23**).

---

[3] There is supposed to be a distinction between a partial fee agreement and a discounted conditional fee agreement, but it is not a distinction that is important: a partial fee agreement is supposed to create two retainers, one of which is payable privately and the other of which is payable conditionally.

Discounted CFA Lite

Other names

9.16   This is often shortened to 'dCFA Lite'; it is a variety of 'guaranteed fee agreement'. The term 'insurers' CFA' is also gaining currency.

Payment terms

9.17   The oxymoronic phrase 'discounted CFA Lite' is used to describe a type of agreement which is now commonplace in commercial litigation. It is an agreement under which a discounted fee is payable regardless of whether the case is won or lost but any fees in addition to that guaranteed minimum will ordinarily be limited to those costs recovered in the litigation.

Pros and cons

9.18   The legal representative has the comfort of knowing that he will be paid something regardless of the outcome of the litigation and the client has the comfort of knowing that ordinarily he will not have to pay any more than those discounted fees. This client gets the additional advantage of knowing that his solicitors have an incentive to win. The pros and cons are otherwise similar to discounted conditional fee agreements in general (see **9.14**).

Notes

9.19   This type of agreement is particularly popular with commercial litigators and with solicitors who have a predominately insurance-based practice (including practices funded by BTE insurance). The discounted fees are usually set at such a level that the 'ordinary' fees are, for all practical purposes, a bonus when compared with the fees that had been payable historically. The fact that a success fee may be payable can be used to put pressure on an opponent to settle or discontinue: some legal representatives see that as a significant advantage.

Damages-based agreements

Other names

9.20   The acronym 'DBA' is gaining currency.[4] The term 'contingency fee agreement' is also used, but this is a term that is apt to cause confusion as it can mean different things in different circumstances (see **9.35**); unless the contrary is obvious from the context, the term 'damages-based agreement' is used in this book.

Payment terms

9.21   A damages-based agreement is an agreement by which the amount of the legal representative's fee is quantitatively linked to the amount of damages or debt recovered

---

[4]   See, for example, the comments in *Regulating Damages-based agreements* CP 10/09 (Ministry of Justice, 1 July 2009), p 3.

(or in non-contentious matters to the price received, the premium, etc). At the time of writing[5] s 58AA of the Courts and Legal Services Act 1990 (as amended) provided the following statutory definition:[6]

> '(a) a damages-based agreement is an agreement between a person providing advocacy services, litigation services or claims management services and the recipient of those services which provides that—.
>
> (i)   the recipient is to make a payment to the person providing the services if the recipient obtains a specified financial benefit in connection with the matter in relation to which the services are provided, and
>
> (ii)   the amount of that payment is to be determined by reference to the amount of the financial benefit obtained.'

Pros and cons

9.22   The main benefit of a damages-based agreement is that the client will pay costs which are proportionate to the benefit received. The main disadvantage is that the costs actually paid may bear no relation to the work undertaken; this can result in over- or under- remuneration and in rare cases can result in clients or solicitors being treated unfairly. Some commentators also take the view that damages-based agreements give rise to a greater potential for conflict of interest than conditional fee agreements.

Notes

9.23   Whilst there is authority to suggest otherwise,[7] damages-based agreements are widely believed to be unlawful at common law in contentious matters. Where the work is non-contentious, however, the common law tolerates such agreements; as an example of this, they have been used in the Employment Tribunal for very many years. As of 7 April 2010 such agreements have been regulated;[8] at the time of writing regulated agreements could be used only in the Employment Tribunal, but the ambit of statutory interventions will, at a date yet to be confirmed, be widened to include any sort of proceedings for resolving disputes.[9]

Collective conditional fee agreements

Other names

9.24   All of the types of agreement mentioned above have their collective counterparts. Thus, in addition to ordinary CCFAs, there are also CCFA Lites, dCCFAs, dCCFA Lites, etc.

---

5   At the time of writing, the Legal Aid, Sentencing and Punishment of Offenders Bill had just been given Royal Assent; clause 44 of which amends s 58AA of the Courts and Legal Services Act 1990 (as amended) so as to enlarge its ambit.

6   Section 58AA(3)(a) of the Courts and Legal Services Act 1990, as amended by s 154 of the Coroners and Justice Act 2009.

7   See, for example, *Benaim (UK) Ltd v Davies Middleton & Davies Ltd* [2004] EWHC 737 (TCC).

8   The enabling Act is the Courts and Legal Services Act 1990, s 58AA (as amended by Coroners and Justice Act 2009, s 154); the regulations are the Damages-Based Agreements Regulations 2010 (SI 1020/1206).

9   See s 42 of the Legal Aid, Sentencing and Punishment of Offenders Bill.

Payment terms

9.25 The terms may mirror any of those which may apply to an individual conditional fee agreement.

Pros and cons

9.26 The advantage of collective conditional fee agreements is that they are administratively easy to implement on a case-by-case basis (although the original agreement needs to be crafted with care, and this is not an easy task).

Notes

9.27 As with CFA Lites (see **9.10**), the ambit of the term has widened since 1 November 2005. The term was originally used to refer to an agreement which purported to comply with the Collective Conditional Fee Agreements Regulations 2000 (SI 2000/2988) (as amended) ('the CCFA Regulations 2000'), but now that those regulations have been revoked, the term is used to refer to any form of conditional retainer in which the terms are contained in an umbrella agreement (often referred to as the 'collective element') that applies to clients in general (or to a class of clients). Although they have now been revoked, reg 3(1) of the CCFA Regulations 2000 provided the following definition:

> '(1) Subject to paragraph (2) of this regulation, a collective conditional fee agreement is an agreement which—
>
> > (a) disregarding section 58(3)(c) of the Courts and Legal Services Act 1990, would be a conditional fee agreement; and
> > (b) does not refer to specific proceedings, but provides for fees to be payable on a common basis in relation to a class of proceedings, or, if it refers to more than one class of proceedings, on a common basis in relation to each class.'

Speccing agreements

Other names

9.28 The more descriptive term 'undeclared CFA' is also occasionally used, although this term may encompass other types of retainer. This type of agreement includes *Thai Trading* agreements (see below), but arguably differs in that a speccing agreement may or may not be a sham agreement, whereas a *Thai Trading* agreement is generally an openly declared arrangement.

Payment terms

9.29 This phrase used to mean a type of conditional fee agreement whereby the solicitor would act for an impecunious client who has no prospect of paying the solicitor's fees unless costs were recovered from an opponent.[10] It describes an informal and often undeclared conditional fee agreement where the conditionality arises out of a mutual understanding rather than a written agreement under which the conditionality arises out of a mutual understanding rather than a written agreement. Over recent years the phrase has taken on a wider meaning relating to informal insurance (see **9.31**).

---

[10] See, for example, the description in M Cook *Cook on Costs 2006* (LexisNexis Butterworths, 2006), para 42.9.

Pros and cons

9.30   Unless the agreement is formalised (or, at the very least, reduced into writing), it will be unenforceable.

Notes

9.31   Over recent years the term 'speccing agreement' has been used to mean something more than a contract of retainer in that it has been used to describe an agreement by which the legal representative provides an informal type of insurance.[11] This used to be regarded as being a somewhat sinister and potentially unlawful arrangement, but this is no longer the case (see **8.289** *et seq*).

Thai Trading agreements

Other names

9.32   A *Thai Trading* agreement can be categorised as a speccing agreement. Whilst some would say that the two terms are identical, a *Thai Trading* agreement arguably differs from a speccing agreement in that there is usually no attempt to conceal its terms.

Payment terms

9.33   The phrase '*Thai Trading* agreement' derives from *Thai Trading Co (a firm) v Taylor* [1998] 1 Costs LR 122; the agreement in that case was an informal conditional fee agreement under which payment would be demanded only if the client won the case, and then only to the extent that she recovered costs from her opponent.[12]

Pros and cons

9.34   Unless the agreement is formalised (or, at the very least, reduced into writing), it will be unenforceable.

Contingency fee agreements

9.35   The term 'contingency fee agreement' can be used to mean different things in different contexts; this can cause difficulties because the two most common usages mean radically different things. As is explained above, the term is often used to mean a subset of conditional fee agreements (as widely defined) under which the legal representative's fee is calculated by reference to the amount of money that is recovered for the client.[13] A non-contentious example would be where the legal representative sought to recover a percentage of the price of sale of a business; an example in a contentious setting would be where the fee was a percentage of the damages or debt recovered (this being a 'damages-based agreement', see **9.20-9.23**). In this book the phrase 'contingency fee agreement' is reserved for agreements where there is no litigation or contemplated litigation (ie, the first of the two examples given above) but there is no reason why the other types could not also be referred to as contingency fee agreements. The other way

---

[11]   See, for example, M Pace *The insurance mediation rules – traps for the unwary* (2007) JPI Law 1, pp 109–113.
[12]   *Thai Trading Co (a firm) v Taylor* [1998] 1 Costs LR 122 at 124.
[13]   See 'Criminal solicitors gear up for mile-high club' (2002) 99 LSG 11, p 41 for an example of the emergence of this usage.

in which the phrase 'contingency fee agreement' is used is to mean *any* conditional fee agreement of *any* sort[14] (that being a wider definition than that given to 'conditional fee agreement' rather than a narrower one). There is nothing wrong with that usage, but in order to avoid confusion, it is not adopted in this book.

Conditional retainers

9.36   This rarely-used phrase embraces the entire spectrum of retainers referred to above. It is a convenient way of referring to a conditional contract of retainer. Its most common usage is where a paying party knows that a success fee is being claimed but does not know the nature of the retainer under which it is being claimed (ie where it is not known whether the agreement is a conditional fee agreement or a collective conditional fee agreement). The term has another role to play: where there is a need to distinguish between the written instrument that creates a conditional fee agreement and the contract itself (such as where it is contended that the written instrument does not reflect the true bargain struck between the counterparties), the phrase can be used to refer to the true bargain struck.

THE LANGUAGE OF CONDITIONAL FEE AGREEMENTS

9.37   The law of conditional fee agreements has its own vocabulary. The following are some of the words and phrases which may be encountered. Where possible, examples of usage are given. Some of the words and phrases set out below are informal and not universally accepted.

Additional liability

9.38   'Additional liability' relates to both conditional fee agreements and ATE policies; CPR, r 43.2(o) provides the following definition:

> '"[A]dditional liability" means the percentage increase, the insurance premium, or the additional amount in respect of provision made by a membership organisation, as the case may be.'

Base costs

9.39   The CPD defines base costs in this way (CPD, art 2.2):

> '"[B]ase costs" means costs other than the amount of any additional liability.'

The term 'basic costs' is also often heard.

---

[14]   See for example, the Solicitors' Code of Conduct 2007, which defined a contingency fee as being "... defined in rule 24 (Interpretation) as any sum (whether fixed, or calculated either as a percentage of the proceeds or otherwise) payable only in the event of success.' The SRA Code of Conduct 2011 seems to use the phrase in that way too, but it is not possible to be sure of this because it contains no express definition.

Collective element

9.40 This is a term which refers to that part of a collective conditional fee agreement which contains the terms of the agreement; under the CCFA Regulations 2000, it was that part of the agreement which was referred to by reg 4 and (where the agreement provides for a success fee) reg 5.

Funder

9.41 Regulation 1(2) of the CCFA Regulations 2000 provides the following definition:

> '"[F]under" means the party to a collective conditional fee agreement who, under that agreement, is liable to pay the legal representative's fees.'

The word has nothing to do with the use of the same word in the context of maintenance and non-party costs orders.

Percentage increase

9.42 Regulation 3(3) of the CFA Regulations 2000 affords the following definition:[15]

> '"percentage increase" means the percentage by which the amount of the fees which would be payable if the agreement were not a conditional fee agreement is to be increased under the agreement.'

A very similar definition is provided by CPR, r 43.2(l):

> '"percentage increase" means the percentage by which the amount of a legal representative's fee can be increased in accordance with a conditional fee agreement which provides for a success fee.'

The difference between a success fee and a percentage increase is that the former is a sum of money whereas the latter is expressed in terms of a percentage. In practice, the two terms are often used interchangeably.

Postponement charge

9.43 This is also known as 'the postponement element'[16] and 'charge for postponement'.[17] It is that part of the success fee which compensates the legal representative for the fact that where his fees are payable conditionally, he will not be able to issue interim bills. Regulation 3(1)(b) of the CFA Regulations 2000 contains the following definition:

> '[That part] of the percentage increase, if any, [which] relates to the cost to the legal representative of the postponement of the payment of his fees and expenses.'

In so far as this book is concerned the phrase is used to refer both to the charge itself, and to the percentage which is used to calculate it.

---

[15] This definition is almost identical to that which appears at reg 5(3) of the Collective Conditional Fee Agreements Regulations 2000.

[16] For an example of this phrase being used see *Sidhu v Sandu* [2008] EWHC 90108 (Costs) at [19].

[17] See, for example, *Utting v McBain* [2007] EWHC 90085 (Costs) at [23].

Quantum risk

9.44   This is a risk that arises out of a conditional fee agreement providing for no payment of base costs in the event of the client failing to secure a result which is more advantageous to him than an opponent's Part 36 offer.[18]

Success fee

9.45   Section 58A(2)(b) of the Courts and Legal Services Act 1990 (as amended) provides:

> 'A conditional fee agreement provides for a success fee if it provides for the amount of any fees to which it applies to be increased, in specified circumstances, above the amount which would be payable if it were not payable only in specified circumstances.'

So a success fee will be a fee which is payable only in specified circumstances (which almost always means that the case has been won) and which exceeds the amount which would have been payable if it were not payable only in specified circumstances.

CONDITIONAL FEE AGREEMENTS AND THE STATUTORY LAW

Statutory definition

9.46   As of 1 April 2000 (with savings as to existing cases) the relevant statutory provisions are ss 58 and 58A of the Courts and Legal Services Act 1990 (as amended by the Access to Justice Act 1999). CLSA 1990, s 58(2)(a) provides:

> '[A conditional fee agreement is an] agreement with a person providing advocacy or litigation services which provides for his fees and expenses, or any part of them, to be payable only in specified circumstances.'

Thus, the statutory definition of a conditional fee agreement is that:

* it is with a person providing litigation services or advocacy services; and
* it provides that his fees, or any part of them, are payable only in specified circumstances.

9.47   The definition will consequently depend on the meaning of 'litigation services' and 'advocacy services'. These are defined by CLSA 1990 thus:[19]

— 'litigation services' means any services which it would be reasonable to expect a person who is exercising, or contemplating exercising, a right to conduct litigation in relation to any proceedings, or contemplated proceedings, to provide; and
— 'advocacy services' means any services which it would be reasonable to expect a person who is exercising, or contemplating exercising, a right of audience in relation to any proceedings, or contemplated proceedings, to provide.

Both of these definitions depend on the meaning of 'proceedings'.

---

[18]   For an example of it being used, see *Haines v Sarner* [2005] EWHC 90009 (Costs) at [15].
[19]   CLSA 1990, s 119 (as amended); these definitions have been unaffected by the amendments made by the Legal Services Act 2007.

9.48 For the purposes of CLSA 1990 in general, 'proceedings' are defined as 'proceedings in any court'.[20] So, if the definition were to be based on only those things that have been described above, the meaning of 'proceedings' would be narrow (which would mean that the class of retainers which would fall within the category of conditional fee agreements would be correspondingly narrow). CLSA 1990 widens the ambit by replacing the narrow definition of 'proceedings' with a much wider one for the purposes of ss 58 and 58A:[21]

> 'In section 58 and this section (and in the definitions of "advocacy services" and "litigation services" as they apply for their purposes) "proceedings" includes any sort of proceedings for resolving disputes (and not just proceedings in a court), whether commenced or contemplated.'

Thus, CLSA 1990, ss 58 and 58A will apply to *any* class of proceedings[22] for resolving disputes, and not just those in a court.[23] The definition will not cover retainers which do not relate to disputes or which relate to disputes but do not relate to proceedings.

9.49 The CPR adopt the statutory definition. It does so by making specific provision for costs to be recovered pursuant to conditional fee agreements, and then by linking that provision to the statutory definition mentioned above. CPR, r 43.3(3) reads:

> 'Where advocacy or litigation services are provided to a client under a conditional fee agreement, costs are recoverable under Parts 44 to 48 notwithstanding that the client is liable to pay his legal representative's fees and expenses only to the extent that sums are recovered in respect of the proceedings, whether by way of costs or otherwise.'

The CPR then go on to define a conditional fee agreement as being an agreement which satisfies all the conditions applicable to it by virtue the statutory provisions mentioned above.[24] For all practical purposes, then, the CPR definition of a conditional fee agreement is the same as the statutory definition. The CPD, unsurprisingly, reflects the CPR.[25]

9.50 The next question is how the statutory definition of a conditional fee agreement is to be applied in practice. An issue that commonly arises is whether a retainer has inadvertently become a conditional fee agreement by reason of a conditional waiver (ie a putative agreement to waive fees if the case is unsuccessful); that waiver may have been made by the solicitor in the client care letter or elsewhere.

9.51 That problem will usually be academic if the retainer was made after 1 November 2005; this is because the document which effected the waiver would usually itself meet the minimal statutory requirements that remained after the revocation of the CFA Regulations 2000. Retainers made before that date would rarely meet the then

---

[20] CLSA 1990, s 119 (as amended).
[21] CLSA 1990, s 58A(4) (as amended).
[22] The definition is somewhat circular because it defines 'proceedings' by reference to a definition which includes that very same word; there is no authority on how that word is to be interpreted. In particular, there is no authority on the issue of whether it would include work which is traditionally regarded as being non-contentious, such as work in tribunals.
[23] Until CLSA 1990, s 58 was amended by the Access to Justice Act 1999, conditional fee agreements that related to arbitral proceedings did not fall within the statutory regime: *Bevan Ashford (a firm) v Geoff Yeandle (Contractors) Ltd (in liquidation)* [1999] Ch 239.
[24] CPR, r 43.2(4).
[25] See CPD, art 2.2.

requirements, so in those circumstances a finding that a retainer was a conditional fee agreement within the meaning of CLSA 1990, s 58(2)(a) would often render it unenforceable.

9.52 Just such a case presented itself to Dyson LJ; he dealt with the matter by interpreting the phrase 'contemplated proceedings' in CLSA 1990, s 58A(4) in a pragmatically narrow way. The client care letter contained the following waiver:[26]

> 'If your claim is disputed by your opponent and you decide not to pursue your claim then we will not make a charge for the work we have done to date.'

Dyson LJ found that as a matter of construction, work carried out before the decision to proceed with a contested claim cannot be characterised as being 'litigation services'. He found that the waiver was intended to apply to fees for modest pre-litigation services. He reminded himself that CLSA 1990, s 119(1) defined litigation services by reference to whether there were 'contemplated proceedings'; he made the following observations:[27]

> '"contemplated proceedings" are proceedings of which it can be said that there is at least a real likelihood that they will be issued. Until the potential defendant disputes the claim, it is not possible to say that proceedings are contemplated. Advising a client as to whether he or she has a good prima facie case and writing a letter of claim are not enough to amount to litigation services.'

Dyson LJ explained that the matter was one of contractual interpretation rather than a matter which turned on the nature of the work which had actually been carried out. Thus, it would not be right to say that a retainer escaped the provisions of the 1990 Act merely because the litigation did not get beyond the letter of claim stage.

9.53 As with the interpretation of any contract, the court is not restricted to looking solely at the four corners of the written instrument. Where appropriate, it may take into account other material, such as other documents, including correspondence, and standard terms and conditions.[28] Whilst dealing with a slightly different point (ie the effect of a retainer rather than whether a retainer was a conditional fee agreement), Waller LJ (with whom Longmore LJ and Hughes LJ agreed) found that a client care letter and a conditional fee agreement could be taken into account in deciding how the retainer would operate in practice:[29]

> 'I can see no reason why the court should not look at the whole package produced by the solicitor, the CFA agreement, the Rule 15 letter explaining to the client the effect of the agreement, and indeed the insurance policy recommended by the solicitor.'

9.54 Other examples exist.[30] There is no reason to believe that, in an appropriate case, the court would adopt a different approach when considering whether a retainer was a conditional fee agreement within the meaning of CLSA 1990, s 58(2)(a).

---

[26] *Gaynor v Central West London Buses Ltd* [2006] EWCA Civ 1120.
[27] Paragraph 17.
[28] See, for example, *Munkenbeck & Marshall v Harold* [2005] EWHC 356 (TCC), in which industry standard terms and conditions were incorporated into an agreement.
[29] *Jones v Wrexham Borough Council* [2007] EWCA Civ 1356 at [17]; other examples exist. Although he ultimately came to the conclusion that the agreement was unenforceable, in *Utting v McBain* [2007] EWHC 3293 (QB) at [21]–[24] Blake J took into account a letter which had been sent to the client at about the same time that the conditional fee agreement was made.
[30] See, for example, *Forde v Birmingham City Council* [2009] EWHC 12 (QB) at [73]–[78].

9.55 In summary, for all practical purposes the definition of a conditional fee agreement is that contained in CLSA 1990, s 58(1): it is that section to which the CPR, etc refer. The process of determining whether a retainer falls within that definition is a question of contractual interpretation.

Basic requirements of all enforceable conditional fee agreements

9.56 Even today (after the revocation of the CFA Regulations 2000, etc) the starting point is CLSA 1990, s 58(1):

'A conditional fee agreement which satisfies all of the conditions applicable to it by virtue of this section shall not be unenforceable by reason only of its being a conditional fee agreement; but (subject to subsection (5))[31] any other conditional fee agreement shall be unenforceable.'

9.57 The 'conditions' which must be satisfied are set out at CLSA 1990, s 58(3):

'The following conditions are applicable to every conditional fee agreement—

(a) it must be in writing;
(b) it must not relate to proceedings which cannot be the subject of an enforceable conditional fee agreement; and
(c) it must comply with such requirements (if any) as may be prescribed by the Lord Chancellor.'

The relevant 'requirements' are contained in delegated legislation. Those requirements have changed since the revocation of the CFA Regulations 2000, etc); the various regimes that have existed from time to time are each discussed below.

9.58 In order to be enforceable, a conditional fee agreement to which CLSA 1990, s 58(3) relates:

- must be in writing;
- must not relate to proceedings which cannot be the subject of an enforceable conditional fee agreement; and
- must comply with the applicable delegated legislation.

The first two of these topics is dealt with in turn. The last is a substantial topic which is discussed at **9.66–9.273**.

The requirement to be in writing

9.59 Whether a conditional fee agreement is in writing will be a matter of fact. It is worth mentioning that, whilst there is no authority directly on the point, it would seem that any conditional fee agreement which is not in writing would be unenforceable regardless of whether it is in respect of contentious or non-contentious work; the reasons for this are explained at **9.305**.

---

[31] The issues meant by the reference to 'subsection 5' are discussed at **8.278** and **9.238**; they relate to non-contentious work.

Prohibited conditional fee agreements

9.60   The types of proceedings which cannot be the subject of an enforceable conditional fee agreement are set out in CLSA 1990, s 58A(1); they are:

(a)   criminal proceedings (apart from proceedings under s 82 of the Environmental Protection Act 1990); and

(b)   family proceedings.

Proceedings under s 82 of the Environmental Protection Act 1990 are brought in the magistrates' court for an order abating a statutory nuisance. For the reasons set out below, whilst a conditional fee agreement in that type of claim is permissible, it may not provide for a success fee. The definition of family proceedings is complex.[32]

Further requirements where there is a success fee

9.61   A conditional fee agreement may – and at the time of writing usually did – provide for a success fee. That type of agreement is defined by CLSA 1990, s 58(2)(b):

> '[A] conditional fee agreement provides for a success fee if it provides for the amount of any fees to which it applies to be increased, in specified circumstances, above the amount which would be payable if it were not payable only in specified circumstances.'

The Jackson reforms will, once implemented, abrogate the ability to recover success fees between opposing parties; whilst this will probably mean that success fees will be less commonly encountered, most of the law set out below will be unchanged.

9.62   In addition to those conditions stipulated in CLSA 1990, s 58(3), the following further conditions which apply to a conditional fee agreement which provides for a success fee are set out in s 58(4):

> 'The following further conditions are applicable to a conditional fee agreement which provides for a success fee—
>
> (a)   it must relate to proceedings of a description specified by order made by the Lord Chancellor;
>
> (b)   it must state the percentage by which the amount of the fees which would be payable if it were not a conditional fee agreement is to be increased; and
>
> (c)   that percentage must not exceed the percentage specified in relation to the description of proceedings to which the agreement relates by order made by the Lord Chancellor.'

9.63   The proceedings to which a conditional fee agreement providing for a success fee must relate are the proceedings which can be the subject of an enforceable conditional fee agreement, except proceedings under s 82 of the Environmental Protection Act 1990.[33]

---

[32]   Family proceedings are defined are defined by CLSA 1990, s 58A(2) as being proceedings under the following: the Matrimonial Causes Act 1973; the Adoption and Children Act 2002; the Domestic Proceedings and Magistrates' Courts Act 1978; Part III of the Matrimonial and Family Proceedings Act 1984; Parts I, II and IV of the Children Act 1989; Part IV of the Family Law Act 1996; Civil Partnership Act 2004, Pt 2, ch 2 (proceedings for dissolution etc of civil partnership), Sch 5 (financial relief in the High Court or a county court etc), Sch 6 (financial relief in magistrates' courts etc), Sch 7 (financial relief in England and Wales after overseas dissolution etc of a civil partnership); and the inherent jurisdiction of the High Court in relation to children.

[33]   Conditional Fee Agreements Order 2000 (SI 2000/823), art 3. A draft statutory instrument (the Draft Conditional fee Agreements Order (Amendment) Order 2010) was laid on 4 March 2010 with the intention

9.64   The percentage increase must not be exceeded 100%.[34] If this percentage is exceeded, the retainer is unenforceable.[35] The measure of the percentage increase is not the costs at risk, but the fees that would have been charged had the agreement not been a conditional fee agreement.[36] This may be relevant in the event that the agreement is a 'discounted conditional fee agreement'. An example illustrates this: if the amount which would have been charged had the agreement not been a conditional fee agreement is £100 per hour, and if the amount which is charged in the event of a loss is £25 per hour, the maximum permissible success fee would be 100% of £100 per hour, rather than 100% of the costs at risk (ie £75 per hour).

9.65   In summary, therefore, a conditional fee agreement as defined in CLSA 1990, s 58(2)(a) will be enforceable, but only if the following conditions are met:

- it is in writing;
- it does not relate to a family or criminal matter (other than proceedings under s 82 of the Environmental Protection Act 1990);
- where it provides for a success fee, it does not relate to proceedings under s 82 of the Environmental Protection Act 1990;
- where it provides for a success fee, it states the percentage increase;
- where it provides for a success fee, the percentage increase does not exceed 100%.

9.66   Whether other requirements apply will depend on the period in which the agreement was made:

- where the agreement was made on or after 1 November 2005, the conditions above are the only conditions that have to be met;[37]
- where a conditional fee agreement was entered into on or after 1 April 2000 and before 1 November 2005, either the CFA Regulations 2000 or the CCFA Regulations 2000 will apply, depending on the nature of the retainer; that period can be further subdivided: this is because significant amendments were made on 2 June 2003;[38]
- where the agreement was entered into before 1 April 2000, older (and now rarely encountered) regulations applied.

Where they apply, all of the regulations make stipulations as to what the written instrument of retainer should contain or not contain, but the regulations relating to individual retainers are, as one would expect, geared towards providing consumer protection for individual clients and make provision for the client to be given pre-contract counselling. It must be stressed that these regulations do not apply to conditional fee agreements entered into today.

Individual conditional fee agreements

9.67   The law which is expounded below applies only to conditional fee agreements that were entered into on or after 1 April 2000 and before 1 November 2005 (although

---

of limiting success fees in defamation cases to 10 percent; on 6 April 2010, however, the then Leader of the Commons Harriet Harman confirmed that the then government would not be proceeding with the proposal.
[34]   SI 2000/823, art 4.
[35]   See *Jones v Caradon Catnic Ltd* [2005] EWCA 1821.
[36]   *Evans v Gloucestershire County Council* [2008] EWCA Civ 21 at [27].
[37]   Conditional Fee Agreements (Revocation) Regulations 2005 (SI 2005/2305), reg 2.
[38]   Conditional Fee Agreements (Miscellaneous Amendments) Regulations 2003 (SI 2003/1240), reg 1.

some of the law relating to agreements entered before that period is also mentioned); the law in this section does not apply to other conditional fee agreements, nor does it apply to collective conditional fee agreements.

9.68   Although, technically, the law set out in this section could apply to agreements for fixed costs payable under the CPR, that law will be irrelevant; this is because fixed costs are recoverable regardless of the operation of the indemnity principle.[39]

9.69   Despite the fact that some years have passed since the relevant delegated legislation was revoked, the law continues to be clarified by decided cases; therefore, the reader should regard this section as being an aid to further research rather than as a comprehensive description of the law. With one or two exceptions, no attempt has been made to refer to cases which are not binding.

9.70   The 'requirements' stipulated in CLSA 1990, s 58(3)(c) are the Conditional Fee Agreements Regulations 2000 ('the CFA Regulations 2000'). If those requirements are not met, the conditional fee agreement will be unenforceable.[40] Whether a putative breach of the regulations will have that result will depend on whether the breach is a 'material' breach. Materiality is a doctrine which arises from case law; it is not mentioned in the CFA Regulations 2000 themselves.

9.71   It is convenient to deal with materiality in some detail, but in order to allow the reader to see the wood for the trees, it is worth considering the overall method by which a putative breach is considered. The following forensic sieve is a useful framework, although it may not be appropriate in every case:

- Is the retainer an individual conditional fee agreement to which the CFA Regulations 2000 relate and, if it is, which specific regulations apply?
- If so, is there a need to consider whether a 'genuine issue' arises in the context of the putative breach under consideration and, if there is, has such an issue been made out upon the facts?
- Is the retainer, properly construed, in breach of one or more the requirements of the CFA Regulations 2000?
- If so, has the particular departure from the CFA Regulations 2000, either on its own or in conjunction with any other such departure in this case, had a materially adverse effect either upon the protection afforded to the client or upon the proper administration of justice?

The components of this sieve are considered at **9.89–9.236**, followed by a brief discussion of the effect that a material breach will have upon the agreement at **9.237–9.246**.

9.72   It is worth mentioning at this stage that a number of cautionary comments have been made about the risk of over-zealously interpreting the CFA Regulations 2000; whilst only two are mentioned, many others exist. The first were made by Latham LJ in a case that did not deal with the CFA 2000 Regulations themselves, but which have been widely referred to in that context:[41]

---

[39]   *Nizami v Butt* [2006] EWHC 159.
[40]   See CLSA 1990, s 58(1).
[41]   *Times Newspapers Ltd v Burstein* [2002] EWCA Civ 1739 at [29].

'... The Deputy Costs Judge is to be commended for ensuring that the detailed assessment did not become an excuse for further expensive litigation at the behest of a disappointed but persistent litigant. Satellite litigation about costs has become a growth industry, and one that is a blot on the civil justice system. Costs Judges should be astute to prevent such proceedings from being protracted by allegations that are without substance.'

Citing those comments with approval in another case, Brooke LJ added the following remarks of his own:[42]

'The court should be watchful when it considers allegations that there have been breaches of the Regulations. The parliamentary purpose is to enhance access to justice, not to impede it, and to create better ways of delivering litigation services, not worse ones. These purposes will be thwarted if those who render good service to their clients under CFAs are at risk of going unremunerated at the culmination of the bitter trench warfare which has been such an unhappy feature of the recent litigation scene.'

9.73   The other side of the coin is that the intention of Parliament ought not to be thwarted. The court has often reminded itself that it cannot be said to be irrational that Parliament chose to impose a harsh regime upon those who are charged with ensuring that their clients are properly protected, as Dyson LJ said (in the context of a discussion on materiality):[43]

'Parliament was painting with a broad brush ... Parliament considered that the need to safeguard the interests of clients was so important that it should be secured by providing that, if any of the conditions were not satisfied, the CFA would not be enforceable and the solicitor would not be paid. To use the words of Lord Nicholls again [in *Wilson v First County Trust Ltd (No 2)* [2003] UKHL 40, [2004] 1 AC 816], this is an approach of punishing solicitors pour encourager les autres. Such a policy is tough, but it is not irrational.'

Similar comments have been made by Law LJ (also in the context of materiality).[44]

9.74   There are three other topics which may be relevant when interpreting the CFA Regulations 2000; they are:

(i)   the difference, if any, that is made by the fact that the challenge is brought by the paying party rather than the client;
(ii)   whether a restrictive (narrow) interpretation would be appropriate when considering regulations with a potentially punitive effect; and
(iii)   the importance of clarity.

These three issues are discussed in turn.

Same approach regardless of indemnity of challenger

9.75   Hughes LJ has confirmed that the construction of the agreement is not inflicted by the source of the challenge: the contractual position as between the solicitor and the

---

[42]   *Hollins v Russell* [2003] EWCA Civ 718 at [224], cited with approval by Clarke LJ in *Tankard v John Fredricks Plastics Ltd* [2008] EWCA Civ 1375 at [51].
[43]   *Myatt v National Coal Board* [2006] EWCA Civ 1017 at [30].
[44]   See *Jones v Caradon Catnic Ltd* [2005] EWCA 1821 at [33]–[36], referred to with approval by Dyson LJ in *Myatt v National Coal Board* [2006] EWCA Civ 1017 at [40]–[41].

client must be the same, whoever takes the point.[45] (This does not mean that the paying party will necessarily be permitted to take the same points that a client would be able to take: see **11.20–11.32**.) The fact that many clients show no real interest in the advice being given to them is not a good reason for not giving effect to the intention of Parliament.[46]

Non-restrictive approach

9.76 It is commonly the case, where legislation is capable of inflicting punitive or harsh consequences upon individuals, that it is interpreted in such a way that the obligations it imposes are read narrowly. It is also commonly the case that where the purpose of legislation is to protect consumers, those obligations will be read widely. In so far as the CFA Regulations 2000 are concerned, these factors pull in opposite directions. Dyson LJ (giving judgment of the court) found that the need for a narrow interpretation did not outweigh the need for a wide interpretation:[47]

> 'The purpose of the Regulations is to protect clients, not the financial interests of solicitors. In our judgment, the Regulations should be construed by giving the plain language in which they are expressed its normal and natural meaning.'

Clarke MR has stated much the same thing, namely that the CFA Regulations 2000 should be interpreted in such a way as to promote, rather than detract from, consumer protection.[48]

Clarity

9.77 Although the Court of Appeal has yet to find that an agreement is unenforceable for want of clarity, on almost every occasion that the issue of the CFA Regulations 2000 has come before it, the court has commented that a lack of clarity would place an agreement at risk of being found to be unenforceable.[49]

9.78 The topics identified in the forensic sieve above will shortly be addressed, but, before that is done, the reader is referred to the full recital of the CFA Regulations 2000 at the end of this chapter. They were twice amended in 2003,[50] and those amendments have resulted in significant changes.

9.79 The most important aspect of the CFA Regulations 2000 lies in the fact that, if they are breached, the conditional fee agreement will be unenforceable. Whilst any form of breach may be encountered from time to time, breaches commonly found in practice are (in no particular order):

---

[45] *Jones v Wrexham Borough Council* [2007] EWCA Civ 1356 at [83].

[46] *Garrett v Halton Borough Council; Myatt v National Coal Board* [2006] EWCA Civ 1017 at [102].

[47] *Garrett v Halton Borough Council; Myatt v National Coal Board* [2006] EWCA Civ 1017 at [92].

[48] *Tankard v John Fredricks Plastics Ltd* [2008] EWCA Civ 1375 at [43].

[49] As an example, see *Tankard v John Fredricks Plastics Ltd* [2008] EWCA Civ 1375 at [45] (discussion about whether inconsistent advice about panel membership would amount to a breach) and *Dunn v Ward; Hollins v Russell* [2003] EWCA Civ 718 at [152]–[154] (discussion about the importance of the clarity of the Law Society Conditions).

[50] See the Conditional Fee Agreements (Miscellaneous Amendments) Regulations 2003 (SI 2003/1240) and the Conditional Fee Agreements (Miscellaneous Amendments) (No 2) Regulations 2003 (SI 2003/3344); they were also amended by the Collective Conditional Fee Agreements Regulations 2000 (SI 2000/2988).

(a) a failure adequately to quantify the postponement charge (see below for a definition of this term);

(b) a failure to sign the agreement; and

(c) a failure to give appropriate advice pursuant to reg 4 of the CFA Regulations 2000.

The first two are examples of drafting errors, whilst the last is often referred to as a 'qualitative breach' (this being because it relates to the quality of pre-contract advice given to the client).

Materiality

9.80 For a breach of the CFA Regulations 2000 to be found to be unenforceable, it must be a 'material' breach, ie it must have had a materially adverse effect either upon the protection afforded to the client or upon the proper administration of justice.[51] The Court of Appeal has given the following guidance:[52]

> 'Costs judges should ask themselves the following question: "Has the particular departure from a regulation or requirement in section 58 [of the 1990 Act], either on its own or in conjunction with any other such departure in this case, had a materially adverse effect either upon the protection afforded to the client or upon the proper administration of justice?".'

9.81 The enforceability of the agreement is determined on the date it was made. Drawing an analogy with consumer credit cases,[53] Dyson LJ said:[54]

> 'We see no reason for departing from the general rule that the legal character of a contract must be determined (or determinable) at its commencement.'

9.82 In considering whether a breach is material, it is the potential rather than the actual consequences[55] of the breach which are relevant. Causation and harm are irrelevant (save to the extent that actual harm may shed light on the potential for loss), so the court does not need to find that there has been actual detriment in order to find that there has been a material breach. Dyson LJ (giving judgment of the court) explained the rationale behind this:[56]

> '[It] is fallacious to say that a breach is trivial or not material because it does not in fact cause loss to the client in the particular case. The scheme has the wider purpose of providing for client protection (as well as the proper administration of justice).'

9.83 Thus, if, for example, there has been a failure to make adequate enquiries about the possible existence of alternative means of funding, the fact that no alternative means of funding actually existed would be irrelevant for the purposes of considering

---

51 *Hollins v Russell* [2003] EWCA Civ 718 at [107] and [221].

52 It seems as if Lord Woolf MR foresaw the test of materiality long before Hollins: in *Hodgson & Ors v Imperial Tobacco* [1998] 1 WLR 1056 at 1065 he said (of a CFA), 'If it materially departs from the legislative requirements it will not be enforceable.'

53 Specifically, he referred to *MacMillan Williams v Range* [2004] EWCA Civ 294.

54 *Myatt v National Coal Board* [2006] EWCA Civ 1017 at [36].

55 *Myatt v National Coal Board* [2006] EWCA Civ 1017 at [27]–[39]; the first instance of this was in *Jones v Caradon Catnic Ltd* [2005] EWCA Civ 1821, in which a breach was found to be material on the basis that it had the potential for causing harm to the administration of justice.

56 *Myatt v National Coal Board* [2006] EWCA Civ 1017 at [32].

materiality. However, it might be helpful to have regard to what actually happened, because that may shed light on the potential consequences of a breach.[57]

9.84   The concept of materiality has its limitations; in particular, Laws LJ has commented that it must not be allowed to undermine the force of CLSA 1990, s 58(1).[58] This seems to be particularly relevant in cases where the breach is binary, in the sense that it either has been committed or it has not, with no room for gradations of severity between those two extremes.[59]

9.85   Although the Court of Appeal has not, as yet, found it necessary to rule on whether the concept of materiality is merely an expression of the principle that the law is not concerned with very small things,[60] it is clear from the way in which the Court of Appeal has decided cases relating to materiality that only breaches that are 'literal but trivial and immaterial' or 'marginal' will be regarded as being immaterial.[61]

9.86   Breaches which are not immaterial for other reasons would rarely be immaterial solely because they are very small; in the context of declarable interests under reg 4(2)(e), for example, Clarke MR has commented that it would be difficult to envisage of such a situation.[62] That said, Brooke LJ has confirmed that the maxim that the law does not care about very small matters must be applied when a court considers whether there has been compliance with the CFA Regulations 2000.[63] When considering whether the effect of multiple breaches is material, it is permissible to consider them in aggregate, rather than just individually.[64]

9.87   The test of materiality is a manifestation of the doctrine of substantial compliance.[65] It has been argued that the test of materiality is being allowed to stray away from the confines of what is permissible under that doctrine, and that it should be viewed in 'a wider habitat'. Whilst some judges have found that approach to be of assistance,[66] many have not; in particular, Mann J has concluded that that approach did not shed any significant illumination as to how the test of materiality should be applied.[67]

9.88   The first two questions posed in the forensic sieve mentioned above are now considered in turn.

---

57   *Myatt v National Coal Board* [2006] EWCA Civ 1017 at [39].
58   *Jones v Caradon Catnic Ltd* [2005] EWCA Civ 1821 at [34].
59   Whilst not binding, an example is *Preece v Caerphilly County Borough Council*, 15 August 2007, Cardiff County Court, para 18, a decision of HHJ Hickinbottom (now Hickinbottom J) concerning a total failure to sign an agreement.
60   *Myatt v National Coal Board* [2006] EWCA Civ 1017 at [31].
61   See *Myatt v National Coal Board* [2006] EWCA Civ 1017 at [31] and *Jones v Caradon Catnic Ltd* [2005] EWCA Civ 1821 at [34].
62   *Tankard v John Fredricks Plastics Ltd* [2008] EWCA Civ 1375 at [47].
63   *Hollins v Russell* [2003] EWCA Civ 718 at [50].
64   *Fosberry v HMRC* [2007] EWHC 2249 (Ch) at [46]; this case has also acquired a second Neutral Citation number, that being [2008] EWHC 3344 (Ch) and is also often reported as being [2007] EWHC 3344 (Ch).
65   See, for example, *Hollins v Russell* [2003] EWCA 718 at [106], in which Brooke LJ said that 'conditions are sufficiently met when there has been substantial compliance with, or in other words no material departure from, what is required'.
66   See, for example, *Preece v Caerphilly County Borough Council*, 15 August 2007, Cardiff County Court, HHJ Hickinbotton.
67   *Fenton v Holmes* [2007] EWHC 2476 (Ch) at [40].

Do the CFA Regulations 2000 apply?

9.89 The first question is whether the retainer is a conditional fee agreement within the meaning of CLSA 1990, s 58(2)(a). This is an issue that is dealt with under the subheading 'statutory definition' (above). This is not an issue that will present any difficulty in the majority of cases. Difficulties may arise where transitional provisions need to be considered, however.

9.90 If the retainer was entered into after 1 November 2005, then the CFA Regulations 2000 will not apply, because they were revoked on that date.[68] Difficulties may arise where a conditional fee agreement was entered into before 1 November 2005 but where a further conditional fee agreement was made after that date. The relevant transitional provision is:[69]

'3.(1) The [CFA Regulations 2000] shall continue to have effect for the purposes of a conditional fee agreement entered into before 1 November 2005.'

9.91 Thus, whilst there is no authority directly on the point, the test seems not to be whether *any* conditional fee agreement was entered into before 1 November 2005, but whether the particular conditional fee agreement in question was entered into before that date.[70] So it is possible to have in the same claim an 'old' retainer to which the CFA Regulations 2000 do apply, and a 'new' retainer which is not governed by those regulations. Disputes may arise in respect of retainers where the 'old' and 'new' retainers are very similar or identical (or, in extreme cases, merely re-signed). Although there is no guidance on the point from the higher courts, that issue is likely to be a question mixed of fact and law as to whether the new agreement is, in fact, genuinely a new agreement.

9.92 Disputes may also arise where the 'new' retainer purports retroactively to replace the 'old' retainer in such a way as to make compliance with the CFA Regulations 2000 irrelevant. These issues are discussed in detail at **9.408–9.420**, and are also touched upon at **10.14–10.31**.

9.93 Agreements which were entered into before 1 April 2000 may occasionally be encountered in practice; where this is so, the CFA Regulations 2000 will not apply. The Access to Justice Act 1999 (Transitional Provisions) Order 2000 makes the following transitional provisions:

'1. This Order may be cited as the Access to Justice Act 1999 (Transitional Provisions) Order 2000 and shall come into force on 1 April 2000.

(2) In this Order a reference to a section by number alone means the section so numbered in the Access to Justice Act 1999.

2.(1) Section 58A(6) and (7) of the Courts and Legal Services Act 1990 shall not apply, as regards a party to proceedings, to:

(a) any proceedings in relation to which that party entered into a conditional fee agreement before 1 April 2000; or
(b) any proceedings arising out of the same cause of action as any proceedings to which sub-paragraph (a) refers.

---

[68] The Conditional Fee Agreements (Revocation) Regulations 2005 (SI 2005/2305), regs 1 and 2.
[69] SI 2005/2305, reg 3(1).
[70] This position has to be contrasted with the Access to Justice Act 1999 (Transitional Provisions) Order 2000 (SI 2000/900), for example, which is worded in a much broader way.

(2) The coming into force of section 27 [of the Access to Justice Act 1999] shall not affect the validity of any conditional fee agreement entered into before 1 April 2000, and any such agreement shall continue to have effect after that date as if section 27 had not come into force.

(3) In paragraphs 1(a) and (2) "conditional fee agreement" has the same meaning as in section 58 of the Courts and Legal Services Act 1990 as that section stands immediately before the coming into force of section 27 of the Access to Justice Act 1999.'

The effect of these transitional provisions is that if a conditional fee agreement was entered into before 1 April 2000, the CFA Regulations 2000 will not apply (although earlier regulations will: see below); if a new conditional fee agreement was entered into after this date, the existence of an old agreement made prior to that date will preclude the recovery of a success fee on a between the parties basis. This issue is dealt with in more detail at **30.11**.

9.94 As with the transitional provisions regulating the revocation of the CFA Regulations 2000, difficulties may arise where the 'old' and 'new' conditional fee agreements are very similar or identical; in practice, however, such problems rarely occur because the CFA Regulations 2000 were more onerous than the regulations they replaced, so (in view of the fact that no success fee would be recoverable from the paying party) there was no incentive for litigants to re-cast their retainers to be compliant with the CFA Regulations 2000. Moreover, for all practical purposes the CFA Regulations 2000 added to rather than differed from the requirements that existed before 1 April 2000.

9.95 Where the agreement is one to which the CFA Regulations 2000 apply, the next issue will be to determine whether the agreement in question must comply with the CFA Regulations as they were originally made, or whether they need comply only with the regulations introduced on 2 June 2003 regulating CFA Lites. The latter are significantly less burdensome, in that whilst reg 3A will apply to a CFA Lite, regs 2, 3 and 4 will not.

9.96 Unsurprisingly, a factor that needs to be taken into account in deciding that issue is whether the agreement was made on or after 2 June 2003. There are no transitional provisions relating directly to reg 3A, so the court is required to draw such inferences as to how the amendments were intended to apply to transitional cases as, in the light of the interpretative criteria, it considers Parliament to have intended.[71] The delegated legislation which created the CPR does contain transitional provisions concerning a provision which impliedly refers to reg 3A,[72] by providing that the changes in the CPR have effect only where the agreement was entered into on or after 2 June 2003.[73] It is a reasonable inference, then, that the same applies to the regulations themselves.

9.97 The relevant parts of the CFA Regulations 2000 are set out above. The CFA Lite provisions will apply where the following conditions are met:

•   that, disregarding the ATE premium and save as is set out below, the client is liable to pay his legal representative's fees and expenses (including disbursements)[74] only to the extent that sums are recovered in respect of the relevant proceedings, whether by way of costs or otherwise; and

---

[71]   See (in a context other than costs) *Cardshops Ltd v John Lewis Properties Ltd* [1983] QB 161.
[72]   CPR, r 43.2(7).
[73]   The Civil Procedure (Amendment No 2) Rules 2003 (SI 2003/1242), para 6.
[74]   See *Jones v Wrexham Borough Council* [2007] EWCA Civ 1356 at [51].

- that the exceptions to this fetter do not go beyond the following circumstances:
  - where the client fails to co-operate with the legal representative (this includes where the client asks the solicitor to work in an improper way, and where the client deliberately misleads the solicitor,[75] but would not necessarily include rejecting the solicitor's advice concerning settlement);[76]
  - where the client fails to attend any medical or expert examination or court hearing which the legal representative reasonably requests him to attend;
  - where the client fails to give necessary instructions to the legal representative;
  - where the client withdraws instructions from the legal representative;
  - where the client is an individual who is adjudged bankrupt or enters into an arrangement or a composition with his creditors, or against whom an administration order is made;
  - where the client is a company for which a receiver, administrative receiver or liquidator is appointed; or
  - where the client dies and where his estate becomes liable for the fees.

9.98 The court may take into account all of the relevant circumstances in deciding whether these conditions have been met rather than just what is written in the written instrument (see **10.37–10.70** for a general discussion of this topic). This may include documents other than the agreement itself, such as the client care letter (**10.67–10.70**). Waller LJ (with whom Hughes and Longmore LJJ agreed) has commented:[77]

> 'The important point is that if and insofar as [the paying party] would seek to look at the CFA on its own, and construe that CFA strictly, I would reject that approach ... The correct approach in my view is to ask the question, has the solicitor produced an arrangement for a CFA under which the client would not be liable for any own-side costs or expenses (apart from the circumstances defined by [regulation 3(5)], other than those that are actually recovered from the other side or from insurers.'

On the facts of the case before him, Waller LJ found that when the agreement was read in conjunction with the client care letter, the client was insulated from paying his solicitor's profit costs.

9.99 One particular circumstance that may arise is where the liability for costs may be covered by ATE insurance which sits alongside the agreement. This may be relevant because it is not usual for ATE policies to cover a party's own costs in such a way that the client is not exposed to the risk of having to pay those costs. If a policy of that type is combined with a conditional fee agreement which insulates the client from the risk of paying profit costs, then the overall effect may be the same as a CFA Lite. This, however, would only be the case if the monies recoverable under the ATE policy could be taken into account.

9.100 Waller LJ found that those monies could be taken into account. The issue turned on whether the words 'or otherwise' in reg 3A(1) of the CFA Regulations 2000 included the proceeds of an ATE policy. Waller LJ summarised his views in this way:[78]

---

75   *Jones v Wrexham Borough Council* [2007] EWCA Civ 1356 at [49].
76   *Jones v Wrexham Borough Council* [2007] EWCA Civ 1356 at [54]; Hughes LJ at [96]–[97] came to the conclusion that on the facts of the case before him (in which the solicitor had a very high degree of control over the claim) that a failure to accept a recommendation concerning an offer could amount to a failure to co-operate.
77   *Jones v Wrexham Borough Council* [2007] EWCA Civ 1356.
78   *Jones v Wrexham Borough Council* [2007] EWCA Civ 1356 at [27].

> 'I can see no reason why the court should not look at the whole package produced by the solicitor, the CFA agreement, the Rule 15 letter explaining to the client the effect of the agreement, and indeed the insurance policy recommended by the solicitor.'

The possibility of the insurer avoiding its liabilities is not to the point.[79]

9.101 In summary, whether the CFA Regulations 2000 apply will be a question of fact and law, and in essence will turn on the court's findings as to the nature of the agreement (or, in appropriate cases, the nature of the overall funding package) and on when the conditional fee agreement was made.

Genuine issues

9.102 The paragraphs which follow focus on the way in which the *Bailey* presumption applies to conditional fee agreements. If the reader is not familiar with the general principles, this section ought to be read in conjunction with **11.20–11.32**.

9.103 In brief, the Court of Appeal has explained that the presumption in *Bailey v IBC Vehicles Ltd*[80] should not extend to the written instrument of a conditional fee agreement made under the CFA Regulations 2000 (it is a moot point whether it applies to other types of agreement).[81] Thus, in so far as the CFA Regulations 2000 are concerned, there is a need to distinguish between those regulation which depend on the written instrument for compliance (ie regs 2, 3, 3A and 5), and those which turn on other factors (ie the reg 4(1)–(6)). The receiving party will be able to rely on the *Bailey* presumption in respect of the latter, but not in respect of the former.

The written instrument

9.104 In *Hollins v Russell*,[82] Brooke LJ identified five reasons why the principle in *Bailey* should not apply to the written instrument of a conditional fee agreement, and explained why the receiving party should normally be put to his election in relation to the conditional fee agreement itself. Those reasons can be summarised as follows.

Significance of argument

9.105 The challenge in *Bailey* was only to a part of the profit costs (the hourly rate), but challenges in respect of conditional fee agreements usually go to the entirety of the profit costs. Challenges in respect of conditional fee agreements are, therefore, more significant, as Brooke LJ remarked:

> 'The challenge to a bill of costs must surely move several ratchets up the scale once the challenge changes from a challenge to the figures produced to a challenge to the principle of paying anything at all.'

---

[79] *Jones v Wrexham Borough Council* [2007] EWCA Civ 1356 at [13]–[22] and [42].
[80] [1998] 3 All ER 570.
[81] A decision in the county court has confirmed that collective conditional fee agreements ought to be dealt with in a similar way: *Woollam v Cleanaway Ltd* (unreported) 26 July 2004, Chester County Court, HHJ Halbert.
[82] [2003] EWCA Civ 718.

Complexity of the issues

9.106 With a non-conditional retainer the matters which are normally the subject of a certificate are conventional matters; this is not so with compliance with the Conditional Fee Agreements Regulations 2000, as these introduced a level of complexity which was unknown when *Bailey* was decided.

Legitimate interest in the terms

9.107 The CPR and the CPD require that only extremely basic information is given about a conditional fee agreement;[83] the paying party may reasonably require more. For example, the paying party might need to know how a 'win' has been defined.

Not solely matters of fact

9.108 The question of whether a conditional fee agreement is enforceable is principally a matter of law. This is distinct from whether costs are properly claimed in cases not involving conditional fee agreements, as such issues are generally questions of fact and are likely to be within a solicitor's peculiar expertise. In view of this difference, the certificate may not be sufficient in the context of conditional fee agreements.

Policy and efficient use of court time

9.109 There are policy reasons for not extending the *Bailey* decision to conditional fee agreements. Given the complexity of the issues, Brooke LJ thought that it was not appropriate to impose on costs judges the responsibility of acting as a filter to see that the relevant regulations had been complied with in every respect, as this would inevitably be a time-consuming task.

9.110 In view of these factors, Brooke LJ came to the conclusion that the *Bailey* decision should not be extended beyond the facts with which it was dealing, ie that of a conventional bill. He went on to say:[84]

> '[Where] there is a [conditional fee agreement], a costs judge should normally exercise his discretion under the Costs Practice Direction and the *Pamplin* procedure [ie the process of election] so as to require the receiving parties (subject to their right of election preserved by paragraph 40.14 of the Costs Practice Direction and the *Goldman* case)[85] to produce a copy of their [conditional fee agreements] to the paying parties.'

9.111 A decision in the county court has confirmed that collective conditional fee agreements ought to be dealt with in a similar way.[86]

9.112 What is not clear is whether the decision not to extend the *Bailey* presumption to conditional fee agreement cases will apply to cases in which the conditional fee agreement was entered into after the revocation if the CFA Regulations 2000. Clearly, many of the reasons given by Brooke LJ for disapplying the principle in *Bailey* will not apply to such agreements. The matter can be argued either way, and there have been

---

[83]   The Rule Committee responded to Brooke LJ's remarks by proposing amendments to the CPD; see below.
[84]   *Hollins v Russell* [2003] EWCA Civ 718 at [71].
[85]   *Goldman v Hesper* [1988] 1 WLR 1238.
[86]   *Woollam v Cleanaway Ltd* (unreported) 26 July 2004, Chester County Court, HHJ Halbert.

conflicting first instance decisions on the point.[87] Changes to the CPD were mooted, but they did not materialise.[88] The position in law is not wholly clear, therefore, but there remains wisdom in the words quoted with reverence by Brooke LJ[89] and initially spoken by Louis Brandeis J shortly before he was nominated to the Supreme Court of the United States:[90]

> 'Sunlight is said to be the best of disinfectants; electric light the most efficient policeman.'

9.113 Clearly, Brooke LJ intended to encourage parties to go about dealing with the indemnity principle in a transparent way. But, where disclosure is not given voluntarily, the court is still required to exercise its discretion. As a result, a receiving party cannot be put to his election until such time as the court has considered the matter judicially. Although not binding on any court, there have been decisions in which it has been found that a receiving party cannot be put to his election until after points of dispute have been served.[91] If this is the true state of the law, then the practical effect is that a receiving party will be able to defer deciding whether to give disclosure until after he knows the paying party's case.

9.114 What is not clear is whether the decision not to extend the *Bailey* presumption to conditional fee agreement cases will apply to those in which the conditional fee agreement was entered into after the Conditional Fee Agreements Regulations 2000 were revoked. This is a matter that could be argued either way.

9.115 The agreement may be disclosed in redacted form.[92] It is, however, implicit from the way in which the Court of Appeal has commented upon redaction that the court ought to be put in a position to decide whether it is fair;[93] this would usually mean providing an un-redacted copy of the retainer for the court.

Matters other than the written instrument

9.116 A paying party will often wish to see not only the written instrument of the agreement, but also evidence of compliance with reg 4 of the CFA Regulations 2000. Where those are the circumstances, the *Bailey* presumption will apply, ie the paying party must make out a 'genuine issue'. The costs judge should not require attendance notes to be disclosed unless there is a genuine issue as to whether there has been compliance with reg 4.[94] The Court of Appeal commented that the adequacy of the explanation given to the client is largely a matter of fact, so that it is appropriate that the

---

[87] See *Vinayak & Anor (t/a Doctors Chambers) v Lovegrove & Eliot (a firm)* [2007] EWHC 90096.
[88] It was proposed to introduce a new CPD, art 32.5(1)(d), which would have read:
     'If the conditional fee agreement is not disclosed (and the Court of Appeal has indicated that it should be the usual practice for a conditional fee agreement – redacted where appropriate – to be disclosed for the purpose of costs proceedings in which a success fee is claimed) a statement setting out the following information from the conditional fee agreement so as to enable the paying party and the court to determine the level of risk undertaken by the solicitor:
     i.   The definition of "win" and (if applicable) "lose";
     ii. Details of the receiving party's liability to pay costs if he or she wins or loses; and
     iii. Details of the receiving party's liability to pay costs if he or she fails to beat a Pt 36 offer.'
[89] *Hollins v Russell* [2003] EWCA Civ 718 at [71].
[90] L Brandeis *Other People's Money – and How the Bankers Use It* (1914, Brandeis School of Law); only the first half was quoted by Brooke LJ.
[91] See *Cole v News Group Newspapers* (unreported) 18 October 2006, SCCO, Master Howarth.
[92] See, for example, *Hollins v Russell* [2003] EWCA Civ 718 at [72].
[93] *Hollins v Russell* [2003] EWCA Civ 718 at [80].
[94] *Hollins v Russell* [2003] EWCA Civ 718 at [81].

paying party should have to rebut the presumption arising from the fact that the receiving party's solicitor, an officer of the court, has signed the certificate of accuracy. Whilst common sense dictates that there is a limit to the extent to which such evidence can be taken into account before a finding of a 'genuine issue' becomes inescapable, it would seem that evidence may be adduced for the purposes of rebutting an allegation that a 'genuine issue' exists.[95]

9.117 In summary, a receiving party will normally be put to his election in respect of the written instrument of the conditional fee agreement, but the court will usually have to be satisfied that there is a genuine issue before putting the receiving party to his election in relation to material other than the written instrument.

Individual regulations: breach and materiality

9.118 This section deals with breaches of each of the CFA Regulations 2000; it addresses the last two parts of the forensic sieve mentioned above: ie whether there has been a breach and, if so, whether that breach is material. Each of the regulations (which Phillips MR has described as 'extremely detailed')[96] is addressed in turn.

Regulation 2(1)

9.119 This regulation requires that the agreement defines its own ambit and that it incorporates a number of provisions clarifying its effect. It therefore goes to the written instrument of the agreement.

9.120 The regulation provides:

'2.(1) A conditional fee agreement must specify—

(a)   the particular proceedings or parts of them to which it relates (including whether it relates to any appeal, counterclaim or proceedings to enforce a judgment or order),

(b)   the circumstances in which the legal representative's fees and expenses, or part of them, are payable,

(c)   what payment, if any, is due—
(i)   if those circumstances only partly occur,
(ii)   irrespective of whether those circumstances occur, and
(iii)   on the termination of the agreement for any reason, and

(d)   the amounts which are payable in all the circumstances and cases specified or the method to be used to calculate them and, in particular, whether the amounts are limited by reference to the damages which may be recovered on behalf of the client.'

The regulation applies to all conditional fee agreements (other than CFA Lites), including those which are made with an additional legal representative, those which do not provide for a success fee, and those where the legal representative is a membership organisation.

9.121 The following issues may arise in practice.

---

[95]   See, for example, *Thornley (a child) v MoD* [2010] EWHC 2584 (QB) at [27], per HHJ Behrens, sitting as a judge of the High Court.

[96]   *Thornley v Lang* [2003] EWCA Civ 1484 at [11].

The meaning of the word 'specify' and implied terms

9.122 The requirement to 'specify' is to be read as meaning that the thing must be stated explicitly.[97] For the reasons set out below, this can be achieved either by the agreement dealing expressly with the matter in terms which reflect the above requirements, or by the way in which the agreement operates as a whole.[98]

Clarity

9.123 The court may be influenced by the clarity with which the agreement is expressed. In a case in which he was able to interpret the agreement in a way which was favourable to the legal representative, Brooke LJ commented that his findings might have been different had the agreement been less clear.[99]

Provisions relating to termination

9.124 In a case in which the agreement failed to specify what would happen in the event of termination prior to the conclusion of the claim, Mann J found that there had been a breach. In coming to this conclusion he reminded himself that the requirement was to 'specify'; he found that the process he was being asked to accept was 'close to a process of implication rather than mere construction'.[100] He did not need to express a view as to whether that breach was material.

Unexpected developments and provisions relating to appeals

9.125 Whilst only a decision refusing permission to appeal and therefore not a decision that should be cited to any court, Maurice Kay LJ refused permission for a paying party to argue that the conditional fee agreement in question ought to have been drafted in such a way as to embrace all areas into which the claim may develop.[101] Although obiter, Mann J explained that there was nothing objectionable about an agreement which did not expressly refer to whether it covered an appeal brought by an opponent; he came to this view because it was clear from the provisions that the legal representative was contractually bound to act in the client's bests interests, and that this extended to representing the client on an appeal brought by an opponent.[102]

Provisions relating to hourly rates

9.126 Retainers often make provision for hourly rates to be increased, but may fail to state the mechanism by which that increase will be calculated. Eady J noted (obiter, but without disapproval) that a costs judge had found that the requirement was satisfied by an implied term that any increase would be fair and reasonable.[103] In view of

---

[97] See the comments of Brooke LJ in *Hollins v Russell* [2003] EWCA Civ 718 at [125], in which he drew upon *BWE International Ltd v Jones* [2003] EWCA Civ 298 at [29] as being an example of that approach.

[98] See also *Myler v Williams* [2003] EWHC 1587 (QB) at [23], per Crane J.

[99] *Hollins v Russell* [2003] EWCA Civ 718 at [128].

[100] *Fosberry v HMRC* [2007] EWHC 2249 (Ch) at [43]; this case has also acquired a second Neutral Citation number, that being [2008] EWHC 3344 (Ch) and is also often reported as being [2007] EWHC 3344 (Ch).

[101] *Blair v Danesh* [2009] EWCA Civ 516.

[102] *Fenton v Holmes* [2007] EWHC 2476 (Ch) at [58]–[63].

[103] *Cox v MGN Ltd* [2006] EWHC 1235 (QB) at [75].

Brooke LJ's comments about the meaning of the word 'specify', that decision (as described to Eady J) ought to be treated with some caution (although the same conclusion can be reached in other ways).

Method by which amounts are calculated

9.127 Crane J has emphasised that the regulations choose the word 'method' rather than, for example, the word 'formula' or some such word. He said that no formula is required; and that in his view a method which relied on the old 'A plus B' analysis was compliant.[104]

Need to state whether there is a cap when there is no cap

9.128 Brooke LJ rejected the argument that the requirement was to state the existence of a damaged-based cap only if there was a cap.[105] (The effect of this finding was significantly ameliorated by his other findings in relation to the cap: see below.)

Failure to state a cap

9.129 Where there has been literal non-compliance with the requirement to state whether there is a damages-based cap, it may be that the court finds that such a breach lacks materiality. Brooke LJ found (obiter) that where an agreement was otherwise clear as to its effect (i e it was clear that there was no cap), any failure expressly to refer to the absence of a cap was immaterial.[106]

Early Law Society model agreements

9.130 Brooke LJ has specifically commented that no problem will arise where the post-July 2000 version of the Law Society model agreement is used.[107] The version which existed between April and July 2000 was less felicitously drafted, in that it read:

> 'If you win your claim, you pay our basic charges, our disbursements and a success fee. The amount of the success fee is not based on or limited by reference to the damages.'

When read in isolation, this provision failed to comply with the requirement to state whether there was a damages-based cap; this is because it specified only whether the success fee was limited by reference to the damages, rather than whether the costs generally were limited. Brooke LJ went on to explain that the agreement must be read as whole, and that other provisions made it clear that there was no cap.[108] There was, therefore, no breach.

---

[104] *Myler v Williams* [2003] EWHC 1587 (QB) at [32].
[105] In particular, Brooke LJ rejected the notion that there was significance in the fact that the Conditional Fee Agreements Regulations 1995 required solicitors to state 'whether or not' there was a cap, but the Conditional Fee Agreements Regulations 2000 referred only to 'whether' there was a cap: see *Hollins v Russell* [2003] EWCA Civ 718 at [123]–[124].
[106] *Hollins v Russell* [2003] EWCA Civ 718 at [120] *et seq.*
[107] *Hollins v Russell* [2003] EWCA Civ 718 at [118].
[108] In particular, para 4 of the standard terms and conditions made it clear that the client was liable for all of the legal representative's basic charges and success fee; see *Hollins v Russell* [2003] EWCA Civ 718 at [126]–[127].

9.131 In summary, whilst the requirement to specify certain things is a requirement to state those things expressly, in practice the court looks at the whole of the agreement in deciding whether there has been a breach and (in particular) in deciding whether that breach was material.

Regulation 2(2)

9.132 This regulation imposes a requirement that the agreement must contain a statement that the relevant requirements of reg 4 have been complied with. This is usually done by way of a brief statement in the body of the agreement:

> '2.(2) A conditional fee agreement to which regulation 4 applies must contain a statement that the requirements of that regulation which apply in the case of that agreement have been complied with.'

9.133 This regulation applies to all conditional fee agreements to which reg 4 applies; this means it applies to all agreements except CFA Lites and those between legal representatives and an additional legal representative.

9.134 As far as the writer is aware, there have been no authoritative decisions in which a breach of this regulation has, of itself, led to an agreement being found to be unenforceable.

Regulation 3(1)(a)

9.135 This regulation stipulates that the agreement must specify the reasons for setting the percentage increase at the level stated:

> '3.(1) A conditional fee agreement which provides for a success fee—
>
> (a)   must briefly specify the reasons for setting the percentage increase at the level stated in the agreement ...'

It applies to all agreements which provide for a success fee other than CFA Lites; this includes those with an additional legal representative and those where the legal representative is a membership organisation. The requirements of this regulation are usually met by including a brief risk assessment, which may or may not have been drafted specifically for the case in hand.

9.136 Wilson LJ has confirmed that compliance with reg 3(1)(a) is an issue that could be decided with regard to the background (which, in the case before him, included the fact that the client was assisted by a shrewd and intelligent lawyer);[109] in those circumstances, references to 'the fact that if you lose, we will not earn anything' and 'our assessment of the risks of your case' were regarded as being sufficient.

Regulation 3(1)(b)

9.137 In so far as drafting errors are concerned, breaches of this regulation are probably the most common cause of conditional fee agreements being found to be

---

[109] *Bray Walker Solicitors (A Firm) v Silvera* [2010] EWCA Civ 332 at [25].

unenforceable. This regulation relates to the 'postponement charge' (defined at **9.43**); it requires the agreement to specify the percentage increase which is used to calculate the postponement charge:

> '3.(1)   A conditional fee agreement which provides for a success fee—
>
> . . .
>
> (b)   must specify how much of the percentage increase, if any, relates to the cost to the legal representative of the postponement of the payment of his fees and expenses.'

It applies to all agreements (other than CFA Lites) which provide for a success fee, including those with an additional legal representative and those where the legal representative is a membership organisation.

9.138   The court will, in general, approach the issue of compliance by reference to the agreement as properly interpreted rather than by reference to what is literally set out in the agreement. That process has been referred to as 'prior interpretation' or 'anterior interpretation'. Although there is no authority on the point, it is probably true to say that the process of interpretation should not be permitted to develop into a process of implication.[110]

9.139   Two topics arise:

- the effect of failing entirely to state the postponement charge; and
- the effect of a postponement charge which is unclear or unintelligible.

Each if these topics is discussed in turn.

Complete failure

9.140   Blake J has confirmed that the duty to state the postponement charge exists even if there is no intention to levy it. That, however, was in the context of the agreement making reference to the postponement charge; he commented that his conclusion might have been different if the agreement had been entirely silent on that matter.[111]

9.141   The court is not limited to looking at the body of the agreement when deciding whether the postponement charge has been specified. An example of the court going beyond the corpus is where Burton J held that the details given in the schedule were, when properly interpreted, sufficiently clear to satisfy the requirement.[112] Where the court finds that there has been a complete failure to state the postponement charge and where the court finds that this does amount to a breach, it may be relevant to the issue of materiality that, in general, a party is not entitled to benefit from his own breach.[113]

---

[110]   Mann J dealt with similar issues in *Fosberry v HMRC* [2007] EWHC 2249 (Ch) at [43]; this case has also acquired a second Neutral Citation number, that being [2008] EWHC 3344 (Ch) and is also often reported as being [2007] EWHC 3344 (Ch).

[111]   *Utting v McBain* [2007] EWHC 3293 (QB) at [9]–[11].

[112]   *Sidhu v Sandhu* (unreported) 5 May 2009, QBD, Burton J.

[113]   In a setting other than costs, see *Micklefield v SAC Technology Ltd* [1990] 1 WLR 1002; *Richco International Ltd v Alfred C Toepfer GmbH* [1991] 1 Lloyd's Rep 136; and *Little v Courage* [1995] CLC 164 at 168, Millett LJ.

Ambiguity or inconsistency

9.142 It is not uncommon for an agreement to contain terms concerning the postponement charge which are in conflict, which are unclear or, in an extreme case, which are unintelligible. Whilst the last of these circumstances would usually be beyond rescue, the process of prior interpretation may offer a route by which the court may find compliance in appropriate cases.

9.143 The process of prior interpretation may go to breach or materiality,[114] ie it may lead to the court finding that:

(i)   properly interpreted, the agreement can be said to specify the postponement charge; or
(ii) the ambiguity or inconsistency cannot be said to expose the client or the administration of justice to the risk of harm.

It is convenient to deal with inconsistency and ambiguity separately.

Inconsistency

9.144 An early example of prior interpretation was a case in which there was an inconsistency between what was said in the body of the agreement and what was recorded in the risk assessment; the former said that the postponement charge was nil, but the latter mentioned delay as being a factor which seemingly had been taken into account when setting the success fee.[115] The paying party said that the ambiguity could not be resolved; the Court of Appeal expressed its disagreement in fairly forceful terms.[116] Brooke LJ (giving judgment of the court) made the following finding:[117]

> 'Taken together, [the terms in the body] prevail over the risk assessment schedule, and thus on its true construction the CFA in this case complies with the Regulations.'

(One could argue that on the facts of that case it would have been possible to have come to the same conclusion by focusing on materiality rather than breach; this is because Brooke LJ also found that no court would have dreamt of allowing a postponement charge.)

Ambiguity

9.145 In a case which was at the opposite end of the spectrum the receiving party elected not to contend for a process of prior interpretation; perhaps this was because the agreement was too disorganised to permit of any sense being made of it. Rather than the terms being inconsistent (in which case the task would have been to choose between the competing terms), the provisions were ambiguous (which meant that the process

---

114   An example of the court finding that a breach of reg 3(1)(b) was immaterial was *Brennan v Association Asphalt Ltd* [2006] EWHC 90052 (Costs), but it is important to note that an appeal from that decision was allowed by consent, thereby diminishing the persuasive value of that case.

115   *Tichband v Hurdman* [2003] EWCA Civ 718, which was one of the cases heard at the same time as *Hollins v Russell*; the corpus of the agreement said that the postponement charge was nil, but the risk assessment indicated that it had been taken into account in calculating the success fee.

116   Brooke LJ called the paying party's arguments 'as unattractive as they are unmeritorious': see *Tichband v Hurdman* [2003] EWCA Civ 718 at [132].

117   *Tichband v Hurdman* [2003] EWCA Civ 718 at [134].

would have been more demanding and the result even less predictable). The body of the agreement made it clear that the postponement charge existed and was chargeable, but it was impossible to discern what that charge was intended to be. Brooke LJ (with whom Parker and Kay LJJ agreed) found (obiter) that the court below had been entitled to find that there had been a breach.[118]

9.146 Other examples exist of the court finding that provisions which are ambiguous do not satisfy the requirements of reg 3(1)(b).[119] Mann J found that a risk assessment which recorded that postponement was a factor which had been taken into account when calculating the success fee was capable of giving rise to an inference that a postponement charge existed; he commented that if that charge is unquantified, that may amount to a material breach.[120]

9.147 In summary, the court will often seek to interpret the meaning of an agreement before deciding whether there has been a failure to specify the postponement charge. As is usually the case with contractual interpretation, inconsistencies are generally less troublesome to resolve than ambiguities.

Regulation 3(2)

9.148 This regulation stipulates three provisions, the first of which goes to advance waiver of privilege, and the second and third of which go to the 'reverse of the indemnity principle' (as Blake J has called it[121] – this reference was to the requirement that the agreement must stipulate that unless the court orders otherwise, the success fee should be limited to that which is recoverable from the opposing party):

'3.(2) If the agreement relates to court proceedings, it must provide that where the percentage increase becomes payable as a result of those proceedings, then—

   (a)   if—
       (i)   any fees subject to the increase are assessed, and
       (ii)   the legal representative or the client is required by the court to disclose to the court or any other person the reasons for setting the percentage increase at the level stated in the agreement,
   he may do so,
   (b)   if—
       (i)   any such fees are assessed, and
       (ii)   any amount in respect of the percentage increase is disallowed on the assessment on the ground that the level at which the increase was set was unreasonable in view of facts which were or should have been known to the legal representative at the time it was set,
   that amount ceases to be payable under the agreement, unless the court is satisfied that it should continue to be so payable, and
   (c)   if—
       (i)   sub-paragraph (b) does not apply, and
       (ii)   the legal representative agrees with any person liable as a result of the proceedings to pay fees subject to the percentage increase that a lower amount than the amount payable in accordance with the conditional fee agreement is to be paid instead,

---

[118] *Spencer v Wood* [2004] EWCA Civ 352 at [17].
[119] See, for example, *Utting v McBain* [2007] EWHC 3293 (QB) at [21]–[25].
[120] *Fosberry v HMRC* [2007] EWHC 2249 (Ch) at [46]; this case has also acquired a second Neutral Citation number, that being [2008] EWHC 3344 (Ch) and is also often reported as being [2007] EWHC 3344 (Ch).
[121] *Bray Walker Solicitors (A Firm) v Silvera* [2008] EWHC 3147 (QB) at [71].

the amount payable under the conditional fee agreement in respect of those fees shall be reduced accordingly, unless the court is satisfied that the full amount should continue to be payable under it.'

Regulation 3(2) applies only to agreements which both provide for a success fee and which relate to court proceedings. It applies regardless of whether the agreement is with an additional legal representative or whether it is with a membership organisation. It does not apply to CFA Lites.

9.149 A number of issues may arise in practice, as follows.

Total failure to include disclosure provision

9.150 A total failure to include the disclosure provisions will give rise to a material breach. Mann J rejected the argument that the provisions were immaterial because they were solely for the benefit of the legal representative (in the sense that non-compliance would do no more than to impair the legal representative's ability to recover a high success fee). He found that the disclosure provisions had a role to play in the administration of justice:[122]

> 'Assuming that any written assessment is a privileged document, absent reg 3(2)(a), the receiving party would have the option of disclosing it in order to assist its case, or not disclosing it and proving the case otherwise. It might be that, by refusing to disclose the document, the case of that party would be damaged ... [Regulation 3(2)(a)] probably has the effect of overruling such privilege as might otherwise have existed in any risk assessment documents germane to the CFA. It effectively requires the client to consent in advance to the disclosure of the material. That being the practical purpose of the reg 3(2)(a) provision and, therefore, of reg 3(2)(a) itself, it seems to me that the legal purpose ... is that it furthers the administration of justice.'

The extent of the limiting provisions

9.151 It has been argued that the limiting provisions do not – as implied above – relate only to the success fee, but that they also relate to base costs. That argument has had a degree of success at first instance (although not to the extent that any breach has ever been found to be material), but it has not been developed or pursued for many years.[123]

Partial failure to include limiting provisions

9.152 In a different case Mann J found that an agreement which included the first limiting provision but not the second was in breach of reg 3(2); he was not persuaded by the fact that the agreement stated that the success fee might be limited by agreement.[124]

---

[122] *Fenton v Holmes* [2007] EWHC 2476 (Ch) at [46]–[49].
[123] See *Ghannouchi v Houni Ltd & Ors* [2004] EWHC 9002 (Costs); it seems that the last time this point was mentioned in the SCCO was 2006 (see *Oyston v The Royal Bank of Scotland plc* [2006] EWHC 90053), which was also the last time it was mentioned in legal journals (see A Gore 'Access to justice in personal injury cases' (2006) JPI Law 2, pp 189–198).
[124] *Fosberry v HMRC* [2007] EWHC 2249 (Ch) at [43]; this case has also acquired a second Neutral Citation number, that being [2008] EWHC 3344 (Ch) and is also often reported as being [2007] EWHC 3344 (Ch).

Regulation 3A

9.153 These paragraphs should be read in conjunction with the relevant parts of the section on 'Do the CFA Regulations 2000 apply?' above.

9.154 The provisions of reg 3A are set out in full, as it was amended very shortly after it was created:

'3A.(1)   This regulation applies to a conditional fee agreement under which, except in the circumstances set out in paragraph (5) and (5A), the client is liable to pay his legal representative's fees and expenses only to the extent that sums are recovered in respect of the relevant proceedings, whether by way of costs or otherwise.

(2)   In determining for the purposes of paragraph (1) the circumstances in which a client is liable to pay his legal representative's fees and expenses, no account is to be taken of any obligation to pay costs in respect of the premium of a policy taken out to insure against the risk of incurring a liability in the relevant proceedings.

(3)   Regulations 2, 3 and 4 do not apply to a conditional fee agreement to which this regulation applies.

(4)   A conditional fee agreement to which this regulation applies must—

   (a)   specify—
      (i)   the particular proceedings or parts of them to which it relates (including whether it relates to any appeal, counterclaim or proceedings to enforce a judgment or order); and
      (ii)   the circumstances in which the legal representative's fees and expenses, or part of them, are payable; and

   (b)   if it provides for a success fee—
      (i)   briefly specify the reasons for setting the percentage increase at the level stated in the agreement; and
      (ii)   provide that if, in court proceedings, the percentage increase becomes payable as a result of those proceedings and the legal representative or the client is ordered to disclose to the court or any other person the reasons for setting the percentage increase at the level stated in the agreement, he may do so.

(5)   A conditional fee agreement to which this regulation applies may specify that the client will be liable to pay the legal representative's fees and expenses whether or not sums are recovered in respect of the relevant proceedings, if the client—

   (a)   fails to co-operate with the legal representative;
   (b)   fails to attend any medical or expert examination or court hearing which the legal representative reasonably requests him to attend;
   (c)   fails to give necessary instructions to the legal representative;
   (d)   withdraws instructions from the legal representative;
   (e)   is an individual who is adjudged bankrupt or enters into an arrangement or a composition with his creditors, or against whom an administration order is made; or
   (f)   is a company for which a receiver, administrative receiver or liquidator is appointed.

(5A)   A conditional fee agreement to which this regulation applies may specify that, in the event of the client dying in the course of the relevant proceedings, his estate will be liable for the legal representative's fees and expenses, whether or not sums are recovered in respect of those proceedings.

(6)   Before a conditional fee agreement to which this regulation applies is made, the legal representative must inform the client as to the circumstances in which the client or his estate

may be liable to pay the legal representative's fees and expenses, and provide such further explanation, advice or other information as to those circumstances as the client may reasonably require.'

9.155 Regulation 3A creates a mechanism whereby a simplified agreement (known as a 'CFA Lite') may be created. It will apply to all CFA Lites, including those with additional legal representatives and to those where the legal representative is a membership organisation. There is provision in the CPR which allows costs to be recovered under a CFA notwithstanding that the client is liable to pay his legal representative's fees and expenses only to the extent that sums are recovered in respect of the litigation, whether by way of costs or otherwise;[125] that provision is not relevant for the purposes of regulatory compliance because it only deals with the position between opposing parties.

9.156 Regulation 3A contains a number of conditions ('the conditions') which must be satisfied before the agreement can be said to be a CFA Lite (thereby disapplying regs 2, 3 and 4). Once those conditions have been met, then a number of requirements ('the requirements') will apply; the requirements are similar to, but less onerous than, the requirements of the other regulations. Put another way, the requirements are reduced: hence the label 'CFA Lite'.

9.157 Disputes about reg 3A are often about whether the conditions have been met; this is an issue which is discussed elsewhere in this chapter.[126] A failure to satisfy the conditions will mean that the agreement is not a CFA Lite. It is possible for an agreement to satisfy the conditions but not the requirements, in which case it will still be a CFA Lite, but it will be an unenforceable CFA Lite.

9.158 Broadly speaking, reg 3A has two functions: (i) it regulates the circumstances in which a legal representative is able to look to the client for payment under a CFA Lite; and (ii) it imposes a number of requirements which (when viewed in the context of the client's liability being otherwise limited to what is recovered) afford a degree of protection which is not dissimilar to that afforded by the CFA Regulations 2000 in general.

9.159 Regulation 3A(1) creates the most important aspect of the conditions, which, essentially, is that the client must not be liable for the legal representative's fees beyond those which are recovered in the litigation.

9.160 Regulations 3A(5) and (5A) provide that the client may be required personally to pay the legal representative's fees and expenses, but only in certain stipulated circumstances, such as a failure on the part of the client to co-operate with the legal representative, or where he fails to give necessary instructions. It is by stipulating those circumstances that the conditions are fully defined.

9.161 The requirements are set out in regs 3(4) and (6). In common with regs 2, 3 and 4, a legal representative entering into a CFA Lite must ensure that certain information is given to the client and that certain provisions have been incorporated into the agreement itself.[127] In particular, a CFA Lite must include:

---

[125] CPR, r 43.2(3), which brings into force the provisions in s 51(2) of the Senior Courts Act 1981, as amended by AJA 1999, s 31.

[126] See the section on 'Do the CFA Regulations 2000 apply?'

[127] See reg 3A(6) and (4) of the Conditional Fee Agreements Regulations 2000 (as amended), respectively.

- a provision which specifies the particular proceedings or parts of them to which the agreement relates, including whether it relates to:
  - any appeal;
  - any counterclaim; or
  - any proceedings to enforce a judgment or order; and
- a provision which specifies the circumstances in which the legal representative's fees and expenses, or part of them, are payable.

9.162 Before a CFA Lite is signed, the legal representative must inform the client as to the circumstances in which the client or his estate may be liable to pay the legal representative's fees and expenses, and provide such further explanation, advice or other information about those circumstances as the client may reasonably require.

9.163 Where it provides for a success fee, a CFA Lite must also include the following:

- a brief statement of the reasons for setting the percentage increase at the level stated in the agreement; and
- a provision that that if the percentage increase becomes payable as a result of court proceedings, then
  - if any fees subject to the increase are assessed, and
  - if the legal representative or the client is required by the court to disclose to the court or any other person the reasons for setting the percentage increase at the level stated in the agreement,

  he may do so.

There is no binding authority dealing with these requirements in the specific context of reg 3A, but there is no reason to believe that the principles relating to regs 2, 3, and 4 would not apply.

Regulation 4(2) (in general)

9.164 Regulation 4 imposes a number of obligations; it is convenient first to take an overview, and then to consider each obligation in turn. There is a certain amount of overlap between the obligations.

9.165 Regulation 4(2) must be read in conjunction with reg 4(1): the latter creates a requirement that the client receives information, and reg 4(2) states what that information should be. There is also a requirement that if the client reasonably requires any further explanation, advice or other information, it should be provided. A number of generalisations can be made about reg 4(2), as follows.

Situations where reg 4(2) will not apply

9.166 There are three situations where reg 4(2) will either not apply or, if it applies, will be entirely redundant.

Membership organisations

9.167 Where the legal representative is a body to which s 30 of the Access to Justice Act 1999 applies (ie where a body is a membership organisation),[128] and where there are no circumstances in which the client may personally be liable to pay any costs in respect of the proceedings, then reg 4(1) will not apply;[129] this has the effect of making reg 4(2) redundant. This provision caters for organisations which wish to support its members via its own in-house legal staff rather than by engaging external lawyers through a collective conditional fee agreement; such organisations are allowed to enter into conditional fee agreements in such a way that is administratively comparable to a collective arrangement.

Additional legal representatives

9.168 Regulation 4 (in general) does not apply to agreements made between a legal representative and an additional legal representative.

CFA Lites

9.169 As is explained in the section on reg 3A at **9.153–9.163**, reg 4 will not apply to agreements which are CFA Lites.

Delegation

9.170 Subject to certain safeguards, a legal representative is permitted to delegate functions under reg 4 to an unqualified person.

9.171 More than a century before the CFA Regulations 2000 were even thought of, Lord Blackburn had the following to say about delegation in general:[130]

> 'There are some matters as to which though he may delegate them and need not do them in person but may employ a clerk, yet he would be required to see that that clerk had competent knowledge.'

9.172 After having reminded himself of what Lord Blackburn had said, Brooke LJ came to the conclusion that delegation under reg 4 is permissible, provided the person to whom the task is delegated is competent and appropriately supervised:[131]

> 'Each situation must be considered on its own facts. Parliament wishes to foster new ways of rendering litigation services, and provided that the performance of the regulation 4 duties is appropriately delegated, and the duties are properly performed under appropriate supervision, we cannot see that Parliament's intentions are being thwarted if the solicitor delegates more widely than is allowed for in [the paying parties'] primary argument before us.

---

[128] Thirteen organisations have been approved since the powers were introduced. They are: AA Legal Service, British Cycling Federation, Defence Police Federation, Durham Colliery Overmen Deputies and Shotfirers Retired Members Group, Engineering Employers' Federation, Police Federation of England and Wales, RAC Motoring Services, the Cyclist Touring Club, the London Cycling Campaign, British Triathlon Federation, the Co-operative Group, the National Union of Students and the British Association of Social Workers.

[129] See reg 4(4) of the Conditional Fee Agreements Regulations 2000.

[130] *Law Society v Waterlow* (1883) 8 App Cas 407 at 415, quoted in *Hollins v Russell* [2003] EWCA Civ 718 at [178].

[131] *Hollins v Russell* [2003] EWCA Civ 718 at [195].

We would not wish to be prescriptive about the form which that supervision should take, provided that an appropriate system has been set up.'

9.173 Sub-delegation is also permissible; Brooke emphasised that it was essential that the legal representative had a degree of supervisory control over the sub-delegates:[132]

'Quality control, however, is all important, and if a solicitor abjures his duty to maintain supervisory responsibility, through an established framework for reporting and accountability, over the ... representatives when they visit his client's home on his behalf, it is likely that it would be found that it was not he who gave the information he was required by regulation 4 to give, and that the regulation has therefore been broken.'

Advice based on a mistake of law

9.174 Irwin J has concluded that it would not be compliant with reg 4 to give advice which was based on an error of law, even where that error was understandable in human terms.[133]

Relevance to enforceability

9.175 Regulation 4(2) relates to requirements which must be satisfied before the conditional fee agreement is made. It has been argued that those requirements should be regarded as being something distinguishable from the agreement itself and that, therefore, a failure to satisfy those requirements does not put the agreement at risk. Brooke LJ rejected that argument, essentially on policy grounds (namely that pre-contract warnings are an important part of a regime which goes to consumer protection); he also rejected it on textual grounds.[134] Thus, if there has been a material breach of reg 4(2), the agreement will be unenforceable.

9.176 In summary, compliance with reg 4 is relevant to the issue of enforceability. There are three situations where reg 4(2) will either not apply or will be entirely redundant: where the agreement is a CFA Lite, where it is with an additional legal representative, and where it is with a membership organisation and the agreement does not put the client personally at risk of having to pay costs. Finally, the functions under reg 4 may be delegated to unqualified persons.

Regulation 4(2)(a)

9.177 This regulation, when read in conjunction with reg 4(1), stipulates that the client must be told of the circumstances in which he may be liable to pay the costs of the legal representative in accordance with the agreement:

'4.(1) Before a conditional fee agreement is made the legal representative must—

---

132 *Hollins v Russell* [2003] EWCA Civ 718 at [217].
133 *Crook v Birmingham City Council* [2007] EWHC 1415 (QB) at [28]; in the case he was dealing with the breach related to reg 4(2)(c), but there is no reason to believe that the principle does not also apply to the other sub-regulations.
134 He cited three reasons (see *Hollins v Russell* [2003] EWCA Civ 718 at [111]):
   (1) section 58A(3)(a) of the CLSA 1990 (as amended) clearly characterises the requirements in the CFA Regulations 2000 as among those with which the agreement must comply;
   (2) the words 'applicable to it' (as used in CLSA 1990, s 58(1)) are able to encompass steps taken by one of the parties before the agreement is made; and
   (3) regulation 2(2) requires a CFA to state that reg 4 has been complied with, thus making compliance part of the obligation under the CFA.

    (a)   inform the client about the following matters, and

    (b)   if the client requires any further explanation, advice or other information about any of those matters, provide such further explanation, advice or other information about them as the client may reasonably require.

  (2)   Those matters are—

    (a)   the circumstances in which the client may be liable to pay the costs of the legal representative in accordance with the agreement ...'

The information must be given orally (whether or not it is also given in writing).[135] Regulation 4(2)(a) applies to all conditional fee agreements, except those mentioned at **9.167–9.169**.

9.178 The duty is to explain the circumstances in which costs may be payable under the agreement rather than to explore hypothetical situations which might arise in the litigation.[136]

Regulation 4(2)(b)

9.179 This regulation, when read in conjunction with reg 4(1) stipulates that the client must be told the circumstances in which he may seek assessment of the fees and expenses of the legal representative and the procedure for doing so:

'4.(1)   Before a conditional fee agreement is made the legal representative must—

    (a)   inform the client about the following matters, and

    (b)   if the client requires any further explanation, advice or other information about any of those matters, provide such further explanation, advice or other information about them as the client may reasonably require.

  (2)   Those matters are—

    ...

    (b)   the circumstances in which the client may seek assessment of the fees and expenses of the legal representative and the procedure for doing so ...'

The information must be given orally (whether or not it is also given in writing).[137] Regulation 4(2)(b) applies to all conditional fee agreements, except the three circumstances mentioned at **9.167–9.169**.

Regulation 4(2)(c)

9.180 This regulation, when read in conjunction with reg 4(1) requires the legal representative to say whether he considers that the client's risk of incurring liability for costs in respect of the proceedings to which agreement relates is insured against under an existing contract of insurance:

'4.(1)   Before a conditional fee agreement is made the legal representative must—

    (a)   inform the client about the following matters, and

---

[135] Regulation 4(5) of the Conditional Fee Agreements Regulations 2000.

[136] *Bray Walker Solicitors (A Firm) v Silvera* [2008] EWHC 3147 (QB) at [75] affirmed by [2010] EWCA Civ 332.

[137] Regulation 4(5) of the Conditional Fee Agreements Regulations 2000.

    (b)   if the client requires any further explanation, advice or other information about any of those matters, provide such further explanation, advice or other information about them as the client may reasonably require.

(2)   Those matters are—

...

    (c)   whether the legal representative considers that the client's risk of incurring liability for costs in respect of the proceedings to which agreement relates is insured against under an existing contract of insurance ...'

The information must be given orally (whether or not it is also given in writing).[138] Regulation 4(2)(c) applies to all conditional fee agreements, except those mentioned at **9.167–9.169**.

9.181 The burden of considering the availability of BTE insurance lies with the legal representative rather than the client, so, unless the circumstances permit (see below), the client should not be asked the 'ultimate question' (as Dyson LJ put it) of whether the client had BTE insurance which would cover the legal expenses of bringing the claim.[139] Indeed, in some, but not all, cases the client should simply be asked to produce any home and motor insurance policies that he may have.[140]

9.182 A 'calibrated' approach ought to be taken when considering the issue of what is reasonably required; Dyson LJ identified five categories of factor which may be relevant, as follows.[141]

Category one: nature of the client

9.183 Some litigants may be sufficiently knowledgeable and intelligent to be able to answer the 'ultimate question' (see above); few will fall into this category. The legal representative must form a view as to whether the client's answers can reasonably be relied upon.

Category two: the circumstances of the instructions

9.184 The legal representative is not required to carry out investigations which would be unreasonable in the circumstances of the case in question. By way of example, Brooke LJ described as 'ridiculous' the notion that full BTE enquiries were required for an 80-year-old woman who was still in hospital after recently having been discharged from an intensive therapy unit.[142]

Category three: the nature of the claim

9.185 If it is unlikely that standard BTE policies would apply to the claim in question, this may justify the legal representative taking fewer steps to ascertain the position than might otherwise have been the case.

---

[138] Regulation 4(5) of the Conditional Fee Agreements Regulations 2000.
[139] *Myatt v National Coal Board* [2006] EWCA Civ 1017 at [55], [62] and [72].
[140] *Myatt v National Coal Board* [2006] EWCA Civ 1017 at [78].
[141] *Myatt v National Coal Board* [2006] EWCA Civ 1017 at [71]–[76].
[142] *Pratt v Bull; Hollins v Russell* [2003] EWCA Civ 718 at [138], cited by Dyson LJ in *Myatt v National Coal Board* [2006] EWCA Civ 1017 at [73].

Category four: the cost of ATE cover

9.186 The cost of ATE cover is a relevant factor.[143]

Category five: previous enquiries

9.187 Where the claim has been referred by a referral agency, it may be relevant that the agency has already investigated the question of the availability of BTE. Whether it is reasonable to rely on that information will be a matter for the legal representative to decide, using his own judgment. Further details are given at **9.170–9.173**.

9.188 Dyson LJ emphasised that this list of categories was not intended to be exhaustive.

9.189 The standard of enquiries is not the same as that required for purposes of considering whether ATE insurance is required (those enquiries often being referred to as '*Sarwar* enquires').[144] Dyson LJ has made it clear that the two are not a single standard:[145]

> '[It] follows that the regulation 4(2)(c) duty does not require solicitors slavishly to follow the detailed guidance given by this court in [*Sarwar v Alam* [2001] EWCA Civ 1401, which dealt with the standard applicable to ATE]. In particular, the statement at para 45 that a solicitor should normally invite a client to bring to the first interview any relevant policy should be treated with considerable caution. It has no application in high volume low value litigation conducted by solicitors on referral by claims management companies.'

A number of specific problems may arise in practice, as follows.

Timing

9.190 Although not binding decisions, Master Wright has found that the requirement that advice is given before the agreement is made does not mean that it must be given at the same time as the agreement is made,[146] and HHJ Stewart QC has found that where the requisite enquiries were carried out after the agreement had been made, that deprived the client of proper advice and amounted to a material breach.[147]

Expired BTE and insurance other than BTE

9.191 In a case in which the costs incurred had already exceeded the level of cover under a pre-existing BTE policy, HHJ Behrens (sitting as a judge of the High Court) found that the there was no obligation to advise that BTE cover existed.[148] Whilst not binding, HHJ MacDuff (now MacDuff J) has found that the duty to make enquiries under reg 4(2)(c) is not limited to making enquiries about BTE insurance, but will, in

---

[143] Dyson LJ noted that this was also a factor relevant to the standard of enquiries required for the purposes of ATE insurance.

[144] After *Sarwar v Alam* [2001] EWCA Civ 1401.

[145] *Myatt v National Coal Board* [2006] EWCA Civ 1017 at [70]; on this issue generally see *Myatt* at [66]–[70] and *Hollins v Russell* [2003] EWCA Civ 718 at [139].

[146] *White v Revell* [2006] EWHC 90054 (Costs).

[147] *Cooper v Morgan*, 29 September 2006, Liverpool County Court.

[148] *Thornley (a child) v MoD* [2010] EWHC 2584 (QB) at [20]–[28].

appropriate circumstances, include a duty to make enquiries about the existence of ATE insurance that may already have been incepted.[149]

ATE insurance already incepted

9.192 In a similar vein, Waller LJ has clarified (obiter) that the onus to give advice would exist even where it was known that ATE insurance had already been incepted.[150]

Regulation 4(2)(d)

9.193 This regulation, when read in conjunction with reg 4(1), requires the legal representative to state whether other methods of financing the costs of the claim are available, and, if so, how they apply to the client and the proceedings in question:

> '4.(1) Before a conditional fee agreement is made the legal representative must—
>
> > (a)   inform the client about the following matters, and
> > (b)   if the client requires any further explanation, advice or other information about any of those matters, provide such further explanation, advice or other information about them as the client may reasonably require.
>
> (2) Those matters are—
>
> ...
>
> > (d)   whether other methods of financing those costs are available, and, if so, how they apply to the client and the proceedings in question ...'

The information must be given orally (whether or not it is also given in writing).[151] Regulation 4(2)(d) applies to all conditional fee agreements, except those three types mentioned at **9.167–9.169**. A number of issues may arise in practice, as follows.

BTE insurance already in existence

9.194 The duty to give advice will exist even where the client has pre-existing insurance (ie even where the client has BTE insurance). In those circumstances, the client must be given advice about whether that insurance is appropriate.[152]

ATE insurance already incepted

9.195 In a similar vein, Waller LJ has clarified (obiter) that the onus to give advice would exist even where it was known that ATE insurance had already been incepted.[153]

Impracticable funding options

9.196 Irwin J has commented that reg 4(2)(d) does not impose a duty to give advice about methods of funding, which, for all practical purposes, would not be available.[154]

---

[149]   *Berry v Spousals*, 24 April 2007, Birmingham County Court.
[150]   *Jones v Wrexham Borough Council* [2007] EWCA Civ 1356 at [62].
[151]   Regulation 4(5) of the Conditional Fee Agreements Regulations 2000.
[152]   *Jones v Wrexham Borough Council* [2007] EWCA Civ 1356 at [62].
[153]   *Jones v Wrexham Borough Council* [2007] EWCA Civ 1356 at [62].
[154]   *Crook v Birmingham City Council* [2007] EWHC 1415 (QB) at [34].

Complex funding options

9.197 In circumstances in which funding options were complex, Christopher Clarke J has said (albeit obiter) that it is reasonable to look at the matter in the round and whether the advice was reasonable advice in all the circumstances.[155]

Timing

9.198 Whilst not in a binding decision, Master Wright has found that the requirement that advice is given before the agreement is made does not mean that it must be given at the same time as the agreement is made.[156] Also not in a binding decision, HHJ Stewart QC has found that, where the requisite enquiries were carried out after the agreement had been made, that deprived the client of proper advice and amounted to a material breach.[157]

English not the client's first language

9.199 Blake J declined to find that there had been a breach of reg 4(2) by reason of the fact that the client (whose first language was Italian) was given a written explanation in English, especially where he had the benefit of a translator easily to hand.[158]

Failure to give advice about protection from adverse costs

9.200 Irwin J has commented (obiter) that if the breach was such that the client had been given inadequate advice about how to manage the possibility of an adverse costs order, then that would amount to a material breach, unless the advice was only minimally deficient.[159]

Failure to give advice about the availability of public funding

9.201 This issue tends to arise only in housing disrepair claims and clinical negligence claims; this is because, for present purposes, these are the two most common types of claims where legal aid continues to apply. There are examples of the court finding that a failure to give advice about the minutiae of public funding would not amount to a material breach;[160] equally, an affirmative and reasonable decision not to burden the client with detailed advice would not amount to a breach.[161] Many examples of material breach, however, do exist.[162]

---

[155] *Forde v Birmingham City Council* [2009] EWHC 12 (QB) at [200].
[156] *White v Revell* [2006] EWHC 90054 (Costs).
[157] *Cooper v Morgan*, 29 September 2006, Liverpool County Court.
[158] *Bray Walker Solicitors (A Firm) v Silvera* [2008] EWHC 3147 (QB) at [73] (affirmed on other grounds at [2010] EWCA Civ 332 at [25]); it was probably relevant that the client was a relatively sophisticated businessman.
[159] *Crook v Birmingham City Council* [2007] EWHC 1415 (QB) at [35].
[160] *Crook v Birmingham City Council* [2007] EWHC 1415 (QB).
[161] *Forde v Birmingham City Council* [2009] EWHC 12 (QB).
[162] These include *Bowen v Bridgend County Borough Council* [2004] EWHC 9010 (Costs) and *Hughes & Ors v London Borough of Newham* [2005] EWHC 90019 (Costs), neither of which is binding.

Regulation 4(2)(e)

9.202 The purpose of reg 4(2)(e), when read in conjunction with reg 4(1) is to ensure that the legal representative acts and gives advice independently of his own interest:[163]

> '4.(1) Before a conditional fee agreement is made the legal representative must—
>
> (a)   inform the client about the following matters, and
> (b)   if the client requires any further explanation, advice or other information about any of those matters, provide such further explanation, advice or other information about them as the client may reasonably require.
>
> (2)   Those matters are—
>
> ...
>
> (e)   whether the legal representative considers that any particular method or methods of financing any or all of those costs is appropriate and, if he considers that a contract of insurance is appropriate or recommends a particular such contract—
>   (i)   his reasons for doing so, and
>   (ii)   whether he has an interest in doing so.'

Regulation 4(2)(e) applies to all conditional fee agreements, except those mentioned at **9.167–9.169**.

9.203 Unlike the other sub-regulations in reg 4(2), the information must be given orally *and* in writing.[164] Provided that it is sufficiently clear, the latter requirement may be met by a written explanation that is part of the agreement itself.[165]

9.204 There is no reason to interpret the requirement to declare any interest as narrowly as meaning only a direct financial interest.[166] The applicable test is an objective one; Clarke MR (giving judgment of the court) has clarified that a legal representative has a declarable interest if a reasonable person with knowledge of the relevant facts would think that the existence of the interest might affect the advice given by the legal representative to his client. If a reasonable person with knowledge of the relevant facts would think that there might be a risk that the legal representative's advice has been influenced by the interest, the client must be informed of that interest.

9.205 The following miscellaneous topics may present themselves in practice (topics relating to panel membership are discussed with at **9.215–9.224**).

No interest

9.206 The requirement to declare an interest in reg 4(2)(e)(ii) does not extend to declaring the absence of an interest: the word 'whether' in the regulation ought to be read as meaning 'if'. Brooke LJ explained the rationale behind that interpretation:[167]

> 'The mischief which this regulation was introduced to remedy was the risk that the client's legal representative might induce the client to enter into insurance arrangements in which he had an interest. If he had no interest, then there was no identified mischief.'

---

[163]   *Tankard v John Fredricks Plastics Ltd* [2008] EWCA Civ 1375 at [13]–[15].
[164]   Regulation 4(5) of the Conditional Fee Agreements Regulations 2000.
[165]   Although dealing with a different aspect of reg 4(2), there is no reason to believe that the analysis in *Dunn v Ward; Hollins v Russell* [2003] EWCA Civ 718 at [152]–[154] would not also apply.
[166]   *Garrett v Halton Borough Council; Myatt v National Coal Board* [2006] EWCA Civ 1017 at [91].
[167]   *Dunn v Ward; Hollins v Russell* [2003] EWCA Civ 718 at [144].

ATE insurance already incepted

9.207 Waller LJ has clarified (obiter) that the onus to give advice pursuant to reg 4(2)(e) exists even where insurance is already in place.[168]

BTE insurance already in existence

9.208 The duty to give advice pursuant to reg 4(2)(e) exists even where the client has pre-existing insurance (ie even where the client has BTE insurance). In those circumstances, the client must be given advice about whether the insurance is appropriate to use.[169]

Timing

9.209 There is no reason to believe that the points made in the sections above concerning the other sub-paragraphs in reg 4(2) do not also apply to reg 4(2)(e).

Incorrect statement of interest

9.210 The obligation to state whether a legal representative has an interest is an obligation to state those details correctly; it will not be sufficient merely to state whether there is an interest if that statement is incorrect, even if the legal representative believed that to be the true position.[170]

Clarity

9.211 As is the case with reg 4 in general, any advice which is given must be clear; inconsistent advice (such as the client being told about the existence of an interest but the agreement saying something different) will not be sufficient to discharge the legal representative's duty.[171]

Complexity and materiality

9.212 On the facts of a palpably complicated matter, Irwin J found that a failure to give advice about the detail of funding lacked materiality because the correct advice would have been so complex, with risks and opportunities 'all hedged about with uncertainty', that it would not have made any difference to the client's decision as to how to fund the claim.[172]

The Conduct of Business Rules

9.213 Whilst Dyson LJ did not say that the two standards were the same, he made obiter comments to the effect that compliance with the requirements imposed by the Solicitors' Financial Services (Conduct of Business) Rules 2001 (which coincided with

---

[168] *Jones v Wrexham Borough Council* [2007] EWCA Civ 1356 at [62].
[169] *Jones v Wrexham Borough Council* [2007] EWCA Civ 1356 at [62].
[170] *Garrett v Halton Borough Council; Myatt v National Coal Board* [2006] EWCA Civ 1017 at [94].
[171] *Tankard v John Fredricks Plastics Ltd* [2008] EWCA Civ 1375 at [45].
[172] *Crook v Birmingham City Council* [2007] EWHC 1415 (QB) at [28].

the CFA Regulations for about 10 months in 2005) would have been sufficient to comply with the obligations under reg 4(2)(e)(ii).[173] The first of these standards is discussed at **30.133–30.141**.

9.214 In summary, the test is an objective one, ie whether a reasonable person with knowledge of the relevant facts would think that the existence of the interest might have affected the advice given by the legal representative to his client.

Panel membership

9.215 The points made in this section concern panel membership. It should be read in conjunction with the section immediately above.

9.216 A number of different types of panel exist, the two most common being an 'insurance panel' (which is where the legal representative is, by virtue of his membership, able to obtain a particular contract of insurance for his clients) and a 'referral panel' (which is where the legal representative receives referrals from a referral agency and is usually required to recommend a particular contract of insurance in return). The term 'membership panel' is also often used to refer to an insurance panel, but that term must be viewed in context, because it is also capable of referring to other types of panel. Panel membership may also bring with it 'delegated authority', which is the power to bind the insurer by incepting a contract of insurance without the direct reference to the insurer.

9.217 Clarke MR (giving judgment of the court) has confirmed that the fact that a legal representative is a member of a panel does not necessarily mean that there is a declarable interest.[174] Every type of panel membership is capable of generating a declarable interest, so each case ought to be considered on its own facts. At one end of the spectrum, where a legal representative is dependent on referrals as the 'lifeblood' of his practice (to use a word adopted by Dyson LJ), that would create an indirect, but declarable, interest;[175] at the other end of the spectrum, where the panel membership is principally for the purposes of obtaining high quality insurance for the benefit of clients, that would not usually amount to a declarable interest.[176]

9.218 It is possible to identify the following factors as being relevant to the issue of whether panel membership gives rise to a declarable interest:

* the motive for a legal representative's membership of the panel, including whether the legal representative was attracted to the panel by the high quality of the insurance: [20] and [30];[177]
* the motive of the panel organisation for requiring panel membership, including whether the concern of the underwriter was merely to avoid adverse selection of cases: [23];
* the extent to which the legal representative is dependent on the referrals. It should not be forgotten that the profit generated by referrals is likely to be of greater significance than the monies received in commission ([18]), but it also ought not to

---

[173] *Garrett v Halton Borough Council; Myatt v National Coal Board* [2006] EWCA Civ 1017 at [103].
[174] *Tankard v John Fredricks Plastics Ltd* [2008] EWCA Civ 1375 at [17]–[18].
[175] *Garrett v Halton Borough Council; Myatt v National Coal Board* [2006] EWCA Civ 1017 at [97].
[176] See *Tankard v John Fredricks Plastics Ltd* [2008] EWCA Civ 1375 at [17]–[20].
[177] The numbers in brackets are paragraph numbers in *Tankard v John Fredricks Plastics Ltd* [2008] EWCA Civ 1375.

be forgotten that many referred cases will not be worth pursuing ([30]) and that those cases will impose their own burden of irrecoverable costs of investigation: [31];

- whether failure to comply with recommending a policy would lead to a cessation of referral of cases: [18];
- whether there have been reviews to ensure that continued membership of the panel was in clients' bests interests ([20]); the relevance of this is that reviews may be indicative of the motive for remaining on the panel; and
- the closeness of the business relationship between the legal representative and the referrer: [18].

This list is nothing more than the writer's interpretation of the authorities; it is not intended to be exhaustive.

9.219 Clarke MR has clarified (obiter) that, where a declarable interest does exist, it will not be sufficient to declare the existence of the interest without giving any indication as to its nature. The requisite standard entails explaining to the client the nature of the benefits to the legal representative in remaining on the panel, and doing so with sufficient clarity for the client to understand what those benefits are and to be able to assess their significance.[178] It would not be sufficient for a legal representative merely to inform the client that he is recommending a policy because that is the only policy which he is free to recommend, as this tells the client nothing of the benefit that accrues to the legal representative through continuing membership of the panel.[179]

9.220 There are a number of miscellaneous topics which may arise in the context of panel membership, as follows.

Exclusivity agreement

9.221 The fact that a legal representative is required exclusively to use a particular insurer is not, of itself, something which creates a declarable interest; Clarke MR explained that this was because such an arrangement might be necessary in order to avoid adverse selection of cases and that, in any event, it does not affect the advice which is given to the client.[180]

Rebates

9.222 Some panels operate a rebate scheme, whereby a membership fee is payable upon subscription to the panel but a rebate or partial rebate is given in the event of a certain number of policies being incepted. Clarke MR has implicitly confirmed that in principle this could amount to a declarable interest, but qualified this by saying that the court must look at the size of the rebate in the context of the legal representative's turnover; on the facts of the case before him (an Accident Line Protect case), he found that the rebate was a 'minute fraction of turnover'.[181]

---

[178] *Tankard v John Fredricks Plastics Ltd* [2008] EWCA Civ 1375 at [37], [38] and [43].

[179] *Tankard v John Fredricks Plastics Ltd* [2008] EWCA Civ 1375 at [44]; any dicta to the contrary in *Garrett v Halton Borough Council; Myatt v National Coal Board* [2006] EWCA Civ 1017 should not be followed.

[180] *Tankard v John Fredricks Plastics Ltd* [2008] EWCA Civ 1375 at [25]–[26], referring to *Rogers v Merthyr Tydfil CBC* [2006] EWCA Civ 1134 at [113]–[114].

[181] *Tankard v John Fredricks Plastics Ltd* [2008] EWCA Civ 1375 at [32]–[33]; the rebate was in the order of £250.

Bare declaration of panel membership

9.223 The mere fact that the client has been made aware of a legal representative's panel membership would not be sufficient declaration of the type of interest mentioned immediately above. This is because a client could not be expected to infer from that information that the recommendation may be dictated by the legal representative's financial interests. Indeed, a lay person might believe that panel membership was a mark of quality control.[182]

Evidence of causal link

9.224 Waller LJ has clarified (obiter) that where a firm is obliged to recommend a particular form of insurance, it is an 'obvious inference not requiring any evidence' that ignoring that provision would cause damage to the legal representative's business relationship with the person to whom that promise was made.[183]

Regulation 4(3)

9.225 This regulation stipulates that before an agreement is made the legal representative must explain its effect to the client:

> '4.(3) Before a conditional fee agreement is made the legal representative must explain its effect to the client.'

The regulation applies to all conditional fee agreements, except those made between a legal representative and an additional legal representative[184] and CFA Lites.[185] It will apply regardless of whether the legal representative is a membership organisation. The explanation must be given both orally *and* in writing.[186]

9.226 There is no reason to believe that the general points made in the discussion on reg 4(2) about reasonableness, timing, etc do not also apply to reg 4(3). These points are not repeated. In essence, each case must be decided on its own facts, and the requisite standard will be one of reasonableness.

9.227 Once the requisite standard has been established, compliance is generally a matter of fact; an example of a case in which the requisite standard was not met is where a new agreement was made without the client being told that it did not cap the fees in the way that his original agreement did.[187] The issues will not always be questions of fact, however, as there may be a dispute about what the agreement means. In these circumstances, the process of prior interpretation may be relevant. Whilst he did not refer to it by that name, Stanley Burnton J carried out that process in a case where the client had been told that the agreement would be effective from one date, but the agreement itself had been backdated and bore a different date. He found that there had been a literal breach but that it was not material; he came to this conclusion because on

---

[182] *Garrett v Halton Borough Council; Myatt v National Coal Board* [2006] EWCA Civ 1017 at [99]–[100].
[183] *Jones v Wrexham Borough Council* [2007] EWCA Civ 1356 at [66].
[184] Regulation 4(6) of the Collective Conditional Fee Agreements Regulations 2000 (SI 2000/2988).
[185] SI 2000/2988, reg 3A(3).
[186] SI 2000/2988, reg 4(5).
[187] *Langsam v Beachcroft LLP & ors* [2011] EWHC 1451 (Ch), per Roth J.

a true interpretation of the agreement the date from which it was effective and the date which the client had been told about were one and the same.[188]

9.228 It has been argued that where an agreement contains inconsistent terms, this would give rise to an inadequate written explanation for the purposes of complying with reg 4(3). In the context of an agreement which failed to set out all the material terms and which had to be read in conjunction with another document, Mann J described the suggestion that this amounted to a breach as a 'bad point'.[189]

9.229 Stanley Burnton J commented (obiter) that if the circumstances were that the client had been given incorrect advice about the scope of the agreement, it would have been open to the court to have found that there was no material breach; this would have been on the grounds that if the client had been given the correct advice, any sensible client would have agreed to what was being proposed.[190]

Regulation 5

9.230 This regulation requires that the agreement is signed by both the client and the legal representative:

> '5.(1)   A conditional fee agreement must be signed by the client and the legal representative.
>
> (2)   This regulation does not apply in the case of an agreement between a legal representative and an additional legal representative.'

This regulation applies to all conditional fee agreements, except those between the legal representative and an additional legal representative.[191]

9.231 Although not in a binding decision, HHJ Hickinbottom (now Hickinbottom J) has found that a total failure to sign a conditional fee agreement would amount to a material breach; as to materiality, he found that if an agreement is not signed, then a less scrupulous legal representative might, for example, seek to enforce his right to be paid in the event of the claim failing.[192] In a similar case[193] Mann J came to a very similar conclusion:[194]

> 'I am afraid that I have difficulty in seeing how a failure to sign important contractual documentation can ever be capable of falling within [the definition of being immaterial]. Parliament not only prescribed that a CFA be in writing ... it also required that it be in writing and signed by both parties. There are clear policy considerations underlying both of these requirements. They achieve that the terms of the agreement (which are capable of impacting not only on the parties to it, but upon a paying party in litigation) are clear and

---

188   *Holmes v Alfred McAlpine Homes (Yorkshire) Ltd* [2006] EWHC 110 (QB) at [21]; the judgment does not record the reasons why Stanley Burnton J did not conclude that there had been no breach at all, which (on the face of it) was a finding that was open to him.

189   *Fenton v Holmes* [2007] EWHC 2476 (Ch) at [65].

190   *Holmes v Alfred McAlpine Homes (Yorkshire) Ltd* [2006] EWHC 110 (QB) at p [21]; it is not clear whether this point was extensively argued before Stanley Burnton J, so those comments should be treated with some caution.

191   SI 2000/692, reg 5(2) (as amended).

192   *Preece v Caerphilly County Borough Council*, 15 August 2007, Cardiff County Court, para 18.

193   The case Mann J was dealing with did not concern the agreement itself, but a letter which the receiving party was forced to rely upon in order to prove compliance with one of the other requirements of the Conditional Fee Agreements Regulations 2000 (as amended).

194   *Fenton v Holmes* [2007] EWHC 2476 (Ch) at [55].

clearly subscribed to. These considerations clearly have implications, both in terms of consumer protection for the client and in terms of the administration of justice.'

9.232 In most legal contexts the issue of whether a document has been signed is a question not merely of fact, but of both fact and law. This is because not all signatures need to be in manuscript. Although in a different context from conditional fee agreements, there is authority for the proposition that printed signatures, rubber stamps, etc are sufficient. It could be argued that parallels could be drawn with the requirement to sign a bill (ie an invoice rendered to a client). These topics are fully discussed at **17.59–17.66**.

9.233 As with any document, the signature must be in a place which governs the document.[195]

Regulation 6

9.234 This regulation imposes an obligation which arises only where the agreement is amended to cover further proceedings or parts of them; an example would be where an agreement is amended to cover an appeal brought by the client against a final order:

'6. Where an agreement is amended to cover further proceedings or parts of them—

(a)   regulations 2, 3, 3A and 5 apply to the amended agreement as if it were a fresh agreement made at the time of the amendment, and

(b)   the obligations under regulation 4 apply in relation to the amendments in so far as they affect the matters mentioned in that regulation.'

This regulation continues to have effect for the purposes of agreements made between 1 April 2000 and 1 November 2005.[196] If the issue of amendment were to arise in respect of such an agreement, it would almost always be prudent to enter into a new agreement rather than to run the risk, however slight, of perpetuating or creating an unenforceable agreement.

9.235 Where the agreement is varied, the following will apply:

•   regulations 2, 3, 3A and 5 will apply to the amended agreement as if it were a fresh agreement made at the time of the amendment; and

•   the obligations under reg 4 will apply in relation to the amendments in so far as they affect the matters mentioned in that regulation.

9.236 Whilst there is no authority on the point, it would appear that the agreement should be treated as if it were a new agreement made under the CFA Regulations 2000, save that the need to explain the agreement pursuant to reg 4 is limited to the need to explain the effect of the amendment. Other interpretations are possible, however.

---

[195]   *Caton v Caton* (1867) LR 2 HL 127.

[196]   See reg 3(1) of the Conditional Fee Agreements (Revocation) Regulations 2005 (SI 2005/2305); it could be argued, however, that the words 'fresh agreement' in reg 6(1) of the Conditional Fee Agreements Regulations 2000 (as amended) release the legal representative from some of the obligations imposed by that regulation.

The effect of a breach of the CFA Regulations 2000

9.237 The position is most easily examined first as between legal representative and client, and then as between opposing parties.

Legal representative and client

9.238 effect of a material breach of the CFA Regulations 2000 is to render the agreement unenforceable.[197] The only exception to this is if the agreement is a non-contentious business agreement which is complaint with s 57 of the Solicitors Act 1974.[198]

9.239 For all practical purposes there is a further exception in that where fixed recoverable costs apply, an opposing party will be liable for those costs regardless of the enforceability of the agreement. Whilst Simon J has explained the policy behind this principle,[199] it is not wholly clear how the legal representative is able to claim those costs from the client. It is possible that the client may hold those costs on constructive trust for the legal representative, but that analysis is far from perfect when looked at in any detail,[200] as are most other analyses.[201] Nonetheless, no client has had sufficient strength of feeling to generate any authority on the point.

9.240 Brooke LJ has confirmed that there is no basis for the proposition that the extent to which the agreement is to be rendered unenforceable is to be tailored so that it is proportionate to the culpability of the breach.[202]

Between opposing parties

9.241 Other than as set out above (fixed recoverable costs)[203] the indemnity principle applies to conditional fee agreements. It is not correct to say that the statutory provisions concerning enforceability are operative only between solicitor and client rather than between opposing parties.[204]

9.242 Some types of disbursements (most noticeably paid disbursements) may be recoverable notwithstanding a breach of the indemnity principle, so it is worth dealing with recoverable and irrecoverable costs in turn.

Recoverable costs

9.243 Where disbursements are recoverable by a mechanism other than via an unenforceable agreement, the enforceability of the agreement will be irrelevant. An

---

[197] CLSA 1990 (as amended), s 58(1).
[198] CLSA 1990 (as amended), s 58(5).
[199] *Nizami v Butt* [2006] EWHC 159 (QB) at [23]–[25].
[200] Not least because it would be an equitable remedy that would go against the grain of CLSA 1990, s 58(1).
[201] Another possibility is that the order of the court in some way affords the legal representative a proprietorial right to the costs, in the sense that the costs are to be paid to the legal representative rather than to the client, but there is nothing in Section II of CPR, Part 45 which suggests that that is the correct analysis; a further analysis is that whilst the agreement may be unenforceable, the legal representative is able to claim a right to any monies which come into his hands by other means.
[202] *Spencer v Wood* [2004] EWCA Civ 352.
[203] There is also an exception created by CPR, r 43.2(3), but for present purposes that can be disregarded, as it has no bearing on unenforceable retainers.
[204] *Hollins v Russell* [2003] EWCA 718 at [92]–[95].

example is where an ATE premium is recoverable under a contract of insurance.[205] Another is where the client is directly responsible for the payment of the fees or expenses of a third party (e g where a client has agreed to pay an expert directly); that situation can occur notwithstanding the fact that the solicitor may have had a role to play in instructing the third party.

9.244 Where they have been paid by the client or by the solicitor out of the client's funds, disbursements will be recoverable.[206] The facility to recover disbursements paid in such a way is of real relevance in practice, because many claims are funded by way of a disbursement funding loan, which often will have been used to pay the disbursements as and when they were incurred.

Irrecoverable costs

9.245 Unless and to the extent that fixed recoverable costs are recoverable, all profit costs incurred under an unenforceable agreement will be irrecoverable. Disbursements other than those mentioned above are also not recoverable. Whilst some conditional fee agreements with additional legal representatives do attempt to provide for a direct liability between the client and the additional legal representative, the vast majority do not, so the fees of the additional legal representative will stand or fall with the fees of the legal representative.

9.246 In summary, with one or two exceptions (such as paid disbursements and fixed recoverable costs), an unenforceable agreement will result in non-recovery of costs both between legal representative and client and between opposing parties.

Conditional fee agreements made before 1 April 2000

9.247 Between 5 July 1995 and 1 April 2000, conditional fee agreements were governed by the Conditional Fee Agreements Regulations 1995 (SI 1995/1675). These will rarely be encountered in present day practice, but they are reproduced at the end of this chapter.[207] The principles of compliance are similar to those which have been described in the context of the CFA Regulations 2000.

9.248 Transitional provisions apply (see below); in essence, no success fee will be recoverable in respect of proceedings where the receiving party entered into a conditional fee agreement before 1 April 2000, or in any proceedings arising out of the same cause of action as those proceedings. That restriction will apply even if there was a break in the period during which the matter was conditionally funded such that the matter was not conditionally funded on 1 April 2000.[208] The transitional provisions are as follows:[209]

'(1)   Section 58A(6) and (7) of the Courts and Legal Services Act 1990 shall not apply, as regards a party to proceedings, to:

(a)   any proceedings in relation to which that party entered into a conditional fee agreement before 1 April 2000; or

---

205   *Hollins v Russell* [2003] EWCA 718 at [114].
206   *Hollins v Russell* [2003] EWCA 718 at [115].
207   See **9.421**.
208   *C v M* [2003] EWHC 250 (Fam).
209   The Access to Justice Act 1999 (Transitional Provisions) Order 2000 (SI 2000/900), reg 2.

(b)   any proceedings arising out of the same cause of action as any proceedings to which sub-paragraph (a) refers.

(2)   The coming into force of section 27 (Conditional fee agreements) shall not affect the validity of any conditional fee agreement entered into before 1 April 2000, and any such agreement shall continue to have effect after that date as if section 27 had not come into force.

(3)   In paragraphs 1(a) and (2) "conditional fee agreement" has the same meaning as in section 58 of the Courts and Legal Services Act 1990 as that section stands immediately before the coming into force of section 27 of the Access to Justice Act 1999.'

A description of the effect of these provisions is contained in the CPD at art 57.8. In order to avoid repetition, it is not set out here.

Collective conditional fee agreements

9.249   This section deals principally with collective conditional fee agreements which were made between 30 November 2000 and 1 November 2005. Such agreements must comply with the Collective Conditional Fee Agreements Regulations 2000 (as amended) ('the CCFA Regulations 2000'). There is no requirement that they comply with the CFA Regulations 2000.[210]

9.250   The terminology has already been defined at **9.38–9.45**. Those definitions should be read in conjunction with this section. The CCFA Regulations 2000 (in their most recent guise) are set out in full at **9.421**.

The structure of a collective conditional fee agreement

9.251   A collective conditional fee agreement involves persons acting in three capacities: the funder, the client and the legal representative. The funder may also be the client. There is no requirement that the agreement refers to specific clients[211] (indeed, specific clients are only very rarely mentioned).

9.252   As with individual conditional fee agreements, a collective conditional fee agreement may provide for a success fee.[212] A collective conditional fee agreement may be a CCFA Lite.[213] The qualifying criteria for an agreement being a CCFA Lite are very similar to those which apply to CFA Lites.[214]

9.253   Any collective conditional fee agreement will contain a collective element, which is the framework document setting out the terms agreed between the funder and the legal representative. By definition, the collective element will not refer to specific proceedings; instead, it provides for fees to be payable on a common basis in relation to a class of proceedings, or, if it refers to more than one class of proceedings, on a common basis in relation to each class.[215]

---

[210]   Conditional Fee Agreements Regulations 2000 (as amended), reg 8; see also *Thornley v Lang* [2003] EWCA Civ 1484 at [13], [17], [18] and [20].

[211]   Collective Conditional Fee Agreements Regulations 2000 (SI 2000/2988) (as amended), reg 3(2).

[212]   SI 2000/2988 (as amended), reg 5.

[213]   See the amendments made by Conditional Fee Agreements (Miscellaneous Amendments) Regulations 2003 and Conditional Fee Agreements (Miscellaneous Amendments) (No 2) Regulations 2003.

[214]   SI 2000/2988 (as amended), reg 5(5), (6) and (7).

[215]   SI 2000/2988 (as amended), reg 3(1).

9.254 In isolation, the collective element cannot form a retainer where the client is not a counterparty to it (which will be in the vast majority of cases). Furthermore, in isolation, it will not refer to any particular claim. Therefore, it must in some way be applied to the claim in hand: some step must be taken to form a retainer; the exact mechanism by which this is achieved is a moot point, but one aspect of the matter is beyond question: the retainer which is formed is not a conditional fee agreement in the sense that it must comply with the CFA Regulations 2000. The two regulatory regimes are mutually exclusive,[216] so when a collective conditional fee agreement is said to have been 'applied' to the matter in hand, this does not mean that it has formed something other than a collective conditional fee agreement.

9.255 Phillips MR has commented that the retainer comes into being as a result of the funder agreeing to use it in an individual case with the authority of the client; he mentioned an alternative, that being that the agreement is ratified by the client.[217] Gray J seems to have accepted that analysis.[218] Regardless of the exact mechanism by which the agreement is applied, the end result is that both the client and the funder have a dual liability for the legal representative's fees.[219] The retainer can probably best be thought of as being a tripartite agreement where, for the time being, the client has agreed to be bound by the terms of the collective element.

The relevant regulations

9.256 The requirements under the CCFA Regulations 2000 are much less exacting than those under the CFA Regulations 2000.[220] For the reasons set out below, they regulate the collective element rather than the way in which the retainer itself is to be formed. The requirements can be split into four groups, as follows.

Any collective conditional fee agreement

9.257 Any collective conditional fee agreement must satisfy the following requirements:[221]

- it must specify the circumstances in which the legal representative's fees and expenses, or part of them, are payable;[222] and
- it must provide that, after accepting instructions in relation to any specific proceedings, the legal representative must confirm his acceptance of instructions in writing to the client.

---

[216] Conditional Fee Agreements Regulations 2000 (as amended), reg 8; see also the comments of Phillips MR in *Thornley v Lang* [2003] EWCA Civ 1484 at [13], [17], [18] and [20].

[217] *Thornley v Lang* [2003] EWCA Civ 1484 at [20], drawing on the line of authority which is described at **11.52–11.66**.

[218] *Kitchen v Burwell Reed & Kinghorn Ltd* [2005] EWHC 1771 (QB) at [16].

[219] *Thornley v Lang* [2003] EWCA Civ 1484.

[220] *Thornley v Lang* [2003] EWCA Civ 1484 at [11], per Phillips MR.

[221] Collective Conditional Fee Agreements Regulations 2000 (SI 2000/2988) (as amended), reg 4.

[222] Those circumstances may include the fact that the legal representative's fees and expenses are payable only to the extent that sums are recovered in respect of the proceedings, whether by way of costs or otherwise: see SI 2000/2988 (as amended) reg 4(1A).

Any collective conditional fee agreement other than an agreement with an additional legal representative

9.258 Such an agreement must satisfy the following requirements:[223]

- it must provide that, when accepting instructions in relation to any specific proceedings the legal representative must inform the client as to the circumstances in which the client or his estate may be liable to pay the costs of the legal representative; and
- it must, if the client requires any further explanation, advice or other information about those matters, provide such further explanation, advice or other information about it as the client may reasonably require.

Any collective conditional fee agreement which provides for a success fee

9.259 Any such agreement must satisfy the following requirements:[224]

'(1) Where a collective conditional fee agreement provides for a success fee the agreement must provide that, when accepting instructions in relation to any specific proceedings the legal representative must prepare and retain a written statement containing—

    (a) his assessment of the probability of the circumstances arising in which the percentage increase will become payable in relation to those proceedings ("the risk assessment");

    (b) his assessment of the amount of the percentage increase in relation to those proceedings, having regard to the risk assessment; and

    (c) the reasons, by reference to the risk assessment, for setting the percentage increase at that level.

(2) If the agreement relates to court proceedings it must provide that where the success fee becomes payable as a result of those proceedings, then—

    (a) if—

        (i) any fees subject to the increase are assessed, and

        (ii) the legal representative or the client is required by the court to disclose to the court or any other person the reasons for setting the percentage increase at the level assessed by the legal representative,

he may do so ...'

Any collective conditional fee agreement which provides for a success fee but which is not CCFA Lite

9.260 Such an agreement must satisfy the following requirements:[225]

- If the agreement relates to court proceedings, it must provide that where the success fee becomes payable as a result of those proceedings, then, if any such fees are assessed by the court, and if any amount in respect of the percentage increase is disallowed on the assessment on the ground that the level at which the increase was set was unreasonable in view of facts which were or should have been known to the legal representative at the time it was set, that amount ceases to be payable under the agreement, unless the court is satisfied that it should continue to be so payable.

---

[223] SI 2000/2988 (as amended), reg 4.
[224] SI 2000/2988 (as amended), reg 5.
[225] SI 2000/2988 (as amended) regs 5(2)(b) and (c), and (4).

- The agreement must provide that if the situation mentioned in the bullet point above does not apply, and if the legal representative agrees with any person liable as a result of the proceedings to pay fees subject to the percentage increase that a lower amount than the amount payable in accordance with the conditional fee agreement is to be paid instead, the amount payable shall be reduced accordingly, unless the court is satisfied that the full amount should continue to be payable under it.

9.261 If a collective conditional fee agreement is defective, then the consequences can be far-reaching (this is because the error may have a bearing on a large number of claims). In view of this, great care should be taken when considering the issue of compliance. The reader should refer to the CCFA Regulations 2000 themselves for the definitive exposition of the requirements.

The effect of a breach of the regulations

9.262 For the reasons set out below, where the collective element has been drafted competently, it will almost never happen that a retainer is rendered unenforceable for want of compliance with the CCFA Regulations. If the client was not made aware of the existence of the collective conditional fee agreement, then it is arguable that no obligation for payment would arise, but that is a proposition which is unsupported by authority and could well be wrong.

9.263 It would be possible for a collective element to be incompetently drafted in the sense that it failed to comply with the regulations. In those circumstances the collective conditional fee agreement would be unenforceable.[226] That would not necessarily mean that the legal representative would be burdened by an unenforceable retainer in every case. Although there is no authority on the point, it is possible that the court would find that where the collective element is unenforceable, any instructions received after 1 November 2005 should be regarded as being outwith the agreement, and that the enforceability of the retainer is to be judged on that basis.

9.264 In order to be compliant with the CCFA Regulations 2000, the collective element must contain the contractual provisions mentioned at **9.257**. In effect, the contract must provide that the client is to be told of the fact that the legal representatives have accepted instructions under a collective conditional fee agreement. While he was sitting in the county court rather than the High Court, Field J found that non-performance of those obligations does not result in unenforceability by reason of the operation of the CCFA Regulations 2000.[227]

9.265 Therefore, if a failure to comply with those provisions is to have any effect at all, one must look at the contract itself rather than the CCFA Regulations 2000. Gray J has found that the obligations which are required to be set out in the collective element are not conditions precedent for the formation of a retainer.[228] Whilst not in a binding decision, Master Wright has found that non-performance of those contractual obligations would not preclude the legal representative from enforcing the obligation that he be paid his fees.[229] Gray J has said (obiter) that non-performance of those

---

[226] CLSA 1990, s 58(1) (as amended).
[227] *Various Claimants v Gower Chemicals Ltd* (unreported) 28 February 2007, Swansea County Court.
[228] *Kitchen v Burwell Reed & Kinghorn Ltd* [2005] EWHC 1771 (QB) at [17].
[229] *Various Claimants v Gower Chemicals Ltd* (unreported) 12 March 2008, SCCO.

contractual obligations might give rise to an entitlement on the part of the client to repudiate the retainer or might sound in damages.[230]

9.266 Where the collective element has been competently drafted, it is difficult to think of circumstances in which the retainer would be rendered unenforceable by reason of non-compliance with the CCFA Regulations 2000 or non-performance of any of the contractual obligations which arise under those regulations. Indeed, the function of the CCFA Regulations 2000 appears to be to afford the client contractual remedies rather than to render retainers unenforceable.

9.267 Whether the contractual obligations mentioned above have been performed will be a matter of the construction of the correspondence sent by the legal representative to the client.[231] There is no need for the detail of the proposal to be set out; the client's agreement may be inferred from his tacit acceptance of the proposal and his continued instructions.[232]

9.268 The indemnity principle applies to collective conditional fee agreements; the regulations and statutory provisions mentioned above do not create a right which allows the paying party to be paid independently of the indemnity principle.[233] For the reasons set out above, however, it would rarely be the case that the court would find that the indemnity principle had been breached.

9.269 In summary, it would rarely be the case that a retainer created by a collective conditional fee agreement would be found to be unenforceable for want of compliance with CCFA Regulations 2000.

The present day

9.270 The writer's experience is that the use of collective conditional fee agreements is becoming increasingly widespread.[234] Many solicitors continue to use agreements drafted before the revocation of the CCFA Regulations 2000, whilst others are choosing to draft new agreements.

9.271 It is not only claimant solicitors who are benefiting from the administrative efficiency of collective conditional fee agreements. Liability insurers and local government organisations commonly require legal services to be provided under such agreements. This is particularly so where they wish to formalise previously unlawful arrangements by which a discounted hourly rate was paid in the event of costs not being recovered from an opposing party; once that informal arrangement has been formalised by way of a dCCFA, it will be lawful.[235]

---

[230]　*Kitchen v Burwell Reed & Kinghorn Ltd* [2005] EWHC 1771 (QB) at [17]; this was an analysis also adopted by Field J in *Various Claimants v Gower Chemicals Ltd* (unreported) 28 February 2007, Swansea County Court.
[231]　*Kitchen v Burwell Reed & Kinghorn Ltd* [2005] EWHC 1771 (QB) at [13], per Gray J; it is clear from that judgment that the correspondence needs only to refer to the collective conditional fee agreement, rather than to the details of the retainer.
[232]　*Kitchen v Burwell Reed & Kinghorn Ltd* [2005] EWHC 1771 (QB) at [15].
[233]　*Thornley v Lang* [2003] EWCA Civ 1484 at [19].
[234]　Indeed, some solicitors are extending the concept in that they are using framework documents in the absence of a funder; a document such as that would probably be best thought of as a set of standard terms and conditions rather than as a true collective conditional fee agreement.
[235]　*Gloucestershire County Council v Evans* [2008] EWCA Civ 21.

9.272 Whilst not yet commonplace, collective conditional fee agreements are now becoming a part of counsel's practice, especially where a solicitor habitually instructs the same chambers.[236]

9.273 In summary, there is no reason to believe that the use of collective conditional fee agreements is diminishing following the revocation of the CCFA Regulations 2000.

Regulated damages-based agreements

9.274 This section deals with those damages-based agreements to which specific legislation applies. At the time of writing this was limited to those agreements made after 7 April 2010[237] relating to employment matters,[238] but within a short period following publication it is likely that the ambit of the relevant legislation will expand to include all damages-based agreements.[239] Those agreements not relating to employment matters are presently governed by a combination of s 58 of the Courts and Legal Services Act 1990 and the common law; this is addressed at **9.309-9.320**. The amendments in waiting are addressed at **42.49**.

9.275 The relevant primary legislation is s 58AA of the Courts and Legal Services Act 1990 (as amended). For the purposes of that section, a damages-based agreement is an agreement between a person providing advocacy services, litigation services or claims management services[240] and the recipient of those services which provides both (i) that the recipient is to make a payment to the person providing the services if the recipient obtains a specified financial benefit in connection with the matter in relation to which the services are provided, and (ii) that the amount of that payment is to be determined by reference to the amount of the financial benefit obtained. Thus, the ambit of that section is not limited to only those agreements where a percentage of the damages is payable.[241] The reference to 'payment' is to be construed widely.[242]

9.276 A damages-based agreement which relates to an employment matter and satisfies the conditions in referred to below will not be unenforceable by reason only of its being a damages-based agreement, but a damages-based agreement which relates to an

---

[236] See M Goodridge 'On Target?' (2006) *Counsel*, January, pp 24–25.

[237] This being the date upon which the Damages-Based Agreements Regulations 2010 (SI 2010/1206) came into force; nothing in the primary legislation will apply to an agreement entered into before 7 April 2010: see s 58AA(8) of the Courts and Legal Services Act 1990 (as amended).

[238] This is defined in s 58AA(3)(b) as a matter in relation to which the services are provided is, or could become, the subject of proceedings before an employment tribunal.

[239] See the Legal Aid, Sentencing and Punishment of Offenders Bill, s 42; this received Royal Assent very shortly before this book went to press.

[240] This phrase has the same meaning as in Part 2 of the Compensation Act 2006 (see s 2 of that Act): see s 58AA(7) of the Courts and Legal Services Act 1990 (as amended).

[241] Indeed, it is arguable that an ordinary conditional fee agreement that takes offers into account may, in some circumstances, fall within the ambit of s 58AA. In any event, the Law Society offer the following guidance (Practice Note: Damages-based Agreements Regulations – 27 May 2010): 'You should be aware, however, that a conditional fee agreement may amount to a DBA for the purposes of the Act where the amount of the costs and/or of any success fee payable under the agreement is to be determined by reference to the amount of any financial award obtained. This would be the case if a conditional fee agreement provided for different levels of success fee dependent on the size of the financial award or capped the costs and/or success fee by reference to the level of that award'.

[242] In particular, it includes a transfer of assets and any other transfer of money's worth: see s 58AA(7) of the Courts and Legal Services Act 1990 (as amended).

employment matter and does not satisfy those conditions will be unenforceable.[243] The conditions set out in the primary legislation are that the agreement:[244]

- must be in writing;
- must not provide for a payment above a prescribed amount or for a payment above an amount calculated in a prescribed manner;
- must comply with such other requirements as to its terms and conditions as are prescribed; and
- must be made only after the person providing services under the agreement has provided prescribed information.

The prescribed matters are set out in delegated legislation, specifically the Damages-Based Agreements Regulations 2010.[245] Those regulations bear a resemblance to the Conditional Fee Agreements Regulations 2000. Each major provision is deal with in turn.

Regulation 2

9.277 This regulation requires that the agreement defines its own ambit and that it incorporates a number of provisions clarifying its effect. It therefore goes to the written instrument of the agreement. The agreement must specify:[246]

- the claim or proceedings or parts of them to which the agreement relates;
- the circumstances in which the representative's payment, expenses and costs, or part of them, are payable; and
- the reason for setting the amount of the payment at the level agreed, including having regard to, where appropriate, whether the claim or proceedings is one of several similar claims or proceedings.

Regulation 3

9.278 Regulation 3 imposes a number of obligations, nearly all of which are reminiscent of reg 4 of the Conditional Fee Agreements Regulations 2000. There are two parts to reg 3: firstly, reg 3(1) creates a requirement that the client receives information in writing and, and secondly, reg 3(2) states what that information should be. There is also a requirement that if the client must be given any further explanation, advice or other information that he may request.[247]

9.279 The requirements governed by reg 3 have little to do with the written instrument of any agreement (ie they are materially separate from the retainer) and they relate to advice that has to be given before any agreement is made (ie they are separate in time).[248] In the analogous context of conditional fee agreements it has been argued that requirements such as those should be regarded as being separate from the agreement itself, and that, therefore, a failure to satisfy those requirements should not put the

---

[243] See s 58AA(1) and (2) of the Courts and Legal Services Act 1990 (as amended by s 154 of the Coroners and Justice Act 2009).

[244] Section 58AA(4) of the Courts and Legal Services Act 1990 (as amended).

[245] SI 2010/1206.

[246] Subparagraphs 2(a), 2(b) and 2(c) of the the Damages-Based Agreements Regulations 2010 respectively.

[247] Regulation 3(1) of the Damages-Based Agreements Regulations 2010 (SI 2010/1206).

[248] See s 58AA(4)(d), which says that a damages-based agreement may be made only after the person providing services has provided the prescribed information.

impinge upon the agreement. Brooke LJ rejected that argument, essentially on policy grounds (namely that pre-contract warnings are an important part of a regime which goes to consumer protection).[249] It is likely that the same line of thinking would apply to damages-based agreements; this is especially likely given the terms of s 58AA(4)(d), which states that an agreement may be made 'only after the person providing services under the agreement has provided [the] prescribed information'; this, it could be argued, is an express provision which creates a secure nexus between the agreement and condition precedent. To the extent that it is admissible as an extrinsic aid to interpretation, it is notable that Lord Bach, speaking in the House of Lords during a motion to approve the regulations made it clear that the relevant advice had to be given before the agreement was made.[250]

9.280 It is likely that subject to certain safeguards, a legal representative is permitted to delegate functions under reg 3 to an unqualified but properly supervised person.[251]

Regulation 3(2)(a)

9.281 This regulation, when read in conjunction with reg 3(1), stipulates that the client must be told in writing of the circumstances in which the client may seek a review of the costs and expenses:

> '3(1) The information prescribed for the purposes of section 58AA(4)(d) of the Act is—
>
> (a)   information, to be provided to the client in writing, about the matters in paragraph (2); and
>
> (b)   such further explanation, advice or other information about any of those matters as the client may request.
>
> (2) Those matters are—
>
> (a)   the circumstances in which the client may seek a review of the costs and expenses of the representative and the procedure for doing so.'

The reference to 'expenses' is a reference to disbursements,[252] but the reference to 'costs' is less straight forward; this is because that word is defined in the following way:[253]

> '"costs" means the total of the representative's time reasonably spent, in respect of the claim or proceedings, multiplied by the reasonable hourly rate of remuneration of the representative.'

Costs are different from the 'payment', which is defined in this way:

> '"payment" means a part of the sum recovered in respect of the claim or damages awarded that the client agrees to pay the representative and excludes expenses.'

---

[249]   He cited several reasons (see *Hollins v Russell* [2003] EWCA Civ 718 at [111]):
(1)   section 58A(3)(a) of the CLSA 1990 (as amended) clearly characterises the requirements in the CFA Regulations 2000 as among those with which the agreement must comply;
(2)   the words 'applicable to it' (as used in CLSA 1990, s 58(1)) are able to encompass steps taken by one of the parties before the agreement is made; and
(3)   regulation 2(2) requires a CFA to state that reg 4 has been complied with, thus making compliance part of the obligation under the CFA.
[250]   Lords Hansard, 25 Mar 2010: Column 1153.
[251]   See, by analogy with the Conditional Fee Agreements Regulations 2000, **9.170–9.173**.
[252]   See reg 1(2) of the Damages-Based Agreements Regulations 2010 (SI 2010/1206), which provides that 'expenses' means disbursements incurred by the representative, including counsel's fees and the expense of obtaining an expert's report.
[253]   See reg 1(2) of the Damages-Based Agreements Regulations 2010 (SI 2010/1206).

9.282 Thus it would seem that the legal representative is required only to explain the procedure relating to those fees that are paid on a time basis rather than the procedures (such as they are) that also relate to the payment (which, to avoid confusion, will be referred to herein as the 'contingent payment'). This may be an oversight, but equally, it may be a reflection of the fact that if a client has agreed a contingent payment and if that payment is enforceable, it would be difficult for the amount of that payment subsequently to be challenged; put another way, it is possible that Parliament intended that clients are not to be given false hope by being told that they are able to challenge contingent payments at a later stage when in fact this is likely to be very difficult.

9.283 By analogy with the Conditional Fee Agreements Regulations 2000, it is likely that the duty is to explain the circumstances in which costs may be payable under the agreement rather than to explore hypothetical situations which might arise in the litigation.[254]

Regulation 3(2)(b)

9.284 When read in conjunction with reg 3(1), this regulation stipulates that the client must be told in writing about the dispute resolution service provided by the Advisory, Conciliation and Arbitration Service ('ACAS') in regard to actual and potential claims:

'3(1) The information prescribed for the purposes of section 58AA(4)(d) of the Act is—

(a)   information, to be provided to the client in writing, about the matters in paragraph (2); and

(b)   such further explanation, advice or other information about any of those matters as the client may request.

(2) Those matters are . . .

(b)   the dispute resolution service provided by the Advisory, Conciliation and Arbitration Service (ACAS) in regard to actual and potential claims.'

9.285 There is no guidance as to what the client must be told, but common sense dictates that at the very least the client must be told of the existence of these services. It is not clear, however, whether the client must also be told whether they are available as a means of resolving the specific claim to which the proposed damages-based agreement relates.

Regulation 3(2)(c)

9.286 This regulation, when read in conjunction with reg 3(1), requires the legal representative to state in writing whether other methods of pursuing the claim or financing the proceedings exist and if so, how they relate to the claim or proceedings in question:

'3(1) The information prescribed for the purposes of section 58AA(4)(d) of the Act is—

(a)   information, to be provided to the client in writing, about the matters in paragraph (2); and

(b)   such further explanation, advice or other information about any of those matters as the client may request.

(2) Those matters are . . .

---

[254]   *Bray Walker Solicitors (A Firm) v Silvera* [2008] EWHC 3147 (QB) affirmed at [2010] EWCA Civ 332.

(a) whether other methods of pursuing the claim or financing the proceedings, including—

 (i) advice under the Community Legal Service,
 (ii) legal expenses insurance,
 (iii) pro bono representation, or
 (iv) trade union representation,

are available, and, if so, how they apply to the client and the claim or proceedings in question.'

9.287 It is likely that, by analogy with the Conditional Fee Agreements Regulations 2000, the burden of considering the availability of BTE insurance, etc, lies with the legal representative. These issues are addressed detail at **9.181-9.192**.

9.288 The Law Society offers the following advice:[255]

'[A solicitor should] discuss with [his] client other methods of funding which may be available to the client including any public funding and/or pro bono help. This would also include funding by a conditional fee agreement or on an hourly rate, depending on what would be in the client's best interest and on [the solicitor's] willingness to undertake the case on that basis.'

It is not clear whether the need to advise about the availability of pro bono funding extends to making enquiries of the providers of such services; it is arguable that such enquiries ought to be carried out in cases where this would be a reasonable funding option.

Regulation 3(2)(d)

9.289 This regulation, when read in conjunction with reg 3(1), requires the legal representative to state in writing the point at which expenses (ie, disbursements) become payable:

'3(1) The information prescribed for the purposes of section 58AA(4)(d) of the Act is—

(a) information, to be provided to the client in writing, about the matters in paragraph (2); and
(b) such further explanation, advice or other information about any of those matters as the client may request . . .
(d) the point at which expenses become payable.'

9.290 Regulation 1(2) defines 'expenses' as meaning disbursements incurred by the representative, including counsel's fees and the expense of obtaining an expert's report.

Regulation 3(2)(e)

9.291 The purpose of reg 3(2)(e), when read in conjunction with reg 3(1) is to ensure that the legal representative provides a fully inclusive estimate of expenses:[256]

'3(1) The information prescribed for the purposes of section 58AA(4)(d) of the Act is—

(a) information, to be provided to the client in writing, about the matters in paragraph (2); and

---

[255] Practice Note on Damages-Based Agreements Regulations, 27 May 2010.
[256] *Tankard v John Fredricks Plastics Ltd* [2008] EWCA Civ 1375 at [13]–[15].

(b)   such further explanation, advice or other information about any of those matters as the client may request . . .

(e)   a reasonable estimate of the amount that is likely to be spent upon expenses, inclusive of VAT.'

It is worth noting that there is no requirement to provide an estimate of either the contingent payment or, if there are any, the time-based costs.

Regulation 4

9.292 Regulation 4 relates to certain types of amendment; it reads as follows:

'Any amendment to a damages-based agreement to cover additional causes of action must be in writing and signed by the client and the representative.'

There would appear to be no express requirement to revisit any of the matters in regulation 3 in the event of an amendment being made.

Regulation 5

9.293 Regulation 5 provides that the amount prescribed for the purposes of s 58AA(4)(b) of the Act (ie, the maximum amount of the contingent payment) is the amount which, including VAT, is equal to 35% of the sum ultimately recovered by the client in the claim or proceedings. The amount of the contingent payment must include any transfer of assets and any other transfer of money's worth.[257]

9.294 The Law Society have this to say about the effect of this cap:[258]

'The cap of 35 per cent applies to the amount recovered by the client and not the award. Consequently, you will not be able to recover any costs from the client without first recovering all or part of the award from the unsuccessful opponent.'

There is a respectable argument that this guidance is not correct as a matter of strict legal interpretation, but it is, no doubt, correct as a matter of practice. The Law Society's guidance continues:

'This figure [ie, the cap] need not include counsel's fees or other disbursements but if these are to be charged separately you must state this in the agreement.'

To the extent that it is admissible as an extrinsic aid to interpretation, when speaking to the draft regulations in the House of Lords, Lord Bach explained that the cap excluded counsel's fees.[259]

Regulation 6

9.295 Regulation 6 imposes a number of restrictions on what can and cannot be done if one of the parties is considering terminating the agreement:

---

[257]   See s 58AA(7) of the Courts and Legal Services Act 1990 (as amended by s 154 of the Coroners and Justice Act 2009.

[258]   Practice Note on Damages-Based Agreements Regulations, 27 May 2010.

[259]   Lords Hansard, 25 Mar 2010 : Column 1153.

'6 Terms and conditions of termination

(1) The additional requirements prescribed for the purposes of section 58AA(4)(c) of the Act are that the terms and conditions of a damages-based agreement must be in accordance with paragraphs (2), (3) and (4).

(2) If the agreement is terminated, the representative may not charge the client more than the representative's costs and expenses for the work undertaken in respect of the client's claim or proceedings.

(3) The client may not terminate the agreement—

    (a)   after settlement has been agreed; or
    (b)   within seven days before the start of the tribunal hearing.

(4) The representative may not terminate the agreement and charge costs unless the client has behaved or is behaving unreasonably.

(5) Paragraphs (3) and (4) are without prejudice to any right of either party under the general law of contract to terminate the agreement.'

9.296 These provisions are self-explanatory. The reference to 'costs' is a reference to time-based costs.[260] The need to prevent termination by the client after settlement or within seven days of the tribunal hearing is to prevent clients from taking the benefit of the legal representatives' efforts and then converting the method of payment to a time-based method by the simple expedient of terminating the agreement.

9.297 The Law Society offers the following guidance as to what might constitute unreasonable conduct sufficient to justify termination:[261]

> The definition of 'unreasonable' is likely to include circumstances in which a client refuses to accept an appropriate settlement, and requires you to act in a way which is contrary to the Code of Conduct. There are many other examples of 'unreasonable' behaviour and it may be appropriate for you to explain these to the client at the start of the case.

If a client refused to accept an appropriate settlement it would not necessarily be in the solicitor's interest to terminate the agreement, this being because time-based costs may be less than he believes is appropriate. As such, the power to terminate is by no means as powerful a sanction as it is in the context of conditional fee agreements.

Breaches of the Damages-Based Agreements Regulations 2010

9.298 Whilst there is no authority on the point, it is likely that putative breaches of the Damages-Based Agreements Regulations 2010 would be subject to a test of materiality similar to that which is described at **9.80-9.88**.

---

[260]   See reg 1(2) of the Damages-Based Agreements Regulations 2010 (SI 2010/1206).
[261]   Practice Note on Damages-Based Agreements Regulations, 27 May 2010.

CONDITIONAL FEE AGREEMENTS AND THE COMMON LAW

9.299 If statutory legislation is disregarded, conditional fee agreements are, on a traditional analysis, unlawful. Denning MR described traditional thinking in the following way (he used the word 'contingency' where the word 'conditional' is usually used today):[262]

> 'English law has never sanctioned an agreement by which a lawyer is remunerated on the basis of a "contingency fee", that is that he gets paid the fee if he wins, but not if he loses. Such an agreement was illegal on the ground that it was the offence of champerty.'

In the past, the common law has held conditional normal fee agreements to be unenforceable,[263] and has even held that an agreement to give a one-fifth discount in the event of failure was contrary to public policy and therefore unenforceable.[264]

9.300 It is quite possible that the common law has moved on since the policy described by Denning MR was first formulated and it may well be that the common law does now tolerate some forms of conditional fee agreement.[265] This is largely irrelevant, however, because the common law has been totally eclipsed by statute, so the matters discussed in the remainder of this paragraph are relevant only in jurisdictions where s 58 of the Courts and Legal Services Act 1990 (as amended) does not apply. In 2003, the Privy Council considered an appeal from one of those jurisdictions (the Turks and Caicos Islands); Lord Carswell commented on an agreement which was arguably a normal-fee conditional fee agreement:[266]

> 'It then has to be considered whether the fee agreement ... constituted a conditional fee agreement. In approaching this issue, their Lordships wish to make it plain that they are not to be taken as accepting without question the traditional doctrine of the common law that all such agreements are unenforceable on grounds of public policy. The content of public policy can change over the years, and it may now be time to reconsider the accepted prohibition in the light of modern practising conditions.'

Lord Carswell went on to refer to the well-known (but wrongly decided) case of *Thai Trading Co v Taylor* [1998] QB 781, in which the Court of Appeal had found that a normal-fee conditional fee agreement was lawful at common law. When freed from the constraints of statute (or, in the case of Court of Appeal, when it is believed that they have been so freed), two of the most senior courts in the land have, therefore, expressed the view that there is nothing objectionable about normal-fee conditional fee agreements.

---

[262] *Wallersteiner v Moir (No 2)* [1975] 1 All ER 849 at 860; it is worth noting that Denning MR went on to find that the retainer was lawful; it was the other two members of the court (Buckley and Scarman LJJ) who found that conditional fee agreements should remain unlawful at common law.

[263] *British Waterways Board v Norman* (1993) 26 HLR 232; the correctness of this decision was doubted in *Thai Trading Co (a firm) v Taylor* [1998] 3 All ER 65 at 71, but *Thai Trading* itself was found to be wrongly decided on the basis that the court had not taken into account professional rules which banned such agreements (*Awwad v Geraghty & Co* [2000] 1 Costs LR 105).

[264] *Aratra Potato Co Ltd v Taylor Joynson Garrett (a firm)* [1995] 4 All ER 695; this case was also said to be 'wrongly decided' in *Thai Trading Co (a firm) v Taylor* [1998] 3 All ER 65 at 73; indeed, Millett LJ said (at 72), 'If this is the law then something has gone badly wrong'.

[265] See the footnotes immediately above; see in particular *Thai Trading Co (a firm) v Taylor* [1998] 3 All ER 65 at 69; and *Kellar v Williams* [2004] UKPC 31 at [21].

[266] *Kellar v Williams* [2004] UKPC 31 at [21]; Gray J has approved of those comments (obiter) in the context of a collective conditional fee agreement: *Kitchen v Burwell Reed & Kinghorn Ltd* [2005] EWHC 1771 (QB).

9.301 In England and Wales such considerations are of academic interest only, although it is worth noting that CLSA 1990, s 58(1) provides that a conditional fee agreement which satisfies all the relevant conditions shall not be unenforceable 'by reason *only* of its being a conditional fee agreement' (emphasis added). Thus, if a conditional fee agreement is unenforceable for some other reason, compliance with s 58 will not restore enforceability.

9.302 In view of this, it is worth examining the following three topics:

- Where costs relate to work which is non-contentious and which is carried out under a non-contentious business agreement.
- Where the common law (or equity) acts to make a conditional fee agreement unenforceable regardless of whether that agreement is compliant with the relevant statutory regime.
- Where the costs relate to work carried out by persons other than those with rights to conduct litigation or those with rights of audience.

Each of these three topics is addressed in turn, but the discussion of the second is limited to a consideration of damages-based agreements; this is because other aspects of the common law (such as undue influence, duress, misrepresentation) are either beyond the scope of this book or are considered in other chapters.[267] It will be seen that in so far as legal representatives are concerned, the role of the common law has dwindled almost to disappearing point.

Conditional fee agreements in non-contentious business

9.303 This section discusses conditional fee agreements in non-contentious business, including those agreements often referred to a 'contingency fee agreements'; in this section that phrase is used to mean agreement by which the legal representative's fees are linked to the outcome of the subject matter of the agreement. The role of the common law is limited to placing emphasis on statutory compliance as being the factor which determines whether the agreement is enforceable. The analysis set out in this section is tortuous and technical, but the conclusion is very simple: the combined effect of the common law and legislation is that any conditional fee agreement which complies with either SA 1974, s 57 or CLSA 1990, s 58(1) will be enforceable, but other agreements will not.

9.304 In order to put the common law in context, it is necessary to explain the statutory law. CLSA 1990, s 58(1) (as amended) provides as follows:

> 'A conditional fee agreement which satisfies all of the conditions applicable to it by virtue of this section shall not be unenforceable by reason only of its being a conditional fee agreement; but (subject to subsection (5)) any other conditional fee agreement shall be unenforceable.'

And CLSA 1990, s 58(5) makes the following provision:

> 'If a conditional fee agreement is an agreement to which section 57 of the Solicitors Act 1974 (non-contentious business agreements between solicitor and client) applies, subsection (1) shall not make it unenforceable.'

---

[267] In particular, undue influence is discussed at **10.3–10.11**.

Thus, if a conditional fee agreement is a non-contentious business agreement to which SA 1974, s 57 applies, CLSA 1990, s 58(1) (as amended) will not make it unenforceable.[268] This means that such an agreement will be enforceable to the extent that it complies with the requirements of CLSA 1990, s 58, or SA 1974, s 57 (or both), but only to the extent that it is not made unenforceable for some other reason, and in particular, as a result of the operation of the common law.

9.305 The wording of SA 1974, s 57 is set out at **8.122**. There is nothing within that section which expressly relates to enforceability; this means that the enforceability of an agreement will turn on what is permitted under the common law (and, of course, by CLSA 1990, s 58). As has already been discussed on the subject of 'oral retainers', unwritten agreements in non-contentious work are generally unenforceable;[269] this applies regardless of whether the agreement is a conditional or a non-conditional agreement. There is, however, no common law restriction on a conditional fee agreement in non-contentious business per se; this is because principles which hold contentious agreements to be unenforceable have their origins in champerty, and champerty does not apply to non-contentious business. This applies to contingency fee agreements as well as other types of conditional fee agreements.

9.306 One of the main requirements of a non-contentious business agreement within the meaning of SA 1974, s 57 (as already discussed) is that it must be in writing, so, since 1 November 2005, the requirements of SA 1974, s 57 and of CLSA 1990, s 58 have been almost coterminous; it is difficult to envisage an agreement that would be compliant with the former but not the latter. The effect of this is that since that date the enforceability of conditional fee agreements in non-contentious work is, for most practical purposes, not influenced by the common law. Again, this is true of contingency fee agreements as well as other types of conditional fee agreements.

9.307 The same is not true of agreements before that date, however. This is because it was then easily possible for a conditional fee agreement to be compliant with SA 1974, s 57 but not CLSA 1990, s 58. In those circumstances, the enforceability of the agreement would be governed by the common law and, for the reasons set out above, would not be rendered unenforceable as a result of being a conditional fee agreement.

9.308 This tortuous route has led to an easily understood conclusion: the combined effect of the common law and legislation is that any conditional fee agreement (including any contingency fee agreement) which complies with either SA 1974, s 57 or CLSA 1990, s 58(1) will be enforceable, but other agreements will not.

Unregulated damages-based agreements

9.309 Damages-based agreements (which are agreements in the fees are quantitatively linked to the sums recovered as damages, debt, or price paid)[270] are often referred to as 'contingency fee agreements'; this phrase should be used with caution, however, because it has other usages.[271] The phrase damages-based agreement is preferred in this book.

---

[268] To this extent, the common law relating to such agreements survives, because a non-contentious business agreement which does not comply with CLSA 1990, s 58(1) will be enforceable only to the extent that the common law permits it to be.

[269] In *In re a Solicitor* [1956] 1 QB 157, for example, Pearson J found that a client could not rely on an oral agreement that his solicitor would charge less than the ordinary rate of remuneration.

[270] See **9.21**.

[271] See **9.35**.

The phrase 'contingency fee agreement' is best reserved for agreements where the amount of fees is linked to results, but only where the subject matter of the agreement is non-contentious in the sense that there is no litigation or contemplated litigation (ie, no damages).[272] This section deals with damages-based agreements in so far as they are governed by the common law and by general legislation not specifically aimed at such agreements. Agreements that are governed by specific legislation are addressed at **9.274** *et seq*; at the time of writing, this category was limited only to agreements in employment matters, but it is likely that in the near future it will relate to all agreements regarding disputes.[273] If so, then what is set out in this section may become old law.

9.310 Two questions arise: the first is whether damages-based agreements that are compliant with the general legislation governing conditional fee agreements[274] are rendered unlawful at common law by virtue of being damages-based agreements, and the second is the ambit and effect of the law relating to non-contentious contingency fee agreement.[275]

The influence of legislation

9.311 It has been argued that CLSA 1990, s 58(1) preserves the common law to the extent that the court may find that a conditional fee agreement which is compliant with that Act should still be found unenforceable by reason of it being champertous. Put simplistically, the argument is that it is against public policy to allow legal representatives to take a share of the spoils.

9.312 HHJ Rich QC (sitting in the High Court) said the following on this topic:[276]

> '[The] mere fact that an arrangement was a conditional fee agreement, as defined in the Act, was accepted by Parliament when the 1990 Act was passed, as enough to make it unenforceable for champerty, whatever the basis of remuneration for which it provided. [Section] 58(1) relieves the party from such unenforceability in respect of such an agreement, which satisfies all the relevant conditions ... There is, in my judgment, no room for treating it, nonetheless, as unenforceable for champerty. The requisite conditions remain satisfied, even if the percentage uplift is calculated by reference to the amount recovered, provided only that it does not exceed 100 per cent.'

Thus, if this is correct, any agreement which is compliant with CLSA 1990, s 58 will not be unenforceable solely by reason of it being a form of conditional fee agreement; if HHJ Rich QC is correct, common law considerations have been excluded entirely, albeit general legislation not specifically directed at damages-based agreements.

9.313 Some commentators have questioned the correctness of HHJ Rich QC's decision. They point to the fact that in its most recent Consultation Paper on the topic, the Ministry of Justice has said that damages-based agreements are not lawful:[277]

---

[272] This description has been chosen in preference to the ordinary definition of non-contentious work in anticipate of the amendments likely to be made by s 42 of the Legal Aid, Sentencing and Punishment of Offenders Bill which will mean that damages-based agreements are those that relate to 'proceedings for resolving disputes (and not just proceedings in a court), whether commenced or contemplated'.

[273] See the footnote immediately above.

[274] Specifically, it is assumed that the agreement in question is compliant with the requirements of the CLSA 1990, s 58(1) (as amended) and that s 58AA of that Act does not apply.

[275] Courts and Legal Services Act 1990, s 58AA, as inserted by s 154 of the Coroners and Justice Act 2009.

[276] *Benaim (UK) Ltd v Davies Middleton & Davies Ltd* [2004] EWHC 737 (TCC).

[277] *Regulating Damages-based agreements* CP 10/09 (Ministry of Justice, 1 July 2009), p 3.

'[Damages-based agreements] ... are not permitted in litigation ... Extending DBAs to litigation would be a major step which raises a number of issues, not least costs shifting and the apportionment of costs between parties. We have no current plans to extend the use of DBAs more widely, but it makes sense to include a provision to allow for this should that be considered to be in the public interest.'

9.314 It is not clear what the true law is, but it has to be said that some of the Ministry's legal reasoning is not as clear as it could be.[278] It would, however, seem that the Ministry's analysis is based primarily on what is permitted under statute,[279] rather than on what is permitted under the common law.

9.315 To summarise, it seems likely that the issue of the legality of damages-based agreements turns on what is and is not permitted under statute; this is because the common law seems to have been ousted by statute. If this is wrong, then it may be necessary to look at what the common law says about damages-based agreements.

The underlying common law

9.316 The common law prohibition against damages-based agreements arose out of the law of champerty, which is discussed in more detail at **9.325** onwards. Whilst champerty itself is an ancient concept, it was not until the 1860s that the court focused on the issue of lawyers' retainers. This was just one of the issues that arose out of a profound crisis between 1859 and 1863 concerning the conduct of the Bar, and in particular, five notorious cases of counsel's misconduct. (The resultant litigation not only clarified the law in respect of contingency fees,[280] but also clarified other points of law, such as the principle that counsel's retainer is non-contractual.[281])

9.317 The relevance of this historical perspective is that the principle that damages-based agreements are unlawful arose out of a crisis and it may well be that the policy considerations that applied during that crisis do not apply now. In this regard it is worth mentioning, perhaps, that in some other common law jurisdictions, the law has developed in such a way as to permit damages-based agreements, and this is in circumstances in which they were previously believed to be prohibited by statute.[282] Contingency fees in personal injury litigation in the United States, for example, are the norm rather than the exception.[283]

9.318 As long ago as 1994 Lord Mustill commented (obiter) that the rule against damages-based agreements was in the course of attenuation and that it survived 'so far as it survive[d] at all', largely as a rule of professional conduct.[284]

---

[278] In particular, it would seem that that the Ministry believes that SA 1974, s 59 prohibits damages-based agreements; the reader will be able form his own view as to whether that is correct: see *Regulating Damages-based agreements* CP 10/09 (Ministry of Justice, 1 July 2009), para 18.

[279] And, in particular, what is permitted under SA 1974, s 59.

[280] WW Pue 'Moral panic at the English Bar: Paternal vs commercial ideologies of legal practice in the 1860s' (1990) *Law and Social Inquiry* 15(1), pp 49–118.

[281] *Kennedy v Broun* (1863) 32 L J (CP) 137.

[282] See, for example, the Canadian cases of *Bergel & Edson v Wolf* (2000) 50 OR (3d) 777 (SCJ), per Justice Spiegel, and *McIntyre Estate v Ontario (Attorney-General)* [2001] OJ 713 (SCJ), per Justice Wilson.

[283] See the American Bar Association Model Rules of Professional Conduct (2004), rule 1:5 (fees).

[284] *Giles v Thompson* [1994] 1 AC 142 at [15]; Phillips MR has criticised Lord Mustill's analysis, but that was largely on the basis that Lord Mustill was focusing on the common law rather than the statutory law: *R v Secretary of State for Transport ex p Factortame* [2002] EWCA Civ 932 at [44].

9.319 Perhaps the only conclusion that can be reached is that the common law is not something which is set in stone, and that what may have been unlawful many years ago may now be seen as being acceptable, or even desirable.[285]

9.320 In summary, there is some doubt as to whether damages-based agreements are lawful, but in any event, the Ministry of Justice is currently looking at the matter, and this, no doubt will result in legislation in the near future. Therefore, even if the common law does have a part to play now, it is unlikely to in the very near future.

Conditional fee agreements and persons other than lawyers

9.321 Persons who do not have rights to conduct litigation or rights of audience are not authorised litigators. Section 58(1) of the Courts and Legal Services Act 1990 (as amended) applies only to authorised litigators, for the following reasons:[286]

- this is the natural reading of CLSA 1990, s 58(1);
- this conclusion is supported by the delegated legislation which was made under that Act, which reads as if the term 'legal representative' applied to a person conducting litigation or exercising rights of audience on behalf of a litigant;
- reference to *Hansard*[287] shows that the provisions of CLSA 1990, s 58 were not intended to apply to those who were not conducting the litigation or appearing as advocates; and
- there is good reason why principles of maintenance and champerty should apply with particular rigour to those conducting litigation or appearing as advocates.

Thus, the common law (and, in particular, the law of champerty) will apply to those who are not authorised litigators. Each case must be decided on its own facts. The law of champerty is briefly discussed below.

9.322 Whilst persuasive rather than binding, an example of a champertous arrangement is a case in which Master Hurst found that an unqualified cost negotiator was acting as a champerter: his retainer provided that his fees were based on the reduction in costs that he was able to secure.[288] Examples of the court declining to make a finding of champerty are commonplace, however; they include contingency fees claimed by a surveyor for carrying negotiations,[289] and surveyors' fees which were conditional on successfully obtaining planning permission.[290]

9.323 A word of caution should be inserted here: it cannot be assumed that because a person is not an authorised litigator that they will be completely unregulated. An example would be where fees are charged by persons providing claims management services, which are regulated by the Compensation Act 2006, Part 2 and associated delegated legislation.[291] So it should not be assumed that just because a person is not an authorised litigator that the only question that needs to be asked is whether their retainer is champertous.

---

[285] See, for example, the comments of Steyn LJ in *Giles v Thompson* [1993] 3 All ER 321 at 331–332.
[286] *R (Factortame Ltd) v Transport Secretary (No 8)* [2002] EWCA Civ 932 at [54].
[287] *Hansard*, HC Deb, 26 January 1999, pp 962 and 964.
[288] *Ahmed v Powell* [2003] EWHC 9011 (Costs).
[289] *Pickering v Sogex Services (UK) Ltd* [1982] 1 EGLR 42.
[290] *Picton Jones & Co v Arcadia Developments Ltd* [1989] 1 EGLR 43.
[291] Compensation (Claims Management Services) Regulations 2006 (SI 2006/3322).

9.324 In summary, persons who are not authorised litigators are not bound by CLSA 1990, s 58(1), so the enforceability of such a person's retainer is to be gauged principally by the common law, most notably the law of champerty. Other legislation may supervene, however, depending on the status of the person and the nature of the work they are carrying out.

Champerty and maintenance

9.325 Many years ago these topics were highly relevant to the law of costs, but this is no longer the case. The range of circumstances in which champerty or maintenance continue to have any practical relevance has dwindled. The following is a non-exhaustive list of such circumstances:

- where a non-party has meddled in the litigation and where a non-party costs order is sought against him;
- where a contract of retainer is said to be champertous by reason of the retainer providing for an objectionable method of remuneration;[292]
- where a contract of retainer is said to be tinged with illegality by reason of the legal representative having an objectionable interest in the litigation;[293]
- where a person other than a legal representative seeks payment for services rendered, and where that payment is sought as costs but is said not to be recoverable by reason of it being based on an objectionable method of remuneration;[294] and
- where a person other than a legal representative seeks payment for services rendered, and where that payment is sought as costs but is said not to be recoverable by reason of that person's champertous involvement in the litigation.

The first of these items is addressed in detail **7.136–7.204**. The second is dealt with in general terms here, but is also in more detail at **9.309–9.320** and **30.20–30.21**.

9.326 The relevance of the topics in even this short list may be undergoing a process of attenuation; in particular, the ascendancy of litigation funding (or third-party funding) may further reshape public policy and may ultimately diminish the relevance of maintenance and champerty almost to vanishing point. At present, however, costs practitioners need to know the law of maintenance and champerty, or at least need to know where to find that law.

Maintenance

9.327 The doctrines of maintenance and champerty developed in order to combat abuses in late medieval England; unscrupulous nobles and royal officials would lend their names to bolster the credibility of doubtful and fraudulent claims.[295] Speaking extrajudicially in the early seventeenth century, Lord Chief Justice Coke described the origins of maintenance:[296]

---

[292] See, for example, *Benaim (UK) Ltd v Davies Middleton & Davies Ltd* [2004] EWHC 737 (TCC).
[293] See, for example, *Dix v Townend & Anor* [2008] EWHC 90117 (Costs).
[294] See, as a counter-example, *Pirie v Ayling* [2003] EWHC 9006 (Costs).
[295] PH Winfield 'The history of maintenance and champerty' (1919) Law QR 35, p 50.
[296] 1 *Coke Litt* 368b.

'Maintenance, *manutenentia*, is derived from the verb *manutenere*, and signifieth in law a taking in hand, bearing up, or upholding of quarrels and sides, to the disturbance or hindrance of common right.'

These comments were made in context of the court previously having been anxious to prevent a wide range of maintenance; indeed, in times past the phrase 'maintenance' had been used to apply not just to those who gave support in civil claims, but also to those who sought to maintain robbers, heretics and even 'a new sect coming from beyond the sea, clad in white garments'.[297] Clearly, the ancient law of maintenance had very different aims to the modern law. Indeed, LCJ Coke himself made a distinction between 'special' and 'general' maintenance, which is not susceptible to modern analysis,[298] so, while scrutiny of the ancient law is fascinating, it is not always of practical use.

9.328 Maintenance was a misdemeanour[299] and was also a tort for which damages were recoverable. In the mid-twentieth century legislation was enacted which abolished both the tort and the crime,[300] but law relating to the enforceability of contracts for maintenance was expressly preserved.[301] To that extent, the common law does remain relevant.

9.329 In modern times, Lord Denning MR described maintenance thus:[302]

'Improperly stirring up litigation and strife by giving aid to one party to bring or defend a claim without just cause or excuse'.

Having got over its fears about robbers and heretics, the modern law of maintenance focuses upon those who meddle in the disputes of others. That policy was described by Fletcher Moulton LJ[303] in the following terms (recently cited with approval by Lord Mustill):[304]

'It is directed against wanton and officious intermeddling with the disputes of others in which the [maintainer] has no interest whatever, and where the assistance he renders to one or the other party is without justification or excuse.'

9.330 What amounts to maintenance will depend on the facts of the case. In ancient times, maintenance might have been by word, writing, countenance or deed;[305] in the late eighteenth century the law even went so far as to allow that volunteering information would suffice.[306] Whilst exceptions exist,[307] anything of this nature would not normally be regarded as being maintenance today. Maintenance generally now focuses on financial aid, such as direct funding or the provision of legal services. It is the

---

[297] Parliamentary Rolls III 125b and III 428a (1399), cited in PH Winfield *The History of Conspiracy and Abuse of Legal Procedure* (Beard Books, 1921), p 134.

[298] PH Winfield *The History of Conspiracy and Abuse of Legal Procedure* (Beard Books, 1921), pp 136–138.

[299] Champerty Act 1275 (3 Ed I (St West I) c 25).

[300] Criminal Law Act 1967, ss 13(1) and 14(1).

[301] Specifically, s 14(2) of the Criminal Law Act 1967 provided that s 14(1) 'shall not affect any such rule of law as to the cases in which a contract is to be treated as contrary to public policy or otherwise illegal'.

[302] *Re Trepca Mines Ltd (No 2)* [1963] Ch 199 at 219.

[303] *British Cash and Parcel Conveyors Ltd v Lamson Store Service Co Ltd* [1908] 1 KB 1006 at 1014.

[304] *Giles v Thompson* [1994] 1 AC 142 at 161; see also *Alabaster v Harness* [1895] 1 QB 339, CA at 342, per Lord Esher MR; *Wallis v Duke of Portland* (1797) 3 Ves 494.

[305] 2 Co Inst 212, per LCJ Coke.

[306] *Master v Miller* (1791) 4 Term Rep 320 at 340.

[307] See, for example, *Fraser v Buckle* [1996] 2 IRLM 34 and other cases given as examples below.

latter that is usually the link between maintenance (or, more usually, champertous maintenance) and a retainer, ie the provision of legal services in the context of maintenance may taint the contract of retainer with illegality.

9.331 There is one further way in which a person can be found to be guilty of maintenance in a way which is relevant to costs, and that is where a claim is assigned from one person to another. The common law abhorred the assignment of a bare cause of action; this was because this would allow a doubtful or fraudulent claim to be transferred to a person of influence or power, who (in a legal system which was still influenced by patronage) could then expect a sympathetic hearing in court proceedings.[308] Where the agreement to assign is struck down as being champertous, there are many ways in which the receiving party could be denied costs. Whilst there is no authority on the point, the range of mechanisms extends from the court finding that the maintainer has been meddling in a claim which had not been assigned to him and therefore was not his, to the court merely finding that the retainer is tainted with illegality.

9.332 Not every act of meddling will amount to maintenance; even in ancient times assistance with litigation was permissible when the assistor had a legitimate interest in the outcome of the claim (or if he had a reasonable belief in such an interest).[309] This was not confined to cases where he had a financial or commercial interest in the outcome. It extended to other circumstances where social, family, or other ties justified the maintainer in supporting the litigation.[310] Viscount Haldane had this to say about who could be regarded as having a legitimate interest:[311]

> 'Such an interest is held to be possessed when in litigation a master assists his servant, or a servant his master, or help is given to an heir, or a near relative, or to a poor man out of charity, to maintain a right which he might otherwise lose.'

Examples and counter-examples of legitimate interests are given at **9.351–9.374**. The interest must not arise out of the agreement to provide assistance,[312] ie it must be a pre-existing interest. Where the likely benefit is far greater than the interest, the court may find that no legitimate interest exists.[313]

9.333 In addition to 'community of interest' (as a shared financial interest is often called), assistance may be justified on the basis that it is provided as an act of charity,[314] or on the basis that it is provided out of kinship[315] or religious ties.[316] Financial institutions are permitted to fund litigation where this is part of the service that they

---

[308] See *Giles v Thompson* [1993] 3 All ER 321 at 328, cited by Baroness Hale in *Massai Aviation Services v Attorney-General* [2007] UKPC 12 at [15].

[309] See *Alabaster v Harness* [1895] 1 QB 339, CA.

[310] *Thai Trading Co (a firm) v Taylor* [1998] 3 All ER 65 at 69, per Millett LJ.

[311] *Neville v London Express Newspaper Ltd* [1919] AC 368 at 389; see also *Bradlaugh v Newdegate* (1883) 11 QBD 1 at 11, in which Lord Coleridge CJ spoke of 'the interest which consanguinity or affinity to the suitor give to the man who aids him, or the interest arising from the connection of the parties, eg as master and servant ...'; see also *Condliffe v Hislop* [1996] 1 WLR 753, in which it was held that it was not unlawful for a mother to provide limited funds to finance her bankrupt son's action for defamation; see also *Thai Trading Co (a firm) v Taylor* [1998] 3 All ER 65 at 70.

[312] *Giles v Thompson* [1993] 3 All ER 321 at 333 (which was appealed, but on other grounds).

[313] *Advanced Technology Structures Ltd v Cray Valley Products Ltd* [1993] BCLC 723, CA.

[314] See *Jennings v Johnson* (1873) LR 8 CP 425 and *Holden v Thompson* [1907] 2 KB 489.

[315] As to the limits of this doctrine, see *Burke v Greene* (1814) 2 Ball & B 517 and *Bradlaugh v Newdegate* (1883) 11 QBD 1 at 11.

[316] *Rothewel v Pewer* (1431) YB 9 Hen 6, p 64, pl 713.

provide: this is the mechanism which permits a bank to offer a disbursement funding loan, and is the mechanism by which a legal expenses insurer is able to fund the provision of legal services.[317] Although there is no authority on the point, it is probably by this mechanism that litigation (third-party) funding avoids the label of maintenance.[318]

9.334 From the beginning of the twentieth century (and probably much earlier), it was recognised that public policy must change with the times,[319] as Danckwerts LJ remarked:[320]

'The law of maintenance depends upon the question of public policy, and public policy is not a fixed and immutable matter. It is a conception which, if it has any sense at all, must be alterable by the passage of time.'

9.335 In modern times the law became much more tolerant of the intervention by one person in the claim of another.[321] By the late twentieth century the stage had been reached where, for example, a car hirer was able to conduct a road traffic accident claim for the purposes of recovering his fees.[322] The change in the law of champerty (which is discussed below) has been equally as noticeable.

9.336 The law of maintenance and champerty is not confined to proceedings in court.[323] It does not apply to all forms of dispute resolution procedures, however; eg it has been found not to apply to licensing magistrates.[324]

9.337 The issue of whether there has been maintenance will largely be a matter for the tribunal of fact. A number of examples are given at **9.351–9.374**. When considering a contract (including a contract of retainer), the matter will not simply be one of contractual interpretation: in particular, the court may go behind a written agreement and draw its own conclusions as to the parties' intentions.[325]

9.338 Legal issues may arise, however, such as the measure of what is and what is not contrary to public policy. In this regard, the common law can take its lead from statue;[326] an example is a case in which the court was asked to declare whether a conditional fee agreement in arbitral proceedings was lawful (at that time, statute did not apply to arbitral proceedings). Sir Richard Scott V-C drew an analogy with the

---

[317] See, for example, *Martell v Consett Iron Co Ltd* [1955] Ch 363 at 416.

[318] See the discussion of 'commercial funders' at **7.175–7.180** and of 'public policy' at **41.3–41.15**; see *Arkin v Borchard* [2005] EWCA Civ 655.

[319] See, for example, *British Cash and Parcel Conveyors Ltd v Lamson Store Service Co Ltd* [1908] 1 KB 1006 at 1013.

[320] *Hill v Archbold* [1968] 1 QB 686 at 697.

[321] See, for example, *Thai Trading Co (a firm) v Taylor* [1998] 3 All ER 65 at 69, per Millett LJ; this case is no longer good law, but it was found to be wrong on bases other than the discussion of what amounts to champertous maintenance. That said, Lord Neuberger MR has urged caution in respect of this case generally: see *Morris v London Borough of Southwark* [2011] EWCA Civ 25 at [24].

[322] *Giles v Thompson* [1994] 1 AC 142 at 161.

[323] See, for example, *In re Trepca Mines Ltd (No 2)* [1963] Ch 199 at 220, 225 and 226.

[324] *Saville Bros Ltd v Langman* (1898) 79 LT 44, CA.

[325] *Rees v De Bernardy* [1896] 2 Ch 437.

[326] 'There is, of course, no more cogent evidence of a change of public policy than the expression of the will of Parliament', per Steyn LJ in *Giles v Thompson* [1993] 3 All ER 321 at 331.

statutory provisions relating to court proceedings and, effectively, found that any agreement which would have met those statutory requirements would be free from any public policy objection.[327]

9.339 In summary, where a person meddles in an another person's claim, the facility does exist for the court to find that the retainer relating to that meddling is unenforceable, but the scope for the court making such a finding has been diminishing over the decades and is now restricted.

Champerty

9.340 Champerty is generally regarded as being a subspecies of maintenance;[328] it is generally said to be maintenance where there is a notion of division of the spoils. It is convenient to use the phrase 'champertous maintenance' to describe that state of affairs.[329] That said, Lord Neuberger MR has point out that it is possible to have champerty without maintenance, this being because the latter involves an element of assisting one of the parties 'without justification or excuse', yet this is not a necessary ingredient of champerty.[330] This distinction is more relevant than it might first appear, this being because one of the most important modern-day applications of champerty is in the context of legal representatives acting in that capacity, and both Lord Phillips[331] and Lord Neuberger MR[332] have explained that such a person can hardly be said to providing assistance without justification or excuse. Put another way, modern notions of champerty draw a distinction between alleged champerters who are also legal representatives acting in that capacity and those who are not legal representatives, and it is not necessary to show that a legal representative is a maintainer for the purposes of showing that he is a champerter.

9.341 Lord Mustill has commented that champerty is so ancient that its 'origins can no longer be traced'.[333] What can be said, however, is that the focus of concern has shifted over the centuries. In the fourteenth century the concern was to combat unprincipled nobles and royal officials lending their names to strengthen the credibility of doubtful and fraudulent claims in return for a share of the property recovered.[334] By the nineteenth century the focus had shifted from the person who was being sued to the person whose claim it was; in particular, there was concern that where such people were unable to litigate for want of finance, they might be tempted to enter into an

---

[327] *Bevan Ashford (a firm) v Geoff Yeandle (Contractors) Ltd (in liquidation)* [1999] Ch 239; this case applied authority (ie *Thai Trading Co (a firm) v Taylor* [1998] 3 All ER 65) which was subsequently found to be wrongly decided and so was probably itself wrongly decided, but it remains illustrative of the principle that public policy can be influenced by statute.

[328] See *Morris v London Borough of Southwark* [2011] EWCA Civ 25 at [52], per Lord Neuberger MR.

[329] See Pearson LJ's comments in *Re Trepca Mines Ltd (No 2)* [1963] Ch 199 at 226; see also *Hickman v Kent or Romney Marsh Sheepbreeders' Association* (1920) 151 LT Jo 5, CA, in which it was said that 'every champerty is maintenance'; see also *Ellis v Torrington* [1920] 1 KB 399 at 412.

[330] *Morris v London Borough of Southwark* [2011] EWCA Civ 25 at [53].

[331] *R v Secretary of State for Transport ex p Factortame* [2002] EWCA Civ 932 at [76].

[332] *Morris v London Borough of Southwark* [2011] EWCA Civ 25 at [53].

[333] *Giles v Thompson* [1994] 1 AC 142 at 153; the earliest solid reference the writer can find is the Champerty Act 1275 (3 Ed I (St West I) c 25), but it is generally thought that statute merely increased the punishment for champerty and that it had existed for many centuries before it was mentioned in statutes or ordinances: see PH Winfield *The History of Conspiracy and Abuse of Legal Procedure* (Beard Books, 1921), p 138.

[334] PH Winfield 'The history of maintenance and champerty' (1919) Law QR 35 at p 50.

'improvident bargain' which would unfairly diminish their rights.[335] Modern-day concerns focus principally on the administration of justice, as Steyn LJ commented:[336]

> 'The doctrine of champerty serves to protect only the integrity of English public justice. It is based not on grounds of morality but on a concern to protect the administration of civil justice in this country.'

9.342 In addition to this change in its aims, public policy has, in recent years, also focused on access to justice: both Lord Hoffmann[337] and Baroness Hale[338] have commented on the fact that the illegality of champertous funding agreements may act to deter poor persons from obtaining legal redress.

9.343 Whilst maintenance must be present for champerty to exist, there are some features of maintenance that are particularly relevant where champerty is alleged. One such feature is the fact that the champerter will not have a legitimate interest in the claim. Lord Mustill has noted that that aspect of champerty can still be well described as 'a wanton and officious intermeddling without justification or excuse'.[339] The phrase 'wanton and officious intermeddling' can be traced at least as far back as the end of the eighteenth century,[340] and has become shorthand for one of the two main ingredients of champerty (the other being division of the spoils). Another phrase which is often heard is that the champerter might be tempted, for his own personal gain 'to inflame the damages, to suppress evidence, or even to suborn witnesses'; those famous words were originally spoken by Denning MR in the mid-1960s,[341] and have been instrumental in shaping the law of champerty ever since.[342]

9.344 Whilst there can be no champerty where there is no maintenance, it is not necessary that the maintenance must, of itself, be unlawful: this is because the public policy which informs the two doctrines is different and allows for different exceptions.[343] So an act of maintenance may be acceptable when carried out in isolation, but may become objectionable when it is combined with the notion of division of the spoils.[344] An example is providing assistance as an act of charity: such assistance may take on an altogether less innocent air if the maintainer puts altruism to one side and demands his share of the proceeds.

9.345 The mere fact that litigation services have been provided in return for a promise in the share of the proceeds is not by itself sufficient to justify a finding of champerty.[345]

---

[335] *Hutley v Hutley* (1873) LR 8 QB 112; see also *Rees v De Bernardy* [1896] 2 Ch 437.
[336] *Giles v Thompson* [1993] 3 All ER 321 at 332; See also *Papera Traders Co Ltd v Hyundai (Merchant) Marine Co Ltd (No 2)* [2002] 2 Lloyd's LR 692.
[337] *Norgeln Ltd v Reeds Rains Prudential Ltd* [1999] 2 AC 1 at 11.
[338] *Massai Aviation Services v Attorney-General* [2007] UKPC 12 at [13].
[339] *Giles v Thompson* [1994] 1 AC 142 at 153 and 161; the phrase was used by Fletcher Moulton LJ in *British Cash and Parcel Conveyors Ltd v Lamson Store Service Co Ltd* [1908] 1 KB 1006 at 1014.
[340] *Wallis v Duke of Portland* (1797) 3 Ves 494.
[341] *Trepca Mines Ltd (No 2)* [1963] 1 Ch 199 at 219.
[342] See, for example, *R v Secretary of State for Transport ex p Factortame* [2002] EWCA Civ 932 at [36].
[343] *Thai Trading Co (a firm) v Taylor* [1998] 3 All ER 65 at 69, per Millett LJ; this case is no longer good law, but it was found to be wrong on bases other than the discussion of what amounts to champertous maintenance.
[344] An example is where assistance is provided by a person whose only interest in the matter is that they are acting out of kinship or to assist the poor; where that person seeks to take a share of the profits, any defence arising out of that interest will no longer be available: see *Cole v Booker* (1913) 29 TLR 295 and *Hutley v Hutley* (1873) LR 8 QB 112.
[345] *R (Factortame) Ltd v Secretary of State for Transport (No 8)* [2003] QB 381; see also Underhill J's analysis in *Mansell v Robinson* [2007] EWHC 101 (QB).

9.346 As has been noted in the discussion of maintenance, public policy is not static but is something that evolves:[346] Lord Phillips said that 'because the question of whether maintenance and champerty can be justified is one of public policy, the law must be kept under review as public policy changes'.[347] Champerty used to be a crime and a tort for which damages were recoverable. Sections 13(1) and 14(1) of the Criminal Law Act 1967 abolished both the tort and the crime, but the law relating to the enforceability of contracts was preserved. In modern times the pendulum has swung in the direction of making the scope of what is champertous more restricted than previously,[348] but it should not be assumed that the pendulum will not swing back again. In Hong Kong, for example, champerty and maintenance were long thought to have been obsolete concepts relegated to textbooks on legal history, but they have been revived in recent years, this being in response to the prevalence of 'recovery agents' (who are a particularly aggressive species of claims farmer). Whilst the arguments have so far failed to find favour, defendants to class actions in Australia have been seeking to rely on arguments closely related to champerty for the purpose of arguing against litigation funding.[349]

9.347 The modern approach to champerty has been explained by Phillips MR:[350]

> 'Where the law expressly restricts the circumstances in which agreements in support of litigation are lawful, this provides a powerful indication of the limits of public policy in analogous situations. Where this is not the case, then we believe one must today look at the facts of the particular case and consider whether those facts suggest that the agreement in question might tempt the allegedly champertous maintainer for his personal gain, to inflame the damages, to suppress evidence, to suborn witnesses or otherwise to undermine the ends of justice.'

The correct approach is not to ask whether the agreement has in fact caused the corruption of public justice; instead, the court must consider the tendency of the agreement to tempt the putatively champertous maintainer for his personal gain, to inflame the damages, to suppress evidence, to suborn witnesses or otherwise to undermine the ends of justice.[351] A flexible approach is required. Some judges have commented that the court is reluctant to make a finding of champerty.[352]

9.348 In so far as the indemnity principle is concerned, the focus is mostly on the retainer in question rather than the claim as a whole; this principle has two consequences:

(1)   It is not permissible to disregard the champertous contract of retainer and look at what would have happened had it not existed. In particular, Atkin LJ has confirmed that where a person is engaged to carry out work under a champertous

---

[346]   In the context of champerty rather than just maintenance, see *R v Secretary of State for Transport ex p Factortame* [2002] EWCA Civ 932 at [31]–[33].

[347]   *R v Secretary of State for Transport ex p Factortame* [2002] EWCA Civ 932 at [32].

[348]   See, for example, *Thai Trading Co (a firm) v Taylor* [1998] 3 All ER 65 at 69, per Millett LJ; this case is no longer good law, but it was found to be wrong on bases other than the discussion of what amounts to champertous maintenance.

[349]   See **41.12**.

[350]   *R v Secretary of State for Transport ex p Factortame* [2002] EWCA Civ 932 at [36].

[351]   Whilst the decision was appealed on other grounds, see *Giles v Thompson* [1993] 3 All ER 321 at 333 and *Trendtex Trading Corp v Crédit Suisse* [1982] AC 629.

[352]   See *London and Regional (St George's Court) Ltd v Ministry of Defence* [2008] EWHC 526 (TCC) at [103], in which Coulson J cited with approval *Papera Traders Co Ltd v Hyundai (Merchant) Marine Co Ltd (No 2)* [2002] 2 Lloyds LR 692.

contract, he cannot seek payment on the basis of quantum meruit or on the basis of an earlier, non-champertous, agreement.[353]

(2) The client's motives and methods need not necessarily be taken into account when considering the issue of whether the contract of retainer is champertous. In particular, a retainer will not be tinged with illegality merely because the solicitor knows that his client has made a champertous agreement to share the proceeds with a third party. The solicitor would have to participate in the champertous arrangement for the retainer to be champertous. Denning LJ has indicted that the participation must be active participation in the sense that the solicitor must voluntarily carry out a positive act of assistance,[354] but his comments were made in the context of champerty being a criminal offence; it is entirely possible that the court would view the matter differently today.

The second of these things does not mean that the court is unable to look beyond the retainer. Although there is no authority on the point, it is easy to envisage circumstances in which a retainer could be found to be unenforceable by reason of the conduct of the solicitor, eg where he has knowingly referred clients to a person who would fund the claim in a way which was champertous.

9.349 Christopher Nugee QC (setting as a deputy judge of the High Court) has commented (obiter) that whilst the court is able to make a finding of champerty of its own volition, it should do so only where it can clearly see that the contract is illegal.[355]

9.350 In summary, whilst the law of champerty continues to exist and continues to be relevant to the issue of enforceability of retainers, in practice it is rarely invoked. The court's task is to consider whether the arrangement might tempt the allegedly champertous maintainer, for his personal gain, to inflame the damages, to suppress evidence, to suborn witnesses or otherwise to undermine the ends of justice. If so, then mechanisms do exist which would allow the court to find that the retainer was unenforceable.

Case examples

9.351 The following are examples and counter-examples of maintenance and champertous maintenance. Very old cases have been disregarded. Only the briefest of descriptions of the facts is given, as an aid to, rather than a substitute for, further legal research. It should be borne in mind that many of the following examples would now be regarded as being lawful (and possibly even in line with public policy) by reason of the intervention of statute.

Provision of legal services by lawyer for share of the proceeds (early twentieth century)

9.352 Where a solicitor agreed to represent a client for a share of the proceeds, the solicitor was found to have entered into a champertous agreement.[356] Whilst an extreme

---

[353] *Wild v Simpson* [1919] 2 KB 544.

[354] *In re Trepca Mines Ltd (No 2)* [1963] Ch 199.

[355] *Ladiaev v Vallen* [2008] EWHC 1271 (Ch) at [105].

[356] *Wild v Simpson* [1919] 2 KB 544; see also *Haseldine v Hosken* [1933] All ER Rep 1 and the cases cited in that case, which include *Earle v Hopwood* (1861) 30 LJCP 217 and *Ford v Radford* (1920) 36 TLR 658; for a discussion of this topic in the context of the CLSA 1990 (as amended) see **9.309–9.320** and **30.20–30.21**.

example, Waller LJ found that there was 'no clearer case of wanton and officious intermeddling' than a case in which a solicitor had initiated, funded, and personally directed the proceedings.[357]

Financial support in commercial context (late nineteenth century)

9.353 A 'genuine pre-existing financial interest in maintaining the solvency of the person whose action he maintains' may be sufficient to avoid a finding of champerty.[358] Where, for example, litigation was funded by brokers who had a 4–5% interest in the placement of the contracts that were being litigated, no champerty existed, as their involvement came 'nowhere near' being wanton and officious intermeddling.[359] At the other end of the spectrum, a director gave financial support to a specialist to bring a libel action for adverse comments made about his own comments about the director's company's products.[360] That was found to amount to maintenance.

Litigation support in a trade union setting (early twentieth century)

9.354 A union funded a libel claim against a member's employer, that not being a stated benefit of membership.[361] That was found to be maintenance.

Litigation support in the context of a charity or other beneficial organisation (early twentieth century)

9.355 A charity funded an action and provided litigation services to an examiner who wished to bring a defamation claim.[362] That was found to be maintenance.

Litigation support in the context of a commercial interest (early twenty-first century)

9.356 In response to the recognition that an overzealous application of the law of maintenance is capable of denying persons access to justice, the concept of a 'genuine commercial interest' has developed.[363] A contract between persons who had entered into a joint venture that one would provide the other with assistance in unrelated litigation was held not to be champertous; this was because the joint venture would have been adversely affected by a poor outcome in that litigation, so the supposed champerter had a genuine commercial interest in the matter.[364]

---

[357] *Nordstern Allgemeine Versicherungs AG v Internav Ltd* [1999] 2 Lloyd's Rep 139.
[358] *Trendtex Trading Corp v Credit Suisse* [1982] AC 629, per Oliver LJ.
[359] *Stocznia Gdanska SA v Latvian Shipping Co* [2001] BCC 174.
[360] *Alabaster v Harness* [1895] 1 QB 339, CA.
[361] *Greig v National Amalgamated Union of Shop Assistants, Warehousemen and Clerks* (1906) 22 TLR 274; see also *Oram v Hutt* [1914] 1 Ch 98, CA, but also see *Hill v Archbold* [1968] 1 QB 686, in which *Greig* and *Oram* were doubted.
[362] *Scott v National Society for Prevention of Cruelty to Children and Parr* (1909) 25 TLR 789.
[363] See the discussion by Baroness Hale in *Massai Aviation Services v Attorney-General* [2007] UKPC 12 at [17].
[364] *Crittenden v Bayliss* [2002] All ER (D) 92.

Assignment of a bare cause of action (early and mid-twentieth century)

9.357 It has been held that the assignment of a bare right to bring a claim can be struck down as a transaction savouring of maintenance.[365] Where the facts permit, this can be the case even where the rights are debts which must be sued upon in order to be able to benefit from them.[366]

Assignment of a cause of action where the assignee has a commercial interest (late twentieth and early twenty-first centuries)

9.358 An example of a genuine commercial interest was where a co-defendant settled as against the claimant, but took the claimant's claim against the other co-defendants.[367] Another example would be a 'borrowing' arrangement where a subcontractor borrows the name of the main contractor for the purposes of pursuing a claim in which he has an interest.[368]

Assignment of an associated cause of action (early twentieth century)

9.359 Assignment of an associated right to bring a claim (such as where it is associated with a property transaction or a legitimate business interest) is not maintenance.[369]

Trafficking in litigation (late twentieth century)

9.360 Where an assignment of a cause of action would have been permissible by reason of the assignee having a legitimate business interest in the matter, it would amount to maintenance if the assignee were to take it for the purposes of reassigning it to a third party with no interest in the matter.[370]

Assignment of a bare cause of action by a trustee or liquidator (late twentieth century)

9.361 A trustee in bankruptcy or liquidator is in a privileged position in that it will not be contrary to public policy for such a person to assign a cause of action or realising its value for the purposes of satisfying the demands of creditors.[371] A transaction such as that would not be maintenance. Where such a transaction is carried out, it would not be open to the court to make a pre-emptive order that a trustee in bankruptcy who assigned the claim will not be liable for costs of a successful defendant if the assigned claim failed.[372]

---

[365]   *Glegg v Bromley* [1912] 3 KB 474, CA.
[366]   *Laurent v Sale & Co (a firm)* [1963] 2 All ER 63; compare with *Camdex International Ltd v Bank of Zambia* [1996] 1 WLR 721.
[367]   See, for example, *Brownton v Edward Moore Inbucon Ltd* [1985] 3 All ER 499.
[368]   For a discussion of this see L Patterson *Identity Crisis* (2008) 23 *Building* 69; see also *London and Regional (St George's Court) Ltd v Ministry of Defence* [2008] EWHC 526 (TCC).
[369]   See the discussion in *Trendtex Trading Corpn v Crédit Suisse* [1982] AC 629 and *Martell v Consett Iron Co Ltd* [1954] 3 All ER 339.
[370]   *Trendtex Trading Corpn v Crédit Suisse* [1982] AC 629.
[371]   *Circuit Systems Ltd (In Liquidation) v Zuken-Redac (UK) Ltd* [1999] 2 AC 1 at 2.
[372]   *Hunt (trustee in bankruptcy of Harb) v Harb and ors* [2011] EWCA Civ 1239 at 19], [26], [28]

Funding insolvent persons (late twentieth century)

9.362 Whilst liquidators and trustees in bankruptcy may be able to assign a cause of action for payment of a sum of money in return, it does not follow that a person may fund an insolvent person to bring a claim. That would, in appropriate circumstances, amount to maintenance.[373]

Funding a liquidator (late twentieth century)

9.363 The funding of a liquidator to bring a claim against the directors of the liquidated company was found to be capable of amounting to maintenance (especially where the funders had a degree of control over the litigation).[374]

Supply of information for the purposes of litigation (late nineteenth century)

9.364 It will not necessarily be maintenance (or, at least, not champertous maintenance) to supply information in return for a share of the proceeds,[375] but it may become maintenance if the agreement itself involves court proceedings.[376]

Assisting with a dispute resolution procedure other than litigation (late twentieth century)

9.365 Providing services for the purpose of representing a person in a valuation court in return for a conditional fee was not maintenance (or, at least, not champertous maintenance); this is because the dispute resolution procedure was found to be administration rather than litigation.[377] The provision of services by a surveyor in a planning inquiry for a conditional fee was held not to be maintenance for similar reasons.[378]

Deduction of legal costs (late twentieth century)

9.366 In the context of family law, in a claim against a husband who was better able to fund the litigation than was the wife, Wilson J held that an agreement to deduct legal costs of proceedings from a divorce award was not champertous or unlawful.

Calculating ATE premiums on the basis of the sums recovered (early twenty-first century)

9.367 Although not in a binding decision, Master Hurst has found that calculating an ATE premium as being 20% of the damages awarded in a road traffic accident claim was not champertous; he found that the insurer was seeking to profit from the insurance rather than from the litigation.[379]

---

[373]   *Grovewood Holdings plc v James Capel & Co Ltd* [1995] Ch 80.
[374]   *Re Oasis Merchandising Services Ltd* [1998] Ch 170.
[375]   *Hutley v Hutley* (1873) LR 8 QB 112. Even in ancient times there was nothing objectionable about an agreement merely to give information in return for a share of the proceeds where the informant took no further part in the litigation; see *Stanley v Jones* (1831) 7 Bing 369; *Spyre v Porter* (1856) 7 E & B 58.
[376]   See the Irish case of *Fraser v Buckle* [1996] 2 IRLM 34.
[377]   *Pickering (t/a City Agents) v Sogex Services (UK) Ltd* [1982] 1 EGLR 42.
[378]   *Picton Jones & Co v Arcadia Developments Ltd* [1989] 1 EGLR 43.
[379]   *Pirie v Ayling* [2003] EWHC 9006 (Costs).

Provision of support services to an expert (early twenty-first century)

9.368 Where a firm of accountants had agreed to provide services on a contingency fee basis, but where they were not acting as experts and where they had limited their role to providing support services for other accountants who were acting as experts, their involvement was not champertous.[380]

Provision of investigative services (early twenty-first century)

9.369 Underhill J declined to find that an agreement made by a journalist to use his investigative skills to assist a person to bring a claim in return for a percentage of the damages was champertous.[381]

Expert witnesses and professional assistance (early twenty-first century)

9.370 Phillips MR has commented (obiter) that the dangers of allowing an expert to be funded on a conditional basis were great, so it would be 'very rare indeed' that the court would be prepared to consent to an expert being funded in such a way.[382] In contrast, Cresswell J found that the involvement of a marine recovery specialist on a contingent basis was not champertous, this being for several reasons, one of which was the fact that the activities of the specialist were subject to the control of the claimant's solicitors, and therefore the specialists had only a limited opportunity to influence the outcome.[383]

Beneficial associations (late twentieth century)

9.371 Where an organisation exists in order to provide benefits for its members, it may have an interest in funding its members claims; an example would be where a trade union brought actions on behalf of its members for damages arising out of industrial accidents,[384] or where a union funded liable actions.[385]

Shared interest in a pastime: (mid-twentieth century)

9.372 Where the members of an angling club gave assistance to a claim which dealt with the pollution in a river, they were held to have a genuine interest in the matter.[386]

Interest in land (early twenty-first century)

9.373 Where a person has an interest in property and where that interest may be affected by the litigation, he may have a sufficient interest to justify providing assistance in that litigation.[387]

---

[380] *R v Secretary of State for Transport ex p Factortame* [2002] EWCA Civ 932.
[381] *Mansell v Robinson* [2007] EWHC 101 (QB).
[382] *R v Secretary of State for Transport ex p Factortame* [2002] EWCA Civ 932 at [72]–[73]; compare this, however, with Chadwick LJ's comments in *Hamilton v Al Fayed and others* [2002] EWCA Civ 665 at [69].
[383] *Papera Traders Co Ltd v Hyundai (Merchant) Marine Co Ltd (No 2)* [2002] 2 Lloyds LR 692.
[384] See *Bourne v Colodense Ltd* (1998) *The Times*, February 4, and *Allen v Francis* [1914] 3 KB 1065, CA at 1067.
[385] *Hill v Archbold* [1968] 1 QB 686; but see *Greig v National Amalgamated Union of Shop Assistants, Warehousemen and Clerks* (1906) 22 TLR 274 and *Oram v Hutt* [1914] 1 Ch 98, CA.
[386] *Martell v Consett Iron Co Ltd* [1955] Ch 363 at 387.
[387] *London and Regional (St George's Court) Ltd v Ministry of Defence* [2008] EWHC 526 (TCC); *Alabaster v Harness* [1894] 2 QB 897; in the context of liability to pay rent, see *Findon v Parker* (1843) 11 M & W 675.

9.374 In summary, whilst the importance of maintenance and champerty has diminished significantly over the past few decades, some agreements (including some retainers) may be found to be unenforceable as a result of a person maintaining a claim for a share in the proceeds. Each case will turn on its own facts.

The history of conditional fee agreements

9.375 Very little of what follows here remains good law: it is included in this book only for interest and to allow older authorities to be put in their correct context. The focus is on the modern history, so ancient law is mentioned only briefly.

History: early twentieth century (and before)

9.376 Judges of pre-eminence have commented that English common law has never sanctioned conditional fee agreements;[388] it is, however, far from certain that this is correct. Whilst there are cases of some antiquity which give credence to that view,[389] there are examples of even the higher courts tolerating what appears to be overt conditional funding.[390] As recently as the early twentieth century, the Court of Appeal expressed no disapproval of an informal conditional fee agreement in a case that was subsequently specifically approved of in *Gundry v Sainsbury*.[391] In the late nineteenth century the Court of Common Pleas found that an agreement by an attorney with a client 'to charge him nothing if he lost the action, and to take nothing for costs out of any money that might be awarded to him in such action' was entirely unobjectionable; indeed, Bovill CJ went so far as to say that 'a promise not to charge anything for costs is not champerty'.[392] (At least one twenty-first century judge has sought to categorise those cases as being examples of solicitors agreeing to waive their fees.)

History: mid-twentieth century

9.377 By the mid-twentieth century the modern notion that conditional fee agreements had always been abhorrent had become ingrained.[393] From 1936 onwards the Law Society issued rules governing solicitors which forbade conditional fee agreements; this created an implied statutory prohibition of such agreements. That said, even Lord Denning MR (who many would regard as having been a proponent of that view) suggested that public policy should favour conditional fee agreements in certain circumstances.[394] The perception was that statutory intervention would be required to allow lawful conditional fee agreements to be made.

---

[388] See, for example, the comments of Lord Denning MR in *Wallersteiner v Moir (No 2)* [1975] QB 373 at 393.
[389] Indeed, by as early as 1870 there was statutory recognition that conditional fee agreements were unenforceable; in particular, in 1870 the equivalent of the Solicitors Act 1974 provided that: 'nothing [herein] ... shall give validity to ... any agreement by which a solicitor retained or employed to prosecute any action, suit or other contentious proceeding, stipulates for payment only in the event of success in that action, suit or proceeding ...'
[390] See *Clare v Joseph* [1907] 2 KB 376; *Ladd v London Road Car Co* [1900] LT 80; and *Jennings v Johnson* (1873) LR 8 CP 425.
[391] See *Clare v Joseph* [1907] 2 KB 376.
[392] *Jennings v Johnson* (1873) LR 8 CP 425; see also *Ladd v London Road Car Co* [1900] LT 80; however, see the comments of Kennedy LJ in *Wells v Barnsley Metropolitan Borough Council* (1999) *The Times*, November 12, QBD, where he says of *Ladd* that the only thing that was approved of was the willingness of the solicitor to act for an impecunious client who would probably not be able to pay if he were to lose.
[393] As an early example see *In re A Solicitor ex p Law Society* [1912] 1 KB 302; see also Lord Esher MR's comment in *Pittman v Prudential Deposit Bank Ltd*, 13 TLR 110 at 111.
[394] Those circumstances being derivative actions: see *Wallersteiner v Moir (No 2)* [1975] QB 373 at 395G.

9.378 In 1966 the Law Commission proposed that maintenance and champerty should be decriminalised, but they refused to recommend making conditional fee agreements lawful; they suggested that this was a question 'upon which the professional bodies as well as the public must have further time for reflection before any solutions can or should be formulated'.[395] Parliament accepted the recommendation not to alter the law of conditional fee agreements.[396] After due reflection and consultation, it was decided to take the matter no further.[397]

History: 1970s

9.379 Giving judgment in the mid-1970s Lord Denning MR rejected the proposal that the fact that champerty had been decriminalised in some way gave legitimacy to conditional fee agreements; he took the opportunity to explain that, in his view, the common law viewed such agreements with abhorrence. He also explained that the Law Society's rule against conditional fee agreements was a reflection of public policy[398] (as opposed to being a self-standing reason to imply a prohibition). In 1979, the Royal Commission on Legal Services examined the topic and concluded that there would be a conflict of interest between litigants and their lawyers if conditional fee agreements were to be permitted.

History: 1980s

9.380 A very similar view was taken in 1987 by a Law Society working party which concluded that 'it would be impossible to overcome the ethical and consumer protection problems [posed by such funding arrangements]'. Shortly thereafter, however, the position began to change. In 1988, the Report of the Review Body on Civil Justice[399] suggested a re-examination of the topic. In 1989, the view of the executive began to change,[400] as did that of the Law Society. Indeed, the latter asked to seek an opportunity to remove the statutory bars on contingency fees.

History: 1990s

9.381 Within a short time, the legislature concluded that changes were required. The statutory mechanism by which enforceable conditional fee agreements could be made was put in place in 1990.[401] The necessary delegated legislation did not come into force until 1995,[402] and then it only permitted conditional fee agreements to be made in a limited range of proceedings.[403] The common law continued to apply to agreements that did not fall with that range, which resulted in a number of agreements being found to be unenforceable.[404]

---

[395] *Proposals for Reform of the Law Relating to Champerty and Maintenance* (Law Com No 7), para 19.
[396] Section 14(2) of the Criminal Law Act 1967 read as follows: 'The abolition of criminal and civil liability under the law of England and Wales for maintenance and champerty shall not affect any rule of that law as to the cases in which a contract is to be treated as contrary to public policy or otherwise illegal'.
[397] The Law Commission (Law Com No 47), Sixth Annual Report 1970–1971, pp 7–8, paras 33–35.
[398] In *Wallersteiner v Moir (No 2)* [1975] QB 373 at 393.
[399] (Cm 394), paras 384–389.
[400] See The Lord Chancellor's Green Paper on 'Contingency Fees' (1989) (Cm 571) and the White Paper, 'Legal Services: A Framework for the Future' (1990) (Cm 740).
[401] Section 58 of the Courts and Legal Services Act 1990 (as unamended).
[402] See the Conditional Fee Agreements Regulations 1995 (SI 1995/1675) and the Conditional Fee Agreements Order 1995 (SI 1995/1674).
[403] The first Order was brought into force on 5 July 1995; this limited conditional fee agreements to personal

9.382 In 1998, the Court of Appeal decided a case which gave rise to the term '*Thai Trading* agreement'[405] (that being an informal agreement that the client will not be charged if the claim is not successful). The court found that the agreement was enforceable, but this was because the parties had failed to direct the court's attention to the implied statutory prohibition arising out of the Law Society's rules (see above). However, *Thai Trading* did give an insight into what the court would have said had it not been encumbered by the implied statutory prohibition. In particular, Millett LJ (with whom Hutchinson and Kennedy LJJ agreed) had the following to say:

> 'The fear that lawyers may be tempted by having a financial incentive in the outcome of litigation to act improperly is exaggerated, and that there is a countervailing public policy in making justice readily accessible to persons of modest means. Legislation was needed to authorise the increase in the lawyer's reward over and above his ordinary profit costs. It by no means follows that it was needed to legitimise the long-standing practice of solicitors to act for meritorious clients without means, and it is in the public interest that they should continue to do so.'

That analysis was followed for brief period of time,[406] but before long it soon came to light that it was wrong.[407] In any event, in more recent times, Lord Neuberger MR has commented that *Thai Trading* is an anomalous case that is inconsistent with subsequent decisions of the Court of Appeal, particularly where the question is whether a legal representative acting in that capacity is a champerter.[408]

9.383 When the Court of Appeal came to consider the issue again (this time in the light of the implied statutory prohibition), Schiemann LJ had this to say:[409]

> 'I share Lord Scarman's reluctance[410] to develop the common law at a time when Parliament was in the process of addressing those very problems. It is clear from the careful formulation of the statutes and regulations that Parliament did not wish to abandon regulation altogether and wished to move forward gradually. I see no reason to suppose that Parliament foresaw significant parallel judicial developments of the law ... I would therefore hold that acting for a client in pursuance of a conditional normal fee agreement, in circumstances not sanctioned by statute, is against public policy.'

Thus, the court deferred to Parliament. It is worth noting, however, that Schiemann LJ was careful to point out that his findings were limited to findings on the law as it stood in 1993; there are those who say that conditional fee agreements (or, at least, conditional fee agreements which do not provide for a success fee) are no longer unlawful at common law. This issue is discussed in more detail at **9.300**.

9.384 At about the same time (1999) a study was published by the Nuffield Foundation which showed that clients did not generally fully understand conditional fee

---

injury cases, insolvency cases and cases before the European Court of Human Rights. In July 1998 the range of proceedings was extended as far as possible under CLSA 1990 to all civil proceedings, other than family cases.

[404] See, for example, *British Waterways Board v Norman* (1993) 26 HLR 232 and *Aratra Potato Co Ltd v Taylor Joynson Garrett* [1995] 4 All ER 695.

[405] *Thai Trading Co v Taylor* [1998] QB 781.

[406] See, for example, *Bevan Ashford (a firm) v Geoff Yeandle (Contractors) Ltd (in liquidation)* [1999] Ch 239.

[407] See *Hughes v Kingston upon Hull City Council* [1999] QB 1193; see also *Leeds City Council v Carr* (1999) *The Times*, November 12, DC, in which a differently constituted Divisional Court doubted *Thai Trading*.

[408] *Morris v London Borough of Southwark* [2011] EWCA Civ 25 at [39].

[409] *Awwad v Geraghty & Co (a firm)* [2001] QB 570 at 593.

[410] In *Wallersteiner v Moir (No 2)* [1975] QB 373.

agreements.[411] Also in 1999 the Law Society issued more detailed and demanding guidance for solicitors, which required them to give more information, and to give some of that information both orally and in writing.[412] In September 1999, the Lord Chancellor issued a new consultation paper,[413] which focused more on the mechanics of conditional fee agreement rather than their desirability. This was in the context of government planning to phase out public funding for most types of claims.[414]

History: 2000s

9.385 The way had been paved for a more widespread implementation of conditional fee agreements. In February 2000, the Lord Chancellor published the government's conclusions following his 1999 consultation. Although the Law Society and the senior costs judge had said that the rules recently introduced by the Law Society ensured that clients would be given adequate information, the government decided to make it a regulatory requirement that a certain level of information be given (those requirements mirroring the Law Society's requirements). This gave rise to the Conditional Fee Agreements Regulations 2000.

9.386 A timetable for reforming public funding had already been set; it left little time – some would say insufficient time – for consideration of the proposed regulations, which came into force in April 2000. There had been no opportunity for consultation. The 'costs war' began a few months later when paying parties began to rely on a doctrine which had previously been a relative rarity in costs litigation, ie the indemnity principle. An attempt was made in 2003 to amend the regulations in such a way as to make compliance with the regulations easier,[415] but those amendments had little impact. The regulations were revoked entirely in November 2005.[416] For practical purposes the only restriction on conditional fee agreements is that the success fee should not exceed 100% and they should not be used in criminal and family matters.

9.387 In summary, the history of conditional fee agreements is that whilst in ancient times they had been tolerated by the courts, in the early part of the twentieth century the court formed the view that the common law had always abhorred conditional means of payment. It may well be the case that the common law has changed but, in any event, public policy as expressed in statute has overshadowed the common law, and over the past two decades there has been an incremental attenuation of the extent to which conditional fee agreements are regulated.

CONTRACTUAL ISSUES CONCERNING CONDITIONAL FEE AGREEMENTS

9.388 This section deals with miscellaneous issues concerning not the enforceability of conditional fee agreements, but the way in which they may apply to the case in question; the questions to be considered are:

---

[411] S Yarrow and P Abrams *Nothing to Lose? Clients' Experiences of Using Conditional Fees*, Summary Report (University of Westminster, 1999).

[412] The Law Society *Solicitors' Costs Information and Client Care Code* (September 1999).

[413] *Conditional Fees: Sharing the Risks of Litigation.*

[414] See the Access to Justice Act 1999, the relevant parts of which did not come into force until 2000.

[415] Conditional Fee Agreements (Miscellaneous Amendments) Regulations 2003 (SI 2003/1240).

[416] Conditional Fee Agreements (Revocation) Regulations 2005 (SI 2005/2305).

- the approach to be taken when it is said that a conditional fee agreement is not capable of applying to the claim in question; and
- the approach to be taken when interpreting whether the definition of a 'win' has been met.

Scope

9.389 This discussion should be read in conjunction with **8.31–8.40** on 'Ambit', which deals with retainers in general, whereas this section deals with those issues which are specific to conditional fee agreements. There is a certain degree of duplication between these two sections.

9.390 The issues to be addressed here are whether the services provided by a legal representative can be said to fall within the ambit of the conditional fee agreement and, if not, what effect this will have on the legal representative's ability to recover his fees. Unlike non-conditional retainers, the principles in this section apply to all legal representatives, including counsel.

9.391 In view of the fact that conditional fee agreements tend to be complex documents which have the potential to contain many qualifying terms, there is an abundance of ways in which an agreement may fail to apply to the claim to which it was intended to relate; examples are where:

- the client is incorrectly identified;
- the legal representative is incorrectly identified;
- the opponent is incorrectly identified;
- the claim is incorrectly described or where the description is for a claim which is different from that for which costs are sought.

The general approach is the same regardless of the details of the putative error. Each is considered in turn.

Client

9.392 It is not uncommon for conditional fee agreements to name the 'wrong' client (ie a person other than the receiving party); commonly encountered situations include where:

- there has been an administrative mistake;
- the name of a director of a company has been substituted for that of his company or vice versa;
- the agreement is with a person who is acting in a representative capacity but where either the agreement should have been with the client himself (eg where it is overlooked that a patient has regained capacity); and
- the agreement is with a person acting in a representative capacity but where it should have been with a different representative person (eg where the agreement is with a child's mother, but his litigation friend is his father).

There are many ways in which the court may deal with the first and second of these issues: these are dealt with in Chapter 10. The third and fourth merit further discussion.

9.393 There are certain arguments which may be deployed which apply only to conditional fee agreements; in particular, it may be said that it is not open to the court to find that there is an implied retainer (on the same terms as the agreement), as there is no such thing as an enforceable unwritten conditional fee agreement. Although there is no binding authority on the point, a number of arguments can be deployed by the receiving party to counter that argument. The first – and simplest – is that the person acting in the representative capacity was acting as the receiving party's agent. Another is that the receiving party holds the rights under the costs order on constructive trust for the representative, and it would be both proper and reasonable for the receiving party to discharge the representative's fees. The matter can also be analysed in terms of restitution. There is no authority to confirm whether these analyses are correct, although, while he was speaking in a different context, Pill LJ has indicated that issues concerning unjust enrichment may arise where a person who has been funded by a third party is entitled to costs but does not pay those costs to the funder.[417]

9.394 There are many other arguments that the parties may wish to deploy, some of which are articulated in the consideration of 'Ambit' at **8.31–8.40**. Further discussion can be found in Chapter 10.

Legal representative

9.395 A legal representative may change his status (perhaps from an ordinary partnership to a limited liability partnership) but overlook the need to change or assign the retainer in order to accommodate that change of status. Very similar principles may apply to those discussed above.

9.396 It will often be the case that there has been an assignment of the rights and obligations from the 'old' entity to the 'new'. The first question that arises is whether, as a matter of law, a retainer is capable of being assigned, because of the fact that (generally speaking) it is only the benefit of a contract that can be assigned to an assignee; the obligations (such as the obligation to provide legal services) are not normally capable of assignment.[418] Rafferty J has found[419] that contracts of retainer fall within an exception to the general rule that obligations cannot be assigned.[420] Therefore, conditional fee agreements are, in principle, capable of being assigned. The next question will be whether the assignment has actually taken place; this will turn on the facts, but s 136 of the Law of Property Act 1925 may assist:[421] compliance with the provisions set out there will generally mean that an assignment has taken place. Thirdly, the retainer itself ought to be examined in order to ensure that there is no provision within it which prohibits assignment.

Opponent

9.397 Very similar principles to those which apply to the 'wrong' client will apply when the issue is whether the opponent has been correctly named. The court has greater scope for interpreting the contract widely when it is said that the wrong opponent has been

---

[417] *Pepin v Watts* [2002] EWCA Civ 958 at [18].

[418] See *Young v Kitchin* (1878) 3 Ex D 127.

[419] *Jenkins v Young Brothers Transport Ltd* [2006] EWHC 151 (QB).

[420] See *Rhone v Stephens* [1994] 2 AC 310 at 322 as an example of this doctrine in practice.

[421] See *Jenkins v Young Brothers Transport Ltd* [2006] EWHC 151 (QB) at [14]; broadly speaking, the requirements are: (i) that the assignment is absolute; (ii) that it must be in writing under the hand of the assignor; and (iii) that express notice in writing thereof must be given to the debtor (ie the client).

named than it would have where it is said that the client has been incorrectly described; this is because the putative error would relate to something less fundamental than the identity of the counterparties. Thus, the court might be more willing to find that as the case progressed the agreement had been impliedly varied to include a further opponent (for example) than it would to infer that the counterparties are not as stated on the face of the agreement.

9.398 An example (albeit not binding) of a similar approach is a case in which Master Gordon-Saker found that a reference to a company which was handling a claim on behalf of an opponent should be taken as being a reference which included the opponent; the effect of this was that the scope of the retainer included the work which had been carried out, notwithstanding the fact that the name of the person against whom the claim was brought was different from the opponent named in the agreement.[422] Contrary examples exist, two of which are discussed in the paragraphs on 'Ambit'.

9.399 It does not automatically follow that no liability will attach when fees are incurred beyond the ambit of the retainer. As mentioned above, the court may find that there is an implied retainer; it may also simply rely on the rebuttable presumption that a person who instructs a solicitor will be liable for the solicitor's reasonable costs.[423] However, where the work has been carried out on a conditional fee basis, it would usually not be possible for the receiving party to rely on the existence of an implied retainer, because it is a statutory requirement that conditional fee agreements are in writing.[424] Contrary examples do exist, however.[425]

The claim

9.400 The process of considering whether a claim (or a part of a claim) falls within the ambit of a conditional fee agreement is a matter of contractual interpretation; the usual principles of contractual interpretation will apply, and to that extent the court's approach will be similar to those set out above (and in the paragraphs on 'Ambit' at **8.31–8.40**; see also Chapter 10).

9.401 The whole of the document should be taken into account. This was illustrated by the way in which Mann J interpreted a conditional fee agreement which (the paying party alleged) did not apply to an appeal.[426] Mann J found (obiter) that the solicitor's duty extended to representing the client on the appeal, this being because of the existence of provisions requiring the solicitor to act in the client's best interests.[427] He found that the existence of that duty (which arose from a provision in the agreement itself) justified a finding that the agreement would apply work done in discharging that duty.

9.402 Although a slightly different topic, Mann J discussed the possibility that the discrepancy between what the agreement was being used for and what it said upon its

---

[422] *Brierley v Prescott* [2006] EWHC 90062 (Costs).

[423] As an example, see *Meretz Investments Ltd v ACP Ltd* [2007] EWHC 2635 (Ch).

[424] See CLSA 1990, s 58(3)(a) (as amended).

[425] *Law v Liverpool City Council*, 10 May 2005, Liverpool County Court, HHJ Stewart QC, where the base costs were held to be recoverable, but that seems to have been as a result of an agreement between the parties.

[426] That was in the context of an alleged breach of reg 2(1)(a) of the of Conditional Fee Agreements Regulations 2000 rather than in the context of the receiving party seeking to recover the costs of an appeal.

[427] *Felton v Holmes* [2007] EWHC 2476 (Ch) at [58]–[60].

face was a breach of reg 2(1)(a) of the Conditional Fee Agreements Regulations 2000; where the agreement was made before 1 November 2005 that regulation is an additional factor which may need to be taken into account.

9.403 A similar approach was taken in a case in which it was argued that the Law Society's model conditional fee agreement did not apply to 'costs only' proceedings (ie proceedings brought pursuant to CPR, r 44.12A). The agreement said that it would apply to the following:

> 'Your claim ... Any appeal by your opponent ... Any appeal you make against an interim order during the proceeding [and] ... Any proceedings you take to enforce a judgment, order or agreement.'

Brooke LJ analysed the matter in this way:[428]

> 'It follows [from the way in which "win" was defined] that the agreement contemplates that the claim will normally be "won" by achieving a result whereby the client is to recover her damages, basic charges, success fee and disbursements from his/her opponent in a quantified amount. Indeed, [the terms and conditions of the agreement] refer to some of the consequences which are to be provided for "if the court carries out an assessment of our charges" on what is clearly, from the context, an assessment between the parties. We are therefore satisfied that this CFA, on its proper construction, embraces the costs only proceedings within the "claim" for which it provides coverage.'

The court, therefore,took into account the whole of the agreement when interpreting its meaning and effect, rather than restricting itself to looking at the narrow issue of what was said upon its face.

'Win'

9.404 Whether the circumstances are such that the definition of 'win' or 'success' has been met will be a matter of contractual interpretation. The ordinary principles of contractual interpretation will apply.

9.405 An argument that may be raised is that the agreement may define 'win' by reference to monies being recovered rather than merely awarded. Coleman J rejected that argument in robust terms:[429]

> 'The suggestion that "recover" in this context means receive actual payment is, in my view, simply unarguable. To recover an ... award does not mean to receive both publication and satisfaction of it: the meaning is simply that award was made.'

9.406 However, each case will turn on its own facts and, in particular, on the way in which the agreement is worded. A rather extreme example (which is not binding, but merely illustrative) is a case in which Master Rogers found that the definition of a win had not been met because the agreement said that damages should be 'awarded', but the damages were, in the event, paid by consent.[430]

---

[428] *Halloran v Delaney* [2002] EWCA Civ 1258 at [20].
[429] *Arkin v Borchard Lines* (unreported), 19 June 2001, QBD.
[430] *Beckham v First News Ltd*, 8 November 2006, SCCO, Master Rogers.

9.407 In summary, the ambit of a conditional fee agreement will be a matter of contractual interpretation, which (broadly speaking) the court will approach in much the same way as it would approach the interpretation of any other contract.

RETROSPECTIVITY AND CONDITIONAL FEE AGREEMENTS

9.408 The question arises of whether a conditional fee agreement can have a retrospective effect (ie whether it is capable of applying to costs which were incurred before it was made). Whether a success fee can be recovered retrospectively is discussed at **30.103–30.111**. The issues addressed here are:

- whether a client can retrospectively bind himself as between solicitor and client;
- whether that would have any bearing on the liability of an opponent; and
- whether 'backdating' is tolerated.

Solicitor and client

9.409 From the solicitor and client point of view, there is nothing inherently objectionable about a conditional fee agreement having retrospective effect; such agreements are lawful.[431] Indeed, it will often be in the client's interests retrospectively to replace a retainer with a conditional retainer: by designating pre-agreement work as being conditional, the client's liability for costs will be contingent upon the outcome of the litigation, and many clients would see this as being an advantage.[432]

9.410 A conditional fee agreement is a contract of retainer and, like any other contract, there is at common law no objection in principle to the parties agreeing that it should be retrospective.[433]

9.411 There is nothing within the CLSA 1990 (as amended), nor in the secondary legislation made under it, which precludes conditional fee agreements from being retrospective.[434] In any event, on one analysis, a conditional fee agreement can be thought of as being a type of contentious business agreement,[435] and s 59(1) of the Solicitors Act 1974 specifically provides that such an agreement may be retrospective in effect.

9.412 Therefore, the issue will not usually be whether the counterparties are at liberty to enter into a retrospective agreement in principle,[436] but whether the agreement makes

---

[431] *Motto & Ors v Trafigura Ltd & Anor (Rev 3)* [2011] EWCA Civ 1150 at [61]. See also *Forde v Birmingham City Council* [2009] EWHC 12 (QB) at [123]–[127]; as an early example of the court tolerating retrospective agreement see *Arkin v Borchard Lines* (unreported) 19 June 2001, QBD, Coleman J; see also *King v Telegraph Group Ltd* [2005] EWHC 90015 (Costs).

[432] *Forde v Birmingham City Council* [2009] EWHC 12 (QB) at [123]–[127].

[433] Indeed, the well-established principle of novation is based on the freedom of parties to enter into a retroactive agreement.

[434] It could be argued that if de facto a retainer was always a conditional retainer, and that if the legal representative failed to discharge his duty to give advice about the effect of the retainer until it was formalised, such a failure could amount to a breach of the Conditional Fee Agreements Regulations 2000.

[435] See *Hollins v Russell* [2003] 1 WLR 2487 at 2501.

[436] An exception to this is where it is suggested that the solicitor has acted improperly, in which case issues of undue influence and informed approval may arise.

provision for retrospective application. That will be a matter of contractual interpretation. In this regard, Lord Neuberger MR had this to say:[437]

> '[A]ny CFA which limits the client's liability to work done after the CFA is entered into, cannot extend to work done before that date. Equally, although of course solicitors and their clients can agree terms otherwise the natural presumption in a contract by which a person engages a solicitor to act for him must be, in the absence of such a term, that he is agreeing to pay for work done in the future, not for work already done.'

9.413 Most conditional fee agreements (including, in particular, those based on the Law Society models) apply to those legal services which have been supplied from 'now';[438] the question, therefore, is what is meant by 'now'. Stanley Burnton J has confirmed that it is a reference to the date on which the agreement is made (which may or may not be the date which appears on the face of the agreement).[439] Where an agreement does apply from 'now', pre-agreement work will usually be claimed under an express or implied private retainer and will, therefore, be payable regardless of the outcome of the claim and will not attract a success fee: where these are the circumstances, the agreement will not be retrospective in effect.

9.414 Not all conditional fee agreements are worded in this way, however. A conditional fee agreement may expressly or impliedly cover work carried out before the agreement was made. An agreement which covers 'all work from the date of instruction, including work carried out before this agreement was made' will have made express provision for a retrospective application. It may be possible for the court to find retrospective application by reason of an implied term. Although there is no authority on the point, the court may be able to imply such a term in circumstances where the client has been assured that he would not pay any costs beyond those which were recoverable from the other side. That said, whist retrospective effect may be implied into a contract (including a conditional fee agreement), the circumstances must demonstrate that this was clearly the intention of the parties.[440]

9.415 Thus, each agreement must be interpreted on its own terms but, in principle, there is no reason why a conditional fee agreement may not bind solicitor and client with retrospective effect.

Between the parties

9.416 Although disputes about base costs may arise from time to time (see below), disputes between opposing parties about retrospective conditional fee agreements tend to focus on the recoverability of the success fee. This is a topic which is addressed at **30.103–30.111**.

9.417 It is most unlikely that the court would allow costs which came into existence as the result of the receiving party voluntarily accepting a liability after he became entitled to costs. While he was discussing contentious business agreements rather than conditional fee agreements, Irwin J made the following (obiter) comments:[441]

---

[437] *Motto & Ors v Trafigura Ltd & Anor (Rev 3)* [2011] EWCA Civ 1150 at [61].

[438] This being a consequence of the way in which base costs are defined.

[439] *Holmes v Alfred McAlpine Homes (Yorkshire) Ltd* [2006] EWHC 110 (QB) at [20]. See also *Motto & Ors v Trafigura Ltd & Anor (Rev 3)* [2011] EWCA Civ 1150 at [61].

[440] *Trollope & Colls v Atomic Power Construction Ltd* [1963] 1 WLR 333 at 339.

[441] *Crook v Birmingham City Council* [2007] EWHC 1415 (QB) at [36].

'I would be hesitant to conclude that any CBA entered into by a Claimant, after an adverse Costs Order had been made ... could be held to alter retrospectively the rights and obligations as between claimant and solicitor. The reason is obvious. To uphold a retrospective rearrangement in circumstances like that, would be to uphold the retrospective revision of – or even creation of – the defendant's costs liability.'

So, if the supposedly retrospective agreement was made after the entitlement to costs had already been decided, it is highly doubtful if that would have any bearing at all on the paying party's liability. This would certainly apply to a success fee, but it may well also apply to base costs. Whilst not binding, there are persuasive decisions which point in that direction.[442]

9.418 Beyond this, there is no particular reason to believe that base costs which are sought under a retrospective conditional fee agreement should be treated any differently from base costs which were sought under any other type of retainer: from the paying party's point of view the nature of the retainer is usually irrelevant, so the only issues that will need to be decided are those which would apply between solicitor and client (see above).

Backdating

9.419 Stanley Burnton J had the following to say about backdating (ie placing a date upon the agreement which predates the date on which it was actually made):[443]

'I would emphasise ... that the back-dating of documents as was done in this case is generally wrong. It is wrong to seek to give an agreement retrospective effect by back-dating it. If it is agreed that a written agreement should apply to work done before it is entered into, it should be correctly dated with the date on which it is signed and expressed to have retrospective effect, ie to apply to work done before its date. Back-dating is liable to mislead third parties, and is liable to lead to the suspicion that it was done in order to mislead third parties, including a court before which the agreement is to be placed.'

Intentional backdating would, therefore, be improper.

9.420 In summary, while special considerations may apply to the success fee, the issue of whether a conditional fee agreement applies retrospectively is generally nothing more than a question of contractual interpretation.

THE RELEVANT REGULATIONS

9.421 The following are the most important regulations discussed in this chapter.

The Conditional Fee Agreements Regulations 1995

Citation, commencement and interpretation

1.(1)   These Regulations may be cited as the Conditional Fee Agreements Regulations 1995 and shall come into force on the day after the day on which they are made.

---

[442] See, for example, *Kellar v Williams* [2004] UKPC 30 and *Oyston v Royal Bank of Scotland* [2006] EWHC 90053 (Costs).

[443] *Holmes v Alfred McAlpine Homes (Yorkshire) Ltd* [2006] EWHC 110 (QB) at [23].

(2)   In these Regulations—

> 'agreement', in relation to an agreement between a legal representative and an additional legal representative, includes a retainer;
> 'legal aid' means representation under Part IV of the Legal Aid Act 1988;
> 'legal representative' means a person providing advocacy or litigation services.

Agreements to comply with prescribed requirements

2.   An agreement shall not be a conditional fee agreement unless it complies with the requirements of the following regulations.

Requirements of an agreement

3.   An agreement shall state—

- (a) the particular proceedings or parts of them to which it relates (including whether it relates to any counterclaim, appeal or proceedings to enforce a judgment or order);
- (b) the circumstances in which the legal representative's fees and expenses or part of them are payable;
- (c) what, if any, payment is due—
    - (i) upon partial failure of the specified circumstances to occur;
    - (ii) irrespective of the specified circumstances occurring; and
    - (iii) upon termination of the agreement for any reason;
- (d) the amount payable in accordance with sub-paragraphs (b) or (c) above or the method to be used to calculate the amount payable; and in particular whether or not the amount payable is limited by reference to the amount of any damages which may be recovered on behalf of the client.

Additional requirements

4.(1)   The agreement shall also state that, immediately before it was entered into, the legal representative drew the client's attention to the matters specified in paragraph (2).

(2)   The matters are—

- (a) whether the client might be entitled to legal aid in respect of the proceedings to which the agreement relates, the conditions upon which legal aid is available and the application of those conditions to the client in respect of the proceedings;
- (b) the circumstances in which the client may be liable to pay the fees and expenses of the legal representative in accordance with the agreement;
- (c) the circumstances in which the client may be liable to pay the costs of any other party to the proceedings; and
- (d) the circumstances in which the client may seek taxation of the fees and expenses of the legal representative and the procedure for so doing.

Application of regulation 4

5.   Regulation 4 shall not apply to an agreement between a legal representative and an additional legal representative.

Form of agreement

6.   An agreement shall be in writing and, except in the case of an agreement between a legal representative and an additional legal representative, shall be signed by the client and the legal representative.

Amendment of agreement

7. Where it is proposed to extend the agreement to cover further proceedings or parts of them regulations 3 to 6 shall apply to the agreement as extended.

The Conditional Fee Agreements Regulations 2000

Citation, commencement and interpretation

1.(1) These Regulations may be cited as the Conditional Fee Agreements Regulations 2000.

(2)   These Regulations come into force on 1 April 2000.

(3)   In these Regulations—

    'client' includes, except where the context otherwise requires, a person who—

      (a)   has instructed the legal representative to provide the advocacy or litigation services to which the conditional fee agreement relates, or

      (b)   is liable to pay the legal representative's fees in respect of those services; and

    'legal representative' means the person providing the advocacy or litigation services to which the conditional fee agreement relates.

Requirements for contents of conditional fee agreements: general

2.(1)   A conditional fee agreement must specify—

    (a)   the particular proceedings or parts of them to which it relates (including whether it relates to any appeal, counterclaim or proceedings to enforce a judgment or order),

    (b)   the circumstances in which the legal representative's fees and expenses, or part of them, are payable,

    (c)   what payment, if any, is due—

      (i)   if those circumstances only partly occur,

      (ii)   irrespective of whether those circumstances occur, and

      (iii)   on the termination of the agreement for any reason, and

    (d)   the amounts which are payable in all the circumstances and cases specified or the method to be used to calculate them and, in particular, whether the amounts are limited by reference to the damages which may be recovered on behalf of the client.

(2)   A conditional fee agreement to which regulation 4 applies must contain a statement that the requirements of that regulation which apply in the case of that agreement have been complied with.

Requirements for contents of conditional fee agreements providing for success fees

3.(1)   A conditional fee agreement which provides for a success fee—

    (a)   must briefly specify the reasons for setting the percentage increase at the level stated in the agreement, and

    (b)   must specify how much of the percentage increase, if any, relates to the cost to the legal representative of the postponement of the payment of his fees and expenses.

(2)   If the agreement relates to court proceedings, it must provide that where the percentage increase becomes payable as a result of those proceedings, then—

    (a)   if—

      (i)   any fees subject to the increase are assessed, and

(ii)   the legal representative or the client is required by the court to disclose to the court or any other person the reasons for setting the percentage increase at the level stated in the agreement,

he may do so,

(b)   if—

(i)   any such fees are assessed, and

(ii)   any amount in respect of the percentage increase is disallowed on the assessment on the ground that the level at which the increase was set was unreasonable in view of facts which were or should have been known to the legal representative at the time it was set,

that amount ceases to be payable under the agreement, unless the court is satisfied that it should continue to be so payable, and

(c)   if—

(i)   sub-paragraph (b) does not apply, and

(ii)   the legal representative agrees with any person liable as a result of the proceedings to pay fees subject to the percentage increase that a lower amount than the amount payable in accordance with the conditional fee agreement is to be paid instead,

the amount payable under the conditional fee agreement in respect of those fees shall be reduced accordingly, unless the court is satisfied that the full amount should continue to be payable under it.

(3)   In this regulation 'percentage increase' means the percentage by which the amount of the fees which would be payable if the agreement were not a conditional fee agreement is to be increased under the agreement.

Requirements where the client's liability is limited to sums recovered

3A.(1)   This regulation applies to a conditional fee agreement under which, except in the circumstances set out in paragraph (5) and (5A), the client is liable to pay his legal representative's fees and expenses only to the extent that sums are recovered in respect of the relevant proceedings, whether by way of costs or otherwise.

(2)   In determining for the purposes of paragraph (1) the circumstances in which a client is liable to pay his legal representative's fees and expenses, no account is to be taken of any obligation to pay costs in respect of the premium of a policy taken out to insure against the risk of incurring a liability in the relevant proceedings.

(3)   Regulations 2, 3 and 4 do not apply to a conditional fee agreement to which this regulation applies.

(4)   A conditional fee agreement to which this regulation applies must—

(a)   specify—

(i)   the particular proceedings or parts of them to which it relates (including whether it relates to any appeal, counterclaim or proceedings to enforce a judgment or order); and

(ii)   the circumstances in which the legal representative's fees and expenses, or part of them, are payable; and

(b)   if it provides for a success fee—

(i)   briefly specify the reasons for setting the percentage increase at the level stated in the agreement; and

(ii)   provide that if, in court proceedings, the percentage increase becomes payable as a result of those proceedings and the legal representative or the client is ordered to disclose to the court or any other person the reasons for setting the percentage increase at the level stated in the agreement, he may do so.

(5)   A conditional fee agreement to which this regulation applies may specify that the client will be liable to pay the legal representative's fees and expenses whether or not sums are recovered in respect of the relevant proceedings, if the client—

(a)   fails to co-operate with the legal representative;

(b)   fails to attend any medical or expert examination or court hearing which the legal representative reasonably requests him to attend;

(c)   fails to give necessary instructions to the legal representative;

(d)   withdraws instructions from the legal representative;

(e)   is an individual who is adjudged bankrupt or enters into an arrangement or a composition with his creditors, or against whom an administration order is made; or

(f)   is a company for which a receiver, administrative receiver or liquidator is appointed.

(5A)   A conditional fee agreement to which this regulation applies may specify that, in the event of the client dying in the course of the relevant proceedings, his estate will be liable for the legal representative's fees and expenses, whether or not sums are recovered in respect of those proceedings.

(6)   Before a conditional fee agreement to which this regulation applies is made, the legal representative must inform the client as to the circumstances in which the client or his estate may be liable to pay the legal representative's fees and expenses, and provide such further explanation, advice or other information as to those circumstances as the client may reasonably require

Information to be given before conditional fee agreements made

4.(1)   Before a conditional fee agreement is made the legal representative must—

(a)   inform the client about the following matters, and

(b)   if the client requires any further explanation, advice or other information about any of those matters, provide such further explanation, advice or other information about them as the client may reasonably require.

(2)   Those matters are—

(a)   the circumstances in which the client may be liable to pay the costs of the legal representative in accordance with the agreement,

(b)   the circumstances in which the client may seek assessment of the fees and expenses of the legal representative and the procedure for doing so,

(c)   whether the legal representative considers that the client's risk of incurring liability for costs in respect of the proceedings to which agreement relates is insured against under an existing contract of insurance,

(d)   whether other methods of financing those costs are available, and, if so, how they apply to the client and the proceedings in question,

(e)   whether the legal representative considers that any particular method or methods of financing any or all of those costs is appropriate and, if he considers that a contract of insurance is appropriate or recommends a particular such contract—

(i)   his reasons for doing so, and

(ii)   whether he has an interest in doing so.

(3)   Before a conditional fee agreement is made the legal representative must explain its effect to the client.

(4)   In the case of an agreement where—

(a)   the legal representative is a body to which section 30 of the Access to Justice Act 1999 (recovery where body undertakes to meet costs liabilities) applies, and

(b)   there are no circumstances in which the client may be liable to pay any costs in respect of the proceedings, paragraph (1) does not apply.

(5) Information required to be given under paragraph (1) about the matters in paragraph (2)(a) to (d) must be given orally (whether or not it is also given in writing), but information required to be so given about the matters in paragraph (2)(e) and the explanation required by paragraph (3) must be given both orally and in writing.

(6) This regulation does not apply in the case of an agreement between a legal representative and an additional legal representative.

Form of agreement

5.(1) A conditional fee agreement must be signed by the client and the legal representative.

(2) This regulation does not apply in the case of an agreement between a legal representative and an additional legal representative.

Amendment of agreement

6. Where an agreement is amended to cover further proceedings or parts of them—

    (a)   regulations 2, 3, 3A and 5 apply to the amended agreement as if it were a fresh agreement made at the time of the amendment, and

    (b)   the obligations under regulation 4 apply in relation to the amendments in so far as they affect the matters mentioned in that regulation.

Revocation of 1995 Regulations

7. The Conditional Fee Agreements Regulations 1995 are revoked.

Exclusion of collective conditional fee agreements

8. These Regulations shall not apply to collective conditional fee agreements within the meaning of regulation 3 of the Collective Conditional Fee Agreements Regulation 2000.

The Collective Conditional Fee Agreements Regulations 2000[444]

Citation, commencement and interpretation

1.(1) These regulations may be cited as the Collective Conditional Fee Agreements Regulations 2000, and shall come into force on 30 November 2000.

(2) In these Regulations, except where the context requires otherwise—

    'client' means a person who will receive advocacy or litigation services to which the agreement relates;
    'collective conditional fee agreement' has the meaning given in regulation 3;
    'conditional fee agreement' has the same meaning as in section 58 of the Courts and Legal Services Act 1990;
    'funder' means the party to a collective conditional fee agreement who, under that agreement, is liable to pay the legal representative's fees;
    'legal representative' means the person providing the advocacy or litigation services to which the agreement relates.

---

[444] The CCFA Regulations 2000 have been amended twice, by the Conditional Fee Agreements (Miscellaneous Amendments) Regulations 2003 (SI 2003/1240) and the Conditional Fee Agreements (Miscellaneous Amendments) (No 2) Regulations 2003 (SI 2003/3344); this is the most up-to-date version (prior to revocation).

Transitional provisions

2. These Regulations shall apply to agreements entered into on or after 30 November 2000, and agreements entered into before that date shall be treated as if these Regulations had not come into force.

Definition of 'collective conditional fee agreement'

3.(1) Subject to paragraph (2) of this regulation, a collective conditional fee agreement is an agreement which—

(a)   disregarding section 58(3)(c) of the Courts and Legal Services Act 1990, would be a conditional fee agreement; and

(b)   does not refer to specific proceedings, but provides for fees to be payable on a common basis in relation to a class of proceedings, or, if it refers to more than one class of proceedings, on a common basis in relation to each class.

(2)   An agreement may be a collective conditional fee agreement whether or not—

(a)   the funder is a client; or

(b)   any clients are named in the agreement.

Requirements for contents of collective conditional fee agreements: general

4.(1)   A collective conditional fee agreement must specify the circumstances in which the legal representative's fees and expenses, or part of them, are payable.

(1A)   The circumstances referred to in paragraph (1) may include the fact that the legal representative's fees and expenses are payable only to the extent that sums are recovered in respect of the proceedings, whether by way of costs or otherwise.

(2)   A collective conditional fee agreement must provide that, when accepting instructions in relation to any specific proceedings the legal representative must—

(a)   inform the client as to the circumstances in which the client or his estate may be liable to pay the costs of the legal representative; and

(b)   if the client requires any further explanation, advice or other information about the matter referred to in sub-paragraph (a), provide such further explanation, advice or other information about it as the client may reasonably require.

(3)   Paragraph (2) does not apply in the case of an agreement between a legal representative and an additional legal representative.

(4)   A collective conditional fee agreement must provide that, after accepting instructions in relation to any specific proceedings, the legal representative must confirm his acceptance of instructions in writing to the client.

Requirements for contents of collective conditional fee agreements providing for success fees

5.(1)   Where a collective conditional fee agreement provides for a success fee the agreement must provide that, when accepting instructions in relation to any specific proceedings the legal representative must prepare and retain a written statement containing—

(a)   his assessment of the probability of the circumstances arising in which the percentage increase will become payable in relation to those proceedings ('the risk assessment');

(b)   his assessment of the amount of the percentage increase in relation to those proceedings, having regard to the risk assessment; and

(c)   the reasons, by reference to the risk assessment, for setting the percentage increase at that level.

(2)   If the agreement relates to court proceedings it must provide that where the success fee becomes payable as a result of those proceedings, then—

(a)   if—
- (i)   any fees subject to the increase are assessed, and
- (ii)   the legal representative or the client is required by the court to disclose to the court or any other person the reasons for setting the percentage increase at the level assessed by the legal representative,

he may do so,

(b)   if—
- (i)   any such fees are assessed by the court, and
- (ii)   any amount in respect of the percentage increase is disallowed on the assessment on the ground that the level at which the increase was set was unreasonable in view of facts which were or should have been known to the legal representative at the time it was set

that amount ceases to be payable under the agreement, unless the court is satisfied that it should continue to be so payable, and

(c)   if—
- (i)   sub-paragraph (b) does not apply, and
- (ii)   the legal representative agrees with any person liable as a result of the proceedings to pay fees subject to the percentage increase that a lower amount than the amount payable in accordance with the conditional fee agreement is to be paid instead,

the amount payable under the collective conditional fee agreement in respect of those fees shall be reduced accordingly, unless the court is satisfied that the full amount should continue to be payable under it.

(3) In this regulation 'percentage increase' means the percentage by which the amount of the fees which would have been payable if the agreement were not a conditional fee agreement is to be increased under the agreement.

(4) Sub-paragraphs (b) and (c) of paragraph (2) do not apply to a collective conditional fee agreement under which, except in the circumstances set out in paragraph (6) and (7), the client is liable to pay his legal representative's fees and expenses only to the extent that sums are recovered in respect of the proceedings, whether by way of costs or otherwise.

(5) In determining for the purposes of paragraph (4) the circumstances in which a client is liable to pay his legal representative's fees and expenses, no account is to be taken of any obligation to pay costs in respect of the premium of a policy taken out to insure against the risk of incurring a liability in the relevant proceedings.

(6) A collective conditional fee agreement to which paragraph (4) applies may specify that the client will be liable to pay his legal representative's fees and expenses whether or not sums are recovered in respect of the relevant proceedings, if the client—

(a)   fails to co-operate with the legal representative;

(b)   fails to attend any medical or expert examination or court hearing which the legal representative reasonably requests him to attend;

(c)   fails to give necessary instructions to the legal representative;

(d)   withdraws instructions from the legal representative.

(e)   is an individual who is adjudged bankrupt or enters into an arrangement or a composition with his creditors, or against whom an administration order is made; or

(f)   is a company for which a receiver, administrative receiver or liquidator is appointed.

(7) A collective conditional fee agreement to which paragraph (4) applies may specify that, in the event of the client dying in the course of the relevant proceedings, his estate will be liable for the legal representative's fees and expenses, whether or not sums are recovered in respect of those proceedings.

Form and amendment of collective conditional fee agreement

6.(1)   Subject to paragraph (2), a collective conditional fee agreement must be signed by the funder, and by the legal representative.

(2)   Paragraph (1) does not apply in the case of an agreement between a legal representative and an additional legal representative.

(3)   Where a collective conditional fee agreement is amended, regulations 4 and 5 apply to the amended agreement as if it were a fresh agreement made at the time of the amendment.

Chapter 10

ERRORS IN RETAINERS

10.1 This chapter addresses the question of how a retainer containing an error can be managed. Its focus is necessarily on the remedial steps that a receiving party (or his legal representative) may take. The topic is dealt with in three parts:

- the position between solicitor and client;
- remedial steps that may be taken before the entitlement to costs has arisen; and
- remedial steps that may be taken after the entitlement to costs has arisen.

The words 'remedy' and 'remedial' are used loosely and refer to solutions and palliations, rather than any formal notion of legal remedy.

THE POSITION BETWEEN SOLICITOR AND CLIENT

10.2 Subject to any contrary statutory, common law or regulatory provision, the counterparties may agree to be bound by any obligations that they care to negotiate; this means that (in principle) there is no reason why a retainer cannot be repaired or replaced with retrospective effect. Some of these issues have already been discussed in the chapter on conditional fee agreements (**9.408–9.420**). There are, however, two aspects of the matter that merit further scrutiny. The first is the issue of undue influence, and the second that of consideration.

Undue influence

10.3 Where a legal representative believes that his retainer is at risk of being unenforceable, he may ask his client to take steps to remedy the situation (either by rectifying or amending the defective retainer, or by entering into a replacement retrospective retainer). In most cases the client would be asked voluntarily to assume a liability that otherwise he might not have had; all other things being equal, this might be seen as asking the client to agree to act against his own rational self-interest.

10.4 In the absence of justification, these circumstances could give rise to a defence on the part of the client of 'undue influence'. Undue influence is a ground of relief developed by the courts of equity; the objective is to ensure that the influence of one person over another is not abused. If a party enters into a transaction in the context of a relationship of trust and confidence, the law may scrutinise the manner in which the agreement to enter into the transaction was obtained; the purpose of this would be to gauge whether the transaction arose by reason of an abuse of that relationship. If the transaction was procured by unacceptable means, the law will not permit it to stand.[1]

---

[1] *Huguenin v Baseley* (1807) 14 Ves 273 at 300.

10.5 Undue influence may be actual or presumed. Presumed undue influence arises in certain classes of relationship between two persons in which one has acquired over another a measure of influence, or ascendancy; where those are the circumstances the ascendant person is then in a position to take unfair advantage.[2] A solicitor and client relationship is an example of such a relationship.[3] In the context of solicitor and client, an irrebuttable presumption of influence will apply.[4]

10.6 Unlike actual undue influence (where something has to be done to twist the mind of a complainant), presumed undue influence may arise as a result of inactivity, ie once the relationship of trust has been demonstrated to exist, the issue may turn on what has *not* been done, such as impartial advice not having been given to the client.[5]

10.7 The court may conclude that there is no undue influence if the client's decision was as a result of 'ordinary motives';[6] Christopher Clarke J found that a willingness on the part of a client to assist in the recovery of costs from a paying party can be said to arise from ordinary motives:[7]

> 'The ordinary motives of ordinary persons do not exclude doing the decent thing, even if some persons would not be minded to do so.'

Notwithstanding the fact that he found that there had been no undue influence in the case before him, he found that there was no reason in principle why a paying party should not be able to assert that there has been undue influence.[8]

10.8 A retainer obtained as a result of undue influence is voidable, not void. It remains effective until it is set aside; such relief may be given on terms (such as payment of a reasonable sum for services actually rendered).[9] Christopher Clarke J declined (obiter) to hold that a failure by a solicitor to put his client's interests first would have the effect of making any retainer resulting from that failure into a prohibited contract; he commented that such a finding would have an effect of which Draco would have approved, and that it would give rise to a myriad of disputes.[10] It is implicit in those comments that a party who seeks to rely on undue influence is likely to face an uphill struggle.

10.9 It has been said that Christopher Clarke J's attention was not drawn to the long line of authorities (predating statutory intervention concerning business agreements) which dealt with the way in which the common law viewed agreements that attempted to restrict a client's right to an assessment. Those authorities supposedly demonstrate that the common law often found such agreements to be unenforceable, this being on bases that were almost indistinguishable from presumed undue influence.[11] It was generally

---

2   *Royal Bank of Scotland v Etridge (No 2)* [2002] 2 AC 773 at [8]–[18].
3   This was accepted before Christopher Clarke J in *Forde v Birmingham City Council* [2009] EWHC 12 (QB).
4   *Royal Bank of Scotland v Etridge (No 2)* [2002] 2 AC 773 at [18] and *Willis v Barron* [1902] AC 271, HL.
5   *Daniel v Drew* [2005] EWCA 507.
6   See *National Westminster Bank plc v Morgan* [1985] AC 686 at 704, approved in *Etridge* and applied in *Forde v Birmingham City Council* [2009] EWHC 12 (QB).
7   *Forde v Birmingham City Council* [2009] EWHC 12 (QB) at [106].
8   *Forde v Birmingham City Council* [2009] EWHC 12 (QB) at [110]; whilst it is not wholly clear from the judgment, it seems that Christopher Clarke J made these comments after having had his attention drawn (at [114]) to *Garbutt v Edwards* [2006] 1 WLR 2907.
9   See *Forde v Birmingham City Council* [2009] EWHC 12 (QB) at [111], citing *Johnson v EBS Pensioner Trustees Ltd* [2002] EWCA Civ 164 and *O'Sullivan v Management Agency & Music Ltd* [1985] 1 QB 429.
10 *Forde v Birmingham City Council* [2009] EWHC 12 (QB) at [114].
11 See **8.118–8.120**.

not the retainers themselves that were found to be unenforceable, however, but the agreements as to the way in which the costs were to be quantified; it is, therefore, debatable whether Christopher Clarke J would have derived much assistance from those authorities.

10.10 Christopher Clarke J found that there is nothing unfair about a solicitor asking for payment of his fees, this having the effect of rendering the Unfair Terms in Consumer Contracts Regulations 1999[12] irrelevant.[13] His decision was limited to the facts of the case before him, but it is difficult to imagine circumstances when a similar conclusion would not also be inevitable.

10.11 In summary, it will not commonly be the case that a legal representative will be found guilty of undue influence for asking a client to remedy a defective retainer.

Consideration

10.12 There is nothing objectionable in principle with a legal representative and client agreeing that one retainer should be replaced with another. The fact that the solicitor would continue to act for the client would, in general, be consideration.[14] Likewise, if the second retainer is on terms more favourable to the client than the first, that would amount to consideration.[15]

10.13 If they were concerned about consideration, the counterparties would be at liberty to make the replacement retainer by way of deed; that would remove the need for consideration entirely. This is briefly discussed below (**10.18** *et seq*).

---

[12] SI 1999/2083.

[13] *Forde v Birmingham City Council* [2009] EWHC 12 (QB) at [158]–[162].

[14] The notion of the continued provision of legal services amounting to good consideration is nothing new: see Duke LJ's dissenting judgment in *Wild v Simpson* [1919] 2 KB 544; in a more modern context, see *Forde v Birmingham City Council* [2009] EWHC 12 (QB) at [81]–[92].

[15] *Forde v Birmingham City Council* [2009] EWHC 12 (QB) at [81]–[92]; Clarke J distinguished *Foakes v Beer* (1884) 9 App Cas 605; he relied on the reasoning in *Williams v Roffey Bros & Nicholls (Contractors) Ltd* [1991] 1 QB 1, in which the following comments were made: 'Consideration there must still be but, in my judgment, the courts nowadays should be more ready to find its existence so as to reflect the intention of the parties to the contract.'

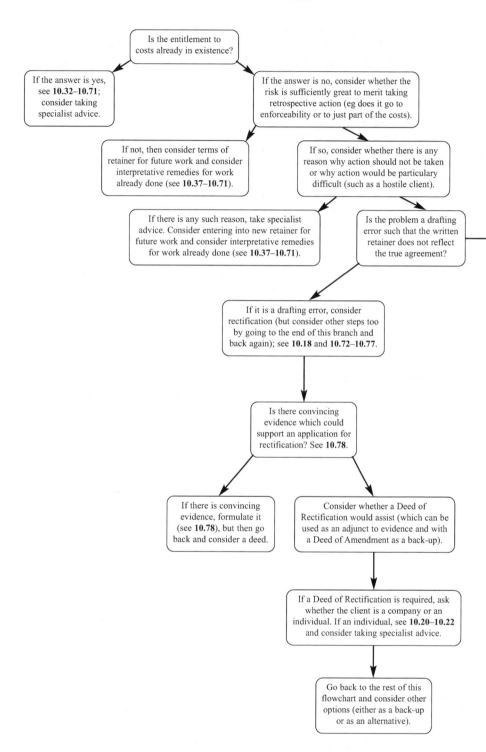

Is the entitlement to costs already in existence?

If the answer is yes, see **10.32–10.71**; consider taking specialist advice.

If the answer is no, consider whether the risk is sufficiently great to merit taking retrospective action (eg does it go to enforceability or to just part of the costs).

If not, then consider terms of retainer for future work and consider interpretative remedies for work already done (see **10.37–10.71**).

If so, consider whether there is any reason why action should not be taken or why action would be particulary difficult (such as a hostile client).

If there is any such reason, take specialist advice. Consider entering into new retainer for future work and consider interpretative remedies for work already done (see **10.37–10.71**).

Is the problem a drafting error such that the written retainer does not reflect the true agreement?

If it is a drafting error, consider rectification (but consider other steps too by going to the end of this branch and back again); see **10.18** and **10.72–10.77**.

Is there convincing evidence which could support an application for rectification? See **10.78**.

If there is convincing evidence, formulate it (see **10.78**), but then go back and consider a deed.

Consider whether a Deed of Rectification would assist (which can be used as an adjunct to evidence and with a Deed of Amendment as a back-up).

If a Deed of Rectification is required, ask whether the client is a company or an individual. If an individual, see **10.20–10.22** and consider taking specialist advice.

Go back to the rest of this flowchart and consider other options (either as a back-up or as an alternative).

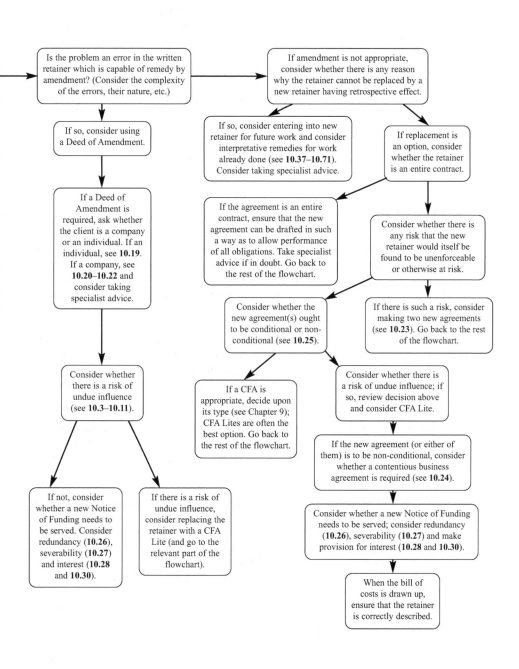

Is the problem an error in the written retainer which is capable of remedy by amendment? (Consider the complexity of the errors, their nature, etc.)

If so, consider using a Deed of Amendment.

If a Deed of Amendment is required, ask whether the client is a company or an individual. If an individual, see **10.19**. If a company, see **10.20–10.22** and consider taking specialist advice.

Consider whether there is a risk of undue influence (see **10.3–10.11**).

If not, consider whether a new Notice of Funding needs to be served. Consider redundancy (**10.26**), severability (**10.27**) and interest (**10.28** and **10.30**).

If there is a risk of undue influence, consider replacing the retainer with a CFA Lite (and go to the relevant part of the flowchart).

If amendment is not appropriate, consider whether there is any reason why the retainer cannot be replaced by a new retainer having retrospective effect.

If so, consider entering into new retainer for future work and consider interpretative remedies for work already done (see **10.37–10.71**). Consider taking specialist advice.

If the agreement is an entire contract, ensure that the new agreement can be drafted in such a way as to allow performance of all obligations. Take specialist advice if in doubt. Go back to the rest of the flowchart.

Consider whether the new agreement(s) ought to be conditional or non-conditional (see **10.25**).

If a CFA is appropriate, decide upon its type (see Chapter 9); CFA Lites are often the best option. Go back to the rest of the flowchart.

If replacement is an option, consider whether the retainer is an entire contract.

Consider whether there is any risk that the new retainer would itself be found to be unenforceable or otherwise at risk.

If there is such a risk, consider making two new agreements (see **10.23**). Go back to the rest of the flowchart.

Consider whether there is a risk of undue influence; if so, review decision above and consider CFA Lite.

If the new agreement (or either of them) is to be non-conditional, consider whether a contentious business agreement is required (see **10.24**).

Consider whether a new Notice of Funding needs to be served; consider redundancy (**10.26**), severability (**10.27**) and make provision for interest (**10.28** and **10.30**).

When the bill of costs is drawn up, ensure that the retainer is correctly described.

REMEDIAL STEPS WHICH MAY BE TAKEN BEFORE THE ENTITLEMENT TO COSTS HAS ARISEN

10.14 The following paragraphs examine the way in which a retainer can be amended or replaced in the event of it being found to be at risk; the focus is on contentious business, but most of the points which are made will also apply to retainers for non-contentious business.

10.15 The principles are broadly the same regardless of the type of retainer in question. Where the replacement retainer is a conditional fee agreement that provides for a success fee, thought ought to be given to the likelihood of recovering the success fee (see **30.103–30.111**).

10.16 Whilst each case must be considered on its own facts, the process for finding the appropriate remedy may be summarised by the flowchart above (which is not intended to be a substitute for specialist advice, but merely an aid to management in less complex cases).

10.17 As can be seen, many of the relevant issues are dealt with elsewhere in this book. The 'interpretative remedies' are discussed in the next section. The remaining topics are briefly addressed here.

Rectification by deed

10.18 If the error is simply a typographical or printing error, then it may be possible to rectify the agreement by way of a deed of rectification. This is different from rectifying on evidence (see **10.72**). It is also different from amending (or varying) a document: rectification will apply where the written instrument contains a mistake which must be rectified so as to reflect the true agreement between the counterparties whereas an amendment will change that agreement itself.

10.19 Formalities apply to rectification by deed (**10.19–10.21**). In respect of deeds made by an individual, the old common law requirements concerning the types of materials on which a deed must be written how it must be sealed have been abolished.[16] As of 31 July 1990, where the deed is made by an individual, the statutory requirements found in s 1 of the 1989 Act state:

- that the deed makes it clear on its face that it is intended to be a deed by the person making it or, as the case may be, by the parties to it (whether by describing itself as a deed or expressing itself to be executed or signed as a deed or otherwise);
- that it is validly executed as a deed:
  - (i) by that person or a person authorised to execute it in the name or on behalf of that person, or
  - (ii) by one or more of those parties or a person authorised to execute it in the name or on behalf of one or more of those parties;
- that it has been signed by the individual in the presence of a witness who attests the signature (or at his direction and in his presence and the presence of two witnesses who each attest the signature); and
- that it is delivered as a deed.

---

[16]   Law of Property (Miscellaneous Provisions) Act 1989 (as amended), s 1(1).

10.20 The position concerning registered companies (including LLPs) is more complex, as the common law continues to apply, rather than the less complex statutory provisions set out above. Moreover, the Memoranda and Articles of Association may prescribe additional formalities.[17] Under the common law, a deed made by a company must be made under seal, but the effect of this requirement is significantly diminished by the fact that a company registered under the Companies Act 1985 is no longer required to have a common seal.[18] Generally speaking, where a deed has been signed by a director and the secretary of a company or by two directors, and where it has been expressed to be executed by the company, that document has the same effect as if it had executed under the common seal of the company.

10.21 Other formalities exist.[19] In view of the fact that the exact formality requirements may depend on the type of corporation and in what is written in the Memoranda and Articles of Association (or other document setting out the constitution or the corporation), advice must be taken before a deed is executed on behalf of a corporation.

10.22 Finally, care also ought to be taken to ensure that any formalities are complied with in respect of the rectified agreement; in theory, rectification will operate *ab initio*, but a cautious legal representative would wish to work on the basis that the effect of the deed may be unintentionally to create an amendment or even a new retainer. Therefore, it may be necessary to consider whether Notice of Funding ought to be (re-)served. For older matters it may be necessary to consider the potential effect of the Conditional Fee Agreements Regulations 2000.

One retainer or two

10.23 (The discussion at **10.23–10.29** should be read in conjunction with the diagram referred to at **10.16**.) Where there is a possibility that the retrospective element of the replacement retainer may be unlawful or unenforceable (perhaps because of an unusual aspect of the case which makes a finding of undue influence a real possibility), thought ought to be given to making two replacement retainers rather than one. The first retainer (which is often a contentious business agreement) would apply to costs which have already been incurred, and the second (which is often a CFA Lite, but can be any type of contractual retainer) would apply to costs yet to be incurred. Many combinations of retainer are available.

Contentious business agreement or other type of agreement

10.24 Each case will turn on its own facts but, generally speaking, where the new retainer is not intended to be a conditional fee agreement, then it would be sensible to enter into a contentious business agreement rather than a non-statutory (ie ordinary) private retainer. This is because there is express statutory provision which confirms that a contentious business agreement may be retrospective.[20]

---

[17] See *Clarke v Imperial Gas Light and Coke Co* (1832) 4 B & Ad 315 at 324.
[18] See s 36A of that Act.
[19] See, for example, the Law of Property Act 1925, s 74A (as amended).
[20] See s 59(1) of the Solicitors Act 1974.

Conditional or non-conditional replacement

10.25 Where the original retainer is a conditional fee agreement, thought should be given to whether the replacement is to be a conditional or non-conditional retainer. If the reality is that the success fee is not likely to be recovered and if the reality is that the condition of a 'win' is almost certainly going to be met, then the counterparties may prefer to enter into a retrospective contentious business agreement (**10.24**) rather than run the risk, however slight, that the court might find some difficulty arising out of the use of a conditional fee agreement.

Redundancy

10.26 Consideration ought to be given to incorporating redundant (ie a back-up) provisions in the replacement retainer; this can be done in one of two ways. The first is to stipulate that if the replacement is found to be unenforceable, inapplicable, or void, then the counterparties agree to rely on the original retainer as if the changes had never been made.[21] The second approach is to make the replacement itself redundant in the sense that it comes into play only if a finding is made that the original retainer is found to be unenforceable, inapplicable, or void; this is not recommended as it may lead to the replacement retainer being formed only after the entitlement to costs has arisen (see **10.32** *et seq*).

Severability clauses, assignment clauses, etc

10.27 Thought ought to be given to including a severability clause. The replacement retainer is likely to be the subject of intense scrutiny, and as such, it is best to make sure that it is as robust as possible. As such, it is normally advisable to include provisions concerning all eventualities, such as assignment, insolvency, jurisdiction, etc (see **8.90–8.102**).

Interest

10.28 The original retainer may have made provision for the payment of interest in the event of non-payment; if this is the case, then it may be necessary to make provision within the new retainer for ensuring that that liability does not arise solely by reason of the client's willingness to assist his legal representatives.

Consumer regulations

10.29 Replacement retainers are often made at arm's length, so there is the possibility that distance selling regulations may apply (see **8.377** *et seq*). At the other end of the spectrum, a legal representative may be so keen to ensure that the client co-operates that he may visit the client at home; where this happens, doorstep selling regulations may come into play (**8.324** *et seq*).

10.30 It is easy for a busy and hard-pressed generalist to make mistakes when dealing with these issues; it would usually be sensible to take specialist advice, but this should be done in full recognition of the fact that the costs of that advice are not likely to be recovered from an opposing party. A receiving party would be well advised not to claim

---

[21]   See, for example, *Forde v Birmingham City Council* [2009] EWHC 12 (QB) at [79]–[80].

the costs of taking remedial steps in the bill of costs as this may give the paying party an unwelcome insight into the receiving party's affairs.

10.31 A final point is that it would be improper to submit a bill of costs which gives a misleading impression: CPD, art 4.5(3) requires that the bill of costs should set out 'a brief explanation of any agreement or arrangement between the receiving party and his solicitors which affects the costs claimed in the bill'. Although there is no authority on the point, common sense dictates that that requirement should not be interpreted so narrowly as to mislead by omission.

REMEDIAL STEPS WHICH MAY BE TAKEN AFTER THE ENTITLEMENT TO COSTS HAS ARISEN

10.32 If the entitlement to costs has already crystallised, there is not a great deal that can usefully be done to change the retainer. This is because any changes would usually be ineffective as against the paying party. Whilst not binding, Lord Carswell has explained this principle:[22]

> 'It was quite open to the [receiving party] and his attorneys to vary the fee agreement ... if they so wished ... If, however, [the variations] were likely to produce a larger costs bill than the original framework ... the [paying party] would be entitled simply to refuse to accept the amended basis and require the respondent to revert to the original framework ... [The paying party] could do so on the ground ... that that amendment had come into existence subsequent to the making of the costs basis and so could be disregarded by the paying party if he wished.'

10.33 It is not wholly clear how the law works to have this effect; the following are both plausible mechanisms:

- that the making of a costs order crystallises the entitlement to costs at the time that it was made, so any subsequent increase in the costs would be irrelevant; and
- that changing the retainer after the entitlement to costs has arisen is unreasonable and gratuitous, so any costs which are supposedly incurred or restored by that change must be disallowed on the basis of reasonableness.

10.34 Where a party finds himself with a potentially defective retainer in circumstances in which he has already become entitled to costs, there are, for all practical purposes, only two ways in which he might be able to recover costs. Firstly, he could try to persuade the court that the retainer is enforceable and effective, and secondly, he could attempt to recover costs by some other mechanism.

10.35 The second of these options can be addressed in short order. Rare situations aside,[23] the only mechanism by which costs may be recovered independently of the retainer is by quantum meruit. This topic is addressed at **11.77–11.84**. As can be seen, quantum meruit is rarely available in the context of a failed retainer.

---

[22]   *Kellar v Williams (Appeal No 13 of 2003)* [2004] UKPC 30 at [20].

[23]   Such as set-off of costs against monies owed by the solicitor to the client; the arguments are complex: *Cosslett (Contractors) Ltd v Bridgend County Borough Council* [2001] UKHL 58 would be a good place to start.

10.36 This means that the receiving party must concentrate on seeking costs under the retainer, either by persuading the court to interpret the contract of retainer in a way that is favourable to him, or by asking the court to rectify the agreement upon evidence. The inelegant term 'interpretative remedy' has been applied to the first of these options, but perhaps the term 'remedy of construction' is better. Rectification will rarely be appropriate where the right to costs has already crystallised, but – for the sake of completeness – it is discussed at the end of this chapter (**10.72** *et seq*).

The remedy of construction

10.37 The term 'remedy of construction' is used merely to describe the process of interpreting a putatively defective retainer is such a way as to permit the recovery of costs. It is not a remedy in the sense that equity uses that term. The discussion in this book is only the briefest of introductions; texts on contractual interpretation ought to be consulted for a full discussion of that topic.

The interpretative approach in general

10.38 Where a contract permits of more than one interpretation, and where one of the competing interpretations would produce a contract that would be unenforceable or unlawful, then the court will, in general, prefer a competing interpretation that does not lead to this result.[24] In so far as costs litigation is concerned, this is relevant because the court has repeatedly confirmed that it is legitimate to interpret a contract of retainer as part of the process of deciding whether it is enforceable. This topic has already been addressed at **9.138–9.147**, where, in the context of regulatory compliance, it was referred to as 'prior interpretation'; it is addressed here in more general terms. It is an example of the court taking into account the state of the law as being part of the background against which the retainer is to be interpreted, this being a well-established method by which (in the words of Lord Hoffmann) the court 'takes into account that the parties are unlikely to have intended to agree to something unlawful or legally ineffective'.[25] This is discussed in more detail at **10.43–10.45**.

10.39 An example of prior interpretation is *Tichband v Hurdman*,[26] in which the Court of Appeal resolved a conflict between what was said in the body of a conditional fee agreement and what was said in the risk assessment; the court applied the Conditional Fee Agreements Regulations 2000 ('the CFA Regulations 2000') to the agreement as interpreted, thereby saving the agreement. The court considered the enforceability of the retainer not on the basis of what it said upon its face in literal terms, but on the basis of what – roperly interpreted – it was understood to mean. Other examples exist.[27]

10.40 Having established that prior interpretation is a legitimate judicial tool, it is useful to rehearse one or two of the basic principles of contractual interpretation. The basic method of contractual interpretation was explained by Lord Hoffmann in the seminal case of *Investors Compensation Scheme v West Bromwich Building Society*:[28]

---

24 See, for example, *Kredietbank Antwerp v Midland Bank plc* [1998] Lloyd's Rep Bank 173; see also *Solly v Forbes* (1820) 2 Brod & Bing 38 at 48 and *Haigh v Brooks* (1839) 10 Ad & El 309.

25 *Bank of Credit and Commerce International SA (in liquidation) v Ali* [2001] UKHL 8 at [39].

26 [2003] 1 WLR 2487.

27 See, for example, *Jones v Wrexham Borough Council* [2007] EWCA Civ 1356; for an example of the limits of the approach of prior interpretation, see *Jones v Caradon Catnic Ltd* [2005] EWCA Civ 1821.

28 [1998] 1 WLR 896, HL at 912.

'(1) Interpretation is the ascertainment of the meaning which the document would convey to a reasonable person having all the background knowledge which would reasonably have been available to the parties in the situation in which they were at the time of the contract.

(2) The background was famously referred to by Lord Wilberforce as the "matrix of fact", but this phrase is if anything an understated description of what the background may include. Subject to the requirement that it should be reasonably available to the parties and to the exception mentioned next, it includes absolutely anything which would have affected the way in which the language of the document would have been understood by a reasonable man.

(3) The law excludes from the admissible background the previous negotiations of the parties and their declarations of subjective intent. They are admissible only in an action for rectification. The law makes this distinction for reasons of practical policy and, in this respect only legal interpretation differs from the way we interpret utterances in ordinary life ...

(4) The meaning which a document (or any other utterance) would convey to a reasonable man is not the same thing as the meaning of its words. The meaning of words is a matter of dictionaries and grammars; the meaning of a document is what the parties using those words against the relevant background would reasonably have been understood to mean ...

(5) The rule that words should be given their "natural and ordinary meaning" reflects the common-sense proposition that we do not easily accept that people have made linguistic mistakes, particularly in formal documents. On the other hand, if one would nevertheless conclude from the background that something must have gone wrong with the language, the law does not require judges to attribute to the parties an intention which they plainly could not have had ...'

10.41 In the context of the interpretation of retainers, the avoidance of unreasonable results and the notion that the contract should make commercial sens e may be of particular relevance.[29] Speaking in the context of a commercial matter, Lord Diplock said:[30]

'If a detailed semantic and syntactical analysis of words in a commercial contract is going to lead to a conclusion that flouts business common sense, it must be made to yield to business common sense.'

In similar vein, Lord Bingham said this:[31]

'The task of the court is to ascertain and give effect to the intentions of the contracting parties, so that a business sense will be given to business documents ... [The court] must seek to give effect to the contract as intended, so as not to frustrate the reasonable expectations of businessmen.'

10.42 The court will strive to interpret a contract (including a contract of retainer) in such a way as to be commercially coherent while seeking to avoid a plainly unreasonable result; Lord Reid had this to say on the point:[32]

---

[29] As an example of this, see *Manning v Kings College Hospital NHS Trust* [2011] EWHC 2954 (QB) (see **30.26**).

[30] *Antaios Compania Naviera v Salen Rederierna* [1985] AC 191 at 221.

[31] *The Starsin* [2004] 1 AC 715, HL at [9]–[12].

[32] *L Schuler AG v Wickman Machine Tools Sales Ltd* [1974] AC 235.

'The fact that a particular construction leads to a very unreasonable result must be a relevant consideration. The more unreasonable the result the more unlikely it is that the parties can have intended it, and if they do intend it the more necessary it is that they shall make that intention abundantly clear.'

The court will avoid an interpretation that renders the contract ineffective; speaking in the context of offers rather than retainers, Rix LJ had this to say:[33]

'Another principle or maxim of construction . . . is that words should be understood in such a way that the matter is effective rather than ineffective (*verba ita sunt intelligenda ut res magis valeat quam pereat*) . . . There are numerous instances of the application of this maxim. This is how *Chitty on Contracts*, 30th ed, 2008, Vol 1, at para 12-081 refers to this rule:

> "If the words used in an agreement are susceptible of two meanings, one of which would validate the instrument or the particular clause in the instrument, and the other render it void, ineffective or meaningless, the former sense is to be adopted. This rule is often expressed in the phrase ut res magis valeat cum [sc. quam] pereat. Thus, if by a particular construction the agreement would be rendered ineffectual and the apparent object of the contract would be frustrated, but another construction, though by itself less appropriate looking to the words only, would produce a different effect, the latter interpretation is to be applied, if that is how the agreement would be understood by a reasonable man with a knowledge of the commercial purpose and background of the transaction. So, where the words of a guarantee were capable of expressing either a past or a concurrent consideration, the court adopted the latter construction, because the former would render the instrument void. If one construction makes the contract lawful and the other unlawful, the former is to be preferred ...".'

10.43 The court can take into account only that 'knowledge which would reasonably have been available to the parties in the situation in which they were at the time of the contract'.[34] These background facts may include the state of the law.[35] Lord Hoffmann has commented (obiter) that the parties are unlikely to have intended to agree to something that was inherently unlawful or legally ineffective;[36] those comments often have particular resonance where the dispute concerns the enforceability of a retainer, especially where the challenge is brought by a stranger to the contract (ie the paying party).

10.44 Notwithstanding the court's desire to avoid unreasonable results, Peter Gibson LJ has reminded himself that there are limits to the extent that the court is able to depart from what is written in the instrument of the contract:[37]

'The court is entitled to look at those consequences because the more extreme they are, the less likely it is that commercial men will have intended an agreement with that result. But the court is not entitled to rewrite the bargain which they have made merely to accord with what the court thinks to be a more reasonable result.'

---

[33]   *C v D* [2011] EWCA Civ 646 at [55].
[34]   *Zoan v Rouamba* [2000] 2 All ER 620 at [36]; that said, see *White v White* [2001] UKHL 9, [2001] 2 All ER 43.
[35]   *Zoan v Rouamba* [2000] 2 All ER 620 at [36].
[36]   *Bank of Credit and Commerce International SA (in liquidation) v Ali* [2001] UKHL 8 at [39].
[37]   *Kazakstan Wool Processors (Europe) Ltd v Nederlandsche Credietverzekering Maatschappij* [2000] 1 All ER (Comm) 708 at 719.

Thus, the court is not entitled to rewrite the contract. That said, where appropriate, the court may be inclined to generosity in this regard.[38]

10.45 Where there are competing interpretations and where one of the interpretations may lead to a commercially sound result (such as a retainer being enforceable), the court will usually prefer the commercially coherent result over an incoherent result (such as a retainer being unenforceable). The court will seek to avoid any interpretation which destroys the contract.[39]

Inconsistent terms

10.46 A problem that often arises in the context of costs litigation is where the retainer contains an inconsistent term; this usually happens because standard terms and conditions have been unthinkingly incorporated without the drafter standing back to look at the effect of the totality of his efforts. Steyn J had this to say about the issue of inconsistent terms (albeit in a context other than costs litigation):[40]

> 'This question must be approached on the basis that the court's duty is to reconcile seemingly inconsistent provisions if that result can conscientiously and fairly be achieved.'

Likewise, Rix LJ endorsed the following extract from a well-known textbook:[41]

> 'The court is reluctant to hold that parts of a contract are inconsistent with each other, and will give effect to any reasonable construction which harmonises such clauses.'

10.47 Where there are inconsistent terms, the first port of call will be the retainer itself: many retainers will make express provision for the resolution of conflicts caused by drafting errors. Indeed, standard terms often contain a provision which expressly defers to the instrument into which they have been incorporated.

10.48 In any event, the court will strive to give effect to the term which records the true intentions of the counterparties.[42] Whilst they should not be afforded the status of rules and should always be viewed in the context of Lord Hoffmann's guidance, a number of principles can be stated. They are as follows.

Bespoke terms

10.49 Generally speaking, where a standard term conflicts with a bespoke term, the latter will prevail.[43] Thus, if the body of a client care letter provides for one hourly rate, but standard terms and conditions provide for a different hourly rate, the former will usually prevail over the latter.

---

[38] As an example of this, see *Manning v Kings College Hospital NHS Trust* [2011] EWHC 2954 (QB) (see **30.26**).

[39] See, for example, *Kredietbank Antwerp v Midland Bank plc* [1998] Lloyd's Rep Bank 173.

[40] *The Brabant* [1967] 1 QB 588 at 589.

[41] *C v D* [2011] EWCA Civ 646 at [51], endorsing Lewison, *The Interpretation of Contracts* (4th edn, 2004) at para 9.13

[42] *Love v Rowtor Steamship Co Ltd* [1916] 2 AC 527 at 535.

[43] *Glynn v Margetson & Co* [1893] AC 351; see also *Robertson v French* (1803) 4 East 130; compare this with *Smith v Royce Properties Ltd* [2001] EWCA 949, in which Tuckey LJ was careful to point out that there is no presumption of law.

Incorporation

10.50 In a similar vein, where a contract incorporates the terms of another document and the terms of that other document conflict with the terms of the contract, the terms of the contract will generally prevail.[44]

Term repugnant to the contract as a whole

10.51 Where a term is repugnant to the contract as a whole, it may, in appropriate circumstances, be rejected.[45] In the context of costs, an example might be where a typographical error has led to a supposed hourly rate of nil.

Later repugnant clause

10.52 Where a clause in a contract is followed by a later clause which destroys the effect of the first clause, the later clause is generally rejected as repugnant. If, however, the later clause can be read as qualifying rather than destroying the effect of the first clause, then the two are to be read together and effect given to both.[46] An example might be where a non-contentious retainer makes provision for payment by way of an hourly rate and a value charge, but where that provision is supposedly destroyed by a later clause which provides for payment on the basis of just an hourly rate. If the latter seemingly destroyed the entitlement to the value charge, then the former would probably prevail, but if they were capable of being read together, the former would probably be read as if it had been qualified by the latter.

Terms as to quantum

10.53 A contract which provides for two mutually inconsistent measures of quantum is not unusual (in the context of costs, this could be where it provides for two inconsistent hourly rates). It is usually possible to decide that one is to be preferred over the other without the contract itself being at risk.[47] This may be relevant if it is argued that the retainer is void for uncertainty.

Costs case examples

10.54 Most authorities relate to contracts other than retainers, but there are one or two examples that relate specifically to contracts of retainer. For example, Hodge J had to decide what to make of a conditional fee agreement that had been adapted to provide for a bespoke definition of 'win' with such ineptitude that term was afforded two mutually inconsistent definitions. Hodge J resolved the conflict by preferring the interpretation which best suited the unusual purpose to which the retainer had been put; as a result, the costs were recoverable in accordance with the true intentions of the counterparties.[48]

---

[44] See the comments of Buckley LJ in *Modern Building Wales Ltd v Limmer and Trinidad Co Ltd* [1975] 1 WLR 1281, CA; see also *Sabah Flour and Feed Mills Sdn Bhd v Comfez Ltd* [1988] 2 Lloyd's Rep 18, CA, and *Adamastos Shipping Co Ltd v Anglo-Saxon Petroleum* [1959] AC 133 at 178.

[45] *Adamastos Shipping Co Ltd v Anglo-Saxon Petroleum* [1959] AC 133; see also *Glynn v Margetson & Co* [1893] AC 351, per Lord Halsbury, LC.

[46] *Forbes v Git* [1922] 1 AC 256, per Lord Wrenbury.

[47] *Love v Stewart Ltd v Rowtor Steamship Co Ltd* [1916] 2 AC 527, HL.

[48] *Wood v Worthing & Southlands Hospitals NHS Trust* (unreported) 18 October 2004, QBD, Hodge J. Another similar example has already been mentioned at **10.38**.

10.55 In summary, where terms are inconsistent, it is often possible to choose between them in such a way as to give effect to the true intentions of the counterparties.

Ambiguous terms

10.56 Ambiguous terms are more troublesome; this is because the court's task is often more complex and nuanced than merely choosing between two competing terms. The principles are as set out at **10.39–10.45**. There are many rules and examples that may be found in textbooks on contract, but the reality is that each case will be decided on its own facts.

10.57 It will often be the case that ambiguity arises only by reason of a microscopic forensic examination of the retainer by a paying party. Where this is the case, it may be appropriate to ensure that the examination of the retainer does not descend into an inappropriate level of detail. Speaking in a context other than costs, Neill LJ indicated:[49]

> 'Construction is a composite exercise neither uncompromisingly literal nor unswervingly purposive. The instrument must speak for itself but must do so in situ and not be transported to the laboratory for microscopic analysis.'

Those comments may well have resonance in cases where the facts cry out for a common sense approach rather than an overly legalistic one.

10.58 Another principle which may occasionally be of assistance is *contra proferentem*;[50] this principle (which is not a rule of law, but merely an aid to interpretation) is that where a contract is ambiguous, the ambiguity should be resolved against the proferens (ie the person who drafted it).[51] In the context of retainers that will almost always be the legal representative. It is very much a principle of last resort.[52]

Mistakes

10.59 The principles discussed in this section have been described as 'common law rectification';[53] they are to be distinguished from the principles discussed at **10.72–10.80** on equitable rectification, which are entirely different.

10.60 If there has been an obvious mistake, the court may be able to interpret the contract in such a way as to disregard it; non-costs examples include where the contract named the wrong party,[54] or where it mis-named one of the parties.[55] Brightman LJ had this to say on the topic:[56]

> 'It is clear on the authorities that a mistake in a written instrument can, in limited circumstances, be corrected as a matter of construction without obtaining a decree in an action for rectification. Two conditions must be satisfied: first, there must be a clear mistake

---

[49]   *International Fina Services AG v Katrina Shipping Ltd, The Fina Samco* [1995] 2 Lloyd's Rep 344 at 350; see also *Sinochem v Mobil* [2000] 1 All ER (Comm) 474.

[50]   'Against (*contra*) the one bringing forth (the *proferens*)'.

[51]   See *Tam Wing Chuen v Bank of Credit and Commerce Hong Kong Ltd* [1996] 2 BCLC 69; see also para 7(2) of Unfair Terms in Consumer Contracts Regulations 1999 (SI 1999/2083).

[52]   *Sinochem v Mobil* [2000] 1 All ER (Comm) 474 at 483.

[53]   G McMeel *The Construction of Contracts* (Oxford, 2007), paras 17.02–17.20.

[54]   *Wilson v Wilson* (1854) 5 HL Cas 40.

[55]   *Nittan (UK) Ltd v Solent Steel Fabrications Ltd* [1981] 1 Lloyd's Rep 633.

[56]   *East v Pantiles Plant Hire Ltd* [1982] 2 EGLR 111 at 116.

on the face of the instrument: secondly, it must be clear what correction ought to be made in order to cure the mistake. If those conditions are satisfied, then the correction is made as a matter of construction. If they are not satisfied, then either the Claimant must pursue an action for rectification or he must leave it to a court of construction to reach what answer it can on the basis that the uncorrected wording represents the manner in which the parties decided to express their intention.'

10.61 As has been discussed above, the court tends to prefer a commercially coherent interpretation to an incoherent and unreasonable one, and Lord Steyn has confirmed that it is open to the court, in appropriate cases, to conclude that the parties must, for whatever reason, have used the wrong words or syntax.[57] It may even be possible for the court to read a contract as if it contained a name which had been omitted from the final draft.[58]

10.62 Where a term has been mistakenly incorporated and where that term is inconsistent with the specific purpose of the contract, the court may decline to give that term effect, Lord Halsbury said:[59]

'Looking at the whole of the document, and seeing what one must regard ... as its main purpose, one must reject words, indeed whole provisions, if they are inconsistent with what one assumes to be the main purpose of the contract.'

Thus, if a retainer mistakenly contained a provision which suggested that legal services would be provided for no charge, the court may, in appropriate circumstances, decline to give effect to that provision.

10.63 The court recognises that mistakes may easily arise in complex documents drafted at short notice;[60] some retainers are certainly complex, and in the context of commercial litigation, they may also be entered into with considerable urgency.

Missing terms

10.64 A retainer may be challenged on the basis that an essential term (such as a term which identifies the counterparties) is absent. This may be particularly relevant where a term is required for the purposes of complying with the Conditional Fee Agreements Regulations 2000 ('CFA Regulations 2000').

10.65 By analogy with cases relating to formalities of other types of written instrument, it is not always the case that detail is required if the requisite elements can be implied. In some cases it may be possible for the court to find that, because the parties are identified, other details are to be implied.[61] This can be of use where the 'retainer' is little more than an introductory letter. In other circumstances it may be sufficient to identify the subject matter of the contract in order to allow other details to be implied.[62] In so far as the CFA Regulations 2000 are concerned, this approach has its limitations; this is because many of those regulations require that the agreement

---

[57]   *Mannai Investment Co Ltd v Eagle Star Life Assurance Co Ltd* [1997] 3 All ER 352, cited with approval by Lord Hoffmann in *ICS v West Bromwich Building Society* [1998] 1 WLR 896, HL at 912.
[58]   Although now a very old case, see *Lord Say and Seals Case* (1711) 10 Mod Rep 40; see also *Protank Shipping Inc v Total Transport Corpn, The Protank Orinoco* [1997] 2 Lloyd's Rep 42 at 46.
[59]   *Glynn v Margetson & Co* [1893] AC 351.
[60]   *Static Control Components (Europe) Ltd v Egan* [2004] EWCA Civ 392.
[61]   *Potter v Duffield* (1874) LR 18 Eq 4 and *Rossiter v Miller* (1878) 3 App Cas 1124.
[62]   *Caddick v Skidmore* (1857) 2 De G&J 52 and *Plant v Bourne* [1897] 2 Ch 281.

'specifies' certain things: Brooke LJ has explained that the word 'specify' is to be read as meaning that the thing must be stated explicitly.[63]

10.66 In contexts far removed for the law of costs, the court has permitted counterparties to demonstrate compliance with formalities by the related mechanisms of 'waiver' and 'submission'. These concepts are mentioned more for the sake of completeness than because they are likely to be of practical relevance. Where a requisite term has been omitted and where that term would have been entirely in favour of one of the counterparties, that person may 'waive' the benefit of the omitted term and enforce the contract notwithstanding the omission.[64] This concept is of limited use in the context of costs because material terms may not be waived.[65] The converse of waiver is submission: where, if it had been included, an omitted term would have been wholly for another person's benefit, a person may submit to that term as if it had been included.[66] it is possible that such an analysis may be of use if a receiving party seeks to waive or submit for the purposes of demonstrating compliance with the indemnity principle, but such analyses would be entirely unsupported by any prior authority and, in any event, would add very little to the other analyses mentioned above.

Joinder

10.67 A useful judicial tool is the ability of the court to take other written instruments into account when construing the retainer; this is based on the premise that where documents form part of the same transaction, they should be interpreted together.[67]

10.68 Although this facility has only recently been affirmed in the context of a retainer,[68] it is by no means a new concept; indeed, it is a well-established principle, and has even come to the aid of counterparties in the face of legislation which expressly contemplated the inclusion of all the relevant terms in one document.[69]

10.69 Ideally, where documents are to be joined, one document should refer to the other,[70] but if this is not the case, it may be possible to introduce oral or other evidence to establish the nexus.[71]

10.70 Costs examples exist.[72] Whilst it was based on a concession, Mann J accepted that a letter could be joined to a conditional fee agreement for the purposes of complying with a requirement of the CFA Regulations 2000.[73]

---

[63] See the comments of Brooke LJ in *Hollins v Russell* [2003] EWCA Civ 718 at [125], in which he drew upon *BWE International Ltd v Jones* [2003] EWCA Civ 298 at [29] as being an example of that approach.

[64] *North v Loomes* [1919] 1 Ch 378.

[65] *Hawkins v Price* [1947] Ch 645.

[66] For obvious reasons, such an approach would not find universal favour, as is evidenced by the fact that, even in contexts other than costs, it is a principle which is often rejected by the court: see *Martin v Pycroft* (1852) 2 De GM&G 785; *Burgess v Cox* [1951] Ch 383; and *Scott v Bradley* [1971] Ch 850.

[67] *Burchell v Clark* (1876) 2 CPD 88.

[68] *Jones v Wrexham Borough Council* [2007] EWCA Civ 1356; some commentators would disagree with the suggestion that this was an example of joinder.

[69] See, for example, *Pearce v Gardener* [1897] 1 QB 688, in which a letter was coupled with the envelope in which it was delivered.

[70] See, for example, the discussion in *Boydell v Durmmond* (1809) 11 East 142 at 158.

[71] See, for example, the obiter analysis of Jenkins LJ in *Timmins v Moreland Street Property Ltd* [1958] Ch 110 at 120.

[72] *Jones v Wrexham Borough Council* [2007] EWCA Civ 1356 at [17]; other examples exist: whilst ultimately he

Severance

10.71 It is, in principle, open to the court to find that a retainer can be salvaged by the court severing the objectionable part from the unobjectionable remainder. In support of this notion, Christopher Clarke J has made obiter comments to the effect that he could see no reason why, in an appropriate case, the court could not place its blue pencil through the objectionable provision.[74] Most cases will not be appropriate, however. This is because where the retainer is objectionable by reason of it being contrary to public policy, it would – in general – itself be contrary to public policy to permit severance.[75]

Rectification

10.72 Rectification is an equitable remedy which may be available in cases where the written instrument does not accurately record what the counterparties intended it to say; in effect, the court rectifies the document so that it reflects the true intentions of the counterparties. The following paragraphs deal largely with rectification on evidence; rectification by deed is addressed at **10.18–10.22.**

10.73 Cozens-Hardy MR described rectification in this way:[76]

> 'The essence of rectification is to bring the document which was expressed and intended to be in pursuance of a prior agreement into harmony with that prior agreement.'

10.74 It is important to distinguish between rectification and interpretation (or 'common law rectification': see **10.59–10.63**). Where the argument is that the factual circumstances of the case are such that the only reasonable conclusion is that a particular term meant something other than what it at first appears to say, the argument is then one of interpretation rather than rectification. The issue of construction ought to be addressed before any attempt is made to rectify the document.[77] However, there is no reason in principle why the arguments cannot be advanced in the alternative.

10.75 The fact that the antecedent agreement is unenforceable by reason of its failure to comply with a statutory provision will not prevent it from being capable of rectification.[78] It is not known whether the same applies when the issue is whether there has been compliance with regulations concerning retainers.

10.76 The court will grant relief only where relief is required, and will not grant it where it is not required; that said, the fact that there may be no dispute between the counterparties is not a bar to the granting of relief.[79] (This will often be relevant in the

---

came to the conclusion that the agreement was unenforceable, Blake J took into account a letter which had been sent to the client at about the same time as the conditional fee agreement was made: *Utting v McBain* [2007] EWHC 3293 (QB) at [21]–[24].

[73]   *Fenton v Holmes* [2007] EWHC 2476 (Ch) at [24]–[27].

[74]   *Forde v Birmingham City Council* [2009] EWHC 12 (QB) at [151], relying on *The Great Peace* [2002] EWCA Civ 14 and *Brennan v Bolt Burdon* [2004] EWCA Civ 1017.

[75]   See *Aratra Potato Co Ltd v Taylor Joynson-Garrett* [1995] 4 All ER 695 at 701, per Garland J; see also *Awwad v Geraghty* [2001] QB 570 at 600, where Shiemann LJ noted that it would be contrary to public policy to go beyond that which Parliament has provided. Whilst not binding, see *Oyston v The Royal Bank of Scotland plc* [2006] EWHC 90053 (Costs) at [54].

[76]   *Lovell and Christmas Ltd v Wall* (1911) 104 LT 85.

[77]   *Sloggett and Perry v Stroud* (unreported) 25 May 2000, Chadwick LJ at para 19.

[78]   See *United States v Motor Trucks Ltd* [1924] AC 196.

[79]   See *Seymour v Seymour* (1989) *The Times*, February 16.

context of costs because the dispute is frequently brought on by a stranger to the contract, rather than by the counterparties themselves.)

10.77 The remedy of rectification will not extend to subject matter that the parties did not consider at the time the contract was made; this is so even if it can be shown that they *would* have come to the requisite agreement *if* they had turned their minds to the matter.[80] In practical terms, this often presents a considerable obstacle in costs cases; this is because the 'mistaken' provision in the antecedent document is often, in truth, a consequence of a lack of intention rather than an inaccurately expressed intention.

10.78 The antecedent document will not be ignored, and 'convincing proof' is required to contradict it.[81] Again, this may cause difficulties in the context of costs: if, for example, the correspondence was vague and inconclusive, a claim for rectification may fail for want of evidence as to what the parties really meant by their agreement.

10.79 Rectification may not be available where it impinges upon the rights of a third party. There is a respectable argument for saying that this would include the paying party.[82] However, where the interest has not been acquired for value, a claim for rectification would not necessarily be defeated by the existence of a third party.[83] The issue of whether rectification is available for the purposes of restoring a paying party's liability arising out of a mistaken retainer is very much a moot point.[84]

10.80 In summary, rectification is fraught with legal difficulties and it is often challenging from the factual point of view; it really is an option of last resort.

---

[80] See *Harlow Development Corpn v Kingsgate (Clothing Productions) Ltd* (1973) 226 EG 1960.

[81] *Thomas Bates v Wyndham's (Lingerie) Ltd* [1981] 1 WLR 505 at 521.

[82] In particular (and in addition to the principles already mentioned arising from *Kellar*, etc), the court will not rectify a document where a third party has purchased an interest for value without notice (*Garrard v Frankel* (1862) 30 Beav 445), and the provision of an indemnity by a third party may qualify as an interest (see *Nurdin & Peacock plc v DB Ramsden & Co* [1999] 1 All ER 941).

[83] See *Load v Green* (1846) 15 M & W 216.

[84] Irwin J was asked to express an obiter view on this issue, but he declined, presumably because he felt that the issue merited more than just an obiter comment: *Crook v Birmingham CC* [2007] EWHC 1415 (QB).

Chapter 11

THE INDEMNITY PRINCIPLE

THE INDEMNITY PRINCIPLE IN GENERAL

11.1 The indemnity principle may be summarised in the following way:[1] an order for costs between parties allows the receiving party to claim from the paying party only an indemnity in respect of the costs covered by the order; receiving parties may not recover a sum in excess of their liability to their own legal advisors, experts, etc.

Historical perspective

11.2 Although the origins of the indemnity principle go back into antiquity,[2] its modern form was first expounded in 1860, when Bramwell B said:[3]

> 'Costs as between party and party are given by the law as an indemnity to the person entitled to them; they are not imposed as a punishment on the party who pays them, nor given as a bonus to the party who receives them. Therefore, if the extent of damnification can be found out, the extent to which costs ought to be allowed is also ascertained.'

This laid down the principle that a litigant should not profit from litigation.

11.3 A decade later, this principle was given statutory force when the following provision was enacted:[4]

> 'The client who has entered into such [an] agreement shall not be entitled to recover from any other person under any order for the payment of any costs which are the subject of such agreement more than the amount payable by the client to his own attorney or solicitor under the same'.

A provision not dissimilar to this provision remains on the statute books today (albeit only in relation to contentious business agreements).[5]

11.4 At the turn of the twentieth century the Court of Appeal found that the rule laid down by Bramwell B had remained undisturbed for 50 years and that it should not be disturbed. Fletcher Moulton LJ found that, while not purely declaratory, the statutory

---

[1] The definition is adapted from that given in *Practice Direction (Taxation: Indemnity Principle)* [1998] 1 WLR 1674.

[2] See, for example, Pollock's Act, which provided that parties should be entitled to recover 'such full and reasonable indemnity as to all costs, charges, and expenses incurred in and about any action, suit or other legal proceedings as shall be taxed by the proper officer on that behalf'.

[3] *Harold v Smith* (1860) 5 H&N 381 at 385.

[4] Section 5 of the Attorneys and Solicitors Act 1870 (33 & 34 Vict c 28).

[5] Section 60(3) of the Solicitors Act 1974.

provision referred to above was a statutory expression of settled common law principle.[6] By that stage, the indemnity principle had become established as the bedrock upon which other costs law was based.

An attenuating principle?

11.5   It is often said that the indemnity principle is a doctrine undergoing a long process of attenuation.[7] As is discussed below, there is certainly some truth in that in the sense that statute has intervened to disapply the indemnity principle in certain specified circumstances. Some liability insurers have agreed to an informal code by which challenges to the indemnity principle must be brought within a very narrow window of opportunity.[8] It is also true to say that there is no judicial appetite for some of the more ruthless challenges brought by paying parties. Nonetheless, there are those who make out a powerful case for cherishing certain aspects of the indemnity principle. Speaking extrajudicially, Sir Anthony May, President of the Queen's Bench Division, remarked:[9]

> 'I rather think that a plea for reasonable costs, unrelated to a commercial rate or amount which is agreed to be payable by the client to the lawyer, risks steering the boat towards at least one whirlpool. In a world of "no win no fee" agreement, where is the measure of what are reasonable costs? Up to now, the main reference for what is reasonable is that which lawyers charge their clients in the market place ... If there were no such market, what is the measure of reasonableness?'

Thus, there are those in senior judicial posts who wish to preserve the indemnity principle for the purposes of maintaining some linkage between what is allowed between opposing parties and what the market in general will bear.[10]

11.6   Notwithstanding this, in the late 2000s there were plans to abrogate the indemnity principle entirely. Speaking extrajudicially, Jackson LJ explained that this proposal was for a number of reasons, but, in particular, he was concerned about satellite litigation 'with no perceptible benefit either to court users or to society'. He proposed that CPR, r 44.4(1) be amended so as to make it clear that costs would be assessed by reference to reasonableness and, where appropriate, proportionality rather than also by reference to the contractual relations between the receiving party and his legal advisors. That proposal was not implemented, but it is possible that this was due to lack of time rather than for policy reasons.

---

[6]   *Gundry v Sainsbury* [1910] 1 KB 645 at 651.

[7]   See, for example, the comments of Gray J in *Kitchen v Burwell Reed & Kinghorn Ltd* [2005] EWHC 1771 (QB) at [29].

[8]   The Personal Injury Multi-Track Code (2008) is a collaborative initiative between the Association of Personal Injury Lawyers, the Forum of Insurance Lawyers, various liability insurers and the Motor Insurers' Bureau; it applies to most personal injury claims (excluding asbestos claims and clinical negligence) where the accident occurred after 1 July 2008 and damages are expected to be over £250,000. Paragraphs 5.1 and 5.2 provide that challenges may be made only within 28 calendar days of the letter of claim.

[9]   Costs Conference, Cardiff, 19 June 2009.

[10]   There are those who say that this view is misguided because it fails to take into account the fact that litigation is increasingly conducted on a CFA Lite basis (where there is no linkage at all between the amount the court allows and the amount the client would have been prepared to pay out of his own pocket). That criticism is misplaced: this is because Sir Anthony May was not suggesting that it is desirable to have linkage in every case, but merely that there needs to be a sufficient prevalence of linkage to afford the court some measure of what is and is not reasonable.

No profit

11.7   Despite the fact that the indemnity principle is rarely employed for the purposes of defeating a claim for unjust remuneration, the court has repeatedly emphasised its role of preventing parties from profiting from litigation.[11] That principle of restraint seems to have developed hand-in-hand with other principles of restraint, namely, that not all losses incurred as a result of litigation will be afforded the status of costs (see **5.3–5.4)**, and that the court will assess costs rather than charges (see **5.6)**.

Principle of individual application

11.8   By the end of the twentieth century the indemnity had become well established as a general concept. What remained unclear was whether the indemnity principle operated only as a cap on the overall figure as assessed, or whether it applied to each individual item in a bill of costs. The answer is the latter: May LJ found that the proper application of the indemnity principle demands that the court looks at the detail of the work done rather than merely the total.[12] In particular, the hourly rate between the parties should never exceed that charged to the client.

11.9   The principle of individual application applies not only to formal written retainers, but also where other relationships exist between legal advisor and client, and this is so even where there is an unwritten agreement or an understanding arising from a long-standing relationship. Tucker J explained the rationale for this:[13]

> 'It is desirable that there should be uniformity in approaches to taxation, and highly undesirable and confusing for different approaches to be adopted according to whether any agreement can be brought within the statutory definition of a [contentious business agreement].'

11.10   The principle of individual application will usually present no conceptual difficulties; if, for example, the retainer limits the maximum hourly rate payable for the solicitor's work, that agreement will provide both the measure and the ceiling for the hourly rate. Difficulties may arise where the retainer provides for the payment of a single gross sum without specifying how that sum has been calculated; in those circumstances, it might be appropriate to make an apportionment of that sum.[14] An example would be where an order for costs relates to only part of the work done under the retainer.

11.11   The principle of individual application ought not to be carried to extremes. In a case where a law firm was charging in a foreign currency (Euros), Mann J pragmatically rejected the argument that the indemnity principle required that the costs be paid in the same currency to avoid overpayments arising out of fluctuations in the exchange rate.[15] Moreover, whilst it is a judicial technique that has its limits (see **28.78)**, where the court wishes to allow a composite hourly rate, some judges will occasionally afford themselves a certain amount of leeway (**28.77–28.79)**.

---

[11]   See, for example, *Harold v Smith* (1860) 5 H&N 381 at 385.
[12]   *The General of Berne Insurance Company v Jardine Reinsurance Management Ltd* [1998] 2 All ER 301.
[13]   *Nederlandse Reassurantie Groep Holding N V v Bacon & Woodrow (No 4)* [1998] 2 Costs LR 32.
[14]   See *The General of Berne Insurance Company v Jardine Reinsurance Management Ltd* [1998] 2 All ER 301 at 310, overruling *Universal Thermosensors Ltd v Hibben* (unreported) 6 March 1992, Sir Donald Nicholls V-C.
[15]   *Schlumberger Holdings Ltd V Electromagnetic Geoservices AS* [2009] EWHC 775 (Pat).

Exceptions to the indemnity principle

11.12 Over the years, Parliament has created a number of exceptions to the indemnity principle. Until recently, these exceptions have been limited; they are as follows.

Litigants in person

11.13 The first exception to the indemnity principle was made in April 1976 when the Litigants in Person (Costs and Expenses) Act 1975 came into force; s 1(1) of that Act permitted the recovery of costs by a litigant in person for work that he has carried out himself in pursuance of his case. This was (and still is) an exception to the indemnity principle in the sense that the costs are payable as compensation rather than as an indemnity.

Public funding

11.14 The next exception was made in February 1994 when provision was made for lawyers representing a publicly funded client to recover costs, and to do so regardless of any rule of law which limited the costs recoverable to the amount which the client was liable to pay his legal representatives.[16] This was (and still is) an exception to the indemnity principle in the sense that the costs are limited only by the measure of reasonableness rather than also by the extent of the client's liability for his lawyer's fees.

11.15 A potentially greater but as yet largely unrealised intervention was made on 2 June 2003. This was as a result of the amendment made to s 51(2) of the Senior Courts Act 1981 (as amended),[17] which now reads:

> 'Without prejudice to any general power to make rules of court, such rules may make provision for regulating matters relating to the costs of those proceedings including, in particular, prescribing scales of costs to be paid to legal or other representatives or for securing that the amount awarded to a party in respect of the costs to be paid by him to such representatives is not limited to what would have been payable by him to them if he had not been awarded costs.

Thus, the Rule Committee is given the power to make rules which permit payment of costs which are unfettered by the indemnity principle.

11.16 In the early days following this amendment there was concern about whether the Rule Committee could lawfully be given the vires to interfere with something as fundamental as the indemnity principle;[18] in particular, there were concerns that the Rule Committee was set up to make rules 'governing ... practice and procedure'[19] and that the indemnity principle transcends those things. Those concerns may have hit the mark, because the Rule Committee has so far made only very limited use of this vires. If CPR, Part 45 is put to one side for the moment, the only time that the Rule Committee has used its powers is to make a 'belt-and-braces' provision in respect of CFA Lites.[20]

---

[16] See reg 107B(1), (3)(b) of the Civil Legal Aid (General) Regulations 1989 (SI 1989/339), as amended.

[17] This amendment was effected by s 31 of the AJA 1999 and the Access to Justice Act 1999 (Commencement No 10) Order 2003 (SI 2003/1241), art 2; confusion can arise because it is often the case that a provision is referred to by reference to the Act which made the amendment, rather than to the Act which was amended.

[18] See, for example, Master O'Hare's paper presented to the Costs Forum entitled *In Defence of the Indemnity Principle*, 30 November 2001.

[19] See s 1 of the Civil Procedure Act 1997.

[20] See CPR, r 43.2(3) which provides that: 'Where advocacy or litigation services are provided to a client under a conditional fee agreement, costs are recoverable under Parts 44–48 notwithstanding that the client is liable

11.17 That said, Simon J has relied upon s 51(2) of the Senior Courts Act 1981 (as amended) to dismiss an appeal in which he held that the indemnity principle does not apply where the Rule Committee has made provision for fixed costs.[21]

11.18 Finally, it is worth clarifying that s 51(2) does not permit the Rule Committee to abolish the indemnity principle (as opposed to set it aside in accordance with the provisions of the CPR): it is generally accepted that primary legislation would be required to achieve that purpose.[22]

Agreements to disapply the indemnity principle

11.19 It is possible for the parties to agree to disapply the indemnity principle; where this is done, it would require very clear words before expenditure which a client could not be required to meet under the terms on which he engaged solicitors could nonetheless be recovered from the paying party.[23] Thus, an agreement to disapply the indemnity principle would, in general, not allow a receiving party to claim costs that fell outside the ambit of the agreement with his solicitor.

EVIDENCING THE INDEMNITY PRINCIPLE

11.20 In order to prove compliance with the indemnity principle it is necessary to demonstrate the existence of an enforceable retainer which supports all the costs that are claimed. This can be done in one of two ways:

- by relying upon one or both of two presumptions; or
- by producing evidence (usually, but not necessarily, in the form of a written retainer).

11.21 Three issues need to be addressed. The first is the extent to which a receiving party may rely solely on the presumptions to prove his retainer; the second is the extent to which a receiving party is required to adduce evidence of his retainer; and the third is the way in which the court would weigh any evidence which is adduced.

The two presumptions

11.22 A knowledge of the process of election is assumed. If the reader is not familiar with that process, reference should be made to Chapter 24 before reading the remainder of this chapter. The law relating to non-conditional retainers differs from that relating to conditional fee agreements; each type of retainer is considered separately.

---

to pay his legal representative's fees and expenses only to the extent that sums are recovered in respect of the proceedings, whether by way of costs or otherwise'; it is described as being a 'belt-and-braces' provision because it is far from certain that CFA Lites breach the indemnity principle at all.

[21] *Nizami v Butt* [2006] EWHC 159 (QB).

[22] See, for example, *The Indemnity Principle – Programme of Change* (Lord Chancellor's Department, November 2002).

[23] *Motto & Ors v Trafigura Ltd & Anor (Rev 3)* [2011] EWCA Civ 1150 at [62], per Lord Neuberger MR.

Non-conditional retainers

11.23 There are two presumptions upon which a receiving party may rely; in practice, the second is by far the more important of the two.

11.24 The first presumption is that a client is liable for the fees of a solicitor whom he engages.[24] This presumption is rebuttable by evidence. Lloyd J explained the presumption in these terms:[25]

> 'Once it was shown ... that [the receiving party] was indeed the client, then a presumption arose that he was to be personally liable for the costs. That presumption could, however, be rebutted if it were established that there was an express or implied agreement, binding on the solicitor, that [the receiving party] would not have to pay those costs in any circumstances.'[26]

11.25 This presumption has its limitations, however, and in practice it is not as valuable to receiving parties as it might first appear: these issues are dealt with in more detail at **8.199–8.216**. The presumption is usually taken as being a presumption that goes to the indemnity principle itself: that is, it is usually accepted that proof of the primary fact (that the client has instructed the solicitor) will imply the secondary fact (that there is an enforceable retainer).[27] It is arguable that this is an overly simplistic analysis of the law: it is arguable that the secondary fact is not that there is presumed to be an *enforceable* retainer, but that there is presumed just to be a retainer, and that generally there would be no reason to doubt its enforceability.[28] It can be seen from the cases referred to in Chapter 8 that, in practice, the presumption can be afforded significant weight, but that tends to be only where the facts suggest the existence of a private, contractual retainer. Indeed, one could argue that the presumption is merely a presumption of fact rather than of law; that is, the presumption may merely be an expression of the fact that that where the client has given instructions and has not agreed that the solicitor will go unpaid, those are circumstances which would naturally lend themselves to the existence of an implied but enforceable private retainer.[29]

11.26 The second presumption (which, as already mentioned, is by far the more important of the two) is created by a solicitor lending his signature to the certificate to a bill of costs; in so doing, a presumption is created that there has been no breach of the indemnity principle. An evidential analysis would be that there is a presumption that proof of the primary fact (that the bill of costs has been certified) will imply the secondary fact (that there has been no breach of the indemnity principle), unless the contrary can be shown. The presumption, which is usually referred to as 'the *Bailey*

---

[24] See *Adams v London Improved Motor Builders Ltd* [1921] 1 KB 495 at 501; see also *R v Miller (Raymond)* [1983] 1 WLR 1056 at 1059–1062, which was cited with approval in *Bailey v IBC Vehicles Ltd* [1998] 3 All ER 570 at 574. See also *Hazlett v Sefton Metropolitan Borough Council* [2000] 4 All ER 887.

[25] *R v Miller* [1983] 1 WLR 1057 at 1061; after having been elevated, Lloyd LJ reaffirmed this principle in *Ghadami v Lyon Cole Insurance Group Limited* [2010] EWCA Civ 767 at [10].

[26] The need to show 'an agreement ... not to have to pay those costs in any circumstances' is not a test of universal applicability; it only applies in cases in which the facts imply the existence of a retainer. See the discussion about *Byrne v Kunkel & Kunkel* [1999] 1 CL 349 elsewhere in this work.

[27] See at **11.56**, for example, the way in which Banks LJ developed the notion of implied agency arising out of the fact of instruction by the member of a union. As an extreme example, see *Harrington v Wakeling* [2007] EWHC 1184 (Ch).

[28] Indeed, one could argue that the presumption is merely a presumption of fact rather than of law.

[29] Similar presumptions may arise in the context of conditional fee agreements; thus, the giving of instructions may be evidence of ratifying a collective conditional fee agreement: *Kitchen v Burwell Reed & Kinghorn Ltd* [2005] EWHC 1771 (QB) at [16].

presumption',[30] is rebuttable by evidence, and is probably best described as a rebuttable presumption of law. *Bailey* was a pre-CPR decision, but there is no doubt that it remains good law.[31]

11.27 The effect of the presumption was explained by Henry LJ:[32]

'The Court can (and should unless there is evidence to the contrary) assume that his signature to the bill of costs shows that the indemnity principle has not been offended.'

Henry LJ went on to give his explanation why a solicitors' signature should be given weight:[33]

'In so signing he [the solicitor] certifies that the contents of the bill are correct. That signature is no empty formality ... The signature of the bill of costs under the Rules is effectively the certificate by an officer of the Court that the receiving party's solicitors are not seeking to recover in relation to any item more than they have agreed to charge their client.'

With the benefits bestowed by the *Bailey* presumption come responsibilities, however. This was also explained by Henry LJ:[34]

'[The] other side of a presumption of trust afforded to the signature of an officer of the Court must be that breach of that trust should be treated as a most serious disciplinary offence.'

In a similar vein, Judge LJ emphasised that the responsibility extends to ensuring that the court is not misled:[35]

'As officers of the court, solicitors are trusted not to mislead or to allow the court to be misled. This elementary principle applies to the submission of a bill of costs. If a cap or similar arrangement had applied in this case, I should have expected [the receiving party's solicitors] to have disclosed that fact ...'

11.28 The *Bailey* presumption does not always apply (in the sense that it does not always arise). In particular, it does not apply where costs have been incurred under certain conditional fee agreements (see below). In addition, it may apply, only to be rebutted by evidence. The presumption will not be rebutted merely by putting the receiving party to proof of the secondary fact (ie that there has been no breach of the indemnity principle):[36] instead, a 'genuine issue' (otherwise known as a 'genuine concern') must be made out. This principle was stated by the Divisional Court (Lord Bingham CJ and Harrison J)[37] in a way which has since been approved by the Privy Council.[38] Harrison J, giving the judgment of the court, expounded the principle:[39]

---

30 After *Bailey v IBC Vehicles Ltd* [1998] 3 All ER 570.
31 See, for example, *Burnstein v Times Newspapers Ltd* [2002] EWCA Civ 1739 at [26].
32 *Bailey v IBC Vehicles Ltd* [1998] 3 All ER 570 at 575.
33 *Bailey v IBC Vehicles Ltd* [1998] 3 All ER 570 at 575.
34 *Bailey v IBC Vehicles Ltd* [1998] 3 All ER 570 at 576.
35 *Bailey v IBC Vehicles Ltd* [1998] 3 All ER 570 at 574.
36 *Burnstein v Times Newspapers Ltd* [2002] EWCA Civ 1739 at [28] and *Hazlett v Sefton Metropolitan Borough Council* [2000] 4 All ER 887 at 893.
37 *Hazlett v Sefton Metropolitan Borough Council* [2000] 4 All ER 887.
38 The practice was approved by the Privy Council in *Kellar v Williams* [2004] UKPC 30 at [23].
39 *Hazlett v Sefton Metropolitan Borough Council* [2000] 4 All ER 887 at 893.

'The need for a [receiving party] to give evidence to prove his entitlement to costs rather than relying on the presumption in his favour will not, however, arise if the defendant simply puts the [receiving party] to proof of his entitlement to costs. The [receiving party] would be justified in relying on the presumption in his favour. It would be necessary for the defendant to raise a genuine issue as to whether the [receiving party] is liable for his solicitors' costs before the [receiving party] would be called upon to adduce evidence to show that he is entitled to his costs.'

11.29 The evidence must be sufficient to displace the secondary fact (or at least to question it). There is a dearth of authority on what amounts to a 'genuine issue'; it may be that the absence of authority on the point is a reflection of the fact that the phrase speaks for itself (although another possible explanation is given in the footnotes[40]). It could be argued that the test is that the paying party 'must show that there is a genuine reason for believing that it is not a proper [retainer]' (per Harrison J),[41] ie the paying party must raise a prima facie case. One could raise an equally credible argument that the test is simply that there must be an issue which requires adjudication and that it must be genuine.

11.30 There are one or two case examples that might assist. Where a paying party is able to prove impecuniosity on the part of the receiving party, that will not, of itself, give rise to a genuine issue.[42] The fact that the receiving party has received assistance from a third party (e g where an employer supports an employee by providing the assistance of its in-house legal staff) would not, of itself, be sufficient to amount to a genuine issue.[43] It is, therefore, clear that hopeless arguments would not raise a genuine issue.

Conditional fee agreements

11.31 The first presumption (that the giving of instructions implies the existence of an enforceable retainer) is not capable of applying to conditional fee agreements; this is because there can be no such thing as an enforceable implied conditional fee agreement.[44]

11.32 As to the *Bailey* presumption, the Court of Appeal has found that it should not extend to the written instrument of any agreement made under the Conditional Fee Agreements Regulations 2000. This is discussed at **9.102–9.103**.

Scrutiny by the court

11.33 Although a receiving party may elect not to disclose his retainer to his opponent, he has less freedom in so far as production of the retainer to the court is concerned.

11.34 CPD, art 40.2(i) provides that where there is a dispute about the receiving party's liability to pay costs to his solicitors, a request for a detailed assessment hearing must be

---

[40] The lack of authority could well reflect the fact that if the court where to find a genuine issue and if the receiving party were to be required to adduce evidence of the retainer, the cat would already be out of the bag by that stage, so an appeal would be pointless; as such, the only truly effective appeal would be one brought immediately after the decision to put the receiving party to his election. Such appeals are rare because they usually require the appellant to ask the court below to adjourn pending the appeal, and that is a request that no party would relish making.

[41] *Hazlett v Sefton Metropolitan Borough Council* [2000] 4 All ER 887 at 894.

[42] *Burnstein v Times Newspapers Ltd* [2002] EWCA Civ 1739.

[43] See, for example, *Pepin v Watts* [2002] EWCA Civ 958 at [15]–[19].

[44] This is discussed in detail at **9.299–9.387**.

accompanied by: 'any agreement, letter or other written information provided by the solicitor to his client explaining how the solicitor's charges are to be calculated'. Where a matter is being funded by an insurer, the requisite documents would include those establishing a retainer between a solicitor and an insurer.[45]

11.35 It has been argued that in order for there to be a 'dispute' within the meaning of CPD, art 40.2, the paying party must raise a prima facie case that there has been a breach of the indemnity principle.[46] There is no authority as to whether this argument is correct, nor, in particular, as to whether a 'dispute' would be created by a paying party merely putting the receiving party to proof on the indemnity principle. If there is a need to prove that there is a 'dispute', the requisite threshold is, in practice, a low one.[47]

11.36 It would be possible for a receiving party to refuse to comply with this requirement, but (for obvious reasons) the more a receiving party protests, the more apprehensive both the court and the paying party will become. Depending on how he explains his actions, a receiving party's refusal to give disclosure to the court may result in him being put to his election in relation to the retainer (which would mean that he would have to consider unveiling the retainer to the paying party, as well as to the court).[48] This situation should be distinguished from that where the receiving party elects not to give voluntary disclosure of the retainer to the paying party: common sense dictates that the bare fact of such a refusal is not capable of being the causative reason for putting the receiving party to his election, because that would make the 'genuine issue' test meaningless.

11.37 The act of giving disclosure to the court is different from the act of relying on the retainer; the first is merely the act of offering the document for inspection, the latter is the act of using the document for the purposes of establishing an affirmative case. The former would not entitle the paying party to see the retainer in the same way that the latter would. This issue is considered in detail at **24.6–24.22** and **24.53**.

11.38 In summary, the receiving party would find it difficult to avoid offering up the retainer for inspection by the court, and any attempt to do so would expose the receiving party to the risk of losing credibility.

Procedural issues

11.39 Where the question of a genuine issue is raised by the paying party, the receiving party must be given adequate notice of the points which are going to be taken; Harrison J has explained that that notice should be sufficient to allow the receiving party to deal with the points properly and without the need for an adjournment.[49] It is implicit from the way in which Harrison J dealt with this problem that a paying party would be at risk on costs if the receiving party was taken by surprise.

---

[45] See *Ilangaratne v British Medical Association* [2005] EWHC 1096 (Ch) at [38]–[39].
[46] See *Ilangaratne v British Medical Association* [2005] EWHC 1096 (Ch) at [37].
[47] See *Ilangaratne v British Medical Association* [2005] EWHC 1096 (Ch) at [37], where Warren J found that 'a surprisingly high rate' was sufficient to amount to a dispute.
[48] As an example of the way in which this can happen in practice, see *Ilangaratne v British Medical Association* [2005] EWHC 1096 (Ch).
[49] *Hazlett v Sefton Metropolitan Borough Council* [2000] 4 All ER 887 at 893.

11.40 While it will usually be the paying party who seeks to persuade the court that a genuine issue has been made out, the court is entitled to make such a finding of its own volition, as Lloyd J explained (albeit in the context of the first presumption, rather than the *Bailey* presumption):[50]

> 'In practice, of course, the taxing officer will have before him on the taxation the whole of the solicitor's file. If it appears to the taxing officer that there is doubt whether there was an express or implied agreement, binding on the solicitors, not to seek to recover the cost from the client, the taxing officer should ask for further evidence. It must then be for the taxing officer to come to a conclusion on the whole of the facts presented to him.'

11.41 Indeed, the court is under a duty properly to consider the relevant material, as Judge LJ discussed:[51]

> 'The taxing officer is exercising a judicial function, with substantial financial consequences for the parties. To perform it, he is trusted properly to consider material which would normally be protected from disclosure under the rules of legal professional privilege. If, after reflecting on the material available to him, some feature of the case alerts him to the need to make further investigation or causes him to wonder if the information with which he is being provided is full and accurate, he may seek further information. No doubt he would begin by asking for a letter or some form of written confirmation or reassurance as appropriate. If this were to prove inadequate he might then make orders for discovery or require affidavit evidence. It is difficult to envisage circumstances in which the party benefiting from the order for costs will not have been anxious to provide the required information, but if all else fails, it would theoretically be open to him to order interrogatories.'

11.42 Disclosure, when given, may be in the form of redacted documents.[52] It is implicit from the way in which the Court of Appeal has commented upon redaction that the court ought to be put in a position to decide whether the redaction is fair;[53] common sense dictates that this would usually mean providing an unredacted copy of the retainer for the court.

11.43 As is discussed at **24.58–24.59**, disclosure of the retainer would (with limited exceptions) be for the purposes of the detailed assessment only.

The ethos of the CPR

11.44 For the reasons set out above, both the paying party and the receiving party have certain legal rights which they can enforce if they wish, although the court has repeatedly encouraged parties to act co-operatively and reasonably in resolving any dispute about the indemnity principle. In so far as paying parties are concerned, Judge LJ issued the following guidance:[54]

> 'An emphatic warning must be added against the over enthusiastic deployment of [the court's power to investigate the indemnity principle], particularly at the behest of the party against whom the order for costs has been made ... [The] danger of "satellite litigation" is acute. As far as possible consistent with the need to arrive at a decision which does broad justice

---

50   *R v Miller* [1983] 1 WLR 1057 at 1061.
51   *Bailey v IBC Vehicles Ltd* [1998] 3 All ER 570 at 572.
52   See, for example, *Hollins v Russell* [2003] EWCA Civ 718 at [72].
53   *Hollins v Russell* [2003] EWCA Civ 718 at [80].
54   *Bailey v IBC Vehicles Ltd* [1998] 3 All ER 570 at 573.

between the parties, it must be prevented or avoided, and the additional effort required of the parties kept to the absolute minimum necessary for the taxing officer properly to perform his function.'

It is implicit in this guidance that paying parties should not seek to bring disproportionate challenges.

11.45 Likewise, receiving parties are also encouraged to act in a reasonable and co-operative way by Judge LJ:[55]

> '[In] view of the increasing interest taken in this issue by unsuccessful parties to litigation, coupled with the developing practice in relation to conditional fees, the extension of the "client care" letter and contentious business agreements ... in future, copies of the relevant documents (where they exist) or a short written explanation of the kind eventually provided in this case ... should normally be attached to the bill of costs. This will avoid skirmishes which add unnecessarily to the costs of litigation.'

This means that whilst a receiving party is not legally obliged to disclose evidence of his retainer, he is encouraged to do so. Warren J has suggested that the onus to give voluntary disclosure of the relevant material is even greater under the CPR than it was when *Bailey* was decided.[56]

Evidential issues

11.46 If a receiving party is put to his election in respect of a retainer, he will have to choose whether to rely upon that retainer or whether to prove compliance with the indemnity principle in some other way. There may be entirely valid reasons why a receiving party would choose not to rely upon the retainer itself, in which case evidence will usually be in the form of a witness statement given by the conducting solicitor or the client (or both). That said, if a receiving party fails to explain why he has elected not to rely upon his written retainer, he will (for obvious reasons) have difficulty in discharging the burden of proving that it is enforceable. The fact that a client makes a witness statement evidencing the retainer will not always be sufficient; Scott Baker J has found that a costs judge is, in appropriate circumstances, entitled to view such evidence with some scepticism.[57]

11.47 Where a genuine issue has been made out, it will not necessarily follow that the court will allow a paying party to test the evidence with all the rigour that might be appropriate in substantive litigation. The comments of Judge LJ have already been noted. Other judges have said much the same thing; in a case in which the paying party sought permission to cross-examine the receiving party's solicitor, Latham LJ (giving the judgment of the court) said:[58]

> 'If there is no prospect that cross-examination could either undermine or further elucidate the respondent's case, to refuse to accede to the application will not be unfair and it would not breach the requirement of the overriding objective that the parties are on equal footing but would save expense and deal with the issues proportionately and expeditiously.'

---

55   *Bailey v IBC Vehicles Ltd* [1998] 3 All ER 570, at 575.
56   See *Ilangaratne v British Medical Association* [2005] EWHC 1096 (Ch) at [40].
57   *R (Ecclestone) v Legal Aid Board* [2001] EWHC 9008 (Costs).
58   *Burnstein v Times Newspapers Ltd* [2002] EWCA Civ 1739 at [28].

11.48 Where the receiving party gives disclosure of a retainer at a hearing, and where that disclosure prompts the paying party to raise factual which are contentious and which require determination, Mann J has commented that the receiving party ought to be given adequate time to adduce evidence to prove his case.[59]

11.49 Where the receiving party has been put to his election, the issue is whether he has a liability to his legal representative for costs, not whether he has actually paid those costs. In view of this, it would not usually be the case that a receiving party would be expected to produce evidence of payment. Robert Walker J has suggested (obiter) that there is no automatic right to see solicitor and client invoices.[60] Moreover, where work is done under a private retainer prior to entering into a conditional fee agreement, the fact that invoices are not rendered to clients is not of itself sufficient for the court to infer that there was no enforceable retainer.[61]

11.50 To date, the Court of Appeal has not found it necessary to rule on whether a retainer is a privileged document.[62] Rimer J has suggested that client care letters (or, at least, client care letters that do not give legal advice) are not privileged; that said, those comments were obiter.[63] Given that the process of election operates regardless of whether the retainer is privileged, this point would be academic in most instances.

THE INDEMNITY PRINCIPLE IN PRACTICE

11.51 This section addresses those disputes about the indemnity principle which are focused on issues other than the retainer itself. If the dispute is primarily about the retainer, then the relevant issues are covered in Chapter 8.

Dual liability for costs

11.52 It is often the case that organisations such as legal expense insurers, motoring organisations, unions and employers agree fund litigation on behalf of their clients, members, or employees. The written retainer, if there is one, is often with the funder rather than the litigant. It is not unusual for there to be no written retainer.[64]

11.53 Unless it can be proven that there was an agreement that the litigant would not in any circumstances be liable for the solicitors' costs (or that the retainer is unenforceable for other reasons), there will have been no breach of the indemnity principle.[65] As will be explained in the examples given below, the matter can be analysed either in terms of agency, ratification, or in terms of 'dual liability'. It is the last of these analyses which is usually preferred in practice but, in reality, there is a great deal of overlap between these analyses.

---

59   *Fosberry v HMRC* [2007] EWHC 2249 (Ch) at [46] (this case has also acquired a second Neutral Citation number, that being [2008] EWHC 3344 (Ch) and is also often reported as being [2007] EWHC 3344 (Ch)); see also *Hazlett v Sefton Metropolitan Borough Council* [2000] 4 All ER 887 at 893.
60   In *Mainwaring v Goldtech Investments Ltd* [1997] 1 All ER 467.
61   *Griffiths v Solutia (UK) Ltd* [2001] 1 Costs LR 99 at 106 (this case went on appeal, but not on this point).
62   See *Hollins v Russell* [2003] EWCA Civ 718 at [79].
63   *Dickinson v Rushmer* [2002] 1 Costs LR 128 at 132.
64   See, for example, *Ilangaratne v British Medical Association* [2007] EWHC 920 (Ch) at [30] onwards. See also *Ghadami v Lyon Cole Insurance Group Limited* [2010] EWCA Civ 767, in which the documentation was not complaint with the Solicitors' Code of Conduct 2007.
65   See **11.56**.

11.54 Similar analyses apply to collective conditional fee agreements (which are governed by written instruments that the client often does not see and does not sign). In those circumstances the client's liability will be created as a result of the funder acting within his authority; an alternative view is that the client ratifies the agreement.[66] Provided that the client is aware of the fact that his solicitors are instructed under such an agreement, his acceptance of the solicitors' services will be sufficient to imply that he has ratified or accepted his liability under that agreement.[67]

11.55 The remainder of this discussion is concerned primarily with non-conditional retainers, but many of the principles will also apply to conditional retainers. The topic is dealt with from the viewpoint of a number of different types of funder: unions, insurers, motoring organisations, employers and the state.

Unions

11.56 In the context of a claim funded by a union, Banks LJ offered the following analysis (which is based on agency, but could have been phrased in terms of dual liability):[68]

> 'It is said here that the plaintiff is not in a position to claim an indemnity, for two reasons, as I understand: one is that the firm who purported to act as his solicitors were not his solicitors at all; all they were were the solicitors for the union, and their only instructions were to act as solicitors for the union. The other is that, assuming the union instructed the solicitors to act as solicitors for the plaintiff, yet it was upon the terms that the solicitors should look solely to the union and not to the plaintiff for payment of their costs. Sankey J [the judge below] held that neither contention was well founded upon facts. He came to the conclusion that the solicitors were engaged to act as solicitors for the plaintiff by the union and that in so engaging the solicitors, the union were acting as agents of the plaintiff. In my opinion that view is correct. The learned Judge also found that there had been no arrangement either by the union or by the solicitors or by the plaintiff, that the solicitors should not under any circumstances, look to the plaintiff for payment of their costs. With that conclusion upon the facts I also agree.'

He went on to mention a further step:[69]

> 'When once it is established that the solicitors were acting for the plaintiff with his knowledge and assent, it seems to me that he became liable to the solicitors for costs and that liability would not be excluded merely because the union undertook to pay the costs. It is necessary to go a step further and prove that there was a bargain, either between the union and the solicitors or between the plaintiff and the solicitors, that under no circumstances was the plaintiff to be liable for costs.'

11.57 Although obiter, Atkin LJ analysed the same issue in terms of dual liability (ie where both the funder and the litigant have a liability for the solicitors' fees):[70]

> 'In these circumstances I think that it is highly probable, though the matter has not been discussed, that the solicitors have a personal right against the trade union to receive a proper remuneration for their services. It has not been discussed, and we do not know the precise terms of the relationship between the trade union and the solicitors, but I assume there exists

---

[66] *Thornley v Lang* [2004] 1 WLR 378 at [19].
[67] *Kitchen v Burwell Reed & Kinghorn Ltd* [2005] EWHC 1771 (QB) at [16].
[68] *Adams v London Improved Motor Coach Builders* [1919] 1 KB 495 at 500.
[69] *Adams v London Improved Motor Coach Builders* [1919] 1 KB 495 at 501.
[70] *Adams v London Improved Motor Coach Builders* [1919] 1 KB 495 at 505.

such an obligation. Nevertheless there is nothing inconsistent in that obligation co-existing with an obligation on the part of the plaintiff to remunerate the solicitors.'

11.58 Regardless of how the situation is analysed, the paying party will not usually be able to make out a breach of the indemnity principle. This will not always be the case, however. Although there is some doubt as to whether it remains good law, the court has found that a union was acting as a maintainer in circumstances in which the support that was being provided was not mentioned in the members' handbook.[71] Even if this does remain good law, such cases will be rare.

Insurers

11.59 In a case involving an insurer as funder, it was argued that no costs had been incurred by the successful defendant as the insurer was bound to pay the costs. That argument was rejected; Viscount Dilhorne explained why:[72]

> 'In this case the solicitors, no doubt first instructed by the insurance company, were the solicitors on record as solicitors for the respondent. They acted for him, and in the absence of proof of an agreement between him and them, or between them and the insurance company that he would not pay their costs, they could look to him for payment of the work done and his liability would not be excluded by the fact that the insurance company had itself agreed to pay their costs.'

A similar conclusion is reached when the matter is analysed in terms of subrogation; see **11.64–11.66**. It is not always necessary for the agreement between the insurer and the legal representative to be in writing.[73] Where insurance is subject to an excess, and where that excess is the only amount that that insured has been told he must pay, Lloyd LJ has confirmed that in the absence of agreement to limit the fees to that amount, the indemnity principle will not act as a limit on the sums that must be paid.[74]

Motoring organisations

11.60 A similar conclusion was reached in circumstances where the funder was a motoring organisation; Lord Denning explained:[75]

> '[it was suggested that the fees were not incurred by the receiving party] but were incurred by the Automobile Association because the Automobile Association undertook the appeal and instructed their solicitors and paid them. I cannot accept this suggestion. It is clear that [the receiving party] was in law the party to the appeal. He was the person responsible for the costs. If the appeal had failed, he would be the person ordered to pay the costs. If the costs had not been paid, execution would be levied against him and not against the Automobile Association. The truth is that the costs were incurred by [the receiving party], but the

---

[71]   *Greig v National Amalgamated Union of Shop Assistants, Warehousemen and Clerks* (1906) 22 TLR 274; see also *Oram v Hutt* [1914] 1 Ch 98, CA, but also see *Hill v Archbold* [1968] 1 QB 686, in which these *Greig* and *Oram* were doubted.

[72]   *Davies v Taylor (No 2)* [1974] AC 225 at 230.

[73]   *Ilangaratne v British Medical Association* [2007] EWHC 920 (Ch) at [30] onwards: Briggs J found that negotiations may be admitted as being evidence of the fact of an agreement, even if they would be inadmissible for the purposes of its interpretation. The agreement in that case was that there was a long-standing understanding that instructions sent to the legal representative by the insurer would give rise to a retainer between the insured and the legal representative on terms already agreed.

[74]   *Ghadami v Lyon Cole Insurance Group Limited* [2010] EWCA Civ 767 at [25] and [26].

[75]   *Lewis v Avery (No 2)* [1973] 2 All ER 229 (this case was doubted in *Davies v Taylor (No 2)* [1974] AC 225, but this was on a different point).

Automobile Association indemnify him against the costs ... that is sufficient to satisfy the requirement that the costs were "incurred by him".'

Employers

11.61 Lloyd J considered the situation where the funder is an employer (the case is also notable for the fact that it related to criminal rather than civil costs, but nothing turns on that):[76]

> 'I would hold, following *Adams* and the other cases I have mentioned, that costs are incurred by a party if he is responsible or liable for those costs, even though they are in fact paid by a third party, whether an employer, insurance company, motoring organisation or trade union and even though the third party is also liable for those costs. It is only if he has agreed that the client shall in no circumstances be liable for the costs that they cease to be costs incurred by him, as happened in *Gundry v Sainsbury*. In practice, of course, the taxing officer will have before him on the taxation the whole of the solicitors file. If it appears to the taxing officer that there is doubt whether there is an express or an implied agreement, binding on the solicitors, not to seek to recover the costs from the client the taxing officer should ask for further evidence. It must then be for the taxing officer to come to a conclusion on the whole of the facts presented to him. Unless those facts establish a clear agreement express or implied that in no circumstances will the solicitor seek to obtain payment from their client then the basic presumption stands ...'

11.62 In a similar vein, Pill LJ declined to find that a genuine issue had been raised by virtue of the fact that a litigant (a policeman) had chosen to be represented by his employer's solicitors.[77]

The state

11.63 The fact that publicly funded clients are funded by the state does not undermine the indemnity principle.[78]

Subrogation

11.64 Subrogation is an equitable remedy which is based on restitution. It arises when an insurer admits a liability to the insured[79] and pays him the amount due under the contract of insurance:[80] subrogation will then operate in such a way as to allow the insurer to be placed in the position of the insured. The insurer must sue or defend in the name of the insured, not in its own name.[81] This distinguishes subrogation from assignment. The insurer must provide the insured with an indemnity against the costs of any proceedings the insurer commences or defends.[82]

11.65 It has been argued that, where a liability insurer brings a claim pursuant to its right of subrogation, that insurer cannot recover costs because any award of costs would

---

76 *R v Miller* [1983] 1 WLR 1056 at 1061.
77 See, for example, *Pepin v Watts* [2002] EWCA Civ 958 at [15]–[19].
78 *Daley v Diggers Ltd* [1951] 1 KB 661 and *Starkey v Railway Executive* [1951] 2 All ER 902.
79 *Page v Scottish Insurance Corpn Ltd* (1929) 140 LT 571, CA.
80 *Castellain v Preston* (1883) 11 QBD 380, CA at 389.
81 See *Clark v Blything Inhabitants* (1823) 2 B & C 254.
82 *Dane v Mortgage Insurance Corpn* [1894] 1 QB 54 at 61.

be in the name of the insured rather than the insurer. There are two ways in which this matter can be analysed. The first arises out of the way in which the Canadian judge, Middleton J, dealt with the issue:[83]

> 'The costs awarded are in the same way the costs of the insurance company, though awarded in the name of the insured.'

The effect of this (if it is good law, which it is usually accepted to be) is that if the insured is awarded costs of a subrogated claim, the insurer will be entitled to the benefit of that award of costs. This is in keeping with the way subrogation operates in litigation other than costs. In particular, subrogation will usually arise regardless of the nature of the legal right against the third party; it will, for example, arise when that right is tortious,[84] contractual[85] or statutory.[86] There is no reason to believe that it would not apply to a right to costs which may be regarded as being statutory[87] or contractual[88] (or both), as the case may be. In any event, for the reasons set out above, the fact that the insurer may be liable for the solicitors' costs will not undermine the indemnity principle.[89]

11.66 The second way in which this issue may be analysed is as an instance of 'dual liability'; in this regard, Moore-Bick LJ had this to say:[90]

> '[44] It is important to remember that although the proceedings are being conducted at the behest of the insurers, the parties to the litigation are in fact [the insured and his opponent]. Accordingly, any solicitors instructed in the matter were acting for him and he became liable for their costs: see *Davies v Taylor (No 2)* [1974] AC 225, [1973] 1 All ER 959, [1973] 2 WLR 610 and *Thornley v Lang* [2003] EWCA Civ 1484, [2004] 1 WLR 378, to which Ward LJ has referred. However, since the insurers were entitled to direct the conduct of the litigation, they were entitled to decide whom he should instruct to act on his behalf ...

> '[45] As between [the insured and his opponent] the existence of a policy of insurance under which he had already been indemnified against his loss is in law irrelevant – it is *res inter alios acta*,[91] as it used to be said. The fact that the insurers are bound to indemnify him against the costs of the proceedings does not provide the council with a defence to a claim to recover the costs, any more than it provides it with a defence to a claim for the damage caused to his house.'

Thus, the arrangements between the insured and the insurer are no concern to the paying party and they do not give rise to a defence to a claim for costs; if this is correct, a right of subrogation is not necessary for the purposes of proving compliance with the indemnity principle and, whilst there is no authority on the point, it would seem that dual liability would exist even where that right was a contingent right (ie, if solicitors were instructed before the right of subrogation arose).

---

[83] *Gough v Toronto & York Radial Railway Co* (1918) 42 OntLR 415; this is similar to the way in which rights in substantive litigation are transferred to the insurer (see, for example, *Finlay v Mexican Investment Corpn* [1897] 1 QB 517).

[84] See, for example, *Lister v Romford Ice and Cold Storage Co Ltd* [1957] AC 555.

[85] See, for example, *Castellain v Preston* (1883) 11 QBD 380.

[86] See, for example, *Ellerbeck Collieries Ltd v Cornhill Insurance Co Ltd* [1932] 1 KB 401.

[87] That is, a right to costs made pursuant to s 51 of the Senior Courts Act 1981.

[88] Where there is an agreement to pay costs.

[89] See, in particular, the discussion concerning *Davies v Taylor (No 2)* [1974] AC 225.

[90] *Sousa v London Borough of Waltham Forest Council* [2011] EWCA Civ 194 at [44].

[91] A thing done between others.

Miscellaneous issues

11.67 Generally speaking, the issue of the indemnity principle will turn on the enforceability of the contract of retainer; i e if the retainer is found to be enforceable, it will usually follow that there has been compliance with the indemnity principle. This will not always be the case, however, because it is possible for the counterparties to come to an agreement which is enforceable, but which either fails to create a liability for costs or fails to pass that liability on to the paying party. The following topics merit discussion.

Waiver of fees

11.68 If a legal representative waives his fees, then that waiver may, in theory, be passed along the line to the paying party in such a way as to diminish or extinguish the amount that the paying party has to pay. In practice, however, waiver (or, more accurately, acts comparable to waiver) will not necessarily have this effect. This is not only because the waiver may fail for want of consideration (see **27.57**), but also for the following reasons.

Agreement not to enforce

11.69 Mann J has found that if a legal representative agrees to forgo enforcement of his entitlement by court proceedings, this will not amount to a total extinguishment of the client's liability in the sense that it will relieve the paying party of the burden of paying costs. That agreement was merely an agreement not to enforce liability in one particular way.[92]

Bad debt

11.70 Patten J has found that if solicitors write off costs as being a bad debt, the contractual liability to pay costs will continue and, accordingly, the solicitors will be entitled to continue to rely on their lien.[93] One could construct an argument that the same applies to the indemnity principle. In any event, although there is no authority on the point, it could be argued that costs should be assessed as they were at the moment the costs order was made and that, unless a subsequent waiver can be taken as being evidence of the unreasonableness of the costs sought, the fact that the solicitor and client have come to some sort of commercial compromise is irrelevant for the purposes of assessing the costs.

Solicitor acting on credit

11.71 In a case in which it was suggested that a third party was maintaining the claim the receiving party's solicitor ledged an affidavit saying that he (personally) had been conducting the action on credit. Mustill LJ found that in those circumstances there was no maintenance; moreover, no adverse comment was made about the propriety of that situation.[94]

---

[92] *Harrington v Wakeling* [2007] EWHC 1184 (Ch).
[93] *Slatter v Ronaldsons* [2002] 2 Costs LR 267.
[94] *Singh & Anr v Observer Ltd* [1989] 3 All ER 777. This appeal was allowed by consent.

CFA Lites

11.72 The enforceability of CFA Lites[95] has already been addressed in Chapter 9. It has been argued that CFA Lites are inherently flawed and that they necessarily result in the indemnity principle being breached. This argument had some success in a case before a VAT tribunal in which a solicitor had agreed to charge only those costs received from the other side (if any); Macpherson J held that no order for costs could be made in those circumstances as there was nothing in respect of which an indemnity could apply. His reasoning was based on the premise that in the absence of an award of costs, the client had no liability and therefore no costs could be recovered.[96]

11.73 That case concerned the incidence of costs rather than the assessment of costs, but it is clear that Macpherson J very much had the indemnity principle in mind. His analysis has been criticised on the basis that it relies on circular reasoning. Commentators have also pointed out that the process of awarding and assessing costs does not create the liability but merely discovers the amount due.[97] Regardless of whether Macpherson J's analysis was correct on the facts of the case before him, it is not binding on any court and is rarely followed.[98]

11.74 In any event, where costs fall to be assessed under the CPR and where the agreement was made on or after 2 June 2003,[99] the concerns raised by Macpherson J will not arise. This is because CPR, r 43.2(3) makes the following provision:

> 'Where advocacy or litigation services are provided to a client under a conditional fee agreement, costs are recoverable under Parts 44 to 48 notwithstanding that the client is liable to pay his legal representative's fees and expenses only to the extent that sums are recovered in respect of the proceedings, whether by way of costs or otherwise.'

It is a moot point whether this provision is necessary; this is because it is possible to draft a CFA Lite in such a way as to avoid the concerns raised by Macpherson J.[100] Nonetheless, it is also possible to make inadvertent errors in the drafting of a CFA Lite, and CPR, r 43.2(3) may be relevant in those circumstances. It should not be regarded as setting aside the indemnity principle entirely: it merely prevents a CFA Lite from being unenforceable by reason of the fact that liability is linked to recovery. If a CFA Lite is unenforceable for other reasons, the indemnity principle will apply.

Problems concerning the effect of the retainer

11.75 It is possible for an enforceable retainer to fail – as a matter of contract – to create a liability which satisfies the indemnity principle. It may be, for example, that the retainer is enforceable but that it does not to apply to the claim in question. It may also be that it is a conditional fee agreement in which the definition of 'win' has not been met. These issues are dealt with at **8.31–8.40**.

---

[95] This discussion of 'CFA Lites' is intended not only to include those agreements which fall within the category of cases to which regulation 3A of the Conditional Fee Agreements Regulations 2000 refers, but to any agreement where the liability of the client is limited to those sums which are recovered in the litigation.

[96] *Commissioners of Customs & Excise v Vaz* (1995) STC 14 (Macpherson J).

[97] See, for example, Kings Costs Team 'Costs Law Brief' (2007) 157 NLJ 7278, pp 890–891 (the author was one of those commentators).

[98] See *Harrington v Wakeling* [2007] EWHC 1184 (Ch) at [14], where it was distinguished on the facts.

[99] See the Civil Procedure (Amendment No 2) Rules 2003 (SI 2003/1242), r 6.

[100] This can be done by phrasing the 'Lite' provision in terms of waiver.

11.76 It can be seen from what is set out in those paragraphs that the court is reluctant to find that there has been a breach of the indemnity principle arising out of a contractual anomaly, but that in some circumstances – such as where a conditional fee agreement names the wrong opponent – the court may be forced to make such a finding.

Quantum meruit

11.77 A claim for quantum meruit is a claim for payment for a reasonable sum for services provided. The term 'quantum meruit' will usually refer to a right to payment arising from the unjust enrichment by one party at the expense of another; that right is an example of a restitutionary remedy. The term may also be used to refer to a contractual remedy, which in effect is an implied contractual term to pay a reasonable rate.

11.78 In so far as the law of costs of concerned, the issue of quantum meruit may arise in the following three situations:

- where there is a written retainer, but it fails to specify the basis upon which the legal representative will be paid;
- where there is no written retainer; and
- where a contract of retainer has, for some reason, been found wanting.

11.79 The first two situations will, in general, present no conceptual difficulties. It will usually be self-evident that the agreement between the legal representative and the client was not intended to be gratuitous; in those circumstances, the law will imply an agreement that a reasonable fee be paid.[101] Lloyd J's presumption (see **11.24**) may be relevant. Even where the court does indulge the legal representative in this way (thereby vicariously indulging the receiving party), not everything will be plain sailing; the court may, for example, decline to uplift the allowable rate to take account of the complexity of the work.[102] Nontheless, it will rarely be the case that the court will find that there has been a breach of the indemnity principle in general terms. At **8.199–8.216** the topic is analysed as a point of contractual law: the topic could be analysed in terms of quantum meruit just as easily.

11.80 The third situation is less straightforward. It is trite law that a claim in quantum meruit cannot arise if there is an existing and enforceable contract to pay an agreed sum,[103] but what is less clear is whether such a claim can arise in circumstances where the retainer exists, but is not an enforceable contract.

11.81 It would seem that in those circumstances, no claim in quantum meruit will arise. If the retainer is a contract which has been found to be unenforceable by reason of it being contrary to public policy, then no claim can be made in quantum meruit. This was made clear by Schiemann LJ:[104]

> 'If the court, for reasons of public policy refuses to enforce an agreement that a solicitor should be paid it must follow that he cannot claim on a quantum meruit ... In the present

---

[101]   See *Kellar v Williams* [2004] UKPC 30, in which the Privy Council applied *Way v Latilla* [1937] 3 All ER 759 at 763; for further discussion, see **8.199–8.216**.

[102]   See *Adams v MacInnes* [2001] EWHC 9014 (Costs).

[103]   *The Olanda* [1919] 2 KB 728.

[104]   *Awwad v Geraghty & Co* [2001] QB 570 at 596; see also *Wild v Simpson* [1918–19] All ER Rep 682 at 693 (Duke LJ dissenting, albeit on other grounds).

case, what public policy seeks to prevent is a solicitor continuing to act for a client under a conditional normal fee arrangement. That is what [the solicitor] did. That is what she wishes to be paid for. Public policy decrees that she should not be paid.'

11.82 Whilst his comments were obiter and based on hypothetical facts, Christopher Clarke J made similar comments in the context of an unenforceable conditional fee agreement. In essence, he found that a client is not *unjustly* enriched in circumstances where the enrichment has been as a result of the operation of statute.[105]

11.83 It occasionally happens that a legal representative accepts instructions on the assumption that a particular type of funding exists (eg public funding), but it later transpires that he had made a mistake. Burton J considered this issue in a case in which, through no fault of his own, the solicitor had carried out work outwith the scope of the legal aid certificate. Burton J had this to say:[106]

> 'Whatever inroads there now are into that indemnity principle as a result of express agreements between a solicitor and his client ... I do not consider that there is, at any rate yet, and certainly was not in this case between 1989 and 1997, any kind of implication in what was otherwise a legal aid arrangement that the client would be liable to his solicitor to make payment in respect of his costs in the event of there being no legal aid, but only in the event that he should be successful in recovering his costs against the opposite party. Or put another way, I do not consider that the plaintiff "freely accepted" the defendant's services on that basis.'

A particular difficulty with the solicitor's argument was that the claim for quantum meruit was, in effect, a claim for payment of costs under an informal (and therefore unenforceable) conditional fee agreement. Whether a claim for quantum meruit can be made in other circumstances (such as where it is wrongly believed that a funder would pay the costs) is a moot point.

11.84 In summary, unless the facts are such that the court can find that there is an implied retainer (or something very similar to an implied retainer), the remedy of quantum meruit will rarely be an answer to an argument that there has been a breach of the indemnity principle.

Estoppel

11.85 Estoppel may arise in many guises, but in the present context there are two arguments which are most relevant:

- the first is that because the paying party has agreed to pay costs, then he is estopped from contending that costs are not payable for want of compliance with the indemnity principle; and
- the second is that the notion of 'fair conduct'[107] would prevent the legal representative's client from taking the point that an agreement was unenforceable, and that, as a result, the paying party should also be estopped from taking the point.[108]

---

[105] *Forde v Birmingham City Council* [2009] EWHC 12 (QB) at [206]. He was unpersuaded that changes to the rules which govern solicitors had altered the lie of the land.
[106] *Bridgewater v Griffith* [2000] 1 WLR 524 at 530.
[107] See *Panchaud Frères Établissement Grains* [1970] 1 Lloyd's Rep 53.
[108] As articulated in *Panchaud Frères SA v Établissements General Grain Company* [1970] 1 Lloyd's Rep 53.

As to the first, whilst it is possible to envisage situations in which a paying party would be estopped from relying on the indemnity principle, those situations rarely arise in practice. In particular, it would rarely be the case that the receiving party would have volunteered the information that there was a problem with his retainer, so no estoppel would arise because the paying party would not have been put in a position in which he was able to acquiesce to that knowledge.[109]

11.86 As to the second of the two arguments mentioned above, Schiemann LJ had this to say:[110]

'[Counsel] submits that the principle of fair conduct … prevents [the client] from now taking the point that … the agreement was champertous. I disagree for a number of reasons. One will suffice. The principle in that case does not prevent [the client] from asserting facts in his evidence. If those facts lead the court to the conclusion that the agreement was champertous then the court will refuse to enforce it whatever [the client's] attitude. Points on illegality are taken by the court of its own motion, not because of any consideration of fairness as between the two parties to the dispute but on wider considerations.'

Thus, the notion of 'fair conduct' has no real part to play. Schiemann LJ's comments were made in the context of a solicitor and client dispute; they are likely to apply a fortiori to a dispute between the parties.

11.87 In summary, it would rarely be the case that a paying party would be estopped from relying on the indemnity principle; estoppel will certainly not arise out of the mere fact that the paying party has agreed to pay costs.

EMPLOYERS

11.88 Another topic to be considered is whether a receiving party can recover costs for services rendered by persons who are also the receiving party's employees and, if so, how those costs are to be assessed; the term 'in-house' will be used to refer to such employees.

11.89 The discussion distinguishes between legal and non-legal in-house staff. In so far as the former are concerned (ie legal in-house staff), it should be noted that different considerations apply where the employer is in the business of providing legal services; that topic is dealt with at **38.79–38.85**.

Legal staff

11.90 Where costs are claimed for work done by in-house legal staff, those staff are – in a nutshell – given a notional status as independent practitioners; this achieves a rough approximation of the costs of employing them and, therefore, achieves justice without requiring the court to carry out the often disproportionate and difficult task of ascertaining the actual cost of employment.[111] The idea of notional fees being ascribed to lawyers carrying out work in circumstances where they are not instructed in an independent capacity is nothing new.[112]

---

[109] *Bridgewater v Griffith* [2000] 1 WLR 524 at 530 relying on *Chitty on Contracts* (27th edn, 1994), vol 1, p 223, para 3-081.

[110] *Awwad v Geraghty & Co* [2001] QB 570 at 595.

[111] See the comments of Arden J in *Stubblefield v Kemp* [2001] 1 Costs LR 30 at [25].

[112] See *Crown & Stafford Stone v Eccleshall Magistrates' Court* [1988] 1 All ER 430 (in which a solicitor was

11.91 Russell LJ (with whom Stamp and Lawton LJJ agreed) laid down the following principles:[113]

- the proper method of assessment is to assess the bill as though it were the bill of an independent solicitor;
- the hourly rate is assessed in the same way as it would if the bill were the bill of an independent solicitor;
- it is a sensible and reasonable presumption that the figure arrived at on this basis will not infringe the indemnity principle; and
- there may be special cases in which it appears reasonably plain that the indemnity principle will be infringed if the above method is used, but it would be impracticable and wrong to require a total exposition and breakdown of the activities and expenses of the in-house department with a view to ensuring that the principle is not infringed, and it is doubtful whether by any method certainty on the point could be reached.

11.92 Russell LJ explained his reasoning in the following way:[114]

'Suppose a solicitor in independent practice with an assistant solicitor, two legal executives, clerks and typists and other overheads, who in year 1 works in fact exclusively for corporation X. For year 2 it is arranged that his whole office and staff is taken over as a department of corporation X, the solicitor also becoming an employee of the corporation at a salary commensurate with the profit made by him in year 1 doing the corporation's legal work. Suppose that in year 1 the corporation was successful in a piece of litigation in which in fact one of the legal executives did all the work: in taxing the corporation's costs the taxing master would apply the A and B conventional method and the figure for the discretionary item would be £75. Suppose in year 2 the corporation is successful in exactly comparable litigation, again with the legal executive doing the work: if the method of taxation adopted in this case were followed, only A (£45) would be allowed for the item, though the change would not have effected any saving to the corporation, who, instead of paying the profit to the solicitor in respect of that litigation, would have paid to him the equivalent in the form of a proportion of his salary. This example seems to us to demonstrate that there must be something wrong in an approach which uses only the A of the A B conventional method in the case of an employed solicitor.'

11.93 Russell LJ's method came under attack in a case in which the paying party argued that, though it may be correct to assign in-house staff a notional status, the actual quantum of costs should reflect the fact that the costs of running an in-house legal department may be lower than the costs of running an independent practice. It was argued that overheads must be lower because, for example, in-house solicitors do not have to incur the costs of advertising. It was also said that there should be no uplift because the in-house staff would receive the same salary regardless of the complexity or difficulty of the case. Recognising that Russell LJ's judgment was binding, the paying party said that these factors could be taken into account by adopting an 'A plus B' approach, but by assessing 'B' at nil. Elias J pithily rejected this argument:[115]

'It is little short of fiction to say one is apply the same method [as applied by Russell LJ] if in fact [one] is always allocating nothing under the B element.'

---

allowed his notional fees for appearing in his own case in a magistrates' court) and *R v Boswell, R v Halliwell* [1987] 2 All ER 513 (in which a barrister was allowed a notional fee for attending an appeal in respect of his own fees).

[113] *In re Eastwood, deceased; Lloyds Bank Ltd v Eastwood* [1975] Ch 112 at 132.
[114] *In re Eastwood, deceased; Lloyds Bank Ltd v Eastwood* [1975] Ch 112 at 131.
[115] *Maes Finance Ltd v WG Edwards & Partners* [2000] 2 Costs LR 198 at 200.

Elias J went on to acknowledge that there might be 'special' cases in which it would not be appropriate to assess the in-house costs as if they were those of an independent practitioner, but the case before him (which was not remarkable in any way) was not such a case.

11.94 It will occasionally be the case that the receiving party will, of its own volition, adduce accountancy evidence or produce a calculation similar to an Expense of Time calculation. In a case in which this happened, the paying party argued that where such evidence was before the court, it should be taken into account. Buxton LJ (with whom Hooper J agreed) rejected that argument.[116] Buxton LJ pointed to the considerable difficulty that would be caused by attempting to take such evidence into account in any meaningful way. That said, like Elias J he too commented (obiter) that the usual method could be departed from in a special case. No guidance exists as to what might make a case special.

11.95 Although not in a binding decision, Master Campbell has found that the fact that a party is also represented by independent solicitors does not preclude the recovery of costs in respect of in-house staff.[117]

11.96 In summary, the costs of in-house legal staff will generally be treated as if the work had been carried out by independent solicitors, but (in theory at least) the court can depart from that principle in special cases.

Non-legal staff

11.97 In order to deal briefly with the recoverability of costs for services rendered by employees who are not (or who are not supervised by) legal staff, it is necessary to stray slightly from the topic of the indemnity principle.

11.98 It is trite law that costs are limited to legal costs.[118] Subject to certain exceptions, this means that a litigant is unable to recover the costs of work done by himself which might otherwise have been carried out by a solicitor. It is convenient to call this principle 'the general prohibition'. The general prohibition is widely accepted as being correct, having been accepted in many other common law jurisdictions.[119]

11.99 At this point it is worth pausing to consider the mechanisms by which a party can avoid the operation of the general prohibition; this is helpful because it allows a distinction to be made between the indemnity principle and the other ways in which the costs of in-house staff (lawyers or otherwise) may be recovered. In so far as they are relevant, the exceptions to the general prohibition are:

- where the costs are the costs of a litigant in person recoverable under the Litigants in Person (Costs and Expenses) Act 1975;
- where the costs are the costs of solicitor litigants: this is now governed by CPR, r 48.6 and the CPD;
- where the costs are the costs of employed solicitors who are acting in the course of their employment; and

---

[116] *Cole v British Telecommunications plc* [2000] 2 Costs LR 310.
[117] *Ultraframe (UK) Ltd v Eurocell Building Plastics Ltd & Anor* [2006] EWHC 90069 (Costs).
[118] *London Scottish Benefit Society v Chorley* (1884) 12 QBD 452.
[119] See, for example, the Irish case of *Henehan v Allied Irish Banks plc* (unreported) 19 October 1984, Findlay P, and *Dawson & anor t/a AE Dawson & Sons v Irish Brokers Association* [2002] IESC 36.

- where the costs are the costs of a limited number of categories of incidental work carried out by non-lawyers.

The relevance of these things is that where the work might otherwise have been carried out by a legal representative, the costs will be recoverable if they fall within any one of the first three categories (only the first of which relates to non-lawyers), but in all other circumstances it would be recoverable only if it fell within the last category.

11.100   Whether this is so will depend on the facts of each case. In particular, it will depend on factors such as the nature of the work being undertaken, whether the receiving party is a litigant in person, etc. These matters go well beyond the topic of the indemnity principle and are considered elsewhere in this book (in particular, Chapters 5, 28, 29, and 38), but their relevance to the indemnity principle is that it is clear from the way in which the court has dealt with such issues that there must actually be a loss: where there is no loss, there will be no costs.

11.101   In summary, the costs of in-house non-legal staff may be recoverable in certain circumstances, but it will always be the case that a loss must be shown.

PRO BONO

11.102   A pedant would say that the topic of pro bono funding has no place in a chapter on the indemnity principle; this – the pedant would say – is because the awards discussed below are not for 'costs' at all, but are for monies payable in lieu of costs. Whilst this doctrinaire distinction may occasionally be important (see **11.109**), for most purposes an award in lieu of costs can be thought of as being a type of costs order which is made pursuant to a statutory exception to the indemnity principle.

11.103   'Pro bono funding' is an oxymoronic phrase which describes a system of funding in which a legal representative provides services without receiving or expecting to receive a fee, gain or reward, and in which an award in lieu of costs may be made by the court in its discretion. Where an award is made, it is made in favour of a 'prescribed charity' rather than the client.

11.104   Pro bono funding is governed by s 194 of the Legal Services Act 2007 ('LSA 2007'), that section having been in force since 1 October 2008; the facility to make an award will apply only to legal services provided after that date.[120]. The Act refers to the legal representative[121] and the client by the letters 'R' (for representative) and 'P' (for party). The legal representative must provide representation free of charge, in whole or in part, but he may continue to be a legal representative within the meaning of s 194 regardless of whether P has also been paid for legal services.[122] 'Free of charge' means that R provides services not for or in expectation of fee, gain, or reward.[123]

---

[120] Legal Services Act 2007, s 194(11). Pro bono funding in the Supreme Court will be governed by s 62 of the Legal Aid, Sentencing and Punishment of Offenders Bill; at the time of writing, it had just received Royal Assent but was not yet in force.

[121] Which is defined as a person exercising a right of audience or conducting litigation on the party's behalf: see LSA 2007, s 194(10).

[122] LSA 2007, s 194(1)(a) and (2).

[123] LSA 2007, s 194(10).

11.105 Where these conditions are met, the court may order any person to make a payment to the prescribed charity in respect of R's representation of P (or, if only part of R's representation of P was provided free of charge, in respect of that part).[124] The order is not made for the benefit of P, but directly for the benefit of the prescribed charity.[125] Where an order has been made, it is P's responsibility to send a copy of the order to the prescribed charity within 7 days of receipt.[126]

11.106 A 'prescribed charity' is a charity prescribed by order;[127] at present, the only prescribed charity is the Access to Justice Foundation.[128] That organisation distributes the monies received to 'Regional Legal Support Trusts' (although monies may also be distributed to other pro bono projects). The Regional Legal Support Trusts will in turn distribute to local advice agencies and law centres.

11.107 In considering whether to make an award, the court must have regard to whether an order would have been made if R had not been acting pro bono;[129] the CPR makes it clear that the court may take into account the same factors as would have been taken into account when considering the incidence of costs generally.[130] It is notable that LSA 2007 does not say that the court must disregard the fact that R is acting pro bono,[131] so it seems that Parliament intended that the court is entitled to take that factor into account when deciding what order to make. That impression is entirely consistent with CPR, r 44.3C(2), which reads:

'(2) Where the court makes an order under section 194(3) of the 2007 Act—

(a) the court may order the payment to the prescribed charity of a sum no greater than the costs specified in Part 45 to which the party with pro bono representation would have been entitled in accordance with that Part and in respect of that representation had it not been provided free of charge; or

(b) where Part 45 does not apply, the court may determine the amount of the payment (other than a sum equivalent to fixed costs) to be made by the paying party to the prescribed charity by—

(i) making a summary assessment; or

(ii) making an order for detailed assessment,

of a sum equivalent to all or part of the costs the paying party would have been ordered to pay to the party with pro bono representation in respect of that representation had it not been provided free of charge.'

Therefore, while the court is limited in the sense that it cannot award more than would have been awarded had the services not been provided pro bono, it does not necessarily have to award the same amount.

11.108 There is no guidance as to which factors the court can take into account when deciding whether to make an award. Although there is no authority on the point, it may be that the court is able to consider whether it is fair that the losing party is ordered to make a payment which is not intended to meet the interests of justice in the particular

---

[124] LSA 2007, s 194(3).
[125] CPR, r 44.3C(3).
[126] CPR, r 44.3C(4).
[127] LSA 2007, s 194(8).
[128] See the Legal Services Act 2007 (Prescribed Charity) Order 2008 (SI 2008/2680), art 2.
[129] LSA 2007, s 194(4).
[130] CPR, r 44.3C(5).
[131] This is different from public funding, where such a provision does exist.

case in hand, but to achieve access to justice in the community as a whole. It could well be that one issue to be given particular emphasis is the financial strength of the losing party, and whether he is insured.

11.109   As mentioned above, it is a moot point whether an award under LSA 2007, s 194 is an order for 'costs'; if it is a costs order, it is a special type of costs order which is made for the benefit of someone other than the parties. The relevance of this is that it seems likely that the parties would not be able to claim set-off in respect of cross-orders; this may be a significant disadvantage to the paying party, because a person who is receiving pro bono advice is not likely to be able to satisfy an order for costs. It can also work to P's disadvantage, because P may prefer his liability to be diminished or extinguished by way of set-off rather than to have an undischarged costs order hanging over his head. If, therefore, the court wishes to take competing entitlements into account in such a way as to make an order for the net balance (which may be nil), this is best done at the stage of deciding the entitlement to costs rather than at a later stage, ie it is best for the court to make a single order which meets the justice of the situation generally. It is for this reason that the Access to Justice Foundation encourages pro bono representatives to ask the court to reserve orders for costs until the conclusion of the matter.

11.110   A person who is being represented by R will have a limited degree of costs protection (similar to that enjoyed by publicly funded clients); no order may be made against such a person in respect of services provided pro bono by R acting for an opponent.[132]

11.111   The award may be quantified by detailed assessment,[133] but the court will make a summary assessment unless there is good reason not to do so.[134] The amount of the award is limited to the amount that would have been awarded under a conventional costs order. There is no guidance as to whether additional liabilities can be taken into account when determining that sum, but it is likely that only base costs should be taken into account (not least because the paying party would not have received Notice of Funding).

11.112   Litigants receiving pro bono services and who intend to recover costs are obliged to serve estimates in the usual way; the estimates are to be based on the costs that would have been charged had the services not been provided pro bono.[135]

11.113   Where the award is sought by way of a summary assessment, a Statement of Costs must be drafted as if the costs had been incurred by a lawyer who was not acting pro bono.[136] Where the award is submitted for detailed assessment, the bill must be divided into parts which distinguish between work which was provided pro bono and work which was not.[137]

Legal Services Act 2007, s 194

11.114   The wording of the pro bono section of the LSA 2007 is as follows:

---

[132]   LSA 2007, s 194(5) and (6).
[133]   CPR, r 44.3A(2)(b) and CPD, art 10A.1.
[134]   CPD, arts 10A.1 and 13.2.
[135]   CPD, art 6.2(b).
[136]   CPD, art 10A.2.
[137]   CPD, art 4.2(1A).

194 Payments in respect of pro bono representation

(1) This section applies to proceedings in a civil court in which—

  (a) a party to the proceedings ('P') is or was represented by a legal representative ('R'), and
  (b) R's representation of P is or was provided free of charge, in whole or in part.

(2) This section applies to such proceedings even if P is or was also represented by a legal representative not acting free of charge.

(3) The court may order any person to make a payment to the prescribed charity in respect of R's representation of P (or, if only part of R's representation of P was provided free of charge, in respect of that part).

(4) In considering whether to make such an order and the terms of such an order, the court must have regard to—

  (a) whether, had R's representation of P not been provided free of charge, it would have ordered the person to make a payment to P in respect of the costs payable to R by P in respect of that representation, and
  (b) if it would, what the terms of the order would have been.

(5) The court may not make an order under subsection (3) against a person represented in the proceedings if the person's representation was at all times within subsection (6).

(6) Representation is within this subsection if it is—

  (a) provided by a legal representative acting free of charge, or
  (b) funded by the Legal Services Commission as part of the Community Legal Service.

(7) Rules of court may make further provision as to the making of orders under subsection (3), and may in particular—

  (a) provide that such orders may not be made in civil proceedings of a description specified in the rules;
  (b) make provision about the procedure to be followed in relation to such orders;
  (c) specify matters (in addition to those mentioned in subsection (4)) to which the court must have regard in deciding whether to make such an order, and the terms of any order.

(8) 'The prescribed charity' means the charity prescribed by order made by the Lord Chancellor.

(9) An order under subsection (8) may only prescribe a charity which—

  (a) is registered in accordance with section 3A of the Charities Act 1993 (c 10), and
  (b) provides financial support to persons who provide, or organise or facilitate the provision of, legal advice or assistance (by way of representation or otherwise) which is free of charge.

(10) In this section—

  'legal representative', in relation to a party to proceedings, means a person exercising a right of audience or conducting litigation on the party's behalf;
  'civil court' means the civil division of the Court of Appeal, the High Court, or any county court;
  'free of charge' means otherwise than for or in expectation of fee, gain or reward.

(11) The court may not make an order under subsection (3) in respect of representation if (or to the extent that) it is provided before this section comes into force.

Chapter 12

POINTS OF LAW

12.1 This chapter addresses a number of miscellaneous points of law, namely agency, plural liability, set-off, finality of litigation in costs, limitation and delay, and human rights.

AGENCY

12.2 The law of agency will apply where a person (the agent) is authorised to act as the representative of another person (the principal) such that the agent has the authority to create legal relations between the principal and third parties.[1] The agreement which is created is a principal–agent relationship. That relationship may be express or implied,[2] or may be created retrospectively by ratification.[3] In the present context (ie the costs of persons said to be agents), an 'agent' is a person (often another solicitor) who, rather than being employed by the solicitor (or other authorised representative), is engaged by a solicitor to carry out work on his behalf; the third party to this principal–agent relationship is the client, who will be responsible for payment for the services rendered by the agent.

12.3 It is convenient to refer to 'the solicitor principal', 'the non-solicitor agent' and 'the solicitor agent' to describe the various persons who might be involved.

12.4 The main topic which is addressed in this section is whether an agent's fees are recoverable as the solicitor principal's fees or on some other basis, ie as a disbursement. The question is relevant for two reasons: first, it is relevant to the manner in which costs are to be presented in the bill of costs (ie as profit costs or disbursements) and, secondly, it can have a bearing on the quantum of costs in that a profit may be made on work not charged as a disbursement (see **12.8–12.17**).

12.5 This latter issue has in recent times become a noteworthy point; this is for two reasons:

(1)   a solicitor principal may, by charging the agent's services as if he had provided them himself, be able to make a considerable profit on services provided by an agent (this is because, in appropriate cases, a success fee may be charged); and
(2)   the question of whether a fee can be regarded as having been incurred as a disbursement may have a bearing on its recoverability under the fixed costs regimes in CPR, Part 45.

---

[1]   *Re Nevill ex p White* (1871) 6 Ch App 397, CA.
[2]   *Pole v Leask* (1863) 33 LJ Ch 155.
[3]   In a slightly different context, see **25.22**.

Solicitor agents

12.6 A solicitor who is instructed by a client will, in general, have authority to instruct a solicitor agent.[4] There will, unless otherwise agreed, be no privity between the client and the solicitor agent[5] and as such the agent will not be able sue the client for his costs.[6] Instead, the solicitor principal will be liable for the agent's costs.[7] If the client wishes to have the agent's fees assessed, this will be in the context of those being costs claimed by the principal.[8] If profit costs are incurred by a solicitor agent, the mere fact that the work has been delegated by the solicitor principal to the solicitor agent does not justify the agent's fee being regarded as a disbursement. This much is made clear by Stirling J:[9]

> 'It is well settled that between the client and the London agent of the country solicitor there is no privity. The relationship of solicitor and client does not exist between the client and the London agent. What is done by the London agent is part of the work done by the country solicitor for the client. The country solicitor does or may do part of the work personally. He does or may do part of his work through clerks whom he employs in the country. Or, if necessary ... he may do part of his work through a London agent. But as between the country solicitor and the client, the whole of the work is done by the country solicitor. It follows, therefore, that the items which make up the London agent's bill are not mere disbursements, but are items taxable in the strictest sense as between the client and the country solicitor, just as much as items in respect of work done by the country solicitor personally, or by the clerk whom he employs in the country.'

These comments remain good law today.[10]

12.7 Where appropriate, the solicitor agent's fees will be charged as being the principal's profit costs; this is confirmed by CPD, art 4.16(6), which provides:

> 'Agency charges as between a principal solicitors and their agents will be dealt with on the principle that such charges, where appropriate, form part of the principal solicitor's charges. Where these charges relate to head (1) in paragraph 4.6 (attendances at court and on counsel) they must be included in their chronological order in that head. In other cases they must be included in head (9) (attendances on London and other agents).'

It seems implicit in this provision that whilst the agency fees should form part of the principal's own fees, the fact that an agent was engaged ought to be stated in the bill of costs. That said, the mere fact that there was an agreement that the supposed agent would be paid by the supposed principal would not give rise to a principal–agent relationship; if the agreement contemplates that the supposed agent will carry out work

---

4   See *Re Bishop, ex p Langley, ex p Smith* (1879) 13 Ch D 110, CA. See also *Solley v Wood* (1852) 16 Beav 370. The solicitor would not impliedly have permission to instruct a different solicitor to act in his stead: *Re Becket, Purnell v Paine* [1918] 2 Ch 72, CA.

5   *Cobb v Becke* (1845) 6 QB 930 and *Robbins v Fennell* (1847) 11 QB 248; see also *Gordon v Dalzell* (1852) 15 Beav 351.

6   See *Ward v Lawson* (1890) 43 Ch D 353 at 360, CA, per Cotton LJ; see also *Scrace v Whittington* (1823) 2 B & C 11.

7   *Scrace v Whittington* (1823) as reported in 2 B & C 11; this does not apply if the agent is an Irish Solicitor: *Hyndman v Ward* (1899) 15 TLR 182. Because the principal solicitor is liable for the agent's fees and can be required to pay them regardless of whether the client has paid them, the solicitor principal is permitted to keep any interest recovered: *Ward v Lawson* (1890) 43 Ch D 353, CA.

8   *Wildbore v Bryan, ex p Wildbore* (1820) 8 Price 677.

9   *In re Pomeroy & Tanner* [1897] 1 Ch 287.

10   See *Agassi v Robinson* [2006] 1 All ER 900 at [74] and *Crane v Canons Leisure Centre* [2007] EWCA Civ 1352 at [7].

on his own behalf, then no agency will be created.[11] Thus, the agent's fees should be charged as the principal's fees only where this is appropriate; an example in which this may not be appropriate would be where the putative agent was instructed directly by the lay client without the involvement of the principal. Another example would be where he was providing services (such as expert evidence) which could not be characterised as legal in nature. Each case would have to be decided on its own facts.

Non-solicitor agents

12.8 For the reasons set out above, services provided by solicitor agents are, in appropriate cases, to be charged as if they had been provided by the solicitor principal. What is less clear is how the costs of a non-solicitor agent should be classified. The receiving party may, at different times, have reason to advance diametrically opposed arguments depending on the circumstances in which the costs are claimed.

12.9 The starting point is that a payment made by a solicitor may, in principle, be treated as a disbursement incurred through the agency of the solicitor.[12] There will be cases in which the payment will be a disbursement.

12.10 In certain circumstances the work of a non-solicitor agent may be regarded as being equivalent to that of a fee earner employed by the solicitor. Indeed, May LJ has commented that the distinction between solicitor agents and non-solicitor agents is not as relevant to the issue of the nature of their fees as it might, at first blush, appear:[13]

> 'I do not think that the classification of the cost of this work [ie the costs done by a non-solicitor agent] can sensibly depend on whether [the solicitor principals] did the work themselves, whether they delegated it to another solicitor or whether they delegated it to [agents] who were not solicitors'

It is implicit in this extract that one factor that is relevant is the nature of the services which are being provided.

12.11 The case that, until recently, was usually cited as the main authority in support of the proposition that non-solicitor agent's fees are charged as if they were the solicitor principal's fees is *Smith Graham v Lord Chancellor's Department*.[14] This was an assessment in which the fees of an enquiry agent (a retired police officer) were allowed as if he were a fee earner. *Smith Graham* was often cited despite the fact that it involved a question of regulatory interpretation, ie whether the work done by the enquiry agent fell within the scope of a particular regulatory definition.[15]

12.12 There was, until 2007 (see **12.13**), a divergence of judicial opinion as to the effect of *Smith Graham*. Hallett J had made it clear that each case turns on its own facts, and some judges seized upon this to limit and distinguish *Smith Graham*;[16] others embraced

---

[11] Although a non-costs case, see *Handley Page Ltd v Customs and Excise Comrs and Rockwell Machine Tool Co Ltd* [1971] 2 Lloyd's Rep 298, CA.

[12] If authority were needed on the point, it can be implied from the way in which the Court of Appeal dealt with certain disbursements in *In Re Blair & Girling* [1906] 2 KB 131.

[13] *Crane v Canons Leisure Centre* [2007] EWCA Civ 1352 at [15].

[14] [1999] 2 Costs LR 1.

[15] Regulation 2 of the Legal Aid in Criminal and Care Proceedings (Costs) Regulations 1989 (SI 1989/343).

[16] See, for example, Master Hurst's comments in *Claims Direct Test Cases Tranche 2* [2003] EWHC 9005 (Costs) at [115].

the notion that agent's fees were capable of being charged as the principal's fees.[17] The point usually arose in the context of whether a success fee was payable on costs draftsmen's fees, so that it was a point which was often argued at first instance with some fervour.

Relevance of supervision

12.13 In 2002, Master Hurst commented that a relevant factor was whether the solicitor principals had personal responsibility for the work that was being carried out.[18] Five years later the Court of Appeal gave judgment in the case which is now the main authority on the point (*Crane v Canons Leisure Centre*), and they too came to the conclusion that this was a relevant factor (per May LJ):[19]

> 'If [solicitor principals] properly choose to delegate their own work, they remain entitled to charge on their own account and the proper amount of the charge is not necessarily the same as the amount which they agree to pay to their subcontractor. It could be more or it could be less. In my view, the appellants are right to concentrate on whether the work is solicitors' work; and Master Hurst was right to say that a characteristic of such work is whether the solicitor remains responsible to the client for its proper conduct.'

It is implicit in this passage that it will not always be the case that the work done by a person other than a solicitor will be regarded as being the costs of the solicitor who instructs him. Clearly, the work has to be legal work for it to be characterised as profit costs (it is for this reason that the costs of an expert could never be regarded as profit costs). Likewise, counsel's fees are not regarded as profit costs.[20] Where other persons are instructed, however, the issue will turn on the facts of the case, and in particular on the nature of the work and the extent to which the solicitor principal remains responsible for the services which are provided.

12.14 The fact that there is an agreement between the putative principal and agent does not necessarily mean that a relationship of agency exists; where the agreement contemplates that the latter will carry out work on his own behalf, then no such relationship will be created.[21] In particular, where the solicitor merely 'rubber stamps' the work (to use Lord Jauncey's phrase), the work probably would be regarded as being a disbursement.[22]

Relevance of the retainer

12.15 The extent to which the solicitor principal remains responsible for the work done may depend on the wording of the retainer. There is no reason why a retainer should not expressly provide that work done by, say, a paginating bureau is a service for which the solicitor principal will (or will not) be responsible.[23] Whilst there is no authority on the

---

[17]   See, for example, *Stringer v Copley (17 May 2002) Kingston on Thames CC*, HHJ Cook.

[18]   See *Claims Direct Test Cases Tranche 2* [2003] EWHC 9005 (Costs) at [80].

[19]   [2007] EWCA Civ 1352 at [14].

[20]   See the comments of Maurice Kay LJ in *Crane v Canons Leisure Centre* [2007] EWCA Civ 1352 at [28].

[21]   Although a non-costs case, see *Handley Page Ltd v Customs and Excise Comrs and Rockwell Machine Tool Co Ltd* [1971] 2 Lloyd's Rep 298, CA.

[22]   *R v Legal Aid Board ex p Bruce* [1992] 3 All ER 321 at 326.

[23]   In support of this, see the way Master Gordon-Saker addressed the issue of pagination agencies in *Ahmed v Aventis Pharma Ltd (Rev 1)* [2009] EWHC 90152 (Costs) (19 November 2009) at [12].

point, it is likely that such a factor would be given significant weight in deciding the nature of the resultant fee (assuming, of course, that the provision in the retainer was not a sham).

12.16 Whilst his was a dissenting judgment, it is clear from the way in which Maurice Kay LJ dealt with the issue of whether a success fee is payable on work done by a costs draftsman that another factor to be taken into account is the extent to which it is just and fair that the solicitor principal makes a profit.[24] On the facts of the case before him, his brother judges did not agree with his analysis, but it may be that that is a factor which can be taken into account in other situations, most notably the issue of reasonableness.

12.17 In particular, the fact that the costs of a non-solicitor agent are, in principle, the costs of the solicitor principal does not necessarily mean that the court will allow those costs in full. This is because the test of reasonableness will apply. If the court is satisfied that it was unreasonable of the solicitor principal to engage the services of a person whose costs would be charged as the principal's costs, then it is arguable that the costs may be restricted accordingly. Although there is no authority on the point, an example might be where a solicitor advocate was engaged in circumstances where counsel would have been a cheaper and more appropriate option. Furthermore, a person cannot do through agency something that he cannot do himself;[25] thus, an enquiry agent cannot be instructed to take a statement from an opponent or carry out any other task that the solicitor principal would not be able to do.[26]

Relevance of the authorisation

12.18 Finally, it is worth saying a word or two about principals who are not themselves entitled to conduct litigation. Where counsel has been instructed by a person who was not entitled to conduct litigation, counsel's fees cease to be recoverable in that litigation.[27] Whilst it should not be forgotten that, strictly speaking, counsel is not instructed as an agent (see **12.24**), this seems to a reflection of the doctrine that a person cannot do through agency something that he cannot do himself.[28] There is no reason to believe that the position would be any different for service providers other than counsel.

12.19 In summary, where a solicitor principal engages a non-solicitor to provide services, the services may or may not be part of the solicitor principal's fees, depending on the facts. Factors that will be relevant will include the nature of the work, the terms of engagement, the degree of supervision, and the terms of the retainer.

Specific relationships

12.20 The following are examples only. Each case will turn on its own facts and there may be exceptions to the general points which are made out. If, for example, a costs draftsman were to provide an expert opinion in a professional negligence case, a compelling case could be made out for the draftsman's fees not to be treated as being those of the solicitor principal.

---

[24] *Crane v Canons Leisure Centre* [2007] EWCA Civ 1352 at [14].
[25] *Bateman v Mid-Wales Rly Co* (1866) LR 1 CP 499.
[26] See, for example, para 15 of the guidance to rule 10.04 of the Solicitors' Code of Conduct 2007.
[27] This is as a result of the operation of s 25 of the Solicitors Act 1974; see *Westland Helicopters Ltd v Al-Hejailan* [2004] EWHC 1625 (Comm).
[28] *Bateman v Mid-Wales Rly Co* (1866) LR 1 CP 499.

Costs draftsmen

12.21   A costs draftsman's fees are to be dealt with in exactly the same way as would the fees of any other non-solicitor agent. Given the nature of the services and responsibility that the solicitor principal must bear for the costs draftsman's work, it is not surprising that the services will generally be treated as if they had been provided by a solicitor principal. This was confirmed by Hallett LJ:[29]

> '[To] determine whether or not these costs are properly described as base costs or disbursements, one must focus on the nature of the work done (whether it is solicitors' work) and where responsibility for the work lies. In my view, the work done by [the costs draftsmen] was undoubtedly solicitors' work. It was the type of work [the solicitors] were retained to do. [The solicitors] may have chosen to delegate their work, but they never relinquished control of it and responsibility for it. At every stage of the process [the costs draftsmen's] work was under [the solicitor's] supervision ... [Had] there been any failure on the part of [the costs draftsmen], [the solicitors] could have been held accountable. Given that background, for my part, I am satisfied that [the costs draftsmen's] work is properly described as work done "on behalf of the solicitors" and their fees are properly described as base costs ...'

12.22   However, the decision of the court was not unanimous. Whilst May and Hallett LJJ opined that a costs draftsman's fees are profit costs, Maurice Kay LJ believed otherwise. He recognised that his views might give rise to an anomalous and adventitious result in the way in which non-solicitor agents' fees are dealt with, but he justified this on the basis that he would 'prefer an anomalous conclusion to an unjust one'. Other senior judges have expressed similar views, albeit extrajudicially.[30]

12.23   In any event, where the services provided by a costs draftsman are charged as profit costs, the bill of costs in which they are charged will usually make it clear that the work has been done by a costs draftsman. Indeed, on one reading of the CPD, this is mandatory.[31]

Counsel

12.24   For the reasons set out above, counsel's fees will not generally be regarded as services provided by the solicitor principal; that is, it is the received view that they are disbursements.[32] This includes any success fee charged by counsel.

Experts

12.25   Unless the expert is, in truth, merely carrying out administrative work for the solicitor, the services provided by an expert are not generally claimable as services provided by the solicitor principal. Whilst there is no authority on the point, one factor that is likely to be relevant is the fact that the services would not generally be capable of being said to be legal services.

---

29   *Crane v Canons Leisure Centre* [2007] EWCA Civ 1352 at [35]–[36].
30   See R Jackson *Review of Civil Litigation Costs: Final Report* (TSO, December 2009), para 10.5.25.
31   See CPD, art 4.5.
32   See the comments of Maurice Kay LJ in *Crane v Canons Leisure Centre* [2007] EWCA Civ 1352 at [28].

Medical agencies

12.26 It is not clear whether the services provided by medical agencies are to be treated as the work done by the solicitor principal or as a disbursement. One of the reasons it is not clear is because the need for authority on the point has waned in the light of an agreement known as the *Woollard* agreement; this is discussed at **31.67–31.68**. Some medical agencies provide pagination services (ie they sort and paginate medical records); those fees are often claimed as disbursements, but for the reasons set out above (**12.15**), this would not necessarily be the correct way in which they should be claimed. If the solicitor were to retain responsibility for the paginator's work (which would usually be the case), then those costs could reasonably be charged as profit costs.[33]

PLURAL LIABILITY: JOINT AND SEVERAL LIABILITY AND CONTRIBUTIONS

12.27 Where a liability or entitlement to costs attaches to more than one person, that liability or entitlement may be:

(a)   joint;
(b)   several; or
(c)   joint and several.

The term 'plural liability' (or 'plural entitlement', as the case may be) is used to describe these things. Where such a state of affairs exists, issues of apportionment may also arise: that topic is dealt with at **8.417–8.426** (in the context of retainers) and **34.125–34.159** (in the context of assessing costs).

12.28 As most of the authorities which are referred to in this discussion derive from legal disciplines other than the law of costs, they ought to be viewed with some caution. Where a difficult point arises, research beyond what is set out herein will be required.

12.29 Whilst the principles are explained with the focus on plural liability, they will apply just as much to plural entitlement. The focus on plural liability is solely for illustrative purposes and to avoid repetition.

Types of plural liability distinguished

Joint liability

12.30 Joint liability is where two or more persons are ordered to pay the same costs (eg 'the first and second defendants will pay the claimant's costs jointly'). Put another way, whilst the joint costs debtors may be two or more, they share only a single obligation to pay costs. Special and often counter-intuitive rules apply to joint liability (see **12.44–12.51**); in particular, payment by one joint costs debtor may or may not discharge the other joint costs debtors from their costs debts. Thus, if A and B owe a joint liability for payment of costs of £1,000 to C, payment of £1,000 by A to C will

---

[33]   Whilst not binding, see *Ahmed v Aventis Pharma Ltd (Rev 1)* [2009] EWHC 90152 (Costs) (19 November 2009) at [19] per Master Gordon-Saker.

discharge B's costs debt. Joint liability must be distinguished from joint and several liability: this is because the aforementioned special rules will not apply where the liability is joint and several.

Several liability

12.31 Several liability is where two or more persons are, by the same instrument or by linked instruments, ordered to pay or receive costs which are not the same (eg 'the first defendant will pay the claimant's costs up to the 1 January, and the second defendant will pay the claimant's costs thereafter'); the effect is as if there were two or more costs orders. Full payment by one paying party of his costs debt will not impact on the liability of the other paying parties to pay their costs debts. Thus, if A and B each owe a several liability to C of £500, payment by A of his £500 will have no bearing on B's costs debt.

Joint and severable liability

12.32 Joint and severable liability is where two or more persons are ordered to pay the same costs not only jointly but also individually (eg 'the first and second defendants will pay the claimant's costs jointly and severally'). As with joint liability, the costs debtors may be numerous, but there is only one obligation to pay costs. The principal difference between the two forms of plural liability is that the special rules which apply to joint liability do not apply to joint and severable liability.

Interpretation of plural costs awards

12.33 The issue of whether liability for costs is: (a) joint, (b) several, or (c) joint and several is a matter of interpretation of the instrument giving rise to an entitlement to costs. The usual canons of interpretation will apply.

12.34 The nature of an award involving more than one costs debtor or creditor will generally be apparent from the plain meaning of the language, ie an award will often specifically state that a liability is to be borne jointly, or jointly and severally. It will rarely be the case that awards will specifically state that a liability is to be borne severally: this is because that conclusion is usually self-evident from the context. Thus, where the award is that A will pay the costs of the claim and B will pay the costs of a specified issue, that will create a severable liability in respect of the costs of that specified issue; it would be otiose explicitly to state the several nature of B's liability.

12.35 The interpretation of plural costs awards is, however, not always so undemanding. A common situation is where a claim is successfully brought against two defendants, both of whom have defended the claim under separate and independent defences; if the claimant is awarded costs against both but is able to pursue only one (because, say, the other defendant is insolvent), the court may have to decide whether he can recover against one the costs of the other defendant's defence. Whilst there is still room for argument on the point, the law is probably as explained by Lord Esher MR, who found that the liability of the defendants was not joint, but several. He said that to compel the other defendant to pay those costs would be 'absolutely contrary to natural justice'. Fry LJ disagreed with Lord Esher's analysis, preferring instead to say that the issue was one of discretion for the trial judge, rather than a matter which should be decided by the costs judge when he comes to interpret the order:[34]

> 'If natural justice requires that one defendant should not be liable for the costs occasioned solely by the act of the other defendant ... justice will be done if the Court or judge be asked to do it, but it cannot be done by the master. In my opinion the effect of the rule which has been laid down by the Master of the Rolls would be to vest in the master a discretion which by virtue of the rule belongs only to the judge.'

12.36 That was more than a century ago. In more recent times, Davies J found that the judgment of Lord Esher should be preferred and that over the years it had become generally accepted that Fry LJ's judgment was the dissenting judgment.[35] Thus, where a costs order is made against two defendants who each defend the claim under their own separate defences, the costs judge has the power to interpret an order that the claimant should have his costs as applying severally to each defendant in relation to the costs of his own defence.

12.37 Each entitling instrument ought to be interpreted individually. There are certain aids to interpretation which may be relevant, but they offer only limited assistance and are rarely determinative. General trends can be identified, however, an example being the outcome in the case mentioned above in which Lord Esher and Fry LJ disagreed; that was probably a reflection of the general canon – if it can be put as high as being a canon – that an instrument will be interpreted according to the interests of the parties[36] (ie if their interests are joint the instrument will generally be interpreted as joint, but if their interests are several the instrument will generally be interpreted as being several).

12.38 There are one or two general rules which may assist (some of which relate to agreements rather than costs orders, but the principles are broadly the same, especially where the order was made by consent); they include the following (see **12.39–12.42**).

Silence as to severance

12.39 Under common law, a contract which provides for two or more persons to pay the same debt without that agreement making any provision for severance, is a contract for a joint liability.[37] The fact that an order has been made by consent may be a relevant factor.

Firms

12.40 Where the costs award has been made in respect of a firm, the liability of the partners of a firm is joint, not joint and several.[38]

---

[34] *Stumm v Dixon & Co and Knight* (1889) 22 QBD 529 at 536.
[35] *CIBC Mellon Trust Co v Mora Hotel Corporation NV* [2003] EWHC 9037 (Costs).
[36] *Sorsbie v Park* (1843) 12 M & W 146.
[37] *White v Tyndall* (1888) 13 App Cas 263.
[38] Partnership Act 1890, s 9.

Irrelevance of impecuniosity

12.41 The ability of the parties to pay is usually an irrelevant factor; in particular, the ordinary meaning of the instrument must not be disregarded for reasons of convenience or hardship.[39]

Fast track trial costs

12.42 In a fast track trial, where there is more than one claimant but only one defendant, the court may make only one award to the defendant of fast track trial costs, for which the claimants are jointly and severally liable.[40]

Joint liability

12.43 In the context of costs, there are two types of joint liability:

(a)   where a costs creditor (ie a receiving party) is owed a costs debt by more than one joint costs debtors (ie paying parties); and
(b)   where a costs debtor is owed a debt by more than one joint costs creditors.

As has been mentioned at **12.29**, the focus is on joint liability, but this is only for illustrative purposes. With the necessary changes the points made below would also apply to joint entitlement.

12.44 The special rules which are set out in this section relate solely to joint liability: most do not relate to joint and several liability. Indeed, this fact is the most prominent feature distinguishing the two.

12.45 Full payment of costs to only one of a number of joint costs creditors will discharge the costs debt to the others;[41] likewise, full payment of costs by one of a number of joint costs debtors will discharge the debt owed by the others.[42] Payment in either of these circumstances may give rise to a right of contribution between the joint debtor/creditors, but this will usually be a matter that is for those persons themselves and would not usually be addressed in the order for costs.

12.46 The same is not necessarily true of circumstances in which there has been a partial payment by one of the cost debtors, but where there has been an agreement between some but not all of the parties that the payment will be in full satisfaction of the costs debt; whether that agreement binds the other parties will depend on the construction of that agreement.

12.47 Where one of a number of joint costs creditors grants a release of the obligation to be paid costs, that release discharges the debt owed to all of the joint costs debtors.[43] Likewise, where a release is given by a receiving party to one of a number of joint costs

---

[39]   *White v Tyndall* (1888) 13 App Cas 263.
[40]   CPR, r 46.4(5).
[41]   *Powell v Brodhurst* [1901] 2 Ch 160 (albeit in the general rather than costs context).
[42]   *Mainwaring v Goldtech Investments Ltd (No 2)* [1999] 1 WLR 745; and (in the general context) *Thorne v Smith* (1851) 10 CB 659 and *Re EWA* [1901] 2 KB 642, CA.
[43]   *Ruddock's Case* (1599) 6 Co Rep 25a.

debtors, the release discharges the debt owed by all the joint costs debtors.[44] This will not be the case if the release is given with a reservation of a right to claim against the other costs debtors.[45]

12.48 A release may be purchased, in which case it is referred to as 'accord and satisfaction' (see **19.43–19.44**). Where the liability is joint, the same principles apply to accord and satisfaction as will apply to release in general; in particular, accord and satisfaction with one of a number of joint costs creditors will discharge the debt to the others;[46] accord and satisfaction with one of a number of joint costs debtors will also discharge the debt, unless there has been a reservation of right to pursue the other paying parties.[47]

12.49 The payment of costs will count as consideration for the accord and satisfaction.[48] In practical terms, this means that if a costs creditor accepts payment of part of his costs from one joint costs debtor on the basis that that payment will discharge that paying party's liability for costs, he must reserve the right to pursue the other costs debtors for the balance if that is his intended course of action.

12.50 Where judgment is obtained against one joint costs debtor, there is no reason why an assessment should not be continued against the other joint costs debtors.[49] This principle will apply where a receiving party obtains a default costs certificate against a paying party whose ability to pay is in doubt (such as an insolvent paying party who has failed to file points of dispute). If the reality is that such an order amounts to accord and satisfaction, then the receiving party may well have compromised his right to pursue the other paying parties for the balance.[50] An example would be where A and B are jointly liable to C for costs; if (for whatever reason) an order is made assessing the costs payable by A at nil, that order will also apply to B. In this regard, Pill LJ commented:[51]:

> 'This may be considered an undeserved windfall for [B] but appears to me the least unsatisfactory result following the serious default [C] by their solicitors. It would only be in an extreme case, such as the present, in which a taxing officer would wholly disallow costs against a party and there can be no legitimate complaint if the joint debtor is also released.'

12.51 In summary, joint costs debts are dealt with in just the same way as other joint debts.

Several liability

12.52 There will usually be no difficulty in identifying several liability. No special rules apply. For all practical purposes, each several liability can be regarded as being its own, separate costs order.

---

[44]   *Deanplan Ltd v Mahmoud* [1993] Ch 151.
[45]   *Tolstoy v Aldington* (1993) *The Times*, December 16, CA.
[46]   *Wallace v Kelsall* (1840) 7 M & W 264.
[47]   *Watters v Smith* (1831) 2 B & Ad 889.
[48]   *Thompson v Percival* (1834) 5 B & Ad 925.
[49]   Civil Liability (Contribution) Act 1978, s 3.
[50]   *Morris v Wentworth-Stanley* [1999] 2 WLR 470, CA.
[51]   *Mainwaring v Goldtech Investments Ltd (No 2)* [1999] 1 WLR 745.

Joint and several liability

12.53 The special rules which are set out at **12.44–12.51** relating to joint liability do not apply to joint and several liability. If, nonetheless, there is doubt as to whether an order provides for joint liability or joint and several liability, then it would usually be prudent to assume that those rules apply before approving the wording of any proposed compromise or consent order.

12.54 If costs are payable jointly and severally, and if there is accord and satisfaction in relation to the liability of one of the paying parties, that will not release the other paying parties from their liability to pay, but it will diminish their liability by the amount that has been paid. For example, if A and B are jointly and severally liable to C for costs of £1,000, and if C releases A from all further liability on the basis that A makes a contribution of £450, then C may pursue B for the remaining £550. In practice, this would mean that there would be an assessment of the full £1,000, and B would be ordered to pay C the assessed sum less £450.

12.55 In summary, joint and several costs debts are dealt with in just the same way as other joint and several debts.

Contributions

12.56 Where a joint costs debtor wishes partially or fully to discharge a joint costs debt, he may wish to seek a partial or full contribution from the other joint costs debtors. The starting point is the Civil Liability (Contribution) Act 1978 ('CL(C)A 1978'), s 1 of which reads:

> '(1) Subject to the following provisions of this section, any person liable in respect of any damage suffered by another person may recover contribution from any other person liable in respect of the same damage (whether jointly with him or otherwise).
>
> (2) A person shall be entitled to recover contribution by virtue of subsection (1) above notwithstanding that he has ceased to be liable in respect of the damage in question since the time when the damage occurred, provided that he was so liable immediately before he made or was ordered or agreed to make the payment in respect of which the contribution is sought.
>
> (3) A person shall be liable to make contribution by virtue of subsection (1) above notwithstanding that he has ceased to be liable in respect of the damage in question since the time when the damage occurred, unless he ceased to be liable by virtue of the expiry of a period of limitation or prescription which extinguished the right on which the claim against him in respect of the damage was based.
>
> (4) A person who has made or agreed to make any payment in bona fide settlement or compromise of any claim made against him in respect of any damage (including a payment into court which has been accepted) shall be entitled to recover contribution in accordance with this section without regard to whether or not he himself is or ever was liable in respect of the damage, provided, however, that he would have been liable assuming that the factual basis of the claim against him could be established.
>
> (5) References in this section to a person's liability in respect of any damage are references to any such liability which has been or could be established in an action brought against him in England and Wales by or on behalf of the person who suffered the damage.'

12.57 CL(C)A 1978, s 2 goes on to provide that the assessment of the contribution shall be such as may be found by the court to be just and equitable having regard to the extent of that person's responsibility for the damage in question.

12.58 As to the applicability of CL(C)A 1978, s 6 provides:

> 'A person is liable in respect of any damage for the purposes of this Act if the person who suffered it ... is entitled to recover compensation from him in respect of that damage (whatever the legal basis of his liability, whether tort, breach of contract, breach of trust or otherwise).'

12.59 CL(C)A 1978, therefore, refers to damages rather than costs. It also draws a distinction between 'damages' and 'damage' (see s 6(1)), so a point which may arise is whether a contribution in respect of costs may be sought under that Act.

12.60 There are competing arguments on the point. In brief, the issue is whether costs can be said to have arisen from the original damage, or whether they are merely a necessary incident of the subsequent claim.

12.61 There is no easy answer to this question. It is necessary to examine a number of authorities (some of which apply only by analogy). The conclusion that is reached is that a contribution of costs may be made where a contribution in respect of damages is also awarded, but there is doubt as to whether a contribution may be awarded solely in respect of costs.

12.62 It is best to deal with the authorities in the order they were decided; only the more recent case law is discussed.[52] It is convenient to start with the following obiter comments of HHJ Lloyd QC (sitting as a judge of the High Court):[53]

> 'Costs in a case such as this arise from the defendant's decision not to accept liability and not from the original cause of action ... Even on a wide interpretation of either section 1 or section 2 of [the Act] costs could not, therefore, form part of the loss or damage with respect to which a party is entitled to contribution.'

Davies J came to a similar conclusion in a different case.[54]

12.63 Whilst adopting a different line of thinking and dealing with a slightly different point, Brooke LJ (with whom Beldham LJ agreed) found that Davies J's judgment should not be followed;[55] presumably, he would have said the same about HHJ Lloyd's analysis. Brooke LJ's comments were obiter and related to the word 'payment' in CL(C)A 1978, s 1(4), but there is no reason to believe that a different interpretation should apply to the use of the word 'damages' elsewhere in the Act.

12.64 In a different case Henry LJ dealt with the issue of 'damages' generally, and he came to much the same conclusion as Brook LJ:[56]

> '[E]ven if part of the payment was expressed to be made in respect of BICC's costs, we are not persuaded that the words of sections 2 or 6(1) of the Act preclude the making of a contribution order in respect of that part. Section 1(1) defines the person who is entitled "... to recover contribution ..." and the person from whom it may be recovered. Section 2(1) does not expressly limit the amount of contribution to the amount payable in respect of

---

[52] This does not mean that earlier case law does not exist; whilst dealing with a different point, in *Biggin & Co Ltd v Permanite Ltd* [1951] 2 KB 314 Lloyd LJ said: 'Reasonable settlements are to be encouraged (which invariably means that costs are taken into account in arriving at the figure).'
[53] *Sainsbury plc v Broadway Malyan* [1998] 61 Con LR 31 at para 8.3.
[54] *Police Federation v Ryder* (1990) The Times, July 30.
[55] See *Adams v Associated Newspapers Ltd et al* (1999) EMLR 26.
[56] *BICC Ltd v Parkman Consulting Engineers (a firm)* [2001] EWCA Civ 1621, (2002) BLR 64 at [121].

liability "... for the damage in question ..." – section 2(3) might, but would not necessarily have this effect; and section 6(1) again defines the person who can claim contribution, without expressly limiting his recovery to the "compensation" he is liable to pay to the injured person.'

12.65 Brooke LJ's analysis was not drawn to Henry LJ's attention, but if it had been, it would probably have served only to bolster his view. Henry LJ went on to add the following comments:[57]

'Our present view is that the 1978 Act enables the party claiming contribution to recover a contribution towards a payment made in respect of the injured party's costs: but it is sufficient for the purposes of the present case that the judge [in the court below] was entitled to have regard to the whole of the settlement figure paid in respect of "all claims".'

Henry LJ, therefore, seems to have limited his conclusion to circumstances in which the compensation paid to the injured party was made up of both costs and damages, so it could be argued that his comments do not apply where the contribution is solely for costs. Ramsey J came to much the same conclusion as Henry LJ, that being in a case in which a lump sum was paid in respect of both costs and damages.[58]

12.66 Thus, a contribution may be awarded where it is also awarded for damages, but it is not clear whether a contribution can be awarded solely for costs; it probably can, but there is some doubt about this. Where a contribution is payable, it will be for the party who seeks it to show that the amount claimed is reasonable.[59]

SET-OFF

12.67 Where there are mutual liabilities for costs (ie A is liable for B's costs and vice versa), set-off may operate to allow the smaller claim to be deducted from the larger claim, thereby leaving the party with the larger of the two to pay the balance. Mr Leggatt QC (setting as a Deputy Judge of the High Court) summarised the principles in this way:[60]

'(1) Where one party has a claim against another party who has a cross-claim, the two claims cannot be netted off so as to extinguish each liability to the extent of the other except by agreement or a judgment of the court and once both liabilities have been established by agreement or judgment.

(2) Where, however, the two claims are for sums of money which are due and certain in amount, each party may raise a defence to the extent of its own claim in proceedings brought by the other (legal set-off).

(3) In addition, where the two claims are (i) made reasonably and in good faith and (ii) so closely connected that it would be manifestly unjust to allow one party to enforce payment

---

[57]   *BICC Ltd v Parkman Consulting Engineers (a firm)* [2001] EWCA Civ 1621, (2002) BLR 64 at [123].
[58]   *Mouchel Ltd v Van Oord (UK) Ltd (No 2)* [2011] EWHC 1516 (TCC).
[59]   See *German Property 50 Sarl v Summers-Inman Construction & Property Consultants LLP* [2009] EWHC 2968 (TCC) at [16] per Coulson J, citing the pre-CPR case of *Biggin & Co Ltd v Permanite Ltd* (1951) 2 KB 314, CA.
[60]   *Fearns v Anglo-Dutch Paint & Chemical Company Ltd* [2010] EWHC 2366 (Ch) at [50].

without taking into account the crossclaim, neither party may exercise any rights contingent on the validity of its claim except in so far as it exceeds the other party's claim (equitable set-off).

(4) Under CPR r.40.13 and the court's inherent jurisdiction, the court has a discretion to order any judgment sum to be set off (in the sense of netted off) against any other such sum. The date at which such a set-off should be effected is the date on which the existence and amount of the two liabilities is or was established.

(5) The approach which the court should adopt when ordering such a set-off between amounts payable in different currencies is: (i) to assess and add to each principal amount any interest accruing up to the date of the setoff;(ii) to convert the smaller amount into the currency of the larger amount at the exchange rate prevailing at that date; and (iii) to order payment of the balance.'

Set-off is in the discretion of the court; if there is no order for set-off, then each claim may be enforced independently.

12.68 In the context of costs, the topic of set-off would usually arise when the court makes cross-orders as to costs. It is that situation which is considered in this section. Set-off (or, more accurately, 'abatement', which is a common law right distinct from set-off)[61] may also apply in a solicitor and client setting, where it can operate as a species of defence to a claim for unpaid solicitors' fees. This is discussed at **27.26–27.30**.

Jurisdiction

12.69 Whilst an oversimplification, set-off traditionally has the following two origins:

*   *At law*: The power to make an order for set-off at law is statutory.[62] It was a right to set-off liabilities which were mutual (ie between the same parties and in the same interest),[63] which were due and payable,[64] and which could be quantified.[65] The competing liabilities do not need to arise at the same time.[66]
*   *In equity as preserved by statute*: Historically the power to make an order for equitable set-off operated to restrain a claimant proceeding in a claim where there was equity which negated the claim; that power is now preserved by statute.[67] Equity has developed by analogy with set-off at law.[68] Where the right to set-off arises at law, equity will recognise it, unless to do so would be inequitable.[69]

Denning MR has commented that these two strands have flowed together and combined so as to be indistinguishable.[70]

---

[61] *Mondel v Steel* (1841) 8 M & W 858.
[62] See now the Senior Courts Act 1981, s 49(2), which derived from the Supreme Court of Judicature (Consolidation) Act 1925 (repealed); in the county court see s 72 of the County Courts Act 1984.
[63] *Inca Hall Rolling Mills Co Ltd v Douglas Forge Co* (1882) 8 QBD 179 and 183.
[64] *Stein v Blake* [1996] AC 243.
[65] *Hanak v Green* [1958] 2 QB 9.
[66] *Day & Dent Constructions Pty Ltd v North Australian Properties Pty Ltd* (1986) 150 CLR 85.
[67] See s 49(2) of the Senior Courts Act 1981, which refers to equitable defences.
[68] See *Halsburys Laws of England*, paras 659–660; and see *Rawson v Samuel* (1841) Cr & Ph 161.
[69] *Re Whitehouse & Co* (1878) Ch D 595.
[70] *Federal Commerce and Navigation Co Ltd v Molena Alpha Inc* [1978] QB 927 at 974.

12.70 This traditional way of looking at set-off does not apply when the court is exercising its discretion as to the incidence of costs (save as a guide). Instead, that matter is very much a matter of discretion; the court's power to make an award of set-off may analysed in two ways:

- *Section 51*: Scott LJ has commented that in so far as set-off involving only costs is concerned, the jurisdiction to make an order for set-off may be thought of as arising from s 51 of the Senior Courts Act 1981; he went on to say that that analysis does not hold good where costs are set-off against damages.[71]
- *Inherent jurisdiction*: Many judges have concluded that the court has an inherent jurisdiction to make an order that costs be set-off against costs;[72] Neuberger J has found that this gives the court greater flexibility than it would have when applying the usual statutory and equitable principles (see **12.83**). Brooke LJ (giving judgment of the court) agreed with that analysis (see **12.84**).[73]

12.71 Regardless of which analysis best suits the case in hand, the court has greater freedom over costs than it does when dealing with other types of set-off. In particular, the requirements of mutuality, etc (which will be referred to in this chapter as 'the requirements in *Hanak*')[74] (see below) do not need to be satisfied before the court can order that costs be set-off. Nonetheless, those requirements would normally be met because most (if not nearly all) cross-orders for costs will:

(i)   be made in circumstances where they will relate to the same parties and the same interests;

(ii)   they will almost always be quantifiable; and

(iii)   they will usually arise and become payable at the same time.

Therefore, the fine distinctions mentioned above are usually little more than of academic interest.

12.72 The CPR provide the mechanism by which orders for set-off may be made. CPR, r 16.6 makes provision for pleading set-off, but that provision is of only limited application to costs. In the present context the more important provision is at r 44.3(9)(a):

> (9)   Where a party entitled to costs is also liable to pay costs the court may assess the costs which that party is liable to pay and either—
>
> (a)   set off the amount assessed against the amount the party is entitled to be paid and direct him to pay any balance ...'

This provision permits set-off of costs in its traditional sense (ie where a quantified sum is subtracted from another quantified sum); for the reasons set out above, the court will not be constrained by the requirements in *Hanak* when making an order under this provision.

---

[71]   *Lockley v National Blood Transfusion Service* [1992] 1 WLR 492 at 496.

[72]   *Izzo v Philip Ross* (unreported) 31 July 2001, Neuberger J; see also *Edwards v Hope* (1885) 14 QBD 922; *Reid v Cupper* [1915] 2 KB 147; and *R (on the application of Burkett) v Hammersmith and Fulham London Borough Council* [2004] EWCA Civ 1342 at [44].

[73]   *R (on the application of Burkett) v Hammersmith and Fulham London Borough Council* [2004] EWCA Civ 1342 at [38].

[74]   After *Hanak v Green* [1958] 2 QB 9.

12.73 The court has an even greater freedom, however, because – contrary to older practices[75] – CPR, r 44.3(6) and (7) also permit the court to take set-off into account when making an order that a party be awarded only part of his costs. In those circumstances, the court is unfettered in its discretion to do justice between the parties; the relevant principles are set out at **7.19–7.26**.

12.74 There is no reason why set-off should not apply to an order which has been made on a general issues-based approach.[76]

12.75 The way in which a party is funded is not something that would deprive the court of the jurisdiction to make an order of set-off. In particular, the fact that the LSC may have a proprietorial right arising out of the statutory charge will not prevent an order for set-off being made; in particular, in so far as the *Hanak* rules apply, there will be no lack of mutuality arising out of the fact that the LSC has a right to a statutory charge.[77] The same seems not to be true of awards made in respect of pro bono representation: see **11.109**.

12.76 In summary, the court has wide powers to make an order for set-off and, whilst the requirements in *Hanak* may be a guide as to how the court should exercise its discretion, those requirements do not fetter the court.

Procedure

12.77 Where an application for set-off is made at the same time as the costs order itself, that application will merely form part of the parties' submissions and so there will be no applicable formalities. It will rarely be the case that a party seeking set-off would need to plead that contention in formal pleadings. Nevertheless, the CPR make provision for set-off to be pleaded as a defence (regardless of whether that entitlement to costs is also brought as a Part 20 claim),[78] and that may be appropriate where it is envisaged that the set-off will involve the costs that are the subject matter of the claim.

12.78 Although there is no authority on the point, there is nothing within the CPR to suggest that the power to make an order for set-off vests only in the judge making the costs order. Indeed, the wording of r 44.3(9) seems specifically to envisage that the court may decide whether to make such an order after the costs have been assessed. It would, therefore, seem that a costs judge has the power to make an order for set-off in respect of those costs of which he is seized.

12.79 There is nothing within the CPR which expressly requires a party seeking set-off to state its case in points of dispute. Such a party would be well advised to do so, however, as this would not only alert the court to the need to allocate the bills of costs to the same judge, but would also alert the court to the need not to make an order of its own volition for a payment on account without first taking set-off into account.

---

[75] See, for example, *Chell Engineering Ltd v Unit Tool and Engineering Co Ltd* [1950] 1 All ER 378.

[76] *Graham Calvert v William Hill Credit Ltd* [2008] EWCA Civ 888.

[77] *R (on the application of Burkett) v Hammersmith and Fulham London Borough Council* [2004] EWCA Civ 1342, following *Lockley v National Blood Transfusion Service* [1992] 1 WLR 492 and overruling *Re A Debtor* (1981) The Times, February 19 and *Anderson v Hills Automobiles (Woodford) Ltd* [1965] 1 WLR 745; see also *Hill v Bailey* [2003] EWHC 2835 (Ch) and *Re Neckles* [2003] EWHC 685 (Ch).

[78] CPR, r 16.6.

12.80 Where the issues concerning set-off place the matter beyond the jurisdiction of the county court, the matter may be transferred to the High Court.[79] Where a party wishes to set-off costs in different courts, written notice must be given to the courts concerned. The matter may then be transferred to a single court for the purposes of dealing with set-off.[80] Where, in the county court, the orders have yet to be made, the counterpart court must send a copy of the order to the court which is dealing with the application.[81]

12.81 In summary, in so far as costs are concerned, from a practical viewpoint there are almost no formalities relating to set-off.

Discretion

12.82 Whether to make an order for set-off is a question for the court's discretion.[82]

The breadth of the court's discretion

12.83 For the reasons set out at **12.71**, the court is not constrained by the requirements in *Hanak*. Neuberger J has explained that this is because the power to order that costs be set-off against costs arises from the court's inherent jurisdiction rather than solely from the doctrines of equitable or statutory set-off.[83] In the case before him, for example, Neuberger J observed (albeit obiter) that the court's inherent jurisdiction would have permitted him to make an order notwithstanding the fact that on a *Hanak* analysis there might have been a lack of mutuality in terms of the parties' identity.

12.84 Brooke LJ agreed with Neuberger J's analysis:

'In [*Lockley v National Blood Transfusion Service* [1992] 1 WLR 492] the court appears also to have been addressed on the basis of the rules as to set-off as a defence, and despite its perception ... that the "set-off" with which it was concerned was different and discretionary in nature, it reviewed those rules ... In truth, that step was not necessary, because the set-off ordered by Newman J, and by this court in *Lockley*, and by our predecessors in *Reid v Cupper* [[1915] 2 KB 147], is of a quite different nature from the type of set-off to which the rules of mutuality apply.'

12.85 One of the passages in *Lockley* to which Brooke LJ referred was the following, in which Scott LJ analysed the matter by reference to the requirements in *Hanak*:[84]

'The broad criterion for the application of set-off is that the plaintiff's claim and the defendant's claim are so closely connected that it would be inequitable to allow the plaintiff's claim without taking into account the defendant's claim. As it has sometimes been put, the defendant's claim must, in equity, impeach the plaintiff's claim.'

12.86 Brooke LJ made it clear that whilst the matter could be analysed in that way, this was not necessary:[85]

---

[79]   SCA 1981, s 75.
[80]   SCA 1981, s 75.
[81]   County Courts Act 1984, s 72.
[82]   *Currie & Co v The Law Society* [1977] QB 990 at 1000, per May J.
[83]   *Izzo v Philip Ross* (unreported) 31 July 2001, Neuberger J.
[84]   *Lockley v National Blood Transfusion Service* [1992] 1 WLR 492 at 496.
[85]   *R (on the application of Burkett) v Hammersmith and Fulham London Borough Council* [2004] EWCA Civ 1342 at [46].

'None of this has anything at all to do with a discretionary balance between two sums of costs. First, it is for the judge to decide, in his discretion, what costs order is appropriate. The exercise of striking a fair balance between such payments is quite different from the judge's task in a case of equitable set-off as just discussed, where he has to decide as a matter of law, not of discretion, what claims can be asserted, and then, but only then, decide whether the rules governing equitable set-off permit the one claim to be set-off against the other. Secondly, and illustrative of the point just made, no right to costs arises until the judge decides that the right exists. Since he has discretion in creating the right, so he has discretion in deciding the amount in which, and the form in which, that right should be enforced.'

Brooke LJ went on to explain that technical objections to set-off founded on the notion of lack of mutuality 'simply beat the air'.[86]

12.87 Where the court is deciding the issue of set-off at the same time as deciding what costs order to make, the requirements in *Hanak* do not apply. There is no authority on the issue of whether the same applies when the topic of set-off is addressed at some later time. For the reasons set out at **12.71**, however, that would rarely present any difficulties; this is because the requirements in *Hanak* would usually be met in circumstances where cross-orders as to costs had already been made.

The form and effect of an order for set-off

12.88 There is nothing to prevent a court from making an order for set-off in respect of only a part of a party's costs. Where, for example, the litigation has lent itself to an issues-based order, the court may order set-off in respect of only those issues in beteen which there is a nexus.[87]

12.89 An order for set-off does not place the person against whom it is asserted under any obligation to pay; it merely reduces the amount that he can recover.[88] Pre-CPR authority suggests that a party cannot be compelled to claim set-off.[89] It may be that this principle has not survived the introduction of the CPR. In any event, the power to make percentage awards, etc, affords the court alternative means of dealing with the situation where there are competing rights to costs.

The exercise of discretion

12.90 As to the way in which the court should exercise its discretion, pre-CPR authority was that, unless there were special circumstances, the court would lean towards making an order for set-off in appropriate cases.[90] Although obiter, Neuberger J seems to have found that those authorities continue to have resonance under the CPR;[91] nevertheless, there are other types of award which may achieve a similar or equally fair result (often in a more efficient manner), and those will usually be borne in mind as alternatives (see **7.19–7.23**)

---

[86] *R (on the application of Burkett) v Hammersmith and Fulham London Borough Council* [2004] EWCA Civ 1342 at [47].

[87] *Hashem v Shayif* [2009] EWHC 864 (Fam).

[88] *Hicks v Russell Jones & Walker (27 October 2000), CAT* at para 11; *Hill v Bailey* [2004] 1 All ER 1210; and *R (on the application of Burkett) v Hammersmith and Fulham London Borough Council* [2004] EWCA Civ 1342 at [50].

[89] In the non-costs setting, see *Laing v Chatham* (1808) 1 Camp 252; *Jenner v Morris* (1861) 3 De GF & J 45; *Davis v Hedges* (1871) LR 6 QB 687; *Re Sturmey Motors Ltd, Rattray v Sturmey Motors Ltd* [1913] 1 Ch 16.

[90] *Puddephatt v Leith (No 2)* [1916] 2 Ch 168 and *Curry & Co v The Law Society* [1977] QB 990.

[91] *Izzo v Philip Ross* (unreported) 31 July 2001, Neuberger J.

12.91 In so far as claims and counterclaims are concerned, CPR, r 40.13 makes the following provisions relating to set-off:

> '(1) This rule applies where the court gives judgment for specified amounts both for the claimant on his claim and against the claimant on a counterclaim.
>
> (2) If there is a balance in favour of one of the parties, it may order the party whose judgment is for the lesser amount to pay the balance.
>
> (3) In a case to which this rule applies, the court may make a separate order as to costs against each party.'

Potter LJ has confirmed that paragraph (3) makes provision for the court to make a separate order for costs against each party according to its view of the justice of the case.[92]

12.92 Scott LJ has confirmed that the fact that a party is in receipt of public funding makes set-off no different from and no more extensive than the set-off available to or against parties who are not publicly funded.[93]

Factors to be taken into account

12.93 The following circumstances may have a bearing on whether an order for set-off will be made. Some of the considerations will be encountered more commonly than others; indeed, it can be seen that in the context of costs, some of the circumstances (such as a claim for costs being time barred) are extremely unlikely to arise. They are mentioned only for the sake of completeness.

Insolvency

12.94 Where a party is likely to be unable to pay costs, it would, in the absence of persuasive factors to make an order for set-off, be counter to common notions of good sense and justice to require the other party to pay, as opposed to set-off, its costs.[94]

Assignment

12.95 Where one of the parties has assigned his right to costs to a third party, equity may, in certain circumstances, intervene to prevent set-off diminishing the third party's rights;[95] this is because it would be unconscionable to allow that entitlement to be negated.[96] Much will depend on timing and notice: these are issues that are dealt with in texts on equity.

---

[92] *Boynton v Willers* [2003] EWCA Civ 904 at [39].
[93] *Lockley v National Blood Transfusion Service* [1992] 1 WLR 492 at 496.
[94] In the costs setting, see *Revenue & Customs Commissioners v Xicom Systems Ltd* [2008] EWHC 1945 (Ch) and *Fearns v Anglo-Dutch Paint & Chemical Company Ltd* [2010] EWHC 2366 (Ch); in a more general setting, see *Re Debtor (No 21 of 1950) (No 1)* [1951] Ch 313.
[95] See, as a costs example, *Izzo v Philip Ross* (unreported) 31 July 2001, Neuberger J, where a *McKenzie* friend's entitlement to costs arising out of an order which had been assigned took precedence.
[96] See *Re Whitehouse & Co* (1878) 9 Ch D 595; *Re Paraguassu Steam Tramroad Co* (1872) 8 Ch App 254; *Mercer v Graves* (1872) LR 7 QB 499.

Legal expenses insurance

12.96 A factor that may be relevant is whether set-off would have a bearing on whether a claim could be made under a policy of legal expenses insurance.

No mutuality and interest of justice

12.97 Where there is a lack of mutuality (such as where the cross-orders related to wholly separate issues,[97] or where they arose in claims where parties were acting in different capacities) the court may decline to order set-off; for the reasons set out above this would be a matter of discretion rather than as a result of a failure to meet the requirements in *Hanak*. By way of example, both Neuberger J and Blofeld J have commented that, on the facts of the case before them, an order for set-off would not have been appropriate where the cross-orders related to entirely separate issues in the litigation.[98] In a case in which the claimant was a lead claimant in group litigation, Owen J refused to set-off the claimant's proportionate share of the costs of trial of the generic issues against the claimant's damages, this being because this would not be fair and just: this is because he had sustained injury and consequential loss and damage, and he would have have succeeded in that action whether or not the generic issues had been litigated.[99]

Inchoate claims, unquantified claims, and foreign currencies

12.98 Where a party has been awarded costs but is not in a position to quantify those costs (such as where the court has declined to make a forthwith order, or where the fees of an expert are required before the bill of costs can be finalised), it may not be appropriate – or, in some cases, even possible – to make an order for set-off at that time. Similarly, where costs are large and where the court has no bills of costs to assist it, it may be appropriate to defer any decision as to set off until once more is known about the sums involved.[100] It may be set off needs to be made of one currency against another; the approach is to assess and add to each principal amount any relevant interest up to the date of the set-off, then convert the lesser sum into the currency of the greater sum at the exchange rate prevailing at that date, and then to order payment of the balance.[101]

Time barred

12.99 Where one of the party's claims for costs is time barred, the court may require that party to pursue his claim independently so as to afford the other party the opportunity to plead limitation.[102]

---

[97] See, for example, *Hashem v Shayif* [2009] EWHC 864 (Fam), in which the court made an order for set-off in respect of the costs of some of the issues, but not all.

[98] *Zappia Middle East Construction Co Ltd v Clifford Chance (a firm)* [2001] EWCA Civ 946, per Neuberger J commenting on a previous decision by Blofeld J in the same case.

[99] *O v Ministry of Defence* [2006] EWHC 990 (QB).

[100] See *Amin v Amin* [2010] EWHC 827 (Ch) at [51].

[101] *Fearns v Anglo-Dutch Paint & Chemical Company Ltd* [2010] EWHC 2366 (Ch) at [50] onwards, per Leggatt QC (sitting as a Deputy Judge of the High Court).

[102] A claim by way of set-off is deemed to be a separate action which commenced on the same date as the original action: see LA 1980, s 35(1)(b) and (2).

Third parties

12.100   The positions of third parties other than assignees may be relevant (such as where a commercial funder may be denied monies if the funded party's costs were to be diminished by reason of set-off, or where the rights of a *McKenzie* friend need to be taken into account).[103] That said, the fact that the financial burden on the Legal Services Commission would be increased by an order for set-off is irrelevant, this being because it was their choice fund the claim.[104]

Unpaid solicitors

12.101   One particular type of third party merits particular mention, namely, solicitors. Where a receiving party has failed to pay his solicitor, the solicitor may take lien over the costs order in the hope that monies paid by the paying party will be recovered. If there are cross-orders as to costs and if the other party claims set-off, the court will have to decide whether to give precedence to the solicitor's lien or whether the rights of the paying party should prevail. Whilst there are older authorities to the contrary, the solicitor's lien would not normally disturb the paying party's right to set-off.[105] This will not always be so. In a case in which orders for costs were the fruits of the solicitor's labour and in which there were no good reasons to allow the solicitor's interest to be defeated, Pumfrey J declined to make an order for set-off.[106]

12.102   In summary, the court has a very wide discretion as to whether to order set-off, and that discretion is not constrained by the requirements in *Hanak*. An order for set-off may apply to all of a party's costs or to only a part of them. Many factors may be taken into account (even if they are to be afforded no or little weight), but the following are commonly found to be relevant:

- the solvency of the parties;
- the rights of third parties (including the rights of assignees and – rarely – of a party's solicitor);
- the position concerning legal expenses insurance;
- mutuality; and
- whether a claim for costs is inchoate.

FINALITY OF LITIGATION IN COSTS

12.103   The following discussion[107] examines the topic of when a decision becomes final in the sense that a party is precluded from controverting or reopening a decision which has been, or which ought to have been, made previously. It assumes that the order in question has not been appealed or revised: those topics are addressed at **23.15**, **6.8–6.12**, and **7.413–7.421**. The topics which are the focus of this subchapter are:

- *res judicata* estoppel (including cause of action estoppel and issue estoppel);

---

[103]   *Izzo v Philip Ross* (unreported) 31 July 2001, Neuberger J.
[104]   *Ahmad v Brent London Borough Council* [2011] EWHC 378 (QB) at [12] per Supperstone J.
[105]   *Puddephatt v Leith (No 2)* [1916] 2 Ch 168.
[106]   *Rohm Haas Co v Collag Ltd* [2002] IPD 25007.
[107]   The writer is grateful to J Handley for his helpful comments. J Handley is co-author of Spencer Bower and Handley: *Res Judicata* (LexisNexis Butterworths, 4th edn, 2009).

- abuse of process; and
- tardy arguments and preclusion by proportionality.

The relevance of these concepts to costs is twofold: first, they may have a bearing on the ability of a costs judge to enquire into that which has, or should have been, previously determined in the substantive litigation; and secondly, they may have a bearing on the extent to which a costs judge may hear arguments which were, or which ought to have been, articulated at the time the costs order was made. Topics concerning finality of costs within costs proceedings (such as whether a further bill of costs may be presented after the first has already been assessed) are also briefly touched upon (see **12.134**).

12.104 From ancient times, it has been a goal of the law that litigation must be capable of being brought to an end. Save for appellate proceedings, the law seeks to discourage the same issues being litigated more than once.[108] To achieve this goal, costs orders are regarded as being final judgments (see **6.8–6.12**) and restrictions are to be imposed on the extent to which parties are able to ask the court to examine issues which have been, or on occasion which should have been, examined before. It is this which is the focus of this chapter.

12.105 Unfortunately, there is a dearth of authority on that topic; this means that it is usually necessary to seek guidance from the way similar issues are dealt with in substantive litigation. The writer is grateful to the Australian judge Handley J (co-author of *Res judicata*) for his kind assistance in indentifying appropriate authorities.[109] Analogous authorities have been addressed with caution, but the reader should be aware that costs litigation can differ markedly from substantive litigation; in particular, costs litigation has a much greater emphasis on adjectival law than is the case in substantive litigation, and this is especially true following the introduction of the CPR.

12.106 Towards the end of this subchapter one or two topics are addressed for the purposes of explaining that the supposed rule in *Aaron v Shelton*)[110] is no longer good law. If the reader is already able to put that authority out of his mind, then the relevant paragraph (**12.138**) can be disregarded.

Res judicata

12.107 *Res judicata* is used as a term to cover a number of different doctrines, including *res judicata* estoppel. It is, however, a term which is used inconsistently, especially in older authorities.[111] In this book it is used to refer to *res judicata* estoppel. That concept subdivides into 'cause of action estoppel' (or, to use a useful American phrase, 'claim preclusion') and 'issue estoppel' (or 'issue preclusion'). These concepts are wholly different from abuse of process, which is addressed later in this subchapter. They are also different from the concept of preclusion by proportionality (see **12.140**). Whilst the distinction between cause of action estoppel and issue estoppel is described, in the context of costs litigation there is a great deal of overlap and it is often a distinction which is of little practical relevance. This is different from substantive litigation, in which the distinction can be of some importance.

---

[108] *Arthur JS Hall v Simons* [2000] 3 All ER 673 at 701, per Lord Hoffmann.
[109] Spencer Bower and Handley: *Res Judicata* (LexisNexis Butterworths, 4th edn, 2009).
[110] [2004] EWHC 1162 (QB).
[111] In particular, it is often used to refer to 'merger of the cause of action' (*transit in rem judicatam*) which, whilst of importance in substantive litigation, is of little relevance to costs.

Cause of action estoppel (or claim preclusion)

12.108   Cause of action estoppel acts to ensure that a person is not vexed by the same claim twice. In its most essential form, it will act to estop an entire cause of action. In the context of substantive litigation it is usually described alongside 'merger of the cause of action in the judgment',[112] but in so far as costs litigation is concerned, this latter concept has little relevance. Instead, its relevance is the fact that the estoppel will preclude a party from controverting points of law or fact which were necessarily decided by the earlier proceedings;[113] this would be as a result either of a determination which was expressly made, or as a result of an inferred judicial determination.

12.109   Whilst there is no costs authority on the point, an example might be where a claim is successfully brought in negligence in a road traffic accident and the paying party (the defendant) seeks to argue during the costs proceedings that the accident did not take place and that no costs should be allowed in respect of it. The receiving party would respond by saying that the paying party is estopped from raising that point because the existence of the accident is a fact which was a necessary part of the claim. From the point of view of costs litigation the effect would often be the same regardless of whether the estoppel were cause of action estoppel of issue estoppel, but this would not always be the case, especially if new material had come to light during the course of the assessment (see **12.122**).[114]

12.110   Cause of action estoppel will apply regardless of the correctness of the decision relied upon.[115] This is of particular relevance to costs litigation because it will often be the case that the parties will come to question the correctness of a decision as a result of material which was not available to the trial judge (or to the parties when they agreed a consent order), but which becomes available on the detailed assessment. The earlier decision will be binding upon the parties (unless overturned on appeal or otherwise set aside). Whilst giving judgment in a context other than costs litigation, Millett J had the following to say:[116]

'*Res judicata* ... gives effect to the policy of the law that the parties to a judicial decision should not afterwards be allowed to re-litigate the same question, even though the decision may be wrong.'

12.111   Thus, if, in the example given above, documentation came to light during the detailed assessment which showed, for example, that the claimant had freely admitted that the car was not his, the defendant would not be able to argue that the court should disregard the prior judgment. This is a topic which is addressed at **12.117**. (In practice, however, a costs judge would be able to give great weight to the new information, in that the judge would not allow as being reasonable costs which had been incurred in putting forward a false case.)

12.112   The court's task in deciding whether a party is estopped is to identify the fact that is in question and then to decide whether that fact is included within the judgment on the claim. Such facts will generally be limited to those issues which have necessarily

---

[112]   See Spencer Bower, Turner and Handley *The Doctrine of Res Judicata* (Butterworths, 1996), paras 176–183.

[113]   See *Gregory v Molesworth* (1747) 3 Ark 626 for an early example of the application of this principle.

[114]   See the discussion of this in Spencer Bower, Turner and Handley *The Doctrine of Res Judicata* (Butterworths, 1996), chapter 7.

[115]   In a setting other than costs; see *Myers v Casey* (1913) 17 CLR 90 at 114.

[116]   *Crown Estate Commissioners v Dorset County Council* [1990] Ch 297 at 305.

been decided by the claim.[117] This will include points which have not been expressly set out in the judgment but which must have been decided for the court to make the finding that it made.[118] The ambit of the estoppel is narrow: the court will generally look only to those facts which, when examined with precision, can be said to have been necessarily included within the judgment on the claim.[119] Thus, cause of action estoppel would apply to a contention that the claimant was present at the scene of the accident mentioned above, but it would not apply to a contention that the colour of the car was blue, and this would be so even if this was the most contentious point decided at trial. That, however, would be something to which the wider doctrines mentioned below might apply.

12.113 The effect of a judgment for a claimant will usually be greater than for a defendant. This is because a defendant is able to succeed if it is successful on only one point, but a claimant must prove an entire cause of action in order to succeed. The consequence of this is that where a defendant wishes to rely on his success in defending the claim he must prove that the previous claim was decided on a basis that afforded him a defence in the subsequent claim.[120]

12.114 The ambit of cause of action estoppel will be decided primarily on the judgment on the claim, including, in an appropriate case, the reasons for the judgment.[121] Where there is ambiguity or uncertainty, it may be determined by examining the transcript of the hearing, the judge's notes, etc,[122] but where the judgment has clear meaning, no evidence (including the pleadings or the procedural history) is admissible to contradict that meaning.[123] Likewise, evidence may not be used for the purposes of denying a fact that has been pleaded and which must be taken to have been included within the judgment on the claim.[124] To use the road traffic case mentioned at **12.109** as an example, if alternative causes of action were pleaded (such as negligence and a deliberate act) the transcript may help the costs judge to identify which cause of action succeeded, but it may not be used to demonstrate that the judge accepted in oral argument that the accident did not take place. It is worth pausing here to add that where a claimant seeks more than one remedy, and where he wins but is not successful in all of them, he will be presumed to have been denied the remedies he has not been awarded, and will not generally be able to claim them on a subsequent occasion.[125]

12.115 The earlier court (or tribunal[126] or arbitrator)[127] must have had jurisdiction to make its decision for estoppel to arise.[128] Judgment may have been made obtained by consent,[129] by an admission,[130] or by default,[131] but were the last of these the case, the

---

[117] *New Brunswick Rly Co v British and French Trust Corpn Ltd* [1938] 4 All ER 747.

[118] *Patchett v Sterling Engineering Co Ltd* (1953) 71 RPC 61, which was reversed on other grounds ([1955] AC 534).

[119] *New Brunswick Rly Co v British and French Trust Corpn Ltd* [1938] 4 All ER 747.

[120] *Isaacs & Sons v Salbstein* [1916] 2 KB 139.

[121] For a detailed discussion of this point, see Spencer Bower and Handley *Res Judicata* (LexisNexis Butterworths, 4th edn, 2009) at paras 7.16 and 8.29.

[122] See, for example, *Randolph v Tuck* [1961] 1 All ER 814.

[123] *Gordon v Gonda* [1955] 2 All ER 762.

[124] *Patchett v Sterling Engineering Co Ltd* (1953) 71 RPC 61, which was reversed on other grounds ([1955] AC 534).

[125] *Blake v O'Kelly* (1874) IR 9 Eq 54.

[126] *Munir v Jang Publications Ltd* [1989] ICR 1.

[127] *Associated Electric and Gas Insurance Services Ltd v European Reinsurance Co of Zurich* [2003] UKPC 11.

[128] *Rogers v Wood* (1831) 2 B & Ad 245.

[129] *Palmer v Durnford Ford (a firm)* [1992] 2 All ER 122; see also *Kinch v Walcott* [1929] AC 482 at 493, in which

effect of the judgment will be interpreted narrowly.[132] The effect of this is, for example, that where a party has judgment in default entered against him, estoppel will generally extend no further than the material facts as set out in the pleadings.[133] Where judgment is consensually entered with a reservation (such as a reservation that liability had not been admitted), it is arguable that the party who made the reservation would be able to rely on it even if it was inconsistent with the judgment.[134] Thus, in the example mentioned above, if judgment were entered by consent without an admission of liability, it would, in theory, be open to the defendant to present his case on the assessment on the basis that he had not been responsible for the accident.

12.116   Whilst judgment entered by consent will give rise to cause of action estoppel, the situation is less clear where the claim has been brought to an end by compromise (including acceptance of a Part 36 offer). Under the RSC it was established that where a claim had been concluded by the acceptance of the then equivalent of a Part 36 offer, whilst that would estop a similar claim being brought,[135] that would not estop the defendant from subsequently asserting matters which contravene the material facts pleaded in the particulars of claim.[136] This is because a compromise is generally seen as being a device by which the proceedings are brought to an end.[137] The relevance of this from the costs point of view is that if the entitlement to costs arose by reason of a Part 36 offer being accepted, it would be consistent with these principles if the defendant were to be permitted to deny the facts of the claim (although, of course, the court would be able to take into account the fact that the defendant did not seek to prove that version of events by ensuring that the matter did not settle).

12.117   It may be that fresh evidence comes to light during the assessment (or at some other time after the earlier judgment). In substantive litigation, the existence of fresh evidence would not ordinarily be an answer to cause of action estoppel[138] (unless, of course, that came to light during the existing proceedings and an appeal was brought or a new trial ordered). It is not known whether the same is true of costs litigation, not least because it is not known whether detailed assessment proceedings are the same proceedings as those which gave rise to the costs. If estoppel does apply, then if, in the running example mentioned at **12.109**, a document came to light which showed that the car did not belong to the claimant and that he was not entitled to the damages awarded in respect of the car, it would not be open to the defendant to argue that the claimant had failed to make out that part of his claim. (The costs judge could, of course, take the new document into account in other ways and, in particular, he could find that it was not reasonable for the claimant to incur the costs of that aspect of his claim in circumstances where he had failed to note the true facts; it is because of the existence of these wider powers that the issue of cause of action estoppel does not commonly arise in

---

Lord Blandesburgh said: 'in relation to this pleas of estoppel it is of no advantage to the appellant that the order [his opponent relied upon] ... was a consent order.'

[130]   *Boileau v Rutlin* (1848) 2 Exch 665.

[131]   *Huffer v Allen* (1866) LR 2 Exch 15.

[132]   See, for exmple, *New Brunswick Rly Co v British and French Trust Corpn Ltd* [1939] AC 1, [1938] 4 All ER 747, HL.

[133]   See, for example, *Howlett v Tarte* (1861) 10 CBNS 813.

[134]   See, for example, in a context other than costs, the Australian case of *Isaacs v Ocean Accident* (1957) 58 SRNSW 69; compare this with *SCF Finance Co Ltd v Masri (No 3)* [1987] QB 1028, CA.

[135]   *Reardon Smith v Cayzer Irvine* (1929) Com Cas at 280 and *Hills v Co-operative Wholesale* [1940] 2 KB 435, CA.

[136]   See *Rigge v Burbidge* (1846) 15 M & W 598.

[137]   *Coote v Ford* [1895–99] All ER Rep 673.

[138]   See the discussion of this in *Arnold v National Westminster Bank plc* [1988] 3 All ER 977; it may be possible to make out special circumstances in order to avoid the operation of the estoppel.

costs litigation.) In a similar vein, Lord Millett has made it clear that the fact that a decision may be wrong will not prevent a party from relying on that decision for the purposes of establishing estoppel of cause of action.[139] If the new evidence related to a fact which was not necessarily decided by the prior proceedings, then issue estoppel may apply; this is discussed at **12.222**). It is commonly said that fraud unravels everything in that a judgment obtained by fraud may be treated as being a nullity,[140] but it should not be forgotten the judgment will remain binding until set aside.[141] Nonetheless, if a costs judge were to find that a document had been deliberately concealed, he would usually focus on his powers under CPR, rr 44.5 and 44.14, and the issue of estoppel may well not arise.

12.118   There are no special rules concerning procedure. The burden of proof lies with the party who seeks to rely on the estoppel,[142] so he must raise the point in such a way that not only is he able to adduce evidence, but that his opponent is able to adduce evidence in response. In substantive litigation, where a party says that his opponent is estopped from raising a point, the estoppel may be decided either in advance of the trial by way of an application to strike out, or he may plead the estoppel and ask the court to deal with the matter at the end of the trial in argument.[143] If the same applies to costs litigation, then the estoppel should be set out in the points of dispute or the replies and thought ought to be given to deciding the question as a preliminary issue.

Issue estoppel (or issue preclusion)

12.119   In so far as costs litigation is concerned, issue estoppel is similar to cause of action estoppel, but it relates to any finding made in the earlier proceedings rather than just those which were part of the cause of action. This means that it is a wider doctrine than cause of action estoppel. However, the issue must have been a necessary part of the judgment, and not merely collateral to it.[144] In the example set out at **12.109**, if the claimant were able to demonstrate that the court found that the car was blue, then the defendant would be issue estopped from saying otherwise, but only if that was a primary part of the prior judgment.

12.120   The goal of issue estoppel is to prevent the same issue being litigated twice. Where an issue has arisen in litigation and where a party has had a finding made against him, that party is precluded from controverting that finding on a subsequent occasion.[145] The issue in question must have been the same one as that which was decided previously, and it must arise between the same parties (or their privies).[146] The issue must have been decided finally,[147] with certainty,[148] and by a court with

---

[139]   *Crown Estates Commissioners v Dorset County Council* [1990] Ch 297 at 305.

[140]   *Shedden v Patrick* (1854) 1 Macq 535, HL.

[141]   For a discussion of this point in detail, see Spencer Bower and Handley *Res Judicata* (LexisNexis Butterworths, 4th edn, 2009) at chapter 17.

[142]   *Isaacs & Sons v Salbstein* [1916] 2 KB 139, CA.

[143]   *Carl Zeiss Stiftung v Rayner and Keeler Ltd (No 3)* [1969] 3 All ER 897.

[144]   See, for example, *Barrs v Jackson* (1842) 1 Y&C Ch Cas 585 at 596, per Knight Bruce V-C.

[145]   *Mills v Cooper* [1967] 2 QB 459, [1967] 2 All ER 100. Similarly, where a separate issue is tried before the other issues in the case, the decision on the separate issue is binding on the parties and the court in the later stages of the case. Diplock LJ said in *Fidelitas Shipping* [1966] QB 630, CA at 642: 'Where the issue separately determined is not decisive of the suit the … suit continues. Yet I take it to be too clear to need citation of authority that the parties to the suit are bound by the determination of the issue. They cannot subsequently in the same suit advance an argument or adduce further evidence directed to showing that the issue was wrongly determined.'

[146]   *Blake v O'Kelly* (1874) IR 9 Eq 54.

[147]   *Bobolas v Economist Newspaper Ltd* [1987] 3 All ER 121.

jurisdiction.[149] Issue estoppel will exist regardless of whether the finding was made as a result of argument or not,[150] and regardless of whether it is an issue of fact, law or both.[151]

12.121   In determining the scope of estoppel, the court must determine the nature of the issue which was decided by the earlier proceedings. The following are admissible in this regard: the judgment;[152] the pleadings;[153] oral evidence,[154] and therefore presumably transcripts. The court must also determine whether the issue was fundamental or collateral to the prior judgment.[155] This can be of significant importance in substantive litigation, but it would be rare for a costs judge to controvert a finding of the trial judge unless there were a good reason to do so (such as new information coming to light).

12.122   This final point is worth expanding upon. Unlike cause of action estoppel, the court is at liberty to find that the parties should not be fettered by issue estoppel if new evidence has come to light which would make it unfair for that fetter to exist.[156] The circumstances have to be 'special', and the evidence must be such that it could not, with due diligence on the part of the party who seeks to avoid the estoppel, have been put before the court during the earlier proceedings.[157] Ignorance of the matter previously omitted may be sufficiently special in substantive litigation;[158] it is not known whether this concept applies to costs litigation, but, if it does, then it may be that if a costs judge discovers a document during the detailed assessment which controverts a finding of fact previously made, he may be at liberty to release the paying party from the fetter of estoppel. (In practice, the court would rarely analyse the matter in this way because a just outcome could usually be achieved on the conceptually less complex grounds of reasonableness. Thus, if in the example mentioned at **12.109** the new document showed that the car had in fact only recently been painted blue, the court could disallow the cost of dealing with that issue if the court found that that document had been unreasonably withheld and that, if it had been disclosed, the costs of that issue would have been avoided.)

12.123   Issue estoppel may operate between co-defendants; the traditional teaching is that this will be the case only if the following conditions are satisfied:[159]

(1)   where there is an issue between them which gives rise to a conflict of interest;

(2)   where resolution of that issue was something that was necessary for the purposes of deciding the claimant's claim; and

---

[148]   See *Re Wright, Blizard v Lockhart* [1954] Ch 347, [1954] 2 All ER 98; and *Re Koenigsberg, Public Trustee v Koenigsberg* [1949] Ch 348.

[149]   *Rogers v Wood* (1831) 2 B & Ad 245.

[150]   See *Re Koenigsberg, Public Trustee v Koenigsberg* [1949] Ch 348.

[151]   *Jones v Lewis* [1919] 1 KB 328.

[152]   *Shoe Machinery Co v Cutlan* [1896] 1 Ch 667.

[153]   *Cribb v Freyberger* [1919] WN 22, CA.

[154]   *Flitters v Allfrey* (1874) LR 10 CP 29.

[155]   One test that has been suggested is that of whether the issue was capable of being appealed: see Spencer Bower, Turner and Handley *The Doctrine of Res Judicata* (Butterworths, 1996), paras 202–205.

[156]   See the principal speech given by Lord Keith in *Arnold v National Westminster Bank plc* [1991] 2 AC 93 at 106; see also *Chamberlain v DCT* (1988) 164 CLR 502.

[157]   For an example of the court finding that due diligence could have resulted in the fresh material being put before the court in a context other than costs, see *McIlkenny v Chief Constable of West Midlands Police Force* [1980] QB 283 at 320.

[158]   The older authorities on this point were Scottish, but Lord Keith has clarified that Scots law and English law are the same: *Arnold v National Westminster Bank plc* [1991] 2 AC 93 at 108.

[159]   *Munni Bibi v Tiroloki Nath* (1931) LR 58 Ind App 158, PC.

(3)   where that issue has been finally decided.

12.124   Whilst some commentators have doubted this traditional view,[160] there is modern authority (albeit in a context other than costs) to confirm that co-defendants who are sued but who did not seek contributions during the earlier proceedings may be issue estopped on a subsequent occasion when one of the co-defendants seeks damages from the other.[161] It is not known whether the same is true in relation to costs, but if it is, then the paying party in the example mentioned above (ie the defendant who had been condemned in costs) would not be able assert that the accident was caused by a co-defendant and that his costs ought to be assessed on that basis.

Abuse of process

12.125   The next doctrine is wider still: it is abuse of process. This is discussed only briefly and chiefly for the purposes of highlighting that it will rarely be relevant. In particular, it will not arise in the sense that the rule in *Henderson v Henderson*[162] will operate as between trial judge and costs judge (see below).

12.126   Whether there is an abuse of process will turn on the facts of each case, but one important aspect of the doctrine which distinguishes it from *res judicata* estoppel is that it may preclude a party from raising an issue which was not raised during the earlier proceedings but which ought to have been. Turning to the running example mentioned at **12.112**, if the defendant were to say that he should not pay the costs of proving that the car had a red strip down the side, and if he were to raise that issue for the very first time during the assessment itself, it may be open to the court to find that he should have raised that argument before the trial judge when the court was considering the colour of the car generally, and that he should be precluded from raising it on an assessment. For the reasons set out below (in this section and the next) it can be seen that whilst the costs judge will sometimes be precluded from hearing such late arguments, it will rarely be on the basis of abuse of process.

12.127   Nonetheless, abuse of process may apply in other circumstances (such as where it is said that an argument ought to have been raised at an earlier stage of the assessment); in view of this, the relevant law is set out in outline (see **12.128–12.129**). The rule in *Henderson v Henderson*[163] is addressed for similar reasons (**12.130–12.135**).

Abuse of process in general

12.128   Some commentators have referred to abuse of process as an extended doctrine of *res judicata*.[164] There is undoubtedly a degree of overlap.[165] This probably arose out of the tendency for the narrower concept of *res judicata* to be assimilated by the wider concept of abuse of process,[166] but they are best treated as being related but distinct. This is not least because there is authority that the principles of *res judicata* ought not to

---

[160]   See *Halsbury's Law of England: Civil Procedure* (vol 12), para 1202 for a discussion of this issue.
[161]   See, for example, *North West Water Ltd v Binnie & Partners (a firm)* [1990] 3 All ER 547.
[162]   *Henderson v Henderson* (1843) 3 Hare 100.
[163]   *Henderson v Henderson* (1843) 3 Hare 100.
[164]   See P Barnett *Res Judicata, Estoppel, and Foreign Judgments* (Oxford University Press, May 2001) para 6.02, where the author implies that this nomenclature is in use but is not to be recommended.
[165]   See, for example, *Lloyds TSB Bank Ltd v Cooke-Arkwright (a firm)* [2001] All ER (D) 127 (Oct), in which both were found to be available.
[166]   See, for example, the comments of Toulson J in *Baker v Ian McCall International Ltd* [2000] CLC 189 at 196.

be extended beyond their present scope.[167] The onus of proving that an argument is an abuse of process rests with the person making that assertion.[168]

12.129   Unlike *res judicata* estoppel, the doctrine of abuse of process does not depend on the earlier court having made a finding; ie a party may be precluded from advancing an issue if the circumstances of the claim in general (as opposed to just the components of the claim or just the judgment) were such that that would be appropriate. In particular, inconsistency may amount to an abuse of process (ie where one version of events is asserted at one stage, and then a different version at a later stage).[169] In the running example mentioned at **12.114**, if his entire case was based on the premise that he could not have seen and did not see the defendant's car, the court might preclude the claimant from arguing that he should be awarded the costs of obtaining expert evidence proving the efficacy of his brakes. Whilst it would be possible to analyse that situation in terms of abuse of process (ie it is an abuse of the court to allow it to be used to recover costs which contradict the receiving party's own case), it is not difficult to see that it would usually be far simpler to analyse the matter in terms of reasonableness.

The rule in Henderson v Henderson

12.130   For the reasons set out above, in substantive litigation abuse of process may be relevant where a party is precluded from advancing an issue on the grounds that he had opportunity to advance it on a previous occasion but failed to avail himself of that opportunity. In particular, where an issue could have been adjudicated upon during earlier proceedings, then the doctrine of abuse of process will, in appropriate circumstances, preclude that issue from being considered during the subsequent proceedings. This principle is usually referred to as being the rule in *Henderson v Henderson*.[170]

12.131   Waller LJ has explained that the rule in *Henderson v Henderson* does not apply to costs litigation in the sense that if, at the time the costs order is made, a party remains silent about some fact or circumstance he will be precluded from relying on that fact or circumstance at the detailed assessment.[171] In so far as Jack J promulgated a different view in *Aaron v Shelton*,[172] he was mistaken.

12.132   Waller LJ had this to say about the interaction between CPR, r 44.3 (the trial judge's role) and CPR, r 44.5 (the costs judge's role):[173]

'In my view 44.3 and 44.5 are intended to work in harmony and it is intended that the parties' conduct (for example) may have to be considered under both. If what is sought is a special order as to costs which a costs judge should follow that obviously should be sought from the trial judge. If it is clear that a costs judge would be assisted in the assessment of costs by some indication from the trial judge about the way in which a trial has been

---

[167]   *Howlett v Tarte* (1861) 10 CBNS 813; see also *Carl Zeiss Stiftung v Rayner & Keeler Ltd (No 2)* [1967] 1 AC 853.
[168]   *Sweetman v Nathan* [2003] EWCA Civ 1115 at [34].
[169]   In a context other than costs, see *Bradford and Bingley Building Society v Seddon* [1999] 4 All ER 217.
[170]   *Henderson v Henderson* (1843) 3 Hare 100.
[171]   *Drew v Whitbread* (unreported) 9 February 2010, CA at [30], which expanded on Waller LJ's comments made previously in *Northstar Systems Ltd v Fielding* [2006] EWCA Civ 1660.
[172]   [2004] EWHC 1162 (QB).
[173]   *Drew v Whitbread* (unreported) 9 February 2010, CA at [37].

conducted, a request for that indication should be sought. But none of this needs a rule as per *Henderson v Henderson* that a failure to raise a point before the trial judge will preclude the raising of a point before the costs judge.'

12.133 As is explained below, there will still be circumstances where a failure to raise a point before the trial judge will mean that it cannot be raised before the costs judge, but this will not be on the basis of abuse of process. Instead, it is based on preclusion by proportionality. This is discussed at **12.136–12.141**.

12.134 The rule in *Henderson v Henderson* still has relevance in the sense that it will be capable of applying to interactions within detailed assessment proceedings (that is, between costs judge and costs judge). This can be illustrated by referring to damages as an analogy: damages (other than provisional damages) must be assessed once and for all.[174] There is no reason to believe that costs are to be dealt with any differently. If the once-and-for-all principle does apply to costs, then that would explain why a receiving party would not be able to present a bill of costs for part of his costs, and then, without the agreement of the paying party or an order of the court, present another bill of costs for the remainder.[175] The rule could also apply in other circumstances, such as where a party applies to a costs judge for relief from sanctions, and subsequently seeks to apply for similar but not identical relief on a subsequent occasion.

12.135 The rule in *Henderson v Henderson* applies where judgment has been entered by consent and, in appropriate circumstances, to settlements generally.[176] Thus, presumably, if a bill of costs was presented and settled without reservation, this would prevent the receiving party from presenting a further bill of costs.

Late arguments and proportionality

12.136 For the reasons set out above, the rule in *Henderson v Henderson* does not apply between trial judge and costs judge. This does not mean, however, that arguments may be whimsically raised before a costs judge regardless of whether the trial judge was given opportunity to comment. This is not only because there will be the potential for estoppel in respect of anything which has already been decided (see **12.107–12.124**), but also because the doctrine of preclusion by proportionality may apply (see **12.140**).

12.137 It may be that a party wishes to raise an argument which was not raised before the trial judge. This invites the question of whether the costs judge would be able to hear it. In certain circumstances, a party would be precluded from raising a new argument: there is nothing new in this as it has always been the case that there has been some regulation of the interaction between trial judge and costs judge.[177] For the reasons set out below, however, such preclusion would be rare and would not be based on abuse of process. The topic is best considered by looking at three issues: conduct, proportionality, and special orders.

---

[174] *Conquer v Boot* [1928] 2 KB 336, DC.

[175] Christopher Clarke J found that this was not permissible: *Harris v Moat Housing Group South Ltd* [2007] EWHC 3092 (QB).

[176] See *Johnson v Gore Wood & Co (a firm)* [2001] 1 All ER 481.

[177] See, for example, *In re Frape ex p Perrett (No 2)* [1894] 2 Ch 295, in which the court found: 'The right of the client to dispute the solicitor's retainer as to this bill in toto was not reserved in the order as it ought to have been, if he was to have that right'; see also *Skuse v Granada Television Limited* [1994] 1 WLR 1156, in which Drake J found that (on the facts of that particular case) the paying parties' failure to raise the issue of alleged maintenance at the time a costs order was made prevented them from raising the issue on the assessment.

Conduct: rule in *Aaron v Shelton*

12.138   In so far as conduct is concerned, it used to be believed that there was a rule – the rule in *Aaron v Shelton*[178] – which restricted the extent to which a costs judge could take conduct into account in circumstances where it had not been raised before the trial judge. Jack J explained that rule in this way:[179]

> 'In my judgment, where a party wishes to raise in relation to costs a matter concerning the conduct of his opposing party (either before the litigation or during it), it is his duty to raise it before the judge making the costs order where it is appropriate to do so ... If he does not do so, it is not open to him when the costs come to be assessed to raise the same matter under CPR 44.5(3) as a ground for the reduction of the costs which he would otherwise have to pay ... Otherwise a party who thinks he has achieved an order which will get him his costs subject to the reasonableness of the amount, may on the assessment face an argument intended to deprive him of what he justifiably thought he had obtained.'

This rule is no longer good law. The true law began to emerge 2 years after Jack J gave his guidance when Waller LJ said that it was 'too broadly stated';[180] 3 years after that, Waller LJ expanded on his previous comments and confirmed that the rule was not good law:[181]

> 'In my view it would not be consistent with the express provisions of 44.3 and 44.5 and with the court's duty to see that costs are proportionate and reasonable to preclude a party raising a point highly material to that question because it had not been raised before the judge under 44.3.'

Thus, a costs judge may take all aspects of the parties' conduct into account, regardless of whether it was raised before the costs judge. This is different from the position in analogous situations in substantive litigation,[182] but this is probably a reflection of the fact that the process of detailed assessment is a much more nuanced affair than comparable processes in substantive litigation.

12.139   There is nothing in Waller LJ's guidance that should discourage a party from airing issues before the trial judge and from seeking his guidance. Waller LJ has advised that if it is clear that the costs judge would be assisted by some indication from the trial judge about the way in which a trial had been conducted, a request for that indication should be sought.[183] Whilst he was giving judgment at a time when the rule in *Aaron v Shelton* was still believed to be good law, Tomlinson J has confirmed that a trial judge is able to give guidance either in the order, or in response to written questions; whilst it rarely happens, he also noted that a trial judge could, in an appropriate case, sit with the costs judge on the assessment.[184]

---

[178]   After *Aaron v Shelton* [2004] EWHC 1162 (QB).

[179]   *Aaron v Shelton* [2004] EWHC 1162 (QB) at [20].

[180]   *Northstar Systems v Fielding* [2006] EWCA Civ 1660 at [32] and [34].

[181]   *Drew v Whitbread* (unreported) 9 February 2010, CA at [41]; at [31] Waller LJ explained that whilst Neuberger LJ had approved of Jack J's judgment (see *Gray v Going Places Leisure Travel Ltd* [2005] EWCA Civ 189), that was in the context of considering the right time to deal with a wasted costs' order.

[182]   In chancery proceedings, for example, where an account is ordered, any special matter affecting the account should be brought forward at the trial, and if this is not done it cannot be raised 'during the mechanical operation of taking an ordinary account': *Sanguineti v Stuckey's Banking Co (No 2)* [1896] 1 Ch 502 at 506.

[183]   *Drew v Whitbread* (unreported) 9 February 2010, CA at [37].

[184]   *Three Rivers District Council v Bank of England* [2006] EWHC 816 (Comm): it should be noted that the comment about sitting with the costs judge was made in the context of an exceptionally complex matter.

Preclusion by proportionality

12.140 Whilst it has its legal foundations firmly in the overriding objective rather than abuse of process, there is a mechanism by which a costs judge can decline to hear an argument which ought to have been put before the trial judge. Waller LJ explained that mechanism in the following way:

> 'There may not be circumstances in which a costs judge may be entitled to say, in the interests of keeping the costs of assessment proportionate, that a matter should have been brought up before the trial judge and a special order sought; for example, if it is to be argued that a witness in a long trial should never have been called because the evidence was irrelevant, a costs judge should not be required effectively to retry the case in order to adjudicate on the point; obviously a special order should be sought from the trial judge. But that is different from there being some form of rule founded on *Henderson v Henderson*, that a failure to raise a matter before the judge for 44.3 purposes precludes the raising of the matter for 44.5 purposes.'

Thus, where the issue to be decided is so deeply inearthed in the substance of the trial that it would be inappropriate to require the costs judge to unearth it, it will stay where it lies. What is not clear is whether it *must* stay where it lies (by reason of the costs judge having lost jurisdiction) or whether it *may* stay where it lies (by reason of the costs judge exercising his discretion). The wording of Waller LJ's judgment suggests the former. In any event, even if it is the former, the decision would depend on a discretionary matter (ie whether it was proportionate to hear the argument), so the distinction between the two is probably more theoretical than practical.

Special orders

12.141 It is implicit in Waller LJ's analysis (see **12.132**) that there will be occasions where a 'special order' is required. Such an order will not be required merely for the purposes of reserving the right to argue some point about conduct (see **12.138–12.139**), but it may be required if the court is to be asked to quantify the costs in a way which is distinguishable from an ordinary assessment of costs. Thus, if a paying party wished to argue that the claim had been exaggerated, for example, no special order would be required, but if the argument was that fixed costs should apply,[185] or that a percentage reduction should be made,[186] then a special order would be required.

LIMITATION, DELAY, AND COSTS

12.142 The main topic which is addressed in this section is delay occurring in the context of the detailed assessment process, but delay of other sorts, such as delay in obtaining or enforcing a costs order, is also touched upon.

12.143 It is assumed that the reader is familiar with the time limits for commencing detailed assessment proceedings and for requesting a detailed assessment hearing. These topics are dealt with in detail at **21.54** *et seq* and **21.193**. Delay in the context of appeals is addressed at **23.23**. Delay in the context of solicitor and client disputes is addressed at **18.36** and **18.37**.

---

[185] See *Drew v Whitbread* (unreported) 9 February 2010, CA at [36].
[186] Whilst on a slightly different point, see *Lahey v Pirelli* [2007] 1WLR 998.

Delay generally

12.144 Most receiving parties are only too eager to have their costs quantified and paid but, surprisingly, that is not always the case. Indeed, the problem of delay has blighted the processes for ascertaining costs since well before the introduction of the CPR.

12.145 There is a spectrum of consequences that may be visited upon a party who has delayed, some of which are more theoretical than real. In particular, whilst the issue of limitation is a topic which has the potential to arise, it does so exceptionally infrequently: it is included here only for the sake of completeness. The same is true of the section on laches.

12.146 In so far as between-the-parties costs are concerned, the spectrum of consequences is as follows:

- disallowance of interest (this topic is dealt with at **35.30–35.34**);
- the imposition of costs sanctions (this topic is dealt with in general in Chapters 6 and 7);
- disallowance of part or all of the costs claimed pursuant to CPR, r 44.14 (misconduct) (see **12.151–12.173**); and
- disallowance of costs as a result of the claim for costs being statutorily time barred.

This list is not exhaustive. Those towards the top of the list are far more frequently encountered than those at the bottom.

12.147 There is very little authority on the issue of limitation in the context of costs, so it would be best to regard the analysis of that topic as being only a starting point for the purposes of further legal research. The same is true of the topic of laches; indeed, it is far from certain that the defence of laches is capable of applying to a claim for costs arising out of a costs order at all.

12.148 Whether a receiving party has been guilty of delay worthy of sanction will turn on the facts of each case, but not every instance of tardiness will result in sanction. It is not always practicable (or, occasionally, even possible) for a receiving party to comply with the time limits in the CPR; in particular, where the bill of costs is substantial, it may take longer to draft than the 3-month time limit in CPR, r 47.7 allows. Thus, the following pre-CPR comments of Walton J continue to have resonance:[187]

> 'Unless such time limit is to become an instrument of oppression – and there can be no conceivable logic or fairness in a deliberate act of oppression ... this time limit will be approached by the [costs judge] with due consciousness of its inappropriateness in many cases.'

12.149 Whilst many cases concerning delay will not be cases where relief from sanctions are sought, the list of factors mentioned in CPR, r 3.9(1) can be a useful guide to the type of issues that the court will take into account. Those factors are paraphrased at **21.125**.

---

[187] *Papathanassiou v Dutch Communication Co Ltd* (unreported) 9 May 1985.

Interest

12.150 Where there has been delay in commencing detailed assessment proceedings or where there has been delay in requesting a detailed assessment hearing, the court has the power to disallow the interest on costs.[188] That is an issue which must be addressed in the context of the court's discretion as to interest generally: this topic is discussed at **36.30–36.34**.

Misconduct and delay

12.151 CPR, rr 47.7 and 47.14(2) stipulate time limits during which the receiving party must commence detailed assessment proceedings and request a detailed assessment hearing (see **21.54** *et seq* and **21.193** respectively). Generally speaking, the receiving party has 3 months to do each; this means that he will typically have a total of 6 months between the date on which the costs order is made and the date by which a request for a detailed assessment should have been made.

12.152 As mentioned above, delay in meeting these requirements may result in a disallowance of interest. Where the extent of the delay is such that a mere disallowance of interest would fail to meet the justice of the situation, the court is able to invoke its powers for dealing with misconduct (see CPR, r 44.14). Where the court invokes those powers the costs themselves (rather than just interest) are at risk.

12.153 The fact that interest may be disallowed is relevant to the issue of whether the court should invoke the power to disallow the costs themselves; this is because the court may be able to impose a significant sanction by exercising its full powers concerning interest, and this may be preferable to making a finding of misconduct (see **12.162**). In order fully to understand the way in which the court exercises its discretion, it is necessary to know something of the history of the law, as otherwise the true significance of older authorities may be overlooked.

The place of pre-CPR authority

12.154 As will be explained below, the language of the authorities dealing with the CPR is similar to the language of the RSC. Both of those vocabularies refer to delay as being 'inordinate' and 'inexcusable'. This makes pre-CPR guidance seem relevant as – on the face of it – the corresponding pre-CPR regime has the allure of being both analogous and well charted. That temptation should be resisted;[189] this is because there are significant differences between the present regime and the corresponding prior regime, and those differences may escape the reader when presented with case reports which are taken out of historical context.

12.155 In particular, the CPR make provision for the paying party to obtain an 'unless order' requiring the receiving party to commence detailed assessment proceedings.[190] The corresponding provision under the RSC was different in that the paying party was

---

[188] See CPR, r 47.8(3) and r 47.14(5) respectively.
[189] Indeed, Longmore LJ has said that little guidance can be gleaned from older authorities decided under the CPR: *Haji-Ioannou v Frangos* [2006] EWCA Civ 1663 at [11].
[190] See CPR, r 47.8(2).

able to apply to begin the proceedings directly.[191] This means that the opportunity to lay blame for delay solely at the feet of the receiving party is not the same under the CPR as it was under the RSC.

12.156 Moreover, the rules were in a state of flux even during the currency of the RSC. Very old cases, for example, were decided under a regime that would, to modern eyes, appear inflexible in the way it regards interest.

12.157 Rule changes are a matter of record and accordingly can be taken into account when considering older authorities, but there is one further factor that is less easy to recognise: namely, the court's attitude to prejudice. The court's stance subtly changed in the 15 or so years before the introduction of the CPR; prejudice used to be a condition precedent for the imposition of a sanction but, following recommendations in a report chaired by the then equivalent of the Senior Cost Judge,[192] not only were changes made to the RSC, but there was also a shift in the judicial approach towards the putative requirement of prejudice.[193] Indeed, shortly before the introduction of the CPR it was often the case that in so far as that requirement continued to exist, prejudice could be inferred from the delay itself.[194]

12.158 Pre-CPR authorities should, therefore, be avoided (unless, of course, those authorities have been affirmed in more recent cases). This chapter does not ignore pre-CPR cases entirely, however: where they give guidance on topics which are likely not to have changed as a result of the introduction of the CPR – such as the court's attitude to how long it ought to take to draft a bill of costs – then they are cautiously included. Moreover, in recognition of the fact that the reader is likely to happen across pre-CPR authorities when carrying out legal research, a brief summary of the pre-CPR law is given in the footnotes.[195]

---

[191] See RSC, Ord 62, r 29(3).

[192] See the report dated 25 January 1983 of a working party on RSC, Ord 62 chaired by Master Horne.

[193] See, for example, *Pamplin v Fraser (No 2)* [1984] 2 All ER 694 and *Jones v Roberts* (1986) *The Times*, August 2, which were two of the first cases in which it was held that it is not a prerequisite for the paying party to show prejudice.

[194] *London Borough of Enfield v P* [1996] 1 FLR 629.

[195] Order 62, r 28(4) provided as follows:
'Where a party entitled to costs—
(a) fails without good reason to commence or conduct proceedings for the taxation of those costs in accordance with this Order or any direction, or
(b) delays lodging a bill of costs for taxation,
the taxing office may—
(i) disallow all or part of the costs of taxation that he would otherwise have awarded that party; and
(ii) after taking into account all the circumstances (including any prejudice suffered by any other party as a result of such failure or delay, as the case may be, and any additional interest payable under section 17 of the Judgments Act 1838 because of the failure or delay), allow the party so entitled less than the amount he would otherwise have allowed on taxation of the bill or wholly disallow the costs.'
Holman J summarised the law as it was shortly before the introduction of the CPR in the following way (*London Borough of Enfield v P* [1996] 1 FLR 629 at 638):
'(1) Subparagraphs (a) and (b) are conditions precedent or "triggers" to the exercise of the powers under (i) and (ii).
(2) They are alternative triggers. (a) requires the absence of "good reason" but (b) does not. Delay alone suffices to trigger the power. Accordingly,
(3) The delay does not have to be "inordinate and inexcusable" before the power is triggered.
(4) If a trigger in either (a) or (b) applies, then the taxing officer has a discretion under (ii) to reduce the amount which would otherwise be allowed on taxation or to disallow the costs entirely.
(5) The court is not limited to compensating prejudice to the paying party but can, in an appropriate case, make a further disallowance even if this confers a benefit on the paying party greater than pure compensation for his prejudice or loss. This is sometimes referred to as a "fine" or "punitive element". I think these terms are perhaps a little misleading. The essence of the court's task is to make an order which

The provisions under the CPR

12.159 In so far as it is relevant to the issue of delay, CPR, r 44.14 reads as follows:

'(1) The court may make an order under this rule where—

   (a) a party or his legal representative, in connection with a summary or detailed assessment, fails to comply with a rule, practice direction or court order; or

   (b) it appears to the court that the conduct of a party or his legal representative, before or during the proceedings which gave rise to the assessment proceedings, was unreasonable or improper.

(2) Where paragraph (1) applies, the court may—

   (a) disallow all or part of the costs which are being assessed ...'

Relationship between interest and misconduct

12.160 There is no halfway house between disallowing interest pursuant to CPR, r 47.8(3) (or r 47.14(5)) and disallowing costs pursuant to CPR, r 44.14; this means that in the absence of a finding of misconduct, the court is not able to impose a sanction which is greater than a mere disallowance of interest.[196] In so far as commencement delay[197] is concerned, the bar against other sanctions exists by reason of CPR, r 47.8(3), which reads as follows:

'(3) If—

   (a) the paying party has not made an application [for an order requiring the paying party to commence detailed assessment proceedings]; and

   (b) the receiving party commences the proceedings later than the period specified in rule 47.7,

the court may disallow ... [interest]

...

but must not impose any other sanction except in accordance with rule 44.14 (powers in relation to misconduct).'

Similar provisions, concerning delay in requesting a hearing, are made at CPR, r 47.14(5).

12.161 In a thorough review of the issue of misconduct and delay, Longmore LJ commented that there is a tension between CPR, r 47.8 and r 44.14, and that the clue to

---

meets the overall justice of the case. But it is important to bear in mind that at least from the perspective of the receiving party and his solicitor any reduction beyond pure compensation will feel punitive.

(6) Even a reduction in the costs calculated to compensate the paying party may have a "punitive" effect when viewed from the position of the receiving party.

(7) In exercising the discretion the taxing office must take into account all the circumstances.

(8) Relevant circumstances include the duration of the delay and the extent to which it is explained or excusable.

(9) Relevant circumstances also include any, and if so what degree of, prejudice suffered by any other party and any additional interest payable under s 17 of the Judgments Act 1838 because of the delay. In an appropriate case prejudice can be inferred from the fact of delay even if no specific prejudice is established. However, prejudice is not a prerequisite to the exercise of the power.'

[196] Where the delay relates to commencing detailed assessment proceedings, it is arguable that the prohibition against 'imposing any other sanction' would apply only where: (a) no application has been made in accordance with CPR, r 47.8(1), and (b) it is the receiving party who has commenced detailed assessment proceedings; there is no authority for this proposition, however.

[197] That is, delay in commencing detailed assessment proceedings: see **21.54** *et seq*.

resolving that tension is in the word 'misconduct' in the title of the latter. Those words point to the nature of the court's discretion. He commented that some breaches of the rules can be more readily described as misconduct than others, and that the rules contemplate costs judges being trusted to recognise misconduct when it occurs.[198]

12.162 In the same appeal, Arden LJ observed that the prescribed sanction of disallowance of interest is likely to be less controversial than disallowance of the costs themselves. This was for two reasons: first, it is more likely that opposing parties could agree a reduction in interest than a reduction in the costs themselves and, secondly, a finding of misconduct may cause disputes between solicitor and client as to who should bear the burden of the disallowed costs.[199] Longmore LJ explained that the court should hesitate before exercising any powers beyond the disallowance of interest (see **12.169**), but it seems implicit in his analysis (and that of Arden LJ) that the court should, where appropriate, make full use of those powers concerning interest.

Jurisdictional threshold

12.163 In exploring the issue of what amounts to 'misconduct' in the context of delay, Longmore LJ used language that would not have been out of place under the RSC; in particular, he remarked:[200]

> 'An inordinate and inexcusable delay which has prejudiced the paying party may well come within this category; excusable, although inordinate delay may not, especially if it has caused no prejudice. The important point is that, while a non-compliance with a rule, practice direction or court order is the only jurisdictional requirement for the exercise of the power contained in Rule 44.14, it will usually be appropriate as a matter of discretion to consider the extent of any misconduct which has occurred in the course of such non-compliance.'

Thus, the mere fact that delay is inordinate would not meet the jurisdictional threshold, but where the delay is also inexcusable, that threshold may well be met. Prejudice may be a factor, but it does not appear to be a necessary ingredient. Longmore LJ emphasised that the test is whether the delay amounts to misconduct: other findings may also be made (such as the delay being exceptional), but they do not define the requisite threshold. In particular, whilst Longmore LJ did not disagree with Warren J's analysis that there must be 'exceptional circumstances' before mere delay would justify the court invoking CPR, r 44.14,[201] he emphasised that the delay must properly be categorised as being misconduct for any sanctions to be imposed.

12.164 For the reasons set out at **12.154–12.158**, care is required when seeking guidance from pre-CPR authorities. Nonetheless, the task of preparing a bill of costs under the RSC was not dissimilar to the same task under the CPR, so some guidance may be found from examining the way in which such a delay was classified as 'inordinate' under the RSC. It must be borne in mind, however, that the test is not whether the delay has been inordinate, but whether the delay amounts to misconduct: the issue of whether the delay is inordinate is merely a factor to be taken into account. Indeed, linguistically, a test of inordinacy is a fairly low threshold.[202]

---

[198] *Haji-Ioannou v Frangos* [2006] EWCA Civ 1663 at [10]; see also the comments of Dyson LJ in *Lahey v Pirelli Tyres Ltd* [2007] EWCA Civ 91 at [29].

[199] *Haji-Ioannou v Frangos* [2006] EWCA Civ 1663 at [18].

[200] *Haji-Ioannou v Frangos* [2006] EWCA Civ 1663 at [10].

[201] See *Less v Benedict* [2005] EWHC 1643 (Ch).

[202] The relevant entry in the *Oxford English Dictionary* (3rd edn, 1989) (inordinate, *a.* 2) is that inordinate means: 'not kept within orderly limits, immoderate, intemperate, excessive'.

Elasticity

12.165 Bearing these qualifications in mind, it is worth noting that Megarry V-C asserted that for the delay to be inordinate, it must be shown that the period of time which has elapsed is materially longer than the period of time which is usually regarded by the courts and the profession as an acceptable period of time.[203] Some pre-CPR case examples are given in the footnotes, but they are, at best, no more than a guide as to the period of time during which a party can be expected to draft a bill of costs.[204] Whilst a pre-CPR case, Walton J acknowledged that it would not always be possible to commence proceedings for assessment within 3 months, and that this time limit was treated with a certain amount of 'elasticity';[205] it would be surprising if a similar approach were not to apply under the CPR, especially where larger bills fall to be considered.

No preclusion arising out of unless orders

12.166 There is one factor that may be dismissed as being irrelevant for the purposes of determining whether the court is able to exercise its jurisdiction under CPR, r 44.14, and that is whether an application for an unless order has been made. The jurisdiction under r 44.14 differs from that concerning interest, where it is possible that the court may be fettered by such an application.[206] Notwithstanding this, whether an application for an unless order has been made may be relevant to the exercise of the court's discretion.

12.167 In summary, whilst issues such as the extent of the delay, whether it was inordinate or inexcusable, and whether it has caused prejudice may all be relevant, the test of whether the jurisdictional threshold has been met is simply a test of whether the delay can be properly characterised as misconduct.

Discretion

12.168 If the jurisdictional threshold is met, then the court must consider how it is to exercise its discretion. It should be emphasised that Longmore LJ did not state that the process is a two-stage process (ie a jurisdictional stage followed by a discretionary stage); the matter is analysed in this way only for the sake of analysis and description. In most instances, there would be no reason why the court would not deal with these two things at the same time.

---

[203] *Chapman v Chapman* [1985] 1 WLR 599 at 607.

[204] In *Papathanassiou v Dutch Communication Co Ltd* (unreported) 9 May 1985 a delay period of 3 months was not inordinate but a delay of 2 years 7 months was held to be inordinately long; in *Drake & Fletcher Ltd v Clark* (1968) 112 SJ 95 a period of 3½ years delay was held to be inordinate. Similarly, in *Pamplin v Fraser (No 2)* (1984) 2 All ER 694, 10 months delay was held to be inordinate.

[205] *Papathanassiou v Dutch Communication Co Ltd* (unreported) 9 May 1985; see also *Pauls Agriculture Ltd v Smith* (1993) 3 All ER 122 at 125, in which Walton J set out his views on this topic: 'I am fully aware that the 3-month period is not strictly adhered to by the profession and the courts in our jurisdiction. In fact, delay for about 3 months is quite normal and acceptable in the courts in which I preside. From the cases cited above, the period of 16 months delay, as has occurred in this case, is not within the limit of 'elasticity' that may be acceptable in this jurisdiction and I therefore hold that such delay was inordinate.'

[206] The argument concerning interest relies on a strict reading of CPR, r 47.8(3): it is possible to read that provision as saying that the court has the jurisdiction to disallow interest only where the paying party has not made an application for an unless order. This topic is discussed in more detail at **21.88–21.89**. No such strict reading is possible in respect of CPR, r 44.14.

Loss of interest is the normal sanction

12.169   Longmore LJ deliberately refrained from giving detailed guidance as to when the court should exercise its powers under CPR, r 44.14. He did, however, explain that the court should make use of its powers to disallow interest – which is what he described as being the normal sanction for delay – but should hesitate before going any further:[207]

> 'Of course delay is to be deprecated but where the relevant rule not only gives to the party at the receiving end of the delay the option of preventing further delay by himself taking the initiative but also spells out the normal sanction for penalising such delay (as Rule 47.8 does), it seems to me that the court should be hesitant to exercise further powers to impose further penalties by way of reducing otherwise allowable costs.'

Longmore LJ's guidance has overshadowed older CPR decisions concerning delay and misconduct: indeed, he commented that a detailed analysis of those cases would serve no useful purpose.[208] Nonetheless, one or two of those cases will be encountered from time to time in practice, and for this reason they are briefly mentioned.

Older cases decided under the CPR

12.170   (For the reasons set out at **12.169**, the extent to which the cases referred to in this paragraph remain helpful is limited.) In a case where there had been significant commencement delay which was not all the blame of the receiving party, Richards J found that no disallowance of costs ought to be made.[209] Factors that Richards J took into account were the fact that the paying party had not availed itself of the opportunity to apply for an unless order and the fact that a fair assessment was still possible notwithstanding the delay. In a different case, Park J considered how the court should exercise its discretion where costs were payable by LSC in respect of services provided to an assisted person: he found that delay in those circumstances was, if anything, positively beneficial to the LSC, and that whilst a delay of more than 4 years met the jurisdictional threshold, it was wrong to disallow the costs entirely.[210] Longmore LJ commented that Park J's analysis depended largely on provisions applicable to the assessment of publicly funded costs.[211] Finally, there is a case which has achieved some notoriety as a result of the commencement delay being about 20 years; had the assessment taken place, some of the costs that would have been assessed would have been incurred 40 years previously. The delay had caused the paying party to be hampered in terms of evidence. Unsurprisingly, Chadwick LJ ruled that 'there must be finality in litigation' and ordered that assessment should not go ahead.[212]

12.171   In summary, whilst each case will turn on its own facts, even where the jurisdictional threshold has been met, the court should be hesitant to impose a sanction which goes beyond the disallowance of interest.

---

[207]   *Haji-Ioannou v Frangos* [2006] EWCA Civ 1663 at [17].

[208]   *Haji-Ioannou v Frangos* [2006] EWCA Civ 1663 at [11].

[209]   *Botham v Khan* [2004] EWHC 2602 (QB).

[210]   *Re Homes Assured plc* [2002] Costs LR 71.

[211]   *Haji-Ioannou v Frangos* [2006] EWCA Civ 1663 at [11].

[212]   *Weston v Weston* [2006] EWCA Civ 1554.

Procedure

12.172 There is no express requirement either in the CPR or in the CPD that an application for disallowance of costs for delay should be made on application. Nonetheless, the CPD provides that the court must give the party or legal representative in question a reasonable opportunity to answer a case of misconduct;[213] unless the relevant persons are already at court, it would generally be that the party against whom the sanction is sought would be given notice of the hearing. In any event, it would always be sensible to inform the court of the fact that an application is likely to be made; this is because this would avoid the matter being allocated to an authorised court officer (who would lack the power to invoke CPR, r 44.14: see **4.15**).[214]

12.173 Where the court has imposed a sanction under CPR, r 44.14(2), and where the receiving party is not present in person when the sanction is imposed, that party's solicitor must notify his client in writing no later than 7 days after the solicitor receives notice of the order imposing the sanction.[215] The solicitor may be required to prove that he took reasonable steps to comply with that obligation.[216]

Limitation

12.174 Whilst there are several Acts pertaining to limitation,[217] in so far as the law of costs is concerned, the only relevant one is the Limitation Act 1980 ('LA 1980'); it is the effect of this Act which is discussed in this section. The focus is on contentious business, but similar principles also apply to non-contentious business.

12.175 The following topics will be discussed:

- whether a solicitor is able to enforce a claim for fees long after the work was done;
- whether a client is able to seek assessment of costs long after the work was done;
- whether a litigant is able to obtain an order for costs where the opportunity to ask for that order arose long ago;
- whether limitation would have any bearing on the court's ability to assess costs; and
- whether a receiving party is able to enforce an order long after it was made.

It is convenient, first, to explain the position as between solicitor and client; this is because that law, to an extent, governs the position between opposing parties.

Solicitor and client

Jurisdiction

12.176 A solicitor's right to recover his fees will generally arise out of a simple contract (which is a contract which has not been made by deed and which is not the very formal type of contract known as a contract of record). The applicable section is s 5 of the LA 1980. That section imposes a limitation period of 6 years beginning on the date the cause of action accrued:

---

213 See CPD, art 18.1.
214 See CPR, r 47.3(1)(b)(i).
215 See CPR, r 44.14(3).
216 See CPD, art 18.3.
217 See the Foreign Limitation Periods Act 1984 and the Limitation (Enemies and War Prisoners) Act 1945.

'An action founded on simple contract shall not be brought after the expiration of six years from the date on which the cause of action accrued.'

Jurisdiction under a non-contractual retainer

12.177   Some contracts of retainer are expressly permitted by statute in the sense that where certain conditions are met, statute makes express provision for the payment of fees;[218] where this is the case it is arguable that LA 1980, s 9(1) should apply (that section dealing with sums recoverable by statute),[219] but the counter-argument is that most statutory provisions relating to costs do not create a cause of action, they merely stipulate the procedure. Regardless of which argument is correct, nothing will turn on the point because the limitation period is the same as that under LA 1980, s 5.

12.178   It will occasionally happen that a solicitor will seek to enforce a non-contractual right to payment by his client (such as where quantum meruit is claimed); in cases where the court does not deal with argument by finding that there is an implied simple contract, it would be open to the court, in appropriate cases, to apply an express statutory limitation period other than that which relates to simple contract,[220] or alternatively to apply the contractual limitation period by analogy.[221]

No discretion

12.179   Regardless of the way in which the solicitor's right to costs is analysed, it will almost always be the case that a 6-year limitation period will apply. In the context of a solicitor and client relationship, the court has no discretion to disapply the limitation period (the only exceptions to this are where the limitation period has been extended or postponed by reason of disability, fraud, etc: see **12.219–12.225**). Thus, unless it has been acknowledged (see **12.213–12.218**), the issue of whether a claim is statute barred will usually depend solely on whether the 6-year limitation period has expired. That is a mixed question of fact and law.

When time begins to run

12.180   Time will begin to run from the date on which the cause of action accrued (or, more accurately, the day after, as the day on which the cause of action arose is excluded).[222] Ward LJ has recently confirmed that the following long-standing definition of 'cause of action' remains good law:[223]

'Every fact which it would be necessary for the plaintiff to prove, if traversed, in order to support his right to the judgment of the court.'

12.181   The issue of when the cause of action accrued is a potentially difficult point in the context of solicitor and client costs because there are many stages in that

---

[218]   See, for example, s 65(2) of the Solicitors Act 1974.
[219]   That section reads as follows: '(1) An action to recover any sum recoverable by virtue of any enactment shall not be brought after the expiration of six years from the date on which the cause of action accrued.'
[220]   See, for example, LA 1980, s 21(3), which applies to non-fraudulent breach of trust; caution must be exercised when the trust is said to be a constructive trust, as a limitation period will not always apply.
[221]   In a context other than costs see *De Seguros Imperio v Heath (REBX) Ltd* [2001] 1 WLR 112.
[222]   *Marren v Dawson Bentley & Co Ltd* [1961] 2 QB 135.
[223]   *Legal Services Commission v Rasool* [2008] EWCA Civ 154 at [16], citing with approval *Coburn v Colledge* [1897] 1 QB 702.

relationship which may, at first blush, appear to be an appropriate trigger point; in so far as contentious work is concerned, these might include:

- the completion of an individual item of work;
- the completion of sufficient work to give rise to a natural break;
- the termination of the contract of retainer;
- the date of delivery of the bill of costs;
- the expiry of the one month following the date of the delivery of the bill of costs; and
- the date on which costs are quantified by assessment or agreement.

In the context of conditional fee agreements, the points at which the claim is won or at which costs are assessed or paid may be added to this list.

12.182   The answer to the question of when time begins to run is that it begins at the moment the solicitor's right to be paid accrues: procedural factors – such as the need to allow a month to expire after serving a bill of costs – are of no relevance.[224] In particular:

- whilst it is true to say that a solicitor cannot ordinarily sue a client for costs until the expiration of one month after delivery of a signed bill,[225] time runs against a solicitor from the time the solicitor has completed the work which allows him contractually to raise a bill, and not from the delivery of the bill;[226] and
- the fact that costs must be quantified (by assessment or by agreement) before they can be paid is a procedural issue only, so the fact that costs have not been quantified does not prevent time from starting to run.[227]

12.183   Lord Esher MR explained the relevance (or, rather, irrelevance) of the requirement to allow one month to expire before issuing proceedings:[228]

> 'It does not provide that no solicitor shall have any cause of action in respect of his costs or any right to be paid till the expiration of a month from his delivering a signed bill of costs, but merely that he shall not commence or maintain any action for the recovery of fees, charges, or disbursements until then.'

12.184   Procedural steps having been discounted as potential trigger points, the next question is how the court determines when the solicitors' right to be paid arose. Each case will be decided on its own merits: this is because each retainer will be different, and the right to payment may arise in diverse ways. The retainer may or may not be an entire contract.[229] Where, for example, the retainer is a private retainer to provide services over a short period of time, the right to be paid is likely to arise immediately upon that work being complete.[230] Where an appeal is brought in the litigation that was the subject of

---

[224]   As to the relevance of procedural provisions in general (ie not solely as they relate to costs), see *O'Connor v Isaacs* [1956] 2 All ER 417.

[225]   Solicitors Act 1974, s 69(1).

[226]   *Coburn v Colledge* [1897] 1 QB 702, CA.

[227]   This is a necessary implication of *Coburn v Colledge* [1897] 1 QB 702; it is also the analysis advanced by Aldous LJ in the analogous situation involving costs payable by the LSC (see *Legal Services Commission v Rasool* [2008] EWCA Civ 154).

[228]   *Coburn v Colledge* [1897] 1 QB 702 at 706.

[229]   See **8.9–8.30**; see *Underwood, Son & Piper v Lewis* [1894] 2 QB 306 for a discussion of this issue by Lord Esher MR.

[230]   See, for example, *Baile v Baile* (1872) LR 13 Eq 497 and *Bonser v Bradshaw* (1860) 25 JP 483.

the retainer, it may be the case that the right does not arise until the conclusion of that appeal;[231] on the other hand, where the retainer is sufficiently lengthy to permit of natural breaks, then the right may arise piecemeal each time such a break occurs.[232] Termination of the retainer will start time running,[233] as will express or implied agreement that costs are due.[234] Whether time has begun to run under a conditional fee agreement will depend on the terms of the agreement: in some cases the cause of action may accrue the moment the claim is won, but in others, it may accrue at some later stage, such as when the costs against an opponent have been assessed or agreed.

The effect of incidental work such as costs proceedings

12.185   It will often be the case that the retainer has concluded, but that work incidental to the retainer then needs to be carried out (such as dealing with the costs, or dealing with receipt of damages). The nature of each retainer will turn on the facts, but generally such incidental work would be disregarded in the sense that it would not prevent time running in respect of the earlier work.[235]

More than one type of costs debt

12.186   It will not always be the case that a retainer will cover only one type of work; where a solicitor carries out work which touches upon differing matters, time will begin to run not in respect of the retainer as a whole, but in respect of each aspect of it.[236] If only some of the items included in the bill are statute barred, the solicitor may claim for those items which are free of that barrier:[237] this, presumably, would apply where there have been natural breaks, interim invoices, etc.

Effect of a successful limitation defence

12.187   The effect of a successful limitation defence is that the solicitor cannot enforce a claim for costs; the right itself continues to exist,[238] but the remedy of claim or legal set-off[239] is extinguished. The practical effect of this is that a bar will apply only where limitation is successfully raised as a defence to a claim: where it is not raised, the claim may be enforced in the usual way.[240]

---

[231]   See, for example, *Harris v Quine* (1869) LR 4 QB 653; the issue will turn on the terms of the retainer.

[232]   See **17.23–17.30**; see, in particular, the analysis of Sir George Jessel MR in *In re Hall v Barker* (1893) 9 Ch D 538 at 545.

[233]   See, for example, *Martindale v Falkner* (1846) 2 CB 706; see also *Underwood, Son and Piper v Lewis* [1894] 2 QB 306, CA.

[234]   See **8.45–8.56** and **17.20**; see in particular, Lord Roskill's analysis in *Davidsons v Jones-Fenleigh* (1980) Costs LR (Core vol) 70 at 75.

[235]   *Rothery v Munnings* (1830) 1 B & Ad 15; *Phillips v Broadley* (1846) 9 QB 744; and *Re Nelson, Son and Hastings* (1885) 30 Ch D 1, CA.

[236]   See *Phillips v Broadley* (1846) 9 QB 744.

[237]   See *Rothery v Munnings* (1830) 1 B & Ad 15; *Blake v Hummell* (1884) 51 LT 430; and *Wilkinson v Smart* (1875) 24 WR 42.

[238]   See *Curwen v Milburn* (1889) 42 Ch D 424, CA at 434, per Cotton LJ.

[239]   See *Smith v Betty* [1903] 2 KB 317, CA; the right to claim equitable set-off would not necessarily be extinguished; see *Filcross Securities Ltd v Midgeley* (unreported) 21 July 1998, CA.

[240]   See CPR, PD 16, para 13.1, which requires a defendant to particularise the basis of his defence.

Trusts

12.188 Where a solicitor has acted for a trust and where his claim for costs has become statute barred, the trustees are at liberty (subject to any contrary provision in the trust) to pay those costs notwithstanding the fact that they would be entitled to refuse to do so.[241]

Lien and security

12.189 A creditor's lien is not something which is capable of becoming time barred.[242] Thus, a solicitor's lien for a statute-barred debt is not affected by the fact that the debt has become statute barred.[243]

12.190 Where his claim for costs is time barred, a solicitor is not able to obtain a charging order pursuant to s 73 of the Solicitors Act 1974.[244]

Late request for assessment of paid costs and accounts

12.191 Where a client has paid his solicitor but wishes to have those costs assessed long after the work was done, the solicitor may wish to argue that the right to an assessment is statute barred. There is no authority on the issue of whether an application for an assessment is capable of being statute barred, which is probably a reflection of the fact that it would almost never be the case that a solicitor would need to rely on such an argument. This is because he would be able to rely on the fact that the court has no discretion to order that costs be assessed where more than 12 months have expired since payment[245] (see **18.4**). (The issue would not arise where the costs had not been paid, because in those circumstances it would be the client rather than the solicitor who would be relying on the expiry of the limitation period.) If, in some preternatural circumstances the issue did arise, then in view of the fact that LA 1980, s 38 provides that 'action' includes any proceeding in a court of law, there is no reason to believe that detailed assessment proceedings could not, in principle, be time barred.[246]

12.192 The time within which a client must assert his right to an account is not limited to 6 years, or to any other definite period.[247]

12.193 In summary, a solicitor's claim for his fees will generally be statute barred within 6 years of the right to payment arising, and the fact that certain tasks need to be carried out after the main work had been completed will not prevent time running.

Seeking an order for costs

12.194 The issue here is whether a party who believes that he is entitled to costs may apply for an order long after the circumstances arose in which it was open to him to make that application. For obvious reasons this issue will arise where the putative right

---

[241] *Budgett v Budgett* [1895] 1 Ch 202.
[242] See *Spears v Hartly* (1800) 3 Esp 81.
[243] *Higgins v Scott* (1831) 2 B & Ad 413 and *Re Carter, Carter v Carter* (1885) 55 LJ Ch 230.
[244] See s 73(2) of the Solicitors Act 1974.
[245] *Harrison v Tew* [1990] 2 AC 523.
[246] It may be relevant that the 1980 Act does not apply to claims based on the court's inherent power over solicitorrs: *Bray v Stuart A West & Co* [1989] NLJR 753.
[247] *Cheese v Keen* [1908] 1 Ch 245.

to costs arose before the claim was issued, so it would generally arise only as a result of an alleged compromise (which could either be a specific agreement to pay costs, or an agreement to compromise the claim generally). It would not arise where a Part 36 offer was accepted or where a claim was discontinued: this is because in those circumstances an order for costs will be deemed to have been made.

12.195 As with costs between solicitor and client, more than one potential trigger point may be identified; in particular, it may be argued that time does not begin to run until after the costs have been quantified.

12.196 An analogous situation to a claim arising out of an alleged compromise would be where the LSC were attempting to recover costs from a formerly assisted person whose certificate had been revoked.[248] Dealing with just such a case, Ward LJ (with whom Smith and Wilson LJJ agreed) considered the issue of whether it was a requirement that costs should be assessed before a cause of action would accrue; after having drawn upon non-costs cases in which quantification of a sum was not found to be necessary to start time running[249], he concluded:[250]

> 'In my judgment the fact that declaratory relief is available demonstrates to me that the process of ascertainment of the amount of costs is a mere procedural requirement, not an inherent element of the cause of action itself.'

These comments suggest that time begins to run from the point not later than the moment that the receiving party was put in a position to apply for a costs order. That point will depend on the facts of each case, but where (as will almost always be the case) it arose as a result of a compromise, time will run from the date on which that compromise was made.

Contributions

12.197 Whilst there is no costs-specific authority on the point, the analysis set out above would not necessarily apply where a party sought a contribution towards its liability for costs under the Civil Liability (Contribution) Act 1978. In this regard, LA 1980, s 10(1) makes the following provisions:

> 'Where under section 1 of the Civil Liability (Contribution) Act 1978 any person becomes entitled to a right to recover contribution in respect of any damage from any other person, no action to recover contribution by virtue of that right shall be brought after the expiration of two years from the date on which that right accrued.'

12.198 Therefore, a party has two years from the time when he becomes 'entitled to a right to recover a contribution' during which to bring his claim for a contribution; there are three reasons for believing that time does not begin to run until the costs in respect of which the contribution is sought have been assessed:

---

[248] The analogy is not perfect: (i) most of the arguments addressed to Ward LJ were based on regulations which do not apply in other types of case; (ii) the costs were recoverable by virtue of an enactment rather than by way of a contract of compromise; and (iii) Ward LJ specifically mentioned the LSC's ability to seek a declaration; the thrust of Ward LJ's analysis is likely to apply by analogy notwithstanding these imperfections.

[249] In particular, *Hillingdon London Borough Council v ARC Ltd* [1999] Ch 139.

[250] *Legal Services Commission v Rasool* [2008] EWCA Civ 154 at [29].

(1)   An analogy may be drawn with the situation where costs are payable between parties (where time does not begin to run until the costs have been quantified); in those circumstances Aldous LJ has found that there was 'nothing to enforce until the amount of costs had been certified', and that 'payment cannot be enforced without knowledge of what should be paid'.[251] Although the contrary is arguable (see below), a similar logic could apply to a party's right to seek a contribution.

(2)   In respect of damages, time begins to run from the date of the assessment of quantum;[252] it could be argued that it would be curious if a different rule were to apply to costs.

(3)   By the operation of CPR, r 47.1 the general rule will be that costs will not be assessed until the conclusion of proceedings. If time began to run from the date of the costs order rather than the date of quantification, a paying party could find itself in the invidious position of having to seek a contribution before it had the right to apply for a hearing to have its own liability quantified.

12.199   However, the true law could be that costs are dealt with differently from damages, and that a paying party is required to obtain an order for a contribution first and then deal with issues concerning quantum. There is no authority on the point. The problems outlined at **12.59–12.66** may also be relevant.

12.200   In summary, the 6-year limitation period will apply to a right to recover costs, and time will begin to run as soon as the cause of action accrues. The position may be different in so far as contributions are concerned.

Assessing costs

12.201   There is no authority on whether the expiry of a limitation period would have an impact on the way in which costs are assessed, so what is said here should be seen as nothing more than a framework for further legal research.

12.202   For the reasons set out in the next section, a receiving party would not be at risk of being barred from enforcing his costs order until 6 years after the court has assessed the costs. Therefore, the only issue that will arise is whether the effect of the law as between solicitor and client has a bearing – as a result of the operation of the indemnity principle – on the position between the parties. Put another way, the question is whether a paying party is relieved of the burden of payment by virtue of the receiving party's solicitor's right to costs becoming statute barred.

12.203   It will rarely be the case that a solicitor's bill of costs will have remained unpaid for a period of 6 years, and it will be even more rarely the case that the paying party would know about that state of affairs, even where it were to exist. The situation could arise, however, where the solicitors are acting for an impecunious client in the hope that he would be able to discharge their fees out of the proceeds of the claim.

12.204   A paying party would have to overcome a number of problems before he could succeed in proving a breach of the indemnity principle; those would include the following:

---

[251]   *Chohan v Times Newspapers Ltd* [2001] EWCA Civ 964 at [33].
[252]   *Aer Lingus plc v Gildacroft Ltd* [2006] EWCA Civ 4.

- the paying party would not find it easy to find out when invoices were rendered and whether they remained unpaid;
- the paying party would have to prove that there was a 'genuine issue' as to whether there had been a breach of the indemnity principle; more than mere assertion would be required in that regard;[253]
- the paying party would have to prove that the debt had not been acknowledged by the client; and
- the court would have to be satisfied that it was open to a paying party to take such a point, given the fact that limitation will operate only when it is raised as a defence.[254]

In support of its argument on the last of these topics, the receiving party could point to the fact that in the analogous situation of payment of statute-barred costs out of a trust, there is no principle that would prevent a trustee from declining to raise a limitation defence.[255]

12.205   In summary, a paying party would have difficulty in persuading the court to disallow costs by reason of those costs allegedly being statute barred as between solicitor and client.

Bringing an action for an order for costs

12.206   The next question is whether a party who believes that he is entitled to costs can bring an action for an order for costs long after it was made. This is different from enforcement:[256] various means by which an order may be enforced are briefly discussed at **21.310–21.321**. There are rules about enforcing judgments out of time;[257] essentially, those rules provide that the permission of the court is required after the expiry of 6 years. Permission is not normally granted in contexts other than costs and there is no reason to believe that costs should be treated any differently.

12.207   Section 24 of the LA 1980 provides:

'(1)   An action shall not be brought upon any judgment after the expiration of six years from the date on which the judgment became enforceable.

(2)   No arrears of interest in respect of any judgment debt shall be recovered after the expiration of six years from the date on which the interest became due.'

The limitation period applies regardless of the nature of the claim and, in particular, regardless of whether the original claim was advanced in law or in equity.[258]

12.208   Therefore, there is a limitation period of 6 years (in respect of both the costs and interest), after which no proceedings may be brought upon the order. As with the other circumstances discussed here, there is more than one potential trigger point. In

---

[253]   See *Hazlett v Sefton Metropolitan Borough Council* [2000] 4 All ER 887 for a general discussion of this topic.

[254]   See, by way of analogy, *Garbutt v Edwards* [2005] EWCA Civ 1206, in which Arden LJ found that it was not ordinarily open to a paying party to take the point that an estimate of costs provided to a client should limit the costs payable between the parties; see also (in a non-costs context) *King v Victoria Insurance Co* [1896] AC 250, PC at 254 concerning the ability of a stranger to intervene.

[255]   *Budgett v Budgett* [1895] 1 Ch 202.

[256]   See *Lowsley v Forbes* [1999] AC 329.

[257]   The provisions are an example of one of the few provisions of the RSC and CCR which are still in force; they are RSC, Ord 46, r 8 and CCR, Ord 25 and Ord 26.

[258]   *Dunne v Doyle* (1860) 10 I Ch R 502.

particular, the trigger could be the date upon which the order was made, or the date upon which the court issues a final costs certificate.

12.209 In contrast to the other circumstances mentioned above, Aldous LJ (with whom Walker and Parker LJJ agreed) found that time does not begin to run until the costs have been quantified and certified.[259] In coming to this conclusion Aldous LJ noted that in a different case Brandon J had found that the word 'enforceable' means enforceable by claim on the judgment, not by execution;[260] he found that that analysis was too restrictive, and that time will run from the date when judgment becomes enforceable by action or otherwise.[261] He concluded:[262]

> 'The word "enforceable" must mean enforceable in a practical way according to law. There cannot be a right to bring an action which would amount to an abuse of process. Further, in the present case there was nothing to enforce until the amount of costs had been certified ... Payment cannot be enforced without knowledge of what should be paid.'

Whilst he did not comment on the point, Aldous LJ's analysis is entirely in keeping with the restrictions imposed by CPR, r 47.8(3)[263] and r 47.15(5).[264]

12.210 Where the costs are to be assessed by detailed assessment, an order for costs will become statute barred only 6 years after the issue of the final costs certificate. For obvious reasons, this will not apply where costs are assessed by summary assessment. Although there is no authority on the point, it is also probably the case that Aldous LJ's reasoning does not apply to foreign judgments.[265]

12.211 Where a costs order is statute barred, the bar will apply to a statutory demand as well as to other means of enforcement.[266]

12.212 In summary, whilst an order for costs cannot be enforced after the expiry of the 6-year limitation period, that period does not run until the costs have been assessed.

Acknowledgement and part payment

12.213 A fresh accrual of a claim may arise where a debt of costs is acknowledged or part paid;[267] this may have the effect of extending a limitation period (and may do so repeatedly), but it will not have the effect of reviving a claim which has already become time barred.[268]

---

[259] *Chohan v Times Newspapers Ltd* [2001] EWCA Civ 964; this was a case dealing with pre-CPR procedure, but there is no reason to believe that it does not remain good law. Whilst only illustrative, Lord Neuberger MR came to a very similar conclusion in a case in which the Legal Services Commission sought to recoup fees overpaid to a barrister: see *Legal Services Commission v Henthorn* [2011] EWCA Civ 1415 at [56].

[260] See *Berliner Industriebank Aktiengesellschaft v Jost* [1971] 1 QB 278 at 293.

[261] *Chohan v Times Newspapers Ltd* [2001] EWCA Civ 964 at [18].

[262] *Chohan v Times Newspapers Ltd* [2001] EWCA Civ 964 at [33].

[263] Which stipulates that the court may not impose any sanction for delay in commencing detailed assessment proceedings other than a disallowance of interest and any sanction made in accordance with CPR, r 44.14.

[264] Which stipulates very similar restrictions relating to delay in requesting a detailed assessment hearing.

[265] For a discussion of foreign judgment generally, see *Berliner Industriebank Aktiengesellschaft v Jost* [1971] 2 QB 463 at 470.

[266] *Re a Debtor (No 647-SD-1999)* (2000) The Times, April 10.

[267] See LA 1980, s 29(5).

[268] See LA 1980, s 29(7).

12.214   In so far as it is relevant to the law of costs, LA 1980, s 29 provides as follows:

'(5)   Subject to subsection (6) below, where any right of action has accrued to recover—

(a)   any debt or other liquidated pecuniary claim; or

(b)   any claim to the personal estate of a deceased person or to any share or interest in any such estate;

and the person liable or accountable for the claim acknowledges the claim or makes any payment in respect of it the right shall be treated as having accrued on and not before the date of the acknowledgement or payment.

(6)   A payment of a part of the rent or interest due at any time shall not extend the period for claiming the remainder then due, but any payment of interest shall be treated as a payment in respect of the principal debt.

(7)   Subject to subsection (6) above, a current period of limitation may be repeatedly extended under this section by further acknowledgements or payments, but a right of action, once barred by this Act, shall not be revived by any subsequent acknowledgement or payment.'

12.215   The potential importance of a part payment made by a client to a solicitor is that the client may lose the opportunity to assert a limitation defence. The same would rarely be true of interim payments between opposing parties (made pursuant to either CPR, r 44.3(8) or r 47.15); this is because those payments would usually be made only in the interval between the costs order being made and the costs being assessed, which is a period during which time does not begin to run in any event.

12.216   When determining whether a payment amounts to an acknowledgement of a debt, the court will look not at the analysis that the court would place upon that payment after having had the benefit of legal argument, but at the position as it was understood by the parties at the time of the payment.[269] Therefore, a payment may be regarded as being a part payment, even if the monies were used for some other purpose (such as paying counsel).

12.217   A request for particulars of costs is capable of being an acknowledgement; Cotton LJ, for example, found that a letter containing the following phrase was an acknowledgement: 'Our client only requires you to deliver particulars of any unsettled bill of costs you may have against him.'[270]

12.218   In summary, whilst the issues of acknowledgement and part payment apply to debts of costs in just the same way as they apply to other debts, for practical purposes they are relevant only to the position between solicitor and client.

Where limitation will not be permitted to stand as a defence

12.219   There are several circumstances in which the court may deny a party a limitation defence. Those circumstances are a mixed bag, and no attempt is made to deal with the issues in any detail or in any particular order: what is set out below is no more than an aid to further legal research. The circumstances are as follows.

---

[269]   *Kleinwort Benson Ltd v South Tyneside Metropolitan Borough Council* [1994] 4 All ER 972.

[270]   *Curwen v Milburn* (1889) 42 Ch D 424.

Lack of capacity

12.220 If, on the date on which a cause of action accrued, the party to whom it had accrued was under a disability, time will not begin to run until that person ceases to be under a disability or dies.[271]

Children

12.221 If, on the date on which a cause of action accrued, the party to whom it had accrued was under the age of 18,[272] time will not begin to run until that person reaches majority or dies.[273]

Estoppel

12.222 The fact that the parties have been engaged in negotiation will not, of itself, prevent the paying party from relying on limitation as a defence,[274] but where the paying party has agreed a 'limitation holiday',[275] or where the paying party has given assurances that the receiving party will not be prejudiced by the delay caused by negotiation,[276] the paying party may be estopped from relying on limitation as a defence. The principles involved are those applicable to any estoppel and can be found in any textbook on equity. A promise not to rely on a limitation defence may result in the promisor being estopped from doing otherwise.[277] Such a promise may be given particular effect when it can also be interpreted as being an acknowledgement of the debt; in particular, a promise not to rely on a limitation defence combined with an acknowledgement of the costs may start time running afresh.[278]

Mediation

12.223 By no later than 11 May 2011 the United Kingdom must give effect to a European Directive[279] which provides, in essence, that parties must not be prevented from issuing proceedings as a result of delay caused by an attempt to mediate; this may require some modification of the present law.

Fraud

12.224 It may happen that a party finds that it has not asserted a right to costs by reason of a fraud being visited upon that party. Where this is the case, time will not begin to run until that party has discovered the fraud (or was in a position to discover the fraud by exercising reasonable diligence).[280]

---

[271] See LA 1980, s 28(1).

[272] See Family Law Reform Act 1969, s 1.

[273] See LA 1980, s 28(1).

[274] *Hewlett v LCC* (1908) 72 JP 136.

[275] See, for example, *James Carleton Seventh Earl of Malmesbury v Strutt and Parker (a partnership)* [2008] EWHC 424 (QB).

[276] See, for example, *Seechurn v Ace Insurance Sa-Nv* [2002] EWCA Civ 67.

[277] *Paterson v Glasgow Corporation* (1908) 46 SLR 10.

[278] *Gardner v M'Mahon* (1842) 3 QB 561.

[279] European Parliament and Council Directive 2008/52/EC (OJ L136, 25.5.2008), p 3.

[280] LA 1980, s 32(1) (as amended).

12.225 In summary, whilst the court has no statutory discretion to disapply a limitation period, it is, in appropriate cases, open to the court to find that the debt has been acknowledged or that there are other circumstances which will prevent the defence of limitation from applying.

Laches and abuse of process

12.226 The issue of laches arises (very) rarely in the context of costs; this means that there is very little authority on the topic. Thus, this discussion ought to be regarded as a starting point for further legal research rather than as a full analysis of the law.

Laches

12.227 Laches[281] is an exclusively equitable defence, which may arise when a party has 'gone to sleep on its rights'.[282]

12.228 It is an ancient doctrine predating statutory limitation, but which is expressly preserved by LA 1980.[283] There are two circumstances (which are not mutually exclusive) in which it may arise:

- it may arise where a party's delay has made it impossible for the court fairly to hear the issues which are in dispute (perhaps because of the loss of evidence); in this respect it is a doctrine that has much in common with the procedural facility to strike claims out for want of prosecution; and
- the doctrine may also arise where the delay has induced the other party to act on the assumption that the claim will not be pursued, in which case it has much in common with the doctrines of acquiescence and estoppel.

Whilst these are the circumstances in which the doctrine may arise, the essential ingredients are substantial delay coupled with a notion that it would be unfair or unconscionable to allow the party guilty of delay to assert its rights.

12.229 It is of pivotal relevance that where statute provides a limitation period (either directly or by analogy), the doctrine of laches is excluded.[284] This is particularly relevant in the context of costs, as a statutory limitation period would almost always apply between solicitor and client; this means that the doctrine of laches would almost never arise where a solicitor has delayed in respect of his own costs.

12.230 Specifically, the defence of laches is not available where a statutory limitation period applies (either directly or by analogy in equity). Where a statutory limitation period does apply, the person who asserts the beneficial right (ie the receiving party) will be entitled to the benefit of the full limitation period.[285] A paying party would not be able to argue that the doctrine of laches should relieve him of the burden of paying costs

---

[281] Meaning 'unconscionable delay', derived from the Old French *lachesse*.

[282] The doctrine is expressed in the phrase *Ie vigilantibus et non dormientibus lex succurrit* (equity aids the vigilant, not the indolent): see *Marquis of Cholmondeley v Lord Clinton* (1820) 2 Jac & W 1 at 140.

[283] See s 36(2), which reads: 'Nothing in this Act shall affect any equitable jurisdiction to refuse relief on the ground of acquiescence or otherwise.'

[284] See *P&O Nedlloyd BV v Arab Metals Co* [2006] EWCA Civ 1717; historically, see *Archbold v Scully* (1861) 9 HL Cas 360 at 383.

[285] *Archbold v Scully* (1861) 9 HL Cas 360 at 383 per Lord Wensleydale; and *Re Birch, Roe v Birch* (1884) 27 Ch D 622.

in circumstances where the right is a legal right. In view of the fact that there is no such thing as an equitable costs order, it can be seen that the doctrine of laches has almost no relevance to the law of costs.

12.231 In any event, in view of the restrictions imposed by CPR, r 47.8(3)[286] and r 47.15(5),[287] it is arguable that even if it applied in principle, the CPR have excluded the doctrine of laches from detailed assessment in that the court is not permitted to impose a sanction for delay in the assessment process other than the two sanctions specifically identified in the CPR.[288]

12.232 However, circumstances may arise from where the doctrine would not be excluded. The only example the writer is able to cite is where a party issues a claim, is successful in that claim, but then leaves it many years before asking the court to make a costs order. In such a case, no limitation period would apply because the claim would already have been issued. It is far from certain whether the laches doctrine would apply in even those unusual circumstances; it also has to be said that the court would almost certainly prefer not to invoke the doctrine, but would probably follow the more straightforward route of taking the delay into account when exercising its general discretion as to costs under CPR, r 44.3, so, even if the doctrine were available as a matter of principle, as a matter of practice it is not necessary for the court to invoke it.

12.233 Where the court does choose to invoke it, the modern approach is not to look at decided cases and see if there is a case on point, but to take a broad view of the matter and to decide whether it would be unconscionable for the party concerned to assert his beneficial rights.[289] Two issues are relevant in the context of costs: acquiescence and change of position. Each of these is considered in turn.

Acquiescence

12.234 Where there has been a significant lapse of time, the lapse itself is capable of being evidence of acquiescence.[290] Whilst each case will turn on its own facts,[291] unless there are other factors at play the delay will ordinarily have to be considerable, such as 20 years.[292] A much shorter period would suffice where there has been a change of position on the part of the party against whom the beneficial right is asserted (see below).

12.235 There can be no acquiescence unless the person who asserts the beneficial right (ie the party who seeks to receive costs) has been made aware of the existence of that beneficial right (ie the opportunity to seek an order for costs); that party must also have been in a position to complain about infringement of those rights.[293] It is not necessary that the party knows the exact nature of the beneficial rights.[294]

---

[286] Which stipulates that the court may not impose any sanction for delay in commencing detailed assessment proceedings other than a disallowance of interest and any sanction made in accordance with CPR, r 44.14.
[287] Which stipulates very similar restrictions relating to delay in requesting a detailed assessment hearing.
[288] It is also arguable that the equitable defence of laches is something that does not give rise to 'sanctions', as the issue is not whether the right to costs should be cut back, but whether it is conscionable for that right to be enforced.
[289] *JJ Harrison (Properties) Ltd v Harrison* [2001] EWCA Civ 1467.
[290] *Life Association of Scotland v Siddal, Cooper v Greene* (1861) 3 De GF & J 58 at 72, per Turner LJ.
[291] See *Smith v Clay* (1767) 3 Bro CC 639.
[292] See, for example, *Byrne v Frere* (1828) 2 Mol 157 at 176, per Hart LC.
[293] *Marker v Marker* (1851) 9 Hare 1 at 16.
[294] *Lindsay Petroleum Co v Hurd* (1874) LR 5 PC 221 at 241.

Change of position

12.236 It is often argued that delay may cause a degradation of the evidence by which a beneficial right may be measured.[295] Whilst there is no authority on the point, in the context of costs this would probably include the loss of the papers which would allow the paying party to prepare its own case. The loss of those papers may be relevant even though they go only to the quantification of costs: this is because the court may decide that it would be unfair to order that a party should pay costs where, as a result of delay, he would have one hand tied behind his back if those costs were ever to come before a costs judge.[296]

Abuse of process

12.237 In a similar vein, a party who asserts that delay has been so extreme as to make proceedings abusive will find that he has an uphill struggle. In the context of a claim brought by the Legal Services Commission for overpayment of fees, Lord Neuberger MR had this to say:

> 'There is, in my view, nothing in that point. Where a claim is based on a statutory right subject to a limitation period, which has not yet expired, it seems to me that it would require wholly exceptional facts before an abuse argument merely based on delay could have any chance of success.'

Lord Neuberger MR went on to say, however, that it would be different if the abuse was also based on some sort of express or implied promise or clear indication that no claim would be brought, especially if that was relied upon.

HUMAN RIGHTS

12.238 This section focuses on human rights in so far as the practice of costs is concerned; it does not deal with access to funding, nor does it deal with human rights and the incidence of costs. The writer is grateful to Regional Costs Judge David Harris for his assistance with this section.

The place of human rights law in the assessment of costs

12.239 Issues concerning human rights are capable of arising in almost any legal dispute, but in so far as the law of costs is concerned, they tend to arise in the following contexts:

- wasted costs (**7.211** and **7.214**);
- security for costs (**16.5, 16.55, 16.65** and **16.96**);
- costs against the Courts Service (**40.3**);
- Privilege and election (**24.31**);
- access to Justice; and
- additional liabilities.

---

[295]   *Bright v Legerton* (1861) 2 De GF & J 606, CA at 617, per Lord Campbell LC.
[296]   *Legal Services Commission v Henthorn* [2011] EWCA Civ 1415 at [58].

Only the last two are addressed in this chapter; the other topics are addressed in the paragraphs indicated.

Jurisdiction and governing bodies

12.240 The starting point is the Convention for the Protection of Human Rights and Fundamental Freedoms 1950; this is almost always referred to as the European Convention on Human Rights ('ECHR'). It is an international treaty by which all member states of the Council of Europe are bound. It was opened for signature in Rome on 4 November 1950 and was entered into force on 3 September 1953.

The European institutions

12.241 The European Court of Human Rights ('ECtHR') was established under the ECHR for the purposes of hearing alleged violations of the human rights enshrined in the ECHR and its protocols. Applications can be made by individuals or by contracting states; the court may also issue advisory opinions. As of 1 June 2010 the European Commissioner for Human Rights has been allowed to intervene in applications as a third party;[297] the office of Commissioner is an independent institution within the Council of Europe. His remit is to promote the awareness of and respect for human rights in member states; he has no judicial role.

12.242 The ECtHR is not part of the European Union ('EU')[298] and should not be confused with the European Court of Justice[299] ('ECJ'). (The ECJ is the judicial institution of the EU which is responsible for ensuring the uniform application and interpretation of European Union law rather than the ECHR.) That said, the ECJ often regards the ECHR as being a guiding principle, and as such, its decisions are often woven with principles from the ECHR. The two courts are geographically separate in that the ECtHR is a supranational court based in Strasbourg whereas the ECJ sits in Luxembourg.

12.243 Applications can be made to the ECtHR only after domestic remedies have been exhausted; this means that the applicant must have taken his case to the highest possible level of domestic jurisdiction. Applications must be lodged within six months following the last domestic judicial decision in the case. The applicant must be personally and directly a victim of a violation of the ECHR, and must have suffered a significant disadvantage as a result.

12.244 The ECtHR is divided into Sections and Chambers. A Section is an administrative entity and a Chamber is a judicial formation of the court within a given Section. Court fees are not charged. At the time of writing the ECtHR had a backlog of over 120,000 cases and listing time was several years; this is relevant in so far as costs law is concerned because supposedly recent decisions may relate to costs regimes that are either obsolete or nearly obsolete.

---

[297]   See Protocol 14 of the ECHR.
[298]   The EU now has a single legal identity and, by virtue of protocol 14 of the ECHR is now able to accede to the ECHR and be regulated as if it were a member state, but at the time of writing had yet to do so.
[299]   Or more formally, the Court of Justice of the European Union; by virtue of the Treaty of Lisbon 2009, the court changed its name to the Court of Justice alongside its two subordinate chambers: the General Court (formerly the Court of First Instance) and the Civil Service Tribunal.

The benefits conferred by the ECHR

12.245   The ECHR is split into Parts and is supplemented by several protocols. The articles in Part 1 of the ECHR create rights which are referred to as 'guaranteed rights'. The rights that are of most relevance in the context of the law of costs are Art 6 (right to a fair trial), Art 8 (right to privacy) and, to lesser extent, Art 10 (right to freedom of expression). Rights can be classified in the following ways:

- **Express and implied rights**: The rights referred to above are express rights. The ECHR is a 'living instrument' which is capable of growth and expansion,[300] and as a result, there are, in addition to the express or core rights, a number of implied rights. An example of an implied right is the right to effective access to the court (see **12.31**), this being a right implied by the right to a fair trial.
- **Absolute, limited and qualified rights:** Whilst some rights are 'absolute' in the sense that they shelter the individual entirely from interference which is detrimental to him but beneficial for the majority, most are 'qualified' in the sense that they may, in appropriate circumstances, be lawfully interfered with where the needs of the majority would justify such a step (see **12.15–12.27**). In the context of the law of costs, an example (albeit a controversial one) might be a requirement to pay a success fee (see **12.38** *et seq*). Other rights are 'limited' in the sense that they are limited under express and defined circumstances.

With the exception of privilege, absolute and limited rights have no real part to play in the context of the law of costs. Qualified rights do occasionally play a part (albeit it only very rarely); the question will not usually be whether any given right exists or whether there has been interference with it, but whether the interference in question is lawful. This is addressed in **12.25–12.29** below.

The Human Rights Act 1998

12.246   The Human Rights Act 1998 ('HRA 1998') came into force on 2 October 2000. Section 6 of the HRA 1998 provides that public bodies (including the court)[301] must act in a way that is compatible with the ECHR. In so far as the law of costs is concerned, the most significant provision is that which relates to the interpretation of legislation: unless it is not possible to do otherwise, both primary and delegated legislation must be read so as to be compatible with the ECHR (see **12.14–12.16** below). This requirement is relevant in the context of the law of costs because, firstly, the vires to award costs is nearly always statutory and, secondly, the procedure by which costs are assessed is typically governed by delegated legislation. In particular, the CPR are delegated legislation (see **3.20**).

Persons who may rely on the HRA

12.247   Section 7 of the HRA 1998 provides that a person who has a claim based on a breach of ECHR may bring proceedings against the public body in question or may rely on the relevant rights in legal proceedings. Only 'victims' are able to do this;[302] in general, that category of persons will not include core public authorities (such as local

---

[300] See *Brown v Stott* [2003] UKHL 21.
[301] See HRA 1998, s 6(3)(a).
[302] For guidance as to who is a victim, see Art 34 of the ECHR. It is a category of persons that is interpreted more narrowly than the category of persons able to apply for judicial review.

authorities)[303] or representative bodies (such as trade unions).[304] Persons whose place of residence is outside the European Union may still be 'victims'.[305]

12.248 The fact that claims may be brought only by victims rarely presents any problem in disputes concerning costs. This is because issues concerning both human rights and costs law usually arise in the context of interpretation of legislation in general rather than in the context of a specific claim brought under s 6 of the HRA 1998. Put otherwise, when issues arise, they tend to focus on the law rather than the litigants themselves. In any event, it is moot point as to whether a person needs to be a victim in order to require the court to interpret legislation in a way that is compatible with the ECHR.[306]

ECtHR authority and conflicts

12.249 Section 2 of the Human Rights Act 1998 requires (amongst other things) the domestic courts to take account of decisions of the ECtHR. The House of Lords has repeatedly held that unless there are special circumstances, 'clear and constant reasoning' in ECtHR authorities should be followed even though they are not binding.[307] The doctrine of (domestic) precedent remains binding upon the lower courts, and where there is conflict between ECtHR authority and domestic authority, the latter will prevail.[308] The higher courts have greater freedom, however. In particular, where the Court of Appeal concludes that one of its previous decisions is inconsistent with a subsequent decision of the ECtHR, it may be able to depart from its previous decision.[309]

Effects, rights and remedies

12.250 In so far as the law of costs is concerned, a putative breach of the ECHR may have the following effects or consequences:

- It may result in the court interpreting a rule, regulation or provision in a way so as to avoid the putative breach;
- It may result in the court making a declaration of incompatibility; or
- It may result in the court awarding some other remedy, such as damages.

Interpretation

12.251 Section 3(1) of the HRA 1998 provides that in so far as it is possible, both primary and secondary legislation must be interpreted in a way that is compatible with ECHR rights and freedoms. Lord Nicholls had this to say on the topic:[310]

---

[303] See *Aston Cantlow and Wilmcote with Billesley Parochial Church Council v Wallbank* [2003] UKHL 37; their Lordships commented, however, that hybrid public authorities that exercise both public and private functions may fall within the category of being a victim.

[304] See *Director General of Fair Trading v Proprietary Association of Great Britain* [2001] EWCA Civ 1217.

[305] See *Farrakhan v Secretary of State for the Home Department* [2001] EWHC 781 (Admin).

[306] *R (on the application of Rusbridger) v Attorney General* [2003] UKHL 38 at [21], per Steyn.

[307] *R (Alconbury Developments Ltd) v Secretary of State for the Environment, Transport and the Regions* [2001] UKHL 23.

[308] *Kay v Lambeth London Borough Council* [2006] UKHL 10.

[309] *R (RJM (FC)) v Secretary of State for Work and Pensions* [2008] UKHL 63.

[310] *Re S (Care Order: Implementation of Care Plan)* [2002] UKHL 10.

'[Section 3] is a powerful tool whose use is obligatory. It is not an optional canon of construction. Nor is its use dependent on the existence of ambiguity. Further the section applies retrospectively.'

Whilst there is no authority on the point, it is likely that these principles apply to the CPD and Pre-action Protocols. The relevant wording of s 3 of the HRA 1998 is as follows:

'(1) So far as it is possible to do so, primary legislation and subordinate legislation must be read and given effect in a way which is compatible with the Convention rights.

(2) This section—

(a)		applies to primary legislation and subordinate legislation whenever enacted;

(b)		does not affect the validity, continuing operation or enforcement of any incompatible primary legislation; and

(c)		does not affect the validity, continuing operation or enforcement of any incompatible subordinate legislation if (disregarding any possibility of revocation) primary legislation prevents removal of the incompatibility.'

The ECtHR has explained that interpretation of ECHR should strike a fair balance between the demands of the general interest of the community and the requirements of the protection of the individuals' fundamental rights.[311]

12.252	There are several mechanisms by which a legislative provision may be read in such a way as to be compatible with those rights. Respected commentators have noted that permissible techniques include 'reading down' words (ie, giving words a narrow meaning), 'reading broadly', and 'reading words in'.[312] Lord Nicholls has explained that s 3(1) of the HRA 1998 may require the court to depart from the *un*ambiguous meaning the legislation in question would otherwise bear;[313] thus, it is an exercise that may significantly differ from the traditional exercise of legislative interpretation, which is normally an exercise of interpreting words that are not unambiguous.

12.253	There are, however, limits to the extent to which the court may depart from the words used. In particular, s 3 of the HRA 1998 is concerned with interpretation of legislation, not amendment. Lord Nichols had this to say on the topic:[314]

'Not all provisions in primary legislation can be rendered Convention compliant by the application of s 3(1). . . . In applying s 3 courts must be ever mindful of this outer limit. The Human Rights Act reserves the amendment of primary legislation to Parliament . . . Interpretation of statutes is a matter for the courts; the enactment of statutes, and the amendment of statutes, are matters for Parliament.'

---

[311]	*Sporrong and Lönnroth v Sweden* (1982) 5 EHRR 35, ECtHR, at [69].
[312]	Lester, Pannick & Herberg *Human Rights Law and Practice* (3rd edn, LexisNexis).
[313]	*Ghaidan v Godin-Mendoza* [2004] UKHL 30, [2004] 2 AC 557, at [30], per Lord Nicholls.
[314]	In *Re S (Care Order: Implementation of Care Plan)* [2002] UKHL 10, [2002] 2 AC 291, at [37]–[40], per Lord Nicholls.

Declarations of incompatibility, etc

Primary legislation

12.254 The court has repeatedly reminded itself that judges will not act as legislators;[315] thus, if primary legislation is incapable of being interpreted in a way that is consistent with ECHR rights and freedoms, the operation and enforcement of that legislation will continue to be valid.[316]

12.255 Where it is impossible to interpret primary legislation in a way that is compatible with the ECHR the court may issue a 'declaration of incompatibility', thereby inviting Parliament to correct the legislation by way of a remedial order.[317]

Secondary legislation

12.256 If secondary legislation is inconsistent as a result of it restrictions imposed by primary legislation, it too will continue to be valid; again, a declaration of incompatibility may be made. If, on the other hand, secondary legislation is inconsistent as a result of something other than restrictions imposed by primary legislation, the court is able directly to set aside the secondary legislation.[318] Not all judges have the power to do this.

Other remedies

12.257 Section 8 of the HRA 1998 provides that where the court finds illegality of the sort contemplated above the court may grant such relief or remedy, or make such order as it considers just and appropriate. This may include an award of damages.

Determining incompatibility

12.258 Whilst an oversimplification, an act of interference with a qualified right (which includes a failure to act)[319] will be lawful only if the following three conditions are met:

- it is prescribed by law;
- it is done for the purposes of securing a permissible aim; and
- it is 'necessary in a democratic society' (see **12.25**), which means that it must (i) serve a pressing social need, (ii) pursue a legitimate aim and (iii) be proportionate to the aims being pursued;

Each of these is considered in turn. In the context of the law of costs, the first two question will rarely present any difficulty, and the question will usually focus on whether the putative interference is an unlawful interference with a guaranteed right.[320]

---

[315] See, for example, *R v A* [2001] UKHL 25 at [103], per Lord Hope.
[316] HRA 1998, s 3(2)(b).
[317] See s 4 of the HRA and CPR, r 40.20.
[318] Under s 6(1) of HRA 1998.
[319] See s 6(6) of HRA 1998.
[320] Examples include the right to privacy (the right) and the need to put a receiving party to his election (the putative interference), or the right to access to justice (the right), and the need to fund the administration of justice by charging court fees (the putative interference).

Prescribed by law

12.259   There are three questions that must be answered when deciding whether an act is prescribed by law; they were described by Lord Hope in this way:[321]

> 'The first is whether there is a legal basis in domestic law for the restriction. The second is whether the law or rule in question is sufficiently accessible to the individual who is affected by the interference, and sufficiently precise to enable him to understand its scope and foresee the consequences of his actions so that he can regulate his conduct without breaking the law. The third is whether, assuming that these two requirements are satisfied, it is nevertheless open to the criticism on the Convention ground that it was applied in a way that was arbitrary because, for example, it has been resorted to in bad faith or in a way that is not proportionate.'

12.260   Where the act in question is prescribed by legislation (such as a requirement to allow fixed costs), then no difficulty will arise, but there are two species of rule that may cause problems in the context of costs litigation:

- **codes, protocols and guidelines**: It may not be immediately obvious whether an act that is prescribed by a code, a guideline or a protocol will be prescribed by law. In general, if the code, guideline or protocol is underpinned by legislation and if they are readily accessible, then they will be prescribed by law.[322] Of equal importance, however, is that a breach of a code, protocol or guideline may give rise to an inference that the act in question is not prescribed by law; and[323]
- **common law:** It is possible for an act to be prescribed by the common law,[324] but difficulties can arise if the law in question is in a state of development of flux (which is not unusual in the context of the law of costs). In particular, if the law is not wholly certain, argument can arise as to whether the law is sufficiently accessible and precise.[325]

Permissible aim

12.261   There must be a legitimate objective which justifies the means.[326] Whether the act is done for the question of securing that objective will depend on the circumstances.

Necessity and proportionality

12.262   An interference with a right must be proportionate to the legitimate aim pursued[327] (or, put another way, there must be a reasonable relationship of proportionality between the means employed and the aim pursued);[328] Three criteria can be identified:[329]

---

[321]   *R (on the application of Rottman) v Metropolitan Police Comr* [2002] UKHL 20 at [35].
[322]   See, for example, *R (on the application of Matthias Rath BV) v the Advertising Standards Authority Ltd* [2001] EMLR 22.
[323]   See, for example, *R v Mason* [2002] EWCA Crim 385, in which a breach of Home Office guidelines found to be relevant.
[324]   See, for example, *R (on the application of Rottman) v Metropolitan Police Comr* [2002] UKHL 20 at [63].
[325]   See, for example, *Douglas v Hello! Ltd* [2005] EWCA Civ 595 at [147].
[326]   *Fayed v United Kingdom* (1994) 18 EHRR 393, ECtHR, at [71].
[327]   *Handyside v United Kingdom* (1976) 1 EHRR 737, ECtHR, at [49].
[328]   *R v Dimsey* [2001] UKHL 46.
[329]   *De Freitas v Permanent Secretary of Ministry of Agriculture, Fisheries, Lands and Housing* [1999] 1 AC 69, PC, at 80C–80H, per Lord Clyde.

- The legislative objective must be sufficiently important to justify limiting the guaranteed right;
- The measures designed to meet the legislative objective must be rationally connected to that objective, and in particular, they must not be arbitrary, unfair or based on irrational considerations; and
- Those measures must be no more than is necessary to accomplish the legitimate objective; in particular, the more severe the detrimental effects of a measure,[330] the more important the objective must be if the measure is to be justified in a democratic society.

The word necessary 'is not synonymous with indispensable, neither has it the flexibility of such expressions as admissible, ordinary, useful, reasonable or desirable . . . it implies the existence of a "pressing social need"'.[331]

12.263 The court does not review the system of the domestic law *in abstracto* but instead will form a view as to whether 'the manner in which this system was applied to or affected the applicants gave rise to any violations of rights.[332] In the context of costs law, this would probably mean looking at the whole of the law, including the CPD, protocols, etc, rather than just the isolated provision in question.

12.264 The court should strive to give effect to the general principle that there is a need to strike a fair balance between the demands of the general interest of the community and the requirements of the protection of the individuals' guaranteed rights.[333] This will turn on whether the interference is 'proportionate to the legitimate aim pursued'.[334] Proportionality as used in this context is wholly different from the concept of proportionality as used in the CPR.

Margin of appreciation

12.265 A wide margin in afforded to those who make legislation, and it will not be every interference with a victim's rights that will be unlawful. Where interference produces an excessive burden on an individual, the requisite balance will not be found:[335] put another way, where there are exceptional circumstances and when a 'threshold of hardship' has been crossed, the court will find that there has been a violation of the victim's rights.[336]

12.266 Whilst it is not for the UK courts to apply the margin of appreciation – that being a matter for the ECtHR – it is important that its existence is recognised domestically. This is for two prime reasons: firstly, it should be recognised that judges may lack the information or expertise to deal with the issue; and secondly, when the question requires the balancing of political factors, the executive will generally be better placed to deal with such things than the judiciary.[337]

---

[330] *R (Farrakhan) v Secretary of State for the Home Department* [2002] EWCA Civ 606, [2002] QB 1391, at [77].

[331] *Buckley v United Kingdom* (1996) 23 EHRR 101, ECtHR, at para 76; and Application 27238/94: *Chapman v United Kingdom* (2001) 33 EHRR 399, ECtHR, at [92], and at [110].

[332] *Hakansson and Sturesson v Sweden* (1990) 13 EHRR 1, ECtHR, at [46]. See similarly *Young, James and Webster v United Kingdom* (1981) 4 EHRR 38, ECtHR, at para 53; and *Buckley v United Kingdom* (1996) 23 EHRR 101, ECtHR, at [59].

[333] *Sporrong and Lönnroth v Sweden* (1982) 5 EHRR 35, ECtHR Applications 7151/75, 7152/75 at [69].

[334] *Handyside v United Kingdom* (1976) 1 EHRR 737, ECtHR, at [49].

[335] *James and Others v The United Kingdom* (1986), ECtHR Application No 8793/79 at [50]

[336] *Velikovi and Others v Bulgaria* (2009) 48 EHRR 27, [2007] ECHR 213, 48 EHRR 27 at [50].

[337] *Secretary of State for Home Department v Rehman* [2001] UKHL 47.

Specific topics relevant to the law of costs

12.267 In theory, any human right may arise in the context of the law of costs (especially where the primary issue is right of access to the court), but in practice, only Art 6 (right to a fair trial) and Art 8 (right to privacy) have any general relevance. Art 10 (right to freedom of expression) is also relevant to the issue of additional liabilities.

Access to justice

12.268 The right to a fair trial (Art 6) is an absolute right which is given a broad and purposive interpretation,[338] but rights ancillary to it – which include the right of access to the court – will be subject to the balancing exercise referred to in **12.21** and **12.25**. Notwithstanding the fact that it is not an absolute right,[339] the right of access to the court – or, more accurately, the right of *effective* access to a court[340] – is regarded as being of especial importance.[341] The ECtHR has said this on the topic:[342]

> 'It would not be consistent with the rule of law in a democratic society or with the basic principle underlying art 6 para 1 – namely that civil claims must be capable of being submitted to a judge for adjudication – if ... a state could, without restraint or control by the Convention enforcement bodies, remove from the jurisdiction of the courts a whole range of civil claims or confer immunities from civil liability on large groups or categories of persons . . .'

Arguments concerning Art 6 are more common in cases before the ECtHR than their incidence in domestic law would suggest. This is surprising given the fact that 'the ECHR is intended to guarantee not rights that are theoretical or illusory but rights that are practical and effective'.[343]

Case examples

12.269 Non-UK examples include the following:

- **State funding**: It has repeatedly been held that there will be cases in which an absence of legal representation (ie an absence of state funding of some type) will deny effective access to the court;[344]
- **Fixed court fees**: The imposition of a substantial and fixed court fee is capable of amount to a disproportionate restriction on access to court;[345]
- **Stamp duty:** A requirement to pay a substantial stamp duty as a prerequisite to access to the court has been held to amount to a disproportionate restriction on access to court;[346]

---

[338] *Delcourt v Belgium* (1970) 1 EHRR 355, ECtHR, at [25].
[339] In *Golder v United Kingdom* (1975) 1 EHRR 524, ECtHR, at [38] the ECtHR said that 'By its very nature calls for regulation by the state, regulation which may vary in time and place according to the needs and resources of the community and of individuals'.
[340] See, for example *Airey v Ireland* (1979) 2 EHRR 305, ECtHR, at [26].
[341] *Sunday Times v United Kingdom* (1979) 2 EHRR 245, ECtHR Application 6538/74 at [65].
[342] *Fayed v United Kingdom* (1994) 18 EHRR 393, ECtHR, at [65].
[343] Application 6289/73: *Airey v Ireland* (1979) 2 EHRR 305, ECtHR, at [24].
[344] See *Airey v Ireland* (1979) 2 EHRR 305.
[345] *Jedamski and Jedamska v Poland* (2007) 45 EHRR 47; see also likewise, see *Kreus v Poland* (2001) ECtHR Application 28249/95.
[346] *Weissman v Romania* (2006) ECtHR Application 63945/00.

- ***Sliding-scale court fees:*** A requirement to pay a court fee calculated as a high fixed percentage of the sums claimed has been found to be capable of being a disproportionate restriction on access to court;[347] and
- ***Blanket ban on waivers of court fees:*** A blanket ban on granting waivers from liability for court fees is capable of being unlawful.[348]

12.270 By contrast, the number of UK cases is very limited. There are cases that concern the availability of legal aid,[349] but there are very few cases that deal with costs other than in the setting of public funding. They include:

- ***Costs and expenses:*** The ECtHR has commented that the costs should not effectively bar access to court for impecunious litigants;[350] and
- ***Inequality of arms:*** The ECtHR has confirmed that an inequality of arms should not act as a bar to effective access to justice, be that as a result of an absence of representation,[351] or as a result of inadequate representation;[352] that said, the mere fact that one side has leading counsel and the other lacks the funding to do likewise would not amount to an unlawful breach of Art 6.[353]

12.271 Where the putative breach has caused a party not to be represented, the tribunal in question will have to decide whether it can fairly dispose of the matter; given the fact that it can constantly remind itself of the need to be fair and to make allowances, it is very much a matter for the tribunal in question.[354] The skill and experience of the litigant may be relevant in this regard.[355]

12.272 It has been held that the court will exercise 'particularly rigorous scrutiny' in cases where the issue is not access to justice over liability, but instead is access to justice over some ancillary matter (in that instance, enforcement).[356]

Right to privacy

12.273 The relevance of Art 8 is that the right to a private life includes the right to assert legal professional privilege.[357] It was for this reason that shortly after the introduction of the CPR, CPR, r 48.7(3) was found to be *ultra vires*; this rule used to provide that the court may direct that privileged documents were to be disclosed for the

---

[347] *Stankov v Bulgaria* (2009) 49 EHRR 7, [2007] ECHR 582.

[348] *Tudor-Comert v Moldova* (2008), ECtHR Application 27888/04.

[349] These include *R (Jarrett) v Legal Services Commission* [2001] EWHC 389 (Admin), *McLean v Procurator Fiscal, Fort William* [2001] 1 WLR 2425, and *Perotti v Collyer-Bristow (a firm)* [2003] EWCA Civ 1521. The threshold that the victim has to cross is a very high threshold (see *Perottii* at [31]), but examples do exist where the court has found that funding was mandatory (see, for example, *Alliss v Legal Services Commission* [2002] EWHC 2079 (Admin).

[350] *Faulkner v United Kingdom* (2000) *The Times*, 11 January, ECtHR.

[351] *Steel and Morris v United Kingdom* (2005) 41 EHRR 403 Application 68416/01.

[352] *R v Thakrar* [2001] EWCA Crim 1096.

[353] See *AG's Reference No 82A of 2000* [2002] EWCA Crim 215 at [14].

[354] *Re B and T (care proceedings: legal representation)* [2001] FCR 512.

[355] See *Pine v Solicitors' Disciplinary Tribunal* [2001] EWCA Crim 1574 in which the Court of Appeal found that a solicitor was not at a disadvantage representing himself before his professional body.

[356] *Apostol v Georgia* (2006) ECtHR Application No 40765/02.

[357] *R (on the application of Morgan Grenfell & Co Ltd) v Special Commissioners of Income Tax* [2002] UKHL 21.

purposes of dealing with applications for wasted costs, but it was revoked[358] after Toulson J found that it was incompatible with the right to a private life and declared it to be *ultra vires*.[359]

12.274   The procedure of election pursuant to CPD art 40.14 is compatible with the ECHR; this is addressed at **24.30** and **24.31**.

Additional liability

12.275   The question here is whether the system of shifting the burden of paying for unsuccessful litigation on to paying parties via the medium of additional liabilities is lawful. There is a conflict between the conclusion of the House of Lords on this topic (which is binding) and the conclusion of the ECtHR (which is not binding); for the reasons set out in **12.12**, it is the former that must prevail (albeit only to the extent that domestic authority is binding).

12.276   The issue arose in the context of Art 10 (the right of freedom of expression). It arose not in the context of the assessment of costs, but in the context of a newspaper publisher seeking a prospective declaration. The newspaper said that the Sword of Damocles that was the success fee would have a chilling effect on the ability of the press to speak freely. Their Lordships rejected that argument (which arose at first instance before them).[360] Their Lordships were unimpressed with the argument that the newspaper's opponent could easily afford to fund the litigation without recourse to conditional fee agreements (see **30.240**).

12.277   More than half a decade later, the same case reached the Fourth Chamber of the ECtHR;[361] the newspaper argued that the UK government had breached its human rights by allowing its opponent to recover a success fee. By that stage, Sir Rupert Jackson had written his final report, and as such, there was a great deal of material that could be used for the purposes of attacking the fairness of additional liabilities.

12.278   The ECtHR took into account Sir Rupert's criticisms, and in doing so it took into account factors that went well beyond the facts of the case that had originally been before the House of Lords. This has led some commentators to observe that the decision of the ECtHR appears to be an indictment of the system of recoverable additional liabilities generally rather than only in the context of freedom of speech; Moore-Bick LJ has, however, confirmed that the House of Lords' decision continues to be good law.[362] To that extent, everything that is set out below must be treated with some caution.

12.279   The ECtHR phrased the question it intended to answer in this way:[363]

> 'The Court will examine whether success fees recoverable against unsuccessful defendants are 'necessary in a democratic society' to achieve that aim. In particular, it must consider the proportionality of requiring an unsuccessful defendant not only to pay the reasonable and proportionate costs of the claimant, but also to contribute to the funding of other litigation

---

[358]   Civil Procedure (Amendment No 3) Rules 2000 (SI 2000/1317).
[359]   *General Mediterranean Holding SA v Patel* [1999] 2 Costs LR 10.
[360]   *Campbell v MGN Ltd* [2004] UKHL 22.
[361]   *MGN Limited v The United Kingdom* [2011] ECHR 66, Application No 39401/04.
[362]   *Sousa v London Borough of Waltham Forest Council* [2011] EWCA Civ 194 at [54].
[363]   At para 198.

and general access to justice, by paying up to double those costs in the form of recoverable success fees. The applicant did not complain about having had to pay any ATE premiums of the claimant.'

As to proportionality (in the costs sense) the court had this to say:[364]

'While those provisions [in the CPR and the CPD] addressed the reasonableness of base costs given matters such as the amount at stake, the interests of the parties and the complexity of the issues, Lord Hope underlined that the separate control of the reasonableness of success fees essentially concerned the review of the percentage uplift on the basis of the risk undertaken in the case and that, in an evenly balanced case such as the present, success fees were inevitably 100% ... Such safeguard provisions could not, therefore, as Lord Hoffman confirmed, address the applicant's rejection in principle of recoverable success fees calculated as a percentage of reasonable base costs.'

In so far as Sir Rupert's report was concerned, the ECtHR had the following to say:[365]

'[O]ne of the particularities of the present case is that this general scheme and its objectives have themselves been the subject of detailed and lengthy public consultation notably by the Ministry of Justice since 2003. While most of this process transpired after the House of Lords judgment in the second appeal in the present case (2005), it highlighted fundamental flaws underlying the recoverable success fee scheme, particularly in cases such as the present.'

As to the relevance of the Jackson reforms, the court had this to say:[366]

'Moreover, these safeguards relied on by the Government were available throughout the period of public consultation at the end of which the Ministry of Justice accepted that costs were disproportionate, especially in publication cases, so that a drastic reduction in the maximum success fee was required.'

Perhaps the nub of the judgment can be found in the following comments about 'the system':[367]

'[T]he Court considers that the depth and nature of the flaws in the system, highlighted in convincing detail by the public consultation process, and accepted in important respects by the Ministry of Justice, are such that the Court can conclude that the impugned scheme exceeded even the broad margin of appreciation to be accorded to the State in respect of general measures pursuing social and economic interests.'

12.280 Thus, whilst other interpretations are possible, it would be reasonable to interpret the ECtHR decision in the following way:

- in the context of publication cases, the system of allowing very high success fees between opposing parties is an interference of the rights of expression guaranteed by Art 10 of the ECHR; and
- that interference did have a legitimate aim (namely, to facilitate access to justice), but the requirement that a paying party pays a success fee was disproportionate having regard to that legitimate aim of achieving access to justice, this being for the following reasons:

---

[364] Ibid.
[365] At para 203.
[366] Ibid.
[367] At para 217.

— the CPR and the CPD were not adequate for the purposes of limiting the success fee, this being because they fostered 'costs races';
— the separate control of success fees (ie control on the basis of risk rather than proportionality) was not effective at controlling costs; and
— the Ministry of Justice had accepted (via the reasoning set out in Sir Rupert's report) that the overall burden of costs was disproportionate.

12.281 It has to be said that some commentators have criticised the way in which the ECtHR analysed the matter.[368] In any event, as Moore-Bick LJ has explained, the position in the domestic courts will be to follow the House of Lords' decision.[369]

> '[U]nless the liability to pay a success fee can be said to infringe the defendant's rights under the Convention ... questions of proportionality and reasonableness do not arise. It is for Parliament to decide what arrangements viewed overall will best serve the general requirement for access to justice. Moreover, the submission is contrary to the decision of the House of Lords in *Campbell v MGN (No 2)*, which remains binding on this court.'

---

[368] Whilst it is only the writer's opinion, it would be fair to say that the court did fail expressly to direct itself that Sir Rupert's report was not at the time UK Government policy.
[369] *Sousa v London Borough of Waltham Forest Council* [2011] EWCA Civ 194 at [54].

Chapter 13

THE BASES OF ASSESSMENT (INDEMNITY BASIS AND STANDARD BASIS)

13.1 This chapter describes the law relating to the bases of assessment; the emphasis is on costs between opposing parties, but some of the principles would also be applicable where a solicitor seeks payment from his client. For a specific explanation as to the bases on which solicitor and client costs are assessed, see **26.4–26.20**.

THE DIFFERENCE BETWEEN THE TWO BASES OF ASSESSMENT

13.2 Under the CPR, costs are assessed either on the standard basis or on the indemnity basis. The standard basis is by far the commoner of the two. The relevant provisions in the CPR are as follows:

'**44.4**(1) Where the court is to assess the amount of costs (whether by summary or detailed assessment) it will assess those costs—

(a) on the standard basis; or
(b) on the indemnity basis,

but the court will not in either case allow costs which have been unreasonably incurred or are unreasonable in amount.

...

(2) Where the amount of costs is to be assessed on the standard basis, the court will—

(a) only allow costs which are proportionate to the matters in issue; and
(b) resolve any doubt which it may have as to whether costs were reasonably incurred or reasonable and proportionate in amount in favour of the paying party.

(Factors which the court may take into account are set out in rule 44.5)[1]

(3) Where the amount of costs is to be assessed on the indemnity basis, the court will resolve any doubt which it may have as to whether costs were reasonably incurred or were reasonable in amount in favour of the receiving party.

(4) Where—

(a) the court makes an order about costs without indicating the basis on which the costs are to be assessed; or
(b) the court makes an order for costs to be assessed on a basis other than the standard basis or the indemnity basis, the costs will be assessed on the standard basis.'

---

[1]   That is, the 'seven pillars of wisdom'.

13.3   Each of the bases encompasses a range of approaches to the ascertainment of costs; thus, it is not possible to define what is '*the* standard basis' or '*the* indemnity basis'. Costs on the standard basis, for example, may be subject to a test either of reasonableness or necessity, depending on whether the costs are proportionate. Likewise, costs on the indemnity basis may, in some circumstances, be subject to certain presumptions, some of which may have a substantial bearing on the outcome of the assessment.[2]

13.4   It is, however, generally true to say that the two bases of assessment differ in the following ways:

•   **The issue of doubt**: On the indemnity basis, any doubt as to whether costs were reasonably incurred or reasonable in amount will be resolved in favour of the receiving party, but on the standard basis, the paying party will be the beneficiary.
•   **Proportionality**: The test of proportionality will apply on the standard basis but will not apply on the indemnity basis.

(The topic of proportionality is dealt with at **34.1–34.41**.)

13.5   Woolf CJ explained the effect of these things in this way:[3]

> 'The differences are two-fold. First, the differences are as to the onus which is on a party to establish that the costs were reasonable. In the case of a standard order, the onus is on the party in whose favour the order has been made. In the case of an indemnity order, the onus of showing the costs are not reasonable is on the party against whom the order has been made. The other important distinction between a standard order and an indemnity order is the fact that, whereas in the case of a standard order the court will only allow costs which are proportionate to the matters in issue, this requirement of proportionality does not exist in relation to an order which is made on the indemnity basis. This is a matter of real significance. On the one hand, it means that an indemnity order is one which does not have the important requirement of proportionality which is intended to reduce the amount of costs which are payable in consequence of litigation. On the other hand, an indemnity order means that a party who has such an order made in their favour is more likely to recover a sum which reflects the actual costs in the proceedings.'

Regardless of the basis upon which costs are to be assessed, the court will not allow costs which have been unreasonably incurred or are unreasonable in amount.[4]

13.6   The difference between the two bases of assessment is often not as great as practitioners and parties often imagine. Indeed, while speaking extrajudicially and before the introduction of the CPR, a former Chief Taxing Master expressed his views on the matter in these pithy terms:[5]

> 'If there is no doubt, there is no difference.'

13.7   That comment was made at a time when the court did not have to apply the test of proportionality, but Lord Scott has made the following comments (albeit obiter)

---

2   See, for example, CPR, r 48.8(2).
3   *Excelsior Commercial & Industrial Holdings Ltd v Salisbury Hamer Aspden & Johnson (Costs)* [2002] EWCA Civ 879 at [15].
4   CPR, r 44.4(1).
5   M Cook *Cook on Costs* (Butterworths, 1st edn, 1991), p 8.

which suggest that, even following the introduction of the CPR, the difference between the two bases is, as he put it, 'not very great':[6]

> '[It] needs to be understood that the difference between costs at the standard rate and costs on an indemnity basis is, according to the language of the relevant rules, not very great. According to CPR 44.5(1), where costs are assessed on the standard basis the payee can expect to recover costs "proportionately and reasonably incurred" or "proportionate and reasonable in amount"; and where costs are assessed on the indemnity basis the payee can expect to recover all his costs except those that were "unreasonably incurred" or were "unreasonable in amount". It is difficult to see much difference between the two sets of criteria, save that where an indemnity basis has been ordered the onus must lie on the payer to show any unreasonableness.'

13.8   Although Lord Scott discussed the matter in terms of onuses lying on one side or the other, it should be noted that the issue of doubt has no part to play in the court's determination of issues of fact. If, for example, the issue is whether the conducting fee earner was (as a matter of fact) a Grade A fee earner or a Grade B fee earner, this issue should be determined according to the evidence by the court sitting as a tribunal of fact: the issue of doubt would have no part to play. This would be an entirely different exercise from that which would determine whether the claim *should* have been allocated to a Grade A or a Grade B fee earner; in these circumstances, the issue of doubt might have a considerable part to play.

THE CIRCUMSTANCES IN WHICH AN AWARD ON THE INDEMNITY BASIS MIGHT BE MADE

13.9   Under the CPR, costs may not be assessed on anything other than the standard basis or the indemnity basis.[7] Should the court make an order for costs to be assessed on a basis which is other than one of these two bases, the costs will, by default, be assessed on the standard basis.[8] More commonly, the basis of assessment might not be stated, in which case the costs will, again, be assessed on the standard basis.[9] Likewise, if costs-only proceedings fail to specify the basis upon which costs are to be assessed, the costs will be treated as having been claimed on the standard basis.[10]

13.10   Broadly speaking, there are two ways in which a party engaged in litigation may be ordered to pay costs on the indemnity basis. The first is as a result of the court exercising its discretion against a party under CPR, r 44.3, and the second is as a result of a defendant failing to beat a claimant's Part 36 offer. Each of these situations is dealt with below.

---

[6]   *Fourie v Le Roux* [2007] UKHL 1 at [39], per Lord Scott.

[7]   This provision does not apply to a solicitor's remuneration in respect of non-contentious business regulated by any general orders made under the Solicitors Act 1974 (see CPR, r 44.4(6)). Costs payable under a contract are in a special category, which (unless the contract provides otherwise) is similar to the indemnity basis, but not referred to as such in the CPR; see CPR, rr 44.4(1) and 48.3.

[8]   See CPR, r 44.4(4)(b), negating the decision in *EMI Records Ltd v Wallace* [1983] 1 Ch 59; this provision probably does not oust the court's power to decide, as a matter of construction, whether the court making the costs order intended costs to be assessed on the indemnity basis.

[9]   CPR, r 44.4(4)(a).

[10]   CPD, art 17.3(5).

13.11 The indemnity basis will also apply in certain other situations, such as where the costs to be assessed are the costs payable by a client to his own solicitor[11] and where the costs of a trustee or personal representative are to be paid out of the relevant trust fund or estate.[12] These situations are dealt with in Chapters 26 and 37 respectively.

Orders to pay costs on the indemnity basis pursuant to CPR, r 44.3

The origin and extent of the jurisdiction

13.12 CPR, r 44.3 does not expressly confer a power to make an award of costs on the indemnity basis, but r 44.3(1)(b) does provide that the court has a discretion as to the amount of costs; when read in conjunction with r 44.4(4), it is implicit that this provision enables the court to make an award of costs on the indemnity basis.[13]

13.13 The jurisdiction to make an award on the indemnity basis is subject to certain restrictions, but these are so rare that they can safely be disregarded. They are as follows.

Pre-1994 legal aid

13.14 Costs may not be recovered on the indemnity basis if the receiving party is a legally aided party whose legal aid certificate was granted before February 1994;[14] this is because the indemnity principle would apply and the costs of such a legally aided litigant's solicitor could be assessed only on a standard basis.[15] This restriction does not apply to publicly funded litigants whose certificates were issued after February 1994;[16] as a result, it will now very rarely be the case that this restriction will be relevant.

Restriction in the retainer

13.15 If, as occasionally happens,[17] the retainer expressly provides that costs will be assessed on the standard basis, then by operation of the indemnity principle, costs will be recoverable only to that extent.

The circumstances in which the jurisdiction will or will not be exercised

13.16 The discretion to make an award on the indemnity basis has to be exercised judicially, having regard to the matters referred to in CPR, r 44.3(4) and (5).[18] It does not need to relate to the whole of the costs in question, but where practicable, it may instead be made in respect of only certain issues.[19]

---

[11]   See CPR, r 48.8(2) and CPD, art 54.2(1).
[12]   CPR, r 48.4(3).
[13]   *Reid Minty (a firm) v Taylor* [2001] EWCA Civ 1723 at [27].
[14]   See *Willis v Redbridge Health Authority* [1996] 1 WLR 1228 and *Brawley v Marczynski & Anor (No 2)* [2002] EWCA Civ 1453 at [17].
[15]   Civil Legal Aid (General) Regulations 1989 (SI 1989/339) (as unamended), reg 107.
[16]   *Brawley v Marczynski & Anor (No 2)* [2002] EWCA Civ 1453.
[17]   Such restrictions are (generally) found only in standard agreements between liability insurers and their solicitors, and even then only rarely.
[18]   *Reid Minty (a firm) v Taylor* [2001] EWCA Civ 1723 at [27].
[19]   See *Webster v Ridgeway Foundation School* [2010] EWHC 318 (QB) at [7], per Nichol J.

13.17 Neither the CPR nor the CPD provide any express guidance as to when an award of costs on the indemnity basis should be made under CPR, r 44.3. Waller LJ formulated the following question:[20]

> 'The question will always be: is there something in the conduct of the action or the circumstances of the case which takes the case out of the norm in a way which justifies an order for indemnity costs?'

As with most issues concerning costs, hindsight should be avoided.[21]

13.18 Beyond this, it is not desirable to be prescriptive about the factors to be taken into account or the circumstances in which an indemnity basis costs order might be appropriate. Woolf CJ had this to say in response to an invitation to give general guidance:[22]

> 'In my judgment it is dangerous for the court to try and add to the requirements of the CPR which are not spelt out in the relevant parts of the CPR. This court can do no more than draw attention to the width of the discretion of the trial judge and re-emphasise the point that has already been made that, before an indemnity order can be made, there must be some conduct or some circumstance which takes the case out of the norm. That is the critical requirement.'

As Barling J has noted, it is possible to summarise the law without being prescriptive; he had this to say on the point:[23]

> '[O]ver the years some guidance has been forthcoming. First of all, the normal order is an order for standard costs. In deciding whether to order indemnity costs, ultimately the question will always be whether there is something in the conduct of the action or in the circumstances of the case which takes the case out of the normal in a way which justifies an order for indemnity costs: ... Secondly, it is now clear that indemnity costs are not reserved for cases where there has been a lack of probity or conduct deserving of moral condemnation: ... Thirdly, an award of indemnity costs is not penal but compensatory, the question in all cases being, what is fair and reasonable in all the circumstances of the case.'

Culpability

13.19 Thus, under the CPR, unlike under the RSC, an award of costs on the indemnity basis would not necessarily imply a degree of culpability on the part of the party against whom the award was made. This would clearly be the case where the award is made under CPR, r 36.14 (see **13.45** onwards), but—as the Court of Appeal have repeatedly emphasised—it would also be the case where an award is made under r 44.3. Nonetheless, for the reasons set out below, in practice it is rare for an award of costs on the indemnity basis to be made pursuant to r 44.3 unless there has been an element of unreasonable conduct on the part of the person against whom the order is made.

---

[20] *Excelsior Commercial & Industrial Holdings Ltd v Salisbury Hamer Aspden & Johnson (Costs)* [2002] EWCA Civ 879 at [39].

[21] *Healy-Upright v Bradley & Another* [2007] EWHC 3161 (Ch), per Jonathan Gaunt QC sitting as a deputy judge of the High Court; see also *Dee v Telegraph Media Group Ltd* [2010] EWHC 1939 (QB) at [3], per Sharpe J.

[22] *Excelsior Commercial & Industrial Holdings Ltd v Salisbury Hamer Aspden & Johnson (Costs)* [2002] EWCA Civ 879 at [32].

[23] *Catalyst Investment Group Ltd v Max Lewisohn, Maximillian and Co (a firm)* [2009] EWHC 3501 (Ch) at [18].

13.20 One of the first cases to deal with the issue of culpability under CPR, r 44.3 was *Reid Minty (a firm) v Taylor*.[24] Having previously made an offer that the claim be discontinued with costs, the defendant went on successfully to defend the claim. The trial judge declined to make an award of costs on the indemnity basis, commenting that:

> '... costs should only be awarded on an indemnity basis if there has been some sort of moral lack of probity or conduct deserving of moral condemnation on the part of the paying party.'

The Court of Appeal held that the judge had misdirected himself:[25]

> 'Under the CPR, it is not ... correct that costs are only awarded on an indemnity basis if there has been some sort of moral lack of probity or conduct deserving moral condemnation on the part of the paying party. The court has a wide discretion under Rule 44.3 which is not constrained, in my judgment, by authorities decided under the rules which preceded the introduction of the CPR.'

13.21 A few months later, a differently constituted Court of Appeal sought to clarify what had been said in *Reid Minty*. Simon Browne LJ said:[26]

> 'I for my part, understand the Court [in *Reid Minty*] to have been deciding no more than that conduct, albeit falling short of misconduct deserving of moral condemnation, can be so unreasonable as to justify an order for indemnity costs. With that I respectfully agree. To my mind, however, such conduct would need to be unreasonable to a high degree; unreasonable in this context certainly does not mean merely wrong or misguided in hindsight. An indemnity costs order made under Rule 44 (unlike one made under Rule 36) does, I think, carry at least some stigma. It is of its nature penal rather than exhortatory.'

13.22 In a subsequent case before the Court of Appeal, both Waller LJ (who had agreed with Simon Browne LJ in *Victor Kiam*) and Woolf CJ were keen to emphasise that there would still be cases in which an award of costs on the indemnity basis would be made even where there was no unreasonable conduct on the part of the party condemned in costs. In particular, Waller LJ said that Simon Browne LJ's language was not apposite to all circumstances.[27] Although Woolf CJ declined to give general guidance (see **13.18**), he did give the following illustrative examples of when an award may be made without culpable conduct:[28]

> 'I give as an example a situation where a party is involved in proceedings as a test case although, so far as that party is concerned, he has no other interest than the issue that arises in that case, but is drawn into expensive litigation. If he is successful, a court may well say that an indemnity order was appropriate, although it could not be suggested that anyone's conduct in the case had been unreasonable. Equally there may be situations where the nature of the litigation means that the parties could not be expected to conduct the litigation in a proportionate manner. Again the conduct would not be unreasonable and it seems to me that the court would be entitled to take into account that sort of situation in deciding that an indemnity order was appropriate.'

---

[24] [2001] EWCA Civ 1723.
[25] *Excelsior Commercial & Industrial Holdings Ltd v Salisbury Hamer Aspden & Johnson (Costs)* [2002] EWCA Civ 879 at [27], per May LJ (with whom Kay and Ward LJJ agreed).
[26] *Victor Kiam v MGN Ltd* [2002] EWCA Civ 66 at [12].
[27] *Excelsior Commercial & Industrial Holdings Ltd v Salisbury Hamer Aspden & Johnson (Costs)* [2002] EWCA Civ 879 at [38].
[28] *Excelsior Commercial & Industrial Holdings Ltd v Salisbury Hamer Aspden & Johnson (Costs)* [2002] EWCA Civ 879 at [31].

These examples are helpful, not least because they illustrate how rare it would be for the court to make, under r 44.3, an award of costs on the indemnity basis in the absence of unreasonable conduct.

13.23 It is worth noting that both Lord Roger and Lord Carswell have expressed (obiter) concern about making an award of costs on the indemnity basis in circumstances in which there has been no unreasonable conduct.[29] Although his was a dissenting speech, Lord Hope went so far as to interpret the judgment in *Reid Minty* as showing that an 'award of costs on [the indemnity] basis will not be justified unless the conduct of the paying party can be said in some respect to have been unreasonable'.[30] It would be wrong to read too much into these comments, not least because their Lordships were at pains to emphasise that the responsibility for overseeing costs awards lay with the Court of Appeal rather than with the House of Lords, but these comments do illustrate the fact that the jurisdiction under CPR, r 44.3 to make an award on the indemnity basis in the absence of unreasonable conduct is one which rarely arises.

Case examples

13.24 Whilst each case will turn on its own facts, the following case-specific examples (and counter-examples) are helpful. It should not be forgotten, however, that general guidance purporting to place a gloss on the CPR may be unhelpful (see **13.18**); it would be wrong, therefore, to afford these case examples too much weight.

Failure to respond co-operatively to attempts to resolve a dispute

13.25 Kay LJ had this to say about the approach of the CPR in general:[31]

'The approach of the CPR is a relatively simple one: namely, if one party has made a real effort to find a reasonable solution to the proceedings and the other party has resisted that sensible approach, then the latter puts himself at risk that the order for costs may be on an indemnity basis.'

Thus, a refusal to consider solutions other than fighting will put the unregenerate party at risk. That said, if the attempt to resolve the dispute 'was close to an invitation by a defendant to the claimant to throw his hand in' it is likely that it would not be given much weight.[32] Furthermore, the act of rejecting a defendant's offer will not usually of itself be sufficient, even where the defendant has put forward other reasonable offers.[33] Unreasonably refusing an offer of mediation is capable of leading to an award of costs on the indemnity basis, especially where the offer was in respect of a court-sanctioned scheme.[34] In a similar vein, a refusal to respond to judicial encouragement to settle may

---

[29] *Fourie v Le Roux* [2007] UKHL 1 at [46] and [49].

[30] *Fourie v Le Roux* [2007] UKHL 1 at [10].

[31] *Reid Minty (a firm) v Taylor* [2001] EWCA Civ 1723 at [37], per Kay LJ; as a case example, see *EQ Projects Ltd v Alavi* [2006] EWHC 29 (TCC).

[32] *Reid Minty (a firm) v Taylor* [2001] EWCA Civ 1723 at [30], per May LJ; as an example of this happening in practice, see *Waites Construction Limited v HGP Greentree Alchurch Evans Limited* [2005] EWHC 2174 (TCC).

[33] See *Epsom College v Pierse Contracting Southern Ltd (formerly Biseley Construction Ltd) (in liq)* [2011] EWCA Civ 1449 at [72], per Rix LJ. *Franks v Sinclair (Costs)* [2006] EWHC 3656 (Ch), [2007] WTLR 785 (David Richards J) is often cited as being authority for the proposition that a refusal of two reasonable offers will justify an award of costs on the indemnity basis, but Rix LJ explained that this was only one factor amongst others (this implication being that it was not of itself sufficient to justify an award on the indemnity basis).

[34] *Virani v Manuel Revert y Cia Sa* [2003] EWCA Civ 1651.

lead to an award of costs on the indemnity basis (although Potter LJ expressed some doubt about the notion of the court giving weight to such issues).[35]

Mere rejection of an offer

13.26 In *Victor Kiam*, the respondent to an appeal (who was found to be in an analogous position to a defendant) had made an offer which, had it been accepted, would have been more advantageous to the appellant than the actual outcome. This was not sufficient to justify an award on the indemnity basis. Simon Brown LJ explained his reasoning:[36]

> '[It] will be a rare case indeed where the refusal of a settlement offer will attract under Rule 44 not merely an adverse order for costs, but an order on an indemnity rather than standard basis. Take this very case. No encouragement in the way of an expectation of indemnity costs was required ... [The offer's] object was to protect the respondent against a standard costs order were the Court, say, to reduce the damages to that level.'

13.27 Thus, a defendant who makes an offer should not expect to be awarded costs on the indemnity basis if he subsequently 'beats' that offer; instead, it is sufficient that the offer affords protection against an adverse costs order.[37] That said, if the court finds, as it occasionally does, that it was unreasonable of the claimant to fail to accept the offer, then the court may be persuaded to make an award on the indemnity basis.[38]

Pursuing a weak claim and failing to make concessions

13.28 Pursuing a claim that is 'Macawber-ish in the hope that something might turn up' (per Laddie J) is a high risk strategy that is likely to lead to an award on the indemnity basis.[39] Advancing an unarguable case is likely to give rise to an order for costs on the indemnity basis.[40] As to claims that are arguable but weak, Tomlinson J had this to say:[41]

> 'Where a claim is speculative, weak, opportunistic, or thin, a claimant who chooses to pursue it is taking a high risk and can expect to pay indemnity costs if it fails'.[42]

Nicol J has commented that a losing case is not to be equated with unreasonable conduct but there does come a point at which a claim is so hopeless that its pursuit can

---

[35]   *Boynton v Willers* [2003] EWCA Civ 904 at [44].

[36]   *Victor Kiam v MGN Ltd* [2002] EWCA Civ 66 at [13].

[37]   See also *HLB Kidsons (a firm) v Lloyds Underwriters subscribing to Lloyd's Policy No 621/PKIDOO101* [2007] EWHC 2699 (Comm).

[38]   See, for example, *D Morgan plc v Mace & Jones (a firm)* [2011] EWHC 26 (TCC), per Coulson J. In a similar vein, see *Southwark LBC v IBM UK Ltd (Costs)* [2011] EWHC 653 (TCC) (Akenhead J) and *Barr v Biffa Waste Services Ltd (Costs)* [2011] EWHC 1107 (TCC), (Coulson J), both cited with apparent approval by Rix LJ in *Epsom College v Pierse Contracting Southern Ltd (formerly Biseley Construction Ltd) (in liq)* [2011] EWCA Civ 1449 at [72].

[39]   *IPC Media v Highbury Leisure Publishing Ltd* [2005] EWHC 283 (Ch) at [24].

[40]   *Mahme Trust Reg and others v Lloyds TSB Bank plc* [2006] EWHC 1782 (Ch).

[41]   *Three Rivers District Council & Ors v The Governor & Company of the Bank of England* [2006] EWHC 816 (Comm) at [25], per Tomlinson J. See also *Excelsior Commercial & Industrial Holdings Ltd v Salisbury Hamer Aspden & Johnson (Costs)* [2002] EWCA Civ 879 and, as an example in practice, *Waites Construction Limited v HGP Greentree Alchurch Evans Limited* [2005] EWHC 2174 (TCC).

[42]   *Three Rivers District Council & Ors v Bank of England* [2006] EWHC 816 (Comm) at [25], per Tomlinson J. See also *Excelsior Commercial & Industrial Holdings Ltd v Salisbury Hamer Aspden & Johnson (Costs)* [2002] EWCA Civ 879 and, as an example in practice, *Waites Construction Ltd v HGP Greentree Alchurch Evans Ltd* [2005] EWHC 2174 (TCC).

be properly characterised as unreasonable conduct.[43] Similar principles will apply where the claim is a counterclaim.[44] Misjudging the merits of a case may lead to an award on the indemnity basis.[45] Advancing a case which is merely unlikely to succeed would not, of itself, ordinarily be sufficient reason for making an award on the indemnity basis,[46] nor would losing as a result of a party's evidence deteriorating in cross-examination.[47] That said, if a claim is so undermined by the other side's case that part of it needs to be abandoned, the residuum may be deemed to be misjudged notwithstanding the fact that the claim as originally brought was satisfactory.[48] In cases concerning public law, an unmeritorious application to set aside a protective costs order will usually result in an award of costs on the indemnity basis.[49] In a case in which he found that the denial of liability was 'unreasonable to a marked extent', David Steel J felt it was appropriate to make an award of costs on the indemnity basis up to the date on which an admission was eventually made.[50]

Abandonment of case or issues

13.29　In a case in which the application was not one that could be said have been hopeless or improper, Mann J found that the mere fact that a litigant had abandoned its application to strike out was not reason to order costs against it on the indemnity basis.[51] Likewise, where a party abandons a point because, upon reviewing the evidence, he realises it is a bad point, it does not follow that an award on the indemnity basis will be made.[52]

Overenthusiastic pursuance of a case (including the pursuance of costs)

13.30　Overburdening the court with documents and chasing every conceivable point is capable of resulting in an award of costs on the indemnity basis.[53] Likewise, pursing a weak case for a collateral purpose will put the pursuer at risk.[54] Pursuing 'highly aggressive tactics in the conduct of the litigation' may contribute to the making of an order on the indemnity basis.[55] Whilst she did not elaborate on what she meant, Sharpe J has indicated that a certain amount of leeway should be afforded to parties who are represented under conditional fee agreements and there is 'costs pressure' (as she put it);[56] presumably this means that the fact that the lawyers had an interest in matter is a

---

[43]　*Webster v The Ridgeway Foundation School* [2010] EWHC 318 (QB) at [7].

[44]　*Chantrey Vellacott v The Convergence Group plc* [2007] EWHC 1774 (Ch), per Rimer J.

[45]　*Wall v Lefever* [1998] 1 FCR 605 at 614, where an order was made by Lord Woolf MR just before the introduction of the CPR.

[46]　*Shania Investment Corp v Standard Bank London Ltd* (unreported) 2 November 2001.

[47]　*Fitzpatrick Contractors Ltd v Tyco Fire & Integrated Solutions (UK) Ltd* [2008] EWHC 1391 (TCC).

[48]　*Barr v Biffa Waste Services Limited* [2011] EWHC 1107 (TCC) in which Coulsen said (at [40]) that the residuum claims in group litigation 'could not sustain the increased weight that they inevitably would have to bear'.

[49]　*R (on the application of Corner House Research) v Secretary of State for Trade and Industry* [2005] EWCA Civ 192 at [79].

[50]　*Colour Quest Ltd v Total Downstream UK Plc* [2009] EWHC 823 (Comm).

[51]　*Ikos Cif Ltd v Hogan Lovells International LLP* [2011] EWHC 2724 (Ch).

[52]　*Fabio Perini SPA v LPC Group plc* [2010] EWCA Civ 525 at [122], per Lord Neuberger MR.

[53]　This was one factor amongst others in *Sager House (Chelsea) Ltd, R (on the application of) v First Secretary of State & Anor* [2006] EWHC 1251 (Admin).

[54]　As an example of this, see *Mahme Trust Reg and others v Lloyds TSB Bank plc* [2006] EWHC 1782 (Ch) at [15] *et seq*, per Evans-Lombe J

[55]　See *Hussain v Cooke* (unreported) 15 February 2010, Ch D (Companies Court), David Donaldson QC (sitting as a Deputy High Court Judge).

[56]　*Dee v Telegraph Media Group Ltd* [2010] EWHC 1939 (QB) at [3], per Sharpe J.

factor to be taken into account. An overly aggressive attitude towards the recovery of costs can backfire and is capable to contributing to an award on the indemnity basis.[57]

Resounding success

13.31 The fact of success, no matter how resounding, will generally not of itself be sufficient to justify an award of costs on the indemnity basis.[58] In a similar vein, Lewison J has found that there is nothing out of the ordinary about making an order for summary judgment in a case where that was the very application before the court, and that an award on the indemnity basis would not be made solely by reason of summary judgment being entered.[59]

Inflammatory behaviour and dishonest conduct

13.32 Unlawful conduct may result in an award of costs on the indemnity basis, especially where it is for an improper purpose, such as an attempt to take over a competitor's business.[60] Launching an unjustified attack on an opponent's integrity could well lead to an award of costs on the indemnity basis.[61] Likewise, launching a gratuitous personal attack on a witness during cross-examination might also lead to such an award.[62] Dishonesty may also suffice; Waller LJ had this to say on that topic:[63]

> 'The best method by which a court can mark its disapproval [of dishonest conduct on the part of the paying party] when, as here, the Claimant would be the paying party, is by making an order for indemnity costs. I for my part have no hesitation in saying that, where insurers establish that a claim has been brought dishonestly, they should on the whole be entitled to an order for indemnity costs not just because of the extra cost they may incur in defending such a claim – though that is considerable – but so that others are discouraged. It is both in the interests of insurers and indeed any Defendants, and in the interests of the court, that persons should be discouraged from bringing dishonest claims and from supporting dishonest claims by lies.'

That said, dishonesty will not always result in an award of indemnity basis costs being made; in a case in which a senior employee of a company had lied in evidence, Ramsey J declined to make an award of costs on the indemnity basis because there was no evidence systemic fraud.[64] Dishonest conduct can also deprive a party of the indemnity basis costs in that a party who might otherwise have been awarded costs on the indemnity basis may lose that benefit if he is himself found guilty of knowingly advancing a false case.[65]

---

[57]   *Hudson v New Media Holding Co LLC* [2011] EWHC 3068 (QB) at [30], per Eady.
[58]   *Amoco (UK) Exploration Co v British American Offshore Ltd* [2002] BLR 135; see also *Balmoral Group Ltd v Borealis (UK) Ltd* [2006] EWHC 2531 (Comm).
[59]   *Easyair Limited (Trading As Openair) v Opal Telecom Limited* [2009] EWHC 779 (Ch).
[60]   See *QBE Management Services (UK) Ltd v Dymoke* [2012] EWHC 116 (QB).
[61]   *Somatra Ltd v Sinclair Roche & Temperley* [2002] EWHC 1627 (Comm).
[62]   Although a pre-CPR case, *Clarke v Associated Newspapers Ltd* (1998) *The Times*, January 28, Lightman J, is still cited as authority in this regard.
[63]   *Quarcoo v Esure Services Ltd* [2009] EWCA Civ 595.
[64]   *BSkyB Limited v HP Enterprise Services UK Limited* [2010] EWHC 862 (TCC) at [42]–[44].
[65]   See, for example, *Bank of Tokyo-Mitsubishi UFJ Ltd v Baskan Gida Sanayi Ve Pazarlama AS* [2009] EWHC 1696 (Ch), per Briggs J; see also *Digicel (St Lucia) v Cable & Wireless plc* [2010] EWHC 774 (Ch), per Morgan J.

Allegations of fraud and exaggeration

13.33 It is commonly the case that a failure to prove fraud will result in an award of costs on the indemnity basis if the allegations prove to have been unreasonably brought.[66] This is a possibility even if the allegations are withdrawn rather than disproved.[67] Allegations that are scandalous (in the legal sense of that word)[68] will put the party who made the allegations at risk.[69] Allegations of exaggeration which are unsupported or contradicted by the evidence may lead to an award of costs on the indemnity basis, especially if those allegations are enthusiastically pursued all the way to cross-examination.[70] Sir Anthony Coleman made an award on the indemnity basis in a case in which a party failed properly to 'load test' (as he put it) an allegation of dishonesty by considering motive.[71] Allegations brought for tactical reasons (ie, with a view to influencing behaviour rather than resolving the dispute) will put the party making the allegations at particular risk.[72]

Changing the case to fit the circumstances

13.34 Changing the case to suit the circumstances may result in an award of costs on the indemnity basis,[73] especially where the case itself is weak.[74]

Where there is a real issue over proportionality or conduct

13.35 If a judge is minded to leave the issue of whether costs have been incurred disproportionately to a costs judge, it would not be appropriate to make an order on the indemnity basis, as this would preclude considerations of proportionality on the assessment.[75] The trial judge has a duty to assist the costs judge in the assessment of costs, and this duty should not be vanquished by the potentially paying party offering to pay costs on an indemnity basis while reserving the right to argue that the costs are extravagant.[76]

Failing to make reasonable enquiries

13.36 Lindsay J had this to say about failing to make proper enquiries:[77]

---

[66] Although both pre-CPR, the cases that are usually cited in this regard are *Bank of Baroda v Panesar* [1987] 2 WLR 208 and, in a personal injury setting, *Cooper v P&O Stena Line Ltd* [1999] 1 Lloyd's Rep 734.

[67] See, for example, *Secretary of State for Trade and Industry v Gee* (2006) BCC 384.

[68] The legal lexicographer Bryan Garner defines scandal in this way: 'Scandal consists in the allegation of anything [that] is unbecoming the dignity of the court to hear, or is contrary to decency or good manners, or which charges some person with a crime not necessary to be shown in the cause … and [which] is is also irrelevant to the case.' (Black's Law Dictionary (2009) 9th edn, Garner BA, ISBN 976-0-314-19949-2).

[69] *Maini v Maini* [2009] EWHC 3036 (Ch) at [14], per Proudman J.

[70] *Clarke v Maltby (Costs)* [2010] EWHC 1856 (QB), per Owen J; the allegations in that case were particularly distressing because the claimant was a solicitor, so the allegation would have serious consequences for her if found to be true.

[71] *National Westminster Bank Plc v Rabobank Nederland* [2007] EWHC 1742 (Comm) at [44].

[72] *Irish Response Ltd (a company incorporated under the laws of the Republic of Ireland) v (1) Direct Beauty Products Ltd)* [2011] EWHC 608 (QB) at [37] *et seq*, per HHJ Richard Seymour QC sitting as Judge of the High Court.

[73] *Three Rivers District Council v Bank of England* [2006] EWHC 816 (Comm) and *ABCI v Banque Franco-Tunisienne & Ors* [2003] EWCA Civ 205.

[74] See, for example, *IPC Media v Highbury Leisure Publishing Ltd* [2005] EWHC 283 (Ch) at [24], per Laddie J.

[75] *Simms v Law Society* [2005] EWCA Civ 849 at [28].

[76] *Three Rivers District Council v Bank of England* [2006] EWHC 816 (Comm).

[77] *Beynon v Scadden* [1999] IRLR 700, EAT.

'A party who, despite having had an apparently conclusive opposition to his case made plain to him, persists with the case down to the hearing in the "Micawberish" hope that something might turn up and yet who does not even take such steps open to him to see whether anything is likely to turn up, runs a risk, when nothing does turn up, that he will be regarded as having been at least unreasonable in the conduct of his litigation.'

Lindsay J was dealing with incidence of costs in an Employment Tribunal rather than the basis of costs in the civil court, but the test he was applying was not dissimilar to that which is presently under discussion.

Failure to comply with a pre-action protocol

13.37 If non-compliance with a pre-action protocol has led to the commencement of proceedings which might otherwise have been unnecessary, or if it has led to costs being incurred in the proceedings which might otherwise have not been incurred, the orders the court may make include an order that the party at fault pay those costs on an indemnity basis.[78] Cox J made an order of indemnity basis costs in a case in which the defendant (the Home Office) was said to be in the habit of not engaging with negotiations until the day before trial; she was not persuaded by the defendant's submissions that making such an order would discourage compromises at a late stage.[79]

Failure to comply with procedural requirements

13.38 Serious procedural errors (such as making an application on a without notice basis when it should have been made with notice) are capable of resulting in awards of costs on the indemnity basis.[80] That said, mishaps of a technical nature (such as typographical errors in the pleadings) do occur, and whilst not normal, are not outside the norm in the sense that they would merit an award of costs on the indemnity basis.[81]

Failures on the part of experts

13.39 Roderick Evans J made an award on the indemnity basis in a case in which a party's experts had been severely criticised for not having addressed their responsibilities and not having conducted themselves in a manner which is expected of expert witnesses.[82] Where the expert evidence merits such a step, it is possible for the court to order that only the costs of the expert are to be paid on the indemnity basis, with the rest of the costs being on the standard basis.[83]

Breach of fiduciary duty

13.40 Where a trustee wrongly applied money owned by a person to whom he owed a fiduciary duty, Richard Sheldon QC (sitting as a deputy judge of the High Court) found that it was appropriate to make an order against him on the indemnity basis.[84]

---

[78] Practice Direction – Protocols, art 2.3(2).
[79] *Youdjeu v Home Office* [2011] EWHC 2002 (QB) at [19].
[80] *Franses (Liquidator of Arab News Network Ltd) v Al Assad* [2007] EWHC 2442 (Ch).
[81] *Irish Response Ltd (a company incorporated under the laws of the Republic of Ireland) v (1) Direct Beauty Products Ltd)* [2011] EWHC 608 (QB) at [47] *et seq*, per HHJ Richard Seymour QC sitting as Judge of the High Court; the judge awarded indemnity basis costs for other reasons, however (see **13.33**).
[82] *Williams v Jevis* [2009] EWHC 1837 (QB).
[83] See, for example, *Balmoral Group Ltd v Borealis (UK) Ltd* [2006] EWHC 2531 (Comm).
[84] *Curtis v Pulbrook* [2009] EWHC 1370 (Ch).

Courting publicity and collateral causes

13.41 Where a party actively seeks to court publicity in support of its serious allegations both before and during the trial, and where those allegations prove to be unfounded, an award on the indemnity basis might be appropriate.[85] Whilst there were many other reasons why the award was made, Coulson J ordered indemnity basis costs against a claimant who pursued a 'bizarre vendetta that bedevilled the West Wirral Conservative Association': the claimant used the claim as a vehicle to pursue a collateral aim, namely, the aforesaid vendetta.[86] Also see **13.33**.

Contractual and collateral entitlements

13.42 Where a contractual right to costs exists (arising, for example, out of a mortgage or lease), the court's discretion should ordinarily be exercised so as to reflect that contractual right.[87] Thus, where the contract provides for costs on the indemnity basis, this will ordinarily result in an award of costs on the indemnity basis, as will a provision that 'all' costs will be paid.[88] As to the collateral rights of auditors to recover from the assets, see **37.6–37.7**.

Anti-suit provisions, arbitration provisions and jurisdiction clauses

13.43 Where a losing party had brought a claim in defiance of an anti-suit provision, Coleman J found that an award on the indemnity basis was appropriate; this was for the purpose of restoring the parties to the position they would have been in had that provision not been breached.[89] Coleman J commented that the same logic would apply to breaches of jurisdiction clauses[90] and arbitration clauses.[91]

Litigation solely about costs

13.44 The fact that the parties are litigating solely about costs will not, of itself, necessarily merit an award on the indemnity basis.[92]

Orders to pay costs on the indemnity basis as a result of having made Part 36 offers

13.45 This section deals only briefly with the issue of Part 36 offers, the discussion being limited to the type of offer that may give rise to an order for costs on the indemnity basis (ie, claimants' Part 36 offers). A more in-depth discussion of Part 36 offers in general can be found in the next chapter, albeit in the context of defendants' Part 36 offers.

13.46 On 5 April 2007 the provisions of CPR, Part 36 were substantially changed;[93] the phrases 'old Part 36' and 'new Part 36' are used accordingly. This book discusses the

---

[85] *Three Rivers District Council v Bank of England* [2006] EWHC 816 (Comm) at [25], per Tomlinson J.
[86] *Noorani v Calver (No 2)* [2009] EWHC 592 (QB) at [19] *et seq.*
[87] *Gomba Holdings Ltd v Minories Finance Ltd* [1993] Ch 171.
[88] *Fairview Investments Ltd v Sharma* (unreported) 14 October 1999, CA.
[89] *National Westminster Bank plc v Rabobank Nederland* [2007] EWHC 3163 (Comm), per Colman J.
[90] Ibid.
[91] *A v B (No 2)* [2007] EWHC 54 (Comm), [2007] 1 All ER (Comm) 633.
[92] *Zissis v Lukomski* [2006] EWCA Civ 341.
[93] Pursuant to the 44th update to the CPR, the Civil Procedure (Amendment No 3) Rules 2006 (SI 2006/3435).

'new' Part 36, but necessarily does so by reference to a number of authorities decided under the 'old' Part 36. To this extent, caution must be exercised. Unless the contrary is specifically stated, references to Part 36 are to provisions in the 'new' Part 36. Transitional provisions exist.[94]

13.47　There are certain formalities and general principles that apply to Part 36 offers; they are discussed at **14.13–14.21**.

Claimants' Part 36 offers

13.48　In so far as it is relevant, CPR, r 36.14 provides:

'(1)　This rule applies where upon judgment being entered—

(a)　…
(b)　judgment against the defendant is at least as advantageous to the claimant as the proposals contained in a claimant's Part 36 offer.

(2)　…

(3)　Subject to paragraph (6), where rule 36.14(1)(b) applies, the court will, unless it considers it unjust to do so, order that the claimant is entitled to—

(a)　interest on the whole or part of any sum of money (excluding interest) awarded at a rate not exceeding 10% above base rate for some or all of the period starting with the date on which the relevant period expired;
(b)　his costs on the indemnity basis from the date on which the relevant period expired; and
(c)　interest on those costs at a rate not exceeding 10% above base rate·

(4)　In considering whether it would be unjust to make the orders referred to in paragraphs (2) and (3) above, the court will take into account all the circumstances of the case including—

(a)　the terms of any Part 36 offer;
(b)　the stage in the proceedings when any Part 36 offer was made, including in particular how long before the trial started the offer was made;
(c)　the information available to the parties at the time when the Part 36 offer was made; and
(d)　the conduct of the parties with regard to the giving or refusing to give information for the purposes of enabling the offer to be made or evaluated.

(5)　…

(6)　Paragraphs (2) and (3) of this rule do not apply to a Part 36 offer—

(a)　that has been withdrawn;
(b)　that has been changed so that its terms are less advantageous to the offeree, and the offeree has beaten the less advantageous offer;
(c)　made less than 21 days before trial, unless the court has abridged the relevant period.

(Rule 44.3 requires the court to consider an offer to settle that does not have the costs consequences set out in this Part in deciding what order to make about costs.)'

---

[94]　See SI 2006/3435, r 7(2), which reads 'Where a Part 36 offer or Part 36 payment was made before 6 April 2007, if it would have had the consequences set out in the Rules of Court contained in Part 36 as it was in force immediately before 6 April 2007, it will have the consequences set out in rr 36.10, 36.11 and 36.14 after that date.'

13.49   The effect of CPR, r 36.14 is that where a claimant secures an award at trial that is 'at least as advantageous' to him as the proposals contained in his own prior Part 36 offer, then, unless the court considers it unjust to do so, it may make an award of costs on the indemnity basis. In these circumstances, the claimant is often said to have 'beaten' his Part 36 offer; this is a useful shorthand (and one which is used in this book), but it should be borne in mind that the test is more sophisticated and wide ranging than the simple issue of whether the offer has been 'beaten' (see **13.52–13.62**). It is also worth bearing in mind that there some doubt whether enhanced interest is payable in the county court: see **36.51** *et seq.*

13.50   It is worth noting that the fact that a claimant has beaten his own Part 36 offer would not deprive the court of its discretion as to the incidence of costs. Although based on the 'old' Part 36, Rix LJ has found that the phrase 'his costs' in what was then CPR, r 36.21(3)(a) (which is analogous to the present CPR, r 36.14(3)(b)) should not be read as if it said 'all his costs'; therefore, if the court wishes to deprive an otherwise successful litigant of costs of, say, an unsuccessful issue, then the fact that that claimant has beaten a Part 36 offer will not prevent the court from doing so.[95]

13.51   In so far as the costs provisions in CPR, r 36.14(1)(b) are concerned, two issues arise: first, the circumstances in which r 36.14(1)(b) will apply; and secondly, the circumstances in which it would be unjust to make an award of costs on the indemnity basis.

The circumstances in which a claimant's offer will be 'beaten'

13.52   CPR, r 36.14(1)(b) will apply where, upon judgment being entered, the terms are at least as advantageous to the claimant as the proposal contained his Part 36 offer.

13.53   It will usually be obvious whether the conditions in CPR, r 36.14(1)(b) have been satisfied, but difficulties can arise from time to time. Whilst by no means an exhaustive list, the following topics can arise in practice.

'Upon judgment being entered'

13.54   It used to be the case that under the 'old' Part 36, CPR, r 36.21 (which was the equivalent of the 'new' CPR, r 36.14(1)(b)) would apply only where the claim was disposed of 'at trial'. That condition would not have been met where, for example, summary judgment was given under CPR, Part 24.[96] It would seem that that restriction no longer applies; this is because (under the 'new' Part 36) CPR, r 36.14(1)(b) applies 'upon judgment being entered' without there being any mention of this being 'at trial'. There is not a great deal of authority on what the word 'judgment' means. That said, on a related point Coulson J has found that an indemnity costs presumption should not be imported into CPR, r 36.10; in particular, he has found that there is no rebuttable presumption that such costs will be recovered in circumstances where a claimant's Part 36 offer is accepted out of time.[97] In any event, it should not be forgotten that where r 36.14(1)(b) does not apply, the court would, in appropriate cases, still have the power to make an award of costs on the indemnity basis pursuant to r 44.3.

---

[95]   *Kastor Navigation Co Ltd v AXA Global Risks (UK) Ltd* [2004] EWCA Civ 277 at [135]–[139].
[96]   *Petrotrade Inc v Texaco Ltd (Note)* [2002] 1 WLR 947 at [58].
[97]   *Fitzpatrick Contractors Ltd v Tyco Fire & Integrated Solutions (UK) Ltd* [2009] EWHC 274 (TCC) at [28].

Offers made prior to the issue of proceedings

13.55 The 'old' CPR, r 36.2(4)(a) provided that a Part 36 offer could be made at any time after proceedings had started. Notwithstanding the fact that the court was specifically empowered to take such offers into account,[98] it was argued that this rule meant that an offer made before the issue of proceedings was not to be regarded as being a Part 36 offer. The Court of Appeal rejected this argument.[99] In any event, CPR, r 36.3(2)(a) now specifically provides that a Part 36 offer may be made at any time, including before the commencement of proceedings.

Appeals

13.56 CPR, r 36.3(2)(a) specifically provides that a Part 36 offer may be made in appeal proceedings. It remains the case (as it was under the 'old' Part 36) that, to be effective, a Part 36 offer must be made in respect of the appeal proceedings themselves, rather than in respect of the proceedings which gave rise to the appeal. Brooke LJ had this to say:[100]

> '[There] is no hint that the rulemakers [of the CPR] ever considered that a claimant might make a portmanteau Part 36 offer which would provide him with the protection of the code in CPR 36.21 both at first instance and on a subsequent appeal. If he wants to protect himself as to the costs of an appeal, he must make a further offer in the appeal proceedings.'

The 'new' CPR Part 36 makes express provision to the same effect.[101]

'Near misses'

13.57 As of 1 October 2011, the law has been as set out in CPR, r 36.14(1A):[102]

> '(1A) For the purposes of paragraph (1), in relation to any money claim or money element of a claim, "more advantageous" means better in money terms by any amount, however small, and "at least as advantageous" shall be construed accordingly.'

Thus a 'near miss' will not confer the benefit of the offer on the offeror, no matter close it might be; this rule was introduced to reverse the decision in *Carver v BAA plc*[103] (see **14.35–14.38**). In theory *Carver* still applies to offers made before 1 October 2011 (albeit in an attenuated form[104]), but Tomlinson LJ has explained that it would, in any event, rarely be the case that a *Carver* approach would be appropriate where the offeror was claimant.[105] Nonetheless, the court would still have its powers under CPR, r 44.3, so if the circumstances permitted, the court would be able to mark a 'near miss' with an award of indemnity costs even without invoking *Carver*.

---

[98]   See the 'old' CPR, r 36.10(1).

[99]   *Huck v Robson* [2002] EWCA Civ 398 at [55].

[100] *P & O Nedlloyd BV v Utaniko Ltd* [2003] EWCA Civ 174 at [6]; these comments relate to the 'old' Part 36. See also *KR v Bryn Alyn Community (Holdings) Ltd (in liquidation)* [2003] EWCA Civ 383.

[101] CPR, r 36.3(4).

[102] This was inserted by Civil Procedure (Amendment No 2) Rules 2011 (SI 2011/1979).

[103] *Carver v BAA plc* [2008] EWCA Civ 412.

[104] See **14.38**.

[105] *Acre 1127 Ltd (Formerly known as Castle Galleries Ltd) v De Montfort Fine Art Ltd* [2011] EWCA Civ 130.

'Equalling' an offer

13.58 A claimant's offer will be said to have been beaten where he achieves a result by judgment[106] which is exactly the same as his offer. Such a result would (under the 'new' Part 36) be regarded as being 'at least as advantageous' as the offer. Even under the 'old' Part 36 (where the test was whether the claimant had been awarded more or whether he had secured a judgment which was more advantageous), the court often exercised its discretion pursuant to CPR, r 44.3; where the court did this, it would often find that an award on the indemnity basis was justified.[107]

Non-monetary claims

13.59 In deciding whether a claimant has secured a result as least as advantageous to him as the offer, non-monetary factors, where they exist and where they are relevant, should be taken into account. Thus, where a claimant had offered to accept four collectable cars but in the result obtained six, the result was more advantageous to her than the offer.[108] Under the 'new' Part 36 the approach in non-money claims and money claims is broadly similar, and both will involve the court examining all the relevant factors, rather than just the financial value of the offer and the benefit ultimately derived.[109] For further details, see **14.45–14.47**.

Offers beaten by consent

13.60 Tugendhat J has found that where a claimant beats an offer by reason of a commercial settlement, it would not necessarily follow that he should be afforded the benefit of his offer; in coming to this conclusion he commented that the provisions of Part 36 are there to promote a commercial approach to litigation in accordance with the overriding objective, not to reward claimants who pursue claims where the costs outweigh the benefit.[110]

Offers to forgo costs or higher rate interest

13.61 Under the 'old' Part 36, when deciding whether a claimant had secured a result that was more advantageous to him than his offer, offers to accept discounted costs were generally disregarded,[111] as were offers to accept a discount on the 'uplift' element of any interest payable pursuant to the 'old' CPR, r 36.21(3)(b).[112] (Such offers could, of course, be taken into account when considering whether an award of costs on the indemnity basis was to be made under CPR, r 44.3.)[113] There is no authority as to how the court would approach such offers under the 'new' Part 36, but it could be argued

---

[106] The related point of how the court should deal with late acceptance of an offer is discussed at **14.65**.

[107] *Read v Edmed* [2004] EWHC 3274 (QB).

[108] *Neave v Neave* [2003] EWCA Civ 325; although this was a non-monetary claim, the court did seek to analyse the matter in financial terms. This case was decided under the 'old' Part 36.

[109] See *Carver v BAA plc* [2008] EWCA Civ 412.

[110] *D Pride & Partners v Institute for Animal Health* [2009] EWHC 1817 (QB) at [33]; on a different but related point (ie late acceptance of an offer) see *Fitzpatrick Contractors Ltd v Tyco Fire & Integrated Solutions (UK) Ltd* [2009] EWHC 274 (TCC) at [28].

[111] *Mitchell v James* [2002] EWCA Civ 997; under the 'new' provisions, see *Williams v Jervis* [2009] EWHC 1838 (QB), where Roderick Evans J declined to take such an offer into account; see also *Eiles v Southwark London Borough Council* [2006] EWHC 2014 (TCC).

[112] *Ali Reza-Delta Transport Co v United Arab Shipping Co* [2003] EWCA Civ 811.

[113] See, for example, *Eiles v Southwark London Borough Council* [2006] EWHC 2014 (TCC), in which Ramsay J gave weight to an offer to discount costs which he had found not to be a Part 36 offer but was an admissible offer.

that it would be in keeping with the openly textured language of the 'new' Part 36[114] for such offers to be taken into account in determining whether judgment was 'at least as advantageous' as a claimant's own Part 36 offer.

Interest and CRU

13.62 When deciding whether a claimant has bettered a Part 36 payment, it is necessary to compare like with like. This means that interest has to be taken into account when considering whether an offer has been beaten.[115] Special provisions apply when considering the effect of interest and recoupable state benefits; these are discussed at **14.48–14.52**.

The circumstances in which it would be unjust to make an award

13.63 The language of the 'new' Part 36 (at CPR, r 36.14(4)) is very similar to the language of the 'old' Part 36 (at CPR, r 36.21(5)). To this extent, the authorities dealing with the 'old' Part 36 remain of assistance.

13.64 CPR, r 36.14(4) provides that, when considering whether it would be unjust to make an award of costs on the indemnity basis pursuant to r 36.14(1)(b), the court will take into account all the circumstances of the case, including:

- the terms of any Part 36 offer;
- the stage in the proceedings when any Part 36 offer was made, including, in particular, how long before the trial started the offer was made;
- the information available to the parties at the time when the Part 36 offer was made; and
- the conduct of the parties with regard to the giving or refusing to give information for the purposes of enabling the offer to be made or evaluated.

These issues are discussed in more detail at **14.53–14.57** and are not repeated here. However, the following issues may be particularly relevant when considering a claimant's Part 36 offer.

Awards under CPR, r 36.14 are not penal

13.65 In deciding whether it would be unjust to make such an award of costs on the indemnity basis, it should be remembered that an award under CPR, r 36.14 does not carry punitive overtones. Chadwick LJ had the following to say about the 'old' CPR, r 36.21 (which was the equivalent of the 'new' r 36.14(1)(b)):[116]

> 'To make the order carries no implied disapproval of the defendant's conduct; nor any stigma. Properly understood, the making of such an order in a case to which CPR 36.21 applies indicates only that the court, when addressing the task which it is set by that rule, has not considered it unjust to make the order for indemnity costs for which the rule provides.'

---

[114] See *Carver v BAA plc* [2008] EWCA Civ 412.

[115] While dealing with the 'old' regime, see *Blackham v Entrepose UK* [2004] EWCA Civ 1109.

[116] *McPhilemy v Times Newspapers Ltd* [2001] EWCA Civ 993 at [9], echoing the comments of Lord Woolf MR in *Petrotrade Inc v Texaco Ltd* [2001] 4 All ER 853 at [62]–[64].

Offers to accept modest discounts

13.66 It is often the case that where primary liability and contributory negligence are at large, a claimant will offer to compromise the issue of liability on the basis of a modest discount. At the most extreme end of the spectrum a claimant might offer to accept a 99:1 split in his favour.

13.67 In a case (decided under the 'old' Part 36) in which the offer was to accept 95% of the full value of the claim, the Court of Appeal was divided as to what effect, if any, such an offer should have on the basis upon which costs were awarded: perhaps this was a reflection of the fact that the offer was close to being an offer to accept a *de minimis* reduction. Jonathan Parker LJ (dissenting) remarked:[117]

> 'In order to qualify for the incentives provided by paragraphs (2) and (3) of the rule a claimant's Part 36 offer must represent at the very least a genuine and realistic attempt by the claimant to resolve the dispute by agreement. Such an offer is to be contrasted with one which creates no real opportunity for settlement but is merely a tactical step designed to secure the benefit of the incentives. That is not to say that the offer must be one which it would be unreasonable for the defendant to refuse; that would be too strict a test ... In some cases, an offer which allows only a small discount from 100 per cent success on the claim may be a genuine and realistic offer; in other cases, it may not. It is for the judge in every case to consider whether, in the circumstances of that particular case, and taking into account the factors listed in paragraph (5) of rule 36.21, it would be unjust to make the order sought.'

13.68 Schiemann LJ and Tuckey LJ took a different view; in particular, Schiemann LJ went on to emphasise that where a claimant has made and beaten an offer to accept only a very small discount, the question is not whether it would be unjust to award costs on the indemnity basis, but whether it would be unjust *not* to award costs on the indemnity basis. He opined that it would have been unjust to deprive the offeror of the benefit of the offer mentioned above, but he went on to say:

> '[C]ircumstances can exist where, notwithstanding that a claimant has recovered in full after making a Part 36 offer for marginally less, he will not be awarded costs on the indemnity basis. I do not consider that Part 36 was intended to produce a situation in which a claimant was automatically entitled to costs on the indemnity basis provided only that he made an offer pursuant to Part 36.10 in an amount marginally less than the claim.'

Tuckey LJ added these comments:

> 'I would however add that if it was self-evident that the offer made was merely a tactical step designed to secure the benefit of the incentives provided by the Rule (e g an offer to settle for 99.9% of the full value of the claim) I would agree with Jonathan Parker LJ that the judge would have a discretion to refuse indemnity costs.'

13.69 Thus, in general, an offer to accept a modest discount would not result in an award of costs on the indemnity basis if it was merely a 'tactical step',[118] but otherwise it should not be disregarded. It seems that this continues to be the law under the 'new' Part 36; in this regard, Henderson J had this to say:[119]

---

[117] *Huck v Robson* [2002] EWCA Civ 398 at [63].
[118] Indeed, such an offer was dismissed as being tactical in *Fotedar v St George's Healthcare NHS Trust (No 2)* [2005] All ER (D) 33 (QB).
[119] *AB v CD and others* [2011] EWHC 602 (Ch) at [22].

'The concept of an "offer to settle" is nowhere defined in Part 36. I think it clear, however, that a request to a defendant to submit to judgment for the entirety of the relief sought by the claimant cannot be an "offer to settle" within the meaning of Part 36. If it were otherwise, any claimant could obtain the favourable consequences of a successful Part 36 offer, including the award of indemnity costs, by the simple expedient of making an "offer" which required total capitulation by the defendant. In my judgment the offer must contain some genuine element of concession on the part of the claimant . . .'

Thus, Henderson J came to much the same conclusion as in the cases referred to above, but he did this by a different route, namely, that a putative offer which does not contain some genuine element of concession on the part of the offeror is not a Part 36 offer at all.

13.70 In summary, the court has discretion when considering the justice of the proposed order on the indemnity basis, and there are many factors which may be taken into account when exercising that discretion.

Chapter 14

ACCEPTANCE OF PART 36 OFFERS, 'BEATING' DEFENDANT'S PART 36 OFFERS, ETC

14.1 This chapter deals with issues concerning acceptance of Part 36 offers made under Section I of Part 36 and with defendants' Part 36 offers made under that section in general. In so far as they relate to awards of costs on the indemnity basis, claimants' offers are dealt with in Chapter 13. Section II of Part 36 (offers in respect of low-value road traffic accident claims[1]) is addressed in Chapter 33. Unless the contrary is obvious, references herein are to Section I offers only.

14.2 On 5 April 2007, the provisions in CPR Part 36 changed;[2] as in the preceding chapter, the phrases 'old Part 36' and 'new Part 36' are used accordingly. This book discusses the 'new' Part 36, but necessarily does so by reference to a number of authorities decided under the 'old' Part 36. To this extent, caution must be exercised. Unless the contrary is specifically stated, references to Part 36 are to provisions in the 'new' Part 36.

THE ORIGIN AND HISTORY OF THE JURISDICTION

14.3 If the offer was made before 5 April 2007, the regime that existed at that time may apply; such circumstances are rare, and as such, the relevant law is relegated to the footnotes.[3] The rest of that which follows is largely of historical interest.

---

[1] See CPR, r 36.A1(3).

[2] Pursuant to the 44th update to the CPR; see the Civil Procedure (Amendment No 3) Rules 2006 (SI 2006/3435).

[3] Where an offer was made before 5 April 2007, it is necessary to know something of the history of the jurisdiction; this is for the following two reasons:

(1) where an offer has been made under the 'old' Part 36 regime, it may be necessary to bear those provisions in mind so as to know the reasonableness of any decision not to accept that offer at the time it was made; this may be relevant to the exercise of the court's discretion under CPR, r 36.14(4); and

(2) transitional provisions provide that offers made under the 'old' Part 36 will have the consequences set out under the 'new' Part 36, but only if it would have had the consequences set out in Part 36 as it was in force immediately before 6 April 2007(see SI 2006/3435, r 7(2)). It seems as if the court gives only little weight to the procedural differences between the two regimes and, in particular, the court seems not to give weight to the fact that an offeror may have appropriately decided not to make a Part 36 payment: see *Cunningham v AST Express Ltd* [2009] EWCA Civ 767 at [33]; and see **14.27**.

Payments into court

14.4   Prior to the introduction of the CPR, if a defendant wished to secure a degree of costs protection in a money claim, he had to make a payment into court. Giving judgment in the mid-1980s, the now obsolete law was articulated by Oliver LJ:[4]

> 'In the case of the simple money claim, a defendant who wishes to avail himself of the protection afforded by an offer must, in the ordinary way, back his offer with cash by making a payment in and speaking for myself, I should not, as at present advised, be disposed in such a case to treat a *Calderbank* offer as carrying the same consequences as payment in.'

14.5   In 1995, Lord Woolf proposed a system of offers which would not be reliant on payments into court;[5] the details are set out in the footnotes.[6] The then equivalent of the Rule Committee did not accept these recommendations (or, more accurately, it took the Rule Committee many years to adopt the same line of thinking). In particular, in its original guise the CPR did not make express provision for weight to be given to Part 36 offers which were not backed up by Part 36 payments.[7] If a provision to give weight to such offers existed, it would be necessary to find that it had been implied.

Move away from payments into court

14.6   The court was initially hostile to that notion that the court should give weight to offer not accompanied by a payment into court. In an early case (2001) Sir Anthony Evans held that it was wrong to afford a Part 36 offer the same status as a Part 36 payment; Simon Brown LJ explained that there was a number of reasons why payments into court had their advantages, citing many of the reasons previously given by the Law Society.[8]

14.7   Shortly thereafter (also 2001) Clarke LJ made similar comments in a different case, but he too reminded himself of the need to take into account all the

---

4   *Cutts v Head* [1984] Ch 290 at 312.
5   *Access to Justice – Interim Report*, June 1995, chapter 24.
6   The system he envisaged would make greater use of offers akin to *Calderbank* letters. The Law Society, amongst others, did not agree with those proposals: they pointed to the fact that a payment into court was a useful way of allowing the offeree to satisfy himself of the genuineness of the offeror's intent and of the substance of the offer. In his final report (in 1996), Lord Woolf stuck to his guns, but he did make one concession: he accepted that the system of payments into court should not be abolished altogether. Nonetheless, he made the following recommendation (*Access to Justice – Final Report*, July 1996, chapter 11, para 4):
     '[I recommend] in respect of defendants' offers, that the making of the offer itself should be the critical step, while the backing of a payment in will be secondary and optional. This means that [the common law rule] which prevents the making of a *Calderbank* offer where a payment into court can be made, will no longer apply under the [CPR].'
7   In particular, the 'old' CPR, r 36.3(1) provided that, 'Subject to rules 36.2A(2), 36.5(5) and 36.23, an offer by a defendant to settle a money claim will not have the consequences set out in this Part unless it is made by way of a Part 36 payment'.
8   *Amber v Stacey* [2001] 1 WLR 1225; see also *Hardy v Sutherland* [2001] EWCA Civ 976.

circumstances;[9] after having done this, he refused to disturb an order in which a trial judge had given effect to a Part 36 offer which had not been backed up by a concurrent Part 36 payment.[10]

14.8 This marked the beginning of a gradual move towards giving weight to Part 36 offers not backed up by Part 36 payments, but it was not until the mid-2000s that the existing state of affairs began to change in any significant way. That change came partly as a result of influential organisations (most notably the NHS Litigation Authority) habitually making Part 36 offers which were not backed up by corresponding Part 36 payments. Their argument was simple but compelling: the NHS was good for the money, and the funds were put to better use treating patients than languishing in court.

14.9 In 2005, Dyson LJ looked at the matter afresh; he concluded that the court was at liberty to find that a Part 36 offer not backed up by a Part 36 payment is to have the same costs consequences as an offer which is backed up by a payment.[11] This prompted a consultation by the Department of Constitutional Affairs,[12] the result of which was the abolition of Part 36 payments and the introduction of the present-day provisions (ie the 'new' Part 36). Transitional provisions exist;[13] in certain circumstances offers made under the 'old' provisions may be taken into account notwithstanding the fact that it was not accompanied by a payment in.[14]

THE POWER TO MAKE PART 36 OFFERS

14.10 Broadly speaking, Part 36 imposes restrictions only on the form which a Part 36 offer must take (see **14.13**) rather than the substance. In particular, as is explained at **14.11–14.12**, there are no express restrictions on when a Part 36 offer can be made or on the subject matter to which it may relate. The only noticeable express provision is that Section I of Part 36 will not apply where Section II applies.[15] This topic is addressed in Chapter 33.

---

9   Even in the early days of the CPR the court had a discretion to take into account offers which were not Part 36 payments (or, for that matter, offers which did not comply with Part 36 at all); the court's vires to do that arose from the provisions in CPR, r 44.3(4), which remain in existence today, and are discussed at **6.53–6.71**.

10 *The Maersk Colombo* [2001] 2 Lloyd's Rep 275; for the sake of accuracy, it should be recorded that a payment had been made, but it was late.

11 *Stokes Pension Fund v Western Power Distribution (South West) plc* [2005] EWCA Civ 854.

12 'Civil Procedure Rules Part 36: offers to settle and payments into court' (2006), CP 02/06.

13 See SI 2006/3435, r 7(2), which reads 'Where a Part 36 offer or Part 36 payment was made before 6 April 2007, if it would have had the consequences set out in the Rules of Court contained in Part 36 as it was in force immediately before 6 April 2007, it will have the consequences set out in rr 36.10, 36.11 and 36.14 after that date.'

14 Whilst technically obiter, see *French v Groupama Insurance Co Ltd* [2011] EWCA Civ 1119 at [35]–[39], per Rix LJ Rix LJ recited that the conditions that must be met are as follows: (1) the offer must be expressed in clear terms so that there is no doubt as to what is being offered; (2) the offer should be open for acceptance for at least 21 days and otherwise accord with the substance of a *Calderbank* offer; (3) the offer should be genuine and not a 'sham or non-serious in some way' (pre Waller in *Stokes* at [41]); and (4) the defendant should clearly have been good for the money when the offer was made.

15 See CPR, r 36.A1(2), CPR, r 36.1(1) and CPR, r 36.19(1). Section II applies to an offer to settle made in accordance with that section where the parties have followed the RTA Protocol and started proceedings under Part 8 in accordance with Practice Direction 8B.

Timing

14.11 A Part 36 offer is made when it is served on the offeree.[16] An offer may be made at any time and, in particular, it may be made before the commencement of proceedings or during an appeal.[17] An offer which is made or accepted before the issue of a claim form is capable of acceptance as a Part 36 offer; in that regard, the reference to 'proceedings' in CPR, r 36.10 is to be given a wide interpretation.[18] An offer which is made during proceedings which are subsequently appealed will need to be remade if it is to have a bearing on the costs of the appeal.[19]

Subject matter

14.12 It is necessary that an offer is authentic in the sense that it involves some genuine element of concession on the part of the offeror (see **13.69**). There is nothing within Part 36 to prevent an offer being made in non-monetary disputes or in respect of non-monetary issues. Even where the dispute is about money, it is permissible for an offer to relate to non-monetary aspects of the claim; indeed, the CPR expressly provide that offers may be made dealing with issues[20] or going to liability.[21] The offer will usually relate to something that is immediately in the control of the offeror, but this need not be the case; Henderson J has confirmed that an offer may relate to an advantage or form of relief which the claimant would only be able to obtain at some later stage.[22] Goldring LJ has found that an offer in respect of contributory negligence may be construed as being an offer in respect of liability, thereby bringing it within the category of a Part 36 offer.[23] Part 36 offers may be made on appeals from a VAT and duties tribunal.[24]

THE FORM OF AN OFFER AND PROCEDURE

14.13 The following formalities apply to all Part 36 offers (both claimant and defendant):

- the offer must be in writing;
- the offer must state on its face that it is intended to have the consequences of Section I[25] of Part 36;
- the offer must state whether it relates to the whole of the claim, to part of it or to an issue that arises in it and, if so, to which part or issue; and
- the offer must state whether it takes into account any counterclaim.

---

[16] CPR, r 36.7(1).
[17] CPR, r 36.3(2).
[18] See *Thompson (a minor) and ors v Bruce* [2011] EWHC 2228 (QB) at [38], per John Leighton Williams QC, disapproving the contrary finding of HHJ Platts in *Solomon v Cromwell Group Plc* (unreported) 2 August 2010, Manchester County Court; approved (in a different context) in *Solomon v Cromwell Group plc* [2011] EWCA Civ 1584.
[19] CPR, r 36.3(4).
[20] CPR, r 36.2(2)(d).
[21] CPR, r 36.2(5).
[22] *AB v CD and others* [2011] EWHC 602 (Ch) at [23].
[23] *Onay v Brown* [2009] EWCA Civ 775 at [28].
[24] *Blue Sphere Global Ltd v Revenue & Customs Commissioners* [2010] EWCA Civ 1448.
[25] It is frequently the case that the words 'Section I of' do not appear in Part 36 offers; whilst there is no authority on the point, it would be difficult to construct an argument that a failure to use these words was, of itself, of any consequence.

The rules for formal service of documents as contained in CPR, Part 6 do not apply to Part 36 offers; instead, service will be effected if a written offer is received by the offeree.[26] Offers may contain provisions that are not those specified by Part 36; thus, a reference to a need to agree a Tomlin order as matter of recording the bargain would not be fatal to the offer being a Part 36 offer.[27] It is, on the other hand, almost certainly the case that a provision that was incompatible with Part 36 would invalidate the offer, this being for the reasons set out in **14.25–14.27**.

Defendant offers

14.14 The requirement to make a Part 36 payment no longer exists (see **14.4–14.9**). Where an offer is made by a defendant and where it is an offer to pay a sum of money in settlement of a claim, it must be to pay a single sum of money.[28]

The 'relevant period', late offers and time limits

14.15 The offer must specify a period of not less than 21 days within which the defendant will, if the offer is accepted, be liable for the claimant's costs in accordance with CPR, r 36.10.[29] That period is one of the factors used to determine a period known as the 'relevant period' (this being the period during which an offer can be accepted on the basis that the claimant is automatically paid costs); the relevant period is calculated as follows:[30]

- in the case of an offer made not less than 21 days before trial, the period stated immediately above or such longer period as the parties agree; or
- in all other cases, it is the period up to end of the trial or such other period as the court has determined.

In view of the fact that an offer is required to state upon its face that it is intended to have the consequences set out in Section I of Part 36, a Part 36 offer must not contain terms that are incompatible with the provisions of that Section; one of those provisions is that an offer may be accepted at any time (see **14.65**). This invites the question of whether an offer that refers to a time limit is capable of being a Part 36 offer. Rix LJ has confirmed that whilst the 'new' Part 36 regime is incapable of accommodating offers that are genuinely time limited,[31] the approach is to avoid such an interpretation wherever possible (see **14.25–14.27** for a discussion of the general approach to interpretation).[32] Thus the words 'open for 21 days' should not be read as limiting the offer itself, but instead should be read as meaning that the offer will not be withdrawn within those 21 days.[33] Rimer LJ explained that those words were intended to convey the meaning that the offeror will not seek the court's permission to withdraw offer during the stated period.[34] Likewise, the phrase 'we ... diarise expiry' is to be regarded as being

[26]   *Charles v NGL Group Ltd* [2002] EWCA Civ 2004.
[27]   *In the matter of Kilopress Ltd* (unreported) 22 April 2010, Norris J, Ch D.
[28]   CPR, r 36.4(1); an offer that includes an offer to pay all or part of the sum, if accepted, at a date later than 14 days following the date of acceptance will not be treated as a Part 36 offer unless the offeree accepts the offer (see CPR, r 36.4(2)).
[29]   CPR, r 36.2(2).
[30]   CPR, r 36.3(1)(c).
[31]   *C v D* [2011] EWCA Civ 646 at [35]–[44], per Rix LJ.
[32]   *C v D* [2011] EWCA Civ 646 at [54] *et seq*; see also *Onay v Brown* [2009] EWCA Civ 775, at [27], per Goldring LJ.
[33]   *C v D* [2011] EWCA Civ 646 at [54].
[34]   *C v D* [2011] EWCA Civ 646 at [77].

a reference to the 'relevant period' rather than to the offer itself.[35] A reference to an 'acceptance period' would almost certainly be interpreted in a similar way.[36]

Personal injury claims

14.16 Where the offer is a personal injury claim, additional requirements may apply where there is a claim for future pecuniary loss, a claim for provisional damages, or where benefits may be deducted. Each is described in turn.

Future pecuniary loss

14.17 An offer which relates to a claim for future pecuniary loss must comply with the following:[37]

- it must state the amount of any offer to pay the whole or part of any damages in the form of a lump sum, and may state:
    - (i)   what part of the lump sum, if any, relates to damages for future pecuniary loss, and
    - (ii) what part relates to other damages to be accepted in the form of a lump sum;
- it must state what part of the offer relates to damages for future pecuniary loss to be paid or accepted in the form of periodical payments and must specify:
    - (i)   the amount and duration of the periodical payments,
    - (ii) the amount of any payments for substantial capital purchases and when they are to be made, and
    - (iii) that each amount is to vary by reference to the retail prices index (or to some other named index, or that it is not to vary by reference to any index); and
- it must state either that any damages which take the form of periodical payments will be funded in a way which ensures that the continuity of payment is reasonably secure in accordance with s 2(4) of the Damages Act 1996 or how such damages are to be paid and how the continuity of their payment is to be secured.

Provisional damages

14.18 Where the offer is made in respect of a claim which includes a claim for provisional damages, it must specify whether or not the offeror is proposing that the settlement shall include an award of provisional damages;[38] where the offeror is offering to make an award of provisional damages, the offer must also state:[39]

(a)   that the sum offered is in satisfaction of the claim for damages on the assumption that the injured person will not develop the disease or suffer the type of deterioration specified in the offer;

(b)   that the offer is subject to the condition that the claimant must make any claim for further damages within a limited period; and

(c)   what that period is.

---

[35]   *Epsom College v Pierse Contracting Southern Ltd (formerly Biseley Construction Ltd) (in liq)* [2011] EWCA Civ 1449 at [66], per Rix LJ.

[36]   *C v D* [2011] EWCA Civ 646 at [24], per Rix LJ; see also *Onay v Brown* [2009] EWCA Civ 775, at [27], per Goldring LJ.

[37]   CPR, r 36.5.

[38]   CPR, r 36.6(1) and (2).

[39]   CPR, r 36.6(3).

Where benefits may be deducted

14.19 In brief, the offer should state whether it is inclusive of CRU or exclusive; if the former, it should state:[40]

(a) the amount of gross compensation;
(b) the name and amount of any deductible amount by which the gross amount is reduced; and
(c) the net amount of compensation.

Clarity and adequacy of information

14.20 An offeree ought to be able to evaluate an offer by reference to a rational assessment of his own case (including the risk of incurring unrecoverable costs if he continues the litigation).[41] Two issues arise (although, in practice, they may be barely distinguishable). The first is the effect of the offerer not giving the offeree adequate information, and the second is the effect of an offer lacking in clarity. As to the first, whilst a lack of adequate information is an issue which may be relevant to the exercise of the court's discretion (see **14.56**), it would (save perhaps in an extreme case where the information was actually misleading) not in itself be capable of nullifying an otherwise effective Part 36 Offer. In this regard, Henderson J had this to say:[42]

> '[It] would in my view be productive of much uncertainty if the validity, as opposed to the costs and interest consequences, of a Pt 36 offer were to depend on something as difficult to ascertain as the adequacy of the information supplied by the offeror to the offeree. In many cases it may well be reasonable for the offeror to supply no, or only limited, information when the offer is made, and to leave it to the offeree to come back with a request for further information. Any such request should then be dealt with in a spirit of co-operation, and (if it is not) the offeree is free to apply to the court for an order under r 36.8. Alternatively, the offeree can decide whether or not to accept the offer as it stands, and if he decides to refuse it, but later fails to match or improve on it, he can argue that the usual adverse consequences should not follow, or should at least be mitigated, in reliance on r 36.14(4)(d). This is in my judgment a coherent and workable scheme, which respects the "demands of clarity and certainty in the operation of Pt 36" to which Moore-Bick LJ referred in Gibbon v Manchester City Council at 18.'

As to clarity, Aldous J has confirmed, albeit in a pre-CPR decision, that in order to be effective, an offer must be expressed in reasonably clear terms.[43] Whilst the contrary is arguable, it is entirely plausible that a lack of information is a point of fact that goes to discretion whereas a lack of clarity is a point of law that goes to interpretation. In any event, in so far as the incidence of costs is concerned, it is a distinction of limited practical relevance because it would be open to the court to decline to give effect to an unclear offer as a matter of discretion,[44] thereby achieving much the same result as would have been achieved if the offer had been found not to be an offer at all.

---

[40] CPR, r 36.15(3) and (6).
[41] *AB v CD and others* [2011] EWHC 602 (Ch) at [23], per Henderson J, who was interpreting the application of the obiter of Moore-Bick LJ in *Gibbon v Manchester City Council* [2010] EWCA Civ 726 at [40].
[42] *AB v CD and others* [2011] EWHC 602 (Ch) at [49].
[43] *C&H Engineering v F Klucznic & Son Ltd* [1992] FSR 667.
[44] *Ford v GKR Construction Ltd* [2000] 1 WLR 1397; although a pre-CPR case, see *Burgess v British Steel plc* [2000] PIQR Q240, in which it was found that the knowledge of the offeree was sufficiently good to know whether to accept the offer. See **14.57**.

Disclosure to the court

14.21 A Part 36 offer will be treated as 'without prejudice except as to costs'.[45] The fact that a Part 36 offer has been made must not be communicated to the trial judge or to the judge (if any) allocated in advance to conduct the trial until the case has been decided; this restriction will not apply, however, where:[46]

- the defence of tender before claim has been raised;
- the proceedings have been stayed under r 36.11 following acceptance of a Part 36 offer; or
- the offeror and the offeree agree in writing that it should not apply.

This prohibition against disclosure is directory, not compulsory; thus, the court would have the discretionary power to continue to hear the case notwithstanding the fact that it has inadvertently been told about an offer.[47] Henderson J has said (albeit obiter) that in split trial cases, the effect of the prohibition against disclosure is that questions of costs would have to be reserved until the conclusion of the whole claim, this being despite the fact that it would usually be desirable to deal with the costs at the end of each stage. He commented that a possible solution might be, in appropriate cases, to interpret the aforesaid prohibition as referring to the conclusion of each stage. This would allow the court to be told of the existence of the any relevant Part 36 offer; he expressed doubt, however, as to whether it was likely that the court would be able to make any rulings on costs at that stage.[48]

TECHNICAL SHORTCOMINGS

14.22 Where an offer substantially fails to comply with the requirements set out above (**14.13–14.20**) it will not have the consequences that would ordinarily flow from having made a Part 36 offer.[49] Nonetheless, a non-compliant offer may be taken into account as being an 'admissible offer' pursuant to CPR, r 44.3(4)(c); the practical effect can be very similar to that of a Part 36 offer. This topic is addressed at **6.53–6.71**. Likewise, an offer that is not a Part 36 offer may still be capable of acceptance notwithstanding its failed status.[50]

14.23 The court is able to overlook minor shortcomings in the format of an offer; there are two ways in which this may be achieved although the second is by far the more important; the first is as a result of the court exercising its discretion, and the second is as a matter of construction. Indeed, it is possible that the second has now wholly superseded the first.

---

[45]   CPR, r 36.13(1).
[46]   CPR, r 36.13(2).
[47]   *Garratt v Saxby* [2004] EWCA Civ 341; this case was decided under the 'old' Part 36, but Henderson J has confirmed (albeit obiter) that it remains good law under the 'new' Part 36 (see *AB v CD and others* [2011] EWHC 602 (Ch) at [16]).
[48]   *AB v CD and others* [2011] EWHC 602 (Ch) at [18]–[20]).
[49]   CPR, r 36.1(2); specifically, it will not have the consequences specified in CPR, rr 36.10, 36.11 and 36.14.
[50]   See, for example, *Carillion JM Ltd v PHI Group Ltd* [2011] EWHC 1581 (TCC), per Akenhead J at [17], which was successfully appealed on other bases: see [2012] EWCA Civ 588.

Discretion and substantial compliance

14.24 Whilst there are limits to such an approach (see **6.72**) and whilst the approach set out in **14.25–14.27** is preferable, there is authority that where an offer falls short of being a Part 36 offer by reason of a minor defect which caused no real uncertainty and no prejudice, the court is able to make a discretionary award that is equivalent to that which would have been made had the offer been free of technical defects. A similar approach was taken under the 'old' Part 36.[51] Whilst this approach probably remains good law in the sense that the discretion continues to exist, Rix LJ has made it clear that if the relevant formalities have not been observed, the mechanistic rules in Part 36 should not be applied;[52] thus, an equivalent award should be made only where this is justified on the merits.[53] An offeror may have particular difficulty in justifying such an award where he seeks an award of costs on the indemnity basis (see **13.25** and **13.26**). Whilst there is no authority that uses the language of substantial compliance,[54] it is likely that this is another means by which minor technical shortcomings can be prevented from depriving an offeror of the benefits of having made an offer. Where the court rejects that approach and also rejects the notion of making an equivalent award, it does not follow that the offer will be disregarded entirely; whilst the offeror may not get the full benefit of the offer, he may still be awarded some valuable benefit (see **6.72**, **14.73** and **14.74**).

Construction

14.25 Offers under the 'old' Part 36 are addressed in the footnotes.[55] In so far as the 'new' provisions are concerned, Carnwath LJ has said that where the Part 36 jurisdiction is expressly invoked, the court should generally take that statement at face value and, as far as possible, give effect to the consequences of CPR Part 36 as envisaged by the rules.[56] Rix LJ had this to say on the topic:[57]

---

[51] *Hertsmere Primary Care Trust v Rabindra-Anandh* [2005] EWHC 320 (Ch), per Lightman J. This contrasts with *Brown v Mcasso Music Production* [2005] EWCA Civ 1546 in which Neuberger LJ found that an offer was defective it too many ways to be regarded as being equivalent to an Part 36 offer, albeit under the 'old' Part 36: the shortcomings included uncertainty as to whether it was without prejudice save as to costs and the fact that it was open for only 7 days.

[52] *French v Groupama Insurance Co Ltd* [2011] EWCA Civ 1119 at [41]. Also see *Epsom College v Pierse Contracting Southern Ltd (formerly Biseley Construction Ltd) (in liq)* [2011] EWCA Civ 1449 at [54] *et seq*, per Rix LJ. Even before this guidance was given, Underhill J had commented that an equivalent award would not be appropriate in every case where there were technical defects, even if they could be characterised as causing no prejudice: *Huntley v Simmonds* [2009] EWHC 406 (QB).

[53] Ramsay J has commented that a factor that can be taken into account is whether the offeree raised the issue of any technical shortcoming at the time the offer was made: *Eiles v Southwark London Borough Council* [2006] EWHC 2014 (TCC) at [51].

[54] That said, in *Harper v Hussain* (unreported) 19 March 2008, Birmingham County Court HHJ McDuff QC (now McDuff J) analysed a case in way that could have been phrased in terms of substantial compliance. The offer in that case failed to state whether it took into account any counterclaim, that being in a claim in which there was no counterclaim; HHJ McDuff QC found that it ought to be treated as being a Part 36 offer.

[55] Whilst a requirement to make a Part 36 payment no longer exists, offers made under the 'old' regime will need to be considered from time to time. A practical approach is taken to such matters; while each case will turn on its own facts, Smith LJ has said that where an offer made under the 'old' Part 36 was made in good faith and held open for 21 days, it would put the claimant at risk on costs notwithstanding the fact that it was not backed up with a Part 36 payment; (see *Cunningham v AST Express Ltd* [2009] EWCA Civ 767 at [33]); Smith LJ also indicated that such an offer should be considered in the light of CPR, r 44.3(3) (ie the 'general rule'). Thus, the advances made in the understanding of the law prior to the introduction of the 'new' Part 36 (see **14.4–14.9**) seem to be relevant if and when the court looks back on an offer made under the 'old' 'old' Part 36. The flexibility of approach will apply even where no payment in was made (see the footnotes to **14.9**), but there are limits; see, for example, *Brown v Mcasso Music Production* [2005] EWCA Civ 1546 in which Neuberger LJ found that the defects (including ambiguity as to whether the offer was without prejudice save as to costs) were too great allow it to be regarded as being a quasi-Part 36 offer.

[56] *Onay v Brown* [2009] EWCA Civ 775, [2010] 1 Costs LR 29 at [33].

'Such a construction would save the Part 36 offer as a Part 36 offer and would also give to both parties the clarity and certainty which both Part 36 itself, and the offer letter . . . aspire to . . . Another principle or maxim of construction which is applicable in the present circumstances is that words should be understood in such a way that the matter is effective rather than ineffective (*verba ita sunt intelligenda ut res magis valeat quam pereat*).'

Thus, Rix LJ interpreted the offer before him in such a way as to preserve the object of its stated intention, namely, that it be a Part 36 offer; where an offer has been unhappily worded, this appears to be the guiding principle.

14.26 The question is how a reasonable solicitor would have understood the offer in the context the dispute as it stood at the time it was made;[58] the subjective intentions of the parties are irrelevant.[59] It is likely that the court would take into account the way in which the parties dealt with and reacted to the offer.[60] As to ambiguity, Rimer LJ had this to say:[61]

'The relevance . . . [of an] expressed intention to make [an] offer a Part 36 offer is that, if there are any ambiguities in it raising a question as to whether the offer does or does not comply with the requirements of Part 36, the reasonable man will interpret it in a way that is so compliant. That is because, objectively assessed, that is what the offeror can be taken to have intended.'

Stanley Burnton LJ put matter more pithily:[62]

'Any ambiguity in an offer purporting to be a Part 36 offer should be construed so far as reasonably possible as complying with Part 36.'

The words of an offer should be regarded as being effective rather than ineffective.[63] Rix LJ has cited with approval an extract from *Chitty on Contracts*[64] that propounded that if one interpretation makes the contract lawful and another makes it unlawful, the former is to be preferred.[65]

14.27 There are, however, limits to the extent to which the court can overlook supposedly technical shortcomings. Some offers will by their very substance be incompatible with Part 36; an offer that was exclusive of costs, for example, would in general not be a Part 36 offer,[66] nor would an offer that imposed a restriction on the

---

[57]   *C v D* [2011] EWCA Civ 646 at [54] and [55].
[58]   *C v D* [2011] EWCA Civ 646 at [45] pre Rix LJ, relying on *ICS v West Bromwich Building Society* [1998] 1 WLR 896 (HL)
[59]   *C v D* [2011] EWCA Civ 646 at [83], per Stanley Burnton LJ.
[60]   In *Seeff v Ho* [2011] EWCA Civ 401 at [12] Thomas LJ (giving judgment of the court) gave weight to the fact that the putative offer said on its face that if it was in any way defective or non-compliant, the offeree should inform the offeror straight away; the offeree raised no concerns in this regard, and this was a factor that persuaded Thomas LJ to accept that a somewhat poorly drafted offer came within the ambit of Part 36.
[61]   *C v D* [2011] EWCA Civ 646 at [75].
[62]   *C v D* [2011] EWCA Civ 646 at [84]; this extract was cited with approval by Rix LJ in *Epsom College v Pierse Contracting Southern Ltd (formerly Biseley Construction Ltd) (in liq)* [2011] EWCA Civ 1449 at [66].
[63]   This being the maxim verba ita sunt intelligenda ut res magis valeat quam pereat.
[64]   *C v D* [2011] EWCA Civ 646 at [55], citing with approval Chitty on Contracts (30th edn, 2008) Vol 1, at para 12-081. 'If one construction makes the contract lawful and the other unlawful, the former is to be preferred ...'.
[65]   *C v D* [2011] EWCA Civ 646 at [55].
[66]   *Howell v Lees-Millais* [2011] EWCA Civ 786 at [23], per Neuberger MR.

entitlement to costs.[67] Lloyd LJ has confirmed that if there has been a failure to state any period at all that was capable of being interpreted as being in compliance with CPR, r 36.2(2)(c), that would preclude the offer from being a Part 36 offer.[68] This is in contrast to specifying a period of 21 days as 'the relevant acceptance period'[69] or stating that 'this offer will be open for 21 days from the date of this letter, [that being] the relevant period',[70] both of which were, on a proper construction, found to be compliant. Lloyd LJ said this on the topic:[71]

> '[Counsel] submitted that [the] offer in the present case should be construed so as to find an implicit specification of a 21 day period for the purposes of rule 36.2(2)(c). I cannot accept that argument. The requirement in the rule that a period of not less than 21 days must be specified requires some explicit identification of a period of 21 or more days. Ambiguity may come in, and with it the principle of construction described, if a period is specified but there is some doubt as to the purpose for which it is specified. Here no period was specified at all, so there is no ambiguity which falls to be resolved.'

Thus, if a suitable period is stated but there is ambiguity as to what was meant, it may be possible to resolve that ambiguity in such a way as to preserve compliance, but if the offer is silent as to such a period, the offer will be beyond rescue.[72]

THE EFFECT OF FAILING TO BEAT A DEFENDANT'S PART 36 OFFER

14.28   The effect of failing to beat a claimant's Part 36 offer is addressed at **13.45–13.70**; only defendant offers are dealt with in this chapter. In a nutshell, the principles can be stated in this way: where a claimant fails to obtain a judgment that is more advantageous to him than the proposals contained in his opponent's prior Part 36 offer, then (unless the court considers it unjust to do so) an award of costs may be made in the defendant's favour, starting from the date on which the relevant period expired.

14.29   If the discretion afforded by CPR, r 44.3(4)(c) is disregarded for a moment (as it must be if the offer in question is a Part 36 offer), the vires to take a defendant's offer into account arises from the combined effects of CPR, r 36.14(1)(a) and (2):

'(1)   This rule applies where upon judgment being entered—

(a)   a claimant fails to obtain a judgment more advantageous than a defendant's Part 36 offer;

…

(2)   Subject to paragraph (6), where rule 36.14(1)(a) applies, the court will, unless it considers it unjust to do so, order that the defendant is entitled to—

(a)   his costs from the date on which the relevant period expired; and

---

67   *London Tara Hotel Limited v Kensington Close Hotel Limited* [2011] EWHC 29 (Ch) at [27] per Roth J. See also *Elliott v Shah* [2011] EW Misc 8.
68   See *PHI Group Ltd v Robert West Consulting Ltd* [2012] EWCA Civ 588 at [27] to [33].
69   *Onay v Brown* [2009] EWCA Civ 775.
70   *C v D* [2011] EWCA Civ 646 at [75].
71   *PHI Group Ltd v Robert West Consulting Ltd* [2012] EWCA Civ 588 at [30].
72   HHJ Behrens (sitting as Judge of the High Court) found that an offer which 'remains open for acceptance for a period of 21 days' lacked the necessary words to comply with CPR, r 36.2(2)(c) (see *Thewlis v Groupama Insurance Company Ltd* [2012] EWHC 3 (TCC) [28] and [29]). That decision was subject to academic criticism (see D Regan D 'Is it or isn't it' *New Law Journal*, February 2012) and in the light of Lloyd LJ's guidance it ought now not to be followed.

(b)   interest on those costs.'

CPR, r 36.14(6) adds the following qualifications:

'Paragraphs (2) and (3) of this rule do not apply to a Part 36 offer—

(a)   that has been withdrawn;

(b)   that has been changed so that its terms are less advantageous to the offeree, and the offeree has beaten the less advantageous offer;

(c)   made less than 21 days before trial, unless the court has abridged the relevant period.'

Thus the date from which the defendant will be awarded costs is generally the date on which the relevant period expired. Where an offer needs to be clarified, the expiry of the relevant period may be adjusted accordingly.[73] There is nothing in any of these provisions to oust the court's jurisdiction to make a discretionary award of costs on the indemnity basis.[74]

Test of unjustness

14.30   The principles underlying an award of costs under Part 36 are not the same as those which govern an award of costs under CPR, r 44.3. Where a party is entitled to costs as a result of the provisions in Part 36, Mann J has found (albeit under the 'old' Part 36) that an ordinary issues-based approach (ie, under CPR, r 44.3) would have no relevance to the application of these provisions; instead the court would have to be persuaded that there was something unjust in giving the offeror the benefit of the offer.[75] If this remains good law (and there is no reason to believe otherwise: see **14.53** *et seq*), it indicates a different approach from that which applies where the court is minded to make an issues-based order in the context of a claimant having beaten a claimant's Part 36 offer (see **13.40**):[76] this is a consequence of the fact that a claimant's offer reflects in the basis of costs, whereas a defendant's offer reflects in the incidence of costs.

Appeals

14.31   CPR, r 36.3(4) provides that a Part 36 offer will have a bearing only on the costs of the proceedings in respect of which it is made, and not on the costs of any appeal from the final decision in those proceedings.[77] This express provision reflects the way in which Brooke LJ had interpreted the 'old' Part 36.[78]

14.32   There is no authority on the topic of whether the costs consequences mentioned above would apply if a defendant's offer were to be beaten by judgment being entered by consent.[79] It would be possible to draw an analogy with the way in which the court deals

---

[73]   *Colour Quest Ltd v Total Downstream UK plc* [2009] EWHC 823 (Comm) at [32], per David Steel J; this case concerned claimants' offers, but the principles can only be the same.

[74]   Indeed, the offer itself can lead to an award of costs on the indemnity basis if the court is satisfied that it was unreasonable (as opposed to merely misjudged) not to accept it; see, for example, *D Morgan plc v Mace & Jones (a firm)* [2011] EWHC 26 (TCC), per Coulson J.

[75]   *Fulham Leisure Holdings Ltd v Nicholson Graham & Jones* [2006] EWHC 2428 (Ch).

[76]   See *Kastor Navigation Co Ltd v AXA Global Risks (UK) Ltd* [2004] EWCA Civ 277 at [135]–[139].

[77]   See CPR, r 36.3(4).

[78]   *P & O Nedlloyd BV v Utaniko Ltd* [2003] EWCA Civ 174 at [6].

[79]   For the related issue of where an offer is accepted out of time or as a result of it being renewed, see **14.65–14.66**.

with claimant's Part 36 offers,[80] but, equally, it could be argued that the policy considerations concerning defendants' Part 36 offers are different,[81] and that this analogy is not appropriate.

THE CIRCUMSTANCES IN WHICH A DEFENDANT'S OFFER WILL BE BEATEN

14.33 The following discussion focuses on a defendant's Part 36 offers, but, by parity of reasoning, many of the principles also relate to claimants' Part 36 offers. The topics to be addressed are:

- 'near misses' in monetary claims;
- barely beating an offer;
- offers beaten by consent;
- assessing the value of non-monetary claims;
- interest; and
- deductible benefits.

'Near misses' in monetary claims

14.34 Where there has been a 'near miss' (ie where the defendant has, on the face of it, failed to beat his offer, but only by a narrow margin), two issue may arise:

(1) the court may have to determine whether the offer really has been beaten; and
(2) the court may have to determine whether the offer should be taken into account when exercising its discretion as to costs.

These two topics are linked almost to the extent that they are opposite sides of the same coin; in the discussion which follows they are treated separately, but in many cases the distinction will be artificial.

Determining whether the offer has been beaten

14.35 As of 1 October 2011, the law has been as set out in CPR, r 36.14(1A):[82]

'(1A) For the purposes of paragraph (1), in relation to any money claim or money element of a claim, "more advantageous" means better in money terms by any amount, however small, and "at least as advantageous" shall be construed accordingly.'

This rule was introduced to reverse the decision in *Carver v BAA plc*,[83] that being a case in which the Court of Appeal had dallied with the idea of deciding the issue of whether an offer had been 'beaten' in a flexible way that took into account factors other than

---

[80]   *D Pride & Partners v Institute for Animal Health* [2009] EWHC 1817 (QB) at [33]; for a different but related point see *Fitzpatrick Contractors Ltd v Tyco Fire & Integrated Solutions (UK) Ltd* [2009] EWHC 274 (TCC) at [28].

[81]   Not least because it would be in accordance with the overriding objective to discourage claimants from pursuing disproportionate claims which are capable of compromise (see *D Pride & Partners v Institute for Animal Health* [2009] EWHC 1817 (QB) at [33]), it could be argued that defendants should be encouraged to make realistic offers.

[82]   This was inserted by Civil Procedure (Amendment No 2) Rules 2011.

[83]   *Carver v BAA plc* [2008] EWCA Civ 412.

Civil Costs: Law and Practice

those related directly to the subject matter of the offer. As of 1 October 2011, CPR, r 36.14(1A) makes it clear that in a money claim, that approach is no longer good law. That said, that rule applies only to Part 36 offers made on or after 1 October 2011;[84] as such, the rule in *Carver* may apply to offers made before that date. All of what follows relates to offers made before that date (or, more accurately, between 5 April 2007 and 1 October 2011. The following table summarises the position:

	Test to be applied	Claimant does marginally better in numerical terms	Defendant does marginally better in numerical terms	Result is the same as the offer
Defendant's offer (pre 1 October 2011)	The claimant fails to obtain a judgment more advantageous than a defendant's Part 36 offer	In a very exceptional case, the claimant will be regarded as having failed to beat the offer, in which case, the court will award the defendant the benefit of the offer (see **14.37**); in all other cases, the court will exercise its discretion as a 'near miss' under CPR, r 44.3 (see **14.39**).	The court will award the defendant the benefit of offer unless it would be unjust to do so (see **14.43**).	The court will award the defendant the benefit of offer unless it would be unjust to do so.
Defendant's offer (post 1 October 2011)	The claimant fails to obtain a judgment more advantageous – by any amount, however small – than a defendant's Part 36 offer	The court will exercise its discretion under CPR, r 44.3 (**14.35**) as a 'near miss' (see **14.39**).	The court will award the defendant the benefit of offer unless it would be unjust to do so (**14.43**).	The court will award the defendant the benefit of offer unless it would be unjust to do so.
Claimant's offer (pre 1 October 2011)	The judgment against the defendant is at least as advantageous to the claimant as the proposals contained in a claimant's Part 36 offer	The court will award the claimant the benefit of offer unless it would be unjust to do so.	In theory, the claimant may be regarded as having beaten the offer in rare cases, but in practice, the court will exercise its discretion under CPR, r 44.3 (**13.57**).	The court will award the claimant the benefit of offer unless it would be unjust to do so (**13.58**).

---

[84] Civil Procedure (Amendment No 2) Rules 2011, r 1(4).

Claimant's offer (post 1 October 2011)	The judgment against the defendant is at least as advantageous – by any amount, however small – to the claimant as the proposals contained in a claimant's Part 36 offer	The claimant will have beaten the offer; the court will award the claimant the benefit of offer unless it would be unjust to do so.	The court will exercise its discretion under CPR, r 44.3 **(13.57)**.	The court will award the claimant the benefit of offer unless it would be unjust to do so **(13.58)**.

Offers made between 5 April 2007 and 1 October 2011

14.36 Under the 'old' Part 36 (ie, pre-5 April 2007) it was generally thought that exceeding a Part 36 payment by even a modest monetary amount was sufficient for the purposes of 'beating' that offer.[85] One of the reasons for taking that view was because the test under the 'old' Part 36 was whether a claimant had 'failed to better' the payment';[86] that language implied a pure monetary comparison, ie it implied a test that was restricted to whether the award was higher or lower than the offer. The language of the 'new' Part 36 is that the claimant will be at risk if he 'fails to obtain a judgment more advantageous' than the defendant's Part 36 offer.[87] This open-textured terminology led to an approach by which the court would take into account all aspects of the matter when considering whether a defendant's offer had been beaten, including non-monetary matters. This was thought to bring the language of the rules on money claims into line with the language pertaining to non-money claims (which, for obvious reasons, could not be evaluated by way of a monetary comparison, even under the 'old' regime).

14.37 In particular, Ward LJ (with whom Rix and Keene LJJ agreed) had this to say:[88]

'Are the concepts of bettering a Part 36 payment and obtaining a judgment more advantageous than the Part 36 offer synonymous? Posed in that way, perhaps they are. But in the context of the new Part 36, where money claims and non-money claims are to be treated in the same way, "more advantageous" is ... an open-textured phrase. It permits a more wide-ranging review of all the facts and circumstances of the case in deciding whether the judgment, which is the fruit of the litigation, was worth the fight.'

Thus, the issue of whether a claimant had failed to obtain a result as least as advantageous as the defendant's offer was based on a test that was capable of taking into account any factor, including irrecoverable costs of the litigation and the emotional cost of litigation; if a claimant had achieved a result that was for an amount only marginally higher than that offered by the defendant, then he would have been at risk of being found not to have 'beaten' the offer.

14.38 It soon became apparent that such an approach would cause difficulties: judges were required to wrestle with the nebulous issue of whether the game was worth the candle rather than with the well-defined issue of whether the offer had been beaten in numerical terms. Those difficulties caused a differently constituted Court of Appeal to

---

[85] See the discussion of this issue by Ward LJ in *Carver v BAA plc* [2008] EWCA Civ 412 at [3].
[86] See the 'old' CPR, r 36.20.
[87] CPR, r 36.14(1)(a).
[88] *Carver v BAA plc* [2008] EWCA Civ 412 at [30].

limit the above approach such that it was to be applied in only the most exceptional of cases.[89] This is probably the current state of the law in relation to offers made by defendants after 5 April 2007 and before 1 October 2011.

The exercise of discretion

14.39 Where there has been a near miss (ie, where a claimant has beaten a defendant's Part 36 offer by a modest margin), the court is at liberty to exercise its discretion pursuant to CPR, r 44.3.[90] One factor to be taken into account is whether any offers have been made.[91] The court has freedom in those circumstances to exercise its discretion to make an order which meets the justice of the situation.

14.40 Where the court elects to exercise its discretion in this way, one or more of the parties may contend that the dispute would have settled if the other side had acted in a way more conducive to negotiation; arguments such as this may be put with particular force when there has been a 'near miss'. Waller LJ said on this topic (albeit in the context of the 'old' CPR Part 36):[92]

> 'If the judge is finding that the case would have settled as opposed to finding that there was a chance it would have settled, that could not have been other than a speculation. In my view it does not come well from a defendant who has paid money into court to argue that if a claimant had been more reasonable he would have offered more. An investigation as to how negotiations would have gone is precisely the form of investigation which should be avoided. In a case about money a defendant has the remedy in his own hands where a claimant is being intransigent. He can pay into court the maximum sum he is prepared to pay.'

14.41 Chadwick LJ expressed a similar view and, in particular, his concern about the possibility of the court being drawn into 'a potentially lengthy, inquiry on incomplete material into "what would have happened if ...?"'.[93]

14.42 In appropriate cases, it is open to the court to make a percentage order.[94] Indeed, that approach was not wholly unknown, even under the 'old' Part 36 regime.[95]

Barely beating an offer

14.43 A near miss (see **14.39**) should be distinguished from the situation where there is a narrow failure on the part of the offeree to beat the offer. In those circumstances the offeror will be entitled to the benefits of the offer unless that would be unjust;[96] that is an entirely different situation from that discussed immediately above.

Offers beaten by consent

14.44 Tugendhat J has found that where a claimant beats an offer by reason of a commercial settlement, it would not necessarily follow that he should be afforded the

---

[89] *L G Blower Ltd v Reeves* [2010] EWCA Civ 726.
[90] *Straker v Tudor Rose (a firm)* [2007] EWCA Civ 368 at [3].
[91] CPR, r 44.3(4)(c); and see *Straker v Tudor Rose (a firm)* [2007] EWCA Civ 368 at [5].
[92] *Straker v Tudor Rose (a firm)* [2007] EWCA Civ 368.
[93] *Johnsey Estates (1990) Ltd v Secretary of State for the Environment* [2001] EWCA Civ 535 at [32].
[94] See, for example, *Owners, Demise Charters & Time Charterers of 'Western Neptune'* [2009] EWHC 1522 (Admlty).
[95] See, for example, *Firle v Datapoint* [2001] EWCA Civ 1106.
[96] See, by way of analogy, *Fulham Leisure Holdings Ltd v Nicholson Graham & Jones* [2006] EWHC 2428 (Ch).

benefit of his offer; in coming to this conclusion he commented that the provisions of Part 36 are there to promote a commercial approach to litigation in accordance with the overriding objective, not to reward claimants who pursue claims where the costs outweigh the benefit.[97]

Assessing the value of an offer in non-money claims

14.45 Ward LJ made the following remark (which was obiter) about the general approach in non-money claims:[98]

'It is quite clear that in non-money claims where there is no yardstick of pounds and pence by which to make the comparison, all the circumstances of the case have to be taken into account.'

This comment would, presumably, apply in circumstances which do not permit the court to evaluate the non-monetary items in financial terms. Where a financial evaluation is possible, then that may be an appropriate yardstick. In a case involving the recovery of motor vehicles, for example, Chadwick LJ found that it was appropriate to analyse the 'advantage' in financial terms.[99]

14.46 Where a non-financial approach is required, the following comments of Sir Thomas Bingham MR may apply:[100]

'The judge must look closely at the facts of the particular case before him and ask: who, as a matter of substance and reality, has won? Has the plaintiff won anything of value which he could not have won without fighting the action through to a finish? Has the defendant substantially denied the plaintiff the prize which the plaintiff fought the action to win?'

These comments were made in the context of a defamation claim. Similar considerations may arise in claims regarding non-monetary disputes about land,[101] chattels, etc.

14.47 Some claims will involve both monetary and non-monetary aspects. Again, the correct approach is to take into account all of the facts. This may mean that an offer is found wanting by reason of it having addressed one aspect of the claim, but not others. In a claim involving the rights to music, for example, Neuberger LJ found that it was open to the court to find that the offer had not been beaten where the defendant secured a more advantageous result in respect of the monetary aspects but not the non-monetary aspects.[102]

---

[97] *D Pride & Partners v Institute for Animal Health* [2009] EWHC 1817 (QB) at [33]; on a different but related point (ie late acceptance of an offer) see *Fitzpatrick Contractors Ltd v Tyco Fire & Integrated Solutions (UK) Ltd* [2009] EWHC 274 (TCC) at [28].

[98] *Carver v BAA plc* [2008] EWCA Civ 412 at [29].

[99] Although decided under the 'old' provisions, see *Neave v Neave* [2003] EWCA Civ 325.

[100] *Roache v Newsgroup Newspapers Ltd* [1998] EMLR 161 (Eady J has confirmed that these comments remain good law under the CPR: see *Jones v Associated Newspapers Ltd* [2007] EWHC 1489 at [14]).

[101] While it dealt with admissible offers rather than Part 36 offers, see *MBI Incorporated v Riminex Investments Ltd* [2002] EWHC 2856 (QB).

[102] *Brown v Mcasso Music Production* [2005] EWCA Civ 1546.

Interest

14.48 Interest has to be taken into account when considering whether an offer has been beaten;[103] this is necessary in order to allow like to be compared with like. There is no express facility under Part 36 to make an offer which is exclusive of interest; instead, offers are presumed to include interest. In this regard, CPR, r 36.3(3) provides:

> '(3) A Part 36 offer which offers to pay or offers to accept a sum of money will be treated as inclusive of all interest until – (a) the date on which the period stated under rule 36.2(2)(c) expires; or (b) if rule 36.2(3) applies, a date 21 days after the date the offer was made.'

CPR, r 36.2(3) applies if the offer is made less than 21 days before the start of the trial.

14.49 Where the offer and the judgment sum are sufficiently close to each other as to create doubt as to whether the offer has been beaten, it may be necessary to calculate the amount that would have been allowed had interest been calculated to the applicable date. In this regard, Brooke LJ endorsed the following extract from the 1999 edition of the *White Book*[104] (the extract is worded in pre-CPR language, but Brooke LJ has confirmed that what is said remains good law under the CPR):

> '[If] the trial Judge awards £x by way of damages and the defendant has paid into Court £y, which exceeds £x, then a calculation may have to be made as to what the amount of interest would have been if judgment were given for £x at the date of the payment into Court. If such figure amounts to £a, and if £x + £a exceeds £y, the result would be that the amount recovered by the plaintiff will have exceeded the amount paid into Court by the defendant, so that the plaintiff will be entitled to be awarded the whole costs of the action. But it is thought that this calculation would not be very difficult and is likely to arise comparatively rarely.'

Brooke LJ commented that this formulaic approach is to be preferred to a more general exercise of discretion; he explained that the latter was not to be preferred because it would lead to inconsistencies between courts and between judges in the same court.

Deductible benefits

14.50 The measure of whether an offer has been beaten is based on the applicable sums net of deductible benefits (usually known as 'CRU').[105]

14.51 Offers may be expressed to be exclusive of deductible benefits,[106] but where this is not the case, an adjustment will need to be made for deductible benefits.

14.52 Determining the net sum of the offer ought to present no problems; this is because it should have been stated in the offer.[107] The net sum of the judgment sum is derived by subtracting deductible amounts identified in the judgment.[108]

---

[103] Although dealing with the 'old' regime, see *Blackham v Entrepose UK* [2004] EWCA Civ 1109.
[104] *Blackham v Entrepose UK* [2004] EWCA Civ 1109.
[105] CPR, r 36.15(8); see also *Blackham v Entrepose UK* [2004] EWCA Civ 1109, in which Brooke LJ has said that the like-for-like rule should be in relation to CRU.
[106] CPR, r 36.15(3).
[107] CPR, r 36.15(6).
[108] CPR, r 36.15(8).

THE CIRCUMSTANCES IN WHICH IT WOULD BE UNJUST TO MAKE AN AWARD

14.53 With certain exceptions[109], the court will make an order giving a successful offeror the benefit of the offer unless it considers it would be unjust to do so;[110] while it is possible that their comments do not remain good law under the 'new' Part 36, both Schiemann LJ and Tuckey LJ (Jonathan Parker LJ dissenting) have indicated that the test is not whether it would be unjust to make the award, but whether it would be unjust *not* to make it.[111] That jurisdiction is not, however, an unfettered jurisdiction in the sense that the court can exercise its discretion as it would when making an award under CPR, r 44.3;[112] indeed, it is a jurisdiction that must be decided independently of CPR, r 44.3 in that 'Part 36 trumps Part 44'.[113] In particular, where a party's entitlement to costs has arisen by reason of him having beaten a Part 36 Offer, the court would have to be persuaded that there was something unjust in applying the normal rule.[114] It is not enough that a party demonstrates what would have happened under CPR, r 44.3.[115] (This does not prevent the court from taking the factors in CPR, r 44.3(4) into account, however, as they may serve as being a guide to the types of factors that are relevant to the exercise of the court's discretion under CPR, r 36.14.[116])

14.54 CPR, r 36.14(4) gives specific guidance as to the factors that the court will take into account when considering whether or not it is just to make the award; those factors are:

- the terms of any Part 36 offer;
- the stage in the proceedings when any Part 36 offer was made, including, in particular, how long before the trial started the offer was made;
- the information available to the parties at the time when the Part 36 offer was made; and
- the conduct of the parties with regard to the giving or refusing to give information for the purposes of enabling the offer to be made or evaluated.

This list is not an exhaustive list; indeed, CPR, r 36.14(4) says in terms that the court will take into account 'all the circumstances of the case'. There are instances, for example, of the court depriving the offeror of some of all of the benefits of his offer on the grounds of his poor conduct.[117] One factor that is not on this list (because it is an inadmissible factor) is the amount of the costs claimed by the parties; whilst he expressed considerable regret at having to make such a finding, Ward LJ has confirmed that the court is not permitted to take that factor into account.[118] Each case will turn on its own facts, but it is worth saying a word or two about conduct, confusing offers, and inadequate information.

---

[109] They are set out in CPR, r 36.14(6); see **14.29**.
[110] CPR, r 36.14(2) (for defendants) and CPR, r 36.14(3) (for claimants).
[111] *Huck v Robson* [2002] EWCA Civ 398 at [63].
[112] *Matthews (a patient) v Metal Improvements Co Inc* [2007] EWCA Civ 215, per Chadwick LJ. This case was decided under the 'old' Part 36, so it should be approached with some caution. It would probably not be helpful to draw any point of principle from it beyond the very general statement made above.
[113] See *Shovelar v Lane* [2011] EWCA Civ 802 at [52], per Ward LJ.
[114] *Fulham Leisure Holdings Ltd v Nicholson Graham & Jones* [2006] EWHC 2428 (Ch).
[115] See *Walsh v Singh (aka Buddha and Walsh)* [2011] EWCA Civ 80 at [7], per Arden LJ
[116] See *Walsh v Singh (aka Buddha and Walsh)* [2011] EWCA Civ 80 at [7], per Arden LJ.
[117] See, for example, *Walsh v Singh (aka Buddha and Walsh)* [2011] EWCA Civ 80 in which the offeror was denied part of his costs to take account of his poor conduct.
[118] *Shovelar v Lane* [2011] EWCA Civ 802 at [53], per Ward LJ.

Conduct

14.55 There are instances of the court depriving the offeror of some of all of the benefits of his offer on the grounds of his poor conduct.[119] As mentioned above, the court would have to be persuaded that there was something unjust in applying the normal rule;[120] it is not enough that a party demonstrates what would have happened had the court been exercising its powers under CPR, r 44.3.[121]

Confusing offers

14.56 Although it may also be analysed in terms of whether an offer has been beaten, the court may find that it would be unjust to allow an offeror to take the benefit of a baffling offer. In particular, Arden LJ has confirmed that where an offer is found to be difficult to evaluate and confusing, it is within the discretion of the court to find that a party cannot be penalised for not having accepted it.[122] (It is also possible for the court to find that an offer is so unclear that it was not a Part 36 offer at all: see **14.20**.)

Inadequate information

14.57 It may be that an offeree is unable to evaluate an offer because he does not have the requisite information. Where those are the circumstances, Lord Woolf MR has confirmed that it is open to the court not to award the offeror the benefit of the offer.[123] In the context of an offeree reasonably requiring time to consider expert evidence, Toulson J allowed protection from the effect of the offer, but only up to that stage by which the offeree had been afforded a reasonable opportunity to examine the evidence.[124] More recent decisions have tended to place more of an emphasis on negotiation, ADR and the need for the offeree to ask for clarification. Ward LJ, for example, had this to say on the point:[125]

> 'It is almost inevitable in all litigation that the nature of the outcome cannot be certainly predicted until after the evidence has been given and even then there is no certainty as to the outcome until the judge has decided the case on that evidence. In this litigation the [evidence was such that] the litigation [was] all the more speculative. Far from there being a reason not to apply Part 36, it is in my judgment all the more reason for parties faced with that dilemma to make or to accept proper offers under Part 36. Not to beat the Part 36 offer has hazardous consequences as this case demonstrates. In these circumstances it is better to mediate than to litigate.'

As such, an offeree who declines to accept an offer on the grounds that he is not able to assess the value of the claim may be adopting a risky strategy. That said, each case will turn on its own facts, and there will, no doubt, continue to be cases in which the court's sympathy will lie with the offeree.

---

[119] See, for example, *Walsh v Singh (aka Buddha and Walsh)* [2011] EWCA Civ 80 in which the offeror was denied part of his costs to take account of his poor conduct.
[120] *Fulham Leisure Holdings Ltd v Nicholson Graham & Jones* [2006] EWHC 2428 (Ch).
[121] See *Walsh v Singh (aka Buddha and Walsh)* [2011] EWCA Civ 80 at [7], per Arden LJ.
[122] *Rio Properties Inc v Gibson Dunn & Crutcher* [2005] EWCA Civ 534.
[123] *Ford v GKR Construction Ltd* [2000] 1 WLR 1397; although a pre-CPR case, see *Burgess v British Steel plc* [2000] PIQR Q240, in which it was found that the knowledge of the offeree was sufficiently good to know whether to accept the offer.
[124] *R v Secretary of State, Ex Parte Factortame* (unreported) 18 October 2000, QBD.
[125] *Shovelar v Lane* [2011] EWCA Civ 802 at [53], [54] per Ward LJ. This was on the grounds that costs would be assessed at a reasonable sum on assessment.

ACCEPTANCE OF OFFERS

14.58 Acceptance of an offer may be in any one of three circumstances:

(1)   within the relevant period (see **14.15** for an explanation of that term);
(2)   following the expiry of the relevant period; and
(3)   following the expiry of the relevant period but after renewal of the offer.

Each of these is discussed in turn.

Acceptance within the relevant period

14.59 In the following circumstances, the court's permission is required to accept a Part 36 offer:[126]

- where the offer has been made by one or more, but not all, of a number of defendants, and neither of the conditions in CPR, r 36.12(2) or (3) has been met (see the footnotes);[127]
- where the offer includes deductible benefits, the relevant period has expired and further deductible amounts have been paid to the claimant since the date of the offer;[128]
- where an apportionment is required under CPR, r 41.3A;[129] and
- where the trial has started.[130]

Rix LJ has confirmed that a significant change of circumstances would not give rise to a general ground on which the court's permission is required to accept a Part 36 offer.[131] Likewise, Coulson J has confirmed that there is no implied term that an offer cannot be accepted once the trial has started; he doubted if there was ever a basis for coming to such a conclusion and explained that even if there was, it would run counter to the provisions in CPR, r 36.9(3)(d).[132]

14.60 Where the permission of the court is required, the court will, in default of agreement, make an order dealing with costs.[133] Where the court's permission is not required, a Part 36 offer may be accepted by serving written notice of the acceptance on

---

[126]   CPR, r 36.9(3).
[127]   See CPR, r 39.9(3)(a) and CPR, r 36.12, relevant parts of the latter of which reads as follows:
  '(2)   If the defendants are sued jointly or in the alternative, the claimant may accept the offer if—
  (a)   he discontinues his claim against those defendants who have not made the offer; and
  (b)   those defendants give written consent to the acceptance of the offer.
  (3)   If the claimant alleges that the defendants have a several liability to him, the claimant may—
  (a)   accept the offer; and
  (b)   continue with his claims against the other defendants if he is entitled to do so.
[128]   See CPR, r 36.9(3)(b) and CPR, r 36.15(3)(b).
[129]   See CPR, r 36.9(3)(c) and CPR, r 41.3A; this relates to claims under the Fatal Accidents Act 1976 and Law Reform (Miscellaneous Provisions) Act 1934.
[130]   See CPR, r 36.9(3)(d); this provision reflects Brooke LJ's view under the 'old' Part 36 that it was doubtful whether an offer could be accepted after the hearing to which it related had begun: *Hawley v Luminar Leisure plc* [2006] EWCA Civ 30.
[131]   See *C v D* [2011] EWCA Civ 646 at [20].
[132]   Which reads 'The court's permission is required to accept a Part 36 offer where . . . the trial has started'. See *Sampla v Rushmoor Borough Council* [2008] EWHC 2616 (TCC) at [39]–[41].
[133]   CPR, r 36.9(4).

the offeror.[134] Unless the parties are in agreement, an offer may not be accepted if the trial has concluded.[135] The costs consequences of such an acceptance will depend on the circumstances, as follows.

Whole of the claim and not less than 21 days before trial

14.61 Where the offer is in respect of the whole of the claim[136] and where the offer was made not less than 21 days before the start of trial,[137] acceptance will result in the claimant being entitled to costs on the standard basis[138] up to the date of service of notice of acceptance;[139] there is no scope within the CPR for the court to exercise its discretion in that regard and, in particular, there is no scope for the court to make an award of costs on the indemnity basis.[140]

Less than 21 days before the start of trial

14.62 Where the offer was made less than 21 days before the start of trial, acceptance will leave the costs at large, to be determined by the court in default of agreement.[141]

Part of claim

14.63 Where the offer is in respect of part of the claim, that part will be stayed and the court will decide the appropriate order for costs.[142] If the claimant abandons the balance of the claim, then, unless the court orders otherwise, the claimant will be entitled to the costs of the whole of the claim up to the date of serving notice of acceptance. It will, however, not always be obvious whether a party can be said to have abandoned an issue. In a case in which the defendant had made an offer putatively in respect of only one aspect of the claimant's injuries (this being on the basis that the other injuries had allegedly been caused by someone else), Stadlen J found that the offer was capable of being accepted in respect of the whole claim and that the Claimant was entitled to her costs accordingly.[143]

14.64 If the Part 36 offer states that it takes into account the counterclaim, the claimant's costs will include the costs incurred in dealing with the defendant's counterclaim.[144]

Acceptance following expiry of the relevant period

14.65 CPR, r 36.9(2) states in terms that where the court's permission is not required (see **14.59**), a Part 36 Offer may be accepted at any time; this includes the period after the expiry of the relevant period. Rix LJ has confirmed that a Part 36 offer does not

---

[134] CPR, r 36.9(1).
[135] CPR, r 36.9(5).
[136] CPR, r 36.10(1) and (2).
[137] CPR, r 36.10(1) and (2)(b).
[138] CPR, r 36.10(3).
[139] CPR, r 36.10(1).
[140] If the offeree wants to argue for costs on the indemnity basis, it would be permissible to wait until immediately after the expiry of the relevant period before accepting the offer; this would allow the matter to be put before the court.
[141] CPR, r 36.10(4)(a).
[142] CPR r 36.11(3)(a) and (b).
[143] *Sutherland v Turnbull* [2010] EWHC 2699 (QB) at [29]–[32].
[144] CPR, r 36.10(6).

cease to be capable of acceptance after the expiry a reasonable period time: it closes only with express withdrawal.[145] Where, in the absence of agreement, an offeree wishes to accept an offer out of time he may do so, but the costs will remain at large to be decided by the court.[146] Unless the court 'orders otherwise', the claimant will be entitled to the costs of the proceedings up to the date on which the relevant period expired; the offeree will be liable for the offeror's costs for the period from the date of expiry of the relevant period to the date of acceptance.[147] Lang J had this to say about the relevant test:[148]

> '[The test] is similar to that set out in rule 36.14. The test which I apply is whether the usual costs order set out in Rule 36.10 (5) should be departed from because it would be unjust for the [offeree] to pay the [offeror's] costs after the expiry of the relevant period, in the particular circumstances of this case. Such a departure would be the exception rather than the rule.'

An example of circumstances in which the court has 'ordered otherwise' is where the offeree was a litigant in person who accepted the offer after having been reminded of the existence of the offer by the offeror.[149] Lang J has commented that the fact that the offeree is a patient would not be sufficient, of itself, to justify 'ordering otherwise', although this may be factor to be taken into account.[150]

Renewed offer

14.66 Where a claimant's Part 36 offer has been 'equalled' (to use a useful colloquialism) as a result of it having been renewed (or as a result of an identical offer having been made by the defendant), and where that offer is accepted within the renewed relevant period, the claimant will be entitled to costs up to the date of service of the notice of acceptance. Coulson J has found that, in those circumstances, an indemnity costs presumption should not be imported into CPR, r 36.10.[151]

REJECTION OF OFFERS

14.67 A Part 36 offer is not capable of being rejected in the sense that rejection will determine the offeree's right subsequently to accept it. It has been argued that the common law continues to apply to the extent that the notion of rejection of offers applies to Part 36 in just the same way as it applies to any other type of offer,[152] but first

---

[145] See *C v D* [2011] EWCA Civ 646 at [57].
[146] CPR, r 36.10(4).
[147] CPR, r 36.10(5).
[148] *Lumb v Hampsey* [2011] EWHC 2808 (QB) at [6]; in formulating his view, Lang J referred to *Matthews v Metal Improvements* [2007] EWCA Civ 215 with apparent approval
[149] *Kunaka v Barclays Bank plc* [2010] EWCA Civ 1035.
[150] *Lumb v Hampsey* [2011] EWHC 2808 (QB) at [4].
[151] *Fitzpatrick Contractors Ltd v Tyco Fire & Integrated Solutions (UK) Ltd* [2009] EWHC 274 (TCC) at [28]; see CPR, r 36.10(3).
[152] That argument was based on an analogy with withdrawals under the 'old' Part 36; broadly speaking, Aldous LJ found that the common law did apply in the absence of an express provision that it should not: *Scammell v Dicker* [2001] 1 WLR 631. This is to be contrasted with payments into court, which were entirely procedural and not governed by the common law (see *Cumper v Pothecary* [1941] 2 KB 58 at 67, which was affirmed as being good law post-CPR in *Flynn v Sougall* [2004] EWCA Civ 873 at [26]).

Coulson J[153] and then Moore-Bick LJ (with whom Sir Anthony May P and Carnwath LJ agreed)[154] rejected this analysis. Moore-Bick LJ had this to say on the point:[155]

> 'Basic concepts of offer and acceptance clearly underpin Pt 36, but that is inevitable given that it contains a voluntary procedure under which either party may take the initiative to bring about a consensual resolution of the dispute. Such concepts are part of the landscape in which everyone conducts their daily life. It does not follow, however, that Pt 36 should be understood as incorporating all the rules of law governing the formation of contracts, some of which are quite technical in nature. Indeed, it is not desirable that it should do so. Certainty is as much to be commended in procedural as in substantive law, especially, perhaps, in a procedural code which must be understood and followed by ordinary citizens who wish to conduct their own litigation.'

Thus, in strictly legal terms, a rejection of a Part 36 offer is of no effect (save, perhaps, as being a background fact for the purposes of subsequently deciding the incidence of costs); 'rejections' may continue to be made for the purposes of negotiation, however.

WITHDRAWAL OF OFFERS

14.68 Before expiry of the relevant period, a Part 36 offer may be withdrawn or its terms changed to be less advantageous to the offeree, but only if the court gives permission.[156] There is, as yet, no authority as to how the court's discretion should be exercised, but if any analogy with the 'old' Part 36 can be drawn, the discretion is unfettered.[157] It is likely that one factor the court will take into account is whether the offeree has tried to accept the offer and in what circumstances.[158]

14.69 After expiry of the relevant period, permission of the court is not required: provided that the offeree has not previously served notice of acceptance, the offeror may withdraw the offer or change its terms.[159] This is achieved by serving notice of withdrawal or notice of change, as the case may be.[160] There is no such thing as an implied withdrawal; this was made clear by Moore-Bick LJ in the following terms:[161]

> 'In my view that leaves no room for the concept of implied withdrawal; it requires express notice in writing in terms which bring home to the offeree that the offer has been withdrawn. If justification for that requirement is sought, it can be found . . . in the need for clarity and certainty in the operation of the Pt 36 procedure. [In] order to avoid uncertainty [the notice] should include an express reference to the date of the offer and its terms, together with some words making it clear that it is withdrawn. There may, of course, be cases in which the terms of the notice are less clear than might be wished so that there is room for argument about whether the notice fulfils the requirements of the rule. However, that is a different question.'

---

[153] *Sampla v Rushmoor Borough Council* [2008] EWHC 2616 (TCC).
[154] *Gibbon v Manchester City Council* [2010] EWCA Civ 726.
[155] *Gibbon v Manchester City Council* [2010] EWCA Civ 726 at [6].
[156] CPR, r 36.3(5).
[157] See *Capital Bank plc v Stickland* [2004] EWCA Civ 1677; see also *Cumper v Pothecary* [1941] 2 KB 58. Permission will be by no means automatic; under the old provisions, May LJ found that a defendant had, by making an early offer, secured the advantage of an earlier payment and that this should be given a degree of weight: *Flynn v Scougall* [2004] EWCA Civ 873
[158] Whilst decided under the 'old' provisions, see *Flynn v Scougall* [2004] EWCA Civ 873.
[159] CPR, r 36.3(6).
[160] CPR, r 36.3(7).
[161] *Gibbon v Manchester City Council* [2010] EWCA Civ 726 at [17].

The effect of this is that an offer can be accepted even though it has become obvious to all concerned that it was no longer an appropriate offer.[162] Likewise, it is not possible both to comply with Part 36 and to contain within the offer a withdrawal that will be effective after a stated period of time (ie, an offer that is akin to a time-limited offer);[163] on the whole, such an offer will be interpreted as being an open-ended offer which has the superadded component that no application to withdraw it will be made within the stated period (see **14.25–14.27**).

14.70 Difficulties may arise where the defendant wishes to withdraw or reduce a Part 36 offer during the 21 days for which it must remain open for acceptance. In these circumstances, the parties may get embroiled in 'an unseemly adversarial scramble' (as May LJ put it),[164] in which the offeree races to accept the offer before the offeror is able to obtain permission to withdraw it.

14.71 While he was dealing with the topic in the context of Part 36 payments rather than offers, May LJ explained the solution:[165]

'... [It] would be most unfortunate if [the offeree] were able to defeat [the offeror's] application for leave to withdraw a payment in by giving notice of acceptance before the [offeror's] summons could be heard. Since [the offeree's] acceptance would not have terminated the action, but merely stayed it, I think that the court may notionally remove the stay and proceed to hear the application. [The offeree's] acceptance does not prevent the court from allowing [the offeror] to withdraw, but is obviously an important consideration to be taken into account in deciding whether he should be given leave to do so.'

As to procedure, May LJ went on to give the following guidance:

'If, exceptionally, [the offeror] wishes within the 21 days to withdraw or reduce a Part 36 payment, he should apply for permission to do so and inform [the offeree] of his application. If [the offeree] wishes to accept the Part 36 payment within the 21 days without permission, he should give the requisite written notice of acceptance. The stage is then set for the court to decide [the offeror's] application in the light of [the offeree's] notice of acceptance.'

14.72 Although the court tends to apply a more flexible approach under the CPR than was applied previously,[166] the pre-CPR test that there must be 'a sufficient change of circumstance since the money was paid to make it just that the defendant should have an opportunity of withdrawing or reducing his payment'[167] has been adopted as consistent with the overriding objective.[168]

---

[162] See, for example, *Mahmood v Elmi* [2010] EWHC 1933 (QB) in which Cox J found that an offer had been accepted notwithstanding the fact that it had become clear that the value of the claim was more than eight times the amount of the offer.

[163] *C v D* [2011] EWCA Civ 646 [35]–[44], per Rix LJ.

[164] *Flynn v Sougall* [2004] EWCA Civ 873 at [30].

[165] In which May LJ adopted a passage from the judgment of HH Judge John Newey QC in *Manku v Seehra* (1987) 7 Con LR 90.

[166] See, for example, *Marsh v Frenchay Healthcare (1 February 2001)*, Curtis J and *MRW Technologies v Cecil Holdings (22 June 2001)*, Garland J, both of which feature in May LJ's judgment in *Flynn*.

[167] Per Goddard LJ in *Cumper v Pothecary* [1941] 2 KB 58.

[168] *Flynn v Sougall* [2004] EWCA Civ 873 at [39].

14.73 If a Part 36 offer is withdrawn, it will not mechanistically have the consequences set out in Part 36.[169] This does not mean, however, that such an offer will be of no relevance at all when the court comes to exercise its discretion as to costs; this is because a withdrawn Part 36 offer is a species of 'admissible offer'.[170] Indeed, under the present costs regime,[171] the same is true of any offer that has been withdrawn, regardless of whether it was a Part 36 offer or an admissible offer. Ward LJ made the following comments about the effect of withdrawn offers:[172]

> '... The principal error in my judgment, was not to distinguish between the question whether the *Calderbank* letter was still on the negotiating table and the question whether its terms materially related to the result of the appeal. That it had lapsed, whether by rejection, non acceptance within a reasonable time, or its withdrawal, matters not. It remained material as a fact in the history of litigation. Had it been accepted within a reasonable time after it was made, and the learned Judge correctly found that it should have been because the Plaintiff eventually did less well than they had been offered, then there would have been no need for the appeal at all. An appeal became necessary because, without it, the wrong order would have stood uncorrected.'

Thus, a withdrawn offer remains relevant as it is part of the relevant history of the proceedings.

14.74 Ward LJ was giving judgment in a pre-CPR decision, but there are several decision made under the CPR that confirm the position. Whilst it was a decision relating to the 'old' CPR Part 36 (see **13.45**), Longmore LJ made it clear that the court should not disregard an offer merely because it may have been withdrawn.[173] Dyson LJ has confirmed that Ward LJ's analysis remains of strong persuasive force under the CPR.[174] In a catastrophic injuries case which was upheld on appeal on a different point,[175] MacDuff J referred to a withdrawn offer as continuing to have 'costs potency'.[176] Teare J came to much the same conclusion in an admiralty case[177] and Rix LJ came to a similar conclusion in a dispute concerning negligent construction work.[178] Thus, there can be little doubt that a withdrawn Part 36 offer is capable of influencing the incidence of costs.

14.75 When faced with a 'potent' but withdrawn offer, an offeree may argue that there would be injustice in allowing that offer – which he can no longer accept – to sit in the

---

[169] *French v Groupama Insurance Co Ltd* [2011] EWCA Civ 1119 at [41] quoted at 6.69A. Also see *Epsom College v Pierse Contracting Southern Ltd (formerly Biseley Construction Ltd) (in liq)* [2011] EWCA Civ 1449 at [54] *et seq*, per Rix LJ at [54], per Rix LJ.

[170] *Epsom College v Pierse Contracting Southern Ltd (formerly Biseley Construction Ltd) (in liq)* [2011] EWCA Civ 1449 at [54] *et seq*, per Rix LJ.

[171] Under the RSC the position was less clear; see *Bristol and West Building Society v Evans and Bullock* (unreported) 5 February 1996, CA. and compare this with *The Toni* [1974] 1 Lloyd's Reports 489 at 496–497 in which Megaw LJ declined to give weight to an open offer that had been withdrawn. It is possible that the earlier cases would still apply in tribunals in which the CPR does not apply, but this seems not to be borne out in practice (see, for example, *Owners and/or Bareboat Charterers and/or Sub Bareboat Charterers of the Ship Samco Europe v Owners of the Ship MSC Prestige* [2011] EWHC 1580 (Admlty), at [27]).

[172] *Bristol and West Building Society v Evans and Bullock* (unreported) 5 February 1996, CA.

[173] *Farag v Commissioner of Police of the Metropolis* [2005] EWCA Civ 1814.

[174] *Stokes Pension Fund v Western Power Distribution (South West) plc* [2005] EWCA Civ 854.

[175] The appeal being *Pankhurst v (1) White and (2) Motor Insurers Bureau* [2010] EWCA Civ 1445: see **30.33** and **36.52**.

[176] *Pankhurst v White* [2010] EWHC 311 (QB), per Macduff J at [40],

[177] *Owners and/or Bareboat Charterers and/or Sub Bareboat Charterers of the Ship Samco Europe v Owners of the Ship MSC Prestige* [2011] EWHC 1580 (Admlty), at [26].

[178] *Epsom College v Pierse Contracting Southern Ltd (formerly Biseley Construction Ltd) (in liq)* [2011] EWCA Civ 1449 at [54] *et seq*.

background operating against him. MacDuff J has acknowledged those concerns, but he rejected the argument by saying that if an offeree had failed to accept a reasonable offer which had subsequently been withdrawn, the offeree should appreciate his costs risk and take protective steps by making his *own* offer.[179] Teare J has explained that there is no reason why an offeree cannot protect himself against future costs by making an offer in exactly the same terms as the one that puts him at risk.[180] Whilst there is no authority on the point, where an offeree becomes an offeror in this way, it is likely that the court would deal with the matter by making different orders covering different periods (see CPR, r 44.3(6)(c)). If, however, the original offeror is unable to give a cogent explanation as to why he is now unable to bear the terms of what in effect was his own offer, it would be open to the court to find that less weight should be given to the initial offer. Each case must be decided on its own facts.

14.76 More details about the effect of admissible offers in general may be found at **6.53–6.71**.

TIME-LIMITED OFFERS

14.77 There is, under the 'new' Part 36, no room for a time-limited offer or for any type of offer that lapses by reason of its own terms (see **14.15** and **14.25–14.27**).[181] Rix LJ explained that this was for the following reasons:[182] (i) when read in conjunction with CPR, r 36.3(5), (6) and (7), the wording of CPR, r 36.9(2) (that an offer may be accepted at any time) indicates that a Part 36 offer may come to an end by withdrawal rather than by its own terms, and that after the relevant period has expired, the offeror can withdraw the offer *only* by serving notice of withdrawal on the offeree (ii) the policy of Part 36 is such that for the benefits and sanctions therein to work, the offer must be kept open, and (iii) it would be unfair if a claimant were to be able to maintain the benefit of a Part 36 offer which had lapsed but not able to maintain the benefit of an offer which had been withdrawn.

14.78 The issue of whether an offer that putatively contains a time limit is to be construed as being a time-limited offer or a Part 36 offer is addressed above (**14.25–14.73**). Where such an offer cannot be interpreted as being a Part 36 offer, it will, however, be an 'admissible offer' (see, by way of analogy, **14.73**). As to admissible offers in general, see **6.53–6.71**.

PROCEEDINGS BROUGHT TO AN END

14.79 Whilst based on a concession by counsel, Kenneth Parker J appeared to accept that where proceedings have been brought to an end (whether on the merits or by reason of procedural default), it is no longer possible for an offeree to accept a Part 36 offer.[183]

---

[179] *Pankhurst v White* [2010] EWHC 311 (QB), per Macduff J at [36]; this reasoning was endorsed (albeit obiter) by Teare J in *Owners and/or Bareboat Charterers and/or Sub Bareboat Charterers of the Ship Samco Europe v Owners of the Ship MSC Prestige* [2011] EWHC 1580 (Admlty) at [23] and [26].

[180] *Owners and/or Bareboat Charterers and/or Sub Bareboat Charterers of the Ship Samco Europe v Owners of the Ship MSC Prestige* [2011] EWHC 1580 (Admlty) at [26].

[181] *C v D* [2011] EWCA Civ 646 at [40].

[182] *C v D* [2011] EWCA Civ 646 at [35]–[44].

[183] *Joyce v West Bus Coach Services Ltd* [2012] EWHC 404 (QB) at [33].

As to the situation where this has happened as a result of the claim being struck out under an 'unless' order, he had this to say:[184]

> 'The reason why the dismissal of the claim or the entry of judgment precludes the acceptance of a Part 36 offer is that on dismissal or entry of judgment the claim is to all intents and purposes at an end. But that is also the position where a statement of case or claim has been struck out under an "unless" order. The purpose of the "unless" order is to avoid the need for any further application or hearing to obtain dismissal of the claim.'

Kenneth Parker J went on to say that the fact that the defaulting party might have made an application for relief from sanctions did not result in the offer being held 'on life support ... awaiting the ministering dispensation of relief by the Court so as to obviate final extinction'.[185]

---

[184] *Joyce v West Bus Coach Services Ltd* [2012] EWHC 404 (QB) at [34].
[185] *Joyce v West Bus Coach Services Ltd* [2012] EWHC 404 (QB) at [35].

Chapter 15

COSTS CAPPING, BUDGETING AND PROTECTIVE COSTS ORDERS

15.1   Costs capping orders are orders which pre-emptively restrict the amount of costs that a party can recover in litigation. The CPR provide the following definition:[1]

> 'A costs capping order is an order limiting the amount of future costs (including disbursements) which a party may recover pursuant to an order for costs subsequently made.'

The costs which are pre-emptively capped are referred to as future costs.[2] Once it has been made, unless it is varied, a costs capping order will limit the costs recoverable by the party to whom it relates to the amount stated in the order.[3] This is one of the ways in which costs capping orders differ from costs budgeting (see **15.65**).

THE HISTORY OF THE JURISDICTION

15.2   Although costs capping orders are now regulated by rules of court (CPR, rr 44.18–44.20), those provisions describe a regime which (with one possible exception)[4] is noticeably similar to the judge-made regime which preceded it. This means that older authorities are likely still to have a part to play. In order to know their true relevance, it is necessary to know the context in which those authorities were decided. Thus the history of the jurisdiction remains relevant.

15.3   Immediately prior to the introduction of the CPR the court articulated – but did not exercise – a jurisdiction to make pre-emptive orders limiting a party's liability to pay costs (although this was only in certain public law cases).[5] Despite the fact that pre-emptive costs orders were not unknown under the RSC,[6] in the private law setting, costs capping was not perceived as being generally available.[7] To a large extent, this was as a result of the court giving precedence to the principle that the winner should be compensated in costs.[8]

---

[1]   CPR, r 44.18(1).
[2]   CPR, r 44.18(2); that term excludes additional liability.
[3]   CPR, r 44.18(7).
[4]   There is one potential exception, in that the CPD seems to have introduced a test of exceptionality; this is discussed below.
[5]   See 'Public interest challenges' below.
[6]   See, as probably the first example, *Davies v Eli Lilly & Co* [1987] 1 WLR 1141.
[7]   In *MacDonald v Horn* [1995] ICR 685, for example, Hoffman LJ commented that 'It is difficult to imagine a case falling within the general principle in which it would be possible for the court properly to exercise its discretion in advance of the substantive decision.'
[8]   For a detailed exposition of this history of costs in this regard, see *R (on the application of Corner House Research) v Secretary of State for Trade and Industry* [2005] EWCA Civ 192 at [6]–[23].

15.4   The landscape changed with the introduction of the CPR, but it was striking that when they were first introduced, the CPR lacked express provision for costs capping orders. This was despite the fact that the concept of 'costs budgeting' had widely been canvassed during consultation; as is explained below (see **15.66**), this was largely because the concept of case management was believed to be preferable to costs management.

15.5   This omission contrasted with the situation in arbitral proceedings, in which specific statutory provision had existed since 1996; those provisions empowered arbitrators to direct that the recoverable costs of the arbitration, or of any part of the arbitral proceedings, should be limited to a specified amount.[9]

15.6   Given the fact that the express provisions in arbitral proceedings were formulated at roughly the same time as the CPR, it was thought by some that the absence of express provision within the CPR was a deliberate omission indicating that the court did not have the power to impose a costs cap.

15.7   A series of decisions, both at first instance and on appeal, proved this view to be incorrect. It is now established law that costs capping orders are available in both private and public law cases. In so far as private law is concerned, the first reported case to deal with costs capping (albeit only as an obiter comment) was *Griffiths v Solutia UK Ltd*, in which Sir Christopher Staughton, after having reminded himself of the provisions in arbitral proceedings, made the following remarks:[10]

> '[Surely] case management powers will allow a judge in the future to exercise the power of limiting costs, either indirectly or even directly, so that they are proportionate to the amount involved.'

15.8   Shortly thereafter the concept of costs capping moved from that which was being proposed to that which was being imposed. The first orders were made in public law cases,[11] but these were soon followed by decisions in private law cases. In clinical negligence group litigation Gage J held that the court's general powers of case management were sufficiently wide to encompass the making of a costs capping order both in group litigation (with which he was then concerned) and in other actions.[12] Hallett J agreed with that proposition.[13]

15.9   In 2007 the Court of Appeal was presented with the opportunity to clarify the law. Buxton LJ explained that the court had drafted a 'comprehensive set of principles', but that after discussion with the Master of Rolls and the Deputy Head of Civil Justice, it was decided not to incorporate those principles in a judgment.[14] Any development of the law was to be a matter for the Rule Committee.

15.10   The Rule Committee set up a subcommittee whose remit was to examine all aspects of the matter other than protective costs orders. A consultation paper was published in 2008,[15] which was followed by responses in early 2009. On 6 April 2009, the

---

9   Arbitration Act 1996, s 65.
10   [2001] EWCA Civ 736 at [29].
11   See *R v Prime Minister ex p CND* [2002] EWHC 2712 (Admin).
12   *AB v Leeds Teaching Hospitals NHS Trust* [2003] EWHC 1034 (QB).
13   *Ledward Claimants v Kent & Medway Health Authority* [2003] EWHC 2551 (QB).
14   *Willis v Nicolson* [2007] EWCA Civ 199 at [24].
15   *Civil Procedure Rules: Costs Capping Orders* (Ministry of Justice, 11 September 2008).

new rules came into force;[16] whilst they are not expressed as being such, to a large extent they are a codification of the pre-existing law.

THE SOURCE OF THE JURISDICTION

15.11 As with almost all modern costs orders, the power by which costs capping orders are made ultimately derives from statute. Section 51(3) of the Senior Courts Act 1981 provides that a court shall have 'full power to determine by whom and to what extent costs are to be paid'; there is nothing within that Act which limits the court to exercising this power only retrospectively.[17]

15.12 The power to make a pre-emptive costs order (such as a costs capping order) is subject to the prevailing rules of court. Although more general vires probably continue to exist,[18] specific provision for costs capping orders is made in CPR, rr 44.18–44.20. Those provisions are described in the relevant paragraphs below. Those provisions do not relate to protective costs orders;[19] to that extent, the residual general vires mentioned above appear to continue to have relevance.

GENERAL PROVISIONS

15.13 A costs capping order may pertain to the whole litigation or any issues which are ordered to be tried separately.[20] It is also possible to make a costs capping order relating to the costs of particular steps or issues.[21]

15.14 The court may make a costs capping order against any or all of the parties at any stage of proceedings;[22] an order against all the parties is often referred to as a 'mutual capping order'.

15.15 The CPR provide that a costs capping order may be made only where the following conditions are met:[23]

- that it is in the interests of justice to make such an order;
- that there is a substantial risk that, without such an order, costs will be disproportionately incurred; and
- that the court is not satisfied that that risk can be adequately controlled by:
  - case management directions or orders made under Part 3; and
  - detailed assessment of costs.

---

[16] Civil Procedure (Amendment No 3) Rules 2008 (SI 2008/3327), r 9.
[17] *AB v Leeds Teaching Hospitals NHS Trust* [2003] EWHC 1034 (QB).
[18] That power being that which derives from CPR, r 3.1(2)(m); see *King v Telegraph Group Ltd* [2005] 1 WLR 2282 at [82].
[19] CPR, r 44.18(3).
[20] CPR, r 44.18(4).
[21] In *A&E Television Networks LLC v Discovery Communications Europe Ltd* [2011] EWHC 1038 (Ch) at [17] in which Mann J made a costs capping order limiting the costs of certain work that a solicitor wished to do in house to no more than would have been incurred had it been done by an outside agency.
[22] CPR, r 44.18(5).
[23] CPR, r 44.18(5)(a), (b) and (c).

As will be explained over the next few pages, these conditions are almost exactly the same as those which already existed as a result of judge-made law.

15.16 The need to consider whether the conditions have been met means that the court must make a number of findings and must then exercise its discretion. The following factors may be relevant to the exercise of the court's discretion:[24]

- whether there is a substantial imbalance between the financial position of the parties;
- whether the costs of determining the amount of the cap are likely to be proportionate to the overall costs of the litigation;
- the stage which the proceedings have reached; and
- the costs which have been incurred to date and the future costs.

Whilst there is no authority on the point, the wording of the CPR suggests that it is mandatory for the court to take these factors into account. The CPD makes provision for the court to be provided with the requisite estimates, schedules, etc, to enable it to discharge that duty.[25]

15.17 The CPD states that a costs capping order will be made only in 'exceptional circumstances'.[26] This is the one area in which the new regime differs from the judge-made law; this is because Gage J – who many would regard as being the architect of judge made costs capping orders – has on more than one occasion emphasised that exceptional circumstances are not a condition for making a costs capping order.[27]

15.18 This creates a degree of uncertainty as to what the law is. This is because the CPD has not been made by the Civil Procedure Rule Committee, it has not been laid before Parliament and it has no legislative force.[28] It could be argued, in view of the fact that the CPR themselves carefully preserve the judge-made law, that the CPD is ultra vires in its attempt to do otherwise. Equally, it could be argued that costs capping orders are wholly procedural in nature, and that the CPD is, therefore, simply performing its natural function of regulating procedure. The point is arguable either way.

15.19 Another possibility (which is unsupported by any authority) is that the need for 'exceptionality' will be treated in much the same way as it is in applications for protective costs orders, ie that it should not be seen as an additional threshold criteria, but merely as a prediction as to the effect of applying the true threshold criteria;[29] for reasons set out below, however, at least one case decided shortly after the introduction of the new regime seems not to have been decided in this manner.[30]

---

[24]   CPR, r 44.18(6)(a)–(d).
[25]   See CPD, arts 23A.3 and 23A.4.
[26]   CPD, art 23A.1.
[27]   See, for example, *Smart v East Cheshire NHS Trust* [2003] EWHC 2806 at [22] and *AB v Leeds Teaching Hospitals NHS Trust* [2003] EWHC 1034 (QB) at [19].
[28]   See, in particular, *Ku v Ungi* [2005] EWCA Civ 475 at [47]; see also **3.31–3.40**.
[29]   *R (Compton) v Wiltshire Primary Care Trust* [2008] EWCA Civ 749 at [24], per Waller and Smith LJJ (Buxton LJ dissenting).
[30]   See *Peacock v MGN Ltd* [2009] EWHC 769 (QB) at [22].

IN WHAT CIRCUMSTANCES SHOULD A COSTS CAPPING ORDER BE MADE?

15.20 It is possible to identify five categories of case. They are: 'ordinary' claims; defamation claims; claims inviting partial orders; group litigation; and public law challenges. Each is considered in turn, but the last is sufficiently distinct from the other categories to merit being discussed separately at the end of this chapter. In addition, there are special provisions in proceedings relating to trusts; this is addressed at **37.14**.

'Ordinary' claims

15.21 This category includes (but will not automatically include) claims in the run of ordinary claims that are not group litigation and that are not defamation claims. As will be explained below, each case will turn on its own facts and it is not possible to say with any certainty what will be categorised as an 'ordinary' claim.

15.22 The approach to costs capping in ordinary cases was first articulated by Gage J in these terms:[31]

> 'In my judgment, the court should only consider making a costs-cap order in such cases [ie ordinary cases] where the applicant shows by evidence that there is a real and substantial risk that without such an order costs will be disproportionately or unreasonably incurred; and that this risk may not be managed by conventional case management and a detailed assessment of costs after a trial; and it is just to make such an order. It seems to me that it is unnecessary to ascribe to such a test the general heading of exceptional circumstances. I would expect that in the run of ordinary actions it would be rare for this test to be satisfied, but it is impossible to predict all the circumstances in which it may be said to arise.'

It can be seen that all of these principles have their counterparts in the new provisions:[32] the new provisions are slightly different in their wording, but (subject to what is said below) they are essentially the same. To that extent, the authorities decided before the new provisions were introduced could well still be relevant.

15.23 As has already been mentioned, there is uncertainty about whether the CPD has introduced a test of exceptionality; this ought to be borne in mind when considering authorities decided before 6 April 2009.

15.24 Although he seems not to have heard any argument about vires, Eady J regarded the exceptionality principle as being a significant fetter upon his discretion. While he began his judgment – in a case he had described as being a 'ding dong' dispute – on the footing that the need for exceptional circumstances was merely an expression of the fact that suitable cases for costs capping will be rare, his analysis led him to the conclusion that it was, in truth, a more restrictive principle:[33]

> 'If I had a free hand ... I should be strongly inclined to impose a costs cap and to refer the matter to a costs judge to address hourly rates ... [but] consistency in these matters is important and I do not have a free hand. I am inhibited both by the "exceptionality" principle and by the fact that I am satisfied that the risk of disproportionality could be adequately controlled by a costs judge at the stage of detailed assessment. While I take into

---

[31] *Smart v East Cheshire NHS Trust* [2003] EWHC 2806 at [22].
[32] See CPR, r 44.18(5).
[33] *Peacock v MGN Ltd* [2009] EWHC 769 (QB) at [22].

account [one of the party's] concerns arising from the "arms race", which I have just identified, I believe that his client should not be prejudiced on either hourly rates or leading counsel, if the costs judge is sufficiently robust, as has proved to be the case in the past.'

15.25 Where the case is an 'ordinary' case, it is a necessary criterion that there is a substantial risk that, without a costs capping order, costs will be disproportionately incurred; it is also a necessary criterion that the risk of disproportionate costs cannot be adequately controlled by case management directions, by orders made under CPR, Part 3, or by detailed assessment of costs.

15.26 No particular difficulty arises out of the first of these criteria: whether a case presents a risk of disproportionately incurred costs is a matter which will be decided on a case-by-case basis on the evidence available. The second criterion can be more problematic. This is because the very purpose of the detailed assessment procedure is (retrospectively) to manage costs so that they are reasonable; if the court assumes (as it usually will) that costs judges are able to achieve this objective, it will rarely be the case that this second criterion will be satisfied.

15.27 Indeed, Mann J had the following to say about what he called 'the normal role of the costs judge':[34]

'It is the normal role of the costs judge to filter out the sort of extravagant costs which have in fact, in some cases, led to the making of a costs-capping order. One should continue to expect them to be able to do that ... [One] would have thought that the exercise of doing that retrospectively (the costs judge's job) would be easier than doing it prospectively (the function of the costs-capping judge).'

15.28 This approach – pragmatic as it may be – is not without its problems. This is because the court's willingness or ability to make costs capping orders will be inverse to the perceived efficacy of the detailed assessment process. Given the fact that the detailed assessment process is, in theory if not always in practice, a process that is effectual at cutting unreasonable costs down to size, it is easy to see how the jurisdiction to make costs capping orders in ordinary cases would itself be cut down to nil.

15.29 In practice, the reality is that the jurisdiction in 'ordinary' cases has almost been cut down to nil. There are one or two arguments which can be raised, but they will infrequently present themselves and even less frequently succeed. One argument that is available is that a detailed assessment will not stop an 'arms race'; for example, if the claimant instructs a particularly costly counsel, then so will the defendant; costly counsel will expect to be attended at trial by his instructing solicitors and will expect a consultation; these costs might be entirely avoidable, but it is unlikely that they would be disallowed on assessment. That is a respectable argument, but even that rarely succeeds.[35]

15.30 For most practical purposes, on the basis of the law as it presently stands, the only circumstances in which the court is likely to make a costs capping order is if a case can be categorised as not being an 'ordinary' case (ie it is a defamation case or a group litigation case). That said, the new regime has only recently been introduced, and it could well be that future cases will clarify the law in such a way as to mark out cases

---

34 *Knight v Beyond Properties Pty Ltd* [2006] EWHC 1242 (Ch).
35 See, for example, *Peacock v MGN Ltd* [2009] EWHC 769 (QB) at [22].

which are suitable for a costs capping order. Indeed, it is wholly possible that the test of 'exceptionality' will develop in such a way as to increase, rather than decrease, the scope for making such orders.

15.31 It is worth pausing here to comment on *Sheppard v Essex Strategic Health Authority*.[36] This was a case which heralded what, with hindsight, must now be seen as a false dawn; Hallett J said:[37]

> '[It] is plain to me that, whether or not the CPR themselves made provision for cost-capping, there is a clear trend ... to active case management on the question of costs. The courts are moving, at whatever pace, toward a system of pre-emptive strikes in order to avoid the costs of litigation spiralling out of control, and becoming unreasonable or disproportionate. In my judgment, it is far better for the court to attempt control and budget for costs where appropriate, than to allow costs to be incurred and then have them submitted to detailed assessment after the event; an assessment, of course, that is meant to take place with the benefit of hindsight. It seems to me that such an approach is entirely in accordance with the spirit and the letter of the CPR.'

Hallett J did not focus on any threshold criteria; instead, she considered that she was able to deal with the matter on the merits of the individual case and to do what was most effective. Given that the threshold criteria are now mandatory, it is likely that *Sheppard* is of historical interest only.

Defamation claims

15.32 Defamation claims are in a category of their own. This is because:

(a)   the financial compensation is often very modest in comparison to the costs which are ultimately incurred;

(b)   such claims are often funded by way of conditional fee agreements which provide for a high success fee;

(c)   they are often pursued by claimants who are unable or unwilling to obtain insurance to cover the other side's costs in the event that the claim is lost; and

(d)   the potential high cost has a potential impact on defendant's ability to exercise its right of freedom of expression.

As is explained in **15.65** *et seq*, defamation claims are now the subject of a mandatory costs budgeting scheme. As such, much of what is set out below is largely redundant. It does, however, apply to cases issued before 1 October 2009 (see **15.68**).

15.33 Brooke LJ summarised this state of affairs:

> 'What is in issue ... is the appropriateness of arrangements whereby a defendant publisher will be required to pay up to twice the reasonable and proportionate costs of the claimant if he loses or concedes liability, and will almost certainly have to bear his own costs ... if he wins. The obvious unfairness of such a system is bound to have the chilling effect on a newspaper exercising its right to freedom of expression ...'

---

[36]   [2005] EWHC 1518 (QB).
[37]   *Sheppard v Essex Strategic Health Authority* [2005] EWHC 1518 (QB) at [60].

15.34 Against this backdrop, Brooke LJ (with whom Maurice Kay LJ and Jonathan Parker LJ agreed) felt that there was a need to make a costs capping order:[38]

> 'There are three main weapons available to a party who is concerned about extravagant conduct by the other side, or the risk of such extravagance. The first is a prospective costs capping order ... The second is a retrospective assessment of costs conducted toughly in accordance with CPR principles. The third is a wasted costs order against the other party's lawyers ... In my judgment recourse to the first of these weapons should be the court's first response when a concern is raised by defendants of the type to which this part of this judgment is addressed. The service of an over-heavy estimate of costs with the response to the allocation questionnaire may well trigger off the need for such a step to be taken in future.'

Brooke LJ went on to say:[39]

> 'If defamation proceedings are initiated under a CFA without ATE cover, the master should at the allocation stage make an order analogous to an order under section 65(1) of the [Arbitration Act 1996]. In the ordinary course of things this order would cover the normal costs of the litigation ...'

15.35 Thus, under the judge-made law, a costs capping order can be seen as being the 'court's first response'; now, of course, the first line of defence would be costs budgeting.

Partial costs capping orders

15.36 Where a claim is likely to involve a stage or an issue that is thought to involve particular expense, it is possible to make a costs capping order relating to the costs of that particular step or issue.[40] The precise jurisdiction under which such orders are made has not been clarified, but it is probably under CPR, r 3.1. CPR, r 44.18(4)(b) also expressly provides that an order may be made in respect of the costs of any issues which are ordered to be tried separately.

Group litigation

15.37 Group litigation can be particularly expensive. The Woolf report specifically identified group litigation as being an area in which costs budgeting would be appropriate.[41] Against this background, it was hardly surprising that group litigation was one of the first types of claim to be subject to costs capping orders. What is surprising, perhaps, is that group litigation claims have not yet been made the subject of a costs budgeting pilot.

15.38 Although possibly now of only historical interest (see below), the first group litigation case to be the subject of a costs cap was *AB v Leeds Teaching Hospitals NHS Trust*, in which Gage J said:[42]

---

[38]   *King v Telegraph Group Ltd* [2005] 1 WLR 2282 at [105]–[106].
[39]   *King v Telegraph Group Ltd* [2005] 1 WLR 2282 at [93].
[40]   In *A&E Television Networks LLC v Discovery Communications Europe Ltd* [2011] EWHC 1038 (Ch) at [17] in which Mann J made a costs capping order limiting the costs of certain work that a solicitor wished to do in house to no more than would have been incurred had it been done by an outside agency.
[41]   *Access to Justice – Final Report* (July 1996) Lord Woolf MR, chapter 7, para 39.
[42]   [2003] EWHC 1034 (QB) at [19].

'In my judgment, in cases where [group litigation orders] are concerned the desirability of ensuring that costs are kept within bounds makes it unnecessary for the court to require exceptional circumstances to be shown before exercising its discretion to make a costs cap order. I note that in claims in [public interests claims] it has been held that there must be exceptional circumstances before a pre-emptive order for costs is made ... However, I see no reason for such a requirement where a costs cap order is sought in a [group litigation order], particularly where there is a risk that costs may become disproportionate and excessive.'

15.39 It is, perhaps, worth noting that the party to whom the proposed cap would apply did not object in principle to the order being made. Likewise, in *Ledward Claimants v Kent and Medway Health Authority and East Kent Hospitals NHS Trust*,[43] Hallett J made a costs capping order but, again, it was (for all practical purposes) by consent.

15.40 The notion of making costs capping orders in group litigation had (prior to the introduction of CPR, rr 44.18–44.20) become ingrained as unremarkable practice. The rationale behind this was explained (obiter) by Gage J:[44]

'For the avoidance of doubt, I should add that these observations [relating to "ordinary" cases] are confined to actions other than those where group litigation is involved. The latter raise entirely different factors and problems. Past experience shows that the costs in group actions have a tendency to spiral out of control. The generic issues are usually managed by one firm of solicitors acting for all potential claimants whether specifically instructed by those claimants or instructed by solicitors acting on behalf of other claimants. In my judgment the court has a clear duty in such cases to manage the litigation from an early stage in such a way that one or other party does not allow costs to spiral out of control.'

15.41 It is not known how the court will deal with group litigation under the new regime. During consultation there were calls for specific provisions relating to group litigation,[45] but it seems as if that suggestion was rejected. The result is that group litigation cases are now subject to the same threshold criteria as other cases; this would appear to be a significant change in the law, with the possible result that the cases mentioned above are no longer good law.

15.42 It is possible that the court will find that when the threshold criteria are applied, the usual nature of group litigation will result in them being readily met. Equally, it is possible that parties will see the benefits of capping costs in group litigation and will consent to caps being made. Another possibility is that specific provisions have been temporarily put to one side pending the outcome of the Jackson review.

Procedure

15.43 The procedure relating to protective costs orders is set out at the end of this chapter. An application for a costs capping order must be made on notice in accordance with Part 23.[46] The following mandatory requirements are imposed:[47]

---

[43] [2003] EWHC 2551 (QB).
[44] *Smart v East Cheshire NHS Trust* [2003] EWHC 2806 (QB) at [23].
[45] See *Civil Procedure Rules: Costs Capping Orders, Summary of Responses* (Ministry of Justice, 23 February 2009), p 8.
[46] CPR, r 44.19(1).
[47] CPR, r 44.19(2).

- the application notice must set out whether the costs capping order is in respect of the whole of the litigation or a particular issue which is ordered to be tried separately; and
- the application notice must explain why a costs capping order should be made; and
- the application notice must be accompanied by an estimate of costs setting out:
  - the costs (and disbursements) incurred by the applicant to date, and
  - the costs (and disbursements) which the applicant is likely to incur in the future conduct of the proceedings; and
- that estimate must be in the form of Precedent H.[48]

Estimates are required to include estimates of the overall costs to be incurred on the assumption that the case will not settle, and not merely estimates of future costs up to some (unspecified) date on which it is thought that the case is likely to, or might, settle.[49]

15.44 The court is able to give directions requiring the applicant to file a schedule of costs in the prescribed form;[50] the prescribed form is different from Precedent H, and is not the same as the requisite form of the estimate mentioned above. The prescribed form is a three-column document which deals with the costs in the same order as in Precedent H; the columns must then be populated in this way:[51]

- column one must contain each sub-heading as it appears in the applicant's estimate of costs;
- column two must contain, alongside each sub-heading, the amount claimed by the applicant in the applicant's estimate of costs; and
- column three must contain the amount that the respondent proposes should be allowed under each sub-heading.

The schedule must be supported by a statement of truth.

15.45 The court may give directions concerning written submissions, etc.[52] Although it is not a formal requirement, where it is appropriate the applicant should give thought to filing and serving evidence of his financial means.

The stage at which to exercise the jurisdiction

15.46 CPD, art 23A.2 offers the following guidance:

> 'An application for a costs capping order must be made as soon as possible, preferably before or at the first case management hearing or shortly afterwards. The stage which the proceedings have reached at the time of the application will be one of the factors the court will consider when deciding whether to make a costs capping order.'

Thus, applications ought to be made at an early stage. In so far as the judge-made law remains relevant, that too stipulated that applications should be timely.[53] However, it is possible to make an application too early; Dobbs J, for example, allowed an appeal

---

[48]   CPD, art 23A.3.
[49]   *Leigh v Michelin Tyres* [2004] 1 WLR 847 at [37].
[50]   CPR, r 44.19(3)(a).
[51]   CPD, art 23A.4.
[52]   CPR, r 44.19(3).
[53]   *King v Telegraph Group Ltd* [2005] 1 WLR 2282 at [80], per Brooke LJ, as emphasised by Eady J in *Tierney v News Group Newspapers Ltd* [2006] EWHC 3275 (QB) at [2].

against an order which had been made at a stage when the court was not in a position to examine all the appropriate management options.[54]

15.47 An application for a costs capping order made very late in the day might be rejected even though the claim was one which otherwise would have been a prime candidate for a costs capping order. In a case in which the application was (through no fault of the applicant) made only a few days before trial, Gray J found that the making of a costs capping order would in effect penalise the capped party when, as has often been said, the purpose of a capping order is to enable the capped party to plan ahead the appropriate level of expenditure to bring the case to trial at a cost which is in line with the amount of the cap.[55]

The scope and effect of the order

15.48 CPR, r 44.18(7) describes the effect of a costs capping order:

> 'A costs capping order, once made, will limit the costs recoverable by the party subject to the order unless a party successfully applies to vary the order.'

A costs capping order does not limit the expenditure of the capped party: it merely limits the amount which can be recovered from the other side in the event of success.[56]

15.49 Generally speaking, costs capping orders operate prospectively and not retrospectively,[57] but retrospective orders have been made in the past, usually with the consent of the parties.[58]

15.50 Although it is not uncommon for restrictions to be imposed on only one party, it is commonly the case that they cap all or both of the parties. Eady J has commented that there is something to be said for the latter approach, this being because it is capable of imposing effective discipline.[59]

15.51 While each case will turn on its own merits, it would not ordinarily be appropriate for separate provision to be made for the costs of interim applications.[60]

Variation of the order

15.52 A costs capping order may be varied, but only where:[61]

- there has been a material and substantial change of circumstances since the date when the order was made; or
- there is some other compelling reason why a variation should be made.

---

[54] *Eli Lilly & Co Ltd v James* [2009] EWHC 198 (QB).

[55] *Henry v British Broadcasting Corporation* [2005] EWHC 2503 (QB) at [39].

[56] *Tierney v News Group Newspapers Ltd* [2006] EWHC 3275 (QB) at [16].

[57] See *King v Telegraph Group Ltd* [2005] 1 WLR 2282 at [80], per Brooke LJ, and *Weir v Secretary of State for Transport (20 April 2005) (Ch D)* at [28], per Lindsay J.

[58] See, by way of example, *AB v Leeds Teaching Hospitals NHS Trust* [2003] EWHC 1034 (QB).

[59] See *Tierney v News Group Newspapers Ltd* [2006] EWHC 3275 (QB) at [3].

[60] *Tierney v News Group Newspapers Ltd* [2006] EWHC 3275 (QB) at [39].

[61] CPR, r 44.18(7).

The quantum of the cap

15.53 Prior to the introduction of CPR, rr 44.18–44.20, the task of setting the level of a cap was generally a matter which was carried out by a costs judge,[62] but the new regime makes specific provision for the court to sit with an assessor,[63] so it will not always be the case that the involvement of a costs judge necessitates a separate hearing.

15.54 As to the factors to be taken into account, CPD, art 23A.5 makes these provisions:

> 'When assessing the quantum of a costs cap, the court will take into account the factors detailed in rule 44.5 and the relevant provisions supporting that rule in this Practice Direction. The court may also take into account when considering a party's estimate of the costs they are likely to incur in the future conduct of the proceedings a reasonable allowance on costs for contingencies.'

15.55 The factors set out in CPR, r 44.5 (ie the 'seven pillars of wisdom') are relevant both to the costs which have already been incurred (which may be taken into account in some circumstances) and the costs yet to be incurred.[64] The base costs and additional liability must be assessed separately.[65] That said, the court should prescribe a total amount of recoverable costs, which will be inclusive, so far as a conditionally funded party is concerned, of any additional liability.[66]

15.56 The following miscellaneous points can be made.

Value of the claim

15.57 The value of the claim is a relevant factor, but it is only one factor amongst others.[67] Non-monetary factors may be taken into account, but the monetary value of the claim would usually be the starting point for estimating the claim's worth.[68]

Conduct

15.58 The conduct of the other side may be relevant: in particular, if it leads to disproportionate expenditure or expenditure on irrelevant matters, this should be taken into account.[69]

Comparators

15.59 In gauging the reasonableness of the costs proposed, the costs to be incurred by the other side may provide a guide, and in some respects a good guide.[70]

---

[62] *King v Telegraph Group Ltd* [2005] 1 WLR 2282 at [94].
[63] See CPR, r 44.19(3)(c); see also *Matadeen v Associated Newspapers (17 March 2005)*, Master Eyre (not binding).
[64] *Tierney v News Group Newspapers Ltd* [2006] EWHC 3275 (QB) at [17].
[65] *Tierney v News Group Newspapers Ltd* [2006] EWHC 3275 (QB) at [18].
[66] *King v Telegraph Group Ltd* [2005] 1 WLR 2282 at [101].
[67] See *Tierney v News Group Newspapers Ltd* [2006] EWHC 3275 (QB) at [10].
[68] *King v Telegraph Group Ltd* [2005] 1 WLR 2282 at [95].
[69] See the example in *Tierney v News Group Newspapers Ltd* [2006] EWHC 3275 (QB) at [35], where the defendant failed to admit that a photograph was that of the claimant, thus putting the claimant to the expense of proving this fact.
[70] *AB v Leeds Teaching Hospitals NHS Trust* [2003] EWHC 1034 (QB), per Gage J.

Success fee

15.60 CPD, art 11.9 is also relevant, in that a percentage increase will not be reduced simply on the ground that, when added to base costs which are reasonable and (where relevant) proportionate, the total appears disproportionate.[71]

Postponement of payment

15.61 It has been held that in circumstances where the risk assessment has not been disclosed, it would be wrong to restrict the level of the success fee to take account of that part of the success fee that is attributable to the postponement of payment of fees and expenses[72] (this is relevant because that part of the success fee is not recoverable between opposing parties). This is not to say, however, that a costs judge could not take this factor into account if the relevant information is available.

The costs of the application

15.62 The costs of the costs capping application itself should not have any impact on the capped figure, but should be treated separately.[73]

Defamation claims

15.63 One or two points need to be made about defamation claims; these are in a class of their own because the costs can be high, especially when compared to the likely award of damages. It is also relevant that very high costs may have a 'chilling effect on press freedom', as Brooke LJ put it.[74] The court has a desire to cut down costs which have that tendency. That desire does not sit easily with the principle that the court will not reduce a success fee solely on the basis that when added to the base costs the total appears disproportionate. Brooke LJ has commented that these conflicting principles give rise to a need 'to square the circle'; his view is that there is a need to apply the regime of conditional funding in such a way as to minimise the chilling effect mentioned above:[75]

> 'If the introduction of this novel costs-capping regime means that a claimant's lawyers may be reluctant to accept instructions on a CFA basis unless they assess the chances of success as significantly greater than evens (so that the size of the success fee will be to that extent reduced), this in my judgment will be a small price to pay in contrast to the price that is potentially to be paid if the present state of affairs is allowed to continue.'

It has been argued that this is wrong, because to treat defamation claims differently would be to make a rule that could only properly be made by Parliament.[76] There is authority to support this view,[77] but it seems to be well established that there is a need

---

[71] *Tierney v News Group Newspapers Ltd* [2006] EWHC 3275 (QB) at [17].
[72] *Tierney v News Group Newspapers Ltd* [2006] EWHC 3275 (QB) at [42].
[73] See Master Hurst's view, as echoed by Eady J in *Tierney v News Group Newspapers Ltd* [2006] EWHC 3275 (QB) at [14].
[74] *King v Telegraph Group Ltd* [2005] 1 WLR 2282 at [101].
[75] *King v Telegraph Group Ltd* [2005] 1 WLR 2282 at [102].
[76] For an analysis of the competing arguments, see *Tierney v News Group Newspapers Ltd* [2006] EWHC 3275 (QB) at [21]–[25].
[77] See Lord Hoffmann's speech in *Campbell v MGN Ltd (No 2)* [2005] 1 WLR 3394 at [37], where he concluded that: 'In the end, therefore, it may be that a legislative solution will be needed to comply with Article 10.'

for a 'palliative' (to use Lord Hoffmann's terminology). In particular, Lord Hoffmann has expressed a view that Brooke LJ's guidance ought to be followed.[78]

The costs of the capping exercise

15.64 The costs of the costs capping exercise will be dealt with by the court in the usual way. It is, however, within the court's power to make a forthwith order in respect of those costs.[79]

COSTS BUDGETING

15.65 There is, as yet, no formal definition of costs budgeting, but it can be described as being the process by which court hearing the substantive matter will manage the costs of the litigation as well as the case itself.[80] It is a far wider concept that costs capping. The objective of costs management is to control the costs of litigation in accordance with the overriding objective.[81] Costs budgeting may be carried out during 'costs management conferences',[82] but costs budgeting is not limited to such hearings.[83] An order approving a costs budget is known as a 'costs management order'.[84]

History

15.66 Costs management (as it was then called) was one of the central features and recommendations of Lord Woolf's *Final Report on Access to Justice*; that was in 1996. Sir Rupert Jackson (speaking extrajudicially) has commented that the ills of the civil justice system were then thought mainly to be due to procedural distortions arising out of the adversarial design of the system.[85] Perhaps as a result, whilst Lord Woolf considered cost management as an option,[86] his emphasis was on *case* management rather than *costs* management. Thus, when they were first introduced, the CPR did not contain any express provisions concerning costs management.

15.67 It soon became apparent that case management was not controlling costs. The need for some form of costs management was mentioned judicially by Dyson LJ in 2003:[87]

'It seems to us that the prospective fixing of costs budgets is likely to achieve that objective [of controlling costs] far more effectively. The question of costs budgets was raised before the Civil Procedure Rule Committee in June 2001. It is contentious and important. The

---

[78] *Campbell v MGN Ltd (No 2)* [2005] 1 WLR 3394 at [34].
[79] *Tierney v News Group Newspapers Ltd* [2006] EWHC 3275 (QB) at [45]–[46].
[80] This being implied by PD 51G, para 4.1, PD 51G, para 2, and PD 51G, para 5.1.
[81] PD 51G, para 4.2.
[82] PD 51G, para 2.
[83] See, for example, PD 51G, para 4.3.
[84] See PD 51G, para 1.2.
[85] See Jackson R, Review of Civil Litigation Costs, Preliminary Report (2009) Ch 48 para 1.1
[86] Lord Woolf did consider costs budgetting, but he ultimately rejected it: this was for the following reasons: 'The paper occasioned a general outcry from the legal profession. Prospective budget-setting was seen as unworkable, unfair and likely to be abused by the creation of inflated budgets. The ability of judges to be involved in the hard detail of matters such as cost was generally doubted. The imposition of fixed fees, even relating only to inter partes costs, was seen as unrealistic and as interference with parties' rights to decide how to instruct their own lawyers.' (See Woolf, Final Report, July 1996, paras 16 and 17).
[87] *Leigh v Michelin Tyre plc* [2003] EWCA Civ 1766 at [34].

committee decided to explore the issue, but has not reached any conclusion about it. We invite the committee to re-examine the provisions relating to costs estimates to see whether they should be amended to make them more effective in the control of costs; and also to reach a conclusion on the issue of cost budgets.'

These comments echoed obiter comments made by Latham LJ two years earlier.[88] Academics said much the same thing.[89] The courts experimented with costs capping (see **15.2–5.10**), but little came of that. It was not until 2009 when Sir Rupert Jackson reopened the issue in his Preliminary Report[90] that the issue of costs budgeting started to move up the agenda.

Jurisdiction

15.68 There are two limbs to the jurisdiction under the CPR: a specific jurisdiction under pilot schemes,[91] and a general jurisdiction.

The Pilots

15.69 There are two pilots:

- **The mercantile pilot:** At the time of writing, a pilot scheme ('the mercantile pilot') was running in all Mercantile Courts and Technology and Construction Courts;[92] it applied to cases in which the first case management conference was heard on or after 1 October 2011.[93] The mercantile pilot started as a voluntary scheme on 1 June 2009[94] and was due to run until 30 September 2012.[95] The pilot was expressly stated to be without prejudice to the court's general management powers under CPR, r 3.1.[96] The reader will have to carry out his own legal research to see if that pilot still exists.
- **The Defamation pilot:** In addition, another pilot[97] ('the defamation pilot') was also running in the Royal Courts of Justice and the District Registry at Manchester; it applied to cases in which there were allegations of libel, slander and/or malicious falsehood,[98] but only where the claim was started on or after 1 October 2009.[99] It too was due to run until 30 September 2012.[100] It started on 1 October 2009 but, unlike the mercantile pilot, it was mandatory from the start.[101]

---

[88]   See *Griffiths v Solutia (UK) Ltd* [2001] EWCA Civ 736 at [29].
[89]   See, for example, Zuckerman on Civil Procedure (Sweet & Maxwell, second edition, 2006), chapter 26; Professor Zuckerman's editorial note at (2007) 26 CJQ 271 and Peysner J, *Predictability and Budgeting* [2004] 23 CJQ 15
[90]   Jackson R, Review of Civil Litigation Costs, Preliminary Report (2009) Ch 48.
[91]   The general power to create pilot schemes derives from CPR, r 51.2.
[92]   Costs Management in Mercantile Courts and Technology and Construction Courts Scheme.
[93]   See PD 51G, para 1.1.
[94]   See Jackson R, Review of Civil Litigation Costs, Final Report (2010) Ch 40, para 21.
[95]   Ibid.
[96]   See PD 51G, para 1.4.
[97]   Defamation Proceedings Costs Management Scheme.
[98]   See PD 51D, paras 1.1 and 1.2.
[99]   See PD 51G, para 1.1.
[100] See PD 51G, para 1.1.
[101] See Jackson R, Review of Civil Litigation Costs, Final Report (2010) Ch 40 para 3.1.

General jurisdiction

15.70 It is difficult to see which, if any, of the powers that are referred to in the pilots could not also be exercised under the court's general case management powers; it is implicit that some of those powers exist, because otherwise it would not have been necessary for the mercantile pilot to specifically state that it was without prejudice to the court's general powers under CPR, r 3.1.[102] Sir Rupert Jackson, speaking extrajudicially,[103] has commented that Coulson J – a judge known for his interest in costs – made a form of costs management order as long ago as 2009;[104] whilst he was speaking extrajudicially, he obviously approved of that approach. It is likely, therefore, that the court has a general jurisdiction to make costs management orders in any case in which such a step would be justified.

15.71 Sir Rupert Jackson summarised the position in this way (again, speaking extrajudicially):[105]

> 'Although not spelt out in terms within the CPR, the jurisdiction for costs management already exists. Within the CPR judges are given an armoury of powers which collectively enable cases to be managed not only by reference to the steps that may be taken in the given proceedings, but also by reference to the level of costs to be incurred.'

The remainder of the subchapter focuses on the pilots.

Costs budgets

15.72 Under both pilots the court is unable to approve costs incurred before the date of the first costs management order, but the court is able to record its comments on those costs and is able to take those costs into account when considering the reasonableness and proportionality of all subsequent costs.[106]

Mercantile Pilot

15.73 Under the mercantile pilot, the requirement to file and serve an estimate of costs in the form illustrated in Precedent H[107] is replaced with a requirement to file and exchange costs budget substantially in the form set out in Precedent HB.[108] The first page of Precedent HB has five columns. The first column is a "work done/to be done" column: it categorises costs into 'stages', such as the costs of issuing the claim, costs of case management conferences, costs of disclosure, etc. In addition, Precedent HB contains rows for 'contingent costs'. The next column allows the parties to record any assumptions that have been made, and the last three columns record the disbursements, the profit costs and the total. At the foot of the first page there are boxes for recording those costs that have not been included within the budget, such as costs of any detailed assessment proceedings, success fees, ATE premiums, etc. The second page of the precedent is where the data is entered, this being in the form of a separate cell for each grade of fee earner and for each stage. Disbursements and counsel's fees also have their own cells.

---

[102] See PD 51G, para 1.4.
[103] See Jackson R, Review of Civil Litigation Costs, Final Report (2010) Ch 40 para 7.5.
[104] *Barr v Biffa Waste Services Ltd* [2009] EWHC 2444 (TCC) at [53]–[60].
[105] See Jackson R, Review of Civil Litigation Costs, Preliminary Report (2009) Ch 48 para 2.1
[106] See PD 51G, para 1.3 and PD 51D, para 5.3A.
[107] This being in the Schedule of Costs Precedents annexed to the CPD.
[108] Which is annexed to PD 51G.

15.74 Each party should include separately in its costs budget reasonable allowances for (1) intended activities: eg, disclosure (if appropriate, showing comparative electronic and paper methodology), preparation of witness statements, obtaining experts' reports, mediation or any other steps which are deemed appropriate to the particular case; (2) identifiable contingencies, eg, specific disclosure application or resisting applications made or threatened by an opponent; and (3) disbursements, in particular court fees, counsel's fees and any mediator or expert fees.[109]

15.75 A party submitting a costs budget under the mercantile pilot is not required to disclose that budget to any other party save by way of exchange. The parties should however discuss their costs budgets during the costs budget building process and before each case management conference, costs management hearing, pre-trial review or trial.[110] One of the main purposes of that discussion is to ensure that the budgets are prepared in a way that allows like to be compared with like.[111]

15.76 If the court decides to make a costs management order it will, after making any appropriate revisions, record its approval of a party's budget.[112]

Defamation Pilot

15.77 Similar provisions apply under the defamation pilot. Other than litigants in person,[113] each party must prepare a costs budget or revised costs budget in the form of Precedent HA;[114] this must be done in advance of any case management conference or costs management conference, for service with the pre-trial checklist, and at any time as ordered to by the court.[115] The items to be included are very similar to those required under the Mercantile pilot.[116] Again, there is a requirement that the parties discuss matters before exchanging their budgets, and in particular, they are encouraged to discuss the assumptions and the timetable upon which their respective costs budgets are based.[117]

15.77 The defamation pilot provides that when approving or disapproving a budget, the court will not attempt to undertake a detailed assessment in advance, but will consider whether the budgeted totals for each stage of the work are within the broad range of reasonable and proportionate costs.[118]

Reviews and revisions

15.79 Under both pilots the parties are at liberty to ask the court to review the budget.[119] Likewise, under both pilots, the parties' lawyers are under an obligation to

---

[109]   See PD 51G, para 3.2.
[110]   See PD 51G, para 5.
[111]   Wainwright P, *Counting the Pennies* (2012) 162 NLJ 26.
[112]   See PD 51G, para 4.4.
[113]   See PD 51D, para 3.2.
[114]   See PD 51D, para 2.
[115]   See PD 51D, para 3.1
[116]   See PD 51D, para 3.3.
[117]   See PD 51D, para 4.1.
[118]   See PD 51D, para 5.3B.
[119]   PD 51D, para 5.5 and PD 51G, para 6.

communicate the court's decisions back to the clients.[120] Under the defamation budget the parties' solicitors are also required to liaise on a monthly basis to check that the budgets are not being exceeded.[121]

- **The mercantile pilot:** After having made a costs management order, under the mercantile pilot the court may order attendance at a subsequent costs management hearing (by telephone if appropriate) in order to monitor expenditure.[122] Any party may apply to the court if that party considers another party is behaving oppressively in seeking to cause that party to spend money disproportionately on costs.[123]
- **The defamation pilot:** Under the defamation pilot the parties must update their budgets for each case management conference or costs management conference and for the pre-trial review. This should enable the judge to review the updated figures, in order to ascertain what departures have occurred from each side's budget and why.[124] At any case management conference, costs management conference or pre-trial review, the court will, to the extent the budgets are not agreed between the parties, record approval or disapproval of each side's budget and, in the event of disapproval, will record the court's view.[125]

Effect of budgets

15.80 The defamation pilot records that at any case management conference, costs management conference or pre-trial review, the court will have before it the detailed costs budgets of both parties for the litigation, updated as necessary, and will take into account the costs involved in each proposed procedural step when giving case management directions.[126]

Both pilots make the following provisions in relation to detailed assessments:[127]

> 'When assessing costs on the standard basis, the court –
>
> (1)   will have regard to the receiving party's last approved budget; and
> (2)   will not depart from such approved budget unless satisfied that there is good reason to do so.'

The future

15.81 Not everyone approves of costs budgeting. Her Majesty's Council of Circuit Judges had this to say on the topic:[128]

> 'We view with trepidation and antipathy yet another area of out of court invigilation which it might be suggested the judiciary should take on. Consideration of parties' budgets would be a very significant and difficult exercise. It would also be very time consuming. If a Judge is worrying his way through two rival litigation budgets, assuming he had somehow acquired the expertise to do so, he will not be trying cases. Judicial productivity would be likely to fall

---

[120]   PD 51G, para 7 and PD 51D, para 5.4.
[121]   See PD 51D, para 5.5.
[122]   See PD 51G, para 4.4.
[123]   See PD 51G, para 4.5.
[124]   See PD 51G, para 3.4.
[125]   See PD 51D, para 5.3.
[126]   See PD 51D, para 5.2.
[127]   See PD 51D, para 5.6.and PD 51G, para 8.
[128]   See Jackson R, Review of Civil Litigation Costs, Final Report (2010) Ch 40, para 6.2.

as fast as morale if we are required to do this work. It is work at which (whatever training may be provided) a judge is likely to be far less competent than the solicitors whose budgets are being managed. If the budget management was badly done it could cripple the proper preparation of a case. It would be likely to result in much ancillary litigation. We are not in favour of moving down this road, however beguilingly professors may argue for a quasi business approach to litigation 'projects'. The best way to minimise costs is for skilled people to work briskly and economically because they want to, not because somebody is trying to control them.'

The Bar Council has taken a similar view. The Law Society, on the other hand, has been supportive of the idea.[129]

15.82 The mercantile pilot in Birmingham has been a considerable success (not least because of the enthusiasm of HHJ Simon Brown QC); Professor Dominic Regan has prepared a report on that pilot which, it is said, has reinvigorated Sir Rupert Jackson's enthusiasm to extend the pilot widely. Respected commentators such as Michael Cook have commented that they believe that costs budgeting will eventually apply to all multi-track cases.[130] This would seem likely, as Sir Rupert Jackson continues to take an active interest in the pilots and is said to be drafting new rules based on the experience gained therefrom.

PUBLIC LAW CHALLENGES

15.83 A public law challenge can be defined in this way:[131]

'The essential characteristics of a public law challenge are that it raises public law issues which are of general importance, where the applicant has no private interest in the outcome of the case.'

The equivalent of costs capping orders in public law challenges are protective costs orders (or 'PCOs'). The court has a wider ambit of discretion than is commonly available in private law cases; in particular, the order may not only cap costs, but it may be that a party will not be liable for costs at all. CPR, rr 44.18–44.20 do not apply to PCOs; this means that the threshold criteria imposed by those rules also do not apply. As with all pre-emptive costs orders, each case will turn on its own facts.[132]

15.84 PCOs are different from other categories of costs capping orders in (in general) that they are not intended to control disproportionate expenditure: there is no need to show that there is a risk that disproportionate costs might be incurred. PCOs are intended to protect litigants who reasonably bring public law proceedings in the public interest from having to pay costs (or significant costs) if they lose. In many ways, PCOs are an extension of the trend in administrative court not to award costs against those who act for the benefit of the public rather than themselves.

---

[129]   See Jackson R, Review of Civil Litigation Costs, Final Report (2010) Ch 40, paras 6.5 and 6.6.
[130]   See M Cook *Cook on Costs* (2012, LexisNexis) at [10.23].
[131]   *R v Lord Chancellor ex p Child Poverty Action Group* [1998] 2 All ER 755 at 756.
[132]   *Re Evans (deceased)* [1986] 1 WLR 101; see also *National Anti-Vivisection Society Ltd v Duddington* (1989) *The Times*, November 23, Mummery J, which confirms that the discretion must be exercised judicially.

Jurisdiction and principles

15.85 The principles guiding PCOs were established by Dyson J in the pre-CPR case of *R v Lord Chancellor ex p Child Poverty Action Group*.[133] Those principles were affirmed under the CPR by Richards J, who accepted that he should:[134]

> '... seek to give effect to the overriding objective and should have particular regard to the need, so far as practicable, to ensure that the parties are on an equal footing and that the case is dealt with in a way which is proportionate to the financial position of each party.'

15.86 Richards J went on to summarise the relevant principles. Those principles have been restated (with only minor revisions) by Phillips MR[135] and can be summarised in the following way:

- A PCO may be made at any stage of the proceedings, on such conditions as the court thinks fit, provided that the court is satisfied that:
  - the issues raised are of general public importance;
  - the public interest requires that those issues should be resolved;
  - the applicant has no private interest in the outcome of the case;[136]
  - having regard to the financial resources of the applicant and the respondent(s) and to the amount of costs that are likely to be involved it is fair and just to make the order; and
  - if the order is not made, the applicant will probably discontinue the proceedings and will be acting reasonably in so doing.
- If those acting for the applicant are doing so pro bono, this will be likely to enhance the merits of the application for a PCO.
- It is for the court, in its discretion, to decide whether it is fair and just to make the order in the light of the considerations set out above.

In environmental claims, it may be necessary to take further factors into account: see **15.97**.

15.87 The jurisdiction is one which 'should be exercised only in the most exceptional circumstances';[137] the Court of Appeal confirmed that this remains the case, but has commented that the notion that there must be exceptional circumstances does not assist in identifying those circumstances;[138] ie the need for 'exceptionality' should not be seen as an additional criterion to those set out above, but a prediction as to the effect of applying those principles.[139]

---

[133]   [1998] 2 All ER 755.
[134]   *R v London Borough of Hammersmith and Fulham ex p CPRE* [2000] ENVLR 544.
[135]   *R (on the application of Corner House Research) v Secretary of State for Trade and Industry* [2005] EWCA Civ 192 at [74].
[136]   See **15.89**.
[137]   *R v Prime Minister ex p CND* [2002] EWHC 2712 (Admin) at [3], per Simon Brown LJ, and *R v Lord Chancellor ex p Child Poverty Action Group* [1998] 2 All ER 755 at 757.
[138]   *R (on the application of Corner House Research) v Secretary of State for Trade and Industry* [2005] EWCA Civ 192 at [72].
[139]   *R (Compton) v Wiltshire Primary Care Trust* [2008] EWCA Civ 749 at [24], per Waller and Smith LJJ (Buxton LJ dissenting).

Formulation

15.88 Phillips MR has given the following guidance as to how PCOs should be formulated:[140]

- An order which caps the costs rather than releases a party from all liability to pay costs is likely to be required in all cases other than where the party's lawyers were acting pro bono.[141]
- When making any PCO where the applicant is seeking an order for costs in his favour if he wins, the court should prescribe by way of a capping order a total amount of the recoverable costs, inclusive of any additional liability.
- The purpose of the PCO will be to limit or extinguish the liability of the applicant if he loses, and as a balancing factor the liability of the defendant for the applicant's costs if the defendant loses will thus be restricted to a reasonably modest amount. The applicant should expect the capping order to restrict the costs to solicitors' fees and a fee for a single advocate of junior counsel status; the amounts which will be allowed will be modest.
- The overriding purpose of the jurisdiction is, in cases of general public importance and where it is in the public interest that an order should be made, to enable the applicant to present his case with a reasonably competent advocate and without being exposed to such serious financial risks as would deter him from advancing his case at all. The beneficiary of a PCO must not expect the capping order that will accompany the PCO to permit anything other than modest representation, and must arrange his legal representation (when its lawyers are not willing to act pro bono) accordingly.

It is implicit in the last of these points that a PCO is intended to act not only between opposing parties, but also between solicitor and client (in the sense that a beneficiary of a PCO would be expected, if not legally obliged, to limit his costs in accordance with the order). This is another way in which PCOs differ from other costs capping orders.

No private interest

15.89 By a majority decision[142] the Court of Appeal has held that the requirements set out above should not be read restrictively.[143] The requirement that there be no private interest has, in particular, generated some seemingly conflicting decisions,[144] not to mention critical extra-judicial comments[145] and pleas for the Rule Committee to clarify

---

[140] *R (on the application of Corner House Research) v Secretary of State for Trade and Industry* [2005] EWCA Civ 192 at [76].

[141] It is not clear what effect, if any, the notion of pro bono funding will have on this aspect of the Master of the Rolls' guidance.

[142] Waller and Smith LLJ (Buxton LJ dissenting).

[143] *R (Compton) v Wiltshire Primary Care Trust* [2008] EWCA Civ 749. See also *Weaver v London Quadrant Housing Trust* [2009] EWCA Civ 235.

[144] These include , *Wilkinson v Kitzinger* [2006] EWHC 835 (Fam) in which Sir Mark Potter P found that the requirement that there be no private interest was a 'flexible element in the court's consideration' (this was cited with approval in *R (Compton) v Wiltshire Primary Care Trust* [2008] EWCA Civ 749). See *R (England) v Tower Hamlets LBC* [2006] EWCA Civ 1742 at [14] in which Carnwath LJ expressed concerns about the workability of the private interest condition. See also *R (Buglife) v Thurrock Gateway Development Corp and another* [2008] EWCA Civ 1209 and *Campaign Against Arms Trade v BAE Systems plc* [2007] EWHC 330 (QB).

[145] As a working group convened by Liberty and chaired by Maurice Kay LJ pointed out (Litigating the Public Interest, July 2006 at [80]), no individual could simultaneously allege that they were the victim of a human

the law.[146] Whilst early cases indicated that the law took a restrictive approach to the private interest requirement (as advocated by Moore-Bick LJ[147] and Buxton LJ[148]), more recent decisions have shown that this has given way to a more 'flexible approach'; in particular, Carnwath LJ has commented that a private interest should not be a disqualifying factor, but 'its weight or importance in the overall context' should be treated as 'a flexible element' in the judge's consideration.[149] This approach is in keeping with the approach advocated in reports prepared (extrajudicially) by Marice Kay LJ and Sullivan J.[150] Both of those reports have received favourable judicial comment and have undoubtedly had a role in shaping the current law.[151] The current law is as described by Carnwath LJ:[152]

> 'On a strict view, it could be said, Goodson [one of the earlier cases advocating a restrictive approach] remains binding authority in this court as to the application of the private interest requirement. It has not been expressly overruled in this court. However, it is impossible in our view to ignore the criticisms of this narrow approach referred to above ... Although they were directly concerned with other aspects of the Corner House guidelines, the "flexible" approach which they approved seems to us intended to be of general application.'

Public interest

15.90 As to the need to show 'general public importance', Waller LJ commented that the two-stage tests of general public importance and the public interest in the issue being resolved are difficult to separate.[153] Smith LJ had further observations to make:

> 'First, there is no absolute standard by which to define what amounts to an issue of general public importance. Second, there are degrees to which the requirement may be satisfied; some issues may be of the first rank of general public importance, others of lesser rank although still of general public importance. Third, making the judgment is an exercise in which two judges might legitimately reach a different view without either being wrong.'

15.91 The need to show that an issue is of general public importance does not mean that it needs to be of national importance,[154] as Waller LJ said:[155]

---

rights violation, and that they also lacked a private interest in the claim they had brought. See also Ensuring Access to Environment Justice in England and Wales, May 2008, this being the report of a committee chaired by Sullivan J.

[146] *Morgan and another v Hinton Organics (Wessex) Ltd* [2009] EWCA Civ 107 at [40].

[147] Moore-Bick LJ said that the requirement is an unqualified requirement (ie, there must be no private interest, and it is not sufficient that the public interest transcends or wholly outweighs the private interest): *R (on the application of Goodson) v Bedfordshire & Luton Coroner* [2005] EWCA Civ 1172 at [27].

[148] See above.

[149] Per Carnwath LJ (in *Morgan and another v Hinton Organics (Wessex) Ltd* [2009] EWCA Civ 107 at [38] and [39]) citing with apparent approval the comments of Lloyd Jones J in *R (Bullmore) v West Hertfordshire Hospitals NHS Trust* [2007] EWHC 1350 (Admin); see also *R (Buglife) v Thurrock Gateway Development Corp and another* [2008] EWCA Civ 1209.

[150] See the earlier footnotes in the paragraph.

[151] See *R (England) v Tower Hamlets LBC* [2006] EWCA Civ 1742 at [14], in which Carnwath LJ (with the agreement of Neuberger LJ) commented that the Kay report (see the footnotes above) was a 'valuable discussion'; this was in the context of an application for permission to appeal, but the court took the view that their comments were of wider significance, and as such, took the exceptional step of authorising reference to their judgment where relevant in other proceedings (see [17])

[152] *Morgan and another v Hinton Organics (Wessex) Ltd* [2009] EWCA Civ 107 at [39].

[153] *R (Compton) v Wiltshire Primary Care Trust* [2008] EWCA Civ 749 at [21].

[154] *R (Compton) v Wiltshire Primary Care Trust* [2008] EWCA Civ 749 at [77], per Smith LJ.

[155] *R (Compton) v Wiltshire Primary Care Trust* [2008] EWCA Civ 749 at [24].

'I do not read the word "general" as meaning that it must be of interest to all the public nationally. On the other hand I would accept that a local group may be so small that issues in which they alone might be interested would not be issues of "general public importance". It is a question of degree and a question which *Corner House* would expect judges to be able to resolve.'

Where an issue can be shown to be important only to some members of the community (such as a focus group), the requisite standard may not be met. For example, the Court of Appeal did not express any adverse comment on a case in which Lloyd Jones J declined to make a PCO on the basis that the application represented a particular interest of a focus group rather than the interest of the community at large; the court did say, however, that such circumstances would not necessarily preclude a PCO.[156]

Financial position of applicant

15.92 As to the financial position of the persons involved, the Supreme Court has ruled that if the Legal Services Commission decided to fund a litigant, that decision ordinarily had to be seen to carry with it something close to an assurance that it would continue to support him in any subsequent appeal by the unsuccessful party;[157] their Lordships found that it was unlawful for the LSC to stipulate that a PCO must be made as a condition of funding, and they declared that the LSC must continue to provide public funding for the purposes of an appeal brought by their client's opponent.

Otherwise discontinue

15.93 In looking at whether the applicant will discontinue, it is permissible to look at whether a person other than the applicant would continue the litigation if the applicant were to discontinue by reason of not obtaining an PCO; in a case in which he was satisfied that if the applicant charity discontinued, a private individual would continue the litigation, Mann J found that he was justified in not making an order.[158]

PCOs on Appeals

15.94 There is no reason why an application cannot be made on appeal.[159] Where an application is made for a PCO in an appeal before the Court of Appeal, it should be for that court to determine whether such an order should be made and, if so, the level of the cap.[160] The way in which the court will deal with the matter will turn on whether the person who seeks the PCO is the appellant or the respondent:[161]

- where the application is made by the party who wishes to appeal to the Court of Appeal, the issue of a PCO should be considered afresh by the Court of Appeal upon its merits; and

---

[156]   *R (on the application of Bullmore) v West Hertfordshire Hospitals NHS Trust* [2007] EWHC 1350 (Admin), considered in *Compton*.
[157]   *R (on the application of E) v Governing Body of JFS and the Admissions Appeal Panel of JFS* [2009] UKSC 1.
[158]   *R (on the application of Action Against Medical Accidents) v General Medical Council* [2009] EWHC 2522 (Admin).
[159]   *R (on the application of Goodson) v Bedfordshire & Luton Coroner* [2005] EWCA Civ 1172, per Moore-Bick LJ R [15].
[160]   *R (Compton) v Wiltshire Primary Care Trust* [2008] EWCA Civ 749 at [28].
[161]   *R (Compton) v Wiltshire Primary Care Trust* [2008] EWCA Civ 749 at [47].

- where the beneficiary of a PCO has succeeded in the court at first instance, it will ordinarily be the case that a PCO will also apply in the Court of Appeal.

Other than this, similar principles will apply to those in other courts.[162]

Form and amount of order

15.95 The label of PCO encompasses a range of possible orders; in this regard, Smith LJ has given the following guidance:[163]

> 'At one end of the scale, the judge may make a PCO which imposes on a defendant the burden of bearing its own costs even though it wins on the merits and does not relieve it of the prospective burden of paying the applicant's costs in the event that the applicant succeeds ... That is the "strongest" form of order which will usually be made. It puts the defendant at a major disadvantage; on costs it is in a "heads you win tails I lose" position. At the other end of the scale, the court can make a much more modest order, whereby the claimant's liability to pay the defendant's costs is capped not at nil but at a specified level and where the defendant is given a guarantee that it will not be required to pay any of the claimant's costs ... If the claimant were to win, the defendant would not have to pay any of the claimant's costs ... Under that order, the defendant has the comfort of knowing that it cannot be required to meet any bill of costs other than its own and, over that, it has a large measure of control.

A PCO will often be made in a specific sum or as a cap, as the case may be. Contrary to the practice in private law cases,[164] it would usually be for the judge who makes the order to set the cap, rather than a costs judge.[165] The level of the cap is ordinarily limited to the fees of the solicitor and one junior counsel.[166] When imposing a cap, it is legitimate to take into account the financial means of those who are supporting the application.[167]

15.96 PCOs will not always be implemented in such a way as to remove the protected party from risk. It may often be right to expose him (or those he represents) to a degree of risk, so that all can see what the risk is.[168] In any event, the protected party will be at risk if his opponent makes an application to set aside a PCO;[169] however, if an appeal is lodged against a PCO and if a PCO is sought on that appeal, the usual order would be no order for costs on the application for a PCO.[170]

---

[162] *R (on the application of Goodson) v Bedfordshire & Luton Coroner* [2005] EWCA Civ 1172, per Moore-Bick LJ R [15].

[163] *R (on the application of Compton) v Wiltshire Primary Care Trust* [2008] EWCA Civ 749 at [86].

[164] The need not to involve a costs judge is probably a reflection of the fact that the level of any cap will assume that only modest costs will be incurred; furthermore, given the nature of the costs which would need to be considered, the administrative court would probably have at least as much relevant experience as a costs judge.

[165] *R (on the application of Corner House Research) v Secretary of State for Trade and Industry* [2005] EWCA Civ 192 at [78].

[166] *R (Compton) v Wiltshire Primary Care Trust* [2008] EWCA Civ 749 at [86], per Smith LJ.

[167] *R (Compton) v Wiltshire Primary Care Trust* [2008] EWCA Civ 749 at [27].

[168] *R (Compton) v Wiltshire Primary Care Trust* [2008] EWCA Civ 749 at [27].

[169] *R (on the application of Corner House Research) v Secretary of State for Trade and Industry* [2005] EWCA Civ 192 at [78].

[170] *R (Compton) v Wiltshire Primary Care Trust* [2008] EWCA Civ 749 at [49].

Environmental cases

15.97 It has been argued that environmental cases are in a different class to other claims. This is because of the existence of a Directive that requires that procedures to which it refers should be fair, equitable and timely and 'not prohibitively expensive' (see **34.163**); that Directive referred to the Aarhus Convention on Access to Information, Public Participation in Decision-making and Access to Justice in Environmental Matters—'the Aarhus Convention'; the cases that fall within its ambit are often referred to as 'Aarhus cases'. Sullivan LJ explained that in such a case the conditions set out in *Corner House* had to be modified insofar as it was necessary to secure compliance with the Directive and the Convention, but only insofar as it was necessary to secure such compliance.[171] He found that the general importance and public interest criteria were of less importance in such cases.[172] In so far as the requirement that the proceedings be 'not prohibitively expensive' was concerned, Sullivan LJ found that a purely subjective approach is not consistent with the objectives underlying the directive; as such, the law as it presently stands is a test that takes into account both objective and subjective elements.[173] That said, the same issue arose before the Supreme Court in a different case, and their Lordships determined that the answer was not clear from the Directives; their Lordships accordingly made a referral to the Court of Justice of the European Union for a preliminary ruling on that point.[174]

Procedure

15.98 Procedurally, a party seeking a PCO should apply for the order in the claim form; that application should be supported by the requisite evidence, which should include a schedule of the claimant's future costs of and incidental to the full judicial review application.

15.99 If the defendant wishes to resist the application for a PCO or any of the sums set out in the claimant's schedule, he should set out his reasons in the acknowledgement of service filed pursuant to CPR, r 54.8. If the defendant successfully resists the application, then it is likely that he will be awarded costs, but only in a modest amount.[175]

15.100 Where the application is made in an appeal to the Court of Appeal, the appropriate procedure should, in so far as it is practicable, be the same. Where the applicant for the PCO is also the appellant, the application for a PCO should be lodged with the application for permission to appeal; the defendant should then have an opportunity of providing written reasons why a PCO would be inappropriate. The decision will be taken on paper by the single Lord Justice.[176]

15.101 It is often the case that a PCO is made on paper without the attendance of the parties. Such orders may be reviewed on oral application by the defendant, but the PCO will be overturned only if the defendant is able to show 'compelling reasons' why that

---

[171] *R (on the application of Garner) v Elmbridge Borough Council* [2010] EWCA Civ 1006 at [32]–[34].

[172] *R (on the application of Garner) v Elmbridge Borough Council* [2010] EWCA Civ 1006 at [39]–[40]

[173] On the basis of the law as it presently stands, evidence of the risk of prohibitive expense is required: *Austin v Miller Argent (South Wales) Ltd* [2011] EWCA Civ 98 at [65].

[174] *R (on the application of Edwards and another) v Environment Agency (Cemex UK Cement Ltd, intervening)* [2010] UKSC 57 at [36].

[175] *Mount Cook Land Ltd v Westminster City Council* [2003] EWCA Civ 1346 at [76(1)].

[176] *R (Compton) v Wiltshire Primary Care Trust* [2008] EWCA Civ 749 at [48].

should be so.[177] The effect of this is that a claimant who is refused a PCO has the right to renew the application at an oral hearing without constraint, but a defendant who has a PCO made against him has to establish compelling reasons.[178]

15.102 Unless there is agreement between the parties that the application could have been decided on paper, the power to set aside a PCO derives from CPR, rr 23.8 and 3.3; this fact does not deter from the need (on the part of the defendant) to show compelling reasons.[179]

15.103 Whilst their Lordships were dealing with the rules of court that govern the Supreme Court rather than the CPR, the Supreme Court has ruled that where applications to reduce or cap a party's liability had been made and rejected by the court, it was not open to a costs officer subsequently to achieve that same result through the detailed assessment process.[180]

---

[177] *R (on the application of Corner House Research) v Secretary of State for Trade and Industry* [2005] EWCA Civ 192 at [79].

[178] *R (Compton) v Wiltshire Primary Care Trust* [2008] EWCA Civ 749 at [42]; this has been justified on the basis that the claimant, who may have been refused a PCO, should have more latitude, because without a PCO no proceedings will be brought at all, whereas the existence of a PCO will not prevent a defendant defending the merits of the case if the PCO is set aside; Smith LJ has explained that a further justification is that there is a need to impose a procedure that would avoid drawn-out preliminary skirmishes (see *Compton* at [90]).

[179] *R (Compton) v Wiltshire Primary Care Trust* [2008] EWCA Civ 749 at [32]–[42] and [90].

[180] *R (on the application of Edwards and another) v Environment Agency (Cemex UK Cement Ltd, intervening)* [2010] UKSC 57.

Chapter 16

SECURITY FOR COSTS

16.1   This chapter discusses security for costs, which is a discretionary interim remedy by which a litigant (usually a claimant) may be ordered to provide security as a condition for continuing to have a role in the litigation.

16.2   A degree of vigilance ought to be kept when seeking guidance from authorities; this is because the basis upon which orders were made was changed on 1 October 2009 in that a statutory jurisdiction was annulled, leaving in its place only those powers conferred by the CPR (see **16.8**). This means that cases decided before that date may refer to provisions which no longer apply (although cases dealing with general principles will remain instructive, if not binding). Caution ought to be exercised whilst reading commentaries on the topic because not all of the standard textbooks acknowledge the change in the law.[1]

AVAILABILITY AND PHILOSOPHY

16.3   There are two types of jurisdiction.[2] These will be referred to as the 'primary jurisdiction' and the 'secondary jurisdictions' (the latter taking the plural because it has two distinct components: see **16.17**). A party may be ordered to give security for costs in the following situations (but only where it is just to do so):

- where he is the claimant or the appellant[3] and where he is not resident in a contracting state;[4]
- where it is the claimant or the appellant, and where it is a company or other body and there is reason to believe that it will be unable to pay the defendant's costs if ordered to do so;[5]

---

[1]   See, for example, M Cook *Cook on Costs 2010* (Butterworths LexisNexis), chapter 13.
[2]   There may also be a residual power to make an award under the court's inherent jurisdiction, but there is no modern authority on the point; one of the last occasions it was mentioned was by Dillon LJ in *CT Bowring & Co (Insurance) Ltd v Corsi & Partners Ltd* [1995] 1 BCLC 148, CA. He commented that it would be difficult to envisage the court creating a new category of case where a party could be required to give security, without leaving that to the Rule Committee or Parliament.
[3]   This includes a respondent who also appeals: see CPR, r 25.15(1)(b).
[4]   CPR, r 25.13(2)(a). A contracting state is a Brussels Contracting State, a Lugano Contracting State or a Regulation State, as defined in s 1(3) of the Civil Jurisdiction and Judgments Act 1982: see CPR, r 25.13(2)(a)(ii). The relevant states are: Austria, Belgium, Denmark, Finland, France, Germany, Greece, Iceland, Ireland, Italy, Luxemburg, Netherlands, Norway, Poland, Portugal, Spain, Sweden, Switzerland, and the United Kingdom. The Isle of Man is not a contracting state: *Greenwich Ltd v National Westminster Bank plc* [1999] 2 Lloyd's Rep 308.
[5]   CPR, r 25.13(2)(c).

- where he is the claimant or the appellant and has changed his address since the claim was commenced with a view to evading the consequences of the litigation, or he has failed to give his address in the claim form, or gave an incorrect address in that form;[6]
- where he is the claimant or the appellant and is acting as a nominal claimant and there is reason to believe that he will be unable to pay the defendant's costs if ordered to do so;[7]
- where he is the claimant or the appellant and has taken steps in relation to his assets that would make it difficult to enforce an order for costs against him;[8]
- where he is an appellant and where he is a limited company and there is reason to believe it will be unable to pay the costs of the other parties to the appeal should its appeal be unsuccessful;[9]
- where he is a third party and has assigned the right to the claim to the claimant with a view to avoiding the possibility of a costs order being made against him;[10] and
- where he is a third party and has contributed or agreed to contribute to the claimant's costs in return for a share of any money or property which the claimant may recover in the proceedings.[11]

In addition, a party may be required to pay a sum of money into court in the following circumstances:

- where he has, without good reason, failed to comply with a rule, practice direction or a relevant pre-action protocol;[12] and
- where the court makes an order, and where the court has made it subject to conditions, including a condition to pay a sum of money into court.[13]

16.4   The underlying principle is illustrated by the first of these situations: Donaldson MR explained that an order for security would be warranted by the notion that it would be unjust if a claimant not resident in a contracting state, who by virtue of his location of residence is more or less immune to the consequences of a costs order against him, were to be allowed to proceed without providing security within the jurisdiction against which such an order could be enforced.[14]

JURISDICTION

International

16.5   Provided that persons resident in other contracting states are not burdened with orders which could not be made against persons within this jurisdiction,[15] and provided

---

6   CPR, r 25.13(2)(d) and (e).
7   CPR, r 25.13(2)(f).
8   CPR, r 25.13(2)(g).
9   CPR, r 25.15(2).
10   CPR, r 25.14(2)(a).
11   CPR, r 25.14(2)(b).
12   CPR, r 3.1(5).
13   CPR, r 3.1(3).
14   *Corfu Navigation Co v Mobil Shipping Co Ltd* [1991] 2 Lloyd's Rep 52, CA.
15   *Data Delecta AB v MSL Dynamics Ltd: C-43/95* [1996] All ER (EC) 961, ECJ: a contracting state will be a Brussels Contracting State, a Lugano Contracting State or a Regulation State, as defined in s 1(3) of the Civil Jurisdiction and Judgments Act 1982. See also *Thune v London Properties Ltd* [1990] 1 All ER 972, CA.

that discretion is exercised on objectively justifiable grounds, then the jurisdiction to make orders for security for costs is compatible with the European Convention on Human Rights.[16]

16.6 There are some specialist types of claim (mostly involving travel) where the jurisdiction is excluded by international convention; those exclusions will be well known to those who practice in those areas of the law; the details are relegated to the footnotes.[17]

Primary jurisdiction

16.7 The primary jurisdiction arises under delegated legislation (ie the CPR). In particular, CPR Part 25 II provides as follows:[18]

'(1)   A defendant to any claim may apply under this Section of this Part for security for his costs of the proceedings.

(Part 3 provides for the court to order payment of sums into court in other circumstances. Rule 20.3 provides for this Section of this Part to apply to Part 20 claims)

(2)   An application for security for costs must be supported by written evidence.

(3)   Where the court makes an order for security for costs, it will—

    (a)   determine the amount of security; and
    (b)   direct—
        (i)   the manner in which; and
        (ii)   the time within which
the security must be given.'

This jurisdiction does not apply in family proceedings in the High Court or county courts.[19] It applies in all other civil cases and in all cases in the Civil Division of the Court of Appeal, even in respect of appeals against orders made in family proceedings.[20]

16.8 There used to be a statutory jurisdiction arising under s 726(1) of the Companies Act 1985, but that section was repealed on 1 October 2009[21] with no replacement being enacted; this was because the 1985 provisions were believed to be otiose given the existence of the powers under CPR Part 25 II.

16.9 In order for the jurisdiction to arise, the costs in respect of which the order is sought must be litigation costs.[22]

---

[16]   *Nasser v United Bank of Kuwait* [2001] EWCA Civ 556 at [56]–[61], per Mance LJ; see also *Al-Koronky and another v Time Life Entertainments Group Ltd* [2005] EWHC 1688 (QB) at [21]–[28], per Eady J.

[17]   Whilst not yet in force in the United Kingdom, the following conventions have been ratified and do exclude an order for security for costs: Carriage of Goods by Rail (Berne) 1952 (see Art 55); Carriage of Passengers by Rail (Berne) 1961 Art 56; Carriage of Goods by Road (Geneva) 1956, Art 31; Carriage of Passengers by Road Convention, Art 41; and Third Party Liability in the Field of Nuclear Energy (Paris) 1960, Art 14 (as amended).

[18]   CPR, r 25.12(1).

[19]   Matrimonial and Family Proceedings Act 1984, s 40(1).

[20]   *Radmacher v Granatino* [2008] EWCA Civ 1304 at [33], per Wilson LJ.

[21]   It was repealed in 2009: See Companies Act 2006, s 1295 and Sch 16 and see Companies Act 2006 (Commencement No 8, Transitional Provisions and Savings) Order (SI 2008/2860), arts 4 and 5; Sch 1, Pt 1; Sch 2, para 1 (as amended).

[22]   Coulson J, for example, found that on the facts of the case before him he lacked the power to make an order in respect of costs of a failed pre-issue mediation: *Lobster Group Ltd v Heidelberg Graphic Equipment Ltd* [2008] EWHC 413 (TCC) at [15] onwards.

Claimants

16.10 The primary jurisdiction is, in general, not available to claimants (unless a counterclaim is brought: see **16.11**). It is a moot point whether a claimant is able seek an order under the primary jurisdiction where it becomes the respondent to an application made in the context of a claim. If pre-CPR authority is any guide, then the answer is in the negative; this is because the jurisdiction will arise only where the applicant is a defendant 'to a claim', and that phrase is generally read as meaning proceedings arising out of a cause of action.[23] The contrary is arguable, however.

Counterclaimants

16.11 Where a counterclaim can be said to have an independent vitality of its own that goes beyond it being a mere matter of defence, then the power to make an order against the counterclaimant (ie the defendant) under the primary jurisdiction would arise.[24] If, on the other hand, the counterclaim were merely an 'automatic counterpart of the defence' (as Dillon LJ put it),[25] then that jurisdiction would not arise.[26] Whilst a pre-CPR case, Bingham LJ clarified that the test is one of substance rather than form:[27]

> 'So the question may arise, as a question of substance, not formality or pleading: is the defendant simply defending himself, or is he going beyond mere self-defence and launching a cross-claim with an independent vitality of its own?'

16.12 The fact that a counterclaim is based on the same facts as the claim is a factor in favour of it being a counterpart of the defence,[28] but is not determinative of the matter.[29] The fact that a counterclaim may overtop the claim is also factor to be taken into account, but again is not determinative of the issue.[30] The nature of a counterclaim may change as the claim progresses, or may, at the time the application is made, not be known.[31]

16.13 Lawton LJ has clarified that where both parties claim to have suffered damages, and where it was mere chance that one started the claim before the other could get in a claim, both should be treated alike;[32] this may mean that security is ordered against neither or both.

---

[23]   *Re B (infants)* [1965] 2 All ER 651, per Pennycuick J.
[24]   *Jones v Environcom Ltd and another* [2009] EWHC 16 (Comm) at [24]–[26]; see also the discussion in *Hutchison Telephone (UK) Ltd v Ultimate Response Ltd* [1993] BCLC 307 at 316, per Dillon LJ, where the issue of equitable set-off is addressed. Likewise, see *C T Bowring & Co (Insurance) Ltd v Corsi & Partners Ltd* [1995] 1 BCLC 148 at 153, per Dillon LJ, and *Autoweld Systems Ltd v Kito Enterprises LLC* [2010] EWCA Civ 1469 at [31], [32] and [35], per Black LJ.
[25]   *Hutchison Telephone (UK) Ltd v Ultimate Response Ltd* [1993] BCLC 307 at 316.
[26]   *Samuel J Cohl Co v Eastern Mediterranean Maritime Ltd, The Silver Fir* [1980] 1 Lloyd's Rep 371; see also *Hutchison Telephone (UK) Ltd v Ultimate Response Ltd* [1993] BCLC 307 at 317.
[27]   *Hutchison Telephone (UK) Ltd v Ultimate Response Ltd* [1993] BCLC 307 at 317. See also *Mapleson v Masini* (1879) 5 QBD 144 at 147, per Field J: 'The substantial position of the parties must always be looked at'.
[28]   Whilst a pre-CPR case, see *Ashworth v Berkeley-Walbrood Ltd* (1989) *The Independent*, October 9, CA.
[29]   *Samuel J Cohl Co v Eastern Mediterranean Maritime Ltd, The Silver Fir* [1980] 1 Lloyd's Rep 371; see also *Hutchison Telephone (UK) Ltd v Ultimate Response Ltd* [1993] BCLC 307 at 317.
[30]   *Hutchison Telephone (UK) Ltd v Ultimate Response Ltd* [1993] BCLC 307 at 317, per Bingham LJ.
[31]   *Camden London Borough Council v Makers UK Ltd* [2009] EWHC 605 (TCC) at [47], per Akenhead J.
[32]   *Samuel J Cohl Co v Eastern Mediterranean Maritime Ltd, The Silver Fir* [1980] 1 Lloyd's Rep 371 at 374. See *Hutchison Telephone (UK) Ltd v Ultimate Response Ltd* [1993] BCLC 307 at 317, per Bingham LJ, confirming *Neck v Taylor* [1893] 1 QB 560 at 562, per Esher MR; and see *Thistle Hotels Ltd v Gamma Four Ltd* [2004] EWHC 322 (Ch) at [30], per Sonia Proudman QC (sitting as a High Court judge).

Part 20 claims

16.14 The primary jurisdiction applies to Part 20 claims in that a defendant is able to seek an order against a Part 20 claimant.[33]

Appeals

16.15 The primary jurisdiction applies to appeals in that an order may be made against an appellant or against a respondent who also brings an appeal.[34] A defendant to a claim will not cease to be a defendant merely because judgment has been entered and he has become a judgment debtor; this means that if a defendant brings an appeal, an order may be made in his favour for his costs below.[35] (An order may also be made where a party seeks permission to appeal, but this would be under the secondary jurisdictions: see **16.17–16.21** and, in particular, **16.20**.) May LJ has confirmed that the jurisdiction to make an award in respect of the costs on an appeal would not extend to costs which had been incurred before the claim became an appeal.[36]

Third parties

16.16 An order for security may be made against persons other than the claimant where that person has assigned the right to the claim to the claimant with a view to avoiding the possibility of a costs order being made against him, or where he has contributed or agreed to contribute to the claimant's costs in return for a share of any money or property which the claimant may recover in the proceedings.[37] The claimant may be required to provide the name and address of a funder (see **16.107**). See also the related topic of nominal claimants at **16.37–16.39**.

Secondary jurisdictions

16.17 The secondary jurisdictions also arise under the CPR, but they arise under the general powers in CPR Part 3 rather than under the specific powers in CPR Part 25 II. The relevant provisions are in CPR, r 3.1:

'(2) Except where these Rules provide otherwise, the court may—

...

(m) take any other step or make any other order for the purpose of managing the case and furthering the overriding objective.

(3) When the court makes an order, it may—

(a) make it subject to conditions, including a condition to pay a sum of money into court; and

(b) specify the consequence of failure to comply with the order or a condition.

(4) Where the court gives directions it will take into account whether or not a party has complied with the Practice Direction (Pre-Action Conduct) and any relevant pre-action protocol.

---

[33] See CPR, r 25.12(1) and r 20.3.

[34] See CPR, r 25.15; see also *Antonelli v Allen* [2001] EWCA Civ 1563.

[35] *Dar International FEF Co v Aon Ltd* [2003] EWCA Civ 1833, per Mance LJ; in a similar vein, if a claimant is successful but the defendant brings an appeal, the court may, pending the appeal, stay the payment out of monies previously paid in as security: *Stabilad Ltd v Stephens & Carter Ltd* [1999] 1 WLR 1201.

[36] *Ahmed v Blackburn & Co* [2001] EWCA Civ 141 at [8].

[37] CPR, r 25.14(2); for the history of the jurisdiction, see *Abraham v Thompson* [1997] 4 All ER 362, CA and *Condliffe v Hislop* [1996] 1 All ER 431, CA.

(5)   The court may order a party to pay a sum of money into court if that party has, without good reason, failed to comply with a rule, practice direction or a relevant pre-action protocol.

(6)   When exercising its power under paragraph (5) the court must have regard to—

(a)   the amount in dispute; and
(b)   the costs which the parties have incurred or which they may incur.

(6A)   Where a party pays money into court following an order under paragraph (3) or (5), the money shall be security for any sum payable by that party to any other party in the proceedings.'

16.18   Moore-Bick LJ has emphasised that CPR, r 3.1 gives rise to two distinct jurisdictions:[38]

- **CPR, r 3.1(3):** Moore-Bick LJ has described this jurisdiction as being designed to control the future conduct of the party on whom it is imposed.[39] It is a parasitic jurisdiction, in that when the court makes an order, it may operate parasitically on it to make that order subject to conditions, including a condition to pay a sum of money into court.[40] Moore-Bick LJ has explained that when the rule speaks about the court making an order, it is referring to a direction that a party act in a certain way or that a certain state of affairs should exist, not to the instrument used to give effect to one or more such directions;[41] thus, it is a jurisdiction that will not support the making of a free-standing order for security for costs.
- **CPR, r 3.1(5):** This is a jurisdiction that is intended to give the court power to manage a party whose past conduct has been found wanting.[42] Unlike the jurisdiction under CPR, r 3.1(3), it is such that the court may make a free-standing order. Where party has, without good reason, failed to comply with a rule, practice direction or a relevant pre-action protocol, then that party may be ordered to pay money into court.[43] Dyson LJ had this to say about that jurisdiction:[44]

   'Rule 3(3) in terms allows the court to make any order conditional on (amongst other things) the payment of money into court. Yet more specifically rule 3(5) empowers the court to order a non-compliant party to pay money into court and rule 3(6) requires the court in exercising that power to have regard to the costs incurred or to be incurred.'

The court must have regard to the amount in dispute and the costs which the parties have incurred or which they may incur.[45]

16.19   Where a party pays money into court following an order under either of these jurisdictions, the money shall be security for any sum payable by that party to any other party in the proceedings.[46]

---

[38]   *Hushcroft v P&O Ferries Ltd* [2010] EWCA Civ 1483 at [18].
[39]   *Hushcroft v P&O Ferries Ltd* [2010] EWCA Civ 1483 at [17].
[40]   CPR, r 3.1(3).
[41]   *Hushcroft v P&O Ferries Ltd* [2010] EWCA Civ 1483 at [18].
[42]   *Hushcroft v P&O Ferries Ltd* [2010] EWCA Civ 1483 at [17].
[43]   CPR, r 3.1(5).
[44]   *Olatawura v Abiloye* [2002] EWCA Civ 998 at [20].
[45]   CPR, r 3.1(6).
[46]   CPR, r 3.1(6A).

16.20 The secondary jurisdictions come into their own where, procedurally, the powers under the primary jurisdiction are unavailable.[47] Moore-Bick LJ has cautioned that it would be wrong to regard the secondary jurisdictions as being a convenient means of circumventing the requirements of the primary jurisdiction, thereby providing a less demanding route by which security for costs may be obtained.[48] That said, secondary jurisdictions are capable of plugging gaps in a wide range of circumstances.[49] Examples include an application for permission to appeal,[50] an application for summary judgment,[51] on an application to strike out,[52] and when giving directions.[53] This is by no means an exhaustive list.

Existing liabilities

16.21 The secondary jurisdictions should be distinguished from the power to stay the claim pending payment of existing liabilities (such as existing costs orders): an application dependent on orders which have already been made will turn on different bases than those which govern applications for security for costs.[54]

Detailed assessments

16.22 It is not clear whether the primary jurisdiction would empower the court to make an order for security for costs in respect of a detailed assessment. An analogous situation would be where a defendant seeks an enquiry as to damages; under a comparable jurisdiction in a pre-CPR case, Dillon LJ found that the power to make an order would not arise in those circumstances, this being primarily on the basis that the assessment was made at the behest of the defendant, who could not be said to be in the position of a claimant for the purposes of the assessment[55] (see **16.10–16.11**). It is possible that the same applies to detailed assessments. It is, nonetheless, also possible that an order could be made under the court's secondary jurisdictions.

PRINCIPLES AND DISCRETION

16.23 Whether an order for security for costs is made is a matter of discretion. In so far as the primary jurisdiction is concerned, an order will be made only if it is just to make such an order and if certain conditions have been satisfied. In this regard, CPR, r 25.13(1) provides as follows:

> '(1) The court may make an order for security for costs under rule 25.12 if—

---

[47] See *Great Future Ltd v Sealand Housing Corpn* [2003] EWCA Civ 682: CPR Part 25 II did not apply at the material time because permission to appeal had not been granted.

[48] *Hushcroft v P&O Ferries Ltd* [2010] EWCA Civ 1483 at [14].

[49] Whilst there are no reported examples of the power being used in isolation, Simon Brown LJ has implied that there is a power under CPR, r 3.1(2)(m) which, if it exists as a discrete vires, would be a widely applicable power: see *Olatawura v Abiloye* [2002] EWCA Civ 998 at [25]. See also *Great Future Ltd v Sealand Housing Corpn* [2003] EWCA Civ 682.

[50] *Mulford Holding & Investment Ltd v Greatex Ltd* [2010] EWCA Civ 1178, per Lloyd LJ; *Great Future International Ltd and others v Sealand Housing Corporation* [2003] EWCA Civ 682.

[51] *Jacobs UK Ltd v Skidmore Owings & Merrill LLP* [2008] EWHC 2847 (TCC).

[52] *Ashfield and another v Union Pensions Trustees Ltd* [2004] All ER (D) 103 (Dec).

[53] *Ali v Hudson (trading as Hudson Freemen Berg (a firm))* [2003] EWCA Civ 1793.

[54] This is an issue which goes beyond the scope of this book, but it is discussed in *CIBC Mellon Trust Co v Mora Hotel Corpn NV* [2002] EWCA Civ 1688.

[55] *CT Bowring & Co (Insurance) Ltd v Corsi & Partners Ltd* [1995] 1 BCLC 148, CA; the jurisdiction arose under the now revoked s 726(1) of the Companies Act 1985.

(a)   it is satisfied, having regard to all the circumstances of the case, that it is just to
        make such an order; and
(b)
        (i)   one or more of the conditions in paragraph (2) applies, or
        (ii)   an enactment permits the court to require security for costs.'

16.24 The secondary jurisdictions are less well structured. Each of the jurisdictions is
considered in turn.

Conditions (primary jurisdiction)

16.25 The conditions which are most frequently relied upon are set out in CPR,
r 25.13(2);[56] they apply to both claimants and appellants (or to respondents who also
appeal):[57]

'(2)   The conditions are—

(a)   the claimant is—
        (i)   resident out of the jurisdiction; but
        (ii)   not resident in a Brussels Contracting State, a State bound by the Lugano
                Convention or a Regulation State, as defined in section 1(3) of the Civil
                Jurisdiction and Judgments Act 1982;
(c)   the claimant is a company or other body (whether incorporated inside or outside
        Great Britain) and there is reason to believe that it will be unable to pay the
        defendant's costs if ordered to do so;
(d)   the claimant has changed his address since the claim was commenced with a view
        to evading the consequences of the litigation;
(e)   the claimant failed to give his address in the claim form, or gave an incorrect
        address in that form;
(f)   the claimant is acting as a nominal claimant, other than as a representative
        claimant under Part 19, and there is reason to believe that he will be unable to pay
        the defendant's costs if ordered to do so;
(g)   the claimant has taken steps in relation to his assets that would make it difficult
        to enforce an order for costs against him.

(Rule 3.4 allows the court to strike out a statement of case and Part 24 for it to give
summary judgment)'

16.26 In addition, there are further provisions (CPR, r 25.15(2)) which relate only to
appellants (and respondents who also appeal, but not to persons who only seek
permission to appeal):[58]

'(2)   The court may also make an order under [the primary jurisdiction] where the
appellant, or the respondent who also appeals, is a limited company and there is reason to
believe it will be unable to pay the costs of the other parties to the appeal should its appeal
be unsuccessful.'

16.27 It is possible for a defendant to seek an order against a person other than a
claimant; CPR, r 25.14 makes the requisite provisions:

---

[56]   CPR, r 25.13(2)(b) has been repealed and not replaced.
[57]   CPR, r 25.15(1), which reads: '(1) The court may order security for costs of an appeal against— (a) an
       appellant; (b) a respondent who also appeals, on the same grounds as it may order security for costs against
       a claimant under this Part.'
[58]   *Kevythalli Design v Ice Associates* [2010] EWCA Civ 379 at [3], per Aikens LJ; where the application is
       wrongly made under the primary jurisdiction, it is open to the court to allow the appliction notice to be
       amended to substitute the correct (ie secondary) jurisdiction: see, for example, *Mulford Holding &
       Investment Ltd v Greatex Ltd* [2010] EWCA Civ 1178, per Lloyd LJ.

'(1) The defendant may seek an order against someone other than the claimant, and the court may make an order for security for costs against that person if—

(a) it is satisfied, having regard to all the circumstances of the case, that it is just to make such an order; and

(b) one or more of the conditions in paragraph (2) applies.

(2) The conditions are that the person—

(a) has assigned the right to the claim to the claimant with a view to avoiding the possibility of a costs order being made against him; or

(b) has contributed or agreed to contribute to the claimant's costs in return for a share of any money or property which the claimant may recover in the proceedings; and

is a person against whom a costs order may be made.'

16.28 Thus, the primary jurisdiction is available where any of the conditions listed at **16.25–16.27** is met. Each of those conditions is addressed in turn.

Residence: CPR, r 25.13(2)(a)

16.29 The question here is whether the claimant is not resident in a contracting state (CPR, r 25.13(2)(a). This will be a matter of fact to be determined on the evidence. A list of contracting states can be found in the footnotes of **16.3**.

16.30 This condition will turn on the interpretation of the word 'resident'. The comparable words 'ordinarily resident' are, in other contexts, usually given their ordinary and natural meaning,[59] and there is no reason to believe that the word 'resident' in this context should be treated differently.[60] Where the person is a corporation, its residency will depend on where its central management and control lies.[61] The fact that a company may not have paid corporation tax in the United Kingdom is a factor relevant to the issue of whether it is resident outside the jurisdiction;[62] presumably, the same applies to other contracting states.

16.31 For the reasons set out more fully at **16.55–16.56**, the mere fact of residency outside a contracting state would not be sufficient to justify the court exercising its discretion in favour of the defendant.

16.32 The fact that a person may have other residences in places other than a contracting state will not prevent the court from finding that they are resident within a contracting state.[63] A person resident outside a contracting state is not able to evade the

---

[59] See, for example, *R v Barnett London Borough Council ex p Shah* [1983] 2 AC 309, HL.

[60] As originally worded, CPR Part 25 II used the words 'ordinarily resident' (see Civil Procedure (Amendment No 2) Rules 2002); whilst the contrary is arguable, it is generally accepted that the loss of the word 'ordinarily' was only stylistic, this being because the Explanatory Notes to the aforesaid amendment state the reason was for other reasons (namely, to comply with the guidance given in *De Beer v Kanaar & Co (a firm)* [2001] EWCA Civ 1318).

[61] *Re Little Olympian Each-Ways Ltd* [1994] 4 All ER 561, Ch D.

[62] *Texuna International Ltd v Cairn Energy plc* [2004] EWHC 1102 (Comm) at [8], per Gross J. See also *Re Little Olympian Each-Ways Ltd (No 2)* [1995] 1 BCLC 48.

[63] See *Somerset-Leeke and another v Kay Trustees* [2003] EWHC 1243 (Ch) at [1], per Jacob J; authorities decided before 2001 ought to be viewed with care, because the wording of the rules changed on this point in that year.

jurisdiction simply by the expedient of moving assets into a contracting state.[64] A person will not be regarded as being resident abroad merely because he has made a decision to move abroad.[65]

Ability of company to pay costs: CPR, r 25.13(2)(c)

16.33 The question here is whether the claimant is a company and there is reason to believe that it will be unable to pay the defendant's costs if ordered to do so (CPR, r 25.13(2)(c)). This is a question of fact and degree which may require expert evidence. With appropriate modifications, the principles set out at **16.37–16.39** apply.

Change of address: CPR, r 25.13(2)(d)

16.34 The question here is whether the claimant changed his address with a view to evading the consequences of the litigation (CPR, r 25.13(2)(d)). This is a question of fact and degree. To satisfy this condition there is a need to show a subjective intention to evade the consequences of the litigation; Moore-Bick J has explained that 'the consequences of the litigation' are not confined solely to the debt or damages sought.[66]

16.35 Where a natural person changes address for bona fide personal reasons, that may be sufficient explanation to avoid an order being made.[67] Presumably, the same is true if a company changes its addresses for bona fide business reasons.

Failure to give correct address: CPR, r 25.13(2)(e)

16.36 This factor is whether the claimant has failed to give his address correctly (CPR, r 25.13(2)(e)). Whether this condition is satisfied is a matter of fact and degree. Whilst the rule does mention intention, it is likely that the court would take into account factors such as whether the incorrect address was given by reason of mistake, who made the mistake, whether it was done for tactical purposes, etc.

Nominal claimants: CPR, r 25.13(2)(f)

16.37 The issue here is whether the claimant is acting as a nominal claimant and there is reason to believe that he will be unable to pay the defendant's costs if ordered to do so (CPR, r 25.13(2)(f)). Whether the claimant is acting as a nominal claimant will be a matter of fact, degree and law. Whilst his comments were made prior to the introduction of the CPR, Kennedy LJ has confirmed that the concept of a 'nominal claimant' should be narrowly interpreted and restricted to cases where there was an element of duplicity or window-dressing.[68] In a similar vein, Buckley LJ said:[69]

> 'It is a rule that a plaintiff ... cannot be called on to give security for costs merely because he is poor, it being deemed right and expedient that a court of justice should be open to every

---

[64] *De Beer v Kanaar & Co (a firm)* [2001] EWCA Civ 1318.

[65] *Appah v Monsen* [1967] 1 WLR 893.

[66] *Aoun v Bahri* [2002] EWHC 29 (Comm) at [18]. Compare this with *Re Myer Wolff & Manley* (unreported) 23 April 1985, CA, in which a person's return to the jurisdiction was found to be bona fide.

[67] *Aoun v Bahri* [2002] EWHC 29 (Comm) at [27].

[68] *Envis v Thakkar* [1997] BPIR 189; see also *Semler v Murphy* [1968] 1 Ch 183, where an order was made notwithstanding the fact that a narrow test was applied. In days gone by, a test of whether the claimant was 'a mere shadow of another person' was applied (see 1885 Law Times Rep LIII 484/2).

[69] *White v Butt* [1909] 1 KB 50 at 55.

one. An exception, however, from that rule is that, if a plaintiff is what has been called a "nominal plaintiff" or what, by way of alternative expression, I will call a "fictitious plaintiff", and is without means, security for costs will be ordered. An example of the kind of case in which that expression "nominal plaintiff" is applicable is where a person in whom a cause of action was vested, not being minded to bring an action himself, has assigned that cause of action to another, whom he puts forward for the purpose of suing, but who has no beneficial interest in the subject-matter of the litigation.'

16.38 Decisions concerning nominal claimants are highly fact-sensitive, but case examples are, nonetheless, illustrative of the court's approach. A claimant who had assigned the benefit of the claim to a third party without retaining any interest in the matter himself was found to be a nominal claimant.[70] On the other hand, a bankrupt to whom the trustee had assigned the right to claim damages was not found to be a nominal claimant, largely because the trustee retained a one-third interest in the benefit of the claim. The court came to a similar conclusion in the context of corporate insolvency, where the liquidator retained a 50% interest in the benefit of a claim.[71]

16.39 The topic of whether the claimant would be unable to pay the defendant's costs if ordered to do so is covered at **16.42–16.47**. Whilst a different topic, the matters set out at **16.16** (concerning third parties) may also be relevant.

Asset sequestration: CPR, r 25.13(2)(g)

16.40 The issue here is whether the claimant has taken steps to put his assets beyond reach (CPR, r 25.13(2)(g)). This will be a matter of fact and degree.[72] Ferris J has explained that there is no need to show subjective intention to avoid the consequences of the litigation[73] (although, presumably, this would be a factor to be taken into account when the court exercises its discretion). The mere fact that a person has been guilty of dishonesty in the past would not, of itself, be reason to find that the requisite threshold had been met.[74] Likewise, Park J has explained that the court will be most unlikely to exercise its discretion if the steps taken by the claimant were ones to which no realistic objection could be taken, like paying his own costs of the litigation.[75] HHJ Pelling QC (sitting as a Judge of the High Court) has indicated that it would only be in the rarest of circumstances that the court would exercise its discretion to make an order for security solely by reference to an assignment of rights under a loan agreement.[76] A refusal on the part of the claimant to give details about his finances may result in the court drawing adverse inferences about his motives and assets.[77]

---

[70] See, for example, *Lloyd v Hathern Station Brick Co Ltd* (1901) 85 LT 158 and *Semler v Murphy* [1967] 2 All ER 185, but compare this with *Cook v Whellock* (1890) 24 QBD 658.

[71] *Farmer v Moseley (Holdings) Ltd* (2001) BCLC 572.

[72] Roth J has summarised the relevant law in *Ackerman v Ackerman* [2011] EWHC (Ch) at [16].

[73] *Harris v Wallis* [2006] EWHC 630 (Ch) at [22].

[74] *Chandler v Brown* (2001) CP Rep 103 (Ch D) at [20]–[23], per Park J.

[75] *Chandler v Brown* (2001) CP Rep 103 (Ch D) at [23], per Park J.

[76] *In the Matter of Abbington Hotel Ltd sub nom D'angelo v Digrado et al* [2010] EWHC 1628 (Ch) at [12], per HHJ Pelling QC.

[77] As an example, see *Dubai Islamic Bank PJSC v PSI Energy Holding Co Bsc & Ors* [2011] EWCA Civ 761 in which the claimant claimed his seemingly substantial income was mostly loans from 'family, family-affiliated companies and third parties'; in those circumstances, it was possible to infer that there were undisclosed assets.

16.41 Ferris J has found that there is no basis for implying some temporal limitation on the steps which are referred to in CPR, r 25.14; thus, if a person took steps to avoid enforcement of a costs order, those steps may be taken into account notwithstanding the fact that they were taken many years ago.[78]

Appeals and inability to bear costs: CPR r 25.15(2)

16.42 The question here, which applies only to appellants and respondents who also appeal, is whether the appellant (or appealing respondent) will be unable to pay the costs of the other parties to the appeal should its appeal be unsuccessful (CPR, r 25.15(2)). The issue of whether the claimant will be able to meet an adverse costs order is a matter of fact and degree; expert evidence may be required. This condition is atypical in that it applies only to appeals rather than to claims and appeals (although a very similar test may be relevant in the context of corporate claimants and nominal claimants who bring claims: see **16.33** and **16.37–16.39** respectively). Arden LJ has confirmed that the court must take into account all the relevant facts and that the matter is to be decided on the balance of probabilities rather than on the basis of whether there is a risk:[79]

> 'The phrase "the company will be unable to pay" requires more than simply that there is doubt whether the company will pay. Otherwise the second limb would have to say "the company may be unable to pay the costs". Secondly ... the court must have regard to conflicting evidence. The court must reach its conclusion as to whether the conditions in the statute are satisfied by reference to the totality of the evidence.'

These comments were not made under the CPR,[80] but Rattee J has confirmed they continue to apply by analogy.[81]

16.43 Whilst it seems not to have been elevated to the status of a presumption of fact, the fact that a company is in liquidation is capable of being prima facie evidence of the fact it would be unable to meet a costs order.[82]

16.44 Timing may be important in two regards. First, if the claimant's financial position is likely to change, that may be taken into account.[83] Secondly, the court will look at the question of whether the claimant will be able to pay *when* ordered to do so. This raises questions concerning liquidity. Park J has approved of the following pre-CPR comments of Nicholls V-C:[84]

> '... the question is, will the company be able to meet the costs order at the time when the order is made and requires to be met?'

---

[78] *Harris v Wallis* [2006] EWHC 630 (Ch) at [22].

[79] *Jirehouse Capital v Beller* [2008] EWCA Civ 908 at [24]. See too *Unisoft Group Ltd (No 2)* [1993] BCLC 532; *Texuna International Ltd v Cairn Energy plc* [2004] EWHC 1102 (Comm) at [13], per Gross J.

[80] They were made under the now revoked provisions mentioned at **16.8**.

[81] *Ovlas Trading SA v Strand (London) Ltd* [2008] EWHC 3236 (Ch) at [9].

[82] *Smith v UIC Insurance Co Ltd* [2001] BCC 11.

[83] By way of example, Kennedy LJ refused to interfere with a decision not to make an order in circumstances where the claimant was likely to be awarded a substantial sum in another action before any enforcement proceedings would be likely to be required on behalf of the defendant: *Cripps v Heritage Distribution Corporation* (1999) *The Times*, November 10, CA.

[84] *Longstaff International Ltd v McKenzie* [2004] EWHC 1852 (Ch) at [18], quoting from *Re Unisoft Group Ltd (No 2)* [1993] BCLC 532 at 534; see also the comment of Sonia Proudman QC (sitting as a High Court judge) in *Thistle Hotels Ltd v Gamma Four Ltd* [2004] EWHC 322 (Ch) at [11].

16.45 Thus, regardless of whether his assets would be sufficient to discharge any relevant costs debt, an order may be made against a claimant where those assets are illiquid to such an extent that they could not be realised in time to pay. (In practice, however, many claimants prefer to borrow against the assets or to obtain a bank guarantee rather than have an order made against them.)

16.46 The court may have regard to the finances of persons who are sufficiently close to the claimant to be expected to make a contribution towards any costs debt. In this regard, Rimer LJ had this to say:[85]

> 'Nowadays the court has to have regard not just to whether the corporate appellant can itself provide security, but whether those behind it can put it in funds to do so.'

16.47 The existence of ATE insurance may be a relevant factor: the comments made at **16.63** would apply.

Assignment with a view of evasion: CPR, 25.14(2)(a)

16.48 The question here is whether a person has assigned the right to the claim to the claimant with a view to avoiding the possibility of a costs order being enforced against him (CPR, r 24.14(2)(a)). The issue of whether there has been an assignment will be largely a question of law. There is no authority addressing unsuccessful attempts to assign, but where those were the facts, it may be that the court would consider invoking the secondary jurisdictions.

16.49 In order to invoke the primary jurisdiction, the court must, in addition to finding that there has been an assignment, be satisfied that there was a subjective intention on the part of the claimant to avoid the possibility of a costs order being enforced against him.[86] That will be a question of fact and degree.

Funders: CPR, r 25.14(2)(b)

16.50 The issue here is whether any person has contributed (or has agreed to contribute) to the claimant's costs in return for a share of the proceeds: (CPR, r 25.14(2)(b)). It is because of this provision, amongst others (see **7.175-7.180**), that most litigation funders will insist on the client having after the event insurance (see **41.25**). Whether there is an agreement to contribute in return for a share of the proceeds of the claim will be a matter of fact. It used to be the case that applications under this ground were commonly accompanied by applications to stay the proceedings on the grounds of champertous maintenance, but this is less common now that the law of champerty has been put in its highly fact-sensitive modern context (see **9.325-9.350**).

Discretion (primary jurisdiction)

16.51 The court's task is to make an order which is just.[87] The test is whether the court is satisfied, having regard to all the circumstances of the case, that it is just to make an

---

[85]   *Meridian International Services Ltd v Richardson* [2008] EWCA Civ 490 at [16]. See also *Keary Developments Ltd v Tarmac Construction Ltd and Another* [1995] 3 AER 534 at 540, per Peter Gibson LJ.

[86]   *Eurocross Sales Ltd v Cornhill Insurance plc* [1995] 1 WLR 1517; see also Ferris J's obiter comments in *Harris v Wallis* [2006] EWHC 630 (Ch) at [22].

[87]   *Fernhill Mining Ltd v Kier Construction Ltd* (unreported) 27 January 2000, CA, at [52], per Evans LJ.

order for security for costs.[88] The court will not exercise its discretion to order security merely on the basis that one of the preconditions mentioned above has been satisfied.[89]

16.52 Whilst it has repeatedly been confirmed that the court has the freedom to take into account any admissible circumstances which it deems to be relevant,[90] the power should not be used to discriminate against persons on grounds unrelated to enforcement.[91] Each case will be decided on its own facts, but it is informative to consider a number of factors which may be relevant. They are addressed in no particular order.

Counterclaims

16.53 In commercial litigation, the question of whether a party is a claimant or a defendant is largely a matter of simply who won the race to issue proceedings; in recognition of this the court may exercise its discretion against making an order if the effect of the order would be simply to give the defendant the right to begin.[92] Hamblen J has explained that as a general rule, the court will not make an order for security of the costs of a claim if the same issues arise on the claim and counterclaim and the costs incurred in defending that claim would also be incurred in prosecuting the counterclaim.[93] There are exceptions, however:

- **Differences in the facts relied upon:** Where the claim raises substantial factual inquiries which are not the subject of the counterclaim, an order for security may be appropriate notwithstanding the fact that the claim provides a defence to the counterclaim;[94] such an order will normally be limited to the costs of addressing additional issues raised only by the claim.[95]
- **Differences in amounts claimed:** In cases where the claim and counterclaim raise additional issues, it may also be relevant to consider whether the quantum of the claim in respect of which security is sought is substantially greater than the applicant's claim.[96]

Plural litigants

16.54 The fact that a claimant has a co-claimant who is resident in the jurisdiction will not, of itself, preclude an order being made.[97] The fact that a co-claimant would be able

---

88   CPR, r 25.13(1)(a).
89   See *Nasser v United Bank of Kuwait* [2002] EWCA Civ 556 at [56]–[61]; see also *Kahangi v Nourizadeh* [2009] EWHC 2451 (QB) at [11], per Eady J.
90   Whilst pre-CPR cases, *Sir Lindsay Parkinson & Co Ltd v Triplan Ltd* [1973] 2 All ER 273 at 286 and *Keary Developments Ltd v Tarmac Construction Ltd* [1995] 3 All ER 534 at 539 are both frequently cited on this point; see also *Dominion Brewery v Foster* (1897) 77 LT 507.
91   *Nasser v United Bank of Kuwait* [2002] EWCA Civ 556 at [56]–[61].
92   *Crabtree (B J) (Insulation) Ltd v GPT Communications Systems Ltd* (1990) 59 BLR 43. See also *Anglo Petroleum v TFB* [2003] EWHC 1177, per Park at [32]: 'In general, the courts recognise that, where there are cross-proceedings, the position is as I have described, and the courts do not order a person in the position of A to provide security for the costs of the claim he is making himself'.
93   *Dumrul v Standard Chartered Bank* [2010] EWHC 2625 (Comm) at [5]; see also *Mapleson v Masini* (1879-80) LR 5 QBD 144 QBD and *Anglo Irish Asset Finance Plc v Brendan Flood* [2011] EWCA Civ 799.
94   *Shaw-Lloyd v ASM Shipping* [2006] EWHC 1958 (QB); *Newman v Wenden* [2007] EWHC 336 (TCC).
95   *Dumrul v Standard Chartered Bank* [2010] EWHC 2625 (Comm) at [8].
96   *Newman v Wenden*; *Hutchison Telephone v Ultimate Response* [1993] BCLC 307.
97   *Slazengers Ltd v Seaspeed Ferries International Ltd* [1987] 3 All ER 967, CA; this will be particularly so where the person within a contracting state has been added solely for the purposes of defeating an

to proceed with the claim even if an order were to be made against another co-claimant would not be a reason for not making an order.[98]

Residency

16.55 Although residence outside a contracting state may be a necessary condition to the application, this alone would not be sufficient to justify an order for security.[99] Such an approach would be discriminatory and contrary to Art 14 of the European Convention for the Protection of Human Rights; the court has now adopted a more flexible approach in that discretion should be exercised on objectively justified grounds relating to obstacles to or the burden of enforcement in the context of the particular country concerned.[100]

16.56 Mance LJ has explained that the mere absence of reciprocal arrangements or legislation providing for enforcement of foreign judgments could not of itself justify an inference that enforcement would not be possible.[101] Nonetheless, there is no need to adduce evidence of the obvious: Mance LJ noted that there are some parts of the world where the natural assumption would be that there would not just be substantial obstacles to enforcement, but that enforcement may be impossible. He also noted that there are other areas where enforcement would be difficult and would involve an additional burden of costs or delay.[102] The language that Mance LJ used suggested that these facts could be established by way of judicial notice without inquiry. It may, on occasion, be difficult to find a witness (usually a local lawyer) who is willing to give evidence about the relevant legal system; Eady J appeared to accept that this was a factor which may be taken into account when evaluating the evidence.[103] Where this is the case, publications of international commentators, courts, and trade publications may be taken into account.[104]

Assets within a contracting state

16.57 Where a claimant is resident outside a contracting state but has assets within a contracting state, then the court will take into account the integrity of the claimant; if that is not in doubt, the court will, in general, not conclude that there is a risk that steps will be taken to put the assets beyond reach. If the claimant's integrity is in doubt, then the court will examine the nature of the assets in order to form a view as to how easily they may be put beyond reach.[105] The court may consider making an order that the assets are not to be removed from the contracting state without the consent of the defendant or an order of the court.[106]

---

application for security for costs: whilst on a slightly different point, see *Jones and Saldanha v Gurney* [1913] WN 72, per Swinfen Eady J. See also *John Bishop (Caterers) Ltd v National Union Bank* [1973] 3 All ER 707.

[98]   *Okotcha v Voest Alpine Intertrading GmbH* [1993] BCLC 474.

[99]   See *Al-Koronky and another v Time Life Entertainments Group Ltd* [2005] EWHC 1688 (QB) at [23], per Eady J, referring to *Nasser v United Bank of Kuwait* [2001] EWCA Civ 556; see also *Berkeley Administration Inc v McClelland* [1990] 2 QB 407, CA, and *Somerset-Leeke and another v Kay Trustees* [2003] EWHC 1243 (Ch) at [9]–[12], per Jacob J.

[100]   *Nasser v United Bank of Kuwait* [2002] EWCA Civ 556 at [56]–[61].

[101]   *Nasser v United Bank of Kuwait* [2001] EWCA Civ 556 at [65].

[102]   *Nasser v United Bank of Kuwait* [2001] EWCA Civ 556 at [64].

[103]   *Kahangi v Nourizadeh* [2009] EWHC 2451 (QB) at [13]–[20], per Eady J; the learned judge took into account evidence from a local lawyer which was anonymous.

[104]   For an example of the type of material which may be relied upon, see *Kahangi v Nourizadeh* [2009] EWHC 2451 (QB) at [14] onwards.

[105]   *Leyvand v Barasch* [2000] All ER (D) 181 at [6], per Lightman J.

[106]   See, for example, *De Bry v Fitzgeral* [1990] 1 WLR 552 and *Kevorkian v Burney (No 2)* [1937] 4 All ER 468.

Merits of the claim

16.58 If the strengths and weaknesses of the claim can be discerned without prolonged examination of voluminous evidence, the court may take the merits of the case into account.[107] On occasion, this may be a significant factor; an example would be that it is ordinarily the case that no order will be made where the claimant is highly likely to succeed.[108]

16.59 In so far as the strengths and weaknesses of a claim (as opposed to an appeal) are concerned, the court should not descend into the detail unless it can clearly be demonstrated that there is a high degree of probability of success or failure.[109] As to the extent of the investigation into merits, Browne-Wilkinson V-C had this to say (albeit in a pre-CPR case):[110]

> 'Undoubtedly, if it can clearly be demonstrated that the plaintiff is likely to succeed, in the sense that there is a very high probability of success, then that is a matter that can properly be weighed in the balance. Similarly, if it can be shown that there is a very high probability that the defendant will succeed, that is a matter that can be weighed. But for myself I deplore the attempt to go into the merits of the case unless it can be clearly demonstrated one way or another that there is a high degree of probability of success or failure.'

16.60 A similar point was made (under the CPR) by Eady J:[111]

> 'A vitally important principle for me to have in mind in the instant case (and the importance of which I do not believe has been diminished by the advent of the Human Rights Act 1998) is that the court should not, upon such an application, enter into the merits of the case in any detail, save in the exceptional case where one party or the other can demonstrate a high degree of probability of success.'

16.61 The position is not the same in so far as an appeal is concerned; this is because the court will already know a great deal about the claim. In this regard, Briggs J had this to say:[112]

> 'The starting point is not that the court simply has no idea [about the merits] ... I bear in mind that there is an appeal which is not suggested to be fanciful or lacking any real prospect of success. Against those conclusions the court does not, as it usually does in a first instance security case, start with there having been no investigation of the merits by any tribunal at any level at all.'

16.62 Browne-Wilkinson V-C has confirmed that the court may take into account any open offer,[113] this being potentially indicative of the parties' belief in the strength or

---

[107] *Porzelack KG v Porzelack (UK) Ltd* [1987] 1 All ER 1074.
[108] See, for example, *Al-Koronky and another v Time Life Entertainments Group Ltd* [2005] EWHC 1688 (QB) at [33]; see also *Keary Developments Ltd v Tarmac Construction Ltd* [1995] 3 All ER 534 at 539 and 540 and *Kahangi v Nourizadeh* [2009] EWHC 2451 (QB) at [8], per Eady J.
[109] This is a long-established principle: see *Porzelack KG v Porzelack (UK) Ltd* [1987] 1 All ER 1074 at 1077, per Browne-Wilkinson V-C and *Keary Developments Ltd v Tarmac Construction Ltd* [1995] 3 All ER 534 at 540, per Peter Gibson LJ.
[110] *Porzelack KG v Porzelack (UK) Ltd* [1987] 1 All ER 1074 at 1077.
[111] *Al-Koronky and another v Time Life Entertainments Group Ltd* [2005] EWHC 1688 (QB) at [33]; see also *Keary Developments Ltd v Tarmac Construction Ltd* [1995] 3 All ER 534 at 539 and 540.
[112] *Calltel Telecom Ltd and another v HM Revenue & Customs* [2008] EWHC 2107 (Ch) at [17]; see also *Ahmed v Blackburn & Co* [2001] EWCA Civ 141 at [10], in which May LJ took into account that the judge who gave permission to appeal did not give 'undue encouragement' to the appellant.
[113] See *Porzelack KG v Porzelack (UK) Ltd* [1987] 1 WLR 420 at 423.

their respective cases. For obvious reasons, the court will not take into account inadmissible offers (see **16.106**). When it does choose to take an offer into account, the court will bear in mind that the offer may have been made for commercial reasons, as opposed to for reasons which reflect the advice that the parties have received.[114] Denning MR made similar comments pre-CPR.[115]

Funding

16.63 The fact that a claimant has ATE insurance may be relevant; this is because this may provide a source from which a costs order can be met. The court may disregard the policy if there is a high risk that there was material non-disclosure of the relevant facts.[116] The nature of the insurance is relevant, however, as are its terms. If, for example, the whole case turns on whether the claimant is telling the truth, a policy which precluded indemnity in circumstances where the insured had lied would not afford any real comfort to the defendant.[117] Likewise, the court may find that a policy that can be cancelled at any time for no reason should not be regarded as affording any comfort to the defendant.[118]

16.64 It may be relevant that a claim is being funded by way of a conditional fee agreement; there are two ways in which this may be so. First, a conditional fee agreement may relieve the claimant from the burden of having to pay his own costs in the event of the claim being lost (thereby increasing the monies available for meeting an adverse costs order) and, secondly, the court may find that the success fee has the effect of exerting unfair pressure on the defendant. Eady J has confirmed that where there is no ATE insurance (or no proper ATE insurance), the court is likely to give particular weight to the second of these factors.[119]

Impecuniosity and illiquidity

16.65 In so far as impecuniosity is concerned, there are two competing factors at play.[120] On the one hand (and subject to what is said below), the court will seek to prevent an impecunious claimant using his inability to pay as a weapon in the litigation,[121] but, on the other hand, the court will seek not to make an order which will stifle the claim. The second of these topics is discussed in detail at **16.71–16.79**.

16.66 The extent to which the court is able to give effect to the first of these factors has been diminished by the Human Rights Act 1998 ('HRA 1998') and by modern attitudes towards access to justice.[122] Mance LJ has explained that the modern emphasis on access to justice means that the court will not make an order on the bare fact that a claimant would be unable to meet a costs order made against it. He has explained that

---

[114] Ibid.

[115] *Sir Lindsay Parkinson & Co Ltd v Triplan Ltd* [1973] 2 All ER 273 at 286.

[116] Whilst a Scottish case, see *Monarch Energy Ltd v Powergen Retail Ltd* [2006] CSOH 102.

[117] See, for example, *Al-Koronky and another v Time Life Entertainments Group Ltd* [2005] EWHC 1688 (QB); see also *Belco Trading Ltd v Kordo* [2008] EWCA Civ 205.

[118] See, for example, *Michael Phillips Architects Ltd v Riklin* [2010] EWHC 834 (TCC) at [29], per Akenhead J.

[119] *Al-Koronky and another v Time Life Entertainments Group Ltd* [2005] EWHC 1688 (QB) at [30]; see also *Nasser v United Bank of Kuwait* [2001] EWCA Civ 556 at [60].

[120] *Keary Developments Ltd v Tarmac Construction Ltd* [1995] 3 All ER 534 at 540.

[121] This is a long-established principle; see *Pearson v Naydler* [1977] 3 All ER 531 at 537 and *Keary Developments Ltd v Tarmac Construction Ltd* [1995] 3 All ER 534 at 540.

[122] For a general discussion of a related topic, see *Hamilton v Al Fayed (No 2)* [2002] 3 All ER 641 at 658–659, per Simon Brown LJ.

instead the court is concerned about the extra burden (in both time and expense) that enforcement abroad may place upon the defendant.[123]

16.67 Where a claimant seeks to resist an order on the basis of his own impecuniosity, the onus is on him to prove that fact; in so doing, he would be expected to make full and frank disclosure.[124] That requirement is not incompatible with Art 6 of the ECHR.[125] If he chooses not to disclose up-to-date accounts, then he may fail to prove that he has sufficient liquidity to discharge an order as and when it fell due.[126] Where the defendant has caused or contributed to the claimant's impecuniosity, that is a factor that the court is able to take into account;[127] whilst a pre-CPR case, Bowen LJ highlighted the injustice of allowing a defendant to benefit from having wrongly caused the claimant to become impecunious:[128]

> 'Suppose the Plaintiff in that case had been right on the point of law, his insolvency would have arisen from the wrongful act complained of in the action. To have required a security for costs on the ground of an insolvency which (if the Plaintiff was right) the Defendant had wrongly caused might have been a denial of justice.'

16.68 The court may take into account the relative financial strengths of the parties.[129]

16.69 In considering whether the claimant would be able to provide security, the court is able to take into account the resources of third parties who could reasonably be expected to assist; this may, in the case of a corporate claimant, include shareholders or associated companies or, in the case of an individual claimant, friends and relatives.[130] Briggs J has commented that a factor to be taken into account is the likelihood that the third party in question would be likely to make the payment voluntarily if an adverse costs order were made.[131]

Wealth

16.70 In the same way that impecuniosity will not be determinative of whether an order for security should be made, wealth on the part of the claimant will not afford a claimant a complete answer to an application; this is because the court will take into account all the relevant factors, including the burden that might be imposed on the defendant if he had to enforce an order for costs (see **16.55–16.56**).[132]

---

[123] *Nasser v United Bank of Kuwait* [2001] EWCA Civ 556 at [34] in particular.

[124] *M V Yorke Motors (a firm) v Edwards* [1982] 1 All ER 1024 at 1027, per Lord Diplock, affirmed post-CPR in *Anglo-Eastern Trust Ltd and another v Kermanshahchi* [2002] EWCA Civ 198.

[125] *Mahan Air v Blue Sky One Ltd* [2011] EWCA Civ 544 at [38], per Stanley Burnton LJ.

[126] *Trade Storage Ltd v Papanicola* [2011] EWHC 598 (Ch).

[127] Whilst a pre-CPR case, see *Farrer v Lacy, Hartland & Co* (1885) 28 Ch D 482 at 485, per Bowen LJ; see also *Aquilla Design (GRP Products) Ltd v Cornhill Insurance plc* [1988] BCLC 134 at 137, per Fox LJ and *Keary Developments Ltd v Tarmac Construction Ltd* [1995] 3 All ER 534 at 540.

[128] *Farrar v Lacy v Hartland & Co* (1885) 28 Ch D 482 at 485; see also *Calltel Telecom Ltd and another v HM Revenue & Customs* [2008] EWHC 2107 (Ch) at [16], per Briggs J, and *Keary Developments Ltd v Tarmac Construction Ltd* [1995] 3 All ER 534 at 540.

[129] *Classic Catering Ltd v Donnington Park Leisure Ltd* [2001] 1 BCLC 537, per HHJ Weeks sitting as a judge of the High Court.

[130] Whilst obiter, see the comments of Rimer LJ in *Conroy v National Westminster Bank* [2009] EWCA Civ 1199 at [31]. See also *Brimko Holdings Ltd v Eastman Kodak Company* [2004] EWHC 1343 (Ch), per Park J; see also *Al-Koronky and another v Time Life Entertainments Group Ltd* [2005] EWHC 1688 (QB) at [32].

[131] *Calltel Telecom Ltd and another v HM Revenue & Customs* [2008] EWHC 2107 (Ch) at [23].

[132] *Kahangi v Nourizadeh* [2009] EWHC 2451 (QB) at [12], per Eady J.

The possibility of stifling the claim

16.71 As explained at **16.65**, the court will strive not to act oppressively by making an order which will stifle the claim. Peter Gibson LJ had this to say about the possibility of oppression (albeit prior to the introduction of the HRA 1998 and the CPR):[133]

> 'The court must carry out a balancing exercise. On the one hand it must weigh the injustice to the plaintiff if prevented from pursuing a proper claim by an order for security. Against that, it must weigh the injustice to the defendant if no security is ordered and at the trial the plaintiff's claim fails and the defendant finds himself unable to recover from the plaintiff the costs which have been incurred by him in his defence of the claim.'

16.72 He went on to say this:[134]

> 'The court will properly be concerned not to allow the power to order security to be used as an instrument of oppression, such as by stifling a genuine claim by an indigent company against a more prosperous company, particularly when the failure to meet that claim might in itself have been a material cause of the plaintiff's impecuniosity ... But it will also be concerned not to be so reluctant to order security that it becomes a weapon whereby the impecunious company can use its inability to pay costs as a means of putting unfair pressure on the more prosperous company.'

16.73 Where the claimant seeks to avoid an order on the grounds that it would stifle the claim, the onus is on him to prove that assertion.[135] A claimant does not need to show with certainty that his claim will be stifled: it would be sufficient to show that this was more likely than not.[136] The claimant would have to show something more than a mere discouraging effect: it has been established since well before the introduction of the CPR that the possibility or probability that the claimant will be deterred from pursuing its claim by an order for security is not without more a sufficient reason for not ordering security.[137]

16.74 Rix LJ has confirmed that the court may take into account not only the financial position of the claimant, but the relative positions of the parties and the conduct of the defendant; if the defendant has sought, by its conduct, to the stifle the claim, then that may be a factor to take into account.[138]

---

[133] *Keary Developments Ltd v Tarmac Construction Ltd* [1995] 3 All ER 534 at 540; this was pre-CPR case, but it was cited with approval by Eady J in *Al-Koronky and another v Time Life Entertainments Group Ltd* [2005] EWHC 1688 (QB) at [28].For a post-HRA example of the court not making an order because of concern about Art 6 of the ECHR, see *Golubovich v Golubovich* [2011] EWCA Civ 528.

[134] *Keary Developments Ltd v Tarmac Construction Ltd* [1995] 3 All ER 534 at 540.

[135] *Kuenyehia v International Hospitals Group Ltd* [2007] EWCA Civ 274 at [26]–[27], per Tuckey LJ. See *Radu v Houston* [2006] EWCA Civ 1575 at [19]; see also *Keary Developments Ltd v Tarmac Construction Ltd* [1995] 3 All ER 534 at 540–541 and *Aquila Design (GRB) Products Ltd v Cornhill Insurance plc* [1988] BCLC 134, CA.

[136] *Trident International Freight Services Ltd v Manchester Ship Canal Co* [1990] BCLC 263, CA.

[137] See *Okotcha v Voest Alpine Intertrading GmbH* [1993] BCLC 474 at 479, per Bingham LJ and *Keary Developments Ltd v Tarmac Construction Ltd* [1995] 3 All ER 534 at 540, per Gibson LJ.

[138] *Pablo Star Ltd v Emirates Integrated Telecommunications Co* [2009] EWCA Civ 616 at [29]. As an example of this, see *Mastermailer Stationery Ltd v Sandison*, (unreported) 20 April 2011, Ch D, in which Vos J found that the application for security had been geared to defeat the claim.

16.75 The court is permitted to take into account financial support that the directors, shareholders or other backers may be able to provide; because these are things which are peculiarly within the respondent's knowledge, he will bear the burden of proving matters in that regard.[139]

16.76 The fact that a company is continuing to raise finance for the purposes of trading may be relevant; Moore-Bick LJ, for example, was persuaded that, despite a claimant's finances being in a parlous state, the fact that it was still trading was evidence that an order would not stifle the claim.[140]

16.77 Longmore LJ has explained that because a stay immediately before a trial is similar in effect to an unless order, the court will be more inclined to accept that a claim is likely to be stifled if that assertion is made in the context of an application shortly before trial.[141] If the application is made in the context of an extant appeal where the judgment below is stayed pending the appeal, and if lifiting the stay on that judgment would stifle the appeal, it is an option to modify the stay so as to grant the respondent a degree of security for costs.[142]

16.78 As to the nature of evidence required, Eady J had this to say:[143]

> 'There needs to be full, frank, clear and unequivocal evidence before I should draw any conclusion that a particular order will have the effect of stifling. The test is whether it is more likely than not.'

It is not uncommon to see expert evidence on the point.[144]

Late applications

16.79 Where an application is made very late (ie shortly before trial), that is be a factor that the court is able to take into account. One way in which such applications have been disposed of in the past (albeit only by consent) has been for security to be given in a form that can always be given immediately, namely, a personal guarantee;[145] the result might be that the party making the application has to bear the risk as to the worthlessness of the personal guarantee, but that would only be fair if that party is responsible for the fact that the application was made so late.

The nature of the costs for which security is sought

16.80 The court has the vires to make an order in respect of pre-action costs, but Coulson J has explained that the court should be slow to do so. He expressed concern that if the pre-issue phase of the litigation was lengthy the costs might be high, and that an order for security for costs may become penal in nature. He also explained that particular caution ought to be exercised where the costs in respect of which the security

---

[139] This is a principle which precedes the CPR; see *Flender Werft AG v Aegean Maritime Ltd* [1990] 2 Lloyd's Rep 27, per Saville J and *Keary Developments Ltd v Tarmac Construction Ltd* [1995] 3 All ER 534 at 541. Whilst obiter, see also *Kahangi v Nourizadeh* [2009] EWHC 2451 (QB) at [9], per Eady J.

[140] *Daley v Environmental Recycling Technologies plc* [2009] EWCA Civ 1088 at [21]–[22].

[141] *Vedatech Corporation v Crystal Decisions (UK) Ltd* [2002] EWCA Civ 356 at [25]. See also *Spy Academy Ltd v Sahar International Inc* [2009] EWCA Civ 481.

[142] *North Shore Ventures Ltd v Anstead Holdings Inc* [2010] EWCA Civ 1634.

[143] *Al-Koronky and another v Time Life Entertainments Group Ltd* [2005] EWHC 1688 (QB) at [31].

[144] As and example of this, *see Chemistree Homecare Ltd v Roche Products Ltd* [2011] EWHC 1579 (Ch).

[145] *Inventors Friend Ltd v Leathes Prior* (unreported) 12 January 2011, QBD.

is sought were incurred long before the proceedings were commenced; this was primarily because he believed that such costs were more likely to be disputed.[146]

Cross liabilities, etc

16.81 The fact that the defendant may already have an order in his favour (such as an order made in other proceedings) will not diminish the court's jurisdiction to make an order for security.[147] Where, on the other hand, the effect of a pre-existing freezing order is to provide sufficient security, this may be reason to decline to make an order.[148] Likewise, if the defendant has made admissions which equal or exceed the appropriate amount of security, it would be open to the court to decline to make an order on the basis that the defendant is, in effect, providing his own security.[149]

Specific types of claimant

16.82 Each case will be decided on its own facts, but it is worth focusing on three specific types of litigant: liquidator and receivers, children, and litigant friends. As will be seen, ancient rules and practices do not necessarily apply today.

16.83 First, liquidators and receivers. A liquidator does not have a duty to ensure that the company can meet the defendant's costs order; Lawrence Collins LJ has explained that a defendant's protection would lie in making an application against the company rather than against the liquidator or receiver personally.[150]

16.84 Second, children. There is ancient authority that security for costs ought not to be ordered against children, even where the litigation friend is insolvent.[151] It is not known whether that thinking survives under the CPR, but one of the principles underlying it is still relevant today, and that is that a child usually has no voice in the litigation, which is usually brought on his behalf by others.[152] It is for this reason, amongst others, that the law focuses on the litigation friend rather than the child (see below).

16.85 Finally, litigant friends. There is an ancient rule in Chancery that it would be dangerous to displace a litigation friend for poverty;[153] this developed into a rule against requiring security for costs from the litigation friend of a child.[154] Towards the end of the nineteenth century that rule began to be eroded[155] and, even before this, it was often

---

[146] *Lobster Group Ltd v Heidelberg Graphic Equipment Ltd* [2008] EWHC 413 (TCC) at [11]–[12].

[147] Whilst a pre-CPR case, see *Flender Werft AG v Aegean Maritime Ltd* [1990] 2 Lloyd's Rep 27, QBD, in which it was held that the fact that a defendant had an arbitral award against the claimant did not prevent the court from making an order for security for costs.

[148] *Hitachi Shipbuilding & Engineering Co Ltd v Viafel Compania Navieran SA* [1981] 2 Lloyd's Re 468, CA.

[149] *Hogan v Hogan (No 2)* [1924] 2 IR 14; this is a pre-CPR case, but there is no reason to believe that the principle does not apply under the CPR. See also *Sir Lindsay Parkinson & Co Ltd v Triplan Ltd* [1973] 2 All ER 273 at 286.

[150] *Mills v Birchall* [2008] EWCA Civ 385 at [84]–[88], per Lawrence Collins LJ; see also *Metalloy Supplies Ltd v MA (UK) Ltd* [1997] 1 WLR 1613 at 1718, per Waller LJ.

[151] *Yarnworth's Case* (1823) 2 Dow & Ry KB 423 and *Anon* (1813) 1 Marsh 4.

[152] *Re Payne, Randle v Payne* (1883) 23 Ch D 288 at 289, per Cotton LJ.

[153] See *Squirrel v Squirrel* (1792) 2 Dick 765.

[154] See, for example, *Fellows v Barrett* (1836) 1 Keen 119 and *St John v Earl of Bessborough* (1819) 1 Hog 41.

[155] See, for example, *Martano v Mann* (1880) 14 Ch D 419 and *Jones v Evans* (1886) 31 Sol Jo 11.

circumvented.[156] Under the CPR there is no mention of litigation friends in the context of orders for security for costs. It is probably the case that the court is now unencumbered by the ancient rule mentioned above, and that it will simply decide each case on its own facts.[157]

Discretion (secondary jurisdictions)

16.86 As has been explained above (**16.18**), each of the secondary jurisdictions needs to be considered separately as the two are wholly different:

- **CPR, r 3.1(3):** Moore-Bick LJ has explained that the power under CPR, r 3.1(3) should not be exercised solely on the grounds that the party in question is not conducting the litigation in good faith, nor should it be exercised on the sole grounds that there is a history of repeated failures to comply with orders of the court[158]; instead, before exercising the power given by that rule the court should identify the purpose of imposing a condition and satisfy itself that the condition it has in mind represents a proportionate and effective means of achieving that purpose having regard to the order to which it is to be attached.[159]
- **CPR, r 3.1(5):** Clarke LJ gave the following guidance (which related primarily to CPR, r 3.1(5) but may:[160]

  'The correct general approach may be summarised as follows:

  i)   it would only be in an exceptional case (if ever) that a court would order security for costs if the order would stifle a claim or an appeal;
  ii)   in any event,
        a)   an order should not ordinarily be made unless the party concerned can be shown to be regularly flouting proper court procedures or otherwise to be demonstrating a want of good faith; good faith being understood to consist (as Simon Brown LJ put it) of a will to litigate a genuine claim or defence (or appeal) as economically and expeditiously as reasonably possible in accordance with the overriding objective; and
        b)   an order will not be appropriate in every case where a party has a weak case. The weakness of a party's case will ordinarily be relevant only where he has no real prospect of succeeding.'

There are also principles that apply to both of the secondary jurisdictions. Moore-Bick LJ has explained that when the court is asked to consider making an order

---

[156]   Where, for example, a litigation friend was in poverty, it was open to the court to stay the claim until a litigation friend with means was appointed: see *Hind v Whitmore* (1856) 4 WR 379 and *Elliot v Ince* (1857) 5 WR 465.

[157]   In support of this proposition, it is noticeable that the law distinguished between different types of litigation friend even when the aforesaid rule was still observed. Where, for example, a woman sued through one litigation friend and then brought a fresh action through another litigation friend without having discharged the costs debt outstanding from the first proceedings, Cotton LJ found that she had sufficient say in the litigation to make it fair to order that the second proceedings should be stayed pending payment of that debt. He commented that the situation would have been different if the litigant had been a child; this, he commented, would have been because the child would have lacked sufficient voice in the litigation to influence the litigation (see *Re Payne, Randle v Payne* (1883) 23 Ch D 288 at 289, per Cotton LJ; as an example of the court refusing to make an order in the case of a child, see *Murrell v Clapham* (1836) 8 Sim 74).

[158]   *Hushcroft v P&O Ferries Ltd* [2010] EWCA Civ 1483 at [18] overruling *Halabi v Fieldmore Holdings* [2006] EWHC 1965 (Ch) Rimer J.

[159]   *Hushcroft v P&O Ferries Ltd* [2010] EWCA Civ 1483 at [18].

[160]   *Ali v Hudson (trading as Hudson Freemen Berg (a firm))* [2003] EWCA Civ 1793 at [40].

under either of the secondary jurisdictions, it should bear in mind the principles underlying CPR, r 25.12 and CPR, r 25.13.[161] Moreover, Clarke LJ's guidance about not stifling the claim (above) is almost certainly applicable under both of the secondary jurisdictions.

16.87 Simon Brown LJ has explained that the court should be alert and sensitive to the risk that by making an order for security it might be denying the party concerned the right to access to justice; in this regard he commented that this was true regardless of the jurisdiction under which the vires was exercised.[162] He explained that relevant considerations included the ability of the person concerned to pay, his conduct of the proceedings (including in particular his compliance or otherwise with any applicable rule, practice direction or protocol) and the apparent strength of his case (be it claim or defence).[163]

16.88 Notwithstanding the broad range of circumstances in which the secondary jurisdictions may arise, it seems that they are jurisdictions which will be invoked only infrequently. Sir Andrew Morritt has commented that it is a remedy of last resort.[164] Simon Brown LJ had this to say (in respect of CPR, r 3.1(5)):[165]

> 'A party only becomes amenable to an adverse order for security under r 3.1(5) (or perhaps r 3.1(2)(m)) once he can be seen either to be regularly flouting proper court procedures (which must inevitably inflate the costs of the proceedings) or otherwise to be demonstrating a want of good faith – good faith for this purpose consisting of a will to litigate a genuine claim or defence as economically and expeditiously as reasonably possible in according with the overriding objective.'

He went on to explain that it is not to be thought that an order for security for costs will be appropriate in every case where a party appears to have a somewhat weak claim or defence.[166]

16.89 As to conduct, Patten J found that a failure to comply with an order concerning disclosure was not enough to amount to regular flouting of court procedures.[167]

Re-application and variation

16.90 Clarke MR has confirmed that the court is able to order further security if there has been a material change of circumstances:[168]

> 'The correct approach ... is that where the court has awarded security in respect of, say, the whole of an action or application, it will not make a further order in the absence of a

---

[161] *Hushcroft v P&O Ferries Ltd* [2010] EWCA Civ 1483 at [14]; as an example of the principles in CPR Part 25 II being applied by analogy, see *Allen v Bloomsbury Publishing plc* [2011] EWHC 770 (Ch) (upheld on appeal).

[162] *Olatawura v Abiloye* [2002] EWCA Civ 998 at [22].

[163] *Olatawura v Abiloye* [2002] EWCA Civ 998 at [24].

[164] *Uddington Business Ltd v Browne* (unreported) (2011) 9 December, Ch D, in which *Asiansky Television Plc v Bayer-Rosin (A Firm)* (2001) EWCA Civ 1792, (2002) CPLR 111 was followed.

[165] *Olatawura v Abiloye* [2002] EWCA Civ 998 at [25]; see also Buckley J's judgment in *Mealey Horgan plc v Horgan* [1999] All ER (D), which Simon Brown LJ quoted with approval.

[166] *Olatawura v Abiloye* [2002] EWCA Civ 998 at [26].

[167] *Ashfield and another v Union Pensions Trustees Ltd* [2004] All ER (D) 103 (Dec).

[168] *Republic of Kazakhstan v Istil Group Inc* [2005] EWCA Civ 1468 at [32]. See also the comments of Beldam LJ in *Kristjansson v R Verney & Co Ltd* (unreported) 18 June 1998, CA, on p 12 of the official transcript.

material change of circumstances. However, it will or may do so if there has been a material change of circumstances ... That principle applies where a court makes an order for security for costs and is asked to make a further order. Moreover, it applies whether the first order is made with or without the consent of the parties. Thus it applies, for example, where the parties consent to an order. Subject to the express terms of the agreement it also applies where the parties agree that security will be provided and security is provided pursuant to an agreement without an order.'

16.91 If the circumstances change such that security is no longer required, an application may be made for the order to be varied or set aside.[169]

Unless orders

16.92 Waller LJ explained that if an unless order is made at the time the order for security is made, then either it ought not to be made as a first order, or the claimant ought to be granted a generous period of time for compliance:[170]

'The obtaining of an order for security for costs is a rather special form of order. It is intended ... to give a claimant a choice as to whether he puts up security and continues with his action or withdraws his claim. That choice is meant to be a proper choice ... The making of an order for security is not intended to be a weapon by which a defendant can obtain a speedy summary judgment without a trial.'

16.93 Practices vary from court to court. In the commercial court it is unusual for an unless order to be made (at least when the order for security is first made); in other courts an unless order may be the usual order, this reflecting the wording of the standard court form.[171]

Quantum and form of security

16.94 The court has freedom to make an award in any amount which is justified (other than a purely nominal amount); there is no presumption that the amount will be substantial.[172] Whilst a pre-CPR case, McCowan LJ has held that sufficient security for costs does not mean complete security, but security of a sufficiency in all the circumstances of the case as to be just.[173]

16.95 Broadly speaking, there are two measures which may be used to set the amount of the security. The first is the amount of costs over which the security is reasonably sought (usually the likely costs of the case), and the second is the reasonable monetary value of the extra burden of enforcement outside the zone of contracting states.[174] (It used to be the case that a rule of thumb was used where the court awarded a fixed proportion of the costs likely to be incurred up to the relevant stage of the litigation;

---

[169]   Whilst pre-CPR, see *Cordano Building Contractors v Burgess* [1988] 1 WLR 890.

[170]   *Radu v Houston* [2006] EWCA Civ 1575 at [18].

[171]   PF44.

[172]   Whilst pre-CPR authorities, see *Roburn Construction Ltd v William Irwin (South) & Co Ltd* [1991] BCC 726 and *Keary Developments Ltd v Tarmac Construction Ltd* [1995] 3 All ER 534 at 540.

[173]   *Innovare Displays plc v Corporate Broking Services Ltd* [1991] BCC 174, CA.

[174]   *Texuna International Ltd v Cairn Energy plc* [2004] EWHC 1102 (Comm) at [29]–[32], per Gross J.

that is no longer recommended practice.)[175] In any event, fixing the appropriate figure for security was not an exact science and would of necessity be approached robustly.[176]

16.96 The first of these measures is a matter of assessment (for the judge making the order) based on the sums claimed. The only fetter is that an order which the claimant lacks the means to pay may amount to a breach of Art 6(11) of the European Convention on Human Rights.[177] Where, however, the court is not persuaded that it has been given a full account of the claimant's resources, it has a discretion to set an amount according to its best estimate of what the claimant can afford.[178] It is generally the case that success fees are taken into account for the purposes of deciding quantum,[179] but Rimer LJ has found that it may be unjust to do that in circumstances where the applicant has not disclosed his conditional fee agreement.[180] In the context of an application for a freezing injunction, Gloster J found that it would be unfair to take into account the full amount of an ATE premium, this being because this would shift the preponderance of risk onto the party giving security and, in effect, would be to require that party to give security for its own costs.[181]

16.97 The second of these measures (the costs of enforcement) is a question of fact and discretion. The measure will usually be the additional burden of enforcing in the claimant's country of residence.[182] This will be the case regardless of whether the claim falls within the Brussels Convention 1968; this because it is a measure that arises of the anti-discrimination provisions in the ECHR, and access to the court is not to be restricted on grounds of the residence (regardless of where the claimant resides).[183] Set-off by a foreign court will not normally be regarded as an addition burden.[184] Where the claimant's assets are in a country which is different from his place of residence, then the court will take into account the additional burden of enforcing in the country where the assets are rather than in the country of residency.[185] Gross J has confirmed that where it is effectively impossible to enforce an order for payment of costs, then this situation would provide 'an objective justification for the court exercising its discretion to make an order for payment of the full amount of the costs likely to be ordered against a claimant if unsuccessful in the litigation'.[186]

16.98 It may be that the court has to determine the quantum of orders for both sides' costs; the court need not vex itself with any rule similar to that in *Medway Oil and Storage Company Ltd v Continental Contractors Limited*[187] (see **7.18**). Where a counterclaim is founded on the same body of facts as the claim itself, there is no justification for limiting the security to those exclusively referable to the counterclaim.

---

[175] *Al-Koronky and another v Time Life Entertainments Group Ltd* [2005] EWHC 1688 (QB) at [26]–[27], per Eady J; see also *Procon (GB) Ltd v Provincial Building Co Ltd* [1984] 2 All ER 368, CA.

[176] *Autoweld Systems Ltd v Kito Enterprises LLC* [2010] EWCA Civ 1469 at [64], per Black LJ.

[177] *Asi-Mouhoub v France, Reports of Judgments and Decisions*, 1998-VIII, p 3214, ECHR.

[178] *Al-Koronky v Time-Life Entertainment Group Ltd* [2006] EWCA Civ 1123.

[179] *Kahangi v Nourizadeh* [2009] EWHC 2451 (QB) at [26], per Eady J.

[180] *Meridian International Services Ltd v Richardson* [2008] EWCA Civ 490 at [16].

[181] *Guerrero and others v Monterrico Metals plc* [2009] EWHC 2475 (QB) at [40].

[182] *Nasser v United Bank of Kuwait* [2001] EWCA Civ 556 at [61], per Mance LJ

[183] *Relational LLC v Hodges* [2011] EWCA Civ 774 at [15].

[184] *Relational LLC v Hodges* [2011] EWCA Civ 774 at [17] *et seq.*

[185] *Kazakhstan Investment Fund Ltd v Aims Asset Management* (unreported) 22 May 2002, Ch D, Mr Gabriel Moss QC, sitting as a deputy judge of the High Court.

[186] *Texuna International Ltd v Cairn Energy plc* [2004] EWHC 1102 (Com); see also *Al-Koronky and another v Time Life Entertainments Group Ltd* [2005] EWHC 1688 (QB) at [25], per Eady J.

[187] [1929] AC 88.

Instead, the entirety of the costs of the counterclaim may be included, regardless of whether they were common to both the claim and the counterclaim.[188]

16.99 Whilst a pre-CPR case, Griffiths LJ has commented that if there is a paucity of information which is put before the court to allow it to estimate costs, then it will be reasonable to make a large discount, particularly when it is borne in mind that, if the security proves inadequate as litigation progresses, it is always possible for a further application to be made for more security.[189] Roth J has impliedly confirmed that the court may take a broad-brush approach to quantum if it finds that the costs are disproportionate.[190]

16.100 Denning MR has held that where a person is in receipt of public funding, the amount he can be ordered to pay in security must not exceed the amount that he would be required to pay if he were to lose;[191] put another way, the costs protection afforded by the public funding must be taken into account. Presumably, the same would apply if the person were in receipt of pro bono funding (see **11.110**).

16.101 There are many forms which security can take; indeed, the court has the power to order that more than one type of security may be given.[192] The usual method is payment into court,[193] but alternatives include:

•	after the event insurance (the existence of which may also be a reason for not making an order: see **16.63–16.64**);[194]
•	monies held to order by the claimant's solicitors;
•	security by way of undertaking to pay costs;[195]
•	security by way of a personal guarantee;[196] and
•	security by way of a guarantee given by a bank.[197]

16.102 The last of these is particularly relevant because the court usually orders that a guarantee be given by a bank in preference to a charge or mortgage: this is on the basis that if the property has real value, a guarantee ought to be reasonably easy to obtain.[198] This would not prevent the court from accepting a charge where that was appropriate; factors the court may take into account are the value of the property (and whether that value is like to remain sufficient) and the ease with which its value could be realised.[199]

---

[188]	*Jones v Environcom Ltd and another* [2009] EWHC 16 (Comm) at [24]–[26]; see also *Petromin SA v Secnav Marine Ltd* [1995] 1 Lloyd's Rep 603, QBD.
[189]	*Procon (GB) Ltd v Provincial Building Co Ltd* [1984] 2 All ER 368 at 379.
[190]	*Ackerman v Ackerman* [2011] EWHC (Ch) at [32].
[191]	*Wyld v Silver (No 2)* [1962] 2 All ER 809, CA, per Denning MR. It used to be the case that no order at all would be made against a publicly funded client (see *Conway v George Wimpey & Co Ltd* [1951] 1 All ER 56), but Denning MR confirmed that the fact of public funding is just a factor to be taken into account.
[192]	See, for example, *Belco Trading Ltd v Kordo* [2008] EWCA Civ 205.
[193]	If monies are paid into court, they should not be viewed as being property recovered or preserved for the purposes of a solicitors' charging order: *Wadsworth, Re, Rhodes v Sugden* (1885) 29 Ch D 517. See **20.84–20.104**.
[194]	See, for example, *Belco Trading Ltd v Kordo* [2008] EWCA Civ 205.
[195]	*Hawkins Hill Co v Want* (1893) 69 LT 297.
[196]	See, for example, *Inventors Friend Limited v Leathes Prior* [2011] EWHC 2840 (QB), per Simon L; this was ordered because there was insufficient time before trial to allow a more orthodox type of security to be obtained.
[197]	See, for example, *Rosengrens Ltd v Safe Deposit Centres Ltd* [1984] 1 WLR 1334.
[198]	*AP (UK) Ltd v West Midlands Fire and Civil Defence Authority* [2001] EWCA Civ 1917.
[199]	*Havai v Solland* [2008] EWHC 2514 (Ch).

Procedure

16.103   CPR, r 25.12 reads as follows:

'(1)   A defendant to any claim may apply under this Section of this Part for security for his costs of the proceedings.

(Part 3 provides for the court to order payment of sums into court in other circumstances. Rule 20.3 provides for this Section of this Part to apply to Part 20 claims)

(2)   An application for security for costs must be supported by written evidence.

(3)   Where the court makes an order for security for costs, it will—

(a)   determine the amount of security; and
(b)   direct—
(i)   the manner in which; and
(ii)   the time within which
the security must be given.'

16.104   Surprisingly, there is no practice direction relating to applications for security for costs. Commentators advise that a skeleton bill of the costs ought to be appended to the application;[200] this would certainly seem sensible. In the writer's experience it is often sufficient to rely on a schedule in the form of Precedent H, but with additional detail in appended schedules where appropriate.

Evidence and disclosure

16.105   Applications are made on notice supported by evidence. Jacob J has said that in applications for security, the relevant ground should always be identified and the relevant evidence aimed at that ground.[201]

16.106   Whilst an obvious point, without prejudice negotiations should not be taken into account without the consent of those concerned.[202]

16.107   Where it is said that a claim is being funded by a third party, and where that is admitted or proved, the court has the power to order the claimant to disclose the name of the funder.[203]

---

[200]   See, for example, M Cook *Cook on Costs 2010* (Butterworths LexisNexis), [13.30].
[201]   *Somerset-Leeke and another v Kay Trustees* [2003] EWHC 1243 (Ch) at [5].
[202]   *Simaan General Contracting Co v Pilkington Glass Ltd* [1987] 1 All ER 345, CA.
[203]   *Reeves v Sprecher* [2007] EWHC 3226 (Ch), Rattee J.

Part III

THE PRACTICE OF COSTS (SOLICITOR AND CLIENT)

Chapter 17

INVOICES AND BILLS

17.1　An invoice is a written instrument by which a solicitor claims monies for services rendered (or occasionally to be rendered) or for disbursements disbursed (or to be disbursed). Beyond this, whilst non-payment may give rise to legal consequences, an invoice *per se* has no legal status. The word 'bill' is, where unqualified, often used synonymously with the word 'invoice'.

17.2　In invoice may or may not be a bill within the meaning of s 69(2) of the Solicitors Act 1974 (as amended) ('SA 1974'); the term 'statute bill' is used in this book to describe a bill bona fide compliant with that section. An instrument which is a statute bill will have significant legal status, not least because it will be the document upon which the solicitor will be able to found a claim for his fees.

17.3　Some invoices will, by intention, not be statute bills; this may be particularly true of invoices rendered part way through a retainer (so called 'interim invoices' or 'interim invoices'). Invoices that are intended not to be bona fide compliant with SA 1974 are merely requests for payments on account, so they are referred to in this book as 'interim invoices on account'.

17.4　Disputes often arise as to the status of interim invoices: there may be a dispute as to whether the invoice is an interim invoice on account or an interim statute bill. The relevance of this is that the status of the bill will determine whether the solicitor is able to sue upon it and whether time has begun to run for the purposes of the client's right to a detailed assessment (which, as will be explained below, is a right which diminishes over time).

INTERIM STATUTE BILLS

17.5　Interim statute bills must be distinguished from interim invoices on account; an interim statute bill is a bill bona fide compliant with the requirements of SA 1974, s 69(2) and, whilst interim, it is a discrete and entire bill in its own right. In particular, subject to certain procedural requirements, the solicitor can sue upon an interim statute bill and the client can apply to have it assessed; neither of these steps can be taken if the invoice is an interim invoice on account.

17.6　For reasons set out below, an interim statute is a final bill in the sense that it is complete and, once rendered, cannot readily be withdrawn, replaced or amended. It is interim only in the sense that it is rendered during the currency of the retainer; the description of it being 'interim' does not meant that it is provisional or temporary.

17.7　The requirements that apply to statute bills generally will apply to interim statute bills; those requirements are discussed in detail in the following pages.

17.8   Interim statute bills may be rendered only if and to the extent that the retainer permits this (be that expressly, or impliedly, or as a result of a type of implication known as a 'natural break': see **8.61** *et seq*).

INTERIM INVOICES ON ACCOUNT

17.9   Interim invoices on account (or, as they are often called, 'requests for payment on account') are not bills upon which a solicitor can found a claim for payment. Instead, an interim invoice on account is merely an interim invoice on account of a future statute bill.

17.10   An interim invoice on account may be for costs which have already been incurred, or it may be for (or include) a reasonable allowance for costs yet to be incurred.[1]

17.11   Although a solicitor cannot bring a claim on an interim invoice on account, such invoices may, in certain circumstances, be of significance in other ways. If, for example, an interim invoice on account is for a very high sum, it might precipitate an application for delivery of a statute bill (see below). If, on the other hand, a client refuses to make a reasonable interim payment on account, this may amount to good cause to terminate the retainer pursuant to SA 1974, s 65(2), which reads as follows:

> 'If a solicitor who has been retained by a client to conduct contentious business requests the client to make a payment of a sum of money, being a reasonable sum on account of the costs incurred or to be incurred in the conduct of that business and the client refuses or fails within a reasonable time to make that payment, the refusal or failure shall be deemed to be a good cause whereby the solicitor may, upon giving reasonable notice to the client, withdraw from the retainer.'

There does not need to be an agreement to this effect in respect of contentious work.[2]

17.12   Because an interim invoice on account is an informal document, the formalities which are described in the following pages do not apply; this means that there is no requirement that an interim invoice on account should contain a narrative, or that it be signed, etc. It must be for no more than a reasonable sum, however:[3] Crane J has found that this means that it must be for an amount which it is reasonable to request at that particular time.[4]

17.13   If the solicitor claims more than a reasonable sum, he may not be able to rely upon the request for the purposes of withdrawing his services pursuant to SA 1974, s 65(2). This may result in the solicitor being in breach of contract if he subsequently withdraws those services. Toulson J has found (obiter) that a request by a firm of solicitors for 90% of its costs was unreasonable in the context of those costs being disputed and that, as a consequence, the subsequent termination of the retainer was unlawful.[5]

---

[1]   In so far as contentious business is concerned, see SA 1974, s 65(1).
[2]   See SA 1974, s 65(2).
[3]   *Collyer Bristow v Robichaux* (unreported) 20 July 2001, QBD.
[4]   *Collyer Bristow v Robichaux* (unreported) 20 July 2001, QBD.
[5]   See *Wong v Vizards* [1997] 2 Costs LR 46 at 52.

DISTINGUISHING INTERIM STATUTE BILLS FROM BILLS FOR A PAYMENT ON ACCOUNT

17.14 Whether a bill is an interim statute bill or a invoice for a payment on account is an issue that will turn on the facts of each case, as Lord Esher explained:[6]

> 'In the case of a series of bills each bill has been sent in as a final bill, or whether they are mere statements of account shewing how far the expenses have gone up to the time of sending them in, is a question of fact to be determined on the evidence in each case, and it is a question which cannot be determined in any case upon the finding of the Court in any other case.'

17.15 Whilst far from being an exhaustive list, the following factors may be relevant in distinguishing an interim statute bill from an interim invoice on account.

The retainer

17.16 The starting point should always be the retainer, which will often expressly state whether an interim invoice is to be regarded as an interim invoice on account or an interim statute bill. A retainer will often provide that an interim invoice is not to be treated as being an interim statute bill unless it says upon its face that it is a final bill: this provision is commonly written into solicitors' terms and conditions in order to allow revisions to be made upon conclusion of the retainer. Some firms (especially larger firms with more sophisticated accounting facilities) will use retainers that say exactly the opposite: the reason for this is because it allows a claim to be brought promptly if a client fails to pay.

The information given to the client

17.17 Where a client has not been told that he will be sent an interim statute bill (which is relevant because it starts time running in respect of SA 1974, s 70(2)), then that will be a factor against the bill being an interim statute bill; Fulford J made the following points about consumer protection:[7]

> 'In particular the party must know what rights are being negotiated and dispensed with in the sense that the solicitor must make it plain to the client that the purpose of sending the bill at that time is that it is to be treated as a complete self-contained bill of costs to date'.

The absence or presence of natural breaks

17.18 If a retainer makes no express provision for interim statute bills and if bills are rendered at times which cannot be said to be natural breaks, then that will be a factor against those bills being interim statute bills.[8] This issue is considered more fully at **17.23–17.30**.

---

[6]   In *Re Romer & Haslam* [1893] 2 QB 286 at 293.
[7]   *Adams v Al Malik* [2003] EWHC 3232 (QB) at [48].
[8]   See, for example, *In re Hall v Barker* (1893) 9 Ch D 538, in which a series of bills was found to have been rendered at natural breaks.

The form of the bill

17.19 Where an invoice bears upon its face a description of its intended effect, then this will be a factor to be taken into account. An invoice may say that it is a final bill (or that it is not). This will be particularly relevant if the retainer says that an interim invoice will be an interim statute bill only if the invoice says upon its face that it is a final bill (see above).

The parties' conduct

17.20 Roskill LJ has emphasised that the reaction of the parties is a factor relevant to whether an invoice should be treated as being an interim statute bill:[9]

> 'If the client's reaction is to pay the bill in its entirety without demur it is not difficult to infer an agreement that that bill is to be treated as a complete self-contained bill of costs to date.'

The content of the bill

17.21 Where an invoice is for work yet to be done or (with one or two exceptions)[10] for a disbursement yet to be paid, it can only be a request for payment on account. If an invoice excludes mark-up on the hourly rate in circumstances were a mark-up would be expected (such as where it is provided for in the retainer), then that too would suggest that it is an invoice for a payment on account.

Carrying forward a balance

17.22 Where there is a series of invoices, the fact that a balance is carried forward from one invoice to the next will suggest that it is a series of invoices for payment on account.[11] It is the carrying forward that is relevant, not the fact that credit may have been given for sums already paid. Where the series comprises a running account, it may, when properly analysed, constitute a single statute bill which is finally delivered only upon completion of the series.[12]

NATURAL BREAKS

17.23 One of the factors mentioned above is the issue of whether there has been a natural break in the matter to which the retainer relates. See **8.61–8.70** for a discussion of that topic: the following is only a brief summary, with the focus firmly on the nature of the invoice.

17.24 The time-honoured position at common law was that a retainer was a contract entire; this meant that the solicitor could not charge for his services unless and until he had performed the entirety of his obligations. In long-running cases this was capable of causing injustice, not only because the solicitor was kept out of his fees until the

---

9   *Davidsons v Jones-Fenleigh* (1980) Costs LR (Core vol) 70 at 75.
10   An invoice may have been incurred notwithstanding the fact that it may not have been paid: if, for example, an solicitor declines to afford his client any credit, a request for payment may be made on the basis that the solicitor is merely acting as agent for the client.
11   See, for example, *In Re Romer & Haslam* [1893] 2 QB 286.
12   See, for example, *Chamberlain v Boodle & King* [1982] 1 WLR 1443.

conclusion of the claim, but also because he may have been unable to secure payment at all if, for some reason, he was prevented from discharging his obligations.

17.25 That potential for injustice is now ameliorated by the doctrine of the 'natural break'. Sir George Jessel MR explained the need for that doctrine by posing the following rhetorical question:[13]

> '[E]ven if it were right [that a retainer is an entire contract], there must be a break somewhere. In the case of a Chancery suit I have shewn what sort of break you may have. In the case of winding up there are all sorts of breaks. Is it to be supposed that, because a few matters are undisposed of, the solicitor is not to be paid until the final termination?'

Sir George Jessel MR went on to answer that question in the negative.

17.26 Giving judgment at about the same time but in a different case, Lord Esher MR explained the mechanism of the doctrine:[14]

> '[When] the award was given there was a break – that is, such a conclusion of a definite and distinct part of the legal transaction as would entitle the solicitors to send in a final bill of costs, such as might in Chancery be sent in at the stage of decree.'

17.27 As to whether a bill is a final statute bill or merely an interim invoice on account, Lord Esher MR said:[15]

> 'In the case of a series of bills each bill has been sent in as a final bill, or whether they are mere statements of account shewing how far the expenses have gone up to the time of sending them in, is a question of fact to be determined on the evidence in each case, and it is a question which cannot be determined in any case upon the finding of the Court in any other case.'

17.28 The issue is, therefore, a question of fact and law. The law will be relevant in that the terms of the retainer may shed light on the nature of the interim invoice,[16] but that will usually be only one factor amongst others. Another way of looking at the doctrine is to regard a natural break as being implied by the combination of an invoice which does not exclude the delivery of interim statute bills and of circumstances which make it appropriate that such a bill be delivered.

17.29 Whether there has been a natural break will, to some extent, depend on the way in which the solicitor and client comported themselves when the invoice was rendered. That is a factor to be taken into account, but Simon Brown LJ has explained that it should not be given so much weight that the solicitor is, in effect, allowed to create a natural break at will.[17]

17.30 Although there is no authority specifically on the point, the court will often bear in mind the fact that clients are dependent on their legal advisors for proper advice as to

---

[13] *Hall v Barker* (1893) 9 Ch D 538 at 545.
[14] *In Re Romer & Haslam* [1893] 2 QB 286 at 293.
[15] *Hall v Barker* (1893) 9 Ch D 538 at 545.
[16] An extreme example would be where the bill was rendered under a provision in a conditional fee agreement which allowed for immediate payment of costs of a successful hearing: in those circumstances, the nature of the retainer itself would strongly – possibly conclusively – indicate that such a bill was an interim statute bill.
[17] *Abedi v Penningtons* [2000] 2 Costs LR 205.

the status of any invoice that is delivered. Judge LJ had this to say (obiter) about the need for there to be express agreement about the terms upon which payments would be made:[18]

> 'The desirability of such arrangements is likely to be reinforced by the increasing impact of the Civil Justice Reforms on a client's entitlement to be kept properly informed of his escalating financial obligations at each stage of the proceedings. As clients should know exactly where they stand throughout the process, it is reasonable to anticipate that questions of their own costs, and payment, should be arranged at an early stage in the process.'

If a solicitor has failed to heed this guidance, he must bear the risk that the court finds that the bill he intended to sue upon is, in truth, an interim invoice on account.

STATUTE BILLS GENERALLY

17.31 A solicitor may render a statute bill for services rendered in contentious or non-contentious business; that bill may be either a gross sum bill (ie a bill which summarises the costs as a whole) or a detailed bill.

17.32 To a large extent, the law is the same for all statute bills – contentious or non-contentious, gross sum or detailed – but there are certain requirements that are specific to certain types of bill. It is convenient to deal with the general principles first, followed by the specific topics.

THE REQUIREMENTS OF A STATUTE BILL

17.33 The relevant law derives from SA 1974, s 69; those provisions relate to bills for services rendered in both contentious and non-contentious business.

17.34 The 1974 Act sets out the circumstances in which a solicitor may bring a claim for his fees; this prescribes the requirements for a statute bill. Since 7 March 2008,[19] the relevant provisions have read as follows:

> **'69   Action to recover solicitor's costs**
>
> (1)   Subject to the provisions of this Act, no action shall be brought to recover any costs due to a solicitor before the expiration of one month from the date on which a bill of those costs is delivered in accordance with the requirements mentioned in subsection (2); ...
>
> (2)   The requirements referred to in subsection (1) are that the bill must be—
>
> > (a)   signed in accordance with subsection (2A), and
> > (b)   delivered in accordance with subsection (2C).
>
> (2A)   A bill is signed in accordance with this subsection if it is—
>
> > (a)   signed by the solicitor or on his behalf by an employee of the solicitor authorised by him to sign, or

---

18   *Abedi v Penningtons* [2000] 2 Costs LR 205 at 221.
19   If the older law is required, then the unamended statute ought to be consulted: see the Legal Services Act 2007, s 177 and Sch 16, Pt 1, paras 1, 64(1) and (3); transitional provisions apply (see LSA 2007, Sch 22, para 14).

(b)   enclosed in, or accompanied by, a letter which is signed as mentioned in paragraph (a) and refers to the bill.

(2B)   For the purposes of subsection (2A) the signature may be an electronic signature.

(2C)   A bill is delivered in accordance with this subsection if—

(a)   it is delivered to the party to be charged with the bill personally,

(b)   it is delivered to that party by being sent to him by post to, or left for him at, his place of business, dwelling-house or last known place of abode, or

(c)   it is delivered to that party—

     (i)   by means of an electronic communications network, or

     (ii)   by other means but in a form that nevertheless requires the use of apparatus by the recipient to render it intelligible,

and that party has indicated to the person making the delivery his willingness to accept delivery of a bill sent in the form and manner used.

(2D)   An indication to any person for the purposes of subsection (2C)(c)—

(a)   must state the address to be used and must be accompanied by such other information as that person requires for the making of the delivery;

(b)   may be modified or withdrawn at any time by a notice given to that person.

(2E)   Where a bill is proved to have been delivered in compliance with the requirements of subsections (2A) and (2C), it is not necessary in the first instance for the solicitor to prove the contents of the bill and it is to be presumed, until the contrary is shown, to be a bill bona fide complying with this Act.

(2F)   A bill which is delivered as mentioned in subsection (2C)(c) is to be treated as having been delivered on the first working day after the day on which it was sent (unless the contrary is proved).

...

(5)   In this section references to an electronic signature are to be read in accordance with section 7(2) of the Electronic Communications Act 2000 (c 7).

(6)   In this section—

"electronic communications network" has the same meaning as in the Communications Act 2003 (c 21);

"working day" means a day other than a Saturday, a Sunday, Christmas Day, Good Friday or a bank holiday in England and Wales under the Banking and Financial Dealings Act 1971 (c 80).'

Thus, there are express statutory requirements that a bill must be signed (electronically or otherwise) and that it must be delivered (electronically or otherwise).

17.35 Compliance with those express requirements will not necessarily result in the bill being a statute bill bona fide compliant with the SA 1974. This is because of the operation of s 69(2E), which states that a bill which complies with those requirements will be a bill bona fide complying with the 1974 Act 'unless the contrary is shown'. Put another way, compliance with the express requirements will create a presumption of compliance with s 69 in general, but that presumption may be rebutted. This is because, in addition to the express requirements, there are implied requirements; in particular, a statute bill must be reasonably complete (see **17.38–17.40**), and there must be a sufficient narrative (see **17.41–17.58**).

17.36 Where a solicitor seeks to bring a claim upon a bill, there can be no bill other than a statute bill. Chitty J made it clear that it is wrong to say a bill which is not bona fide compliant with the 1974 Act has the status of a bill in a different legal sense[20] (although, of course, it may be a 'bill' which lacks legal status in that it is a invoice for a payment on account: see **17.1–17.4**); specifically, an account stated[21] will not suffice to allow a solicitor to sue unless it is a valid bill[22] (or, of course, a valid agreement).[23]

17.37 It is convenient first to deal with the implied requirements (ie the completeness of the statute bill and the sufficiency of the narrative), and then to consider the express requirements (ie the signature and delivery).

Reasonably complete

17.38 A statute bill must be reasonably complete. If, for example, an invoice is rendered to a client which is for only the shortfall in the recovery in costs which have otherwise been paid by a third party, that document would not be a reasonably complete bill.[24] A statute bill must be adequate to serve its purpose of informing the client of the basis upon which it was prepared and to enable the court to investigate its propriety.[25] An invoice that particularised a number of items but which specified a putatively agreed charge in respect of some of them was found not be sufficient in that regard.[26]

17.39 This does not mean that if a statue bill is delivered, it must contain all the costs of the matter to which it relates. Hobhouse LJ found nothing objectionable about a solicitor rendering a statute bill which did not contain counsel's fees, and then subsequently rendering a further (ie additional) statute bill which did contain them; on the facts of the case before him the client had been told why counsel's fees had not been included in the first bill (this being because they were disputed), and the two bills taken together were not liable to mislead.[27]

17.40 The fact that a statute bill contains items it ought not to contain will not negative that bill; the solicitor's claim may be maintained for the residue.[28]

Sufficiency of the narrative

17.41 The narrative is a description of the work to which the bill relates. It should not be confused with the detail in a detailed bill (although the two may overlap or even be the same). A gross sum bill may have an informative narrative running to many pages, but in the absence of a breakdown of the fees, it will still be a gross sum bill.

---

[20]   *In re Bayliss* [1896] 2 Ch 107 at 110.
[21]   An account stated is statement between a costs creditor and a costs debtor that a certain sum is owing.
[22]   *Eicke v Nokes* (1834) 1 M & Rob 359 and *Re Baylis* [1896] 2 Ch 107 at 111.
[23]   If an oral retainer is made and then the agreed sum is acknowledged in the form of an account stated after payment has been made by deduction, that acknowledgement will not be sufficient to give rise to a retrospective business agreement: *Re Fernandes* [1878] WN 57.
[24]   *Cobbett v Wood* [1908] 2 KB 420.
[25]   *Cobbett v Wood* [1908] 2 KB 420; see also *Philby v Hazle* (1860) 8 CBNS 647 (bill containing only some of the items which were agreed to form part of the services rendered).
[26]   *Wilkinson v Smart* (1875) 24 WR 42; see also *Blake v Hummel* (1884) 1 TLR 22.
[27]   *Aaron v Okoye* [1998] Costs LR 6.
[28]   *Pilgrim v Hirschfeld* (1863) 3 New Rep 36.

17.42 Whilst not an express statutory requirement, the need to provide a sufficient narrative is not merely a matter of good practice but is also a matter of principle: in order for a bill to be bona fide compliant with SA 1974, it must have a sufficient narrative for that purpose.[29]

17.43 SA 1974 (as amended) is silent as to what constitutes a sufficient narrative. Other than what is set out in s 69, there is no hint or help in the Act to determine what is or is not bona fide compliant with it.[30] The details of the requirement are judge made. Ward LJ has summarised the appropriate test:[31]

> '... [T]he burden on the client under section [69(2E) of the 1974 Act] to establish that a bill for a gross sum in contentious business will not be a bill "bona fide complying with the 1974 Act" is satisfied if the client shows:
>
> (a)   that there is no sufficient narrative in the bill to identify what it is he is being charged for, and
> (b)   that he does not have sufficient knowledge from other documents in his possession or from what he has been told reasonably to take advice whether or not to apply for that bill to be taxed.'

17.44 Thus (subject to what is set out below about non-contentious business), when considering the adequacy of a narrative of a putative bill the court is not constrained to examining only what is found on the face of that document, but may also take into account the client's own knowledge of the work for which fees are sought. This is an approach which had been articulated by the courts since at least the mid-nineteenth century[32] and continues to be the case today.[33]

17.45 This is certainly the case where the putative bill is for services rendered in contentious business, but it is not wholly clear whether Ward LJ's test applies to bills for non-contentious business. This is because, on the face of it, Ward LJ specifically limited his test to the former.

17.46 It should also be noted that Denning LJ had articulated a different test (albeit obiter) for bills relating to non-contentious business:[34]

> '[T]he question is: what must a solicitor's bill for non-contentious business now contain? It need not contain detailed charges as it used to do before 1920 ... But I think that it must contain a summarised statement of the work done, sufficient to tell the client what it is for which he is asked to pay.'

Thus, Denning LJ's test appears to be a significantly more demanding test from the solicitor's point of view than that articulated by Ward LJ; in particular, Denning LJ's test does not seem to take into account the client's own knowledge.

17.47 Whilst the contrary is arguable, it seems that Ward LJ's test is the correct test in a modern setting even for bills for non-contentious work. Ward LJ made the following

---

[29]   *Garry v Gwillim* [2002] EWCA Civ 1500 at [59]–[60]; see also *Haigh v Ousey* (1857) 7 El & Bl 578 and *Cook v Gillard* (1852) 1 E & B 26.
[30]   *Garry v Gwillim* [2002] EWCA Civ 1500 at [15].
[31]   *Garry v Gwillim* [2002] EWCA Civ 1500 at [70].
[32]   See, for example, *Cook v Gillard* (1852) 1 E & B 26.
[33]   See, for example, *Barclays plc v Villers* [2000] 1 All ER (Comm) 357 at 367.
[34]   *Re a Solicitor: In Re a taxation of costs* [1955] 2 QB 252.

comments, which suggest that Denning LJ's test should be regarded as obiter made without the benefit of full legal argument:[35]

> 'For my part, I do not feel bound to treat Denning LJ's dictum as binding upon me though it is obviously hugely persuasive. I have already explained why it was obiter. Given the way the question was addressed, I cannot believe Lord Denning was laying down an exhaustive statement of the principle or intending to say that the client's knowledge was immaterial. He did not have the benefit of argument addressed to him on the rulings in *Haigh v Ousey* and the other cases to which I have referred.'

It is also worth noting that Ward LJ mentioned two cases in which Denning LJ's test had been applied to invoices for services rendered in contentious business;[36] in doing so, he made no effort to suggest that one test should apply to contentious business but another test should apply to non-contentious business. This seems to suggest that there is only one test.

17.48 In any event, Mance LJ has made it clear that Ward LJ's test (which was based on an analysis of older authorities) may not always be appropriate in every case:[37]

> 'In some future case [it may] be relevant to consider how far interpretation of the concept and purpose of "a gross sum bill" ... can be determined by reference to Victorian authority.'

17.49 Although it should be borne in mind that older authorities may have had their day and may no longer be good law, it is worth reciting some case examples (not least because the older authorities do crop up from time to time in practice).

Computer printouts

17.50 A computer printout may, in appropriate circumstances, be or supplement a narrative (in the case before Nourse LJ, the narrative itself was just for 'general matters', but the printout provided all the necessary detail).[38]

Narrative omitted by implied agreement

17.51 Where a sophisticated client forgoes his right to a narrative, the fact that there is no narrative will not necessarily preclude the court from finding that the invoice is a statute bill.[39]

Numerous errors

17.52 An invoice containing a large number of obviously erroneous details was found to be a document which could not properly be assessed.[40]

---

[35] *Garry v Gwillim* [2002] EWCA Civ 1500 at [62].
[36] *Re A Solicitor* (unreported) 10 October 1994, QBD, Mr Christopher Clarke QC sitting as a deputy judge, and *Ring Sights Holding Co Ltd & Another v Lawrence Graham* (unreported) 8 October 2001, Ch D, Nigel Davis J.
[37] *Garry v Gwillim* [2002] EWCA Civ 1500 at [76]–[78].
[38] *Eversheds (a firm) v Osman* [2000] 1 Costs LR 54.
[39] *Barclays plc v Villers* [2000] 1 All ER (Comm) 357 at 367.
[40] *Slingsby v Attorney-General* [1918] P 236.

'For professional services'

17.53 In the absence of other compensating material, a supposed bill that merely states that it was 'for professional services' would usually be inadequate.[41]

Enable client to judge the bill's fairness

17.54 There is old authority to the effect that a bill should enable the client to judge its fairness, and should enable a legal representative to give advice upon it and to judge the propriety of the items claimed.[42] In view of the matters set out above (**17.41–17.49**) and in view of the fact that it predated the ability to render a gross sum bill, it would seem that it is authority that is largely now of only historical interest.

Different courts

17.55 A bill containing a number of items of work relating to different courts was found to be adequate: the individual items were clearly described.[43]

Client's own knowledge

17.56 A bill which had been split into parts relating to work in different courts did have a sufficient narrative in the light of the client's own knowledge of the work carried out.[44]

Superfluous information

17.57 A bill which failed to mention the name of the court in which the business was transacted was held to be valid because it was clear that the client neither wanted nor needed that information to be set out in the bill.[45]

17.58 Finally, the burden of proving that the narrative is insufficient lies with the client (see **17.43**).[46]

Signature

17.59 The law concerning signatures is now set out in SA 1974, s 69(2A):

'(2A)   A bill is signed in accordance with this subsection if it is—

(a)   signed by the solicitor or on his behalf by an employee of the solicitor authorised by him to sign, or

(b)   enclosed in, or accompanied by, a letter which is signed as mentioned in paragraph (a) and refers to the bill.'

---

[41]   The authority that has for many years been cited in support of this proposition is *Re Kingsley* (1978) 122 Sol Jo 457, but the case report makes no real mention of the issue in hand. Nonetheless, whilst obiter, Swift J has confirmed that if the only material available to the client was such sparse detail as 'for professional services', that would plainly be insufficient as a narrative: *Carter-Ruck (a firm) v Mireskandari* [2011] EWHC 24 (QB) at [80]–[86].

[42]   *Haigh v Ousey* (1857) 7 E & B 578.

[43]   *Keene v Ward* (1849) 13 QB 513. In so far as they suggest the contrary, neither *Martindale v Falkner* (1846) 2 CB 706 nor *Ivimey v Marks* (1847) 16 M & W 843, 153 ER 1433 remain good law.

[44]   *Cook v Gillard* (1852) 1 E & B 26.

[45]   *Cozens v Graham* (1852) 12 CB 398.

[46]   See SA 1974, s 69(2E) (as amended) and *Garry v Gwillim* [2002] EWCA Civ 1500 at [70].

From 7 March 2008[47] this has replaced the old SA 1974, s 69(2)(a), which, in effect, provided that only a solicitor or a partner could sign the bill. Transitional provisions apply.[48]

17.60 It should be noted that even under the old provisions, Irwin J has found that the requirement that a bill be signed is directory rather than mandatory;[49] he explained that his conclusion was based on a purposive interpretation of SA 1974.[50] Even before Irwin J clarified the law in this way, a liberal approach was not unknown. Where fees were sought by a 'recognised body' within the meaning of the Administration of Justice Act 1985, for example, an employee of that body was permitted to sign[51]. Victorian authority suggests that a signature by an employee in the firm's name was not a sufficient signature to satisfy the requirements of legislation.[52] The legislation now expressly provides that employees are able to sign, but even under the pre-7 March 2008 provisions, it is questionable whether the Victorian approach remains good law.

17.61 Electronic signatures are now permitted. SA 1974 Act now makes specific provision for a bill to be signed electronically (s 69(2B) and (5)). An electronic signature is:[53]

> '... so much of anything in electronic form as—
>
> (a)   is incorporated into or otherwise logically associated with any electronic communication or electronic data; and
>
> (b)   purports to be so incorporated or associated for the purpose of being used in establishing the authenticity of the communication or data, the integrity of the communication or data, or both.'

17.62 A signature placed by means of a rubber stamp containing a facsimile representation of a suitable signature was found to be sufficient to satisfy the purposes of s 65 of the Solicitors Act 1932;[54] there is no reason to believe that the law has become any more restrictive in this regard. Although contrary examples do exist, it may be relevant that a printed signature is capable of being regarded as sufficient in contexts other than the law of costs.[55] An unsigned bill accompanied by a signed letter is capable of being sufficient if there is a nexus between the letter and the bill.[56]

17.63 A signature in the solicitor's business name was a good signature by the solicitor for the purposes of SA 1932.[57] Likewise, a recognisable abbreviation of the solicitor's firm's name would be sufficient (although the Court of Appeal has said that it is sensible

---

47   See Legal Services Act 2007, s 177, Sch 16, Pt 1, paras 1, 64(1) and (3).
48   LSA 2007, Sch 22, para 14.
49   *Megantic Services Ltd v Dorsey & Whitney* [2008] EWHC 2662 (QB); some commentators have questioned the correctness of this decision in the light of *R v Soneji* [2006] 1 AC 340, which seems to discourage the distinction between mandatory and directory requirements.
50   See *Zuliani v Veira* [1994] 1 WLR 1149 PC (UK).
51   Administration of Justice Act 1985, Sch 2, para 29.
52   *In re Frape ex p Perrett* [1893] 2 Ch 284 at 291, citing with approval *Evans v Hoare* [1892] 1 QB 593; see also *Angell v Tratt* (1883) 1 Cab & El 118.
53   Electronic Communications Act 2000, s 7(2).
54   *Goodman v J Eban Ltd* [1954] 1 QB 550.
55   See, for example, *Schneider v Norris* (1814) 2 M&S 286.
56   *Penley v Anstruther* (1883) (1) 52 L J (Ch) 367.
57   *Goodman v J Eban Ltd* [1954] 1 QB 550.

to use a firm's full name).[58] Again, there is no reason to believe that the law has become any more restrictive in this regard, especially in the light of Irwin J's clarification of the law (see **17.60**).

17.64 Where a solicitor has died, become bankrupt, or has assigned his rights to another, the executor, administrator and assignee of the solicitor may sign the bill.[59] This is so even if that person is a layman.[60]

17.65 Where an unsigned bill is delivered, it is open to the court to find that the client should be taken, through his conduct, to have accepted that the bill was signed.[61] Whilst dealing with a case in a context other than costs, Roxburgh J found that the court can investigate the circumstances to see whether a document came into being as a perfect instrument, and that, if, on the evidence, it finds that it did, the court is not prevented from so holding by any impediment in law.[62]

17.66 The general law relating to requirements to sign written instruments ought not to be forgotten (although not all of it will apply to signatures to bills). In particular, the court often adopts a purposive approach when considering whether there has been compliance with legislation that requires a signature.[63] As with any written instrument, the signature must be in a place which governs the document,[64] although that would rarely be contentious, because bills tend to be fairly compact documents.

Delivery

17.67 SA 1974, s 69(2C) and (2D) (as amended) provide as follows:

'(2C)   A bill is delivered in accordance with this subsection if—

    (a)   it is delivered to the party to be charged with the bill personally,

    (b)   it is delivered to that party by being sent to him by post to, or left for him at, his place of business, dwelling-house or last known place of abode, or

    (c)   it is delivered to that party—

        (i)   by means of an electronic communications network, or

        (ii)   by other means but in a form that nevertheless requires the use of apparatus by the recipient to render it intelligible,

and that party has indicated to the person making the delivery his willingness to accept delivery of a bill sent in the form and manner used.

(2D)   An indication to any person for the purposes of subsection (2C)(c)—

    (a)   must state the address to be used and must be accompanied by such other information as that person requires for the making of the delivery;

    (b)   may be modified or withdrawn at any time by a notice given to that person.'

---

[58]   *Bartletts de Reya v Byrne* (1983) 127 Sol Jo 69, CA.
[59]   SA 1974, s 68(3).
[60]   *Ingle v M'Cutchan* (1884) 12 QBD 518 and *Penley v Anstruther* (1883) (1) 52 L J (Ch) 367; *Medlicott v Emery* (1933) All ER Rep 655 is often quoted as being authority on this point, but this seems to be an error.
[61]   *Re Gedge* (1851) 14 Beav 56 and *Young v Walker* (1847) 16 M&W 446.
[62]   *Leeman v Stocks* [1951] Ch 941; but see *Firstpost Homes Ltd v Johnson* [1996] 1 WLR 67, which suggests that the principle in that case is not to be applied more widely than it currently is.
[63]   See, for example, *Wood v Smith* [1992] 3 WLR 583; but see *Firstpost Homes Ltd v Johnson* [1996] 1 WLR 67.
[64]   *Caton v Caton* (1867) LR 2 HL 127.

This amended section replaces the old SA 1974, s 69(2)(b),[65] which contained provisions which were almost identical to those now contained in s 69(2C)(b). To this extent, the law relating to the old s 69(2)(b) is preserved.

17.68 Where a series of instruments is properly regarded as being one statute bill delivered in parts, delivery will not take place until the whole bill (ie the entirety of its parts) has been delivered.[66] Time will not start to run for the purposes of SA 1974, s 70 until the last part of the bill has been delivered.[67] As to delivery of bills after payment has been made, see **18.21**.

17.69 Delivery may be to an agent of the client or to the party chargeable.[68] An employee or servant of the client may take delivery at a person's business or home.[69] Delivery to a liability insurer is capable, in appropriate circumstances, of being delivery to the insured.[70]

17.70 A bill containing a qualification or a condition may still be delivered, even if that qualification is that the bill may be replaced at a later stage by another bill.[71]

17.71 Where a former client has instructed new solicitors, delivery to those new solicitors will suffice only if the client has given authority that this may be done,[72] or if the court has so ordered.[73]

17.72 Where a number of parties are jointly liable to pay the bill, delivery to one is capable of being delivery to each.[74]

Erroneous bills: amendment, withdrawal, and substitution

17.73 A solicitor is bound by the bill which he has delivered and, except by operation of SA 1974, s 64(2), or by consent or order of the court, he cannot withdraw it, strike it out or vary or add items.[75] This is true even where a bill has been delivered but not signed.[76] One of the principal justifications for this is that the court wishes to prevent solicitors from abusing the rights of clients by, for example, lodging a bill which they believe to be

---

[65]   The changed took place on 7 March 2008; if the older law is required, then the unamended statute ought to be consulted: see the Legal Services Act 2007, s 177 and Sch 16, Pt 1, paras 1, 64(1) and (3); transitional provisions apply (see LSA 2007, Sch 22, para 14).

[66]   *Chamberlain v Boodle & King* [1982] 1 WLR 1443 at 1446.

[67]   See *Re Cartwright* (1873) LR 16 Eq 469.

[68]   *Daubney v Phipps* (1849) 18 LJQB 337 and *Re Bush* (1844) 8 Bear 66.

[69]   *Macgregor v Keily* (1849) 3 Ex 794.

[70]   *Solicitors Indemnity Fund Ltd v Hewitson & Harker* [2010] EWCA Civ 147 at [12].

[71]   *In Re Thompson* (1885) 30 Ch D 441.

[72]   *Spier v Barnard* (1863) 8 LT 396.

[73]   *Vincent v Slaymaker* (1810) 12 East 372.

[74]   *Mant v Smith* (1859) 4 H&N 324 and *Crowder v Shee* (1808) 1 Camp 437; obviously, this rule would be subject to the prevailing rules of the court.

[75]   *Rezvi v Brown Cooper (a firm)* [1997] Costs LR 109 at 120, approving a passage from *Cordery on Solicitors*; see also *Saad v Griffin* [1908] 2 KB 510, CA, *Davis v Dysart* [1855] 25 LJ Ch 122, , *Re Heather* (1870) LR 5 Ch App 694; and *Re Thompson* (1885) 30 Ch D 441 at 448; of historical interest, also see *In re Carven* (1845) 8 Beav 436 at 438 .

[76]   *Re Jones* (1886) 54 LT 648.

unjustifiable, but then – only when the client takes legal advice and complains – withdrawing it and submitting a bill which is easier to defend.[77] Lord Romilly MR put it this way:[78]

> 'The reason and justice of this is obvious, and it appears to me to rest not less on principle than on practice. If one species of alteration be made, any other might. Who is to determine what alteration might or might not be made and if any alteration may be made? and if any alteration may be made, it is clear that a bill could be altered to meet the turn which the taxation was taking.'

17.74 These general rules are subject to the provisions in SA 1974, s 64(2). In particular, where a solicitor renders a gross sum bill for contentious work and where a client requests a detailed bill in lieu of a gross sum bill, the detailed bill will stand in place of the gross sum bill, which will then be of no effect. This is considered in more detail at **17.82–17.91**. The detailed bill may be for a greater amount than the original gross sum bill.[79]

17.75 Where a solicitor has delivered a gross sum bill, there is nothing to prevent him from delivering a detailed breakdown of that bill.[80] In those circumstances, the detailed breakdown would not replace the gross sum bill, but would merely be an aid for the purposes of assessing the costs claimed therein. This illustrates the fact that a detailed breakdown is not necessarily the same as a detailed bill.

17.76 A solicitor may reserve the right to withdraw the bill or to alter it on conditions;[81] this can be done only if those conditions are both fair, and clearly and fully stated to the client. An example might be where the bill is provisional by reason of a need to estimate counsel's fees. Where the condition is, in reality, an unjustified reservation of a right to re-deliver a different bill (or, as Cotton LJ drily put it, to render 'a bill which contains charges which I [the solicitor] cannot sustain on taxation'), that condition will usually be rejected, leaving the solicitor to be bound by the original bill.[82]

17.77 A client may give his consent to a bill being withdrawn, and such consent may be impliedly given where he consents to an assessment of a new bill delivered in substitution of a previous bill.[83] Where this happens, the court may take the old bill into account when carrying out the assessment.

17.78 Whilst it was originally the case that the court had no jurisdiction to allow a solicitor to withdraw his bill,[84] that rule ceased to be absolute at the turn of the last century and now the court does have a discretion in that regard. There is authority to the effect that typographical errors in a bill may be corrected by the court but omissions

---

[77] *Rezvi v Brown Cooper (a firm)* [1997] Costs LR 109 at 119.
[78] *Re Catlin* (1854) 18 Beav 508 at 519–520.
[79] *In re Taxation of Costs In re Solicitors* [1943] KB 69.
[80] See SA 1974, s 64(4) (as amended) and CPR, r 48.10(2).
[81] See, as a modern example, *Aaron v Okoye* [1998] Costs LR 6.
[82] *In Re Thompson* (1885) 30 Ch D 441.
[83] *Rezvi v Brown Cooper (a firm)* [1997] Costs LR 109: see, in particular,the discussion at 118 and 119 regarding *Loveridge v Botham* (1797) 1 Bos & P 49 772.
[84] See, for example, *Re Catlin* (1854) 18 Beav 508 at 520, per Romilly MR and *Re Thompson* (1885) 30 Ch D 441 at 448, per Cotton LJ.

may not;[85] it is not clear whether this latter constraint remains good law as it seems a rather anachronistic rule that has not been applied for over a century.[86]

17.79 Notwithstanding these general principles which, at the very least, discourage amendments and corrections, the court has a wide discretion to make an order which avoids injustice. Where, for example, a bill contains an accidental omission, the court may, in exceptional circumstances, allow that bill to be withdrawn and substituted.[87] In this regard, Lord Nolan (sitting in the Privy Council) had this to say:[88]

> '[It] by no means follows that an action brought on a bill which fails to satisfy one or more of the statutory requirements or which contains erroneous items must necessarily be dismissed without consideration of the merits. It has long been established that a court, confronted with a defective bill, is entitled to look into all the circumstances of the case and in appropriate cases to allow the solicitor to withdraw the bill and to deliver a fresh one.'

Stanley Burnton LJ has, however, made it clear that it is a jurisdiction which should be exercised only where there has been a genuine mistake or error on the part of the solicitor when preparing his original bill.[89]

17.80 If the court does order substitution of a bill (other than as a result of SA 1974, s 64(2)), the court will be able to take that into account when the costs of the assessment fall to be determined. Whether or not the court can take a gross sum bill into account when it has been replaced by a detailed bill pursuant to s 64(2) is a moot point: this is because the 1974 Act says that the gross sum bill will be of 'no effect'.

17.81 For the avoidance of doubt, it is worth stating that these general rules apply only to assessments made under SA 1974. They do not apply to assessments between opposing parties[90] or where court has merely referred a solicitor's charges to a costs judge for an assessment of a reasonable charge for the work done.[91] Indeed, CPD, art 40.10 specifically states that, unless the court orders otherwise, on a between-the-parties assessment a party may vary his bill of costs without requiring the permission of the court.

GROSS SUM BILLS AND REQUESTS FOR BILLS CONTAINING DETAILED ITEMS

17.82 The modern position is now governed by SA 1974, s 64, which makes the following provisions:[92]

---

85 *In re Grant, Bulcraig & Co* [1906] 1 Ch 124.
86 See, in particular, *Polak v Machioness of Winchester* [1956] 2 All ER 660; *Zuliani v Veira* [1994] 1 WLR 1149, PC; and CPR, r 3.1(m).
87 *Polak v Marchioness of Winchester* [1956] 2 All ER 660 at 668, per Jenkins LJ; see also *Chappell v Mehta* [1981] 1 All ER 349.
88 *Zuliani v Veira* [1994] 1 WLR 1149. The WLR is only a short report; this extract is taken from (1994) 45 WIR 188 at 194.
89 *Bilkus v Stockler Brunton (a firm)* [2010] EWCA Civ 101 at [57]–[59].
90 See CPD, art 40.10 and (historically) *Davis v Dysart (No 2)* (1855) 21 Beav 124 at 132.
91 *Lumsden v Shipcote Land Co* [1906] 2 KB 433 and *Rollinsone v Eversheds* (unreported) 11 May 1993, CA.
92 Minor terminological changes were, at the time of writing, due to be made by the Legal Services Act 2007, s 177 and Sch 16, Pt 1, paras 1 and 60; at the time of writing those changes had not been made, but they are incorporated herein because it is likely that they will have been made by the time the book comes to be read; the reader should check this for himself, however. None of the changes alter the meaning of the extract.

'(1)   Where the remuneration of a solicitor in respect of contentious business done by him is not the subject of a contentious business agreement, then, subject to subsections (2) to (4), the solicitor's bill of costs may at the option of the solicitor be either a bill containing detailed items or a gross sum bill.

(2)   The party chargeable with a gross sum bill may at any time—

    (a)   before he is served with a writ or other originating process for the recovery of costs included in the bill, and

    (b)   before the expiration of three months from the date on which the bill was delivered to him,

require the solicitor to deliver, in lieu of that bill, a bill containing detailed items; and on such a requirement being made the gross sum bill shall be of no effect.

(3)   Where an action is commenced on a gross sum bill, the court shall, if so requested by the party chargeable with the bill before the expiration of one month from the service on that party of the writ or other originating process, order that the bill be assessed.

(4)   If a gross sum bill is assessed, whether under this section or otherwise, nothing in this section shall prejudice any rules of court with respect to assessment, and the solicitor shall furnish the costs officer with such details of any of the costs covered by the bill as the costs officer may require.

Thus, where work is contentious and where there is no contentious business agreement,[93] a solicitor may elect either to deliver a gross sum bill or to deliver a bill containing detailed items (which is usually referred to simply as a 'detailed bill'). It used to be the case that a solicitor had an implied right to render a gross sum bill in non-contentious work, in which case the gross sum bill would stand as the final bill without a right to a more detailed bill, but there is a good argument for saying that the right to render a gross sum bill in non-contentious work no longer exists.[94] That said, a contrary analysis is that the reason s 64 of the SA 1974 relates solely to contentious business is because the common law has always permitted gross sum bills in non-contentious work.[95] In the absence of authority on the point, a cautious solicitor would do well to ensure that he renders only reasonably detailed bills for non-contentious work.

17.83   In so far as contentious work is concerned, a detailed bill delivered pursuant to SA 1974, s 64(2) should not be confused with a detailed breakdown served pursuant to s 64(4) and to CPR, r 48.10(2). If a gross sum bill falls to be assessed, the court will often order the solicitor to prepare a detailed breakdown pursuant to r 48.10(2). That

---

[93]   Contentious business agreements often provide for fixed or partially fixed costs, so the provisions concerning detail are less relevant.

[94]   The implied right came about in the following way: 'By the Order of 1920 . . . a solicitor was authorised to charge a gross sum for non-contentious business, in lieu of detailed charges, but it was provided that the client could insist within six months on a detailed bill of charges, just as if no gross sum were permissible. In 1953 a new order, the Solicitors' Remuneration Order, 1953, was made, which made great alterations in the method of charging for non-contentious business. The solicitor is now entitled . . . to "Such sum as may be fair and reasonable, having regard to all the circumstances of the case . . ." This, I think, means a lump sum as before, but, whereas previously the client could afterwards insist on a detailed bill of charges, he now has no right to have the lump sum split up into items. He is, however, given a valuable new right. He can require the solicitor to put the bill before the Law Society, so that the Law Society can see whether the sum charged is fair and reasonable': *Re A Solicitor* [1955] 2 All ER 283 at 287, per Denning MR. The implied ability to render a gross sum bill was dependant on the words "such sum as may be fair and reasonable", but the present incarnation of the relevant legislation (the Solicitors' (Non-Contentious Business) Remuneration Order 2009) no longer contains those words. As such, it is, at the very least, arguable that the ability to render gross sum bills for non-contentious work no longer exists.

[95]   Whilst not binding, see, for example, the Australian case of *Patel v Sica* [1982] VR 273 at 276, 277.

would not entitle the solicitor to submit a new bill; it would be the same bill (ie the original gross sum bill) rather than the breakdown that will be the subject of assessment. It will often be the case that the detailed breakdown is capable of justifying costs which are higher than those claimed in the bill; if this is the case, then the costs will be limited to those sums claimed in the bill.[96]

17.84 If the solicitor chooses to deliver a gross sum bill relating to contentious work, the client may, within certain time limits, request a detailed bill. If the client makes such a request, the detailed bill will replace the gross sum bill, which will then be of no effect;[97] this may mean that the solicitor can recover an amount which exceeds the amount originally charged.[98] It follows that a client who requests a detailed bill may ultimately pay more than he would have paid had he dealt with the matter on the basis of a gross sum bill.

17.85 A request for greater detail may, on the one hand, be characterised as a request for a detailed bill or, on the other, merely as a request for clarification of the gross sum bill; for the reasons set out above, the distinction can be important. This question is determined by looking at the substance of the demand; it would not be right to allow an overly technical interpretation of the language to defeat the purpose of the request.[99] This is particularly so where the author of the request is a layman.[100]

17.86 Megarry J offered some guidance about how to categorise demands for detail which are said to be requests for a detailed bill:[101]

'It seems to me that before proviso (a) of section 64 is brought into play there must be something which can fairly be described as a request or requirement that the solicitors should deliver to the client a detailed bill to replace the gross sum bill already delivered: and although I do not think that any particular form of words need be employed, the substance of what is relied upon must amount to a request or requirement of this kind.'

17.87 For the reasons explained above, a finding that a request is a request for a detailed bill would usually be to the client's disadvantage. This is a factor that the court can take into account when resolving doubt as to whether a request is a request for a detailed bill. Sir John Vinelott gave the following guidance about the resolution of doubt:[102]

'If there is doubt as to the way in which the letter should be interpreted, the doubt should be resolved in favour of the client for whose protection these provisions were enacted.'

17.88 Where the solicitor is in doubt as to what his client is requesting, Megarry J explained that he should seek clarification from his client:[103]

---

[96] It is good practice to make this clear on the face of the detailed breakdown (an example would be: 'this breakdown supports costs of £x, but the amount claimed is limited to £y in accordance with the bill delivered on ...').
[97] *Madurasinghe v Penguin Electronics (a firm)* [1993] 1 WLR 989.
[98] *In re Taxation of Costs In re Solicitors* [1943] KB 69; see also *Polak v Machioness of Winchester* [1956] 2 All ER 660.
[99] *Penningtons (a firm) v Brown* (unreported) 30 April 1998, CA.
[100] *Penningtons (a firm) v Brown* (unreported) 30 April 1998, CA.
[101] *Carlton v Theodore Goddard & Co* [1973] 1 WLR 623.
[102] *Penningtons (a firm) v Brown* (unreported) 30 April 1998, CA.
[103] *Carlton v Theodore Goddard & Co* [1973] 1 WLR 623.

'If in doubt ... the solicitors, before embarking on the work, can always inquire whether some equivocal communication that they have received is or is not intended to be a requirement under the proviso.'

The absence of such an inquiry would be a factor that might be taken into account in an appropriate case.[104]

17.89 There are, nonetheless, limits to the extent to which the court will shield the client as a consumer. In particular, the client's knowledge or understanding of the law (or lack thereof) will not prevent the court from categorising a request for detail (as opposed to clarification) as being a request for a detailed bill.[105] Pill LJ has found that the court should not be influenced in its construction of a request for detail by the fact that a client may be condemned to pay a greater sum than he would have paid had he not made the request.[106]

17.90 One or two case examples illustrate the court's approach:

- The following statement (which had been drafted by the client's new solicitors) was found not to amount to a request for a detailed bill because it could not be said to be a request or a requirement:[107]

    'Accordingly, it would seem that there is no alternative but for your bill to be prepared and lodged for taxation.'

- A request for 'a full breakdown of your firm's bill' did amount to a request for a detailed bill, even in circumstances where that request also indicated an intention to have 'the bill' (ie the gross sum bill) assessed.[108]

17.91 Where a detailed bill is delivered in circumstances in which the client has made no request, the assessment will proceed on the basis of the original gross sum bill.[109] The solicitor will not be able to withdraw and substitute the gross sum bill unless either the client consents or the court so orders. That said, the superfluous detailed bill may still be of use, in that it may be able to stand as the breakdown of costs pursuant to CPR, r 48.10(2).

THE CONSEQUENCES OF FAILING TO COMPLY WITH SECTION 69 OF THE SOLICITORS ACT

17.92 Should a bill fail to meet the requirements of SA 1974, s 69, then s 69(1) provides that no claim shall be brought to recover any costs due, so the bill is unenforceable.

17.93 If a claim is brought on a defective bill, the court has a discretionary power to allow the solicitor to withdraw the bill and to bring a new claim. There is also authority that the court may allow a solicitor to replace a bill without bringing new

---

[104] See, for example, *Penningtons (a firm) v Brown* (unreported) 30 April 1998, CA, in which Pill LJ implicitly adopted this line of thinking.
[105] *Penningtons (a firm) v Brown* (unreported) 30 April 1998, CA.
[106] *Penningtons (a firm) v Brown* (unreported) 30 April 1998, CA.
[107] *Carlton v Theodore Goddard & Co* [1973] 1 WLR 623.
[108] *Penningtons (a firm) v Brown* (unreported) 30 April 1998, CA.
[109] *Carlton v Theodore Goddard & Co* [1973] 1 WLR 623.

proceedings;[110] that authority is a decision of the Privy Council which relies on a foreign statutory provision with no obvious counterpart in English law, so may not be persuasive. Nonetheless, it is possible that CPR, r 3(1)(m) permits the court to allow a bill to be replaced without the need for new proceedings.

17.94 Whilst no claim may be brought on a defective bill, the solicitor's fees and disbursements may be capable of being recovered in other ways (see the next four paragraphs). In practice, however, it is rare that the court would find that a bill was a defective statute bill (as opposed to something else, such as an interim invoice on account), and it is even rarer for the court to refuse a request to withdraw the bill.

Loss of protection

17.95 The client may lose the benefit of the protection afforded by SA 1974, s 69(1). Where, for example, a solicitor and client compromise a claim for the solicitor's costs and state an account showing a balance in the solicitor's favour, a claim may be brought by the solicitor for that balance; this is because the compromised sum would be for more that the mere remuneration in issue, and as such the compromise falls outside the ambit of the SA, s 69(1).[111] Likewise, a solicitor may sue upon a promissory note given in respect of costs,[112] or he may foreclose a mortgage taken as security on the costs.[113] A solicitor may be able to sue on a dishonoured cheque, but this will not always be the case, as consumer protection issues may arise.[114]

Statutory demand

17.96 It may or may not be the case that a solicitor is permitted to serve a statutory demand in respect of a defective bill. This issue frequently arises in practice because solicitors commonly seek to take active steps against former clients before the expiry of the one-month time limit in SA 1974, s 69(1). There is authority that service of a statutory demand for payment of solicitor's costs does not constitute the bringing of an action.[115] That may be true, but it has been successfully argued that a solicitor's bill is not, prior to an assessment, a 'liquidated debt' for the purposes of bankruptcy proceedings.[116] This is dealt with in more detail at **19.23–19.33**.

Payment

17.97 The fact that a bill is not compliant with SA 1974, s 69 will not render a bill incapable of being paid. In particular, where a bill fails to comply with the requirements of s 69 and where that bill has been paid for more than 12 months, the court will have no power to order an assessment.[117] Likewise, such a bill will not be incapable of

---

[110]   *Zuliani v Veira* [1994] 1 WLR 1149, PC; see also *Tearle & Co (a firm) v Sherring* (unreported) 29 October 1993, Wright J, which concerned an accidental failure to comply with SA 1974, s 67.

[111]   *Turner v Willis* [1905] 1 KB 468. If the agreement merely relates to the costs, then the client will usually not lose protection: *Re Fernandes* [1878] WN 57 and **18.21**.

[112]   *Jeffreys v Evans* (1845) 14 M&W 210.

[113]   *Thomas v Cross* (1864) 29 JP 4.

[114]   *Martin Boston & Co (a firm) v Levy* [1982] 1 WLR 1434.

[115]   *In re A Debtor (No 88 of 1991)* [1993] Ch 286 (Sir Donald Nicholls V-C went on to say (obiter) that a bankruptcy petition probably should be regarded as being an action for the purposes of s 69(1).

[116]   See *Turex v Toll* [2009] EWHC 369 (Ch); *Klamer v Kyriakides & Braier (a firm)* [2005] BPIR, Ch D (which is not binding, as it was a Master's decision); and s 267(2)(b) of the Insolvency Act 1986.

[117]   *In re Sutton & Elliot* (1883) 11 QBD 337.

assessment.[118] Indeed, where a bill has been delivered but not signed, it cannot be withdrawn without the leave of the court.[119]

Set-off

17.98 Where a solicitor is a debtor to a client who has outstanding fees, he may set off the sum due to him even though he has not complied with the requirements of SA 1974, s 69.[120] This is a discretionary remedy which may be refused.[121]

HOW DISBURSEMENTS ARE TREATED IN A STATUTE BILL

17.99 SA 1974, s 67 makes the following provisions:

> 'A solicitor's bill of costs may include costs payable in discharge of a liability properly incurred by him on behalf of the party to be charged with the bill (including counsel's fees) notwithstanding that those costs have not been paid before the delivery of the bill to that party; but those costs—
>
> (a) shall be described in the bill as not then paid; and
> (b) if the bill is assessed, shall not be allowed by the costs officer
>
> unless they are paid before the assessment is completed.'

The words 'properly incurred by him on behalf of the party to be charged with the bill' have the effect of defining disbursements for the purposes of this section. Other definitions of disbursements exist; they are only peripherally relevant for present purposes and are dealt with in Chapter 31. Payments which neither law nor custom require a solicitor to make (such as purchase monies for land) ought not to be categorised as disbursements, and should appear in the cash account rather than the bill.[122] Agents' fees should appear in the bill, but this will be generally as profit costs rather than disbursements;[123] this includes costs draftsmen's fees.[124]

17.100 Disbursements which have been paid ought to be entered into the bill where appropriate,[125] even where they have been paid directly by the client,[126] such as where the client has offered a cheque made payable to counsel.[127]

17.101 Unpaid disbursements merit particular attention. If disbursements are unpaid at the time of assessment, they will be disallowed.[128] This includes counsel's fees; indeed, because of the non-contractual nature of counsel's fees, there will be no enforceable debt

---

[118] *Ex parte D'Aragon* (1887) 3 TLR 815.

[119] *Re Jones* (1886) 54 LT 648.

[120] *Ex parte Cooper* (1854) 14 CB 663; *Harrison v Turner* (1847) 10 QB 482; *Brown v Tibbits* (1862) 11 CBNS 855.

[121] See, for example, *Currie & Co v Law Society* [1977] QB 990.

[122] See *Re Remanant* (1849) 11 Beav 603 (purchase money); *Re Buckwell* [1902] 2 Ch 596 (security for costs); *Prothero v Thomas* (1815) 6 Tuant 196 (monies payable to an opponent).

[123] *Pomeroy v Tanner* [1897] 1 Ch 285.

[124] *Crane v Cannons Leisure* [2007] EWCA Civ 1352.

[125] *Re Seal ex p Crickett* (1893) 37 Sol Jo 842, CA.

[126] *Re Metcalfe* (1862) 30 Beav 406.

[127] *Devereux v White & Co* (1896) 13 TLR 52.

[128] Of historic interest, see *Smith v Howes* [1922] 1 KB 592, which dealt with the then rules of court which were very similar to SA 1974, s 67; it can be seen that the provision was introduced to avoid the stringency of the decision in *Sadd v Griffin* [1908] 2 KB 510, which effectively prevented the recovery of any disbursements which were unpaid at the time the bill was delivered. See also *Re A Taxation of Costs* [1936] 1 KB 523. Other

at all until counsel's fees have been paid.[129] Although there is no authority on the point, there is no particular reason to believe that this rule does not apply to counsel's fees where counsel has been instructed under a conditional fee agreement.[130] It is commonly the case that unpaid disbursements are, accidentally or otherwise, not always described within the bill as being unpaid. The court has the power to order that such a bill is withdrawn and substituted with a revised bill, but there is pre-CPR authority to suggest that the court also has the power to allow such a bill to be amended to include the necessary words.[131] However, some commentators have questioned the existence of that power under the CPR.[132]

17.102 Acton J has confirmed that a client cannot evade liability by instructing the solicitor not to pay disbursements which have been properly incurred. That is, disbursements are recoverable from the client even though the payment is made by the solicitor after the client has stated that he does not propose to pay the disbursement.[133]

POWER TO ORDER DELIVERY OF A BILL

17.103 SA 1974, s 68 gives the court the power to order a solicitor to deliver a bill:

'(1) The jurisdiction of the High Court to make orders for the delivery by a solicitor of a bill of costs, and for the delivery up of, or otherwise in relation to, any documents in his possession, custody or power, is hereby declared to extend to cases in which no business has been done by him in the High Court.

(2) A county court shall have the same jurisdiction as the High Court to make orders making such provision as is mentioned in subsection (1) in cases where the bill of costs or the documents relate wholly or partly to contentious business done by the solicitor in that county court.

(3) In this section and in sections 69 to 71 "solicitor" includes the executors, administrators and assignees of a solicitor.'

The court may be asked to exercise this power in circumstances such as where a solicitor has paid himself by deduction, or where he proposes to take sums paid on account as being final payment without. The application is often combined with an application to deliver a cash account. A solicitor principal may require a solicitor agent to deliver a bill.[134]

17.104 The orders that the court is able to make are set out in CPR, r 67.2(1):

'Where the relationship of solicitor and client exists or has existed, the orders which the court may make against the solicitor, on the application of the client or his personal representatives, include any of the following—

(a)　to deliver a bill or cash account;

---

common law jurisdictions have followed *Sadd* (see, for example, *Vilensky v Banning* (unreported, WA Sup Ct, Kennedy, Ipp and Rowland JJ, 20 June 1996, No Ful 35 of 1995), a decision of the Full Court of Western Australia).

129　*Re Taxation of Costs, Re A Solicitor* [1936] 1 KB 523.
130　For the avoidance of doubt, the provisions concerning unpaid counsel's fee apply only on a solicitor and client assessment; it has no role to play between opposing parties.
131　*Tearle & Co (a firm) v Sherring* (unreported) 29 October 1993, Wright J.
132　See *Greenslade on Costs*, para G.048.
133　*Medlicott v Emery* [1933] All ER 655.
134　*Re A Solicitor* (1909) 54 Sol Jo 67.

(b)   to pay or deliver up any money or securities;

(c)   to deliver a list of the moneys or securities which the solicitor has in his possession or control on behalf of the applicant;

(d)   to pay into or lodge in court any such money or securities.'

17.105   Where the solicitor alleges that he has a claim for costs against the client, the court may make an order securing the payment of the costs, or protecting the solicitor's lien.[135]

17.106   Whether the court makes an order under SA 1974, s 68 is matter of discretion.[136] The power to order delivery of a bill is wider than the power to refer a bill for assessment. The court may order delivery of a bill notwithstanding the fact that the court may not have jurisdiction to order that the bill be assessed.[137] The power to order delivery has always been exercised irrespective of the question whether the bill may be submitted for assessment;[138] the two jurisdictions are quite distinct.[139] The court should bear in mind that it will be for the client to consider, after he has received the bill, whether he will or will not apply for an assessment.[140]

17.107   The court may refuse to exercise its discretion to order delivery; an example would be where a client has left it very late (6 years) to make his application.[141] The court will not make orders which are pointless: this means that if there has been an agreement as to the costs,[142] or if costs have been settled by a third party, the need for a bill will no longer exist.[143] In this regard, Lord Evershed MR had the following to say:[144]

'It seems, therefore, quite plain to me that as a matter of general principle it is not right to say that a client, who has made an agreement for paying a lump sum for non-contentious business, has an unqualified right to come and ask for a bill. His right to require a bill is limited to cases where he can show, on the facts of the particular case, to the satisfaction of the court that there is something which as a matter of general principle or private right, or both, the court ought to look into.'

17.108   Costs must exist before the court can order delivery. Thus, where a solicitor had left it so long to draw up his bill that he was unable to do so and where he had relinquished his right to be paid, no order was made.[145] Likewise, no order would be made where a solicitor declines to raise a charge.[146] Even in those circumstances, the solicitor may be ordered to provide a cash account.[147] That said, pre-CPR authority indicates that if the solicitor claims no costs and swears that that he has no client monies and has retained no client monies, he will generally not be required to furnish a cash account.[148]

---

[135]   CPR, r 67.2(3).

[136]   *In re Solicitor, In re a Taxation of Costs* [1953] Ch 480.

[137]   *Duffet v McEvoy* (1885) 10 App Cas 300.

[138]   *In re West Kings & Adams ex p Clough* [1892] 2 QB 102 at 108.

[139]   *Duffet v McEvoy* (1885) 10 App Cas 300.

[140]   *In Re Blackmore* (1851) 13 Beav 154.

[141]   *In re a Solicitor, In re Taxation of Costs* [1947] Ch 274.

[142]   *In re Van Laun ex p Chatterton* [1907] 1 KB 155 (see also [1907] 2 KB 23, where the Court of Appeal confirmed that, in respect of different bills rendered between the same parties, a trustee could require delivery in order to know the sums to be paid from the estate).

[143]   *Re Chapman* (1903) 20 TLR 3, CA.

[144]   *Rutter v Sheridan-Young* [1958] 1 WLR 444 at 453. See also *Re Palmer* (1890) 45 Ch D 291.

[145]   *In Re Landor (a solicitor)* [1899] 1 Ch 818.

[146]   *Re Griffith* (1891) 7 TLR 268 and *Sparrow v Johns* (1838) 3 M & W 600, 150 ER 1284.

[147]   CPR, r 67.2(1)(a).

[148]   *Re Landor* (1899) 1 Ch 818.

17.109 The costs must be legal costs: if the work which has been done is work that cannot properly be regarded as professional work, the party chargeable will not have the right to apply for delivery of a bill.[149]

17.110 If the application for an order is made within existing proceedings, it must be made by application notice in accordance with CPR, Part 23. Where it is not made in existing proceedings, it is made by the Part 8 procedure.[150] The application will usually be made to the Senior Courts Costs Office, but this need not necessarily be the case.[151]

17.111 If the court allows the application, it will make an order in the form of Precedent K of the Schedule of Costs Precedents annexed to the CPD.

---

[149] *Re Fanshaw* [1905] WN 64.
[150] CPR, r 67.2(2).
[151] PD 67, para 2.1(2).

Chapter 18

SOLICITOR AND CLIENT ASSESSMENTS

18.1   This chapter addresses the procedural aspects of solicitor and client assessments. The law relating to solicitor and client costs and the principles of quantification are dealt with in Chapter 17 and in Part V.

18.2   The antiquated language of solicitor and client costs law has now been brought into line with the language of assessments generally;[1] from 1 January 2010, for example, the process of ascertaining the quantum of costs has been referred to as an 'assessment' rather than a 'taxation'.[2] The new terminology is used in this book.

ON THE APPLICATION OF THE PARTY CHARGEABLE OR THE SOLICITOR

18.3   The law governing the right to solicitor and client assessments derives from s 70 of the Solicitors Act 1974:

'(1)   Where before the expiration of one month from the delivery of a solicitor's bill an application is made by the party chargeable with the bill, the High Court shall, without requiring any sum to be paid into court, order that the bill be assessed and that no action be commenced on the bill until the assessment is completed.

(2)   Where no such application is made before the expiration of the period mentioned in subsection (1), then, on an application being made by the solicitor or, subject to subsections (3) and (4), by the party chargeable with the bill, the court may on such terms, if any, as it thinks fit (not being terms as to the costs of the assessment), order—

(a)   that the bill be assessed; and

(b)   that no action be commenced on the bill, and that any action already commenced be stayed, until the assessment is completed.

(3)   Where an application under subsection (2) is made by the party chargeable with the bill—

(a)   after the expiration of 12 months from the delivery of the bill, or

(b)   after a judgment has been obtained for the recovery of the costs covered by the bill, or

(c)   after the bill has been paid, but before the expiration of 12 months from the payment of the bill,

no order shall be made except in special circumstances and, if an order is made, it may contain such terms as regards the costs of the assessment as the court may think fit.

(4)   The power to order assessment conferred by subsection (2) shall not be exercisable on an application made by the party chargeable with the bill after the expiration of 12 months

---

1   See the Legal Services Act 2007, Sch 16.

2   Legal Services Act 2007 (Commencement No 6, Transitory, Transitional and Saving Provisions) Order 2009 (SI 2009/3250), para 2(f).

from the payment of the bill.'

18.4   Thus, the ease with which a party chargeable (see **18.6–18.12**) may obtain an order for assessment diminishes with the effluxion of time after delivery or payment of the bill. This can be summarised in following way:

- if an application for an assessment is made within one month of the delivery of the bill, the court will order that the bill be assessed as a matter of right (**18.25**);
- if the application is made after the expiry of one month but before 12 months have passed, the court has an unfettered discretion to order an assessment (**18.26**);
- if the application is made after the expiry of 12 months, the court may order an assessment, but only if 'special circumstances' can be made out; likewise, if the bill has been paid for a period of less than 12 months (or judgment has been obtained), then special circumstances must be made out (**18.27–18.47**); and
- if the application is made after the expiry of 12 months from the payment of the bill, the court has no power to order an assessment under SA 1974.

If the last of these circumstances applies, then that is an absolute bar to an assessment under SA 1974.[3] The court may, however, have a non-statutory power to quantify the costs in some other way: see **19.18–19.22**.

18.5   A number of issues arise:

- the meaning of 'party chargeable with the bill' (**18.6–18.12**);
- the time of delivery (**18.13–18.15**);
- the meaning of 'payment' (**18.16–18.23**);
- the meaning of 'one month' and of '12 months' (**18.24**);
- the court's discretion (**18.25–18.26**);
- special circumstances (**18.27–18.47**); and
- procedural issues (**18.48–18.54**).

The meaning of 'party chargeable with the bill'

18.6   The identification of the party chargeable will usually be a question of fact, but points of law may arise from time to time (see, for example, **18.9–18.11**). Usually no problems will arise in identifying the party chargeable; he will be the person who has entered into a contract of retainer with a solicitor and who has been charged for that solicitor's services. He may or may not be the person who has been in receipt of the legal services.

18.7   The following circumstances merit specific discussion:

- where the client is a professional client (**18.8**);
- where there is group litigation with the sharing of common costs (**18.9**);
- where there are joint contracts of retainer involving joint costs debtors (**18.10**);
- where the party chargeable is acting in a representative capacity or as a trustee (**18.11**); and

---

3   See s 70(4) of SA 1974 and *Harrison v Tew* [1990] 2 AC 523. This applies where the application is made by a liquidator following payment made by the now-insolvent company: *Forsinard Estate Ltd v Dykes* [1971] 1 WLR 232. For the rights of a cestui que trust in respect of a bill delivered to his trustee, see *Re Downes* (1844) 5 Beav 425 and *Re Brown* (1867) LR 4 Eq 464.

- where the assessment is a quantification of the solicitor's claim against assets (**18.12**).

Professional clients

18.8   The fact that the solicitor's client is himself a solicitor is no bar to him being a party chargeable. Where a solicitor instructs another solicitor as his agent, the instructing solicitor may be a party chargeable notwithstanding the principal–agent relationship.[4] Likewise, where a solicitor is a trustee entitled under the trust to charge for his professional services and where he delivers a bill to a co-trustee, the co-trustee is a party chargeable.[5]

Group litigation

18.9   Where individual retainers exist in group litigation, it will usually be the case that each party will be the party chargeable in respect of his individual costs and in respect of his share of the common costs. Thus, there will be more than one party chargeable with the common costs. In order to prevent a multiplicity of assessments, the court will, so far as possible, direct a single assessment in the presence of all the relevant parties.[6] See **39.58** for further comments on the management of such matters.

Joint retainers

18.10   Where a retainer is joint (ie where there is one debt of costs, and each client is liable for the whole of it: see **12.43–12.51**), any client may be the party chargeable, regardless of whether the co-clients refuse to join or object to the assessment.[7]

Joint representatives and trustees

18.11   A party chargeable may include a personal representative,[8] a trustee in bankruptcy,[9] or a liquidator[10] of the client. In a similar vein to the point made above (**18.10**), any one of a number of trustees can obtain an order for assessment of work done for the trust, regardless of whether the co-trustee refuses to join or raises an objection.[11]

Quantification of claim against assets

18.12   Where the purpose of the exercise is solely to ascertain the amount of the solicitor's claim against the assets, it is possible that the court is permitted to carry out an assessment under the general jurisdiction of the court rather than under SA 1974; if

---

4   *In re Wilde (a solicitor)* [1910] 1 Ch 100; see also *Jones v Roberts* (1838) 8 Sim 397 and *Toghill v Grant, Re Boord* (1840) 2 Beav 261.
5   *In re HP Davies & Son* [1917] 1 Ch 216.
6   Whilst a very old case, see by analogy *In re Salaman* [1894] 2 Ch 201.
7   *Lockhard v Hardy* (1841) 4 Beav 224. ; see also *Re Hair* (1847) 10 Beav 187 and *Re Lewin* (1853) 16 Beav 608.
8   *Jefferson v Warrington* (1840) 7 M&W 137.
9   *Re Allingham* (1886) 32 Ch D 36, CA.
10   *In re Foss, Bilbrough, Plaskitt & Foss* [1912] 2 Ch 161.
11   *Hazard v Lane* (1817) 3 Mer 285 at 290.

this is correct, the issue of whether the party seeking the assessment is party chargeable will not arise.[12] It is not wholly clear whether this remains good law; it is arguable either way.[13]

The time of delivery

18.13 The time of delivery will usually be predominantly a matter of fact to be determined on the evidence. Points of law may arise in a number of circumstances, two of which merit particular mention (namely, where the bill is one of a series of requests for payment, and where the client is a company in the process of being wound up). Other points of law may arise from time to time (see **17.67–17.72**).

Series of bills

18.14 It may be necessary to examine the nature of the retainer in order to determine when a bill was delivered in law (see **17.68**). If the bill related to an entire contract[14] and if it comprised a series of invoices which could properly be regarded as forming a single bill, time will not begin to run until delivery of the final bill.[15] This is because the bill is not delivered until the last part of it has been delivered. That type of bill is sometimes referred to as a '*Chamberlain* bill'.[16] The types of circumstance in which a *Chamberlain* bill will exist are where the parts of the bill were delivered at times that were not natural breaks, over a short period of time and with a nexus between them (such as where a running total is carried over from one invoice to the next).[17]

Winding up

18.15 Where a bill is delivered to a company which is subsequently wound up, time is counted from the date of winding up. If a bill was delivered more than 12 months before winding up, there will be a need to show special circumstances,[18] but if the bill was delivered less than 12 months before winding up, there will be no need to show special circumstances, and this will be so even if more than 12 months has elapsed between delivery and application.[19]

The meaning of 'payment'

18.16 There are conditions that must be satisfied before a transfer of money can properly be said to be a payment within the meaning of SA 1974, s 70:

(1)   there must have been delivery of a statute bill;[20] and

---

12   *In re Foss, Bilbrough, Plaskitt & Foss* [1912] 2 Ch 161 and *In re Palace Restaurants* [1914] 1 Ch 492.

13   See *Harrison v Tew* [1990] 2 AC 523; compare with *Turner & Co v Palomo SA* [2000] 1 WLR 37; the situation is arguably comparable to the latter, in which case the jurisdiction will exist.

14   This will, in general, not be a finding open to the court where the retainer is a general retainer (i e a retainer that does not relate to a single case): see *Warmingtons v McMurray* [1936] 2 All ER 745.

15   *Chamberlain v Boodle & King* [1982] 1 WLR 1443; see also *Re Street* (1870) LR 10 Eq 165 and, as to timing, *Warmingtons v McMurray* [1936] 2 All ER 745.

16   After *Chamberlain v Boodle & King* [1982] 1 WLR 1443.

17   See, for example, the facts of *Chamberlain* itself.

18   *James, Re, ex p Quilter* (1850) 4 De G & Sm 183.

19   *Re Park, Cole v Park* (1888) 41 Ch D 326; *Re Brabant* (1879) 23 Sol Jo 779; *Marseilles Extension Rly and Land Co, Re, ex p Evans* (1870) LR 11 Eq 151; *Re James, ex p Quilter* (1850) 4 De G & Sm 183; and *In re Foss, Bilbrough, Plaskitt & Foss* [1912] 2 Ch 161.

20   *Re Foster* [1920] 3 KB 306; see also *Re West King & Adams* [1892] 2 QB 102.

(2)   the client must have knowledge that the putative payment has been made.[21]

Both of these are issues of fact; the following case examples illustrate the way in which the court addresses those issues.

No bill

18.17   There can be no payment in the absence of a statute bill.[22] This is true even if there has been an agreement as to the amount payable.[23] Lord Romilly wearily explained this point:[24]

> 'I have held over and over again that there can be no payment ... before the bill has been delivered and the client has had the opportunity of seeing the items.'

As to delivery of bills after payment has been made, see **18.21**.

Payment by deduction and the client's knowledge

18.18   There can be no payment without the client's knowledge. If a solicitor pays his bills by deduction without the knowledge of his client, that will not amount to payment within the meaning of SA 1974, s 70.[25] Mere acquiescence on the part of the client would not suffice.[26] Payment by deduction with the client's knowledge may, on the other hand, be regarded as being payment.[27]

Partial payment

18.19   In the absence of accord and satisfaction (see **19.43–19.44**), where a payment is only partial (ie a costs debt is not extinguished by the payment), it is not a payment within the meaning of SA 1974, s 70 but is merely a payment on account.[28]

Negotiable instruments

18.20   Presenting a negotiable instrument will amount to payment only if and when it is honoured.[29] The date of payment is the date on which it is honoured rather than the date on which it is presented.[30] A solicitor cannot evade his obligation to deliver a statute bill by taking a bill of exchange from his client for an agreed amount.[31]

---

[21]   See *In Re Bignold* (1845) 9 Beav 269 at 270; see also the other footnotes in the case examples.
[22]   *Re Foster* [1920] 3 KB 306.
[23]   *In re Frape ex p Perrett* [1893] 2 Ch 284; see also *In re Baylis* [1896] 2 Ch 107.
[24]   *In re Street* (1870) Law Rep 10 Eq 165, CA at 167. See also *In re Blackmore* (1851) 13 Beav 154 and *In re Stogdon* (1887) 56 LJ (Ch) 420, where Chitty J approved and followed *In re Street*. See also *In re Bayliss* [1896] 2 Ch 107, in which the Court of Appeal upheld Chitty J's analysis.
[25]   *In re Jackson* [1915] 1 KB 371 at 381 and 383 and *In Re Stogdon* (1887) 56 LJ (Ch) 420.
[26]   See *Re Ingle* (1855) 25 LJ Ch 169; *Re West, King & Adams* [1892] 2 QB 102 ; *Re Foss, Bilborough & Co* [1912] 2 Ch 161.
[27]   *Forsinard Estates v Dykes* [1971] 1 WLR 237; see also *Re David* (1861) 30 Beav 278; *Hitchcock v Stretton* [1892] 2 Ch 343 and *Re Thompson* [1894] 1 QB 462.
[28]   *Re Callis* (1901) 49 WR 316 and *Re Woodard* (1869) 18 WR 37.
[29]   *Sayer v Wagstaff* (1844) 14 LJ Ch 116.
[30]   *Re Romer & Haslam* [1893] 2QB 286 and *Ray v Newton* [1913] 1 KB 249 at 256.
[31]   *Ray v Newton* [1913] 1 KB 249.

Subsequent delivery

18.21 Provided that the monies were at all times referable to the bill in question,[32] where the bill has been delivered after the monies were paid or deducted the court is able to find that there has been payment notwithstanding the fact that delivery came after the transfer of monies.[33] There are limits to this approach, however: whilst persuasive rather than binding, there is Australian authority confirming that delivery of a putative bill after payment will not cure the original failure to deliver a proper bill.[34]

Charges and mortgages

18.22 The giving of a mortgage with a covenant to pay is not equivalent to payment of the bill.[35]

Putative compromise

18.23 Disputes about whether there has been a payment often arise in a context in which it is said that the payment compromised the dispute between the solicitor and client. These issues are dealt with at **19.34–19.46**.

The meaning of 'one month' and of '12 months'

18.24 The reference to one month is a reference to one calendar month.[36] The day of delivery is excluded, as is the day on which proceedings are commenced.[37] The period ends when an application for an assessment is made: Carnwath LJ has made it clear that what is required is an actual application for an assessment.[38]

Assessment as of right

18.25 Where the application is made before the expiry of a month since the delivery of the bill, the client's right to an assessment is absolute; there can be no defence on the merits.[39] It would be wrong to impose conditions (such as a requirement to make an interim payment).[40]

The court's discretion

18.26 Where the application is made after the first month but where the need to show special circumstances has not yet arisen, the matter will be in the court's discretion. Many of the factors listed under 'special circumstances' at **18.27–18.47** will be relevant

---

[32] See, for example, *Re Simmons & Politzer* [1954] 2 QB 296 in which the monies related to 'business done, or to be done, in any action': that was not regarded as being payment.

[33] *In re Thompson ex p Baylis* [1894] 1 QB 463; see also *Hitchcock v Stretton* [1892] 2 Ch 352; compare with *Re Simmons & Politzer* [1954] 2 QB 296.

[34] *Woolf v Trebilco* [1933] VLR 180 at 190. In a similar vein, if an oral retainer is made and then the agreed sum is acknowledged in the form of an account stated after payment has been made by deduction, that acknowledgement will not be sufficient to give rise to a retrospective business agreement: *Re Fernandes* [1878] WN 57.

[35] *In re Val Laun ex p Chatterton* [1907] 1 KB 155.

[36] Interpretation Act 1978, Sch 1.

[37] *Blunt v Heslop* (1838) 4 A&E 577.

[38] *Solicitors Indemnity Fund Ltd v Hewitson & Harker* [2010] EWCA Civ 147 at [12].

[39] *Szekeres v Alan Smeath & Co* [2005] EWHC 1733 (Ch), per Pumfrey J.

[40] *Re Brockman* [1908–10] All ER Rep 364.

by analogy. Lord Cozens-Hardy MR has commented that the court is able to take into account the power to order the client to make a payment on account or to pay money into court.[41]

Special circumstances

18.27 Where special circumstances exist the client may be entitled to an assessment notwithstanding the fact that the application for an assessment has been made more than 12 months after delivery or following payment within the first 12 months after delivery.

18.28 Special circumstances are not confined to pressure, overcharge, or fraud: the existence of such circumstances is a matter of degree and of discretion to be exercised in the circumstances of the particular case.[42] Circumstances need to be considered in context.[43] Special means 'special', not 'exceptional'.[44] Lewison J had this to say on the topic:[45]

> 'Whether special circumstances exist is essentially a value judgment. It depends on comparing the particular case with the run of the mill case in order to decide whether a detailed assessment in the particular case is justified, despite the restrictions contained in Section 70(3).'

18.29 When the court is asked to consider more than one factor, it should consider those factors in aggregate, rather than individually.[46]

Third parties

18.30 Where the application is brought by a third party under s 71 of the Act, SA 1974, s 71(2) states that the court may take into account circumstances which affect the applicant but do not affect the party chargeable with the bill. Langley J has confirmed that the mere fact that the third party did not have control over the litigation would not be sufficient to amount to special circumstances.[47]

Case examples

18.31 The following case examples are not intended to be a statement of the law (indeed, some of them are decisions of costs judges and are therefore not binding). They are meant only to be illustrative.

---

[41]   *Re Brockman* [1908–10] All ER Rep 364.
[42]   See *In re Hirst & Capes* [1908] 1 KB 982, affirmed by the House of Lords at [1908] 1 AC 416.
[43]   See *Kris Motor Spares Ltd v Fox Williams LLP* [2009] EWHC 2813 (QB), in which Holroyde J declined to find special circumstances arising out of a reservation of a right to assessment because the client had sought an assessment only after the solicitor had refused to provide legal services on favourable terms.
[44]   *Riley v DLA, sub nom A v BCD (a firm)* (unreported) 5 June 1997, Sedley J.
[45]   *Falmouth House Freehold Co Ltd v Morgan Walker LLP* [2010] EWHC 3092 (Ch) at [13].
[46]   *Sanders v Isaacs* [1971] 1 WLR 240; and *Kundruth v Henry Kwatia & Gooding* [2005] 2 Costs LR 279.
[47]   *Barclays plc v Villers* [2000] 1 All ER (Comm) 357 at 369.

Excessive costs

18.32 Special circumstances may exist where a client shows that costs are unreasonably large,[48] that there has been overcharging,[49] or that costs are such that they call for an explanation.[50] An explicably high level of fees will not, however, amount to special circumstances.[51]

Pressure brought to bear

18.33 Where a client is put under pressure not to seek an assessment in a case where the recovery of costs was questionable, the court may find that special circumstances had been made out.[52] In general, the client should be able to specific the areas where there has been alleged overcharging.[53]

Incorrect advice about the process of assessment

18.34 Where solicitors wrongly advised a client that in order to have her costs assessed she would have had to have made an upfront payment of 40% of the costs as claimed, the court found that special circumstances had been made out by reason of the misleading advice that the client had received.[54]

Errors in the bill

18.35 The presence of gross errors or blunders in the bill may give rise to special circumstances.[55] The presence of costs charged as a result of a mistake as to the law may do the same.[56]

Unavoidable delay

18.36 If a client has applied for a remuneration certificate and if the remuneration procedure has taken more than 12 months to complete, that may amount to a special circumstance.[57] The remuneration certificate procedure no longer exists, but the same principle also applies to other unavoidable delays, such as those caused by an appellate process.[58] It is possible that the same principle would also apply where it was necessary to make a complaint to the Legal Ombudsman.

Prejudice caused by delay

18.37 Where a client has delayed in making an application for an assessment, the presence or absence of prejudice caused by that delay may be a relevant factor; indeed, it has been said (obiter) that delay alone would not be fatal to an application for an

---

[48] *Re Norman* (1886) 16 QBD 673.
[49] *Re a Solicitor* [1961] Ch 491.
[50] *Re Robinson* (1867) LR 3 Ex 4.
[51] See *Winchester Commodities Group Ltd v RD Black & Cl* [2000] BCC 310 in which the high level of fees was explicable on the grounds of the specialist nature of the work; see also *Re Cartwright* (1873) LR 16 Eq 469.
[52] *Kralj v Birkbeck Motague* (unreported) 18 February 1988, CA.
[53] *Re Boycott* (1885) LR 29 Ch D 571.
[54] *Kundruth v Henry Kwatia & Gooding* [2005] 2 Costs LR 279.
[55] *Re Norman* (1886) 16 QBD 673.
[56] *Re G* (1909) 53 SJ 469.
[57] *Riley v DLA, sub nom A v BCD (a firm)* (unreported) 5 June 1997, Sedley J.
[58] *Pine v Law Society* (unreported) 26 October 2004, QBD, HHJ Maddocks sitting as a High Court judge.

assessment unless the respondent solicitors could prove prejudice.[59] Where the solicitors have themselves caused or contributed to the delay (by, for example, taking a long time to prepare a detailed breakdown of costs), that is a factor that can be taken into account.[60]

Reservation as to right to assess

18.38 Special circumstances may arise where a client pays a bill with an express reservation of the right to assess.[61] Of itself, a reservation may not be sufficient to amount to special circumstances, but taken in conjunction with other factors (such as the solicitor asserting lien), special circumstances may be made out.[62]

Agreement to assess (or not)

18.39 Where there has been an agreement between the parties that there would be a detailed assessment of solicitors' costs, such agreement is as powerful a special circumstance as it is possible to get.[63] A mutual understanding (as opposed to an express agreement) that the bill would be assessed is also capable of amounting to a special circumstance.[64] On a related note, it is no defence to an application for an assessment made by a client to say that there has been a verbal agreement as to the quantum of costs.[65]

Delivery of bill with reservations

18.40 Where a bill is delivered with a reservation that a further bill may follow, that is capable of amounting to special circumstances.[66]

Poor client care

18.41 A refusal on the part of a solicitor to give further details about his costs has been held not to amount to special circumstances,[67] but incorrect advice about the assessment process might amount to special circumstances.[68]

Sophisticated client

18.42 The fact that the client is an experienced litigant acting on the advice of experienced solicitors may be relevant.[69]

---

[59]   *Kundruth v Henry Kwatia & Gooding* [2005] 2 Costs LR 279. See also *Arrowfield Services Ltd v BP Collins (a firm)* [2003] EWHC 830 (Ch), [2005] 2 Costs LR 171.

[60]   *Barnes v Stones (a firm)* [2007] EWHC 90069 (Costs), Master Simons (this is not binding).

[61]   *Re Tweedie* [1909] WN 110; and *Re Solicitors* (1934) 50 TLR 327.

[62]   *Sanders v Isaacs* [1971] 1 WLR 240. See also *Kris Motor Spares Ltd v Fox Williams LLP* [2009] EWHC 2813 (QB), per Holroyde J.

[63]   *Arrowfield Services Ltd v BP Collins (a firm)* [2003] EWHC 830 (Ch), [2005] 2 Costs LR 171.

[64]   *Barnes v Stones (a firm)* [2007] EWHC 90069 (Costs), Master Simons; see also *BFS Investments plc v Manches plc* [2007] EWHC 90082 (Costs), Master Gordon-Saker. Neither of these is binding.

[65]   In relation to contentious costs, see *In Re Russell Son & Scott 30 Ch D 114*, and in relation to non-contentious costs, *In Re West Kings & Adams ex p Clough* [1892] 2 QB 106.

[66]   *Harris v Yarm* [1960] Ch 256.

[67]   *Re Metal Distributors (UK) Ltd* [2004] EWHC (Ch).

[68]   *Kundruth v Henry Kwatia & Gooding* [2005] 2 Costs LR 279.

[69]   *Ingrams v Sykes* (1987) 137 NLJ 1135.

Payment

18.43 The fact that the client paid the bills without demur is a factor to be taken into account.[70] That said, where the payment is made in circumstances where the client was actively seeking an assessment, the fact of payment would rarely count against him.[71]

Unpaid disbursements

18.44 The fact that disbursements may not have been paid at the time the bill was delivered has been held not to amount to a special circumstance.[72] Non-payment of counsel's fees by a solicitor agent has been held not to constitute special circumstances.[73]

Personal stress and associated health problems

18.45 Where a client complained that the dispute with her solicitors had caused her considerable personal stress and (unspecified) health problems, the court found that no special circumstances had been made out (although the court took into account the fact that the client was herself a solicitor and that she had been given clear advice as to how and when to apply for an assessment).[74]

18.46 It is worth noting that an experienced costs judge (Master Rogers) has commented that the court is often prepared to find special circumstances where, in the past, special circumstances would not have been found.[75] If this is correct, older cases, such as some of those set out above, should be approached with some caution.

Appeals

18.47 An appeal court will not readily interfere with a decision as to special circumstances[76] (especially where the court at first instance was a specialist cost judge)[77] but successful appeals are not entirely unknown under the CPR.[78]

Procedural issues

The claim (or application)

18.48 The application for an assessment is made by the CPR, Part 8 procedure (or, in existing proceedings, on application).[79] The claim (or application) must be accompanied by the bill and, where there is one, the conditional fee agreement,[80] but by analogy with other types of litigation, it is likely that a procedural error will not necessarily lead to the claim being struck out.[81] If the claim is uncontested (ie if the parties agree that there

---

[70]   *Barclays plc v Villers* [2000] 1 All ER (Comm) 357 at 369.
[71]   On a slightly different point, see *Re Simmons and Politzer* [1954] 2 All ER 811.
[72]   *Re Massey* (1909) 101 LT 517.
[73]   *Re Nelson, Son and Hastings* (1885) 30 Ch D 1, CA.
[74]   *Sharif v The Law Society* [2005] EWHC 90018 (Costs).
[75]   See Master Roger's comments in *Sharif v The Law Society* [2005] EWHC 90018 (Costs) at [23]. This case is not binding.
[76]   *Re Ward Bowie & Co* (1910) 102 LT 881; see also *Re Cheeseman* [1891] 2 Ch 289, CA.
[77]   *Falmouth House Freehold Co Ltd v Morgan Walker LLP* [2010] EWHC 3092 (Ch) at [13].
[78]   See, for example, *Kundruth v Henry Kwatia & Gooding* [2005] 2 Costs LR 279.
[79]   CPR, r 67.3(2).
[80]   CPD, art 56.2.
[81]   See, for example, *Parnall v Hurst* (2003) *The Times*, 10 July in which HHJ Peter Langan QC declined to

should be an assessment), then there is no need to file evidence with the Part 8 claim.[82] An application for an assessment must be made in the matter of that solicitor.[83] Where the retainer is wholly disputed[84] (see **18.49**) or where it is said that there has been a compromise,[85] then these aspects of the claim should ordinarily be pleaded (ie pleaded in the claim itself as opposed to being held over for the points of dispute). The same is true where the client seeks more than a mere assessment of costs.[86]

Disputed retainers and the interpretation of retainers

18.49   Where the client disputes the existence of the retainer (as opposed to merely its terms), then he may wish to dispute the entirety of the bill. Where the application for an assessment has been made by the solicitor, then the client is at liberty to argue this point on the assessment itself (ie he is at liberty to plead this point for the first time in the points of dispute).[87] Where, however, the application has been made by the client, then there is authority (albeit pre-CPR authority) that without a special order the client is precluded from raising such an argument in that way.[88] It is entirely possible that under the CPR this is no longer good law, but notwithstanding this, a client who disputes the retainer will do well to plead his case fully in the claim form: this will allow the court either to address that issue at trial, or to make a special order that the costs judge is entitled to address this issue on the detailed assessment. Where the issue is merely the interpretation of the retainer the costs judge has jurisdiction to determine those issues for the purposes of the detailed assessment,[89] but that jurisdiction is not an exclusive jurisdiction.[90]

Formalities and applications by informal means

18.50   Although an application for an assessment should normally be made formally, it is possible for it to be made informally (eg by letter);[91] that said, it must amount to an actual application.[92] A mere reference to the fact that an application will be made would be sufficient to amount to an application.[93] There used to be a requirement that where a claim for an assessment is made by a solicitor, that solicitor must provide a certificate of compliance with SA 1974.[94] This requirement no longer exists under the CPR, but it would be sensible to confirm compliance in the pleadings.

---

strike out a Part 8 claim where the evidence in support had not been served along with the claim form. Also see *Szekeres v Alan Smeath & Co* [2005] EWHC 1733 (Ch) in which Pumfrey J refused to dismiss a claim in which the claim form contained a number of minor discrepancies.

[82]   PD 67, para 4.
[83]   SA 1974, s 72(1).
[84]   See, for example, *Re Inderwick* (1884) LR 25 Ch D 279.
[85]   *Re Lymn* (1910) 130 LTJ 9.
[86]   See, for example, *Baker & Lees & Co* [1903] 1 KB 189.
[87]   Whilst now rather old, see (*Re Jones* (1887) 36 Ch D 105; *Re Graham & Wigley* (1908) 52 SJ 684; *Re Wingfield & Blew* (1904) 2 Ch 665 at 675.
[88]   *Re Herbert* (1887) 34 Ch D 504 and *Re Frape* [1894] 2 Ch 290.
[89]   See, for example, *Re Hirst & Capes* [1908] AC 416.
[90]   *Mosley v Kitson* (1912) 57 SJ 12.
[91]   *Connolly v Harrington (Liquidator of Chelmsford City Football Club (1980) Ltd)* (unreported) 17 May 2002, QB, HH Judge Chapman.
[92]   *Solicitors Indemnity Fund Ltd v Hewitson & Harker* [2010] EWCA Civ 147 at [12].
[93]   *Turex v Toll* [2009] EWHC 369 (Ch) at [42].
[94]   RSC, Ord 106, r 5A.

Venue

18.51 The claim (or application) must be made in the High Court unless the costs relate to contentious business done in a county court and the amount to be assessed is within the financial limit (currently £5,000)[95] specified in SA 1974, s 69(3), in which case the assessment may (but not must)[96] proceed in *that* county court.[97] The fact that the solicitor may have made an application in a county court for a charging order under s 73 of the Act does not mean that the claim for the assessment may subsequently be issued in that court.[98]

18.52 If the matter is suitable for the county court, then (if that court is in London) it must be commenced at the Senior Courts Costs Office.[99] Other county court matters may (but not must) be issued in the Senior Courts Costs Office.[100] An application made in the wrong court can, in theory, be struck out, but in practice is likely to be transferred.[101]

The order for an assessment

18.53 Where a solicitor sues upon a bill and where the only dispute between the parties is quantum, the court may order the bill to be assessed and that judgment be entered for the amount assessed.[102] This is often referred to as a *Smith v Edwardes* order. Such an order should, as a matter of good practice, preserve the right of the parties to take the benefit of the one-fifth rule.

The hearing

18.54 SA 1974, s 70(8) specifically provides that if, after due notice of any assessment, either party fails to attend, the officer may proceed with the assessment notwithstanding the absence of the party or parties in question. Whilst the context was wholly different (namely, non-attendance following a debarring order in an assessment between opposing parties), Langley J has commented that it would never be appropriate merely to 'rubber-stamp' costs; he found that an assessment must take place regardless of who attending to make submissions.[103]

THE SCOPE OF THE ASSESSMENT

18.55 Usually, an assessment will be in respect of the whole of the bill, but SA 1974, s 70(5) and (6) empower the court to restrict the ambit of the assessment:

---

[95] See SA 1974, s 69(3), as amended by the High Court and County Courts Jurisdiction Order 1991 (SI 1991/724), art 2(7) and (8) and Part 1 of the Schedule.
[96] CPR, r 67.3(3)(c)(ii).
[97] See CPR, r 67.3(1)(a).
[98] *Jones v Twinsectra Ltd* [2002] EWCA Civ 668.
[99] CPD, art 31.1A.
[100] PD 67, para 2.1(2).
[101] CPR, r 30.1(2)(c).
[102] *Smith v Edwardes* (1888) 22 QBD 103; such an order is probably not strictly required under the SA 1974, because s 72(4) appears to give the costs judge the power to enter judgment.
[103] *Days Healthcare UK Ltd v Pihsiang Machinery Manufacturing Co Ltd* [2006] EWHC 1444 (QB) at [30].

'(5)   An order for the assessment of a bill made on an application under this section by the party chargeable with the bill shall, if he so requests, be an order for the assessment of the profit costs covered by the bill.

(6)   Subject to subsection (5), the court may under this section order the assessment of all the costs, or of the profit costs, or of the costs other than profit costs and, where part of the costs is not to be assessed, may allow an action to be commenced or to be continued for that part of the costs.'

Thus, the party chargeable is at liberty to elect to limit the assessment to profit costs only; subject to this right, the court has a discretionary power to order that all of the costs, or the profit costs, or the costs other than profit costs be assessed. Where only part of the costs are to be assessed, the court can order that any claim in respect of the undisputed part may be commenced or continue.

18.56   The significance of this facility to limit the assessment to only a part of the bill is that only that part will be subject to the one-fifth rule (which is explained below).[104] The effect of this can have a dramatic bearing on the risks of an adverse costs order being made at the conclusion of the assessment, and can make the difference between an assessment being economically viable or not.

18.57   The following (unrealistic) example illustrates this: if the bill entire is £10,000 (prior to assessment), but £8,001 of this relates to undisputed disbursements, it would be impossible for the party chargeable to satisfy the one-fifth rule. By obtaining an order that only the profit costs (of £1,999) are assessed, the prospects of satisfying the one-fifth rule are restored.

THE COSTS OF THE ASSESSMENT

18.58   In so far as it is relevant to the costs of the assessment, SA 1974, s 70 provides:[105]

'(7)   Every order for the assessment of a bill shall require the costs officer to assess not only the bill but also the costs of the assessment and to certify what is due to or by the solicitor in respect of the bill and in respect of the costs of the assessment.

(8)   ...

(9)   Unless—

    (a)   the order for assessment was made on the application of the solicitor and the party chargeable does not attend the assessment, or

    (b)   the order for assessment or an order under subsection (10) otherwise provides,

the costs of an assessment shall be paid according to the event of the assessment, that is to say, if the amount of the bill is reduced by one fifth, the solicitor shall pay the costs, but otherwise the party chargeable shall pay the costs.

(10)   The costs officer may certify to the court any special circumstances relating to a bill or to the assessment of a bill, and the court may make such order as respects the costs of the assessment as it may think fit.

(11)   ...

---

[104]   See SA 1974, s 70(12), which expressly states that the one-fifth rule will relate only to the costs being assessed.

[105]   The points made previously about the use of the provisions amended by the Legal Services Act 2007 are repeated.

(12) In this section "profit costs" means costs other than counsel's fees or costs paid or payable in the discharge of a liability incurred by the solicitor on behalf of the party chargeable, and the reference in subsection (9) to the fraction of the amount of the reduction in the bill shall be taken, where the assessment concerns only part of the costs covered by the bill, as a reference to that fraction of the amount of those costs which is being assessed.'

At the heart of these provisions is the 'one-fifth rule', which, in effect, provides that where the amount of the bill is reduced by one-fifth, the solicitor pays the costs of the assessment, but otherwise the party chargeable pays the costs. This is subject to the court finding special circumstances, in which case the court may make some different order.

One-fifth rule

18.59 A number of points can be made about the measure of the one-fifth rule.

Disbursements and the one-fifth rule

18.60 Save where the scope of the assessment has been restricted to exclude them, the one-fifth rule will be applied to the costs inclusive of disbursements.[106]

Discounted bill and the one-fifth rule

18.61 If a bill has been discounted, it is the undiscounted figure that is used for the purposes of applying the one-fifth rule.[107] However, the fact that the solicitor was prepared to give a discount may be relevant as giving rise to special circumstances.[108] The rationale behind this rule was explained by Baggallay LJ:[109]

'I think it would be exceedingly pernicious to lay down a rule which would enable a solicitor whose bill exceeded what could be allowed on taxation, to oblige his client, by a device of this kind [ie a discount], to have his bill taxed at a greater risk as to costs than if a bill had been delivered for the amount which the solicitor had stated his willingness to accept.'

Gross sum bill and the one-fifth rule

18.62 In the same vein, where a gross sum bill is being assessed with the benefit of a detailed breakdown, it is the gross sum bill (and the reductions thereto) that are relevant for the purposes of applying the one-fifth rule.[110]

More than one bill and the one-fifth rule

18.63 Where a number of bills have been delivered under the same retainer, but only some of which are the subject of assessment, only the costs in those which are being assessed will be taken into account for the purposes of applying the one-fifth rule.[111]

---

[106]   *Re Haigh* (1849) 12 Beav 307.
[107]   *In re Carthew, In re Paull* (1884) 27 Ch D 485; see also *Re McKenzie* (1894) 69 LT 751.
[108]   *In re Paull* (1884) 27 Ch D 485, although, in that case, the court did not depart from the rule that costs should follow the assessment.
[109]   *In re Carthew, In re Paull* (1884) 27 Ch D 485 at 494.
[110]   See obiter comments in *Re McKenzie* (1894) 69 LT 751.
[111]   *Devereaux v White* (1896) 13 TLR 52.

Excluded items and the one-fifth rule

18.64 Items in the cash account are excluded.[112] Where items are disallowed at the instance of the client because the business to which the items relate was never included in any retainer, those items cannot be taken into consideration for the purpose of applying the one-fifth rule.[113] It seems, however, that the reasoning behind this principle would not extend to the situation where costs are disallowed for want of an *enforceable* retainer. The relevant reasoning was described by Scott LJ:[114]

> 'We think that the phrase "[assessed] off" contained in the Solicitors Act ... means a reduction of the bill by [costs officer] where the business involved is within the retainer, and not where the client says: "This is business with which I have no concern, it ought never to have been in the bill at all".'

The decision to disregard the non-retainer costs was based on the fact that they were incurred beyond the scope of the client's instructions – or beyond the scope of the retainer – rather than because they were disallowed as a result of a defective retainer.

More than one solicitor's costs and the one-fifth rule

18.65 Where a solicitor includes another solicitor's costs in his own bill, it will be the combined total that will be relevant for the purposes of applying the one-fifth rule. This will be so even if the solicitor's own costs are reduced by less than one-fifth.[115]

Costs already assessed and paid and the one-fifth rule

18.66 Costs are not excluded from the one-fifth rule merely by virtue of their having been already assessed[116] and paid.[117] Where the monies in question are actual disbursements (see **31.2**), then even where the client has himself paid those monies (such as where the client has sent a cheque directly to counsel), those monies must appear in the bill; put otherwise, the payment must, where appropriate, be entered as credit in the cash account rather regarded as being expunged from the bill.[118]

VAT and the one-fifth rule

18.67 Whilst there is no binding authority on the point, VAT is generally excluded[119] as being something beyond the solicitor's control.

Non-attendance

18.68 Where the assessment was made on the application of the solicitor, the one-fifth rule would not apply if the party chargeable were to fail to attend. Given the fact that SA 1974 is silent as to how the court should exercise its discretion in those

---

[112] *Re Haigh* (1849) 12 Beav 307.
[113] *Re Taxation of Costs; Re a Solicitor* [1936] 1 KB 523; see also *White v Milner* (1794) 2 H Bl 357 and *Mills v Revett* (1834) 1 A&E 856.
[114] *Re Taxation of Costs; Re a Solicitor* [1936] 1 KB 523 at 532.
[115] *In re Fletcher and Dyson* [1903] 2 Ch 688.
[116] This may happen where, for example, an assessment has been carried out on behalf of the client, but then a further assessment is carried out for a person making an application under SA 1974, s 71.
[117] *Re Osborn and Osborn* [1913] 3 KB 862.
[118] *Re Osborn & Osborn* [1913] 3 KB 862 at 869 and *Re Richards* [1912] 1 Ch 49 at 53.
[119] This is the view expressed by the editors of the *White Book*.

circumstances, it is probable that the court has a wide discretion which can be exercised in the usual way (ie pursuant to CPR, r 44.3). Other textbooks advise that if a solicitor accepts a client's invitation to make a solicitor's application for an assessment and if the client subsequently chooses not to attend, the solicitor will be penalised, because the court will make no order for costs; this, it is said, is reason enough why solicitors should not apply for an assessment of their own costs.[120] For the reasons set out immediately above, this would appear to be incorrect. However, there are usually many other reasons why a solicitor may choose not to make application for an order to assess his own costs.

Special circumstances

18.69 SA 1974 gives no guidance as to what may constitute 'special circumstances'. Where special circumstances are made out, the court has:[121]

'... a general power to vary the ordinary statutory rule [ie the one-fifth rule], and where it is inequitable in the special circumstances certified that the statutory rule should be applied, the Court should exercise its discretion in favour of the solicitor or the client as the case may be.'

The following are case examples (of which there are surprisingly few).

Properly made offers

18.70 Where an offer is made at what Parker J called the 'proper time' (which in the modern day would be likely to mean reasonably early), that could amount to special circumstances capable of reversing the presumption arising from the one-fifth rule.[122]

Inopportune offers

18.71 Where an offer is made which is not made at the proper time or where it is unclear, that may negate the effect of that offer. By way of example, an offer which does not state the costs consequences of its acceptance may be given less weight as a result.[123]

Items claimed in error

18.72 Where disbursements have been claimed in the bill in error but in such a way as to mislead no one, the fact that the one-fifth rule would have been satisfied had the error not been made may amount to special circumstances.[124]

Failure to mediate or negotiate

18.73 A failure to engage in mediation or to attempt to negotiate is capable of giving rise to special circumstances.[125]

---

[120] See *Cook on Costs 2010* (Butterworths, 2009), para [5.22].
[121] Per Parker J in *In re Davies* [1912] 1 Ch 49 at 54.
[122] *Angel Airlines (a Romanian company in liquidation) v Dean & Dean* [2008] EWHC 1513 (QB).
[123] Whilst not dealing with the one-fifth rule, see *Tramountana Armadora SA v Atlantic Shipping Co SA (The Vorros)* [1978] 2 All ER 870 (Comm).
[124] *In re Davies* [1912] 1 Ch 49.
[125] *Allen v Colman Coyle LLP* [2007] EWHC 90075 (Costs), Master Simons.

18.74 Each case will turn on its own facts, so the above should be treated only as illustrative examples.

ON THE APPLICATION OF THIRD PARTIES

18.75 SA 1974 (as amended) distinguishes between those persons who have primary liability for the costs, and those who have secondary liability; the former persons are referred to as 'the party chargeable' and the latter as 'third parties'.[126]

18.76 The relevant law is set out in SA 1974, s 71 (as amended):[127]

'(1) Where a person other than the party chargeable with the bill for the purposes of section 70 has paid, or is or was liable to pay, a bill either to the solicitor or to the party chargeable with the bill, that person, or his executors, administrators or assignees may apply to the High Court for an order for the taxation of the bill as if he were the party chargeable with it, and the court may make the same order (if any) as it might have made if the application had been made by the party chargeable with the bill.

(2) Where the court has no power to make an order by virtue of subsection (1) except in special circumstances it may, in considering whether there are special circumstances sufficient to justify the making of an order, take into account circumstances which affect the applicant but do not affect the party chargeable with the bill.

(3) Where a trustee, executor or administrator has become liable to pay a bill of a solicitor, then, on the application of any person interested in any property out of which the trustee, executor or administrator has paid, or is entitled to pay, the bill, the court may order—

(a)   that the bill be taxed on such terms, if any, as it thinks fit; and
(b)   that such payments, in respect of the amount found to be due to or by the solicitor and in respect of the costs of the taxation, be made to or by the applicant, to or by the solicitor, or to or by the executor, administrator or trustee, as it thinks fit.

(4)   In considering any application under subsection (3) the court shall have regard—

(a)   to the provisions of section 70 as to applications by the party chargeable for the taxation of a solicitor's bill so far as they are capable of being applied to an application made under that subsection;
(b)   to the extent and nature of the interest of the applicant.

(5)   If an applicant under subsection (3) pays any money to the solicitor, he shall have the same right to be paid that money by the trustee, executor or administrator chargeable with the bill as the solicitor had.

(6)   Except in special circumstances, no order shall be made on an application under this section for the taxation of a bill which has already been taxed.

(7)   If the court on an application under this section orders a bill to be taxed, it may order the solicitor to deliver to the applicant a copy of the bill on payment of the costs of that copy.'

Where a third party obtains an order for assessment, the fact that he has that order will not enlarge his potential liability for the sums for which he may be liable.[128] Where an

---

[126]   The term 'third party' in this sense should not be confused with an 'entitled third party' as defined in art 2 of the Solicitors' (Non-contentious Business) Remuneration Order 2009: the two are entirely different.
[127]   The points made previously about the amendments made by the Legal Services Act 2007 are repeated.
[128]   *Re Negus* [1895] 1 Ch 73 and *Re Gray* [1901] 1 Ch 239 at 245–246, 248; see also *Re Denne & Secretary of State for War* (1884) 51 LT 657.

assessment takes place under s 71(1), the person chargeable may raise the points that the client may have raised, but no more: thus, in so far as the court's assessment of quantum is concerned, the result will – for those items that are assessed – be precisely the same as if the assessment had been requested by the client.[129] But the court may omit items for which the person chargeable has no liability; when this happens, such items are left out of the assessment altogether; this means that the solicitor remains entitled to pursue the client for those monies.[130] If the monies have already been agreed and paid by the client, this will leave the person chargeable in a difficult position on an assessment; his remedy in those circumstances would lie against the client in the form of an account.[131]

18.77 A number of points arise:

- the difference between applications made under SA 1974, s 71(1) and (3);
- the meaning of 'a person other than the party chargeable with the bill'; and
- the meaning of 'a person interested'.

Each is considered in turn.

The difference between applications made under s 71(1) and (3)

18.78 There is a distinction to be drawn between an application made pursuant to SA 1974, s 71(1) and an application made pursuant to s 71(3). Applications made under s 71(1) are made by persons who are 'as if he were the party chargeable' (that is, an applicant steps into the shoes of the person chargeable). Section 71(2) provides that in so far as there is a need to consider special circumstances, the court can take into account factors which affect the applicant but do not affect the party chargeable.

18.79 SA 1974, s 71(1) gives the court the same powers in the case of an applicant under s 71(1) as the court would have had if the application had been made by the person chargeable under s 70. These powers would be limited, where appropriate, by the absolute bar on ordering an assessment of any bills which had been paid for more than 12 months.[132]

18.80 The same is not true, however, of application made under SA 1974, s 71(3). Such an application is made by 'a person interested' in the property out of which the bill is to be paid, rather than by a person 'as if he were the party chargeable', so different considerations apply.

18.81 In particular, it has been held that the absolute limit on ordering an assessment of any bills which had been paid for more than 12 months does not apply to applications made under SA 1974, s 71(3).[133] Section 71(4)(a) specifically requires the court to have regard to the provisions of s 70 so far as they are capable of being applied to an application by a person interested in chargeable property. HHJ Rich QC (sitting as a deputy High Court judge) offered his guidance:

---

[129] *Tim Martin Interiors Ltd v Akin Gump LLP* [2011] EWCA Civ 1574 at [82], per Lloyd LJ.

[130] *Tim Martin Interiors Ltd v Akin Gump LLP* [2011] EWCA Civ 1574 at [95] *et seq*, per Lloyd LJ.

[131] *Re Abbott* (1861) 4 LT 576 and *Tim Martin Interiors Ltd v Akin Gump LLP* [2011] EWCA Civ 1574 at [31] and [98], per Lloyd LJ.

[132] SA 1974, s 70(4).

[133] *McIlwraith v McIlwraith* [2002] EWHC 1757 (Ch), HHJ Rich QC sitting as a deputy High Court judge.

'I have decided that there is a discretion [to order assessment of a bill on application under section 71(3) notwithstanding the fact that that bill has been paid for more than 12 months]. It is, however, a discretion to be exercised in circumstances where the Court is required to have regard to the fact that there would be no power to order a taxation on the application of the chargeable party. It will, therefore, in my judgment, be for the Applicant, who is interested in the chargeable property, to persuade the Court that it should nonetheless order a taxation at his request, and that the considerations of finality which justify the rule in respect of the chargeable party should not prevail upon the present application.'

18.82 Where the application is made under SA 1974, s 71(3), it is specifically provided by s 71(4)(b) that the court is to have regard to the extent and nature of the interest of the applicant. Thus, for example, if an applicant under s 71(3) were liable to pay only a small part of the costs sought, that would be a factor to take into account.

18.83 Regardless of whether the application is made 'as if he were the party chargeable' (s 71(1)) or by 'a person interested' (s 71(3)), the court will need to find special circumstances before ordering an assessment (or, rather, reassessment) of a bill which has already been assessed.[134]

18.84 Finally, where the court orders an assessment by a third party (be it under its powers conferred by SA 1974, s 71(1) or by s 71(3)), the assessment itself will proceed as if it were at the request of the party chargeable.[135] Whilst only persuasive rather than binding, the Supreme Court of Victoria has found that the legislation is aimed at the relationship between solicitor and party chargeable, not at that between solicitor and the third party.[136]

The meaning of 'a person other than the party chargeable with the bill'

18.85 Robert Walker LJ has emphasised the general applicability of SA 1974, s 71(1):[137]

'Section 71 is of general application. It recognises that the person chargeable with the bill may not be ultimately liable to pay the costs thereby claimed. Its evident purpose is to confer on one with a secondary liability for those costs a right comparable to that possessed by the person primarily liable. Given that, for the reasons I have already explained, the Law Society is entitled to have the bills taxed under section 70 Parliament is unlikely to have intended that there should be degrees of secondary liability, some of which are excluded from the ambit of section 71.'

18.86 Examples of those who might successfully make an application under this section include:

— a person who has provided a guarantee for another person's costs;[138]
— a tenant who is contractually liable to pay his landlord's costs;
— a mortgagor who is liable to pay the mortgagee's costs;
— solicitors who are liable to meet the costs intervention in their practices;[139]

---

[134] SA 1974, s 71(6).
[135] *R Massey* (1865) 34 LJ Ch 492.
[136] *Re Lawler* (1878) 4 VLR 8.
[137] *Pine v Law Society* [2002] EWCA Civ 175 at [27].
[138] See the obiter examples given by Cockburn CJ in *In re Heritage ex p Docker* (1878) 3 QBD 726.
[139] See, for example, *Pine v Law Society* [2002] EWCA Civ 175.

— a person who agrees to pay costs as between solicitor and client as part of a compromise[140] or other agreement;[141] and
— liquidators of companies.

Indeed, Rolt LJ has said 'that if a person who is not chargeable thinks fit to pay the bill it is open to him to do so, and if he does so, he should be entitled to have that bill assessed as the party chargeable therewith might himself have done'.[142]

18.87 The fact that the contract under which the person who applies for the assessment is itself the subject of a dispute will not necessarily prevent that person from applying for an assessment. In particular, questions as to the construction of the agreement to pay costs would not ordinarily be a bar to an assessment.[143]

18.88 Despite the wide applicability of SA 1974, s 71(1), not everyone who believes that they are liable to pay costs would be able successfully to make an application. Examples include:

— a party who voluntarily accepts a liability for another person's costs;[144]
— a person who is liable to pay costs solely as a result of being a taxpayer;[145]
— a person who agreed to pay a fixed sum to an opponent's solicitor for that solicitor's trouble in promoting a composition between himself and his creditors;[146] and
— a person who agrees to pay a sum to his opponent's solicitors on discontinuing proceedings.[147]

If a person is unable to bring himself within the category of a person other than the party chargeable with the bill, he cannot bring himself within the category of a party chargeable by pointing to the fact that the solicitors had made him into a 'quasi-client' by virtue of the fact that they had kept him up-to-date with what services they were providing.[148]

The meaning of 'any person interested in the property'

18.89 This relates to s 71(3) of the SA 1974; that section relates to any person interested in any property out of which a trustee, executor or administrator has paid, or is entitled to pay, a solicitor's bill. This would include a creditor who, seeking assessment of a bill paid by the deceased, has obtained a judgment in an administration.[149]. It does not extend so far as to permit a bankrupt to obtain an assessment of a bill paid by the trustee in bankruptcy.[150]

---

[140] *Re Chapman* (1903) 20 TLR 3.
[141] *Re Grundy, Kershaw & Co* (1881) 17 Ch D 108.
[142] *Re Newman* (1867) 2 Ch App 707.
[143] *In re Hirst & Capes* [1908] 1 KB 982.
[144] *Re Becke* (1843) 5 Beav 506; see also *Langford v Nott* (1820) 1 Jac & W 291 and *Re Cookson* (1886) 30 SJ 305.
[145] *Re Barber* (1845) 14 M&W 720.
[146] *In re Heritage ex p Docker* (1878) 3 QBD 726.
[147] *Re Morris* (1872) 27 LT 554.
[148] *Barrett v Rutt-Field* [2006] TLR 1505.
[149] *Re Jones & Everett* [1904] 2 Ch 363.
[150] *In re Leadbitter* (1878) 10 Ch D 388.

THE ASSESSMENT HEARING AND PROCEDURE LEADING UP TO THE ASSESSMENT HEARING

18.90 Where the court orders a solicitor and client assessment, it will follow the guidance given in CPR, r 48.10:

'(1) This rule sets out the procedure to be followed where the court has made an order under Part III of the Solicitors Act 1974 for the assessment of costs payable to a solicitor by his client.

(2) The solicitor must serve a breakdown of costs within 28 days of the order for costs to be assessed.

(3) The client must serve points of dispute within 14 days after service on him of the breakdown of costs.

(4) If the solicitor wishes to serve a reply, he must do so within 14 days of service on him of the points of dispute.

(5) Either party may file a request for a hearing date—

    (a)   after points of dispute have been served; but
    (b)   no later than 3 months after the date of the order for the costs to be assessed.

(6) This procedure applies subject to any contrary order made by the court.'

On the face of it, these directions appear to be mandatory: both the CPR and the CPD refer to these steps as being ones which must be taken.[151] The contrary is arguable, however. In any event, there is nothing within either the CPR or the CPD to prevent the court from amending the directions.

18.91 The court will usually also make an order in the form of Precedent L (or, if the application has been made by the solicitor, Precedent K). The form of Precedent L has been the subject of judicial criticism: Morgan J has found that Precedent L ought to reflect the wording of SA 1974, s 70(2)(b) (ie 'no action be commenced on the bill, and … any action already commenced on the bill be stayed, until the assessment is completed'). Unfortunately, Precedent L fails to do this.[152] Practitioners may wish to ask the court to depart from Precedent L accordingly.

18.92 The breakdown of costs referred in CPR, r 48.10(2) is a document which contains the following:[153]

- *Detailed breakdown*: Unless the bill itself is a detailed bill, the breakdown must contain details of the work done under each of the bills sent for assessment.[154]
- *Cash account*: In applications under SA 1974, s 70, the breakdown must include a cash account.[155]

A model breakdown is provided at Precedent P of the Schedule of Costs Precedents annexed to the CPD.

---

[151] See CPR, r 48.8 and CPD, art 56.4.

[152] *Mastercigars Direct Ltd v Withers LLP* [2007] EWHC 2733 (Ch) at [145].

[153] CPD, art 56.5.

[154] Where the bill relates to contentious business, the requirement to serve a detailed breakdown in respect of a gross sum bill is not only set out in at CPR, r 48.10(2); it is also set out at SA 1974, s 64(4).

[155] A cash account is an account which includes money received by the solicitor to the credit of the client and sums paid out of that money on behalf of the client, but excludes outgoing payments which were made in satisfaction of the bill (or any items contained therein).

18.93 Copies of counsel's fee notes and the fee notes of any experts should also be served. Written evidence as to any other disbursement exceeding £250 should be provided; this will usually mean the appropriate vouchers or receipted invoices.

18.94 Points of dispute will, as far as practicable, comply with the requirements for between-the-parties assessments.[156]

18.95 The time for requesting a detailed assessment hearing is within 3 months of the date of the order for costs to be assessed; unlike the corresponding between-the-parties provision, this provision is contained only in the CPD[157] rather than in the CPR itself. No penalty is mentioned in the event of default. The request must be in a prescribed form (N258C) which must contain an estimate of the length of the hearing and must be accompanied by the following:[158]

- the order sending the bill for assessment;
- the bill;
- the solicitor's breakdown of costs and any invoices or accounts served with that breakdown;
- a copy of the points of dispute, annotated as necessary to show which items have been agreed and their value and to show which items remain in dispute;
- as many copies of the points of dispute so annotated as there are other parties entitled to attend the assessment;
- a copy of the replies, if any; and
- a statement signed by the party filing the request or his legal representative giving the names and addresses for service of all parties to the proceedings.

Upon receipt of the request, the court may either set the matter down for directions or for the assessment.[159]

18.96 Unless the court gives permission, it will hear only the solicitor whose bill it is and those parties who have served points of dispute.[160]

18.97 Permission is not required to vary a breakdown of costs, points of dispute or a reply, but the court may disallow the variation or permit it only upon conditions, including conditions as to the payment of any costs caused or wasted by the variation.[161] The power to vary a bill is highly restricted, as is explained at **17.73–17.81**.

18.98 Unless the court directs otherwise, the solicitor must file the papers in support of the bill not less than 7 days and not more than 14 days before the date for the assessment hearing.[162] The solicitor has 14 days from the end of the hearing to calculate, complete, and file the bill.

18.99 After the detailed assessment hearing is concluded, the court will perform the following functions:[163]

---

[156]   CPD, art 56.8.
[157]   At CPD, art 56.9.
[158]   See CPD arts 56.11 and 56.10.
[159]   CPD, art 56.12.
[160]   CPD, art 56.13(c), which makes reference to CPR, r 47.14(6) and (7).
[161]   CPD, art 56.14.
[162]   CPD, art 56.15.
[163]   CPD, art 56.18(2).

- complete the court copy of the bill so as to show the amount allowed;
- determine the result of the cash account;
- award the costs of the detailed assessment hearing in accordance with SA 1974, s 70(8); and
- issue a final costs certificate showing the amount due.

Unless the court orders otherwise, the final costs certificate will include an order to pay the sum it certifies.[164]

COSTS CERTIFICATES IN SOLICITOR AND CLIENT ASSESSMENTS AND INTERIM PAYMENTS

18.100 The court has the power to issue both interim[165] and final costs certificates in solicitor and client assessments. The power to issue an interim certificate is in addition to the power to make an interim award pursuant to the combined effect of SA 1974, s 70(6)[166] and CPR, r 25.1(1)(k);[167] that power is limited to making an award of those monies which the court holds that the client is liable to pay, so may not be as broad as the power to issue an interim costs certificate. It is probably best to regard the power under r 25.1(1)(k) as being complementary to the power to issue an interim costs certificate rather than being equivalent it. Where an order is made for only a part of the costs which are claimed to be assessed, the power under r 25.1(1)(k) may be used to award the solicitor the undisputed costs (which is not something which could be achieved by way of an interim costs certificate, because those the costs judge would not be seized of those costs).

18.101 The court is able to issue an interim costs certificate in favour of the client;[168] this may happen, for example, where the cash account shows that the client has overpaid.

18.102 There is no provision within the CPR for a default costs certificate to be issued in solicitor and client assessments.[169] However, if a party simply refuses to co-operate, SA 1974 specifically provides that the costs officer may hear the assessment ex parte.[170]

18.103 The solicitor must file a completed bill within 14 days of the conclusion of the assessment hearing; the court will then issue the final costs certificate.[171] The certificate will include an order to pay the sum it certifies.[172]

---

[164] CPD, art 56.19.

[165] See CPD, art 56.17, which refers to CPR, r 47.15 as being applicable to solicitor and client assessments.

[166] Which allows a claim to be commenced or continued for parts of the bill which are not to be the subject of an assessment.

[167] CPR, r 25.1(1)(k) permits payment by a defendant on account of 'any damages, debt or other sum (except costs) which the court may hold the defendant liable to pay': rightly or wrongly, the reference to 'except costs' is generally interpreted as being a reference to costs of the claim, rather than costs which are the subject of the claim.

[168] CPD, art 56.17(2).

[169] See CPD, art 56.7.

[170] SA 1974, s 70(8).

[171] CPR, r 47.16(1).

[172] CPD, arts 56.18 and 56.19; and CPR, r 47.16(1).

18.104   Unless it is set aside or amended, the costs certificate will be final; unless the retainer is disputed,[173] the costs officer is able to enter judgment for the amount certified.[174]

---

[173]   This qualification arises from SA 1974, s 74(2). It is not wholly clear what it means; one interpretation is that it refers to the situation where the issue of enforceability of the retainer is to be decided at trial, and the assessment is only a quantification exercise.

[174]   SA 1974, s 72(4).

Chapter 19

COMPROMISE AND ALTERNATIVES TO STATUTORY ASSESSMENTS

19.1 This chapter examines a miscellaneous group of topics which can be said to be alternatives to statutory assessments; this includes the most attractive alternative of all, compromise.

REMUNERATION CERTIFICATES (NOW OBSOLETE)

19.2 A remuneration certificate was a certificate issued by the Legal Complaints Service ('LCS') on behalf of the Law Society; it gave an opinion as to the amount properly chargeable. It is now an obsolete procedure; the current-day equivalent (which has applied since 11 August 2009)[1] is described at **19.48–19.56**. The old procedure may still be relevant from time-to-time today, however – such as if a client contends that a solicitor failed to obtain a remuneration certificate – and as such, it is briefly described below (**19.4–19.14**).[2] In any event, the old requirements to give notice under the old procedure may still be relevant (see **19.15–19.16**).

19.3 The certificate was binding upon the solicitor and client in that the sum payable was the sum stated in the remuneration certificate.[3] The process of obtaining a remuneration certificate was free (both to the client and the solicitor), but was available only in respect of non-contentious work, and even then only in certain circumstances.

Procedure (now obsolete)

19.4 The relevant law derived from the now revoked Solicitors' (Non-Contentious Business) Remuneration Order 1994 (SI 1994/2616)[4] and, in particular, from art 4, which provided:

> '(1) Without prejudice to the provisions of sections 70, 71, and 72 of the Solicitors Act 1974 ... an entitled person may, subject to the provisions of this Order, require a solicitor to obtain a remuneration certificate from the Council in respect of a bill which has been delivered where the costs are not more than £50,000.
>
> (2) The remuneration certificate must state what sum, in the opinion of the Council, would be a fair and reasonable charge for the business covered by the bill (whether it be the sum charged or a lesser sum). In the absence of taxation the sum payable in respect of such costs is the sum stated in the remuneration certificate.'

---

[1] See Solicitors' (Non-Contentious Business) Remuneration Order 2009 (SI 2009/1931), art 1(3).
[2] See, for example, also *R (on the application of Scott Halborg, trading under the style of Halborg & Co, Solicitors) v Law Society* [2010] EWHC 38 (Admin).
[3] The Solicitors' (Non-Contentious Business) Remuneration Order 1994 (SI 1994/2616), art 4(2).
[4] Made under s 56 of the Solicitors Act 1974.

19.5   The procedure was that the client asked the solicitor to obtain a remuneration certificate.[5] The solicitor would complete an application and send it to the client so that he could add his comments. The solicitor then returned the completed forms to the LCS along with the solicitor's file of papers (this was mandatory).[6] A caseworker then assessed the file and prepared a report: a provisional assessment was then sent to the client and the solicitor. The client had 14 days to ask for a review; if a review was requested, the matter would be referred by the LCS to an external adjudication panel. If no review was requested, a remuneration certificate was issued and the solicitor's file was returned to his firm.

19.6   The LCS sought to deal with applications within 5 months of receipt, but they warned that this might not always be possible.[7]

19.7   The remuneration certificate procedure was not appropriate to the following issues: questions of law; questions of negligence; questions as to whether instructions had been given; disputes as to the quality of legal advice that had been given; issues concerning VAT; or whether all or part of the bill was payable by another person.

19.8   A person who was entitled to request a remuneration certificate was referred to as an 'entitled person'. This meant the client or an 'entitled third party'. The relevant provisions are in the footnotes.[8] A personal residuary beneficiary would not be an entitled third party if one or more of the personal representatives was a lay person.

19.9   Save as set out above, a paying party (ie an opponent who has been ordered to pay costs) was not an entitled third party. Nonetheless, the LCS guidance indicated that a certificate could be provided if the paying party obtained the client's consent.[9]

19.10   Unless sufficient monies had already been paid, the client had to pay a sum towards the solicitor's costs as a condition of obtaining a remuneration certificate. That sum would have been equivalent to the paid disbursements and the VAT, together with 50% of the profit costs. The relevant provisions are in the footnotes.[10] This sum did not need to be paid if either the solicitor or the LCS agreed in writing that it should not be paid.[11]

---

[5]   See also *R (on the application of Scott Halborg, trading under the style of Halborg & Co, Solicitors) v Law Society* [2010] EWHC 38 (Admin) at [33], per Keith J.

[6]   SI 1994/2616, art 15.

[7]   *Remuneration certificates – Information for clients and people who are entitled to them* (The Law Society, 14 February 2006), para 4.

[8]   SI 1994/2616, art 2 defined an entitled third party as:
  '[A] residuary beneficiary absolutely and immediately (and not contingently) entitled to an inheritance, where a solicitor has charged the estate for his professional costs for acting in the administration of the estate, and either
  (a) the only personal representatives are solicitors (whether or not acting in a professional capacity); or
  (b) the only personal representatives are solicitors acting jointly with partners or employees in a professional capacity.'

[9]   *Remuneration certificates – Information for clients and people who are entitled to them* (The Law Society, 14 February 2006).

[10]   The relevant provisions were at SI 1994/2616, art 11:
  '(1)   On requiring a solicitor to obtain a remuneration certificate a client must pay to the solicitor the paid disbursements and value added tax comprised in the bill together with 50% of the costs unless—
  (a) the client has already paid the amount required under this article, by deduction from monies held or otherwise; or
  (b) the solicitor or (if the solicitor refuses) the Council has agreed in writing to waive all or part of this requirement.
  (2)   The Council shall be under no obligation to provide a remuneration certificate, and the solicitor may

19.11 The LCS indicated that it would grant a waiver only in exceptional circumstances, such as where the solicitor had failed to give costs information, the solicitor had given an estimate which was subsequently exceeded, or the solicitor was the subject of disciplinary proceedings or intervention. Financial difficulty on the part of the client was not usually regarded as being sufficient to justify a waiver.[12]

19.12 The right to a certificate was capable of being lost, especially by the effluxion of time.[13] A client might have lost the right to a certificate if he had paid the bill (other than by deduction), if he left it too long to ask for a certificate, if he had entered into a non-contentious business agreement, if he had obtained an order that the bill be assessed, or if he had not complied with his obligations to pay a sum towards the costs.

19.13 An entitled third party lost the right to a certificate if he left it too long to ask for it or if the court had already ordered that the bill should be assessed (the details are in the footnotes).[14]

19.14 The solicitor and client were able to agree that the client was entitled to a remuneration certificate notwithstanding the fact that the bill might have been paid or the application made out of time.[15] Payment of the bill after the application had been made would not invalidate that application.[16]

Notification requirements

19.15 Whilst the procedure set out above is now obsolete, the issue of whether the requisite notices were given may occasionally arise. This is because the solicitor was obliged to give certain information to the client, and in particular, before a solicitor could bring proceedings to recover costs against a client on a bill for non-contentious business, he was (except where the bill had been assessed)[17] required to inform the client in writing of certain matters specified in SI 1994/2616, art 8:

---

take steps to obtain payment of his bill, if the client, having been informed of his right to seek a waiver of the requirements of paragraph (1), has not—

(a) within one month of receipt of the information specified in article 8, either paid in accordance with paragraph (1) or applied to the Council in writing for a waiver of the requirements of paragraph (1); or

(b) made payment in accordance with the requirements of paragraph (1) within one month of written notification that he has been refused a waiver of those requirements by the Council.'

[11] See art 11(1)(b) of SI 1994/2616.

[12] See http://www.legalcomplaints.org.uk/how-we-handle-complaints.page.

[13] In this regard SI 1994/2616, art 9 made the following provisions:

'A client may not require a solicitor to obtain a remuneration certificate—

(a) after a bill has been delivered and paid by the client, other than by deduction;

(b) where a bill has been delivered, after the expiry of one month from the date on which the client was informed in writing of the matters specified in article 8 or from delivery of the bill if later;

(c) after the solicitor and client have entered into a non-contentious business agreement in accordance with the provisions of section 57 of the Solicitors Act 1974;

(d) after a court has ordered the bill to be taxed;

(e) if article 11(2) applies.'

[14] The provisions relating to entitled third parties at SI 1994/2616, art 10 were as follows:

'An entitled third party may not require a solicitor to obtain a remuneration certificate—

(a) after the prescribed time (within the meaning of article 7(2)(b)) has elapsed without any objection being received to the amount of the costs;

(b) after the expiry of one month from the date on which the entitled third party was (in compliance with article 7) informed in writing of the matters specified in article 8 or from notification of the costs if later;

(c) after a court has ordered the bill to be taxed.'

[15] SI 1994/2616, art 12(2).

[16] SI 1994/2616, art 12(1).

[17] SI 1994/2616, art 6.

'When required by articles 6 or 7, a solicitor must inform an entitled person in writing of the following matters—

    (a)   where article 4(1) applies—

          (i)   that the entitled person may, within one month of receiving from the solicitor the information specified in this article or (if later) of delivery of the bill or notification of the amount of the costs, require the solicitor to obtain a remuneration certificate; and

          (ii)   that (unless the solicitor has agreed to do so) the Council may waive the requirements of article 11(1), if satisfied from the client's written application that exceptional circumstances exist to justify granting a waiver;

    (b)   that sections 70, 71 and 72 of the Solicitors Act 1974 set out the entitled person's rights in relation to taxation;

    (c)   that (where the whole of the bill has not been paid, by deduction or otherwise) the solicitor may charge interest on the outstanding amount of the bill in accordance with article 14.'

19.16 Likewise, there was an obligation to give the aforesaid information where costs were paid by deduction:[18]

'(1)   If a solicitor deducts his costs from monies held for or on behalf of a client or of an estate in satisfaction of a bill and an entitled person objects in writing to the amount of the bill within the prescribed time, the solicitor must immediately inform the entitled person in writing of the matters specified in article 8, unless he has already done so.

(2)   In this article ... "the prescribed time" means—

    (a)   in respect of a client, three months after delivery of the relevant bill, or a lesser time (which may not be less than one month) specified in writing to the client at the time of delivery of the bill, or

    (b)   in respect of an entitled third party, three months after delivery of notification to the entitled third party of the amount of the costs, or a lesser time (which may not be less than one month) specified in writing to the entitled third party at the time of such notification.'

Payments

19.17 Where a certificate was issued in a sum less than that taken by the solicitor, the solicitor was obliged to give a refund.[19]

---

[18]   SI 1994/2616, art 7.

[19]   This was in accordance with SI 1994/2616, art 13:

'(1)   If a solicitor has received payment of all or part of his costs and a remuneration certificate is issued for less than the sum already paid, the solicitor must immediately pay to the entitled person any refund which may be due (after taking into account any other sums which may properly be payable to the solicitor whether for costs, paid disbursements, value added tax or otherwise) unless the solicitor has applied for an order for taxation within one month of receipt by him of the remuneration certificate.

(2)   Where a solicitor applies for taxation, his liability to pay any refund under paragraph (1) shall be suspended for so long as the taxation is still pending.

(3)   The obligation of the solicitor to repay costs under paragraph (1) is without prejudice to any liability of the solicitor to pay interest on the repayment by virtue of any enactment, rule of law or professional rule.'

NON-STATUTORY ASSESSMENTS (*TURNER & CO V PALOMO* QUANTIFICATIONS)

19.18 Whether the court is able to carry out an assessment pursuant to s 70 (or s 71) of the Solicitors Act 1974 (a 'statutory assessment') will depend on a number of factors, including whether the bill has been paid and the period of time which has expired between the delivery of the bill and the application for an assessment (see **18.4**). Circumstances will exist in which the court is precluded from making an order for a statutory assessment;[20] where this is the case, the court may order a non-statutory ascertainment of the quantum of costs (which will be referred to as a 'non-statutory assessment').

19.19 The jurisdiction to make such an order stems from the fact that a claim brought by a solicitor for his fees is a claim for a reasonable (unliquidated) sum. The court is, therefore, able to rule on the reasonableness of the sums claimed in much the same way as it would in any other claim for payment for services rendered. The jurisdiction was first exercised under the RSC[21] and, unsurprisingly, continues to exist under the CPR.[22] Whilst there is no authority directly on the point,[23] it is probable that the jurisdiction also exists by reason of the fact that, unless there is statutory provision to the contrary, the court has inherent jurisdiction to secure that the solicitor, as an officer of the court, is remunerated properly and no more for the work he has done.[24] It is possible that there is a separate jurisdiction that permits a solicitor principal to have the costs of a solicitor agent assessed, this being by under the court's jurisdiction to regulate officers of the court;[25] there is, however, no modern authority on that point.

19.20 Where practicable, the assessment should be heard by a costs judge; the costs judge's task will be to assess the costs and to enter judgment for the assessed amount.[26] Where it would be unfair to transfer the matter to a costs judge (such as where the application to transfer the matter to a costs judge has been made very late in the day), the matter may be heard by a trial judge.[27]

19.21 Although there is no authority on the point, common sense dictates that the client ought not to be able to escape an assessment on the indemnity basis simply by placing himself in a position where he was unable to ask for a statutory assessment. Anecdotally, non-statutory assessments are a less rigorous process than statutory assessments in that the court tends to paint with a broader brush and is less inclined to hear detailed argument (especially from the client) than it would on a statutory assessment. If this is correct, the client would be ill-advised to allow his right to a statutory assessment to lapse on the carefree assumption that a non-statutory assessment will be similar to a statutory assessment.

---

[20] See, for example, *Harrison v Tew* [1990] 2 AC 523.
[21] *Thomas Watts & Co (a firm) v Smith* [1998] 2 Costs LR 59 and *Turner & Co (a firm) v O Palomo SA* [2000] 1 WLR 37.
[22] See, for example, *Truex v Toll* [2009] EWHC 396 (Ch) and *King v Rothschild Trust* [2002] EWHC 1346 (Ch).
[23] The authority referred to below (*Sutton v Sears* [1959] 3 All ER 545) related to sums payable under a legal aid certificate rather than to sums payable under a private contract of retainer.
[24] See *Sutton v Sears* [1959] 3 All ER 545 at 550.
[25] See *Storer & Co v Johnson* (1890) 15 App Cas 203, HL.
[26] *Thomas Watts & Co (a firm) v Smith* [1998] 2 Costs LR 59 at 74.
[27] *King v Rothschild Trust* [2002] EWHC 1346 (Ch).

19.22 The parties will not be afforded the automatic protection of the one-fifth rule (although it is possible that the court would bear that rule in mind when deciding the incidence of costs). Other factors that the court may take into account are the client's delay, the efforts that have been taken to settle the dispute, and the fact that the parties are at liberty to make offers without being impeded by the need to show special circumstances before the court can take those offers into account.

STATUTORY DEMANDS AND BANKRUPTCY PROCEEDINGS

19.23 When a solicitor is faced with a client who will not pay, one option that might go through his mind would be to serve a statutory demand. Whether a solicitor is able to do this will turn on the facts of each case, but (for the reasons set out below) it is an option which would exist only very infrequently.

Statutory demands

19.24 A statutory demand is a precursor to a petition for bankruptcy.[28] There are a number of conditions which must be satisfied at the date of presentation. For the purposes of most solicitor and client disputes, they are:

- that the costs debt (ie the amount outstanding) is at least equal to £750;
- that the costs debt which is relied upon is a liquidated sum;
- that the costs debt is one which the costs debtor (ie the client or the party chargeable) has no reasonable prospect of being able to pay; and
- that there is no outstanding application to set aside the statutory demand.

Usually the matter will turn on whether the costs debt which is relied upon is a liquidated sum. For the reasons set out below, this is a condition which is rarely met.

Liquidated versus unliquidated

19.25 An unassessed bill which is entirely free of agreement is not a bill for a liquidated sum. Where this is so, it is not possible to serve a statutory demand for the full amount of the bill.[29] The fact that a client may have acknowledged the solicitor's invoices does not turn an unliquidated costs debt into a liquidated costs debt, nor does it give rise to estoppel.[30]

19.26 Some bills will have been agreed; in particular, where a business agreement exists, there may be agreement as to part of the costs (such as hourly rates, etc). There are conflicting authorities on whether a statutory demand can be issued under those

---

[28]   It is issued pursuant to s 268 of the Insolvency Act 1986. See also s 267 of that Act.
[29]   See *Klamer v Kyriakides & Braier (a firm)* [2005] BPIR 1142, Ch D, a decision of Master Simmonds; see also *Turex v Toll* [2009] EWHC 369 (Ch), in which Proudman J accepted without demur the agreement between the parties that such a bill is not for a liquidated sum. See also *In Re Laceward Ltd* [1981] 1 WLR 133 at 137; this approach is in line with the analogous law in relation to accountants' bills, where Vinelott J held that it would be an abuse of process for a firm of accountants to serve a statutory demand for the amount of their bill: see *Re a Debtor No 32 of 1991 (No 2)* [1994] BCC 524 at 527. See also *Wallace LLP v Yates* (unreported) 2 March 2010, Ch D, in which Morgan J found that the meaning of 'immediately payable' in s 268 of the Insolvency Act 1986 referred to sums that had to be both liquidated and payable immediately.
[30]   *Truex v Toll* [2009] EWHC 396 (Ch).

circumstances. In the past, the court took a view as to whether the undisputed amount exceeded the threshold; indeed, in ancient times there was a practice of sending the costs for a provisional assessment before a costs judge to determine that point.[31] Proudman J has found that a solicitor may not issue a statutory demand even where the supposed agreement relates to costs which exceed the £750 threshold. She commented that her conclusion was at odds both with standard Chancery practice and previous decisions,[32] and that she was 'hesitant' about it.[33] However, at least one Chancery Master has come to a similar conclusion.[34]

19.27 It may well be that the modern approach differs from that which used to exist in times past,[35] but there are contrary arguments which have yet to be decided.[36]

Conversion to a liquidated sum

19.28 An unliquidated costs debt can be converted into a liquidated costs debt by agreement or conduct. Proudman J said that this may happen in the following circumstances:[37]

- An agreement for consideration, that is to say:
  - an agreement as to a fixed amount;
  - an agreement as to hourly rates and time spent in consideration of future services;
  - a compromise agreement; or
- Conduct giving rise to an estoppel according to established principles.

The agreement would not have to be for an expressly stated sum: a costs debt will not be unliquidated merely by virtue of the fact that an arithmetical calculation needs to be performed in order to ascertain the sums due.[38]

19.29 It seems implicit in Proudman J's reasoning that an agreed costs debt will be liquidated notwithstanding the fact that the court has the power set the agreement aside (see **8.115**). Where there is a dispute about whether there has been a compromise, the court may have to determine that dispute. That topic is addressed at **19.34–19.46**, but one aspect of that topic needs particular emphasis as it is commonly encountered in practice: a mere admission of the fees unsupported by consideration or estoppel would ordinarily be insufficient to convert a costs debt into a liquidated sum.[39]

---

[31] See, for example, *Re Ford* (1838) 3 Deac 494, Mont & Ch 97.

[32] See, for example, *Re a debtor No 833 of 1993 and No 834 of 1993* [1994] NPC 82, in which Vinelott J found that the mere fact that the costs might be reduced was not a reason to set aside a statutory demand if the reduced amount would still be above £750.

[33] *Turex v Toll* [2009] EWHC 369 (Ch) at [38].

[34] *Klamer v Kyriakides & Braier (a firm)* [2005] BPIR 1142, Ch D.

[35] One of Proudman J's reasons for departing from previous decisions was because those decisions were made before it was established that the quantum of a solicitor's bill could be investigated even if an assessment under the Solicitors Act 1974 had been precluded: see *Turex v Toll* [2009] EWHC 369 (Ch) at [24] *et seq*, relying on cases such as *In Turner & C v O Palomo SA* [2000] 1 WLR 37.

[36] In particular, if Proudman J's analysis is correct, it would seem to be at odds with the position relating to limitation, in respect of which a claim for a solicitor's fees is capable of being a liquidated claim within the meaning of s 29(5) of the Limitation Act 1980: see *Byatt v Nash* [2002] All ER (D) 353.

[37] *Turex v Toll* [2009] EWHC 369 (Ch) at [26]–[40] and, in particular, [30].

[38] *Re a Debtor No 32 of 1991 (No 2)* [1994] BCC 524 at 527.

[39] *Turex v Toll* [2009] EWHC 369 (Ch) at [36].

One-month period

19.30 It is, for the sake of completeness, worth recording that service of a statutory demand does not constitute the bringing of a claim and that the solicitor is not, therefore, precluded from issuing a statutory demand by the provisions concerning the one-month period stipulated in SA 1974, s 69(1).[40] That narrow point remains good law but, for the reasons set out above, it is rarely of practical relevance.

Bankruptcy proceedings

19.31 The following points are made subject to the points made above; much of what is set out below would be academic in most cases because no statutory demand could be issued.

19.32 There is nothing innate about a solicitor's costs which would prevent him from issuing a bankruptcy petition in an effort to recover unpaid costs; it need not be the case that the solicitor is in a position to bring a claim for his costs.[41] That said, the solicitor will have to prove the costs debt, and in appropriate cases the court may order that a bill be drawn up and that the costs be assessed. There is, however, no requirement that a bill be delivered in every case:[42] if the circumstances permit (such as where there is a fixed sum retainer), the court may accept that the solicitor has proved the costs debt without delivering a bill.[43] Where this is done, the court may enlist the assistance of a costs judge in deciding the correctness of the solicitor's assertions.[44]

19.33 In summary, there are only limited circumstances in which a solicitor is able to issue a statutory demand founded on an unpaid and unassessed bill.

DISPUTED COMPROMISE

19.34 A disputed compromise will exist where one of the parties says that the amount due has been agreed but the other says that this is not so.

19.35 Most of the authorities cited in the next few paragraphs are ancient. It could easily be the case that those authorities are no longer good law. In particular, the concept of consumer protection probably plays a much greater role today than it did in times past. This is relevant because (unlike in disputed compromise in other spheres of the law) the effect of the putative agreement does not turn solely on the law, as it is often also a matter of discretion (see below). In view of these things, what is set out below ought to be regarded as setting the boundaries of what the law will permit as opposed to being a guide to what a present-day court would actually decide.

---

[40]   *In re A Debtor (No 88 of 1991)* [1993] Ch 286 (Sir Donald Nicholls V-C went on to say (obiter) that a bankruptcy petition probably should be regarded as being an action for the purposes of s 69(1).

[41]   See *Ex parte Sutton* (1805) 11 Ves 163 and, in more modern times, *Re a debtor No 833 of 1993 and No 834 of 1993* [1994] NPC 82.

[42]   *Re Potts ex p Établissements Callot and De Schrijver v Leonard Tubbs & Co and Official Receiver* [1934] Ch 356 at 362 and 364, per Farwell J.

[43]   *Eicke v Nokes* (1829) Mood & M 303.

[44]   Whilst ancient authority, see *Re Woods ex p Ditton* (1880) 13 Ch D 318.

19.36 The counterparties to a contract of retainer may reach agreement (or, from a consumer protection point of view, may negotiate away their rights) in a number of ways,[45] including:

- a written agreement forming a contentious or non-contentious business agreement;
- an oral agreement as to the amount to be charged;
- a compromise of the bill (not being accord and satisfaction);
- accord and satisfaction;
- a promise giving rise to promissory estoppel; and
- subsequent promise.

Each is discussed in turn. There is considerable overlap between these categories; indeed, it could be argued that the distinction between some of them is so fine as to be artificial.

Disputed business agreements, etc

19.37 Whether there has been a written agreement which forms a contentious or non-contentious business agreement will be a matter of fact and law to be determined on the evidence and in accordance with the principles set out at **8.114–8.198**. The following case examples may be relevant in the present context (ie where there is a dispute as to whether there was intended to be agreement):

- a memorandum signed by the client and the solicitor may be sufficient to amount to contentious business agreement;[46]
- a memorandum signed retrospectively is capable of amounting to a contentious business agreement, even though a lower amount had initially been agreed;[47]
- where there is no consideration, an admission that the costs debt exists or a promise to pay it would not be sufficient to preclude a subsequent assessment;[48]
- a receipt given for monies paid in 'full and final settlement of all outstanding costs' would, in general, not preclude an assessment in circumstances where the monies were paid for the purposes of securing a release of papers held under lien;[49] and
- a signed memorandum is capable of binding a party chargeable, even though it was the client (rather than the party chargeable) who had affixed his signature.[50]

19.38 Many of these cases were decided not on the basis of whether there was an agreement in principle, but on the basis of whether it was fair to allow that agreement to bind the parties; the statutory provisions which allow the court to exercise its discretion in this way continue to exist.[51] The court, therefore, has considerable freedom to arrive at a conclusion which meets the justice of the situation. Where no bill had been delivered, agreements to compromise a costs debt for a fixed sum were enforceable if the

---

45   Other mechanisms would include composition with creditors, and account stated or release by deed.

46   *Bake v French (No 2)* [1907] 2 Ch 215, following *Re Jones* [1895] 2 Ch 719, applied in *In re Thompson ex p Baylis* [1894] 1 QB 463; *Bake* doubted the earlier case of *Pontifex v Farnham* (1892) 62 LJQB 344.

47   *In re Thompson ex p Baylis* [1894] 1 QB 462; this case was criticised in *Re Simmons and Politzer* [1954] 2 All ER 811, but that criticism was based on a provision that no longer exists (ie the need for an agreement to be approved before it can be enforced).

48   *Turex v Toll* [2009] EWHC 369 (Ch) at [36].

49   *Re Simmons and Politzer* [1954] 2 All ER 811.

50   *Turner v Hand* (1859) 27 Beav 561; in a similar vein see *Re Stogdon ex p Baker* (1887) 51 JP 565, but compare this with *Re Blackmore* (1851) 13 Beav 154.

51   See SA 1974, ss 57(5) and 61(4).

solicitor could show that the agreement had been made fairly and with proper knowledge on both sides;[52] that said, the relationship between solicitor and client is a fiduciary relationship, and as such, the burden of proving these things is no easy burden to shift.[53]

Disputed oral agreements

19.39 Whether there has been a binding oral agreement is a matter of fact and law to be determined on the evidence and in accordance with the principles set out at **8.217–8.230**; as can be seen from that discussion, there is a distinction between contentious and non-contentious business.

19.40 In the days before the court drew that distinction it was established that an oral agreement by a solicitor to take a gross sum from his client in lieu of costs was not void, although it was regarded by the court 'with jealousy' (which, in more modern language, means that it would have been viewed with some circumspection).[54] Thus, even in ancient times, the court was not overly ready to allow an oral agreement to be enforced in such a way as to cause detriment to the client. Whilst there remains room for argument on the point, a reasonably accurate generalisation is that an oral agreement as to non-contentious work is not enforceable against either of the parties,[55] and an oral agreement as to contentious work is not enforceable against the client[56] (see **8.222–8.225**). It has to be said, however, that there is uncertainty as to whether these principles remain good law; other common law jurisdictions have moved towards examining such agreements on an ordinarily contractual basis: see **8.223**. In any event, where no bill has been delivered, that would be a factor that the court could take into account.[57]

Disputed agreements relating to a bill

19.41 This category is larger than the two categories mentioned above in that it is the alleged compromise of the bill itself which falls to be considered rather than any putative agreement about what that bill should contain. The question of whether a bill has been compromised will be an issue of fact and law. The fact that a purported compromise could, in certain circumstances,[58] be said to be a retrospective contentious or non-contentious business agreement is relevant because, if the court finds that the

---

52 *Stedman v Collett* (1854) 17 Beav 608; and *Clare v Joseph* [1907] 2 KB 369 at 376.

53 *Tyrrell v Bank of London* (1862) 10 HLC 26 at 44 and *Re Van Laun; Ex parte Chatterton* [1907] 2 KB 23 at 29.

54 *In re Whitcombe* (1844) 8 Beav 140.

55 In *In re a Solicitor* [1956] 1 QB 157, for example, Pearson J found that a client could not rely on an oral agreement that his solicitor would charge less than the ordinary rate of remuneration.

56 *Chamberlain v Boodle & King* (1980) 124 SJ 186, subsequently upheld on appeal at [1982] 1 WLR 1443; *Martin Boston & Co (a firm) v Levy* [1982] 1 WLR 1434 (arguable defence to a claim by solicitors for fees for contentious work under an oral agreement).

57 *West King & Adams* [1892] 2 QB 102; see also *Re Ingle* (1855) 25 LJ Ch 169, in which the court gave particular weight to the fact that the client was poorly educated.

58 There is authority that a compromise can operate independently of the Solicitors Act 1974 (*Re Morris* (1872) 27 LT 554), but it is doubtful if this remains good law and, in any event, does not accord with the modern approach, which is generally determined on the basis of discretion (see *Re Heritage ex p Docker* (1878) 3 QBD 726 and *Ingrams v Sykes* (1987) 137 NLJ 1135; see also *Barclays plc v Villers* [2000] 1 All ER (Comm) 357 at 367).

agreement is a business agreement, it has the power to set it aside.[59] The modern approach seems to be to decide these issues on a discretionary basis.[60]

19.42 An early example (circa 1860) of the principle of consumer protection is where the court found that a compromise was not binding because the bill which had been delivered did not comply with the then statutory requirements for a statute bill.[61]

Accord and satisfaction

19.43 In the present context, 'accord and satisfaction' means that a client has purchased his release from the obligation to discharge his costs debt, and that he has done so by means of valuable consideration which is not payment of the debt in full. It is akin to an agreed partial payment. Subject to what is said below, partial payment of a debt (in general, as opposed to a costs debt) will not normally suffice as satisfaction because there would have been no consideration for the remainder of the debt;[62] this would normally be true even where part payment would be commercially useful to the creditor for reasons of cash flow.[63] Costs debts are treated differently; this is because most costs debts are for unliquidated sums;[64] where this is so, payment of a sum agreed between the parties is capable of amounting to good consideration.[65]

19.44 This means that it is relatively easy for the parties to negotiate a compromise which amounts to accord and satisfaction. That said, there are no modern authorities on this point; this is probably a reflection of the fact that where evidence exists which would support a finding of accord and satisfaction, that evidence would also support a finding that there is a business agreement for the agreed sum. This would be a much more attractive finding from the court's point of view because it would mean that the court would have the discretionary power to set the agreement aside. Where, on the other hand, the purchase of the release is made with something which is entirely extraneous to the costs, a finding of accord and satisfaction may be the only finding open to the court.

Promissory estoppel

19.45 Estoppel is a discretionary equitable remedy whereby a promisor may be prevented (ie estopped) from disputing the quantum of the costs debt; this may happen where he has made a promise (such as a promise to pay that debt in a particular sum) and where that promise has caused the promisee adversely to alter his position. A detailed discussion of this topic is beyond the scope of this book. There are no authorities directly on costs debts,[66] but there are many authorities dealing with

---

[59]   See SA 1974, ss 57(5) and 61(4); as an early example, see the comments of Sir George Jessel MR in *Re Attorneys & Solicitors Act* (1870) 1 Ch D 575.

[60]   See *Barclays plc v Villers* [2000] 1 All ER (Comm) 357 at 367; as older examples, see *Re Heritage ex p Docker* (1878) 3 QBD 726 and *Ingrams v Sykes* (1987) 137 NLJ 1135.

[61]   *Philby v Hazle* (1860) 8 CBNS 647; see also *Wilkinson v Smart* (1875) 24 WR 42.

[62]   *Pinnel's Case* (1602) 5 Co Rep 117a.

[63]   *Foakes v Beer* (1884) 9 App Cas 605; but see *Williams v Roffey Bros & Nicholls (Contractors) Ltd* [1991] 1 QB 1: 'Consideration there must still be but, in my judgment, the courts nowadays should be more ready to find its existence so as to reflect the intention of the parties to the contract.'

[64]   See *Thomas Watts & Co (a firm) v Smith* [1998] 2 Costs LR 59 and *Turner & Co (a firm) v O Palomo SA* [2000] 1 WLR 37.

[65]   *Wilkinson v Byers* (1834) 1 Ad & El 106.

[66]   There is a negative authority in which it was found that there was no estoppel: see *Truex v Toll* [2009] EWHC 396 (Ch).

promissory estoppel in general.[67] The absence of specific authority could be a reflection of the fact that a solicitor asserting estoppel would probably face difficulties arising out of the fact that it would be seen as being an attempt to circumvent the consumer protection afforded by SA 1974. In any event, Proudman J has confirmed that seeking to enforce a costs debt is not of itself a sufficient alteration of position to found an estoppel: otherwise, there would be an estoppel in almost every case.[68]

19.46 In summary, although it is possible for a costs debt to be compromised in the sense that the court's jurisdiction no longer applies, in practice the court would often have a discretionary power to set the compromise aside.

Subsequent promise

19.47 Whilst unrelated to promissory estoppel in terms of its legal foundations, the effect of a subsequent promise (ie, a promise or ratification after the original bargain has been struck) will often lead to a result that is very similar to the operation of promissory estoppel. Whilst not binding, the Australian judge Anderson J has explained the principles in this way:[69]

> 'In [*Kennedy v Brown*[70]] it was held that the request to perform the services, followed by performance, created an implied contract to pay a reasonable amount; and that the subsequent promise to pay a stipulated amount (or to pay at a stipulated rate) is in the nature of an admission by the promisor of what is a reasonable amount, ie the subsequent promise is evidence against the promisor of what is a reasonable amount. In [*Re Casey's Patents; Stewart v Casey*[71]], it was held that the subsequent promise was "a positive bargain which fixes the amount of that reasonable remuneration on the faith of which the service was originally rendered". In both these explanations the later express promise to pay a specified sum was treated as nothing more than a refinement of the earlier implied promise to pay a reasonable sum, the consideration for both promises being the actual performance of the work.'

Similarly, whilst relating to a topic other than costs, the Privy Council have confirmed that 'an act done or service performed before the giving of a promise to make a payment can be consideration for the promise'.[72] That said, a subsequent acknowledgment of an agreed fee will not necessarily result in a favourable outcome from the solicitor's point of view as it will not necessarily result in an oral retainer being converted into a business agreement.[73] In a similar vein, an assurance or putative waiver given by the solicitor will not necessarily produce a favourable outcome from the client's point of view as it may fail for want of consideration (see **27.57**).

---

[67] See the *High Trees* principles as explained in *Central London Property Trust Ltd v High Trees House Ltd* [1947] KB 130.

[68] *Turex v Toll* [2009] EWHC 369 (Ch) at [41].

[69] *D'Alessandro & D'Angelo v Cooper* (unreported, WASC, Full Ct, Kennedy, Rowland and Anderson JJ, Lib No 960334, 2 June 1996 at p 9 of the reasons.

[70] *Kennedy v Broun* (1863) 13 CBNS 677, 143 ER 268.

[71] *Re Casey's Patents; Stewart v Casey* [1892] 1 Ch 104 at 115–116.

[72] *Pao On v Lau Iu Long* [1980] AC 614.

[73] If an oral retainer is made and then the agreed sum is acknowledged in the form of an account stated after payment has been made by deduction, that acknowledgement will not be sufficient to give rise to a retrospective business agreement: *Re Fernandes* [1878] WN 57.

LEGAL OMBUDSMAN AND SRA

19.48   There are, in essence, two mechanisms by which a dissatisfied client may pursue a complaint about his solicitors' fees.[74] They are:

- The Solicitors Regulation Authority ('SRA'); and
- The Legal Ombudsman (previously known as the Legal Services Ombudsman).

The SRA is able to investigate breaches of the SRA Code of Conduct 2011, but will not investigate issues concerning poor services (such as excessive fees) unless the services are supplied in such a way as to give rise to a breach of the Code. In particular, only the Legal Ombudsman has the power of redress (ie to award compensation or reduce fees).[75] The focus of the next few paragraphs is mainly on the Legal Ombudsman.

Governance

19.49   The SRA is governed by the Legal Services Board ('LSB') and is thereby accountable to Parliament. The Legal Ombudsman is established by the Office for Legal Complaints ('OLC'), which in turn is also accountable to the LSB and thereby to Parliament.

The Legal Ombudsman's Jurisdiction

19.50   The following points can be made about the Legal Ombudsman's jurisdiction:

- *Nature of the complaint:* A complaint is excluded from the jurisdiction if the complainant has not first used the respondent's complaints procedures.[76] The complaint must be about services provided to the complainant either directly or at the request of an intermediary, such as the complainant's solicitor.[77]
- *Complainants:* Individuals and most business are able to make complaints, but public bodies and their agents may not.[78]
- *Respondents:* Whilst the focus of this sub-chapter is on solicitors' fees, the Legal Ombudsman is able to consider complaints against any 'authorised person' (see **5.34**). It is a moot point as to whether the Legal Ombudsman has jurisdiction to deal with a complaint about unregulated legal practitioners (such as unqualified costs draftsmen); the writer's personal communications with the Legal Ombudsman indicates that the following approach would be taken (although it has to be stressed that this personal communication must not be taken as being authoritative):[79]

  > 'If the consumer had engaged the unqualified costs adviser directly the situation would be more complicated. Assuming that the work was on a paid basis and related to costs litigation then the draftsman has probably been conducting litigation. The Act says this is "reserved legal activity" and that to do it without proper qualification or

---

[74]   This book focuses solely on the use of those mechanisms for the purpose of dealing with a dispute about costs: it makes no attempt to deal with the wider regulatory aspects of the matter.

[75]   See the Legal Services Act 2007, s 157.

[76]   See the Legal Services Act 2007, s 126.

[77]   See the Legal Services Act 2007, s 128(4). There are additional provisions allowing beneficiaries of an estate or trust to complain about administration, etc.

[78]   See the Legal Services Act 2007, s 128(5)(b).

[79]   Note by Anthony Rich, General Counsel, the Legal Ombudsman prepared on 2 February 2012.

authorisation is a criminal offence. In practice the Ombudsman would look at whether the costs draftsman had led the client to believe they were authorised to do the work. If they suggested they were [sic] would be likely to accept their claim that they were authorised, and so within [the Ombudsman's] jurisdiction. It might be unappealing for a costs draftsman to argue they were not within the Ombudsman's jurisdiction because what they were doing was in fact an offence. At least one consequence is that they would lose any entitlement to their fees.'

- *Employees:* Any act or omission by a person in the course of the person's employment is to be treated as also an act or omission by the person's employer, whether or not it was done with the employer's knowledge or approval.[80]
- *Legal Proceedings:* The Legal Ombudsman may summarily dismiss a complaint if it would be better dealt with by legal proceedings or if it has previously been dealt with by legal proceedings.[81] Neither the complainant nor the respondent may institute or continue legal proceedings in respect of a matter which was the subject of a complaint, after the time when a determination by becomes binding and final.[82]

Every month the Legal Ombudsman publishes an article in the Law Society's Gazette in which he gives an indication of the type of cases he refers and how he decides those cases.

Charges and fees

19.51 Unless a costs order is made against him (see below), the Legal Ombudsman's service is free to the complainant. The respondent, however, will generally be charged; the relevant provisions are in the footnotes.[83]

Powers

19.52 The ombudsman may dismiss a complaint without consideration of the merits if he considers that:[84]

- the complaint or part to be frivolous or vexatious or totally without merit:
- the complaint or part would be better dealt with under another ombudsman scheme, by arbitration or by other legal proceedings;
- there has been undue delay;
- the subject of the complaint or part has previously been dealt with under another ombudsman scheme, by arbitration or by other legal proceedings; or
- there are other compelling reasons why it is inappropriate for the complaint to be dealt with under the ombudsman scheme.

---

80   See the Legal Services Act 2007, s 131.
81   See the Legal Services Act 2007, s 133(4).
82   See the Legal Services Act 2007 s 140(11).
83   This is governed by s 136 of the Legal Services Act 2007: '136 Charges payable by respondents. (1) Scheme rules must require respondents, in relation to complaints under the ombudsman scheme, to pay to the OLC such charges as may be specified in the rules. (2) The rules must provide for charges payable in relation to a complaint to be waived (or wholly refunded) where— (a) the complaint is determined or otherwise resolved in favour of the respondent, and (b) the ombudsman is satisfied that the respondent took all reasonable steps to try to resolve the complaint under the respondent's complaints procedures.'
84   See the Legal Services Act 2007, s 133(4)

The Legal Ombudsman has wide procedural powers,[85] including the power to compel parties to attend to give evidence and to produce documents.[86]

19.53 The powers of the Legal Ombudsman upon determination are as follows:[87]

'137 Determination of complaints

(1) A complaint is to be determined under the ombudsman scheme by reference to what is, in the opinion of the ombudsman making the determination, fair and reasonable in all the circumstances of the case.

(2) The determination may contain one or more of the following—

(a)   a direction that the respondent make an apology to the complainant;

(b)   a direction that—

    (i)   the fees to which the respondent is entitled in respect of the services to which the complaint relates ("the fees") are limited to such amount as may be specified in the direction, and

    (ii)   the respondent comply, or secure compliance, with such one or more of the permitted requirements as appear to the ombudsman to be necessary in order for effect to be given to the direction under sub-paragraph (i);

(c)   a direction that the respondent pay compensation to the complainant of such an amount as is specified in the direction in respect of any loss which has been suffered by, or any inconvenience or distress which has been caused to, the complainant as a result of any matter connected with the complaint;

(d)   a direction that the respondent secure the rectification, at the expense of the respondent, of any such error, omission or other deficiency arising in connection with the matter in question as the direction may specify;

(e)   a direction that the respondent take, at the expense of the respondent, such other action in the interests of the complainant as the direction may specify.

(3) For the purposes of subsection (2)(b) "the permitted requirements" are—

(a)   that the whole or part of any amount already paid by or on behalf of the complainant in respect of the fees be refunded;

(b)   that the whole or part of the fees be remitted;

(c)   that the right to recover the fees be waived, whether wholly or to any specified extent.

(4) Where—

(a)   a direction is made under subsection (2)(b) which requires that the whole or part of any amount already paid by or on behalf of the complainant in respect of the fees be refunded, or

(b)   a direction is made under subsection (2)(c),

the direction may also provide for the amount payable under the direction to carry interest from a time specified in or determined in accordance with the direction, at the rate specified in or determined in accordance with scheme rules

(5) The power of the ombudsman to make a direction under subsection (2) is not confined to cases where the complainant may have a cause of action against the respondent for negligence.'

---

85   See the Legal Services Act 2007, s 133.

86   See the Legal Services Act 2007, s 133(3)(e), but see the limit at s 133(5), those limits being that the Ombudsman may not compel the giving of evidence of the production of a document which that person could not be compelled to produce in court proceedings.

87   See the Legal Services Act 2007, s 137.

19.54 The powers mentioned above are limited, this being in accordance with s 138 of the Legal Services Act 2007:

> **'138 Limitation on value of directions under the ombudsman scheme**
>
> (1) Where a determination is made under the ombudsman scheme in respect of a complaint, the total value of directions under section 137(2)(c) to (e) contained in the determination must not exceed £30,000.
>
> (2) For this purpose the total value of such directions is the aggregate of—
>
>   (a)   the amount of any compensation specified in a direction under subsection (2)(c) of section 137, and
>
>   (b)   the amount of any expenses reasonably incurred by the respondent when complying with a direction under subsection (2)(d) or (e) of that section.
>
> (3) For the purposes of determining that total value, any interest payable on an amount within subsection (2)(a) of this section, by virtue of section 137(4), is to be ignored.'

Costs orders

19.55 The Legal Ombudsman has the power to award costs against the respondent in favour of the complainant;[88] he also has power to award costs against the complainant, but only if in his opinion that person acted so unreasonably that it is appropriate in all the circumstances of the case to make such an award.[89] Interest may be added to the costs.[90]

Acceptance of rejection of the determination

19.56 The Legal Ombudsman must notify the parties of his determination.[91] If the complainant notifies the ombudsman that the determination is accepted by the complainant, it is binding on the respondent and the complainant and is final.[92] It may be enforced via the court.[93]

---

[88]   See the Legal Services Act 2007, s 133(3)(h).
[89]   See the Legal Services Act 2007, s 133(3)(i).
[90]   See the Legal Services Act 2007, s 133(6).
[91]   See the Legal Services Act 2007, s 139.
[92]   See the Legal Services Act 2007, s 140(4).
[93]   See the Legal Services Act 2007, s 141.

Chapter 20

SOLICITORS' RIGHTS AND REMEDIES: PROCEEDINGS, LIEN, AND CHARGING ORDERS

20.1   This chapter describes the rights that a solicitor may assert when faced with a client who either will not pay or who cannot pay. Statutory demands are dealt with in **19.23–19.30**, but for the reasons set out therein, this is not an option which would commonly be available. Rights against legal expenses insurers are addressed at **21.322** and **30.251**.

SUING FOR RECOVERY OF COSTS

20.2   This discussion addresses the topics of whether, how and when a solicitor can bring a claim for his costs. Prior to 11 August 2009 there were minor differences between the procedure for contentious and non-contentious business, but since that date, those differences have ceased to exist. Nevertheless, there are one or two procedural considerations which relate only to contentious business which, while not mandatory, ought to be borne in mind for the purposes of the efficient management of the claim.

General principles

20.3   Subject to certain exceptions (see **20.5**), a solicitor may not bring a claim for his costs before the expiration of one month from the date on which a statute bill for those costs has been delivered. The topics of what constitutes a statute bill and what constitutes delivery are addressed at **17.33** *et seq* and **17.67–17.72** respectively.

One-month period

20.4   The reference to one month is a reference to one calendar month.[1] The day of delivery is excluded, as is the day on which proceedings are commenced.[2]

20.5   There are exceptions to the general rule that the client is afforded a month's grace. They are set out in the Solicitors Act 1974, s 69(1):[3]

'If there is probable cause for believing that the party chargeable with the costs—

---

[1]   Interpretation Act 1978, Sch 1.
[2]   *Blunt v Heslop* (1838) 4 A&E 577.
[3]   Minor terminological changes were, at the time of writing, due to be made by the Legal Services Act 2007, s 177 and Sch 16, Pt 1, paras 1 and 60; at the time of writing those changes had not been made, but they are incorporated herein because it is likely that they will have been made by the time the book comes to be read; the reader should check this for himself, however.

(a)   is about to quit England and Wales, to become bankrupt or to compound with his creditors, or

(b)   is about to do any other act which would tend to prevent or delay the solicitor obtaining payment,

the High Court may, notwithstanding that one month has not expired from the delivery of the bill, order that the solicitor be at liberty to commence an action to recover his costs and may order that those costs be assessed.'

20.6   Where an application for an assessment has been made within one month of the bill being delivered, the court will, as of the client's right rather than as a matter of discretion, order both that the bill be assessed and that no claim may be commenced until the assessment has been completed.[4] SA 1974 does not expressly provide that a claim already commenced will be stayed but, given the fact that no claim should be commenced during this period without the leave of the court,[5] such a provision would be otiose.

20.7   Where an application is made following the expiry of a one-month period since the bill was delivered, the court has the discretionary power to order that there be an assessment; where the makes such an order, no claim may be commenced on the bill and any existing claim will be stayed.[6] Jurisdictional and discretionary issues are discussed at **18.3–18.54**; as is explained therein, it may happen that the court is obliged to find that there have been special circumstances before an order can be made for an assessment.

Claims based on dishonoured cheques, etc

20.8   Whilst most claims for fees are brought on the basis of the debt created by the retainer, this will not always be the case; where, for example, a client's cheque is dishonoured, the solicitor may wish to sue on the cheque. Warner J has held that it is arguable[7] that the consumer protection afforded by the requirement to wait a month following delivery of a statute bill would be defeated if a solicitor were to be permitted to do this within that period of grace.[8] Likewise, it seems that a solicitor cannot evade his obligation to deliver a bill of costs by taking a bill of exchange from his client for an agreed amount.[9]

Distinction between claim for assessment and claim for payment

20.9   A claim brought by a solicitor for his costs is not a claim for an assessment. This means that the procedural requirements under CPR, r 67.3(1) do not apply, and a solicitor is free to choose his venue. Nonetheless, in furtherance of the overriding objective thought ought to be given to the fact that the client could well bring a counterclaim for an assessment, thereby excluding certain courts from subsequently dealing with the matter; the factors to be taken into account in that regard will depend on whether the work is contentious or non-contentious (see **20.13** and **20.15**).

---

[4]   SA 1974, s 70(1).
[5]   SA 1974, s 69(2).
[6]   SA 1974, s 70(2) and (3).
[7]   The application before him was an application to set aside default judgment.
[8]   *Martin Boston & Co (a firm) v Levy* [1982] 1 WLR 1434.
[9]   *Ray v Newton* [1913] 1 KB 249, CA.

Procedure

20.10 As to procedure, it is not wholly clear whether a claim for unpaid fees may be brought by a CPR, Part 7 claim. CPR, r 67.3(2) provides that a claim for 'an order under Part III of the Act' must be made by Part 8 claim form (unless it is made in existing proceedings), but it is arguable that a claim for unpaid fees is not an order under Part III of SA 1974 (this being because that Act does not create the cause of action, it merely qualifies it). Regardless of this, the CPR, Part 8 procedure would, in any event, almost always be the appropriate procedure as a matter of convenience.

Non-contentious work (pre 11 August 2009)

20.11 In addition to the restrictions mentioned above, art 6 of the Solicitors' (Non-Contentious Business) Remuneration Order 1994 (SI 1994/2616) makes the following provisions (which relate only to bills rendered before 11 August 2009):[10]

> 'Before a solicitor brings proceedings to recover costs against a client on a bill for non-contentious business he must inform the client in writing of the matters specified in article 8, except where the bill has been taxed.'

20.12 Slade J has said that the phrase 'proceedings to recover costs on ... a bill for non-contentious business' is to be construed in such a way that no client or former client should have a claim brought against them without having been informed of his right under SI 1994/2616, art 8; he also commented that the phrase is wide enough to include any proceedings where costs are sought to be recovered, including a winding-up petition.[11] The requisite information set out in art 8 is:

> 'When required by articles 6 or 7, a solicitor must inform an entitled person in writing of the following matters—
>
> (a)   where article 4(1) applies—
>
>   (i)   that the entitled person may, within one month of receiving from the solicitor the information specified in this article or (if later) of delivery of the bill or notification of the amount of the costs, require the solicitor to obtain a remuneration certificate; and
>
>   (ii)   that (unless the solicitor has agreed to do so) the Council may waive the requirements of article 11(1), if satisfied from the client's written application that exceptional circumstances exist to justify granting a waiver;
>
> (b)   that sections 70, 71 and 72 of the 1974 Act set out the entitled person's rights in relation to taxation;
>
> (c)   that (where the whole of the bill has not been paid, by deduction or otherwise) the solicitor may charge interest on the outstanding amount of the bill in accordance with article 14.'

These provisions do not apply to bills delivered on or after 11 August 2009; therefore, since that date, only the general provisions (common to both contentious and non-contentious business) will apply (see **20.3–20.10**).

20.13 A claim brought by a solicitor for his costs is not a claim for an assessment, so the procedural requirements under the CPR, r 67.3(1) do not apply. If, however, the court were to order that the costs be assessed, that assessment would have to proceed in

---

[10]   Solicitors' (Non-Contentious Business) Remuneration Order 2009, art 1(3).
[11]   *In re Laceward Ltd* [1981] 1 WLR 136.

the High Court.[12] Unless an assessment is unlikely (such as where the costs were incurred under a non-contentious business agreement for a fixed fee), it would often be prudent to bring the claim in the High Court. The practice of deliberately bringing the claim in the 'wrong' court in an attempt to discourage a detailed assessment is contrary to the overriding objective and is to be deplored.

Contentious work

20.14 Where a contentious business agreement does more than just provide for remuneration by reference to an agreed hourly rate, the costs incurred under that agreement shall not be subject to assessment[13] (unless, of course, the court sets the agreement aside). This is discussed in detail at **8.139–8.198**.

20.15 The points made at **20.13** about the appropriate court are repeated; where the claim relates to contentious business done in a county court and were the claim is within the financial limit of the county court's jurisdiction (ie less than £5,000),[14] that county court will be able to hear the assessment.[15] This may be a factor to take into account when deciding where proceedings should be issued. Errors can mean that the court lacks vires to make the order sought:[16] see **8.196**.

Summary judgment

20.16 Where the claim is resisted on a point of principle (as opposed to merely on quantum) and where the client has no real prospect of success, the court may give summary judgment in favour of the solicitor. The test is whether the client has no real prospect of successfully defending the claim or issue.[17]

20.17 An application may be based on:[18]

- a point of law (including a question of construction of a document);
- the evidence which can reasonably be expected to be available at trial or the lack of it; or
- a combination of these things.

Unless the court acts of its own initiative, it would be for the solicitor to make an application on notice.[19] Save where the court gives permission, the application must not be made until the client has filed an acknowledgement of service or a defence. Written evidence must be served in advance of the hearing.[20]

---

[12]	See CPR, r 67.3(1)(b).
[13]	SA 1974, s 60(1).
[14]	See SA 1974, s 69(3), as amended by the High Court and County Courts Jurisdiction Order 1991 (SI 1991/724), art 2(7) and (8) and Part 1 of the Schedule.
[15]	CPR, r 67.3(1)(a).
[16]	See also *R (on the application of Srinivasans Solicitors) V Croydon County Court* [2011] EWHC 3615 (Admin).
[17]	CPR, r 24.2(a)(ii).
[18]	PD 24, para 1.3.
[19]	See PD 24, para 2 for the relevant procedure.
[20]	CPR, r 24.5(1)–(4).

20.18 Case examples are surprisingly uncommon. Turner J gave summary judgment in a case in which the client repeatedly changed her case, proceeding with each new argument only when the previous argument had been shown to be untenable.[21]

Default judgment

20.19 A default judgment is a judgment which is entered as a result of the client having failed to file an acknowledgement of service or a defence within the requisite time period.[22] Although there is no authority on the point, there are two reasons why a solicitor would, in general, be well advised not to make an application for default judgment. They are as follows.

Not a specified amount of money

20.20 It used to be the case that where a default judgment was sought, judgment was entered for the amount claimed; there is now doubt as to whether this is the correct procedure. This is because of the growing body of case law relating to the statutory demands (see **17.96**); that case law makes it clear that claims for solicitors' fees are not liquidated sums.[23] Although there are arguments to the contrary,[24] it would be a reasonable point of view to say that it would be inconsistent if one rule were to apply to statutory demands but another to civil claims.

Abuse of process

20.21 Default judgments may not be made in claims brought by way of the CPR, Part 8 procedure;[25] for the reasons set out above, it is arguable that CPR, r 67.3(2) is drafted in sufficiently wide terms as to preclude a claim for a solicitor's cost being brought by the Part 7 procedure. If that argument is correct, then it could be argued that it would be an abuse of process to allow default judgment to be entered in a claim which has been brought in defiance of a mandatory rule.

20.22 If both of these arguments are wrong, then default judgment may be obtained in the sum claimed; if only the second argument is wrong, then default judgment may be obtained only for an 'amount of money to be decided by the court'.[26] Few solicitors would wish for such an order, this being because the potential for dispute as to its meaning would be significant. The only exception to this would (perhaps) be where a previously agreed sum was claimed pursuant to a contentious or non-contentious business agreement.

---

[21] *Penningtons (a firm) v Abedi*, 30 July 1999, QBD.

[22] CPR, rr 12.1 and 12.3(1) and PD 12, para 1.1.

[23] See *Klamer v Kyriakides & Braier (a firm)* [2005] BPIR Ch D, a decision of Master Simmonds; see also *Truex v Toll* [2009] EWHC 369 (Ch), in which Proudman J accepted without demur the agreement between the parties that such a bill is not for a liquidated sum; see also *In Re Laceward Ltd* [1981] 1 WLR 133 at 137.

[24] It could be argued that unless the fees were obviously excessive it would be an abuse of process to afford the defendant the opportunity to have the fees assessed, as this would undermine the provisions in SA 1974, s 70; it could also be argued that the cases concerning statutory demands can be distinguished on the basis that they relate to an enforcement procedure, as opposed to a civil claim, which (at the stage of default judgment) is a procedure of ascertainment rather than enforcement.

[25] CPR, r 12.2(b).

[26] CPR, r 12.4(1).

20.23 In any event, the solicitor would be unable to apply for summary judgment in any of the following circumstances:[27]

- where the client has applied to strike out the claim;
- where the client has applied for summary judgment;
- where the client has satisfied the whole claim (including the costs); or
- where the client has filed an admission together with a request for time to pay.

20.24 If the court were to make order for an amount of money to be decided by the court, then it would either allocate the matter to a track, or would give directions (or both).[28]

PAYMENTS ON ACCOUNT

20.25 The most secure form of security that a solicitor can have is possession of cash: there is no reason why a client should not be asked to pay part or all of the costs debt pending an assessment.[29] Indeed, it is commonly the case that the court will make an order to this effect, that order being a condition for the continuance of the assessment.[30] These issues are addressed at **18.100–18.104**.

20.26 If relations between the solicitor and client have reached the nadir that the client will not tolerate the solicitor having use of the money, an escrow account[31] may prove to be an acceptable compromise, with the monies being released only with the consent of both parties or upon order of the court. The following factors might be relevant to the issue of whether a voluntary payment on account should be made.

Interest

20.27 A payment on account would stop interest running; this would usually be to the client's benefit.

Subsequent effect of voluntary payment

20.28 Although payment without demur may be a factor which may count against a client who subsequently seeks an assessment,[32] it will rarely be the case that a voluntary payment will count against the client if it is made without prejudice to the right to seek an assessment.[33] This will be especially true if the payment is only a part payment.[34]

---

[27] CPR, r 12.3(3).

[28] CPR, r 12.7(2).

[29] If a remuneration certificate is available and if the client wants to take advantage of that scheme, he is required to pay at least half of the costs debt: see **19.2–19.17**.

[30] See, for example, *Re Brockman* [1908–10] All ER Rep 364.

[31] In this context, an escrow account is an account where money is held until specific conditions are met.

[32] *Barclays plc v Villers* [2000] 1 All ER (Comm) 357 at 369.

[33] See, for example, *Re Simmons and Politzer* [1954] 2 All ER 811, in which payment to secure release of papers did not preclude an assessment.

[34] *Re Callis* (1901) 49 WR 316 and *Re Woodard* (1869) 18 WR 37.

Overpayment

20.29 The court has the power to order the solicitor to return any monies which have been overpaid.[35]

LIEN

20.30 This book is about costs rather than solicitors, and there is therefore a limit to the extent to which the subject of a solicitor's lien can be addressed. The following overview is intended to assist costs practitioners and generalists; specialists in the law pertaining to solicitors will need to consult other texts.[36]

20.31 The common law gives a solicitor the right, in certain circumstances, to retain the costs debtor's property pending discharge of the costs debt in general. Such a lien is called a 'retaining lien', and is an example of a general lien.[37]

20.32 In addition to this general lien, there is also a particular lien[38] over the property which has been recovered in the litigation[39] (but not negotiation)[40] in which the solicitor was retained; it is a right which is similar to, but distinct from, the statutory rights described below.[41] This type of lien is referred to in this book as a 'particular lien'.

20.33 A particular lien is far less frequently encountered than a retaining lien: unless the contrary is indicated, unqualified references to 'lien' are to the latter rather than former.

The effect of a retaining lien

20.34 Where a solicitor holds a retaining lien, he may retain property against the client and against all persons claiming through the client; he may do this until the full costs debt is discharged.[42]

20.35 The starting point is that a solicitor with a retaining lien is entitled to refuse access to the retained property, be that by the client or his successors,[43] or by any new solicitor instructed by the client; where that property is the client's file (or any other file of documents belonging to the client), he may refuse to allow any copies to be taken[44] or to allow the documents to be inspected.[45] This can apply even in family cases.[46]

---

[35]   *Barclays plc v Villers* [2000] 1 All ER (Comm) 357 at 367.

[36]   A more detailed account can be found in *Halsbury's Laws of England*, vol 68 (5th edn, 2008).

[37]   A general lien allows a person in possession of property to retain that property until all of the owner's debts owed to the person (in general) have been satisfied.

[38]   A particular lien is a right to retain particular property pending payment of the charges incurred in respect of that property.

[39]   *Re Sullivan v Pearson ex p Morrison* (1868) LR 4 QB 153.

[40]   *Megeurditchian v Lightbound* [1917] 2 KB 298, CA.

[41]   *Re Clarke's Settlement Fund* [1911] WN 39 at 40.

[42]   *Re Hawkes, Ackerman v Lockhart* [1898] 2 Ch 1, CA.

[43]   Such as personal representatives (*Re Watson* (1884) 53 LJ Ch 305), trustee in bankruptcy (*Re Watters* (1881) 7 LR Ir 531) or, in the case of a company, liquidator (*Re Aveling Barford Ltd* [1988] 3 All ER 1019).

[44]   See *Leo Abse & Cohen v Evan G Jones (Builders) Ltd* (1984) 128 Sol Jo 317; see also *Hemsworth ex p Underwood* (1845) de G 190.

[45]   See *Leo Abse & Cohen v Evan G Jones (Builders) Ltd* (1984) 128 Sol Jo 317 and *Re Biggs and Roche* (1897) 41 Sol Jo 277.

The effect of a particular lien

20.36 Particular lien relates to the proceeds of litigation. It is distinct from retaining lien in that it must be actively enforced[47] (ie it requires a court order,[48] without which it may not be asserted).[49] Unlike a retaining lien, a particular lien does not extend to the costs debt generally, but only to that part of the costs debt which pertains to the recovery of the property in question.[50]

20.37 The principal benefit of a particular lien is that where notice is given to the party liable to discharge the order for costs, damages, etc, that person would be at risk of being held accountable to the solicitor if he were to comply with that order in disregard of the lien.[51]

The extent and acquisition of lien

20.38 As a general rule, a retaining lien may extend to any money,[52] deed,[53] paper,[54] or personal chattel[55] which, with the client's consent,[56] has come into the solicitor's possession;[57] the solicitor must, at the relevant time, have been acting in the course of his engagement as a solicitor on behalf of the costs debtor or his successors.[58] Lien may attach regardless of whether the property has intrinsic value.[59]

20.39 Generally speaking, a solicitor will not acquire retaining lien in the following circumstances.

Not acting as a solicitor

20.40 Where the property comes into the solicitor's possession in his personal rather than his professional capacity, then a retaining lien will not attach. If a solicitor acts as a mortgagee for the client, the property upon which the mortgage was secured would typically have come into his possession in a personal rather than a professional capacity.[60] In a similar vein, the debt must have a arisen as a result of the solicitor acting in that capacity;[61] where the debt has arisen as a result of a mere loan, a retaining lien would not ordinarily attach.[62]

---

[46] *Hughes v Hughes* [1958] P 224.
[47] *Bozon v Bolland* (1839) 4 My & Cr 354.
[48] *Re Fuld (No 4)* [1968] P 727.
[49] *James Bibby Ltd v Woods and Howard* [1949] 2 KB 449.
[50] *Re Bayly's Estate ex p Humphrey* (1860) 12 I Ch R 315.
[51] *Ross v Buxton* (1889) 42 Ch D 190.
[52] *Re Phoenix Life Assurance Co, Howard and Dolman's Case* (1863) 1 Hem & M 433 at 444.
[53] *Re Dee Estates Ltd, Wright v Dee Estates Ltd* [1911] 2 Ch 85, CA.
[54] *Re Markby ex p Markby Assignees* (1864) 11 LT 250.
[55] *Friswell v King* (1846) 15 Sim 191, where lien extended to evidence which was to be relied upon at trial.
[56] *Gibson v May* (1853) 4 De GM & G 512.
[57] It is the legal entity that took possession which is relevant: *Re Forshaw* (1847) 16 Sim 121; a solicitor's successors may also take possession: *Pelly v Wathen* (1849) 7 Hare 351.
[58] *Re Long ex p Fuller* (1881) 16 Ch D 617.
[59] *Hughes v Hughes* [1958] P 224.
[60] *Vaughan v Vanderstegen* (1854) 2 Drew 408; compare this with *Re Riddell, Public Trustee v Riddell*, as reported in [1936] 2 All ER 1600.
[61] See, for example, *Re Walker, Meredith v Walker* (1893) 68 LT 517, in which the solicitor acted as a land agent; lien was found not to attach.
[62] *Re Taylor, Stileman and Underwood* [1891] 1 Ch 590.

Solicitor as trustee

20.41 Where the property comes into the solicitor's possession as trustee, then a retaining lien will generally not apply;[63] likewise, a retaining lien would not extend to property held by a solicitor who, subsequent to receipt, has constituted himself as a trustee.[64] (If property is held on trust but is subsequently retained by the solicitor for other purposes, then a retaining lien may attach.)[65]

Escrow accounts

20.42 Where monies are paid into an escrow account controlled by the solicitor, such monies are akin to monies paid into court. This means that the solicitor is acting as a bare trustee and will, therefore, not be entitled to assert a retaining lien.[66] (Where monies come to be paid out of the account, a particular lien may attach at that point.)[67]

Wills

20.43 A retaining lien will not ordinarily extend to the costs debtor's will.[68]

Public records

20.44 A retaining lien will not typically extend to public records, such as court orders.[69]

No personal liability

20.45 The client must be personally liable for the costs debt; where this is not the case, no lien will attach.[70]

20.46 The principles applying to particular lien are different. The property must have been recovered in the litigation in respect of which the solicitor was retained.[71] Recovery by way of negotiation would not suffice.[72] A particular lien may attach to almost any form of property except maintenance payments[73] and real property.[74] In particular, it may extend to an award of costs[75] and to money paid into court as security for costs.[76]

---

[63] *Halvanon Insurance Co Ltd v Central Reinsurance Corpn* [1988] 3 All ER 857 and *Hicks v Wrench* (1821) 6 Madd 93.

[64] *Lloyd v Gough* (1894) 70 LT 725 and *Re Clark ex p Newland* (1876) 4 Ch D 515.

[65] *Re Mid-Kent Fruit Factory* [1896] 1 Ch 567.

[66] *Halvanon Insurance Co Ltd v Central Reinsurance Corporation* [1988] 1 WLR 1122.

[67] *Halvanon Insurance Co Ltd v Central Reinsurance Corporation* [1988] 1 WLR 1122; see also *Knight v Knight* [1925] Ch 835.

[68] *Balch v Symes* (1823) 1 Turn & R 87.

[69] *Bird v Heath* (1848) 6 Hare 236.

[70] *Lightfoot v Keane* (1836) 1 M & W 745.

[71] *Re Sullivan v Pearson ex p Morrison* (1868) LR 4 QB 153.

[72] *Megeurditchian v Lightbound* [1917] 2 KB 298, CA.

[73] *Cross v Cross* (1880) 43 LT 533.

[74] *Shaw v Neale* (1858) 6 HL Cas 581.

[75] *Campbell v Campbell and Lewis* [1941] 1 All ER 274, CA; and see *Pounset v Humphreys* (1837) Coop Pr Cas 142.

[76] *Hall v Hall* [1891] P 302, CA.

Relief from lien

20.47 Difficulties may arise where, in the midst of litigation, the solicitor asserts lien over the client's file of papers. In those circumstances the court may afford the client relief from lien by ordering delivery up of the file. Whether the court would do this will depend on the circumstances. For the purposes of analysis, the following scenarios should be distinguished from each other:

- where the solicitor discharges himself from the retainer (see **20.51–20.57**);
- where the retainer is still extant and where the solicitor continues to act (see **20.58**); and
- where the client has determined the retainer by withdrawing instructions (see **20.59** *et seq*).

The distinction between these three scenarios will usually be a question of fact, but occasionally points of law may arise; these are dealt with at **20.48–20.50**, following which each of the three circumstances mentioned above will be addressed in turn.

Want of payment

20.48 If termination has arisen as a result of the solicitor determining the retainer for want of payment, this would typically be characterised as discharge by the solicitor rather than by the client;[77] this would be so regardless of whether the solicitor's right to interim payments was express or implied.[78]

Dissolution of the solicitor's firm

20.49 Dissolution of a firm would generally amount to determination of the retainer by the solicitor.[79]

Constructive determination

20.50 Discharge by the client as a result of misconduct on the part of the solicitor would ordinarily be capable of amounting to constructive discharge by the solicitor.[80] Although there is no authority on the point, the converse is also probably true (ie that misconduct by the client may amount to constructive determination by him).

Lien where the solicitor discharges himself

20.51 Lord Eldon pithily summed up the fact that a solicitor's rights are restricted:[81]

'A solicitor cannot, by virtue of his lien, prevent the king's subject from obtaining justice.'

20.52 Save in exceptional cases, where a solicitor terminates the retainer during ongoing litigation, the court will make a mandatory order obliging him to deliver up the

---

[77]   *Robins v Goldingham* (1872) LR 13 Eq 440, which was approved in *Gamlen Chemical Co (UK) Ltd v Rochem Ltd* [1980] 1 WLR 614 and *Ismail v Richards Butler (a firm)* [1996] 2 All ER 506; as an earlier example, see *Webster v Le Hunt* (1861) 9 WR 804.

[78]   *Bluck v Lovering & Co* (1886) 35 WR 232.

[79]   *Griffiths v Griffiths* (1843) 2 Hare 587.

[80]   *Hannaford v Hannaford* (1871) 24 LT 86.

[81]   *Commerell v Poynton* (1818) 1 Swan 1 at 2.

client's papers; this would normally be against an undertaking by the new solicitor to preserve the lien of the original solicitor. This practice was described by Templeman LJ:[82]

> '[The] practice of the court ... in order to save the client's litigation from catastrophe, [is to order] the solicitor to hand over the client's papers to the client's new solicitors, provided the new solicitors undertake to preserve the original solicitor's lien and to return the papers to the original solicitor, for what they are worth, after the end of the litigation.'

20.53 Templeman LJ did not suggest a particular form of the mandatory order, but the order made in that case has become the standard form; it includes the following provisions:

- that the new solicitor will hold the documents delivered to him subject to the first solicitor's lien;
- that the new solicitor will allow the original solicitor and his costs draftsman reasonable access to the documents for the purpose of preparing his bill of costs;
- that the new solicitor will progress the litigation in an active manner; and
- that the new solicitor will restore the said documents to the original solicitor upon conclusion of the litigation.

20.54 A mandatory order will not be made in every case, nor will it always be made in the standard form.[83] Roch LJ has commented (obiter) that the court's task is to weigh the principle that a client should not be deprived of material relevant to the conduct of his case and so be 'driven from the judgment seat' against the principle that litigation should be conducted with due regard to the interest of the solicitor. He implied that it was relevant that a solicitor is one of the court's own officers, and that he should not be left without payment of that which is due to him.[84]

20.55 Each case will turn on its own facts. Goff LJ has confirmed that much would depend on the nature of the case, the stage which the litigation has reached, the conduct of the solicitor and of the client, and the 'balance of hardship' which might result from the order the court is asked to make.[85]

20.56 Where the new solicitor accepts the standard obligations, that would ordinarily be the only security to which the old solicitor would be entitled; in exceptional cases, the court may order that further security is also given.[86]

20.57 Where the standard obligations (or any obligations) are accepted by way of an undertaking, the court will lack the vires to relieve the new solicitor of the burden of compliance.[87]

---

[82] *Gamlen Chemical Ltd v Rochem Ltd* [1980] 1 WLR 614 at 624.
[83] *Gamlen Chemical Ltd v Rochem Ltd* [1980] 1 WLR 614 at 625; see also *A v B* [1984] 1 All ER 265.
[84] *Bentley v Gaisford* [1997] QB 627.
[85] *Gamlen Chemical Ltd v Rochem Ltd* [1980] 1 WLR 614 at 625, in which the Court of Appeal approved the speech of Lord Cottenham LC in *Heslop v Metcalfe* (1837) 3 M & C 183 at 190: 'I think the principle should be, that the solicitor claiming the lien, should have every security not inconsistent with the progress of the cause.'
[86] *Ismail v Richards Butler (a firm)* [1996] 2 All ER 506.
[87] *Hughes v Hughes* [1958] P 224.

Lien where the solicitor is still acting

20.58 Where the solicitor continues to act, the issue of lien will be more academic than practical; this is because the client will not feel the effect of the lien as his claim will proceed with the benefit of the papers. Although there is no authority on the point, if the client were to make an application for delivery up, the court would probably treat that as if the client had terminated (or was about to terminate) the retainer.

Lien where the client terminates the retainer

20.59 Where the retainer has been determined by the client, the solicitor will not ordinarily be ordered to deliver up the client's file. Hodson LJ explained the relevant principles:[88]

> 'There is no doubt that a solicitor who is discharged by his client during an action, otherwise than for misconduct, can retain any papers in the cause in his possession until his costs have been paid.'

There are exceptions to this position; there are two mechanisms by which the court may order delivery up (or something very similar to delivery up).

Mechanisms by which delivery up may be ordered

Equitable jurisdiction

20.60 The court has an equitable jurisdiction to order delivery up if, as a matter of conscience, it would be inappropriate for the lien to be enforced.[89]

Rules of court

20.61 CPR, r 25.1(1)(m) provides that the court may make 'an order permitting a party seeking to recover personal property to pay money into court pending the outcome of the proceedings and directing that, if he does so, the property shall be given up to him'. There is a surprising lack of authority on the point, but Hart J has accepted that the jurisdiction does exist to make an order overriding lien.[90]

Case examples concerning delivery up

20.62 Regardless of which jurisdiction applies, the exceptions tend to apply where the rights of third parties would be affected by the lien. Each case will turn on its own facts, but the following are examples.

Documents required for trust managed by the court

20.63 The Court of Appeal in Chancery found that solicitors for the trustees of an estate under the administration of the court should be ordered to produce documents required for the management of the estate.[91]

---

[88] *Hughes v Hughes* [1958] P 224 at 227.
[89] *Slatter v Ronaldsons* [2002] 2 Costs LR 267 at 274.
[90] *Paragon Finance plc v Rosling King* (unreported) 26 May 2000, Ch D.
[91] *Belaney v Ffrench* (1872) 8 Ch 918.

Rights owed by client to third parties

20.64 A solicitor's lien is only available as against his client and persons claiming through him; it does not enable him to refuse production to anyone to whom his client was bound to produce the documents.[92] This is an example of the principle that between the solicitor and third parties the solicitor has no greater right to refuse production of documents on which he has a lien than his client would have if the documents were in his own possession.[93]

Representative claims

20.65 The solicitor may be ordered to deliver up where the property is required for the purposes of a representative claim.[94]

Law Society guidance concerning delivery up

20.66 Regardless of the position de jure, the Law Society has recently gave the following guidance that, whilst no longer part of the prevailing Code of Conduct, is still sage advice:[95]

> 'When you cease acting for a client, you will need to consider what should be done with the paperwork. You must hand over the client's files promptly on request subject to your right to exercise a lien in respect of outstanding costs. You should try to ensure the client's position is not prejudiced, and should also bear in mind his or her rights under the Data Protection Act 1998. Undertakings to secure the costs should be used as an alternative to the exercise of a lien if possible. There may be circumstances where it is unreasonable to exercise a lien, for example, where the amount of the outstanding costs is small and the value or importance of the matter is very great.'

A failure on the part of a solicitor to comply with his professional obligations would not, of itself, ordinarily be grounds for the court exercising its equitable discretion to order delivery up.[96]

Loss of lien

Case examples of loss of lien

20.67 A solicitor may lose his lien in a number of ways. The following are examples (each of which is dealt with in turn): discharge, waiver, parting possession (including, in some circumstances, where this is done for the purposes of preserving property) and, in some circumstances, silence.

Discharge

20.68 First and foremost, lien will be lost upon payment of the costs debt.[97] In practice, this is often the only way in which a client can secure release of papers where he has

---

[92]   *Furlong v Howard* (1804) 2 Sch & Lef 115.
[93]   *In re Hawkes Ackerman v Lockhart* [1898] 2 Ch 1.
[94]   *Simmonds v Great Eastern Rly Co* (1868) 3 Ch App 797 and *Ross v Laughton* (1813) 1 Ves & B 349.
[95]   See para 11 of the guidance to rule 2.01 in the *Solicitors' Code of Conduct 2007*.
[96]   *Slatter v Ronaldsons* [2002] 2 Costs LR 267 at 277.
[97]   *Re Emma Silver Mining Co, Re Turner* (1875) 24 WR 54.

terminated the retainer. The payment must be a full payment; this is because (in the absence of accord and satisfaction) a debt cannot be discharged by payment of a lesser sum.[98] Payment must be made, not merely ordered.[99]

20.69 While it is doubtful that it remains good law, there is ancient authority to the effect that upon discharge, the solicitor must deliver up not only the file, but also the working papers (such as drafts and copies).[100] It is likely that the modern interpretation would be that the working papers belong to the solicitor as his property and that they could be retained.[101]

Waiver (alternative securities)

20.70 A solicitor may lose lien by way of waiver (or, as it sometimes called, 'abandonment'). This can be done expressly or impliedly. One way in which implied waiver can come into existence is by a solicitor taking alternative security for his costs (such as a charge over a client's house) without explaining to the client that he intends to reserve his lien.[102] This is not a rule of law, but an inference to be drawn from the facts, Kay LJ explained:[103]

> 'I take it that the true rule is ... that in every case where you have to consider whether a lien has been waived you must weigh all the circumstances of that particular case ... A solicitor has a duty to perform towards his client to represent to his client all the facts of the case in a clear and intelligible manner and to inform him of his rights and liabilities, and where you find a solicitor dealing with his client and taking from him such a security as was given in this case, not expressly reserving his right of lien ... the inference ought to be against the continuance of the lien.'

20.71 As is explained below, it will not always be the case that taking alternative security will amount to waiver.

Parting possession

20.72 A solicitor may lose lien if he parts with possession of the property,[104] but this will not be true in every circumstance in which possession passes to someone else. In particular, it might not happen:

• where an undertaking is given and the undertaker holds the property to the solicitors account (see **20.80–20.83**);

• where the property is given for the purposes of allowing an arbitrator to make an award;[105]

• where the circumstances show that the lien was being expressly or impliedly reserved;[106] and

---

[98] *Beer v Foakes* (1883) 11 QBD 221.
[99] *Re Aikin's Estate* [1894] 1 IR 225.
[100] *Re Horsfall* (1827) 7 B&C 528.
[101] See, by analogy, *Leicestershire County Council v Michael Faraday & Partners Ltd* [1941] 2 KB 205; see also *Chantrey Martin (a firm) v Martin* [1953] 2 QB 286 and *Wentworth v de Montfort* (1988) 15 NSWLR 348.
[102] See, for example, *In re Taylor, Stileman & Underwood* [1891] 1 Ch 591; see also *In re Galland* (1885) 31 Ch D 296; *Cowell v Simpson* 16 Ves 275; and *In re Douglas Norman & Co* [1898] 1 Ch 199.
[103] *Taylor, Stileman & Underwood* [1891] 1 Ch 591 at 600.
[104] *Re Phoenix Life Assurance Co, Howard and Dollman's Case* (1863) 1 Hem & M 433.
[105] *Whalley v Halley* (1829) 8 LJOSKB 6.
[106] *Watson v Lyon* (1855) 7 de GM & C288.

- where the court has made an order requiring the solicitor to part with the property on the basis that lien is preserved.[107]

Preservation of property

20.73 Where, in order to preserve the property it is necessary to order that it be delivered up, the court may make such an order, but the solicitor's security would ordinarily be preserved by the client being required to make a suitable payment into court[108] (or an escrow account).

Silence when proving the costs debt

20.74 Lien may be lost if the solicitor is silent about it when he proves the costs debt in insolvency proceedings.[109]

Counter-examples concerning loss of lien

20.75 As counter-examples, the following are circumstances in which lien would not ordinarily be lost: writing off bad debts, taking consistent securities, taking specific securities for costs, and the effluxion of time.

Bad debts

20.76 Writing off costs as bad debt would not ordinarily result in a loss of lien; this would be so even if the solicitor's liability for tax had been adjusted accordingly.[110]

Consistent securities

20.77 Where securities other than the lien are taken, but where there is no inconsistency between those securities and the lien, that would not amount to waiver.[111]

Taking security for specific costs

20.78 In a similar vein, where a client gives securities for the purpose of securing payment of particular costs (such as counsel's fees), the lien in general is unaffected.[112]

Limitation

20.79 The fact that the costs debt is statute barred will not result in the loss of retaining lien[113] or particular lien.[114]

---

[107] *Re Till ex p Parsons* (1871) 19 WR 325.
[108] *Richards v Platel* (1841) 10 LJ Ch 375.
[109] *Re Safety Explosives Ltd* [1904] 1 Ch 226.
[110] *Slatter v Ronaldsons* [2002] 2 Costs LR 267.
[111] See the discussion, per Christopher Nugee QC in *Clifford Harris & Co v Solland International Ltd* [2005] EWHC 141 (Ch); and see *Balch v Symes* (1823) 1 Turn & R 87.
[112] *In re John Morris* [1908] 1 KB 473.
[113] *Re Broomhead* (1847) 5 Dow & L 52.
[114] *Higgins v Scott* (1831) 2 B & Ad 413.

Undertakings to hold to order

20.80 Where solicitor A has a retaining lien over documents handed over to solicitor B, solicitor A may specify that the documents be 'held to order' (or 'held to account', which means much the same thing). Where this is so, the legal possession of the documents remains with solicitor A, thus preserving his lien. An undertaking may arise in two ways:

- *Express undertaking*: An express undertaking may be made orally or in writing. Obligations ought to be well thought out, because the court lacks the vires to relieve the solicitor B of the burden of compliance.[115]
- *Implied undertaking*: An implied acceptance of an undertaking may arise if solicitor B retains documents that have been offered conditionally on an undertaking.[116]

20.81 Where an undertaking is given over the client's papers, it may be that there is no express agreement as to the extent to which solicitor B may use and distribute those papers. The value of solicitor A's lien might be substantially negated if solicitor B were to use the papers in a way which advanced the client's claim. If this were to happen, the lien would continue to exist, but its value would be diminished. There is, therefore, a distinction to be drawn between the fact of solicitor A's lien and its value.

20.82 Although Sir Richard Scott V-C dissented, Roch and Henry LJJ have held that the use solicitor B could make of the documents was impliedly limited so as to preserve to solicitor A every security not inconsistent with the progress of the client's litigation. They held that unless it was necessary for the purposes of the litigation, it would be a breach of the undertaking to copy the documents to the client wholesale.[117]

20.83 A breach of an undertaking will not necessarily sound in damages (or other relief). This is because the jurisdiction to order compensation will normally be exercised only where the conduct of the solicitor is inexcusable and such as to merit reproof.[118] That said, the court normally affords undertakings given by solicitors significant weight.

SOLICITORS' CHARGING ORDERS

Under the Solicitors Act 1974, s 73

20.84 A solicitors' charging order will be available where, in course of court proceedings, a solicitor is instrumental in recovering money on behalf of his client; the usual order is that the solicitor will be given a charge over a between-the-parties costs order.

20.85 The relevant statutory provisions are contained in SA 1974, s 73:

'(1) Subject to subsection (2), any court in which a solicitor has been employed to prosecute or defend any suit, matter or proceedings may at any time—

---

[115] *Hughes v Hughes* [1958] P 224.

[116] *Caldwell v Sumpters* [1972] 1 Ch 478.

[117] *Bentley v Gaisford* [1997] QB 627 at 643; Roch LJ effectively adopted the test to be applied when an application is made to the court for release of documents following termination of the retainer by the solicitor: *Heslop v Metcalfe* (1837) 3 M & C 183.

[118] *Udall v Capri Lighting Ltd* [1988] 1 QB 907 at 917, per Balcombe LJ.

(a)   declare the solicitor entitled to a charge on any property recovered or preserved through his instrumentality for his assessed costs in relation to that suit, matter or proceeding; and

(b)   make such orders for the assessment of those costs and for raising money to pay or for paying them out of the property recovered or preserved as the court thinks fit;

and all conveyances and acts done to defeat, or operating to defeat, that charge shall, except in the case of a conveyance to a bona fide purchaser for value without notice, be void as against the solicitor.

(2)   No order shall be made under subsection (1) if the right to recover the costs is barred by any statute of limitations.'

20.86 '*Any Court*': 'Any court' means any civil court.[119] Thus, money recovered by other means (such as by being recovered by the police as a result of a criminal investigation) would not be chargeable.[120] The phrase 'any court' is not intended to distinguish between levels of judge; a judge is not limited to dealing only with proceedings and costs in his own court.[121]

20.87 '*Been employed*': The phrase 'been employed' does not mean that the solicitors' retainer has to have been with the person against whom the charge is sought (although this will usually be the case).[122] The words 'shall be employed' are not used in the future tense. The use is conditional; they do not tie the employment down to any particular time.[123]

20.88 '*Property*': 'Property' includes both real and personal property.[124] That word is to be construed widely and to encompass choses in action; this may include an order for costs where no assessment has yet taken place.[125]

20.89 '*Recovered or preserved*': It is a statutory prerequisite to making a charging order that property is 'recovered or preserved'.[126] The following are examples where this was found to be so:

•   where a sum of money is recovered for costs (but not by compromise);[127]
•   where a sum of money is recovered for costs with no other monies being recovered;[128]
•   where a sum of money is recovered for damages;[129] and
•   where a beneficial interest is obtained in real property held under a trust for sale.[130]

---

[119]   *Re Humphreys ex p Lloyd-George and George* [1898] 1 QB 520, CA at 525.
[120]   *Re Humphreys* [1898] 1 QB 520.
[121]   *Re Deakin* [1900] 2 QB 489 and *Mastercigars Direct Ltd v Withers LLP* [2007] EWHC 2733 (Ch) at [137].
[122]   *Bonser v Bradshaw* (1860) 30 LJ Ch 159, in which the retainer was with a litigation friend but the order was sought against a person who, when the retainer was made, was a child.
[123]   *Colver v Adams* (1881) 6 QBD 622, per Grove J.
[124]   *Redfern & Son v Rosenthall Bros* (1902) 86 LT 855, CA.
[125]   *Fairfold Properties Ltd v Exmouth Docks Co Ltd (No 2)* [1993] Ch 196.
[126]   *Re Blake, Clutterbuck v Bradford* [1945] Ch 61.
[127]   *Campbell v Lewis* [1941] 1 All ER 274; see also *Al-Abbas v As-Dabbagh* [2002] EWCA Civ 1962.
[128]   *Re Blake, Clutterbuck v Bradford* [1945] 1 Ch 61.
[129]   *Marie Gartz (No 2)* [1920] 1 P 460.
[130]   *National Westminster Bank Ltd v Stockman* [1981] 1 WLR 67.

20.90 In contrast, the following are examples where it was found that monies were not recovered or preserved:[131]

- where money has been paid into court as security for costs of proceedings which were later abandoned;[132]
- where an administration order had been made but not executed;[133]
- where a costs order was made by compromise;[134] and
- where money was paid into court with a denial of liability but the client proceeded with the claim and recovered a smaller sum.[135]

20.91 Property may be preserved even though the value of it diminishes while under the solicitor's control; this would be so even if the property yielded little or nothing for the client.[136] The fact that a fund had been lodged prior to a solicitor being retained would not preclude the solicitor preserving the fund.[137] The fact that a fund has been diminished by way of a collusive compromise will not preclude the solicitor taking a charge.[138] Money paid into court as security for costs would not be property which had been recovered or preserved.[139]

20.92 As to the exercise of the court's discretion, a solicitor must make out a prima facie case that without the charging order he will not obtain his costs.[140] Where the solicitor makes out this prima facie case, the court will generally make the order unless there is reason for not doing so.[141] The court will take the interests of the client into account. This may be reflected in the form that the order takes.[142]

20.93 The solicitor's conduct is relevant to the exercise of the court's discretion: it may decline to make the order if the solicitor's conduct or inactivity would make it unjust that the interest of other parties should come second to his interests.[143]

Miscellaneous points concerning solicitors' charging orders

20.94 The following miscellaneous points can be made.

Waiver (inconsistent securities)

20.95 The right to a charging order may be lost if the solicitor seeks a remedy which is inconsistent with the continuance of the charging order. This may happen, for example, if a solicitor seeks and accepts security for costs.[144]

---

[131] For a full treatment of this issue, see *Halsbury Law of England*, vol 44(1), para 264, from which these examples are taken.
[132] *The Dirigo* [1920] P 425.
[133] *Pinkerton v Easton* (1873) LR 16 Eq 490.
[134] *Al-Abbas v As-Dabbagh* [2002] EWCA Civ 1962 at [25].
[135] *Westacott v Bevan* [1891] 1 QB 774, DC.
[136] *Re Turner* [1907] 2 Ch 126; see also *White v Hyde* [1933] P 105.
[137] *Wimbourne v Fine* [1952] 2 All ER 681.
[138] *Twynam v Porter* (1870) LR 11 Eq 181; see also *Moxon v Sheppard* (1890) 24 QBD 627.
[139] *Rhodes v Sugden* (1885) 29 Ch D 517.
[140] *Harrison v Harrison* (1888) 13 PD 180, CA at 184.
[141] *Dallow v Garrold ex p Adams* (1884) 13 QBD 543.
[142] *Jackson v Smith ex p Digby* (1884) 53 LJ Ch 972 at 975.
[143] *Higgs v Higgs* [1934] 1 P 95.
[144] *Groom v Cheesewright* (1885) 1 Ch 730.

No mandatory need for an assessment

20.96   Notwithstanding the use of the phrase 'assessed costs' in SA 1974, s 73(1)(a), there is no need for the court to order that there is a solicitor and client assessment of costs.[145]

No need to wait until the expiry of one month

20.97   Morgan J has clarified that the bar against commencing proceedings within one month of delivery of a bill does not apply to an application for a charging order.[146]

Set-off

20.98   Where a party seeks set-off which would diminish or negative the value of a solicitor's charging order, the court should bear the solicitor's position in mind. The protectable interest conferred by statute should be upheld unless there are good reasons to the contrary. This would be the case notwithstanding the fact that an order for set-off would not prejudice the party for whom the solicitors were acting: that factor is irrelevant.[147]

Child clients

20.99   A charging order may be obtained even where the work was done on behalf of a child.[148]

Assignment

20.100   An assignee of a solicitor's right to costs may apply for a charging order.[149]

Notice by way of injunction

20.101   Whilst technically it has more to do with particular lien than charging orders, the court seems to retain an ancient jurisdiction to make an injunction restraining the client from receiving payment in the litigation without giving notice to the solicitor.[150]

Procedure relating to solicitors' charging orders

20.102   Unless there are already existing proceedings, the application is made by way of a CPR, Part 8 claim.[151]

20.103   A costs judge has the jurisdiction to hear an application for a charging order.[152]

---

[145]   *Fairfold Properties Ltd v Exmouth Docks Co Ltd (No 2)* [1993] Ch 196.
[146]   *Mastercigars Direct Ltd v Withers LLP* [2007] EWHC 2733 (Ch) at [144]–[146].
[147]   *Rohm & Haas Co v Colllag Ltd* (2002) IPD 25007.
[148]   *Baile v Baile* (1872) LR 13 Eq 497; see *Greer v Young* (1881–85) All ER Rep 513 and *Bonser v Bradshaw* (1860) 25 JP 483.
[149]   *Briscoe v Briscoe* [1892] 3 Ch 543.
[150]   *Hobson v Shearwood* (1845) 8 Beav 486.
[151]   CPR, r 67.3(2).
[152]   *Mastercigars Direct Ltd v Withers LLP* [2007] EWHC 2733 (Ch) at [139].

20.104 A costs judge sitting in the Senior Courts Costs Office will have jurisdiction to hear an application notwithstanding the fact that he has not heard the proceedings in respect of which the solicitors were instructed.[153] The High Court may make an order in respect of arbitral proceedings.[154] The power to make an order is capable of being delegated to a registrar in bankruptcy.[155]

Charing orders under Charging Orders Act 1979

20.105 Where a solicitor obtains judgment against a former client for his costs, he may ask the court to make a charging order in respect of those monies.[156] The details of this subject are beyond the scope of this work. What may be relevant, however, is the fact that the court lacks vires to make a charging order absolute where the sums claimed are unassessed costs.[157]

SOLICITORS' SECURITY FOR COSTS

20.106 While it will be of value only where its use is contemplated before the work is done, SA 1974, s 65(1) makes provision for security to be taken for the solicitor's fees for contentious work:

> '(1) A solicitor may take security from his client for his costs, to be ascertained by assessment or otherwise, in respect of any contentious business to be done by him.'

20.107 Article 4 of the Solicitors' (Non-Contentious Business) Remuneration Order 2009 (SI 2009/1931) makes a similar provision for security in non-contentious business:

> '(3) A solicitor may take from his client security for the payment of any costs, including the amount of any interest to which the solicitor may become entitled under article 14 [of that Order].'

20.108 Solicitors considering taking security for costs should consider the following guidance given by the SRA:[158]

> 'Whilst you are entitled to take security for costs you should be aware of the risk of the court finding undue influence. Before you do take a charge over a client's property it is advisable, therefore, to suggest the client consider seeking independent legal advice. Such advice would not normally be essential unless the terms of the proposed charge are particularly onerous or would give you some unusual benefit or profit. It is, however, important always to ensure that the client understands that a charge is being taken and the effect of such a charge.'

This advice was given under the Solicitors' Code of Conduct 2007 (which have been replaced by the SRA Code of Conduct 2011), but there is no reason to believe that the general thrust of what was said no longer applies.

---

153 *Mastercigars Direct Ltd v Withers LLP* [2007] EWHC 2733 (Ch) at [137]–[139], drawing on CPR, rr 67.1(1)(b) and 67.3(3); PD 67, paras 2.1(2) and 3.2.
154 Arbitration Act 1996, s 44.
155 *Re Wood ex p Fanshawe* [1897] 1 QB 314.
156 Charging Orders Act 1979, s 1(1).
157 *Monte Developments Ltd (In Administration) of Court Management Consultants Ltd* [2010] EWHC 3071 (Ch).
158 *Solicitors Code of Conduct 2007*, guidance to rule 3, 'Conflict of interests', para 43.

20.109   If a first legal charge is to be obtained over a client's property, care should be taken to ensure that the solicitor does not inadvertently enter into a regulated mortgage contract as a lender. Standard textbooks on financial regulation should be consulted on this matter.

20.110   An agreement for security which is not an agreement as to the amount or method of payment does not need to comply with the formalities relating to contentious and non-contentious business agreements.[159]

20.111   Obtaining security for costs can, in certain circumstances, result in loss of lien (see **20.70**). This will be particularly likely if there is no express reservation of lien.

---

[159]   *In re an undertaking by Wingfields, Halse and Trustram, Jonesco v Evening Standard Company* [1932] 2 KB 340.

Part IV

THE PRACTICE OF COSTS (BETWEEN THE PARTIES)

Chapter 21

DETAILED ASSESSMENTS BETWEEN OPPOSING PARTIES

21.1 This chapter describes the procedural aspects of costs litigation between opposing parties. It begins with a summary of the assessment process, that summary being cross-referenced to the more detailed analysis which follows. The detailed analysis broadly follows the structure of CPR, Part 47.

SUMMARY OF THE ASSESSMENT PROCESS

21.2 A detailed assessment is a judicial process by which costs are quantified. The following summary applies to an assessment of costs payable between the parties. It does not apply where costs are payable out of a fund (such as the LSC fund) or where costs are payable on a solicitor and client basis.

Summary: commencement

21.3 As a general rule, detailed assessment proceedings may be commenced no earlier than the conclusion of the proceedings to which the costs relate (see **21.41**).[1] If they are to be commenced earlier than this, the receiving party will need to obtain an order colloquially known as a 'forthwith order' (see **21.42–21.53**).

21.4 Proceedings are commenced by the receiving party serving a notice of commencement and a copy bill of costs on the other parties (see below).[2] Unlike most other types of civil proceedings, there is no involvement of the court at the stage of commencement: this is because the relevant documents are merely served rather than lodged at, or issued by, the court.

21.5 Certain documents should accompany the notice of commencement, one of which is a statement giving the name and address of any person upon whom the receiving party intends to serve the notice of commencement. The CPD provides that, unless the bill of costs is in respect of additional liability only, it must also be accompanied by copies of fee notes and disbursements vouchers (see **21.40**).[3]

21.6 Where additional liabilities are claimed, 'relevant details' must also be served,[4] which means that in essence the receiving party must identify all the costs upon which a success fee will be claimed, together with the reasons for claiming the success fee at the

---

[1] See CPR, r 47.1.
[2] See CPR, r 47.6.
[3] See CPD, art 32.3.
[4] The requisite details are listed at CPD, art 32.5.

level sought (see **30.92**);[5] where an ATE premium is claimed, a copy of the insurance certificate should also be served (see **30.141**). Corresponding provisions apply where a notional premium is sought (see **30.227**).[6]

21.7 Time limits apply; broadly speaking, proceedings must be commenced within 3 months of the entitlement to costs arising (see **21.54**). In particular, where the entitlement to costs is as a result of a judgment, order or direction, the detailed assessment proceedings should be commenced within 3 months of that judgment, order or direction being made.[7] Similar provisions apply to deemed costs orders (such as those that arise upon discontinuance, acceptance of a Part 36 offer, etc).

21.8 It is often the case that detailed assessment proceedings are not commenced within the stipulated time limits, especially if the bill of costs is for a large sum. The parties may agree that an extension of time should be granted or the court may grant one (see **21.57–21.60**). Permission is not required to commence detailed assessment proceedings out of time,[8] but adverse consequences may follow tardy commencement (see **21.82–21.89**).

21.9 Occasionally, a detailed assessment may stall (or, more accurately, never get off the ground) in the sense that the receiving party fails entirely to serve notice of commencement. Where this is so, the paying party may apply for an unless order (see **21.81–21.89**).

Summary: disputing the costs

21.10 If the paying party wishes to dispute the costs which are claimed, he should serve points of dispute on the receiving party (see **21.102–21.113**).[9]

21.11 Points of dispute should be short and to the point.[10] They should identify each item in the bill of costs which is disputed, and in each case they should state concisely the nature and grounds of dispute. Where practicable, the paying party should make offers for the disputed items (see **21.90–21.100**). The points of dispute should be signed by the paying party or by his solicitors.[11] They may include Part 18 requests about the costs which are claimed (see **21.98–21.99**).[12]

21.12 With one or two exceptions, the period for serving points of dispute is 21 days after service of the notice of commencement (see **21.103**).[13] This period may be extended by consent[14] or by order of the court (see **21.106**).[15]

21.13 If a party serves points of dispute after the requisite period, he may not be heard further in the detailed assessment proceedings unless the court gives permission (see

---

5   CPD, art 32.5(1).
6   CPD, art 32.5(2).
7   CPR, r 47.7.
8   CPD, art 33.4.
9   CPR, r 47.9.
10 CPD, art 35.2.
11 CPD, art 35.3.
12 CPD, art 35.7.
13 CPR, r 47.9(2).
14 CPD, art 33.1.
15 CPD, art 33.2.

21.102).[16] If the period of time for serving points of dispute has expired and if points of dispute have not been served, then the receiving party may file a request for a default costs certificate (see **21.114–21.118**).[17] Default costs certificates can be set aside (see **21.119–21.129**), and very often are.

21.14 If points of dispute are served, the receiving party is at liberty to serve replies (or 'replies to the point of dispute', as they are sometimes known);[18] the CPR state that the receiving party may do so within 21 days after service on him of the points of dispute,[19] but in practice there is no sanction for the late service of replies (see **21.142–21.143**). Replies are optional. They must be signed by the party serving them, or by his solicitor.[20]

Summary: requesting a hearing

21.15 Where points of dispute are served and where the matter has not settled, the receiving party should file a request for a detailed assessment hearing. He must file a request within 3 months of the expiry of the period for commencing assessment proceedings (see **21.193**).[21] The request must be accompanied by a number of documents (see **21.199–21.203**), which include those which were served along with the notice of commencement together with the points of dispute, the replies (if any), relevant orders (if any) and documentation relating to the receiving party's retainer.[22]

21.16 Where a receiving party fails to file such a request within the stipulated time, the paying party may apply to the court for an unless order (see **21.208**).[23] Upon receipt of such an application the court may order that, unless the receiving party requests a detailed assessment hearing within a time specified by the court, all or part of the costs to which the receiving party would otherwise be entitled will be disallowed.[24]

21.17 Once the request for a detailed assessment hearing has been made, the court is at liberty to issue an interim costs certificate for such a sum as it considers appropriate; that certificate may be amended or cancelled at any time (see **21.284–21.287**). The court may also order the costs certified in the interim certificate to be paid into court.[25]

21.18 Once that stage has been reached many, but not all, county courts will direct the parties to meet and to confer in an attempt to narrow the issues.[26] If the court makes such an order it would usually be made of the court's own initiative, and will include a provision for the parties to be heard upon that point, if they so wish.[27] In some courts (Leeds, York and Scarborough County Courts), where the base costs are £25,000 or less and where the assessment proceedings started on or after 1 October 2010, the costs may

---

[16] CPR, r 47.9(3).
[17] CPR, r 47.9(4).
[18] CPR, r 47.13(1).
[19] CPR, r 47(2).
[20] CPD, art 39.1(3).
[21] CPR, r 47.14(1) and (2).
[22] CPD, art 40.2; there are further requirements for bills of costs in respect of LSC funded clients: see CPD, art 40.2(l).
[23] CPR, r 47.14(3).
[24] CPR, r 47.14(4).
[25] CPR, r 47.15.
[26] This practice originated in or around Manchester and is often called 'the Manchester Direction'.
[27] CPR, r 3.3(5).

be provisionally assessed under a pilot scheme running in those courts.[28] That scheme is due to end on 30 September 2012, but it is likely to be extended thereafter.

Summary: preparing for the hearing

21.19 The CPD provides that unless the court directs otherwise the receiving party must file the papers in support of the bill of costs not less than 7 days before the date for the detailed assessment hearing and not more than 14 days before that date (see **21.215**).[29]

21.20 The following provisions apply in respect of the papers to be filed in support of the bill of costs (see **21.199–21.203**):[30]

'(a)   If the claim is for costs only without any additional liability, the papers to be filed, and the order in which they are to be arranged are as follows:

(i)   instructions and briefs to counsel arranged in chronological order together with all advices, opinions and drafts received and response to such instructions;

(ii)   reports and opinions of medical and other experts;

(iii)   any other relevant papers;

(iv)   a full set of any relevant pleadings to the extent that they have not already been filed in court; and

(v)   correspondence, files and attendance notes.

(b)   Where the claim is in respect of an additional liability only, such of the papers listed at (a) above, as are relevant to the issues raised by the claim for additional liability;

(c)   Where the claim is for both base costs and an additional liability, the papers listed at (a) above, together with any papers relevant to the issues raised by the claim for additional liability.'

Summary: the hearing

21.21 The detailed assessment hearing will usually take place before a costs judge, a district judge, or an authorised court officer (see **21.70–21.81**).

21.22 Hearings originating from claims in county courts in London will usually be transferred automatically to the SCCO (see **21.64**); other assessments may be transferred to the SCCO, either at the request of the parties, or upon the order of the court. It is not unusual for costs judges or costs officers to travel to sit in venues outside London, but the need for this has declined over recent years because of the existence of regional costs judges (see **21.74–21.76**).

21.23 Assessments will be allocated to an authorised court officer only if the hearing is in the SCCO and the sums claimed are less than £75,000 (see **21.77–21.81**). The parties may agree that the assessment should not be heard by an authorised court officer.[31] If there is disagreement between the parties on this point, an application may be made to the court for directions.[32]

---

[28]   See Practice Direction 51E – County Court Provisional Assessment Pilot Scheme.
[29]   CPD, art 40.11.
[30]   CPD, art 40.12.
[31]   CPD, art 30.1(3).
[32]   CPD, art 30.1(4).

21.24 Hearings are in public. Unless the court orders otherwise, no one but the parties will be heard on the detailed assessment (see **21.217**).[33]

21.25 The court will usually rule on each of the points of dispute item by item (see **21.218–21.219**). Unless the court gives permission, only those items specified in the points of dispute may be raised at the hearing.[34]

21.26 The court may direct the receiving party to produce any document which in its opinion is necessary to enable it to reach its decision. Any such document will in the first instance be produced to the court, but the court may ask the receiving party to elect whether to disclose that document to the paying party, or whether to decline disclosure and instead to rely on other evidence.[35] This process is known as election, and is discussed in detail at **24.26–24.62**.

21.27 The bill of costs, points of dispute and replies may be varied (see **21.101**); if a party wishes to do this, then the amended or supplementary document must be filed with the court, and copies of it must be served on all other relevant parties.[36] Permission is not required, but the court may disallow the variation or permit it only upon conditions, including conditions as to the payment of any costs caused or wasted by the variation.[37]

Summary: the costs of the assessment

21.28 There is a presumption that the receiving party is entitled to his costs of the detailed assessment unless the court makes some other order (see **21.232**).[38] The most common situation in which the court will make some other order is where a paying party has made a Part 47 offer (which is akin to a Part 36 offer in substantive litigation) and the paying party has achieved a result which is more advantageous to him than the terms of that offer (see **21.247–21.261**).[39] Where an offer has been made, the fact of the offer must not be communicated to the court until the question of costs of the detailed assessment proceedings falls to be decided.[40]

21.29 The court must have regard to the following when deciding the incidence of the costs of the assessment (ie when deciding whether to make some other order):[41]

- the conduct of all the parties;
- the amount, if any, by which the bill of costs has been reduced; and
- whether it was reasonable for a party to claim the costs of a particular item or to dispute that item.

---

[33] CPR, r 47.14(6).
[34] CPR, r 47.14(7).
[35] CPD, art 40.14.
[36] CPD, art 40.10(1).
[37] CPD, art 40.10(2).
[38] CPR, r 47.18.
[39] CPR, r 47.19(1)(b).
[40] CPR, r 47.19(2).
[41] CPR, r 47.18(2).

Summary: after the hearing

21.30 Once the detailed assessment hearing has ended, it is the responsibility of the receiving party or his lawyers to remove the papers from court.[42] The bill of costs must then be completed (ie calculations must be entered to show the amount due following the detailed assessment of the costs) (see **21.289–21.303**).[43] The court will issue a final costs certificate in the assessed amount.[44]

21.31 If a party is dissatisfied with the outcome of an assessment, he may seek to appeal (see Chapter 23). Where the assessment has been heard by an authorised court officer, no permission is required and the appeal will proceed by way of rehearing before a costs judge (see **23.2**).[45] In all other circumstances, permission will be required and the appeal will be by way of review.

Summary: settled proceedings and discontinued proceedings

21.32 If costs are agreed, then either party may apply for a costs certificate in the agreed amount (see **21.131**).[46] Where there is a dispute as to whether there has been an agreement, an application may be made to the court for a determination of the issue (see **21.139–21.140**).[47] If a detailed assessment settles after a request for a detailed assessment hearing has been made, the receiving party must inform the court immediately, preferably by fax.[48]

21.33 It is possible for a receiving party to discontinue the detailed assessment proceedings in accordance with CPR, Part 38 (see **21.304–21.309**).[49] If a detailed assessment hearing has already been requested, the court's permission is required.[50] However, a bill of costs may be withdrawn by consent regardless of whether a detailed assessment hearing has been requested.

FORM AND CONTENT OF THE BILL OF COSTS

21.34 The form and content of a bill of costs is governed by Section 4 of the CPD, art 4.1 of which reads as follows:

'4.1 A bill of costs may consist of such of the following sections as may be appropriate:

(1)   title page;
(2)   background information;
(3)   items of costs claimed under the headings specified in paragraph 4.6;
(4)   summary showing the total costs claimed on each page of the bill;
(5)   schedules of time spent on non-routine attendances; and
(6)   the certificates referred to in paragraph 4.15.'

---

[42]   CPD, art 40.16.
[43]   CPR, r 47.16(1).
[44]   CPR, r 47.16(3).
[45]   CPR, rr 47.20 and 47.23.
[46]   CPR, r 47.10; the application is made pursuant to r 40.6.
[47]   CPD, art 36.2.
[48]   CPD, art 40.9(2).
[49]   CPD, art 36.5(1).
[50]   CPD, art 36.5(3).

In practice, bills of costs are generally drafted in the following design (or something very like it):

- Title page (**21.35**);
- Background information (**21.35**) and rates (see **28.31–28.35**);
- Statement of reasons for setting the success fee at the level claimed (see **30.98**);
- Chronological entries (**21.35**), which will include attendances such as court hearings, consultations and conferences;
- Attendances on the receiving party (**21.37** and **29.42–29.44**);
- Attendances on the paying party and/or any other party (**21.37**);
- Attendances on witnesses (including expert witnesses) (**21.37**);
- Attendances on and by agents (**21.37** and **12.6–12.7**);
- Attendances on others;
- Non-chronological attendances on the court (**21.37** and **29.47**);
- Non-chronological attendances on counsel (**21.37** and **29.46**);
- Documentary work (which is usually a summary of the time claimed in a schedule) (**21.37** and **29.60–29.73**);
- Success fees (**21.39**) and ATE premiums;
- Costs of preparing and cheeking the bill of costs (**21.39**);
- Summary of costs claimed (**21.35**);
- Certificates (**21.35**); and
- Schedules (**21.35**).

The anatomy of a bill of costs can be dissected in the following way (where each items is a component of the last): (i) the bill of costs as a whole; (ii) the parts of the bill of costs; (iii) the heads of costs; and (iv) items and entries.

The bill of costs as a whole

21.35 The following points can be made about the overall structure of bill of costs:

- **Title page:** The title page must set out the following:[51](1) the full title of the proceedings; (2) the name of the party whose bill of costs it is and a description of the document granting the right to an assessment;[52] (3) the VAT number of the

---

[51] See CPD art 4.4.
[52] These are defined at CPD art 40.4 in the following way:
   'The document giving the right to detailed assessment' means such one or more of the following documents as are appropriate to the detailed assessment proceedings:
   (a) a copy of the judgment or order of the court giving the right to detailed assessment;
   (b) a copy of the notice served under rule 3.7 (sanctions for non-payment of certain fees) where a claim is struck out under that rule;
   (c) a copy of the notice of acceptance where an offer to settle is accepted under Part 36 (Offers to settle);
   (d) a copy of the notice of discontinuance in a case which is discontinued under Part 38 (Discontinuance);
   (e) a copy of the award made on an arbitration under any Act or pursuant to an agreement, where no court has made an order for the enforcement of the award;
   (f) a copy of the order, award or determination of a statutorily constituted tribunal or body;
   (g) in a case under the Sheriffs Act 1887, the sheriff's bill of fees and charges, unless a court order giving the right to detailed assessment has been made;
   (h) a notice of revocation or discharge under Regulation 82 of the Civil Legal Aid (General) Regulations 1989.
   (j) In the county courts certain Acts and Regulations provide for costs incurred in proceedings under those Acts and Regulations to be assessed in the county court if so ordered on application. Where such an application is made, a copy of the order.'

legal representative or other person in respect of whom VAT is claimed; and (4) details of all relevant legal aid certificates, LSC certificates and relevant amendment certificates.

- **Background information:** Background information is often referred to as 'the narrative' (which must be distinguished from 'the narrative column': see below). It should contain the following:[53] (1) a brief description of the proceedings up to the date of the notice of commencement; (2) a statement of the status of the solicitor or solicitor's employee in respect of whom costs are claimed[54] and (if those costs are calculated on the basis of hourly rates) the hourly rates claimed for each such person, and (3) a brief explanation of any agreement or arrangement between the receiving party and his solicitors which affects the costs claimed in the bill.

- **Chronological entries:** This is part of the bill is often referred to as 'the chronology'. It is made up of items such as the court fees, conferences, court hearings, etc. It should include items which will assist the court even though they bear no charge (so called 'non-chargeable items'); this would include orders and other major chronological landmarks.[55]

- **Columns:** The numbered items of cost may be (and in practice always are) set out on paper divided into columns.[56] The column on the extreme left is the 'narrative column' (ie that column in which the items are described).[57] The remaining columns are the 'arithmetic columns' (ie those columns that contain the amounts claimed).[58] There are three columnar formats in ordinary usage,[59] but the first is by far the most common. They are:

  — *A three-column format:*[60] in this format profit costs are claimed in the left arithmetic column, disbursements in the middle, and VAT in the right column;

  — *A four-column format:* in this format the two leftmost arithmetic columns contain profit costs and disbursements in one column and VAT in the other, and the two rightmost arithmetic columns are left blank for a record the amounts allowed; and

  — *A six-column format:* this may either be an expanded version of the four-column format (ie, with profit costs and disbursements each occupying one column each) or it may be a version in which on set of arithmetic columns relates to claims against the paying party and the other relates to claims against the LSC (see **21.203**).

Details of legal aid bills are set out in the footnotes.[61]

---

[53] See CPD art 4.5.

[54] Other than guidance as to the use of the term 'legal executive' (see **28.32**) the CPD does not prescribe the way in which the status of the fee earners should be described; that said, it is almost universally the case this is done by reference to Grades A to D (see **28.31–28.35**).

[55] In this regard, CPD art 4.10 provides as follows:
'4.10 In each part of the bill of costs which claims items under head (1) (attendances on court and counsel) a note should be made of:
(1) all relevant events, including events which do not constitute chargeable items;
(2) any orders for costs which the court made (whether or not a claim is made in respect of those costs in this bill of costs).'

[56] See CPD art 4.11.

[57] See CPD art 4.17 for a usage of this phrase.

[58] Ibid.

[59] Precedents A, B, C and D in the Schedule of Costs Precedents annexed to the CPD illustrate various model forms of bills of costs; all three types are illustrated there.

[60] The narrative column is disregarded when describing a bill by reference to the number of columns it contains.

[61] It is not mandatory that a six-column bill of costs is used in circumstances where costs are claimed against a paying party and the LSC; in this regard CPD art 4.3 provides as follows: 'Where a party claims costs against another party and also claims costs against the LSC only for work done in the same period, the costs

- **Summary:** At the end of the bill of costs there must be a summary that summarises the total costs claimed. The summary must show the total profit costs and disbursements claimed separately from the total VAT claimed.[62] Where the bill of costs is divided into parts, the summary must also give totals for each part. If each page of the bill gives a page total, the summary must also set out the page totals for each page;[63] it is not, however, mandatory that pages have page summaries.

- **Certificates:** The bill of costs must contain signed[64] 'appropriate certificates';[65] this will always including the following:
  - — certificate as to accuracy and as to the indemnity principle;[66] and
  - — certificate as to interest and payments.[67]

  Where appropriate, the certificates will usually include the following:
  - — certificate in respect of disbursements not exceeding £500;[68] and
  - — certificate as to recovery of VAT.[69]

  In addition, there may be a certificate in accordance with CPD art 20.6 (where a legal representative wishes to claim a higher success fee from his client that is recovered from the paying party).[70] Further provisions apply where the receiving party was publically funded.[71]

- **Schedules:** If the number of attendances and communications (other than routine communications) in any one head of costs is twenty or more, the claim for the costs of those items in that section of the bill of costs should be for the total only and should refer to a schedule in which the full record of dates and details is set out.[72] On a strict reading of the CPD this does not include attendances on court or counsel (presumably because the CPD envisages that most of these items will be in the chronology). If the bill of costs contains more than one schedule each schedule should be numbered consecutively.[73]

---

claimed against the LSC only can be claimed either in a separate part of the bill or in additional columns in the same part of the bill. Precedents C and D in the Schedule of Costs Precedents annexed to this Practice Direction show how bills should be drafted when costs are claimed against the LSC only.' CPD art 49.5 provides as follows: 'If the bill of costs contains additional columns setting out costs claimed against the LSC only, the schedule may be set out in a separate document or, alternatively, may be included in the additional columns of the bill.' Finally, CPD art 4.17(2) provides as follows: 'Where a claim is made against the LSC only and includes enhancement and where a claim is made in family proceedings and includes a claim for uplift or general care and conduct, the amount of enhancement uplift and general care and conduct must be shown, in respect of each item upon which it is claimed, as a separate amount either in the appropriate arithmetic column or in the narrative column. (For an example, see Precedent C.)'

[62] See CPD art 4.14.
[63] See CPD art 4.14.
[64] As to who should sign, see **29.117**.
[65] See CPD art 4.15.
[66] See precedent (1) in Schedule F in the Schedule of Costs Precedents annexed to the CPD.
[67] See precedent (2) in Schedule F.
[68] See precedent (5) in Schedule F.
[69] See precedent (6) in Schedule F.
[70] See **21.202**. A precedent can be found in Chapter 44.
[71] In all cases in which the client is publicly funded, the certificates must include the following a certificate as to interest of assisted person/LSC funded client pursuant to reg 119 of the Civil Legal Aid (General) Regulations 1989; where appropriate, it will also contain consent to the signing of the certificate within 21 days of detailed assessment pursuant to regs 112 and 121 of the Civil Legal Aid (General) Regulations 1989. See precedents (3) and (4) in Schedule F.
[72] See CPD art 4.12.
[73] See CPD art 4.12.

Division of the bill of costs into parts

21.36 The CPD gives guidance as to when a bill of costs ought to be divided into parts. That guidance reads as follows:

> '4.2 Where it is necessary or convenient to do so, a bill of costs may be divided into two or more parts, each part containing sections (2), (3) and (4) above. Circumstances in which it will be necessary or convenient to divide a bill into parts include:
>
> (1) Where the receiving party acted in person during the course of the proceedings (whether or not that party also had a legal representative at that time) the bill must be divided into different parts so as to distinguish between;
>
> > (a)   the costs claimed for work done by the legal representative; and
> > (b)   the costs claimed for work done by the receiving party in person.
>
> (1A) Where the receiving party had pro bono representation for part of the proceedings and an order under section 194(3) of the Legal Services Act 2007 has been made, the bill must be divided into different parts so as to distinguish between:
>
> > (a)   the sum equivalent to the costs claimed for work done by the legal representative acting free of charge; and
> > (b)   the costs claimed for work done by the legal representative not acting free of charge.
>
> (2) Where the receiving party was represented by different solicitors during the course of the proceedings, the bill must be divided into different parts so as to distinguish between the costs payable in respect of each solicitor.
>
> (3) Where the receiving party obtained legal aid or LSC funding in respect of all or part of the proceedings the bill must be divided into separate parts so as to distinguish between;
>
> > (a)   costs claimed before legal aid or LSC funding was granted;
> > (b)   costs claimed after legal aid or LSC funding was granted; and
> > (c)   any costs claimed after legal aid or LSC funding ceased.
>
> (4) Where value added tax (VAT) is claimed and there was a change in the rate of VAT during the course of the proceedings, the bill must be divided into separate parts so as to distinguish between;
>
> > (a)   costs claimed at the old rate of VAT; and
> > (b)   costs claimed at the new rate of VAT.
>
> (5) Where the bill covers costs payable under an order or orders under which there are different paying parties the bill must be divided into parts so as to deal separately with the costs payable by each paying party.
>
> (6) Where the bill covers costs payable under an order or orders, in respect of which the receiving party wishes to claim interest from different dates, the bill must be divided to enable such interest to be calculated.'

Each part of a bill of costs is usually ended by way of a summary of the costs claimed; each such summary will then itself be summarised in the grand summary at the end of the bill of costs.[74]

Heads of costs

21.37 The following heads of costs are defined at CPD art 4.6:

---

[74]   See CPD art 4.14.

'4.6 The bill of costs may consist of items under such of the following heads as may be appropriate:

(1) attendances on the court and counsel up to the date of the notice of commencement;

(2) attendances on and communications with the receiving party;

(3) attendances on and communications with witnesses including any expert witness;

(4) attendances to inspect any property or place for the purposes of the proceedings;

(5) attendances on and communications with other persons, including offices of public records;

(6) communications with the court and with counsel;

(7) work done on documents: preparing and considering documentation, including documentation necessary to comply with Practice Direction (Pre-Action Conduct) or any relevant pre-action protocols where appropriate, work done in connection with arithmetical calculations of compensation and/or interest and time spent collating documents;

(8) work done in connection with negotiations with a view to settlement if not already covered in the heads listed above;

(9) attendances on and communications with London and other agents and work done by them;

(10) other work done which was of or incidental to the proceedings and which is not already covered in the heads listed above.'

Where appropriate, agency charges will form part of the principal solicitor's charges (see **12.2** *et seq*). Where these charges relate to attendances at court and on counsel, they must be included in chronological order under the relevant head. Otherwise they must be included as a separate head under 'attendances on London and other agents'.[75] The reason for this requirement is to ensure that the court is not wrongly led into believing that work carried out by agents was carried out by the principal solicitors.

Items of costs and other individual entries

21.38 The following detail must be provided:[76]

'In respect of each of the heads of costs:

(1) "communications" means letters out e-mails out and telephone calls;

(2) communications, which are not routine communications, must be set out in chronological order;

(3) routine communications must be set out as a single item at the end of each head.'

21.39 Each item must be consecutively numbered.[77] Directions are given in respect of the following types of item:

• **Routine communications:** Routine outgoing letters, routine outgoing e-mails and routine telephone calls (either outgoing or incoming) will in general be allowed on a unit basis of six minutes each (see **29.53**). Other electronic communications may be allowed on a time basis (see **29.55**). As set out above, CPD art 4.7 provides that routine communications must be set out as a single item at the end of each head; this is usually interpreted as meaning that the number of letters, e-mails and telephone should be shown separately as well as cumulatively.

---

75 See CPD art 4.16(6).

76 CPD art 4.7.

77 See CPD art 4.9.

- **Success fee:** Where a claim is made for a success fee, the amount of the percentage increase must be shown separately from the base fee, either in the appropriate arithmetic column or in the narrative column.[78]
- **Costs of preparing the bill of costs:** Other than the costs of preparing and checking it, the bill must not contain any costs relating solely to the detailed assessment proceedings.[79]

COMMENCEMENT AND WHEN TO COMMENCE THE ASSESSMENT

21.40 Detailed assessment proceedings are commenced by the receiving party serving notice of commencement.[80] If the detailed assessment is in respect of costs without any additional liability, the receiving party must serve the proceedings on the paying party and on all the other relevant persons;[81] the documents must include a notice of commencement in the prescribed form,[82] a copy of the bill of costs, a statement giving the name and address for service of any person upon whom the receiving party intends to serve the notice of commencement, and copies of certain supporting documents, such as fee notes and vouchers.[83] The Senior Courts Costs Office informally requests that e-mail addresses are included in the statement of parties.[84] The notice of commencement should state the date upon which points of dispute must be served.[85] If the detailed assessment is in respect of an additional liability only, the documents are more limited[86] but must still include relevant details of the additional liability.[87] Where both base costs and addition liability are claimed, the requirements are combined accordingly.[88]

---

[78]   See CPD art 4.17(1). For an example see Precedent A or Precedent B in the Schedule of Costs Precedents annexed to the CPD.

[79]   See CPD art 4.13.

[80]   CPR, r 47.6(1). The receiving party must also serve a copy of the notice of commencement and the bill on any other relevant persons specified in the costs practice direction (see CPR, r 47.6(2)).

[81]   CPD, art 32.10 provides as follows: '(1) For the purposes of rule 47.6(2) a "relevant person" means: (a) any person who has taken part in the proceedings which gave rise to the assessment and who is directly liable under an order for costs made against him; (b) any person who has given to the receiving party notice in writing that he has a financial interest in the outcome of the assessment and wishes to be a party accordingly; (c) any other person whom the court orders to be treated as such. (2) Where a party is unsure whether a person is or is not a relevant person, that party may apply to the appropriate office for directions. (3) The court will generally not make an order that the person in respect of whom the application is made will be treated as a relevant person, unless within a specified time he applies to the court to be joined as a party to the assessment proceedings in accordance with Part 19 (Parties and Group Litigation).

[82]   See CPD, art 32.8, which reads: '(1) The Notice of Commencement should be in Form N252. (2) Before it is served, it must be completed to show as separate items: (a) the total amount of the costs claimed in the bill; (b) the extra sum which will be payable by way of fixed costs and court fees if a default costs certificate is obtained.

[83]   CPD, art 32.3 reads as follows: 'If the detailed assessment is in respect of costs without any additional liability, the receiving party must serve on the paying party and all the other relevant persons the following documents: (a) a notice of commencement; (b) a copy of the bill of costs; (c) copies of the fee notes of counsel and of any expert in respect of fees claimed in the bill; (d) written evidence as to any other disbursement which is claimed and which exceeds £250; (e) a statement giving the name and address for service of any person upon whom the receiving party intends to serve the notice of commencement.'

[84]   Request made to members of the ALCD on about 26 January 2010.

[85]   CPD, art 32.9 makes provision for foreign paying parties: '(1) This paragraph applies where the notice of commencement is to be served outside England and Wales. (2) The date to be inserted in the notice of commencement for the paying party to send points of dispute is a date (not less than 21 days from the date of service of the notice) which must be calculated by reference to Section IV of Part 6 as if the notice were a claim form and as if the date to be inserted was the date for the filing of a defence.'

[86]   CPD, art 32.4 reads as follows: 'If the detailed assessment is in respect of an additional liability only, the receiving party must serve on the paying party and all other relevant persons the following documents: (a) a

The earliest a detailed assessment can be commenced

21.41 A detailed assessment should be commenced in time, i e not too soon or too late. Sanctions may be imposed if a detailed assessment is commenced too late (see **12.144–12.173**). Where costs are to be ascertained by detailed (as opposed to summary) assessment, the general rule is that the assessment should take place only upon the conclusion of the proceedings to which they relate. CPR, r 47.1 makes the following provisions:

> 'The general rule is that the costs of any proceedings or any part of the proceedings are not to be assessed by the detailed procedure until the conclusion of the proceedings but the court may order them to be assessed immediately.'

Forthwith orders

21.42 An order which provides for an earlier assessment is generally known as a 'forthwith order' (see **7.64–7.73**). A forthwith order would usually be made at the same time as the order making the award, but a forthwith order may also be made by a costs judge. Whilst there is no authority on the point, CPD, art 28.1(5) appears to be worded in such a way as to restrict the costs judge to making such an order only where there is no realistic prospect of the claim continuing. The CPD is not a source of law, however, and the putative restriction may be little more than an acknowledgement of the fact that a costs judge would only be likely to make a forthwith order where he was able to find that the litigation was at an end. An alternative interpretation is that the CPD is merely continuing the long-standing common law principle that costs will not be assessed until the conclusion of the claim.[89] Regardless of which interpretation is correct, the court will take into account all the relevant factors (see immediately below).

21.43 Guidance about when proceedings are concluded is given in CPD, art 28.1:

> '(1) For the purposes of rule 47.1, proceedings are concluded when the court has finally determined the matters in issue in the claim, whether or not there is an appeal.
>
> (2) For the purposes of this rule, the making of an award of provisional damages under Part 41 will be treated as a final determination of the matters in issue.
>
> (3) The court may order or the parties may agree in writing that, although the proceedings are continuing, they will nevertheless be treated as concluded.
>
> (4)
>
>   (a)   A party who is served with a notice of commencement (see paragraph 32.3 below) may apply to a costs judge or a district judge to determine whether the party who served it is entitled to commence detailed assessment proceedings.
>
>   (b)   On hearing such an application, the orders which the court may make include: an order allowing the detailed assessment proceedings to continue, or an order setting aside the notice of commencement.

---

notice of commencement; (b) a copy of the bill of costs; (c) the relevant details of the additional liability; (d) a statement giving the name and address of any person upon whom the receiving party intends to serve the notice of commencement.'

[87]   See **30.92**, **30.141** and **30.227** for details.

[88]   CPD, art 35.7 provides as follows: 'If a detailed assessment is in respect of both base costs and an additional liability, the receiving party must serve on the paying party and all other relevant persons the documents listed in paragraph 32.3 and the documents giving relevant details of an additional liability listed in paragraph 32.5.'

[89]   That principle was based on the *maxim unica directio fiat damnorum* (which meant that there should be only one certification of the damages). This rule arose at a time when damages were considered to include costs, and as such came to apply to costs as well as damages: see *Phillips v Phillips* (1879) 5 QBD 60.

'(5) A costs judge or a district judge may make an order allowing detailed assessment proceedings to be commenced where there is no realistic prospect of the claim continuing.'

Thus, the parties may agree that the proceedings are to be treated as concluded even where they have not concluded. If there is dispute about whether the proceedings have concluded, the paying party may make an application for a determination. Likewise, if the receiving party believes that a claim has stalled, he may make an application for a forthwith order. Whilst of persuasive value only, the SCCO Guide stipulates that where an application is made to a costs judge for permission to continue a detailed assessment, the court may take into account the fact that no corresponding application has been made to the court making the original order.[90]

Appeals

21.44 Appeals may present problems of their own. It used to be the case that appeals in the Court of Appeal were regarded as being separate proceedings,[91] but this seems no longer to be the case, at least as a matter of practice.[92] In any event, the following pre-CPR guidance remains good law:[93]

'When there is doubt as to whether or not an order results in the "conclusion or the cause or matter" the wise course is to ask the court … for consent to proceed to taxation forthwith.'

21.45 Where an interim appeal on a discrete point has resulted in a costs order being made, and where that appeal will not dispose of the claim as a whole, the appeal court will often order that the costs of the appeal be assessed forthwith.[94]

21.46 It will often be the case that a party wishes to bring an appeal which, if successful, might alter the incidence of costs. Where a party has permission to bring such an appeal, it does not follow that the assessment proceedings are automatically stayed; this is made clear by CPR, r 47.2:

'Detailed assessment is not stayed pending an appeal unless the court so orders.'

Therefore, in the absence of an order which says otherwise, a receiving party would not have to wait until the conclusion of the appeal in order to request a detailed assessment. The overriding objective may, however, require that a receiving party acts sensibly in this regard.

21.47 The court has the power to order a stay, an application for which may be made either to the court whose order is being appealed or to the court which will hear the appeal.[95]

---

90 See *Bottin (International) Investments Ltd v Venson Group plc* [2005] EWHC 90005 (Costs), Master Campbell.
91 See the discussion by Morritt LJ in *Morris v Bank of America National Trust (appeal against striking out)* [2001] 1 All ER 954.
92 Although not a binding decision, this was the conclusion of Master Campbell in *Bottin (International) Investments Ltd v Venson Group plc* [2005] EWHC 90005 (Costs) at [44].
93 *Harrods (Buenos Aires) Ltd* (unreported) 10 March 1993, CA, cited in *Bottin* by Sir Mervyn Davies.
94 *Morris v Bank of America National Trust (Appeal Against Striking Out)* [2000] 1 All ER 954.
95 CPD, art 29.1(2).

Additional liability

21.48 Success fees may also present problems; this is because a receiving party would usually be reluctant to disclose the risk assessment until the conclusion of the case. CPD, art 14.5 makes the following provision:

> 'Where there has been a trial of one or more issues separately from other issues, the court will not normally order detailed assessment of the additional liability until all issues have been tried unless the parties agree.'

This allows the receiving party to keep his risk assessment secret until the appropriate stage has been reached.

Group litigation

21.49 Finally, group litigation can also create difficulties; this is because it is a type of litigation which is prone to tie up resources for many years. This will not, however, generally be a reason to make a forthwith order; Morland J had the following to say on the topic:[96]

> 'In ... almost all group litigation cases there should be no need for any detailed assessment of costs until the conclusion of the group litigation. Solicitors engaged in group litigation will be specialists and experienced in the field. Solicitors for claimants are fully entitled to an adequate cash flow from the defendants once the general issue of liability has been admitted or determined in the claimants' favour, similarly on determination of generic issues in the claimants favour and on the assessment or settlement of awards of damages to individual or batches of claimants.'

Thus, whilst it is true to say that it would not usually be desirable for a forthwith order to be made prior to the conclusion of group litigation,[97] it would not be unusual for a paying party to be ordered to make an interim payment.

Case examples

Where there may be set-off

21.50 Where a paying party's liability for costs may be diminished as a result of set-off, this may be a factor to be taken into account when deciding whether it is fair to make a forthwith order.[98]

Where both parties are entitled to costs

21.51 Where both parties are entitled to costs, the court may take into account the fact that only one party seeks a forthwith order in deciding whether it is fair to make such an order.[99]

---

[96] *Giambrone v JMC Holidays Ltd (formerly Sunworld Holidays Ltd)* [2002] EWHC 2932 (QB) at [10], per Morland J.

[97] Contrary examples are easy to find, however, especially where the litigation is very long-running. See, for example, the *British Coal Respiratory Disease Litigation*, in which forthwith orders were repeatedly made over the best part of an entire decade.

[98] *Hicks v Russell Jones & Walker* [2001] CP Rep 25, CA.

[99] See *Bottin (International) Investments Ltd v Venson Group plc* [2005] EWHC 90005 (Costs), Master Campbell.

Outstanding issues

21.52 Although a pre-CPR case, where accounts remained outstanding in a partnership dispute the Court of Appeal found that the proceedings had not yet concluded.[100] A contrary example (also pre-CPR) is a case in which a claimant had obtained an order for an enquiry as to damages: the Patents Court ruled that the proceedings could be treated as being concluded.[101]

Poverty and access to justice

21.53 Whilst it was a very old case decided under a jurisdiction entirely different to the CPR,[102] Hardwick LC ordered that a claimant should have her costs if, by reason of her poverty, she would otherwise not have been able to continue the litigation.[103]

The latest a detailed assessment may be commenced

The relevant period of time

21.54 As a rule of thumb, the period for beginning detailed assessment proceedings is 3 months from the date on which the receiving party became entitled to costs:[104]

Source of right to detailed assessment	Time by which detailed assessment proceedings must be commenced
Judgment, direction, order, award or other determination	3 months after the date of the judgment etc. Where detailed assessment is stayed pending an appeal, 3 months after the date of the order lifting the stay
Discontinuance under Part 38	3 months after the date of service of notice of discontinuance under rule 38.3; or 3 months after the date of the dismissal of application to set the notice of discontinuance aside under rule 38.4
Acceptance of an offer to settle under Part 36	3 months after the date when the right to costs arose

21.55 The CPR does not stipulate what should happen where the proceedings are ongoing but there is no forthwith order. There are two schools of thought: the first is that the receiving party must serve notice of commencement within the stipulated 3-month period and then take no steps to request a hearing until the conclusion of the proceedings, and the second is that the receiving party must wait until the conclusion of the proceedings before serving notice of commencement. A party faced with having to decide between these two schools could take comfort in the fact that it would be rare for a court to impose sanctions as a result of a party reasonably preferring one interpretation of the law over another.

---

[100] *Small v Cohen* (1992) *The Times*, September 7, CA.
[101] *Mölnlycke AB v Proctor & Gamble Ltd (No 6)* [1993] FSR 154, Patents Ct.
[102] That jurisdiction was the inherent jurisdiction of the Courts of Chancery.
[103] *Jones v Coxeter* (1742) 2 Atk 400.
[104] See CPR, r 47.7.

The measure of time for starting assessment proceedings

21.56 The 3-month period is measured in calendar months.[105] It is implicit from CPD, art 33.3 that time will stop running upon compliance with CPR, r 47.6(1) (ie service of a notice of commencement and a copy of the bill of costs). CPD, art 33.3 reads:

> 'Attention is drawn to rule 47.6(1). The detailed assessment proceedings are commenced by service of the documents referred to.'

Variation of the period for starting assessment proceedings

21.57 Both the court and the parties have the power to vary the 3-month period. This may happen upon application, retrospectively, or by consent.

Upon application

21.58 Where a party wishes to vary the time for commencing detailed assessment proceedings in default of agreement to that effect, the court has power pursuant to CPR, Part 3 to make the appropriate order. CPD, art 33.2 makes the following provision:

> 'A party may apply to the appropriate office for an order under rule 3.1(2)(a) to extend or shorten that time.'

The court will take into account the overriding objective. In cases of complexity, the court may take into account the matters listed in CPR, r 3.9 (relief from sanctions),[106] but this will not always be mandatory.[107]

Retrospective application

21.59 CPR, r 3.1(2)(a) stipulates that the application for an extension may be made after the time for compliance has expired. This would often be otiose, however, because permission to commence assessment proceedings out of time is not required.[108] Where a decision is required, then (presumably) the court would take into account the matters listed in CPR, r 3.9 (relief from sanctions) (see **21.58**).

By consent

21.60 The parties may agree to vary the period of time for serving notice of commencement; this will often happen where either the bill of costs is large and will take more than 3 months to draft, or where the parties are in active negotiation about the costs. This power is exercisable under CPR, r 2.11, as is made clear by CPD, art 33.1:

> 'The parties may agree under rule 2.11 (Time limits may be varied by parties) to extend or shorten the time specified by rule 47.7 for commencing the detailed assessment proceedings.'

The court has the power to make a different order from that which the parties have agreed,[109] but in practice this would almost never happen because the extension would usually be agreed prior to the court's involvement.

---

[105] See CPR, r 2.10.

[106] *Sayers v Clarke Walker* [2002] EWCA Civ 645.

[107] *Robert v Momentum Services Ltd* [2003] EWCA Civ 299.

[108] CPD, art 33.4.

[109] In a context other than costs, see *Ropac Ltd v Inntrepreneir Pub Co* [2001] CP Rep 31.

VARIATION OF THE BILL OF COSTS

21.61 A bill of costs may be varied without permission of the court (although the court may order otherwise).[110]

VENUE FOR DETAILED ASSESSMENT

The 'appropriate office'

21.62 CPR, r 47.4 refers to assessments being dealt with by the 'appropriate office'. This is the court office which will deal with the administrative aspects of the assessment; it may or may not be the court which will be judicially responsible for the assessment.[111] The CPR makes provision for cases to be referred to or between courts.[112]

Provinces

21.63 Where the originating court is outside London, the 'appropriate office' will be:[113]

* the court which was dealing with the matter when the receiving party became entitled to costs;
* the court to which the matter has been transferred; or
* in all other cases, the SCCO.

London

21.64 The practice in the London Group of County Courts is that in general the SCCO will be the appropriate office.[114]

---

[110] See CPD art 40.10; historically, see *Davis v Dysart (No 2)* (1855) 21 Beav 124 at 132.

[111] There is a difference between an assessment being transferred to a court and a case being referred to a court as the appropriate office (see CPR, r 47.4(4); the former will mean that the assessment and any subsequent appeal will be heard at the destination court, but the latter means that whilst the assessment would usually be heard at the destination court, any subsequent appeal would revert back to the originating court.

[112] See CPR, r 47.4, which provides:
'(1) All applications and requests in detailed assessment proceedings must be made to or filed at the appropriate office.
(The costs practice direction sets out the meaning of "appropriate office" in any particular case)
(2) The court may direct that the appropriate office is to be the Senior Courts Costs Office.
(3) A county court may direct that another county court is to be the appropriate office.
(4) A direction under paragraph (3) may be made without proceedings being transferred to that court.
(Rule 30.2 makes provision for any county court to transfer the proceedings to another county court for detailed assessment of costs)'

[113] See CPD, art 31.1, which provides:
'For the purposes of rule 47.4(1) the "appropriate office" means—
(1) the district registry or county court in which the case was being dealt with when the judgment or order was made or the event occurred which gave rise to the right to assessment, or to which it has subsequently been transferred; or
(1A) where a tribunal, person or other body makes an order for the detailed assessment of costs, a county court (subject to paragraph 31.1A(1)); or
(2) in all other cases, including Court of Appeal cases, the Senior Courts Costs Office.'

[114] CPD, art 31.1A makes the following provisions:
'(1) This paragraph applies where the appropriate office is any of the following county courts:
Barnet, Bow, Brentford, Bromley, Central London, Clerkenwell, Croydon, Edmonton, Ilford, Kingston, Lambeth, Mayors and City of London, Romford, Shoreditch, Uxbridge, Wandsworth, West London,

SCCO

21.65 Regardless of where it originated, any court has the power to refer an assessment to the SCCO;[115] the following will be relevant to the exercise of the court's discretion:[116]

- the size of the bill of costs;
- the difficulty of the issues involved;
- the likely length of the hearing;
- the cost to the parties; and
- any other relevant matter.

Whether a court is able to refer an assessment to a local regional costs judge is another factor which can, perhaps, be added to this list. The points made at **21.69** would probably also apply, if only by analogy.

Transfer between county courts

21.66 Any county court has the power to refer the matter to another county court.[117] The relevant procedure for specifying the appropriate office is set out in CPD, art 31.2, which provides:

'(1) A direction under rule 47.4(2) or (3) specifying a particular court, registry or office as the appropriate office may be given on application or on the court's own initiative.

(2) Before making such a direction on its own initiative the court will give the parties the opportunity to make representations.'

(Special provisions apply where the matter concerns determination proceedings under the Community Legal Service (Costs) Regulations 2000 (SI 2000/441).)[118]

Willesden and Woolwich.
(2) Where this paragraph applies—
(i) the receiving party must file any request for a detailed assessment hearing in the Senior Courts Costs Office and, for all purposes relating to that detailed assessment, the Senior Courts Costs Office will be treated as the appropriate office in that case; and
(ii) unless an order is made under rule 47.4(2) directing that the Senior Courts Costs Office as part of the High Court shall be the appropriate office, an appeal from any decision made by a costs judge shall lie to the Designated Civil Judge for the London Group of County Courts or such judge as he shall nominate. The appeal notice and any other relevant papers should be lodged at the Central London Civil Justice Centre.'
[115] See CPR, r 47.4(2).
[116] See CPD, art 31.2(3), which provides as follows:
'(3) Unless the Senior Courts Costs Office is the appropriate office for the purposes of Rule 47.4(1) an order directing that an assessment is to take place at the Senior Courts Costs Office will be made only if it is appropriate to do so having regard to the size of the bill of costs, the difficulty of the issues involved, the likely length of the hearing, the cost to the parties and any other relevant matter.'
[117] See CPR, r 47.4(3).
[118] CPD, art 23.2: in this section of this Practice Direction 'appropriate court office' means:
'(1) the district registry or county court in which the case was being dealt with when the Section 11(1) order [made under the Access to Justice Act 1999] was made, or to which it has subsequently been transferred; or
(2) in all other cases, the Senior Courts Costs Office.'
CPD, art 23.2A:
'(1) This paragraph applies where the appropriate office is any of the following county courts:
Barnet, Bow, Brentford, Bromley, Central London, Clerkenwell, Croydon, Edmonton, Ilford, Kingston, Lambeth, Mayors and City of London, Romford, Shoreditch, Uxbridge, Wandsworth, West London, Willesden and Woolwich.
(2) Where this paragraph applies—
(i) a receiving party seeking an order specifying costs payable by an LSC funded client and/or by the Legal Services Commission under this section must file his application in the Senior Courts Costs Office and, for all purposes relating to that application, the Senior Courts Costs Office will be treated as the appropriate

Transferral

21.67 An assessment may be transferred to a new court rather than merely sent to that court as the appropriate office; if a case is transferred, then the effect is to transfer not only the assessment itself, but also any subsequent appeal.

21.68 CPR, r 30.2 deals with transfers generally; in so far as it is relevant to detailed assessments, it makes the following provisions:

'(1) A county court may order proceedings before that court, or any part of them ... to be transferred to another county court if it is satisfied that—

   (a)   an order should be made having regard to the criteria in rule 30.3; or
   (b)   proceedings for—
       (i)   the detailed assessment of costs;
       (ii)   ...
   could be more conveniently or fairly taken in that other county court.

(2) ...

(3) An application for an order under paragraph (1) or (2) must be made to the county court where the claim is proceeding.

(4) The High Court may, having regard to the criteria in rule 30.3, order proceedings in the Royal Courts of Justice or a district registry, or any part of such proceedings (such as a counterclaim or an application made in the proceedings), to be transferred—

   (a)   from the Royal Courts of Justice to a district registry; or
   (b)   from a district registry to the Royal Courts of Justice or to another district registry.

(5) A district registry may order proceedings before it for the detailed assessment of costs to be transferred to another district registry if it is satisfied that the proceedings could be more conveniently or fairly taken in that other district registry.

(6) An application for an order under paragraph (4) or (5) must, if the claim is proceeding in a district registry, be made to that registry.'

21.69 CPR, r 30.3 gives guidance as to the factors to be taken into account when considering whether a matter should be transferred:

'(1) Paragraph (2) sets out the matters to which the court must have regard when considering whether to make an order under—

   (a)   section 40(2), 41(1) or 42(2) of the County Courts Act 1984 (transfer between the High Court and a county court);
   (b)   rule 30.2(1) (transfer between county courts); or
   (c)   rule 30.2(4) (transfer between the Royal Courts of Justice and the district registries).

(2) The matters to which the court must have regard include—

   (a)   the financial value of the claim and the amount in dispute, if different;
   (b)   whether it would be more convenient or fair for hearings ... to be held in some other court;
   (c)   the availability of a judge specialising in the type of claim in question;

office in that case; and
(ii) unless an order is made transferring the application to the Senior Courts Costs Office as part of the High Court, an appeal from any decision made by a costs judge shall lie to the Designated Civil Judge for the London Group of County Courts or such judge as he shall nominate. The appeal notice and any other relevant papers should be lodged at the Central London Civil Justice Centre.'

(d) whether the facts, legal issues, remedies or procedures involved are simple or complex;

(e) the importance of the outcome of the claim to the public in general;

(f) the facilities available at the court where the claim is being dealt with and whether they may be inadequate because of any disabilities of a party or potential witness;

(g) whether the making of a declaration of incompatibility under section 4 of the Human Rights Act 1998 has arisen or may arise;

(h) in the case of civil proceedings by or against the Crown, as defined in rule 66.1(2), the location of the relevant government department or officers of the Crown and, where appropriate, any relevant public interest that the matter should be tried in London.'

Allocation within the judiciary

21.70 There are three species of tribunal specialising in the ascertainment of civil costs: costs judges; regional costs judges; and authorised court officers. Generalist district judges will also hear a significant number of detailed assessments. Only issues concerning allocation are addressed in this chapter; jurisdictional issues are addressed in Chapter 4.

Costs judges

21.71 The post of taxing master (now referred to as a costs judge) was created by the Court of Chancery Act 1842.[119] Specialist chancery taxing masters used to exist up until the early 1900s, but that post has now been abolished as a separate appointment.

21.72 A 'costs judge' is defined by CPR, r 43.2(b) as being a 'taxing master of the Supreme Court'; all such judges (be they full-time or part-time) are based in the Senior Courts Costs Office. In recognition of their status, costs judges (including a lady costs judge) are usually addressed as 'Master'.

21.73 Where the occasion demands, a costs judge will sit as a deputy district judge of the Principal Registry of the Family Division, or as deputy district judge of a county court. Where a costs judge sits in one of those capacities, he will be vested of all the powers of the court in question.[120]

Regional costs judges

21.74 Regional costs judges are district judges who have officially nurtured an interest in costs. A regional costs judge may sit either in the county court or in the appropriate District Registry of the High Court.

21.75 The criteria for referral to a regional costs judge are as follows:[121]

'... the time estimate for the detailed assessment exceeds one day; and/or the sum claimed exceeds £50,000; and/or complex arguments on points of law, or an issue affecting a group of similar cases, are identified in the points of dispute or the reply or are referred to in argument at a detailed assessment hearing.'

---

[119] 5 & 6 Vict c 103.

[120] CPR, r 2.4.

[121] *SCCO Guide 2006*, para 1.1(c).

21.76 The following guidance is given on procedure:[122]

> 'Once a request for detailed assessment in Form N258 has been filed at court the bill will be referred to a District Judge who will consider whether it falls within the criteria for reference to a Regional Costs Judge. If it does, the bill will be referred to the appropriate Regional Costs Judge who will then decide whether to accept it and will give any directions required, including directions as to listing.
>
> If a party wishes to make submissions as to whether any particular detailed assessment fulfils the criteria for reference to a Regional Costs Judge, or as to the most convenient court for any hearing before a Regional Costs Judge, they should first consult the other parties or their legal representatives before making submissions to the court. It is helpful if such submissions are filed with the court when the request for detailed assessment is lodged. If possible the parties should attempt to agree the reference to the Regional Costs Judge, any directions and the most convenient venue.'

At the time of writing, there were 22 regional costs judges; no circuit was without a regional costs judge.

Authorised court officers

21.77 An authorised court officer is a civil servant who hears those detailed assessments which are deemed apt for an unqualified tribunal. The correct title is 'court officer', but common usage has corrupted the term to 'costs officer'. Senior court officers are referred to as 'principal officers'; less senior court officers are referred to as 'senior executive officers' (or 'SEOs').

21.78 There are no authorised court officers outside the SCCO. Assessments are allocated to authorised court officers only if the sums claimed are less than £75,000 (inclusive of additional liability but exclusive of VAT). The parties may agree that the assessment should not be heard by an authorised court officer.[123] If there is disagreement on this point, an application may be made for directions.[124]

21.79 CPD, art 30.1 gives the following guidance:

> '(1) The court officers authorised by the Lord Chancellor to assess costs in the Senior Courts Costs Office and the Principal Registry of the Family Division are authorised to deal with claims for costs not exceeding £30,000 (excluding VAT) in the case of senior executive officers, or their equivalent, and £75,000 (excluding VAT) in the case of principal officers.
>
> (2) In calculating whether or not a bill of costs is within the authorised amounts, the figure to be taken into account is the total claim for costs including any additional liability.
>
> (3) Where the receiving party, paying party and any other party to the detailed assessment proceedings who has served points of dispute are agreed that the assessment should not be made by an authorised court officer, the receiving party should so inform the court when requesting a hearing date. The court will then list the hearing before a costs judge or a district judge.
>
> (4) In any other case a party who objects to the assessment being made by an authorised court officer must make an application to the costs judge or district judge under Part 23 (General Rules about Applications for Court Orders) setting out the reasons for the objection and if sufficient reason is shown the court will direct that the bill be assessed by a

---

[122]   Ibid.
[123]   See CPD, art 30.1(3).
[124]   See CPD, art 30.1(4).

costs judge or district judge.'

21.80 In deciding whether or not a case is suitable for an authorised court officer, it may be relevant to consider the powers that they have. Those powers are set out in CPR, r 47.3:

'(1) An authorised court officer has all the powers of the court when making a detailed assessment, except—

    (a) power to make a wasted costs order as defined in rule 48.7;

    (b) power to make an order under—

        (i) rule 44.14 (powers in relation to misconduct);

        (ii) rule 47.8 (sanction for delay in commencing detailed assessment proceedings);

        (iii) paragraph (2) (objection to detailed assessment by authorised court officer); and

    (c) power to make a detailed assessment of costs payable to a solicitor by his client, unless the costs are being assessed under rule 48.5 (costs where money is payable to a child or protected party).

(2) Where a party objects to the detailed assessment of costs being made by an authorised court officer, the court may order it to be made by a costs judge or a district judge.

(The costs practice direction sets out the relevant procedure).'

Thus, an authorised court officer does not have penal powers, nor (for all practical purposes) is he able to hear solicitor and client assessments. The restrictions relating to delay are not limited to misconduct: they also prevent an authorised court officer from adjudicating on the disallowance of interest.

21.81 CPR, r 3.2 empowers an authorised court officer to refer a juridical step to a judge.[125] It permits only part of an assessment to be referred; if, for example, there is a dispute about the indemnity principle, a court officer may refer that part of the assessment only to a judge but reserve the rest of the assessment to himself.

SANCTION FOR DELAY IN COMMENCING PROCEEDINGS AND 'UNLESS ORDERS'

21.82 Tardiness on the part of the receiving party may be said to be delay in commencing detailed assessment proceedings, or delay in requesting a detailed assessment hearing, or both. Where either or both of these things happen, a paying party has two remedies available to him: first, he can apply for an unless order and, secondly, he can seek sanctions against the receiving party.

21.83 This discussion considers the first of these issues; the topic of sanctions is addressed in Chapter 12. For the reasons set out below, one interpretation of the CPR is that the two remedies are mutually exclusive.

21.84 CPR, r 47.8(1) provides as follows:

---

[125] It provides as follows:
    'Where a step is to be taken by a court officer—
    (a) the court officer may consult a judge before taking that step;
    (b) the step may be taken by a judge instead of the court officer.'

'Where the receiving party fails to commence detailed assessment proceedings within the period specified—

(a)   in rule 47.7; or

(b)   by any direction of the court,

the paying party may apply for an order requiring the receiving party to commence detailed assessment proceedings within such time as the court may specify.'

21.85 This rule allows the court to make one component of an unless order; the other component arises out of CPR, r 47.8(2):

'On an application under paragraph (1), the court may direct that, unless the receiving party commences detailed assessment proceedings within the time specified by the court, all or part of the costs to which the receiving party would otherwise be entitled will be disallowed.'

Almost identical provisions govern delay in requesting a detailed assessment hearing.[126]

Discretion

21.86 The fact that the court has the vires to make an unless order does not mean that it will exercise that power. An unless order would ordinarily visit significant consequences on the defaulting party, this being without further judicial scrutiny; as such, it is not a trivial species of order. Moore-Bick LJ had this to say on the topic (albeit it in a context other than the law of costs):[127]

'[A further] consequence is that before making conditional orders, particularly orders for the striking out of statements of case or the dismissal of claims or counterclaims, the judge should consider carefully whether the sanction being imposed is appropriate in all the circumstances of the case. Of course, it is impossible to foresee the nature and effect of every possible breach and the party in default can always apply for relief, but a conditional order striking out a statement of case or dismissing the claim or counterclaim is one of the most powerful weapons in the court's case management armoury and should not be deployed unless its consequences can be justified. I find it difficult to imagine circumstances in which such an order could properly be made for what were described in *Keen Phillips v Field*[128] as "good housekeeping purposes".'

There is no reason to believe that the power to make an order in detailed assessment proceedings should be exercised any differently: thus an unless order will not be made unless 'its consequences can be justified'.

Relief

21.87 If the court were to be asked to grant relief from the effect of an unless order, this should normally be considered at a hearing;[129] a refusal to grant relief would be

---

[126] See CPR, r 47.14(3) and (4), which provides as follows:
'(3) Where the receiving party fails to file a request in accordance with paragraph (2), the paying party may apply for an order requiring the receiving party to file the request within such time as the court may specify.
(4) On an application under paragraph (3), the court may direct that, unless the receiving party requests a detailed assessment hearing within the time specified by the court, all or part of the costs to which the receiving party would otherwise be entitled will be disallowed.'

[127] *Marcan Shipping (London) Ltd v Kefalas* [2007] EWCA Civ 463 at [36].

[128] [2006] EWCA Civ 1524, [2007] 1 WLR 686.

[129] See *Vernon v Spoudeas* [2010] EWCA Civ 666 at [25] (per Ward LJ) citing *Collier v Williams* [2006] EWCA Civ 20 at [38], per Dyson LJ.

vitiated if the court failed to give reasons.[130] Knowingly failing to comply with an unless order would often result in the court not granting relief.[131] That said, it is not unknown for parties to agree to unless orders as a convenient procedural accommodation for the purposes of case management; where these were the circumstances, non-compliance would ordinarily be correspondingly less serious, and would rarely be decisive.[132]

21.88 CPR, r 47.8(3) makes the following further provisions:

'If—

(a)   the paying party has not made an application in accordance with paragraph (1); and

(b)   the receiving party commences the proceedings later than the period specified in rule 47.7,

the court may disallow all or part of the interest otherwise payable to the receiving party under—

(i)   section 17 of the Judgments Act 1838; or

(ii) section 74 of the County Courts Act 1984,

but must not impose any other sanction except in accordance with rule 44.14 (powers in relation to misconduct).'

The effect of this provision is ambiguous. In particular, the effect of the words 'if the paying party has not made an application' is not clear. These words could be read as meaning that the act of making an application for an unless order would preclude the court from disallowing interest. Equally, the rule as a whole could be read as giving the court the power to impose whatever sanction it adjudges to be appropriate. There is no authority on which interpretation is correct.

21.89 If the correct interpretation is that the court has no power to disallow interest once an application for an unless order has been made, then that would not give rise to any particular unfairness; this is for the reasons set out in the footnotes.[133] It should be noted, however, that there is no authority to confirm that that line of thinking is correct. To make matters even more complicated, it is possible that the provisions relating to interest are ultra vires in the county court: see **36.12**.

POINTS OF DISPUTE AND CONSEQUENCES OF NOT SERVING

Contents

21.90 Points of dispute contain the paying party's objections to the costs which are claimed (see below). In practice, it is often a hybrid between a counter-schedule and an

---

130   *Vernon v Spoudeas* [2010] EWCA Civ 666 at [31] *et seq* (per Ward LJ)

131   See, for example, *Eden v Rubin* [2011] EWHC 3090 (QB) at [51], per Coulson J; see also *Rybak and others v Langbar International Ltd* [2010] EWHC 2015 (Ch), per Morgan J (deliberately destroying computer files).

132   *Pannone LLP v Aardvark Digital Ltd* [2011] EWCA Civ 803 at [33], per Tomlinson LJ.

133   That interpretation could be justified on the basis that a paying party who is faced with an apparently tardy opponent has a choice: either he can make an application to the court (in which case he would give up his rights concerning interest, but may benefit by way of an immediate order), or he can let the matter rest (in which case he would not benefit by way of an immediate order, but may benefit by interest being disallowed).

abbreviated skeleton argument. It should be borne in mind, however, that the CPD requires only that objections are stated (together with grounds), not that full arguments are articulated.

21.91 CPD, art 35.3 gives guidance as to the contents of points of dispute:

'Points of dispute must—

(1) identify each item in the bill of costs which is disputed,

(2) in each case, state concisely the nature and grounds of dispute,

(3) where practicable suggest a figure to be allowed for each item in respect of which a reduction is sought, and

(4) be signed by the party serving them or his solicitor.'

21.92 Points of dispute are commonly are set out in the form of a tabular schedule containing both columns and rows. Each objection is usually contained in its own row. One column (or, in some cases, two columns) on the left hand side will identify the objection by number (or by item number in the points of dispute together with the corresponding item number in the bill of costs). The middle column typically contains the objection, and the right-hand column is typically left blank for the insertion of the receiving party's replies.

21.93 Where practicable, each objection should be accompanied by a corresponding offer:[134] where the item objected to is a disbursement, the offer will usually be a monetary figure, but where the objection relates to profit costs, the offer will usually be for an allowance of time (or, in the case of routine communications, a specified number of units).

21.94 Although there is no prescribed structure, the following sequence of objections is commonly encountered (but only in so far as the topics arise):

- any issue arising out of the certificates;
- any issue concerning misconduct and delay in the assessment proceedings;
- the indemnity principle;
- proportionality;
- estimates;
- hourly rates; and
- the individual items in the order they are claimed in the bill of costs.

21.95 Where it is claimed, some draftsmen would deal with the success fee out of sequence as if it were a point of principle.

21.96 Where the paying party intends the court to take into account an estimate of costs, the points of dispute must make a statement setting out his case.[135]

21.97 The writer's precedent on points of dispute can be found at the end of this book. That precedent tries to achieve a balance between brevity and detail, but these things are a matter of judgment, to which there is no 'right' answer. The level of detail to be included in the points of dispute is a matter which, where possible, ought to be tailored according to the likes and dislikes of the court which is likely to hear the matter. There are competing considerations: it should always be borne in mind that the court has the

---

[134] CPD, art 35.3(3).

[135] CPD, art 6.5A(2).

power to refuse to hear arguments which are not articulated in the points of dispute,[136] but it should also be borne in mind that the CPD encourages brevity. It also states that points of dispute should follow as closely as possible Precedent G of the Schedule of Costs Precedents annexed to the CPD:[137] that precedent is significantly pithier than the points of dispute encountered in practice.

21.98 Where a paying party wishes to make a request about alternative means of funding, that request may be made in the points of dispute; CPD, art 35.7 makes the following provisions:

'(1) Where the receiving party claims an additional liability, a party who serves points of dispute on the receiving party may include a request for information about other methods of financing costs which were available to the receiving party.

(2) Part 18 (further information) and the Practice Direction Supplementing that part apply to such a request.'

21.99 Part 18 will apply to that request; this means that the request must be concise and strictly confined to matters which are reasonably necessary and proportionate to enable the paying party to prepare his own case or to understand the case he has to meet.[138] In so far as it is relevant, PD 18, para 1.6 gives the further following guidance:

'(1) A Request ... must—

    (a)   . . .
    (b)   ... state that it is a Request made under Part 18, identify the [party making the request and the party receiving the request] and state the date on which it is made,
    (c)   set out in a separate numbered paragraph each request for information or clarification,
    (d)   ...
    (e)   state the date by which the first party expects a response to the Request.

(2)

    (a)   A Request ... may, if convenient, be prepared in such a way that the response may be given on the same document.
    (b)   To do this the numbered paragraphs of the Request should appear on the left hand half of each sheet so that the paragraphs of the response may then appear on the right.
    (c)   Where a Request is prepared in this form an extra copy should be served for the use of the second party.'

21.100 Where points of dispute have been prepared on a computer, a copy of the computer file must be provided free of charge upon request; CPD, art 35.6 makes the following provisions:

'(1) This paragraph applies in cases in which points of dispute are capable of being copied onto a computer disk.

(2) If, within 14 days of the receipt of the points of dispute, the receiving party requests a disk copy of them, the paying party must supply him with a copy free of charge not more than 7 days after the date on which he received the request.'

---

[136] See *Ilangaratne v British Medical Association* [2005] EWHC 2096 (Ch) at [18]; the objection was raised only 48 hours before the hearing.
[137] CPD, art 35.2.
[138] See PD 18, para 1.2.

Variation

21.101   If the paying party wishes to raise an argument which has not been articulated in the points of dispute, they may be varied. Permission is not generally required, as is made clear by CPD, art 40.10:

'(1) If a party wishes to vary his ... points of dispute ... an amended or supplementary document must be filed with the court and copies of it must be served on all other relevant parties.

(2) Permission is not required to vary ... points of dispute ... but the court may disallow the variation or permit it only upon conditions, including conditions as to the payment of any costs caused or wasted by the variation.'

Service

21.102   CPR, r 47.9 lays down the relevant procedure:

'(1)   The paying party and any other party to the detailed assessment proceedings may dispute any item in the bill of costs by serving points of dispute on—

(a)   the receiving party; and
(b)   every other party to the detailed assessment proceedings.

(2)   The period for serving points of dispute is 21 days after the date of service of the notice of commencement.

(3)   If a party serves points of dispute after the period set out in paragraph (2), he may not be heard further in the detailed assessment proceedings unless the court gives permission.

(The costs practice direction sets out requirements about the form of points of dispute).'

21.103   Where the paying party resides inside England and Wales, the time for serving points of dispute is generally 21 days; this is made clear by CPD, art 35.4:

'(1) The normal period for serving points of dispute is 21 days after the date of service of the notice of commencement.

(2) Where a notice of commencement is served on a party outside England and Wales the period within which that party should serve points of dispute is to be calculated by reference to Part 6 Section III as if the notice of commencement was a claim form and as if the period for serving points of dispute were the period for filing a defence.'

21.104   Where it is expressed as being a number of days, the time for serving points of dispute is computed in 'clear days'; CPR, r 2.8 provides:

'(2)   A period of time expressed as a number of days shall be computed as clear days.

(3)   In this rule "clear days" means that in computing the number of days—

(a)   the day on which the period begins; and
(b)   if the end of the period is defined by reference to an event, the day on which that event occurs

are not included.'

21.105   In view of the fact that the relevant period is almost always more than 5 days, Saturdays, Sundays, Bank Holidays, Christmas Days and Good Fridays are included within the calculation,[139] but where the last day is a day on which the court office is closed, service may be effected in time if made on the next day on which the court office is open.[140]

21.106　The time for serving points of dispute may be varied by consent or by order of the court; CPD, art 35.1 provides:

> 'The parties may agree under rule 2.11 (Time limits may be varied by parties) to extend or shorten the time specified by rule 47.9 for service of points of dispute. A party may apply to the appropriate office for an order under rule 3.1(2)(a) to extend or shorten that time.'

21.107　The paying party must serve points of dispute on all of those persons listed in the statement of interested persons served by the receiving party with the bill of costs; CPD, art 35.5 makes the following provision:

> 'A party who serves points of dispute on the receiving party must at the same time serve a copy on every other party to the detailed assessment proceedings, whose name and address for service appears on the statement served by the receiving party in accordance with paragraph 32.3 or 32.4 above.'

Thus, usually points of dispute must be served on the receiving party and on any other paying party.

21.108　Service may be effected in a number of ways. In addition to service by way of delivery of a hard copy, the following may suffice.

Service by e-mail (generally)

21.109　Service may be effected by e-mail. Restrictions apply. Broadly speaking, the receiving party must have expressly indicated in writing that he is willing to accept service by electronic means[141]; the unqualified inclusion of an e-mail address in the receiving party's headed paper or statement of parties would amount to such an indication.[142] Where a party seeks to serve a document by electronic means, he should first seek to clarify with the party who is to be served whether there are any limitations to the recipient's agreement to accept service by such means, including the format in which documents are to be sent and the maximum size of attachments that may be received.[143] Where a document is served by electronic means, the party serving the document is not obliged also to effect service in hard copy.[144]

Service by e-mail (mandatory requirement)

21.110　It is possible that, in some circumstances, there is a mandatory requirement for service by e-mail. On a strict reading of the CPR, where the points of dispute contain Part 18 Requests those requests must be served by e-mail.[145] However, that requirement is mandatory only where service by e-mail is reasonably practicable. Moreover, it could be argued that the requirement would apply only to the Part 18 Requests themselves rather than to the rest of the points of dispute.

---

[139]　CPR, r 2.8(4).
[140]　CPR, r 2.8(5).
[141]　PD 6A, para 4.1(1).
[142]　PD 6A, para 4.1(2)(b).
[143]　PD 6A, para 4.2.
[144]　PD 6A, para 4.3.
[145]　PD 18, para 1.7.

Fax

21.111 Service may be effected by fax, in which case it need not also be effected in hard copy.[146] The receiving party must have expressly indicated in writing that he is willing to accept service by fax and must have provided the requisite fax number.[147] The unqualified inclusion of a fax number in the receiving party's headed paper or statement of parties would amount to such an express indication.[148]

Failure to serve points of dispute

21.112 If a party fails to serve points of dispute, the receiving party may request a default costs certificate (see below).

21.113 If a paying party has had a default costs certificate issued against it, any application to set aside that certificate must be accompanied by a draft of the points of dispute he proposes to serve if that application is successful.[149]

DEFAULT COSTS CERTIFICATES

21.114 A default costs certificate certifies the amount that the paying party must pay consequent upon him having failed to file points of dispute. It is issued in an amount which is based on the sum claimed in the bill of costs rather than a sum which the court has found to be reasonable.

21.115 A default costs certificate will be effective only against the paying party: it will not be effective against the LSC.[150] The default costs procedure does not apply to solicitor and client assessments.[151]

Issue

21.116 A default costs certificate is issued on application.[152] The jurisdiction is defined by CPR, r 47.9:[153]

'(4) The receiving party may file a request for a default costs certificate if—

(a)   the period set out in rule 47.9(2) for serving points of dispute has expired; and

(b)   he has not been served with any points of dispute.

(5) If any party (including the paying party) serves points of dispute before the issue of a default costs certificate the court may not issue the default costs certificate.'

It is implicit from these provisions that the receiving party must inform the court if points of dispute are received after a request for a default costs certificate has been made but before a certificate has been issued.

---

[146] PD 6A, para 4.3: whilst this provision refers to 'electronic means' rather than 'fax or electronic means' it is generally regarded as applying to both.
[147] PD 6A, para 4.1.
[148] PD 6A, para 4.1(2)(a).
[149] CPD, art 38.2(3).
[150] CPD, art 37.5.
[151] CPD, art 56.7.
[152] The procedure is governed by CPR, Part 47, Section III and by CPD, art 37.
[153] CPR, r 47.9.

21.117 The model form of request for a default costs certificate contains two certificates:[154]

- a certificate confirming that the paying party has been served with the notice of commencement, the bill of costs and a copy of the document giving rise to the detailed assessment; and
- a certificate confirming that points of dispute have not been served.

It is mandatory that the model form is used; it must be signed by the receiving party or his solicitor.[155] The request must be accompanied by the document giving rise to the detailed assessment[156] (which will usually be a costs order). No further evidence is required.

21.118 Unless the court orders otherwise, fixed costs are payable upon the issue of a default costs certificate.[157]

Setting aside a default costs certificate and requesting a stay

21.119 If the receiving party discovers that the notice of commencement did not reach the paying party at least 21 days before the default costs certificate was issued, the onus is on him to take active steps to have it set aside.[158] In all other circumstances, the onus is on the paying party to make an application for the certificate to be set aside. CPR, r 47.12 gives the following guidance:

'(1) The court must set aside a default costs certificate if the receiving party was not entitled to it.

(2) In any other case, the court may set aside or vary a default costs certificate if it appears to the court that there is some good reason why the detailed assessment proceedings should continue.

(3) Where—

(a) the receiving party has purported to serve the notice of commencement on the paying party;

(b) a default costs certificate has been issued; and

(c) the receiving party subsequently discovers that the notice of commencement did not reach the paying party at least 21 days before the default costs certificate was issued,

the receiving party must—

(i) file a request for the default costs certificate to be set aside; or

(ii) apply to the court for directions.

(4) Where paragraph (3) applies, the receiving party may take no further step in—

(a) the detailed assessment proceedings; or

(b) the enforcement of the default costs certificate,

until the certificate has been set aside or the court has given directions.

(The costs practice direction contains further details about the procedure for setting aside a default costs certificate and the matters which the court must take into account).'

---

[154] N254.
[155] CPD, art 37.1.
[156] CPD, art 37.1.
[157] CPD, arts 25.1, 25.2 and 37.8.
[158] CPR, r 47.12(3).

21.120　Thus, there are two bases upon which a paying party may bring an application to set aside a default costs certificate:

- where the receiving party was not entitled to it; and
- where there is 'some good reason' why the detailed assessment proceedings should continue.

Each is considered in turn.

Not entitled to default costs certificate

21.121　If the receiving party was not entitled to the default costs certificate, then the court has no option but to set it aside.[159] This will be so in the following circumstances:[160]

- where there had been a failure to serve a notice of commencement;
- where the certificate was issued before the requisite period[161] had expired; or
- where points of dispute were served before the certificate was issued.

This list is not exhaustive; other similar circumstances might include where the bill of costs was grossly defective or where there had been an agreement between the parties that a default costs certificate would not be issued.

21.122　The certificate may contain an error which, if uncorrected, would award the receiving party costs to which he was not entitled. That would not necessarily be reason to set it aside[162] (but it would, of course, be reason to vary it).

Good reason to set aside a default costs certificate

21.123　An application to set aside for good reason must be supported by evidence.[163] It is implicit within the provisions of the CPD that the application ought to be accompanied by the following:[164]

- a copy of the bill of costs;
- a draft of the points of dispute; and
- a copy of the default costs certificate.

21.124　An application to set aside for good reason is an application for relief from sanctions; this means that CPR, r 3.9 applies. The well-known factors set out therein will be relevant and (in line with practices in litigation other than costs) must each be considered,[165] but this does not mean that the court must expressly address each an every factor; this is especially when the court is giving judgment *ex tempore*.[166]

---

[159]　CPR, r 47.12(1).
[160]　CPR, r 47.9(4).
[161]　CPR, r 47.9(2); this period is 21 days after service of the Notice of Commencement.
[162]　See the comments in *Meghani v Nessfield Ltd* [2008] EWHC 2827 (Ch) at [7], which indicate that on an earlier occasion Collins J rejected the argument that a miscalculation was reason to set aside the certificate.
[163]　CPD, art 38.2(1); see also CPR, r 3.9(2).
[164]　CPD, art 38.2(3).
[165]　See *Bansal v Cheema* [2001] CP Rep 6 and *Woodhouse v Consignia plc* [2002] EWCA Civ 275.
[166]　*Khatib v Ramco International* [2011] EWCA Civ 605 at [64], per Lloyd LJ.

21.125   In practice, certain factors are (in the writer's experience) regarded as being particularly relevant, including:

- the promptitude with which the application to set aside was made;[167]
- the reasons why points of dispute were not served in time and whether this failure was intentional or accidental;[168]
- whether there was a good explanation for the failure to serve points of dispute on time;[169]
- the extent to which the points of dispute were out of time and the efforts (or lack of efforts) that were made by the receiving party to prompt the paying party to serve them;
- the merits of the bill and, in particular, whether the objections in the draft points of dispute are likely to result in a significant reduction in the allowable costs;[170]
- whether the application was accompanied by the bill of costs, draft points of dispute and a default costs certificate;[171]
- the amount of costs claimed and whether it would be proportionate to allow a detailed assessment to proceed;[172]
- the effect that granting relief would have on the parties;[173] and
- the overall justice of the situation, and whether any prejudice can be compensated for by an award of costs.[174]

21.126   Brooke LJ had the following to say (obiter) about the last of these factors:[175]

'The overriding objective necessarily implied that dealing with a case justly included actually dealing with the case. If the deputy judge had made any other order, he would have shut out the council entirely from pursuing the disputed points in relation to costs, and both sides agreed that the amount of costs were very substantial indeed.'

21.127   Only one or two reported case examples exist. They include the following.

Promptitude

21.128   On the facts of the case before him (in which the paying party was hampered by practical problems), Gibbs J commented that it was difficult to imagine a more prompt application to set aside than 3 days.[176] This indicates that the court will take into account the paying party's circumstances, including any difficulties that he may encounter (but see below). It also, perhaps, gives a broad indication of the time scales that would be regarded as being sufficiently prompt.

---

[167]   CPD, art 38.2(2); see CPR, r 3.9(1)(b); see also the unnamed case mentioned in *Seray-Wurie v London Borough of Hackney* [2002] EWCA Civ 909 at [10]; see also *Bagley v Branch* [2007] EWHC 2344 (Ch), Kitchen J.
[168]   *Smolen v Solon Co-operative Housing Services Ltd* [2005] EWCA Civ 1567.
[169]   CPD, art 38.2(2); and see *Smolen v Solon Co-operative Housing Services Ltd* [2005] EWCA Civ 1567.
[170]   *Ford v Labrador* [2003] UKPC 41 and *Seray-Wurie v London Borough of Hackney* [2002] EWCA Civ 909.
[171]   CPD, art 38.2(3); see also CPR, r 3.9(1)(e).
[172]   *Ford v Labrador* [2003] UKPC 41.
[173]   *Ford v Labrador* [2003] UKPC 41.
[174]   *Ford v Labrador* [2003] UKPC 41.
[175]   *Seray-Wurie v London Borough of Hackney* [2002] EWCA Civ 909 at [11].
[176]   Unreported case mentioned in *Seray-Wurie v London Borough of Hackney* [2002] EWCA Civ 909 at [10].

Procrastination

21.129   Where a paying party (who acted in person throughout) failed entirely to serve points of dispute, Jack J declined to allow an appeal against the decision not to set the certificate aside. He found (obiter) that procrastination by the paying party may be factor to be taken into account, even if the paying party is disadvantaged as a result of illness.[177] Thus, this indicates that there is a limit to the extent to which the court will take the paying party's circumstances into account.

PROCEDURE WHERE COSTS ARE AGREED

21.130   The following discussion contemplates the procedure to be adopted where there is uncontested agreement as to the costs payable; and the procedure when there is a dispute as to whether there has been agreement (ie where the purported compromise is contested) is addressed at **21.139**.

Uncontested agreement as to costs

21.131   If detailed assessment proceedings are settled, the receiving party must give notice of that fact to the court immediately, preferably by fax.[178] CPD, art 46.3 provides the following guidance:

> 'Where an offer to settle is accepted, an application may be made for a certificate in agreed terms, or the bill of costs may be withdrawn, in accordance with rule 47.10 (Procedure where costs are agreed).'

21.132   Thus, there are two expressly recommended mechanisms by which agreement may be effected: by applying for a final costs certificate and by withdrawing the bill of costs on terms. In practice, there are two further mechanisms which ought to be borne in mind; they are discontinuance and the Tomlin order.

Final costs certificate

21.133   CPR, r 47.10 provides guidance as to how to proceed in the event of uncontested agreement as to costs:

> '(1)   If the paying party and the receiving party agree the amount of costs, either party may apply for a costs certificate (either interim or final) in the amount agreed.
>
> (Rule 47.15 and rule 47.16 contain further provisions about interim and final costs certificates respectively)
>
> (2)   An application for a certificate under paragraph (1) must be made to the court which would be the venue for detailed assessment proceedings under rule 47.4.'

21.134   In so far as it is relevant, CPD, art 36 provides the following additional guidance:

> '**36.1** Where the parties have agreed terms as to the issue of a costs certificate (either interim or final) they should apply under rule 40.6 (Consent judgments and orders) for an order that

---

[177]   *Smolen v Solon Co-Operative Housing Services Ltd* [2005] EWCA Civ 1567.
[178]   CPD, art 40.9(2).

a certificate be issued in terms set out in the application. Such an application may be dealt with by a court officer, who may issue the certificate.

36.4 Nothing in rule 47.10 prevents parties who seek a judgment or order by consent from including in the draft a term that a party shall pay to another party a specified sum in respect of costs.'

21.135   Thus where the parties wish to conclude matters in the most formal way, an application may be made for a final costs certificate.

Tomlin orders

21.136   If the compromise embraces matters of which the court is not seized (which is not uncommon in commercial disputes), a Tomlin order can be a convenient way of encapsulating the compromise.[179] A potential disadvantage of this is that the parties may have to return to court for the purposes of enforcing the compromise (this is because the schedule of a Tomlin order gives rise to contractual rights rather than rights which have been ordered by the court).

Withdrawal and discontinuance

21.137   A further way of recording a compromise is to withdraw or discontinue the detailed assessment proceedings upon the agreed terms. Neither of these can be recommended. This is for two reasons: first, these mechanisms would lead to difficulties if there was a need to take a matter back before the court, and secondly, neither of them automatically precludes further detailed assessment proceedings. If the parties are unable or unwilling to agree that a final costs certificate is to be issued, a Tomlin order is generally to be preferred to withdrawal.

21.138   If, notwithstanding the above, the proceedings are to be brought to an end by withdrawal or discontinuance, then CPD, art 36.5 provides the following guidance:

'(1) The receiving party may discontinue the detailed assessment proceedings in accordance with Part 38 (Discontinuance).

(2) Where the receiving party discontinues the detailed assessment proceedings before a detailed assessment hearing has been requested, the paying party may apply to the appropriate office for an order about the costs of the detailed assessment proceedings.

(3) Where a detailed assessment hearing has been requested the receiving party may not discontinue unless the court gives permission.

(4) A bill of costs may be withdrawn by consent whether or not a detailed assessment hearing has been requested.'

CONTESTED AGREEMENTS

21.139   A contested agreement will arise where one party believes that there has been a binding agreement as to the amount of costs payable but the other party (or parties) says otherwise.

21.140   CPD, art 36 provides the following procedural guidance:

---

[179]   A form of wording can be found at **7.55**.

'**36.2** Where in the course of proceedings the receiving party claims that the paying party has agreed to pay costs but that he will neither pay those costs nor join in a consent application under paragraph 36.1, the receiving party may apply under Part 23 (General Rules about Applications for Court Orders) for a certificate either interim or final to be issued.

36.3 An application under paragraph 36.2 must be supported by evidence and will be heard by a costs judge or a district judge. The respondent to the application must file and serve any evidence he relies on at least two days before the hearing date.'

21.141   Whether there has been a compromise will be a matter of fact and law;[180] that topic is addressed at **19.34** *et seq.*

REPLIES

21.142   Replies are a receiving party's comments on the objections raised in the points of dispute. They are optional.[181] Replies may be presented as a separate document prepared by the receiving party *de novo*, or they may be included within the same document as the points of dispute.[182] Replies must be served on the party who has served the points of dispute and on every other party to the detailed assessment proceedings.[183] The time for doing so is within 21 days after service of the points of dispute[184] but, in practice, late service will not usually result in any adverse consequences other than costs consequences (see below). Replies must be signed by the party serving it or by his solicitor.[185]

21.143   Unless he has disobeyed a specific order, no default sanction will be imposed for the late service of replies. This does not mean that a receiving party may ignore the facility with impunity; if he fails to serve replies in circumstances where such sensible intervention would have saved costs, he may find that he has to bear the costs thrown away.

21.144   There are other more specific instances where a failure to serve replies may result in adverse consequences. In particular, failing to reply to an objection to counsel's success fee may result in a finding against the receiving party. This is because CPD, art 20.4 makes the following provisions which suggest that not responding may be taken as being a tacit acceptance of the challenge raised:

'(1) Where detailed assessment proceedings have been commenced, and the paying party serves points of dispute … which show that he is seeking a reduction in any percentage increase charged by counsel on his fees, the solicitor acting for the receiving party must within 3 days of service deliver to counsel a copy of the relevant points of dispute and the bill of costs or the relevant parts of the bill.

(2) Counsel must within 10 days thereafter inform the solicitor in writing whether or not he will accept the reduction sought or some other reduction. Counsel may state any points he wishes to have made in a reply to the points of dispute, and the solicitor must serve them on the paying party as or as part of a reply.

---

[180]   Many of the relevant principles are mentioned at **19.34–19.46**. None of the special rules set out therein which apply to solicitor and client disputes will apply to purported compromises between opposing parties; therefore, the effect of the consumer protection provisions in the Solicitors Act 1974 should be disregarded.
[181]   CPR, r 47.13(1).
[182]   CPD, art 39.1(2).
[183]   CPD, art 39.1(1).
[184]   CPR, r 47.13(2) and CPD, art 39.1(1).
[185]   CPD, art 39.1(3).

(3) Counsel who fails to inform the solicitor within the time limits set out above will be taken to accept the reduction unless the court otherwise orders.'

PROVISIONAL ASSESSMENTS (SELECTED COURTS ONLY)

21.145   A provisional assessment (often referred to as a 'PA') is a paper exercise by which the court carries out an initial assessment on the basis of the bill of costs, the points of dispute, the replies, and certain other documents. It is 'provisional' in the sense that if a party is dissatisfied with the result, he can seek an oral hearing. There is a sting in the tail, however, in that if that party fails to achieve a result that is significantly more advantageous to him than the provisionally assessed figure, he is likely to be condemned in costs.

The past, the present and the future

21.146   Provisional assessments have been a feature of English costs litigation for decades,[186] but over recent years they have featured only in legal aid and in forums such as the Privy Council[187] and the Supreme Court.[188] A similar procedure has been used in Hong Kong since 2009[189] where an 'order *nisi*' may be set aside following an oral assessment.[190]

Selected courts only: Leeds, York and Scarborough

21.147   At the time of writing provisional assessments of costs under the CPR were limited to a pilot running in the Leeds, York and Scarborough County Courts. The pilot began on 1 October 2010 and is due to run until 30 September 2012; it applies only where proceedings were commenced on or after 1 October 2010 and the base costs claimed are £25,000 or less.[191]Anecdotally it has been so popular that litigants from outside Leeds, York and Scarborough have been commencing litigation there in order to be part of the pilot.

Plans for the future

21.148   The pilot has been reported to be a success.[192] Sir Rupert Jackson has recommended that it be rolled out nationally for 'all bills up to £25,000'.[193] It is intended that the procedure will, in future, be improved by having a facility for Part 36 offers and for better automation (which will include self-calculating bills of costs).[194] Whilst not strictly speaking a provisional assessment, there are also plans to make provision for dealing with disbursement-only disputes in the absence of the parties.[195]

---

[186]   See, for example, RSC Ord 62, r 31.
[187]   See para 14 of the Judicial Committee of the Privy Council: Practice Direction 8, Costs.
[188]   The Supreme Court of the United Kingdom, Practice Direction 13, para 14.
[189]   See R Jackson *Report on the Provisional Assessment Pilot*, 13 January 2012.
[190]   See Ord 62, r.21B(1)–(3) of Hong Kong Rules of the High Court.
[191]   See Practice Direction 51E – County Court Provisional Assessment Pilot Scheme, art 1.
[192]   See R Jackson *Report on the Provisional Assessment Pilot*, 13 January 2012.
[193]   See R Jackson *Report on the Provisional Assessment Pilot*, 13 January 2012, para 4.1.
[194]   See R Jackson *Report on the Provisional Assessment Pilot*, 13 January 2012, paras 3.2 and 4.3.
[195]   The proposed wording is at a new CPD, art 40.5A: 'Unless the court otherwise orders, if the only dispute between the parties concerns disbursements, the hearing shall take place in the absence of the parties on the basis of the documents filed and the court will issue'.

Jurisdiction

21.149 Under the aforesaid pilot the jurisdiction to carry out a provisional assessment derives from Practice Direction 51E. That practice direction itself derives its power from CPR, r 51.2 such that it 'modifies or disapplies' the CPR;[196] the relevance of this is that the Practice Direction has an elevated status as a source of law rather than being a mere direction as to practice (see **3.34**).

21.150 Part 47 continues to apply, but in a modified way. The pilot seeks to modify Part 47 by referring to which rules are included, but so many rules fall within that category that it is easier to refer to what does not, namely, CPR, r 47.14(6) and (7);[197] thus, as one would expect, the excluded provisions are those that relate to procedure at detailed assessment hearings. The CPD is treated in a similar way.[198]

Procedure

21.151 Under the pilot, when the receiving party files the request for a detailed assessment hearing, in addition to the bill of costs, Notice of Commencement, etc, he must also file an additional copy of the bill and a statement of the costs of the detailed assessment; that statement must be drawn on the assumption that no party will subsequently request an oral hearing following a provisional assessment.[199] Within 6 weeks of receipt of those documents the court will undertake a provisional assessment based on the information contained in the bill of costs, the points of dispute and the replies. The court will take into account the papers filed with the bill of costs, but the receiving party's file of papers is not lodged. No party will be permitted to attend the provisional assessment.[200]

21.152 If the court takes the view that the matter is unsuitable for a provisional assessment, the court will direct that the matter must be listed for hearing; where this happens, the pilot scheme ceases to apply.[201]

21.153 If, on the other hand, the court continues with the provisional assessment, it will send a copy of the bill as provisionally assessed to each party with a notice stating that either party may request the court to list the matter for full argument on any aspect of the provisional assessment within 21 days of receipt of the notice.[202]

21.154 Unless the only dispute is the amount of the costs of the assessment as provisionally assessed, then either party may, within 21 days of receipt of the notice and provisionally assessed bill, aks for an oral hearing; the court will then fix a date for the hearing and give at least 14 days' notice of thereof.[203] If the only dispute is the amount of the costs of the assessment as provisionally assessed, then the court will invite written submissions on that point.[204]

---

[196]   See CPR, r 51.2.
[197]   See PD 51E, art 2.
[198]   The following provisions in the CPD are excluded: CPD arts 40.5–40.7, 40.9, 40.11 and 40.16; again, those provisions all relate to procedure at the detailed assessment hearing.
[199]   See PD 51E, art 3.
[200]   See PD 51E, art 4.
[201]   See PD 51E, art 5
[202]   See PD 51E, art 6.
[203]   See PD 51E, art 7.
[204]   See PD 51E art 9.

The costs of the assessment

21.155 Unless the court otherwise, the costs of the assessment are dealt with in the following way:

- **Costs awarded to the paying party:** If the costs as finally assessed are 80% or less than the amount provisionally assessed, or if the receiving party was the one who asked for the hearing and the amount allowed is not more than 120% of the amount provisionally assessed, the costs of the assessment will be awarded to the paying party:[205]
- **Costs awarded to the receiving party:** If the costs as finally assessed are 120% or more than the amount provisionally assessed, or if the paying party was the one who asked for the hearing and the amount allowed is more than 80% of the amount provisionally assessed, the costs of the assessment will be awarded to the receiving party:[206]
- **No order for costs:** Where both parties asked for the hearing, and where the amount allowed is greater than 80% but less than 120% of the sum which had been provisionally assessed, then neither party will be awarded their costs.[207]

The costs of the provisional assessment are excluded for the purposes of applying the rules set out above.[208]

Wording

21.156 The wording of the relevant provisions is as follows:[209]

'1 This Practice Direction is made under rule 51.2. It provides for a pilot scheme (the County Court Provisional Assessment Pilot Scheme) to—

    (1)   operate from the 1 October 2010 to 30 September 2012;

    (2)   operate in the Leeds, York and Scarborough County Courts;

    (3)   apply to detailed assessment proceedings

        (a)   which are commenced on or after 1 October 2010; and

        (b)   in which the base costs claimed are £25,000 or less.

2 Under this pilot scheme CPR Part 47 will apply with modifications. The following provisions of Part 47 and the Costs Practice Direction will continue to apply—

    (1)   rules 47.1, 47.2, 47.4 to 47.13, 47.14 (except paragraphs (6) and (7)), 47.15, 47.16, 47.18 and 47.19; and

    (2)   sections 28, 29, 31 to 39, 40 (with the exception of paragraphs 40.5 to 40.7, 40.9, 40.11 and 40.16), 41, 42, 45 and 46 of the Costs Practice Direction.

3 In cases falling within the scope of this pilot scheme, when the receiving party files the request for a detailed assessment hearing, that party must not only file the request in Form N258 together with the documents set out at paragraph 40.2 of the Costs Practice Direction but must also file with them an additional copy of the bill and a statement of the costs claimed in respect of the detailed assessment drawn on the assumption that (unless any of the following paragraphs apply) no party will subsequently request an oral hearing following a provisional assessment.

---

[205]   See PD 51E, art 8(1).
[206]   See PD 51E, art 8(2).
[207]   See PD 51E, art 8(2).
[208]   See PD 51E, art 8(1), (2) and (3).
[209]   PD 51E.

4 On receipt of the request for detailed assessment and the supporting papers, the court will within 6 weeks undertake a provisional assessment based on the information contained in the bill and supporting papers and the contentions set out in the points of dispute and any reply. No party will be permitted to attend the provisional assessment.

5 If, having commenced a provisional assessment, the court takes the view that the matter is unsuitable for a provisional assessment, the court will direct that the matter must be listed for hearing and thereafter the pilot scheme will cease to apply to it.

6 If the court completes a provisional assessment, it will send a copy of the bill as provisionally assessed to each party with a notice stating that either party may request the court to list the matter for full argument on any aspect of the provisional assessment within 21 days of receipt of the notice.

7 Unless paragraph 9 applies, either party may, within 21 days of receipt of the notice and provisionally assessed bill, request the court by letter to list the matter for an oral hearing. On receipt of a request for an oral hearing the court will fix a date for the hearing and give at least 14 days notice of the time and place of the detailed assessment hearing to all parties who are entitled to be heard.

8 Unless the court otherwise orders the costs of and incidental to an oral hearing convened under paragraph 7 above, shall be awarded as follows—

(1)   Costs may be awarded to a paying party if the amount allowed is reduced to a sum which is 80% or less than the sum which had been provisionally assessed (excluding costs of the provisional assessment), or if the oral hearing was requested by a receiving party only and the amount allowed is not increased to a sum which is 120% or more than the sum which had been provisionally assessed (excluding costs of the provisional assessment).

(2)   Costs may be awarded to a receiving party, if the amount allowed is increased to a sum which is 120% or more than the sum which had been provisionally assessed (excluding costs of the provisional assessment), or if the oral hearing was requested by a paying party only and the amount allowed is not reduced to a sum which is 80% or less than the sum which had been provisionally assessed (excluding costs of the provisional assessment).

(3)   Where requests for an oral hearing are made by a receiving party and also by a paying party no order for the costs of and incidental to the oral hearing will be made if the amount allowed is greater than 80% but less than 120% of the sum which had been provisionally assessed (excluding costs of the provisional assessment).

9 If a party wishes to be heard only as to the amount provisionally assessed in respect of the receiving party's costs of the provisional assessment, the court will invite each side to make written submissions and the amount of the costs of the provisional assessment will be finally determined without a hearing.'

OFFERS TO SETTLE (PART 47 OFFERS)

21.157   The topic of offers and the incidence of the costs of the detailed assessment is addressed at **21.230–21.266**. The present discussion deals with the complementary topic of the form, content, and acceptance of offers. Where appropriate, the two sections should be read in conjunction.

21.158   CPR, r 47.19 implicitly provides that the parties may each make offers to settle the detailed assessment proceedings and that those offers may be made without prejudice save as to the costs of the detailed assessment proceedings. The term 'Part 47 offer' is used to refer to such an offer.

The time for making an offer

21.159 For the reasons set out below, there are (within reason) no restrictions on when a Part 47 offer can be made.

Early offers

21.160 There is no prohibition against a Part 47 offer being made prior to service of the notice of commencement.[210]

Late offers

21.161 Neither the CPR nor the CPD specifies a restrictive time limit within which a Part 47 offer must be made. The CPD directs (as opposed to mandates) that where it is made by the paying party, an offer should be made within 14 days of service of the notice of commencement and, where it is made by the receiving party, it ought to be made within 14 days of service of the points of dispute.[211] 'Days' are clear days, but include weekends and bank holidays.[212] These directions are often not heeded; this is because the paying party would usually wish to wait until he has drafted points of dispute before making an offer.

21.162 There is no reason in principle why an offer cannot be made after the expiry of the periods mentioned above. That said, an offer outwith those periods may be afforded less weight:[213] this topic is discussed at **21.230–21.266**.

The form and scope of the offer

21.163 It is implicit from CPR, r 47.19(1) that a Part 47 offer is required to be in writing and to be expressed to be without prejudice save as to costs of the detailed assessment proceedings. In a pre-CPR case, Roderick Evans J held that a failure to comply with the then requirements under the RSC did not prevent the court from taking that offer into account (albeit as a *Calderbank* offer);[214] there is no reason to believe that this would not also be the case under the CPR.

Interest, VAT, etc

21.164 An offer should specify whether it is intended to be inclusive of interest, value added tax and the costs of preparation of the bill. An offer which is silent on these monies will be deemed to include them.[215] This reflects the pre-CPR position.[216]

---

[210] Whilst a pre-CPR case, see *Platt v GKN Kwikform Ltd* [1992] 1 WLR 465.

[211] CPD, art 46.1.

[212] CPR, r 2.8(3) and (4).

[213] CPD, art 46.1 and *Wills v Crown Estate Commissioners* [2003] EWHC 1718 (Ch) at [31].

[214] *Morris v Wiltshire and Woodspring District Council* [2002] 1 Costs LR 167 at [24].

[215] CPD, art 46.2.

[216] *Bell v Mahoney, 17 May 1991, ChD*: an offer that was 'in full settlement of your claim for costs' was deemed to be inclusive of interest.

Part 47 offers and costs-only proceedigns

21.165 Where a Part 47 offer is for the costs of a claim which settled without the need for the issue of proceedings, it will not by default be taken to include the costs of any subsequent cost-only proceedings.[217]

Partial and conditional Part 47 offers

21.166 Where a significant point of principle exists (such as a point concerning the indemnity principle), an offer may be expressed in conditional terms (e g 'subject to you proving that there has been no breach of the indemnity principle, the defendant offers the sum of £———'). A pedant would argue that such an offer is not a true Part 47 offer; this may be so, but regardless of its taxonomy, there is no reason to believe that it would not be taken into account.

21.167 The rules for formal service of documents as contained in CPR, Part 6 do not apply to Part 36 offers.[218] There is no reason to believe that Part 47 offers should be treated any differently.

Offers other than Part 47 offers

21.168 A written offer which is without prejudice save as to the costs of the detailed assessment will, in general, be a Part 47 offer. This will not always be the case, however.

21.169 The categories of offer that may be made in detailed assessment proceedings are:

- Part 47 offers;
- 'admissible offers' akin to that described in CPR, r 44.3(4)(c);
- *Calderbank* offers;
- commercial offers (or without prejudice offers); and
- (in rare circumstances) Part 36 offers.

There is overlap between these categories; each category is considered in turn (other than Part 47 offers, which are addressed at **21.230–21.266**).

Admissible offers

21.170 The term 'admissible offer' derives from CPR, r 44.3(4)(c); strictly speaking, those provisions do not apply to detailed assessments,[219] but the terminology may be used by analogy. An offer which has failed to comply with the formalities mentioned above (**21.163–21.164**) may fall into the category of being an admissible offer. An offer which includes something other than the costs of the proceedings which gave rise to the detailed assessment may be treated in a similar manner.[220] It is a moot point whether an 'all inclusive' offer (ie an offer inclusive of the costs of the assessment) is a Part 47 offer or an admissible offer. Whilst not binding on any court, HHJ Hughes QC has found that a Part 47 offer should not include anything other than the costs claimed in the

---

[217] *Crosbie v Munroe* [2003] EWCA Civ 350.
[218] *Charles v NGL Group Ltd* [2002] EWCA Civ 2004.
[219] The incidence of costs of detailed assessment is governed by CPR, r 47.18 rather than r 44.3.
[220] See, for example, *Morris v Wiltshire and Woodspring District Council* [2002] 1 Costs LR 167 at [24].

bill.[221] This would accord by analogy with the way in which Part 36 is interpreted.[222] Regardless of how it is categorised, it would often be difficult to take an all-inclusive offer into account in determining incidence of costs;[223] the practical effect of this is that an all-inclusive offer will afford the offeree a lesser degree of costs protection than an offer which excludes those costs. This disadvantage has to be balanced against the benefit that, if accepted without qualification, an all-inclusive offer would bring an end to the detailed assessment.

Calderbank offers

21.171   In the present context there is, for all practical purposes, no difference in principle between a *Calderbank* offer and an admissible offer.[224]

Commercial offers (or without prejudice offers)

21.172   It may be that an offeror wishes to make an offer which is not intended to afford any costs protection, but is made solely for the purposes of disposing of the matter on a commercial basis. Such an offer would not be admissible in the question of costs and would often be expressly stated to be without prejudice (as opposed to without prejudice save as to costs). There are as many motives for making a commercial offer as there are offerors: an example would be where an offer is made in the context of mediation or where the offeror wants to emphasise that the offer is made in a genuine spirit of compromise rather than in an attempt to garner a tactical advantage. Whilst not in a binding decision, HHJ Hughes QC has found that in the absence of reason to believe otherwise, a commercial offer should be taken to include the costs of the negotiation which led to it being made.[225]

Part 36 offers

21.173   It may be appropriate to make a Part 36 offer rather than a Part 47 offer; indeed, Sir Rupert Jackson has said that this is being considered as the default position.[226] Where such an offer is made, it will be necessary to explain that the receiving party is analogous to the claimant and the paying party is analogous to the defendant.

21.174   There is no reason why an offer cannot be stated to fall into more than one of these categories. If, for example, the offeror is unsure about the nature of the offer, it may be stated to be 'a Part 47 offer or in the alternative an admissible offer and/or a *Calderbank* offer'.

---

[221]   *Longman v Feather & Black (a firm), 18 March 2008, Southampton County Court*, HHJ Hughes QC at para 52; compare this with the pre-CPR case of *Morris v Wiltshire and Woodspring District Council* [2002] 1 Costs LR 167 at 176, in which Roderick Evans J seems to have entertained a different analysis.

[222]   See *Mitchell v James* [2002] EWCA Civ 997, in which it was found that a Part 36 offer could not be inclusive of costs.

[223]   This is because the court would have to estimate the value of the costs at the detailed assessment at the time the offer was made.

[224]   A pedant would say that an admissible offer is a term of art which refers to CPR, r 44.3(4)(c) and that, as that provision does not apply to the costs of detailed assessments, the term *Calderbank* offer is to be preferred.

[225]   See *Longman v Feather & Black (a firm), 18 February 2008, Southampton County Court*; HHJ Hughes QC rejected the submission that in so far as *Ross v Owners of the Bowbelle* [1997] 1 WLR 1159 at 1163 (per Leggatt LJ) was authority for the proposition that acceptance of an offer carried with it an implied right to the costs of negotiation, it was no longer good law under the CPR.

[226]   KPMG Forensic Law Lecture 2012, 25 January 2012.

Withdrawal, amendment, rejection and limitation of Part 47 offers

21.175 Offers may be withdrawn (or revoked), varied, rejected or limited. Part 47 imposes no fetters in this regard; this means that the ordinary principles of contract will apply. Each topic is addressed in turn.

Express withdrawal of Part 47 offers

21.176 Provided it has not been accepted, an offer may be expressly withdrawn at any time.[227] What is unclear is whether an offeror may subsequently rely upon a withdrawn offer for the purposes of influencing the court's decision as to the incidence of costs. There is no authority on the point, but it may be that a withdrawn offer can to be taken into account in such a way as to afford it less weight than would have been the case had it not been withdrawn.

Implied withdrawal of Part 47 offers

21.177 There are no formalities for withdrawing a Part 47 offer (or any of the other offers mentioned above other than Part 36 offers). Whilst there is no affirmative authority on the point, the absence of formalities leaves the way open for Part 47 offers to be withdrawn informally by implication.[228] In particular, there is nothing in the CPR which would prevent the court from finding that an offer had been impliedly withdrawn by the effluxion of time (see **21.182**).

Variation of Part 47 offers

21.178 Any offer can be varied, but a variation which is disadvantageous to the offeree may be seen as being an implied withdrawal of the original offer.[229] If, on the other hand, the variation is on such terms as to costs that it affords the offeree a further chance to accept the original offer, that may be seen as being a form of a renewal;[230] in appropriate circumstances that may add to the weight subsequently to be given to that offer.

Rejection of Part 47 offers

21.179 As with any offer of a general contractual nature, a clear and unambiguous rejection of an offer will determine the offeree's ability to accept it.[231] Whilst a trite point, it is worth reciting that a counter-offer is usually interpreted as being an implied rejection.[232]

---

[227] In a context other than costs, see *Payne v Cave* (1789) 3 Term Rep 148.
[228] Ibid.
[229] In a context other than costs, see *Gilkes v Leonino* (1858) 4 CBNS 485.
[230] In a context other than costs, see *Dunlop v Higgins* (1848) 1 HL Cas 381.
[231] In a context other than costs, see *Thornbury v Bevill* (1842) 1 Y & C Ch Cas 554.
[232] See *Hyde v Wrench* (1840) 3 Beav 334 at 337 and *Norfolk County Council v Dencare Properties Ltd* (unreported) 9 November 2005, CAT; see also the discussion in *Halsbury's Laws of England* (9th edn), vol 9(1), para 663.

Express limitation of Part 47 offers

21.180   An offer may terminate at a time specified in the offer.[233] It is not uncommon to see offers stated to be open for acceptance for a period of 21 days.

Implied limitation of Part 47 offers

21.181   An offer may contain an implied term that it may not be accepted after a particular stage in the proceedings has been reached. By analogy, it is very likely that an offer cannot be accepted after commencement of the detailed assessment hearing,[234] and there is almost no doubt that an offer cannot be accepted after the conclusion of the hearing.[235] Other determining events also exist: though well beyond the scope of this book, these would include death, incapacity, and insolvency.

Effluxion of time and Part 47 offers

21.182   In general (ie in contexts other than costs), an offer will expire after a reasonable period of time.[236] What amounts to a reasonable period of time will be a matter for the tribunal of fact; it is an issue which will turn on factors such as the nature of the offer[237] (and, in particular, on whether it was inclusive of costs)[238], the subsequent conduct of the parties, and whether there was any implied renewal of the offer.[239] It is quite possible that true Part 47 offers (ie offers which do not include any costs) never expire solely by reason of the effluxion of time: that is a point which is arguable either way.

Acceptance of an offer

21.183   There are no formalities governing the acceptance of Part 47 offers, so an offer may be accepted by any method, such as by written acceptance, by oral acceptance, or by the offeree's conduct. With one important exception, the acceptance must be communicated to the offeror. The exception is 'the posting rule', which, as every law student knows, is a rule which stipulates that when a written acceptance is delivered by post, it will generally be effective from the moment it is posted.[240]

21.184   An offer may be accepted by the offeree's agent[241] (such as his costs draftsman). Where there is a dispute as to whether the offeree (principal) has been bound by the putative acceptance of an offer by his supposed agent, it may be necessary to examine the authority (both actual and ostensible) of the agent. This is an issue which is beyond the scope of this book.

---

[233]   The authority which is often cited in this regard is persuasive only (because it is not English): *Barrick v Clark* [1951] SCR 177, [1950] 4 DLR 529, Can SC.

[234]   While dealing with CPR, Part 36 rather than CPR, Part 47, see *Hawley v Luminar Leisure plc* [2006] EWCA Civ 30 at [26].

[235]   In a non-costs context, see *Bright v Low* 1940 SC 280.

[236]   See, for example, *Meynell v Surtees* (1855) 25 LJ Ch 257.

[237]   In a context other than costs, see *Ramsgate Victoria Hotel Co Ltd v Montefiore* (1866) LR 1 Exch 109.

[238]   In a context other than costs, see *Wakefield (t/a Wills Probate and Trusts of Weybridge) v Ford* [2009] EWHC 122 (QB).

[239]   In a context other than costs, see *Dunlop v Higgins* (1848) 1 HL Cas 381.

[240]   *Henthorne v Fraser* [1892] 2 Ch 27.

[241]   *Earl v Mawson* (1973) 228 Estates Gazette 529; affd (1974) 232 Estates Gazette 1315, CA.

21.185 Acceptance of a Part 47 offer will result in a compromise of the costs to which the offer relates. Three points merit specific mention.

Interest, VAT and the costs of preparing the bill

21.186 If the offer is silent as to the costs of preparing the bill, interest and value added tax, acceptance of the offer will compromise any entitlement that the receiving party may have had.[242]

Part 8 proceedings and acceptance of Part 47 offers

21.187 Unless there is reason to believe otherwise, acceptance of a Part 47 offer made in the context of costs-only proceedings will not compromise the costs of the Part 8 proceedings.[243]

Costs of negotiation and acceptance of Part 47 offers

21.188 Whilst not binding, HHJ Hughes QC has found that, unless there is reason to believe otherwise (such as the offeree stating that he reserves the right to raise a further claim), acceptance of a commercial offer will compromise the costs of negotiation.[244]

21.189 In some circumstances (such as where one of the parties is a child or a patient), the court's approval may be required before the compromise is enforceable; these issues are touched upon (albeit only briefly) elsewhere in this book.

Offers at the hearing

21.190 Neither the fact nor the terms of a Part 47 offer may be communicated to the court until the stage is reached where the court will hear submissions as to the costs of the detailed assessment.[245] Unlike the analogous provisions in Part 36, no express exceptions to this rule are made in Part 47. That said, common sense dictates that the exceptions set out in Part 36 will also apply to Part 47 offers; they are:

- where it is said that the assessment has been compromised (in which case CPD, art 36.2 may apply);
- where the proceedings have been stayed following acceptance of an offer; and
- where the offeror and the offeree agree in writing that the court may be told of the fact of the offer.

21.191 If, without proper cause, the fact of an offer is communicated to the court, that may or may not be grounds for recusal. Whilst dealing with the issue of recusal in a context other than costs, Lord Hope has described the appropriate test as being whether a fair-minded and informed observer, having considered the facts, would conclude that

---

[242] CPD, art 46.2.
[243] Which reads: 'a written offer to settle the costs of the proceedings which gave rise to the assessment proceedings'.
[244] See *Longman v Feather & Black (a firm)* 18 February 2008, Southampton County Court.
[245] CPR, r 47.19(2).

there was a real possibility that the tribunal would be biased.[246] Whether inadvertent disclosure of an offer would lead to the possibility of bias would depend on the facts of the case.

REQUESTING A HEARING

21.192   Costs proceedings are an atypical example of civil litigation in the sense that they are commenced without the involvement of the court, ie they are commenced by way of proceedings being served on the paying party rather than proceedings being filed at or issued by the court. This means that the court will play a role only where requested to do so. That request would take the form of a request for a detailed assessment hearing. Either of the parties may ask for the court's assistance, but the requests that they are permitted to make are not the same.

The receiving party's role

21.193   The onus to request a hearing lies with the receiving party. Where points of dispute have been served, the receiving party must file a request for a detailed assessment hearing.[247] That request must be filed within 3 months of the expiry of the period during which detailed assessment proceedings must be commenced.[248]

The paying party's remedies and delay

21.194   The paying party cannot himself apply for a hearing. Instead, where the receiving party has failed to apply for a hearing within the period mentioned above, he may file a request for an order requiring the receiving party to file a request.[249] The court may direct that, unless the receiving party requests a detailed assessment hearing within a certain time, all or part of the costs to which the receiving party would otherwise be entitled will be disallowed.[250] Such an order is usually referred to as an 'unless order'.

21.195   There is no reason why the guidance given by Moore-Bick LJ about unless orders in general would not apply (see **21.87**);[251] he reminded himself that an unless order is one of the most powerful weapons in the court's case management armoury and that it should be deployed only if 'its consequences can be justified'. He also reminded himself that it would be difficult to imagine circumstances in which such an order could properly be made for 'good housekeeping purposes'. Notwithstanding that guidance, it is commonplace for unless orders to be made against receiving parties who recidivistically fail to progress matters.

21.196   Where the receiving party has filed a request for a hearing later than the period specified in CPR, r 47.14 and where the paying party has not filed a request for an order,

---

[246]   *Magill v Weeks* [2001] UKHL 67.
[247]   CPR, r 47.14(1).
[248]   CPR, r 47.14(2) and CPD, art 40.1.
[249]   CPR, r 47.14(3) and CPD, art 40.7(1).
[250]   CPR, r 47.14(4).
[251]   *Marcan Shipping (London) Ltd v Kefalas* [2007] EWCA Civ 463 at [36].

the court is permitted to disallow interest on the costs, but (in the absence of misconduct) must not impose any other sanction.[252] This is discussed in more detail at **21.208–21.209**.

Documents for requesting a hearing

21.197 A request for a detailed assessment hearing is made by way of standard form;[253] a separate style of standard form must be used for publicly funded work.[254] Copies of a number of documents must accompany the form; the requirements differ, depending on whether the court is to assess publicly funded costs.

No publicly funded costs

21.198 The following provisions apply to any non-publicly funded costs, including where the court is asked to assess costs payable out of a fund other than the Community Legal Services Fund.[255]

21.199 The request for a hearing must be accompanied by:[256]

- the bill of costs;
- the notice of commencement;
- the document giving the right to detailed assessment (ie the costs order, Part 36 offer and acceptance, the tribunal's award, etc);
- the points of dispute from each person who has served them;
- the replies, if any;
- all orders relating to the costs which are to be assessed;
- relevant details of any additional liability claimed[257] (see below);
- a certificate in accordance with CPD, art 20.6, if appropriate (see below);
- fee notes and other written evidence as served on the paying party in accordance with CPD, art 32.3;
- where there is a dispute as to the indemnity principle, any agreement, letter or other written information provided by the solicitor to his client explaining how the solicitor's charges are to be calculated; and
- a statement signed by the receiving party or his solicitor giving the name, address for service, reference and telephone number and fax number, if any, of:
  - the receiving party;
  - the paying party; and
  - any 'relevant person' as defined in CPD, art 32.10(1)(b);
  and giving a time estimate for the detailed assessment hearing.

21.200 Where appropriate, the points of dispute must be annotated to show which items have been agreed and their value.[258]

---

[252] CPR, r 47.14(5).
[253] N258.
[254] N258A.
[255] Where that is the case, an N258B must be used.
[256] CPD, art 40.2 and art 20.6.
[257] This item is listed on the standard form but is missing from the CPD itself; this, presumably, is merely an oversight.
[258] CPD, art 40.2(d).

21.201 The relevant details of an additional liability are as follows:[259]

(1) Where there is a conditional fee agreement (including a collective conditional fee agreement) which provides for a success fee, the following are relevant:
- a statement showing the amount of costs which have been summarily assessed or agreed, and the percentage increase which has been claimed in respect of those costs; and
- a statement of the reasons for the percentage increase given in accordance with reg 3(1)(a) of the Conditional Fee Agreements Regulations or reg 5(1)(c) of the Collective Conditional Fee Agreements Regulations 2000.
    (As of 1 November 2005, these regulations have been revoked,[260] so this latter requirement will have only limited applicability.)
(2) Where the additional liability is an insurance premium, the following are relevant:
- a copy of the insurance certificate showing whether the policy covers:
    – the receiving party's own costs;
    – his opponents costs; or
    – his own costs and his opponent's costs; and
- the maximum extent of that cover; and
- the amount of the premium paid or payable.
    (It may be the case that the certificate itself does not bear all of these details on its face; if so, then it would be sensible to provide them somewhere else.)
(3) Where the additional liability is a notional premium (ie an additional amount payable under s 30 of the Access of Justice Act 1999), a statement setting out the basis upon which the receiving party's liability for the additional amount is calculated must be provided.

21.202 The combination of the CPD, art 4.15 and Precedent F of the Schedule of Costs Precedents annexed to the CPD makes it clear that the bill of costs should be properly certified (see **21.35**). CPD, art 20.6[261] makes provision for an additional certificate to be served where a success fee is disputed.[262] It is not wholly clear at which stage of the proceedings that certificate would be required, but it would probably be when the solicitor intends to recover from his own client any success fee not recovered from the paying party (ie where there is a shortfall in the success fee). The certificate must state the following:

- that the amount of the percentage increase is disputed, either in respect of counsel's fees or the solicitor's fees;
- whether the solicitor will make an application for an order that the aforesaid shortfall remains payable by his client;
- that the solicitor has given his client an explanation in accordance with CPD, art 20.5; and

---

[259] CPD, art 32.5.

[260] Conditional Fee Agreements (Revocation) Regulations 2005 (SI 2005/2305).

[261] Which reads: 'Where the solicitor acting for a receiving party files a request for a detailed assessment hearing it must if appropriate, be accompanied by a certificate signed by him stating: (1) that the amount of the percentage increase in respect of counsel's fees or solicitor's charges is disputed; (2) whether an application will be made for an order that any amount of that increase which is disallowed should continue to be payable by his client; (3) that he has given his client an explanation in accordance with paragraph 20.5; and (4) whether his client wishes to attend court when the amount of any relevant percentage increase may be decided.'

[262] There is no precedent for that certificate in the Schedule of Costs Precedents; the writer's suggested precedent appears at the end of this book.

- whether his client wishes to attend court when the amount of any relevant percentage increase is to be decided.

Publicly funded costs

21.203 The following provisions apply only if the court is to assess publicly funded costs (ie costs of an assisted person or LSC funded client). Where this is the case, copies of the following documents must be filed in addition to those mentioned above:[263]

- the legal aid certificate, LSC certificate and relevant amendments thereto, together with any authorities and any certificates of discharge or revocation;
- a certificate in accordance with the precedent at Precedent F(3) of the Schedule of Costs Precedents (ie a certificate of the funded person's interests);
- if the assisted person has a financial interest in the detailed assessment hearing and wishes to attend the hearing, the postal address of that person;
- if the rates payable out of the LSC fund are prescribed rates, a schedule to the bill of costs setting out all the items in the bill which are claimed against other parties calculated at the legal aid prescribed rates with or without any claim for enhancement: (see CPD, art 48); and
- a copy of any relevant default costs certificate.

Where documents in the list above relate to public funding, the documents must be the latest relevant version and in any event must not be more than 2 years old (at the time of filing).[264] If those documents have been filed previously, then they need not be filed again, but the receiving party must specify the case number under which the court may locate the documents.[265]

Fees for requesting a hearing

21.204 The Ministry of Justice is empowered to levy a fee for the court's services.[266] It is the Ministry's stated aim that court fees should be set, so far as possible, at levels that reflect the full cost of the process involved.[267]

21.205 The fees for detailed assessment used to be modest but, following consultation,[268] they have, since 1 May 2008, significantly increased.[269] Where the only costs to be assessed are publicly funded costs, a fee of £120 is payable in the Senior Courts Costs Office, or £105 in the county court,[270] In all other cases a sliding scale will apply, that scale being based on the sums claimed:[271]

---

[263] CPD, art 40.2(i).
[264] CPD, art 40.3(1).
[265] CPD, art 40.3(2).
[266] Courts Act 2003, s 92.
[267] See para 2 of *Civil Court Fees 2008*, Consultation Paper, CP31/08.
[268] *Civil Court Fees 2008*, Consultation Paper, CP 5/07.
[269] Civil Proceedings Fees Order 2008 (SI 2008/1053), art 1(1).
[270] SI 2008/1053, Sch 1, Fee 5, para 5.1.
[271] SI 2008/1053, Sch 1, Fee 5, para 5.2.

Sums claimed	*Fee payable*
does not exceed £15,000:	£300
exceeds £15,000 but does not exceed £50,000:	£600
exceeds £50,000 but does not exceed £100,000:	£900
exceeds £100,000 but does not exceed £150,000:	£1,200
exceeds £150,000 but does not exceed £200,000:	£1,500
exceeds £200,000 but does not exceed £300,000:	£2,250
exceeds £300,000 but does not exceed £500,000:	£3,750
exceeds £500,000:	£5,000

21.206   Where the bill contains both publicly funded costs and costs payable between the parties, the fees will be attributed proportionately on the basis of the amounts allowed.[272]

Other procedural issues

21.207   Once it has received a request for a detailed assessment hearing, the court will fix a date. Alternatively, the court will give directions or fix a date for a preliminary appointment.[273]

SANCTION FOR DELAY IN REQUESTING A HEARING

21.208   Where the receiving party has filed a request for a hearing later than the period specified in CPR, r 47.14 and where the paying party has not filed a request for an order pursuant to r 47.14(3), the court may disallow interest, but (in the absence of misconduct) must not impose any other sanction.[274] There is a possibility that this power does not exist in the county court: see **36.12**.

21.209   The provisions referred to above are capable of being read restrictively in the sense that the court is not able to disallow interest if the paying party has filed a request for an order pursuant to CPR, r 47.14(3). There is no authority on that point, but if that interpretation is correct, then where the detailed assessment has ground to a halt after service of the bill of costs, the paying party must make an election: either he can make an application and forgo disallowance of interest, or he can bide his time and ask the court to disallow interest if and when the assessment is revived. If this analysis is correct, the least attractive option would be to allow many months to pass and then to make an application.

---

[272] SI 2008/1053, Sch 1, Fee 5, para 5.2.
[273] CPD, art 40.5.
[274] CPR, r 47.14(5); see also CPD, art 40.7(2).

THE HEARING

21.210   The hearing will be in public unless the court orders otherwise[275] or unless the court is determining the liability of a publicly funded client.[276]

21.211   The court will, in due course, give at least 14 days' notice of the hearing.[277] Any request to vary the date of the hearing must be made in accordance with CPR, Part 23.[278] Likewise, a request to vary directions must be made upon application[279] (even if the variation is sought by consent).[280] In practice, this latter requirement is not always rigidly enforced.

Special notice provisions

21.212   Special notice provisions may apply from time to time; in particular, notice must be given where there is an allegation of misconduct or where the receiving party's solicitor intends to recover a shortfall in the success fee.

21.213   If the court intends to rule on whether there has been misconduct within the meaning of CPR, r 44.14, it must give the party or legal representative in question a reasonable opportunity to attend a hearing to give reasons why it should not make such an order.[281]

21.214   If the receiving party's solicitor intends to recover any shortfall in the success fee from his client, he must inform his client within 7 days of receipt of the notice. If counsel seeks his shortfall, he must be informed too.[282]

Filing papers in support of the bill

21.215   The CPD provides that unless the court directs otherwise, the receiving party must file the papers in support of the bill of costs not less than 7 and not more than 14 days before the hearing date.[283] A number of county courts have their own practices

---

[275] See CPR, r 39.2 and PD 39A, para 1.2; the circumstances in which the court may order otherwise are limited in the following way (CPR, r 39.2(3)):
  'A hearing, or any part of it, may be in private if—
  (a)   publicity would defeat the object of the hearing;
  (b)   it involves matters relating to national security;
  (c)   it involves confidential information (including information relating to personal financial matters) and publicity would damage that confidentiality;
  (d)   a private hearing is necessary to protect the interests of any child or protected party;
  (e)   it is a hearing of an application made without notice and it would be unjust to any respondent for there to be a public hearing;
  (f)   it involves uncontentious matters arising in the administration of trusts or in the administration of a deceased person's estate; or
  (g)   the court considers this to be necessary, in the interests of justice.'
[276] CPR, r 23.8.
[277] CPD, art 40.6(1).
[278] CPD, art 40.9(1)(b) and (3).
[279] CPD, art 40.9.
[280] CPD, art 40.9(1)(c) and (4).
[281] CPD, art 18.1.
[282] CPD, art 20.7(1). One reason for this is because a very large number of seemingly contested detailed assessments settle shortly before the detailed assessment hearing.
[283] CPD, art 40.11.

which local costs practitioners will be expected to know; in particular, some courts will discourage early filing, preferring instead for the papers to be made available on the day of the assessment itself.

21.216   Unless the court orders otherwise, there is no need to file or serve a statement of costs of the detailed assessment.[284] There are, however, plans to change the CPD in such a way as to bring detailed assessments into line with other types of hearing.

Submissions at the hearing

21.217   Unless the court gives permission, only the following persons may be heard on the detailed assessment:[285]

- the receiving party;
- the paying party; and
- any party who has served points of dispute under CPR, r 47.9.

Where counsel seeks to recover a shortfall in his success fee, he too is entitled to be heard or to make written submissions[286] (presumably limited to the issues in which he has an interest).

21.218   Although there is no prescriptive rule on the point, the court will generally work through the objections in the points of dispute sequentially. Items may be taken out of turn where the court so directs: an example might be where the court leaves the issue of hourly rates until the later stages of the hearing.[287] Only items specified in the points of dispute may be raised at the hearing, unless the court gives permission.[288] That said, the court should give due weight to the need to allow the parties to be heard; in this regard Peter Smith J found that it was wrong not to hear a paying party on a 'totally new' point even though an adjournment had been granted previously to allow the same party to put a different 'totally new' point.[289]

Judgments in the context of detailed assessment

21.219   A reasoned judgment must be given: although dealing with criminal rather than civil costs, Richards LJ has confirmed that when the court disallows costs, it is incumbent on the costs judge to provide some explanation, however brief.[290] Where a party is concerned that inadequate reasons have been given, he should generally invite the judge to consider whether to amplify upon those reasons before complaining about their inadequacy to an appeal court.[291]

21.220   The court will usually give judgment on each item individually. In keeping with the general principle that a judgment takes effect from the time when the judge

---

[284]   CPD, art 45.3.
[285]   See CPR, r 47.14(6) and CPD, art 40.6(3).
[286]   CPD, art 20.7(2).
[287]   See, for example, J Duerden 'Detailed Assessment: A Judge's Advice on Preparation' (2008) 66 PILJ June, pp 2–5.
[288]   CPR, r 47.14(7).
[289]   *Rye v The Liquidator of Ashfield Nominees Ltd* [2005] EWHC 1189 (Ch).
[290]   *Budgens Stores Ltd v Hastings Magistrates Court* [2009] EWHC 1646 (Admin); in a more general context, see *English v Emery Reimbold & Strick Ltd* [2002] EWCA Civ 605.
[291]   *Paulin v Paulin* [2009] EWCA Civ 221 at [30].

pronounces it and the subsequent entry of it is in obedience to the rules of court,[292] time for lodging an appellant's notice runs from the moment judgment is given rather than from the conclusion of the assessment.[293] The court (ie the costs judge) often grants an extension of time until the conclusion of hearing. While there is no authority on the point, it seems that the lower court (ie the costs judge) has power to order that the time for filing an appellant's notice is to be whatever period the court directs, but that only the appeal court can vary that time limit.[294] Therefore, it would seem that if the lower court is to allow a party more than the default 21-day period from the time of the decision, this must be done at the time the decision is made, rather than subsequently.

21.221   The court will make a note in the bill of any disallowances or reductions that it has made.[295] The CPD requires the court to record the disallowance or reduction of the sums claimed,[296] but more often than not, the court will record the time which has been allowed rather than the actual sums.

Determination of issues of fact

21.222   Occasionally, an issue of fact will need to be decided on the basis of formal evidence (or, more accurately, on the basis of formal evidence beyond that which is contained within the receiving party's file of papers). The 'general rule' is that evidence will be by witness statement unless the court directs otherwise.[297]

21.223   Where cross-examination is not merited, the general rule will apply and the court will refuse permission. Indeed, it is uncommon for a costs judge to allow witnesses to be cross-examined unless there is substance in the allegations of fact. Latham LJ had the following to say on the topic:[298]

> 'The mere fact that [an] issue has been raised is not of itself sufficient. If there is no prospect that cross-examination could either undermine or further elucidate the respondent's case, to refuse to accede to the application will not be unfair and it would not breach the requirement of the overriding objective that the parties are on equal footing but would save expense and deal with the issues proportionately and expeditiously.'

The court will take into account the cogency of the points to which the disputed facts relate; in a case in which the costs judge had found that the paying party's allegations of an unlawful retainer were ill-founded, Underhill J found that the costs judge had been entitled to refuse permission to cross-examine the receiving party's solicitor.[299]

21.224   Where cross-examination is merited, it will not always be appropriate for it to be heard in the context of a detailed assessment rather than a trial. Neuberger J commented on the range of issues that may be encountered:[300]

---

[292]   *Holtby v Hodgson* (1889) 24 QBD 103.
[293]   *Kasir v Darlington & Simpson Rolling Mills Ltd* [2001] 2 Costs LR 228, Popplewell J.
[294]   See CPR, r 52.4(2), which allows the appellant to file an appellant's notice within 'such period as may be directed by the lower court'; and compare this with r 52.6(1), which provides that 'an application to vary the time limit for filing an appeal notice must be made to the appeal court'.
[295]   CPD, art 42.1.
[296]   CPD, art 42.2.
[297]   CPR, r 32.6(1).
[298]   *Burnstein v Times Newspapers Ltd* [2002] EWCA Civ 1739 at [28].
[299]   *Chaffe v Kingsley* [2006] EWHC 3412 (QB).
[300]   *Rosling King v Rothschild Trust* [2002] EWHC 1346 (Ch) at [20].

'[There were issues] more appropriate for a High Court judge than a costs judge, in some respects equally appropriate for a High Court judge and a costs judge, and in some respects more appropriate for a costs judge.'

Where an assessment involves weighty issues (such as where a professional person's integrity is impugned), it is possible for the adjudication of that matter to be referred to a trial judge for a trial of those issues.[301] In practice, this very rarely happens.

21.225 It will often be the case in costs litigation that evidence will be hearsay. Hearsay evidence is generally admissible in civil proceedings, but a party proposing to adduce it is obliged to give notice of his intention to do so in accordance with the rules of court.[302] CPR, r 33.3 provides, however, that that requirement does not apply to evidence at hearings other that trials, and as such, the requirement to serve a hearsay notice will almost never arise in the context of costs litigation. That said, PD 32, para 18.2(2) provides that a witness statement must indicate 'the source for any matters of information or belief', so to that extent, notice of hearsay evidence does need to be given.

Miscellaneous matters concerning detailed assessment

21.226 If either party wishes to make an application in the detailed assessment proceedings, the provisions of CPR, Part 23 (General Rules about Applications for Court Orders) apply.[303]

21.227 It may be that the receiving party's legal representatives wish to recover part or all of the success fee not recovered from the paying party; where that is the case the court will deal with the assessment between the opposing parties first, and then with the position as between solicitor (or counsel) and client.[304] The court may proceed without an adjournment, but only if the client is present in court, the persons affected agree to there being no adjournment, and if the court is satisfied that the issue can be fairly decided in that way.[305] In any other case, the court will give directions and fix a date for the hearing of the issues between solicitor and client.[306]

21.228 Once the detailed assessment hearing has ended, it is the responsibility of the legal representative appearing for the receiving party or the receiving party in person to remove the papers filed in support of the bill of costs.[307]

21.229 The procedure on the conclusion of the hearing is described at **21.289–21.303**.

LIABILITY FOR COSTS OF DETAILED ASSESSMENT PROCEEDINGS

21.230 The incidence of costs of the detailed assessment is generally a topic of some importance to the parties. Where a party is ordered to bear the costs of the assessment,

---

[301] This could be done under CPR, r 30.5 or r 3.1(2)(m).
[302] See s 2(1) of the Civil Evidence Act 1995.
[303] CPD, art 40.8.
[304] CPD, art 20.8(1).
[305] CPD, art 20.8(2).
[306] CPD, art 20.8(3).
[307] CPD, art 40.16.

this can result in that party failing to realise any net economic benefit from those proceedings, and may result in that party suffering a net economic detriment.

21.231   This discussion addresses the factors relevant to the incidence of costs of the detailed assessment. It assumes that there has been no misconduct.

The factors to be taken into account

21.232   The starting point is that there is a rebuttable presumption in favour of the receiving party: the CPR provides that the receiving party is entitled to the costs of the detailed assessment except where any Act, rule or practice direction provides otherwise, or where the court orders otherwise.[308] It is arguable that a similar presumption also exists at common law.[309]

21.233   In deciding whether to make some other order, the court must have regard to all the circumstances, including:[310]

- the conduct of all the parties;
- the amount, if any, by which the bill of costs has been reduced; and
- whether it was reasonable for a party to claim the costs of a particular item or to dispute that item.

Although there is no authority on the point, the wording of the CPR is such that the requirement to take these factors into account appears to be mandatory rather than directory.

21.234   Where it has been made, the court will take a Part 47 offer into account in deciding who should pay the costs of the detailed assessment proceedings.[311] Again, the wording of the CPR appears to be mandatory.

21.235   There are two circumstances in which the incidence of costs of the assessment will be decided on different principles from those described above.

Pro bono

21.236   First, the aforementioned presumption will not apply where the receiving party has pro bono representation in the detailed assessment proceedings; however, that party may apply for an order in respect of that representation under s 194(3) of the Legal Services Act 2007.[312] This is an issue which is dealt with in more detail at **11.102–11.114**.

Legally aided

21.237   Second, unless the court orders otherwise, the provisions relating to Part 47 offers do not apply where the receiving party is a funded client or an assisted person. This topic is dealt with in further detail at **21.203**.

---

[308]   CPR, r 47.18; see also CPD, art 45.1.
[309]   See, for example, *Horsford v Bird* [2006] UKPC 55, in which the Privy Council approved of *Chrulew v Borm-Reid & Co* [1992] 1 WLR 176.
[310]   CPR, r 47.18(2); see also r 45.4.
[311]   CPR, r 47.19(1).
[312]   CPR, r 47.18(1A).

21.238   Each of the topics mentioned at **21.233** and **21.234** is dealt with in turn. In so far as Part 47 offers are concerned, the focus is on the effect they will have on the incidence of costs rather than on their form and nature; those issues are discussed at **21.157–21.207**.

Conduct and the costs of the detailed assessment

21.239   The CPR does not qualify the statement that the court may take the conduct of the parties into account, so it is impossible to be prescriptive about the types of conduct that may be relevant. The discussion in Chapter 7 on 'orders' probably applies to detailed assessments (with, of course, the necessary adaptations to take account of the specialist nature of the proceedings).

21.240   An example of the type of conduct that might be relevant is a failing to make an application at the time that it ought to have been made.[313] Common sense dictates that on the grounds of relevance alone the court should be slow to take into account conduct during the proceedings which gave rise to the bill of costs. If, however, belligerent conduct has been carried forward into the assessment, then that might be relevant (see, by analogy, **6.76–6.82**).

21.241   A factor that will often be given weight is an offeree's willingness to enter into negotiations once an offer has been made.[314] However, whilst not a binding decision, the Privy Council has commented that on the facts of the case before them the receiving party's failure to make a counter-offer was not, of itself, sufficient to deprive him of his costs.[315] Each case will turn on its own facts.

Amount of reduction and the costs of the detailed assessment

21.242   Each case must be decided on its own facts: it is not possible to say that a reduction beyond a fixed percentage will displace the presumption that the receiving party will be awarded his costs. In particular, there is no basis in principle for drawing an analogy with the regime governing solicitor and client assessments (where the incidence of costs is largely governed by the one-fifth rule). The two regimes are based on wholly different underlying policies and, in any event, are procedurally dissimilar.

21.243   With the comments made immediately above firmly in mind, it is worth noting that HHJ Griggs declined to interfere with a decision to deprive the receiving party of his costs in a case where the amount recovered was about 65% of the amount claimed.[316] On the facts of the case before him (which was not particularly remarkable) HHJ Griggs believed that it was within the ambit of the court's discretion to give weight to a reduction of 35%. Mitting J found that a reduction of 25% (largely attributable to a reduction in hourly rates) was a factor that should count against the receiving party in so far as the costs of the assessment were concerned.[317] Likewise, Christopher Clarke J

---

[313]   See, for example, *Manning (Personal Representatives) v King's College Hospital NHS Trust* [2011] EWHC 3054 (QB) at [38]–[42] in which the claimant lost 25 percent of its costs as a result of failing to apply for relief from sanctions at the appropriate time.

[314]   See, for example, *Bufton v Hill* [2002] EWHC 9024 (Costs), in which Silber J addressed this issue in the context of publicly funded persons; he found that whilst he could not take the offers themselves into account, he could take into account the parties' conduct in responding to those offers.

[315]   *Horsford v Bird* [2006] UKPC 55 at [15].

[316]   *Palmer v Milbrook Beds Ltd* (unreported) 23 February 2007, Torquay County Court.

[317]   *Lewis v The Royal Shrewsbury Hospital* (unreported) 20 May 2005, QBD (summarised as SCCO Summary

declined to interfere with a decision to deprive the receiving parties of their costs where their bill had been reduced by 60% (this being where the reductions were made primarily because of the absence of attendance notes); he provided the following explanation:[318]

> 'Here the reduction was very large and the reason for the reduction was in large measure because the solicitors had failed to keep attendance notes. Such a failure materially contributes to the length and cost of assessment proceedings ... [It] leads to a scrambling around among the papers when the costs are queried to seek to work out what was done at different stages often without any clear answer, followed by a guessing game on the part of the costs judge.'

Thus, there seems to have been a degree of overlap between the reduction and the receiving parties' conduct.

21.244   It is open to the court to make allowances for the fact that a ruling on a point of principle has had a significant bearing on the amount of costs ultimately allowed.[319]

'Reasonable to claim' and the costs of the detailed assessment

21.245   Whether it is reasonable for a party to claim the costs of a particular item or to dispute that item is an issue which will turn on the facts of each case.

21.246   It is implicit in the CPR that the court may make an order for the costs of the assessment which takes into account the costs of issues. In appropriate cases the court is able to reflect the costs of issues in a variety of different ways (such as by making a percentage order or by allowing costs from a specified date).

Part 47 offers and the costs of the detailed assessment

21.247   A Part 47 offer may have a considerable effect on the incidence of the costs of the detailed assessment, especially where the offer has been made by the paying party. In essence, if a paying party makes an offer at a reasonably early stage of the assessment and if he achieves a result which is more advantageous from his point of view (that is, if he 'beats' the offer, to use a useful colloquialism), he may be awarded the costs of the assessment.[320] Offers made by the receiving party may have a similar effect, but given the fact that a receiving party would already have the benefit of the presumption that he will be awarded his costs, its effect is usually masked.

21.248   The following miscellaneous topics may arise from time to time.

The measure of the Part 47 offers

21.249   A Part 47 offer which is silent as to the cost of preparation of the bill, interest, and VAT will be treated as being inclusive of those monies.[321] Adjustments may have to

---

No 15 of 2005). The order he made was no order for costs, but this took into account other factors, such as the fact that the Claimant had lost a significant point (namely, the hourly rates).

[318]   *Fattal v Walbrook Trustees (Jersey) Ltd* [2009] EWHC 1674 at [61].

[319]   Whilst not binding, see *Horsford v Bird* [2006] UKPC 55 at [15].

[320]   The importance of this factor was highlighted by Master O'Hare who, speaking extrajudicially, labelled it as being one of his 'top ten mistakes' for a paying party not to have made a sensible offer: O'Hare 'Detailed Assessments: The top ten mistakes' (2000) 149 *NLJ* 6919, pp 51–52.

[321]   See CPD, art 46.2.

be made to ensure that like is compared with like. When making adjustments for interest, it is the amount of interest payable at the time of the offer which is relevant, not the interest which (absent the offer) would have been payable at the time of the assessment. Unless there is reason to believe otherwise, the appropriate date on which the offeree could reasonably have accepted the offer is often taken as being 7 days after the date of the offer.[322]

Offers which are inclusive of the costs of the assessment

21.250 Offers may be stated to be 'fully inclusive' or 'all inclusive', in which case they may (in appropriate circumstances) be regarded as being inclusive of the costs of assessment.[323] This may cause the offeror some difficulties; if the analogous situation under CPR, Part 36 sheds any light on the topic, it can be seen that the court is generally slow to agree to make complex and speculative findings solely for the purpose of deciding whether the offer has been beaten.[324] For the reasons set out at **21.170** it is doubtful whether such an offer can be categorised as being a Part 47 offer. It may, however, be classified as being an admissible offer, in which case it would often be afforded at least some weight. Offers that are inclusive of costs tend to expire after the effluxion of a reasonable period of time.[325]

Costs-only proceedings and Part 47 offers

21.251 Unless there is reason to believe otherwise, a Part 47 offer should not be taken as being inclusive of the costs of bringing costs-only proceedings.[326] The offer may have a bearing on both the costs of the assessment and the costs of the Part 8 claim.[327]

Early Part 47 offers and the costs of the assessment

21.252 Pre-CPR authority confirms that offers may be taken into account if they were made before the bill of costs was served.[328] There is no reason to believe that the same is not true under the CPR. Where appropriate, a paying party may wish to argue that the offer was made at such an early stage that it had not been given the information necessary to be able to evaluate it; that argument would stand little chance of succeeding unless the offeror had refused to allow a subsequent acceptance of the offer.

Late Part 47 offers and the costs of the assessment

21.253 The CPD expressly provides that where a Part 47 offer is made after the expiry of the 14-day period mentioned at **21.161**, and where there is no 'good reason' why this was so, the offer is likely to be given less weight than otherwise would have been the case.[329] Peter Smith J had the following to say about the policy behind that principle:[330]

---

[322] See, for example, *Morris v Wiltshire* [2002] 1 Costs LR 167.
[323] See *Morris v Wiltshire* [2002] 1 Costs LR 167 for a discussion of how such an offer ought to be interpreted.
[324] See, by way of analogy, *Mitchell v James* [2002] EWCA Civ 997.
[325] *Wakefield (t/a Wills Probate and Trusts of Weybridge) v Ford* [2009] EWHC 122 (QB).
[326] *Crosbie v Munroe* [2003] EWCA Civ 250.
[327] *Crosbie v Munroe* [2003] EWCA Civ 250.
[328] *Platt v GKN Kwikform Ltd* [1992] 1 WLR 465.
[329] CPD, art 46.1.
[330] *Wills v Crown Estate Commissioners* [2003] EWHC 1718 (Ch) at [31].

'This appeal emphasises the need for paying parties who wish to protect themselves against the costs consequences of CPR 47.19 to make realistic settlement offers at the beginning of the detailed assessment proceedings and not at the end. The Court is bedevilled with late settlements. The procedures in CPR 47.19 are designed to promote early reasonable offers and parties should bear this in mind in the future.'

In practice, however, the court is usually sympathetic to the practical considerations mentioned at **21.161**. In any event, Butterfield J ruled that it an offer made about 13 days before trial ought to have been taken into account;[331] thus it would seem that a late offer should merely be given less weight, rather than no weight at all. Indeed, there are those who question whether the principle referred to in the CPD is good law.

Withdrawn offers and the costs of the assessment

21.254 This topic is addressed at **21.175–21.177**; in essence, the court is able to take the offer into account, but in doing so it may give it less weight than would have been the case had it not been withdrawn.

'Near misses' and the costs of the assessment

21.255 It may be the case that a paying party fails to beat his offer by a narrow margin. Where those are the circumstances, the principles which are discussed at **14.34–14.42** on 'near misses' in the context of Part 36 offers may be relevant (with appropriate modifications). The court does not need to paint in only black and white: it may, in appropriate circumstances, make no order for costs of the assessment, or may award one of the parties only part of his costs.

Technically deficient offers and the costs of the assessment

21.256 It may be that an offer fails, in some minor way, to comply with the requirements of CPR, r 47.19. While dealing with the analogous provisions under the RSC, Roderick Evans J found that a minor technical shortcoming would not necessarily deprive the offer of effect.[332]

Offers against funded persons and the costs of the assessment

21.257 The CPR provides that in so far as a funded person is concerned, a Part 47 offer will not have the consequences specified under CPR, r 47.19 unless the court so orders.[333] Silber J appears to have accepted (obiter) the consensual view of the parties that Part 47 offers are of no relevance as against a funded person.[334] Whether the parties were correct to come to that view is a moot point, but Silber J did explain that, while the offers themselves may not be of relevance, the court was able look at the conduct of the receiving party in choosing to accept or reject the offer.[335] A funded person is therefore not able to dismiss offers with impunity.

---

[331] *Stephens v Tesco Stores Ltd* (unreported) 5 November 2010, QBD at [19].
[332] *Morris v Wiltshire* [2002] 1 Costs LR 167.
[333] This provision is made by CPR, r 47.19 deferring to the CPD, which then lays down the relevant rule at CPD, art 46.4.
[334] *Bufton v Hill* [2002] EWHC 9024 (Costs).
[335] This approach, if correct, is similar to the effect of CPR, r 27.14(2A), which states, in relation to costs on the small claims track, that 'A party's rejection of an offer in settlement will not of itself constitute unreasonable behaviour under paragraph (2)(d) but the court may take it into consideration when it is applying the unreasonableness test.'

Set-off and Part 47 offers

21.258   Although each case will turn on its own facts, the effect of an offer will not be diminished merely because it contains a provision for set-off of other sums which are not in dispute.[336]

Offers by receiving parties and the costs of the assessment

21.259   A receiving party who beats his own offer will not ordinarily benefit in the sense that he will be awarded costs that he otherwise might not have been awarded. This is because in the ordinary run of things he would be entitled to costs even if the offer were to be disregarded. The benefit to a receiving party of making an offer is subtle. The fact that an offer has been made may be used to defeat an argument that there was a reluctance to negotiate, or it may be a factor to be taken into account when one or more factors in CPR, r 47.18 conspire to deprive him of costs. In some circumstances, it may be a factor which would justify an award of costs on the indemnity basis (although this should not be seen as being the ordinary consequence of a receiving party beating his offer). In any event, the making of offers is commercially sensible and is in accordance with the overriding objective.

The effect of a beaten offer on the costs of the assessment

21.260   It is a curious feature of detailed assessments that where a paying party has beaten his offer, he is often awarded the entire costs of the assessment rather than only those costs which post-date the offer. If this practice is correct, the following points (which are not supported by authority) could be said in its justification:

(1)   The practice could merely be a reflection of the fact that, where a paying party makes a Part 47 offer within the 14-day period stipulated in the CPD,[337] the costs of the assessment would usually be nil or close to nil.
(2)   The requirement to pay the whole of the paying party's costs could be seen as being a fair levy to pay for the presumption in the receiving party's favour.

However, whilst not binding, the Privy Council seems to have treated an offer as having a bearing on the incidence of costs-only from the date when the offer should reasonably have been accepted.[338] It is certainly within the court's discretion to treat an offer in that way.

21.261   Roderick Evans J has commented that where the court is minded to make an order which differentiates between costs incurred before and after the offer, the relevant date is not the date of the offer, but a date which is based on the offeree having had a reasonable period of time – 7 days on the facts of the case before him – to consider the offer.[339]

---

[336]   *Morris v Wiltshire and Woodspring District Council* [2002] 1 Costs LR 167 at 173.
[337]   CPD, art 46.1.
[338]   *Horsford v Bird* [2006] UKPC 55.
[339]   *Morris v Wiltshire and Woodspring District Council* [2002] 1 Costs LR 167 at [25].

Interest on the costs of the assessment

21.262   The pre-CPR position was that interest on the costs of the assessment was payable from the date on which the receiving party was awarded the costs which appear in the bill of costs.[340] This is no longer the case, as CPD, art 45.5(1) makes the following provision:

> 'In respect of interest on the costs of detailed assessment proceedings, the interest shall begin to run from the date of the default, interim or final costs certificate as the case may be.'

Procedure for assessing the costs of the assessment

21.263   There is no need for the parties to file statements of costs in advance of the hearing.[341] As a general rule, the court will assess the receiving party's costs of the detailed assessment proceedings and add them to the bill of costs.[342] If the costs of the detailed assessment proceedings are awarded to the paying party, the court will either assess those costs by summary assessment or make an order for them to be decided by detailed assessment.[343]

The wording of the relevant provisions relating to the costs of assessment

21.264   The wording of CPR, r 47.18 is as follows:

> '(1)   The receiving party is entitled to the costs of the detailed assessment proceedings except where—
>
> (a)   the provisions of any Act, any of these Rules or any relevant practice direction provide otherwise; or
> (b)   the court makes some other order in relation to all or part of the costs of the detailed assessment proceedings.
>
> (1A)   Paragraph (1) does not apply where the receiving party has pro bono representation in the detailed assessment proceedings but that party may apply for an order in respect of that representation under section 194(3) of the Legal Services Act 2007.
>
> (2)   In deciding whether to make some other order, the court must have regard to all the circumstances, including—
>
> (a)   the conduct of all the parties;
> (b)   the amount, if any, by which the bill of costs has been reduced; and
> (c)   whether it was reasonable for a party to claim the costs of a particular item or to dispute that item.'

21.265   CPR, r 47.19 makes the following provisions:

> '(1)   Where—
>
> (a)   a party (whether the paying party or the receiving party) makes a written offer to settle the costs of the proceedings which gave rise to the assessment proceedings; and
> (b)   the offer is expressed to be without prejudice save as to the costs of the detailed assessment proceedings, the court will take the offer into account in deciding who should pay the costs of those proceedings.

---

[340]   *Ross v Bowbelle (Owners)* [1997] 1 WLR 1159.
[341]   CPD, art 45.2.
[342]   CPD, art 45.1A.
[343]   CPD, art 45.2.

(2)   The fact of the offer must not be communicated to the costs officer until the question of costs of the detailed assessment proceedings falls to be decided.'

21.266   The CPD gives the following further guidance:

'**45.1** As a general rule the court will assess the receiving party's costs of the detailed assessment proceedings and add them to the bill of costs.

45.2 If the costs of the detailed assessment proceedings are awarded to the paying party, the court will either assess those costs by summary assessment or make an order for them to be decided by detailed assessment.

45.3 No party should file or serve a statement of costs of the detailed assessment proceedings unless the court orders him to do so.

45.4 Attention is drawn to the fact that in deciding what order to make about the costs of detailed assessment proceedings the court must have regard to the conduct of all parties, the amount by which the bill of costs has been reduced and whether it was reasonable for a party to claim the costs of a particular item or to dispute that item.

45.5

(1)   In respect of interest on the costs of detailed assessment proceedings, the interest shall begin to run from the date of the default, interim or final costs certificate as the case may be.

(2)   This provision applies only to the costs of the detailed assessment proceedings themselves. The costs of the substantive proceedings are governed by rule 40.8(1).'

PAYMENTS ON ACCOUNT OF COSTS

21.267   A payment on account of costs is not the same as an interim costs certificate (see **21.284**)). An order for a payment on account of costs is made in the litigation itself under CPR, Part 44, whereas an interim costs certificate is issued in the assessment proceedings under CPR, Part 47. The terms are often used incorrectly and inconsistently in the authorities, as is the term 'interim payment'; in this chapter, the phrase 'payment on account of costs' is used to mean a payment made pursuant to CPR, r 44.3(8), and the term 'interim costs certificate' is used to mean a certificate awarded pursuant to CPR, r 47.15.

Judicial approach and jurisdiction

21.268   The power[344] to make an order for a payment on account of costs arises from CPR, r 44.3(8):

'Where the court has ordered a party to pay costs, it may order an amount to be paid on account before the costs are assessed.'

The test to be applied under that jurisdiction differs depending on whether the application is made to the trial judge (which in this context means the judge who has made the costs order in the context of having heard a trial or disposal hearing) or to some other judge.

---

[344]   Section 32(5) of the Senior Courts Act 1981 (which prevents the court making an interim payment in respect of costs) is disapplied for the purposes of costs proceedings by s 32(4) of that Act.

21.269 Giving guidance in the context of an application to a trial judge, Jacob J said:[345]

> 'Where a party has won and has got an order for costs the only reason that he does not get the money straightaway is because of the need for a detailed assessment. Nobody knows how much it should be. If the detailed assessment were carried out instantly he would get the order instantly. So the successful party is entitled to the money. In principle he ought to get it as soon as possible. It does not seem to me to be a good reason for keeping him out of some of his costs that you need time to work out the total amount. A payment of some lesser amount which he will almost certainly collect is a closer approximation to justice. So I hold that where a party is successful the court should on a rough and ready basis also normally order an amount to be paid on account, the amount being a lesser sum than the likely full amount.'

21.270 Elias LJ has explained that the notion that the receiving party should not be kept out if his money should not be afforded the status of being a presumption; instead, the fact that a party has an entitlement to costs is simply a factor to be taken into account.[346]

21.271 The court must take into account all the circumstances of the particular case. Jacob J commented that these might include the fact that a party wishes to appeal, the conduct of the parties, their financial positions, etc.[347] The fact that the entitlement has been diminished by set-off may be relevant.[348] Laddie J has commented that other relevant factors might include the ability of the receiving party to make a repayment if it is found at the end of the day that the payment on account of costs was excessive.[349]

21.272 Whilst it is only to be expected that a judge who has made an award of costs following a trial would be inclined to make an order that a payment on account of costs be made, the same may not be true of judges who have had a lesser involvement in the case, as Laddie J commented:[350]

> 'It seems to me that whatever the normal rule should be where there has been a full trial, different considerations may apply where there has not been a full trial. As is apparent in this case, there is a world of difference between a judge's ability to make a fair and rational assessment of costs for payment under the provisions of CPR 44.3(8) when he has heard the whole trial, or the whole inquiry as to damages, compared with his ability to do that when he has heard virtually nothing.'

Laddie J noted the powers of a costs judge to issue an interim costs certificate (see below), and that a costs judge would have the advantage over other judges because a costs judge would have more material upon which to base his interim assessment.

21.273 The fact that the costs judge may have more material before him than would the trial judge should not be given disproportionate weight. In a case in which the trial judge had heard extensive evidence concerning allegations of fraud, Gloster J found that

---

[345] *Mars UK Ltd v Teknowledge Ltd (No 2)* [1999] 2 Costs LR 44 at 46.
[346] *Blakemore v Cummings* [2009] EWCA Civ 1276.
[347] *Mars UK Ltd v Teknowledge Ltd (No 2)* [1999] 2 Costs LR 44 at 46.
[348] See *Commission for Equality & Human Rights v Griffin* [2011] EWHC 675 (Admin) at [16], per Moore-Bick LJ.
[349] *Dyson Appliances Ltd v Hoover Ltd* [2003] EWHC 624 (Ch) at [33], per Laddie J.
[350] *Dyson Appliances Ltd v Hoover Ltd* [2003] EWHC 624 (Ch) at [15], per Laddie J.

it would be 'unreal' to expect a costs judge to be in a better position to take a view on the quantum of a payment on account than the trial judge.[351]

21.274 Relevant factors may include the financial resources of the parties.[352] For obvious reasons the financial resources of the receiving party often feature large, but the resources of the paying party may also be relevant. In a case in which there was a possibility that the paying party would not be able to satisfy its liability for costs, Laddie J regarded as relevant the fact that an order for a payment on account of costs may encourage settlement and may relieve the parties of the financial burden of having to prepare for a detailed assessment.[353]

21.275 The following miscellaneous topics may present themselves from time to time.

Payment by instalments and failure to pay

21.276 Langley J has confirmed that if a paying party fails to meet is obligations under an order for payments on account of costs, the court is able to exercise its inherent jurisdiction, as preserved by CPR, r 3.1(1), to debar a paying party from taking any further part in the detailed assessment pending compliance with the order.[354] Langley J went on to say that such an order could also be justified as being the exercise of the general power of the court to debar a party in contempt.[355] Whilst there is no authority directly on the point, it is likely that the general principles relating to unless orders apply (see **21.87**), and that in particular, no order should require a payment that was so large that there was no prospect of it being paid.[356] If a paying party would have difficulty in making payments, then by analogy with orders for payments made under CPR, r 44.3(8), there is no reason why the court cannot order that payments on account of costs be made in instalments.[357] Again by analogy, the fact that there are grave doubts about the honesty and bona fides of the paying party would generally not of itself be sufficient justification for making an unless order.[358]

Costs-only proceedings and payments on account

21.277 It is not clear whether the court has jurisdiction to make an order that a payment on account is made in costs-only proceedings.[359] This is a moot point, which could be argued either way.

---

[351] *Petromec Inc v Petroleo Brasileiro* [2006] EWHC 3518 (Comm).

[352] See *German Property 50 Sarl v Summers-Inman Construction & Property Consultants LLP* [2009] EWHC 2968 (TCC) at [11], per Coulson J.

[353] *Allason v Random House UK Ltd* [2002] EWHC 1030 (Ch) at [12].

[354] *Days Healthcare UK Ltd v Pihsiang Machinery Manufacturing Co Ltd* [2006] EWHC 1444 (QB) at [18]–[20], [23], and [25]–[27]. See also *Hammond Suddard Solicitors v Agrichem International Holdings Ltd* [2001] EWCA Civ 2065 at [48], per Clarke LJ.

[355] *Days Healthcare UK Ltd v Pihsiang Machinery Manufacturing Co Ltd* [2006] EWHC 1444 (QB) at [23].

[356] See, by way of analogy, *Anglo-Eastern Trust Ltd and another v Kermanshahchi* [2002] EWCA Civ 198 at [22], per Park J (in the Court of Appeal).

[357] *Nova Productions Ltd v Mazooma Games Ltd* [2006] EWHC 189 (Ch).

[358] See, by analogy, *Lexi Holdings plc v Luqman* [2007] EWHC 2410 (Ch) at [44], per Briggs J.

[359] *Banchio v Lai* [2003] EWHC 9038 (Costs).

Stay and payments on account

21.278   Where circumstances merit such a step (such as where an appeal is being brought) there is no reason why an order for a payment on account of costs cannot be stayed:[360] Warren J has confirmed that it is not a contradiction in terms to grant a stay pending the outcome of some event.[361]

Appropriate tribunal

21.279   Morland J has indicated that (in group litigation at least) applications should be made to the judge who will be hearing the trial, where at all possible.[362]

Amount of payment on account of costs

21.280   As to the amount of the payment on account of costs, the measure that Jacob J used was an amount that the receiving party would almost certainly collect;[363] in a similar vein, Laddie J allowed 'the absolute bare minimum' that the receiving party could hope to recover.[364] Awards based on that measure are typically between 35% and 60% of the amount claimed (although it has to be stressed that there is no 'standard' percentage). Other measures are occasionally used. For example, Norris J sitting in the Patents Court has said that in appropriate cases the court should seek to reach a figure which would discourage the prosecution of an assessment;[365] presumably, this would result in an award which would be higher than the absolute bare minimum. It is entirely possible that that approach is limited to commercial disputes. Vos J and Warren J have shown a preference for using and estimate of the amount most likely to be allowed;[366] by using this measure, Warren J reduced an award from 95% of that which is claimed to 70%.[367]

21.281   Where the receiving party's recovery of costs was at risk by reason of a credible challenge as to the enforceability of the retainer, this may be a factor.[368] Likewise, the court may take into account the fact that there is doubt as to what the contractual terms of the retainer are and what effect they will have.[369] The amount claimed by the paying party is not an appropriate measure.[370]

21.282   There are examples of the court ordering a relatively generous payment on account of costs (effectively a summary assessment) which could be followed by a

---

[360]   See, for example, *Renewable Power & Light plc v Renewable Power & Light Services Inc* [2008] EWHC 3584 (QB).

[361]   *Amin v Amin* [2011] EWHC 641 (Ch) at [18].

[362]   *Giambrone v JMC Holidays Ltd (formerly Sunworld Holidays Ltd)* [2002] EWHC 2932 (QB) at [11]–[12], per Morland J.

[363]   *Mars UK Ltd v Teknowledge Ltd (No 2)* [1999] 2 Costs LR 44 at 46; see also *Shovelar v Lane* [2011] EWCA Civ 802 at [58].

[364]   *Allason v Random House UK Ltd* [2002] EWHC 1030 (Ch) at [14].

[365]   *Les Laboratoires Servier v Apotex Inc* [2008] EWHC 2563 (Pat) at [7].

[366]   See *United Airlines Inc v United Airways Ltd* (2011) EWHC 2411 (Ch) (post-hearing discussion) and *Gollop v Pryke* (unreported) 19 November 2011, Ch D respectively.

[367]   *Gollop v Pryke* (unreported) 19 November 2011, Ch D.

[368]   *Munkenbeck & Marshall v Harold* [2005] EWHC 356 (TCC) at [31] per Richard Harvey QC sitting as a Deputy Judge of the High Court.

[369]   See, for example, *Beattie v Smailes* [2011] EWHC 3865 (Ch), in which Norris J took into account the fact that there was doubt as to what effect a conditional fee agreement would have in relation to costs incurred before it was made.

[370]   *Shovelar v Lane* [2011] EWCA Civ 802 at [59].

detailed assessment if the receiving party believed that more was payable;[371] those examples are limited to the early days of the CPR, and it is not an approach which has found general favour. It could be argued that it is an unlawful practice.

Wording of the relevant provisions

21.283 CPR, r 44.3(8) reads:

> 'Where the court has ordered a party to pay costs, it may order an amount to be paid on account before the costs are assessed.'

There is no guidance in the CPD which is specific to the topic.

INTERIM COSTS CERTIFICATES

21.284 An interim costs certificate is an order for an interim payment of costs which is made after the receiving party has filed a request for a detailed assessment hearing. An payment made pursuant to an interim costs certificate should be distinguished from a payment on account (see **21.267**).

21.285 CPR, r 47.15 provides:

> '(1) The court may at any time after the receiving party has filed a request for a detailed assessment hearing—
>
> (a) issue an interim costs certificate for such sum as it considers appropriate;
> (b) amend or cancel an interim certificate.
>
> (2) An interim certificate will include an order to pay the costs to which it relates, unless the court orders otherwise.
>
> (3) The court may order the costs certified in an interim certificate to be paid into court.
>
> (4) Where the court—
>
> (a) issues an interim costs certificate; or
> (b) amends or cancels an interim certificate,
>
> in detailed assessment proceedings pursuant to an order under section 194(3) of the Legal Services Act 2007, the receiving party must send a copy of the interim costs certificate or the order amending or cancelling the interim costs certificate to the prescribed charity.'

The court has no power[372] to issue an interim costs certificate until the receiving party has filed a request for a detailed assessment hearing.[373]

21.286 The fact that a party is entitled to costs is simply a factor to be taken into account; it does not give rise to a presumption that the receiving party is entitled to an interim award.[374] There is no reason to believe that the factors already discussed at **21.268–21.274** would not be relevant to interim costs certificates; in practice the court

---

[371] *Mabey & Johnson Ltd v Ecclesiastical Insurance Office plc (Costs)* [2000] CLC 1470.
[372] Section 32(5) of the Senior Courts Act 1981 (which prevents the court making an interim payment in respect of costs) is disapplied for the purposes of costs proceedings by s 32(4) of that Act.
[373] See CPD, art 41.1(2) and CPR, r 47.15(1).
[374] *Blakemore v Cummings* [2009] EWCA Civ 1276. In *German Property 50 Sarl v Summers-Inman Construction & Property Consultants LLP* [2009] EWHC 2968 (TCC) at [11] Coulson J appears to have said the opposite, but his attention seems not to have been drawn to *Blakemore v Cummings*.

takes into account the same factors regardless of whether the application is for an interim costs order or on order for a payment on account of costs.

21.287   The relevant procedure is to make an application under CPR, Part 23.[375] Further procedural guidance is given by CPR, r 47.15, which provides:

> '(1)   The court may at any time after the receiving party has filed a request for a detailed assessment hearing—
>
>> (a)   issue an interim costs certificate for such sum as it considers appropriate;
>> (b)   amend or cancel an interim certificate.
>
> (2)   An interim certificate will include an order to pay the costs to which it relates, unless the court orders otherwise.
>
> (3)   The court may order the costs certified in an interim certificate to be paid into court.
>
> (4)   Where the court—
>
>> (a)   issues an interim costs certificate; or
>> (b)   amends or cancels an interim certificate,
>
> in detailed assessment proceedings pursuant to an order under section 194(3) of the Legal Services Act 2007, the receiving party must send a copy of the interim costs certificate or the order amending or cancelling the interim costs certificate to the prescribed charity.'

21.288   If a paying party wishes to apply for a stay of enforcement of an interim costs certificate, he may apply to a costs judge or district judge of the court office which issued the certificate, or (if it is a different court) to the court which has general jurisdiction to enforce the certificate.[376] Enforcement proceedings may not be issued in the Senior Courts Costs Office.[377] Langley J has explained that if a paying party fails to meet his obligations pursuant to an order to make a payment on account of costs, he can be debarred from taking any further part in the detailed assessment pending discharge of those obligations (see **21.276**);[378] there is no reason to suspect that the position would be any different if the obligation arose under an interim costs certificate.

FINAL COSTS CERTIFICATES AND THE CONCLUSION OF THE ASSESSMENT

Calculations

21.289   The CPD provides that the court must make a note in the bill of any disallowances or reductions it has made;[379] the receiving party must make clear the correct figures agreed or allowed in respect of each item and must recalculate the summary of the bill appropriately.[380] Once those details have been noted to it, that bill is referred to as the 'completed bill'.[381]

---

[375]   CPD, art 41.1(1).
[376]   CPD, art 42.11.
[377]   CPD, art 42.12.
[378]   *Days Healthcare UK Ltd v Pihsiang Machinery Manufacturing Co Ltd* [2006] EWHC 1444 (QB) at [18]–[20], [23], and [25]–[27]; see also *Hammond Suddard Solicitors v Agrichem International Holdings Ltd* [2001] EWCA Civ 2065 at [48], per Clarke LJ.
[379]   CPD, art 42.1.
[380]   CPD, art 42.2.
[381]   CPR, r 47.16(1).

Final filing

21.290   The completed bill must be filed with the court within 14 days of the end of the hearing.[382] At the same time as filing the completed bill, the receiving party must (with one or two exceptions) also file receipted fee notes and receipted accounts in respect of all disbursements.[383] The exceptions are disbursements other than counsel's fees which do not exceed £500 and which have been duly discharged.[384]

21.291   Once these things have been attended to, the court will consider issuing a final costs certificate. This is a document which will state the amount of costs which have been assessed, and, unless the court orders otherwise, will include an order to pay the costs to which it relates.[385] A separate certificate will be issued for each person entitled to costs.[386]

21.292   There are two circumstances in which the court may defer issuing a final costs certificate:

- *Unpaid fees*: The court will not issue a final costs certificate until all relevant court fees payable on the assessment have been paid.[387]
- *Unpaid costs*: Where a party is both entitled to costs and is required to pay costs, CPR, r 44.3(9)(b) permits a costs judge to delay the issue of a party's final costs certificate until he has paid the amount which he is liable to pay. CPR, r 47.16(4) echoes that provision.

21.293   Form N256 is the model form of final costs certificate.[388] The certificate must show the amount of costs which have been agreed or which have been allowed on detailed assessment and, where applicable, the amount agreed or allowed in respect of VAT.[389] There is no need separately to record the amounts of profit costs and disbursements (although those figures would ordinarily be recorded in the completed bill). The model form gives the court the option of separately recording the amount allowed for the costs of the detailed assessment; this may be necessary where interest on those costs runs from a different date from interest on the remainder of the costs. There is also provision for the court separately to state the relevant dates.

21.294   The following miscellaneous topics may, from time to time, present themselves.

Payments already made

21.295   If the court makes an order that costs be paid, there is also provision for the court to set out amounts which have already been paid on account, and to state the balance which remains due.

---

[382]   CPD, art 42.3 and CPR, r 47.16(2).
[383]   CPD, art 42.4.
[384]   See Precedent F(5) in the Schedule of CPD, which is referred to by CPD, art 42.4.
[385]   CPR, r 47.16(5).
[386]   CPD, art 42.9.
[387]   CPD, art 42.5.
[388]   CPD, art 42.10.
[389]   CPD, art 42.7.

Payments outstanding

21.296   If the court is aware that previous orders or interim costs certificates have gone unpaid, the certificate may contain an endorsement, such as:[390]

> '... and, no sums having been paid under the order of Mr Justice X dated ... or under the interim certificate dated ...'

VAT rate changes

21.297   Where there has been a change in the rate of VAT, and where that change has been made between the end of the detailed assessment and the court issuing the final costs certificate, an application may be made for the detailed assessment to be varied so as to take account of that change of rate. Once the final costs certificate has been issued, no such variation will be permitted.[391]

Delay in filing the completed bill

21.298   It will occasionally happen that the receiving party will fail to file a completed bill; in practice, this will usually be where the bill has been assessed at a figure which is lower than sums already paid on account. Where the receiving party is delaying things in this way, the paying party may make an application seeking an appropriate order under CPR, r 3.1 (ie the court's general powers of management).[392]

Pro bono work and completion

21.299   Where a person has been represented pro bono and the court has made an order on a detailed assessment for the benefit of a prescribed charity (ie under s 194(3) of the Legal Services Act 2007), the receiving party must send a copy of the final costs certificate to the prescribed charity.[393]

Stay of enforcement of the final costs certificate

21.300   If a paying party wishes to apply for a stay of enforcement of a final costs certificate, he may apply to a costs judge or district judge of the court office which issued the certificate, or to the court (if it is a different court) which has general jurisdiction to enforce the certificate.[394]

21.301   If the final costs certificate includes an order that costs be paid, that order may be enforced in the usual way;[395] the receiving party will have become a judgment creditor and the paying party a judgment debtor.[396] These issues are briefly dealt with at **21.310–21.321**.

21.302   CPR, r 47.16 provides:

---

[390]   *Supreme Court Costs Office Guide 2006*, para 12.3; reproduced with kind permission.
[391]   CPD, art 5.8.
[392]   CPD, art 42.6.
[393]   CPR, r 47.16(6).
[394]   CPD, art 42.11.
[395]   CPR, r 70.1(2)(d).
[396]   CPR, r 70.1(2)(a) and (b).

'(1)   In this rule a completed bill means a bill calculated to show the amount due following the detailed assessment of the costs.

(2)   The period for filing the completed bill is 14 days after the end of the detailed assessment hearing.

(3)   When a completed bill is filed the court will issue a final costs certificate and serve it on the parties to the detailed assessment proceedings.

(4)   Paragraph (3) is subject to any order made by the court that a certificate is not to be issued until other costs have been paid.

(5)   A final costs certificate will include an order to pay the costs to which it relates, unless the court orders otherwise.

(The costs practice direction deals with the form of a final costs certificate)

(6)   Where the court issues a final costs certificate in detailed assessment proceedings pursuant to an order under section 194(3) of the Legal Services Act 2007, the receiving party must send a copy of the final costs certificate to the prescribed charity.'

21.303   The wording of Part 42 of the CPD is as follows:

'**42.1** At the detailed assessment hearing the court will indicate any disallowance or reduction in the sums claimed in the bill of costs by making an appropriate note on the bill.

42.2 The receiving party must, in order to complete the bill after the detailed assessment hearing make clear the correct figures agreed or allowed in respect of each item and must recalculate the summary of the bill appropriately.

42.3 The completed bill of costs must be filed with the court no later than 14 days after the detailed assessment hearing.

42.4 At the same time as filing the completed bill of costs, the party whose bill it is must also produce receipted fee notes and receipted accounts in respect of all disbursements except those covered by a certificate in Precedent F(5) in the Schedule of Costs Precedents annexed to this Practice Direction.

42.5 No final costs certificate will be issued until all relevant court fees payable on the assessment of costs have been paid.

42.6 If the receiving party fails to file a completed bill in accordance with rule 47.16 the paying party may make an application under Part 23 (General Rules about Applications for Court Orders) seeking an appropriate order under rule 3.1 (The court's general powers of management).

42.7 A final costs certificate will show:

   (a)   the amount of any costs which have been agreed between the parties or which have been allowed on detailed assessment;

   (b)   where applicable the amount agreed or allowed in respect of VAT on the costs agreed or allowed.

This provision is subject to any contrary provision made by the statutory provisions relating to costs payable out of the Community Legal Service Fund.

42.8 A final costs certificate will include disbursements in respect of the fees of counsel only if receipted fee notes or accounts in respect of those disbursements have been produced to the court and only to the extent indicated by those receipts.

42.9 Where the certificate relates to costs payable between parties a separate certificate will be issued for each party entitled to costs.

42.10 Form N257 is a model form of interim costs certificate and Form N256 is a model form of final costs certificate.

42.11 An application for an order staying enforcement of an interim costs certificate or final costs certificate may be made either:

(1)   to a costs judge or district judge of the court office which issued the certificate; or

(2)   to the court (if different) which has general jurisdiction to enforce the certificate.

42.12 Proceedings for enforcement of interim costs certificates or final costs certificates may not be issued in the Senior Courts Costs Office.'

DISCONTINUING COSTS PROCEEDINGS AND WITHDRAWAL

21.304   It will occasionally be the case that a receiving party will wish to terminate the detailed assessment proceedings. This topic has already been addressed in the context of compromise at **21.131–21.138**; the present discussion addresses the topic in a wider, more general context.

21.305   Whether the proceedings should be determined by discontinuance or withdrawal will, as a matter of practice, depend on whether the paying party consents to the receiving party's proposal.

No consent as to determination

21.306   Detailed assessment proceedings may be discontinued by the CPR, Part 38 procedure,[397] which is a procedure which may be brought to bear at any time and at any stage in the proceedings.[398] The paying party will ordinarily be entitled to the costs of the assessment,[399] but an application may be made for a different order.[400] Permission will be required in the following circumstances:

• where an application has already been made for a hearing date;[401]
• where a payment on account has been made or ordered, and where an interim costs certificate has been issued;[402] and
• where there is more than one receiving party and it is not the case that all the other receiving parties agree.[403]

Permission is not required solely because there is more than one paying party and the receiving party wishes to discontinue against some, but not all, of them.[404]

21.307   Where detailed assessment proceedings are discontinued, the paying party will ordinarily be entitled to the costs of the assessment,[405] but an application may, in appropriate cases, be made for a different order.[406]

---

[397]   CPD, art 36.5(1).
[398]   CPR, r 38.2(1).
[399]   CPR, r 38.6.
[400]   CPD, art 36.5(2).
[401]   CPD, art 36.5(3).
[402]   CPR, r 38.2(b).
[403]   CPR, r 38.2(c).
[404]   CPR, r 38.2(3).
[405]   CPR, r 38.6.
[406]   CPD, art 36.5(2).

Consent as to determination

21.308   Where the parties consent, the bill of costs may be withdrawn; the advantage of this is that the court's permission is not required.[407] In view of the fact that withdrawal is procedurally less cumbersome than discontinuance, withdrawal would often be the preferred option. It should be borne in mind that, while the CPR makes express provision for subsequent proceedings to be brought in the case of discontinuance,[408] there is no such provision in the case of withdrawal. This does not mean that new proceedings cannot be brought following withdrawal, but parties who are contemplating compromise should be aware that there might be dispute about this if it is the receiving party's intention to bring new proceedings.

21.309   CPD, art 36.5 provides:

'(1) The receiving party may discontinue the detailed assessment proceedings in accordance with Part 38 (Discontinuance).

(2) Where the receiving party discontinues the detailed assessment proceedings before a detailed assessment hearing has been requested, the paying party may apply to the appropriate office for an order about the costs of the detailed assessment proceedings.

(3) Where a detailed assessment hearing has been requested the receiving party may not discontinue unless the court gives permission.

(4) A bill of costs may be withdrawn by consent whether or not a detailed assessment hearing has been requested.'

The relevant part of CPR, Part 38 is relegated to the footnotes.[409]

ENFORCEMENT AND RIGHTS AGAINST LEGAL EXPENSES INSURERS

21.310   This book does not attempt to deal with the issue of enforcement in any detail. Only a brief introduction to the subject is offered.

---

[407]   CPD, art 36.5(4).
[408]   CPR, r 38.7.
[409]   '38.2(1)   A claimant may discontinue all or part of a claim at any time.
(2)   However—
(a)   a claimant must obtain the permission of the court if he wishes to discontinue all or part of a claim in relation to which—
(i)   the court has granted an interim injunction(GL); or
(ii)   any party has given an undertaking to the court;
(b)   where the claimant has received an interim payment in relation to a claim (whether voluntarily or pursuant to an order under Part 25), he may discontinue that claim only if—
(i)   the defendant who made the interim payment consents in writing; or
(ii)   the court gives permission;
(c)   where there is more than one claimant, a claimant may not discontinue unless—
(i)   every other claimant consents in writing; or
(ii)   the court gives permission.
(3)   Where there is more than one defendant, the claimant may discontinue all or part of a claim against all or any of the defendants.'

Means of enforcing a costs debt

21.311 A costs order for a stated amount is an enforceable judgment debt.[410] Where such an order exists, the receiving party will have become a judgment creditor and the paying party a judgment debtor.[411]

21.312 The enforcement of costs certificates is broadly the same as the enforcement of any other form of order, so a costs order may be enforced by any of the following methods:

- a writ of fieri facias or warrant of execution;[412]
- a third-party debt order;[413]
- a charging order, stop order or stop notice;[414]
- in a county court, an attachment of earnings order;[415]
- the appointment of a receiver;[416] and
- by way of insolvency proceedings (although technically this would not be a form of enforcement).

21.313 Broadly speaking, the decision as to how to enforce a costs order will depend on the nature of the judgment debtor's assets. The following is a summary:

- where goods and chattels are owned by the judgment debtor, a warrant of execution would be appropriate;
- where fixed assets are owned by the judgment debtor, a charging order would be appropriate;
- where the judgment debtor is employed, an attachment of earnings order may be appropriate; and
- where the judgment debtor has savings or other monies in the bank, a third party debt order may be appropriate.

Where the nature of the debtor's assets is not known, an application may be made for an oral examination of his assets and liabilities.

21.314 The following is a (very) brief description of the various methods of enforcement.

Warrant of execution

21.315 A warrant of execution is an order that gives a bailiff the authority to take goods from the judgment debtor's home or business. If the sum outstanding is more than £5,000, the county court is not able to issue a warrant.

---

[410] CPR, r 70.1(2)(d).
[411] CPR, r 70.1(2)(a) and (b).
[412] RSC Ords 46 and 47 and CCR Ord 26.
[413] CPR, Part 72.
[414] CPR, Part 72.
[415] CCR Ord 27.
[416] Part 69.

Attachment of earnings

21.316 An attachment of earnings order is an order which is sent to the judgment debtor's employer ordering him to take money from the debtor's earnings and to pay them to the creditor (via the court). Obviously, this method may not be used in respect of a debtor who is unemployed or self-employed.

Third-party debt order

21.317 A third-party debt order is an order requiring a third party who owes money to the judgment debtor to pay an appropriate sum to the judgment creditor. The order usually applies to a building society or bank which holds an account in the debtor's name.

Charging order

21.318 A charging order prevents the judgment debtor from disposing of his assets (usually land) without discharging his judgment debt. In some circumstances, this may lead to an order for sale of the assets. The court lacks vires to make a charging order absolute where the sums claimed are unassessed costs.[417]

Statutory demand

21.319 In view of the fact that an order for a stated amount is for a liquidated sum, another option would be to issue a statutory demand;[418] this would be as a precursor to a bankruptcy petition (in the case of an individual) or to a winding-up petition (in the case of a company). This would be an option only if the outstanding monies were in excess of £750.

21.320 Enforcement proceedings may not be issued in the Senior Courts Costs Office.[419]

21.321 If a paying party wishes to apply for a stay of enforcement of a final costs certificate, he may apply to a costs judge or district judge of the court office which issued the certificate, or to the court (if it is a different court) which has general jurisdiction to enforce the certificate.[420]

Rights against legal expenses insurers

21.322 It may be that costs creditor (such as a receiving party or a solicitor) is unable to enforce against the costs debtor (such as a paying party or a client) because of the latter's insolvency. Where this is the case and where the debtor had the benefit of legal expenses insurance, there are several mechanisms by which the creditor may try to recover his monies directly from the insurer; as is explained below, on the basis of the law as it stood at the time of writing, any such attempt would be an uphill struggle.

---

[417] *Monte Developments Ltd (In Administration) of Court Management Consultants Ltd* [2010] EWHC 3071 (Ch).

[418] Insolvency Act 1986, s 123(1)(a) or s 222(1)(a).

[419] CPD, art 42.12 (in respect of a final or interim costs certificate) and CPD, art 37.7 (in respect of a default costs certificate).

[420] CPD, art 42.11 (in respect of a final or interim costs certificate) and CPD, art 37.6 (in respect of a default costs certificate).

Third parties (rights against insurers) Acts

21.323 If a person having an insurance policy becomes liable to a third party for monies covered by the policy, the third party would ordinarily be able to claim against the insured, and that liability would be covered by the insurer. If the insured became insolvent, however, the third party would not at common law be able to proceed against the insured; he would simply become a general creditor. The Third Parties (Rights against Insurers) Act 1930 ('the 1930 Act') will, in certain circumstances, transfer the insured's rights to the third party so that he can proceed directly against the insurer. The relevant provisions of the Act are set out in the footnotes.[421]

21.324 The usefulness of the 1930 Act in the context of legal expenses insurance is limited. This is because it applies only where a person or company takes out *liability* insurance;[422] in this regard, Toulson J made the following findings (and in doing so he expressed his regret):[423]

> 'I have to choose between construing the words 'where a person is insured against liabilities to third parties which he may incur' as limited to insurance against liabilities which may be imposed on that person by operation of law, whether for breach of contract or in tort, or as including the underwriting of liabilities voluntarily undertaken by that person, ie the payment of contract debts. I do not believe that the words were intended to include the latter. So with regret on the facts of the present case, I would hold that the claimant has no right of claim against the insurers under the 1930 Act.'

This decision is generally regarded as precluding reliance on the 1930 Act in any circumstances where a person with BTE insurance becomes insolvent (although it is possible that the situation is different with ATE insurance).[424] New legislation (the Third Parties (Rights against Insurers) Act 2010 – 'the 2010 Act') has been passed; at the time of writing it had yet to be appointed,[425] but if and when it is, it will repeal and replace the 1930 Act. Transitional provisions will apply.[426]

---

[421] Section 1 of the 1930 Act provides as follows;
'(1) Where under any contract of insurance a person (hereinafter referred to as the insured) is insured against liabilities to third parties which he may incur, then—
(a) in the event of the insured becoming bankrupt or making a composition or arrangement with his creditors; or
(b) in the case of the insured being a company, in the event of a winding-up order ... being made, or a resolution for a voluntary winding-up being passed, with respect to the company, or of the company entering administration, or of a receiver or manager of the company's business or undertaking being duly appointed, or of possession being taken, by or on behalf of the holders of any debentures secured by a floating charge, of any property comprised in or subject to the charge or of a voluntary arrangement proposed for the purposes of Part I of the Insolvency Act 1986 being approved under that Part;
if, either before or after that event, any such liability as aforesaid is incurred by the insured, his rights against the insurer under the contract in respect of the liability shall, notwithstanding anything in any Act or rule of law to the contrary, be transferred to and vest in the third party to whom the liability was so incurred.'
[422] See s 1(1) of the 1930 Act.
[423] *Tarbuck v Avon Insurance plc* [2001] 2 All ER 503 at 509.
[424] Whilst there was no analysis of the point in the judgment and whilst it is not clear if Tarbuck was drawn to the court's attention, David Steel J heard an application under the 1930 Act where the insurer had underwritten an ATE policy; he ultimately dismissed that application on the facts, but he seemed impliedly to accept that the claim was arguable as a matter of law: see *Persimmon Homes Ltd and another v Great Lakes Reinsurance (UK) plc* [2010] EWHC 1705 (Comm) at [2].
[425] At the time of writing, no such day has been appointed.
[426] In so far as it is relevant, Sch 3, para 3 of the 2010 Act provides that the 1930 Act will continue to apply in relation to cases where the bankruptcy or insolvency and the liability under the policy both arose before commencement day.

The new legislation (not yet in force)

21.325   This book does not deal with the 2010 Act in any detail; only an outline is given. One of the most important differences between that Act and the 1930 Act, however, is the fact that under the 2010 Act it is irrelevant whether or not the liability of the insured is or was incurred voluntarily;[427] this means that the new Act is not limited to liability insurance. Whilst there is no authority on the point, it is likely that this will mean that the 2010 Act will allow solicitors and receiving parties to look directly to legal expenses insurers in the event of insolvency of the insured.

21.326   The 2010 Act defines a 'relevant person', who – in essence – is the person who has become bankrupt or otherwise insolvent; there are provisions relating both to natural persons[428] and to corporate bodies.[429] The Act also defines a 'third party', this being the person to whom the rights of the relevant person under the contract against the insurer in respect of the liability[430] are transferred.[431] In essence, if a 'relevant person' incurs a liability against which he is insured, or if (ii) a person who is subject to such a liability becomes a 'relevant person', then the rights of the relevant person are transferred to and vest in the third party. The insurer is able to assert any defence that he would have been able to assert against the insured.[432] Moreover, where the liability of the insured to the third party is less than the liability of the insurer to the insured, no rights are transferred in respect of the difference.[433] The third party may bring

---

[427]   See s 16 of the 2010 Act.

[428]   Section 4(1) of the 2010 makes the following provisions: '(1) An individual is a relevant person if any of the following is in force in respect of that individual in England and Wales—(a) a deed of arrangement registered in accordance with the Deeds of Arrangement Act 1914, (b) an administration order made under Part 6 of the County Courts Act 1984, (c) an enforcement restriction order made under Part 6A of that Act, (d) subject to subsection (4), a debt relief order made under Part 7A of the Insolvency Act 1986, (e a voluntary arrangement approved in accordance with Part 8 of that Act, or (f) a bankruptcy order made under Part 9 of that Act.'

[429]   Sections 6(1) and (2) of the 2010 makes the following provisions: '(1) A body corporate or an unincorporated body is a relevant person if— (a) a compromise or arrangement between the body and its creditors (or a class of them) is in force, having been sanctioned in accordance with s 899 of the Companies Act 2006, or (b) the body has been dissolved under section 1000, 1001 or 1003 of that Act, and the body has not been— (i) restored to the register by virtue of section 1025 of that Act, or (ii) ordered to be restored to the register by virtue of section 1031 of that Act. (2) A body corporate or an unincorporated body is a relevant person if, in England and Wales — (a) a voluntary arrangement approved in accordance with Part 1 of the Insolvency Act 1986 is in force in respect of it, (b) an administration order made under Part 2 of that Act is in force in respect of it, (c) there is a person appointed in accordance with Part 3 of that Act who is acting as receiver or manager of the body's property (or there would be such a person so acting but for a temporary vacancy), (d) the body is, or is being, wound up voluntarily in accordance with Chapter 2 of Part 4 of that Act, (e) there is a person appointed under section 135 of that Act who is acting as provisional liquidator in respect of the body (or there would be such a person so acting but for a temporary vacancy), or (f) the body is, or is being, wound up by the court following the making of a winding-up order under Chapter 6 of Part 4 of that Act or Part 5 of that Act.'

[430]   Section 1(4) of the 2010 Act providest that ' liability is established only if its existence and amount are established; and, for that purpose, "establish" means establish— (a) by virtue of a declaration under section 2 or a declarator under section 3, (b) by a judgment or decree, (c) by an award in arbitral proceedings or by an arbitration, or (d) by an enforceable agreement.' The third party may bring proceedings to enforce the rights against the insurer without having established the relevant person's liability; but the third party may not enforce those rights without having established that liability: see subs 1(3) of the 2010 Act.

[431]   See s 1(2) of the 2010 Act.

[432]   In this regard, s 2(4) of the 2010 Act reads as follows: 'Where proceedings are brought under subs (2)(a) the insurer may rely on any defence on which the insured could rely if those proceedings were proceedings brought against the insured in respect of the insured's liability to P.' There are also provisions concerning set-off (see s 10).

[433]   See s 8 of the 2010 Act.

proceedings against the insurer for either or both of the following: (a) a declaration as to the insured's liability; and (b) a declaration as to the insurer's potential liability.[434]

Contracts (Rights of Third Parties) Act 1999

21.327 The Contracts (Rights of Third Parties) Act 1999[435] ('the 1999 Act') will, in certain circumstances, apply to contracts of insurance. That Act makes provision for a person who is not a party to a contract to enforce the contract; it will apply only (i) where the contract expressly provides that the third party may enforce it, or (ii) where there is a term that purports confer a benefit on him.[436] The third party must be expressly identified in the contract by name, or as a member of a class, or as answering a particular description.[437] It is doubtful whether the 1999 would assist a third party seeking to enforce against an legal expenses insurer: thus Toulson J found it to be of little assistance in a case in which a solicitor sought to enforce his fees against a BTE insurer of an insolvent insured.[438]

Other mechanisms

21.328 There are several other mechanisms by which a third party (such as a solicitor) may try to enforce an insurer's obligations under a legal expenses policy. They include the following:

- **Implied contract:** Whist relating primarily to insurance in respect of adverse costs, it has been argued that where a solicitor agrees to refer a client to an insurer and write the policy on behalf of the insurer, and where in doing so the solicitor agrees to enter into a conditional fee agreement to provide legal services to the client, a contractual obligation is created pursuant to which the solicitor can enforce the insurer's obligation to honour its obligations under the policy. Cooke J rejected that argument; he likened the solicitors to 'cover holders': there was nothing unusual in an arrangement that a person is given authority to arrange insurance. He found that no such term could be implied by reference to either the business efficacy or officious bystander test.[439]

- **Implied term within policy, restitution and the Civil Liability (Contribution) Act 1978:** In the case referred to above, the solicitors (who had already made significant payments in respect of adverse costs that they said ought to have been paid by the insurers) submitted that there was an implied agreement between them and the insurer as surety and debtor and/or that they were entitled to payment by reason of the Civil Liability (Contribution) Act 1978 and/or the law of restitution. Cooke J agreed. He made no finding as to which of those mechanisms was the correct mechanism (that being 'a matter of indifference') but he explained that the insurers did have a duty that the law would enforce.[440]

---

[434] See s 2(2) of the 2010 Act.

[435] It applies to contracts entered into or renewed after 11 May 2000.

[436] Unless on a proper construction of the contract it appears that the parties did not intend the term to be enforceable by the third party: see s 1(1) and (2) of the Contracts (Rights of Third Parties) Act 1999.

[437] See s 1(3) of the Contracts (Rights of Third Parties) Act 1999.

[438] *Tarbuck v Avon Insurance plc* [2001] 2 All ER 503 at 509

[439] *Greene Wood McLean LLP (in Administration) v Templeton Insurance Ltd* [2010] EWHC 2679 (Comm) at [33], [42], [44] and [45], and [48]–[50].

[440] *Greene Wood McLean LLP (in Administration) v Templeton Insurance Ltd* [2010] EWHC 2679 (Comm) at [65]–[72].

- **Declaration:** A solicitor who seeks to ensure that he is appointed under a contract of insurance held by one of his would-be clients is entitled to seek a declaration to that effect.[441]
- **Trust:** It is possible for a third party to gain rights as a result of the operation of a trust;[442] there is, however, no authority for the proposition that such a mechanism would assist a costs creditor in obtaining payment from a legal expenses insurer.
- **Road traffic cases:** Likewise, provisions exist concerning the rights of third parties involved in road traffic cases[443] but there is no authority to suggest that they are relevant in the present context.

COSTS-ONLY PROCEEDINGS

21.329 Costs-only proceedings were introduced to facilitate the resolution of disputes in which the parties have, prior to the issue of proceedings, reached agreement on all issues save the amount of costs.

Jurisdiction

21.330 Costs-only proceedings allow recovery of those costs which would have been recoverable in the proceedings if they had been commenced.[444] Costs-only proceedings may be brought using the CPR, Part 8 procedure;[445] in some circumstances, that is the only procedure which may be used (see the footnotes).[446] Separate provisions relate to low-value road traffic accident claims (see the footnotes).[447]

21.331 In the days before costs-only proceedings, the receiving party would have had to issue a substantive claim (either on the original claim or on the compromise) solely for the purposes of obtaining a costs order. For obvious reasons that was undesirable. The existence of costs-only claims is intended to enhance rather than restricts the

---

[441] This is implied by *Brown-Quinn & Anor v Equity Syndicate Management Ltd & Anor* [2011] EWHC 2661 (Comm) at [28]; this was following a decision that was made following argument, but which is not recorded in the written judgment.

[442] See, for example, *Bowskill v Dawson* [1955] 1 QB 13, [1954] 2 All ER 649, CA (which was an express trust) and *Hepburn v A Tomlinson (Hauliers) Ltd* [1966] AC 451, [1966] 1 All ER 418, HL (where the party was a bailee).

[443] See Road Traffic Act 1988, s 151.

[444] *Callery v Gray* [2001] EWCA Civ 1117 at [54], per Woolf CJ.

[445] CPR, r 44.14A(1) and (2).

[446] See CPD, art 25A.10, which provides: 'If the parties agree the amount of the fixed recoverable costs and the only dispute is as to the payment of, or amount of, a disbursement or as to the amount of a success fee, then proceedings should be issued under rule 44.12A in the normal way and not by reference to Section II of Part 45'.

[447] '**Costs-only application after a claim is started under Part 8 in accordance with Practice Direction 8B**
44.12C (1) This rule sets out the procedure where
(a) the parties to a dispute have reached an agreement on all issues (including which party is to pay the costs) which is made or confirmed in writing; but
(b) they have failed to agree the amount of those costs; and
(c) proceedings have been started under Part 8 in accordance with Practice Direction 8B.
(2) Either party may make an application for the court to determine the costs.
(3) Where an application is made under this rule the court will assess the costs in accordance with rule 45.34 or rule 45.37.
(4) Rule 48.3 (amount of costs where costs are payable pursuant to a contract) does not apply to an application under this rule.
(Practice Direction 8B sets out the procedure for a claim where the parties have followed the Pre-Action Protocol for Low Value Personal Injury Claims in Road Traffic Accidents.)'

parties' access to the courts: in particular, there is nothing to prevent a party from suing on an agreement made in settlement of a dispute where that agreement makes provision for costs, nor is there anything to prevent that party from claiming an order for costs or a specified sum in respect of costs.[448]

21.332 Costs-only proceedings are consensual: either party may issue costs-only proceedings[449] but, if the claim is opposed, it must be dismissed.[450] A claim will be treated as opposed if the defendant files an acknowledgement of service stating that he intends to contest the making of an order for costs or to seek a different remedy; it will not be treated as opposed if the defendant files an acknowledgement of service stating that he disputes the amount claimed.[451] The fact that a claim may have been dismissed as a result of it being opposed does not prevent the claimant from issuing another claim.[452]

21.333 The fact that a paying party has the absolute right to ask the court to dismiss a costs-only claim does not mean that he can exercise that right with impunity; although there is no authority on the point, a paying party who unreasonably defends costs-only proceedings may be at risk on costs if and when the matter comes before the court via a different route.

Procedure

21.334 A costs-only claim imposes few procedural demands on the parties. As with all CPR, Part 8 claims, formal pleadings are not required.[453] The claim form needs to do little more than to perform the following administrative functions:[454]

- it should identify the claim or dispute to which the agreement to pay costs relates;
- it should state the date and terms of the agreement on which the claimant relies;
- it should set out or have attached to it a draft of the order which the claimant seeks;
- it should state the amount of the costs claimed;
- it should state whether the costs are claimed on the standard or indemnity basis (if no basis is specified, the costs will be treated as being claimed on the standard basis);
- where CPR, Part 45, II applies and where the receiving party seeks costs which exceed fixed costs, it must state details of the exceptional circumstances which the receiving party considers justifies the additional costs;[455]
- where CPR Part 45, II applies, it must state details of any disbursements or success fee the receiving party wishes to claim[456] (including any details of the particular feature of the dispute which necessitated a claim under CPR, r 45.10(2)(d));[457]

---

[448] CPD, art 17.11.
[449] CPR, r 44.12A(2).
[450] CPR, r 44.12A(4)(b). CPD, art 36.2 has no applicability as it relates to putative compromises of the costs which are claimed, as opposed to putative compromises leading to an entitlement to costs.
[451] CPD, art 17.9(1).
[452] CPD, art 17.9(2).
[453] CPR, r 8.9(a)(ii).
[454] CPD, art 17.3, CPR, r 8.2 and PD 8A, para 4.2.
[455] CPD, art 25A.8.
[456] CPD, art 17.2.
[457] CPD, art 25A.9.

- if the claimant is claiming in a representative capacity, it should state what that capacity is;[458] and
- if the defendant is sued in a representative capacity, it should state what that capacity is.[459]

The claim form must contain or be accompanied by the agreement that entitles the receiving party to costs, or, where that agreement was not in written form, it should contain or be accompanied by a confirmation in writing.[460] By analogy with litigation other than costs, it would seem that procedural errors will not necessarily lead to the claim being struck out.[461]

21.335   The following miscellaneous topics may arise from time to time.

Venue

21.336   The claim form should not be issued in the High Court unless the dispute to which the agreement relates was of such a value or type that, had proceedings been begun, they would have been commenced in the High Court.[462] If the claim form needs to be issued in the RCJ, it should be issued in the SCCO.[463]

Fixed costs

21.337   Costs-only proceedings cannot be used to circumvent the fixed costs provisions in CPR, Part 45, II.[464] Where the claimant is claiming an amount of costs which exceeds the amount of the fixed recoverable costs, he must state details of the exceptional circumstances which he considers justifies the additional costs.[465] The receiving party must also include details of any disbursements or success fee he wishes to claim. If the disbursement falls within CPR, r 45.10(2)(d) (ie disbursements that have arisen due to a particular feature of the dispute), the receiving party must give details of the particular feature of the dispute and why he considers the disbursement to be necessary.[466]

Smaller claims

21.338   The small claims provisions do not apply to costs-only proceedings; this is because the claim is treated as if it had not been allocated.[467]

---

[458]   CPR, r 8.2.
[459]   CPR, r 8.2.
[460]   CPR, r 44.12A(3) and CPD, art 17.4.
[461]   See, for example, *Parnall v Hurst* (2003) *The Times*, 10 July in which HHJ Peter Langan QC declined to strike out a Part 8 claim where the evidence in support had not been served along with the claim form.
[462]   CPD, art 17.1.
[463]   CPD, art 17.2.
[464]   CPR, r 44.12A(4A).
[465]   CPD, art 25A.8.
[466]   CPD, art 25A.9.
[467]   See CPD, art 17.10(1), which overrides CPR, r 8.9(c).

Undefended claims

21.339   If the claim is uncontested, the claimant (who would usually be the receiving party) may request an order in the terms of his claim; that request may be made by letter rather than formal application.[468]

Basis upon which costs are payable

21.340   The fact that there has been agreement as to the incidence of costs does not mean that costs are payable under contract in the sense that CPR, r 48.3 applies.[469] Therefore, there is no basis for saying that costs are payable pursuant to contract on indemnity basis.

The relevant wording

21.341   CPR, r 44.12A provides:

'(1) This rule sets out a procedure which may be followed where—

(a)   the parties to a dispute have reached an agreement on all issues (including which party is to pay the costs) which is made or confirmed in writing; but
(b)   they have failed to agree the amount of those costs; and
(c)   no proceedings have been started.

(2)   Either party to the agreement may start proceedings under this rule by issuing a claim form in accordance with Part 8.

(3)   The claim form must contain or be accompanied by the agreement or confirmation.

(4)   Except as provided in paragraph (4A), in proceedings to which this rule applies the court—

(a)   may
    (i)   make an order for costs to be determined by detailed assessment; or
    (ii)   dismiss the claim; and
(b)   must dismiss the claim if it is opposed.

(4A)   In proceedings to which Section II[470] of Part 45 applies, the court shall assess the costs in the manner set out in that Section.

(5)   Rule 48.3 (amount of costs where costs are payable pursuant to a contract) does not apply to claims started under the procedure in this rule. (Rule 7.2 provides that proceedings are started when the court issues a claim form at the request of the claimant)

(Rule 8.1(6) provides that a practice direction may modify the Part 8 procedure).'

21.342   CPD, art 17 provides:

'**17.1** A claim form under this rule should not be issued in the High Court unless the dispute to which the agreement relates was of such a value or type that had proceedings been begun they would have been commenced in the High Court.

17.2 A claim form which is to be issued in the High Court at the Royal Courts of Justice will be issued in the Senior Courts Costs Office.

17.3 Attention is drawn to rule 8.2 (in particular to paragraph (b)(ii)) and to rule 44.12A(3). The claim form must:

---

[468]   CPD, art 17.6.
[469]   CPR, r 44.12A(5).
[470]   At the time of writing it was proposed the words 'or Section VI' be inserted.

(1)   identify the claim or dispute to which the agreement to pay costs relates;
(2)   state the date and terms of the agreement on which the claimant relies;
(3)   set out or have attached to it a draft of the order which the claimant seeks;
(4)   state the amount of the costs claimed; and,
(5)   state whether the costs are claimed on the standard or indemnity basis. If no basis is specified the costs will be treated as being claimed on the standard basis.

17.4 The evidence to be filed and served with the claim form under Rule 8.5 must include copies of the documents on which the claimant relies to prove the defendant's agreement to pay costs.

17.5 A costs judge or a district judge has jurisdiction to hear and decide any issue which may arise in a claim issued under this rule irrespective of the amount of the costs claimed or of the value of the claim to which the agreement to pay costs relates. A costs officer may make an order by consent under paragraph 17.7, or an order dismissing a claim under paragraph 17.9 below.

17.6 When the time for filing the defendant's acknowledgement of service has expired, the claimant may by letter request the court to make an order in the terms of his claim, unless the defendant has filed an acknowledgement of service stating that he intends to contest the claim or to seek a different order.

17.7 Rule 40.6 applies where an order is to be made by consent. An order may be made by consent in terms which differ from those set out in the claim form.

17.8

(1)   An order for costs made under this rule will be treated as an order for the amount of costs to be decided by a detailed assessment to which Part 47 and the practice directions relating to it apply. Rule 44.4(4) (determination of basis of assessment) also applies to the order.
(2)   In cases in which an additional liability is claimed, the costs judge or district judge should have regard to the time when and the extent to which the claim has been settled and to the fact that the claim has been settled without the need to commence proceedings.

17.9

(1)   For the purposes of rule 44.12A(4)(b)—
       (a)   a claim will be treated as opposed if the defendant files an acknowledgement of service stating that he intends to contest the making of an order for costs or to seek a different remedy; and
       (b)   a claim will not be treated as opposed if the defendant files an acknowledgement of service stating that he disputes the amount of the claim for costs.
(2)   An order dismissing the claim will be made as soon as an acknowledgement of service opposing the claim is filed. The dismissal of a claim under rule 44.12A(4) does not prevent the claimant from issuing another claim form under Part 7 or Part 8 based on the agreement or alleged agreement to which the proceedings under this rule related.

17.10

(1)   Rule 8.9 (which provides that claims issued under Part 8 shall be treated as allocated to the multi-track) shall not apply to claims issued under this rule. A claim issued under this rule may be dealt with without being allocated to a track.
(2)   Rule 8.1(3) and Part 24 do not apply to proceedings brought under rule 44.12A.

17.11 Nothing in this rule prevents a person from issuing a claim form under Part 7 or Part 8 to sue on an agreement made in settlement of a dispute where that agreement makes provision for costs, nor from claiming in that case an order for costs or a specified sum in respect of costs.'

21.343   CPD, arts 25A.8 and 25A.9 (which apply to fixed costs) provide:

> '**25A.8** Costs-only proceedings are commenced using the procedure set out in rule 44.12A. A claim form should be issued in accordance with Part 8. Where the claimant is claiming an amount of costs which exceed the amount of the fixed recoverable costs he must include on the claim form details of the exceptional circumstances which he considers justifies the additional costs.
>
> **25A.9** The claimant must also include on the claim form details of any disbursements or success fee he wishes to claim. The disbursements that may be claimed are set out in rule 45.10(1). If the disbursement falls within 45.10(2)(d) (disbursements that have arisen due to a particular feature of the dispute) the claimant must give details of the particular feature of the dispute and why he considers the disbursement to be necessary.'

Chapter 22

SUMMARY ASSESSMENTS

MEANING OF SUMMARY ASSESSMENT

22.1 Summary assessment is a procedure whereby the court makes an award for a stated amount of costs rather than for costs to be assessed or for fixed costs. CPR, r 43.3 defines summary assessment in this way:

> '"Summary assessment" means the procedure by which the court, when making an order about costs, orders payment of a sum of money instead of fixed costs or "detailed assessment".'

ENTITLEMENT TO A SUMMARY ASSESSMENT

22.2 The court's power to make a summary assessment is contained in CPR, r 44.7:

> 'Where the court orders a party to pay costs to another party (other than fixed costs) it may either—
>
> (a)   make a summary assessment of the costs; or
> (b)   order detailed assessment of the costs by a costs officer,
> unless any rule, practice direction or other enactment provides otherwise.
>
> (The costs practice direction sets out the factors which will affect the court's decision under this rule).'

Other than one or two provisions concerning additional liabilities (see **22.24**), most of the detail of the jurisdiction is contained in Section 13 the CPD rather than in the CPR.

22.3 There is a 'general rule' that costs will be summarily assessed at the end of certain types of hearing. The CPD expresses that rule in the following way:

> '**13.2** The general rule is that the court should make a summary assessment of the costs:
>
> (1)   at the conclusion of the trial of a case which has been dealt with on the fast track, in which case the order will deal with the costs of the whole claim, and
> (2)   at the conclusion of any other hearing, which has lasted not more than one day, in which case the order will deal with the costs of the application or matter to which the hearing related. If this hearing disposes of the claim, the order may deal with the costs of the whole claim;
> (3)   in hearings in the Court of Appeal to which Paragraph 14 of the Practice Direction supplementing Part 52 (Appeals) applies;
>
> unless there is good reason not to do so eg where the paying party shows substantial grounds for disputing the sum claimed for costs that cannot be dealt with summarily or there is insufficient time to carry out a summary assessment.'

22.4   The reference to para 14 of PD 52 is a reference to a further list of types of hearing during which costs are likely to be summarily assessed:

> '14.1 Costs are likely to be assessed by way of summary assessment at the following hearings [in the Court of Appeal]:
>
> (1)   contested directions hearings;
> (2)   applications for permission to appeal at which the respondent is present;
> (3)   dismissal list hearings in the Court of Appeal at which the respondent is present;
> (4)   appeals from case management decisions; and
> (5)   appeals listed for one day or less.'

22.5   Thus, a summary assessment of costs can be expected at the conclusion of the following types of hearing:

- any fast track trial;
- any hearing lasting less than one day (or any hearing listed in the Court of Appeal for one day or less);
- any contested directions hearing in the Court of Appeal;
- any application for permission to appeal in the Court of Appeal where the respondent is present;
- any dismissal list hearings in the Court of Appeal where the respondent is present; and
- any appeals from case management decisions in the Court of Appeal.

In addition, CPR Part 45 VII provides that (with certain expectations) all costs in the Patents County Court will be assessed by way of summary assessment: see **33.176**.

22.6   The court's power to carry out a summary assessment is not limited to these situations; CPD, art 13.1 makes the following general provision:

> 'Whenever a court makes an order about costs which does not provide for fixed costs to be paid the court should consider whether to make a summary assessment of costs.'

22.7   Thus, the court has general discretion summarily to assess costs in any case which does not provide for fixed costs. There is no presumption against the court carrying out a detailed assessment following a case which lasted more than one day.[1] An award in respect of pro bono representation may be assessed summarily.[2]

22.8   Where an application is dealt with by consent, the applicant ought not to attend court expecting his costs to be summarily assessed as of right; he should, instead, seek to agree those costs. The CPD gives the following guidance:[3]

> 'Where an application has been made and the parties to the application agree an order by consent without any party attending, the parties should agree a figure for costs to be inserted in the consent order or agree that there should be no order for costs. If the parties cannot agree the costs position, attendance on the appointment will be necessary but, unless good reason can be shown for the failure to deal with costs as set out above, no costs will be allowed for that attendance.'

---

[1]   *Q v Q (Family Division: Costs; Summary Assessment)* [2002] 2 FLR 668.
[2]   CPR, r 44.3C(2)(b).
[3]   CPD, art 13.4.

22.9 There are exceptions to the general rule set out above; they are:

- where the receiving party is an assisted person or LSC funded client;[4]
- where the receiving party is a child or protected party (unless the solicitor acting for the child or protected party has waived the right to further costs, in which case a summary assessment may take place);[5] and
- where the receiving party is a mortgagee who does not seek his costs from a third party, but only where the costs were incurred in possession proceedings or other proceedings relating to a mortgage.[6]

In the first two of these situations the court will not carry out a summary assessment; in so far as the third is concerned, the matter is in the court's discretion. The bar on carrying out a summary assessment applies only where costs are payable to a child or protected party; the CPD expressly provides that the court has the power to make a summary assessment of costs payable by a child or protected party.[7]

DISCRETIONARY POWER TO ORDER THAT THERE BE NO SUMMARY ASSESSMENT

22.10 The court has the discretionary power not to assess costs summarily;[8] whilst not binding, the CPD states that there must be 'good reason' not to assess the costs summarily.[9] The following miscellaneous points can be made about the exercise of the court's discretion not to carry out a summary assessment.

Lack of time

22.11 Lack of time would be a good reason for not summarily assessing costs,[10] but mere weariness would not; this is made clear by the Judicial Studies Board in its advice given to judges:[11]

> 'You may be tired at the end of a case and lack enthusiasm for dealing with the costs, but this does not entitle you to order detailed assessment, which may be to the detriment of the lay clients on both sides. The receiving party will have to involve himself in the additional expenditure of preparing a bill, and will be kept out of his money for longer than he need be. If enforcement is necessary it is preferable to be able to pursue the total of the judgment debt and costs, instead of first recovering the debt, and several months later having to start once more on the enforcement process, this time for the costs. By then the paying party may have successfully divested himself of assets, paid other creditors, or disappeared. As regards the paying party, he also may incur further expense in instructing his lawyers to deal with the bill, whilst interest on the costs will continue to accrue.'

---

[4] CPD, art 13.9.
[5] CPD, art 13.11(1).
[6] CPD, art 13.3, which provides: 'The general rule in paragraph 13.2 does not apply to a mortgagee's costs incurred in mortgage possession proceedings or other proceedings relating to a mortgage unless the mortgagee asks the court to make an order for his costs to be paid by another party ...'
[7] CPD, art 13.11(2).
[8] It is arguable that the court lacks the vires to make such an order in the Patents County Court: see **33.178**.
[9] CPD, art 13.2.
[10] CPD, art 13.2.
[11] Civil Bench Book, para 8.42.

This guidance is not in any way binding, but it does set out the potential consequences of not carrying out a summary assessment (those being further cost, delay and the potential for a multiplicity of enforcement proceedings).

Substantial costs

22.12 Costs of a complex and weighty claim may not be suitable for summary assessment. The Guide to the Summary Assessment of Costs gives the following advice:[12]

> 'It may not be appropriate to carry out a summary assessment if a case lasts more than half a day or involves leading Counsel since in those circumstances the case is likely to be complex and weighty. It will often be unwise for the court summarily to assess costs in a matter which is not simple and straightforward, unless the difference between the parties is comparatively small, or unless the correct allowance appears clear.'

This guidance is given in the context of hearings in the Court of Appeal, but there is no reason to believe that it would not also have resonance in other circumstances.

Substantial objections

22.13 The CPD states that where the paying party shows substantial grounds for disputing the sum claimed, that may amount to good reason for not assessing the costs summarily.[13]

Complex objections

22.14 Complex legal arguments about the costs themselves might justify a detailed assessment. In a case where there were arguments over the hourly charging rates of employed solicitors, for example, a detailed assessment was thought appropriate.[14]

Challenges to the indemnity principle

22.15 In a similar vein, a serious challenge to the indemnity principle would not normally be suitable for summary assessment.[15]

Conditional fee agreements

22.16 The Judicial Studies Board advises that the existence of a conditional fee agreement or other funding arrangement would not of itself be a good reason to order a detailed assessment.[16]

---

[12]   See para 65(1) of the Guide to the Summary Assessment of Costs 2005.
[13]   CPD, art 13.2.
[14]   *R v Cardiff City Council ex p Brown* (unreported) 11 August 1999, QBD.
[15]   *R v Cardiff City Council ex p Brown* (unreported) 11 August 1999, QBD.
[16]   Civil Bench Book, para 8.42.

Litigant in person

22.17 Where a litigant in person wishes to demonstrate pecuniary loss,[17] that may justify a detailed assessment.

No fetter

22.18 Where the rules mentioned above provide that a summary assessment is the ordinary method by which costs will be assessed, a decision to summarily assess the costs will rarely be corrected on appeal. In a case involving a £22,000 statement of costs which provided a paucity of detail, the Court of Appeal refused to find that the judge had been wrong not to order that the costs be sent for detailed assessment.[18]

PROCEDURE (GENERALLY)

22.19 The parties are expected to assist the court by preparing for a summary assessment. CPD, arts 13.5 and 13.6 give the following guidance:

'**13.5** (1) It is the duty of the parties and their legal representatives to assist the judge in making a summary assessment of costs in any case to which paragraph 13.2 above applies, in accordance with the following paragraphs.

(2) Each party who intends to claim costs must prepare a written statement of the costs he intends to claim showing separately in the form of a schedule:

(a)   the number of hours to be claimed,

(b)   the hourly rate to be claimed,

(c)   the grade of fee earner;

(d)   the amount and nature of any disbursement to be claimed, other than counsel's fee for appearing at the hearing,

(e)   the amount of solicitor's costs to be claimed for attending or appearing at the hearing,

(f)   the fees of counsel to be claimed in respect of the hearing, and

(g)   any value added tax (VAT) to be claimed on these amounts.

(3) The statement of costs should follow as closely as possible Form N260 and must be signed by the party or his legal representative. Where a litigant is an assisted person or is a LSC funded client or is represented by a solicitor in the litigant's employment the statement of costs need not include the certificate appended at the end of Form N260.

(4) The statement of costs must be filed at court and copies of it must be served on any party against whom an order for payment of those costs is intended to be sought. The statement of costs should be filed and the copies of it should be served as soon as possible and in any event not less than 24 hours before the date fixed for the hearing.

(5) Where the litigant is or may be entitled to claim an additional liability the statement filed and served need not reveal the amount of that liability.

13.6 The failure by a party, without reasonable excuse, to comply with the foregoing paragraphs will be taken into account by the court in deciding what order to make about the costs of the claim, hearing or application, and about the costs of any further hearing or detailed assessment hearing that may be necessary as a result of that failure.'

---

[17]   *Neil v Stephenson* [2001] EWCA Civ 627.

[18]   *Bryen & Langley Ltd v Boston* [2005] EWCA Civ 973.

PROCEDURE (FAILURE BY PARTY TO SERVE STATEMENT)

22.20 It may be that the receiving party has failed to file and serve a statement of costs in accordance with these provisions. Neuberger J has given detailed guidance about how the court should deal with such a situation.[19] That guidance can be summarised in the following way:

- the court should ask itself what, if any, prejudice has been caused by that failure; if there is no prejudice, then the court should summarily assess the costs in the normal way; or
- if there has been prejudice, one of the following may be appropriate:
  - the paying party may be afforded a short adjournment to consider the statement of costs, following which the costs will be summarily assessed; the court should bear in mind the fact that the paying party has not had much time to consider the statement, so where there is doubt, the court should err in favour of a light rather than a heavy figure;
  - the matter may be sent for a detailed assessment on the basis that there are appropriate sanctions as to costs; or
  - the matter may be stood over for a summary assessment at a later date (either on the basis of paper submissions or otherwise).

Neuberger J explained that, if there were aggravating factors, it might be correct to deprive a defaulting party of his costs entirely. It might also be relevant that CPD, art 13.6 enables the court to take into account an unexcused failure to file and serve a statement in accordance with the provisions set out above.

22.21 It should be borne in mind that it would not be an option in the circumstances described above (or, indeed, in any circumstances), to remit the matter to a costs judge for a *summary* assessment. This is because of a provision in CPD, art 13.8:

> 'The court awarding costs cannot make an order for a summary assessment of costs by a costs officer. If a summary assessment of costs is appropriate but the court awarding costs is unable to do so on the day, the court must give directions as to a further hearing before the same judge.'

Thus, if the court is minded to remit the matter to a costs judge, this must be for a detailed assessment rather than a summary assessment.

22.22 Indeed, the only judge who is in a position to carry out a summary assessment is the judge who has made the order, as explained by Sir Swinton Thomas:[20]

> 'The important words in 13.8 are the words "a further hearing before the same judge". The reasoning behind that rule is clear. It is that only the person who has actually heard the case and knows about it is in a position to make a summary assessment of costs.'

This means that if there is going to be an adjournment for a summary assessment at a later date, it must be reserved to the judge who made (or who intends to make) the costs order.

---

[19] *MacDonald v Taree Holdings Ltd* [2001] 1 Costs LR 147.

[20] *Mahmood v Penrose* [2002] EWCA Civ 457. However, the rule that only the judge who made the order can summarily assess the costs has, from time to time, been broken by the Court of Appeal itself: in *Bryen & Langley Ltd v Boston* [2005] EWCA Civ 973, for example, the court indicated that if the quantum of costs in the court below had not been agreed, it would have been minded to assess those costs.

PROCEDURE (ADDITIONAL LIABILITY)

Summary assessment at conclusion of proceedings

22.23 Where, at the conclusion of proceedings a party seeks to have his additional liability summarily assessed, he should ensure that all relevant documentation is to hand and is available for the court. The relevant guidance is given by the CPD:

'**14.9** In order to facilitate the court in making a summary assessment of any additional liability at the conclusion of the proceedings the party seeking such costs must prepare and have available for the court a bundle of documents which must include—

(1) a copy of every notice of funding arrangement (Form N251) which has been filed by him;

(2) a copy of every estimate and statement of costs filed by him;

(3) a copy of the risk assessment prepared at the time any relevant funding arrangement was entered into and on the basis of which the amount of the additional liability was fixed.

The court will take account of the risk assessment,[21] will assess the appropriate success fee, and then apply that to the whole of the costs. Common sense dictates that the bundle should contain all of the costs which the party seeks to claim.

Assessment of costs incurred while the claim is ongoing

22.24 Additional liability poses a potential problem when costs are summarily assessed prior to the conclusion of proceedings; this is for the following reasons:

- first, the court will not know whether the proceedings will be determined in favour of the receiving party, and therefore it may not be known whether a success fee will be payable; and
- second, the receiving party may have a legitimate interest in keeping confidential the quantum of the success fee.

These are the reasons why the assessment of additional liability is usually postponed until the conclusion of the proceedings.

22.25 CPR, r 44.3A provides:

'(1) The court will not assess any additional liability until the conclusion of the proceedings, or the part of the proceedings, to which the funding arrangement relates.

("Funding arrangement" and "additional liability" are defined in rule 43.2)

(2) At the conclusion of the proceedings, or the part of the proceedings, to which the funding arrangement relates the court may—

(a) make a summary assessment of all the costs, including any additional liability;

(b) make an order for detailed assessment of the additional liability but make a summary assessment of the other costs; or

(c) make an order for detailed assessment of all the costs.

(Part 47 sets out the procedure for the detailed assessment of costs).'

---

[21] The CPD appears to require the receiving party to disclose a risk assessment to the court; it could be argued that the CPD is ultra vires in this regard as the court lacks the power to order a party to waive privilege; see, by way of analogy, *General Mediterranean Holdings SA v Patel* [1999] 2 Costs LR.

22.26 The CPD gives the following further guidance:

> '**13.12** (1) Attention is drawn to rule 44.3A which prevents the court from making a summary assessment of an additional liability before the conclusion of the proceedings or the part of the proceedings to which the funding arrangement relates. Where this applies, the court should nonetheless make a summary assessment of the base costs of the hearing or application unless there is a good reason not to do so.'

22.27 Thus, the court is encouraged to summarily assess the base costs even if the additional liability is to be held over to another time. An example of this happening is a case in which the assessment of the success fee raised issues of some complexity; Floyd J decided that a costs judge would be in a better position to conduct a proper investigation into the risks that were present at the time the risk assessment was carried out.

22.28 In much the same vein, CPD gives the following further guidance:

> '**14.1** The existence of a conditional fee agreement or other funding arrangement within the meaning of rule 43.2 is not by itself a sufficient reason for not carrying out a summary assessment.
>
> **14.2** Where a legal representative acting for the receiving party has entered into a conditional fee agreement the court may summarily assess all the costs (other than any additional liability).'

22.29 There are many options available to the court at the conclusion of the matter, but one option which is not open is to make a summary assessment of the success fee and then to remit the base costs to a costs judge for a detailed assessment. This is confirmed by CPD, art 3.1:

> 'Rule 43.3 defines summary assessment. When carrying out a summary assessment of costs where there is an additional liability the court may assess the base costs alone, or the base costs and the additional liability.'

22.30 As explained above, the rationale behind the restriction on the court assessing additional liability during the currency of the claim is not simply in order to prevent the paying party from knowing what success fee is claimed (and thereby gaining a potentially unfair insight into his opponent's view of the litigation risks), but is also because the receiving party might not 'win' the claim generally, in which case the success fee might not be payable. Indeed, it is possible (albeit unlikely) that if a party wins an interim hearing but loses generally, no costs would be payable at all, even in respect of the successful interim hearing. In view of this, the CPD makes the following provisions:

> '**14.3** Where costs have been summarily assessed an order for payment will not be made unless the court has been satisfied that in respect of the costs claimed, the receiving party is at the time liable to pay to his legal representative an amount equal to or greater than the costs claimed. A statement in the form of the certificate appended at the end of Form N260 may be sufficient proof of liability. The giving of information under rule 44.15 (where that rule applies) is not sufficient.
>
> **14.4** The court may direct that any costs, for which the receiving party may not in the event be liable, shall be paid into court to await the outcome of the case, or shall not be enforceable until further order, or it may postpone the receiving party's right to receive payment in some other way.'

Thus, if the paying party objects to paying the costs during the currency of the claim on the basis that the receiving party's conditional fee agreement may not provide for payment of base costs in the event of the claim not being successful overall, the court may order payment of the cost into court, or may make some other order deferring payment of the cost until the conclusion of the claim.

22.31 If the assessment of the additional liability is held over, it is not necessarily the case that it should be assessed by way of detailed assessment; if, however, the additional liability is summarily assessed at the conclusion of the proceedings, that assessment must relate to the whole of the additional liability, rather than just that relating to the final hearing. This is made clear by the CPD:

> '**14.7** Where the court makes a summary assessment of an additional liability at the conclusion of proceedings, that assessment must relate to the whole of the proceedings; this will include any additional liability relating to base costs allowed by the court when making a summary assessment on a previous application or hearing.'

22.32 If there is agreement as to base costs, but no agreement as to additional liability, the court may either send the additional liability for a detailed assessment, or it may summarily assess it. The relevant provision in this regard is CPD, art 14.8:

> 'Paragraph 13.13 applies where the parties are agreed about the total amount to be paid by way of costs, or are agreed about the amount of the base costs that will be paid. Where they disagree about the additional liability the court may summarily assess that liability or make an order for a detailed assessment.'

22.33 On a practical level, CPD, art 13.12(2) gives the following guidance:

> 'Where the court makes a summary assessment of the base costs all statements of costs and costs estimates put before the judge will be retained on the court file.'

Presumably, this provision is made in order to assist the court in the event of further summary assessments being carried out, or to assist the costs judge in the event of the matter coming back before the court for a detailed assessment of the additional liability.

22.34 CPD, art 14.6 makes provisions which, again, appear to be for the benefit of the costs judge who carries out the detailed assessment of the additional liability:

> '**14.6** Rule 44.3A(2) sets out the ways in which the court may deal with the assessment of the costs where there is a funding arrangement. Where the court makes a summary assessment of the base costs:
>
> (1) The order may state separately the base costs allowed as (a) solicitor's charges, (b) counsel's fees, (c) any other disbursements and (d) any VAT;
> (2) the statements of costs upon which the judge based his summary assessment will be retained on the court file.'

THE ASSESSMENT ITSELF

22.35 Other than being shorter and more broad-brush, a summary assessment is not dissimilar to a detailed assessment. The pre-eminent costs counsel Jeremy Morgan QC has commented that summary assessments are often difficult hearings to get right;[22] if an assessment is to be a condensed version of a fully contested detailed assessment that would undoubtedly be correct. Generally speaking, the advocate for the paying party will make points on the following topics (and usually in this order):

---

[22] K Scott *Summary Assessment of Costs* (Oxford University Press, 2006), para 1.02.

- the indemnity principle;
- proportionality;
- hourly rates;
- the attendances;
- the documentary time;
- counsel's fees
- other disbursements; and
- additional liability.

The receiving party will then respond to these points. The court will often give judgment on all the points that have been put, although some judges will deal with each point in turn. Judgments are usually brief;[23] Burton J has held that the court should give sufficient reasons for the receiving party to know why costs have been disallowed.[24]

22.36 The CPD, gives the following guidance as to the approach to be taken on the summary assessment of costs:

'**13.13** The court will not give its approval to disproportionate and unreasonable costs. Accordingly:

(a)   When the amount of the costs to be paid has been agreed between the parties the order for costs must state that the order is by consent.

(b)   If the judge is to make an order which is not by consent, the judge will, so far as possible, ensure that the final figure is not disproportionate and/or unreasonable having regard to Part 1 of the CPR. The judge will retain this responsibility notwithstanding the absence of challenge to individual items in the make-up of the figure sought. The fact that the paying party is not disputing the amount of costs can however be taken as some indication that the amount is proportionate and reasonable. The judge will therefore intervene only if satisfied that the costs are so disproportionate that it is right to do so.'

It would seem, therefore, that a judge carrying out a summary assessment has a wide discretion as to overall figure allowed.

Ascertainment of quantum on a summary assessment

General approach

22.37 The court's task is to focus on the heads of costs claimed and to form the best judgment it can as to what proportion of those costs it is reasonable for the paying party to pay.[25] The approach is more rough and ready than in the detailed assessment.[26] Black LJ had this to say about the balance between broad-brush and fine-brush:[27]

'[I]t is very important for the judge to take a global view of the proportionality of the costs incurred but, before he fixes a figure for costs, he must advance from that to an item by item consideration of the individual elements of the bill by way of a summary assessment or

---

[23]   Although of only descriptive value, see K Scott *Summary Assessment of Costs* (Oxford University Press, 2006), para 2.05.

[24]   *Sterling Publications Ltd v Burroughs* [2000] 2 Costs LR 155.

[25]   *Bryen & Langley Ltd v Boston* [2005] EWCA Civ 973 at [54].

[26]   Ibid. See also *Naylor v Monahan* [2011] EWHC 1412 (QB) at [12(a)] in which Coulson J declined to give permission to appeal from a summary assessment, this being because he found that a judge is not 'obliged to go through a box-ticking exercise, in which he or she is forced to comment in detail upon each item of the draft bill'.

[27]   *Morgan v Spirit Group Ltd* [2011] EWCA Civ 68 at [27], per Black LJ.

alternatively, he must direct a detailed assessment which will fulfil that task. Naturally, any judge carrying out a summary assessment appropriately focused on the detailed breakdown of costs will have firmly in mind that the court's discretion when carrying out such an assessment is very wide and that a minute examination of detail is not always required and a broad brush can, where appropriate, be used. It would be a great pity if the summary assessment procedure were to become bedevilled by formulaic and time consuming intricacy which would often be wholly disproportionate to the exercise being carried out and the nature of the litigation in hand.'

The court will not give its approval to disproportionate and unreasonable costs.[28]

Proportionality

22.38 The two-stage approach under *Lownds v Home Office*[29] applies.[30] Whilst there is no authority on that point, some commentators have noted that the powers described by CPD, art 13.13 are, if anything, wider than those which are available to a costs judge conducting a detailed assessment.

Excessive costs

22.39 Jonathan Parker LJ made the following comments about the correct approach to costs which appear to be excessive:[31]

'Having dealt with the costs by reference to the detailed items in the statement of costs which is before it, the court may find it helpful to look at the total sum at which it has arrived in order to see whether that sum falls within the bounds of what it considers reasonable and proportionate. If the court considers the total sum to be unreasonable or disproportionate, it may wish to look again at the various detailed items in order to see what further reductions should be made.'

These comments preceded *Lownds v Home Office*, but it is an approach which is consistent with the guidance given in that case.

Comparators

22.40 It would be wrong not to focus on the individual arguments and instead to rely on a comparison with the other party's costs. Rimer J (sitting in the Court of Appeal) has noted that those costs may provide a helpful cross-check, but that it would be wrong in principle for the court to conclude that, because the paying party's costs are much the same as the receiving party's costs, the latter can be assumed to be reasonable.[32]

---

[28] CPD, art 13.13.
[29] [2002] EWCA Civ 365.
[30] *Bryen & Langley Ltd v Boston* [2005] EWCA Civ 973 at [51]–[52]; *Morgan v Spirit Group Ltd* [2011] EWCA Civ 68 at [38], per Black LJ.
[31] *1-800 Flowers Inc v Phonenames Ltd* [2001] EWCA Civ 712 at [114].
[32] *Bryen & Langley Ltd v Boston* [2005] EWCA Civ 973 at [54].

No tariff

22.41 It would not be appropriate for a judge to set a tariff. Jonathan Parker LJ commented that it would be wrong in principle for the court to apply its own tariff to the case which was arrived at without carrying out any detailed examination or analysis of the costs actually incurred.[33]

Acquiesence as to costs

22.42 It is implicit in CPD, art 13.13 that the court would not be bound by the fact that the paying party raises no objections to the costs which are being claimed. The fact that no objection has been raised can be taken as some indication that the amount is proportionate and reasonable, but the absence of objection will not change the fact that the court will not give its approval to disproportionate and unreasonable costs.

---

[33]   *1-800 Flowers Inc v Phonenames Ltd* [2001] EWCA Civ 712; see also *Morgan v Spirit Group Ltd* [2011] EWCA Civ 68 at [27], per Black LJ.

Chapter 23

APPEALS

23.1   There are, under the CPR, two entirely distinct appeal regimes relating to costs. This is because there is a specific regime that applies where the appeal is from the decision of an authorised court officer. That regime is unique to costs, whereas other decisions are subject to the general appeals regime as set out in CPR Part 52. A degree of knowledge of the general appeals regime is assumed.

APPEALS FROM AUTHORISED COURT OFFICERS

The appeal in general

23.2   An appeal from a decision of an authorised court officer differs from other appeals under the CPR in the following ways:[1]

- the appellant is able to appeal as of right (ie no permission to appeal is required);[2]
- the appeal will be by way of a rehearing rather than a review;[3] and
- the destination court will be a court which itself had an ordinary jurisdiction to hear the original assessment, rather than a higher court.[4]

Thus, an appeal will proceed as if it were an assessment: it is a second bite at the cherry. In practice, both the court and the parties will often refer to the hearing below, but the court is in no way bound by that decision. In particular, there is no requirement that the appeal court must find that the decision of the court below was 'wrong' in order to allow the appeal.

23.3   The applicable procedure is governed principally by CPR Part 47 VIII rather than Part 52.[5] (CPR, r 47.20 refers to Part 52 setting out general rules in respect of appeals, but for all practical purposes the governing provisions are CPR Part 47 VIII and the associated articles in the CPD.)

Timing

23.4   An appellant's notice must be filed within 21 days of the authorised court officer's decision;[6] it is the date of the decision itself that is relevant, not the conclusion

---

[1]   Although there is no authority on the point, these differences are probably a reflection of the fact that an authorised court officer is not a judge in the sense that he or she is required to have both legal qualifications and experience of legal practice (see **4.14–4.15**, and **21.289–21.293**).

[2]   This is implied by CPR, r 47.20 and made explicit by CPD, art 47.2.

[3]   CPR, r 47.23(a) and CPD, art 48.2.

[4]   CPR, r 47.21 and CPD, art 48.2.

[5]   CPD, art 47.1.

[6]   CPR, r 47.22.

of the assessment.[7] The appellant's notice will be in the same form as in other appeals (ie an N161).[8] The appellant does not need to serve the appellant's notice on the other parties, as this is something that the court will do.[9]

Record of hearing below

23.5   Where possible, a suitable record of the judgment of the authorised court officer must be obtained.[10] What amounts to a suitable record of judgment is dealt with in more detail in the footnotes at **23.34**, but it may be any one of the following:

- an approved transcript;
- a written judgment (including the comments written on the bill); or
- an agreed and approved note.

23.6   Where reasons given for the decision have been officially recorded by the court, an approved transcript should be filed along with the appellant's notice. Photocopies should not be used in substitution for the original transcript.[11] There is no requirement to obtain written reasons from the authorised court officer.[12]

Litigants in person

23.7   Where a litigant in person wishes to appeal and where there is no transcript, the respondent's advocate, if there is one, must make his note freely available to the appellant. The appellant should then submit the notes to the appeal court.[13]

Publicly funded appellants

23.8   CPR, r 47.20(2) states that an LSC funded client or an assisted person is not a party to the detailed assessment for the purposes of CPR, Part 47 VIII. Although there is no authority on the point, this would appear to mean that a publicly funded client must bring an appeal under CPR, Part 52 rather than CPR, Part 47 VIII. It could be conjectured that this may be a provision which is intended to discourage appeals funded at public expense.

APPEALS OTHER THAN FROM AUTHORISED COURT OFFICERS

23.9   Appeals from persons other than authorised court officers follow the appeals procedure in CPR Part 52. CPR Part 47 VIII has no part to play in such an appeal. A knowledge of Part 52 in general is assumed; the following discussion focuses only on those aspects of appeals which pertain to detailed assessments and to costs in general.

---

7   *Kasir v Darlington & Simpson Rolling Mills Ltd* [2001] 2 Costs LR 228; and see CPR, r 47.22(1).
8   CPD, art 48.1.
9   CPR, r 47.22(2).
10   CPD, arts 48.3 and 48.4; it may not always be possible to obtain that record within the time in which the appellant's notice must be filed; where this is the case, the appellant's notice should be completed to the best of the appellant's ability; it may then be amended with the permission of the costs judge or district judge hearing the appeal.
11   CPD, art 48.3.
12   CPR, r 47.20(1) and CPD, art 47.2.
13   PD 52, para 5.12(3) and CPD, art 48.3.

The applicable standard

23.10 Generally speaking, an appeal will be by way of review rather than a rehearing.[14] The court will allow an appeal if the decision of the lower court was 'wrong' or 'unjust because of a serious procedural or other irregularity in the proceedings'.[15] The second of these reasons very rarely arises in the context of costs and is not discussed any further as specialist advice would always be required before bringing or defending such an appeal.[16]

23.11 The general approach to appeals by way of review was described by Woolf LJ:[17]

'Before the court can interfere it must be shown that the judge has either erred in principle in his approach or has left out of account or has taken into account some feature that he should or should not have considered or that his decision was wholly wrong because the court is forced to the conclusion that he has not balanced the various factors fairly in the scales.'

23.12 As a rule, the appeal court will be loath to interfere with a decision on costs; Wilson LJ had the following to say about the ethos which underlies that approach:[18]

'This is an appeal ... in relation to costs. As such, it is overcast, from start to finish, by the heavy burden faced by any appellant in establishing that the judge's decision falls outside the discretion in relation to costs ... For reasons of general policy, namely that it is undesirable for further costs to be incurred in arguing about costs, this court discourages such appeals by interpreting such discretion very widely.'

23.13 Having stated the general approach, a number of more specific circumstances are now considered.

Appeals concerning the incidence of costs

23.14 An appellant who seeks to challenge a finding as to the incidence of costs will find that he has a heavy burden to shift; Waller LJ explained that the appellant must show that the court below had gone seriously wrong before he could expect to succeed:[19]

'It is well known that this court will be loath to interfere with the discretion exercised by a judge in any area but so far as costs are concerned that principle has a special significance. The judge has the feel of a case after a trial which the Court of Appeal cannot hope to replicate and the judge must have gone seriously wrong if this court is to interfere.'

---

[14] CPR, r 52.11(3)(b); this topic was considered by the Court of Appeal in *Audergon v La Baguette Ltd* [2002] EWCA Civ 10; it is clear for the matter to proceed as a rehearing that there must be some element of injustice of a serious procedural or other irregularity; however, in a second appeal of real importance the court may hear costs appeals by way of a rehearing; examples include *U v Liverpool County Council* [2005] EWCA Civ 475 and *Rogers v Merthyr Tydfil County Borough Council* [2006] EWCA Civ 1134.

[15] CPR, r 52.11(3).

[16] For a discussion of this topic, see *Storer v British Gas plc* [2000] 2 All ER 440; see also *Tanfern Ltd v Cameron-MacDonald* [2000] 2 All ER 801 at 809.

[17] *AEI Rediffusion Music Limited v Phonographic Performance Limited* [1999] 1 WLR 1507 at 1523; see also the comments of by Brooke LJ in *Tanfern Ltd v Cameron-Macdonald* [2000] 1 WLR 1311 at 1317.

[18] *SCT Finance v Bolton* [2002] EWCA Civ 56 at [1].

[19] *Straker v Turner Rose (a firm)* [2007] EWCA Civ 368 at [2].

23.15 Sir Murray Stuart-Smith explained the circumstances in which the appeal court might be persuaded to interfere:[20]

> 'Costs are in the discretion of the trial judge, and this court will only interfere with the exercise of that discretion on well-defined principles. As I said in *Roache v News Group Newspapers Ltd* [1998] EMLR 161, 172:
>
>> "Before the court can interfere it must be shown that the judge has either erred in principle in his approach, or has left out of account, or taken into account, some feature that he should, or should not, have considered, or that his decision is wholly wrong because the court is forced to the conclusion that he had not balanced the various factors in the scale".'

Thus, the appeal court will interfere in an appropriate case, but that would usually be on the basis that the court below had made an error in its method, such as taking into account an irrelevant factor, failing to take into account a relevant factor, or something of that nature. In theory, an appeal could also succeed on the basis that the court below came to a conclusion that was beyond the ambit of decisions reasonably available to it, but in view of the breadth of that ambit in issues pertaining to the incidence of costs, that would not be a conclusion that the court would readily reach. There are, however, examples of appeals being allowed on the basis that the court below exceeded the available ambit.[21]

Appeals concerning the amount of costs

23.16 Appeals concerning the amount of costs are also notoriously challenging from the appellant's point of view. There are many cases decided under the CPR[22] which confirm that the following comments of Lord Fraser remain good law; as can be seen, Lord Fraser brings to light the difference between a finding which is wrong and a finding which is merely an alternative imperfect solution to that which would have been adopted by the appeal court:[23]

> 'Certainly it would not be useful to inquire whether different shades of meaning are intended to be conveyed by words such as "blatant error" used by the President in the present case, and words such as "clearly wrong", "plainly wrong" or "simply wrong" used by other judges in other cases. All these various expressions were used in order to emphasise the point that the appellate court should only interfere when they consider that the judge of first instance has not merely preferred an imperfect solution, which is different from an alternative imperfect solution which the Court of Appeal might or would have adopted, but has exceeded the generous ambit within which a reasonable disagreement is possible.'

23.17 In a similar vein, Buckley J had these oft-cited observations to make about the approach generally taken in appeals concerning the quantum of costs:[24]

---

[20]   *Adamson v Halifax plc* [2002] EWCA Civ 1134 at [16]; see also Viscount Cave LC in *Donald Campbell & Co Ltd v Pollak* [1927] AC 732.

[21]   An example of this is *Lowe v W Machell Joinery Limited* [2011] EWCA Civ 798, in which the Court of Appeal allowed an appeal despite having commented that 'the legitimate ambit of the discretion afforded by the rules to the court determining the question of costs is unusually wide' (at [12]).

[22]   See, for example, *Griffiths v Solutia UK Ltd* [2001] EWCA Civ 736; and *Higgs v Camden & Islington Health Authority* [2003] EWHC 15 (QB).

[23]   *G v G (minors: custody appeal)* [1985] 1 WLR 647 at 652.

[24]   *Mealing-McLeod v Common Professional Examination Board* [2000] 2 Costs LR 223 at 224.

'A Judge will allow an appeal ... if satisfied that the decision of the Costs Judge was wrong ... That is easy to apply to matter of principle or construction. However, where the appeal includes challenges to the details of the assessment, such as hours allowed in respect of a particular item, the task in hand is one of assessment or judgment rather than principle. There is no absolute answer ... I would regard it as inappropriate for the Judge on appeal to be drawn into an exercise calculated to add a little here or knock off a little there. If the Judge's attention is drawn to items which with the advice of Assessors he feels should, in fairness, be altered, doubtless he will act. That is a matter for his good judgment.'

The fact that the court will be cautious does not mean that the court will not reverse the decision of the court below where it is appropriate to do so. By way of example, in the case referred to above, Buckley J went on to make about a dozen adjustments, some of which were as modest as allowing an extra 15 minutes.

Appeals where the court below failed to give reasons or failed to cite the law

23.18 In the context of an appeal where it was said that the court at first instance had not fully appreciated the law, Ward LJ quoted the following passage from a speech of Lord Hoffmann, adding his own emphasis:[25]

'The exigencies of daily court room life are such that reasons for judgment will always be capable of having been better expressed. This is particularly true of an unreserved judgment such as the judge gave in this case but also of a reserved judgment based upon notes, such as was given by the District Judge. *These reasons should be read on the assumption that, unless he has demonstrated the contrary, the judge knew how he should perform his functions and which matters he should take into account. This is particularly true when the matters in question are* [well known]. An appellate court should resist the temptation to subvert the principle that they should not substitute their own discretion for that of the judge by a narrow textual analysis which enables them to claim that he misdirected himself.'

23.19 It ought to be apparent from a judgment why one side has lost and the other has won, and a failure to give reasons is itself capable of standing as a ground of appeal.[26] As to the duty to give reasons in respect of a cost order, Woolf CJ said:[27]

'As is to be expected, the decision of the judge in relation to costs was expressed succinctly. A judge is not expected to give a detailed decision as to why he is making an order. However, if he is going to make an order for costs which is not the normal order expected under the particular provisions of the CPR, then the parties are entitled to know the basis of that order and the judge is required to explain that so far as is necessary to do.'

Those comments were made in the context of litigation in general, but they also apply to costs. Burton J, for example, has made similar comments in the context of the duty to give reasons for disallowance made during a summary assessment.[28] Where a judge makes an issues-based order, the reasons will normally be readily apparent from the judgment in the substantive matter.[29] In so far as the assessment of costs is concerned, Hart J has commented that it will sometimes be impossible – and sometimes undesirable

---

25 *Cambertown Timber Merchants Ltd v Sidhu* [2011] EWCA Civ 1041 at [35], citing Lord Hoffmann from *Piglowska v Piglowski* [1999] 1 WLR 1360 at 1372.
26 *English v Emery Reimbold & Strick Ltd* [2002] EWCA Civ 605.
27 *Excelsior Commercial & Industrial Holdings Ltd v Salisbury Hamer Aspden & Johnson (Costs)* [2002] EWCA Civ 879.
28 *Sterling Publications Ltd v Burroughs* [2000] 2 Costs LR 155.
29 *Early Red Corporation NV v Glidepath Holdings BV* [2005] EWCA Civ 525.

– for the costs judge to spell out the exact process of reasoning which has led to the final figure; he commented that a decision as to quantum will frequently be the result of 'a triangulation' between a variety of relatively unfixed possible positions, and that that process is based very much on expert 'feel'.[30] For obvious reasons, an appeal court would be reluctant to find that a judge had erred simply by reason of not having described every step taken in that process. Similarly, Peter Smith J has said that the appellate court should not be tempted into a detailed analysis of each and every reason or argument put forward and allegedly not dealt with by the judge at first instance.[31]

Appeals in respect of interim decisions

23.20 Costs orders made in general litigation are atypical in the sense that enduring decisions may be taken during the litigation rather than at the end. This may cause litigants to ask the court to reconsider its earlier decisions in the light of the outcome of the case. A request to reconsider earlier orders ought to be made by way of an appeal rather than application (see **7.416** *et seq*), but even if the correct procedure is followed to the letter, the court is not likely to be receptive to such an appeal; it would often be dismissed as being an attempt to re-litigate an interim costs order with the benefit of hindsight.[32] A claimant is not able to extinguish the jurisdiction to appeal an interim costs order by the expedient of discontinuing the claim.[33]

Appeals against decisions where lower court did not hear the substantive claim

23.21 Where the parties have settled everything but the costs, and where the parties ask the lower court to rule on costs without that court having heard the substantive issues, the appeal court will (in the absence of an error of principle) be highly reluctant to interfere with that decision. Wilson LJ has explained that the parties can reasonably be expected to accept the court's decision unless it could be shown that the decision was 'manifestly unjust'.[34] Where there has been an error of principle, however, the appeal court may interfere.[35]

Procedure

23.22 The following miscellaneous procedural points may be made (which are broadly in the order that they would arise in the appeal process).

Time

23.23 Unless the court directs otherwise, the appellant's notice must be filed within 21 days of the decision of the court below.[36] Time for lodging an appellant's notice runs from the time judgment is given rather than from the conclusion of the assessment.[37] Brooke LJ has explained that when considering an application for an extension of time for appealing, in a case of any complexity the court should have regard to the checklist

---

[30]   *Jemma Trust Company Ltd v Liptrott & Ors (No 2)* [2004] EWHC 1404 (Ch) at [26].
[31]   *Sibley & Co v Reachbyte Ltd* [2008] EWHC 2665 (Ch) at [39].
[32]   *Koshy v Deg-Deutsche Investitions und Entwicklungs Gesellschaft Gmbh* [2003] EWCA Civ 1718.
[33]   See *Safeway v Twigger* [2010] EWCA Civ 1472, per Pill LJ at [58].
[34]   *BCT Software Solutions Ltd v C Brewer & Sons Ltd* (2003) EWCA Civ 939.
[35]   See, for example, *Lay v Drexler* [2007] EWCA Civ 464.
[36]   CPR, r 52.4(2).
[37]   *Kasir v Darlington & Simpson Rolling Mills Ltd* [2001] 2 Costs LR 228, Mr Justice Popplewell.

in CPR, r 3.9.[38] Once time has begun to run, the lower court's power to vary the time for lodging the appellant's notice derives from the power to direct when the appellant's notice is to be filed;[39] that power is not negated by the provision that an application to vary the time limit for filing an appellant's notice must be made to the appeal court.[40] The lower court should not exercise that power if an appellant's notice has been filed at the appeal court,[41] and in any event, should exercise that power only if there is 'good reason' to do so.[42] The lower court should bear in mind the checklist in CPR, r 3.9, and should always have in mind that it could leave the question of any extension to the appeal court.[43] Save in 'wholly exceptional circumstances' (to use Law LJ's phrase),[44] extreme delay will defeat an application for permission to appeal.[45]

No automatic stay

23.24 If a party brings an appeal against a costs order, that appeal will not stay the detailed assessment of any costs which have been ordered by the court below.[46] If a party appeals an assessment, the order (or certificate) of the court will not be stayed unless and until the court so orders.[47]

Destination court and 'leapfrog' procedure

23.25 Destination courts are set out in Table 1 of PD 52; the following is only a brief summary. Table 1 distinguishes between 'interim decisions' and 'final decisions'.[48] An order made on summary or detailed assessment of costs is not a final decision (see below), but an order concerning the incidence of costs may or may not be, depending on the context:

- *The incidence of costs (county court):* The destination will depend on the level of judge and on whether the decision was or was not part of a final decision:[49]
  1. *District judges:* A decision of a district judge in a claim other than a multi-track claim will be appealed to a circuit judge, as will an interim

---

38   *Sayers v Clarke Walker (a firm)* [2002] EWCA Civ 645, per Brooke LJ.
39   That being CPR, r 52.4(2); see *Aujla v Sanghera at* [2004] EWCA Civ 121, per Arden LJ at [14].
40   See CPR, r 52.6(1).
41   *Aujla v Sanghera at* [2004] EWCA Civ 121 [14], per Arden LJ at [18].
42   Ibid at [17], per Arden LJ.
43   Ibid at [17]–[19].
44   *Compagnie Noga D'Importation et D'Exportation SA v Abacha* [2003] EWCA Civ 1101 at [7].
45   In the case referred to immediately above, for example, there had been a delay of over four years in asking for permission to appeal an interim costs order; permission was (robustly) refused.
46   See CPR, r 47.2 and CPD, art 29.1.
47   CPR, r 52.7.
48   Access to Justice Act 1999 (Destination of Appeals) Order 2000, art 1(2)(c) defines a final decision as being '…a decision of a court that would finally determine (subject to any possible appeal of detailed assessment of costs) the entire proceedings whichever way the court decided the issues before it.'. In so far as it is relevant, PD 52 provides as follows:
'2A.2 A "final decision" is a decision of a court that would finally determine (subject to any possible appeal or detailed assessment of costs) the entire proceedings whichever way the court decided the issues before it
...
2A.3 A decision of a court is to be treated as a final decision for routes of appeal for purposes where it: (1) is made at the conclusion of part of a hearing or trial which has been split into parts; and (2) would, if it had been made at the conclusion of that hearing or trial, have been a final decision. Accordingly, a judgment on liability at the end of a split trial is a 'final decision' for this purpose and the judgment at the conclusion of the assessment of damages following a judgment on liability is also a 'final decision' for this purpose.
Moore-Bick LJ has confirmed that decision as to cost may be regarded as being a part of trial for the purposes of PD 52, para 2A.3 (see *Fox v Foundation Piling Group Ltd* [2011] EWCA Civ 104 at [26].
49   See the Access to Justice Act 1999 (Destination of Appeals) Order 2000, art 3.

decision of a district judge in a multi-track claim; a final decision in a multi-track claim will be appealed to the Court of Appeal. Any decision by a district judge in a Part 8 claim will be appealed to a circuit judge, as will any decision in a claim or pre-action application started otherwise than by a Part 7 or Part 8 claim (for example an application under Part 23).

2. *Circuit judges:* A decision of a circuit judge in a claim other than a multi-track claim will be appealed to a single judge of the High Court, as will an interim decision of a circuit judge in a multi-track claim; a final decision in a multi-track claim will be appealed to the Court of Appeal. Any decision by a circuit judge in a Part 8 claim will be appealed to a single judge of the High Court, as will any decision in a claim or pre-action application started otherwise than by a Part 7 or Part 8 claim (for example an application under Part 23).

Were the only matter in dispute is the incidence of costs of the proceedings, an order dealing with that point will be a final decision.[50]

- **The incidence of costs (High Court):** The destination will depend on the level of judge and on whether the decision was or was not part of a final decision:[51]

  1. *Masters, district judges sitting in a district registry, etc:*[52] A decision in a claim other than a multi-track claim will be appealed to a single judge of the High Court, as will an interim decision in a multi-track claim; a final decision in a multi-track claim will be appealed to the Court of Appeal. Any decision in a Part 8 claim will be appealed to a circuit judge, as will any decision in a claim or originating or pre-action application started otherwise than by a Part 7 or Part 8 claim (for example an application under Part 23).

  2. *High Court judges:* A decision of a High Court will be appealed to the Court of Appeal.

Were the only matter in dispute is the incidence of costs of the proceedings, an order dealing with that point will be a final decision.[53]

- **Free-standing matters:** Sometimes a decision concerning costs (such as wasted costs orders) will be free-standing from the claim to which it relates; where this is so, it will be decided by reference to the level of judge rather than to the claim in which the issue arose.[54]

- **Detailed and summary assessments:** An order made on a summary or detailed assessment of costs is not a final decision;[55] the effect of this is that, in general, on a first appeal from an assessment a decision of a district judge in the county court will be appealed to a circuit judge and a decision of a district judge or master in the High Court will be appealed to a single judge of the High Court.

- **Appeals from masters in the SCCO:** Where a master or deputy master hears a detailed assessment which has been referred to the Senior Courts Costs Office

---

[50]	*Fox v Foundation Piling Group Ltd* [2011] EWCA Civ 104 at [11], per Moore-Bick LJ (heard at the same time as *Thorne v Courtier & Ors* [2011] EWCA Civ 104).

[51]	See the Access to Justice Act 1999 (Destination of Appeals) Order 2000, art 2.

[52]	This includes or any other judge referred to in art 2 of the Access to Justice Act 1999 (Destination of Appeals) Order 2000: art 2(a) includes a person holding an office referred to in Part II of Sch 2 of the Senior Courts Act 1981.

[53]	*Fox v Foundation Piling Group Ltd* [2011] EWCA Civ 104 at [11] (heard at the same time as *Thorne v Courtier & Ors* [2011] EWCA Civ 104).

[54]	*Gray v Going Places Leisure Travel Ltd* [2005] EWCA Civ 189 at [19].

[55]	PD 52, para 2A.4(1) reads: 'An order made: (1) on a summary or detailed assessment of costs ... is not a "final decision" ...'; see also *Dooley v Parker & Anor* [2002] EWCA Civ 96 at [7], per Brooke LJ (clarifying *Tanfern Ltd v Cameron-Macdonald & Anor* [2000] EWCA Civ 3023 at [17]). See also s 16(1) of the Senior Courts Act 1981 (as amended); s 77(1) of the County Courts Act 1984 (as amended); and the Access to Justice Act 1999 (Destination of Appeals) Order 2000 set out the provisions governing routes of appeal).

from a county court (see **21.65–21.66**), the route of first appeal will be to a circuit judge of the court from which it was referred. Otherwise, an appeal will generally be to a single judge of the High Court.

• *Appeals from costs officers in the SCCO:* The destination court will be a costs judge: see **23.2–23.8**.

• *Second appeals:* Second appeals are to the Court of Appeal.[56]

• *Leapfrog procedure:*[57] Where the court from or to which an appeal is made, or from which permission to appeal is sought, considers that an appeal which is to be heard by a county court or the High Court would raise an important point of principle or practice, or where it considers that there is some other compelling reason for the Court of Appeal to hear it, that court may order the appeal to be transferred to the Court of Appeal;[58] this procedure is known as the 'leapfrog' procedure. Whilst Lord Phillips MR has pointed out that it is only the appeal itself that may be transferred rather than the application for permission to appeal,[59] in cases of doubt, there is a statutory provision[60] which permits the matter to be referred to the Master of the Rolls for his consideration.[61] The practical effect of this is that the lower court must either decide the issue of permission for itself, or it must refer the matter to the Master of Rolls. If the lower court refuses permission to appeal, it lacks the vires to direct that any subsequent appeal should be heard in the Court of Appeal.[62]

Venue

23.26 CPD, art 31.1A(2)(ii) provides:

'unless an order is made under rule 47.4(2) directing that the Senior Courts Costs Office as part of the High Court shall be the appropriate office, an appeal from any decision made by a costs judge shall lie to the Designated Civil Judge for the London Group of County Courts or such judge as he shall nominate. The appeal notice and any other relevant papers should be lodged at the Central London Civil Justice Centre.'

Appellant's notice and grounds

23.27 The appellant's notice must be filed at the appeal court[63] along with the supporting documentation.[64] The grounds of appeal should set out clearly the reasons why the appeal should be allowed and, for each ground, should specify whether the ground raises an appeal on a point of law or is an appeal against a finding of fact.[65]

---

[56] PD 52, para 4.9; see also the Access to Justice Act 1999 (Destination of Appeals) Order 2000, art 5.
[57] See s 57 of the Access to Justice Act 1999.
[58] See CPR, r 52.14(1); it is a power conferred by s 57 of the Access to Justice Act 1999.
[59] See *In the Matter of Claims Direct Test Cases* [2002] EWCA Civ 428 at [23].
[60] Section 57(1)(a) of the Access to Justice Act 1999.
[61] See *Clark (Inspector of Taxes) v Perks* [2001] 1 WLR 17 at 9.
[62] *7E Communications Ltd v Vertex Antennentechnik GmBH* [2007] EWCA Civ 140.
[63] CPR, r 52.4(2).
[64] PD 52, para 5.6; these include the following: two additional copies of the appellant's notice for the appeal court; one copy of the appellant's notice for each of the respondents; one copy of his skeleton argument for each copy of the appellant's notice that is filed; a sealed copy of the order being appealed; a copy of any order giving or refusing permission to appeal, together with a copy of the judge's reasons for allowing or refusing permission to appeal; any witness statements or affidavits in support of any application included in the appellant's notice; and a copy of the order allocating a case to a track (if any).
[65] PD 52, para 3.2.

Respondent's notice

23.28 A respondent may file a respondent's notice and must do so if he is seeking permission to appeal from the appeal court or if he wishes to ask the appeal court to uphold the order of the lower court for reasons different from or additional to those given by the lower court.[66]

Permission to appeal (generally)

23.29 As a rule, permission to appeal will be required in all costs appeals (other than those from an authorised court officer: see **23.2**). This will generally be so even if permission is not required to appeal the matter to which the costs relate.[67] An application may be made to the lower court at the time the decision appealed against is made, or it may be made to the appeal court in the appellant's notice.[68] If the lower court refuses permission, the application may be renewed to the appeal court.[69] If the appeal court refuses permission on paper (as it very often does in costs cases), the appellant has the right to request an oral hearing; this is done by sending a request (usually in the form of a letter) within 7 days after service of the notice that permission has been refused.[70] Permission to appeal will be granted only where the court considers that the appeal would have a real prospect of success, or where there is some other compelling reason why the appeal should be heard.[71] Buckley J has emphasised that permission to appeal should not be granted 'simply to allow another trawl through the bill, in the absence of some sensible and significant complaint'.[72] Moreland J made a similar point, but in terms that were more forceful:[73]

> '[There is] a trend in litigation, which in my judgment I condemn as deplorable, satellite litigation about costs which is hugely wasteful of both professional time and expensive resources. If the trend were allowed to continue, it would tend to render nugatory the "overriding objective" of the CPR.'

23.30 Where the judge granting permission has been misled, permission to appeal may be revoked.[74]

Permission to appeal (conditions)

23.31 The court may impose conditions on the granting of permission to appeal, and this is not uncommon in costs litigation. If, for example, the appellant's insurer wishes to clarify the law, permission may be granted on the condition that the appellant bears the costs of the appeal regardless of the outcome.[75] Where a judge at first instance has conditionally granted a party permission to appeal, that party could not appeal against the terms; the only courses of action open to it would be (i) to abandon the prospective

---

[66] CPR, r 52.5.
[67] See, for example, *Hosking v Michaelides* [2003] EWHC 3029 (Ch), in which it was held that permission was required to appeal a summary assessment of costs in insolvency proceedings, even though permission would not have been required to appeal the proceedings themselves.
[68] CPR, r 52.3(2).
[69] CPR, r 52.3(3).
[70] CPR, r 52.3(4) and (5).
[71] CPR, r 52.3(6).
[72] *Mealing-McLeod v Common Professional Examination Board* [2000] 2 Costs LR 223 at 224.
[73] *Giambrone v JMC Holidays Ltd (formerly Sunworld Holidays Ltd)* [2002] EWHC 2932 (QB) at [3], per Morland J.
[74] *Angel Airlines SA v Dean & Dean Solicitors* [2006] EWCA Civ 1505.
[75] As happened, for example, in *Jones v Caradon Catnic Ltd* [2005] EWCA Civ 1821.

appeal, (ii) to accept the terms, or (iii) to treat the conditional permission as a refusal of permission to appeal, and to make a fresh application for permission to the appellate court.[76]

Permission to appeal (submissions)

23.32 Respondent's submissions should only be filed at the permission stage if they are addressed solely to the question of whether the appeal satisfied the relevant threshold test or if there was some material inaccuracy in the papers placed before the court; submissions on the merits should be left to the appeal itself.[77] Attendance by the respondent at an oral hearing should only be necessary where a written submission would not, for whatever reason, be sufficient. Where the court does not request submissions from or attendance by the respondent, costs will not normally be allowed to a respondent who volunteers submissions or attendance.[78]

Permission to appeal (refusal)

23.33 No appeal may be brought from a decision to refuse permission to appeal.[79] The inherent jurisdiction of the court to review decisions of officials of the court did not extend to permit the Court of Appeal to review the decision of a High Court judge who refused to give permission to appeal.[80]

Hearings, bundles, etc

23.34 In so far as procedure is concerned, an appeal in respect of costs is exactly the same as any other appeal; the provisions can be found in CPR, Part 52 and PD 52. The only papers that the appeal court will need will be those that are mentioned in PD 52;[81]

---

[76] *R (ex p Medical Justice) v Secretary of State for the Home Department* [2011] EWCA Civ 269 at [8], per Lord Neuberger MR.

[77] *Jolly v Jay* [2002] EWCA Civ 277.

[78] PD 52, para 4.23.

[79] See Access to Justice Act 1999, s 54(4) and CPR, r 52.3(3); see *R (on the application of Sivasubramaniam) v Wandsworth County Court* [2002] EWCA Civ 1738.

[80] *Riniker v University College London* [2001] 1 Costs LR 20; Robert Walker LJ (with whom Brooke LJ agreed) commented that by no stretch of language or thought could a High Court judge's refusal to grant permission to appeal be regarded as a decision taken as a delegate of the Court of Appeal. In this regard, the court of appeal reminded itself that its jurisdiction is wholly statutory, and that it has no original jurisdiction.

[81] In this regard, PD 52, para 5.6A provides as follows:

'(1)   An appellant must include in his appeal bundle the following documents:

(a)   a sealed copy of the appellant's notice;

(b)   a sealed copy of the order being appealed;

(c)   a copy of any order giving or refusing permission to appeal, together with a copy of the judge's reasons for allowing or refusing permission to appeal;

(d)   any affidavit or witness statement filed in support of any application included in the appellant's notice;

(e)   a copy of his skeleton argument;

(f)   a transcript or note of judgment (see paragraph 5.12), and in cases where permission to appeal was given by the lower court or is not required those parts of any transcript of evidence which are directly relevant to any question at issue on the appeal;

(g)   the claim form and statements of case (where relevant to the subject of the appeal);

(h)   any application notice (or case management documentation) relevant to the subject of the appeal;

(i)   in cases where the decision appealed was itself made on appeal (e g from district judge to circuit judge), the first order, the reasons given and the appellant's notice used to appeal from that order;

(j)   ...

(l)   any other documents which the appellant reasonably considers necessary to enable the appeal court to

there is no need to file the receiving party's file of papers (as would happen in a detailed assessment). A suitable record of the judgment appealed will be required.[82]

Appeals against legal aid assessments

23.35 Appeals against Legal Aid assessment must be notified to the Ministry of Justice. This rule will not be applied in such a way as to cause injustice.[83]

Interest on overpaid costs

23.36 Where an appeal results in a reversal of a costs order, and where costs have already been paid under that order, the court may order the party who has to repay costs also to pay interest on those costs.[84] This topic is addressed in more detail at **36.73–36.77**.

---

reach its decision on the hearing of the application or appeal; and

(m)   such other documents as the court may direct.

(2)   All documents that are extraneous to the issues to be considered on the application or the appeal must be excluded. The appeal bundle may include affidavits, witness statements, summaries, experts' reports and exhibits but only where these are directly relevant to the subject matter of the appeal.

(3)   Where the appellant is represented, the appeal bundle must contain a certificate signed by his solicitor, counsel or other representative to the effect that he has read and understood paragraph (2) above and that the composition of the appeal bundle complies with it.'

The 'other documents' (para 5.6A(1)(l) would usually include the notice of commencement, the bill of costs, points of dispute and replies, the final costs certificate, and any orders made pertaining to the assessment.

[82]   PD 52, art 5.12 provides as follows:

'**5.12**   Where the judgment to be appealed has been officially recorded by the court, an approved transcript of that record should accompany the appellant's notice. Photocopies will not be accepted for this purpose. However, where there is no officially recorded judgment, the following documents will be acceptable:

Written judgments

(1)   Where the judgment was made in writing a copy of that judgment endorsed with the judge's signature.

Note of judgment

(2)   When judgment was not officially recorded or made in writing a note of the judgment (agreed between the appellant's and respondent's advocates) should be submitted for approval to the judge whose decision is being appealed. If the parties cannot agree on a single note of the judgment, both versions should be provided to that judge with an explanatory letter. For the purpose of an application for permission to appeal the note need not be approved by the respondent or the lower court judge.

Advocates' notes of judgments where the appellant is unrepresented

(3)   When the appellant was unrepresented in the lower court it is the duty of any advocate for the respondent to make his/her note of judgment promptly available, free of charge to the appellant where there is no officially recorded judgment or if the court so directs. Where the appellant was represented in the lower court it is the duty of his/her own former advocate to make his/her note available in these circumstances. The appellant should submit the note of judgment to the appeal court.

Reasons for Judgment in Tribunal cases

(4)   A sealed copy of the Tribunal's reasons for the decision.

[83]   In *Edwards & Ors v Roche Products Ltd* [2003] EWHC 9022 (Costs) Fulford J permitted a funded party (in reality, his counsel) to recover the costs of an appeal pursuant to reg 113(2) of the Civil Legal Aid (General) Regulations 1989 (as amended), notwithstanding the fact that the Lord Chancellor's Department had not been kept informed of the appeal to the extent that they should have been; Fulford J did not impose any sanction because the Lord Chancellor's Department (the forerunner of the Ministry of Justice) had indicated that they did wish to intervene and, as a result, there was no prejudice.

[84]   *Bim Kemi AB and Blackburn Chemicals Ltd* [2003] EWCA Civ 889.

Topics likely to arise during an appeal hearing

New evidence

23.37 Unless the court gives permission, the appeal court will not receive evidence which was not before the lower court;[85] it will, in general, give permission only if the following criteria are met:[86]

- where the evidence is such that it could not have been obtained with 'reasonable diligence' for use in the assessment;
- where the evidence is such that, if given, it would probably have an important influence on the outcome of the appeal (although it need not be decisive); and
- where the evidence is such as is presumably to be believed.

New points

23.38 In a similar vein, if a point was not taken during the detailed assessment, the appeal court may refuse to hear the point.[87] An appellant will bear a heavy burden when trying to persuade the appeal court to hear a point not taken or abandoned in the court below; in this regard, Peter Gibson LJ had this to say:[88]

> 'In general the court expects each party to advance his whole case at the trial. In the interests of fairness to the other party this court should be slow to allow new points, which were available to be taken at the trial but were not taken, to be advanced for the first time in this court. That consideration is the weightier if further evidence might have been adduced at the trial, had the point been taken then, or if the decision on the point requires an evaluation of all the evidence and could be affected by the impression which the trial judge receives from seeing and hearing the witnesses. Indeed it is hard to see how, if those circumstances obtained, this court, having regard to the overriding objective of dealing with cases justly, could allow that new point to be taken.'

Thus, the appellant must seek to discharge the burden of showing that the case would not have been conducted differently had the points which are raised on appeal been raised in the court below;[89] where those points are factual and where the court below heard live evidence, that burden will be difficult to shift. At the other end of spectrum will be where the appellant seeks to raise a new point of law; where, for example, the new point goes to jurisdiction, then the court is more likely to be persuaded to the hear the new point.[90] The burden lies with the appellant rather than the respondent; Arden LJ explained the court cannot reasonably expect the respondent to be specific about the evidence he would have adduced had the point been raised earlier. She explained that if

---

[85]   CPR, r 52.11(2).

[86]   *Ladd v Marshall* [1954] 1 WLR 1489, which was confirmed to be good law under the CPR in *Hertfordshire Investments Ltd v Bubb* [2000] All ER (D) 1052; the description of the criteria has been adapted to a costs context.

[87]   In the context of costs litigation, see *Ross v Stonewood Securities Ltd* [2004] EWHC 2235 (Ch) at [29], per Lewison J.

[88]   *Jones v MBNA International Bank* [2000] EWCA Civ 514 at [38]. See also *Australia and New Zealand Banking Group Ltd v Société Générale* [2000] 1 All ER (Comm) 682 which confirmed the approach taken in *Jones v MBNA*.

[89]   For a discussion of this see *Lowe v W Machell Joinery Ltd* [2011] EWCA Civ 794 at 59 *et seq*; see also *Mullarkey v Broad (in the matter of Southill Finance Limited, in liquidation)* [2009] EWCA Civ 2 at [49].

[90]   See, by way of example, *Hardy v Sefton Metropolitan Borough Council* [2006] EWHC 1928 (Admin), per Walker J. See also *Pittalis v Grant* [1989] QB 605.

there is any area of doubt, the benefit of it must be given to the respondent; it is the party who should have raised the point at trial who should bear any risk of prejudice.[91]

Much will also turn on the way in which the case was put in the court below; if, for example, the point had been raised and then abandoned, much will depend on the stage that had been reached at the time of abandonment. In a case in which the putatively new point had been raised in pleadings but expressly disavowed at an early stage of trial (ie, before the evidence had been heard) Lloyd LJ said this:[92]

> 'A party who seeks to advance a different case, in circumstances such as this, bears a heavy burden as regards showing that the case could not have been conducted differently, in any material respect, as regards the evidence.'

If, on the other hand, the point is abandoned after the evidence had been heard (such as during closing submissions), that burden will be easier to discharge.[93] In so far as costs litigation is concerned, where the new point goes to the incidence of costs, it would rarely be the case that the submissions on costs would have been conducted differently had the arguments been different: this because the vast majority of costs orders are decided without the court hearing evidence specifically on that point. Detailed assessments, however, are likely to be in a different category; this is because one point often follows on from the next, and decisions as to what to elect to show the court and what to concede are often influenced by what has gone before.

Findings of fact

23.39 The appeal court will ordinarily not interfere with the lower court's findings of fact unless the decision which was reached was a decision which no reasonable court would have reached on the material available, or unless pivotal factors which ought to have been taken into account were not taken into account.[94]

Material not referred to in the judgment

23.40 The appeal court will be reluctant to find that the lower court took into account factors which were not referred to in the judgment.[95] This may be particularly relevant in appeals from detailed assessments because the costs judge is likely to have had access to the receiving party's entire file; this means that unless it is referred to in his judgment, it will not always be clear which material the costs judge applied his mind to and took into account.

Assessors

23.41 The appeal court may sit with assessors,[96] and usually will do so when the appeal is from a costs judge.[97] One of the assessors will usually be a costs judge and the other will often be a practising barrister or solicitor, depending on the nature of the case.

---

[91]   *Crane v Sky In-home Ltd* [2008] EWCA Civ 978 at [21].
[92]   *Mullarkey v Broad (in the matter of Southill Finance Limited, in liquidation)* [2009] EWCA Civ 2 at [49].
[93]   See, for example, *Slack & Partners Ltd v Slack* [2010] EWCA Civ204.
[94]   *Designers Guild Ltd v Russell Williams (Textiles) Ltd* [2001] 1 All ER 700, HL.
[95]   *MacDonald v Taree Holdings* [2001] 1 Costs LR 147 at 150.
[96]   CPR, r 35.15.
[97]   See para 13.5 of the SCCO Guide 2006.

Circuit judges hearing appeals from district judges may or may not sit with an assessor:[98] practices vary from court to court.

23.42 Not less than 21 days before making any such appointment, the court will notify each party in writing of the name of the proposed assessor, of the matter in respect of which the assistance of the assessor will be sought and of the qualifications of the assessor to give that assistance; if so advised, any party may object to the assessor.[99]

23.43 It would ordinarily be the court's responsibility to make arrangements for the attendance of assessors, rather than that of the parties. In view of this, Leggatt LJ described as 'surprising' a circuit judge's decision not to grant an adjournment to enable assessors to sit with him except on terms that the paying party (whose appeal it was) paid the costs thrown away.[100]

Second appeals

23.44 Second appeals are to the Court of Appeal.[101] For all but the most exceptional costs case, the Court of Appeal will be the final court of appeal; this is because the responsibility for overseeing costs litigation rests primarily with that court rather than with the Supreme Court. This was explained by Lord Bingham:[102]

> 'The responsibility for monitoring and controlling the developing practice in a field such as this lies with the Court of Appeal and not the House, which should ordinarily be slow to intervene. The House cannot respond to changes in practice with the speed and sensitivity of the Court of Appeal.'

23.45 The Court of Appeal will not give permission to bring a second appeal unless it considers that the appeal would raise an important point of principle or practice or unless there is some other compelling reason for hearing it.[103]

23.46 The Court of Appeal has no jurisdiction to hear an application for permission to appeal in a case where the court at first instance and a judge hearing a subsequent application have both refused permission; this is so even where it is said that the Court of Appeal should hear the matter by reason of an inherent jurisdiction.[104] However, where the subject of the second application is a decision ancillary to it (such as a decision on the costs of the application), those may be regarded as being separate decisions in respect of which a further application may be made.[105]

---

[98] See s 63 of the County Courts Act 1984 (as amended).

[99] PD 35, paras 7.1 and 7.2.

[100] *Laurence v Singh* [1997] 1 Costs LR 58 at 61.

[101] PD 52, paras 4.9 and 4.10. The Court of Appeal used to be barred from hearing appeals in discretionary costs matters unless the court below had been given permission (see, originally, s 49 of the Judicature Act 1873), but the scope of that scope of this restriction was cut back by the court taking a narrow view as to what was 'discretionary' (see *Jones v Curling* (1884) 13 QBD 262 at 267 and 271). In any event, the restriction was abolished entirely by the Courts and Legal Services Act 1990, ss 7(2), 125(7) and Sch 20, repealing s 18(1)(f) of the Senior Courts Act 1981.

[102] *Callery v Gray* [2002] UKHL 28 at [8]; see also *Girvan v Inverness Farmers Dairy 1998 SC (HL) 1* at 21D–21G.

[103] CPR, r 52.13.

[104] *Riniker v University College London* [2001] 1 WLR 13, applying s 54(4) of the Access to Justice Act 1999; see also (in a more general setting than the law of costs) *Clark (Inspector of Taxes) v Perks* [2001] 1 WLR 17 at 20.

[105] *Riniker v University College London* [2001] 1 WLR 13; see also *Jolly v Jay* [2002] EWCA Civ at [51]–[52].

Judicial review

23.47 Occasionally, a costs judge or a county court judge will exercise a jurisdiction which is not amenable to appeal within the regime mentioned above. This will usually be in the context of criminal costs, but it could also include examples of the court acting in an arbitral role, such as where the court is assessing the costs of a non-statutory inquiry. Another example is where the court has refused permission to appeal and there is no further route of appeal. Where the usual route of appeal is unavailable, the question may arise as to whether the costs judge's decision is amenable to judicial review.

23.48 Decisions of judges in the county court are amenable to judicial review;[106] this includes refusals to grant permission to appeal,[107] but this will not include cases where the application is based on the merits of the original appeal.[108] Generally speaking, the decisions of costs judges' in the High Court are not susceptible to challenge by way of judicial review; this is because the court does not judicially review its own decisions.[109] That said, where there is 'a gap in the rules', the High Court has an inherent jurisdiction to control the exercise of the authority of the court where that authority has been delegated to a costs judge.[110]

23.49 Maurice Kay LJ has emphasised that the jurisdiction will be exercised sparingly,[111] but it may be exercised if there has been a 'real injustice'.[112] Nonetheless, case examples do exist where no 'real injustice' was expressly identified.[113] The jurisdiction is a wide one, it cannot be invoked in such a way as to do something which is inconsistent with the CPR.[114]

23.50 The Supreme Court has held that judicial review by the High Court of a refusal by the Upper Tribunal of permission to appeal to itself was available, but that it was limited to the application of the criteria for second-tier appeals, namely where either the proposed appeal raises some important point of principle or practice, or there was some other compelling reason.[115]

---

[106] *R (on the application of Strickson) v Preston County Court and ors* [2007] EWCA Civ 1132 and *R v His Honour Judge Sir Donald Hurst, ex p Smith* [1960] 2 All ER 385; see also *R (on the application of Srinivasans Solicitors) v Croydon County Court* [2011] EWHC 3615 (Admin).

[107] *R (on the application of Strickson) v Preston County Court and ors* [2007] EWCA Civ 1132 and *R (on the application of Sivasubramaniam) v Wandsworth County Court* [2002] EWCA Civ 1738.

[108] *R (on the application of Sivasubramaniam) v Wandsworth County Court* [2002] EWCA Civ 1738.

[109] *R v SCTO ex p John Singh & Co* [1997] 1 Costs LR 49.

[110] *R v Taxing Officer ex p Bee-Line Roadways International Ltd* (1982) *The Times*, February 11; the *Times* report is very brief; lengthier extracts from Woolf J's judgment can be found in *In re Macro (Ipswich) Ltd* [1997] 1 Costs LR 128 at 136.

[111] See also *Brewer v SCCO* [2009] EWHC 986 (QB), which involved the same parties in which the lower court's decision was quashed by reason of its failure to conduct a hearing.

[112] *R v SCTO ex p John Singh & Co* [1997] 1 Costs LR 49 at 51; see also, for example, *R (on the application of Brewer) v Supreme Court Costs Office* [2006] EWHC 1955 (Admin).

[113] *In re Macro (Ipswich) Ltd* [1997] 1 Costs LR 128 at 139, per Ferris J. It is not clear whether this authority remains good law (see *R (on the application of Strickson) v Preston County Court and ors* [2007] EWCA Civ 1132, which suggests that the test is different to that applied by Ferris J).

[114] *Tombstone Ltd v Raja* [2008] EWCA Civ 1444.

[115] *R (on the application of Cart) v Upper Tribunal; R (on the application of MR (Pakistan)) v Upper Tribunal (Immigration and Asylum Chamber) and another* [2011] UKSC 28.

Chapter 24

EVIDENTIAL ISSUES

INTRODUCTION

24.1 This chapter describes the fact-finding process in detailed assessments. An understanding of the rudiments of evidential law (such as the varieties of evidence, burdens of proof, relevance and admissibility) is assumed. Evidential disputes in costs litigation usually turn on the selection of evidence rather than on admissibility or relevance; in view of this, it is appropriate to start with the procedural law, namely filing and election, rather than the substantive law of evidence. Most evidence in detailed assessments is documentary and it is this which is the focus of this chapter; a brief discussion of the role of testimony and hearsay evidence can be found at **21.222–21.225**. Evidential issues arising on appeals are dealt with at **27.3–27.10**.

ELECTION, FILING AND DISCLOSURE

24.2 Costs litigation is litigation without disclosure of the type familiar in other civil litigation. This is because the subject matter of the assessment is often privileged, either in its entirety or at least in part.

24.3 Apart from certain narrow exceptions (such as fraud), the court lacks the vires to order a party to disclose privileged material. Instead of a process of disclosure, costs litigation has, first, a mandatory process of filing and, secondly, an optative process known as election. Before these topics are addressed in detail, a brief overview is given.

Filing

24.4 Filing is the process of offering up material for inspection so that the court is able to read it either during or in advance of the hearing; material is often filed several days before the hearing, often by the receiving party's entire file being lodged at court (see **21.215**). It is a moot point whether a receiving party is under a duty to file material which undermines his case: this is discussed in detail at **24.9–24.20**. The fact that material has been filed does not mean that the receiving party should be taken to have expressed an intention to rely on it; that is a decision which will be taken only by the receiving party indicating that intention in the context of the process of election (see below).

Election

24.5 Election is the process by which the receiving party chooses (ie elects) whether to rely on documentary material; if he chooses not to rely on it, he may continue to assert privilege over it, but if he elects to rely on it, he waives privilege *pro tem* for the purposes of the assessment, in which case the document will become material that his opponent is permitted to see and to comment upon. These topics are addressed in detail at **24.26–24.62**.

FILING

24.6   CPD, art 40.11 makes the following provisions which impose an obligation on a receiving party to file material in support of his bill:

> 'Unless the court directs otherwise the receiving party must file with the court the papers in support of the bill not less than 7 days before the date for the detailed assessment and not more than 14 days before that date.'

24.7   The following papers need to be filed, and in the stated order:[1]

- Where there is no success fee and no insurance premium:
    - instructions and briefs to counsel arranged in chronological order together with all advices, opinions and drafts received and response to such instructions;
    - reports and opinions of medical and other experts;
    - any other relevant papers;
    - a full set of any relevant pleadings to the extent that they have not already been filed in court; and
    - correspondence, files and attendance notes.
- Where the claim is in respect of a success fee and/or an insurance premium only, such of the papers listed above as are relevant to the issues raised by that claim.
- Where the claim is for both base costs and a success fee and/or an insurance premium, then all of the above need to be filed.

These are the documents which must be filed prior to the hearing, and will be additional to those which will already have been filed at the time the hearing was requested; therefore, this list ought to be read in conjunction with the list at **21.15**. Of particular note is the requirement that where the indemnity principle is in dispute, the request for a detailed assessment should have been accompanied by any agreement, letter, or other written information comprising the retainer.[2]

24.8   The requirement to file documents in accordance with CPD, art 40.11 invites the question of whether the receiving party is under a compulsion to file material which is adverse to his case. That is not an easy question to answer.

Duty to file adverse material

24.9   To address that question it is necessary to examine the recent history of the law. Under the RSC, Aldous LJ held that the duty to lodge material with the court was 'a duty … to disclose to the taxing master all relevant papers … [including] those which support the claim and those which undermine the claim'.[3] Thus, there was a judge-made duty to file adverse material (or, more accurately, there was a duty arising out of the

---

[1]   CPD, art 40.12; some courts ask that a bundle is prepared, but most do not.
[2]   See CPD, art 40.2.
[3]   *Bourns Inc v Raychem Corporation* [1999] 3 All ER 154 at 162.

court's broad interpretation of the then rules of court). It is worth looking first at the law generally, and then focusing on the law relating to retainers.

Duty to file written documents other that the retainer

24.10 Despite the CPR's emphasis on openness and transparency, it is not clear whether the duty to file adverse material continues to exist. There is no express reference to such a duty in either the CPR or the CPD. Indeed, CPD, arts 40.11 and 40.12 relate to papers *in support* of a bill of costs; it could be argued that that excludes (or, at least, does not include) documents which undermine the bill. Whilst that interpretation is not entirely in harmony with the overriding objective, it is a sound and logical interpretation; this is because an absence of an express duty to file adverse material could be said to be a reflection of the fact that a receiving party cannot be compelled to produce privileged material. This means that the absence of an express requirement cannot be dismissed as a mere oversight.

24.11 Nonetheless, there are three mechanisms by which a duty to file adverse material (or, at least, a duty not to conceal the existence of adverse material) may continue to exist; they are as follows.

Judge-made duty

24.12 The aforesaid judge-made duty may continue to exist regardless of the fact that the rules of court have changed from being the RSC to the CPR (this analysis would be consistent with the court's duty to take into account adverse material: see **24.21** *et seq*).

Overriding objective

24.13 It could be argued that CPR, r 1.2 requires the court to give effect to the overriding objective when considering any rule of court, so that the provisions concerning filing must be read in such a way as require transparency (ie the words 'in support of the bill' in CPD, art 40.11 should be read as being a reference to papers which underpin rather than merely bolster a bill of costs).

Professional duty

24.14 There is a professional duty not to mislead the court: there would be a very fine line between not filing the entirety of the relevant parts of a file, and filing a file which has been filleted so as to give a misleading impression.

24.15 It should be stressed that there is no authority dealing with any of these supposed mechanisms, and it could well be the case that the duty to file adverse material simply does not exist under the CPR. That said, the points made about a solicitor's professional duty are beyond dispute.

Duty to file written instruments of retainer

24.16 Written instruments of retainer (such as client care letters, terms and conditions, conditional fee agreements, etc) are treated differently from other documents; this is because the CPD expressly provides that where there is a dispute about the indemnity principle, a request for a hearing should be accompanied by[4] '*any* agreement, letter or other written information' (emphasis added). This means that the court would expect to see that material and, if it is not supplied, the court is likely to make enquiries. This would be the case even if, ultimately, the receiving party had a right not to rely upon it.

24.17 Although there is no authority on the point, a refusal to file adverse material could be analysed in many ways, with the following two at opposite ends of the spectrum.

That a refusal is permitted

24.18 It could be said that, provided the court is not misled, a refusal is unobjectionable because it is nothing more than an advance election not to rely on the documents which have not been filed.

That a refusal is not permitted

24.19 Alternatively, it could be said that a refusal is not permitted and that, unless the receiving party has a change of heart, the court may impose sanctions, such as dismissing the request for a hearing on the basis that the request was not properly made.

24.20 One could argue for either of these points of view (or for many other similar analyses). Regardless of exactly what the duty is, the points made above about not misleading the court apply (see **24.14**). If a solicitor were, for example, to fillet a file of all adverse material, and if he were to present it to the court without explanation and in such a way as potentially to mislead the court, he might not only find himself having to answer to the court, but he might also have committed a disciplinary offence.

The effect of filing adverse material

24.21 Where the court discovers a document or an omission in a receiving party's file which causes it concern, the court will begin a process which can usefully be called an escalator of enquiry. The escalator exists because the court has a duty to ensure fairness between the parties. The court's concerns may be adequately dealt with by brief informal enquiries, but where those enquiries do not satisfy the court or in order to meet the needs of justice, it may be necessary to move to the next level.

24.22 Judge LJ (with whom Butler-Sloss and Henry LJJ agreed) discussed the topic in this way:[5]

> 'The taxing officer is exercising a judicial function ... he is trusted properly to consider material which would normally be protected from disclosure under the rules of legal professional privilege. If ... some feature of the case alerts him to the need to make further investigation or causes him to wonder if the information with which he is being provided is full and accurate, he may seek further information. No doubt he would begin by asking for a letter or some form of written confirmation or reassurance as appropriate. If this were to prove inadequate he might then make orders for discovery or require affidavit evidence. It is difficult to envisage circumstances in which the party benefiting from the order for costs will not have been anxious to provide the required information, but if all else fails, it would theoretically be open to him to order interrogatories. However, if the stage has been reached

---

[4]   CPD, art 40.2(i).
[5]   In the context of privilege in relation to retainers in *Bailey v IBC Vehicles Ltd* [1998] 3 All ER 570 at 572.

where interrogatories might reasonably be ordered, the conclusion that the receiving party had not been able to satisfy the taxing officer about the bill, or some particular aspect of it, would seem inevitable.'

24.23 Judge LJ's comments were made under the RSC, but there is no reason to believe that they do not continue to apply under the CPR. Whilst there is no authority which fully describes the various steps, it could, in a suitable case, include the following:

- the receiving party may be put to his election in respect of the relevant documents;
- if election does not satisfy the court, then the receiving party may be asked to provide an informal explanation via his representative;
- if that does not satisfy the court, then the court may require the receiving party to provide an explanation in a witness statement or (in more serious cases) by affidavit;
- if that does not satisfy the court, the receiving party may be required to answer Part 18 Questions or to offer his witnesses for cross-examination; and
- if the court remains dissatisfied (or if the receiving party has refused to assist the court), it may either draw an adverse inference or may find that the receiving party has not shifted the evidential burden of proving his claim for costs, whichever is appropriate.

This escalator is only an example of what the court might do; an entirely different escalator might be appropriate, depending on the circumstances of the case in hand. As to the inferences that the court would be able to draw, see **24.60–24.62**.

Material mistakenly filed

24.24 Where the court happens upon a document it was not supposed to see (such as a Part 47 offer or a document giving advice about the assessment itself), it will be the court's task to ensure that the parties are not prejudiced as a result; Hobhouse J commented:[6]

'The trained legal mind normally has no difficulty in preventing irrelevant or improper material from influencing its decision. Occasionally a master may feel embarrassed by what he has seen, and knows that the respondent has not seen, and cannot be told about. In such a case, the master can [order] that the taxation of one or more items be dealt with by another taxing master'.

24.25 If the court were to recuse itself as a result of one the parties having filed material which ought not to have been filed, then that party (or that party's legal representatives) would be at risk of having to bear the costs thrown away.

ELECTION: THE PRINCIPLES

24.26 It is fair to say that election is to costs litigation what disclosure is to substantive litigation, but the similarities end there. This is because the two are markedly different in terms of both procedure and philosophy.

---

[6] *Pamplin v Express Newspapers Ltd* [1985] 1 WLR 689 at 697.

24.27 Election is a method whereby the court ensures that neither party is able to have his cake and eat it. The receiving party's right to claim privilege and the paying party's right to see the material his opponent is relying upon are both respected in the sense that the receiving party may not claim privilege on a document at the same time as relying upon it. The receiving party must elect which of these two rights he will hold to himself.

24.28 The process of election was devised by Hobhouse J in the mid-1980s.[7] The CPD contains the present-day manifestation, which is merely a pithy reincarnation of Hobhouse J's method; it reads as follows:[8]

> 'The court may direct the receiving party to produce any document which in the opinion of the court is necessary to enable it to reach its decision. These documents will in the first instance be produced to the court, but the court may ask the receiving party to elect whether to disclose the particular document to the paying party in order to rely on the contents of the document, or whether to decline disclosure and instead rely on other evidence.'

24.29 Thus, the procedure is that the court may put the receiving party to his election. Where this happens, he must choose whether to continue to assert privilege over the document in question (in which case it will be disregarded) or whether he will waive privilege (in which case it will be taken into account).

24.30 This procedure takes into account that in the last resort the right of the paying party to know the material put before the court must prevail over the right of the receiving party to claim privilege. It is fundamental to the method of election that it does not balance the two rights in the sense that each party has a less than full version of his right: instead, the court has compared the two rights and found that the right to see material prevails over the right to privacy, but that the latter must be preserved if possible. Thus, whilst the paying party's right prevails over the right to assert privilege, this would (absent fraud) never lead to the receiving party being ordered to disclose privileged material.

24.31 Pumfrey J has confirmed that the method of election presents no incompatibility with the principles articulated by the European Court of Human Rights.[9]

The procedure of election and the court's discretion

The informal approach

24.32 One of the most striking things about the process of election is that, in practice, it is rarely encountered. This is because most, if not nearly all, detailed assessments are dealt with on an informal basis whereby the paying party suspends his formal rights and places trust in the costs judge to be fair in his examination of the receiving party's privileged material. In practical terms, this means that the receiving party will hand privileged material to the costs judge who will examine it and form a view; he may or may not informally place it before the paying party on the tacit understanding that privilege has not been waived; he may or may not read aloud from selected passages, thereby orally redacting those parts which are not read out; he will usually give

---

[7] *Pamplin v Express Newspapers Ltd* [1985] 1 WLR 689 at 695; it is possible that Hobhouse J was merely describing a process which had already arisen before taxing masters.

[8] CPD, art 40.14.

[9] *South Coast Shipping Co Ltd v Havant Borough Council* [2002] 3 All ER 779 at 793, referring to the European Convention for the Protection of Human Rights and Fundamental Freedoms 1950 (as set out in Sch 1 to the Human Rights Act 1998).

judgment without the issue of election ever being mentioned. This courteous and efficient fact-finding procedure will suffice for all but the most contentious of assessments.

24.33 Davies J has described this informal procedure as 'sensible, pragmatic and time and cost saving';[10] he also highlighted the fact that where a party unnecessarily departs from it, he can be penalised in costs.[11]

24.34 The benefits of the informal approach were recognised even by the judge who devised the formal approach; he (Hobhouse J) had this to say:[12]

> '[It will be] very rare for the full formality of these steps [relating to election] to be gone through. Most [paying parties] appreciate that once they have drawn to the master's attention the possibility that an item of charge may be unnecessary or may be being overvalued, their interests are best served by allowing the master to look at the relevant documents and form his own judgment. The [paying party] will normally achieve little or nothing by asking to see the documents as well. The master is well aware of the criteria he has to apply and is highly experienced in the exercise of assessment he has to undertake.'

The court will actively (rather than merely passively) encourage the informal approach; in particular, the Court of Appeal has said that a costs judge should use 'all his expertise and tact' to avoid a party being put to his election.[13] The Court of Appeal has suggested that the costs judge should consider alternatives, such as partial disclosure, or disclosure given only to an opponent's lawyers.

The formal approach

24.35 Cases will arise from time to time in which the informal approach is not appropriate. Where that is so, the court's task is to identify the stage at which the receiving party has to be put to his election (or must be taken to have waived privilege); that stage may never be reached but, if it is, the matter will then proceed on a formal footing.

24.36 That stage is not reached when documents are filed at court pursuant to the CPD (see **24.6–24.23**). The fact that the costs judge goes through the documents filed at court does not raise any problems of natural justice; this is because the costs judge is able to disregard documents if the receiving party subsequently chooses not to rely on them.[14]

24.37 That stage may be reached during the course of the assessment itself. Once it has been reached, the costs judge has a duty to put the receiving party to his election, as was explained by Hobhouse J:[15]

> 'An issue of fact may emerge which necessitates ... making formally or informally a finding of fact. In such a situation, the master may have to ask the [receiving party] what evidence he

---

[10] *Gower Chemicals Group Litigation* [2008] EWHC 735 (QB) at [15]; see also *Pamplin v Express Newspapers Ltd* [1985] 1 WLR 689.

[11] *Gower Chemicals Group Litigation* [2008] EWHC 735 (QB) at [34].

[12] *Pamplin v Express Newspapers Ltd* [1985] 1 WLR 689 at 697.

[13] *Goldman v Hesper* [1988] 1 WLR 1238 at 1245; this was a pre-CPR case, but it is doubtful if this aspect of the law is any different under the CPR.

[14] See *Pamplin v Express Newspapers Ltd* [1985] 1 WLR 689 at 695, which, although a pre-CPR authority, remains authoritative on this point.

[15] *Pamplin v Express Newspapers Ltd* [1985] 1 WLR 689 at 696.

wishes to rely upon in support of the contested allegation of fact. The [paying party] may then take the stand that if the claimant wishes to adduce evidence, he [the paying party] wishes to see it and comment on or contradict it. This will mean that the [receiving party] will then have to elect whether he wants to use the evidence and waive his privilege or seek to prove what he needs in some other way.

... [I]t is the duty of the master, if the respondent raises a factual issue, which is real and relevant and not a sham or fanciful dispute, to require the claimant to prove the facts upon which he relies.'

24.38 In a post-CPR case, Rimer J came to much the same conclusion:[16]

'[The situation] was one which involved an issue of fact which the costs judge had to decide. It appears to me to be obvious that as soon as it became clear that the [receiving party] was proposing to support his own case on the point by reference to documents which he was not willing to disclose to the [paying party], the costs judge should have considered whether that course was consistent with one of the most basic principles of natural justice, namely the right of each side to know what the other party's case is and to see the documentary material that he is relying on so that he can make his own comments on it.'

24.39 Pumfrey J suggested that election is not limited by the nature of the document, but may arise where the document is of sufficient importance for the judge to take it into account:[17]

'Once the document is of sufficient importance to be taken into account in arriving at a conclusion as to recoverability, then, unless otherwise agreed, it must be shown to the paying party or the receiving party must content itself with other evidence.'

The other side of the coin (whether the court may decline to put a party to his election on the basis that the document is of insufficient importance to be taken into account) is discussed at **24.44** and **24.48–24.50**.

24.40 The stage at which a party should be put to his election will be reached only if there is a need to adjudicate upon a contentious issue. No such issue will arise if the receiving party is able to rely on a presumption in his favour. It is for this reason that the receiving party could expect not to be put to his election over a private retainer (unless, of course, the presumption is rebutted: see below).

24.41 The stage at which a receiving party should be put to his election will not be reached if its purpose is merely to test his evidence; this was noted by Rimer J:

'It does not seem to me that the principles set out above require privileged material available to the receiving party to be disclosed for the purpose of testing the evidence given ... The solution is imperfect, but is dictated by the existence of the privilege: ... either both or neither can deploy the privileged material. The familiar rule that the other party is entitled to see the disclosable material even if the party which possesses it does not deploy it can have no application when the material is privileged.'

Thus, the process of election cannot be used to force disclosure of documents upon which the receiving party does not intend to rely.

---

16   *Dickinson v Rushmer* [2002] 1 Costs LR 128 at 144.
17   *South Coast Shipping Co Ltd v Havant Borough Council* [2002] 3 All ER 779 at 793.

Factors to be taken into account

24.42 The following factors may be relevant to the issue of whether the stage has been reached where the receiving party should be put to his election.

Irrelevance

24.43 There is no authority on the point, but common sense dictates that if a document is deemed to be irrelevant, the court could fairly decline to require the receiving party to elect whether to rely upon it. (In this context 'irrelevance' would mean that it was neither probative nor disprobative of the issue in hand rather than that it was a document which did not cause the court to alter its view.)

De minimis material

24.44 Again, common sense dictates that the court must be able to find that material is *de minimis* in the sense that it could not be taken into account in deciding any of the issues which are before the court. *De minimis* is not the same as merely having a small monetary effect: whether the court is able to decline to put a receiving party to his election on grounds of proportionality is discussed at **24.48–24.50**.

Blanket election

24.45 The court will generally not tolerate blanket applications for a party to be put to his election (such as an unfocused application in respect of the receiving party's whole file).[18]

Waiver limited to assessment

24.46 The fact that a receiving party is (usually) able to reassert privilege in subsequent contexts is a factor the court is permitted to take into account.[19]

24.47 It is a moot point whether the court should see the document before deciding whether the receiving party should be put to his election in respect of it. The CPD suggests that this is permissible, but it ought to be remembered that the CPD is not itself a source of law (especially where, as here, it merely describes a judge-made procedure). Where a document is particularly contentious, the court would often wish to avoid seeing it before reaching its decision (this would be so that the court would not subsequently have the difficult task of putting the document out of its mind). That is, the court would hear submissions about the document and then decide the issue without examining it. This approach would be particularly suitable where the court takes the view that the threshold for putting the receiving party to his election is likely to be reached without sight of the document.[20]

---

[18] See, for example, *Pamplin v Express Newspapers Ltd* [1985] 1 WLR 689, which is an example of this.

[19] *South Coast Shipping Co Ltd v Havant Borough Council* [2002] 3 All ER 779 at 785j.

[20] See, for example, *Gower Chemicals Group Litigation* [2008] EWHC 735 (QB) at [31]–[33], in which Davies J seems to have approved of that method in a case where the document in question was unusually contentious.

Proportionality and election

24.48 In a case concerning a disputed retainer, Pumfrey J made the following observations, which at first blush seem to suggest that a costs judge is at liberty to decline to put a party to his election on the grounds of proportionality:[21]

> 'I would expect that in the great majority of cases the paying party would be content to agree that the costs judge alone should see privileged documents. Only where it is necessary and proportionate should the receiving party be put to his election.'

24.49 Rimer J came to a conclusion which seems to be at odds with Pumfrey J's analysis:[22]

> 'I do not attach much weight to [the] submissions as to the need for proportionality in relation to the procedure applicable on a detailed assessment of costs. I interpret the substance of this submission to be that a detailed assessment of costs is essentially ancillary to the main litigation and so justifies the court in adopting something of a broad-brush approach to the performance of the exercise. I do not subscribe to that view. A claim by one party to recover costs from another may well in practice prove to be just as important, perhaps even more so, to one or other or both sides as the resolution of the substantive issues in the action.'

24.50 These seemingly antagonistic observations are reconcilable: proportionality will play a role where the costs judge is using 'all his expertise and tact' to avoid the need to put a party to his election but, once that need is made out, the process of election will not be cut back on grounds of proportionality. This analysis can be supported on the easily understood basis that if a document is worth putting before the court at all, then it is of sufficient importance to respect the paying party's right to see it if it is going to be relied upon. This does not mean that a paying party is able to insist with impunity on the court putting the receiving party to his election in respect of every letter, attendance note and file note: at the very least, a paying party who took that approach would be at risk of being condemned in costs.

Implied waiver of privilege

24.51 Whilst there is a great deal of overlap between implied acceptance of election and waiver of privilege, and whilst most authorities do not make any distinction between them, they are not the same:

- *Implied acceptance of election* may occur where the receiving party can be taken to have attached sufficient weight to a document that it is fair to conclude that he has impliedly accepted that he should be put to his election over it.
- *Implied waiver of privilege* may occur where it is fair to conclude that the receiving party has elected to rely upon the document in question; if the receiving party has not already been put to his election, a finding of implied waiver will include a finding of implied acceptance of election.

One way of analysing the matter is to look upon these things as being stages: the first would be reached where there is an implied acceptance of the need to elect, and the second would be reached where the receiving party has impliedly elected actually to rely

---

[21] *South Coast Shipping Co Ltd v Havant Borough Council* [2002] 3 All ER 779 at 793j.
[22] *Dickinson v Rushmer* [2002] 1 Costs LR 128 at 143.

on the document in question. In practical terms, the difference between the two is that the opportunity to withdraw the document in question is present with the first but not the second. For convenience, these two topics will be referred to collectively as 'unintended waiver'.

24.52 As with election, unintended waiver is addressed by identifying the stage at which the receiving party must be taken to have impliedly accepted the waiver. Hobhouse J had the following to say:[23]

> '[It] will normally be a matter of express waiver only. It should always be possible to avoid having to get involved with implied waiver … A [receiving party] should not have imposed on him an unintended waiver unless fairness to both parties really does necessitate that result.'

24.53 The way in which a receiving party would avoid having an unintended waiver imposed upon him is by being given the opportunity to withdraw the document in question, as explained by Gray J:[24]

> 'When a party lodges a privileged document for detailed assessment in order to claim the costs of it, if the other party wishes to see it to dispute that claim for costs the [receiving party] must be given the right to elect to withdraw it and not claim costs or he must disclose it.'

This means that a receiving party would not be taken to have waived privilege or accepted election merely because he has filed a document at court. What is less clear is whether the fact of handing a document to the costs judge during a detailed assessment is capable of amounting to unintended waiver.

24.54 Rimer J has held that if a receiving party voluntarily chooses to hand a document to the judge in support of his case, then this would pre-empt the decision as to whether the receiving party should be put to his election (that is, it would be the first of the two types of unintended waiver). After having reminded himself that in the case before him certain documents had been voluntarily handed up to the costs judge, he continued:[25]

> 'The costs judge did not *direct* the production to him of the relevant documents, and so the procedure contemplated by that rule [ie CPD, art 40.14] was strictly not engaged at all. The judge saw the documents because the [receiving party] voluntarily chose to hand them to him in support of his case … [This] was a simple situation in which the [receiving party] chose to prove his version of a disputed issue of fact by reference to certain documents. In my view, the basic principle is that, if he wanted to do so, fairness required him also to disclose the documents to the [paying party].'

24.55 It is commonly the case that documents relating to the retainer are handed up to the costs judge in the expectation that those documents will not be shown to the paying party unless and until the court finds that a 'genuine issue' has been made out. Such a practice is unwise, as it may give rise to unintended waiver. This was explained by Rimer J:[26]

---

[23] *Pamplin v Express Newspapers Ltd* [1985] 1 WLR 689 at 698.
[24] *Adams v MacInnes* [2001] EWHC 9014 (Costs).
[25] *Dickinson v Rushmer* [2002] 1 Costs LR 128 at 144 and 145.
[26] *Dickinson v Rushmer* [2002] 1 Costs LR 128 at [31].

'A paying party raises an issue about [the indemnity principle] by advancing factual assertions which serve to put it in question ... Faced with those assertions, the [receiving party] had a choice as to what course to follow. He could have asked the costs judge to direct whether he regarded the [paying party] as having raised an issue on which he, the [receiving party] needed to provide further evidence ... Alternatively, he could, as he did, pre-empt any decision by the judge on that point ... The fact that the [receiving party] thought it appropriate to adopt the latter course is perhaps the best indication that the issue the [paying party] had raised was a genuine one – or at least the [receiving party] so regarded it.'

24.56 Likewise, Gray J has indicated (obiter) that where a client care letter is affirmatively relied upon, it ought to be 'standard practice' that it be made available to the paying party.[27] A receiving party who wishes to avoid disclosing a retainer to his opponent would usually best achieve this aim not by affirmatively relying upon it, but merely by making the retainer available to the court in compliance with CPD, art 40.2(i). Where the documents are in the hands of the judge solely as a result of the procedure envisaged by CPD, art 40.2(i), there will have been no waiver of privilege or implied acceptance of election.[28]

Withdrawal of waiver of privilege

24.57 It is possible to withdraw a waiver of privilege, which may be effective if it is made before the waiver has resulted in documents being inspected by the paying party.[29]

The consequences of electing to disclose documents

24.58 Any disclosure of privileged documents for the purposes of the assessment is, with very limited exceptions, for that purpose only; this means that voluntary waiver or disclosure by a costs judge on an assessment would not prevent the owner of the document from reasserting his privilege in any subsequent context.

24.59 This principle was memorably illustrated by Aldous LJ by reference to 'Mr Bloch's cat':[30]

'As to Mr Bloch's "cat" [Mr Bloch being one of the advocates], in all cases where there is disclosure upon terms the "cat is out of the bag". There is no need to put it back. Documents disclosed for a limited purpose can only be used for that purpose. Of course difficulties arise, but that is not the fault of the person making the disclosure nor the law which protects the confidences of the person disclosing the documents.'

Thus, there will be no need to put the cat back in the bag for the purposes of a subsequent (non-costs) dispute or hearing; this is because the cat would not have been let out of that particular bag in the first place.

---

[27]   *Adams v MacInnes* [2001] EWHC 9014 (Costs).
[28]   *Giambrone v JMC Holidays Ltd* [2002] 2 Costs LR 294 at 302.
[29]   *Goldman v Hesper* [1988] 1 WLR 1238 at 1240.
[30]   *Bourns Inc v Raychem Corp* [1999] 3 All ER 154 at 159.

The consequences of electing not to disclose documents

Burden of proof

24.60 A decision not to disclose a document will place the receiving party at the disadvantage of relying on what inevitably will be imperfect evidence. Where the burden of proof lies with the receiving party (which will almost always be the case where he has been put to his election), that disadvantage may cause the receiving party to fail to prove the issue in question.

No adverse inferences

24.61 It is a general principle that, if a party declines to waive privilege, it would be wrong to regard that refusal as giving rise to an adverse inference in respect of the issue in question;[31] there is no authority to suggest that this general rule should be disregarded for the purposes of costs litigation.

No assumptions

24.62 In a similar but wider context, where a receiving party elects not to disclose a document, it would be wrong to make assumptions about the receiving party's motives; in particular, the court will usually bear in mind that the receiving party may have a legitimate interest in not adducing the most obvious or complete evidence.[32]

DISCLOSURE IN CASES OF FRAUD

24.63 The court will not tolerate fraud. Where it is necessary for the purposes of defeating fraud, the receiving party may be ordered to disclose privileged material without being given the option of electing not to rely upon it. Where fraud is alleged, the party seeking disclosure must provide 'strong evidence' before the court will order disclosure.[33]

DISCLOSURE OF NON-PRIVILEGED MATERIAL

24.64 The paying party may argue that a certain document is not privileged and that it ought to be disclosed without the receiving party being given the option of withdrawing it. There is no binding authority to confirm that the court is able to accede to such a request, but there are instances of the lower courts doing so.[34]

Is the document privileged?

24.65 Where the topic arises, the court may have to determine whether a document is or is not privileged. Broadly speaking, there are, in the present context, two types of privilege: litigation privilege and advice privilege.

---

[31]   See, for example, *Reed Executive plc v Reed Business Information Ltd* [2004] EWCA Civ 887 at [36].

[32]   *Pamplin v Express Newspapers Ltd* [1985] 1 WLR 689 at 697.

[33]   *Skuse v Granada Television* [1994] 1 WLR 1156 at 1166, relying on the principle set out in *Derby & Co Ltd v Weldon (No 7)* [1990] 1 WLR 1156; by analogy, see **6.53–6.71**.

[34]   See, for example, *Stables v York City Council, 13 October 2008, Leeds County Court*, HHJ Grenfell.

Litigation privilege

24.66 Communications made for the purposes of preparing for litigation, and items referred to or enclosed with such communications will generally be covered by 'litigation privilege';[35] this is so regardless of whether they were between the receiving party and his lawyers, or between his lawyers and a third party (such as an expert).

Advice privilege

24.67 Communications passing between the receiving party and his legal representatives made for the purposes of obtaining legal advice are in general covered by 'advice privilege'.[36] The communications must have been confidential. They must also have been made in the context of a professional lawyer–client relationship.[37] Legal professional privilege will not attach to communications between an accountant and his client, even if the purpose of those communications was to obtain legal advice.[38]

24.68 Other types of privilege exist, but may be discounted for present purposes.[39] The following points can be made about documents commonly encountered in the context of costs.

Specific types of documents

Bills

24.69 In general, bills are privileged. Turner V-C held that this is on the ground that 'an attorney's bill of costs is, in truth, his history of the transaction in which he has been concerned'.[40] In more recent times, Turner V-C's comments seem still to be good law: Aldous J, for example, appears to have accepted a concession made by leading counsel that bills were privileged. He commented that 'the reasonable solicitor would have been in no doubt that the legal bills were privileged documents'.[41] Rimer J also seems to have accepted this as being the correct position, but he went on to say that calculations made in relation to bills are not privileged.[42]

Client care letters

24.70 A client care letter may be privileged, depending on the nature of its contents and the context in which it is written.[43] Rimer J commented (obiter) that a letter merely setting out the terms on which the solicitor will act is not privileged.[44] If only parts of the letter relate to legal advice, it would not be right to try to hive off the rest of the letter as not being privileged.[45]

---

[35] See *Three Rivers District Council v Governor and Company of the Bank of England* [2004] UKHL 48 at [10].
[36] *Balabel v Air India* [1988] Ch 317.
[37] *Minter v Priest* [1930] AC 558; see also *Wilden Pump Engineering Co v Fusfeld* (1985) FSR 159 CA (Civ Div).
[38] *R (on the application of (1) Prudential Plc v Special Commissioner of Income Tax* [2010] EWCA Civ 1094.
[39] A third type, privilege against self-incrimination may arise in theory, but in practice it would almost never arise in the context of a detailed assessment.
[40] *Chant v Brown* (1851) 9 Hare 790 at 794. Whilst in a wholly different context, Tindall CJ has found that 'the attorney's bill may be called the history of the cause': *Waller v Lacey* (1840) 133 ER 245 at 251.
[41] *International Business Machines Corpn v Phoenix International (Computers) Ltd* [1995] 1 All ER 413 at 424.
[42] *Dickinson v Rushmer* [2002] 1 Costs LR 128 at 132.
[43] For general guidance, see *Balabel v Air India* [1988] Ch 317, in particular at 330.
[44] *Dickinson v Rushmer* [2002] 1 Costs LR 128 at 133.
[45] See *Balabel v Air India* [1988] Ch 317.; see also *The Sagheera* [1997] 1 Lloyd's Rep 160 at 168.

Administrative records

24.71 Brooke LJ has confirmed that not every document generated in the course of a retainer will be privileged.[46] Whilst not a binding decision, HHJ Grenfell has found that automated records of time spent are not privileged.[47] In the context of a criminal matter, Bingham CJ has found that records of the times of attendances were not privileged.[48]

Insurance policies

24.72 This is addressed at **30.222**.

Communications made prior to litigation

24.73 Privilege may be claimed in respect of professional communications made in a professional capacity, even if those communications were not made in anticipation of litigation.[49] Whilst an obvious point, instructions given by the client to his solicitor are privileged.[50]

Communications for purposes other than litigation

24.74 In general, communications with persons other than the client for purposes other than obtaining legal advice will not be covered by privilege.[51] That said, there might be other reasons why they cannot be disclosed (such as the privilege which attaches to without prejudice material).

Litigation funding (third-party agreements)

24.75 In the context of an application for security of costs, Sir Donald Rattee addressed the issue of whether a litigation funding agreement should be disclosed; his decision was that it should not be disclosed, but it was notable that at no stage did he contemplate that the agreement might be privileged.[52]

Procedure

24.76 The topics of timing and of whether the document in question should be shown to the court before a ruling is made are both dealt with above (see **24.35–24.38** and **24.47**).

24.77 In general, there are no procedural formalities pertaining to election; this is because the issue of whether the receiving party should be put to his election will arise as

---

[46]   *Hollins v Russell* [2003] 1 WLR 2487 at [77].

[47]   *Stables v York City Council, 13 October 2008, Leeds County Court*, HHJ Grenfell.

[48]   *R v Manchester Crown Court ex p Rogers* [1999] 1 WLR 832.

[49]   *Lawrence v Campbell* (1859) 4 Drew 485.

[50]   *Bristol Corporation v Cox* (1884) 26 Ch D 678.

[51]   *Alfred Crompton Amusement Machines Ltd v Customs and Excise Comrs (No 2)* [1974] AC 405; in a costs context see *Hollins v Russell* [2003] 1 WLR 2487 at [77].

[52]   *Reeves v Sprecher* [2007] EWHC 3226 (Ch).

an integral part of the detailed assessment. Receiving parties are, however, encouraged to consider giving advance disclosure in appropriate cases. The SCCO Guide 2006 offers the following advice:[53]

> 'The production of documents at a detailed assessment hearing may well cause substantial delay to that hearing and may prejudice or embarrass any appeal made in the proceedings in which the costs were awarded or in any similar proceedings between the same parties. Receiving parties should therefore consider in advance what voluntary disclosure to their opponents they are willing to make and how such disclosure can be achieved before the detailed assessment hearing without substantially damaging any privilege they wish to retain.'

That guidance goes on to say that in appropriate cases the court may order that the issue of election be tried as a preliminary issue; where this is so, the issues to be tried should be clearly defined and, where appropriate, reduced into writing.[54]

---

[53]   Paragraph 10.5.
[54]   *Lahey v Pirelli Tyres* [2007] EWCA Civ 91 at [5]; see also J O'Hare *Applications about CFAs in detailed assessments* (2007, Sweet & Maxwell Professional Conference), p 6.

Chapter 25

REPRESENTATION AND RIGHTS
OF AUDIENCE

INTRODUCTION

25.1   This chapter discusses the rights of costs practitioners to conduct costs litigation and to be heard in court. This chapter also touches on the issues of advocates who wish to be heard on their own fees. The analysis focuses on the current law (namely, the Legal Services Act 2007, referred to herein as 'LSA 2007'), but reference is also made to the old law (namely, the Courts and Legal Services Act 1990 as amended, referred to herein as 'CLSA 1990'). The old yielded to the new on 1 January 2010.

25.2   The acts of conducting litigation and exercising a right of audience are both 'reserved legal activities' within the meaning of the LSA 2007.[1] As of 1 January 2010,[2] the question of whether a person is entitled to carry out such an activity is to be determined solely in accordance with the provisions of LSA 2007.[3] Whilst there is no authority relating specifically to that Act, it is likely that the definition of what is meant by 'conducting litigation' is to be read narrowly (see **5.55**). A person is entitled to carry on a reserved legal activity where he is an 'authorised person' or an 'exempt person' in relation that activity.[4] It is an offence for a person to carry on such an activity without being entitled to do so.[5] Certain persons may be exempt, depending on whether the relevant activity is conducting litigation or exercising a putative right of audience; these topics are addressed at **5.59** and **5.60** respectively. The fact that a person has a right to be heard will not preclude the court refusing to hear him;[6] the court must give its reasons for so doing.[7] The court may also hear a person who otherwise would not have a right to be heard.[8]

---

[1]   Section 12(1) of the Legal Services Act 2007.

[2]   Before this date, the issues were governed by the Courts and Legal Services Act 1990 (as amended). The relevant provisions were introduced in a staged way; the majority of the provisions came into force on 1 January 2010 (see the Legal Services Act 2007 (Commencement No 6, Transitory, Transitional and Saving Provisions) Order 2009, SI 2009/3250), but in so far as s 12 of the Act defines the term 'reserved legal activity' for the purposes of ss 1, 207, 69(4), Sch 1 para 2(3)–(5), Sch 15, para 2(3), (4), and Sch 22, para 2(6), (7)(b)), the relevant date was 7 March 2008 (see Legal Services Act 2007 (Commencement No 1 and Transitory Provisions) Order 2008, SI 2008/222), and in so far as s 12 defines that term for the purposes of the Administration of Justice Act 1985, ss 9, 32A), the relevant date was 31 March 2009 (see Legal Services Act 2007 (Commencement No 4, Transitory and Transitional Provisions and Appointed Day) Order 2009, SI 2009/503).

[3]   See s 13(1) of the Legal Services Act 2007.

[4]   See the Legal Services Act, s 13(2).

[5]   See the Legal Services Act, s 14(1).

[6]   See **5.59** and **5.60**.

[7]   LSA 2007, s 192(2).

[8]   Legal Services Act 2007, Sch 3, para 1(3).

25.3   A person is an 'authorised person' if he is authorised by a relevant 'approved regulator' to carry on the relevant activity.[9] Regulators are themselves regulated by complex provisions.[10]Those who are authorised persons in relation to the practice of law generally will be able to conduct litigation and exercise a right of audience; this will include solicitors, barristers, etc. In addition, there is an approved regulator relating specifically to the practice of costs; that body is the Association of Costs Lawyers[11] (previously known as the Association of Law Costs Draftsmen). As of 31 October 2011 that body has delegated its regulatory role to the Costs Lawyer Standards Board.

UNAUTHORISED PERSONS

25.4   The term 'unauthorised person' is used in this chapter to describe a person who is not an authorised person in the sense that his status does not give him the right to carry on the relevant activity in question (see **25.2**). The term 'authorised person, on the other hand, is used to mean a person who does have such a right (such as a costs lawyer, solicitor, barrister, etc). In the context of the practice of costs, the most important category of unauthorised person is costs draftsmen (as distinct from costs lawyers). This does not mean that costs draftsmen are necessarily unqualified or that they lack experience; it is not uncommon for costs draftsmen to be educated in law up to degree level and to have considerable experience. At the other end of the scale are costs draftsmen who have no formal training and very little experience. For the reasons set out at **5.63–5.66**, a distinction needs to be drawn between independent costs draftsmen and costs draftsmen who are employed by a firm of solicitors; the latter may be afforded rights of audience vicariously (ie by reason of his being employed by a qualified advocate) but, even where this is so, his rights of audience will, as is explained at **25.7**, be limited.

25.5   The general approach to the issue of representation by unauthorised persons was addressed by Woolf CJ:[12]

> 'It is very important that courts, without going into the matter in a disproportionate way, do satisfy themselves that it is right to extend rights of audience to those who are not properly qualified. The courts are at a disadvantage and the public can be at a disadvantage if rights of audience are too readily given to those who do not have the necessary qualifications.'

This extract confirms that the court is vigilant to ensure that only qualified or otherwise suitable persons appear before it for the purpose of representing others. These concerns continue to apply today (see **5.66**).

25.6   In practice, the court's concerns tend to focus on whether there is a proper chain of command from the client (or insurer, as the case may be), through an authorised person, to the person who seeks to be heard.[13] This is relevant because it is only by reason of such a chain of command that any authorised body is able to exert an

---

9   See the Legal Services Act 2007, s 18(1)(a).
10   See the Legal Services Act 2007, Part 4.
11   See the Association of Law Costs Draftsmen Order 2006, SI 2006/3333.
12   *Clarkson v Gilbert & Ors* [2000] EWCA Civ 3018 at [24] of the transcript.
13   Put another way, the court will be interested in whether the person is employed or otherwise engaged by a 'qualified litigator' to assist in the conduct of litigation: see CLSA 1990, s 27(2)(e).

influence over the authorised person (or those who instruct him). Although not binding on any court, the following comments of Master Hurst illustrate the way in which this issue is often addressed:[14]

> 'There is nothing in my view inherently wrong in a requirement by an insurance company that, when costs come to be determined, a particular firm of costs draftsmen should be instructed. Those instructions must come from the instructing solicitors who have themselves been properly instructed and who are required to consider the claim for costs and advise the client. It is abundantly clear in this case that [the unauthorised persons] were attempting to run the detailed assessment proceedings without reference to the Defendant's solicitors under the umbrella of the correspondence to which I have referred, which does not, for the reasons I have given, achieve its objective.'

Other judges have expressed similar sentiments (see **5.66**). On the facts of the case before him, Master Hurst declined to hear the unauthorised person, but, if particularly unimpressed, the court may go further; there are, for example, instances of the court visiting costs sanctions on the party who had failed to ensure that the person who appeared on his behalf was properly able to represent him.[15]

25.7   Where a person has right of audience as a result of being employed or otherwise engaged by an authorised person, those rights will generally be limited to being heard in chambers.[16] This is discussed in more detail at **5.66**. In so far as costs draftsmen are concerned, a person who is not contractually employed by his instructing solicitor is often regarded as being temporarily employed for the purposes of the case;[17] it is not wholly clear whether that analysis continues to be correct under the LSA 2007. In any event, in the absence of a contrary order, the right of audience will be limited to being heard in chambers; it is because of this restriction that an unauthorised person would not ordinarily be able to represent his client on an appeal, even where he appeared in the court below. The court does, however, have discretionary power to grant rights in relation to reserved activities.[18] An example of this having happened on appeal was where Dyson LJ gave a costs draftsman permission to go on the record in the Court of Appeal, this being on the grounds that it would save costs.[19]

25.8   Where an unauthorised person has been instructed by a litigant in person for the purposes of assisting him in litigation, the court has the power to allow that person to be heard.[20] That person is often referred to as a *McKenzie* friend.[21] He may be qualified in the sense that he is a member of a body other than an approved regulator; in some circumstances this would allow the litigant to recover his costs under affirmative power conferred by the CPR, but only where the work was the provision of expert assistance in assessing costs, and only where he was:[22]

---

[14]   *Ahmed v Powell* [2003] EWHC 9011 (Costs) at [36].
[15]   *Salmons v Perch* (unreported) 30 April 2002, SCCO, Master Hurst.
[16]   See the Legal Services Act 2007, Sch 3, para 1(7): see **5.65**.
[17]   See, for example, *Claims Direct Test Cases Tranche 2* [2003] EWHC 9005 (Costs) at [115] and *Crane v Canons Leisure Centre* [2007] EWCA Civ 1352 at [12], per May LJ.
[18]   See Legal Services Act 2007, Sch 3, para 1(3).
[19]   See *Cumming v Blakemore* [2009] EWCA Civ 404, where Dyson LJ gave permission to a costs draftsman on the basis that it would result in a saving in costs, this being under the old provisions (namely, the Courts and Legal Services Act 1990, s 27(2)(c)).
[20]   See Legal Services Act 2007, s 19 and Sch 3, para 1(2) (or, before 1 January 2010, pursuant to CLSA 1990, ss 27(2)(b) and 28(2)(c) respectively).
[21]   *McKenzie v McKenzie* [1971] P 33.
[22]   CPR, r 48.6(3)(c); see also CPD, art 52.1.

- a barrister, solicitor or Fellow of the Institute of Legal Executives;[23]
- a Fellow of the Association of Law Costs Draftsmen;[24]
- a law costs draftsman who is a member of the Academy of Experts; or
- a law costs draftsman who is a member of the Expert Witness Institute.

AUTHORISED PERSONS

25.9   Solicitors, counsel and Fellows of the Institute of Legal Executives (FILEXs) are able to carry on most reserved legal activities, including nearly all of those that relate to the law of costs (at least at first instance). Up until 31 December 2011 there were three categories of authorised costs practitioners,[25] but as of that date, there has been only one, namely, the costs lawyer.

25.10   The rights which a costs lawyer is able to enjoy are set out in a Statement of Rights issued in July 2007 by the ALCD (now called the Association of Costs Lawyers).[26] The following extract is reproduced with the kind permission of the ACL:

'**Statement of Rights Granted To Fellows Holding a Current ALCD Practising Certificate**

(i)   **Rights of audience** in all proceedings being conducted under Parts 43–48 of the Civil Procedure Rules 1999 ('CPR') and under Part 52 of those rules with regard to appeals from detailed assessment hearings before a High Court Judge or a Circuit Judge such rights to exclude and issue of entitlement to costs under CPR 44.3 and entitlement to wasted costs order arising solely under CPR 44.14(1)(b) or CPR, rule 48.7 other than in connection with proceedings under (vi) and (vii) below.

(ii)   **Right of audience** on all determinations of costs under the Community Legal Services and Criminal Defence Services regulations.

(iii)   **Right of audience** on all determinations of costs under s 16 of the Prosecution of Offences Act 1985 and the Costs in Criminal Cases (General) Regulations 1986.

(iv)   **Right of audience** in proceedings at first instances relating to costs before the House of Lords.

(v)   **Right of audience** in all costs proceedings at first instance before Her Majesties Privy Council.

(vi)   **The right to litigate** in all proceedings under Parts 43–48 of the CPR and under Part 52 of those rules with regard to appeals from detailed assessment to the listed before a High Court Judge or a Circuit Judge.

---

[23]   Obviously these persons are authorised persons in any event.

[24]   This has not been updated to refer to the Association of Costs Lawyers; it is likely that the court would now interpret this as meaning costs lawyer.

[25]   These being Associates of the Association of Law Costs Draftsmen (AALCDs), Fellows of the Association of Law Costs Draftsmen (FALCDs), and costs lawyers (who were FALCDs who had undertaken advocacy training).

[26]   That statement was issued pursuant to The Association of Law Costs Draftsmen Order 2006, which came into force on 1 January 2007

(vii)   **The right to litigate** under sections 64(3) and (4), 68, 69, 70, 71 and 74 of the Solicitors Act 1974 or any subsequent enactment of the provisions thereof.

(viii)   **The right to administer** oaths and take affidavits under section 113 of the Courts and Legal Services Act 1990.

July 2007'

25.11   Thus, a costs lawyer has the right to conduct most types of costs litigation, and he also has the right to be heard in most courts which are likely to be relevant to his practice. This will be so regardless of whether he has been instructed by a solicitor. Where that right does not exist by reason of a costs lawyer's status (such as at an appeal in the Court of Appeal), the court may exercise its discretion to grant the appropriate rights.[27] Moreover, whilst only a decision on application for permission to appeal,[28] Burnett J has found that a costs lawyer is able to delegate the task of appearing in court to an employee under his direct supervision.[29]

RESTRICTION OF RIGHTS OF AUDIENCE

25.12   The court has the power to refuse to hear from a person who would otherwise have enjoyed a right of audience; the relevant provisions are as follows:[30]

'192 Powers of court in respect of rights of audience and conduct of litigation

(1) Nothing in this Act affects the power of any court in any proceedings to refuse to hear a person (for reasons which apply to that person as an individual) who would otherwise have a right of audience before the court in relation to those proceedings.

(2) Where a court refuses to hear a person as mentioned in subsection (1), it must give its reasons for refusing.

(3) Where—

    (a)   immediately before the commencement of section 13 (entitlement to carry on reserved legal activities), or

    (b)   by virtue of any provision made by or under an enactment passed subsequently,

a court does not permit the appearance of advocates, or permits the appearance of advocates only with leave, no person may exercise a right of audience before the court, in relation to any proceedings, solely by virtue of being entitled to do so under this Act.

(4) But a court may not limit the right to appear before the court in any proceedings to only some of those who are entitled to exercise that right by virtue of this Act.

(5) A court may not limit the right to conduct litigation in relation to proceedings before the court to only some of those who are entitled to exercise that right by virtue of this Act.

(6) In this section "advocate", in relation to any proceedings, means a person exercising a right of audience as a representative of, or on behalf of, any party to the proceedings.'

---

[27]   See CLSA 1990, s 27(2)(c) (or s 28(2)(c) in respect of rights to conduct litigation). See **25.7**.
[28]   The court does not encourage such decisions being cited: *Clark v University of Lincolnshire and Humberside* [2000] 3 All ER 752 at 762 f, per Lord Woolf MR.
[29]   *Kynaston v Carroll* [2011] EWHC 2179 (QB) [6]–[8].
[30]   This being s 192 of the Legal Services Act 2007.

INTERESTED ADVOCATES

25.13 In the present context, the term 'interested advocate' is used to mean a person who seeks to be heard on the issue of his own fees (or on the issue of fees in respect of which he has had a close involvement). He may or may not be a qualified representative.

25.14 There is a lack of judicial consensus as to whether interested advocates may be heard on a detailed assessment. The court usually tolerates (and occasionally encourages) the attendance of solicitors, but where counsel seeks to justify his fees, the court has been known to take a less generous view. There are competing factors which may affect counsel's ability to assist the court: counsel will usually know a great deal about the claim and would be able to assist the court in that regard, but he might lack objectivity, especially if he has a financial interest in the matter. It was this latter factor that troubled Cazalet J:[31]

> 'Mr B, who was junior counsel in the main case, also appeared before us in this review of taxation. As was to be expected of him, he made his submissions in a balanced and measured way. However, I do not consider that, as a general rule, counsel who has appeared in the substantive case should be instructed to appear at taxation of costs review concerning the same case and involving his own fees. Although we do not suggest that there is any professional impropriety in this, such a course could lead to submissions being confused with evidence and possible loss of objective assessment.'

25.15 Leveson J, however, did not agree. Giving judgment in a case concerning criminal costs, he believed that counsel could assist:[32]

> 'Whatever might have been the position in 1995 [when Cazalet J made the comments above], and with very great respect to [him], I do not accept that his concerns have the same validity today. After all, summary assessment of costs (albeit at a much reduced level) not infrequently requires counsel to justify their own brief fee or challenge that of an opponent ... Furthermore, solicitors regularly appear on assessments to justify their own costs (with or without the assistance of costs draftsmen) and there is no reason to believe that barristers are less able sensibly to justify their own fees. Obviously, if any member of the bar (or indeed a solicitor for the rules are the same) feels so emotionally involved in a case that he wishes to instruct and advocate to appear on his behalf, he is perfectly entitled to do so. However, it does not seem to me that this should justify his being indemnified against the costs of so doing (over and above that which he would himself have been entitled to recover) ...'

25.16 The comments of Leveson J are not binding, not least because they relate to a criminal case. The difference between criminal and civil costs is significant and ought not to be overlooked.[33] Perhaps the law is that each case must be decided on its own facts and that the court should take into account all of the factors mentioned both by Cazalet J and by Leveson J. Regardless of whether counsel is able to be heard, there can usually be no objection to counsel preparing a signed note to be handed to the costs

---

[31] *F v F* [1995] 2 FLR 702 at 713D.
[32] *Jackson v Lord Chancellor* [2003] EWHC 626 (QB).
[33] In particular, in a criminal case, counsel will usually be engaged in a well-defined exercise, the purpose of which will be apparent to all concerned (ie he will be fighting his corner for the purposes of getting paid). The same would not necessarily be true in a civil matter, because counsel may or may not have an interest in the matter (or, at the very least, he may fear that he is at risk of not getting paid even if the legal niceties suggest otherwise).

judge: whether such a note is to be regarded as evidence or a submission is a moot point, but there is little doubt that, in principle, the court is entitled to take such a note into account.[34]

AUTHORITY OF COSTS PRACTITIONERS

25.17 The remainder of this chapter deals with the issue of whether a person who represents a client has the authority to bind the client. The following discussion does not attempt a detailed analysis of the issue of agency: it deals with this issue only from the standpoint of costs litigation. Whilst the context is different from the matter presently in hand, a brief discussion of the language and principles of agency can be found at **12.2** onwards.

25.18 Where a person is represented by counsel or a solicitor, then, unless there is reason to believe otherwise, both the court and his opponent are entitled to assume that he has actual authority both to represent and to bind the person who instructs him. A solicitor retained under a 'general retainer' will have actual authority for the purposes of preserving and protecting his client's interests; this would be so even where there was an absence of specific instructions.[35] The ambit of authority in other cases must be determined on the facts. That said, an agent will have implied authority to carry out all those acts which are necessary or ordinarily incidental to the exercise of his express authority: therefore, the agent's authority will not be limited solely to the principal's precise commands.[36]

25.19 Where there is an absence of actual authority, the court may find that the representative has 'ostensible' or 'apparent' authority[37]; this would allow the court to interpret the actions of the representative as if he had actual authority in relation to those actions. In the context of company law rather than costs, Lord Hatherly explained the concept of ostensible authority:[38]

> 'When there are persons conducting the affairs of the company in a manner which appears to be perfectly consonant with the articles of association, those so dealing with them externally are not to be affected by irregularities which may take place in the internal management of the company.'

25.20 Where a solicitor or counsel negotiates a compromise, he will, in the ordinary run of things, have ostensible authority to do so; this will be so unless the compromise takes in matters collateral to the claim. A matter would not be collateral to the claim unless it took in extraneous subject matter (such as a compromise of a claim for damages which took into account a debt entirely unrelated to the claim); a compromise would not take in matters collateral to the claim merely because it resulted in the parties coming to an agreement that the court could not itself have ordered.[39]

---

[34] See *Armitage v Nurse* [2000] 2 Costs LR 231.
[35] *Donsland Ltd (a firm) v Van Hoogstraten* [2002] EWCA Civ 253.
[36] See, for example, *Gavaghan v Edwards* [1961] 2 QB 220, [1961] 2 All ER 477, CA, in which the legal representatives were found to have authority to make a memorandum recording an agreement.
[37] See *Royal British Bank v Turquand* (1856) 6 E&B 327 and *Criterion Properties plc v Stratford UK Properties LLC* [2004] UKHL 28. Circumstances may also exist where agency by estoppel may be created, which, in the present context, is similar to a finding of ostensible authority: see the discussion of this concept in *Rama Corpn Ltd v Proved Tin and General Investments Ltd* [1952] 2 QB 147.
[38] *Mahoney v East Holyford Mining Co* (1875) LR 7 HL 869.
[39] *Waugh v HB Clifford & Sons Ltd* [1982] Ch 374.

25.21 The position in respect of persons who hold themselves out as 'costs draftsmen' is less clear-cut. This is because such a person may be anything from a costs lawyer through to an entirely unqualified person. Therefore, neither the court nor an opponent can be sure that person who describes himself as a costs draftsman is under any form of professional duty, still less that he owes a duty to ensure that he has authority. Neill LJ made the following obiter comments about the issue of ostensible authority of costs draftsmen:[40]

> 'On the facts of the present case, however, I do not find it necessary to reach a final decision as to the ostensible authority of an independent costs draftsman, but I am inclined to the view that where a solicitor sends a costs draftsman to a taxation the other parties to the litigation are entitled to assume in the absence of any information to the contrary or unless the sums involved are very large, that the costs draftsman has the same authority as the solicitor would have had to consent to orders which are not plainly collateral to the matters before the taxation officer.'

Evans LJ agreed, and added the following comments of his own:

> 'As regards the authority, actual or apparent, of an independent costs draftsman who attends before the taxing officer, it should be remembered that he can appear on behalf of the party only as a duly authorised representative of the solicitor who has instructed him to be there. The scope of his apparent authority would be the same, in my judgment, as that of any costs draftsman employed by the firm.'

These comments seem to have narrowed the gap between the authority of employed draftsmen and of independent costs draftsmen. In so far as costs lawyers are concerned, it might be relevant that they are subject to a professional duty to keep clients properly informed as to the progress of their instructions.[41]

25.22 Thus, unless there is reason to believe otherwise or unless the sums involved are very large, a costs draftsman will be regarded as having authority to speak for and bind the person who instructs him, as will a costs lawyer. Another way of analysing the matter would be to say that costs draftsmen have implied authority to act in accordance with the customs of their profession, and that would include having authority to bind their clients.[42] Even where a representative does not have actual or ostensible authority, the subsequent conduct of the person who instructed him may ratify the actions of the representative.[43] Ratification must be by adoption of the agent's acts or by acquiescence thereto;[44] ratification may be express, or it may be implied, usually by conduct.[45] This means that it is not always the case that the costs draftsman would need to have had actual authority at the time the agreement, offer or concession was made.

CONFLICT OF INTEREST

25.23 The court may prevent the advocate from acting where, by reason of an advocate's connection with the other side or one of their witnesses, there is a risk of

---

[40] *Waterston Hicks v Eliopoulos* (1995) Costs LR, Core vol 363.
[41] See rule 6.8 of the Code of Conduct of the Association of Costs Lawyers 2011.
[42] Whilst a non-costs case, see *Lienard v Dresslar* (1862) 3 F & F 212.
[43] See *OPM Property Services Ltd v Venner* [2004] EWHC 427 (Ch). See also *Re Vimbos Ltd* [1900] 1 Ch 470.
[44] *Lythgoe v Vernon* (1860) 5 H & N 180.
[45] *Soames v Spencer* (1822) 1 Dow & Ry KB 32.

disclosure of confidential information or there is a risk of irregularity which would be grounds for ordering a re-trial.[46] The following issues are relevant to the species of law in question:

- **Solicitors**: The court has power to remove a solicitor from the record.[47] A solicitor has a duty not to make any use of confidential without the client's (or former client's) consent.[48]
- **Counsel**: Unless all relevant persons consent, a barrister must not accept instructions if there is or appears to be a conflict or risk of conflict either between the interests of the barrister and some other person.[49] A barrister may not accept instructions to act against his former client where the barrister is in receipt of potentially relevant t confidential information. This is as a matter of law as well as a matter of professional conduct.[50] Injunctive relief may be granted in an appropriate case.[51]
- **Costs Lawyers:** A costs lawyer must act at all times to ensure the client's interest is paramount except where this conflicts with his duties to the court or where otherwise permitted by law. A costs lawyer must decline to act if it would not be in the client's best interests or if that client's interests conflict directly with his own or with those of another client.[52]

---

[46] *Geveran Trading Co Ltd v Skjevesland* [2002] EWCA Civ 1567.
[47] *Re L (minors) (care proceedings: solicitors)* [2001] 1 WLR 100.
[48] *Bolkiah v KPMG (a firm)* [1999] 2 AC 222, [1999] 1 All ER 517, HL
[49] Code of Conduct of the Bar of England and Wales (8th edn, 2004), para 603(e).
[50] *Earl of Cholmondeley v Lord Clinton* (1815) 19 Ves 261 at 275 per Lord Eldon.
[51] *Geveran Trading Co Ltd v Skjevesland* [2002] EWCA Civ 1567 at [38].
[52] See Principle 3, para 3.1 of the Code of Conduct published by the Costs Lawyer Standards Board, effective from 31 October 2011.

Part V

THE QUANTUM OF COSTS (SOLICITOR AND CLIENT)

This part of the book addresses the quantum of costs between solicitor and client. Unlike the rest of this book, Chapter 26 assumes a fair degree of knowledge on the part of the reader. If it is believed that the requisite knowledge is lacking, then that chapter should be read in tandem with the corresponding parts of Part VI; the book has been written in this way in order to avoid repetition.

Chapter 26

THE BASIS OF ASSESSMENT BETWEEN SOLICITOR AND CLIENT

26.1   Whilst most commentators would focus on the similarities rather than the differences,[1] the quantification of solicitor and client costs can be said to comprise not one, but two, separate topics; the first being the assessment of contentious costs and the assessment of non-contentious costs. This distinction arises not because of differences in the law itself, but because of differences in the way the law is applied and in the circumstances in which the costs are likely to have been incurred. This was noted by Longmore LJ:[2]

> 'There are significant differences in the circumstances in which charges are made for contentious and non-contentious business and the approach to such charges can properly differ even though the same factors fall to be taken into account.'

26.2   Solicitor and client costs are assessed on the indemnity basis; this means that any doubt as to reasonableness is resolved in favour of the solicitor and that the concept of proportionality does not apply.

26.3   A general description of the indemnity basis has already been given in Chapter 13; there are, however, subtle differences between the way in which contentious and non-contentious costs are assessed. Each is dealt with in turn.

CONTENTIOUS COSTS

26.4   The indemnity basis is modified for the purposes of the assessment of solicitor and client costs (both contentious and non-contentious) in that a number of presumptions are created which give weight to two factors: firstly, they give weight to what was agreed between the solicitor and his client and, secondly, they give weight to the solicitor's duty to ensure that his client is properly advised. Those presumptions predate the CPR,[3] but are now expressed in CPR, r 48.8:

> '(1)   This rule applies to every assessment of a solicitor's bill to his client except a bill which is to be paid out of the Community Legal Service Fund under the Legal Aid Act 1988 or the Access to Justice Act 1999 – and

---

[1]   See, for example, M Cook *Cook on Costs 2010*, para 21.1, in which the author says that the similarities between contentious and non-contentious costs are much greater than the differences, and that the differences need to be considered only as and when they arise.

[2]   *Jemma Trust Co Ltd v Liptrott* [2004] 1 WLR 646 at 656.

[3]   RSC Ord 62, r 15.

(1A)   Section 74(3) of the Solicitors Act 1974(a) applies unless the solicitor and client have entered into a written agreement which expressly permits payment to the solicitor of an amount of costs greater than that which the client could have recovered from another party to the proceedings.

(2)   Subject to paragraph (1A), costs are to be assessed on the indemnity basis but are to be presumed—

(a)   to have been reasonably incurred if they were incurred with the express or implied approval of the client;

(b)   to be reasonable in amount if their amount was expressly or impliedly approved by the client;

(c)   to have been unreasonably incurred if—

(i)   they are of an unusual nature or amount; and

(ii)   the solicitor did not tell his client that as a result he might not recover all of them from the other party.

(3)   Where the court is considering a percentage increase, whether on the application of the legal representative under rule 44.16 or on the application of the client, the court will have regard to all the relevant factors as they reasonably appeared to the solicitor or counsel when the conditional fee agreement was entered into or varied.

(4)   In paragraph (3), "conditional fee agreement" means an agreement enforceable under section 58 of the Courts and Legal Services Act 1990 at the date on which that agreement was entered into or varied.'

For practical purposes, CPR, r 48.8 creates two sets of rules, which can be referred to as the solicitor and client presumptions, and the county court procedural restriction.

The solicitor and client presumptions

26.5   CPR, r 48.8(3) provides that costs shall be assessed on the indemnity basis; this means that CPR, r 44.4(3) applies. It reads as follows:

'Where the amount of costs is to be assessed on the indemnity basis, the court will resolve any doubt which it may have as to whether costs were reasonably incurred or were reasonable in amount in favour of the receiving party.'

26.6   These provisions concerning the resolution of doubt are modified by the presumptions in CPR, r 48.8(2); in particular:

• costs are assumed to have been reasonably incurred if they were incurred with the express or implied approval of the client;

• costs are assumed to be reasonable in amount if their amount was expressly or impliedly approved by the client; and

• costs are assumed to have been unreasonably incurred if:

– they are of an unusual nature or amount; and

– the solicitor did not tell his client that as a result he might not recover all of them from the other party.

26.7   At first blush, it would appear that these presumptions are not rebuttable (ie that they are irrebuttable presumptions of law, or 'conclusive presumptions' as such pre-emptions are often called); certainly, there is nothing in the CPR or its predecessor which expressly gives the court the power of rebuttal.[4] This was a topic which vexed Holland J when he was considering the pre-CPR version of these presumptions. He found that the first two presumptions (concerning approval) were theoretically rebuttable but went to comment that he could conceive no basis upon which such a rebuttal could take place.[5] Holland J expressed concern that, if left unmitigated, a presumption which could not be rebutted could lead to injustice. An unscrupulous solicitor, for example, could cajole his client into approving rates which were not only unreasonable, but outlandish. He was, therefore, unable to find anything in the notion of rebuttal which afforded the client any refuge. In compensation for this, Holland J discovered the concept of 'informed approval':

'I talked of "informed" approval and even with reflection I adhere to that concept. To rely on the [clients'] approval the solicitor must satisfy me that it was secured following a full and fair exposition of the factors relevant to it so that the [clients], lay persons as they are, can reasonably be bound by it.'

26.8   Thus, the client's protection lies not in the court's discretion to find that the presumption had been rebutted, but in the requirement that the client must have given 'informed approval' rather than merely unqualified approval. If the client had not given informed approval, then the court is able to assess the costs unhindered by the presumptions mentioned above.

26.9   On the facts of the case before him (in which an hourly charging rate of £300 per hour was claimed at a time when such rates were highly unusual) Holland J found that the information which had been given to the clients was insufficiently frank and detailed to make their approval 'informed'. The following factors featured in his reasoning:

- the fact that the client had not been given a fair and full explanation of the likely recovery of costs on a between the parties assessment;
- his finding that there was no logical basis for charging the hourly rate that was claimed (the solicitors had increased their hourly rate in a seemingly arbitrary way); and
- the fact that the clients had not been told how the higher rate would impact upon the sums that they would have to pay generally.

In view of his findings, Holland J found that costs should be assessed without reference to the presumptions.

The county court procedural restriction

26.10   CPR, r 48.8(1A) provides that, unless it is disapplied by agreement (see **26.13**), s 74(3) of the Solicitors Act 1974 will apply; that section imposes a restriction on the amount of costs recoverable in the county court. It reads as follows:

'(3) The amount which may be allowed on the assessment of any costs or bill of costs in respect of any item relating to proceedings in a county court shall not, except in so far as rules of court may otherwise provide, exceed the amount which could have been allowed in respect of that item as between party and party in those proceedings, having regard to the nature of the proceedings and the amount of the claim and of any counterclaim.'

---

[4]   It is possible that two competing presumptions would conflict; if this were so, then it would be open to the court to find that they had cancelled each other out; in a non-costs setting, see *Monkton v Tarr* (1930) 23 BWCC 504, CA.

[5]   *MacDougall v Boote Edgar Estekin* [2001] 1 Costs LR 118 at 122.

Thus, in so far as it applies, SA 1974, s 74(3) limits the amount that the client has to pay to the amount which could have been allowed had the costs been payable between opposing parties.

26.11 This seemingly wide-ranging restriction has been held to apply only where the CPR imposes limits as to the level of costs recovery; this was explained by Hughes J:[6]

> 'I am satisfied that section 74(3) exists to apply a cap where there are limits under the rules to the level of costs recoverable as between the parties. The subsection remains in the same form as it has in 1974. At that time, costs in the County Court were in most cases recovered on one or other of five scales, according to the amount of money in dispute ... The section was designed to limit the costs between solicitor and client to those scales, in the same way as the scales limited costs recoverable as between the parties ... Under the [CPR] the express reference to section 74(3) which appears in rule 48.8(1A), shows that the section does not simply survive but is intended still to bite. And bite it does whenever there are fixed costs ...'

Thus, the restriction applies where there is a principled limit to the sums which may be recovered between the parties; it will not apply where the putative limit would merely be an incidental part of the ordinary assessment of costs.

26.12 SA 1974, s 74(3) can be disregarded, therefore, for the purposes of most assessments. It is of potential relevance where a solicitor seeks to recover more than fixed costs in a case in which fixed costs would apply. Most fixed costs relate to pre-issue work (which is non-contentious), so even this limited sphere of influence is not as great as it first appears.

26.13 Moreover, CPR, r 48.8(1A) provides a mechanism by which the restriction can be disapplied by consent; it reads as follows:

> 'Section 74(3) of the Solicitors Act 1974(a) applies unless the solicitor and client have entered into a written agreement which expressly permits payment to the solicitor of an amount of costs greater than that which the client could have recovered from another party to the proceedings.'

In practice, many (if not most) well-written retainers contain a provision which addresses this point, so – for all practical purposes and taking into account the matters set out above – it would be an atypical case in which SA 1974, s 74(3) had an influence on the amount that a client had to pay his solicitor.

NON-CONTENTIOUS COSTS

26.14 Non-contentious costs are assessed on what can be termed the 'fair and reasonable basis'.[7] In reality, however, that basis is merely a sub-category of the indemnity basis (and is usually referred to as such: indeed, the phrase 'fair and reasonable basis' is rarely heard in practice). Nonetheless, whilst part of the same family,

---

[6]   *Lynch v Paul Davidson Taylor (a firm)* [2004] EWHC 89 (QB) at [15]–[19].

[7]   The term 'fair and reasonable basis' derives from art 3 of the Solicitors' (Non-Contentious Business) Remuneration Order 2009 and its predecessors; a pedant may object to the term on the basis that it does not describe the basis upon which costs are to be assessed, but merely one measure which comprises the appropriate basis. The term has in the past been used to describe other bases of assessment, so some caution must be exercised when it is encountered in older authorities.

it is distinguishable from other bases of assessment. Specifically, CPR, rr 44.4(3) and 44.5(3) are disapplied by r 44.4(6), which reads:

> 'Where the amount of a solicitor's remuneration in respect of non-contentious business is regulated by any general orders made under the Solicitors Act 1974, the amount of the costs to be allowed in respect of any such business which falls to be assessed by the court will be decided in accordance with those general orders rather than this rule and rule 44.5.'

26.15 Thus, the assessment of non-contentious costs does not have its foundations in the 'seven pillars of wisdom' in CPR, r 44.5(3), but in the very similar nine factors in art 3 of the Solicitors' (Non-Contentious Business) Remuneration Order 2009[8] ('the 2009 Order'):

> 'A solicitor's costs must be fair and reasonable having regard to all the circumstances of the case and in particular to—
>
> (a)   the complexity of the matter or the difficulty or novelty of the questions raised;
> (b)   the skill, labour, specialised knowledge and responsibility involved;
> (c)   the time spent on the business;
> (d)   the number and importance of the documents prepared or considered, without regard to length;
> (e)   the place where and the circumstances in which the business or any part of the business is transacted;
> (f)   the amount or value of any money or property involved;
> (g)   whether any land involved is registered land within the meaning of the Land Registration Act 2002;
> (h)   the importance of the matter to the client; and
> (i)   the approval (express or implied) of the entitled person or the express approval of the testator to—
>
> > (i)   the solicitor undertaking all or any part of the work giving rise to the costs; or
> > (ii)   the amount of the costs.'

It is worth noting that other jurisdictions have very similar lists; one of the most complete is a 12-point list used in United States.[9]

26.16 It can be seen that with one exception (namely, conduct), each of the seven pillars also appears in the nine factors (conduct does not apply because in most instances there would be no opposing parties and therefore there would be no occasion where issues of conduct may arise). The three further factors the court is to take into account are, firstly, the number and importance of the documents prepared or perused (without regard to

---

8   SI 2009/1931. Very similar provisions appeared in the Solicitors' Remuneration Order 1972 and the Solicitors' (Non-Contentious Business) Remuneration Order 1994.

9   That list is as follows (*Johnson v Georgia Highway Express* 488 F 2d 714 (1974)):

'(a) The time and labour required;
(b) The novelty and difficulty of the questions involved;
(c) The skill requisite to perform the legal service properly;
(d) The fact that acceptance of the case made it impossible to take on other cases;
(e) Any customary fee for similar work;
(f) Whether the fee was fixed or contingent;
(g) Any degree of urgency imposed by the client or the circumstances;
(h)The amount of money involved or awarded and the results obtained;
(i) The experience, reputation and ability of the attorney;
(j)The undesirability of being associated with the case;
(k)The nature and length of the professional relationship of the attorney with the client;
(l) Awards in similar cases.'

length),[10] secondly, whether any land involved is registered land and, thirdly, any approval given by the client (or person paying).

26.17 This last factor is amplified in CPR, r 48.8 which (in so far as it relates to non-contentious costs) makes the following provisions:

> '(1)   This rule applies to every assessment of a solicitor's bill to his client except a bill which is to be paid out of the Community Legal Service Fund under the Legal Aid Act 1988 or the Access to Justice Act 1999 – and
>
> (1A)   ...
>
> (2)   ... [C]osts are to be assessed on the indemnity basis but are to be presumed—
>
> > (a)   to have been reasonably incurred if they were incurred with the express or implied approval of the client;
> >
> > (b)   to be reasonable in amount if their amount was expressly or impliedly approved by the client;
> >
> > (c)   to have been unreasonably incurred if—
> >
> > > (i)   they are of an unusual nature or amount; and
> > >
> > > (ii)   the solicitor did not tell his client that as a result he might not recover all of them from the other party.'

(The presumptions created by CPR, r 48.8(2) are dealt with at **26.6**.)

26.18 Curiously, CPR, r 48.8 refers to the indemnity basis, yet the only definition of the indemnity basis in the CPR is in r 44.4 (which, as mentioned above, is a rule which specifically disapplies itself for the purposes of assessing non-contentious costs: see **26.14**). This is not a conundrum which is capable of causing any real interpretative difficulty, however, as there can be no doubt about what is meant by the indemnity basis.

26.19 For most practical purposes the basis of assessment of non-contentious costs is the same as that of contentious costs; the only significant difference is that the court needs to take into account nine factors rather than seven (see **26.16**). It is, perhaps, because of this similarity that the term 'fair and reasonable basis' is so infrequently heard (see **26.14**).

26.20 Although the *basis* of assessment of non-contentious costs might be almost the same as the basis on which contentious costs are assessed, the *method* of assessment is often markedly different. In particular, much greater emphasis is often placed on the value of money or property involved. This factor is often reflected in an element of charge known as the 'value element', which, if significant, will overshadow all other aspects of the assessment. Thus, whilst the law may be much the same regardless of whether the costs are contentious or non-contentious, the way in which the law is applied often varies markedly. That issue is considered in detail at **27.2–27.61**.

---

[10]   The prohibition against taking the length of documents into account has its origins in the need to deal with the problem which vexed ancient courts of lawyers writing overly long documents in order to enhance their fees; this is discussed in Chapter 1.

Chapter 27

QUANTUM BETWEEN SOLICITOR AND CLIENT

INTRODUCTION

27.1   The quantification of costs of contentious work is similar to that between opposing parties; this is a topic which is discussed elsewhere in this book (Part VI). The only significant differences between the methods described in Part VI and the methods of assessment between solicitor and client are, first, that the basis of assessment will be more generous between solicitor and client (see Chapter 26) and, second, that the court will look to the retainer rather than to section 4 of the CPD for guidance as to what is and what is not payable. This means that items such as incoming correspondence, photocopying, postage, etc, may or may not be chargeable, depending on the terms of the retainer. The assessment on non-contentious costs, however, is markedly different from the assessment of other species of costs (this being because of the existence of a type of charge known as the 'value charge': see **27.9**), and it is the topic of non-contentious costs which is the focus of the rest of this chapter.

The two components: hourly rates and value charges

27.2   Although there are many ways in which a solicitor may calculate his fees, two prevail as being the received methods; they are the hourly rate and the value charge. The term 'value charge' requires some explanation; this is because it needs to be distinguished from a related but distinct concept, namely the factor described by art 3(f) of the Solicitors' (Non-Contentious Business) Remuneration Order 2009.[1] That factor – the value of the money or property involved – may be reflected in a fee which is separate from and additional to the hourly rate, or it may be reflected in the hourly rate itself. In this chapter, the term 'value charge' is used to refer to the separate fee, and the term 'value element' to refer to the factor described by art 3(f) of the 2009 Order. This nomenclature is not standard and is adopted only for the purposes of description: the two terms are used interchangeably in other texts and in the authorities.

27.3   The next few paragraphs focus on the hourly rates and value charges individually, but it should be remembered that they are both facets of the same entity (ie fees for legal services) and that they must be ascertained collectively as well as individually. While there will inevitably be overlap between the hourly rate and the value charge, it is necessary to ensure that there is no duplication. Duplication may be disguised; where, for example, an allowance had already been made for complexity, value, time, and responsibility, Donaldson J found that it would be wrong also to give weight to the number of documents, as that would be to count those factors twice over.[2] Likewise, it is

---

[1]   SI 2009/1931.

[2]   *Property and Reversionary Investment Corpn Ltd v Secretary of State for the Environment* [1975] 2 All ER 436 at 442.

important to stand back and look at the overall charge so as to ensure that the total is not excessive;[3] to that extent, the hourly rates and the value charge will have to be assessed collectively. Longmore LJ had this to say (in the context of probate):[4]

> 'In an estate of small or medium value, it may be appropriate for a solicitor to limit his charges to a percentage of the estate's value or to charge a percentage together with an appropriately modest hourly rate. For a high-value estate it may also be appropriate to charge a percentage together with an hourly rate because, if one is to take value into account ... that will mean that the charges will have one element of comparative certainty. An hourly rate, although certain of itself, is subject to the variable that the number of hours worked cannot be ascertained until the business is completed. It must always be remembered that, once the business is completed, it is the solicitor's duty to have charged no more than is fair and reasonable in all the circumstances and the costs judge will be able to look at the matter in the round.'

The limited role of authority and comparators

27.4   Each case will be decided on its own facts. Donaldson J has explained that comparable cases are to be used only as a cross-check of the fairness and reasonableness of sums charged; it would be wrong in principle to seek to find a comparable case and then to adjust and correct it so that it can be used as a primary indicator of value.[5] To an extent this is true of all issues concerning costs, but it is especially true of non-contentious costs; this is because non-contentious costs turn more on what was agreed between solicitor and client than do other species of costs, which tend more to turn on what is inherently reasonable.

HOURLY RATES

27.5   Hourly rates are dealt with in detail in Part IV of this book; that discussion focuses on rates between the parties (see **28.1–28.79**) but in most regards the principles also apply to other species of costs such as those between solicitor and client. Regardless of the context (between the parties or otherwise) practitioners are encouraged to set a single rate inclusive of 'care and conduct'.[6] If the bases of assessment are put to one side for a moment, there is no great difference between the assessment of the hourly rate between opposing parties and the assessment of costs between solicitor and client. This is true of both contentious and non-contentious costs. The only other difference is that liability is governed by the retainer rather than by the CPD (although rates may be implied if not set out expressly),[7] and this may result in costs being levied for items such as incoming correspondence.

27.6   Notwithstanding these similarities in principle, the bases of assessment (and the presumptions in CPR, r 48.8 in particular: see **26.6**) make a significant difference in practice. In particular, if the hourly rates were agreed with the client, the presumption in CPR, r 48.8(2)(b) will weigh heavily in the solicitor's favour. For the reasons given in the previous chapter, that presumption is likely not to be rebuttable (see **26.7**). Given the fact that most hourly rates are set out in the client care letter together with a full

---

3   See *Treasury Solicitor v Regester* [1978] 1 WLR 446 at 450; see also, by analogy with the 'A plus B approach', *Leopold Lazarus Ltd v Secretary of State for Trade and Industry* (1976) Costs LR, Core vol 62.
4   *Jemma Trust Co Ltd v Liptrott* [2004] 1 WLR 646 at [24].
5   *Treasury Solicitor v Regester* [1978] 2 All ER 920 at 924.
6   See, for example, *Non-contentious costs: Practice Advice Service* (Law Society, August 2009), p 10.
7   *Ghadami v Lyon Cole Insurance Group Limited* [2010] EWCA Civ 767 at [27], per Lloyd LJ.

explanation of the proposed fees, it can, in practice, be very difficult for a client to avoid that presumption. The concept of 'informed approval' (see **26.7–26.8**) may afford some refuge, as (in extreme cases) would the doctrine of presumed undue influence (see **10.3–10.7**), but though the legal burden may lie with the solicitor for both of these things, in practice, a client would bear a heavy evidential burden of proving a prima facie case.

27.7 Another significant difference – concerning non-contentious costs, at least – is that the value element can be a significant factor. If the money or property involved is valuable, this may result in a high hourly rate or it may be result in a separate value charge (see below). There is a considerable degree of overlap between the hourly rate and the value charge in that they may both take into account similar factors, but they ought not to take into account the same factors; in particular, they should not both take into account the value element (see **27.3**).

27.8 The other relevant factors are those in the 2009 Order. Of those, two merit special attention: they are 'the adrenalin factor' (which is a factor arising out of a need to work under a time pressure: **27.14**), and 'the bath-time factor' (which is a factor which takes into account the contribution that a professional person's musings outside business hours – such as 'in the train or car home, or in the bath, or even whilst watching television'[8] – can make to the legal services provided: **27.16**). These are described in the context of the value charge, but they can also have a bearing on the hourly rate.

THE VALUE CHARGE

27.9 This topic is addressed in three parts: first, the principle of and justification for the value charge; second, factors other than value; and, third, the value element (ie the factor described in art 3(f) of the Solicitors' (Non-Contentious Business) Remuneration Order 2009). It is important to bear in mind the distinction between the value charge and the value element (see **27.2**).

Principle

27.10 The ascertainment of costs is simply a matter of measurement. Like all measurements, the starting point is to identify the relevant number of dimensions. Many species of costs are two dimensional (ie hourly rate and time spent), but non-contentious costs are often three dimensional (ie hourly rate, time spent, and value charge). The existence of this three-dimensional model means that different factors will be reflected to differing extents along one or more of the dimensions in such a way as to lead to a fee which, overall, is fair and reasonable. Thus, in a case which is low value but intensive of labour, the fee will be predominantly made up of a time charge (ie the product of the hourly rate and the time spent); in a case where large sums are involved and where time is a luxury, the time charge may be dwarfed by the value charge. The existence of the third dimension makes for a very flexible system of charging.

27.11 The notion of the value charge is ancient, but in recent times it has been challenged as being so ancient as to be anachronistic. It was said that the value element can be reflected in the hourly rate, this being the more modern way of measuring costs. The Court of Appeal rejected that argument. In essence, Longmore LJ noted that there

---

[8]   *Maltby v DJ Freeman & Co* [1978] 1 WLR 431 at 435, per Walton J.

are significant differences between contentious and non-contentious business and that those differences explain and justify the value charge.[9] Whilst recognising that value charges continued to have a role to play, he cautioned that the solicitor must address himself to whether the overall remuneration is fair and reasonable, taking into account all the relevant factors set out in (the then equivalent of) the 2009 Order.

27.12 As to the need to avoid over-preoccupation with the twin dimensions of time spent and rate charged, Donaldson J had the following to say:[10]

> 'The magnetic attraction of [the time spent] as a foundation for assessment of fair and reasonable remuneration is that, in the absence of an approved scale applied to value, it is the only figure which is readily calculable. It is an attraction which must be sternly resisted in cases of this sort where one or more of the other factors is such as to dwarf it into insignificance.'

Thus, there is a need to give appropriate weight to all of the factors in the 2009 Order:[11] it would be a mistake to focus solely on time. Donaldson J continued:

> 'This is not to say that the calculation [of time] has no value. It has a real value in all cases. Thus, if calculated accurately, it informs a solicitor of the minimum figure which he must charge if he is not to make an actual loss on the transaction. Second, it gives him an idea of the relationship between the overheads attributable to the transaction and the profit accruing to him. This latter point is plainly relevant in the broad sense that the nature of some transactions will justify much larger profits than others of a more routine type. But we must stress that it is only one of a number of crosschecks on the fairness and reasonableness of the final figure. The final figure will result from an exercise in judgment, not arithmetic, whatever arithmetical cross-checks may be employed.'

The correct approach is a matter of judgment rather than logic; it is to take into account all of the relevant circumstances without giving inappropriate weight to any of them.

The weight to be given to factors other than value

27.13 The value charge will usually take into account the value of the money or property involved, but value is not the only aspect of the business which is relevant. Any one of the factors listed in the Solicitors' (Non-Contentious Business) Remuneration Order 2009 might be germane (see **26.15**). Two aspects in particular are often afforded weight: they are 'the adrenalin factor' and 'the bath-time factor'. Each is considered in turn:

The adrenalin factor

27.14 The adrenalin factor is that factor which becomes relevant when the solicitor is required to work under a time pressure with little or no margin for error. It can be

---

9   In summary, Longmore LJ noted that with contentious business it is usually difficult to ascribe a 'value' to the money or property involved; he also commented that in contentious business it is ordinarily necessary to know the charges at the outset (because that information will be required for providing costs estimates, recovering the costs of interim hearings, etc), whereas the same is not true of non-contentious work, where the charges can be assessed at conclusion on a basis which is fair and reasonable in all the circumstances.

10 *Treasury Solicitor v Regester* [1978] 1 WLR 446 at 450.

11 This sentiment was recently affirmed by the Court of Appeal: *Jemma Trust Co Ltd v Liptrott* [2004] 1 WLR 646 at 656.

categorised within either art 3(e) of the 2009 Order (place and circumstance) or art 3(h) (importance), or both. Donaldson J described it in this way:[12]

> '[W]hat was the factor or factors, if any, which distinguished this transaction from the general run of such transactions. The answer was clearly the "adrenalin" factor. By this we mean that the solicitor had not only to work fast but had absolutely no margin for error. The transaction had to be completed by 31 July, come what might ... This caused us to look towards the top rather than the bottom of the bracket. In a different case, we might have found that there was plenty of time and that the transaction was very similar to one with which the solicitors had previously been concerned for the same client. This would have caused us to look in a reverse direction.'

27.15 The adrenalin factor may be reflected in the hourly rate or the value charge; the latter would be particularly appropriate when, as would often be the case, the time pressure was such that the solicitor did not have the luxury of being able to devote as much time to the matter as he would have liked.

Bath-time factor

27.16 The bath-time factor can be categorised as being within art 3(b) of the 2009 Order (ie the skill, labour, specialised knowledge and responsibility involved), but it could also be said to be a time charge in a different guise (ie art 3(c)). It was described by Walton J in these terms:[13]

> 'In a good many cases – although by no means all – [the actual time recorded] the logical starting point, in that it gives in itself a good indication of the weight of the matter as a whole. I would, however, make one gloss; however meticulously time records are kept, this will always, save in the plainest of all possible cases, represent an undercharge. No professional man, or senior employee of a professional man, stops thinking about the day's problems the minute he lifts his coat and umbrella from the stand and sets on the journey home. Ideas – often very valuable ideas – occur in the train or car home, or in the bath, or even whilst watching television. Yet nothing is ever put down on a time sheet – or can be put down on a time sheet – adequately to reflect this out of hours devotion of time. Thus, it will be a rare bill which can be simply compounded of time and value; there must always be a third element – usually under the second head.'

27.17 Thus, the bath-time factor reflects the fact that no matter how accurate a solicitor's time recording system might be, it will not record time spent thinking about the client's affairs while going about other business. Donaldson J held a similar view, but he expressed it by cautioning against giving excessive weight to the time which has been recorded rather than by recommending that an affirmative adjustment be made for time not recorded:[14]

> 'It also follows that it is wrong always to start by assessing the direct and indirect expense to the solicitor, represented by the time spent on the business. This must always be taken into account, but it is not necessarily, or even usually, a basic factor to which all others are related. Thus, although the labour involved will usually be directly related to, and reflected by, the time spent, the skill and specialised knowledge involved may vary greatly for different parts of that time. Again not all time spent on a transaction necessarily lends itself to being recorded, although the fullest possible records should be kept.'

---

[12]   *Treasury Solicitor v Regester* [1978] 2 All ER 920 at 926.
[13]   *Maltby v DJ Freeman & Co* [1978] 1 WLR 431 at 435.
[14]   *Property and Reversionary Investment Corporation Ltd v Secretary of State for the Environment* [1975] 1 WLR 1504, recited by Donaldson J in *Treasury Solicitor v Regester* [1978] 1 WLR 446.

27.18 As with the adrenalin factor, the bath-time factor may be reflected in either the hourly rate or the value charge. For the reasons set out at **27.3** it would usually not be appropriate to reflect it in both.

The weight to be given to value

27.19 The Law Society recommends that in certain areas, such as probate, mortgages, commercial leases and domestic conveyancing, it may be appropriate to include a value element in the method of charging.[15] The value element may be included within the hourly rate or as a separate charge, but that it ought not to be reflected in both (see **27.3**).

27.20 The Law Society recommends that where there is no specific guidance in the individual subject area, the following charges – known as the 'general regressive scale' – may assist in formulating an overall charging structure:

Value band	Percentage
Up to £400,000	0.5 percent
On next £600,000 (maximum value £1 million)	0.375 percent
On next £1,500,000 (maximum value £2.5 million)	0.25 percent
On next £2,500,000 (maximum value £5 million)	0.125 percent
On next £5,000,000 (maximum value £10 million)	0.1 percent

27.21 The following practice areas merit particular mention: probate and estates, domestic conveyancing, leasehold work, and acting on a mortgage (or remortgage).

Probate and estates

27.22 The Law Society recommends[16] that the estate is divided into two parts: the value of the deceased's residence and the value of the rest of the estate. Where the solicitor is not acting as an executor, a value charge of 1% of the value of the gross estate less residence plus 0.5% of the value of the residence would be reasonable. Where the solicitor is acting as an executor, these figures could reasonably rise to 1.5% and 0.75% respectively. Where the estate has a high value, then the following regressive scale may be appropriate:[17]

Value	Percentage
Up to £1 million	1.5 percent
£1 million to £4 million	0.5 percent

---

15   *Non-contentious costs: Practice Advice Service* (Law Society, August 2009), p 8.
16   *Non-contentious costs: Practice Advice Service* (Law Society, August 2009), pp 10 and 11.
17   *Jemma Trust Co Ltd v Liptrott* [2004] 1 WLR 646 at 656, affirming the approach originally articulated by Walton J in *Maltby v D J Freeman & Co* [1978] 1 WLR 431.

Value	Percentage
£4 million to £8 million	0.1666 percent
£8 million to £12 million	0.0833 percent
Over £12 million	0.0416 percent

(This scale is based on work done in 2003. Presumably, it will be updated from time to time.)

Domestic conveyancing

27.23 The Law Society recommends[18] either taking a broad view of the circumstances, or applying the general regressive scale (above).

Leasehold work

27.24 It would be reasonable to charge an hourly rate and a value charge. The value charge can be calculated by taking half the yearly rent, multiplying it by the unexpired term of the lease (limited to 20 years), then adding any premium payable by the lessee and deducting any payable by the lessor, and then applying the general regressive scale (above). The resultant figure should then be reviewed to ensure that it is fair and reasonable, having regard to all the circumstances.[19]

Acting on a mortgage or remortgage

27.25 Many lenders have their own scales, but where this is not the case the Law Society suggests the following may be appropriate in cases other than very high value cases:[20]

When acting for purchaser/mortgagor	0.25 percent
When acting for the mortgagee alone	0.5 percent
When acting for purchaser/mortgagor	0.25 percent
When acting for the mortgagee alone	0.5 percent

SHODDY WORK

27.26 It has long been established that a legal representative cannot recover his costs from his client where deficient professional performance has negated the benefit of that work;[21] this is an example of the doctrine of abatement. The right of abatement will arise where a trader claims fees, but the customer has an unliquidated counterclaim

---

18 *Non-contentious costs: Practice Advice Service* (Law Society, August 2009), pp 11 and 12.
19 *Non-contentious costs: Practice Advice Service* (Law Society, August 2009), p 12.
20 *Non-contentious costs: Practice Advice Service* (Law Society, August 2009), p 13.
21 *In re Massey and Carey* (1884) 26 Ch D 459; as a modern example of this (albeit it one concerning a barrister

against him arising out of a breach of the contract for the supply of those services; where those are the circumstances, the customer may be entitled to deduct his counterclaim. It is a right which is a true defence at common law,[22] and is distinct from set-off.[23] (That said, there would be no reason why set-off could not be pleaded in the alternative.) Where a client wishes to rely on a right of abatement, he must show that the breach of contract directly reduced the value of the services rendered;[24] therefore, not all counterclaims arising out of a solicitor – client relationship would suffice, but a counterclaim for shoddy work would ordinarily be capable of passing that test.

27.27 Abatement is an ancient doctrine, but in a modern context the solicitor's fees would either be diminished by a counterclaim, or they would be assessed as being nil or close to nil as a result of the value of the work being negated by the solicitor's shortcomings. The principles set out above would not operate to diminish the costs incurred prior to the provision of deficient services.[25] Some retainers seek to preclude the client from claiming abatement or set-off for shoddy work (or at all); such provisions are probably not enforceable.[26]

SA 1974, s 63(3)

27.28 There is another mechanism by which the court is able to take shoddy work into account, but it is available only where the work has been carried out under a contentious business agreement, and, even then, only when the client changes solicitors before the solicitor has fully performed his obligations. In those circumstances SA 1974, s 63(3) may apply. That subsection reads:

> 'If [where the client changes solicitors] an order is made for the assessment of the amount due to the solicitor in respect of the business done under the agreement, the court shall direct the costs officer to have regard to the circumstances under which the change of solicitor has taken place, and the costs officer, unless he is of the opinion that there has been no default, negligence, improper delay or other conduct on the part of the solicitor, or any of his employees, affording the client reasonable ground for changing his solicitor, shall not allow to the solicitor the full amount of the remuneration agreed to be paid to him.'

27.29 This provision permits the court to take account of default or negligence, so presumably it allows the court to take account of substandard work. It is clear that negligence can be taken into account in such a way as to reduce the solicitor's fees to a level which is lower than they would have been had the agreement been fully performed. What is less clear is whether the court is able to take that conduct into account in such a way as to allow a figure which is lower than the amount which is a reasonable amount: it is arguable that the court does have this power, but there is no authority to confirm that.

---

instructed directly rather than a solicitor) see *Dunn v Glass Systems (UK) Ltd* [2007] EWHC 1901 (QB) in which fees were disallowed on the basis that they were for drafting prolix pleadings that would have led to the litigation being unmanageable.

22   Although there is no modern authority relating to solicitors, it is probable that the true defence mentioned above is unaffected by the laws relating to limitation: see Limitation Act 1980, s 35(3).

23   See *Mondel v Steel* (1841) 8 M & W and *Aries Tanker Corpn v Total Transport Ltd* [1977] 1 WLR 185, HL; as to the principles by which legal set-off may operate as a defence, see *Hanak v Green* [1958] 2 QB 9 at 16.

24   *Mellowes Archital Ltd v Bell Properties Ltd* (1997) 87 BLR 26, CA.

25   *Lewis v Samuel* (1846) 8 QB 685.

26   Although not a costs case, see *Hong Kong & Shanghai Banking Corpn v Kloeckner & Co AG* [1990] 2 QB 514.

Ombudsman

27.30 Although not a remedy which is within the power of the court, a facility exists by which a client may complain to the Legal Ombudsman (previously known as the Legal Services Ombudsman) for the purposes of obtaining a reduction in the fees payable. The relevant provisions are discussed at **19.48–19.56**. This procedure was introduced at broadly the same time as the long-standing provisions concerning inadequate professional services were revoked;[27] this was probably no coincidence as it is clear that the Ombudsman has the powers to deal with shoddy work.

ESTIMATES AND ASSURANCES ON A SOLICITOR AND CLIENT BASIS

27.31 The following discussion explicates two topics: first, the extent to which a client is able to rely on the fact that an estimate has been exceeded (or not been given when it ought to have been, as the case may be) and, secondly, the extent to which a client is able to rely on an assurance (be it express or implied) that legal services would be provided in a particular manner (such as by a particular grade of fee earner or by a particular person).

Duty to give an estimate

27.32 There are many ways in which a duty to provide an estimate may arise. It may be a professional duty; it may arise as a result of the giving of specific instructions or under the rules of court; it may arise under the common law; and, finally, it may arise under an agreed term in the retainer. Any of these duties may be relevant to the assessment of costs, but the first (professional duty) is particularly relevant. This is because it will exist in all cases. The extent and nature of the professional duty will turn on when the estimate was, or should have been, given.

Pre-1 July 2007 professional duties

27.33 Prior to 1 July 2007 a solicitor's obligations arose out of the Solicitors' Costs Information and Client Care Code 1999 ('the 1999 Code'). The solicitor in question was under an obligation to give the client the 'best information possible' about the likely overall costs, including a breakdown between fees, VAT and disbursements.[28] There was a requirement that all information given orally was confirmed in writing.[29]

27.34 Where the fee was based on time spent, the solicitor was under an obligation to explain clearly the time that was likely to be spent in dealing with a matter.[30] Giving 'the best information possible' would have included:[31]

- agreeing a fixed fee;
- giving a realistic estimate;

---

[27] Those provisions were contained in SA 1974, s 37A, and were repealed by the Legal Services Act 2007, ss 177 and 210, Sch 16, Part 1, paras 1 and 39 and Sch 23; this happened on 1 January 2009.

[28] Paragraph 4(a) of the Solicitors' Costs Information and Client Care Code 1999 ('the 1999 Code').

[29] The 1999 Code, paras 3(a)–(c).

[30] The 1999 Code, para 4(b).

[31] The 1999 Code, para 4(c).

- giving a forecast within a possible range of costs; or
- explaining to the client the reasons why it is not possible to fix, or give a realistic estimate or forecast of, the overall costs, and giving instead the best information possible about the cost of the next stage of the matter.

27.35 Where the client was a privately paying client, the solicitor was at liberty to tell him that he could set an upper limit on the solicitor's costs for which he might be liable without further authority; this would appear not to have been a mandatory requirement. Where such a limit was set, it should not have been (and still should not be) exceeded without first obtaining the client's consent.[32] The solicitor ought to have made it clear at the outset if an estimate, quotation or other indication of cost was not intended to be fixed.[33]

27.36 A cost-benefit analysis ought to have been carried out, and the solicitor in question was required to discuss whether the likely outcome in a matter justified the expense or risk involved.[34]

27.37 The solicitor ought to have kept the client properly informed about costs as the matter progressed and, in particular:[35]

- unless agreed otherwise, the solicitor ought to have said how much the costs were; this ought to have been done at regular intervals (at least every 6 months);
- the solicitor ought to have explained any changed circumstances which were likely to have had a bearing on the amount of costs, the degree of risk involved, or the cost-benefit to the client of continuing with the matter; and
- the solicitor ought to have informed the client in writing as soon as it appeared that a costs estimate or agreed upper limit might or would be exceeded.

Professional duties between 1 July 2007 and 5 October 2011

27.38 Between 1 July 2007 and 5 October 2011 the matter has been governed by the Solicitors' Code of Conduct 2007 ('the 2007 Code'). During that period the solicitor continued to have a duty to give the best information possible about the likely overall cost of a matter at the outset. Any information about costs ought to have been clear and confirmed in writing[36] and ought to have been given as soon as possible after the solicitor had agreed to act.[37] In so far as estimates were concerned, the solicitor was required to:[38]

- advise the client of the basis and terms of the solicitor's charges;
- advise the client if charging rates are to be increased;
- advise the client of likely payments which may need to be made; and
- discuss with the client how the client will pay, in particular:
    - whether the client may be eligible and should apply for public funding; and

---

[32] The 1999 Code, para 4(d).
[33] The 1999 Code, para 4(e).
[34] The 1999 Code, para 4(k).
[35] The 1999 Code, paras 6(a)–(d).
[36] Paragraph 2.03(5) of the Solicitors' Code of Conduct 2007 ('the 2007 Code') and para 27 of the notes thereto.
[37] Paragraph 18 of the notes to para 2.03 of the Solicitors' Code of Conduct 2007.
[38] The 2007 Code, para 2.03(1).

  –   whether the client's own costs are covered by insurance or may be paid by
        someone else, such as an employer or trade union.

There was a requirement to carry out a cost-benefit analysis; In particular, the solicitor
was required to discuss with his client whether the potential outcomes of the case
justified the expense or risk involved, including, if relevant, the risk of having to pay an
opponent's costs.[39] The solicitor was not required to give information where it was
inappropriate to do so.[40]

Professional duties on and after 6 October 2011

27.39 The present-day provisions are contained in the SRA Code of Conduct 2011;
they are not as prescriptive as the provisions that preceded them. They are as follows:

> 'You must achieve these outcomes:
>
> **O(1.12)** clients are in a position to make informed decisions about the services they need,
> how their matter will be handled and the options available to them;
>
> **O(1.13)** clients receive the best possible information, both at the time of engagement and
> when appropriate as their matter progresses, about the likely overall cost of their matter;
>
> ...
>
> Acting in the following way(s) may tend to show that you have achieved these outcomes and
> therefore complied with the *Principles*:
>
> **IB(1.13)** discussing whether the potential outcomes of the client's matter are likely to justify
> the expense or risk involved, including any risk of having to pay someone else's legal fees;
>
> **IB(1.14)** clearly explaining your fees and if and when they are likely to change;
>
> **IB(1.15)** warning about any other payments for which the client may be responsible;
>
> **IB(1.16)** discussing how the client will pay, including whether public funding may be
> available, whether the client has insurance that might cover the fees, and whether the fees
> may be paid by someone else such as a trade union;
>
> **IB(1.17)** where you are acting for a client under a fee arrangement governed by statute, such
> as a conditional fee agreement, giving the client all relevant information relating to that
> arrangement;
>
> **IB(1.18)** where you are acting for a publicly funded client, explaining how their publicly
> funded status affects the costs;
>
> **IB(1.19)** providing the information in a clear and accessible form which is appropriate to the
> needs and circumstances of the client.'

27.40 It is not known how the court will interpret these provisions. Notwithstanding
the shift from a prescriptive approach to an outcome-based approach, similarities with

---

[39]   The 2007 Code, para 2.03(6).
[40]   Paragraph 18 of the notes to para 2.03 of the 2007 Code.

the previous incarnations of the Code of Conduct are far greater than the differences. Solicitors would be storing up trouble for themselves if they were not to set themselves high standards in this regard.[41]

Non-professional duties

27.41 In addition to the professional duties mentioned above, there are other ways in which a duty to give estimates may (or may not) arise; these include the following

Contract (duty to give estimate)

27.42 In the ordinary run of things, the fact that the aforesaid professional duties exist would not give rise to a corresponding implied contractual duty[42] (see **27.56**). Each case will turn on its own facts and duties may arise out of express or implied terms within the retainer.

Contract (limitation of retainer)

27.43 Again, in the ordinary run of things, a failure to comply with the aforesaid professional duties would not limit ambit of the retainer.[43]

Rules of court and practice directions

27.44 Where an estimate is served and filed in court proceedings, the CPD provides that the solicitor must also serve the estimate on the client;[44] this includes the circumstances where the estimate is served by reason of a change in the funding arrangement.[45] Where an estimate is of the sort used for costs budgeting, further provisions apply (see **15.79**), albeit it to estimates that have been approved by the court.

General consumer law

27.45 A solicitor is under an obligation not to give an unrealistic estimate in order to secure the work. If he fails in this regard, then he will be guilty of a criminal offence.[46] This does not give rise to a duty affirmatively to give an estimate, however.

---

[41]   By way of example, in *Darby v Law Society* [2003] EWHC 2270 (Admin) at [27], Auld LJ (sitting the Divisional Court) said that there was a heavy onus on a solicitor to establish that his client is so sophisticated in matters of litigation, and so attentive to the cost implications of the litigation in question, that the then requirements (under the SPR 1990) to give information about costs could be disregarded.

[42]   *Mastercigars Direct Ltd v Withers LLP* [2007] EWHC 2733 (Ch) at [107]–[111].

[43]   *Mastercigars Direct Ltd v Withers LLP* [2007] EWHC 2733 (Ch) at [107]–[111].

[44]   CPD, art 6.4(1). The relevant provision read as follows:'(1) When –
(a) a party to a claim which is outside the financial scope of either the small claims track or the fast track files an allocation questionnaire; or
(b) a party to a claim which is being dealt with on the fast track or the multi track files a pre-trial check list (listing questionnaire),
that party must also file an estimate of costs and serve a copy of it on every other party, unless the court otherwise directs. Where a party is represented, that party's legal representative must in addition serve a copy of the estimate on that party.
(2) Where a party who is required to file and serve a new estimate of costs in accordance with Rule 44.15(3), is represented; and the legal representative must in addition serve the new estimate on that party.
(3) This paragraph does not apply to litigants in person.'

[45]   See CPD, art 6.4(2) and CPR, r 44.15(3).

[46]   See Part III of the Consumer Protection Act 1987, ss 20 and 21 which deals with misleading price indications.

Instructions

27.46 Where the client gives instructions which expressly or impliedly require that an estimate be given, that will create a duty which may be relevant, especially if the client can show reliance.

Relevance of estimate

27.47 It will rarely be the case that a figure intended to be an estimate would be regarded as being a binding quote.[47] The relevance of any such figure would be a matter of contractual interpretation, to be decided on the facts of the matter in hand.

27.48 While a pedant would say that the law was merely clarified rather than changed, in 2007 there was a shift in the juridical approach towards cases in which estimates had been exceeded.[48] In order to understand that shift, it is necessary to know something of the history of the law. The starting point is the approach adopted by Toulson J in (*Wong v Vizards*),[49] that case being unusual only by reason of the fact that an estimate had been exceeded; Toulson J found that it was permissible to reduce the allowable costs to the level of the estimate, and then to add back an allowance which 'effectively allowed to the solicitor a margin of approximately 15% over the worst case estimate.' This gave rise to a method of assessing costs on a solicitor and client assessment where the court would allow the figure stated in the estimate plus a margin, typically between 10% and 20%.[50]

27.49 In 2007, Morgan J clarified the law in such a way as to discourage the use of that method. He explained that Toulson J was not expounding a point of principle;[51] he held that where an estimate has been exceeded, the approach is not to allow the figure in the estimate to be adjusted by a margin, but to use the estimate as a yardstick by which the reasonableness of the costs finally claimed may be measured:[52]

> 'This is not to say that I would reject altogether the idea that a margin might offer something useful. As I indicated earlier, when saying that an excess of the final bill over the estimate calls for an explanation, this reaction is heavily dependent upon the extent of the excess. A modest excess does not call for much explanation and a substantial excess calls for a great deal of explanation.'

Morgan J was at pains to point out that his comments were not in any way at odds with what Toulson J had said previously.[53]

27.50 Morgan J's approach appears at first to be different from the approach between opposing parties (where the CPD specifically mentions a margin of 20%), but in truth they are the same. This is because the 20% is simply a threshold beyond which an explanation is required; if that explanation is unsatisfactory, then the amount by which

---

[47] *Wong v Vizards* [1997] 2 Costs LR 46 at 48.

[48] Some commentators have said that the law has not been clarified, but that there is simply a divergence of judicial option; see, for example, Morgan J 'Estimating the Damage' (2009) *Litigation Funding* 60, April, pp 14–15.

[49] [1997] 2 Costs LR 46.

[50] See, for example, *Reynolds v Stone Rowe Brewer (a firm)* [2008] EWHC 497 and *Anthony v Ellis & Fairburn (a firm)* [2000] 2 Costs LR 277.

[51] *Mastercigars Direct Ltd v Withers LLP* [2007] EWHC 2733 (Ch) at [118].

[52] *Mastercigars Direct Ltd v Withers LLP* [2007] EWHC 2733 (Ch) at [104].

[53] See *Wong v Vizards* [1997] 2 Costs LR 46 at 49.

the estimate has been exceeded will be a factor that the court will take into account. It will not operate as a cap, either on a solicitor and client basis,[54] or between opposing parties.

27.51 Morgan J's approach invites the obvious question of whether the court is at liberty to allow an amount which is lower than the amount that would be justified on a line-by-line assessment; whilst obiter, he confirmed that it was:[55]

> '[E]ven if the solicitor has spent a reasonable time on reasonable items of work and the charging rate is reasonable, the resulting figure may exceed what it is reasonable in all the circumstances to expect the client to pay and, to the extent that the figure does exceed what is reasonable to expect the client to pay, the excess is not recoverable.'

Thus, the test is what it is reasonable to expect the client to pay. To that extent, the client does not need to show that he relied upon the estimate for the court to take the estimate into account. Where, presumably, the client is able to show reliance, then the court would give greater weight to that estimate.

27.52 The following miscellaneous points can be made about estimates.

Revised estimates

27.53 Where a revised estimate is given in an attempt to correct an underestimate (as opposed to being given as a result of a change in the facts), then it is open to the court to find that weight should be given to the original rather than to the revised estimate.[56]

Qualified estimates

27.54 In a case in which the client sought to justify his failure to pay an interim invoice on the grounds that an estimate had been exceeded, Ward LJ had to consider the effect of the following qualification:[57]

> 'We only give estimates as a guide. Thus we will make every attempt to ensure their accuracy, we cannot guarantee that the final charge will not exceed the estimate. This is because there are many factors outside our control which may affect the level of costs'

Ward LJ had the following to say about the effect of this qualification:[58]

> 'The complaint that the bill exceeded the estimate cannot stand in the face of the fact that [the above provision] made [it] plain ... that estimates were not intended to be fixed or binding and that other factors might mean that the estimate would be varied from time to time.'

It would be wrong to read too much into this ratio. This is because Ward LJ was dealing with a refusal to pay interim invoices in a case in which there were very good reasons for the estimate having been exceeded; that is a very different from the more common situation in which the estimate was not adequately revised or was palpably unrealistic

---

54   *Mastercigars Direct Ltd v Withers LLP* [2007] EWHC 2733 (Ch) at [106].
55   *Mastercigars Direct Ltd v Withers LLP* [2007] EWHC 2733 (Ch) at [102].
56   *Reynolds v Stone Rowe Brewer (a firm)* [2008] EWHC 497 at [67] *et seq.*
57   *Cawdery Kaye Fireman & Taylor v Minkin* [2012] EWCA Civ 546 at [7].
58   *Cawdery Kaye Fireman & Taylor v Minkin* [2012] EWCA Civ 546 at [336].

from the very outset. In the context of a conditional estimate (that being an estimate such as 'if the matter settles after exchange of pleadings ...') Sir Oliver Poppelwell found that the conditionality of the estimate did not give rise to implied authority that it may be exceeded with impunity.[59]

Incomplete estimates

27.55 While dealing with the interpretation of a contract rather that the effect of an estimate, Hughes LJ has indicated that if a client is not told about a potential liability for costs, he will not be required to pay them.[60] The extent to which this applies to estimates is not known.

The effect of a failure to give a revised estimate

27.56 Although each case will turn on its own facts, Morgan J found that there was no basis for saying that the requirements to provide updated costs information were impliedly incorporated within the retainer with the effect that the solicitor was contractually obliged to provide updated costs information.[61] The facts of the case before Morgan H were unremarkable, so whilst he was not laying down a principle of law, there would be no reason to believe that similarly quotidian cases would be dealt with any differently. Morgan J went on to find that the ambit of the retainer was not limited in such a way that the estimate defined the work for which a charge might be made.[62] Thus a failure to give a revised estimate would seem to be nothing more than a factor to be taken into account.

Putative waiver

27.57 Whilst waiver of fees would clearly be a factor that the court could take into account for assessing the amount payable, if a client is to rely on waiver as negating the solicitor's contractual right to payment, the waiver must be supported by consideration. In this regard Tugendhat J has held that the mere fact that a promise not to raise a fee would was capable of being advantageous to the promisor did not amount to consideration.[63] Likewise, the act of writing-off costs for taxation purposes would not extinguish the contractual right to payment.[64]

Assurances about how services will be provided

27.58 In the same way that a client can expect to be given reasonably accurate information about costs, he is also entitled to receive reasonably accurate information about the way in which it is proposed that the legal services be provided. In particular, he should be told the status of the person who is carrying out the work.[65] Although only of persuasive value, the notes to the 2007 Code give the following guidance:[66]

---

[59] *Anthony v Ellis & Fairburn (a firm)* [2000] 2 Costs LR 277 at 283.
[60] In *Jones v Wrexham Borough Council* [2007] EWCA Civ 1356 at [94].
[61] *Mastercigars Direct Ltd v Withers LLP* [2007] EWHC 2733 (Ch) at [107]–[111].
[62] *Mastercigars Direct Ltd v Withers LLP* [2007] EWHC 2733 (Ch) at [112].
[63] *Ashia Centur Ltd v Barker Gillette LLP* [2011] EWHC 148 (QB) at [20].
[64] *Slatter v Ronaldsons* [2002] 2 Costs LR 267.
[65] The 2007 Code, para 2.02(2).
[66] See para 19 of the Guidance to para 2.02 of the 2007 Code; a similar provision existed prior to 1 July 2007 (see r 15(2)(a) of the Solicitors Practice Rules 1990).

'The status of the person dealing with your client must be made absolutely clear, for legal and ethical reasons. For example, a person who is not a solicitor must not be described as one, either expressly or by implication. All staff having contact with clients, including reception, switchboard and secretarial staff, should be advised accordingly.'

27.59 There are two circumstances in which this requirement may become relevant to the issue of costs: the first is where the client has made a specific request concerning the provision of legal services and that request is not met, and the second is where the solicitor's conduct has led to a reasonable expectation about the way in which legal services will be provided: each is dealt with in turn.

Specific request

27.60 Failure to comply with a specific request made by the client may result in total non-performance of the solicitor's obligations under the contract of retainer. Where the client had asked for a solicitor but got an unqualified fee earner, Schiemann LJ found that the solicitors were at fault in that the client ought to have been told of the status of the fee earner who was doing the work. He found that the fact that the client had asked to see a solicitor had resulted in the retainer being a contract for the provision of legal services *by a solicitor*; he found that the purported performance of the contract by someone other than a solicitor was no performance at all, and that therefore no costs were payable.[67] Underhill J has found that, in an appropriate case, the question will turn on the client's knowledge both at the time he first gave instructions and throughout the retainer generally; the implication of this is that if a client becomes aware of the true status of the person providing the legal services, and if he continues to accept those services without demur, he will find it difficult to persuade the court that the services were not the same as those he required.[68] As to the types of evidence that might be relevant, see **27.61**. Underhill J also raised the question of whether adequate supervision by a solicitor may, in certain circumstances, amount to the provision of legal services by a solicitor; he made no findings in that regard, but he implied that this was possible.[69]

Solicitor's conduct

27.61 The expectation that the work be done in a certain way or by a certain person may arise from the conduct of the solicitor. In a case where a fee earner had said he was a practising solicitor when in fact he was not, Brooke LJ found that the fee earner had misrepresented his status and that this had created a situation similar to that which is mentioned above (see **27.60**).[70] Whilst he was dealing with a case in which there had been a specific request, Underhill J explained that the court's findings will be based on all of the circumstances and not just that which is in the client care letter;[71] the facts he took into account included the following: the fee earner's standard professional practice as to whether he would explain his status to his clients; the client's reaction on learning of the true status of the fee earner; and any note about the fee earner's status on the firm's letterhead.[72]

---

[67]   *Pilbrow v Pearless de Rougement & Co* [1999] 3 All ER 355.
[68]   *Manches LLP v Green (tla Green Denman & Co)* [2008] EWHC 917 (QB) at [71], per Underhill J.
[69]   *Manches LLP v Green (tla Green Denman & Co)* [2008] EWHC 917 (QB) at [70], per Underhill J.
[70]   *Adrian Alan Ltd v Fuglers* [2002] EWCA Civ 1655.
[71]   *Manches LLP v Green (tla Green Denman & Co)* [2008] EWHC 917 (QB) at [83], per Underhill J.
[72]   *Manches LLP v Green (tla Green Denman & Co)* [2008] EWHC 917 (QB) at [84], per Underhill J.

INTEREST BETWEEN SOLICITOR AND CLIENT

27.62 The following paragraphs should be read in conjunction with Chapter 36; these comments are a coda to that chapter in that they add one or two specific points about interest that relate to solicitor and client.

27.63 Unless interest is allowed under the court's statutory powers to make a discretionary award (see **36.35–36.36**), interest will be payable on a contractual basis in accordance with the terms of the retainer. In so far as non-contentious costs are concerned, there is also delegated legislation which allows interest to be awarded on unpaid fees (see **27.65–27.67**). It is a moot point whether that right is enforceable as a direct right conferred by legislation or indirectly by way of an implied contractual right; it is probably the former.[73]

27.64 Mr Nugee QC (sitting as a deputy judge of the High Court) has determined that unless he had informed his client that the law would not otherwise enable him to claim such a rate, a solicitor is not able to enforce a provision for interest at a rate markedly higher than would allowed by the court under s 35A of the Senior Courts Act 1981.[74] A solicitor is not able to divert monies paid on account in such a way as to leave disbursements unpaid (and therefore attracting interest).[75]

Interest on non-contentious costs

27.65 In so far as bills delivered on or after 11 August 2009 are concerned, art 5 of the Solicitors' (Non-Contentious Business) Remuneration Order 2009 makes the following default provisions:

'Interest

5(1)   A solicitor may charge interest on the unpaid amount of his costs plus any paid disbursements and value added tax, subject to the remainder of this article.

(2)   Where an entitlement to interest arises under paragraph (1), and subject to any agreement made between a solicitor and client, the period for which interest may be charged runs from one month after the date of delivery of a bill.

(3)   Subject to any agreement made between a solicitor and client, the rate of interest must not exceed the rate for the time being payable on judgment debts.

(4)   Interest charged under this article must be calculated, where applicable, by reference to—

    (a)   the amount specified in a determination of costs by the Law Society under Schedule 1A to the Solicitors Act 1974;

    (b)   the amount ascertained on taxation if an application has been made for the bill to be taxed.'

As such, a client is afforded a period of grace of one month.

27.66 It is possible for a client to agree interest in such a way as to create a non-contentious business agreement relating to interest; such an agreement may be

---

[73]   See *Walton v Egan* [1982] 3 WLR 352.
[74]   *Clifford Harris & Co v Solland International Ltd* [2005] EWHC 141 (Ch) at [50].
[75]   *Hartland v Murrell* (1873) LR 16 Eq 285.

enforced in just the same way as any other non-contentious business agreement.[76] The relevance of this is that the one-month period of grace referred to immediately above may not apply.[77]

27.67 In so far as bills rendered before 11 August 2009 are concerned, art 14 of the Solicitors' (Non-Contentious Business) Remuneration Order 1994 provides:

'**Interest**

14.(1) After the information specified in article 8 has been given to an entitled person in compliance with articles 6 or 7, a solicitor may charge interest on the unpaid amount of his costs plus any paid disbursements and value added tax, subject to paragraphs (2) and (3) below.

(2) Where an entitlement to interest arises under paragraph (1), and subject to any agreement made between a solicitor and client, the period for which interest may be charged may run from one month after the date of delivery of a bill, unless the solicitor fails to lodge an application within one month of receipt of a request for a remuneration certificate under article 4, in which case no interest is payable in respect of the period between one month after receiving the request and the actual date on which the application is lodged.

(3) Subject to any agreement made between a solicitor and client, the rate of interest must not exceed the rate for the time being payable on judgment debts.

(4) Interest charged under this article must be calculated, where applicable, by reference to the following—

    (a)   if a solicitor is required to obtain a remuneration certificate, the total amount of the costs certified by the Council to be fair and reasonable plus paid disbursements and value added tax;

    (b)   if an application is made for the bill to be taxed, the amount ascertained on taxation;

    (c)   if an application is made for the bill to be taxed or a solicitor is required to obtain a remuneration certificate and for any reason the taxation or application for a remuneration certificate does not proceed, the unpaid amount of the costs shown in the bill or such lesser sum as may be agreed between the solicitor and the client, plus paid disbursements and value added tax.'

Wyn Williams J has found that where interest is claimed in compliance with the provisions of art 14 of the Solicitors' (Non-Contentious Business) Remuneration Order 1994, those provisions do not confer upon the court a discretionary power to disallow that interest or reduce its amount.[78]

Interest on contentious costs

27.68 It is a moot point whether interest is necessarily payable on unpaid contentious costs. If the retainer makes provision for interest, then it will be payable in accordance with those provisions, but it is often the case that no provision is made. Where no such provision is made, then interest cannot be claimed as of right, but would have to be awarded pursuant to either the Senior Courts Act 1981, s 35A, or the County Courts Act 1984, s 69(1).

---

[76]   See *Walton v Egan* [1982] 3 WLR 352; this related to the 1972 equivalent of the Solicitors' (Non-Contentious Business) Remuneration Order 2009.

[77]   See subpara (2) in the regulation cited at **27.65**.

[78]   *Lake v Hunt Kid Law Firm LLP (in administration)* [2011] EWHC 766 (QB) at [26]; Wyn Williams J found it very difficult to read s 35A of the Senior Courts Act 1981 as conferring a power to reduce or extinguish interest which is payable as a consequence of a provision wholly independent of that section.

Judgment debt interest

27.69 Judgment debt interest may accrue on debts for which there is already a judgment, but in the county court this will be subject to the £5,000 limit mentioned at **36.13**. As to the time from which interest runs, art 2(2) of the County Courts (Interest on Judgment Debts) Order 1991 reads as follows:

> '(2) In the case of a judgment or order for the payment of a judgment debt, other than costs, the amount of which has to be determined at a later date, the judgment debt shall carry interest from that later date.'

At first blush this appears to mean that interest is payable on costs from the moment that there is an order for costs to be assessed (which would be the position between opposing parties: see **36.22**) rather than from the date of the certificate quantifying those costs. This is probably not the correct interpretation; it is more likely that the reference to 'costs' is a reference to 'costs awarded pursuant to s 51 of the Senior Courts Act 1981'. This would not only accord with the common-sense view that a solicitor's unpaid fees should be treated in exactly the same way as anyone else's unpaid fees, but it also accords with the notion that art 2(2) is written in this way merely to reflect the fact that the incipitur rule applies to costs awarded by the court whereas the allocatur rule applies to all other monies (see **36.22–36.23**).

Discretion generally

27.70 For the reasons set out in **27.66**, it will commonly be the case that the court will lack the vires to reduce or extinguish interest where that interest is payable as a consequence of compliance with art 14 of the Solicitors' (Non-Contentious Business) Remuneration Order 1994. Where interest is payable under contract, or where interest is payable as a result of the operation of legislation similar to art 14 of the Solicitors' (Non-Contentious Business) Remuneration Order 1994, it is difficult to see why any other reasoning would apply. As such, the exercise of ascertaining the amount of interest payable between solicitor and client will typically be limited to finding the start date and the end date (both being questions of mixed fact and law), and to determining the applicable rate or rates (this being question of interpretation). These steps will be equivalent to layers two and three in the scheme described at **36.1**. Put otherwise, the wide-ranging discretion (ie, layer four) will generally not apply.

27.71 Where a general discretion does arise, however, the relevant factors will be much the same as those described in Chapter 36. Whilst obiter, Wyn Williams J has confirmed that the court's primary purpose when making an award of interest is to compensate the recipient for the fact that he has been precluded from obtaining a return on the money rightfully kept from him; Wyn Williams J explained that the fact that the party liable for that interest may have been out of pocket for whatever reason (in that case because a payment into court had been made) would not generally count as a sufficient reason to justify a reduction in the interest properly payable.[79]

---

[79] *Lake v Hunt Kid Law Firm LLP (in administration)* [2011] EWHC 766 (QB) at [34] and [35]; Wyn Williams J cited with approval the decision of Christopher Clarke J in *Fattal v Walbrook Trustees (Jersey) Ltd & Another* [2009] EWHC 1674 (Ch) at [26].

Part VI

THE QUANTUM OF COSTS (BETWEEN THE PARTIES)

Whilst this Part of the book focuses primarily on the quantum of costs between opposing parties, that is an issue which may turn on what is allowable between solicitor and client (this being because of the operation of the indemnity principle). There are some topics which turn on the amounts allowable between solicitor and client, but which almost always arise only in the context of assessments between opposing parties. Where this is so, in an effort to avoid duplication and too much page turning, one or two solicitor and client topics are addressed in this Part rather than in Part V.

Chapter 28

HOURLY RATES

THE APPROACH IN GENERAL

28.1 Although an oversimplification, the assessment of hourly rates depends on the following factors:

- the time when the work was done (**28.30**);
- the status of the person who did the work (that status usually being referred to as the grade of fee earner) (**28.31–28.35**);
- the place where the work was done (**28.36–28.59**); and
- other factors, such as the complexity of the work, the value of the matter, etc (**28.60–28.76**).

These factors must be addressed as a matter of fact (ie who did the work, where it was done, etc), and then as a matter of discretion (ie whether it was reasonable for the work to be done by the person who did it, for it to be done where it was done, etc). Where quantitative findings are made, the former will limit the latter;[1] if, for example, the work was carried out by a trainee solicitor in Grimsby, the amount allowed will be limited to that trainee's rate even if the work could reasonably have been carried out by a senior partner in London.

The relevance of guideline rates

28.2 Guideline rates are published every year or so in the form of a table which marshals localities together into 'bands'.[2] Those tables refer to the applicable guideline rate for any given 'grade' of fee earner (from Grade A to Grade D)[3] in any given band during any given year (further details are given below). It has repeatedly been said that the guideline rates are not binding; indeed, many judges take the view that they are of no use at all in the context of detailed assessments. Be that as it may, the method of describing rates according to grades and years is a useful taxonomy, not least because it is standardised and universally understood. Out of deference to this, the language of guideline rates is used in this book, but this should not be taken to be an endorsement of the usage of guideline rates in detailed assessments.[4]

---

[1] See *The General of Berne Insurance Company v Jardine Reinsurance Management Limited* [1998] 2 All ER 301.

[2] The most recent incarnation of the guidelines does not use the word 'bands', but the old terminology persists.

[3] Rather confusingly, the most recent incarnation of guideline rates refers to the grades of fee earner as being bands, but that terminology is rarely used.

[4] Even when the case is such that guideline rates would assist, in any particular area the Designated Civil Judge may supply more exact guidelines for rates in that area (see the narrative to the guideline rates).

Statistical analyses

28.3   The Advisory Committee on Civil Costs – that being the committee that advises the Master of Rolls about guideline rates – has tried to match guideline rates to market rates by carrying out surveys. There are those who say that that committee's good intentions have been thwarted by unreliable data; they would probably make the following observations:

- *Insignificant response rate:* A recent attempt (2008) to match the guideline rates to market rates was based on a survey in which the response rate was less than 8%;[5]
- *Absence of random selection:* There seems to be an absence of evidence showing that data was randomly selected;
- *Skewed data:* The data appears to have been skewed in that a better response was received from those who tend to receive costs than those who tend to pay costs;[6]
- *Unrepresentative samples:* Reference was made to the evidence of individual firms without any published evidence demonstrating that those firms are representative of the market;[7]
- *Amplification of errors*: In more recent years the rates have been updated by reference to private sector 'wage index' rather than by reference to reliable sampling, thereby amplifying errors made in previous years;[8] and
- *Lack of proper statistical analysis*: There is a lack absence of any statistical analysis of the data, and in particular, there is a lack of confidence intervals.

Notwithstanding these methodological difficulties, in 2010, the committee felt able to reject the suggestion that London guideline rates were higher than the actual market rate and that provincial guideline rates were lower; the committee also rejected the suggestion that 20 to 35 percent difference between the rates paid to claimant firms and the rates charged defendant firms was not justified.[9] The precise statistical bases upon which the committee reached these conclusions appears not to be in the public domain.

Use of guideline rates

28.4   It is commonplace for the court to be referred to guideline rates. Often a receiving party will argue for rates which exceed the applicable guideline rates. This will usually be on the basis that the applicable guideline rates should be uplifted, but it is not uncommon for receiving parties to argue that the guideline rates should be disregarded entirely. However the argument is put, the court's decision will be a matter of discretion, albeit a discretion which ought to be exercised in a structured way. The seven factors in CPR, r 44.5(3) will be relevant, but beyond this, the applicable law becomes somewhat ill-defined.

---

[5]   See The Derivation of New Guideline Hourly Rates, a report produced by the Advisory Committee on Civil Costs dated about 9 December 2008.

[6]   Only 26 insurers and local authorities responded, as against a total of 129 respondents. Whilst there is detail about the geographical distribution of the requests for data, there is no corresponding detail about the response.

[7]   See Guideline Hourly Rates, Conclusions, Advisory Committee on Civil Costs, March 2010 at para 2: there is no mention of any evidence that the firms referred to therein were representative. See also the 2008 report, where one firm submitted separate responses from each of its offices.

[8]   See 'Why We Recommend Uprating the 2009 GHRs', Advisory Committee on Civil Costs, March, 2010; the committee has been unable to produce any evidence to demonstrate a link between the index used and the legal services industry.

[9]   See Guideline Hourly Rates, Conclusions, Advisory Committee on Civil Costs, March 2010.

28.5 Although not an exhaustive list, receiving parties frequently rely on the following to justify a high hourly rate:

- the complexity of the work;
- the particular experience of the fee earner who did the work;
- the specialism involved;
- the importance of the matter to the parties;
- the urgency of the work;
- the conduct of the parties; and
- the special expertise of the firm involved in comparison to other firms in the area.

The fact that this list reflects the factors set out in CPR, r 44.5(3) demonstrates the importance of those factors. Firms specialising in personal injury and clinical negligence also point to the fact that they often have to pay referral fees.[10] Claimant firms also point to the costs of case screening (which are usually irrecoverable), the costs associated with delay in payment, the costs of dealing with less knowledgeable clients, and the costs associated with a volatile supply of work.[11]

28.6 One would have hoped that so long after the introduction of the CPR, the legal principles involved in setting hourly rates would be established and precise. Regrettably, this is far from being the case. This could be because the court has a wide ambit of discretion; perhaps the very existence of that wide discretion has allowed a multiplicity of different methods to flourish and has discouraged dissatisfied parties from seeking to clarify the law. Regardless of the cause of the absence of authority, the truth is that there is a need to grapple with a variety of different methods without knowing which is the correct (or even preferred) approach for the case in hand.

28.7 One notable feature of the topic of hourly rates is the frequent (but inconsistent) use that is made of pre-CPR law. Some commentators say that this is a reflection of the lack of any forensic structure under the CPR for setting hourly rates. Regardless of whether it is correct to refer to pre-CPR law, it is necessary to know something of it, in particular, of the relevant pre-CPR terminology.

28.8 For all these reasons, this book acknowledges the existence of both the guideline rates and the pre-CPR law. Many readers will disagree with that approach (especially in view of the concerns expressed at **28.3**), but it is necessary to describe the relevant principles in some detail because, in reality, they are often used in practice.

PRE-CPR TERMINOLOGY

28.9 The pre-CPR approach to the ascertainment of hourly rates involved the combination of two components: the 'A factor', and the 'B factor'. The A factor and the B factor were combined to make the hourly charging rate. Thus, the pre-CPR method was referred to as the 'A plus B' approach. The A factor was an approximation of the costs of carrying out the work in question (such as the costs of employing staff, providing premises, administration, etc), and the B factor represented the solicitor's remuneration (ie profit, hence the term 'profit costs'). The A factor and the B factor

---

[10] See 'Why We Recommend Uprating the 2009 GHRs', Advisory Committee on Civil Costs, March, 2010 at para 2; there is no authority to suggest that this is a factor that ought to be taken into account.

[11] Ibid. The committee that advises on guideline rates has taken all of these factors into account.

were combined by multiplying the A factor by the B factor and then adding this figure back to the A factor to give an 'hourly charging rate'; for example, an A factor of £100 per hour when combined with a B factor of 85% would have given an hourly charging rate of £185 per hour. Further details (including the history) are given in the footnotes.[12]

28.10 For the remainder of this discussion, the following terminology will be used: 'hourly charging rate', 'A factor', 'B factor' and (to refer to modern day rates) 'guideline rates'. The use of these terms does not mean that the pre-CPR law applies. Where appropriate, the phrase 'hourly rate' refers to the rate that would be allowed in an assessment under the CPR.

The A factor

28.11 The next few paragraphs continue to describe the pre-CPR law. Some aspects of the pre-CPR law remain relevant under the CPR, but the discussion of what falls within that category does not begin until **28.24**.

28.12 In essence, the A factor was the hourly cost of running relevant aspects of the solicitor's practice calculated by reference to the fee earner in respect of whom costs were claimed. Brightman J put it this way:[13]

> '[The A factor is] the proper cost per hour of the time so spent having regard to a reasonable estimate of the overhead expenses of the solicitors' firm including (if the time spent is that of an employee) the reasonable salary of the employee or (if the time spent is that of a partner) a notional salary.'

---

[12] The A plus B approach was first described by Brightman J in about 1975 (*In re Eastwood, decd; Lloyds Bank Ltd v Eastwood* [1975] Ch 112 at 119):
'The [receiving party's solicitor] submits (A) what is the proper cost per hour of the time so spent having regard to a reasonable estimate of the overhead expenses of the solicitors' firm including (if the time spent is that of an employee) the reasonable salary of the employee or (if the time spent is that of a partner) a notional salary. The firm will also submit ... (B) what is a proper additional sum to be allowed over and above (A) by way of further profit costs.'
Shortly after the introduction of the terms 'A factor' and 'B factor', the terminology grew and became more refined (and also more confusing). In 1976 Kerr J explained that the 'A factor' was the 'direct cost' to the firm of carrying out the work, and should be sufficient 'to cover the salary and the appropriate share of the general overheads' of the person doing the work (*Leopold Lazarus Ltd v Secretary of State for Trade and Industry* (1976) Costs LR, Core vol 62); thus (for a short while) the 'A factor' became known as the 'direct costs'. It also became known as the 'hourly expense rate' (which should not be confused with the hourly charging rate).
In about 1980 the phrase 'broad average direct costs' became the preferred term (*R v Wilkinson* [1980] 1 All ER 597 at 604, Goff J); this was to reflect the fact that the A factor should be based on a broad range of the costs of running a firm in a particular area, rather than the actual costs applicable to the individual firm whose fees are the subject of the assessment (see below). In 1996, however, the Court of Appeal said that the term 'comparable direct costs' was to be preferred (*L v L* [1997] 1 Costs LR 9). This was because it was felt that the word 'average' was capable of misunderstanding in that it might lead to assessments being made by an arithmetical calculation rather than by the exercise of judicial assessment.
Like the A factor, the B factor has also had a number of labels over the years, the most commonly used of which is 'care and conduct'. Other terms include: 'care and attention', 'care, skill and attention', 'mark-up', 'profit element', 'service increment' or just 'uplift'. Where the work is non-contentious work the phrase 'value element' is often used: this is not entirely the same as 'care and conduct', but it is sufficiently similar to be thought of as the non-contentious equivalent.
[13] *In re Eastwood, dec'd; Lloyds Bank Ltd v Eastwood* [1975] Ch 112 at 119.

Expense of Time Calculations

28.13 This factor differed from fee earner to fee earner. It was a calculation which had its roots in the Law Society's 1967 booklet entitled *Know What it Costs You*. That booklet had been written in an attempt to allow solicitors to assess what it cost to carry out work; as such it was intended to be a practice management tool rather than an aid to assessing costs. In due course, it evolved into *The Expense of Time*. This too was intended to be a practice management tool. That publication still exists, but it expressly distances itself from the assessment of costs.[14]

28.14 The *Expense of Time* calculation is described in the footnotes.[15] The results are highly influenced by figures which must be assumed rather than measured. It is, for example, possible to derive extravagant or frugal rates from the same data simply by altering the figure which is assumed for the number of hours billed per year.[16] This presents no difficulty when using the calculation for its original intended purpose (ie practice management) because consistent assumptions can be made across the whole practice, but the same is not true when it is used for assessing costs. This is because different firms will (for entirely legitimate reasons) make different assumptions at different times. It is primarily for this reason that *The Expense of Time* booklet cautions against using the calculation as a means of calculating costs.

28.15 Notwithstanding this, the figures derived from the *Expense of Time* calculation became almost synonymous with the A factor. Indeed, there was a time when the court tolerated solicitors submitting their own *Expense of Time* calculations on a case-by-case basis. That practice soon fell by the wayside; the details are set out in the footnotes[17] but, in essence, the task of ascertaining the A factor ceased to be based on the facts of the case in hand, but became a task to be carried out generically by the court using its own

---

14   The current edition warns that: 'the procedure used in this booklet will enable you [ie the solicitor] to calculate what each matter has cost you ... It is not a means of calculating the charge to be made to the client'.

15   Broadly speaking, the *Expense of Time* calculation involved ascertaining the expenses of a practice, and then apportioning those expenses amongst the fee earners within that firm in accordance with their actual (or, in the case of non-salaried partners, notional) salaries. The result was that it was possible to estimate how much it cost to employ and support an individual fee earner over any given period of time. If that cost was then divided by the number of hours for which that fee earner had been able to render fees, his cost-per-hour could be calculated. For the purposes of calculating costs, a notional figure was used (because otherwise a hard-working fee earner would be rewarded with an artificially low rate). Therefore, a number of factors had to be assumed, including the notional salary and the number of hours for which a full-time fee earner could have been expected to raise a fee.

16   This figure is often taken as being 1,100, but (more realistically) is often taken as being 1,500. It would be rare for a fee earner to bill more than 1,800 hours per year.

17   In 1976 Kerr J emphasised that the assessment of the expense rate was a task for the costs judge and that the assessment was to be based on the costs judge's general knowledge of costs in the locality, as Kerr J said (*Leopold Lazarus Ltd v Secretary of State for Trade and Industry* (1976) Costs LR, Core vol 62):
       '[The A factor] would be based on the [costs judge's] knowledge and experience of the average solicitor or executive employed by the average firm in the area concerned.'
       In *R v Wilkinson* [1980] 1 All ER 598 at 608 Goff J cast doubt on the suitability of the Expenses of Time calculation as a basis for calculating costs:
       '... I have come to the conclusion that The *Expense of Time*, laudable though it is in many ways, does not in its present form provide a reliable basis for the taxation of costs; and I also conclude that it will be difficult in practice for any such system to form such a basis without some prior monitoring by an appropriate body.'
       The need to look at the average rather than the specific was reaffirmed by Hirst J in 1988 in the following terms (*Stubbs v Board of Governors of the Royal National Orthopaedic Hospital* (unreported) 21 December 1988, QBD):
       'It is ... a matter which is properly approached by reference to averages since it is unlikely that there will be a very wide divergence between comparable firms of solicitors operating in similar fields or work in similar geographical areas'.

knowledge of local solicitors' charges. There were exceptions to this,[18] some of which remain relevant today.[19] In times gone by, the main concern was that the court tended to allow rates which were too low. In response, guidance was given that the A factor was to be ascertained in a realistic way; attempts to inflate the B factor for the purpose of compensating for an unreasonably low A factor were to be discouraged.[20]

28.16 The fact that the use of individual *Expense of Time* calculations was discouraged continues to have resonance even today; this is because this highlights the difference between costs and charges. Evans J had this to say on the topic:[21]

> 'There remains the question ... of what weight, if any, the [costs judge] should give to *Expense of Time* calculations, if they are produced in a particular case. The answer, in my judgment, is that, if the figures for an individual solicitor, or firm, are produced for the purposes of the assessment in that case, then they should be given very little weight ... The "market" is for charges, not for costs.'

Expense rates surveys

28.17 Partly as a result of Evans J's comments and partly as a result of the realisation that A factors were being allowed at rates which were artificially low (see **28.15**), a practice of local Law Societies carrying out 'Expense Rate Surveys' flourished. This was a practice in which data would be collected from a number of representative firms in a locality; that data would then be averaged and published for use in detailed assessments. The use of that data became part of the process of assessing the hourly rate.[22] The present-day relevance of this is that that data no longer exists (or, more accurately, very rarely exists).[23] This means that a strict adherence to the A plus B approach is not only undesirable, but usually not even possible (see **28.3**).

The B factor

28.18 Again, the following few paragraphs describe the pre-CPR law; the discussion of the CPR law begins at **28.24**. The exercise of ascertaining the B factor was not a fact-finding exercise, but a matter of judgment and discretion. The B factor was usually expressed as a percentage of the A factor.[24] Broadly speaking, in a run-of-the-mill claim it would be 50%, rising to 100% and beyond in exceptional claims (see **28.21–28.23**). Contrary to present-day practices, different B factors (and therefore different hourly charging rates) would be applied to different types of work within the same bill.[25] When

---

[18] *Finley v Glaxo Laboratories Ltd* (1989) Costs LR, Core vol 106 at 110, in which Hobhouse J took account of an Expense of Time calculation in calculating the appropriate hourly rate.

[19] See *Jones v Secretary of State for Wales* [1997] 1 WLR 1008.

[20] See *Loveday v Renton (No 2)* (1991) Costs LR, Core vol 204.

[21] *Johnson v Reed Corrugated Cases Ltd* [1992] 1 All ER 169 at 180.

[22] Those surveys were only a factor to be taken into account by the costs judge: *L v L* [1997] 1 Costs LR 9 at 13, per Neill LJ.

[23] Some local Law Societies still publish data. There are those who seek to derive an A factor from the guideline rates by subtracting a third (which equates to a B factor of 50%). Whether this is legitimate is debatable; this is because the guideline rates are not based on local data. There are, however, examples of this approach being adopted (see *Higgs v Camden and Islington Health Authority* [2003] EWHC 15 (QB)).

[24] The percentage was not the percentage of hourly charging rate, but of the A factor. Thus, if, in a run-of-the-mill claim the B factor is 50% and the hourly charging rate is £150 per hour, the A factor would be £100 per hour rather than £75 per hour.

[25] Pre-CPR B factors, usually of less than 50%, applied to some aspects of a solicitor's work. Thus, travelling tended not to attract any B factor at all, and sitting behind counsel or attending upon counsel would attract a lower B factor than other work.

'the' B factor was referred to, this was generally a reference to the figure which applied to the work which attracted the highest percentage increment.

Seven Pillars of Wisdom

28.19 On a between-the-parties basis, the B factor was based on those factors which are now listed in CPR, r 44.5(3) (this being 'the Seven Pillars of Wisdom'):[26]

- the conduct of all the parties;
- the amount or value of any money or property involved;
- the importance of the matter to all the parties;
- the particular complexity of the matter or the difficulty or novelty of the questions raised;
- the skill, effort, specialised knowledge and responsibility involved;
- the time spent on the case; and
- the place where and the circumstances in which work or any part of it was done.

The level of the uplift

28.20 Evans J explained the appropriate method in the following way:[27]

'I approach the assessment on the following basis. I am advised that the range for normal, i e nonexceptional, cases starts at 50%, which the [costs judge] regarded, rightly in my view, as an appropriate figure for "run-of-the-mill" cases. The figure increases above 50% so as to reflect a number of possible factors ... but only a small percentage of accident cases results in an allowance over 70%. To justify a figure of 100% or even one closely approaching 100% there must be some factor or combination of factors which mean that the case approaches the exceptional. A figure above 100% would seem to be appropriate only when the individual case, or cases of the particular kind, can properly be regarded as exceptional, and such cases will be rare.'

28.21 A B factor of in excess of 100% has always been a level of uplift which required justification, as explained by Hobhouse J:[28]

'To justify an uplift of 100 percent it is necessary ... to demonstrate that the case is exceptional. There has been a tendency among some firms of solicitors to put forward grossly inflated percentages by way of uplift and a failure to appreciate that to justify an uplift even as high as 100 percent requires the demonstration that the case is exceptional.'

28.22 B factors of significantly higher than 100% are correspondingly difficult to justify, as Cazalet J commented:[29]

'In my view to justify a percentage uplift of 150 percent a case would not have to be just exceptional but extraordinary. To achieve an uplift of 100 percent a case would indeed have to be exceptional.'

---

[26] Pre-CPR the relevant factors were marginally different: in particular, the conduct of the parties was not a factor specifically to be taken into account.

[27] *Johnson v Reed Corrugated Cases Ltd* [1992] 1 All ER 169 at 183.

[28] *Loveday v Renton (No 2)* (1991) Costs LR, Core vol 204.

[29] *Foroughi v Foroughi* (unreported) 30 July 1993, Cazalet J, but recited by Cazalet in *Re Children Act 1989 (Taxation of Costs)* [1994] 2 FLR 934 at 953.

28.23 The following are case examples:

- Hobhouse J allowed an uplift of 75% in a clinical negligence case involving alleged vaccine damage;[30] and
- Hobhouse J allowed an uplift of 125% in a group litigation case concerning the damage done by whooping cough vaccine, and involved 'technical evidence which differed in degree, though not in kind, from that experienced in other cases involving scientific or medical disputes' and in which 'the volume of documentation was very large indeed'.[31]

THE RELEVANCE OF PRE-CPR LAW UNDER THE CPR

28.24 It is undoubtedly the case that under the CPR both practitioners and the courts are encouraged to express hourly charging rates as a single figure (eg £150 per hour rather than £100 per hour plus a B factor of 50%). Indeed, there are those who say that the A plus B approach has no part to play under the CPR. In support of this position, they would point to a consultation paper by the Lord Chancellor's Department in which it was explained that solicitors would be required to provide an inclusive charging basis, 'thereby abolishing the uplift for care and conduct element claimed in a bill of costs'.[32]

The role of A plus B under the CPR

28.25 A contrary view is that the A plus B approach (or something very similar to it) is not only permissible under the CPR, but is necessary. There is support for this view in that the A plus B approach is little more than an expression of the fact that professional charges – all professional charges – will contain an element of cost and an element of profit. Those who advocate that view would say that whilst the CPR might have abolished the practice of describing these two components separately, they still exist and, in the absence of a better analytical tool for dealing with hourly rates, it will be appropriate from time to time to consider rates from the A plus B perspective. That view is based on authority. Eady J had the following to say on this matter:[33]

> 'It is important to have in mind the observation in *Cook [on Costs]*: "Whether or not the A and B factors are identified or concealed in a charging rate, they will still be there. Any commercial enterprise must base its prices and charges on costs plus profit and it is naive to think that the legal profession could operate in some other way".'

28.26 Moreover, Fulford J did not object to an A plus B analysis being applied to costs incurred under the CPR (albeit in the early days of the CPR: 2003). The case before him was a clinical negligence claim in which the claimant suffered a quadriplegic cerebral palsy with dyskinetic features.[34] Liability was in dispute until only 3 weeks before trial. It settled for £3.5m. The claimant's solicitors were based in the City of London (an EC1 postcode).[35] The costs were incurred between 1999 and 2001 by a fee earner of more than 20 years' experience. An hourly rate of £300 per hour was claimed. The costs judge

---

[30] *Finley v Glaxo Laboratories Ltd* (1989) Costs LR, Core vol 106 at 112.
[31] *Loveday v Renton (No 2)* (1991) Costs LR, Core vol 204.
[32] Controlling Costs: A Lord Chancellor's Department Consultation Paper, May 1999.
[33] *Cox v MGN* [2006] EWHC 1235, QB.
[34] *Higgs v Camden and Islington Health Authority* [2003] EWHC 15 (QB).
[35] Some of these details are not in the judgment; they have been kindly provided by Anne Winyard, a partner of the firm involved.

carried out an A plus B analysis by deriving an A factor from the guideline rates; he accepted the rate as claimed as representing an A factor of £150 per hour plus a B factor of 100%.

28.27 The paying party (the defendant) argued that this was not a legitimate way of dealing with the hourly rate. The defendant argued that a single (composite) rate was appropriate because this is what was encouraged by the Lord Chancellor's consultation paper.[36] Fulford J disagreed with these submissions; he reminded himself that the rates set out in the *Guide to the Summary Assessment of Costs* were only guideline rates and went on to make the following findings concerning the A plus B analysis:

'The CPR and the Costs Practice Direction discourage the use of the A plus B calculation, and commend the claiming of costs on the basis of a single charging rate. I fully accept the advantages that the single hourly rate has for both the paying and the receiving party. However I am not persuaded that the learned judge did more than use the A plus B method as one of the measures and indicators to ensure that he was able to gauge the propriety or otherwise of a figure of £300 per hour ... I am unable to accept the submission that the learned judge misdirected himself in considering the A plus B basis. It may well be that reliance on that method of calculation will rapidly diminish, but in this case I consider the learned judge did not misdirect himself when he took it into consideration.'

Conversion to and from A plus B

28.28 As to Fulford J's prediction that reliance on the A plus B approach would diminish over time, Master Gordon-Saker has made the following observations (in 2008):[37]

'I suspect that now ... may be time to bury concepts such as expense rates, mark-ups, A figures and B figures, for we must by now have sufficient experience of the single hourly rates that have been claimed and allowed since 1999.'

That view is certainly not one which can be criticised, but it is not universally held. In particular, many judges still use the A plus B approach (or, rather, aspects of it) as a cross-check. Where such an approach is used, the following table may assist with calculations:

Hourly rate converter[38]

To convert Guideline to 'A plus B'		To convert 'A plus B' to Guideline	
% above Guideline	'B' factor	Intended 'B' factor	Required increase in Guideline rate
0%	50%	50%	0%
2%	53%	60%	7%
5%	58%	65%	10%
7½%	61%	70%	13%
10%	65%	75%	17%

---

[36] Controlling Costs: A Lord Chancellor's Department Consultation Paper, May 1999.
[37] *Holliday v EC Realisations Ltd* [2008] EWHC 90103 (Costs).
[38] Reproduced with the kind permission of Master Colum Leonard.

15%	73%	80%	20%
20%	80%	85%	23%
25%	88%	90%	27%
30%	95%	95%	30%
33%	100%	100%	33%
40%	110%	105%	37%
45%	118%	110%	40%
50%	125%	115%	43%
55%	133%	125%	50%
60%	140%	130%	53%
67%	151%	135%	57%
80%	170%	140%	60%
85%	178%	145%	63%
90%	185%	150%	67%

This table is based on the assumption that the relevant guideline rate includes a B factor of 50%. This assumption could well be wrong; it is impossible to say whether it is right or wrong because there is no reliable data by which the A factor can be discovered. This means that the role of the A plus B analysis is limited to being a cross-check or a tool for comparing rates;[39] it should not be used as a means of calculating rates *de novo*.

THE MODERN APPROACH

28.29 Eady J has summarised the modern approach in this way:[40]

> 'The court is required to take into account all the circumstances including, in particular, the factors listed at CPR Pt 44.5(3), which are sometimes referred to as the "Seven Pillars of Wisdom". It is necessary to have regard to the solicitor's particular skill, effort, specialised knowledge and responsibility. Obviously, also, the case in hand must be assessed for importance, complexity, difficulty or novelty. All the while the court will apply the test of proportionality.

Thus, there are certain factors the court is required to take into account (ie the seven pillars of wisdom); these are almost always considered in the context of the factors set out at **28.1**. To this extent, the court's discretion is exercised in a structured way, but it would be wrong to believe that the court will explicitly and individually take each factor into account. Most experienced costs judges prefer to focus only on the factors which are relevant to the case in hand rather than to painstakingly work through each factor in turn. The resultant rate will be limited to amount allowed for in the retainer, but it is not necessary for the retainer expressly to record the rates.[41]

---

[39] Comparison of rates by the A plus B method is unobjectionable. In particular, if a judge is in the habit of allowing a particular rate for run-of-the-mill work for solicitors in his locality, it would be difficult to object to him using the A plus B analysis for the purposes of adjusting that rate for more difficult cases. Indeed, such a method could be commended on the basis that it brings structure and consistency to a process which otherwise may lack these attributes.

[40] *Cox v MGN* [2006] EWHC 1235 (QB) at [55].

[41] *Ghadami v Lyon Cole Insurance Group Limited* [2010] EWCA Civ 767 at [27], per Lloyd LJ.

The time when the work was done

28.30   The costs must be assessed as at the time the work was done[42] with no allowance being made for the passing of the years.[43] There will usually be no factual dispute as to when the work was carried out; if there is, the court would have to determine the issue sitting as a tribunal of fact (and in doing so it would give due weight to the presumption afforded by the certificate to the bill). It would rarely be the case that the court would have to determine the reasonableness of when the work was done;[44] timing is, therefore, usually an uncomplicated point of fact.

The grade of person who did the work

28.31   As has been mentioned at **28.2–28.3**, it is now almost universally received practice to refer to fee earners as being one of four Grades (usually referred to as Grades A to D)[45] Recent editions[46] of the *Guide to the Summary Assessment of Costs* describe that grading system in this way:

> 'The grades of fee earner have been agreed between representatives of the Supreme Court Costs Office, the Association of District Judges and the Law Society. The categories are as follows:
>
> 1. Solicitors with over eight years post qualification experience including at least eight years litigation experience.
> 2. Solicitors and legal executives with over four years post qualification experience including at least four years litigation experience.
> 3. Other solicitors and legal executives and fee earners of equivalent experience.
> 4. Trainee solicitors, para legals and other fee earners.

In so far as the use of the term 'Legal Executive' is concerned, the *Guide* has the following to say (this being very similar to the guidance given in the CPD on the point):[47]

> '"Legal Executive" means a Fellow of the Institute of Legal Executives. Those who are not Fellows of the Institute are not entitled to call themselves legal executives and in principle are therefore not entitled to the same hourly rate as a legal executive.
>
> Unqualified clerks who are fee earners of equivalent experience may be entitled to similar rates and in this regard it should be borne in mind that Fellows of the Institute of Legal Executives generally spend two years in a solicitor's office before passing their Part 1 general examinations, spend a further two years before passing the Part 2 specialist examinations and then complete a further two years in practice before being able to become Fellows. Fellows have [sic] therefore possess considerable practical experience and academic achievement. Clerks without the equivalent experience of legal executives will be treated as being in the bottom grade of fee earner i e trainee solicitors and fee earners of equivalent experience. Whether or not a fee earner has equivalent experience is ultimately a matter for the discretion of the court.'

---

[42]   See, for example, *Finley v Glaxo Laboratories Ltd* (1989) Costs LR, Core vol 106 at 111.

[43]   Whilst the matter would depend on the wording of the retainer, it could be argued that the correct measure is not when the work was done but the date upon which the invoice for the work was rendered, or could have been rendered; with conditional fee agreements, that would be long after the work was done; it is surprising that there is no authority on that point.

[44]   It usually arises in the context of longstanding group litigation where the court has set out a detailed roadmap of what should be done and when.

[45]   This is notwithstanding the fact that the *Guide to the Summary Assessment of Costs* refers to the four Grades as being 1, 2, 3 and 4, and that in its most recent incarnation the guide refers to the grades as being 'bands'.

[46]   This extract is taken from the 2007 version; from 2009 this guidance has been omitted, but it is clear from the way in which the present guideline rates were formulated that the classification was to remain unchanged.

[47]   See CPD, art 4.5.

28.32 The CPD gives similar guidance, albeit that it is limited to what is meant by the phrase 'legal executive'. Whilst the CPD makes no express mention of the need to refer to Grades A to D in the background information (ie, the narrative) of a bill of costs,[48] the fact that the guidance concerning legal executives is so similar to that used in the *Guide to the Summary Assessment of Costs* implies that, at the very least, the latter is acceptable under the CPR. Indeed, that scheme is almost always used in practice.

Factual issues

28.33 There may be a dispute as to which fee earner actually carried out the work, but such disputes should be rare because CPD, art 4.5(2) provides that the background information included in the bill should set out the relevant details:

> '[A] statement of the status of the solicitor or solicitor's employee in respect of whom costs are claimed and (if those costs are calculated on the basis of hourly rates) the hourly rates claimed for each such person.
>
> It should be noted that "legal executive" means a Fellow of the Institute of Legal Executives.
>
> Other clerks, who are fee earners of equivalent experience, may be entitled to similar rates. It should be borne in mind that Fellows of the Institute of Legal Executives will have spent approximately 6 years in practice, and taken both general and specialist examinations. The Fellows have therefore acquired considerable practical and academic experience. Clerks without the equivalent experience of legal executives will normally be treated as being the equivalent of trainee solicitors and para-legals.'

28.34 If there is a dispute as to who actually carried out the work, the court would have to resolve that issue sitting as a tribunal of fact (and in doing so it would give due weight to the presumption afforded by the certificate to the bill). By far the commonest dispute, however, is whether it was reasonable for the work in question to have been carried out by the person who did it. That is a matter of discretion to be decided on the basis of all the circumstances, including the fee earner's expertise.[49] The types of circumstances and factors the court may take into account are addressed at **28.60–28.76**.

28.35 A frequently encountered argument is that the work should have been allocated to a lower grade of fee earner, but the contrary argument may arise from time to time, namely that a junior fee earner was punching above his weight and that this should be reflected in the hourly rate. That type of argument may cross over into being an argument about a fee earner having special expertise (see **28.50**). These issues will be decided on a case-by-case basis, having regard to the factors in CPR, r 44.5(3) and (on the standard basis) to proportionality.

The place where work was done

28.36 Although it would be rare for there to be a factual dispute over the identity of the locus where the work was done, disputes commonly arise over where the instructions might have been placed. Occasionally it will be the receiving party who says that a rate higher than the local norm would be appropriate because if he had so desired, he could have instructed solicitors in a pricier area and still remained within the bounds of that

---

[48] CPD, art 4.5(2).
[49] Although they are criminal cases, see *R v Halcrow and R v Ali* (1984), Taxing Masters Compendium, published by the Supreme Court Taxing Office in 1984.

which was reasonable; that argument will usually fail[50] (unless, of course, it is part of another submission, such as an assertion that the local firm needed to bear higher overheads in order to maintain a specialism[51]). Arguments about the locus of instructions are, however, usually raised by paying parties, and the archetypal objection is that it was unreasonable to instruct London solicitors when provincial solicitors could have received the instructions just as competently. The urban centre is not always London, however, so rather than using labels such as 'the City', 'London' and 'the provinces', this book use the more generic terms 'town' and 'local'.

28.37 Each case will turn on its own facts, but there is a degree of guidance available from the authorities (some of which are pre-CPR). In so far as the pre-CPR authorities give guidance on issues unrelated to the A plus B analysis, they are usually regarded as still being good law. The principles are broadly the same regardless of whether the receiving party brought or defended the claim.[52]

Wraith

28.38 The town-versus-local argument is colloquially referred to as the '*Wraith* argument' after *Wraith v Sheffield Forgemasters Ltd*.[53] The final appeal in *Wraith* was heard along with another case, *Truscott v Truscott*. It is worth dealing with the facts of both *Wraith* and *Truscott* in some detail because those facts are often referred to in practice. Mr Wraith was injured in an accident at his workplace in Sheffield; he brought a claim funded by his union. As was their habit, the union instructed specialist personal injury solicitors in London. Proceedings were commenced in London but transferred to Sheffield. Mr Wraith was awarded substantial damages.

28.39 Mr Truscott was pursued by his former wife for maintenance payments. He lived in Tunbridge Wells and had previously instructed solicitors in East Grinstead (also in Kent). Although the order was enforceable only in the magistrates' court, his former wife's solicitors obtained an order for sale of his house. Acting on a recommendation made by a friend, he instructed a firm of solicitors in central London. His new solicitors obtained an order striking out the order for sale; Mr Truscott was awarded costs. At the assessment, he was awarded London rates but, at the first appeal, these were reduced to local rates.

28.40 The Court of Appeal allowed both appeals (ie Mr Wraith was restricted to local rates, but Mr Truscott was allowed town rates). Kennedy LJ found that a paying party could object to a receiving party's choice of lawyer if that choice had been a 'luxury' – a word that is often used in such arguments:[54]

> '[Costs may be disallowed if they have] not been "reasonably incurred" to the extent that they had been augmented by employment of a solicitor who, by reason of his calibre, normal area of practice, status or location, amounts to an unsuitable or "luxury" choice, made on grounds other than grounds which would be taken into account by an ordinary reasonable litigant concerned to obtain skilful competent and efficient representation in the type of litigation concerned.'

---

[50] See *Re Ajanaku* (unreported) 28 October 1991, Eastham J; this is a pre-CPR authority, but it is usually accepted as still being good law.
[51] See **28.67** onwards.
[52] See *Walbrook Properties Ltd v Severn Trent Water Ltd & Ors* [2002] EWHC 9016 (Costs), in which a defendant's hourly rate was reduced from London rates to Birmingham rates.
[53] [1998] 1 WLR 132.
[54] *Wraith v Sheffield Forgemasters Ltd* [1998] 1 WLR 132 at 142.

Kennedy LJ went on to emphasise that the heart of the issue was the reasonableness of the decision to instruct town solicitors:[55]

> '[The] focus is primarily upon the reasonable interests of the [claimant] in the litigation so that, in relation to broad categories of costs, such as those generated by the decision of a [claimant] to employ a particular status or type of solicitor or counsel, or one located in a particular area, one looks to see whether, having regard to the extent and importance of the litigation to a reasonably minded [claimant], a reasonable choice or decision has been made.'

Factors to be taken into account when considering geographical issues

28.41 Kennedy LJ identified a number of factors which were relevant. The wording of his judgment is given in the footnotes,[56] but if the fact-specific aspects of his guidance are disregarded, the following factors can be identified as being of relevance generally:

- the importance of the matter to the client;
- the legal and factual complexities involved (in so far as the client could reasonably be expected to understand them);
- the location of the client's home, his place of work, and the location of the court;
- the client's previous experience of local solicitors;
- any advice that the client might have received (including, presumably, recommendations);
- the location of the town solicitors, their accessibility, and their readiness to attend at the relevant court; and
- what, if anything, the client could be expected to know of the difference in rates charged by town and local solicitors.

Both Moses J and Tugendhat J have commented that the list in *Wraith* must not be read as a comprehensive or exclusive list applicable to all cases.[57] Factors not on this list, for example, might include the age of the client and the urgency with which the instructions must be placed.[58] In short, each case is to be decided on its own facts.

Client's subjective knowledge about difference in rates

28.42 Whilst the court will take into account the client's actual knowledge, Kennedy LJ has confirmed that knowledge may be imputed to the client.[59] Thus, whilst as a matter

---

[55]   Ibid.
[56]   [1998] 1 WLR 132 at 141: 'The following are matters which, as it seems to me, the judge should have regarded as relevant when considering the reasonableness of Mr Truscott 's decision to instruct ATC [his solicitors]. (1) The importance of the matter to him. It was obviously of great importance. It threatened his home. (2) The legal and factual complexities, in so far as he might reasonably be expected to understand them. Due to the incompetence of MFC the matter had taken on an appearance of some complexity. (3) The location of his home, his place of work and the location of the court in which the relevant proceedings had been commenced. (4) Mr Truscott's possibly well-founded dissatisfaction with the solicitors he had originally instructed, which may well have resulted in a natural desire to instruct solicitors further afield, who would not be inhibited in representing his interests. (5) The fact that he had sought advice as to whom to consult, and had been recommended to consult ATC. (6) The location of ATC, including their accessibility to him, and their readiness to attend at the relevant court. (7) What, if anything, he might reasonably be expected to know of the fees likely to be charged by ATC as compared with the fees of other solicitors whom he might reasonably be expected to have considered.'
[57]   *Higgins v Ministry of Defence* [2010] EWHC 654 (QB) at [14] and [24], per Tugdenhat; Moses J's comments are referred to at [22] where Tugendhat refers to the unreported case of *Rana v Harrar*.
[58]   *Higgins v Ministry of Defence* [2010] EWHC 654 (QB) at [24].
[59]   *Wraith v Sheffield Forgemasters Ltd* [1998] 1 WLR 132 at 142.

of fact the client may not have had the information necessary to allow him to make a reasoned decision, he may be taken to have had that information if it was reasonably available and if he could have been expected to have found out about it.

Objectivity of the appropriate test

28.43 The need to examine the matter from an objective viewpoint rather than from a subjective viewpoint was emphasised by May LJ in *Sullivan v Co-operative Insurance Society*; litigants are entitled to engage any lawyer they choose and from a subjective point of view the choice may be entirely reasonable, but the question is to be judged objectively.[60] The test is not an entirely objective one, however, as Latham LJ made clear in a different case:[61]

'It seems to me that the conclusion that one can properly reach from the judgment of Kennedy LJ [in *Wraith*] is that, whereas it is clear that the test must involve an objective element when determining the reasonableness or otherwise of instructing the particular legal advisers in question, nonetheless that must always be a question which is answered within the context of the particular circumstances of the particular litigants with whom the court is concerned.'

Thus, the test is an objective test, but it must be applied within the context of the circumstances of the particular litigants in question.

Relevance of instructions arising out of habit

28.44 Both May LJ and Kennedy LJ have confirmed that the fact that a union or other organisation habitually instructs a particular firm of solicitors is a relevant factor, but of limited relevance on assessment in an individual case.[62] Notwithstanding this guidance, there are many first instance decisions in which the court has found that the firm's familiarity with the funder's working practices had resulted in savings in the time spent, and that this justified the use of town solicitors (see, on a related point, **28.47** and **28.50**).

Relevance of locus, geographical convenience, etc

28.45 May LJ has explained that the fact that a case has no obvious connection with the area in which solicitors were instructed is a relevant factor, the more so if the case did not require expertise only to be found there.[63]

28.46 It may be that a claim is so well rooted in a particular location that it can be said, for example, to be 'a Manchester case'; May LJ has confirmed that this would be a relevant factor.[64] Judge LJ added:[65]

---

[60]   *Sullivan v Co-operative Insurance Society Limited* [1999] 2 Costs LR 158 at 165 onwards.

[61]   *Griffiths v Solutia UK Limited* [2001] EWCA Civ 736 at [16].

[62]   *Sullivan v Co-operative Insurance Society Limited* [1999] 2 Costs LR 158 at 167, per May LJ, and *Wraith v Sheffield Forgemasters Ltd* [1998] 1 WLR 132 at 142, per Kennedy LJ.

[63]   *Sullivan v Co-operative Insurance Society Limited* [1999] 2 Costs LR 158 at 167. Whilst obiter, see also *Higgins v Ministry of Defence* [2010] EWHC 654 (QB) at [26]

[64]   The facts were that the claim was an asbestosis case without extraordinary legal complication or special features. The claimant lived in Manchester, the cause of action arose in Manchester, the lay witnesses lived in or around Manchester, one of the claimant's experts practised close to Manchester, the defendant was based in Manchester, and there were many firms of solicitors in the Manchester area who were well capable of handling the claim. May LJ found that it was 'pre-eminently a Manchester case with no obvious connection with London: *Sullivan v Co-operative Insurance Society Limited* [1999] 2 Costs LR 158 at 167.

'In reality this was a Manchester case. The cause of action arose from the plaintiff's employment by the defendants in Manchester and his consequent fault exposure to asbestos which caused him serious personal injury. Even as the case developed through the identification of witnesses and the selection of experts and discovery, the case remained a Manchester case with no, or no relevant, connection at all with London.'

28.47 The matter is not limited to geographical convenience as the court must take into account all the circumstances, including those which do not pertain to geography. In a case in which London solicitors had been instructed to carry out a search and seize order in Manchester, HHJ Hegarty QC (sitting as a High Court judge) found that this was reasonable given the urgency of the situation, the fact that the client was based outside the UK, and the fact that the solicitors who were instructed were familiar with the claimants' business and needs.[66]

28.48 In a similar vein, Latham LJ has found that the absence of a connection with the town in question is not, of itself, sufficient to make the decision to instruct solicitors there an unreasonable decision; in the case before him, Latham LJ took into account all of the facts, rather than just those relating to geography.[67]

Relevance of geographical differences in rates

28.49 The differential between town and local rates may not only be a factor, but in an appropriate case it may be a factor which must be taken into account. This was explained by Sir Christopher Staughton:[68]

> 'It does not appear that the costs judge or the deputy judge on appeal were told what the difference was between the costs of London solicitors and Manchester solicitors. But how can one answer the question whether it was reasonable to engage a London solicitor unless one at least takes into account the answer to that question? In this case we did ask and we were told ... This ... is a matter of some importance.'

These comments were made in the context of group litigation in which the rising costs were a particular concern. Given that in *Wraith* Kennedy LJ emphasised that the test is what the *client* knew or ought to have known (see **28.41**), it cannot be the case that the differential will be relevant in every case. Indeed, Teare J has implied that it would only be in appropriate cases that a reasonable litigant could be expected to acquaint himself with the difference between town and local hourly rates.[69] Tugendhat J has said that a reasonable litigant will normally be expected to investigate the hourly rates of solicitors whom he might instruct and to take advice thereupon before choosing whom to instruct; he said that other relevant factors that the client would be expected to take into account would include the time and costs associated with geographical location.[70] Notwithstanding those high expectations, Tugendhat J found that the other factors in the case before him (namely, the urgency of the matter and the age of the client) justified the decision of the receiving party in the case before him to instruct town solicitors; he was at pains to point out that each case must be decided on its own facts rather than in a formulaic way.[71]

---

[65]   *Sullivan v Co-operative Insurance Society Limited* [1999] 2 Costs LR 158.
[66]   *Fisher Price Inc & Mattel UK Ltd v RSW Group plc* [2004] EWHC 1610 (Ch).
[67]   *Griffiths v Solutia UK Limited* [2001] EWCA Civ 736 at [20], per Latham LJ.
[68]   *Griffiths v Solutia UK Limited* [2001] EWCA Civ 736 at [24].
[69]   *A v Chief Constable of South Yorkshire* [2008] EWHC 1658 (QB) at [27].
[70]   *Higgins v Ministry of Defence* [2010] EWHC 654 (QB) at [26].
[71]   *Higgins v Ministry of Defence* [2010] EWHC 654 (QB) at [14] and [24].

Geographical variations in specialist expertise

28.50 Whilst an obvious point, if a solicitor has specialist expertise which is not available elsewhere, that would be a factor to be taken into account in deciding whether it was reasonable to instruct him. (For a discussion of the relevance of specialist experts in general, see **28.66–28.72**.) A solicitor's expertise would be a relevant factor even where it has been gained as a result of prior experience of the case in question.[72]

Paying party's conduct concerning locus and geography

28.51 Mance LJ has commented that if a paying party remained silent about the fact that the receiving party had instructed town solicitors, then that would be a factor that the court could take into account.[73] In practice, however, most claimants will have already instructed solicitors before their opponents are given any opportunity to comment.

Proportionality and distant solicitors

28.52 In giving judgment in an appeal where proportionality did not apply, Sir Christopher Staughton made it clear that his decision might have been different if that test had applied.[74] The clear implication is that it is possible for a decision to instruct town solicitors to be reasonable but disproportionate.

28.53 The following miscellaneous points at **28.54–28.59** can be made about the *Wraith* argument generally.

Experience of local solicitors

28.54 The fact that the client's experience of local solicitors may be relevant was commented upon in *Wraith* (see **28.41**). The fact that it is a factor which may be afforded considerable weight was demonstrated in *Ryan v Tretol Group Limited*.[75] This was a case in which Wright J found[76] that it was reasonable for a claimant with an asbestos-related claim to dis-instruct local solicitors in preference for London solicitors. A notable feature of this case is the fact that the injury was not life-threatening and there were many solicitors outside London who could have dealt with the claim; this suggests that a client who is dissatisfied with his first choice of solicitors is not always required to shop around for suitable specialist county solicitors. See, however, Eady J's comments in a different case about the potential effect of the availability of specialist advice from the bar (recited at **28.57**).

---

[72] *Griffiths v Solutia UK Limited* [2001] EWCA Civ 736 at [33], per Mance LJ.

[73] *Griffiths v Solutia UK Limited* [2001] EWCA Civ 736 at [33].

[74] *Griffiths v Solutia UK Limited* [2001] EWCA Civ 736 at [27]. This case was decided before *Lownds v Home Office* [2002] EWCA 365, but there is nothing in *Lownds* which undermines Sir Christopher Staughton's reasoning.

[75] [2002] All ER (D) 156.

[76] It should be noted that to a large extent the appeal was allowed by consent in that it was conceded that if it was reasonable for the receiving party to dis-instruct his solicitor in Nottingham it would have been reasonable for him to instruct solicitors in London; thus, Wright J did not have to consider the issue of whether Mr Ryan had acted reasonably in instructing solicitors in London, as opposed to Sheffield, or Manchester or Leeds.

Knowledge of local solicitors

28.55 Teare J has found that in an appropriate case a litigant can be expected to make reasonable enquiries as to the availability of local specialist expertise.[77]

Recommendations and support groups

28.56 Advice given by support groups may be relevant.[78]

Geographical availability of a specialist bar

28.57 A factor that might be relevant is the availability of a specialist bar. *Gazley v Wade*[79] concerned a man who was wrongly identified as paedophile by a national newspaper. He initially instructed local solicitors, but after he grew dissatisfied with their services, he instructed specialist solicitors in London. Eady J had this to say:

> 'It is important to recognise that in order to have the necessary or the proportionate expertise available one does not always need to instruct London specialist solicitors. An important factor is that any competent litigation solicitor in the country can call upon specialist members of the bar at very short notice. Indeed, as I have already said, [the claimant's solicitors] themselves took advice from counsel.'

Travelling as a factor

28.58 Whilst she was dealing with a costs-capping application rather than an assessment, Hallett J has implied that the court may take the costs of travelling into account.[80] HHJ Behrens (sitting as a Judge of the High Court) has commented that where a complex case involves a great deal of travelling (which, he observed, is an activity that does not involve difficult work), then either the travelling ought to be reflected in a generally lower rate for all of the work or a differential hourly rate for travel; in the case before him, he allowed those rates published in *Guide to the Summary Assessment of Costs*.[81]

City rates

28.59 Master Hurst has had this to say about City rates (ie rates applicable to the City of London itself):[82]

---

77 *A v Chief Constable of South Yorkshire* [2008] EWHC 1658 (QB) at [27].
78 Astill J, for example, allowed town rates in an asbestos-related disease case where one of the main reasons for instructing town solicitors was because a local support group had recommended those solicitors (*Patterson v Cape Darlington & Ors* [2001] EWHC 9005 (Costs)).
79 [2004] EWHC 2675 (QB).
80 *Ledward v Kent & Medway Health Authority* [2003] EWHC 2551 (QB) at [22]. On the facts of that case, the town solicitors were actually cheaper than the local solicitor and the issue was whether those savings justified the travelling time.
81 *Thornley (a child) v Ministry of Defence* [2010] EWHC 2584 (QB) at [67]–[76], per HHJ Behrens, sitting as a Judge of the High Court.
82 *King v Telegraph Group plc* [2005] EWHC 90015 (Costs) at [92]. (These comments are not binding, but given the fact that hourly rates, and other issues of quantum, are matters which are particularly within Master Hurst's realm of expertise, they must be regarded as being highly persuasive.) See, however, *KPMG Peat Marwick McLintock v HLT Group Ltd* [1995] 2 All ER 180, in which Auld J allowed City rates in a case which was not a commercial case, but 'had commercial undertones'; this case, however, was decided before the jurisdiction established by the line of cases following *Wraith* had matured; it was also pre-CPR.

'City rates for City solicitors are recoverable where the City solicitor is undertaking City work, which is normally heavy commercial or corporate work. Defamation is not in that category, and, particularly given the reduction in damages awards for libel, is never likely to be. A City firm which undertakes work, which could be competently handled by a number of Central London solicitors, is acting unreasonably and disproportionately if it seeks to charge City rates.'

Other factors

28.60 The 'other factors' which can have a bearing on the hourly rate are numerous. Almost any aspect of a claim can be relevant, including arguments about uplift. The factors which used to be relevant to the old B factor (see above) continue to be relevant under the CPR notwithstanding the fact that they are frequently not phrased in pre-CPR language. The following factors merit particular attention:

- complexity;
- specialist expertise;
- unusually low overheads; and
- the use of comparators.

Complexity

28.61 Complexity is a factor to be taken into account; indeed, it is one of the factors listed in CPR, r 44.5(3). The following miscellaneous points can be made.

Factual complexity

28.62 Both Hallett J and Lewison J have implied (albeit briefly) that factual complexity will not necessarily merit the high rates claimed by specialist lawyers: something more is usually required.[83]

Legal complexity

28.63 Legal complexity is a factor to be taken into account. It is open to the court to take into account a note prepared by counsel explaining the difficulties that were encountered.[84]

Emotional complexity

28.64 Hallett J has said (obiter) that it is doubtful if the difficulty and unpleasantness of extracting allegations in an emotionally charged case would merit an unusually high hourly rate.[85]

---

[83] *Ledward v Kent & Medway Health Authority* [2003] EWHC 2551 (QB) at [42], per Hallett J; *Ross v Stonewood Securities Ltd* [2004] EWHC 2235 (Ch) at [31], per Lewison J.

[84] *A v Chief Constable of South Yorkshire* [2008] EWHC 1658 (QB) at [22]–[23]. Teare J found that such a note is admissible notwithstanding the fact that it may partly be opinion. He went on to say that the court is not obliged to accept the opinion of counsel, as the court must decide matters in dispute for itself.

[85] *Ledward v Kent & Medway Health Authority* [2003] EWHC 2551 (QB) at [42].

Group litigation

28.65 Where work is being carried out on individual (non-lead) claims which form part of group litigation, it might be appropriate to award a lower rate for that work than would be allowed for the generic work.[86] On the other hand, Lord Neuberger MR has implied that the costs of obtaining clients and getting business may be a factor that could be reflected in the hourly rate in group litigation.[87]

Specialist expertise

28.66 There are four aspects to the issue of specialist expertise. The first is whether the hourly rate should be uplifted to take account of the costs of maintaining a specialism (ie higher overheads), the second is whether the rate should be uplifted generally to reflect specialist expertise (ie discretionary uplift), the third is the way in which the costs incurred by teams of fee earners should be assessed, and the last is the extent to which the specialisation (or lack thereof) of counsel might be relevant.

Higher overheads arising out of specialism

28.67 The first issue may arise in any context,[88] but it most commonly arises when a specialist solicitor practising in the provinces wishes to claim a higher rate than the local norm because of the higher overheads of maintaining a specialism (such as the costs of employing specialist staff, of maintaining a specialist library, etc). This argument is often referred to as a '*Jones* argument'.[89] Whilst it is a different argument from the argument that there should be a discretionary uplift to reflect the expertise (see **28.70**); the two arguments are not mutually exclusive.

28.68 A *Jones* argument would be based on the premise that a specialist firm would have higher overheads than the average provincial firm; they may, for example, have to pay their assistant solicitors and other staff higher salaries, or they may have to provide extra facilities for demanding clients.[90] The increased overheads have to be proved by evidence; in *Jones* itself the receiving party's claim for a higher rate failed because that evidence was not put before the court.

28.69 Eady J has impliedly confirmed that the requirement for evidence has survived the introduction of the CPR. In a case in which a lawyer sought to justify a very high rate on the basis of his supposedly fearsome reputation, Eady J made the following remarks:[91]

> '[The paying party] argued as follows: "If you wish to take yourself out of the norm you have to provide the court with evidence to enable you to do so. You may have a niche practice, and you may be able to persuade celebrities that you are the solicitor to go to at

---

[86]   *Giambrone v JMC Holidays Ltd* [2002] 2 Costs LR 294 at 300.

[87]   *Motto & Ors v Trafigura Ltd & Anor* [2011] EWCA Civ 1150 at [110].

[88]   See, for example, *Cox and Carter v MGN Ltd* [2006] EWHC 1235 (QB), where the issue arose in relation to a solicitor practising in central London.

[89]   After *Jones v Secretary of State for Wales* [1997] 1 WLR 1008.

[90]   A hypothetical example which is often cited is a firm which specialises in representing foreign commercial clients; one would expect such a firm's overheads to be higher as a result of the need to keep the office open to take calls from clients in different time zones.

[91]   *Cox and Carter v MGN Ltd* [2006] EWHC 1235 (QB at [61]).

whatever rate you choose to charge them, but without evidence that your overheads are out of the ordinary there is no basis for holding that a *Jones* increase should apply". I find his reasoning persuasive.'

Discretionary enhancement for specialist expertise

28.70 A receiving party may seek to be awarded a discretionary enhancement (which under the A plus B model would be an increase in B rather than A). If the argument is limited in this way, and if it is not based on an assertion that there are increased overheads, then evidence would not usually be required. The justification for a discretionary enhancement is usually based on the premise that a specialist lawyer would complete the task in hand with greater frugality of time than a generalist. There are examples of the court accepting such an argument,[92] but the expertise has to be relevant in the sense that it may assist in disposing of the claim, and in that regard it has to be more than merely desirable.[93]

Teams and distribution of responsibility

28.71 Where work is being carried out by a team which is made up of senior members who bear a greater burden of responsibility than the junior members, the key to determining the appropriate rates is the level of responsibility borne. This means that it may be appropriate to allow differential enhancements above the rates which would have been allowed to generalists.[94] Morland J has commented that if a single enhancement is contemplated, it ought to reflect the average level of responsibility borne rather the highest.[95]

Counsel's specialisation

28.72 The availability of a specialist bar has already been mentioned (see **28.57**): while speaking in the context of whether it was reasonable to instruct solicitors in a particular locality, Eady J commented that any solicitor is able to call upon the services of specialist counsel.[96] Therefore, the availability of a local specialist bar (or lack thereof) may be relevant.

Unusually low overheads

28.73 It may be the case that the paying party seeks a reduction in the hourly rates because of unusually low overheads. There is authority for this proposition.[97] In a case

---

[92] Although dealing with legal aid enhancement, Sullivan J allowed an enhanced rate to take account of a fee earner's expertise gained outside his legal practice (in that case, as a dentist); this was on the basis that the fee earner's expertise saved time: see *Diacou v Staden* [2000] EWHC 9003 (Costs).

[93] In a case which involved psychiatric issues, issues concerning ethnicity and claims against the police, Teare J found that although counsel would have been assisted by the fact that his instructing solicitors were specialists in these areas, experienced personal injury counsel could have been expected to bring the claim to a successful conclusion without that additional assistance: *A v Chief Constable of South Yorkshire Police* [2008] EWHC 1658 at [23].

[94] *Giambrone v JMC Holidays Ltd* [2002] 2 Costs LR 294 at 299.

[95] Ibid.

[96] In *Gazley v Wade* [2004] EWHC 2675 (QB).

[97] *Stubblefield v Kemp* [2001] 1 Costs LR 30: that authority was in the context of solicitor–litigants rather than litigants represented by solicitors. Nonetheless, it was decided on a more general basis than whether the two-thirds cap as set out in CPR, r 48.6(2) should apply. The solicitor–litigants in question claimed a full

in which that argument succeeded, Arden J referred to *London Scottish Benefit Society v Chorley* and, in particular, to the following extract from Brett MR's judgment:[98]

> 'The unsuccessful adversary of a solicitor appearing in person cannot be charged for what does not exist'.

Arden J found that the costs judge had been correct to assess the hourly rate on the basis that no allowance should be made for overheads which did not exist. The case before Arden J involved a solicitor–litigant: it is not known whether the same analysis would apply to the assessment of costs where the receiving party was represented. There is (ancient) authority to suggest that it would, albeit in a context other than hourly rates.[99]

Urgency and pressure of time

28.74 The need for the urgent supply of legal services may justify a higher hourly rate. Peter Smith J, for example, allowed £400 ph as against a guideline rate of £317 ph, this being because 'given the nature of the application and the urgency a figure higher than the guideline figure [was] justified; the application was to commit a party to prison for failure to comply with the terms of a freezing order'.[100]

THE USE OF COMPARATORS AND PRECEDENTS

28.75 The amounts charged by a party's previous solicitors might be an appropriate comparator,[101] as might rates charged by an opponent. A comparison with rates paid by those who instruct defendant firms may not be a helpful comparator; Hallett J explained that this is because 'their "clout" in the market place is such that they can drive down lawyers' fees and still benefit from the assistance of experienced solicitors'.[102] The Advisory Committee on Civil Costs came to much the same conclusion following a survey which referred to costs incurred in 2007; that survey came to the following conclusions:[103]

> '[The researchers found] a large gap between the rates charged by claimants' solicitors and those charged by defendants' solicitors for Personal Injury (PI) or Clinical Negligence (CN) cases. No such gap exists for Chancery (CH) or Employment Tribunal (ET) cases. In PI/CN cases the rates charged by claimants' solicitors were around the GHRs, those charged by defendants' solicitors were 20–35 percent lower.'

In their 2010 report, the committee found that the difference between the rates charged by claimant firms and firms working for insurers is capable of being accounted from on

---

hourly rate for work on their own claims (rather than claims brought or defended on behalf of their firms); the issue was whether the rate should be restricted to take account of the fact that the solicitor–litigants did not have any overheads.

98 *Stubblefield v Kemp* [2001] 1 Costs LR 30 at 37; the original extract (of Brett MR) was from *London Scottish Benefit Society v Chorley* (1884) 13 QBD 872.

99 *Henderson v Merthyr Tydfil Urban District Council* [1900] 1 QB 434 at 437.

100 *Global Marine Drillships Ltd v La Bella* [2010] EWHC 2498 (Ch) at [8].

101 *Ross v Stonewood Securities Ltd* [2004] EWHC 2235 (Ch) at [31], per Lewison J.

102 *Ledward v Kent & Medway Health Authority* [2003] EWHC 2551 (QB) at [32]; see also *Mainwaring v Goldtech Investments Ltd* [1997] 1 All ER 467.

103 See *The Derivation of New Guideline Hourly Rates*, a report produced by the Advisory Committee on Civil Costs dated about 9 December 2008, p 2, para (vi); These figures should be read in the context of the criticism made at **28.3**, however, as they are derived from the same data which is, to say the least, questionable.

the basis that claimant firms have to bear the costs of case screening, they have to deal with less knowledgeable clients, have to wait longer to be paid and have to cope with a volatile flow of work.[104] That committee's methodology and conclusions are not universally accepted.[105]

28.76 As to the rates allowed in other cases, the court has repeatedly stressed that each case is to be decided on its own facts. In the context of the court below having declined to give weight to a decision recently decided by another judge, Lewison J said:[106]

> 'He was rightly unimpressed with the attempt to use [that case] as a comparator. [That case] was a decision on its own facts, and did not establish any general rule about the appropriate level of charging rates, even in specialised cases.'

COMPOSITE RATES

28.77 Composite rates are a blend of unequal hourly rates (usually applicable to different time periods). If, for example, a bill claims relatively modest sums in the period 2001 to 2007, it might be seen as being proportionate and sensible to apply a single composite rate throughout rather than three or four different rates, each applicable to a different time period. The composite rate may be based on an arithmetical mean, or they may be based on midpoint (ie a 2004 rate in the example above). Weighted average may be appropriate in some circumstances.[107]

28.78 Evans J has confirmed the legality of such an approach in principle; he had the following to say:[108]

> 'Whether he [the costs judge] takes an average figure covering a number of years or an annual figure which he applies to the work done in each particular year is a matter of convenience and entirely a question for him, in the particular circumstances of the individual case.'

It should be noted that Evans J was referring to what the *costs judge* was able to do, not what the *parties* were able to do: whilst an assessment based on a composite rate is nothing more than a judicial shortcut, the same may not be true if a composite rate is claimed in the bill of costs. This is because of the 'principle of individual application' (see **11.8–11.11**) which means that the indemnity principle applies to each-and-every item, rather than as a cap.

28.79 Although there is no specific requirement within either the CPR or the CPD precluding the use of composite rates, some judges find such rates objectionable (not

---

[104] Advisory Committee on Civil Costs; Guideline Hourly Rates – Conclusion, March 2010, paras 2(i) to (iv).

[105] The 2010 report, for example, seems not to provide any proper explanation as to why the cost of screening cases was not covered by success fees; moreover, no proper explanation was given as to why the cost of dealing with less knowledgeable clients should be reflected in the rate as opposed to the time. Also, whilst the committee refers to the evidence of specific firms, there is nothing to suggest that those firms are themselves representative of the market as a whole.

[106] *Ross v Stonewood Securities Ltd* [2004] EWHC 2235 (Ch) at [30], per Lewison J.

[107] A weighted average would be particularly appropriate where the work was not spread out evenly over the periods in question. Thus, if twice as much work was done in 2001 than in the other years, that year may be afforded a double share when the average is calculated.

[108] *Johnson v Reed Corrugated Cases Ltd* [1992] 1 All ER 169 at 178. These comments were made prior to the introduction of the CPR.

least because of the infringement of the principle of individual application). The court will often express its disapproval (usually by allowing rates which are based on the lowest of the component rates rather than the composite rate), but it will rarely allow itself to be used as a vehicle for the advancement of pedantry. Master Wright, for example, rejected a challenge to a composite rate on the basis that it would have been impracticable to allow differential rates; he rejected the notion that the bill should be redrawn.[109]

---

[109]   *Abu v MGN* [2004] EWHC 9043 (Costs) at [82].

Chapter 29

ASSESSMENT OF TIME

THE APPROACH IN GENERAL

29.1 Many of the points which follow go to very small items, sometimes as small as whether three or six minutes is the appropriate allowance. Small items soon add up to a much larger total, so their importance should not be overlooked; indeed, Denning MR suggested, in his inimitable way, that every minute merits proper accounting:[1]

> 'These rates are over a pound a minute. It would seem that there must be a very good system of timing – almost by stopwatch – if that is to be the rate of payment.'

That said, this book is not intended to promote a laborious approach to the quantification of costs. The fact that the law permits time to be scrutinised in minute detail does not mean that every assessment should proceed in that way. What is set out below is intended to be a reference, not a manual of instruction.

Principles of accounting for time

Sachs's sensible solicitor

29.2 The correct vantage point from which to gauge the reasonableness of the time spent was explained by Sachs J:[2]

> 'The correct viewpoint to be adopted by a taxing officer is that of a sensible solicitor sitting in his chair and considering what in the light of his then knowledge is reasonable in the interests of his lay client ... [It] is wrong for a taxing officer to adopt an attitude akin to a revenue official called upon to apply rigorously one of those Income Tax Act Rules as to expenses which have been judicially described as "jealously restricted" and "notoriously rigid and narrow in their operation." I should add that, as previously indicated, the lay client in question should be deemed a man of means adequate to bear the expense of the litigation out of his own pocket – and by "adequate" I mean neither "barely adequate" nor "superabundant."'

Whilst these comments can apply to any item of costs, they are particularly relevant to profit costs; this is because profit costs are the costs over which a solicitor has most control.

Duty to examine material

29.3 Where profit costs are challenged, the receiving party will usually put material before the court in support of the costs claimed; this may be formally (as a result of the

---

[1] *Chamberlain v Boodle & King* [1982] 1 WLR 1443 at 1445.
[2] *Francis v Francis and Dickerson* [1956] P 87 at 91.

court exercising its discretion to put the receiving party to his election) or, more usually, informally without the issue of election ever arising (see Chapter 24 and, in particular, **24.32**). The following points can be made about the court's duty to examine the relevant material.

Need for an adequate examination

29.4   Whilst the case before him related to the assessment of criminal costs rather than civil costs, Maurice Kay LJ (sitting in the Divisional Court) explained that where a costs judge finds that costs are to be admitted in principle, the documentation relating to those costs must be adequately examined before an assessment of quantum is made.[3]

Extrapolating from a sample

29.5   Where costs are made up of a number of items (such as a documentary schedule) the court may take a broad-brush approach which is based on an extrapolation of the results of the assessment of a sample of the items; Park J has commented that where such an extrapolation is carried out the court should be aware of the fact that if the sample is unrepresentative errors may be made which would serve to substantially distort the accuracy of that test.[4]

Approximation of the discount

29.6   In a similar vein but in the context of the court seeking to disallow the costs of pursuing an exaggerated claim, Kennedy LJ found that it would be wrong to apply a percentage discount in lieu of an item-by-item assessment; he commented that the correct approach was to go through the bill on an item-by-item basis and only then (if appropriate) to apply a percentage reduction.[5]

Estimated time

29.7   Estimated time is time which is claimed notwithstanding the absence of a contemporaneous time recording. It is time which has been estimated retrospectively, either by the solicitor or by the costs draftsman who prepared the bill. Two points arise: first, whether costs based on estimated time are recoverable in principle and, second, if so, how the appropriate allowance is assessed.

29.8   Before these points are addressed, it is worth mentioning that, ideally, the need to estimate time ought to be avoided in the first place by keeping a proper record of the time spent (either manually on file notes, or electronically on a practice management system). Notwithstanding its procedural obsolescence, the following guidance from a 1986 practice direction still has resonance in this regard:[6]

'Properly kept and detailed time records are helpful in support of a bill provided they explain the nature of the work as well as recording the time involved. The absence of such records

---

[3]   *R (on the application of Brewer) v Supreme Court Costs Office* [2006] EWHC 1955 (Admin) at [24]–[26].

[4]   See, for example, *Arab Monetary Fund v Hashim* (unreported) 30 June 2000, Ch D, Park J, in which the costs judge allowed 80% of a senior grade fee earner's time but, on closer scrutiny, an allowance of 90% was the appropriate extrapolation.

[5]   *Booth v Britannia Hotels Ltd* [2002] EWCA Civ 579.

[6]   Note 13 in the Practice Direction (Supreme Court Taxing Office) No 1 of 1986.

may result in the disallowance or diminution of the charges claimed. They cannot be accepted as conclusive evidence that the time recorded either has been spent or if spent, is "reasonably" chargeable.'

29.9 There is – surprisingly – no requirement within either the CPR or the CPD that estimated time should be stated to be such in the bill; it is, nonetheless, good practice to state the fact that time has been estimated. This is usually done by marking the entry with an 'e' or some other suitable symbol. Best practice would be also to state the basis upon which the time has been estimated (eg '12 mins (e); estimate based on two-page attendance note').

Recoverability in principle

29.10 There will be occasions when it is not possible to record time. Parker J gave as an example an exceptionally complex case in which short but important discussions arose in an environment of exigency.[7] He found that it would be 'wholly impractical in some instances to keep [attendance] notes'. He found that there is no reason in principle why the court should not accept that actual time was spent notwithstanding the absence of a contemporaneous time recording. Brooke J came to a similar conclusion; he found that the general rule is that costs are not made irrecoverable solely by reason of being based on estimated time.[8]

29.11 Where time is estimated, the court will usually require the receiving party to explain the basis upon which the estimate was made; this may involve the receiving party being put to his election in respect of the material upon which the estimate is based. Whether or not the court allows the time will be a matter of fact to be decided on the evidence, but the material the court may take into account is not limited to the presence or absence of attendance notes; this was explained by Parker J:[9]

> 'The right to charge cannot depend upon the question whether discussions are recorded or unrecorded. It must depend, initially, upon whether they in fact took place and occupied the time claimed. If they are recorded in attendance notes, this will no doubt ordinarily be accepted as sufficient evidence of those facts. If they are not so recorded it may well be that the claimant is unable to satisfy the taxing officer or master as to the facts. But neither the presence nor the absence of an attendance note is conclusive.'

29.12 The amount of time that will be allowed will depend on the nature of the claim which is made; in particular, it will depend on the cogency of the evidence concerning the length of the attendance and the scope and complexity of the work carried out.

Estimated time: short letters and emails

29.13 For obvious reasons (ie that the correspondence will speak for itself), a solicitor is not required to record the time spent preparing routine correspondence. That said, CPD, art 4.16(2) provides that the court may, in its discretion, allow a time charge for preparation of emails sent by solicitors, but only if the time taken has been recorded.

---

7   *In re Frascati* (unreported) 2 December 1981, quoted in *Brush v Bower Cotton & Bower* [1993] 4 All ER 741 at 753.

8   Although a pre-CPR case, the authority which is usually cited on this point is *Brush v Bower Cotton & Bower* [1993] 4 All ER 741 at 753, in which Brooke J reviewed the authorities on the point.

9   *In re Frascati* (unreported) 2 December 1981.

Estimated time: 'padding' of the bill

29.14 Whilst a colloquial expression, a bill may be said to be 'padded' if it contains multiple claims for short attendances or other work which are not recorded but which are said to be implied by the nature of the work being carried out. An example would be where short file reviews are habitually claimed before writing routine letters. Whilst he did not refer to it by that name, Evans J found that the court is entitled to disallow costs which are the result of padding. He did so on the basis that there is no presumption that the time which is recorded in a file is an under-recording of the time actually spent.[10]

Estimated time: short attendances

29.15 It is implicit in what is said at **29.16** about long attendances that the court will not necessarily be perturbed by the fact that there is no record of the time spent in short attendances (although, of course, the award may be less generous than it might have been). A complete absence of a record of the fact of the attendance will rarely be overlooked, however: Parker J opined that an allowance should only be made in those circumstances where it would have been impracticable to have kept a record.[11]

Estimated time: long attendances

29.16 Brooke J has warned that claims for unrecorded long attendances are likely to be 'viewed with very considerable care' and that it would only be in an unusual case that any substantial allowance would be made for unrecorded time.[12]

Repeated failure to record time

29.17 Where there is an habitual failure to record the time spent, very significant reductions are the norm. In a case in which 350 hours of unrecorded time were claimed, Park J described an allowance of 100 hours as 'generous'.[13]

29.18 Most of the cases referred to above are pre-CPR; given the fact that neither the RSC nor the CPR have anything significant to say about estimated time, they probably remain good law. That said, as with all pre-CPR cases, they ought to be viewed with appropriate caution.

Methods of working

29.19 There is considerable diversity in the methods by which legal services are provided; in particular, some solicitors will place more emphasis on teamwork than others. A number of issues will arise where legal services are provided by a team rather than by an individual. Those issues arise out of the fact that members of a team will need to spend time communicating with each other for the purposes of delegation, supervision and general liaison.

---

[10] *Johnson v Reed Corrugated Cases Ltd* [1992] 1 All ER 169 at 187, per Evans J; this was in response to the suggestion that *Maltby v D J Freeman & Co* [1978] 2 All ER 913 at 916 was authority for the proposition that an allowance ought to be routinely made for unrecorded time.

[11] *In re Frascati* (unreported) 2 December 1981.

[12] *Brush v Bower Cotton & Bower* [1993] 4 All ER 741 at 742.

[13] *Arab Monetary Fund v Hashim* (unreported) 30 June 2000, Ch D, Park J.

Delegation and supervision

29.20 Delegation occurs where a duty is entrusted to another, and supervision occurs where the execution or performance of a task is superintended. The former will usually arise in the context of the person who has conduct of the matter enlisting the help of a more junior colleague, and the latter may arise in that context or in that of the person who has conduct of the matter asking for help from a more senior colleague.

29.21 Delegation and supervision give rise to the same potential problem in that both require a degree of interaction between colleagues; the time spent interacting may be objected to on the basis that it was not required or on a more intrinsic basis that such work is not chargeable in principle.

29.22 That intrinsic objection arises out of the fact that some types of supervision are properly characterised as being the costs of running a practice rather than the costs of litigation. Whilst he was dealing with a criminal case, Mustill J had this to say on the topic:[14]

> 'Every senior solicitor will wish to keep an eye on what is going on in his office, to make sure that it is operating efficiently, and that the standards set by the senior solicitor, who bears the ultimate responsibility for the proper conduct of all work carried out by the practice, are being scrupulously maintained. Again, a senior solicitor who has proper regard for his broader responsibilities will find it necessary to discuss matters with his more junior staff, as a method of practical instruction, with a view to making them better fitted to perform their allotted work. Very often in both of these spheres the solicitor may occupy some time on a particular case. It would not, however, by any means necessarily follow that this time would be attributed to the preparation of that case, so as to entitle the solicitor to remuneration under [the relevant Regulation]. It would simply be part of the overhead expense incurred by the solicitor in the proper conduct of his practice.'

29.23 As can be seen, Mustill J made no mention of reasonableness. Thus, the court may disallow costs, not because they were unreasonably incurred (such as where there has been duplication of effort), but because they are irrecoverable in principle. There is no generally received way of referring to that principle, but the phrases 'costs which are absorbed within the overhead' and 'costs of running a practice' are as good as any.

29.24 There is a limit to the amount of work which will be disallowed in this way; where the work is such that it passes the threshold of no longer being the costs of running a practice, then a receiving party will have to demonstrate that they were reasonably incurred. Mustill J stated that the burden will lie with the receiving party to provide an explanation as to why the delegation or supervision was reasonably required.[15]

Delegation

29.25 Although there is no authority on the point, common sense dictates that where they are allowed in principle, the costs of delegation will be recoverable only to the extent that the overall costs do not exceed those which would have been incurred had the delegation not taken place (see, by way of analogy, **29.27**). That will be an issue of fact.

---

[14] *R v Sandhu* (1984) 29 November, Taxing Masters Compendium (published by the SCTO in 1984); that the principles referred to in that case have survived the introduction of the CPR is suggested by the fact that it was extensively relied upon by Master O'Hare in *In Re Radcliffe* [2004] EWHC 90039 (Costs).

[15] Ibid.

An allowance will generally be made for the delegatee to familiarise himself with the necessary material.[16] Indeed, Edwards-Stuart J impliedly made an allowance for the fact that a very junior fee earner might not have been fully familiar with the relevant procedure (this being in the context of the procedure being an unusual one, namely commercial arbitration).[17]

Supervision by the person with conduct of the file

29.26 Supervision may be provided by the person who has conduct of the matter; where this is so, the points made immediately above would apply. It would be open to the court to allow the supervisee a lower rate than would have been allowed if he had been entrusted to carry out the task in hand without supervision (ie if he had been a delegatee rather than a supervisee)[18] (see **28.71**).

Supervision of the person with conduct of the file

29.27 Where the person with conduct of the file is supervised by a more senior colleague, the court will usually consider the effect of that supervision on the costs overall. If, for example, the fact that the supervision has taken place has resulted in the matter being allocated to a more junior fee earner than would otherwise have been the case, the costs of supervision may well be justifiable. Mustill J had these comments to make on the issue:[19]

> 'There must be many cases where, once the case has been allocated to a fee earner of the appropriate grade he or she can be allowed to carry on the work unaided, without any need for intervention by someone more senior. On the other hand, there may equally be cases where, if and when the matter is in the hands of someone who could ordinarily be considered competent to deal with it, there might be an unexpected turn of events where the senior solicitor's extra experience and weight would be an essential reinforcement.'

Mustill J went on to say that costs may be allowable if there has been an unexpected turn of events where the senior fee earner's extra experience and weight would be 'an essential reinforcement'.

Costs of office memoranda and discussions between fee earners

29.28 Whilst not binding, Master O'Hare offered this opinion on the costs of communications between colleagues in the same firm:[20]

> 'In my judgment it is always, or almost always, inappropriate for a claim to be made for letters sent by one fee earner to another fee earner in the same firm. The allocation of tasks between them is part of the irrecoverable overhead of the firm. If the senior fee earner needs to be informed of some aspect of a matter he should simply read the relevant attendance notes when the file is sent to him.'

These comments were made in the context of work having been delegated, but they would probably also apply where there has been no delegation.

---

[16]   Whilst a criminal case, see, for example, *R v Sandhu* (1984) 29 November, Taxing Masters Compendium.
[17]   *Price v Carter* [2010] EWHC 1737 (TCC) at [11].
[18]   *Giambrone v JMC Holidays Ltd* [2002] 2 Costs LR 294 at 299.
[19]   *R v Sandhu* (1984) 29 November, Taxing Masters Compendium, quoted by Master O'Hare in *In Re Radcliffe* [2004] EWHC 90039 (Costs).
[20]   *In Re Radcliffe* [2004] EWHC 90039 (Costs); see also SCCO Practice Direction No 2 of 1992, para 1.8.

29.29 It likely that the court would make similar comments where there is discussion between colleagues in the same firm (as opposed to where there has been an exchange of memoranda). It would, however, be open to the court to make an allowance for the time that would have been spent by the relevant fee earner reading into the file.

Unqualified staff and administrative work

29.30 For the reasons set out at **5.34–5.56**, an employed fee earner's unqualified status will not preclude a charge being made for his work. That said, work carried out by the most junior members of a team may be administrative in nature, in which case it may be objectionable on the basis that it was not fee earners' work.

29.31 Subject to the terms of the retainer, it is the nature of the work which is relevant, not the fact that it had been carried out by an unqualified person. Brooke J has confirmed that where the work can properly described as clerical or administrative work, it must go unremunerated. Where, on the other hand, there were features of the work which would have been properly charged had it been carried out by the solicitor, then to that extent it ought to be allowed.[21] Each case will turn on its own facts, to be decided by on evidence.[22]

Costs incurred at particular times

29.32 Costs incurred during certain stages of litigation, such as prior to issue of proceedings, after the costs order has been made, and during a stay are dealt with at **29.33–29.39**. To an extent, these issues will depend on the wording of the costs order; the analyses which follow assume that there is nothing atypical about the costs order which could limit its ambit in any way.

Costs incurred prior to issue

29.33 Whilst there can be no liability for costs incurred without authority before the retainer was made,[23] the court has long had the discretion to determine whether costs incurred prior to issue were reasonably required for the attainment of justice and, if they were, to allow them.[24] This may apply even if part of that which was sought was agreed prior to the issue of proceedings.[25] It has been argued that the words 'of and incidental to proceedings' in s 51(a) of the Senior Courts Act 1981 (as amended) qualify costs orders such that pre-issue costs are not recoverable; this is not so, as (whilst different

---

[21] *Brush v Bower Cotton & Bower* [1993] 1 WLR 1328 at 1353.

[22] On a related point, the need to produce evidence of allegedly high overheads was recognised by Eady J in *Cox and Carter v MGN Ltd* [2006] EWHC 1235 (QB) at [59]–[60], where the judge commented favourably on *Various Claimants v TUI UK Ltd* (unreported) 11 August 2005, SCCO, Master Hurst; presumably, the same would apply by analogy.

[23] *Re Watson, ex p Phillips* (1887) 19 QBD 234, CA; the practical effect of this rule is limited, this being because authority will usually be implied by virtue of instructions being given: see *Bolden v Nicholay* (1857) 3 Jur NS 884 and **11.23** *et seq*.

[24] *Société Anonyme Pêcheries Ostendaises v Merchants Marine Insurance Co* [1928] 1 KB 750; see also *Gibson's Settlement Trusts* [1981] Ch 179; and *Roach v Home Office* [2009] EWHC 312 (QB).

[25] An example of this is *Lee v Birmingham City Council* [2008] EWCA Civ 891 in which Hughes LJ (giving judgment of the court) took into account repairs which had been effected before the claim was issued: in this regard, he had this to say (at [34]): 'the effect of the claim is to get the work done, then providing that the landlord was liable for the disrepair the tenant ought to recover the reasonable costs of achieving that result.'

words used in the order may have a different meaning)[26] these are words of extension rather than words of restriction.[27] Lord Harnworth MR said this on the topic:[28]

> 'It appears to me ... that there is power in the Master to allow costs incurred before action brought, and that if the costs are in respect of materials ultimately proving of use and service in the action, the Master has a discretion to allow these costs, which he probably will exercise in favour of the party incurring them, because they have been made use of during the course of the action.'

Lord Harnworth MR's words continue to have resonance today; in particular, it remains the case that costs need not necessarily have been incurred in contemplation of the actual proceedings which were ultimately brought; instead, the court is permitted to focus on the use to which they were put, rather than the use for which they were originally intended;[29] this does not offend against the rule precluding the use of hindsight because the question is whether it was reasonable to make use of the work which had already been carried out (the alternative being to re-do the work).

29.34 Where costs are incurred under a pre-action protocol, Lord Woolf CJ has explained that this is a factor which goes to those costs being recoverable in principle:[30]

> 'Where an action is commenced and a costs order is then obtained, the costs awarded will include costs reasonably incurred before the action started, such as costs incurred in complying with the pre-action protocol.'

This seems to be reflected in the CPD[31] and has been confirmed in several authorities.[32] This is not surprising given the emphasis on 'front loading' which seems to be a focus of the CPR and the ever-growing collection of pre-action protocols.

29.35 The fact that the receiving party is a defendant in no way negates his ability to recover pre-issue costs.[33] That said, HHJ Coulson QC (now Coulson J) has confirmed that costs incurred in responding to issues subsequently not included from the claim would not ordinarily be recoverable; he explained that they would become recoverable only in exceptional circumstances.[34] Whilst he was dealing with the incidence of costs rather than the assessment of costs, Tugendhat J ruled that in a case where the claimant brought an abusive claim, the defendant should not have its costs pre-issue because it would not have been able to seek an order for those costs if the abusive claim had not

---

[26] See, for example, *Newall v Lewis* [2008] EWHC 910 (Ch), in which Briggs J found that the order in question referred to 'costs of' rather than 'costs of and incidental'.

[27] *Gibson's Settlement Trusts* [1981] Ch 179 at 184, per Megarry V-C, thereby limiting *Re Fahy's Will Trusts* [1962] 1 All ER 73 to its own facts.

[28] *Société Anonyme Pêcheries Ostendaises v Merchants Marine Insurance Co* [1928] 1 KB 750 at 757; see also *Frankenburg v Famous Lasky Film Service Ltd* [1931] 1 Ch 428.

[29] See *Admiral Management Services Ltd v Para-Protect Europe Ltd* [2002] EWHC 233 (Ch), in which Stanley Burton J found that costs incurred before solicitors had been instructed were, in principle, recoverable if they resulted in material which was ultimately used.

[30] *Callery v Gray* [2001] EWCA Civ 1117 at [54(ii)]. See also *Lee v Birmingham City Council* [2008] EWCA Civ 891 [11] to [16] per Hughes LJ giving judgment of the court.

[31] See CPD, art 4.6(7), which provides that a bill of costs may include documentation necessary to comply with Practice Direction (Pre-Action Conduct) or any relevant pre-action protocols, where appropriate.

[32] See *McGlinn v Waltham Contractors Ltd* [2005] EWHC 1419 (TCC) at [6], per HHJ Coulson QC (now Coulson J), *Roundstone Nurseries Ltd v Stephenson Holdings Ltd* [2009] EWHC 1431 (TCC) at [48], per Coulson J, and *Citation Plc v Ellis Whittam Ltd* [2012] EWHC 764 (QB) at [16], per Tugendhat J (who emphasised that pre-action costs *may* be recoverable, not that they will always be recoverable).

[33] *Bright's Trustee v Sellar* [1904] 1 Ch 370.

[34] *McGlinn v Waltham Contractors Ltd* [2005] EWHC 1419 (TCC) at [11].

been brought;[35] perhaps this is best regarded as being an illustration of the fact that each case must be determined on its own facts.

Costs incurred after the order for costs was made

29.36 Where proceedings have been brought to an end by way of a final costs order, the receiving party may have to carry out further work for the purposes of concluding the claim. After having reviewed competing authorities on the point, Sir Christopher Staughton came to the following conclusion:[36]

'In my judgment, the fees of [the receiving party's] solicitors reasonably incurred in procuring that the settlement be carried out can fairly be described as being party of the costs of the action.'

29.37 That case was pre-CPR, but the fact that such costs continue to be recoverable is confirmed by CPD, art 4.6(1), which states that a bill may include:

'Attendances on the court and counsel up to the date of the notice of commencement.'

(The reference to 'attendances on the court and counsel' is a rather obscure way of referring to the chronology in a bill of costs: it is not intended to give rise to some sort of limitation.)

Costs incurred during a stay

29.38 The court has the power to stay the whole or part of any proceedings or judgment, either generally or until a specified date or event.[37] The CPR defines a stay in the following terms:[38]

'A stay imposes a halt on proceedings, apart from taking any steps allowed by the Rules or the terms of the stay. Proceedings can be continued if a stay is lifted.'

29.39 That definition is similar to pre-CPR definitions, so these comments of Lord Harnworth MR probably remain good law:[39]

'Then comes the more important point upon which the appeal has been presented to us. MacKinnon J has held, apparently, that the stay of proceedings included in the order for ship's papers prevents any costs incurred while that stay was operative from being recovered. I take note that the stay is of "All further proceedings." It is not a stay of activities, the steps which prudence dictates are not forbidden. The question whether the steps that are taken are or are not premature is a matter for the Taxing Master. I agree with the answer made by Sir George King in these terms: "I do not understand that the order entirely paralyses the plaintiff so that he cannot do anything by way of preparation for his real proceedings. If this is so, the question whether any act by the plaintiff during that period is or is not premature must be like every other question about premature acts, a question of reasonableness to be decided by me." I think that Sir George King has rightly answered the objection carried in.'

---

35   *Citation Plc v Ellis Whittam Ltd* [2012] EWHC 764 (QB) at [28].
36   *Wallace v Brian Gale & Associates (a firm)* [1998] 2 Costs LR 53 at 56; see also *Krehl v Park* (1875) 10 Ch App 334; compare with *Thomas v Cunard Whitestar Line* [1950] 2 All ER 1157.
37   CPR, r 3.1(2)(f).
38   Glossary to the CPR.
39   *Société Anonyme Pêcheries Ostendaises v Merchants Marine Insurance Co* [1928] 1 KB 750 at 757; see also *Whiteley Exerciser Ltd v Gamage* [1898] 2 Ch 405.

The stay, therefore, transitorily brings the proceedings to a halt, but it does not bring a halt to the gamut of activities that a solicitor may need to engage in for the purposes of managing the claim. Costs reasonably incurred in managing the claim will, in principle, continue to be recoverable notwithstanding the stay. This will be particularly true if the purpose of the stay is to enable the parties to attempt to reach a compromise.

Specific categories of work

Costs of drafting attendances notes

29.40 Provided that the time claimed is reasonable, there is no reason why time cannot be claimed for drafting attendance notes; Brooke J said:[40]

> 'Work properly and reasonably done in furthering the client's interests may reasonably include the preparation of attendance and file notes recording what work has been done. The time spent in preparation of these notes should be recorded. The emphasis must always be on the question whether this work is reasonable.'

29.41 This does not mean that time will always be allowed in addition to the time allowed for the attendance itself. Whilst speaking in the context of costs capping rather than the assessment of costs, Hallett J has indicated that additional note-drafting time should not ordinarily be allowed in the following circumstances:[41]

- where the note could have been drafted during the course of the attendance itself;
- where the note could have been drafted while travelling; and
- where there is more than one fee earner in attendance.

Costs of attendance on the client

29.42 The topic of the costs of travelling to see a client is addressed at **29.70–29.73**. Beyond this, no special principles apply.

29.43 That said, there are certain anecdotal measures – which some would say are entirely spurious – which may be encountered in practice. One of them has found its way into the *Guide to the Summary Assessment of Costs* (albeit in the context of appeals):

> '(6) Although the solicitor may have spent many hours with the client, the client should have been warned that little of this time is recoverable against a losing party. Reasonable time spent receiving instructions and reporting events should not greatly exceed the time spent on attending the opponents.'

29.44 This is one of many ratios and measures that are said to be of use in assessing the costs of attendance upon the client. Another anecdotal measure (which the writer has found to be surprisingly reliable) is that if the number of telephone calls to a client exceeds one-half of the number of letters, then this suggests a degree of duplication or a degree of solicitor and client work. Another is that the total time spent on attending upon the client is usually less than one-half of the documentary time. None of these rules are supported by authority and are nothing more than a method by which a paying party can be alerted to the possibility of unreasonable or irrecoverable costs.

---

[40]   *Brush v Bower Cotton & Bower* [1993] 1 WLR 1328 at 1349.
[41]   *Ledward v Kent & Medway Health Authority* [2003] EWHC 2551 (QB) at [50].

Costs of attendance on court and counsel

Attendances at court for the purposes of issuing

29.45 In general, the costs of personal attendance at court to issue documents would be largely disallowed on the basis that that the same chore could be carried out by post. Where, however, the receiving party can show a degree of urgency, an allowance may be made. Thus, in a case in which there was a degree of urgency which was compounded by the fact that 'local experience [was that applications] can take several days to be processed', Edwards-Stuart J made an allowance for personal attendance.[42]

Attendances upon counsel in chambers

29.46 It is a time-honoured practice that attendances on court and counsel are dealt with as being closely related items; this has its origins in the notion that counsel's duty is to the court. Attendances on counsel are treated in the same way as any other attendance; Brooke J has made it clear that it is irrelevant whether counsel raises a fee, and it is irrelevant whether counsel has specific instructions on the point being discussed.[43] (The second of these factors may be highly relevant to counsel's fee, however: see **32.47–32.49**.)

Attendances upon the court

29.47 The costs of attending upon the court are recoverable under the CPR in just the same way as are the costs of any other attendance. The notion that costs of communicating with the court should be subsumed within costs generally is an obsolete doctrine that applied to the intricate scale of fees which existed before 1986 (see **1.28–1.29**).[44] Where there is more than one claimant or more than one defendant, and where there is no conflict between them, then the costs of separate representation may not be justified.[45]

Sitting behind counsel (professional obligations)

29.48 Whether it is reasonable for a solicitor to sit behind counsel will depend on the facts of each case, if but it would be easier to justify such an attendance if the solicitor was professionally obliged to attend.[46] For work done between 1 July 2007 and 5 October 2011 the Solicitors' Code of Conduct 2007 gave the following guidance (which has been quoted selectively to disregard those provisions relating to criminal matters):[47]

> '8. Whenever you instruct an advocate – whether counsel or a solicitor advocate – you will need to decide whether it is in the interests of your client and the interests of justice for you, or a responsible representative of your firm, to attend the proceedings. In reaching this decision you will need to consider what is necessary for the proper conduct of the case, taking into account the nature and complexity of the case and the capacity of the client to understand the proceedings. For example, you, or your representative, should normally attend:

---

[42] *Price v Carter* [2010] EWHC 1737 (TCC) at [9].

[43] *Brush v Bower Cotton & Bower* [1993] 1 WLR 1328 at 1352.

[44] See *Brush v Bower Cotton & Bower* [1993] 1 WLR 1328 at 1352 for a discussion of this point.

[45] *Birmingham City Council v H (a minor)* [1994] 2 WLR 31 at 33, per Lord Keith.

[46] That said, see *Motto & Ors v Trafigura Ltd & Anor* [2011] EWCA Civ 1150 at [112]; Lord Neuberger MR has explained that the mere fact that a solicitor is obliged to do something does not mean that the costs of that task are recoverable between opposing parties.

[47] Guidance to rule 11 – Litigation and advocacy of the Solicitors' Code of Conduct 2007.

    ...
    (c)   where the client may have difficulty in giving or receiving instructions or in understanding the proceedings, for example if the client is a child, has inadequate knowledge of English, or suffers from a mental illness or some other disability;
    (d)   where the client is likely to disrupt proceedings if the advocate appears alone;
    (e)   where the advocate is representing more than one party to the hearing;
    ...
    (g)   where there are a large number of witnesses in the case;
    (h)   ...; or
    (i)   where issues are likely to arise which question the client's character or your conduct of the case.'

For obvious reasons, the vast majority of hearings will be far removed from the situations mentioned above; more commonplace reasons for permitting the attendance of solicitors at trial are where there is a need to care for witnesses or where there is a need to keep a handwritten note, etc. Particular provisions apply to fast track trials (see **33.126**).

Sitting behind counsel at trial

29.49 The rule that a solicitor had to attend counsel at trial[48] was amended as of 3 April 2001. There is now no professional rule which requires counsel to be attended by his instructing solicitors in court, either at trial or at all.

Sitting behind counsel in the Court of Appeal

29.50 While dealing with the issues of costs in the context of summary assessment, the *Guide to the Summary Assessment of Costs* gives the following guidance:[49]

    'Although it is usually reasonable to have a senior fee earner sitting with Counsel in the Court of Appeal, it is not usually reasonable to have two fee earners. The second fee earner may be there for training purposes only.'

Where there is more than one appellant or respondent, and where there is no conflict between them, then the costs of separate representation may not be justified;[50] this is particularly so in the context of appeals because the issues will be well defined. Lord Keith has commented that, where appropriate, it is the duty of counsel and solicitors carefully to consider this issue.[51]

Appointments in the Court of Appeal

29.51 In respect of appointments in the Court of Appeal, the following further guidance is given:[52]

---

[48]   Solicitors' Practice Rules 1990, r 20.04.
[49]   See para 65 of the *Guide to the Summary Assessment of Costs*, 2005.
[50]   *Birmingham City Council v H (a minor)* [1994] 2 WLR 31 at 33, per Lord Keith.
[51]   Ibid.
[52]   See para 66 of the *Guide to the Summary Assessment of Costs*, 2005; that document suggests actual figures for the following types of hearing in the Court of Appeal:
    • Contested Directions Hearings
    • Applications for Permission to Appeal at which the Respondent is Present
    • Appeals from Case Management Decisions
    • Dismissal List Hearing at which the Respondent is Present
    The reader is referred to the current edition of the Guide for the up-to-date figures.

'Although many appointments in the Court of Appeal merit the attendance of a senior fee earner familiar with the case, the most minor appointments may not. For example, on an application in the dismissal list in a case tried in Newcastle, if Counsel who was briefed for the trial attends it may be unreasonable for a solicitor familiar with the case to travel from Newcastle to attend also. In order to arrive at a notional figure to represent the instruction of and costs of an agent, it may be appropriate to disallow most of the travel time and travelling expenses claimed by the solicitor.'

Costs of communication, etc

29.52 Communications are defined as letters out and telephone calls; incoming correspondence and emails are in a different category because they are either discretionary (emails) or not recoverable at all (routine incoming correspondence).

Routine communications

29.53 Routine communications are outgoing letters, outgoing emails and telephone calls (either received or made) which, because of their simplicity, should not be regarded as letters or emails of substance, or telephone calls which properly amount to an attendance.[53] Such communications will in general be allowed on a unitary basis of 6 minutes each, the charge being calculated by reference to the appropriate hourly rate.[54]

Timed communications

29.54 The term 'real communications' is occasionally used to mean communications which are not routine communications.[55] They are assessed on a time basis. They may include an allowance for electronic communications other than email.

SMS texts, etc

29.55 Perhaps as a result of long-standing criticism that it did not reflect modern practice,[56] CPD, art 4.16(2) has been updated so that it deals with electronic communications other than email; this would include short messaging service communications (ie 'text messages' or 'SMS'), multimedia messaging service communications ('MMS'), but probably not faxes and telexes. The new provisions read as follows:

> 'The court may, in its discretion, allow an actual time charge for preparation of electronic communications other than e-mails sent by solicitors, which properly amount to attendances provided that the time taken has been recorded.'

There are no transitional provisions in respect of the new provisions.

Incoming correspondence

29.56 In general, no costs are allowed for incoming correspondence (including emails). This is because the allowance for outgoing letters will include an allowance for perusing and considering incoming correspondence. The CPD specifically provides that no

---

[53] CPD, art 4.8.
[54] CPD, art 4.16(1).
[55] See, for example, J Harrison 'Costs a bomb' (2007) 137 NLJ 56.
[56] See, for example, J Harrison 'Costs a bomb' (2007) 137 NLJ 56.

separate charge should be made for incoming letters,[57] but it is a moot point whether this applies to all or just routine correspondence; most judges interpret the rule to mean the latter.

Short letters

29.57 Whilst not binding, Master O'Hare has found that, in certain circumstances, letters of an administrative nature (such as a covering letter) may justify an allowance of three minutes rather than a full allowance of a full six minutes.[58]

Circular letters

29.58 In group litigation involving anything more than a handful of litigants there will often be a need to dispatch volleys of letters which differ very little from litigant to litigant. Such letters are often referred to as being circular letters. Each case will turn on its own facts, but in a case where the letters were substantially the same, Nelson J found that a full allowance of 6 minutes would be inappropriate. Nonetheless, he found that that some allowance ought to be made for 'thinking time', and (on the facts of the case before him) he allowed 2 minutes per letter.[59] A part of this allowance will be for printing and postage costs; where a significant number of letters is involved then this becomes the predominant cost. Where this is so, one option is for the court to allow a stated amount of costs (often in the order of £5) rather than an amount of time.

Wording of relevant provisions

29.59 The wording of the relevant provisions in the CPD is in the footnotes.[60]

Documentary work

29.60 The CPD provides that, in principle, a bill of costs may contain the following documentary work:[61]

> 'Work done on documents: preparing and considering documentation, including documentation necessary to comply with Practice Direction (Pre-action Conduct) or any relevant pre-action protocols where appropriate, work done in connection with arithmetical

---

[57]   CPD, art 4.16(1).

[58]   *In Re Walker* (unreported) November 2002, SCCO, Master O'Hare, a decision he confirmed as being correct in *In Re Radcliffe* [2004] EWHC 90039 (Costs).

[59]   *Giambrone v JMC Holidays Ltd* [2002] Costs LR 294.

[60]   '4.7 In respect of each of the heads of costs:
(1) 'communications' means letters out e-mails out and telephone calls;
(2) communications, which are not routine communications, must be set out in chronological order;
(3) routine communications must be set out as a single item at the end of each head;
4.8   Routine communications are letters out, e-mails out and telephone calls which because of their simplicity should not be regarded as letters or e-mails of substance or telephone calls which properly amount to an attendance.
4.16   The following provisions relate to work done by solicitors:
(1) Routine letters out routine e-mails out and routine telephone calls will in general be allowed on a unit basis of 6 minutes each, the charge being calculated by reference to the appropriate hourly rate. The unit charge for letters out and e-mails out will include perusing and considering the relevant letters in or e-mails in and accordingly no separate charge is to be made for in-coming letters or e-mails.
(2) The court may, in its discretion, allow an actual time charge for preparation of electronic communications other than e-mails sent by solicitors, which properly amount to attendances provided that the time taken has been recorded.

[61]   CPD, art 4.6(7).

calculations of compensation and/or interest and time spent collating documents.'

29.61 Generally speaking, documentary time will be assessed without regard to any special rules or principles.

Short documents

29.62 Buxton LJ has confirmed that short documents do not draft themselves,[62] the implication being that work is required to achieve pithiness.

Reading in

29.63 While each case will turn on its own facts, time spent by one fee earner reading into a file after having received the file from another fee earner is usually not recoverable. Although of nothing more than persuasive value, this is confirmed by the *Guide to the Summary Assessment of Costs*.[63]

Collating documents

29.64 CPD, art 4.6(7) specifically provides that the costs of time spent collating documents are, in principle, recoverable under the CPR. It is not wholly clear what is meant by 'collate'; it is often regarded as referring to sorting and marshalling documents, but the *Oxford English Dictionary* suggests that when used in its legal sense, it means bringing documents together for comparison in order to ascertain points of agreement and difference.[64] If the latter were the correct meaning, then recoverable costs would be limited to bringing documents together for the purposes of working on them. There is no authority on which meaning is correct.

Disorganised documentation and opponents' prolixity

29.65 Edwards-Stuart J has implied that where a party causes another party to carry out work because of the disorganised nature of the documentation he serves, this is a factor that may be taken into account;[65] he went on to say the same about prolix documentation.[66]

The relevance of heavy documentation

29.66 It has been argued that differences in the wording between the RSC and the CPR mean that the court is unable to give particular weight to the fact that a case was heavy in terms of documentary work. Lloyd J rejected that submission; in an appropriate case the court is able to give weight to the amount of documentary work involved,[67] and this may be so in terms of both the documentary time itself, and the seven pillars of wisdom.

---

[62]   *R (on the application of Roudham & Larling Parish Council) v Breckland Council* [2008] EWCA Civ 714 at [28].

[63]   See the *Guide to the Summary Assessment of Costs*, para 65(7).

[64]   *Oxford English Dictionary* (3rd edn, 1989), collate, v.2.

[65]   *Price v Carter* [2010] EWHC 1737 (TCC) at [15].

[66]   Ibid at [16]–[18]

[67]   *Ortwein v Rugby Mansions* [2003] EWHC 2077 (Ch) at [24], per Lloyd J.

Work done over a long period of time

29.67 Where a claim is long-running, work may necessarily be carried out piecemeal. Donaldson J had the following to say about multiple small items of work carried out over a long period of time:[68]

> 'The bill of costs showed that the solicitors were engaged for 30 hours in the relevant period. Most of this time was made up of short items spread over a period. This did not mean that what was done was of little importance or required little skill. Far from it ... It is in some ways more difficult to pick up the thread continually over a period than to do the same work more or less continuously.'

It should be noted that this was a pre-CPR case concerning non-contentious costs: its relevance in the present context is merely to illustrate the fact that it is not necessarily unreasonable to incur costs in multiple, short bursts.

Duplicated work and prolixity

29.68 If work duplicates the work performed by counsel, then the time may be disallowed; although of no more than persuasive value, this is confirmed by the *Guide to the Summary Assessment of Costs*.[69] Unjustifiable prolixity may result in costs being disallowed.[70]

Decision not to use counsel

29.69 It is open to the court to take into account the amount that would have been charged by counsel if he had been instructed to carry out the work; this too is confirmed by the *Guide to the Summary Assessment of Costs*.[71]

Travelling time

29.70 Under the CPR, travelling time is claimed at the same rate as other work (unless, of course, the retainer provides for a lower rate);[72] this is made clear by CPD, art 4.16(3):

> 'Where travelling and waiting time is claimed, this should be allowed at the rate agreed with the client unless this is more than the hourly rate on the assessment.'

29.71 Hallett J (sitting with Master Hurst as an assessor) has confirmed that unless the client is housebound or in hospital, it is normal for a client to visit the solicitor at the office;[73] whilst each case will turn on its own facts, it would be reasonable to infer that the costs of travelling to see a client who is not housebound or in hospital would, absent justification, be irrecoverable.

---

[68]   *Property and Reversionary Investment Corporation Ltd v Secretary of State for the Environment* [1975] 1 WLR 1504.

[69]   See the *Guide to the Summary Assessment of Costs*, para 65(5).

[70]   Whilst it concerned a barrister instructed directly rather than a solicitor, see *Dunn v Glass Systems (UK) Ltd* [2007] EWHC 1901 (QB) in which fees were disallowed on the basis that they were for drafting prolix pleadings that would have led to the litigation being unmanageable.

[71]   See the *Guide to the Summary Assessment of Costs*, para 65(5).

[72]   Although a criminal case, see, by analogy *R (on the application of Schwartz) v Highbury Corner Magistrates Court* [2009] EWHC 1397 (Admin).

[73]   *Ledward v Kent & Medway Health Authority* [2003] EWHC 2551 (QB) at [24].

29.72 In considering the reasonableness of the time claimed, the court is entitled to examine the entirety of the costs and, in particular, is entitled to look at the savings that may have been made as a result of the travelling. Thus, where travelling has reduced the need to engage agents, this is a factor that can be taken into account.[74] Likewise, if travelling has meant that the use of a distant solicitor has reduced the hourly rate, then this too is a factor which may be taken into account.[75] Likewise, if the travelling could have been avoided by the use of technology, the time may be disallowed. Whilst not dealing specifically with costs, Carnwath LJ had this to say on the topic:[76]

> 'It is incumbent on those advising parties appearing before this, or any, court to take all the steps they can in accordance with CPR Rules 1.1 and 1.3 to reduce the cost of the proceedings. This includes taking advantage of such cost-saving facilities as video-conferencing whenever they are available and it is appropriate to use them.'

29.73 Where public transport is reasonably easily available and where it would be more efficient in terms of time, it would be open to the court to find that the costs of travelling by private car were allowable only if and to the extent that this resulted in a saving in costs.[77]

COSTS OF SPECIFIC ACTIVITIES

29.74 This subchapter deals with the costs of certain specified activities; first, however, it is necessary to set out 'the *Gibson* principles' (see **29.75–29.77**). It should be emphasised that whilst costs will usually be assessed in accordance with the principles set out below, it is rare for those principles to be referred to expressly.

The *Gibson* principles

29.75 Although in present-day practice it is rare for express reference to be made to them, Megarry V-C identified the three strands of reasoning that the court will take into account when gauging whether costs are allowable in principle;[78] they may be referred to as the *Gibson* principles (after the name of the case in which they were articulated). Originally they related equally to profit costs and disbursements, but they have come to have particular resonance where the issue is whether profit costs can be recovered for an identifiable type of work, or for work done for a specified purpose.[79]

29.76 Megarry V-C's three strands of reasoning are:

- whether the work was of use and service in the claim;
- whether the work was of relevance to an issue in the claim; and
- whether the need for the work can be attributed to the paying party's actions or omissions.

---

[74]   See, by way of analogy, the guidance mentioned at **29.51**.
[75]   *Ledward v Kent & Medway Health Authority* [2003] EWHC 2551 (QB) at [17].
[76]   *Black v Pastouna & Anor* [2005] EWCA Civ 1389 at [14].
[77]   Whilst a criminal case, see *R v Slessor* (1984), Taxing Masters Compendium.
[78]   See *Re Gibson's Settlement Trusts* [1981] Ch 179 at 185, in which Megarry V-C drew on *Frankenburg v Famous Lasky Film Service Ltd* [1931] 1 Ch 428 and *Société Anonyme Pêcheries Ostendaises v Merchants Marine Insurance Co* [1928] 1 KB 750.
[79]   See, for example, *Ross v Owners of the Bowbelle (Review of Taxation under Ord 62 r 35)* (1997) 2 Lloyd's Rep 196 (Note) QBD (Admlty) and *Roach v Home Office* [2009] EWHC 312 (QB).

Each of these strands of reasoning must be decided in the receiving party's favour if the costs in question are to be recoverable.

29.77 The last of these strands requires clarification; some authorities (including *Re Gibson's Settlement Trusts* itself) refer to the third strand as pertaining to the 'conduct' of the paying party. The way in which Megarry V-C applied that test makes it clear that the issue is not whether the receiving party has been vexed by poor conduct, but whether the need for the work can be attributed to the paying party's endeavours.

Costs of marshalling the facts

29.78 The phrase 'marshalling the facts' is used to refer to the task of gathering and organising evidence. It does not refer to the costs of actually formulating the evidence and exercising professional judgment in selecting which parts of it will be relied upon, but only to the task of gathering together the material that will allow those tasks to be completed.

29.79 The topic commonly arises in one of two guises; first, it may arise in the context of the work having been carried out by the solicitor (in which case the issues will be simply whether it is, by its nature, irrecoverable) and, secondly, it may arise where the work has been carried out by the receiving party, or his employees or agents, personally (in which case there will be the additional consideration of whether that person is able to recover costs at all – see **5.57–5.69**).

29.80 Although it is arguable that it has been overtaken by the CPR,[80] the general rule is that the costs of marshalling the facts are not recoverable because they are not 'legal costs'. This is because they are the costs of being a litigant, rather than the costs of litigation;[81] as Bingham J put it, they are the costs 'a litigant must bear ... to prove his own case'.[82]

29.81 This does not mean that such work would always be irrecoverable. Each case will turn on its own facts.

Technical or expert marshalling of facts

29.82 If the work was of a technical nature or if it had an expert flavour to it, then an allowance may be made.[83]

Academic work and marshalling the facts

29.83 The principle mentioned immediately above would not extend to work which merely had an academic flavour to it; in a case in which the receiving party had to

---

[80] See, for example, *Papera Traders Co Ltd & Ors v Hyundai Merchant Marine Co Ltd & Anor* [2003] EWHC 9018 (Costs) at [73] *et seq*, where it was said that *Amec Process & Energy Ltd v Stork Engineers & Contracts (No 3)* [2002] All ER (D) suggested that *Re Nossen's Patent* and *Richards & Wallington (Plant Hire) Ltd v Monk & Co* had been overtaken. For the converse view, see *Sisu Capital Fund Ltd and others v Tucker* [2005] EWHC 2321 (Ch), in which Warren J declined to follow *Amec*.

[81] See the extensive discussion in *London Scottish Benefit Society v Chorley* [1884] 13 QBD 872 at 877; see also Chapter 5.

[82] *Richards & Wallington (Plant Hire) Ltd v Monk & Co* (1984) Costs LR, Core vol 79 at 83.

[83] See *Re Nossen's Patent* [1969] 1 All ER 775, in which Lloyd-Jacob J contemplated making an allowance for work of a technical nature.

prepare a schedule of academic books lost as a result of the paying party's negligence, Douglas Brown J declined to find that the costs of carrying out that work were recoverable.[84]

Non-legal professional work and marshalling the facts

29.84 The mere fact that the work was carried out by persons who were professionals or office holders would not displace the general rule that costs of marshalling the facts are not recoverable.[85]

Extensive work relating to factual material

29.85 In a family case[86] in which the wife had asked complex questions about the husband's accounts, Bennett J determined that the test to be applied was 'whether the instruction of [a lawyer] to draft the answers and all such necessary work to enable him to do that, was reasonable' (most of the work related to factual material rather than drafting). Bennett J asked himself whether the receiving party could be expected to collate, marshal and present the information without expert assistance. He found that it was reasonable to engage a lawyer to carry out the work in question.

Costs of funding

29.86 For present purposes, it is useful to distinguish between the following:

- financing costs (such as interest on a disbursement funding loan);
- administrative costs (such as the costs of preparing invoices, paying cheques, etc); and
- the profit costs arising from professional advice concerning the methods of funding the claim ('costs of funding advice').

It is the costs of funding advice (ie the third of these categories) that is the focus of the immediate discussion. It is well established that the first cannot be recovered from an opposing party[87] and that the second could not properly be characterised as being legal costs at all.[88]

29.87 After a long period of there having been no binding authority on the issue of the recoverability of the costs of funding advice, Lord Neuberger MR has now confirmed that such costs are not recoverable.[89]

---

[84] *Stockinger v Highdorn Co Ltd* (unreported) 5 April 2001, QBD.

[85] *Sisu Capital Fund Ltd and others v Tucker* [2005] EWHC 2321 (Ch) (office holders not entitled to recover fees); although not binding, see *Cuthbert v Gair* (unreported) 26 September 2009, SCCO, Master Haworth (loss adjusters not entitled to recover fees).

[86] *D v D* [2002] 2 Costs LR 312.

[87] See *Hunt v RM Douglas (Roofing) Ltd* (1987) *The Times*, November 23, CAT, cited by the Court of Appeal in *Claims Direct Test Cases* [2003] EWCA Civ 136 at [35]; see also *Bushwell Properties v Vortex Properties* [1975] 2 All ER 214 (per Evans J).

[88] See the extensive discussion in *London Scottish Benefit Society v Chorley* (1884) 13 QBD 872 at 877; see also Chapter 5.

[89] *Motto & Ors v Trafigura Ltd & Anor* [2011] EWCA Civ 1150 at [104]–[114].

29.88 In a pre-CPR case which has been affirmed as still being good law,[90] Purchas LJ said:[91]

'[B]y established practice and custom funding costs have never been included in the category of expenses, costs or disbursements envisaged by ... statute or [the then rules of court].'

Part of Purchas LJ's reasoning was that costs of funding are not costs. This analysis is still good law (see the footnotes)[92], but Lord Neuberger MR's analysis is more easily understood in the context of modern legal practice:[93]

'The time, expertise and effort devoted by solicitors to identifying a potential claimant, and negotiating the terms on which they are to be engaged by the claimant, in connection with litigation, cannot, in my view, be properly described as an item incurred by the client for the purposes of the litigation. Until the CFA is signed, the potential claimant is not merely not a claimant: he is not a client. When advising a potential claimant on the terms and effect of the CFA, the solicitors are acting for themselves, not for the potential claimant: the solicitors are negotiating with him as a prospective client, not for him as an actual client.'

29.89 The fact that funding advice must be given as a matter of professional conduct is not sufficient to render the costs associated with that work recoverable: in this regard, Lord Neuberger MR has explained that mere fact that a solicitor is obliged to do something by the SRA Code of Conduct 2011 does not mean that he can charge for it.[94]

29.90 The costs of giving advice about legal expenses insurance is similarly irrecoverable between opposing parties; Lord Neuberger MR has explained that such costs are not so much a cost of the litigation as a cost which was collateral to litigation, being a cost incurred to ensure that the client was not at risk on costs.[95]

Costs of legal research

29.91 Legal research is work which is carried out for the purposes of discovering the law; it should be distinguished from work carried out for the purposes of applying the law.[96]

---

[90]   The confirmation was given by Brooke LJ in *Claims Direct Test Cases* [2003] EWCA Civ 136 at [35] and then again in *Motto & Ors v Trafigura Ltd & Anor* [2011] EWCA Civ 1150 at [105]

[91]   *Hunt v RM Douglas (Roofing) Ltd* (1987) *The Times*, November 23, CAT.

[92]   The receiving party argued that the particular monies in question (interest) were capable of quantification, and that this, therefore, undermined the conclusion that they were not costs; this the receiving party argued – was because part of Bowen LJ's seminal analysis of what are and are not costs was the question of whether the monies in question could readily be quantified (see **5.8**) Purchas LJ rejected this analysis, finding that to categorise measurable costs of funding as costs 'would be an extension of the existing category of 'legal costs' which is not under the prevailing circumstances warranted'.

[93]   *Motto & Ors v Trafigura Ltd & Anor* [2011] EWCA Civ 1150 at [108].

[94]   See *Motto & Ors v Trafigura Ltd & Anor* [2011] EWCA Civ 1150 at [112]. It is worth noting that it does not always follow that because work is mandatory, it will be remunerated; see, for example, *In Re Radcliffe* [2004] EWHC 90039 (Costs) at [16], in which Master O'Hare described the costs of certain mandatory requirements in the Court of Protection as being work which had to be carried out 'in order to obtain the right to undertake the work which is remunerated'.

[95]   *Motto & Ors v Trafigura Ltd & Anor* [2011] EWCA Civ 1150 at [114].

[96]   Time claimed for applying the law is recoverable: *Loveday v Renton (No 2)* [1992] 3 All ER 184 at 190.

29.92 Each case will be decided on its own facts but, in general, the costs of legal research will not be allowed if the solicitor could have been expected to have known the law in question. Lord Donaldson MR explained this by referring to legal knowledge as the solicitor's 'stock in trade':[97]

> 'Solicitors, like barristers and Judges, are not to be expected to carry a knowledge of all the law in their heads. They have to consider rules, regulations, text books and authorities or get others to undertake the research for them. If the problem is difficult or outside the scope of their experience, they will wish to discuss it with others who are more qualified (whether professionally or otherwise) and in some circumstances may have to remunerate those who they consult. But knowledge of the law, however acquired or recalled, is their stock in trade ... In so far as expenses involved in added to or replenishing this stock in trade, it is an overhead expense and not something which can be charged to the client ...'

29.93 Although his decision relates to counsel's fees rather than profit costs, Garland J observed that there may be cases which give rise to legal issues which are so unusual or infrequent that time ought to be allowed for discovering the law; he stressed that each case should be decided on its own facts and according to the lawyer's professed expertise.[98] A factor which may be relevant is the judicial level at which the matter is to be heard; it is, for example, not unknown for a modest allowance to be made for researching the law in the Court of Appeal.[99] In a similar vein, Swinton Thomas LJ has noted that counsel cannot be expected to be 'a walking law library'.[100] Presumably, the same applies to solicitors.

29.94 Costs of legal research will not be transformed into something else merely by reason of the solicitor instructing a specialist to carry out the work; where this is done and where the law is such that the solicitor could reasonably have been expected to know it without seeking specialist advice, then the cost will usually be disallowed. Arden J has commented that such costs are incurred by the solicitor using the specialist for his own purposes, ie replenishing his own stock in trade.[101]

'Solicitor and client' work

29.95 A person has the right to retain the solicitor of his choice[102] and (subject to rules of professional conduct), he has the right to give him whatever instructions he likes; where this results in costs being disallowed as being 'solicitor and client' in nature, this arises not by the operation of an exclusory principle, but because there is a fissure between that which it is reasonable for a client to pay his solicitor and that which it is reasonable for a paying party to pay a receiving party.

29.96 The fissure is there by design rather than happenstance. This was explained by Malins V-C:[103]

---

[97] *R v Legal Aid Board ex p Bruce* [1991] 1 WLR 1231; this case went to the House of Lords, where Lord Jauncey approved of selected parts of this extract ([1992] 3 All ER 321 at 326).

[98] *Perry v Lord Chancellor* (1994) *The Times*, May 26, QBD.

[99] See, for example, *Hornsby v Clarke Kenneth Leventhal (a firm)* [2000] 2 Costs LR 295.

[100] *Johnson v Valks* (unreported) 15 March 2000, CA.

[101] *In the Matter of Tina Jayne Cloughton* (unreported, 1999), Arden J.

[102] See *Watts v Official Solicitor* [1936] 1 All ER 249, CA; see also *Oswald Hickson Collier & Co v Carter-Ruck* [1984] AC 720n CA in which it was held that a restraint of trade clause in a contract was contrary to public policy, this being because it sought to prevent a client from instructing the solicitor of his choice. See also *Edwards v Worboys* [1984] AC 724.

[103] *Smith v Buller* (1875) LR 19 Eq 473 at 474.

'It is of great importance to litigants who are unsuccessful that they should not be oppressed into having to pay an excessive amount of costs ... I adhere to the rule which has already been laid down that the costs chargeable under a taxation as between party and party are all that are necessary to enable the adverse party to conduct the litigation and no more. Any charges merely for conducting litigation more conveniently may be called luxuries and must be paid by the party incurring them.'

Speaking extra-judicially in a peer reviewed journal, Master Hurst has confirmed that what Malins V-C had to say remains relevant under the CPR.[104]

29.97 Convenience is not the only motivation which may lead a receiving party to incur costs which are ultimately deemed to be solicitor and client costs. Hallett J has indicated that the costs of acting as counsellor in an emotionally charged matter might not be recoverable against the paying party.[105] That type of work is often referred to as 'hand-holding', but the fact that it has this label does not mean that it is rendered irrecoverable as a result; as with all work which is said to be solicitor and client in nature, the issue is one of reasonableness and degree rather than principle, and there is no authority for the proposition that an exclusory principle can be made out.

Costs of isolated counterclaim

29.98 Where a counterclaimant is awarded costs, the appropriate measure of costs will depend on whether he is also ordered to pay costs. If he has been ordered to pay costs, then the principles set out at **7.1–7.25** will apply. If he has not been ordered to pay costs, then the costs of a counterclaim could legitimately include costs relating to the perusal and consideration of issues in the claim; this is because he will need to keep abreast of the claim for the purposes of managing the counterclaim.[106]

Costs of preparing material which was not used

Prematurity

29.99 Speaking of a costs regime long since passed, Lord Hanworth referred to the following extract from a Master's certificate[107] dealing with material thrown away:[108]

'We have always acted upon the principle that the costs of all work in preparing, briefing, or otherwise relating to affidavits or pleadings, reasonably and properly and not prematurely done, down to the time of any notice which stops the work, are allowable; and ... the Taxing Master, having regard to the circumstances of each case, must decide whether the work was reasonable and proper and the time for doing it had arrived.'

This extract illustrates the fact that it is possible to carry out work prematurely; if the benefit of that work is ultimately thrown away, the costs may be disallowed on the basis that the work ought not to have been carried out until it was known whether there was a need for it.

---

[104] 'Going round in circles' (2006) CJQ 25 (Oct), pp 546–556; Master Hurst commented that this was despite the fact that the test of necessity to which Malins V-C referred has been replaced by a test of reasonableness.

[105] *Ledward v Kent & Medway Health Authority* [2003] EWHC 2551 (QB) at [54].

[106] *Re a Company (No 004081 of 1989)* [1995] 2 All ER 155 at 162, per Lindsay J.

[107] This was a formal document used to state some aspect of the law or practice.

[108] See the certificate referred to in *Harrison v Leutner* (1881) 16 Ch D 559 as being 'a working rule which properly exhibits the discretion which is entrusted to the Masters' by Lord Hanworth MR in *Société Anonyme Pêcheries Ostendaises v Merchants Marine Insurance Co* [1928] 1 KB 750 at 758.

Subsequent conduct and amendments

29.100 It is trite law that costs must not be assessed with hindsight. That said, it is possible to negate an entitlement to costs by subsequent conduct. A decision not to use a witness statement for no good reason could, for example, be interpreted as being a waiver of the right to claim the associated costs. Likewise, the costs of amendments will often be disallowed, either by disallowing the costs thrown away, or by disallowing the costs of carrying out the amendment, or a combination of the two.

Costs of dealing with the media

29.101 Proceedings in court may attract a degree of media attention; it may be that costs are claimed for liaison with the media or for advice about media relations.

29.102 In a judgment which preceded the CPR, Clarke J confirmed that there are three strands of reasoning which are relevant to the issue of whether the costs of dealing with the media are recoverable.[109] Those strands rely heavily on the *Gibson* principles set out at **29.76**:

- whether the work was of use and service in the claim;
- whether the work was of relevance to an issue in the claim; and
- whether the need for the work can be attributed to the paying party's conduct.

In practice, these three strands of reasoning amount to a three-part test. Clarke J explained that the work of protecting the receiving party from what may be unwelcome pressure from different parts of the media may well satisfy that test, depending on the facts.

29.103 In some cases (especially high-profile cases), such costs may be said not to be a necessary incident of the claim, but to be an integral part of it in the sense that the media were being used as a method of putting pressure on an opponent; Clarke J has made it clear that costs incurred in that way are not likely to be recoverable:[110]

'Civil claims should be pursued in the civil Courts and not through the media.'

Costs of inquests and other proceedings in the context of a civil claim

29.104 It may be necessary for a party to attend proceedings other than the civil claim (such as an inquest, criminal proceedings, etc); this may be specifically in contemplation of a civil claim, or it may be for other purposes. The question may then arise of whether the costs of the non-costs bearing proceedings were 'of and incidental' to the costs bearing proceedings (this being the wording of s 51 of the Senior Courts Act 1981 (as amended)).

29.105 It has been argued that the court lacks the power to make an award of costs incurred in proceedings other than the civil claim. It has also been argued that the fact

---

[109] *Ross v Owners of the Bowbelle (Review of Taxation under Ord 62 r 35)* (1997) 2 Lloyd's Rep 196 (Note) QBD (Admlty) at 210; the three strands were drawn from Megarry V-C's analysis in *Re Gibson's Settlement Trusts* [1981] Ch 179.

[110] *Ross v Owners of the Bowbelle (Review of Taxation under Ord 62 r 35)* (1997) 2 Lloyd's Rep 196 (Note) QBD (Admlty) at 210.

that the tribunal in the non-costs bearing proceedings lacks the vires to make an award of costs is relevant in the sense that the civil court should not make an order that the other tribunal would be unable to make. Davis J rejected these submissions; he found that costs of attending non-costs bearing proceedings may be of and incidental to the costs bearing proceedings[111] and that attending other proceedings may very often be the most efficient way of investigating the claim. He also found that, while the receiving party's purpose of attending the non-costs bearing proceedings may be a factor to be taken into account, it cannot be determinative of the matter.[112]

29.106   There are, nevertheless, limits to the extent to which costs of non-costs bearing proceedings can be regarded as being of and incidental to the costs bearing proceedings. In particular, the costs of the other proceedings must be 'subordinate costs'; this was explained by Arden LJ:[113]

> 'The expression "of and incidental to" is a time-hallowed phrase in the context of costs [which] has received a limited meaning, [in particular] the words "incidental to" have been treated as denoting some subordinate costs to the costs of the action. If [counsel for the receiving party] was right in this action it would mean that the costs of some very substantial proceedings would be treated as costs of and incidental to other proceedings.'

Examples abound of the court declining to find that costs of other proceedings are subordinate to the civil claim; a small number of examples are given at **29.107–29.111**.

Papers prepared in other proceedings

29.107   The costs of providing documents to counsel in proceedings at first instance could not be regarded as costs 'incidental to' the proceedings in the Court of Appeal and therefore did not form part of the costs of the appeal. The costs had been incurred in the lower court and the bundle of documents was simply passed on to counsel for use in the appeal.[114]

Statutory and non-statutory inquiries

29.108   Jupp J has held that on the facts of the case before him, the costs of an inquiry held pursuant to a reference to the Secretary of State were not costs 'incidental' to the claim in which the reference was made.[115]

Other civil claims

29.109   Donaldson MR has held that costs of an action ordered to be paid by a charterer to a subcharterer were not costs 'incidental to' the charterer's defence of an action by the owner, even though the unsuccessful proceedings against the subcharterer were the inevitable consequence of the owner's unsuccessful action against the charterer.[116]

---

[111]   This being the wording of the general power to award costs in s 51 of the Senior Courts Act 1981.
[112]   *Roach v Home Office* [2009] EWHC 213 (QB), in particular at [57].
[113]   *Contractreal Limited v Davies* [2001] EWCA Civ 928 at [41]; see also *In Re Llewellin* (1887) 37 Ch D 317.
[114]   *Wright v Bennett* [1948] 1 QB 601, CA.
[115]   *Department of Health v Envoy Farmers Ltd* [1976] 1 WLR 1018.
[116]   *Aiden Shipping v Interbulk Ltd* [1985] 1 WLR 1222 at 1226.

Administration of an estate

29.110 In a case where success in a claim resulted in a need to carry out administrative estate work that otherwise would not have been required, Willmer J found that the fact that the administrative work had been carried out after the conclusion of the proceedings demonstrated that those costs were in no way necessary to enable him to conduct the claim.[117] This decision was pre-CPR and ought to be approached with appropriate caution, but whether the work was carried out before or after the conclusion of the claim must still be a factor that the court is able to take into account.

29.111 Where a person's attendance at proceedings other than the civil claim is as a result of an opponent's default, and where costs have been incurred which are not likely to be recoverable as costs, then it may be possible to claim those costs as damages; this topic is addressed in general terms at **5.27–5.33**.

Costs of negotiation and mediation

29.112 In principle, the costs of negotiation may be included within a bill of costs;[118] this is true even if the negotiation went to interim solutions such as security for costs, interim custody of the property that is the subject of the claim, etc.[119] There is no reason to believe that costs of mediation should be treated in a different way. Notwithstanding this, many mediation agreements will make provision for the costs of mediation, and this may have a bearing on whether those costs can be recovered.

29.113 There is no authority as to the effect that a mediation agreement has on the recoverability of the costs of the mediation; it is, however, established law that where there is a contract making provision for costs, the court will generally exercise its discretion in such a way as to give effect to that contract.[120]

29.114 The whole of the mediation agreement (including any attached schedules) must be taken into account; many agreements contain a standard provision which at first blush appears to impose an obligation on each party to bear his own costs of the mediation, but on closer inspection of the agreement it can often be seen that that provision is qualified in such a way as to make that nothing more than the starting position. It will often be necessary to interpret the costs order alongside the mediation agreement in order to determine the true meaning of the order (this, of course, assuming that the mediation agreement is admissible).

29.115 Although it related to an application for security for costs rather than a detailed assessment, Coulson J has found that the costs of a failed mediation which took place prior to issue were not likely to be recoverable as costs payable in the claim;[121] in a separate judgment in the same case he explained that they may be recoverable if they were incurred in an attempt to comply with pre-action protocols.[122]

---

[117] *Thomas v Cunard Whitestar Line* [1950] 2 All ER 1157.
[118] CPD, art 4.6(8), which provides that the bill may contain 'work done in connection with negotiations with a view to settlement if not already covered in the heads listed above.'
[119] *National Westminster Bank v Kotonou* [2009] EWHC 3309 (Ch), per Briggs J.
[120] See **37.2–37.3**, and *Gomba Holdings Ltd v Minories Finance Ltd* [1993] Ch 171 in particular.
[121] *Lobster Group Ltd v Heidelberg Graphic Equipment Ltd* [2008] EWHC 413 (TCC).
[122] *Lobster Group Ltd v Heidelberg Graphic Equipment Ltd* [2008] EWHC 413 (TCC).

THE COSTS OF PREPARING AND CHECKING THE BILL OF COSTS

29.116　The costs of preparing and checking the bill are recoverable between the parties.[123] The following miscellaneous points can be made (see **29.117–29.119**).

Status of signatory

29.117　Where a receiving party has been represented by a firm of solicitors, the issue may arise as to whether it needs to be signed by a partner (or a director, as the case may be). The requirement that a partner certifies the bill of costs was a pre-CPR requirement which no longer applies.[124] CPD, art 4.15 states that a bill of costs must contain certificates based on Precedent F of the Schedule of Costs Precedents annexed to the CPD; that precedent straightforwardly stipulates that the bill of costs must be signed by a solicitor. Therefore, where a junior solicitor has had conduct of the claim, that person is able to certify the bill of costs regardless of his status within his firm.

More than one firm

29.118　Where a receiving party has been represented by more than one solicitor or firm, the question may arise as to whether the paying party is liable for the costs of preparation of only one certificate, or for the costs of the preparation of a certificate for each solicitor or firm. It is implicit from the guidance given in Precedent F that the latter is correct.[125]

Time claimed for checking the bill

29.119　It is not uncommon for only peppercorn times to be allowed for checking the bill of costs, but this will not always be the case. Hooper J found that 30 minutes was insufficient for checking two bills of costs where there was a need to carry out a degree of cross-checking between the two. Indeed, he allowed several hours for the task.[126]

Costs of preparing the bill

Hourly rate

29.120　Whilst only persuasive rather than binding, the Privy Council refused to disturb a rate for drafting work of £160 per hour (relating to costs incurred in about 2005);[127] the judgment does not make it clear whether their Lordships had the benefit of a costs assessor. Many judges are less generous than this and will allow a different (lower) rate for drafting bills of costs than they will allow for costs advocacy. A rate

---

[123]　See CPD, art 4.18.
[124]　See RSC Ord 62, r 29(7)(c)(iii); and r 13(iii) of the Matrimonial Causes (Costs) Rules 1988 – Form and contents of bills of costs lodged in Principal Registry as from 3 October 1988.
[125]　That guidance reads: 'Where the bill claims costs in respect of work done by more than one firm of solicitors, certificate (1) [of Precedent F], appropriately completed, should be signed on behalf of each firm.'
[126]　*Pritchard and Riccio v Ford Motor Co Ltd* [1997] 1 Costs LR 39; this was a pre-CPR case, so ought to be treated with some caution because there was no allowance for preparing the bill of costs under the RSC, when the regime was not the same as it is at present.
[127]　*Horsford v Bird* [2006] UKPC 55.

equivalent to a Grade D (or occasionally Grade C) is not unusual for routine bills of costs, with higher rates being reserved for weightier bills.

Appeals from assessments of time

29.121 The amount of costs for preparing the bill of costs is a matter which lies peculiarly within the expertise of the costs judge and it would, therefore, be difficult to disturb such a decision on appeal.[128]

Success fee

29.122 Where the solicitor is engaged under a conditional fee agreement which provides for a success fee and where the costs draftsman is engaged by the solicitor rather than by the client directly, the success fee will be recoverable on the costs draftsman's fees for preparing the bill of costs.[129] This topic is addressed in detail at **12.2–12.26**.

---

[128] *Horsford v Bird* [2006] UKPC 55.
[129] *Crane v Canons Leisure Centre* [2007] EWCA Civ 1352.

Chapter 30

ADDITIONAL LIABILITIES

30.1   The first quarter of this chapter focuses on the amount of success fees. Issues that go to whether a success fee should be allowed in principle are addressed in the second quartern; in particular, alternative means of funding are addressed at **30.101**, retrospectivity is addressed at **30.103**, and failure to give notice of funding is addressed at **30.88**. After the event insurance ('ATE') is addressed in the second half of this chapter, beginning at **30.123**.

SUCCESS FEES

30.2   A pedant would draw a strict distinction between a percentage increase and a success fee. The former is a percentage and the latter is a sum of money (see **2.81** and **2.103**). In practice, however, percentages are almost always referred to as 'success fees'. Unless the contrary is obvious from the context, this is the way in which that term is used in this book.

30.3   The quantification of success fees is an issue which turns very much on the facts. Legal research may be necessary to find cases which can be held out as being similar to the case in hand. Whilst one or two examples are given, this book does not contain case reports; on-line databases must be consulted in that regard.

Jurisdiction and regulatory restrictions

30.4   Success fees are a creation of statute and are governed by the Courts and Legal Services Act 1990 (as amended) ('CLSA 1990'); whilst not technically binding, the Privy Council has confirmed that they are not recoverable in the absence of specific statutory authority.[1] The CLSA 1990 provides that certain conditions must be met before a conditional fee agreement may lawfully provide for a success fee;[2] these are addressed below. Generally speaking, non-compliance with the requirements of CLSA 1990 will result in the entire agreement being struck down for want of enforceability (see Chapter 9).

The jurisdiction to allow a success fee and regulatory restrictions

30.5   In so far as a success fee is concerned, the agreement must state the percentage by which the amount of the fees which would be payable if it were not a conditional fee

---

[1]   The Privy Council came to this decision on the basis that the addition of a success fee to a fee that was reasonable and proportionate would almost certainly render the resultant fee unreasonable and disproportionate: *Seaga v Harper* [2009] UKPC 26.

[2]   CLSA 1990, s 58(4) (as amended).

agreement is to be increased; it is that percentage which is known as the 'percentage increase'.[3] When it is applied to the base costs, the product is the 'success fee'.

30.6 The starting point is CLSA 1990, s 58A(6), which deals with the recoverability of success fees in principle:[4]

> 'A costs order made in any proceedings may, subject in the case of court proceedings to rules of court, include provision requiring the payment of any fees payable under a conditional fee agreement which provides for a success fee.'

Thus, success fees are, subject to rules of court, recoverable between opposing parties.

30.7 The rules governing the assessment of success fees are themselves founded upon CLSA 1990, s 58A(7), which reads as follows:

> 'Rules of court may make provision with respect to the assessment of any costs which include fees payable under a conditional fee agreement (including one which provides for a success fee).'

Thus, success fees may be assessed (as is the case with other costs), and that process is subject to the applicable rules of court.

30.8 Delegated legislation made under CLSA 1990 provides that the success fee must not exceed 100%.[5] Notwithstanding the powers mentioned above, the restrictions imposed by rules of court are limited: other than where they fix the percentage increase (CPR Part 45), the only significant restrictions in the CPR are those which relate to notice of funding.[6] Whilst he commented that it was an obvious point, Brooke LJ has confirmed that fixed success fees do not apply to claims that predate the relevant fixed regimes[7].

Criminal, quasi-criminal and family matters

30.9 Success fees are proscribed in some types of litigation (see **9.62–9.63**). In particular, proceedings under s 82 of the Environmental Protection Act 1990 may be funded by way of a conditional fee agreement, but they may not be funded by an agreement which provides for a success fee.[8]

30.10 Conditional fee agreements are proscribed entirely in criminal or family matters (see **9.60**).

Agreements entered into before 1 April 2000

30.11 Whilst such agreements will now be encountered rarely, if at all, where a conditional fee agreement was made before the coming into force of the provisions mentioned at **30.6** and **30.7**, transitional provisions will apply in such a way as to prevent

---

3 See also CPR, r 43.2(1)(l), which makes a similar provision.
4 It is worth stating that Jackson LJ (speaking extrajudicially) has recommended the abrogation of the recovery of success fees between the parties: R Jackson *Review of Civil Litigation Costs: Final Report* (December 2009), chapter 10.
5 See CLSA 1990, s 58(4)(a) (as amended) and art 4 of the Conditional Fee Agreements Order 2000 (SI 2000/823).
6 This is discussed in detail at **30.88–30.97**.
7 *Atack v Lee* [2004] EWCA Civ 1712 at [12].
8 See CLSA 1990, s 58A(1)(a) and art 3 of the Conditional Fee Agreements Order 2000.

the recovery of a success fee (see **9.93–9.95**). In particular, success fees will not be recoverable by a party in the following types of proceedings:[9]

'(a) any proceedings in relation to which that party entered into a conditional fee agreement before 1 April 2000; or

(b) any proceedings arising out of the same cause of action as any proceedings to which sub-paragraph (a) refers.'

The effect of these transitional provisions is that if a conditional fee agreement was entered into before 1 April 2000, the recovery of a success fee on a between the parties basis will be precluded.[10] This will be so whether the pre-2000 CFA was made in the same proceedings, or any proceedings arising out of the same cause of action. That restriction will apply even if there was a break in the period during which the matter was conditionally funded such that on 1 April 2000 no conditional fee agreement was in existence.[11]

Types of success fee

Single-stage success fees

30.12 A single-stage success fee is the conventional type of success fee where the same percentage increase will apply throughout the claim (including the detailed assessment). Where a single-stage success fee is claimed, that is the only type of success fee that the court is able to allow. That is, the court lacks the vires to order that the percentage increase be adjusted so that different percentage increases apply at different times.[12] Likewise, it is not permissible simply to adopt and apply the relevant allowances in Part 45[13] although examples do exist of the court taking those allowances into account, presumably as a cross-check.[14]

30.13 In general, a single-stage success fee will be assessed by identifying the entire risk in the claim (including, where appropriate, the risks relating to quantum and the risk posed by the costs proceedings which might follow the claim), and then by gauging the appropriate percentage increase which best suits that risk. This is described in detail below.

Two- or multi-stage success fees

30.14 A two- or multi-stage success fee is a fee which will change at certain pre-defined stages in the litigation. It is also often called a 'sliding scale'.

30.15 The percentage increase will usually rise as the claim progresses, but there is no reason in principle why it should not decrease. An example would be where the percentage increase would be abated if liability was admitted within a certain period.

---

[9] Access to Justice Act 1999 (Transitional Provisions) Order 2000, art 2(1).

[10] The Access to Justice Act 1999 (Transitional Provisions) Order 2000 (SI 2000/900) does not expressly prohibit a party who has not entered into a conditional fee agreement before 1 April 2000 from recovering a success fee for work done prior to that date, but it is likely that the court would regard this as being such an obvious lacuna that it has been omitted because it would have been a statement of the obvious, and that success fees cannot be recovered for work done prior to 1 April 2000.

[11] *C v M* [2003] EWHC 250 (Fam) (also known as *Cowley v Mersey Regional Ambulance Services NHS Trust*.

[12] *U v Liverpool City Council (Practice Note)* [2005] EWCA Civ 475 at [49]; see **30.112–30.113**.

[13] *Atack v Lee* [2004] EWCA Civ 1712 at [52], per Brooke LJ.

[14] See, for example, *Thornley (a child) v Ministry of Defence* [2010] EWHC 2584 (QB) at [50], per HHJ Behrens, sitting as a Judge of the High Court.

30.16 The rationale for two-stage or multi-stage success fees was explained by Woolf CJ:[15]

> 'It can properly be assumed that if, notwithstanding the compliance with the protocol, the other party is not prepared to settle, or not prepared to settle upon reasonable terms, there is a serious defence.'

Woolf CJ went on to explain that the fact that the full success fee would be payable if the matter did not settle at an early stage would act as an incentive to defendants rigorously to examine the merits of the claim.

30.17 Brooke LJ has repeatedly supported this approach,[16] and in particular, he has pointed to another advantage of two- and multi-stage success fees (from the legal representative's point of view), namely, that if the case does not settle, a high success fee will be more readily defensible than otherwise might have been the case.[17]

30.18 There is no recognised mathematical formula for calculating two- or multi-stage success fees, but Woolf CJ explained that even if the matter settles at an early stage, a success fee will still be payable (ie it would not be zero). This was because:[18]

- the legal representatives would be entitled to be compensated for accepting a retainer on a no-win-no-fee basis, with the inevitable risk that that would involve; and
- an appropriate success fee would contribute towards those cases where no fees are payable because they end unsuccessfully.

At the other end of the scale is where liability has been admitted; in a case in which the agreement did put the solicitors at risk from Part 36 offers, Sir Robert Nelson found that a second-stage success fee of 100% could not be justified because the admission had removed a large part of the risk. He found that the first stage (claimed at 25% was itself not justified given the risks and that it was not an appropriate platform for the second-stage fee).[19]

Revisable success fees

30.19 A revisable success fee is where the contract between the client and the legal representative is such that the latter can revise the success fee at some point in the future, usually if and when a Part 36 offer is made. It will often be combined with an agreement which allows the legal representative to withdraw from the agreement if he believes that the risks of continuing do not justify the costs.

Contingent success fees

30.20 A conditional fee agreement will provide for a contingent success fee if the level of the percentage uplift is based on the outcome of the litigation. An example would be where the success fee was linked to the amount of damages; that would be a form of

---

[15] *Callery v Gray* [2001] EWCA Civ 1117 at [108].
[16] See, for example, *Atack v Lee* [2004] EWCA Civ 1712 at [7]–[11] and *Halloran v Delaney* [2002] EWCA Civ 1258 (as clarified in *Claims Direct Test Cases* [2003] EWCA Civ 136 at [101].
[17] *U v Liverpool City Council (Practice Note)* [2005] EWCA Civ 475 at [21].
[18] *Callery v Gray* [2001] EWCA Civ 1117 at [110].
[19] *Fortune v Roe* [2011] EWHC 2953 (QB) at [18], [36]–[37], [46], [51]–[53].

damages-based agreement, which is discussed in detail in Chapter 9. There is authority to suggest that such arrangements are lawful,[20] but that is not a universally held view (see **9.309–9.320**).

30.21 A provision which may be of particular relevance to an agreement which provides for a contingent success fee is the wording of CLSA 1990, s 58(4)(b):

> '[A conditional fee agreement which provides for a success fee] must state the percentage by which the amount of the fees which would be payable if it were not a conditional fee agreement is to be increased.'

Whilst there is no authority on the point, it would seem that a success fee which is not in the form of a percentage increase would fail to meet this criterion. An example might be where a lump sum is payable on the recovery of more than a certain sum, or a success fee calculated as a percentage of the damages. Arrangements such as those are laden with risk (in the sense that the law is uncertain) and are best avoided.

Prematurity and early risk assessments

30.22 It is well established that a legal representative is able to enter into a conditional fee agreement and set his success fee at an early stage of the litigation. Woolf CJ had the following to say on the topic:[21]

> 'We do not consider [that it is] mandatory for the claimant to delay entering into a CFA or taking out ATE insurance in order to enable his legal representative to acquire a greater knowledge of the circumstances of the case than that provided to him by the claimant. In the type of claim with which these appeals are concerned, the circumstances of the case will often lead the legal representative to assess the risk of failure, not only on the basis of particular features of the case, but on his general experience that claims which appear to have every prospect of success none the less occasionally founder as a result of matters which are unforeseen.'

Woolf CJ explained that one of the reasons he had arrived at this conclusion was because that would make it less likely that the burden of paying for unsuccessful claims would fall on the few with strong defences rather than on the many with defences of varying strength; he said that it would be more equitable that success fees be apportioned in relatively small amounts among many unsuccessful defendants rather than be borne in much larger amounts by those unsuccessful defendants who persist in contesting liability.[22]

30.23 There are those who have argued that the right to set a success fee at an early stage is limited to modest road traffic claims (this being because such claims are often, as a class, much the same, so that they 'do not turn on the peculiar features of the claim itself').[23] There is a divergence of judicial opinion as to how a success fee set at an early stage ought to be assessed. There can be no little doubt that a success fee based on an assessment of risk on enquiry will be easier to justify than an initial assessment based on

---

[20]   *Benaim (UK) Ltd v Davies Middleton & Davies Ltd* [2004] EWHC 737 (TCC).
[21]   *Callery v Gray* [2001] EWCA Civ 1117 at [96]–[97].
[22]   *Callery v Gray* [2001] EWCA Civ 1117 at [99].
[23]   *Callery v Gray* [2001] EWCA Civ 1117 at [84].

the absence of information,[24] but there have been differing approaches as to how the latter should be addressed. In the context of a clinical negligence case Jack J said:[25]

> '[Some may say] that a solicitor should not enter an agreement at an early stage. However, as I have said, he is entitled to do so. It follows inevitably from that entitlement that he will be in a position of ignorance compared with that when he has the medical records and expert advice. But he is likely to be experienced in the field and he will have some knowledge of the claim. His "ignorance" is relative. He may have taken on a winner: he does not know. But equally he may have taken on a case where greater knowledge would show the chances were well below 50 percent.'

Thus, Jack J was influenced by the risk of not yet knowing what the evidence, upon enquiry, would hold. Whilst he was also influenced by this factor (albeit to a lesser degree), Mackay J refused to follow Jack J's analysis in full, this being on very similar facts; Mackay J concluded that if a success fee is set at a stage which was too early for a full assessment of risk to be made, then weight ought to be given to the facts that firstly, it would have been open to the legal representative to have set a staged success fee,[26] and secondly, it would usually be possible to terminate the agreement if subsequent enquires showed the case to be laden with risk.[27] Regardless of which analysis is correct, it is likely that no legal representative can shut his eyes to evidence that would easily be available at the time the risk assessment was made; in this regard, it is relevant that Brooke LJ found that on the facts of the case before him, a solicitor ought to have made a telephone call to ascertain certain facts.[28] Some judges have gone further and disallowed success fees entirely (albeit not on the basis of prematurity *per se,* but on the basis that excessive haste can result in a failure to try to resolve the dispute). In a case in which the receiving party had acted hurriedly in the sense that it did not trouble itself with the pre-action protocol, Akenhead J found that no success fee should be recoverable; there were several grounds for that finding[29], but one of them was that compliance with the protocol might have resolved the dispute.[30] That type of finding is rare, and perhaps ought to be regarded as being assessment under CPR, r 44.3(5) (ie an assessment based on conduct) rather than an assessment based on risk.

Risk and success fees

30.24 Where a success fee is based on the perceived merits (as opposed to being a sliding scale or a fixed success fee) the factors pertinent to the level of the percentage increase may be divided into those going to risk and those not going to risk. The latter include the 'postponement charge' and the 'disbursement charge' and are dealt with at **30.79–30.87**. Those going to risk are addressed at **30.25–30.77**.

---

[24]   Whilst not binding, see *Barhan v Athreya and (2) Barking, Havering & Redbridge NHS Trust* (unreported) 16 June 2007, Central London County Court, HHJ Dean QC at [53].

[25]   *Oliver v Whipps Cross University NHS Trust* [2009] EWHC 1104 (QB) at [17]. It is, perhaps, worth noting that Jack J had before him data which had been prepared by the receiving party's solicitors; that data showed that about half of the clinical negligence cases which were initially investigated ultimately failed. Therefore, by assessing risks at a very early stage the solicitor was not merely having a stab in the dark, but was purposively placing the case in a category about which data existed and in respect of which risks could be ascertained.

[26]   *McCarthy v Essex Rivers Healthcare NHS Trust* (unreported) 13 November 2009, QBD at [18].

[27]   *McCarthy v Essex Rivers Healthcare NHS Trust* (unreported) 13 November 2009, QBD at [8]; that is, this was the analysis in the court below, and Mackay J did not interfere with it.

[28]   *Ellerton v Harris* [2004] EWCA Civ 1712 at [49], per Brooke LJ

[29]   The other reasons were lack of risk, lack of evidence as to whether there had been a success, and a need to amend the claim.

[30]   *Buildability Ltd v O'Donnell Developments Ltd* [2009] EWHC 3196 (TCC) at [27]. For a discussion as to the difference between disallowing a success fee and assessing it at nil, see **30.43**.

30.25 Risks can be categorised according to the nature of the event to which they relate; thus, a risk of the case being lost entirely may be called a 'liability risk', the risk of failing to achieve a better result than a Part 36 offer may be a 'quantum risk', etc. This categorisation is useful for the purposes of describing the various types of risk which might pertain in any given case, but the percentage uplift is usually based on the overall, entire risk rather than the sum of individual risks (see **30.30–30.32**).

Risk in general

30.26 The CPD provides as follows:[31]

'In deciding whether a percentage increase is reasonable relevant factors to be taken into account may include:

(a)   the risk that the circumstances in which the costs, fees or expenses would be payable might or might not occur ...'

Thus, it is necessary to identify the circumstances in which the legal representative may fail to recover his fees. This will turn on how 'win' or 'success' is defined in the agreement, and in this regard, it may be necessary to look at the circumstances in which the agreement was made as well as the agreement itself.[32] The CPD goes on to provide guidance about the measure of risk:[33]

'Subject to paragraph 17.8(2),[34] when the court is considering the factors to be taken into account in assessing an additional liability, it will have regard to the facts and circumstances as they reasonably appeared to the solicitor or counsel when the funding arrangement was entered into and at the time of any variation of the arrangement.'

Brooke LJ has confirmed that where the risk assessment recorded by the legal representative is inadequate, the court must substitute its own assessment, this being from the standpoint of a reasonably careful legal representative assessing the risk on the basis of what was known him at the time.[35]

30.27 Moore-Bick LJ articulated the applicable test in this way:[36]

'The success fee must reflect a reasonable and rational assessment of the risks facing the solicitor at the time when the agreement was entered into.'

30.28 There are no significant rules limiting the factors that the court may take into account when assessing the nature and level of the relevant risk (or risks). The court cannot take hindsight into account (although the outcome of the litigation is, from time to time, used as a cross-check in the sense that it is evidence of what the parties believed

---

[31]   CPD, art 11.8(1).
[32]   In *Manning v Kings College Hospital NHS Trust* [2011] EWHC 2954 (QB), for example, Spencer J found that an agreement which state that 'win' would include any award of damages did not mean that the case had already been won by reason of certain admissions that had already been made at the time the agreement was made.
[33]   CPD, art 11.7.
[34]   The reference to paragraph 17.8(2) is a reference to a provision which applies only to costs-only proceedings; that provision is possibility ultra vires, but in any event can be disregarded for the moment.
[35]   *Atack v Lee* [2004] EWCA Civ 1712 at [37].
[36]   *C (a patient acting by her litigation friend Jocelyn Fox) v W* [2008] EWCA Civ 1459 at [8].

the merits to be,[37] and retrospective experience of other cases may, occasionally, be relevant[38]). In an appropriate case, the court might be assisted by statistical data,[39] but Mackay J had this to say on that topic:[40]

'[A] complex statistical analysis of the cases dealt with by these [the firms in question] will not help me resolve this appeal and nor should such evidence need to be put before costs judges every time they have to assess such cases. I agree with her that that would be an undesirable and onerous task and should not be encouraged.'

30.29 Risks are generally expressed in numerical terms, but pinpoint accuracy would be spurious; in this regard, Lord Neuberger MR had this to say:[41]

'When it comes to determining the prospects of a claim succeeding, there is ... a risk of becoming beguiled by the apparent accuracy of an assessment which is expressed in figures and appears to be logically based. In the end, however, the determination is a matter of judgment, which involves arriving at an overall assessment by weighing up various factors, which are inherently difficult to quantify, not least because the quantification will be a matter of opinion on which reasonable people could differ (sometimes quite substantially), and because the factors are not as independent of each other as might first appear.'

Liability risks are generally expressed as the chance of success (or failure) quantified as a percentage. Quantum risks are often expressed in terms of the proportion of the fees that are perceived to be put at risk by reason of the operation of CPR Part 36.[42] That said, there is no right or wrong way of describing or quantifying risk, and – in an appropriate case – different methods might be appropriate.

30.30 An example might assist. A quantitative risk assessment in a case where the agreement provides for a quantum risk might read:

'The chances of succeeding in this claim are generally good (say, 70 percent); if the claim is successful, then on average I would expect to lose 10 percent of my costs as a result of Part 36 offers. When both risks are taken into account, I would expect to be awarded 63 percent of my total fees, on average.'

It would be equally appropriate to express the risk in other terms, such as qualitatively:

'The prospects of success are reasonably good but not excellent, and there is a small risk that we will fail to beat the other side's Part 36 Offer. The overall prospects can be said to be fair to good.'

Regardless of the way in which the risk is described, the ideal is that ultimately a single, global figure is placed upon the risk in general. Given the way in which most ready reckoners are set out, it is best if that figure is an estimate of the amount of costs which

---

[37]   Whilst not binding, see *Designer Guild Ltd v Russell Williams (Textiles) Ltd (t/a Washington DC) (No 2)* [2003] EWHC 9024 (Costs), in which Master Hurst had the following to say: 'There is an argument for saying that in any case which reached trial a success fee of 100% is easily justified because both sides presumably believed that they had an arguable and winnable case. In this case we have no doubt at all that the matter was finely balanced and that the appropriate success fee is therefore 100%.' See also **30.48** and **30.49**.

[38]   See *Motto & Ors v Trafigura Ltd & Anor* [2011] EWCA Civ 1150 at [128], per Lord Neuberger MR.

[39]   See, for example, *Oliver v Whipps Cross University NHS Trust* [2009] EWHC 1104 (QB) at [17].

[40]   *McCarthy v Essex Rivers Healthcare NHS Trust* (unreported) 13 November 2009, QBD at [19].

[41]   *Motto & Ors v Trafigura Ltd & Anor* [2011] EWCA Civ 1150 at [127].

[42]   *C (a patient acting by her litigation friend Jocelyn Fox) v W* [2008] EWCA Civ 1459 at [17].

is likely to be recovered, expressed as a percentage of the total costs claimed. Thus, if the only risk is liability risk and if that risk is 60%, the global recovery is 60%. If, on the other hand, there is an additional risk that 10% of those costs will be disallowed as a result of Part 36 offers, the global recovery will fall to 54% (ie 60% discounted by 10%). Other ways of expressing risk exist, but the use of a single global figure is both supported by authority[43] and easy to work with in terms of subsequent calculations.

30.31 The weight to be given to the receiving party's own assessment of risk will depend on the facts of the case and the quality of the risk assessment, but the following comments of Lord Nicholls suggest that the success fee which has been agreed should not be afforded the same weight as would a fee which had been negotiated in the context of an open, competitive market:[44]

> 'It is extremely difficult to say whether the actual "premium" [ie the success fee] paid by the client was reasonable or not. This is because the client does not pay the "premium" ... The transaction therefore lacks the features of a normal insurance, in which the transaction takes place against the background of an insurance market ... Since the client will in no event be paying the success fee out of his pocket or his damages, he is not concerned with economic rationality. He has no interest in what the fee is ... [The solicitor's] interest centres entirely upon whether the agreed success fee will or will not exceed what the costs judge is willing to allow.'

30.32 Once risk has been quantified, it needs to be converted into a percentage uplift. The theory underlying that process was explained by Jack J:[45]

> 'The rationale behind the percentage mark up as it is applied in our courts is that the successful cases should pay for the unsuccessful ones. The theory runs as follows. If a solicitor acts in two cases with 50% chances of success, he will win one and lose one, and so he needs a success fee, or mark up, on the costs in the successful action of 100% to recover the costs of both. If he acts in three cases each with a one third chance of success, he will win one and lose two. So in the winning case he needs a mark up of 200%. But the maximum allowed in law is 100%. If he acts in three cases each with a two thirds chance of success, he will win two and lose one. So in each winning case he needs a mark up of 50%. If he acts in five cases with a 60% chance of success, he should win three and lose two, so he needs a mark up of two thirds (or 67% as Master Campbell took it) on each of the three to pay for the two. It can be seen that a small decrease in the chances of success, results in a comparatively large increase in the mark up required.'

Whilst the calculation of success fees is a matter of justice rather than mere calculation, the essence of Jack J's analysis can be expressed in terms of a formula (see **30.35**).

30.33 Finally, it is worth pointing out that some judges have expressed disquiet about a regime where legal fees are determined not by a market, but by an adversarial approach before a tribunal. The House of Lords articulated those sentiments in *Callery v Gray*.[46] A pithy synopsis of those concerns was expressed by Eady J:[47]

---

[43] *Redwing Construction Ltd v Wishart* [2011] EWHC 19 (TCC) at [15(c)]; *Smiths Dock Limited v Edwards* [2004] EWHC 116 (QB) at [35]–[36]; and *C (a patient acting by her litigation friend Jocelyn Fox) v W* [2008] EWCA Civ 1459 at [17] and [34].

[44] *Callery v Gray* [2002] UKHL 28 at [25]; Lord Nichols went on to say (at [34]): 'Solicitors will charge whatever is currently allowed and exert upward pressure to be able to charge more. But that will not tell anyone whether the fees paid to the solicitors represent reasonable value for money.'

[45] *Oliver v Whipps Cross University NHS Trust* [2009] EWHC 1104 (QB) at [2].

[46] [2002] 2 Costs LR 205, HL.

[47] *Cox v MGM* [2006] EWHC 1235 (QB) at [34].

'One must always therefore be alert to identify "a success uplift grossly disproportionate to any fair assessment of the risks of failure" (to adopt the words of Lord Bingham [in *Callery v Gray* [2002] 2 Costs LR 205]). The object is often to obtain as much as possible from the other side. This is a new phenomenon, which costs judges clearly need to have very much in consideration when attempting to achieve a fair outcome. Careful analysis accompanied by a healthy dose of scepticism is likely to be appropriate.'

Exaggerated success fees are a matter of grave judicial concern,[48] and a failure properly to identify and acknowledge the absence of risk can lead to savage and very public judicial criticism.[49]

30.34 The following types of risks are now discussed in turn:

(1)   liability risk;
(2)   quantum risk;
(3)   recovery risk; and
(4)   enforcement risk.

This list is such that each risk will tend to include the risks which are higher up in the list. Thus, quantum risk (2) will include the liability risk (1); and (3) will include both (1) and, where relevant, (2). The reason for this Russian Doll effect is because a party cannot be at risk from a Part 36 offer unless he has won the case in general, and he cannot find himself at risk of not being able to recover unless he has won and been awarded his costs. Whether a particular category of risk is relevant is a matter of contractual interpretation; it has nothing to do with the nature of the case, which will go to the degree of risk rather to its relevance.

Liability risk

30.35 If the only risk in question is the liability risk (ie the risk of losing), then it is generally accepted that the following formula is appropriate for converting risk into a percentage uplift:[50]

---

[48]   See the Times Law Report of *Begum v Klarit* [2005] EWCA Civ 210 (ie (2005) *The Times*, 18 March); the words 'grave judicial concern' do not appear in the judgment, so presumably were said during submissions.
[49]   See, for example, *Pankhurst v (1) White and (2) Motor Insurers Bureau* [2010] EWCA Civ 1445 at [54] in which Jackson LJ famously condemned the funding arrangments as 'grotesque'; see also *Begum v Klarit* [2005] EWCA Civ 210 at [5] in which Brooke LJ said that he found 'it hard to understand how responsible counsel could have agreed with responsible solicitors [to agree funding that would] discredit and devalue the whole arrangements for conditional fee agreements'.
[50]   This formula is only an approximation; this is because most conditional fee agreements will deprive the legal representative of his success fee in the event of his client failing to beat a Part 36 offer; it is possible to include that factor in the calculation, but there is no authority to suggest that this should be done.

$$s = \frac{f}{(1-f)}$$ Where s is the success fee expressed as a fraction and f is the risk of failure expressed as a fraction.

This is the formula that is used to calculate the well – known 'ready reckoner' that is often found in publications on success fees.

30.36 Another way of expressing exactly the same formula (but using percentages rather than fractions, and by focusing on the prospects of success rather than the risks of failure) is:

$$s_\% = \frac{(100 - p_\%)}{p_\%}$$ Where $s\%$ and $p\%$ are the success fee and prospects of success, both expressed as percentages.

30.37 These formulae are nothing more than an algebraic way of expressing the notion that the success fee is (a) that proportion of the total base costs which, on average, will go unpaid as a result of the risk in question divided by (b) that proportion of the base costs which will be paid. This is a manifestation of the 'neutrality principle', namely, that the success fee compensates for lost income.

30.38 It may be that there is a need to work backwards to derive the risks from the success fee. Assuming that the only risk in question is the risk of losing, the following formula allows this to be done:

$$p_\% = \frac{1}{(1 + s_\%)}$$

30.39 The analysis set out above assumes that it is possible to estimate the risks. It may be, however, that there is so little information that it is difficult even to assess the risk. In those circumstances, the case may be categorised as having 'uncertain prospects' (to use Jack J's phrase).[51] Where this is the case, a high success fee may or may not be justified, depending on the facts.[52] Moore-Bick LJ has suggested that if the risks are very difficult to assess, it may be appropriate to enter into a variant of a two-stage agreement where the risks are to be reassessed if an offer is made.[53] Mackay J has confirmed that if the solicitor has the opportunity to abandon the claim if the prospects of success become too bleak, then that is something that can be reflected in the success fee (see **30.45**).

---

[51] *Oliver v Whipps Cross University NHS Trust* [2009] EWHC 1104 (QB) at [17]. See, however, *McCarthy v Essex Rivers Healthcare NHS Trust* (unreported) 13 November 2009, QBD at [17]–[21], in which Mackay J questions the correctness of Jack J's analysis.

[52] On the facts of the case before him, Jack J allowed a success fee of 100%, but he did not intend to create any precedent in that regard. It is, perhaps, worth noting that although Jack J said that the risk was uncertain, on the facts of the case before him this finding immediately put the case into a larger category of similar cases in respect of which there was data which quantified the risk; thus, one could argue that the 'uncertain' risks could perhaps better be described as 'less certain than would ideally be the case'.

[53] *C (a patient acting by her litigation friend Jocelyn Fox) v W* [2008] EWCA Civ 1459 at [24].

30.40   The following miscellaneous points can be made about liability risks.

Admissions, denials and the risk of withdrawals

30.41   The fact that liability has already been admitted would not preclude the claimant from entering into a conditional fee agreement; where this is the case, and where it is not possible to infer that the agreement related to risks other than those that had been negated by the admission (see **30.26**), the success fee should be low as a reflection of the absence of significant risk.[54] Moore-Bick LJ has explained that if weight is to be given to the risk that an admission might be withdrawn, there must be some basis for believing that this might happen.[55] A denial of liability is a factor to which some weight may be attached.[56]

Complexity

30.42   HHJ Behrens (sitting as a Judge of the High Court) has commented that it is important not to confuse complexity with risk; the complexity of the case may justify a higher hourly rate, but it does not necessarily justify a higher success fee.[57]

Low risk litigation

30.43   There is no such thing as an entirely risk free claim.[58] Brooke LJ has explained that where prospects of success approach 100%, the success fee ought not to tend to 0% but instead should not ordinarily fall below about 5%.[59] There are, however, exceptions. Akenhead J was one of the first judges to refuse to allow a success fee[60] and now such decisions are not uncommon.[61]

Possibility of withdrawal of instructions

30.44   Moore-Bick LJ has indicated that an allowance for the possibility of withdrawal of instructions should not be made unless there is a basis for believing that this will happen; furthermore, the agreement must be such that the client would, by withdrawing instructions, avoid liability for the costs incurred.[62]

---

[54]   *C (a patient acting by her litigation friend Jocelyn Fox) v W* [2008] EWCA Civ 1459 at [18]; as an extreme example of this (i e where judgment had been entered in favour of the receiving party) see *Pankhurst v Whilte* [2001] EWCA Civ 1445. See also *Thornley (a child) v MoD* [2010] EWHC 2584 (QB).

[55]   *C (a patient acting by her litigation friend Jocelyn Fox) v W* [2008] EWCA Civ 1459 at [14].

[56]   See, for example, Brooke LJ's comments in *Atack v Lee* [2004] EWCA Civ 1712 at [38].

[57]   *Thornley (a child) v Ministry of Defence* [2010] EWHC 2584 (QB) at [48], per HHJ Behrens, sitting as a Judge of the High Court.

[58]   See the Court of Appeal's apparent acceptance of counsel's concession in *Callery v Gray* [2001] EWCA Civ 1117 at [127], and *Halloran v Delaney* [2002] EWCA Civ 1258 at [31].

[59]   *Halloran v Delaney* [2002] EWCA Civ 1258, and clarified by Brooke LJ in *Claims Direct Test Cases, Re* [2003] EWCA Civ 136 at [99]–[101].

[60]   The first was *Buildability Ltd v O'Donnell Developments Ltd* [2009] EWHC 3196 (TCC) at [27]; that was a decision based largely on conduct, however. In *Redwing Construction Ltd v Wishart* [2011] EWHC 19 (TCC) at [15(c)] Akenhead J commented that it was open to the court to allow nil success fee. It is not clear whether, in either of these cases, Akenhead J's attention had been drawn to *Halloran v Delaney* [2002] EWCA Civ 1258 .

[61]   Whilst not binding, there are instances of specialist judges finding that success fees ought to be nil. See, for example, *Collett v (1) Smith and (2) Middlesborough Football and Athletic Company (1986) Ltd* (unreported) 20 May 2011, SCCO (from the QBD), Master Haworth. See also *Thornley (a child) v Ministry of Defence* [2010] EWHC 2584 (QB) at [58], per HHJ Behrens, sitting as a Judge of the High Court.

[62]   *C (a patient acting by her litigation friend Jocelyn Fox) v W* [2008] EWCA Civ 1459 at [21]–[22].

Client's solvency

30.45 Moore-Bick LJ has confirmed that unless the conditional fee agreement provides that a client may terminate the retainer without liability for any fees, concerns about the client's solvency are irrelevant for the purposes of considering the success fee.[63]

Size of the claim

30.46 The size of the claim *per se* is not a factor which would merit an increase in the success fee independently of it giving rise to an identifiable increase in the risk; this was explained by Moore-Bick LJ:[64]

'It is probably true in general that high value claims tend to be more complex and to involve a greater amount of work than claims of lower value, but that does not of itself increase the risk of losing. If more work is done the base fees are inevitably higher, but the application of a percentage success fee means that the amount recovered by the solicitor if the claim succeeds is correspondingly greater. It may be the case that the more complex the litigation, the larger the number of potential pitfalls, but the right way to allow for that is to adjust the chance of success and by that means the success fee.'

Size of the firm

30.47 Sole practitioners and smaller firms often say that they are exposed to greater risk than larger entities because they are less able to cushion themselves against the financial insult of losing. Whilst not in a binding decision, Master O'Hare rejected this argument on the basis that the risk remained the same regardless of the nature of or the identity of the legal representative.[65]

Costs only proceedings

30.48 CPD, art 17.8(2) reads as follows:

'In cases in which an additional liability is claimed, the costs judge or district judge should have regard to the time when and the extent to which the claim has been settled and to the fact that the claim has been settled without the need to commence proceedings.'

30.49 In an extract which has been approved by the Court of Appeal, Master Hurst had this to say on the effect of this provision when read in conjunction with CPD, art 11.8(2):[66]

'The combined effect of these two paragraphs is to prevent the costs officer from using hindsight in arriving at the appropriate success fee, and to prevent excessive claims for success fees in cases which settle without the need for proceedings when it was clear, or ought to have been clear from the outset, that the risk of having to commence proceedings was minimal.'

---

[63] *C (a patient acting by her litigation friend Jocelyn Fox) v W* [2008] EWCA Civ 1459 at [21].
[64] *C (a patient acting by her litigation friend Jocelyn Fox) v W* [2008] EWCA Civ 1459 at [14].
[65] *Omnibridge Consulting Ltd v Clearsprings (Management) Ltd* (unreported) 10 October 2005, SCCO. That said, his attention was not drawn to the topic of 'risk premiums' (see **30.74–30.77**).
[66] See *Halloran v Delaney* [2002] EWCA Civ 1258, in which Brooke LJ approved of an extract from *Bensusan v Freedman* [2001] EWHC 9001 (Costs), [2001] All ER (D) 212 (Oct).

Thus, in a case which settles at such an early stage as to avoid the need to issue proceedings, the outcome may, in an appropriate case, be seen as being evidence of the risks which pertained at the outset.

Rear end shunts

30.50 Comparisons are often drawn with the archetypal rear end shunt. It is, therefore, worth noting what Woolf CJ had to say about such cases:[67]

> 'The Court of Appeal concluded that: "After careful consideration and having reflected on the reasoning in the judgments below in the two appeals, we have concluded that, where a CFA is agreed at the outset in such cases, 20% is the maximum uplift that can reasonably be agreed ..." It assumes that there is no special feature that raises apprehension that the claim may not prove to be sound.'

It is notable that the figure of 20% was the maximum percentage uplift that could reasonably be agreed, not the ordinary percentage uplift which could reasonably be agreed.

Passenger claims

30.51 In a claim where the claimants were passengers (and therefore unlikely to be to blame), Richards J made the following comment about the risks:[68]

> 'The fact that the claimants had been passengers and were plainly not themselves to blame was an important consideration. But there remained the possibility that this was an accident for which no-one was to blame, or that the blame lay with an untraced driver, or that the claimants would not be able to establish who was to blame.'

On the facts of the case before him (which was atypical because there were two potential defendants), he found that a range of between 33% and 50% would be appropriate.

Risk arising out of costs litigation

30.52 Eady J has found that it is permissible to take into account risks arising out of the detailed assessment in setting the success fee generally.[69] Likewise, in the early days of recoverable success fees, Brooke LJ found uncertainty as to the law to be a relevant factor.[70]

Risk of suing the wrong defendant and risks arising out of insurance issues

30.53 Where the defendant had already been identified and his insurer had already impliedly accepted indemnity (in that an admission of liability had been made), Moore-Bick LJ found that it was not appropriate to make a separate allowance in the success fee for the risk of having identified the wrong dependant or for the possibility of

---

[67]	*Callery v Gray* [2001] EWCA Civ 1117 at [104].
[68]	*Burton v Kingsbury* [2005] EWHC 1034 (QB) at [21].
[69]	*Cox v MGM* [2006] EWHC 1235 (QB) at [45]; see also *Halloran v Delaney* [2002] EWCA Civ 1258 at [31] and [33].
[70]	*Halloran v Delaney* [2002] EWCA Civ 1258 at [33].

insurance issues arising; that said, this was very much on the facts of the case, and it is doubtful if Moore-Bick intended to create any law in this regard.[71]

Contributory negligence

30.54 Contributory negligence is a risk which goes to quantum; it is not a liability risk.[72] That said, it may have a bearing on the liability risk (in that it reduces it); this was explained by Woolf CJ:[73]

> 'In this category of litigation, the prospect of some success on liability is increased because of the ability of a court to make a reduced award on account of contributory negligence.'

Uncertainty in the law and technical points

30.55 It is permissible to take into account a risk that relates to uncertainty in the law; it seems that this could include uncertainties in the law of costs.[74] Whilst technical points are unattractive and are usually disliked by the court, they should not be forgotten about entirely; this is because technical points can succeed, especially where the need for consistency, clarity and adherence to the established principles is greater than the avoidance of a technical rule.[75] There is no authority to suggest that technical points ought to be disregarded for the purposes of setting the success fee.

Relevance of acceptance of responsibility for disbursements

30.56 Eady J has explained that the fact that a firm has agreed to fund disbursements is a factor which can be taken into account, but it cuts both ways. This is because there are two competing factors at play. The first is the additional financial risk posed by the disbursements, but the second is the fact that if the solicitors felt sufficiently confident about the claim to fund disbursements, they must have thought that the prospects of success were reasonably good.[76] This topic is discussed further at **30.81–30.87**.

Relevance of advice given to the client and counsel's advices

30.57 The court is entitled to give weight to the advice that was given to the client, even if this differs from the assessment of risk as set out in the risk assessment. Eady J had this to say on the topic:[77]

> 'When one is advising the client on the likelihood of overall success or failure, one should be applying the same criteria to exactly the same information as when one is assessing the same risks for the purposes of deciding on the terms of a CFA. The chances of success do not suddenly diminish because one turns to the calculation of a success fee. A solicitor may wish to take other factors into account when deciding whether to proceed on a CFA basis, or when defining "success", but the overall merits remain the same and do not expand or shrink like Alice.'

---

[71] *C (a patient acting by her litigation friend Jocelyn Fox) v W* [2008] EWCA Civ 1459 at [16].
[72] *C (a patient acting by her litigation friend Jocelyn Fox) v W* [2008] EWCA Civ 1459 at [17], per Moore-Bick LJ.
[73] *Callery v Gray* [2001] EWCA Civ 1117 at [103].
[74] See *Halloran v Delaney* [2002] EWCA Civ 1258 at [31] and [33].
[75] See, for example, *Millburn-Snell v Evans* [2011] EWCA Civ 577 in which the claimants were found not to have title to sue because they did not have letters of administration.
[76] *Cox v MGM* [2006] EWHC 1235 (QB) at [34] and [41].
[77] *Cox v MGM* [2006] EWHC 1235 (QB) at [46].

In so far as counsel's advices are concerned, Lord Neuberger MR has commented that it would also be unrealistic not to acknowledge that many members of the Bar tend to err on the side of caution when advising (although – he commented – a significant proportion of barristers may tend the other way).[78]

Adverse selection

30.58 It may be that a client chooses conditional funding over private funding because he has insufficient confidence in the merits of the claim to fund it himself. This may lead to 'adverse selection',[79] especially where such a client was less than forthcoming about the facts which led to his concern about the merits. Thus, clients with weak cases may be more likely to select conditional funding than clients with a strong cases.[80] There is no authority dealing with the issue of adverse selection in the context of success fees, but in the analogous topic of ATE insurance it is established that insurers are permitted to take steps to prevent it, and that the costs of those steps may be reflected in the additional liabilities allowed between opposing parties (see **30.177–30.181**). It may be that a similar approach would apply to success fees, but the arguments against that are cogent, and some would say compelling (see the footnotes).[81]

Discounted agreements (liability risk)

30.59 A relatively recent phenomenon is the discounted conditional fee agreement (see **9.12–9.19**). The principle of the algebra is the same, but the formulae used to manipulate the figures are different. This is because a discounted conditional fee agreement introduces a further factor known as the discount factor (which is the percentage or fraction of base fees which will be payable in the event of a loss).

30.60 While it has to be stressed that the formula has not been approved by any court, it is possible to adapt the formulae mentioned above in such a way as to take account of the fact that discounted costs will be payable in the event of a loss. The adapted formula is as follows (again, f represents the chance of failure expressed as a fraction, and s is the percentage uplift expressed as a fraction: see **30.35**):

$$s = \frac{f(1-d)}{(1-f)}$$

The fraction of the base costs that is the discounted costs is represented by d in this formula.

---

[78]   *Motto & Ors v Trafigura Ltd & Anor* [2011] EWCA Civ 1150 at [129].

[79]   In the present context this phrase may be defined as a tendency for the chances of a person choosing conditional funding being negatively correlated with the chances of success.

[80]   An example might be where a client has information that the solicitor does not have (that information being called 'asymmetric information'), and that information is such that if the solicitor had known about it, he would either have charged a higher success fee or he would have declined the instructions altogether. Another way in which adverse selection might affect conditional fee agreements is where the prospects of a client selecting (or the solicitor offering) a high success fee is negatively correlated with the likelihood of a case being successful. This could arise as a result of the client being more guarded about weak cases.

[81]   The first argument would be that the need to allow the costs of adverse selection in ATE insurance arises out of the need to examine the reasonable needs of the market as a whole – so-called macroeconomics – rather than the reasonable needs of the individual client; the argument would be that there is no such thing as macroeconomics in the context of success fees. A further argument would be that the paying party should not be paying for risks caused by clients not being open with their legal advisors.

30.61 This formula is another manifestation of the principle expressed at **30.37**. The same formula can be expressed in terms of percentages and prospects of success (again, $p_\%$ represents the prospect of success expressed as a percentage and $s_\%$ represents the percentage uplift expressed as a percentage: see **30.36**):

$$S_\% = \frac{(100 - p_\%)(100 - d_\%)}{p_\%}$$ Where $d_\%$ represents the percentage of the base costs which is payable in the event of failure.

A worked example would be where, in the event of a loss, the solicitor would be paid 60% of his fees, and where the prospects of winning are 75%, the applicable success fee would be 25% (ie 100% less 75%) multiplied by 40% (ie 100% less 60%) divided by 75%; this gives a total of 13%.

30.62 The discounted figures appear on the ready reckoner on the back cover. If the discount factor and the liability risk are known, the appropriate success fee can be derived.

Quantum risk

30.63 Quantum risk is the risk of costs being disallowed as a result of the party in question failing to beat a Part 36 offer (see **9.44**). Whether a conditional fee agreement puts the legal representative at risk on quantum is a matter of contractual interpretation. If the agreement says that the legal representative will not be paid his base costs in the event that his client fails to beat a Part 36 offer, then the agreement provides for a quantum risk. If there is no such provision, then this will generally not be the case,[82] but such a provision may be implied by the circumstances.[83]

30.64 Whilst quantum risk will often simply be subsumed within the success fee without any need to give thought to it as a separate entity,[84] Moore-Bick LJ has given guidance as to how quantum risk should be analysed where it does justify specific attention:[85]

'The task facing [the legal representatives] was to assess, as best they could, the risk of losing part of their fees for reasons of that kind, and then expressing that as a percentage of the total fees likely to be earned to trial. Only by doing so could they calculate a success fee expressed as a percentage uplift on the whole of their profit costs.'

Thus, the quantum risk is expressed as a percentage (see below). Moore-Bick LJ referred to the overall risk as being a risk 'equivalent to failure overall'.[86]

30.65 The following is an example of how a quantum risk may be reflected in a success fee. If Part 36 offers posed a 30% risk that half of the fees would be disallowed, it would

---

[82]   *Atack v Lee* [2004] EWCA Civ 1712 at [38].
[83]   See *Manning v Kings College Hospital NHS Trust* [2011] EWHC 2954 (QB) at [97]–[147], per Spencer J, applying *Investors Compensation Scheme Ltd v West Bromwich Building Society (No 1)* [1998] 1 WLR 896.
[84]   See, for example, *Ellerton v Harris* [2004] EWCA Civ 1712 at [49] in which Brooke LJ found that 'the only significant risk related to the possibility of the Claimant accepting her solicitor's advice and then not beating a payment in' and that 'this [was] just one of the rare risks which justified a success fee set as high as 20% in the simplest of claims.'
[85]   *C (a patient acting by her litigation friend Jocelyn Fox) v W* [2008] EWCA Civ 1459 at [17].
[86]   *C (a patient acting by her litigation friend Jocelyn Fox) v W* [2008] EWCA Civ 1459 at [24].

be fair to say that 15% of the costs were at risk in this way. If the prospects of success generally were 80%, then a single, global figure for risk (or an 'equivalent' figure, to use Moore-Bick LJ's terminology) would be 85% of 80%, which is 68% (say 70% for ease of calculation). If that figure is put into the ready reckoner, the appropriate success fee would be 42%.

30.66 It can be seen that all of these risks are somewhat nebulous and, at the very least, difficult to assess; this means that there is little point in aiming for spurious accuracy. In view of this, the ready reckoner on the back cover includes three columns marked 'high', 'medium' and 'low': these represent an entirely arbitrary assumption that these categories of risk can be assessed as putting 30%, 20% and 10% of the costs at risk of non-recovery by reason of Part 36 offers. The formula used to create this table is as follows ($p_\%$ represents the prospect of success expressed as a percentage and $s_\%$ represents the percentage uplift expressed as a percentage: see **30.36**):

$$s_\% = \frac{100 - \left(\frac{p_\% q_\%}{100}\right)}{\frac{p_\% q_\%}{100}} \quad \text{Where } q\% \text{ is that proportion of the costs which are at risk as a result of Part 36 offers.}$$

The applicable figures do not represent the percentage that would be disallowed in a case where an offer had been beaten, but the percentage that would be disallowed as a result of quantum risk on average.

30.67 The fact that a risk may exist in principle does not mean that it will exist as a matter of course, as Moore-Bick LJ remarked:[87]

> 'The chance that [the legal representatives] would advise [the claimant] to reject an offer which she subsequently failed to beat at trial is difficult to assess, but one would not expect highly experienced solicitors practising in this field to differ very widely in their assessment of the bracket in which an award would be likely to fall, provided they had access to the same information.'

30.68 It should also be borne in mind that for a quantum risk to eventuate, the offer has to be made and then beaten. This makes that risk relatively remote (which tends to drive the size of the success fee down). If, however, a case is particularly risky in terms of quantum, high success fees might well be justified. Crane J, for example, refused to interfere with a success fee of 87% in a case which he described as 'very far from straightforward'.[88]

Recovery risk

30.69 Recovery risk is the risk that costs will not be awarded notwithstanding the fact that the case has been won and the traps posed by Part 36 offers have been successfully avoided. The risk will be relevant only if the conditional fee agreement provides that the legal representative, rather than the client, will bear the risk that costs may not be awarded; whether this is so will be a matter of contractual interpretation. A recovery risk will usually arise in the context of an agreement whereby the legal representative's

---

[87]   *C (a patient acting by her litigation friend Jocelyn Fox) v W* [2008] EWCA Civ 1459 at [17].
[88]   *Smiths Dock Limited v Edwards* [2004] EWHC 116 (QB) at [35].

full entitlement to fees is that which the paying party is ordered to pay (that is, a CFA Lite – see **9.9–9.11**); but this will not always be the case.

30.70 Indeed, there are many different types of recovery risk. At the most conservative end of the spectrum the legal representative can agree to forgo any costs in respect of which an order is not made (such as where the costs of an issue are disallowed or where a percentage award is made); at the other end of the spectrum is where the entitlement is limited to the actual figures awarded by the court (which would mean that the legal representative would be at risk not only by reason of an unfavourable decision on the incidence of costs, but also by reason of costs being reduced by way of assessment).

30.71 Regardless of which end of the spectrum the case lies, subject to the point made immediately below, there is no reason to believe that the method described above under 'quantum risk' would not apply, ie the task is to arrive at a single, global figure for risk, and then to convert that into a percentage uplift.

30.72 The exception is the fact that a case might be at risk of being non-costs bearing by reason of it being a small claim, as Brooke LJ noticed:[89]

> 'In a claim as small as this, it is not reasonable that the defendant should have to pay the claimant's solicitor a higher success fee against the risk that the value of the claim was so low that legal costs would not be recoverable at all: this is a risk the solicitor must bear himself if he is willing to act at all.'

It is possible that other exceptions exist, such as the risk of non-recovery arising out of factors which were wholly within the receiving party's control.

Enforcement risk

30.73 An enforcement risk will exist where, in addition to bearing a recovery risk, the legal representative bears the risk of not being able to enforce the award against the paying party. This is the most risk-laden type of conditional fee agreement that there is. Although there is no authority on the point, the principles of ascertainment are likely to be as set out under quantum risk and recovery risk.

Risk premium

30.74 A risk premium is a premium payable to compensate the risk-taker for having borne the risk. Thus, if there is a 33% chance of losing, a success fee of 50% would compensate the solicitor for the loss of income in those cases which are lost, but it would do nothing to compensate him for bearing the risk in the first place. Risk premiums are a common feature in actuarial calculations, but they seem to have been largely overlooked in the calculation of success fees. There is an absence of authority on the point. Therefore, their inclusion as a relevant factor may or may not be correct. The following discussion assumes that it is correct to include a risk premium.

30.75 It is possible to explain risk premiums mathematically, but (as will be seen) it ultimately depends on a value judgment by which an allowance is made on an entirely discretionary basis. There are those who say that the assessment of success fees is a judicial art rather than an actuarial science; if they are correct, then the discretionary

---

[89]   *U v Liverpool City Council (Practice Note)* [2005] EWCA Civ 475 at [24].

nature of the risk premium would allow that view to sit in harmony with a scientific analysis rather than to be in conflict with it.

30.76 Whilst it is a discretionary entity, the risk premium is most easily described in formulaic terms. If it is assumed that the only risk is a liability risk, and if no allowance is made for a risk premium, then the success fee is calculated on the basis of the formula at **30.35**. If a risk premium (*r*) is then factored in, that formula becomes:

$$s = \left(\frac{f}{(1-f)}\right) + r$$ Where s is the success fee expressed as a fraction and f is the risk of failure expressed as a fraction.

30.77 It is possible to express the risk premium in ways which become increasingly complex and involved, but, given the fact that the whole calculation of the success fee is based on discretion and assumptions rather than data, there is a limit to the extent that this is desirable. Instead, it is sufficient to make the following comments.

Issues other than risk

30.78 There are two issues other than risk that are worth mentioning: delay and liability for disbursements.

Delay

30.79 A success fee may contain an element which relates to the cost to the legal representative of the postponement of the payment of his fees and expenses;[90] that element is referred to herein as 'the postponement charge'.

30.80 Prior to 1 October 2009, the postponement charge was not recoverable between the parties, but the court has, on the face of it, now been given the power to order otherwise.[91] In view of the fact that the court may decline to permit it to be recovered, it would be prudent to state it separately from the remainder of the percentage uplift.[92] In any event, it is arguable that the new provisions in the CPR do nothing to override the principle that the costs of financing a claim are not recoverable between opposing parties and that, therefore, the court ought not to exercise its discretion in favour of allowing a postponement charge.

30.81 There is no authority establishing the correct principle of quantifying the postponement charge. If it were to be assumed that the correct measure was the amount of interest that would have been paid on borrowing the monies, then calculating it is merely a matter of arithmetic, though it is very difficult to know in advance what delay in payment is likely to occur.

---

[90]   See, for example, reg 3(1)(b) of the Conditional Fee Agreements Regulations 2000, which makes specific reference to such an element.

[91]   CPR, r 44.3B(1)(a); the changes which were made on 1 October 2009 were to insert the words 'unless the court orders otherwise'.

[92]   Prior to 1 November 2005 this was a regulatory requirement in respect of non-collective conditional fee agreements: see reg 3(1)(b) of the Conditional Fee Agreements Regulations 2000.

30.82 Various methods have been proposed for estimating the postponement charge,[93] but it is also possible accurately to calculate the interest that would have been paid by using standard actuarial methods. The calculation itself is too complex to be applied on a case-by-case basis, but proceeds as follows. If the total fee receivable is F, the annual rate of interest rate is i and the case lasts for n years (where n can be anything from 0 upwards, including fractions of years), then the adjusted fee allowing for interest is:

$$(F/n)(((1+i)^n) - 1)/\log(1+i)$$

Subtracting F gives the amount of the increase over the fee F, and dividing by F gives a standardised increase. The appropriate formula is:

$$(((1+i)^n) - (1))/n log(1+i)) - 1$$

30.83 The results of the calculation can be summarised in a table. Whilst it must be stressed that there is no authority for this method, the following table summarises those results:

Estimated duration of claim (years)	Interest rate (percent per year)				
	2%	**4%**	**6%**	**8%**	**10%**
1	1.0%	2.0%	3.0%	3.9%	4.9%
2	2.0%	4.0%	6.1%	8.1%	10.2%
3	3.0%	6.1%	9.3%	12.5%	15.8%
4	4.1%	8.3%	12.6%	17.1%	21.7%
5	5.1%	10.5%	16.1%	22.0%	28.1%
6	6.2%	12.7%	19.7%	27.1%	34.9%
7	7.3%	15.1%	23.5%	32.5%	42.2%
8	8.4%	17.5%	27.4%	38.2%	50.0%
9	9.5%	19.9%	31.5%	44.2%	58.3%
10	10.6%	22.4%	35.7%	50.6%	67.2%

These figures are appropriate only where the accumulation of fees will, in general, be constant throughout the duration of the claim. Where this condition is not met, adjustments will need to be made.

---

[93] A plausible method is to use standard actuarial tables to discount the fees for an estimated term certain, and then to work out the percentage uplift required to negate that discount; it would be entirely logical to apply that discount to only one half of the fees, this (by analogy to special damages) to take account of the fact that the fees will accrue steadily as the case progresses.

Liability for disbursements

30.84 If the legal representative is bearing the risk of paying for the disbursements, the success fee may be enhanced to take account of this. CPD, art 11.8(1) makes the following provision:

> 'In deciding whether a percentage increase is reasonable relevant factors to be taken into account may include—
>
> ...
>
> (b)   the legal representative's liability for any disbursements.'

30.85 There is no guidance in either the CPR or the CPD as to how the appropriate uplift ought to be calculated, but one method is to estimate the disbursements as a percentage of base profit costs, and then to adjust the success fee so that the success fee covers not only the profit costs of unsuccessful cases, but also the disbursements. This is an easy calculation; of the proportion of disbursements to base profit costs is $b_\%$ (expressed as a percentage), and if the percentage uplift is $p_\%$ (also expressed as a percentage), the percentage uplift adjusted to take account of disbursements ($p_{(disb)\%}$) is as follows:

$$p_{(disb)\%} = \left(\frac{(100+b_\%)}{100}\right) \times p_\%$$

30.86 If, for example, the pre-disbursements success fee were 50%, and the disbursements were 25% the size of the base profit costs, the percentage uplift adjusted to take account of disbursements would be 62.5%.

30.87 Eady J has noted a point that might have a bearing on the issue, albeit it is a point with which many receiving parties would vehemently disagree (see **30.56**). He has said that where a firm has accepted the risk of disbursements, that this is a factor which is capable of cutting both ways; this is because, while funding disbursements increases the potential liability, it can be taken as being an indicator that the legal representative was sufficiently confident as to the prospects of success that he was prepared to accept that additional burden.[94] For obvious reasons, each case would have to be decided on its own facts, but this might be a factor to take into account in appropriate cases. Equally, the facts might demonstrate that the decision to fund disbursements had nothing to do with the merits of the claim, but was merely the funding policy of the firm in question.

Notice of funding and failure to serve

30.88 The next few paragraphs focus on success fees, but the principles apply equally to ATE premiums. When read in conjunction with its associated practice directions and pre-action protocols, the CPR have always required that a party who intends to recover an additional liability[95] must inform his opponent of that fact; where there has been a failure to comply with that requirement, the court may disallow the additional liability, often by default.

---

[94]   *Cox v MGM* [2006] EWHC 1235 (QB) at [34] and [41].
[95]   This is defined in CPD, art 19.1(2):
   '(2)   In the following paragraphs a party who has entered into a funding arrangement is treated as a person who intends to recover a sum representing an additional liability by way of costs.'

30.89 As of 1 October 2009, the following restrictions in CPR, r 44.3B have applied to the recovery of additional liabilities:

> '(1)   Unless the court orders otherwise, a party may not recover as an additional liability—
>
> ...
>
> (c)   any additional liability for any period in the proceedings during which that party failed to provide information about a funding arrangement in accordance with a rule, practice direction or court order
>
> ...
>
> (Paragraph 9.3 of the Practice Direction (Pre-action Conduct) provides that a party must inform any other party as soon as possible about a funding arrangement entered into before the start of proceedings.)
>
> (Rule 3.9 sets out the circumstances the court will consider on an application for relief from a sanction for failure to comply with any rule, practice direction or court order).'

Spencer J has explained that this provision does not impose a blanket penalty rendering irrecoverable each and every additional liability for the period during which notice was not served, but that it applied only to the specific additional liability which was the subject of the default.[96]

30.90 CPR, r 44.15 sets out the need not only to give initial notice of funding, but also to renew notice of funding in the event of a change which renders the initial notice of funding inaccurate:

> '(1)   A party who seeks to recover an additional liability must provide information about the funding arrangement to the court and to other parties as required by a rule, practice direction or court order.
>
> (2)   Where the funding arrangement has changed, and the information a party has previously provided in accordance with paragraph (1) is no longer accurate, that party must file notice of the change and serve it on all other parties within 7 days.
>
> (3)   Where paragraph (2) applies, and a party has already filed—
>
> (a)   an allocation questionnaire; or
> (b)   a pre-trial check list (listing questionnaire)
> he must file and serve a new estimate of costs with the notice.
> (The costs practice direction sets out—
> •   the information to be provided when a party issues or responds to a claim form, files an allocation questionnaire, a pre-trial check list, and a claim for costs;
> •   the meaning of estimate of costs and the information required in it)
> (Rule 44.3B sets out situations where a party will not recover a sum representing any additional liability).'

30.91 In so far as success fees are concerned, the information which needs to be given in defined by CPD, arts 19.4(1) and (2):

> '(1) Unless the court otherwise orders, a party who is required to supply information about a funding arrangement must state whether he has –
>
> •   entered into a conditional fee agreement which provides for a success fee within the meaning of section 58(2) of the Courts and Legal Services Act 1990;
> •   taken out an insurance policy to which section 29 of the Access to Justice Act 1999 applies;

---

[96]   *Manning v Kings College Hospital NHS Trust* [2011] EWHC 2954 (QB) at [93].

- made an arrangement with a body which is prescribed for the purpose of section 30 of that Act;

or more than one of these.

(2) Where the funding arrangement is a conditional fee agreement, the party must state the date of the agreement and identify the claim or claims to which it relates (including Part 20 claims if any).'

The corresponding requirements relating to ATE premium may be found at **30.148**. There is no requirement to state the amount of additional liability.[97]

30.92 The requirements to give notice of funding are as follows:

- Upon the order of the court in any particular case.[98]
- 'As soon as possible' after entering into a funding agreement[99] (as of 1 October 2009 the provisions were amended to make it clear that the requirement is mandatory, not directory): this provision changed on 9 April 2009[100] and then again on 1 October 2009; transitional provisions apply.[101]
- In any event, in the letter of claim,[102] specific provisions apply to personal injury[103] and disease and illness claims.[104]

---

[97] CPD, art 19.1(1) reads as follows:
'A party who wishes to claim an additional liability in respect of a funding arrangement must give any other party information about that claim if he is to recover the additional liability. There is no requirement to specify the amount of the additional liability separately nor to state how it is calculated until it falls to be assessed. That principle is reflected in rules 44.3A and 44.15, in the following paragraphs and in Sections 6, 13, 14 and 31 of this Practice Direction. Section 6 deals with estimates of costs, Sections 13 and 14 deal with summary assessment and Section 31 deals with detailed assessment.'

[98] CPR, r 45.15(1).

[99] See art 9.3 of Practice Direction – Pre-Action Protocols (which came into force only on 9 April 2009 and was amended on 1 October 2009; in its present form, it reads:
'Where a party enters into a funding arrangement within the meaning of rule 43.2(1)(k), that party must inform the other parties about this arrangement as soon as possible and in any event either within 7 days of entering into the funding arrangement concerned or, where a claimant enters into a funding arrangement before sending a letter before claim, in the letter before claim.'
In its pre-1 October 2009 form, it read as follows:
'Where a party enters into a funding arrangement within the meaning of rule 43.2(1)(k), that party should inform the other parties about this arrangement as soon as possible.'
There was uncertainty as to whether this was directory or mandatory: see *Metcalf v Clipston* (unreported) 6 April 2004, SCCO.

[100] Prior to 9 April 2009 the recommendation that is now contained in para 9.3 of Practice Direction – Pre-Action Protocols took a different form (ie para 4A.2 of the Practice Direction – Protocols); it was worded as follows:
'4A.1 Where a person enters into a funding arrangement within the meaning of rule 43.2(1)(k) he should inform other potential parties to the claim that he has done so.
4A.2 Paragraph 4A.1 applies to all proceedings whether proceedings to which a pre-action protocol applies or otherwise.'
Whilst obiter, Brooke LJ has commented that the word 'proceedings' in para 4A.2 should be read as meaning the substantive claim, regardless of whether proceedings are issued (*Crosbie v Munroe & Anor* [2003] EWCA Civ 350 at [37]).

[101] CPD, art 19.6 reads as follows:
'The amendments to the parenthesis below paragraph 19.2 [ie the insertion of the word "must"] … do not apply where the funding arrangement was entered into before 1 October 2009 and the parenthesis below paragraph 19.2 … in force immediately before that date will continue to apply to that funding arrangement as if those amendments had not been made.'

[102] See art 9.3 of Practice Direction – Pre-Action Protocols.

[103] From 1 April 2005, para 3.2 of the Pre-Action Protocol for Personal Injury Claims has made the following provision in relation to the letter of claim:
'Where the case is funded by a conditional fee agreement (or collective conditional fee agreement), notification should be given of the existence of the agreement and where appropriate, that there is a success fee and/or insurance premium, although not the level of the success fee or premium.'

- In the claim:[105]
  - for a claimant, with his claim form;
  - for a defendant, with his 'first document', such as an acknowledgement of service, a defence, or any other document, such as an application to set aside a default judgment;
  - in all cases, within 7 days of entering into the agreement.[106]
- On any change if the information he has previously provided is no longer accurate.[107]
- There is no need to give notice of an agreement with an additional legal representative.[108]

It is probably not necessary to given notice of funding in respect of an appeal where notice has been given at first instance and the appeal is brought against the party who has entered into the conditional fee agreement.[109] Spencer J has held that there is a requirement to give notice of funding where the legal representative makes an agreement in the same claim but with a new client.[110]

---

[104] Paragraph 6.2 of the Pre-Action Protocol for Disease and Illness Claims has made the following provision in relation to the letter of claim:
'Where the case is funded by a conditional fee agreement, notification should be given of the existence of the agreement and where appropriate, that there is a success fee and insurance premium, although not the level of the success fee or premium.'

[105] See CPD, art 19.2, which reads as follows:
'(1) In this paragraph, 'claim form' includes petition and application notice, and the notice of funding to be filed or served is a notice containing the information set out in Form N251.
(2)(a) A claimant who has entered into a funding arrangement before starting the proceedings to which it relates must provide information to the court by filing the notice when he issues the claim form.
(b) He must provide information to every other party by serving the notice. If he serves the claim form himself he must serve the notice with the claim form. If the court is to serve the claim form, the court will also serve the notice if the claimant provides it with sufficient copies for service.
(3) A defendant who has entered into a funding arrangement before filing any document—
(a) must provide information to the court by filing notice with his first document. A "first document" may be an acknowledgement of service, a defence, or any other document, such as an application to set aside a default judgment.
(b) must provide information to every party by serving notice. If he serves his first document himself he must serve the notice with that document. If the court is to serve his first document the court will also serve the notice if the defendant provides it with sufficient copies for service.
(4) In all other circumstances a party must file and serve notice within 7 days of entering into the funding arrangement concerned.
(Practice Direction (Pre-Action Conduct) provides that a party must inform any other party as soon as possible about a funding arrangement entered into prior to the start of proceedings.)'

[106] See, also, art 9.3 of Practice Direction – Pre-Action Protocols.

[107] See CPD, art 19.3, which reads:
'(1) Rule 44.15 imposes a duty on a party to give notice of change if the information he has previously provided is no longer accurate. To comply he must file and serve notice containing the information set out in Form N251. Rule 44.15(3) may impose other duties in relation to new estimates of costs.
(2) Further notification need not be provided where a party has already given notice:
(a) that he has entered into a conditional fee agreement with a legal representative and during the currency of that agreement either of them enters into another such agreement with an additional legal representative; or
(b) of some insurance cover, unless that cover is cancelled or unless new cover is taken out with a different insurer.
(3) Part 6 applies to the service of notices.
(4) The notice must be signed by the party or by his legal representative.'

[108] CPD, art 19.3(2)(a).

[109] Whilst no transcript is available, this is reportedly what the Court of Appeal said during oral argument at the conclusion of *Bexbes LLP v Beer* [2009] EWCA Civ 628.

[110] *Manning v Kings College Hospital NHS Trust* [2011] EWHC 2954 (QB) at [81]: in the case before Spencer J the new agreement was with the personal representative of the original claimant, who had died part way through the claim.

30.93 If a party who seeks to recover an additional liability fails to serve notice of funding (or fails to serve it timeously), then he should consider making an application for relief from sanctions; see CPD, art 10, which provides:

> '**10.1** In a case to which rule 44.3B(1)(c) or (d) applies the party in default may apply for relief from the sanction. He should do so as quickly as possible after he becomes aware of the default. An application, supported by evidence, should be made under Part 23 to a costs judge or district judge of the court which is dealing with the case. (Attention is drawn to rules 3.8 and 3.9 which deal with sanctions and relief from sanctions).
>
> **10.2** Where the amount of any percentage increase recoverable by counsel may be affected by the outcome of the application, the solicitor issuing the application must serve on counsel a copy of the application notice and notice of the hearing as soon as practicable and in any event at least 2 days before the hearing. Counsel may make written submissions or may attend and make oral submissions at the hearing. (Paragraph 1.4 contains definitions of the terms "counsel" and "solicitor".)'

30.94 The application for relief from sanctions must be made on evidence;[111] given the fact that the court is required to take into account each of the factors listed in CPR, r 3.9(1),[112] it is usually convenient to formulate the evidence with those factors in mind.

30.95 Whether relief is granted will turn on the facts of each case, as Floyd J remarked (obiter):[113]

> 'Relief from sanctions should not be granted lightly and any party who fails to comply with the CPR runs a significant risk that he will be refused relief. Thus if a party does not have a good explanation, or the other side is prejudiced by his failure, relief from sanctions will usually be refused. It is vitally important to the administration of justice that the rules of procedure are observed.'

Likewise, Akenhead J has explained that the notification requirements relating to funding arrangements were important. The reason, he explained, was that a potential paying party might wish to make its dispositions as soon as it knew formally what costs risk it faced; those dispositions might include simply admitting liability or making an offer. Unless there is a good reason for non-notification in accordance with the CPR, the default as set out in CPR, r 44.3B(1) should apply. Thus, generally, the successful party should not recover its success fee for the period during which notice ought to have been given but had not been given.[114]

30.96 In a similar vein, HHJ Hamilton QC has said (in a judgment that is only persuasive rather than binding) that an absence of prejudice on the part of the paying party is not, of itself, necessarily sufficient to justify relief from sanctions.[115]

30.97 It is often the case that formal notice of funding (ie in the form of N251) is not given (or is given late), but informal notice of the existence of a funding arrangement is

---

[111] See CPR, r 3.9(2).

[112] *Bansal v Cheema* [2001] CP Rep 6 and *Woodhouse v Consignia plc* [2002] EWCA Civ 275; whilst the court will take each factor into account, there is no requirement that the court must expressly address each an every factor when giving judgment; this is especially when the court is giving judgment *ex tempore*: see *Khatib v Ramco International* [2011] EWCA Civ 605 at [64], per Lloyd LJ.

[113] *Supperstone v Hurst* [2008] EWHC 735 (Ch) at [39].

[114] *Redwing Construction Ltd v Wishart* [2011] EWHC 19 (TCC) at [15(f)].

[115] *Connor v Birmingham City Council* (unreported) 16 March 2005, Birmingham County Court, HHJ Hamilton QC.

given in correspondence (usually the letter of claim). Langley J had the following to say about the court's approach to those circumstances:[116]

> '... in my judgment, [the paying party] has from the outset had the information to which it was entitled and I cannot see any conceivable prejudice to [the paying party] from the breaches of the practice directions ... In those circumstances I think [the receiving parties] are entitled to relief from the sanction provided for by Rule 44.3(B)(i)(c) and so are not to be deprived of the opportunity in principle to recover the agreed success fee.'

Statement of reasons and failure to serve

30.98 If an additional liability is claimed in a bill of costs, then the receiving party must serve on the paying party the 'relevant details'.[117] In so far as conditional fee agreements are concerned, those details are as follows:[118]

> '(1) In the case of a conditional fee agreement with a success fee:
>
> (a)   a statement showing the amount of costs which have been summarily assessed or agreed, and the percentage increase which has been claimed in respect of those costs;
>
> (b)   a statement of the reasons for the percentage increase given in accordance with Regulation 3(1)(a) of the Conditional Fee Agreements Regulations or Regulation 5(1)(c) of the Collective Conditional Fee Agreements Regulations 2000. [Both sets of regulations were revoked by the Conditional Fee Agreements (Revocation) Regulations 2005 but continue to have effect in relation to conditional fee agreements and collective conditional fee agreements entered into before 1 November 2005].'

30.99 CPR, r 44.3B(1) imposes a restriction on recovery of an additional liability where the statement of reasons (ie (b) immediately above) has not been served:

> 'Unless the court orders otherwise, a party may not recover as an additional liability—
>
> ...
>
> (d)   any percentage increase where that party has failed to comply with—
> (i)   a requirement in the costs practice direction; or
> (ii)   a court order,
> to disclose in any assessment proceedings the reasons for setting the percentage increase at the level stated in the conditional fee agreement.'

30.100 Relief from sanctions may be sought (see **30.88–30.97**). It is common for relief from sanctions to be granted, but this will not invariably be the case; whilst not binding, HHJ Rubery has found that where a receiving party failed without good reason to serve a statement of reasons in support of an additional liability, it was (on the facts of that case, where there had been opportunity to remedy matters) wrong to afford relief from sanctions.[119]

Alternative means of funding

30.101 Where a suitable alternative means of funding existed, the court is able to disallow the success fee on the basis that it was not reasonably incurred. CPD, art 11.8 gives the following guidance:

---

[116]   *Montlake and Ors v Lambert Smith Hampton Group Limited* [2004] EWHC 1503 (Comm) at [15].
[117]   CPD arts 32.4 and 32.7.
[118]   CPD, art 32.5.
[119]   *Szfranski v Twyfords Ltd* (unreported) 2 October 2008, Stoke-on-Trent County Court.

'(1) In deciding whether a percentage increase is reasonable relevant factors to be taken into account may include:

(a)   the risk that the circumstances in which the costs, fees or expenses would be payable might or might not occur;

(b)   the legal representative's liability for any disbursements;

(c)   what other methods of financing the costs were available to the receiving party.'

Whether alternative means of funding existed will either be a question of fact, or, if there is an issue going to the ambit of the putative alternative means, a mixed question of fact and law. The principles set out at **30.174** apply just as much to success fees as they do to ATE insurance.

30.102   The existence of an alternative means of funding will not always mean that the success fee is not recoverable. By way of example, in a case where a legal expense insurance (in that instance, an after-the-event policy) contained provision for funding counsel's fees, Master O'Hare found that it was reasonable to instruct counsel on a conditional fee agreement, given the relatively low limit of cover.[120] In a similar vein, if the indemnity under a before-the-event policy has been exhausted, it would be reasonable to incur a success fee.[121]

Recovery of success fees retrospectively

30.103   As is discussed at **9.408–9.420**, a solicitor and client may agree whatever arrangement they like (provided it falls within the statutory scheme created by s 58(1) of the Courts and Legal Services Act 1990 (as amended)).That said, Christopher Clarke J has confirmed that the court may take into account the interests of the paying party.[122]

30.104   The argument against recovery of retrospective success fees between opposing parties is that the CPR requires that notice of funding be given[123] (see **30.88–30.97**); the argument is that it would run contrary to the spirit of this requirement if a success fee could be recovered for work which was done before a conditional fee agreement was made.[124] These arguments are addressed below.

30.105   A receiving party may seek to recover a success fee retrospectively in a number of circumstances depending on the nature of the pre-existing retainer (if any) and the period in respect of which the success fee is sought. The most often encountered circumstances are addressed below.

Transfer of liabilities from a private retainer to a conditional fee agreement

30.106   A client's existing liability for fees incurred under a private retainer may, by agreement, be transferred such that they are payable conditionally under a conditional

---

[120]   *Hennessy v Burger King* (unreported) 8 September 2005, SCCO, Master O'Hare.

[121]   *Thornley (a child) v Ministry of Defence* [2010] EWHC 2584 (QB) at [35], per HHJ Behrens, sitting as a Judge of the High Court.

[122]   See *Forde v Birmingham City Council* [2009] EWHC 12 (QB) at [134].

[123]   See CPR, r 44.15(1) and (2); Section 19 of the CPD; and Protocols Practice Direction para 4A.

[124]   Indeed, whilst only persuasive, CPD, art 57.9(3) provides: 'Nothing in the legislation referred to above [ie CLSA 1990 (as amended), etc] makes provision for a party who has entered into a funding arrangement to recover from another party any amount of an additional liability which relates to anything done or any costs incurred before the arrangement was entered into.'

retainer. Christopher Clarke J found that there was nothing objectionable about such a transfer, this being largely because the court has the ability to disallow unreasonably incurred success fees.[125] He also explained that the appropriate standpoint for gauging the success fee would not be the time instructions were received, but the time that the agreement was made. It was not possible for Christopher Clark J to deal with all aspects of retrospectivity, so it is possible that his guidance will, in due course, either be qualified or further clarified.[126]

Revision of success fee

30.107   Where a new success fee is agreed which retrospectively replaces the success fee which was originally agreed, the success fee may be said to have been revised.[127] Christopher Clarke J implied that such a success fee is recoverable in principle, but that the court would be able to disallow it on the grounds of reasonableness, in appropriate circumstances.[128] The receiving party may face arguments arising out the interpretation of the agreements and, in an extreme instances, he may face an argument that the success fee should be disallowed by reason of presumed undue influence. The second of these arguments would be unlikely to succeed (see **10.3–10.13**).

Retrospective claim for a success fee for a period prior to 1 November 2005

30.108   There is nothing wrong in principle with the notion of a post-1 November 2005 agreement providing for a success fee which covers work carried out prior to that date.[129]

Retrospective claim for a success fee for a period prior to 1 April 2000

30.109   Article 2 of the Access to Justice Act 1999 (Transitional Provisions) Order 2000 prevents recovery of success fees in proceedings (or related proceedings) where a party entered into a conditional fee agreement before 1 April 2000. Although that order does not expressly say that a success fee may not be recovered retrospectively before this date, it would be difficult to argue the contrary.

Retrospective claim where a costs entitlement has already materialised

30.110   It will rarely be the case that the court will allow costs which have come into being as the result of the receiving party voluntarily accepting a liability after he has

---

[125]   *Forde v Birmingham City Council* [2009] EWHC 12 (QB) at [150]; some commentators have pointed out that Christopher Clarke J's attention seems not to have been drawn to the encouragement given by the then Practice Direction – Protocols to give notice of funding pre-issue; however, his judgment seems not to have turned on the issue of when notice was given.

[126]   One factor that seems not to have been drawn to Christopher Clarke J's attention was the fact that where a fixed success fee applies, the court has no discretion to disallow it on the basis of reasonableness (*Kilby v Gawith* [2008] EWCA Civ 812); therefore, the 'armoury' to which he referred would often have a bare rack; Christopher Clarke J has not addressed the difficulty which arises out of the fact that if a retrospective success fee is recoverable in principle, it is arguable that a claimant could enter into a conditional fee agreement in the most manifestly unreasonable circumstances – such as after judgment but before the costs order has been made – and still recover a success fee for the whole of the claim.

[127]   If, for example, a legal representative was entitled to terminate an agreement because of the risks of the litigation changing adversely, but if he then agrees to enter into a new agreement which provides for a higher success fee, then that would be an example of a success fee being revised.

[128]   *Forde v Birmingham City Council* [2009] EWHC 12 (QB) at [150] and [151].

[129]   *Forde v Birmingham City Council* [2009] EWHC 12 (QB) at [153]–[157].

become entitled to costs. Whilst he was discussing contentious business agreements rather than conditional fee agreements, Irwin J said:[130]

> 'I would be hesitant to conclude that any CBA entered into by a Claimant, after an adverse Costs Order had been made ... could be held to alter retrospectively the rights and obligations as between claimant and solicitor. The reason is obvious. To uphold a retrospective rearrangement in circumstances like that, would be to uphold the retrospective revision of – or even creation of – the defendant's costs liability.'

Other cases have pointed in much the same direction.[131]

30.111 Finally, there is a curious provision which merits brief mention. In a section at the very end of the CPD under the heading 'transitional provisions' resides CPD 57.9(3), which reads as follows:

> 'Nothing in the legislation referred to above [ie the CLSA 1990 (as amended, etc)] makes provision for a party who has entered into a funding arrangement to recover from another party any amount of an additional liability which relates to anything done or any costs incurred before the arrangement was entered into.'

It has been argued that this provision prevents the recovery of retrospective success fees. Whilst there is no authority on the point, the better analysis is that this is a provision which appears to do little more than to state the effect of other legislation: ie it states (correctly) that there is nothing in the aforesaid legislation which expressly deals with retrospective success fees. It is likely that this provision was intended to do nothing more than to highlight the fact that it was not possible retrospectively to replace a pre-2000 conditional fee agreement with an agreement which provided for a success fee which was recoverable between the parties. Therefore, it can probably now be ignored.

Different rates for different periods

30.112 It used to be the case that CPD, art 11.8(2) permitted the court to allow different percentage uplifts for different items of costs and for different periods during which costs were incurred. That provision was found to be ultra vires; Brooke LJ explained why:[132]

> 'The approach [of allowing different rates for different periods] negates the whole purpose of assessing at the outset the risks involved in pursuing a claim. The solicitor did not have the contractual power or the professional duty to do what [was] suggested, namely to renegotiate the success fee once it became clear that the risks were now very small and that there was no longer any need to fear a "worst case scenario" such as might have been in the solicitor's mind when the CFA was initially agreed.'

30.113 This principle applies to the fees of a costs draftsman engaged as agent for the purposes of a detailed assessment.[133] In principle, the success fee is not only recoverable when a costs draftsman is engaged to deal with the costs at the conclusion of a claim, but also when costs-only Part 8 proceedings are brought.[134]

---

[130] *Crook v Birmingham City Council* [2007] EWHC 1415 (QB) at [36].
[131] See, for example, *Kellar v Williams* [2004] UKPC 30 and *Oyston v Royal Bank of Scotland* [2006] EWHC 90053 (Costs).
[132] *U v Liverpool City Council (Practice Note)* [2005] EWCA Civ 475 at [36]; see also [42] and [49].
[133] *Crane v Canons Leisure Centre* [2007] EWCA Civ 1352.
[134] *Halloran v Delaney* [2003] 1 WLR 28.

Fixed success fees

30.114 Fixed success fees may apply in the following types of claims:

- road traffic accidents;
- employers' liability claims; and
- industrial disease claims.

These are issues which are discussed at length in Chapter 33.

Costs draftsmen

30.115 Although Maurice Kay LJ dissented, May LJ and Hallett LJ have found that costs draftsmen's fees are profit costs rather than disbursements, this having the effect that a success fee is payable on those fees.[135] There is no reason to believe that the same logic does not apply to agents in general.

Solicitor and client issues

30.116 Prior to 1 November 2005, all conditional fee agreements contained a provision which meant that clients would not have to pay any percentage increase which was disallowed on assessment because it was unreasonably high in view of facts which were or should have been known at the time it was set.[136] The court had the power to order otherwise (see below), but it was very rare that it was asked to do so. Similar provisions applied if the costs were agreed rather than assessed.[137] Those regulatory requirements no longer exist, but a professional custom has arisen whereby clients are almost always still afforded the benefit of such a provision.

30.117 CPR, r 44.16 gives the court the power to order that the client remains liable for all or part of the success fee notwithstanding the fact that it has been reduced as against the paying party:

'(1) This rule applies where the Conditional Fee Agreements Regulations 2000 or the Collective Conditional Fee Agreements Regulations 2000 continues to apply to an agreement which provides for a success fee.

(2) Where—

(a) the court disallows any amount of a legal representative's percentage increase in summary or detailed assessment proceedings; and

(b) the legal representative applies for an order that the disallowed amount should continue to be payable by his client,

the court may adjourn the hearing to allow the client to be—

(i) notified of the order sought; and

(ii) separately represented ...'

The procedure will depend on whether the costs between the parties have been assessed by summary or detailed assessment (see below). It should be pointed out that the issue will arise only where there is a shortfall in the success fee as a result of the court

---

[135] *Crane v Canons Leisure Centre* [2007] EWCA Civ 1352.

[136] See reg 3(2)(b) of the Conditional Fee Agreements Regulations 2000 and reg 5(2)(b) of the Collective Conditional Fee Agreements Regulations 2000.

[137] See reg 3(2)(c) of the Conditional Fee Agreements Regulations 2000 and reg 5(2)(c) of the Collective Conditional Fee Agreements Regulations 2000.

reducing the success fee because it was excessive: if the shortfall is caused by the existence of a postponement charge, then those monies are payable by the client without the procedure contemplated by CPR, r 44.16 being invoked.

Summary assessment

30.118 Where the issue arises at the conclusion of a summary assessment, the court may choose between dealing with the matter then and there or remitting it to a costs judge for a determination. CPD, art 20.3 makes the following provisions:

> '(1) If the court disallows any amount of a legal representative's percentage increase, the court will, unless sub-paragraph (2) applies, give directions to enable an application to be made by the legal representative for the disallowed amount to be payable by his client, including, if appropriate, a direction that the application will be determined by a costs judge or district judge of the court dealing with the case.
>
> (2) The court that has made the summary assessment may then and there decide the issue whether the disallowed amount should continue to be payable, if:
>
> > (a) the receiving party and all parties to the relevant agreement consent to the court doing so;
> >
> > (b) the receiving party (or, if corporate, an officer) is present in court; and
> >
> > (c) the court is satisfied that the issue can be fairly decided then and there.'

Detailed assessment

30.119 Detailed assessments differ from summary assessments in that the objections are known in advance (this is because they are set out in the Points of Dispute); this means that the legal representative is able to take steps which will enable the court to deal with the matter in a single hearing, where appropriate.

30.120 The first of those steps is that the legal representative must inform the client of the fact that a shortfall will be sought against him. The legal representative will be alerted to the need to do this by the fact that the Points of Dispute will raise a challenge in respect of the success fee. The procedure is set out in CPD, arts 20.5 and 20.6:

> '**20.5** Where the paying party serves points of dispute seeking a reduction in any percentage increase charged by a legal representative acting for the receiving party, and that legal representative intends, if necessary, to apply for an order that any amount of the percentage disallowed as against the paying party shall continue to be payable by his client, the solicitor acting for the receiving party must, within 14 days of service of the points of dispute, give to his client a clear written explanation of the nature of the relevant point of dispute and the effect it will have if it is upheld in whole or in part by the court, and of the client's right to attend any subsequent hearings at court when the matter is raised.
>
> **20.6** Where the solicitor acting for a receiving party files a request for a detailed assessment hearing it must if appropriate, be accompanied by a certificate signed by him stating:
>
> > (1) that the amount of the percentage increase in respect of counsel's fees or solicitor's charges is disputed;
> >
> > (2) whether an application will be made for an order that any amount of that increase which is disallowed should continue to be payable by his client;
> >
> > (3) that he has given his client an explanation in accordance with paragraph 20.5; and,
> >
> > (4) whether his client wishes to attend court when the amount of any relevant percentage increase may be decided.'

30.121   The second step the receiving party's solicitor must take is, where appropriate, to inform counsel of the challenge to his success fee. Where this is done, the onus is on counsel to inform the solicitor that he wishes to recover the shortfall. If he fails to do this, then unless the court orders otherwise he will be deemed to have accepted the reduction. CPD, art 20.4 makes the following provisions:

> '(1) Where detailed assessment proceedings have been commenced, and the paying party serves points of dispute (as to which see Section 34 of this Practice Direction), which show that he is seeking a reduction in any percentage increase charged by counsel on his fees, the solicitor acting for the receiving party must within 3 days of service deliver to counsel a copy of the relevant points of dispute and the bill of costs or the relevant parts of the bill.

> (2) Counsel must within 10 days thereafter inform the solicitor in writing whether or not he will accept the reduction sought or some other reduction. Counsel may state any points he wishes to have made in a reply to the points of dispute, and the solicitor must serve them on the paying party as or as part of a reply.

> (3) Counsel who fails to inform the solicitor within the time limits set out above will be taken to accept the reduction unless the court otherwise orders.'

30.122   The third step is that within 7 days of receiving notice of the date of the assessment hearing the solicitor must notify his client and, if appropriate, counsel in writing of the date, time and place of the hearing.[138] CPD, art 20.8 provides that the hearing itself will be conducted in the following way:[139]

> '(1) At the detailed assessment hearing, the court will deal with the assessment of the costs payable by one party to another, including the amount of the percentage increase, and give a certificate accordingly.

> (2) The court may decide the issue whether the disallowed amount should continue to be payable under the relevant conditional fee agreement without an adjournment if:

> | (a) | the receiving party and all parties to the relevant agreement consent to the court deciding the issue without an adjournment, |
> | (b) | the receiving party (or, if corporate, an officer or employee who has authority to consent on behalf of the receiving party) is present in court, and |
> | (c) | the court is satisfied that the issue can be fairly decided without an adjournment. |

> (3) In any other case the court will give directions and fix a date for the hearing of the application.'

Counsel does not need to attend in person: he may make his representations in writing.[140]

ATE POLICIES AND FORMALITIES

30.123   After the event ('ATE') insurance protects against costs liability (which may include the insured's own costs) in specific proceedings; policies are incepted after the dispute has arisen, hence the name. Whilst legal expense insurance is a type of general insurance, it is in a separate class for purposes of authorisation.[141] This section discusses the relevant formalities; the assessment of after the event premiums is discussed at

---

[138]   CPD, art 20.7(1).
[139]   CPD, art 20.7(8).
[140]   CPD, art 20.7(1).
[141]   Financial Services and Markets Act 2000 (Regulated Activities) Order 2001, SI 2001/544, art 3(1), Sch 1 Pt 1 para 17.

30.143 onwards. In general, when a solicitor recommends a contract of insurance he must comply with certain regulatory requirements. Failure to comply with those requirements would allow the court to find that the policy is unenforceable against the client; this would have the effect of rendering the premium irrecoverable from the paying party. It is for this reason that the issue of formalities is addressed in this book. This book does not attempt to address that issue from a regulatory point of view: other texts must be consulted for that purpose. Whether a non-compliant policy is enforceable against the client is in the discretion of the court (see **30.131**).

The Financial Services and Markets Act 2000

30.124 The Financial Services and Markets Act 2000 ('FSMA 2000') creates a 'general prohibition' forbidding unauthorised and non-exempt persons from engaging in certain activities known as 'regulated activities'. The general prohibition is phrased in the following terms:[142]

> '(1) No person may carry on a regulated activity in the United Kingdom, or purport to do so, unless he is—
>
> (a) an authorised person; or
> (b) an exempt person.
>
> (2) The prohibition is referred to in this Act as the general prohibition.'

What is and is not a regulated activity is defined by the Financial Services and Markets Act 2000 (Regulated Activities) Order 2001 (SI 2001/544) ('the RAO'). On 14 January 2005, the RAO was amended in such a way that it now provides that giving advice about ATE insurance is a regulated activity.

30.125 Certain persons are exempted from the general prohibition, but only if:[143]

- that person is a member of a profession (or controlled or managed by one or more such members);
- that person accounts to his client for any commission received;
- the relevant activities are 'incidental to the provision by him of professional services';
- the relevant activities are of a certain permitted type, and are not of a prohibited type; and
- the relevant activities are the only regulated activities carried on by that person (other than regulated activities in relation to which he is an exempt person).

30.126 These provisions permit solicitors to be treated as 'exempt'. Such persons are permitted to carry on activities known as 'exempt regulated activities' without being regulated by the Financial Services Authority; instead, they are under the supervision of the SRA, which is known as a 'designated professional body'. Such a body is required to make rules that govern the exempt person; those rules are discussed below.

The SRA Financial Services (Scope) Rules 2001

30.127 In accordance with the requirement to make rules governing regulated activities (see above), in 2001 the Law Society made the Solicitors' Financial Services (Scope)

---

[142] See s 19 of the FSMA 2000.
[143] See s 327 of the FSMA 2000.

Rules 2001[144] ('the Scope Rules'); these have now been adopted by the SRA and, since 6 October 2011, have been known as the SRA Financial Services (Scope) Rules 2001. The Scope Rules include:

- a list of prohibited activities;
- basic conditions which must be satisfied; and
- other restrictions relating to particular types of activities.

30.128 Like the RAO, the Scope Rules were amended on 14 January 2005 to encompass ATE insurance. In so far as the law of costs is concerned, the most important provisions of the Scope Rules are:

- that a solicitor may provide 'insurance mediation activities' only if registered with the FSA;
- that the relevant activity must arise out of, or be complementary to, the provision of a particular professional service to a particular client; and
- that the solicitor must account to a client for any pecuniary reward or other relevant advantage received from a third party.

The first of these provisions needs no explanation: whilst a solicitor does not need to be regulated by the FSA, he does need to be registered. The second of these provisions would rarely be relevant in the context of the law of costs.[145] The third may be relevant in that it is not unusual for solicitors to be paid a commission for recommending a particular contract of insurance; if that commission is not accounted for correctly, then the entire premium may be put at risk.

30.129 The issue of commissions has already been addressed at **8.311** and **8.312**: in essence, a solicitor needs to account for all commissions, regardless of size; he may be permitted to keep a commission, but only if the client consents to this.

30.130 A breach of the Scope Rules may result in disciplinary proceedings or – in extreme circumstances – criminal proceedings under FSMA 2000, s 23.

30.131 Where a contract is made in contravention of the general prohibition by an unauthorised person, it will be unenforceable;[146] that said the court does have discretion in the matter, that discretion being exercised in the following way:[147]

'(3) If the court is satisfied that it is just and equitable in the circumstances of the case, it may allow—

    (a)   the agreement to be enforced; or
    (b)   money ... paid ... under the agreement to be retained.

(4) In considering whether to allow the agreement to be enforced or (as the case may be) the money ... paid ... under the agreement to be retained the court must—

---

[144] Those rules being made under ss 31, 79 and 80 of the Solicitors Act 1974, ss 9 and 9A of the Administration of Justice Act 1985 and s 83 of the Legal Services Act 2007, with the approval of the Legal Services Board under para 19 of Sch 4 to the Legal Services Act 2007.

[145] It could become relevant if a solicitor were to become overly involved in distributing and marketing a particular form of insurance; it might also become relevant if a solicitor were to be in the habit of conspiring to write 'ghost insurance'.

[146] See FSMA 2000, ss 26 and 27 makes similar provisions concerning contracts made through an unauthorised person.

[147] See s 38 of FSMA 2000.

(a)   if the case arises as a result of section 26 [ie where the contract has been made by an authorised person], have regard to the issue mentioned in subsection (5); or

(b)   if the case arises as a result of section 27 [ie where the contract has been made through an authorised person], have regard to the issue mentioned in subsection (6).

(5)   The issue is whether the person carrying on the regulated activity concerned reasonably believed that he was not contravening the general prohibition by making the agreement.

(6)   The issue is whether the provider knew that the third party was (in carrying on the regulated activity) contravening the general prohibition.

(7)   If the person against whom the agreement is unenforceable—

(a)   elects not to perform the agreement, or

(b)   as a result of this section, recovers money paid or other property transferred by him under the agreement,

he must repay any money and return any other property received by him under the agreement.'

30.132   Thus, the test is what is just and equitable, and in this regard the court will take into account whether the solicitor knew that he was acting in breach of the general prohibition.

The SRA Financial Services (Conduct of Business) Rules 2001

30.133   In addition to the Scope Rules, the Law Society has made the Solicitors' Financial Services (Conduct of Business) Rules 2001 ('the Conduct Rules'). Like the Scope Rules, these were amended on 14 January 2005 to include ATE insurance and these continue to apply notwithstanding the introduction of the SRA Code of Conduct 2011.

30.134   In many ways the Conduct Rules bear comparison with the now-revoked Conditional Fee Agreements Regulations 2000. In particular, the solicitor is required to give the client a degree of pre-contract counselling. One of the topics that must be addressed is 'status disclosure'; this means that the solicitor must give the client the following information in writing:[148]

•   a statement that the firm is not authorised by the FSA;

•   the name and address of the firm;

•   the nature of the regulated activities carried on by the firm, and the fact that they are limited in scope;

•   a statement that the firm is regulated by the Law Society; and

•   a statement explaining that complaints and redress mechanisms are provided through Law Society regulation.

The following statement must be made in writing:[149]

'[This firm is]/[We are] not authorised by the Financial Services Authority. However, we are included on the register maintained by the Financial Services Authority so that we can carry on insurance mediation activity, which is broadly the advising on, selling and administration of insurance contracts. This part of our business, including arrangements for complaints or

---

[148]   See para 3 of the SRA Financial Services (Conduct of Business) Rules 2001.

[149]   See para 3(3) of the SRA Financial Services (Conduct of Business) Rules 2001.

redress if something goes wrong, is regulated by Solicitors Regulation Authority. The register can be accessed via the Financial Services Authority website at www.fsa.gov.uk/register.'

(The guidance notes to the Conduct Rules suggest that this information may be made in the client care letter.)

30.135 The Conduct Rules require that certain records must be kept.[150] In essence, records need to be kept of the instructions received from the client, the instructions given by the solicitor to another person to effect a transaction, of the commissions received, and of how the solicitor has accounted to the client for those commissions. These records must be kept for at least 6 years.[151]

30.136 In so far as ATE insurance is concerned, a solicitor must comply with the provisions of 'Appendix 1'.[152] Broadly speaking, that appendix requires solicitors to do three things: they must disclose certain information, they must consider whether the ATE insurance is suitable, and they must prepare a 'demands and needs statement'. Each of these requirements is considered in turn.

Disclosure

30.137 The solicitor must take reasonable steps to communicate information to the client in a way that is 'clear, fair and not misleading'.[153]

30.138 The solicitor must declare the basis upon which his recommendation is made.[154] In particular:

- where a solicitor recommends an ATE policy, he must inform the client whether he has given advice on the basis of a 'fair analysis' of a sufficiently large number of insurance contracts available on the market to enable him to make a recommendation regarding which contract of insurance would be adequate to meet the client's needs;[155] and
- if the answer to the question above is in the negative, the solicitor must:
  - advise whether he is contractually obliged to conduct insurance mediation activities with only one or more insurance undertakings;
  - advise the client that he can request details of the insurance undertakings with which the solicitor conducts business; and
  - provide the client with such details on request.[156]

30.139 Thus the Conduct Rules recognise that a solicitor's recommendation might be influenced by commercial realities. Indeed, the Law Society's guidance on the Conduct Rules expressly recognises this:[157]

'The Law Society is aware that some firms have entered into contracts with introducers whereby they are obliged to effect for their client a particular type of insurance contract e g if

---

[150]   See paras 5 and 6 of the SRA Financial Services (Conduct of Business) Rules 2001.
[151]   See para 9 of the SRA Financial Services (Conduct of Business) Rules 2001.
[152]   See para 8A of the SRA Financial Services (Conduct of Business) Rules 2001.
[153]   See Art 1 of the Appendix of the SRA Financial Services (Conduct of Business) Rules 2001.
[154]   See Art 1(2) and (3) of the Appendix of the SRA Financial Services (Conduct of Business) Rules 2001.
[155]   See Art 1(2) of the Appendix of the SRA Financial Services (Conduct of Business) Rules 2001.
[156]   See Art 1(3) of the Appendix of the SRA Financial Services (Conduct of Business) Rules 2001.
[157]   See at para 9.7 of that guidance.

there is a conditional fee agreement. These arrangements are acceptable provided, of course, that the particular insurance policy is suitable for the client's needs and the solicitor has informed the client of the constraint.'

30.140　The above information must be provided to the client on paper or on any other durable medium available and accessible to the client.[158]

Suitability

30.141　Before a solicitor recommends an ATE policy, he must take reasonable steps to ensure that the recommendation is suitable to the client's demands and needs. Solicitors must:[159]

- consider relevant information already held;
- obtain details of any relevant existing insurance;
- identify the client's requirements and explain to the client what he needs to disclose;
- assess whether the level of cover is sufficient for the risks that the client wishes to insure; and
- consider the relevance of any exclusions, excesses, limitations or conditions.

Where the solicitor recommends a contract of insurance that does not meet the needs of the client and where this is because no such contract is available in the market, the client must be told of those things.[160]

Demands and needs

30.142　The solicitor must give the client a 'demands and needs statement'.[161] This must be provided to the client before the contract of insurance is finalised. That statement must:[162]

- set out the client's demands and needs on the basis of the information provided by the client;
- explain the reason for recommending that contract of insurance;
- reflect the complexity of the insurance contract being proposed; and
- be on paper or on any other durable medium available and accessible to the client.

ATE PREMIUMS

30.143　This section focuses on the relevance of after the event ('ATE') insurance to the law of costs, and in particular on the assessment of ATE premiums. It may need to be read in conjunction with the discussion immediately above (on ATE formalities). Other texts must be consulted for a detailed discussion of the actuarial aspects of insurance.

---

[158]　See Art 1(4) of the Appendix of the SRA Financial Services (Conduct of Business) Rules 2001.
[159]　See Art 2 of the Appendix of the SRA Financial Services (Conduct of Business) Rules 2001.
[160]　Ibid.
[161]　See Art 3 of the Appendix of the SRA Financial Services (Conduct of Business) Rules 2001.
[162]　Ibid.

30.144   The CPR defines an ATE premium in this way:[163]

> '"insurance premium" means a sum of money paid or payable for insurance against the risk of incurring a costs liability in the proceedings, taken out after the event that is the subject matter of the claim.'

Thus, the premium payable for before the event ('BTE') insurance will not be regarded as being a premium for the purposes of assessing costs.

Jurisdiction

30.145   Under the common law, ATE premiums are not recoverable between opposing parties.[164] Statute intervened on 1 April 2000[165] when s 29 of the Access to Justice Act 1999 ('AJA 1999') came into force; it reads as follows:

> 'Where in any proceedings a costs order is made in favour of any party who has taken out an insurance policy against the risk of incurring a liability in those proceedings, the costs payable to him may, subject in the case of court proceedings to rules of court, include costs in respect of the premium of the policy.'

(At the time of writing, proposals had recently been made to reverse the changes made by s 29.)[166]

30.146   Phillips MR has clarified that the phrase 'liability in those proceedings' means liability for legal costs.[167] He has also explained that the words 'insurance against the risk of incurring a costs liability' should be read as meaning 'insurance against the risk of incurring a costs liability that cannot be passed on to the opposing party'.[168] This means that the costs of 'own costs cover' are, in principle, recoverable from a paying party. This includes an element for covering the risk of being unable to recover the premium as a consequence of losing the action.[169]

Costs-only proceedings

30.147   The fact that the proceedings are costs-only proceedings rather than substantive proceedings does not diminish the jurisdiction to recover an ATE premium; this is for the reasons set out immediately above, and also because an ATE premium is recoverable notwithstanding the fact that it was taken out before proceedings were commenced.[170]

---

[163]   CPR, r 43.2(1)(m); see also CPD, art 2.2.

[164]   See *Seaga v Harper* [2009] UKPC 26 (Jamaica) for an indication of the position under the common law; transitional provisions apply.

[165]   Transitional provision apply; art 3 of the Access to Justice Act 1999 (Transitional Provisions) Order 2000 reads: 'Section 29 (Recovery of insurance premiums by way of costs) shall not apply, as regards a party to proceedings, to: (a) any proceedings in relation to which that party took out an insurance policy of the sort referred to in section 29 before 1 April 2000; or (b) any proceedings arising out of the same cause of action as any proceedings to which sub-paragraph (a) refers.'

[166]   R Jackson *Review of Civil Litigation Costs: Final Report* (December 2009), chapter 9.

[167]   *Callery v Gray* [2001] EWCA 1246 at [7].

[168]   *Callery v Gray* [2001] EWCA 1246 at [59].

[169]   *Callery v Gray* [2001] EWCA 1246 at [63].

[170]   *Callery v Gray* [2001] EWCA Civ 1117 at [54], per Woolf CJ.

Notice of funding and the rules of court generally

30.148   The effect of AJA 1999, s 29 is subject to rules of court; there are only two rules of any note:

(1)   As of 1 October 2009,[171] CPR, r 44.3B(1)(e) has provided as follows:

> 'Unless the court orders otherwise, a party may not recover as an additional liability . . . any insurance premium where that party has failed to provide information about the insurance policy in question by the time required by a rule, practice direction or court order.'

Thus a party will not be able to recover any insurance premium where he has failed to give his opponent notice of funding (see **30.88–30.97**; the principles are broadly the same as those relating to success fee). The notice requirements are set out in the footnotes.[172] There is also a requirement to serve a copy of the certificate at the time the bill of costs is served;[173] the very similar issue of failure to supply a statement of reasons in respect of the success fee has already been dealt with at **30.98–30.100** and those principles are not repeated here.

(2)   CPR 44.12B imposes a specific restriction in 'publication cases' (ie defamation, malicious falsehood, etc); this is discussed at **30.183**.

The role of the common law

30.149   For the reasons set out above, ATE policies are largely governed by legislation; the common law seems to have very little residual relevance. Whilst not binding, Master Hurst found that there was nothing, in principle, objectionable about the notion of the level of a premium being linked to the damages recovered.[174] If this is correct, the law of champerty has no part to play in this area of the law.

Components of the premium and the language of ATE insurance

30.150   A premium may be made up of the following four elements, all of which are recoverable in principle: burning costs, risk/profit costs, administrative costs and distribution commission.[175]

---

[171]   Prior to this date there was no CPR, r 44.3B(1)(e); this led to confusion because the other provision in CPR, r 44.3B(1) related to percentage increases and periods, and as such were not well suited to governing premiums.

[172]   CPD, art 19.4(3): 'Where the funding arrangement is an insurance policy, the party must—
(a)   state the name and address of the insurer, the policy number and the date of the policy and identify the claim or claims to which it relates (including Part 20 claims if any);
(b)   state the level of cover provided by the insurance; and
(c)   state whether the insurance premiums are staged and, if so, the points at which an increased premium is payable.'

[173]   CPD, art 32.5(2): 'If the additional liability is an insurance premium: a copy of the insurance certificate showing whether the policy covers the receiving party's own costs; his opponents costs; or his own costs and his opponent's costs; and the maximum extent of that cover, and the amount of the premium paid or payable.'

[174]   *Pirie v Ayling* [2003] EWHC 9006 (Costs).

[175]   *Callery v Gray* [2001] EWCA 1246 at [21]–[26]; see also CPD, art 11.10.

Burning costs

30.151 Burning costs are the cost of meeting claims; it may also be called the 'basic pure underwriting cost'. Broadly speaking there are two ways in which they may be calculated: 'individual rating' (where the risk is assessed in each case or each category of risk and the premium set accordingly), and 'block rating' (where a uniform premium, or series of premiums, is charged for any case which is deemed to have adequate prospects of success).[176] The term 'individual assessment' is also often used.

Risk/profit costs

30.152 This will include the insurer's profit, but will not necessarily be limited to that; instead, it may include the costs of reinsurance (see **30.159**).

Administrative costs

30.153 These include items such as personnel, premises, issuing costs, processing costs, and claims administration.

Distribution commission

30.154 These cover advertising, marketing and commissions paid to brokers, underwriting agents or other intermediaries.

30.155 In addition, there may be monies claimed in the lump sum which may be referred to as being a premium but which cannot properly be categorised in that way. Those monies are discussed under the heading 'deconstruction' at **30.223–30.225**.

30.156 The court does not seek to be its own actuarial advisor. Indeed, Buxton LJ has emphasised the breadth of the discretion conferred on the costs judge by CPR, r 44.4 and that it is a discretion which cannot be exercised with mathematical nicety.[177] Unless a specific case merits expert evidence, there is (at present, at least) no need for the court to decide issues of reasonableness by reference to actuarial method. Nonetheless, there is no harm in knowing the language of ATE insurance,[178] nor is there any harm in knowing the fundamentals of the concepts by which premiums are calculated. The following is only the most rudimentary of guides to these issues and (with one or two very limited exceptions) it is not intended for use as an aid to assessing the reasonableness of a premium. The reader is referred to standard actuarial textbooks for a more detailed exposition of this topic.[179]

---

[176] Block rating is a phrase that is used to describe a portfolio or book of claims, of the same or a similar type, where it is expected that the claims will be insured on or before a particular point in time (such as before sending a letter of claim). This approach is based on the insurance principle of 'the many paying for the few' so that there is a spread of risk within a basket of cases that are expected to be insured. This approach is adopted where there is a large number of claims, and is, therefore, particularly suitable for cases dealt with by delegated authority.

[177] *Sharratt v London Central Bus Company and other cases (No 2) The Accident Group Test Cases* [2004] EWCA Civ 575 at [37].

[178] A useful synopsis of this topic can be found in C Bennett *Dictionary in Insurance* (Prentice Hall, 2nd edn, 2004).

[179] A Schwepcke *Reinsurance* (Verlag Versicherungswirtschaft GmbH, 2nd edn, 2004); T Mikosch *Non-life insurance mathematics: an introduction with stochastic processes* (Springer, 2003).

30.157   The mechanism by which a premium is set is called 'rating'. The premium will relate to a pool of policies which will be accounted for as a group and which is called a 'book'; the composition of the book will be such that assumptions known as 'underwriting assumptions' may be made about the book and about the cases within it. There are many different methods of rating, and an insurer may use more than one method to arrive at and then check a premium. The methods which are commonly used are 'experience rating' (where historical data, known as 'claims experience', is taken into account) and 'rating based on assumed distributions' (where estimates are made of the risks, and assumptions are used to calculate the way in which that risk is distributed).[180]

30.158   There are two significant concepts which are relevant to the issue of rating. The first is 'gross net premium income' (which is usually referred to as 'GNPI'); it is the amount of premiums recovered before any adjustment. The second is 'burning cost' (which is sometimes known as 'burn costs'), which are the basic costs of underwriting, ie the cost of paying claims (see **30.151**). The insurer will seek to balance the books in such a way as to allow GNPI to pay for the benefits and for running the business. This goal is called 'adequacy'. In addition, insurers will seek to achieve 'equity' (ie a fair price), not least because that is the method most likely to attract customers.[181] Once the premium has been set at a level which achieves adequacy and equity, then monies must be put to one side to cover adverse outcomes. Those monies are called 'reserves' and the method used to calculate them is called 'valuation'.[182]

30.159   There are many methods by which an insurer may seek to balance its books. The most obvious is to set premiums that are high enough to achieve adequacy. That said, insurance is all about risk, and this means that an alternative is to manage the risk rather than merely to charge enough to cover it. An insurer may seek to limit risk by stipulating a level of cover, or he may seek to spread the risk by obtaining reinsurance.[183] Limits of cover are not necessarily limited to the limit in any given case, but where a number of policies are linked, they can be aggregate limits (ie '£— in one claim, but no more than £——— overall'. Reinsurance is insurance that the insurer buys to provide a further layer of insurance; an example would be where an insurer wanted to insure against the risk of having to pay out more than a certain amount. Many actuarial calculations regard the cost of reinsurance as being part of the insurer's profit; whilst an oversimplification, this is on the basis that an alternative to reinsurance is simply to hold a floating fund, and if the burning cost has been calculated correctly, that floating fund would, over a very large number of claims, be left untouched.

30.160   The methods by which the burning risks are estimated are more complex and subtle than merely taking the estimated size of the adverse costs and multiplying that by the estimated risk that an adverse costs order will be made. That, however, is the essence of an entirely acceptable actuarial method (albeit a basic one) known as the deterministic model. Greater sophistication may be achieved by applying a stochastic model, which assigns probabilities to certain categories of loss. It is by doing this that statistical methods may be brought to bear.[184] It is this method which allows different categories of risk to be identified, a relevant example being where staged ATE premiums are charged (thereby dealing separately with those cases which do not settle at an early stage).

---

[180]   A Schwepcke *Reinsurance* (Verlag Versicherungswirtschaft GmbH, 2nd edn, 2004), p 301.
[181]   S Promislow *Fundamentals of Acturial Mathematics* (Wiley-Blackwell, 2005), para 1.5.
[182]   See MV Wüthrich *Market-consistent Actuarial Valuation* (Springer, 2007).
[183]   A Schwepcke *Reinsurance* (Verlag Versicherungswirtschaft GmbH, 2nd edn, 2004), section 6.
[184]   S Promislow *Fundamentals of Acturial Mathematics* (Wiley-Blackwell, 2005), paras 1.4 and 1.5.

30.161   As mentioned above, two commonly used methods of estimating those two parameters are experience rating and rating based on assumed distributions. The latter is a matter of judgment whereas the former is a matter of analysing data. Experience rating uses data gleaned either during or after a period known as the observation period; that data is then used to predict what is likely to happen during the period of cover (which is known as the rating period). For experience rating to work well, three conditions must be met: first, historical data must exist; secondly, it must relate to claims which are representative of claims in the rating period; and, thirdly, any changes which have taken place between the observation period and the rating period must be such that allowances can be made. It is the process of making allowances which is where actuarial skill becomes particularly relevant. Allowances may be made for almost anything, such as inflation, changes in the law, changes in economic conditions, etc.[185]

30.162   For all the reasons set out above, historical data and claims experience are both invaluable resources from an ATE insurer's point of view. This is because claims experience and experience of detailed assessment will respectively allow the twin goals of adequacy and equity to be achieved. The converse is that the absence of that type of experience means that it can be difficult to balance the books in a fledgling market. It is, perhaps, because of this that the court (to date, at least) has not shown a great willingness to examine the reasonableness of the underwriting assumptions made for the purposes of rating the premium.

Types

30.163   There are many different types of policy providing for many different types of premium. The following is a brief and non-exhaustive list; it has been prepared with the kind assistance of Mr Rocco Pirozzolo (a well-respected expert on the ATE market).

Single premium

30.164   A policy which provides for a single premium is an ordinary ATE policy which provides for a single premium payable in full regardless of the outcome of the claim.

Staged premium

30.165   A staged premium is a premium which is quantified by reference to the stage at which the claim concludes; it is also often called a 'stepped premium' or a 'rebated premium'. The amount payable increases if the litigation fails to settle before certain pre-defined steps. It may be calculated by way of a diminishing discount or an escalating price: the effect is broadly the same regardless of which it is. A premium is usually referred to as being staged or stepped where it is deferred (ie where there is an escalating price). The term 'rebated' is usually reserved for premiums which have been paid at inception on the basis that it will be partially refunded if the claim settles early (ie it is a policy which provides for a diminishing discount).

Deferred premium

30.166   A deferred premium is a premium (which may be single or staged) which is not payable upon inception, but instead is payable either upon conclusion of the claim or upon termination of the policy, whichever occurs first. A deferred premium is often

---

[185]   A Schwepcke *Reinsurance* (Verlag Versicherungswirtschaft GmbH, 2nd edn, 2004), p 309.

combined with own-premium cover (see below). The phrase 'deferred premium' is often loosely used to refer to a premium which is payable only if the claim is successful; whilst it is true to say that such a premium is a deferred premium, this term is also used to describe many other types of premium, and it is therefore not a usage to be encouraged.

Own-premium cover

30.167   Own-premium cover will exist where the policy provides cover for non-recovery of the premium.[186] The premium may be deferred, but it may also be payable upon inception. Where it is payable on inception it would usually be covered by a disbursement funding loan which will be paid off by the insurer in the event of an adverse outcome. Own-premium cover is also called premium shortfall waiver and premium indemnity guarantee (often shorted to PIG by those who dislike the concept of own-premium cover).[187]

Own disbursements cover

30.168   This is a policy which provides cover for the insured's own disbursements (either including, or excluding counsel). What is and is not a disbursement will be a matter of contractual interpretation. The word 'disbursement' may be defined in the policy as including the ATE premium itself; this is one mechanism by which own-premium cover (above) might be provided.

Both sides' costs

30.169   This is an extended form of the category above, but rather than the cover being limited to the insured's disbursements, it includes cover for the insured's other costs. It is an alternative to funding by way of conditional fee agreements. Mr Pirozzolo confirms that whilst it is a small market, it does exist.[188]

Delegated authority

30.170   Delegated authority modifies the administrative process by which a policy comes into existence. A solicitor with delegated authority is able to incept a policy without having first to obtain case-specific authority from the insurer or from an intermediary. It is often combined with block rating (see **30.151**). Delegated authority will arise out of an authorisation agreement between the insurer and the solicitor; that agreement will almost always include provisions which are intended to avoid adverse selection (see **30.177–30.181**). Mr Pirozzolo confirms that delegated authority schemes are common for personal injury and clinical negligence claims, but that they are also available for other types of claim.[189]

---

[186]   Hughes LJ was obviously impressed by this type of policy as he has commented that it was 'remarkable': *Jones v Wrexham Borough Council* [2007] EWCA Civ 1356 at [75].
[187]   Amey M, PIG of a Problem, Litigation Funding (2010) No 68 August, pp 20–21.
[188]   Personal communication with Mr Rocco Pirozzolo, 25 November 2009.
[189]   Ibid.

The assessment of ATE premiums

30.171 This topic is addressed in two parts: first, the issue of quantum in general and, second, deconstruction (which is a process whereby the premium is broken down into its constituent parts).

30.172 It should be said at the outset that while it is possible to analyse premiums in great detail, it is rarely the case that the court will entertain a challenge beyond considering whether it was reasonable to take out the policy and checking that it is not grossly out of line with the market norm. Simon J has explained that challenges to ATE premiums must be resolved on the basis of evidence and analysis, rather than by assertion and counter-assertion. The issues should be identified promptly and, where necessary, there should be directions for the proper determination of specific issues. This might involve the costs judge looking at the proposal; and the receiving party providing a note as to the method used to calculate the premium (this being so regardless of whether the premium is a one-off ATE premium or a staged premium).[190]

Inception and reasonableness

30.173 Whether it was reasonable to take out a policy will depend on the facts of each case, but for the reasons mentioned below, those facts may extend beyond the individual case to include the wider context of the ATE market itself. That wider context has been referred to as 'insurance macroeconomics'. There are four topics which merit discussion: the relevance of alternative means of funding, the relevance of supposed absence of risk, adverse selection, and timing. Whilst premiums are – like all costs – assessed under CPR, r 44.4, the method of assessment is unique under the CPR in that costs may be allowed as being both reasonable and proportionate notwithstanding the fact that they may not have been reasonably required for the purposes of funding the case in question.

Alternative means of funding

30.174 If a receiving party unreasonably eschewed an alternative means of funding in favour of an ATE policy, then it would be open to the court to disallow the premium on the basis that it was a cost which had been unreasonably incurred.[191] Alternative means of funding would include before the event insurance (BTE insurance), trade union funding, legal aid, etc. The CPD specifically mentions pre-existing insurance as being a relevant factor;[192] the availability of BTE insurance is discussed in detail at **30.239–30.258**. The fact that an alternative means of funding was available would not necessarily mean that it would be unreasonable not to use it. This is because it might not be suitable. If, for example, the BTE cover insisted on the use of far-flung panel solicitors, then it might, in certain circumstances, be reasonable to reject that as a means of funding. Again, these issues are addressed at **30.239–30.258**.

Agreement between the parties

30.175 It will occasionally happen that the need for additional liabilities (and ATE in particular) will be diminished or negated by agreement between the parties as to how the litigation should be managed. It is, for example, not unknown for defendants in clinical negligence disputes to agree not to seek costs, this being in return for the claimant's

---

[190] *Kris Motor Spares Ltd v Fox Williams LLP* [2010] EWHC 1008 (QB) at [46].
[191] See CPR, r 44.4.
[192] CPD, art 11.10(2).

agreement not to incept ATE insurance. Such arrangements may apply to more than one case and may even be properly described as being protocols. An example of this is that of a consultant urogynaecologist who caused some 400 cases to be brought against his former employer: a formal protocol was agreed which may ultimately have the effect of reducing the burden of additional liabilities by as much as £8m.[193]

Absence of risk

30.176   The lower the risk that an adverse costs order may be made, the less pressing the need for ATE insurance. There are examples of the court finding that the risk was so low that no insurance was required at all,[194] but it would not often be the case that the level of risk would be the sole determining factor. In particular, it may be that the receiving party's solicitor is obliged to recommend a policy as a condition of his delegated authority (this is known as obligatory recommendation). Many delegated authority schemes impose an obligation of this type in an effort to avoid adverse selection. This is discussed in more detail below. Akenhead J has explained that it is important that claimants do not use ATE insurance as a commercial threat to defendants; he has explained that where the risks are low, it is legitimate for the court to ask itself whether, in any particular case, it was reasonable and proportionate to take out insurance.[195] The implication in Akenhead J's logic is that if the court believes that the policy was taken out for the purposes of gaining a tactical advantage, the premium may be disallowed.

Adverse selection and macroeconomics

30.177   Adverse selection is cherry picking (or, more accurately, it is what is left on the tree after the best cherries have been picked). It results from the solicitor electing not to recommend insurance in those cases in which the risks are very low. If the insurer's underwriting assumptions have been based on data where there has been no adverse selection, then those assumptions will be undermined by the fact that the risk will be much greater, on average, than envisaged. This can lead to a failure to charge an adequate premium and, in extreme cases, can even lead to GNPI being less than the burning risk.

30.178   These considerations do not relate to the individual litigant or to the case in question, but to the insurer and *its* economic needs. Lord Scott has used the word 'macroeconomics' to describe that topic.[196] There can be no doubt that it is reasonable and legitimate for an insurer to have concerns about the macroeconomic position of the insurance book in question. Indeed, Woolf CJ has even gone so far as to say that delegated authority schemes will not work unless there are safeguards against adverse selection.[197] He has explained that if a solicitor is – without restraint – permitted to choose which cases merit ATE insurance and which do not, then the principle that the many will pay for the few will become distorted. He went on to find that the need to avoid adverse selection might amount to reasonable justification of a decision to take an

---

[193]   D Locke 'New lease of life' *New Law Journal* (2010) Vol 160 No 7418, pp 717–718; the figures were provided by Mr Locke in January 2011.

[194]   As an illustration, see *Dhanoia v Mehmi*, 17 October 2007, Bristol County Court, in which a district judge found that so little was in dispute that it was unreasonable to take out ATE insurance, notwithstanding the modest size of the premium.

[195]   *Redwing Construction Ltd v Wishart* [2011] EWHC 19 (TCC) at [16].

[196]   *Callery v Gray* [2002] UKHL 28 at [114].

[197]   *Callery v Gray* [2001] EWCA Civ 1117 at [67].

ATE policy. This would be a significant development in the law of costs because it would mean that costs could be recovered notwithstanding the fact that the case itself (taken in isolation) did not justify those costs being incurred; this is discussed further at **30.181**.

30.179   Although Woolf CJ's judgment was not overturned on appeal, Lord Nicholls expressed doubt as to whether this would continue to be the case in the future. He commented that in a mature market where premiums had been adjusted so as to avoid underfunding, the need for obligatory recommendation in all cases is something which may need to be kept under review.[198] It was implicit in his reasoning, however, that adverse selection would be a factor to be taken into account, even if it were not determinative of the matter.

30.180   It is informative to note what Lord Scott had to say in his dissenting judgment; this is because it highlights the difference between the assessment of costs in isolation and in a macroeconomic context:[199]

'The question whether the paying party should be required to meet a particular item of expenditure is a case specific question. It is not a question to which the macroeconomics of the ATE insurance market has any relevance. If the expenditure was not reasonably required for the purposes of the claim, it would, in my opinion, be contrary to long-established costs recovery principles to require the paying party to pay it.'

30.181   In other contexts costs are assessed solely on the facts of the case in hand. It is a striking departure from the customary method of assessment to assess a premium by reference to other facts (ie to facts unrelated to the claim itself). There are many instances in which costs are claimed as a result of a contractual obligation to pay for services which were required only transiently or which were believed to be required but eventually were not required;[200] it is, however, difficult to think of any other instance where an item of expenditure is allowable where there was never any need for it at all. It is, perhaps, because of this that Lord Nicholls was so careful to make it clear that the current practice (of giving weight to the need to avoid adverse selection) is something which needs to be kept under review and that it may not be a permanent state of affairs.

Timing (prematurity and late application)

30.182   The next issue is whether it would be appropriate to object to a premium on the basis that the policy was taken out too early (early inception) or too late (late application). It could never be the case that a policy had been taken out so prematurely that it fell beyond the jurisdiction of AJA 1999. This is because the act permits recovery of the premium even where the policy was taken out only in contemplation of proceedings and before they were commenced.[201] The issue is, therefore, not a jurisdictional one, but a question of reasonableness.

30.183   Woolf CJ has given the following reasons why it would be reasonable to take out ATE insurance at an early stage:[202]

---

[198]   *Callery v Gray* [2002] UKHL 28 at [41].
[199]   *Callery v Gray* [2002] UKHL 28 at [114].
[200]   Examples would include booking fees and cancellation fees.
[201]   *Callery v Gray* [2001] EWCA Civ 1117 at [54], per Woolf CJ.
[202]   *Callery v Gray* [2001] EWCA Civ 1117 at [99].

- premiums will produce cover which would benefit defendants in the sense that there would be a means by which costs awarded in their favour would be paid;
- the interests of defendants could, with the assistance of the court, be preserved by restricting premiums to amounts which are reasonable having regard to overall requirements of the scheme created by AJA 1999;
- claimants would be able to know at the outset that a satisfactory arrangement had been made to provide cover for an adverse costs order;
- access to justice would be enhanced by legal representatives being about to offer claimants a service that includes all of these benefits; and
- there is a risk that unless a policy is taken out before it is known whether liability is going to be contested, the premium might rise substantially, or no policy might be available at all.

Woolf CJ's comments were made in the context of modest road traffic accident cases; the relevance of this is that it is not necessarily the case that the same logic would apply to less quotidian types of claim. Indeed, the fact that the CPR deals with one type of claim (publication claims) in such a way as to discourage early inception, suggests that different considerations apply to other types of claim. The details of publication claims are addressed in the footnotes.[203]

30.184   At the other end of the spectrum is where it is said that the receiving party left it so late to apply for ATE insurance that he has made himself unable to obtain insurance at modest cost. Simon J has explained that late inception may (in some cases) indicate that a contractual premium was an unreasonable cost, but that there is no principle that the premium on a late incepting policy is irrecoverable as an unreasonable cost.[204] He explained that each case is likely to depend on its facts.[205] Where the deferral

---

[203]   Publication claims include claims in defamation and malicious falsehood. They are notoriously expensive. Where a publication claim settles prior to the issue of proceedings, the CPR imposes significant restrictions on the recoverability of premiums; those restructions were recommended by the Civil Justice Council following consultation resulting in the 'Theobalds Park Plus Agreement' (see Consultation Paper CP 16/07). Although those restrictions are not phrased in the language of prematurity and reasonableness, it must be the case that they have a bearing on that issue because they can only be a strong disincentive to litigants taking out ATE insurance at a stage which is earlier than the expiry of the prescribed periods. Those restriction are set out in CPR, r 44.12B:
'(1)   If in proceedings to which rule 44.12A applies it appears to the court that—
(a)   if proceedings had been started, they would have been publication proceedings;
(b)   one party admitted liability and made an offer of settlement on the basis of that admission;
(c)   agreement was reached after that admission of liability and offer of settlement; and
(d)   either—
(i)   the party making the admission of liability and offer of settlement was not provided by the other party with the information about an insurance policy as required by the Practice Direction (Pre-Action Conduct); or
(ii)   that party made the admission of liability and offer of settlement before, or within 42 days of, being provided by the other party with that information,
no costs may be recovered by the other party in respect of the insurance premium.
(2)   In this rule, "publication proceedings" means proceedings for—
(a)   defamation;
(b)   malicious falsehood; or
(c)   breach of confidence involving publication to the public at large.'
To a certain extent these provisions place the issue of his liability for premiums in the hands of the paying party.
[204]   *Kris Motor Spares Ltd v Fox Williams LLP* [2010] EWHC 1008 (QB) at [41].
[205]   Ibid. It is worth noting that the points made about macroeconomics at **30.177–30.181** would not apply in these circumstances; whilst the point was not mentioned by Simon J, this is likely to be one of the reasons why cases of late inception turn on their own facts.

was for good reason (such as an attempt to limit costs until they became unavoidable), it is not likely that the court would find fault.[206]

Quantum (other than deconstruction)

Measure and judicial approach

30.185 There are two ways in which the reasonableness of a premium may be gauged: first, it may be measured in terms of its overall reasonableness and, second, it may be broken down into its constituent parts. The latter is called 'deconstruction' and is considered at **30.223–30.225**.

30.186 The first point to make is that it is trite costs law that the court will not allow costs which are unreasonable; this means that the court is able to take a robust view and to reduce a premium if it is unreasonable.[207] For the reason set out below, reductions will not be common without case-specific evidence, but they are not unknown.[208]

30.187 On the whole, however, reductions will be made on the basis of case-specific or macroeconomic evidence. In this regard, CPD, art 11.10 gives the following guidance about the appropriate factors to be taken into account:

'In deciding whether the cost of insurance cover is reasonable, relevant factors to be taken into account include:

(1) where the insurance cover is not purchased in support of a conditional fee agreement with a success fee, how its cost compares with the likely cost of funding the case with a conditional fee agreement with a success fee and supporting insurance cover;

(2) the level and extent of the cover provided;

(3) the availability of any pre-existing insurance cover;

(4) whether any part of the premium would be rebated in the event of early settlement; [and]

(5) the amount of commission payable to the receiving party or his legal representatives or other agents.'

(A conspicuous omission from this list is risk; this is discussed at **30.203–30.208**.) Simon J has explained that there is no presumption that the premium is reasonable unless the contrary is shown.[209] He went on to explain that notwithstanding this, it is for the paying party to raise the contention that the premium is unreasonable, and the evidential burden is on the paying party to advance at least some material in support of that contention.[210] Simon J said that this is not to reverse the burden of proof, this being because if, having heard the evidence and the argument, there is still a doubt about the reasonableness of the premium, that doubt must be resolved in favour of the paying party.[211]

---

[206] See, for example, *RSA Pursuit Test Cases, Re* [2005] EWHC 90003 (Costs) at [365]–[374]. In *Kris Motor Spares Ltd v Fox Williams LLP* [2010] EWHC 1008 (QB), for example, Simon J found that the decision to take out insurance at a very late stage was reasonable because the insured's opponent had instructed leading counsel, thereby increasing the risk in terms of costs.

[207] *Callery v Gray* [2001] EWCA 1246 at [11].

[208] See, for example, *Smith v Interlink Express Parcels Ltd* [2007] EWHC 90095 (Costs).

[209] *Kris Motor Spares Ltd v Fox Williams LLP* [2010] EWHC 1008 (QB) at [35].

[210] *Kris Motor Spares Ltd v Fox Williams LLP* [2010] EWHC 1008 (QB) at [44].

[211] Ibid. There is, of course, a fundamental difference between the burden of proof and the provisions concerning resolution of doubt, but presumably Simon J was merely illustrating his point by reference to the latter rather than suggesting that that is the mechanism that avoids reversal of the evidential burden.

Comparison with conditional funding

30.188 A comparison with conditional funding[212] will be relevant in those cases where no success fee is claimed. The task is to compare the premium with the additional liability that would have been charged had the receiving party's solicitors acted under a conditional fee agreement which provided for a success fee. Presumably, this means that the court should form a view about the level of success fee that would have been charged if a conditional fee agreement had been made at the time the policy was incepted.

30.189 Like must be compared with like and, in any event, it would be a mistake to try to deal with the comparison with any degree of mathematical nicety.[213]

The level of cover

30.190 The level of cover is a factor that may be taken into account. There are two ways in which it may be relevant:

- first, the level of cover may be said to have been excessive, and that a cheaper policy with a lower level of cover ought to have been used; and
- secondly, it may be said that the premium was excessive, given the level of cover (that is, that the premium was over-rated).

Both of these are topics which may call for the expertise of an expert broker or an expert actuary, but this will not always be the case: where the over-rating is obvious, the court may draw upon its own knowledge and its own experience (see **30.186**).

30.191 The point at which the court abjures any notion of its own actuarial competence is quickly reached, and it would generally be only in cases of gross over-rating of the premium that the court would claim the ability to intervene. Brooke LJ had the following to say:[214]

> '[The court does not have] the expertise to judge the reasonableness of a premium except in very broad brush terms, and the viability of the ATE market will be imperilled if they regard themselves (without the assistance of expert evidence) as better qualified than the underwriter to rate the financial risk the insurer faces.'

30.192 Whilst their limitations must at all times be borne in mind, it is helpful to know something of the relevant actuarial principles (see **30.156–30.162**); this is because a back-of-the-envelope calculation may be used as a screening test in some cases, and as a cross-check in others. Where there is no suitable factual or expert evidence, it may also be a judicial method of last resort.[215] It is possible to estimate the burning costs by looking at the level of cover and the risks in the litigation generally; once the burning costs have been estimated, an allowance may then be made for the costs of administration, etc. It is possible to arrive at a rough approximation of what the premium should be, based on the assumptions which led to the relevant figures being selected.

---

[212] See CPD, art 11.10(1).
[213] *Sharratt v London Central Bus Company and other cases (No 2) The Accident Group Test Cases* [2004] EWCA Civ 575 at [33]–[37].
[214] *Rogers v Merthyr Tydfil County Borough Council* [2006] EWCA Civ 1134 at [111]; see also [117].
[215] See, for example, *Smith v Interlink Express Parcels Ltd* [2007] EWHC 90095 (Costs).

30.193 Whilst over-reliance or inappropriate reliance on back-of-the-envelope calculations will lead to error, such calculations do have a role; in particular, they can legitimately demonstrate that actuarial calculations may give rise to results which are surprising and counter-intuitive. This can be demonstrated by the following example. Suppose a paying party complains that the premium is close to or even exceeds the level of cover. Intuitively, that premium would seem to be excessive. If, however, the policy provides for own-premium cover (see **30.167**), then the premium that would otherwise have been charged would itself need to be added to the costs which comprise the burning costs. This can have the effect of nearly doubling the premium. When an allowance of, say, 50% is then added for administration, profit, reinsurance, etc, it can be seen that a premium which exceeds the level of cover is by no means unjustifiable (although, of course, it may be objectionable on other grounds, such as equity).

30.194 In summary, back-of-the-envelope calculations do have a role to play, but this is usually as a screening test or as a cross-check. They may be used as a judicial method of last resort.

The availability of alternative means of funding

30.195 This topic is addressed at **30.240**. Whilst it usually goes to recoverability in principle, the availability of pre-existing insurance cover is capable of going to the issue of quantum. This is because BTE cover may have been available up to a certain limit. If the costs exceed the limit of a BTE policy and if it was not used, then it could be argued that the premium would have been lower had the BTE policy been used to fund part of the claim.

Staged/rebated premiums

30.196 The term 'staged premium' will be used to refer generically to those types of premiums described at **30.165** (ie premiums which increase as the claim progresses). The underlying rationale is that riskier cases are selected by virtue of the fact that they do not settle, and that it is, therefore, appropriate to levy higher premiums in those cases to take account of the higher-than-average risk.

30.197 Common sense dictates that the fact that a rebate was available during the early part of the proceedings would be a factor the court could take into account when assessing the reasonableness of the premium. The receiving party would argue that under a staged-premium model, the source of the GNPI had shifted from those claims which settled early to those claims which had not. This shift is between claims rather than within claims: this means that it would not be legitimate to compare final-stage with the premium (hereinafter referred to as 'the unrebated premium') which would applied under a single-premium model.[216] Notwithstanding this, there are examples of the court looking at the reasonableness of the individual stages,[217] albeit with obvious reluctance.

30.198 There is no guidance in the CPR or elsewhere as to how stage premiums should be assessed. It can, however, be demonstrated by elementary mathematics that the final-stage premium can be surprisingly high when compared with the unrebated premium. If no adjustment is made for differential rates of failure, then where the

---

[216] *Rogers v Merthyr Tydfil County Borough Council* [2006] EWCA Civ 1134 at [111].
[217] See, for example, *Smith v Interlink Express Parcels Ltd* [2007] EWHC 90095 (Costs).

proportion of cases which go to trial is t and where the lower premium is d of the unrebated premium, the factor by which the unrebated premium (P_r) must be increased is as follows:

$$P_r = 1 + \frac{(1-d)(1-t)}{(1-t)}$$

30.199   If, for example, the first-stage premium is 75% of the unrebated premium, and if only 5% of cases reach trial, the final-stage premium must be 5.75 times higher than the unrebated premium (and this assumes that the cases which go to trial will be no more likely to lose than the average case). If the insurer wishes to reduce the lower premium to 50% of the unrebated premium, the higher premium must rise to 10.5 times higher than the unrebated premium in order to preserve GNPI. Thus, small changes can have very large effects. The relevance of this is that it can be difficult to form a view as to the reasonableness of staged premiums.

30.200   One factor that may be relevant is that the risk associated with first-stage premiums will usually be very much lower than that associated with final-stage premiums. Lord Scott made the following comment about this (albeit in a dissenting judgment):[218]

> 'It is important to notice that this risk cannot arise unless litigation is commenced.'

This is relevant because it affords the insurer an opportunity to manage risk, that is the lower premium can be crafted so that it covers virtually no risk at all, but is still available to make up the reserves for other cases. This makes the topic even more complex, however, as it means that any rating calculation must take into account the different risks which pertain to the different premiums. It is at that point that the calculations move from being simple deterministic calculations into being stochastic ones, and that is unquestionably a topic which can be addressed only with the benefit of expert evidence.

Commission

30.201   Commission is money the insurer pays to a third party for the purposes of obtaining business. The CPD does not refer to commission in general, but only to commission payable to the receiving party or his legal representatives or other agents.[219] This type of commission is dealt with separately because, in general, it is not payable by the paying party. By way of example, if out of a premium of £450 a commission of £50 is payable to the receiving party's solicitor, the maximum indemnity that the paying party could be asked to provide would be £400, this being because the receiving party would be able to ask his solicitor to account to him for the commission of £50 (see **30.129**).

30.202   Other types of commission (ie ones payable to persons other than the receiving party or his legal representatives or other agents) are probably best regarded as being part of the insurer's general overhead and therefore of no more significance than any

---

[218]   *Callery v Gray* [2002] UKHL 28 at [70].
[219]   CPD, art 11.10(5).

other expenditure.[220] This does not mean that they are wholly irrelevant, however; this is because they will be part of the overall costs of the business and, as Phillips MR has explained, if an insurer incurs extravagant expenditure, its premiums are likely to be uncompetitive and not recoverable in full.[221]

Risk

30.203   A noticeable omission from the CPD's list of relevant factors is the risk that a claim may be made on the policy. Brooke LJ has confirmed, however, that it is a relevant factor.[222] Risk is often taken into account for the purposes of making a rough estimate of the burning costs, which is generally used as a cross-check for confirming (or refuting) the reasonableness of the premium.[223]

30.204   Where the premium is block rated then the risk in the individual case will be an irrelevance because the premium would have been calculated without reference to that risk, but where the premium has been individually rated it may be a relevant factor. The relevance of risk, and the many and complex ways in which it may be measured, has been addressed at **30.150–30.162**. It can be seen that it would be naive and occasionally plainly wrong to say that a risky case justifies a high premium. Where, however, there is evidence that it is relevant to the way in which the premium has been calculated then it will be a factor to be taken into account. Akenhead J has said that it had to be a reasonable presumption that premiums were linked to an assessment of risks. He opined that the allowable premium can be adjusted downwards to reflect the fact that at the time when the insurance was entered into the prospects of success were good or high.[224]

30.205   The risk includes any risk which may be covered by insurance falling within the ambit of AJA 1999, s 29. In particular, there is no objection in principle to a premium being based on a risk that the insured may fail to beat a Part 36 offer and may be required to pay costs as a result.[225]

30.206   Risk is difficult to measure, and therefore premiums based on an estimate of risk are difficult to monitor. This means that there is the potential for profiteering. That potential ought to be limited by the concept of equity (see **30.158**), but – in insurance generally – the ultimate moderating influence is the market. In the ATE insurance business the market is skewed by the fact that very often (if not most often) the insurer will look to a stranger for payment of his premium rather than to his own client. This potential for abuse was noted by Lord Bingham in the following terms:[226]

'A … possible abuse [of the system of funding by way of CFAs and ATE] was that claimants, although able to obtain after the event insurance, would be able to do so only at an unreasonably high price, the after the event insurers having no incentive to moderate a

---

[220]   As an example of such a commission being allowed see *Re Claims Direct Test Cases* [2003] EWCA Civ 136 at [47].

[221]   *Callery v Gray* [2001] EWCA 1246 at [13].

[222]   *Rogers v Merthyr Tydfil County Borough Council* [2006] EWCA Civ 1134 at [108].

[223]   For example, see *Tyndall v Battersea Dogs Home* [2005] EWHC 90011 (Costs) at [80]–[98] in the context of a block rated premium and *Rogers v Merthyr Tydfil County Borough Council* [2006] EWCA Civ 1134 in the context of an individually rated premium.

[224]   *Redwing Construction Ltd v Wishart* [2011] EWHC 19 (TCC) at [15(d)]. Notwithstanding the fact that such an approach would afford the court a good deal of freedom, it has to be said that this method of assessment has been widely adopted. Indeed, there are those who suggest that Akenhead J's judgment on this point should be regarded as being restricted to its own facts.

[225]   *Callery v Gray* [2001] EWCA 1246 at [31].

[226]   *Callery v Gray* [2002] UKHL 28 at [5].

premium which would be paid by the defendant or his insurers and which might be grossly disproportionate to the risk which the insurer was underwriting.'

30.207   Brooke LJ seems to have placed greater faith in the ability of the market to regulate ATE premiums; however, he had this to say:[227]

'Although the claimant very often does not have to pay the premium himself, this does not mean that there are no competitive or other pressures at all in the market. As the evidence before this court shows, it is not in an insurer's interest to fix a premium at a level which will attract frequent challenges.'

Brooke LJ's analysis is entirely in keeping with the principle of equity (ie the professional goal of rating a premium at a level which is fair: see **30.158**). There are, however, those who say that it is hard to reconcile Brooke LJ's analysis with the following comments of Lord Nicholls:[228]

'ATE insurers do not compete for claimants, still less do they compete on premiums charged. They compete for solicitors who will sell or recommend their product. And they compete by offering solicitors the most profitable arrangements to enable them to attract profitable work. There is only one restraining force on the premium charged and that is how much the costs judge will allow on an assessment against the liability insurer.'

30.208   Although the two analyses may at first appear to be directly contradictory, on closer analysis they are not. This is because Lord Nicholls was speaking about a general, theoretical concern about policies which fund themselves wholly from the monies recovered as costs. Brooke LJ, on the other hand, was giving judgment on the basis of evidence going to the state of a particular market at a particular time. Put another way, the extent to which the court can rely on the market as a moderating influence will depend on the circumstances of the market in question.

Proportionality

30.209   Akenhead J has confirmed that the basic costs rules and practice about reasonableness and proportionality apply to ATE premiums; to the extent that a premium was unreasonable or disproportionate, it should be disallowed, at least on a standard basis assessment.[229] The question of whether an additional liability is proportionate must be considered separately from the question of whether base costs are proportionate.[230] This does not mean that an ATE premium will escape the test of proportionality: indeed, there are instances of the court reducing premiums solely on the grounds of proportionality (usually by finding that the particular choice of premium was disproportionate).[231]

30.210   The test of proportionality applies in a way which takes into account the macroeconomic factors mentioned above (see **30.177–30.181**). In simplistic terms, the court recognises as a matter of pragmatism that if, for good macroeconomic reasons, the market dictates that it will not offer less expensive policies, then it will be 'necessary'

---

[227]   *Rogers v Merthyr Tydfil County Borough Council* [2006] EWCA Civ 1134 at [105]; see also *Kris Motor Spares Ltd v Fox Williams LLP* [2010] EWHC 1008 (QB) at [44] where Simon J impliedly confirms that the same principles have continued to apply even after the passage of some years.

[228]   *Callery v Gray* [2002] UKHL 28 at [43].

[229]   *Redwing Construction Ltd v Wishart* [2011] EWHC 19 (TCC) at [15].

[230]   CPD, art 11.5.

[231]   See, for example, *Baker* in *RSA Pursuit Test Cases, Re* [2005] EWHC 90003 (Costs). This case is not binding.

(within the meaning of the test in *Lownds v Home Office*)[232] for the receiving party to take out a policy which is less than ideally priced. Brooke LJ had the following to say on the topic:[233]

> 'Necessity ... may be demonstrated by the application of strategic considerations which travel beyond the dictates of the particular case. Thus, it may include the unavoidable characteristics of the market in insurance of this kind. It does so because this very market is integral to the means of providing access to justice in civil disputes in what may be called the post-legal aid world.'

30.211   In practical terms, this means that if a solicitor is tied to recommending a particular contract of insurance to all his clients with viable claims, and if the receiving party can show that that was as a result of a legitimate need to avoid adverse selection, then the premium is likely to be allowed.

30.212   One method of ensuring proportionality of premiums is to link them to the value of the claim. Whilst not binding, Master Hurst has found that such an approach is not, in principle, champertous.[234] A similar method is to link the premium to the level of costs generally. Again, Master Hurst has found that such a premium is untouched by the law of champerty.[235]

Evidence and comparators

Judicial notice and judges' personal knowledge

30.213   That a judge is permitted to take personal knowledge into account when assessing a premium was confirmed by Phillips MR:[236]

> 'When considering whether a premium is reasonable, the Court must have regard to such evidence as there is, or knowledge that experience has provided, of the relationship between the premium and the risk and also of the cost of alternative cover available.'

In view of the narrow view that the court takes of evidence of reasonableness (see below), it is likely that Phillips MR was referring to personal knowledge of the market in general rather than to knowledge of specific types of insurance. Nonetheless, there are instances of the court drawing upon its knowledge of specific types of policy in order to fill in gaps in the evidence.[237] The basis upon which the court does this is not entirely clear. It certainly cannot be said that knowledge of the ATE insurance market could fall within either of the categories of judicial notice (those being notice upon enquiry and notice of notorious and commonly known facts). That said, Lord Buckmaster has held that 'properly applied, and within reasonable limits' the court is entitled to use its own knowledge of matters which were commonly known within the locality;[238] it is only a small step to expand this principle so that a court with a particular specialism is entitled

---

[232] [2002] EWCA Civ 365.

[233] *Rogers v Merthyr Tydfil County Borough Council* [2006] EWCA Civ 1134 at [105].

[234] *Pirie v Ayling* [2003] EWHC 9006 (Costs); this case is not binding. See the discussion at **30.149**.

[235] See *RSA Pursuit Test Cases, Re* [2005] EWHC 90003 (Costs) at [283]–[297] and, in particular, [260]. On the facts of that case where the premium was in the same order of magnitude as the costs, he found that for that approach to work, the costs upon which the premium is based must themselves be proportionate. This case is not binding, but is usually accepted as being highly persuasive.

[236] *Callery v Gray* [2001] EWCA Civ 1246 at [69].

[237] See *Sharratt v London Central Bus Company and other cases (No 2) The Accident Group Test Cases* [2004] EWCA Civ 575 at [30].

[238] See *Keane v Mount Vernon Colliery Co Ltd* [1933] AC 309 at 317; see also *Reynolds v Llanelly Associated*

to take into account that which is commonly known within that specialism. Even if this is wrong, it is well established that as long as the judge does not give evidence to himself which contradicts the evidence adduced, a judge is entitled to draw on specialised knowledge when evaluating evidence.[239]

Comparators

30.214 A paying party will often seek to challenge a premium on the basis that an apparently cheaper alternative was available at the material time. While each case will turn on its own facts and whilst global comparisons may prove persuasive from time to time,[240] such challenges tend to be fraught with difficulties. This is not only because of problems in adducing relevant and sufficiently persuasive evidence (see below), but also because the court recognises that receiving parties' solicitors will not always be able to pick and choose from a variety of products and offer different policies to different clients. Brooke LJ had this to say on the point:[241]

> 'For block rating to work the insurer needs to be sure that it is receiving a full and fair selection of cases, ranging from those where liability is unlikely to be in doubt to those where it is contested. In order to avoid adverse selection it is standard practice for ATE insurers to require solicitors to insure all available cases with the ATE provider. In practice, therefore, claimants' solicitors cannot simply pick and choose from a variety of products and offer different policies to different clients. This approach is, in any event, incompatible with block rating.'

30.215 Unlike most issues concerning the assessment of costs, the court will, as a rule, insist on an exacting standard of evidence if it is to entertain a challenge to the reasonableness of an ATE premium, and whilst there are no specific exclusory rules, it is only a narrow range of evidence that the court will regard as being probative of a challenge.

Market

30.216 Experience or evidence of the market are factors that can be taken into account.[242] Evidence must be case-specific. This means that (unless the evidence is for a purpose such as showing the general state of the market or for making a point about macroeconomics), it must show not what was available in the market generally, but what was available to the receiving party on the facts of the particular claim in question.[243] A case-specific report would often be required, usually from an expert broker.

Tinplate Co Ltd [1948] 1 All ER 140, CA; these cases were decided under the Workmen's Compensation Acts, but the principles were confirmed to be of general applicability in *Mullen v Hackney London Borough Council* [1997] 1 WLR 1103.

[239] Whilst it related to criminal evidence rather than civil costs, see *Wetherall v Harrison* [1976] QB 773, per Widgery CJ.

[240] See, for example, *Sharratt v London Central Bus Company and other cases (No 2) The Accident Group Test Cases* [2004] EWCA Civ 575 at [34].

[241] *Rogers v Merthyr Tydfil County Borough Council* [2006] EWCA Civ 1134 at [33].

[242] *Callery v Gray* [2001] EWCA 1246 at [13].

[243] *Rogers v Merthyr Tydfil County Borough Council* [2006] EWCA Civ 1134 at [108]–[112], approving of *RSA Pursuit Test Cases, Re* [2005] EWHC 90003 (Costs) at [235].

Efficiency

30.217 Evidence of extravagant expenditure may prove that a policy is uncompetitive, with the result that the premium is not recoverable in full.[244] Evidence that the insurer lost money on the transaction is irrelevant to the issue of whether the premium was reasonable.[245]

Actuarial method

30.218 Phillips MR has confirmed that it is open to an insurer to adduce evidence as to the reasonableness of the premium sought, but he emphasised that it was not the court's task to carry out an audit of the insurer's business.[246]

Evidence in support

30.219 The points made above about the need to adduce evidence in support of a challenge to the quantum of a premium do not mean that evidence must be adduced in support of an unchallenged premium; compliance with the CPD is generally regarded as being sufficient. Service of the bill of costs ought to be accompanied by a copy of the insurance certificate showing the following:[247]

- whether the policy covers the receiving party's own costs, his opponent's costs, or his own costs and his opponent's costs;
- the maximum extent of that cover; and
- the amount of the premium paid or payable.

If a receiving party wishes to go further, however, he may; if he anticipates a challenge to the premium, it is open to him to adduce evidence as to the reasonableness of the premium sought. If he does so, and if the evidence is detailed, he would place himself at risk of impliedly accepting a deconstructive approach (see **30.223–30.225**); it is for this reason that there is often reluctance on the part of receiving parties to adduce detailed evidence.

30.220 Nonetheless, the receiving party may wish to prove that, after having made reasonably diligent enquiries, the policy was the most appropriate that he could find. Alternatively, he may wish to prove that extensive enquiries would have been disproportionate in the particular circumstances of the claim. Such evidence need not be elaborate, as was explained by Brooke LJ:[248]

> '[If] an issue arises about the size of a ... premium, it will ordinarily be sufficient for a claimant's solicitor to write a brief note for the purposes of the costs assessment explaining how he came to choose the particular ATE product for his client, and the basis upon which the premium is rated – whether block rated or individually rated.'

Brooke LJ went on to imply that expert evidence might be required in some circumstances. In a different case, Simon J has said that where a real issue was raised,

---

[244] *Callery v Gray* [2001] EWCA 1246 at [13].
[245] *Sharratt v London Central Bus Company and other cases (No 2) The Accident Group Test Cases* [2004] EWCA Civ 575 at [33].
[246] *Callery v Gray* [2001] EWCA 1246 at [16].
[247] CPD, art 32.5(2).
[248] *Rogers v Merthyr Tydfil County Borough Council* [2006] EWCA Civ 1134 at [117].

the court envisaged the hearing of expert evidence as to the reasonableness of the premium.[249] Akenhead J has implied much the same thing, but he went on to say that on a summary assessment such evidence would be disproportionate.[250] It is fair to say, however, that expert evidence on any assessment – even the most involved of detailed assessments – is a considerable rarity.

30.221   Factual evidence is not unusual, however, but care ought to be taken not to refer to irrelevant matters. By way of example, the following would be irrelevant:[251]

- evidence that other forms of insurance might have been more expensive (as opposed to evidence that there were no cheaper policies available);
- evidence that the receiving party's solicitor secured a commercially favourable package with the insurer; and
- evidence that the insurers lost money on the transactions.

The policy

30.222   Gray J has indicated (obiter) that ATE policies ought not to be privileged and that they ought to be disclosed 'as a matter of course';[252] whilst his comments can be read in other ways, it seems likely that what he meant was that if it is foreseeable that an opponent will reasonably wish to see it, an ATE policy ought to be drafted in such a way that the issue of privilege does not arise. Notwithstanding this, it is probably the case that the court lacks the vires to require a party to disclose its ATE policy (unless, of course, there are grounds on which the court can find that it is not privileged);[253] in a detailed assessment, however, the court can put the receiving party to his election. Indeed, in some circumstances the court may even impose a condition of disclosure (which is not an order to disclose, but an order to choose whether to disclose or to bear the consequences of not disclosing) during the substantive case itself.[254]

Deconstruction

30.223   Deconstruction is the process of dismantling a premium for the purposes of examining its constituent parts.[255] It would be possible to deconstruct a premium simply for the purposes of examining the reasonableness of each component, but that is not usually its intended purpose. Instead, deconstruction is usually carried out for the purposes of isolating and excluding monies which are not true premium monies and which are to be subtracted from the amount claimed.[256]

---

[249]   *Kris Motor Spares Ltd v Fox Williams LLP* [2010] EWHC 1008 (QB) at [44].

[250]   *Redwing Construction Ltd v Wishart* [2011] EWHC 19 (TCC) at [15].

[251]   *Sharratt v London Central Bus Company and other cases (No 2) The Accident Group Test Cases* [2004] EWCA Civ 575 at [33].

[252]   *Henry v British Broadcasting Corporation* [2005] EWHC 2503 (QB) at [26].

[253]   Although a non-costs case, see *West London Pipeline & Storage Ltd v Total UK Ltd* [2008] EWHC 1296 (Comm).

[254]   Such as a condition for the continuance of group litigation: see *Barr v Biffa Waste Services Ltd* [2009] EWHC 1033 (TCC).

[255]   *Sharratt v London Central Bus Company and other cases (No 2) The Accident Group Test Cases* [2004] EWCA Civ 575 at [17].

[256]   *Callery v Gray* [2001] EWCA 1246 at [12].

30.224   In order to know what is to be excluded, it is necessary to know what is to be included; this means that it is necessary to have a definition of what is a premium. The following definition is generally received as being appropriate in the context of ATE insurance:[257]

'The consideration required of the assured in return for which the insurer undertakes his obligation under the contract of insurance.'

Thus, a premium is a sum paid to the insurer; this does not include monies paid to an intermediary (unless, of course, it is received by the intermediary on behalf of the insurer). An intermediary cannot make his fee into a premium by the mere expedient of calling it a premium.[258]

30.225   The following are examples of monies which might be disallowed upon deconstruction, depending on the circumstances:

- money paid for the right to be included within a claims management scheme;[259]
- referral fees;[260]
- the costs of 'ring-fencing' damages;[261] and
- voluntary payments made by claims management companies to an underwriter for the purposes of securing extra capacity.

Monies which are not true premium monies may be irrecoverable for reasons unconnected with or additional to those mentioned above. Where, for example, a fee is an *unlawful* referral fee, it would become irrecoverable by reason of implied statutory prohibition against the enforceability of that fee; this would be an additional reason for its disallowance.[262]

MEMBERSHIP ORGANISATIONS AND NOTIONAL PREMIUMS

30.226   A notional premium[263] is an amount charged by a membership organisation as compensation for bearing the responsibility for meeting adverse costs orders made against its members. It is akin to an ATE premium, but is payable to a membership organisation instead of an insurer. This means that there is no market capable of directly exerting any moderating influence on the amount claimed. For the reasons set out below, the procedure by which such premiums are assessed creates a link with the

---

[257]   This definition is taken from *MacGillivray* (9th edn), and was approved of in both *Claims Direct litigation* [2003] EWCA Civ 136 at [25] and *Sharratt v London Central Bus Company and other cases (No 2) The Accident Group Test Cases* [2004] EWCA Civ 575 at [17].

[258]   *Sharratt v London Central Bus Company and other cases (No 2) The Accident Group Test Cases* [2004] EWCA Civ 575 at [17]; see also *Re Claims Direct Test Cases* [2003] EWCA Civ 136 at [35]–[46].

[259]   See, for example, *Re Claims Direct Test Cases* [2003] EWCA Civ 136.

[260]   See, for example, *Sharratt v London Central Bus Company and other cases (No 2) The Accident Group Test Cases* [2004] EWCA Civ 575 at [39]–[42].

[261]   See, for example, *Re Claims Direct Test Cases* [2002] All ER (D) 76 at [214], per Master Hurst; this case is not binding; the decision was affirmed on appeal (*Re Claims Direct Test Cases* [2003] EWCA Civ 136) but not on this specific point.

[262]   See, for example, *Sharratt v London Central Bus Company and other cases (No 2) The Accident Group Test Cases* [2004] EWCA Civ 575 at [39]–[42].

[263]   The term 'self insurance premium' is also often used, but this ought not to be confused with self-insuring policies, which fund themselves by recovery of enhanced premiums payable only in the event of success.

ATE market; by creating that link, the ATE market is used by way of analogy as a measure (or, more accurately, a cap) of the allowable sums (see **30.235**).

The statutory framework

30.227 AJA 1999, s 30[264] (as amended) makes the following provisions which create the jurisdiction under which notional premiums may be claimed:

> **'Recovery where body undertakes to meet costs liabilities**
>
> (1) This section applies where a body of a prescribed description undertakes to meet (in accordance with arrangements satisfying prescribed conditions) liabilities which members of the body or other persons who are parties to proceedings may incur to pay the costs of other parties to the proceedings.
>
> (2) If in any of the proceedings a costs order is made in favour of any of the members or other persons, the costs payable to him may, subject to subsection (3) and (in the case of court proceedings) to rules of court, include an additional amount in respect of any provision made by or on behalf of the body in connection with the proceedings against the risk of having to meet such liabilities.
>
> (3) But the additional amount shall not exceed a sum determined in a prescribed manner; and there may, in particular, be prescribed as a manner of determination one which takes into account the likely cost to the member or other person of the premium of an insurance policy against the risk of incurring a liability to pay the costs of other parties to the proceedings.
>
> (4) In this section "prescribed" means prescribed by regulations made by the Lord Chancellor by statutory instrument; and a statutory instrument containing such regulations shall be subject to annulment in pursuance of a resolution of either House of Parliament.
>
> (5) Regulations under subsection (1) may, in particular, prescribe as a description of body one which is for the time being approved by the Lord Chancellor or by a prescribed person.'

The regulations mentioned in s 30(1) were, originally, the Access to Justice (Membership Organisations) Regulations 2000[265] ('the 2000 Regulations'), but the 2000 Regulations were revoked (with saving provisions) by the Access to Justice (Membership Organisation) Regulations 2005[266] ('the 2005 Regulations'). The saving provisions provide that the 2000 Regulations shall continue to have effect for the purposes of arrangements entered into before 1 November 2005;[267] this means that it is necessary to know about both sets of regulations.

30.228 The 2005 Regulations make the following provisions:

---

[264] Transitional provisions apply. Article 4 of the Access to Justice Act 1999 (Transitional Provisions) Order 2000 reads: 'Section 30 (Recovery where body undertakes to meet costs liabilities) shall not apply, as regards a party to proceedings, to: (a) any proceedings in relation to which that party gave an undertaking before 1 April 2000 which, if it had been given after that date, would have been an undertaking to which section 30(1) applied; or (b) any proceedings arising out of the same cause of action as any proceedings to which sub-paragraph (a) refers.' See also CPR, r 57.8(1), which makes similar provisions.

[265] SI 2000/693.

[266] SI 2005/2306.

[267] See reg 2(2) if the Access to Justice (Membership Organisation) Regulations 2005.

'Bodies of a prescribed description

3. The bodies which are prescribed for the purpose of section 30 (recovery where body undertakes to meet costs liabilities) are those bodies which are for the time being approved by the Secretary of State for that purpose.

Requirements for arrangements to meet costs liabilities

4.(1)   Section 30(1) applies to arrangements which satisfy the following conditions.

(2)   The arrangements must be in writing.

(3)   The arrangements must contain a statement specifying the circumstances in which the member may be liable to pay costs of the proceedings.

Recovery of additional amount for insurance costs

5.(1)   Where an additional amount is included in costs by virtue of section 30(2) (costs payable to a member of a body or other person party to the proceedings to include an additional amount in respect of provision made by the body against the risk of having to meet the member's or other person's liabilities to pay other parties' costs), that additional amount must not exceed the following sum.

(2)   That sum is the likely cost to the member of the body or, as the case may be, the other person who is a party to the proceedings in which the costs order is made of the premium of an insurance policy against the risk of incurring a liability to pay the costs of other parties to the proceedings.'

30.229   The 2000 Regulations were not dissimilar to the 2005 Regulations.[268] The main difference is that some of the more cumbersome provisions have been replaced by a simple requirement that the arrangements must be in writing and must contain a statement specifying when a member would become liable to pay the costs of the proceedings. The now old provisions (which no longer apply except under the saving provisions mentioned at **30.125**) were as follows:

'Requirements for arrangements to meet costs liabilities

3(1)   Section 30(1) of the Access to Justice Act 1999 applies to arrangements which satisfy the following conditions.

(2)   The arrangements must be in writing.

(3)   The arrangements must contain a statement specifying—

(a)   the circumstances in which the member or other party may be liable to pay costs of the proceedings,
(b)   whether such a liability arises—
    (i)   if those circumstances only partly occur,
    (ii)   irrespective of whether those circumstances occur, and
    (iii)   on the termination of the arrangements for any reason,
(c)   the basis on which the amount of the liability is calculated, and
(d)   the procedure for seeking assessment of costs.

(4)   A copy of the part of the arrangements containing the statement must be given to the member or other party to the proceedings whose liabilities the body is undertaking to meet as soon as possible after the undertaking is given.'

---

[268] The Explanatory Memorandum to the 2005 Regulations says that, notwithstanding the similarities, it was thought that it would be clearer and simpler to replace the 2000 Regulations rather than to issue more complex amending regulations. Regulation 5 of the 2005 Regulations mirrors reg 4 of the 2000 Regulations, and reg 3 of the 2005 Regulations is all but identical to reg 2 of the 2000 Regulations.

30.230   The Explanatory Memorandum to the 2005 Regulations gave the following reasons for discarding the old provisions:[269]

> 'The existing requirements [i e the 2000 Regulations] are designed to ensure that the client is aware of the arrangements for payment of the solicitor's costs. However, given that the membership organisation will in nearly all circumstances be indemnifying the member for any costs liability, it has been concluded that the amount of detail required by the current regulation 3 was unnecessary and cumbersome and of no real value to the member. Therefore the requirements will be simplified in the new regulation 4 to the need for a written explanation (for those rare circumstances where an indemnity would not apply).'

Whilst there is no authority on the point, it is possible that these comments would be of relevance if the court were to decide whether a putatively petty breach of the 2000 Regulations should be disregarded (either on the basis of materiality or on the basis of substantial compliance, or on some other basis).

30.231   In any event, neither AJA 1999 nor the regulations made under s 30 of that Act state what should happen in the event of non-compliance with those regulations. It is, perhaps, for this reason that there has been little litigation on the issue of regulatory compliance. Non-compliance would probably mean that the receiving party would be precluded from recovering his notional premium, but there is no authority to support the contention that it would have any greater effect than this. Whilst there is no authority on the point, the mechanism by which the notional premium would be rendered irrecoverable would probably be on the straightforward basis that the receiving party ought not to be afforded the benefit of legislation with which he has failed to comply.

30.232   It is worth pausing here to say that compliance with the regulations made under AJA 1999, s 30 has nothing to do with collective conditional fee agreements. In particular, there is no requirement that only bona fide membership organisations may enter into collective conditional fee agreements. Most membership organisations tend to prefer collective conditional fee agreements, but that is a matter of administrative and commercial convenience rather than as a result of the operation of the law.

Membership organisation

30.233   An organisation must be approved before it can hold itself out as a membership organisation; a civil servant known as the certification officer will keep a record of those organisations which have been approved. All unions listed by the certification officer are automatically approved; in addition, about thirteen other organisations have been approved, including a number of professional organisations and cycling organisations.[270]

30.234   In deciding whether to approve an organisation, the Lord Chancellor will take into account the following:[271]

---

[269]   At para 7.3 of the Explanatory Memorandum.

[270]   They are: AA Legal Service, British Cycling Federation, Defence Police Federation, Durham Colliery Overmen Deputies and Shotfirers Retired Members Group, Engineering Employers' Federation, Police Federation of England and Wales, RAC Motoring Services, the Cyclist Touring Club, the London Cycling Campaign, British Triathlon Federation, the Co-operative Group, the National Union of Students and the British Association of Social Workers (personal communication with I Akhtar, Ministry of Justice, 20 July 2009).

[271]   Personal communication with I Akhtar, Ministry of Justice, 20 July 2009.

- whether it exists to protect, defend, represent and promote the interest of its members;
- whether it has an exclusive range of benefits for members;
- whether it offers litigation funding as one of those benefits and on a discretionary basis, at no additional charge;
- whether it publishes annual accounts;
- whether it invests its membership payment within the organisation for the benefit of the members and the organisation; and
- whether it covers all those deemed eligible by the organisation (not only members).

The fact that an organisation is a membership organisation does not preclude it from taking out ATE insurance as opposed to claiming a notional premium. Indeed, some unions prefer to do just that.[272]

Notional premiums

30.235 Notice must be given of an intention to claim a notional premium;[273] whilst there is no authority on the point, the principles already discussed pertaining to notice of funding in other circumstances are likely to apply (see **30.98** and **30.148**). As explained above, reg 5 of the 2005 Regulations provides that the amount payable by an opponent must not exceed the likely cost of 'an insurance policy against the risk of incurring a liability to pay the costs of other parties to the proceedings'. This means that a notional premium ought not to exceed the sum the market would bear for an ATE policy.[274] This restriction is echoed in AJA 1999 itself[275] and in the CPD.[276] The wording of these provisions suggests that the appropriate measure would be premiums for policies providing cover for only the other side's costs, rather than premiums for policies also providing cover for the member's own disbursements; it is debateable, however, whether the difference between the amounts generally charged for the two types of policy would amount to much.

30.236 As of 1 October 2009 CPR, r 44.3B(1)(b) has read as follows:

'Unless the court orders otherwise, a party may not recover as an additional liability ... any provision made by a membership organisation which exceeds the likely cost to that party of the premium of an insurance policy against the risk of incurring a liability to pay the costs of other parties to the proceedings.'

The words 'unless the court orders otherwise' are a new addition; the way in which that amendment has been implemented gives the impression that notional premiums have been caught in the crossfire of an amendment aimed at another target (see **30.89**) and that the court has not been given the vires to exercise its discretion on this point. This is

---

[272] This is particularly common where the union funds a large number of employers' liability cases. They often do so because they believe that it is not possible to claim the costs of covering their own disbursement under a notional premium (see **30.238**).

[273] See CPD, art 32.5(3), which reads: 'If the receiving party claims an additional amount under Section 30 of the Access of Justice Act 1999: a statement setting out the basis upon which the receiving party's liability for the additional amount is calculated.'

[274] Historically, ATE premiums have tended to be higher than notional premiums; this, unfortunately, can lead to somewhat circular arguments about what the appropriate measure should be.

[275] AJA 1999, s 30(3) provides that the notional premium shall not exceed a sum determined in a prescribed manner and that 'there may, in particular, be prescribed as a manner of determination one which takes into account the likely cost to the member or other person of the premium of an insurance policy against the risk of incurring a liability to pay the costs of other parties to the proceedings.'

[276] CPD, arts 32.6 and 11.11.

because the 2005 Regulations have not been amended so as to echo the amendment to the CPR. Although there is no authority on the point, it is likely that reg 5 of the 2005 Regulations prevails (as being the *status quo*) and that the mandatory cap based on the ATE market continues to exist.

30.237 As to the factors to be taken into account, CPD, art 11.11 gives the following guidance:

> 'Where the court is considering a provision made by a membership organisation ... the court will, when assessing the additional liability, have regard to the factors set out in paragraph 11.10 above, in addition to the factors set out in rule 44.5.'

Thus, not only is the notional premium limited to the amount of an equivalent ATE premium, but it is also to be assessed by reference to the same criteria. The court would not have the benefit of an actual premium as to the starting point, so (unless there was evidence as to the going rate) the court, presumably, would have to draw upon its own experience of the ATE market (see **30.213**).

30.238 Not all membership organisations charge notional premiums. Some take the view that it is in their interests (or those of their members) to take out ATE insurance instead. This is often on the basis that an ATE premium will allow recovery for own-disbursement cover whereas notional premiums do not (see **30.235**). Whether this is a good reason for preferring ATE insurance over a notional premium will depend on the facts.[277]

BTE INSURANCE AND ALTERNATIVE MEANS OF FUNDING

30.239 The following discussion addresses alternative means of funding and, in particular, before the event ('BTE') insurance (otherwise known as legal expenses insurance or LEI); it does so in the context of whether the availability of suitable alternative means of funding would have a bearing on the recoverability of an additional liability. The phrase 'funding arrangements' will be used to refer to methods of funding which provide for an additional liability;[278] this includes conditional fee agreements, collective conditional fee agreements, ATE policies and arrangements with membership organisations.

Types of alternative means of funding

30.240 An alternative means of funding is, in the present context, a reference to a means of funding which is not the funding arrangement under consideration. At its broadest (and excluding other funding arrangements), it is a category which may encompass any one of the following:

- private funding (including pre-existing liability insurance) and conditional fee agreements which do not provide for a success fees;
- BTE insurance;
- trade union funding;
- funding through employers;

---

[277] Paying parties usually argue that own-disbursement cover is something that can be taken into account when setting the success fee.
[278] CPR, r 43.2(k).

- public funding;
- litigation funding (ie, third-party funding);
- altruistic funding; and
- pro bono funding.

The relevance of this list is that such a method of funding may, if available, be preferable to a funding arrangement by reason of the alternative means not giving rise to an additional liability. If the court were to find that an alternative means of funding had been unreasonably rejected, the additional liability may be disallowed on the basis that it was unreasonably incurred. It is very likely that the court would find that it was unreasonable to prefer a funding arrangement over any of the last three methods, so, for present purposes, these can be disregarded. The first category (private funding) can also be disregarded; this is because a person is at liberty to enter into such an agreement notwithstanding the fact that he could afford to fund the claim privately (ie there is no means test for funding arrangements).[279] Likewise, the fact that a person has the benefit of liability insurance would not prevent him from reasonably entering into a conditional fee agreement via his insurer.[280] Of the remainder, BTE insurance and trade union funding are the most relevant, as they are the two which are most frequently encountered.

BTE insurance

30.241 Before the event (BTE) insurance protects an insured against the risk of an adverse costs award in the event that he becomes involved in litigation; it is taken out before the dispute arises, hence the name. If BTE insurance was available and suitable for the matter in hand, then the court may disallow or reduce the additional liabilities accordingly. Before the court will do this, the court must be satisfied that a BTE policy existed, that it was reasonably discoverable, and that it was suitable for the purposes of funding the matter in hand. Whether a BTE policy existed will be a matter of fact to be decided on evidence. The paying party is entitled to raise CPR Part 18 Questions on the point,[281] and those are often contained in the points of dispute. Master Hurst has found that the questions which may reasonably and proportionately be asked are: first, whether the receiving party had insurance; secondly, with whom; and thirdly whether he had any legal expenses insurance.[282] Master Hurst's findings were in the context of a modest, unremarkable personal injury claim; they are of persuasive value only.

30.242 The fact that BTE insurance existed would not be determinative of the matter (even if it were suitable: see **30.250**). This is because the receiving party may say that he did not know about it, and that he could not reasonably have been expected to discover it. In order to address that point it is necessary to know the extent and nature of the enquires that a receiving party's solicitor might be expected to make (see below); in that regard, it is useful to know something about the prevalence of BTE insurance.

The prevalence of BTE insurance

30.243 The concept of BTE insurance originated in Continental Europe. It was initially sold by companies who specialised in legal expenses insurance, but in the early

---

[279] *Campbell v MGN Ltd (No 2)* [2005] UKHL 61 at [27].
[280] *Sousa v Waltham Forest London Borough Council* [2011] EWCA Civ 194 [28]–[39].
[281] See CPD, art 35.7.
[282] *Hutchings v The British Transport Police Authority* [2006] EWHC 90064 (Costs) at [23].

1980s it began to be offered by other types of insurer.[283] Associations between insurers became closer, and it became common (as it still is) that it was offered as an adjunct to other financial products, such as household insurance. In the United Kingdom BTE insurance tends to be bundled with motor insurance policies, household insurance policies,[284] and credit card agreements. Stand-alone policies are available, and may be purchased to provide cover to families, landlords, small businesses, commercial organisations, and boat owners.

30.244 BTE insurance purchased as an add-on to household policies will typically afford cover for the following:[285]

- personal injury claims, fatal accident claims and claims for clinical negligence;
- contractual disputes arising out of consumer transactions;
- property disputes (including boundary disputes, nuisance, landlord and tenant, etc); and
- employment disputes, including proceedings in the Employment Tribunal.

Other types of BTE insurance may differ, depending on the circumstances in which they were sold; boat-owners' insurance, for example, might provide cover for marine disputes. BTE insurance, however purchased, may include cover that goes beyond providing benefits for the person who purchased the policy. Policies purchased as an adjunct to motor insurance will often provide cover not only for the driver, but also for passengers. The same may be true of insurance purchased to provide liability cover for a public service vehicle. Members of the same household may be entitled to cover, even where they are not members of the same family. The breadth of cover is probably a reflection of the fact that BTE insurers see value in persons who have viable claims, and that they may be able to charge fees for referring claims to their panel solicitors.[286]

BTE inquiries

30.245 Speaking extrajudicially, Jackson LJ made the following comments about the importance of BTE inquiries in the context of modern litigation:[287]

> 'The first question which any litigation solicitor should, and would, ask of a client with a claim in the categories mentioned in paragraph **[30.237]** above is whether the client has household insurance and, if so, what are its terms. Indeed solicitors are required, as a matter of professional conduct, to discuss with their clients at the outset whether the client's costs are covered by insurance.'

The extent to which a solicitor is expected to conduct speculative enquiries for the purposes of discovering suitable BTE insurance will depend on the facts and, in particular, will depend on the amount at stake.[288] Phillips MR has given guidance on

---

[283] For a full historical perspective, see D Jenkins *The History of Insurance* (Pickering & Chatto (Publishers) Ltd, 2000).

[284] Of the 25m households in the United Kingdom in 2008, between 10m and 15m have BTE insurance as an add-on to household insurance: see R Jackson *Review of Civil Litigation Costs: Final Report* (TSO, December 2009), para 8.5.1.

[285] R Jackson *Review of Civil Litigation Costs: Final Report* (TSO, December 2009), para 8.5.2.

[286] See the discussion of this in R Jackson *Review of Civil Litigation Costs: Final Report* (TSO, December 2009), chapter 20.

[287] R Jackson *Review of Civil Litigation Costs: Final Report* (TSO, December 2009), para 8.5.5; the reference to professional obligations was a reference to para 2.03(1)(d)(ii) of the *Solicitors Code of Conduct 2007*.

[288] *Sarwar v Alam* [2001] EWCA Civ 1401 at [46]; while the test being addressed was itself not the same as the

this topic, but it is limited to unremarkable, modest road traffic accident cases and should not to be treated as being an inflexible code.[289] He had the following to say:[290]

> '[P]roper modern practice dictates that a solicitor should normally invite a client to bring to the first interview any relevant motor insurance policy, any household insurance policy and any stand-alone BTE insurance policy belonging to the client and/or any spouse or partner living in the same household as the client.'

30.246 The exact nature of the enquires would need to be adapted to suit the circumstances. Dyson LJ has explained that Phillips MR's guidance would have no application in high-volume, low-value work of the type referred by claims management companies.[291] Phillips MR himself was at pains to point out that solicitors were not obliged to conduct treasure hunts.[292]

30.247 In so far as credit cards are concerned, Phillips MR gave the following advice:[293]

> 'So far as credit cards and charge cards are concerned ... [we] are inclined to think that the time taken by a solicitor in assisting a client to identify and pursue such cover would at present be likely to result in this course proving more expensive than an ATE premium in this class of case.'

Whilst he indicated that the financial landscape might, at some point, change so as to justify such enquiries, there is nothing to suggest that this has yet happened.

30.248 The standard of the requisite enquiries is not the same as the standard of enquiries required by reg 4 of the Conditional Fee Agreements Regulations 2000,[294] nor is it the same as the standard applicable to claims in negligence.[295] Presumably, the same applies to the professional standard. However, it is unlikely that a failure to achieve a proper professional standard would be regarded as being reasonable, so to that extent the professional standard is of some relevance. Prior to 6 October 2011 the requisite standard was to discuss with the client 'whether [his] liability for another party's costs may be covered by existing insurance;[296] this did not add a great deal to an unadorned test of reasonableness. The same is true of the provisions on and after 6 October 2011.[297]

---

present test, *Myatt v National Coal Board* [2006] Civ 1017 at [73]–[76] gives some guidance as to factors which may be relevant, such as the nature of the circumstances in which the solicitor was instructed, the nature of the claim, and the cost of the alternative (ie ATE insurance).

[289] *Sarwar v Alam* [2001] EWCA Civ 1401 at [50].

[290] *Sarwar v Alam* [2001] EWCA Civ 1401 at [45].

[291] *Myatt v National Coal Board* [2006] EWCA Civ 1017 at [70].

[292] *Sarwar v Alam* [2001] EWCA Civ 1401 at [46].

[293] *Sarwar v Alam* [2001] EWCA Civ 1401 at [49].

[294] *Myatt v National Coal Board* [2006] EWCA Civ 1017 at [70].

[295] *Sarwar v Alam* [2001] EWCA Civ 1401 at [51]; this is of practical relevance because it means that a client who failed to recover his ATE premium by reason of inadequate BTE inquiries might be able to bring a claim against his solicitor.

[296] *Solicitors Code of Conduct 2007*, para 2.03(1)(g).

[297] IB(1.16) of the SRA Code of Conduct 2011 reads requires the solicitor to discuss 'how the client will pay, including whether public funding may be available, whether the client has insurance that might cover the fees, and whether the fees may be paid by someone else such as a trade union.'

30.249 Enquiries should not be curtailed or avoided merely because the person of whom they are made is also an opposing party (such as where the claimant was injured in a car being driven by the defendant). Phillips MR explained that each case must turn on its own facts:[298]

> 'Now that motor insurance often contains provision for BTE cover for a claim brought by a passenger, the solicitor should ordinarily ask the client passenger to obtain a copy of the driver's insurance policy, if reasonably practicable. Whether it is reasonably practicable to comply with the solicitor's request is likely to be fact-sensitive.'

Suitability

30.250 The existence of a BTE policy will be relevant only if it would have been a suitable method of funding the claim in question. Whether a BTE policy was suitable would be a matter of both contractual interpretation and reasonableness. This is because there may be factual or legal restrictions on the way in which it can be used. In particular, the insurer may stipulate that a panel solicitor should have conduct of the claim rather than the solicitor who was the client's first choice. This is a subject where the facts can readily overshadow the niceties of the law (see **30.251–30.253**). In particular, the receiving party may find that, notwithstanding his rights in law, he has been unable to enforce those rights because of a lack of co-operation on the part of the BTE insurer. These issues are usually highly fact-sensitive.

Restrictions on the use of BTE insurance

30.251 By the operation of an EU directive,[299] a person who has the benefit of BTE insurance must be able to choose the lawyer who will act for him.[300] That directive is given domestic implementation by secondary legislation,[301] namely, the Insurance Companies (Legal Expenses Insurance) Regulations 1990;[302] those regulations will apply to the most commonly-encountered types of BTE insurance.[303] For present purposes, the most relevant provisions are at reg 6:[304]

---

[298] *Sarwar v Alam* [2001] EWCA Civ 1401 at [47].

[299] This was originally, EU Council Directive 87/344/EEC; that Directive will be prospectively repealed with effect from 1 November 2012. It will be replaced with EC Directive 2009/138. It is anticipated that the new Directive will be implemented into domestic law in 2013 and will become fully operative in January 2014: see the *Financial Times*, 5 October 2011, p 21. The differences between the old and new Directives is not significant for the purposes of the matters discussed in this chapter.

[300] The wording of the relevant part of that directive is as follows:
'6(1) Where under a legal expenses insurance contract recourse is had to a lawyer (or other person having such qualifications as may be necessary) to defend, represent or serve the interests of the insured in any inquiry or proceedings, the insured shall be free to choose that lawyer (or other person).
(2) The insured shall also be free to choose a lawyer (or other person having such qualifications as may be necessary) to serve his interests whenever a conflict of interests arises.
(3) The above rights shall be expressly recognised in the policy.'

[301] That legislation is made under s 2(2) of the European Communities Act 1972.

[302] SI 1990/1159.

[303] The exceptions are: (i) legal expenses insurance contracts concerning disputes or risks arising out of, or in connection with, the use of sea-going vessels, (ii) where the cover is for the purpose of defending or representing the insured in an inquiry or proceedings which is at the same time done in the insurer's own interest under such cover, or (iii) cover provided by an assistance insurer where that cover is provided under a contract of which the principal object is the provision of assistance for persons who fall into difficulties while travelling, while away from home or while away from their permanent residence and where the costs are incurred outside the state in which the insured normally resides: see reg 3.

[304] This regulation does not apply to insurance in relation to seagoing vessels, to insurance provided as a benefit to motorists of being in organisations such as the AA or the RAC (see reg 7).

'(1) Where under a legal expenses insurance contract recourse is had to a lawyer (or other person having such qualifications as may be necessary) to defend, represent or serve the interests of the insured in any inquiry or proceedings, the insured shall be free to choose that lawyer (or other person).

(2) The insured shall also be free to choose a lawyer (or other person having such qualifications as may be necessary) to serve his interests whenever a conflict of interests arises.

(3) The above rights shall be expressly recognised in the policy.'

The regulations go on to provide that policies must mention the right of the insured to have recourse to arbitration in the event of a dispute arising between him and the insurer.[305] They also stipulate the structure of the policy,[306] and they make provision for managing potential conflict of interest.[307]

30.252 The European Court of Justice has confirmed that an insured has a right to engage a lawyer[308] of his own choice.[309] That decision (*Eschig v UNIQA Sachversicherung AG*) is frequently cited, but often incorrectly; the following is a summary of what the ECJ actually said (and, more importantly, of what it did not say):[310]

- firstly, contrary to what is often reported, there was *no* express discussion about the stage at which a right to choose accrues;
- the court did, however, distinguish between a number of distinct rights of election:
  — A specific individual right of election which arises in every case where proceedings are issued (which can be referred to as 'the right in proceedings');
  — A specific individual right of election which arise in every case where there is a conflict of interest (hereinafter referred to as 'the right in conflict'); and

---

[305] See reg 8.

[306] Legal expenses cover must be contained in a separate policy (reg 4(a)) or, where that cover is provided under a policy relating to one or more other classes of general insurance business, a separate section of the policy relating to that cover only (reg 4(b)) and specifying the nature of that cover (reg 4).

[307] Regulation 5 reads as follows: '(1) An insurance company carrying on legal expenses insurance business shall adopt at least one of the following arrangements.
(2) The company shall ensure that no member of staff who is concerned with the management of claims under legal expenses insurance contracts, or with legal advice in respect of such claims, carries on at the same time any similar activity—
(a) in relation to another class of general insurance business carried on by the company, or
(b) in any other insurance company, having financial, commercial or administrative links with the first company, which carries on one or more other classes of general insurance business.
(3) The company shall entrust the management of claims under legal expenses insurance contracts to an undertaking having separate legal personality, which shall be mentioned in the separate policy or section referred to in regulation 4.
If that undertaking has financial, commercial or administrative links with another insurance company which carries on one or more other classes of general insurance business, members of the staff of the undertaking who are concerned with the processing of claims, or with providing legal advice connected with such processing, shall not pursue the same or a similar activity in that other insurance company at the same time.
(4) The company shall, in the policy, afford the insured the right to entrust the defence of his interests, from the moment that he has the right to claim from the insurer under the policy, to a lawyer of his choice or, to the extent that the law of the relevant forum so permits, to any other appropriately qualified person.'

[308] HHJ Seymour (sitting as a judge of the High Court) has confirmed that this would include counsel in the context of direct public access: *Pine v DAS Legal Expenses Insurance Co Ltd* [2011] EWHC 658 (QB).

[309] *Eschig v UNIQA Sachversicherung AG* (2009) Case C-199/08, ECJ.

[310] This summary is the author's interpretation of Eschig; it ought not be given any greater status than that.

— A conditional right which will arise if the domestic regulator and/or the insurer chooses one particular method of avoiding conflict of interest (hereinafter referred to as 'the conditional right');

• the principal argument that the ECJ had to decide was whether the right in proceedings was in some way tied to the conditional right in such a way as to make them both conditional;[311] the court rejected that argument;

• in coming to that conclusion, the ECJ specifically commented on the fact that the various rights were distinct; and

• finally, the ECJ stated that any contractual terms which sought to limit the right of election would be in breach of the directive.

Thus *Eschig* is not authority for the proposition that an insured is always permitted to exercise a right to choose his lawyer; indeed, the fact that the ECJ distinguished between the various ways in which the right may arise goes against the proposition that there is a blanket right that will apply in all circumstances. It is not surprising that *Eschig* is often mis-cited given the fact that when it was handed down, the Financial Services Authority (FSA) gave guidance that needed to be retracted and corrected (see the footnotes for details).[312] In any event, the ECJ has, in a subsequent case, clarified that the right to choose may be curtailed in some circumstances.[313] There have also been domestic decisions of note; in particular, Burton J has ruled that if a client exercises a right to choose, the fees payable by the insurer to the lawyer will be assessed in a way that he descried as being 'a hybrid, neither an ordinary assessment, only taking account of the factors in CPR 44, nor an assessment specifically adopting [the rate that the insurer usually pays]'.[314] It has yet to be seen what effect this approach will have on the industry at large.[315]

30.253 At the time of writing, most BTE insurers were continuing to resist attempts by clients to exercise a pre-issue right to choose. Speaking extrajudicially, Jackson LJ has

---

[311] Specifically, the question the ECJ set itself was as follows: 'Is Article 4(1) of Council Directive 87/344 ... to be interpreted to the effect that it precludes a clause, contained in the standard terms and conditions of insurance of a legal expenses insurer, which entitles the insurer, in respect of insurance claims concerning losses suffered by a large number of insured persons as a result of the same event (for example the insolvency of an investment services undertaking), to select a legal representative and which thereby restricts the right of the individual insured person to choose his own lawyer (so-called 'mass torts clause')?'

[312] Prior to *Eschig*, the Financial Services Ombudsman interpreted the 1990 regulations as meaning that the right to choose is triggered only when negotiations have been completed and proceedings have to be begun (see the decisions of the Insurance Ombudsman against Cornhill Insurance plc of 3 May 2002 and against DAS, of 17 June 2002). The FSA's reaction to Eschig was to overstate its effect (see the letter from Mr K Hogg to insurers dated July 2010), and in particular, it wrongly stated that *Eschig* was authority for the proposition that the right to choose arose before proceedings had been begun. This needed to be corrected following criticism by the insurance industry (see, for example, M Lee 'Freedom Fighters' *Solicitors Journal*, 4 October 2010). That correction was effected by way of the FSA issuing a revised letter (dated 12 August 2010) which included explanatory footnotes. Those footnotes are not entirely clear, and this has led some commentators to say that even now, the FSA's guidance is confused and ambiguous.

[313] *Stark v DAS Oesterreiche Algemeine Rechtsschutzversicherung AG* [2011] Case C-293/10, in which the court said this (at [33]): 'Consequently, freedom of choice ... does not mean that Member States are obliged to require insurers, in all circumstances, to cover in full the costs incurred in connection with the defence of an insured person, irrespective of the place where the person professionally entitled to represent that person is established in relation to the court of administrative authority with jurisdiction to deal with a dispute, on condition that that freedom is not rendered meaningless. That would be the case if the restriction imposed on the payment of those costs were to render de facto impossible a reasonable choice of representative by the insured person. In any event, it is for the national courts, if an action is brought before them in this regard, to determine whether or not there is any such restriction.'

[314] *Brown-Quinn & Anor v Equity Syndicate Management Ltd & Anor* [2011] EWHC 2661 (Comm) at [27].

[315] Burton J gave permission to appeal; that appeal was lodged in November 2011.

urged a change in the regulations to give clients greater choice,[316] but at the time of writing, no such changes had been made. This means that unless proceedings have already been issued, an insured will find it difficult to persuade his insurer to allow him to exercise a right to choose; given the fact that very few claims will have been issued at the stage when the client gives his first instructions to a lawyer, the practical effect of restricting the right to choose in his way is significant. In particular, a client with BTE insurance may – for all practical purposes – be required to choose between using his insurance cover and instructing a panel firm, or not using it but instead instructing a lawyer of his own choice under a conditional fee agreement.[317] If he chooses the latter, and if the court subsequently finds that he ought to have chosen the former, he is likely to fail to recover additional liabilities. Each case will turn on its own facts, however, and the restrictions imposed by the insurer may have consequences that would make it reasonable for the receiving party to reject BTE funding. An example might be where there were no panel solicitors who were reasonably local to the receiving party.[318] The considerations at **28.41** (concerning hourly rates) might well be relevant by analogy. The size of the claim is also likely to be a relevant factor.[319]

Suitability generally

30.254 Phillips MR has explained that if a claimant possesses pre-existing BTE cover which appears to be suitable, then in the ordinary course of events the claimant should be referred to the BTE insurer. He made it clear that that guidance was specifically limited to small, personal injury claims in which the value of the claim would be likely to be no more than about £5,000.[320]

30.255 It may be that the limit of cover is too low to fund the whole of the claim. Where this is so, it may be reasonable to set up a different form of funding entirely, but, equally, it may be reasonable to exhaust the policy first. Another option would be to combine the policy with other methods of funding.[321] Each case will turn on its own facts. Policies may also include conditions that make it difficult or impossible to make a claim for the purposes of the matter in hand; that said it is not uncommon for the court to read such conditions restrictively.[322]

---

[316] R Jackson *Review of Civil Litigation Costs: Final Report* (TSO, December 2009), para 8.6.3. The change he advocated was not one of his formal recommendations.

[317] Burton J has found that an insured has the right to change lawyers (see *Brown-Quinn & Anor v Equity Syndicate Management Ltd & Anor* [2011] EWHC 2661 (Comm) at [29] *et seq*); he gave permission to appeal that decision. At the time of writing, that appeal was pending.

[318] *Chappell v De Bora's of Exeter (A Firm)* [2004] EWHC 90020 (Costs), per HHJ Overend; despite the 'EWHC' reference, this was a county court case and is not binding.

[319] In this regard, Philips MR had this to say (*Sarwar v Alam* [2001] EWCA Civ 1401 at [56]): 'We are not … persuaded by the … contention that there is such a strong public interest in maintaining a client's freedom of choice of legal adviser that this should override the appropriateness of a claim as small as that with which we are concerned on this appeal being handled by a BTE insurer with or without the assistance of a panel solicitor. The philosophy contained in CPR, r 1.1(2)(c), and the express provisions of CPR, r 44.5, require the court to ensure that no costs are incurred which are not reasonable and proportionate.' See also *R v Legal Aid Board ex p Duncan* [2000] COD 159 which dealt with a similar issue in the context of public funding.

[320] *Sarwar v Alam* [2001] EWCA Civ 1401 at [41].

[321] See, for example, *Smith v Interlink Express Parcels Ltd* [2007] EWHC 90095 (Costs), where counsel's success fee was justified on the basis that it was reasonable to use the limited BTE cover on counsel, but instead to fund counsel by way of a conditional fee agreement. This case is not binding.

[322] An example is *Laker Vent Engineering Ltd v Templeton Insurance Ltd* [2009] EWCA Civ 62, in which the policy stipulated that the insurer be notified as soon as the insured became aware of any event which had given or was likely to give rise to a construction claim; Aikens LJ found that that stage would be reached only where adjudication, arbitration or litigation was likely to be required to resolve the dispute.

30.256   An issue that may arise is whether a claimant may reasonably reject funding afforded by the defendant's BTE policy. In the context of low-value, modest personal injury claims Phillips MR has said that the claimant would be expected not to reject that form of funding, but that if the defendant were to fail to co-operate, that would be sufficient reason to justify eschewing it.[323] Again, each case will turn on its own facts.[324]

Trade union funding

30.257   Trade unions and professional organisations often provide, as a benefit of membership, legal assistance for their members and families of their members. In most cases, the body concerned would both seek a notional premium under AJA 1999, s 30 and a success fee, so it is arguable that the availability of such a form of funding should make no difference to the recoverability of any additional liability.

Employer funding

30.258   Employers may provide legal expenses funding as a perquisite but, unless the employer is itself a firm of solicitors, that benefit is usually provided in the form of BTE insurance. The fact that the employee has to pay tax on the benefit received has made employer funding a relative rarity.

---

[323]   *Sarwar v Alam* [2001] EWCA Civ 1401 at [48].
[324]   *Sarwar v Alam* [2001] EWCA Civ 1401 at [48].

Chapter 31

DISBURSEMENTS

INTRODUCTION

31.1 'Disbursements are money paid on behalf of the client'.[1] This is true of most disbursements, but it does not include all types of disbursements, and perhaps a better definition is disbursements are those monies that are not profit costs[2] or taxes but that can properly be included within a bill of costs.[3] In so far as costs between opposing parties are concerned, disbursements include the following:

- monies paid by the solicitor for goods or services which the solicitor is by law or by custom required to disburse ('actual disbursements', also often known as professional disbursements);
- fees charged by persons other than the solicitor (such as an expert) which the solicitor passes on directly to the client ('services disbursements');
- the solicitor's rechargeable expenses (such as the costs of photocopying carried out by a bureau) ('true expenses');
- expenses of a similar nature to those mentioned above, but incurred by the client (such as where a client pays an expert directly) ('client's disbursement'); and
- expenses charged by the solicitor for administrative services (such as charges for photocopying carried out in house) ('office disbursements').

This categorisation does not exist in law, but exists only for the purpose of describing the law. There is considerable overlap between these categories: in particular, the first category (actual disbursements) includes both services disbursements and true expenses (see the diagram below). Each category is considered in turn.

---

[1] *Browne v Barber* [1913] 2 KB 553 at 573, per Vaughan Williams LJ.
[2] This would now have to include success fees.
[3] See *Joel v Barnato* (1929) 45 TLR 167.

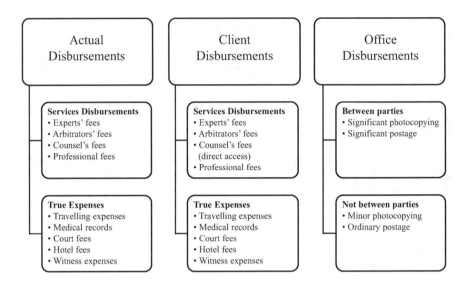

Actual disbursements

31.2   Actual disbursements may be identified as being those payments a solicitor is bound either by law or by custom to make.[4] Whilst there is no judicial authority on the point, it is said that in the absence of express authority from the client, they are disbursements that may be incurred with the client's implied authority.[5] They include stamp duty,[6] purchase money,[7] estate duty[8] and deposits.[9] Confusingly, monies described as being actual disbursements in some authorities may also include monies which would not be regarded as being costs,[10] but those can be disregarded for present purposes. The distinction between what is and is not an actual disbursement was explained by Langdale MR:[11]

> 'It appears to me, that it is the practice of solicitors, who may have to pay or advance money on behalf of their clients, carefully to distinguish such professional disbursements as ought to be entered in their bill of costs, from such other advances or payments, as ought to be entered only in their cash accounts, as cash payments or advances. And it seems to me a very reasonable and proper rule, that those payments only, which are made in pursuance of the professional duty undertaken by the solicitor, and which he is bound to perform, or which are sanctioned as professional payments, by the general and established custom and practice of the profession, ought to be entered or allowed as professional disbursements in the bill of costs.'

---

4   See, for example, *Re Remnant* (1849) 11 Beav 603 at 611.
5   See R Quick *Quick on Costs* (Thomson Reuters) at [2.920].
6   *Re Blair and Girling* [1906] 2 KB 131.
7   *Re Remnant* (1849) 11 Beav 603.
8   *Re Kingdon and Wilson* [1902] 2 Ch 242.
9   *Re Buckwell and Berkeley* [1902] 2 Ch 596.
10   Such as debt or damages; see *Re Fletcher and Dyson* [1903] 2 Ch 688 and *Prothero v Thomas* (1815) 6 Taunt 196.
11   *In re Remnant* (1849) 11 Beav 603 at 613; this decision was endorsed by the Court of Appeal in *Buckwill v Berkley* [1902] 2 Ch D 596.

Thus, a payment made by a solicitor on behalf of a client will not become a disbursement merely by reason of it being made by the solicitor rather than the client.[12] Where the solicitor is not bound by law or custom to make it, a payment made on behalf of the client would not be a disbursement and it would not appear in the solicitor's bill; instead, it will merely appear as an entry in the client account.

Services disbursements

31.3 Services disbursements are monies paid to third parties for services. It is a category that overlaps the category of actual disbursements in that were the solicitor pays for services in circumstances in which custom or professional etiquette requires him to make that payment, it will be an actual (professional) disbursement.[13] There is also overlap with client disbursements in that services disbursements may be monies for which the client is responsible (see **31.5**). Examples of services disbursement would include experts' fees, accountancy fees, counsel's fees, etc. Services disbursements must be distinguished from those monies paid by a solicitor to an agent for the procurement of services which are then accounted for as if they had been provided by the solicitor himself (see **12.8–12.19**); those monies will be absorbed by the solicitor's own practice as being practice expenses. A solicitor may wish to account for those services in this way because he may be able to make a profit, both in terms of enhanced base costs[14] and in terms of a success fee.[15] Whether a solicitor is entitled to account for services in this way (or is required to do so) will depend on the nature of the services (ie they must be legal services which the solicitor could have provided himself); there must also be a degree of supervision; this was explained by May LJ:[16]

> '[A] characteristic of such work [ie work which may be recharged as profit costs] is whether the solicitor remains responsible to the client for its proper conduct.'

This is a topic which is explored in more detail in Chapter 12 (at **12.2–12.19** in particular).

True expenses

31.4 The label 'true expenses' is self-explanatory. It is a category which includes out-of-pocket expenses such as hotel bills, parking fees, tolls, etc. Where the sums involved are modest, true expenses may be challenged on the basis that, given the hourly rate, the solicitor can be expected to bear the costs himself.[17] The CPD makes provision for this in respect of local travelling expenses, postage and copying fees.[18] The CPD does not govern the position between solicitor and client, however: that is governed by the terms of the retainer. Thus, it is entirely plausible that an expense may be categorised as being a true expense as between solicitor and client, but not between opposing parties.

---

[12] The act of giving express authority will not make a disbursement into an actual disbursement: *Re Page (No 3)* (1863) 32 Beav 487; 55 ER 190; *Re Blair & Girling* [1906] 2 KB 131 at 137–138; *Re Fletcher & Dyson* [1903] 2 Ch 688 at 693; and *Re Porter Amphlett & Jones* [1912] 2 Ch 98.

[13] This is not an immutable category; it has been held, for example, that fees for shorthand notes are monies that have become payable by the solicitor who requests them, and that as such, they are actual disbursements: *Cocks v Bruce Searl & Good* (1904) 21 TLR 62.

[14] *Smith Graham v Lord Chancellor's Department* [1999] 2 Costs LR 1.

[15] *Crane v Cannons Leisure Centre* [2007] EWCA Civ 1352.

[16] *Crane v Cannons Leisure Centre* [2007] EWCA Civ 1352 at [14], Maurice Kay LJ dissenting.

[17] This is often referred to as absorbing the expenses within the solicitor's overhead.

[18] Local travelling expenses (CPD, art 4.16(3)); postage and courier's fee (CPD, art 4.16(4)); and copying charges (CPD, art 4.16(5)).

Client's disbursements

31.5   A client's disbursement (which, when paid via the agency of a solicitor, is known as a non-professional disbursement[19]) is a sum of money paid by the client (either personally, or by some other person acting on his behalf) for services of provisions pertaining to the litigation. An example would be where the client had agreed to pay an expert directly, or where he agreed to bear a witness's travel expenses. Client's disbursements are recoverable regardless of whether there is an enforceable retainer.[20] They may be paid through the agency of the solicitor; where this is done, they may be distinguished from an actual disbursement by virtue of the fact that the solicitor will have no duty to disburse the disbursements.[21] If there is a dispute as to whether an item included within a bill is an actual disbursement or a client disbursement, then the burden will lie with the solicitor to prove that it is properly chargeable as an actual disbursement.[22] Client disbursements will, where appropriate, appear in the cash account, but the cash account itself does not have a bearing on whether a disbursement is an actual disbursement or a client disbursement;[23] in particular, the fact that a client has put his solicitor in funds for a disbursement (such as counsel's fees) will not generally have a bearing on whether that disbursement is or is not an actual disbursement.[24]

Office disbursements

31.6   Offices disbursements are notional sums charged by the solicitor for the supply of goods or services which are ancillary to the supply of professional legal services. Office disbursements include charges for services like in-house photocopying. It is a moot point whether office disbursements are true disbursements at all; it could be said that they are a type of profit cost which is not based on time.[25] There is a degree of overlap with true expenses, and the points made at **31.4** also apply to office disbursements. Indeed, some charges may be placed in either category (such as mileage or rounded-up postal charges).

EXPERT WITNESSES

31.7   An expert is a person who has expertise beyond that which is possessed by laymen. An expert may be an expert witness or an advisory expert. The former will prepare a report which will be relied upon by the party instructing him (or, if he is a joint expert, by both parties) and which may be used as evidence, whereas the latter will advise the party by whom he is instructed (about matters such as the merits of the claim, cross-examination, etc), but will not give evidence.

---

[19]   See, for example, R Quick R *Quick on Costs* (Thomson Reuters) at [2.930].

[20]   *Hollins v Russell* [2003] EWCA Civ 718 at [114]–[115].

[21]   *See In re Remnant* (1849) 11 Beav 603 at 613 and *Re Buckwell and Berkley* [1902] 2 Ch D 596; see **31.2**.

[22]   *Re Blair & Girling* [1906] 2 KB 131 at 139. If a disbursement has been included in bills which have been assessed, then that will be compelling evidence that the disbursement is an actual disbursement: *Re Blair & Girling* [1906] 2 KB 131 at 138.

[23]   *Re Remnant* (1849) 11 Beav 603 at 612.

[24]   *Re Seal; Ex parte Crickett* (1893) 37 SJ 685 at 842 and *Devereux v White* (1896) 13 TLR 52.

[25]   The relevance of this is that it is arguable that a success fee might be payable on them.

Recoverability of experts' fees in principle

31.8 An expert's fee is recoverable in principle as a disbursement;[26] the costs of attending upon him are recoverable as profit costs.[27] A number of miscellaneous points are made about experts' fees in general.

Restrictions by way of order

31.9 The court may impose a restriction on an expert's fees at the time the costs order is made. In particular, the court has the power to limit the expert's fees, or, where the expert fails to answer CPR Part 35 Questions, to disallow his fees altogether.[28] Likewise, if fees were incurred at a time when there was no permission and necessity for expert evidence, then the court may disallow those fees.[29]

Area of expertise

31.10 It is trite law that an expert must confine his evidence to matters within the area of his expertise.[30] If he fails to do this, it will be open to the court to disallow his fees on the bases of relevance and reasonableness.

No need for retainer with expert

31.11 There is no need for the receiving party to prove the existence of a retainer with the expert; this is because the solicitor is personally liable as a matter of professional good practice and etiquette to discharge the fees of any expert he has engaged.[31]

In-house experts

31.12 The fact that an advisory expert may be in-house would not necessarily preclude recovery of his fees (assuming, of course, that the work done was not merely marshalling the facts).[32] Where the costs of engaging that person are not recoverable as costs, then it is possible that they may be recovered as damages; that is an issue which is beyond the scope of this book, but the relevant authorities are mentioned in the footnotes.[33]

Conditional or contingency funding of experts

31.13 Lord Phillips MR has explained that it would be 'very rare indeed' for the court to permit an expert witness to be remunerated in such a way that his fees would be dependent on his client's success (this being because such an arrangement would be

---

[26] *Crane v Cannons Leisure Centre* [2007] EWCA Civ 1352 at [7] and *Re Remnant* (1849) 11 Beav 603 at 613.

[27] CPD, art 4.6(3) specifically provides that time is allowed for attending upon experts.

[28] See CPR, rr 35.4(4) and 35.6(4).

[29] See, for example, *LPI (Hotels) Ltd v Technical & General Guarantee Co SA* [2010] EWHC 2049 (TCC), in which Akenhead J found that the fees had been speculatively incurred.

[30] *Whitehouse v Jordan* [1981] 1 WLR 246 at 256.

[31] *Young v Leighton* (unreported) 1969, QBD, Mocatta J.

[32] *Re Nossen's Patent* [1969] 1 All ER 775; see *Richards & Wallington (Plant Hire) Ltd v Monk & Co* (1984) Costs LR, Core vol 79 at 83, where the costs were found to be irrecoverable by reason of the work being marshalling factual evidence; see **29.78–29.85** for a further discussion.

[33] See **5.27–5.33** for a general discussion; see also *Admiral Management Services Ltd v Para-Protect Europe Ltd* [2002] EWHC 233 (Ch); *R+V Versicherung AG v Risk Insurance and Reinsurance Solutions SA (No 3)* [2006] EWHC 42 (Comm); and *Aerospace Publishing Ltd v Thames Water Utilities Ltd* [2007] EWCA Civ 3.

champertous). Advisory experts are in a different position: where a professional's role is limited to advisory work, then (whilst each case will be decided on its own facts) it would not necessarily be unlawful for that person to be paid on a conditional basis. Indeed, it may even be permissible for payment to be based on the amount recovered.[34]

Agreements to limit experts' fees

31.14 Phillips J has accepted as being desirable an agreement that an expert would limit his fees to those which where are assessed by the court; although the point was not argued before Phillips J, this would, in an appropriate case, need to be on the basis that the expert would be paid regardless of whether the case was won or lost (otherwise the law of champerty may make that agreement unlawful: see **31.13**).[35]

Medical and reporting agencies

31.15 This topic is addressed at **31.62–31.69**.

Whether it was reasonable to instruct the expert

31.16 The court has an affirmative duty to restrict expert evidence to that which is reasonably required to resolve the proceedings.[36] Alternatives to the traditional order that both parties have their own experts include the following: (i) that there be single joint experts,[37] (ii) that there be one expert and written questions,[38] (iii) that there be experts who meet and prepare a joint statement,[39] (iv) that there be experts who 'hot-tub',[40] (v) that there be no experts and that the court relies on assessors instead.[41] Whether it was reasonable to instruct (or reinstruct) the expert will turn on the facts of each case, but one factor which is particularly relevant is whether the receiving party had permission to rely on the expert and, if so, in what capacity (see **31.23–31.26**). In this regard, CPR, r 35.4 may be relevant:

'(1) No party may call an expert or put in evidence an expert's report without the court's permission.

(2) When parties apply for permission they must identify—

(a) the field in which expert evidence is required; and
(b) where practicable, the name of the proposed expert.

(3) If permission is granted under this rule it shall be in relation only to the expert named or the field identified under paragraph (2).'

Thus, the assessment of an expert's costs may need to take into account not only the fact of his instruction, but also his identity (see **31.26**) and the field his evidence covers.

---

[34] *R (on the application of Factortame) v Secretary of State for Transport (No 2)* [2002] EWCA Civ 932; the 'very rare' extract is at [73].
[35] *Cementation Construction Ltd v Keaveney* (1988) *The Independent*, July 12.
[36] CPR, r 35.1.
[37] CPR, r 35.7.
[38] CPR, r 35.6.
[39] CPR, r 35.12.
[40] This means that experts are examined at the same time: see J Ames 'Hot-tubbing: cutting costs and time: will experts appearing together in the witness box help to simplify complex trials' *The Times*, March 10, 2011, Law 59.
[41] CPR, r 35.15.

31.17 The fact that a party had permission to rely on an expert does not mean that all, or indeed any, of the expert's fees will necessarily be allowed; the topic of when expert evidence is reasonably required is beyond the scope of this book, but the following points can be made.

Relevance of pre-action protocols

31.18 Where a pre-action protocol contemplates the use of an expert, the court may take that guidance into account when deciding whether it was reasonable to instruct an expert. Hughes LJ has commented that each case must be decided on its own facts, and that guidance such as that would not be determinative of the matter.[42]

Replacing experts and obtaining further expert evidence

31.19 A party may be dissatisfied with his expert's evidence (or with the evidence of an expert he has jointly instructed). Where this is so, he may wish to instruct a further expert. Whilst he was dealing with substantive litigation rather than costs, Neuberger J identified the following factors as being relevant to whether it would be reasonable to seek further expert evidence:[43]

- the nature of the issue or issues;
- the number of issues between the parties;
- the reason for requiring the new expert;
- the amount at stake or the nature of the issues at stake and their importance;
- the effect of permitting one party to call further expert evidence on the conduct of the trial;
- any delay caused in the proceedings;
- any other special features; and
- the overall justice to the parties in the context of the litigation.

Whilst there is no authority on the point, this list seems ideal for the purpose of considering the costs of a further expert.

Multiple experts

31.20 Even before the introduction of the CPR, the court was loath to tolerate a multiplicity of experts; as long ago as the early twentieth century it was noted that the costs of three experts in one discipline could be justified only in exceptional cases.[44] Under the CPR the court has an affirmative duty to restrict expert evidence to that which is reasonably required to resolve the proceedings.[45] That said, the court also has a duty to ensure a level playing field (see **31.22**). Particular restrictions apply on the small claims track and the fast track.[46]

---

[42]   *BCC v Avril Lee* [2008] EWCA Civ 891 at [37(iii)].

[43]   *Cosgrove v Pattison* (2001) *The Times*, February 13.

[44]   *Graigola Merthyr Co Ltd v Swansea Corporation* [1927] WN 30, per Tomlin J; Lord Hanworth MR made it clear that Tomlin J's comments should not be taken to be setting a tariff, but he reaffirmed the court's desire to restrict the use of experts to those who are necessary (*Frankenburg v Famous Lasky Film Service Ltd* [1931] 1 Ch 428).

[45]   CPR, r 35.1.

[46]   CPR, r 35.3A reads: 'Where a claim has been allocated to the small claims track or the fast track, if permission is given for expert evidence, it will normally be given for evidence from only one expert on a particular issue.'

Unused expert material and mulitiple draft reports

31.21 The fact that a witness's evidence is not used is a factor to be taken into account, but it does not preclude the recovery of fees.[47] Although it related to the incidence of costs rather than the ascertainment of costs, Smith LJ found that the costs of medical reports which had been abandoned because the expert had been 'outclassed and outgunned' by an opponent's expert ought not to be recoverable.[48] Peter Smith J declined to interfere with reductions made where an expert repeatedly was asked to redraft reports by the lawyers who instructed him; indeed, Peter Smith J was critical of such conduct.[49]

Comparison with opponent's experts

31.22 The CPR is based on the premise that the parties play on a level playing field. Where an opponent has instructed more than one expert in a particular discipline, or where an opponent has access to persons who may give expert or quasi-expert assistance, then the court would be able to take those facts into account when deciding the reasonableness of the receiving party's actions.[50]

Experts instructed without the court's permission

31.23 Where permission is required to rely on a witness (expert or otherwise) and where the receiving party incurs costs without having obtained permission, it is open to the court to find that those costs were not reasonably incurred.[51] This means that the provisions relating to permission are relevant to the issue of costs.

31.24 Permission is required to rely on expert evidence[52] and the CPR provides that it should be restricted to that which is reasonably required to resolve the proceedings.[53] The court may limit the amount of the expert's fees and expenses that the party who wishes to rely on the expert may recover from any other party.[54]

31.25 Where a party has instructed an expert before the court has ruled on whether permission should be granted, the starting point would be that unless there is reason for not having a joint expert, there would be only a joint expert;[55] if the receiving party has ignored this guidance he would be at risk as to the expert's fees if the court were subsequently to decide that a joint expert should be instructed.[56]

---

[47] *Fulham Leisure Holdings Ltd v Nicholson Graham & Jones* [2006] EWHC 2428 (Ch) at [15]; see also *London Chatham and Dover Rly Co v South Eastern Rly Co* (1889) 60 LT 753.

[48] *Hall v Stone* [2007] EWCA Civ 1354 at [47] and [79].

[49] *Sibley & Co v Reachbyte Ltd* [2008] EWHC 2665 (Ch) at [57]–[59].

[50] Although dealing with permission rather than costs, see *S v Chesterfield & North Derbyshire Royal Hospital NHS Trust* [2003] EWCA Civ 1284.

[51] See, by way of analogy with factual witnesses, *Leeds Forge Co Ltd v Deighton's Patent Flue and Tube Co Ltd* [1903] 1 Ch 475.

[52] CPR, r 35.4(1).

[53] CPR, r 35.1.

[54] CPR, r 35.3(4).

[55] *Peet v Mid Kent Healthcare NHS Trust* [2001] EWCA Civ 1703, per Woolf CJ; see also *Daniels v Walker* [2000] 1 WLR 1382.

[56] *Thomas Johnson Ciker v Barkkand Clearing Co* (1999) TLR, December 6, CA.

31.26 Where permission is given to use an expert identified by name, that permission will not extend to another expert in the same discipline.[57] Where a receiving party has instructed an expert who is not the expert named in the order, then that is a factor that the court will be able to take into account.

Measure of experts' fees

31.27 The court will allow fees which are reasonable in amount (or, on the standard basis, reasonable and proportionate in amount). In ascertaining the correct amount, the court may have regard to the duties of the expert. If the expert has been instructed for the purposes of giving evidence, then those duties can be summarised in the following way:[58]

- expert evidence presented to the court should be, and should be seen to be, the independent product of the expert uninfluenced by the exigencies of litigation;
- an expert witness should provide independent assistance to the court by way of objective and unbiased opinion on matters within his expertise;
- an expert witness should never assume the role of an advocate;
- an expert witness should state the facts or assumptions on which his opinion is based;
- an expert witness should not omit to consider material facts which could detract from his concluded opinion;
- an expert witness should make it clear when a particular question or issue falls outside his expertise;
- if an expert's opinion is not properly researched because he considers that insufficient data are available, then this must be stated; and
- if, after exchange of reports, an expert changes his view on a material matter, having read the other side's expert's report or for any other reason, such change of view should be communicated to the other side without delay and, when appropriate, to the court.

The court would be entitled to take any infringement of the duties into account when assessing an expert's fees.

31.28 The following specific points can be made about the types of fees which may be allowed.

Reading-in time for experts

31.29 It has long been held that experts are allowed an allowance for reading-in and for familiarising themselves with the factual material.[59] Occasionally, the costs of such work will be claimed as a separate fee.

---

[57] *Hajigeorgeiou v Vasiliou* [2005] EWCA Civ 236.

[58] *National Justice Compania Naviera SA v Prudential Life Assurance Co Ltd (No 1)* [1995] 1 Lloyd's Rep 455.

[59] See, for example, *Smith v Buller* (1875) LR 19 Eq 473.

Experts' qualifying fee

31.30 A 'qualifying fee' is a type of booking fee which in principle is allowable,[60] even if it was paid before the issue of proceedings.[61] A qualifying fee differs from the allowance for reading-in in that it is not necessarily paid for reading factual material, but may be paid simply to retain the expert. Qualifying fees are rarely encountered nowadays, and may, therefore, be difficult to justify on a between the parties assessment.

Experts' cancellation fees

31.31 A cancellation fee is payable in the event of a witness's attendance being cancelled at short notice; in a pre-CPR case, Bingham J opined that parties who leave it to the last minute to settle must expect to pay for that privilege.[62] This continues to be true under the CPR. Holland J has stressed the desirability of good experts being able to commit themselves to attending hearings for the purposes of assisting the court.[63] He had this to say on the point:[64]

> 'The essential point is that it is the busy person who is the expert that one wants to have in court. Even at the Bar I was always impressed by the expert who wanted to get away because there was a lot to do somewhere else. I was always worried by those who were content to sit around waiting to hear the judgment.'

Cancellation fees are also often justified on the basis that the expert had to book annual or exceptional leave from his salaried position in order to be available to attend court.

Non-expert professional services

31.32 An expert's fees must not include the fees of providing ordinary professional services to his client; by way of example, in a case concerning a company's finances, an accountant's fee was reduced because part of the work carried out by the expert was merely putting his client's books in order.[65]

Experts' travelling expenses

31.33 Experts' travelling expenses are allowable in principle. Although of only persuasive value, the guidance in the Crown Court is that first class travel will be allowed for expert witnesses.[66] By analogy with factual witnesses, the expenses of an overseas expert could, in principle, include those of travelling to this country.[67] Guidance in the Crown Court is that whilst the court may take into account 'cheap fares', the court should be realistic. That guidance also says that the court may take into account the time saved by travelling by air.[68] This guidance is not binding in any way in the civil courts, but may well have resonance.

---

[60]　See, for example, *A-G v Birmingham Drainage Board* (1908) 52 Sol Jo 855.

[61]　*Jones v D Davies & Sons Ltd* [1914] 3 KB 549.

[62]　*Reynolds v Meston* (unreported) 24 February 1986, QBD.

[63]　*Martin v Holland & Barrett Ltd* [2002] 3 Costs LR 530.

[64]　*Martin v Holland & Barrett Ltd* [2002] 3 Costs LR 530 at [23].

[65]　*Great Western Rly Co v Carpalla United China Clay Co Ltd (No 2)* [1909] 2 Ch 471, 79 LJ Ch 55.

[66]　D Carter *Guide to Allowances Under Part V of the Costs in Criminal Cases (General) Regulations 1986* (Ministry of Justice, June 2007), para 8.2.

[67]　*Picasso v Maryport Harbour Trustees* (1884) WN 85.

[68]　D Carter *Guide to Allowances Under Part V of the Costs in Criminal Cases (General) Regulations 1986* (Ministry of Justice, June 2007), paras 8.3 and 8.4.

Stand-by expert reports

31.34 Whilst each case will turn on its own facts, Mann J has indicated that he did not think it was reasonable to have a stand-by report which had been prepared in anticipation of the possibility that the litigation might change direction.[69]

31.35 Most experts will charge on a time basis. In a heavy case (that is, in a case where the expert's fees are considerable), evidence as to market rate may be admissible; indeed, the expert himself may be permitted to give evidence on the point.[70]

Experts' hourly rates

Status and standing

31.36 CPR, r 44.5(3)(e) will apply (ie the court may take into account the skill, effort, specialised knowledge and responsibility involved). Even before the CPR, the expert's status was a factor to be taken into account.[71]

Experts' overhead costs

31.37 Where a technical or scientific expert is instructed to give evidence which necessitates investigatory work, the court is entitled to take into account the fact that the expert would have overhead expenses in running his laboratory, employing staff, etc. A reasonable allowance should be made for that, as well as a profit element on such expenditure.[72]

More than one role for the expert

31.38 Where an expert has more than one role to play in the litigation, it may be appropriate to allow different rates for each role.[73]

Availability of other forms of professional assistance

31.39 Where the expert's involvement is for the purposes of assisting the receiving party rather than giving evidence (that is, where the expert is an advisory expert), the court is entitled to look at whether the work done by the expert could have been carried out by a person of lower status.[74]

---

[69] *Fulham Leisure Holdings Ltd v Nicholson Graham & Jones* [2006] EWHC 2428 (Ch) at [19].

[70] *Cementation Construction Ltd v Keaveney* (1988) *The Independent*, July 12.

[71] *Railways Comr v O'Rourke* [1896] AC 594.

[72] *Nossen's Letter Patent* [1969] 1 WLR 638, per Lloyd-Jacob J. Whilst this is a pre-CPR case, it is often still relied upon.

[73] Whilst not binding, see *McCann v Department for Social Development*, Land Tribunal (NI), 30 October 2007.

[74] See, for example, *BCC v Avril Lee* [2008] EWCA Civ 891 at [37(iii)] in which Hughes LJ noted that the task of preparing a schedule of repairs in a housing disrepair claim could have been lower if a builder had been used rather than a surveyor.

Trade conventions and statements

31.40 Conventions concerning expert's fees are not binding on the court and are merely factors to be taken into account.[75] Presumably, the same would apply if guidance as to fees had been published by the expert's professional body or union.

Jointly instructed experts and questions to experts

31.41 The CPR makes provision for experts to be jointly instructed by the parties.[76] Where the court gives permission for a joint expert, it has the power to give directions about his fees.[77] Unless there is reason to do otherwise, the principle of equal apportionment would ordinarily apply.[78]

31.42 By analogy with factual witnesses, where an expert is jointly instructed in such a way that his fees are shared, the receiving party would be entitled to recover his share in the bill of costs upon conclusion of the claim.[79] This is a common occurrence in practice.

31.43 Unless the court orders otherwise, where CPR Part 35 questions are put to an expert, the party instructing the expert must pay the expert's fee; that rule does not in any way tie the court's hands over the issue of who should ultimately pay those costs.[80] If an expert fails to respond to Part 35 questions, the court is able to order that his fees will not be recoverable.[81]

FACTUAL WITNESSES

31.44 There is a long-established principle that witnesses' expenses are recoverable as costs between opposing parties.[82] Compliance with the indemnity principle can usually be demonstrated by one or both of two following mechanisms.

- *The solicitor's liability*: The communications which take place for the purposes of securing the witness's attendance at trial will readily give rise to an implied contract that the solicitor will discharge the witness's expenses.[83] (That said, the mere act of serving a witness summons would not always be sufficient for that purpose.)[84]
- *The client's liability*: The fact that a party allows a witness to attend to give evidence is ordinarily sufficient to demonstrate a promise by the receiving party to pay his expenses.[85]

---

[75] *Morgan v Hinton Organics (Wessex Ltd)* [2009] EWCA Civ 107.
[76] CPR, r 35.7.
[77] CPR, r 35.8(3)(a).
[78] This is addressed in detail at **34.125–34.145**.
[79] *Allen v Yoxall* (1844) 1 Car & Kir 315.
[80] CPD, art 5.3.
[81] CPR, r 35.6(4).
[82] Although a pre-CPR case, see *Atkins v Johnson Matthey & Co Ltd* (unreported) 12 November 1970, QBD.
[83] See, for example, *Miller v Appleton* (1906) 50 Sol Jo 192, in which the court found that the solicitors' conduct created an implied contract.
[84] *Robins v Bridge* (1837) 3 M & W 114.
[85] See *Pell v Daubeny* (1850) 5 Exch 955 and *Hallet v Mears* (1810) 13 East 15.

Conduct money

31.45 A witness may be compelled to attend court by way of a summons, in which case he will be paid conduct money (which is an advance payment of expenses paid for the purposes of securing his attendance). Although the CPR do not refer to conduct money by that name,[86] they make provision for it:[87]

> 'At the time of service of a witness summons the witness must be offered or paid—
>
> (a) a sum reasonably sufficient to cover his expenses in travelling to and from the court; and
>
> (b) such sum by way of compensation for loss of time as may be specified in the relevant practice direction.'

Some commentators have said that these provisions give rise to an important change in that it permits recovery of costs for loss of time.[88] A better analysis is that these expenses are not intended to compensate the witness for the loss of time *per se*, but for financial losses suffered as a result of the loss of time.[89]

31.46 PD 34A, para 3 makes the following provisions:

> '3.1 When a witness is served with a witness summons he must be offered a sum to cover his travelling expenses to and from the court and compensation for his loss of time.
>
> 3.2 If the witness summons is to be served by the court, the party issuing the summons must deposit with the court:
>
> (1) a sum sufficient to pay for the witness's expenses in travelling to the court and in returning to his home or place of work, and
>
> (2) a sum in respect of the period during which earnings or benefit are lost, or such lesser sum as it may be proved that the witness will lose as a result of his attendance at court in answer to the witness summons.
>
> 3.3 The sum referred to in 3.2(2) is to be based on the sums payable to witnesses attending the Crown Court.'

Thus, there is link with the method of assessment in the Crown Court. Whilst it is not clear whether that method is to be followed, it is worth explaining that method.

The Crown Court method

31.47 For the reasons set out above, there is a link between the expenses which are allowed in the Crown Court and the sums to be allowed in the civil courts. That link depends on conduct money being an approximation of witness expenses. Garland J has held that conduct money does not *limit* the amount that the receiving party is entitled to recover.[90] Similarly, in the context of family law, conduct money is not taken as being

---

[86] It seems to be a term of ancient origin; it did not appear in the RSC or the CCR, but did last appear in *Practice Direction (Costs: Taxation: Procedure) (No 2 of 1992)* [1993] 1 All ER 263.

[87] CPR, r 34.7.

[88] See, for example, Civil Procedure (the White Book Service) (Sweet & Maxwell, 2010), Vol 1, para 34.7.1.

[89] See para 2.2 of D Carter *Guide to Allowances Under Part V of the Costs in Criminal Cases (General) Regulations 1986* (Ministry of Justice, June 2007) (to which the CPD indirectly refers: see below), which reads: 'A financial loss allowance is payable to an ordinary witness to compensate for any expenditure (other than travelling, lodging or subsistence) to which the witness would not otherwise have been subject, or for any loss of earnings or benefit under the enactments relating to National Insurance.'

[90] *JH Shannon v Country Casuals Holdings plc* (1997) *The Times*, June 16 (this is because conduct money is an estimate of expenditure and it may not ultimately prove to be accurate); in the context of family law, see *M v M* [2006] All ER (D) 58 (Jun).

the measure of a witness's *actual* expenses.[91] Nonetheless, there is a link, even if it is imperfect. It is reasonable to work on the basis that the Crown Court method is relevant, but it should be borne in mind that it is not known whether it is binding, persuasive or merely a factor to be taken into account.

31.48 There are two sets of regulations governing witnesses in the Crown Court, one for witnesses in general[92] and another for the Crown Prosecution Service.[93] Established custom favours the former.[94] The sums allowable are revised from time to time and are currently as follows:[95]

Item	*Allowance*
Financial loss allowance for period of absence not exceeding 4 hours	A maximum of £33.50
Financial loss allowance for period of absence exceeding 4 hours	A maximum of £67.00
Subsistence allowance for period of absence not exceeding 5 hours	A maximum of £2.25
Subsistence allowance for period of absence exceeding 5 hours but not exceeding 10 hours	A maximum of £4.50
Subsistence allowance for period of absence exceeding 10 hours	A maximum of £9.75
Hotel (London, Birmingham, Manchester, Leeds, Liverpool or Newcastle Upon Tyne city centres)	A maximum of £95.00
Hotel (elsewhere)	A maximum of £65.00
Overnight stay with family or friends	A maximum of £25.00
Public transport rate (motor cycles and cars)	25 pence per mile
Standard rate (motor cycles and cars)	45 pence per mile
Parking fees	Amount reasonably incurred
Pedal cycle	20 pence per mile

---

[91]   In *M v M* [2006] All ER (D) 58 (Jun) Peter Hughes QC (sitting as a deputy judge of the High Court) found, in the context of a family case, that a witness who attended in response to a subpoena was entitled to his or her costs in complying with the subpoena, in addition to conduct money; it is not clear whether he was asked to decide this point following argument.

[92]   Costs in Criminal Cases (General) Regulations 1986 (SI 1986/1335) and, in particular, Part V; those regulations are made under the Prosecution of Offences Act 1985.

[93]   Crown Prosecution Service (Witnesses' etc Allowances) Regulations 1988 (SI 1988/1862).

[94]   See, for example, the appropriate entry in Civil Procedure (the White Book Service), Vol 1.

[95]   See D Carter *Guide to Allowances Under Part V of the Costs in Criminal Cases (General) Regulations 1986* (Ministry of Justice, June 2007).

The 'standard rate' is allowed where the use of a private motor vehicle was necessary (e g because no public transport was available), or where a considerable saving of time is made.[96] An alternative to the travelling allowance is to allow the amount actually spent on public transport; where a rail fare is claimed, it will normally be limited to the standard fare.[97]

31.49 There are two exceptions to the general rules governing payment of travelling expenses. Where, in the opinion of the court, a person is suffering from a serious illness, and where heavy exhibits have to be carried to court. Where either of these are the circumstances an amount in excess of the normal allowances may be paid.[98]

Miscellaneous matters concerning factual witnesses

No permission to rely on factual witness

31.50 Where permission is required to rely on a person as witness and where the receiving party incurs costs without having obtained that permission, it is open to the court to find that that person's expenses were not reasonably incurred.[99]

Non-attendance of factual witness

31.51 Where the receiving party chooses not to call a witness or use his evidence, that may be a factor to be taken into account.[100]

Non-attendance and conduct money

31.52 Where a witness has been paid conduct money but is subsequently not required at court, the conduct money would, in theory, be recoverable only if a reasonable effort had been made to ask for its return and if it had not been repaid.[101] In practice, however, the costs of making that request would often exceed the conduct monies themselves (especially if a success fee were payable). It is often open to the court to allow conduct money regardless of whether the witness has been asked to return it.

Travelling expenses of factual witnesses

31.53 If the travelling was for purposes other than the matter in hand, then the monies ought to be apportioned.[102] In appropriate cases, a witness may be allowed expenses for travelling from abroad.[103]

---

[96] See D Carter *Guide to Allowances Under Part V of the Costs in Criminal Cases (General) Regulations 1986* (Ministry of Justice, June 2007), paras 8.7–8.9.

[97] See D Carter *Guide to Allowances Under Part V of the Costs in Criminal Cases (General) Regulations 1986* (Ministry of Justice, June 2007), para 8.2.

[98] See D Carter *Guide to Allowances Under Part V of the Costs in Criminal Cases (General) Regulations 1986* (Ministry of Justice, June 2007), para 8.12.

[99] See, by way of analogy with factual witnesses, *Leeds Forge Co Ltd v Deighton's Patent Flue and Tube Co Ltd* [1903] 1 Ch 475.

[100] *London Chatham and Dover Rly Co v South Eastern Rly Co* (1889) 60 LT 753.

[101] *Martin v Andrews* (1856) 7 E&B 1.

[102] *Griffin v Hoskyns* (1856) 1 H & N 95.

[103] *Picasso v Maryport Harbour Trustees* (1884) WN 85.

Overnight expenses of factual witnesses

31.54 Where a witness seeks overnight expenses, the court may take into account the nature of his evidence and the probability that he will be recalled.[104]

Factual witnesses and the costs of legal advice

31.55 Where a witness has been summonsed to attend court and where he needs to take advice on the summons, then the costs of taking advice are, in principle, recoverable.[105]

Witness and receiving party the same person

31.56 Where the witness is also the receiving party, he is, in theory, treated in a similar manner to any other witness.[106] This, however, is subject to the important qualification that he may not recover the costs of being a litigant[107] and, in particular, he may not recover his travelling expenses.[108] In many cases, the costs of being a litigant and the costs of being a witness will be one and the same, in which case no monies be recoverable.

Professional witnesses of fact

31.57 A professional witness is a witness of fact, but one whose evidence is given in his professional capacity rather than in his personal capacity. This is relevant because a professional witness is likely to incur expenses arising out of the loss of time occasioned by his involvement in the litigation (those expenses including loss of earnings, monies paid to a locum tenens, or both).

31.58 Professional witnesses are factual witnesses, and this means that the points made about the possible relevance of conduct money and the Crown Court method of assessing expenses must be repeated: see **31.45–31.49** (those points being that that method may be relevant, but it is not known whether it is binding, persuasive or merely a factor to be taken into account). There are two factors which suggest that that method is not to be afforded much weight where the witness is a professional witness. The first is that the court will often allow a professional witness his ordinary professional rates (an example being a solicitor witness, who is entitled to fees to be assessed in the ordinary way).[109] The second is that the distinction between a professional witness and an expert witness is not always easy to define, and there are instances of the court treating professional witnesses as if they were expert witnesses.[110] Although there is no authority on the point, it is probable that the Crown Court guidance is merely a factor to be taken

---

[104] *Railways Comr v O'Rourke* [1896] AC 594.
[105] *J H Shannon v Country Casual Holdings plc* (1997) *The Times*, June 16, per Garland J.
[106] *Davey v Durrant* (1858) 24 Beav 493.
[107] *London Scottish Benefit Society v Chorley* (1884) 13 QBD 872.
[108] *R v Legal Aid Board (Merseyside) Area Office ex p Eccleston* [1998] 1 WLR 1279; this is based on the same principles as those by which the costs of attending a legal or medical advisor are not recoverable: *Atkins v Johnson Matthew & Co* (1970) (unreported), Donaldson J.
[109] See *Hamilton v Colhoun* [1906] 2 IR 104 and *Butler v Hobson* (1838) 5 Bing NC 128.
[110] See, for example, *Aktieselskabet de Danske Sukkerfabriker v Bajamar Cia Naviera SA, The Torenia* [1983] 2 Lloyd's Rep 210 at 233, in which Hobhouse J found that a professional witness is a species of expert witness.

into account, and that it would be most useful in cases where there is no other material upon which the court could base its assessment. In so far as it is relevant, the current guidance is as follows:[111]

Item	Allowance (no locum engaged)	Allowance (locum engaged)
Professional witness allowance for period of absence not exceeding 2 hours	A maximum of £83.50	A maximum of £89.00
Professional witness allowance for period of absence exceeding 2 hours but not exceeding 4 hours	A maximum of £117.00	A maximum of £125.00
Professional witness allowance for period of absence exceeding 4 hours but not exceeding 6 hours	A maximum of £174.00	A maximum of £250.00
Professional witness allowance for period of absence exceeding 6 hours	A maximum of £234.00	A maximum of £250.00
Other expenses	As per factual witnesses plus £21.00 'Night Subsistence Allowance' and £5.00 'Personal Incidental Allowance' if at a Hotel with effect from 1 June 2005	As opposite

MEDICAL RECORDS

31.59 The Data Protection Act 1998 creates a qualified right of access to medical records. Delegated legislation made under that Act limits the fee which can be charged for providing medical records; that fee is referred to as a 'subject access fee'. It is that fee which is usually claimed as being the cost of obtaining medical records, although an agency fee may also be charged (see **31.62–31.69**).

---

[111] See D Carter *Guide to Allowances Under Part V of the Costs in Criminal Cases (General) Regulations 1986* (Ministry of Justice, June 2007).

31.60 The maximum subject access fee is £50, but there is a sliding scale which is based on the number of pages copied;[112] that scale is as follows:

Number of pages of information comprising the copy	Maximum fee	Number of pages of information comprising the copy	Maximum fee
fewer than 20	£1	100–149	£10
20–29	£2	150–199	£15
30–39	£3	200–249	£20
40–49	£4	250–299	£25
50–59	£5	300–349	£30
60–69	£6	350–399	£35
70–79	£7	400–449	£40
80–89	£8	450–499	£45
90–99	£9	500 or more	£50

OTHER TYPES OF PERSONAL RECORDS

31.61 Credit records and educational records are treated in a similar way to medical records (see **31.59–31.60**). Other records containing personal data must be supplied to the person to whom they relate for a subject access fee of no more than £10.[113]

MEDICAL AGENCIES

31.62 Solicitors often instruct medical agencies to carry out the administrative tasks of obtaining medical reports and medical records. Medical agencies are unregulated, but a non-statutory association exists (the Association of Medical Reporting Organisations) which encourages membership and publishes a code of conduct.

Agency fees

31.63 Where an agency is used, the fee charged is often a single, composite fee which includes both the agency's fee and the fee paid to the expert, clinic, or practice.

31.64 There is no binding authority as to the recoverability of the agency element of the fee, but the following comments of HHJ Cook are usually regarded as being persuasive:[114]

> 'I am satisfied that there is no principle which precludes the fees of a medical agency being recoverable between the parties, provided it is demonstrated that their charges do not exceed the reasonable and proportionate costs of the work if it had been done by the solicitors.'

---

[112] See reg 6(2) and the Schedule to the Data Protection (Subject Access) (Fees and Miscellaneous Provisions) Regulations 2000 (SI 2000/191) (as amended).

[113] Data Protection (Subject Access) (Fees and Miscellaneous Provisions) Regulations 2000 (as amended), reg 3 and Data Protection Act 1998, s 7(1).

[114] *Stringer v Copley* (17 May 2002) Kingston on Thames County Court, at p 7, per HHJ Cook; May LJ referred to this judgment with apparent approval in *Crane v Cannons Leisure Centre* [2007] EWCA Civ 1352 at [7].

A pedant would say that the agency element ought to be claimed as profit costs rather than as a disbursement; the pedant would be correct in many instances, but in practice such fees are often presented as disbursements (often to the advantage of the paying party, who escapes paying a success fee on the agency element of the fee).

31.65 Receiving parties are often reluctant to reveal details concerning the agency element. HHJ Cook deprecated that attitude:[115]

> 'To demonstrate the point by taking an extreme, if the doctor's fee was only £75 and [the agency's] charges £300, the total of £375 would undoubtedly be unreasonable and disproportionate. It does therefore seem to be important that, whilst there is much to commend the use of medical agencies, it is important that their invoices (or "fee notes") should distinguish between the medical fee and their own charges, the latter being sufficiently particularised to enable the costs officer to be satisfied they do not exceed the reasonable and proportionate costs of the solicitors doing the work.'

Agency fees and fixed costs

31.66 An issue that commonly used to arise was the interaction between agency fees and predictable costs. Where predictable costs were payable and where work that could have been carried out by the solicitor had in fact been delegated to an agency, the court often used to be vexed by the issue of whether the agency element could be recovered, or whether the predictable costs regime precluded its recovery. For the reasons set out below, this point now arises only rarely.

31.67 Whilst there is no binding authority on this issue, there is an informal consensus which is so rarely disregarded as to be almost a rule of practice. That consensus arose out of an appeal from a decision of Master Hurst;[116] that appeal was disposed of by way of a mediated agreement which is known as the *Woollard* agreement (or, more recently, as the MRO agreement, the contraction standing for Medical Reporting Organisation).[117] Many defendant insurers[118] and medical agencies[119] are content to abide by that agreement.

31.68 The amounts payable under the *Woollard* agreement depend on the length of the period during which the agency's fees remain unpaid. The sums payable (exclusive of VAT) are set out in the following table:

---

[115] *Stringer v Copley* (17 May 2002) Kingston on Thames County Court, at p 8, per HHJ Cook.

[116] *Woollard & Anor v Fowler* [2005] EWHC 90051 (Costs); despite its neutral citation reference, this case was heard in 2006.

[117] Which originally was dated 11 May 2007 and a very similar agreement was made on 2 April 2009.

[118] Which originally were Zurich, Aviva, Allianz, Fortis, HSBC, AXA, Churchill, Direct Line, National Insurance, and UK Insurance, but now include many more.

[119] Which originally were Doctors Chambers Limited, e-Reporting Group Limited, Mobile Doctors Limited, Medical-Legal Reporting, Premex Services Limited, Premier Medical Limited, Speed Medical Examination Services Limited, and UK Independent Medical Services Limited, but now include Aman Health-care Ltd, Aslam Mohammed Limited, First Legal Support, Inquiry QED Ltd, Insurance Medial Reporting Ltd, and others.

	Rate A: payable if paid within 90 days	Rate A: payable if not paid within 90 days
General practitioner report – no medical records	£195	£220
Review of medical records by general practitioner	£50	£55
Orthopaedic report – including review of medical records	£425	£465
Accident and Emergency report – including review of medical records	£375	£410
Addendum	Cost plus £25	Cost plus £30
Costs of obtaining each set of medical records	Cost plus £25	Cost plus £30

The *Woollard* agreement relates solely to cases in which predictable costs apply, so it would ordinarily be correct to rely on these figures as comparators in other types of case.

Value added tax and agency fees

31.69 Although it is now unusual for there to be a dispute about the fees themselves, there is occasionally dispute about the amount of VAT to be paid on those fees. This is because the VAT provisions relating to the agency element may be different from those relating to the rest of the costs. Where the fees were incurred before 1 May 2007, VAT would usually be payable only on the agency element. The agency (or the solicitor) could elect whether to pay VAT on the balance. Whilst not binding, there have been instances of the court disallowing VAT where the solicitor had elected to claim VAT in circumstances where he was not obliged so to do.[120] In view of the fact that since 1 May 2007 VAT is payable on most medical reports (see **35.16**), this is likely soon to be of only historical interest.

COPYING CHARGES

31.70 CPD, art 4.16(5) provides as follows:

'The cost of making copies of documents will not in general be allowed but the court may exceptionally in its discretion make an allowance for copying in unusual circumstances or where the documents copied are unusually numerous in relation to the nature of the case. Where this discretion is invoked the number of copies made, their purpose and the costs

---

[120] See, for example, *Sutton v Selwyns Travel* (8 August 2008), Birkenhead County Court (Regional Costs), Smedley J.

claimed for them must be set out in the bill.'

Whilst not binding, Master Gordon-Saker has confirmed that the court is able to take into account the overall costs claimed; thus, if the overall costs are small, it would be open to the court to find that even relatively small amounts of copying fall into the category of being exceptional.[121]

31.71 Evans J had the following to say (in a pre-CPR case):[122]

'[Counsel for the receiving party] submitted that the maximum number of pages which might require copying in a personal injury case of a normal kind would be 1,000, and that therefore this case did involve an unusual number. I sympathise with this submission, but I am troubled that neither the plaintiffs nor the registrar have made an allowance for the number which in the normal case would form part of the solicitor's general overheads.'

Therefore, where the threshold is reached where charges are recoverable, it is only the excess beyond that threshold (or some other suitable figure) which is recoverable, rather than the total.

Copying charges in the Court of Appeal

31.72 Copying charges for appeals in the Court of Appeal are often treated differently from copying charges in other arenas; this is because the allowance for copying which is included in the hourly rate will have been used up in the lower court. The Guide to the Summary Assessment of Costs has this to say on the point:[123]

'(9) In most appeals it will be appropriate to make an allowance for copy documents. The allowance for copying which is included in the solicitor's hourly rates will have already been used up or exceeded in the lower court. An hourly rate charge is appropriate for selecting and collating documents and dictating the indices. If the paperwork is voluminous much of this should be delegated to a trainee. Note that:

(a)   (for the copying itself, a fair allowance is 10p per page, i e £100 per 1,000 sheets. This includes an allowance for checking the accuracy of the copying.

(b)   Time spent standing at the photocopier and time spent taking the papers to a local photocopy shop is not recoverable. Such work is not fee earner work; it is secretarial.'

Amounts of copying charges

31.73 Hallett J has commented (with reference to criminal costs rather than civil costs) that where the court is inclined to allow a commercial rate for photocopying, that rate should take into account the fact that a solicitor who regularly uses the services of commercial copying bureaux ought to be able to negotiate a commercial rate.[124] The implication is that a realistic rate ought to be allowed for copying carried out in-house.

---

[121]   *Ahmed v Aventis Pharma Ltd (Rev 1)* [2009] EWHC 90152 (Costs) (19 November 2009) at [19].
[122]   *Johnson v Reed Corrugated Cases Ltd* (1990) Costs LR, Core vol 180 at 185.
[123]   At para 65(9).
[124]   *Landau & Cohen v Lord Chancellor's Department* [1999] 2 Costs LR 5; Hallett J noted that the commercial rate may be as low as 4 pence per page.

COURIERS, POSTAGE, ETC

31.74 CPD, art 4.16(4) stipulates that the cost of postage and couriers will in general not be allowed, but the court may exceptionally in its discretion allow such expenses in unusual circumstances or where the cost is unusually heavy.

31.75 Presumably, Evans J's comments referred to at **31.71** also apply to courier charges and postage (that is, it is probable that once the threshold has been reached, it is only the excess beyond the threshold which is payable).

HOTEL EXPENSES

31.76 Hotel expenses are recoverable as disbursements. If a room is paid for but not used, the test will be whether it was likely to have been required.[125]

31.77 Whilst only persuasive, the Privy Council has held that where expenses are claimed for a period longer than is necessary, the hotel expenses may be apportioned accordingly.[126] Although its applicability is limited to factual witnesses, guidance exists for assessing hotel expenses in the Crown Court. That guidance is described at **31.48**; it can be seen that it is arguable whether it is binding, persuasive or merely a factor to be taken into account.

TRAVELLING EXPENSES

31.78 Local travelling expenses are not recoverable under the CPR, but the court has discretion as to what is meant by 'local'. CPD, art 4.26(3) makes the following provisions:

> 'Local travelling expenses incurred by solicitors will not be allowed. The definition of "local" is a matter for the discretion of the court. While no absolute rule can be laid down, as a matter of guidance, "local" will, in general, be taken to mean within a radius of 10 miles from the court dealing with the case at the relevant time. Where travelling and waiting time is claimed, this should be allowed at the rate agreed with the client unless this is more than the hourly rate on the assessment.'

31.79 Hallett J has stated that unless the client is housebound or in hospital, it is normal for him to visit the solicitor rather than the other way around;[127] it would be reasonable to infer from this that the expenses of travelling to see a client who is not housebound or in hospital would, absent justification, be irrecoverable.

31.80 In considering the reasonableness of the expenses claimed the court is entitled to examine the whole costs and, in particular, is entitled to look at the savings that may have been made by reason of the travelling. Thus, where travelling has resulted in savings elsewhere (such as by avoiding the need to instruct agents or a saving in the hourly rate),[128] the court may take those savings into account.

---

[125]   See, by way of analogy with witness expenses, *Railways Comr v O'Rourke* [1896] AC 594.
[126]   *Horsford v Bird* [2006] UKPC 55.
[127]   *Ledward v Kent & Medway Health Authority* [2003] EWHC 2551 (QB) at [24].
[128]   *Ledward v Kent & Medway Health Authority* [2003] EWHC 2551 (QB) at [17].

31.81 Whilst its applicability is limited to factual witnesses, guidance exists for assessing travelling expenses in the Crown Court (see **31.48**). One particular aspect on which that guidance focuses is whether public transport was reasonably available for use by the witness; where it was, it would be open to the court to find that the costs of travelling by private car were not allowable unless this resulted in a saving in costs.[129]

DISBURSEMENT FUNDING LOANS

31.82 Disbursement funding loans (or, more accurately, the interest on and the costs of setting up and managing the loan) are not recoverable between opposing parties; they are mentioned in this context primarily to make the point that they are irrecoverable because they are not properly characterised as being legal costs.[130]

31.83 From a solicitor and client perspective, compliance with the relevant consumer protection regulations is usually a prerequisite for enforceability.[131] Whilst there is no authority on the point, some commentators have suggested that loans which de facto are funded by the fruits of the claim may be champertous.[132]

COURT FEES

Issue fee

31.84 The issue fee is payable on a sliding scale increasing with the value of the claim;[133] if the claim has been overvalued, the court may take that into account in assessing the fee.

Pre-trial checklist (listing questionnaire)

31.85 Where it was paid before 1 May 2008, the court is able to disallow the listing fee if the case settled more than 14 days before trial. This is because the claimant could have reclaimed the fee.[134] After that date, different provisions applied (see below). In essence, the listing fee could not have been recovered, but the much larger hearing fee could.

Hearing fee

31.86 Where the fee was paid after 1 May 2008, the listing fee could not be refunded, but the much larger hearing fee could, depending on how long before trial the matter

---

[129] Although a criminal case, see *R v Slessor* (1984), Taxing Masters Compendium.

[130] *Hunt v RM Douglas (Roofing) Ltd* (1987) *The Times*, November 23, CAT.

[131] See Consumer Credit Act 1974 as amended by Consumer Credit Act 2006, and the relevant delegated legislation; see also the provisions mentioned at **8.324–8.401**.

[132] D Capper *Litigation funding for 'big money' divorces: an assessment of legal risk* (2007) CJQ 26, October, pp 447–465. It may be that a disgruntled client would be able to take that point if he was successful in the litigation but wished to avoid repaying the loan.

[133] Civil Proceedings Fees Order 2008 (SI 2008/1053), Sch 1, para 1.1.

[134] Civil Proceedings Fees Order 2004 (SI 2004/3121), Sch 1, para 2.3.

settled. Where the court receives notice in writing from the party who paid the hearing fee that the case has been settled or discontinued, the following percentages of the hearing fee will be refunded:[135]

- 100% if the court is notified more than 28 days before the hearing;
- 75% if the court is notified between 15 and 28 days before the hearing; and
- 50% if the court is notified between 7 and 14 days before the hearing.

If a refund has gone unclaimed, then it is not likely that the court would require the paying party to bear those fees.

Group litigation

31.87 Listing questionnaire fees are not payable on individual claims listed after a GLO has been made.[136]

Commencement fee

31.88 The bill must not contain any court fees which relate solely to the detailed assessment proceedings[137] (unless, of course, the costs are those of a detailed assessment).

Benefits

31.89 Receiving parties who were on state benefits at the material time may not have been required to pay court fees.[138] If that was the case, the court may disallow the fee on the grounds that it was not reasonably incurred.

FOREIGN LAWYERS

31.90 Where the receiving party's costs reasonably include the fees of a lawyer in another jurisdiction, the correct measure of those fees is the method by which they would have been assessed in the lawyer's home jurisdiction.[139] This would be the case even where costs were payable according to a scale.[140]

31.91 Diplock J has commented that where the bill contains a foreign lawyer's fees, it ought to include a detailed statement of the circumstances which required the services of the foreign lawyer; presumably, if the court were to find that the involvement of a foreign lawyer was not justified, the court would make an allowance based on the costs which would have been incurred had the work been carried out domestically. Diplock J

---

[135] SI 2008/1053, Sch 1, para 2.3.
[136] SI 2008/1053, Sch 1, para 2.2.
[137] CPD, art 4.13.
[138] For details, see the Civil Proceedings Fees Order 2004.
[139] Master Gordon-Saker made a (non-binding) analysis of the authorities on this point in *Societa Finanziaria Industrie Turistiche SpA v Manfredi Lefebvre D'Ovidio De Clunieres Di Balsorano & Anor* [2006] EWHC 90068 (Costs).
[140] See *Slingsby v Attorney-General* [1918] P 236 (a pre-CPR case).

also commented that it is the receiving party's responsibility to provide a sufficiently detailed breakdown within the bill to allow the local costs regime to be applied.[141]

31.92 It should not be forgotten that several jurisdictions exist in even the British Isles; they include:

- *Scotland*: the Rules of the Court of Session 1994.
- *Northern Ireland*: the Rules of the Supreme Court (Northern Ireland) 1980.
- *Isle of Man*: the Advocates Act 1995; the Advocates (Prescribed Fees) Regulations 1995; Advocates (Law Society Assessment of Fees) Regulations 2000; and the Advocates Practice Rules 2001.

INTERPRETERS

31.93 Where a party or a witnesses needs the assistance of an interpreter, those costs are recoverable in principle.[142]

---

[141] *McCullie v Butler* [1962] 2 QB 309.
[142] *Thomas v Parry* (1880) WN 184.

Chapter 32

COUNSEL'S FEES

32.1   This chapter focuses on those aspects of counsel's practice and remuneration that are relevant to the law of costs (both between opposing parties and, to a lesser extent, amongst solicitor, counsel and client). Issues concerning counsel's professional obligations are addressed only to the limited extent to which they are relevant to costs.

32.2   Save for paragraphs **32.34–32.36**, this chapter relates to barristers in independent practice (ie barristers who hold themselves out as being practising barristers and who are not employed barristers acting in the course of their employment).[1] For purposes of costs, employed barristers are best regarded as being a species of fee earner (ie they are best regarded as being subject to the principles set out in Chapters 28 and 29).

THE NATURE OF COUNSEL'S RIGHT TO PAYMENT

32.3   The common law provides that counsel is not able to enter into a contract for the supply of professional services[2] but, despite the abolition of this rule by statute (see **32.6**), there remains a tradition of counsel electing not to enter into contractual arrangements. The type of fee that is usually paid is, therefore, an honorarium.[3] This used to be based on the courteous understanding that counsel acting in a non-contractual capacity could neither sue nor be sued, but given the fact that counsel can now be sued for professional negligence, this justification no longer exists. It is now a decision which is made on other grounds, such as a desire not to get embroiled in debt recovery litigation.

32.4   The (now abolished) position at common law was described by Swinfen Eady LJ:[4]

> 'It is settled beyond all question that counsel's fee is not a debt but an honorarium, the fees are payable as a matter of honour and not of legal obligation.'

32.5   This rule was based on counsel's lack of capacity; this was explained by Lopes LJ:[5]

---

1   See paras 201 and 1001 of the Code of Conduct of the Bar.
2   The modern law on this point is stated in *Kennedy v Broun* (1862) 32 LJ (CP) 137, but (under common law) can be traced back to *Moor v Row* (1629) 1 Rep Ch 38; it can be traced back further under Roman Law (see Lex Cincia c 204 BC); the non-contractual nature exists even if the services are provided in a different jurisdiction: *R v Doutre* (1884) 9 App Cas 745, PC at 752.
3   The *Oxford English Dictionary* (2nd edn, 1989) defines this word as 'an honorary reward; a fee for services rendered, esp. by a professional person'.
4   *Wells v Wells* [1914] 1 P 157 at 162.
5   *In re Le Brasseur and Oakley* [1896] 2 Ch 487.

'[*Kennedy v Broun* (1862) 32 LJ (CP) 137] establishes the unqualified doctrine that the relation of counsel and solicitor renders the parties mutually incapable of making any legal contract of hiring and service in regard to litigation. That rule has existed for a long time, and, speaking for myself, I should be very sorry to see it in any way impugned.'

32.6   On 1 January 1991, statute intervened in the form of s 61 of the Courts and Legal Services Act 1990:

'Right of barrister to enter into contract for the provision of his services

(1)   Any rule of law which prevents a barrister from entering into a contract for the provision of his services as a barrister is hereby abolished.

(2)   Nothing in subsection (1) prevents the General Council of the Bar from making rules (however described) which prohibit barristers from entering into contracts or restrict their right to do so.'

32.7   Thus, counsel's ability to enter into a contract for the supply of legal services is subject to the rules made by the General Council of the Bar. Broadly speaking,[6] those rules permit counsel to enter into the following arrangements:

- non-contractual agreements with solicitors;
- contractual agreements with solicitors;
- contractual agreements with professionals who are not solicitors; and
- contractual agreements with lay clients.

Each of these arrangements is considered in turn.

Non-contractual agreements with solicitors

32.8   Where counsel receives instructions from a solicitor and chooses not to enter into a contract for the supply of services, the default position is that the arrangement is not an enforceable contract. Counsel would be able to look to his instructing solicitors for payment as a matter of custom of the profession;[7] this is by reason of the *Terms of Work on Which Barristers Offer Their Services to Solicitors* ('the Terms of Work'), which are published as part of the Withdrawal of Credit Scheme 1998. The relevant provisions read as follows:

'(2)   Any solicitor who sends a brief or instructions to a barrister will be deemed to instruct that barrister on these Terms unless and to the extent that the barrister and the solicitor have agreed in writing in relation to the particular matter or generally (a) that the Contractual Terms on which Barristers Offer their Services to Solicitors 2000 shall apply, or (b) to exclude or vary these Terms.

...

---

[6]   These may be subject to change following the coming into force of the Legal Services Act 2007; the reader is advised to carry out his own legal research for the up-to-date position.

[7]   See *Hobart v Butler* (1859) 9 ICLR 157; see also *Re Seal ex p Crickett* (1893) 37 Sol Jo 685; the professional rules governing solicitors used to provide that non-payment of fees was a disciplinary offence, but that express provision did not appear in the Solicitors Code of Conduct 2007, nor does it appear in the SRA Code of Conduct 2011.

(25) Neither the General Council of the Bar in authorising these Terms nor a barrister in offering his services to a solicitor on these Terms has any intention to create legal relations or to enter into any contract or other obligation binding in law.

(26) Neither the sending by a solicitor of a brief or instructions to a barrister nor the acceptance by a barrister of a brief or instructions nor anything done in connection therewith nor the arrangements relating thereto (whether mentioned in these Terms or in the Bar Code of Conduct or to be implied) nor these Terms or any agreement or transaction entered into or payment made by or under them shall be attended by or give rise to any contractual relationship rights duties or consequences whatsoever or be legally enforceable by or against or be the subject of litigation with either the barrister or the General Council of the Bar.'

32.9 As mentioned at **32.4**, in so far as his instructing solicitor was concerned, counsel was, under common law, debarred from recovering his fee as a debt[8] and he was prevented from suing on the basis of a representation that he would be paid.[9] The fact that his instructing solicitor might have been placed in funds counted for nothing before the court.[10] The Terms of Work appear to preserve these principles, although the exact mechanism by which they achieve that is debatable.[11]

32.10 In so far as the relationship between counsel and the lay client is concerned, the Terms make the following provision:

'(3) By the established custom of the profession a barrister looks for payment of his fees to the solicitor who instructs him and not to his lay client.'

32.11 With one or two exceptions,[12] counsel's instructions will not create an agreement directly between counsel and his lay client (or if there is an agreement, it is not an enforceable agreement).[13] Thus, subject to those exceptions, counsel cannot sue his lay client for his fees. Counsel's clerk is also unable to sue the lay client for his own fees.[14]

32.12 For the sake of completeness, it is worth mentioning that whilst counsel cannot sue for his fees as if he were a debtor, the court is able to order a solicitor to pay counsel's fees in the exercise of its administrative jurisdiction to supervise solicitors as officers of the court. The circumstances in which the court would make such an order would be few and far between;[15] it is most unlikely that the court would make such an order where counsel had brought a claim specifically in respect of his own fee.[16]

---

[8]   *Wells v Wells* [1914] P 157 and *Re Sandiford (No 2)* [1935] Ch 681.
[9]   *Hobart v Butler* (1859) 9 ICLR 157.
[10] *Re Sandiford (No 2)* [1935] Ch 681.
[11] One analysis is that the Terms have created a contract which, by express agreement between the counterparties, is not enforceable at law.
[12] See paras 31.29–31.31. There is ancient authority that where counsel has communicated directly with the lay client, a promise that counsel would be paid was a promise that could be enforced at law (*Marsh and Rainsford's Case* (1687) Leon 111), but it is very doubtful whether this authority is still good law, not least because it would cut across modern consumer protection provisions.
[13] Support for the first of these analyses is gained from authority which suggests that a solicitor does not act as his lay client's agent when he instructs counsel: *Mostyn v Mostyn* (1870) LR 5 Ch App 457.
[14] Whilst an ancient authority, *Ex parte Cotton* (1846) 9 Beav 107 probably remains good law; counsel's clerk can, however, sue counsel: *Lyster v Spearman* (1882) 72 LT Jo 391.
[15] An example would be where a trustee in bankruptcy is paid counsel's fees, but refuses to pass them on to counsel: see *Ex parte James* LR 9 Ch 609 and *Ex parte Simmonds, In re Carnac* (1885) 16 QBD 308; see also *Re Farman* (1883) 18 L Jo 352; *Re A Solicitor ex p Incorporated Law Society* (1894) 63 LJQB 397, DC.
[16] See, for example, *A Solicitor ex p Incorporated Law Society* (1909) *The Times*, January 27.

32.13 The following points can be made about fees payable under the Withdrawal of Credit Scheme 1988.

Basis of payment

32.14 The Terms of Work provide that counsel may agree either a fee or a charging rate before commencing work, but that in default of agreement a reasonable professional rate shall be payable.[17]

Terms of payment

32.15 Fees should be paid within one month of receipt of the fee note regardless of whether the case is on-going.[18] If counsel's fees go unpaid, interest will be payable, but only where the principle of payment of interest has been agreed.

Enforcement of payment

32.16 Where fees remain unpaid, counsel's remedy is to invoke the procedure set out in the Withdrawal of Credit Scheme 1998. This scheme provides that a defaulting solicitor (referred to as a 'notified solicitor') may ultimately be denied credit by the Bar in general. This would have the effect that the notified solicitor could instruct counsel only if: (i) he had secured public funding; (ii) if fees had been agreed and paid before counsel starts work; or (iii) if counsel has agreed to work pro bono.[19] To invoke the Withdrawal of Credit Scheme 1988 the barrister must send the solicitor two reminder letters. The first (known as 'the A Letter') must be sent no earlier than one month after the first fee note, and the second (known as 'the B Letter') must be sent 3 months after the first fee note was sent. Both letters must be in a prescribed form or a reasonable adaptation thereof.[20] If the fees remain unpaid, the barrister may report the facts to the Chairman of the General Council of the Bar, who will send a further reminder letter ('the C Letter'). In the absence of a satisfactory response, the Chairman will write to the solicitor saying that unless written representations are received by him within 14 days, he will issue a direction. That direction will state that no barrister may without the written consent of the Chairman knowingly accept instructions from the notified solicitor unless one of the conditions set out above ((i)–(iii)) is met.[21] The Chairman may also refer the solicitor to the SRA.[22]

Challenging fees

32.17 The solicitor may challenge the fee (be this on the grounds that it is excessive, on an issue of competence, or otherwise). If, within the appropriate time limits (see **32.19**), the solicitor makes written representations about the disputed fee, the matter will be referred to a tribunal (known as the joint tribunal); the joint tribunal will consist of a barrister nominated by the Chairman and a solicitor nominated by the President of the Law Society. The tribunal will act in an expert rather than arbitral capacity, and its decision shall be conclusive, final and binding for all purposes between the solicitor and

---

[17] Terms of Work, para 10(1).
[18] Terms of Work, paras 8 and 13.
[19] Terms of Work, para 9.
[20] Terms of Work, para 15.
[21] Terms of Work, para 17.
[22] Terms of Work, para 18.

the barrister.[23] The tribunal has issued standing orders[24] which provide that the parties must supply a Statement of Case and a Statement of Response. Additional material or a Statement of Reply may be supplied, but only in exceptional circumstances. The tribunal will notify the parties of the date of the determination. The determination may be by way of oral hearing.

Time limits and waiver

Barrister

32.18 Save in exceptional circumstances, the Chairman will not consider a complaint from a barrister if that complaint is made about a fee which has been outstanding for more than 2 years or, in the case of a publicly funded fee, where the complaint has been made more than 2 years since the event which gave rise to the right to assessment or, in the case of a conditional fee agreement, more than 2 years after the termination of the agreement or the end of the case.[25]

Solicitor

32.19 The solicitor's challenge must be made in writing within 3 months after the first fee note relating to the disputed fee has been sent, or within one month after the A Letter has been sent, whichever is the later; Morland J has found that if he fails to do this, the solicitor will be taken to have assented to and to have accepted as payable the fee as claimed.[26] If a fee is disputed, the solicitor must within 14 days agree to submit the issue or dispute giving rise to the challenge to the decision of a tribunal and to abide by and forthwith give effect to the decision of the tribunal. Unless the solicitor complies with these requirements, no challenge may be made[27] and the fees will be payable in full (without set-off) in the amount set out in the relevant fee note.[28]

32.20 A solicitor may be found to have impliedly waived the right to challenge counsel's fee; Morland J has found that if a solicitor files a signed bill of costs in which counsel's fee is claimed, he must be taken to have assented to and to have accepted as payable the fee as claimed;[29] that finding was made in the context of a detailed assessment, but is likely to be a factor that the joint tribunal could take into account.

Contractual agreements with solicitors

32.21 Where a barrister is instructed by a solicitor, and where both the barrister and the solicitor have agreed in writing that the agreement between them shall be contractually binding, a contract enforceable at law will be created. Some barristers take the view that

---

23 See para 14(3) of the Terms of Work together with the section on 'definitions and consequential provisions' from para 21 onwards.
24 Joint Tribunal Standing Orders.
25 Bar Council – Fees Collection Committee Guidelines, para 7.
26 *Spath Holmes Ltd v Chairman of the Greater Manchester and Lancashire Rent Assessment Committee* [1998] 1 Costs LR 40 at 46.
27 Terms of Work, para 14(1) and (2).
28 Terms of Work, para 14(4).
29 *Spath Holmes Ltd v Chairman of the Greater Manchester and Lancashire Rent Assessment Committee* [1998] 1 Costs LR 40 at 47.

this is not only a sensible thing to do from a business perspective, but it is also fair; this is because the old gentlemen's agreement that counsel could not sue but could be sued[30] is no longer tenable under modern law.

32.22 Unless they agree different terms, the Contractual Terms of Work on Which Barristers Offer Their Services to Solicitors 2001 ('the Contractual Terms') will apply.[31] The Contractual Terms disapply certain provisions in the Terms of Work and, in so doing, they create a retainer that continues to exist under the Withdrawal of Credit Scheme 1988, but which is also a contract.

32.23 The Contractual Terms provide that counsel may agree either a fee or a charging rate before commencing work, but that in default of agreement a reasonable professional rate shall be payable.[32] Fees must be paid within one month of receipt of the fee note, in default of which simple interest (which is usually stipulated to be 2% above base rate) is payable.

32.24 The fact that counsel has entered into a contractual agreement with his instructing solicitor will not prevent him from invoking the Withdrawal of Credit Scheme 1988 (as amended) in the event of non-payment.[33]

Contractual agreements with professionals other than solicitors

32.25 A scheme, known as the licensed access scheme, exists which permits barristers to accept instructions from professionals other than solicitors.[34] That scheme seeks to maximise client access to the legal profession while at the same time ensuring that the Bar retains its identity as a referral profession.[35]

32.26 Before he can instruct counsel directly, a professional who is not a solicitor must obtain a licence from the Access to the Bar Committee.[36] The following professionals are entitled to apply for a licence: accountants, insolvency practitioners, architects, surveyors, town planners, engineers, valuers, actuaries, chartered secretaries, and insurers.

32.27 The Licensed Access Terms of Work apply, which provide that the licensed access client is contractually liable for the barrister's fee due in respect of work carried out by the barrister under any instructions, and that where the matter concerns a lay client, the

---

[30] *Turner v Philipps* (1792) Peake 166.
[31] These terms apply only to agreements made on or after 24 March 2001 (see para 28 of the Contractual Terms); agreements made before that date are probably unenforceable.
[32] See para 9(1) of the Contractual Terms.
[33] See para 14 of the Contractual Terms.
[34] There are other circumstances in which counsel might be instructed by someone other than a solicitor. Pursuant to s 28 of the Courts and Legal Services Act 1990 (as amended) the General Council of the Bar is authorised to grant the right to conduct litigation, and it has done so in respect of employed barristers where they are acting for their employer, or, if their employer is a solicitor, for a client of their employer. Section 104(2) of the Patents Act 1977 permits Patent Agents to instruct counsel for the purpose of conducting patent appeals. Indeed, some patent agents are allowed the right to conduct any kind of litigation involving intellectual property. Section 15 of the Criminal Justice and Court Services Act 2000 permits officers of the Children and Family Court Advisory and Support Service to instruct counsel in certain circumstances.
[35] See the Licensed Access Guidance Handbooks for Barristers And Chambers and Licensed Access Clients, para 2.1.
[36] See the Licensed Access Recognition Regulations.

licensed access client is solely and exclusively liable to the barrister for the fees. The agreement between the barrister and the licensed access client is contractual.[37]

32.28 The Withdrawal of Credit Scheme 1988 does not apply to work accepted under the licensed access scheme (this being because there is no credit to withdraw).

Contractual agreements with lay clients

32.29 Provided that it is in the best interests of the client, appropriately qualified barristers may accept instructions directly from a lay client rather than through a solicitor or a licensed access client. This is known as public access.

32.30 Not all barristers are eligible to undertake public access work. To qualify, a barrister must have been in practice for a period of not less than 3 years from the completion of pupillage, he must have complied with certain training requirements, and he must have notified the General Council of the Bar that he intends to do public access work.

32.31 The arrangement between the client and the barrister will be by way of written agreement in which the barrister must set out the fees he proposes to charge, or the basis on which his fee will be calculated.[38] The agreement will be a contract enforceable at law.

LIABILITY FOR FEES AS BETWEEN COUNSEL AND HIS INSTRUCTING SOLICITOR

Set-off

32.32 Unless there has been agreement to the contrary or unless the solicitor has formally challenged the fees, a solicitor is not entitled to set off counsel's fee. The Contractual Terms provide that counsel's fees will be payable without any deductions or set-off whatsoever,[39] and the Terms of Work make similar provision.[40]

Agents

32.33 Where counsel is instructed by an agent, the agent is responsible for discharging counsel's fees.[41]

COUNSEL NOT IN INDEPENDENT PRACTICE

32.34 In general, this chapter assumes that where a barrister seeks payment, it will be as a barrister in independent practice; that said, there are two other circumstances which merit mention.

---

[37] See reg 5 of the Licensed Access Rules and Recognition Regulations and para 3.22 of the Licensed Access Guidance Handbooks for Barristers And Chambers and Licensed Access Clients.
[38] See the Public Access Rules, para 6(g).
[39] Paragraph 12(4) of the Contractual Terms.
[40] Paragraph 14(4) of the Terms of Work.
[41] *Re Nelson, Son and Hastings* (1885) 30 Ch D 1 at 10.

Not practising as a barrister

32.35 A person qualified as a barrister may provide legal services in a capacity other than as a barrister in independent practice.[42] Examples might include an employed barrister, or a barrister who holds himself out as a non-practising barrister providing legal services in another capacity (such as a costs consultant). In these circumstances, that person's remuneration will usually be dependent on a contract, and his fees will be assessed by reference to the capacity in which the legal services are supplied.

Not supplying legal services

32.36 A barrister in independent practice may supply services which are not legal services, in which case counsel would usually be able to sue the recipient of those services for any unpaid fees. Examples include acting as an arbitrator,[43] as a returning officer,[44] a lecturer, an umpire, or as a judge. The modern position is dealt with by the Code of Conduct,[45] para 1001 of which defines 'legal services':

> '"[L]egal services" includes legal advice representation and drafting or settling any statement of case witness statement affidavit or other legal document but does not include:
>
> (a)   sitting as a judge or arbitrator or acting as a mediator;
>
> (b)   lecturing in or teaching law or writing or editing law books articles or reports;
>
> (c)   examining newspapers, periodicals, books, scripts and other publications for libel, breach of copyright, contempt of court and the like;
>
> (d)   communicating to or in the press or other media;
>
> (e)   exercising the powers of a commissioner for oaths;
>
> (f)   giving advice on legal matters free to a friend or relative or acting as unpaid or honorary legal adviser to any charitable benevolent or philanthropic institution; [or]
>
> (g)   in relation to a barrister who is a non-executive director of a company or a trustee or governor of a charitable benevolent or philanthropic institution or a trustee of any private trust, giving to the other directors trustees or governors the benefit of his learning and experience on matters of general legal principle applicable to the affairs of the company institution or trust.'

For obvious reasons it will generally be the case that fees for providing services other than legal services will not be the subject of assessment.

COUNSEL'S FEES IN GENERAL

Counsel's fees between opposing parties

32.37 A number of points can be made about the way counsel's fees are assessed between opposing parties; some of the conclusions that have been reached are not easy to reconcile.

---

[42]   Paragraph 201 of the Code of Conduct.

[43]   See *Norjarl K/S A/S v Hyundai Heavy Industries Co Ltd* [1991] 3 All ER 211; *Virany v Warne* (1801–1804) 4 Esp 47; *Hoggins v Gordon* (1842) 3 QB 466 and *Sinclair v Great Eastern Railway Company* (1870) 21 LT 752.

[44]   *Egan v Kensington Union Guardians* (1841) 3 QB 935.

[45]   That is, the 8th edition of the Code of Conduct of the Bar of England & Wales 2004.

Nature of fees

32.38 Counsel's fees are recoverable as disbursements; this is true regardless of the fact that the solicitor could have instructed someone other than counsel to carry out the work and could have charged for that work as if he had carried it out himself.[46]

Indemnity principle

32.39 In so far as privately payable fees are concerned, the fact that counsel cannot enforce his fees against the solicitor does not present the paying party with an opportunity to say that there has been a breach of the indemnity principle.[47] This is because it is the liability between the solicitor and the client that is relevant, not the liability between counsel and solicitor; once counsel has been paid, the solicitor is able to enforce the debt against the client irrespective of whether his agreement with counsel is one that the latter can enforce.

Unpaid counsel's fees

32.40 Where counsel's fees are unpaid at the time a solicitor and client bill is assessed, those fees will not be allowed.[48] This is a procedural impediment, however, and does not have a bearing on the right to payment. It is questionable whether a paying party would ever be able to rely on non-payment of counsel's fees in a modern-day assessment. This is because there would be no breach of the indemnity principle unless the court were satisfied that the receiving party would not be liable for the legal representative's fees in any circumstances;[49] it could be argued that this could never be the case because the receiving party's solicitor would be able to enforce the debt immediately upon disbursing counsel's fees.[50]

Conditional fee agreements

32.41 The law set out in Chapter 9 of this book applies to counsel's fees. There are two additional points that merit attention.

Unintended conditional fee agreements

32.42 Where, as commonly happens, counsel naively makes an oral agreement to accept one fee if the case is won but a lower fee (or no fee) if the case is lost, the agreement will be unenforceable for the reasons set out at **8.217–8.230**.

Regulatory breach

32.43 Where, before 1 November 2005, counsel entered into a conditional fee agreement at a time when his instructing solicitors had not done likewise, the agreement would be enforceable only if he could show compliance with *all* the requirements of the Conditional Fee Agreements Regulations 2000 (as opposed only to those which relate to

---

[46]   *Crane v Cannons Leisure Centre* [2007] EWCA Civ 1352.
[47]   *Morris v Hunt* (1819) 1 Chit 544.
[48]   *Re Taxation of Costs, Re A Solicitor* [1936] 1 KB 523. See paras 17.99–17.102.
[49]   See **11.20–11.50**, and *R v Miller* [1983] 1 WLR 1057 at 1061 in particular.
[50]   See *Morris v Hunt* (1819) 1 Chit 544, which confirms that the solicitor can enforce counsel's fees once they have been disbursed.

additional legal representatives). This is because counsel would, in those circumstances, not have been acting as an additional legal representative.

Apportioning fees

32.44 Where a paying party is responsible for paying only part of counsel's fee, then the court will have to decide how that part is to be quantified. Where the fee is a simple un-staged fee, Hallett J found that the correct measure is to decide what proportion of the brief fee is payable; she found that it was permissible to take into account not only the work done during the period for which fees were payable, but also the fact that during that period counsel would have committed himself to carrying out further work.[51] Patten J has found that where a brief fee is payable in stages, the stage payments became costs incurred as and when they were paid and, unless the court decided otherwise, they would be apportioned on that basis.[52]

The basis of charging

32.45 It used to be the case that counsel was required to charge a separate fee for each discrete item of work,[53] but this is no longer the case as there is now no rule to prescribe the method by which counsel may charge (other than a prohibition against payment by a wage or salary).[54] Indeed, there is an affirmative rule which permits counsel to charge in any way which is lawful.[55] That rule is reflected in the Terms of Work.[56]

32.46 The following bases of charging are encountered in practice:

- brief fees (see **32.55**);
- refreshers (see **32.106**);
- hourly charging (see **32.110**);
- fees per item (see **32.116**); and
- retainers (or commitment fees) (see **32.118**).

Each of these is addressed in turn but, first, two points of principle are addressed: the scope of counsel's instructions and the evidence by which counsel's fees may be proved.

Scope of instructions

32.47 Counsel carries out work on instructions. Regardless of the nature of the work, counsel is entitled to be paid only for that work which he has been instructed to do. Any

---

[51] *Bowcott v Walding* [2003] EWHC 9042 (Costs).
[52] *Cantor Fitzgerald International v Tradition (UK) Ltd* [2003] EWHC 1907 (Ch).
[53] As to the 'item-by-item' approach, see the Code of Conduct for the Bar of England and Wales (4th edn, 1989): this rule has now been withdrawn.
[54] Code of Conduct, para 405.
[55] In particular, para 405 of the Code of Conduct provides: 'Subject to paragraph 307 a self-employed barrister may charge for any work undertaken by him (whether or not it involves an appearance in Court) on any basis or by any method he thinks fit provided that such basis or method: (a) is permitted by law; [and] (b) does not involve the payment of a wage or salary.'
[56] Paragraph 8 of the Terms of Work provides that: '(8) Save in the case of publicly funded work or in the case of a Notified Solicitor a barrister and solicitor may (subject to any rules regarding contingent fees) make such agreement or arrangement between them as to the time or times whether at the time of delivery of the brief or instructions or subsequently thereto or otherwise at which the barrister's fees shall be paid as they may think fit and the barrister's fees shall be paid by the solicitor accordingly PROVIDED that every such agreement or arrangement shall be in writing.'

work which goes beyond his instructions will go unremunerated. This principle has survived the introduction of the CPR and may, on occasion, result in significant reductions in counsel's fees.[57]

32.48 Hobhouse J explained that this rule does not mean that counsel must carry out work for no pay; it merely means that counsel must negotiate a fee that is sufficient to cover any work that needs to be done. Hobhouse J also explained that where this has not been done, counsel must either make some other arrangement for the delivery of supplementary instructions, or he must agree an additional fee (or both).[58] In a similar vein, Brooke J explained that if, after having discussed the matter with his instructing solicitors, counsel realises that he needs to carry out work which is not covered within the four corners of his present instructions, he must seek additional instructions.[59] Brooke J made it clear that this would not be a rule to be applied inflexibly; in practice, it is not uncommon for the court to find that the requirement for instructions has been met by, for example, a brief exchange of emails.

32.49 It will occasionally happen that counsel not only strays from the four corners of his instructions, but that he disobeys those instructions altogether. Where this is the case, his entire fees may be a risk, including those for work done before the disobedience.[60]

Evidencing counsel's fees

32.50 The points made about evidence in detailed assessment generally apply to counsel's fees; the issues addressed in this discussion are limited to those which pertain to counsel. Other than his instructions, etc, there are three types of evidence which are commonly put before the court in support of counsel's fees, as follows.

Contemporaneous records

32.51 Since July 2000, barristers in independent practice have been required to make and retain records supporting their fees.[61] There is no requirement that these are to be produced on a detailed assessment, but there is a requirement that counsel makes the records available to his client,[62] who may then choose whether to put them before the court. The admissibility of such evidence has been confirmed by Fulford J.[63]

---

[57] See, for example, *Sibley & Co v Reachbyte Ltd* [2008] EWHC 2665, per Peter Smith J.

[58] *Loveday v Renton (No 2)* (1991) Costs LR, Core vol 204 at 210, in which Hobhouse J disallowed charges made by counsel for work at the weekend on the basis that they had not been instructed to carry out that work.

[59] *Brush v Bower Cotton & Bower (a firm)* [1993] 4 All ER 741 at 765.

[60] *Re Harrisson* [1908] 1 Ch 282.

[61] Paragraph 701(f) of the Code of Conduct reads: '[the barrister] must ensure that adequate records supporting the fees charged or claimed in a case are kept at least until the last of the following: his fees have been paid, any taxation or determination or assessment of costs in the case has been completed, or the time for lodging an appeal against assessment or the determination of that appeal, has expired'.

[62] Ibid.

[63] *Edwards & Ors v Roche Products Ltd* [2003] EWHC 9022 (Costs).

Notes from counsel

32.52 Counsel may seek to place a note before the court in support of his fees.[64] The admissibility and relevance of material such as that was confirmed by Lloyd J, who had this to say in the context of an assessment of substantial fees:[65]

> 'It would certainly be helpful to the court and wise from the point of view of counsel to furnish at least some substantial additional material at the stage of the detailed assessment as to why the substantial fees ought to be regarded as proper. It may, for example, be a useful practice for counsel to prepare a short note in the course of, or at the conclusion of the case, to be submitted to the solicitors with fee notes for the purposes of the legal aid assessment.'

Lewison J has pointed out that Lloyd J's comments were not intended to create a legal duty to supply a note; instead, Lloyd J was merely highlighting the fact that if counsel does not supply a note, his fees may be at risk.[66]

32.53 There is no prescribed format, but according to guidance issued by the General Council of the Bar, the contents of the note may usefully address the following:[67]

- the seniority, reputation and relevant expertise of counsel;
- the complexity of the case;
- the amount of preparation required in advance of the hearing;
- counsel's commitment to a fixed hearing date, if any;
- the expected length of the case and, therefore, the time reserved for it in counsel's diary;
- the urgency of the matter when counsel was briefed;
- the amount of work required out of court and in the preparation of any kind of written submission during the hearing; and
- the importance of the case to the parties or any of them, or to the public interest.

Written work

32.54 The admissibility of counsel's written work in support of his fees for that work is beyond doubt; indeed, if it were not produced on cue, the court would probably be concerned about its absence. It is not essential that counsel's written work is produced, however, and even an extreme lack of documentation will not automatically preclude recovery. Where, for example, counsel failed to give disclosure of the written work which he had been specifically ordered to produce, Evans-Lombe J found that the court was still entitled to find as a matter of fact that the work had been done.[68]

---

[64] This is something which is often formally encouraged: see, for example, para 26.7 of the Practice Directions Applicable to Judicial Taxations in the House of Lords (March 2007).

[65] *Armitage v Nurse* [2000] 2 Costs LR 231.

[66] *Ross v Stonewood Securities Ltd* [2004] EWHC 2235 (Ch) at [39], per Lewison J. A serious failure to assist in the recovery of his fees could result in a finding of inadequate professional services against the barrister: Professional Standards and Remuneration Committee of the Bar Council (March 2000), para 6.

[67] Professional Standards and Remuneration Committees Guidance, 22 March 2000.

[68] *Melvin v England Palmer (A Firm)* [2004] EWHC 90019 (Costs).

THE QUANTUM OF COUNSEL'S FEES

Brief fees

32.55 A brief is a document drawn up for the purposes of instructing counsel who is to conduct the matter in court;[69] a brief fee is the fee paid for the appearance. It may be a single fee, or (as is often the case with larger trials) it may be a fee payable in stages, each stage payment becoming payable at a set stage in the litigation.

The 'hypothetical counsel' test

32.56 The starting point for the assessment of any brief fee (and, arguably, for the assessment of any fee charged by counsel) is the 'hypothetical counsel' test, originally articulated by Pennycuick J:[70]

> 'One must envisage a hypothetical counsel capable of conducting the particular case effectively but unable or unwilling to insist on the particularly high fee sometimes demanded by counsel of pre-eminent reputation. Then one must estimate what fee this hypothetical character would be content to take on the brief ... There is, in the nature of things, no precise standard of measurement. The taxing master, employing his knowledge and experience, determines what he considers the right figure.'

32.57 This test remains the correct approach under the CPR.[71] Although Hobhouse J did not expressly refer to the hypothetical counsel test, he made the following comments, which sit alongside that test without any disharmony:[72]

> 'In assessing the brief fee one also has to take into account what will be earned by way of refreshers and what will be the totality of the work that will be required from counsel in the proper discharge of their obligations to protect the interests of their client and the extent to which that work will not be separately remunerated.'

32.58 It is, accordingly, permissible to look at the totality of counsel's fees associated with the hearing rather than just the brief fee. Jackson J built on this approach by saying that where a brief fee includes a skeleton argument, the correct method is to look at the fees which have been provisionally allowed for the hearing and the skeleton argument, and then (as a cross-check) to consider the total amount. The context in which Jackson J was speaking was in respect of costs in the Court of Appeal, but there is no reason to believe that his approach would not be appropriate for any hearing where a brief fee includes a specific item of written work, such as a skeleton argument. Jackson J had the following to say:[73]

> 'Stage 1: The fee for the skeleton argument should be assessed. In the ordinary run of cases, this can be done largely by reference to the amount of time which counsel has reasonably and proportionately devoted to reading the documents, researching the law and drafting the skeleton argument.
>
> Stage 2: The brief fee should be assessed. This exercise involves considering both the amount of time properly spent and many other factors ... In relation to a brief fee in the Court of

---

69   'Brief, n.' 7.a.Law, *Oxford English Dictionary* (2nd edn, 1989).
70   *Simpsons Motor Sales (London) v Hendon Borough Council* [1965] 1 WLR 112 at 117.
71   See, for example, *Orwin v British Coal Corporation* [2003] EWHC 757 (Ch) at [12] and *Higgs v Camden and Islington Health Authority* [2003] EWHC 15 (QB) at [56].
72   *Loveday v Renton (No 2)* [1992] 3 All ER 184 at 194.
73   *Hornsby v Clark Kenneth Leventhal (a firm)* [2000] 4 All ER 567 at 572.

Appeal [where skeleton arguments are required] it is important to avoid double payment. Insofar as counsel prepared himself/herself whilst drafting the skeleton argument, that preparation time should not be paid for in the brief fee.

Stage 3: Having arrived at an appropriate skeleton argument fee and brief fee, a cross check should then be done. The two figures should be aggregated to see whether the total appears too large or too small for the overall conduct of the case in the Court of Appeal. If the total figure seems to be disproportionately large or disproportionately small, then an appropriate adjustment should be made to the brief fee or the skeleton fee.'

32.59 In summary, the test is an objective test which assumes that counsel is unable or unwilling to insist on the particularly high fees sometimes demanded by counsel of pre-eminent reputation; in applying this test the court is entitled to take into account all of the facts, including the fees for work other than the hearing itself, but associated with it.[74]

The scope of the brief fee

32.60 The ambit of the brief fee is a central issue for two reasons: first, both counsel and his instructing solicitor must, for the purposes of negotiating it, be aware of what the fee is intended to include and, secondly, the ambit of the fee may be relevant on the assessment of costs if is it said that a fee other than the brief fee ought to be disallowed because the work it relates to has been included within the brief fee.

32.61 The effect of principles set out at **32.45** is that (subject to one or two constraints) counsel may negotiate whatever form of remuneration he likes. This was not the case when many of the older authorities on the topic were decided.[75] Where counsel has negotiated a different form of remuneration, it would be open the court to look at the total amount claimed in respect of a hearing and then to assess that total as if it were a brief fee. The following points are made on the assumption that either the fee in question is a traditional brief fee, or that the court has decided to assess the total claimed as if it were a traditional brief fee.

32.62 Hobhouse J has explained that a brief fee covers work done by way of preparation for representation at the hearing and attendance on the first day of the hearing.[76] In addition, PD 52, para 14 gives further guidance:[77]

'Advocates' brief (or, where appropriate, refresher) fee includes:

(1)   remuneration for taking a note of the judgment of the court;
(2)   having the note transcribed accurately;
(3)   attempting to agree the note with the other side if represented;
(4)   submitting the note to the judge for approval where appropriate;
(5)   revising it if so requested by the judge;
(6)   providing any copies required for the appeal court, instructing solicitors and lay client; and
(7)   providing a copy of his note to an unrepresented appellant.'

---

[74]   Ibid.
[75]   This is because many of those cases were decided under regulations which, for all practical purposes, limited counsel to charging a traditional brief fee.
[76]   *Loveday v Renton (No 2)* [1992] 3 All ER 184 at 190.
[77]   These provision follow *Practice Note (Barrister: Fees)* [1994] 1 WLR 74, which in turn was based on *Practice Direction of 9 May (Barrister: Fees)* [1989] 1 WLR 605.

32.63 The following additional points relate only to the scope of the brief fee; factors relevant to quantum are discussed below.

Conferences

32.64 Cooke J has found that unless there are exceptional circumstances which change the whole nature of the dispute, the brief fee includes conferences after delivery of the brief.[78]

Skeleton arguments

32.65 Unless the case is an exceptional one of considerable complexity,[79] a brief fee will include the fee for a skeleton argument.[80] This analysis assumes, of course, that the skeleton argument is for the purposes of the hearing.

Judgment

32.66 A brief fee does not include attending at a later date when judgment is given.[81]

After-care

32.67 Where appropriate, a brief fee includes an allowance for explaining the outcome of the case; Jackson J has referred to that type of work as 'after-care'.[82] It seems that Jackson J was not referred to the principle stated immediately above; there is a tension between these two principles which will have to be resolved on a case-by-case basis.

Additional material

32.68 There is ancient authority that if additional material is sent to counsel such that counsel has to carry out work which was not envisaged when the brief fee was negotiated, then an additional fee may be allowable.[83] In practice, the additional work would usually be addressed by counsel renegotiating his fee, or by the court assessing the totality of the costs as if counsel had renegotiated his fee.

Work occasioned by a material change in the case

32.69 On a related point, if there is a material change in the case such that counsel has to carry out work which was not envisaged when the brief fee was negotiated, then an additional fee may be allowable, where appropriate; an example would be where a hearing was unexpectedly opposed when it was previously believed to be unopposed.[84]

32.70 These last two points (at **32.68** and **32.69**) are based on old authority, and in the light of the guidance of the more modern authorities mentioned at **32.64** and **32.65**, the

---

[78] *XYZ v Schering Health Care: Oral Contraceptive Litigation* [2004] All ER (D) 577 (Mar), Cooke J.
[79] *Chohan v Times Newspapers Ltd* (unreported) 7 September 1998, QBD, per Nelson J.
[80] *Loveday v Renton (No 2)* [1992] 3 All ER 184 at 191.
[81] *Practice Note (Barristers' Fees)* [1994] 1 WLR 74, para 2; see also *Practice Note: Brief Fees* [1989] 1 WLR 605, CA.
[82] *Hornsby v Clark Kenneth Leventhal (a firm)* [2000] 4 All ER 567 at 572.
[83] *Wakefield v Brown* (1874) LR 9 CP 410.
[84] *Stephens v Lord Newborough* (1848) 11 Beav 403.

events which prompted the additional or renegotiated fee would probably have to be unusual or possibly even exceptional before the court would regard the extra fees as being recoverable.

Delivery, going short, and abatement

The stage at which it can be said that counsel's brief was delivered

32.71 As between counsel and his instructing solicitor there are no fetters capable of limiting the stage at which a brief will be said to be delivered.[85] Bespoke commercially minded arrangements are commonplace, such as staged fees (where counsel's fee will be incurred, and usually paid, at certain predefined stages in the litigation) or escalating fees (where counsel's brief fee will sequentially increase up to the full amount if the matter does not settle). Thus, it may be difficult (or impossible) to define 'the' stage when the brief was said to be delivered.

32.72 The fact that a brief may have been delivered as between counsel and his instructing solicitor does not mean that the court will necessarily find that that was reasonable. In particular, Danckwerts J considered a case in which it was said that counsel's brief had been delivered prematurely (ie during on-going negotiations); on the facts of that case he rejected this submission (placing reliance on the fact that counsel was conducting those negotiations, and the brief fee was his only means of remuneration),[86] but it was implicit from his judgment that premature delivery is, in principle, possible.

32.73 A finding that a brief has or has not been delivered in no way ties the court's hands; this is because the court has significant freedom to allow a reasonable fee regardless of delivery. In particular:

Where the court finds that there has been delivery

32.74 Jack J has found that 'the old, the very old, rule' that brief fees were payable immediately upon delivery does not fetter the court and had the following to say about the modern approach:[87]

> 'In short it is today appropriate to take a realistic and practical approach rather than to apply rigidly the old rule that a brief fee becomes payable on delivery of the brief.'

Where the court finds that there has been no delivery

32.75 Although there is no authority specifically on the point, where the court has disallowed the brief fee for want of delivery, the court would be able to rely on the Withdrawal of Credit Scheme 1988 for the purposes of allowing a reasonable fee for the work done.[88]

---

[85]   This, of course, assumes that the solicitor it not a notified solicitor under the Withdrawal of Credit Scheme 1988.
[86]   *Re Holberton's Settlement Trusts* [1953] 2 All ER 506 at 507.
[87]   *Miller v Hales* [2006] EWHC 1717 at [7].
[88]   This would be consistent with para 10 of the Withdrawal of Credit Scheme 1988, which provides that counsel will be entitled to a reasonable professional rate for work not covered by an agreed fee.

32.76 While the court has considerable freedom to assess the fee without being fettered by any finding of fact as to the date of delivery, that finding is a background fact which may be taken into account in ascertaining the proper fee. An example would be where delivery meant that counsel had to set aside time and rearrange his diary. Whether the brief has been delivered may also be relevant in the sense that it may have a bearing on the liability as between counsel and his instructing solicitor; it may, therefore, determine the maximum amount payable between opposing parties.

The approach where the brief has been delivered at a late stage

32.77 A paying party may argue that work done prior to delivery of a brief ought to go unremunerated. That argument would go against the provisions of the Withdrawal of Credit Scheme 1988[89] but, in any event, the fact that the brief was delivered late is irrelevant to the ascertainment of counsel's fee, as Hobhouse J noted:[90]

> 'It is not uncommon ... that the actual brief is delivered late and the barrister has to start his preparation for his appearance at the trial on the faith of the solicitor's statement that he will deliver a brief; this does not prejudice the assessment of the proper brief fee when the brief is later delivered.'

The effect of carrying out the work before a brief fee has been agreed

32.78 On a related point, it may be that the brief was delivered but there has been a failure to agree a fee before the work was carried out. A paying party might argue that this precludes recovery of any fee which is subsequently claimed in the bill. This would go against the provisions of the Withdrawal of Credit Scheme 1988, which specifically provides that counsel is entitled to a reasonable fee.[91]

32.79 Morland J has found that a brief fee can be impliedly and retrospectively agreed. In particular, a solicitor is to be taken to have agreed a fee if he includes it in a signed bill of costs.[92] Morland J did not have to address the argument that agreements going to quantum cannot be made after the receiving party has become entitled to costs, but that argument could be met by saying that there was no new agreement, but merely discovery of the level of fees that were payable under a pre-existing agreement.

32.80 There is a further mechanism by which the court may find that there has been an implied agreement; this is because the solicitor will lose the right to object to the fee if he chooses not to raise an objection during the 3-month period after receipt of the fee note (see **32.19**).[93]

32.81 Finally, there is no requirement that the fee be marked on the brief; there is no basis under the CPR or the Withdrawal of Credit Scheme 1988 for arguing that the absence of the fee on the brief precludes recovery.

---

[89]   See footnote 84.
[90]   *Loveday v Renton (No 2)* [1992] 3 All ER 184 at 192.
[91]   See para 10(1) of the Terms of Work in the Withdrawal of Credit Scheme 1988.
[92]   *Spath Holmes Ltd v Chairman of the Greater Manchester and Lancashire Rent Assessment Committee* [1998] 1 Costs LR 40 at 46 and 47.
[93]   See **32.21–32.24**.

The effect of adjournments

32.82 It may be that counsel is denied a fee because a hearing has been adjourned. Although counsel would be entitled to a fee for the work actually done and thrown away by the adjournment, the fact that he has lost the opportunity to earn the full fee is only a background fact; this was explained by Hobhouse J:[94]

> 'The brief fee [relating to the vacated hearing] can only remunerate counsel for the work done on the brief delivered and lost opportunities can only be taken into account as a general background fact to the level of barristers' fees overall in the same way as their overhead expenses and lost time. It is however legitimate for counsel to point to the commitment of time that it involves both for preparation and in the reservation of time for the trial.'

It is not wholly clear what weight should be given to that type of background fact; in some cases the loss of opportunity would be very relevant, even if it were relegated to the status of being a background fact. Nonetheless, with smaller cases the practice is to give only marginal weight to loss of opportunity, focusing instead on the work actually done and thrown away. In cases where adjournment was foreseeable, it is open to the court to find that a fee should have been agreed in advance for the contingency of the matter being adjourned.[95]

The effect of late compromise

32.83 On a related point, it may be that a hearing is vacated because the claim, or part of it, has settled. The starting point is that if a brief has been delivered, the full brief fee is payable.[96] This is only the starting point, as an abatement may be appropriate.

Abatement between counsel and his instructing solicitor

32.84 The Bar Council encourages counsel to renegotiate fees in cases where it would be appropriate. The renegotiated fee would take into account both the work done and (between counsel and his instructing solicitor) loss of opportunity.

Abatement between opposing parties

32.85 If the matter settles before trial, the court is able to abate counsel's fee to reflect the fact that he did not attend the hearing to which the fee relates. In a matter analogous to late compromise,[97] Hallett J found that the correct measure is not whether counsel had carried out the work, but what proportion of the brief fee is payable; she found that it was reasonable to take into account the fact that counsel had to commit time to the hearing and that a commitment fee (as she called it) was payable.[98] Likewise, Mitting J has confirmed that the brief fee for a full trial or an aborted trial covered the

---

[94]   *Loveday v Renton* [1992] 3 All ER 184 at 194. It should be noted that (obiter) comments made by Leggatt LJ in *Norjarl K/S A/S v Hyundai Heavy Industries Co Ltd* [1991] 3 All ER 211 at 222 have suggested that loss of opportunity is something which can be taken into account.

[95]   *Sibley & Co v Reachbyte Ltd* [2008] EWHC 2665 (Ch) at [64]–[66], per Peter Smith J.

[96]   See *Re Holberton's Settlements Trusts* [1953] 1 WLR 1080.

[97]   A Part 36 offer had been made, which meant that the paying party was liable for costs up to a point shortly before trial; the matter did not settle until after the trial had started, however.

[98]   *Bowcott v Walding* [2003] EWHC 9042 (Costs).

commitment for that trial plus preparation and any negotiations before the trial.[99] He commented that it is irrelevant whether or not counsel was able to take on other work and that it would be wrong to assume that he would be able to do so.[100] Whilst obiter, Legatt LJ has explained that in a case set down for a lengthy hearing, an abated brief fee would normally include an element of compensation for possible loss of refreshers.[101]

The following examples illustrate the approach in practice.

One to two weeks before the hearing

32.86 In a matter that settled 13 days before a 3-day trial, Holland J allowed just under a third of the full brief fee,[102] this being in addition to a conference fee. Holland J commented that the two ought to be considered together; if this approach is taken, he allowed just over a third of the total of the brief fee and the conference fee. It should be noted that Holland J did not state the amount of the unabated brief fee; as such, the reduction may include an element that is not abatement.

Two to three weeks before the hearing

32.87 In a matter set down for a longer period of time than 3 days[103] which (for present purposes)[104] can be taken to have settled about 18 days before trial, Hallett J allowed half of the full brief fee. In a clinical negligence claim that settled three weeks before trial[105] and at a stage when little preparation had been carried out, Mitting J found that half the brief fee should be allowed.[106]

32.88 There is nothing in any of these cases to suggest that they were intended to set a tariff or to establish any points of principle. Indeed, if anything, they demonstrate that each case must be decided on its own facts.

The effect of hearings going short

32.89 It may be that a hearing goes short (either because the matter is settled at the doors of the court, or for some other reason). Where this is the case, counsel would ordinarily be entitled to his full brief fee.[107] This can be justified as being a payment based on the principle of swings and roundabouts (that is, some hearings go short, but some last longer than was originally envisaged).

---

[99]   *Lewis v The Royal Shrewsbury Hospital* (unreported) 20 May 2005, QBD (summarised as SCCO Summary No 15 of 2005).
[100] *Lewis v The Royal Shrewsbury Hospital* (unreported) 20 May 2005, QBD (summarised as SCCO Summary No 15 of 2005).
[101] K/S Norjarl A/S v Hyundai Heavy Industries Co Ltd [1991] 3 All ER 211 at 222
[102] *Martin v Holland & Barrett Ltd* [2002] 3 Costs LR 530.
[103] *Bowcott v Walding* [2003] EWHC 9042 (Costs); the case report does not state the exact length.
[104] *Bowcott v Walding* [2003] EWHC 9042 (Costs); the matter was more complex than a straightforward settlement, but those complexities are not relevant to the topic in hand.
[105] Unfortunately the case summary does not state the length of the trial.
[106] *Lewis v The Royal Shrewsbury Hospital* (unreported) 20 May 2005, QBD (summarised as SCCO Summary No 15 of 2005).
[107] See, for example, *Re a Company (No 004081 of 1989)* [1995] 2 All ER 155; see also *Charman v Brandon* (1900) 82 LT 369.

The relevance of time

32.90 It is often said that counsel's fees are not based on an arithmetical analysis of the time spent: indeed, some commentators have put that point with vigour.[108] It is undoubtedly the case that brief fees are not assessed in the same way as solicitors' fees (ie by mathematically applying a reasonable hourly rate to a reasonable allowance of time), and it is also undoubtedly the case that there is 'no precise standard of measurement' of brief fees, to use Pennycuick J's words. Thus, time is not a factor which should determine the fee and, to that extent, those commentators are correct.

32.91 It is, however, a moot point whether time is as unimportant as it was a decade or so ago. In a relatively recent case, Cooke J confirmed that whilst it was not appropriate to determine a brief fee by having regard solely to an hourly rate, time was a factor to be taken into account when determining the appropriate fee.[109] Indeed, there are recent examples of the court determining in a *quantitative* way the time that would have been reasonably spent in preparation, and then using that figure to ascertain the appropriate fee;[110] this approach was rarely seen a decade or so ago.

32.92 Even if time is a factor which is becoming increasingly important, care must be taken not to give disproportionate weight to the time reasonably spent. Although not dealing specifically with counsel, CPD, art 11.3 gives the following guidance:

> 'Where a trial takes place, the time taken by the court in dealing with a particular issue may not be an accurate guide to the amount of time properly spent by the legal or other representatives in preparation for the trial of that issue.'

32.93 In summary, time is a factor to be taken into account, but it would be wrong to afford it greater weight than it deserves.

The use of comparators

32.94 Many other comparisons may be made, but three types of comparator are often relied upon in practice: the first is the amount charged by opposing counsel, the second is the amount charged by other lawyers on the same side, and the last is the amount previously charged by the barrister whose fees are being assessed.

Comparators (opponents)

32.95 The fee charged by opposing counsel is relevant, but it should not be given disproportionate weight, as Pennycuick J emphasised:[111]

> '[The fee charged by an opponent] is certainly a factor of weight but not, I think, by any means conclusive. In the ordinary course of events it often happens that the clerks to counsel of comparable degree ask for rather different fees, but I do not think that in these circumstances one is justified without more ado in saying that one counsel has asked too

---

[108] See Butterworths Costs Service, J:III:202, where HHJ Peter Birts QC explains the benefits of charging by the item rather than by the hour.

[109] *XYZ v Schering Health Care: Oral Contraceptive Litigation* [2004] All ER (D) 577 (Mar); see also *Global Marine Drillships Ltd v La Bella* [2010] EWHC 2498 (Ch) at [13], per Peter Smith J.

[110] *Orwin v British Coal Corporation* [2003] EWHC 757 (Ch) at [11]–[14]; see also *Hornsby v Clark Kenneth Leventhal (a firm)* [2000] 4 All ER 567 at 573.

[111] *Simpsons Motor Sales (London) v Hendon Borough Council* [1965] 1 WLR 112 at 119

much. It can equally be said that the other has asked too little. The truth is that there is no exact figure which can be said to represent the proper fee.'

32.96 As with any comparator, like should be compared with like. It may be necessary to consider the appropriateness of the comparator as well as the weight that it should be afforded. Care should be taken where the comparator counsel has had the benefit of being able to read his opponent's submissions before beginning his own preparation.[112] Sir Charles Gray has warned that where comparators are taken into account, it is necessary to consider them carefully in order to exclude those which are inappropriate or misleading.[113]

32.97 It would be wrong to give disproportionate weight to an opponent's fees; nevertheless, this does not mean that comparators will be only a minor factor. In a pre-CPR case, Romer J found that there were circumstances in which it could be implied that counsel whose fees were being assessed had done at least as much work as his opponent, and that his fee should, therefore, not be lower.[114] Where inexplicable differences exist between the fees in question and the comparator's fees, that is a factor which may be afforded weight.[115] Commenting on the changes brought about by the CPR, Lawrence Collins J indicated that summary assessment has led to comparison being a more important factor than it was in the past, and that this was also true of detailed assessments.[116]

Comparators (same side)

32.98 Where leading and junior counsel are both instructed, it is often the case that the junior counsel's fee is allowed as a fixed proportion of that of the leading counsel. This topic is addressed in more detail at **32.120–32.124**. Occasionally, it will be appropriate to take into account the fees charged by counsel's instructing solicitors (but usually only in a way that affords them very little weight). The *Guide to the Summary Assessment of Costs* makes the following observations about counsel's fees in the Court of Appeal:[117]

'(2) Where both Counsel and solicitors have been instructed, the reasonable fees of Counsel are likely to exceed the reasonable fees of the solicitor.'

Presumably, if counsel's fees were lower than those of his instructing solicitors, the court might take this into account as being an indicator that his fees were reasonable.

Comparators (fees previously charged)

32.99 There used to be a custom that brief fees in the Court of Appeal were to be the same as those in the court below;[118] that custom seems to have fallen by the wayside (although it stills seems to be relevant in so far as refreshers are concerned).[119] The fee claimed previously is now merely a factor that the court may take into account in

---

[112] See *Hornsby v Clark Kenneth Levental (a firm)* [2000] 4 All ER 567 at 573 (relating to fees of counsel on the same side).
[113] *Lord Chancellor v Rees* [2008] EWHC 3168 (QB); by way of example, at [63] Sir Charles Gray found that it was not appropriate to use privately-payable fees as comparators for publically funded work.
[114] *Re Bennett (Viscount), Barclays Bank Ltd* [1950] 1 All ER 435.
[115] *Lord Chancellor v Wright* [1993] 1 WLR 1561.
[116] *Orwin v British Coal Corporation* [2003] EWHC 757 (Ch) at [12].
[117] At para 65.
[118] *Sunnucks v Smith* [1950] 1 All ER 550.
[119] *Hornsby v Clark Kenneth Leventhal (a firm)* [2000] 4 All ER 567 at 574.

appropriate circumstances. The *Guide to the Summary Assessment of Costs* makes the following observations about counsel's fees in the Court of Appeal:[120]

> '(3)   The fact that the same Counsel appeared in the lower court does not greatly reduce the reasonable fee unless, for example, the lower court dealt with a great many more issues than are raised on the appeal. It is reasonable for Counsel to spend as much time preparing issues for the Court of Appeal hearing as he spent preparing those issues for the lower court hearing.'

Other factors relevant to quantum

'Going rate'

32.100   Whilst it is a difficult factor to identify and describe, both judicial[121] and extrajudicial[122] comments support the notion that the court takes into account a 'going rate'. This, presumably, is a way of referring to the judge's own experience.

London counsel and local bar

32.101   The availability of a local bar may be a factor to be taken into account,[123] but there is authority to show that where the local bar is able to offer only a small number of suitable counsel, the instruction of London counsel can be justified.[124]

Work outside business hours

32.102   There is authority for the proposition that counsel is expected to work at unsociable hours from time to time and that no extra remuneration is to be allowed for this.[125] That said, the urgency of the work may be a factor to be taken into account, and where urgent work needs to be done in the long vacation, a higher fee may be appropriate to take account of the fact that counsel may be kept waiting for a judge.[126]

Researching the law

32.103   This is a topic which is addressed in detail at **29.91–29.94**: the principles for solicitor and counsel are broadly the same. Common sense dictates that counsel who is instructed as a specialist will be deemed to know a greater part of the relevant law than those who instruct him.

Travelling

32.104   Although the context was public funding, Sachs J has confirmed that an allowance may be made if counsel is required to travel to attend court.[127] That said,

---

[120]   At para 65.
[121]   See, for example, the comments of Cazalet J in *H v H (financial relief: costs)* [1995] 1 FCR 718, sub nom *Re H (a minor)* [1995] 2 FCR 733 and in *F v F (ancillary relief: costs)* [1995] 2 FLR 702 at 710.
[122]   See Butterworths Costs Service, J:III:266, where HHJ Birts QC has indicated that this is a factor that is habitually taken into account.
[123]   See, for example, Wallington J's obiter in *Young v Young and Kohler* [1955] 1 All ER 796 and *Eaves v Eaves and Powell* [1956] P 154.
[124]   *Self v Self* [1954] 2 All ER 550 at 551 and *Raybould v Raybould* [1968] 1 All ER 608.
[125]   *R v Mills and Morris* [1997] 1 Costs LR 49.
[126]   *Global Marine Drillships Ltd v La Bella* [2010] EWHC 2498 (Ch) at [8] and [14], per Peter Smith J.
[127]   *Self v Self* [1954] 2 All ER 550 at 551.

Mitting J has commented that counsel could ordinarily be expected to work whilst on a train journey and that no time ought ordinarily to be allowed for travelling; he accepted, however, that there will be times when travelling times could not be usefully spent.[128] In practice, Sach J's approach seems generally to be preferred (not least because counsel is able to decline instructions if the fee is insufficient to cover the expenses he will incur).[129] There are limits to what counsel can claim, however, and in particular there is no legal basis for counsel being allowed a 'special fee' to compensate him for inconvenient travel.[130]

Overlap between cases

32.105 There is old authority that if counsel has more than one case in the same court, his fee would be assessed on the basis that the only case he had was the case in question.[131] Each case must be decided on its own facts, however, and there would be no reason why the court could not take into account the factual background created by counsel's involvement in the other case or cases.

REFRESHERS

32.106 According to the dramatist Reynolds, 'barristers ... can only be kept alive by refreshers'.[132] The word 'refresher' used to be used to refer to a fee paid on an adjournment,[133] but its use is now limited to a fee payable for appearing on the second or subsequent days of a hearing. To an extent, the points made about brief fees apply to refreshers. The following additional points may be made.

Abated refresher

32.107 It has long been established that it is open to the court to find that a refresher should be reduced if a case lasts only a short part of a day. Where the court does this, the allowance should be based on a fair fee, and should not be a mere mechanical calculation based on the number of hours actually spent in court.[134]

Comparators (fees previously charged)

32.108 Jackson J has commented that the refreshers charged in the lower court may be relevant to the refresher claimed in an appeal court;[135] this may be a particularly helpful comparator because the level and intensity of the work would usually be directly comparable, especially in a second appeal.

---

[128] *Lewis v The Royal Shrewsbury Hospital* (unreported) 20 May 2005, QBD (summarised as SCCO Summary No 15 of 2005).

[129] Code of Conduct, para 604(b)(iii).

[130] *The Warkworth* (1885) 1 TLR 659, CA; such fees used to be required by circuit rules: see *Payne v Schmidt* [1949] 2 All ER 741 for a discussion of this.

[131] *Isaacs v Isaacs* [1955] 2 All ER 811 at 812.

[132] F Reynolds *A Playwright's Adventures* (Longman, Rees, Orme, Brown, & Green, 1831), p 108.

[133] 'f. refresh v. + -er1', *Oxford English Dictionary* (2nd edn, 1989).

[134] Although decided under the 'five hour rule', the analysis set out in *Re Mercury Model Aircraft Supplies Ltd* [1956] 1 WLR 1153 still has resonance under the CPR.

[135] *Hornsby v Clark Kenneth Leventhal (a firm)* [2000] 4 All ER 567 at 574.

Obsolete authorities

32.109   Refreshers used to be determined by the application of 'the five hour rule'.[136] That rule has no counterpart under the CPR, but it is worth being aware of it for two reasons. First, obsolete authorities ought to be recognised as such; and, second, it has given rise to a number of decisions about what is and is not time spent 'in court'. Denning MR, for example, found that the lunch hour is not time spent in court;[137] another example is that the time with the judge in chambers is equivalent to time in court.[138] The relevance of these cases under the CPR is peripheral at best, but they may occasionally be encountered when the court assesses the appropriate refresher on the basis of the time spent in court.[139]

HOURLY CHARGING

32.110   Much of counsel's working day is spent carrying out work which will be charged by the hour. In particular, drafting pleadings, drafting advices, advising in conference, etc, will usually be charged on this basis. Even if they have not been charged on this basis, it would be open to the court to assess the reasonable costs by reference to the time spent (but only as one factor amongst others: see **32.90–32.93**).

Advices

32.111   The distinction between preliminary opinions and advices[140] is obsolete and ought not to be made under the CPR; in particular, there is no rule that preliminary opinions will, in general, not be allowed.

Conferences and consultations

32.112   Conferences are usually charged at an hourly rate,[141] but conferences which take place after delivery of the brief may be covered by the brief fee.[142] The same is true of consultations with leading counsel.

Counsel's view

32.113   A counsel's 'view' is a site visit. Unless it is part and parcel of the brief fee, a reasonable fee may be charged on the basis of time spent.[143]

Skeleton arguments

32.114   These may be charged by the hour or on an item-by-item basis; they may also be charged as being part of a brief fee (see **32.58**). Toulson LJ has noted that there is a tendency towards prolixity; he described 132-page document before him as being: 'a

---

[136]   RSC Ord 65, r 27(48).
[137]   *Wright v Bennett* [1947] KB 828.
[138]   *Lawson v Tiger* [1953] 1 WLR 503.
[139]   See, for example, *Sibley & Co v Reachbyte Ltd* [2008] EWHC 2665 (Ch) at [67], per Peter Smith J.
[140]   See *Practice Direction (Counsel's Fees)* [1957] 1 WLR 839.
[141]   If authority were needed on the point, it can be found in *Re Cosedge* (1885) 29 SJ.
[142]   *XYZ v Schering Health Care: Oral Contraceptive Litigation* [2004] All ER (D) 577 (Mar), Cooke J.
[143]   If authority were needed on the point, it can be found at *Leeds Forge Company Ltd v Deighton's Patent Flue and Tube Co Ltd* [1903] 1 Ch 475.

grotesque example of a tendency to burden the court with documents of grossly disproportionate quantity and length.'[144] The full costs of such documents are not likely to be recoverable. In a similar vein, Mummery LJ said this:[145]

'We remind practitioners that skeleton arguments should not be prepared as verbatim scripts to be read out in public or as footnoted theses to be read in private. Good skeleton arguments are tools with practical uses: an agenda for the hearing, a summary of the main points, propositions and arguments to be developed orally, a useful way of noting citations and references, a convenient place for making cross references, a time–saving means of avoiding unnecessary dictation to the court and laborious and pointless note–taking by the court.'

Specific provisions apply where the skeleton argument is for an appeal. The cost of preparing a skeleton argument which does not comply with those requirements will not be allowed on assessment except to the extent that the court otherwise directs;[146] those requirements are set out in the footnotes.[147] Similarly, if a skeleton argument for an appeal was not filed within the time limits provided by PD 52 (or any further time granted by the court), then the costs will be disallowed save to the extent that the court orders otherwise.[148]

Other documents

32.115 Not all work carried out by counsel will be capable of being neatly compartmentalised into a category such as those mentioned above; the fact that work is of an unusual nature will not, of itself, prevent a fee being charged.[149]

FEES PER ITEM

32.116 Another method of ascertaining counsel's costs is on an item-by-item basis. The time spent is often a major factor in determining the appropriate fee, but there will be occasions where this is not the predominant factor. An example would be where a skeleton argument has been prepared for a hearing, but has been prepared so far in advance of the hearing that a separate fee has been charged; the reason a simple hourly rate would not be appropriate is because of the possibility of overlap between the work done in preparing the skeleton argument and the work done in preparing for the hearing. This was explained by Jackson J:[150]

'The process of drafting a skeleton argument has the effect of at least partially preparing an advocate to argue his case in court. Thus, there is an overlap between the work which is

---

[144] *Midgulf International Ltd v Groupe Chimiche Tunisien* (2010) EWCA Civ 66 at [71] onwards.

[145] *Tombstone Limited v Raja* [2008] EWCA Civ 1444 at [125].

[146] See PD 52, para 5.10(6)(a).

[147] PD 52, para 5.10 '(1) A skeleton argument must contain a numbered list of the points which the party wishes to make ... Each point should be stated as concisely as the nature of the case allows. (2) A numbered point must be followed by a reference to any document on which the party wishes to rely. (3) A skeleton argument must state, in respect of each authority cited – (a) the proposition of law that the authority demonstrates; and (b) the parts of the authority (identified by page or paragraph references) that support the proposition. (4) If more than one authority is cited in support of a given proposition, the skeleton argument must briefly state the reason for taking that course.'

[148] See PD 52 5.10(6)(b).

[149] See, for example, *D v D* [2002] EWHC 2511 (Fam), where counsel was allowed a fee for drafting an accountancy schedule.

[150] *Hornsby v Clark Kenneth Leventhal (a firm)* [2000] 4 All ER 567 at 572.

covered by a skeleton argument fee and the work which is covered by a brief fee. If the skeleton argument is drafted shortly before the hearing, then the overlap is greater than it would be if the skeleton argument is drafted far in advance of the hearing.

32.117   While he did not purport to lay down any point of principle, Jackson J's approach to assessing a fee for a skeleton argument prepared in advance of the hearing was as follows:[151]

* he found as a matter of fact the number of hours spent in preparing it;
* he reduced that figure to a reasonable and proportionate figure;
* he allowed a figure which was based on all the factors, including the figure mentioned above and the fee which was claimed; and
* he carried out a 'cross-check', in that he ensured that when the brief fee and the skeleton argument were combined, they did not exceed a sum which was reasonable and disproportionate.

As can be seen, although Jackson J's approach was not limited to ascertaining a reasonable time, the time reasonably spent was a significant factor in his adjudication.

RETAINERS (OR COMMITMENT FEES)

32.118   A retainer is a near-obsolete payment made to retain counsel; 'general retainers' used to be paid (which secured the right to a refusal of counsel's services generally), but the term is now restricted to retainers paid to retainer counsel for a specific purpose, in which case the phrase 'common retainer'[152] is appropriate, but rarely used. The payment is to compensate counsel for placing the matter in his diary and for not accepting other instructions (especially from an opponent). It would, in an appropriate case, be open to the court to disallow a retainer on the basis that it was a solicitor and client expense.

32.119   While speaking in the context of retainers for arbitrators rather than counsel, Stuart-Smith LJ has made it clear that once a retainer has been agreed and paid, a further retainer would be justified only if there was a change of circumstances. In the same case, Legatt LJ made the following comments about a proposal to charge a retainer of 100% for a period of 60 days:[153]

> 'The arbitrators' original requirement of a 100% commitment fee was more than was required to protect them against loss. In those circumstances to refer to the commitment fee as "earned" by the instalments demanded was an abuse of language. A fee is only earned if and in so far as a hearing takes place. Yet payment was demanded for being available to conduct it, irrespective of whether the arbitrators did any work or not, or ... as protection against the risk of *not* working ... The notion that, if the arbitration were settled before it started, these particular arbitrators would find themselves unemployed for the whole of the period set aside (assuming that they then held themselves out as available to accept instructions) seems little short of absurd.'

---

[151]   *Hornsby v Clark Kenneth Leventhal (a firm)* [2000] 4 All ER 567 at 573 and 574.
[152]   *The Penny Cyclopædia of the Society for the Diffusion of Useful Knowledge*, XXI. 272/1, referred to under 'retainer', *Oxford English Dictionary* (2nd edn, 1989).
[153]   *Norjarl K/S A/S v Hyundai Heavy Industries Co Ltd* [1991] 3 All ER 211 at 222.

It is clear from what Leggatt LJ had to say that retainers must be reasonable, and that it would not be reasonable to treat retainers is if they were brief fees.

LEADING COUNSEL

32.120 Giving judgment in the Divisional Court, Woolf LJ explained that the appropriate test is whether the receiving party acted reasonably in instructing his choice of counsel, and not whether more junior counsel could adequately have dealt with the case.[154] Henriques J has found that where costs fall to be assessed on the standard basis, this test must be applied according to the two-stage test in *Lownds v Home Office*[155] (see **34.9–34.10**).[156]

32.121 The following relevant factors were listed by Evans J (albeit in the context of whether both leading and junior counsel were required):[157]

'(a) the nature of the case;

(b) its importance for the client;[158]

(c) the amount of damages likely to be recovered;

(d) the general importance of the case, e g as affecting other cases;

(e) any particular requirements of the case, e g the need for legal advice, or for special expertise, e g witnesses; and

(f) other claims why experienced and senior advocate may be required.'

32.122 Evans J went on to say that in personal injury claims the following may be relevant:

'(1) The nature and severity of the plaintiff's injury.

(2) The likely duration of the trial.

(3) Difficult questions regarding the quantum of damages including medical evidence and questions of law.

(4) Difficult questions of fact, including expert engineering evidence, or issues as to causation.'

32.123 Whether the other side has instructed a leader is relevant, but not conclusive.[159]

---

[154] *R v Dudley Magistrates' Court ex p Power City Stores Limited* (1990) 154 JP 654.

[155] [2002] EWCA Civ 365.

[156] *Young v JR Smart (Builders) Ltd* [2004] EWHC 90018 (Costs).

[157] *Juby v LFCDA and Saunders v Essex CC* (unreported) 24 April 1990.

[158] As an example of a higher fee being allowed on the basis of importance (amongst other factors), see *Global Marine Drillships Ltd v La Bella* [2010] EWHC 2498 (Ch) at [13], in which Peter Smith J allowed a high fee on the basis that whilst the application was short, it concerned a person's liberty.

[159] *British Metal Corporation Ltd v Ludlow Bros* [1938] Ch 987.

32.124   Each case will turn on its own facts, but there are some circumstances where leading counsel's involvement would be hard to justify. In particular, Lindsay J has commented that it could not be said to be necessary, or even usual, for leading counsel to attend a hearing when all that was required was a simple assent on his client's behalf to terms already agreed.[160] As to the quantum of leading counsel's fees, counsel who has recently taken silk would often charge as if he were still a junior, but there is no rule that would compel him to do this, either during the first year after taking silk or otherwise.

TWO COUNSEL

32.125   There is no prohibition against two juniors being instructed,[161] but it is usual that, where two counsel are instructed, at least one of them will be leading counsel. Where this is so, the points made immediately above would be relevant. After having set out the questions mentioned at **32.121** and **32.122**, Evans J went on to explain that there may be many reasons why a junior would be necessary for proper conduct of the case, such as to provide the following types of assistance:[162]

> '(a) to assist the court proceedings either by taking an active part (examining or cross-examining some witnesses or dealing with a discreet part of the case, eg expert evidence, damage, etc) or by keeping a full note of the evidence, editing transcripts, etc;
>
> (b) dealing with documents generally, particularly when the junior counsel has taken part in discovery;
>
> (c) to carry out legal and other research, eg on matters on which expert evidence is given;
>
> (d) to assist leading counsel in negotiations with the other party, particularly when, as in many accident cases, junior counsel has already advised the litigant in person and has become known to him. The lay client might well fail to understand why the junior who has dealt with the case up to the trial should no longer be present when his claim is settled by negotiation or dealt with by judgment.'

32.126   It may be relevant to the issue of reasonableness that where more than one counsel is instructed, they have a duty to consider whether it would be in the best interest of their lay client for fewer of them to be instructed.[163] For obvious reasons, counsel's conclusion would not bind the court, but where there was evidence that counsel had considered this issue and concluded that more than one counsel was required, it would be open to the court to take that fact into account. Where there are co-parties, and where there is no conflict between them, then the costs of separate representation may not be justified;[164] this is particularly so in the context of appeals because the issues will be well defined. Lord Keith has commented that, where appropriate, it is the duty of counsel carefully to consider this issue.[165]

---

[160]   *Re a Company (No 004081 of 1989)* [1995] 2 All ER 155 at 157.
[161]   *Douglas v Associated Newspapers* (1922) 67 Sol Jo 48.
[162]   *Juby v LFCDA and Saunders v Essex CC* (unreported) 24 April 1990.
[163]   See the Code of Conduct, para 606.2.
[164]   *Birmingham City Council v H (a minor)* [1994] 2 WLR 31 at 33, per Lord Keith; more recently, see *Commission for Equality & Human Rights v Griffin* [2011] EWHC 675 (Admin) at [16], per Moore-Bick LJ.
[165]   Ibid.

32.127   In contrast to criminal costs,[166] there is no rule in civil cases setting any ratio determining the amount of leading and junior counsel's fees.[167] There used to be a convention in civil litigation that the junior's fee should be either a half or two-thirds that of his leader,[168] but this was merely a custom rather than a rule of law.

32.128   Nonetheless, whilst it is not a rule of law, that ratio is often used as a rule of thumb. Where the court does apply it, a ratio of between one-half and two-thirds would usually be taken as being the appropriate measure. Nonetheless, Garland J has explained that the court should look at the time spent and the work actually carried out.[169] In a similar vein, Cazalet J explained that each case must be decided on its own facts:[170]

> 'In a normal case I would expect 50% broadly to reflect the division of responsibility, effort and the other factors ... There will be cases, however, where the burden of the preparation and argument is borne by leading counsel and where junior counsel has performed little more than a noting function. In these cases 50% of leading counsel's fee will be well beyond the remuneration for junior counsel ... Moving to the other extreme there will be cases in which junior counsel may carry out the vast proportion of the preparation for trial and make a most substantial input to the case. In such circumstances 50% would be unlikely to reflect his contribution and a fee of or approaching two-thirds of leading counsel's fee could well be appropriate.'

32.129   The *Guide to the Summary Assessment of Costs*, for example, gives the following guidance about summary assessments in the Court of Appeal:[171]

> '(4)   If the case merits leading Counsel it may merit also the instruction of a junior to assist him. The junior's fees should be allowed at one half of the leader's fees unless:
>
> - the junior is a senior junior and the case merited both a leader and a senior junior.
> - The junior took a responsibility which was equal to or larger than that taken by the leader.
> - The junior undertook work not covered by the brief.'

Although it would be uncommon, it is not unknown for the junior's fee to equal or even exceed that of his leader.[172]

32.130   Whilst each case will turn on its own facts, the following points can be made about the use of two counsel:

- *Arbitration*: it is unusual for more than one counsel to be allowed on a reference for arbitration;[173] and
- *Unopposed claims*: whilst it would be a factor to take into account, the fact that a claim is unopposed would not necessarily result in disallowance of the fee of second counsel.[174]

---

[166]   See, for example, CPS Fees Guidance (1 April 1995), para 5.
[167]   There is, however, some authority that 50% is the starting point: see *Perloff v Gordon Dadds & Co* (1989) *The Independent*, November 20, Webster J.
[168]   See, for example, *Practice Direction (Refresher Fees to Counsel)* [1959] 1 WLR 350.
[169]   *Matthews v Dorkin* [2000] All ER (D) 1584.
[170]   *F v F (ancillary relief: costs)* [1995] 2 FLR 702 at 710.
[171]   *Guide to the Summary Assessment of Costs*, para 65.
[172]   See, for example, *Matthews v Dorkin* [2000] All ER (D) 351, per Garland J.
[173]   *Drew v Josolyne* (1888) 4 TLR 717, DC.
[174]   *Friend v Solly* (1847) 10 Beav 329.

INFORMAL ARRANGEMENTS FOR TWO COUNSEL (DEVILLING)

32.131   It will occasionally be the case that counsel will seek assistance from another barrister (often a pupil or very junior barrister) for the purposes of examining factual material, carrying out legal research, etc; this practice is called 'devilling'.[175] Where counsel devils work to another barrister, he is entitled to charge the other barrister's fee as if it were his own (although he will be responsible for paying the other barrister).[176] This means that the devil's fee would usually be subsumed: it would rarely be the case that a devil's fee would appear as a separate item, either in counsel's fee note or in the bill of costs.

MORE THAN TWO COUNSEL

32.132   In general, the court will be reluctant to allow the fees of more than two counsel at any one hearing.[177] Indeed, even on a solicitor and client basis, the costs of instructing more than two counsel would require justification; in particular, it would often be regarded as being 'unusual' for the purposes of CPR, r 48.8(2).[178]

32.133   The decision will ultimately be for the costs judge, but where three counsel have been instructed, the trial judge will often express a view as to whether that was reasonable.[179]

32.134   Whether it was reasonable to instruct three or more counsel is a topic which is particularly fact sensitive. The following are examples of the types of cases were three counsel may be justified:

- on-going group litigation lasting many years;[180]
- cases requiring significant legal research;[181]

- cases involving extremely lengthy and detailed pleadings;[182] and

- on-going cases involving significant examination of scientific experts.[183]

32.135   The following would not generally be regarded as justifying the employment of three counsel:

---

[175]   See 'devil n 5b, c; devil v. 3' in *Oxford English Dictionary* (2nd edn, 1989).

[176]   Code of Conduct, rule 406.

[177]   See, for example, *Mercedes Daimler Motor Co Ltd v FIAT Motor Cab Co Ltd* (1913) 31 RPC 8.

[178]   See *Re Broad and Broad* (1885) 15 QBD 252, DC.

[179]   This was the guidance of the Court of Appeal in *Fluflon Ltd v William Frost & Sons Ltd* [1965] RPC 574. As an example of this, see *Mahme Trust Reg and others v Lloyds TSB Bank plc* [2006] EWHC 1782 (Ch) at [30], per Evans-Lombe J.

[180]   *AB and Ors v British Coal Corporation* [2006] EWCA Civ 987, where the litigation (or, more accurately, a court-managed compensation scheme) lasted for over a decade.

[181]   See, for example, *Carl Zeiss Stiftung v Rayner & Keeler Ltd (No 2)* [1965] Ch 596, [1965] 1 All ER 300, CA, where the issues involved wasted costs and conflict of law.

[182]   As an example of this, see *Mahme Trust Reg and others v Lloyds TSB Bank plc* [2006] EWHC 1782 (Ch) at [30], per Evans-Lombe J, although it should be noted that costs in that case were payable on the indemnity basis.

[183]   See, for example, *Great Western Rly Co v Carpalla United China Clay Co Ltd (No 2)* [1909] 2 Ch 471, where counsel had to prepare 'examination of varied scientific theories and investigations'.

- concerns about counsel's availability;[184]
- junior counsel originally instructed taking silk;[185] and
- as a result of a professional rule or custom.[186]

Evans-Lombe J has implied that the use of three counsel should be kept under review, especially as the issues are narrowed and the intensity of the work is reduced.[187]

---

[184] *Perry & Co Ltd v Hessin & Co* (1913) 108 LT 332.

[185] *Betts v Cleaver* (1872) 20 WR 732.

[186] *Payne v Schmidt* [1949] 2 All ER 741.

[187] *Mahme Trust Reg and others v Lloyds TSB Bank plc* [2006] EWHC 1782 (Ch) at [30], per Evans-Lombe J.

Chapter 33

FIXED COSTS, COSTS ON THE SMALL CLAIMS TRACK, AND FAST TRACK COSTS

This chapter addresses the following:

- Fixed commencement costs (**33.1–33.22**).
- Fixed recoverable costs (**33.23–33.41**).
- Fixed success fees in road traffic accident claims (**33.43–33.53**), employers' liability claims (**33.54–33.60**); employers' liability disease claims (**33.61–33.75**).
- Costs on the small claims track (**33.76–33.103**).
- Fast track trial costs (**33.104–33.132**).
- Low value road traffic accident claims (**33.133–33.175**).
- Scale costs for claims in a patents county court (**33.176–33.180**).
- Fixed Costs: HM Revenue and Customs (**33.181–33.183**).

The writer is grateful to Kevin Latham for his assistance with this chapter.

FIXED COMMENCEMENT COSTS

Generally

33.1 This section discusses CPR Part 45 I, which includes fixed commencement costs (at **33.7**), fixed costs on entry of judgment (at **33.18**), miscellaneous fixed costs, and fixed enforcement costs (at **33.22**). Save where is otherwise obvious from the context, this group of entitlements is referred to collectively as 'fixed commencement costs'.

33.2 Care ought to be exercised when reading commentary about fixed commencement costs; this is because some commentators refer to pre-CPR schedules of fixed costs as if they were still applicable.[1] This is not the case as those provisions were revoked on 1 April 2005.[2] Only the CPR are relevant.

33.3 Chancery practitioners may be familiar with a *Table of Fixed Costs Published by the Senior Master (Queen's Bench Divisions) and the Chief Master (Chancery Division)*. At first blush that table does not tally with the CPR, but, in fact, it does; the reason the figures are not the same is because the figures in that table are inclusive of court fees. This is why the figures in that table display many more incremental steps than do the tables in CPR Part 45 I.

---

[1] See M Cook *Cook on Costs 2010* (Butterworths) at [25.15].
[2] See Civil Procedure (Amendment No 4) Rules 2004, r 17.

Applicability

33.4 Broadly speaking, fixed costs will apply where a claim is for a specified amount of money and where that claim is short-lived by reason of it settling or being dealt with by default or by summary judgment (see **33.5** for the details). In these circumstances, fixed commencement costs will be payable (see **33.7**), with or without fixed costs on entry of judgment, depending on the circumstances (see **33.18**). Other costs may be payable in addition.

33.5 CPR, r 45.1(2) sets out the circumstances in which fixed costs are to apply; that rule reads as follows:

'This Section applies where—

    (a)   the only claim is a claim for a specified sum of money where the value of the claim exceeds £25 and—
        (i)   judgment in default is obtained under rule 12.4(1);
        (ii)   judgment on admission is obtained under rule 14.4(3);
        (iii)   judgment on admission on part of the claim is obtained under rule 14.5(6);
        (iv)   summary judgment is given under Part 24;
        (v)   the court has made an order to strike out a defence under rule 3.4(2)(a) as disclosing no reasonable grounds for defending the claim; or
        (vi)   rule 45.3 applies;
    (b)   the only claim is a claim where the court gave a fixed date for the hearing when it issued the claim and judgment is given for the delivery of goods, and the value of the claim exceeds £25;
    (c)   the claim is for the recovery of land, including a possession claim under Part 55, whether or not the claim includes a claim for a sum of money and the defendant gives up possession, pays the amount claimed, if any, and the fixed commencement costs stated in the claim form;
    (d)   the claim is for the recovery of land, including a possession claim under Part 55, where one of the grounds for possession is arrears of rent, for which the court gave a fixed date for the hearing when it issued the claim and judgment is given for the possession of land (whether or not the order for possession is suspended on terms) and the defendant—
        (i)   has neither delivered a defence, or counterclaim, nor otherwise denied liability; or
        (ii)   has delivered a defence which is limited to specifying his proposals for the payment of arrears of rent;
    (e)   the claim is a possession claim under Section II of Part 55 (accelerated possession claims of land let on an assured shorthold tenancy) and a possession order is made where the defendant has neither delivered a defence, or counterclaim, nor otherwise denied liability;
    (f)   the claim is a demotion claim under Section III of Part 65 or a demotion claim is made in the same claim form in which a claim for possession is made under Part 55 and that demotion claim is successful; or
    (g)   a judgment creditor has taken steps under Parts 70 to 73 to enforce a judgment or order.'

33.6 It is worth noting that several of the aforesaid circumstances will arise only were 'fixed commencement costs ... [are] stated on the claim form'. It seems, therefore, that to this limited extent a claimant may elect whether or not to seek those costs.[3] If this is right, and if a claimant were unreasonably to elect not to claim fixed costs, it is likely

---

3   Indeed, CPR, r 45.1(4) states that 'the claim form may include a claim for fixed commencement costs'; this impliedly confirms the claimant's right to choose.

that the court would have the power to award costs as if fixed commencement costs had been claimed[4]. Each case would have to be decided on its own facts, but it would be difficult to object to the court taking fixed costs into account as being a measure (amongst others) of what reasonable costs should be.

Fixed commencement costs

33.7   Fixed commencement costs will apply only to claims for a specified sum of money where the value of the claim is more than £25. These provisions also apply on the small claims track (see CPR, r 27.14(2)(a)), so it is likely that if the claim was worth less than £25, the court would simply make no award for the costs of commencement.

33.8   Fixed costs will apply only if the claim is for a specified sum. Damages (or debt) may be claimed as a sum to be assessed, but the defendant might say that those monies should have been claimed as a specified sum. An archetypal example of this is where repairs are claimed in a 'bent metal' road traffic accident claim in circumstances where the repairs have been carried out and invoices have already been delivered for those repairs. The claimant will say that the damages are to be assessed (and therefore that fixed commencement costs do not apply), but the defendant will say that the amount of the repairs was a fixed sum (ie the amount claimed in the invoice). The resolution of that dispute would turn on examining the nature of the claim.

33.9   There is no authority on the point, but the distinction between liquidated and unliquidated damages may be of relevance. *Halsbury*'s has this to say about that difference:[5]

> 'The parties may agree by contract that a particular sum is payable on the default of one of them. If the agreement is not obnoxious as a "penalty", such a sum constitutes "liquidated damages" and is payable by the party in default. The term is also applied to sums expressly made payable as liquidated damages under a statute. In every other case, where the court has to quantify or assess the damages or loss, whether pecuniary or non-pecuniary, the damages are "unliquidated".'

Thus, the issue may turn on whether the court has to quantify or assess the monies claimed: on the basis of the law as it is presently understood, each case must be decided on its own facts.

33.10   It has been argued that damages arising out of a claim for negligence could never be regarded as being for fixed sums because there is always the possibility that the damages would be reduced by reason of contributory negligence and/or a (partial) causation defence. Whether this argument is one which will find judicial favour is currently unknown.

The court's discretion

33.11   Generally speaking, where the conditions set out in CPR, r 45.1(2) are met, the claimant's costs of the claim will be limited to fixed costs (plus court fees). The court has a discretion in this regard, however. In particular, CPR, r 45.1(1) implies that the court has a general discretion to allow costs other than (or in place of) fixed costs:

---

[4]   There is no authority directly on this point, but *Drew v Whitbread plc* [2010] EWCA Civ 53 and *O'Beirne v Hudson* [2010] EWCA Civ 52 seem to make this point by analogy.

[5]   *Halsbury's Laws of England*, vol 12(1) (reissue), para 808.

'This Section sets out the amounts which, unless the court orders otherwise, are to be allowed in respect of solicitors' charges in the cases to which this Section applies.'

33.12 Likewise, CPR, r 45.3 confers a discretion in cases where the defendant has paid the sums claimed within a short period of time after commencement:

'(1)   Where—

(a)   the only claim is for a specified sum of money; and
(b)   the defendant pays the money claimed within 14 days after service of particulars of claim on him, together with the fixed commencement costs stated in the claim form,
the defendant is not liable for any further costs unless the court orders otherwise.'

33.13 There archetypal example of where the court 'orders otherwise' is where the defendant articulates a seemingly cogent defence – thereby putting the claimant to the trouble of 'front loading' the claim – only then to change his stance capriciously and without explanation immediately upon being served with proceedings.[6]

The amount of fixed commencement costs

33.14 The amount of fixed commencement costs depends on whether the claim is for money (or property) or for land (or demotion). Where the claim is for money (or property), Table 1 applies (see CPR, r 45.2); where the claim is for land (or demotion), Table 2 applies. In both cases, an additional amount under Table 4 may be payable if the circumstances are appropriate. The relevant court fee is payable in addition (see CPR, r 45.1(3)).

33.15 Table 1 provides as follows:

Fixed costs on commencement of a claim for the recovery of money or goods

Relevant band	Where the claim form is served by the court or by any method other than personal service by the claimant	Where— • the claim form is served personally by the claimant; and • there is only one defendant	Where there is more than one defendant, for each additional defendant personally served at separate addresses by the claimant
Where— • the value of the claim exceeds £25 but does not exceed £500	£50	£60	£15

---

[6]   See, for example, *Amber Construction Services Ltd v London Interspace HG Ltd* [2007] EWHC 3042 (TCC).

Fixed costs on commencement of a claim for the recovery of money or goods

Where—			
• the value of the claim exceeds £500 but does not exceed £1,000	£70	£80	£15

Where—			
• the value of the claim exceeds £1,000 but does not exceed £5,000; or • the only claim is for delivery of goods and no value is specified or stated on the claim form	£80	£90	£15

Where—			
• the value of the claim exceeds £5,000	£100	£110	£15

33.16 Table 2 provides as follows:

Fixed costs on commencement of a claim for the recovery of land or a demotion claim

Where the claim form is served by the court or by any method other than personal service by the claimant	Where— • the claim form is served personally by the claimant; and • there is only one defendant	Where there is more than one defendant, for each additional defendant personally served at separate addresses by the claimant
£69.50	£77.00	£15.00

33.17 Table 4 permits further miscellaneous allowances in cases where the costs of service are higher than the norm:

Miscellaneous Fixed Costs

For service by a party of any document required to be served personally including preparing and copying a certificate of service for each individual served	£15.00

Miscellaneous Fixed Costs

Where service by an alternative method is permitted by an order under rule 6.8 for each individual served	£53.25

Where a document is served out of the jurisdiction—	

(a)	in Scotland, Northern Ireland, the Isle of Man or the Channel Islands;	£68.25

(b)	in any other place	£77.00

Fixed judgment costs

33.18 Fixed judgment costs will apply to a claim where fixed commencement costs are recoverable but where the court is required to enter judgment.

33.19 Where the claim is for money (or property), the applicable rule will be CPR, r 45.4, which reads as follows:

'Where—

(a) the claimant has claimed fixed commencement costs under rule 45.2; and
(b) judgment is entered in a claim to which rule 45.1(2)(a) or (b) applies in the circumstances specified in Table 3, the amount to be included in the judgment for the claimant's solicitor's charges is the total of—
    (i) the fixed commencement costs; and
    (ii) the relevant amount shown in Table 3.'

33.20 Table 3 reads as follows:

Fixed Costs on Entry of Judgment in a claim for the recovery of money or goods

	Where the amount of the judgment exceeds £25 but does not exceed £5,000	Where the amount of the judgment exceeds £5,000
Where judgment in default of an acknowledgement of service is entered under rule 12.4(1) (entry of judgment by request on claim for money only)	£22	£30
Where judgment in default of a defence is entered under rule 12.4(1) (entry of judgment by request on claim for money only)	£25	£35
Where judgment is entered under rule 14.4 (judgment on admission), or rule 14.5 (judgment on admission of part of claim) and claimant accepts the defendant's proposal as to the manner of payment	£40	£55

Fixed Costs on Entry of Judgment in a claim for the recovery of money or goods

	Where the amount of the judgment exceeds £25 but does not exceed £5,000	Where the amount of the judgment exceeds £5,000
Where judgment is entered under rule 14.4 (judgment on admission), or rule 14.5 (judgment on admission of part of claim) and court decides the date or time of payment	£55	£70
Where summary judgment is given under Part 24 or the court strikes out a defence under rule 3.4(2)(a), in either case, on application by a party	£175	£210
Where judgment is given on a claim for delivery of goods under a regulated agreement within the meaning of the Consumer Credit Act 1974 and no other entry in this table applies	£60	£85

33.21 Where the claim is for land (or demotion), the applicable rule will be CPR, r 45.4A, which reads as follows:

'(1) Where—

(a) the claimant has claimed fixed commencement costs under rule 45.2A; and
(b) judgment is entered in a claim to which rule 45.1(2)(d) or (f) applies, the amount to be included in the judgment for the claimant's solicitor's charges is the total of—
(i) the fixed commencement costs; and
(ii) the sum of £57.25.

(2) Where an order for possession is made in a claim to which rule 45.1(2)(e) applies, the amount allowed for the claimant's solicitor's charges for preparing and filing—

(a) the claim form;
(b) the documents that accompany the claim form; and
(c) the request for possession,
is £79.50.'

Fixed enforcement costs

33.22 Certain fixed costs are allowed upon enforcement (see CPR, r 45.6); the relevant sums are set out in Table 5:

Fixed Enforcement Costs

For an application under rule 70.5(4) that an award
may be enforced as if payable under a court order,
where the amount outstanding under the award:

exceeds £25 but does not exceed £250	£30.75
exceeds £250 but does not exceed £600	£41.00
exceeds £600 but does not exceed £2,000	£69.50
exceeds £2,000	£75.50

On attendance to question a judgment debtor (or officer of a company or other corporation) who has been ordered to attend court under rule 71.2 where the questioning takes place before a court officer, including attendance by a responsible representative of the solicitor	for each half hour or part, £15.00 (When the questioning takes place before a judge, he may summarily assess any costs allowed.)

On the making of a final third party debt order
under rule 72.8(6)(a) or an order for the payment to
the judgment creditor of money in court under
rule 72.10(1)(b):

if the amount recovered is less than £150	one-half of the amount recovered
otherwise	£98.50

On the making of a final charging order under rule 73.8(2)(a):	£110.00

	The court may also allow reasonable disbursements in respect of search fees and the registration of the order.
Where a certificate is issued and registered under Schedule 6 to the Civil Jurisdiction and Judgments Act 1982, the costs of registration	£39.00

Where permission is given under RSC Order 45,
rule 3 to enforce a judgment or order giving
possession of land and costs are allowed on the
judgment or order, the amount to be added to the
judgment or order for costs—

(a) basic costs	£42.50
(b) where notice of the proceedings is to be to more than one person, for each additional person	£2.75

Fixed Enforcement Costs

Where a writ of execution as defined in the RSC Order 46, rule 1, is issued against any party	£51.75
Where a request is filed for the issue of a warrant of execution under CCR Order 26, rule 1, for a sum exceeding £25	£2.25
Where an application for an attachment of earnings order is made and costs are allowed under CCR Order 27, rule 9 or CCR Order 28, rule 10, for each attendance on the hearing of the application	£8.50

FIXED RECOVERABLE COSTS

33.23 Fixed recoverable costs fall within the ambit of CPR Part 45 II. As is explained in more detail below, they apply to road traffic accident claims. At the time of writing the Ministry of Justice was in the process of developing a new process of dealing with road traffic accident claims where fixed costs would apply to the whole claim where liability had been admitted and the value of the claim was no more than £10,000. Hopes and concerns seem to have been expressed about that scheme in equal measure, but perhaps the most striking comment was the following from Jackson LJ (speaking extrajudicially):[7]

> '[One of my] concern[s] is the sheer complexity of the process. Over 80 pages of new material will be added to the rule book, in order to deal with the simplest category of litigation which exists, namely low value RTA claims where liability is admitted. I fear that collectively these procedures might possibly open up a new theatre for the costs war.'

Fortunately, the present regime is far less daunting. It is described below.

Scope

33.24 Fixed recoverable costs apply where the following conditions are met:[8]

- the claim has been commenced under the costs-only procedure (CPR, r 44.12A) or is a claim for approval of a settlement under CPR, r 21.10(2);
- the dispute arises from a road traffic accident which occurred on or after 6 October 2003;
- the agreed damages include damages in respect of personal injury, damage to property, or both;
- the total value of the agreed damages does not exceed £10,000;
- if a claim had been issued for the amount of the agreed damages:
  - the small claims track would not have been the normal track for that claim, and
  - the claimant is not a litigant in person; and

---

[7] R Jackson *Review of Civil Litigation Costs: Final Report, December 2009*, chapter 22, para 4.3.

[8] CPR, r 45.7(1), (2) and (3), and CPD, arts 25A.1, 25A.2 and 25A.4.

- the claim is not a claim which falls within the scope of the Untraced Drivers Agreement dated 14 February 2003.

Moore-Bick LJ has explained that the fact that the claim may have been compromised by way of the procedure in Part 36 does not avoid the operation of fixed recoverable costs regime.[9] Likewise, the requirement that the claim be commenced under the costs-only procedure does not prevent the provisions applying to a dispute where no proceedings have yet to be issued: fixed recoverable costs apply to those cases also (unless, of course, there is no agreement in the claim).[10]

Small claims requiring the court's approval

33.25 Where the claim is brought under CPR, r 21.10(2) for approval, the claim will automatically be allocated to the multi-track (see CPR, r 8.9(c)); this means that where the claim is one that, had it not needed approval would have been allocated to the small claims track, there is a tension between those provisions that pull towards the small claims track regime and those that pull towards the multi-track. Patten LJ resolved that tension by finding that where a claim that otherwise would have been a small claims track claim is brought before the court for approval, the order for costs will be an order for costs to be assessed (ie under CPR, r 44.5), and in those circumstances, the court is able to exercise its discretion as to what is reasonable and proportionate:[11]

> '[T]he costs judge is entitled to take into account the size and complexity of the claim under CPR. What he is required to do is to look realistically at the underlying claim for damages which has been settled and consider whether the costs claimed in the Part 21.10(2) proceedings are proportionate to the issues involved. In practice the issues raised in the approval proceedings are unlikely to be any more or less complex than those which would have existed had the damages claim been issued and tried. Although the claimants are children, I accept [the paying party's] submission that in a simple and straightforward case (which these are) not involving serious injuries and with no real issues about liability or quantum the court is likely to have allocated the claim to its normal track and to have been able to deal with the case on that basis. This will obviously be highly material to a consideration of whether it was proportionate for the claimant to have employed solicitors to handle the approval proceedings beyond providing a written advice on the merits of the settlement in accordance with the Practice Direction.'

Put otherwise, the court is entitled to look at the matter in the round, and if the court is satisfied that the matter would have been allocated to the small claims track, the court is entitled to allow costs by reference to that track, but this being as a matter of discretion rather than as a matter of the direct operation of CPR, r 27.14.

Definitions

33.26 The CPR define the following words and phrases:

- 'personal injuries' includes any disease and any impairment of a person's physical or mental condition;[12]

---

9   See *Solomon v Cromwell Group plc* [2011] EWCA Civ 1584 at [22]–[26].
10   Although not binding on any court, see *Lloyds TSB Group plc v Allen* (unreported) 20 October 2005, Medway County Court, HHJ Cryan, in which fixed recoverable costs were denied for want of agreement.
11   *Dockerill v Tullett* [2012] EWCA Civ 184 at [37]–[42].
12   CPR, r 2.3.

- 'road traffic accident' means an accident resulting in bodily injury to any person or damage to property caused by, or arising out of, the use of a motor vehicle on a road or other public place in England and Wales;[13]
- 'motor vehicle' means a mechanically propelled vehicle intended for use on roads;[14] and
- 'road' means any highway and any other road to which the public has access and includes bridges over which a road passes.[15]

By analogy with legislation using similar language to that used in CPR, r 45.7, what amounts to a 'road', 'motor vehicle', etc, is a matter of fact to be determined by the tribunal of fact properly directing itself as to the law.[16]

33.27 Although the CPR define the words and phrases set out above, there is no definition of the word 'use' in the phrase 'use of motor vehicle'; there is room for disagreement as to what it means. If, for example, a lorry carrying explosive material explodes, causing injury to bystanders, the applicability of the fixed recoverable costs regime could be argued either way. Some guidance can, perhaps, be obtained by looking at the way in which similar phrases have been interpreted when they have been used in the Road Traffic Acts. The Court of Appeal considered a case in which a person had run out of petrol, got out of her car to cross the road to reach a colleague, and was killed by a passing car. The issue was whether the death arose out of the use of the deceased car. Rose LJ held that it did[17] and, in giving judgment, impliedly approved of an Australian decision in which Windeyer J had said:[18]

> 'The words "injury caused by or arising out of the use of the vehicle" postulate a causal relationship between the use of the vehicle and the injury. "Caused by" connotes a direct or proximate relationship of cause and effect. "Arising out of" extends this to a result that is less immediate; but it still carries a sense of consequence. It excludes cases of bodily injury in which the use of a vehicle is a merely causal concomitant not considered to be, in a relevant causal sense, a contributing factor.'

Rose LJ also commented that one factor which may be relevant to the issue is the injured person's reasons or motive for carrying out the activity which led to the injury.

33.28 The Road Traffic Acts may also assist in the interpretation of other words. The House of Lords has found that an ordinary meaning of the word 'road' should be applied.[19] The meaning of the phrase 'to which the public have access' may be relevant to the definition of a road; that is, to a large extent, a question of fact[20]; whilst the law may also be relevant, a finding that a place is privately owned will not be determinative of issue.[21] It should be borne in mind that whilst there are similarities between

---

[13]   CPR, r 45.7(4)(a).
[14]   CPR, r 45.7(4)(b).
[15]   CPR, r 45.7(4)(c).
[16]   *Cutter v Eagle Star Insurance Company Ltd* [1998] 1 WLR 1647.
[17]   *Dunthorne v Bentley* (1996) RTR 428, CA; this was in respect of s 145(3)(a) of the Road Traffic Act 1988. In a similar vein, whilst not binding, see *Scheider v Door2Door PTS Ltd*, [2011] EWHC 90210 (Costs) in which Master Campbell found that it was no necessary for there to be vehicular movement for there to be a road traffic accident for the purposes of CPR Part 45 II.
[18]   *Government Insurance Office of New South Wales v R J Green & Lloyd Pty Ltd* (1966) 114 CLR 437.
[19]   *Cutter v Eagle Star Insurance Company Ltd* [1998] 1 WLR 1647. This too was in respect of s 145(3)(a) of the Road Traffic Act 1988, but also took into account the effects of Road Traffic Act 1991, ss 1 and 2.
[20]   See *Cox v White* [1976] RTR 248 at 248, per Kilner Brown J.
[21]   See *Harrison v Hill* (1931) SLT 598, per Lord Blackburn. On the similar and linked topic of what is a 'public place', see *Paterson v Ogilvy* [1957] JC 42 (field used in connection with an agricultural show was a public

CPR Part 45 II and certain sections in the Road Traffic Acts, the latter was enacted for a purpose far removed from the issue of whether fixed costs should apply: caution should be exercised before a direct comparison is drawn between the two legislative regimes.

The amount of fixed recoverable costs

33.29 Where fixed recoverable costs apply, the only costs which are recoverable are:[22]

- fixed recoverable costs;
- disbursements allowed in accordance with CPR, r 45.10; and
- a success fee allowed in accordance with CPR, r 45.11.

33.30 Subject to the matters set out below, fixed recoverable costs are calculated on the basis of a fixed sum plus a variable percentage of the value of the claim. The amount is the total of:[23]

- £800;
- 20% of the damages agreed up to £5,000; and
- 15% of the damages agreed between £5,000 and £10,000.

These figures are exclusive of VAT. These sums are recoverable independently of the indemnity principle.[24]

33.31 The following provisions apply when calculating the amount of damages:[25]

- account must be taken of both general and special damages and interest;
- any interim payments made must be included;
- where the parties have agreed an element of contributory negligence, the amount of damages attributed to that negligence must be deducted; and
- CRU must not be included.

The amount allowable may be increased by 12.5% in cases in which the claimant lives or works in and around London; those areas are listed in the footnotes.[26]

33.32 A success fee may also be claimed if the claimant has entered into a funding arrangement of a type specified in CPR, r 43.2(k)(i). This is recoverable regardless of whether the conditional fee agreement is enforceable.[27] The amount of the success fee is 12.5%, but this not payable on the additional amount allowed by virtue of location (see immediately above).[28]

---

place; see also *Rodger v Normad* [1995] SLT 411 on a similar point concerning a school playground); *Bowman v DPP* [1991] RTR 263 (multi-storey car park was a public place); *DPP v Coulman* [1993] RTR 230 (immigration lane at dockyard was a public place); *R (on application of Lewis) v DPP* [2004] EWHC 3081 (Admin) (a public house car park was a public place); and *May v DPP* [2005] EWHC 1280 (a customer car park was a public place); *Rodger v Normad* [1995] SLT 411.

22   CPR, r 45.8.
23   CPR, r 45.9 and CPD, art 25A.5.
24   *Nizami v Butt* [2006] EWHC 159 (QB).
25   CPD, art 25A.3.
26   CPD, art 25A.6.
27   *Nizami v Butt* [2006] EWHC 159 (QB).
28   CPR, r 45.11.

33.33 There are restrictions on the disbursements that may be allowed.[29] The court may allow disbursements that have arisen due to a particular feature of the dispute. Other than this, in a claim other than on involving a child or a protected party as defined in Part 21, the only allowable disbursements are the costs associated with:

- medical records;
- a medical report;
- a police report;
- an engineer's report;
- a search of the records of the Driver and Vehicle Licensing Agency; and
- ATE premium (or notional premium, as the case may be).

Where they were necessarily incurred by reason of the claimant being a child or protected party, the court may allow fees payable for instructing counsel and court fees.[30] In so far as counsel's fees for attending the hearing are concerned, Patten LJ had this to say:[31]

> '[F]or counsel's fees for attending a hearing to be recoverable there must, I think, be some complexity in the case which justified their being instructed to appear on the approval hearing. It is not enough to say that counsel would help to remove the stress of the occasion … Many of these cases … do not involve difficult issues and can be dealt with shortly on the basis of the written advice on the merits. In such cases the convenience of having counsel attend the hearing has, I think, to be borne by the solicitors as part of their costs just as they would have had to meet the costs of instructing a local agent.'

The effect of the test of necessity has caused some solicitors seek to avoid the need for court approval by settling on the basis of a 'parental indemnity';[32] HHJ Stewart QC has impliedly criticised this practice.[33]

33.34 Where there is more than one potential claimant and two or more claimants instruct the same solicitor or firm of solicitors, the provisions mentioned above apply in respect of each claimant.[34]

Exceptional cases

33.35 An application may be made for an amount exceeding fixed recoverable costs (excluding any success fee or disbursements), but there are penalties if that application fails. The claimant must make out 'exceptional circumstances' to justify an award greater than fixed recoverable costs, in which case the court will either assess his costs or make an order that they be assessed.[35] There is no definition of 'exceptional circumstances' in the CPR; the *Oxford English Dictionary* defines 'exceptional' in this way:

> 'Of the nature of or forming an exception; out of the ordinary course, unusual, special.'

---

[29] CPR, r 45.10.
[30] See CPR, r 45.10(c).
[31] *Tubridy v Sarwar* [2012] EWCA Civ 184 at [54]–[56] (heard at the same time as *Dockerill v Tullett* [2012] EWCA Civ 184).
[32] See D Ellis 'The Right Price' *Solicitors Journal* (2010) Vol 154 No 17, p 14.
[33] *Coles v Keklik* (unreported) 30 June 2008, Liverpool County Court, HHJ Stewart QC.
[34] CPD, art 25A.7.
[35] CPR, r 45.12.

To the extent that it is admissible as an extrinsic aid to interpretation – and this is highly doubtful – it is of note that the industry representatives who negotiated CPR Part 45 II commented that the criteria for opting out 'should be strict';[36] this implies that CPR Part 45 II was intended to be of very wide application. In any event, case examples of 'exceptional circumstances' are rare: one involved a child who had possibly suffered a severe eating disorder as a result of the accident,[37] and another was a claim in which the court found that the defendant had given the claimant 'the run-around'.[38]

33.36 If the court does not consider that exceptional circumstances have been made out, it must make an order for fixed recoverable costs only. Furthermore, if the costs are assessed and are found to be in an amount which is less than 20% greater than the amount of the fixed recoverable costs, the court will allow the lesser of that amount and the fixed recoverable costs. If the application fails, or if the amount allowed does not exceed fixed recoverable costs, the court must order the claimant to pay the costs of costs only proceedings.[39]

Procedure and fixed recoverable

33.37 Where disbursements are claimed, they must be included on the claim form, as must any details concerning the particular features of the dispute which are going to be relied upon for the purposes of recovering those disbursements.[40]

33.38 If the parties agree the amount of the fixed recoverable costs and the only dispute is as to the payment of, or amount of, a disbursement or as to the amount of a success fee, then proceedings should be issued under CPR, r 44.12A and not by reference to Part 45 II (for the wording of which see **33.133**).[41]

Premature issue and fixed recoverable costs

33.39 A particular difficulty that has arisen in certain parts of the country is the alleged practice of issuing claims prematurely for the purposes of circumventing the fixed recoverable costs regime. Where that is the case, the court often assesses the costs as if that regime applied, this being on the basis that it would have applied had the claimant dealt with the matter in a reasonable and sensible way. Before 9 April 2009, reliance was often placed on the following guidance given in Practice Direction – Protocols, para 2.4:

> 'The court will exercise its powers ... with the object of placing the innocent party in no worse a position than he would have been in if the protocol had been complied with.'

Since that date, Practice Direction – Pre-Action Conduct has applied; it does not contain an express counterpart of this guidance, but it is likely to be implied in para 4.5:

> 'The court will look at the overall effect of non-compliance on the other party when deciding whether to impose sanctions.'

33.40 When faced with such an argument, claimants often say that the court should not speculate as to what would have happened had proceedings not been issued when they

---

[36] This was the Civil Justice Council's Costs Form II held on 12–14th December 2002; this gave rise to the 'Milton Hill House Agreement'.
[37] See *Carlon v Domino's Pizza Group Ltd*, Birmingham County Court, 27 August 2010, DJ Wyatt.
[38] *Udogaranya v Nwagw* [2010] EWHC 90186 (Costs) at [23], per Master Haworth.
[39] CPR, r 45.14.
[40] CPD, art 24A.9.
[41] CPD, art 25A.10.

were; in this regard they often rely on *Straker v Turner Rose (a firm)*[42] (see **14.40**). Whilst not binding on any court, HHJ Stewart has found that the court is able to take a view as to what would have happened; this was on the basis of the guidance set out immediately above, that guidance being – in his view – sufficient reason to distinguish *Straker*.[43]

33.41 Arguments concerning alleged premature issue often focus on what is and is not reasonable under the Pre-action Protocol for Personal Injury Claims. In particular, defendants will say that Notes of Guidance accompanying that protocol require claimants to afford a reasonable opportunity to negotiate a settlement of the claim. This may be a factor that the court takes into account.

FIXED PERCENTAGE INCREASES AND SUCCESS FEES

33.42 Fixed percentage increases (which are usually colloquially referred to as 'fixed success fees') may be payable in the followings classes of claim:

- road traffic accident claims (CPR Part 45 III);
- employers' liability claims (CPR Part 45 IV); and
- employers' liability disease claims (often known as industrial disease claims) (CPR Part 45 V).

Road traffic accident claims

33.43 Fixed percentage increases in road traffic claims are governed by CPR Part 45 III (for the wording of which see **33.133**). There are no corresponding provisions in the CPD.

Scope and application

33.44 A fixed percentage increase will apply where a dispute has arisen from a road traffic accident which occurred on or after 6 October 2003 (see **33.23–33.41**) and where the claimant has entered into a funding arrangement of a type specified in CPR, r 43.2(k)(i).[44] The definition afforded by CPR, r 43.2(k)(i) is for a funding arrangement, not an *enforceable* funding arrangement; this means that fixed recoverable costs will be recoverable independently of the indemnity principle.[45]

33.45 Fixed percentage increases do not apply to a claim which has been allocated to the small claims track or to a claim not allocated to a track, but for which the small claims track would be the normal track.[46]

33.46 A fixed percentage increase under CPR Part 45 III will not apply in cases to which CPR Part 45 II applies (ie fixed recoverable costs: see above).[47] This will be so even if the court allows a sum more than fixed recoverable costs; this is because success

---

[42]   [2007] EWCA Civ 368.
[43]   *Ellison v Fairclough* (unreported) 13 July 2007, Liverpool County Court.
[44]   CPR, r 45.15(2) and CPR, r 45.15(4)(c).
[45]   Although dealing with CPR Part 45 II, see *Nizami v Butt* [2006] EWHC 159 (QB).
[46]   CPR, r 45.15(4)(a) and (b).
[47]   CPR, r 45.15(3).

fees are expressly excluded from the provisions permitting the court to allow those greater sums.[48] The issue is largely academic, however, because a success fee of 12.5% would be allowed in any event (see **33.32**); the only practical effect of CPR Part 45 III not applying is that there is no provision under Part 45 II for the court to allow a higher percentage increase.

The amount of the fixed percentage increase (solicitors)

33.47 In so far as solicitors are concerned, the fixed percentage increase will be 100% where the claim concludes at trial, and 12.5% where the claim concludes before trial has commenced or the dispute is settled before the claim is issued.[49] This invites the obvious question of how the court is to gauge whether the claim has concluded at trial.

33.48 'Trial' is a reference to the final contested hearing or to the contested hearing of any issue ordered to be tried separately; a reference to a claim concluding at trial is a reference to a claim concluding by settlement after the trial has commenced or by judgment.[50] Slade J has confirmed that a case will conclude at trial only if it does so after the trial has been opened;[51] it is not sufficient that it settles on the day listed for trial.[52] It has been argued that the word 'trial' should not be given its ordinary meaning and that it should be regarded as being fully defined by the words 'final contested hearing'. Wilson LJ disagreed with that proposition (albeit in an application for permission to appeal as opposed to a fully argued appeal).[53]

33.49 An application may be made for a percentage increase which is higher or lower than 12.5%.[54] Such an application may be made only when one of the following conditions is met:[55]

- the parties agree damages of an amount greater than £500,000, or the court awards damages of an amount greater than £500,000; or
- the court awards damages of £500,000 or less, but would have awarded damages greater than £500,000 if it had not made a finding of contributory negligence; or
- the parties agree damages of £500,000 or less, and it is reasonable to expect that if the court had made an award of damages, it would have awarded damages greater than £500,000, disregarding any reduction the court may have made in respect of contributory negligence.

The £500,000 does not need to be by way of a lump sum: periodical payments of equivalent value will suffice.[56] Where one of these conditions has been met, the court must either assess the percentage increase or make an order that it be assessed (there is no need to show 'exceptional circumstances' or anything similar). If the percentage increase, once assessed, is less than 7.5% or more than 20%, the court must allow 12.5%; where this is so, the costs of the application shall be paid by the applicant.[57]

---

48   CPR, r 45.12(1).
49   CPR, r 45.16.
50   CPR, r 45.15(6).
51   *Amin & Anor v Mullings & Anor* [2011] EWHC 278 (QB).
52   *Amin & Anor v Mullings & Anor* [2011] EWHC 278 (QB). Whilst not binding, *Sitapuria v Khan*, 10 December 2007, Liverpool CC, HHJ Stewart QC is also often cited as authority on the same point.
53   *Thenga v Quinn*, 28 January 2009, RCJ.
54   CPR, r 45.18(2).
55   CPR, r 45.18(2).
56   CPR, r 45.18(3)
57   CPR, r 45.19.

33.50 Other than this, the court has no power to disallow or reduce the fixed percentage increase on a discretionary basis or on the grounds of reasonableness. In particular, if acceptance of a Part 36 offer would have resulted in a claim not reaching trial, and if at trial the claimant fails to obtain a result that is more advantageous to him than that offer, the court has no power to allow the percentage increase that would have applied had the offer been accepted.[58] Likewise, if a claimant already had alternative means funding (such as a BTE policy), the fixed percentage uplift could not be disallowed on the ground that it was unreasonable to enter into a conditional fee agreement.[59]

The amount of the fixed percentage increase (counsel)

33.51 The provisions relating to counsel's percentage increase are more complex than those relating to solicitors; in essence, counsel's percentage increase sequentially increases as trial approaches. The provisions are to be found in CPR, r 45.17 (see **33.133**).

33.52 The meaning of the word 'trial' in this context has been discussed at **33.48**, but that meaning is not important for the purposes of determining counsel's percentage uplift, because the measure is not trial itself, but the date fixed for trial. 'Trial period' means a period of time fixed by the court within which the trial is to take place and, where the court fixes more than one such period in relation to a claim, means the most recent period to be fixed.[60]

33.53 Where the fixed percentage increase would otherwise be 12.5%, an application may be made for a higher percentage increase: the provisions are identical to those which apply to solicitors' percentage increase (see **33.49**).

Employers' liability claims

33.54 Fixed percentage increases in employers' liability claims are governed by CPR Part 45 IV (for the wording of which see **33.133**). There are no corresponding provisions in the CPD.

Scope and application

33.55 A fixed percentage increase will apply where the following conditions are met:[61]

- the dispute is between an employee and his employer;
- the dispute arises from a bodily injury sustained by the employee in the course of his employment;
- the claimant has entered into a funding arrangement of a type specified in CPR, r 43.2(k)(i);
- that injury does not relate to a disease and CPR Part 45 V does not apply;
- that injury was not sustained before 1 October 2004;
- the dispute does not arise out of a road traffic accident; and

---

[58] *Lamont v Burton* [2007] EWCA Civ 429.
[59] *Kilby v Gawith* [2008] EWCA Civ 812.
[60] CPR, r 45.15(6)(d).
[61] CPR, r 45.20(1) and (2).

- the claim has not been allocated to the small claims track, or if it is a claim not allocated to a track, the small claims track would not be the normal track to which it should be allocated;

33.56 The definition of 'road traffic accident' for the purposes of CPR Part 45 IV is the same as it is for CPR Part 45 II. The definition of 'employee' is the same as that given in s 2(1) of the Employers' Liability (Compulsory Insurance) Act 1969:[62]

> '[An] individual who has entered into or works under a contract of service or apprenticeship with an employer whether by way of manual labour, clerical work or otherwise, whether such contract is expressed or implied, oral or in writing.'

33.57 This invites the questions of what is a 'contract of service' and what is a 'contract of apprenticeship'. For present purposes the two may be regarded as being similar (ie an apprentice may be regarded as being a species of employee). The modern approach to the issue of whether a contract is a contract of employment is what is called the 'multiple test'; there have been no decisions as to whether that test applies to CPR Part 45 IV, but there is no reason to believe that it does not. There are three components to the multiple test:[63]

- whether the worker undertook to provide his own work and skill in return for remuneration;
- whether there was a sufficient degree of control over the worker to enable the worker to be called an employee; and
- whether there were any features of the case which were inconsistent with the contract being a contract of employment.

33.58 There is no definition of what amounts to a 'bodily injury' in the CPR; in particular, it is not known whether this definition would include psychiatric injury or injury to the brain. Assistance may be drawn from cases dealing with the words 'bodily injury' in Art 17 of the Warsaw Convention; the House of Lords has found that the phrase means injury to a person's body, and that this includes injury to a person's brain or central nervous system. Shock, anxiety, fear, distress, grief and other emotional disturbances are not included within that definition.[64] In practice, the exclusion of psychiatric conditions from the definition of 'bodily injury' does not present too many problems; this is because most compensable psychiatric conditions will be classified as being diseases, so CPR Part 45 V would apply.

The amount of the fixed percentage increase

33.59 The provisions relating to road traffic accident claims apply, save that the minimum success fee (for both counsel and solicitors) is higher, ie the 12.5% mentioned in those provisions will be replaced by 25% in respect of both solicitors and counsel. If a membership organisation has undertaken to meet the claimant's liabilities for legal costs in accordance with AJA 1999, s 30, that figure rises to 27.5%, but only in respect of solicitors.[65]

---

[62]   CPR, r 45.20(3)(a).
[63]   *Ready-Mixed Concrete (South East) Ltd v Minister of Pensions and National Insurance* [1968] 2 QB 497.
[64]   *King v Bristow Helicopters Ltd* [2002] UKHL 7.
[65]   CPR, r 45.21.

33.60 Likewise, the provisions relating to applications for an alternative percentage increase are the same as those relating to road traffic claims, save that in order to avoid the percentage increase of 25% (or 27.5%, as the case may be), the court must find that a percentage increase of 40% or more, or 15% or less would be appropriate.[66]

Employers' liability disease claims

33.61 Fixed percentage increases in employers' liability claims are governed by CPR Part 45 V (for the wording of which see **33.133**) and CPD, art 25B.1.

Scope and application

33.62 A fixed percentage increase will apply where the following conditions are met:[67]

- the dispute is between an employee (or, if the employee is deceased, the employee's estate or dependants) and his employer (or a person alleged to be liable for the employer's alleged breach of statutory or common law duties of care);
- the dispute relates to a disease with which the employee is diagnosed that is alleged to have been contracted as a consequence of the employer's alleged breach of statutory or common law duties of care in the course of the employee's employment;
- the claimant has entered into a funding arrangement of a type specified in CPR, r 43.2(k)(i);
- the letter of claim was not sent before 1 October 2005; and
- the claim has not been allocated to the small claims track, or if it is a claim not allocated to a track, the small claims track would not be the normal track to which it should be allocated.

'Letter of claim' is impliedly defined as being a letter containing a summary of the facts on which the claim is based and main allegations of fault before 1 October 2005.[68]

33.63 The definition of 'employee' is the same as that given in s 2(1) of the Employers' Liability (Compulsory Insurance) Act 1969:[69]

> '[An] individual who has entered into or works under a contract of service or apprenticeship with an employer whether by way of manual labour, clerical work or otherwise, whether such contract is expressed or implied, oral or in writing.'

This definition has already been addressed at **33.56**.

The amount of the fixed percentage increase (solicitors)

33.64 The applicable percentage uplift will depend on the nature of the claim. Claims are categorised into three Types:[70]

- 'Type A claim' means a claim relating to a disease or physical injury alleged to have been caused by exposure to asbestos;

---

[66]   CPR, r 45.22.
[67]   CPR, r 45.23(1) and (2).
[68]   CPR, r 45.23(2)(a).
[69]   CPR, r 45.20(3)(a).
[70]   CPR, r 45.23(3).

- 'Type B claim' means a claim relating to—
  - a psychiatric injury alleged to have been caused by work-related psychological stress,
  - a work-related upper limb disorder which is alleged to have been caused by physical stress or strain, excluding hand/arm vibration injuries; and
- 'Type C claim' means a claim relating to a disease not falling within either Type A or Type B.

33.65 The following table appears at CPD, art 25B.1; it is a non-exhaustive list of the conditions which fall within Types A and B:

Claim type	Description
A	Asbestosis
	Mesothelioma
	Bilateral Pleural Thickening
	Pleural Plaques
B	Repetitive Strain Injury/WRULD
	Carpal Tunnel Syndrome caused by Repetitive Strain Injury
	Occupational Stress

33.66 If the claim concludes at trial, a percentage increase of 100% is payable. Otherwise, the percentage increase will depend on the type of case. If it is a Type B claim, it will be 100% regardless of when it concludes. If it is a Type A claim, the percentage increase will be 27.5% (or 30% if a membership organisation has undertaken to meet the claimant's liabilities for legal costs in accordance with AJA 1999, s 30). A Type C claim will attract a 62.5% increase (or 70% if a membership organisation has undertaken to meet the claimant's liabilities for legal costs).[71]

33.67 An application may be made for an alternative percentage increase (but not in respect of the percentage increase allowable for a claim which concludes at trial).[72] Such an application may be made only when one of the following conditions is met:[73]

- the parties agree damages of an amount greater than £250,000 or the court awards damages of an amount greater than £250,000; or
- the court awards damages of £250,000 or less but would have awarded damages greater than £250,000 if it had not made a finding of contributory negligence; or
- the parties agree damages of £250,000 or less and it is reasonable to expect that if the court had made an award of damages, it would have awarded damages greater than £250,000, disregarding any reduction the court may have made in respect of contributory negligence.

The £250,000 does not need to be by way of a lump sum: periodical payments of equivalent value will suffice.[74] Where one of these conditions has been met, the court

---

[71] CPR, r 45.24.
[72] CPR, r 45.26.
[73] CPR, r 45.26, which modifies the effect of CPR, r 45.18.
[74] Ibid.

must either assess the percentage increase or make an order that it be assessed (there is no need to show 'exceptional circumstances' or anything similar).

33.68 Where the £250,000 threshold has been met, the outcome of an application for an alternative percentage will be determined by reference to the following table:[75]

Type of claim	Amount allowed	
A	If the percentage increase is assessed as greater than 40% or less than 15%, the percentage increase that is assessed by the court.	If the percentage increase is assessed as no greater than 40% and no less than 15%— (i) 27.5%; and (ii) the costs of the application and assessment shall be paid by the applicant.
B	If the percentage increase is assessed as less than 75%, the percentage increase that is assessed by the court.	If the percentage increase is assessed as no less than 75%— (i) 100%; and (ii) the costs of the application and assessment shall be paid by the applicant.
C	If the percentage increase is assessed as greater than 75% or less than 50%, the percentage increase that is assessed by the court.	If the percentage increase is assessed as no greater than 75% and no less than 50%— (i) 62.5%; and (ii) the costs of the application and assessment shall be paid by the applicant.

The amount of the fixed percentage increase (counsel)

33.69 The applicable percentage uplift will depend on the nature of the claim (ie Types A, B or C: see above).

33.70 Where the claim concludes at trial, the percentage increase will be 100%.[76]

33.71 Where the claim has been allocated to the fast track and does not conclude at trial, the percentage increase will be determined by reference to the following table:[77]

---

[75]   CPR Part 45, Table 8.
[76]   CPR, r 45.25(1)(a).
[77]   CPR, r 45.25(2)(a) and Table 6 of CPR Part 45.

Claims allocated to the fast track

	If the claim concludes 14 days or less before the date fixed for commencement of the trial	If the claim concludes more than 14 days before the date fixed for commencement of the trial or before any such date has been fixed
Type A claim	50%	27.5%
Type B claim	100%	100%
Type C claim	62.5%	62.5%

33.72 Where the claim has been allocated to the multi-track and does not conclude at trial, the percentage increase will be determined by reference to the following table:[78]

Claims allocated to the multi-track

	If the claim concludes 21 days or less before the date fixed for commencement of the trial	If the claim concludes more than 21 days before the date fixed for commencement of the trial or before any such date has been fixed
Type A claim	75%	27.5%
Type B claim	100%	100%
Type C claim	75%	62.5%

33.73 In calculating the periods of time, the day fixed for the commencement of the trial (or the first day of the trial period, where appropriate) is not included.[79]

33.74 Where a trial period has been fixed and the claim concludes on or after the first day of that period but before commencement of the trial, the figures in the first column in the tables above will apply.[80]

33.75 Where a claim concludes before the first day of a period fixed for trial but before a new period is given, the first day of that period is treated as the date fixed for the commencement of the trial. If a new period has been given, then the first date of that new period is the date to be used.[81]

COSTS ON THE SMALL CLAIMS TRACK

General provisions

33.76 As a general rule, the court's power to make an award of costs on the small claims track is significantly restricted; the relevant provisions are in CPR, r 27.14(2):

---

[78]   CPR, r 45.25(2)(a) and Table 6 of CPR Part 45.
[79]   CPR, rr 45.25(3) and 45.17(5).
[80]   CPR, rr 45.25(3) and 45.17(2)–(5).
[81]   CPR, rr 45.25(3) and 45.17(2)–(5).

'The court may not order a party to pay a sum to another party in respect of that other party's costs, fees and expenses, including those relating to an appeal , except—

(a)   the fixed costs attributable to issuing the claim which—
   (i)   are payable under Part 45; or
   (ii)   would be payable under Part 45 if that Part applied to the claim;
(b)   in proceedings which included a claim for an injunction or an order for specific performance a sum not exceeding the amount specified in Practice Direction 27 for legal advice and assistance relating to that claim;
(c)   any court fees paid by that other party;
(d)   expenses which a party or witness has reasonably incurred in travelling to and from a hearing or in staying away from home for the purposes of attending a hearing;
(e)   a sum not exceeding the amount specified in Practice Direction 27 direction for any loss of earnings or loss of leave by a party or witness due to attending a hearing or to staying away from home for the purposes of attending a hearing;
(f)   a sum not exceeding the amount specified in Practice Direction 27 direction for an expert's fees; and
(g)   such further costs as the court may assess by the summary procedure and order to be paid by a party who has behaved unreasonably; and
(h)   the Stage 1 and, where relevant, the Stage 2 fixed costs in rule 45.29 where –
   (i)   the claim was within the scope of the Pre-Action Protocol for Low Value Personal Injury Claims in Road Traffic Accidents ('the RTA protocol');
   (ii)   the claimant reasonably believed that the claim was valued at more than the small claims track limit in accordance with paragraph 4.1(4) of the RTA protocol; and
   (iii)   the defendant admitted liability under the process set out in the RTA protocol; but
   (iv)   the defendant did not pay those Stage 1 and, where relevant, Stage 2 fixed costs.'

These limits apply not only to 'costs' in the general sense of that word, but also to fees rendered by a lay representative for acting on behalf of a party to the proceedings (see CPR, r 27.14(4)).

33.77   The following figures may be relevant:

- expert's fees are recoverable, but are limited to £200 for each expert;[82]
- the amount which a party may be ordered to pay for loss of earnings (or loss of leave) is £50 for each other party or witness;[83] and
- the amount which a party may be ordered to pay for legal advice and assistance in claims including an injunction or specific performance[84] is a sum not exceeding £260.

The applicability of the small claims restriction

33.78   The matters relevant to allocation are set out in CPR, r 26.8:

'(1) When deciding the track for a claim, the matters to which the court shall have regard include—

(a)   the financial value, if any, of the claim;
(b)   the nature of the remedy sought;

---

[82]   CPD, art 7.3(2).
[83]   CPD, art 7.3(1).
[84]   CPR, r 27.14(2)(b).

(c)   the likely complexity of the facts, law or evidence;
(d)   the number of parties or likely parties;
(e)   the value of any counterclaim or other Part 20 claim and the complexity of any matters relating to it;
(f)   the amount of oral evidence which may be required;
(g)   the importance of the claim to persons who are not parties to the proceedings;
(h)   the views expressed by the parties; and
(i)   the circumstances of the parties.

(2) It is for the court to assess the financial value of a claim and in doing so it will disregard—

(a)   any amount not in dispute;
(b)   any claim for interest;
(c)   costs; and
(d)   any contributory negligence.

(3) Where—

(a)   two or more claimants have started a claim against the same defendant using the same claim form; and
(b)   each claimant has a claim against the defendant separate from the other claimants,

the court will consider the claim of each claimant separately when it assesses financial value under paragraph (1).'

Whilst these factors will usually already have been decided before any issues concerning costs may arise, they may be relevant if a costs judge is considering exercising his discretion in the manner described at **6.9**.

33.79 Guidance on the interpretation of these provisions is set out in PD 26, para 7. That guidance stresses that whilst the court will regard the parties' views as an important factor, the allocation decision is matter for the court; thus, the court will not be bound by any agreement or common view of the parties.[85] The following guidance (PD 26, para 7.4) is may be particularly relevant:

'"any amount not in dispute"

In deciding, for the purposes of rule 26.8(2), whether an amount is in dispute the court will apply the following general principles:

(1)   Any amount for which the defendant does not admit liability is in dispute,
(2)   Any sum in respect of an item forming part of the claim for which judgment has been entered (for example a summary judgment) is not in dispute,
(3)   Any specific sum claimed as a distinct item and which the defendant admits he is liable to pay is not in dispute,
(4)   Any sum offered by the defendant which has been accepted by the claimant in satisfaction of any item which forms a distinct part of the claim is not in dispute.

It follows from these provisions that if, in relation to a claim the value of which is above the small claims track limit of £5,000, the defendant makes, before allocation, an admission that reduces the amount in dispute to a figure below £5,000 (see CPR Part 14), the normal track for the claim will be the small claims track. As to recovery of pre-allocation costs, the claimant can, before allocation, apply for judgment with costs on the amount of the claim that has been admitted (see CPR rule 14.3 but see also paragraph 15.1(3) of the Costs Practice Direction supplementing Parts 43 to 48 under which the court has a discretion to allow pre-allocation costs).'

---

[85]   PD 26, paras 7.3 and 7.4.

Where the case involves more than one money claim (for example where there is a Part 20 claim or there is more than one claimant each making separate claims) the court will not generally aggregate the claims; instead it will generally regard the largest of them as determining the financial value of the claims.[86]

Pre-allocation

33.80 Where a claim has yet to be allocated, no special restriction will apply. This is made clear by CPD, art 15.1(1):

> 'Before a claim is allocated to one of those tracks the court is not restricted by any of the special rules that apply to that track.'

33.81 Hughes LJ has confirmed that it is open to the court to take into account the value of the claim at the time the letter of claim was sent, rather than the value at the time proceedings were issued. This will be relevant where the defendant takes steps to diminish the value of the claim. The example that was before Hughes LJ was where a claim for disrepair initially included a claim for specific performance, but where the repairs were carried out on a certain date prior to the claim being made; Hughes LJ found that the appropriate order in that instance was that the costs should be determined on the fast track up to that date, and that the small claims regime would apply thereafter.[87]

33.82 The fact that a claim may not have been allocated to the small claims track would not, in an appropriate case, prevent the court from making an award that is consistent with the small costs regime: see **33.93–33.98**. This is true even if the costs are being assessed rather than if the court is ruling on the incidence of costs (see **33.93**).

Upon allocation

33.83 Allocation to the small claims track usually results in the small claims costs restriction applying. CPR, r 27.14(1) provides that r 27.14 will apply to any case which has been allocated to the small claims track unless: (a) the financial value of a claim exceeds the limit for the small claims track, and (b) the parties have agreed not only that the matter should be allocated to the small claim track, but also that fast track costs provisions should continue to apply.

33.84 Generally speaking, the effect of allocation (as opposed to re-allocation) is retrospective; this is made clear by CPR, r 44.9(2):

> 'Once a claim is allocated to a particular track, those special rules shall apply to the period before, as well as after, allocation except where the court or a practice direction provides otherwise.'

There are very few instances where a practice direction does indicate otherwise.

33.85 CPD, art 15.1(3) makes the following provisions about claims which are allocated to the small claims track solely as a result of a defendant making a partial admission:

---

[86] PD 26, para 7.7.
[87] *BCC v Avril Lee* [2008] EWCA Civ 891 at [36].

'(i) This paragraph applies where a claim, issued for a sum in excess of the normal financial scope of the small claims track, is allocated to that track only because an admission of part of the claim by the defendant reduces the amount in dispute to a sum within the normal scope of that track.

(See also paragraph 7.4 of the practice direction supplementing CPR Part 26)

(ii) On entering judgment for the admitted part before allocation of the balance of the claim the court may allow costs in respect of the proceedings down to that date.'

33.86 However, costs orders made prior to allocation will still stand; this is made clear by CPR, r 44.11(1):

'Any costs orders made before a claim is allocated will not be affected by allocation.'

33.87 The combined effect of CPR, rr 44.9(2) and 44.11(1) is explained at CPD, art 15.1(2):

'Where a claim has been allocated to one of those tracks, the special rules which relate to that track will apply to work done before as well as after allocation save to the extent (if any) that an order for costs in respect of that work was made before allocation.'

Thus, the effect of allocation is generally retrospective.

Re-allocation

33.88 The effect of re-allocation is, however, not generally retrospective; this is made clear by CPR, r 44.11(2):

'Where—

(a) a claim is allocated to a track; and

(b) the court subsequently re-allocates that claim to a different track,

then unless the court orders otherwise, any special rules about costs applying—

    (i)   to the first track, will apply to the claim up to the date of re-allocation; and

    (ii)   to the second track, will apply from the date of re-allocation.'

33.89 CPR, r 27.15 makes a very similar provision relating to claims which are re-allocated upwards from the small claims track to another track:

'Where a claim is allocated to the small claims track and subsequently re-allocated to another track, rule 27.14 (costs on the small claims track) will cease to apply after the claim has been re-allocated and the fast track or multi-track costs rules will apply from the date of re-allocation.'

33.90 Where this happens (ie where a claim is re-allocated from the small claims track to another track) the court must decide whether any party should pay costs already incurred in accordance with the rules about costs contained in CPR Part 27; this is made clear by CPD, art 16:

'**16.1** This paragraph applies where the court is about to make an order to re-allocate a claim from the small claims track to another track.

16.2 Before making the order to re-allocate the claim, the court must decide whether any party is to pay costs to any other party down to the date of the order to re-allocate in accordance with the rules about costs contained in Part 27 (The Small Claims Track).

16.3 If it decides to make such an order about costs, the court will make a summary assessment of those costs in accordance with that Part.'

Misallocation

33.91 Where a claim was misallocated to the multi-track as a result of the defendant keeping in play a counterclaim which ought never to have been brought, and where the claim would have been allocated to the small claims track if the counterclaim had not been brought, Goldring LJ found that this was conduct which should be given weight when the court was exercising its discretion under CPR, r 44.3,[88] ie when the opportunity to assess the costs under the small claims regime had passed, the fact that that loss of that opportunity had been caused by one of the parties is a factor to be taken into account.

Exceptions

33.92 CPR, r 27.14(6) provides that where the parties agree that the fast track costs provisions are to apply pursuant to r 27.14(5), the claim and any subsequent appeal will be treated for the purposes of costs as if it were proceeding on the fast track. There is one important difference, however: the trial costs will be in the discretion of the court and (rather than being fixed) they will not exceed the amount set out for the value of claim in r 46.2.

Deemed applicability

33.93 The small claims costs regime can be relevant even where the claim has not been allocated to the small claims track; it would be wrong to treat the absence of allocation as being conclusive. If circumstances permit, the absence of allocation to the small claims track will not prevent the court from making an award that is consistent with the small costs regime. This is true even if the receiving party has an award for costs to be assessed; whilst the small claims regime ought not to be applied in those circumstances, the costs judge would be able to take the existence of that regime into account when assessing the reasonableness of the costs, and by that route he would be entitled to assess the profit costs at a level that is commensurate with the small claims regime.[89]

33.94 The issue of deemed applicability will arise in cases which settle before allocation. Dealing with an unallocated claim in which the value of the claim was put at more than the small claims limit but should have been pleaded at below the small claims limit, Judge LJ (with whom Dyson LJ agreed) made the following comment:[90]

'... [In] the absence of any specific factors suggesting otherwise, in a case like this where, if sought, an allocation would have been made to small claims track the normal rule should be that small claims costs regime for costs should apply.'

---

[88]   *Peackman v Linbrooke Services Ltd* [2008] EWCA Civ 1239; see also *Singh v Aqua Descaling Ltd* (unreported) 12 June 2008, Walsall County Court, HHJ Oliver-Jones QC.

[89]   *O'Beirne v Hudson* (unreported) 9 February 2010, CA at [19], per Waller LJ; see also the comments of Hooper LJ at [22]. See also, in a different context, *Lahey v Pirelli* [2007] 1WLR 998 at [19]–[22], per Dyson LJ.

[90]   *Voice and Script International Ltd v Ashraf Alghafar* [2003] EWCA Civ 736 at [21].

33.95 Judge LJ was at pains to point out that his judgment was not intended to affect the way in which costs are dealt with in cases which had been allocated to the fast track, but failed on the evidence to produce an award in excess of the small claims limit:[91]

> 'Costs issues in such cases are resolved day-by-day up and down the country without difficulty, and I intend to say nothing which could or possibly be regarded as affecting the ordinary conduct of such litigation.'

33.96 The usual circumstances, however, in which the small claims restrictions will be deemed to apply are where a claim has been exaggerated and, but for that exaggeration, would have been allocated to the small claims track. In particular, if it can be shown that the claim was pleaded at a level above the small claims limit because of exaggeration, then the court will usually have no difficulty in imposing the small claims costs regime.[92] It might well do likewise if it can be shown that the claim has been pleaded above the small claims limit because of mistake, oversight, or carelessness. Both culpable and innocent exaggeration are discussed at **6.138–6.154**.

33.97 When deciding whether a claim has been pleaded at an inappropriately high level, there is authority to suggest that the settlement figure (if any) is a factor that can be taken into account. An example of such an approach is *E Ivor Hughes Educational Foundation v Leach*,[93] in which Peter Smith J said:

> 'It is appropriate that the costs which the claimant recovers ... should be measured by its recovery. They have recovered £5,000. Once again, they chose to take the £5,000. If they were not happy with that or they wanted to protect their costs position further, they could have proceeded to trial to ... to establish liability beyond that. They have chosen not to do so.'

It is trite costs law that costs should not be assessed with the benefit of hindsight, so presumably the settlement figure can be taken into account only where it can fairly be said to indicate the true value of the claim as it ought to have been perceived at the time of allocation.

33.98 A claim and a counter-claim will not be relegated to the small claims track merely because the net amount due after set-off is below the small claims limit; the court will look at the matter in the round rather than at the net effect.[94]

Unreasonable behaviour on the small claims track

33.99 What amounts to unreasonable behaviour will depend on the facts of each case. There is no reason to believe that the approach to this issue would be any different from the way it would be approached in any other case. Whilst allowances would almost certainly be appropriate in cases where litigants are unrepresented, there are circumstances in which compliance with the relevant pre-action protocol would be a factor.[95]

---

[91] *Voice and Script International Ltd v Ashraf Alghafar* [2003] EWCA Civ 736 at [17].
[92] *Devine v Franklin* [2002] EWHC 1846 (QB), per Gray J; see also *E Ivor Hughes Educational Foundation v Leach* [2005] EWHC 1317 (Ch).
[93] [2005] EWHC 1317 (Ch).
[94] *Boynton v Willers* [2003] EWCA Civ 904 at [41].
[95] See, for example, *BCC v Avril Lee* [2008] EWCA Civ 891 at [33].

33.100   Few small claims are appealed on the issue of costs, which means that there is a dearth of authority on the point, but the writer's researches[96] suggest that an award of costs on the small claims track is a 'genuine rarity' (to use the words of a regional costs judge);[97] the writer has been told that the district bench recognises the policy behind the restriction on costs in the small claims track, and seeks to give effect to that policy. Costs will be awarded in circumstances such as the following:

- failing to comply with orders for directions (such as orders to give disclosure or to serve evidence);
- wilfully exaggerating a claim;
- defending a claim which has no defence;
- failing to respond to correspondence;
- obstructing attempts to settle the claim; and
- lack of objectivity on the part of professional advisers.

33.101   Each case will turn on its own facts, but there are one or two legal principles specific to the exercise of discretion on the small claims track. CPR, r 27.14(3) provides:

'A party's rejection of an offer in settlement will not of itself constitute unreasonable behaviour under paragraph (2)(g) but the court may take it into consideration when it is applying the unreasonableness test.'

This rule is relevant because CPR Part 36 does not apply to claims allocated to the small claims track.

33.102   Hughes LJ has confirmed that a failure to settle will also not usually amount to unreasonable behaviour. He gave two reasons: first, to categorise a failure to settle on particular terms as unreasonable conduct would open up wide questions with ramifications for other forms of litigation; and, secondly, the investigation of whether an offer of settlement was reasonable or not would require the trial of the case, which would be inconsistent with the objectives of the CPR.[98]

33.103   The small claims provisions apply to the costs of an appeal brought against a decision in a small claim.[99]

FAST TRACK TRIAL COSTS

33.104   From 6 April 2009 the fast-track trial limit was raised,[100] thereby increasing the importance of the fast track.

---

[96]   Personal communications with the District Bench in the North West of England.
[97]   Personal communication with RCJ Duerden, 24 July 2009.
[98]   *BCC v Avril Lee* [2008] EWCA Civ 891 at [32].
[99]   See CPR, r 27.14(2), which reads: 'The court may not order a party to pay a sum to another party in respect of that other party's costs, fees and expenses, including those relating to an appeal, except [those allowed under the small claims regime].'
[100]   The new criteria read as follows (CPR, r 26.6):
   (4)   Subject to paragraph (5), the fast track is the normal track for any claim—
   (a)   for which the small claims track is not the normal track; and
   (b)   which has a value—
   (i)   for proceedings issued on or after 6th April 2009, of not more than £25,000; and
   (ii)   for proceedings issued before 6th April 2009, of not more than £15,000.
   (5)   The fast track is the normal track for the claims referred to in paragraph (4) only if the court considers

Scope and application

33.105   CPR Part 46 deals with the amount of costs which the court may award for the advocate preparing for and appearing at a fast track trial.[101]

33.106   These provisions apply only where, at the date of the trial, the claim is allocated to the fast track. They do not apply in any other case, irrespective of the final value of the claim.[102] In particular, they do not apply to the hearing of a claim which is allocated to the small claims track with the consent of the parties given under r 26.7(3), nor do they apply to any disposal hearing at which the amount to be paid under a judgment or order is decided by the court.[103]

33.107   'Fast track trial costs' means the costs of a party's advocate for preparing for and appearing at the trial, but does not include:

- any other disbursements; or
- value added tax.[104]

33.108   'Advocate' means a person exercising a right of audience as a representative of, or on behalf of, a party; the definition is not limited to counsel.[105]

33.109   'Trial' includes a hearing where the court decides an amount of money or the value of goods following a judgment under CPR Part 12 (Default judgment) or CPR Part 14 (Admissions) but does not include the following:[106]

- the hearing of an application for summary judgment (under CPR Part 24); or
- the court's approval of a settlement (under CPR, r 21.1).

The amount of fast track trial costs

33.110   Where the receiving party is a litigant in person, the costs will be assessed in the usual way (see **38.53–38.85**).[107] Otherwise, the amount of costs depends on the value of the claim in accordance with the following table.[108]

33.111   For costs incurred on or after 1 October 2007, the appropriate amounts are as follows:

---

that—
(a)   the trial is likely to last for no longer than one day; and
(b)   oral expert evidence at trial will be limited to—
(i)   one expert per party in relation to any expert field; and
(ii)   expert evidence in two expert fields.
[101]   CPR, r 46.1 and CPD, art 26.1.
[102]   CPD, art 26.2.
[103]   CPD, art 26.3; see para 12.8 of the Practice Direction which supplements Part 26 (Case Management – Preliminary Stage).
[104]   CPR, r 46.1(2)(b).
[105]   CPR, r 46.1(2)(a).
[106]   CPR, r 46.1(2)(c).
[107]   CPR, r 46.3(5).
[108]   CPR, r 46.2(1).

Value of the claim	Amount of fast track trial costs which the court may award
No more than £3,000	£485
More than £3,000 but not more than £10,000	£690
More than £10,000 but not more than £15,000	£1,035
For proceedings issued on or after 6 April 2009, more than £15,000	£1,650

33.112   For costs incurred prior to 1 October 2007, the amounts were as follows:

Value of the claim	Amount of fast track trial costs which the court may award
No more than £3,000	£350
More than £3,000 but not more than £10,000	£500
More than £10,000	£750

33.113   The measure of the value of the claim varies, depending on whether the claim is a money claim and on whether the receiving party is the claimant or the defendant.[109]

Money only (claimant)

33.114   For the purposes of evaluating a money-only claim where costs are payable to a claimant, the figure is the amount of the judgment, but interest and costs are disregarded, as is any reduction made for contributory negligence.

Money only (defendant)

33.115   For the purposes of evaluating a money-only claim where costs are payable to a defendant, the figure is the amount specified in the claim form, but interest and costs are disregarded. If no amount is stated in the claim form, then the figure is the maximum amount the claimant reasonably expected to recover according to the statement of value included in the claim form under CPR, r 16.3. If the claim form states that the claimant cannot reasonably say how much he expects to recover, then the amount is £15,000.

Non-money only (claimant and defendant)

33.116   Where the claim is only for a remedy other than the payment of money, then unless the court orders otherwise the value of the claim is deemed to be more than £3,000 but not more than £10,000.

---

[109]   CPR, r 46.2(3), (4) and (5).

Both money and non-money (claimant and defendant)

33.117   Where the claim includes both a claim for the payment of money and for a remedy other than the payment of money, the value of the claim is deemed to be the higher of:

- the value of the money claim (decided as above); or
- the deemed value of the other remedy (decided as above).

The court may order otherwise, however.

33.118   Where the court assesses the costs of a claim which has been allocated to the fast track but which has settled before the start of the trial, it may not allow, in respect of the advocate's costs, an amount that exceeds the amount of fast track trial costs which would have been payable had the trial taken place. When deciding the amount to be allowed in respect of the advocate's costs, the court shall have regard to when the claim was settled and when the court was notified that the claim had settled.[110]

33.119   As to valuation where there is more than one claimant or defendant, see **33.127–33.132.**

33.120   Where a defendant has made a counterclaim against the claimant which has a higher value than the claim, and where the claimant succeeds at trial both on his claim and the counterclaim, the value of the claim is the value of the defendant's counterclaim calculated in accordance with the provisions set out above.[111]

Power to award more or less than the amount of fast track trial costs

33.121   The court may not award more or less than the amount shown in the table except where:

- it decides not to award any fast track trial costs, or
- one of the circumstances set out below applies,

but the court may apportion the amount awarded between the parties to reflect their respective degrees of success on the issues at trial.[112]

Unreasonable conduct

33.122   Where the court considers that the party to whom fast track trial costs are to be awarded has behaved unreasonably or improperly during the trial, it may award that party an amount less than would otherwise be payable for that claim, as it considers appropriate.[113]

---

[110]   CPR, r 44.10 and CPD, art 26.4.
[111]   CPR, r 46.2(6).
[112]   CPR, r 46.2(2).
[113]   CPR, r 46.3(7).

Improper conduct

33.123 Where the court considers that the party who is to pay the fast track trial costs has behaved improperly during the trial, the court may award such additional amount to the other party as it considers appropriate.[114]

Multiple trials

33.124 Where there is more than one trial (for example, a trial on limitation followed by a trial generally), the court may award an additional amount in respect of the additional trial, but the amount must not exceed two-thirds of the amount payable for that claim, subject to a minimum award of £485 (or £350 before 1 October 2007).[115]

Cross-orders as to costs

33.125 Where a defendant has made a counterclaim against the claimant, and the claimant has succeeded on his claim and the defendant has succeeded on his counterclaim, the court will quantify the amount of the award of fast track trial costs to which:

- but for the counterclaim, the claimant would be entitled for succeeding on his claim, and
- but for the claim, the defendant would be entitled for succeeding on his counterclaim,

and make one award of the difference, if any, to the party entitled to the higher award of costs.[116]

Necessary to be attended

33.126 If the court believes that it was 'necessary' for another legal representative to attend the trial to assist the advocate, the court may award an additional £345 in respect of that person's attendance (or £250 before 1 October 2007).[117] (See **29.48–29.49** for a discussion of a solicitor's professional obligations concerning attending counsel.)

Fast track trial costs where there is more than one claimant or defendant

33.127 Where one advocate is acting for more than one claimant, and where each claimant has a separate claim against the defendant, the value of the claim is as follows.[118]

Money only (claimant)

33.128 Where the only claim of each claimant is for the payment of money, if the award of costs is in favour of the claimants, the value of the claim is the total amount of the judgment made in favour of all the claimants jointly represented.

---

[114] CPR, r 46.3(8).
[115] CPR, r 46.3(3) and (4).
[116] CPR, r 46.3(6).
[117] CPR, r 46.3(2).
[118] CPR, r 46.4(3) and CPR, r 46.4(6).

Money only (defendant)

33.129   Where the award is in favour of the defendant, the value of the claim is the total amount claimed by the claimants, and in either case, quantified in accordance with the principles set out at **33.112–33.118**.

Non-money only (claimant and defendant)

33.130   Where the only claim of each claimant is for a remedy other than the payment of money, the valued of the claim is deemed to be more than £3,000 but not more than £10,000.

Both money and non-money (claimant and defendant)

33.131   Where the claims of the claimants include both a claim for the payment of money and for a remedy other than the payment of money, the value of the claim will be deemed to be more than £3,000 but not more than £10,000; or, if greater, the value of the money claims calculated in accordance with the provisions above.

33.132   Once the value of the claim has been gauged, the costs will be awarded on the following bases:

- Where the same advocate is acting for more than one party, the court may make only one award in respect of fast track trial costs payable to that advocate. The parties for whom the advocate is acting are jointly entitled to any fast track trial costs awarded by the court.[119]
- Where there is more than one defendant, and any or all of the defendants are separately represented, the court may award fast track trial costs to each party who is separately represented.[120]
- Where there is more than one claimant but only one defendant, the court may make only one award to the defendant of fast track trial costs, for which the claimants are jointly and severally liable.[121]

LOW VALUE PERSONAL INJURY CLAIMS IN ROAD TRAFFIC ACCIDENTS

33.133   In October 2009, after having consulted widely, the Ministry of Justice published a policy report which confirmed plans to implement a new method of resolving low-volume road traffic accidents involving personal injury. The new process, known as the Road Traffic Accident Protocol ('the RTA protocol') took effect from 30 April 2010.[122]

---

[119]   CPR, r 46.4(1).
[120]   CPR, r 46.4(4).
[121]   CPR, r 46.4(5).
[122]   See Civil Procedure (Amendment) Rules 2010, r 1(2).

The effect of the RTA protocol

The effect of the RTA protocol on the burden of costs

33.134 It is, perhaps, worth beginning with an overview of the effect of the RTA protocol. The following table (which was originally created by Kevin Latham)[123] sets out the ultimate costs burden in a number of different types of claims. Scenarios one to three settle; scenario four does not settle.

Scenario	Value (see notes)	RTAP Costs	Fixed Costs	Estimated Standard Basis Costs
1[124]	**£1,500 general damages plus notional special damages**	**£1,200.00 profit costs** plus disbursements pursuant to CPR 45.30	**£1,110.00 profit costs** plus disbursements pursuant to CPR 45.10	**£1,422.00 profit costs** 9 hours at Grade C £158 plus reasonable disbursements
2[125]	**£4,000 general damages plus £1,000 special damages**	**£1,350.00 profit costs** plus disbursements pursuant to CPR 45.30	**£1,687.50 profit costs** plus disbursements pursuant to CPR 45.10	**£2,133.00 profit costs** 12 hours at Grade C £158 plus 12.5% success fee plus reasonable disbursements
3[126]	**£7,500 general damages plus £2,500 special damages**	**£1,200.00 profit costs** plus disbursements pursuant to CPR 45.30	**£2,550.00 profit costs** plus disbursements pursuant to CPR 45.10	**£2,212.00 profit costs** 14 hours at Grade C £158 plus reasonable disbursements

---

[123] K Latham 'Following Protocol' *Personal Injury Law Journal* (2010) No 86 June, pp 9–14.

[124] Scenario 1: RTA involving soft tissue injury to the neck. Solicitors instructed on a private retainer. Case settles when the Defendant makes an offer of £1,500 general damages plus £50 special damages upon receipt of the medical report and supporting special damages documentation which is accepted by the Claimant within 21 days.

[125] Scenario 2: RTA involving soft tissue injury to the neck. Solicitors instructed under a Conditional Fee Agreement. Case settles when the Defendant makes an offer of £4,000 general damages plus £1,000 special damages after some limited negotiation following disclosure of the medical report and supporting special damages documentation, which is accepted by the Claimant within 21 days.

[126] Scenario 3: RTA involving soft tissue injury to the neck. Solicitors instructed on a private retainer. Case settles when the Defendant makes an offer of £7,500 general damages plus £2,500 special damages after some 6 weeks protracted negotiation following disclosure of the medical report and supporting special damages documentation.

Sce-nario	Value (see notes)	RTAP Costs	Fixed Costs	Estimated Standard Basis Costs
4[127]	**Case goes to hearing (general damages assessed at £5,000)**	**£1,700.00 profit costs** plus £500 Advocate's fee plus disbursements pursuant to CPR 45.30	N/A	**£5,056.00 profit costs** 16 hours at Grade C £158 plus 100% success fee] plus reasonable disbursements

33.135 As these examples show, where lower-value claims settle (which will be the fate of the vast majority of claims) the difference between costs under the RTA protocol and costs under other regimes is minimal. For very modest claims, it will result in a higher costs burden than ordinary fixed costs. Over a very large number of cases the differences between the seemingly similar figures soon become significant.

The effect of non-compliance with the RTA protocol

33.136 Much of the RTA protocol is contained in protocols annexed to the CPR (see **33.138**); as such, not all of the protocol can be regarded as being a source of law. It is, nonetheless, relevant in that – as with any pre-action protocol – it creates obligations and expectations which, if disregarded, may sound in costs; in this regard, CPR, r 44.5(5)(a) defines relevant conduct for the purposes of deciding the incidence of costs as including the extent to which the parties followed any relevant pre-action protocol (see **6.83–6.88**). This general principle is reinforced by the preamble to the RTA protocol, which specifically states that in an appropriate case the RTA protocol describes the behaviour that the court will normally expect of the parties.[128]

33.137 In addition to this general path by which the RTA protocol can sound in costs, there is a specific provision in that the RTA protocol[129] – or, more accurately, CPR Part 45 VI – provides as follows:[130]

> '45.27(1) This Section applies to claims that have been or should have been started under Part 8 in accordance with Practice Direction 8B ("the Stage 3 Procedure").'

Thus, in so far as Stage 3 is concerned, the RTA protocol will apply if the court finds that the claim ought to have been in accordance with the Stage 3 Procedure (see **33.170–33.173**). It is not known whether this deemed applicability would operate in a mandatory way or only at the court's discretion, but the wording of CPR Part 45 VI suggests the former.[131] The RTA protocol makes provision for the court to take into account non-compliance with the RTA protocol, and in particular, the court may take into account the fact that the claimant has failed to give the requisite information about the claim, where the claimant overvalued the claim, or where the claimant has in some

---

[127] Scenario 4: RTA involving soft tissue injury to the neck. Solicitors instructed under a Conditional Fee Agreement. Case proves incapable of settlement between the parties and must be determined by the Court at a Stage 3 Hearing/Disposal Hearing.

[128] See para 2.1 of the RTA Protocol para under the heading 'preamble'.

[129] See, for example, *Drew v Whitbread* [2010] EWCA Civ 53.

[130] See CPR, r 45.27(1).

[131] See CPR, r 45.36(2), which appears to impose a limit on the amount that the defendant will be required to pay in certain circumstances, one of which is where the claimant has overvalued the claim.

other way caused the RTA protocol process to be discontinued.[132] Where the court makes such a finding, the defendant's liability for costs will be limited (not fixed) to the amount that would have been paid had the claim progressed under the RTA protocol.[133]

Jurisdiction

33.138   The RTA protocol is a heterogeneous jurisdiction. It exerts its effect in three stages and by no fewer than three legal mechanisms: the first two stages work via the protocol itself, but the third operates via CPR Part 45 VI and PD 8B. Consequential and supplementary provisions are distributed throughout the CPR and the associated practice directions.

Scope

33.139   The RTA protocol applies to claims for damages arising from road traffic accidents occurring on or after 30 April 2010.[134] It applies where the claim was started under the RTA protocol and where it continues under it. The RTA Protocol is also relevant where the claim should have been, but was not, started under the Stage 3 Procedure (see **33.137**).[135]

Types of claim

33.140   To fall within the ambit of the RTA protocol the claim must include a claim for damages for personal injury,[136] must not be a case for which the small claims track would be the normal track, and must be of a value of no more than £10,000.[137] Vehicle-related damages[138] are excluded for the purposes of valuing the claim.[139] The RTA protocol ceases to apply if the claimant notifies the defendant that the claim has been re-valued at more than the threshold figure.[140] Vehicle-related damage will ordinarily be dealt with outside the RTA protocol[141] (in the early stages, at least: see **33.168**), although as a matter of administrative convenience, requests for payment may include those damages.

Smaller claims

33.141   There is no provision for a claim to join the RTA protocol part-way through, so although there may be opportunity to review an approbative decision to engage the RTA protocol, there is no opportunity to review a decision not to do so. This means that where there is doubt about whether a claim is substantial enough to qualify, the

---

[132]   See CPR, r 45.36(2).
[133]   See CPR, r 45.36(2).
[134]   See the RTA Protocol para 4.1.
[135]   See CPR, r 45.27(1), which appears to make it unnecessary to rely by analogy on cases such as *Drew v Whitbread* [2010] as application is a matter of express provision rather than impliedly as a matter of reasonableness.
[136]   See the RTA Protocol para 4.1(3); for reasons that are not wholly clear, para 1.1(10) of the protocol defines RTAs according to bodily, not personal, injury.
[137]   See para 4.1 of the RTA Protocol.
[138]   This includes pre-accident value, vehicle repair charges, insurance excess and vehicle hire charges: see para 1.1(6).
[139]   See para 4.3 of the RTA Protocol.
[140]   See para 4.2 of the RTA Protocol.
[141]   See para 6.4 of the RTA Protocol.

claimant's representative would be well advised to engage the RTA protocol and the review the matter at a later stage. If he does this, there are several options then available to the parties:

- ***Claimant:*** If the choice were between staying within the RTA protocol and being relegated to the small claims track, few claimants would choose the latter; thus most claimants would be anxious to remain with the RTA protocol. Up to the point that his opponent arrests engagement of the RTA protocol (see below), a claimant may remain within its ambit if he 'reasonably believes' that the claim is valued between £1,000 and £10,000.[142] Whether the claimant's valuation was reasonable will be a question of fact to be determined on the evidence. The wording of the relevant provisions is such that it can safely be presumed that hindsight will not apply.
- ***Defendant:*** The defendant has the right to arrest engagement of the RTA protocol on the grounds that he values the claim as being suitable for the small claims track. If the defendant says that he considers the claim to be a small claims track case, the claim will no longer continue under the RTA protocol.[143] Such a step would expose the defendant to risk that if the claim is ultimately found to fall outside the small claims track, he will have lost the costs protection which the RTA protocol would otherwise have afforded him.

Larger claims

33.142   Where the claim is at the other end of the spectrum, the claimant will have to decide whether to engage the RTA protocol or to seek to have the claim allocated to the fast track; if he unreasonably chooses the latter, then CPR Part 45 VI provides that the court may limit the claimant's costs to those recoverable under the RTA protocol.[144]

Excluded claims

33.143   The following claims are excluded from the RTA protocol:

- claims made to the Motor Insurer's Bureau (MIB) pursuant to the Untraced Drivers Agreement 2003[145] (although claim under the Uninsured Drivers Agreement are not excluded);
- claims where one of the parties is deceased or is a protected party;[146]
- claims where the claimant is bankrupt;[147]
- claims where the defendant's vehicle is registered outside the UK;[148]
- employers' liability claims;[149] and

---

142   See para 5.9 of the RTA Protocol.
143   See para 6.15 of the RTA Protocol.
144   CPR, r 45.36.
145   See para 4.4(2) of the RTA Protocol.
146   See para 4.4(3) of the RTA Protocol.
147   See para 4.4(4) of the RTA Protocol.
148   See para 4.4(5) of the RTA Protocol.
149   Which include those arising from breach of the Control of Substances Hazardous to Health Regulations 2002 (SI 2002/2677); Lifting Operations and Lifting Equipment Regulations 1998 (SI 1998/2307); Management of Health and Safety at Work Regulations 1999 (SI 1999/3242); Manual Handling Operations Regulations 1992 (SI 1992/2793); Personal Protective Equipment at Work Regulations 1992 (SI 1992/2966); Provision and Use of Work Equipment Regulations 1998 (SI 1998/2306); Work at Height Regulations 2005 (SI 2005/735); and Workplace (Health, Safety and Welfare) Regulations 1992 (SI 1992/3004).

- claims which were started under the RTA protocol but which did not continue under it.[150]

For all practical purposes, the costs-related aspects of the RTA protocol do not apply where the claimant is a litigant in person.[151]

Stages at which the RTA protocol can be exited

33.144   There are many mechanisms by which the parties are able to bring engagement of the RTA protocol to an end.

Exclusion at the outset

33.145   Exclusion at the outset is so easy that that the decision to engage the RTA protocol is something close to being a matter of consent:

- *Claimant:* Nothing in the RTA protocol imposes a mandatory requirement that the claimant must use it; that said, a failure to use it may have a bearing on costs.[152]
- *Defendant:* The RTA protocol will apply only where liability has been admitted and where contributory negligence has not been alleged.[153] Although there is no authority on the point, the court would probably disfavour a defendant who kept liability in issue solely for the purpose of avoiding the operation of the RTA protocol; this would almost certainly sound in costs, but there is no mechanism by which the court is able to order that the claim should be placed back within the ambit of the RTA protocol.

Leaving the RTA protocol)

33.146   Again, both parties have ample opportunity to bring the RTA protocol to an end. It should be borne in mind, nonetheless, that parties may be penalised in costs for inappropriately exiting the RTA protocol.[154] The options for leaving the RTA protocol are as follows:

- *Claimant:* the claimant may exit the RTA protocol if the defendant fails to pay costs in accordance with the provisions in Stage 1; the claimant must do this within ten days of the expiry of the period during which payment ought to have been made.[155] Similar provisions apply to the payment of damages in Stage 2.[156] There are many other routes by which a claimant may leave the RTA protocol; if, for example, the claimant believes that 'there are complex issues of fact or law in

---

[150]   See para 5.11 of the RTA Protocol.
[151]   See para 4.5 of the RTA Protocol.
[152]   It cannot be assumed that it would never be reasonable not to use the RTA Protocol where it is available. In particular, the difference between the costs allowed under the RTA Protocol and those allowed under CPR Part 45 II is often small. This raises the possibility that one or both of the parties may reasonably reject the RTA Protocol on the grounds that compliance would do nothing to save costs.
[153]   See para 6.15 of the RTA Protocol.
[154]   Whilst not binding, see *Patel v Fortis Insurance Ltd*, Leicester County Court, 23 December 2011
[155]   See paras 6.18 and 6.19 of the RTA Protocol.
[156]   See para 7.23 of the RTA Protocol.

relation to the vehicle-related damages', he is able to give notice to the defendant that will result in the claim automatically exiting the RTA protocol.[157]

- *Defendant:* if insufficient information has been provided by the claimant, the defendant can state that the claim should no longer continue under the RTA protocol;[158] where this happens, the court may, when exercising its discretion as to costs, take the claimant's failure into account.[159] Presumably, the court would also take into account the defendant's conduct if the defendant had unreasonably decided that insufficient information had been given. Additionally, the defendant may disapply the RTA protocol if, during Stage 2, he concludes that the small claims track would be the normal track for the claim or if the admission of causation is withdrawn.[160]

The three-stage process and the monies payable

33.147   The RTA protocol provides for payments in three separate stages. This issue will first be addressed from the point of view when the relevant types of costs fall due (ie base profit costs, disbursements and additional liabilities). Once that issue has been examined, each of the three stages is addressed in turn.

Base profit costs

33.148   Profit costs are fixed with no escape provisions.[161] They may be summarised as follows:[162]

Fixed costs in relation to the RTA protocol		
Stage 1	Legal Representative's Fixed Costs	£400*
Stage 2	Legal Representative's Fixed Costs	£800*
Stage 3	Legal Representative's Fixed Costs	£250*
	Advocate's Costs	£250
	Costs of Child Quantum Advice	£150

*These amounts will be increased by 12.5% if the claimant lives and instructs a legal representative who practices in an area set out in the Costs Practice Direction.[163]

---

[157]   See para 7.67 of the RTA Protocol.
[158]   See para 6.8 of the RTA Protocol.
[159]   See para 6.9 of the RTA Protocol and CPR, r 45.36(2).
[160]   See para 7.32 of the RTA Protocol.
[161]   See CPR, r 45.29(4).
[162]   See CPR, rr 45.29 and 45.30.
[163]   See CPR, r 45.29(5); they are: Barnet, Bow, Brentford, Bromley, Central London, Clerkenwell, Croydon, Edmonton, Ilford, Kingston, Lambeth, Mayors and City of London, Romford, Shoreditch, Uxbridge, Wandsworth, West London, Willesden and Woolwich.

Disbursements

33.149 These are limited to fees for a medical report (or reports) and for obtaining medical records, engineer's report fees, DVLA or MIB search fees, court fees, or any other disbursement that has arisen due to a particular feature of the case.[164]

Additional liabilities

33.150 Both parties are able to recover a success fee:

• *Claimant:* The success fee is fixed with no escape provisions.[165] Only a party who has entered into funding arrangement of the type specified in CPR 43.2(1)(k)(i) may recover a success fee; the default percentage uplift is 12.5%.[166] This is the amount which will be payable on claims which settle in stages one or two. If the end result is determined by the court and if that result is that the claimant has been awarded more than the defendant's RTA protocol offer, the percentage uplift on the Stage 3 costs will rise to 100%, but only on the fees for that stage.[167]

• *Defendant:* If the defendant enters into a funding arrangement of the type specified in CPR 43.2(1)(k)(i) and the damages awarded at a Stage 3 determination are less than or equal to the defendant's RTA protocol offer, then the defendant is entitled to a 100% success fee on the relevant Stage 3 fixed costs.

ATE and notional premiums

33.151 ATE insurance premiums (or an additional amount pursuant to s 30 of the Access to Justice Act 1999) are recoverable as disbursements.[168]

The three-stage process stage-by-stage

Stage 1

33.152 Stage 1 is the process by which the parties set out their respective cases. It also provides for an interim payment of costs.

Starting claims: the Claims Notification Form

33.153 Claims are started under the RTA protocol by the claimant's solicitor completing a lengthy document known as a Claims Notification Form or 'CNF'.[169] That is an electronic document[170] which is automatically transmitted to the defendant's

---

[164] See CPR, r 45.30.
[165] See CPR, r 45.31; uniquely under the CPR, express provision is made for success fees to be charged by defendants as well as claimants. This is probably a reflection of the fact that many defendant solicitors have, over the years, begun to provide legal services under discounted collective conditional fee agreements.
[166] CPR, r 45.32(6).
[167] That is, different success fees may be payable for costs incurred during different parts of the claim. In cases which determined at stage three (be that on the papers or at a stage three hearing) the claimant will be entitled to a 12.5% uplift on stage one fixed costs and stage two fixed costs, and will be entitled to a 100% uplift on stage three fixed costs.
[168] CPR, r 45.30.
[169] See the RTA Protocol, para 6.1.
[170] There are two ways of completing the form: using a standard web browser (www.rtapiclaimsprocess.org.uk) or using an application-to-application interface.

insurer. At the same time (or as soon as practicable thereafter) a 'defendant-only CNF' – a similar form but with slightly less information – should be sent to the defendant by first-class post.[171]

Responding to claims: the insurer response

33.154   The defendant's insurer must send an electronic acknowledgment the day after receiving the CNF.[172] Assuming the defendant's insurer acknowledges the claim, it will then have 15 business days to complete the 'insurer response' section of the CNF and to return it to the claimant;[173] where the claim is against the MIB, the insurer response must be completed and returned within 30 business days.[174]

Early exit and integration with other protocols

33.155   There are five circumstances which will result in a claim automatically exiting the RTA protocol.[175] These are when, within the 15 or 30-day period mentioned above, the defendant:

- makes an admission of liability, but alleges contributory negligence (other than in relation to the claimant's admitted failure to wear a seatbelt);
- does not complete and send the insurer response;
- does not admit liability;
- notifies the claimant that he considers there to be inadequate mandatory information in the CNF; or
- notifies the claimant that he considers the matter to be a small claims track case.

Where any of these conditions exist, claims will exit the RTA protocol and proceed under the existing Pre-action Protocol for Personal Injury Claims, starting at para 3.7 (or para 3.1 if the claim exits the protocol by reason of there having been inadequate information on the CNF); this will provide the defendant with a maximum of three months to investigate the claim. If the case settles, then CPR 45 Section II will, where appropriate, apply.

Admissions and early payments

33.156   Where liability is admitted (or admitted along with an allegation that the claimant failed to wear a seatbelt), the defendant must pay Stage 1 fixed costs within ten business days of sending the insurer response.[176] Where a defendant fails to do this, the claimant may give written notice that the claim will no longer continue under the RTA protocol;[177] any such notice must be given within ten business days of the defendant's failure, in default of which claim will continue under the RTA protocol.[178] If the claimant exercises that right unreasonably, the court is able to take that conduct into account when deciding the issue of costs.[179]

---

[171]   See the RTA Protocol, para 6.1.
[172]   See the RTA Protocol, para 6.10.
[173]   See the RTA Protocol, para 6.11.
[174]   See the RTA Protocol, para 6.13.
[175]   See the RTA Protocol, para 6.15.
[176]   See the RTA Protocol, para 6.18.
[177]   See the RTA Protocol, para 6.19.
[178]   Ibid.
[179]   See CPR, r 45.36.

Medical Evidence

33.157   The claimant is required to obtain a medical report[180] and to check its factual accuracy before the same is sent to the defendant;[181] no further opportunity will be afforded to the claimant to do this once the report has been disclosed.[182] Where appropriate, the claimant may obtain a report from two medical experts of different disciplines;[183] if a further report is needed from an expert in another specialism, then this must be on expert recommendation rather than solely on the advice of the claimant's solicitors.[184] A maximum of a total of six reports may be obtained from experts in four disciplines.[185] If further medical reports are required, the RTA protocol provides that the party should agree to stay the process for a suitable period.[186]

33.158   Where a claimant obtains medical evidence which exceeds that for which the RTA protocol provides, he will be at risk of not recovering the relevant fees.[187]

Interim Payments

33.159   A notable feature of the RTA protocol is the fact that it makes provision for very early interim payments; early interim payments relate primarily to damages, but they are relevant because they may influence the costs. The process begins when the claimant's representative serves the Interim Settlement Pack (ISP), in which the claimant is able to request an interim payment.

33.160   The request may be for £1,000 or for more:[188]

- **£1,000:** If the claimant requests an interim payment of £1,000, the defendant must make such interim payment within 10 business days of receiving the ISP.[189] Failure to do so will result in the claimant being entitled to exit the RTA protocol. Notice of an intention to quit the RTA protocol must be given within 10 business days of the expiry of the defendant's time to pay; if this is not done, the claim will continue under the RTA protocol.[190]
- **More than £1,000:** If the claimant requests an interim payment of more than £1,000, the request must be explained.[191] Once this has been done, the defendant must, within 15 business days of receiving the ISP:[192]
    (a)   pay the full amount requested (less any deductible benefits);
    (b)   pay £1,000 and explain why the requested figure has not been agreed; or
    (c)   pay more than £1,000 but less than the requested sumand explain why the requested figure has not been be agreed.

---

180   RTA Protocol, para 7.1.
181   RTA Protocol, para 7.2.
182   RTA Protocol, para 7.2
183   RTA Protocol, para 7.4.
184   RTA Protocol, para 7.6
185   RTA Protocol, paras 7.4–7.6
186   RTA Protocol, para 7.7.
187   RTA Protocol, para 7.24.
188   There seems to be no provision which allows the Claimant to request less than £1,000.
189   RTA Protocol, para 7.13
190   RTA Protocol, para 7.23.
191   RTA Protocol, para 7.11
192   RTA Protocol, para 7.14

If anything other than the full amount is paid, the claimant is able to elect to exit the RTA protocol;[193] if the claimant does this but is subsequently awarded no more than the amount the defendant had offered, the claimant's costs will be limited to Stage 1 and 2 fixed costs, disbursements and, if appropriate, the success fee.[194]

The above provisions do not apply to child claimants.[195]

Stage 2

33.161   Within 15 business days of the claimant approving the final medical report, a Stage 2 Settlement Pack ('S2 Pack') must be submitted to the defendant.[196] A defendant will not know when the claimant gave his approval, so it is unclear how this aspect of the timetable will be policed. It is implicit that the claimant is required to make an offer when sending the S2 Pack to the defendant.[197] The defendant is given a second opportunity to arrest the engagement of the protocol on the grounds that the claim is a small claims track case.[198]

33.162   The parties are given 35 business days to agree settlement, this being 'the total consideration period'); within 15 business days of receiving the S2 Pack the defendant must either accept the claimant's offer or make a counter-offer; that period of time is 'the initial consideration period'.[199] Failure to respond within that period results in automatic exit from the RTA protocol. The parties are explicitly given the ability to agree extensions of time.[200]

33.163   The defendant's counter-offer must propose an amount for each head of loss and may make a total offer which is more than the sum of the individual parts.[201] Thereafter the parties can use the remaining time to negotiate settlement, this being 'the negotiation period'. If a party makes an offer 5 business days or fewer before the end of the consideration period, there will be a further 5 day period for the offeree to consider the offer, this being 'the further consideration period'; no further offers can be made during that period.[202]

33.164   Where a claimant receives a counter offer, he will have until the end of the total consideration period to accept or reject the offer.[203] It is theoretically possible for a claimant to postpone rejection of the offer until the last day of the total consideration period, thereby ensuring entry into Stage 3. If the claimant has acted unreasonably in that regard, his opponent may be successful in challenging entitlement to Stage 3 costs; there is no authority on that point, however.

---

[193]   RTA Protocol, para 7.22.
[194]   CPR, r 45.36(3); in particular, no stage 3 costs will be payable.
[195]   The RTA Protocol, paras 7.19–17.20: Part 7 proceedings must be commenced and an application made to the court.
[196]   See para 7.26 of the RTA Protocol.
[197]   See, for example, para 7.31, 'Within the initial consideration period … the defendant must either accept the offer made by the Claimant on the Stage 2 Settlement Pack Form or make a counter-offer using that form'.
[198]   See RTA Protocol, para 7.32(a).
[199]   See RTA Protocol, para 7.28.
[200]   Pursuant to RTA Protocol, para 7.29
[201]   RTA Protocol, para 7.34.
[202]   RTA Protocol, para 7.30.
[203]   RTA Protocol, para 7.36

33.165   Where, following the expiry of the total consideration period (or further consideration period), a party withdraws an offer made in the S2 Pack, the claim automatically exits the RTA protocol.[204] There is the potential for abuse in this regard.[205]

Settlement at Stage 2

33.166   Where settlement is achieved (except where the claimant is a child) the defendant must pay (a) agreed damages, less CRU and interim payments; (b) any unpaid Stage 1 fixed costs; (c) Stage 2 fixed costs; (d) disbursements as applicable; and (e) success fee as applicable. This must be done within 10 business days of the end of the relevant period during which agreement was reached.[206]

Costs protection during Stage 2

33.167   The offers contained within S2 Pack, and those made during the total and further consideration periods are not ordinary Part 36 offers as they will not comply with the requirements set out in CPR, r 36.2; this is because the S2 Pack form does not contain the necessary notices. Moreover, they will not have effect as Part 36 Section II offers until Stage 3 is commenced.[207] It is, therefore, not wholly clear how a defendant can garner costs protection. One method would be to repeat every offer made the S2 Pack as a separate Part 36 offer, but this would be cumbersome and it would afford protection only if the claim were subsequently to exit the RTA protocol.[208]

Vehicle-related damages

33.168   Where they were originally dealt with outside the protocol but subsequently brought within it, vehicle-related damages are referred to as 'additional damages'. Once the total consideration period (or the further consideration period) has expired, if both the 'original damages' (ie those damages set out in the S2SP) and the additional damages remain outstanding, the claimant must incorporate those losses into the existing claim by amending the S2SP.[209] If vehicle related damages were included in the S2SP from the outset, they remain classified as 'original damages'. The following table summarises what may happen where additional damages are claimed.

---

[204]   RTA Protocol, para 7.39

[205]   There is a risk that less scrupulous claimants will make offers which are unlikely to be accepted by defendants, only to withdraw them following the total consideration period and thus obtain costs assessed on the standard basis when Part 7 proceedings are issued. It seems that the new regime offers the defendant very little protection from this potential abuse. It would seem that the only way in which a defendant can protect himself against this unsatisfactory position, is to replicate every offer made within the S2 Pack and subsequent total consideration period in correspondence as a fully compliant Part 36 offer.

[206]   RTA Protocol, para 7.40. See, however, the RTA Protocol, paras 7.41–7.42 where at the date of the acceptance of an offer in the Stage 2 Settlement Pack, the defendant does not have a certificate of recoverable benefits that will remain in force for at least 10 days.

[207]   See CPR, r 36.18.

[208]   See CPR, r 36.20(1) and (2).

[209]   RTA Protocol, paras 7.43–7.46.

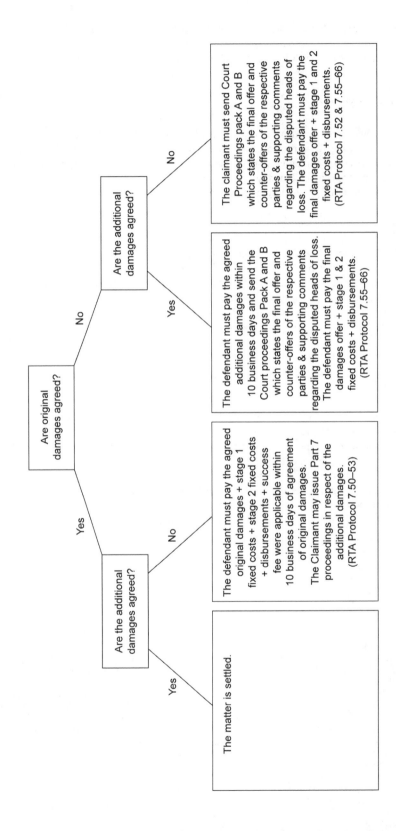

33.169 If the defendant fails to pay the sums set out in boxes 3rd and 4th boxes from the left within the 15-day period specified,[1] then the claimant may elect to exit the claim from the RTA protocol and commence proceedings under Part 7[2].

Stage 3

33.170 Stage 3 is the litigation stage of the RTA protocol.

33.171 Where the claim has not been capable of settlement following the procedure in Stage 2, the claimant should issue proceedings pursuant to CPR Practice Direction 8B. The claim form must state:

- that the claimant followed the RTA protocol;
- the date that Court Proceedings Pack (CPP) Parts A and B have been sent to the defendant;
- whether the claim should be determined by the court on the papers or at a Stage 3 hearing;
- dates to avoid for the Stage 3 hearing; and
- the value of the claim.

The claim form must be filed with the following items:

- CPP Part A;
- CPP Part B in a sealed envelope;
- copies of medical reports;
- evidence of special damages;
- evidence of disbursements; and
- notice of funding.

33.172 Service of the CPP Parts A and B on the defendant remains part of Stage 2. Stage 3 begins when the Part 8 claim form and the documents set out above are filed at court.[3] The final S2 Pack offer for each side, now contained within CPP Part B, becomes an effective 'RTA protocol Offer' pursuant to CPR, rr 36.17 and 36.18. If proceedings have been started, any such offer may be withdrawn only with the permission of the court.[4]

33.173 RTA protocol offers must not be communicated to the court during the currency of the claim and other offers must not be communicated to the court at all.[5] Where a claimant achieves a result that is less than or equal to the defendants RTA protocol Offer, the claimant will pay the fixed costs[6] in CPR, r 45.38 (plus interest).[7] but where he achieves a result for more than his own offer, he will be awarded fixed costs, plus enhanced interest on both the costs and damages.[8]

---

[1] This period is specified at para 7.63 of the RTA Protocol.
[2] RTA Protocol, para 7.66.
[3] RTA Protocol, para 6.2
[4] See PD 8, para 10.1.
[5] See CPR, rr 36.20(1) and (2).
[6] See CPR, r 36.21(2)(a)
[7] See CPR, r 36.21(2)(b); the interest starts to run from the first business day after the deemed date of the RTA Protocol offer under CPR, r 36.18.
[8] See CPR, r 36.21(4); the interest must not exceed 10 percent above base rate.

Costs consequences of a Stage 3 determination

33.174   Where the claimant obtains a judgment for an amount less than or equal to the defendant's RTA protocol offer, the claimant will be ordered to pay the following:[1]

- the appropriate type of Stage 3 fixed costs (the claimant having already been paid Stage 1 and Stage 2 fixed costs);
- disbursements; and
- a success fee.

Where the claimant obtains a judgment for an amount more than the defendant's RTA protocol offer, but less than the claimant's RTA protocol offer, the defendant will be ordered to pay the following:[2]

- any outstanding Stage 1 or Stage 2 fixed costs;
- the appropriate type of Stage 3 fixed costs;
- disbursements; and
- a success fee.

Where the claimant obtains a judgment for an amount equal to or more than the claimant's own RTA protocol offer, the court will order the defendant to pay the following:[3]

- any outstanding Stage 1 or Stage 2 fixed costs;
- the appropriate type of Stage 3 fixed costs;
- disbursements;
- a success fee; and
- enhanced interest on damages and costs.

Approval of child settlements

33.175   The RTA protocol retains the need for court approval of settlements made on behalf of a child claimant.[4]. The relevant provisions are contained in PD 8B. Costs will be awarded pursuant to CPR, r 45.33(2). Where the proposed settlement is not approved, the court will order a second approval hearing. If approved at the second hearing, the court will award the claimant his Stage 3 type B fixed costs in respect of one of the two hearings only, but may, in its discretion, award Stage 3 type B fixed costs in respect of the other hearing to either party. If the proposed award is not approved at the second hearing, the court will give directions and the matter will proceed as a Part 7 claim.

Scale costs for claims in the a Patents Count Court

33.176   This section deals with scale costs in the Patents County Court (see Part 45 VII). Those scale costs form part of a package of measures introduced on 1 October

---

[1]   CPR, r 36.21 and CPR, r 45.38.
[2]   CPR, r 36.21 and CPR, r 45.32.
[3]   CPR, r 36.21.
[4]   See, for example, the RTA Protocol, para 7.40.

2010[1] to reform the procedure in the Patents County Court. That package consists of new rules in Part 63 (procedure), Part 30 (transfers), and Part 45 (costs).

Scope and application

33.177 CPR, r 45.41 provides as follows:

'(1) Subject to paragraph (2) this Section applies to proceedings in a patents county court.

(2) This Section does not apply where—

    (a)   the court considers that a party has behaved in a manner which amounts to an abuse of the court's process; or

    (b)   the claim concerns the infringement or revocation of a patent or registered design the validity of which has been certified by a court in earlier proceedings.

(3) The court will make a summary assessment of the costs of the party in whose favour any order for costs is made. Rules 44.3(8), 44.3A(2)(b) and (c), 44.7(b) and Part 47 do not apply to this Section.

(4) 'Scale costs' means costs as defined in rule 43.2(1)(a).'

In addition, CPR, r 45.43 makes the following provisions:

'Summary assessment of the costs of an application where a party has behaved unreasonably

Costs awarded to a party under rule 63.26(2) are in addition to the total costs that may be awarded to that party under rule 45.42.'

The package of measures referred to above is intended to apply as a whole. This means that scale costs do not apply to costs incurred in circumstances in which the rest of the package of measures did not apply.[2] Costs incurred in the High Court before transfer to the patents county court will be assessed without reference to scale costs.[3]

Procedure and application

33.178 By CPR, r 45.41(3) the court will make a summary assessment of the costs of the party in whose favour any costs order is made. This applies whether or not the trial has taken a single day or has taken more time. HHJ Birse QC has commented that in the Patents County Court all costs are to be subject to summary assessment.[4]

33.179 The amount of scale costs which may be ordered is governed by CPR, r 45.42 which reads as follows:

'(1) Subject to rule 45.43 the court will not order a party to pay total costs of more than—

    (a)   £50,000 on the final determination of a claim in relation to liability; and

    (b)   £25,000 on an inquiry as to damages or account of profits.

(2) The amounts in paragraph (1) apply after the court has applied the provision on set off in accordance with rule 44.3(9)(a).

---

[1]   This followed the publication of the Final Report of the IPCUC's Working Group on Proposals for Reform of the Patents County Court, section 5.

[2]   *Westwood v Knight* [2011] EWPCC 011, per HHJ Birse QC at [13] and *Technical Fibre* [2010] EWPCC 011 at [8]; see also *Caljan Rite-Hite Ltd v Sovex Ltd* [2010] EWHC 669 (Ch), per Kitchin J.

[3]   *Westwood v Knight* [2011] EWPCC 011, per HHJ Birse QC at [13] and [38].

[4]   *Westwood v Knight* [2011] EWPCC 011, per HHJ Birse QC.

(3) The maximum amount of scale costs that the court will award for each stage of the claim is set out in the Costs Practice Direction.

(4) The amount of the scale costs awarded by the court in accordance with paragraph (3) will depend on the nature and complexity of the claim.

(5) Where appropriate, value added tax (VAT) may be recovered in addition to the amount of the scale costs and any reference in this Section to scale costs is a reference to those costs net of any such VAT.'

(The tables are not set out here for want of space.)

33.180 Notwithstanding the fact that they are called scale costs, these provisions merely limit costs. That limit works in two ways. First there is a global cap,[1] and second there are caps at various stages in the proceedings. Those provisions are to be applied in a broad way that is not limited by the fact that they appear to be chronologically ordered.[2] The global cap applies after any set-off.[3] In every case the amount of the scale costs awarded by the court will depend on the nature and complexity of the claim.[4] The limits are net of VAT.[5]

FIXED COSTS: HM REVENUE AND CUSTOMS

33.181 Fixed Costs: HM Revenue and Customs are governed by CPR Part 45 VIII. That Section applies where the only claim is conducted by an HMRC Officer[6] in the county court for recovery of a debt[7] and the Commissioners obtain judgment on the claim. The costs, known as 'HMRC charges' are not the costs in the traditional sense, but are monies payable for the work carried out by an HMRC Officer; as such, they are a species of litigant in person costs. They are, nonetheless, treated as if they were solicitors' profit fees.[8] They are 'fixed' only in the sense that they are default figures: the court is able to 'order otherwise',[9] which presumably means that the court is able to exercise its discretion according to CPR, rr 44.3 and 44.5.

33.182 Court fees and fixed commencement costs may be claimed;[10] the latter, however, comprise the HMRC charges, and are calculated on the basis of the following table in accordance with the value of the claim as stated on the claim form:[11]

Fixed costs on commencement of a County Court claim conducted by an HMRC Officer

---

[1]   CPR, r 45.42(2)(a).
[2]   *Westwood v Knight* [2011] EWPCC 011 at [30], per HHJ Birse QC.
[3]   See CPR, r 45.42(3).
[4]   See CPR, r 45.42(4).
[5]   See CPR, r 45.42(5).
[6]   'HMRC Officer' means a person appointed by the Commissioners under s 2 of the Commissioners for Revenue and Customs Act 2005 and authorised to conduct county court proceedings for recovery of debt under s 25(1A) of that Act: see CPR, r 45.44(2).
[7]   'Debt' means any sum payable to the Commissioners under or by virtue of an enactment or under a contract settlement: see CPR, r 45.44(2).
[8]   CPR, r 45.44(3) provides that HMRC charges shall, for the purpose of CPR Part 45 VIII, be claimed as 'solicitor costs' on relevant court forms.
[9]   CPR, r 45.44(1).
[10]   See CPR, rr 45.44(5) and (6) respectively.
[11]   See CPR, 45.45.

Where the value of the claim exceeds £25 but does not exceed £500	£33
Where the value of the claim exceeds £500 but does not exceed £1,000	£47
Where the value of the claim exceeds £1,000 but does not exceed £5,000	£53
Where the value of the claim exceeds £5,000 but does not exceed £15,000	£67
Where the value of the claim exceeds £15,000 but does not exceed £50,000	£90
Where the value of the claim exceeds £50,000 but does not exceed £100,000	£113
Where the value of the claim exceeds £100,000 but does not exceed £150,000	£127
Where the value of the claim exceeds £150,000 but does not exceed £200,000	£140
Where the value of the claim exceeds £200,000 but does not exceed £250,000	£153
Where the value of the claim exceeds £250,000 but does not exceed £300,000	£167
Where the value of the claim exceeds £300,000	£180

33.183 Where judgment in entered, 'fixed costs on entry of judgment' are added; those are £15 if the value of the claim does not exceed £5,000 and £20 if it does.[1] If, on the other hand, the full amount of the claim and the fixed costs on commencement are paid within 14 days of service of the particulars of claim, nothing else is payable unless the court orders otherwise.[2]

THE WORDING OF THE RELEVANT PROVISIONS

CPR Parts 45 II–V

33.184

II   ROAD TRAFFIC ACCIDENTS – FIXED RECOVERABLE COSTS

45.7   Scope and interpretation

(1)   This Section sets out the costs which are to be allowed in—

   (a)   costs-only proceedings under the procedure set out in rule 44.12A; or
   (b)   proceedings for approval of a settlement or compromise under rule 21.10(2),

in cases to which this Section applies.

(2)   This Section applies where—

   (a)   the dispute arises from a road traffic accident;
   (b)   the agreed damages include damages in respect of personal injury, damage to property, or both;
   (c)   the total value of the agreed damages does not exceed £10,000; and

---

[1]   See CPR, 45.46.
[2]   See CPR, 45.47.

(d)   if a claim had been issued for the amount of the agreed damages, the small claims track would not have been the normal track for that claim.

(3)   This Section does not apply where the claimant is a litigant in person.

(Rule 2.3 defines 'personal injuries' as including any disease and any impairment of a person's physical or mental condition)

(Rule 26.6 provides for when the small claims track is the normal track)

(4)   In this Section—

(a)   'road traffic accident' means an accident resulting in bodily injury to any person or damage to property caused by, or arising out of, the use of a motor vehicle on a road or other public place in England and Wales;

(b)   'motor vehicle' means a mechanically propelled vehicle intended for use on roads; and

(c)   'road' means any highway and any other road to which the public has access and includes bridges over which a road passes.

45.8   Application of fixed recoverable costs

Subject to rule 45.12, the only costs which are to be allowed are—

(a)   fixed recoverable costs calculated in accordance with rule 45.9;

(b)   disbursements allowed in accordance with rule 45.10; and

(c)   a success fee allowed in accordance with rule 45.11.

(Rule 45.12 provides for where a party issues a claim for more than the fixed recoverable costs)

45.9   Amount of fixed recoverable costs

(1)   Subject to paragraphs (2) and (3), the amount of fixed recoverable costs is the total of—

(a)   £800;

(b)   20% of the damages agreed up to £5,000; and

(c)   15% of the damages agreed between £5,000 and £10,000.

(2)   Where the claimant—

(a)   lives or works in an area set out in the relevant practice direction; and

(b)   instructs a solicitor or firm of solicitors who practise in that area,

the fixed recoverable costs shall include, in addition to the costs specified in paragraph (1), an amount equal to 12.5% of the costs allowable under that paragraph.

(3)   Where appropriate, value added tax (VAT) may be recovered in addition to the amount of fixed recoverable costs and any reference in this Section to fixed recoverable costs is a reference to those costs net of any such VAT.

45.10   Disbursements

(1)   The court—

(a)   may allow a claim for a disbursement of a type mentioned in paragraph (2); but

(b)   must not allow a claim for any other type of disbursement.

(2)   The disbursements referred to in paragraph (1) are—

(a)   the cost of obtaining—
(i)   medical records;
(ii)   a medical report;

       (iii)   a police report;
       (iv)   an engineer's report; or
       (v)   a search of the records of the Driver Vehicle Licensing Authority;

(b)   the amount of an insurance premium; or, where a membership organisation undertakes to meet liabilities incurred to pay the costs of other parties to proceedings, a sum not exceeding such additional amount of costs as would be allowed under section 30 in respect of provision made against the risk of having to meet such liabilities;

('membership organisation' is defined in rule 43.2(1)(n))

(c)   where they are necessarily incurred by reason of one or more of the claimants being a child or protected party as defined in Part 21—
       (i)   fees payable for instructing counsel; or
       (ii)   court fees payable on an application to the court;

(d)   any other disbursement that has arisen due to a particular feature of the dispute.

('insurance premium' is defined in rule 43.2)

45.11   Success fee

(1)   A claimant may recover a success fee if he has entered into a funding arrangement of a type specified in rule 43.2(k)(i).

(2)   The amount of the success fee shall be 12.5% of the fixed recoverable costs calculated in accordance with rule 45.9(1), disregarding any additional amount which may be included in the fixed recoverable costs by virtue of rule 45.9(2).

(Rule 43.2(k)(i) defines a funding arrangement as including a conditional fee agreement or collective conditional fee agreement which provides for a success fee)

45.12   Claims for an amount of costs exceeding fixed recoverable costs

(1)   The court will entertain a claim for an amount of costs (excluding any success fee or disbursements) greater than the fixed recoverable costs but only if it considers that there are exceptional circumstances making it appropriate to do so.

(2)   If the court considers such a claim appropriate, it may—

(a)   assess the costs; or
(b)   make an order for the costs to be assessed.

(3)   If the court does not consider the claim appropriate, it must make an order for fixed recoverable costs only.

45.13   Failure to achieve costs greater than fixed recoverable costs

(1)   This rule applies where—

(a)   costs are assessed in accordance with rule 45.12(2); and
(b)   the court assesses the costs (excluding any VAT) as being an amount which is less than 20% greater than the amount of the fixed recoverable costs.

(2)   The court must order the defendant to pay to the claimant the lesser of—

(a)   the fixed recoverable costs; and
(b)   the assessed costs.

45.14   Costs of the costs-only proceedings or the detailed assessment

Where—

(a)   the court makes an order for fixed recoverable costs in accordance with rule 45.12(3); or
(b)   rule 45.13 applies,

the court must—

> (i)   make no award for the payment of the claimant's costs in bringing the proceedings under rule 44.12A; and
>
> (ii)   order that the claimant pay the defendant's costs of defending those proceedings.

III   FIXED PERCENTAGE INCREASE IN ROAD TRAFFIC ACCIDENT CLAIMS

45.15   Scope and interpretation

(1)   This Section sets out the percentage increase which is to be allowed in the cases to which this Section applies.

(Rule 43.2(1)(l) defines 'percentage increase' as the percentage by which the amount of a legal representative's fee can be increased in accordance with a conditional fee agreement which provides for a success fee)

(2)   This Section applies where—

> (a)   the dispute arises from a road traffic accident; and
>
> (b   the claimant has entered into a funding arrangement of a type specified in rule 43.2(k)(i).

(Rule 43.2(k)(i) defines a funding arrangement as including an arrangement where a person has entered into a conditional fee agreement or collective conditional fee agreement which provides for a success fee).

(3)   This Section does not apply if the proceedings are costs only proceedings to which Section II of this Part applies.

(4)   This Section does not apply—

> (a)   to a claim which has been allocated to the small claims track;
>
> (b)   to a claim not allocated to a track, but for which the small claims track is the normal track; or
>
> (c)   where the road traffic accident which gave rise to the dispute occurred before 6 October 2003.[1]

(5)   The definitions in rule 45.7(4) apply to this Section as they apply to Section II.

(6)   In this Section—

> (a)   a reference to 'fees' is a reference to fees for work done under a conditional fee agreement or collective conditional fee agreement;
>
> (b)   a reference to 'trial' is a reference to the final contested hearing or to the contested hearing of any issue ordered to be tried separately;
>
> (c)   a reference to a claim concluding at trial is a reference to a claim concluding by settlement after the trial has commenced or by judgment; and
>
> (d)   'trial period' means a period of time fixed by the court within which the trial is to take place and where the court fixes more than one such period in relation to a claim, means the most recent period to be fixed.

45.16   Percentage increase of solicitors' fees

Subject to rule 45.18, the percentage increase which is to be allowed in relation to solicitors' fees is—

> (a)   100% where the claim concludes at trial; or

---

[1]   At the time of writing it was proposed that the following words be added: 'or (d) to a claim to which Section VI of this Part applies'.

(b)   12.5% where—
    (i)   the claim concludes before a trial has commenced; or
    (ii)   the dispute is settled before a claim is issued.

45.17   Percentage increase of counsel's fees

(1)   Subject to rule 45.18, the percentage increase which is to be allowed in relation to counsel's fees is—

(a)   100% where the claim concludes at trial;
(b)   if the claim has been allocated to the fast track—
    (i)   50% if the claim concludes 14 days or less before the date fixed for the commencement of the trial; or
    (ii)   12.5% if the claim concludes more than 14 days before the date fixed for the commencement of the trial or before any such date has been fixed;
(c)   if the claim has been allocated to the multi-track—
    (i)   75% if the claim concludes 21 days or less before the date fixed for the commencement of the trial; or
    (ii)   12.5% if the claim concludes more than 21 days before the date fixed for the commencement of the trial or before any such date has been fixed;
(d)   12.5% where—
    (i)   the claim has been issued but concludes before it has been allocated to a track; or
    (ii)   in relation to costs-only proceedings, the dispute is settled before a claim is issued.

(2)   Where a trial period has been fixed, if—

(a)   the claim concludes before the first day of that period; and
(b)   no trial date has been fixed within that period before the claim concludes,

the first day of that period is treated as the date fixed for the commencement of the trial for the purposes of paragraph (1).

(3)   Where a trial period has been fixed, if—

(a)   the claim concludes before the first day of that period; but
(b)   before the claim concludes, a trial date had been fixed within that period,

the trial date is the date fixed for the commencement of the trial for the purposes of paragraph (1).

(4)   Where a trial period has been fixed and the claim concludes—

(a)   on or after the first day of that period; but
(b)   before commencement of the trial,

the percentage increase in paragraph (1)(b)(i) or (1)(c)(i) shall apply as appropriate, whether or not a trial date has been fixed within that period.

(5)   For the purposes of this rule, in calculating the periods of time, the day fixed for the commencement of the trial (or the first day of the trial period, where appropriate) is not included.

45.18   Application for an alternative percentage increase where the fixed increase is 12.5%

(1)   This rule applies where the percentage increase to be allowed—

(a)   in relation to solicitors' fees under the provisions of rule 45.16; or
(b)   in relation to counsel's fees under rule 45.17,

is 12.5%.

(2)   A party may apply for a percentage increase greater or less than that amount if—

(a)   the parties agree damages of an amount greater than £500,000 or the court awards damages of an amount greater than £500,000; or

(b)   the court awards damages of £500,000 or less but would have awarded damages greater than £500,000 if it had not made a finding of contributory negligence; or

(c)   the parties agree damages of £500,000 or less and it is reasonable to expect that if the court had made an award of damages, it would have awarded damages greater than £500,000, disregarding any reduction the court may have made in respect of contributory negligence.

(3)   In paragraph (2), a reference to a lump sum of damages includes a reference to periodical payments of equivalent value.

(4)   If the court is satisfied that the circumstances set out in paragraph (2) apply it must—

(a)   assess the percentage increase; or

(b)   make an order for the percentage increase to be assessed.

45.19   Assessment of alternative percentage increase

(1)   This rule applies where the percentage increase of fees is assessed under rule 45.18(4).

(2)   If the percentage increase is assessed as greater than 20% or less than 7.5%, the percentage increase to be allowed shall be that assessed by the court.

(3)   If the percentage increase is assessed as no greater than 20% and no less than 7.5%—

(a)   the percentage increase to be allowed shall be 12.5%; and

(b)   the costs of the application and assessment shall be paid by the applicant.

IV   FIXED PERCENTAGE INCREASE IN EMPLOYERS LIABILITY CLAIMS

45.20   Scope and interpretation

(1)   Subject to paragraph (2), this Section applies where—

(a)   the dispute is between an employee and his employer arising from a bodily injury sustained by the employee in the course of his employment; and

(b)   the claimant has entered into a funding arrangement of a type specified in rule 43.2(1)(k)(i).

(2)   This Section does not apply—

(a)   where the dispute—
    (i)   relates to a disease;
    (ii)   relates to an injury sustained before 1 October 2004; or
    (iii)   arises from a road traffic accident (as defined in rule 45.7(4)(a)); or
    (iv)   relates to an injury to which Section V of this Part applies; or

(b)   to a claim—
    (i)   which has been allocated to the small claims track; or
    (ii)   not allocated to a track, but for which the small claims track is the normal track.

(3)   For the purposes of this Section—

(a)   'employee' has the meaning given to it by section 2(1) of the Employers' Liability (Compulsory Insurance) Act 1969; and

(b)   a reference to 'fees' is a reference to fees for work done under a conditional fee agreement or collective conditional fee agreement.

45.21 Percentage increase of solicitors' and counsel's fees

In the cases to which this Section applies, subject to rule 45.22 the percentage increase which is to be allowed in relation to solicitors' and counsel's fees is to be determined in accordance with rules 45.16 and 45.17, subject to the modifications that—

(a) the percentage increase which is to be allowed in relation to solicitors' fees under rule 45.16(b) is—

  (i) 27.5% if a membership organisation has undertaken to meet the claimant's liabilities for legal costs in accordance with section 30 of the Access to Justice Act 1999; and

  (ii) 25% in any other case; and

(b) the percentage increase which is to be allowed in relation to counsel's fees under rule 45.17(1)(b)(ii), (1)(c)(ii) or (1)(d) is 25%.

('membership organisation' is defined in rule 43.2(1)(n))

45.22 Alternative percentage increase

(1) In the cases to which this Section applies, rule 45.18(2)–(4) applies where—

(a) the percentage increase of solicitors' fees to be allowed in accordance with rule 45.21 is 25% or 27.5%; or

(b) the percentage increase of counsel's fees to be allowed is 25%.

(2) Where the percentage increase of fees is assessed by the court under rule 45.18(4) as applied by paragraph (1) above—

(a) if the percentage increase is assessed as greater than 40% or less than 15%, the percentage increase to be allowed shall be that assessed by the court; and

(b) if the percentage increase is assessed as no greater than 40% and no less than 15%—

  (i) the percentage increase to be allowed shall be 25% or 27.5% (as the case may be); and

  (ii) the costs of the application and assessment shall be paid by the applicant.

V FIXED RECOVERABLE SUCCESS FEES IN EMPLOYER'S LIABILITY DISEASE CLAIMS

45.23 Scope and interpretation

(1) Subject to paragraph (2), this Section applies where—

(a) the dispute is between an employee (or, if the employee is deceased, the employee's estate or dependants) and his employer (or a person alleged to be liable for the employer's alleged breach of statutory or common law duties of care); and

(b) the dispute relates to a disease with which the employee is diagnosed that is alleged to have been contracted as a consequence of the employer's alleged breach of statutory or common law duties of care in the course of the employee's employment; and

(c) the claimant has entered into a funding arrangement of a type specified in rule 43.2(1)(k)(i).

(2) This Section does not apply where—

(a) the claimant sent a letter of claim to the defendant containing a summary of the facts on which the claim is based and main allegations of fault before 1 October 2005; or

(b) rule 45.20(2)(b) applies.

(3) For the purposes of this Section—

(a)   rule 45.15(6) applies;

(b)   'employee' has the meaning given to it by section 2(1) of the Employers' Liability (Compulsory Insurance) Act 1969;

(c)   'Type A claim' means a claim relating to a disease or physical injury alleged to have been caused by exposure to asbestos;

(d)   'Type B claim' means a claim relating to—

    (i)   a psychiatric injury alleged to have been caused by work-related psychological stress;

    (ii)   a work-related upper limb disorder which is alleged to have been caused by physical stress or strain, excluding hand/arm vibration injuries; and

(e)   'Type C claim' means a claim relating to a disease not falling within either type A or type B.

(The Table annexed to the Practice Direction supplementing Part 45 contains a non-exclusive list of diseases within Type A and Type B).

45.24   Percentage increase of solicitors' fees

(1)   In the cases to which this Section applies, subject to rule 45.26, the percentage increase which is to be allowed in relation to solicitors' fees is—

(a)   100% if the claim concludes at trial; or

(b)   where—

    (i)   the claim concludes before a trial has commenced; or

    (ii)   the dispute is settled before a claim is issued,

to be determined by rule 45.24(2).

(2)   Where rule 45.24(1)(b) applies, the percentage increase which is to be allowed in relation to solicitors' fees is—

(a)   in type A claims—

    (i)   30% if a membership organisation has undertaken to meet the claimant's liabilities for legal costs in accordance with section 30 of the Access to Justice Act 1999; and

    (ii)   27.5% in any other case;

(b)   in type B claims, 100%; and

(c)   in type C claims –

    (i)   70% if a membership organisation has undertaken to meet the claimant's liabilities for legal costs in accordance with section 30 of the Access to Justice Act 1999; and

    (ii)   62.5% in any other case.

('Membership organisation' is defined in rule 43.2(1)(n)).

45.25   Percentage increase of counsel's fees

(1)   In the cases to which this Section applies, subject to rule 45.26, the percentage increase which is to be allowed in relation to counsel's fees is—

(a)   100% if the claim concludes at trial; or

(b)   where—

    (i)   the claim concludes before a trial has commenced; or

    (ii)   the dispute is settled before a claim is issued,

to be determined by rule 45.25(2).

(2)   Where rule 45.25(1)(b) applies, the percentage increase which is to be allowed in relation to counsel's fees is—

(a)   if the claim has been allocated to the fast track, the amount shown in Table 6; and

(b)   if the claim has been allocated to the multi-track, the amount shown in Table 7.

(3)   Where a trial period has been fixed, rules 45.17(2) to 45.17(5) apply for the purposes of determining the date fixed for the commencement of the trial.

TABLE 6
Claims allocated to the fast track

	If the claim concludes 14 days or less before the date fixed for commencement of the trial	If the claim concludes more than 14 days before the date fixed for commencement of the trial or before any such date has been fixed
Type A claim	50%	27.5%
Type B claim	100%	100%
Type C claim	62.5%	62.5%

TABLE 7
Claims allocated to the multi-track

	If the claim concludes 21 days or less before the date fixed for commencement of the trial	If the claim concludes more than 21 days before the date fixed for commencement of the trial or before any such date has been fixed
Type A claim	75%	27.5%
Type B claim	100%	100%
Type C claim	75%	62.5%

45.26   Alternative percentage increase

(1)   In cases to which this Section applies and subject to paragraph (2) below, rules 45.18(2) to (4) apply where the percentage increase is the amount allowed under rules 45.24 and 45.25.

(2)   For the purposes of this section, the sum of £250,000 shall be substituted for the sum of £500,000 in rules 45.18(2)(a) to (c).

(3)   Where the percentage increase of fees is assessed by the court under rule 45.18(4), as applied by paragraph 1 above, the percentage increase to be allowed shall be the amount shown in Table 8.

(4)   The percentage increase cannot be varied where the case concludes at trial.

TABLE 8

Type of claim	Amount Allowed		
		If the percentage increase is assessed as no greater than 40% and no less than 15%—	
A	If the percentage increase is assessed as greater than 40% or less than 15%, the percentage increase that is assessed by the court.	(i) 27.5%; and	
		(ii)	the costs of the application and assessment shall be paid by the applicant.

TABLE 8

Type of claim	Amount Allowed		
B	If the percentage increase is assessed as less than 75%, the percentage increase that is assessed by the court.	If the percentage increase is assessed as no less than 75%—	
		(i)	100%; and
		(ii)	the costs of the application and assessment shall be paid by the applicant.
C	If the percentage increase is assessed as greater than 75% or less than 50%, the percentage increase that is assessed by the court.	If the percentage increase is assessed as no greater than 75% and no less than 50%—	
		(i)	62.5%; and
		(ii)	the costs of the application and assessment shall be paid by the applicant.

CPR Part 45 VI

33.185 At the time of writing, it was proposed that a new section be added to CPR Part 45 dealing with low-value road traffic accident claims; the draft which was being considered at the time is set out below. **This is only a draft and may be different from the actual provisions: the reader ought not to rely in any way on this draft.**

SECTION VI – PRE-ACTION PROTOCOL FOR LOW VALUE PERSONAL INJURY CLAIMS IN ROAD TRAFFIC ACCIDENTS

45.27 Scope and Interpretation

(1) This Section applies to claims that have been or should have been started under Part 8 in accordance with Practice Direction 8B ('the Stage 3 Procedure').

(2) Where a party has not complied with the RTA protocol rule 45.36 will apply.

(3) 'RTA protocol' means the Pre-Action Protocol for Personal Injury Claims in Road Traffic Accidents.

(4) A reference to 'Claim Notification Form' is a reference to the form used in the RTA protocol.

45.28 Application of fixed costs, disbursements and success fee

The only costs allowed are—

    (a)   fixed costs in rule 45.29;
    (b)   disbursements in accordance with rule 45.30; and
    (c)   a success fee in accordance with rule 45.31.

45.29 Amount of fixed costs

(1) Subject to paragraph (4), the amount of fixed costs is set out in Table 1.

(2) In Table 1—

    (a)   'Type A fixed costs' means the legal representative's costs;
    (b)   'Type B fixed costs' means the advocate's costs; and
    (c)   'Type C fixed costs' means the costs for the advice on the amount of damages where the claimant is a child.

(3) 'Advocate' has the same meaning as in rule 46.1(2)(a).

(4) Subject to rule 45.36(2) the court will not award more or less than the amounts shown in Table 1.

(5) Where the claimant—

(a)   lives or works in an area set out in the Costs Practice Direction; and
(b)   instructs a legal representative who practises in that area,

the fixed costs will include, in addition to the costs set out in Table 1, an amount equal to 12.5% of the Stage 1 and 2 and Stage 3 Type A fixed costs.

(6) Where appropriate, value added tax (VAT) may be recovered in addition to the amount of fixed costs and any reference in this Section to fixed costs is a reference to those costs net of any such VAT.

Table 1 – Fixed costs in relation to the RTA protocol		
Stage 1 fixed costs—		£400
Stage 2 fixed costs—		£800
Stage 3—		
	Type A fixed costs—	£250
	Type B fixed costs—	£250
	Type C fixed costs—	£150

45.30   Disbursements

(1)   The court—

(a)   may allow a claim for a disbursement of a type mentioned in paragraph (2); but
(b)   must not allow a claim for any other type of disbursement.

(2)   The disbursements referred to in paragraph (1) are—

(a)   the cost of obtaining—
　　(i)   medical records;
　　(ii)   a medical report or reports as provided for in the RTA protocol;
　　(iii) an engineer's report;
　　(iv)   a search of the records of the—
　　　　(aa)   Driver Vehicle Licensing Authority;
　　　　(bb)   Motor Insurance Database;

(b)   the amount of the insurance premium or, where a membership organisation undertakes to meet liabilities incurred to pay the costs of other parties to proceedings, a sum not exceeding such additional amount of costs as would be allowed under section 30 of the Access to Justice Act 1999 in respect of provision made against the risk of having to meet such liabilities;
(c)   court fees as a result of Part 21 being applicable;
(d)   court fees payable where proceedings are started as a result of a limitation period that is about to expire;
(e)   court fees in respect of the Stage 3 Procedure;
(f)   any other disbursement that has arisen due to a particular feature of the dispute.

(insurance premium is defined in rule 43.2(1)(m).)

(membership organisation is defined in rule 43.2(1)(n).)

45.31   Success fee

(1)   A party who has entered into a funding arrangement of a type specified in rule 43.2(1)(k)(i) in respect of any element of the fixed costs in rule 45.29 may recover a success fee on that element of the fixed costs.

(2)   A reference to a success fee in this Section is a reference to a success fee in accordance with paragraph (1).

(3)   Where the court—

(a)   determines the claim at a Stage 3 hearing or on the papers; and
(b)   awards an amount of damages that is more than the defendant's RTA protocol offer,

the amount of the claimant's success fee is—

(i)   12.5% of the Stage 1 and 2 fixed costs; and
(ii)   100% of the relevant Stage 3 fixed costs.

(RTA protocol offer is defined in rule 36.17.)

(4)   Where the court—

(a)   determines the claim at a Stage 3 hearing or on the papers;and
(b)   awards an amount of damages that is equal to or less than the defendant's RTA protocol offer,

the amount of the defendant's success fee is 100% of the relevant Stage 3 fixed costs.

(5)   Where the claimant is a child and the court—

(a)   does not approve a settlement at a settlement hearing;
(b)   determines the claim at a Stage 3 hearing; and
(c)   awards an amount of damages that is more than the amount of the settlement considered by the court at the first settlement hearing;

the amount of the claimant's success fee is—

(i)   12.5% of the Stage 1 and 2 fixed costs;
(ii)   100% of the relevant Stage 3 fixed costs.

(6)   Where paragraphs (3) to (5) do not apply the success fee is—

(a)   12.5% of Stage 1 and 2 fixed costs; and
(b)   12.5% of the relevant Stage 3 fixed costs.

(7)   The amount of the success fee set out in paragraphs (3) to (6) will be calculated without regard to any additional amount which may be included in the fixed costs by virtue of rule 45.29(5).

45.32   Where the claimant obtains judgment for an amount more than the defendant's RTA protocol offer

Where rule 36.21(1)(b) or (c) applies, the court will order the defendant to pay—

(a)   where not already paid by the defendant, the Stage 1 and 2 fixed costs;
(b)   where the claim is determined—

(i)   on the papers, Stage 3 Type A fixed costs;
(ii)   at a Stage 3 hearing, Stage 3 Type A and B fixed costs; or
(iii) at a Stage 3 hearing and the claimant is a child, Type A, B and C fixed costs;

(c)   disbursements allowed in accordance with rule 45.30; and
(d)   a success fee in accordance with rule 45.31(3).

45.33   Settlement at Stage 2 where the claimant is a child

(1)   This rule applies where—

    (a)   the claimant is a child;

    (b)   there is a settlement at Stage 2 of the RTA protocol; and

    (c)   an application is made to the court to approve the settlement.

(2)   Where the court approves the settlement at a settlement hearing it will order the defendant to pay—

    (a)   the Stage 1 and 2 fixed costs;

    (b)   the Stage 3 Type A, B and C fixed costs;

    (c)   disbursements allowed in accordance with rule 45.30; and

    (d)   a success fee in accordance with rule 45.31(6).

(3)   Where the court does not approve the settlement at a settlement hearing it will order the defendant to pay the Stage 1 and 2 fixed costs.

(4)   Paragraphs (5) and (6) apply where the court does not approve the settlement at the first settlement hearing but does approve the settlement at a second settlement hearing.

(5)   At the second settlement hearing the court will order the defendant to pay—

    (a)   the Stage 3 Type A and C fixed costs for the first settlement hearing;

    (b)   disbursements allowed in accordance with rule 45.30;

    (c)   the Stage 3 Type B fixed costs for one of the hearings; and

    (d)   a success fee in accordance with rule 45.31(6) on the Stage 1 and 2 fixed costs and the Stage 3 Type A, B and C fixed costs.

(6)   The court in its discretion may also order—

    (a)   the defendant to pay—

        (i)   an additional amount of either or both the Stage 3—

            (aa)   Type A fixed costs;

            (bb)   Type B fixed costs; and

        (ii)   a success fee in accordance with rule 45.31(6) on the additional Stage 3 fixed costs in sub-paragraph (a)(i); or

    (b)   the claimant to pay an amount equivalent to either or both the Stage 3—

        (i)   Type A fixed costs;

        (ii)   Type B fixed costs.

45.34   Settlement at Stage 3 where the claimant is a child

(1)   This rule applies where—

    (a)   the claimant is a child;

    (b)   there is a settlement after proceedings are started under the Stage 3 Procedure;

    (c)   the settlement is more than the defendant's RTA protocol offer; and

    (d)   an application is made to the court to approve the settlement.

(2)   Where the court approves the settlement at the settlement hearing it will order the defendant to pay—

    (a)   the Stage 1 and 2 fixed costs;

    (b)   the Stage 3 Type A, B and C fixed costs;

    (c)   disbursements allowed in accordance with rule 45.30; and

    (d)   a success fee in accordance with rule 45.31(6).

(3)   Where the court does not approve the settlement at the settlement hearing it will order the defendant to pay the Stage 1 and 2 fixed costs.

(4)   Paragraphs (5) and (6) apply where the court does not approve the settlement at the first settlement hearing but does approve the settlement at the Stage 3 hearing.

(5)   At the Stage 3 hearing the court will order the defendant to pay—

    (a)   the Stage 3 Type A and C fixed costs for the settlement hearing;

(b)   disbursements allowed in accordance with rule 45.30;

(c)   the Stage 3 Type B fixed costs for one of hearings; and

(d)   a success fee in accordance with rule 45.31(6) on the Stage 1 and 2 fixed costs and the Stage 3 Type A, B and C fixed costs.

(6)   The court in its discretion may also order—

(a)   the defendant to pay—

    (i)   an additional amount of either or both the Stage 3—

        (aa)   Type A fixed costs;

        (bb)   Type B fixed costs; and

    (ii)   a success fee in accordance with rule 45.31(6) on the additional Stage 3 fixed costs in sub-paragraph (a)(i); or

(b)   the claimant to pay an amount equivalent to either or both the Stage 3—

    (i)   Type A fixed costs;

    (ii)   Type B fixed costs.

(7)   Where the settlement is not approved at the Stage 3 hearing the court will order the defendant to pay the Stage 3 Type A fixed costs.

45.35   Where the court orders the claim is not suitable to be determined under the Stage 3 Procedure and the claimant is a child

Where—

(a)   the claimant is a child; and

(b)   at a settlement hearing or the Stage 3 hearing the court orders that the claim is not suitable to be determined under the Stage 3 Procedure,

the court will order the defendant to pay—

    (i)   the Stage 1 and 2 fixed costs; and

    (ii)   the Stage 3 Type A, B and C fixed costs.

**45.36   Failure to comply or electing not to continue with the RTA protocol –
costs consequences**

(1)   This rule applies where the claimant—

    (a)   does not comply with the process set out in the RTA protocol; or

    (b)   elects not to continue with that process,

and starts proceedings under Part 7.

(2)   Where a judgment is given in favour of the claimant but—

(a)   the court determines that the defendant did not proceed with the process set out in the RTA protocol because the claimant provided insufficient information on the Claim Notification Form;

(b)   the court considers that the claimant acted unreasonably—

    (i)   by discontinuing the process set out in the RTA protocol and starting proceedings under Part 7;

    (ii)   by valuing the claim at more than £10,000, so that the claimant did not need to comply with the RTA protocol; or

    (iii) except for paragraph (2)(a), in any other way that caused the process in the RTA protocol to be discontinued; or

(c)   the claimant did not comply with the RTA protocol at all despite the claim falling within the scope of the RTA protocol;

the court may order the defendant to pay no more than the fixed costs in rule 45.29 together with the disbursements allowed in accordance with rule 45.30 and success fee in accordance with rule 45.31(3).

(3)   Where the claimant starts proceedings under paragraph 7.22 of the RTA protocol and the court orders the defendant to make an interim payment of no more than the interim

payment made under paragraph 7.14(2) or (3) of that Protocol the court will, on the final determination of the proceedings, order the defendant to pay no more than—

(a)   the Stage 1 and 2 fixed costs;
(b)   the disbursements allowed in accordance with rule 45.30; and
(c)   a success fee in accordance with rule 45.31(3).

45.37   Where the parties have settled after proceedings have started

(1)   This rule applies where an application is made under rule 44.12C (costs-only application after a claim is started under Part 8 in accordance with Practice Direction 8B).

(2)   Where the settlement is more than the defendant's RTA protocol offer the court will order the defendant to pay—

(a)   the Stage 1 and 2 fixed costs where not already paid by the defendant;
(b)   the Stage 3 Type A fixed costs;
(c)   disbursements allowed in accordance with rule 45.30; and
(d)   a success fee in accordance with rule 45.31(6).

(3)   Where the settlement is less than or equal to the defendant's RTA protocol offer the court will order the defendant to pay—

(a)   the Stage 1 and 2 fixed costs where not already paid by the defendant;
(b)   disbursements allowed in accordance with rule 45.30; and
(c)   a success fee in accordance with rule 45.31(6).

(4)   The court may, in its discretion, order either party to pay the costs of the application.

45.38   Where the claimant obtains judgment for an amount equal to or less than the defendant's RTA protocol offer

Where rule 36.21(1)(a) applies, the court will order the claimant to pay—

(a)   where the claim is determined—
   (i)   on the papers, Stage 3 Type A fixed costs; or
   (ii)   at a hearing, Stage 3 Type A and B fixed costs;
(b)   disbursements allowed in accordance with rule 45.30; and
(c)   a success fee in accordance with rule 45.31(4).

45.39   Adjournment

Where the court adjourns a settlement hearing or a Stage 3 hearing it may, in its discretion, order a party to pay—

(a)   an additional amount of the Stage 3 Type B fixed costs; and
(b)   any court fee for that adjournment.

45.40   Account of payment of Stage 1 fixed costs

Where a claim no longer continues under the RTA protocol the court will, when making any order as to costs including an order for fixed recoverable costs under Section II of this Part, take into account the Stage 1 fixed costs together with any success fee on those fixed costs that have been paid by the defendant.

CPR Part 46

33.186

46.1 Scope of this Part

(1) This Part deals with the amount of costs which the court may award as the costs of an advocate for preparing for and appearing at the trial of a claim in the fast track (referred to in this rule as 'fast track trial costs').

(2) For the purposes of this Part—

  (a)   'advocate' means a person exercising a right of audience as a representative of, or on behalf of, a party;

  (b)   'fast track trial costs' means the costs of a party's advocate for preparing for and appearing at the trial, but does not include—
    (i)   any other disbursements; or
    (ii)   any value added tax payable on the fees of a party's advocate; and

  (c)   'trial' includes a hearing where the court decides an amount of money or the value of goods following a judgment under Part 12 (default judgment) or Part 14 (admissions) but does not include—
    (i)   the hearing of an application for summary judgment under Part 24; or
    (ii)   the court's approval of a settlement or other compromise under rule 21.10.

(Part 21 deals with claims made by or on behalf of, or against, children and protected parties)

46.2 Amount of fast track trial costs

(1) The following table shows the amount of fast track trial costs which the court may award (whether by summary or detailed assessment).

Value of the claim	Amount of fast track trial costs which the court may award
No more than £3,000	£485
More than £3,000 but not more than £10,000	£690
More than £10,000 but not more than £15,000	£1,035
For proceedings issued on or after 6 April 2009, more than £15,000	£1,650

(2) The court may not award more or less than the amount shown in the table except where—

  (a)   it decides not to award any fast track trial costs; or
  (b)   rule 46.3 applies,

but the court may apportion the amount awarded between the parties to reflect their respective degrees of success on the issues at trial.

(3) Where the only claim is for the payment of money—

  (a)   for the purpose of quantifying fast track trial costs awarded to a claimant, the value of the claim is the total amount of the judgment excluding—
    (i)   interest and costs; and
    (ii)   any reduction made for contributory negligence.

  (b)   for the purpose of quantifying fast track trial costs awarded to a defendant, the value of the claim is—

(i)   the amount specified in the claim form (excluding interest and costs);

(ii)   if no amount is specified, the maximum amount which the claimant reasonably expected to recover according to the statement of value included in the claim form under rule 16.3; or

(iii) more than £15,000, if the claim form states that the claimant cannot reasonably say how much is likely to be recovered.

(4)   Where the claim is only for a remedy other than the payment of money the value of the claim is deemed to be more than £3,000 but not more than £10,000, unless the court orders otherwise.

(5)   Where the claim includes both a claim for the payment of money and for a remedy other than the payment of money, the value of the claim is deemed to be the higher of—

(a)   the value of the money claim decided in accordance with paragraph (3); or

(b)   the deemed value of the other remedy decided in accordance with paragraph (4),

unless the court orders otherwise.

(6)   Where—

(a)   a defendant has made a counterclaim against the claimant;

(b)   the counterclaim has a higher value than the claim; and

(c)   the claimant succeeds at trial both on the claim and the counterclaim,

for the purpose of quantifying fast track trial costs awarded to the claimant, the value of the claim is the value of the defendant's counterclaim calculated in accordance with this rule.

46.3   Power to award more or less than the amount of fast track trial costs

(1)   This rule sets out when a court may award—

(a)   an additional amount to the amount of fast track trial costs shown in the table in rule 46.2(1); and

(b)   less than those amounts.

(2)   If—

(a)   in addition to the advocate, a party's legal representative attends the trial;

(b)   the court considers that it was necessary for a legal representative to attend to assist the advocate; and

(c)   the court awards fast track trial costs to that party,

the court may award an additional £345 in respect of the legal representative's attendance at the trial.

(Legal representative is defined in rule 2.3)

(2A)   The court may in addition award a sum representing an additional liability.

(The requirements to provide information about a funding arrangement where a party wishes to recover any additional liability under a funding arrangement are set out in the costs practice direction)

('Additional liability' is defined in rule 43.2)

(3)   If the court considers that it is necessary to direct a separate trial of an issue then the court may award an additional amount in respect of the separate trial but that amount is limited in accordance with paragraph (4) of this rule.

(4)   The additional amount the court may award under paragraph 3 must not exceed two-thirds of the amount payable for that claim, subject to a minimum award of £485.

(5)   Where the party to whom fast track trial costs are to be awarded is a litigant in person, the court will award—

(a)   if the litigant in person can prove financial loss, two-thirds of the amount that would otherwise be awarded; or

(b)   if the litigant in person fails to prove financial loss, an amount in respect of the time spent reasonably doing the work at the rate specified in the costs practice direction.

(6)   Where a defendant has made a counterclaim against the claimant, and—

(a)   the claimant has succeeded on his claim; and

(b)   the defendant has succeeded on his counterclaim,

the court will quantify the amount of the award of fast track trial costs to which—

(i)   but for the counterclaim, the claimant would be entitled for succeeding on his claim; and

(ii)   but for the claim, the defendant would be entitled for succeeding on his counterclaim,

and make one award of the difference, if any, to the party entitled to the higher award of costs.

(7)   Where the court considers that the party to whom fast track trial costs are to be awarded has behaved unreasonably or improperly during the trial, it may award that party an amount less than would otherwise be payable for that claim, as it considers appropriate.

(8)   Where the court considers that the party who is to pay the fast track trial costs has behaved improperly during the trial the court may award such additional amount to the other party as it considers appropriate.

46.4   Fast track trial costs where there is more than one claimant or defendant

(1)   Where the same advocate is acting for more than one party—

(a)   the court may make only one award in respect of fast track trial costs payable to that advocate; and

(b)   the parties for whom the advocate is acting are jointly entitled to any fast track trial costs awarded by the court.

(2)   Where—

(a)   the same advocate is acting for more than one claimant; and

(b)   each claimant has a separate claim against the defendant,

the value of the claim, for the purpose of quantifying the award in respect of fast track trial costs is to be ascertained in accordance with paragraph (3).

(3)   The value of the claim in the circumstances mentioned in paragraph (2) is—

(a)   where the only claim of each claimant is for the payment of money—

(i)   if the award of fast track trial costs is in favour of the claimants, the total amount of the judgment made in favour of all the claimants jointly represented; or

(ii)   if the award is in favour of the defendant, the total amount claimed by the claimants,

and in either case, quantified in accordance with rule 46.2(3);

(b)   where the only claim of each claimant is for a remedy other than the payment of money, deemed to be more than £3,000 but not more than £10,000; and

(c)   where claims of the claimants include both a claim for the payment of money and for a remedy other than the payment of money, deemed to be—

(i)   more than £3,000 but not more than £10,000; or

(ii)   if greater, the value of the money claims calculated in accordance with sub paragraph (a) above.

(4)   Where—

    (a)   there is more than one defendant; and

    (b)   any or all of the defendants are separately represented,

the court may award fast track trial costs to each party who is separately represented.

(5) Where—

    (a)   there is more than one claimant; and

    (b)   a single defendant,

the court may make only one award to the defendant of fast track trial costs, for which the claimants are jointly and severally liable (GL).

(6) For the purpose of quantifying the fast track trial costs awarded to the single defendant under paragraph (5), the value of the claim is to be calculated in accordance with paragraph (3) of this rule.

Practice Direction 46

33.187

SECTION 26   SCOPE OF PART 46: RULE 46.1

26.1 Part 46 applies to the costs of an advocate for preparing for and appearing at the trial of a claim in the fast track.

26.2 It applies only where, at the date of the trial, the claim is allocated to the fast track. It does not apply in any other case, irrespective of the final value of the claim.

26.3 In particular it does not apply to:

    (a)   the hearing of a claim which is allocated to the small claims track with the consent of the parties given under rule 26.7(3); or

    (b)   a disposal hearing at which the amount to be paid under a judgment or order is decided by the court (see paragraph 12.8 of the Practice Direction which supplements Part 26 (Case Management – Preliminary Stage)).

Cases which settle before trial

26.4 Attention is drawn to rule 44.10 (limitation on amount court may award where a claim allocated to the fast track settles before trial).

SECTION 27   POWER TO AWARD MORE OR LESS THAN THE AMOUNT OF FAST TRACK TRIAL COSTS: RULE 46.3

27.1 Rule 44.15 (providing information about funding arrangements) sets out the requirement to provide information about funding arrangements to the court and other parties. Section 19 of this Practice Direction sets out the information to be provided and when this is to be done.

27.2 Section 11, of this Practice Direction explains how the court will approach the question of what sum to allow in respect of additional liability.

27.3 The court has the power, when considering whether a percentage increase is reasonable, to allow different percentages for different items of costs or for different periods during which costs were incurred.

Chapter 34

POINTS OF PRINCIPLE

34.1 This chapter addresses a number of miscellaneous points of principle which, when they arise, are often most conveniently decided either at the beginning of the detailed assessment or at a preliminary issues hearing. It begins with a discussion of proportionality as it applies to detailed assessments;[1] it then moves on to the related topics of how the court should take estimates into account and of how the court assesses conduct and misconduct. There is then a brief discussion of apportionment of costs: that discussion necessarily makes reference to other parts of this book. Finally, there is mention of number of statutory restrictions on the recovery of costs.

PROPORTIONALITY

34.2 Proportionality is a principle upon which the effectiveness of the CPR depends.[2] It reflects the policy that litigation should be conducted in a proportionate manner and, where possible, at a proportionate cost.[3] It is convenient to refer to that policy as 'the general policy'.

34.3 Whilst there may be some overlap,[4] proportionality is conceptually distinct from reasonableness; reasonable expenditure, nonetheless, is usually a necessary condition of proportionate expenditure.[5]

34.4 Proportionality played no part in the assessment of costs prior to the introduction of the CPR:[6] the only test then available to the court was that of reasonableness. According to Lord Woolf MR, the problem with that was that it tended to use as its yardstick the costs charged by the legal profession, thereby institutionalising those costs as being the appropriate amount to allow. It seems that Woolf MR intended to avoid that seemingly self-serving method of measuring costs by requiring the court to have a second, shorter yardstick to hand, namely proportionality.

The general policy and the proportionate management of claims

34.5 The general policy is reflected in CPR, r 1.1, which provides:

---

1   Summary assessments are discussed in Chapter 22.
2   *Lownds v Home Office* [2002] EWCA Civ 365 at [1], per Lord Woolf CJ.
3   Ibid.
4   *Simms v The Law Society* [2005] EWCA Civ 849 at [24], per Carnworth LJ.
5   *Rogers v Merthyr Tydfil CBC* [2006] EWCA Civ 1134 at [104], per Brooke LJ.
6   See, however, *Finley v Glaxo Laboratories Ltd* (1989) Costs LR, Core Vol 106 at 111, per Hobhouse J: 'the district registrar is quite right that at the end of any assessment of this kind he should stand back for a moment and consider the implications and the overall picture presented by his decision on the detail.' See also the criminal case of *R v SCTO ex p John Singh & Co* [1997] 1 Costs LR 49, in which Henry LJ approved of the practice of 'making a sensible assessment of the consequences of aggregation [of individual items] in the light of the overall complexities in the case'.

'(1) These Rules are a new procedural code with the overriding objective of enabling the court to deal with cases justly.

(2) Dealing with a case justly includes, so far as is practicable—

    (c)   Dealing with the case in ways which are proportionate
        (i)   to the amount of money involved;
        (ii)   to the importance of the case;
        (iii)   to the complexity of the issues; and
        (iv)   to the financial position of each party;'

34.6   In order to give effect to the general policy, it is necessary to recognise at an early stage those cases in which it is anticipated that costs might be disproportionate.[7] As to the management of those cases, Lord Woolf endorsed the following approach, which had originally been articulated by HHJ Alton:[8]

'In modern litigation, with the emphasis on proportionality, there is a requirement for parties to make an assessment at the outset of the likely value of the claim and its importance and complexity, and then to plan in advance the necessary work, the appropriate level of person to carry out the work, the overall time which would be necessary and appropriate spend on the various stages in bringing the action to trial and the likely overall cost. While it was not unusual for costs to exceed the amount in issue, it was, in the context of modest litigation such as the present case, one reason for seeking to curb the amount of work done, and the cost by reference to the need for proportionality.'

Lord Woolf said that he hoped that by allowing only those costs which are necessary for the proportionate management of the claim, parties will be encouraged to conduct litigation in a proportionate manner.[9]

The application of the general policy to the assessment of costs

34.7   In so far as the assessment of costs is concerned, proportionality applies only to those costs which are to be assessed on the standard basis. CPR, r 44.4(2) provides:

'Where the amount of costs is to be assessed on the standard basis, the court will—

    (a)   only allow costs which are proportionate to the matters in issue; and
    (b)   resolve any doubt which it may have as to whether costs were reasonably incurred or reasonable and proportionate in amount in favour of the paying party.

(Factors which the court may take into account are set out in rule 44.5)'

34.8   The factors set out in CPR, r 44.5 are the 'seven pillars of wisdom', which are set out in r 44.5(3):

'The court must also have regard to—

    (a)   the conduct of all parties, including in particular—
        (i)   conduct before, as well as during, the proceedings; and
        (ii)   the efforts made, if any, before and during the proceedings in order to try to resolve the dispute;
    (b)   the amount or value of any money or property involved;
    (c)   the importance of the matter to all the parties;
    (d)   the particular complexity of the matter or the difficulty or novelty of the questions raised;

---

[7]   See *Lownds v Home Office* [2002] EWCA Civ 365 at [23].
[8]   *Jefferson v National Freight Carriers plc* [2001] EWCA Civ 2082.
[9]   *Lownds v Home Office* [2002] EWCA Civ 365 at [8].

(e)   the skill, effort, specialised knowledge and responsibility involved;

(f)   the time spent on the case; and

(g)   the place where and the circumstances in which work or any part of it was done.'

Whilst now encountered in only the longest running of cases, transitional provisions exist; in essence, they provide that proportionality should not result in a reduction in the allowance made for costs incurred prior to the introduction of the CPR.[10]

The Lownds test

34.9   The way in which the test of proportionality is to be applied was explained by Lord Woolf in *Lownds v Home Office*; the applicable test is usually known as the '*Lownds* test' or the 'two-stage test'. This latter name applies because a two-stage approach should be taken in which the first stage determines the test to be applied on the second:[11]

> '[What] is required is a two-stage approach. There has to be a global approach and an item by item approach. The global approach will indicate whether the total sum claimed is or appears to be disproportionate having particular regard to the [seven pillars of wisdom]. If the costs as a whole are not disproportionate according to that test then all that is normally required is that each item should have been reasonably incurred and the cost for that item should be reasonable. If on the other hand the costs as a whole appear disproportionate then the court will want to be satisfied that the work in relation to each item was necessary and, if necessary, that the cost of the item is reasonable.'

34.10   Lord Woolf went on to give guidance as to procedure:[12]

> 'In a case where proportionality is likely to be an issue, a preliminary judgment as to the proportionality of the costs as a whole must be made at the outset. This will ensure that the costs judge applies the correct approach to the detailed assessment. In considering that question the costs judge will have regard to whether the appropriate level of fee earner or counsel has been deployed, whether offers to settle have been made, whether unnecessary experts had been instructed and the other matters set out in Part 44.5(3). Once a decision is reached as to proportionality of costs as a whole, the judge will be able to proceed to consider the costs, item by item, applying the appropriate test to each item.'

Thus, if at the outset the totality of the costs is, or appears to be, disproportionate, then, when the court goes on to assess the individual items within the bill, the court will apply a test of necessity rather than reasonableness.

34.11   Moreland J has commented that a finding that the costs are disproportionate does not penalise the receiving party, nor does it determine the amount of the assessment. It merely regulates the manner of the detailed assessment and requires the receiving party to justify each item in the bill as being both necessary and reasonable.[13] Lewison J has commented that a finding of disproportionality does not shut out the

---

10   PD 51A, para 18(2) '... the general presumption is that no costs for work undertaken before 26 April 1999 will be disallowed if those costs would have been allowed in a costs taxation before 26 April 1999'; and see *Lownds v Home Office* [2002] EWCA Civ 365 at [17].

11   *Lownds v Home Office* [2002] EWCA Civ 365 at [28]; in order to give effect to the CPR concept of proportionality, the Court of Appeal found it necessary to resurrect the pre-CPR concept that the court would allow only those costs which were 'necessary for the proper attainment of justice' (see RSC Ord 28(2)).

12   *Lownds v Home Office* [2002] EWCA Civ 365 at [36].

13   *Giambrone v JMC Holidays Ltd* [2003] 2 Costs LR 189 at [32]–[33], per Moreland J.

receiving party from obtaining the costs of the exercise in question; instead, it requires him to demonstrate that the costs were necessary.[14]

34.12 Eady J has commented that the general policy does not always mean that corners need to be cut; in a case involving grave allegations, it may be that justice requires that significant time and money are spent in arriving at the right answer.[15]

The first stage: whether the costs are disproportionate

34.13 The issue of whether the costs claimed are, or appear to be, disproportionate should be decided having regard to the seven pillars of wisdom (ie CPR, r 44.5(3): see **34.8**).[16]

34.14 Many judges will rely on their own experience in determining the appropriateness of the totality of the costs.[17] It is not necessary or reasonable to expect an experienced costs judge, having recently read the papers, to go through the seven pillars of wisdom as a checklist.[18] However, a failure to apply the two-stage test in *Lownds* is capable of being a procedural irregularity of a serious nature.[19]

The test to be applied

34.15 Lewison J has commented that the decision as to whether the costs are disproportionate is one of judgment and 'feel': in the case of an experienced costs judge it will be based on his experience of litigation generally.[20] There is no requirement that disproportionality has to 'jump off the page' or that the costs need to be obviously disproportionate.[21] Whilst not binding, Master Hurst has suggested that the following test of stepping into the client's shoes may, in an appropriate case, be of assistance:[22]

> 'One way of testing the proportionality of the costs is to ask whether a litigant, paying the costs out of his own pocket, would have been prepared to pay that level of costs in order to achieve success. For the purpose of the test the Claimant must be deemed to be a person of adequate means. That is someone whose means are neither inadequate nor super abundant ...'

Lord Neuberger MR had this to say:[23]

> '[T]he value of a claim in monetary terms, even where it is the only relief claimed, cannot be the sole guide to proportionality, although it will be a rare case where it is not a significant factor.'

---

14   *Ross v Stonewood Securities Ltd* [2004] EWHC 2235 (Ch) at [26], per Lewison J.
15   *Abu v MGN* [2002] EWHC 2345 (QB) (NB Eady J was not dealing with proportionality in the context of costs, but in a more general context).
16   See *Lownds v Home Office* [2002] EWCA Civ 365 at [36] and CPD, art 11.6.
17   By way of example, while he was talking in a context other than proportionality, Thorpe LJ has indicated that the costs of an appeal on a point of law lasting about half a day would ordinarily not exceed £15,000: *Moore v Moore* [2009] EWCA Civ 737.
18   *Ortwein v Rugby Mansions Ltd* [2003] EWHC (Ch) 2077 at [23], per Lloyd J.
19   *Lloyds TSB Bank plc v Lampert* [2003] EWHC 249 (Ch).
20   *Ross v Stonewood Securities Ltd* [2004] EWHC 2235 (Ch) at [27], per Lewison J.
21   *Giambrone v JMC Holidays Ltd* [2003] 2 Costs LR 189 at [53], per Moreland J.
22   *King v Telegraph Group Ltd* [2005] EWHC 90015 (Costs) at [54].
23   *Motto & Ors v Trafigura Ltd & Anor* [2011] EWCA Civ 1150 at [42].

34.16 When considering the quantum of costs, the issue is whether it is just to require the paying party to pay the sums that are claimed; the court should not be concerned with the position between solicitor and client.[24]

34.17 The relationship between the costs incurred and the value of the claim may not be a reliable guide to whether the costs are disproportionate. CPD, art 11.1 provides:

> 'In applying the test of proportionality the court will have regard to rule 1.1(2)(c). The relationship between the total of the costs incurred and the financial value of the claim may not be a reliable guide. A fixed percentage cannot be applied in all cases to the value of the claim in order to ascertain whether or not the costs are proportionate.'

This guidance does more than merely express the fact that the court will take into account all the relevant circumstances; it also makes it clear that each case must be decided on its own facts rather than on the basis of a preconceived notion of what is and what is not proportionate. Black LJ has pointed out that the operative word in this guidance is that the relationship between the total of the costs incurred and the financial value of the claim *may* not be a reliable guide, the implication being that in some circumstances it will be a reliable guide.[25]

34.18 It is the whole of the costs that needs to be considered: the bill of costs may not be broken down into parts for individual consideration.[26] Arden LJ has commented that the exercise is more complex than comparing the costs with the value of the claim and scaling down the costs accordingly.[27]

34.19 In every case there will be costs which are necessary for the conduct of the claim; in recognition of this, CPD, art 11.2 makes the following provisions:

> 'In any proceedings there will be costs which will inevitably be incurred and which are necessary for the successful conduct of the case. Solicitors are not required to conduct litigation at rates which are uneconomic. Thus in a modest claim the proportion of costs is likely to be higher than in a large claim, and may even equal or possibly exceed the amount in dispute.'

Thus, in a modest claim the proportion of costs is likely to be higher than in a large claim and may even equal or possibly exceed the amount in dispute. This reflects the fact that there is a degree of work which is required to manage any claim, regardless of its size.

The resolution of doubt pertaining to the first stage

34.20 The test is whether the costs claimed are, or appear to be, disproportionate;[28] thus, the presumption in CPR, r 44.4(2)(b) will apply.[29] Any doubt as to whether the costs are disproportionate must be resolved in favour of the paying party; Moreland J has confirmed that in the unlikely event that a costs judge is unable to say whether the

---

[24] *Habib Bank Ltd v Ahmed* [2004] EWCA Civ 805 (the Court of Appeal were carrying out a summary assessment, but, notwithstanding this, it is clear that they applied the two-stage *Lownds* test).
[25] *Morgan v Spirit Group Limited* [2011] EWCA Civ 58 at [38].
[26] *Motto & Ors v Trafigura Ltd & Anor* [2011] EWCA Civ 1150 at [50], per Lord Neuberger MR.
[27] *Contractreal Ltd v Davies* [2001] EWCA Civ 928; those comments preceded *Lownds*, however, and should be treated with some caution.
[28] *Lownds v Home Office* [2002] EWCA Civ 365 at [28], per Woolf MR.
[29] That provision will always apply because the test of proportionality will apply only where the costs are assessed on the standard basis.

bill viewed as a whole is proportionate or disproportionate, he will be obliged to carry out a detailed assessment applying the dual test of necessity and reasonableness.[30]

The measure of value for the purposes of the first stage

34.21 Where the claim is a money claim[31] the value of the claim will be the amount of money involved, the measure of which will depend on whether the receiving party is a claimant or a defendant:[32]

- proportionality of the costs incurred by the claimant is determined having regard to the sum that it was reasonable for him to believe that he might recover at the time he made his claim; and
- proportionality of the costs incurred by the defendant is determined having regard to the sum that it was reasonable for him to believe that the claimant might recover, should the claimant succeed in his claim; a defendant would ordinarily be entitled to take the claimant's claim at face value, so the appropriate measure is normally the amount which has been claimed.

The measure of costs for the purposes of the first stage

34.22 The following points may be made about the way in which the amount of costs may be measured.

VAT

34.23 By established practice,[33] the costs which are to be taken into account are the base costs (including disbursements), but exclusive of VAT. The exclusion of VAT is because it could have had no bearing on the steps taken in the litigation or the cost of those steps.

Additional liability

34.24 In deciding whether the costs claimed are proportionate, the court will consider additional liability separately from base costs.[34] In practice, this means that unless there is a specific challenge to the proportionality of the success fee or the ATE premium, the court will disregard the additional liability entirely.

Pre-CPR costs

34.25 For the purposes of applying stage one of the two-stage test, pre-CPR should be taken into account when considering whether the costs claimed are proportionate, but

---

30   *Giambrone v JMC Holidays Ltd* [2003] 2 Costs LR 189 at [33], per Moreland J.
31   For non-money claims, see **34.26**.
32   See *Lownds v Home Office* [2002] EWCA Civ 365 at [39].
33   Now supported by authority: *Giambrone v JMC Holidays Ltd* [2003] 2 Costs LR 189 at [43], per Moreland J.
34   CPD, art 11.5.

they will not themselves be subject to a test of necessity;[35] Moreland J has commented that it would be wrong not to take those costs into account, since they must form part of the global view.[36]

Miscellaneous topics concerning the first stage

Non-monetary factors

34.26 Not all claims are for nothing but money, so it may be necessary to take non-monetary factors into account.[37] Whilst there is no authority on the point, the principles at **14.45–14.47** may, by analogy, have a bearing.

Settlements and hindsight

34.27 Where a claimant has settled a claim for an amount which is palpably less than he was seeking, the settlement sum may be good evidence of the true value of the claim. In a slightly different context (whether the small claims regime should apply),[38] Peter Smith J had the following to say about a claim which had been exaggerated:[39]

> 'It is appropriate that the costs which the claimant recovers on the expense claim should be measured by its recovery. They have recovered £5,000. Once again, they chose to take the £5,000. If they were not happy with that or they wanted to protect their costs position further, they could have proceeded to trial to seek an account and to seek to establish liability beyond that. They have chosen not to do so.'

Whilst an obvious point, this approach would not be permitted to make inroads into the principle that the court may not use hindsight. Lord Neuberger MR had this to say about the rule against hindsight:[40]

> '... that does not mean that one simply ignores the amount actually recovered, as it can provide some sort of reality check. For instance, where the sum eventually awarded or agreed is substantially less than the amount claimed, that may (and I emphasise "may") call into question the notion that the claim was genuinely or reasonably thought to be worth what it was claimed to be worth when it was first raised and while it was being prosecuted.'

Notes from counsel

34.28 A party may seek to rely on a note prepared by counsel (ie counsel who was involved in the claim) for the purposes of persuading the court that the costs are proportionate or disproportionate, as the case may be. While dealing with such a note in the context of hourly rates rather than proportionality, Teare J has found that such notes are admissible notwithstanding the fact that they may be partly opinion.[41]

---

35   PD 51, para 18(2).
36   *Giambrone v JMC Holidays Ltd* [2003] 2 Costs LR 189 at [41], per Moreland J, echoing the approach previously adopted in the Senior Courts Costs Office in *Clyde v Thompson Holidays* (unreported) 9 October 2002, SCCO.
37   *Cox v Carter v MGN Ltd* [2006] EWHC 1235 (QB) at [28], per Eady J.
38   The incidence of costs.
39   *E Ivor Hughes Educational Foundation v Leach* [2005] EWHC 1317 (Ch) at [25].
40   *Motto & Ors v Trafigura Ltd & Anor* [2011] EWCA Civ 1150 at [42].
41   *A v Chief Constable of South Yorkshire* [2008] EWHC 1658 (QB) at [22]–[23].

Individually disproportionate items

34.29 Contrary to what was originally believed,[42] where the costs are globally proportionate the court is not permitted to find that individual items are to be subjected independently to the dual test of necessity and reasonableness.

Capped costs

34.30 Where the costs claimed in a bill of costs have been limited or capped in some way, Lloyd J has commented (obiter) that the court should look at the proportionality or otherwise of the amount claimed, rather than the original amount that might have been claimed had the cap or limit not been applied.[43]

Group litigation

34.31 Moreland J has explained that whilst it cannot be expected that group litigation involving very small claims should result in very small costs, there should be economies of scale even when each individual claimant has to be dealt with individually (see **39.46**).[44] The test of proportionality applies to interim assessments in group litigation[45] (although, in practice, the court may have difficulty in applying the first stage of the two-stage test if the totality of the costs is not known to the judge who is carrying out the assessment, this being a common occurrence where the litigation settles piecemeal).

Impecuniosity

34.32 A paying party's impecuniosity could well be relevant to the case management of a claim, but it has no bearing on the application of the test of proportionality.[46]

Dishonesty

34.33 Whilst he was dealing proportionality in a context other than the application of the two-stage test in a detailed assessment, Waller LJ has made it clear that there is no general rule that a losing party who can establish dishonesty must receive all his costs of establishing that dishonesty, however disproportionate they may be.[47]

Procedural issues

Appropriate use of court time

34.34 Moreland J has explained that a costs judge is not required to 'plough through [a] gargantuan mass of material' solely for the purposes of deciding whether the costs

---

[42] See *Giambrone v JMC Holidays Ltd (formerly Sunworld Holidays Ltd)* [2002] EWHC 2932 (QB) at [54], per Morland J and *Cox v Carter v MGN Ltd* [2006] EWHC 1235 (QB) at [26], per Eady J; those paragraphs are no longer good law.

[43] *Ortwein v Rugby Mansions Ltd* [2003] EWHC 2077 (Ch) at [31], per Lloyd J.

[44] *Giambrone v JMC Holidays Ltd (formerly Sunworld Holidays Ltd)* [2002] EWHC 2932 (QB) at [52].

[45] *Giambrone v JMC Holidays Ltd (formerly Sunworld Holidays Ltd)* [2002] EWHC 2932 (QB) at [48], per Morland J.

[46] *Ilangaratne v British Medical Association* [2005] EWHC 2096 (Ch) at [10]; on a related point, see also the pre-CPR case of *MB Building Contractors Ltd v Ahmed* (1998) *The Independent*, November 23.

[47] *Ultraframe (UK) Limited v Fielding* [2006] EWCA Civ 1660 at [36]; this lengthy judgment has, in this context, been summarised by Briggs J in *Bank of Tokyo-Mitsubishi UFJ Ltd v Baskan Gida Sanayi Ve Pazarlama AS* [2009] EWHC 1696 (Ch) at [15]–[19].

are or are not disproportionate; even in complex litigation, an experienced costs judge ought not to be required to spend more than an hour or two on the issue.[48]

Chains of Part 20 claims

34.35 Where there is a chain of Part 20 claims, and where the costs liability passes down the chain to a single order at the end, the chain of bills should be assessed at the same time and with reference to each other.[49]

Appeals

34.36 Moreland J has expressed a firm view that appeals against decisions about the proportionality of costs are to be discouraged.[50]

The second stage: the test of necessity

34.37 Once the court has determined that the costs are disproportionate, the test of necessity applies to every item in the bill of costs; it is not open to the court to find that certain items are proportionate.[51] The requisite standard of necessity is not a fixed standard, but a variable standard – or a 'sensible' standard, as Lord Woolf MR put it.[52] Although the requisite standard is higher than that of reasonableness (or, in Moreland J's word, more 'stringent'),[53] it is still a standard that a competent practitioner should be able to achieve without undue difficulty.[54] In a similar vein, Lord Neuberger MR had this to say on the point:[55]

> 'It does not seem to me to be a profitable or useful exercise for this court to describe in abstract the difference between assessing whether an item has been necessarily incurred and assessing whether an item has been reasonably incurred, save to confirm that the former hurdle is higher, but it does not carry with it the strictest sense of necessity.'

34.38 In deciding what is necessary, the conduct of the paying party (or any other opponent) is relevant. If he was unco-operative, then that may have rendered necessary costs which would otherwise have been unnecessary.[56] (As a matter of practice, where a paying party's conduct has caused costs to be incurred, that is a factor which would often be reflected in a finding that the costs claimed are not disproportionate rather than in a finding that the costs are disproportionate but were incurred out of necessity, but this is not always the case, especially where the court discovers the true nature of the parties' conduct only part way through the assessment.)

---

[48]   *Giambrone v JMC Holidays Ltd* [2003] 2 Costs LR 189 at [37]–[38], per Moreland J. It is not always easy to deal with issues so quickly; see, for example, Master Wright's comments in *Holland v PKF (a firm)* [2004] EWHC 9043 (Costs) at [58].

[49]   *SCT Finance v Bolton* [2002] EWCA Civ 56 at [56], per Waller LJ.

[50]   Moreland J in *Giambrone & Ors v JMC Holidays* [2003] 2 Costs LR 189 at [56] and Henriques J in *Young v JR Smart (Builders) Ltd* [2004] EWHC 103.

[51]   *Motto & Ors v Trafigura Ltd & Anor* [2011] EWCA Civ 1150 at [46].

[52]   *Lownds v Home Office* [2002] EWCA Civ 365 at [37].

[53]   *Giambrone v JMC Holidays Ltd (formerly Sunworld Holidays Ltd)* [2002] EWHC 2932 (QB) at [33], per Morland J.

[54]   *Lownds v Home Office* [2002] EWCA Civ 365 at [37].

[55]   *Motto & Ors v Trafigura Ltd & Anor* [2011] EWCA Civ 1150 at [52].

[56]   *Lownds v Home Office* [2002] EWCA Civ 365 at [38].

34.39 There is authority to suggest that if the court applies the two-stage test but finds that after the application of that test the costs continue to be disproportionate, then the correct approach is not to reduce the costs to a level that appears to be proportionate, but to revisit the item-by-item assessment in an effort to achieve further reductions.[57] It is unquestionably true that the court cannot reduce the costs globally, but (unless the court made it clear at the outset that it was carrying out only a provisional assessment), it is a moot point whether the court is able to revisit items to any significant extent.[58]

34.40 There is nothing to prevent the court from applying a test of necessity to an additional liability.[59] Nonetheless, a success fee should not be reduced simply on the grounds that, when it is added to reasonable and proportionate base costs, the total appears disproportionate.[60]

34.41 In summary, a test of proportionality will apply where costs fall to be assessed on the standard basis. It is a two-stage test, in which the first stage determines whether a standard of necessity will apply on the second stage.

ESTIMATES OF COSTS

Estimates on a between the parties basis

34.42 There are two ways in which a paying party may seek to rely on an estimate (or an alleged failure to provide an estimate); the first is where the estimate was, or should have been, given between the parties, and the second is where the estimate was, or should have been, given to the receiving party by his solicitor. The following discussion deals principally with the former. The latter is addressed at **27.31–27.61**.

The duty to provide an estimate

34.43 The duty to provide estimates is set out in Section 6 of the CPD. By 'estimate', that section refers, first, to an estimate of base costs (including disbursements) already incurred and, secondly, to base costs (including disbursements) yet to be incurred.[61] These will be referred to as 'past estimates' and 'future estimates' respectively.

34.44 Unless the person in question is a litigant in person,[62] there are four circumstances in which an estimate must be filed and served; they are: when an allocation questionnaire is filed, when a listing questionnaire is filed, when there has been a change of funding arrangement, and upon the order of the court. Each is dealt with in turn.

---

[57] *Hosking v Michaelides* [2003] EWHC 3029 (Ch).
[58] Not least because each decision on an assessment is regarded as being a self-contained decision: see *Kasir v Darlington & Simpson Rolling Mills Ltd* [2001] 2 Costs LR 228.
[59] Although not binding, Master Hurst's analysis in *King v Telegraph Group plc* [2005] EWHC 90015 (Costs) at [17]–[19] seems to support this view. Master Hurst concluded: 'Both the base costs and the success fee separately must be assessed at reasonable and proportionate figures but, if the two figures taken together appear, as they inevitably will, to be disproportionate, that is not a factor to be taken into account.'
[60] CPD, art 11.9.
[61] CPD, art 6.2.
[62] CPD, art 6.4(3).

Allocation questionnaire

34.45 Unless the claim is within the financial scope of the small claims track, an estimate must be filed and served at the time the allocation questionnaire is filed;[63] the relevant provisions are set out at **27.44**. (Where a party is represented, the legal representative must in addition serve an estimate on the party he represents.[64]) Dyson LJ has emphasised the importance of the estimate which accompanies the allocation questionnaire; he noted that the estimates are part of the material that is placed before the court to enable it to form a view as to what measures it should take in order to manage and control the case in the interests of what is reasonable and proportionate.[65]

Listing questionnaire

34.46 Where a party to a claim which is being dealt with on the fast track or the multi track, or under Part 8, files a pre-trial check list (listing questionnaire), he must also file an estimate of costs and serve a copy of it on every other party, unless the court otherwise directs.[66] (Where a party is represented, the legal representative must in addition serve an estimate on the party he represents.)[67]

Change of funding arrangement

34.47 Where a funding arrangement changes such that a new notice of funding must be served, and where an estimate has already been filed with the allocation or listing questionnaire, a new estimate must be served.[68]

Other times

34.48 The court may order that an estimate is to be filed and served at other times; where no time limit is specified, the estimate should be filed and served within 28 days of the date of the order.[69] Gray J has indicated that it is up to the parties to keep themselves informed of their opponents' estimated costs, if necessary by making an application to the court for an order that an estimate be provided.[70] In a similar vein, Newman J has found that, in the absence of a court order to the contrary, there is no obligation upon a party to bring in an estimate other than at those times stipulated above.[71]

34.49 The court is able to order that estimates be given in the alternative; in particular, where the court is contemplating which would be the most appropriate choice out of a number of alternative case-management plans, it may direct that the estimate be prepared in such way as to demonstrate the likely effects of each.[72]

---

[63] CPD, art 6.4(1).
[64] CPD, art 6.4(1).
[65] *Leigh v Michelin Tyre plc* [2003] EWCA Civ 1766 at [16]–[17].
[66] CPD, art 6.4(1).
[67] CPD, art 6.4(1).
[68] CPR, r 44.15(3); see also CPD, art 19.3.
[69] CPD, art 6.3.
[70] *Henry v British Broadcasting Corporation* [2005] EWHC 2503 (QB) at [36].
[71] *Tee-Hillman v Heppenstalls (A Firm)* [2004] EWHC 90024 (Costs).
[72] CPD, art 6.3.

34.50 The fact that a person is represented pro bono does not release him from the duty to file an estimate (unless, of course, he does not wish to recover any costs).[73]

Procedure for bringing an estimate in

34.51 The format of the estimate is that it should be substantially in the form illustrated in Precedent H in the Schedule of Costs Precedents annexed to the CPD.[74]

34.52 The estimates must be those which the party intends to seek to recover from any other party under an order for costs.[75] A future estimate should be based on the assumption that the case will not settle; it should not be merely an estimate of future costs up to some (unspecified) date on which it is thought that the case is likely to, or might, settle.[76]

34.53 There is no requirement to state the amount of the additional liability.[77] The CPD does not state whether an estimate is required to be inclusive or exclusive of VAT, although this will usually be obvious if the format of the estimate follows Precedent H.

Procedure where an estimate has been exceeded

34.54 Where an estimate has been exceeded, the parties should state what, if anything, they say should be the result. In particular:[78]

- if there is a difference of 20% or more between the base costs claimed by a receiving party on detailed assessment and the costs shown in an estimate of costs filed by him, he must provide a statement of the reasons for the difference with his bill of costs; and
- if a paying party claims that he reasonably relied on an estimate of costs filed by a receiving party, or if he wishes to rely upon the costs shown in the estimate in order to dispute the reasonableness or proportionality of the costs claimed, then he must serve a statement setting out his case in this regard in his points of dispute.

The effect of exceeding an estimate where there has been no reliance

34.55 The court may take an estimate into account as a factor among others when assessing the reasonableness and proportionality of any costs claimed; the court may take into account the receiving party's own estimate or the estimate of any other party.[79] In particular, where there is a difference of 20% or more between the base costs claimed

---

[73] CPD, art 6.2(b) provides:
      '(b) in proceedings where the party has pro bono representation and intends, if successful in the
      proceedings, to seek an order under section 194(3) of the Legal Services Act 2007, an estimate of the sum
      equivalent to—
      (i) the base costs (including disbursements) that the party would have already incurred had the legal
      representation provided to that party not been free of charge; and
      (ii) the base costs (including disbursements) that the party would incur if the legal representation to be
      provided to that party were not free of charge.'
[74] CPD, art 6.5.
[75] CPD, art 6.2.
[76] *Leigh v Michelin Tyre plc* [2003] EWCA Civ 1766 at [37].
[77] CPD, art 6.2(2).
[78] CPD, art 6.5A.
[79] CPD, art 6.6(1).

by a receiving party and the costs shown in his estimate, and where the receiving party has not provided a satisfactory explanation for that difference, the court may regard the difference between the costs claimed and the costs shown in the estimate as evidence that the costs claimed are unreasonable or disproportionate.[80] The usual mechanism by which an estimate is taken into account (if at all) is that it is taken as being evidence of disproportionate costs expenditure, which leads to a finding that a test of necessity is to be applied rather than the lower standard of reasonableness.[81]

34.56 Although he was addressing an older version of the CPD than exists today, Dyson LJ had the following to say about the relevance of an estimate where there has been no reliance:[82]

> '[The] estimates ... should usually provide a useful yardstick by which the reasonableness of the costs finally claimed may be measured. If there is a substantial difference between the estimated costs and the costs claimed, that difference calls for an explanation. In the absence of a satisfactory explanation, the court may conclude that the difference itself is evidence from which it can conclude that the costs claimed are unreasonable.'

These comments probably remain apposite notwithstanding the changes to the CPD.

34.57 Dyson LJ went on to explain that there was another mechanism by which the estimate could be taken into account, that being where the court concludes that it would probably have given different case management directions if a realistic estimate had been given.[83] It is not clear whether this remains a factor that can be taken into account under the present CPD; even if the court cannot take this factor into account directly, it is likely that it could take very similar factors into account when considering the reasonableness of the steps taken by the receiving party.

The effect of exceeding an estimate where there has been reliance

34.58 Where there is a difference of 20% or more between the base costs claimed by a receiving party and the costs shown in his estimate, and where the paying party reasonably relied on the estimate of costs, the court may regard the difference between the costs claimed and the costs shown in the estimate as evidence that the costs claimed are unreasonable or disproportionate.[84] Whilst the contrary is arguable, the wording of the CPD suggests that the court is able to look at the matter in this way even where the receiving party is able to supply an explanation as to why the estimate was exceeded.

34.59 Dyson LJ had this to say about the relevance of an estimate where there has been reliance:[85]

> '[The] court may take the estimated costs into account if the other party shows that it relied on the estimate in a certain way. An obvious example would be where A shows that he relied on the relatively low estimate given by B not to make an offer of settlement, but carried on with the litigation on the basis that his potential liability for costs was likely to be of the order indicated in B's estimate. In our judgment, it would be a proper use of [the then

---

80   CPD, art 6.6(2).
81   CPD, art 6.6(2).
82   *Leigh v Michelin Tyre plc* [2003] EWCA Civ 1766 at [26].
83   *Leigh v Michelin Tyre plc* [2003] EWCA Civ 1766 at [28].
84   CPD, art 6.6(2).
85   *Leigh v Michelin Tyre plc* [2003] EWCA Civ 1766 at [27].

provisions in the CPD] to take such a factor into account in deciding what costs it was reasonable to require A to pay B on an assessment.'

These comments were made under an older version of the CPD, but as a general observation, they are likely to remain relevant.

34.60 Where he could reasonably have been expected to ask for an updated estimate, a paying party may find it difficult to gain the court's sympathy for having relied on an inaccurate estimate. Warren J made the following comments (obiter):[86]

> 'When a case develops (and grows in scale) in a way which clearly was not foreseen when the original costs estimate was given by one party, the other party must realise, or be taken to realise, that the estimate is not to be relied upon. He can take steps to obtain an updated estimate. What, in my judgment, he cannot do is to say, when a costs order is eventually made against him, that the early estimate should result in a large reduction in the amount which he has to pay.'

34.61 While merely illustrative rather than binding, in a case where a 'surprisingly low' estimate had been given, Master Gordon-Saker rejected the submission that it ought to have been obvious to the paying party that it was too low;[87] this was in circumstances where there was no adequate explanation for the estimate being incorrect.

The failure to give a solicitor-and-client estimate on recovery of costs between opposing parties

34.62 Where the paying party wishes to challenge the costs on the basis that the solicitor had in some way failed to provide his client (the receiving party) with proper and accurate estimates in accordance with the Solicitors' Code of Conduct 2007 ('the 2007 Code') or the SRA Code of Conduct 2011 ('the 2011 Code'), then he would be seeking to rely on the arguments set out at **27.31–27.61**. The issue addressed in the following paragraphs is the extent to which the paying party is permitted to step into the client's shoes in this way.

34.63 That question was addressed by Arden LJ in the context of the obligations arising under the Solicitors Costs Information and Client Care Code 1999 ('the 1999 Code'); nothing turns on the fact that she was addressing the 1999 Code rather than the 2007 Code or the 2011 Code:[88]

> '[The 1999 Code] is there to protect the legitimate interests of the client, and the administration of justice, rather than to relieve paying parties of their obligations to pay costs which have been reasonably incurred.'

Arden LJ explained that where the paying party has grounds for saying that had an estimate been given a lower amount of costs would have been incurred, he can ask the costs judge to require the receiving party to prove that such an estimate was given; the procedure as described at **24.32–24.41** would then become relevant. It would, however, be open to the court to give weight to the certificate as to accuracy in much the same way as it would in respect of a challenge to a retainer. Arden LJ explained that there

---

[86] *Ilangaratne v British Medical Association* [2005] EWHC 2096 (Ch) at [20].
[87] *Tribe v Southdown Gliding Club Ltd* [2007] EWHC 90080 (Costs).
[88] *Garbutt v Edwards* [2005] EWCA Civ 1206 at [31].

must be a 'real basis' for the paying party's contention that the receiving party should be required to prove that there was an estimate, or an adequate estimate.[89]

34.64 If the paying party succeeds in making out a 'real basis' for his concerns, and if the receiving party fails to satisfy the court that an adequate estimate had been given, then the court will take that information into account in deciding the amount of the costs.[90] The way in which the court will do this will depend on whether the estimate was absent or merely inadequate; each of those scenarios is now dealt with in turn.[91]

No estimate

34.65 Where there was no estimate, the court would usually consider whether and, if so, to what extent the costs claimed would have been significantly lower if an adequate estimate had been given when it ought to have been given.

Inadequate estimate (or inadequately updated estimate)

34.66 Where an estimate was given but not adequately updated (or where it was inadequate for some other reason), the estimate would provide a yardstick by which the reasonableness of the costs finally claimed might be measured; in the absence of a satisfactory explanation, the court may conclude that the difference between the costs claimed and the estimate is evidence from which it may conclude that the costs claimed are unreasonable.

34.67 Thus, the estimate (or absence thereof) may be relevant to quantum. Arden LJ rejected the submissions that the obligation to give an estimate is at the heart of the 1999 Code and that a contract of retainer in which no estimate had been given was unenforceable for want of performance. Likewise, she rejected the notion that the court should take into account the sanctions which could have been awarded against the solicitor. Other common law jurisdictions have come to similar conclusions in analogous situations.[92]

CONDUCT AND MISCONDUCT

Conduct as one of the seven pillars

34.68 Even the most perfunctory of detailed assessments will, in some way or another, take into account the parties' conduct. That is one of the factors which distinguish an assessment from a simple accounting exercise. The CPR afford conduct the status of being the first of the seven pillars, and they complete that pillar with the following entasis:[93]

> 'The court must also have regard to—
>
>   (a)   the conduct of all the parties, including in particular—
>
>   (i)   conduct before, as well as during, the proceedings; and
>
>   (ii)   the efforts made, if any, before and during the proceedings in order to try

---

[89]   *Garbutt v Edwards* [2005] EWCA Civ 1206 at [41]–[42].
[90]   *Garbutt v Edwards* [2005] EWCA Civ 1206 at [42].
[91]   *Garbutt v Edwards* [2005] EWCA Civ 1206 at [43]–[44].
[92]   See, for example, *Boyne v Dublin Bus* [2006] IEHC 209.
[93]   CPR, r 44.5(3)(a).

to resolve the dispute.'

The ways in which conduct may be taken into account are as diverse as the ways in which parties may choose to comport themselves, but four topics merit special attention: first, principles applying to conduct in general; secondly, conduct prior to the issue of the claim; thirdly, exaggeration; and, lastly, misconduct. The mechanisms by which a costs judge may take poor conduct into account are discussed in the context of exaggeration (see **34.87–34.97**), but the principles are of general applicability.

Conduct in general

The effect of the order

34.69 For the reason set out above, the parties' conduct will be a central part of any detailed assessment. This is not to say, however, that the costs judge will always be permitted to take into account all aspects of the parties' behaviour, without fetter; this is because a costs order may restrain the costs judge from considering certain issues pertaining to conduct. This situation may arise either because the order expressly or impliedly imposes a constraint, or because issues of double jeopardy arise, or because the court concludes that the topic in question ought to have been raised at the time the order was made. These matters are addressed at **34.83–34.83, 34.83** and at **34.87–34.97**. It should be borne in mind that it would be an atypical case in which the costs judge was constrained by the order: the vast majority of assessments are conducted on the basis that the costs judge is entitled (and required) to take into account all relevant aspects of the parties' behaviour, without constraint.

No hindsight

34.70 It is trite costs law that costs should not be assessed with hindsight.[94] In particular, it would be wrong to assess the costs on the basis of the outcome of the claim. Thus, where a party was awarded the costs of a preliminary issue, it would be wrong to assess those costs as being nil solely because subsequent proceedings showed that the claim itself was misconceived.[95] This is because it is necessary not only to note that the parties would have been ignorant of the outcome of the litigation, but also that they might not have had as clear a view of the facts as might have existed at the time the costs fell to be assessed. Although speaking in a different context from the seven pillars, Sir Hugh Griffiths said:[96]

'Ordinary experience of life frequently teaches us that which is plain for all to see once the dust of battle has subsided was far from clear to the combatants once they took up arms.'

All the parties

34.71 Whilst an obvious point, the appropriate test is the conduct of all of the parties, not just the paying party.

---

[94] *Francis v Francis and Dickerson* [1956] P 87 at 91.
[95] Although it was not phrased in terms of hindsight, see Mann J's analysis in *Business Environment Bow Lane v Deanwater Estates Ltd* [2009] EWHC 2014 (Ch).
[96] In *E T Marler v Robertson* [1974] ICR 72, NIRC; the context was the incidence of costs in an Employment Tribunal.

Pre-issue conduct and pre-action protocols

34.72 For reasons set out at **29.32–29.39** and **29.75–29.77**, pre-issue costs are recoverable, but only to the extent that they are attributable to the paying party's actions or omissions. Some of the authorities on that point speak of 'conduct' rather than actions and omissions, but the meaning is the same.

34.73 The CPR specifically refer to the court having a mandatory duty to have regard to the parties' conduct before the proceedings, and to the efforts that were made in order to try to resolve the dispute[97] (see **34.68**). This is in keeping with the emphasis on 'front loading' of costs and, in particular, is consistent with the notion that pre-issue management will, in many cases, be governed by pre-action protocols.

34.74 In principle, costs incurred for the purposes of complying with a pre-action protocol will be recoverable as being costs of the claim.[98] Conversely, non-compliance with a pre-action protocol may result in the disallowance of costs. The following four general points can be made: litigation should be seen as being the option of last resort; the parties are under a duty to seek to narrow the issues; there must be co-operation in relation to certain types of disclosure; and obstructive behaviour may lead to sanctions being imposed. Each of these is briefly addressed in turn.

'Last resort'

34.75 Most of the pre-action protocols contain a paragraph similar to the following (which has been taken from the Pre-action Protocol for Defamation):[99]

> 'The parties should consider whether some form of alternative dispute resolution procedure would be more suitable than litigation, and if so, endeavour to agree which form to adopt. Both the Claimant and Defendant may be required by the Court to provide evidence that alternative means of resolving their dispute were considered. The Courts take the view that litigation should be a last resort, and that claims should not be issued prematurely when a settlement is still actively being explored. Parties are warned that if the protocol is not followed (including this paragraph) then the Court must have regard to such conduct when determining costs.'

Thus, a failure to consider ADR could result in a disallowance of costs. The protocols which contain a similar provision are those in personal injury,[100] disease and illness claims,[101] clinical negligence,[102] professional negligence,[103] and judicial reviews.[104]

---

[97] CPR, r 44.5(3)(a).
[98] See the obiter comment of Woolf CJ in *Callery v Gray* [2001] EWCA Civ 1117 at [54(ii)].
[99] Pre-Action Protocol for Defamation, para 3.7.
[100] Pre-Action Protocol for Personal Injury Claims, para 2.16.
[101] Pre-Action Protocol for Disease and Illness Claims, para 2A.1.
[102] Pre-Action Protocol for the Resolution of Clinical Disputes, para 5.1.
[103] Pre-Action Protocol for Professional Negligence, para B1.6.
[104] Pre-Action Protocol for Judicial Review, para 3.1.

Narrow the issues

34.76 One particular aspect of claims conducted under a pre-action protocol is that it affords the parties a chance to narrow the issues.[105] If the conduct of one of the parties prevents this, then that would be a factor which may be taken into account.

Unreasonable delay in providing medical records

34.77 The pre-action protocols relating to clinical negligence[106] and industrial disease claims[107] provide that the court may take into account any unreasonable delay in providing medical records.

34.78 While non-compliance with the relevant pre-action protocol might lead to adverse costs consequences, so can overly rigid compliance, especially where it is used as a tactic for generating costs. Practice Direction – Pre-action Conduct provides:[108]

> 'The parties must not use this Practice Direction as a tactical device to secure an unfair advantage for one party or to generate unnecessary costs.'

34.79 That said, reasonable and proper compliance with a pre-action protocol will generally be a factor in favour of the recovery of the costs. Indeed, such compliance may even bring costs within the ambit of the costs order where otherwise they would have lain beyond it.[109]

Obstructive behaviour

34.80 Obstructive behaviour may be taken into account either generally, or as misconduct; in this regard, CPD, art 18.3 makes the following provision:

> 'Conduct before or during the proceedings which gave rise to the assessment which is unreasonable or improper includes steps which are calculated to prevent or inhibit the court from furthering the overriding objective.'

Therefore, serious non-compliance with a pre-action protocol may lead to a finding of misconduct (see **34.98–34.124**).

34.81 In general, where a defendant successfully repels a claim such that a different claim is pursued against him when proceedings are eventually issued, the court will lack the vires to award him his costs in respect of the abandoned claim.[110] Whilst only an obiter comment, Coulson J has implied that where 'exceptional circumstances' exist – which, presumably, would include exceptional circumstances resulting from the

---

[105] See Practice Direction – Pre-Action Conduct, Annex, A, para 6.1, which states that 'At the very least, it should be possible to establish what issues remain outstanding so as to narrow the scope of the proceedings and therefore limit potential costs'.

[106] Pre-Action Protocol for the Resolution of Clinical Disputes, para 3.12.

[107] Pre-Action Protocol for Disease and Illness Claims, para 4.5.

[108] Practice Direction – Pre-Action Conduct, Annex A, para 6.2.

[109] *Lobster Group Ltd v Heidelberg Graphic Equipment Ltd* [2008] EWHC 1431 (TCC); this related to the costs of a failed mediation which, in an earlier judgment ([2008] EWHC 413 (TCC)) Coulson J had found were not costs which would ordinarily be costs of the proceedings.

[110] This is because they are not incidental to the proceedings and, therefore, do not fall within the ambit of s 51 of the Senior Courts Act 1981.

claimant's poor conduct – the court may acquire a jurisdiction to make an award.[111] That is, exceptional circumstances may widen the category of costs which can be said to pertain to the claim which was issued rather than the claim which was mooted. This, perhaps, is a further mechanism by which an adverse costs order may be visited upon a party who is guilty of obstructive behaviour.

Exaggeration

34.82 The topic of exaggeration has already been addressed at **6.138–6.154**. Much of what is said therein – in the context of the incidence of costs – also applies to the assessment of costs. The following discussion builds on what is said in Chapter 6, but it addresses only those topics which are peculiar to the assessment of costs. In particular, it examines the mechanisms by which the costs judge may take exaggeration into account (see **34.87–34.97**).

Double jeopardy

34.83 A receiving party must not be subjected to double jeopardy; in particular, if exaggeration has been reflected in the costs order, that should be taken into account when assessing the costs. Whether the court will allow or disallow the costs of pursuing the exaggerated claim will be a matter of interpretation of the order (see Chapter 12 and, in particular, **12.136–12.141**). Each case will turn on its own facts, but Waller LJ has explained that where there has been dishonesty on the part of the receiving party and where that has been reflected in a percentage reduction, the natural construction of the costs order would be that the costs judge would not allow the costs of advancing a dishonest claim.[112]

Misallocation

34.84 Where, through exaggeration, a claim has been allocated to a track, and where, absent that exaggeration, it would have been allocated to a lower track, the judge assessing the costs may confine the claimant to those costs to which he would have been entitled if there had not been that exaggeration.[113] This may lead to costs being restricted to those that are allowed under the small claims track regime.[114] In none of those situations should the costs judge directly apply the costs regime of the lesser track, but he would be entitled to take it into account when determining the reasonableness of the costs incurred (see **6.9**).[115]

Supposed failure of paying party to stop deception

34.85 Where a receiving party is accused of exaggeration, it may be the case that the paying party had it within its powers to put an end to the receiving party's deception by, for example, disclosing surveillance evidence. Jonathan Parker LJ said that in the

---

[111] See Coulson J's (obiter) comments about 'exceptional cases' in *McGlinn v Waltham Contractors Ltd* [2005] EWHC 1419 (TCC) at [11].
[112] *Northstar Systems v Fielding* [2006] EWCA Civ 1660 at [33].
[113] *Devine v Frankilin* [2002] EWHC 1846 (QB), per Gray J; see also *Drew v Whitbread* [2010] EWCA Civ 53 at [41]; *E Ivor Hughes Educational Foundation v Leach* [2005] EWHC 1317 (Ch); and *David Peakman v Linbrooke Services Ltd* [2008] EWCA Civ 1239, CA.
[114] *O'Beirne v Hudson* [2010] EWCA Civ 52 at [19], per Waller LJ.
[115] *O'Beirne v Hudson* [2010] EWCA Civ 52 at [19], per Waller LJ; see also the comments of Hooper LJ at [22].

absence of special circumstances (which he did not define) a receiving party could not be heard to complain about the paying party's decision not to put an end to the deception.[116]

Effect of offers

34.86 For the reasons set out at **6.141–6.150**, an exaggerator may afford himself a degree of protection from the costs consequences of his exaggeration if he makes offers which are more realistic than his claim. Whilst this is plainly a factor to be taken into account, it is of less relevance to the assessment of costs than it is to the incidence of costs. This is because the offer will usually neither prove nor disprove the reasonableness of the costs incurred in pursuing the exaggerated claim.

Mechanisms by which the assessment takes in exaggeration

34.87 The discussion which follows focuses on exaggeration, but much of what is said will also apply in other situations, such as where there has been obstructive behaviour or dishonesty. Where the court finds that the receiving party's conduct is such that it ought to be reflected in the amount of costs allowed, the court must decide upon the appropriate mechanism by which this may be achieved. In all cases the exaggeration will be taken into account as being one of the seven pillars; this may have a number of consequences, the most wide-ranging of which would be that the costs were found to be generally disproportionate. Whilst there is no recognised nomenclature for the mechanisms by which the court may disallow (or seek to disallow) the costs of an exaggerator, the following list is as good as any:

(i)   individual disallowance;
(ii)   complete disallowance as a matter of principle;
(iii) abatement (ie allowing only a percentage or a proportion of the costs);
(iv)   deletion (ie deleting a part of the costs, such as the costs from a certain date);
(v)   structured disallowance (ie making individual reductions in a structured way);
(vi)   substitution (ie allowing those costs which ought to have been incurred rather than those which were incurred); and
(vii) disallowances pursuant to CPR, r 44.14 (misconduct).

For the reasons set out below, some of these mechanisms are, in the absence of a finding of misconduct, unlawful or of questionable legality; they are mentioned in order to underline that fact. Those which are unlawful are (ii) complete disallowance as a matter of principle and (iii) abatement (see **34.88–34.90**). Substitution (vi) is probably lawful within certain limits (see **34.96**). This leaves (i) individual disallowance, (iv) deletion and (v) structured disallowance as being mechanisms which are unquestionably lawful (see **34.91–34.95**). Exaggeration may or may not be accompanied by misconduct (vii); the discussion at **34.88–34.97** assumes that there has been no misconduct, and the subsequent discussion assumes that misconduct is an issue.

Individual disallowance and complete disallowance as a matter of principle

34.88 The term 'individual disallowance' refers to the item-by-item disallowance of costs on the basis that they were unreasonably or disproportionately incurred: it is the ordinary process of assessment. Where many individual disallowances are made, they

---

[116] *Booth v Britannia Hotels Ltd* [2002] EWCA Civ 579 at [32].

may be referred to collectively as 'deletion' or to 'structured disallowances', depending on the circumstances (see below): despite the different names, they are all the exercise of the same jurisdiction. Complete disallowance as a matter of principle is at the other end of the spectrum in that the court disallows all of the costs. Such a step would usually be contrary to the true interpretation of the costs order to allow no costs at all.[117] That said, complete disallowance as a matter of reasonableness is permitted, as Waller LJ explained:[118]

> 'There is a real distinction between directing at the outset that nothing but small claims costs will be awarded and giving items on a bill very anxious scrutiny to see whether costs were necessarily or reasonably incurred, and thus whether it is reasonable for the paying party to pay more than would have been recoverable in a case that should have been allocated to the small claims track. Was it for example necessary to have had lawyers and is it reasonable for the paying party to have to pay for lawyers are questions that should arise where a claim should have been allocated to the small claims track.'

Abatement

34.89 Abatement is where costs are reduced globally (such as by a percentage or a fraction) at the outset of the assessment. A judge making the order for costs is entitled to abate the costs (such as where he makes a percentage order), but the costs judge exercising his ordinary jurisdiction lacks that vires in that he is bound to assess the entirety of the costs which have been awarded. Dyson LJ had the following to say on this topic:[119]

> 'There is a real distinction between (a) carrying out an assessment and deciding as part of the assessment to reduce the bill by a percentage and (b) deciding in advance of the assessment that the receiving party will only receive a percentage of the assessed costs. The figure that results from (a) represents 100% of the assessed costs. In deciding as part of the assessment to reduce the bill by a percentage, the costs judge is giving effect to an order that the successful party is entitled to his costs, to be assessed if not agreed. The figure that results from (b) represents less than 100% of the assessed costs. In deciding in advance of the assessment that the receiving party will only receive a percentage of the assessed costs, the costs judge is not giving effect to an order that the successful party is entitled to his costs, to be assessed if not agreed.'

The Supreme Court considered these comments and came to much the same conclusion (albeit technically in the context of the rules that govern that court rather than the CPR). Lord Hope had this to say on the topic:[120]

> 'The test of reasonableness which [costs officers] must apply is directed to their assessment of the costs incurred by the receiving party: see CPR 44.5 as to the factors to be taken into account by the costs judge when exercising his discretion as to costs. It is not directed to the entirely different question of whether the cost to the paying party would be prohibitively expensive, which is what the Aarhus test is concerned with.'

---

[117]   Although on a slightly different point, see *Business Environment Bow Lane v Deanwater Estates Ltd* [2009] EWHC 2014 (Ch); see also the point made at **34.89–34.90**. If the receiving party's conduct was such that complete disallowance would meet the justice of the situation, then there are two ways in which that could be achieved: first, the paying party could bring an appeal against the costs order and, secondly, the paying party could make an application to the original court to have the costs order varied or set aside (see *Business Environment Bow Lane v Deanwater Estates Ltd* at [40].

[118]   *O'Beirne v Hudson* (unreported) 9 February 2010, CA at [19].

[119]   *Lahey v Pirelli Tyres Ltd* [2007] EWCA Civ 91 at [19].

[120]   *R (on the application of Edwards and another) v Environment Agency and others* [2010] UKSC 57 at [25].

34.90 Thus, a costs judge is not entitled to reduce a bill of costs by abating it at the outset of the assessment by a percentage or a fraction (although he can achieve a similar result if he makes the reductions as part of the process of assessment: see **34.91** and **34.151**).

Deletion

34.91 For the reasons set out above, abatement is not permissible, but much the same effect can be achieved by different means, which are within the costs judge's vires. In particular, the bill of costs may be assessed by way of deletion. Deletion is where whole parts of the bill are disallowed on a reasoned common basis. An example would be where, on the grounds of reasonableness, the court disallowed the the costs of issuing proceedings. Dyson LJ had the following to say on the topic:[121]

> '[The receiving party] concedes (rightly) that in an appropriate case, the costs judge can disallow entire sections of a bill of costs. If the costs judge considers that the claimant acted unreasonably in refusing an offer to settle made before proceedings were issued, he is entitled to disallow all the costs post-issue on the footing that they were costs "unreasonably incurred": rule 44.4(1). Similarly, where he decides that a party was unreasonable to raise and pursue an issue, the costs judge is entitled to disallow the costs relating to that issue on the grounds that they were unreasonably incurred.'

In an appropriate case the whole of the bill may be deleted,[122] but this would be lawful only if it was on the grounds of reasonableness: it would not be lawful if the bill was struck out as a matter of entitlement to costs.

34.92 As has been explained at **6.7–6.12**, the costs judge is required to stay within the four corners of the costs order and is required not to contradict it. The extent to which he is able to embark on a process of deletion will be a matter of interpretation of the order. Kennedy LJ had this to say:[123]

> 'I accept of course that the district judge must work within the ambit of the order made in relation to costs, whether it be a consent order or an order made after a contested hearing. But such an order does not in any way deprive the district judge of the powers expressly granted to her by [the pre-CPR equivalent of CPR, r 44.4(2)].'

34.93 In a similar vein, Chadwick LJ has explained that a costs judge may disallow the costs of an issue which was not pursued at trial;[124] there is no reason to believe that a similar approach cannot be taken where the costs judge wishes to disallow the costs of an issue for other reasons, such as where a discrete issue was pursued solely as a result of exaggeration.

34.94 The vires to reduce a bill of costs by deletion may be tempered by estoppel (see **12.119–12.124**) but not by a finding that the exercise of that vires would be abusive (see **12.125–12.135**).

---

[121] *Lahey v Pirelli Tyres Ltd* [2007] EWCA Civ 91 at [23].
[122] See, for example, *O'Beirne v Hudson* [2010] EWCA Civ 52, CA at [19].
[123] *Lahey v Pirelli Tyres Ltd* [2007] EWCA Civ 91 at [23].
[124] *Shirley v Caswell* [2000] Lloyds Rep PN 955 (CA), para 60; Dyson LJ has explained that this is nothing more than an example of the costs judge disallowing costs which have been unreasonably incurred (see *Lahey v Pirelli Tyres Ltd* [2007] EWCA Civ 91 at [21]).

Structured disallowance

34.95 Deletion may be objectionable on more quotidian grounds that those mentioned immediately above, namely, that the brush may be too broad to paint a fair picture. Indeed, unless it has been drafted with the possibility of deletion in mind, few bills of costs would lend themselves to such an approach. Where an item-by-item assessment is necessary, there is no reason why the court cannot make a finding that there will be a structured disallowance of costs. An example would be where the court finds (as a matter of reasonableness rather than entitlement) that the costs of instructing a particular expert should be disallowed.

Substitution

34.96 The court may conclude that the receiving party ought to have adopted a different case-management plan to that which was actually implemented. It may be, for example, that if there had been no exaggeration, different or fewer experts would have been instructed. Where the court believes this to be the case, the court may find itself having to choose between assessing the costs on the basis of the work which was done, and assessing the costs on the basis of the work which would have been done had the claim been managed reasonably and proportionately. The latter can lead to costs being 'substituted'.

34.97 There is ample authority to confirm that the court is at liberty to *restrict* costs to those which would have been incurred had the claim been managed properly. If, for example, the claim has been misallocated as a result of the claimant's exaggeration, then the costs may be limited accordingly.[125] Likewise, at the other end of the spectrum it is well established that the court cannot simply make a stock 'one-size-fits-all' allowance for managing the claim.[126] What is less clear is the extent to which the court is able to substitute costs which have been disallowed with costs which would have been incurred had the claim been appropriately managed. This is an issue which could be argued either way. It is difficult to see why there should be any sensible objection to the court allowing, for example, the costs of a video conference (a disbursement) in lieu of the profit costs of travelling to a face-to-face conference. There is, however, no authority to confirm that this would be lawful. Indeed, there is authority which would allow one to argue that it is a breach of the indemnity principle (see **11.8–11.11**).

Misconduct

34.98 It has always been the case that the court has had powers to make reductions in a bill of costs to reflect poor conduct. In 1884, for example, costs might have been 'expunged for scandal and impertinency';[127] the language may now be less graceful, but the court's powers relating to misconduct remain. In the present context there are two types of misconduct. The first is misconduct during the claim which gave rise to the bill of costs, and the second is misconduct during the assessment (or the negotiations) which preceded it.

---

[125] See the discussion of this topic at **34.82–34.86**.
[126] See *1-800 Flowers Inc v Phonenames Ltd* [2001] EWCA Civ 712 at [114].
[127] (1884) Law Times LXXVIII. 115/2.

Misconduct during the claim

34.99 The law of misconduct is in need of clarification but, for reasons that will be addressed below, the uncertainties in the law do not, in general, present any practical problems. It is convenient to begin by referring to the way in which CPR, r 44.14 is worded:

'(1)   The court may make an order under this rule where—

    (a)   a party or his legal representative, in connection with a summary or detailed assessment, fails to comply with a rule, practice direction or court order; or

    (b)   it appears to the court that the conduct of a party or his legal representative, before or during the proceedings which gave rise to the assessment proceedings, was unreasonable or improper.

(2)   Where paragraph (1) applies, the court may—

    (a)   disallow all or part of the costs which are being assessed; or

    (b)   order the party at fault or his legal representative to pay costs which he has caused any other party to incur.

(3)   Where—

    (a)   the court makes an order under paragraph (2) against a legally represented party; and

    (b)   the party is not present when the order is made,

the party's solicitor must notify his client in writing of the order no later than 7 days after the solicitor receives notice of the order.'

34.100   Thus, in so far as the assessment of costs is concerned (ie the powers under CPR, r 44.14(2)(a)), there are two limbs:[128] there is a limb pertaining to misconduct during the claim itself (r 44.14(1)(b)), and there is a limb pertaining to misconduct during the assessment (r 44.14(1)(a)). It is the former that is the focus of this section; the latter is addressed at **34.116**.

34.101   A finding of misconduct must be made in two stages. First, the court must determine whether the relevant threshold criteria have been met (ie whether there has been improper or unreasonable behaviour) and, secondly, the court must consider whether it would be just to impose a discretionary sanction.[129]

Unreasonable behaviour

34.102   Longmore LJ has found that although CPR, r 44.14 does not itself contain the word 'misconduct', that word is contained in the title, and that title points to the nature of the court's discretion.[130] Dyson LJ has commented (obiter) that the word 'unreasonable' in r 44.14(1)(b) is to be construed 'quite narrowly' in much the same way

---

[128]   These two limbs should not be confused with the other aspects of CPR, r 44.14, ie the powers concerning the incidence of costs under r 44.14(2)(b), a topic addressed at **7.215–7.217**: the two topics are not the same.

[129]   *Haji-Ioannou v Frangos* [2006] EWCA Civ 1663 at [10]; Longmore LJ's comments related to CPR, r 44.14(1)(a) (ie misconduct during the assessment) rather than r 44.14(1)(b), but there is no reason to believe that different principles apply.

[130]   See *Haji-Ioannou v Frangos* [2006] EWCA Civ 1663 at [10], referred to with approval in *Lahey v Pirelli Tyres Ltd* [2007] EWCA Civ 91 at [28]; Dyson LJ noted that there was some tension between comments made by Lord Woolf MR under the corresponding pre-CPR provisions (*Burrows v Vauxhall Motors Ltd* [1998] PIQR P48 (CA), which dealt with RSC Ord 62, r 10(1)), but Longmore LJ's analysis was to be preferred.

as it is construed in the context of wasted costs.[131] He concluded that the meaning of the word should not vary depending on whether it is the client or the legal representative whose conduct is under consideration.[132]

Improper behaviour

34.103 There is no authority dealing with the meaning of the word 'improper' in the context of CPR, r 44.14, but if it is correct to deal with the word 'improper' in the same way that Dyson LJ treated the word 'unreasonable', then guidance can be gleaned from authorities concerning wasted costs. This analysis creates its own difficulties because that definition focuses solely on professional obligations,[133] which, of course, the party himself would not bear. In practice, however, most parties are legally represented, so conduct which was said to be improper could usually be measured against that standard.

34.104 Whether either of these threshold criteria has been met will depend on the facts of each case, as will the identification of the factors relevant to the exercise of the court's discretion. These things present no conceptual difficulty, but the same is not true of the next stage (ie the stage of formulating a sanction), where the law is somewhat unclear.

Sanctions

34.105 In order to address this topic, it is necessary to know something the history of the relevant law. The power to impose sanctions arising out of unreasonable or improper conduct is a continuation of a long-standing power[134] that, three decades ago, vested only in the judge who made the entitling costs order. Contrary to the wishes of the Law Society, that power was delegated in the first instance to masters,[135] and then to all costs judges[136] (other than authorised court officers).[137] The relevance of this is that the power to impose a sanction derives from a power which originally was vested in the trial judge. It is also worth pausing to say that the power to impose a sanction was just that: as Michael Cook said in 1995, it was a power to impose something which was 'not just compensatory ... but [a] punishment'.[138] This was something which was entirely in keeping with the fact that the power originally vested in the trial judge. Where a penalty was made, it commonly took the form of a percentage discount or flat reduction.[139]

34.106 Thus, the pre-CPR law was that misconduct could lead to sanctions in the form of a disallowance of part or all of the costs. Given the fact that the CPR have preserved the power to impose sanctions (and that the CPR expressly refer to a power to 'disallow all or part of the costs which are being assessed'), it would be surprising if the court's

---

[131] *Lahey v Pirelli Tyres Ltd* [2007] EWCA Civ 91 at [29]; he commented that it was unlikely that the draftsman intended that a legal representative could be ordered to pay costs under CPR, r 44.14 in circumstances where a wasted costs order could not be made.

[132] *Lahey v Pirelli Tyres Ltd* [2007] EWCA Civ 91 at [29].

[133] See *Ridehalgh v Horsefield* [1994] Ch 205, in which Lord Bingham MR said that improper 'covers ... conduct which would ordinarily be held to justify disbarment, striking off, suspension from practice or other serious professional penalty'.

[134] See RSC Ord 62, r 28.

[135] This was as a result of comments made by Megarry V-C in *Re Solicitors* [1982] 2 All ER 683 at 688.

[136] See M Cook *Cook on Costs* (2nd edn, 1995), p 239 for a discussion of this topic.

[137] See CPR, r 47.3.

[138] See M Cook *Cook on Costs* (2nd edn, 1995), p 240.

[139] See, for example, *Chapman v Chapman* [1985] 1 WLR 599 and *Morrow v Naddeem (No 2)* (1990) *The Times*, March 23, QB.

powers to impose a sanction were any less liberal. In view of this, the following
comments of Dyson LJ come as a surprise:[140]

> 'The short answer to the defendant's submission [that the cost should be reduced by a
> percentage] is that the costs judge has no power to vary the costs order that is deemed to have
> been made. In our judgment, this is a complete answer to [the paying party's] submissions,
> whether based on rules 44.4 and 44.5 or 44.14. It follows that the costs judge has no
> jurisdiction to make an order of the kind contended for by the defendant in this case.'

At first blush, it seems as if Dyson LJ has ruled out the exact form of penalty that one
would expect to be imposed as a result of misconduct (ie a reduction in the receiving
party's entitlement to costs). Dyson LJ made a distinction between making a percentage
reduction before the assessment and making a reduction during the assessment; he said
that a costs judge lacked the vires to make the former but he could make the latter; it is
not clear exactly what the significance of this is, however, as he also went on to say that
the power to make a percentage reduction was not required, because it was otiose by
reason of the costs judge's powers generally[141] (that is, the judge could achieve a similar
effect by exercising his general powers).

34.107   It is not wholly clear how the court is to exercise its discretion once the
threshold criteria have been met. There can be no doubt that the court is permitted to
disallow those costs which have been incurred as a result of the misconduct, but that
power adds very little to the power that the costs judge would have had under CPR,
r 44.5 in any event. What is not clear is whether the court is able to go any further and to
impose a sanction.

34.108   It is possible that the answer lies in comments made by Longmore LJ about
causation; he has made it clear that (unlike the misconduct-during-the-assessment limb
of CPR, r 44.14), the power to disallow costs by reason of poor conduct during the
claim is limited to those costs which were incurred as a result of that conduct.[142] This
assists because it highlights the need to read Dyson LJ's comments in context (which
was that he was dealing with misconduct during the claim, rather than with misconduct
during the assessment). Therefore, it may be that the two limbs of r 44.14 are entirely
distinct, and that the long-standing powers to impose sanctions continue to exist, but in
the misconduct-during-the-assessment limb of r 44.14 rather than the limb relating to
conduct during the claim itself.

34.109   In summary, there is no doubt that a costs judge has the power to disallow
those costs which have been incurred as a result of misconduct. While this would not
add a great deal to his powers under CPR, r 44.5, it is, perhaps, a broader, bolder test
which would allow more far-reaching reductions to be made. Beyond this, the law is
unclear; in particular, it is not clear whether and, if so, how the costs judge can impose
sanctions for misconduct during the claim. This uncertainty is unlikely to create any real
difficulties in practice, however. This is because the main purpose of the
misconduct-during-the-claim limb of CPR, r 44.14 is to allow the costs judge to take
account of any misconduct which is discovered during the course of the assessment and
which was not known at the time the costs order was made. The powers described above
would almost always allow this to be done. Therefore, the uncertainties are largely
academic.

---

140   *Lahey v Pirelli Tyres Ltd* [2007] EWCA Civ 91 at [22].
141   *Lahey v Pirelli Tyres Ltd* [2007] EWCA Civ 91 at [19] and [23].
142   *Haji-Ioannou v Frangos* [2006] EWCA Civ 1663 at [8].

Case examples of misconduct during the claim

34.110 The following are examples of the type of conduct which may (or may not) be said to amount to misconduct.

Obstructive behaviour

34.111 The CPD confirms that where a party takes steps which are calculated to prevent or inhibit the court from furthering the overriding objective, he would be engaging in conduct which may be said to be unreasonable or improper.[143]

Withholding information

34.112 In a case in which relevant information capable of leading to resolution of the claim had been withheld, Lord Woolf MR commented that the court had the power on an assessment to disallow all or part of the claimant's costs;[144] that decision was based on the predecessor to CPR, r 44.14 and should, therefore, be viewed with caution, but it is still cited from time to time as being an enlightening case example.[145]

Failure to comply with practice directions

34.113 Although he was dealing with the incidence provisions of CPR, r 44.14 rather than the assessment provisions (see **7.215–7.217**), Wall J has found that a complete and unexplained failure to comply with a practice direction is capable of amounting to unreasonable conduct.[146] Lesser failures may not justify such a finding; by way of example, Arden LJ declined to find that a failure properly to comply with certain practice directions concerning costs estimates was insufficient to amount to misconduct.[147]

Failure to comply with rules of professional conduct

34.114 The case referred to immediately above also touched upon rules of professional conduct,[148] (that is, the receiving party's lawyer was, technically, in breach of his professional obligations). The fact that there was no misconduct demonstrates that a breach of the rules of professional conduct will not necessarily amount to misconduct.

Criminality

34.115 Although he did not have to decide the issue, Phillips MR raised no objection to the suggestion that an act of criminal conduct would be capable of amounting to misconduct.[149]

---

[143] CPD, art 18.2.
[144] *Burrows v Vauxhall Motors Ltd* [1998] PIQR P48 (CA); the continuing relevance of this case has been doubted; see the obiter postscript to *Haji-Ioannou v Frangos* [2006] EWCA Civ 1663.
[145] That is, it dealt with RSC Ord 62, r 10(1) and r 28(1).
[146] *Re CH (a minor)* (2000) *The Times*, June 6; the failure to comply meant that Wall J was forced to conduct a trial in a family matter with virtually no papers.
[147] *Garbutt v Edwards* [2005] EWCA Civ 1206 at [47].
[148] *Garbutt v Edwards* [2005] EWCA Civ 1206 at [47].
[149] *Earl of Portsmouth v Hamilton* (2000) *The Independent*, October 27; in that instance the alleged criminality was using papers stolen from an opponent's lawyers.

Misconduct during the assessment

34.116   The following paragraphs deal with the misconduct-during-the-assessment limb of CPR, r 44.14; for the reasons set out at **34.108** it seems that this is an entirely different entity to the misconduct-during-the-claim limb.

34.117   The threshold test is whether a party or his legal representative, in connection with a summary or detailed assessment, has failed to comply with a rule, practice direction, or court order. It is, therefore, a narrower test than the test under the misconduct-during-the-claim limb. That said, the very first rule in the CPR is the overriding objective; almost any questionable behaviour capable of having an adverse effect on the assessment proceedings could be said to be a failure to comply with that rule. Thus, whilst narrowly worded, the misconduct-during-the-assessment limb of CPR, r 44.14 is of wide application. Whilst there is no authority directly on the point, it is likely that the appropriate threshold is that of misconduct.[150]

34.118   Once the threshold criteria have been met, the matter becomes one of discretion (see below). Longmore LJ has made it clear that, whilst the misconduct-during-the-claim limb requires there to be a causative link between the defaulting party's conduct and the costs which are ordered to be paid, the misconduct-during-the-assessment limb does not.[151] He approved of the reasoning in the court below, in which Lindsay J had said:[152]

> 'There is no express reference to any causative connection being required in 44.14(2)(a), that there is, as far as we can see, no necessity to imply any such requirement, that the draftsman shows, from the nature of the provisions he makes in 44.14(2)(b), that when he intends a causative link he knows how to provide one and that the *expressio unius* canon of construction therefore suggests that no causative link was intended under 44.14(2)(a).'

34.119   As to discretion, Longmore LJ commented:[153]

> 'The important point is that, while a non-compliance with a rule, practice direction or court order is the only jurisdictional requirement for the exercise of the power contained in Rule 44.14, it will usually be appropriate as a matter of discretion to consider the extent of any misconduct which has occurred in the course of such non-compliance.'

Although he expressly declined to given any general guidance, it is clear from Longmore LJ's method that prejudice is a factor to be taken into account in the exercise of the court's discretion. The relevance of this is that while the court is not fettered by a need to show causation, a factor which may be relevant to the exercise of the court's discretion is prejudice.

34.120   In summary, once the threshold criteria are met, the matter becomes one of discretion, in respect of which the court is not fettered by a need to prove a causal link between the misconduct and the costs in question. This, of course, is entirely as would be expected: this is because any misconduct would have taken place after the costs had been incurred, so it would generally be impossible to show a causal link.

---

150   See, by analogy, the comments made about the misconduct-during-the-claim limb at **34.102**.
151   *Haji-Ioannou v Frangos* [2006] EWCA Civ 1663 at [8].
152   *Haji-Ioannou v Frangos* [2005] EWHC 279 (Ch).
153   *Haji-Ioannou v Frangos* [2006] EWCA Civ 1663 at [10].

34.121 It is a moot point how the court would give effect to a decision to impose a sanction. The most obvious way of doing this would be to impose a percentage or a flat reduction. For the reasons set out at **34.109** it is likely that (unlike under the misconduct-during-the-claim limb of CPR, r 44.14) the court is, in appropriate cases, able to impose a percentage discount or flat reduction.

Case examples of misconduct during the assessment

Delay

34.122 The most frequently encountered allegation of misconduct during the assessment is delay. This topic is addressed in detail at **12.151–12.173**.

Overzealous negotiation

34.123 Towards the end of the last decade the district bench in certain areas of the country noted a number of cases in which without prejudice schedules for costs were submitted which were significantly greater than the amounts which were ultimately claimed (or claimable) in the bill of costs. A well-respected regional costs judge has made it clear (albeit extrajudicially) that such conduct is capable of attracting a sanction.[154]

Procedure

34.124 Where the court makes an 'order' under CPR, r 44.14, it must observe certain procedural requirements. A mere disallowance of costs during the course of the assessment is probably not an order, but (arguably) a percentage or flat reduction is. Where they apply, the requirements are as follows:

- before making an 'order' under CPR, r 44.14 the court must give the party or legal representative in question a reasonable opportunity to attend a hearing to give reasons why it should not make such an order;[155] and
- where the conduct complained of is an omission, the CPD provides that the court may, by order, require the solicitor to produce to the court evidence that he took reasonable steps to comply with the obligation.[156]

Presumably, this power stops short of requiring the solicitor to produce privileged material.[157]

APPORTIONMENT

34.125 The following discussion deals with apportionment of costs,[158] that is, it deals with the seemingly simple question of how much a party should pay (or receive, as the

---

[154] J Duerden 'The costs-only minefield' (2009) 62 *Litigation Funding*, August, pp 12 and 14.
[155] CPD, art 18.1.
[156] CPD, art 18.3.
[157] See, on a related topic, *General Mediterranean Holdings SA v Patel* [1999] 2 Costs LR, which confirms that secondary legislation and practice directions do not have the vires to require a party to waive privilege.
[158] The topics addressed in the following paragraphs are entirely different from the question of how costs are to

case may be) where two or more persons have an interest in the same order for costs. Often the most demanding aspect of this topic is identifying the precise nature of the question that needs to be answered. This book seeks to analyse the topic in terms of four 'layers' (see **34.126–34.129**): the retainer is the first layer, the incidence of costs is the second, the meaning of the order is the third, and the fourth concerns issues of quantum. By working methodically through these layers, the correct questions will be identified and no relevant question will be left out. Whilst an oversimplification, the four layers allow the following questions to be answered:

- What is the receiving party's liability on a solicitor and client basis?
- What order should be made?
- What, in principle, is the receiving party entitled to receive according to the terms of the order?
- How much is the receiving party entitled to receive from all the persons involved?

There is a considerable degree of overlap between these layers, and the extent to which they play a role (if at all) will differ from case to case.

Layer one: solicitor and client apportionment

34.126   Solicitor and client apportionment relates to the retainer and is addressed at **8.402–8.434**. It is a question of law. Where the question is apportionment of costs between the parties, its relevance is that a paying party will not be required to pay any more than the amount for which the receiving party is himself liable;[159] thus, for example, if A and B instructed the same solicitor in the same proceedings against C, and if A was awarded costs against C but B was unsuccessful and received no costs, C's liability for costs incurred jointly by A and B would be limited by (and may be determined by) A's own liability for those costs to his solicitor. If those were the circumstances, then layer one would be the most important of the four layers. If, on the other hand, the receiving party's retainer were a sole retainer which involved no one else, then it would be the least important of the four layers.

Layer two: the incidence of costs

34.127   This layer is a discretionary layer rather than a layer which is dictated by the law; it is determined when the court decides which order to make.[160] Where the question is apportionment on a detailed assessment, layer two will rarely be of relevance because the incidence of costs will already have been decided (in which case it will be the meaning of the costs order which will be relevant, as opposed to any question as to which order the court should make). That said, there is overlap between all four of the layers, and it is, therefore, touched upon below.

---

be distributed according to the issues in the litigation (such as where an issues-based order is contemplated, or where there has been a successful claim and a successful counterclaim). The topic of issues apportionment is dealt with at **6.100–6.127**.

[159] It is worth expanding on the reasons why layer one (solicitor and client apportionment) has a bearing on layer four (quantum). There can be a significant overlap between apportionment of the liability under the retainer and apportionment between opposing parties. Where the co-litigant is receiving costs, it will often be necessary to determine the position as between solicitor and client before a view can be taken as to the position between opposing parties. This is because a receiving party who is a co-litigant may be awarded no more than his share of the costs.

[160] In view of the fact that it is an issue which usually arises in the context of group litigation, the discussion of how the court should exercise its discretion is addressed at length at **39.12** onwards.

Layer three: the meaning of the order

34.128   The third layer is the meaning and effect of the costs order. It is a matter of law as opposed to a matter of discretion. A discussion of the relevant law can be found at **12.33** onwards. If, for example, the issue is whether payment by one jointly liable paying party will discharge the debt owed by the other, then **12.43–12.55** would be the appropriate place to start. Apportionment that is not between parties would follow similar prinicples.

Layer four: co-litigant apportionment

34.129   The final layer is co-litigant apportionment; it is a process of quantification and therefore a matter of fact and degree, although it may occasionally involve questions of law. It turns on the principles of apportionment (see below).

The interaction of the four layers

34.130   Each of the four layers is governed by the doctrine of equal apportionment (or, in the case of layer three, something very similar to equal apportionment). Thus, layer one (solicitor and client apportionment) relies on equal apportionment as a tenet for the interpretation of the contract of retainer (see **8.417**); layer two (the incidence of costs) is governed by the principle that there will be equal apportionment unless there is an order or agreement to the contrary (see **39.15**); layer three (plural liability) does not refer to equal apportionment by that name, but it relies heavily on a presumption of several obligations, which is a strikingly similar concept (see **12.35**); and, finally, layer four (co-litigant apportionment) is wholly dictated by the concept of equal apportionment (see below).

34.131   Notwithstanding this common link, there is a fundamental difference between solicitor and client apportionment and co-litigant apportionment, and it would be a mistake to believe that the four layers can be amalgamated into one. Where the issue arises between solicitor and client (layer one), the question is generally a matter of contractual interpretation (ie the court's task is to decide where the liabilities of the counterparties to the contract of retainer lie and what the retainer says about who bears which share); where, on the other hand, the task is to apportion costs between litigants (layer two and layer four), the matter is discretionary and will turn on the provisions of CPR, r 44.3 (or r 44.5, as the case may be). That discretion is subject to the indemnity principle, but is not dictated by it (see below); put another way, the terms of the contract of retainer are relevant, but not determinative (as they are in layer one). When considering layer four, it is necessary to do so with reference to layer one because otherwise the amount which is awarded to the receiving party may exceed the amount that he is required to pay his own solicitors.

34.132   This discussion is concerned with apportionment between opposing parties (that is, it looks at layer four and, where appropriate, all the other layers). Two examples will illustrate the importance of looking at all four layers as if they posed questions in a forensic sieve. The first is that mentioned at **34.126**; the principle of equal apportionment may well limit the amount payable by C as a result of the operation of the first layer. For one reason or another A may be awarded only part of his costs (layer two). At the assessment, the court may discover that the vast majority of the work was carried out in respect of B's claim and at the behest of B, in which case, the court may deviate from the principle of equal apportionment and find that only a small part of the costs is payable by C. A contrary scenario might be where X brings a claim against Y and Z, but only Z is condemned in costs. It may be that (for one reason or another) layers three to four suggest that the vast majority of the claim work was attributable to the claim against Z; on the other hand, it might be that the retainer (layer one) makes it clear that costs are to be apportioned equally between the two claims.[161]

The layers in practice, and the doctrine of equal apportionment

34.133   On a detailed assessment the trial judge will usually have made a ruling as to the incidence of costs (layer two); therefore, this is usually a convenient starting point. The first task will be to determine whether there is anything in that order which affects the other layers (such as an indication that the court has already seen the retainers and has ruled accordingly). Assuming this not to be the case, then it would ordinarily be appropriate to determine the position as between solicitor and client (layer one). This is illustrated by the examples given above.

34.134   Unless the court is able to find an express term as to apportionment,[162] the starting point is that there will be equal apportionment; this is a principle which Donaldson MR has commented has age-old respectability, being based 'upon the Rhodian Law, the Rolls of Oleron and the maritime law of general average'.[163]

34.135   The principle of equal apportionment is simply one of equal shares (see **8.417** for a detailed analysis of this topic). It can be seen that it is a principle which is centuries old. In a difficult case, the reader should turn to Chapter 8 for the purposes of considering layer one.

34.136   Common sense dictates that the court would be hampered if the receiving party chose not to present his retainer to the court for scrutiny. The paying party would, no doubt, also wish to see it, not least because its interpretation is a matter of law upon which he may wish to make submissions. Whilst there is no authority on the point, one could formulate an argument that because the interpretation of the retainer is a matter of law rather than fact, the receiving party ought to be put to his election as a matter of course in much the same way as he would be if he were relying on a pre-November 2005 conditional fee agreement (see **9.108**).

34.137   There may be a need to distinguish between common costs (ie those which need to be apportioned) and individual costs (ie those which do not need to be apportioned). This distinction may apply even at layer one; this is because Kelly CB has confirmed that if there was a joint contract of retainer between the solicitor and his clients, each client would be jointly liable for the whole costs, but if there were separate contracts, each would be liable for his own costs and his own portion of the joint costs.[164] That said, Amphlett B has clarified that the fact that the litigation may have

---

[161]   Where a solicitor acts for more than one client in the same claim, the clients' liability for the solicitor's fees will principally depend on what is said in the contracts of retainer. If there is a joint contract of retainer which expressly provides that each client is jointly liable for all the costs incurred, then the position will be clear. Often, however, there are separate retainers which make no mention of the issue of apportionment; in those circumstances, the court must make a ruling as to how those costs are to be apportioned.

[162]   Where there is an agreement as to apportionment, that may be a factor that the court can take into account even when the paying party is not a counterparty to that agreement: see **34.140–34.145** and see *Coys of Kensington Ltd V Woollcombe Beer Watts (a firm)*, 18 February 1999, QBD, Gardland J.

[163]   *Davies v Eli Lilly & Co* [1987] 1 WLR 1136.

[164]   *Burridge v Bellew* (1875) 32 LT 807 at 812.

been conducted jointly would not necessarily make the liability joint;[165] in other words, the fact that co-litigants bring a claim jointly does not mean that each of them will bear a liability for the whole of the costs.

34.138 An oft-quoted example of equal apportionment is *Beaumont v Senior and Bull*,[166] which illustrates the fact that equal apportionment has a bearing on all of the layers such that unless there is reason to believe otherwise, there will be equal apportionment throughout. The Divisional Court found that in the absence of any agreement between the litigants as to how the costs of the litigation should be shared, the receiving parties were each liable for an equal proportion of the costs of the litigation (this being layer one), and that as this was the position between solicitor and client, in the absence of reason to believe otherwise, that was also the position between the parties (layers two to four).

34.139 This is only the starting point, however. This is because, in an appropriate case, the court may deviate from equal apportionment.

Deviation from equal apportionment

34.140 The principle of equal apportionment is capable of leading to injustice and, in view of this, there is a certain flexibility in the way in which that principle is applied. There are, however, significant limits to the extent to which the court is able to deviate from equal apportionment.

34.141 The case that is usually quoted as being an example of the flexible approach is *Korner v H Korner & Co Ltd*,[167] in which the Court of Appeal found that the general principle of equal apportionment was a rule of thumb which was convenient to apply in ordinary cases, but should not be applied in every case. The court found that the principle of equal apportionment was not appropriate in the case before them; this, amongst other things, was because of the differences in the defences which had been raised by the defendants.

34.142 Singleton LJ explained the court's reasoning in this way:[168]

> 'I do not know of any authority which compels the court to follow the rule [of equal apportionment] which I have mentioned in every class of case, and even if to follow it would result in injustice. To do so would be to fly in the teeth of the generally accepted principle as stated in [*Ellingsen*] "that the successful party is to be recompensed the liability he has reasonably incurred in defending himself".'

It should be noted that Singleton LJ did not say that an adjustment should be made so as to meet the justice of the situation: the adjustment that he made was based on the nature of the case each litigant advanced and the different costs attributable thereto rather than on a broader discretionary basis of what was fair and just.

34.143 More recently, Chadwick J has reviewed the authorities; his conclusions can be summarised as follows:[169]

---

[165] *Burridge v Bellew* (1875) 32 LT 807 at 813 and 814.
[166] [1903] 1 KB 282.
[167] [1951] Ch 11.
[168] *Korner v H Korner & Co Ltd* [1951] Ch 11 at 17.
[169] *Bayliss v Kelly and Ors* [1997] 2 Costs LR 54.

- where a solicitor acts for a number of clients in the same claim on separate retainers, each client is entitled to have a separate bill, and to have that bill assessed as between himself and the solicitor;
- when assessing a client's bill the court is to have regard to the overriding principle that the client is to be charged only for those costs properly attributable to the conduct of his claim;
- any costs relating solely to the claim of one client should be charged to him, to the exclusion of the other clients;
- the court must have regard to the nature of the claims raised in order to determine whether there were distinct issues in relation to particular clients; if so, the costs relating to those issues (so far as they can be indemnified) should be attributed accordingly;
- the general costs of the claim (ie the costs which cannot be attributed to particular clients on the basis of separate claims or distinct issues) must be apportioned pro-rata; and
- it is irrelevant that the effect of an apportionment may be that the solicitor cannot recover some part of the apportioned costs (because, for example, one or more clients are insolvent).

Chadwick J was addressing the position between solicitor and client (layer one) but (subject to what is said below) there is no reason why his guidance would not apply to the other layers.

34.144   That qualification arises out of the following points made by Chadwick J:[170]

> '[There is] no support in [the authorities] for the proposition that a pro-rata apportionment of the general costs of the action should be modified or "adjusted" on the ground that one client is more important, or more prominent in the litigation, than others. If costs cannot be attributed to particular clients on the basis of separate defences or separate issues, then they must be apportioned equally between all those clients for whose benefit they have been incurred.'

Thus, Chadwick J found that there was no support for the proposition that the adjustment should take into account the relative importance or prominence of the parties: he found that it should be based solely on the issues raised and the costs which could be attributed to those issues. This is undoubtedly true on a solicitor and client basis (layer one), but it is not true on a between the parties basis (layers two to four). As is explained below and in Chapter 39, these issues can be taken into account in the exercise of the court's discretion as to the incidence of costs (layer two), and they would usually be reflected in layer four simply by virtue of the fact that demanding clients take up more time than those who are less demanding.

34.145   The exercise of adjustment will be a largely factual exercise.[171] As can be seen from one of the authorities which are discussed below (*BCCI v Ali & Ors*), where a party has incurred costs that cannot fairly be attributed to his co-litigants, the court can take that fact into account, but only in a limited way. It should also be said that where inequality is an express term of the retainer, that may be a factor that the court can take into account even when the paying party is not a counterparty to that agreement.[172]

---

170   *Bayliss v Kelly and Ors* [1997] 2 Costs LR 54 at 60.
171   See *Meretz Investments Ltd v ACP Ltd* [2007] EWHC 2635 (Ch).
172   See **34.146–34.150**; see also *Coys of Kensington Ltd V Woollcombe Beer Watts (a firm)*, 18 February 1999, QBD, Gardland J.

Discretionary matters

34.146 The cases mentioned above focus on the principle of equal apportionment in so far as it pertains to the client's liability to his solicitor for his own costs (layer one). Similar methodology may be appropriate when exercising a discretion as to costs on a between the parties basis.[173] This is discussed in more detail at **39.20–39.37**.

34.147 Where the facts permit of such a finding, there is nothing to prevent the court from ordering that apportionment should be unequal.[174] If, for example, a claimant was found to have been guilty of having advanced a fraudulent case, the court could find that no part of those costs could be fairly attributed to the other claims and that therefore that litigant should personally bear the whole of those costs. Whilst he declined to exercise that power, Park J found that it existed.[175] The power to order unequal apportionment is based on the relative contributions made as a result of the issues raised by the parties and on whether those issues can properly be regarded as being common costs; as Park J pointed out, it would be wrong to regard the court's discretion as being penal or punitive. In an extreme case, an order may be for costs that 'relate exclusively' to a certain party or issue; where that was the case, then there would be no apportionment at all, and only those costs that could properly be attributed to the person or issue by division would be payable.[176]

34.148 As has been mentioned at **34.144**, the court has a greater breadth of discretion in relation to costs between opposing parties than it does in relation to costs between solicitor and client; that greater freedom is evident in the way that the court deals with such cases, especially group litigation. In a difficult case or in a case involving group litigation, the reader is encouraged to turn to Chapter 39.

34.149 The position between the parties may be summarised by referring to the comments made by Darling LJ:[177]

> '[A]lthough each of the four plaintiffs may be liable to the solicitor for the whole of the costs common to all of them, still as between themselves, each is liable to contribute one-fourth. From this it follows that ultimately each of the plaintiffs is only liable to pay one-fourth of the common costs, and that, therefore, as costs are given as an indemnity only, one-fourth is all that the defendant should be called upon to pay to one plaintiff. To order the defendant to pay to the successful plaintiff more than one-fourth would be to order him to pay an amount in relief of the amount that the unsuccessful plaintiffs ought to pay.'

34.150 The discussion above has primarily addressed apportionment on a detailed assessment (that is, layers one, three and four), but the potential effect of the indemnity principle should be borne in mind when a costs order is formulated (layer two). If this is not done, the eventual award of costs can be very different from what the court intended when it made the order. Unintended consequences may be avoided if the order makes it

---

[173] See, for example, *Ward v Guinness Mahon plc* [1996] 1 WLR 894.
[174] Although he declined to exercise the power, Warren J found that the principle of equal apportionment was only a general rule which should not be allowed to produced injustice: *Meretz Investments Ltd v ACP Ltd* [2007] EWHC 2635 (Ch).
[175] This was in the context of group litigation in which the lead claimants were accused of dishonesty in the litigation itself (*BCCI v Ali & Ors* [2000] 2 Costs LR 243).
[176] *Hay v Szterbin* [2010] EWHC 1967 (Ch) at [13], per Newey J.
[177] *Keen and Others v Towler TLR* (28 November 1924).

clear either that the paying party is to pay the costs attributable to a stated person's claims, or that a stated proportion of the costs incurred can properly be attributed to the issues in the paying claimant's claim.

The role of costs sharing agreements

34.151 For the reasons set out above, the apportionment of costs will be subject to the indemnity principle, but will not be dictated by it. To that extent, the retainer will be relevant on the assessment of costs between opposing parties. The matter may be made more complex if there is a contract dealing with the issue of how co-litigants (that is, litigants who were on the same side) should share the burden of their costs. That agreement may be in the retainers themselves, or it may be in a separate costs sharing agreement.

34.152 The existence of a costs sharing agreement will usually have a bearing on the apportionment between co-litigants, but, for the reasons set out at **34.158**, it may also have a bearing on apportionment between opposing parties (not least because it may modify the retainer); this means that the agreement may need to be taken into account by the costs judge during the assessment. In any event, it is not uncommon for the costs judge to be charged not only with the task of assessing the costs between opposing parties, but also between co-litigants (especially where one co-litigant has settled the costs, but one or more of the others has not).

34.153 Where such an agreement exists, the court must ask itself how it should be regarded and whether it is bound by the agreement. The answer seems to be that (in so far as co-litigants are concerned, at least) the court would not be bound by such an agreement, but would very rarely make an order which would depart from it. In *BCCI v Ali & Ors*,[178] Park J had to decide how to apportion solicitor and client costs where there had been no written costs sharing agreement. The costs related to a single issue, in respect of which five lead claimants were selected. All of these claims failed; the non-lead claimants said that this was as a result of the alleged dishonesty on the part of the lead claimants. Having made no order for costs as against the defendants, Park J had to decide how the claimants should bear their own costs. (This was in the context of the incidence of costs – layer two – but there is no reason to believe that different principles would apply to the other layers.)

34.154 He found that the costs should be borne by all of the claimants in equal measure. He decided the matter on the basis that there was an implied agreement – or 'clear understanding' – that the lead claimants' costs would be shared. Whilst obiter, Park J commented on whether he would have had the vires to deal with the costs other than in accordance with the agreement; his conclusion was that he did:

> 'The answer [to the question of jurisdiction] would be yes, though it would be a very rare case where the judge would make an order which departed from what the group litigants had agreed.'

34.155 In making these comments, he commented that the situation was similar to that in *Gomba Holdings (UK) Ltd v Minories Financne Ltd*,[179] but rather than the agreement

---

[178]   [2000] 2 Costs LR 243.
[179]   [1993] Ch 172.

being between opposing parties (as it was in *Gomba*), it was between parties on the same side. He summarised the position as follows:

> '[If] there is an agreement about the apportionment between group litigants of costs of proceedings, like a test case, the existence of the agreement does not exclude the statutory discretion of the court to make its own order, including an order which binds group litigants which are not strictly parties to the test case. However, where there are contractual rights and obligations the court's discretion should ordinarily be exercised so as to reflect those contractual rights and obligations.'

34.156 Park J ultimately refused to depart from the terms of the 'clear understanding' that each claimant would bear a proportionate part of the lead claimant's costs. Amongst the many reasons he gave for coming to this decision was his desire not to set a precedent for lead claimants being stripped of the protection that costs sharing gave them; such a precedent, he explained, would be harmful to group litigation generally. In commenting on the discreditable conduct of the lead claimants, he said that:

> 'to withdraw costs sharing on this ground would be the equivalent of fining the test case employees because of their discreditable conduct ... The process before me is not a penal process, and it would be wrong for me to exercise my discretion for penal purposes.'

34.157 The exact nature of the solicitor's right to payment will not usually be relevant, even where the costs sharing agreement is between co-litigants with different types of retainer. In particular, Wright J has found that (in so far as group litigation is concerned) there is no distinction to be drawn between claimants who have legal aid and those who are funded by way of conditional fee agreements.[180] Again, this decision related to the incidence of costs (layer two), but there is no reason to believe that it would not also apply to the other layers.

34.158 Although the existence of a costs sharing agreement will not usually be relevant to entitlement to costs between opposing parties (as opposed to between co-litigants), this will not always be the case (especially where the agreement goes to costs incurred in jointly instructing the same legal representatives). For example, Garland J has found that where there is a costs sharing agreement between a defendant who was entitled to costs and a defendant who was not entitled to costs, that agreement might result in the paying party (the claimant) being liable for the entitled defendant's share of conducting the defendants' defence.[181] One way of analysing that decision is to regard the costs sharing agreement as having modified the retainer, thereby having a bearing on layer one.

34.159 In summary, where a costs sharing agreement exists the court will usually seek to apportion costs in such a way as to respect it and, in any event, it may be taken into account as being an agreement which fashions or qualifies the retainer.

---

[180] *Hodgson v Imperial Tobacco Ltd (No 2)* [1998] 2 Costs LR 27.
[181] *Coys of Kensington Ltd V Woollcombe Beer Watts (a firm)*, 18 February 1999, QBD, Gardland J; on the facts of that case the costs sharing agreement was academic because it was an agreement for equal apportionment, so merely confirmed the position that would have existed if there had been no agreement.

LEGISLATIVE FETTERS ON THE RECOVERY OF COSTS

34.160   Whilst they tend to relate only to certain types of litigation, there are a small number of legislative restrictions which are capable of having a bearing on the amount of costs.[182] They tend to be specific, and as such, they tend to take precedence over more general statutory provisions concerning the amount of costs.[183] The only commonly encountered example is 'the county court procedural restriction'; this has already been described at **26.10–26.13** and for the reasons set out therein is not likely to give rise to any limit on the recovery of costs beyond those which would apply for other reasons.

34.161   The Slander of Women Act 1891 makes specific provision for the recovery of damages for words which impute unchastity or adultery to any woman or girl. Section 1 of that Act imposes the following restriction:

> '[In] any action for words spoken and made actionable by this Act, a plaintiff shall not recover more costs than damages, unless the judge shall certify that there was reasonable ground for bringing the action.'

Thus, where the Slander of Women Act 1891 applies, save where the court provides a certificate of reasonableness, the amount of costs will be limited to the amount of damages. This provision is, surprisingly, still in force,[184] but its relevance is likely to be negated by the fact that it would probably be open to a costs judge to provide the requisite certificate. In any event, it is questionable whether the court is permitted to enforce such a provision, given the fact that it applies only to women and could therefore be said to be discriminatory within the meaning of Art 14 of the European Convention on Human Rights.

34.162   Where a patents claim is commenced in the High Court and where it could have been brought in the county court, the costs may be restricted to those allowable in the county court; this is as a result of s 290 of the Copyright, Designs and Patents Act 1988, which provides:

> '(1)   Where an action is commenced in the High Court which could have been commenced in a patents county court and in which a claim for a pecuniary remedy is made, then, subject to the provisions of this section, if the plaintiff recovers less than the prescribed amount, he is not entitled to recover any more costs than those to which he would have been entitled if the action had been brought in the county court.
>
> (2)   For this purpose a plaintiff shall be treated as recovering the full amount recoverable in respect of his claim without regard to any deduction made in respect of matters not falling to be taken into account in determining whether the action could have been commenced in a patents county court.
>
> (3)   This section does not affect any question as to costs if it appears to the High Court that there was reasonable ground for supposing the amount recoverable in respect of the plaintiff's claim to be in excess of the prescribed amount.
>
> (4)   The High Court, if satisfied that there was sufficient reason for bringing the action in the High Court, may make an order allowing the costs or any part of the costs on the High Court scale or on such one of the county court scales as it may direct.

---

[182]   The restriction on the recovery costs in the CPR (such as the small claims regime and fixed costs) are not included because they have been made by delegated legislation rather than statute.

[183]   *Hasker v Wood* (1885) 54 LJQB 419, CA; *Reeve v Gibson* [1891] 1 QB 652, CA; *Re Butler's Will ex p Metropolitan Board of Works* (1912) 106 LT 673.

[184]   It was amended by Statute Law Revision Act 1908, but otherwise has remained untouched.

(5)   This section does not apply to proceedings brought by the Crown.

(6)   In this section "the prescribed amount" means such amount as may be prescribed by Her Majesty for the purposes of this section by Order in Council.

(7)   No recommendation shall be made to Her Majesty to make an Order under this section unless a draft of the Order has been laid before and approved by a resolution of each House of Parliament.'

The 'prescribed amount' is £30,000.[185] In practice, the difference between the two costs regimes is limited (which is very different from the position which pertained at the time the restriction was first enacted); thus, this is a restriction which lacks teeth.

34.163   Some restrictions arise out of European law. An example is Art 15A of Council Directive 96/61/EC of 24 September 1996 concerning integrated pollution prevention and control. That Article was inserted by Arts 3(7) and 4(4) of Council Directive 2003/35/EC of 26 May 2003 to implement provisions which first appeared in the Convention on Access to Information, Public Participation in Decision-Making and Access to Justice in Environmental Matters of 25 June 1998 ('the Aarhus Convention'). Among the provisions as to access to justice in Art 9 of the Aarhus Convention is a requirement that the procedures to which it refers should be fair, equitable and timely and 'not prohibitively expensive'. Lord Hope has explained that whilst a costs officer is not able to take that article into account when assessing costs, the court is able to do so when making an order for costs.[186]

---

[185]   See art 2(5) of the High Court and County Courts Jurisdiction Order 1991.
[186]   *R (on the application of Edwards and another) v Environment Agency and others* [2010] UKSC 57.

Chapter 35

VALUE ADDED TAX

35.1   Value added tax ('VAT') is a form of consumption tax which all member states of the European Union must charge.[1] This chapter addresses its recoverability between opposing parties, both in principle and in terms of quantum. It also addresses VAT between solicitor and client. Whilst the writer has taken accountancy advice when writing this chapter, he is not an accountant, and the reader must take his own advice for the purposes of taxation.

Whether and to what extent a paying party is liable for VAT will depend on a number of factors:

- whether the receiving party's legal representatives are obliged to charge VAT as 'output tax';
- whether disbursements attract VAT when they are first disbursed or whether they attract VAT as a result of being recharged to the client via the legal party's legal representatives;
- whether VAT, or any part thereof, can be recovered by the receiving party as 'input tax'; and
- whether it is reasonable for the receiving party to claim VAT from the paying party.

LIABILITY FOR VAT

35.2   In the present context 'output tax' means VAT on supplies made by a 'taxable person'[2] (this being a person who is or who ought to be registered for VAT).[3] 'Input tax' is the VAT on the supply to a taxable person of any goods or services.[4] Thus, from the point of view of the lawyer supplying the services, 'output tax' is VAT on output supplies and which must be paid to HM Revenue and Customs ('HMRC'), and 'input tax' is VAT on input supplies and may be claimed reclaimed or deducted.[5]

Whether VAT is chargeable by the receiving party's lawyers

35.3   Most legal representatives will be registered for VAT, so their services will be subject to output tax. A handful of lawyers will not be VAT registered, the most common example being recently called counsel.[6] If a solicitor instructs counsel who is not registered for VAT, his services will be deemed to be part of the service provided by

---

[1]   Directive 2006/112/EC.
[2]   See s 24(2) of the Value Added Tax Act 1994.
[3]   See s 3(1) of that Act.
[4]   See s 24(1) of the Value Added Tax Act 1994.
[5]   See the Value Added Tax Regulations 1995, reg 29.
[6]   Since April 2011 the threshold for compulsory registration is £73,000

his or her instructing solicitor[7] and, therefore, VAT will, in principle, be payable. In practice, however, the HMRC permits the solicitor to 're-address' counsel's fee note,[8] such that it is payable directly by the lay client as a 'qualifying disbursement' (see **35.11**). The effect of this is that VAT can be avoided reasonably easily; this means that a receiving party will not normally recover VAT on the fees of counsel who is not registered for VAT. Other types of lawyer may also not be VAT registered. Whilst an obvious point, no VAT is chargeable on the costs of lawyers who are employed in-house.[9] Likewise, if a lawyer is acting on his own behalf, he is not treated for the purposes of VAT as having supplied a service, so no VAT would be chargeable.

The time when VAT falls due: tax points

Solicitors

35.4   A liability for output tax will arise upon the creation of a 'basic tax point' or an 'actual tax point':

- *Basic tax points:* A basic tax point[10] is generally created on completion of the work:[11] HMRC give the following advice about basic tax points:[12]

  > 'The majority of supplies by a solicitor are single supplies, albeit the supply may involve work undertaken over an extended period of time. A good example of this is litigation. The basic tax point occurs when the services have been fully completed. But it can be difficult sometimes to establish precisely when this might be, especially where the matter has taken a number of years to be resolved.

  > 'Some solicitors make supplies on a regular basis to an individual client. In most cases this will represent a series of separate supplies, each of which will be subject to its own basic tax point ... Only in exceptional circumstances, such as where a solicitor is retained and remunerated as a permanent legal adviser or to act as the client's legal office, might this kind of relationship represent a continuous supply of services.'

  Thus a basic tax point is the date on which the supply of services has been fully completed; this is addressed in in the next paragraph.

- *Actual tax points:* A basic tax point may be overridden by an actual tax point, be that before or after the basic tax point; an actual tax point may be created upon payment or upon issue of a VAT invoice, whichever is the earlier.[13] HMRC has issued further guidance on legally aided work.[14]

---

[7] This is a matter of accountancy rather than costs law; it is an entirely different issue to those discussed at **12.2–12.26**.

[8] This agreement was first published in the Law Society Gazette on 4 April 1973; it is now recorded at para 1.2.2 of *VAT Guide 1996* (Revenue Law Committee of the Law Society, December 1996).

[9] See para 1.9.3 of *VAT Guide 1996* (Revenue Law Committee of the Law Society, December 1996).

[10] See Value Added Tax Act 1994, s 6(3).

[11] VATTOS8540 draws a distinction between contentious and non-contentious work; non-contentious costs will give rise to a basic tax point when it is complete and any subsequent solicitor and client assessment will be accounted for by an adjustment, but where the fees are to be paid by a paying party the basic tax point will arise upon conclusion of the assessment. See also para 2.1.9 of *VAT Guide 1996* (Revenue Law Committee of the Law Society, December 1996).

[12] See VATTOS8520 – Tax points for specific categories of supplier: solicitors: basic tax point.

[13] See para 2.2 of VAT change: Reversion of the standard rate to 17.5 per cent (Law Society, 15 December 2009).

[14] See VATTOS8560 – Tax points for specific categories of supplier: solicitors: legal aid work (contracting arrangements).

35.5 As a matter of general principle, the supply of services will, subject to certain exceptions,[15] be treated as taking place at the time when the services are performed.[16] Special provisions relate to solicitors, however, and in this regard, HMRC draws a distinction between contentious and non-contentious work:[17]

> **'Contentious work (non-Legal Aid)**: The losing party to the legal action may be ordered to pay costs. Where this is the case, the solicitor for the successful party prepares a bill which is then either agreed with the solicitor for the loser, or is referred to the Court for scrutiny under the taxation procedures. Settling of the costs in these circumstances is part and parcel of the solicitor's overall supply to the client. A basic tax point does not therefore occur until either the costs have been agreed between the solicitors or the taxation procedure is complete.
>
> **Non-contentious (non-Legal Aid)**: By law a client may ask the Law Society to scrutinise a solicitor's bill to ensure that it is fair and reasonable. Under this procedure the Law Society can reduce the amount payable by the client. None of this action forms part of the supply by the solicitor to the client and the basic tax point will have occurred when all the work, except the invoicing, was completed. Where this has resulted in tax being accounted for in advance of a reduction to the bill, the solicitor may subsequently adjust the amount accounted for subject to the normal rules regarding credits.'

If a solicitor's fees are not known at or before the time when the services were supplied, the supply may be treated as taking place at the time of the issue of the VAT invoice rather than upon completion of the work to which the fees relate. There is a longstop of 3 months after the date of performance of the services. The supply of services does not include the time spent preparing the invoice to the client.[18]

Barristers

35.6 Barristers are often paid months or even years after they carried out the work, and to take account of this they are permitted to defer liability for output tax until receipt of payment.[19] Thus, the tax point will normally be the date on which fee notes are receipted. In this regard, reg 92 of the Value Added Tax Regulations 1995 reads as follows:

> '92 Services supplied by a barrister ... acting in that capacity, shall be treated as taking place at whichever is the earliest of the following times—
>
> (a)   when the fee in respect of those services is received by the barrister or advocate, .
> (b)   when the barrister or advocate issues a VAT invoice in respect of them, or .
> (c)   the day when the barrister or advocate ceases to practise as such.'

Rates of VAT

(The issue of changes to the rate of VAT is addressed later in this chapter.)

---

15 See 6(4)–(14) of the Value Added Tax Act 1994. Subsection 6(4) reads provides that a person making the supply may elect whether, in certain circumstances, the supply shall, to the extent covered by the invoice or payment, be treated as taking place at the time the invoice is issued or the payment is received.

16 See 6(3) of the Value Added Tax Act 1994.

17 See VATTOS8540 – Tax points for specific categories of supplier: solicitors: adjustments to fees.

18 See VATTOS8540 and the Law Society's Practice Note: VAT change: Reversion of the standard rate to 17.5 per cent – 15 December 2009 at para 2.1.

19 The power derives from reg 92 of the Value Added Tax Regulations 1995 (SI 1995/2518).

Standard, reduced, zero and exempt rating

35.7   Not all services provided by legal representatives will attract a standard rate of VAT. The following table summarises the position:

Rate	Example
Standard Rate	Supply of legal services to persons in the UK (other than relating to land outside the UK) and to private (ie non-business) clients in the EU Disbursements that are not 'qualifying disbursements' or zero rated or exempt, such as taxi fares, tolls (privately operated), hotel bills, etc
Reduced Rate	There are no legal supplies within this category
Zero Rate	Disbursements relating to public transport, such as rail fares
Exempt	Some disbursements, such as postal services and (prior to about 1 May 2007), medical experts' fees
Outside scheme	Services supplied outside the EU Services supplied by non-taxable person Tolls (publically operated) and the congestion charge Statutory fees, such as court fees

Place where persons 'belong'

35.8   Services provided to persons 'belonging'[20] to a place outside the EU will be zero rated[21] (other than where those services relate to UK land),[22] as will services provided for business purposes to persons belonging outside the UK.[23] An individual receiving the services for non-business purposes belongs where he has his usual place of residence.[24] Otherwise, the person will belong (a) where he has his only place of business or other fixed establishment; (b) if he has no such place or establishment, where he has his usual place of residence;[25] (c) if he has business or fixed establishments in more than one country, where the establishment at which or for the purposes of which the services are to be used is located. A person carrying on a business through a branch or agency in any country shall be treated as having a business establishment there.[26]

---

[20]   Article 7(11) of the Value Added Tax (Place of Supply of Services) Order 1992 (SI 1992/3121).

[21]   Section 4(1) of the Value Added Tax Act 1994.

[22]   For a discussion of the law, see *W H Payne & Co (1995) VAT decision 13668*; for a description of the effect of the law, see Appendix 1 of *VAT Guide 1996* (Revenue Law Committee of the Law Society, December 1996).

[23]   Value Added Tax Act 1994, s 9; and see para 1.7 of *VAT Guide 1996* (Revenue Law Committee of the Law Society, December 1996).

[24]   See s 9 of the Value Added Tax Act 1994 and Art 9 of the Sixth Council Directive (77/388/EEC).

[25]   This will be the place where it is legally constituted if the person is a corporation: see s 9(5)(b) of the Value Added Tax Act 1994.

[26]   Section 9(5)(a) of the Value Added Tax Act 1994.

Resolution of disputes regarding rating

35.9 If there is a dispute as to whether a service is zero rated or exempt, CPD, art 5.6 provides that the receiving party is to obtain the view of HM Revenue and Customs, and that that view should be made available to the court at the hearing at which the costs are assessed.

Self-supply of legal services

35.10 Whilst no VAT is chargeable on the costs of employed in-house solicitors (see **35.3**), VAT may be charged where one entity within a group of companies supplies services to another. This will not always be the case, however: Government Departments who use their own staff to provide legal services (such as the Treasury Solicitor) cannot claim from the paying party VAT relating to those legal services.[27]

Expenses and disbursements

35.11 HM Revenue and Customs use the word 'disbursement' to mean something wholly different from that which is meant when a lawyer uses that word. To avoid confusion, the term 'qualifying disbursement' will be used in this book. Broadly speaking, for VAT purposes a qualifying disbursement is an amount of money paid to a third party by the solicitor acting as agent of the client, but this will be so only where the client's account is debited for precisely the same amount as was paid to the third party.[28] If, however, these monies have been paid in order to allow a solicitor to provide a service to his or her client, then (for VAT purposes), those monies are not regarded as being a qualifying disbursement (in which case they will be known as 'non-qualifying expenses' or 'petty disbursements').[29] If an expense is classified as being a qualifying disbursement, then no VAT will be payable, but if it is a non-qualifying expense, then it is treated as being part of the supply of legal services, and VAT is added in the ordinary way.[30]

35.12 A solicitor may treat a payment to a third party as being a qualifying disbursement for VAT purposes if all of the following conditions are met:[31]

- the solicitor was acting as the agent of the client (this condition will almost always be met);
- the client actually received and used the goods or services provided by the third party (this condition usually prevents the solicitor's own travelling and subsistence expenses, telephone bills, postage, and other costs being treated as disbursements for VAT purposes);
- the client[32] was responsible for paying the third party (examples might include estate duty and stamp duty payable by the client on a contract to be made by the client);

---

[27] CPD, art 5.20.
[28] See Art 79(c) of the EC Directive 2006/112/EC.
[29] See CPD, art 5.11.
[30] That is, the supply is treated as having been made by the solicitor under s 47(3) of the Value Added Tax Act 1994. See CPD, arts 5.11 and 5.12 for a discussion of the practical effect of the law discussed in this section.
[31] See para 25.1.1 of *Notice 700: the VAT Guide* (HMRC, April 2002).
[32] Whilst not binding on any court, Master Pollard found that the fact that monies would be payable out of public funds rather than directly by the client does not mean that this condition is not met: *R v Findlay and MacGregor* [2002] 2 Costs LR 322.

- the client authorised the solicitor to make the payment on his or her behalf, and the client knew that the goods or services would be provided by a third party (if there has been compliance with the Solicitors Costs Information and Client Care Code 1999, this condition will usually have been met);
- the solicitor's outlay is separately itemised when the client is invoiced;
- the solicitor recovers only the exact amount which he or she paid to the third party; and
- the goods or services are clearly additional to the supplies which the solicitor makes to his or her client on his or her own account.

35.13 Examples of what are and are not qualifying disbursements are given in the following table (the examples are necessarily very general, and the classification may vary from case to case).

Qualifying disbursements	Non-qualifying expenses
VAT is not chargeable (unless, of course, VAT is charged by the third party)	*VAT is chargeable*
Photocopying bureau charges (unless the copying is done to allow the solicitor to provide a service)	Photocopies made in the office
Counsel's fees (but only where the fee note is re-addressed)[33]	Counsel's fees (where the fee note is not re-addressed)
Courier charges (but only where the service is provided to or for the benefit of the client)	All other courier charges
Oath fees paid to another solicitor or commissioner for oaths[34]	CHAPS/TT fees,[35] bank charges for supplying a bankers' draft, and administration charges[36]
Search fees relating to searches carried out by post and supplied directly to the client[37]	Search fees relating to searches carried out personally (including on-line searches); mining search fees[38]
Fees for police reports[39]	Travelling expenses,[40] hotel and accommodation expenses

---

[33] See **35.4**.

[34] See para 1.1.2.4.2 of *VAT Guide 1996* (Revenue Law Committee of the Law Society, December 1996); for fees for oaths administered, see para 3.2.3.1 of that guide.

[35] *Shuttleworth & Co v Commissioners of Customs and Excise (LON/94/986A)*.

[36] See *National Transit Insurance Co Ltd v Customs and Excise Commissioners* [1975] STC 35.

[37] See para 1.1.2.4.1 of *VAT Guide 1996* (Revenue Law Committee of the Law Society, December 1996).

[38] See para 1.6 of *VAT Guide 1996* (Revenue Law Committee of the Law Society, December 1996).

[39] See para 1.1.2.4.2 of *VAT Guide 1996* (Revenue Law Committee of the Law Society, December 1996).

[40] See *Rowe & Maw v Customs and Excise Commissioners* [1975] STC 340.

Qualifying disbursements	Non-qualifying expenses
VAT is not chargeable (unless, of course, VAT is charged by the third party)	*VAT is chargeable*
Fees for medical reports[41]	Telephone call charges and postage (these would usually be absorbed within the solicitors' overhead in any event)[42]
Court fees and witness fees[43]	Telephone conference fees
Insurance premiums (IPT is, however, payable)	Lexis (and similar) charges (again, these would usually be absorbed within the solicitors' overhead)

35.14 It can be seen that the classification of monies as qualifying disbursements or non-qualifying expenses is not wholly intuitive. For example, if a company search is made personally by the solicitor, it is the solicitor rather than the client who receives the supply and the fee cannot properly be regarded as being a qualifying disbursement. If, on the other hand, exactly the same search is requested via post and the results are then passed on to the client for his or her own use, then the fee can properly be regarded as being a qualifying disbursement. Fortunately, the advice of practising accountants is that there is a certain amount of flexibility in this regard.[44]

35.15 If the third party charges VAT, this can properly be passed on to the client and will in principle be payable by the paying party. Thus, if an accountant prepares an expert report, the VAT charged by the accountant will in principle be recoverable from the paying party irrespective of whether accountant's fees are to be regarded as a qualifying disbursement.

MEDICAL AND DENTAL REPORTS AND RECORDS

Medical and dental experts

35.16 The VAT status of medical and dental experts has changed over recent years. In general, the services of medical and dental experts are exempt from VAT if the following conditions are met:[45]

- the services consist of care, diagnosis, treatment or assessment of a patient;
- the services are within the discipline in which the expert is registered to practice; and

---

[41] See para 1.1.2.4.2 of *VAT Guide 1996* (Revenue Law Committee of the Law Society, December 1996).
[42] See CPD, art 5.12.
[43] Ibid.
[44] It is said that where the invoice is not in the client's name then HMRC do not object to the agent recovering the input tax and issuing a tax invoice to the client and accounting for the corresponding output tax; this has the same overall effect as if the expense had been treated as a disbursement, but provides the client with a VAT invoice in their name to enable recovery of the VAT: see *VAT Treatment of Disbursements* (Lovewell Blake, Spring 2009).
[45] See para 2.2 of VAT Notice 701/57.

- performance of those services requires the application of knowledge, skills and judgment acquired in the course of the expert's professional training.

35.17 Until about 1 May 2007, the provision of medical or dental reports was regarded as fulfilling these criteria. Only work which was predominantly the supply of legal services (such as arbitration, mediation, negotiation, etc) would have attracted VAT. In 2003, the ECJ ruled that the first of the requirements referred to above related to 'services intended principally to protect (including maintain or restore) the health of an individual'.[46] Following consultation, HM Revenue and Customs amended the relevant schedule of the Value Added Tax Act 1994[47] so as to fall in line with that decision. Therefore, since 1 May 2007, medical or dental reports prepared for legal purposes are subject to VAT.[48]

Medical and dental records

35.18 The situation with medical and dental records is more complex. Two issues arise: firstly, whether the supply of such records is exempt for VAT purposes at the point of supply to the solicitor, and secondly, whether the solicitor is required to charge VAT as a result of the records being part and parcel of his supply of legal services. This second point turns on whether or not records are qualifying disbursements.

- *Whether exempt:* The supply of medical and dental records is generally exempt from VAT. Where the request is made under the Data Protection Act 1998, the Access to Medical Reports Act 1988 or the Access to Health Records Act 1990, then that activity is beyond the scope of VAT.[49] Where a copy of a health record is provided in circumstances that do not fall within one of these statutory obligations, that is a taxable supply,[50] but it is difficult to imagine circumstances in which that could reasonably apply in a legal context.
- *Qualifying disbursements*: Judge David Demack sitting in the First-Tier Tribunal Tax Chamber has found that it was merely administrative convenience which led to solicitors paying for the medical records, and that when those sums were re-charged to the client, they were qualifying disbursements.[51] He found that the records were obtained for the interest of the client, not the lawyer; the client needed them to establish his claim.

The effect of the above is that VAT is not charged on medical or dental records obtained for the purpose of personal injury claims.

Medical agencies

35.19 An area of uncertainty is where a solicitor uses a medical agency to obtain a medical report. That part of the fee that relates to the medical report itself ought not to

---

[46] *Peter d'Ambrumenil, Dispute Resolution Services Ltd and Commissioners of Customs and Excise* [2003] EWECJ C307/01.
[47] That is, Group 7 (Health and Welfare) of Sch 9 (Exemptions) to the Value Added Tax Act 1994, item 1(a).
[48] The Value Added Tax (Health and Welfare) Order 2007 (SI 2007/206).
[49] HMRC Reference: Notice 701/57 (January 2007), para 3.1.
[50] Ibid.
[51] *Barratt, Goff and Tomlinson v Revenue and Customs Commissioners (Law Society intervening)* [2011] UKFTT 71 (TC) at [40] and [52]–[58].

attract VAT (see **35.18**), but that part of the fee that relates to the agency's administrative is arguably in a different category. There is, however, no authority on the point.

VAT BETWEEN OPPOSING PARTIES

General principles

35.20 Whilst not expressly included within the definition of 'costs' within the CPR,[52] VAT is recoverable between opposing parties.[53] If VAT can be recovered by the receiving party as input tax, it ought not to be claimed from the paying party as costs;[54] this is because he would have suffered no net loss in respect of that VAT.[55] Where the receiving party is able to obtain credit from HMRC for a proportion of the VAT as input tax, only that proportion which is not eligible for credit should be included in the claim for costs.[56] The CPD makes it clear that it is the receiving party who is responsible for ensuring that VAT is claimed only in so far as the receiving party is unable to recover VAT as input tax;[57] the irrecoverable VAT ought, therefore, to be excluded from the bill. Where VAT is properly claimed, it cannot be recovered by the paying party as input tax (not least because no services would have been supplied to the paying party).[58]

Resolution of disputes regarding input tax

35.21 Where there is a dispute as to whether (or to what extent) VAT can be recovered as input tax, CPD, art 5.5 provides that the receiving party must provide a certificate as to recovery of VAT. This must be signed either by the receiving party's solicitors or by the receiving party's auditors who must certify the extent to which the receiving party is able to recover VAT as input tax. Although the CPD lays down no hard and fast rules in this regard, it is clear from Precedent F (ie the model certificates annexed to the CPD) that the receiving party's solicitors or auditors are expected to base their opinion on the receiving party's most recent VAT return.

Subrogated claims, indemnities and insurers

35.22 It is the ability of the receiving party himself to recover VAT as input tax that is relevant. If an insurer conducts a subrogated claim in the name of an insured or if he provides an indemnity, it is irrelevant for the purposes of assessing the paying party's liability for VAT whether the insurer is able to recover VAT.[59] If the insured is unable to claim input tax for any reason, the solicitor's invoice may be sent directly to the insurer, but this must not be treated as a VAT invoice which gives rise to a right on the part of the insurer to claim input tax: put another way, input tax cannot be claimed by the back door.[60] Where, on the other hand, the insured is able to claim input tax, then a VAT invoice may be sent directly to the insured with the insurer paying the non-VAT

---

[52] See CPR, r 43.2(a).
[53] This is implied by Section 5 of the CPD.
[54] See CPD, art 5.3.
[55] See para 1.9.1.2.2 of *VAT Guide 1996* (Revenue Law Committee of the Law Society, December 1996).
[56] See CPD, art 5.3.
[57] See CPD art 5.3.
[58] *N O Turner (trading as Turner Agricultural) v Commissioners of Customs & Excise* [1992] STC 621.
[59] See para 1.9.4 of *VAT Guide 1996* (Revenue Law Committee of the Law Society, December 1996).
[60] See para 1.9.4.5 of *VAT Guide 1996* (Revenue Law Committee of the Law Society, December 1996).

element.[61] Where the insurer is itself the litigant, then it is commonly the case that it is able to claim only a tiny fraction of the VAT as input tax; this may mean that VAT between opposing parties will be reclaimed at a rate that is different from the prevailing standard rate.

Reasonableness

35.23 It will rarely be the case that a receiving party has the option of avoiding VAT, so the issue of reasonableness will arise only infrequently. An opportunity to make an election may arise if there is a change of rate (see below); if VAT is charged at a higher rate than is reasonably required, the court will order the paying party to pay that rate only if the receiving party is able to justify the decision not to elect to charge at the lower rate.[62]

35.24 In practice, where a decision has been taken to charge at a higher rate, this is often for sound accountancy reasons pertaining to the receiving party's solicitors, and in those circumstances, the court may be satisfied that the election to charge that rate was reasonable, as the alternative would have been to incur the costs of instructing new solicitors. Examples do exist, however, of VAT being disallowed as a result of it being incurred voluntarily.[63]

Proportionality

35.25 Generally speaking, VAT ought to be disregarded for the purpose of considering whether the costs are proportionate (see **34.23**).

Part 47 offers

35.26 Unless stated otherwise, a Part 47 offer will be deemed to be inclusive of VAT.[64] If recoverability of VAT is in dispute, it would be sensible for parties to make it clear beyond doubt whether their offers include or exclude VAT.

Changes of the rate of VAT

35.27 The following rates of VAT have applied over recent years:

• Prior to 1 December 2008	17½%
• Between 1 December 2008 and 31 December 2009[65]	15%
• Between 1 December 2010 and 4 January 2011	17½%
• After 3 January 2011	20%

35.28 This invites the obvious question of how such changes in rate are to be dealt with between opposing parties. This is largely a matter of examining the options that are or

---

[61] See para 1.9.4.8 of *VAT Guide 1996* (Revenue Law Committee of the Law Society, December 1996).
[62] CPD, art 5.8.
[63] See, for example, *Sutton v Selwyns Travel (8 August 2008)*, Birkenhead CC, Regional Costs Judge Smedley.
[64] CPD, art 46.2.
[65] The Value Added Tax (Change of Rate) Order 2008: this Order, which came into force on 1 December 2008, reduces the rate of Value Added Tax by 142/7% to effect a reduction from 17.5% to 15% and makes a consequential change to the Value Added Tax Act 1994. This Order had effect from 1 December 2008 to 30 November 2009.

were available to the receiving party's solicitor and then deciding which was the most reasonable course of action. If VAT is charged at a higher rate than is reasonably required, the court will order the paying party to pay that rate only if the receiving party is able to justify the decision not to elect to charge at the lower rate.[66]

Changes of rate before the assessment

35.29 Whilst an oversimplification, solicitors are permitted to elect to use either the rate of VAT in force at the time of the basic tax point (ie at the time the services were completed) or the prevailing rate at the time of the actual tax point (ie the date of issue of the bill). The CPD summarises the position in this way:

> **'Form of bill of costs where VAT rate changes**
>
> '5.7 Where there is a change in the rate of VAT, suppliers of goods and services are entitled by ss. 88 (1) and 88(2) of the VAT Act 1994 in most circumstances to elect whether the new or the old rate of VAT should apply to a supply where the basic and actual tax points span a period during which there has been a change in VAT rates.
>
> 5.8 It will be assumed, unless a contrary indication is given in writing, that an election to take advantage of the provisions mentioned in paragraph 5.7 above and to charge VAT at the lower rate has been made. In any case in which an election to charge at the lower rate is not made, such a decision must be justified to the court assessing the costs.'

Legislative provisions

35.30 In so far as it is relevant, s 88 of the Value Added Tax Act 1994 provides as follows:

> **'88 Supplies spanning change of rate etc.**
>
> (1) This section applies where there is a change in the rate of VAT in force under section 2 or 29A or in the descriptions of exempt, zero-rated or reduced-rate supplies or exempt, zero-rated or reduced-rate acquisitions.
>
> (2) Where—
>
> > (a)   a supply affected by the change would, apart from section 6(4), (5), (6) or (10), be treated under section 6(2) or (3) as made wholly or partly at a time when it would not have been affected by the change; or
> >
> > (b)   a supply not so affected would apart from section 6(4), (5), (6) or (10) be treated under section 6(2) or (3) as made wholly or partly at a time when it would have been so affected,
>
> the rate at which VAT is chargeable on the supply, or any question whether it is zero-rated or exempt or a reduced-rate supply], shall if the person making it so elects be determined without regard to section 6(4), (5), (6) or (10)
>
> (3) Any power to make regulations under this Act with respect to the time when a supply is to be treated as taking place shall include power to provide for this section to apply as if the references in subsection (2) above to section 6(4), (5), (6) or (10) included references to specified provisions of the regulations. ...
>
> (6) No election may be made under this section in respect of a supply to which section 6(9) or paragraph 7 of Schedule 4 applies. ...
>
> (8) References in this section—

---

[66]   CPD, art 5.8.

(a)   to a supply being a reduced-rate supply, or

(b)   to an acquisition being a reduced-rate acquisition,

are references to a supply, or (as the case may be) an acquisition, being one on which VAT is charged at the rate in force under section 29A.'

35.31 The reference to ss 6(4), (5), (6) or (10) of the Value Added Tax Act 1994 is a reference to the following:

'6 Time of supply

(4) If, before the time applicable under subsection (2) or (3) above, the person making the supply issues a VAT invoice in respect of it or if, before the time applicable under subsection (2) (a) or (b) or (3) above, he receives a payment in respect of it, the supply shall, to the extent covered by the invoice or payment, be treated as taking place at the time the invoice is issued or the payment is received.

(5) If, within 14 days after the time applicable under subsection (2) or (3) above, the person making the supply issues a VAT invoice in respect of it, then, unless he has notified the Commissioners in writing that he elects not to avail himself of this subsection, the supply shall (to the extent that it is not treated as taking place at the time mentioned in subsection (4) above) be treated as taking place at the time the invoice is issued. .

(6) The Commissioners may, at the request of a taxable person, direct that subsection (5) above shall apply in relation to supplies made by him (or such supplies made by him as may be specified in the direction) as if for the period of 14 days there were substituted such longer period as may be specified in the direction. ...

(10) The Commissioners may, at the request of a taxable person, by direction alter the time at which supplies made by him (or such supplies made by him as may be specified in the direction) are to be treated as taking place, either—

(a)   by directing those supplies to be treated as taking place—

    (i)   at times or on dates determined by or by reference to the occurrence of some event described in the direction; or

    (ii)   at times or on dates determined by or by reference to the time when some event so described would in the ordinary course of events occur,

the resulting times or dates being in every case earlier than would otherwise apply; or

(b)   by directing that, notwithstanding subsections (5) and (6) above, those supplies shall (to the extent that they are not treated as taking place at the time mentioned in subsection (4) above) be treated as taking place—

    (i)   at the beginning of the relevant working period (as defined in his case in and for the purposes of the direction); or

    (ii)   at the end of the relevant working period (as so defined).'

35.32 Thus, there is a right of election such that the solicitor can choose whether to apply the rate at the time the work was completed (but see below about work done over a period of time), or the rate at the time invoice was raised, this being subject to a longstop of 3 months from the date of completion of the work.

35.33 This invites the obvious question of what is to happen in cases where the prevailing rate at the time the work was done was different to that which applied at the conclusion of the claim. In this regard, the Law Society have given the following guidance:[67]

---

[67]   See the Law Society's Practice Note: VAT change: Increase in the standard rate to 20 per cent – 24 November 2010.

'3. Special change of rate rules

Under the normal rules, standard rated supplies with tax points created by payments received or VAT invoices issued on or after 04 January 2011 will be liable to the 20 per cent rate. However, there are optional change of rate rules that you may wish to apply:

- Where you issue a VAT invoice or receive a payment on or after 04 January 2011 for work that was completed before 04 January 2011 you may account for VAT at 17.5 per cent.
- Where work commenced after 01 January 2010 and before 04 January 2011 but will not be completed until on or after 04 January you can apportion the supply between that liable to 17.5 per cent and that liable to 20 per cent.

You can apply the rules selectively to different clients and you can adopt them without notifying HMRC. If your client is VAT registered and able to recover the VAT charged in full, the use of the special rules will not save them any tax.'

35.34 Thus, the applicable rate is, should the solicitor so chose, that which pertained at the time the work was done. The CPD gives the following further guidance:

'Apportionment

'5.9 All bills of costs, fees and disbursements on which VAT is included must be divided into separate parts so as to show work done before, on and after the date or dates from which any change in the rate of VAT takes effect. Where, however, a lump sum charge is made for work which spans a period during which there has been a change in VAT rates, and paragraphs 5.7 and 5.8 above do not apply, reference should be made to paragraphs 8 and 9 of Appendix F of Customs' Notice 700 (or any revised edition of that notice), a copy of which should be in the possession of every registered trader. If necessary, the lump sum should be apportioned. The totals of profit costs and disbursements in each part must be carried separately to the summary.

5.10 Should there be a change in the rate between the conclusion of a detailed assessment and the issue of the final costs certificate, any interested party may apply for the detailed assessment to be varied so as to take account of any increase or reduction in the amount of tax payable. Once the final costs certificate has been issued, no variation under this paragraph will be permitted.'

Disbursements

35.35 The relevant date in respect of disbursement will be the date on which the invoice is issued, regardless of when the disbursement was incurred.[68]

Counsel

35.36 As to counsel's fees, the Law Society has given the following advice:[69]

'Normally, the tax point for Counsel's services will be determined by payment and not delivery of a fee note. On payment, Counsel's clerk will add the VAT number of Counsel and other particulars required under Regulation 13 of the VAT Regulations 1995 to constitute a document as a VAT invoice so that the receipted fee note is a VAT invoice.

---

[68] See the Law Society's Practice Note: VAT change: Reversion of the standard rate to 17.5 per cent – 15 December 2009 at para 3.5.

[69] See the Law Society's Practice Note: VAT change: Reversion of the standard rate to 17.5 per cent – 15 December 2009 at para 3.6.

Fees received on or after 01 January 2010 will be liable to VAT at 17.5 per cent. However, if you pay fees after 01 January for cases completed before that, these can still be subject to VAT at 15 per cent. Similarly, if you pay a fee after 01 January 2010 which covers services partly performed while the 15 per cent VAT rate applied, these the fees may be apportioned so that the rate of 15 per cent applies to those fees accrued before 01 January 2010. You should clarify the VAT treatment of the fees with Counsel's clerk before payment.'

The Bar Council's advice is similar:[70]

'17. In general, barristers can choose to charge and account for VAT at either the rate in force when the work was done or the rate in force when the fee is received. Assuming barristers will wish to charge the lowest rate (and ignoring prepayments and flat-rate scheme), this means:

(a)   Work before 1st December 2008 can be charged with VAT at 17.5%;
(b)   Work between 1st December 2008 and 1st January 2010 can be charged with VAT at 15%.
(c)   Work done on or after 1st January 2010 and 3rd January 2011 can be charged with VAT at 17.5%.
(d)   Work done on or after 4th January 2011 must be charged at 20%.
(e)   Where work on a single matter spans a change in rate, the fee can be apportioned.'

Changes of rate after the assessment

35.37 Should there be a change in the rate between the conclusion of a detailed assessment and the issue of the final costs certificate, any interested party may apply for the detailed assessment to be varied so as to take account of any increase or reduction in the amount of tax payable. Once the final costs certificate has been issued, no variation under this paragraph will be permitted.[71]

WORDING OF RELEVANT PROVISIONS

35.38 The wording of section 5 of the CPD is as follows:

'**5.1** This section deals with claims for value added tax (VAT) which are made in respect of costs being dealt with by way of summary assessment or detailed assessment.

VAT Registration Number

5.2 The number allocated by HM Revenue and Customs to every person registered under the Value Added Tax Act 1983 (except a Government Department) must appear in a prominent place at the head of every statement, bill of costs, fee sheet, account or voucher on which VAT is being included as part of a claim for costs.

Entitlement to VAT on Costs

5.3 VAT should not be included in a claim for costs if the receiving party is able to recover the VAT as input tax. Where the receiving party is able to obtain credit from HM Revenue and Customs for a proportion of the VAT as input tax, only that proportion which is not eligible for credit should be included in the claim for costs.

---

[70]   Standard Rate VAT Increase, Bar Council Guide, 4 January 2011.
[71]   CPD, art 5.10.

5.4 The receiving party has responsibility for ensuring that VAT is claimed only when the receiving party is unable to recover the VAT or a proportion thereof as input tax.

5.5 Where there is a dispute as to whether VAT is properly claimed the receiving party must provide a certificate signed by the solicitors or the auditors of the receiving party substantially in the form illustrated in Precedent F in the Schedule of Costs Precedents annexed to this Practice Direction. Where the receiving party is a litigant in person who is claiming VAT, reference should be made by him to HM Revenue and Customs and wherever possible a Statement to similar effect produced at the hearing at which the costs are assessed.

5.6 Where there is a dispute as to whether any service in respect of which a charge is proposed to be made in the bill is zero rated or exempt, reference should be made to HM Revenue and Customs and wherever possible the view of HM Revenue and Customs obtained and made known at the hearing at which the costs are assessed. Such application should be made by the receiving party. In the case of a bill from a solicitor to his own client, such application should be made by the client.

Form of bill of costs where VAT rate changes

5.7 Where there is a change in the rate of VAT, suppliers of goods and services are entitled by ss 88(1) and 88(2) of the VAT Act 1994 in most circumstances to elect whether the new or the old rate of VAT should apply to a supply where the basic and actual tax points span a period during which there has been a change in VAT rates.

5.8 It will be assumed, unless a contrary indication is given in writing, that an election to take advantage of the provisions mentioned in paragraph 5.7 above and to charge VAT at the lower rate has been made. In any case in which an election to charge at the lower rate is not made, such a decision must be justified to the court assessing the costs.

Apportionment

5.9 All bills of costs, fees and disbursements on which VAT is included must be divided into separate parts so as to show work done before, on and after the date or dates from which any change in the rate of VAT takes effect. Where, however, a lump sum charge is made for work which spans a period during which there has been a change in VAT rates, and paragraphs 5.7 and 5.8 above do not apply, reference should be made to paragraphs 8 and 9 of Appendix F of Customs' Notice 700 (or any revised edition of that notice), a copy of which should be in the possession of every registered trader. If necessary, the lump sum should be apportioned. The totals of profit costs and disbursements in each part must be carried separately to the summary.

5.10 Should there be a change in the rate between the conclusion of a detailed assessment and the issue of the final costs certificate, any interested party may apply for the detailed assessment to be varied so as to take account of any increase or reduction in the amount of tax payable. Once the final costs certificate has been issued, no variation under this paragraph will be permitted.

Disbursements

5.11 Petty (or general) disbursements such as postage, fares etc which are normally treated as part of a solicitor's overheads and included in his profit costs should be charged with VAT even though they bear no tax when the solicitor incurs them. The cost of travel by public transport on a specific journey for a particular client where it forms part of the service rendered by a solicitor to his client and is charged in his bill of costs, attracts VAT.

5.12 Reference is made to the criteria set out in the VAT Guide (Customs and Excise Notice 700 – 1 August 1991 edition paragraph 83, or any revised edition of that Notice), as to expenses which are not subject to VAT. Charges for the cost of travel by public transport, postage, telephone calls and telegraphic transfers where these form part of the service rendered by the solicitor to his client are examples of charges which do not satisfy these criteria and are thus liable to VAT at the standard rate.

Legal Aid/LSC Funding

5.13

    (1)   VAT will be payable in respect of every supply made pursuant to a legal aid/LSC certificate where—

        (a)   the person making the supply is a taxable person; and

        (b)   the assisted person/LSC funded client—

            (i)   belongs in the United Kingdom or another member state of the European Union; and

            (ii)   is a private individual or receives the supply for non-business purposes.

    (2)   Where the assisted person/LSC funded client belongs outside the European Union, VAT is generally not payable unless the supply relates to land in the United Kingdom.

    (3)   For the purpose of sub-paragraphs (1) and (2), the place where a person belongs is determined by section 9 of the Value Added Tax Act 1994.

    (4)   Where the assisted person/LSC funded client is registered for VAT and the legal services paid for by the LSC are in connection with that person's business, the VAT on those services will be payable by the LSC only.

5.14 Any summary of costs payable by the LSC must be drawn so as to show the total VAT on Counsel's fees as a separate item from the VAT on other disbursements and the VAT on profit costs.

Tax invoice

5.15 A bill of costs filed for detailed assessment is always retained by the Court. Accordingly if a solicitor waives his solicitor and client costs and accepts the costs certified by the court as payable by the unsuccessful party in settlement, it will be necessary for a short statement as to the amount of the certified costs and the VAT thereon to be prepared for use as the tax invoice.

Vouchers

5.16 Where receipted accounts for disbursements made by the solicitor or his client are retained as tax invoices a photostat copy of any such receipted account may be produced and will be accepted as sufficient evidence of payment when disbursements are vouched.

Certificates

5.17 In a costs certificate payable by the LSC, the VAT on solicitor's costs, Counsel's fees and disbursements will be shown separately.

Litigants acting in person

5.18 Where a litigant acts in litigation on his own behalf he is not treated for the purposes of VAT as having supplied services and therefore no VAT is chargeable in respect of work done by that litigant (even where, for example, that litigant is a solicitor or other legal representative).

5.19 Consequently in the circumstances described in the preceding paragraph, a bill of costs presented for agreement or assessment should not claim any VAT which will not be allowed on assessment.

Government Departments

5.20 On an assessment between parties, where costs are being paid to a Government Department in respect of services rendered by its legal staff, VAT should not be added.

Payment pursuant to an order under section 194(3) of the Legal Services Act 2007

5.21 Where an order is made under section 194(3) of the Legal Services Act 2007 any bill presented for agreement or assessment pursuant to that order must not include a claim for VAT.'

Chapter 36

INTEREST BETWEEN OPPOSING PARTIES

36.1 An award of interest will involve answering a number of separate questions; in this chapter those question are described as being layers of discretion. They are:

- *Layer one (jurisdiction and principle)*: whether the power to make an award of interest exists and whether that power should be exercised;
- *Layer two (period)*: what date interest should start to run and whether there is a date (other than the date of payment) on which it should stop running;
- *Layer three (rates)*: what rate of interest is payable and which method of calculation should be used to apply that rate; and
- *Layer four (adjustments and discounts)*: whether a discount or other adjustment should be applied, and if so, what that discount or adjustment should be.

36.2 Under the common law and prior to the enactment of the Judgments Act 1838, interest was, in general, irrecoverable on costs payable between opposing parties.[1] With limited exceptions (see **36.75–36.76**), the court has no power to award interest on costs beyond those which are conferred by statute.[2] The exceptions will arise only infrequently. This means that the layers of discretion are largely a matter of interpreting and then applying legislation. At the time of writing there was uncertainty about the effect of some of that legislation[3] so the reader must carry out his own research.

36.3 There is no wholly satisfactory system of taxonomy for interest. This book distinguishes between 'judgment debt interest' (ie interest which accrues on an unsatisfied judgment debt) and 'pre-judgment interest' (ie interest which accrues before the award of costs is made). This classification combines a jurisdictional category (judgment debt interest) with a descriptive category (pre-judgment interest); this lacks mutual exclusivity, but it is a pragmatic way of classifying interest, and it is used in this book because it lends itself to solving real-life problems.

JUDGMENT DEBT INTEREST

36.4 When judges and lawyers talk of 'interest on costs', they are usually referring to judgment debt interest: this is by far the most common form of interest awarded on costs.

36.5 Judgment debt interest is interest on undischarged judgment debt; it therefore tends to relate only to post-judgment interest (ie to interest which has accrued after

---

[1] *Nykredit Mortgage Bank plc v Edward Erdman Group Ltd (No 2)* [1997] 1 WLR 1627 at 1635.

[2] Ibid; see also *London, Chatham and Dover Railway Co v South Eastern Railway Co* [1893] AC 429.

[3] The case of *Simcoe v Jacuzzi UK Group Plc* [2012] EWCA Civ 137 had been decided in the Court of Appeal; the defendant sought to bring a further appeal the Supreme Court.

judgment has been given). This is not always the case, however. In particular, powers originally created for the purposes of allowing the court to make an award of post-judgment interest are now understood to have a wider role.

36.6   Each of the layers of discretion mentioned at **36.1** is considered in turn.

Layer one: jurisdiction and principle

36.7   An order for payment of costs ranks as a judgment.[4] It is for this reason that judgment debt interest applies to orders that costs be paid.[5] Lord Neuberger MR has confirmed that the starting point is that interest is payable from the date on which a party becomes entitled to costs.[6]

36.8   The relevant legislation differs from court to court; in particular, there is a need to draw a distinction between the High Court and the county court.

Judgment debt interest in the High Court

36.9   Judgment debt interest in the High Court carry is governed by s 17 of the Judgments Act 1838 (as amended):

'**17   Judgment debts to carry interest**

(1)   ... Every judgment debt shall carry interest at the rate of [8 per cent per annum] from such time as shall be prescribed by rules of court ... until the same shall be satisfied, and such interest may be levied under a writ of execution on such judgment.

(2)   Rules of court may provide for the court to disallow all or part of any interest otherwise payable under subsection (1).'

The starting point is that judgment debt interest in the High Court starts run from the date on which a party becomes entitled to costs (**36.21** *et seq*).

Judgment debt interest in the county court

36.10   The equivalent legislation in the county court is s 74 of the County Courts Act 1984 (as amended):

'**74   Interest on judgment debts etc**

(1)   The Lord Chancellor may by order made with the concurrence of the Treasury provide that any sums to which this subsection applies shall carry interest at such rate and between such times as may be prescribed by the order.

(2)   The sums to which subsection (1) applies are—

    (a)   sums payable under judgments or orders given or made in a county court, including sums payable by instalments; and

---

4   *Nykredit Mortgage Bank plc v Edward Erdman Group Ltd (No 2)* [1997] 1 WLR 1627 at 1635.
5   Likewise, it is for this reason that an agreement to pay costs which is contained within the schedule of a Tomlin order will not bear interest; see, by analogy, *Horizon Technologies International v Lucky Wealth Consultants Ltd* [1992] 1 WLR 24.
6   *Simcoe v Jacuzzi UK Group Plc* [2012] EWCA Civ 137 at [35]–[48].

(b)   sums which by virtue of any enactment are, if the county court so orders, recoverable as if payable under an order of that court, and in respect of which the county court has so ordered.

(3)   The payment of interest due under subsection (1) shall be enforceable as a sum payable under the judgment or order.

(4)   The power conferred by subsection (1) includes power—

(a)   to specify the descriptions of judgment or order in respect of which interest shall be payable;

(b)   to provide that interest shall be payable only on sums exceeding a specified amount;

(c)   to make provision for the manner in which and the periods by reference to which the interest is to be calculated and paid;

(d)   to provide that any enactment shall or shall not apply in relation to interest payable under subsection (1) or shall apply to it with such modifications as may be specified in the order; and

(e)   to make such incidental or supplementary provisions as the Lord Chancellor considers appropriate.

(5)   Without prejudice to the generality of subsection (4), an order under subsection (1) may provide that the rate of interest shall be the rate specified in section 17 of the Judgments Act 1838 as that enactment has effect from time to time.

(5A)   The power conferred by subsection (1) includes power to make provision enabling a county court to order that the rate of interest applicable to a sum expressed in a currency other than sterling shall be such rate as the court thinks fit (instead of the rate otherwise applicable).

(6)   The power to make an order under subsection (1) shall be exercisable by statutory instrument subject to annulment in pursuance of a resolution of either House of Parliament.'

36.11   The order to which this section refers is the County Courts (Interest on Judgment Debts) Order 1991.[7] The combined effect of that order and the County Courts Act 1984 is that the rate of interest will be the same as that specified in s 17 of the Judgments Act 1838.[8] There are, however, three ways in which the jurisdiction in the county court differs from that in the High Court.

CPR is ultra vires

36.12   Lord Neuberger MR has explained that art 2(2) of the County Courts (Interest on Judgment Debts) Order provides that interest runs from the date of the costs order, and that the CPR, r 40.8 is *ultra vires* in so far as any contrary position is concerned.[9] This means that the county court lacks the power to order that interest runs from any other date.[10] Whilst the contrary is arguable, the same probably applies to other provisions in the CPR concerning interest in the county court; this would almost certainly include CPR, r 44.3(6)(g), but it is possible that it would also include those provisions in CPR Part 47 concerning delay[11] and possibly even those provision in

---

[7]   SI 1991/1184 (as amended).

[8]   See art 5 of the County Court (Interest on Judgment Debts) Order 1991.

[9]   *Simcoe v Jacuzzi UK Group Plc* [2012] EWCA Civ 137 at [23]–[31].

[10]   The reason for this is that the only delegated legislation that can modify the aforesaid order is that which is made with the concurrence or the Treasury (see s 74(1) of the County Courts Act 1984), and the CPR was not made in that way: see *Simcoe v Jacuzzi UK Group Plc* [2012] EWCA Civ 137 at [23]–[31].

[11]   See **21.208–21.209** and **12.50**; the counter argument in this regard is that those provision relate to the disallowance of interest rather than the date on which interest starts to run.

CPR Part 36 concerning enhanced interest.[12] This is a developing area of the law, and the reader ought to carry out his own up-to-date legal research into this point.

No interest on small sums in county court

36.13 Interest in the county court is generally not payable on sums of money of less than £5,000. Article 2(1) of the County Courts (Interest on Judgment Debts) Order 1991 provides that interest will be payable only in respect of a 'relevant judgment'. Article 1(2) of that Order defines a relevant judgment in the following way:

> '"[R]elevant judgment" means a judgment or order of a county court for the payment of a sum of money (a) of not less than £5,000 or (b) in respect of a debt which is a qualifying debt for the purposes of the Late Payment of Commercial Debts (Interest) Act 1998 and, in relation to a judgment debt, means the judgment or order which gives rise to the judgment debt.'

36.14 The measure of the sums of money involved is the aggregate of the costs and the damages; thus, if a claimant recovers £3,000 in damages and £3,000 in costs, he will be entitled to judgment debt interest on the costs notwithstanding the fact that individually both the damages and the costs are below £5,000.[13]

36.15 This restriction on the recovery of interest will not apply to judgments below £5,000 where the judgment is either due to or from the Crown.[14]

Suspension of interest during enforcement proceedings

36.16 In the county court interest will be suspended during any period when enforcement proceedings are brought, but only if those proceedings are successful. Article 4(1) of the County Courts (Interest on Judgment Debts) Order 1991 provides:

> 'Where a judgment creditor takes proceedings in a county court to enforce payment under a relevant judgment, the judgment debt shall cease to carry interest thereafter, except where those proceedings fail to produce any payment from the debtor in which case interest shall accrue as if those proceedings had never been taken.'

This, presumably, is to avoid the possibility of enforcement proceedings being brought in respect of a moving target.

36.17 In a similar vein, where an administration order or an attachment of earnings order is made, interest shall not accrue during the time the order is in force.[15]

Layer two: the date upon which interest begins to run

36.18 CPR, r 40.8 (which is a general provision rather than a provision relating solely to costs) provides:

> '(1) Where interest is payable on a judgment pursuant to section 17 of the Judgments Act 1838 or section 74 of the County Courts Act 1984, the interest shall begin to run from the date that judgment is given unless—
>
> > (a)   a rule in another Part or a practice direction makes different provision; or

---

[12]   See **36.51** *et seq.*
[13]   *Twigg Farnell v Wildblood* (1998) PNLR 211.
[14]   See Crown Proceedings Act 1947, s 24.
[15]   See County Courts (Interest on Judgment Debts) Order 1991, art 4(3).

(b)   the court orders otherwise.

(2)   The court may order that interest shall begin to run from a date before the date that judgment is given.'

Lord Neuberger MR has found that CPR, r 40.8 is *ultra vires* in the county court; as such, the matters set out between **36.20** and **36.26** do not apply in the county court.[16] It would, however, be easy for the Treasury to take certain steps that would make the rule valid,[17] and as such, the reader must carry out his own research on this point.

36.19   CPR, r 44.3(6)(g) makes a similar provision which is specifically in respect of costs:

'The orders which the court may make under this rule include an order that a party must pay—

...

(g)   interest on costs from or until a certain date, including a date before judgment.'

Lord Neuberger MR has confirmed that the starting point is that interest is payable from the date on which a party becomes entitled to costs.[18] In the county court, this is only order that the court can make (see **36.12**). In the High Court the court has the vires to order that interest should run from an earlier date or, increasingly commonly, a later date.

Jurisdiction in the High Court

36.20   The power to make an award of interest running from a date before the date of judgment derives from an amendment made in 1998 to s 17 of the Judgments Act 1838.[19] Prior to that amendment, that power did not exist. Where the court makes an award of interest running from before the date of judgment, it is usually under this provision (see **36.35–36.40**).

The exercise of discretion in the High Court

36.21   Christopher Clarke J has explained there is no requirement that the case be 'exceptional' before the court could make such an order.[20] Lord Neuberger MR added the following points:[21]

'We were referred to *Fattal v Walbrook Trustees (Jersey) Ltd* [2009] EWHC 1674 (Ch), [2009] 4 Costs LR 591, paras 25-30, in which Christopher Clarke J held, in summary terms, that the effect of CPR 40.8 was that (a) the general rule is that interest on costs runs from the incipitur date, (b) a departure from that general rule is justified if it is "what justice requires"; (c) the notion that a departure can only be justified in "exceptional" cases is an unhelpful guide; (d) the primary purpose of an award of interest is "to compensate the recipient for [having] been precluded from obtaining a return on [his] money"; (e) "[s]ince the payment of solicitors' costs involves the payment of money which could otherwise have been profitably employed, the overwhelming likelihood is that justice requires some recompense in the form of interest".

---

16   *Simcoe v Jacuzzi UK Group Plc* [2012] EWCA Civ 137 at [23]–[31].
17   *Simcoe v Jacuzzi UK Group Plc* [2012] EWCA Civ 137 at [31].
18   *Simcoe v Jacuzzi UK Group Plc* [2012] EWCA Civ 137 at [35]–[48].
19   The Civil Procedure (Modification of Enactments) Order 1998 (SI 1998/2940), art 3.
20   *Fattal v Walbrook Trustees (Jersey) Ltd* [2009] EWHC 1674 (Ch) at [28].
21   *Simcoe v Jacuzzi UK Group Plc* [2012] EWCA Civ 137 at [47]–[48].

I agree with all those observations, but would add two precautionary comments on his observations. First, I would discourage too detailed an approach into the facts of the particular case in hand for the purpose of determining the date from which interest should run. As Lord Ackner's speech in *Hunt* [1990] 1 AC 398 implies, when making such a determination, the court should take a broad view of the position. Prolonged argument, let alone detailed evidence, on the issue must be avoided. There will often be no perfect date, and the decision inevitably will, indeed should, be broad brush. Further, if interest was to run from different dates on different components of the costs, it would, in many cases, lead to arguments which would do the legal system no credit. The second observation is that I would not necessarily agree with the suggestion, at [2009] 4 Costs LR 591, para 30, that it may be inappropriate to award interest on costs where the case is being funded by a third party entirely voluntarily or otherwise free of any cost. I would have thought that, following the logic of reason (v) in para 11 above (and see para 46 above), if interest on costs is payable from the *incipitur* date, the party to whom it is paid may have to account for it to the third party, and, if that is correct, there would seem to me to be a powerful argument for saying that the third party should get interest on costs in the normal way . . .'

In practice it tends to be long-running cases and cases in which the costs burden is noticeably heavy in which orders for interest predating the date of the costs order are made. An example is group litigation in which Akenhead J awarded interest for a period when the prevailing base rate was conspicuously low; he found that the interests of justice would best be met by making an order that interest did not begin to run until 6 months after the costs order had been made.[22] David Steel J came to a very similar conclusion in another group litigation case.[23] Thus, there is a certain degree of flexibility. It should be noted, however, that not all judges would approve of that approach (see **36.28**).

The history of the jurisdiction in the High Court

36.22 In ancient times, practice differed between common law[24] and the courts of chancery.[25] In particular, the rule relating to common law cases (which is often referred to as the '*incipitur* rule') was that interest ran from the date on which judgment was pronounced,[26] hence '*incipitur*' (meaning 'it begins'). In chancery a different rule applied, that being the '*allocatur* rule' under which interest ran from the date of the costs certificate (hence '*allocatur*', meaning 'it is allowed').[27] Lord Ackner explained the difference in this way:[28]

'In the first place, this deeming of the ascertainment of quantum, which in fact may have taken place months or years later, to have occurred on the date of judgment is the origin of the Latin name of the Common Law Rule, the *incipitur* rule. This Latin word has a connotation of reference back to the beginning or origin of the entitlement. The alternative Chancery Rule was known as the *allocatur* rule, which has connotations of the date on which a precise quantification or allocation of money to the previously unquantified sum occurs.'

---

22   *Multiple Claimants v Corby District Council (Corby Group Litigation)* [2009] EWHC 2109 (TCC) at [43].
23   *Colour Quest Ltd v Total Downstream UK plc* [2009] EWHC 823 (Comm).
24   Those being the Court of the Queen's Bench and the Court of Common Pleas.
25   Those being the Court of Chancery and the Court of Exchequer.
26   See *Fisher v Dudding* 9 Dowl. 872 at 874, per Tindal CJ 'the legal meaning of those words must be taken to be the time of signing judgment, or making the entry of the incipitur in the Master's book'; also *Newton v Grand Junction Railway Co* (1846) 16 M & W 139.
27   See the practice referred to in *Boswell v Coaks* (1888) 57 LJ Ch 101 at 105, in which Lindley LJ referred to the Chancery Courts having issued forms of writ of *fi fa* providing for interest to run from the date of the Taxing Master's Certificate.
28   *Thomas v Bunn* [1991] 1 AC 362 at 376.

The Judicature Acts of 1873[29] and 1875[30] fused the hitherto split system of courts; the object of those Acts was to provide for enforcement of the same rule of law in cases where the common law and chancery courts recognised different rules. The then Rules of Court were drafted in such a way as to lead to uncertainty as to the correct law,[31] but after those rules were amended, the general consensus was that the incipitur rule was to be preferred.[32]

36.23 Thus, Chitty J noted that by the late nineteenth century it had become settled practice generally to apply the *incipitur* rule.[33] The Rules of the Supreme Court were revised in 1965, however, and in particular, a footnote that had been pivotal to the interpretation that *incipitur* rule was to be preferred ceased to exist. Lord Denning MR said that 'a little common sense' was required and that the *allocatur* rule should apply.[34] Stephenson LJ agreed, noting that he was 'free to choose the better rule'.[35]

36.24 In 1990 the House of Lords came to the opposite conclusion[36]. This was for the following reasons:

> 'It is the unsuccessful party to the litigation who, *ex hypothesi*, has caused the costs unnecessarily to be incurred. Hence the order made against him. Since interest is not awarded on costs incurred and paid by the successful party before judgment, why should he suffer the added loss of interest on costs incurred and paid after judgment but before the taxing master gives his certificate? Since … payments of costs are likely nowadays to be made to lawyers prior to taxation, then the application of the *allocatur* rule would generally speaking do greater injustice than the operation of the *incipitur* rule. Moreover, the *incipitur* rule provides a further necessary stimulus for payments to be made on account of costs and disbursements prior to taxation, for costs to be more readily agreed, and for taxation, when necessary, to be expedited, all of which are desirable developments. Barristers, solicitors and expert witnesses should not be expected to finance their clients' litigation until it is completed and the taxing master's certificate obtained.'

At the time of writing, the *incipitur* rule prevailed[37] (but see **36.21**). The position relating to costs should be contrasted with the situation in respect of interest on damages: where interest is payable on damages, the *allocatur* rule is to be preferred.[38] The relevance of this is that it is rarely appropriate to seek guidance from authorities on damages as the two jurisdictions are different.

---

[29] Ie the Supreme Court of Judicature Act 1873 36 & 37 Vict c 66.

[30] Ie the Supreme Court of Judicature Act 1875 38 and 39 Vict c 77.

[31] This arose out of the fact that the relevant provision appeared to be contained in something as insubstantial as a footnote to a precedent: see *Schroder v Clough* (1877) 35 LT 850. The fact that that that footnote was amended without explanation did not assist.

[32] See *Pyman & Co v Burt, Boulton & another* [1884] WN 100, per Field J; this was followed in the High Court in *Landowners' West of England and South Wales Land Drainage and Inclosure Co v Ashford* [1884] 33 WR 41 and, subsequently, in the Court of Appeal in *Boswell v Coaks* (1888) 57 LJ Ch 101 at 105.

[33] *In re London Wharfing Company* (1885) 54 LJ Ch 1137 at 1138; contrary findings were made, however: see, for example, *Schroeder v Cleugh* (1877) 46 LJQB 365.

[34] *K v K (Divorce Costs: Interest)* (1977) Fam 39 at 48 and 49; this decision was followed in *Erven Warnink BV v J Townend & Sons (Hull) Ltd.*

[35] *K v K (Divorce Costs: Interest)* (1977) Fam 39 at 53–56.

[36] *Hunt v RM Douglas* [1990] 1 AC 398.

[37] Not only is the *incipitur* rule the default position under the CPR but, in the county court, it is also the default position by reason of other delegated legislation: see art 2(2) of the County Courts (Interest on Judgment Debts) Order 1991 (as amended).

[38] *Thomas v Bunn* [1991] 1 AC 362.

36.25 A costs order may be phrased in such a way as to disapply the *incipitur* rule in preference for the *allocatur* rule, but clear language would be required to achieve such a result; a phrase such as 'costs when taxed or agreed shall be paid' would not be sufficient to do so.[39]

36.26 There is a dearth of authority on when it would be appropriate for the court to deprive a party of interest as a matter of entitlement (as opposed to as a matter of adjustment as per layer four). Christopher Clarke J has explained that the ability of the High Court to depart from the *incipitur* rule (see **36.22**) was conferred in order that the court could take account of the fact that money would often be expended before any judgment. He explained that where, conversely, money had not been expended – such as where the bulk of the costs have been paid at a date long after the relevant judgment – justice may require that the date for the commencement of the interest is postponed beyond the date of that judgment.[40] This, presumably, is a factor that the court is able to take into account.

Layer three: the rate of interest

36.27 In both the High Court and the county courts,[41] post-judgment interest is set at the rate specified by order.[42] The Secretary of State has the power to vary the rate,[43] but it has remained unchanged at 8% per annum since 1 April 1993.[44]

36.28 Save where judgment is given in a currency other than pounds sterling,[45] the statutory rate of post-judgment interest may not be varied.[46] Mann J has confirmed that this applies to interest on costs.[47] It will apply even where a claimant has 'beaten' his own offer.[48] It is possible to disallow interest pursuant to CPR, rr 47.8(3) and 47.14(5), thereby achieving a result similar to a lowering of the rate, but Mann J has expressed disapproval of this, explaining that a fixed rate affords a degree of certainty and clarity, and is capable of providing an incentive for paying sooner rather than later.[49] Coulson J came to a similar conclusion, but he commented that it may be best to defer the application of the statutory rate until after the amount of costs is known;[50] this would

---

[39]   *Electricity Supply Nominees Ltd v Farrell* [1997] 2 All ER 498 at 504, per Kennedy LJ.

[40]   *Fattal v Walbrook Trustees (Jersey) Ltd* [2009] EWHC 1674 (Ch) at [26] and [27].

[41]   See the County Courts (Interest on Judgment Debts) Order 1991, art 5.

[42]   The parent provision is the Judgments Act 1838, s 17(1).

[43]   In the High Court see the Administration of Justice Act 1970, s 44 and in the county court see s 74(1) of the County Courts Act 1984.

[44]   The Judgment Debts (Rate of Interest) Order 1993 (SI 1993/564); previously, the rate had been 15% since 16 April 1985.

[45]   See the Administration of Justice Act 1970, s 44A.

[46]   *Thomas v Bunn* [1991] 1 AC 362, HL. Moreover, whilst now based on old authority, it probably remains the case that where a contract provides for payment of interest on costs at a rate higher than judgment debt rate, the court cannot award interest at that higher rate: *Economic Life Assurance Society v Usborne* [1902] AC 152.

[47]   *Schlumberger Holdings Ltd v Electromagnetic Geoservices AS* [2009] EWHC 773 (Pat); it has to be said that there are instances of the court awarding post-judgment interest at rates other than that prescribed in statute: it is likely that those are instances of the correct law not being drawn to the court's attention.

[48]   Whilst it related to the 'old' Part 36, see *McPhilemy v Times Newspapers Ltd and others (No 2)* [2001] EWCA Civ 933 at [24], per Chadwick LJ.

[49]   *Schlumberger Holdings Ltd v Electromagnetic Geoservices AS* [2009] EWHC 773 (Pat).

[50]   *London Tara Hotel Limited v Kensington Close Hotel Limited* [2011] EWHC 29 (Ch) at [34] *et seq*. This was not dissimilar to the pre-CPR practice of adjusting the period during which interest was payable so as to give rise to equitable overall amount of interest (see *Kuwait Airways Corpn v Iraqi Airways Co (No 2)* [1995] 1 All ER 790); this a practice that was limited to only a very small class of cases, however, namely, successful appeal where there was a need to change and to backdate the original costs order.

have the effect of allowing a lower rate for that period during which the paying party was ignorant of the precise figure he had to pay.

36.29 The rate applicable to pre-judgment interest is addressed at **36.45** onwards.

Layer four: discounts and adjustments

36.30 The interests of justice may require an adjustment to be made to the amount of interest payable. Christopher Clarke J has stated[51] that the most important criterion is that any award should reflect what justice requires.[52] He noted that the primary purpose of an award of interest is to compensate the recipient for the fact that he has been precluded from obtaining a return on the money in question.[53] Whilst obiter and whilst dealing with interest between solicitor and client, Wyn Williams J has explained that the fact that the paying party may, for whatever reason, also have been deprived of the use of that money would not generally be sufficient reason to justify a reduction in the interest properly payable.[54]

36.31 Interest may be disallowed as a result of delay in the detailed assessment. CPR, r 47.8(3) makes the following provisions:

'If—

(a) the paying party has not made an application in accordance with paragraph (1); and

(b) the receiving party commences the proceedings later than the period specified in rule 47.7,

the court may disallow all or part of the interest otherwise payable to the receiving party under—

(i) section 17 of the Judgments Act 1838; or

(ii) section 74 of the County Courts Act 1984,

but must not impose any other sanction except in accordance with rule 44.14 (powers in relation to misconduct).'

Thus, delay in commencing detailed assessment proceedings may result in interest being disallowed. It is possible that this provision is *ultra vires* in the county court (see **36.12**).

36.32 Likewise, CPR, r 47.14(5) makes almost identical provision concerning delay in applying for an assessment hearing. It should be noted, however, that the court is not permitted to exercise this power if the paying party has made an application for an order requiring the receiving party to commence detailed assessment proceedings (see **21.88–21.89**).Likewise, it is possible that this provision is *ultra vires* in the county court (see **36.12**).

---

[51] This was in the context of deciding the date from which interest should run.

[52] *Fattal v Walbrook Trustees (Jersey) Ltd* [2009] EWHC 1674 (Ch) at [26] cited with approval in *Lake v Hunt Kid Law Firm LLP (in administration)* [2011] EWHC 766 (QB) at [34] and [35], per Wyn Williams J.

[53] Christopher Clarke J (giving judgment in *Fattal v Walbrook Trustees (Jersey) Ltd* [2009] EWHC 1674 (Ch) at [26]) referred to *London Chatham & Dover Railway Company v South Easter Railways Company* [1893] AC 429 at 437 and *Earl of Malmsbury v Strutt & Parker* [2008] EWHC 616 (QB) at [5] and [6].

[54] *Lake v Hunt Kid Law Firm LLP (in administration)* [2011] EWHC 766 (QB) at [34] and [35].

36.33 Longmore LJ has described the disallowance of interest as being the 'the normal sanction for penalising delay;' he commented that 'the prescribed sanction of the disallowance of interest is likely to be both comparatively uncontroversial and also calculable without unnecessary dispute'.[55]

36.34 Where delay amounts to misconduct, the sanction may extend beyond the mere disallowance of interest.[56] This topic is addressed at **12.151–12.173**.

PRE-JUDGMENT INTEREST

Layer one: jurisdiction and principle

36.35 There are two, or possibly three, vires by which pre-judgment interest may be awarded. The first is that which relates to judgment debt interest; these have already been addressed (**36.4–36.34**). The second—which is rarely relevant in costs litigation—is under s 35A(1) of the Senior Courts Act 1981 (or, in the county court, under s 69(1) of the County Courts Act 1984).[57] The third is a jurisdiction that certainly exists but is not wholly clear as to its origins (see **36.38**); it is described below.[58] In addition, there are mechanisms by which interest may be recovered as debt or damages; these mechanisms are discussed at **36.45–36.70**.

36.36 The first of these three jurisdictions arises out of the court's power to allow judgment debt interest from a date that precedes the date of judgment. This topic is addressed at **36.4–36.34**, and in particular, at **36.19**.

36.37 For reasons that are relegated to the footnotes, the second of the three vires mentioned above can, for the purposes of considering interest on costs between opposing parties, be disregarded.[59] (Those provisions will, however, be relevant to the recovery of interest on a solicitor and client basis: see **27.62–27.69**.)

36.38 The third vires is, in practical terms, the most important, but it is also the most difficult to understand in terms of its jurisdictional origin. It includes the power to award pre-judgment interest under Part 36 of the CPR. Where judgment is entered against the defendant that is at least as advantageous to the claimant as the proposals contained in that claimant's Part 36 offer, the court may make an award of enhanced interest on the claimant's costs from the date on which the relevant period expired. The rate must not exceed 10% above base rate. This topic is discussed further at **36.51–36.53**; claimants' Part 36 offers in general are addressed at **13.48–13.70**. It seems likely that such an award has at its jurisdictional core the same provisions that relate to judgment debt interest (see **36.4–36.34**), but this analysis gives rise to a clear conflict between the fact that the CPR provide for a rate which is not the same as that which is allowable

---

[55] *Haji-Ioannou v Frangos* [2006] EWCA Civ 1663 at [17]–[18].
[56] CPR, r 44.14(2)(a); and see *Haji-Ioannou v Frangos* [2006] EWCA Civ 1663.
[57] Section 3 of the Law Reform (Miscellaneous Provisions) Act 1934 continues to apply to other courts of record.
[58] It has to stressed that there is no authority to confirm the existence of this third vires.
[59] Lord Nicholls has explained that the discretionary power to award interest conferred by SCA 1981, s 35A (or CCA 1984, s 69(1), as the case may be) does not specifically apply to costs because it is confined to the payment of interest on a debt or damages: *Nykredit Mortgage Bank plc v Edward Erdman Group Ltd (No 2)* [1997] 1 WLR 1627 at 1635, overruling *Kuwait Airways Corp v Iraqi Airways Co (No 2)* [1995] 1 All ER 790 overruled.

under those provisions.[60] It has been argued that pre-judgment interest is awarded under some different vires (such as under the general powers conferred by SCA 1981, s 51 or the CPR generally, or both), but – in the analogous context of pre-judgment interest payable under CPR, r 44.3(6)(g) – Lord Neuberger MR rejected that argument:[61]

> 'The defendant contends the 1997 Act represented a wholly new source of authority for making rules for the County Court, including rules with regard to the payment of interest on sums of money awarded by the court, including costs. I cannot accept that. Section 1 of the 1997 Act states that the CPR should govern the 'practice and procedure' in the English civil courts. This does not suggest that they were intended to empower those courts to have the substantive power to award interest ... My view is supported by CPR 40.8(1) itself, which states in terms that the powers which it confers derive not from the 1997 Act, but from the 1838 Act in the High Court and from the 1984 Act in the County Court.'

Thus, it seems that the third vires is a species of judgment debt interest (see **36.4–36.34**), but is not clear how this can be reconciled with the fact that the court will routinely allow a rate that is very different from the judgment debt rate.

36.39 Likewise, there is uncertainty as to the exact nature of the power to award pre-judgment interest under CPR, r 44.3(6)(g). In any event, other than in the commercial court (see **36.40**), it is a power that is not commonly exercised;[62] this is surprising given the fact that Waller LJ has had this to say of it:[63]

> 'In any event in principle there seems no reason why the Court should not do so [ie make an award of pre-judgment interest] where a party has had to put up money paying its solicitors and been out of the use of that money in the meanwhile.'

In a similar vein, Laddie J said this:[64]

> 'The purpose of a costs order is to compensate the winning party for the real cost of having conducted the litigation and the real cost is not measured simply by adding up mathematically the bills that it has paid to or agreed to pay to its lawyers. A pound paid in 1980 may be the same coin that is paid in 2005, but it is not the same in value. What the award of interest on costs allows the court to do is to ensure that the receiving party is compensated properly for the real cost to it of having conducted the litigation successfully In my view, the discretion to award interest on costs is a broad one. Courts can take into account all the circumstances in coming to a conclusion as to what to do.'

36.40 Unlike the practice in other courts, such awards are not a rarity in the Commercial Court. If anything, it is the rule rather than the exception that interest is awarded on costs from the date (or dates) on which they were paid (or on which payment became due). As long ago as 2002, Langley J had this to say on the topic:[65]

---

[60]   See, for example, *McPhilemy v Times Newspapers Ltd and others (No 2)* [2001] EWCA Civ 933 at [24], where Chadwick LJ refused to allow the then provisions concerning interest payable where a claimant had beaten his own Part 36 offer to interfere with rate prescribed for judgment debt interest.

[61]   *Simcoe v Jacuzzi UK Group Plc* [2012] EWCA Civ 137 at [24].

[62]   Examples of such orders being made are *Earl of Malmesbury v Strytt & Parker (Interest on Costs)* [2008] EWHC 616 (QB), *Lloyd v Svenby* [2006] EWHC 576 (QB) and *Douglas v Hello! Limited* [2004] EWHC 63 (Ch).

[63]   *Bim Kemi AB v Blackburn Chemicals Ltd* [2003] EWCA Civ 889.

[64]   *IPC Media v Highbury Leisure Publishing Ltd* [2005] EWHC 283 (Ch) at [12] and [13].

[65]   *UK Exploration Company v British American Offshore Limited* [2002] BLR 135 at [10].

'For my part, I think it may well be appropriate, at least in substantial proceedings involving commercial interests of significant importance both in balance sheet and reputational terms, that the court should award interest on costs under the rule where substantial sums have inevitably been expended perhaps a year or more before an award of costs is made ...'

There is no requirement that exceptional circumstances must be made out before the court can make such an award. In this regard, Kitchen J said this:[66]

'[I]t seems to me that the court has a broad discretion when deciding whether to award interest on costs from a date before judgment. That discretion must be exercised in accordance with the principles set out in CPR 44.3 and the court must take into account all the circumstances of the case, including such matters as the conduct of the parties and the degree to which a party has succeeded. Further, the discretion must be exercised in accordance with the overriding objective of dealing with the case justly. I am unable to accept the submission that interest on costs should only be awarded in a case which is in some way out of the norm ...'

Akenhead J has confirmed that is open to the court to allow interest notwithstanding the fact that the costs were incurred by a successful party's insurers rather than by that party himself.[67] It does not necessarily follow that this will apply in all instances of funding by third parties: both Akenhead J[68] and Christopher Clarke J[69] have commented (obiter) that a party could be denied interest if they had been funded on a voluntary or favourable basis. Moreover, the prohibition against the recovery of costs of funding may apply. In any event, conventional wisdom is that it is within the court's discretion to set an appropriate rate, but this may not be correct (see **36.45–36.50**).

Layer two: the date upon which interest begins to run

36.41 Where pre-judgment interest is awarded pursuant to CPR, r 36.14(3)(c), it is awarded from the date of the expiry of the 'relevant period' as defined in CPR, r 36.3(c).[70] The court will not be bound to make such an order if it considers it would be unjust to do so; this means that the court is able to defer the effect of a claimant's Part 36 offer.[71] It is worth pausing here to say that it is possible that the power to make an award under CPR, r 36.14(3)(c) does not exist in the county court; this is addressed at **36.12**. The law is in a state of flux, and this is an area in respect of which the reader must conduct his own up-to-date legal research.

36.42 Where it is awarded under provisions other than CPR, r 36.14(3)(c), pre-judgment interest may be awarded from the date upon which the relevant invoices were raised between solicitor and client,[72] from the date on which invoices were actually paid,[73] or from some other date. There seems to be no judicial consensus as to whether the appropriate date is the date of accrual or the date of payment: perhaps each case is to be decided on its own facts.

---

[66]   *Nova Productions v Mazooma Games* [2006] EWHC 189 (Ch) at [16]; see also *Fattal v Walbrook Trustees (Jersey) Ltd* [2009] EWHC 1674 (Ch).

[67]   *Fosse Motor Engineers Limited v Conde Nast and National Magazine Distributors Limited* [2008] EWHC 2527 (QB) at [10].

[68]   Ibid.

[69]   *Fattal v Walbrook Trustees (Jersey) Ltd* [2009] EWHC 1674 (Ch) at [28]–[30].

[70]   This is the combined effect of CPR, rr 36.15(3)(b) and (c).

[71]   As an example of this, see *Epsom College v Pierse Contracting Southern Ltd (formerly Biseley Construction Ltd) (in liq)* [2011] EWCA Civ 1449 at [67], per Rix LJ.

[72]   See, for example, *Bim Kemi AB v Blackburn Chemicals Ltd* [2003] EWCA Civ 889.

[73]   *Douglas & Ors v Hello! Ltd & Ors* [2004] EWHC 63 (Ch).

36.43 The award may be influenced by factors other than when invoices were rendered and when they were paid. In the context of a claim funded by a conditional fee agreement,[74] Ramsay J allowed interest from the date on which the work was done rather than from some later date, this counterbalancing the fact that there would be a delay in paying the success fee.[75]

36.44 Whilst an obvious point, if pre-judgment interest is awarded, it should not be calculated in such a way as to cover the same period as an award of post-judgment interest.[76]

Layers three and four: the rate of interest and discretion generally

36.45 In so far as pre-judgment interest is concerned, the appropriate rate will depend in the circumstances in which the award is made. It is, therefore, convenient to consider layers three and four together. Not only does the court have, where appropriate, discretion as to the rate, but the court may, very occasionally, also have the ability to allow compound interest (see **36.68–36.636.12**). It should be borne in mind that it is possible that most of what follows does not apply in the county court (see **36.12**).

Pursuant to CPR, r 44.3(6)(g)

36.46 It is generally accepted that the rate that applies to pre-judgment interest awarded pursuant to CPR, r 44.3(6)(g) is a discretionary matter. It is not entirely clear that this is correct; this is because it is possible that such awards are made pursuant to s 17 of the Judgments Act 1838 (as amended) (or the corresponding county court provision), and the court's discretion in this regard is fettered (see **36.28**).

36.47 Notwithstanding this, the practice of allowing a discretionary rate has arisen, this being largely by reason of the court drawing guidance from analogous cases dealing with awards of interest on damages (see below).

36.48 Waller LJ has noted that the practice of the commercial court is to award interest at a rate which broadly represents that which the successful party would have had to pay had the money been borrowed commercially.[77] He went on to say that the practice of the commercial court is to allow a rate of 1% above base, but that that rate can be varied up or even down to meet the justice of the situation.[78] An example of a situation in which a higher rate might be appropriate is where the receiving party is a small business; in this regard Waller LJ cited with approval the following judgment of Rix LJ:[79]

'It is right that the defendants who have kept small businessmen out of money to which a court ultimately judges them to be entitled should pay a rate which properly reflects the cost

---

[74] This related to the 'old' CPR Part 36. It is arguable that that case is wrongly decided in so for as the analysis of Part 36 is concerned, but even if there had been an error, the comments about interest were still instructive.

[75] *Eiles v Southwark London Borough Council* [2006] EWHC 2014 (TCC) at [75].

[76] If authority were needed on the point, it can be found in *Douglas & Ors v Hello! Ltd & Ors* [2004] EWHC 63 (Ch).

[77] *Bim Kemi AB and Blackburn Chemicals Ltd* [2003] EWCA Civ 889 at [18]; this case mostly concerned an overpayment of costs, but it also dealt with interest payable to a receiving party.

[78] Ibid at [18(b)].

[79] *Bim Kemi AB and Blackburn Chemicals Ltd* [2003] EWCA Civ 889 at [18], quoting from *Jaura v Ahmed* [2002] EWCA Civ 210 at [26]; *Jaura* was a case concerning damages, but Waller LJ obviously thought that it was analogous on this point.

of borrowing by such a class of businessmen. The law should be prepared to recognise, as I suspect the evidence might well reveal, that the borrowing costs generally incurred by them are well removed from the conventional rate of 1% above base, (and sometimes even less) available to first class borrowers.'

36.49 Waller LJ went on to imply that evidence of actual (rather than hypothetical) expenditure would be required if a higher rate were to be sought: it would be insufficient for a receiving party merely to adduce evidence of what *might* have been charged *if* he had borrowed to fund the litigation. He had this to say (original emphasis):[80]

'The question is whether the evidence in this case demonstrates that a rate greater than 1% above base rate should be applied. Evidence of what a bank might have charged *if* money had been borrowed is not we think sufficient. It is not clear to us what takes [the receiving party] outside the norm to which the 1% above base rate presumption applies.'

36.50 In practice, awards under CPR, r 44.3(6)(g) tend to between 1% and 2% above base rate.[81] In a case in which the receiving party had been compelled to take out loans at a high rate of interest to fund the claim and where costs were payable on the indemnity basis, Sales J found that it was appropriate to allow interest at the rate that the receiving party bore.[82] On the basis of the law as it currently stands, only simple interest may be awarded.

Under Part 36 of the CPR

36.51 Where judgment is entered against the defendant that is at least as advantageous to the claimant as the proposals contained in that claimant's Part 36 offer, the court may, from the date on which the relevant period expired, make an award of 'enhanced interest' (as it is often called) on the claimant's costs; awards of interest under CPR, r 36.14(3)(c) tend to be higher than when made under r 44.3(6)(g), which is why the term 'enhanced' is used. Coulson J has explained that there is no corresponding express power to award enhanced interest to a defendant has beaten his own offer.[83] That said, the enhancement is limited such that the rate must not exceed 10% above base rate;[84] where the court awards enhanced interest and also awards interest on the same sum and for the same period under any other power, the total rate of interest may not exceed 10% above base rate.[85]

36.52 The court will make such an award unless it considers it to be unjust to do so.[86] In considering whether it would be unjust to make such an order, the court will take into account all the circumstances of the case, including: the terms of any Part 36 offer; the stage in the proceedings when any Part 36 offer was made (in particular how long before the trial started the offer was made); the information available to the parties at the time when the Part 36 offer was made; and the conduct of the parties with regard to the giving or refusing to give information for the purposes of enabling the offer to be made

---

[80] Ibid.
[81] See, for example, *Douglas & Ors v Hello! Ltd & Ors* [2004] EWHC 63 (Ch).
[82] *F&C Alternative Investments (Holdings) Ltd v Barthelemy* [2011] EWHC 2807 (Ch) at [77] *et seq.*
[83] *J Murphy & Sons Ltd v Johnson Precast Ltd (No 2) (Costs)* [2008] EWHC 3104 (TCC) at [38]–[40], citing (in relation to the 'old' Part 36) *Excelsior Commercial Industrial Holdings Ltd v Salisbury Hammer Aspden and Johnston* [2002] EWCA Civ 879 at [18], per Lord Woolf.
[84] See CPR, rr 36.14(3)(a) and (3)(c).
[85] See CPR, r 36.14(5).
[86] CPR, r 36.14(3).

or evaluated.[87] Whilst speaking in the context of a case in which the sums claimed were so high as to cause him to refer to the funding arrangements as 'grotesque', Jackson LJ implied that the court is able to look at the total effect of the interest and to disallow or reduce the same if that total would give rise to an unjust burden falling upon the paying party.[88]

36.53 The rationale for making an award of enhanced interest was explained by Chadwick LJ:[89]

'The purpose for which the power to order interest on costs under that paragraph is conferred is, I think, plain. It is to redress, in a case to which CPR 36.21 applies, the element of perceived unfairness which arises from the general rule that interest is not allowed on costs paid before judgment – see *Hunt v R M Douglas (Roofing) Ltd* [1990] 1 AC 398, 415F. So, in the ordinary case, the successful claimant who has made payments to his own solicitor on account of costs in advance of the trial will be out of pocket even if he obtains, at the trial, an order for costs on an indemnity basis. He will get interest on his costs from the date of the order (whether he has actually paid them or not); but he will get nothing to compensate him for the cost of money (or the loss of the use of money) which he has had to bear before trial in relation to payments which he has made on account of costs. An order under paragraph (3)(b) of CPR 36.21 enables the court to achieve a fairer result in that respect.'

Chadwick LJ went on to say that he would be inclined to make an award of interest at a rate which reflects (albeit generously) the cost of money (which he thought could be achieved by making an award of 4% above base rate); he was inclined to order that interest runs from the date upon which the work was done or liability for disbursements was incurred. The court lacks the power to award any rate other than the judgment debt rate on costs following judgment.[90] Otherwise, a rate of about 4–5% above base rate seems not to be an unusual rate.[91]

Contract, tort and damages

36.54 The issue of costs as damages is addressed at **5.27** *et seq.* Where costs (ie expenses incurred in paying lawyers, experts, etc) are recoverable as special damages (or as debt), interest may be recoverable. The same may be true of costs payable under contract.

36.55 It is not always clear whether legal fees are recoverable as costs or as damages (**5.25.2–5.25.38**). Whether such monies are best regarded as being costs or damages will depend on the circumstances. Usually an award of interest on costs as damages will, in reality, be an award of damages which (for convenience) is to be assessed as if it were an award of costs (see **5.38**).

36.56 The relevance of this seemingly arcane point is that it may affect the basis upon which interest is calculated. Interest on costs *as* damages differs from the other types of

---

[87] CPR, r 36.14(4).

[88] *Pankhurst v (1) White and (2) Motor Insurers Bureau* [2010] EWCA Civ 1445 at [54].

[89] *McPhilemy v Times Newspapers (No 4)* [2001] EWCA Civ 933 at [23].

[90] *McPhilemy v Times Newspapers (No 4)* [2001] EWCA Civ 933 at [24].

[91] See, for example, *McPhilemy v Times Newspapers (No 4)* [2001] EWCA Civ 933 at [23]; see also *Linklaters Business Services v Sir Robert Mcalpine Limited et al* [2010] EWHC 3123 (TCC) at [30] in which Akenhead J allowed 5% above base rate almost as a matter of course. See also *Crema v Cenkos Securities plc* [2010] EWCA Civ 10 at [11], per Aikens LJ.

interest in that interest may be recoverable *as* damages, as opposed to *on* damages: this means that—in theory—compound interest may by payable. Three situations are worth examining: where costs are payable under contract, where costs are payable as damages arising out of breach of contract, and were costs are payable as damages arising out of some tortious act or omission.

Costs payable under contract

36.57 It will occasionally be the case that a party will be contractually liable to another party for interest on costs.[92] The amounts of interest payable will depend on the terms of the contract. Where the costs themselves are payable under a contract, the court will usually assess the costs (including any applicable interest) in accordance with the terms of that contract (see **37.2**).[93] Such interest may be compound if the contract so provides.

36.58 Section 69(4) of the County Courts Act 1984 reads:

> 'Interest in respect of a debt shall not be awarded under this section for a period during which, for whatever reason, interest on the debt already runs.'

If, therefore, there is a contractual agreement to pay interest, then the statutory provisions will yield to the contractual provisions.

Breach of contract

36.59 Broadly speaking, special damages arising out of breach of contract may be recovered under two heads:[94] the first is where losses 'may fairly and reasonably be considered arising naturally, ie according to the usual course of things', and the second is where the damages 'may reasonably be supposed to have been in the contemplation of both parties at the time they made the contract'. The second of these heads will almost never apply to costs. Until recently, the House of Lords had found that the first head will not extend to include recovery of interest as damages,[95] but this has recently changed (see **36.68**). Where it does apply, the first head is capable of resulting in an award of compound interest.

36.60 Although interest cannot be recoverable *as* damages, it can, of course, be recovered *on* damages pursuant to SCA 1981, s 35A(1) (or the county court equivalent). The practical effect of the distinction between the two is that interest recoverable on special damages is limited to simple interest, whereas interest recoverable as special damages can (theoretically) be compound.

Tort

36.61 Other than the recovery of costs of mitigation in professional negligence claims and recovery of costs incurred in other jurisdictions, recovery of costs as special damages is a rarity. The recovery of interest on such costs will be governed by the law relating to damages; this is beyond the scope of this book. In practice, however, the method of calculation of interest usually applies to the special damages as a whole (or

---

[92] Such as litigation between a mortgagor and a mortgagee, and under some government run compensation schemes.

[93] *Gomba Holdings Ltd v Minories Finance Ltd* [1993] Ch 171.

[94] See *Hadley v Baxendale* (1854) 9 Exch 341, 156 ER 145.

[95] *London, Chatham and Dover Railway Co v South Eastern Railway Co* [1893] AC 429.

parts of the special damages as a whole) rather than to particular heads of damages. As such, where costs are claimed as special damages, they will – in so far as interest is concerned – usually be subsumed within the special damages generally, and as such, no specific issues will arise.

The Late Payment of Commercial Debts (Interest) Act 1998

36.62 The Late Payment of Commercial Debts (Interest) Act 1998[96] is capable of implying a term into an applicable contract that it will carry simple interest. Broadly speaking, the 1998 Act will apply when payment has been 30 days late.[97]

36.63 From the point of view of costs between opposing parties, it will rarely be the case that the 1998 Act will apply; this is because it will apply only to a contract for the supply of goods or services where the purchaser and the supplier are each acting in the course of a business.[98] In practical terms, the Late Payment of Commercial Debts (Interest) Act 1998 will apply only to solicitor and client costs, and even then only rarely.

36.64 Where the Late Payment of Commercial Debts (Interest) Act 1998 does apply, however, the applicable rate of interest is 8% per annum over 'the official dealing rate'[99] (which is the rate announced from time to time by the Monetary Policy Committee of the Bank of England); compensation for late payment of up to £100 may also be payable.

Pursuant to the equitable jurisdiction of the court

36.65 Interest may be awarded as in respect of equitable remedies such as the taking of an account. Interest may also be awarded where money has been obtained by fraud or misapplication by someone in a fiduciary position.

36.66 The practical relevance of this jurisdiction is that in cases of fraud or misapplication by someone in a fiduciary position, it is commonly the case that the court will make an award of compound interest.[100]

Interest in arbitrations

36.67 Section 49 of the Arbitration Act 1996 specifically permits the award of compound interest. The London Maritime Arbitrators Association reported to the Law Commission that (in respect of damages) it was 'the general practice' to award compound interest 'quite simply because it seems commercially just to do so'.[101] Whether the same applies to awards of costs is not known.

---

[96] As amended by the Late Payment of Commercial Debts Regulations 2002 (SI 2002/1674).

[97] Late Payment of Commercial Debts (Interest) Act 1998, s 4.

[98] Late Payment of Commercial Debts (Interest) Act 1998, s 2(1). Furthermore, a debt does not carry (and shall be treated as never having carried) statutory interest if or to the extent that a right to demand interest on it, which exists by virtue of any rule of law, is exercised; see s 3(2) and (3).

[99] Late Payment of Commercial Debts (Rate of Interest) (No 3) Order 2002 (SI 2002/1675), art 4.

[100] *Westdeutsche Landesbank Girozentrale v Islington London Borough Council* [1996] AC 669. That said, compound interest may be awarded in situations which do not involve fraud or misapplication (see *Sempra Metals Ltd (formerly Metallgesellschaft Ltd) v Inland Revenue Commissioners and another* [2007] UKHL 34).

[101] The Law Commission *Pre-judgment Interest of Debts and Damages*, Law Com No 287 (23 February 2004), footnote 51.

Compound interest

36.68 Until recently[102] it was thought that there was no power to make an award of compound interest save in cases of fraud or misapplication.[103] This was by reason of there being no statutory provision for interest to be paid on interest. The law has now been clarified in such a way that there is the possibility of awards being made of compound interest (albeit not in respect of awards made under statute).

36.69 Lord Nicholls explained the reasoning behind that line of thinking in the following way:

> 'Legal rules which are not soundly based resemble proverbial bad pennies: they turn up again and again. The unsound rule returning once more for consideration by your Lordships' House concerns the negative attitude of English law to awards of compound interest on claims for debts paid late.'

He went on to say:

> 'We live in a world where interest payments for the use of money are calculated on a compound basis. Money is not available commercially on simple interest terms. This is the daily experience of everyone, whether borrowing money on overdrafts or credit cards or mortgages or shopping around for the best rates when depositing savings with banks or building societies. If the law is to achieve a fair and just outcome when assessing financial loss it must recognise and give effect to this reality.'

36.70 It remains to be seen whether these sentiments will result in changes being made to the statutory law.

SPECIAL SITUATIONS

Deemed costs orders

36.71 Deemed costs orders will arise on acceptance of a Part 36 offer; on discontinuance of a claim; and where a claim is struck out for non-payment of fees (see **7.74–7.98**).[104]

36.72 CPR, r 44.12(2) provides:

> 'Interest payable pursuant to section 17 of the Judgments Act 1838 or section 74 of the County Courts Act 1984 on the costs deemed to have been ordered under [the situations set out above] shall begin to run from the date on which the event which gave rise to the entitlement to costs occurred.'

Thus, interest will run from the date of acceptance, discontinuance, or striking out. This provision reverses the effect of a ruling in the House of Lords in which their Lordships rejected the notion that costs should be payable upon acceptance of monies paid into court notwithstanding absence of an order entitling the offeree to costs.[105]

---

[102] See the discussion below about *Sempra Metals Ltd (formerly Metallgesellschaft Ltd) v Inland Revenue Commissioners and another* [2007] UKHL 34.

[103] This is not the case in arbitrations: see Arbitration Act 1996, s 49.

[104] CPR, r 44.12(1).

[105] *Legal Aid Board v Russell* [1991] 2 AC 317.

Reversal of costs orders on appeal

36.73 In a claim in which there had been a successful appeal which had reversed the costs order made in the court below, Waller LJ held that interest on the costs of the ultimately successful party should ordinarily run from the date of the original costs order, rather than from the date of the order on appeal.[106]

36.74 Likewise, where a party is entitled to recoup costs which have been overpaid, he may be entitled to interest (see **3.75–3.77**).

Interest on overpaid costs

36.75 Where a party is found to have overpaid costs to an opponent, the court has the jurisdiction to award interest on that overpayment.[107]

36.76 This jurisdiction to make such an award is under CPR, r 44.3(6)(g). It is, however, worth mentioning the pre-CPR position because this was an example of one of the very limited exceptions to the general rule that interest on costs – or, more accurately, monies very similar to interest – are payable only pursuant to statute. Lord Nicholls dealt with the issue in this way:[108]

> 'This has given rise to the question whether, when ordering repayment, the House has jurisdiction to award interest on the money ordered to be repaid. I am in no doubt that the answer to this question is "Yes". The court has no general, inherent power to order the payment of interest. But the situation now under consideration is not directed at requiring a defendant against whom the plaintiff has a cause of action to pay interest on money to which the plaintiff's cause of action entitles him. Nor is it directed at requiring him to pay interest on unpaid costs. Rather, when ordering repayment the House is unravelling the practical consequences of orders made by the courts below and duly carried out by the unsuccessful party. The result of the appeal to this House was that, to the extent indicated, orders made in the courts below should not have been made. This result could, in some cases, be an idle exercise unless the House were able to make consequential orders which achieve, as nearly as is reasonably practicable, the restitution which this result requires. This requires that the House should have power to order repayment of money paid over pursuant to an order which is subsequently set aside. It also requires that in suitable cases the House should have power to award interest on amounts ordered to be repaid. Otherwise the unravelling would be partial only.'

It is possible that this jurisdiction continues to exist. That said, given the powers under CPR, r 44.3(6)(g), there would never be any need to rely upon it; that said, Lord Nicholls's guidance would continue to be relevant to the issue of discretion.

36.77 Awards are usually made on the basis of simple interest.[109]

Advance and multiple orders for costs

36.78 It is not uncommon for orders for costs to be made at different times. An example would be where there has been a split trial on liability and quantum and

---

[106] *Bim Kemi AB v Blackburn Chemicals Ltd* [2003] EWCA Civ 889.
[107] *Bim Kemi AB v Blackburn Chemicals Ltd* [2003] EWCA Civ 889 at [18].
[108] *Nykredit Mortgage Bank plc v Edward Erdman Group Ltd (No 2)* [1997] 1 WLR 1627 at 1636.
[109] If the jurisdiction mentioned at **36.76** continues to exist, it would be possible to construct an argument that compound interest should apply (see **36.68**). There is no authority for this, however.

separate costs orders have been made in respect of each. Less commonly, a party might become entitled to costs before those costs have been incurred; an example would be where a party is given permission to appeal on a point of general principle but this was on the condition that that party would bear the costs of the appeal in any event.

36.79 Difficulties can arise in such circumstances: there may be a dispute about which order should be the subject of the *incipitur* rule; moreover, a strict application of the *incipitur* rule can lead to injustice. The solution lies in CPR, r 44.3(6)(g), which affords the court the flexibility to make an order that meets the justice of the situation.

36.80 An example of the problems which may arise can be found in *Powell v Herefordshire Health Authority*;[110] this was a claim in tort in which liability had been agreed (together with an entitlement to costs) in 1994. The case did not settle until 2001. If interest had been permitted to run from 1994, not only would the claim for interest have been almost as great as the principal costs, but interest would have been payable on costs which had yet to be incurred. The costs judge's attention had not been drawn to CPR, r 44.3(6)(g) and, as a result, he felt constrained to allow interest in full (ie from 1994). The Court of Appeal found that this was unjust; in allowing the appeal, Kay LJ made the following comments:

> 'There was ... no need in law for [the costs judge] to find himself in the legal straightjacket that the parties had suggested. He had a discretion which enabled him to look at the dates when the costs had been incurred, and to come to a conclusion in relation to the payments of interest that fitted the justice of the circumstances of the particular case.'

36.81 The CPD provides that where the bill of costs includes costs payable under an order or orders, in respect of which the receiving party wishes to claim interest from different dates, the bill of costs should be divided to enable such interest to be calculated.[111]

Interest payable out of a fund

36.82 In *Wills v Crown Estate Commissioners*[112] Peter Smith J considered the issue of whether the court should make an award of interest where costs were payable out of a fund (as opposed to were costs were payable as a result of an adversarial order).

36.83 Peter Smith J confirmed that the nineteenth-century cases of *A-G v Nethercote*[113] and *Re Marsdens Estate*[114] remained good law, and that it would be wrong to interpret the former as being limited to the administration of estates. This means that interest is not normally payable on costs to be paid out of a fund:

> 'It is quite clear that whenever there are funds, out of which costs are paid, there is not an order which attracts interest. The reason for that is that there is not an order of the court in adversarial litigation.'

Therefore, interest is not generally payable on such costs.

---

[110] [2002] EWCA Civ 1786.
[111] See CPD, art 4.2(6).
[112] [2003] EWHC 1718 (Ch).
[113] (1841) 11 SIM 529.
[114] (1889) 40 Ch D 475.

Interest on the costs of assessment

36.84 The pre-CPR position was that interest on the costs of assessment was payable from the date on which the receiving party was awarded the costs which appear in the bill of costs.[115] This is no longer the case, as CPD, art 45.5(1) makes the following provisions:

> 'In respect of interest on the costs of detailed assessment proceedings, the interest shall begin to run from the date of the default, interim or final costs certificate as the case may be.'

Interest on the costs of the detailed assessment will, therefore, tend to run from the date of the relevant default, interim or final costs certificate.

---

[115] *Ross v Bowbelle (Owners)* [1997] 1 WLR 1159.

Part VII

PARTICULAR CIRCUMSTANCES

Chapter 37

CONTRACTS AND TRUSTS

COSTS PAYABLE PURSUANT TO CONTRACT

37.1 It is commonly the case that contracts (particularly mortgage contracts and leasehold contracts) contain provisions that one party (usually the mortgagor or lessee) will indemnify the other for costs incurred. The authority of *Gomba Holdings Ltd v Minories Finance Ltd*[1] is well established as setting out the law, having been cited with apparent approval in the House of Lords.[2] *Gomba* concerned a dispute between a borrower and a mortgagee. After default on the part of the borrower, receivers were appointed. The borrower commenced redemption proceedings and raised sufficient money to satisfy its liabilities, thereby allowing the receivers to be discharged. The borrower disputed the amount of the mortgagee's costs (which were payable on the indemnity basis under a term in the mortgage). A further issue arose out of the fact that during the course of proceedings the mortgagor had been awarded costs, but on the standard basis; the court had to decide whether the costs were payable on the standard basis (under the order) or on the indemnity basis (under the mortgage).

Basic principles

37.2 Scott LJ considered previous authorities, from which he was able to distil the following principles:[3]

(i) An order for the payment of costs of proceedings is always a discretionary order: see the Senior Courts Act 1981, s 51 (but see **37.5**);

---

[1]   [1993] Ch 171.

[2]   It was cited favourably by the House of Lords in *Callery v Gray (Nos 1 and 2) (HL(E))* [2002] UKHL 28.

[3]   [1993] Ch 171 at 194A; these provisions are reflected in CPD, art 50.3, which reads as follows: 'The following principles apply to costs relating to a mortgage—

(1)   An order for the payment of costs of proceedings by one party to another is always a discretionary order: section 51 of the Senior Courts Act 1981.

(2)   Where there is a contractual right to the costs the discretion should ordinarily be exercised so as to reflect that contractual right.

(3)   The power of the court to disallow a mortgagee's costs sought to be added to the mortgage security is a power that does not derive from section 51, but from the power of the courts of equity to fix the terms on which redemption will be allowed.

(4)   A decision by a court to refuse costs in whole or in part to a mortgagee litigant may be—

(a)   a decision in the exercise of the section 51 discretion;

(b)   a decision in the exercise of the power to fix the terms on which redemption will be allowed;

(c)   a decision as to the extent of a mortgagee's contractual right to add his costs to the security; or

(d)   a combination of two or more of these things.

The statements of case in the proceedings or the submissions made to the court may indicate which of the decisions has been made.

(5)   A mortgagee is not to be deprived of a contractual or equitable right to add costs to the security merely by reason of an order for payment of costs made without reference to the mortgagee's contractual or equitable rights, and without any adjudication as to whether or not the mortgagee should be deprived of those costs.'

(ii)	Where there is a contractual right to the costs, the discretion should ordinarily be exercised so as to reflect that contractual right;

(iii)	The power of the court to disallow a mortgagee's costs sought to be added to the mortgage security is a power that does not derive from s 51 but from the power of courts of equity to fix the terms on which redemption will be allowed;

(iv)	A decision by a court to refuse costs, in whole or in part, to a mortgage litigant may be a decision in the exercise of the s 51 discretion or a decision in the exercise of the power to fix the terms on which redemption will be allowed, or a decision as to the extent of a mortgagee's contractual right to add his costs to the security, or a combination of two or more of these things; the pleadings in the case and the submissions made to the judge may indicate which of the decisions to which we have referred has been made; and

(v)	A mortgagee is not to be deprived of a contractual or equitable right to add costs to the security merely by reason of an order for payment of costs made without reference to the mortgagee's contractual or equitable rights and without any adjudication as to whether or not the mortgagee should be deprived of those costs.

37.3	The most wide-ranging of the principles is (ii) (namely, that where there is a contractual right to the costs, the discretion should ordinarily be exercised so as to reflect that contractual right). Notwithstanding this, all the facts ought to be taken into account; it would be wrong to give disproportionate weight to the contractual obligations of the parties.[4] The court should not allow the provisions of the contract to prevail if the outcome would be unjust.[5]

Basis of assessment

37.4	The basis of assessment will be a matter of interpretation of the contract, but there will be a presumption that the costs will be assessed on the indemnity basis (see below). Where an assessment needs to be carried out of the costs as between solicitor and client, there is no reason why that assessment may not take place at the same time as the assessment of the contractual liability.[6] The basis of assessment of the contractual liability will be governed by CPR, r 48.3:

> '(1)	Where the court assesses (whether by the summary or detailed procedure) costs which are payable by the paying party to the receiving party under the terms of a contract, the costs payable under those terms are, unless the contract expressly provides otherwise, to be presumed to be costs which—
>
> (a)	have been reasonably incurred; and
> (b)	are reasonable in amount, and the court will assess them accordingly.
>
> (The costs practice direction sets out circumstances where the court may order otherwise)
>
> (2)	This rule does not apply where the contract is between a solicitor and his client.'

Where a contract provides that a party is entitled to 'all' his costs, the appropriate basis of assessment is the indemnity basis. The word 'all' does not enable or entitle the lessor to recover costs and expenses which are *un*reasonably incurred or which are *un*reasonable in amount.[7] Indeed, the CPD makes specific provision that costs unreasonably incurred or costs which are unreasonable in amount may be disallowed.[8]

4	*Venture Finance plc v Mead* [2005] EWCA Civ 325.
5	See, for example, *Forcelux Ltd v Binnie (Costs)* [2009] EWCA Civ 1077.
6	*Tim Martin Interiors Ltd v Akin Gump LLP* [2010] EWHC 2951 (Ch) at [42], per Lewison J.
7	*Fairview Investments Ltd v Sharma* (unreported) 14 October 1999, CA, at p 12 of the approved transcript.
8	See CPD, art 50.1, which reads: 'Where the court is assessing costs payable under a contract, it may make an

As with the basis of assessment, the ambit of the entitlement is a matter of interpretation of the contract; for example, a provision for costs of steps taken 'in or in contemplation of, or in relation to, any proceedings under the Law of Property Act 1925, s 146' would not include costs of correspondence to the tenant trying to enforce an obligation to undertake repairs.[9] The CPD makes provision for the mortgagor to seek an account, in appropriate cases.[10]

Precedence of other enactments

37.5 In *Fairview Investments Ltd v Sharma*,[11] Chadwick LJ (with whom Thorpe LJ agreed) qualified the first of the five statements of principle in *Gomba*; this was done on the basis that SCA 1981, s 51(1) is expressly made subject to the provisions of any other enactment. In *Fairview*, Chadwick LJ took the view that s 146(3) of the Law of Property Act 1925[12] applied and took precedence. Having made this point, Chadwick LJ went on to say that it is enough to rely on the second statement of principle in *Gomba*: where there is a contractual right to costs, the discretion should ordinarily be exercised so as to reflect that contractual right.

Orders made in ignorance of contractual provisions

37.6 *Elton John v Price Waterhouse*[13] demonstrates that a perfected order that is made in ignorance of a contractual right to costs will not be set aside solely for that reason, but nor will it detract from the contractual right to costs enforceable by other means. The defendants, who were the claimants' auditors, successfully defended a claim brought against them. The defendants initially expressly said that they did not seek costs on the indemnity basis; an order for costs on the standard basis was drawn up and perfected. At a subsequent hearing the defendants sought to reopen the issue of costs; this was because they had discovered that under the articles of association of the claimants they were contractually entitled to costs on the indemnity costs.

37.7 The application was refused. Ferris J found that the court's jurisdiction under SCA 1981, s 51 was exhausted. He accepted that the fact that he had made an order for the standard basis did not detract from any contractual right of the defendants to indemnity costs under the terms of the articles of association of the claimants. He

---

order that all or part of the costs payable under the contract shall be disallowed if it is satisfied by the paying party that costs have been unreasonably incurred or are unreasonable in amount.'

[9] *Agricullo Ltd v Yorkshire Housing Ltd (formerly Yorkshire Community Housing Ltd)* (2010) EWCA Civ 229.

[10] In this regard, CPD, art 50.4 reads as follows: '(1) Where the contract entitles a mortgagee to—
   (a) add the costs of litigation relating to the mortgage to the sum secured by it;
   (b) require a mortgagor to pay those costs, or
   (c) both,
   the mortgagor may make an application for the court to direct that an account of the mortgagee's costs be taken.
   (Rule 25.1(1)(n) provides that the court may direct that a party file an account)
   (2) The mortgagor may then dispute an amount in the mortgagee's account on the basis that it has been unreasonably incurred or is unreasonable in amount.
   (3) Where a mortgagor disputes an amount, the court may make an order that the disputed costs are assessed under rule 48.3.'

[11] *Fairview Investments Ltd v Sharma* (unreported) 14 October 1999, CA.

[12] Which provides that: 'A lessor shall be entitled to recover as a debt due to him from a lessee, and in addition to damages (if any), all reasonable costs and expenses properly incurred by the lessor in the employment of a solicitor and surveyor or valuer, or otherwise, in reference to any breach giving rise to a right of re-entry or forfeiture which, at the request of the lessee, is waived by the lessor, or from which the lessee is relieved, under the provisions of this Act.'

[13] [2002] 1 WLR 953.

commented that under the CPR there probably was a jurisdiction to reopen the issue (as this might save the costs of a fresh claim being brought), but he would be inclined to exercise that jurisdiction only if it were clear that there could be no defence to a contractual claim for indemnity costs, so that if a fresh claim were commenced, summary judgment would be given in favour of the defendant. That was not so in the claim before him. Thus, if they wanted to pursue the full extent of the indemnity, the defendants would have to bring a fresh claim.

TRUSTEES

Costs incurred by trustees

37.8   In general, a trustee is entitled to reimbursement from the trust funds[14] of his costs properly[15] incurred in administering the trust,[16] including remuneration paid to agents.[17] That right has existed since well before the fusion of the administration of the common law and equity by the Judicature Acts, and was expressly preserved by those Acts.[18] A trustee may assert lien over trust property in respect of funds applied by him for preservation of the trust.[19] A trustee will also be entitled to the costs of litigation brought on behalf of the trust but only to the extent that those costs are not recovered or paid by any other person. In this regard, CPR, r 48.4 makes the following provisions:

'(1)   This rule applies where—

   (a)   a person is or has been a party to any proceedings in the capacity of trustee or personal representative; and

   (b)   rule 48.3 does not apply.

(2)   The general rule is that he is entitled to be paid the costs of those proceedings, insofar as they are not recovered from or paid by any other person, out of the relevant trust fund or estate.

(3)   Where he is entitled to be paid any of those costs out of the fund or estate, those costs will be assessed on the indemnity basis.'

(Rule 48.3 will apply if the costs are payable pursuant to a contract: see **37.4**). Thus whilst the court does has the power to order otherwise (that discretion being introduced to deal with the old practice of the Court of Chancery of allowing the trustee his costs as a matter of course),[20] the general rule is that the trustee will be allowed his costs. The CPD confirms that the trustee's costs may include costs awarded against the trustee in favour of another party.[21] The topic of the contract of retainer between a trustee and his solicitor, see **8.438**.

---

[14]   'Trust funds' means income or capital funds of the trust: see the Trustee Act 2000, s 39(1).

[15]   This requirement is ancient and implied (see, for example, *Re Grimthorpe* [1958] Ch 615 at 623); it probably does not add a great deal to the test of reasonableness under CPR, r 44.4.

[16]   Trustee Act 2000, s 31(1).

[17]   Trustee Act 2000, s 32(1).

[18]   See Order 55 of the rules annexed as a schedule to the 1875.

[19]   *Clack v Holland* (1854) 19 Beav 262 at 273.

[20]   The discretion was originally created by Order 65 of the General Order 1883; see *Re Beddoe, Downs v Cottam* [1893] 1 Ch 547 at 554.

[21]   See CPD, art 50A.1, which reads: 'A trustee or personal representative is entitled to an indemnity out of the relevant trust fund or estate for costs properly incurred, which may include costs awarded against the trustee or personal representative in favour of another party.'

Principles of assessment

37.9 It will often be the case that the dispute as to what is and is not payable will be dealt with item-by-item on the assessment rather than as a matter principle at the time a costs order is made. As mentioned above, costs are assessed on the indemnity basis. Costs improperly[22] or unnecessarily[23] incurred will not be payable.[24] In so far as proceedings are concerned, CPD, art 50A.2 gives the following additional guidance:

> 'Whether costs were properly incurred depends on all the circumstances of the case, and may, for example, depend on—
>
> (1)   whether the trustee or personal representative obtained directions from the court before bringing or defending the proceedings;[25]
>
> (2)   whether the trustee or personal representative acted in the interests of the fund or estate or in substance for a benefit other than that of the estate, including his own;[26] and
>
> (3)   whether the trustee or personal representative acted in some way unreasonably in bringing or defending, or in the conduct of, the proceedings.'

Where, prior to his appointment, a trustee has incurred funds setting up the trust or obtaining a statement of costs property, he will be entitled to be reimbursed those monies out of the estate notwithstanding the fact that he was not appointed at the time those monies were disbursed.[27] There is a longstanding practice that where there is more than one trustee, the costs of only one of them will be allowed[28] unless separate representation was necessary (such as where one of them is being subject to a hostile attack,[29] or where one of them is a beneficiary,[30] etc). Under the RSC, costs were presumed to have been unreasonably incurred if they were incurred contrary to the duty of the trustee;[31] this rule is not expressly preserved in the CPR, but that is unlikely to mean that such costs would be recoverable. Where the cost are payable directly out of a fund, special procedural provisions apply (see **37.35–37.40**).

Reimbursement of the costs of proceedings

37.10 This section deals primarily with whether a trustee should be denied his costs out of the fund. The principles as to awards of costs between trustee and beneficiary – including 'the *Buckton* classification' – are addressed at **37.16–37.23**, as are other issues of entitlement. Each case will be decided on its own facts but misconduct on the part of the trustee may result not only in the trustee being denied his costs, but also in him being condemned in costs (see **37.16–37.23**).[32] Where the trustee was acting unreasonably in

---

22   *Hosegood v Pedler* (1896) 66 LJQB 18.

23   *Malcolm v O'Callaghan* (1837) 3 My & Cr 52, CA at 62.

24   Care ought to be exercised when considering what is meant by 'necessary' in pre-CPR cases: that word tends to be used to mean 'required' rather than necessary in the sense that it is used in the second stage of the *Lownds* test.

25   This is a reference to a *Beddoe* application (after *Re Beddoe, Downes v Cottam* [1893] 1 Ch 547), which is an application where a trustee seeks a pre-emptive order: see **37.26**.

26   CPD, art 50A.3 provides the following guidance: 'The trustee or personal representative is not to be taken to have acted in substance for a benefit other than that of the fund by reason only that he has defended a claim in which relief is sought against him personally.'

27   *Harvey v Olliver* (1887) WN 149.

28   See, for example, *Nicholson v Falkiner* (1830) 1 Mol 555.

29   *Bruty v Edmundson* [1918] 1 Ch 112, CA.

30   *Re Love, Hill v Spurgeon* (1885) 29 Ch D 348, CA.

31   RCS Ord 62, r 14.

32   See, for example, *Re Knox's Trusts* [1895] 2 Ch 483, CA. A trustee cannot easily avoid liability by pointing to

bringing or defending a claim, the trustee may be deprived of his costs from the fund.[33] This may extend to the costs of entire proceedings brought unnecessarily.[34] Where the proceedings were not brought or defended in the capacity of trustee, the trustee may or may not be denied his costs, depending on the circumstances (see below). Where the proceedings are brought for his own private benefit, the trustee may be deprived of his costs, or part of them, and may be required to pay costs[35] (see **37.16–37.23**).

Errors as to status and disputed trusts

37.11   Where a person reasonably pursues a claim believing he is a trustee, he may still be entitled to his costs out of the fund (or part of them) even if it is ultimately shown that he was not a trustee.[36]

37.12   Likewise, where there is a disputed trust that is set aside, it will not automatically be the case that the person who was acting as trustee will be deprived of costs.[37] Given the fact that the would-be trustee would usually be the loser and given the fact that there may be no fund upon which to draw, it is not surprising that Kekewich J described the discretion as being 'extremely difficult to exercise'. That said, the modern law is that the would-be trustee would often be penalised in costs as a result of having acted unreasonably;[38] this may be on the grounds that he would have incurred expenditure and liabilities in an unsuccessful effort to prefer one class of beneficiaries (eg the express beneficiaries specified in the trust instrument) over another (eg the trustees in bankruptcy or creditors), thereby acting otherwise than for the benefit of the trust. Each case will be decided on its own facts, however.

Costs of appeals

37.13   A distinction is made between the costs of appeals brought by the trustee and the costs of appeals brought by others. In general, the principle that costs should be paid from the trust regardless of the outcome will only at first instance but not on appeal. Where a trustee brings an appeal concerning the law or administration of the trust, the trustee may be at risk of bearing those costs personally.[39] The trustee will need to show exceptional circumstances in order to recover those costs from the fund; exceptional circumstances may exist where the appeal was in the interests of other persons (such as those yet to be born). Where the appeal is brought by others, he will often be allowed the costs of appearing,[40] especially in the Court of Appeal,[41] and especially where he is supporting a previously made order concerning the administration of the trust.[42] The

---

a specific provision within the trust instrument providing that the beneficiary must bear his share of proceedings instituted by him: see *Re Williams, Williams v Williams* [1912] 1 Ch 399.

[33]   See, by way of example, *Holding Ltd v Property Trust plc* [1989] 1 WLR 1313 (trustee of a maintenance fund for a block flats sought to increase expenditure in a way that was adverse to the tenant's interests and was not supported by either the tenants or the landlord).

[34]   See, for example, *Horner v Wheelwright* (1857) 2 Jur NS 367.

[35]   See, for example, *Re Dargie, Miller v Thornton-Jones* [1954] Ch 16 at 20–21; historically, see *Henley v Philips* (1740) 2 Atk 48.

[36]   *In re Preston's Estate* [1951] 1 Ch 878.

[37]   *Ideal Bedding Co Ltd v Holland* [1907] 2 Ch 157.

[38]   *Alsop Wilkinson (a firm) v Neary* [1996] 1 WLR 1220 at 1225.

[39]   *Re Earl of Radnor's Will Trust* (1890) 45 Ch D 402, CA.

[40]   Each case will be determined on its own facts; one factor that might be relevant is whether the trustee was put on notice that there may be an objection to paying his costs: see *Re Stuart, Johnson v Williams* [1940] 4 All ER 80 at 82, per Clauson LJ.

[41]   *Re Stuart, Johnson v Williams* [1940] 4 All ER 80 at 82, per Luxmoore LJ.

[42]   See, for example, *Chettiar v Chettiar (No 2)* [1962] 2 All ER 238 at 245.

Buckton principles (see **37.16** *et seq*) will not, in general, apply.[43] The difference between appeals and litigation at first instance was described by Carnwath J in the following way:[44]

'So one sees that where there is a genuine difficulty, trustees, and by analogy beneficiaries, may be able to seek authoritative guidance of the High Court at the expense of the fund, but once such guidance has been obtained from the High Court's decision, then in the absence of some special circumstances, such for example as difficulties arising from that decision itself, the parties have the authoritative guidance they need. The fact that they do not like it is not a reason for litigating further at the expense of the fund. That principle would apply equally in this case. The judgment provides the sort of clear guidance which is required under the *Buckton* approach, and the fact that some of the parties do not like it would not justify the costs of the appeal.'

Thus, pre-emptive are unlikely to be made in respect of the costs of appeals[45] (see **37.35**).

Prematurity, aggression and abusive claims

Controlling costs

37.14 Special provisions apply to costs incurred in proceedings in relation to trust funds; they are intended to make it easier for the court to make a costs capping order. Those provisions read as follows:[46]

'Section 23B Costs Capping Orders In Relation to Trust Funds

23B.1 In this Section 'trust fund' means property which is the subject of a trust, and includes the estate of a deceased person.

23B.2 This Section contains additional provisions to enable—

(a)   the parties to consider whether to apply for; and
(b)   the court to consider whether to make of its own initiative,
a costs capping order in proceedings relating to trust funds.
It supplements rules 44.17–20 and Section 23A of this Practice Direction.

23B.3 Any party to such proceedings who intends to apply for an order for the payment of costs out of the trust fund must file and serve on all other parties written notice of that intention together with an estimate of the costs likely to be incurred by that party.

23B.4 The documents mentioned in paragraph 23B.3 must be filed and served—

(a)   in a Part 7 claim, with the first statement of case; and
(b)   in a Part 8 claim, with the evidence (or, if a defendant does not intend to serve and file evidence, with the acknowledgement of service).

23B.5 When proceedings first come before the court for directions the court may make a costs capping order of its own initiative whether or not any party has applied for such an order.'

---

[43] See, for example, *Chessels v British Telecommunications plc* [2002] Pens LR 141 and *HR Trustees Ltd v German & IMG (UK) Ltd* [2010] EWHC 3467 (Ch).
[44] *Laws v National Grid Plc* [1998] PLR 295 at 314.
[45] *Chessels v British Telecommunications plc* [2002] Pens LR 141, per Laddie J.
[46] CPD art 23B.

Costs incurred by beneficiaries

37.15 A beneficiary would normally be entitled to payment of his costs from the estate in accordance with the terms of the trust. Any beneficiary may be entitled to his costs, regardless of his status.[47] Where a beneficiary brings a claim for the administration of the estate, he may be entitled to costs from the trustee personally if the trustee is found to have brought the claim upon himself by reason of his own default or neglect.[48] The same is true if the claim is for an account that the trustee has brought upon himself.[49] Where, on the other hand, the beneficiary is found to have commenced the claim too hastily or without good reason, he may be ordered to bear the costs personally.[50]

Costs of proceedings as between trustee and beneficiary (and others)

37.16 Disputes may be 'friendly'[51] or 'hostile'.[52] Lightman J has identified three types of dispute in which costs may be sought against a trustee (as opposed to where a trustee may be denied his costs from the fund: see **37.10–37.13**);[53] this classification can be combined with the better known taxonomy identified by Kekewich J – known as *Buckton* categorisation[54] – to produce the following:

- ***Trust disputes:*** In general, these are proceedings for the construction of a trust instrument or guidance on some other question of law concerning the administration of the trust; they may include the following:[55]
    — *Buckton category (1):* Amicable claims brought by the trustee (**37.18**);
    — *Buckton category (2):* Amicable claims brought by a person other than the trustee, usually a beneficiary (**37.19**); and
    — *Buckton category (3):* Adverse (or 'hostile') claims brought by person other than the trustee, usually a beneficiary (**37.20**);
- ***Beneficiaries disputes:*** These, in general, are hostile disputes in which the trustee's actions or inactions are challenged; such disputes may, for example, take the form of proceedings for breach of trust and/or for an order removing the trustees; and
- ***Third-party disputes:*** These are disputes with persons other than beneficiaries; an example would be a dispute with a contractor about payment under a contract for services provided to the trust.

37.17 There may be overlap between these categories; moreover, not every case of construction or dispute about the administration of the trust will fall within the *Buckton* categories. Arden LJ has explained that the *Buckton* categories are not closed. She has explained that a further category may exist where the issue of construction is being pursued not simply by a beneficiary in a way that is analogous to category (2) (see **37.19**) but also by a third party for its own separate interests.[56] She implied that more categories may exist. Where a case falls outside the classic *Buckton* categories it may be

---

[47] Where the Attorney-General, acting under a certificate issued to him under s 20 of the Charitable Trusts Act 1853, takes out an originating summons for the determination of a question of construction relating to charitable bequests under a will, as representing the objects of a charity, he is in the same position as any other beneficiary and is entitled to costs out of the estate: *In re Cardwell. A-G v Day* [1912] 1 Ch 779.

[48] See, for example, *Re Skinner, Cooper v Skinner* [1904] 1 Ch 289.

[49] See, for example, *Re Holton's Settlement Trusts, Holton v Holton* (1918) 88 LJ Ch 444.

[50] See, for example, *Re Dartnall, Sawyer v Goddard* [1895] 1 Ch 474, CA.

[51] Such as a dispute as to the true construction of the trust instrument: see **37.18** and **37.19**.

[52] Such as a challenge to the validity of the trust: see **37.20** and **37.21**.

[53] *Alsop Wilkinson (a firm) v Neary* [1996] 1 WLR 1220.

[54] *In re Buckton* [1907] 2 Ch 406.

[55] These being *In re Buckton* [1907] 2 Ch 406.

[56] *Singapore Airlines Ltd & Anor v Buck Consultants Ltd* [2011] EWCA Civ 1542 at [75].

necessary to consider novel ways of meeting the justice of the situation: in the circumstances referred to above, Arden LJ found that the burden of costs ought to be shared between the parties such that the beneficiaries were awarded only part of those costs that they would have had had it been a pure category (2) claim.

Buckton category (1): Amicable claim brought by the trustee

37.18 A category (1) claim is brought for the benefit of both the trustee and the beneficiaries. Regardless of the outcome, the costs of the parties are generally treated as necessarily incurred for the benefit of the trust. An example might be where the parties ask the court to construe the instrument of trust. Kekewich J regarded the costs of the parties in such cases as necessarily incurred for the benefit of the trust; therefore, provided that the claim was reasonable and was brought in good faith, the usual order would be that the trustee's costs be paid out of the fund.

Buckton category (2): Amicable claim brought by a person other than the trustee

37.19 Claims in this category differ only in form, but not in substance, from claims in the first category. They are claims which would fall in category (1) if brought by the trustee, but—for one reason or another—have in fact been brought by someone other than the trustee (usually a beneficiary). Costs are dealt with as per category (1).

Buckton category (3): Adverse claim brought by a beneficiary

37.20 Claims in this category differ in substance from those in the other two categories. They are often also referred to as 'hostile claims' or 'adverse claims'. Such claims are usually made by a beneficiary and may be adverse to other beneficiaries. Kekewich J had this to say:[57]

> 'It is often difficult to discriminate between cases of the second and third classes, but when [a claim falls in the third category] I apply the rule which ought, I think, to be rigidly enforced in adverse litigation, and order the unsuccessful party to pay the costs. Whether he ought to be ordered to pay the costs of the trustees, who are, of course, respondents, or not, is sometimes open to question, but with this possible exception the unsuccessful party bears the costs of all whom he has brought before the Court.'

Thus, where a claim falls within the category (3) the general rule applies (ie the loser pays costs to the winner)[58] but the court is able in an appropriate case to order the loser to pay the trustee's costs. It seems that Kekewich J particularly had mind the situation where two or more beneficiaries raise mutually antagonistic arguments.

37.21 Where a beneficiary argues for one particular construction against the interests of another beneficiary and where this has a bearing on the beneficiaries' respective shares of the fund, it would usually be the case that the costs would be borne by the losing beneficiary. This is because it would be unjust to impose upon the successful beneficiary the burden of paying for the litigation out of fund he has successfully obtained.[59]

---

[57] *In re Buckton* [1907] 2 Ch 406.
[58] See, for example, *Williams v Jones* (1886) 34 Ch D 120.
[59] *In re Halson* [1912] 1 Ch 439.

37.22 Where a trustee pursues a hopeless case, he will do so on the basis that he is at risk on costs.[60]

37.23 Whilst a more robust attitude to costs is appropriate under the CPR than that discussed in *Buckton*, Kekewich J's guidelines remain relevant and have not been superseded.[61] Other pre-CPR authorities must be treated with due caution, however. Appeals are in a class of their own (see **37.13**); where a trustee brings an appeal concerning the law or administration of the trust, as well as being at risk of bearing his own costs personally (see above), he may also be at risk of having personally to bear the other side's costs.

37.24 Where a defaulting trustee is ordered to pay costs, it will usually be on the standard basis.[62] Arden LJ has explained that there is a close analogy between the position of a trustee and a director in this regard. There are exceptions to the standard basis in the case of a defaulting trustee, such as where the trustee has acted wholly unreasonably.[63]

Pre-emptive orders

37.25 The court has an exceptional jurisdiction[64] to make a pre-emptive order as to whether costs should be paid out of the fund in the event of the trustee's entitlement to those costs being challenged. The jurisdiction to make such an order is modern (SCA 1981, s 51(3) and, probably, CPR, r 3.1(2)(m)), but it is based on principles that have a long lineage.[65] Laddie J described the discretion in this way:[66]

> 'For most purposes a trust is treated like any other litigant. If it brings or is embroiled in civil litigation with others, the basic rule that costs follow the event applies. However, whatever the relationship may be between the trust and opponents, special provisions as to costs need to be put in place as between the trust and the trustees. ... The trust is operated by the trustees for the beneficiaries' benefit. It may be appropriate for the trustees to seek the assistance of the court in determining how the trust instrument should be construed or as to the proper administration of the trust so as to enable them to execute their duties properly. They can then act in accordance with that guidance without fear that they are in breach of their duties to the beneficiaries.'

Laddie J went on to explain that there are two types of cases where such a pre-emptive order might be appropriate:[67]

> 'First the trustees may need to advance claims against, or defend against claims brought by, third parties which could affect the estate. If they bring the proceedings or defend them properly for the benefit of the estate, they will be entitled to be reimbursed for their costs from the estate, even if they lose in the litigation. However waiting until the end of the litigation for an order for indemnification to be made could place an unreasonable burden on

---

[60]   *In re Preston's Estate* [1951] 1 Ch 878.

[61]   *D'Abo v Paget (No 2)* (2000) The Times, August 10, Lawrence Collins QC.

[62]   *Bartlett v Barclays Bank Trust Co Ltd* [1980] Ch 515 referred to with apparent approval by Arden LJ in *Carlisle & Cumbria United Independent Supports' Society Limited v CUFC Holding Limited* [2010] EWCA Civ 463 at [23].

[63]   *Carlisle & Cumbria United Independent Supports' Society Limited v CUFC Holding Limited* [2010] EWCA Civ 463 at [23].

[64]   See *Alsop Wilkinson (a firm) v Neary* [1996] 1 WLR 1220.

[65]   *Re Beddoe* [1893] 1 Ch 457.

[66]   *Chessels v British Telecommunications plc* [2002] Pens LR 141 at [45]–[46].

[67]   *Chessels v British Telecommunications plc* [2002] Pens LR 141 at [46] to [48].

the trustees. Therefore it is open to them, and prudent, to make an application to the court for permission to bring or defend the proceedings on the basis of a pre-emptive indemnity out of the estate for the costs of doing so: see *re Beddoe* [1893] 1 Ch 547. It does not matter what the outcome of the litigation is. Because they will be acting for the benefit of the trust estate, they are protected.

… There is a second group of cases in which the trustees can seek an order for costs out of the estate. These are cases in which the trustees want guidance from the court as to their powers or duties. There may not be opponents as such. The trustees' actions are to ensure proper administration of the trust and are therefore for the benefit of the trust as a whole. For that reason, in such cases the trustees are indemnified out of the estate for the cost of seeking help from the court.'

37.26 Where a pre-emptive order is made for the benefit of a trustee in a claim brought by or against a third party, it is often referred to as a *Beddoe* order.[68] The most common type of such order is also that which affords the greatest protection: it is an order by which the trustee is awarded costs out of the fund in any event (i.e., regardless of whether he wins or loses).[69] There is pre-CPR authority to suggest that an application for a pre-emptive order can be made even where proceedings have been begun and the trustees are already parties.[70]

37.27 Pre-emptive orders may be made for the benefit of persons other than the trustee, such as a representative beneficiary.[71] This might be appropriate where a beneficiary with a limited interest seeks to vindicate the right of others or where a beneficiary brings proceedings to determine an administrative issue for the purposes of ensuring the proper running of the trust.[72] A pre-emptive order may be made in respect of a representative notwithstanding the fact that he has not been formally appointed as a representative under CPR, r 19.7(2).[73]

37.28 Four layers of discretion are particularly relevant to the issue of whether a pre-emptive costs order should be made.[74] They are:

- the merits of the claim;
- the likely order as to costs;
- the justice of the matter; and
- other factors.

Each is considered in turn.

The merits

37.29 A pre-emptive order should not be used to require a fund (or any person) unconditionally to pay for a claim which is not brought on reasonable grounds or is

---

[68]   *Re Beddoe* [1893] 1 Ch 457.

[69]   *Re Dallaway (deceased)* [1982] 1 WLR 756.

[70]   *Westdock Realisations Ltd* [1988] BCLC 354.

[71]   See, for example, *In Re AXA Equity & Law Life Assurance Society plc (No 1)* (2001) 2 BCLC 447 and *Wallerstiener v Moir* [1975] QB 373. See also **37.23**.

[72]   For example minority shareholder's actions were treated like *Beddoe* cases in *Wallersteiner v Moir (No 2)* [1975] QB 373.

[73]   *IBM United Kingdom Pensions Trust Ltd v Metcalfe* [2012] EWHC 125 (Ch).

[74]   *Re Biddencare Ltd* [1994] 2 BCLC 160 and *Alsop Wilkinson (a firm) v Neary* [1996] 1 WLR 1220.

brought in bad faith.[75] Where a *Beddoe* order is sought, the trustee is required to make full disclosure of the strengths and weaknesses of his case;[76] the court then assesses whether to give permission. In so doing, it does not determine whether the trustee will win or lose, but only whether the decision to litigate it is a proper exercise of the trustee's duties to the trust.[77]

The likely order to be made as to costs

37.30 In general, a pre-emptive order should be made only if the court is satisfied that at the end of the proceedings no other order regarding costs could properly be made.[78] In this regard, the nature of the litigation is relevant: if the litigation is a 'trust dispute' or a 'third-party dispute' (ie, *Buckton* categories (1) and (2): see **37.16**), then it is likely that the trustee will recover his costs from the fund in any event, but if it is a 'beneficiaries dispute' (category (3)), costs will probably follow the event. In particular, where it is a hostile beneficiaries dispute (ie where it is adverse to the trustee), the court should make a pre-emptive order only if satisfied that the trustee could not properly be deprived of his costs from the fund.[79] Hoffmann LJ has explained that the court may sometimes be sufficiently confident that the claim is within category (1) or category (2) to be able to make a pre-emptive order that parties other than the trustees are to have their costs in any event.[80] The fact that no other order could be made at the end of the proceedings is close to being a condition prerequisite: in particular, Hoffmann LJ has explained that in cases in which it is not clear that the trial judge would be bound to make an order in favour of the applicant, the court would be 'very reluctant to make a prospective order'.[81]

The justice of the matter

37.31 The order should not be one which will defeat the justice of the situation. For example, if a beneficiary brings a claim which, if successful, would result in him winning the property in the trust, it might be unfair to burden the trust pre-emptively with the costs of the trustee if the reality is that this would mean that the successful beneficiary might be indirectly condemned to pay unsuccessful trustee's costs.

---

[75]   *Re Wedstock Realisations Ltd* [1988] BCLC 354; for an example of a claim which failed the merits test, see *Trustee Corporation Ltd v Nadir* (2001) The Independent, January 29.

[76]   See *McDonald v Horn* [1995] 1 All ER 961 at 970, per Hoffmann LJ and *Chessels v British Telecommunications plc* [2002] Pens LR 141 at [47], per Laddie J.

[77]   *Chessels v British Telecommunications plc* [2002] Pens LR 141 at [47], per Laddie J.

[78]   *Chessels v British Telecommunications plc* [2002] Pens LR 141 at [54]; see also *Re Wedstock Realisations Ltd* [1988] BCLC 354. See also *McDonald v Horn* [1995] 1 All ER 961 at 972 in which Hoffmann LJ said: 'I think that before granting a pre-emptive application in ordinary trust litigation or proceedings concerning the ownership of a fund held by a trustee or other fiduciary, the judge must be satisfied that the judge at the trial could properly exercise his discretion only by ordering the applicant's costs to be paid out of the fund. Otherwise the order may indeed fetter the judge's discretion.'

[79]   *Chessels v British Telecommunications plc* [2002] Pens LR 141.

[80]   See *McDonald v Horn* [1995] 1 All ER 961 at 971, per Hoffmann LJ ; such orders have been made at the request of, or with the support of, the trustee or other fiduciary bringing the proceedings: see *Re Exchange Securities and Commodities Ltd (No 2)* [1985] BCLC 392 at 395.

[81]   *McDonald v Horn* [1995] 1 All ER 961 at 971. As an example of a case where an order was not made, see *Re Charge Card Services Ltd* [1986] BCLC 316.

Other factors

37.32 If the existence of the trust is in dispute or if there is a dispute as to whether a litigant is a trustee, then it would usually be inappropriate to make a pre-emptive order.[82]

37.33 If litigation is necessary in order to resolve a large number of similar disputes, or to resolve a representative dispute which might affect a large number of persons, then the interests of justice might require that a party is properly funded. An example of this would be where it is necessary for a representative trustee to be funded for the purposes of testing the arguments of other parties.[83] In this regard, the applicant's access to other means of funding is a relevant factor.[84] Pension funds held in trust are often regarded as being comparable

37.34 For the reasons set out in **37.13,** a litigant is not generally able to rely on the *Buckton* classification on appeal; in particular, proceedings that would, at first instance, have been in either of the *Buckton* categories (1) or (2) would, on appeal, generally cease to be regarded as being brought for the purposes of seeking guidance as to the construction or administration of the trust.[85] It is possible, however, for alternative grounds for a pre-emptive order to be made out; if, for example, the applicant beneficiaries are not volunteers (such as where they are beneficiaries to a pension fund), special principles may apply (see **37.33**).[86] This may apply in both hostile litigation and in cases that, at first instance, would be in one or other of categories (1) and (2).[87]

Costs payable out of a fund

Procedural issues

37.35 Contrary to the general provision at CPR, r 44.13(1) that where an order is silent as to costs, no party is entitled to costs in relation to that order, an order which is silent as to costs will not affect any entitlement of a party to recover costs out of a fund held by him as trustee or personal representative, or pursuant to any lease, mortgage or other security.[88]

37.36 Special provisions apply to assessment of costs payable out of a fund; they are contained in CPR, r 47.17A:

'(1) Where the court is to assess costs which are payable out of a fund other than the Community Legal Service Fund, the receiving party may commence detailed assessment proceedings by filing a request in the relevant practice form.

(2) A request under paragraph (1) must be filed within 3 months after the date when the right to detailed assessment arose.

(3) The court may direct that the party seeking assessment serve a copy of the request on any person who has a financial interest in the outcome of the assessment.

---

[82] See, for example *R v National Anti-Vivisection Society Ltd v Duddington* (1989) The Times, November 23, Mummery J.

[83] See, for example, *In Re AXA Equity & Law Life Assurance Society plc (No 1)* (2001) 2 BCLC 447.

[84] *Trustee Corporation Ltd v Nadir* (2001) The Independent, January 29.

[85] See **37.13**; also see *Chessels v British Telecommunications plc* [2002] Pens LR 141 and *HR Trustees Ltd v German & IMG (UK) Ltd* [2010] EWHC 3467 (Ch).

[86] *McDonald v Horn* [1995] 1 All ER 961 at 973–975.

[87] *HR Trustees Ltd v German & IMG (UK) Ltd* [2010] EWHC 3467 (Ch) at [41]–[52], per Arnold J.

[88] CPR, r 44.13(1)(b).

(4)   The court will, on receipt of the request for assessment, provisionally assess the costs without the attendance of the receiving party, unless it considers that a hearing is necessary.

(5)   After the court has provisionally assessed the bill, it will return the bill to the receiving party.

(6)   The court will fix a date for an assessment hearing if the party informs the court, within 14 days after he receives the provisionally assessed bill, that he wants the court to hold such a hearing.'

Thus, the costs will usually be provisionally assessed without the benefit of points of dispute or replies (in much the same way as CLS-only costs are, save that the costs will be on the indemnity rather than the standard basis). The court may direct that a person – usually a beneficiary – who has a financial interest in the outcome of the assessment may be served with a copy of the request for a detailed assessment.

37.37   The CPD provides additional guidance at CPD, art 44:

'**44.6**

(1)   Where the court has provisionally assessed a bill of costs, it will send to the receiving party, a notice in Form N253 of the amount of costs which the court proposes to allow together with the bill itself. If the receiving party is legally represented the legal representative should, if the provisional assessment is to be accepted, then complete the bill.

(2)   The court will fix a date for a detailed assessment hearing, if the receiving party informs the court within 14 days after he receives the notice in Form N253 of the amount allowed on the provisional assessment, that he wants the court to hold such a hearing.

44.7 Where the court makes an order that a person who has a financial interest is to be served with a copy of the request for assessment, it may give directions about service and about the hearing.

44.8 The court will give at least 14 days notice of the time and place of the detailed assessment hearing to the receiving party and, to any person who has a financial interest in the outcome of the assessment and has been served with a copy of the request for assessment.

44.9 If the receiving party, or any other party or any person who has a financial interest in the outcome of assessment, wishes to make an application in the detailed assessment proceedings, the provisions of Part 23 (General Rules about Applications for Court Orders) applies.

44.10 If the receiving party is legally represented the legal representative must in order to complete the bill after the assessment make clear the correct figures allowed in respect of each item and must recalculate the summary of the bill if appropriate.'

37.38   Thus, the request for a detailed assessment hearing must be accompanied by:

- a copy of the bill;
- the document giving rise to the right to detailed assessment;
- a copy of all orders made by the court relating to the costs which are to be assessed;
- fee notes of both counsel and experts;
- written evidence as to any other disbursement which is claimed and which exceeds £250;
- a statement signed by the receiving party giving his name, address for service, reference, telephone number, fax number;

- a statement of the postal address of any person who has a financial interest in the outcome of the assessment; and
- in respect of each person stated to have such an interest if such person is a child or protected party, a statement to that effect.

37.39 Where the assessment is in the Senior Courts Costs Office (or elsewhere if the court directs), the papers in support of the bill should be filed in accordance with CPD, art 4.12 (see CPD, art 43.3(g)).

37.40 In deciding whether notice should be given to any person with a financial interest in the outcome of the assessment, the court will take into account the size of the fund and the number of persons who have a financial interest. If notice is to be given, the court may (and usually will) give directions about service and the hearing.

Chapter 38

SPECIFIC TYPES OF PARTY

38.1 This chapter focuses on the way in which the court safeguards the rights of vulnerable parties, such as children and persons who lack capacity. It also discusses the issue of the costs of litigants in person.

CHILDREN AND MENTAL INCAPACITY

38.2 The topic of capacity is addressed solely from the viewpoint of costs. The analysis is necessarily rudimentary: if a difficult issue arises, other texts dealing specifically with capacity ought to be consulted. This chapter does not deal with all aspects of capacity; in particular, it does not deal with the issue of capacity and corporations, nor does it deal with insolvency. Again, other texts should be consulted for guidance on that type of issue.

Children

38.3 A person becomes an adult on attaining the age of 18.[1] Prior to this, in the eyes of the law, a person is a child[2] and therefore lacking in capacity. A child will litigate through a litigation friend; a litigation friend is an officer of the court who has been appointed to look after the child's interests[3] and who is bound to do so until released from that role.[4] In the ordinary run of things he is not a party to the proceedings[5] and has no rights to be heard as a party in his own right.[6]

Costs orders

38.4 In view of the child's lack of capacity, the issue of liability for costs generally focuses on the liability of the litigation friend rather than the child personally.[7] Other than this, the modern approach to making orders for costs in litigation involving children is the same as in any other form of litigation. There are ancient authorities on the exercise of the court's discretion, but care must be exercised when seeking guidance

---

[1] Family Law Reform Act 1969, s 1(1).
[2] This is the term used in the Children Act 1989 and the CPR (see CPR, r 21.2); the terms 'minor' and 'infant' are used in statutes prior to 1989.
[3] *Rhodes v Swithenbank* (1889) 22 QBD 577, CA at 579.
[4] *Re E (mental health patient)* [1985] 1 All ER 609 at 616.
[5] *Dyke v Stephens* (1885) 30 Ch D 189 at 190.
[6] *Rhodes v Swithenbank* (1889) 22 QBD 577, CA at 579.
[7] Save in cases of fraud, a child would not usually be ordered to pay costs personally (*Lemprière v Lange* (1879) 12 Ch D 675 at 679, and *Elsey v Cox* (1858) 26 Beav 95); this is a reflection of the principle that a child could not personally make himself liable for an opponent's costs (*Turner v Turner* (1726) 2 Stra 708); there are numerous exceptions to this rule (see, for example, *Brockelbank v Brockelbank and Borlase* (1911) 27 TLR 569), but with the modern facility for the court to ensure that a litigation friend is able to meet a costs order, it would rarely be the case that the court would have to consider those exceptions.

from those cases because many of them deal with the position between the child and his litigation friend, rather than between opposing parties.[8] This is not always apparent from the case reports.

Timing and procedure

38.5 Although it predates the CPR, there is authority to show that where an order is sought against a litigation friend, it must be sought at the time the costs order is made.[9] If the receiving party wishes the court to address the point at some future time, that aspect of the matter ought to be reserved.[10] Regardless of whether these principles have survived the introduction of the CPR, they are undoubtedly guidelines for good practice.

Principles concerning litigation friend

38.6 A child may be awarded costs in just the same way as may any other litigant. In so far as the indemnity principle is concerned, a child is able to recover costs from an opponent by the mechanisms described under the heading 'position between solicitor and child' (see **38.8–38.12**). Where the court is minded to make an order against a child, it would be effective against the litigation friend,[11] who would then be able to claim those costs from the child as expenses[12] (see **38.31–38.35**). Indeed, it is implicit in CPR, r 21.4(3)(c) that a litigation friend acting on behalf of a claimant undertakes to meet any adverse costs order which may be made in the proceedings. In so far as it is relevant, it provides:

> 'If nobody has been appointed by the court ... a person may act as a litigation friend if he ... undertakes to pay any costs which the child or protected party may be ordered to pay in relation to the proceedings, subject to any right he may have to be repaid from the assets of the child or protected party.'

38.7 A similar, but more explicit, provision is made at PD 21, para 2.2(e), which makes provision for the litigation friend to file a written undertaking.[13] A litigation friend may be required to prove compliance with the undertaking upon evidence.[14] The litigation friend's liability is not without end, however. In this regard, CPR, r 21.9(6) makes the following provisions:

---

[8]   There is ancient authority which establishes a principle that a litigation friend will not be required personally to pay the costs of an unsuccessful defence unless he has been guilty of gross misconduct (*Vivian v Kennelly* (1890) 63 LT 778); the modern equivalent of that principle would be that the court would make the order against the litigation friend as if he were any other litigant, but then deal with misconduct in the exercise of its discretion in terms of the litigant friend's expenses.

[9]   *Re Picton, Picton v Picton* [1931] WN 254.

[10]   *Caley v Caley* (1877) 25 WR 528.

[11]   It has long been the case that a where a defendant successfully defends a claim brought by a child, the court has been able to order the litigation friend to pay the costs; there is no reason to believe that the situation is any different under the CPR; see, for example, *Huxley v Wootton* (1912) 29 TLR 132; *Slaughter v Talbott* (1739) Willes 190; and *Catt v Wood* [1908] 2 KB 458, CA at 473.

[12]   The litigation friend may bring a claim against the child for an indemnity in respect of those costs: *Steeden v Walden* [1910] 2 Ch 393; those monies may not be recoverable if the litigation was not brought for the child's benefit (see, for example, *Re Fish, Bennett v Bennett* [1893] 2 Ch 413, CA) or if it was improper litigation (*Re Hicks, Lindon v Hemery* [1893] WN 138).

[13]   That article reads as follows: 'A person who wishes to become a litigation friend without a court order pursuant to r 21.5(3) must file a certificate of suitability in Practice Form N235 ... where the child or protected party is a claimant, undertaking to pay any costs which the child or protected party may be ordered to pay in relation to the proceedings, subject to any right he may have to be repaid from the assets of the child or protected party'.

[14]   See PD 21, para 3.3(4).

'The liability of a litigation friend for costs continues until—

    (a)   the person in respect of whom his appointment to act has ceased serves the notice referred to in paragraph (4); or

    (b)   the litigation friend serves notice on the parties that his appointment to act has ceased.'

Position between solicitor and child

38.8   In the following discussion it should be borne in mind that very often the issue of the retainer between the solicitor and child will not arise (or would be little more than a distraction); this is because there would usually be a retainer with the litigation friend, who would recover his outlay from the child as expenses. There would, in those circumstances, be no need for a retainer with the child because those expenses would be recovered under the CPR rather than under a retainer (see **38.31–38.35**). Where the retainer is with the litigation friend, the child's rights would be preserved not only by the court's supervision of the expenses, but also by his right to apply for an assessment pursuant to s 71 of the Solicitors Act 1974. This is dealt with in more detail at **38.21–38.22**.

38.9   That said, retainers with children are not unknown. With certain exceptions (most notably contracts for 'necessaries'), a contract with a child is generally voidable, but not void.[15] For the reasons set out under the next heading, it is entirely plausible that contracts for legal services are contracts for necessaries (or, rather, are capable of being contracts for necessaries), in which case the difficulties described immediately below would be avoided.

The meaning of voidable

38.10   In this context 'voidable' means one of two things: it may mean either that the contract is not enforceable against the child unless he ratifies it upon reaching majority, or it may mean that the contract may be repudiated by the child while he remains a child and for a reasonable period of time thereafter. There is no authority as to whether a contract of retainer would fall into the former or the latter category, but in view of the fact that the latter category usually pertains to contracts for land, property, etc,[16] it is likely that it would be the former. Unless it is for necessaries,[17] therefore, a contract of retainer is probably unenforceable unless ratified. The contrary – that retainers fall within the latter category – is arguable, however: see **38.20**.

38.11 As has been implied above, a contract with a child will become enforceable against him if ratified when he reaches majority.[18] In a similar vein, a child may, within a reasonable period of time after reaching maturity, elect to become liable under a contract, and he can do this even if he has previously avoided it.[19] Beyond these things, there is, in the present context, no power of election which would result in the contract being enforceable against the child. (This does not mean that the contract is of no effect, however, because in most instances the child is able to elect to enforce the contract

---

[15] *Bruce v Warwick* (1815) 6 Taunt 118 and *Nash v Inman* [1908] 2 KB 1.
[16] See the discussion of this topic at *North Western Rly Co v M'Michael* (1850) 5 Exch 114 at 123.
[17] See **38.9** and **38.13–38.14**.
[18] *Williams v Moor* (1843) 11 M & W 256.
[19] *North Western Rly Co v M'Michael* (1850) 5 Exch 114 at 127.

against the adult,[20] but that is irrelevant for the purposes of the indemnity principle because it would give no power of enforcement to the solicitor.)

38.12 The effect of payment under a retainer with a child is a moot point. If the contract is of the voidable type, ie the second type of contract mentioned at **38.10**, the child may be debarred from recovering monies he has paid out[21] but, for the reasons set out above, it is not likely that a retainer would fall within that category. It is, therefore, likely that if a retainer is unenforceable by reason of the client being a child, the unenforceability will have a similar effect to unenforceability of any other origin.

Necessaries

38.13 It should not be forgotten that the retainer with the child is often merely a distraction (see **38.8**); where this is not the case, and where the receiving party is forced to rely on the existence of an enforceable contract, it may be necessary to look at the law of necessaries. A contract for necessaries would generally be enforceable against the child.[22] Whether services can be said to be necessaries is a question of mixed fact and law.[23] Broadly speaking, necessaries are, as the name implies, things without which an individual cannot reasonably function. Although authority on the point is lacking,[24] there is no reason to believe that, in appropriate circumstances, a contract for the supply of legal services could not be a contract for necessaries. An argument in support of that contention would be particularly persuasive if the legal services related to a claim for an injury that resulted in the lack of capacity. It has been held that the supply of money to purchase necessaries is itself necessary;[25] it may be that the same logic applies where the purpose of the claim is to provide necessaries such as care, accommodation, etc.

38.14 There is, however, a potential problem with relying on the doctrine of necessaries in a case where the retainer is a conditional fee agreement. This is because it is possible that the basis of the liability created by the supply of necessaries is restitutionary rather than contractual.[26] If this is correct, then a paying party would, with some justification, argue that there can be no such thing as a conditional restitutionary remedy in circumstances where Parliament has expressly reserved to itself all control over conditional fee agreements.[27]

Prejudicial contacts

38.15 It is worth making one or two further points about children and contracts. Contracts which are prejudicial to a child are wholly void (as opposed to being merely voidable);[28] in the context of costs such contracts will rarely arise, but some contracts

---

[20] *North Western Rly Co v M'Michael* (1850) 5 Exch 114 and *Re Smith's Trusts* (1890) 25 LR Ir 439.
[21] *Steinberg v Scala (Leeds) Ltd* [1923] 2 Ch 452, CA; in those circumstances, the question will not be whether the child got value for money, but whether there was a total failure of consideration (see p 461).
[22] *Chapple v Cooper* (1844) 13 M & W 252 at 258, per Alderson B; a child who is so young as to be incapable of consent would not be bound by a contract, even if it were for necessaries: *R v Oldham Metropolitan Borough Council ex p G* [1993] 1 FLR 645.
[23] *Ryder v Wombwell* (1868) LR 4 Exch 32 at 38, per Willes J.
[24] The nearest authority is *De Stacpoole v De Stacpoole* (1887) 37 Ch D 139, which confirms that legal advice for certain non-contentious services (drawing a marriage settlement) were necessaries.
[25] *Beavan, Davies, Banks & Co v Beavan* [1912] 1 Ch 196.
[26] See the competing analyses of Fletcher Moulton LJ and Buckley LJ in *Nash v Inman* [1908] 2 KB 1.
[27] See s 58 of the Courts and Legal Services Act 1990 (as amended).
[28] *Slator v Brady* (1863) 14 ICLR 61.

for disbursement funding loans may conceivably fall within such a category.[29] Whether a contract is prejudicial is a matter of balancing the prejudicial aspects against the general benefit that the contract confers upon the child.[30] Likewise, contracts (even for the supply of necessaries) which contain provisions which are harsh or onerous upon the child may be adjudged void.[31] Again, such contracts will be rare in the context of costs litigation, but an example might be a conditional fee agreement that provides for a particularly sizeable postponement charge or an outlandishly high hourly rate.

The position of a paying party

38.16 Where a paying party is ordered to pay a child's costs, the fact the child lacks capacity to enter into a contract may lead to uncertainty as to whether there has been compliance with the indemnity principle. The following points can be made.

Litigation friend

38.17 In the ordinary run of things, the child's litigation friend will have entered into a retainer (often in the form of a contract where he and the child are jointly liable for the solicitor's fees). Where this is the case, compliance with the indemnity principle can usually be proved by reason of the litigation friend's right to seek expenses from the child.[32] That is not a contractual obligation, so issues of the child's capacity do not arise. There is a cap of between 25% and 50% in cases where the amount awarded is £5,000 or less (see **38.31–38.35**).[33]

Ratification on reaching majority

38.18 If a child, upon reaching majority, were to ratify the retainer, then the retainer would become enforceable against him. A paying party could argue that it was unreasonable for the child to ratify the retainer, but it is not likely that the court would accept such an argument. A better argument would be that ratification after the costs order was made ought to be of no effect, but there is no authority to confirm or counter that argument.

Necessaries

38.19 If the receiving party were able to show that the legal services were necessaries, then he might be able to rely on that doctrine to establish a liability on the part of the child. This would not present any problems in the case of a private retainer, but it might give rise to difficulties if the retainer were a conditional retainer. This is because of the reasons mentioned at **38.13–38.14**.

Public policy

38.20 As mentioned at **38.10–38.12**, a category of contracts exists in which a contract would be regarded as being enforceable unless and until the child were to take steps to avoid it. Whether a contract falls within that category seems to be a matter of public

---

[29] See, in relation to loans in general, *Martin v Gale* (1876) 4 Ch D 428.
[30] *Chaplin v Leslie Frewin (Publishers) Ltd* [1966] Ch 71.
[31] *Roberts v Gray* [1913] 1 KB 520.
[32] See CPR, r 21.4(3)(c) and PD 21, paras 2.2(e) and 3.3(4); see also *Re Fish, Bennett v Bennett* [1893] 2 Ch 413 and Practice Direction – Children and Protected Parties, paras 2.2(e) and 3.3(4).
[33] CPR, r 22.12(6).

policy. The public policy underlying the rules regarding children and their contracts is there to protect children against their immaturity and inexperience.[34] It is – to say the least – doubtful that policy would be advanced by allowing it to be used as a vehicle for establishing breaches of the indemnity principle. It is, therefore, arguable that retainers are within that special group of contracts, and that they are enforceable until the child takes steps to avoid them. There is, however, no authority to support that contention. In any event, for the reasons set out at **38.17**, in modern litigation, the point ought not to arise.

Position between solicitor and litigation friend

38.21 Where a litigation friend instructs solicitors, there will, in the absence of an express retainer, ordinarily be an implied term that he will be liable for the solicitors' fees;[35] where the litigation was properly conducted for the child's benefit, the litigation friend would then be able to recover the monies from the child as expenses.[36] Thus, the child would be indirectly responsible for the solicitor's fees. This applies regardless of whether the child is a claimant or a defendant.[37] The child's rights would be preserved not only by the court's supervision of the expenses, but also by his right to apply for an assessment pursuant to s 71 of the Solicitors Act 1974.

Joint contracts of retainer

38.22 The litigation friend and the child may be jointly liable under the same retainer. Where this is so, the friend is not bound by the contract if it can be performed only jointly.[38] If, however, it can be performed by the friend acting alone, then he remains liable under it;[39] this will be the situation with most contracts of retainer. Put another way, the rules relating to contractual joint liability will rarely result in a breach of the indemnity principle, so it usually creates no problems if the child and the litigation friend are counterparties to the same retainer.

Procedural issues

38.23 In general, the procedure relating to children is similar to that relating to adults, but a number of additional provisions apply. In so far as litigation friends, orders, etc are concerned, the relevant procedure is governed by CPR Part 21 and its associated Practice Direction. In addition, CPR Part 48 contains a number of relevant provisions relevant to children.

Statement of interest

38.24 If a person who has an interest in the outcome of an assessment of costs is a child, then a statement to that effect must accompany a request for a detailed assessment hearing.[40]

---

[34] *Latey Report of the Committee on the Age of Majority* (1967), Cmnd 3342, para 289.
[35] *Re Payne, Randle v Payne* (1883) 23 Ch D 288, CA at 289.
[36] See CPR, r 21.4(3)(c) and PD 21, paras 2.2(e) and 3.3(4); see also *Re Fish, Bennett v Bennett* [1893] 2 Ch 413 and Practice Direction – Children and Protected Parties, paras 2.2(e) and 3.3(4).
[37] *Earl of Orford v Churchill* (1814) 3 Ves & B 59 at 71.
[38] *Gill v Russell* (1673) Freem KB 62.
[39] *Chaplin v Leslie Frewin (Publishers) Ltd* [1966] Ch 71.
[40] CPD, art 44.3(c).

Assessment of costs payable to or by a child

38.25 The 'general rule' is that where costs are payable either to or by a child, those costs will be assessed by way of detailed assessment; CPR, r 48.5 makes the following provisions:

'(1)   This rule applies to any proceedings where a party is a child or protected party and—

(a)   money is ordered or agreed to be paid to, or for the benefit of, that party; or

(b)   money is ordered to be paid by him or on his behalf.

("Child" and "protected party" have the same meaning as in rule 21.1(2))

(2)   The general rule is that—

(a)   the court must order a detailed assessment of the costs payable by, or out of money belonging to, any party who is a child or protected party; and

(b)   on an assessment under paragraph (a), the court must also assess any costs payable to that party in the proceedings, unless—

(i)   the court has issued a default costs certificate in relation to those costs under rule 47.11; or

(ii)   the costs are payable in proceedings to which Section II[41] of Part 45 applies.

(3)   The court need not order detailed assessment of costs in the circumstances set out in the costs practice direction.

(4)   Where—

(a)   a claimant is a child or protected party; and

(b)   a detailed assessment has taken place under paragraph (2)(a), the only amount payable by the child or protected party is the amount which the court certifies as payable.

(This rule applies to a counterclaim by or on behalf of a child or protected party by virtue of rule 20.3)'

38.26 Thus, this general rule will not apply in 'the circumstances set out in the costs practice direction'; those circumstances are contained at art 51 of the CPD, and are as follows:

'(a) where there is no need to do so to protect the interests of the child or protected party or his estate;

(b) where another party has agreed to pay a specified sum in respect of the costs of the child or protected party and the solicitor acting for the child or protected party has waived the right to claim further costs;

(c) where the court has decided the costs payable to the child or protected party by way of summary assessment and the solicitor acting for the child or protected party has waived the right to claim further costs;

(d) where an insurer or other person is liable to discharge the costs which the child or protected party would otherwise be liable to pay to his solicitor and the court is satisfied that the insurer or other person is financially able to discharge those costs.'

---

[41]   At the time of writing, it was proposed that the words 'or Section VI' be inserted.

Fixed costs

38.27 In proceedings to which Section II of CPR Part 45 applies (ie where predictable costs are payable), the court will not make an order for detailed assessment of the costs payable to the child, but will assess the costs in the manner set out in that Section.[42]

Summary assessment of costs payable to or by a child

38.28 Corresponding provisions exist in relation to summary assessment; where costs are payable by a child, the court may carry out a summary assessment,[43] but where the costs are payable to a child, the court will not make a summary assessment of the costs unless the solicitor acting for the child has waived the right to further costs.[44]

Contentious business agreements

38.29 Where the costs are payable by a child pursuant to a contentious business agreement which has been entered into by his guardian acting in a representative capacity, the agreement must be laid before the court for the court's approval before payment; failure to do this can result in the guardian being ordered to account to the child.[45] This is dealt with in detail at **8.139–8.193**.

Compromise by a child

38.30 Compromises involving children have to be approved.[46] That said, Clarke MR has confirmed (obiter) that the approval of the court is not required if the terms of the compromise were such that the child would have no interest in the matter.[47] Thus, it would not be necessary to seek the court's approval of a compromise of costs under a CFA Lite. Likewise, it would not be necessary to seek approval in circumstances where the solicitor was willing to waive any monies not recovered from the paying party.

Litigation friend's expenses

38.31 Where a litigation friend enters into a contract of retainer to pursue a claim on behalf of the child, the costs reasonably incurred in that claim will be recoverable from the child, but only to the extent that they are reasonable. Express provision for this is made at CPR, r 21.12:

> '(1) In proceedings to which rule 21.11 applies, a litigation friend who incurs expenses on behalf of a child or protected party in any proceedings is entitled on application to recover the amount paid or payable out of any money recovered or paid into court to the extent that it—
>
> > (a)   has been reasonably incurred; and
> > (b)   is reasonable in amount.
>
> (2) Expenses may include all or part of—
>
> > (a)   an insurance premium, as defined by rule 43.2(1)(m); or

---

[42]   CPR, r 21.10(3).
[43]   CPD, art 13.11(2).
[44]   CPD, art 13.11(1).
[45]   See Solicitors Act 1974, s 62.
[46]   See CPR, r 21.10.
[47]   *Tankard v John Fredricks Plastics Ltd* [2008] EWCA Civ 1375 at [7].

(b)   interest on a loan taken out to pay an insurance premium or other recoverable disbursement.'

Discouragement of multiple assessments

38.32 If costs have already been assessed, the court discourages a further assessment by placing a bar on the recovery costs which have been disallowed on the prior assessment; CPR, r 21.12(3) makes the following provisions:

'(3)   No application may be made under the rule for expenses that—

(a)   are of a type that may be recoverable on an assessment of costs payable by or out of money belonging to a child or protected party; but

(b)   are disallowed in whole or in part on such an assessment.'

(Expenses which are also 'costs' as defined in r 43.2(1)(a) are dealt with under r 48.5(2).)

Basis of assessment

38.33 The CPR do not state a basis on which the expenses will be assessed, but they lay the foundation for an assessment which would be very similar to an assessment of costs:

'(4)   In deciding whether the expenses were reasonably incurred and reasonable in amount, the court will have regard to all the circumstances of the case including the factors set out in rule 44.5(3).

(5)   When the court is considering the factors to be taken into account in assessing the reasonableness of the expenses, it will have regard to the facts and circumstances as they reasonably appeared to the litigation friend or to the child's or protected party's legal representative when the expense was incurred.'

Low-value claims

38.34 Where judgment is given on terms that the amount awarded does not exceed £5,000, the sums which may be recovered in expenses are limited to no higher than 25% of the sums awarded (or, if the court gives permission, up to 50%). CPR, r 22.12 makes the following provision:

'(6)   Where the claim is settled or compromised, or judgment is given, on terms that an amount not exceeding £5,000 is paid to the child or protected party, the total amount the litigation friend may recover under paragraph (1) must not exceed 25% of the sum so agreed or awarded, unless the court directs otherwise. Such total amount must not exceed 50% of the sum so agreed or awarded.'

It is arguable that this limit would, in some circumstances, operate as a cap between opposing parties, but that point would rarely arise because such small claims would often be relegated to the small claims track where, of course, the issue of costs would be unlikely to arise.

Procedure

38.35 From the procedural point of view, PD 21, para 11 makes the following provisions:

'11.1   A litigation friend may make a claim for expenses under rule 21.12(1)—

(1)   where the court has ordered an assessment of costs under rule 48.5(2), at the detailed assessment hearing;

(2)   where the litigation friend's expenses are not of a type which would be recoverable as costs on an assessment of costs between the parties, to the Master or district judge at the hearing to approve the settlement or compromise under Part 21 (the Master or district judge may adjourn the matter to the costs judge); or

(3)   where an assessment of costs under Part 48.5(2) is not required, and no approval under Part 21 is necessary, by a Part 23 application supported by a witness statement to a costs judge or district judge as appropriate.

11.2   In all circumstances, the litigation friend must support a claim for expenses by filing a witness statement setting out—

(1)   the nature and amount of the expense; and

(2)   the reason the expense was incurred.'

Mental capacity

38.36   Persons who lack mental capacity have in the past been referred to as 'lunatics', 'mental patients', and the 'mentally disordered'; some of these terms are still encountered from time to time, but the term 'persons who lack mental capacity' seems, at present, to be most well received. This, perhaps, is because it reflects the language used in recent legislation, the Mental Capacity Act 2005 ('MCA 2005').

38.37   There are three sources of the law relevant to costs: the common law, statute, and codes of practice. The common law establishes a test of capacity and acts in such a way as to protect persons who have entered into contracts they were unable to understand. Statute gives guidance (and, in particular, it lays down five principles) which affects the test of capacity but otherwise broadly reflects the pre-existing common law. Statute also creates mechanisms by which a person's affairs may be managed for them if they lack capacity. Much of the guidance in MCA 2005 is all-encompassing and non-specific, and the need for detailed guidance (if only by analogy) is likely to be met by existing common law authorities.

38.38   The topic is addressed in four parts. First, there is a summary of MCA 2005 and, in particular, of the five presumptions mentioned above; secondly, there is an outline of the common law; thirdly, there is a brief overview of the effect that a person's incapacity will have on his ability to enter into a contract of retainer and, finally, there is a brief account of the steps that must be taken where a person is found to lack capacity, or it is thought that he might lack capacity. It should be borne in mind that the law is still in a state of flux following the coming into force of the 2005 Act, so the reader must carry out his own research in anything but the most obvious of cases.

The Mental Capacity Act 2005

38.39   MCA 2005 came into force in 2007.[48] It is supplemented by a Code of Practice issued by the Lord Chancellor.[49] The Code of Practice acknowledges that the 2005 Act's new definition of capacity is in line with the existing common law authorities; the code goes on to say that judges are at liberty to adopt the new definitions if they think it is

---

[48]   The provisions relevant to the law of costs came into force on 1 October 2007; transitional provisions apply (see Mental Capacity Act 2005 (Transitional and Consequential Provisions) Order 2007 (SI 2007/1898).

[49]   Which was issued by the Lord Chancellor on 23 April 2007 in accordance with MCA 2005, ss 42 and 43.

appropriate.[50] Thus, there is plasticity in the law; this is necessary because the issue of capacity is largely a factual exercise, and the relevant factors will differ from one area of law to another. MCA 2005, s 2 provides the following general definition of incapacity:

> '(1) For the purposes of this Act, a person lacks capacity in relation to a matter if at the material time he is unable to make a decision for himself in relation to the matter because of an impairment of, or a disturbance in the functioning of, the mind or brain.'

38.40 What amounts to impairment or disturbance of the functioning of the mind or brain will depend on the circumstances and the nature and extent of the impairment and, to that extent, some guidance may be obtained from the common law. Notwithstanding the occasional need to refer to the common law, both MCA 2005 and the Code of Practice give a good amount of guidance (much of which mirrors the common law), and it would be very rare for further guidance to be necessary in a detailed assessment or other matter relating to costs.

38.41 MCA 2005 establishes five key principles which empower and protect people who are thought to lack capacity:[51]

* a person must be assumed to have capacity unless it is established that he lacks capacity;
* a person is not to be treated as unable to make a decision unless all practicable steps to help him to do so have been taken without success;
* a person is not to be treated as unable to make a decision merely because he makes an unwise decision;
* an act done, or decision made, under this Act for or on behalf of a person who lacks capacity must be done, or made, in his best interests; and
* before any such act is done, or any such decision is made, regard must be had to whether the purpose for which it is needed can be as effectively achieved in a way that is less restrictive of the person's rights and freedom of action.

38.42 In addition, MCA 2005 stipulates that it does not matter whether the impairment or disturbance is permanent or temporary.[52] A lack of capacity cannot be established merely by reference to a person's age or appearance, or a condition of his, or an aspect of his behaviour, which might lead others to make unjustified assumptions about his capacity.[53] Any question whether a person lacks capacity within the meaning of the 2005 Act must be decided on the balance of probabilities.[54]

38.43 The Act goes on to provide that a person lacks capacity in respect of a decision if he is unable to do the following:[55]

* to understand the information relevant to the decision;
* to retain that information;
* to use or weigh that information as part of the process of making the decision; or
* to communicate his decision (whether by talking, using sign language or any other means).

---

[50] Mental Capacity Act 2005 Code of Practice, para 4.32.
[51] MCA 2005, s 1.
[52] MCA 2005, s 2(2).
[53] MCA 2005, s 2(3).
[54] MCA 2005, s 2.
[55] MCA 2005, s 3.

The common law

38.44 The common law test of capacity is whether or not the person was capable of understanding the nature of the contract into which he was entering:[56] it is the person's capacity to understand the actual contract under consideration that is relevant, rather than his capacity in general.[57] The nature of the contract is, therefore, a relevant factor. Although there is no authority on the point, it is possible that a client may have capacity to understand a simple contract of retainer (such as a 'CFA Lite'), but at the same time lack capacity to understand a more complex retainer (such as a retainer which provides for an hourly rate and a value element).[58] Capacity is time-specific: capacity may be regained, albeit temporarily, during lucid intervals.[59]

The effect of incapacity

38.45 A contract is binding upon the person who lacks capacity unless he can show that the other contracting party knew,[60] or ought to have known,[61] of his lack of capacity. It is not clear whether a paying party would be in a position to prove these things (or, for that matter, to challenge the receiving party's capacity) in circumstances where an allegedly incapable receiving party wishes to rely upon the contract of retainer in order to recover his costs.[62] The following points can be made, none of which make heartening reading for a paying party who wished to rely on his opponent's incapacity. The topic of what happens if a client loses capacity after having previously had capacity is addressed at **8.80**.

Enforceable until proven otherwise

38.46 There is no reason to believe that the *Bailey* presumption (see **11.26**) is to be afforded any less weight simply because one of the issues implicitly covered by the certificate to the bill is the factual issue of capacity. The court is likely to say that capacity is, on the whole, a factual issue and an issue of professional judgment, and that weight ought, therefore, to be afforded to the certificate. The paying party would be hampered by the fact that under MCA 2005 there are presumptions which require cogent evidence before the court could make a finding of incapacity. Whilst there is no authority on the point, there is scope for the court to go further than this and to say that a person who is thought to be incapacitated ought to have been given help to avoid that finding (see the second presumption at **38.41**), and that it would be undesirable to impose a retrospective finding of incapacity in circumstances where the receiving party had not received the assistance that Parliament has said that he ought to have had.

---

[56]   *Boughton v Knight* (1873) LR 3 P & D 64.
[57]   *Boughton v Knight* (1873) LR 3 P & D 64 at 72.
[58]   See, by way of analogy, *Manches v Trimborn* (1946) 174 LT 344, in which a person was found capable of understanding what a cheque was and what it did, but was found not to be capable of understanding the transaction for which a cheque was given in payment.
[59]   *Drew v Nunn* (1879) 4 QBD 661.
[60]   *Imperial Loan Co Ltd v Stone* [1892] 1 QB 599, CA.
[61]   *York Glass Co Ltd v Jubb* (1925) 134 LT 36, CA at 41.
[62]   Whilst not directly on point, the reasoning of the Court of Appeal in *Garbutt v Edwards* [2005] 1 All ER 553 may apply in this regard.

Adoption

38.47 If the incapacity is temporary or if the contract of retainer is validated by a person with capacity who lawfully acts on behalf of the person who lacks capacity, the court has the power to find that a contract has been be adopted and thus validated *ab initio*.[63]

Necessaries (common law)

38.48 Under common law,[64] where a contract for 'necessaries' was entered into by a person who did not have capacity to enter into that contract, that person would nonetheless be required to pay a reasonable price for the services rendered (but only if the circumstances suggest that this would be just).[65] The law relating to necessaries extends to the supply of necessary services.[66] The law of necessaries has already been addressed in the context of children (see **38.13–38.14**).

Necessary services (statute)

38.49 MCA 2005 provides that if necessary services are supplied to a person who lacks capacity to contract for the supply, he must pay a reasonable price for those services. The Act stipulates that 'necessary' means suitable to a person's condition in life and to his actual requirements at the time when the services are supplied.[67] To an extent, this provision reflects the common law (see **38.13**). There is no reason why a contract for the supply of legal services could not fall within this category.

Steps necessary to deal with mental incapacity

38.50 Thought will need to be given to the issue both where a new client is thought to lack capacity, and where an existing client is thought to have lost capacity. It should be noted that the Guidance to the Solicitors' Code of Conduct 2007 states that a retainer will automatically terminate if a client loses mental capacity;[68] this may or may not be correct, but it is worth bearing in mind as, at the very least, a possibility. If a solicitor is concerned that a client may lack capacity to enter into a contract of retainer, the Code of Practice states that it is the solicitor's responsibility to assess the client.[69] The Code of Practice recommends that, in cases of doubt, an opinion from a doctor or other professional expert should be obtained. Where a person's capacity to enter into a contract could later be challenged, the Code of Practice recommends that a formal assessment be carried out;[70] this may be required in any event to establish whether a person needs the assistance of the Official Solicitor or other litigation friend.

---

[63]   *Baldwyn v Smith* [1900] 1 Ch 588. As to the position of creditors once a person's property and affairs have become subject to the court's jurisdiction, see paras 682, 686 and 699.

[64]   Where the 'necessaries' are goods rather than services (as may be the case in respect of some disbursements), s 3 of the Sale of Goods Act 1954 made a very similar provision; in so far as mental capacity is concerned, that section has been repealed in order not to conflict with MCA 2005, s 7.

[65]   *Re Rhodes, Rhodes v Rhodes* (1890) 44 Ch D 94, CA.

[66]   *Re Rhodes, Rhodes v Rhodes* (1890) 44 Ch D 94, CA; *Re Beavan, Davies, Banks & Co v Beavan* [1912] 1 Ch 196 (in the context of the law of costs, it is worth noting that the Court of Appeal found that necessaries may include rent audit expenses; these would seem to be analogous to legal costs).

[67]   MCA 2005, s 7.

[68]   See para 6(a)(iii) of the guidance to rule 2.01.

[69]   Mental Capacity Act 2005 Code of Practice, para 4.40.

[70]   Mental Capacity Act 2005 Code of Practice, para 4.54.

Donees and deputies

38.51 If a person lacks capacity, it is possible for other persons to be given authority to act on his behalf. There are two mechanisms by which this may be done:

- *Donee:* a person who does not have capacity may (while he still has capacity) appoint another person to exercise lasting powers of attorney; that person is called a 'donee'; such an arrangement must comply with certain formalities and must be registered;[71] and
- *Deputy:* where the court finds that a person lacks capacity, the court has the authority to make decisions on that person's behalf, or to appoint another person to make decisions on the incapacitated person's behalf;[72] that person is referred to as a 'deputy'.

Unless there is reason to the contrary, a donee or a deputy may enter into a contract of retainer on behalf of the person who lacks capacity.

Contentious business agreements

38.52 Where the costs are payable by a person who lacks capacity pursuant to a contentious business agreement which has been entered into by a person acting in a representative capacity, the agreement must be laid before the court for the court's approval before payment; failure to do this can result in the representative person being ordered to account to the person who lacks mental capacity.[73] This is dealt with in detail at **8.139–8.193** and **8.198**. It should be borne in mind that a written agreement may easily be a contentious business agreement, even if this was not the intention of the counterparties.

LITIGANTS IN PERSON

Jurisdiction

38.53 Under the common law, a litigant in person (other than a solicitor)[74] is not entitled to claim costs in respect of his time;[75] only out-of-pocket expenses are recoverable.[76] Statute has intervened to allow the recovery of costs for time spent by a litigant in person; that intervention is in the form of the Litigants in Person (Costs and Expenses) Act 1975 (as amended) ('LP(CE)A 1975'), s 1(1) of which reads as follows:

---

[71]   MCA 2005, s 9(2).
[72]   MCA 2005, s 16.
[73]   Solicitors Act 1974, s 62.
[74]   Under the common law a solicitor who appeared as a litigant in person was entitled to costs as a solicitor but only if he would have been able to charge a fee qua a solicitor in the court in question had he been representing a client: see, for example, *H Tolputt & Co Ltd v Mole* [1911] 1 KB 87 and the discussion in *R v Sharpe* (unreported) 10 November 1995, QBD, Dyson J.
[75]   *Buckland v Watts* [1970] 1 QB 27; see also *London Scottish Benefit Society v Chorley, Crawford and Chester* (1884) 12 QBD 452; whilst not binding on any court, the VAT Tribunal has found that the principle of equality in European law did not have a bearing on the principle against the recovery of a litigant in person's costs under common law: *Serpes v Revenue & Customs Commissioners* (unreported) 22 December 2008, V&DTr.
[76]   The effect of the common law was dramatically demonstrated in a case which was decided in the days when a company was not able to be treated as a litigant in person; the receiving party was represented in court by a director, but his costs were not recoverable; this was despite the fact that he had been given a right of audience to represent the company at a trial: *Jonathan Alexander Ltd v Proctor* [1996] 1 WLR 518.

'Where, in any proceedings to which this subsection applies, any costs of a litigant in person are ordered to be paid by any other party to the proceedings or in any other way, there may, subject to rules of court, be allowed on the taxation or other determination of those costs sums in respect of any work done, and any expenses and losses incurred, by the litigant in or in connection with the proceedings to which the order relates.'

The rules of court referred to in that section are the CPR, and in particular CPR, r 48.6[77] and r 46.3(5).

Definition and status

38.54 LP(CE)A 1975 will not apply in all instances, which means that costs for time spent and work done will not be recoverable by all litigants in person, but this will rarely be an issue in most courts and tribunals.[78] There is no definition of a litigant in person in the 1975 Act or the CPR.[79] Peter Gibson LJ has explained that if a person is represented at all (even by an agent), then he may lose his status as a litigant in person.[80] There are exceptions to this:

(1) a person may receive legal advice in the conduct of his claim and still be classified as a litigant in person for those aspects of the claim which he conducted himself;[81]
(2) a litigant in person may, without losing his status, receive help in respect of an assessment from a costs practitioner;[82] and
(3) a person may continue to be a litigant in person notwithstanding the fact that he has instructed counsel under the Licensed Access Scheme.[83]

The first and third of these exceptions are a reflection of the fact that the right of representation is separate from the right to conduct litigation and that, in any event, a person's status will not necessarily be the same throughout the claim.[84]

38.55 Although it stops short of providing a definition of the phrase 'litigant in person', CPR, r 48.6(6) has the effect of widening the ambit of that phrase:

'(6) For the purposes of this rule, a litigant in person includes—

(a) a company or other corporation which is acting without a legal representative; and
(b) a barrister, solicitor, solicitor's employee or other authorised litigator (as defined in the Courts and Legal Services Act 1990 who is acting for himself.'

---

[77] CPR, r 48.6(1); although there is no authority on the point, he is probably relieved of his status as a litigant in person in respect of those aspects of the claim about which he was receiving advice.
[78] The Litigants in Person (Costs and Expenses) Act 1975 applies only to those tribunals in respect of which it is applied by s 1(2) of that Act or by Order; it applies in most costs-bearing tribunals, including all civil courts, the Land Tribunal, the First-tier Tribunal and the Upper Tribunal; where it does not apply, only out-of-pocket disbursements are recoverable (*Customs and Excise Commissioners v Ross* [1990] 2 All ER 65).
[79] Save for some qualifying remarks at CPR, r 48.6(6): see below.
[80] *Jonathan Alexander Ltd v Proctor* [1996] 1 WLR 518 at 525G.
[81] CPR, r 48.6(3)(b).
[82] CPR, r 48.6(3)(c).
[83] *Agassi v Robinson (HM Inspector of Taxes)* [2005] EWCA Civ 1507 at [25].
[84] See the discussion of this topic in *Agassi v Robinson (HM Inspector of Taxes)* [2005] EWCA Civ 1507 at [25].

Thus, companies and certain legal representatives are capable of being litigants in person. The Crown is not able to be a litigant in person.[85]

Quantum

38.56 There are two tiers by which a litigant in person's costs may be assessed; those two tiers are generally regarded as being separate and mutually exclusive. Where a litigant in person is able to prove financial loss, then, subject to certain restrictions, he would be entitled to compensation for that loss; where he is not able to show financial loss, then he would able to recover costs on the basis of a fixed, but almost nominal, hourly rate.

38.57 With one or two exceptions (see **38.73–38.75**), disbursements will be treated in a like manner to disbursements in any other context: in that regard, there is no difference in principle between the two tiers mentioned above.

General principles

38.58 The two tiers mentioned above are created and regulated by CPR, r 48.6:

'(2) The costs allowed under this rule must not exceed, except in the case of a disbursement, two-thirds of the amount which would have been allowed if the litigant in person had been represented by a legal representative.

(3) The litigant in person shall be allowed—

    (a)   costs for the same categories of—
        (i)   work; and
        (ii)   disbursements,

which would have been allowed if the work had been done or the disbursements had been made by a legal representative on the litigant in person's behalf;

    (b)   the payments reasonably made by him for legal services relating to the conduct of the proceedings; and
    (c)   the costs of obtaining expert assistance in assessing the costs claim.

(4) The amount of costs to be allowed to the litigant in person for any item of work claimed shall be—

    (a)   where the litigant can prove financial loss, the amount that he can prove he has lost for time reasonably spent on doing the work; or
    (b)   where the litigant cannot prove financial loss, an amount for the time reasonably spent on doing the work at the rate set out in the practice direction.'

Thus, in so far as costs for time spent are concerned, there is a cap of two-thirds of the amount that would have been allowed had the work been carried out by a legal representative; the policy underlying that restriction has its origins in the fundamental tenet that litigants must not profit from litigation.[86] There is then a further limit if the litigant in person is unable to show financial loss.[87] It is, thus, convenient to consider the law both where there is and where there is not financial loss.

---

[85]   Although the Crown is unable to recover monies as a litigant in person, statutory office holders (such as the official receiver or registrars of births, deaths and marriages) can: *Official Receiver v Brunt, sub nom In re Minotaur Data Systems Ltd* [1999] 1 WLR 1129.

[86]   *Hart v Aga Khan Foundation (UK)* [1984] 1 WLR 994 at 997, per Lloyd J; that is, it is that part of a solicitor's profit costs which represents the costs of running the practice with the profit element discounted.

[87]   CPR, r 48.6(4).

Time (financial loss)

38.59 There are two issues to quantifying costs for time spent where it is said that there has been financial loss. The first is the issue of whether there has been financial loss, and the second is the amount to be allowed.

Proof of financial loss

38.60 The issue of whether there has been pecuniary loss is a question of mixed fact and law.[88] The burden of proving financial loss rests with the receiving party[89] and is to be proved on evidence,[90] but the requisite standard of evidence will vary from case to case, depending on the occupational circumstances in which the work was done. Robert Walker J described the two ends of the spectrum of possible circumstances:[91]

> '[At one extreme ... a self-employed tradesman in a small but profitable way of business who has more customers than he can cope with and can fill every working hour to advantage; at the other extreme, a retired civil servant with an index-linked pension who finds the conduct of litigation a more interesting pastime than bowls or crossword puzzles.'

38.61 Loss of time has long been regarded as capable of equating to loss of income; Mainstay J had this to say (of a solicitor litigant in person):[92]

> 'Time is money to a solicitor; and why should he not be as much entitled to his proper costs, if he affords the time and skill which he brings to bear upon the business where he is a party to the action as he is where he is not a party.'

Professional persons

38.62 In more recent times, Douglas Brown J has implicitly found that loss of a professional's time is capable of amounting to a loss of earnings.[93] The fact that a loss of time is capable of giving rise to financial loss will not shift the evidential burden, however; this is because proof of actual loss is required. Patten J gave the following guidance:[94]

> 'It is not ... enough for the solicitor merely to establish that he or she was in practice during the relevant period. The solicitor must show that he could have charged for the time which he expended on his personal litigation. This does not ... mean that the solicitor in that position will have to prove that for all of the time expended on the litigation he could otherwise have been engaged on other clients' business, nor will it be necessary for the Court to examine in detail how successful or otherwise the solicitor's practice was at the relevant time. The rule is, for purely practical reasons, more broad-brush than that. The Court will assume that it was possible for the solicitor to have hired out his services to clients during the relevant period.

---

[88] *Official Receiver v Brunt, sub nom In re Minotaur Data Systems Ltd* [1999] 1 WLR 1129 at 1137.

[89] Pecuniary loss must be proved by evidence; the litigants in person in both *Mainwaring v Goldtech Investments Ltd* [1997] 1 All ER 467 and *Mealing-McLeod v Common Professional Examination Board* [2000] Costs LR 223 failed to do this.

[90] Where a litigant in person commences detailed assessment proceedings, he should serve copies of written evidence of financial loss (if he intends to prove loss) with the notice of commencement (CPD, art 42.3); he should also serve a copy of that evidence on any party against whom he seeks costs at least 24 hours before the hearing at which the question may be decided (CPD, art 42.2).

[91] *Mainwaring v Goldtech Investments Ltd* [1997] 1 All ER 467.

[92] *London Scottish Benefit Society v Chorley, Crawford and Chester* (1884) 12 QBD 452 at 457; see also *Malkinson v Trim* [2002] EWCA Civ 1273.

[93] *Stockinger v Highdorn Co Ltd* (unreported) 5 April 2001, QBD at [20].

[94] *Joseph v Boyd & Hutchinson* [2003] EWHC 413 (Ch) at [19].

But for his time to be regarded as valuable, the solicitor does, I believe, have to demonstrate that he has used up time in litigation during which he would otherwise have been able to pursue his practice as a solicitor for reward.'

Thus, it is necessary both to show that loss of time was capable of causing financial loss, and that this in fact did happen.

38.63 Douglas Brown J was speaking of a solicitor litigant in person, but there is no reason to believe that the same would not be the case with any other profession or trade where fees are ordinarily calculated on a time basis. Not all losses of a professional person's time would be capable of equating to a loss of income, however: a distinction must be drawn between work carried out in such a way as to reduce a professional's working day and work done during leisure time. Lloyd J has explained that the latter would not be regarded as giving risk to a financial loss.[95]

Determinants other than direct loss of fees

38.64 Loss of a professional's time which otherwise would have been billed to a client is not the only way in which financial loss can be determined; losses can be incurred in a variety of ways other than a direct loss of fees (such as where a person is employed, or where he has to employ a *locum tenens*). The fact that a holder of statutory office is salaried and that his salary would have been paid in any event will not prevent the court from finding that there has been pecuniary loss.[96] Another method of gauging whether there has been loss would include ascribing notional fees to the work done.[97] The relevant determinant will depend on the facts of the case.

Quantification in cases of financial loss

38.65 In the early days of the CPR[98] there was concern that if a litigant in person could show loss, he would be entitled to an amount of two-thirds of the reasonable fee of a notional lawyer regardless of whether his losses justified this.[99] There is some doubt as to whether these concerns were justified given the commonsense way in which the CPR were interpreted,[100] but on 2 December 2002 the CPR were amended[101] so as to put the issue beyond doubt. The appropriate measure is the amount that the litigant in person can prove he has lost for time reasonably spent on doing the work[102] (subject, of course, to being no more than two-thirds the reasonable fees of a notional lawyer).

---

[95]   *Hart v Aga Khan Foundation (UK)* [1984] 1 WLR 994 at 998; compare this with *Malkinson v Trim* [2002] EWCA Civ 1273 at [21], where it was held that work done in the firm's time is recoverable in full.

[96]   *Official Receiver v Brunt, sub nom In re Minotaur Data Systems Ltd* [1999] 1 WLR 1129 at 1138; this was by analogy with *In re Eastwood, decd* [1975] Ch 112.

[97]   See *Crown & Stafford Stone v Eccleshall Magistrates' Court* [1988] 1 All ER 430 (in which a solicitor was allowed his notional fees for appearing in his own case in a magistrates' court) and *R v Boswell, R v Halliwell* [1987] 2 All ER 513 (in which a barrister was allowed a notional fee for attending an appeal in respect of his own fees).

[98]   The method of quantification was restated on 2 December 2002.

[99]   Curiously, the provisions relating to fast track trial costs (CPR, r 46.3(5)) have not been amended so as to be in line with CPR, r 48.6.

[100] See, in particular, *HM Customs and Excise v Chitolie* (unreported) 30 November 2000, in which Robert Walker J made it clear that the amount to be allowed was the lower of the actual losses and the notional lawyer's fees.

[101] Civil Procedure (Amendment) Rules 2002 (SI 2002/2058), r 19.

[102] CPR, r 48.6(4).

38.66 There will be two layers to the court's discretion: the first will be the hourly rate and the second will be the time to be allowed. The first layer will be a process of making a finding as to the losses, and then limiting that rate to two-thirds of the reasonable rate of a notional lawyer. The first of these steps will not always be a matter of looking at the litigant's usual charging rate; this is because his losses may not be the same as would ordinarily be charged. An example is a case in which Arden J found that where a professional person had avoided his usual overheads, the allowable rate could reflect the fact that there was no loss relating to those overheads.[103]

38.67 Although there is no authority on the point, common sense dictates that if the costs are to be assessed on the basis of a notional lawyer's rate, the appropriate measure of time is the time that would have been spent by that notional lawyer (or, put otherwise, the fact that the work has not been carried out by a lawyer does not expand the categories of work for which costs may be allowed. This would be entirely in keeping with the way in which time is assessed where there has been no financial loss (see **38.68–38.70**) and with the express terms of CPR, r 48.6(3).

Time (no financial loss)

38.68 The amount which may be allowed where the litigant in person has suffered no financial loss is £18.00 per hour.[104] It is possible that this is an upper limit[105] but, in practice, there would be no reason to allow a lower rate. For practical purposes the assessment of a litigant in person's costs where he cannot show financial loss focuses on the time rather than the hourly rate.

38.69 Lloyd J (sitting in the Court of Appeal) has explained that the measure of time is that which would have been spent by a solicitor.[106] Buckley J acknowledged that approach, but explained that it was a test which must be applied sensibly:[107]

> 'We wondered whether [Lloyd J] had kept in mind that it is appropriate, in a proper case, to allow a litigant in person more time for a particular task that would be allowed to a solicitor. A solicitor's charging rate includes or takes account of the fact that he has support staff, secretaries, messengers and so forth. A litigant in person, for example, must himself post letters, take files to court and photocopy documents. "The time spent reasonably doing the work ..." mentioned in CPR 48.6(4) permits a reasonable assessment of the time spent by the litigant in person and should reflect those matters.'

Some commentators have implied that Buckley J's comments should be treated with caution,[108] but even if this is correct, the extent of that caution need not be great; this is because Buckley J was merely explaining that, whilst the measure is the time spent by a solicitor, that measure must be applied in the factual circumstances in which the litigant

---

[103] *Stubblefield v Kemp* [2001] 1 Costs LR 30.

[104] CPD, art 52.4; on 1 October 2011 this increased from £9.25 per hour, which had been the rate since 1995.

[105] Jacob J has explained the correct method, which is a follows: 'Find out in respect of the item what, at the litigant in person's charging rate, the total is. Compare that with two thirds of the notional solicitor rate. Give the lower of the two items.' (*Morris v Wiltshire and Woodspring District Council* (unreported) 16 January 1998); that said, the wording of the CPR does not suggest that the court would contemplate allowing a rate lower than the prescribed rate.

[106] *Hart v Aga Khan Foundation (UK)* [1984] 1 WLR 994 at 998 and 1005; more recently, see *R v LSC ex p Wulfsohn* [2002] EWCA Civ 250, in which Rix J impliedly accepted this principle as being correct; see also *Greville v Sprake* [2001] EWCA Civ 234.

[107] *Mealing-McLeod v Common Professional Examinations Board* [2000] 2 Costs LR 223.

[108] See, for example, Civil Bench Book, para 8.75.

found himself. There can be no objection to that. In particular, Buckley J did not say anything that runs contrary to CPR, r 48.6(3)(a):

> '(3) The litigant in person shall be allowed—
>
>   (a)   costs for the same categories of—
>   (i)   work; and
>   (ii)   disbursements,
>   which would have been allowed if the work had been done or the disbursements had been made by a legal representative on the litigant in person's behalf.'

These provisions mean that it would be wrong to make an allowance for work that would not be recoverable if carried out by a solicitor; Buckley J's comments went to the amount of time to be allowed rather than the types of work to which it relates, so there is no conflict. Whilst a solicitor would be hard pressed to persuade a court to allow time claimed for research into procedure, Rimer LJ has confirmed that such work is allowable in principle to a litigant in person.[109]

38.70 Costs which are not recoverable generally will not become recoverable solely by reason of the work having been carried out by the litigant personally. A litigant in person is, for example, not able to recover costs for time spent carrying out expert work beyond his own sphere of expertise.[110]

Disbursements and witness allowances

38.71 The right to payment in respect of disbursements is defined by CPR, r 48.6(3)(a). It is the right to be allowed costs for the same categories of disbursements which would have been allowed if the disbursements had been made by a legal representative on the litigant in person's behalf. Disbursements are allowable without the two-thirds restriction mentioned above (this reflecting the fact that there is no profit in recovering an outlay). For the reasons set out below, only disbursements actually incurred as proper disbursements can be recovered: disbursements cannot be recovered if they were incurred in lieu of work which would have been done by the notional legal representative (see **38.73**). The following points can be made.

Notional disbursements

38.72 A litigant in person is not entitled to notional disbursements; this was explained by Lloyd J, who was addressing the topic in the context of a claim for a notional counsel's fee:[111]

> 'There is a clear contrast between work and disbursements. Disbursements are allowed in full, just as they were before the Litigants in Person (Costs and Expenses) Act 1975, provided they would have been allowed if incurred by a solicitor, and provided they are actually incurred by the litigant in person. Work, on the other hand, is treated as if it had been done by a solicitor, and is then allowed up to two-thirds of the appropriate rate. What a solicitor would have been allowed is, of course, notional; but there is no room for a notional disbursement. Otherwise one would get the absurd position that the litigant in person would

---

[109] *Grand v Gill* [2011] EWCA Civ 902 at [14], citing *R v Legal Services Commission, ex p Wulfsohn* [2002] EWCA Civ 250.

[110] *Sisu Capital Fund Ltd v Tucker* [2005] EWHC 2321 (Ch); this case is useful for illustrating this point, but not all of it remains good law, so it should be treated with caution.

[111] *Hart v Aga Khan Foundation (UK)* [1984] 1 WLR 994 at 997.

be allowed 100 per cent of counsel's notional brief fee as a "disbursement", but only two-thirds of the solicitor's notional fee for attendance.'

Professional fees in lieu of legal representatives' work

38.73 Dyson LJ has explained that if the expenditure is a fee for work which the notional legal representative would normally have done himself, it is not a disbursement within the meaning of CPR, r 48.6(3)(a)(ii), primarily because it is not a disbursement that the legal representative would have incurred.[112] This, of course, applies only where the disbursement is the fee levied by a person who is not a legal representative (such as where the assistance is provided by an accountant or a surveyor); the fees of legal representatives can, in principle, be recovered.[113]

Disbursements in lieu of legal representatives' work

38.74 The same principle applies where the disbursement is for expenditure other than a fee. Pre-CPR authorities on that issue are no longer good law: pre-CPR, the disbursements incurred in lieu of a legal representative's fees would, in principle, have been recoverable[114] but the test under the CPD limits the allowable disbursements to those which would have been allowed if the disbursements had been made by a legal representative on the litigant in person's behalf.[115] Therefore, the points made at **38.73** would apply.

Witness allowances

38.75 A litigant who is allowed costs for attending court to conduct his case is not also entitled to a witness allowance in respect of that attendance.[116]

Payments for legal services

38.76 A litigant in person is entitled to payments reasonably made by him for legal services relating to the conduct of the proceedings.[117] Those monies may or may not be disbursements, depending on the status of the legal representative.

Expert assistance in respect of costs

38.77 Where a litigant in person requires expert assistance with an assessment of costs, he will be entitled to the reasonable fees of a costs practitioner (known as an 'expert assistant').[118]

38.78 In order to qualify as an expert assistant, the person in question must be a barrister, a solicitor, a Fellow of the Institute of Legal Executives, a Fellow of the

---

[112] See *Agassi v HM Inspector of Taxes* [2005] EWCA Civ 1507 at [73]–[76]; see also *United Building and Plumbing Contractors v Kajila* [2002] EWCA Civ 628.
[113] CPR, r 48.6(3)(b).
[114] See for example, *Law Society v Persaud* (1990) Costs LR, Core vol 114, per Hobhouse J.
[115] See *United Building and Plumbing Contractors v Malkit Singh Kajila* [2002] EWCA Civ 628 at [14].
[116] CPR, r 48.6(5).
[117] CPR, r 48.6(3)(b).
[118] See CPR, r 48.6(3)(c).

Association of Law Costs Draftsmen,[119] a law costs draftsman who is a member of the Academy of Experts, or a law costs draftsman who is a member of the Expert Witness Institute.[120]

Lawyers acting for themselves and on behalf of their firms

38.79 Where a lawyer acts for himself or on behalf of his firm, he may wish to avoid being categorised as being a litigant in person; he would wish to do this in order to avoid his fees being restricted as per the regime mentioned above. Different considerations will apply to different species of lawyer, as follows.

Solicitors

38.80 For the reasons set out at **5.34–5.68**, a solicitor litigant is entitled to recover costs as if he had instructed a solicitor to act on his behalf.[121] This principle applies regardless of whether the solicitor acts through himself, or through a partner or firm,[122] or through his employee.[123] This is a principle which has survived the introduction of the CPR.[124] It is not a principle which is based on contract, but is based on a principle of compensation which takes account of the expenditure of time. Chadwick LJ described the relevant policy in this way:[125]

> '[A] partner who is represented in legal proceedings by his firm incurs no liability to the firm; but he suffers loss for which under the indemnity principle he ought to be compensated, because the firm of which he is a member expends time and resources which would otherwise be devoted to other clients. The only sensible way in which effect can be given to the indemnity principle is by allowing those costs.'

38.81 There are some costs which cannot be recovered as a matter of principle, but they are not many in number. A solicitor litigant is not entitled to recover those costs which the fact of his acting has directly rendered unnecessary (such as costs of taking instructions from himself, etc).[126] In view of the fact that the recovery of a litigant in person's costs operates independently of contract, it is unlikely that a success fee would be recoverable.[127]

38.82 CPD, art 52.5 gives the following guidance, which is of particular relevance to solicitors:

> 'Attention is drawn to rule 48.6(6)(b). A solicitor who, instead of acting for himself, is represented in the proceedings by his firm or by himself in his firm name, is not, for the purpose of the Civil Procedure Rules, a litigant in person.'

---

[119] Whist there is no mention of costs lawyers, it is likely that the court would interpret this as being a reference to costs lawyers, this being because FALCDs no longer exist.
[120] CPD, art 52.1.
[121] *London Scottish Benefit Society v Chorley* (1884) 13 QBD 872.
[122] *Bidder v Bridges* (1887) WN 208 at 209, per Stirling J.
[123] *R v Stafford Stone and Eccleshall Magistrate's Court ex p Robinson* [1988] 1 All ER 430 at 432, per Simon Brown J.
[124] *Malkinson v Trim* [2002] EWCA Civ 1273.
[125] *Malkinson v Trim* [2002] EWCA Civ 1273 at [24].
[126] *London Scottish Benefit Society v Chorley* (1884) 13 QBD 872.
[127] *Malkinson v Trim* [2002] EWCA Civ 1273 (in particular, at [23]–[26]); there would, however, be nothing to prevent a solicitor from entering into a conditional fee agreement with his employer if this employer had a separate corporate identity, such as if it were a limited company.

Received teaching is that a firm is permitted to recover its costs via the medium of the work being carried out by one of its solicitors acting in the firm's name, and that this creates the facility whereby the firm avoids the two-thirds limit in CPR, r 48.6(2). It is debatable whether this view is correct and, in particular, it is a moot point whether CPD, art 52.5 achieves what it is said to achieve.[128]

Counsel

38.83 Whilst changes may be made in the near future, counsel in independent practice are not permitted to enter into partnerships, so a barrister in independent practice cannot rely on the mechanism mentioned above; put another way, a practising barrister acting for himself will always be a litigant in person and would never be able to act in the name of his firm.[129] This means that the 'two-thirds' restriction mentioned above would always apply to counsel in independent practice.

38.84 Whilst a criminal case and therefore only persuasive, Mitchell J has found that counsel may recover by way of costs remuneration for work done which required the application of his training, skills and professional experience; what he cannot do, however, is to recover 'costs' by reason of his 'attendance' at any hearing or at any conference or by reason of any 'work' he performed which could have been performed by any intelligent lay client.[130]

Other lawyers

38.85 Mitchell J made these comments (in respect of a claim involving a barrister litigant):[131]

> 'In this special class of case, work involving the time and skills of a practising lawyer for the purposes of legal proceedings to which he is a party is to be treated as an expense properly incurred because, in the event of a successful outcome, not only will he have mitigated his costs, but he is entitled to be indemnified in respect of that professional time and skill.'

These comments, which are *ratio*, are very wide in the sense that they allowed Mitchell J to decide the case before him not on some narrow point relating to specifically to counsel, but on first principles. Therefore, it could well be that they would apply equally well to other species of authorised litigator. In particular, in an appropriate case, they may apply to costs draftsmen.

Public bodies and the Crown

38.86 In most instances there will be little difference between costs litigation brought by or against public bodies or the Crown and those pertaining to other persons. There are, however, a number of particular principles that may arise from time to time. What

---

[128] Although the intention of those who drafted the CPD is clear, it is questionable whether a practice direction is able to qualify the meaning of CPR, r 48.6(6)(b), which says, in terms, that a solicitor or solicitor's employee acting for himself will be a litigant in person. It is arguable that CPD, art 52.5 does not reflect the true meaning of CPR, r 48.6(6)(b), in which case, a solicitor acting for himself would be limited by the 'two-thirds' rule, regardless of whether he acted in his own name or that of his firm.

[129] See CPR, r 48.6(6)(b); employed counsel might be in a different position, but they may find it difficult to prove financial loss.

[130] *Khan v Lord Chancellor* [2003] EWHC 12 (QB) at [78]; his analysis was based on the civil law and was thorough, so must be highly persuasive.

[131] *Khan v Lord Chancellor* [2003] EWHC 12 (QB) at [76].

follows is, in general, a discussion relating to civil litigation under the CPR in the civil courts; in other tribunals the CPR may apply only by analogy or possibly not at all, in which case highly specific statutory or tribunal-made principles may apply. In particular, it is common for the 'general rule' that the loser pays(CPR, r 44.2(a)) to apply only in the indirect sense that success is taken into account as being a factor relevant to the incidence of costs.[132] Whilst one or two such tribunals are referred to for the purposes of illustration, such issues are generally beyond the scope of this book.[133]

Orders against the Crown

38.87 Since 1 January 1948, civil proceedings to which the Crown is a party[134] have been procedurally similar to those brought against any other party.[135] Unless CPR Part 66, a practice direction or any enactment provides otherwise, the CPR apply to civil proceedings by or against the Crown and to other civil proceedings to which the Crown is a party.[136] In this regard, the Administration of Justice (Miscellaneous Provisions) Act 1933 makes the following provisions:[137]

> '7(1) In any civil proceedings to which the Crown is a party in any court having power to award costs in cases between subjects, and in any arbitration to which the Crown is a party, the costs of and incidental to the proceedings shall be in the discretion of the court or arbitrator to be exercised in the same manner and on the same principles as in cases between subjects, and the court or arbitrator shall have power to make an order for the payment of costs by or to the Crown accordingly:
>
> Provided that—
>
> (a)   in the case of proceedings to which by reason of any enactment or otherwise the Attorney-General, a Government department or any officer of the Crown as such is required to be made a party, the court or arbitrator shall have regard to the nature of the proceedings and the character and circumstances in which the Attorney-General, the department or officer of the Crown appears, and may in the exercise of its or his discretion order any other party to the proceedings to pay the costs of the Attorney-General, department or officer, whatever may be the result of the proceedings; and
>
> (b)   nothing in this section shall affect the power of the court or arbitrator to order, or any enactment providing for, the payment of costs out of any particular fund or property, or any enactment expressly relieving any department or officer of the Crown of the liability to pay costs.
>
> (2) In this section the expression "civil proceedings" includes ... proceedings by the Crown in the High Court or a county court for the recovery of fines or penalties, and references to proceedings to which the Crown is a party include references to proceedings to which the Attorney-General or any Government department or any officer of the Crown as such is a party, so, however, that the Crown shall not be deemed to be a party to any proceedings by reason only that the proceedings are proceedings by the Attorney-General on the relation of some other person.'

---

[132] See, for example, *The Racecourse Association v the Respondent et al* [2006] CAT 1 at [8], per Rimer J sitting in the Competition Appeals Tribunal.

[133] The writer has, however, prepared a draft chapter that could not be included for want of space; that draft will be forwarded to any reader upon request.

[134] In the context of the CPR, 'civil proceedings by the Crown. are those described in s 23(1) of the Crown Proceedings Act 1947, but excluding the proceedings described in s 23(3), 'civil proceedings against the Crown' means those proceedings described in s 23(2) of that Act, but excluding the proceedings described in s 23(3), and civil proceedings to which the Crown is a party has the same meaning as it has for the purposes of Parts III and IV of that Act by virtue of s 38(4): see CPR, r 66.1(2).

[135] Crown Proceedings Act 1947.

[136] CPR, r 66.2.

[137] Administration of Justice (Miscellaneous Provisions) Act 1933, s 7(1).

Thus, the main difference between the Crown and other litigants is that (in certain circumstances) there is an express statutory requirement that the court shall have regard to the nature of the proceedings and the character and circumstances in which the Crown appears. In practice, this adds very little as these factors would in any event be taken into account under CPR, r 44.3. This, however, is markedly different to the preceding common law, that was that the Crown neither paid nor received costs.[138]

38.88 In so far as the exercise of discretion is concerned, there is no reason to believe that the principle set out at **38.91–38.94** (namely, that in civil litigation public bodies will not be afforded special protection solely by virtue of their being public bodies); indeed, this much seems to be expressly provided for in the legislation set out above. It may also be relevant that many Government Departments have, where possible, committed themselves to ADR (see **6.172**). The culture of making no order for costs where one party was publicly funded and the other was a public body, on the ground that it would simply amount to transferring funds from one public body to another, was no longer acceptable.[139] The fact that a public body may be overworked is not a factor that can properly be taken into account.[140]

38.89 Where any costs are awarded to or against the Crown in the High Court, interest shall be payable upon those costs unless the court otherwise orders, and any interest so payable shall be at the same rate as that at which interest is payable upon judgment debts due from or to the Crown.[141]

38.90 Other than these points, the differences between costs litigation involving the Crown and that involving only other persons are largely procedural:

- **Place of proceedings:** CPR, r 30.3(2)(h) provides that in the case of civil proceedings by or against the Crown, the court must have regard to the location of the relevant government department or officers of the Crown and, where appropriate, any relevant public interest in the matter, and where appropriate, the matter should be tried in London; it is not clear whether this provision applies to detailed assessments.
- **Payment:** Final and interim costs certificates and orders for costs summarily assessed are not enforced against the Crown in the usual way; instead, a certificate is issued in the relevant amount which is then paid by the department in question. The Crown Proceedings Act 1947 makes specific provision for costs where the order provides for the payment of costs and the costs are required to be assessed, a proper officer may issue the certificate at any time after the costs have been assessed or within 21 days of the order, whichever is the later[142] An application for such a certificate may be made without notice.[143]

---

[138] It has been suggested that this rule came about by reason of the fact that the Statute of Gloucester did not name the Crown, thereby impliedly excluding it from the regime of costs between opposing parties (see Blackstone, Commentaries on the Laws of England (a facsimile of the First Edition of 1765–1769 reprinted by the University of Chicago Press, 1979) Vol 3, p 400; see also *Swift & Co v Board of Trade* [1926] 2 KB 131 at 137).

[139] *Bahta & Ors, R (on the application of) v Secretary of State for the Home Department & Ors* [2011] EWCA Civ 895 at [61], per Pill LJ.

[140] *Bahta & Ors, R (on the application of) v Secretary of State for the Home Department & Ors* [2011] EWCA Civ 895 at [60], per Pill LJ.

[141] Crown Proceedings Act 1947, s 24(2).

[142] See Crown Proceedings Act 1947, s 25(1).

[143] CPR, r 66.6(3).

Public bodies discharging an administrative function

38.91   Where a public body (which may include the Crown) is a litigant by reason of the exercise of some statutory or other public duty, it may be argued that it ought to be afforded a degree of protection against costs. It would seem that in civil litigation the court will reject such a suggestion (see **38.92–38.94**), but that in other tribunals public bodies may be afforded a degree of protection (see **38.95**). It should be noted that in none of those cases cited in the latter category (ie, other tribunals) was the tribunal exercising any powers under s 51 of the Senior Courts Act 1981 (as amended); as such, it is safe to work on the basis that in civil litigation the position is governed by the principles at **38.92–38.94** rather than **38.95**.

38.92   Perhaps the starting point is to state the law as it is now known not to be. The incorrect law was stated by Harman J in these terms:[144]

> 'I think I can properly say that there has grown up something of a practice in the court not to visit upon the department costs incurred by a director who has been proceeded against in a case where there is cause to investigate . . . but, more than that, cause to believe that there is a prima facie case of unfitness to be a director, which prima facie case is then rebutted by the evidence that comes in. So had evidence, being credible evidence and unlikely to be destroyed by cross-examination, shows that the appearance of unfitness was, indeed, no more than an appearance.'

In a scathing judgment with which McCowan and Beldam LJJ agreed, Nourse LJ found that the supposed practice was unlawful.[145] In a different case but in a similar vein, Sedley LJ commented that the public body in question (the Crown Prosecution Service) had no 'special litigation position or status'.[146] Dyson J came to a similar conclusion in an administrative matter.[147] Lord Neuberger MR had this to say (in the context of the public law claim):[148]

> '[I]t may be said that government and public bodies should be encouraged to settle, and should not therefore be penalised in costs if they do so after proceedings have been issued. There are four answers to that. First, if it is a good point, it should apply to any litigation, whether in private law or public law, and in very few, if any, private law cases would such an argument carry any weight. The implication that public authority Defendants should be in a more privileged position than other Defendants in this connection is not, in my view, maintainable. Secondly, it is simply unfair on the Claimant or his lawyers if, at least in the absence of special factors, he does not recover his costs of bringing wholly successful proceedings, provided that they have been properly brought and conducted. Thirdly, while Defendants may be more ready to concede a claim rather than fight it if they know that they will not thereby be liable for the Claimant's costs, it can forcefully be said that the fact that, if Defendants know they will have to pay the Claimant's costs, it would be a powerful

---

[144]   *Re Southbourne Sheet Metal Co Ltd* [1993] 1 WLR 244, where there is an extract taken from the court below, which is reported at [1992] BCLC 361 at 363.

[145]   *Re Southbourne Sheet Metal Co Ltd* [1993] 1 WLR 244 at 245; to the extent that other judges may have adopted the supposed practice, they were wrong to do so, and in that regard the costs relating to *Re Austinsuite Furniture Ltd* [1992] BCLC 1047, per Vinelott J were wrongly decided.

[146]   *Grimes v Crown Prosecution Service* [2003] EWCA Civ 1814 at [30]; see also *R (Bahta and ors) v Home Secretary* [2011] EWCA Civ 895 at [60], per Pill LJ.

[147]   Dyson J (as he then was) in *R v Lord Chancellor, ex p Child Poverty Action Group* [1999] 1 WLR 347. See also *R (on the application of AK & Ors) v Secretary of State for the Home Department & Ors* [2011] EWCA Civ 895.

[148]   *M v Mayor and Burgesses of the London Borough of Croydon* [2012] EWCA Civ 595 at [53].

incentive to concede the claim sooner rather than later. Fourthly, if the Defendants wish to settle, the time to do so is before proceedings are issued: that is one of the main reasons for the introduction of the Protocol.'

On the whole, first instance tribunals exercising a civil (that is, non-regulatory) function have taken a similar view, as have most appellate tribunals;[149] this is discussed in more detail in **38.95–38.96.**

38.93 Brooke LJ has explained that public bodies need to engage in the process of dispute resolution in just the same way as any other litigant. He had this to say:[150]

'But that does not, in my judgment, mean that the CPS were entitled to behave, as litigants far too often behaved before the CPR came in, by simply standing back and saying:

"We will make no offer at all for the court to consider when it decides what order as to costs is a reasonable one to make. We will simply see you in court."'

Brooke LJ went on to criticise the CPS for not having made any offers.

38.94 In a different case Brooke LJ explained that the fact that the public authority may have incurred costs in order to clarify a point of law of particular contemporary concern did not mean that it should be relieved of the burden of paying its opponent's costs if unsuccessful.[151] Likewise, Moses LJ has explained that a public body will not be immune from being ordered to pay costs on the indemnity basis solely by reason of a putative need to protect the public purse; he said this:[152]

'[If] anyone should suffer as a result of HMRC's laudable persistence, it is the taxpayer at large, on whose behalf HMRC fought this particular appeal. It lost, and it is difficult to see why, in those circumstances, a particular trader which vindicated its rights . . . should be deprived of the effect of its Part 36 offer. If the Crown wishes its particular position to be acknowledged in the Rules, then they should seek amendment.'

In a similar vein, Lord Neuberger MR has said that it would 'not be good enough for [a public authority] to say that they had not got round to dealing with the Claimant's claim because of [their] "heavy workload" or "constraints upon [their] resources"'.[153]

38.95 Public bodies will not always be denied special status, however, and this will be particularly so where the public body in question is taking an essentially administrative decision (to use the phraseology of Neuberger MR).[154] In the context of licensing appeals,[155] Bingham CJ has said that where a complainant has successfully challenged an administrative decision by a regulatory authority acting honestly, reasonably, properly and on grounds that reasonably appeared to be sound, in exercise of its public duty, the court should consider, in addition to any other relevant fact or circumstances, both (i) the financial prejudice to the particular complainant in the particular

---

[149] See, for example, in respect of non-penalty cases in the Competition Appeals Tribunal *Racecourse Association v OFT et al* [2006] CAT 1 at [9], per Rimer J.

[150] *Grimes v Crown Prosecution Service* [2003] EWCA Civ 1814 at [21] and [22].

[151] *Bradford Metropolitan District Council v Yorkshire Water Services Ltd* [2001] EWHC 803 (Admin).

[152] *Commissioners for HM Revenue and Customs v Blue Sphere Global Limited* [2010] EWCA Civ 1448 at [11].

[153] *M v Mayor and Burgesses of the London Borough of Croydon* [2012] EWCA Civ 595 at [54], quoting with approval *R (Bahta) v Secretary of State for the Home Department* [2011] EWCA Civ 895 at [63].

[154] See, for example, *R (on the application of Perinpanathan) v City of Westminster Magistrates' Court and another* [2010] EWCA Civ 40, per Lord Neuberger MR at [64].

[155] Which are not conducted under the CPR.

circumstances if an order for costs is not made in his favour; and (ii) the need to encourage public authorities to make and stand by honest, reasonable and apparently sound administrative decisions made in the public interest without fear of exposure to undue financial prejudice if the decision is successfully challenged.[156] In a similar vein, Lord Neuberger MR has explained that this approach may be appropriate where the body in question was performing one of its regulatory functions;[157] he went on the explain that the approach also applied where the body in question was carrying out its functions of seeking a sanction.[158]

38.96 This approach (usually known as 'the *Booth* principle') has been applied in one guise or another in several regulatory contexts. Examples include disciplinary proceedings against accountants[159], disciplinary proceedings against solicitors,[160] proceedings under the Dangerous Dogs Act 1871,[161] vehicle licensing proceedings,[162] proceedings under s 80 of the Environmental Protection Act 1990,[163] proceedings concerning antisocial behaviour orders,[164] and forfeiture proceedings.[165] The *Booth* principle has its limits, however: whilst not binding, Roth J has explained that where there is an appeal from an administrative or regulatory decision, the *Booth* principles will not apply.[166] Examples of that type of tribunal would include the Competition Appeals Tribunal[167] and the Asylum and Immigration Tribunal.[168]

38.97 It is important to note that none of the examples given above relate to the exercise of the court's discretion under CPR, r 44.3; as such they are of very limited application in the context of civil litigation.

---

[156] *Bradford Metropolitan District Council v Booth* (2000) 164 JP 485 at 488; see also *R (on the application of Telford and Wrekin Borough Council) v Crown Court at Shrewsbury* [2003] EWHC 230 (Admin), per Moses J.

[157] *R (on the application of Perinpanathan) v City of Westminster Magistrates' Court and another* [2010] EWCA Civ 40, per Lord Neuberger MR at [65].

[158] *R (on the application of Perinpanathan) v City of Westminster Magistrates' Court and another* [2010] EWCA Civ 40, per Lord Neuberger MR at [71]. Whilst not binding, see also *Eden Brown v Office of Fair Trading* [2011] CAT 29 at [15], per Roth J.

[159] *R (on the application of Gorlov) v Institute of Chartered Accountants in England and Wales* [2001] EWHC 220 (Admin), per Jackson J; this, of course, will be subject to any tribunal-specific rules.

[160] *Baxendale-Walker v Law Society* [2006] EWHC 643 (Admin); this, of course, will be subject to any tribunal-specific rules.

[161] *Swale Borough Council v Boulter* [2002] All ER (D) 378 (Oct), per Maurice Kay J.

[162] *Milton Keynes Council v Edwards* [2004] EWHC 267 (Admin), per Harrison J.

[163] *Waveney District Council v Lowestoft (North East Suffolk) Magistrates' Court* [2008] EWHC 3295 (Admin), per Charles J.

[164] *Manchester City Council v Manchester Crown Court and others* [2009] EWHC 1866 (Admin), per Burton J

[165] *R (on the application of Perinpanathan) v City of Westminster Magistrates' Court and another* [2010] EWCA Civ 40, per Lord Neuberger MR.

[166] *Eden Brown v Office of Fair Trading* [2011] CAT 29 at [15], per Roth J citing *Walker v Royal College of Veterinary Surgeons* [2007] UKPC 20.

[167] See *Eden Brown v Office of Fair Trading* [2011] CAT 29 at [16], per Roth J.

[168] *R (Bahta and ors) v Home Secretary* [2011] EWCA Civ 895 at [60], per Pill LJ.

Chapter 39

SPECIFIC TYPES OF LITIGATION

39.1 This chapter deals with the costs of group litigation, derivative claims, representative claims and public law claims.

GROUP LITIGATION

39.2 It is assumed that the reader is familiar with the principles of apportionment (see **34.125–34.159**). If the reader is not familiar with those principles—the most important of which is the principle of 'equal apportionment' – the relevant parts of Chapter 34 should be read either before or in conjunction with this chapter.

39.3 Broadly speaking, this sub-chapter addresses that type of litigation that is governed by group litigation orders ('GLOs'). There are, however, other ways in which groups of disputants can be case-managed, such as by case consolidation and by appointing representative claims. Those methods have much in common with group litigation, so much of what is said below would apply even in the absence of a GLO.

Terminology

39.4 The CPR define a number of relevant terms.[1] A GLO is defined as an order to provide for the case management of claims which give rise to common or related issues of fact or law (the 'GLO issues'). A 'group litigant' is a claimant or defendant whose claim is entered onto a 'group register', which is a list of persons who are parties to the group litigation. The register is kept either by the court or by one of the parties' solicitors (usually the claimants').

39.5 The 'management court' is the court which has been be appointed to manage the claims on the group register.[2] A judge may be appointed to oversee the GLO: he is the 'managing judge'.

39.6 'Individual costs' are those costs incurred in the pursuit or defence of an individual claim. A 'test claim' is a claim of a person on the group register whose claim is litigated for the purpose of resolving GLO issues; a test claim will often, but not always,[3] be representative of other claims.

---

[1]   See CPR, r 48.6A(2) and CPR Part 19 III.
[2]   CPR, r 19.11.
[3]   That is, where a claimant's claim is the only one of its type and there are no other similar cases in the litigation, that case can (and probably must) proceed as a test case: *Nash v Eli Lilly* [1993] 4 All ER 383 at 414.

39.7 'Common costs' are those costs incurred in pursuing or defending the GLO issues, including the costs of individual claims which are proceeding as test claims. Common costs will include costs incurred by the lead solicitor in administering the group litigation, such as the costs of keeping the group register. These three species of common costs are often referred to as 'GLO costs', 'test-case costs' and 'administration costs' respectively.

39.8 Non-standard terminology may be encountered from time to time. The term 'lead costs' may be used to refer to test-case costs. The term 'generic costs' should be treated with caution; this is because it will often have a specific meaning ascribed to it by the GLO. Where this is not so, it is usually – but not always – used to refer to common costs.

Costs sharing agreements

39.9 Although not defined in the CPR, a 'costs sharing agreement' may be categorised as a 'funding costs sharing agreement' ('FCSA')—which is an instrument which states co-litigants' relative or absolute contributions towards their own costs—and a 'liability costs sharing agreement' ('LCSA'), which is an instrument which states co-litigants' relative or absolute liability for an opponent's costs. The two are often combined in the same written instrument. If no agreement can be reached, then a costs sharing order may be made in lieu. Contractual issues concerning costs sharing agreements are addressed at **8.427–8.431**). A draft agreement (an FCSA) can be found in Chapter 44.

Initial considerations

39.10 It is often appropriate to consider the issue of costs at an early stage in the litigation; where this is so, the following issues frequently arise:

- whether an FCSA (or order in lieu) should be made;
- whether an LCSA (or order in lieu) should be made;
- whether any orders or agreements are required concerning how the costs of test claims are to be borne;[4]
- whether estimates of costs are required and, if so, whether those estimates should relate to common costs, individual costs, or both;
- whether a costs capping order should be made;[5]
- whether there should be quarterly rests for discontinuers and settlers;[6]
- whether the GLO should make other provisions for discontinuers and settlers, and whether it should make provision for late joiners;[7]
- whether there is a need for any category of costs to be accounted for separately, such as administration costs, GLO costs, etc;
- whether the parties who are awarded costs before the conclusion of the litigation should be permitted to have their costs assessed forthwith;
- whether ATE insurance provision is appropriate and adequate; and
- whether litigation funding (ie, third-party funding) should be considered.

---

[4] PD 19B, para 12.4.
[5] See Chapter 15.
[6] See **39.38–39.41**.
[7] In particular, whether any special provisions should apply in relation to discontinuers (see below).

This list is not by any means exhaustive. Costs issues in group litigation can become complex and challenging, and this is particularly likely if the costs issues are not actively managed during the litigation itself. The CPR make express provision for the managing judge to appoint a costs judge to assist him as an assessor; the costs judge may attend case management hearings, where this is appropriate.[8] Costs conditions may be imposed, such as the condition concerning disclosure of an ATE policy.[9]

Lead solicitors

39.11 PD 19B, para 2.2 recommends that where more than one firm is involved in group litigation, a solicitors' group should be formed, and one of their number should be nominated to take the lead role. That solicitor's role should be defined in writing.[10] In very complex claims, different lead roles may need to be allocated to different firms.

Liability, retainers and apportionment

39.12 For the purposes of this sub-chapter, it will be assumed that there is one defendant and many claimants. This is for illustrative purposes only.

39.13 Where many litigants pursue a common cause, a number of issues will arise as to who is liable for costs; those issues may be summarised as follows:

- the extent to which the claimants are each to bear the individual costs incurred in respect of other claimants' claims (see **39.14**);
- the extent to which the claimants are each to bear the GLO costs and administration costs as between themselves (see **39.15–39.19**);
- the extent to which the claimants, and the test claimants in particular, are (between themselves) each to bear the test-case costs (see **39.20–39.25**);
- the extent to which the claimants are each to bear the defendant's costs if ordered to pay those costs (see **39.26–39.32**); and
- the extent to which the defendant is to bear the claimants' costs if ordered to pay the costs of only some of them (see **39.33–39.37**).

Individual costs

39.14 Unless there is an agreement to the contrary, a litigant will be responsible for the costs attributable to his own claim, but he will not be responsible for the costs incurred solely in pursuing someone else's claim (unless that claim is a test claim). These issues are dealt with more fully at **34.125–34.159** but, in essence, any costs relating solely to the claim of one client should be charged to him only and to the exclusion of the other clients.[11]

GLO and administration costs

39.15 Many of the issues concerning liability for the costs of pursuing or defending GLO issues and administration costs have already been addressed at **34.125–34.159**. In essence, unless there is an order or agreement to the contrary, the principle of equal

---

8   PD 19B, para 8.
9   *Barr v Biffa Waste Services Ltd* [2009] EWHC 1033 (TCC).
10 See also CPR, r 19.13(c).
11 *Bayliss v Kelly and Ors* [1997] 2 Costs LR 54.

apportionment will apply.[12] Where there is an agreement dealing with the issue of apportionment (such as an FCSA) the court would not be bound by that agreement, but would rarely depart from its terms.[13]

Default position under the CPR

39.16 There is a default position which will apply even where there is no express provision within a costs sharing agreement or order detailing the litigants' liability for common costs. This is as a result of CPR, r 48.6A(4), which makes the following provisions:

> '(4)   The general rule is that where a group litigant is the paying party, he will, in addition to any costs he is liable to pay to the receiving party, be liable for—
>
> (a)   the individual costs of his claim; and
> (b)   an equal proportion, together with all the other group litigants, of the common costs.'

Thus, there is a 'general rule' that when a litigant is a paying party, he will be liable not only for the costs of his claim, but also for his share of the common costs. To this extent the CPR mirror the common law (ie the principle of equal apportionment).

Default position under the common law

39.17 Even where there is no costs sharing agreement relating to common costs, Smith LJ has explained that a client would be liable to his solicitors for his share of the common costs properly incurred for his benefit:[14]

> 'I am satisfied that there is no requirement for [a costs sharing] agreement relating to generic costs [ie common costs]. The client's entitlement is to recover the costs for which he would have been liable to his solicitor. He would be liable for all costs properly incurred whether they were incurred solely on his behalf or whether they were incurred for the benefit of a large group and he had only to pay an appropriate proportion. There is nothing fundamentally different or special about generic costs; they are simply costs that have been shared for the sensible purpose of keeping the costs of each claim down. I can see no merit in the suggestion that some special rule applies to the generic element of a bill of costs.'

Late joiners, settlers and discontinuers

39.18 Even a principle as straightforward as the principle of equal apportionment can become unwieldy if co-litigants drift in and out of the litigation. CPR, r 48.6A(6) makes the following provision about late joiners:

> 'Where common costs have been incurred before a claim is entered on the group register, the court may order the group litigant to be liable for a proportion of those costs.'

The court *may* (not must) order a late joiner to bear a part of the costs which had already been incurred before he joined; the court has a discretion to depart from the principle of equal apportionment, if the circumstances permit.

---

[12]   *In re Colquhoun* (1854) 5 DM & G 35; *Ellingsen v Det Skandinaviske Compani* [1919] 2 KB 567; and, more recently, *Bayliss v Kelly and Ors* [1997] 2 Costs LR 54.
[13]   *BCCI v Ali & Ors* [2000] 2 Costs LR 243; and *Gomba Holdings (UK) Ltd v Minories Finance Ltd* [1993] Ch 172.
[14]   *Russell Young & Co v Brown & Ors* [2007] EWCA Civ 43.

39.19 CPR, r 48.6A(7) makes similar provision for settlers and discontinuers; this is dealt with at **39.38–39.41**.

Test-case costs

39.20 Unless there is an agreement or order to the contrary, the principle of equal apportionment will apply to liability for the costs of test cases. This is illustrated by *Davies v Eli Lilly & Co*,[15] which was one of the first group action cases in which the issue of costs sharing arose;[16] about 1,500 claimants claimed damages arising out of the use of a drug. The managing judge ordered that the claimants would bear the costs of the test claims on a per capita basis; this was on the advice of an amicus appointed by the court.

39.21 Longmore LJ approved of that approach (ie per capita):[17]

'This resolved an important practical difficulty that, if there was to be one or more legal actions, the claimants in those lead actions would otherwise have had to bear all the costs themselves. Even if such claimants won, the burden of irrecoverable costs would be too great for any claimant, who did not have legal aid, to bear them; moreover, even any legally aided claimant would be liable to find his damages wiped out by the Law Society's charge for costs.'

39.22 In a different case, Donaldson MR also commented favourably on per capita apportionment:[18]

'Those who have practised in the Commercial Court ... will recognise the age old respectability of such an order, based as it clearly is upon the Rhodian Law, the Rolls of Oleron and the maritime law of general average.'

39.23 Test-case costs are common costs and therefore the 'general rule' in CPR, r 48.6A(4) applies (see **39.16**). Likewise, the rules concerning late joiners[19] and early leavers[20] will also apply (see **39.18–39.19**).

Personal position of test-case litigants

39.24 The existence of a fee sharing agreement will not deprive a successful test-case litigant of the benefit of his success, ie by being awarded only part of his costs.[21]

39.25 Test-case costs should not also be categorised as individual costs: this means that the individual litigant to whom the costs relate would not generally be personally liable for the whole of the costs incurred while his claim was proceeding as a test claim. This would usually be true even if the other litigants objected to paying those costs on the

---

[15] [1987] 1 WLR 1136.
[16] See *Aiden Shipping Co Ltd v Interbulk Ltd* [1986] AC 965; GLOs did not exist before the mid-1980s; moreover, it was not until 1986 that it was realised that costs orders could be made in respect of non-parties.
[17] *Afrika & Ors v Cape plc* [2001] EWCA Civ 2017 at [10].
[18] *Ward v Guinness Mahon plc* [1996] 1 WLR 894.
[19] CPR, r 48.6A(6).
[20] CPR, r 48.6A(7).
[21] *Nash v Eli Lilly & Co* [1993] 4 All ER 383 at 415; in practice, in many cases the amount a successful test-case claimant is ultimately awarded may be restricted by the operation of the indemnity principle.

grounds of some perceived impropriety on the part of the test-case litigant; one reason for this common-law rule is to avoid discouraging those who would otherwise put themselves forward as test-case litigants.[22]

Claimants' liability (adverse costs)

39.26 The issue here is the extent to which the co-claimants are to bear the defendant's costs in the event of an adverse costs order being made against them. Again, for the purposes of illustration, it is assumed that there is one defendant and many claimants.

Preliminary rulings

39.27 The court may be asked to make a preliminary ruling at the outset of the litigation dealing with the potential individual liabilities of the co-claimants in the event of an adverse costs order being made. Such an order is not a pre-emptive order in the sense that it determines the incidence of costs, but it is pre-emptive in the sense that it legislates for how costs should be apportioned if and when the incidence of costs is determined against the co-claimants.[23] It is a relatively recent jurisdiction.[24]

Several liability and apportionment

39.28 The need to allow co-claimants to know their potential liability before the litigation is commenced underlies CPR, r 48.6A(3):

> 'Unless the court orders otherwise, any order for common costs against group litigants imposes on each group litigant several liability for an equal proportion of those common costs.'

This provision can, perhaps, be seen as being a codification of the common law; it is worth briefly setting out the common law on the topic.

39.29 In *Ward v Guinness Mahon plc*,[25] a large number of investors claimed damages against the sponsor of a business venture which ultimately failed. Lord Bingham MR commented that the order in *Davies v Eli Lilly & Co*[26] (see **39.20**) was directed to the position of the claimants amongst themselves (ie funding costs) rather than to the position of the co-claimants vis-à-vis the defendant (ie adverse costs). He went on to consider whether he had a jurisdiction to make an order that could 'bite on the defendants', as he put it; he found that he did.

39.30 The defendants argued that each co-claimant (including each test-case claimant) should be jointly liable. The claimants argued that their liability should be restricted (ie several) to a proportionate share of the common costs (which would include the costs of the test claims); without such an order – they argued – there would be reluctance on the part of individual claimants to be selected as test claimants.

---

22 *BCCI v Ali & Ors* [2000] 2 Costs LR 243.
23 *Afrika & Ors v Cape plc* [2001] EWCA Civ 2017 at [15].
24 One of the first instances was *In re Westdock Realisations Ltd* [1988] BCLC 354, albeit not in group litigation; the first instance of the jurisdiction being exercised in group litigation was *Ward v Guinness Mahon plc* [1996] 1 WLR 894.
25 [1996] 1 WLR 894.
26 [1987] 1 WLR 1136.

39.31 Lord Bingham MR preferred the claimants' arguments. He took account of a report published in 1995 by a Law Society working party in which the following recommendation was made:[27]

> 'One point on which there is general agreement is that if defendants win on common issues and costs are ordered against the plaintiffs, the liability of plaintiffs should be several rather than joint. Thus, if a defendant incurs £1m costs defending the common issues of claims brought by 1,000 plaintiffs, the maximum common costs liability of any individual plaintiff will be £1,000 (subject to costs protection for legally-aided claimants). Any other arrangement would make the risk inherent in group actions so great as to limit access to justice solely to those plaintiffs with nothing at all to lose. Regardless of the number of plaintiffs sharing costs, no individual plaintiff could hope to satisfy the private client test. Whilst several liability will make it much harder for defendants to recover their costs when they are successful, we see no real alternative to such a rule.'

Lord Bingham MR rejected the submission that it would be best to wait until the end of the litigation before making any order; he said that that approach would run counter to the need to allow co-claimants to know – before they start – where they stand.

Late joiners, settlers and discontinuers

39.32 The liability costs sharing order may include a period during which a number of co-claimants are taken off the register. There is usually no need for that factor to be specifically taken into account at the time the order is made; this is because the defendant's bill of costs can be split into parts in such a way as to enable the costs to be assessed by reference only to those periods during which any given litigant was on the group register. The same is not true of late joiners, however; this is because the court will need to consider whether to make an order that the late joiner is to bear a part of the common costs already incurred.[28] Therefore, specific provision will usually have to be made, both in the order, and also in the bill of costs.

Defendant's liability

39.33 The issue here is the extent to which the defendant is to bear the claimants' costs if ordered to pay the costs of some but not all of them.

Failed claims

39.34 The defendant's liability will usually be obvious from the context in which the order was made; in particular, the fact that the court has limited the beneficiaries of the order to some but not all of the claimants will usually make it palpably clear that the defendant is not to be liable for the costs of the failed claims. However, the successful claimants may argue that they should be fully indemnified in respect of their costs, and that that indemnity embraces all common costs, rather than merely a proportionate share thereof.

39.35 In most cases such an argument would be defeated by the principle of equal apportionment, which would restrict the defendant's liability by the operation of the indemnity principle. Moreover, even if the successful claimants were able to show that the costs were not restricted as a result of the operation of the indemnity principle, they

---

[27] At para 7.4.2.
[28] CPR, r 48.6A(6).

would still have to demonstrate that the principle of equal apportionment should not apply to the interpretation of the costs order: that would be a difficult to thing to do in circumstances where the court has made an order that some, but not all, of the claimants be awarded their costs.

No costs sharing agreement

39.36 In some cases a defendant may argue that common costs are not recoverable for want of an FCSA. That would be a difficult argument to make good. In particular, Smith LJ has found that where there is no formal GLO and no costs sharing agreement, a client would still have a liability for his share of the common costs properly incurred for his benefit.[29]

Late joiners

39.37 For the reasons set out above (at **39.32**), it may be necessary to consider the position of late joiners. In particular, if one of the successful claimants joined the litigation part way through, the court may need to make an order stating whether the defendant should pay anything towards that claimant's share (if any) of the common costs incurred before his name was entered on the group register.

Rests, settlers and discontinuers

39.38 In the same way that provision is made for late joiners, CPR, r 48.6A(7) makes the following provision for settlers and discontinuers:

> 'Where a claim is removed from the group register, the court may make an order for costs in that claim which includes a proportion of the common costs incurred up to the date on which the claim is removed from the group register. (Part 19 sets out rules about group litigation.)'

Thus where a litigant leaves the litigation early his liability for common costs may be reduced accordingly.

39.39 May J has developed the concept of the cost-sharing order which provides for quarterly rests; this is for the purpose of calculating the costs of settlers and discontinuers. He had this to say:[30]

> 'In principle the plaintiffs, individually and as a group, and the defendants need to know the basis upon which costs liabilities would be spread if an order for costs were made or came into force. The underlying principle should be that costs which it is appropriate to apportion between or for the benefit of plaintiffs should be divided by the total number of relevant plaintiffs. Costs which it is appropriate to apportion could include (a) the defendants' costs, if one or more of the plaintiffs becomes liable to pay them, and (b) plaintiffs' central administration costs and other plaintiffs' costs which are incurred for the benefit of plaintiffs as a whole, rather than for individual plaintiffs. Any plaintiff who joins the group in the future will acquire the benefit of work done in the past and should become potentially liable for apportionable costs liabilities going back to the beginning. Thus the defendant should be potentially liable to each individual plaintiff for that plaintiff's proper individual costs and for a fraction of the plaintiffs' central costs whose denominator is the number of plaintiffs in the group. Each plaintiff should be potentially liable for a fraction of the defendants' costs

---

[29]   *Russell Young & Co v Brown & Ors* [2007] EWCA Civ 43; see **39.17** for Smith LJ's judgment.
[30]   *Foster v Roussel Laboratories* (unreported) 29 October 1997.

whose denominator is the number of plaintiffs in the group. If plaintiffs leave the group by settlement or discontinuance before the conclusion of the litigation when a general costs order is made, a calculation should be made to withdraw from the plaintiffs' central costs and from the defendants' costs a fraction of each of the then totals whose denominator is the number of plaintiffs then in the group before the departing plaintiff leaves. If the departing plaintiff is to pay the defendants' costs, the amount will be the amount of the defendants' costs so withdrawn. If the defendant is to pay the departing plaintiff's costs, the amount will be the amount withdrawn from the plaintiffs' central costs plus the departing plaintiff's proper individual costs. All this would be subject to taxation. This means that costs calculations will need to be made on a quarterly basis, and both the plaintiffs centrally and the defendants need to keep records appropriately.'

39.40 Longmore LJ has commented that there are many reasons why a claimant might discontinue a claim in group litigation other than his claim being without merit, such that a prima facie rule that a discontinuer should pay costs would be too blunt an instrument. He made the following comments about how best to manage discontinuers:[31]

'A prima facie rule tends to become the accepted rule, especially if it is necessary to incur the expense of going to the judge and asking, against opposition, for a different order. It is therefore not merely more sensible but also more consonant with justice that both the recoverability of common costs and the liability (if any) of discontinuing claimants for costs of common issues should be determined at the same time as orders for common costs are made in respect of those common issues. The court then has a full picture and can make whatever order is just in all the circumstances.'

39.41 If the prima facie rule (ie at CPR, r 38.6(1)) is to be set aside, an order will have to be made to the effect (preferably in the GLO).

Quantum

39.42 Costs of group litigation are assessed in the same way as any other costs, but the following miscellaneous issues may merit special attention. They are addressed in no particular order.

The bill

39.43 Group litigants may be added to and removed from the group register at different stages of the litigation.[32] The bill of costs may need to be split into parts appropriately.

Categorisation of costs

39.44 Costs will usually need to be categorised as being common costs or individual costs, and they may need to be further categorised as being GLO costs, administration costs, test-case costs, etc.[33] The categorisation will be a question of mixed fact and law. If there is dispute about categorisation, that dispute can often be resolved by referring to the GLO, which will usually specify the GLO issues and thereby impliedly define the GLO costs. The GLO will also often define the other sub-categories of costs, or at least give an indication as to what they are.[34] Categorisation is sometimes too challenging to

---

[31]   *Sayers v Merck Smithkline Beecham* [2003] 3 All ER 631 at 639.
[32]   CPR, r 19.14.
[33]   This is often necessary because different rates are often allowed for these different types of work: see **39.48**.
[34]   CPR, r 19.11(2)(b).

be resolved by proportionate means, in which case it may be necessary to create a catch-all category (eg 'other costs'), or to define a default position where, if there is doubt, the costs are to be attributed to a particular category.

Issue apportionment

39.45 Where the court has made an order about costs of an application or hearing which involved both GLO issues and issues relevant only to individual claims, the costs judge may have to make a decision as to the relevant proportions.[35] That would not be an exercise dictated by equal apportionment or any legal principles; instead, it would be a straightforward matter of fact.[36]

Proportionality

39.46 Whilst it would be wrong to say that very small claims should result in very small costs, there should be economies of scale, even when each claim requires individual attention.[37] The test of proportionality applies to all costs assessed on the standard basis, including those which are awarded prior to the conclusion of the group litigation.[38] As to proportionality in general, Sir Christopher Staughton had this to say:[39]

> 'It would seem that particular care should be paid to the costs likely to be incurred in group litigation cases if they may, in the course of the proceedings, be likely to become disproportionate to the amount at stake. Such actions, as we have been told, may involve a considerable amount of administrative management which do not perhaps require any particular legal skill. That in itself could give rise to disproportionate expense unless controlled.'

It would not be appropriate to split costs up into segments or parts for the purpose of applying the first stage of the two-stage test (see **34.18**).

Estimates

39.47 It is often the case that claims litigated under a GLO are not the subject of individual allocation to a track. This is because ordinarily every claim is automatically allocated to the multi-track.[40] There will often be no estimates of costs relating to individual costs; where an estimate is required, an order may be made. Estimates are often available for common costs: there is no reason to believe that the court would regard such an estimate any differently from any other estimate in other litigation; as such, CPD, Section 6 would apply (see **34.42–34.67**).

---

[35] CPR, r 48.6A(5) and PD 19B, para 16.2.
[36] CPR, r 48.6A(5) and PD 19B, para 16.2.
[37] *Giambrone v JMC Holidays Ltd (formerly Sunworld Holidays Ltd)* [2002] EWHC 2932 (QB) at [52], per Morland J.
[38] *Giambrone v JMC Holidays Ltd (formerly Sunworld Holidays Ltd)* [2002] EWHC 2932 (QB) at [48], per Morland J.
[39] *Griffiths v Solutia UK Ltd* [2001] EWCA Civ 736.
[40] PD 19B, para 7(1).

Hourly rates

39.48 Differential rates are commonplace: common costs usually merit a higher hourly rate than individual costs, but administration costs do not always merit a high hourly rate. As to geography, an individual litigant may have had little choice but to instruct geographically distant solicitors (this being because he would have little choice but to instruct the solicitors who had conduct of the matter on behalf of the other group litigants).

Wrong court, registers, etc

39.49 GLOs usually provide that claims should be commenced in the management court;[41] where a claim has been commenced in breach of such an order, then the paying party can legitimately object to the additional costs incurred as a consequence. Occasionally a claim will be litigated in circumstances where it could have been entered onto a group register but was not. If those are the circumstances, the paying party may wish to argue that a claim ought to have been litigated within the GLO and that, if this had happened, the costs would have been lower. Where the paying party is unsure of the terms of the GLO to which he wishes to refer, assistance can be obtained from Law Society's Multi Party Action Information Service. In any event, care should be taken to ensure that the claim was not commenced after a cut-off date for entry of claims onto the Group Register;[42] again, the Law Society is often able to assist in this regard.

'Failure' to comply with directions

39.50 Pre-existing directions will be set aside automatically when a claim is entered onto a group register;[43] therefore, it would be wrong to object to costs arising from the apparent 'failure' to comply with those directions.

Circular letters

39.51 It is common to find time claimed for printing and dispatching circular letters. The receiving party may not be entitled to the full 6-minute unit for each letter. See the references to *Giambrone v JMC Holidays Ltd*[44] at **29.58**.

Media and promotion

39.52 The costs of dealing with the media may be a recoverable cost in group litigation;[45] this is dealt with in more detail in discussion of the media at **29.101–29.103**, which describes the applicable three-stage test (ie (i) use and service, (ii) relevance and (iii) attributability). It should be borne in mind that the court may have given directions for publicising the GLO.[46] The costs of publicity will not, however, extend to the costs of promoting the interests of the solicitors. In this regard, Lord Neuberger MR had this to say:[47]

---

41 See CPR, r 19.11(3)(b) and PD 19B, para 9.1.
42 See CPR, r 19.13(e) and PD 19B, para 13.
43 PD 19B, para 7(2).
44 [2002] Costs LR 294.
45 *Ross v Owners of the Bowbelle (Review of Taxation under Ord 62 r 35)* (1997) 2 Lloyd's Rep 196 (Note), QBD (Admlty).
46 CPR, r 19.11(3)(c).
47 *Motto & Ors v Trafigura Ltd & Anor* [2011] EWCA Civ 1150 at [110].

'It seems to me that the expenses of getting business, whether advertising to the public as potential clients, making a presentation to a potential client, or discussing a possible instruction with a potential client, should not normally be treated as attributable to, and payable by, the ultimate client or clients. Rather, such expenses should generally be treated as part of a solicitor's general overheads or expenses, which can be taken into account when assessing appropriate levels of charging, such as hourly rates.'

Travelling

39.53 Although common issues are normally tried at the management court, individual issues may be directed to be tried at other courts whose locality is convenient for the parties.[48]

Costs of funding

39.54 The costs of funding are irrecoverable; this extends to the costs of giving advice about ATE insurance[49] (see **29.86–29.90**). Whether this exclusory principle extends to the costs of giving advice about costs sharing agreements is a moot point.

Procedure

39.55 Procedurally a detailed assessment of group litigation costs will be similar to other detailed assessments; the following issues may, however, arise from time to time.

Preliminary issues hearings

39.56 Where appropriate, the court may order that certain issues are to be determined as preliminary issues. An example is the issue of apportionment between common costs and individual costs, which PD 19B refers to as being suitable for determination before the assessment itself.[50] Such preliminary issues must be clearly defined and reduced into writing.[51]

Case management

39.57 It will occasionally be the case that there will be such a large number of claims that the detailed assessment of those claims will themselves give rise to GLO issues. Where this is the case, then those issues may be managed by an appointed costs judge or by the managing judge. Examples exist of the task being shared between both judges.[52]

Appointed costs judge (or appointed costs court)

39.58 It is not unusual for all of the costs (including the individual costs) to be allocated to a particular court (which may or may not be the management court), or

---

[48] PD 19B, para 15.2.
[49] *Motto & Ors v Trafigura Ltd & Anor* [2011] EWCA Civ 1150 at [104]–[114].
[50] PD 19B, para 16.2.
[51] *Lahey v Pirelli Tyres Ltd* [2007] EWCA Civ 91 at [4].
[52] An example being *AB and Ors v British Coal Corporation* [2006] EWCA Civ 987.

even a particular judge.[53] This was the practice well before the CPR.[54] Where this happens, the court may order that some of the assessments are to proceed as test claims.[55]

Forthwith orders

39.59 Group litigation can create difficulties in that it can tie up the parties' resources for many years. That said, this would not generally be a reason to make a 'forthwith' order in respect of costs awarded prior to the conclusion of the proceedings, as Morland J said:[56]

> 'In … almost all group litigation cases there should be no need for any detailed assessment of costs until the conclusion of the group litigation. Solicitors engaged in group litigation will be specialists and experienced in the field. Solicitors for claimants are fully entitled to an adequate cash flow from the defendants once the general issue of liability has been admitted or determined in the claimants' favour, similarly on determination of generic issues in the claimants' favour and on the assessment or settlement of awards of damages to individual or batches of claimants.'

Interim payments

39.60 As Morland J implied (see above), whilst it would not be usual for a forthwith order to be made prior to the conclusion of group litigation, the court is able to make an order that a payment be made on account or an interim payment made. Applications should be made to the nominated trial judge, where at all possible:[57]

> 'It is to be hoped that in most cases defendants' solicitors would agree to pay at various stages in the group litigation a realistic interim amount on account of a final detailed assessment of costs if necessary. If agreement cannot be reached as to an interim payment of costs, it should be dealt with cheaply and shortly by the nominated trial Judge who will be familiar with the general issues in the case and the realistic overall size of the claim under his powers under CPR 44.3(8).'

39.61 It is not clear whether the court has a jurisdiction to make an order, other than by consent, that a payment on account of costs be made in costs only proceedings in group litigation.[58]

Disclosure

39.62 Where disclosure is given by one person (either in the assessment or in the claim itself), this may cause a dispute about whether that document can be relied upon for the purposes of dealing with costs claimed by or against another person. Where that document relates to a GLO issue, it can be taken to have been disclosed to all parties, unless the court orders otherwise.[59]

---

[53] PD 19B, para 8.
[54] *In re Salaman* [1894] 2 Ch 201.
[55] PD 19B, para 12.3.
[56] *Giambrone v JMC Holidays Ltd (formerly Sunworld Holidays Ltd)* [2002] EWHC 2932 (QB) at [10], per Morland J.
[57] *Giambrone v JMC Holidays Ltd (formerly Sunworld Holidays Ltd)* [2002] EWHC 2932 (QB) at [11]–[12], per Morland J.
[58] *Banchio v Lai* [2003] EWHC 9038 (Costs).
[59] CPR, r 19.12(4).

REPRESENTATIVE CLAIMS

39.63 A representative claim which is brought in the context of group litigation is properly characterised as a test claim, so the matters discussed above will, to that extent, be relevant.

39.64 A representative claim may be brought outwith group litigation; the relevant procedure is in CPR Part 19 II. It is a claim which is brought by a person who acts as a representative of other persons who have an interest shared by the representative claimant.[60]

39.65 Generally speaking, an order made in a representative claim is binding on all persons represented in the claim, but it may be enforced by or against a person who is not a party to the claim only with the permission of the court.[61] That provision invites the question of whether an order for costs made against a representative claimant or defendant is binding on the persons who were represented.

39.66 This issue was addressed by Cox J in a representative claim brought by two members on behalf of an unincorporated association. The claim was dismissed with costs. The costs order was against 'the claimants'; no application had been made for a non-party order against the other members. Cox J rejected the submission that the order bound the other members. She commented that if the receiving party wanted to enforce against the other members, they should have made an application for a non-party costs order.[62]

39.67 Where an application for a non-party costs order is brought, it is far from being a foregone conclusion that it will be made. Each case will turn on its own facts, such as the extent to which the non-parties funded the matter, the extent to which they directed the litigation, the extent to which they had a financial interest in the matter, etc. Whilst obiter, Denning LJ has emphasised the fact that no automatic liability will arise:[63]

> 'In a representative action, the one who is named as a Plaintiff is, of course, a full party to the action. The others who are not named, but whom she represents are also parties to the action. They are all bound by the eventual decision in the case. They are not full parties because they are not liable individually for costs.'

39.68 Where the representative party is acting autonomously, the non-parties may well not be held liable for costs. Vaughan Williams LJ had the following to say on the topic:[64]

> 'The Plaintiff is the self-elected representative of the others. He has not to obtain their consent. It is true that consequently they are not liable for costs, but they will be bound by the estoppel created by the decision.'

39.69 The issue of non-party costs orders is dealt with in detail at **7.136–7.205**. Where an application for a non-party costs order is made, certain procedural rules may apply, depending on the nature of the claim. For the wording of CPR, r 19.8A, see **39.83**.

---

[60]   CPR, r 19.6(1).
[61]   CPR, r 19.6(4).
[62]   *Howells v Dominion Insurance Co Ltd* [2005] EWHC 552 (QB).
[63]   *Moon v Atherton* [1972] 2 QB 435.
[64]   *Markt & Co Ltd v Knight Steamship Company Ltd* [1910] 2 KB 1201 at 1039.

DERIVATIVE CLAIMS

39.70 A derivative claim is a claim where a company, other body corporate, or trade union is said to be entitled to a remedy, and the claim is made by a member of that company, body or union for it to be given that remedy. The definition does not include petitions for protection of members of a company against unfair prejudice made under s 996 of the Companies Act 2006.[65] Where it relates to a company, a derivative claim is a claim in respect of a cause of action arising from an actual or proposed act or omission involving negligence, default, breach of duty or breach of trust by a director of the company.[66]

39.71 The court may order the company, body corporate, or union to indemnify the claimant against liability for costs incurred in the permission application or in the derivative claim (or both).[67] Where a claimant seeks such a pre-emptive costs order from the court, this should be stated in the permission application or claim form (or both), as the case requires.[68]

39.72 The claimant usually has to make out a prima facie case, this being something which must be done at the start of the litigation;[69] the decision whether the claimant's evidence does this will normally be made without submissions from or attendance by the company, body corporate, or union. If without invitation from the court the company, body corporate or union volunteers a submission or attendance, it will not normally be allowed any costs of that submission or attendance.[70]

PUBLIC LAW AND JUDICIAL REVIEW

39.73 This sub-chapter is the briefest of overviews; specialist practitioners should consult specialist textbooks on public law. The incidence of costs in public law cases will not necessarily be governed by identical principles to those which govern private law cases,[71] but many of the principles set out in this book will apply. This subchapter identifies the key factors which distinguish public from private law costs practice. Notwithstanding those differences, it should be borne in mind there is nothing in CPR, Part 54 which removes the discretionary powers given to the court by s 51 of the Senior Courts Act 1981;[72] the similarities, therefore, far outweigh the differences.

Application for permission

39.74 An unsuccessful claimant must expect to pay the defendant's costs of filing an acknowledgment of service.[73] A defendant who chooses to attend and oppose an oral application for permission cannot ordinarily expect to recover its costs of doing so even

---

[65] CPR, r 19.9(1).
[66] Companies Act 2006, s 260(3).
[67] CPR, r 19.9E.
[68] PD 19C, para 2(2).
[69] See Companies Act 2006, ss 261, 262 and 264.
[70] PD 19C, para 5.
[71] *Davey v Aylesbury Vale DC* (2007) EWCA Civ 1166.
[72] *R (on the application of Mount Cook Land Ltd) v Westminster City Council* [2003] EWCA Civ 1346 at [67].
[73] *R (Leach) v Comr for Local Administration* [2001] EWHC 455 (Admin) at [50]; see also *R (on the application of Mount Cook Land Ltd) v Westminster City Council* [2003] EWCA Civ 1346 at [54].

if permission is refused, but it may be awarded costs in exceptional circumstances (see below).[74] This principle is confirmed in PD 54A, which reads as follows:

> '8.5   Neither the defendant nor any other interested party need attend a hearing on the question of permission unless the court directs otherwise.
>
> 8.6   Where the defendant or any party does attend a hearing, the court will not generally make an order for costs against the claimant.'

39.75   Some commentators have commented adversely on this practice direction, saying that it appears to be at odds with established practices and the CPR themselves.[75] Auld LJ gave the following guidance which, amongst other things, explained how the practice direction should be applied in practice:[76]

> '(1)   ... a successful defendant or other party at the permission stage who has filed an acknowledgment of service, pursuant to CPR 54.8, should generally recover the costs of doing so from the claimant, whether or not he attends any permission hearing.
>
> (2)   The effect of para 8.6, when read with para 8.5, of the practice direction, in conformity with the long-established practice of the courts in judicial review ... is that a defendant who attends and successfully resists the grant of permission at a renewal hearing should not generally recover from the claimant his costs of, and occasioned by, doing so.
>
> (3)   A court, in considering an award against an unsuccessful claimant of the defendant's and/or any other interested party's costs at a permission hearing, should depart from the general guidance in the practice direction only if he considers that there are exceptional circumstances for doing so.
>
> (4)   A court considering costs at the permission stage should be allowed a broad discretion as to whether, on the facts of the case, there are exceptional circumstances justifying the award of costs against an unsuccessful claimant.
>
> (5)   Exceptional circumstances may consist in the presence of one or more of the features in the following non-exhaustive list:
>
> > (a)   the hopelessness of the claim;
> > (b)   the persistence in it by the claimant after having been alerted to facts and/or of the law demonstrating its hopelessness;
> > (c)   the extent to which the court considers that the claimant, in the pursuit of his application, has sought to abuse the process of judicial review for collateral ends – a relevant consideration as to costs at the permission stage, as well as when considering discretionary refusal of relief at the stage of substantive hearing, if there is one; and
> > (d)   whether, as a result of the deployment of full argument and documentary evidence by both sides at the hearing of a contested application, the unsuccessful claimant has had, in effect, the advantage of an early substantive hearing of the claim.
>
> (6)   A relevant factor for a court, when considering the exercise of its discretion on the grounds of exceptional circumstances, may be the extent to which the unsuccessful claimant has substantial resources that it has used to pursue the unfounded claim, and that are available to meet an order for costs.'

39.76   In some circumstances the claimant may be able to apply at the permission stage for a protective costs order; this is addressed at **15.83–15.102**. It will occasionally be the case that the defendant will acquiesce to the claimant's claim in such a way that

---

74   *R (on the application of Mount Cook Land Ltd) v Westminster City Council* [2003] EWCA Civ 1346 at [76]; reaffirmed in *Davey v Aylesbury Vale DC* (2007) EWCA Civ 1166.

75   See *Halsbury's Laws of England* (Butterworths) Vol 1, para 178, footnote 5.

76   *R (on the application of Mount Cook Land Ltd) v Westminster City Council* [2003] EWCA Civ 1346 at [76].

proceedings become otiose either before or shortly after the application for permission; where that is the case, then the claimant would ordinarily be entitled to his costs.[77]

Acknowledgements

39.77 Errors concerning acknowledgements of service may be taken into account. Where a person who has been served with proceedings takes part in a hearing, the court may take his failure to file an acknowledgement of service into account when deciding what order to make about costs.[78] An overly detailed acknowledgement may also result in costs sanctions; the allowable costs would usually be limited to those which would have been incurred had only a summary of the grounds been drafted.[79]

Discretion generally

39.78 (The topic of claims that settle leaving only the incidence of costs at large is addressed in the footnotes at **7.104**.) Unless the court orders otherwise, where a defendant incurs costs in opposing a claim, those costs would be recoverable only if the claimant gets permission and ultimately loses.[80] Put another way, costs follow the event.

39.79 Sedley LJ has given the following guidance,[81] which is often referred to as the 'Sedley-Clarke principles':[82]

'(1) On the conclusion of full judicial review proceedings in a defendant's favour, the nature and purpose of the particular claim is relevant to the exercise of the judge's discretion as to costs. In contrast to a judicial review claim brought wholly or mainly for commercial or proprietary reasons, a claim brought partly or wholly in the public interest, albeit unsuccessful, may properly result in a restricted or no order for costs.

(2) If awarding costs against the claimant, the judge should consider whether they are to include preparation costs in addition to acknowledgement costs. It will be for the defendant to justify these. There may be no sufficient reason why such costs, if incurred, should be recoverable.

(3) It is highly desirable that these questions should be dealt with by the trial judge and left to the costs judge only in relation to the reasonableness of individual items.

(4) If at the conclusion of such proceedings the judge makes an undifferentiated order for costs in a defendant's favour:

(a)   the order has to be regarded as including any reasonably incurred preparation costs; but

---

[77]   The principles are much the same as they are in a private law setting (see **7.111–7.118**); as an example in a public law setting see *R v Kensington and Chelsea Royal London Borough Council ex p Ghebregiogis* [1994] COD 502. Late concessions will usually not impress the court (see *R v Islington London Borough Council ex p Hooper* [1995] COD 76. Equally, if discontinuance is required, there must be no delay on the part of the claimant: see *R v Warley Justices ex p Callis* [1994] COD 240.

[78]   See CPR, r 54.9(2).

[79]   *Ewing v ODPM* [2005] All ER (D) 315.

[80]   *R (on the application of Thurman) v Lewisham LBC* (unreported) 1 January 2007, QBD (Admin), approved of in *Davey v Aylesbury Vale DC* (2007) EWCA Civ 1166.

[81]   *Davey v Aylesbury Vale DC* [2007] EWCA Civ 1166 at [21].

[82]   This is because they were approved of by Clarke MR; see *R (Roudham & Larling Parish Council) v Breckland Council* [2008] EWCA Civ 714.

(b)   the 2004 Practice Statement should be read so as to exclude any costs of opposing the grant of permission in open court, which should be dealt with on the *Mount Cook* principles.'

Principle (3) has subsequently been emphasised by other members of the Court of Appeal.[83]

39.80 Clarke MR commented upon these principles by adding the following note of caution:[84]

'It does seem to me that costs should ordinarily follow the event and that it is for the claimant who has lost to show that some different approach should be adopted on the facts of a particular case ... That said, I agree with Sedley LJ's second proposition ... that it will be for the successful defendant to justify preparation costs. That is, however, because (as stated above) he must show that it was reasonable and proportionate to incur such costs. If the claimant wishes to submit that any or all the costs which would be otherwise recoverable should not be recovered, however reasonable and proportionate they were, it is, as I see it, for him to persuade the court to that effect.

Thus, if the claimant wishes to avoid paying costs which are reasonable and proportionate in amount, the burden of persuading the court lies with him rather than the defendant.

Interested parties

39.81 An unsuccessful claimant would not usually be required to pay the costs of more than one of the other parties.[85] This would not always be the case, however, in that the claimant may be asked to meet the costs of an interested party who had to address issues which were discrete from those addressed by the defendant.[86]

Conclusion of proceedings

39.82 An undifferentiated order in favour of a defendant should be read as including costs of preparation but excluding any costs of opposing the grant of permission in open court; those costs should be dealt with on the *Mount Cook* principles (see **39.74**).[87] That approach should not give rise to a risk of defendants recovering more expense than was reasonable at the permission stage. Where an order for costs made on an application for permission to seek judicial review is challenged or where the quantum of such an order is challenged, written submissions should be made.[88]

---

[83]   This was further emphasised in *R (Roudham & Larling Parish Council) v Breckland Council* [2008] EWCA Civ 714.

[84]   *Davey v Aylesbury Vale DC* [2007] EWCA Civ 1166 at [29]–[30].

[85]   *Bolton Metropolitan District Council v Secretary of State for the Environment* [1996] 1 All ER 184; as to the pedigree of that principle, see *R v Industrial Disputes Tribunal ex p American Express Co Inc* [1954] 2 All ER 764.

[86]   See, for example, *R v Panel on Take-overs and Mergers ex p Datafin plc* [1987] QB 815.

[87]   *Practice Statement (QBD (Admin Court): Judicial Review: Costs)* [2004] 1 WLR 1760.

[88]   See *R (on the application of Loucif) V Secretary of State for the Home Department* [2011] EWHC 3640 (Admin) citing *Ewing v ODPM* [2005] All ER (D) 315.

RELEVANT EXTRACTS FROM THE CPR AND PRACTICE DIRECTIONS

CPR, r 19.8A, rr 19.10–19.15 and r 48.6A

39.83 The wording of the CPR provisions relevant to this chapter is as follows:

19.8A Power to make judgements binding on non-parties

(1) This rule applies to any claim relating to—

    (a)   the estate of a deceased person;

    (b)   property subject to a trust; or

    (c)   the sale of any property.

(2) The court may at any time direct that notice of—

    (a)   the claim; or

    (b)   any judgment or order given in the claim,

be served on any person who is not a party but who is or may be affected by it.

(3) An application under this rule—

    (a)   may be made without notice; and

    (b)   must be supported by written evidence which includes the reasons why the person to be served should be bound by the judgment in the claim.

(4) Unless the court orders otherwise—

    (a)   a notice of a claim or of a judgment or order under this rule must be—

        (i)   in the form required by the practice direction;

        (ii)   issued by the court; and

        (iii)   accompanied by a form of acknowledgement of service with any necessary modifications;

    (b)   a notice of a claim must also be accompanied by—

        (i)   a copy of the claim form; and

        (ii)   such other statements of case, witness statements or affidavits as the court may direct; and

    (c)   a notice of a judgment or order must also be accompanied by a copy of the judgment or order.

(5) If a person served with notice of a claim files an acknowledgement of service of the notice within 14 days he will become a party to the claim.

(6) If a person served with notice of a claim does not acknowledge service of the notice he will be bound by any judgment given in the claim as if he were a party.

(7) If, after service of a notice of a claim on a person, the claim form is amended so as substantially to alter the relief claimed, the court may direct that a judgment shall not bind that person unless a further notice, together with a copy of the amended claim form, is served on him.

(8) Any person served with a notice of a judgment or order under this rule—

    (a)   shall be bound by the judgment or order as if he had been a party to the claim; but

    (b)   may, provided he acknowledges service—

        (i)   within 28 days after the notice is served on him, apply to the court to set aside or vary the judgment or order; and

        (ii)   take part in any proceedings relating to the judgment or order.

(9) The following rules of Part 10 (acknowledgement of service) apply—

(a)   rule 10.4; and

(b)   rule 10.5, subject to the modification that references to the defendant are to be read as references to the person served with the notice.

(10)   A notice under this rule is issued on the date entered on the notice by the court.

...

19.10   Definition

A Group Litigation Order ('GLO') means an order made under rule 19.11 to provide for the case management of claims which give rise to common or related issues of fact or law (the 'GLO issues').

19.11   Group Litigation Order

(1)   The court may make a GLO where there are or are likely to be a number of claims giving rise to the GLO issues.

(The practice direction provides the procedure for applying for a GLO.)

(2)   A GLO must—

(a)   contain directions about the establishment of a register (the 'group register') on which the claims managed under the GLO will be entered;

(b)   specify the GLO issues which will identify the claims to be managed as a group under the GLO; and

(c)   specify the court (the 'management court') which will manage the claims on the group register.

(3)   A GLO may—

(a)   in relation to claims which raise one or more of the GLO issues—
    (i)   direct their transfer to the management court;
    (ii)   order their stay until further order; and
    (iii)   direct their entry on the group register;

(b)   direct that from a specified date claims which raise one or more of the GLO issues should be started in the management court and entered on the group register; and

(c)   give directions for publicising the GLO.

19.12   Effect of the GLO

(1)   Where a judgment or order is given or made in a claim on the group register in relation to one or more GLO issues—

(a)   that judgment or order is binding on the parties to all other claims that are on the group register at the time the judgment is given or the order is made unless the court orders otherwise; and

(b)   the court may give directions as to the extent to which that judgment or order is binding on the parties to any claim which is subsequently entered on the group register.

(2)   Unless paragraph (3) applies, any party who is adversely affected by a judgment or order which is binding on him may seek permission to appeal the order.

(3)   A party to a claim which was entered on the group register after a judgment or order which is binding on him was given or made may not—

(a)   apply for the judgment or order to be set aside, varied or stayed; or

(b)   appeal the judgment or order,

but may apply to the court for an order that the judgment or order is not binding on him.

(4)   Unless the court orders otherwise, disclosure of any document relating to the GLO issues by a party to a claim on the group register is disclosure of that document to all parties to claims—

(a)   on the group register; and

(b)   which are subsequently entered on the group register.

19.13   Case management

Directions given by the management court may include directions—

(a)   varying the GLO issues;

(b)   providing for one or more claims on the group register to proceed as test claims;

(c)   appointing the solicitor of one or more parties to be the lead solicitor for the claimants or defendants;

(d)   specifying the details to be included in a statement of case in order to show that the criteria for entry of the claim on the group register have been met;

(e)   specifying a date after which no claim may be added to the group register unless the court gives permission; and

(f)   for the entry of any particular claim which meets one or more of the GLO issues on the group register.

(Part 3 contains general provisions about the case management powers of the court.)

19.14   Removal from the register

(1)   A party to a claim entered on the group register may apply to the management court for the claim to be removed from the register.

(2)   If the management court orders the claim to be removed from the register it may give directions about the future management of the claim.

19.15   Test claims

(1)   Where a direction has been given for a claim on the group register to proceed as a test claim and that claim is settled, the management court may order that another claim on the group register be substituted as the test claim.

(2)   Where an order is made under paragraph (1), any order made in the test claim before the date of substitution is binding on the substituted claim unless the court orders otherwise.'

…

48.6A Costs where the court has made a group litigation order

(1)   This rule applied where the court has made a Group Litigation Order ('GLO').

(2)   In this rule—

(a)   'individual costs' means costs incurred in relation to an individual claim on the group register;

(b)   'common costs' means—

(i)   costs incurred in relation to the GLO issues;

(ii)   individual costs incurred in a claim while it is proceeding as a test claim, and

(iii)   costs incurred by the lead solicitor in administering the group litigation; and

(c)   'group litigant' means a claimant or defendant, as the case may be, whose claim is entered on the group register.

(3)   Unless the court orders otherwise, any order for common costs against group litigants imposes on each group litigant several liability for an equal proportion of those common costs.

(4)   The general rule is that where a group litigant is the paying party, he will, in addition to any costs he is liable to pay to the receiving party, be liable for—

(a)   the individual costs of his claim; and

(b)   an equal proportion, together with all the other group litigants, of the common costs.

(5)   Where the court makes an order about costs in relation to any application or hearing which involved—

(a)   one or more GLO issues; and

(b)   issues relevant only to individual claims,

the court will direct the proportion of the costs that is to relate to common costs and the proportion that is to relate to individual costs.

(6)   Where common costs have been incurred before a claim is entered on the group register, the court may order the group litigant to be liable for a proportion of those costs.

(7)   Where a claim is removed from the group register, the court may make an order for costs in that claim which includes a proportion of the common costs incurred up to the date on which the claim is removed from the group register. (Part 19 sets out rules about group litigation.)'

CPD, art 19.5

39.84   As to notice of funding, CPD, art 19.5 provides as follows:

Where the court makes a Group Litigation Order, the court may give directions as to the extent to which individual parties should provide information in accordance with rule 44.15. (Part 19 deals with Group Litigation Orders.)

PD 19B

39.85   In so far as it relates to costs, PD 19B provides as follows:

16.1 CPR 48 contains rules about costs where a GLO has been made.

16.2 Where the court has made an order about costs in relation to any application or hearing which involved both—

(1)   one or more of the GLO issues; and

(2)   an issue or issues relevant only to individual claims;

and the court has not directed the proportion of the costs that is to relate to common costs and the proportion that is to relate to individual costs in accordance with rule 48.6A(5), the costs judge will make a decision as to the relevant proportions at or before the commencement of the detailed assessment of costs.

Chapter 40

COSTS AGAINST THE COURTS SERVICE

40.1 Her Majesty's Courts Service ('the Courts Service') is able to make *ex gratia* compensation payments for costs thrown away by their error. Such payments are not costs, but compensation; in particular, the Courts Service will not usually agree to an order that it pays costs to be assessed.

THE POWER TO MAKE PAYMENTS

40.2 Although a litigant would have a theoretical right to apply for a non-party costs order against the Courts Service, in practice this is not practicable because of the availability of *ex gratia* payments.

40.3 Prior to the coming into force of the Human Rights Act 1998, the House of Lords had ruled that s 51 of the Senior Courts Act 1981 did not impliedly confer a power on the court to make an order out of central funds to compensate a litigant for costs thrown away as a result of court maladministration.[1] In a case in which the first instance judge was found not be impartial, a disgruntled litigant challenged that position on the grounds that Art 6(1) of the European Convention on Human Rights required the court, as an emanation of the state, to provide an impartial tribunal. That point was not decided, however, because Phillips MR (with whom Brooke and Walker LJJ agreed) found that on the facts of that particular case the disgruntled litigant was not a 'victim' for the purposes of making a claim under s 7(1) of the Human Rights Act 1998. The issue, therefore, remains undecided.[2] In most instances of maladministration, however, the issue of Art 6(1) of the European Convention will be irrelevant; this is because most instances of costs being thrown away are due to mundane clerical errors rather than the lack of an unbiased tribunal.

40.4 Subject to the issues mentioned immediately above, the power to make payments does not arise from s 51 of the Senior Courts Act 1981 (or, for that matter, from any other similar Act), and is probably an instance of the Crown – whose department the Courts Service is – exercising its prerogative power. There is, however, no authority on this point.

40.5 There is no published document that restricts the ambit of the Courts Service's powers to make an *ex gratia* payment; that said, there is a well-established principle that

---

[1]   *Steele Ford & Newton v Crown Prosecution Service* [1994] 1 AC 22, overruling *Re Central Independent Television plc & Ors* [1991] 1 All ER 347 and *R v Bow Street Metropolitan Stipendiary Magistrate ex p Mirror* (unreported) 1992.

[2]   *Director General of Fair Trading v Proprietary Association of Great Britain, In re Medicaments & Related Classes of Goods (No 4)* [2002] 1 WLR 269.

payments will be made only in respect of maladministration rather than judicial errors. The principles underlying *ex gratia* payments are as follows:[3]

> 'Where a public body has failed to get it right and this has led to injustice or hardship, it should take steps to put things right. That means, if possible, returning complainants and, where appropriate, others who have suffered the same injustice or hardship as a result of the same maladministration or poor service, to the position they were in before this took place. If that is not possible, it means compensating complainants and such others appropriately.'

40.6   There are, therefore, three requirements which must be satisfied before a payment can be made in accordance with these principles: there must have been maladministration or poor services; there must be injustice or hardship; and there must be a causal link between the two.

40.7   Although *ex gratia* payments are, in practice, limited to recompensing complainants for costs thrown away, the Courts Service has a discretion to make payments relating to other errors and events, which in appropriate circumstances may include the following:[4]

> 'Financial compensation for direct or indirect financial loss, loss of opportunity, inconvenience, distress, or any combination of these.'

This may be relevant in the sense that a litigant may not be entitled to only his own costs thrown away by maladministration (ie direct financial loss), but also to any costs which he might be ordered to pay as a result of that maladministration (ie indirect financial loss).

THE EXERCISE OF DISCRETION

40.8   It is not always easy to distinguish between maladministration and judicial errors: if, for example, the court makes an order in the absence of the parties and if by reason of maladministration that order caused costs to be throw away, it is possible that the Courts Service would decline to make a payment on the basis that the costs were incurred as a result of a judicial decision rather than maladministration. If there is doubt about whether an error is maladministration, and where the opportunity arises, it is good practice to ask the court (that is, a judge) to make a finding in this regard. This should be done only if the opportunity arises (for example at a hearing to set aside an erroneous order); it should not be done by application, this being because the Courts Service is the recipient of the complaint rather than the tribunal seized of that complaint.

40.9   The matter will be determined in accordance with the *Ombudsman's Principles*, which are published from time-to-time by the Parliamentary Commissioner for Administration (often referred to as 'the Parliamentary Ombudsman'). There are three sets of principles governing the matter: they are the Principles of Good Administration, the Principles for Remedy and the Principles of Good Complaint Handling. All three of these are based on a common six-part framework which is as follows:

---

[3]   *Ombudsman's Principles: Principles of Good Complaint Handling* (Parliamentary and Health Service Ombudsman, 13 February 2009).
[4]   *Ombudsman's Principles: Principles of Good Complaint Handling* (Parliamentary and Health Service Ombudsman, 13 February 2009).

- getting it right;
- being customer focused;
- being open and accountable;
- acting fairly and proportionately;
- putting things right; and
- seeking continuous improvement.

40.10 Each set of principles is dealt with in turn in accordance with this framework.

Principles of Good Administration

40.11 These were first published on 27 March 2007, following a consultation that took place at the end of 2006.[5] They include a number of guiding principles under the headings: 'Getting it right', 'Being customer focused', 'Being open and accountable', 'Acting fairly and proportionately, 'Putting things right' and 'Seeking continuous improvement'. The details are published on the website of the Parliamentary and Health Service Ombudsman.

Principles for Remedy

40.12 These were first published on 11 October 2007, following a consultation that took place in early 2007.[6] They are as follows:

'1   Getting it right

- Quickly acknowledging and putting right cases of maladministration or poor service that have led to injustice or hardship.
- Considering all relevant factors when deciding the appropriate remedy, ensuring fairness for the complainant and, where appropriate, for others who have suffered injustice or hardship as a result of the same maladministration or poor service.

2   Being customer focused

- Apologising for and explaining the maladministration or poor service.
- Understanding and managing people's expectations and needs.
- Dealing with people professionally and sensitively.
- Providing remedies that take account of people's individual circumstances.

3   Being open and accountable

- Being open and clear about how public bodies decide remedies.
- Operating a proper system of accountability and delegation in providing remedies.
- Keeping a clear record of what public bodies have decided on remedies and why.

4   Acting fairly and proportionately

- Offering remedies that are fair and proportionate to the complainant's injustice or hardship.
- Providing remedies to others who have suffered injustice or hardship as a result of the same maladministration or poor service, where appropriate.

---

[5]   *Principles of Good Administration: Response to Consultation, Parliamentary and Health Service Ombudsman,* 27 March 2009.

[6]   *Report on the Consultation on Principles for Remedy, Parliamentary and Health Service Ombudsman,* 11 October 2007.

- Treating people without bias, unlawful discrimination or prejudice.

5   Putting things right

- If possible, returning the complainant and, where appropriate, others who have suffered similar injustice or hardship, to the position they would have been in if the maladministration or poor service had not occurred.
- If that is not possible, compensating the complainant and such others appropriately.
- Considering fully and seriously all forms of remedy (such as an apology, an explanation, remedial action, or financial compensation).
- Providing the appropriate remedy in each case.

6   Seeking continuous improvement

- Using the lessons learned from complaints to ensure that maladministration or poor service is not repeated.
- Recording and using information on the outcome of complaints to improve services.'

Principles of Good Complaint Handling

40.13 These principles should be read in conjunction with the other principles. They are as follows:

'1   Getting it right

- Acting in accordance with the law and relevant guidance, and with regard for the rights of those concerned.
- Ensuring that those at the top of the public body provide leadership to support good complaint management and develop an organisational culture that values complaints.
- Having clear governance arrangements, which set out roles and responsibilities, and ensure lessons are learnt from complaints.
- Including complaint management as an integral part of service design.
- Ensuring that staff are equipped and empowered to act decisively to resolve complaints.
- Focusing on the outcomes for the complainant and the public body.
- Signposting to the next stage of the complaints procedure, in the right way and at the right time.

2   Being customer focused

- Having clear and simple procedures.
- Ensuring that complainants can easily access the service dealing with complaints, and informing them about advice and advocacy services where appropriate.
- Dealing with complainants promptly and sensitively, bearing in mind their individual circumstances.
- Listening to complainants to understand the complaint and the outcome they are seeking.
- Responding flexibly, including co-ordinating responses with any other bodies involved in the same complaint, where appropriate.

3   Being open and accountable

- Publishing clear, accurate and complete information about how to complain, and how and when to take complaints further.
- Publishing service standards for handling complaints.

- Providing honest, evidence-based explanations and giving reasons for decisions.
- Keeping full and accurate records.

4   Acting fairly and proportionately

- Treating the complainant impartially, and without unlawful discrimination or prejudice.
- Ensuring that complaints are investigated thoroughly and fairly to establish the facts of the case.
- Ensuring that decisions are proportionate, appropriate and fair.
- Ensuring that complaints are reviewed by someone not involved in the events leading to the complaint.
- Acting fairly towards staff complained about as well as towards complainants.

5   Putting things right

- Acknowledging mistakes and apologising where appropriate.
- Providing prompt, appropriate and proportionate remedies.
- Considering all the relevant factors of the case when offering remedies.
- Taking account of any injustice or hardship that results from pursuing the complaint as well as from the original dispute.

6   Seeking continuous improvement

- Using all feedback and the lessons learnt from complaints to improve service design and delivery.
- Having systems in place to record, analyse and report on the learning from complaints.
- Regularly reviewing the lessons to be learnt from complaints.
- Where appropriate, telling the complainant about the lessons learnt and changes made to services, guidance or policy.'

40.14   Further details are given in the *Ombudsman's Principles*; most of the guidance contained in that document is not relevant for present purposes, but it does make clear that the Courts Service must act in accordance with its own policy and guidance. In this regard it may be relevant that the Courts Service's own guidance is that processes and procedures will be designed to suit the user rather than the administrator.[7]

QUANTUM

40.15   The Courts Service is not required to take the seven pillars (ie CPR, r 44.5(3)) into account; instead, the following may be taken into account:[8]

- the nature of the complaint;
- the impact on the complainant;
- how long it took to resolve the complaint; and
- the trouble the complainant was put to in pursuing it.

---

[7]   *HMCS Business Strategy* (February 2006), p 4.
[8]   *Ombudsman's Principles: Principles of Good Complaint Handling* (Parliamentary and Health Service Ombudsman, 13 February 2009).

40.16 Compensation may include the costs of making the claim itself; in this regard, the following guidance is given:[9]

> 'Remedies may also need to take account of any injustice or hardship that has resulted from pursuing the complaint as well as from the original dispute.'

40.17 None of the guidance specifically mentions interest, but there is no reason to suppose that this would not be an indirect financial loss. The complainant may need to prove loss in this regard (ie he may need to prove either that he has had to pay interest, or that if he would have earned interest on monies he has had to pay out).

PROCEDURE

40.18 It would be a mistake to make a claim for compensation within litigation; in particular, it ought not to be made upon application or by way of the CPR Part 8 Claim. Instead, a claim should be made by letter sent either to the relevant court, or to:

Customer Service Unit
Post Point 4.01
4th Floor
102 Petty France
London SW1H 9AJ
DX 152380 Westminster 8.

Guidance can be obtained from the Customer Service Unit on 0845 4568770.

40.19 Although there is no prescribed procedure, it would be sensible for a complaint to focus on the three requirements identified at **40.6** (ie whether there has been maladministration/poor services; whether there has been injustice or hardship; and whether there is a causal link between the two).

40.20 The costs themselves could be claimed either by way of an informal Schedule of Costs or a Statement of Costs in the form of Precedent H of the Schedule of Costs Precedents.

40.21 If a complainant is dissatisfied by a response to a claim, then an application may be made to the Parliamentary Commissioner for Administration via the Parliamentary and Health Service Ombudsman. Advice on this can be obtained from the Ombudsman's Helpline on 0345 015 4033.

40.22 The exercise of discretion is justiciable notwithstanding the fact that it is a non-statutory power.[10] Therefore, a refusal to pay compensation may, in theory, be amenable to judicial review. Such things are the preserve of specialists, and advice ought to be taken from a person specialising in administrative law. Strict time limits apply. In

---

[9] *Ombudsman's Principles: Principles of Good Complaint Handling* (Parliamentary and Health Service Ombudsman, 13 February 2009).

[10] See *Council of Civil Service Unions v Minister of State for Civil Service* [1985] AC 374 for a general discussion of this.

any event, the court may dismiss an application on the basis that the complainant has an alternative remedy, ie to apply for a non-party costs order and/or to complain to the Ombudsman.

Chapter 41

LITIGATION FUNDING

41.1   This chapter has been written with the assistance of Mr Rocco Pirozzolo, solicitor and senior underwriter with the insurer QBE.[1] An agreement for litigation funding (this being the preferred name for what used to be called third-party funding) is an agreement whereby a stranger to a dispute provides funding (other than insurance) in return for a share of the proceeds. It also goes by the names of litigation financing, professional funding and, occasionally in older authorities, sponsoring. Speaking extrajudicially, Jackson LJ has defined litigation funding in the following way:[2]

> '[Litigation funding is the] funding of litigation by a party who has no pre-existing interest in the litigation, usually on the basis that (i) the funder will be paid out of the proceeds of any amounts recovered as a consequence of the litigation, often as a percentage of the recovery sum; and (ii) the funder is not entitled to payment should the claim fail.'

41.2   If such an arrangement were to be adjudged by the law as it stood in or before the early 1980s, then with one or two exceptions relating to insolvency (see **41.4**) such an arrangement would have been condemned as being champertous; prior to 1967, the creation of such an agreement may even have been a criminal offence.[3] Champerty, however, is a doctrine based on public policy, and that means that it is far from immutable (see **9.327–9.350**). The chronology set out below explains how public policy has changed so that far from finding funding repugnant, it has now come to embrace certain types of litigation funding.

PUBLIC POLICY AND RELEVANT HISTORY

41.3   It is not possible to point to 'the' authority which confirmed the legality of litigation funding, nor is it possible to point to any such legislation. Instead, litigation funding has become lawful by a piecemeal process which, in part, has been as the result of tacit acceptance and extrajudicial commentary. The prime example of tacit acceptance is *Arkin v Borchard Lines Ltd*,[4] in which the Court of Appeal ruled on an ancillary matter without passing any adverse comment on the fact that the litigation had been funded by way of a litigation funding agreement (see **41.9**). As has been explained in the discussion of champerty at **9.327–9.350**, up until the mid-1960s an arrangement such as a litigation funding agreement would have been not only unenforceable, but also illegal in the criminal sense. (Some very limited forms of 'sponsoring' were permitted in the context of insolvency,[5] but that was limited in scope[6] and in any event only bore a

---

[1]   Mr Pirozzolo was a member of the Civil Justice Council's Working Party which produced the Code of Conduct for Litigation Funders 2011 (see **41.16**); he has, however, assisted in his personal capacity only.

[2]   R Jackson *Review of Civil Litigation Costs: Preliminary Report* (2009), Vol 1, p viii.

[3]   See **9.327–9.328**.

[4]   *Arkin v Borchard Lines Ltd* [2005] EWCA Civ 655.

[5]   In *Guy v Churchill* (1888) 40 Ch D 481 there was an assignment on terms that the assignee would continue

passing resemblance to modern-day litigation funding.) The law has changed beyond recognition since those days. Speaking extrajudicially in 2009,[7] Jackson LJ identified the following benefits of litigation funding that now seem to be generally accepted as justifying its existence:

- litigation funding promotes access to justice by reason of it providing an additional means of funding litigation and, for some, the only means of funding;
- notwithstanding the fact that a successful claimant with litigation funding will be liable to the funder for a percentage of his winnings, that is a better position to be in than to recover no winnings at all;
- the use of litigation funding does not impose additional financial burdens upon paying parties;[8] and
- the screening process used by litigation funders tends to filter out unmeritorious cases; this being of benefit to opposing parties.

Given the fact that other senior judges, such a Lord Neuberger,[9] have commented favourably on litigation funding (again, extrajudicially), and also given the fact that Jackson LJ's comments were made following extensive public consultation, it can safely be said that the policies that underlay the rules of champerty no longer hold sway over the law.

History and comparative law

41.4   In order fully to understand the relevant public policy, it is necessary to look at the history of litigation funding both in this country and in other common law countries;[10] it is also necessary to consider the development of conditional funding generally, and to that extent there is a degree of overlap with the history of conditional fee agreements (see **9.375** *et seq*). The law in other common law jurisdictions is relevant for two reasons: firstly, policymakers now more than ever look at what is happening on other common law jurisdictions, and secondly, funders tend to be global investors rather than domestic entities, and therefore well-equipped to argue that more conservative jurisdictions are behind the times and parochial.

---

the action in his name and pay to the trustee in bankruptcy 25% of any net recovery. Chitty J upheld the assignment. The decision was followed by the Court of Appeal in *Ramsey v Hartley* [1977] 2 All ER 673, [1977] 1 WLR 686 where the trustee assigned a cause of action to the bankrupt in consideration of receiving 35% of any net recovery;

6   In *Grovewood Holdings case* [1994] 2 BCLC 782, [1995] Ch 80 there was no outright assignment of the cause of action but a sponsorship arrangement under which the action was pursued in the name of the company but at the expense of the sponsors and with the assistance but not subject to the control of the liquidator. In the result the action was stayed as champertous. See *Rawnsley v Weatherall Green & Smith North Ltd* [2009] EWHC 2482 (Ch) per HHJ Behrens for a discussion of this area of the law.

7   R Jackson *Review of Civil Litigation Costs: Final Report* (2009), chapter 11, para 1.2; he also commented that third-party funding would become more important if success fees become irrecoverable between opposing parties.

8   As set out in **41.16**, s 58B(8) of the Courts and Legal Services Act 1990 (as amended) does, in fact, contain provision requiring the payment of any amount payable under a litigation funding agreement, but this is not in force and, in the writer's view, is unlikely ever to come into force save, perhaps, in the context of a small barrister-driven contingency legal aid fund.

9   See his comments made in a press release in November 2011 in which he welcomed the Code of Conduct of Litigation Funders.

10   For a full analysis of this topic, see R Mulheron 'Third-party funding: a changing landscape' (2008) 27 CJQ 3, pp 312–341.

Up to and including 1995

41.5 Whilst in the UK the crime of champerty had been abolished in the 1960s, it was not until the 1980s that the UK Parliament felt able to enact legislation making conditional fee agreements lawful (see **9.375–9.387**). At that stage there was no mention of litigation funding, but the acceptance of conditional funding in any form was a significant step which laid the ground for further developments. Despite it being enacted in 1990, that legislation did not come into force until 1995 (see **9.381**); when it did, it was a significant event in that the fact that conditional funding had become a practical reality. With hindsight, it can be seen that the Rubicon had been crossed. Similar developments were happening in other jurisdictions. Whilst the details are unimportant in the present context, in the 1990s Australian legislation was passed that also heralded a change in attitudes towards conditional funding.[11]

41.6 There were also developments in the common law. In 1994 the House of Lords, dealing with issues that bore a degree of similarity to litigation funding,[12] explained that the approach to public policy was more nuanced than had been believed previously; their Lordships established that the question of whether an agreement claiming a stake in litigation was objectionable is whether the agreement under scrutiny has a 'tendency to corrupt public justice'. Their Lordships determined that this issue turns the nature and surrounding circumstances of the agreement in question;[13] the relevance of this is that it meant that a funding agreement would not be automatically struck down as a matter of law merely because it belonged to a certain class of agreement. It must be stressed, however, that at this stage, litigation funding of the type that is seen today was not regarded as lawful.

Early 2000s

41.7 In the late 1990s and early 2000s the court repeatedly demonstrated a flexible and pragmatic approach to cases which previously would have been characterised as champertous.[14] The legal profession became so familiar with the use of conditional funding that it became a quotidian means of funding legal services. Many commentators said that the long-standing objections that had been used to justify the law of champerty relating to funders[15] began to sound hoary and hollow.

41.8 In 2003 the Court of Appeal (in the UK) clarified the law of champerty in such a way as to permit persons other than solicitors to enter into agreements in which payment of their fees was dependent on success; it was established that the mere fact that litigation services have been provided in return for a share of the proceeds was not by itself sufficient to justify a finding of unenforceability.[16] It was at about this time that modern-day litigation funding agreements started to emerge; that said, it was a slow start, not least because litigation funders in other common law jurisdictions suffered a

---

[11]   It would be excessive to give the historic details, but in 1995 administrators and liquidators were given powers that allowed them to dispose of company assets in such a way as to make a profit from something similar to litigation funding.

[12]   A putatively champertous car hire agreement.

[13]   *Giles v Thompson* [1994] 1 AC 142.

[14]   See, for example, *Papera Traders Co Ltd v Hyundai (Merchant) Marine Co Ltd (No 2)* [2002] 2 Lloyd's Rep 692.

[15]   The law of champerty has always been well preserved in so far as legal representatives acting in that capacity are concerned: see **9.348** *et seq.*

[16]   *R (Factortame Ltd and others) v Secretary of State for Transport, Local Government and Regions (No 8)* [2002] EWCA Civ 932.

series of setbacks, this being largely as a result of funders trying to sequester to themselves an excessive degree of control over the litigation.[17]

Mid-2000s

41.9 The legality of litigation funding agreements in the UK was confirmed by the Court of Appeal in 2005, but this was by way of what was *not* said rather than by way of an express ruling. The court heard an application for a third-party costs order in a claim which had plainly be funded by a third-party funder. The court could have disposed of that application by finding that third-party funding was an anathema which should inevitably lead to the funder being condemned in costs to the maximum extent, but instead the court pragmatically weighted the rights of all the persons involved (including the rights of the funder) and determined, in the round, how much, if any, the funder should contribute to his opponent's costs; in particular, the court found that the funder should be potentially liable for costs up to the limit of his investment. The way the court approached that issue implied that litigation funding was in some ways desirable, but more importantly, it strongly implied that it was lawful. Phillips MR explained the benefits of litigation funding (or third-party funding, as it was then known) in the following way:[18]

- professional funders would be likely to cap the funds that they provide in order to limit their exposure to a reasonable amount;
- this would have a salutary effect in keeping costs proportionate; and
- professional funders would also have to consider with even greater care whether the prospects of the litigation are sufficiently good to justify the support that they are asked to give.

Litigation funding had arrived. The same was also happening in Australian courts at about the same time in that the benefits of litigation funding were being recorded in almost exactly the same terms as those used by Phillips MR.[19]

41.10 Indeed, the rise of conditional funding in Australia gathered pace. In 2006 the High Court of Australia[20] handed down decisions that, for all practical purposes, abolished the common law rules against champerty and maintenance;[21] the High Court said this about the age-old concerns that underlay those rules:[22]

> 'to meet these fears by adopting a rule in either form would take too broad an axe to the problems that may be seen to lie behind the fears.'

---

[17]   See, for example, the Australian case of *Clairs Keeley (a Firm) v Treacy & Ors* (2003) 28 WAR 139, where the case was stayed because the court found that the fact that the case had been assigned to the funder meant that the litigation was proceeding without reference to the plaintiff in any way. Likewise, in In *Marston v Statewide Independent Wholesalers Ltd* [2003] NSWSC 816 the funder had contractually prevented communication between the solicitors and the plaintiffs; unsurprisingly this was held to be an abuse of process.

[18]   *Arkin v Borchard Lines Ltd* [2005] EWCA Civ 655.

[19]   See, for example, *Fostif Pty Ltd v Campbells Cash & Carry Pty Ltd* (2005) 63 NSWLR 203; 218 ALR 166; [2005] NSWCA 83, at [100]; *QPSX Ltd v Ericsson Australia Pty Ltd (No 3)* (2005) 219 ALR 1; 66 IPR 277; [2005] FCA 933, at [54]

[20]   This being a court whose decisions are binding on all courts in Australia.

[21]   See *Campbells Cash and Carry Pty Ltd v Fostif Pty Ltd* (2006) 229 CLR 386; 229 ALR 58; [2006] HCA 41; *Mobil Oil Australia Pty Ltd v Trendlen Pty Ltd* [2006] HCA 42.

[22]   *Fostif* (supra) at [91].

Thus, in Australia questions of illegality and public policy would be answered according to the prevailing circumstances (ie, on the facts of each case). This echoed the position in the UK (see **41.9**). The High Court noted that existing substantive and procedural rules were, in general, sufficient to protect court processes.[23]

Late 2000s

41.11 In early 2007 in the UK, the influential Civil Justice Council spoke positively about litigation funding.[24] This reinforced the view that public policy now tolerated such agreements. In that same year the Office of Fair Trading recommended that litigation funding ought to be encouraged in private competition claims (this being a type of litigation that is notoriously difficult to fund);[25] the reason the OFT believed that it was desirable to encourage litigation of that sort because it was hoped that this would discourage anti-competitive practices – this, obviously, being something that was in the public interest.

41.12 In Australia – where funding was used primarily for class actions – defendants were complaining that the involvement of funders was not facilitating the resolution of disputes but allowing lawyers to stir up disputes; defendants also brought a number of technical challenges. On the whole, however, most of the challenges based on policy were rejected.[26]

41.13 Speaking extrajudicially in 2008, the retiring English judge Sir Gavin Lightman said that 'throwing aside the shackles of the past law' on champerty and maintenance 'would release litigants and funders from rules which are positively damaging to the public';[27] the Master of the Rolls made similar comments. Commentators began to discuss why litigation funding was not being more widely adopted.[28] Other commentators noted that recent developments in the law of conditional fee agreements would be a boon to the future development of litigation funding.[29] Thus, the debate in the UK had got to the stage at which policymakers were looking at how litigation funding could be given a more prominent role in the litigation landscape.

41.14 In 2009 the Jackson review called for comments about whether the common law of champerty and maintenance ought to be replaced by a regulatory framework. Following consultation, Jackson LJ (speaking extrajudicially) concluded that whilst it was not necessary to abolish the champerty and maintenance, litigation funding was to be encouraged (see **41.3**); he believed that it was too early to impose a legislative

---

[23] *Fostif* (supra) at [92].
[24] *Improved Access To Justice – Funding Options and Proportionate Costs* (Civil Justice Council, June 2007).
[25] OFT916, *Private Actions in Competition Law: Effective Redress for Consumers and Businesses.*
[26] For example, in *Jeffery and Katauskas Pty Ltd v Rickard Constructions Pty Ltd* (2009) 239 CLR 75, the High Court rejected the argument that a failure by the litigation funder to provide security for costs amounted to an abuse of process; similar, in *Deloitte Touche Tohmatsu v JP Morgan Portfolio Services Limited* (2007) 158 FCR 417, the Full Federal Court summarily rejected arguments by the appellant that there was an abuse of process, essentially relying on *Fostif* and *Trendlen.*
[27] Rose N News 'Radical shake-up needed in funding of litigation' (2008) LS Gaz 20 Mar 5(1).
[28] C Ciumei 'A more open competition' (2008) 158 NLJ 7321, pp 691–692.
[29] S Friel 'Funding Manoeuvres' (2009) 159 NLJ 7369, p 707.

Civil Costs: Law and Practice

regulation, but he did recommend a voluntary code (see below). The issue of regulation arose in other Australia too, albeit in the context of contested cases rather than consultation.[30]

Early 2010s

41.15 The effect of these developments has been to shift the focus towards regulation, this being both in this country and abroad.[31] The Australian courts have concluded that litigation funding arrangements are, where appropriate, to be treated as investment products and that they are to be regulated in that way,[32] but the practical effect of such findings is limited.[33] No specific regulations had – at the time of writing – been made, but this was in the context of an on-going debate on the topic.[34] The Law Council of Australia has noted that despite clear rulings by the High Court as to the legality of litigation funding (see **41.9**), there continues to be satellite litigation on the topic;[35] the Australian courts are, in some ways, a few years ahead of the UK in terms of the arguments that are likely to arise, and it is possible that the UK will follow suit. That said, there is less willingness in the UK to deal with the issue of champerty on a case-by-case basis,[36] and this may be enough to save the UK from that fate. In the UK, the Civil Justice Council has recommended that a voluntary association ought to be established. This was achieved in November 2011 when the Association of Litigation Funders of England & Wales published its rules of membership. The Code of Conduct for Litigation Funders was also published at this time, this being a development that the Master of the Rolls has welcomed.[37]

FUTURE DEVELOPMENTS

Regulation

41.16 Whilst a statutory framework for regulation exists, it is not yet in force and is largely ignored;[38] the writer's opinion is that it will never come into force (or, at least,

---

[30] In *Brookfield Multiplex Ltd v International Litigation Funding Partners Pte Ltd* (2009) 256 ALR 427, the defendant in funded proceedings challenged the propriety of the litigation funding arrangements, citing the lack of regulation as being a relevant factor.

[31] See, for example, *Regulation of third party litigation funding in Australia (Position Paper)*, June 2011, Law Council of Australia; see also *International Litigation Partners Pte Ltd v Chameleon Mining NL* [2011] NSWCA 50 (15 March 2011), in which New South Wales Court of Appeal dealt with a litigation funding agreement as if it were any other financial product.

[32] In *International Litigation Partners Pte Ltd v Chameleon Mining NL* [2011] NSWCA 50, the NSW Court of Appeal found that the funder must hold a financial services licence because the funding agreement was a 'financial product' which involved 'managed risk'.

[33] The practical effect of decisions to treat litigation funders as financial service providers is limited because of ASIC Class Order 10/333, which exempts litigation funders from holding a financial services licence.

[34] In 2011 the Law Council of Australia concluded that only guidelines were necessary for the purpose of regulating lawyers and that either guidelines or regulations would be sufficient for regulating funders: see *Regulation of third party litigation funding in Australia (Position Paper)*, June 2011, Law Council of Australia at para 70.

[35] See *Regulation of third party litigation funding in Australia (Position Paper)*, June 2011, Law Council of Australia at para 54.

[36] See, for example, *Morris v London Borough of Southwark* [2011] EWCA Civ 25 at [57], per Lord Neuberger MR.

[37] See his comments made in a press release in November 2011 in which he welcomed the Code of Conduct of Litigation Funders.

[38] That framework is s 58A of the Courts and Legal Services Act 1990, as amended by s 28 of the Access to

that there are parts of it that will never come into force).[39] Commentators have noted that there is an absence of regulation of litigation funding,[40] but the focus has been on self-regulation rather than legislation. Of particular concern, it is said, is the absence of any solvency requirements.[41] This is in marked contrast to insurers, who have to satisfy the Financial Services Authority as to their solvency. Speaking extrajudicially in 2009, Jackson LJ recommended a voluntary code,[42] this echoing the thoughts of a number of academics.[43] In 2008 the Civil Justice Council published a draft voluntary code of conduct; speaking extrajudicially, Jackson LJ opined that it did not go far enough in terms of consumer protection.[44] A new Code of Conduct for Litigation Funders was also published in November 2011. That code does not apply to funders who are already the subject of statutory regulation; thus, if funding is provided by a bank (and, accordingly, is regulated by the FSA) then the code would not apply.

Justice Act 1999. That framework is as follows:

'58B Litigation funding agreements.

'(1) A litigation funding agreement which satisfies all of the conditions applicable to it by virtue of this section shall not be unenforceable by reason only of its being a litigation funding agreement.

'(2) For the purposes of this section a litigation funding agreement is an agreement under which—

(a) a person ("the funder") agrees to fund (in whole or in part) the provision of advocacy or litigation services (by someone other than the funder) to another person ("the litigant"); and

(b) the litigant agrees to pay a sum to the funder in specified circumstances.

'(3) The following conditions are applicable to a litigation funding agreement—

(a) the funder must be a person, or person of a description, prescribed by the Secretary of State;

(b) the agreement must be in writing;

(c) the agreement must not relate to proceedings which by virtue of section 58A(1) and (2) cannot be the subject of an enforceable conditional fee agreement or to proceedings of any such description as may be prescribed by the Secretary of State;

(d) the agreement must comply with such requirements (if any) as may be so prescribed;

(e) the sum to be paid by the litigant must consist of any costs payable to him in respect of the proceedings to which the agreement relates together with an amount calculated by reference to the funder's anticipated expenditure in funding the provision of the services; and

(f) that amount must not exceed such percentage of that anticipated expenditure as may be prescribed by the Secretary of State in relation to proceedings of the description to which the agreement relates.

'(4) Regulations under subsection (3)(a) may require a person to be approved by the Secretary of State or by a prescribed person.

'(5) The requirements which the Secretary of State may prescribe under subsection (3)(d)—

(a) include requirements for the funder to have provided prescribed information to the litigant before the agreement is made; and

(b) may be different for different descriptions of litigation funding agreements.

'(6) In this section (and in the definitions of "advocacy services" and "litigation services" as they apply for its purposes) "proceedings" includes any sort of proceedings for resolving disputes (and not just proceedings in a court), whether commenced or contemplated.

...

'(8) A costs order made in any proceedings may, subject in the case of court proceedings to rules of court, include provision requiring the payment of any amount payable under a litigation funding agreement.

'(9) Rules of court may make provision with respect to the assessment of any costs which include fees payable under a litigation funding agreement.'

[39] In particular, it is close to inconceivable that the provision permitting recovery of funding monies between opposing parties (see s 58B(8)) will ever come into force.

[40] See, for example, R Pirozzolo 'Opinion: Funder the cosh' *The Lawyer*, 11 August 2009.

[41] Ibid; see also R Jackson *Review of Civil Litigation Costs: Final Report* (2009), Chapter 11.

[42] R Jackson *Review of Civil Litigation Costs: Final Report* (2009), chapter 11, para 6.1. This is an issue which has been considered by the Civil Justice Council.

[43] See, for example, R Mulheron 'Third-party funding: a changing landscape' (2008) 27 CJQ 3, p 312.

[44] R Jackson *Review of Civil Litigation Costs: Final Report* (2009), chapter 11, para 6.1.

41.17 In addition to provisions concerning confidentiality, promotional literature, etc, that code contains provisions relating to solvency,[45] client counselling,[46] and conduct of cases.[47] In addition, it contains the following provisions concerning the contents of any litigator funding agreement:[48]

> '8. The LFA shall state whether (and if so to what extent) the Funder is liable to the Litigant to:
>
> (a)   meet any liability for adverse costs;
> (b)   pay any premium (including insurance premium tax) to obtain costs insurance;
> (c)   provide security for costs;
> (d)   meet any other financial liability.'

And it also provides that:

> '9. The LFA shall state whether (and if so how) the Funder may:
>
> (a)   provide input to the Litigant's decisions in relation to settlements;
> (b)   terminate the LFA in the event that the Funder:
>   (i)   reasonably ceases to be satisfied about the merits of the dispute;
>   (ii)   reasonably believes that the dispute is no longer commercially viable; or
>   (iii)   reasonably believes that there has been a material breach of the LFA by the Litigant.
>
> 10. The LFA shall not establish a discretionary right for a Funder to terminate a LFA in the absence of the circumstances described in clause 9(b).
>
> 11. If the LFA does give the Funder any of the rights described in clause 9 the LFA shall provide that:
>
> (a)   if the Funder terminates the LFA, the Funder shall remain liable for all funding obligations accrued to the date of termination unless the termination is due to a material breach under clause 9(b)(iii);
> (b)   if there is a dispute between the Funder and the Litigant about settlement or about termination of the LFA, a binding opinion shall be obtained from a Queen's Counsel who shall be instructed jointly or nominated by the Chairman of the Bar Council.'

Blurring of the boundaries

41.18 Some commentators have noticed that the boundary between litigation funding and ATE insurance has become blurred in the sense that many funders now limit their funding to adverse costs, and some insurers are prepared to agree to provide an indemnity for the costs of security for costs applications.[49] Indeed, some insurers will

---

45   Paragraph 7(d) provides that the funder will 'maintain at all times adequate financial resources to meet its obligations to fund all of the disputes that it has agreed to fund, and in particular will maintain the capacity: (i) to pay all debts when they become due and payable; and
      (ii) to cover aggregate funding liabilities under all of its LFAs for a minimum period of 36 months.' There are further provision at para 2.
46   Paragraph 7(a) provides that a funder will 'take reasonable steps to ensure that the Litigant shall have received independent advice on the terms of the LFA, which obligation shall be satisfed if the Litigant confirms in writing to the Funder that the Litigant has taken advice from the solicitor instructed in the dispute.'
47   Paragraph 7(b) prevents the funder from taking 'any steps that cause or are likely to cause the Litigant's solicitor or barrister to act in breach of their professional duties', and para 7(c) provides that the funder will 'not seek to influence the Litigant's solicitor or barrister to cede control or conduct of the dispute to the Funder.'
48   Paragraph 8.
49   M Amey 'Litigation Funding' (2009) 61 *Litigation Funding*, June, p 24.

even go so far as to provide security (such as bonds) for the purposes of security for costs.[50] It is certainly possible that the roles will become less distinct in the coming years.

Alternative business structures

41.19 With the introduction of alternative business structures under the Legal Services Act 2007, it is possible that risk may be more widely spread in the future (at least amongst lawyers); this will do nothing to stifle innovation. It is certainly true to say that funders are already seeking to forge links with species of lawyer that previously would not have considered such links, such as barristers in independent practice.

PRESENT LEGISLATIVE CONTROL

41.20 There is, at present, nothing to suggest that the UK is likely to follow the Australian lead and seek to regulate litigation funders by means of the state's general powers to regulate financial service providers (see **41.15**). That said, if funding becomes available to consumers, then they will, where appropriate, become entitled to the protection of the Consumer Credit Act 1974 and the Consumer Credit Act 2006. At present, however, most funding agreements are with commercial organisations, and it seems that voluntary regulation is presently the preferred method of control. The same also seems to be true of the role of solicitors; prior to 6 October 2011 there used to be a provision that prevented solicitors from entering into certain agreements with funders of personal injury claims; the details are in the footnotes.[51] It is noticeable that those provisions have no counterpart in the SRA Code of Conduct 2011;[52] this, presumably, being because claims management services are regulated by other means, namely, the Compensation Act 2006. The effect of the new provision is, *in toto*, that *per se* seems not to be regulated.

AVAILABILITY AND PRACTICE

41.21 Those involved in litigation funding are trading in a nascent market: as of January 2009, less than 100 claims in England and Wales were being funded by litigation

---

[50] See R Pirozzolo 'Opinion: Insurers and third-party funders should work together' *The Lawyer*, 1 December 2008.
[51] Paragraph 9.01 of the Solicitors' Code of Conduct 2007 used to provide as follows:
'(4) You must not, in respect of any claim arising as a result of death or personal injury, either:
(a)enter into an arrangement for the referral of clients with; or
(b)act in association with,
any person whose business, or any part of whose business, is to make, support or prosecute (whether by action or otherwise, and whether by a solicitor or agent or otherwise) claims arising as a result of death or personal injury, and who, in the course of such business, solicits or receives contingency fees in respect of such claims.
(5) The prohibition in 9.01(4) shall not apply to an arrangement or association with a person who solicits or receives contingency fees only in respect of proceedings in a country outside England and Wales, to the extent that a local lawyer would be permitted to receive a contingency fee in respect of such proceedings.
(6) In 9.01(4) and (5) "contingency fee" means any sum (whether fixed, or calculated either as a percentage of the proceeds or otherwise howsoever) payable only in the event of success in the prosecution or defence of any action, suit or other contentious proceedings.'
[52] Indeed, serious thought was given to the relevant provisions being excluded from the Solicitors Code of Conduct 2007: see M Cook *Cook on Costs 2011* (LexisNexis) at [41.18].

funders;[53] this figure has increased significantly (in relative terms) since then, but the numbers are still small. Whilst an oversimplification, litigation funding tends to be available in the following circumstances:[54]

- where the claim is large (six or seven figures: see **41.22**) and where the defendant is assessed to be able to satisfy any judgment made against him;
- where the prospects of success are very good (usually at least 70% likely to succeed: see **41.23**); and
- where the risks can be shared with both an ATE insurer and the client's lawyers (see **41.23**), and where the lawyers are experienced and competent at the type of claim in question.

In the same way that ATE insurers work on the basis of the actuarial principles of adequacy and equity (see **30.151**), litigation funders look to achieving an appropriate return on their investment; the quantification of that return is known as 'gearing'. That is, litigation funders seek to invest in claims which, if successful, will repay their investment together with a reward. The business model which has traditionally been used has sought a reward of about three times its value,[55] this usually being calculated as a percentage of the damages or debt which is the subject matter of the claim (see **41.24**). With new entrants into the market, funders are being more flexible in terms of gearing, but on the whole, funders tend to focus on monetary claims of high value (see **41.22**). To date, the claims that have been funded have been predominantly insolvency claims, professional negligence claims, securities litigation and tax disputes. The following paragraphs (**41.22–41.27**) set out the factors which may be relevant to whether a case is suitable for litigation funding. Each funder will, however, have his own selection criteria.

Minimum values

41.22 Most litigation funders have a threshold for the value of the claim below which they will not offer funding; in early 2010, a selection of minimum values was as follows:[56]

Claims Funding International[57]	£25,000,000
1st Class Legal	£150,000
Allianz Litigation Funding[58]	£500,000
IM Litigation Funding	£500,000
Harbour Litigation Funding	£2,000,000

Trade publications exist which give up-to-date information about the state of the market.[59] The market has grown significantly since early 2010 as new litigation funders continue to enter into the market.

---

[53] Personal communication, R Pirozzolo, 25 November 2009.
[54] The highly respected legal commentator Michael Cook refers to an additional requirement, namely that the costs of pursuing the matter are proportionate to the size of the claim (see *Cook on Costs 2012* (LexisNexis) at [41.4]).
[55] R Pirozzolo 'Opinion: Insurers and third-party funders should work together' *The Lawyer*, 1 December 2008.
[56] R Jackson *Review of Civil Litigation Costs: Preliminary Report* (2009), Vol 1, p 161.
[57] This funder is no longer active in this country.
[58] This funder has now left the UK funding market.
[59] A table of third-party funders and their products can often be found in a table in the Litigation Funding magazine.

Acceptance of cases

41.23 The purpose of commercial funding is to cover costs and make a profit, so it is a condition of funding that the case in question has good prospects of success. Funders will take care in choosing their cases, often electing to carry out their own risk assessments. Some will accept only about 10% of referrals. Most will invest only if there is at least a 70% chance of success.[60] Most will also require the client's solicitor to demonstrate his faith in the strength of the case by agreeing to expose himself to some risk that the funder faces; thus, a solicitor would normally be expected to enter into a discounted conditional fee agreement where at least 30% of his fees were at risk (see **9.12**).

Remuneration

41.24 Remuneration is typically between 10% and 40% of the value of the claim, but may be higher; this is broadly in line with rates paid in other jurisdictions.[61] The market is made up of two types of funder: established professional funders (whose core business is funding) and hedge-fund funders (who usually commit a smaller percentage of their capital assets to funding than established funders). Because a higher proportion of their capital is committed to funding (and therefore at risk), established funders are typically less willing to take risks than hedge-fund funders. It is for this reason that established funders will generally abide by fixed actuarial methods; hedge-fund funders, on the other hand, will often be more willing to negotiate a bespoke package, and which may involve accepting a greater degree of risk.[62]

ATE insurance

41.25 A funder is potentially liable for costs, at least to the extent that he has funded the claim;[63] in view of this it is now almost always a necessary requirement for funding that appropriate ATE insurance is put in place.[64] The premium may or may not be recoverable, depending on the facts.[65] It is worth pausing here to note that insurers and funders are usually able to co-exist in peaceful accord. This is partly due to their having mutual clients, but also because they have complementary roles (ie the funder funds own-costs and disbursements and the insurer indemnifies adverse costs).On the whole, funders and insurers trade in sufficiently dissimilar markets to avoid direct competition.

---

[60] *Arkin v Borchard Lines Ltd* [2005] EWCA Civ 655 at [161].

[61] The percentages in Australia are usually between 25 and 40%: see Standing Committee of Attorneys-General, Litigation Funding in Australia, May 2006, pp 4 and 7.

[62] J Delaney 'Litigation insurance and funding' (2008) 19 Cons Law 6, p 20.

[63] *Arkin v Borchard Lines Ltd* [2005] EWCA Civ 655 at [41]; the court explained that the restriction on the funder's liability will not apply if the agreement falls foul of the policy considerations that render an agreement champertous. In these circumstances, the funder may have an unlimited liability.

[64] R Jackson *Review of Civil Litigation Costs: Preliminary Report* (2009), Vol 1, p 161; exceptions do exist, however: see, for example, *Stone & Rolls Ltd (In Liquidation) v Moore Stephens (A Firm)* [2009] UKHL 39, HL, which was funded without ATE insurance.

[65] Where both ATE insurance and third-party funding is required, and where the former is purchased at the behest of the latter, it is a moot point whether the premium would be recoverable from a paying party; it has been suggested that the premium ought not to be recoverable as the expenditure could be categorised as being part of the funder's business overheads (see G Langdon-Down 'Litigation Funding: Place your bets' (2009) *Law Society Gazette*, 21 May, p 11).

By way of example, whilst litigation funders seek clients with claims which have at least a 70% chance of success (see **41.23**), insurers tend, as a rule, to consider claims that have at least a 60% chance of success.[66]

Independent legal advice

41.26 The Code of Conduct for Litigation Funders 2011 states that a funder will take reasonable steps to ensure that the litigant has received independent advice on the terms of the litigation funding agreement.[67] This is in line with experience from the United States, which suggests that in appropriate cases clients should be advised to take independent legal advice about the proposed method of funding.[68]

Control of litigation

41.27 The Code of Conduct for Litigation Funders 2011 provides that a funder will not seek to influence the litigant's solicitor or barrister to cede control of the dispute to the funder.[69] This provision is probably otiose, however, as fears that their involvement may otherwise be seen as being champertous have generally stopped funders from exercising any significant control over funded litigation.[70]

Contractual provisions

41.28 Litigation funding agreements ought to be drafted only by funding specialists, but the following general points can be made.

Precedence condition

41.29 It is sensible to ensure that the agreement is drafted by a drafter who has had prior sight of the draft contracts of retainer and the ATE policies; the drafter ought to be asked to ensure that there are no conflicts. It is good practice to include a provision which stipulates which document will take precedence in the event of a conflict.

Reporting provision

41.30 Whilst not something that is required by the Code of Conduct for Litigation Funders 2011, it is good practice to include a reporting provision which that states in specific terms what the legal representative is expected to report to the funder. That provision must not require such a level of reporting that it might lead to allegations of 'wanton intermeddling' and champerty.

Management provision

41.31 The Code of Conduct for Litigation Funders 2011 states that agreements should state whether (and if so how) the funder may provide input to the litigant's decisions in

---

[66]   R Pirozzolo 'Opinion: Insurers and third-party funders should work together' *The Lawyer*, 1 December 2008.

[67]   Paragraph 7(a) of the Code of Conduct for Litigation Funders 2011.

[68]   J Wheeler 'Welcome to the Party' (2008) 158 NLJ 7342, pp 1491–1492.

[69]   See para 7(c) of the Code of Conduct for Litigation Funders 2011.

[70]   R Jackson *Review of Civil Litigation Costs: Preliminary Report* (2009), Vol 1, p 163.

relation to settlements. It is good practice to set out, in terms, what the funder cannot do (ie, to limit the funder's influence so that he cannot be accused of controlling the litigation).

Termination provision

41.32 The Code of Conduct for Litigation Funders 2011 sets out the following provisions concerning termination:

> '9. The LFA shall state whether (and if so how) the Funder may:
>
> ...
> (b)   terminate the LFA in the event that the Funder:
>   (i)   reasonably ceases to be satisfied about the merits of the dispute;
>   (ii)   reasonably believes that the dispute is no longer commercially viable; or
>   (iii)   reasonably believes that there has been a material breach of the LFA by the Litigant.'

Importantly, the Code also provides that the agreement shall not establish a discretionary right for a funder to terminate an agreement in the absence of the circumstances described in clause 9(b). The Code then goes on to make the following provision:

> '11. If the LFA does give the Funder any of the rights described in clause 9 the LFA shall provide that:
>
> (a)   if the Funder terminates the LFA, the Funder shall remain liable for all funding obligations accrued to the date of termination unless the termination is due to a material breach under clause 9(b)(iii);

Priorities provision

41.33 Whilst not something that is dealt with in the Code of Conduct for Litigation Funders 2011, it is often helpful to include within an agreement (or as a schedule to an agreement) a record of priorities (ie an agreement which will deal with who is to be paid what if the sums recovered in the litigation are insufficient to satisfy all of the parties' contractual entitlements). This is often referred to as 'the waterfall of priorities'. Where other stakeholders are involved—such as ATE insurers—a separate agreement, known as a priorities agreement, could be appropriate. Paying attention to these issues at the beginning of the litigation will lessen the chances of disputes at the end.

Disputes resolution procedure

41.34 The Code of Conduct for Litigation Funders 2011 provides that if there is a dispute between the funder and the litigant about settlement or about termination of the agreement, a binding opinion shall be obtained from a Queen's Counsel who shall be instructed jointly or nominated by the Chairman of the Bar Council.[71] This requirement does not provide the parties any route of appeal; it is good practice to ensure that both the funder and the litigant are fully aware of this fact before the agreement is made.

---

[71]   See para 11(b) of the Code of Conduct for Litigation Funders 2011.

Adverse event provision, security for costs, etc

41.35 The Code of Conduct for Litigation Funders 2011 states that agreements should state whether the funder will (i) meet any liability for adverse costs, (ii) pay any premium (including insurance premium tax) to obtain costs insurance, (iii) provide security for costs, or (iv) meet any other financial liability. It is usually convenient to set these details out in a schedule to the agreement. Unless the entire risk is borne by the ATE insurer, there also ought to be a record of who pays what and in which circumstances (ie, would be responsible for adverse costs orders, who would pay for top-up insurance, etc).

Chapter 42

THE JACKSON REFORMS

42.1 This chapter reviews those reforms that, at the time of writing, were in the process of being implemented. It is not intended to be a rigorous examination of those reforms; it would be dangerous to attempt such an analysis where the law is neither in force nor in its final form. Instead, this chapter has the more modest objectives of describing the reforms and suggesting a framework by which lawyers with a financial interest in those reforms might prepare for their implementation. The flowcharts at the end of this chapter are intended to assist in this regard. Unlike the rest of this book, this chapter records the writer's opinion on a number of issues; much of this is educated guesswork, and as such ought not to be afforded any greater status than it deserves.

42.2 This chapter is intended to be neutral as to the merits of the reforms. The proposals have caused considerable polarisation within the legal profession, and any attempt to please everyone and offend no-one would result in a useless and anodyne essay. Instead, this chapter is based on the assumption that the reader will want to know how to manage the effect of the reforms, and to that extent it, of necessity, leans towards acceptance thereof.

42.3 When more information is available, an appendix to this chapter will be published on the Internet. The reader must not rely on anything in this chapter (or the appendix) without first carrying out his own research.

42.4 The topics are as follows:

- History and implementation of the reforms (**42.5–42.18**).
- The interaction with other changes in the legal marketplace (**42.11–42.18**).
- Reforms relating to the conduct of substantive litigation.
  - costs management and costs budgeting (**42.31**, but see also **15.65**);
  - case management (and in particular, controlling the costs of disclosure) (**42.20–42.30**);
  - offers under CPR Part 36 (**42.36–42.39**);
  - costs shifting (**42.36–42.39**).
- Funding reforms:
  - the 'myth of full costs recovery' (**42.41–42.45**);
  - damages-based agreements (**42.46–42.53**);
  - litigation (third-party) funding (**42.54–42.56**);
  - contingency legal aid and supplementary legal aid fund (**42.57–42.58**).
- Reforms relating to the amount of costs:
  - additional liabilities (**42.60–42.68**);
  - fixed costs (**42.69**);
  - other issues concerning the amount of costs (**42.70–42.73**).
- Reforms relating to costs procedure.
  - bills of costs (**42.75**)

- detailed assessment (**42.76**)
- summary assessment (**42.77**)
- provisional assessment (**42.76**, but see **21.145–21.156**)
- proportionality (**42.78**)
- Miscellaneous matters: the proposed increase in general damages (**42.79–42.80**).
- How to prepare for the reforms (**42.82** *et seq*).

HISTORY AND IMPLEMENTATION

42.5   A review of the history of the Jackson reforms would normally start with the announcement of the 'Civil Costs Review' in November 2008 (see **2.7**), but it is worth putting matters in historical context. As has been explained at **1.1** above, costs policy tends to be cyclical in that reviews tend to take place every decade or so. This is almost inevitable as policy drifts (and occasionally shifts) between two opposing concerns: on the one hand, there are concerns about access to justice and on the other there are concerns about who should pay for those cases that do not pay for themselves through the recovery of costs between opposing parties). History has repeatedly shown that there is no such thing as the perfect balance: whoever bears that burden – be it the state (e g legal aid and success fees paid by the NHS), the losing party (i e awarded costs), the winning party (i e solicitor and client costs), or society in a more general sense (e g insurance) –the pendulum will eventually swing in the opposite direction.

42.6   Things are different under the Jackson reforms, in that the reforms are not merely about *who* pays, but about *how much* is received, and in particular, the profits being made by the legal services industry. The reforms are partly driven by the concern that there is 'too much money swirling around in the system' (to use Sir Rupert Jackson's words).[1] This focus on profits as opposed to costs is new, and unless one goes back to Bentham's observation that costs are 'the grand instrument of mischief in English practice'[2] and the Leases Act 1845,[3] the Jackson reviews are, for this reason, qualitatively different to previous reviews.

42.7   The story begins on 3 November 2008 when Sir Anthony Clarke MR announced the following review:

> 'The Master of the Rolls has appointed Lord Justice Jackson to lead a fundamental review into the costs of civil litigation. The review will commence in January 2009, and the findings are due to be presented to the Master of the Rolls in December 2009. Lord Justice Jackson will be the sole author of the final report ... The review is being undertaken as the Master of the Rolls, Sir Anthony Clarke, is concerned at the costs of civil litigation and believes that the time is right for a fundamental and independent review of the whole system.'

42.8   This review became known as 'the Jackson Review' or the 'Civil Costs Review' and the still-evolving reforms are generally referred to as 'the Jackson Reforms'. The review had three phases:

- ***Phase 1 (January to April 2009):*** fact finding, preliminary consultation and preparation of Preliminary Report[4] ('the Preliminary Report');

---

[1]   R Jackson *A talk by Lord Justice Jackson to the Cambridge Law Faculty*, 5 September 2011 at p 4.
[2]   See **1.20**.
[3]   See **1.20–1.23**.
[4]   R Jackson *Review of Civil Litigation Costs: Preliminary Report*, May 2009, HMSO, ISBN 9780117064034.

- *Phase 2 (May to July 2009):* consultation; and
- *Phase 3 (September to December 2009):* an analysis of material received and preparation of Final Report[5] ('the Final Report').

In addition to these formal phases, there were (and still are) pilot exercises, such as the pilots relating to costs budgeting (see **15.68**) and to provisional assessments (see **21.145–21.156**).

42.9 The Final Report was published in December 2009 (ie on target). The Government (who, in must be recalled, did not initiate the Jackson Review, but subsequently elected to adopt it) began its own consultation in November 2010. In March 2011 it published its response[6] in which the Secretary of State (Kenneth Clarke) had this to say:

> '[I]n recent years, the system has got out of kilter, fuelled to a significant extent by the way that 'no win, no fee' conditional fee agreements (CFAs) now work. They have played an important role in extending access to justice but they also enable claims to be pursued with no real risk to claimants and the threat of excessive costs to defendants. It cannot be right that, regardless of the extreme weakness of a claim, the sensible thing for the defendant to do is to settle, and get out before the legal costs start running up.'

Thus the political will to implement the reforms was present.

42.10 Implementation is on-going; in particular, a great deal of implementation work is being carried out by committees including the Civil Procedure Rule Committee. Sir Rupert Jackson has been keeping the public up-to-date by giving a series of Implementation Lectures.[7] He has explained that the following three types of implementation will be relevant:

- *Primary legislation:* Some of the reforms will be effected by primary legislation; the necessary Act (the Legal Aid, Sentencing and Punishment of Offenders Bill) received Royal Assent on 1 May 2012;
- *Secondary legislation and rule changes (and in particular, changes to the CPR):* Rule amendments were, at the time or writing, being drafted for approval by the Rule Committee; the intention is that they will be 'then held in escrow until the "big bang" date';[8] and
- *Judicial supervision:* A Judicial Steering Group ('JSG') chaired by the Master of the Rolls is overseeing implementation on behalf of the judiciary;

The Liberal Democrat peer Lord Wallace has confirmed that, subject to Parliamentary approval, the implementation of the reforms will be postponed until April 2013. Several commentators have said that it is unlikely that all the relevant provisions will be in ready by then and that implementation may, in fact, be a piecemeal affair. This, nonetheless, is not the stated intention of the Government.

---

[5] R Jackson *Review of Civil Litigation Costs: Final Report*, December 2009, HMSO, ISBN 9780117064041.
[6] *Reforming Civil Litigation Funding and Costs in England and Wales – Implementation of Lord Justice Jackson's Recommendations, The Government Response*, Cm 8041, March 2011,
[7] Those lectures can be found at http://www.judiciary.gov.uk/media/speeches/2012/index.
[8] R Jackson *Assessment of Costs in the Brave New World: Eighth Lecture* (KPMG Forensic's [sic] Leeds Law Lecture 2012, 25 January 2012 at 1.3.

INTERACTION WITH OTHER CHANGES IN THE LEGAL SERVICES INDUSTRY

42.11 There are many changes in the legal services industry that will have a bearing on the way in which the Jackson reforms will operate; the following are worth examining in some detail:

- the influence of alternative business structures (with particular emphasis on the effect that this will have on charging by the hour) (**42.12–42.15**);
- the political reaction to the putative 'compensation culture'(**42.16–42.17**); and
- the plans for audit (**42.18**).

Alternative business structures

42.12 Some of the most important changes lie outwith the central Jackson reforms; in particular, not only are the reforms taking place shortly after the introduction of alternative business structures, but they are also taking place in the midst of an economic recession. This is a heady mix of economic pressures, as was noted by Lord Neuberger MR:[9]

> 'Three relatively new developments may prove to be spurs to innovation, towards value-pricing rather than time-pricing, and the first development arises from Government policy, and it is the birth of alternative business structures (ABSs). It may be that the ABS business model will sound the death knell of hourly billing, as it will lead to more positive and market-orientated practices. The second development arises from economic change, and it is the present financial constraint on actual and potential clients ... Thirdly, there are the consequences of technological change: it may well be that the internet, and the development of legal price comparison websites, will help drive innovation – giving an impetus to the greater adoption of fixed pricing for legal work.'

Unsurprisingly Lord Neuberger MR was buoyant about the opportunities that the new regime might present, but it would do no harm also to recognize the difficulties and problems that lie in store, especially for those that work in the legal industry. It is, for those purposes, worth distinguishing between the consumer market and the commercial market.

The consumer market

42.13 The following predictions are intended to be conservative and realistic; they are, nonetheless, only the writer's opinions and should not be afforded any greater status than they deserve:

- ***Increased competition for clients:*** From the point of view of legal representatives, the Jackson reforms are likely to decrease the extent to which profit can be extracted from opponents whilst simultaneously increasing the pressure to look to clients for a contribution to profits. The inevitable effect of these pressures will be to increase competition for high-yield client bases ('stack them high and sell them cheap' as it were). In both these regards, well-resourced ABSs will have the edge

---

[9]   *Association of Costs Lawyers' Annual Conference 2012 (Keynote Address): Fourteenth Lecture in the Implementation Programme* (11 May 2012), para 20.

over traditional firms of solicitors, especially if they are well connected in the consumer market (such as retailers) or with referrers (such as BTE insurers).

- ***Reduced reliance on hourly rates***: There is a growing judicial antipathy for hourly billing as the default method by which legal services are purchased (**42.70-42.73**).[10] This may or may not result in a change in the market, but perhaps the greater pressure will come from the market itself. Non-legal investors—unlike many members of the legal profession—are likely to have no reservations about charging for services on the basis of fixed prices; they also have no qualms about reducing prices for the purposes of securing market share. ABSs will, again, have the edge as they will not have the baggage of having been raised on a diet of hourly billing.

- ***Greater incentive to assess***: In view of the non-recoverability of success fees and the increasing pressure to look to clients for a contribution to profits, clients are likely to become increasingly motivated to challenge top-heavy and disproportionate fees. Former clients will, in time, learn to use damages learn to use damages-based agreements for the purposes of bringing claims for solicitor and client assessments. This will mean that those legal representatives who continue to charge by the hour will be noticeably exposed (this being because it is a method of charging that is particularly susceptible to assessment when compared to more innovative methods, such as damages-based agreements and fixed-fees). In time, these things are likely to add to the pressures to abandon the old methods of charging and to focus on the new.

- ***Greater choice, greater confusion***: While consumers are likely to be presented with a wider choice of funding, the complexity of those choices has the potential to be baffling. It is possible that this will give rise to a new breed of middlemen (e g price comparison websites). Where, in the past, lawyers have operated in markets that lack limpidity they have tended to prosper[11] but this has been only where lawyers have competed with other layers. Now they will be competing with consumer-focused business and the result may be different. It could also lead to consumers moving away from traditional practices and towards trusted 'brands'. A recent example of this type of market drift is the way that deregulation of opticians in the 1980s resulted in the decline of independent dispensing opticians and to the rise in opticians as branded retailers; the same could happen to the consumer legal industry.

- ***Winners and losers***: The effect of the above will depend on local factors and on the type of practice in question. In general, changes will fall into one of the following three categories:

  — some businesses will thrive, this being by virtue of high-quality marketing and sagacious pricing (which will almost certainly not be based on hourly rates);
  — some businesses will carve out a niche for themselves in areas away from the cut-and-thrust of mainstream competition; those businesses will probably continue to charge by reference to hourly rates;
  — many businesses will do neither of these things and they will fail to thrive.

Most lawyers will be concerned about falling into the third category but there is no reason why they should not strive to be in the first or the second; it should be stressed that the opportunities are very great indeed.

---

[10] See *Association of Costs Lawyers' Annual Conference 2012 (Keynote Address): Fourteenth Lecture in the Implementation Programme* (11 May 2012); moreover, Sir Rupert Jackson has stated in clear terms that he intends to drive hourly rates down.

[11] An example being the way in which non-contentious business can attract both an hourly rate and a value charge: see **27.2** et seq.

The commercial market

42.14 Changes are already taking place in the commercial market that indicate a move away from the traditional model of supplying legal services as a professional service billable by the hour. By way of example, virtual organizations are already offering subscription-based legal services to commercial clients, and discussions are already taking place between commercial organisations and firms of solicitors that would allow firms greater access to litigation funding (similar to delegated authority in the ATE market). Again, the presence of ABS's is likely to accelerate these changes. It is likely that as that market matures, strategic alliances will be formed between commercial organisations and legal representatives which will be based on certainty of pricing and predictability (which again will make hourly billing all the less attractive).

42.15 That said, the opportunities to carve out niche practices will be greater in the commercial sector than in the consumer sector; in particular, there will always be business that will be prepared to pay for what they regard as being 'the best'. Even niche practices, however, will not be immune to the influence of ABS as ABSs could easily place themselves in a position of being referrers. An example would be similar to the subscription-based model above (namely, the client business pays a subscription that pre-purchasers the supply of legal services up to a certain stage in any given claim but fees thereafter are separately chargeable.

'Compensations culture' and referrers

42.16 It will be recalled that Secretary of State (Kenneth Clarke) has said that access to justice has got out of kilter in that defendants are finding it commercially difficult to defend claims (**2.9**). Those comments were made shortly after Government had published *Common Sense, Common Safety*, a report written by Lord Young on what is commonly described as the 'compensation culture'. The general tone of that controversial report can be gleaned from the following passage:[12]

> 'It may seem unusual to commence a review of health and safety with the state of litigation in the country but I believe that a 'compensation culture' driven by litigation is at the heart of the problems that so beset health and safety today. Last year over 800,000 compensation claims were made in the UK while stories of individuals suing their employers for disproportionately large sums of money for personal injury claims, often for the most trivial of reasons, are a regular feature in our newspapers..'

It is not only politicians who have raised such concerns. Sir Rupert Jackson has had some fairly forthright things to say about the compensation industry too:[13]

> 'In the context of personal injury litigation, one consequence of the recoverability regime [ie the recoverability of additional liabilities] is that there is now far too much money swirling around in the system. This has led to a progressive escalation of the referral fees which lawyers pay to get a share of the business. Thus the beneficiaries are not the accident victims, but usually the referrers and (when no referral fee is paid) the lawyers. The referrers who benefit from this state of affairs are claims management companies, BTE insurers, trades unions and others. At the moment market forces compel personal injury solicitors to hand over a large part of the costs which they receive to claims management companies, BTE insurers etc in the form of referral fees. In other words, these middlemen who add no value to the process are the true beneficiaries of competition. In low value cases more than

---

12   D Young *Common Sense, Common Safety* (Oct 2010), HM Government, at p 11.
13   R Jackson *A talk by Lord Justice Jackson to the Cambridge Law Faculty*, 5 September 2011 at p 4.

half the costs received sometimes go out in referral fees. In high value cases referral fees may be £10,000 or more. In my view such referral fees should be banned, as they were up until March 2004.'

These comments focus attention on a particularly controversial aspect of the compensation industry, namely, the profits being made by middlemen (and in particular, referrers). Such issues are beyond the scope of this book, but it is clear that a political will exists to bring about radical changes.

42.17 The reports and lectures referred to above have caused some commentators to complain that the political pendulum is swinging too far away from claimants and too far towards defendants. One can understand why such fears are being expressed,[14] but an analysis based on that single axis (ie claimant-defendant) is overly simplistic in the context of the present-day legal marketplace. In particular, it is entirely credible that the true political motivation has little to do with that axis, but is to reduce legal fees generally and to encourage greater competition in the legal marketplace.[15] In the context of what is set out above under 'alternative business structures' (**42.12–42.15**) the Jackson reforms could be seen as being an attempt to encourage competition at the point of, this being by shifting the focus of funding away from opponents to the client, whilst at the same time encouraging innovation in the marketplace.

42.18 The relevance of the above is that there are certain parts of the consumer legal services have, by reason of their insatiable desire for new business, become undesirable; the political will exists to reduce the profits made by that sector. Whilst this is almost diametrically opposite to the concerns that were being expressed 15 years ago and whilst it is entirely possible that the pendulum will swing back again at some point in the future, practitioners should be aware of the fact that the pendulum's cycle is measured in decades rather than years. Perhaps more importantly, they should bear in mind the following comments made by Lord Neuberger MR in May 2012:[16]

'One day in the future, it may be that the call to adopt the US costs rule or the German fixed costs regime will become too great to resist. However, we are not there yet …'

This is a clear warning that (unlike in the past) the current reforms are going to be audited for effectiveness. Indeed, Sir Rupert Jackson has repeatedly commented on the need for audit (although he has not referred to it by that name).[17] This is relevant to practitioners because it means that certain sectors of the compensation industry are likely to be under greater scrutiny in future than they would like.

---

[14] Sir Rupert Jackson himself commented that 'No procedural code can achieve in every case the twin objectives of perfect justice and certainty of outcome': see R Jackson *Technical Aspects of Implementation: Third Lecture in the Implementation Programme* (31 October 2011) at para 1.3.

[15] Indeed, this has been expressly stated as being an intended aim: see R Jackson *A talk by Lord Justice Jackson to the Cambridge Law Faculty*, 5 September 2011 on p 4.

[16] *Association of Costs Lawyers' Annual Conference 2012 (Keynote Address): Fourteenth Lecture in the Implementation Programme* (11 May 2012), para 20.

[17] See the Final Report at Chapter 6, para 2.4 and R Jackson *Assessment of Costs in the Brave New World: Eighth Lecture in the Implementation Programme* (KPMG Forensic's [sic] Leeds Law Lecture 2012, 25 January 2012) at 2.3 where Sir Rupert comments on the need for a Costs Council.

REFORMS RELATING TO THE CONDUCT OF SUBSTANTIVE LITIGATION

42.19 The following topics are addressed under this heading:

- case management (and in particular, controlling the costs of disclosure)(**42.20–42. 30**);
- costs management and costs budgeting (**42.31** and **15.65** et seq);
- offers under CPR Part 36 (**42.32–42.35**); and
- costs shifting (**42.36–42.39**).

Some of these topics are beyond the scope of this book and are addressed only briefly.

Case management

42.20 Sir Rupert Jackson's recommendations regarding case management are, on the whole, beyond the scope of this textbook, but it is worth mentioning one or two of the more relevant topics. This is not only because active case management is likely to have a bearing on the level of costs that is likely to be allowed, but also because an understanding of what is proposed is required for the purposes of making decision about how to manage the Jackson reforms in practice.

Active case management

42.21 Sir Rupert Jackson has the following to say about what he called the meaning of 'robust case management':[18]

> 'The concept of robust case management is really a package. It entails:
>
> (i)　The delivery of effective case management directions by a judge with relevant expertise who is on top of the case.
> (ii)　Moving the action along swiftly to settlement or trial.
> (iii)　Firm enforcement of directions once they have been given – ie a "no nonsense" approach.'

42.22 Sir Rupert went on to acknowledge that whilst good case management saves costs, bad case management has the opposite effect.[19] He made the following recommendations:[20]

- that judges be 'docketed';[21]
- that there be greater use of standard directions (templates of which will be published widely);
- that over-long witness statements be discouraged; and

---

[18]　R Jackson *Achieving a Culture Change in Case Management; Fifth Lecture in the Civil Litigation Costs Review Implementation Programme* (22 November 2011) at para 1.5.

[19]　R Jackson *Achieving a Culture Change in Case Management; Fifth Lecture in the Civil Litigation Costs Review Implementation Programme* (22 November 2011) at para 1.9.

[20]　R Jackson *Achieving a Culture Change in Case Management; Fifth Lecture in the Civil Litigation Costs Review Implementation Programme* (22 November 2011) at para 4.2 *et seq*.

[21]　This is a system of assigning a case to one judge from issue up to and including trial. The 'docket' is the collection of cases being managed by the judge in question:: see the Preliminary Report, Chapter 43 at para 5.9

- that disclosure be controlled (see **42.28–42.80**);

42.23 In recognition of the fact that appeals concerning case management are inevitable, Sir Rupert has commented on the need for greater consistency in the Court of Appeal, and to this end he has proposed that two Lords Justices be nominated;[22] he commented that the Court of Appeal might take steps to sit with District Judge assessors in some cases, but as yet, there are no plans to implement such an proposal.[23]

42.24 In his practical, 'hands-on' article in the *New Law Journal* HHJ Simon Brown QC (who is a recognised authority on such matters) outlined the following forensic sieve:[24]

'At the CMC, which is after all a "conference", I explore within the hour allotted, how the case is to be handled by both parties.

- I look at the case "surgically" to find out what is really in dispute via a List of Issues[25] and to see how the whole case can then be more efficiently and quickly disposed of.
- I look to the biggest "Manhattens" normally disclosure and oddly enough, witness statements (they are supposed to be in the witnesses' own words not lawyer speak), and, of course, trial costs.
- I will see which areas can be cut because they do not take the case any further.
- I will query the need for experts, particularly expensive accountants when lawyers should be able to do the quantum calculations if appearing in a mercantile court. I will ask if quotations from experts have been obtained.
- I will ask how many documents are likely to be relevant, i e adverse or supportive of the parties cases and enquire of how electronic documents are to be disclosed and then exchanged and produced to the court (in many cases e-mails have to be de-duplicated and reordered or left in electronic form and invoices for example normally remain in electronic form).
- I look to see if the volume of paper can be restricted.
- I will look at the charging rates and the grades of lawyers actually doing the work.
- I will enquire about apparent double manning of lawyers and what looks excessive hours working. If the budgets look too light, too high or too far apart, I will normally give the parties the opportunity to exchange and submit revised budgets for subsequent approval in writing.'

42.25 HHJ Simon Brown QC went on to say this about how he sees case management in the future:[26]

'If civil litigation practitioners have not prepared themselves they will have a nasty (and expensive) shock in a year's time if they turn up for a routine case management conference (CMC) expecting the judge to rubber stamp their draft directions. They will, instead, find themselves in front of a docketed judge trained by the Judicial College in "active" case

---

[22] R Jackson *Achieving a Culture Change in Case Management; Fifth Lecture in the Civil Litigation Costs Review Implementation Programme* (22 November 2011) at para 4.8.

[23] R Jackson *Achieving a Culture Change in Case Management; Fifth Lecture in the Civil Litigation Costs Review Implementation Programme* (22 November 2011) at para 5.2; Sir Rupert reported that the Master of the Rolls had identified certain logistical issues with district judges sitting as assessors, and that this was to become a medium rather than short term objective.

[24] S Brown 'Costs control' NLJ 162 NLJ 498, 13 April 2012.

[25] This is one of the few areas where Sir Rupert Jackson disagrees with HHJ Brown QC: Sir Rupert has advised against using Lists of Issues.

[26] S Brown 'Costs control' NLJ 162 NLJ 498, 13 April 2012.

management of his cases, demanding the parties to justify the "proportionality" of their itemised and carefully calculated costs budgets in prescribed form, as approved by their respective clients.'

For obvious reasons case management of this nature is likely to have a significant effect on the amounts of costs that are likely to be incurred dealing with issues such as disclosure and the marshalling of evidence.

Expert evidence

42.26 Sir Rupert Jackson reports that the Rule Committee has approved a number of amendments to CPR, r 35.4 and that those amendments 'are being held in escrow until the general implementation date for the Costs Review reforms'.[27] The proposed amendments make provision for (i) the parties to identify the issues at an early stage, and (ii) the parties to obtain early estimates of the costs of obtaining their experts' evidence.[28]

42.27 Sir Rupert has proposed the following methods of controlling costs:[29]

- that the costs of experts be budgeted;
- that the aforesaid estimates be taken into account and monitored (this being something that will happen automatically under costs budgeting); and
- the thought be given to the possible use of concurrent expert evidence at trial.

Disclosure and e-disclosure

42.28 The active case management of disclosure (and in particular, e-disclosure) are likely to be particularly relevant,[30] not least because the proposed reforms may, in the future, have a dramatic effect on the amount of costs that will be claimed in 'document heavy' cases. In the Final Report, Sir Rupert said this:[31]

'(i) E-disclosure as a topic should form a substantial part of (a) CPD for solicitors and barristers who will have to deal with e-disclosure in practice and (b) the training of judges who will have to deal with e-disclosure on the bench.

(ii) A new CPR rule 31.5A should be drafted to adopt the menu option in relation to (a) large commercial and similar claims and (b) any case where the costs of standard disclosure are likely to be disproportionate. Personal injury claims and clinical negligence claims should be excluded from the provisions of rule 31.5A.'

42.29 At the time of writing a draft practice direction was in the process of being approved by the Rule Committee, as was an amended CPR, r 31.5 (that amended rule

---

[27]   See R Jackson *Focusing Expert Evidence and Controlling Costs: Fifth Lecture in the Civil Litigation Costs Review Implementation Programme* (11 November 2011).

[28]   See R Jackson *Focusing Expert Evidence and Controlling Costs: Fifth Lecture in the Civil Litigation Costs Review Implementation Programme* (11 November 2011), Annex 1.

[29]   See R Jackson *Focusing Expert Evidence and Controlling Costs: Fifth Lecture in the Civil Litigation Costs Review Implementation Programme* (11 November 2011), paras 3 and 4.

[30]   This was addressed in R Jackson *Controlling the Costs of Disclosure; Seventh Lecture in the Civil Litigation Costs Review Implementation Programme* (24 November 2011).

[31]   Final Report, Chapter 37, para 4.1.

providing for far more focussed and efficient disclosure).[32] It is also proposed that there be a 'menu option' (this being a menu of possible disclosure orders from which the court should choose).[33]

42.30 As to the future, Sir Rupert Jackson has this to say:[34]

> 'The new disclosure rule is part of a package of case management reforms which will be coming into force on big bang date ... One theme which runs through the reforms is that the first case management conference should be a real event at which the court takes hold of the case and gives directions which will focus the factual evidence, the expert evidence and the disclosed documents on the real issues between the parties.'

From a practical point of view, disclosure and e-disclosure are issues that need to be considered well before the reforms take hold, this being because firms may need to consider the way in which they intend to provide disclosure services, whether they intend to outsource it, and if not, whether they intend to purchase the IT facilities to be able to offer full IT services themselves. All of these issues need to be considered in the context of fees and costs.

Costs management and budgeting

42.31 This is addressed in detail at **15.65** *et seq.*

Offers and Part 36

42.32 This topic is addressed only very briefly, this being because insufficient details were known about the proposals to be able to say anything specific.

42.33 Sir Rupert Jackson proposed a number of changes to Part 36; the Government had this to say on the topic:[35]

> '12 Part 36 of the Civil Procedure Rules (offers to settle) will be amended to equalise the incentives between claimants and defendants to make and accept reasonable offers. This will apply to all civil cases, and the Government will discuss the details with stakeholders in due course. In particular, it will be made clear that where a money offer is beaten at trial, by however small a margin, the costs sanctions applicable under Part 36 will apply. An additional sanction (equivalent to 10% of the value of the claim) will be introduced to be paid by defendants who do not accept a claimant's reasonable offer that is not beaten at trial. The Government is minded to explore an alternative sanction (linked to costs rather than damages) for claims where a remedy other than damages is sought, to avoid satellite litigation around the court's valuation of such claims. '

42.34 The relevant statutory provisions are now contained in s 55 of the Legal Aid, Sentencing and Punishment of Offenders Act 2012; they are set out in the footnotes.[36]

---

[32] See R Jackson *Controlling the Costs of Disclosure; Seventh Lecture in the Civil Litigation Costs Review Implementation Programme* (24 November 2011) at para 4.3.

[33] See R Jackson *Controlling the Costs of Disclosure; Seventh Lecture in the Civil Litigation Costs Review Implementation Programme* (24 November 2011) at para 2.4.

[34] See R Jackson *Controlling the Costs of Disclosure; Seventh Lecture in the Civil Litigation Costs Review Implementation Programme* (24 November 2011) at para 5.3.

[35] *Reforming Civil Litigation Funding and Costs in England and Wales – Implementation of Lord Justice Jackson's Recommendations* (March 2011) Cm 8041 at para 12 under 'The Way Forward'.

[36] '55 Payment of additional amount to successful claimant.'

'(1) Rules of court may make provision for a court to order a defendant in civil proceedings to pay an

In essence, the statute creates a framework for rules to be made that allow for payment of an 'additional amount'; this is an amount not exceeding a prescribed percentage of the amount awarded to the claimant by the court (excluding any amount awarded in respect of the claimant's costs). Thus, the devil will be in the detail.

42.35 Sir Rupert Jackson has argued that any incentive arising out of Part 36 should go to the litigant (ie, should be in the form of damages) rather than his lawyers (ie, in the form of costs).[37] Practitioners may or may not agree; it is entirely possible that they will take the view that those monies can be used to pay any shortfall in the amount of costs recovered from the opponent. On a practical level, lawyers will need to have a policy (preferably a written policy) as to how such monies are distributed, and if such monies are to be used for the purposes of paying costs, thought will need to be given to making the relevant provisions in standard terms and conditions.

---

additional amount to a claimant in those proceedings where—
(a) the claim is a claim for (and only for) an amount of money,
(b) judgment is given in favour of the claimant,
(c) the judgment in respect of the claim is at least as advantageous as an offer to settle the claim which the claimant made in accordance with rules of court and has not withdrawn in accordance with those rules, and
(d) any prescribed conditions are satisfied.
(2) Rules made under subsection (1) may include provision as to the assessment of whether a judgment is at least as advantageous as an offer to settle.
(3) In subsection (1) "additional amount" means an amount not exceeding a prescribed percentage of the amount awarded to the claimant by the court (excluding any amount awarded in respect of the claimant's costs).
(4) The Lord Chancellor may by order provide that rules of court may make provision for a court to order a defendant in civil proceedings to pay an amount calculated in a prescribed manner to a claimant in those proceedings where—
(a) the claim is or includes a non-monetary claim,
(b) judgment is given in favour of the claimant,
(c) the judgment in respect of the claim is at least as advantageous as an offer to settle the claim which the claimant made in accordance with rules of court and has not withdrawn in accordance with those rules, and
(d) any prescribed conditions are satisfied.
(5) An order under subsection (4) must provide for the amount to be calculated by reference to one or more of the following—
(a) any costs ordered by the court to be paid to the claimant by the defendant in the proceedings;
(b) any amount awarded to the claimant by the court in respect of so much of the claim as is for an amount of money (excluding any amount awarded in respect of the claimant's costs);
(c) the value of any non-monetary benefit awarded to the claimant.
(6) An order under subsection (4)—
(a) must provide that rules made under the order may include provision as to the assessment of whether a judgment is at least as advantageous as an offer to settle, and
(b) may provide that such rules may make provision as to the calculation of the value of a non-monetary benefit awarded to a claimant.
(7) Conditions prescribed under subsection (1)(d) or (4)(d) may, in particular, include conditions relating to—
(a) the nature of the claim;
(b) the amount of money awarded to the claimant;
(c) the value of the non-monetary benefit awarded to the claimant.
(8) Orders under this section are to be made by the Lord Chancellor by statutory instrument.
(9) A statutory instrument containing an order under this section is subject to annulment in pursuance of a resolution of either House of Parliament.
(10) Rules of court and orders made under this section may make different provision in relation to different cases.
(11) In this section—
"civil proceedings" means proceedings to which rules of court made under the Civil Procedure Act 1997 apply;
"non-monetary claim" means a claim for a benefit other than an amount of money;
"prescribed" means prescribed by order made by the Lord Chancellor.'

[37] R Jackson *Technical Aspects of Implementation; Third Lecture in the Implementation Programme* (31 October 2011) at para 3.1.

Qualified one-way costs shifting ('QOCS')

42.36 Sir Rupert Jackson had this to say about costs shifting:[38]

> 2.6 *Qualified one way costs shifting.* ATE insurance premiums add considerably to the costs of litigation. Litigation costs can be reduced by taking away the need for ATE insurance in the first place. This can occur if qualified one way costs shifting is introduced, at least for certain categories of litigation in which it is presently common for ATE insurance to be taken out. By "qualified" one way costs shifting I mean that the claimant will not be required to pay the defendant's costs if the claim is unsuccessful, but the defendant will be required to pay the claimant's costs if it is successful. The qualifications to this are that unreasonable (or otherwise unjustified) party behaviour may lead to a different costs order, and the financial resources available to the parties may justify there being two way costs shifting in particular cases.

42.37 Thus qualified one-way costs shifting ('QOCS') is intended to go hand-in-hand with the abolition of recoverable ATE premiums. The Government adopted Sir Rupert's recommendations; as to the details, the Government said this:[39]

> The exceptions will be: (i) on behaviour grounds – where the claimant has acted fraudulently, frivolously or unreasonably in pursuing proceedings – so a reasonable claimant will not be at risk of paying the other side's costs on behaviour grounds; and (ii) on financial means grounds – only the very wealthy would be at risk of paying any costs. The Government will continue to discuss with stakeholders how the rules should be drafted, including whether any minimum payment to a successful defendant's costs should be payable by the losing claimant in order to prevent speculative claims. QOCS will not be extended beyond personal injury at this stage, so the normal costs shifting rules will continue to apply in other cases.'

42.38 In October 2011 Sir Rupert Jackson had this to say:[40]

> 'The Government intends to introduce QOCS for personal injury litigation in the first instance and then to consider extending QOCS later. I hope that QOCS will be extended in the manner recommended in the FR, but that is not on the agenda for today's workshop.'

42.39 The relevant provisions did not, however, find their way into the Legal Aid, Sentencing and Punishment of Offenders Bill; an amendment to the Bill was moved in the House of Lords to introduce a section for QOCS, but it failed. That omission has been widely criticised; indeed one commentator even went so far as to call the Bill 'intellectually bankrupt'.[41] The APIL president has warned of a 'frightening' lack of detail:[42]

> 'The Bill does not contain any provisions for two structural parts of the Jackson reforms—the 10% increase in general damages and qualified one-way cost shifting (QOCS). Amendments to do so failed. The increase in damages is to be the subject of extra statutory regulation and QOCS will be regulated by secondary legislation, but many are unclear as to exactly how these are to be affected and their final form.'

---

[38] Final Report, Executive Summary, para 2.6 page xvii.
[39] *Litigation Funding and Costs in England and Wales, Implementation of Lord Justice Jackson's Recommendations* Consultation Paper CP 13/10 (November 2010) Cm 7947 at para 13.
[40] R Jackson *Technical Aspects of Implementation; Third Lecture in the Implementation Programme* (31 October 2011) at para 4.1.
[41] See, for example, K Manley 'Lords expose intellectual bankruptcy of LASPO Part 2' Law Soc Gazette 31 January 2012
[42] D Green 'The missing links' 162 NLJ 555, 27 April 2012.

One can, perhaps, understand that the concern that underlies these complaints, but QOCS is not something that could be achieved only through primary legislation; as such, it is not entirely surprising that matters have been left to the Rule Committee. No doubt, a draft will be published in due course.

FUNDING REFORMS

42.40 From the point of view of costs law, the proposed reforms concerning funding are of considerable importance. They are also important because it is through those reforms that successful business will make their profit. The following topics are addressed:

- the 'myth of full costs recovery' (**42.41–42.45**);
- damages-based agreements (**42.46**);
- litigation (third-party) funding (**42.54–42.56**); and
- contingency legal aid and supplementary legal aid fund (**42.57–41.58**).

The 'myth of full costs recovery'

42.41 Sir Rupert Jackson has been at pains to point out what he regards as being the 'recent myth' that clients are entitled to full costs recovery. He had this to say on the point:[43]

> 'The principle of full costs recovery is a recent myth. The above summary of APIL's evidence in 1995 neatly illustrates another important proposition. It has for many decades been accepted that a successful litigant does not recover all of his own costs from the other side. Thus throughout the twentieth century a successful claimant always expected to pay out some part of his damages to make up the shortfall in costs recovery. The fact that both parties will have some costs liability, even if they win, has long been accepted as imposing a necessary discipline in litigation. The ancient principle of restitution is, for good policy reasons, embedded in the law of damages but not in the law of costs. This fact does not feature in the Law Society's campaign material.'

42.42 No-one could reasonably challenge the assertion that English law does not and has never stipulated that a successful litigant should be fully compensated in costs, but there are many solicitors who would point to a long and creditable history of not requiring clients to pay the shortfall in recovery of their fees; they may argue that this amounted to *de facto* full costs recovery. That analysis would usually not stand up to scrutiny, however, this being because pre-2000 they would have been able to point to Legal Aid as being a source of income. They would say that whilst they accept that the principle of full costs recovery was a myth, under the proposed regime post-reforms, there will be a hiatus left by the absence of Legal Aid.

42.43 Sir Rupert would probably agree with such sentiments; he has, after all, been a vociferous critic of the proposals to whittle Legal Aid down almost to vanishing point. He would, however, no doubt stand firm on the basic premise of his comment, namely, that clients have no right not to expect to have to make a contribution to the costs of their claims.

---

[43]   R Jackson *A talk by Lord Justice Jackson to the Cambridge Law Faculty*, 5 September 2011 at p 5.

42.44 As a matter of simple economics Sir Rupert is entirely right: regardless of one's views as to the rights and wrongs of the matter, the reality is that costs recovered from opponents in successful cases are, in most cases, not likely to cover the costs of providing legal services in both successful and unsuccessful cases. In all but a tiny minority of practices the economic reality is that clients will have to contribute towards solicitors' fees in order to balance the books.

42.45 There will be exceptions, however; it is possible that some very large firms will be able to rely so heavily on economies of scale that they will be able to offer an essentially free service. It would be a mistake, however, to work on the assumption that this is the ideal to which firms should aspire. As a business model, it is leaves a great deal to be desired. Most firms will be forced to look to their clients for a contribution to fees.

Damages-based agreements

42.46 The relevant history slightly predates the Costs Review in that the first steps were taken by the Ministry of Justice in its 2009 consultation *Regulating Damages Based Agreements.*[44] That consultation ultimately led to an amendment to the Courts and Legal Services Act 1990; that amendment introduced regulated damages-based agreements in employment tribunals.[45]

42.47 In his Final Report, Sir Rupert Jackson adopted much of what the Ministry of Justice had said, but his recommendation was to re-amend the 1990 Act so as to make damages-based agreements lawful in civil litigation generally rather than just litigation in employment tribunals.[46] He opted for the 'Ontario model',[47] which is a scheme under which costs would be recoverable on an hourly rate basis as between opposing parties notwithstanding the existence of a damages-based agreement as between solicitor and client. He commented that damages-based agreements would become particularly important once the recoverability of success fees had been abrogated.[48] He went on to recommend a number of safeguards[49] (not all of which have been adopted).

42.48 Unsurprisingly given this history, the Government largely adopted those recommendations; their response to the Final Report was as follows:[50]

> 'DBAs will provide a useful additional form of funding for claimants, for example in commercial claims. Successful claimants will recover their base costs (the lawyer's hourly rate fee and disbursements) from defendants as for claims, whether funded under a CFA or otherwise, but in the case of a DBA, the costs recovered from the losing side would be set off against the DBA fee, reducing the amount payable by the claimant to any shortfall between the costs recovered and the DBA fee. DBAs will be subject to similar requirements for parties to the agreement as for CFAs. For example, the amount of the payment that lawyers can take from the damages in personal injury cases will be capped (at 25% of damages excluding for further care and loss).'

---

[44] Regulating Damages Based Agreements, Consultation Paper CP 10/09, 1 July 2009.
[45] See s 58AA of the Courts and Legal Services Act 1990 (as amended by 54 of the Coroners and Justice Act 2009, which received Royal Assent on 12 November 2009).
[46] See the Final Report, Chapter 12, para 4.6.
[47] See the Final Report, Chapter 12, para 4.1.
[48] See the Final Report, Chapter 12, para 4.2.
[49] See the Final Report, Chapter 12, paras 4.6–4.11.
[50] *Litigation Funding and Costs in England and Wales, Implementation of Lord Justice Jackson's Recommendations* Consultation Paper CP 13/10 (November 2010) Cm 7947 at para 13.

42.49   These proposals have become s 45 of the Legal Aid, Sentencing and Punishment of Offenders Act (which is set out below[51]). The effect of that section will be to re-amend the Courts and Legal Services Act 1990 so as to give rise to the following:

- to make damages-based agreements lawful across the whole of civil law (save for those disputes that are specified by Order or which are of a type which would preclude the use of a conditional fee agreement);
- to allow damages-based agreements to operate as per the Ontario model (ie, costs would be recoverable on an hourly rate basis as between opposing parties but would be payable on a damages-based basis as between solicitor and client); where costs are recovered between opposing parties, those monies will be off-set against the damages-based fee; and
- to restrict the damages-based fee in personal injury cases to a sum equal to 25% of damages, that restriction being treated in almost exactly the same way as the restriction that applies to success fees.

Contrary to Sir Rupert Jackson's recommendations,[52] there is no requirement for clients to receive independent legal advice before entering into a damages-based agreement.

42.50   Whilst the details of the primary legislation are now known, at the time of writing, no draft regulations had been published.

---

[51]   '45 Damages-based agreements.

(1) Section 58AA of the Courts and Legal Services Act 1990 (damages-based agreements) is amended as follows.

(2) In subsection (1) omit "relates to an employment matter and".

(3) In subsection (2)—

(a) after "But" insert "(subject to subsection (9))", and

(b) omit "relates to an employment matter and".

(4) Omit subsection (3)(b).

(5) After subsection (4)(a) insert—

"(aa) must not relate to proceedings which by virtue of section 58A(1) and (2) cannot be the subject of an enforceable conditional fee agreement or to proceedings of a description prescribed by the Lord Chancellor;".

(6) In subsection (4)(b), at the beginning insert "if regulations so provide,".

(7) In subsection (4)(d) for "has provided prescribed information" substitute "has complied with such requirements (if any) as may be prescribed as to the provision of information".

(8) After subsection (6) insert—

"(6A) Rules of court may make provision with respect to the assessment of costs in proceedings where a party in whose favour a costs order is made has entered into a damages-based agreement in connection with the proceedings.".

(9) After subsection (7) insert—

"(7A) In this section (and in the definitions of "advocacy services" and "litigation services" as they apply for the purposes of this section) (and not just proceedings in a court), whether commenced or contemplated.".

(10) After subsection (8) insert—

"(9) Where section 57 of the Solicitors Act 1974 (non-contentious business agreements between solicitor and client) applies to a damages-based agreement other than one relating to an employment matter, subsections (1) and (2) of this section do not make it unenforceable.".

(10) For the purposes of subsection (9) a damages-based agreement relates to an employment matter if the matter in relation to which the services are provided is a matter that is, or could become, the subject of proceedings before an employment tribunal.".

(11) In the heading of that section omit "relating to employment matters".

(12) In section 120(4) of that Act (regulations and orders subject to parliamentary approval) for "58AA" substitute "58AA(4)".

(13) The amendments made by subsections (1) to (11) do not apply in relation to an agreement entered into before this section comes into force.

[52]   See the Final Report at Chapter 12, para 4.10.

42.51 It has been said that very few solicitors practising in the field of personal injury would regard damages-based agreements as being commercially viable; this is because the limits that apply to the damages-based fee are very similar to those that would apply to a success fee (ie, *just* the success fee) payable under a conditional fee agreement. As such, a solicitor would—it is said—make less profit under a damages-based agreement that under a conditional fee agreement.[53] There is certainly some truth in this, but there are two factors that push in the opposite direction:

- firstly, if a case were to settle very early, then the solicitor would be very much better off under a damages-based agreement than he would be under a conditional fee agreement; and
- secondly, a solicitor who offered damages-based agreements might be able to increase the volume of work he does by virtue of being able to offer his clients more attractive terms than would a solicitor who was prepared to work under only conditional fee agreements.

42.52 In so far as this second point is concerned, Lord Neuberger MR (speaking extrajudicially) had this to say:[54]

'It may be that it would be unattractive from a solicitor's perspective to offer a DBA, rather than a CFA, in a personal injury case. But what one solicitor finds pointless may represent another solicitor's competitive advantage. Given the choice between a solicitor who only offers CFAs and one who offers CFAs and DBAs at more advantageous prices, and perhaps with normal costs calculated by way of fixed fee rather than hourly billing, clients can reasonably be expected to appreciate where their interests lie. In other words, the brave new world of DBAs may well help to encourage a more genuinely competitive market place, in which solicitors are having to become ever more client – or consumer – focused.'

42.53 On a practical level, solicitors will need to ensure that their draft agreements are up to the job. There are three reasons why they should take advice on this topic:

- firstly, damages-based agreements are almost certain to be challenged *by clients,* and the court is likely to be far less forgiving of errors in those circumstances than it was when challenges were brought by opponents during the Costs Wars;
- secondly, challengers are likely to highly motivated, this being because their legal advisors are likely themselves to be funded by damages-based agreements; and
- thirdly, the drafting skill that is required to achieve the 'Ontario model' is far in excess of that which is needed to draft a conditional fee agreement.

There is nothing to prevent counsel from making damages-based agreements. If this happens, however, steps must be taken to ensure that his agreement is compatible with his instructing solicitors' contract of retainer. In particular, steps need to be taken to set out a priorities agreement.

Litigation (third-party) funding

42.54 Sir Rupert Jackson's recommendations concerning litigation funding (or 'third-party funding' as he then called it) were as follows:[55]

---

[53]   See D Regan *Butterworths Personal Injury Litigation Service*, para 3022.
[54]   Association of Costs Lawyers' Annual Conference 2012 (Keynote Address): Fourteenth Lecture in the Implementation Programme (11 May 2012), para 36.
[55]   Final Report Chapter 11, para 6.1.

'6.1 I do not consider that full regulation of third party funding is presently required. I do, however, make the following recommendations:

(i)   A satisfactory voluntary code, to which all litigation funders subscribe, should be drawn up. This code should contain effective capital adequacy requirements and should place appropriate restrictions upon funders' ability to withdraw support for ongoing litigation.

(ii)   The question whether there should be statutory regulation of third party funders by the FSA ought to be re-visited if and when the third party funding market expands.

(iii)   Third party funders should potentially be liable for the full amount of adverse costs, subject to the discretion of the judge.'

42.55 These issues were considered at a number of events during 2010, including a litigation funding conference at Oxford University; this led to the creation of the Litigation Funders Association[56] which ultimately led to the creation of the present voluntary code (see **41.16**). Sir Rupert has commented that his concerns about litigation funding have been met by the terms of that voluntary code.[57] He went on to make the following comments about what he sees as being the future of litigation funding:[58]

'There is likely to be a greater role for litigation funders, if CFA success fees cease to be recoverable ... I express the hope that in the future litigation funders will be able to support a wider range of litigation than at present, including group actions and claims of lower value.

42.56 Discussions are already taking place between litigation funders and larger firms of solicitors aimed at providing facilities to fund group litigation and lower value claims. The relevance of the latter is that it should not be assumed that litigating funding is something exotic that is relevant only to those who practice commercial litigation. It is entirely credible that in the very near future it will be available in personal injury litigation too.

Contingency legal aid and supplementary legal aid

42.57 These are lesser-known aspects of the Jackson reforms. Supplementary legal aid is a form of state funding and as such is beyond the scope of this book. Contingency legal aid (ie a contingency legal aid fund, or CLAF) is a self-funding mechanism of funding for which the statutory framework already exists;[59] Sir Rupert Jackson explained the history of that jurisdiction in this way:[60]

'2.2 In 1978 Justice published its original proposals for a CLAF. Twenty one years later in 1997, in the run-up to the Access to Justice Act 1999 ("the 1999 Act") and removal of personal injury cases from the scope of legal aid, a range of proposals for CLAFs were made by the Bar Council, the Law Society and the Consumer Association. None of these proposals were implemented, as the Government chose instead to promote and enhance CFAs under the 1999 Act reforms. However, provisions were included within the 1999 Act to

---

[56]   See R Jackson *Third Party Funding or Litigation Funding; Sixth Lecture in the Civil Litigation Costs Review Implementation Programme* (23 November 2011) at para 2.6.

[57]   See R Jackson *Third Party Funding or Litigation Funding; Sixth Lecture in the Civil Litigation Costs Review Implementation Programme* (23 November 2011) at para 3.1 to 3.6.

[58]   See R Jackson *Third Party Funding or Litigation Funding; Sixth Lecture in the Civil Litigation Costs Review Implementation Programme* (23 November 2011) at para 3.1 to 3.6.

[59]   See s 58B of the Courts and Legal Services Act 1990 (as amended); this provision is not yet in force.

[60]   R Jackson *Contingency Legal Aid Fund and Supplementary Legal Aid Fund: Second Lecture in the Implementation Programme*: 8 October 2011 at para 2.2.

provide for a CLAF or SLAS scheme: see s. 58B of the Courts and Legal Services Act 1990, which was inserted by s. 28 of the 1999 Act. These provisions have not yet been implemented, but they could be. Proposals for a SLAS emerged more recently, in particular from reports by the Civil Justice Council in 2005 and 2007.

Sir Rupert went on to comment that he saw no reason why a CLAF would not work;[61] he suggested that in the first instance, a CLAF ought to be a small-scale affair.[62] He concluded that these are matter for the legal profession.

42.58 As far as the writer is aware, there are no solid plans to progress these aspects of the Jackson reforms.

REFORMS RELATING TO THE AMOUNT OF COSTS:

42.59 The following topics are addressed in this section:

- additional liabilities (**42.60–42.68**);
- fixed costs (**42.69**); and
- hourly rates (**42.70–42.73**).

Additional liabilities

Success fees

42.60 Sir Rupert Jackson's recommendation is to abolish the recoverability of success fees.[63] He had this to say on the point:

'4.20 In my view the proper course is to abolish recoverability and to revert to … CFAs, as they existed before April 2000. Those arrangements were satisfactory and opened up access to justice for many individuals who formerly had no such access: … During 1996 APIL confirmed that those arrangements provided access to justice for personal injury claimants and that those arrangements were satisfactory: see paragraph 25 of chapter 2 of Lord Woolf's Final Report on Access to Justice.'

42.61 Sir Rupert Jackson went on to suggest the following:

- that there be a cap on the amount of the success fee payable between solicitor and client of 25% of damages (but excluding damages referable to future care or future losses);[64] and
- that there be a 10 per cent increase in general damages for pain, suffering and loss of amenity, the intention being that clients would then be able to use those extra monies to pay success fees as between solicitor and client.

---

[61] R Jackson *Contingency Legal Aid Fund and Supplementary Legal Aid Fund: Second Lecture in the Implementation Programme*: 8 October 2011 at para 2.3.

[62] R Jackson *Contingency Legal Aid Fund and Supplementary Legal Aid Fund: Second Lecture in the Implementation Programme*: 8 October 2011 at para 4.

[63] The topic is dealt with in Chapter 10, pp 94–116 of his Final Report.

[64] Sir Rupert Jackson has said that this should include VAT: see R Jackson *Technical Aspects of Implementation; Third Lecture in the Implementation Programme* (31 October 2011) at para 5.3.

42.62 Sir Rupert Jackson's recommendations were adopted by the Government:[65]

> '5 ... The Government intends to: Abolish the general recoverability of the CFA success fee from the losing side. In future any CFA success fee will be paid by the CFA funded party, rather than the other side. Crucially, this would give individual CFA claimants a financial interest in controlling the costs incurred on their behalf. It returns the position to when CFAs were first allowed in civil litigation in England and Wales in the 1990s.

> 8 The Government believes that claimants who have been compensated for personal injury should have their damages protected from having too much deducted by their lawyer as a success fee. In personal injury cases, there will be a cap on the amount of damages that may be taken as a success fee. The cap will be set at 25% of the damages other than those for future care and loss ...

> 9 The maximum success fee that a lawyer may agree with a client under a CFA will remain at 100% of base costs. However, in personal injury cases this would be subject to the 25% cap on damages (other than those for future care and loss) as described above.'

42.63 The relevant provisions in the Legal Aid, Sentencing and Punishment of Offenders Act are set out in the footnotes.[66]

42.64 As explained above, s 48 provides exceptions to the principle that no success fee may be recovered between opposing parties:

---

[65] *Litigation Funding and Costs in England and Wales, Implementation of Lord Justice Jackson's Recommendations Consultation Paper* CP 13/10 (November 2010) Cm 7947.
[66] '44 Conditional fee agreements: success fees
(1) In section 58 of the Courts and Legal Services Act 1990 (conditional fee agreements), in subsection (2)—
(a) omit "and" after paragraph (a), and
(b) after paragraph (b) insert "and
(c) references to a success fee, in relation to a conditional fee agreement, are to the amount of the increase."
(2) After subsection (4) of that section insert—
(4A) The additional conditions are applicable to a conditional fee agreement which—
(a) provides for a success fee, and
(b) relates to proceedings of a description specified by order made by the Lord Chancellor for the purposes of this subsection.
(4B) The additional conditions are that—
(a) the agreement must provide that the success fee is subject to a maximum limit,
(b) the maximum limit must be expressed as a percentage of the descriptions of damages awarded in the proceedings that are specified in the agreement,
(c) that percentage must not exceed the percentage specified by order made by the Lord Chancellor in relation to the proceedings or calculated in a manner so specified, and
(d) those descriptions of damages may only include descriptions of damages specified by order made by the Lord Chancellor in relation to the proceedings."
(3) In section 58A of that Act (conditional fee agreements: supplementary), in subsection (5) after "section 58(4)" insert ", (4A) or (4B)".
(4) For subsection (6) of that section substitute—
"(6) A costs order made in proceedings may not include provision requiring the payment by one party of all or part of a success fee payable by another party under a conditional fee agreement."
(5) In section 120(4) of that Act (regulations and orders subject to parliamentary approval) after "58(4)," insert "(4A) or (4B),".
(6) The amendment made by subsection (4) does not prevent a costs order including provision in relation to a success fee payable by a person ("P") under a conditional fee agreement entered into before the day on which that subsection comes into force ("the commencement day") if—
(a) the agreement was entered into specifically for the purposes of the provision to P of advocacy or litigation services in connection with the matter that is the subject of the proceedings in which the costs order is made, or
(b) advocacy or litigation services were provided to P under the agreement in connection with that matter before the commencement day.'

'Sections 44 and 46 and diffuse mesothelioma proceedings

(1) Sections 44 and 46 may not be brought into force in relation to proceedings relating to a claim for damages in respect of diffuse mesothelioma until the Lord Chancellor has—

    (a)   carried out a review of the likely effect of those sections in relation to such proceedings, and

    (b)   published a report of the conclusions of the review.

(2) In this section "diffuse mesothelioma" has the same meaning as in the Pneumoconiosis etc (Workers' Compensation) Act 1979.'

It is possible that these exceptions will be only temporary.

42.65 In practical terms, solicitors will have to prepare business plans that are based on the premise that success fees are not recovered between opposing parties. They will need to decide whether to continue using conditional fee agreements or whether to use one of the other methods of funding instead. If a solicitor wishes to continue to use conditional fees agreements, steps must be taken to ensure that any draft agreement makes proper and adequate provision for the aforesaid cap. Moreover, it there is an intention to recoup any part of the 10% increase in general damages (by, for example, choosing not to waive a shortfall in recovered costs), then provision will need to be made for that too.

ATE premiums

42.66 Sir Rupert Jackson proposed abolition of the recoverability of after the event insurance premiums between opposing parties; the Government had this to say on the topic:[67]

'The government intends to ... Abolish the general recoverability of after-the-event (ATE) insurance premiums. In future any ATE insurance premium will be paid by the party taking out the insurance, rather than the other side. Again, this returns the position to that which existed in the 1990s.'

42.67 The machinery for achieving this aim is set out in s 46 of the Legal Aid, Sentencing and Punishment of Offenders Act; it is set out in the footnotes.[68] For all

---

[67]   *Reforming Civil Litigation Funding and Costs in England and Wales – Implementation of Lord Justice Jackson's Recommendations* (March 2011) Cm 8041 at para 5 under 'The Way Forward'.

[68]   '46 Recovery of insurance premiums by way of costs

(1) In the Courts and Legal Services Act 1990, after section 58B insert—

"58C Recovery of insurance premiums by way of costs

(1) A costs order made in favour of a party to proceedings who has taken out a costs insurance policy may not include provision requiring the payment of an amount in respect of all or part of the premium of the policy, unless such provision is permitted by regulations under subsection (2).

(2) The Lord Chancellor may by regulations provide that a costs order may include provision requiring the payment of such an amount where—

(a) the order is made in favour of a party to clinical negligence proceedings of a prescribed description,

(b) the party has taken out a costs insurance policy insuring against the risk of incurring a liability to pay for one or more expert reports in respect of clinical negligence in connection with the proceedings (or against that risk and other risks),

(c) the policy is of a prescribed description,

(d) the policy states how much of the premium relates to the liability to pay for an expert report or reports in respect of clinical negligence ("the relevant part of the premium"), and

(e) the amount is to be paid in respect of the relevant part of the premium.

(3) Regulations under subsection (2) may include provision about the amount that may be required to be paid by the costs order, including provision that the amount must not exceed a prescribed maximum

practical purposes, ATE premiums are irrecoverable between opposing parties save where the case is (i) a clinical negligence claim and (ii) the receiving party has taken out a policy insuring against the risk of incurring a liability to pay for one or more expert report. Even where those two conditions are met, the type of policy and the amount payable are subject to certain restrictions (which are set out in the footnotes).

Notional premiums

42.68 In a similar vein, s 47 of the Legal Aid, Sentencing and Punishment of Offenders Act abolishes recovery of notional premiums; the details are in the footnotes.[69]

Fixed costs

42.69 In the Final Report, Sir Rupert Jackson had the following to say about fixed costs:[70]

> '2.9 *Fixed costs in fast track litigation.* Cases in the fast track are those up to a value of £25,000, where the trial can be concluded within one day. A substantial proportion of civil litigation is conducted in the fast track. I recommend that the costs recoverable for fast track personal injury cases be fixed. For other types of case I recommend that there be a dual system (at least for now), whereby costs are fixed for certain types of case, and in other cases there is a financial limit on costs recoverable (I propose that £12,000 be the limit for pre-trial costs). The ideal is for costs to be fixed in the fast track for all types of claim.
>
> 2.10 There are several advantages to the fixing of costs in lower value litigation. One is that it gives all parties certainty as to the costs they may recover if successful, or their exposure if unsuccessful. Secondly, fixing costs avoids the further process of costs assessment, or disputes over recoverable costs, which can in themselves generate further expense. Thirdly, it ensures that recoverable costs are proportionate. There is a public interest in making litigation costs in the fast track both proportionate and certain.'

---

amount.

(4) The regulations may prescribe a maximum amount, in particular, by specifying— (a) a percentage of the relevant part of the premium;

(b) an amount calculated in a prescribed manner.

(5) In this section—

"clinical negligence" means breach of a duty of care or trespass to the person committed in the course of the provision of clinical or medical services (including dental or nursing services);

"clinical negligence proceedings" means proceedings which include a claim for damages in respect of clinical negligence;

"costs insurance policy", in relation to a party to proceedings, means a policy insuring against the risk of the party incurring a liability in those proceedings;

"expert report" means a report by a person qualified to give expert advice on all or most of the matters that are the subject of the report;

"proceedings" includes any sort of proceedings for resolving disputes (and not just proceedings in court), whether commenced or contemplated.".

(2) In the Access to Justice Act 1999, omit section 29 (recovery of insurance premiums by way of costs).

(3) The amendments made by this section do not apply in relation to a costs order made in favour of a party to proceedings who took out a costs insurance policy in relation to the proceedings before the day on which this section comes into force.'

[69] '47 Recovery where body undertakes to meet costs liabilities

(1) In the Access to Justice Act 1999, omit section 30 (recovery where body undertakes to meet costs liabilities).

(2) The repeal made by subsection (1) does not apply in relation to a costs order made in favour of a person to whom a body gave an undertaking before the day on which this section comes into force if the undertaking was given specifically in respect of the costs of other parties to proceedings relating to the matter which is the subject of the proceedings in which the costs order is made.'

[70] Final Report, Executive Summary; page xviii.

No details have yet been published as to how or when further fixed costs are going to be implemented.

Hourly rates

42.70 As has been explained above **(42.13)**, charging by the hour is likely to become less attractive than it is at present. One of the reasons for this is the fact that there is likely to a downwards pressure on the allowable rates.

42.71 It is proposed that guideline hourly rates should be set by a Costs Council chaired by a judge of suitable experience. Sir Rupert Jackson has made the following recommendations:[71]

> 'If a Costs Council is set up, it should be chaired by a judge or other senior person, who has long experience of the operation of the costs rules and costs assessment. It is appropriate for the Costs Council to include representatives of stakeholder groups. However, its membership should not be dominated by vested interests. It is important that all members be of high calibre and appropriate experience, so that the recommendations of the Costs Council will be authoritative. The Costs Council, like the Civil Procedure Rule Committee, should include a consumer representative. It should also, in my view, include an economist and a representative of the MoJ. It is unrealistic to expect the Costs Council to act on the basis of consensus, because of the conflicting interests which will be represented within it. The chairman will sometimes act as mediator and sometimes as arbitrator between opposing views, so as to ensure that fair and consistent recommendations are made on costs levels.'

42.72 Lord Neuberger MR has commented that he believes that charging by hourly rates will decline as competition in the marketplace (especially from alternative business structures) encourages more economical methods of charging.[72] He had this to say:[73]

> 'An approach to litigation costs based on value-pricing rather than hourly-billing is one which urgently needs to be worked out and applied. Rather than treating time as the commodity which is being sold, we should be adopting an approach where skill and experience are the commodities which are sold.'

42.73 He went on to say this:[74]

> '[H]ourly billing at best leads to inefficient practices, at worst it rewards and incentivises inefficiency. Moreover, it undermines effective competition in the provision of legal services, as it *'penalises ... well run legal business whose systems and processes enable it to conclude matters rapidly.'*

In practical terms, solicitors should keep a careful eye on what is happening in their locality and in their specialism; firms need to take steps to ensure that their infrastructure would cope with charging on a basis other than hourly rates.

---

[71] See the Final Report at Chapter 6, para 2.4 and R Jackson *Assessment of Costs in the Brave New World: Eighth Lecture (KPMG Forensic's* [sic] Leeds Law Lecture 2012, 25 January 2012 at 2.3.
[72] *Association of Costs Lawyers' Annual Conference 2012 (Keynote Address): Fourteenth Lecture in the Implementation Programme* (11 May 2012), para 19.
[73] Ibid.
[74] *Association of Costs Lawyers' Annual Conference 2012 (Keynote Address): Fourteenth Lecture in the Implementation Programme* (11 May 2012), para 17, quoting R Susskind *The End of Lawyers? Rethinking the Nature of Legal Services* (2010) (OUP) at 151.

REFORMS RELATING TO COSTS PROCEDURE

42.74 The following topics are addressed in this section:

- bills of costs (**42.75**);
- detailed assessments (**42.76**); and
- summary assessments (**42.77**).

Bills of costs

42.75 The Final Report recommended (a) the creation of a new form bill of costs and (b) the development of software which will automatically generate schedules of costs or bills of costs at different levels of generality, according to the client's or the court's requirements.[75] The Association of Costs Lawyers has set up a Jackson Working Group to take these proposals forward. The working group produced an interim report in October 2011; it is currently developing an interim format for bills of costs, which will need to be piloted. This aspect of the reforms is very much work in progress.[76]

Detailed assessment: procedure, points of dispute and replies

42.76 The Rule Committee has reportedly accepted the following proposals[77] (although the full changes themselves have yet to be released):

- ***Interim payments:*** The CPD will be amended to provide that whenever the court makes an order for costs to be assessed, the court shall also order an interim payment on account of costs, unless there is good reason not to do so (this effectively reversing the decision of *Blakemore v Cummings* [2009] EWCA Civ 1276).[78]
- ***Points of dispute and points of reply:*** It is intended that points of dispute and points of reply need to be shorter and more focused. The practice of quoting passages from well-known judgments should be abandoned. Sir Rupert Jackson has said that 'the practice of repeatedly using familiar formulae, in Homeric style, should be abandoned'.[79] It is envisaged that there should be no need to plead to every individual item in a bill of costs, nor to reply to every paragraph in the points of dispute. The proposed changes to the CPD are in the footnotes;[80] in

---

[75] See Chapter 45.

[76] R Jackson *Assessment of Costs in the Brave New World: Eighth Lecture in the Implementation Programme* (KPMG Forensic's [sic] Leeds Law Lecture 2012, 25 January 2012) at 3.3.

[77] R Jackson *Assessment of Costs in the Brave New World: Eighth Lecture in the Implementation Programme* (KPMG Forensic's [sic] Leeds Law Lecture 2012, 25 January 2012) at 3.2.

[78] See the Final Report at Chapter 45, para 5.10 and R Jackson *Assessment of Costs in the Brave New World: Eighth Lecture in the Implementation Programme* (KPMG Forensic's [sic] Leeds Law Lecture 2012, 25 January 2012) at 3.1.

[79] R Jackson *Assessment of Costs in the Brave New World: Eighth Lecture in the Implementation Programme* (KPMG Forensic's [sic] Leeds Law Lecture 2012, 25 January 2012) at 3.1.

[80] In so far as points of dispute are concerned, the following changes will be made to the CPD:
    '35.2 Points of dispute have in the past become too long and repetitive. Points of dispute should be short and to the point. The points should identify any points of principle, as well as any specific items, but once a point has been made it should not be repeated in respect of subsequent items in the bill. Points of dispute should follow the amended Precedent G of the Schedule of Costs Precedents annexed to this Practice Direction.
    35.3 Points of dispute must – (1) identify any general points or points of principle which require decision before the individual items in the bill are addressed, and (2) identify specific points stating concisely the nature and grounds of dispute. Once the point has been made it should not be repeated but the item numbers, where the point arises, should be inserted in the left hand box as shown in the amended Precedent

essence, parties are encouraged to make more general points rather than laboriously set out arguments point-by-point.

- **Compulsory offers:** It is proposed that paying parties are to be required to make an offer when they serve their points of dispute. The offer may be contained in the points of dispute or in a separate document.[81] The sum offered may be more or less than the amount of the interim payment ordered by the court.

- **Provisional assessments:** It is proposed that bills of costs for an amount below a certain level will be provisionally assessed. This is addressed at **(21.145–21.156)**.

- **Part 36 offers and the costs of the assessment:** It is proposed that the Part 36 procedure should apply to detailed assessment proceedings. The '14 day' provision at CPD art 46.1 should be repealed. The default position should remain as set out in CPR, r 47.18 but if a paying party makes an offer which the receiving party fails to beat, then the normal consequence should be that receiving party pays the costs after the date when the offer expired. Likewise receiving parties should be rewarded for making sufficient offers, that reward being the enhanced interest and indemnity basis costs of the assessment.[82]

- **Appeals:** It is proposed that unless the court orders otherwise the time for appeal should start to run from the conclusion of the final hearing (thereby effectively overruling *Kasir v Darlington & Simpson Rolling Mills Ltd* [2001] 2 Costs LR 228).[83] It is envisaged that there will be some occasions when it would be appropriate for the court to order otherwise such as where an appeal against a decision on a preliminary issue may have a bearing on the rest of the assessment.

Summary assessment

42.77 It is proposed that a revised statement of costs (N260) is prepared.[84] The draft is not dissimilar to the current version save that there is more detail in respect of both attendances and documentary time.

Proportionality

42.78 In the Third Lecture in the Implementation Programme, Sir Rupert Jackson had this to say:[85]

> '2.1 *No need for elaborate practice direction.* The proposed proportionality rule is set out in FR chapter 3 para 5.15. Subject to any drafting improvements which may be made by the Rule Committee, the rule is sufficiently clear. Apart from making the amendments to the Costs Practice Direction proposed in chapter 3 paras 5.22 to 5.23 (which result in overall shortening) there is no need for any further practice direction.

G. Section 39 of the Costs Practice Direction deals with the optional reply under CPR rule 47.13.'
In so far as replies are concerned, the following subparagraph will be added to CPR art 39.1:
(4) Where replies are served these should be limited to replies to points of principle and concessions only. A simple rejection of the paying party's points of dispute is of no assistance to the court.'

[81] See the Final Report at Chapter 45, para 5.13 and R Jackson Assessment of Costs in the Brave New World: Eight Lecture (KPMG Forensic's [sic] Leeds Law Lecture 2012, 25 January 2012 at 3.1.

[82] See the Final Report at Chapter 45, paras 5.14 and 5.15 and R Jackson *Assessment of Costs in the Brave New World: Eighth Lecture in the Implementation Programme* (KPMG Forensic's [sic] Leeds Law Lecture 2012, 25 January 2012) at 3.1.

[83] See the Final Report at Chapter 45, para 4.16 and R Jackson Assessment of Costs in the Brave New World: Eight Lecture (KPMG Forensic's [sic] Leeds Law Lecture 2012, 25 January 2012 at 3.1.

[84] R Jackson *Assessment of Costs in the Brave New World: Eighth Lecture in the Implementation Programme* (KPMG Forensic's [sic] Leeds Law Lecture 2012, 25 January 2012) at 2.1.

[85] R Jackson *Technical Aspects of Implementation; Third Lecture in the Implementation Programme*: (31 October 2011) at para 1.3.

2.2 *Operation of the proportionality rule.* The rule will have to be applied in a number of different situations. There will be cases in which it is obvious at the outset that the costs claimed are proportionate. In such cases the only issue to consider under rule 44.4 is the reasonableness of individual items. There will be cases where it is obvious at the outset that the costs claimed are disproportionate. J will have to consider the reasonableness of each item in the bill. He will also have to consider how to reduce the bill to a proportionate level. He may do this by reducing particular items or by reducing the overall total in order to achieve proportionality. There will be borderline cases where it is unclear whether the bill is disproportionate until after J has dealt with the reasonableness of individual items. J should not be constrained by a practice direction to approach his task in a particular way. One size does not fit all.

2.3 *Satellite litigation.* Any major civil justice reform is followed by litigation in which parties test the boundaries of the new rule. A few robust Court of Appeal decisions are needed to deal with the points raised. If the rule is supplemented by an elaborate practice direction, opportunities for satellite litigation will increase exponentially, as practitioners explore the relationship between the provisions, possible interstices in the language and so forth. One lesson from the Costs War is that lawyers leave no stone unturned when it comes to arguing about costs.

2.4 *Rarity.* There is comment in the workshop materials that the proportionality rule will rarely lead to cutting down costs. I only agree with this comment if all the other FR recommendations are implemented: fixed costs across the whole fast track; effective costs management in the multi-track; ending recoverable success fees and ATE premiums; etc. If the rest of the FR package is not implemented, the proportionality rule will bite more often.'

As yet, no firm draft rules have been published.

MISCELLANEOUS MATTERS

Increase in general damages

42.79 At paragraph 7 of the section 'The Way Forward' in the Government's response 'Reforming the Civil Litigation Funding and Costs in England and Wales – Implementation of Lord Justice Jackson's Recommendations' published by the Ministry of Justice in March 2011, it stated:

'There will be an increase of 10% in non-pecuniary general damages such as pain, suffering and loss of amenity in tort cases, for all claimants.'

However, this provision has not been included in the Legal Aid, Sentencing and Punishment of Offenders Act, and the Government has stated that it will rely on judges to implement the uplift. This has caused particular concern as the uplift on damages for successful Part 36 claimants is in the Act (s 55).

42.80 Sir Rupert Jackson explained the interaction of the various provisions concerning damages in the following way:[86]

3.2 *Personal injury cases where C makes an effective Part 36 offer.* In personal injury cases C will lose up to 25% of his damages (excluding damages referable to future losses) in the

---

[86]   R Jackson *Technical Aspects of Implementation; Third Lecture in the Implementation Programme*: (31 October 2011) at para 3.2.

success fee which he must pay to his solicitor. C will be assisted in paying this sum this by means of (a) a 10% uplift on general damages + (b) an uplift of 10% on the total damages as a reward for his effective Part 36 offer.

It is worth pausing here to say that the proposed 10% increase in general damages has not found its way into any of the legislation referred to below; if it is going to be introduced, it is possible it will be introduced by way of a judicial adjustment similar to that in *Heil v Rankin*.[87]

HOW TO PREPARE FOR THE REFORMS

42.81 The following guide (which is in the form of a series flow charts) is intended to provide practical assistance to persons who are reasonably familiar with the relevant concepts. It is in no way a substitute for proper legal advice and is used solely at the reader's own risk. This is an area where, if in doubt, specialist legal and accountancy advice should be taken from people who have the appropriate experience.

42.82 The writer is grateful to Ms Elizabeth Love (costs lawyer) and Mr Paul Hughes (barrister) for their help with what is said below.

42.83 The guidance set out below comprises seven 'Charts' in three phases (see the table below). The phases are:

- **Data Collection Phase:** Data is collected and then used (i) to prepare forecasts as to how new methods of funding would generate profit, and (ii) to go towards the first draft of a proposed business plan (or, where more than one new method of generating profit is contemplated, two or three alternative business plans). The starting point is the Initial Chart; this Chart will then usually lead to the DBA Chart or the Fixed Costs Chart (or both). The data collection is usually best carried out by a costs lawyer working in conjunction with an accountant (or the practice's accounts manager).

- **Evaluation Phase**: The next stage is evaluation of the data; this is a process of comparing the draft business plans for each method of funding (or combination thereof) and choosing the one most likely to generate profit, good cash flow and stability. There are three Evaluation Charts: one for personal injury, one for other consumer business, and one for commercial business. Evaluation will include financial modelling that will allow a number of 'what if' scenarios to be tested. Modelling can only go so far, however, and in all but the most straightforward of situations, contracts of retainer will need to be drafted and piloted.

- **Implementation and Audit Phase**: Once the competing methods have been evaluated and the best method (or methods) selected, it is necessary to move on to implementation. This may mean looking at issues that are not directly related to costs but which are likely to have a bearing on profit. Ideally, written policies (such as policies concerning e-disclosure, costs budgeting, provisional assessments, etc,) should be drafted. Staffing changes may also need to be considered at this stage. Finally, a yearly or quarterly audit programme ought to be put in place.

---

[87] *Heil v Rankin* [2000] 2 WLR 1173; see D Regan D 'Here it comes!' 161 NLJ 895, 1 July 2011.

42.84 Some of the proposed methods of funding have yet been made lawful (in particular, DBAs are generally regarded as being unlawful in contentious business). In view of this it may be necessary to carry out the aforesaid review in anticipation of the law being changed. It may not be possible to carry out pilots on 'live' cases; it may be necessary to run a dummy file alongside the real file and to evaluate the new method of funding in that way. It is, however, better to have carried out the work in advance of the reforms rather than to run the risk of being on the back foot when the realities of the reforms begin to hit home. In particular, if the 'what if' part of the Evaluation Phase has been carried out with rigour, the firm will not only know what contingencies to expect, but will also know how to manage them. This will give that firm a significant competitive advantage.

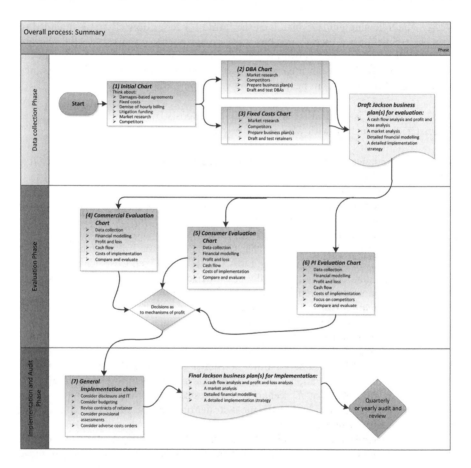

Preparing to begin the review

42.85 Some firms (such as those that practise in a niche area of the law) will be able to run through the Charts very quickly. Most, however, will need to carry out a significant amount of work. The ideal team would be as follows:

- **Overseer**: It is best that there is a single overseer (be that a single person or a committee); in a solicitors' firm the overseer would usually be the managing partner or his delegate;

- ***Costs lawyer***: It would be best to involve a costs lawyer at stages, but in particular, a costs lawyer will be required in the Data Collection Phase and the Evaluation Phase;
- ***Accountant (or accounts manager)***: Accountancy input will be required to: (a) assist the costs lawyer, and (b) advise generally on the accounts in the draft business plans;
- ***Practice manager***: The practice manager will need to deal with issues such as the costs of implementation, staffing and timetabling; many practices managers also have the necessary skills to draft the business plans; and
- ***Costs counsel***: In a large firm, costs counsel would work with the overseer to coordinate the whole exercise, but in most firms this would not be necessary; it would, nonetheless, usually be necessary to ask counsel to draft the relevant contractual documents.

42.86 The Data Collection Phase and the Evaluation Phase are figure-intensive processes in which the territory traditionally occupied by costs lawyers overlaps with the territory traditionally occupied by accountants (see **42.83**). Ideally, the costs lawyer should be able to prepare a model (ie, a spreadsheet) as to what would happen on a case-by-case basis in a variety of circumstances; he should then be able to present that data in such a way as to allow the accountant to take an overview as to what would happen to the firm's profits if those circumstances were to eventuate. This work is very different to ordinary costs work, and the extent to which a costs lawyer will feel comfortable doing this will vary from individual to individual: if the costs lawyer is not confident that he has the skills, it will be necessary to ensure that someone else within the team has.

Starting the review

42.87 The review is carried out by faithfully working through the Charts. Many of the conclusions that a firm will reach will be counterintuitive, and as such it is important that no steps are omitted: a step should be omitted only if it is not relevant as opposed to being omitted because the firm believes it knows the answer. The starting points and the finishing points will be the same for all business. The Initial Chart will always be the starting point; this is a management sieve that sorts business into categories. The General Implementation Chart will always be the finishing point. The Initial Chart helps the business choose the correct route between these two points.

42.88 The first question is whether the firm is a niche firm or a mainstream firm. This is a reference to the nature of the firm's practice rather than to the area of law in which it practices. In particular, it implies a lack of direct competition regarding fees. It is very rare that this can be said to be true: perhaps 1% of firms will fall into that category. If in doubt, it is best to work on the basis that the firm in question is a mainstream firm rather than a niche firm.

42.89 Firms that routinely deal with very large amounts of money (eight figure sums of costs or damages) are filtered out at an early stage; this is because such firms need to consider a range of options that do not appear in these Charts. They will also need to know what their competitors are doing. They should be taking specific advice. They should not, however, assume that they will be unaffected by the Jackson reforms: this could be disastrous for them because, without planning, their practices are likely to be such that they would not be able to respond quickly to unforeseen changes in the market.

42.90 There are then several questions that can only be answered with the benefit of data; the type of data that is required is along the following lines:

- The average ratio of damages to base profit costs;
- The stage at which cases generally settle;
- Whether cases have a tendency to settle 'early' (in the sense that the costs at that stage are low) or whether they have a tendency to settle 'late';
- The effect of charging fixed costs rather than by the hour;
- Market research as to what market want and what the market realistically expects; and
- Information as to what competitors are doing.

42.91 The topics of marshalling the data and evaluating it are addressed below. This will largely be the province of the costs lawyer and the accountant. Market research should be proportionate: an informal survey designed in-house would usually be sufficient.

42.92 At the end of the Initial Chart, the reader will then end up on one of the circles; this will then lead to one or more of the other Charts.

Initial Chart

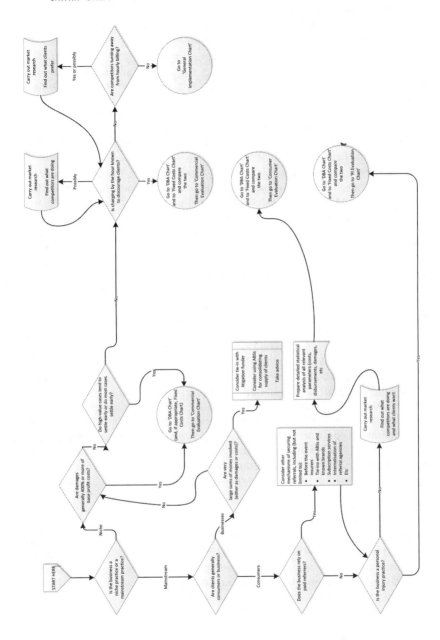

42.93 Whilst it simply highlights the issue, the Initial Chart includes a reminder to firms who rely on referral fees to take steps sooner rather than later to deal with the changes that banning them will bring. There are many ways in which this situation can be managed; the following may be worth thinking about:

- *Change in business model*: Whilst it may be a painful decision for many firms, it may be best to change the business model entirely. If the firm is in the consumer compensation industry, then (for the reasons alluded to at **42.16-42.18** above) serious thought ought to be given to this. Most firms that have been sufficiently well run to prosper in the consumer compensation industry will have the skills to prosper in other sectors too. A great deal will depend on the local market and on the skills of the firm involved.

- *Before the event insurers*: The relative importance of before the event insurers is nearly certain to rise following the reforms; the extent to which this will provide a source of bulk referrals will depend on many factors, but in particular, it will depend on the extent to which BTE insurers will be able to continue to attract customers by keeping premiums to a very low level. Whilst it is possible that non-panel firms will be able to make a reasonable profit out of BTE insurers by forcing them to pay rates that are higher than panel rates (see **30.252**), the law is uncertain in this regard, and there it would be risky to make the acquisition of such work the mainstay of business. As such, it may be best to compete for panel work. Again, a great deal will depend on local factors.

- *Other insurers and funders*: There are many other types of funder, such as motoring organisations and unions. Most of these will already have longstanding relationships with trusted solicitors, but in the market turmoil of the review, they may be willing to look at other suppliers.

- *Subscription organisations*: A recent development is the emergence of subscription organisations. These are organisations that charge persons (presently only commercial concerns) a subscription. If a claim is made by or brought against the subscriber, the subscription will then be used to fund the provision of legal services either in part or in full, but only up to a certain stage (such as allocation). Thereafter, legal services are funded by direct payments (which may or may not be based on fixed fees). Subscription organisations are such a new concept that there is no reason why larger firms could not form their own scheme.

- *Non-commercial referrers*: Not all referrers are commercial concerns. Some referrers (such as Action Against Medical Accidents and INQUEST) refer cases on merit rather than in return for a referral fee.

- *Internalising the referrer*: This is a proposal that, at the time of writing, was creating a fair amount of interest. The idea is that the referrer becomes the firm's marketing department and carries on much as before. There are considerable problems with this approach, but perhaps the most obvious pitfall is that the Government's concerns set out at **42.16-42.18** (above) will not abate, and internalisation of the referrer is likely to pour petrol on the flames rather than water. Given the fact that the Master of Rolls has already hinted at the fact if the Jackson reforms do not work it may be necessary to adopt the US costs rule or the German fixed costs regime (see **42.18**), other options would seem to be preferable.

- *Marketing*: Marketing is less provocative because it is, in general, aimed at increasing market share rather than increasing the size of the market itself.

- *Franchising*: Another recent development is an upsurge in franchising; the idea is that a firm joins a franchise with a trusted brand name (such as Quality Solicitors). Franchising may be aimed at specific areas of the consumer legal industry (such as personal injury) or at the industry as a whole.

Marshalling the data

42.94 The data collection phase and the early part of the evaluation phase is all about collecting data. The objective is to prepare a financial model (ie, a spreadsheet) which predicts income in a representative sample of individual cases, and then—for each competing method of funding—to extrapolate that data so as to be able to predict the firm's entire profit. The model must be such that it allows comparison of the competing methods of funding in a variety of 'what if' scenarios; this means it must allow certain parameters (such as hourly rates, levels of damages-based fees, etc) to be varied empirically.

42.95 There are three types of information that will need to be collected: (i) numerical information that which is collected (such as historical earnings, damages, etc), (ii) non-numerical (or qualitative) information that is collected (such as the stage at which cases tend to settle), and (iii) assumed or estimated parameters (such as projected hourly rates, etc). The following table explains gives an indication of the types of data that might be required (and who should collect it).

	Costs Lawyer (detailed data)	**Costs Lawyer (overview data)**	**Accountant (detailed data)**	**Accountant (overview data)**
Historical Numerical Data	Actual hourly rates		Fee income from opponents and own clients (including cash flow)	
	Actual time spent		Overheads of providing legal services (staff costs, etc)	
	Disburse-ments		Payment of disbursements (including cash flow)	
	Additional liabilities		Costs, overheads, etc	
	Other costs income (such as interest)	Overall historical costs per case (or average thereof)	Bad debts; recovery in general	Overall historical profit and loss and cash flow

			Damages (or average damages)	Ratio of costs to damages (or average thereof)
Historical Qualitative Data	Stage at which cases settle		Qualifications to accounts	
	Types of case in general			
Assumed parameters	Contingency fees (10, 20, 30 % etc.)	Projected costs per case under DBAs (or average thereof)	Data from costs lawyer	Overall projected profit and loss and cash flow for DBAs
	Fixed costs	Projected costs per case under Fixed Costs (or average thereof)	Data from costs lawyer	Overall projected profit and loss and cash flow for Fixd Costs
	Effect of costs budgeting	Projected costs per case if carefully budgeted (or average thereof)	Data from costs lawyer	Overall projected profit and loss and cash flow when budgeted

42.96 The qualitative information will need to be as accurate as possible (and it may be necessary to resort to some numerical measures in order to achieve that accuracy). In particular, it will be important to describe with accuracy the stage at which cases tend to settle; this is because the stage of settlement may have a dramatic effect on the profit that can be taken out of fixed costs of damages-based fees.

42.97 The accountant will have to obtain details of the profit and loss account, the balance sheet and cash flow (or some measure thereof, such as 'aged debt'). Using these figures, it will then be necessary to work out what the firm would have earned had it been using one or more of the various competing methods of funding during the relevant previous accounting periods. This will necessarily involve a degree of rough-and-ready estimation, but ideally, the costs lawyers' data should allow the accountant to predict what effect the competing methods of funding would have had on a typical case (or range of typical cases); this should then allow the accountant to predict the effect of that method of funding on profit and loss generally.

42.98 It would generally not be wise to prepare a model that attempts to calculate the firm's entire profit directly from the representative sample; this is because such a model would be very ambitious and might itself be based on assumptions that are wrong. In any event, such a model would simply lead to excessive reliance being placed on spuriously 'accurate' results. It would usually be better to use the case-by-case calculations as being indicative of profit as opposed to directly leading to a calculation of profit. Such a model would be less objective than a model based solely on calculations, but it would be less prone to modelling errors.

42.99 Unless it is possible to include all relevant cases over a given period of time, it will be necessary to collect data from a representative sample of cases. Ideally that sample ought to be randomly selected, but the nature of the exercise is such that this is not absolutely necessary: indeed, it would be better to have a hand-picked sample that was truly representative of the firm as a whole than a randomly selected sample that was unrepresentative.

The damages-based agreement (DBA) chart

42.100 As many a small business has found out to its cost, cash flow is of supreme importance. As such, it may be desirable for the firm to create two main spreadsheets; the first setting out the profit and loss and the second setting out the cash flow at specific points in time. This may indemnify problem areas for some firms, particularly niche firms, as big cases take a long time to settle.

DBA Chart

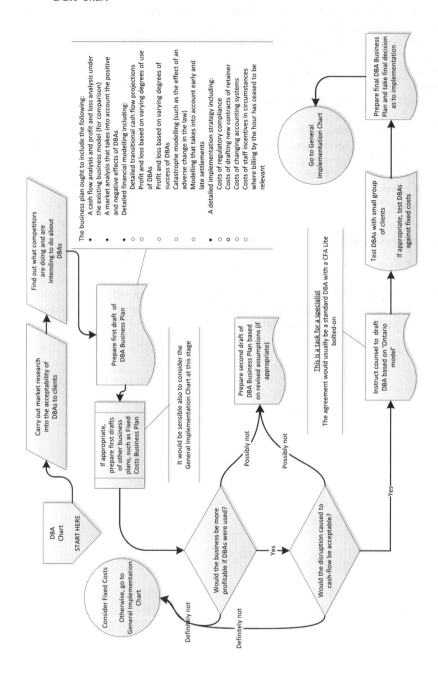

42.101 Most business will need to work their way through the DBA Chart. The first two boxes require the firm to complete its market research in order to find out exactly what competitors are doing and what clients and potential clients want. This would usually be based on an informal survey that can be managed in-house.

42.102 The next box requires the first draft business plan to be drawn up; this will not be a full business plan but will be a series of short reports, financial analyses and projections. The precise format will depend on the size and nature of the firm, but most would include the following:

- A full description of the existing business model (for comparison); this would usually include a profit and loss account and a measure of cash flow (such as an aged debt report);
- A narrative market analysis that takes into account the positive and negative effects of DBAs;
- Detailed financial modelling including:
  - Detailed transitional cash flow projections;
  - Profit and loss accounts based on varying degrees of use of DBAs;
  - Profit and loss accounts based on varying degrees of success of DBAs;
  - Catastrophe modelling (such as the effect of an adverse change in the law); and
  - Modelling that takes into account early and late settlements;
- A detailed implementation strategy including:
  - Costs of regulatory compliance;
  - Costs of drafting new contracts of retainer;
  - Costs of changing accounting systems; and
  - Costs of staff incentives in circumstances where billing by the hour has ceased to be relevant.

Different species of damages-based agreements

42.103 The types of DBA that might be worth considering are the following:

- Transitional DBAs: Whilst there is no authority to confirm that they are lawful,[88] adventurous firms might want to consider using 'transitional DBAs' straight away.[89] A transitional DBA is a non-contentious DBA (or often a DBA Lite: see below) bolted on to a conditional fee agreement (often a CFA Lite); the effect is that if proceedings are issued (ie, if the claim becomes contentious business) the contract automatically transforms ab initio from being a DBA into being a conditional fee agreement. This means that the firms can get the benefit of DBAs in the period during which they are most profitable, namely, the early part of the litigation. The advantage of the early adoption of Transitional DBAs is that adventurous firms may well have a head start over other firms in so far as marketing, client care and other issues are concerned. The disadvantages are that they may occasionally run into problems with the indemnity principle. For many firms, however, the benefit outweighs the risks (especially as the paying party would rarely need to be told about the existence of the DBA).

---

[88] There is doubt as to the enforceability of transitional DBAs under the current law; that said, it is possible to draft the agreements in such a way as to make the risk of non-recovery of costs very small indeed.

[89] They would do so at their own risk (ie, there is a small chance that they will fail to recover their fees from time-to-time).

- DBA Lite: A DBA Lite is a cross between a DBA and CFA Lite; if the claim is successful then the lawyer will get no less than the damages-base fee (ie, the percentage of the damages), but if the client is awarded costs, then he will also be entitled to any further monies that are recovered as costs. At present such agreement are not lawful save in some non-contentious work, but in the future, is likely that most DBAs will be DBA Lites. This type of agreement is also often called 'the Ontario Model' (this being because this is a type of agreement that is used in that jurisdiction: see **42.47**).

- Personal Injury DBAs: It has been said that very few solicitors practising in the field of personal injury would regard DBAs as being commercially viable; this is because the limits that would restrict the damages-based fee are very similar to those that would apply to a success fee (ie, just the success fee) payable under a conditional fee agreement. As such, a solicitor would—it is said—make less profit under a DBA than under a conditional fee agreement.[90] There is certainly some truth in this, but there are two factors that pull in the opposite direction:

  - Firstly, if a case were to settle very early, then the solicitor would be very much better off under a DBA than he would be under a conditional fee agreement; and

  - Secondly, a solicitor who offered DBAs might be able to increase the volume of work he does by virtue of being able to offer his clients more attractive terms than would a solicitor who was prepared to work under only conditional fee agreements.

Pilots and testing

42.104   The last three boxes in the DBA Chart encourage the business to conduct a pilot (but only in appropriate cases). The firm is encouraged to draft a DBA, to test it, and then to revise the business plan to take the pilot into account. This is necessary for the following reasons:

- lessons learnt during the pilot may need to be factored into the financial model;

- errors in the retainer need to be spotted before the draft in question is rolled out across the firm; and

- quotidian housekeeping issues such as whether to issue interim statute bills will need to be addressed.

The pilot ought to be overseen by a specialist.

Fixed costs chart

42.105   The points made above about the DBA Chart apply by analogy to the Fixed Costs Chart.

---

[90]   See D Regan *Butterworths Personal Injury Litigation Service*, para 3022.

Fixed Costs Chart

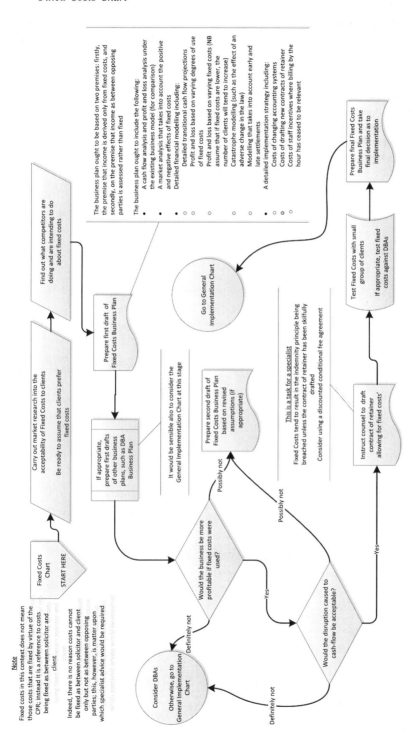

Note

Fixed costs in this context does not mean those costs that are fixed by virtue of the CPR; instead it is a reference to costs being fixed as between solicitor and client.

Indeed, there is no reason costs cannot be fixed as between solicitor and client only but not as between opposing parties; this, however, is matter upon which specialist advice would be required.

Fixed Costs Chart

START HERE

Carry out market research into the acceptability of Fixed Costs to clients

Be ready to assume that clients prefer fixed costs

Find out what competitors are doing and are intending to do about fixed costs

The business plan ought to be based on two premises: firstly, the premise that income is derived only from fixed costs, and secondly, on the premise that income as between opposing parties is assessed rather than fixed

The business plan ought to include the following:
- A cash flow analysis and profit and loss analysis under the existing business model (for comparison)
- A market analysis that takes into account the positive and negative effects of fixed costs
- Detailed financial modelling including:
  ○ Detailed transitional cash flow projections
  ○ Profit and loss based on varying degrees of use of fixed costs
  ○ Profit and loss based on varying fixed costs (NB assume that if fixed costs are lower, the number of clients will tend to increase)
  ○ Catastrophe modelling (such as the effect of an adverse change in the law)
  ○ Modelling that takes into account early and late settlements
- A detailed implementation strategy including:
  ○ Costs of changing accounting systems
  ○ Costs of drafting new contracts of retainer
  ○ Costs of staff incentives where billing by the hour has ceased to be relevant

If appropriate, prepare first drafts of other business plans, such as DBA Business Plan

Prepare first draft of Fixed Costs Business Plan

It would be sensible also to consider the General Implementation Chart at this stage

Prepare second draft of Fixed Costs Business Plan based on revised assumptions (if appropriate)

Go to General Implementation Chart

Would the business be more profitable if fixed costs were used?

Possibly not

Definitely not

Consider DBAs

Otherwise, go to General Implementation Chart

Would the disruption caused to cash-flow be acceptable?

Definitely not

Yes

Possibly not

This is a task for a specialist
Fixed Costs tend to result in the indemnity principle being breached unless the contract of retainer has been skilfully drafted
Consider using a discounted conditional fee agreement

Instruct counsel to draft contract of retainer allowing for fixed costs'

Yes

Test Fixed Costs with small group of clients

If appropriate, test fixed costs against DBAs

Prepare final Fixed Costs Business Plan and take final decision as to implementation

Commercial evaluation chart

42.106   If the draft Jackson business plans have been prepared well, then the evaluation will be a simple task. The financial models should be arranged such that the following can be examined (either by comparing competing models, or by comparing the proposed model against the *status quo*):

*   profit and loss in first, second and third years post-implementation;
*   cash flow at one month, three months, six months and 12 months post-implementation;
*   average effect on average clients' damages; and
*   cost of implementation.

Commercial Evaluation Chart

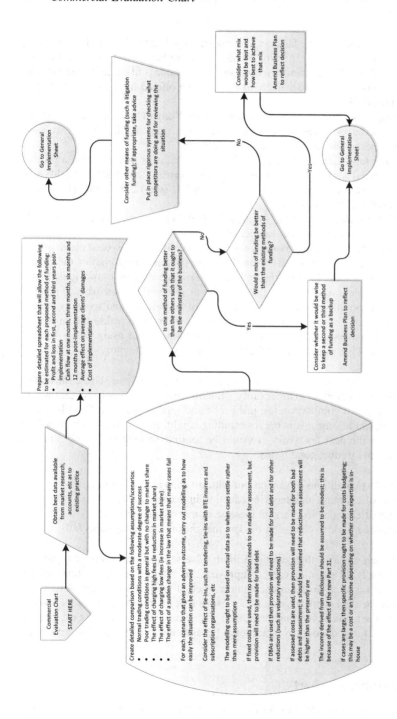

42.107 The following topics should receive particular attention when considering commercial work:

- *Market expectations*: The Jackson reforms are very likely to have an impact on the expectations of clients generally (ie all clients rather than just those that are directly affected by the reforms); charging by the hour is likely to decline (at least to an extent) and clients are likely to expect to be offered fixed fees or DBAs (see **42.13** and **42.71-42.73**).
- *Budgeting*: Costs management and budgeting are likely to limit the extent to which clients will be prepared to tolerate work being carried out where that work generates costs that are not likely to be recovered.
- *Disclosure*: One particular aspect of the Jackson reforms that will have a bearing on commercial work is the fact that the income derived from disclosure is likely to fall; this is because of the effect of the new Part 31 (see **42.28-42.30**). This should be factored into the evaluation.
- *Litigation funding*: Litigation funding is likely to become more prevalent in commercial claims (especially smaller claims).
- *Bad debts*: A surprising amount of commercial litigation is conducted on the basis—which is often concealed from the lawyers—that the solvency of the litigant depends on success in the litigation. The relevance of this is two-fold: firstly, monies payable in the event of failure (such as discounted rates payable under a discounted conditional fee agreement) may not be payable, and secondly, even if the case is won the client's debts might make it difficult to realise the entire fees payable. This is especially relevant to firms thinking about using DBAs because credit control is a particularly difficult with that type of funding.

42.108   Once the financial modelling is complete, the task will be to choose the best of the competing business plans. This is fairly straightforward, but it is important not to carry out a single-axis comparison (eg just profit and loss, or just cash flow) based on normal trading conditions; this is because trading conditions are likely to be anything but normal over the next few years. It would be sensible to look at the following (in addition to normal trading conditions):

- poor trading conditions in general but with no change to market share;
- the effect of charging high fees (ie reduction in market share);
- the effect of charging low fees (ie increase in market share); and
- the effect of a sudden change in the law that means that many cases fail.

42.109   For each scenario that gives rise to an adverse outcome, it would be wise to consider how easily the situation can be improved; this will give an idea of how 'robust' the business plan is likely to be in changing market. If trading conditions deteriorate, robustness may be the key to survival. It is possible that in order to ensure robustness it is necessary to use a mix of funding methods. Thus, it may be necessary to have a mix of DBAs (for profit) and discounted conditional fee agreements (for cash flow and credit control).

Consumer evaluation chart

42.110   The points made above under Commercial Evaluation Chart apply by analogy; the following factors ought to receive specific attention:

- ***Market expectations and robustness***: No one knows what is going to happen to the expectations of consumers. It is possible that clients will continue to believe in the 'myth of full costs recovery' and that they will continue to expect not to have to personally contribute to the costs of litigation. Likewise, it is possible that clients will accept that there is now no Legal Aid and no recoverable success fees, and that this inevitably means that they are going to have to bear some of the costs themselves. The relevance of this uncertainty is that the business model must be robust: it must be able to work (or to adapt so as to work) regardless of whether clients expect to pay or expect not to pay.
- ***Change in market share***: In a similar vein, no one knows what effect franchising, ABSs, the abolition of referral fees, etc, is going to have on the market. Again, the only sensible way of dealing with this is to ensure that the model is robust.
- ***Clarification of the law and cash flow***: In the medium term (ie the next four to five years) it is all but inevitable that the newer methods of funding will result in cases working their way up to the Court of Appeal. This will mean that costs disputes get stayed pending clarification of the law. This is a factor that needs to be factored into the model.

Consumer Evaluation Chart

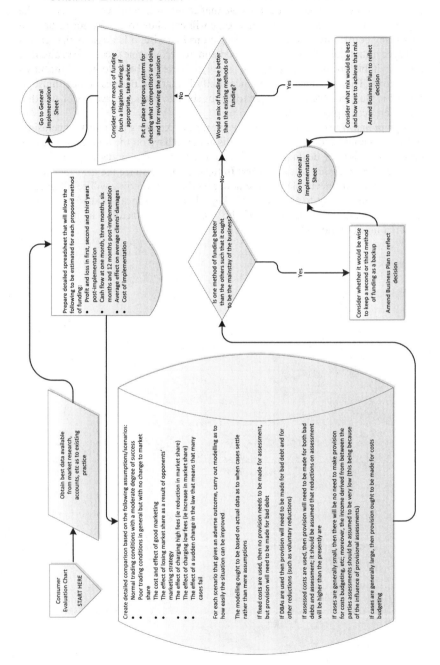

Personal injury evaluation chart

42.111 The points made above apply by analogy (see following).

General implementation chart

42.112 All firms will end up working their way through the General Implementation Chart. It is self-explanatory (see following).

Personal Injury Evaluation Chart

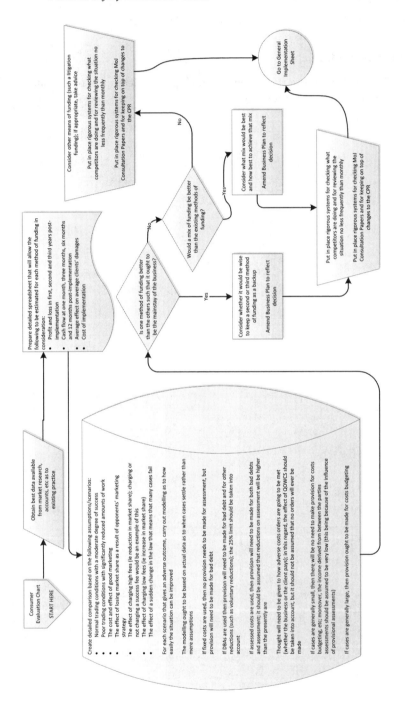

General Implementation Chart

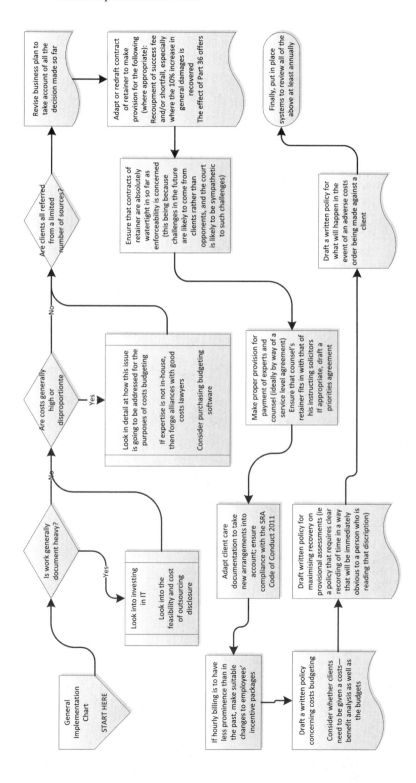

Chapter 43

PRECEDENTS

None of these precedents is intended to be a substitute for proper legal advice; if the reader finds himself not fully understanding what is said (or not said), he should take advice.

CERTIFICATE IN ACCORDANCE WITH CPD, ART 20.6

This certificate may be used where the solicitor wishes to claim a greater percentage increase from his client than that recovered from the paying party.

——— 0 ———

'I hereby certify the following:

- That the amount of the percentage increase in respect of [counsel's fees and/or solicitor's charges] is disputed;
- I intend to make an application that if the percentage increase payable by the [Defendant] or Claimant] is reduced (either by agreement or by assessment), that amount should continue to be payable by my client;
- I confirm that I have given my client an explanation in accordance with article 20.5 of the Costs Practice Direction; and
- I understand that my client [does or does not] wish to attend court when the amount of any relevant percentage increase may be decided.'

STATEMENT IN COMPLIANCE WITH CPD, ART 32.5

The following precedent will need to be changed to suit the case; in particular, certain aspects of the risks may need to be omitted entirely if they did not feature in the original risk assessment. An alternative would be simply to append the risk assessment to the statement.

——— 0 ———

'This statement is made in accordance with CPD article 32.5. By certifying the bill of costs as being accurate, I also confirm the correctness of what is set out below. In particular, I believe that the facts stated below are true.

'I confirm that the bill of costs claims a success fee payable under a [collective] conditional fee agreement. The following costs are those costs which have been summarily assessed or agreed, together with the success fee claimed thereupon (all figures are exclusive of VAT):

	Amount	(Success fee)
1 January 2001	£123-45	£123-45
2 January 2002	£67-89	£67-89
Total	£191-34	£191-34

'Whilst this [collective] conditional fee agreement was not subject to the provisions of the [Collective] Conditional Fee Agreements Regulations 2000, I am happy to provide a statement of the reasons for the percentage increase; those reasons are as follows:

(1) The risk that the claim may fail entirely, and in particular:
[describe the case-specific risks relating to the claim generally]
(2) The risk that the opponent will make a Part 36 Offer and that [he] [she] [it] subsequently secures a result that is more advantageous to [him] [her] [it] than the Part 36 Offer; in particular:
[describe the case-specific risks relating to quantum]
(3) The risk that the court will make an issues-based costs order or a percentage costs order; in particular:
[describe the case-specific risks relating to issues, etc]

'I confirm that no part of the success fee relates to the fact that there would be delay in payment.

[and/or]

'I confirm that the bill of costs claims a premium arising out of an after the event (ATE) insurance policy taken out in respect of this claim; I attach a copy of the relevant certificate, which shows the following:

(1) That the policy covers [the receiving party's own costs] [together with his opponents costs] [only the receiving party's opponent's costs]; and
(2) That the maximum extent of that cover is [£50,000]; and
(3) That the amount of the premium which I seek is [£1,000].

[Or]

'The bill of costs claims an additional amount under section 30 of the Access to Justice Act 1999: the basis upon which my client's liability for the additional amount has been calculated is as follows:

[describe the process by which the amount was calculated and, in particular, state whether the amount is calculated to be appropriate for all cases, or if it is tailored to meet the needs of the particular case in hand.]'

POINTS OF DISPUTE AND REPLIES

The following points of dispute are in the writer's own style; many costs practitioners (and some judges) would probably criticise that style as being too detailed and prolix. If a less involved style is required, then the reader is directed to Precedent G of the Schedule of Precedents at the end of the CPD.

——— 0 ———

IN THE ANYWHERE COUNTY COURT

Claim No: 0AW12345

BETWEEN:

AB

Claimant

- and -

CD

Defendant

POINTS OF DISPUTE

No	Item	Point of Dispute	Replies
1	Certificates	The bill of costs has not been properly certified. The Claimant is asked to ensure that the bill of costs has been properly certified well before the commencement of the detailed assessment hearing.	This has been attended to; the court's copy was signed when it was filed.
2	The indemnity principle	Production of the CFAs is required (including that with counsel). The Claimant will be required to hand up to the court attendance notes proving compliance with regulation 4(2) of the Conditional Fee Agreements Regulations 2000.	Herewith. The paying party must show a 'genuine issue'; this has not been done.
3	Proportionality	The costs are disproportionate both to the limited issues involved and to the value of the claim. The base costs are £27,092 (exclusive of VAT), of which £10,233 are base profit costs. This compares unfavourably with the value of the claim, which was £10,000: CPD article 11.1 cannot even begin to bridge that gap. A test of necessity ought to apply.	The costs are not disproportionate. The Defendant's conduct resulted in much higher costs than would otherwise have been necessary. In particular, the Defendant caused difficulties regarding disclosure.

No	Item	Point of Dispute	Replies
4	**Rates**	The Claimant is required to prove that the rates which are claimed were agreed with the Claimant.	See the CFAs.
		This matter ought to have been allocated to a Grade B fee earner. Guideline rates ought to apply.	Rejected.
		The Defendants offer the following composite rates:	Rejected; the Claimant will accept the following rates:
		Part One (2002 to 2003) £155 per hour Part Two (2003 to 2007) £165 per hour	Part One (2002 to 2003) £175 per hour Part Two (2003 to 2007) £185 per hour
		The Defendant offers £100 per hour for the Litigation Manager. Subject to proof, offers as above	Accepted.
5	**Claimant**	17 October 2002 – Too long was spent on this activity. Offer 1 hour.	Rejected.
		24 September 2002 – This ought to have been a short attendance. Offer 6 minutes.	Accepted.
		24 February 2003 – It would appear that this letter related to funding; such costs are not recoverable on a between-the-parties basis. In any event, the time claimed is unreasonable (by a substantial margin). Offer nil.	Rejected; these costs are recoverable.
		The number of telephone calls is excessive. Offer 3 telephone calls.	Accepted.
		The routine letters can be agreed. Offers as above	Noted.
6	2	The Claimant (substantially) overestimated the value of the claim; this fee ought to have been lower. Offer £400	This applies hindsight. Rejected.

No	Item	Point of Dispute	Replies
7	3	The claim settled more than 14 days before trial. As such, this fee could have been recovered from the court. Offer nil	Accepted.
8	**4 (and all other success fees claimed in the bill of costs)**	If the Claimant is to recover any additional liability, he must confirm (after having made reasonably diligent enquiries) that he did not have any BTE insurance which could have been used to fund this matter. In any event, the success fee is too high. On the facts as they were known at the time the risk assessment was carried out, success was likely (albeit with an element of contributory negligence). An appropriate success fee would be 35 percent. Subject to confirmation, offer 35 percent	Rejected. The Claimant will rely on the statement already made in compliance with CPD article 32.5.
9	6	Production of the Advice is required. The Claimant is required to prove both that it was reasonable to take counsel's advice at this stage and that the sums claimed are reasonable. Offer reserved pending production	The Advice will be produced at the hearing.

No	Item	Point of Dispute	Replies
10	**Claimant**	*Personal attendances*	
		6 March 2003 – This was a duplication of work which was done, or ought to been done, on 17 October 2003. In any event, the time claimed is (substantially) excessive. Offer nil.	Rejected. The Claimant will accept 12 minutes.
		28 July 2005 – it is accepted that there was a need to obtain updated instructions, but the time claimed is in excessive of that which is reasonable. Offer 30 minutes.	Accepted.
		Telephone calls 14 July 2004 – An adequate allowance has already been made for this work in the routine correspondence. This matter did not merit a further long letter. Offer nil.	

No	Item	Point of Dispute	Replies
		24 October 2005 – Production of the letter is required. Offer reserved pending production. 8 December 2005 – This duplicated the issues that would be discussed on 13 December 2005. In any event, the time claimed is excessive. Offer nil.	
		9 December 2005 – *Mutatis mutandis* the points made immediately above are repeated. Offer nil.	
		If all the aforesaid objections are upheld, then the time claimed will fall to about 1 hour 6 minutes. In an effort to save court time, the Defendant offers a total of 1 hour 24 minutes.	Rejected. The Claimant will accept 1 hour 42 minutes.
		The number of both letters and telephone calls is excessive. Offer 15 telephone calls and 35 letters. Offers as above	Accepted.
11	**ATE insurer**	This work related to funding and is therefore not recoverable on a between-the-parties basis. Offer nil	The points made previously about funding are repeated.
12	**Documents**	13 August 2003 – This work related to funding and is therefore not recoverable on a between-the-parties basis. Offer nil.	Rejected.
		6 February 2004 – The points made immediately above are repeated. In any event, an adequate allowance for this work has already been made within the routine correspondence. Offer nil.	Rejected.
		19 May 2004 – First, this work related to funding and is therefore not recoverable on a between-the-parties basis and, secondly, this was routine correspondence, an allowance for which has already been made within the body of the bill of costs. Offer nil.	The points made previously about funding are repeated.
		...	...
		7 July 2005 – This matter did not merit 'nominating' suitable expert witnesses. Offer 6 minutes.	Accepted.

No	Item	Point of Dispute	Replies
		27 July 2005 – This work related to funding. In any event, this was a routine letter, an allowance for which has already been made within the body of the bill of costs. Offer nil.	The points made previously about funding are repeated.
		27 July 2005 (2) – Too long was spent on this activity. Offer 24 minutes.	Rejected. The Claimant will accept 36 minutes.
		If all the aforesaid objections are upheld, then the time claimed will fall to about 17 hours. In an effort to save court time, the defendant offers a total of 18 hours. Offer as above	Rejected. The Claimant will accept 23 hours.
13	43	The costs draftsmen's hourly rate is excessive. £110 per hour would be appropriate for drafting work. The time can be agreed. Offer £880	

....

SERVED this..............day of...............20–

Affirm Solicitors LLP, Anywhere House, Anytown, AB1 2CD

<u>**Solicitors for the Defendant**</u>

COSTS SHARING AGREEMENT

Note: the example given is only the heart of a costs sharing agreement; each agreement must be drafted to suit the needs of the case in hand; most costs sharing agreements will be considerably more complex than the example.

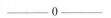 0

'BETWEEN

(1) **THE CLAIMANTS** ("the claimants") listed in the attached Schedule, those persons being claimants entered onto the group register in the **XYZ GROUP LITIGATION**, as defined in paragraph 4 of the Group Litigation Order made by Master Smith dated 1 August 20–.

(2) **AFFIRM SOLICITORS LLP**, ("the solicitors") of Anywhere House, Anytown, AB1 2CD.

'PREAMBLE

(1)   The claimants wish to enter into a costs sharing agreement pertaining to the aforesaid litigation ("the litigation") such that the agreement binds the claimants (and each of them as against each other). The solicitors are to oversee the administration of that costs sharing agreement.

(2)   This agreement deals with the liability for the claimants' own costs, and with the claimants' liability for any costs which may be ordered against them.

(3)   The parties' intention is to share the aforesaid liabilities equitably in that each claimant will bear his own costs of pursuing his own claim and an equal share of the costs of pursuing the group litigation generally; where there is ambiguity or uncertainty, it is to be interpreted in this way.

(4)   It is expressly recorded that this agreement is subject to the court ordering that costs will be shared in some other way; it is also expressly recorded that the parties agree that the court should be invited to give great weight to the terms of this agreement when exercising its discretion.

'DEFINITIONS

"The parties" has the meaning set out above.

"Individual costs" means those costs which are incurred by or in respect of a claimant's own claim. Individual costs may refer to costs incurred by or ordered against a claimant, as the case may be.

"Common costs" means those costs which are incurred by or in respect of the claimants collectively for the purposes of the litigation generally; common costs may refer to costs incurred by or ordered against the claimants (or any of them), as the case may be. Common costs will include test claim costs and costs incurred by the solicitors in administering the litigation.

"GLO issues" means those issues identified as being group litigation issues as defined in paragraph 9 of the Group Litigation Order made by Master Smith dated 1 August 20–.

"Test claim costs" means those costs which are incurred by or in respect of a claimant for the purposes of resolving any GLO issue; test claim costs fall within the category of common costs. Test claim costs may refer to costs incurred by or ordered against a claimant, as the case may be. They may include costs incurred in reasonable anticipation of a claimant becoming a test claim claimant.

"Test claim" means a claim which the court has ordered to be a test claim for the purposes of resolving any GLO issue.

'IT IS AGREED

1.   In so far as the claimants' liability to the solicitors is concerned:

    a.   Individual costs are to be borne severally by the relevant individual claimant.

    b.   Common costs are to be apportioned into shares (see below), and each claimant will be severally liable for his apportioned share.

    c.   Apportionment will take place every quarter (starting on 1 January 20–); the apportionment will be carried out by the solicitors according the following formula:

        i   All common costs incurred during the relevant quarter will be summated including, where appropriate, an appropriate proportion of any costs which may be said to have been incurred both for the benefit of any given individual claimant and the claimants as a group.

ii   The aggregated common costs will be equally apportioned amongst the claimants whose names have appeared on the attached Schedule at any time during the relevant quarter.

iii   Where costs have been incurred which fall due in one quarter but which relate to services or supplies which pertain to several quarters (such as an after the event insurance premium), an adjustment will, where appropriate, be made as if the costs in question had fallen due piecemeal and at regular intervals over the period of time in question. Unless there is reason to do otherwise, it will be assumed that an equal proportion of the costs would have fallen due within each quarter.

iv   Where an individual claimant has entered into a conditional fee agreement, the success fee will be disregarded for the purposes of the aforesaid calculation.

d.   Once the appropriate share has been determined, the solicitors will be at liberty to render an invoice; that invoice will be a request for a payment on account. The solicitors may, in their absolute discretion, elect to charge a lower figure on account.

e.   Where a claimant's name is entered onto the Schedule, he will not (at that stage) be required to make a contribution towards the common costs already incurred.

2.   Where common costs are recovered in the litigation, they will be apportioned in a similar way to that set out above.

3.   Upon conclusion of the litigation, the solicitors will carry out a final calculation (in respect of which the solicitors will seek the approval of the court) which will be based on the aforesaid formula (namely, apportionment following summation). The solicitors will, for each claimant, calculate two figures: the amount of common costs payable by the claimant to the solicitors, and the amount of costs (if any) recovered in the litigation and payable to the claimant. The solicitors are not bound to carry out both calculations at the same time, but may do so if they so wish. The fact that the solicitors have provided either or both of these figures will not prevent further costs accruing (such as costs of a detailed assessment).

4.   In calculating the first of the two figures, the following provisions will apply (in addition to the general principles set out above):

a.   Unless there is good reason to do otherwise, the calculation will be carried out as if the names of all of the claimants had appeared on the Schedule from the outset of the litigation.

b.   Unless there is good reason to do otherwise, where a claimant's name is removed from the Schedule, he will be disregarded for the purposes of the calculation for all subsequent quarters.

5.   In calculating the second of the two figures mentioned in paragraph 3 above, the following provisions will apply (in addition to the general principles set out in paragraphs 1 and 2 above):

a.   Individual costs will be disregarded for the purposes of the calculation.

b.   Where common costs have been awarded both to the claimants and against them, the amounts recoverable and the amounts payable will be accounted for separately following which a net figure due will be derived.

c.   Unless there is good reason to do otherwise, the calculation will be carried out as if the names of all of the claimants had appeared on the Schedule from the outset of the litigation.

d.   Unless there is good reason to do otherwise, where a claimant's name is removed from the Schedule, he will be disregarded for the purposes of the calculation for all subsequent quarters.

6.   In so far as any costs ordered against the Claimants are concerned:

a.   With the appropriate modifications, the general principles set out in paragraph 1 above will apply.

b.   The fact that a claimant may or may not have legal expenses insurance will be disregarded for the purposes of the calculation. In particular, any limits on the extent of cover will be disregarded.

7.   The parties acknowledge and agree that this agreement is not a contentious business agreement within the terms of the Solicitors Act 1974.

8.	This agreement is governed by the law of England and Wales.

9.	In the event that any term or condition or provision of this agreement is held to be a violation of any applicable law or statute or regulation, the same shall be deemed to be deleted from this agreement and shall be of no force and effect and this agreement shall remain in full force and effect as if such term and condition or provision had not originally been contained in this agreement.

10.	It is recorded that prior to signing this agreement, the solicitors explained the following:

	a.	the circumstances in which the client may be liable for the costs and whether the solicitors will seek payment of these from the client, if entitled to do so; and

	b.	the client's right to an assessment of those costs.

11.	It is expressly recorded that this agreement does not require a signature for the purposes of entering a claimant's name onto the Schedule; the solicitors will be authorised to enter a claimant's name immediately upon being given instructions to do so. Retrospective amendments to the Schedule may be made.

12.	To be effective (and unless the court orders otherwise), any variation of or supplement to this agreement must be made in writing.

13.	Where there is disagreement amongst the claimants or between the claimants and the solicitors about what is an appropriate apportionment, the parties (or any of them) will be at liberty to apply to the court for a determination.'

STATEMENT REQUESTING RELIEF FROM SANCTIONS

This is a draft statement intended primarily as a guide for those who are not used to drafting witness statements.

'I, Andrew Norman Other, of Costs and Partners, Anywhere House, Anytown, AB1 2CD will state as follows:

1.	I am an associate of the Association of Law Costs Draftsmen and I have, under the supervision of my instructing solicitors, been managing the detailed assessment proceedings. I make this statement in support of the claimant's application for relief from sanctions. Save where otherwise indicated, the facts contained in this witness statement are within my own personal knowledge and are, to the best of my belief, true.

2.	This statement concerns events which happened before my involvement in this matter. It has not been possible to contact the assistant solicitor who had conduct of this matter at the relevant time as she has left my instructing solicitors' firm. I have, however, carefully been through the file of papers and I am happy that everything that I say is supported by contemporaneous documentation. I have also spoken with Mr Frederick Earner of my instructing solicitors (who was the supervising partner) and he has confirmed that he agrees with what I say.

3.	The claimant's application concerns the claimant's failure to serve notice of funding pertaining to a conditional fee agreement dated 5 May 20–. The claimant says that notice of funding was not required for the vast majority of the duration of this claim, but in the alternative, the claimant seeks relief from sanctions.

4.	The claimant suffered an injury after slipping on ice in a car park belonging to and managed by the defendant. The claimant instructed my instructing solicitors on about 2 May 20–. A lengthy attendance took place on 3 May 20–, during which the claimant gave my instructing solicitors instructions to bring an occupier's liability claim against the defendant. A letter of claim was sent on 5 May 20–. There is now produced and shown to me ANO1, which is a copy of all the relevant correspondence and attendance notes. (In so far as it is necessary, I give notice of the fact that the claimant intends to rely on those extracts from my instructing solicitors' file as a record of business and as documentary hearsay evidence.) The letter of claim can be found at page 1 of that exhibit. It can be seen from the antepenultimate paragraph of that letter that the claimant gave informal notice of funding (that notice being given on the very same day that the conditional fee agreement was made).

5. The claim was issued on 4 September 20 — and served on 12 September 20–. After the event insurance was taken out the day before the claim was served. Formal notice of funding was given, but this unfortunately referred to only the ATE insurance rather than both the ATE insurance and the conditional fee agreement.

6. I have carefully been through the file and I can find no record of any explanation for this. There is nothing to suggest that this was a deliberate omission. Whilst it will be a matter for the court, I work on the basis that the failure to give formal notice of funding was an oversight on the part of the fee earner who had conduct of the matter at the material time.

7. The claim settled on 23 September 20–, only about 10 days after it was served.

8. I was instructed on 1 October 20–, and I noticed the oversight on 4 October 20–, the day before this application was made.

9. My primary case is that there has been substantial compliance with the requirements to give notice of funding. I say that there was no requirement to give notice of funding prior to service of the proceedings, and that the period between service of the proceedings and conclusion was so short that the failure to serve formal notice of funding along with the proceedings was of no real consequence.

10. In the alternative, I ask for relief from sanctions. I do so by addressing the factors set out in CPR rule 3.9(1):

   a. **The interests of the administration of justice:** It is not in the interests of the administration of justice for legal representatives to go under-remunerated for work which, in good faith, they have carried out and carried out well. If the court were minded to acknowledge the claimant's failure to comply with the requirements to give notice of funding, that could adequately be done by imposing a costs sanction upon the claimant; it would, in my respectful submission, be disproportionate to deprive the claimant of the success fee.

   b. **Whether the application for relief has been made promptly:** The application was made the day after the failure to serve formal notice of funding of the conditional fee agreement came to light.

   c. **Whether the failure to comply was intentional:** The failure was not intentional.

   d. **Whether there is a good explanation for the failure:** I accept that there is no good explanation for the failure.

   e. **The extent to which the party in default has complied with other rules, practice directions, court orders and any relevant preaction protocol:** There has been compliance with all other rules, practice direction and court orders.

   f. **Whether the failure to comply was caused by the party or his legal representative:** The failure was caused by the legal representative.

   g. **Whether the trial date or the likely trial date can still be met if relief is granted:** This factor is not relevant.

   h. **The effect which the failure to comply had on each party:** This is an important point. The failure had no bearing whatsoever on the management of the claim or the defendant. This is because informal notice of funding had been given in the letter of claim. It is also because the matter settled so quickly after the service of proceedings that the period during which there was an absence of notice of funding was too short to have any bearing on the overall costs which are claimed.

   i. **The effect which the granting of relief would have on each party:** The effect of granting relief would be to put the parties back in the position that they expected to be. This has to be contrasted with the effect of not granting relief, which would be to award the defendant an unearned windfall.

11. For all these reasons I respectfully ask the court to allow the success fee in full (subject, of course, to it being reasonable in amount).'

PARTICULARS OF CLAIM FOR UNPAID SOLICITORS' FEES

IN THE ANYWHERE COUNTY COURT[1]   **Claim No: 0AW12345**

BETWEEN:

VW LLP   **Claimant**

- and -

XYZ Ltd   **Defendant**

PARTICULARS OF CLAIM

1. The Claimant is and at all material times was a firm of solicitors (incorporated as a limited liability partnership) whose business it was to provide legal services.
2. The Defendant is a former client of the Claimant, and at various times in the period from 1 May 20– instructed the Claimant to provide the following legal services:
    a.   advice and representation in a claim against QRS plc; and
    b.   advice concerning certain generic matters.
    Further details of the legal services may be found in the detailed breakdown of costs ('the bill of costs') dated 1 June 20–, attached hereto.
3. The aforesaid legal services were provided pursuant to a retainer hereinafter referred to as 'the Retainer'.
4. The terms of the Retainer were set out in a letter sent by the Claimant to the Defendant on 1 July 20– The terms of the Retainer permitted the Claimant to charge those hourly rates set out in the bill of costs.
5. In the alternative, if the terms of the Retainer were not as described above, then there was an implied term that the Defendant would pay the Claimant a reasonable professional fee for any work done by the Claimant. In the further alternative, the Claimant was entitled to quantum meruit.
6. It was an express term of the Retainer that the Defendant would pay the Claimant's fees within 30 days of receipt of an invoice.
7. Pursuant to the Retainer, the Claimant provided the legal services summarised in paragraph 2 herein and fully particularised in the bill of costs. As a result, the Claimant became entitled to raise invoices for its fees.
8. The Claimant rendered a number of invoices which are particularised in the Schedule ('the Schedule') annexed hereto. Those invoices were rendered on the dates particularised therein. In so far as any payments or part payments were made, they were for the amounts and were received on the dates particularised therein.
9. The Defendant has had delivery of all of the aforesaid invoices for a period of more than one month.
10. The sum of £23,467.83 was paid, but the sum of £52,399.03 remains unpaid (as particularised in the Schedule). The Claimant is entitled to payment of those unpaid fees (hereinafter referred to as 'the costs debt').
11. In so far as the costs debt relates to invoices which have not yet been paid (either in part or in full), the Claimant will raise no objection to an application for a detailed assessment pursuant to section 70 of the Solicitors Act 1974. For the avoidance of doubt, the Claimant does not itself apply for an assessment.
12. Furthermore, the Claimant claims interest pursuant to section 69 of the County Courts Act 1984 at a rate of 6 percent per year for such periods as the court sees fit.

AND the Claimant claims:

---

[1]   If it is anticipated that the client will request a detailed assessment, then it would usually be good practice to commence in the High Court rather than the county court (see **18.51**).

(1) £52,399.03;
(2) In the alternative, fees to be assessed by the court;
(3) In the alternative, quantum meruit;
(4) Interest as aforesaid; and
(5) Costs.

SERVED this...............day of...............20–

STATEMENT OF TRUTH

The Claimant believes that the facts stated in these Particulars of Claim are true

....

....

PARTICULARS OF CLAIM FOR UNPAID COSTS DRAFTSMEN'S FEES

The following is an example of Particulars of Claim to be used where a costs draftsman is suing for his fees. If the claim is straightforward, thought ought to be given to bringing a Part 8 Claim.

——— 0 ———

IN THE ANYWHERE COUNTY COURT   Claim No: 0AW12345

BETWEEN:

AB   Claimant

- and -

CD (a firm)   Defendant

_____

PARTICULARS OF CLAIM
_____

1. The Claimant is and was a costs draftsman who, at all material times, was practising on his own account.
2. The Defendant is and was a firm of solicitors who at all material times practised as such.
3. In about August 20– and for a period of about 3 years thereafter, the Defendant gave the Claimant instructions to provide legal services pertaining to the recovery of legal costs. The Defendant's instructions were ongoing, and related to the costs of a number of the Defendant's clients.
4. The basis on which those instructions were given was a retainer (hereinafter referred to as 'the Retainer'). The terms of the Retainer were contained in the Claimant's letter ('the letter') dated 21 August 20–. Those terms were:
    a. That the Defendant would pay the Claimant the prevailing guideline rate for a Grade C fee earner in Anywhere County Court (which at the time the letter was written was £130 per hour); and

     b.   That (unless otherwise agreed), the costs of preparing a bill of costs would be limited to 6 percent of the costs as drawn (excluding success fees and ATE premiums).

5.   In the alternative, if the terms of the Retainer were not as described in the letter, then there was an implied term that the Defendant would pay the Claimant a reasonable professional fee for any work done by the Claimant. In the further alternative, the Claimant was entitled to quantum meruit.

6.   It was an implied term of the Retainer that the Defendant would pay the Claimant's fees within a reasonable period of time after receipt of an invoice.

7.   Pursuant to the Retainer, the Claimant supplied legal services in relation to various bills of costs and associated work (both as paying party and as receiving party). As a result, the Claimant became entitled to raise invoices for his fees.

8.   The Claimant rendered a number of invoices which are particularised in Schedules One and Two.

9.   The invoices particularised in Schedule One are invoices for preparing bills of costs, and are therefore limited to 6 percent of the bills as drawn.

10.   The invoices particularised in Schedule Two are for work other than preparing bills of costs, and were therefore not subject to the 6 percent limit.

11.   The invoices were rendered on the dates particularised in the Schedules. The Defendant has had delivery of all of the aforesaid invoices for a substantial period of time, ranging from 4 months to 27 months. The Defendant has therefore been afforded a reasonable opportunity to pay those invoices.

12.   The Defendant has made payments totalling £2,000.00, none of which were in respect of any particular invoice.

13.   The sum of £12,254.64 remains unpaid. The Claimant is entitled to payment of those monies.

14.   For the avoidance of doubt, should the Defendant object to the level of the Claimant's fees, the Claimant will raise no objection to the court assessing those fees on whatever basis it sees fit.

Furthermore, the Claimant claims interest pursuant to section 69 of the County Courts Act 1984 at a rate of 6 percent per year to the date of judgment, which on 1 October 20– was £204.32, and which will increase by £2.01 per day thereafter.

AND the Claimant claims:

(1)   £12,254.64;
(2)   In the alternative, fees to be assessed by the court;
(3)   In the alternative, quantum meruit;
(4)   Interest as aforesaid; and
(5)   Costs.

SERVED this...............day of...............20–

STATEMENT OF TRUTH

The Claimant believes that the facts stated in these Particulars of Claim are true

....

....

DEFENCE TO CLAIM FOR UNPAID SOLICITORS' FEES AND COUNTERCLAIM FOR AN ASSESSMENT

IN THE ANYWHERE COUNTY COURT[2]   Claim No: 0AW12345

IN THE MATTER OF SECTION 70 OF THE
SOLICITORS ACT 1974 AND OF VW LLP
SOLICITORS[3]

BETWEEN:

VW LLP   Claimant

- and –

XYZ Ltd   Defendant

**DEFENCE AND COUNTERCLAIM
(PART 20 CLAIM)**

---

1. The terminology used in the Particulars of Claim is adopted.
2. Paragraphs 1 and 2 of the Particulars of Claim are admitted. The work referred to in sub-paragraph 2(a) and (b) of the Particulars of Claim are referred to herein as 'the contentious work' and 'the non-contentious work' respectively.
3. Paragraph 3 of the Particulars of Claim is admitted.
4. Paragraph 4 of the Particulars of Claim is admitted; it is averred that the Retainer also made express provision (or, in the alternative, implied provision) for the delivery of interim bills on account. It is averred that in so far as the retainer governed the contentious work, it was an entire contract by which a final right to payment would accrue only upon conclusion of the claim ('the Claim') referred to in sub-paragraph 2(a) of the Particulars of Claim. Those being the circumstances, the facility to render interim statute bills was a facility that the Claimant was entitled to use only for the purposes of rendering interim invoices for the non-contentious work. It is averred that all other invoices were for payments on account.
5. Given the admission made in the paragraph immediately above, the alternative cases in paragraph 5 of the Particulars of Claim do not arise. In so far as it they are relevant, they are denied on the basis that the terms of the Retainer were contained entirely within the letter referred to in paragraph 4 of the Particulars of Claim ('the letter'); in the context of a contract where the Defendant was entirely reliant on the Claimants for advice about the Claimant's fees), it was not open to the Claimant to rely on terms which were not expressly entered into the contract.
6. Paragraph 6 of the Particulars of Claim is admitted.
7. As to paragraph 7 of the Particulars of Claim, it is admitted that the Claimant provided legal services to the Defendant. It is averred that, at a time now unknown but very shortly after receipt of the letter, the Defendant specified that the legal services were to be provided by a qualified solicitor; in fact, they were primarily provided by unqualified fee earners (too numerous to particularise herein). It is averred that that was in breach of the Defendant's instructions.
8. In so far as paragraph 8 of the Particulars of Claim, it is admitted that the Claimant rendered a number of invoices as set out in the Schedules. For the avoidance of doubt, the accuracy of the Schedules is admitted. It is averred that in so far as the invoices related to contentious work, they were merely requests for payments on account.

---

[2] The Defendant applies for the matter to be transferred to the High Court: see paragraph 11. Ordinarily, this type of matter would be in the High Court.

[3] It is a moot point whether this is required; s 72(1) of the Solicitors Act 1972 states that a claim for an assessment must be made in the matter of the solicitors whose bill it is, but (unlike under the RSC) the CPR does not lay down any requirements in this regard.

9.   Paragraph 9 of the Particulars of Claim is admitted. It is averred that in so far as the contentious work is concerned, no interim statute bills have been delivered and that as such the Claimant is not entitled to bring proceedings for the recovery of those fees.

10.   Paragraph 10 is admitted and averred: part of the payment was in respect of the invoices for the non-contentious work. Those invoices have been paid in full; those invoices have been identified in the attached schedule. It is admitted that £42,498.96 remains unpaid, but it is denied that the Claimant is entitled to payment (in full, or at all). The Claimant's fees pertaining to the non-contentious work have been discharged in full. The Claimant has no entitlement to any fees for the contentious work: this is because (a) the Claimant wrongly terminated the retainer prior to discharging the whole of his obligations concerning the contentious work, and (b) the Claimant failed to discharge its obligations to provide legal services solely via a qualified solicitor. In view of these things, in so far as the contentious claim is concerned, there has been a complete failure to perform the obligations arising under the contract of retainer.

11.   In so far as paragraph 11 is concerned, the Defendant lawfully and reasonably seeks an assessment of the Claimant's costs pursuant to section 70 of the Solicitors Act 1974.[4] The Defendant applies herein for an order for an assessment of the bills marked as such in the Schedule attached hereto. In accordance with CPR rule 67.3(1), the Defendant applies for this matter to be transferred to the High Court. In so far as the Defendant is required to prove an entitlement to an assessment pursuant to section 70 of the Solicitors Act 1974, the Defendant relies upon the following:

(a)   The fact that the Defendant has reasonably delayed making an application for an assessment pending a complaint to the Legal Complaints Service;

(b)   The fact that sums now claimed significantly exceed the sums that the Defendant reasonably believed that it would be asked to pay;

(c)   The fact that the Defendant raises a credible challenge to entitlement to costs; and

(d)   The fact that the costs which are claimed are unreasonably high.

COUNTERCLAIM (PART 20 CLAIM)

---

12.   Paragraphs 1 to 11 herein are repeated.

13.   The Claimant gave negligent advice about funding as set out below.

PARTICULARS

(a)   The Claimant failed to make any (or any adequate) enquiries as to the Defendant's eligibility for Before the Event (BTE) legal expenses insurance;

(b)   The Claimant wrongly assumed that because the Defendant was a small business, it would not have BTE insurance;

(c)   The Defendant wrongly failed to advise the Defendant that it did have BTE insurance which could have covered this claim;

(d)   In the premises, the Defendant failed to advise the Claimant to use BTE funding rather than to enter into the Retainer and fund the matter itself.

PARTICULARS OF THE EFFECT OF THE NEGLIGENCE

---

[4]   An application for an assessment is sometimes set out in a counterclaim, but this is not a necessity. On a strict reading of the CPR, an application notice has to be served even where an application is made in pleadings (see CPR, rr 67.3(2) and 23.3).

Had the Defendant been properly advised about the availability of BTE funding, it would have elected to fund the proceedings by way of BTE funding rather than privately. As such, the Defendant has suffered a loss in that it has been made liable for fees which otherwise it would have avoided (or in respect of which it would have had the benefit of an indemnity).

14. The Defendant seeks damages to be assessed, such damages to be set off against any fees and disbursements for which the Defendant might otherwise be liable. In the interests of proportionality (and in an effort to allow all matters to be disposed of by the judge hearing the detailed assessment), the Part 20 Claim is limited to a claim for set-off.

15. The Defendant seeks interest on the aforesaid damages pursuant to section 69 of the County Courts Act 1984; again, that claim is limited to a claim for set-off.

AND the Defendant claims:

1. A detailed assessment pursuant to section 70 of the Solicitors Act 1974;
2. Relief in the form of a finding of undue influence;
3. Damages limited to £5,000 and in any event limited to those sums claimed by the Claimant in its claim;
4. Set-off;
5. Interest pursuant to statute; and
6. Costs.

PART 18 REQUESTS FOR FURTHER DETAILS IN RESPECT OF ADDITIONAL LIABILITY

In an appropriate case, the following Part 18 Requests may be made. It should be noted that the court will not always allow these questions to be put, especially where there is no reason to believe that there was alternative means of funding.

'These Questions are put pursuant to CPR Part 18 and should be answered by no later than 4.00 pm on . . . . 20 . . .

'The following questions should receive factual answers rather than assertions about the perceived adequacy of the investigations that were made prior to the Claimant entering into his conditional fee agreement. These questions should be answered on the basis of reasonably diligent factual enquiries.

1. Please state whether, at the time of his accident, the Claimant was a member of a trade union.
2. If the Claimant was a member of a trade union, please state the name of that union and whether that union offered legal assistance to its members.
3. Please state whether the Claimant or any adult member of his household had household contents insurance; if so, please state the name of the insurer and the name of the insurance product.
4. Please state whether the Claimant or any adult member of his household had motor insurance; if so, please state the name of the insurer and the name of the insurance product.
5. If any insurance policy has been identified in the two questions immediately above, please state whether the policy (or policies) in question had any form of BTE attached to them; if so, please state the name of the legal expense insurer and the name of the insurance product.

6.   Please state whether the Claimant or any adult member of his household had any form of stand-alone BTE insurance at the time of his accident.'

——— 0 ———

Finally, neither the author nor Jordans Publishing Ltd accepts any liability whatsoever arising out of the use of these precedents: they may be used only on that basis.

Chapter 44

TABLES AND FIGURES

Hourly rates

Rates are set out in the following bracketed matrix:

Band Number |Grade A Grade B|
                 |Grade C Grade D|

	2003	2005	2007	2008	2009	2010
City of London: EC1, EC2, EC3, EC4	City |342 247| |189 116|	City |359 259| |198 122|	City |380 274| |210 129|	City |396 285| |219 134|	London 1 |402 291| |222 136|	London 1 |409 296| |226 138|
Central London: W1, WC1, WC2, SW1	Central |263 200| |163 105|	Central |276 210| |171 110|	Central |292 222| |181 116|	Central |304 231| |189 121|	London 2 |312 238| |193 124|	London 2 |317 242| |196 126|
Outer London: (All other London post codes: W, NW, N, E, SE, SW and Bromley, Croydon, Dartford, Gravesend and Uxbridge)	Outer |189–221 142–189| |137 100|	Outer |198–232 149–198| |144 105|	Outer |210–246 158–210| |152 111|	Outer |219–256 165–219| |158 116|	London 3 |225–263 169–225| |162 119|	London 3 |229–267 172–229| |165 121|
Accrington	Band 3 |150 135| |115 85|	Band 3 |158 142| |121 90|	Band 3 |167 150| |128 95|	Band 3 |174 156| |133 99|	National 2/3 |198 174| |144 109|	National 2 |201 177| |146 111|
Aldershot	Band 1 |175 155| |130 95|	Band 1 |184 163| |137 100|	Band 2 |183 161| |133 101|	Band 1 |203 180| |151 110|	National 1 |213 189| |158 116|	National 1 |217 192| |161 118|
Altrincham	Band 2 |165 145| |120 90|	Band 2 |173 152| |126 95|	Band 2 |183 161| |133 101|	Band 2 |191 168| |139 105|	National 2/3 |198 174| |144 109|	National 2 |201 177| |146 111|
Aylesbury	Band 2 |165 145| |120 90|	Band 2 |173 152| |126 95|	See Thames Valley	See Thames Valley	See Thames Valley	See Thames Valley
Basingstoke	Band 1 |175 155| |130 95|	Band 1 |184 163| |137 100|	Band 1 |195 173| |145 106|	Band 1 |203 180| |151 110|	National 1 |213 189| |158 116|	National 1 |217 192| |161 118|
Bath	Band 2 |165 145| |120 90|	Band 2 |173 152| |126 95|	Band 2 |183 161| |133 101|	Band 2 |191 168| |139 105|	National 2/3 |198 174| |144 109|	National 2 |201 177| |146 111|
Bedford	Band 2 |165 145| |120 90|	Band 2 |173 152| |126 95|	Band 1 |195 173| |145 106|	Band 2 |191 168| |139 105|	National 2/3 |198 174| |144 109|	National 2 |201 177| |146 111|
Birkenhead	Band 1 |175 155| |130 95|	Band 1 |184 163| |137 100|	Band 1 |195 173| |145 106|	Band 1 |203 180| |151 110|	National 1 |213 189| |158 116|	National 1 |217 192| |161 118|
Birmingham Inner	Band 1 |175 155| |130 95|	Band 1 |184 163| |137 100|	Band 1 |195 173| |145 106|	Band 1 |203 180| |151 110|	National 1 |213 189| |158 116|	National 1 |217 192| |161 118|
Birmingham Outer	Band 3 |150 135| |115 85|	Band 3 |158 142| |121 90|	Band 3 |167 150| |128 95|	Band 3 |174 156| |133 99|	National 2/3 |198 174| |144 109|	National 2 |201 177| |146 111|
Blackburn	Band 3 |150 135| |115 85|	Band 3 |158 142| |121 90|	Band 3 |167 150| |128 95|	Band 3 |174 156| |133 99|	National 2/3 |198 174| |144 109|	National 2 |201 177| |146 111|
Blackpool	Band 3 |150 135| |115 85|	Band 3 |158 142| |121 90|	Band 3 |167 150| |128 95|	Band 3 |174 156| |133 99|	National 2/3 |198 174| |144 109|	National 2 |201 177| |146 111|
Bournemouth (including Poole)	Band 1¹ |175 155| |130 95|	Band 1² |184 163| |137 100|	Band 1 |195 173| |145 106|	Band 1 |203 180| |151 110|	National 1 |213 189| |158 116|	National 1 |217 192| |161 118|

¹ Poole is not mentioned in the Guide, but Poole is usually regarded as attracting the same rate as Bournemouth.
² *Ibid.*

Hourly rates

	2003	2005	2007	2008	2009	2010
Bradford	Band 3 [150 115 / 135 85]	Band 3 [158 121 / 142 90]	Band 3 [167 128 / 150 95]	Band 3 [174 133 / 156 99]	National 2/3 [198 144 / 174 109]	National 2 [201 146 / 177 111]
Bristol	Band 2³ [165 120 / 145 90]	Band 1 [184 137 / 163 100]	Band 1 [195 145 / 173 106]	Band 1 [203 151 / 180 110]	National 1 [213 158 / 189 116]	National 1 [217 161 / 192 118]
Burnley	Band 3 [150 115 / 135 85]	Band 3 [158 121 / 142 90]	Band 3 [167 128 / 150 95]	Band 3 [174 133 / 156 99]	National 2/3 [198 144 / 174 109]	National 2 [201 146 / 177 111]
Bury	Band 2 [165 120 / 145 90]	Band 2 [173 126 / 152 95]	Band 2 [183 133 / 161 101]	Band 2 [191 139 / 168 105]	National 2/3 [198 144 / 174 109]	National 2 [201 146 / 177 111]
Bury St Edmunds	Band 2 [165 120 / 145 90]	Band 2 [173 126 / 152 95]	Band 2 [183 133 / 161 101]	Band 2 [191 139 / 168 105]	National 2/3 [198 144 / 174 109]	National 2 [201 146 / 177 111]
Cambridge City	Band 1 [175 130 / 155 95]	Band 1 [184 137 / 163 100]	Band 1 [195 145 / 173 106]	Band 1 [203 151 / 180 110]	National 1 [213 158 / 189 116]	National 1 [217 161 / 192 118]
Cambridge County	Band 2 [165 120 / 145 90]	Band 2 [173 126 / 152 95]	Band 2 [183 133 / 161 101]	Band 2 [191 139 / 168 105]	National 2/3 [198 144 / 174 109]	National 2 [201 146 / 177 111]
Canterbury	Band 1 [175 130 / 155 95]	Band 1 [184 137 / 163 100]	Band 1 [195 145 / 173 106]	Band 1 [203 151 / 180 110]	National 1 [213 158 / 189 116]	National 1 [217 161 / 192 118]
Cardiff (Inner)	Band 1 [175 130 / 155 95]	Band 1 [184 137 / 163 100]	Band 1 [195 145 / 173 106]	Band 1 [203 151 / 180 110]	National 1 [213 158 / 189 116]	National 1 [217 161 / 192 118]
Cardiff (Outer)	Band 2 [165 120 / 145 90]	Band 2 [173 126 / 152 95]	Band 2 [183 133 / 161 101]	Band 2 [191 139 / 168 105]	National 2/3 [198 144 / 174 109]	National 2 [201 146 / 177 111]
Chelmsford North	Band 2 [165 120 / 145 90]	Band 2 [173 126 / 152 95]	Band 2 [183 133 / 161 101]	Band 2 [191 139 / 168 105]	National 2/3 [198 144 / 174 109]	National 2 [201 146 / 177 111]
Chelmsford South	Band 2 [165 120 / 145 90]	Band 2 [173 126 / 152 95]	Band 1 [195 145 / 173 106]	Band 1 [203 151 / 180 110]	National 1 [213 158 / 189 116]	National 1 [217 161 / 192 118]
Cheltenham	Band 2 [165 120 / 145 90]	Band 2 [173 126 / 152 95]	Band 2 [183 133 / 161 101]	Band 2 [191 139 / 168 105]	National 2/3 [198 144 / 174 109]	National 2 [201 146 / 177 111]
Cheshire	Band 3 [150 115 / 135 85]	Band 2 [173 126 / 152 95]	Band 2 [183 133 / 161 101]	Band 2 [191 139 / 168 105]	National 2/3 [198 144 / 174 109]	National 2 [201 146 / 177 111]
Chester	Band 3 [150 115 / 135 85]	Band 3 [158 121 / 142 90]	Band 2 [183 133 / 161 101]	Band 1 [203 151 / 180 110]	National 1 [213 158 / 189 116]	National 1 [217 161 / 192 118]
Chorley	Band 3 [150 115 / 135 85]	Band 3 [158 121 / 142 90]	Band 3 [167 128 / 150 95]	Band 3 [174 133 / 156 99]	National 2/3 [198 144 / 174 109]	National 2 [201 146 / 177 111]
Cornwall	Band 3 [150 115 / 135 85]	Band 3 [158 121 / 142 90]	Band 3 [167 128 / 150 95]	Band 3 [174 133 / 156 99]	National 2/3 [198 144 / 174 109]	National 2 [201 146 / 177 111]
Coventry	Band 3 [150 115 / 135 85]	Band 3 [158 121 / 142 90]	Band 2 [183 133 / 161 101]	Band 2 [191 139 / 168 105]	National 2/3 [198 144 / 174 109]	National 2 [201 146 / 177 111]
Cumbria	Band 3 [150 115 / 135 85]	Band 3 [158 121 / 142 90]	Band 3 [167 128 / 150 95]	Band 3 [174 133 / 156 99]	National 2/3 [198 144 / 174 109]	National 2 [201 146 / 177 111]
Derbyshire	Band 3 [150 115 / 135 85]	Band 3 [158 121 / 142 90]	Band 2 [183 133 / 161 101]	Band 2 [191 139 / 168 105]	National 2/3 [198 144 / 174 109]	National 2 [201 146 / 177 111]

³ From 2004, Bristol was reclassified as Band 1.

Hourly rates

	2003	2005	2007	2008	2009	2010
Devon	Band 3 | 150 135 / 115 85	Band 3 | 158 142 / 121 90	Band 3 | 167 150 / 128 95	Band 3 | 174 156 / 133 99	National 2/3 | 198 174 / 144 109	National 2 | 201 177 / 146 111
Dewsbury	Band 3 | 150 135 / 115 85	Band 3 | 158 142 / 121 90	Band 3 | 167 150 / 128 95	Band 3 | 174 156 / 133 99	National 2/3 | 198 174 / 144 109	National 2 | 201 177 / 146 111
Doncaster	No specific entry	No specific entry	Band 2 | 183 161 / 133 101	Band 2 | 191 168 / 139 105	National 2/3 | 198 174 / 144 109	National 2 | 201 177 / 146 111
Dorset	Band 2 | 165 145 / 120 90	Band 2 | 173 152 / 126 95	Band 1 | 195 173 / 145 106	Band 1 | 203 180 / 151 110	National 1 | 213 189 / 158 116	National 1 | 217 192 / 161 118
Dudley	Band 3 | 150 135 / 115 85	Band 3 | 158 142 / 121 90	Band 2 | 183 161 / 133 101	Band 2 | 191 168 / 139 105	National 2/3 | 198 174 / 144 109	National 2 | 201 177 / 146 111
East Suffolk	No specific entry	No specific entry	Band 1 | 195 173 / 145 106	Band 1 | 203 180 / 151 110	National 1 | 213 189 / 158 116	National 1 | 217 192 / 161 118
Epsom	Band 1 | 175 155 / 130 95	Band 1 | 184 163 / 137 100	Band 1 | 195 173 / 145 106	Band 1 | 203 180 / 151 110	National 1 | 213 189 / 158 116	National 1 | 217 192 / 161 118
Essex	No specific entry	No specific entry	Band 1 | 195 173 / 145 106	Band 1 | 203 180 / 151 110	National 1 | 213 189 / 158 116	National 1 | 217 192 / 161 118
Evesham	Band 3 | 150 135 / 115 85	Band 3 | 158 142 / 121 90	Band 3 | 167 150 / 128 95	Band 3 | 174 156 / 133 99	National 2/3 | 198 174 / 144 109	National 2 | 201 177 / 146 111
Exeter	Band 3 | 150 135 / 115 85	Band 3 | 158 142 / 121 90	Band 2 | 183 161 / 133 101	Band 2 | 191 168 / 139 105	National 2/3 | 198 174 / 144 109	National 2 | 201 177 / 146 111
Fareham	Band 1 | 175 155 / 130 95	Band 1 | 184 163 / 137 100	Band 1 | 195 173 / 145 106	Band 1 | 203 180 / 151 110	National 1 | 213 189 / 158 116	National 1 | 217 192 / 161 118
Farnham	Band 1 | 175 155 / 130 95	Band 1 | 184 163 / 137 100	Band 1 | 195 173 / 145 106	Band 1 | 203 180 / 151 110	National 1 | 213 189 / 158 116	National 1 | 217 192 / 161 118
Gloucester	Band 2 | 165 145 / 120 90	Band 2 | 173 152 / 126 95	Band 2 | 183 161 / 133 101	Band 2 | 191 168 / 139 105	National 2/3 | 198 174 / 144 109	National 2 | 201 177 / 146 111
Grimsby	Band 3 | 150 135 / 115 85	Band 3 | 158 142 / 121 90	Band 3 | 167 150 / 128 95	Band 3 | 174 156 / 133 99	National 2/3 | 198 174 / 144 109	National 2 | 201 177 / 146 111
Guildford	Band 1 | 175 155 / 130 95	Band 1 | 184 163 / 137 100	Band 1 | 195 173 / 145 106	Band 1 | 203 180 / 151 110	National 1 | 213 189 / 158 116	National 1 | 217 192 / 161 118
Halifax	Band 3 | 150 135 / 115 85	Band 3 | 158 142 / 121 90	Band 3 | 167 150 / 128 95	Band 3 | 174 156 / 133 99	National 2/3 | 198 174 / 144 109	National 2 | 201 177 / 146 111
Hampshire	Band 2 | 165 145 / 120 90	Band 2 | 173 152 / 126 95	Band 1 | 195 173 / 145 106	Band 1 | 203 180 / 151 110	National 1 | 213 189 / 158 116	National 1 | 217 192 / 161 118
Harlow	Band 1 | 175 155 / 130 95	Band 1 [4] | 184 163 / 137 100	Band 1 | 195 173 / 145 106	Band 1 | 203 180 / 151 110	National 1 | 213 189 / 158 116	National 1 | 217 192 / 161 118
Harrogate	Band 2 | 165 145 / 120 90	Band 2 | 173 152 / 126 95	Band 2 | 183 161 / 133 101	Band 2 | 191 168 / 139 105	National 2/3 | 198 174 / 144 109	National 2 | 201 177 / 146 111
Hereford	Band 3 | 150 135 / 115 85	Band 3 | 158 142 / 121 90	Band 3 | 167 150 / 128 95	Band 3 | 174 156 / 133 99	National 2/3 | 198 174 / 144 109	National 2 | 201 177 / 146 111
Hertford	Band 2 | 165 145 / 120 90	Band 2 | 173 152 / 126 95	Band 2 | 183 161 / 133 101	Band 2 | 191 168 / 139 105	National 2/3 | 198 174 / 144 109	National 2 | 201 177 / 146 111

[4] There is no specific mention of Harlow in this edition of the Guide; it is likely to be in Band 1 but the contrary is arguable.

Hourly rates

	2003	2005	2007	2008	2009	2010
Hitchin	Band 2 | 165 145 / 120 90	Band 2 | 173 152 / 126 95	Band 2 | 183 161 / 133 101	Band 2 | 191 168 / 139 105	National 2/3 | 198 174 / 144 109	National 2 | 201 177 / 146 111
Huddersfield	Band 3 | 150 135 / 115 85	Band 3 | 158 142 / 121 90	Band 3 | 167 150 / 128 95	Band 3 | 174 156 / 133 99	National 2/3 | 198 174 / 144 109	National 2 | 201 177 / 146 111
Hull (City)	Band 2 | 165 145 / 120 90	Band 2 | 173 152 / 126 95	Band 2 | 183 161 / 133 101	Band 2 | 191 168 / 139 105	National 2/3 | 198 174 / 144 109	National 2 | 201 177 / 146 111
Hull Outer	Band 3 | 150 135 / 115 85	Band 3 | 158 142 / 121 90	Band 3 | 167 150 / 128 95	Band 3 | 174 156 / 133 99	National 2/3 | 198 174 / 144 109	National 2 | 201 177 / 146 111
Isle of Wight	Band 2 | 165 145 / 120 90	Band 2 | 173 152 / 126 95	Band 1 | 195 173 / 145 106	Band 1 | 203 180 / 151 110	National 1 | 213 189 / 158 116	National 1 | 217 192 / 161 118
Keighley	Band 3 | 150 135 / 115 85	Band 3 | 158 142 / 121 90	Band 3 | 167 150 / 128 95	Band 3 | 174 156 / 133 99	National 2/3 | 198 174 / 144 109	National 2 | 201 177 / 146 111
Kidderminster	Band 3 | 150 135 / 115 85	Band 3 | 158 142 / 121 90	Band 3 | 167 150 / 128 95	Band 3 | 174 156 / 133 99	National 2/3 | 198 174 / 144 109	National 2 | 201 177 / 146 111
Kingston	Band 1 | 175 155 / 130 95	Band 1 | 184 163 / 137 100	Band 1 | 195 173 / 145 106	Band 1 | 203 180 / 151 110	National 1 | 213 189 / 158 116	National 1 | 217 192 / 161 118
Lancaster	Band 3 | 150 135 / 115 85	Band 3 | 158 142 / 121 90	Band 3 | 167 150 / 128 95	Band 3 | 174 156 / 133 99	National 2/3 | 198 174 / 144 109	National 2 | 201 177 / 146 111
Leeds Inner	Band 1 [5] | 175 155 / 130 95	Band 1 [5] | 184 163 / 137 100	Band 1 [6] | 195 173 / 145 106	Band 1 [6] | 203 180 / 151 110	National 1 [6] | 213 189 / 158 116	National 1 [6] | 217 192 / 161 118
Leeds Outer	Band 2 | 165 145 / 120 90	Band 2 | 173 152 / 126 95	Band 2 | 183 161 / 133 101	Band 2 | 191 168 / 139 105	National 2/3 | 198 174 / 144 109	National 2 | 201 177 / 146 111
Leicester	Band 3 | 150 135 / 115 85	Band 3 | 158 142 / 121 90	Band 3 | 167 150 / 128 95	Band 3 | 174 156 / 133 99	National 2/3 | 198 174 / 144 109	National 2 | 201 177 / 146 111
Leigh	Band 2 | 165 145 / 120 90	Band 2 | 173 152 / 126 95	Band 2 | 183 161 / 133 101	Band 2 | 191 168 / 139 105	National 2/3 | 198 174 / 144 109	National 2 | 201 177 / 146 111
Lewes	Band 1 | 175 155 / 130 95	Band 1 | 184 163 / 137 100	Band 1 | 195 173 / 145 106	Band 1 | 203 180 / 151 110	National 1 | 213 189 / 158 116	National 1 | 217 192 / 161 118
Lincoln	Band 3 | 150 135 / 115 85	Band 2 | 173 152 / 126 95	Band 2 | 183 161 / 133 101	Band 2 | 191 168 / 139 105	National 2/3 | 198 174 / 144 109	National 2 | 201 177 / 146 111
Liverpool	Band 1 | 175 155 / 130 95	Band 1 | 184 163 / 137 100	Band 1 | 195 173 / 145 106	Band 1 | 203 180 / 151 110	National 1 | 213 189 / 158 116	National 1 | 217 192 / 161 118
Lowestoft	Band 2 | 165 145 / 120 90	Band 2 | 173 152 / 126 95	Band 2 | 183 161 / 133 101	Band 2 | 191 168 / 139 105	National 2/3 | 198 174 / 144 109	National 2 | 201 177 / 146 111
Ludlow	Band 3 | 150 135 / 115 85	Band 3 | 158 142 / 121 90	Band 3 | 167 150 / 128 95	Band 3 | 174 156 / 133 99	National 2/3 | 198 174 / 144 109	National 2 | 201 177 / 146 111
Luton	Band 2 | 165 145 / 120 90	Band 2 | 173 152 / 126 95	Band 2 | 183 161 / 133 101	Band 2 | 191 168 / 139 105	National 2/3 | 198 174 / 144 109	National 2 | 201 177 / 146 111
Maidstone	Band 1 | 175 155 / 130 95	Band 1 | 184 163 / 137 100	Band 1 | 195 173 / 145 106	Band 1 | 203 180 / 151 110	National 1 | 213 189 / 158 116	National 1 | 217 192 / 161 118

[5] The area was within a 1 km radius of the City Art Gallery.
[6] The area was within a 2 km radius of the City Art Gallery.

Civil Costs: Law and Practice

Hourly rates

	2003	2005	2007	2008	2009	2010
Manchester Central	Band 1 |175 155| |130 95|	Band 1 |184 163| |137 100|	Band 1 |195 173| |145 106|	Band 1 |203 180| |158 110|	National 1 |213 189| |158 116|	National 1 |217 192| |161 118|
Manchester Outer (Oldham, Bolton, Tameside)	Band 2 |165 145| |120 90|	Band 2 |173 152| |126 95|	Band 2 |183 161| |133 101|	Band 2 |191 168| |139 105|	National 2/3 |198 174| |144 109|	National 2 |201 177| |146 111|
Medway	Band 1 |175 155| |130 95|	Band 1 |184 163| |137 100|	Band 1 |195 173| |145 106|	Band 1 |203 180| |151 110|	National 1 |213 189| |158 116|	National 1 |217 192| |161 118|
Milton Keynes	Band 2 |165 145| |120 90|	Band 2 |173 152| |126 95|	No specific entry	No specific entry	No specific entry	No specific entry
Nelson	Band 3 |150 135| |115 85|	Band 3 |158 142| |121 80|	Band 3 |167 150| |128 95|	Band 3 |174 156| |133 99|	National 2/3 |198 174| |144 109|	National 2 |201 177| |146 111|
Newcastle - City Centre[7]	Band 1 |175 155| |130 95|	Band 1 |184 163| |137 100|	Band 1 |195 173| |145 106|	Band 1 |203 180| |151 110|	National 1 |213 189| |158 116|	National 1 |217 192| |161 118|
Newcastle (other than City Centre)	Band 3 |150 135| |115 85|	Band 3 |158 142| |121 90|	Band 2 |183 161| |133 101|	Band 2 |191 168| |139 105|	National 2/3 |198 174| |144 109|	National 2 |201 177| |146 111|
Newport	Band 2 |165 145| |120 90|	Band 2 |173 152| |126 95|	Band 2 |183 161| |133 101|	Band 2 |191 168| |139 105|	National 2/3 |198 174| |144 109|	National 2 |201 177| |146 111|
Norfolk	Band 2 |165 145| |120 90|	Band 2 |173 152| |126 95|	Band 2 |183 161| |133 101|	Band 2 |191 168| |139 105|	National 2/3 |198 174| |144 109|	National 2 |201 177| |146 111|
North Wales	Band 3 |150 135| |115 85|	Band 3 |158 142| |121 90|	Band 2 |183 161| |133 101|	Band 2 |191 168| |139 105|	National 2/3 |198 174| |144 109|	National 2 |201 177| |146 111|
Northampton	Band 3 |150 135| |115 85|	Band 3 |158 142| |121 90|	Band 3 |167 150| |128 95|	Band 3 |174 156| |133 99|	National 2/3 |198 174| |144 109|	National 2 |201 177| |146 111|
Norwich City	Band 1 [8] |175 155| |130 95|	Band 1 [9] |184 163| |137 100|	Band 1 |195 173| |145 106|	Band 1 |203 180| |151 110|	National 1 |213 189| |158 116|	National 1 |217 192| |161 118|
Nottingham	Band 3 |150 135| |115 85|	Band 3 |158 142| |121 90|	Band 2 |183 161| |133 101|	Band 2 |191 168| |139 105|	National 2/3 |198 174| |144 109|	National 2 |201 177| |146 111|
Nottingham City	Band 1 |175 155| |130 95|	Band 1 |184 163| |137 100|	Band 1 |195 173| |145 106|	Band 1 |203 180| |151 110|	National 1 |213 189| |158 116|	National 1 |217 192| |161 118|
Oswestry	Band 3 |150 135| |115 85|	Band 3 |158 142| |121 90|	Band 3 |167 150| |128 95|	Band 3 |174 156| |133 99|	National 2/3 |198 174| |144 109|	National 2 |201 177| |146 111|
Oxford	Band 2 |165 145| |120 90|	Band 2 |173 152| |126 95|	Band 1 |195 173| |145 106|	Band 1 |203 180| |151 110|	National 1 |213 189| |158 116|	National 1 |217 192| |161 118|
Peterborough	Band 2 |165 145| |120 90|	Band 2 |173 152| |126 95|	Band 2 |183 161| |133 101|	Band 2 |191 168| |139 105|	National 2/3 |198 174| |144 109|	National 2 |201 177| |146 111|
Plymouth	Band 3 |150 135| |115 85|	Band 3 |158 142| |121 90|	Band 2 |183 161| |133 101|	Band 2 |191 168| |139 105|	National 2/3 |198 174| |144 109|	National 2 |201 177| |146 111|
Pontefract	Band 2 |165 145| |120 90|	Band 2 |173 152| |126 95|	Band 2 |183 161| |133 101|	Band 2 |191 168| |139 105|	National 2/3 |198 174| |144 109|	National 2 |201 177| |146 111|

[7] The area was within a 2 mile radius of St Nicholas Cathedral.
[8] This rate applied to just 'Norwich', rather than 'Norwich City'.
[9] This rate applied to just 'Norwich', rather than 'Norwich City'.

Hourly rates

	2003	2005	2007	2008	2009	2010
Portsmouth	Band 1 | 175 155 | 130 95	Band 1 | 184 163 | 137 100	Band 1 | 195 173 | 145 106	Band 1 | 203 180 | 151 110	National 1 | 213 189 | 158 116	National 1 | 217 192 | 161 118
Preston	Band 3 | 150 135 | 115 85	Band 3 | 158 142 | 121 90	Band 3 | 167 150 | 128 95	Band 3 | 174 156 | 133 99	National 2/3 | 198 174 | 144 109	National 2 | 201 177 | 146 111
Rawenstall	Band 3 | 150 135 | 115 85	Band 3 | 158 142 | 121 90	Band 3 | 167 150 | 128 95	Band 3 | 174 156 | 133 99	National 2/3 | 198 174 | 144 109	National 2 | 201 177 | 146 111
Reading	See Thames Valley					
Redditch	Band 3 | 150 135 | 115 85	Band 3 | 158 142 | 121 90	Band 3 | 167 150 | 128 95	Band 3 | 174 156 | 133 99	National 2/3 | 198 174 | 144 109	National 2 | 201 177 | 146 111
Reigate	Band 1 | 175 155 | 130 95	Band 1 | 184 163 | 137 100	Band 1 | 195 173 | 145 106	Band 1 | 203 180 | 151 110	National 1 | 213 189 | 158 116	National 1 | 217 192 | 161 118
Rugby	Band 3 | 150 135 | 115 85	Band 3 | 158 142 | 121 90	Band 2 | 183 161 | 133 101	Band 2 | 191 168 | 139 105	National 2/3 | 198 174 | 144 109	National 2 | 201 177 | 146 111
Salford	Band 2 | 165 145 | 120 90	Band 2 | 173 152 | 126 95	Band 2 | 183 161 | 133 101	Band 2 | 191 168 | 139 105	National 2/3 | 198 174 | 144 109	National 2 | 201 177 | 146 111
Scarborough & Ripon	Band 3 | 150 135 | 115 85	Band 3 | 158 142 | 121 90	Band 3 | 167 150 | 128 95	Band 3 | 174 156 | 133 99	National 2/3 | 198 174 | 144 109	National 2 | 201 177 | 146 111
Sheffield	Band 2 | 165 145 | 120 90	Band 2 | 173 152 | 126 95	Band 2 | 183 161 | 133 101	Band 2 | 191 168 | 139 105	National 2/3 | 198 174 | 144 109	National 2 | 201 177 | 146 111
Shrewsbury	Band 3 | 150 135 | 115 85	Band 3 | 158 142 | 121 90	Band 3 | 167 150 | 128 95	Band 3 | 174 156 | 133 99	National 2/3 | 198 174 | 144 109	National 2 | 201 177 | 146 111
Skegness	Band 3[10] | 150 135 | 115 85	Band 3[11] | 158 142 | 121 90	Band 3 | 167 150 | 128 95	Band 3 | 174 156 | 133 99	National 2/3 | 198 174 | 144 109	National 2 | 201 177 | 146 111
Skipton	Band 3 | 150 135 | 115 85	Band 3 | 158 142 | 121 90	Band 3 | 167 150 | 128 95	Band 3 | 174 156 | 133 99	National 2/3 | 198 174 | 144 109	National 2 | 201 177 | 146 111
Slough	Band 2 | 165 145 | 120 90	Band 2 | 173 152 | 126 95	See Thames Valley	See Thames Valley	See Thames Valley	See Thames Valley
South & West Wales	Band 3 | 150 135 | 115 85	Band 3 | 158 142 | 121 90	Band 3 | 167 150 | 128 95	Band 3 | 174 156 | 133 99	National 2/3 | 198 174 | 144 109	National 2 | 201 177 | 146 111
South Yorkshire	Band 2 | 165 145 | 120 90	Band 2 | 173 152 | 126 95	Band 2 | 183 161 | 133 101	Band 2 | 191 168 | 139 105	National 2/3 | 198 174 | 144 109	National 2 | 201 177 | 146 111
Southampton	Band 1 | 175 155 | 130 95	Band 1 | 184 163 | 137 100	Band 1 | 195 173 | 145 106	Band 1 | 203 180 | 151 110	National 1 | 213 189 | 158 116	National 1 | 217 192 | 161 118
Southport	Band 2 | 165 145 | 120 90	Band 2 | 173 152 | 126 95	Band 2 | 183 161 | 133 101	Band 2 | 191 168 | 139 105	National 2/3 | 198 174 | 144 109	National 2 | 201 177 | 146 111
St Albans	Band 2 | 165 145 | 120 90	Band 2 | 173 152 | 126 95	Band 2 | 183 161 | 133 101	Band 2 | 191 168 | 139 105	National 2/3 | 198 174 | 144 109	National 2 | 201 177 | 146 111
St Helens	Band 2 | 165 145 | 120 90	Band 2 | 173 152 | 126 95	Band 2 | 183 161 | 133 101	Band 2 | 191 168 | 139 105	National 2/3 | 198 174 | 144 109	National 2 | 201 177 | 146 111

---

10 Skegness is not specifically mention in this edition of the Guide to Summary Assessment, but given the rates allowed in surrounding areas, it is likely that Skegness is Band 3.

11 As above.

Hourly rates

	2003	2005	2007	2008	2009	2010
Stafford	Band 3 | 150 135 / 115 85	Band 3 | 158 142 / 121 90	Band 3 | 167 150 / 128 95	Band 3 | 174 156 / 133 99	National 2/3 | 198 174 / 144 109	National 2 | 201 177 / 146 111
Stockport	Band 2 | 165 145 / 120 90	Band 2 | 173 152 / 126 95	Band 2 | 183 161 / 133 101	Band 2 | 191 168 / 139 105	National 2/3 | 198 174 / 144 109	National 2 | 201 177 / 146 111
Stoke	Band 3 | 150 135 / 115 85	Band 3 | 158 142 / 121 90	Band 3 | 167 150 / 128 95	Band 3 | 174 156 / 133 99	National 2/3 | 198 174 / 144 109	National 2 | 201 177 / 146 111
Stourbridge	Band 3 | 150 135 / 115 85	Band 3 | 158 142 / 121 90	Band 2 | 183 161 / 133 101	Band 2 | 191 168 / 139 105	National 2/3 | 198 174 / 144 109	National 2 | 201 177 / 146 111
Strafford	Band 3 | 150 135 / 115 85	Band 3 | 158 142 / 121 90	Band 2 | 183 161 / 133 101	Band 2 | 191 168 / 139 105	National 2/3 | 198 174 / 144 109	National 2 | 201 177 / 146 111
Swansea	Band 2 | 165 145 / 120 90	Band 2 | 173 152 / 126 95	Band 2 | 183 161 / 133 101	Band 2 | 191 168 / 139 105	National 2/3 | 198 174 / 144 109	National 2 | 201 177 / 146 111
Swindon	Band 1 | 175 155 / 130 95	Band 1 | 184 163 / 137 100	Band 1 | 195 173 / 145 106	Band 1 | 203 180 / 151 110	National 1 | 213 189 / 158 116	National 1 | 217 192 / 161 118
Tamworth	Band 3 | 150 135 / 115 85	Band 3 | 158 142 / 121 90	Band 3 | 167 150 / 128 95	Band 3 | 174 156 / 133 99	National 2/3 | 198 174 / 144 109	National 2 | 201 177 / 146 111
Taunton	Band 3 | 150 135 / 115 85	Band 3 | 158 142 / 121 90	Band 2 | 183 161 / 133 101	Band 2 | 191 168 / 139 105	National 2/3 | 198 174 / 144 109	National 2 | 201 177 / 146 111
Teesside	Band 3 | 150 135 / 115 85	Band 3 | 158 142 / 121 90	Band 3 | 167 150 / 128 95	Band 3 | 174 156 / 133 99	National 2/3 | 198 174 / 144 109	National 2 | 201 177 / 146 111
Telford	Band 3 | 150 135 / 115 85	Band 3 | 158 142 / 121 90	Band 3 | 167 150 / 128 95	Band 3 | 174 156 / 133 99	National 2/3 | 198 174 / 144 109	National 2 | 201 177 / 146 111
Thames Valley[12]	n/a	n/a	Band 1 | 195 173 / 145 106	Band 1 | 203 180 / 151 110	National 1 | 213 189 / 158 116	National 1 | 217 192 / 161 118
Tunbridge Wells	Band 1 | 175 155 / 130 95	Band 1 | 184 163 / 137 100	Band 1 | 195 173 / 145 106	Band 1 | 203 180 / 151 110	National 1 | 213 189 / 158 116	National 1 | 217 192 / 161 118
Wakefield	Band 2 | 165 145 / 120 90	Band 2 | 173 152 / 126 95	Band 2 | 183 161 / 133 101	Band 2 | 191 168 / 139 105	National 2/3 | 198 174 / 144 109	National 2 | 201 177 / 146 111
Walsall	Band 3 | 150 135 / 115 85	Band 3 | 158 142 / 121 90	Band 2 | 183 161 / 133 101	Band 2 | 191 168 / 139 105	National 2/3 | 198 174 / 144 109	National 2 | 201 177 / 146 111
Warwick	Band 3 | 150 135 / 115 85	Band 3 | 158 142 / 121 90	Band 2 | 183 161 / 133 101	Band 2 | 191 168 / 139 105	National 2/3 | 198 174 / 144 109	National 2 | 201 177 / 146 111
Watford	Band 2 | 165 145 / 120 90	Band 2 | 173 152 / 126 95	Band 1 | 195 173 / 145 106	Band 1 | 203 180 / 151 110	National 1 | 213 189 / 158 116	National 1 | 217 192 / 161 118
Wigan	Band 2 | 165 145 / 120 90	Band 2 | 173 152 / 126 95	Band 2 | 183 161 / 133 101	Band 2 | 191 168 / 139 105	National 2/3 | 198 174 / 144 109	National 2 | 201 177 / 146 111
Wiltshire	Band 2 | 165 145 / 120 90	Band 2 | 173 152 / 126 95	Band 1 | 195 173 / 145 106	Band 1 | 203 180 / 151 110	National 1 | 213 189 / 158 116	National 1 | 217 192 / 161 118
Winchester	Band 1 | 175 155 / 130 95	Band 1 | 184 163 / 137 100	Band 1 | 195 173 / 145 106	Band 1 | 203 180 / 151 110	National 1 | 213 189 / 158 116	National 1 | 217 192 / 161 118

---

[12] This is usually taken to include the following: Aylesbury, Basingstoke, High Wycombe, Maidenhead, Newbury, Reading, Slough, Woking; Bracknell and Oxford have their own specific entries.

Hourly rates

	2003	2005	2007	2008	2009	2010
Wolverhampton	Band 3 |150 135| |115 85|	Band 3 |158 142| |121 90|	Band 2 |183 161| |133 101|	Band 2 |191 168| |139 105|	National 2/3 |198 174| |144 109|	National 2 |201 177| |146 111|
Worcester	Band 3 |150 135| |115 85|	Band 3 |158 142| |121 90|	Band 3 |167 150| |128 95|	Band 3 |174 156| |133 99|	National 2/3 |198 174| |144 109|	National 2 |201 177| |146 111|
Yeovil	Band 3 |150 135| |115 85|	Band 3 |158 142| |121 90|	Band 2 |183 161| |133 101|	Band 2 |191 168| |139 105|	National 2/3 |198 174| |144 109|	National 2 |201 177| |146 111|
York	Band 2 |165 145| |120 90|	Band 2 |173 152| |126 95|	Band 2 |183 161| |133 101|	Band 2 |191 168| |139 105|	National 2/3 |198 174| |144 109|	National 2 |201 177| |146 111|

Civil Costs: Law and Practice

Hourly rates in graphical form

The following graphs set out the hourly rates in graphical form; some of the data points have been extrapolated. The thin black lines are regression analyses (with a coefficient of determination (R²) overlying the regression. The method of regression is (simple) linear for all of the Bands save for Band Three, which has been analysed using polynomial regression.

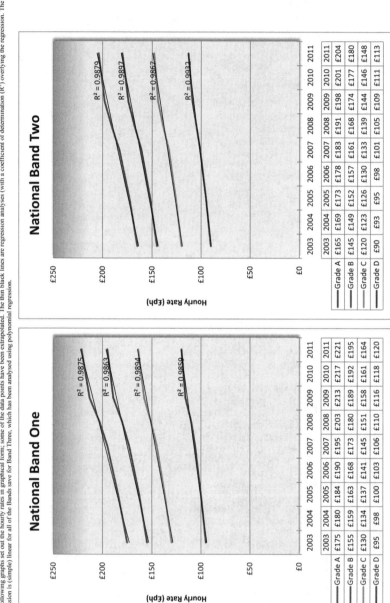

National Band One

$R^2 = 0.9875$
$R^2 = 0.9863$
$R^2 = 0.9894$
$R^2 = 0.9850$

Hourly Rate (£ph)

	2003	2004	2005	2006	2007	2008	2009	2010	2011
Grade A	£175	£180	£184	£190	£195	£203	£213	£217	£221
Grade B	£155	£159	£163	£168	£173	£180	£189	£192	£195
Grade C	£130	£134	£137	£141	£145	£151	£158	£161	£164
Grade D	£95	£98	£100	£103	£106	£110	£116	£118	£120

National Band Two

$R^2 = 0.9879$
$R^2 = 0.9897$
$R^2 = 0.9867$
$R^2 = 0.9932$

Hourly Rate (£ph)

	2003	2004	2005	2006	2007	2008	2009	2010	2011
Grade A	£165	£169	£173	£178	£183	£191	£198	£201	£204
Grade B	£145	£149	£152	£157	£161	£168	£174	£177	£180
Grade C	£120	£123	£126	£130	£133	£139	£144	£146	£148
Grade D	£90	£93	£95	£98	£101	£105	£109	£111	£113

Hourly rates in graphical form

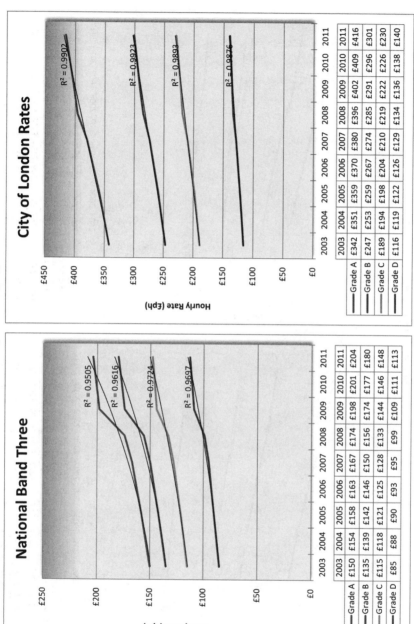

City of London Rates

	2003	2004	2005	2006	2007	2008	2009	2010	2011
Grade A	£342	£351	£359	£370	£380	£396	£402	£409	£416
Grade B	£247	£253	£259	£267	£274	£285	£291	£296	£301
Grade C	£189	£194	£198	£204	£210	£219	£222	£226	£230
Grade D	£116	£119	£122	£126	£129	£134	£136	£138	£140

$R^2 = 0.9902$
$R^2 = 0.9923$
$R^2 = 0.9893$
$R^2 = 0.9876$

National Band Three

	2003	2004	2005	2006	2007	2008	2009	2010	2011
Grade A	£150	£154	£158	£163	£167	£174	£198	£201	£204
Grade B	£135	£139	£142	£146	£150	£156	£174	£177	£180
Grade C	£115	£118	£121	£125	£128	£133	£144	£146	£148
Grade D	£85	£88	£90	£93	£95	£99	£109	£111	£113

$R^2 = 0.9505$
$R^2 = 0.9616$
$R^2 = 0.9724$
$R^2 = 0.9697$

Hourly rates in graphical form

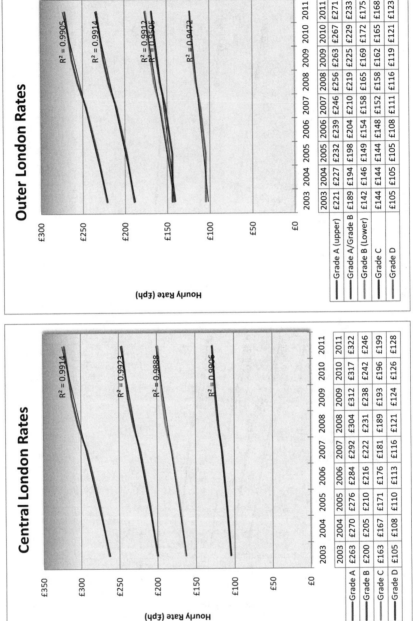

Miscellaneous tables

A+B rate converter

To convert Guideline to "A plus B"		To convert "A plus B" to Guideline	
% above Guideline	"B" factor	Intended "B" factor	Required increase in Guideline rate
0%	50%	50%	0%
2%	53%	60%	7%
5%	58%	65%	10%
7½%	61%	70%	13%
10%	65%	75%	17%
15%	73%	80%	20%
20%	80%	85%	23%
25%	88%	90%	27%
30%	95%	95%	30%
33%	100%	100%	33%
40%	110%	105%	37%
45%	118%	110%	40%
50%	125%	115%	43%
55%	133%	125%	50%
60%	140%	130%	53%
67%	151%	135%	57%
80%	170%	140%	60%
85%	178%	145%	63%
90%	185%	150%	67%

Tax Rates

	VAT	IPT
Prior to 1 December 2008	17½%	5%
Between 1 December 2008 and 31 December 2009	15%	5%
Between 1 January 2010 and 4 January 2011	17½%	5%
After 3 January 2011	20%	6%

Consumer Price Index[13]

	CPI
2012[14]	125
2011	119.6
2010	114.5
2009	110.8
2008	108.5
2007	104.7
2006	102.3
2005	100.0
2004	98
2003	96.7
2002	95.4
2001	94.2
2000	93.1

	2001	2002	2003	2004	2005	2006	2007	2008	2009	2010	2011	2012
2012[14]												
2011												104.5%
2010											104.5%	109.2%
2009										103.3%	107.9%	112.8%
2008									102.1%	105.5%	110.2%	115.2%
2007								103.6%	105.8%	109.4%	114.2%	119.4%
2006							102.3%	106.1%	108.3%	111.9%	116.9%	122.2%
2005						102.3%	104.7%	108.5%	110.8%	114.5%	119.6%	125.0%
2004					102.0%	104.4%	106.8%	110.7%	113.1%	116.8%	122.0%	127.6%
2003				101.3%	103.4%	105.8%	108.3%	112.2%	114.6%	118.4%	123.7%	129.3%
2002			101.4%	102.7%	104.8%	107.2%	109.7%	113.7%	116.1%	120.0%	125.4%	131.0%
2001		101.3%	102.7%	104.0%	106.2%	108.6%	111.1%	115.2%	117.6%	121.5%	127.0%	132.7%
2000	101.2%	102.5%	103.9%	105.3%	107.4%	109.9%	112.5%	116.5%	119.0%	123.0%	128.5%	134.3%

[13] To adjust a fee from its original value to a real value in any given year, the original value is multiplied by the percentage in the appropriate cell.

[14] This is estimated.

Civil Costs: Law and Practice

Medical disbursements

	Mobile Doctors 2012[15] (for fast track cases)	AMRO 2011[16]	AMRO 2010[17]
General medical practitioners			
GP Report (no medical records)	£225.00	£195 if paid within 90 days, otherwise £220	£195 if paid within 90 days, otherwise £220
Review of Medical Records	£55.00	£50 if paid within 90 days, otherwise £55	£50 if paid within 90 days, otherwise £55
Medical specialisms			
Cardiologist or chest physician	From £915.00		
Dermatologist	From £575.00		
Gastroenterologist	From £905.00		
Neurologist	From £775.00		
Paediatrician	From £485.00		
Pain Management Specialist	From £910.00		
Rheumatologist	From £910.00		
Surgical specialisms			
Accident and emergency	£410.00	£375 if paid within 90 days, otherwise £410	£375 if paid within 90 days, otherwise £410
General Surgeon	From £600.00		
Neurosurgeon	From £775.00		
Obstetrician and gynaecologist	From £650.00		
Orthopaedic	£465.00	£425 if paid within 90 days, otherwise £465	£425 if paid within 90 days, otherwise £465
Plastic Surgeon	From £720.00		
Urologist	From £700.00		
Vascular Surgeon	From £600.00		

	Mobile Doctors 2012[15] (for fast track cases)	AMRO 2011[16]	AMRO 2010[17]
Mental health specialisms			
Psychologist or psychiatrist[18]	From £625.00		
Child Psychologist	From £785.00		
Neuropsychologist[19]	From £1,810.00		
Head, neck, eyes and dental			
Dentist	From £595.00		
Ear, nose and throat surgeon	From £600.00		
Ophthalmologist	From £562.00		
Oral and maxillofacial surgeon	From £830.00		
Orthodontist	From £910.00		
Trichologist (hair)	From £665.00		
Miscellaneous			
Supplementary Addendum report	Cost + £30.00	Cost plus £25 if paid within 90 days, otherwise, £30	Cost plus £25 if paid within 90 days, otherwise, £30
First failure to attend	Nil		
Medical Record Fee	Cost + £30.00	Cost charged by data provider plus £25 if paid within 90 days or £30 if not	Cost charged by data provider plus £25 if paid within 90 days or £30 if not
Subsequent failure to attend	£65.00		

---

15 This is based on the published price list effective from December 2011. All prices are stated to "prices from" the given figure.

16 This is based on the agreement dated 2 April 2011; it applies only to certain classes of case which, in broad terms, are similar to fast track claims.

17 This is based on the agreement dated 30 March 2010; it applies only to certain classes of case which, in broad terms, are similar to fast track claims.

18 Including child physiatrist

19 This would usually include a certain number of investigations.

Court fees

Number and description of fee	Amount of fee from 1 October 2007[20]	Amount of fee from 1 May 2008[21]	Amount of fee from 13 July 2009[22]	Amount of fee from 4 April 2011[23]
1 Starting proceedings (High Court and county court)				
1.1 On starting proceedings (including proceedings issued after permission to issue is granted but excluding CPC cases brought by Money Claim OnLine users) to recover a sum of money where the sum claimed:				
(a) does not exceed £300	£30	£30	£30	£35
(b) exceeds £300 but does not exceed £500	£45	£45	£45	£50
(c) exceeds £500 but does not exceed £1,000	£60	£65	£65	£70
(d) exceeds £1,000 but does not exceed £1,500	£70	£75	£75	£80
(e) exceeds £1,500 but does not exceed £3,000	£80	£85	£85	£95
(f) exceeds £3,000 but does not exceed £5,000	£108	£108	£108	£120
(g) exceeds £5,000 but does not exceed £15,000	£225	£225	£225	£245
(h) exceeds £15,000 but does not exceed £50,000	£360	£360	£360	£395
(i) exceeds £50,000 but does not exceed £100,000	£630	£630	£630	£685
(j) exceeds £100,000 but does not exceed £150,000	£810	£810	£810	£885
(k) exceeds £150,000 but does not exceed £200,000	£990	£990	£990	£1,080
(l) exceeds £200,000 but does not exceed £250,000	£1,170	£1,170	£1,170	£1,275
(m) exceeds £250,000 but does not exceed £300,000	£1,350	£1,350	£1,350	£1,475
(n) exceeds £300,000 or is not limited	£1,530	£1,530	£1,530	£1,670

Interest: Where the claimant is making a claim for interest on a specified sum of money, the amount on which the fee is calculated is the total amount of the claim and the interest.

Additional or alternative to a claim for recovery of land or goods (money claims): Where a claim for money is additional or alternative to a claim for recovery of land or goods, only fee 1.4 or 1.5 shall be payable.

Additional or alternative to a claim for recovery of land or goods or goods (non-money claims): Where a claim for money is additional to a non-money claim (other than a claim for recovery of land or goods), then fee 1.1 is payable in addition to fee 1.5; where a claim for money is alternative to a non-money claim (other than a claim for recovery of land or goods), only fee 1.1 shall be payable in the High Court, and, in the county court, fee 1.1 or fee 1.5 shall be payable, whichever is the greater.

More than one non-money claim: Where more than one non-money claim is made in the same proceedings, fee 1.5 shall be payable once only, in addition to any fee which may be payable under fee 1.1.

Amendments: Where the claim or counterclaim is amended, and the fee paid before amendment is less than that which would have been payable if the document, as amended, had been so drawn in the first instance, the party amending the document shall pay the difference.

Solicitors and client assessments: Fees 1.1 and 1.5 shall not be payable where fee 1.8(b) applies;

---

20 The Civil Proceedings Fees (Amendment) (No.2) Order 2007 (SI 2007/2176)
21 The Civil Proceedings Fees Order 2008 (SI 2008/1053)
22 The Civil Proceedings Fees (Amendment) Order 2009 (SI 2009/1498)
23 The Civil Proceedings Fees (Amendment) Order 2011 (SI 2011/586)

Civil Costs: Law and Practice

Court fees

Number and description of fee	Amount of fee from 1 October 2007[20]	Amount of fee from 1 May 2008[21]	Amount of fee from 13 July 2009[22]	Amount of fee from 4 April 2011[23]
Judicial review: Fees 1.1 and 1.5 shall not be payable where fee 1.9(a) applies.				
Miscellaneous: Fees 1.1 and 1.5 shall not be payable where fee 10.1 or fee 3 applies.				
1.2 On starting proceedings to recover a sum of money in Claim Production Centre cases brought by Centre users, where the sum claimed:				
(a) does not exceed £300	£15	£15	£15	£15
(b) exceeds £300 but does not exceed £500	£30	£30	£30	£30
(c) exceeds £500 but does not exceed £1,000	£55	£55	£55	£55
(d) exceeds £1,000 but does not exceed £1,500	£65	£65	£65	£65
(e) exceeds £1,500 but does not exceed £3,000	£75	£75	£75	£75
(f) exceeds £3,000 but does not exceed £5,000	£85	£85	£85	£85
(g) exceeds £5,000 but does not exceed £15,000	£190	£190	£190	£190
(h) exceeds £15,000 but does not exceed £50,000	£310	£310	£310	£310
(i) exceeds £50,000 but does not exceed £100,000	£550	£550	£550	£550
1.3 On starting proceedings to recover a sum of money brought by Money Claim OnLine users where the sum claimed:				
(a) does not exceed £300	£25	£25	£25	£25
(b) exceeds £300 but does not exceed £500	£35	£35	£35	£35
(c) exceeds £500 but does not exceed £1,000	£65	£65	£60	£60
(d) exceeds £1,000 but does not exceed £1,500	£75	£75	£70	£70
(e) exceeds £1,500 but does not exceed £3,000	£85	£85	£80	£80
(f) exceeds £3,000 but does not exceed £5,000	£100	£100	£100	£100
(g) exceeds £5,000 but does not exceed £15,000	£210	£210	£210	£210
(h) exceeds £15,000 but does not exceed £50,000	£340	£340	£340	£340
(i) exceeds £50,000 but does not exceed £100,000	£595	£595	£595	£595
1.4 On starting proceedings for the recovery of land:[24]				
(a) in the High Court;	n/a	n/a	£400	£465
(b) in the county court, other than where fee 1.4(c) applies;	n/a	n/a	£150	£175
(c) using the Possession Claims Online website.	£100	£100	£100	£100
1.5 On starting proceedings for any other remedy (including proceedings issued after permission to issue is granted)—				

[24] The description of these categories and the categories themselves changed over the years; the descriptions given are close approximations to the Orders themselves.

Court fees

Number and description of fee	Amount of fee from 1 October 2007[20]	Amount of fee from 1 May 2008[21]	Amount of fee from 13 July 2009[22]	Amount of fee from 4 April 2011[23]
—in the High Court	£400	£400	£400	£465
—in the county court	£150	£150	£150	£175
1.6 On the filing of proceedings against a party or parties not named in the proceedings[25]	£40	£40	£40	£45
1.7 On the filing of a counterclaim[26]	The same fee as if the remedy sought were the subject of separate proceedings			
1.8 (a) On an application for permission to issue proceedings	£40	£40	£40	£45
(b) On an application for an order under Part III of the Solicitors Act 1974(27) for the assessment of costs payable to a solicitor by his client or on starting costs-only proceedings	£40	£40	£40	£45
1.9(a) On starting proceedings for judicial review	£50	£50	£50	£60
Where the court has made an order giving permission to proceed with a claim for judicial review, there shall be payable by the claimant within 7 days of service on the claimant of that order:				
➤ **1.9(b) if the judicial review procedure has been started**	£180	£180	£180	£215
➤ **1.9(c) if the claim for judicial review was started otherwise than by using the judicial review procedure**	£50	£50	£50	£60
2 General Fees (High Court and county court): allocation and listing				
Counterclaims alone (allocation): Fee 2.1 shall be payable by the claimant except where the action is proceeding on the counterclaim alone, when it shall be payable by the defendant—				
—on the defendant filing an allocation questionnaire; or				
—where the court dispenses with the need for an allocation questionnaire, within 14 days of the date of despatch of the notice of allocation to track; or				
—where the CPR or a Practice Direction provide for automatic allocation or provide that the rules on allocation shall not apply, within 28 days of the filing of the defence to the counterclaim (or the filing of the last defence to the counterclaim if there is more than one party entitled to file a defence to the counterclaim), or within 28 days of the expiry of the time permitted for filing all defences to the counterclaim if sooner.				
Counterclaims alone (listing): Fee 2.2 shall be payable by the claimant except where the action is proceeding on the counterclaim alone, when it shall be payable by the defendant—				
—on the defendant filing a pre-trial checklist (listing questionnaire); or				
—where the court fixes the trial date or trial week without the need for a listing questionnaire, within 14 days of the date of despatch of the notice (or the date when oral notice is given if no written notice is given) of the trial week or the trial date if no trial week is fixed.				
Allocation and reallocation: Where fee 2.1 is payable on the filing of an allocation questionnaire, by the claimant or the defendant as the case may be, the fee payable is based on the track for the case specified in the allocation questionnaire. If the case is subsequently allocated to a track which attracts a higher fee then the difference in fee is payable, by the party liable to pay the fee, within 14 days of the date of despatch				

[25] Fee 1.6 shall be payable by a defendant who adds or substitutes a party or parties to the proceedings or by a claimant who adds or substitutes a defendant or defendants.

[26] No fee is payable on a counterclaim which a defendant is required to make under the CPR because he contends that he has any claim or is entitled to any remedy relating to a grant of probate of a will, or letters of administration of an estate, of a deceased person.

[27] 1974 c.47.

Court fees

of notice of allocation to track. If the case is allocated to a track which attracts a lower fee the difference in fee will be refunded. Fees 2.1 and 2.2 shall be payable as appropriate where the court allocates a case to track for a trial of the assessment of damages.

Group litigation: Fees 2.1 and 2.2 shall not be payable in relation to claims managed under a GLO after that GLO is made.

Payable only once: Fees 2.1 and 2.2 shall be payable once only in the same proceedings.

Part 8 claims: Fee 2.1 shall not be payable where the procedure in Part 8 of the CPR is used.

Early listing: Fee 2.2 shall not be payable where the court fixed the hearing date on the issue of the claim.

Claims for less than £1,500 in the county court: Fee 2.1 shall not be payable in proceedings where the only claim is a claim to recover a sum of money and the sum claimed does not exceed £1,500.

Small claims in the county court: Fee 2.2 shall not be payable in respect of a case on the small claims track.

2.1 On the claimant filing an allocation questionnaire; or

➤ where the court dispenses with the need for an allocation questionnaire, within 14 days of the date of despatch of the notice of allocation to track; or

➤ where the CPR or a Practice Direction provide for automatic allocation or provide that the rules on allocation shall not apply, within 28 days of the filing of the defence (or the filing of the last defence if there is more than one defendant), or within 28 days of the expiry of the time permitted for filing all defences if sooner:

Number and description of fee	Amount of fee from 1 October 2007[20]	Amount of fee from 1 May 2008[21]	Amount of fee from 13 July 2009[22]	Amount of fee from 4 April 2011[23]
(a) if the case is on the small claims track and the claim exceeds £1,500	£35	£35	£35	£40
(b) if the case is on the fast track or multi-track	£200	£200	£200	£220
2.2 On the claimant filing a pre-trial check list (listing questionnaire); or where the court fixes the trial date or trial week without the need for a pre-trial check list, within 14 days of the date of despatch of the notice (or the date when oral notice is given if no written notice is given) or the trial week or the trial date if no trial week is fixed.[28]	n/a	£100	£100	£110

2.3 On the occasion of fee 2.2 becoming payable; or where the claim is on the small claims track, within 14 days of the date of despatch of the notice (or the date when oral notice is given if no written notice is given) of the trial week or the trial date if no trial week the following fees are payable:

	Amount of fee from 1 October 2007[20]	Amount of fee from 1 May 2008[21]	Amount of fee from 13 July 2009[22]	Amount of fee from 4 April 2011[23]
(a) a case on the multi-track	£1,000	£1,000	£1,000	£1,090
(b) a case on the fast track	£500	£500	£500	£545
(c) a case on the small claims track where the sum claimed:				
(i) does not exceed £300	£25	£25	£25	£25
(ii) exceeds £300 but does not exceed £500	£50	£50	£50	£55
(iii) exceeds £500 but does not exceed £1,000	£75	£75	£75	£80
(iv) exceeds £1,000 but does not exceed £1,500	£100	£100	£100	£110
(v) exceeds £1,500 but does not exceed £3,000	£150	£150	£150	£165
(vi) exceeds £3,000 but does not exceed £5,000	£300	£300	£300	£325

---

28 The wording of this provision has changed over the years.

Court fees

Number and description of fee	Amount of fee from 1 October 2007[20]	Amount of fee from 1 May 2008[21]	Amount of fee from 13 July 2009[22]	Amount of fee from 4 April 2011[23]
Counterclaims alone: Fee 2.3 shall be payable by the claimant except where the action is proceeding on the counterclaim alone, when it shall be payable by the defendant—				
—on the defendant filing a listing questionnaire; or				
—where the claim is on the small claims track or the court fixes the trial date or trial week without the need for a listing questionnaire, within 14 days of the date of despatch of the notice (or the date when oral notice is given if no written notice is given) of the trial week or the trial date if no trial week is fixed.				
Settlements and refunds: Where a case is on the multi-track or fast track and, after a hearing date has been fixed, the court receives notice in writing from the party who paid the hearing fee that the case has been settled or discontinued then the following percentages of the hearing fee shall be refunded—				
(i) 100% if the court is notified more than 28 days before the hearing;				
(ii) 75% if the court is notified between 14 and 28 days before the hearing;				
(iii) 50% if the court is notified between 7 and 14 days before the hearing.				
Where a case is on the small claims track and, after a hearing date has been fixed, the court receives notice in writing from the party who paid the hearing fee, at least 7 days before the date set for the hearing, that the case has been settled or discontinued the hearing fee shall be refunded in full.				
Early listing: Fee 2.3 shall not be payable in respect of a case where the court fixed the hearing date on the issue of the claim.				
Appeals, applications, etc				
2.4 In the High Court on filing—				
—an appellant's notice, or				
—a respondent's notice where the respondent is appealing or wishes to ask the appeal court to uphold the order of the lower court for reasons different from or additional to those given by the lower court	£200	£200	£200	£235
2.5 In the county court on filing—				
—an appellant's notice, or				
—a respondent's notice where the respondent is appealing or wishes to ask the appeal court to uphold the order of the lower court for reasons different from or additional to those given by the **lower court:, the fees set out below will be payable.**				
(a) in a claim allocated to the small claims track	£100	£100	£100	£115
(b) in all other claims	£120	£120	£120	£135
Appeals from detailed assessments: Fees 2.4 and 2.5 do not apply on appeals against a decision made in detailed assessment proceedings.				
2.6 On an application on notice where no other fee is specified	£75	£75	£75	£80
2.7 On an application by consent or without notice for a judgment or order where no other fee is specified, the following fees will be payable:				
	£40	£40	£40	£45
Request for judgment on admission: For the purpose of fee 2.7 a request for a judgment or order on admission or in default shall not constitute an application and no fee shall be payable.				
Adjournment by consent: Fee 2.7 shall not be payable in relation to an application by consent for an adjournment of a hearing where the application is received by the court at least 14 days before the date set for that hearing.				
Applications in appeal notices: Fees 2.6 and 2.7 shall not be payable when an application is made in an appeal notice or is filed at the same time as an appeal notice.				

Court fees

Number and description of fee	Amount of fee from 1 October 2007[20]	Amount of fee from 1 May 2008[21]	Amount of fee from 13 July 2009[22]	Amount of fee from 4 April 2011[23]
2.8 On an application for a summons or order for a witness to attend court to be examined on oath or an order for evidence to be taken by deposition, other than an application for which fee 7.2 or 8.3 is payable	£35	£35	£35	£40
2.9 On an application to vary a judgment or suspend enforcement (where more than one remedy is sought in the same application only one fee shall be payable)	£35	£35	£35	£40
2.10 Register of judgments kept under section 98 of the Courts Act 2003—				
On a request for the issue of a certificate of satisfaction	£15	£15	£15	£15
3 Companies Act 1985(29) and Insolvency Act 1986(30) (High Court and county court)[31]				
3.1 On entering a bankruptcy petition:				
(a) if presented by a debtor or the personal representative of a deceased debtor	£150	£150	£150	£175
(b) if presented by a creditor or other person	£190	£190	£190	£220
3.2 On entering a petition for an administration order	£150	£150	£150	£175
3.3 On entering any other petition	£190	£190	£190	£220
3.4(a) On a request for a certificate of discharge from bankruptcy	£60	£60	£60	£70
(b) and after the first certificate, for each copy	£5	£5	£5	£5
3.5 On an application under the Companies Act 1985 or the Insolvency Act 1986 other than one brought by petition and where no other fee is specified	£130	£130	£130	£155
Existing proceedings: Fee 3.5 is not payable where the application is made in existing proceedings.				
3.6 On an application for the conversion of a voluntary arrangement into a winding up or bankruptcy under Article 37 of Council Regulation (EC) No 1346/2000	£130	£130	£130	£155
3.7 On an application, for the purposes of Council Regulation (EC) No 1346/2000, for an order confirming creditors' voluntary winding up (where the company has passed a resolution for voluntary winding up, and no declaration under section 89 of the Insolvency Act 1986 has been made)	£30	£30	£30	£35
3.8 On filing— —a notice of intention to appoint an administrator under paragraph 14 of Schedule B1 to the Insolvency Act 1986 or in accordance with paragraph 27 of that Schedule; or— a notice of appointment of an administrator in accordance with paragraphs 18 or 29 of	£30	£30	£30	£35

(29) 1985 c.6.
(30) 1986 c.45.
31 **Partnerships:** One fee only is payable where more than one petition is presented in relation to a partnership.

Court fees

Number and description of fee	Amount of fee from 1 October 2007[20]	Amount of fee from 1 May 2008[21]	Amount of fee from 13 July 2009[22]	Amount of fee from 4 April 2011[23]
that Schedule				
Administrator: Where a person pays fee 3.8 on filing a notice of intention to appoint an administrator, no fee shall be payable on that same person filing a notice of appointment of that administrator.				
3.9 On submitting a nominee's report under section 2(2) of the Insolvency Act 1986	£30	£30	£30	£35
3.10 On filing documents in accordance with paragraph 7(1) of Schedule A1 to the Insolvency Act 1986	£30	£30	£30	£35
3.11 On an application by consent or without notice within existing proceedings where no other fee is specified	£30	£30	£30	£35
3.12 On an application with notice within existing proceedings where no other fee is specified	£60	£60	£60	£70
3.13 On a search in person of the bankruptcy and companies records, in a county court	£40	£40	£40	£45
Requests and applications with no fee: No fee is payable on a request or on an application to the Court by the Official Receiver when applying only in the capacity of Official Receiver to the case (and not as trustee or liquidator), or on an application to set aside a statutory demand.				
Copy Documents (Court of Appeal, High Court and county court)				
4.1 On a request for a copy of a document (other than where fee 4.2 applies):				
(a) for ten pages or less	£5	£5	£5	£5
(b) for each subsequent page	50p	50p	50p	50p
Fee 4.1 shall be payable for a faxed copy or for examining a plain copy and marking it as an examined copy and shall be payable whether or not the copy is issued as an office copy.				
4.2 On a request for a copy of a document on a computer disk or in other electronic form, for each such copy	£5	£5	£5	£5
Detailed assessments				
5 Determination of costs (Senior (formerly Supreme) Court and county court).				
Court of Protection: Fee 5 does not apply to the determination in the Senior (formerly Supreme) Court of costs incurred in the Court of Protection.				
5.1 On the filing of a request for detailed assessment where the party filing the request is legally aided or is funded by the LSC and no other party is ordered to pay the costs of the proceedings—				
—in the Senior (formerly Supreme) Court	£120	£120	£140	£145
—in the county court	£105	£105	£140	£145
5.2 On the filing of a request for detailed assessment in any case where fee 5.1 does not apply; or on the filing of a request for a hearing date for the assessment of costs payable to a solicitor by his client pursuant to an order under Part III of the Solicitors Act 1974				
where the amount of the costs to be assessed (excluding VAT and disbursements):				

Court fees

Number and description of fee	Amount of fee from 1 October 2007[20]	Amount of fee from 1 May 2008[21]	Amount of fee from 13 July 2009[22]	Amount of fee from 4 April 2011[23]
(a) does not exceed £15,000	£300	£300	£300	£325
(b) exceeds £15,000 but does not exceed £50,000	£600	£600	£600	£655
(c) exceeds £50,000 but does not exceed £100,000	£900	£900	£900	£980
(d) exceeds £100,000 but does not exceed £150,000	£1,200	£1,200	£1,200	£1,310
(e) exceeds £150,000 but does not exceed £200,000	£1,500	£1,500	£1,500	£1,635
(f) exceeds £200,000 but does not exceed £300,000	£2,250	£2,250	£2,250	£2,455
(g) exceeds £300,000 but does not exceed £500,000	£3,750	£3,750	£3,750	£4,090
(h) exceeds £500,000	£5,000	£5,000	£5,000	£5,455
Where there is a combined party and party and legal aid, or a combined party and party and LSC, or a combined party and party, legal aid and LSC determination of costs, fee 5.2 shall be attributed proportionately to the party and party, legal aid, or LSC (as the case may be) portions of the bill on the basis of the amount allowed.				
5.3 On a request for the issue of a default costs certificate—				
— in the Senior (formerly Supreme) Court	£50	£50	£60	£60
— in the county court	£45	£45	£60	£60
5.4 On an appeal against a decision made in detailed assessment proceedings—				
— in the Senior (formerly Supreme) Court	£200	£200	£200	£205
— in the county court	£105	£105	£200	£205
5.5 On applying for the court's approval of a certificate of costs payable from the Community Legal Service Fund—				
— in the Senior (formerly Supreme) Court	£50	£50	£50	£50
— in the county court	£35	£35	£50	£50
Fee 5.5 is payable at the time of applying for the court's approval and is recoverable only against the Community Legal Service Fund.				
5.6 On a request or application to set aside a default costs certificate—				
— in the Senior (formerly Supreme) Court	£100	£100	£100	£105
— in the county court	£65	£65	£100	£105
Court of Protection				
6 Determination in the Senior (formerly Supreme) Court of costs incurred in the Court of Protection				
6.1 On the filing of a request for detailed assessment:				
(a) where the amount of the costs to be assessed (excluding VAT and disbursements)	£100	£100	£100	£110

Court fees

Number and description of fee	Amount of fee from 1 October 2007[20]	Amount of fee from 1 May 2008[21]	Amount of fee from 13 July 2009[22]	Amount of fee from 4 April 2011[23]
does not exceed £3,000				
(b) in all other cases	£200	£200	£200	£220
6.2 On an appeal against a decision made in detailed assessment proceedings	£60	£60	£60	£65
6.3 On a request or application to set aside a default costs certificate	£60	£60	£60	£65
Enforcement in the High Court				
7.1 On sealing a writ of execution/possession/delivery	£50	£50	£50	£60
Where the recovery of a sum of money is sought in addition to a writ of possession and delivery, no further fee is payable.				
7.2 On an application for an order requiring a judgment debtor or other person to attend court to provide information in connection with enforcement of a judgment or order	£50	£50	£50	£50
7.3(a) On an application for a third party debt order or the appointment of a receiver by way of equitable execution	£100	£100	£100	£100
More than one third party: Fee 7.3(a) shall be payable in respect of each third party against whom the order is sought.				
(b) On an application for a charging order	£100	£100	£100	£100
More than one application: Fee 7.3(b) shall be payable in respect of each application issued.				
7.4 On an application for a judgment summons	£100	£100	£100	£100
7.5 On a request or application to register a judgment or order, or for permission to enforce an arbitration award, or for a certificate or a certified copy of a judgment or order for use abroad	£50	£50	£50	£60
Enforcement in the county court				
8.1 On an application for or in relation to enforcement of a judgment or order of a county court or through a county court[32]—				
In cases other than County Court Bulk Centre CCBC) cases brought by Centre users, by the issue of a warrant of execution against goods except a warrant to enforce payment of a fine:	£100	£100	£100	£100
(a) Where the amount for which the warrant issues does not exceed £125	£35	£35	See above	See above
(b) Where the amount for which the warrant issues exceeds £125	£55	£55	See above	See above
In CCBC cases brought by Centre users, by the issue of a warrant of execution against goods except a warrant to enforce payment of a fine:	£70[33]	£70[33]	£70[33]	£70[34]
(a) Where the amount for which the warrant issues does not exceed £125	£25	£25	£25	See above

[32] The description of these categories and the categories themselves changed over the years; the descriptions given are close approximations to the Orders themselves.
[33] This applies to all CCBC applications.
[34] This applies to all CCBC applications.

Court fees

Number and description of fee	Amount of fee from 1 October 2007[20]	Amount of fee from 1 May 2008[21]	Amount of fee from 13 July 2009[22]	Amount of fee from 4 April 2011[23]
(b) Where the amount for which the warrant issues exceeds £125	£45	£45	£45	See above
8.2 On a request for a further attempt at execution of a warrant at a new address following a notice of the reason for non-execution (except a further attempt following suspension and CCBC cases brought by Centre users)	£25	£25	£25	£30
8.3 On an application for an order requiring a judgment debtor or other person to attend court to provide information in connection with enforcement of a judgment or order	£45	£45	£50	£50
8.4(a) On an application for a third party debt order or the appointment of a receiver by way of equitable execution	£55	£55	£100	£100
(b) On an application for a charging order	£55	£55	£100	£100
More than one third party: Fee 7.3(a) shall be payable in respect of each third party against whom the order is sought.				
More than one application: Fee 7.3(b) shall be payable in respect of each application issued.				
8.5 On an application for a judgment summons	£95	£95	£100	£100
8.6 On the issue of a warrant of possession or a warrant of delivery	£95	£95	£95	£110
Where claim is in addition to a money claim: Where the recovery of a sum of money is sought in addition, no further fee is payable.				
8.7 On an application for an attachment of earnings order (other than a consolidated attachment of earnings order) to secure payment of a judgment debt	£65	£65	£100	£100
More than one defendant: Fee 8.7 is payable for each defendant against whom an order is sought.				
Hearing of judgment summons: Fee 8.7 is not payable where the attachment of earnings order is made on the hearing of a judgment summons.				
8.8 On a consolidated attachment of earnings order or on an administration order	For every £1 or part of a £1 of the money paid into court in respect of debts due to creditors – 10p			
Monies paid into court: Fee 8.8 shall be calculated on any money paid into court under any order at the rate in force at the time when the order was made (or, where the order has been amended, at the time of the last amendment before the date of payment).				
8.9 On the application for the recovery of a tribunal award	£35	£35	£35	£40
8.10 On a request for an order to recover a sum that is—				
— a specified debt within the meaning of the Enforcement of Road Traffic Debts Order 1993[35] as amended from time to time; or	£5	£5	£5	£7
— pursuant to an enactment, treated as a specified debt for the purposes of that Order				
No fee is payable on—				
— an application for an extension of time to serve a statutory declaration in connection with any such order; or				

(35)   S.I. 1993/2073; as amended by S.I. 2001/1386.

Court fees

Number and description of fee	Amount of fee from 1 October 2007[20]	Amount of fee from 1 May 2008[21]	Amount of fee from 13 July 2009[22]	Amount of fee from 4 April 2011[23]
—a request to issue a warrant of execution to enforce any such order.				
8A. Service in the county court				
8A.1 On a request for service by a bailiff of an order to attend court for questioning		£30[36]	£100	£100
Sale (county court only)				
9.1 For removing or taking steps to remove goods to a place of deposit	The reasonable expenses incurred			
Animals: Fee 9.1 is to include the reasonable expenses of feeding and caring for any animals.				
9.2 For advertising a sale by public auction pursuant to section 97 of the County Courts Act 1984(37)	The reasonable expenses incurred			
9.3 For the appraisement of goods	5p in the £1 or part of a £1 of the appraised value			
9.4 For the sale of goods (including advertisements, catalogues, sale and commission and delivery of goods)	15p in the £1 or part of a £1 on the amount realised by the sale or such other sum as the district judge may consider to be justified in the circumstances			
9.5 Where no sale takes place by reason of an execution being withdrawn, satisfied or stopped	(a) 10p in the £1 or part of a £1 on the value of the goods seized, the value to be the appraised value where the goods have been appraised or such other sum as the district judge may consider to be justified in the circumstances; and in addition (b) any sum payable under fee 9.1, 9.2 or 9.3			
Bills of Sale (in the High Court only)				
10.1 On filing any document under the Bills of Sale Acts 1878(38) and the Bills of Sale Act (1878) Amendment Act 1882(39) or on an application under section 15 of the Bills of Sale Act 1878 for an order that a memorandum of satisfaction be written on a registered copy of the bill	£25	£25	£25	£25
Searches (High Court only)				
10.2 For an official certificate of the result of a search for each name, in any register or index held by the court; or in the Court Funds Office, for an official certificate of the result of a search of unclaimed balances for a specified period of up to 50 years	£40	£40	£40	£45
10.3 On a search in person of the bankruptcy and companies records, including inspection, for each 15 minutes or part of 15 minutes	£5	£5	£5	£7
Judge sitting as arbitrator (High Court only)				
10.4 On the appointment of:				

36 From 26 November 2008 only; this fee was inserted by the Civil Proceedings Fees (Amendment) Order 2008 SI 2008/2853.

(37) 1984 c.28.
(38) 1878 c.31.
(39) 1882 c.43.

Court fees

Number and description of fee	Amount of fee from 1 October 2007[20]	Amount of fee from 1 May 2008[21]	Amount of fee from 13 July 2009[22]	Amount of fee from 4 April 2011[23]
(a) a judge of the Commercial Court as an arbitrator or umpire under section 93 of the Arbitration Act 1996(40); or	£1,800	£1,800	£1,800	£2,390
(b) a judge of the Technology and Construction Court as an arbitrator or umpire under section 93 of the Arbitration Act 1996	£1,400	£1,400	£1,400	£1,860
10.5 For every day or part of a day (after the first day) of the hearing before:				
(a) a judge of the Commercial Court; or	£1,800	£1,800	£1,800	£2,390
(b) a judge of the Technology and Construction Court, so appointed as arbitrator or umpire	£1,400	£1,400	£1,400	£1,860
No hearing: Where fee 10.4 has been paid on the appointment of a judge of the Commercial Court or a judge of the Technology and Construction Court as an arbitrator or umpire but the arbitration does not proceed to a hearing or an award, the fee shall be refunded.				
Foreign process (High Court only)				
10.6 For the registration and service of process received from abroad41	£60			n/a
Fees payable in Admiralty matters in the Admiralty Registrar and Marshal's Office				
11.1 On the issue of a warrant for the arrest of a ship or goods	£200	£200	£200	£220
11.2 On the sale of a ship or goods (subject to a minimum fee of £200):				
(a) for every £100 or fraction of £100 of the price up to £100,000	£1	£1	£1	£1
(b) for every £100 or fraction of £100 of the price exceeding £100,000	50p	50p	50p	50p
Sale in Court: Where there is sufficient proceeds of sale in court, fee 11.2 shall be taken by transfer from the proceeds of sale in court.				
11.3 On entering a reference for hearing by the Registrar	£50	£50	£50	£70
Affidavits (High Court and Court of Appeal only)				
12.1 On taking an affidavit or an affirmation or attestation upon honour in lieu of an affidavit or a declaration except for the purpose of receipt of dividends from the Accountant General and for a declaration by a shorthand writer appointed in insolvency proceedings—				
—for each person making any of the above	£10	£10	£10	£11
12.2 For each exhibit referred to in an affidavit, affirmation, attestation or declaration for which fee 12.1 is payable	£2	£2	£2	£2
Fees payable in appeals to the Court of Appeal				
13.1(a) Where in an appeal notice permission to appeal or an extension of time for appealing is applied for (or both are applied for)—				

(20) 1996 c.23.
41 in accordance with the Convention of 15 November 1965 on the service abroad of judicial and extra judicial documents in civil or commercial matters signed at the Hague on November 15 1965( )or Council Regulation (EC) No 1348/2000 of 29 May 2000 on the service in the Member States of judicial and extra judicial documents in civil or commercial matters

Court fees

Number and description of fee	Amount of fee from 1 October 2007[20]	Amount of fee from 1 May 2008[21]	Amount of fee from 13 July 2009[22]	Amount of fee from 4 April 2011[23]
— on filing an appellant's notice, or				
— where the respondent is appealing, on filing a respondent's notice	£200	£200	£200	£235
13.1(b) Where permission to appeal is not required or has been granted by the lower court—				
— on filing an appellant's notice, or				
— on filing a respondent's notice where the respondent is appealing	£400	£400	£400	£465
13.1(c) On the appellant filing an appeal questionnaire (unless the appellant has paid fee 13.1(b), or on the respondent filing an appeal questionnaire (unless the respondent has paid fee 13.1(b))	£400	£400	£400	£465
13.2 On filing a respondent's notice where the respondent wishes to ask the appeal court to uphold the order of the lower court for reasons different from or additional to those given by the lower court	£200	£200	£200	£235
13.3 On filing an application notice	£200	£200	£200	£235
Applications in appeal notice: Fee 13.3 shall not be payable for an application made in an appeal notice.				

Rail fares

National Rail Fares (2012)

The figures are prices (£ Sterling) in the following return tickets:

First class
Standard class
Off peak

	London	Birmingham	Bristol	Cambridge	Cardiff	Carlisle	Leeds	Manchester	Newcastle
Birmingham	271 85 50								
Bristol	294 179 65	210 94 48							
Cambridge	58 36 22	265 81 67	326 210 61						
Cardiff	316 199 85	179 78 51	35 16 11	348 232 77					
Carlisle	453 319 103	304 148 79	318 223 127	519 355 102	318 243 131				
Leeds	353 249 165	247 106 56	439 199 101	220 156 75	468 213 108	n/a 65 35			
Manchester	423 296 74	168 71 33	326 149 75	500 364 74	n/a 73 73	188 100 50	n/a 26 20		
Newcastle	402 301 117	443 193 98	597 276 134	309 222 104	609 276 138	n/a 18 18	125 70 54	148 90 69	
Oxford	99 54 25	147 64 33	141 52 21	144 74 48	224 138 52	318 184 104	378 296 171	322 144 66	557 478 319

INDEX

References are to paragraph numbers.